IMMIGRATION AND REFUGEE LAW AND POLICY

FOURTH EDITION

by

STEPHEN H. LEGOMSKY
Charles F. Nagel Professor of International and Comparative Law
Washington University

FOUNDATION PRESS
NEW YORK, NEW YORK
2005

© 1992, 1997, 2002 FOUNDATION PRESS
© 2005 By FOUNDATION PRESS
     395 Hudson Street
     New York, NY 10014
     Phone Toll Free 1–877–888–1330
     Fax (212) 367–6799
     fdpress.com

Printed in the United States of America

ISBN 1–58778–896–9

TEXT IS PRINTED ON 10% POST
CONSUMER RECYCLED PAPER

*To Annie, Katie, and Lorraine,
and in loving memory of my parents, Jack and Pauline*

*

PREFACE TO FOURTH EDITION

"Immigration, it seems, hardens hearts and softens brains like few other issues." The Economist, Sept. 8–14, 2001, at 14.

Why should this be? In the United States, the vast majority of us are either immigrants ourselves or the recent descendants of immigrants. Some Americans, and some of our ancestors, fled hopelessness and poverty. Others came to escape tyranny. A great number sought to unite their families. Still others were brought here forcibly, as slaves.

But whether one's own immigrant heritage is centuries-old or more recent, all who live here now are part of a national community whose character has been sculpted by generations of immigrants. History aside, the law by which a nation selects its members speaks volumes about the nation's values and about the society those values will produce. In this global age, immigration touches *everyone*.

That United States immigration policy permeates every aspect of American life and affects millions of people in far-off lands might alone explain the fervor with which immigration issues tend to be argued. But there are other explanations. Debates in this field ignite core values that excite passion—fundamental beliefs about sovereignty, national security, race, personal autonomy, equal economic opportunity, freedom of association, national community, civil rights and human rights, taxes, jobs, welfare, law enforcement, labor policy, the environment, foreign relations, war, and the distribution of wealth. Those issues and passions are not uniquely American and neither, therefore, is the debate over immigration. The United States has a distinctive immigration history, but globalization and technology have brought the immigration issue to sending and receiving states all over the world.

The first edition of this book appeared in 1992. Its preface described the surging public interest in immigration policy and frenetic change in immigration law. Throughout the preceding decade, the new laws had reflected mixed public sentiments toward immigrants. There had been the usual tough talk about "illegal aliens," the familiar restrictionist rhetoric, and a renewed emphasis on law enforcement. But there had also been the Refugee Act of 1980, a massive legalization program in 1986, and in 1990 a dramatic increase in the annual legal ceiling on professional and other skilled immigration.

In the 1990s, something happened. The United States intensified the interception of Haitian vessels on the high seas and returned the passengers without bothering to sort the refugees from the others. The voters of California passed Proposition 187. Official English movements sprouted nationally and locally. The United States Commission on Immigration Reform proposed large reductions in both family and employment-related immigration. Immigration became a key issue in the 1996 Presidential election, particularly in California and other high-immigration states. Phrases like "illegal aliens" and "criminal aliens" became the standard coin of political discourse. And a series of statutes enacted by Congress in 1996—arguably the harshest changes ever enacted in this field—sent shock waves through immigrant communities.

Immigrants, practitioners, government officials, scholars, NGO leaders, and other experienced immigration professionals suddenly felt that the ground beneath their feet had been swept away. Familiar central precepts were gone. The 1996 legislation broadened the grounds for excluding and expelling noncitizens, narrowed the possibilities for discretionary relief in compassionate cases, truncated many of the adjudication procedures, barred judicial review of important decisions of immigration officials, added new restrictions to asylum, and cut off millions of lawful immigrants from the major welfare programs.

By the late 1990s the climate was starting to thaw. Public opinion polls revealed substantially softer sentiments toward immigrants, and favorable legislative developments blunted at least some of the 1996 restrictions. Until September 11, 2001 there was even serious talk of an expanded guest worker program and an ambitious amnesty.

And then came the terrorist attacks. In immigration as in other areas of public life, everything changed. Proposed immigration liberalizations were suddenly off the table. Taking their place were the USA PATRIOT Act of 2001, the Homeland Security Act of 2002 (transferring almost all functions of the former INS to multiple agencies in the new Department of Homeland Security), controversial new Justice Department regulations intensifying the investigation, apprehension, and detention of noncitizens, the President's Order subjecting various categories of noncitizens to criminal trials before military tribunals without the usual constitutional constraints, and the REAL ID Act of 2005.

We are living in a new era. For the first time in history, the main United States agencies that shape immigration policy are under the auspices of a Department whose defining charge is to safeguard national security, principally against terrorists. The Secretary of Homeland Security understands that the President, the Congress, and the public will judge him, first and foremost, by how successful he is in fighting terrorism. How that political reality will affect future U.S. immigration policy is only beginning to be seen.

But the overriding message that I would personally urge is this: Despite the new home for U.S. immigration agencies, despite the spate of new laws and other policies that treat immigration primarily as a terrorism issue, and despite the alarmist public rhetoric along all points of the ideological spectrum, immigration is not primarily a national security issue. It is about national security, to be sure. But it is also about a lot of other things—family unity, economics, autonomy, community, ethnicity, civil rights, refugee protection, and a range of other themes from which the evolving norms of immigration and refugee law and policy will always draw their lifeblood.

Such is the life of immigration law. The public mood is ever volatile, and so are the resulting rules. Through it all, America for more than 200 years has sustained two venerable traditions. One is to admit immigrants in plentiful numbers. The other is to complain, every step of the way, that today's immigrants just aren't of the same caliber as yesterday's. The irony, of course, is that today's immigrants eventually become the solid citizens with whom tomorrow's immigrants inevitably suffer by comparison.

Something else is different. In the past, Congress typically enacted major immigration legislation every ten to twenty years and let things simmer in between. Starting in the 1980s, the bouts of inactivity shrank. Today, major policy changes take place almost every year. The "immigration issue" is now, and probably will remain forever, a perennial.

The law school world has kept pace with that trend. Twenty years ago, the law school that offered a course in immigration was the exception rather than the norm. Today the reverse is true. Immigration law is taught at virtually every United States law school. Many law schools also offer immigration clinics and specialized courses in refugee law, citizenship law, or business immigration. Scholarship in this once esoteric field is now abundant, sophisticated, and diverse. And in our information age exchanges of ideas now routinely occur across both national boundaries and disciplinary boundaries.

The Pedagogy

Immigration courses are taught in a variety of ways that reflect both the instructors' pedagogical goals and their judgments about the effectiveness of particular teaching methods. My own goals for a course in immigration and refugee law include those that I consider fundamental to legal education generally—honing students' abilities to analyze, evaluate, and synthesize difficult materials; challenging them to think about broader questions of law and social policy; training them to work with, and to develop confidence in their abilities to work with, traditional legal materials such as statutes and cases; sharpening problem-solving skills; enhancing communication skills; and fostering social and ethical responsibility. Beyond those general goals, I believe a survey course in immigration law should strive to accomplish other things: It should expose students to the core principles of immigration law; force them to think critically about immigration policy and the theory that underlies it; use the comprehensive and intricate Immigration and Nationality Act as a vehicle for teaching statutory interpretation techniques; and enable students to acquire a feel for the administrative process so central to immigration. Above all, a successful immigration course should appeal to students' imaginations, encouraging them to embrace ideas from other nations, from other disciplines, and from polar opposite ideologies.

So this coursebook walks a middle ground. It mixes theory, policy, and politics with practice-oriented materials that deal in doctrine, planning, and problem-solving. There is enough of both kinds of material that instructors will be able to give their courses whatever emphasis they think appropriate.

A few distinctive features of the book are worth mentioning:

(1) There is heavy use of fact problems. They generally call upon the student to plan a strategy for helping a hypothetical client or analyze how a case is likely to come out.

(2) There are a number of "Simulation Exercises." Students play the roles of legislative drafters, witnesses testifying for or against proposed reform legislation, immigration lawyers advising clients, lawyers engaged in oral argument before an appellate court, dissenting judges, and members of Congress debating a bill on the House floor. The most ambitious of the simulation exercises is a mock removal hearing (chapter 9) at which the students play the roles of government trial attorneys and the immigrant's counsel. The present edition adds a simulated attorney-client asylum interview. I have found student enthusiasm for these simulations especially keen and the preparation levels unusually high.

(3) Immigration lawyers know that this area of practice involves much more than statutes and appellate court decisions. The materials here attempt, within reasonable limits, to impart the flavor of the administrative process. Substantial space is devoted to the decisions of the Board of Immigration Appeals (BIA), to important principles of administrative law, and to the interplay between the statute and the regulations. To help students appreciate the progression that culminates in a judicial opinion, chapter 9 includes the file in an actual removal case. The file starts with a Notice to Appear and continues with the transcript of the removal hearing, the decision of the immigration judge, the opposing briefs to the BIA, the BIA opinion, the petition for review and opposing briefs to the court of appeals, and the final court decision. Those materials not only provide a glimpse into the administrative process and the role of the attorneys, but also permit an understanding of how a record is developed and where the "facts" that appear in a judicial opinion come from.

(4) The Notes and Questions are *much* more extensive than in most law school coursebooks, and an explanation is in order. My view is that whatever classroom methods a teacher uses—Socratic dialogue, group discussion, lecture, or a combination—the educational gains are greatest when the students have done some hard thinking before they walk into the classroom. Those of us who teach Socratically have a particular problem: The Socratic

method achieves its goals only if the questions are provocative and challenging. If they are, however, students who hear the questions in class for the first time will rarely be able to provide spontaneous answers that do the questions justice. To address that dilemma, I have included in this book the kinds of questions and fact problems—ranging from highly theoretical to highly practical—that can be used as the basis for classroom discussion to the extent the instructor wishes. Spontaneity has its benefits, but too often the flip side is a superficial level of analysis devoid of any lasting educational benefit. When students think critically about specific questions and problems before class, their thoughts can be more contemplative and the resulting class discussion more vibrant and sophisticated. At any rate, most of the questions generate differences of opinion that preserve a good deal of spontaneity.

This book is intended to be used in conjunction with the text of the Immigration and Nationality Act. Several excellent statutory supplements (which also include the texts of the 1951 Refugee Convention, 1967 Protocol, and miscellaneous other documents) are available.

STEVE LEGOMSKY

St. Louis
July 2005

*

ACKNOWLEDGMENTS

It is customary for an author to thank the many people without whose efforts the book could not possibly have been written. That tribute is traditionally followed by a gracious acknowledgment that any errors are, of course, solely the responsibility of the author.

I have always dreamed of writing a book in which I could say: "No one helped me with this book. Any errors are somebody else's fault."

Over the years, a great number of people have shattered that dream. A few deserve special mention. When I wrote the first edition I was just getting my feet wet in refugee and asylum law; Deborah Anker came to my rescue and vastly improved what is now chapter 11. Maria Frankowska has provided an endless stream of encouragement and ideas, and she has diplomatically identified errors in time for me to correct them. Arthur Helton, killed in Baghdad while continuing his life's work of humanitarian service, was and remains a source of ideas and inspiration; his friendship was a gift. Peter Schuck's prolific and provocative feedback has been especially generous. I am grateful to the Honorable Gene McNary for educating me about the immigration bureaucracy and Capitol Hill at monthly meetings during his four-year term as Commissioner of the former INS. I also thank two other special people—Kevin Johnson and Michael Olivas—for their continuing commentary, for alerting me to a glaring (and embarrassing) omission in the first two editions, and most of all for their lasting friendship.

I extend my sincere appreciation to all the friends and colleagues whose generous comments are reflected in successive editions of this book. The list has grown long, but here's my best try: Muneer Ahmad, Lynn Alvarez, Deborah Anker, Rodney Barker, Betsy Bedient, Lenni Benson, Patty Blum, Cindy Buys, Franco Capriotti, Gabriel (Jack) Chin, Michael Churgin, Mary Crock, Clark Cunningham, Nora Demleitner, Valerie Epps, Jason Eyster, the late Joan Fitzpatrick, Eugene Flynn, Susan Saab Fortney, Maria Frankowska, Maryellen Fullerton, Michael Gans, Pamela Goldberg, Iris Gomez, Guy Goodwin-Gill, the late Charles Gordon, Honorable John Gossart, Elwin Griffith, Lucas Guttentag, Kay Hailbronner, Lee Hall, James Hathaway, Dina Haynes, the late Arthur Helton, Berta Hernández-Truyol, Michael Heyman, David Hudson, Linton Joaquin, Kevin Johnson, Mark Jones, Dan Kanstroom, Harvey Kaplan, Linda Kelly, Dan Kowalski, Estelle Lau, Arnold Leibowitz, Warren Leiden, the late Daniel Levy, Michael Maggio, Stanley Mailman, Susan Martin, Angela McCaffrey, Gene McNary, Isabel Medina, Frank Miller, Hiroshi Motomura, Craig Mousin, Jim Nafziger, Gerald Neuman, Michael Olivas, Huyen Pham, Michele Pistone, Judy Rabinovitz, the late Maurice Roberts, the late William Robie, Victor Romero,

Linda Rose, Lory Rosenberg, John Scanlan, Andy Schoenholtz, Phil Schrag, Peter Schuck, Anna Shavers, Roy Simon, Peter Spiro, William Stock, Michael Straus, Michael Teitelbaum, David Thronson, Karen Tokarz, Bernard Trujillo, Jorge Vargas, Leti Volpp, David Weissbrodt, Virgil Wiebe, Leon Wildes, and Steve Yale-Loehr.

I also appreciate the information provided by John Bjurke, Robert Bombaugh, Tomas Curi, Bruce Hake, Michael Hoefer, Honorable Gerald Hurwitz, Rick Inzunza, Mary Ann Mohan, Chester Moyer, David Neal, Charles Oppenheim, Honorable Paul Schmidt, Cornelius D. Scully, Paul Virtue, and Carol Wolchok. Closer to home, I have benefitted from the insights of my friends Suzanne Brown, Larry Carp, Lilian Fernandez, and George Newman.

Locky Nimick (1st edition), Caryn Jackson (2nd edition), Karla Mitchell (1999 Supplement), and Stacie Powderly (4th edition) served as research assistants. All were outstanding. The staff of the Washington University Law Library, and especially Peggy McDermott, deserve the highest praise. The late Mary Ellen Powers, my secretary and dear friend for almost 20 years, was a special person, as all who knew her will attest. Her successor, Jo Hobbs, has also done fabulous work that I have much appreciated. As anyone who has ever written a coursebook well knows, I am greatly indebted to the many students whose questions and ideas have made their way onto the pages of the book. Those of us who teach immigration law also have the most supportive colleagues one could ever hope for. It has sometimes felt as if 100 co-authors and friends were with me as I was working.

Before writing the first edition, I had the advantage of teaching for several years from an excellent coursebook by Alex Aleinikoff and Dave Martin. Since then, the addition of Hiroshi Motomura has only enhanced their fine book. I value their friendship and continue to appreciate their huge positive impact on our field.

In the first edition I thanked my little daughters, Annie and Katie, for their superb assistance with the cutting and pasting. By the time of the second edition, alas, they had grown too old for cutting and pasting. By then, technology and downsizing had eliminated that job anyway. They still contribute nonetheless, in countless ways that they will not fully appreciate until they are blessed with children of their own. Expressing proper appreciation to them, and to my loving wife, Lorraine, is not possible in a few words. They have all tolerated my ridiculous work hours and my mood swings with much more grace than I had a right to expect, and they have provided the love and encouragement that have sustained me through the most grueling periods.

So much for my dream.

The author thanks the many people without whose efforts this book could not possibly have been written. Any errors are, of course, solely the responsibility of the author.

TECHNICAL CONVENTIONS AND ABBREVIATIONS

Deletions from reprinted materials are indicated by three asterisks. If an entire paragraph is being deleted, the asterisks are centered. Footnotes and citations, however, are deleted without notation.

When footnotes in reprinted material are retained, the original footnote numbers are used. My own footnotes to reprinted material are lettered "a,b,c," etc., and the notation "ed." appears at the end of each of these footnotes. My own text is footnoted "1,2,3," etc., within each chapter.

The Immigration and Nationality Act (INA) has been codified as title 8 of the United States Code (8 U.S.C.). Title 8 has not yet been enacted into positive law. The INA and 8 U.S.C. use different sequences of section numbers, and there is no systematic conversion formula. For example, INA §§ 101 and 212 correspond, respectively, to 8 U.S.C. §§ 1101 and 1182. For the sake of uniformity (and because DOJ and DHS regulations are pegged to the INA section numbers that they implement), this book uses only the INA section numbers. References to sections of 8 U.S.C. in the reprinted materials have all been changed to INA section numbers without any notations to that effect. Students using this book should not need the parallel citations to 8 U.S.C., but a conversion chart is provided at the front of each volume of 8 U.S.C.A. for anyone who wants it.

The following abbreviations are used throughout the book:

1951 Convention   Convention Relating to the Status of Refugees, 1989 U.N.T.S. 137, accepted by U.N. Conference of Plenipotentiaries on the Status of Refugees and Stateless Persons, signed at Geneva, July 28, 1951

1967 Protocol   United Nations Protocol Relating to the Status of Refugees, 606 U.N.T.S. 267, 19 U.S.T. 6223, T.I.A.S. No. 6577, done at New York, Jan. 31, 1967

2003 Yearbook of Immigration Statistics
    U.S. Dept. of Homeland Security, Office of Immigration Statistics, 2003 Yearbook of Immigration Statistics (Sept. 2004)

AEDPA   Antiterrorism and Effective Death Penalty Act of 1996, Pub.L. 104–132, 110 Stat. 1214 (Apr. 24, 1996)

AILA   American Immigration Lawyers Association (the main national organization for immigration lawyers in the private sector)

Anker   Deborah E. Anker, Law of Asylum in the United States (3d ed. 1999) (the leading treatise on U.S. asylum law)

BALCA   Board of Alien Labor Certification Appeals (within Dept. of Labor)

BIA   Board of Immigration Appeals (within EOIR, below)

BIB   Bender's Immigration Bulletin

CAT   Convention Against Torture and Other Cruel, Inhuman or Degrading Treatment or Punishment, UNGA Res. 39/46, 39 U.N. GAOR Supp. (No. 51) at 197, U.N. Doc. A/39/51 (adopted 10 Dec. 1984)

CBP   Customs and Border Protection (within DHS, below)

DHS   Department of Homeland Security

EBSVERA   Enhanced Border Security and Visa Entry Reform Act of 2002, Pub. L. 107–173, 116 Stat. 543 (May 14, 2002).

EOIR   Executive Office for Immigration Review (adjudicative tribunal within Dept. of Justice)

F.A.M.   U.S. Dept. of State, Foreign Affairs Manual (updated regularly)

Gordon, Mailman, & Yale-Loehr   Charles Gordon, Stanley Mailman & Stephen Yale-Loehr, Immigration Law and Procedure (the leading treatise on immigration law; multiple volumes updated regularly)

HSA   Homeland Security Act of 2002, Pub. L. 107–296, 116 Stat. 2135 (Nov. 25, 2002)

I. & N. Dec.   United States Dept. of Justice, Administrative

	Decisions under Immigration and Nationality Laws (bound volumes reporting decisions of BIA and sometimes USCIS or former INS)
ICE	Immigration and Customs Enforcement (in DHS)
IIRIRA	Illegal Immigration Reform and Immigrant Responsibility Act of 1996, Pub.L. 104–208, 110 Stat. 3009, Div. C (Sept. 30, 1996)
IR	Interpreter Releases
IJ	Immigration Judge (within EOIR, above)
IMFA	Immigration Marriage Fraud Amendments, Pub.L. 99–639, 100 Stat. 3537 (Nov. 10, 1986)
Imm. Act 1990	Immigration Act of 1990, Pub.L. 101–649, 104 Stat. 4978 (Nov. 29, 1990)
INA	Immigration and Nationality Act, Pub.L. 82–414, 66 Stat. 163 (June 27, 1952), as amended
INS	Immigration and Naturalization Service (now defunct agency replaced by several agencies within DHS)
INS OIs	INS Operations Instructions (internal guidelines, to employees of former INS, refining regulations)
IRCA	Immigration Reform and Control Act, Pub.L. 99–603, 100 Stat. 3359 (Nov. 5, 1986)
LIFE	Legal Immigration and Family Equity Act, Pub.L. 106–553, 114 Stat. 2762, Title 11 (Dec. 21, 2000) and Pub.L. 106–554, 114 Stat. 2763, Title 15, Div. B (Dec. 21, 2000)
LPR	Noncitizen admitted as "lawful permanent resident" of the United States
NACARA	Nicaraguan Adjustment and Central American Relief Act, Pub.L. 105–100, Title II, 111 Stat. 2160, 2193 (Nov. 19, 1997)
OCAHO	Office of the Chief Administrative Hearing Officer (within EOIR, above)
REAL ID Act	REAL ID Act of 2005, Division B of Pub. L. 109–13, 119 Stat. 231 (May 11, 2005)
UNHCR	United Nations High Commissioner for Refugees

UNHCR Handbook

>UNHCR, Handbook on Procedures and Criteria for Determining Refugee Status (Geneva, Sept. 1979)

USA PATRIOT Act of 2001

>Uniting and Strengthening America by Providing Appropriate Tools Required to Intercept and Obstruct Terrorism Act of 2001, Pub.L. 107–56, 115 Stat. 272 (Oct. 26, 2001)

USCIS

>United States Citizenship and Immigration Services (in DHS)

VO

>Visa Office (an office of the Bureau of Consular Affairs, within the State Dept.)

PERMISSIONS

The author acknowledges the permissions kindly granted to reprint excerpts from the following works:

T. Alexander Aleinikoff, *Citizens, Aliens, Membership and the Constitution*, 7 Const. Commentary 9. Copyright © 1990 Constitutional Commentary. Reprinted by permission.

Deborah E. Anker, *Refugee Status and Violence Against Women in the "Domestic" Sphere: The Non-State Actor Question*, 15 Georgetown Immigration L.J. 391 (2001). Copyright © 2001 Deborah E. Anker. Reprinted by permission.

David Bacon, *Be Our Guests*, Reprinted with permission from the September 27, 2004 issue of *The Nation*. For subscription information, call 1–800–333–8536. Portions of each week's Nation magazine can be accessed at http://www.thenation.com.

George J. Borjas, Heaven's Door (1999). Copyright © 1999 Princeton University Press. Reprinted by permission.

Linda S. Bosniak, *Exclusion and Membership: The Dual Identity of the Undocumented Worker under United States law*, 1988 Wisconsin L.Rev. 955. Copyright © 1988 Wisconsin Law Review. Reprinted by permission.

Peter Brimelow, Alien Nation—Common Sense about America's Immigration Disaster (1995). Copyright © 1995 by Peter Brimelow. Reprinted by permission of the Wylie Agency.

Howard F. Chang, *Migration as International Trade: The Economic Gains from the Liberalized Movement of Labor*, 3 UCLA J. Internat'l L. & Foreign Affairs 371 (1998). Copyright © 1998 Howard F. Chang. Reprinted by permission.

Gabriel J. Chin, *Segregation's Last Stronghold: Race Discrimination and the Constitutional Law of Immigration*, originally published in 46 UCLA L.Rev. 1 (1998). Copyright © 1998, The Regents of the University of California. All Rights Reserved.

David Cole, *The Priority of Morality: The Emergency Constitution's Blind Spot*, 113 Yale L.J. 1753 (2004). Copyright © 2004 The Yale Law Journal.

*

SUMMARY OF CONTENTS

PREFACE TO FOURTH EDITION -- v
ACKNOWLEDGMENTS --- xi
TECHNICAL CONVENTIONS AND ABBREVIATIONS ------------------------------------ xiii
PERMISSIONS -- xvii
TABLE OF CASES --- xliii
TABLE OF SECONDARY AUTHORITIES --- lix

Overview of United States Immigration Law ------------------------------ 1

Sec.
A. Terminology -- 1
B. General Regulation of Immigration ------------------------------------- 2
C. Nationality -- 8
D. The Admission of Noncitizens to the United States ---------------------- 9
E. Expulsion -- 11
F. Other Sanctions -- 12

CHAPTER 1 The Immigration Debate: Goals, Strategies, and Impact ------- 13

Sec.
A. The History -- 14
B. The Moral Dimensions of Immigration Control --------------------------- 25
C. Immigration, Race, Culture, and Language ----------------------------- 34
D. The Economic Impact of Immigration ----------------------------------- 61
E. Immigration, Population, and the Environment -------------------------- 75
F. The Politics of Immigration --- 81
G. Immigration and National Security: An Introduction -------------------- 87
H. Immigrants, Self–Identity, and Home ---------------------------------- 88

CHAPTER 2 Immigration and the Constitution --------------------------- 103

Sec.
A. Sources of the Federal Immigration Power ------------------------------ 103
B. Limits to the Federal Immigration Power ------------------------------- 120

CHAPTER 3 Immigrant Priorities --------------------------------------- 238

Sec.
A. The Fundamentals: Quotas and Preferences ------------------------------ 239
B. Family Immigration -- 250
C. Employment–Based Immigration --- 292
D. Diversity Immigrants -- 337

CHAPTER 4 Nonimmigrant Priorities ----------------------------- 345

Sec.

A. Commercial Categories of Nonimmigrants ----------------- 348
B. Educational Categories ------------------------------- 383
C. Tourists -- 394
D. Fiancés and Fiancées -------------------------------- 397
E. A Few Other Nonimmigrant Categories ----------------- 401
F. General Nonimmigrant Problems ----------------------- 403

CHAPTER 5 Exclusion Grounds and Waivers ------------- 410

Sec.

A. Grounds Related to Immigration Control --------------- 422
B. Political and National Security Grounds -------------- 427
C. Criminal Grounds ------------------------------------- 435
D. Economic Grounds ------------------------------------- 438
E. Public Health and Morals ----------------------------- 441

CHAPTER 6 Admission Procedure ----------------------- 444

Sec.

A. The Early Days --------------------------------------- 444
B. Modern Procedure: Preliminary Comments -------------- 450
C. Visa Petitions -------------------------------------- 452
D. Visa Applications ----------------------------------- 461
E. Actual Admission ------------------------------------ 485
F. Adjustment of Status -------------------------------- 490

CHAPTER 7 Deportability Grounds --------------------- 496

Sec.

A. General Considerations ------------------------------- 496
B. The Meaning and Significance of "Entry" and "Admission" ----- 504
C. Deportability Grounds Concerned With Immigration Control ------- 525
D. Crime–Related Deportability Grounds ----------------- 530
E. Political and National Security Grounds -------------- 567
F. Other Deportability Grounds ------------------------- 568
G. Time Limits --- 568

CHAPTER 8 Relief From Deportability ----------------- 572

Sec.

A. Lasting Relief -------------------------------------- 574
B. Limited Relief -------------------------------------- 614
C. Miscellaneous Defenses ------------------------------ 630
D. A Perspective on Relief From Deportability ---------- 632

CHAPTER 9 Deportation Procedure ------------------------------ 633

Sec.
A. Overview -- 634
B. A Sampling of Specific Procedural Ingredients ----------------- 645
C. A Case File: From Initial Notice to Judicial Review ----------- 761
D. A Simulated Removal Hearing ---------------------------------- 817
E. Exceptions to Usual Removal Procedures ----------------------- 833

CHAPTER 10 Immigration and National Security -------------- 843

Sec.
A. The Detention of Noncitizens --------------------------------- 844
B. Intelligence–Gathering -------------------------------------- 866
C. Expansion of Removal Grounds -------------------------------- 875
D. Shrinking Procedural Rights --------------------------------- 875
E. Visas and Other Overseas Policies --------------------------- 885
F. Enhanced Border Enforcement -------------------------------- 890
G. Profiling --- 891
H. Immigration and National Security in Perspective ------------ 900

CHAPTER 11 Refugees --------------------------------------- 915

Sec.
A. Overseas Refugees --- 918
B. Asylum and Nonrefoulement ---------------------------------- 937
C. Beyond Persecution: Protection Against Other Dangers -------- 1144

**CHAPTER 12 Undocumented Migrants and Law Enforce-
ment** --- 1192

Sec.
A. Immigration Offenses -- 1204
B. Employer Misconduct -- 1209
C. Undocumented Migrants and Public Benefits ------------------ 1230

CHAPTER 13 Citizenship ------------------------------------ 1265

Sec.
A. Acquiring Citizenship --------------------------------------- 1266
B. Losing Citizenship -- 1312
C. The Significance of Citizenship ----------------------------- 1350

INDEX --- 1375

*

TABLE OF CONTENTS

PREFACE TO FOURTH EDITION v
ACKNOWLEDGMENTS xi
TECHNICAL CONVENTIONS AND ABBREVIATIONS xiii
PERMISSIONS xvii
TABLE OF CASES xliii
TABLE OF SECONDARY AUTHORITIES lix

Overview of United States Immigration Law 1

Sec.
A. Terminology 1
B. General Regulation of Immigration 2
C. Nationality 8
D. The Admission of Noncitizens to the United States 9
E. Expulsion 11
F. Other Sanctions 12

CHAPTER 1 The Immigration Debate: Goals, Strategies, and Impact 13

Sec.
A. The History 14
   1 Charles Gordon, Stanley Mailman, and Stephen Yale–Loehr, Immigration Law and Procedure 14
   Immigration from Selected Countries and Regions 23
B. The Moral Dimensions of Immigration Control 25
   Roger Nett, The Civil Right We Are Not Ready For: The Right of Free Movement of People on the Face of the Earth 25
   Notes and Questions 29
C. Immigration, Race, Culture, and Language 34
   Peter H. Schuck, Diversity in America—Keeping Government at a Safe Distance 36
   Peter Brimelow, Alien Nation—Common Sense About America's Immigration Disaster 38
   Kevin R. Johnson, Fear of an "Alien Nation": Race, Immigration and Immigrants 44
   Juan F. Perea, "Am I an American or Not?" Reflections on Citizenship, Americanization, and Race, in Noah M.J. Pickus (Ed.), Immigration and Citizenship in the Twenty–First Century 50
   Notes and Questions 54
   Note on the English–Only Movement 57
D. The Economic Impact of Immigration 61
   George J. Borjas, Heaven's Door—Immigration Policy and the American Economy 62
   Howard F. Chang, Migration as International Trade: The Economic Gains From the Liberalized Movement of Labor 66

Sec.

D. The Economic Impact of Immigration—Continued
  James P. Smith & Barry Edmonston (Eds.), National Research Council of the National Academy of Sciences, The New Americans—Economic, Demographic, and Fiscal Effects of Immigration 68
  Notes and Questions 72
E. Immigration, Population, and the Environment 75
  James P. Smith & Barry Edmonston (Eds.), National Research Council of the National Academy of Sciences, The New Americans—Economic, Demographic, and Fiscal Effects of Immigration 76
  Ellen Percy Kraly, Research Paper for the U.S. Commission on Immigration Reform, U.S. Immigration and the Environment: Scientific Research and Analytic Issues 79
  Notes and Questions 81
F. The Politics of Immigration 81
G. Immigration and National Security: An Introduction 87
H. Immigrants, Self–Identity, and Home 88
  Henry Grunwald, Home is Where you are Happy 88
  Berta Esperanza Hernández–Truyol, Natives, Newcomers and Nativism: A Human Rights Model for the Twenty–First Century 92
  Michael A. Olivas, The Chronicles, My Grandfather's Stories, and Immigration Law: The Slave Traders Chronicle as Racial History 93
  Natsu Taylor Saito, Alien and Non–Alien Alike: Citizenship, "Foreignness," and Racial Hierarchy in American Law 94
  Victor C. Romero, Broadening Our World: Citizens and Immigrants of Color in America 96
  Notes and Questions 98

CHAPTER 2 Immigration and the Constitution 103

Sec.

A. Sources of the Federal Immigration Power 103
  1. The Enumerated Powers 104
    a. The Commerce Clause 104
    b. The Migration or Importation Clause 106
    c. The Naturalization Clause 106
    d. The War Clause 107
  2. Implied Constitutional Powers 107
    Chae Chan Ping v. United States (The Chinese Exclusion Case) 108
    Notes and Questions 111
    Stephen H. Legomsky, Immigration and the Judiciary: Law and Politics in Britain and America 114
    Note on the Public Reaction to Asian Immigration 115
  3. Beyond the Constitution 118
  4. Residual State Power 119
B. Limits to the Federal Immigration Power 120
  1. The Foundation Cases 121
    Ekiu v. United States 122
    Questions 123

Sec.

B. Limits to the Federal Immigration Power—Continued

 Fong Yue Ting v. United States ---- 124

 Notes and Questions ---- 137

 2. Modern Developments ---- 144

  a. Procedural Due Process in Exclusion Cases ---- 144

  Shaughnessy v. United States ex rel. Mezei ---- 145

  General Notes and Questions ---- 152

  Notes and Questions on the Exclusion of Returning Residents: Some Cracks in the Plenary Congressional Power ---- 153

  Notes and Questions on the Detention of Excluded Noncitizens ---- 156

  b. Procedural Due Process in Deportation Cases: More Cracks in the Plenary Congressional Power ---- 158

  Yamataya v. Fisher (The Japanese Immigrant Case) ---- 159

  Notes and Questions ---- 161

  c. Substantive Applications of the Plenary Power Doctrine ---- 163

  Harisiades v. Shaughnessy ---- 163

  Notes and Questions ---- 171

  Substantive Cracks in the Plenary Congressional Power ---- 181

  Francis v. INS ---- 181

  Notes and Questions ---- 183

  d. Still More Cracks ---- 186

  INS v. Chadha ---- 186

  Notes and Questions ---- 190

  Zadvydas v. Davis ---- 191

  Notes and Questions ---- 203

  Clark v. Martinez ---- 208

  Demore v. Hyung Joon Kim ---- 211

  Stephen H. Legomsky, *The Detention of Aliens: Theories, Rules, and Discretion* ---- 225

  Notes and Questions ---- 227

  e. Where Are We Now? ---- 229

  Gabriel J. Chin, *Segregation's Last Stronghold: Race Discrimination and the Constitutional Law of Immigration* ---- 232

  Simulation Exercise ---- 234

  Concluding Note on the Plenary Power Over Immigration: Historical Parallels From Across the Atlantic ---- 235

CHAPTER 3 Immigrant Priorities ---- 238

Sec.

A. The Fundamentals: Quotas and Preferences ---- 239

 1. Immigrants Exempt from the General Quotas ---- 239

 2. Immigrants Subject to the General Quotas ---- 241

  a. Programs and Ceilings ---- 241

  Problem 1 ---- 243

  b. Preference Categories and Sub–Ceilings ---- 243

  Problem 2 ---- 246

  c. Selecting Individual Applicants ---- 247

  Questions ---- 249

Sec.

B. Family Immigration 250
   1. The Basics 250
      Problems 3–4 254
   2. Spouses 255
      a. Same–Sex Marriages 255
         Adams v. Howerton 255
         Notes and Questions 258
         Note, An Argument for the Application of Equal Protection Heightened Scrutiny to Classifications Based on Homosexuality 264
         Notes and Questions 265
      b. Fraudulent Marriages 270
         Problems 5–11 275
         Notes and Questions 276
         Notes and Questions on Marriages During Removal Proceedings 278
   3. Other Family Members 280
      Matter of Mourillon 281
      Notes and Questions 283
      Problems 12–15 286
      Note on Foreign Adoptions 286
   4. Family Unification Policy in Perspective 290
      Notes and Questions 290
C. Employment–Based Immigration 292
   1. The First Three Preferences: Superstars, Stars and Others 293
      a. General Eligibility Requirements 293
      b. Labor Certification 295
         i. Displacing American Workers 298
           Matter of Marion Graham 298
           Notes and Questions 302
           David Isaacson, We're All Entitled: The Literary and Cultural Significance of the Dictionary of Occupational Titles 312
         ii. Adversely Affecting the Wages and Working Conditions of American Workers 316
           Industrial Holographics, Inc. v. Donovan 316
           Notes and Questions 319
      c. Perspective on Employment–Based Immigration 321
         Demetrios G. Papademetriou & Stephen Yale–Loehr, Balancing Interests: Rethinking U.S. Selection of Skilled Immigrants 321
         Notes and Questions 331
   2. The Fourth Preference: Certain "Special Immigrants" 333
   3. The Fifth Preference: Immigrant Investors 334
D. Diversity Immigrants 337
   Problem 16 340
   Essay on Diversity Immigrants 341

CHAPTER 4 Nonimmigrant Priorities ------------------------- 345

Sec.
2003 Yearbook of Immigration Statitics ------------------------- 346
A. Commercial Categories of Nonimmigrants ------------------------- 348
  1. Business Visitors ------------------------- 348
    International Union of Bricklayers and Allied Craftsmen v. Meese ------------------------- 348
    Notes and Questions ------------------------- 356
    Problems 1–3 ------------------------- 358
  2. Treaty Traders and Investors ------------------------- 359
    Nice v. Turnage ------------------------- 360
    Notes and Questions ------------------------- 361
  3. Temporary Workers ------------------------- 362
    a. "Specialty Occupations," Athletes, and Entertainers: H–1B's, O's, and P's ------------------------- 362
    b. Lesser Skills and Labor Shortages: H–2's ------------------------- 367
      David Bacon, Be Our Guests ------------------------- 368
      Matter of Artee Corporation ------------------------- 372
      Notes and Questions ------------------------- 374
    c. Trainees: H–3's ------------------------- 376
    d. Miscellaneous Other Temporary Workers ------------------------- 376
      Problems 4–5 ------------------------- 377
  4. Intra–Company Transferees ------------------------- 378
    Karmali v. INS ------------------------- 378
    Notes and Questions ------------------------- 379
  5. Comparing Commercial Categories ------------------------- 381
    Problems 6–7 ------------------------- 381
B. Educational Categories ------------------------- 383
  1. Students ------------------------- 383
  2. Exchange Visitors ------------------------- 387
    Sheku–Kamara v. Karn ------------------------- 389
    Notes and Questions ------------------------- 392
    Problems 8–9 ------------------------- 393
C. Tourists ------------------------- 394
  Matter of Healy and Goodchild ------------------------- 394
  Notes and Questions ------------------------- 397
D. Fiancés and Fiancées ------------------------- 397
  Moss v. INS ------------------------- 398
  Notes and Questions ------------------------- 400
  Problem 10 ------------------------- 401
E. A Few Other Nonimmigrant Categories ------------------------- 401
F. General Nonimmigrant Problems ------------------------- 403
  1. Intent to Remain Permanently ------------------------- 403
    David Weissbrodt and Laura Danielson, Should the Lawyer Tell the Client About a Fixed Intent to Immigrate?, in Immigration Law and Procedure in a Nutshell ------------------------- 405
    Problems 11–13 ------------------------- 406
  2. Change of Nonimmigrant Status ------------------------- 408
    Problem 14 ------------------------- 409

CHAPTER 5   Exclusion Grounds and Waivers 410

Committee on the Judiciary, United States House of Representatives, Grounds for Exclusion of Aliens Under the Immigration and Nationality Act 412

Sec.

A. Grounds Related to Immigration Control 422
    Problems 1–5 426
B. Political and National Security Grounds 427
    Notes and Questions on the Political and National Security Grounds 431
    Problems 6–8 435
C. Criminal Grounds 435
    Problems 9–12 437
D. Economic Grounds 438
    Notes and Questions 441
E. Public Health and Morals 441
    Question 443

CHAPTER 6   Admission Procedure 444

Sec.

A. The Early Days 444
    Him Mark Lai, Genny Lim & Judy Yung, Island—Poetry and History of Chinese Immigrants on Angel Island 1910–1940 444
B. Modern Procedure: Preliminary Comments 450
C. Visa Petitions 452
    Linda Kelly, Stories From the Front: Seeking Refuge for Battered Immigrants in the Violence Against Women Act 454
    Notes and Questions 457
    Florida Bar v. Matus 457
    Notes and Questions 459
    Problems 1–3 460
D. Visa Applications 461
    1 Charles Gordon, Stanley Mailman & Stephen Yale–Loehr, Immigration Law and Procedure 462
    Notes and Questions 465
    James A.R. Nafziger, Review of Visa Denials by Consular Officers 469
    H.R. 2567 473
    Simulation Exercise 475
    Hermina Sague v. United States 475
    Notes and Questions 478
E. Actual Admission 485
    1. At the Border 485
    2. Hearings Before Immigration Judges 486
    3. Appeals From Immigration Judge Decisions 488
    4. Expedited Removal 488
    5. Other Special Removal Procedures 489
        a. National Security and Foreign Policy Cases 489
        b. Terrorism Cases 490
F. Adjustment of Status 490
    Notes and Questions 493
    Problems 4–7 494

CHAPTER 7 Deportability Grounds 496

Sec.
A. General Considerations 496
  1. Historical Overview of American Deportation Policy 498
    3 Charles Gordon, Stanley Mailman, and Stephen Yale–Loehr,
      Immigration Law and Procedure 498
  2. The Theory of Deportation 499
  3. Current Deportability Grounds 500
  4. Deportation and Statutory Interpretation 501
    Fong Haw Tan v. Phelan 501
    Notes and Questions 502
B. The Meaning and Significance of "Entry" and "Admission" 504
  Matter of Ching and Chen 505
  Notes and Questions 508
  Problems 1–3 510
  Rosenberg v. Fleuti 511
  Notes and Questions 519
  Problems 4–6 525
C. Deportability Grounds Concerned With Immigration Control 525
  1. Entry Without Inspection 526
  2. Entry While Inadmissible and Related Issues 526
    Notes and Questions 527
    Problems 7–13 527
  3. Post-entry Conduct Related to Immigration Control 529
D. Crime–Related Deportability Grounds 530
  1. What is a Conviction? 532
    a. Withdrawing Guilty Pleas 533
      United States v. Parrino 533
      Notes and Questions 537
    b. Expungements 538
      Questions 540
    c. Executive Pardons 540
    d. Miscellaneous Collateral Attacks 540
  2. Crimes Involving Moral Turpitude 540
    a. The Meaning of "Crime Involving Moral Turpitude" 540
      Marciano v. INS 540
      Notes and Questions 546
      Problems 14–16 548
    b. "Committed Within Five Years ... After the Date of Ad-
      mission" 549
      Problems 17–18 549
    c. Sentencing Requirements 549
    d. Two Crimes Involving Moral Turpitude 549
      Problem 19 550
    e. Judicial Recommendations Against Deportation 550

Sec.

D. Crime–Related Deportability Grounds—Continued
- 3. Drug Offenses 552
  - Problems 20–21 552
- 4. Aggravated Felonies 553
  - *Leocal v. Ashcroft* 555
  - Notes and Questions 559
  - Problems 22–24 563
- 5. Miscellaneous Criminal Grounds 564
  - Note on Comparative Law, Separation of Powers, and the Making of Immigration Policy 565
- 6. The Merits of Removing Noncitizen Criminal Offenders 566
  - Drafting Exercise 566

E. Political and National Security Grounds 567
F. Other Deportability Grounds 568
G. Time Limits 568
- Problems 25–27 570

CHAPTER 8 Relief From Deportability 572

Sec.

A. Lasting Relief 574
- 1. Cancellation of Removal 574
  - a. Cancellation of Removal: Part A 574
    - i. General Applicability and Scope 574
    - ii. Timing 579
    - iii. Disqualifications 580
    - iv. Discretion 580
      - Questions 580
      - Problems 1–3 581
  - b. Cancellation of Removal: Part B 581
    - i. Continuous Physical Presence 583
      - Questions 585
      - Problem 4 585
    - ii. Hardship 585
      - *INS v. Jong Ha Wang* 588
      - Notes and Questions 591
      - *Hee Yung Ahn v. INS* [before *Wang*] 597
      - *Hee Yung Ahn v. INS* [after *Wang*] 597
      - Notes and Questions 601
    - iii. Other Hurdles: Good Moral Character, Disqualified Groups, Discretion, and Reporting to Congress 604
    - iv. NACARA 605
- 2. Registry 607
- 3. Legalization 607
  - a. General Legalization in 1986 609
  - b. Legalization of Agricultural Workers in 1986 610
  - c. Cubans and Haitians in 1986 610
  - d. Nicaraguans and Cubans in 1997 611
  - e. Haitians in 1998 611
    - Questions 611
- 4. Adjustment of Status 612
- 5. Private Bills 613

Sec.

B. Limited Relief -- 614
  1. Deferred Action-- 614
    Notes and Questions -------------------------------------- 617
  2. Voluntary Departure-------------------------------------- 617
    Questions -- 621
    Problems 5–6 -- 622
  3. Objections to Destination ---------------------------------- 622
    Linnas v. INS -- 625
    Notes and Questions -------------------------------------- 628
    Problem 7 -- 630
  4. Stays of Removal-- 630
C. Miscellaneous Defenses-- 630
D. A Perspective on Relief From Deportability -------------------- 632

CHAPTER 9 Deportation Procedure ---------------------- 633

Sec.

A. Overview -- 634
  1. Apprehension-- 634
  2. Before the Hearing -- 635
  3. The Removal Hearing ------------------------------------ 639
  4. Administrative Review ------------------------------------ 641
  5. Judicial Review -- 642
  6. The Execution of the Removal Order------------------ 643
B. A Sampling of Specific Procedural Ingredients -------------- 645
  1. The Hearing Process: History, the APA, and Separation of
    Functions -- 645
    Sidney B. Rawitz, From Wong Yang Sung to Black Robes ------- 645
    Notes and Questions -------------------------------------- 650
  2. Representation-- 653
    a. Authorization to Practice ------------------------------ 655
      8 C.F.R. §§ 292.1, 292.2 (2004) ---------------------- 655
      Notes and Questions ---------------------------------- 656
    b. Finding Lawyers for the Indigent -------------------- 657
      i. A Constitutional Right to Counsel?------------------ 658
        Aguilera–Enriquez v. INS ------------------------ 658
        Notes and Questions ------------------------------ 663
      ii. Legal Aid -- 665
      iii. Pro Bono Legal Services ------------------------------ 666
      iv. Equal Access to Justice Act ------------------------ 667
        Notes and Questions ------------------------------ 667
    c. Discipline of Immigration Practitioners------------ 668
      8 C.F.R. § 1003.102 (2004) ------------------------ 668
      Notes and Questions ---------------------------------- 670
    d. Ineffective Assistance of Counsel------------------ 671
      People v. Pozo-- 672
      Notes and Questions ---------------------------------- 677
      Matter of Lozada-- 681
      Notes and Questions ---------------------------------- 683

Sec.

    3. Evidence and Proof 685
        a. Admissibility of Evidence 685
            INS v. Lopez–Mendoza 686
            Notes and Questions 700
            Other Illegally Obtained Statements 702
            Note on Judicial Politics 704
        b. Burden of Proof and Sufficiency of the Evidence 705
            Woodby v. INS 705
            Notes and Questions 711
            Problem 1 716
    4. Administrative Review: The Board of Immigration Appeals 717
        Notes and Questions 723
    5. Motions to Reopen or Reconsider 725
        Question 727
    6. Judicial Review of Removal Orders 727
        a. Petitions for Review 731
            i. Crime–Related Removal Orders 734
            ii. Denials of Discretionary Relief 735
            iii. Expedited Removal Orders 739
            iv. Voluntary Departure Regulations 739
            v. Prosecutorial Discretion 740
            vi. Detention Decisions 740
        b. Habeas Corpus 741
            Henry M. Hart, Jr., The Power of Congress to Limit the
               Jurisdiction of Federal Courts: An Exercise in Dialectic   742
            Question 746
            INS v. St. Cyr 746
            Notes and Questions 755
        c. Other Strategies 757
            i. General Federal Question Jurisdiction 757
            ii. Injunctions and Class Actions 757
            iii. Collateral Attack in Criminal Proceedings 759
            iv. Claims of United States Nationality 759
        d. Consolidating Reviewable Claims 759
        e. The Theory and the Consequences of Judicial Review 760
            Question 761
C. A Case File: From Initial Notice to Judicial Review 761
D. A Simulated Removal Hearing 817
E. Exceptions to Usual Removal Procedures 833
    1. Expedited Removal 833
    2. Criminal Cases 834
        a. Prison Hearings 834
        b. Administrative Removal 836
        c. Judicial Removal 837
    3. In Absentia Removal Hearings 838
    4. Noncitizens Reentering after Prior Removals 839
    5. Crew Members 840

Sec.

E. Exceptions to Usual Removal Procedures—Continued

    6. Terrorist Removal Proceedings 840

    7. Rescission of Adjustment of Status 840

       Notes and Questions 841

CHAPTER 10 Immigration and National Security 843

Sec.

A. The Detention of Noncitizens 844

    1. Detention in Connection with Removal Proceedings 844

    2. The PENTTBOM Investigation 847

      a. Disclosure of Information 850

      b. Monitoring of Attorney–Client Conversations 851

    3. The Certification Program 852

       Notes and Questions 853

    4. Detention of "Unlawful Combatants" 854

       Rasul v. Bush 856

       Notes and Questions 862

B. Intelligence–Gathering 866

    1. The Automated Entry–Exit System 866

    2. NSEERS 867

    3. SEVIS and Other Student–Related Programs 868

    4. US VISIT 870

    5. Voluntary Interviews of Noncitizens 872

    6. "Snitch" Visas and the "Responsible Cooperator" Program 873

       Notes and Questions 874

C. Expansion of Removal Grounds 875

D. Shrinking Procedural Rights 875

    1. Arriving Noncitizens 875

    2. The Terrorist Removal Court 876

       Question 879

    3. Closed Removal Hearings 879

    4. Secret Evidence Hearings 880

    5. Military Tribunals 883

       Notes and Questions 884

E. Visas and Other Overseas Policies 885

    1. Country–Specific Strategies 885

    2. Injecting DHS into the Visa Process 886

    3. Heightened Scrutiny and Delay 886

    4. Technological Innovation 887

    5. Restrictions on the Visa Waiver Program 887

    6. Slowdowns in the Admission of Overseas Refugees 890

F. Enhanced Border Enforcement 890

G. Profiling 891

    Peter H. Schuck, A Case for Profiling 893

    Notes and Questions 895

    Simulation Exercise 899

Sec.

H. Immigration and National Security in Perspective ------------------ 900

    Mark Krikorian, Keeping Terror Out—Immigration Policy and Asymmetric Warfare ------------------ 900

    Muzaffar A. Chishti, Doris Meissner, Demetrios G. Papademetriou, Jay Peterzell, Michael J. Wishnie & Stephen W. Yale–Loehr, Migration Policy Institute, America's Challenge: Domestic Security, Civil Liberties, and National Unity After September 11 (2003) ------------------ 908

    David Cole, The Priority of Morality: The Emergency Constitution's Blind Spot ------------------ 910

    Notes and Questions ------------------ 912

CHAPTER 11 Refugees ------------------ 915

Sec.

A. Overseas Refugees ------------------ 918

    Astri Suhrke, Global Refugee Movements and Strategies of Response in Mary M. Kritz (Ed.), U.S. Immigration and Refugee Policy ------------------ 918

    Robert A. Divine, American Immigration Policy, 1924–1952 ---------- 922

    Guy S. Goodwin–Gill, The Refugee in International Law ------------ 924

    Notes and Questions ------------------ 934

B. Asylum and Nonrefoulement ------------------ 937

    1. Persecution or Fear of Persecution ------------------ 941

        Matter of Acosta ------------------ 941

        Notes and Questions ------------------ 947

        Persecution Versus Prosecution ------------------ 954

        Matter of Izatula ------------------ 954

        Notes and Questions ------------------ 958

        Coercive Population Controls as Persecution ---------------- 959

        Question ------------------ 961

    2. "On Account of Race, Religion, Nationality, Membership in a Particular Social Group, or Political Opinion" ------------------ 962

        a. Race, Religion, Nationality ------------------ 962

        b. Political Opinion ------------------ 964

        INS v. Elias–Zacarias ------------------ 964

        Notes and Questions ------------------ 968

        Neutrality as Political Opinion ------------------ 971

        Notes and Questions ------------------ 974

        Refugees Sur Place ------------------ 976

        c. "Particular Social Group" ------------------ 977

            i. General Definition of "Social Group" ------------------ 978

            Matter of Acosta ------------------ 978

            Sanchez–Trujillo v. INS ------------------ 979

            United States Department of Justice, Proposed Rule ----- 980

            Arthur C. Helton, Persecution on Account of Membership in a Social Group as a Basis for Refugee Status 983

            Notes and Questions ------------------ 984

           ii. Sexual Orientation and "Social Group" ------------------ 989

            Matter of Toboso–Alfonso ------------------ 989

            Notes and Questions ------------------ 992

Sec.

B. Asylum and Nonrefoulement—Continued
    iii. Gender and "Social Group" ---------------------------------- 995
        Jacqueline Greatbatch, The Gender Difference: Feminist Critiques of Refugee Discourse ---------------------- 997
        Notes and Questions ---------------------------------- 999
        Fatin v. INS -- 1000
        Notes and Questions ---------------------------------- 1005
        Matter of Kasinga ---------------------------------- 1008
        Notes and Questions ---------------------------------- 1019
        Domestic Violence and the Problem of the Non–State Actor -- 1025
        Jennifer Moore, From Nation State to Failed State: International Protection From Human Rights Abuses by Non–State Agents -------------------------------- 1028
        Deborah Anker, Refugee Status and Violence Against Women in the "Domestic" Sphere: The Non–State Actor Question --- 1030
        Notes and Questions ---------------------------------- 1035
    d. "On Account Of": The Nexus Requirement ---------------- 1037
        Islam v. Secretary of State for the Home Department ---------- 1042
        Notes and Questions ---------------------------------- 1046
    e. Problems -- 1049
        Problems 1–5 --- 1049
  3. "Well–Founded" Fear and "Would be Threatened": The Standards of Proof --- 1050
      Notes and Questions -- 1051
      Problem 6 -- 1053
  4. Methods of Proof -- 1054
    a. Material Facts --- 1054
        i. Membership in a Persecuted Group ------------------- 1054
        ii. Past Persecution ----------------------------------- 1055
    b. Relevant Evidence -- 1056
        i. The Applicant's Own Testimony ---------------------- 1056
            Damaize–Job v. INS ----------------------------------- 1059
            Notes and Questions --------------------------------- 1061
        ii. State Department Opinions ------------------------- 1063
        iii. Advice from UNHCR -------------------------------- 1066
        iv. Other Sources of Information --------------------- 1067
  5. Exceptions to Eligibility ----------------------------------- 1067
    a. Firm Resettlement --- 1068
    b. Past Wrongdoing --- 1069
        Matter of Carballe ----------------------------------- 1070
        Notes and Questions --------------------------------- 1073
  6. Discretion in Asylum Cases --------------------------------- 1077
  7. Procedure --- 1081
    a. General Principles of United States Asylum Procedure ------- 1082
        Notes and Questions --------------------------------- 1091
    b. Barring or Discouraging Access to the Asylum Process -------- 1095
        i. Filing Deadlines --------------------------------- 1096
        ii. Safe Countries of Origin ----------------------- 1096

Sec.

B. Asylum and Nonrefoulement—Continued
  iii. Returning Asylum–Seekers to Third Countries 1097
  iv. Expedited Removal --- 1103
  v. Detention -- 1106
  vi. Criminal Prosecutions of Asylum–Seekers for Illegal Entry --- 1109
  vii. Denying Employment Authorization------------------- 1110
  viii. Sanctioning Frivolous Applications---------------------- 1111
  ix. Application Fees -- 1111
  x. Preinspection -- 1112
  xi. Visas and Carrier Sanctions ----------------------------- 1112
  xii. Interdiction of Vessels on the High Seas----------------- 1112
    Sale v. Haitian Centers Council------------------------- 1115
    Notes and Questions ------------------------------------- 1130
  8. A Simulated Attorney–Client Asylum Interview------------- 1135
    United States Department of State Country Report on Human Rights Practices -- 1135
    Interviewing a Client, Asylum Law Manual, Center for Applied Legal Studies of Georgetown University Law Center ------------ 1137
C. Beyond Persecution: Protection Against Other Dangers ------------- 1144
  1. The Convention Against Torture ----------------------------- 1145
    Convention Against Torture and Other Cruel, Inhuman or Degrading Treatment or Punishment ----------------------- 1148
    Resolution of the United States Senate Ratifying the Convention Against Torture--- 1151
    Foreign Affairs Reform and Restructuring Act of 1998 ------------ 1153
    Notes and Questions-------------------------------------- 1154
    Problems 7–9 --- 1163
  2. Temporary Protection --- 1164
    a. United States Domestic Law: Temporary Protected Status and its Predecessors -------------------------------- 1164
      Notes and Questions ----------------------------------- 1169
    b. Global and Regional Approaches to Temporary Protection --- 1170
      Joan Fitzpatrick, Temporary Protection of Refugees: Elements of a Formalized Regime ----------------------- 1171
      Notes and Questions ----------------------------------- 1179
  3. Other International Law Protection Mechanisms----------------- 1183
    T.I. v. United Kingdom ----------------------------------- 1183
    Notes and Questions-------------------------------------- 1189

CHAPTER 12   Undocumented Migrants and Law Enforcement-- 1192

Sec.

A. Immigration Offenses --- 1204
B. Employer Misconduct --- 1209
  1. Employer Sanctions --- 1209
    United States General Accounting Office, Immigration Reform—Employer Sanctions and the Question of Discrimination -- 1214
    Problems 1–7 --- 1222
  2. Prohibitions on Discrimination---------------------------------- 1223
    Problems 8–12 -- 1229

Sec.
C. Undocumented Migrants and Public Benefits------------------------------ 1230
   1. The Legal and Social Identities of Undocumented Migrants------ 1230
      Linda S. Bosniak, Exclusion and Membership: The Dual Identity of the Undocumented Worker Under United States Law 1230
      Notes-- 1233
   2. Undocumented Migrants and Public Assistance ------------------ 1234
   3. Undocumented Migrants and Public Education ------------------ 1234
      Plyler v. Doe -- 1235
      Notes and Questions-- 1249
      Proposition 187-- 1251
      Notes and Questions-- 1253
      Post–Secondary Education-------------------------------------- 1256
      Notes and Questions-- 1257
   4. Undocumented Migrants and Drivers' Licenses ------------------ 1258
      Margaret D. Stock, Driver Licenses and National Security: Myths and Reality -- 1261
      Questions-- 1264

CHAPTER 13 Citizenship--- 1265

Sec.
A. Acquiring Citizenship -- 1266
   1. Citizenship Acquired at Birth-------------------------------------- 1267
      a. Jus Soli -- 1267
      b. Jus Sanguinis-- 1269
         Robert A. Mautino, Acquisition of Citizenship ------------ 1271
         Problems 1–3 -- 1272
         Jus Sanguinis and the Constitution -------------------------- 1273
   2. Citizenship Acquired After Birth ---------------------------------- 1276
      a. Administrative Naturalization ------------------------------ 1277
         Citizenship USA -- 1279
         Jana Mason, U.S. Committee for Refugees, Citizenship Under Attack: Congress Investigates Motives Behind INS Initiative -- 1279
         i. Substantive Criteria---------------------------------- 1282
            In Re Petition for Naturalization of Vafaei–Makhsoos--- 1284
            Notes and Questions -------------------------------- 1287
         ii. Procedure -- 1289
      b. The Child Citizenship Act and Other Miscellaneous Forms of Naturalization ------------------------------------ 1291
      c. A Swiss Perspective-- 1293
   3. Dual Nationality -- 1294
   4. Statelessness -- 1297
   5. Who Should Be a United States Citizen?---------------------------- 1297
      Peter H. Schuck & Rogers M. Smith, Citizenship Without Consent—Illegal Aliens in the American Polity ------------------ 1297
      Gerald L. Neuman, Book Review [of Schuck and Smith], Back to Dred Scott? -- 1304
      Notes and Questions-- 1309

Sec.

B. Losing Citizenship --- 1312
   1. Revocation of Naturalization -- 1313
     Kungys v. United States --- 1314
     Notes and Questions --- 1331
   2. Expatriation --- 1333
     Vance v. Terrazas --- 1336
     Later Developments -- 1344
     Notes and Questions --- 1345
C. The Significance of Citizenship --- 1350
   Citizenship and Welfare Reform --- 1353
   Questions --- 1358
   Peter H. Schuck, Membership in the Liberal Polity: The Devaluation of American Citizenship, in William R. Brubaker (Ed.), Immigration and the Politics of Citizenship in Europe and North America --- 1359
   T. Alexander Aleinikoff, Citizens, Aliens, Membership and the Constitution -- 1365
   Notes and Questions --- 1369

INDEX -- 1375

TABLE OF CASES

Principal cases are in bold type. Non-principal cases are in roman type. References are to Pages.

A.A., Matter of, 20 I. & N. Dec. 492, Interim Decision (BIA) 3176 (BIA 1992), 555

Abankwah v. I.N.S., 185 F.3d 18 (2nd Cir. 1999), 1020

Abay v. Ashcroft, 368 F.3d 634 (6th Cir. 2004), 1020, 1022

Abbott Laboratories v. Gardner, 387 U.S. 136, 87 S.Ct. 1507, 18 L.Ed.2d 681 (1967), 480

Abdille v. Ashcroft, 242 F.3d 477 (3rd Cir. 2001), 1068

Abourezk v. Reagan, 785 F.2d 1043, 251 U.S.App.D.C. 355 (D.C.Cir.1986), 484

Abreu–Reyes v. I.N.S., 292 F.3d 1029 (9th Cir.2002), 685

Abudu v. I.N.S., 802 F.2d 1096 (9th Cir. 1986), 592

Acosta, Matter of, 19 I. & N. Dec. 211, Interim Decision (BIA) 2986 (BIA 1985), **941,** 948, 949, 950, 951, **978,** 986, 987, 988, 1005, 1020, 1021, 1037, 1039, 1052, 1054

Acosta v. Ashcroft, 341 F.3d 218 (3rd Cir. 2003), 539

Acosta v. Gaffney, 558 F.2d 1153 (3rd Cir. 1977), 631

Adams v. Howerton, 673 F.2d 1036 (9th Cir.1982), **255,** 258, 259, 260, 261, 262, 267, 269, 270

Adetiba, Matter of, 20 I. & N. Dec. 506, Interim Decision (BIA) 3177 (BIA 1992), 550

Afroyim v. Rusk, 387 U.S. 253, 87 S.Ct. 1660, 18 L.Ed.2d 757 (1967), 1335, 1336, 1345

A.G., Matter of, 19 I. & N. Dec. 502, Interim Decision (BIA) 3040 (BIA 1987), 959

Aguilar, United States v., 883 F.2d 662 (9th Cir.1989), 1206

Aguilera–Cota v. United States I.N.S., 914 F.2d 1375 (9th Cir.1990), 1061

Aguilera–Enriquez v. Immigration and Naturalization Service, 516 F.2d 565 (6th Cir.1975), **658,** 663, 664

Ahmed v. Ashcroft, 341 F.3d 214 (3rd Cir. 2003), 953

Ahmed v. Ashcroft, 286 F.3d 611 (2nd Cir. 2002), 521

Ahmetovic v. I.N.S., 62 F.3d 48 (2nd Cir. 1995), 1073

A.L.A. Schechter Poultry Corporation v. United States, 295 U.S. 495, 55 S.Ct. 837, 79 L.Ed. 1570 (1935), 621

Alderete–Deras, United States v., 743 F.2d 645 (9th Cir.1984), 702

Alexander v. Sandoval, 532 U.S. 275, 121 S.Ct. 1511, 149 L.Ed.2d 517 (2001), 58

Ali v. I.N.S., 661 F.Supp. 1234 (D.Mass.1986), 455

Ali v. Reno, 237 F.3d 591 (6th Cir.2001), 1156

Al–Kateb v. Godwin, [2004] HCA 37 (2004), 206

Allende v. Shultz, 845 F.2d 1111 (1st Cir. 1988), 429

Almario v. Attorney General, 872 F.2d 147 (6th Cir.1989), 278

Al–Salehi v. I.N.S., 47 F.3d 390 (10th Cir. 1995), 1074

Alvarez–Machain, United States v., 504 U.S. 655, 112 S.Ct. 2188, 119 L.Ed.2d 441 (1992), 704

Ambach v. Norwick, 441 U.S. 68, 99 S.Ct. 1589, 60 L.Ed.2d 49 (1979), 1353

American Arab Anti–Discrimination Committee v. Meese, 714 F.Supp. 1060 (C.D.Cal. 1989), 177, 178, 181

American–Arab Anti–Discrimination Committee v. Reno, 70 F.3d 1045 (9th Cir. 1995), 177

American Baptist Churches v. Thornburgh, 760 F.Supp. 796 (N.D.Cal.1991), 1085, 1169

Andazola–Rivas, In re, 23 I. & N. Dec. 319, Interim Decision (BIA) 3467 (BIA 2002), 596

Anderson, Matter of, 16 I. & N. Dec. 596, Interim Decision (BIA) 2669 (BIA 1978), 595

Anderson v. Conboy, 156 F.3d 167 (2nd Cir. 1998), 1224

Andreiu v. Ashcroft, 253 F.3d 477 (9th Cir. 2001), 732, 799, 800, 803

Anetekhai v. I.N.S., 876 F.2d 1218 (5th Cir. 1989), 278

Angco v. Haig, 514 F.Supp. 1328 (E.D.Pa. 1981), 248

Application of (see name of party)

Arauz v. Rivkind, 845 F.2d 271 (11th Cir. 1988), 1073, 1074

Ardestani v. I.N.S., 502 U.S. 129, 112 S.Ct. 515, 116 L.Ed.2d 496 (1991), 667

Arguelles–Campos, In re, 22 I. & N. Dec. 811, Interim Decision (BIA) 3399 (BIA 1999), 619

Arguelles–Vasquez v. I.N.S., 786 F.2d 1433 (9th Cir.1986), 701

Arrozal v. I.N.S., 159 F.3d 429 (9th Cir.1998), 604

Artee Corporation, Matter of, 18 I. & N. Dec. 366, Interim Decision 2934 (INS 1982), **372,** 374, 375, 376

A–S–, In re, 21 I. & N. Dec. 1106, Interim Decision (BIA) 3336 (BIA 1998), 1058

Assaad, In re, 23 I. & N. Dec. 553, Interim Decision (BIA) 3487 (BIA 2003), 683, 685

Attorney–General of Canada and Ward, In re, 103 D.L.R.4th 1 (S.C.C.1993), 969, 986

Attorney–General for Canada v. Cain [1906] A.C. 542 (Privy Council), 236

Ayala–Arevalo, In re, 22 I. & N. Dec. 398, Interim Decision (BIA) 3371 (BIA 1998), 436

Azizi v. Thornburgh, 908 F.2d 1130 (2nd Cir.1990), 278

Baehr v. Lewin, 74 Haw. 530, 74 Haw. 645, 852 P.2d 44 (Hawai'i 1993), 261

Baehr v. Miike, 1996 WL 694235 (Hawai'i Cir.Ct.1996), 261

Baker v. Carr, 369 U.S. 186, 82 S.Ct. 691, 7 L.Ed.2d 663 (1962), 190

Balasubramanrim v. I.N.S., 143 F.3d 157 (3rd Cir.1998), 1061

Baldwin v. Hale, 68 U.S. 223, 17 L.Ed. 531 (1863), 142

Baliza v. I.N.S., 709 F.2d 1231 (9th Cir.1983), 685

Balsys, United States v., 524 U.S. 666, 118 S.Ct. 2218, 141 L.Ed.2d 575 (1998), 704

Balzac v. Porto Rico, 258 U.S. 298, 42 S.Ct. 343, 66 L.Ed. 627 (1922), 140

Bark v. Immigration and Naturalization Service, 511 F.2d 1200 (9th Cir.1975), 270

Barker v. Ashcroft, 382 F.3d 313 (3rd Cir. 2003), 737

Barraza Rivera v. I.N.S., 913 F.2d 1443 (9th Cir.1990), 963

Bejjani v. I.N.S., 271 F.3d 670 (6th Cir.2001), 800, 803

Belenzo, Matter of, 17 I. & N. Dec. 374, Interim Decision 2793 (BIA & A.G. 1980 & 1981), 842

Beltran–Zavala v. I.N.S., 912 F.2d 1027 (9th Cir.1990), 1074

Benitez, Matter of, 19 I. & N. Dec. 173, Interim Decision (BIA) 2979 (BIA 1984), 714

Berdo v. Immigration and Naturalization Service, 432 F.2d 824 (6th Cir.1970), 433

Berehe v. I.N.S., 114 F.3d 159 (10th Cir. 1997), 734

Berlin Democratic Club v. Rumsfeld, 410 F.Supp. 144 (D.D.C.1976), 483

Bernal v. Fainter, 467 U.S. 216, 104 S.Ct. 2312, 81 L.Ed.2d 175 (1984), 1352

Bhagat Singh Thind, United States v., 261 U.S. 204, 43 S.Ct. 338, 67 L.Ed. 616 (1923), 1282

Bhandari v. First Nat. Bank of Commerce, 829 F.2d 1343 (5th Cir.1987), 1224

Bhupinder Sigh Kamboi, Matter of, A27 887 288 (BIA 1989), 1080

Bilbao–Bastida, Matter of, 11 I. & N. Dec. 615, Interim Decision (BIA) 1586 (BIA 1966), 717

Blancas–Lara, In re, 23 I. & N. Dec. 458, Interim Decision (BIA) 3477 (BIA 2002), 580

Blanco v. I.N.S., 68 F.3d 642 (2nd Cir.1995), 602

Blanco–Comarribas v. I.N.S., 830 F.2d 1039 (9th Cir.1987), 1061

Blazina v. Bouchard, 286 F.2d 507 (3rd Cir. 1961), 938

Board of Regents of State Colleges v. Roth, 408 U.S. 564, 92 S.Ct. 2701, 33 L.Ed.2d 548 (1972), 143

Bolanos–Hernandez v. I.N.S., 767 F.2d 1277 (9th Cir.1984), 950, 973, 974, 975

Bolling v. Sharpe, 347 U.S. 497, 74 S.Ct. 693, 98 L.Ed. 884 (1954), 171

Booker, United States v., 125 S.Ct. 738, 160 L.Ed.2d 621 (2005), 554

Borrero v. Aljets, 325 F.3d 1003 (8th Cir. 2003), 207

Botezatu v. I.N.S., 195 F.3d 311 (7th Cir. 1999), 617, 740

Boutilier v. Immigration and Naturalization Service, 387 U.S. 118, 87 S.Ct. 1563, 18 L.Ed.2d 661 (1967), 259

Bowers v. Hardwick, 478 U.S. 186, 106 S.Ct. 2841, 92 L.Ed.2d 140 (1986), 267

Brandenburg v. Ohio, 395 U.S. 444, 89 S.Ct. 1827, 23 L.Ed.2d 430 (1969), 177, 179, 432

Brignoni–Ponce, United States v., 422 U.S. 873, 95 S.Ct. 2574, 45 L.Ed.2d 607 (1975), 701

Brownell v. Tom We Shung, 352 U.S. 180, 77 S.Ct. 252, 1 L.Ed.2d 225 (1956), 481

Bugajewitz v. Adams, 228 U.S. 585, 33 S.Ct. 607, 57 L.Ed. 978 (1913), 499, 500, 631

Bulk Farms, Inc. v. Martin, 963 F.2d 1286 (9th Cir.1992), 307

Burrafato v. United States Dept. of State, 523 F.2d 554 (2nd Cir.1975), 483

Bustos–Torres v. I.N.S., 898 F.2d 1053 (5th Cir.1990), 637, 641, 685, 702

Cabell v. Chavez–Salido, 454 U.S. 432, 102 S.Ct. 735, 70 L.Ed.2d 677 (1982), 1353

Cabral–Avila v. Immigration and Naturalization Service, 589 F.2d 957 (9th Cir.1978), 716

Calcano–Martinez v. I.N.S., 533 U.S. 348, 121 S.Ct. 2268, 150 L.Ed.2d 392 (2001), 734, 735

Campos–Asencio, United States v., 822 F.2d 506 (5th Cir.1987), 663

Canas–Segovia v. I.N.S., 970 F.2d 599 (9th Cir.1992), 951, 963, 969

Canjura–Flores v. I.N.S., 784 F.2d 885 (9th Cir.1985), 1061

Carballe, Matter of, 19 I. & N. Dec. 357, Interim Decision (BIA) 3007 (BIA 1986), **1070,** 1073, 1074

Carrillo, Matter of, 17 I. & N. Dec. 30, Interim Decision (BIA) 2717 (BIA 1979), 703

Carty v. Ashcroft, 395 F.3d 1081 (9th Cir. 2005), 735

Castellano–Chacon v. I.N.S., 341 F.3d 533 (6th Cir.2003), 986

Castrinakis, Petition of, 179 F.Supp. 444 (D.Md.1959), 1288

Castro–Louzan, United States ex rel. v. Zimmerman, 94 F.Supp. 22 (E.D.Pa.1950), 663

Castro–O'Ryan v. United States Dept. of Immigration and Naturalization, 847 F.2d 1307 (9th Cir.1987), 664, 1093

Cato v. I.N.S., 84 F.3d 597 (2nd Cir.1996), 579

Center for Nat. Sec. Studies v. United States Dept. of Justice, 331 F.3d 918, 356 U.S.App.D.C. 333 (D.C.Cir.2003), 848, 849, 851

Chae Chan Ping v. United States (The Chinese Exclusion Case), 130 U.S. 581, 9 S.Ct. 623, 32 L.Ed. 1068 (1889), **108,** 111, 113, 115, 116, 117, 121, 122, 124, 132, 137, 139, 141, 144, 236

Chang, Matter of, 20 I. & N. Dec. 38, Interim Decision (BIA) 3107 (BIA 1989), 959, 960, 961

Chaunt v. United States, 364 U.S. 350, 81 S.Ct. 147, 5 L.Ed.2d 120 (1960), 1332

Chavez–Ramirez v. I.N.S., 792 F.2d 932 (9th Cir.1986), 521

Chen, Matter of, 20 I. & N. Dec. 16, Interim Decision (BIA) 3104 (BIA 1989), 947, 1055, 1056

Chen, United States v., 2 F.3d 330 (9th Cir. 1993), 1132

Chen v. United States I.N.S., 195 F.3d 198 (4th Cir.1999), 961

Cheng Fan Kwok v. Immigration and Naturalization Service, 392 U.S. 206, 88 S.Ct. 1970, 20 L.Ed.2d 1037 (1968), 760

Chen Zhou Chai v. Carroll, 48 F.3d 1331 (4th Cir.1995), 509

Chevron U.S.A., Inc. v. Natural Resources Defense Council, Inc., 467 U.S. 837, 104 S.Ct. 2778, 81 L.Ed.2d 694 (1984), 503, 550, 559, 560

Chew Heong v. United States, 112 U.S. 536, 5 S.Ct. 255, 28 L.Ed. 770 (1884), 116, 117

Chiaramonte v. Immigration and Naturalization Service, 626 F.2d 1093 (2nd Cir. 1980), 285

Chiles v. United States, 69 F.3d 1094 (11th Cir.1995), 1255

Chinese Community Center, Matter of, 91–INA–99 (BALCA 1991), 306

Ching and Chen, Matter of, 19 I. & N. Dec. 203, Interim Decision (BIA) 2984 (BIA 1984), **505,** 509, 510

Cho v. Immigration and Naturalization Service, 649 F.2d 867 (9th Cir.1981), 603

Chong Shin Chen v. Ashcroft, 378 F.3d 1081 (9th Cir.2004), 725

Chow v. I.N.S., 113 F.3d 659 (7th Cir.1997), 588

Christopher, United States v., 239 F.3d 1191 (11th Cir.2001), 563

Chy Lung v. Freeman, 92 U.S. 275, 2 Otto 275, 23 L.Ed. 550 (1875), 119, 120, 1253

Cisneros–Gonzalez, Matter of, 23 I. & N. Dec. 668, Interim Decision (BIA) 3500 (BIA 2004), 581

City of (see name of city)

Clark v. Martinez, 125 S.Ct. 716, 160 L.Ed.2d 734 (2005), 158, **208,** 210, 230, 231, 756

Cleanex House Cleaning Service, Inc., Matter of, No. 2003–INA–208 (BALCA 2004), 307

Collado–Munoz, In re, 21 I. & N. Dec. 1061, Interim Decision (BIA) 3333 (BIA 1998), 523, 524

Collins Foods Intern., Inc. v. United States I.N.S., 948 F.2d 549 (9th Cir.1991), 1210, 1211

Columbus Hospital, Matter of, 95–INA–282 (BALCA 1996), 320

Consolo v. Federal Maritime Commission, 383 U.S. 607, 86 S.Ct. 1018, 16 L.Ed.2d 131 (1966), 711

Contopoulos, Matter of, 10 I. & N. Dec. 654, Interim Decision 1370 (INS 1964), 374

Cornejo–Merida v. Ashcroft, 2004 WL 2712643 (9th Cir.2004), 994

Corona–Palomera v. Immigration and Naturalization Service, 661 F.2d 814 (9th Cir. 1981), 714

Correa v. Thornburgh, 901 F.2d 1166 (2nd Cir.1990), 510

Cortes–Castillo v. I.N.S., 997 F.2d 1199 (7th Cir.1993), 576

Cortez, Matter of, 16 I. & N. Dec. 289, Interim Decision (BIA) 2603 (BIA 1977), 184, 717

Cote, Matter of, 17 I. & N. Dec. 336, Interim Decision (BIA) 2783 (BIA 1980), 358

Council of Civil Service Unions v. Minister for the Civil Service [1984] 3 All E.R. 935 (HL 1984), 237

Crammond, In re, 23 I. & N. Dec. 9, Interim Decision (BIA) 3443 (BIA 2001), 554

Cubillos–Gonzalez v. Immigration and Naturalization Service, Los Angeles, Cal., 352 F.2d 782 (9th Cir.1965), 403

Cuello, Matter of, 20 I. & N. Dec. 94, Interim Decision (BIA) 3117 (BIA 1989), 289

Cunanan v. I.N.S., 856 F.2d 1373 (9th Cir. 1988), 686

Curtiss–Wright Export Corporation, United States v., 299 U.S. 304, 57 S.Ct. 216, 81 L.Ed. 255 (1936), 118, 119

C.V.T., In re, 22 I. & N. Dec. 7, Interim Decision (BIA) 3342 (BIA 1998), 580

C.Y.Z., In re, 21 I. & N. Dec. 915, Interim Decision (BIA) 3319 (BIA 1997), 960, 1055

Dalton v. Ashcroft, 257 F.3d 200 (2nd Cir. 2001), 734

Damaize–Job v. I.N.S., 787 F.2d 1332 (9th Cir.1986), **1059,** 1061, 1062

Dass, Matter of, 20 I. & N. Dec. 120, Interim Decision (BIA) 3122 (BIA 1989), 1062

Dastmalchi v. Immigration and Naturalization Service, 660 F.2d 880 (3rd Cir.1981), 717

Dataphase Systems, Inc. v. C L Systems, Inc., 640 F.2d 109 (8th Cir.1981), 800

Dawood–Haio v. I.N.S., 800 F.2d 90 (6th Cir. 1986), 1057

DeCanas v. Bica, 424 U.S. 351, 96 S.Ct. 933, 47 L.Ed.2d 43 (1976), 119, 1352

De Leon v. I.N.S., 115 F.3d 643 (9th Cir. 1997), 732

De Leon–Reynoso v. Ashcroft, 293 F.3d 633 (3rd Cir.2002), 184, 436

Delgadillo v. Carmichael, 332 U.S. 388, 68 S.Ct. 10, 92 L.Ed. 17 (1947), 520

De Los Santos v. I.N.S., 690 F.2d 56 (2nd Cir.1982), 284

Del Rosario, United States v., 902 F.2d 55, 284 U.S.App.D.C. 90 (D.C.Cir.1990), 680

Demore v. Kim, 538 U.S. 510, 123 S.Ct. 1708, 155 L.Ed.2d 724 (2003), 163, 186, 204, **211,** 229, 230, 231, 636, 740, 756, 835, 845, 847

Dennis v. United States, 341 U.S. 494, 71 S.Ct. 857, 95 L.Ed. 1137 (1951), 168, 176, 177

Department of Commerce v. United States House of Representatives, 525 U.S. 316, 119 S.Ct. 765, 142 L.Ed.2d 797 (1999), 1233

Desir v. Ilchert, 840 F.2d 723 (9th Cir.1988), 948, 970

Detroit Free Press v. Ashcroft, 303 F.3d 681 (6th Cir.2002), 880

De Valle v. I.N.S., 901 F.2d 787 (9th Cir. 1990), 988, 1051

Devison, Matter of, 22 I. & N. Dec. 1362, Interim Decision (BIA) 3435 (BIA 2000), 538

Diallo v. I.N.S., 232 F.3d 279 (2nd Cir.2000), 1058

Diaz v. Pan Am. World Airways, Inc., 442 F.2d 385 (5th Cir.1971), 304

Diaz–Escobar v. I.N.S., 782 F.2d 1488 (9th Cir.1986), 975

Dillingham v. I.N.S., 267 F.3d 996 (9th Cir. 2001), 184, 540

Di Pasquale v. Karnuth, 158 F.2d 878 (2nd Cir.1947), 520

Discipio v. Ashcroft, 369 F.3d 472 (5th Cir. 2004), 539

Disu v. Ashcroft, 338 F.3d 13 (1st Cir.2003), 725

D–J–, In re, 23 I. & N. Dec. 572, Interim Decision 3488 (A.G. 2003), 846, 941, 1108

Dominguez v. Ashcroft, 336 F.3d 678 (8th Cir.2003), 814

Downes v. Bidwell, 182 U.S. 244, 21 S.Ct. 770, 45 L.Ed. 1088 (1901), 140

Drakes v. Zimski, 240 F.3d 246 (3rd Cir. 2001), 734

Dred Scott v. Sandford, 60 U.S. 393, 19 How. 393, 15 L.Ed. 691 (1856), 1268

Dunar, Matter of, 14 I. & N. Dec. 310, Interim Decision (BIA) 2192 (BIA 1973), 1050, 1051

D.V., In re, 21 I. & N. Dec. 77, Interim Decision (BIA) 3252 (BIA 1993), 1008

Echeverria–Hernandez v. United States I.N.S., 923 F.2d 688 (9th Cir.1991), 1182

Edwards v. People of State of California, 314 U.S. 160, 62 S.Ct. 164, 86 L.Ed. 119 (1941), 105

E.E.O.C. v. Premier Operator Services, Inc., 113 F.Supp.2d 1066 (N.D.Tex.2000), 59

Ekiu v. United States, 142 U.S. 651, 12 S.Ct. 336, 35 L.Ed. 1146 (1892), **122,** 124, 137, 140, 144, 158, 236

Elder, United States v., 601 F.Supp. 1574 (S.D.Tex.1985), 1206

Elias v. United States Dept. of State, 721 F.Supp. 243 (N.D.Cal.1989), 1274, 1275

Elk v. Wilkins, 112 U.S. 94, 5 S.Ct. 41, 28 L.Ed. 643 (1884), 1268

Ellis v. Carter, 291 F.2d 270 (9th Cir.1961), 602

El Rescate Legal Services, Inc. v. Executive Office of Immigration Review, 941 F.2d 950 (9th Cir.1991), 162

El Rescate Legal Services, Inc. v. Executive Office of Immigration Review, 959 F.2d 742 (9th Cir.1991), 641, 1087

Escobar–Ramos v. I.N.S., 927 F.2d 482 (9th Cir.1991), 684

Escobar Ruiz v. I.N.S., 838 F.2d 1020 (9th Cir.1988), 667

Eslamizar, In re, 23 I. & N. Dec. 684, Interim Decision (BIA) 3502 (BIA 2004), 532

Esperdy, United States ex rel. Piperkoff v., 267 F.2d 72 (2nd Cir.1959), 551

Espinoza v. Farah Mfg. Co., Inc., 414 U.S. 86, 94 S.Ct. 334, 38 L.Ed.2d 287 (1973), 1224

Espinoza–Franco v. Ashcroft, 394 F.3d 461 (7th Cir.2005), 560

Estime, Matter of, 19 I. & N. Dec. 450, Interim Decision (BIA) 3029 (BIA 1987), 457

Estrada v. I.N.S., 775 F.2d 1018 (9th Cir. 1985), 1062

Estrada–Posadas v. United States I.N.S., 924 F.2d 916 (9th Cir.1991), 987, 988

Examining Bd. of Engineers, Architects and Surveyors v. Flores de Otero, 426 U.S. 572, 96 S.Ct. 2264, 49 L.Ed.2d 65 (1976), 1352

Falcon Carriche v. Ashcroft, 335 F.3d 1009 (9th Cir.2003), 725

Fatin v. I.N.S., 12 F.3d 1233 (3rd Cir.1993), 986, **1000,** 1006, 1007, 1020, 1021, 1037, 1046

Fedorenko v. United States, 449 U.S. 490, 101 S.Ct. 737, 66 L.Ed.2d 686 (1981), 1331

Felzcerek v. I.N.S., 75 F.3d 112 (2nd Cir. 1996), 685

Feroz v. I.N.S., 22 F.3d 225 (9th Cir.1994), 1074

Fiallo v. Bell, 430 U.S. 787, 97 S.Ct. 1473, 52 L.Ed.2d 50 (1977), 174, 175, 176, 181, 183, 231, 283

Fidalgo/Velez v. I.N.S., 697 F.2d 1026 (11th Cir.1983), 583

Finau v. I.N.S., 277 F.3d 1146 (9th Cir.2002), 436

Firestone v. Howerton, 671 F.2d 317 (9th Cir.1982), 433

Fisher v. I.N.S., 79 F.3d 955 (9th Cir.1996), 1007

Flemming v. Nestor, 363 U.S. 603, 80 S.Ct. 1367, 4 L.Ed.2d 1435 (1960), 1352

Flores v. Bowen, 790 F.2d 740 (9th Cir.1986), 356

Foley v. Connelie, 435 U.S. 291, 98 S.Ct. 1067, 55 L.Ed.2d 287 (1978), 1353

Fong, Matter of, 17 I. & N. Dec. 212, Interim Decision (BIA) 2749 (BIA 1980), 286

Fong Haw Tan v. Phelan, 333 U.S. 6, 68 S.Ct. 374, 92 L.Ed. 433 (1948), **501,** 503, 594

Fong Yue Ting v. United States, 149 U.S. 698, 13 S.Ct. 1016, 37 L.Ed. 905 (1893), 117, **124,** 137, 139, 140, 142, 144, 153, 156, 161, 162, 180, 236, 631, 701

Francis v. Immigration and Naturalization Service, 532 F.2d 268 (2nd Cir. 1976), **181,** 183, 184, 231, 576, 577, 578, 579

Franklin v. I.N.S., 72 F.3d 571 (8th Cir.1995), 548

Frentescu, Matter of, 18 I. & N. Dec. 244, Interim Decision (BIA) 2906 (BIA 1982), 1073, 1074

G., Matter of, 20 I. & N. Dec. 764, Interim Decision (BIA) 3215 (BIA 1993), 508

G.A., Matter of, 7 I. & N. Dec. 274, Interim Decision (BIA) 808 (BIA 1956), 575, 576, 579

Gagnon v. Scarpelli, 411 U.S. 778, 93 S.Ct. 1756, 36 L.Ed.2d 656 (1973), 663, 664

Galvan v. Press, 347 U.S. 522, 74 S.Ct. 737, 98 L.Ed. 911 (1954), 174, 183, 237

Garberding v. I.N.S., 30 F.3d 1187 (9th Cir. 1994), 184

Garcia, Matter of, 17 I. & N. Dec. 319, Interim Decision (BIA) 2778 (BIA 1980), 702

Garcia–Garrocho, Matter of, 19 I. & N. Dec. 423, Interim Decision (BIA) 3022 (BIA 1986), 1074, 1075

Garcia–Lopez v. Ashcroft, 334 F.3d 840 (9th Cir.2003), 559

Garcia–Martinez v. Ashcroft, 371 F.3d 1066 (9th Cir.2004), 1047

Garner, Matter of, 15 I. & N. Dec. 215, Interim Decision (BIA) 2357 (BIA 1975), 285

Gastelum–Quinones v. Kennedy, 374 U.S. 469, 83 S.Ct. 1819, 10 L.Ed.2d 1013 (1963), 433

Gault, Application of, 387 U.S. 1, 87 S.Ct. 1428, 18 L.Ed.2d 527 (1967), 664, 702

Gebremichael v. I.N.S., 10 F.3d 28 (1st Cir. 1993), 986, 988

Gegiow v. Uhl, 239 U.S. 3, 36 S.Ct. 2, 60 L.Ed. 114 (1915), 421

Gharadaghi, Matter of, 19 I. & N. Dec. 311, Interim Decision (BIA) 3001 (BIA 1985), 1077

Gideon v. Wainwright, 372 U.S. 335, 83 S.Ct. 792, 9 L.Ed.2d 799 (1963), 663

Gill v. Ashcroft, 335 F.3d 574 (7th Cir.2003), 539

Git Foo Wong v. Immigration and Naturalization Service, 358 F.2d 151 (9th Cir. 1966), 520

Gjonaj v. I.N.S., 47 F.3d 824 (6th Cir.1995), 579

G–N–C–, In re, 22 I. & N. Dec. 281, Interim Decision (BIA) 3366 (BIA 1998), 617

Golden Jade Restaurant, Matter of, 88–INA–342 (BALCA 1989), 303

Gomez v. I.N.S., 947 F.2d 660 (2nd Cir.1991), 986

Gomez–Lopez v. Ashcroft, 391 F.3d 1109 (9th Cir.2004), 736

Gonzales–Vela, United States v., 276 F.3d 763 (6th Cir.2001), 554

Gonzalez, Matter of, 19 I. & N. Dec. 682, Interim Decision (BIA) 3071 (BIA 1988), 1074

Gonzalez v. Reno, 212 F.3d 1338 (11th Cir. 2000), 1088

Gonzalez–Oropeza v. United States Atty. Gen., 321 F.3d 1331 (11th Cir.2003), 587

Gonzalez–Rivera v. I.N.S., 22 F.3d 1441 (9th Cir.1994), 702

Gonzalez–Sandoval v. United States I.N.S., 910 F.2d 614 (9th Cir.1990), 550

Goodridge v. Department of Public Health, 440 Mass. 309, 798 N.E.2d 941 (Mass. 2003), 262

Gorbach v. Reno, 2001 WL 34145464 (W.D.Wash.2001), 1314

Gorbach v. Reno, 219 F.3d 1087 (9th Cir. 2000), 1314

Graham v. Richardson, 403 U.S. 365, 91 S.Ct. 1848, 29 L.Ed.2d 534 (1971), 1352, 1358

Graham, Matter of, 88–INA–102 (BALCA 1990), **298,** 302, 304, 305

Graham, United States v., 169 F.3d 787 (3rd Cir.1999), 563

Granados, Matter of, 16 I. & N. Dec. 726, Interim Decision (BIA) 2701 (BIA 1979), 577, 578

Greyhound Lines v. INS, Civ. No. 95–1608(NHJ) (D.D.C.1995), 358

Griffin v. California, 380 U.S. 609, 85 S.Ct. 1229, 14 L.Ed.2d 106 (1965), 716

Griffiths, Application of, 413 U.S. 717, 93 S.Ct. 2851, 37 L.Ed.2d 910 (1973), 1352

Griggs v. Duke Power Co., 401 U.S. 424, 91 S.Ct. 849, 28 L.Ed.2d 158 (1971), 1227

Griswold v. Connecticut, 381 U.S. 479, 85 S.Ct. 1678, 14 L.Ed.2d 510 (1965), 113

Guantanamo Detainee Cases, In re, 355 F.Supp.2d 443 (D.D.C.2005), 864

Guerrero–Perez v. I.N.S., 242 F.3d 727 (7th Cir.2001), 554, 734

Guevara, Matter of, 20 I. & N. Dec. 238, Interim Decision (BIA) 3143 (BIA 1990), 716

Guinac v. I.N.S., 179 F.3d 1156 (9th Cir. 1999), 952

Gunaydin v. United States I.N.S., 742 F.2d 776 (3rd Cir.1984), 527

Gur, Matter of, 16 I. & N. Dec. 123, Interim Decision (BIA) 2560 (BIA 1977), 285, 286

Guzman–Landeros, United States v., 207 F.3d 1034 (8th Cir.2000), 561

Hall v. McLaughlin, 864 F.2d 868, 275 U.S.App.D.C. 46 (D.C.Cir.1989), 307

Hamdi v. Rumsfeld, 124 S.Ct. 2633, 159 L.Ed.2d 578 (2004), 862, 863, 865

Hamid v. Immigration & Naturalization Service, 648 F.2d 635 (9th Cir.1981), 603

Hampton v. Mow Sun Wong, 426 U.S. 88, 96 S.Ct. 1895, 48 L.Ed.2d 495 (1976), 1352

Harisiades v. Shaughnessy, 342 U.S. 580, 72 S.Ct. 512, 96 L.Ed. 586 (1952), **163,** 171, 172, 174, 176, 177, 179, 180, 183, 237, 570, 1370

Hathaway Childrens Services, Matter of, 91–INA–388 (BALCA 1994), 320

He v. Ashcroft, 328 F.3d 593 (9th Cir.2003), 641

Head Money Cases, 112 U.S. 580, 5 S.Ct. 247, 28 L.Ed. 798 (1884), 105, 124

Healy and Goodchild, Matter of, 17 I. & N. Dec. 22, Interim Decision (BIA) 2716 (BIA 1979), **394,** 397

Heckler v. Chaney, 470 U.S. 821, 105 S.Ct. 1649, 84 L.Ed.2d 714 (1985), 482

Hee Yung Ahn v. Immigration & Naturalization Service, 651 F.2d 1285 (9th Cir.1981), **597,** 601, 603, 604

Heitland v. Immigration and Naturalization Service, 551 F.2d 495 (2nd Cir.1977), 583

Henderson v. Mayor of City of New York, 92 U.S. 259, 2 Otto 259, 23 L.Ed. 543 (1875), 105, 119, 120, 1253

Hermina Sague v. United States, 416 F.Supp. 217 (D.Puerto Rico 1976), **475,** 479, 480, 481, 482

Hernandez–Casillas, Matter of, 20 I. & N. Dec. 262, Interim Decision 3147 (BIA & A.G. 1990), 577, 579

Hernandez–Cordero v. U.S. I.N.S., 819 F.2d 558 (5th Cir.1987), 604

Hernandez–Guadarrama v. Ashcroft, 394 F.3d 674 (9th Cir.2005), 685, 686

Hernandez–Herrera, United States v., 273 F.3d 1213 (9th Cir.2001), 510

Hernandez–Montiel v. I.N.S., 225 F.3d 1084 (9th Cir.2000), 980, 987

Hernandez–Ortiz v. I.N.S., 777 F.2d 509 (9th Cir.1985), 950, 1078

Hill v. Lockhart, 474 U.S. 52, 106 S.Ct. 366, 88 L.Ed.2d 203 (1985), 678

Hill v. I.N.S., 714 F.2d 1470 (9th Cir.1983), 260

Hira, Matter of, 11 I. & N. Dec. 824, Interim Decision (BIA) 1647 (BIA 1966), 357, 358

H–M–V–, In re, 22 I. & N. Dec. 256, Interim Decision (BIA) 3365 (BIA 1998), 1148, 1157

Ho, Matter of, 19 I. & N. Dec. 582, Interim Decision (BIA) 3051 (BIA 1988), 457

Hoffman Plastic Compounds, Inc. v. N.L.R.B., 535 U.S. 137, 122 S.Ct. 1275, 152 L.Ed.2d 271 (2002), 1202, 1203

Hosseinpour, Matter of, 15 I. & N. Dec. 191, Interim Decision (BIA) 2349 (BIA 1975), 404

Iao v. Gonzales, 400 F.3d 530 (7th Cir.2005), 720

Iavorski v. United States I.N.S., 232 F.3d 124 (2nd Cir.2000), 726

Idowu, United States v., 105 F.3d 728, 323 U.S.App.D.C. 114 (D.C.Cir.1997), 1205

Ignacio v. I.N.S., 955 F.2d 295 (5th Cir.1992), 803

Industrial Holographics, Inc. v. Donovan, 722 F.2d 1362 (7th Cir.1983), **316,** 319, 320

Information Industries, Matter of, 88–INA–82 (BALCA 1989), 303, 304, 306

In re (see name of party)

I.N.S. v. Abudu, 485 U.S. 94, 108 S.Ct. 904, 99 L.Ed.2d 90 (1988), 592, 705, 726

I.N.S. v. Aguirre–Aguirre, 526 U.S. 415, 119 S.Ct. 1439, 143 L.Ed.2d 590 (1999), 812, 814, 1075

I.N.S. v. Cardoza–Fonseca, 480 U.S. 421, 107 S.Ct. 1207, 94 L.Ed.2d 434 (1987), 1051, 1053

I.N.S. v. Chadha, 462 U.S. 919, 103 S.Ct. 2764, 77 L.Ed.2d 317 (1983), **186,** 190, 191, 204, 231, 605, 760

I.N.S. v. Doherty, 502 U.S. 314, 112 S.Ct. 719, 116 L.Ed.2d 823 (1992), 1080

I.N.S. v. Elias–Zacarias, 502 U.S. 478, 112 S.Ct. 812, 117 L.Ed.2d 38 (1992), **964,** 968, 969, 970, 976, 1037, 1038

I.N.S. v. Jong Ha Wang, 450 U.S. 139, 101 S.Ct. 1027, 67 L.Ed.2d 123 (1981), **588,** 592, 594, 595, 596, 597, 603, 604

I.N.S. v. Lopez–Mendoza, 468 U.S. 1032, 104 S.Ct. 3479, 82 L.Ed.2d 778 (1984), **686,** 700, 701, 702, 704, 705

I.N.S. v. Miranda, 459 U.S. 14, 103 S.Ct. 281, 74 L.Ed.2d 12 (1982), 631, 632, 705

I.N.S. v. Orlando Ventura, 537 U.S. 12, 123 S.Ct. 353, 154 L.Ed.2d 272 (2002), 1053

I.N.S. v. Phinpathya, 464 U.S. 183, 104 S.Ct. 584, 78 L.Ed.2d 401 (1984), 583, 584, 705

I.N.S. v. Rios–Pineda, 471 U.S. 444, 105 S.Ct. 2098, 85 L.Ed.2d 452 (1985), 592, 815

I.N.S. v. St. Cyr, 533 U.S. 289, 121 S.Ct. 2271, 150 L.Ed.2d 347 (2001), 121, 230, 503, 734, **746,** 755, 756, 757

I.N.S. v. Stevic, 467 U.S. 407, 104 S.Ct. 2489, 81 L.Ed.2d 321 (1984), 1051, 1053

I.N.S. v. Yueh–Shaio Yang, 519 U.S. 26, 117 S.Ct. 350, 136 L.Ed.2d 288 (1996), 527

International Union of Bricklayers and Allied Craftsmen v. Meese, 616 F.Supp. 1387 (N.D.Cal.1985), **348,** 356, 357, 503

Iran v. Immigration and Naturalization Service, 656 F.2d 469 (9th Cir.1981), 714

Islam (A.P.) v. Secretary of State for the Home Department, [1999] 2 A.C. 629, [1999] 2 All E.R. 545, [1999] 2 W.L.R. 1015 (U.K.1999), 986, 988, **1042**

Itzcovitz v. Selective Service Local Bd. No. 6, New York, N. Y., 447 F.2d 888 (2nd Cir. 1971), 520

Izatula, Matter of, 20 I. & N. Dec. 149, Interim Decision (BIA) 3127 (BIA 1990), 952, **954,** 958, 962, 968, 969, 975

Jahed v. I.N.S., 356 F.3d 991 (9th Cir.2004), 1047

Jama v. Immigration and Customs Enforcement, 125 S.Ct. 694, 160 L.Ed.2d 708 (2005), 624

Janvier v. United States, 793 F.2d 449 (2nd Cir.1986), 551

Jean v. Nelson, 727 F.2d 957 (11th Cir.1984), 176

Jenkins v. I.N.S., 32 F.3d 11 (2nd Cir.1994), 803

Jewell, United States v., 532 F.2d 697 (9th Cir.1976), 1211

Jie Lin v. Ashcroft, 377 F.3d 1014 (9th Cir. 2004), 988

J–J–, In re, 21 I. & N. Dec. 976, Interim Decision (BIA) 3323 (BIA 1997), 796

Jobson v. Ashcroft, 326 F.3d 367 (2nd Cir. 2003), 503, 561

Johnson, Matter of, No. A72 370 565 (IJ 1995), 1022

Jordan v. De George, 341 U.S. 223, 71 S.Ct. 703, 95 L.Ed. 886 (1951), 546

Joseph, In re, 22 I. & N. Dec. 799, Interim Decision (BIA) 3398 (BIA 1999), 224

Jubilado v. United States, 819 F.2d 210 (9th Cir.1987), 520

Kahane v. Secretary of State, 700 F.Supp. 1162 (D.D.C.1988), 1347

Kahane v. Shultz, 653 F.Supp. 1486 (E.D.N.Y.1987), 1347

Karmali v. United States I.N.S., 707 F.2d 408 (9th Cir.1983), **378,** 380

Karouni v. Gonzales, 399 F.3d 1163 (9th Cir. 2005), 995

Kasinga, In re, 21 I. & N. Dec. 357, Interim Decision (BIA) 3278 (BIA 1996), 952, **1008,** 1019, 1020, 1022, 1023, 1024, 1025, 1037, 1039

Kasravi v. Immigration and Naturalization Service, 400 F.2d 675 (9th Cir.1968), 1065

Kawakita v. United States, 343 U.S. 717, 72 S.Ct. 950, 96 L.Ed. 1249 (1952), 1296

Kellogg, United States ex rel. Ulrich v., 30 F.2d 984 (D.C.Cir.1929), 478, 479, 480, 481, 482, 484

Kennedy v. Mendoza–Martinez, 372 U.S. 144, 83 S.Ct. 554, 9 L.Ed.2d 644 (1963), 1335

Kessler v. Strecker, 307 U.S. 22, 59 S.Ct. 694, 83 L.Ed. 1082 (1939), 180

Khalid v. Bush, 355 F.Supp.2d 311 (D.D.C. 2005), 864

Khodagholian v. Ashcroft, 335 F.3d 1003 (9th Cir.2003), 521

Kids 'R' Us, Matter of, No. 89–INA–311 (BALCA 1991), 319

Kim Ho Ma v. Ashcroft, 257 F.3d 1095 (9th Cir.2001), 205, 755

Kirby, United States v., 74 U.S. 482, 19 L.Ed. 278 (1868), 258

Kleindienst v. Mandel, 408 U.S. 753, 92 S.Ct. 2576, 33 L.Ed.2d 683 (1972), 176, 179, 433, 483, 1275

Knapik v. Ashcroft, 384 F.3d 84 (3rd Cir. 2004), 547

Knauff, United States ex rel. v. Shaughnessy, 338 U.S. 537, 70 S.Ct. 309, 94 L.Ed. 317 (1950), 144, 145, 152, 153, 174, 875

Knezevic v. Ashcroft, 367 F.3d 1206 (9th Cir.2004), 1051

Kofa v. United States I.N.S., 60 F.3d 1084 (4th Cir.1995), 1074

Kohama, Matter of, 17 I. & N. Dec. 257, Interim Decision 2761 (INS 1978), 439

Koloamantangi, Matter of, 23 I. & N. Dec. 548, Interim Decision (BIA) 3486 (BIA 2003), 580

Kovac v. I.N.S., 407 F.2d 102 (9th Cir.1969), 952

Kowalczyk v. I.N.S., 245 F.3d 1143 (10th Cir.2001), 1067

Kozminski, United States v., 487 U.S. 931, 108 S.Ct. 2751, 101 L.Ed.2d 788 (1988), 1203

Kulle, Matter of, 19 I. & N. Dec. 318, Interim Decision (BIA) 3002 (BIA 1985), 1061

Kungys v. United States, 485 U.S. 759, 108 S.Ct. 1537, 99 L.Ed.2d 839 (1988), **1314,** 1332, 1333

Kwong Hai Chew v. Colding, 344 U.S. 590, 73 S.Ct. 472, 97 L.Ed. 576 (1953), 153, 155, 158, 163

L., Matter of, 1 I. & N. Dec. 1 (BIA & A.G. 1940), 575, 576, 577
Ladha v. I.N.S., 215 F.3d 889 (9th Cir.2000), 1058
Landon v. Plasencia, 459 U.S. 21, 103 S.Ct. 321, 74 L.Ed.2d 21 (1982), 154, 155, 158, 159, 163, 231, 705
Lara–Ruiz v. I.N.S., 241 F.3d 934 (7th Cir. 2001), 436
Latu v. Ashcroft, 375 F.3d 1012 (10th Cir. 2004), 436
Laureano, Matter of, 19 I. & N. Dec. 1, Interim Decision (BIA) 2951 (BIA 1983), 270
Lauvik v. I.N.S., 910 F.2d 658 (9th Cir.1990), 404
Lawrence v. Texas, 539 U.S. 558, 123 S.Ct. 2472, 156 L.Ed.2d 508 (2003), 267
Lawyers Committee for Human Rights v. I.N.S., 721 F.Supp. 552 (S.D.N.Y.1989), 434
Lazo–Majano v. I.N.S., 813 F.2d 1432 (9th Cir.1987), 969, 970
Le v. United States Atty. Gen., 196 F.3d 1352 (11th Cir.1999), 559
League of United Latin American Citizens v. Wilson, 908 F.Supp. 755 (C.D.Cal.1995), 1251, 1252, 1253, 1254
Lee Lung v. Patterson, 186 U.S. 168, 22 S.Ct. 795, 46 L.Ed. 1108 (1902), 144
Legal Assistance for Vietnamese Asylum Seekers v. Department of State, 45 F.3d 469, 310 U.S.App.D.C. 168 (D.C.Cir.1995), 484
Lem Moon Sing v. United States, 158 U.S. 538, 15 S.Ct. 967, 39 L.Ed. 1082 (1895), 144
Leng May Ma v. Barber, 357 U.S. 185, 78 S.Ct. 1072, 2 L.Ed.2d 1246 (1958), 939
Lennon, Matter of, 15 I. & N. Dec. 9, Interim Decision (BIA) 2304 (BIA 1974), 184
Lennon v. Immigration and Naturalization Service, 527 F.2d 187 (2nd Cir.1975), 411
Leocal v. Ashcroft, 125 S.Ct. 377, 160 L.Ed.2d 271 (2004), **555,** 559, 560, 561, 734
Lewis v. United States I.N.S., 194 F.3d 539 (4th Cir.1999), 734
L–G–, In re, 21 I. & N. Dec. 89, Interim Decision (BIA) 3254 (BIA 1995), 562
Li v. Ashcroft, 356 F.3d 1153 (9th Cir.2004), 1047
Li, United States v., 206 F.3d 56 (1st Cir. 2000), 704
Licea–Gomez v. Pilliod, 193 F.Supp. 577 (N.D.Ill.1960), 480
Lieggi v. United States Immigration and Naturalization Service, 529 F.2d 530 (7th Cir. 1976), 631
Lignomat USA, Matter of, No. 88–INA–276 (BALCA 1989), 307

Lin, Matter of, 18 I. & N. Dec. 219, Interim Decision (BIA) 2900 (BIA 1982), 509
Linebery v. United States, 512 F.2d 510 (5th Cir.1975), 602
Linnas v. I.N.S., 790 F.2d 1024 (2nd Cir. 1986), **625,** 629
Lombera–Camorlinga, United States v., 206 F.3d 882 (9th Cir.2000), 704
London, United States ex rel. v. Phelps, 22 F.2d 288 (2nd Cir.1927), 478, 479, 482, 483
Longstaff, Matter of, 716 F.2d 1439 (5th Cir. 1983), 259, 260
Lopez v. I.N.S., 184 F.3d 1097 (9th Cir.1999), 839
Lopez v. I.N.S., 775 F.2d 1015 (9th Cir.1985), 975
Lopez–Chavez v. I.N.S., 259 F.3d 1176 (9th Cir.2001), 715
Lopez–Elias v. Reno, 209 F.3d 788 (5th Cir. 2000), 561
Lopez–Meza, Matter of, 22 I. & N. Dec. 1188, Interim Decision (BIA) 3423 (BIA 1999), 548
Loza–Bedoya v. Immigration and Naturalization Service, 410 F.2d 343 (9th Cir.1969), 480
Lozada, Matter of, 19 I. & N. Dec. 637, Interim Decision (BIA) 3059 (BIA 1988), **681,** 683, 684, 685
Lozada v. I.N.S., 857 F.2d 10 (1st Cir.1988), 723
L.S., In re, 22 I. & N. Dec. 645, Interim Decision (BIA) 3386 (BIA 1999), 1074, 1075
Lucky Horse Fashion, Matter of, No. 97–INA–182 (BALCA 2000), 306
Lujan–Armendariz v. I.N.S., 222 F.3d 728 (9th Cir.2000), 539
Lukowski v. I.N.S., 279 F.3d 644 (8th Cir. 2002), 436
Lukwago v. Ashcroft, 329 F.3d 157 (3rd Cir. 2003), 1157
Lutheran Ministries of Florida, Matter of, 20 I. & N. Dec. 185, Interim Decision (BIA) 3132 (BIA 1990), 657
Lwin v. I.N.S., 144 F.3d 505 (7th Cir.1998), 986, 988

M.A. v. United States I.N.S., 899 F.2d 304 (4th Cir.1990), 726, 959, 1084
Mackenzie v. Hare, 239 U.S. 299, 36 S.Ct. 106, 60 L.Ed. 297 (1915), 1334, 1345
Mada–Luna v. Fitzpatrick, 813 F.2d 1006 (9th Cir.1987), 615
Magallanes–Damian v. I.N.S., 783 F.2d 931 (9th Cir.1986), 663
Mahler v. Eby, 264 U.S. 32, 44 S.Ct. 283, 68 L.Ed. 549 (1924), 499, 500
Maldonado–Cruz, Matter of, 19 I. & N. Dec. 509, Interim Decision (BIA) 3041 (BIA 1988), 975

Manwani v. United States Dept. of Justice, I.N.S., 736 F.Supp. 1367 (W.D.N.C.1990), 185, 272, 278

Marbury v. Madison, 5 U.S. 137, 2 L.Ed. 60 (1803), 122

Marcel Watch Corp., United States v., 1 OCA-HO 988 (ALJ 1990), 1228

Marcello v. Bonds, 349 U.S. 302, 75 S.Ct. 757, 99 L.Ed. 1107 (1955), 650

Marciano v. Immigration and Naturalization Service, 450 F.2d 1022 (8th Cir. 1971), **540,** 546, 547

Margalli–Olvera v. I.N.S., 43 F.3d 345 (8th Cir.1994), 681

Marin–Navarette, United States v., 244 F.3d 1284 (11th Cir.2001), 554

Marquez, Matter of, 20 I. & N. Dec. 160, Interim Decision (BIA) 3129 (BIA 1990), 288

Marroquin–Garcia, In re, 23 I. & N. Dec. 705, Interim Decision 3507 (A.G. 2005), 538, 539

Martinez, Matter of, 18 I. & N. Dec. 399, Interim Decision (BIA) 2941 (BIA 1983), 285

Martinez–Perez v. Ashcroft, 393 F.3d 1018 (9th Cir.2004), 560

Martinez–Romero v. Immigration and Naturalization Service, 692 F.2d 595 (9th Cir. 1982), 1164

Martirosyan v. I.N.S., 229 F.3d 903 (9th Cir. 2000), 951

Massieu v. Reno, 915 F.Supp. 681 (D.N.J. 1996), 162

Mathews v. Diaz, 426 U.S. 67, 96 S.Ct. 1883, 48 L.Ed.2d 478 (1976), 25, 1265, 1352, 1358

Mathews v. Eldridge, 424 U.S. 319, 96 S.Ct. 893, 47 L.Ed.2d 18 (1976), 142, 144, 153, 155, 185, 455, 663, 664, 724

Matter of (see name of party)

May, Matter of, 18 I. & N. Dec. 381, Interim Decision (BIA) 2938 (BIA 1983), 285

M–B–A–, In re, 23 I. & N. Dec. 474, Interim Decision (BIA) 3480 (BIA 2002), 1157

McBoyle v. United States, 283 U.S. 25, 51 S.Ct. 340, 75 L.Ed. 816 (1931), 432

McColvin v. Immigration and Naturalization Service, 648 F.2d 935 (4th Cir.1981), 583

McDonnell Douglas Corp. v. Green, 411 U.S. 792, 93 S.Ct. 1817, 36 L.Ed.2d 668 (1973), 1227

McMullen, Matter of, 19 I. & N. Dec. 90, Interim Decision (BIA) 2967 (BIA 1984), 1069

McMullen v. I.N.S., 788 F.2d 591 (9th Cir. 1986), 1076

McNary v. Haitian Refugee Center, Inc., 498 U.S. 479, 111 S.Ct. 888, 112 L.Ed.2d 1005 (1991), 758

Medina, Matter of, 19 I. & N. Dec. 734, Interim Decision (BIA) 3078 (BIA 1988), 1182, 1183

Medina–Morales v. Ashcroft, 362 F.3d 1263 (9th Cir.2004), 737

Mendoza–Lopez, United States v., 481 U.S. 828, 107 S.Ct. 2148, 95 L.Ed.2d 772 (1987), 759, 1205

Mendoza Perez v. United States I.N.S., 902 F.2d 760 (9th Cir.1990), 974

Merkt, United States v., 764 F.2d 266 (5th Cir.1985), 1206

Mester Mfg. Co. v. I.N.S., 879 F.2d 561 (9th Cir.1989), 1210, 1211

Meyer v. Nebraska, 262 U.S. 390, 43 S.Ct. 625, 67 L.Ed. 1042 (1923), 57

Meyers v. Canada, 97 D.L.R.4th 729 (Fed. C.A.1992), 985

M.G., Matter of, 5 I. & N. Dec. 531, Interim Decision (BIA) 538 (BIA 1953), 551

Michel, In re, 21 I. & N. Dec. 1101, Interim Decision (BIA) 3335 (BIA 1998), 436

Michel v. I.N.S., 206 F.3d 253 (2nd Cir.2000), 550

Millard, Matter of, 11 I. & N. Dec. 175, Interim Decision (BIA) 1468 (BIA 1965), 528

Miller v. Albright, 523 U.S. 420, 118 S.Ct. 1428, 140 L.Ed.2d 575 (1998), 1276

Minatsis v. Brown, 713 F.Supp. 1056 (S.D.Ohio 1989), 278

Miranda v. Arizona, 384 U.S. 436, 86 S.Ct. 1602, 16 L.Ed.2d 694 (1966), 637

Miranda v. Reno, 238 F.3d 1156 (9th Cir. 2001), 757

Mireles–Valdez v. Ashcroft, 349 F.3d 213 (5th Cir.2003), 736

Mistretta v. United States, 488 U.S. 361, 109 S.Ct. 647, 102 L.Ed.2d 714 (1989), 621

Mogharrabi, Matter of, 19 I. & N. Dec. 439, Interim Decision (BIA) 3028 (BIA 1987), 1051, 1056, 1164

Mohammed v. Gonzales, 400 F.3d 785 (9th Cir.2005), 685, 986, 1005, 1020, 1024, 1055

Moin v. Ashcroft, 335 F.3d 415 (5th Cir. 2003), 521

Monreal–Aguinaga, In re, 23 I. & N. Dec. 56, Interim Decision (BIA) 3447 (BIA 2001), 595, 596

Montana v. Kennedy, 366 U.S. 308, 81 S.Ct. 1336, 6 L.Ed.2d 313 (1961), 632

Montecino v. I.N.S., 915 F.2d 518 (9th Cir. 1990), 1051, 1089, 1093

Montenegro v. Ashcroft, 355 F.3d 1035 (7th Cir.2004), 533

Montero–Camargo, United States v., 208 F.3d 1122 (9th Cir.2000), 701

Moore v. Ashcroft, 251 F.3d 919 (11th Cir. 2001), 436

Morales–Alvarado v. Immigration and Naturalization Service, 655 F.2d 172 (9th Cir. 1981), 533

Morales–Izquierdo v. Ashcroft, 388 F.3d 1299 (9th Cir.2004), 840

Morales–Morales v. Ashcroft, 384 F.3d 418 (7th Cir.2004), 736

Morrissey v. Brewer, 408 U.S. 471, 92 S.Ct. 2593, 33 L.Ed.2d 484 (1972), 664

Moss v. Immigration and Naturalization Service, 651 F.2d 1091 (5th Cir.1981), **398**

Mourillon, Matter of, 18 I. & N. Dec. 122, Interim Decision (BIA) 2882 (BIA 1981), **281,** 283, 284, 285

Murillo–Espinoza v. I.N.S., 261 F.3d 771 (9th Cir.2001), 539

Murphy v. I.N.S., 54 F.3d 605 (9th Cir.1995), 640, 715

Musgrove v. Chun Teeong Toy [1891] A.C. 272 (Privy Council), 236

Nai Cheng Chen v. Immigration and Naturalization Service, 537 F.2d 566 (1st Cir. 1976), 637

Nakamoto v. Ashcroft, 363 F.3d 874 (9th Cir.2004), 738

Narenji v. Civiletti, 617 F.2d 745, 199 U.S.App.D.C. 163 (D.C.Cir.1979), 184

Nason v. Immigration and Naturalization Service, 394 F.2d 223 (2nd Cir.1968), 550

Naturalization of Vafaei–Makhsoos, In re, 597 F.Supp. 499 (D.Minn.1984), **1284**

Nehme v. I.N.S., 252 F.3d 415 (5th Cir.2001), 734

New El Rey Sausage Co., Inc. v. United States I.N.S., 925 F.2d 1153 (9th Cir. 1991), 1210, 1211

New Jersey, State of v. United States, 91 F.3d 463 (3rd Cir.1996), 1254

Newton v. I.N.S., 736 F.2d 336 (6th Cir. 1984), 184, 631

New York, City of v. United States, 179 F.3d 29 (2nd Cir.1999), 1200

Ng Fung Ho v. White, 259 U.S. 276, 42 S.Ct. 492, 66 L.Ed. 938 (1922), 631, 759

Nguyen v. I.N.S., 533 U.S. 53, 121 S.Ct. 2053, 150 L.Ed.2d 115 (2001), 175, 176, 204, 284, 1276

Ngure v. Ashcroft, 367 F.3d 975 (8th Cir. 2004), 725

Nice v. Turnage, 752 F.2d 431 (9th Cir. 1985), **360**

Nicholas v. Immigration and Naturalization Service, 590 F.2d 802 (9th Cir.1979), 616, 617

Nishikawa v. Dulles, 356 U.S. 129, 78 S.Ct. 612, 2 L.Ed.2d 659 (1958), 1335

N.M.A., In re, 22 I. & N. Dec. 312, Interim Decision (BIA) 3368 (BIA 1998), 1053

North Jersey Media Group, Inc. v. Ashcroft, 308 F.3d 198 (3rd Cir.2002), 879, 880

Nyquist v. Mauclet, 432 U.S. 1, 97 S.Ct. 2120, 53 L.Ed.2d 63 (1977), 1352

O, Matter of, 8 I. & N. Dec. 295, Interim Decision (BIA) 991 (BIA 1959), 455

O, Matter of, 8 I. & N. Dec. 291, Interim Decision (BIA) 992 (BIA 1959), 421

Oden v. Northern Marianas College, 284 F.3d 1058 (9th Cir.2002), 812

O.J.O., In re, 21 I. & N. Dec. 381, Interim Decision (BIA) 3280 (BIA 1996), 586, 595

Olivares v. I.N.S., 685 F.2d 1174 (9th Cir. 1982), 248

Oloteo v. Immigration and Naturalization Service, 643 F.2d 679 (9th Cir.1981), 842

Olowo v. Ashcroft, 368 F.3d 692 (7th Cir. 2004), 1022

Olsen v. Albright, 990 F.Supp. 31 (D.D.C. 1997), 466

Oluloro, Matter of, No. A72 147 491 (IJ 1994), 1022

Onal, Matter of, 18 I. & N. Dec. 147, Interim Decision (BIA) 2886 (BIA 1981), 841

Ontunez–Tursios v. Ashcroft, 303 F.3d 341 (5th Cir.2002), 986, 1155

Onyinkwa v. Ashcroft, 376 F.3d 797 (8th Cir.2004), 737

Orantes–Hernandez v. Meese, 685 F.Supp. 1488 (C.D.Cal.1988), 620

Ord, Matter of, 18 I. & N. Dec. 285, Interim Decision 2916 (INS 1982), 376

Ordonez v. I.N.S., 137 F.3d 1120 (9th Cir. 1998), 602

Orhorhaghe v. I.N.S., 38 F.3d 488 (9th Cir. 1994), 702

Osmani v. I.N.S., 14 F.3d 13 (7th Cir.1994), 628

Osorio v. I.N.S., 99 F.3d 928 (9th Cir.1996), 1061

Osorio v. I.N.S., 18 F.3d 1017 (2nd Cir.1994), 948

Ozbirman v. Regional Manpower Adm'r, United States Dept. of Labor, 335 F.Supp. 467 (S.D.N.Y.1971), 319

O.Z. & I.Z., In re, 22 I. & N. Dec. 23, Interim Decision (BIA) 3346 (BIA 1998), 962

Ozkok, Matter of, 19 I. & N. Dec. 546 (BIA 1988), 532

Pacheco v. Immigration and Naturalization Service, 546 F.2d 448 (1st Cir.1976), 549, 550

Padavan v. United States, 82 F.3d 23 (2nd Cir.1996), 1255

Padilla–Agustin v. I.N.S., 21 F.3d 970 (9th Cir.1994), 724

Palmer v. City of Euclid, Ohio, 402 U.S. 544, 91 S.Ct. 1563, 29 L.Ed.2d 98 (1971), 546

Palmer v. Reddy, 622 F.2d 463 (9th Cir. 1980), 285

Palomino v. Ashcroft, 354 F.3d 942 (8th Cir. 2004), 816

Panama Refining Co. v. Ryan, 293 U.S. 388, 55 S.Ct. 241, 79 L.Ed. 446 (1935), 621

Paris Bakery Corp., No. 88–INA–337 (BALCA 1990), 307

Parrino, United States v., 212 F.2d 919 (2nd Cir.1954), **533,** 538, 677, 680

Pasquini v. Morris, 700 F.2d 658 (11th Cir. 1983), 616

Passenger Cases, 48 U.S. 283, 7 How. 283, 12 L.Ed. 702 (1849), 104, 106, 107, 119

Patel, Matter of, 20 I. & N. Dec. 368, Interim Decision (BIA) 3157 (BIA 1991), 510

Patel, Matter of, 19 I. & N. Dec. 774, Interim Decision (BIA) 3083 (BIA 1988), 713

Patterson v. McLean Credit Union, 491 U.S. 164, 109 S.Ct. 2363, 105 L.Ed.2d 132 (1989), 1224

Pazcoguin v. Radcliffe, 292 F.3d 1209 (9th Cir.2002), 152

Pena v. Kissinger, 409 F.Supp. 1182 (S.D.N.Y.1976), 482

Penuliar v. Ashcroft, 395 F.3d 1037 (9th Cir. 2005), 734

People v. _____ (see opposing party)

Perez, In re, 22 I. & N. Dec. 1325, Interim Decision (BIA) 3432 (BIA 2000), 561

Perez v. Brownell, 356 U.S. 44, 78 S.Ct. 568, 2 L.Ed.2d 603 (1958), 1335, 1371

Perez v. Elwood, 294 F.3d 552 (3rd Cir.2002), 180

Perlera–Escobar v. Executive Office for Immigration, 894 F.2d 1292 (11th Cir.1990), 975

Pesikoff v. Secretary of Labor, 501 F.2d 757, 163 U.S.App.D.C. 197 (D.C.Cir.1974), 304

Petition of (see name of party)

Phelps, United States ex rel. London v., 22 F.2d 288 (2nd Cir.1927), 478, 479, 482, 483

Pickering, In re, 23 I. & N. Dec. 621, Interim Decision (BIA) 3493 (BIA 2003), 538

Pierre, Matter of, 14 I. & N. Dec. 467, Interim Decision (BIA) 2238 (BIA 1973), 508, 510

Pineda, Matter of, 20 I. & N. Dec. 70, Interim Decision (BIA) 3112 (BIA 1989), 283

Pino v. Landon, 349 U.S. 901, 75 S.Ct. 576, 99 L.Ed. 1239 (1955), 533

Pino v. Nicolls, 215 F.2d 237 (1st Cir.1954), 546, 547

Piperkoff, United States ex rel. v. Esperdy, 267 F.2d 72 (2nd Cir.1959), 551

Pitcherskaia v. I.N.S., 118 F.3d 641 (9th Cir. 1997), 951, 994

Plyler v. Doe, 457 U.S. 202, 102 S.Ct. 2382, 72 L.Ed.2d 786 (1982), **1235,** 1250, 1251, 1252, 1254, 1258, 1352

Poll v. Lord Advocate [1899] 1 F. 823 (Ct. of Sessions, Scotland), 236

Pozo, People v., 746 P.2d 523 (Colo.1987), 537, **672,** 678, 679, 680

Pradieu, Matter of, 19 I. & N. Dec. 419, Interim Decision (BIA) 3021 (BIA 1986), 455

Price v. United States I.N.S., 962 F.2d 836 (9th Cir.1991), 1275

Puente–Salazar, In re, 22 I. & N. Dec. 1006, Interim Decision (BIA) 3412 (BIA 1999), 559

Pula, Matter of, 19 I. & N. Dec. 467, Interim Decision (BIA) 3033 (BIA 1987), 1080, 1081

Punu, In re, 22 I. & N. Dec. 224, Interim Decision (BIA) 3364 (BIA 1998), 532, 533

Qu v. Gonzales, 399 F.3d 1195 (9th Cir.2005), 961, 1055

Quan, Matter of, 12 I. & N. Dec. 487, Interim Decision 1802 (INS 1967), 841

R. v. Governor of Brixton Estate, ex parte Soblen [1963] 2 Q.B. 243 (U.K.Ct.App. 1963), 237, 629

R. v. Immigration Appeal Tribunal, ex parte Khan [1983] 2 All E.R. 420 (C.A.), 237

R. v. Secretary of State for Home Affairs, ex parte Duke of Chateau Thierry [1917] 1 K.B. 922 (C.A.), 237

R. v. Secretary of State for the Home Dept., ex parte Adan and Aitseguer [2001] 2 W.L.R. 143 (U.K.2001), 1028, 1185, 1189

R. v. Uxbridge Magistrates' Court, ex parte Adimi [2001] Q.B. 667 (QBD 1999), 1109, 1110

R., Matter of, 6 I. & N. Dec. 444, Interim Decision (BIA) 666 (BIA 1954), 546

R., Matter of, 5 I. & N. Dec. 29, Interim Decision (BIA) 411 (BIA 1952), 622

R.A., In re, 23 I. & N. Dec. 694, Interim Decision 3504 (A.G. 2005), 1027

R.A., In re, 22 I. & N. Dec. 906, Interim Decision 3403 (BIA 1999, A.G. 2001), 968, 970, 1026

Rafeedie v. I.N.S., 795 F.Supp. 13 (D.D.C. 1992), 177

Rafeedie v. I.N.S., 880 F.2d 506, 279 U.S.App. D.C. 183 (D.C.Cir.1989), 155

Ramirez–Ramos v. I.N.S., 814 F.2d 1394 (9th Cir.1987), 1073

Ramirez Rivas v. I.N.S., 899 F.2d 864 (9th Cir.1990), 969

Ramos, In re, 23 I. & N. Dec. 336, Interim Decision (BIA) 3468 (BIA 2002), 559

Ramos v. I.N.S., 695 F.2d 181 (5th Cir.1983), 604

Rao, Matter of, A77 249 526 (IJ 2000), 988

Rasul v. Bush, 124 S.Ct. 2686, 159 L.Ed.2d 548 (2004), 141, 158, 231, 756, **856,** 862, 863, 864, 865

Ratnayake v. Mack, 499 F.2d 1207 (8th Cir. 1974), 304

Ravindran v. I.N.S., 976 F.2d 754 (1st Cir. 1992), 969

Recinos De Leon v. Gonzales, 400 F.3d 1185 (9th Cir.2005), 720

Reid v. Covert, 354 U.S. 1, 77 S.Ct. 1222, 1 L.Ed.2d 1148 (1957), 140

Reid v. Immigration and Naturalization Service, 420 U.S. 619, 95 S.Ct. 1164, 43 L.Ed.2d 501 (1975), 526

Reno v. American–Arab Anti–Discrimination Committee, 525 U.S. 471, 119 S.Ct. 936, 142 L.Ed.2d 940 (1999), 83, 177, 740

Reno v. Flores, 507 U.S. 292, 113 S.Ct. 1439, 123 L.Ed.2d 1 (1993), 184, 636

Renteria–Gonzalez v. I.N.S., 322 F.3d 804 (5th Cir.2002), 539, 551

Resendiz, In re, 105 Cal.Rptr.2d 431, 19 P.3d 1171 (Cal.2001), 680

Reyes–Palacios v. United States I.N.S., 836 F.2d 1154 (9th Cir.1988), 665

Reyes–Reyes v. Ashcroft, 384 F.3d 782 (9th Cir.2004), 1156

Reyes–Vasquez v. Ashcroft, 395 F.3d 903 (8th Cir.2005), 585, 725, 736, 816

Richardson v. Reno, 994 F.Supp. 1466 (S.D.Fla.1998), 524

Richmond Newspapers, Inc. v. Virginia, 448 U.S. 555, 100 S.Ct. 2814, 65 L.Ed.2d 973 (1980), 880

Rivera de Gomez v. Kissinger, 534 F.2d 518 (2nd Cir.1976), 482

Rivera–Jimenez v. I.N.S., 214 F.3d 1213 (10th Cir.2000), 523

Rivera–Rioseco, Matter of, 19 I. & N. Dec. 833, Interim Decision (BIA) 3092 (BIA 1988), 1080

R.M., Matter of (Immigration Court, York County Prison, Penn., May 21, 2001), 653

Robert L. Lippert Theatres, Matter of, No. 88–INA–433 (BALCA 1990), 306

Rodriguez, Matter of, 10 I. & N. Dec. 488, Interim Decision (BIA) 1328 (BIA 1964), 962

Rodriguez v. I.N.S., 204 F.3d 25 (1st Cir. 2000), 270

Rodriguez–Coto, Matter of, 19 I. & N. Dec. 208, Interim Decision (BIA) 2985 (BIA 1985), 1075

Rodriguez–Lariz v. I.N.S., 282 F.3d 1218 (9th Cir.2002), 684

Rodriguez–Padron v. I.N.S., 13 F.3d 1455 (11th Cir.1994), 579

Rodriguez–Ruiz, Respondent, 22 I. & N. Dec. 1378, Interim Decision (BIA) 3436 (BIA 2000), 538

Rodriguez–Tejedor, In re, 23 I. & N. Dec. 153, Interim Decision (BIA) 3454 (BIA 2001), 1292

Rogers v. Bellei, 401 U.S. 815, 91 S.Ct. 1060, 28 L.Ed.2d 499 (1971), 1267, 1273, 1274, 1335, 1336

Roldan–Santoyo, In re, 22 I. & N. Dec. 512, Interim Decision (BIA) 3377 (BIA 1999), 538

Romalez–Alcaide, In re, 23 I. & N. Dec. 423, Interim Decision (BIA) 3475 (BIA 2002), 802, 803, 804, 806, 815, 816

Romero–Torres v. Ashcroft, 327 F.3d 887 (9th Cir.2003), 587, 736

Rosales–Garcia v. Holland, 322 F.3d 386 (6th Cir.2003), 207

Rosenberg v. Fleuti, 374 U.S. 449, 83 S.Ct. 1804, 10 L.Ed.2d 1000 (1963), **511,** 519, 520, 522, 523, 524, 525, 575, 583, 705

Rowoldt v. Perfetto, 355 U.S. 115, 78 S.Ct. 180, 2 L.Ed.2d 140 (1957), 433

Ruiz v. Hull, 191 Ariz. 441, 957 P.2d 984 (Ariz.1998), 58

Ruiz–Lopez, United States v., 234 F.3d 445 (9th Cir.2000), 510

Rumsfeld v. Padilla, 124 S.Ct. 2711, 159 L.Ed.2d 513 (2004), 865

Rusin, Matter of, 20 I. & N. Dec. 128, Interim Decision (BIA) 3123 (BIA 1989), 433

Russian Volunteer Fleet v. United States, 282 U.S. 481, 51 S.Ct. 229, 75 L.Ed. 473 (1931), 140

S.A., In re, 22 I. & N. Dec. 1328, Interim Decision (BIA) 3433 (BIA 2000), 963

Saa, Matter of, No. A28 852 512 (BIA 1989), 487

Saavedra Bruno v. Albright, 197 F.3d 1153, 339 U.S.App.D.C. 78 (D.C.Cir.1999), 483

Salazar–Regino, In re, 23 I. & N. Dec. 223, Interim Decision (BIA) 3462 (BIA 2002), 539

Sale v. Haitian Centers Council, Inc., 509 U.S. 155, 113 S.Ct. 2549, 125 L.Ed.2d 128 (1993), **1115,** 1130, 1131, 1132, 1133, 1134, 1135, 1158

Saleh v. United States Dept. of Justice, 962 F.2d 234 (2nd Cir.1992), 986

Salim, Matter of, 18 I. & N. Dec. 311, Interim Decision (BIA) 2922 (BIA 1982), 1077, 1078

Sanchez–Trujillo v. I.N.S., 801 F.2d 1571 (9th Cir.1986), **979,** 980, 985, 986, 987, 988, 1026, 1042

Sandoval v. I.N.S., 240 F.3d 577 (7th Cir. 2001), 538

Sangha v. I.N.S., 103 F.3d 1482 (9th Cir. 1997), 976

San Pedro v. United States, 79 F.3d 1065 (11th Cir.1996), 680

Santana–Figueroa v. Immigration and Naturalization Service, 644 F.2d 1354 (9th Cir. 1981), 604

Santos, Matter of, 19 I. & N. Dec. 105, Interim Decision (BIA) 2969 (BIA 1984), 702

Santos–Gomez, Matter of, No. A29 564 781 (Immigration Judge 1990), 1183

Sarmadi v. I.N.S., 121 F.3d 1319 (9th Cir. 1997), 588

Sarvia–Quintanilla v. United States I.N.S., 767 F.2d 1387 (9th Cir.1985), 1062

Saunders, Matter of, 16 I. & N. Dec. 326, Interim Decision (BIA) 2610 (BIA 1977), 841

Sayaxing v. I.N.S., 179 F.3d 515 (7th Cir. 1999), 950

Schmidt v. Sec. of State for Home Affairs [1969] 2 Ch. 149 (U.K. Ct. of App.), 237

Schneider v. Rusk, 377 U.S. 163, 84 S.Ct. 1187, 12 L.Ed.2d 218 (1964), 1335

Schneiderman v. United States, 320 U.S. 118, 63 S.Ct. 1333, 87 L.Ed. 1796 (1943), 1313

Schweiker v. Hansen, 450 U.S. 785, 101 S.Ct. 1468, 67 L.Ed.2d 685 (1981), 632

Securities and Exchange Commission v. Chenery Corp., 318 U.S. 80, 63 S.Ct. 454, 87 L.Ed. 626 (1943), 592

Selgeka v. Carroll, 184 F.3d 337 (4th Cir. 1999), 959

Senathirajah v. I.N.S., 157 F.3d 210 (3rd Cir. 1998), 1058

Seven Star, Inc. v. United States, 873 F.2d 225 (9th Cir.1989), 375

Shaker, Matter of, No. A27 560 431 (BIA 1989), 488

Shamp Plumbing and Building, Matter of, 94–INA–530 (BALCA 1996), 305

Shanks v. Dupont, 28 U.S. 242, 3 Pet. 242, 7 L.Ed. 666 (1830), 1333

Sharif v. I.N.S., 87 F.3d 932 (7th Cir.1996), 952

Shaughnessy v. Pedreiro, 349 U.S. 48, 75 S.Ct. 591, 99 L.Ed. 868 (1955), 728

Shaughnessy, United States ex rel. Knauff v., 338 U.S. 537, 70 S.Ct. 309, 94 L.Ed. 317 (1950), 144, 145, 152, 153, 174, 875

Shaughnessy v. United States ex rel. Mezei, 345 U.S. 206, 73 S.Ct. 625, 97 L.Ed. 956 (1953), **145,** 152, 153, 154, 155, 158, 159, 161, 162, 172, 174, 237, 489, 862, 875

Sheku–Kamara v. Karn, 581 F.Supp. 582 (E.D.Pa.1984), **389,** 392

Shimizu v. Dept. of State, No. CV–89–2741–WMB (C.D.Cal.1990), 484

Shirazi–Parsa v. I.N.S., 14 F.3d 1424 (9th Cir.1994), 969

Shoafera v. I.N.S., 228 F.3d 1070 (9th Cir. 2000), 962

Sida v. Immigration and Naturalization Service, 665 F.2d 851 (9th Cir.1981), 602, 603

Sida v. I.N.S., 783 F.2d 947 (9th Cir.1986), 603

Sierra v. Romaine, 347 F.3d 559 (3rd Cir. 2003), 207

Silva, Matter of, 16 I. & N. Dec. 26, Interim Decision (BIA) 2532 (BIA 1976), 184, 576

Singh v. Gonzales, 404 F.3d 1024 (7th Cir. 2005), 737

Singh v. I.N.S., 328 F.3d 1205 (9th Cir.2003), 882

Siverts v. Craig, 602 F.Supp. 50 (D.Hawai'i 1985), 617

Skafte v. Rorex, 191 Colo. 399, 553 P.2d 830 (Colo.1976), 1353

Small, Matter of, 23 I. & N. Dec. 48 (BIA 2002), 554

Smith v. I.N.S., 684 F.Supp. 1113 (D.Mass. 1988), 278

Smriko v. Ashcroft, 387 F.3d 279 (3rd Cir. 2004), 725

Snyder v. Rosales–Garcia, 539 U.S. 941, 123 S.Ct. 2607, 156 L.Ed.2d 627 (2003), 207

Sofinet v. I.N.S., 188 F.3d 703 (7th Cir.1999), 800

Solano–Godines, United States v., 120 F.3d 957 (9th Cir.1997), 716

Solis–Ramirez v. United States Dept. of Justice, 758 F.2d 1426 (11th Cir.1985), 239, 334

Solorzano–Patlan v. I.N.S., 207 F.3d 869 (7th Cir.2000), 561

Song, In re, 23 I. & N. Dec. 173, Interim Decision (BIA) 3455 (BIA 2001), 563

Song v. I.N.S., 82 F.Supp.2d 1121 (C.D.Cal. 2000), 436

Southeastern Capital Corp., Matter of, 88–INA–198 (BALCA 1989), 303

S–S–, In re, 22 I. & N. Dec. 458, Interim Decision (BIA) 3374 (BIA 1999), 1075

State of (see name of state)

Stokes v. United States INS, 74 Civ. 1022 (S.D.N.Y.1976), 455

Stone v. I.N.S., 514 U.S. 386, 115 S.Ct. 1537, 131 L.Ed.2d 465 (1995), 724, 731

Strickland v. Washington, 467 U.S. 1267, 104 S.Ct. 3562, 82 L.Ed.2d 864 (1984), 678, 679

Sugarman v. Dougall, 413 U.S. 634, 93 S.Ct. 2842, 37 L.Ed.2d 853 (1973), 1352, 1353, 1370

Sure–Tan, Inc. v. N.L.R.B., 467 U.S. 883, 104 S.Ct. 2803, 81 L.Ed.2d 732 (1984), 1202

Sussex Engineering, Ltd. v. Montgomery, 825 F.2d 1084 (6th Cir.1987), 375

S.V., In re, 22 I. & N. Dec. 1306, Interim Decision (BIA) 3430 (BIA 2000), 1156

Takao Ozawa v. United States, 260 U.S. 178, 43 S.Ct. 65, 67 L.Ed. 199 (1922), 1282

Tan, Matter of, 12 I. & N. Dec. 564, Interim Decision (BIA) 1825 (BIA 1967), 962

Tapia v. Ashcroft, 351 F.3d 795 (7th Cir. 2003), 523

Tapia–Acuna v. Immigration and Naturalization Service, 640 F.2d 223 (9th Cir.1981), 184, 576

Tarango v. Ridge, No. CV 03–1738–PA (D.Or. 2004), 846

Tashnizi v. I.N.S., 585 F.2d 781 (5th Cir. 1978), 703

Tayabji, Matter of, 19 I. & N. Dec. 264, Interim Decision (BIA) 2994 (BIA 1985), 841

Taylor v. United States, 495 U.S. 575, 110 S.Ct. 2143, 109 L.Ed.2d 607 (1990), 561

Tejeda–Mata v. Immigration and Naturalization Service, 626 F.2d 721 (9th Cir.1980), 162

Tel–Ko Electronics, Inc., Matter of, 88–INA–416 (BALCA 1990), 305

Tesfamichael v. Gonzales, No. 04–61180 (5th Cir.2005), 732

The Florida Bar v. Matus, 528 So.2d 895 (Fla.1988), **457,** 460

The Paquete Habana, 175 U.S. 677, 20 S.Ct. 290, 44 L.Ed. 320 (1900), 1182, 1183

Thomas v. Ashcroft, 359 F.3d 1169 (9th Cir. 2004), 1036, 1047

Thomas v. Gonzales, 409 F.3d 1177 (9th Cir. en banc 2005), 988, 1036, 1047

Thomas v. I.N.S., 35 F.3d 1332 (9th Cir. 1994), 681

T.I. v. United Kingdom, App. No. 43844/98 (Euro.Ct. Human Rts., 3rd Sec.2000), 1028, **1183,** 1189

Tiede, United States v., 86 F.R.D. 227 (U.S.Ct.Berlin 1979), 141

Tineo v. Ashcroft, 350 F.3d 382 (3rd Cir. 2003), 523

Toboso–Alfonso, Matter of, 20 I. & N. Dec. 819, Interim Decision (BIA) 3222 (BIA 1990), **989,** 992, 995

Toll v. Moreno, 458 U.S. 1, 102 S.Ct. 2977, 73 L.Ed.2d 563 (1982), 1352

Torres–Varella, In re, 23 I. & N. Dec. 78, Interim Decision (BIA) 3449 (BIA 2001), 547, 548

Toyota v. United States, 268 U.S. 402, 45 S.Ct. 563, 69 L.Ed. 1016 (1925), 1282

Trias–Hernandez v. I.N.S., 528 F.2d 366 (9th Cir.1975), 685

Trop v. Dulles, 356 U.S. 86, 78 S.Ct. 590, 2 L.Ed.2d 630 (1958), 1335

Tsegay v. Ashcroft, 386 F.3d 1347 (10th Cir. 2004), 725

Tuan Thai v. Ashcroft, 366 F.3d 790 (9th Cir.2004), 206

Turcios v. I.N.S., 821 F.2d 1396 (9th Cir. 1987), 1056, 1062

Turcotte, Matter of, 12 I. & N. Dec. 206, Interim Decision (BIA) 1728 (BIA 1967), 604

Turner, United States ex rel. v. Williams, 194 U.S. 279, 24 S.Ct. 719, 48 L.Ed. 979 (1904), 179

Tuskegee University, Matter of, No. 87–INA–561 (BALCA 1988), 320

Tzimas, Matter of, 10 I. & N. Dec. 101, Interim Decision (BIA) 1251 (BIA 1962), 717

Ulrich, United States ex rel. v. Kellogg, 30 F.2d 984 (D.C.Cir.1929), 478, 479, 480, 481, 482, 484

Unauthorized Practice Committee, State Bar of Texas v. Cortez, 692 S.W.2d 47 (Tex. 1985), 459, 460

United States v. _____ (see opposing party)

United States ex rel. v. _____ (see opposing party and relator)

Urban v. I.N.S., 123 F.3d 644 (7th Cir.1997), 602

Vajtauer v. Commissioner of Immigration (Supreme Court, 1927), 755

Valiyee, Matter of, 14 I. & N. Dec. 710, Interim Decision (BIA) 2292 (BIA 1974), 842

Vance v. Terrazas, 444 U.S. 252, 100 S.Ct. 540, 62 L.Ed.2d 461 (1980), **1336,** 1346, 1347, 1348, 1349

Vargas–Garcia v. I.N.S., 287 F.3d 882 (9th Cir.2002), 724

Vasquez–Velezmoro v. United States I.N.S., 281 F.3d 693 (8th Cir.2002), 539

Velez–Lozano v. Immigration and Naturalization Service, 463 F.2d 1305, 150 U.S.App. D.C. 214 (D.C.Cir.1972), 551

Verdugo–Urquidez, United States v., 494 U.S. 259, 110 S.Ct. 1056, 108 L.Ed.2d 222 (1990), 140, 704

Villanueva–Jurado v. Immigration and Naturalization Service, 482 F.2d 886 (5th Cir. 1973), 1274, 1275

Vizcaino, Matter of, 19 I. & N. Dec. 644, Interim Decision (BIA) 3061 (BIA 1988), 283

Wadman v. Immigration and Naturalization Service, 329 F.2d 812 (9th Cir.1964), 583

Wadud, Matter of, 19 I. & N. Dec. 182, Interim Decision (BIA) 2980 (BIA 1984), 578

Wall v. I.N.S., 722 F.2d 1442 (9th Cir.1984), 702

Walsh and Pollard, Matter of, 20 I. & N. Dec. 60, Interim Decision (BIA) 3111 (BIA 1988), 361

Wang v. Immigration & Naturalization Service, 622 F.2d 1341 (9th Cir.1980), 592, 705, 726

Wards Cove Packing Co., Inc. v. Atonio, 490 U.S. 642, 109 S.Ct. 2115, 104 L.Ed.2d 733 (1989), 1227

Watkins v. I.N.S., 63 F.3d 844 (9th Cir.1995), 595, 602

Wauchope v. United States Dept. of State, 985 F.2d 1407 (9th Cir.1993), 1275

Waziri v. United States Immigration and Naturalization Service, 392 F.2d 55 (9th Cir.1968), 841

Weng v. United States Atty. Gen., 287 F.3d 1335 (11th Cir.2002), 732, 799, 800, 803

Wickard v. Filburn, 317 U.S. 111, 63 S.Ct. 82, 87 L.Ed. 122 (1942), 106

Wije v. Barton Springs/Edwards Aquifer Conservation District, 1995 WL 626204 (O.C.A.H.O.1995), 1228

Williams, United States ex rel. Turner v., 194 U.S. 279, 24 S.Ct. 719, 48 L.Ed. 979 (1904), 179

Windsor v. McVeigh, 93 U.S. 274, 3 Otto 274, 23 L.Ed. 914 (1876), 142

Winship, In re, 397 U.S. 358, 90 S.Ct. 1068, 25 L.Ed.2d 368 (1970), 713

Wong, Matter of, 12 I. & N. Dec. 271, Interim Decision (BIA) 1745 (BIA 1967), 583

Wong Kim Ark, United States v., 169 U.S. 649, 18 S.Ct. 456, 42 L.Ed. 890 (1898), 1269

Wong Wing Hang v. Immigration and Naturalization Service, 360 F.2d 715 (2nd Cir. 1966), 605

Wong Yang Sung v. McGrath, 339 U.S. 33, 70 S.Ct. 445, 94 L.Ed. 616 (1950), 650

Woodby v. Immigration and Naturalization Service, 385 U.S. 276, 87 S.Ct. 483, 17 L.Ed.2d 362 (1966), **705,** 711, 713, 714, 716, 733

Xi v. United States I.N.S., 298 F.3d 832 (9th Cir.2002), 207

X.P.T., In re, 21 I. & N. Dec. 634, Interim Decision (BIA) 3299 (BIA 1996), 960

Yamataya v. Fisher, 189 U.S. 86, 23 S.Ct. 611, 47 L.Ed. 721 (1903), **159,** 161, 162, 163, 231

Yanez–Garcia, In re, 23 I. & N. Dec. 390, Interim Decision (BIA) 3473 (BIA 2002), 562

Yanez–Garcia v. Ashcroft, 388 F.3d 280 (7th Cir.2004), 562

Yarina, In re, 73 F.Supp. 688 (N.D.Ohio 1947), 1287

Yazdani, Matter of, 17 I. & N. Dec. 626, Interim Decision (BIA) 2848 (BIA 1981), 385

Ye v. I.N.S., 214 F.3d 1128 (9th Cir.2000), 561

Yefremov v. NYC Dept. of Transprotation, 1993 WL 502295 (O.C.A.H.O.1993), 1229

Yerkovich v. Ashcroft, 381 F.3d 990 (10th Cir.2004), 737

Y–L–, In re, 23 I. & N. Dec. 270, Interim Decision 3464 (A.G. 2002), 1075

Yniguez v. Arizonans for Official English, 69 F.3d 920 (9th Cir.1995), 58

Y–T–L–, In re, 23 I. & N. Dec. 601, Interim Decision (BIA) 3492 (BIA 2003), 961

Yuen Sang Low v. Attorney General of United States, 479 F.2d 820 (9th Cir.1973), 519

Yui Sing Tse v. Immigration and Naturalization Service, 596 F.2d 831 (9th Cir.1979), 311

Zadvydas v. Davis, 533 U.S. 678, 121 S.Ct. 2491, 150 L.Ed.2d 653 (2001), 158, **191,** 203, 204, 205, 206, 207, 208, 210, 211, 228, 229, 230, 231, 755, 756, 853, 865

Zalawadia v. Ashcroft, 371 F.3d 292 (5th Cir. 2004), 865

Zamora v. Immigration and Naturalization Service, 534 F.2d 1055 (2nd Cir.1976), 1065

Zamora–Morel v. I.N.S., 905 F.2d 833 (5th Cir.1990), 1051

Zardui–Quintana v. Richard, 768 F.2d 1213 (11th Cir.1985), 803

Zavala v. Ridge, 310 F.Supp.2d 1071 (N.D.Cal.2004), 846

Zhang v. Slattery, 55 F.3d 732 (2nd Cir. 1995), 509

Zhao v. Gonzales, 404 F.3d 295 (5th Cir. 2005), 737

Zimmerman, United States ex rel. Castro–Louzan v., 94 F.Supp. 22 (E.D.Pa.1950), 663

Zinnanti v. Immigration & Naturalization Service, 651 F.2d 420 (5th Cir.1981), 533

*

TABLE OF SECONDARY AUTHORITIES

This table includes all books, articles (other than newspaper articles) and reports cited in this book, except for those that are cited only within reprinted materials. Student Notes and Comments are all listed as, and alphabetized under, "Note."

2003 Yearbook of Immigration Statistics [United States Dept. of Homeland Security, Office of Immigration Statistics, 2003 Yearbook of Immigration Statistics (Sept. 2004)]—23, 24, 239, 288, 336, 340, 345, 346, 383, 889, 931, 1085, 1086, 1090, 1205, 1278

Abourezk, James, *The Congressional Veto: A Contemporary Response to Executive Encroachment on Legislative Prerogatives*, 52 Indiana L.Rev. 323 (1977)—190

Abraham, David, International Decisions, *González ex rel. González v. Reno, 212 F.3d 1338 (11th Cir. 2000)*, 95 Amer. J. Internat'l L. 204 (2001)—1088

Abraham, David, *The Good of Banality? The Emergence of Cost–Benefit Analysis and Proportionality in the Treatment of Aliens in the United States and Germany*, 4 Citizenship Studies 237 (2000)—1370

Abrams, Kerry, *Polygamy, Prostitution, and the Federalization of Immigration Law*, 105 Columbia L. Rev. 641 (2005)—118, 264

Abreu, Alice G., *Taxing Exits*, 29 U.C. Davis L.Rev. 1087 (1996)—438, 1349

Abreu, Alice G., *The Difference Between Expatriates and Mrs. Gregory—Citizenship Can Matter*, 10 Tax Notes Internat'l 1612 (May 8, 1995)—1349

Abriel, Evangeline G., *Ending the Welcome: Changes in the United States Treatment of Undocumented Aliens (1986 to 1996)*, 1 Rutgers Race & L. Rev. 41 (1998)—1196

Abriel, Evangeline G., *Presumed Ineligible: The Effect of Criminal Convictions on Applications for Asylum and Withholding of Deportation Under Section 515 of the Immigration Act of 1990*, 6 Georgetown Immigration L.J. 27 (1992)—1073

Abriel, Evangeline G., *Rethinking Preemption for Purposes of Aliens and Public Benefits*, 42 UCLA L. Rev. 1597 (1995)—1255

Abriel, Evangeline G., *The Effect of Criminal Conduct upon Refugee and Asylum Status*, 3 Southwestern J. L. & Trade in the Americas 359 (1996)—1075

Acer, Eleanor & Lyon, Beth, *And the Boat Is Still Rocking: Asylum Practice Update in the Midst of Shifting Regulations and Caselaw: Part Two*, March 1999 Immigration Briefings—1058

Ackerman, Bruce A., Social Justice in the Liberal State (1980)—32

Adams, Laura S., *Divergence and the Dynamic Relationship Between Domestic Immigration Law and International Human Rights*, 51 Emory L.J. 983 (2002)—1191

Adams, Laura S., *Fleeing the Family: A Domestic Violence Victim's Particular Social Group*, 49 Loyola L. Rev. 287 (2003)—1035

Adlerstein, JoAnne C., *Immigration Crimes: A Practitioner's Guide*, Jan. 1989 Immigration Briefings—1206

AGORA, *Military Commissions*, 96 Amer. J. Internat'l L. 320 (2002)—855, 884

Ahmad, Muneer I., *A Rage Shared by Law: Post–September 11 Racial Violence as Crimes of Passion*, 92 California L. Rev. 1259 (2004)—100, 101, 892

AILA, *Boiling the Frog Slowly: Executive Branch Actions Since September 11, 2001*, 7 BIB 1236 (Oct. 15, 2002)—846

AILA, Immigration and Nationality Law Handbook (2000–01)—727

Akram, Susan M., *Orientalism Revisited in Asylum and Refugee Claims*, 12 Internat'l J. of Refugee L. 7 (2000)—83, 100

Akram, Susan M., *Palestinian Refugees and Their Legal Status: Rights, Politics, and Implications for a Just Solution*, 31/3 J. Palestine Studies No. 123, at 36 et seq. (2002)—928

Akram, Susan M., *Reinterpreting Palestinian Refugee Rights Under International Law*, in Naseer Aruri (ed.), Palestinian Refugees–The Right of Return, ch.10 (2001)—1191

Akram, Susan M., *Scheherezade Meets Kafka: Two Dozen Sordid Tales of Ideological Exclusion*, 14 Georgetown Immigration L.J. 51 (1999)—83, 100, 882

Akram, Susan & Johnson, Kevin R., *Race, Civil Rights, and Immigration Law After September 11, 2001: The Targeting of Ar-*

abs and Muslims, 58 NYU Ann. Survey Amer. L. 295 (2003)—892

Akram, Susan M. & Karmely, Maritza, *Immigration and Constitutional Consequences of Post–9/11 Policies Involving Arabs and Muslims in the United States: Is Alienage a Distinction Without a Difference?,* 38 U.C. Davis L. Rev. 609 (2005)—892

Akram, Susan M. & Rempel, Terry, *Temporary Protection as an Instrument for Implementing the Right of Return for Palestinian Refugees,* 22 Boston Univ. Internat'l L.J. 1 (2004)—1168

Aldana–Pindell, Raquel, *The 9/11 "National Security" Cases: Three Principles Guiding Judges' Decision–Making,* 81 Oregon L. Rev. 985 (2002)—914

Aleinikoff, T. Alexander, *Aliens, Due Process and "Community Ties": A Response to Martin,* 44 Univ. Pittsburgh L.Rev. 237 (1983)—31, 153

Aleinikoff, T. Alexander, Between Principles and Politics: The Direction of U.S. Citizenship Policy (1998)—1295

Aleinikoff, T. Alexander, *Citizens, Aliens, Membership and the Constitution,* 7 Const. Commentary 9 (1990)—173, 1365, 1372

Aleinikoff, T. Alexander, *Detaining Plenary Power: The Meaning and Impact of* Zadvydas v. Davis, 16 Georgetown Immigration L.J. 365 (2002)—204

Aleinikoff, T. Alexander, *Legal Immigration Reform: Toward Rationality and Equity,* in Richard D. Lamm & Alan Simpson (eds.), Center for Immigration Studies, Blueprints for an Ideal Legal Immigration Policy, Center Paper 17 (March 2001)—34, 249

Aleinikoff, T. Alexander, *Political Asylum in the Federal Republic of Germany and the Republic of France: Lessons for the United States,* 17 Univ. Michigan J. L. Reform 183 (1984)—1065, 1066, 1084, 1092

Aleinikoff, T. Alexander, Semblances of Sovereignty: The Constitution, the State, and American Citizenship (2002)—103, 139

Aleinikoff, T. Alexander, *The Meaning of "Persecution" in United States Asylum Law,* 3 Internat'l J. Refugee L. 5 (1991)—950

Aleinikoff, T. Alexander, *Theories of Loss of Citizenship,* 84 Michigan L. Rev. 1471 (1986)—1336, 1346, 1347

Aleinikoff, T. Alexander & Chetail, Vincent (eds.), Migration and International Legal Norms (2003)—13, 137, 1170

Aleinikoff, T. Alexander & Klusmeyer, Douglas (eds.), Citizenship Today: Global Perspectives and Practices (2001)—1351

Aleinikoff, T. Alexander & Klusmeyer, Douglas (eds.), From Migrants to Citizens— Membership in a Changing World (2000)—1351

Aleinikoff, T. Alexander & Martin, David A., Immigration Process and Policy (1st ed. 1985)—113, 410, 496, 519, 620, 1166

Aleinikoff, T. Alexander & Rumbaut, Ruben, *Terms of Belonging: Are Models of Membership Self-Fulfilling Prophecies?,* 13 Georgetown Immigration L.J. 1 (1998)—60

Alston, Philip (ed.), The United Nations and Human Rights–A Critical Appraisal (1992)—1191

American Bar Association Commission on Immigration Policy, Practice & Pro Bono, Seeking Meaningful Review: Findings and Recommendations in Response to Dorsey & Whitney Study of Board of Immigration Appeals Procedural Reforms (Oct. 2003)—718, 722, 723

American Friends Service Committee Report, U.S.-Mexico Border Project (Nov. 1999)—1198

Amnesty International, United States of America: Lost in the Labyrinth: Detention of Asylum–Seekers, Rpt. AMR51/51/99 (Sept. 1999)—1108

Anderson, Stuart, *The Multiplier Effect,* Internat'l Educator 13, 15 (Summer 2004)—75

Anderson, Stuart, *Widespread Abuse of H–1Bs and Employment–Based Immigration? The Evidence Says Otherwise,* 73 IR 637 (May 13, 1996)—311, 365

Anker, Deborah E., *A Case Study on the Implementation of Legal Norms in an Unstructured Adjudicatory Environment,* 19 NYU Rev. L. & Social Change 433 (1992)—1084

Anker, Deborah E., *Determining Asylum Claims in the United States—Summary Report of an Empirical Study of the Adjudication of Asylum Claims Before the Immigration Court,* 2 Internat'l J. Refugee L. 252 (1990)—1067, 1087

Anker, Deborah E., *Discretionary Asylum: A Protection Remedy for Refugees Under the Refugee Act of 1980,* 28 Virginia J. Internat'l L. 1 (1987)—939, 1078, 1080

Anker, Deborah E., *Gender and Social Group: Comments to Proposed Regulations,* 6 BIB 185 (Feb. 15, 2001)—1048

Anker, Deborah E., Law of Asylum in the United States (3d ed. 1999)—915, 950, 958, 963, 964, 976, 977, 978, 995, 1052, 1055, 1057, 1067, 1068, 1069, 1081, 1089, 1145

Anker, Deborah E., *Refugee Status and Violence Against Women in the "Domestic" Sphere: The Non–State Actor Question,* 15 Georgetown Immigration L.J. 391 (2001)—1026, 1030, 1035

Anker, Deborah E., *Women Refugees: Forgotten No Longer?,* 32 San Diego L.Rev. 771 (1995)—995

Anker, Deborah E., Blum, Carolyn P. & Johnson, Kevin R., *The Supreme Court's*

Decision in INS v. Elias–Zacarias: Is There any "There" There?, 69 IR 285 (Mar. 9, 1992)—970

Anker, Deborah E., Fitzpatrick, Joan & Shacknove, Andrew, Crisis and Cure: A Reply to Hathaway/Neve and Schuck, 11 Harvard Human Rights J. 295 (1998)—935

Anker, Deborah E., Gilbert, Lauren & Kelly, Nancy, Women Whose Governments are Unable or Unwilling to Provide Reasonable Protection from Domestic Violence May Qualify as Refugees under United States Asylum Law, 11 Georgetown Immigration L.J. 709 (1997)—1027

Anker, Deborah E., Kelly, Nancy & Willshire–Carrera, John, Defining "Particular Social Group" in Terms of Gender: The Shah Decision and U.S. Law, 76 IR 1005 (July 2, 1999)—1049

Anker, Deborah E., Kelly, Nancy & Willshire–Carrera, John, Rape in the Community as a Basis for Asylum: The Treatment of Women Refugees' Claims to Protection in Canada and the United States–Part 2, 2 BIB 608 (Aug. 1, 1997)—1007, 1008

Anker, Deborah, E. & Posner, Michael H., The Forty Year Crisis: A Legislative History of the Refugee Act of 1980, 19 San Diego L. Rev. 9 (1981)—928, 1064, 1066, 1091

Appleman, Irving A., Right to Counsel in Deportation Proceedings, 14 San Diego L.Rev. 130 (1976)—664

Arnold, Fred, Unanswered Questions About the Immigration Multiplier, 23 Internat'l Migration Rev. 889 (1989)—290

Aruri, Naseer (ed.), Palestinian Refugees–The Right of Return (2001)—1191

Augustine–Adams, Kif, The Plenary Power Doctrine After September 11, 38 U.C. Davis L. Rev. 701 (2005)—173

Avery, Christopher, Refugee Status Decision–Making: The Systems of Ten Countries, 19 Stanford J. Internat'l L. 235 (1983)—1091

Bach, Robert L., Building Community among Diversity: Legal Services for Impoverished Immigrants, 27 Univ. Michigan J. Law Reform 639 (1994)—665

Bach, Robert & Meissner, Doris, America's Labor Market in the 1990's: What Role Should Immigration Play? (1990)—290

Bach, Robert L. & Meissner, Doris, Employment and Immigration Reform: Employer Sanctions Four Years Later (1990)—1213, 1220

Bacon, David, Be Our Guests, The Nation (Sept. 27, 2004)—368

Balderrama, Francisco E. & Rodríguez, Raymond, Decade of Betrayal: Mexican Repatriation in the 1930s (1995)—367

Bar–Yaacov, Nissim, Dual Nationality (1961)—1295

Barrington, Lowell W., The Making of Citizenship Policy in the Baltic States, 13 Georgetown Immigration L.J. 159 (1999)—1351

Batchelor, Carol A., Stateless Persons: Some Gaps in International Protection, 7 Internat'l J. Refugee L. 232 (1995)—1297

Bau, Ignatius, This Ground is Holy—Church Sanctuary and Central American Refugees (1985)—1207

Bayefsky, Anne F. & Fitzpatrick, Joan (eds.), Human Rights and Forced Displacement, 4 Refugees & Human Rights (2000)—949

Bean, Frank D., Vernez, George & Keely, Charles B., Rand Corp. & Urban Institute, Opening and Closing the Doors—Evaluating Immigration Reform and Control (1989)—1219

Bell, Alan P., Weinberg, Martin S. & Hammersmith, Sue K., Sexual Preference—Its Development in Men and Women (1981)—266

Benson, Lenni B., Back to the Future: Congress Attacks the Right to Judicial Review of Immigration Proceedings, 29 Connecticut L. Rev. 1411 (1997)—741

Benson, Lenni B., Breaking Bureaucratic Borders: A Necessary Step Toward Immigration Law Reform, 54 Administrative L. Rev. 203 (2002)—452

Benson, Lenni B., By Hook or by Crook: Exploring the Legality of an INS Sting Operation, 31 San Diego L.Rev. 813 (1994)—644

Benson, Lenni B., The Invisible Worker, 27 North Carolina J. Internat'l L. & Commercial Regulation 483 (2002)—1195

Benson, Lenni B., The New World of Judicial Review of Removal Orders, 12 Georgetown Immigration L.J. 233 (1998)—741

Benson, Lenni B. & Bacon, Roxana C., A Practitioner's Guide to Successful Alien Labor Certifications, May 1988 Immigration Briefings—304, 311

Berger, Raoul, The Presidential Monopoly of Foreign Relations, 71 Mich.L.Rev. 1 (1972)—24

Berns, Walter, The Constitution and the Migration of Slaves, 78 Yale L.J. 198 (1968)—106

Bernsen, Sam, Consular Absolutism in Visa Cases, 63 IR 388 (1986)—469

Beyani, Chaloka, Fitzpatrick, Joan, Kälin, Walter & Zard, Monette (eds.), Exclusion from Protection, 12 Internat'l J. Refugee L. (special supp. issue, 2000)—1067

Bhabha, Jacqueline, Demography and Rights: Women, Children and Access to Asylum, 16 Internat'l J. Refugee L. 227 (2004)—1000

Bhabha, Jacqueline, Embodied Rights: Gender Persecution, State Sovereignty, and Refugees, 9 Public Culture 3 (1996)—995, 1008, 1020, 1023

Bhabha, Jacqueline, *European Harmonisation of Asylum Policy: A Flawed Process*, 35 Virginia J. Internat'l L. 101 (1994)—1098

Bhabha, Jacqueline, *Lone Travelers: Rights, Criminalization, and the Transnational Migration of Unaccompanied Children*, 7 Univ. Chicago L. School Roundtable 269 (2000)—936

Bhabha, Jacqueline, *Minors or Aliens? Inconsistent State Intervention and Separated Child Asylum–Seekers*, 3 European J. Migration & L. 283 (2001)—1087

Bhabha, Jacqueline, *"More than Their Share of Sorrows": International Migration Law and the Rights of Children*, 22 St. Louis Univ. Public L. Rev. 253 (2003)—1087

Bhabha, Jacqueline & Young, Wendy A., *Through a Child's Eyes: Protecting the Most Vulnerable Asylum Seekers*, 75 IR 757 (June 1, 1998)—936

Bhagwati, Jagdish & Rao, Milind, *The U.S. Brain Gain—At the Expense of Blacks?*, 39 Challenge 50 (March 1996)—383, 384, 385

Bickel, Alexander M., The Morality of Consent (1975)—1373

Black, Robert N., *Due Process and Deportation—Is there a Right to Assigned Counsel?*, 8 U.C. Davis L.Rev. 289 (1975)—664

Bleichmar, Javier, *Deportation as Punishment: A Historical Analysis of the British Practice of Banishment and Its Impact on Modern Constitutional Law*, 14 Georgetown Immigration L.J. 115 (1999)—499

Blum, Carolyn P., *A Question of Values: Continuing Divergences Between U.S. and International Refugee Norms*, 15 Berkeley J. Internat'l L. 1 (1997)—971

Blum, Carolyn P., *The Ninth Circuit and the Protection of Asylum Seekers Since the Passage of the Refugee Act of 1980*, 23 San Diego L.Rev. 327 (1986)—953

Bodenheimer, Edgar, Oakley, John B., & Love, Jean C., An Introduction to the Anglo–American Legal System (2d ed. 1988)—1287

Bogdan, Attila, *Guilty Pleas by Non–Citizens in Illinois: Immigration Consequences Reconsidered*, 53 DePaul L. Rev. 19 (2003)—537

Bonnerjea, Lucy, Shaming the World—The Needs of Women Refugees (1985)—996

Borjas, George J., Heaven's Door–Immigration Policy and the American Economy (1999)—62, 72, 1357

Bosniak, Linda S., *Citizenship Denationalized*, 7 Indiana J. Global Legal Studies 447 (2000)—1295, 1373

Bosniak, Linda S., *Exclusion and Membership: the Dual Identity of the Undocumented Worker under United States Law*, 1988 Wisconsin L. Rev. 955—1230, 1251

Bosniak, Linda S., *Human Rights, State Sovereignty and the Protection of Undocu-mented Migrants under the International Migrant Workers Convention*, 25 Internat'l Migration Rev. 737 (1991)—1203

Bosniak, Linda S., *Immigrants, Preemption and Equality*, 35 Virginia J. Internat'l L. 179 (1994)—1253

Bosniak, Linda S., *Membership, Equality, and the Difference that Alienage Makes*, 69 NYU L. Rev. 1047 (1994)—103, 1250, 1352

Bosniak, Linda S., *Multiple Nationality and the Postnational Transformation of Citizenship*, 42 Virginia J. Internat'l L. 979 (2002)—1295

Bosniak, Linda S., *Opposing Prop. 187: Undocumented Immigrants and the National Imagination*, 28 Connecticut L. Rev. 555 (1996)—1255

Boswell, Richard A., *Racism and U.S. Immigration Law: Prospects for Reform after "9/11"?*, 7 J. Gender, Race & Justice 315 (2003)—82

Boswell, Richard A., *Restrictions on Noncitizens' Access to Public Benefits: Flawed Premise, Unnecessary Response*, 42 UCLA L. Rev. 1475 (1995)—1196, 1255

Boswell, Richard A., *Rethinking Exclusion—the Rights of Cuban Refugees Facing Indefinite Detention in the United States*, 17 Vanderbilt J.Transnat'l L. 925 (1984)—156

Boyle, Daniel F., *Labor Certification Pitfalls*, 9 BIB 1354 (Nov. 15, 2004)—309

Brady, Michael P., *Asylum Adjudication: No Place for the INS*, 20 Columbia Human Rights L. Rev. 129 (1988)—1091

Brimelow, Peter, Alien Nation–Common Sense about America's Immigration Disaster (1995)—38

Brown, Peter G. & Shue, Henry (eds.), Boundaries–National Autonomy and Its Limits (1981)—31, 32, 33, 1373

Brubaker, William R. (ed.), Immigration and the Politics of Citizenship in Europe and North America (1989)—1295, 1296

Buergenthal, Thomas & Murphy, Sean D., Public International Law in a Nutshell (3d ed. 2002)—940, 1147

Burgess, Susan N., *SEVIS: Is It Academic?*, Feb. 2004 Immigration Briefings—868

Butcher, Kristin F. & Piehl, Anne Morrison, Recent Immigrants: Unexpected Implications for Crime and Incarceration, NBER Working Paper No. 6067 (June 1997)—531

Butterfield, Jeanne A., *The New Asylum Regulations: A Practitioner's Guide*, Jan. 1995 Immigration Briefings—1083

Byrne, Rosemary, Noll, Gregor, & Vested–Hansen, Jens (eds.), New Asylum Countries? Migration Control and Refugee Protection in an Enlarged European Union (2002)—1098

Byrne, Rosemary & Shacknove, Andrew, *The Safe Country Notion in European Asylum*

Law, 9 Harvard Human Rights J. 185 (1996)—1097, 1098

Calavita, Kitty, *Employer Sanctions Violations: Toward a Dialectical Model of White–Collar Crime*, 24 L. & Society Rev. 1041 (1990)—1219

Calvo, Janet M., *A Decade of Spouse–Based Immigration Laws: Coverture's Diminishment, But Not Its Demise*, 24 Northern Illinois Univ. L. Rev. 153 (2004)—275, 453

Calvo, Janet M., *Immigrant Status and Legal Access to Health Care* (1993)—1234

Calvo, Janet M., *Spouse–Based Immigration Laws: The Legacies of Coverture*, 28 San Diego L.Rev. 593 (1991)—274

Calvo, Janet M., *The Violence Against Women Act: An Opportunity for the Justice Department to Confront Domestic Violence*, 72 IR 485 (Apr. 10, 1995)—453, 582

Cameron, Christopher David Ruiz, *How the García Cousins Lost their Accents: Understanding the Language of Title 7 Decisions Approving English–Only Rules as the Product of Racial Dualism, Latino Invisibility, and Legal Indeterminacy*, 85 California L. Rev. 261 (1997)—59

Cao, Lan, Monkey Bridge (1997)—100

Caprara, Alfonso, Engineer, Rumi, & Marcouiller, Barbara (eds.), AILA, Ethics and Your Immigration Practice: Have you Considered . . . ? (1998)—310

Capriotti, Franco, Ramirez, Linda Friedman, Norikay, Leslie & Unger, Rachel, *Small–Time Crime, Big–Time Trouble: The New Immigration Laws*, 13 Crim. Justice #2 (1998)—678

Carens, Joseph H., *Aliens and Citizens: The Case for Open Borders*, 49 Rev. of Politics 251 (1987)—29

Carlier, Jean–Yves & Vanheule, Dirk (eds.), Europe and Refugees: A Challenge? (1997)—915

Carlin, James L., *Significant Refugee Crises since World War II and the Response of the International Community*, 1982 Michigan Yearbook Internat'l Legal Studies 3—925, 926

Carliner, David, *United States Compliance with the Helsinki Final Act: The Treatment of Aliens*, 13 Vanderbilt J. Transnat'l L. 397 (1980)—429

Carliner, David, Guttentag, Lucas, Helton, Arthur C. & Henderson, Wade, The Rights of Aliens and Refugees (2d ed. 1990)—635, 1230, 1351

Carrasco, Gilbert Paul, *Congressional Arrogation of Power: Alien Constellation in the Galaxy of Equal Protection*, 74 Boston Univ. L. Rev. 591 (1994)—1358

Carrasco, Gilbert Paul, *Latinos in the United States–Invitation and Exile*, in Juan F. Perea (ed.), Immigrants Out! The New Nativism and the Anti–Immigrant Impulse in the United States, at 190 et seq. (1997)—82, 367

Carro, Jorge L., *From Constitutional Psychopathic Inferiority to AIDS: What is in the Future for Homosexual Aliens?*, 7 Yale L. & Policy Rev. 201 (1989)—259, 267, 442, 443

Carro, Jorge L., *Municipal and State Sanctuary Declarations: Innocuous Symbolism or Improper Dictates?*, 16 Pepperdine L. Rev. 297 (1989)—1206, 1207

Carro, Jorge L., *Sanctuary: The Resurgence of an Age–Old Right or a Dangerous Misinterpretation of an Abandoned Ancient Privilege?*, 54 Univ. Cincinnati L. Rev. 747 (1986)—1207

Carter, Barry E. & Trimble, Phillip R., International Law (2d ed. 1995)—1147

Chander, Anupam, *Diaspora Bonds*, 76 NYU L. Rev. 1005 (2001)—1373

Chang, Gordon H. (ed.), Asian Americans and Politics (2001)—99

Chang, Howard F., *Immigration and the Workplace: Immigration Restrictions as Employment Discrimination*, 78 Chicago–Kent L. Rev. 291 (2003)—333, 1213

Chang, Howard F., *Immigration Policy, Liberal Principles, and the Republican Tradition*, 85 Georgetown L.J. 2105 (1997)—29, 82

Chang, Howard F., *Liberal Ideals and Political Feasibility: Guest–Worker Programs as Second–Best Policies*, 27 No. Car. J. Internat'l & Commercial Regulation 465 (2002)—372

Chang, Howard F., *Liberalized Immigration as Free Trade: Economic Welfare and the Optimal Immigration Policy*, 145 U. Pa. L. Rev. 1147 (1997)—333

Chang, Howard F., *Migration as International Trade: The Economic Gains from the Liberalized Movement of Labor*, 3 UCLA J. Law & Foreign Affairs 371 (1998)—66, 333

Chang, Howard F., *Public Benefits and Federal Authorization for Alienage Discrimination by the States*, 58 NYU Ann. Survey Amer. L. 357 (2002)—1358

Chang, Howard F., *The Immigration Paradox: Poverty, Distributive Justice, and Liberal Egalitarianism*, 52 DePaul L. Rev. 759 (2003)—372

Chang, Robert S., Disoriented: Asian Americans, Law, and the Nation–State (1999)—99

Chang, Robert S., *Toward an Asian American Legal Scholarship: Critical Race Theory, Post–Structuralism, and Narrative Space*, 81 California L. Rev. 1241 (1993)—99

Cheetham, Janet H. (ed.), Immigration Practice and Procedure under the North American Free Trade Agreement (1995)—377

Chetail, V. & Gowlland–Debbas, Vera (eds.), Switzerland and the International Protection of Refugees (2002)—1026

Chiappari, Ted J., *LCA Wage Regulations: A Can of Worms for the Employer to Open*, 72 IR 1437 (Oct. 23, 1995)—364

Chiappari, Ted J., *Survey of Labor Condition Application Enforcement Proceedings*, 73 IR 673 (May 20, 1996)—364

Chin, Gabriel J., *Is There a Plenary Power Doctrine? A Tentative Apology and Prediction for Our Strange but Unexceptional Constitutional Immigration Law*, 14 Georgetown Immigration L.J. 257 (2000)—229

Chin, Gabriel J., *Segregation's Last Stronghold: Race Discrimination and the Constitutional Law of Immigration*, 46 UCLA L. Rev. 1 (1998)—232

Chin, Gabriel J., *The Civil Rights Revolution Comes to Immigration Law: A New Look at the Immigration and Nationality Act of 1965*, 75 North Carolina L.Rev. 273 (1996)—19

Chin, Gabriel J. & Holmes, Richard W., *Effective Assistance of Counsel and the Consequences of Guilty Pleas*, 87 Cornell L. Rev. 697 (2002)—537

Chishti, Muzaffar A. et al, Migration Policy Institute, America's Challenge: Domestic Security, Civil Liberties and National Unity after September 11 (2003)—908

Christian, Bryan Paul, *Visa Policy, Inspection and Exit Controls: Transatlantic Perspectives on Migration Management*, 14 Georgetown Immigration L.J. 215 (1999)—484

Chuman, Frank F., The Bamboo People (1976)—108, 843

Churgin, Michael J., *Immigration Internal Decisionmaking: A View from History*, 78 Texas L. Rev. 1633 (2000)—14

Churgin, Michael J., *Mass Exoduses: The Response of the United States*, 30 Internat'l Migration Rev. 310 (1996)—1130

Cipriani, Linda, *Gender and Persecution: Protecting Women under International Refugee Law*, 7 Georgetown Immigration L.J. 511 (1993)—995

Clark, Dick, Foreword to Elizabeth Hull, Without Justice For All—The Constitutional Rights of Aliens at ix (1985)—932

Cleveland, Sarah H., *Powers Inherent in Sovereignty: Indians, Aliens, Territories, and the Nineteenth Century Origins of Plenary Power over Foreign Affairs*, 81 Texas L. Rev. 1 (2002)—139

Cleveland, Sarah H., *The Plenary Power Background of Curtiss–Wright*, 70 U. Colorado L. Rev. 1127 (1999)—139

Cole, David, *Enemy Aliens*, 54 Stanford L. Rev. 953 (2002)—431, 844, 892, 896, 897

Cole, David, Enemy Aliens–Double Standards and Constitutional Freedoms in the War on Terrorism (2003)—844, 845, 892, 914

Cole, David, *In Aid of Removal: Due Process Limits on Immigration Detention*, 51 Emory L. Rev. 1003 (2002)—844, 846, 853

Cole, David, *Judging the Next Emergency: Judicial Review and Individual Rights in Times of Crisis*, 101 Michigan L. Rev. 2565 (2003)—865

Cole, David, *Jurisdiction and Liberty: Habeas Corpus and Due Process as Limits on Congress's Control of Federal Jurisdiction*, 86 Georgetown L.J. 2481 (1998)—741

Cole, David, *The Priority of Morality: The Emergency Constitution's Blind Spot*, 113 Yale L.J. 1753 (2004)—910

Cole, Richard P., & Chin, Gabriel J., *Emerging from the Margins of Historical Consciousness: Chinese Immigrants and the History of American Law*, 17 Law & History Rev. 325 (1999)—118

Colon, Jeffrey M., *Changing U.S. Tax Jurisdiction: Expatriates, Immigrants, and the Need for a Coherent Tax Policy*, 34 San Diego L. Rev. 1 (1997)—1349

Commission for the Study of Internat'l Migration and Cooperative Economic Development, Report, Unauthorized Migration: An Economic Development Response (July 1990)—1201

Commission of the European Communities, Proposal for a Council Directive on minimum standards for the qualification and status of third country nationals and stateless persons as refugees or as persons who otherwise need international protection, COM(2001), 510 final, 2001/0207 (CNS) (Dec. 9, 2001)—1028

Committee on Federal Courts, The Surge of Immigration Appeals and Its Impact on the Second Circuit Court of Appeals (2004)—729

Cooper, Bo, *Procedures for Expedited Removal and Asylum Screening under the Illegal Immigration Reform and Immigrant Responsibility Act of 1996*, 29 Connecticut L. Rev. 1501 (1997)—1106

Cornelius, Wayne A., *Evaluating Enhanced U.S. Border Enforcement*, 9 BIB 654 (May 15, 2004)—1198

Costello, Patrick, *Haiti: Prospects for Democracy*, 15 Ref. Survey Q. 1 (1996)—1132

Covington & Burling and National Asian Pacific American Legal Consortium, *Protecting the Rights of Legal Permanent Residents: A First Amendment Analysis of Proposals to Prohibit Campaign Contributions and Expenditures by Legal Permanent Residents*, 3 BIB 16 (Jan. 1, 1998)—1350

Cox, Adam M., *Citizenship, Standing, and Immigration Law*, 92 California L. Rev. 373 (2004)—179

Craig, Barbara H., Chadha—The Story of an Epic Constitutional Struggle (1988)—191

Crawley, Heaven, Refugees and Gender–Law and Process (2001)—995

Crépeau, François & Janik, Kinga, Comparative Study on Immigration and Social Transformation–Canada (2004)—280

Crock, Mary E., *Apart from Us or a Part of Us? Immigrants' Rights, Public Opinion and the Rule of Law*, 10 Internat'l J. Refugee L. 49 (1998)—961

Crock, Mary E., *Contract or Compact: Skilled Migration and the Dictates of Politics and Ideology*, 16 Georgetown Immigration L.J. 133 (2001)—332, 366

Crock, Mary E., Immigration and Refugee Law in Australia (1998)—1234

Currie, David P. & Goodman, Frank I., *Judicial Review of Federal Administrative Action: Quest for the Optimum Forum*, 75 Columbia L.Rev. 1 (1975)—731

D'Emilio, John, Sexual Politics, Sexual Communities—The Making of a Homosexual Minority in the United States 1940–1970 (1983)—267

Daoust, Isabelle & Folkelius, Kristina, *UNHCR Symposium on Gender–Based Persecution*, 8 Internat'l J. Refugee L. 180 (1996)—995

Davis, Martha F., Guttentag, Lucas & Wernick, Allan H., *Report of the Committee on Immigration and Nationality Law of the Association of the Bar of the City of New York: An Analysis of Discrimination Resulting from Employer Sanctions and a Call for Repeal*, 26 San Diego L. Rev. 711 (1989)—1219, 1220

DeConcini, Christina & McKenna, Molly, *BIA Pro Bono Project: Representing Detained Migrants Before the BIA and Uncovering Government Obstacles to Pro Se Detainees Appealing their Cases*, 6 BIB 809 (Aug. 15, 2001)—666

Demleitner, Nora V., *How Much Do Western Democracies Value Family and Marriage?: Immigration Law's Conflicted Answers*, 32 Hofstra L. Rev. 273 (2003)—291

Demleitner, Nora V., *Immigration Threats and Rewards: Effective Law Enforcement Tools in the "War" on Terrorism*, 51 Emory L.J. 1059 (2002)—530, 1208

Demleitner, Nora V., *Power, Perceptions, and the Politics of Immigration and Welfare*, 14 Industrial Development & Social Fabric 9 (1998)—1357

Demleitner, Nora V., *The Fallacy of Social "Citizenship," or the Threat of Exclusion*, 12 Georgetown Immigration L.J. 35 (1997)—1353

Demleitner, Nora V., *The Law at a Crossroads: The Construction of Migrant Women Trafficked into Prostitution*, in David Kyle & Rey Koslowski (eds.), Global Human Smuggling: Comparative Perspectives (2001), ch.10—402, 1207

Deng, Francis Mading, *The Global Challenge of Internal Displacement*, 5 Washington Univ. J. L. & Policy 141 (2001)—937

Developments in the Law, *Immigration Policy and the Rights of Aliens*, 96 Harvard L.Rev. 1286 (1983)—33, 663

Divine, Robert A., American Immigration Policy, 1924–1952 (1957)—921, 922, 924

Dobbs, Dan B., The Law of Torts (2000)—33, 1038, 1052

Dorsey & Whitney LLP, Study Conducted for the American Bar Association Commission on Immigration Policy, Practice and Pro Bono, Re Board of Immigration Appeals: Procedural Reforms to Improve Case Management (July 22, 2003)—718, 723

Dow, Mark, American Gulag—Inside U.S. Immigration Prisons (2004)—229

Dowty, Alan, Closed Borders–The Contemporary Assault on Freedom of Movement (1987)—34

Duignan, Peter & Gann, Lewis H. (eds.), The Debate in the United States over Immigration (1998)—1213

Durst, Ilene, *Lost in Translation: Why Due Process Demands Deference to the Refugee's Narrative*, 53 Rutgers L. Rev. 127 (2000)—1058

Duvall, Donald K.,*Expatriation Under United States Law*, Perez to Afroyim: The Search for a Philosophy of American Citizenship, 56 Virginia L. Rev. 408 (1970)—1336

Einhorn, Bruce J., *Political Asylum in the Ninth Circuit and the Case of Elias–Zacarias*, 29 San Diego L. Rev. 597 (1992)—969

Eisgruber, Christopher L., *Birthright Citizenship and the Constitution*, 72 NYU L. Rev. 54 (1997)—1312

Endelman, Gary, *How to Prevent Loss of Citizenship: Part I*, Nov. 1989 Immigration Briefings—1345

Endelman, Gary, *How to Prevent Loss of Citizenship: Part II*, Dec. 1989 Immigration Briefings—1348

Endelman, Gary, *Mother Knows Best: A New Look at an Old Law*, 13 Immigration J. 29 (Apr.–June 1990)—1275

Endelman, Gary, *Saying Goodbye to Uncle Sam: Formal Renunciation of U.S. Citizenship*, 73 IR 709 (May 24, 1996)—1336, 1344, 1345

Epps, Valerie, *The Validity of the Political Offender Exception in Extradition Treaties in Anglo–American Jurisprudence*, 20 Harvard Internat'l L.J. 61 (1979)—1076

Espenoza, Cecelia M., *No Relief for the Weary: VAWA Relief Denied for Battered Immigrants Lost in the Intersections*, 83 Marquette L. Rev. 163 (1999)—453

Espenoza, Cecelia M., *The Illusory Provisions of Sanctions: The Immigration Reform and Control Act of 1986*, 8 Georgetown Immigration L.J. 343 (1994)—1213

Fallon, Richard H., *Applying the Suspension Clause to Immigration Cases*, 98 Columbia L. Rev. 1068 (1998)—741

Fehlings, Gregory, *Storm on the Constitution: The First Deportation Law*, 10 Tulsa J. Comp. & Internat'l L. 63 (2002)—107

Feller, Erika, *The Evolution of the International Refugee Protection Regime*, 5 Washington Univ. J. of L. & Policy 129 (2001)—935

Feller, Erika, Türk, Volker, & Nicholson, Frances (eds.), Refugee Protection in International Law: UNHCR's Global Consultations on International Protection (2003)—292, 1110

Ferg–Cadima, James A., MALDEF, *Survey of Recent State Law and Legislation during the 2003–04 Legislative Term Aimed at Facilitating Undocumented Student Access to State Universities* (May 18, 2003)—1257

Feroli, James, *Habeas Corpus Subject Matter Jurisdiction over Final Orders of Removal Pursuant to 28 U.S.C.A. § 2241*, Sept. 2004 Immigration Briefings—735

Fitzpatrick, Joan, *Flight from Asylum: Trends Toward Temporary "Refuge" and Local Responses to Forced Migrations*, 35 Virginia J. Internat'l L. 13 (1994)—1171

Fitzpatrick, Joan, *Human Rights and Forced Displacement: Converging Standards*, in Anne F. Bayefsky & Joan Fitzpatrick, Human Rights and Forced Displacement, 4 Refugees & Human Rights 3 (2000)—949

Fitzpatrick, Joan (ed.), Human Rights Protection for Refugees, Asylum–Seekers, and Internally Displaced Persons–A Guide to International Mechanisms and Procedures (2002)—1191

Fitzpatrick, Joan, *Race, Immigration, and Legal Scholarship: A Response to Kevin Johnson*, 2000 Univ. of Illinois L. Rev. 603—101

Fitzpatrick, Joan, *Temporary Protection of Refugees: Elements of a Formalized Regime*, 94 Amer. J. Internat'l L. 279 (2000)—1171

Fitzpatrick, Joan, *The End of Protection: Legal Standards for Cessation of Refugee Status*, 13 Georgetown Immigration L.J. 343 (1999)—936

Fitzpatrick, Joan, *The Gender Dimension of U.S. Immigration Policy*, 9 Yale J. Law & Feminism 23 (1997)—305

Fitzpatrick, Joan, *The Post–Exclusion Phase: Extradition, Prosecution and Expulsion*, 12 Internat'l J. Refugee L. (special issue) at 272 (2000)—1076

Fitzpatrick, Joan, & Bennett, William McKay, *A Lion in the Path? The Influence of International Law on the Immigration*

Policy of the United States, 70 Washington L.Rev. 589 (1995)—232, 442

Fitzpatrick, Joan & Kelly, Katrina, *Gendered Aspects of Migration: Law and the Female Migrant*, 22 Hastings Internat'l & Comparative L. Rev. 47 (1998)—305

Fitzpatrick, Joan & Pauw, Robert, *Foreign Policy, Asylum and Discretion*, 28 Willamette L. Rev. 751 (1992)—933, 1080

Fix, Michael & Hill, Paul T., Enforcing Employer Sanctions: Challenges and Strategies (1990)—1213, 1219, 1220

Fix, Michael, Passel, Jeffrey S. & Sucher, Kenneth, *Trends in Naturalization*, 80 IR 1473 (Oct. 27, 2003)—1278

Fix, Michael & Zimmermann, Wendy, *Patterns of Welfare Use among Immigrants*, 23 Migration World, No. 5, at 15 (1995)—1357

Fleissner, James P. & Shapiro, James A., *Federal Sentences for Aliens Convicted of Illegal Reentry Following Deportation: Who Needs the Aggravation?*, 9 Georgetown Immigration L.J. 451 (1995)—555

Flynn, Eugene, *Countries Which the U.S. Recognizes as Eligible (or soon to be eligible) for E–1 or E–2 Status* (periodically updated)—359

Flynn III, William J. & Patel, Dilip, *Employers, Employees and Ethics*, in Alfonso Caprara, Rumi Engineer & Barbara Marcouiller (eds.), AILA, Ethics and Your Immigration Practice: Have you Considered … ?, at 31 (1998)—310

Forced Migration Project, Open Society Institute, A Proposal to Establish a Temporary Refuge Scheme in the Caribbean Region for Refugee and Migration Emergencies (1995)—935

Fragomen, Austin T., Del Rey, Alfred J. & Bernsen, Sam, Immigration Law and Business (1996)(2 vols.)—311, 348

Fragomen, Austin T., Del Rey, Alfred J. & Bernsen, Sam (law firm), *Proper Standards for Admission in the B–1 Category*, 1990 Immigration & Nationality L.Rev. 363—357

Fragomen, Austin T. & Robosson, Gwendolyn M., *The Foreign Investor: Current Approaches Toward United States Immigration Law*, 18 Vanderbilt J. Transnat'l L. 335 (1985)—334

Francis, John J., *Failure to Advise Non–Citizens of Immigration Consequences of Criminal Convictions: Should This Be Grounds to Withdraw a Guilty Plea?*, 36 Univ. Michigan J. L. Reform 691 (2003)—537

Franck, Thomas M., *Clan and Superclan: Loyalty, Identity and Community in Law and Practice*, 90 Amer. J. Internat'l L. 359 (1996)—1295, 1296

Free, Robert A., *The Lawyer's Role in Consular Visa Refusals*, Nov. 1990 Immigration Briefings—468

Free, Robert A., Paparelli, Angelo A. & Peterson, Jan M., *Consular Processing*, in AILA, 1989(1) Immigration and Nationality Law at 225—468

Freeman, Gary P., & Birrell, Bob, *Divergent Paths of Immigration Politics in the United States and Australia*, 27 Population & Development Rev. 525 (2001)—83

Frelick, Bill, *North America Considers Agreement to Deflect Asylum Seekers*, 7 BIB 1404 (Nov. 15, 2002)—1103

Frelick, Bill, *U.S. Detention of Asylum Seekers: What's the Problem? What's the Solution?*, 10 BIB 564 (Apr. 1, 2005)—1108

Frelick, Bill, *Who's On First? The Canada–U.S. Memorandum of Agreement on Asylum*, 73 IR 217 (Feb. 26, 1996)—1102

Frenzen, Niels W., *National Security and Procedural Fairness: Secret Evidence and the Immigration Laws*, 76 IR 1677 (Nov. 22, 1999)—880, 881, 882

Frey, Barbara & Udagama, Deepika, *Assisting Indigent Political Asylum Seekers in the United States: A Model for Volunteer Legal Assistance*, 13 Hamline L.Rev. 661 (1990)—666

Frickey, Philip P., *Domesticating Federal Indian Law*, 81 Minnesota L.Rev. 31 (1996)—139

Friedland, Bernard & Epps, Valerie, *The Changing Family and the U.S. Immigration Laws: The Impact of Medical Reproductive Technology on the Immigration and Nationality Act's Definition of the Family*, 11 Georgetown Immigration L.J. 429 (1997)—284

Friedler, Edith Z., *From Extreme Hardship to Extreme Deference: United States Deportation of its Own Children*, 22 Hastings Const.L.Q. 491 (1995)—595

Frisch, Max, Überfremdung I, in Schweiz als Heimat?, at 219 (1990)—362

Fullerton, Maryellen, *A Comparative Look at Refugee Status Based on Persecution Due to Membership in a Particular Social Group*, 26 Cornell Internat'l L.J. 505 (1993)—985

Fullerton, Maryellen, *Cuban Exceptionalism: Migration and Asylum in Spain and the United States*, 35 Inter–American L. Rev. 527 (2004)—156

Fullerton, Maryellen, *Failing the Test: Germany Leads Europe in Dismantling Refugee Protection*, 36 Texas Internat'l L.J. 231 (2001)—1098

Fullerton, Maryellen, *Hungary, Refugees, and the Law of Return*, 8 Internat'l J. Refugee L. 499 (1996)—933

Fullerton, Maryellen, *Persecution Due to Membership in a Particular Social Group: Jurisprudence in the Federal Republic of Germany*, 4 Georgetown Immigration L.J. 381 (1990)—984, 985

Fullerton, Maryellen & Kinigstein, Noah, *Strategies for Ameliorating the Immigration Consequences of Criminal Convictions: A Guide for Defense Attorneys*, 23 Amer.Crim.L.Rev. 425 (1986)—530, 531

Fullerton, Maryellen & Nafziger, James A.R., *Draft Declaration on Internally Displaced Persons*, in Immigration Law Conference, Scholarship Panels Works in Progress 187 (1996)—937

Gabor, Francis A., *Reflections on the Freedom of Movement in Light of the Dismantled "Iron Curtain,"* 65 Tulane L. Rev. 849 (1991)—1181

Gabor, Francis A., *The Immigration Reform and Control Act of 1986: An Analysis in the Light of Contemporary International Law*, 23 Internat'l Lawyer 485 (1989)—1181

Gagné, Chris, *POTA: Lessons Learned from India's Anti–Terror Act*, 25 Boston College Third World L. Rev. 261 (2005)—914

Gallagher, Anna Marie, *Immigration Consequences of Criminal Convictions: Protecting Your Client's Immigration Interests in Criminal Proceedings*, April 2001 Immigration Briefings—530, 533

Gallagher, Anna Marie, *Practice and Procedure Before the Board of Immigration Appeals: An Update*, Feb. 2003 Immigration Briefings—717, 718

Galloway, Donald, Immigration Law (1997)—280

Galloway, J. Donald, *The Dilemmas of Canadian Citizenship Law*, 13 Georgetown Immigration L.J. 201 (1999)—1351, 1373

Garcia, Juan R., Operation Wetback, The Mass Deportation of Mexican Undocumented Workers in 1954 (1980)—367

Garcia, Ruben J., *Across the Borders: Immigrant Status and Identity in Law and LatCrit Theory*, 55 Florida L. Rev. 511 (2003)—1224

Garcia, Ruben J., *Ghost Workers in an Interconnected World: Going Beyond the Dichotomies of Domestic Immigration and Labor Laws*, 36 Univ. Michigan J. L. Reform 737 (2003)—1202

Garis, Roy L., Immigration Restriction(1927)—32

Gee, Harvey, *Asian Americans, the Law, and Illegal Immigration in Post–Civil Rights America: A Review of Three Books*, 77 Univ. of Detroit Mercy L. Rev. 71 (1999)—100

Gerety, Tom, *Children in the Labyrinth: The Complexities of Plyler v. Doe*, 44 Univ. Pittsburgh L. Rev. 379 (1983)—1251

Germain, Regina, *Perspectives on the Bush Administration's New Immigrant Guestworker Proposal*, 32 Denver J. Internat'l L. & Policy 747 (2004)—1195

Gibney, Mark (ed.), Open Borders? Closed Societies? The Ethical and Political Issues (1988)—29

Gibney, Matthew J., *Asylum and the Principle of Proximity*, 3 Ethics, Race & Environment 313 (2000)—1180

Gibson, Paul, *Gay Male and Lesbian Youth Suicide*, in 3 Report of the Secretary's Task Force on Youth Suicide 110 (Jan. 1989)—269

Gilbert, Lauren, *When Democracy Dies Behind Closed Doors: The First Amendment and "Special Interest" Hearings*, 55 Rutgers L. Rev. 741 (2003)—880

Gilboy, Janet A., *Administrative Review in a System of Conflicting Values*, 13 L. & Social Inquiry 515 (1988)—637

Gilboy, Janet A., *Implications of "Third–Party" Involvement in Enforcement: The INS, Illegal Travelers, and International Airlines*, 31 L. & Society Rev. 505 (1997)—486

Gilboy, Janet A., *Setting Bail in Deportation Cases: The Role of Immigration Judges*, 24 San Diego L.Rev. 347 (1987)—637

Goddard, Christopher, *Valuing Citizenship: The Case for Retaining a Citizenship–Based Electorate* (unpublished student seminar paper, 2005)—1353

Gold, Eric, *Leyes del "Inglés Solamente" ("English–Only Laws")* (unpublished student seminar paper, 2003)—60

Goldberg, Pamela, *Analytical Approaches in Search of Consistent Application: A Comparative Analysis of the Second Circuit Decisions Addressing Gender in the Asylum Law Context*, 66 Brooklyn L. Rev. 309 (2000)—1051

Goldberg, Pamela, *Anyplace but Home: Asylum in the United States for Women Fleeing Intimate Violence*, 26 Cornell Internat'l L.J. 565 (1993)—995, 1027

Goldberg, Pamela, *Women and Refugee Status: A Review Essay*, 7 Internat'l J. Refugee L. 756 (1995)—995

Goldberg, Pamela & Cissé, Bernadette Pasade, *Gender Issues in Asylum Law after Matter of R–A–*, Feb. 2000 Immigration Briefings—1027

Goldstein, Eugene & Piazza, Victoria, *Naturalization, Dual Citizenship and Retention of Foreign Citizenship*, 75 IR 1613 (Nov. 23, 1998)—1294

Gomez, Iris, *The Consequences of Nonappearance: Interpreting New Section 242B of the Immigration and Nationality Act*, 30 San Diego L.Rev. 75 (1993)—839

González-Baker, Susan, Plascencia, Luis F.B., Freeman, Gary P. & Orozco, Manuel, Tomás Rivera Institute, *The Making of Americans–Results of the Texas Naturalization Survey*, Policy Brief (Aug. 2000)—1282

Goodman, Ryan, Note, *The Incorporation of International Human Rights Standards into Sexual Orientation Asylum Claims: Cases of Involuntary "Medical" Intervention*, 105 Yale L.J. 255 (1995)—949, 951, 994

Goodwin–Gill, Guy S., *Article 31 of the 1951 Convention Relating to the Status of Refugees: Non-penalization, Detention and Protection*, in Erika Feller, Volker Türk & Frances Nicholson (eds.), Refugee Protection in International Law: UNHCR's Global Consultations on International Protection, at 185–252 (2003)—1109

Goodwin–Gill, Guy S., *Judicial Reasoning and Social Group after Islam and Shah*, 11 Internat'l J. Refugee L. 537 (1999)—1049

Goodwin–Gill, Guy S., International Law and the Movement of Persons Between States (1978)—13, 137, 500, 1171

Goodwin–Gill, Guy S., *Non–Refoulement and the New Asylum Seekers*, 26 Virginia J. Internat'l L. 897 (1986)—938, 1182

Goodwin–Gill, Guy S., *The Obligations of States and the Protection Function of the Office of the United Nations High Commissioner for Refugees*, 1982 Michigan Yearbook Internat'l Legal Studies 291—1066

Goodwin–Gill, Guy S., The Refugee in International Law (1983)—924

Goodwin–Gill, Guy S., The Refugee in International Law (2d ed. 1996)—915, 1171

Gordon, Charles, *Recent Developments in Judicial Review of Immigration Cases*, 15 San Diego L.Rev. 9 (1977)—469

Gordon, Charles, *The Citizen and the State: Power of Congress to Expatriate American Citizens*, 53 Georgetown L. Rev. 315 (1965)—1268, 1334, 1336

Gordon, Charles, *The Marriage Fraud Act of 1986*, 4 Georgetown Immigration L.J. 183 (1990)—272, 277

Gordon, Charles, *Who Can Be President of the United States: The Unresolved Enigma*, 28 Maryland L. Rev. 1 (1968)—1267

Gordon, Charles, Mailman, Stanley & Yale–Loehr, Stephen, Immigration Law and Procedure (continually updated)—14, 288, 289, 298, 348, 358, 361, 455, 462, 498, 500, 522, 607, 615, 622, 638, 727, 915, 931, 1168, 1266, 1267, 1268, 1274, 1276, 1283, 1284, 1291, 1297

Gordon, Howard W. & Morawetz, Nancy H., *Special Registration: A Nightmare for Foreign Visitors*, Immigration Law Today (Mar/Apr 2003), at 42—868

Gordon, Jennifer, Suburban Sweatshops–The Fight for Immigrant Rights (2005)—1202

Gotanda, Neil, *"Other Non–Whites" in American Legal History: A Review of* Justice at War, 85 Columbia L. Rev. 1186 (1985)—99

Gragert, Michael D. & Harvey, Kathleen, *Asylum Granted in "Honor Killing" Case*, 7 BIB 513 (May 1, 2002)—997

Grahl–Madsen, Atle, The Status of Refugees in International Law (2 vols., 1966 and 1972)—915, 1171

Graves, Maureen, *From Definition to Exploration: Social Groups and Political Asylum Eligibility*, 20 San Diego L.Rev. 740 (1989)—950, 951, 986

Greatbatch, Jacqueline, the Gender Difference: Feminist Critiques of Refugee Discourse, 1 Internat'l J. Refugee L. 518 (1989)—997

Green, Richard, The "Sissy Boy Syndrome" and the Development of Homosexuality (1987)—266

Greenberg, David F., The Construction of Homosexuality (1988)—266

Griffith, Elwin, *Asylum and Withholding of Deportation—Challenges to the Alien After the Refugee Act of 1980*, 12 Loyola L.A. Internat'l & Comp. L.J. 515 (1990)—939, 1057, 1077

Griffith, Elwin, *Deportation and the Refugee*, 1982 Michigan Yearbook Internat'l Legal Studies 125—938

Griffith, Elwin, *Expatriation and the American Citizen*, 31 Howard L.J. 453 (1988)—1336

Griffith, Elwin, *Problems of Interpretation in Asylum and Withholding of Deportation Proceedings under the Immigration and Nationality Act*, 18 Loyola L.A. Internat'l & Comp. L.J. 255 (1996)—915

Griffith, Elwin, *The Road between the Section 212(c) Waiver and Cancellation of Removal under Section 240A of the Immigration and Nationality Act—The Impact of the 1996 Reform Legislation*, 12 Georgetown Immigration L.J. 65 (1997)—574

Griffith, Elwin, *The Transition Between Suspension of Deportation and Cancellation of Removal for Nonpermanent Residents under the Immigration and Nationality Act: The Impact of the 1996 Reform Legislation*, 48 Drake L. Rev. 79 (1999)—581

Grunwald, Henry, Home Is Where You Are Happy, Time, July 8, 1985, at 100–01—88

Guendelsberger, John W., *Access to Citizenship for Children Born within the State to Foreign Parents*, 40 Amer. J. Comparative L. 379 (1992)—1312

Guendelsberger, John W., *Equal Protection and Resident Alien Access to Public Benefits in France and the United States*, 67 Tulane L. Rev. 669 (1993)—1351

Guendelsberger, John W., *Implementing Family Unification Rights in American Immigration Law: Proposed Amendments*, 25 San Diego L.Rev. 253 (1988)—291

Guendelsberger, John W., *Judicial Deference to Agency Decisions in Removal Proceedings in Light of INS v. Ventura*, 18 Georgetown Immigration L.J. 605 (2005)—503

Guendelsberger, John W., *The Right to Family Reunification in French and United States Immigration Law*, 21 Cornell Internat'l L.J. 1 (1988)—291

Guild, Elspeth, *The Impetus to Harmonize: Asylum Policy in the European Union*, in Frances Nicholson & Patrick Twomey (eds.), Refugee Rights and Realities (1999), at 313 et seq.—1095

Gunning, Isabelle R., *Arrogant Perception, World–Travelling and Multicultural Feminism: The Case of Female Genital Surgeries*, 23 Columbia Human Rights L.Rev. 189 (1992)—1023

Gunning, Isabelle R., *Expanding the International Definition of Refugee: A Multicultural View*, 13 Fordham Int'l L.J. 35 (1989-90)—936, 1170

Gunning, Isabelle R., *Global Feminism at the Local Level: Criminal and Asylum Laws Regarding Female Genital Surgeries*, 3 J. Gender, Race & Justice 45 (1999)—1023

Gunning, Isabelle R., *Modernizing Customary International Law and the Challenge of Human Rights*, 31 Virginia J. Internat'l L. 301 (1991)—1170, 1182

Gunther, Gerald & Sullivan, Kathleen M., Constitutional Law (13th ed. 1997)—171, 174, 1235

Gyory, Andrew, Closing the Gate—Race, Politics, and the Chinese Exclusion Act (1998)—117

Hailbronner, Kay, *Fifty Years of the Basic Law–Migration, Citizenship and Asylum*, 53 Southern Methodist Univ. L. Rev. 519 (2000)—14

Hailbronner, Kay, *Labor Transfer Schemes–In Whose National Interest? Globalization and the Transfer of Labor–The European Experience*, 16 Georgetown Immigration L.J. 773 (2002)—332, 366

Hailbronner, Kay, *New Techniques for Rendering Asylum Manageable*, in 4 Kay Hailbronner, David A. Martin & Hiroshi Motomura (eds.), Immigration Controls (1998), at 59 et seq.—1095

Hailbronner, Kay, *Non-Refoulement and "Humanitarian" Refugees: Customary International Law or Wishful Legal Thinking?*, 26 Virginia J. Internat'l L. 857 (1986)—1182

Hailbronner, Kay, *The Concept of "Safe Country" and Expeditious Asylum Procedures: A Western European Perspective*, 5 Internat'l J. Refugee L. 31 (1993)—1097, 1098

Hailbronner, Kay, Martin, David A. & Motomura, Hiroshi (eds.), Immigration Controls (1998)—1095

Haines, David W. & Rosenblum, Karen E., (eds.), Illegal Immigration in America–A Reference Handbook (1999)—1194

Hake, Bruce A., *A Great Wind: The New INS / EOIR Attorney Discipline Regime*, 5 BIB 885 (Nov. 1, 2000)—671

Hake, Bruce A., *"Attorney Misconduct"—A Rebuttal,* 4 Georgetown Immigration L.J. 727 (1990)—307, 671

Hake, Bruce A., *Dual Representation in Immigration Practice: The Simple Solution is the Wrong Solution,* 5 Georgetown Immigration L.J. 581 (1991)—310

Hall, Lee, *Nomads under the Tent of Blue: Migrants Fuel the U.S. Prison Industry,* 6 Rutgers Race & L. Rev., issue #2 (2003)—847

Hall, Lee, *Shackles and Shareholders: Developments in the Business of Immigration Detentions,* 9 BIB 394 (Apr. 1, 2004)—847

Hall, Lee, *Update to "Shackles and Shareholders: Developments in the Business of Immigration Detentions,"* 9 BIB 565 (May 1, 2004)—847

Hammar, Tomas, *Basic Civil Rights and Dual Citizenship* (unpublished paper at International Conference on Citizenship, State and Identity in a Globalizing World, Bilkent Univ., Ankara, Turkey, June 1–3, 2000)—1295

Hammar, Tomas, *Democracy and the Nation State* (1990)—1295

Hammar, Tomas, *State, Nation, and Dual Citizenship,* in William R. Brubaker (ed.), Immigration and the Politics of Citizenship in Europe and North America, at 81 et seq. (1989)—1295, 1296

Hammond, Denise C., *Immigration and Sexual Orientation: Developing Standards, Options and Obstacles,* 77 IR 113 (Jan. 24, 2000)—269

Hansen, Randall, Martin, Susan, Schoenholtz, Andrew & Weil, Patrick, *Report on the Workshop on Refugee and Asylum Policy in Practice in Europe and North America,* 14 Georgetown Immigration L.J. 801 (2000)—1081

Hansen, Randall & Weil, Patrick, *Dual Nationality, Social Rights and Federal Citizenship in the U.S. and Europe* (2002)—1295

Hansen, Randall & Weil, Patrick (eds.), *Towards a European Nationality–Citizenship, Immigration and Nationality Law in the EU* (2001)—1373

Hart, Henry, *The Power of Congress to Limit the Jurisdiction of the Federal Courts: An Exercise in Dialectic,* 66 Harvard L.Rev. 1362 (1953)—152, 728, 742

Harvard Law Student Advocates for Human Rights & Centro de Justico Global, Keeping the Peace in Haiti? (Mar. 2005)—1132

Hathaway, James C., *A Reconsideration of the Underlying Premise of Refugee Law,* 31 Harvard Internat'l L.J. 129 (1990)—916

Hathaway, James C., *International Refugee Law: The Michigan Guidelines on the Internal Protection Alternative,* 21 Michigan J. Internat'l L. 131 (1999)—1052

Hathaway, James C., *Michigan Guidelines on Nexus to a Convention Ground,* 23 Michigan J. Internat'l L. 210 (2002)—1040, 1041

Hathaway, James C., *The Causal Nexus in International Refugee Law,* 23 Mich. J. Internat'l L. 207 (2002)—1040

Hathaway, James C., *The Law of Refugee Status* (1991)—915, 949, 1171

Hathaway, James C., *The Relationship Between Human Rights and Refugee Law: What Refugee Law Judges Can Contribute,* 8 Human Rights & Refugee L. 80 (1998)—949

Hathaway, James C., *The Right of States to Repatriate Former Refugees,* 20 Ohio State J. Dispute Resolution 175 (2005)—934

Hathaway, James C., Third Colloquium on Challenges in International Refugee Law, *The Michigan Guidelines on Well–Founded Fear,* 26 Michigan J. Internat'l L. 492 (2005)—948

Hathaway, James C., *Who Should Watch Over Refugee Law?,* 14 Forced Migration Rev. 23 (2002)—926

Hathaway, James C. & Cusick, Anne K., *Refugee Rights Are Not Negotiable,* 14 Georgetown Immigration L.J. 481 (2000)—1053

Hathaway, James C. & Foster, Michelle, *The Causal Connection ("Nexus") to a Convention Ground,* 15 Internat'l J. Refugee L. 461 (2003)—1041, 1042

Hathaway, James C. & Harvey, Colin J., *Framing Refugee Protection in the New World Disorder,* 34 Cornell Internat'l L.J. 257 (2001)—1069

Hathaway, James C. & Hicks, William S., *Is There a Subjective Element in the Refugee Convention's Requirement of "Well–Founded Fear?,"* 26 Michigan J. Internat'l L. 505 (2005)—948

Hathaway, James C. & Neve, R. Alexander, *Making International Refugee Law Relevant Again: A Proposal for Collectivized and Solution–Oriented Protection,* 10 Harvard Human Rights J. 115 (1997)—934

Hawley, D.L., *Gays, Lesbians and Immigration,* August 1999 Immigration Briefings—261

Haycraft, Thomas W., *Alien Legislation and the Prerogative of the Crown,* 13 L.Q.Rev. 165 (1897)—237

Haynes, Dina Francesca, *Used, Arrested and Deported: Extending Immigration Benefits to Protect the Victims of Trafficking and to Secure the Prosecution of Traffickers,* 26 Human Rights Q. 221 (2004)—1207

Hebrew Immigrant Aid Society, Faithful but Forsaken: Real ID Act Harms Victims of Religious Persecution (Jan. 24, 2005)—963

Helton, Arthur C., *Harmonizing Political Asylum and International Extradition:*

Avoiding Analytical Cacophony, 1 Georgetown Immigration L.J. 457 (1986)—969

Helton, Arthur C., *Persecution on Account of Membership in a Social Group as a Basis for Refugee Status*, 15 Columbia Human Rights L.Rev. 39 (1983)—949, 983

Helton, Arthur C., *Political Asylum under the 1980 Refugee Act: An Unfulfilled Promise*, 17 Univ. Michigan J. L. Reform 243 (1984)—1065, 1066, 1067

Helton, Arthur C., *Reconciling the Power to Bar or Expel Aliens on Political Grounds with Fairness and the Freedoms of Speech and Association: An Analysis of Recent Legislative Proposals*, 11 Fordham Internat'l L.J. 467 (1988)—429

Helton, Arthur C., *Resistance to Military Conscription or Forced Recruitment by Insurgents as a Basis for Refugee Protection: A Comparative Perspective*, 29 San Diego L. Rev. 581 (1992)—971

Helton, Arthur C., *The CIS Migration Conference: A Chance to Prevent and Ameliorate Forced Movements of People in the Former Soviet Union*, 8 Int'l J. Refugee L. 169 (1996)—937

Helton, Arthur C., The Price of Indifference–Refugees and Humanitarian Action in the New Century (2002)—916

Helton, Arthur C., *The Proper Role of Discretion in Political Asylum Determinations*, 22 San Diego L. Rev. 999 (1985)—1077

Helton, Arthur C. & Nicoll, Alison, *Female Genital Mutilation as Ground for Asylum in the United States: The Recent Case of In re Fauziya Kasinga and Prospects for More Gender Sensitive Approaches*, 28 Columbia Human Rights L. Rev. 375 (1997)—1020

Henkin, Louis, Foreign Affairs and the Constitution (1972)—112, 118

Henkin, Louis, Neuman, Gerald L., Orentlicher, Diane F. & Leebron, David W., Human Rights (1999)—1134, 1190, 1191

Hernández-Truyol, Berta Esperanza, *Borders (En)gendered: Normativities, Latinas, and the LatCrit Paradigm*, 72 NYU L. Rev. 882 (1997)—98

Hernández-Truyol, Berta Esperanza, *Building Bridges: Bringing International Human Rights Home*, 9 La Raza L.J. 69 (1996)—86

Hernández-Truyol, Berta Esperanza, *Building Bridges–Latinas and Latinos at the Crossroads: Realities, Rhetoric and Replacement*, 25 Columbia Human Rights L. Rev. 369 (1994)—86

Hernández-Truyol, Berta Esperanza, *Building Bridges III: Personal Narratives, Incoherent Paradigms, and Plural Citizens*, 19 Chicano-Latino L. Rev. 303 (1998)—87

Hernández-Truyol, Berta Esperanza, *Glocalizing Terror*, 81 Oregon L. Rev. 941 (2002)—914

Hernández-Truyol, Berta Esperanza, *Natives, Newcomers and Nativism: a Human Rights Model for the Twenty-first Century*, 23 Fordham Urban L.J. 1075 (1996)—92, 232

Hernández-Truyol, Berta Esperanza, *Nativism, Terrorism, and Human Rights: The Global Wrongs of Reno v. American–Arab Anti–Discrimination Committee*, 31 Columbia Human Rights L. Rev. 521 (2000)—83

Hernández-Truyol, Berta Esperanza, *On Becoming the Other: Cubans, Castro, and Elian–A LatCritical Analysis*, 78 Denver Univ. L. Rev. 687 (2001)—1089

Hernández-Truyol, Berta Esperanza, *Querying Lawrence*, 65 Ohio State L.J. 1151 (2004)—267

Hernández-Truyol, Berta Esperanza & Johns, Kimberly A., *Global Rights, Local Wrongs, and Legal Fixes: An International Human Rights Critique of Immigration and Welfare "Reform,"* 71 Southern California L. Rev. 547 (1998)—232, 1357

Heyman, Michael G., *Asylum, Social Group Membership and the Non–State Actor: The Challenge of Domestic Violence*, 36 Univ. Michigan J. L. Reform 767 (2003)—985

Heyman, Michael G., *Immigration Law in the Supreme Court: The Flagging Spirit of the Law*, 28 J. of Legislation 113 (2002)—596

Heyman, Michael G., *Judicial Review of Discretionary Immigration Decisionmaking*, 31 San Diego L.Rev. 861 (1994)—595

Heyman, Michael G., *Language and Silence: The Supreme Court's Search for the Meaning of American Denaturalization Law*, 5 Georgetown Immigration L.J. 409 (1991)—1333

Heyman, Michael G., *Redefining Refugee: A Proposal for Relief for the Victims of Civil Strife*, 24 San Diego L.Rev. 449 (1987)—1165, 1166

Higham, John, Send These to Me: Immigrants in Urban America (rev. ed. 1984)—438

Hing, Bill Ong, *Answering Challenges of the New Immigrant–Driven Diversity: Considering Integration Strategies*, 40 Univ. Louisville Brandeis L.J. 861 (2002)—57

Hing, Bill Ong, *Beyond the Rhetoric of Assimilation and Cultural Pluralism: Addressing the Tension of Separatism and Conflict in an Immigration–Driven Multiracial Society*, 81 California L. Rev. 863 (1993)—341

Hing, Bill Ong, *Border Patrol Abuse: Evaluating Complaint Procedures Available to Victims*, 9 Georgetown Immigration L.J. 757 (1995)—1198

Hing, Bill Ong, *Detention to Deportation–Rethinking the Removal of Cambodian Refugees*, 38 U.C. Davis L. Rev. 891 (2005)—937

TABLE OF SECONDARY AUTHORITIES

Hing, Bill Ong, *Estoppel in Immigration Proceedings—New Life from Akbarin and Miranda,* 20 San Diego L.Rev. 11 (1982)—632

Hing, Bill Ong, *Immigration Policies: Messages of Exclusion to African Americans,* 37 Howard L.Rev. 237 (1994)—84, 86, 333

Hing, Bill Ong, Making and Remaking Asian America through Immigration Policy, 1850–1990 (1993)—117, 937

Hing, Bill Ong, *No Place for Angels: In Reaction to Kevin Johnson,* 2000 Univ. Illinois L. Rev. 559—82, 100, 101, 921

Hing, Bill Ong, *Refugee Policy and Cultural Identity: In the Voice of Hmong and Iu Mein Young Adults,* 1 Race & Poverty L.J. 111 (2003)—100

Hing, Bill Ong, *The Dark Side of Operation Gatekeeper,* 7 U.C. Davis J. Internat'l L. & Policy 121 (2001)—1198

Hing, Bill Ong, The Economic Impact of Immigration—A Brief Survey of the Literature (1990)—62, 106, 1196

Hing, Bill Ong, *The Emma Lazarus Effect: A Case Study in Philanthropic Revitalization of the Immigrant Rights Community,*15 Georgetown Immigration L.J. 47 (2001)—1357

Hing, Bill Ong, *Vigilante Racism: The De-Americanization of Immigrant America,* 7 Michigan J. Race & Law 441 (2002)—100

Hirson, David & Mayou, Catherine I., *The Sinking of the Titanic or the Rising of the Phoenix?—An Update on Immigrant Investor Visas,* September 1998 Immigration Briefings—336, 337

Holy Bible, Leviticus—1265

Hopper, Robert & Osuna, Juan P., *Remedies of Last Resort: Private Bills and Deferred Action,* June 1997 Immigration Briefings—613, 614, 617

Horne, Daniel C., *Requests for Evidence,* 8 BIB 1626 (Oct. 15, 2003)—363

Hudson, David M., *Tax Problems for Departing Aliens,* March 1997 Immigration Briefings—1349

Hughes, Joyce A., *Flight from Cuba,* 36 California Western L. Rev. 39 (1999)—158, 933, 1086

Hughes, Joyce A. & Crane, Linda P., *Haitians: Seeking Refuge in the United States,* 7 Georgetown Immigration L.J. 747 (1993)—1130

Hull, Elizabeth, Without Justice for All—The Constitutional Rights of Aliens (1985)—932, 1084

Human Rights First, In Liberty's Shadow—U.S. Detention of Asylum Seekers in the Era of Homeland Security (2004)—1108

Human Rights Watch and Lawyers Committee for Human Rights, Critique—Review of the Department of State's Country Reports on Human Rights Practices for 1987 (1988)—1064

Hurwitz, Agnes, *The Dublin Convention: A Comprehensive Assessment,* 11 Internat'l J. Refugee L. 646 (1999)—1098

Hutchins, Thomas, *Detention of Aliens: An Overview of Current Law,* April 2003 Immigration Briefings—206

Ignatius, Sarah B., *Selected Recent Developments in Family Immigration Law,* Oct. 1996 Immigration Briefings—250

Ignatius, Sarah B. & Stickney, Elisabeth S., Immigration Law and the Family (1995, continually updated)—250

Inniss, Lolita K. Buckner, *California's Proposition 187—Does It Mean What It Says? Does It Say What It Means? A Textual and Constitutional Analysis,* 10 Georgetown Immigration L.J. 577 (1996)—1255

Innis, Lolita K. Buckner, *Tricky Magic: Blacks as Immigrants and the Paradox of Foreignness,* 49 DePaul L. Rev. 85 (1999)—101

Institute for Global Legal Studies, The UN and the Protection of Human Rights, 5 Washington Univ. J. Law & Policy (2001)—1191

Institute for the Study of International Migration of Georgetown University & European Forum for Migration Studies of Univ. of Bamberg, *Transatlantic Workshop on Human Smuggling,* 15 Georgetown Immigration L.J. 167 (2001)—1207

Institute of International Education, Open Doors–Report on International Educational Exchange (2004)—383, 384

International Law Association, Report of the Sixty–Ninth Conference (2000)—937

International Lesbian & Gay Association, World Legal Survey, http://www.ilga.org/Information/legal_survey/summary_information_by_subject.htm—270

Isaacson, David, *We're All Entitled: the Literary and Cultural Significance of the Dictionary of Occupational Titles,* 27 Reference Quarterly 226 (1987)—312

Isgro, Francesco, *Immigration Litigation Update: Constitutionality of Indefinite Detention,* 28 Migration World, issue 1–2, at 46–48 (2000)—203

Isgro, Francesco, *Italy Enacts Law to Protect Basic Human Rights of Foreign Workers,* 1 Georgetown Immigration L.J. 693 (1986)—608, 1221

Isgro, Francisco, *Seeking Relief Under the Convention Against Torture,* 27 Migration World #3 at 44 (1999)—1145

Jacobson, Jon L., *At–Sea Interception of Alien Migrants: International Law Issues,* 28 Willamette L. Rev. 811 (1992)—1134

James, Alan G., *The Board of Appellate Review of the Department of State: The Right to Appellate Review of Administrative De-*

terminations of Loss of Nationality, 23 San Diego L. Rev. 261 (1986)—1345, 1349

Janis, Mark W., An Introduction to International Law (4th ed. 2003)—1146, 1147

Jarvis, Robert J., *Rusting in Drydock: Stowaways, Shipowners and the Administrative Penalty Provision of INA Section 273(d)*, 13 Tulane Maritime L.J. 25 (1988)—1208

Jastram, Kate & Newland, Kathleen, *Family Unity and Refugee Protection*, in Erika Feller, Volker Türk & Frances Nicholson (eds.), Refugee Protection in International Law at 555–603 (2003)—292

Joaquin, Linton, *The 1996 Immigration Act: Grounds of Inadmissibility and Deportability and Available Waivers*, 73 IR 1641 (Nov. 25, 1996)—411

Joaquin, Linton & Cancilla, Braden, *Protecting Immigrants and the Community: A New Approach to Public Charge Determinations*, 76 IR 885 (June 7, 1999)—441

Joaquin, Linton, Silverman, Mark, & Klapal, Lisa, Temporary Protected Status (Nat'l Immigration Law Center, May 1999)—1166

Joaquin, Linton & Wheeler, Charles, *Document Fraud Enforcement the Second Time Around: Will the Right Lessons Be Learned?*, 78 IR 473 (Mar. 12, 2001)—1205

Joe, Harry J., *Ethics in Immigration Law: Immigration Benefit Fraud and the Peril of Conscious Avoidance*, June 2002 Immigration Briefings—406

Joe, Harry J., *Temporary Entry of Business Persons to the United States under the North American Free Trade Agreement*, 8 Georgetown Immigration L.J. 391 (1994)—377

Johnson, Kevin R., *A "Hard Look" at the Executive Branch's Asylum Decisions*, 1991 Utah L. Rev. 279—1095

Johnson, Kevin R., *"Aliens" and the U.S. Immigration Laws: The Social and Legal Construction of Nonpersons*, 28 Univ. Miami Inter–Amer. L. Rev. 263 (1996–97)—1, 1192

Johnson, Kevin R., *An Essay on Immigration Politics, Popular Democracy, and California's Proposition 187: The Political Relevance and Legal Irrelevance of Race*, 70 Washington L. Rev. 629 (1995)—83, 1255

Johnson, Kevin R., *Civil Rights and Immigration: Challenges for the Latino Community in the Twenty-First Century*, 8 La Raza L.J. 42 (1995)—83

Johnson, Kevin R., *Driver's Licenses and Undocumented Immigrants: The Future of Civil Rights Law?*, 5 Nevada L.J. 213 (2004)—1259, 1260

Johnson, Kevin R., *Fear of an "Alien Nation": Race, Immigration, and Immigrants*, 7 Stanford Law & Policy Rev. 111 (1996)—44

Johnson, Kevin R., *Free Trade and Closed Borders: NAFTA and Mexican Immigration to the United States*, 27 U.C. Davis L. Rev. 937 (1994)—377, 1201

Johnson, Kevin R., How Did You Get to Be Mexican? (1999)—98

Johnson, Kevin R., *Immigration and Latino Identity*, 19 Chicano–Latino L.Rev. 197 (1998)—98

Johnson, Kevin R., *International Human Rights Class Actions: New Frontiers for Group Litigation*, 2004 Michigan State L. Rev. 643—367

Johnson, Kevin R., *Judicial Acquiescence to the Executive Branch's Pursuit of Foreign Policy and Domestic Agendas in Immigration Matters: The Case of the Haitian Asylum–Seekers*, 7 Georgetown Immigration L.J. 1 (1993)—1131

Johnson, Kevin R., *Legal Immigration in the 21st Century*, in Richard D. Lamm & Alan Simpson, Center for Immigration Studies, Blueprints for an Ideal Legal Immigration Policy, Center Paper 17 (March 2001)—34

Johnson, Kevin R., *Los Olvidados: Images of the Immigrant, Political Power of Noncitizens, and Immigration Law and Enforcement*, 1993 Brigham Young Univ. L. Rev. 1139—83

Johnson, Kevin R., *"Melting Pot" or "Ring of Fire"?: Assimilation and the Mexican–American Experience*, 85 California L. Rev. 1259 (1997)—56

Johnson, Kevin R., *Open Borders?*, 51 UCLA L. Rev. 193 (2003)—29

Johnson, Kevin R., *Public Benefits and Immigration: The Intersection of Immigration Status, Ethnicity, Gender, and Class*, 42 UCLA L. Rev. 1509 (1995)—1196, 1255

Johnson, Kevin R., *Race and Immigration Law and Enforcement: A Response to Is There a Plenary Power Doctrine?*, 14 Georgetown Immigration L.J. 289 (2000)—229

Johnson, Kevin R., *Race Matters: Immigration Law and Policy Scholarship, Law in the Ivory Tower, and the Legal Indifference of the Race Critique*, 2000 Univ. Illinois L. Rev. 525—101

Johnson, Kevin R., *Race, The Immigration Laws, and Domestic Race Relations: A "Magic Mirror" into the Heart of Darkness*, 73 Indiana L.J. 1111 (1998)—56

Johnson, Kevin R., *Racial Hierarchy, Asian Americans and Latinos as "Foreigners" and Social Change: Is Law the Way to Go?*, 76 Oregon L. Rev. 347 (1997)—99

Johnson, Kevin R., *Racial Profiling After September 11: The Department of Justice's 2003 Guidelines*, 50 Loyola L. Rev. 67 (2004)—899

Johnson, Kevin R., *Responding to the Litigation Explosion: The Plain Meaning of Executive Branch Primacy over Immigration*,

71 North Carolina L. Rev. 413 (1993)—173, 667

Johnson, Kevin R., *September 11 and Mexican Immigrants: Collateral Damage Comes Home*, 52 DePaul L. Rev. 849 (2003)—843, 892

Johnson, Kevin R., *Something Old, Something New, Something Borrowed, Something Blue*, in Juan F. Perea (ed.), Immigrants Out! The New Nativism and the Anti–Immigrant Impulse in the United States at 165 et seq. (1997)—1255

Johnson, Kevin R. *The Antiterrorism Act, the Immigration Reform Act, and Ideological Regulation in the Immigration Laws: Important Lessons for Citizens and Noncitizens*, 28 St. Mary's L.J. 833 (1997)—230, 435

Johnson, Kevin R., *The Case Against Race Profiling in Immigration Enforcement*, 78 Washington Univ. L.Q. 675 (2000)—98, 892

Johnson, Kevin R., *The Case for African American and Latina/o Cooperation in Challenging Racial Profiling in Law Enforcement*, 55 Florida L. Rev. 341 (2003)—87

Johnson, Kevin R., The "Huddled Masses" Myth–Immigration and Civil Rights (2004)—14, 84

Johnson, Kevin R., *U.S. Border Enforcement: Drugs, Migrants, and the Rule of Law*, 47 Villanova L. Rev. 897 (2002)—1199

Jones, Maldwyn A., American Immigration (1960)—32

Juss, Satvinder S., *Free Movement and the World Order*, 16 Internat'l J. Refugee L. 289 (2004)—30

Juss, Satvinder, *Toward a Morally Legitimate Form of Refugee Law: The Uses of Cultural Jurisprudence*, 11 Harvard Human Rights J. 311 (1998)—934

Justman, Rob A., *The Effects of AEDPA and IIRIRA on Ineffective Assistance of Counsel Claims for Failure to Advise Alien Defendants of Deportation Consequences of Pleading Guilty to an Aggravated Felony*, 2004 Utah L. Rev. 701—678

Kälin, Walter, Committee on Refugee Procedures, International Law Association, *Third Interim Report on Temporary Protection*, in International Law Association, Report of the Sixty–Ninth Conference at 902 et seq. (2000)—1181

Kälin, Walter, *Non–State Agents of Persecution and the Inability of the State to Protect*, 15 Georgetown Immigration L.J. 415 (2001)—1026

Kälin, Walter, *Troubled Communication: Cross–Cultural Misunderstandings in the Asylum–Hearing*, 20 Internat'l Migration Rev. 230 (1986)—1091

Kanstroom, Daniel, *Criminalizing the Undocumented: Ironic Boundaries of the Post–September 11th "Pale of Law,"* 29 North Carolina J. Internat'l L. & Commercial Regulation 639 (2004)—1208

Kanstroom, Daniel, *Dangerous Undertones of the New Nativism: Peter Brimelow and the Decline of the West*, in Juan F. Perea, Immigrants Out! The New Nativism and the Anti–Immigrant Impulse in the United States, at 300 et seq. (1997)—57

Kanstroom, Daniel, *Deportation, Social Control, and Punishment: Some Thoughts about Why Hard Cases Make Bad Laws*, 113 Harvard L. Rev. 1890 (2000)—500, 1208

Kanstroom, Daniel, *Hello Darkness: Involuntary Testimony and Silence as Evidence in Deportation Proceedings*, 4 Georgetown Immigration L.J. 599 (1990)—704, 715, 716

Kanstroom, Daniel, *Judicial Review of Amnesty Denials: Must Aliens Bet Their Lives to Get into Court?*, 25 Harvard Civil Rights—Civil Liberties L.Rev. 53 (1990)—758

Kanstroom, Daniel, *Surrounding the Hole in the Doughnut: Discretion and Deference in U.S. Immigration Law*, 71 Tulane L. Rev. 703 (1997)—632, 735

Kanstroom, Daniel, *Wer Sind Wir Wieder? Laws of Asylum, Immigration, and Citizenship in the Struggle for the Soul of the New Germany*, 18 Yale J. Internat'l L. 155 (1993)—341

Kaplan, Harvey, *Immigration Marriage Fraud Practice Advisory* (running column in AILA Monthly Mailings)—272

Kaplan, Harvey, *Immigration Marriage Fraud Practice Advisory*, Feb. 1990 AILA Monthly Mailing 77—279

Kaplan, Harvey & O'Sullivan, Maureen, *The Role of the BIA in Reviewing Negative Credibility Findings: Circumventing the Well–Founded Fear Standard*, 75 IR 1181 (Aug. 31, 1998)—1058

Karlen, Arno, *Homosexuality in History*, in Judd Marmor (ed.), Homosexual Behavior—A Modern Reappraisal (1980) at 75–99—267, 268

Karst, Kenneth L., *Equality and Community: Lessons from the Civil Rights Era*, 56 Notre Dame Lawyer 183 (1980)—31

Kassindja, Fauziya, Bashir, Layli Miller, Do They Hear You When You Cry? (1999)—1019

Kelly, H. Ansgar, *Dual Nationality, the Myth of Election, and a Kinder, Gentler State Department*, 23 Univ. Miami Inter–American L.Rev. 421 (1991–92)—1294, 1344

Kelly, Linda, *Domestic Violence Survivors: Surviving the Beatings of 1996*, 11 Georgetown Immigration L.J. 303 (1997)—453

Kelly, Linda, *Family Planning: American Style*, 52 Alabama L. Rev. 943 (2001)—290

Kelly, Linda, *Preserving the Fundamental Right to Family Unity: Championing Notions of Social Contract and Community Ties in the Battle of Plenary Power versus Aliens' Rights*, 41 Villanova L. Rev. 725 (1996)—103

Kelly, Linda, *Republican Mothers, Bastards' Fathers and Good Victims: Discarding Citizens and Equal Protection through the Failures of Legal Images*, 51 Hastings L.J. 557 (2000)—176

Kelly, Linda, *Stories from the Front: Seeking Refuge for Battered Immigrants in the Violence against Women Act*, 92 Northwestern L. Rev. 665 (1998)—454

Kelly, Linda, *The Alienation of Fathers*, 6 Michigan J. Race & L. 181 (2000)—1276

Kelly, Linda ,*The Fantastic Adventure of Supermom and the Alien: Educating Immigration Policy on the Facts of Life*, 31 Connecticut L. Rev. 1045 (1999)—388

Kelly, Nancy, *Gender–Related Persecution: Assessing the Asylum Claims of Women*, 26 Cornell Internat'l L.J. 625 (1993)—995

Kelly, Nancy & Anker, Deborah E. (directing eds.), Refugee Law Center, 1 Gender Asylum Law in Different Countries–Decisions and Guidelines (1999)—995

Kerwin, Donald M., *Charitable Legal Immigration Programs: Can They Survive?*, 74 IR 813 (May 19, 1997)—657

Kerwin, Donald M., *Charitable Legal Programs for Immigrants: What They Do, Why They Matter and How They Can Be Expanded*, June 2004 Immigration Briefings—654

Kerwin, Donald M., *Counterterrorism and Immigrant Rights Two Years Later*, 80 IR 1401 (Oct. 13, 2003)—914

Kerwin, Donald M., *Don't Give Me Your Tired, Your Poor or Your Huddled Masses: The Impact of Pending Legislation*, 73 IR 181 (Feb. 12, 1996)—657

Kesselbrenner, Dan, *Contesting Deportability: A Strategy for Minor Respondents*, 67 IR 1 (1990)—716

Kesselbrenner, Dan & Rosenberg, Lory D., National Lawyers Guild, Immigration Law and Crimes (updated periodically)—530, 533

King, Timothy, *Immigration from Developing Countries: Some Philosophical Issues*, 93 Ethics 525 (1983)—30

Klasko, Ronald, *American Competitiveness in the 21st Century: H–1Bs and Much More*, 77 IR 1689 (Dec. 11, 2000)—298, 365

Kleven, Thomas, *Why International Law Favors Emigration over Immigration*, 33 U. Miami Inter–Amer. L. Rev. 69 (2002)—34

Knauff, Ellen R., The Ellen Knauff Story (1952)—145

Kneebone, Susan, *Moving Beyond the State: Refugees, Accountability and Protection*, in Susan Kneebone (ed.), The Refugee Convention 50 Years On: Globalisation and International Law, ch. 11, at 281 et seq. (2003)—1026

Kneebone, Susan (ed.), The Refugee Convention 50 Years On: Globalisation and International Law (2003)—1026

Kneebone, Susan, *The Refugee Review Tribunal and the Assessment of Credibility: An Inquisitorial Role?*, 5 Australian J. Administrative L. 78 (1998)—1061

Kneebone, Susan, *Women Within the Refugee Construct: 'Exclusionary Inclusion' in Policy and Practice–The Australian Experience*, 17 Internat'l J. Refugee L. 7 (2005)—999

Koehler, Sean & Yale–Loehr, Stephen, *National Interest Waiver Petitions for Researchers: Demonstrating a Measurable Impact on the Larger Field*, 9 BIB 1341 (Nov. 15, 2004)—295

Koh, Harold Hongju, *Reflections on Refoulement and Haitian Centers Council*, 35 Harvard Internat'l L.J. 1 (1994)—1134

Koh, Harold Hongju, *The "Haiti Paradigm" in United States Human Rights Policy*, 103 Yale L.J. 2391 (1994)—1131, 1134

Koh, Harold Hongju, *The Human Face of the Haitian Interdiction Program*, 33 Virginia J. Internat'l L. 483 (1993)—1134

Kohli, Aarti & Sullivan, Kathleen M., *Intercountry Adoption: A Practitioner's Update*, July 2001 Immigration Briefings—290

Kondo, Atsushi (ed.), Citizenship in a Global World–Comparing Citizenship Rights for Aliens (2001)—1351

Konvitz, Milton R., The Alien and the Asiatic in American Law (1946)—116

Koslowski, Rey, *Changing Norms on Dual Nationality and Military Service* (unpublished draft prepared for German American Summer Institute on Immigration, Incorporation and Citizenship in Advanced Industrialized Democracies, Berlin, July 1997)—1295

Kowalski, Daniel M., *The $99 Border Guard*, 4 BIB 579 (June 1, 1999)—1197

Kraly, Ellen Percy, Research Paper for the U.S. Commission on Immigration Reform, U.S. Immigration and the Environment: Scientific Research and Analytic Issues (1995)—79

Kramer, Mary E. & Novick, Amy R. (eds.), AILA, Immigration Consequences of Criminal Convictions in the Nineties: What Every Immigration and Criminal Lawyer Needs to Know (1995)—530

Kranc, Benjamin A., *The New Canadian Immigration and Refugee Protection Act*, 79 IR 1565 (Oct. 21, 2002)—336

Krieger, Stanley, *Priority Dates—How to Get Them—How to Keep Them*, in AILA, 1990 (2) Immigration and Nationality Law at 284–96—247

Krikorian, Mark, *Keeping Terror Out–Immigration Policy and Asymmetric Warfare*, The National Interest (spring 2004)—900, 912

Kritz, Mary M. (ed.), U.S. Immigration and Refugee Policy (1983)—918

Kurzban, Ira J., *A Critical Analysis of Refugee Law*, 36 Univ. Miami L. Rev. 865 (1982)—1084

Kurzban, Ira J., Kurzban's Immigration Law Sourcebook—A Comprehensive Outline and Reference Tool (9th ed. 2004)—915

Kurzban, Ira J., *Restructuring the Asylum Process*, 19 San Diego L. Rev. 91 (1981)—1086, 1087, 1091

Kwong,Peter, Forbidden Workers: Illegal Chinese Immigrants and American Labor (1999)—100

Kyle, David, & Koslowski, Rey (eds.), Global Human Smuggling: Comparative Perspectives (2001)—402, 1207

LaBrie, Christina, *Lack of Uniformity in the Deportation of Criminal Aliens*, 25 NYU Rev. L. & Social Change 357 (1999)—538

Lafave, Wayne R., Criminal Law (4th ed. 2003)—143, 1052, 1347

Lai, Him Mark, Lim, Genny & Yung, Judy, Island—Poetry and History of Chinese Immigrants on Angel Island 1910–1940 (2d ed. 1986)—444

Lambert, Hélène, *The European Court of Human Rights and the Right of Refugees and Other Persons in Need of Protection to Family Reunion*, 11 Internat'l J. Refugee L. 427 (1999)—292, 1190

Lamm, Richard D. & Simpson, Alan (eds.), Center for Immigration Studies, Blueprints for an Ideal Legal Immigration Policy (2001), http://cis.org/articles/2001/blueprints/toc.html—34, 249

Lau, Estelle T., *Excavating the "Chinese Wall": Towards a Socio–Historical Perspective on the Development of United States Immigration Administration and Chinese Exclusion*, 92 Northwestern Univ. L. Rev. 1068 (1998)—99

Law, Anna O., *The Diversity Visa Lottery: A Cycle of Unintended Consequences in U.S. Immigration Policy*, 21 J. Amer. Ethnic History, issue no. 4, at 3 (2002)—337

Lawyers Committee for Human Rights, Refugee Refoulement: The Forced Return of Haitians Under the U.S.–Haitian Interdiction Agreement (Feb.1990)—1113

Lawyers Committee for Human Rights, Slamming "The Golden Door": A Year of Expedited Removal (1998)—1106

Lawyers Committee for Human Rights, The Alien Blacklist: A Dangerous Legacy of the McCarthy Era (1990)—434

Legal Services Corporation, *The Erlenborn Commission Report*, 15 Georgetown Immigration L.J. 99 (2001)—658, 665

Legomsky, Stephen H., *An Asylum Seeker's Bill of Rights for a Non–Utopian World*, 14 Georgetown Immigration L.J. 619 (2000)—1081

Legomsky, Stephen H., *Dual Nationality and Military Service: Strategy Number Two*, in David A. Martin & Kay Hailbronner (eds.), Rights and Duties of Dual Nationals: Evolution and Prospects (2003), at 79–126—1296, 1297

Legomsky, Stephen H., *E Pluribus Unum: Immigration, Race, and Other Deep Divides*, 21 Southern Illinois Univ. L.Rev. 101 (1996)—84

Legomsky, Stephen H., *Employer Sanctions: Past and Future*, in Peter Duignan & Lewis H. Gann (eds.), The Debate in the United States over Immigration, chap. 6 (1998)—1213

Legomsky, Stephen H., *Fear and Loathing in Congress and the Courts: Immigration and Judicial Review*, 78 Texas L. Rev. 1615 (2000)—727

Legomsky, Stephen H., *Forum Choices for the Review of Agency Adjudication: A Study of the Immigration Process*, 71 Iowa L.Rev. 1297 (1986)—456, 717, 731

Legomsky, Stephen H., *Immigrants, Minorities, and Pluralism: What Kind of Society Do We Really Want?*, 6 Willamette J. Internat'l L. & Dispute Resolution 153 (1998)—55, 102

Legomsky, Stephen H., Immigration and the Judiciary—Law and Politics in Britain and America (1987)—103, 113, 114, 153, 203, 230, 469, 479, 484, 503, 629

Legomsky, Stephen H., *Immigration, Equality and Diversity*, 31 Columbia J. Transnat'l Law 319 (1993)—102, 341

Legomsky, Stephen H., *Immigration Exceptionalism: Commentary on Is There a Plenary Power Doctrine?*, 14 Georgetown Immigration L.J. 307 (2000)—229

Legomsky, Stephen H., *Immigration, Federalism, and the Welfare State*, 42 UCLA L.Rev. 1453 (1995)—1234, 1256, 1357

Legomsky, Stephen H., *Immigration Law and the Principle of Plenary Congressional Power*, 1984 Supreme Ct. Rev. 255—82, 103, 138, 162, 173, 191, 231

Legomsky, Stephen H., *Political Asylum and the Theory of Judicial Review*, 73 Minnesota L. Rev. 1205 (1989)—761, 1095

Legomsky, Stephen H., Recent Development, *Deportation of an Alien for a Marihuana Conviction Can Constitute Cruel and Unusual Punishment*, 13 San Diego L. Rev. 454 (1976)—499

Legomsky, Stephen H., *Reforming the Criteria for the Exclusion and the Deportation of Alien Criminal Offenders*, 12 In Defense of the Alien 64 (1990)—553, 567

Legomsky, Stephen H., *Refugees, Administrative Tribunals, and Real Independence:*

Dangers Ahead for Australia, 76 Washington Univ. L.Q. 243 (1998)—722

Legomsky, Stephen H., *Secondary Refugee Movements and the Return of Asylum Seekers to Third Countries: The Meaning of Effective Protection*, 15 Internat'l J. Refugee L. 567 (2003) (Consultant's Report to Dept. of International Protection, UNHCR)—937, 1099, 1101

Legomsky, Stephen H., Specialised Justice—Courts, Administrative Tribunals, and a Cross-National Theory of Specialization (1990)—679, 1091

Legomsky, Stephen H., *Ten More Years of Plenary Power: Immigration, Congress, and the Courts*, 22 Hastings Const. L.Q. 925 (1995)—103, 232

Legomsky, Stephen H., *The Alien Criminal Defendant*, 14 San Diego L. Rev. 105 (1977)—499

Legomsky, Stephen H., *The Deportation Process, the War on Independence, and Reverse Darwinism: Why We Need Habeas Corpus More than Ever*, 91 Cornell L. Rev., issue #2 (forthcoming 2006)—723, 725, 741

Legomsky, Stephen H., *The Detention of Aliens: Theories, Rules, and Discretion*, 30 Univ. Miami Inter-American L. Rev. 531 (1999)—225, 229, 636, 844, 854

Legomsky, Stephen H., *The Ethnic and Religious Profiling of Noncitizens: National Security and International Human Rights*, 25 Boston College Third World L.J. 161 (2005)—892, 899

Legomsky, Stephen H., *The Haitian Interdiction Programme, Human Rights, and the Role of Judicial Protection*, Int'l J. Refugee L. at 182 (special ed.1990)—1114

Legomsky, Stephen H., *The Making of United States Refugee Policy: Separation of Powers in the Post-Cold War Era*, 70 Washington L. Rev. 675 (1995)—332, 933, 935

Legomsky, Stephen H., *The New Techniques for Managing High-Volume Asylum Systems*, 81 Iowa L.Rev. 671 (1996)—1095

Legomsky, Stephen H., *Why Citizenship?*, 35 Virginia J.Internat'L. 279 (1994)—32, 1289, 1372

Leibowitz, Arnold H., A Time for Decision: Citizenship at the Millennium (Office of Refugee Resettlement, Nov. 1998)—1373

Lemay, Michael & Barkan, Elliott Robert (eds.), United States Immigration and Naturalization Laws and Issues—A Documentary History (1999)—14

Leopold, David W., & Karen Grisez, *The Nuts and Bolts of Federal Court Litigation*, in AILA, Immigration and Nationality Law Handbook 384–96 (2000–01)—727

Lesbian and Gay Immigration Rights Task Force, Task Force Update (Summer & Fall 1996)—260

Levinson, Peter J., *The Facade of Quasi-Judicial Independence in Immigration Appellate Adjudications*, 9 BIB 1154 (Oct. 1, 2004)—718, 722, 723

Levitan, David M., *The Foreign Relations Power: An Analysis of Mr. Justice Sutherland's Theory*, 55 Yale L.J. 467 (1946)—118

Levy, Daniel, *The Child Citizenship Act of 2000*, 6 BIB 293 (Mar. 15, 2001)—1292, 1293

Lewis, Anthony, *A Bad Time for Civil Liberties*, 5 Annual Survey Internat'l & Comp. L. 1 (1999)—1106

Lewis, Hope, *Between Irua and "Female Genital Mutilation": Feminist Human Rights Discourse and the Cultural Divide*, 8 Harvard Human Rights J. 1 (1995)—1023

Lewis, Hope & Gunning, Isabelle R., *Cleaning Our Own House: "Exotic" and Familial Human Rights Violations*, 4 Buffalo Human Rights L. Rev. 123 (1998)—1019

Lichtenberg, Judith, *National Boundaries and Moral Boundaries: A Cosmopolitan View*, in Peter G. Brown & Henry Shue (eds.) National Autonomy and Its Limits (1981)—32, 1373

Lillich, Richard B., The Human Rights of Aliens in Contemporary International Law (1984)—1170, 1350

Loescher, Gil & Scanlan, John A., Calculated Kindness—Refugees and America's Half-Open Door 1945–Present (1986)—932, 933, 1084

Lopez, Gerald P., *Learning about Latinos*, 19 Chicano-Latino L. Rev. 363 (1998)—86

Lopez, Gerald P., *Undocumented Mexican Migration: In Search of a Just Immigration Law and Policy*, 28 UCLA L.Rev. 615 (1981)—82

López, María Pabón, *More than a License to Drive: State Restrictions on the Use of Driver's Licenses by Noncitizens*, 29 Southern Illinois Univ. L.J. 91 (2004)—1260

Loue, Sana, *Alien Rights and Government Authority: An Examination of the Conflicting Views of the Ninth Circuit Court of Appeals and the United States Supreme Court*, 22 San Diego L.Rev. 1021 (1985)—705

Lovo, Mario M., *Nicaraguan Adjustment and Central American Relief Act "NACARA"*, Nov. 1998 Immigration Briefings—606

Lowell, B. Lindsay, & Martin, Susan, *Transatlantic Roundtable on High Skilled Migration: A Report on the Proceedings*, 15 Georgetown Immigration L.J. 649 (2001)—332

Lubet, Steven, *Extradition Reform: Executive Discretion and Judicial Participation in the Extradition of Political Terrorists*, 15 Cornell Internat'l L.J. 247 (1982)—1076

Lubet, Steven & Reed, Jan S., *Extradition of Nazis from the United States to Israel: A*

Survey of Issues in Transnational Criminal Law, 22 Stanford J. Internat'l L. 1 (1986)—629

Luna, Guadalupe T., *"Agricultural Underdogs" and International Agreements: The Legal Context of Agricultural Workers within the Rural Economy,* 26 New Mexico L.Rev. 9 (1996)—368, 1203

Luna, Guadalupe T., *"Zoo Island:" Latcrit Theory, "Don Pepe" and Señora Peralta,* 19 Chicano–Latino L. Rev. 339 (1998)—102

Mackler, Ian & Weeks, James K., *The Fleeing Political Refugee's Final Hurdle—the Immigration and Nationality Act,* 5 Northern Kentucky L.Rev. 9 (1978)—939

Macklin, Audrey, *Cross–Border Shopping for Ideas: A Critical Review of United States, Canadian, and Australian Approaches to Gender–Related Asylum Claims,* 13 Georgetown Immigration L.J. 25 (1998)—1006

Macklin, Audrey, *Disappearing Refugees: Reflections on the Canada–U.S. Safe Third Country Agreement,* 36 Columbia Human Rights L. Rev. 101 (2005)—1103

Maggio, Michael, *Interested Government Agency Exchange Visitor Waivers,* 12 Imm.J. 1 (July–Sept.1989)—393

Maggio, Michael, Rifkin, Larry S. & Starkey, Sheila T., *Immigration Fundamentals for International Lawyers,* 13 Amer. Univ. Internat'l L. Rev. 857 (1998)—466

Maguire, Bernadette, Immigration: Public Legislation and Private Bills (1997)—613

Mailman, Stanley, *California's Proposition 187 and Its Lessons,* New York L.J. 3 (Jan. 3, 1995)—1255

Mailman, Stanley, *The Employer as Immigration Inspector,* 1 BIB #8 at 20–25 (July 1996)—1213

Mailman, Stanley, *The New Adjustment of Status Law: Background and Analysis,* 71 IR 1505 (Nov. 14, 1994)—490

Mailman, Stanley & Yale–Loehr, Stephen, *Controversy over Investor Category,* 3 BIB 491 (May 15, 1998)—336

Mailman, Stanley & Yale–Loehr, Stephen, *Detaining and Criminalizing Asylum Seekers,* 8 BIB 764 (May 1, 2003)—941

Mailman, Stanley & Yale–Loehr, Stephen, *Immigrant Investor Green Cards: Rise of the Phoenix,* 10 BIB 801 (May 15, 2005)—337

Mailman, Stanley & Yale–Loehr, Stephen, *Immigration Appeals Overwhelm Federal Courts,* 10 BIB 45 (Jan. 15, 2005)—729, 730

Mailman, Stanley & Yale–Loehr, Stephen, *Immigration Functions in the Department of Homeland Security,* 8 BIB 663 (Apr. 15, 2003)—3

Mailman, Stanley & Yale–Loehr, Stephen, *The "National Interest" Waiver,* 4 BIB 271 (Apr. 1, 1999)—295

Mailman, Stanley & Yale–Loehr, Stephen, *The Price of Tracking Overstays,* 3 BIB 179 (Mar. 1, 1998)—867

Malpert, Rodney A. & Petersen, Amanda (eds.), Business Immigration Law: Strategies for Employing Foreign Nationals (2000)—348

Mancini, Mark A., *The Carlos Marcello Case,* 1990(2) Immigration and Nationality Law at 2—728

Margulies, Peter, *Asylum, Intersectionality, and AIDS: Women with HIV as a Persecuted Social Group,* 8 Georgetown Immigration L.J. 521 (1994)—995

Margulies, Peter, *Children, Parents, and Asylum,* 15 Georgetown Immigration L.J. 289 (2001)—1088

Margulies, Peter, *Democratic Transitions and the Future of Asylum Law,* 71 Univ. Colorado L. Rev. 3 (2000)—1053

Margulies, Peter, *Difference and Distrust in Asylum Law: Haitian and Holocaust Refugee Narratives,* 6 St. Thomas L.Rev. 135 (1993)—1130

Margulies, Peter, *Stranger and Afraid: Undocumented Workers and Federal Employment Law,* 38 DePaul L. Rev. 553 (1989)—1202

Margulies, Peter, *Uncertain Arrivals: Immigration, Terror, and Democracy After September 11,* 2002 Utah L. Rev. 481 (2002)—914

Marmor, Judd (ed.), Homosexual Behaviour—A Modern Reappraisal (1980)—266, 267

Marmor, Judd, *Overview: The Multiple Roots of Homosexual Behavior,* in Judd Marmor (ed.), Homosexual Behavior—A Modern Reappraisal (1980)—266

Martin, David A., Asylum Case Law Sourcebook (4th ed. 2003)—915

Martin, David A., Book Review, *The Law of Refugee Status,* 87 Amer. J. Internat'l L. 348 (1993)—950

Martin, David A., *Due Process and Membership in the National Community: Political Asylum and Beyond,* 44 Univ. Pittsburgh L.Rev. 165 (1983)—31, 153

Martin, David A., *Effects of International Law on Migration Policy and Practice: The Uses of Hypocrisy,* 23 Internat'l Migration Rev. 547 (1989)—1170

Martin, David A., *Graduated Application of Constitutional Protections for Aliens: The Real Meaning of Zadvydas v. Davis,* 2001 Supreme Ct. Rev. 47—153, 206, 881, 882, 883

Martin, David A., *Immigration Policy and the Homeland Security Act Reorganization: An Early Agenda for Practical Improvements,* 80 IR 601 (Apr. 28, 2003)—3

Martin, David A., *Making Asylum Policy: The 1994 Reforms*, 70 Washington L. Rev. 725 (1995)—1083

Martin, David A., *Membership and Consent: Abstract or Organic?*, 11 Yale J. Internat'l L. 278 (1985)—1312, 1348

Martin, David A., *New Rules on Dual Nationality for a Democratizing Globe: Between Rejection and Embrace*, 14 Georgetown Immigration L.J. 1 (1999)—1295

Martin, David A., *Offshore Detainees and the Role of Courts after Rasul v. Bush: The Underappreciated Virtues of Differentiated Review*, 25 Boston College Third World L. Rev. 125 (2005)—863

Martin, David A., *On Counterintuitive Consequences and Choosing the Right Control Group: A Defense of Reno v. AADC*, 14 Georgetown Immigration L.J. 363 (2000)—178

Martin, David A., *Reforming Asylum Adjudication: On Navigating the Coast of Bohemia*, 138 Univ. Pennsylvania L.Rev. 1247 (1990)—1063, 1064, 1066, 1081, 1083, 1085, 1086, 1087, 1091

Martin, David A., The United States Refugee Admission Program: Reforms for a New Era of Refugee Resettlement (2003)—936

Martin, David A., *Two Cheers for Expedited Removal in the New Immigration Laws*, 40 Virginia J. Internat'l L. 673 (2000)—1106

Martin, David A., *Waiting for Solutions: Extending the Period of Time for Migrants to Apply for Green Cards Doesn't Get at the Real Problem*, Legal Times (May 28, 2001)—493

Martin, David A. & Hailbronner, Kay (eds.), Rights and Duties of Dual Nationals: Evolution and Prospects (2003)—1295, 1296, 1297

Martin, Philip, *Does the U.S. Need a New Bracero Program?*, 9 J. Internat'l L. & Policy 127 (2003)—368

Martin, Susan Forbes, *Forced Migration and Professionalism*, 35 Internat'l Migration Rev. 226 (2001)—926

Martin, Susan Forbes, Refugee Women (2d ed. 2004)—995

Martin, Susan Forbes, Lowell, B. Lindsay, & Martin, Philip, *U.S. Immigration Policy: Admission of High Skilled Workers*, 16 Georgetown Immigration L.J. 619 (2002)—332

Martin, Susan Forbes & Schoenholtz, Andrew I., *Asylum in Practice: Successes, Failures, and the Challenges Ahead*, 14 Georgetown Immigration L.J. 589 (2000)—1081

Martin, Susan, Schoenholtz, Andy & Meyers, Deborah Waller, *Temporary Protection: Towards a New Regional and Domestic Framework*, 12 Georgetown Immigration L.J. 543 (1998)—935

Martínez, George A., *African–Americans, Latinos, and the Construction of Race: Toward an Epistemic Coalition*, 19 Chicano–Latino L. Rev. 213 (1998)—87

Martínez, George A., *Latinos, Assimilation and the Law: A Philosophical Perspective*, 20 Chicano–Latino L. Rev. 1 (1999)—56

Martínez, George A., *Race and Immigration Law: A Paradigm Shift*, 2000 Univ. of Illinois L. Rev. 517—101

Marx, Reinhard & Lumpp, Katharina, *The German Constitutional Court's Decision of 14 May 1996 on the Concept of "Safe Third Countries"—A Basis for Burden-Sharing in Europe*, 8 Internatl'l J. Refugee L. 419 (1996)—1095, 1098

Mason, Jana, U.S. Committee for Refugees, *Citizenship under Attack: Congress Investigates Motives Behind INS Initiative*, 17 Refugee Reports, No. 11, at 1–4 (Nov./Dec. 1996)—1279

Masters, Suzette Brooks, *Environmentally Induced Migration: Beyond a Culture of Reaction*, 14 Georgetown Immigration L.J. 855 (2000)—81

Masters, Suzette Brooks & Ruthizer, Ted, *The H1–B Straitjacket: Why Congress Should Repeal the Cap on Foreign–Born Highly Skilled Workers*, May 2000 Immigration Briefings—366

Mathew, Penelope, *Address–Legal Issues Concerning Interdiction*, 17 Georgetown Immigration L.J. 221 (2003)—1113

Mathew, Penelope, *The High Court and "Particular Social Groups": Lessons for the Future*, 21 Melbourne Univ. L. Rev. 277 (1997)—985

Matsuda, Mari J., *Voices of America: Accent, Antidiscrimination Law, and a Jurisprudence for the Last Reconstruction*, 100 Yale L.J. 1329 (1991)—61

Mautino, Robert A., *Acquisition of Citizenship*, Immigration Briefings (April 1990)—1270, 1271, 1272

Mautino, Robert A., *Naturalization Changes Effected by Immigration Act of 1990*, in AILA, Understanding the Immigration Act of 1990, at 277 (1991)—1289

Mazzoli, Romano L. & Trucios–Haynes, Enid, *Public Sentiment and Congressional Response: 15 Years of Immigration Policymaking*, 73 IR 469 (Apr. 12, 1996)—84

McCaffrey, Angela, *Don't Get Lost in Translation: Teaching Law Students to Work with Language Interpreters*, 6 Clinical L. Rev. 347 (2000)—1087, 1091

McCallum, Ron, *Australian Labor Law, Migration and the Performance of Work*, 16 Georgetown Immigration L.J. 637 (2002)—332

McCormick, Margaret H. & Stanton, David, *Finding the Correct Wage for LCAs: Recent Developments in H–1B Practice*, April 1995 Immigration Briefings—364

McDermid, Lea, *Deportation is Different: Noncitizens and Ineffective Assistance of Counsel*, 89 California L. Rev. 741 (2001)—537

McIlmail, Timothy P., *Toward a More Reasonably Rebutted Presumption: A Proposal to Amend the "Past Persecution" Asylum Regulation-8 C.F.R. § 208.13(b)(1)*, 12 Georgetown Immigration L.J. 265 (1998)—1055

Medina, M. Isabel, *Demore v. Kim–A Dance of Power and Human Rights*, 18 Georgetown Immigration L.J. 697 (2004)—229

Medina, M. Isabel, *Employer Sanctions in the United States, Canada and Mexico: Exploring the Criminalization of Immigration Law*, 3 Southwestern J. L. & Trade in the Americas 333 (1996)—1221

Medina, M. Isabel, *Judicial Review—A Nice Thing? Article III, Separation of Powers and the Illegal Immigration Reform and Immigrant Responsibility Act of 1996*, 29 Connecticut L. Rev. 1525 (1997)—741

Medina, M. Isabel, *Of Constitutional Amendments, Human Rights, and Same-Sex Marriages*, 64 Louisiana L. Rev. 459 (2004)—263

Medina, M. Isabel, *Real Differences and Stereotypes–Two Visions of Gender, Citizenship, and International Law*, 7 N.Y. City L. Rev. 315 (2004)—1276

Medina, M. Isabel, *The Criminalization of Immigration Law: Employer Sanctions and Marriage Fraud*, 5 George Mason L. Rev. 669 (1997)—280, 530, 1208, 1213

Mertus, Julie, *The State and the Post-Cold War Refugee Regime: New Models, New Questions*, 20 Michigan J. Internat'l L. 59 (1998)—933

Miller, Mark J., Employer Sanctions in Western Europe (1987)—1221

Miller, Teresa A., *Blurring the Boundaries Between Immigration and Crime Control After September 11*, 25 Boston College Third World L. Rev. 81 (2005)—530

Miller, Teresa A., *Citizenship and Severity: Recent Immigration Reforms and the New Penology*, 17 Georgetown Immigration L.J. 611 (2003)—530, 1208

Miranda, Carlos Ortiz, *An Agenda for the Commission on Immigration Reform*, 29 San Diego L. Rev. 701 (1992)—87

Miranda, Carlos Ortiz, *Haiti and the United States During the 1980s and 1990s, Refugees, Immigration, and Foreign Policy*, 32 San Diego L.Rev. 673 (1995)—1132

Miranda, Carlos Ortiz, *United States Commission on Immigration Reform: The Interim and Final Reports*, 38 Santa Clara L. Rev. 645 (1998)—87

Money, Jeanette, Fences and Neighbors: The Political Geography of Immigration Control (1999)—83

Money, John, *Genetic and Chromosomal Aspects of Homosexual Etiology*, in Judd Marmor (ed.), Homosexual Behavior—A Modern Reappraisal (1980), at 59—266

Money, John & Ehrhardt, Anke A., Man and Woman, Boy and Girl (1972)—266

Moore, Andrew, *Matter of Jacques Martin*, 7 BIB 1502 (Dec. 1, 2002)—560

Moore, Jennifer, *From Nation State to Failed State: International Protection from Human Rights Abuses by Non–State Agents*, 31 Columbia Human Rights L. Rev. 81 (1999)—1026, 1027, 1028

Moore, Jennifer, *Restoring the Humanitarian Character of U.S. Refugee Law Lessons from the International Community*, 15 Berkeley J. Internat'l L. 51 (1997)—971

Moore, Jennifer, *Whither the Accountability Theory: Second–Class Status for Third–Party Refugees as a Threat to International Refugee Protection*, 13 Internat'l J. Refugee L. 32 (2001)—1189

Morawetz, Nancy, *Detention Decisions and Access to Habeas Corpus for Immigrants Facing Deportation*, 25 Boston College Third World L. Rev. 13 (2005)—865

Morawetz, Nancy, *Predicting the Meaning of INA § 242(b)(9)*, 14 Georgetown Immigration L.J. 453 (2000)—740

Morawetz, Nancy, *Rethinking Retroactive Deportation Laws and the Due Process Clause*, 73 NYU L. Rev. 97 (1998)—180, 570

Morawetz, Nancy, *Understanding the Impact of the 1996 Deportation Laws and the Limited Scope of Proposed Reforms*, 113 Harvard L. Rev. 1936 (2000)—554

Motomura, Hiroshi, *Federalism, International Human Rights, and Immigration Exceptionalism*, 70 Univ. Colorado L. Rev. 1361 (1999)—1191

Motomura, Hiroshi, *Immigration and Alienage, Federalism and Proposition 187*, 35 Virginia J. Internat'l L. 201 (1994)—1253

Motomura, Hiroshi, *Immigration Law After a Century of Plenary Power: Phantom Constitutional Norms and Statutory Interpretation*, 100 Yale L.J. 545 (1990)—230

Motomura, Hiroshi, *Judicial Review in Immigration Cases after AADC: Lessons from Civil Procedure*, 14 Georgetown Immigration L.J. 385 (2000)—740

Motomura, Hiroshi, *The Curious Evolution of Immigration Law: Procedural Surrogates for Substantive Constitutional Rights*, 92 Columbia L.Rev. 1625 (1992)—162

Motomura, Hiroshi, *The Family and Immigration: A Roadmap for the Ruritanian Lawmaker*, 43 Amer.J.Comp.L. 511 (1995)—250, 291

Motomura, Hiroshi, *The Year is 2020: Looking Back on the Elian Gonzalez Case (A Fantasy)*, 77 IR 853 (2000)—1088

Motomura, Hiroshi, *Whose Alien Nation?: Two Models of Constitutional Immigration Law*, 94 Michigan L. Rev. 1927 (1996)—57

Mousin, Craig B., *A Clear View From the Prairie: Harold Washington and the People of Illinois Respond to Federal Encroachment of Human Rights*, 29 Southern Illinois Univ. L. Rev. 285 (2005)—1201

Mousin, Craig B., *Standing with the Persecuted: Adjudicating Religious Asylum Claims after the Enactment of the International Religious Freedom Act of 1998*, 2003 B.Y.U. L. Rev. 541—963

Mulcahy, Elizabeth & Schmidt–Nowara, Mary, *Law Students Work to Repeal Jim Crow–Era Anti–Asian Alien Land Laws*, 6 BIB 611 (June 15, 2001)—99

Musalo, Karen, *Claims for Protection Based on Religion or Belief*, 16 Internat'l J. Refugee L. 165 (2004)—962

Musalo, Karen, *Gender–Based Asylum: An Analysis of Recent Trends*, 77 IR 1533 (Oct. 30, 2000)—995

Musalo, Karen, *In re Kasinga: A Big Step Forward for Gender–Based Asylum Claims*, 73 IR 853 (July 1, 1996)—1019

Musalo, Karen, *Matter of R–A–: An Analysis of the Decision and Its Implications*, 76 IR 1177 (Aug. 9, 1999)—1027

Musalo, Karen, *Revisiting Social Group and Nexus in Gender Asylum Claims: A Unifying Rationale for Evolving Jurisprudence*, 52 DePaul L. Rev. 777 (2003)—1049

Musalo, Karen, *Swords into Ploughshares: Why the United States Should Provide Refuge for Young Men Who Refuse to Bear Arms for Reasons of Conscience*, 26 San Diego L.Rev. 849 (1989)—951, 963

Musalo, Karen, Gibson, Lauren, Knight, Stephen & Taylor, J. Edward, Evaluation of the General Accounting Office's Second Report on Expedited Removal (Oct. 2000)—1104

Musalo, Karen, Gibson, Lauren, Knight, Stephen & Taylor, J. Edward, The Expedited Removal Study, Report on the First Three Years of Implementation of Expedited Removal (May 2000)—1104

Musalo, Karen, Moore, Jennifer & Boswell, Richard A., Refugee Law and Policy: A Comparative and International Approach (2d ed. 2002)—915

Mutharika, A. Peter, The Alien under American Law (2 vols. 1980, 1981, with 1985 Supplement)—1230, 1351

Nafziger, James A.R., *A Commentary on American Legal Scholarship Concerning the Admission of Migrants*, 17 Univ. Michigan J. L. Reform 165 (1984)—137, 1170

Nafziger, James A.R., *A Comparison of Processes for Reforming Migration Laws in Transitional States: China, Kazakhstan, and Albania*, 70 Washington L. Rev. 757 (1995)—87

Nafziger, James A.R., *Review of Visa Denials by Consular Officers*, 66 Washington L.Rev. 1 (1991)—462, 468, 469, 483

Nafziger, James A.R., *The General Admission of Aliens under International Law*, 77 Amer. J. Internat'l L. 804 (1983)—232, 1171

Nafziger, James A.R., & Yimesgen, Michael, *The Effect of Expungement on Removability of Non–Citizens*, 36 Univ. Michigan J. L. Reform 915 (2003)—538

Narvaez–Hasfura, Carlos, Immigration in Mexico and America: Constitutional Reciprocity within a Plenary Power (J.S.D. dissertation, Washington Univ., Dec. 8, 1995)—566

Neal, David L., *The Changing Dynamics of Adjustment of Status*, May and June 1996 Immigration Briefings (2–part article)—490

Neal, David L., *Women as a Social Group: Sex–Based Persecution as Grounds for Asylum*, 20 Columbia Human Rights L.Rev. 203 (1988)—999

Nessel, Lori A., *Undocumented Immigrants in the Workplace: The Fallacy of Labor Protection and the Need for Reform*, 36 Harvard Civil Rights—Civil Liberties L. Rev. 345 (2001)—1202

Nessel, Lori A., *"Willful Blindness" to Gender–Based Violence Abroad: United States' Implementation of Article Three of the United Nations Convention Against Torture*, 89 Minnesota L. Rev. 71 (2004)—1027, 1146

Nett, Roger, *The Civil Right We Are Not Ready For: The Right of Free Movement of People on the Face of the Earth*, 81 Ethics 212 (1971)—25

Neuman, Gerald L., *Aliens as Outlaws: Government Services, Proposition 187, and the Structure of Equal Protection Doctrine*, 42 UCLA L. Rev. 1425 (1995)—1193, 1256

Neuman, Gerald L., Book Review [of Schuck and Smith], *Back to Dred Scott?*, 24 San Diego L. Rev. 485 (1987)—1304

Neuman, Gerald L., *Closing the Guantánamo Loophole*, 50 Loyola L. Rev. 1 (2004)—865

Neuman, Gerald L., *Extraterritorial Violations of Human Rights by the United States*, in Amer. Univ. J. Internat'l L. & Policy and Loyola L.A. Internat'l & Comp. L.J. (eds.), Immigration Law: International Perspectives on Asylum and Refugee Status at 213 (1994)—1134

Neuman, Gerald L., *Federal Courts Issues in Immigration Law*, 78 Texas L. Rev. 1661 (2000)—727

Neuman, Gerald L., *Habeas Corpus, Executive Detention, and the Removal of Aliens*, 98 Columbia L. Rev. 961 (1998)—741

Neuman, Gerald L., *Immigration and Judicial Review in the Federal Republic of Germany*, 23 N.Y.U. J.Internat'l L. & Politics 35 (1990)—237

Neuman, Gerald L., *Jurisdiction and the Rule of Law After the 1996 Immigration Act*, 113 Harvard L. Rev. 1963 (2000)—727

Neuman, Gerald L., *Justifying U.S. Naturalization Policies*, 35 Virginia J. Internat'l L. 237 (1994)—1289, 1296

Neuman, Gerald L., Strangers to the Constitution—Immigrants, Borders, and Fundamental Law (1996)—103

Neuman, Gerald L., *Terrorism, Selective Deportation and the First Amendment after Reno v. AADC*, 14 Georgetown Immigration L.J. 313 (2000)—178

Neuman, Gerald L., *The Constitutional Requirement of "Some Evidence,"* 25 San Diego L. Rev. 631 (1988)—712, 755

Neuman, Gerald L., *The Habeas Corpus Suspension Clause After INS v. St. Cyr*, 33 Columbia Human Rights L. Rev. 555 (2002)—741

Neuman, Gerald L., *The Lost Century of American Immigration Law (1776–1875)*, 93 Columbia L.Rev. 1833 (1993)—15, 104

Neuman, Gerald L., *Whose Constitution?*, 100 Yale L.J. 909 (1991)—141

New York State Inter–Agency Task Force on Immigration Affairs, Workplace Discrimination Under the Immigration Reform and Control Act of 1986: A Study of Impacts on New Yorkers (Nov. 4, 1988)—1219

Newland, Kathleen, *The Impact of U.S. Refugee Policies on U.S. Foreign Policy: A Case of the Tail Wagging the Dog?*, ch. 5 in Michael S. Teitelbaum & Myron Weiner (eds.), Threatened Peoples, Threatened Borders at 199 (1995)—1115, 1131

Newman, Edward & Van Selm, Joanne (eds.), Refugees and Forced Displacement (2003)—915

Newman, Frank & Weissbrodt, David, International Human Rights: Law, Policy, and Process (2d ed. 1996)—1025

Newman, George S., *Considerations in Recruitment of Foreign Scholars for Faculty Appointments*, in AILA, 1990 (2) Immigration and Nationality Law at 195—293

Newton, Andowah A., *Injecting Diversity into U.S. Immigration Policy: The Diversity Visa Program and the Missing Discourse on its Impact on African Immigration to the United States*, 38 Cornell Internat'l L.J. issue 3 (forthcoming 2005)—344

Nicholson, Frances & Twomey, Patrick (eds.), Refugee Rights and Realities (1999)—1095

Noll, Gregor, *Formalism vs. Empiricism: Some Reflections on the Dublin Convention on the Occasion of Recent European Case Law* (unpublished paper, 2001)—1098

Noll, Gregor, *Risky Games? A Theoretical Approach to Burden–Sharing in the Asylum Field*, 16 Internat'l J. Refugee L. 236 (2003)—934

North, David S., Alien Legalization and Naturalization: What the United States Can Learn from Down Under (1984)—608, 1291

North, David S., The Long Gray Welcome—A Study of the American Naturalization Program (1985)—1291

Note, *A Common Sense Reconstruction of the INA's Crime–Related Removal System: Eliminating the Caveats from the Statue of Liberty's Welcoming Words*, 78 Washington Univ. L.Q. 1549 (2000)—567

Note, *An Argument for the Application of Equal Protection Heightened Scrutiny to Classifications Based on Homosexuality*, 57 Southern California L.Rev. 797 (1984)—264

Note, *An Opportunity to be Heard: The Right to Counsel in a Deportation Hearing*, 63 Washington L.Rev. 1019 (1988)—664

Note, *Basing Asylum Claims on a Fear of Persecution Arising from a Prior Asylum Claim*, 56 Notre Dame Lawyer 719 (1981)—976, 977

Note, *Coming to America: The Immigration Obstacle Facing Binational Same–Sex Couples*, 73 Southern Calif. L. Rev. 811 (2000)—270

Note, *Ethical Problems in Representing Aliens Applying for Visas Based on Marriages to United States Citizens*, 28 Santa Clara L.Rev. 709 (1988)—280

Note, *Exclusion and Deportation of Resident Aliens: The Re–Entry Doctrine and the Need for Reform*, 13 San Diego L.Rev. 192 (1975)—519

Note, *Ideological Exclusion, Plenary Power, and the PLO*, 77 California L.Rev. 831 (1989)—179

Note, *Immigration for Investors: A Comparative Analysis of U.S., Canadian, and Australian Policies*, 7 Boston College Internat'l & Comp. L. Rev. 113 (1984)—334

Note, *INS Transfer Policy: Interference with Detained Aliens' Due Process Right to Retain Counsel*, 100 Harvard L. Rev. 2001 (1987)—657

Note, *Judicial Review of Visa Denials: Reexamining Consular Nonreviewability*, 52 N.Y.U. L.Rev. 1137 (1977)—469

Note, *Legal Fictions Mask Human Suffering: The Detention of the Mariel Cubans—Constitutional, Statutory, International Law, and Human Considerations*, 62 Southern California L.Rev. 1733 (1989)—156, 157

Note, *Litigating as Law Students: An Inside Look at Haitian Centers Council*, 103 Yale L.J. 2337 (1994)—1135

Note, *Queer Reasoning: Immigration Policy, Baker v. State of Vermont, and the (Non)Recognition of Same–Gender Relationships*, 10 Law & Sexuality 211 (2001)—263

Note, *The Constitutionality of the INS Sham Marriage Investigation Policy,* 99 Harvard L.Rev. 1238 (1986)—271

Note, *The Propriety of Denying Entry to Homosexual Aliens: Examining the Public Health Service's Authority over Medical Exclusions,* 17 Univ. Michigan J.L. Reform 331 (1984)—259

Note, *The Turning Point Approaches: The Political Offense Exception to Extradition,* 24 San Diego L.Rev. 549 (1987)—969

Novotny, Ann, Strangers at the Door: Ellis Island, Castle Garden, and the Great Migration to America (1971)—444

Nugent, Christopher, *Strengthening Access to Justice: Prehearing Rights Presentations for Detained Respondents,* 76 IR 1077 (July 19, 1999)—666

Ogletree, Jr., Charles J., *America's Schizophrenic Immigration Policy: Race, Class, and Reason,* 41 Boston College L. Rev. 755 (2000)—82

Oldham, James & Wishnie, Michael J., *The Historical Scope of Habeas Corpus and INS v. St. Cyr,* 16 Georgetown Immigration L.J. 485 (2002)—756

Olivas, Michael A., *A Rebuttal to FAIR: States Can Enact Residency Statutes for the Undocumented,* 7 BIB 652 (June 1, 2002)—1257

Olivas, Michael A., *"Breaking the Law" on Principle: An Essay on Lawyers' Dilemmas, Unpopular Causes, and Legal Regimes,* 52 Univ. Pittsburgh. L. Rev. 815 (1991)—936

Olivas, Michael A., *IIRIRA, the DREAM Act, and Undocumented College Student Residency,* 30 J. College & University L. 435 (2004)—1257

Olivas, Michael A., *Immigration Law Teaching and Scholarship in the Ivory Tower: A Response to* Race Matters, 2000 Univ. Illinois 613—102

Olivas, Michael A., *Plyler v. Doe, Toll v. Moreno, and Postsecondary Admissions: Undocumented Aliens and Enduring Disability,* 15 J.L. & Education 19 (1986)—1251

Olivas, Michael A., *Preempting Preemption: Foreign Affairs, State Rights and Alienage Classifications,* 35 Virginia J. Internat'l L. 217 (1994)—1253

Olivas, Michael A., *Storytelling out of School: Undocumented College Residency, Race, and Reaction,* 22 Hastings Constitutional L.Q. 1019 (1995)—1256

Olivas, Michael A., *The Chronicles, My Grandfather's Stories, and Immigration Law: The Slave Traders Chronicle as Racial History,* 34 St. Louis U.L.J. 425 (1990)—93, 367

Olivas, Michael A., *The War on Terrorism Touches the Ivory Tower–Colleges and Universities After September 11,* 30 J. Colleges & Universities L. 233 (2004)—868

Olivas, Michael A., *Unaccompanied Refugee Children: Detention, Due Process, and Disgrace,* 2 Stanford L. & Policy Rev. 159 (1990)—654, 936, 1087

Ontiveros, Maria L., *Immigrant Workers' Rights in a Post–Hoffman World–Organizing Around the Thirteenth Amendment,* 18 Georgetown Immigration L.J. 651 (2005)—1202

Osuna, Juan P., *The 1996 Immigration Act: Employer Sanctions, Antidiscrimination and Work Verification,* 73 IR 1749 (Dec. 20, 1996)—1225

Osuna, Juan P., *The Exclusion from the United States of Aliens Infected with the AIDS Virus: Recent Developments and Prospects for the Future,* 16 Houston J. Internat'l L. 1 (1993)—442

Osuna, Juan P., Understanding the 1996 Immigration Act (1997)—23

Osuna, Juan P. & Mariani, Patricia, *Expedited Removal: Authorities, Implementation, and Ongoing Policy and Practice Issues,* Nov. 1997 Immigration Briefings—1106

Palmer, Geoffrey W.R., Unbridled Power— An Interpretation of New Zealand's Constitution and Government (2d ed. 1987)— 566

Palmer, John R.B., Yale Loehr, Stephen W. & Cronin, Elizabeth, *Why Are So Many People Challenging Board of Immigration Appeals Decisions in Federal Court? An Empirical Analysis of the Recent Surge in Petitions for Review* (unpublished manuscript 2005)—721

Papademetriou, Demetrios G. & Yale–Loehr, Stephen, Balancing Interests: Rethinking U.S. Selection of Skilled Immigrants (1996)—321, 337, 365

Papandrea, Mary–Rose, *Under Attack: The Public's Right to Know and the War on Terror,* 25 Boston College Third World L. Rev. 35 (2005)—880

Paparelli, Angelo A. & Burkemper, J. Ira, *Skeletons in the Closet: LCA Audits in the Age of H–1B Uncertainty,* 73 IR 745 (June 3, 1996), 781 (June 10, 1996)—364

Paparelli, Angelo A. & Tilner, Mitchell C., *A Proposal for Legislation Establishing a System of Review of Visa Refusals in Selected Cases,* 65 IR 1027 (1988)—469

Paral, Rob, *Naturalization: New Demands and New Directions at the INS,* 72 IR 937 (July 17, 1995)—1279

Passel, Jeffrey S., Estimates of the Size and Characteristics of the Undocumented Population (Mar. 21, 2005)—1194, 1195

Passel, Jeffrey S., Recent Efforts to Control Illegal Immigration to the United States (unpublished paper, presented to OECD

Working Party on Migration, Paris, June 13–14, 1996)—1194, 1197

Passel, Jeffrey S., & Clark, Rebecca L., How Much Do Immigrants Really Cost? A Reappraisal of Huddle's "The Cost of Immigrants" (Feb. 1994)—1195

Pauw, Robert, *A New Look at Deportation as Punishment: Why at Least Some of the Constitution's Criminal Procedure Provisions Must Apply*, 52 Administrative L. Rev. 305 (2000)—500, 530

Pauw, Robert, *Gete v. INS: Vehicle Seizure Class Action*, 4 BIB 844 (Aug. 15, 1999)—1197

Pauw, Robert, *Judicial Review of "Pattern and Practice" Cases: What to Do When the INS Acts Unlawfully*, 70 Washington L. Rev. 779 (1995)—758

Pauw, Robert, *Plenary Power: An Outmoded Doctrine that Should Not Limit IIRIRA Reform*, 51 Emory L.J. 1095 (2002)—103

Pauw, Robert & Boos, Greg, *Conveyance Seizures and Forfeitures: Constitutional Limits on Agency Decision-Making*, Apr. 1996 Immigration Briefings—1197

Perea, Juan F., *"Am I an American or Not?" Reflections on Citizenship, Americanization, and Race*, in Noah M.J. Pickus (ed.), Immigration and Citizenship in the Twenty-First Century at 49 et seq. (1998)—50

Perea, Juan F., *Demography and Distrust: An Essay on American Languages, Cultural Pluralism, and Official English*, 77 Minnesota L. Rev. 269 (1992)—61

Perea, Juan F. (ed.), Immigrants Out! The New Nativism and the Anti-Immigrant Impulse in the United States (1997)—57, 82, 367, 1255

Perluss, Deborah & Hartman [Fitzpatrick], Joan F., *Temporary Refuge: Emergence of a Customary Norm*, 26 Virginia J. Internat'l L. 551 (1986)—1171, 1182

Pham, Huyen, *The Inherent Flaws in the Inherent Authority Position: Why Inviting Local Enforcement of the Immigration Laws Violates the Constitution*, 31 Florida State Univ. L. Rev. 965 (2004)—120, 1200

Phuong, Catherine, *Persecution by Non-State Agents: Comparative Judicial Interpretations of the 1951 Refugee Convention*, 4 European J. Migration & L. 521 (2003)—1026, 1028

Piatt, Bill, Only English? Law and Language Policy in the United States (1990)—61

Pickus, Noah M.J. (ed.), Immigration and Citizenship in the Twenty-First Century (1998)—50

Pilcher, Susan L., *Justice Without a Blindfold: Criminal Proceedings and the Alien Defendant*, 50 Arkansas L. Rev. 269 (1997)—679

Pinnix, John L. (ed.), Ethics in a Brave New World (2004)—310

Pistone, Michele R., *A Times Sensitive Response to Professor Aleinikoff's Detaining*

Plenary Power, 16 Georgetown Immigration L.J. 391 (2002)—204

Pistone, Michele R., *Asylum Filing Deadlines: Unfair and Unnecessary*, 10 Georgetown Immigration L.J. 95 (1996)—1096

Pistone, Michele R., *Justice Delayed is Justice Denied: A Proposal for Ending the Unnecessary Detention of Asylum Seekers*, 12 Harvard Human Rights J. 197 (1999)—1108

Pitkin, Thomas M., Keepers of the Gate: A History of Ellis Island (1975)—444

Plascencia, Luis F.B., Freeman, Gary P. & Setzler, Mark, Tomás Rivera Policy Institute, *Restricting Immigrant Access to Employment: An Examination of Regulations in Five States*, Policy Brief (Aug. 1999)—1351

Plender, Richard, International Migration Law (rev. 2d ed.1988)—34, 137, 1171

Portes, Alejandro & Schauffler, Richard, *Language and the Second Generation: Bilingualism Yesterday and Today*, 28 International Migration Rev. 640 (1994)—60

Quinn, Ryan & Yale–Loehr, Stephen, *Private Immigration Bills: An Overview*, 9 BIB 1147 (Oct. 1, 2004)—613, 614

Raffonelli, Lisa, *INS Final Rule to Assist Victims of Trafficking*, 23 Refugee Reports 1 (Apr. 2002)—402, 1207

Ragland, Thomas K., *Presumed Incredible: A View from the Dissent*, 75 IR 1541 (Nov. 9, 1998)—1058

Rawitz, Sidney B., *From Wong Yang Sung to Black Robes*, 65 IR 453 (1988)—645

Rawls, John, *A Theory of Justice* (1971)—33

Reich, Peter L., *Environmental Metaphor in the Alien Benefits Debate*, 42 UCLA L. Rev. 1577 (1995)—1196, 1256

Reich, Peter L., *Jurisprudential Tradition and Undocumented Alien Entitlements*, 6 Georgetown Immigration L.J. 1 (1992)—1234

Reich, Peter L., *Public Benefits for Undocumented Aliens: State Law into the Breach Once More*, 21 New Mexico L. Rev. 219 (1991)—1234

Ressler, Everett M., Boothby, Neil & Steinbock, Daniel J., Unaccompanied Children: Care and Protection in Wars, Natural Disasters, and Refugee Movements (1988)—936

Rice, Marcelle, *Protecting Parents: Why Mothers and Fathers Who Oppose Female Genital Cutting Qualify for Asylum*, Nov. 2004 Immigration Briefings—1022

Rizza, Nicholas J., *INS Detention: The Impact on Asylum Seekers*, 17 Refugee Reports No. 8, at 2 (Aug. 30, 1996)—1109

Robbins, Ira P., *The Revitalization of the Common Law Civil Writ of Audita Quere-*

la as a Post–Conviction Remedy in Criminal Cases: The Immigration Context and Beyond, 6 Georgetown Immigration L.J. 643 (1992)—540

Roberts, Maurice A., The Exercise of Administrative Discretion Under the Immigration Laws, 13 San Diego L.Rev. 144 (1975)—605

Roberts, Maurice A. & Yale–Loehr, Stephen, Employers as Junior Immigration Inspectors: The Impact of the 1986 Immigration Reform and Control Act, 21 Internat'l Lawyer 1013 (1987)—1219

Roberts, Maurice A. & Yale–Loehr, Stephen, Understanding the 1986 Immigration Law (1987)—368, 608, 1210

Robie, William R., The Purpose and Effect of the Proposed Rules of Procedure for Proceedings Before Immigration Judges, 1 Georgetown Immigration L.J. 269 (1986)—641

Robin–Olivier, Sophie, Citizens and Noncitizens in Europe: European Union Measures Against Terrorism After September 11, 25 Boston College Third World L. Rev. 197 (2005)—914

Rochvarg, Arnold, Report to the Administrative Conference—Reforming the Administrative Naturalization Process: Reducing Delays While Increasing Fairness, 9 Georgetown Immigration L.J. 397 (1995)—1291

Rollin, Joseph Justin, Humpty Dumpty Logic: Arguing against the "AggravatedMisdemeanor" in Immigration Law, 6 BIB 445 (May 15, 2001)—553, 563

Romero, Victor C., Alienated–Immigrant Rights, the Constitution, and Equality in America (2005)—103

Romero, Victor C., "Aren't You Latino?": Building Bridges upon Common Misperceptions, 33 U.C. Davis L. Rev. 837 (2000)—87, 100

Romero, Victor C., Asians, Gay Marriage, and Immigration: Family Unification at a Crossroads, 15 Indiana Internat'l & Comp. L. Rev., issue #2 (forthcoming 2005)—262

Romero, Victor C., Broadening Our World: Citizens and Immigrants of Color in America, 27 Capitol Univ. L. Rev. 13 (1998)—96

Romero, Victor C., Critical Race Theory in Three Acts: Racial Profiling, Affirmative Action, and the Diversity Visa Lottery, 66 Albany L. Rev. 375 (2003)—892

Romero, Victor C., Decoupling "Terrorist" from "Immigrant:" An Enhanced Role for the Federal Courts Post 9/11, 7 Univ. of Iowa J. of Gender, Race & Justice 201 (2003)—885

Romero, Victor C., Expanding the Circle of Membership by Reconstructing the "Alien": Lessons from Social Psychology and the "Promise Enforcement" Cases, 32 Univ. Michigan J.L. Reform 1 (1998)—681

Romero, Victor C., Noncitizen Students and Immigration Policy Post 9/11, 17 Georgetown Immigration L.J. 357 (2003)—386, 868, 869, 1256

Romero, Victor C., On Elián and Aliens: A Political Solution to the Plenary Power Problem, 4 NYU J. Legislation & Public Policy 343 (2000–01)—87, 1088

Romero, Victor C., Postsecondary School Education Benefits for Undocumented Immigrants: Promises and Pitfalls, 27 North Carolina J. Internat'l L. & Commercial Regulation 393 (2002)—1256

Romero, Victor C., Proxies for Loyalty in Constitutional Immigration Law: Citizenship and Race After September 11, 52 DePaul L. Rev. 871 (2003)—892, 897

Romero, Victor C., Racial Profiling: "Driving While Mexican" and Affirmative Action, 6 Michigan J. Race & Law 195 (2000)—98, 892

Romero, Victor C., The Child Citizenship Act and the Family Reunification Act: Valuing the Citizen Child as Well as the Citizen Parent, 55 Florida L. Rev. 489 (2003)—1292

Romero, Victor C., The Congruence Principle Applied: Rethinking Equal Protection Review of Federal Alienage Classifications after Adarand Constructors, Inc. v. Pena, 76 Oregon L. Rev. 425 (1997)—1193, 1352

Romero, Victor C., The Domestic Fourth Amendment Rights of Undocumented Immigrants: On Gutierrez and the Tort Law / Immigration Law Parallel, 35 Harvard Civil Rights—Civil Liberties L. Rev. 57 (2000)—701

Romero, Victor C., The Selective Deportation of Same–Gender Partners: In Search of the "Rara Avis," 56 Univ. Miami L. Rev. 537 (2002)—261

Romero, Victor C., Whatever Happened to the Fourth Amendment? Undocumented Immigrants' Rights after INS v. Lopez–Mendoza and United States v. Verdugo–Urquidez, 65 Southern California L. Rev. 999 (1992)—704

Rosati, Kristen B., Article 3 of the United Nations Convention Against Torture: A Powerful Tool to Prevent Removal Just Became More Powerful, 4 BIB 137 (Feb. 15, 1999)—1145, 1147, 1156, 1157, 1159

Rosati, Kristen B., The United Nations Convention Against Torture: A Self-Executing Treaty that Prevents the Removal of Persons Ineligible for Asylum and Withholding of Removal, 26 Denver J. Internat'l L. 533 (1998)—1148

Rosberg, Gerald M., Aliens and Equal Protection: Why Not the Right to Vote?, 75 Michigan L. Rev. 1092 (1977)—1353

Rose, Linda, *De–Mystifying Reduction in Recruitment*, 19 Immigration Law Today 205 (April 2000)—296

Rosenberg, Lory Diana, *Administrative Deportation Proceedings: Accomplishment or Abomination?*, 72 IR 721 (May 25, 1996)—837

Rosenberg, Lory Diana, *Arrests, Jails, and Video Hearings*, 9 BIB 1233 (Oct. 15, 2004)—639

Rosenberg, Lory Diana, *Ask Lory—Clash of Intentions*, 8 BIB 1881 (Dec. 15, 2003)—522

Rosenberg, Lory Diana, *Credibility Determinations in Asylum Cases: Evidentiary Factors and Regulatory Limits Under the Clearly Erroneous Standard*, 8 BIB 573 (Apr. 1, 2003)—721

Rosenberg, Lory Diana, *It's Alive: A Noncitizen's Right to Competent Counsel Before the EOIR and BCIS After Matter of Assaad*, 8 BIB 943 (June 1, 2003)—684, 685

Rosenberg, Lory Diana, *Recognition of Vacation of Conviction and Matter of Pickering: Comity or Tragedy?*, 8 BIB 1103 (July 1, 2003)—538

Rosenberg, Lory Diana, *The Courts and Interception: The United States' Interdiction Experience and Its Impact on Refugees and Asylum Seekers*, 17 Georgetown Immigration L.J. 199 (2003)—834, 1114

Rosenberg, Lory Diana, *Understanding Immigration Consequences: The Elusive Construction of Controlled Substance Possession Convictions*, 7 BIB 1295 (Nov. 1, 2002)—562

Rosenberg, Lory Diana & Sabagh, Denise, *A Practitioner's Guide to INA § 212(c)*, Apr. 1993 Immigration Briefings—574

Rosenberg, Lory Diana & Vargas–Padilla, Nelson, *An Odyssey of Immigration Consequences of Crime: The BIA's 2001 Interpretations*, 78 IR 909 (June 4, 2001)—530, 553

Rosenberg, Lory Diana & Vargas–Padilla, Nelson, *Immigration Consequences of Crimes on the Doorstep of the Twenty-First Century*, 77 IR 685 (May 26, 2000)—530, 553

Rosenfield, Harry N., *Consular Non–Reviewability: A Case Study in Administrative Absolutism*, 41 A.B.A.J. 1109 (1955)—469

Rubenstein, Kim, *Citizenship in Australia: Unscrambling Its Meaning*, 20 Melbourne L. Rev. 503 (1995)—1351

Rubenstein, Kim & Adler, Daniel, *International Citizenship: The Future of Nationality in a Globalized World*, 7 Indiana J. Global Legal Studies 519 (2000)—1295

Rubman, David, *Seizure and Forfeiture of Conveyances Under the INA*, Feb. 1990 Immigration Briefings—1208

Ruse, Michael, Homosexuality—A Philosophical Inquiry (1988)—266

Sadat, Leila Wexler, *Official English, Nationalism and Linguistic Terror: A French Lesson*, 71 Washington L.Rev. 285 (1996)—57

Said, Edward W., Orientalism (1978)—100

Saito, Natsu Taylor, *Alien and Non-alien Alike: Citizenship, "Foreignness," and Racial Hierarchy in American Law*, 76 Oregon L. Rev. 261 (1997)—94

Saito, Natsu Taylor, *Asserting Plenary Power over the "Other": Indians, Immigrants, Colonial Subjects, and Why U.S. Jurisprudence Needs to Incorporate International Law*, 20 Yale L. & Policy Rev. 427 (2002)—139

Saito, Natsu Taylor, *Whose Liberty? Whose Security? The USA PATRIOT Act in the Context of COINTELPRO and the Unlawful Suppression of Political Dissent*, 81 Oregon L. Rev. 1051 (2002)—914

Saito, Natsu Taylor, *Will Force Trump Legality After September 11? American Jurisprudence Confronts the Rule of Law*, 17 Georgetown Immigration L.J. 1 (2002)—844, 850, 855

Salyer, Lucy, Laws Harsh as Tigers: Chinese Immigrants and the Shaping of Modern Immigration Law (1995)—117

Sanger, Carol, *Immigration Reform and Control of the Undocumented Family*, 2 Georgetown Immigration L.J. 295 (1987)—250, 609

Savin–Williams, Ritch C., *Theoretical Perspectives Accounting for Adolescent Homosexuality*, 9 J. Adolescent Health Care 95 (1988)—266, 267

Scanlan, John A., *Aliens in the Marketplace of Ideas: The Government, The Academy, and the McCarran–Walter Act*, 66 Texas L.Rev. 1481 (1988)—179, 429, 433

Scanlan, John A., *American–Arab–Getting the Balance Wrong–Again!*, 52 Administrative L. Rev. 347 (2000)—178

Scanlan, John A., Book Review, *Something Happened: Descent into the Immigration Maelstrom*, 4 Indiana J. Global Legal Studies 239 (1996)—83

Scanlan, John A., *Call and Response: The Particular and the General*, 2000 Univ. of Illinois 639—102

Scanlan, John A. & Kent, O.T., *The Force of Moral Arguments for a Just Immigration Policy in a Hobbesian Universe: The Contemporary American Example*, in Mark Gibney (ed.), Open Borders? Closed Societies? The Ethical and Political Issues, at 61 (1988)—29

Scaperlanda, Michael A., *Are We That Far Gone?: Due Process and Secret Deportation Proceedings*, 7 Stanford L. & Policy Rev. 23 (1996)—876

Scaperlanda, Michael A., *Kulturkampf in the Backwaters: Homosexuality and Immigration Law*, 11 Widener J. Pub. L. 475 (2002)—270, 994

Scaperlanda, Michael A., *Partial Membership: Aliens and the Constitutional Community*, 81 Iowa L. Rev. 707 (1996)—103, 1250, 1352

Scaperlanda, Michael A., *Polishing the Tarnished Golden Door*, 1993 Wisconsin L. Rev. 965—173, 232

Scaperlanda, Michael A., *Who is My Neighbor? An Essay on Immigrants, Welfare Reform, and the Constitution*, 29 Connecticut L. Rev. 1587 (1997)—180

Scharf, Irene, *Commentary by Irene Scharf on Anderson v. Conboy*, 3 BIB 1102 (Nov. 1, 1998)—1224

Scharf, Irene, *Commentary on United States v. Balsys*, 3 BIB 886 (Sept. 1, 1998)—704

Scharf, Irene, *Tired of Your Masses: A History of and Judicial Responses to Early 20th Century Anti-Immigrant Legislation*, 21 Univ. Hawaii L. Rev. 131 (1999)—58, 82

Scharf, Irene & Hess, Christine, *What Process is Due? Unaccompanied Minors' Rights to Deportation Hearings*, 1988 Duke L.J. 114—620

Schauer, Frederick, *Community, Citizenship, and the Search for National Identity*, 84 Michigan L. Rev. 1504 (1986)—1373

Scheppele, Kim Lane, *Other People's PATRIOT Acts: Europe's Response to September 11*, 50 Loyola L. Rev. 67 (2004)—914

Schmidt, Paul W., *Detention of Aliens*, 24 San Diego L.Rev. 305 (1987)—156

Schmidt, Paul W., *Immigration Benefits for Children Born Out of Wedlock and for their Natural Fathers: A Survey of the Law*, 16 San Diego L.Rev. 11 (1978)—284

Schoenholtz, Andrew I., *Aiding and Abetting Persecutors: The Seizure and Return of Haitian Refugees in Violation of the U.N. Refugee Convention and Protocol*, 7 Georgetown Immigration L.J. 67 (1993)—1134

Schoenholtz, Andrew I., *Beyond the Supreme Court: A Modest Plea to Improve Our Asylum System*, 14 Georgetown Immigration L.J. 541 (2000)—1053

Schoenholtz, Andrew I., *Supreme Court Orders Ninth Circuit to Defer to the BIA in Refugee Cases*, 4 BIB 615 (June 15, 1999)—1075

Schoenholtz, Andrew I. & Jacobs, Jonathan, *The State of Asylum Representation: Ideas for Change*, 16 Georgetown Immigration L.J. 739 (2002)—654

Schorr, Naomi & Yale-Loehr, Stephen, *The Odyssey of the J-2: Forty-Three Years of Trying Not to Go Home Again*, 18 Georgetown Immigration L.J. 221 (2004)—388

Schrag, Philip G., *A Well-Founded Fear-The Congressional Battle to Save Asylum in America* (2000)—1081

Schrag, Philip G., *Center for Applied Legal Studies of Georgetown Law Center, Interviewing a Client, Asylum Law Manual* (2005)—1137

Schrag, Philip G., *Don't Gut Political Asylum*, 10 Georgetown Immigration L.J. 93 (1996)—1096

Schrag, Philip G., *The Summary Affirmance Proposal of the Board of Immigration Appeals*, 12 Georgetown Immigration L.J. 531 (1998)—718

Schrag, Philip G. & Pistone, Michele R., *The 1996 Immigration Act: Asylum Application Deadlines and Expedited Removal—What the INS Should Do*, 73 IR 1565 (Nov. 11, 1996)—1096

Schrag, Philip G. & Pistone, Michele R., *The New Asylum Rule: Not Yet a Model of Fair Procedure*, 11 Georgetown Immigration L.J. 267 (1997)—1106

Schuck, Peter H., *A Case for Profiling*, The American Lawyer, January 2002—893

Schuck, Peter H., *Alien Rumination*, 105 Yale L.J. 1963 (1996)—57

Schuck, Peter H., *Citizens, Strangers, and In-Betweens: Essays on Immigration and Citizenship* (1998)—1295

Schuck, Peter H., *Citizenship in Federal Systems*, 48 Amer. J. Comp. L. 195 (2000)—1373

Schuck, Peter H., *Diversity in America* (2003)—36, 54, 60, 337, 344

Schuck, Peter H., *INS Detention and Removal: A "White Paper,"* 11 Georgetown Immigration L.J. 667 (1997)—229, 844

Schuck, Peter H., *Membership in the Liberal Polity: The Devaluation of American Citizenship*, 3 Georgetown Immigration L.J. 1 (1989)—1359

Schuck, Peter H., *Plural Citizenships*, in Peter H. Schuck, Citizens, Strangers, and In-Betweens: Essays on Immigration and Citizenship, ch. 10 (1998)—1295

Schuck, Peter H., *Refugee Burden-Sharing: A Modest Proposal*, 22 Yale J. Internat'l L. 243 (1997)—934

Schuck, Peter H., *The Emerging Political Consensus on Immigration Law*, 5 Georgetown Immigration L.J. 1 (1991)—83, 1196

Schuck, Peter H., *The Message of Proposition 187*, 26 Pacific L.J. 989 (1995)—1255

Schuck, Peter H., *The Politics of Rapid Legal Change: Immigration Policy in the 1980's*, 6 Studies in Amer. Political Development 37 (1992)—83

Schuck, Peter H., *The Re-Evaluation of American Citizenship*, 12 Georgetown Immigration L.J. 1 (1997)—1363

Schuck, Peter H., *The Transformation of Immigration Law*, 84 Columbia L.Rev. 1 (1984)—31, 32, 103, 173, 1251

Schuck, Peter H., *Whose Membership Is It, Anyway? Comments on Gerald Neuman*, 35 Virginia J. Internat'l L. 321 (1994)—1312

Schuck, Peter H. & Elliott, E. Donald, *Studying Administrative Law: A Methodology for, and Report on, New Empirical Re-*

search, 42 Administrative L.Rev. 519 (1990)—484, 760

Schuck, Peter H. & Smith, Rogers M., Citizenship Without Consent—Illegal Aliens in the American Polity (1985)—1269, 1297, 1308, 1312, 1348

Schuck, Peter H. & Smith, Rogers M., *Membership and Consent: Actual or Mythic?*, 11 Yale J. Internat'l L. 545 (1986)—1312

Schuck, Peter H. & Wang, Theodore H., *Continuity and Change: Patterns of Immigration Litigation in the Courts, 1979–1990*, 45 Stanford L.Rev. 115 (1992)—760

Schuck, Peter H. & Williams, John, *Removing Criminal Aliens: The Pitfalls and Promises of Federalism*, 22 Harvard J. L. & Public Policy 367 (1999)—532

Schwartz, Liam, *E-Visa Classification: The Case for a Single Policy on Dual Intent*, 21 Immigration L. Today 691 (Nov. 2002)—360

Schwartz, Liam & Lazerow, Michelle L., *The Consul and the Visas Condor–Closely Scrutinizing*, Immigration Law Today (May/June 2003) at 24—885

Schwartz, Warren F. (ed.), Justice in Immigration (1995)—29

Seltzer, Suzanne, *Demystifying the HHS Waiver Process*, 9 BIB 1165 (Oct. 1, 2004)—393

Shachar, Ayelet, *Whose Republic?: Citizenship and Membership in the Israeli Polity*, 13 Georgetown Immigration L.J. 233 (1999)—1351

Shapiro, Steven R., *Ideological Exclusions: Closing the Border to Political Dissidents*, 100 Harvard L.Rev. 930 (1987)—179, 434

Shusterman, Carl M. & Neal, David L., *Survey and Analysis of H–1B Labor Condition Application Decisions*, 72 IR 49 (Jan. 9, 1995)—364

Silverman, Andrew, *An Historical and Legal Perspective of Mexican Migration*, 1988 Arizona J. Internat'l & Comp. L. 138—82

Silverman, Mark & Joaquin, Linton, *NACARA for Guatemalans, Salvadorans and Former Soviet Bloc Nationals: An Update*, 76 IR 1141 (Aug. 2, 1999)—606

Simon, Julian L., The Economic Consequences of Immigration (2d ed. 1999)—73, 1196

Singer, Audrey (ed.), *Immigrants, Their Families, and Their Communities in the Aftermath of Welfare Reform*, Research Perspectives in Migration (Carnegie Endowment for International Peace 2001)—1357

Singer, Eric H., *United States v. Idowu: Inadmissibility and Unlawful Reentry After Deportation–Still Confused After All These Years*, 29 Southwestern Univ. L. Rev. 301 (2000)—1205

Sinha, S. Prakash, *Asylum and International Law* (1971)—973, 975

Sklar, Morton, *New Convention Against Torture Procedures and Standards*, July 1999 Immigration Briefings—1145

Slocum, Brian G., *The Immigration Rule of Lenity and Chevron Deference*, 17 Georgetown Immigration L.J. 515 (2003)—503

Smith, Debbie and ABC Legal Team, *The ABC Settlement: A Guide for Class Members and Advocates*, 72 IR 1497 (Nov. 6, 1995)—1085

Smith, James F., *A Nation that Welcomes Immigrants? An Historical Examination of United States Immigration Policy*, 1 U.C. Davis J. Internat'l L. & Policy 227 (1995)—14

Smith, James F., *NAFTA and Human Rights: A Necessary Linkage*, 27 U.C. Davis L.Rev. 793 (1994)—377

Smith, James F., *United States Immigration Law As We Know It: El Clandestino, The American Gulag, Rounding Up the Usual Suspects*, 38 U.C. Davis L. Rev. 747 (2005)—1193

Smith, James M., Freedom's Fetters (1956)—427

Smith, James P. & Edmonston, Barry (eds.), National Research Council of the National Academy of Sciences, The New Americans–Economic, Demographic, and Fiscal Effects of Immigration (1997)—68, 76

Smith, Rogers M., Civic Ideals: Conflicting Visions of Citizenship in U.S. History (1997)—1373

Smolla, Rodney A., *The Reemergence of the Right–Privilege Distinction in Constitutional Law: The Price of Protesting Too Much*, 35 Stanford L.Rev. 69 (1982)—144

Song, Julie M., *In re L: Overcoming an Aggravated Felony Conviction through the Common Law Remedy of Coram Nobis*, 77 IR 993 (July 24, 2000)—540

Sopf, Davor, *Temporary Protection in Europe after 1990: The "Right to Remain" of Genuine Convention Refugees*, 6 Washington Univ. J. L. & Policy 109 (2001)—1171

Spiro, Peter J., *Dual Nationality and the Meaning of Citizenship*, 46 Emory L.J. 1411 (1997)—1295, 1296

Spiro, Peter J., Embracing Dual Nationality, Occasional Paper No. 1, Internat'l Migration Policy Program, Carnegie Endowment for International Peace (1998)—1295

Spiro, Peter J., *Explaining the End of Plenary Power*, 16 Georgetown Immigration L.J. 339 (2002)—204

Spiro, Peter J., *Learning to Live with Immigration Federalism*, 29 Connecticut L. Rev. 1627 (1997)—119, 1253

Spiro, Peter J., *Questioning Barriers to Naturalization*, 13 Georgetown Immigration L.J. 479 (1999)—1284

Spiro, Peter J., *The Citizenship Dilemma*, 51 Stanford L. Rev. 597 (1999)—1373

Spiro, Peter J., *The States and Immigration in an Era of Demi–Sovereignties*, 35 Virginia J. Internat'l L. 121 (1994)—119, 1253

Starr, Lynn Acker, *The Ineffectiveness and Impact of the Human Immunodeficiency Virus (HIV) Exclusion in U.S. Immigration Law*, 3 Georgetown Immigration L.J. 87 (1989)—443

Stein, Dan, *Family–Sponsored Immigration*, 4 Georgetown Immigration L.J. 201 (1990)—290

Stein, Dan & Bauer, John, *Interpreting the 14th Amendment: Automatic Citizenship for Children of Illegal Immigrants?*, 7 Stanford L. & Policy Rev. 127 (1996)—1312

Steinbock, Daniel J., *Interpreting the Refugee Definition*, 45 UCLA L. Rev. 733 (1998)—915, 1134

Steinbock, Daniel J., *National Identity Cards: Fourth and Fifth Amendment Issues*, 56 Florida L. Rev. 697 (2004)—1221

Steinbock, Daniel J., *Separated Children in Mass Migration: Causes and Cures*, 22 St. Louis Univ. Public L. Rev. 297 (2003)—1087

Steinbock, Daniel J., *The Admission of Unaccompanied Children into the United States*, 7 Yale L. & Policy Rev. 137 (1989)—936

Steinbock, Daniel J., *The Qualities of Mercy: Maximizing the Impact of U.S. Refugee Resettlement*, 36 Univ. Michigan J. L. Reform 951 (2003)—916

Stevenson, Andrew, *DREAMing of an Equal Future for Immigrant Children: Federal and State Initiatives to Improve Undocumented Students' Access to Postsecondary Education*, 46 Arizona L. Rev. 551 (2004)—1256

Stickney, Beth, *Whither Family Unity? A Post–IIRIRA Update*, Dec. 1998 Immigration Briefings—439

Stock, Margaret D., *Driver Licenses and National Security: Myths and Reality*, 10 BIB 422 (Mar. 1, 2005)—1261

Stock, Margaret D., *The "REAL ID" Act–A Real Nightmare for DoD*, The Officer (Apr. 2005)—1260

Stock, William A., *So, Now What? A Lighthearted Look at Strategies for Dealing with the H–1B Cap*, 10 BIB 471 (Mar. 15, 2005)—365

Stone, Lincoln, *Immigrant Investment in Local Clusters*, 80 IR 837 (June 16, 2003)—335, 337

Storchevoy, Leonard, *The Right to Family Reunification in the Immigration Law of the Commonwealth Caribbean and the United States: A Comparative Study*, 7 Touro Internat'l L. Rev. 177 (1997)—291

Stotzky, Irwin P., Silencing the Guns in Haiti (1997)—1132

Straus, Michael W., *Employment of Aliens: A Guideline for Employers and Employees,* 20 Univ. West L.A. L. Rev. 133 (1988–89)—1210

Strauss, Peter L., *Was There a Baby in the Bathwater? A Comment on the Supreme Court's Legislative Veto Decision*, 1983 Duke L.J. 789—190

Strojny, Andrew M., *Papers, Papers ... Please: A National ID or an Electronic Tattoo*, 72 IR 617 (May 8, 1995)—1221

Suhrke, Astri, Global Refugee Movements and Strategies of Response, in Mary M. Kritz (ed.), U.S. Immigration and Refugee Policy at 163 (1983)—918

Sullivan, Kathleen M., *Commentary on Reno v. American–Arab Anti–Discrimination Committee*, 4 BIB 249 (Mar. 15, 1999)—741

Sullivan, Kathleen M., *Congress Streamlines Procedures for Certain Intercountry "Orphan" Adoptions*, 1 BIB #3 (1996)—289

Sullivan, Kathleen M., *Intercountry Adoption Act Becomes Law*, 5 BIB 977 (Dec. 1, 2000)—289

Sullivan, Kathleen M., *The Year in Detention Law and Policy: Immigration Detention Developments May 2003–April 2004*, 9 BIB 851 (July 15, 2004)—1109

Sullivan, Kathleen M., *When Representations Cross the Line*, 1 BIB No. 11 at 16 (Oct. 1996)—422

Survey on the Constitutional Right to Privacy in the Context of Homosexual Activity, 40 Univ. Miami L.Rev. 521 (1986)—267

Takaki, Ronald T., Strangers from a Different Shore—A History of Asian Americans (1989)—117, 1196

Taylor, Margaret H., *Behind the Scenes of St. Cyr and Zadvydas: Making Policy in the Midst of Litigation*, 16 Georgetown Immigration L.J. 271 (2002)—230

Taylor, Margaret H., *Dangerous by Decree: Detention Without Bond in Immigration Proceedings*, 50 Loyola L. Rev. 149 (2004)—853

Taylor, Margaret H., *Detained Aliens Challenging Conditions of Confinement and the Porous Border of the Plenary Power Doctrine*, 22 Hastings Constitutional L.Q. 1087 (1995)—103, 229, 230, 1250, 1352

Taylor, Margaret H., *Promoting Legal Representation for Detained Aliens: Litigation and Administrative Reform*, 29 Connecticut L. Rev. 1647 (1997)—666

Taylor, Margaret H., *Symbolic Detention*, 20 In Defense of the Alien 153 (1998)—229

Taylor, Margaret H., *The 1996 Immigration Act: Detention and Related Issues*, 74 IR 209 (Feb. 3, 1997)—229

Taylor, Margaret H. & Wright, Ronald F., *The Sentencing Judge as Immigration Judge*, 51 Emory L.J. 1131 (2002)—838

Taylor, Margaret Kuehne, *The Mogharrabi Rule in 1998: A Review of Recent BIA*

Asylum Decisions, 75 IR 901 (July 6, 1998)—1058

Teitelbaum, Michael S., *Political Asylum in Theory and Practice*, 76 Public Interest 74 (1984)—1086

Teitelbaum, Michael S., *Right versus Right: Immigration and Refugee Policy in the United States*, 59 Foreign Affairs 21 (1980)—32

Teitelbaum, Michael S., *Skeptical Noises about the Immigration Multiplier*, 23 Internat'l Migration Rev. 893 (1989)—290, 342

Teitelbaum, Michael S. & Weiner, Myron (eds.), Threatened Peoples, Threatened Borders (1995)—971, 1115, 1131

Teran, Lee J., *Barriers to Protection at Home and Abroad: Mexican Victims of Domestic Violence and the Violence Against Women Act*, 17 Boston Univ. Internat'l L.J. 1 (1999)—582

Teran, Lee J., *Obtaining Remedies for INS Misconduct*, May 1996 Immigration Briefings—1199

Thornberry, Cedric H.R., *Dr. Soblen and the Alien Law of the United Kingdom*, 12 Internat'l & Comp.L.Q. 414 (1963)—237

Thronson, David B., *Kids Will Be Kids? Reconsidering Conceptions of Children's Rights Underlying Immigration Law*, 63 Ohio State L.J. 979 (2002)—286

Ting, Jan C.,*"Other than a Chinaman": How U.S. Immigration Law Resulted from and Still Reflects a Policy of Excluding and Restricting Asian Immigration*, 4 Temple Political & Civil Rights L. Rev. 301 (1995)—100, 118

Ting, Jan C., Testimony to Subcomm. on Immigration, Border Security, and Claims, Comm. on the Judiciary, U.S. House of Reps. (Apr. 29, 2004)—344

Ting, Jan C., *Unobjectionable But Insufficient–Federal Initiatives in Response to the September 11 Terrorist Attacks*, 34 Connecticut L. Rev. 1145 (2002)—852, 880, 889, 892

Tooby, Norton, *Sourcelist of Cases Defining "Crimes of Moral Turpitude" under the Immigration and Nationality Act*, http://www.criminalandimmigration-law.com/cmt/cmt.html—548

Torpey, John, The Invention of the Passport (2000)—14

Tourney, Garfield, *Hormones and Homosexuality*, in Judd Marmor (ed.), Homosexual Behavior (1980), at 41—266

Tribe, Laurence H., American Constitutional Law (2d ed. 1988)—432, 433

Trillin, Calvin, *Making Adjustments*, The New Yorker, May 28, 1984—309

Trucios–Haynes, Enid, *"Family Values" 1990s Style: U.S. Immigration Reform Proposals and the Abandonment of the Family*, 36 Brandeis J. Family L. 241 (1997–98)—290

Trucios–Haynes, Enid, *National Interest Waivers*, July 1995 Immigration Briefings—294

Trucios–Haynes, Enid, *Religion and the Immigration and Nationality Act: Using Old Saws on New Bones*, 9 Georgetown Immigration L.J. 1 (1995)—333, 376

Trucios–Haynes, Enid, *Temporary Workers and Future Immigration Policy Conflicts: Protecting U.S. Workers and Satisfying the Demand for Global Human Capital*, 40 Univ. Louisville Brandeis L.J. 967 (2002)—366

Trucios–Haynes, Enid, *The Legacy of Racially Restrictive Immigration Laws and Policies and the Construction of the American National Identity*, 76 Oregon L. Rev. 369 (1997)—56

Trucios–Haynes, Enid & Shaukat, Lois Gimpel, *Grounds of Inadmissibility under the Illegal Immigration Reform and Immigrant Responsibility Act of 1996*, January & February 1998 Immigration Briefings (2 parts)—411

Trujillo, Bernard, *Immigrant Visa Distribution: The Case of Mexico*, 2000 Wisconsin L. Rev. 713—249

Tucker, Joe A., *Assimilation to the United States: A Study of the Adjustment of Status and the Immigration Marriage Fraud Statutes*, 7 Yale L. & Policy Rev. 20, (1989)—271, 272, 274, 277, 490, 491

Türk, Volker, *Forced Migration and Security*, 15 Internat'l J. Refugee L. 113 (2003)—937

Türk, Volker, *Non-State Agents of Persecution*, in V. Chetail & Vera Gowlland–Debbas (eds.), Switzerland and the International Protection of Refugees, at 95 et seq. (2002)—1026

UNHCR, 2003 Global Refugee Trends (15 June 2004)—915

UNHCR, Centre for Documentation & Research, *Internal Displacement in Africa*, 18 Refugee Survey Q., issue #1 (entire issue) (1999)—937

UNHCR, Executive Committee, Ex. Com. Conclusion 44, *Detention of Refugees and Asylum–Seekers*, No. 44 (XXXVII) (1986)—1107

UNHCR Expert Round Table, Summary Conclusions from Lisbon roundtable, Protecting Refugees, Legal and Protection Policy Research Series, Expert Meetings, Effective Protection (Lisbon, Dec. 2002), www.unhcr.ch—1101

UNHCR, Guidelines on International Protection: Gender–Related Persecution within the context of Article 1A(2) of the 1951 Convention and/or its 1967 Protocol relating to the Status of Refugees, U.N. Doc. HCR/GIP//02/01 (May 7, 2002), reproduced, 81 IR 561 (Apr. 26, 2004)—986, 1005

UNHCR, Guidelines on International Protection: "Membership of a particular social group"within the context of article IA(2) of the 1951 Convention and/or its 1967 Protocol relating to the Status of Refugees, U.N. Doc. HCR/GIP/02/02 (May 7, 2002), reproduced, 81 IR 571 (Apr. 26, 2004)—985, 986, 987, 989, 1005, 1027, 1035, 1036

UNHCR, Revised Guidelines on Applicable Criteria and Standards Relating to the Detention of Asylum–Seekers (Feb. 1999)—1107, 1108

UNHCR, Summary Conclusions from Expert Round Table in Lisbon, www.unhcr.ch, Protecting Refugees, Legal and Protection Policy Research Series, Expert Meetings, Effective Protection (Lisbon, Dec. 2002)—1101

UNHCR, UNHCR Handbook on Procedures and Criteria for Determining Refugee Status (Sept. 1979)—948, 959, 962, 963, 976, 977, 1027, 1054, 1057, 1063, 1068, 1069, 1073, 1075, 1076

UN High Commissioner for Refugees Responds to U.S. Supreme Court Decision in Sale v. Haitian Centers Council, 32 Internat'l Legal Materials 1215 (1993)—1134

United States Census Bureau, The Foreign–Born Population of the United States (Feb. 2005)—55

United States Citizenship and Immigration Services, Affirmative Asylum Procedures Manual (rev. Feb. 2003)—1082

United States Commission on Civil Rights, The Immigration Reform and Control Act: Assessing the Evaluation Process (Sept. 1989)—1219

United States Commission on Immigration Reform, Becoming an American: Immigration and Immigrant Policy (Sept. 1997)—452, 469, 1357

United States Commission on Immigration Reform, Legal Immigration: Setting Priorities (June 1995)—290, 295, 332, 368

United States Commission on Immigration Reform, U.S. Immigration Policy: Restoring Credibility (Sept. 1994)—1213, 1220

United States Commission on Immigration Reform, U.S. Refugee Policy: Taking Leadership (June 1997)—935, 936, 1075, 1106, 1108

United States Commission on International Religious Freedom, Report on Asylum Seekers in Expedited Removal (Feb. 2005)—1104

United States Committee for Refugees, World Refugee Survey 2003 (May 2003)—916

United States Congressional Research Service, 9/11 Commission: Implications for U.S. Immigration Law and Policy (Sept. 30, 2004)—914

United States Congressional Research Service, Illegal Aliens: Analysis and Background, U.S. House Comm. on the Judiciary, 95th Cong., 1st Sess. (1977)—1194

United States Congressional Research Service, Review of U.S. Refugee Resettlement Programs and Policies (Comm. Print, Senate Comm. on the Judiciary, 1980)—926, 928, 1164

United States Dept. of Homeland Security, Office of Immigration Statistics, 2003 Yearbook of Immigration Statistics (Sept. 2004) [See 2003 Yearbook of Immigration Statistics].

United States Dept. of Homeland Security, Office of the Inspector General, An Evaluation of the Security Implications of the Visa Waiver Program, No. OIG–04–26 (Apr. 2004)—889

United States Dept. of Homeland Security, Office of the Inspector General, DHS Challenges in Consolidating Terrorist Watch List Information, No. OIG–04–31 (Aug. 2004)—886

United States Dept. of Homeland Security, Office of the Inspector General, Implementation of the United States Visitor and Immigration Status Indicator Technology Program at Land Border Points of Entry, No. OIG–05–11 (Feb. 2005)—871, 872

United States Dept. of Justice, Office of the Inspector General, Inspection Report, The Potential for Fraud and INS's Efforts to Reduce the Risks of the Visa Waiver Pilot Program, Rpt. No. I–99–10 (Mar. 1999)—888

United States Dept. of Justice, Office of the Inspector General, The September 11 Detainees: A Review of the Treatment of Aliens Held on Immigration Charges in Connection with the Investigation of the September 11 Attacks (April 2003)—848, 849, 850

United States Dept. of Labor, Dictionary of Occupational Titles (4th ed. 1991)—312

United States Dept. of State, Trafficking in Persons Report (June 14, 2004)—1207

United States Dept. of State, Visa Office, Annual Report (2002)—421

United States General Accounting Office, Asylum Approval Rates for Selected Applicants (1987)—654

United States General Accounting Office, Border Security–Implications of Eliminating the Visa Waiver Program, GAO–03–38 (Nov. 2002)—890

United States General Accounting Office, Criminal Aliens—Prison Deportation Hearings Include Opportunities to Contest Deportation, Report No. GAO/GGD–90–79 (1990)—835, 836

United States General Accounting Office, Illegal Aliens—Despite Data Limitations, Current Methods Provide Better Population Estimates, GAO/PEMD–93–25 (Aug. 1993)—1194

United States General Accounting Office, Illegal Aliens—Information on Selected Countries' Employment Prohibition Laws, No. GAO/GGD–86–17BR (Oct. 1985)—1221

United States General Accounting Office, Illegal Aliens: Opportunities to Improve the Expedited Removal Process (Sept. 2000)—1104

United States General Accounting Office, Immigration Reform—Employer Sanctions and the Question of Discrimination, (March 1990)—1214, 1219, 1220

United States General Accounting Office, Naturalized Aliens: Efforts to Determine If INS Improperly Naturalized Some Aliens, GAO/GGD–98–62 (March 1998)—1281

United States General Accounting Office, Report to Congressional Committees, Homeland Security–Justice Department's Project to Interview Aliens after September 11, 2001, No. GAO–03–459 (April 2003)—872, 873

United States House of Representatives, Committee on the Judiciary, Grounds for Exclusion of Aliens under the Immigration and Nationality Act, Serial No. 7 (1988)—412, 428, 429

United States INS, 1987 Statistical Yearbook—931

United States INS, 1988 Statistical Yearbook—287

United States INS, 1989 Statistical Yearbook—287, 931, 932

United States INS, 1994 Statistical Yearbook—608, 1278

United States INS, 1995 Statistical Yearbook—239

United States INS, 1998 Statistical Yearbook—336, 613

United States INS, Gender Guidelines, 72 IR 781 (June 5, 1995)—1006, 1007, 1023

United States INS, Guidelines for Children's Asylum Claims (Dec. 10, 1998), 76 IR 5 (Jan. 1999)—1088

United States INS, Immigration Reform and Control Act: Report on the Legalized Alien Population (1992)—609

United States Office of Personnel Management, Investigations Service, Citizenship Laws of the World, http://www.opm.gov/extra/investigate/IS–01.pdf—1351

United States Select Comm'n on Immigration and Refugee Policy, U.S. Immigration Policy and the National Interest (Final Report) (1981)—334, 420

Van Alstyne, William W., *The Demise of the Right–Privilege Distinction in Constitu-*

tional Law, 81 Harvard L.Rev. 1439 (1968)—144

Van Krieken, Peter J. (ed.), The Asylum Acquis Handbook (2000)—1095

Vanheule, Dirk, *A Comparison of the Judicial Interpretations of the Notion of Refugee*, in Jean–Yves Carlier & Dirk Vanheule (eds.), Europe and Refugees: A Challenge?, chap. 5 (1997)—915

Vargas, Jorge A., *Consular Protection to Illegal Migratory Workers and Mexican Undocumented Minors: Two Sensitive Issues Addressed by the Thirteenth Annual Meeting of the United States–Mexico Binational Commission*, 6 Florida State Univ. J. Transnat'l L. & Policy 143 (1996)—638

Vargas, Jorge A., *Dual Nationality for Mexicans*, 35 San Diego L. Rev. 823 (1998)—1295

Vargas, Jorge A., *NAFTA, the Chiapas Rebellion, and the Emergence of Mexican Ethnic Law*, 25 California Western Int'l L.J. 1 (1994)—377

Vargas, Jorge A., *U.S. Border Patrol Abuses, Undocumented Mexican Workers, and International Human Rights*, 2 San Diego Internat'l L.J. 1 (2001)—1198

Vaughns, Katherine L., *A Tale of Two Opinions: The Meaning of Statutes and the Nature of Judicial Decision–Making in the Administrative Context*, 1995 B.Y.U. L.Rev. 139—484

Vaughns, Katherine L., *Retooling the "Refugee" Definition: The New Immigration Reform Law's Impact on United States Domestic Asylum Policy*, 1 Rutgers Race & L. Rev. 41 (1998)—961

Vaughns, Katherine L., *Taming the Asylum Adjudication Process: An Agenda for the Twenty–First Century*, 30 San Diego L. Rev. 1 (1993)—1089

Vazquez, Carlos M., *The "Self–Executing" Character of the Refugee Protocol's Nonrefoulement Obligation*, 7 Georgetown Immigration L.J. 39 (1993)—1134

Vázquez-Aspiri, A. James & Horne, Daniel C., *The Impotence of Being Earnest: Revisiting the L–1 Controversy*, 8 BIB 1607 (Oct. 15, 2003)—381

Vera Institute of Justice, The Appearance Assistance Program (1998)—229

Vidal, Mavelyn, *Membership of a 'Particular Social Group' and the Effect of Islam and Shah*, 11 Internat'l J. Refugee L. 528 (1999)—1049

Villiers, Janice D., *Closed Borders, Closed Ports: The Plight of Haitians Seeking Political Asylum in the United States*, 60 Brooklyn L. Rev. 841 (1994)—1130

Volpp, Leti, *Blaming Culture for Bad Behavior*, 12 Yale J. L. & Humanities 89 (2000)—1023

Volpp, Leti, *Court–Stripping and Class–Wide Relief: A Response to Judicial Review in Immigration Cases after AADC*, 14

Georgetown Immigration L.J. 463 (2000)—740, 757

Volpp, Leti, *Feminism versus Multiculturalism*, 101 Columbia L. Rev. 1181 (2001)—1023

Volpp, Leti, *'Obnoxious to their Very Nature': Asian Americans and Constitutional Citizenship*, 5 Citizenship Studies 57 (2001)—99

Volpp, Leti, *The Citizen and the Terrorist*, 49 UCLA L. Rev. 1575 (2002)—100

Von Sternberg, Mark R., *Emerging Bases of "Persecution" in American Refugee Law: Political Opinion and the Dilemma of Neutrality*, 13 Suffolk Transnat'l L.J. 1 (1989)—971

Walzer, Michael, *The Distribution of Membership*, in Peter G. Brown & Henry Shue (eds.), Boundaries–National Autonomy and Its Limits, at 1 (1981)—31, 1373

Wani, Ibrahim J., *Truth, Strangers, and Fiction: The Illegitimate Uses of Legal Fiction in Immigration Law*, 11 Cardozo L.Rev. 51 (1989)—113, 156, 520, 701

Warren, Carol, *Homosexuality and Stigma*, in Judd Marmor, Homosexual Behavior—A Modern Reappraisal, at 123 (1980)—266

Watkins, Henry G., *Credibility Findings in Deportation Proceedings: "Bear[ing] Witness Unto the Truth"*, 2 Georgetown Immigration L.J. 231 (1987)—1057

Watkins, Henry G., *Streamlining Deportation Proceedings: Self–Incrimination, Immunity from Prosecution, and the Duty to Testify in a Deportation Context*, 22 San Diego L.Rev. 1075 (1985)—715

Waxman, Nathan A., *New York State Department of Transportation: National Interest Waivers One Year Down the Road*, 76 IR 1641 (Nov. 15, 1999)—295

Weil, Patrick, *Races at the Gate: A Century of Racial Distinctions in American Immigration Policy*, 15 Georgetown Immigration L.J. 625 (2001)—82

Weis, Paul, *The Development of Refugee Law*, 1982 Michigan Yearbook Internat'l Legal Studies 27—920

Weiss, Herbert A., *Employment–Based Immigrant Visa Petitions: An Update*, June 1996 Immigration Briefings—294

Weiss, Herbert A., *Twenty-First Century Developments in Employment–Based (EB) Immigration Law*, May 2003 Immigration Briefings—298

Weissbrodt, David & Danielson, Laura, Immigration Law and Procedure in a Nutshell (5th ed. 2005)—86, 310, 405, 613, 614, 671, 1171, 1204, 1351, 1353

Weisselberg, Charles D., *The Detention and Treatment of Aliens Three Years After September 11: A New New World?*, 38 U.C. Davis L. Rev. 815 (2005)—844

Weisselberg, Charles D., *The Exclusion and Detention of Aliens: Lessons from the Lives of Ellen Knauff and Ignatz Mezei*, 143 Univ. Pennsylvania L.Rev. 933 (1995)—145, 152

Wettstein, Nadine K., *The Chandler Raids: Wake–Up Call or Harbinger of Local Police Enforcement of the INA?*, 3 BIB 101 (Feb. 1, 1998)—1199

Wettstein, Nadine K., *The Peddler Sells His Caps: The EOIR and INS Issue a New Rule on the Suspension/Cancellation Ceiling*, 3 BIB 1083 (Nov. 1, 1998)—583, 611

Wettstein, Nadine K., *Wasted Days and Wasted Nights: INS Visa Processing Delays and How to Combat Them*, 76 IR 1441 (Sept. 30, 1999)—493

Wheeler, Charles, *Affidavit of Support: A Year in Review*, 4 BIB 97 (Feb. 1, 1999)—439

Wheeler, Charles, *The Affidavit of Support and Sponsorship Requirements: A Critical Analysis*, Immigration Briefings (June 1998)—440

Wheeler, Charles, *The New Alien Restrictions on Public Benefits: The Full Impact Remains Uncertain*, 73 IR 1245 (Sept. 23, 1996)—1354

Wheeler, Charles, *Until INS Do Us Part: A Guide to IMFA*, Mar. 1990 Immigration Briefings—272, 274

Whiteman, Marjorie M., Digest of Internat'l Law (1967)—1333

Wildes, Leon, *Consular Nonreviewability—A Reexamination*, 64 IR 1012 (1987)—469

Wildes, Leon, *The Deferred Action Program of the Bureau of Citizenship and Immigration Services: A Possible Remedy for Impossible Immigration Cases*, 41 San Diego L. Rev. 819 (2004)—617

Wildes, Leon, *The Nonpriority Program of the Immigration and Naturalization Service Goes Public: The Litigative Use of the Freedom of Information Act*, 14 San Diego L. Rev. 42 (1976)—615

Wildes, Leon, *The Operations Instructions of the Immigration Service: Internal Guides or Binding Rules?*, 17 San Diego L. Rev. 99 (1979)—616

Wing, Adrien Katherine, *Reno v. American–Arab Anti–Discrimination Committee: A Critical Race Perspective*, 31 Columbia Human Rights L. Rev. 561 (2000)—83

Wishnie, Michael J., *Emerging Issues for Undocumented Workers*, 6 Univ. Pennsylvania J. Labor & Employment L. 497 (2004), reproduced in 9 BIB 1289 (Nov. 1, 2004)—1203

Wishnie, Michael J., *Immigrant Workers and the Domestic Enforcement of International Labor Rights*, 4 Univ. Pennsylvania J. Labor & Employment L. 529 (2002)—1203

Wishnie, Michael J., *Immigrants and the Right to Petition*, 78 NYU L. Rev. 667 (2003)—1202

Wishnie, Michael J., *Laboratories of Bigotry? Devolution of the Immigration Power, Equal Protection, and Federalism*, 76 NYU L. Rev. 493 (2000)—120, 1358

Women's Commission for Refugee Women and Children, An Uncertain Future, A Cruel Present: Women in INS Detention (1996)—1109

Women's Commission for Refugee Women and Children, Liberty Denied: Women Seeking Asylum Imprisoned in the United States (April 1997)—1109

Wood, Charles, *Losing Control of America's Future—The Census, Birthright Citizenship, and Illegal Aliens*, 22 Harvard J. L. & Pub. Policy 465 (1999)—1233

Woodward, David R. & Levin, Ronald M., *In Defense of Deference: Judicial Review of Agency Action*, 31 Administrative L. Rev. 329 (1979)—503

Woodhouse, Barbara Bennett, *"Who Owns the Child?": Meyer and Pierce and the Child as Property*, 33 William & Mary L.Rev. 995 (1992)—58

Wright, R. George, *Federal Immigration Law and the Case for Open Entry*, 27 Loyola L.A. L. Rev. 1265 (1994)—29

Wu, Frank H., *Difficult Decisions During Wartime: A Letter from a Non-Alien in an Internment Camp to a Friend Back Home*, 54 Case Western Reserve L. Rev. 1301 (2004)—99

Wu, Frank H., *Neither Black Nor White: Asian Americans and Affirmative Action*, 15 Boston College Third World L.J. 225 (1995)—99

Wu, Frank H., *The Future of the American Mosaic: Issues in American Immigration Reform*, 7 Stanford L. & Policy Rev. 35 (1996)—103

Wu, Frank H. & Youngberg, Francey Lim, *People from China Crossing the River: Asian American Political Empowerment and Foreign Influence*, in Gordon H. Chang (ed.), Asian Americans and Politics, ch. 12 (2001)—99

Yackle, Larry W., Federal Courts–Habeas Corpus (2003)—741

Yale–Loehr, Stephen, AILA, *Statement on the Operations of the Executive Office for Immigration Review (EOIR) Before the House Committee on the Judiciary Subcommittee on Immigration and Claims* (Feb. 6, 2002)—718, 721, 723

Yale–Loehr, Stephen, *An Overview of INA § 212(c)*, Feb. 1995 Immigration Briefings—574

Yale–Loehr, Stephen, *Foreign Farm Workers in the U.S.: The Impact of the Immigration Reform and Control Act of 1986*, 15 N.Y.U.Rev. L. & Soc. Change 333 (1986–87)—368, 610

Yale–Loehr, Stephen, *USCIS Vows to Improve EB–5 Immigrant Investor Programs*, 10 BIB 169 (Feb. 15, 2005)—337

Yale–Loehr, Stephen, & Hoashi–Erhardt, Christoph, *A Comparative Look at Immigration and Human Capital Assessment*, 16 Georgetown Immigration L.J. 99 (2001)—333

Yale–Loehr, Stephen & Palmer, Brian, Asylum Law Update, 5 BIB 633 (July 15, 2000)—962, 963

Yale–Loehr, Stephen & Palmer, Brian, *Unlawful Presence Update*, 6 BIB 507 (June 1, 2001)—423

Yale–Loehr, Stephen & Palmer, John R.B., *Evidentiary Issues in Asylum Cases*, 6 BIB 595 (June 15, 2001)—1057

Yale–Loehr, Stephen & Reed, Roni, *Preserving Permanent Residency*, 1 BIB No. 9 at 14–20 (1996)—522

Yale–Loehr, Stephen, Sherman, Christina, Hoashi–Erhardt, Christoph & Palmer, Brian, *T, U and V Visas: More Alphabet Soup for Immigration Practitioners*, 6 BIB 113 (Feb. 1, 2001)—401, 402

Yamamoto, Eric K., Interracial Justice: Conflict and Reconciliation in Post-/Civil Rights America (1999)—99

Yamamoto, Eric K. et al, Race, Rights and Reparation: Law and the Japanese American Internment (2001)—99

Yates, Laura S., *Plyler v. Doe and the Rights of Undocumented Immigrants to Higher Education: Should Undocumented Students Be Eligible for In–State College Tuition Rates?*, 82 Washington Univ. L.Q. 585 (2004)—1256

Zall, Barnaby W., *Asylum and Sanctuary—the American Dilemma*, 72 A.B.A.J. 66 (Aug. 1, 1986)—1207

Zappalà, Gianni & Castles, Stephen, *Citizenship and Immigration in Australia*, 13 Georgetown Immigration L.J. 273 (1999)—1351

Zilbershats, Yaffa, *Extraditing Israeli Citizens to the United States–Extradition and Citizenship Dilemmas*, 21 Michigan J. Internat'l L. 297 (2000)—1296, 1351

Zilbershats, Yaffa, The Human Right to Citizenship (2002)—1297

Zolberg, Aristide, Book Review, 21 Population & Development Rev. 659 (1995)—57

Zucker, Norman L. & Zucker, Naomi F., The Guarded Gate—The Reality of American Refugee Policy (1987)—1084

IMMIGRATION AND REFUGEE LAW AND POLICY

*

OVERVIEW OF UNITED STATES IMMIGRATION LAW

The Immigration and Nationality Act (INA), passed in 1952 and amended many times since, is a hideous creature. Its hundreds of pages contain excruciating technical provisions that are often hopelessly intertwined. Other sources of immigration law are similarly byzantine. The extensive inter-relationships make it hard to separate the law into discrete components that newcomers can comprehend without frequent cross-references and asides. This Overview addresses that problem. Superficial as it necessarily is, it acquaints you with a few basic concepts that will hopefully make the later discussion more comprehensible.

As you will see throughout this book, the terrorist attacks of September 11, 2001 had especially far-reaching implications for immigration law. With one major exception, those consequences will be synthesized in chapter 10, which deals specifically with national security and terrorism. The exception is the sweeping reorganization of the government's administrative framework; this will be covered in the present overview.

SECTION A.   TERMINOLOGY

As explained more fully below, the INA defines "aliens" as all people who are not nationals of the United States. It then uses the word "alien" frequently and consistently. The term covers even people who have been admitted as permanent residents and who have lived lawfully in the United States for decades. Further, because the word "alien" is used in the INA and other federal statutes, it also appears often in agency regulations, judicial opinions, and other legal materials. In addition, the word is frequently used in public and academic discourse.

Past editions of this book, striving for precision and for consistency with the statutory terminology, similarly used the word "alien" in that technical sense. (Even the first edition drew the line at the pejorative, irritating, and technically meaningless term "illegal alien" and explained why. See pages 984–85 of the first edition (1992), or pages 1192–93 of the present edition.) But the word "alien," even when not adorned with the modifier "illegal," has always struck a disturbing chord. Many feel that the term connotes dehumanizing qualities of either strangeness or inferiority (space aliens come readily to mind) and that its use builds walls, strips human beings of their essential dignity, and needlessly reinforces an "outsider" status. Some believe that its constant use and repetition also solidify racial and cultural stereotypes. See especially the thoughtful examination of the term "alien" by Professor Kevin R. Johnson, *"Aliens" and the U.S. Immigration Laws: The Social and Legal Construction of Nonpersons*, 28 Univ. of Miami Inter–American L. Rev. 263 (1996–97).

Beginning with the third edition (2002), therefore, this book stopped using the word "alien" except in direct quotations. The word "noncitizen" conveys essentially the same technical meaning without the same baggage. (As explained below, "non-national" is more precise, but the word "noncitizen" is in far more common use and will be employed here.)

One acronym that you will see repeatedly in this book is "LPR." It stands for "lawful permanent resident" and is used here to refer to those noncitizens whom the United States has formally admitted as permanent residents. As proof of their status, LPRs carry so-called "green cards" (which actually have been various colors over the years).

Throughout this book you will also see repeated references to the INA, to certain other crucial statutes that have amended the INA, and to some important international conventions. Because these statutes and conventions are mentioned frequently, the book refers to them in shorthand terms that immigration lawyers commonly use. Among those you will see abbreviated are the REAL ID Act, HSA, the USA PATRIOT Act, Imm. Act 1990, IRCA, IMFA, AEDPA, the Welfare Reform Act, IIRIRA, NACARA, LIFE, CAT, the 1951 Refugee Convention, and the 1967 Refugee Protocol. At first they will blur together, but after repeated exposure they will become old friends. Until that happens, consult the Table of Abbreviations. It contains the full citations to these statutes and conventions, as well as some other immigration jargon.

SECTION B.   GENERAL REGULATION OF IMMIGRATION

Until the late 1800's, United States immigration law was largely a matter for the states. Today it is almost entirely federal (and to an increasing extent international) law, although the fifty states still have some leeway to regulate the activities of noncitizens within their borders. For more than a century, the Supreme Court has held that Congress's power over immigration is exceptionally broad, both relative to the states and relative to the courts.

Several federal agencies have roles in administering the INA. From 1940 until 2003, the lion's share of the responsibility rested with the Attorney General, whose functions in turn were delegated to various Justice Department agencies and officials. The best known of the Department's immigration agencies was the Immigration and Naturalization Service (INS), headquartered in Washington, D.C. Its functions included law enforcement, inspection of arriving passengers, prosecution at administrative hearings, detention of noncitizens in connection with immigration proceedings, and processing applications for various immigration benefits.

The events of September 11, 2001 led eventually to a radical restructuring of the myriad federal government agencies whose missions relate to national security. The Homeland Security Act of 2002 (HSA) brought almost all of those agencies under a single new umbrella, the Department of Homeland Security (DHS). Some 22 federal agencies, 185,000 government employees, and countless specific functions were transferred. See Stanley Mailman & Stephen Yale–Loehr, *Immigration Functions in the Department of Homeland Security*, 8 BIB 663 (Apr. 15, 2003); David A. Martin, *Immigration Policy and the Homeland Security Act Reorganization: An Early Agenda for Practical Improvements*, 80 IR 601 (Apr. 28, 2003). Most relevant here, the Act dissolved the INS and transferred almost all its functions to the DHS. See HSA § 471(a). That change took effect on March 1, 2003. (The one major INS responsibility that was transferred elsewhere was the care of unaccompanied noncitizen children. That duty now belongs to the Office of Refugee Resettlement, within the Department of Health and Human Services. See HSA § 462.)

Even before September 11, ideologically diverse voices had called persistently for splitting the INS into two separate agencies—one for law enforcement, and one for service functions, such as the processing of applications for permanent residence, asylum, naturalization, and other immigration benefits. When Congress passed the HSA, therefore, it divided the immigration enforcement and service functions between two different entities within DHS. See HSA §§ 442, 451. The HSA also authorized the President to modify the statutory departmental structure further, see HSA §§ 872, 1502, with the caveat that neither the two separate entities themselves, nor their specific functions, could be combined. HSA § 471(b). Acting on that authority, the President converted the two original DHS immigration agencies into three—two bureaus for the various enforcement functions, and one other bureau for service functions. See U.S. Department of Homeland Security Press Release, *Border Reorganization Fact Sheet* (Jan. 30, 2003) (DHS Press Release); see generally 6 U.S.C.

The two immigration enforcement entities are the Bureau of Customs and Border Protection (CBP), which is headed by a "Commissioner," and the Bureau of Immigration and Customs Enforcement (ICE), which is headed by an "Assistant Secretary." See 68 Fed. Reg. 35273–82 (June 13, 2003), amending 8 C.F.R. §§ 1.1(d, y, z). Both enforcement bureaus report to the Undersecretary of Border and Transportation Security, who in turn reports directly to the Secretary of Homeland Security. See DHS Press Release, above.

Generally, the two enforcement bureaus—CBP and ICE—are responsible for border enforcement and interior enforcement, respectively. CBP took over the functions of the INS Border Patrol and also consolidated the border inspections that were formerly carried out by the INS, the Customs Service, and the Agricultural Quarantine Program. CBP "border" inspections take place at all "ports of entry"—land borders, airports, and seaports. In contrast, ICE functions mainly in the interior. It is responsible for investigations, intelligence-gathering, detention, certain elements of the deportation process, the registration of noncitizens, and other interior enforcement operations. See DHS Press Release, above. You will see much more on the subject of immigration enforcement in chapter 12 below. At this writing there is some congressional interest in merging CBP and ICE into a single enforcement agency, as the HSA originally envisioned. See 82 IR 483 (Mar. 21, 2005).

The new immigration service entity is called U.S. Citizenship and Immigration Services (USCIS). See HSA § 451; 69 Fed. Reg. 60937 (Oct. 13, 2004) (changing the name). It is headed by a Director, who reports to the Deputy Secretary of Homeland Security. HSA § 451(a)(2)(A); 68 Fed. Reg. 35273–82 (June 13, 2003), amending 8 C.F.R. §§ 1.1(d, x). USCIS handles a variety of applications for immigration benefits. See HSA § 451(b). Like the former INS, USCIS operates through a network of regional and district offices dispersed throughout the United States and, in a few instances, overseas.

A new innovation is the Citizenship and Immigration Services Ombudsman, responsible for handling problems encountered by individuals and employers in their dealings with USCIS. The Ombudsman operates mainly through a network of local offices, is independent of USCIS, and reports directly to the Deputy Secretary. HSA § 452. (There is no analogous office for either of the two immigration enforcement bureaus.)

Another new creation is the post of Director of Shared Services. This official, who reports to the Deputy Secretary of Homeland Security, coordinates and manages the resources that the three DHS immigration bureaus share. These resources include information technology, data records, and standardized forms. See HSA § 475.

Although the Department of Justice has lost the INS, it retains an agency called the Executive Office for Immigration Review (EOIR). In fact the HSA gives the EOIR statutory recognition for the first time. HSA § 1101. (EOIR had been solely a creature of administrative regulation.)

The EOIR does only one thing—adjudication. It comprises three units, all headquartered in Falls Church, Virginia. One unit is the Office of the Chief Immigration Judge. This Office coordinates the work of a cadre of immigration judges dispersed throughout the United States. Their main function is to preside over "removal" hearings. These are formal evidentiary hearings in which immigration judges decide whether to admit noncitizens to the United States and whether to expel certain noncitizens who are already present. A second EOIR unit, the Board of Immigration Appeals (BIA), hears appeals from the decisions of the immigration judges as well as appeals from certain USCIS decisions. A third unit, the Office of the Chief Administrative Hearing Officer (OCAHO), conducts evidentiary hearings in certain cases that involve the unauthorized employment of noncitizens and cases that involve certain forms of job discrimination.

The HSA also codifies the Attorney General's power to direct and regulate the EOIR. See HSA §§ 1101, 1102(3) (adding INA § 103(g)). This power includes the authority to review individual decisions of the BIA. See former 8 C.F.R. § 3.1(h) (2002), indirectly codified by HSA § 1102(3), adding INA § 103(g)(1). Importantly, BIA decisions (and Attorney General modifications of those decisions) are binding on immigration judges; until INS functions were transferred to DHS, they were binding on the INS as well. See former 8 C.F.R. § 3.1(g) (2002). Now that DHS officers make the vast majority of the decisions that the INS used to make—including adjudication of asylum claims and many other benefit applications—the Attorney General has amended the Justice Department regulations to provide explicitly that BIA decisions, as modified by the Attorney General, are binding on all DHS officers and employees (and still, of course, on immigration judges). See 68 Fed. Reg. 9824, 9831–32 (Feb. 28, 2003), adding 8 C.F.R. § 1003.1(g).[1]

The Department of State still plays a major role in the administration of the immigration laws, most notably by issuing or denying visas to noncitizens who wish to enter the United States. Visa applications are decided by consular officers at United States embassies and consulates around the world. See INA §§ 221, 222. Shaken by the State Department's lapses in issuing visas to the individuals who perpetrated the September 11 attacks, however, Congress has given DHS a major role in the visa process. The Secretary of Homeland Security is now principally responsible for the administration and enforcement of the visa process, HSA § 428(b), and may assign DHS employees to consular posts to advise, train, and review the decisions of consular officers, HSA § 428(e). The State Department also plays key roles in the various educational exchange programs and in refugee affairs (the latter through its Bureau of Population, Refugees, and Migration, or PRM).

The role of the Department of Labor is also significant. As you will see in chapter 3, it is normally the first step in the process when a noncitizen seeks admission to the United States on the basis of occupational qualifications.

The Department of Health and Human Services has a more limited role. Its new responsibility for unaccompanied noncitizen children has already been noted. In addition, through its Public Health Service, HHS makes the necessary medical judgments when a noncitizen is alleged to be inadmissible on health-related grounds. See INA § 212(a)(1).

Here is an organization chart for the main federal immigration agencies:

---

1. Congress gave the Secretary of Homeland Security the power to administer all immigration laws *except* insofar as the INA or other laws confer powers on the Attorney General and certain other officials. In doing so, Congress left untouched the provision that renders the Attorney General's rulings on questions of law "controlling." See INA § 103(a)(1), as amended by Consolidated Appropriations Resolution 2003, Pub. L. 108–7, 117 Stat. 11 (Feb. 20, 2003), Div. L, § 105(a)(1), amending HSA § 1102(2).

ORGANIZATION CHART
FEDERAL IMMIGRATION AGENCIES

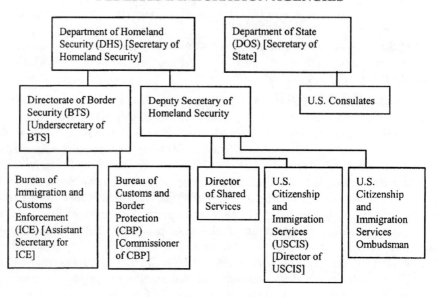

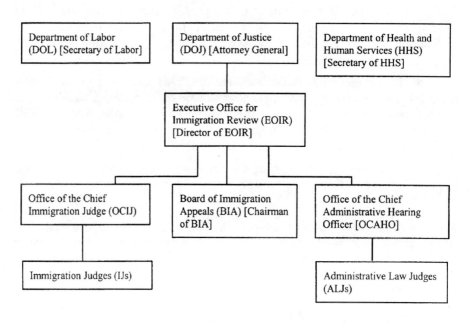

Finally, a few words on the statute and regulations: As noted earlier, the main statute that governs United States immigration law (including refugee law and citizenship law) is the INA, originally enacted in 1952 and amended frequently since then. Its essential provisions are reproduced in title 8 of the United States Code.

The recent reorganization of immigration functions requires two technical warnings. First, even though the HSA transferred almost all INS functions to DHS, both the INA and the agency regulations on immigration are still chock full of references to the "Attorney General," the "Department of Justice," the "Immigration and Naturalization Service," the "Service," the "Commissioner," and other INS officials. Rather than correct every one of these references individually, the HSA did so in one fell swoop. Under HSA § 1517, whenever a federal law refers to a "department, commission, or agency or any officer or office" whose functions the HSA has transferred elsewhere, that law is "deemed" to refer to the Secretary or the particular official or component of the Department to which the function was transferred. For example, with respect to any transferred immigration function, most references to the Attorney General in either the INA or the regulations should be read as if they referred to the Secretary of Homeland Security. References to the INS should be read as if they referred to USCIS, ICE, or CBP, depending on which component has been assigned the particular function. See also HSA § 456(a)(similar technique specifically for USCIS).[2]

Second, the federal immigration regulations have been slightly reorganized. The vast bulk of them appear in title 8 of the Code of Federal Regulations (CFR), as they did before the HSA. Until 2003, all the regulations in that title were issued by the Department of Justice. Now that DHS is responsible for most immigration functions but the Justice Department retains responsibility for the EOIR, the Attorney General wanted to reorganize 8 CFR so that it could contain both departments' immigration regulations. As a stopgap measure, therefore, the Attorney General issued a Final Rule, 68 Fed. Reg. 9824 (Feb. 28, 2003), dividing 8 CFR into "chapters." Before the reorganization, title 8 of CFR had comprised only one chapter (chapter 1). The new rule creates a new chapter 5 to serve as a vessel for almost all the provisions that relate to the continuing powers of DOJ. Chapter 1 was conveyed to DHS. (The Final Rule did not say, but it is assumed that the Secretary of Homeland Security will have the option of creating new chapters 2, 3, and 4 in the future.) Each of the two departments has the freedom to make changes to its respective chapter(s), but consultation is anticipated whenever one department's proposed changes would affect the work of the other department.

Under the reorganized 8 CFR, all the provisions that affect only the former INS (now the province of DHS) stayed in chapter 1. Those that affected only the EOIR were transferred to new chapter 5. And those that affected both INS and EOIR were duplicated; they now appear in both chapters 1 and 5. To ease the transition, all the provisions that were either

---

2. The author thanks Eugene J. Flynn, Esq., for figuring this out and sharing his research. See also 68 Fed. Reg. 35273–82 (June 13, 2003), amending 8 C.F.R. §§ 1.1(c, d, o) (DHS final rule clarifying that references to the INS should be interpreted as referring to the INS's successor bureaus and officials in DHS).

transferred to chapter 5 or duplicated there were assigned their original section numbers of 8 CFR, plus 1000. For example, 8 CFR § 208 (which deals with asylum) was duplicated in chapter 5, where it became 8 CFR § 1208. Eventually the terminology will be cleaned up, the few remaining issues as to the allocation of functions between the two departments will be resolved, most of the duplication will be eliminated, and, undoubtedly, each Department will make periodic substantive changes to its respective chapters. It is emphasized that these regulations are still very much in flux.

So the DHS and DOJ immigration regulations appear in 8 CFR. Generally, the State Department regulations appear in 22 CFR. The relevant Labor Department regulations are in 20 CFR. The regulations that lay out the basic organization of DHS are contained in 6 C.F.R.

SECTION C.   NATIONALITY[3]

According to the Immigration and Nationality Act (the INA), every person in the world is either a United States "national" or an "alien." Nationals are further divided into those who are "citizens" and those who are not. Today almost all nationals of the United States are also citizens; the few who are not are almost entirely natives of American Samoa and Swains Island. Since the number of noncitizen nationals is so small, and since their rights so closely resemble those of citizens anyway, the terms "national" and "citizen" are often used interchangeably. That practice is technically incorrect, but the distinction is rarely important. The INA lays out various categories of citizens (and of non-citizen nationals) and defines "aliens" as everyone else.

The vast majority of United States citizens acquired their citizenship at birth. The most common way in which to acquire citizenship at birth is to be born on United States soil. Several provisions of the INA also bestow citizenship by descent. With varying qualifications, these provisions automatically transmit citizenship from one or two citizen parents to a child born abroad.

Many other people obtain citizenship at some time after birth. They are said to be "naturalized." The INA sets forth a number of prerequisites. With some exceptions, naturalization is something for which one must affirmatively apply. Also with exceptions, the applicant must first become an LPR, must thereafter reside in the United States for at least five years, and must satisfy other requirements concerning physical presence in the United States, age, literacy, knowledge of American history and government, moral character, and attachment to American constitutional principles.

Once acquired, citizenship can be lost. If citizenship was acquired by naturalization, the naturalization order can be revoked because of defects in the original order. Regardless whether citizenship was acquired at birth

---

3.   See chapter 13 below.

or by naturalization, one can voluntarily relinquish citizenship by a process known as expatriation.

Citizenship has important legal consequences, both in domestic United States law and in international law. Apart from its capacity to be transmitted, citizenship can affect one's voting and other political rights, one's tax, military, and jury obligations, one's susceptibility to extradition for crime, and one's eligibility for certain publicly funded programs, for certain government jobs, and for certain occupations. Congress, the state legislatures, and the federal courts have all helped to shape the boundaries. Most important here, United States citizens are not subject to immigration restrictions. They may come, go, and stay as they please. Additionally, as noted below, citizens may sponsor certain of their noncitizen family members for admission to the United States.

SECTION D.   THE ADMISSION OF NONCITIZENS TO THE UNITED STATES[4]

Within the class of noncitizens, the most fundamental distinction drawn by the United States immigration law is between immigrants and nonimmigrants. The INA defines nonimmigrants as those who fall within any of several specifically enumerated categories of (typically) temporary entrants. Common examples are tourists, business visitors, students, and temporary workers, but there are many others as well. By statute, every other noncitizen is an "immigrant." The term includes both those who have been lawfully admitted as immigrants ("LPRs") and those who have not ("undocumented immigrants"). LPRs may reside in the United States permanently and may work, unless found deportable as discussed below.

With some exceptions (relating to temporary workers), the admission of nonimmigrants is numerically unrestricted. To qualify for admission, however, a nonimmigrant must still clear two major hurdles: He or she must fit within one of the statutory pigeonholes, most of which require an intent to leave the United States by the end of the authorized time period. In addition, the person must *not* fall within any of the "inadmissibility" grounds—for example, those that relate to crime, national security, health, or public assistance—unless he or she also fits one of several statutory provisions that authorize waivers of the relevant grounds.

An immigrant similarly has to fit within one of several statutory pigeonholes. The three main programs are family reunification, employment, and "diversity" (more on these below). Generally, each of the qualifying categories is numerically limited. Those limits, sometimes known as quotas, are of two types. First, for each category, no more than a specified number may be admitted worldwide in a given fiscal year. Second, the law limits the number of immigrants who may be admitted from a single country in a given fiscal year. As will be seen in chapter 3, the

---

4.   See generally chapters 3–6 below.

combination of those quotas and the high demand from particular countries has meant that many noncitizens who meet all the qualitative admission criteria must wait several years to get in.

Numerical limits are subject to several exceptions. Two are important enough to mention here. Certain close family members of United States citizens qualify as "immediate relatives;" they are exempt from the numerical constraints. Another group of noncitizens—refugees fleeing statutorily defined forms of persecution at home—are admitted under a separate quota system.

Within the group of those immigrants who are subject to the general quotas, admission is not awarded on a strict first-come, first-served basis. Instead, the INA gives "preference" to various categories of immigrants. Some such preferences are for noncitizens who have certain specified family relationships to United States citizens or to LPRs, but who for various reasons do not qualify as "immediate relatives." Other preference categories are for noncitizens whose occupational skills fill economic needs and for certain individuals who are favored for other economic reasons. A third program admits "diversity immigrants"—noncitizens who come from countries that have sent relatively few immigrants to the United States in recent years.

With some specific exceptions—the most important being refugees—a noncitizen *must* fit one of the above preferences in order to immigrate. Moreover, like the nonimmigrant, even an immigrant who fits one of the qualifying categories will be ineligible if he or she falls within any of the various inadmissibility grounds and does not qualify for a statutory waiver.

The procedure for admitting noncitizens depends on the substantive basis for admission. When an immigrant seeks admission on the basis of a family relationship, the process begins with a "visa petition" filed by the United States citizen or LPR sponsor in a regional office of USCIS, normally in the United States. The purpose of the visa petition is to establish that the beneficiary in fact has the claimed relationship. If USCIS approves the visa petition, the beneficiary in most cases then applies for a visa at whichever United States consulate serves the applicable region of his or her home country. Shortly before the applicant's position in the queue is reached, a consular officer adjudicates the application. The consular officer decides whether the person falls within any of the various inadmissibility grounds. If the application is approved, the consular officer issues an entry document called an immigrant "visa." The applicant eventually presents the visa to a CBP inspector at the port of entry. That official has the authority to duplicate the searching examination conducted abroad by the consular officer, but in practice the border inspection of a person who presents what appears to be a valid visa is much less rigorous.

When an immigrant seeks admission under one of the employment-based categories, a roughly similar process is used. For certain of those categories, however, the immigrant must first obtain from the Department of Labor a certification that (a) the job he or she proposes to take is one for which not enough qualified United States workers are available and (b) the immigrant's employment will not adversely affect the wages and working conditions of United States workers.

In certain instances a noncitizen who is already present in the United States and who meets all the substantive requirements for admission as an immigrant may perform all the necessary steps without leaving the country. The process is called "adjustment of status."

Refugees, generally defined to require a "well-founded fear of persecution on account of race, religion, nationality, membership in a particular social group, or political opinion," are admitted under two separate programs. The overseas refugee program, for which the President annually announces numerical limits, admits refugees who apply from outside United States territory. The asylum program, which is not subject to numerical limits, is used to admit certain refugees who have already arrived at United States ports of entry or the interior on their own. Both programs are discussed in chapter 11.

Ordinarily, nonimmigrants are not required to file visa petitions with USCIS. They generally apply directly to the applicable consulates for visas that they will ultimately present to the immigration inspectors at their points of entry. A few categories of nonimmigrants, however, must go through the visa petition process, and some must first complete the labor certification process as well.

Once admitted as a nonimmigrant, one will sometimes be able to alter the conditions or duration of his or her stay, or change status entirely to a different nonimmigrant category ("change of status") or to an immigrant classification ("adjustment of status"). The processes for accomplishing those changes involve USCIS and, in some instances, the Labor Department.

As you have probably noticed already, there are several stages at which a person seeking admission can be turned down. Depending on the particular stage, the applicant might or might not have a right to a hearing or an appeal. Depending on several other variables, the applicant might or might not be detained by USCIS pending the final outcome of his or her case. The procedural details appear in chapter 6.

In recent years, Congress has created exceptions to the admission process just described. Probably the most significant is "expedited removal," an abbreviated procedure that has its greatest impact on asylum seekers. This and other exceptions will be taken up at various points in the text.

SECTION E. EXPULSION[5]

The INA lists many different grounds for the removal of "deportable" noncitizens. Like the (slightly different) grounds for inadmissibility, the "deportability" grounds reflect a range of national concerns relating to economics, crime, health, morality, politics, and national security. Addition-

---

5. See chapters 7–9 below.

al deportability grounds are designed to secure the integrity of the immigration inspection system itself. The deportability grounds are accompanied by a network of statutory provisions that authorize discretionary waivers of specified grounds when certain circumstances exist. Eligibility for these waivers has shrunk considerably in recent years.

When noncitizens already in the United States are removed, it is usually because they overstayed or otherwise violated the terms of their nonimmigrant visas, or because they never were admitted and are not admissible. But lawfully admitted noncitizens—even LPRs—can also be deported for conduct or circumstances not concerned with the immigration system itself; a criminal conviction is the most common example.

As discussed in detail later, the vast majority of deportable noncitizens apprehended by the government are expelled by means of an informal procedure known as "voluntary departure." In well over 100,000 cases every year, however, formal removal hearings are held. DHS (usually ICE) initiates those proceedings, which entail evidentiary hearings before the immigration judges mentioned earlier. The job of the immigration judge in those proceedings is to determine whether the individual falls within any of the charged "deportability" grounds and, if so, whether he or she is statutorily eligible for, and deserving of, asylum, voluntary departure, or some other form of discretionary relief. In most cases, the principal issues at the hearing concern applications for relief. Either the noncitizen or ICE may appeal the decision of the immigration judge to the BIA. Subject to many recently enacted exceptions, the noncitizen may also obtain judicial review of the BIA decision in the court of appeals.

SECTION F.   OTHER SANCTIONS[6]

The INA and provisions of other federal statutes establish a range of civil and criminal sanctions for immigration-related misconduct. Some such sanctions are imposed on the noncitizens themselves; others are visited upon designated individuals or companies with whom they interact. The best known of the latter are those imposed on employers by the Immigration Reform and Control Act of 1986, popularly known as IRCA. IRCA punishes employers and certain others for knowingly employing noncitizens who are not authorized to work, for hiring persons without observing specified paperwork requirements (even if the employees turn out to be authorized to work), or for discriminating on the basis of national origin or, in certain cases, citizenship status.

Apart from IRCA, the immigration laws create a number of criminal offenses concerned with maintaining a workable system of immigration control. They include illegal entry; transporting, smuggling, or harboring noncitizens who are in the United States unlawfully; and fraud, including marriage fraud. In addition, commercial carriers (airlines, shipping lines, bus companies, railroad companies, etc.) that transport improperly documented noncitizen passengers are subject to civil penalties, usually fines.

---

6.   See chapter 12 below.

CHAPTER 1

THE IMMIGRATION DEBATE: GOALS, STRATEGIES, AND IMPACT

Permanent international migration is a worldwide phenomenon. The United Nations Population Division reports that by the year 2000 some 175,000,000 people—almost 3% of the world's population—had migrated from their countries of birth. See http://www.un.org/esa/population/publications/migstock/2003TrendsMigstock.pdf (last visited Dec. 2004). Such massive population movements present challenges. For the most part, those challenges are managed at the national level. Increasingly, they are becoming the subjects of international cooperation as well.[1]

In the United States, where immigration has been both part of the historical core and a continuing national ethic, the debate over its impact and its future remains contentious. This chapter introduces you to that debate. It deals with the "big picture" policy questions: What is the real meaning of immigration? Are *any* immigration controls morally defensible? What is the proper *mission* of an immigration policy? What sorts of strategies are most likely to further that mission? What are the practical consequences of immigration—racial, cultural, linguistic, sociological, demographic, economic, environmental, and political? What have been the effects of U.S. immigration policy on the immigrants themselves?

Given the breadth of these subjects, this chapter obviously does not attempt comprehensive treatment. The goal here is just broad exposure to some of the issues that have generated public or scholarly debate. Further, this chapter confines itself to the subject of permanent, "voluntary," legal migration; later chapters deal with the admission of temporary visitors (chapter 4), forced migration (refugees, covered in chapter 11), and irregular migration (chapter 12).

---

1. See generally T. Alexander Aleinikoff & Vincent Chetail (Eds.), Migration and International Legal Norms (2003); Guy S. Goodwin–Gill, International Law and the Movement of Persons Between States (1978). The International Organization for Migration (IOM), an intergovernmental association established in 1951, now has 105 member states (including the U.S.) and another 27 observer states, in addition to formal affiliations with a long list of other international organizations and NGOs. Based in Geneva, IOM has more than 200 field offices around the world and an operational staff of more than 4000. It helps governments manage the logistics of large migrations, especially in times of emergency. See http://www.iom.int/en/who/main-members.shtml. In 2004, UN Secretary General Kofi Annan established a Global Commission on International Migration to study the future of both voluntary and involuntary population movements. The work of UNHCR is integral to refugee protection and assistance worldwide and figures prominently in chapter 11 below.

Of course immigration law is also about "little picture" policy questions. Precisely which family priorities, and which labor-related priorities, are optimal? What role, if any, should national origin play in an immigrant selection system? How many refugees should be admitted, and which ones? How should an asylum system work? What should be the criteria for admitting temporary visitors such as tourists, business visitors, students, and guest workers? On what grounds should noncitizens be subject to deportation? What provision should the law make for granting discretionary relief in exceptional cases? Who should receive citizenship? Who should lose it? What should turn on citizenship? What procedures should the law establish for applying all these substantive criteria to individuals? When should immigration-related misconduct be a criminal offense? How great a problem is irregular immigration, and what policy responses are appropriate? Do specific statutory provisions, or specific elements of those provisions, make sense? Those sorts of questions are dispersed throughout the remainder of the book.

SECTION A.   THE HISTORY

Modern U.S. immigration policy cannot be understood without at least brief exposure to its historical roots. The following excerpt from the leading immigration law treatise summarizes the path that led to the current version of the Immigration and Nationality Act. In keeping with the scope of this chapter, this historical summary will focus primarily on the admission of immigrants. Significant developments on such related issues as nonimmigrants, exclusion, and expulsion will also be noted. As you will discover, public attitudes toward immigration have fluctuated. United States history gives both cause for congratulation and cause for shame.[2]

1 Charles Gordon, Stanley Mailman, and Stephen Yale–Loehr, Immigration Law and Procedure

§§ 2.02–2.04 (2004).

[1]—1776–1875: One Hundred Years of Open Frontier

The first one hundred years of our national existence was a period of generally unimpeded immigration. New settlers were important to the

2. On the latter score, see the well-written, highly critical accounts by Kevin R. Johnson, The "Huddled Masses" Myth—Immigration and Civil Rights (2004); and James F. Smith, *A Nation that Welcomes Immigrants? An Historical Examination of United States Immigration Policy*, 1 U.C. Davis J. Internat'l L. & Policy 227 (1995). See also Michael Lemay & Elliott Robert Barkan (Eds.), United States Immigration and Naturalization Laws and Issues—A Documentary History (1999); Reed Ueda, Postwar Immigrant America—A Social History (1994). For a history of passports, see John Torpey, The Invention of the Passport (2000). For a thoughtful account of the history of the INS and its predecessor institutions, see Michael J. Churgin, *Immigration Internal Decisionmaking: A View from History*, 78 Texas L. Rev. 1633 (2000). The analogous German immigration history is well recounted in Kay Hailbronner, *Fifty Years of the Basic Law—Migration, Citizenship and Asylum*, 53 Southern Methodist Univ. L. Rev. 519 (2000).

young nation and immigrants were welcomed. The gates were open and unguarded and all were free to come. This national policy paid rich dividends as the immigrants and their descendants contributed heavily to the growth of our nation.

During this period there was little federal legislation. An early attempt at restriction was the Alien Act of 1798, a part of the Alien and Sedition Laws, which authorized the President to expel from the United States any alien he deemed dangerous. This legislation was very unpopular and was allowed to expire at the end of its two-year term. Subsequent statutes, commencing in 1819, sought to improve conditions on ships bringing immigrants to the United States. As late as 1864, Congress passed legislation designed to encourage immigration, and some of the states had active programs to promote immigration.

* * *

Even during this period of tolerance the policy favoring immigration was by no means unopposed. From the earliest days there were groups counseling restriction. As immigration continued to increase these groups gained adherents, and they were most potent during times of economic depression. Some of the states were disturbed at the influx of immigrants and sought to impose local controls from time to time.[a] However, the Supreme Court declared some of these state statutes unconstitutional as an invasion of the exclusive federal power to regulate foreign commerce.

[2]—1875–1917: Institution of Federal Controls on Immigration

Continued demand for federal action finally resulted in legislation. An 1875 statute barring convicts and prostitutes was quickly followed by the adoption of the first general immigration statute in 1882. The 1882 Act imposed a head tax of 50 cents and excluded idiots, lunatics, convicts, and persons likely to become a public charge. Another important enactment in 1882 was the Chinese Exclusion Act, which remained an important facet of immigration policy until it was repealed in 1943.

In 1885 and 1887, Congress passed the contract labor laws, aimed at the practice of importing cheap foreign labor under labor contracts which depressed the labor market in the United States. * * * [Later statutes expanded the list of exclusion grounds. See chapter 5 below.—Ed.]

* * *

In the first decade of the twentieth century there was a vast increase in immigration, more than doubling the previous decade's arrivals. During four years of this decade annual immigration exceeded a million. In addition, the new immigrants were coming predominantly from southern and eastern Europe, instead of the previous migrations from northern Europe. The antagonisms which previously had been directed against the

---

a. See also Gerald L. Neuman, *The Lost Century of American Immigration Law (1776–1875)*, 93 Columbia L.Rev. 1833 (1993) (emphasizing and describing the many state-imposed immigration restrictions during this period).—Ed.

Irish–Catholic and German migrants were transferred to this "new" immigration. The vast tide of immigrants created uneasiness, which was accentuated during periods of economic crisis. The demand for further restrictions increased.

* * *

[3]—1917–1924: Solidification of Restrictive Immigration Policies

The development of the restrictive immigration policy reached fruition between 1917 and 1924. In 1917 Congress passed another comprehensive revision of the immigration laws over the veto of President Wilson. The most controversial innovation of this legislation was the literacy test, which previously had summoned vetoes by Presidents Cleveland, Taft and Wilson. Another new feature was the creation of an Asiatic Barred Zone to shut out Orientals. Japan alone was not included, since Japanese were dealt with by the so-called Gentleman's Agreement between the Governments of the United States and Japan. * * *

The 1917 Act was followed shortly by the Anarchist Act of 1918, which expanded the provisions for exclusion and deportation of subversive aliens and authorized their expulsion without time limitations.

Until now the law had dealt only with the quality of the aliens who sought to enter. No attempt had been made to limit the number of entrants. At the conclusion of World War I immigration again began to increase. There was widespread fear of inundation by a flood of immigrants from the war-devastated countries of Europe. The isolationist mood of the period and a severe post-war depression augmented the already large sentiment for further restrictions. The result was the Quota Law of 1921, enacted as a temporary measure. This legislation introduced for the first time numerical limitations on immigration. With certain enumerated exceptions it allocated quotas to each nationality totaling 3% of the foreign born persons of that nationality residing in the United States in 1910, for an annual total of approximately 350,000. This law was scheduled to expire in 1922, but was extended to June 30, 1924.

In the meantime Congress enacted a permanent policy of numerical restriction in 1924. The 1924 legislation adopted a national origins formula that eventually based the quota for each nationality on the number of persons of their national origin in the United States in 1920. This formula resulted in a sharp curtailment of immigrants from southern and eastern Europe. Quota immigrants were limited to approximately 150,000 per year. However, natives of Western Hemisphere countries could enter without numerical restriction. Other nonquota groups included alien wives and children of American citizens and returning lawful residents. Aliens seeking to enter were required to obtain immigration visas from American consuls overseas. Those who entered in violation of the visa and quota requirements were deportable without time limitation. Another provision aimed at Orientals barred all aliens ineligible to citizenship, thus affronting the Japanese, who felt that they had dealt with the problem cooperatively through the Gentleman's Agreement.[b]

[4]—1924–1952 Legislation

The Immigration Acts of 1917 and 1924 became the twin elements of immigration policy, the one proclaiming qualitative restrictions and the other numerical limitations. They remained substantially unchanged until 1952. * * * [Statutes passed in 1940 and 1950 expanded the grounds for excluding, and for deporting, those noncitizens thought to be subversive. These and other World War II–Era and McCarthy Era events are taken up in chapter 5, § B below.—Ed.]

* * *

During this period there were some relaxations of the prevailing restrictions in measures generated by World War II and its aftermath. The major liberalization was the Displaced Persons Act. Enacted in 1948 and substantially amended in 1950, this humanitarian program ultimately brought over 400,000 refugees to our shores in three and a half years. They were admitted, however, under a system that mortgaged the quotas for their countries far into the future.

Another relaxation benefited the alien spouses and children and fiancees of World War II American servicemen, facilitating their admission to the United States. One hundred and eighteen thousand aliens were admitted to the United States under the War Brides Act and over 5000 were admitted under the Fiancees Act. * * *

§ 2.03   The Immigration and Nationality Act of 1952

[1]—Consideration and Enactment

The Act of 1952 had its genesis in a two-year study of the Senate Judiciary Committee, then headed by Senator Pat McCarran of Nevada. The resulting legislative proposals were sponsored in the Senate by Senator McCarran and in the House by Representative Francis E. Walter of Pennsylvania, Chairman of the Immigration Subcommittee of the House Judiciary Committee. The bill encountered opposition in both chambers, led in the House by Representative Emanuel Celler, Chairman of the House Judiciary Committee, and in the Senate by Senator Hubert Humphrey of Minnesota and Senator Herbert H. Lehman of New York. However, the bill was approved by substantial majorities in both Houses.

President Truman vetoed the bill. He castigated the national origins quota system that it carried over from the 1924 Act, criticized the severity of the grounds prescribed for exclusion, deportation, and denaturalization,

b. A prior Act had limited naturalization to "free white persons". In Ozawa v. United States, 260 U.S. 178, 43 S.Ct. 65, 67 L.Ed. 199 (1922), the Supreme Court held that persons of Japanese descent were non-white and therefore ineligible for citizenship. The 1924 legislation barring noncitizens who were "ineligible for citizenship" was thus Congress's way of excluding the Japanese.—Ed.

and opposed the limitations on the authority to alleviate hardships. However the McCarran–Walter bill became law when Congress overrode the President's veto, and it was enacted on June 27, 1952, as Pub.L. 414, 82d Cong., 2d Sess. Under its terms the law was designated the Immigration and Nationality Act. * * * Although the McCarran–Walter Act has been repeatedly amended, it is still the basic statute dealing with immigration and nationality. The amendments have been fitted into the structure of the parent statute. * * *

[2]—Basic Features of the 1952 Act

* * *

[c]—Immigrants and Quotas

Every alien seeking to enter the United States was deemed an immigrant unless he established that he was a nonimmigrant. A nonimmigrant is one who establishes that he sought to come temporarily and originally included foreign government and international organization officials, visitors, aliens in transit to other countries, students, crewmen, treaty traders and temporary workers.

Every immigrant is deemed subject to the prescribed numerical limitations unless he is exempted from such limitations. The principal classes exempted from numerical restrictions by the Act of 1952 were alien spouses and children of American citizens, returning lawful residents, and natives of Western Hemisphere countries.

The Act established annual quotas based on a system of national origins for immigrants who came from all countries except those in the Western Hemisphere. It enacted special racial quotas for Asians. The law also established preferences within the quotas for immigrants with specialized skills and certain relatives of American citizens and of resident aliens.

* * *

§ 2.04 Legislative Activity After 1952

* * *

The movement for legislative reform received its major stimulus on July 23, 1963, when President Kennedy submitted to Congress a comprehensive program for revision of the immigration laws. His major proposals were for abolition of the national origins quota system and of discriminations against Asians and allocation of immigrant visas on a first come, first served basis, subject to preferences for relatives of American citizens and persons with special skills.

President Kennedy had long been interested in immigration problems. Moreover, several factors contributed to produce a more favorable climate. In the first place, the most powerful champions of the McCarran–Walter Act had left the scene, since Senator McCarran and Representative Walter were both dead. In addition, Congress had enacted a number of amelioratory laws, described in § 2.04[2]. Nevertheless there was strong resistance to change, and progress was slow and uncertain.

After President Kennedy's death, his proposals for reform of the immigration laws were adopted and pressed by President Johnson. His effort finally achieved fruition in a major revision enacted in 1965, which abolished the national origins quota system. The 1965 amendments are discussed [below].

[2]—1952–1964 Legislation

* * *

The 1961 amendments included:

* * *

- Elimination of ceiling of 2,000 visas that could be issued for countries in the Asia Pacific Triangle;

* * *

[3]—The 1965 Amendments[c]

In 1965, Congress enacted far-reaching legislative changes. In large measure these changes responded to the proposals of Presidents Kennedy and Johnson to eliminate discriminations based on race or national origin. [In that respect, the reforms reflected the spirit of the 1964 Civil Rights Act, passed just one year earlier—Ed.] In other respects, however, the 1965 amendments were restrictive, imposing additional limitations on the entry of persons seeking to perform labor and restrictions on the entry of aliens from the Western Hemisphere. The major revisions of the 1965 enactment:

- Ended the national origins quota system, effective June 30, 1968.
- Abolished the special immigration restrictions relating to Orientals and forbade immigration discriminations because of race, sex, nationality, place of birth, or place of residence.
- Fixed a unified immigration quota, for areas outside the Western Hemisphere, of 170,000 annually. However, no more than 20,000 of these visas could be allocated to the natives of any single foreign state.
- * * * Established the following categories of immigrants exempt from the worldwide numerical restrictions:
  - — *Immediate relatives of United States Citizens.* Defined as the spouses and children of U.S. citizens, and parents of U.S. citizens who are at least 21 years of age.

---

c. The abolition of the national origins quota system dramatically changed the composition of the immigrant stream. For an insightful look at the history of (and assumptions underlying) the 1965 legislation, see Gabriel J. Chin, *The Civil Rights Revolution Comes to Immigration Law: A New Look at the Immigration and Nationality Act of 1965,* 75 North Carolina L.Rev. 273 (1996)—Ed.

— *Special immigrants.* Additional groups formerly designated as nonquota immigrants and including aliens born in Western Hemisphere countries, returning lawful residents, certain former citizens of the United States, ministers of religion, and employees of the United States.

- Abolished the system of quota priorities under the 1952 Act and established new priorities, based on family relationships and selective skills, in issuing immigrant visas within the established numerical limitations for countries other than those in the Western Hemisphere.

* * *

- * * * [Ended] the exemption of Western Hemisphere natives, other than immediate relatives of American citizens, from numerical restrictions. * * * [C]ommencing July 1, 1968 a numerical limitation of 120,000 annually would apply to this class of special immigrants.

- [Barred the admission of most non-family immigrants] if they were coming to perform skilled or unskilled labor unless the Secretary of Labor determined or certified that qualified workers were not available at the place of destination and that the employment of such prospective immigrants would not adversely affect wages and working conditions in the United States. * * *

* * *

[A combination of amendments enacted in 1976 and 1978 eliminated the remaining distinctions between Western and Eastern Hemisphere immigrants. The Eastern Hemisphere immigration criteria became applicable worldwide.—Ed.]

[7]—The Refugee Act of 1980

[Refugees and asylees are discussed in chapter 11 below.—Ed.]

* * *

[The Immigration Reform and Control Act of 1986 made sweeping changes. The most important concerned the imposition of sanctions on employers of undocumented workers; prohibitions on certain forms of discrimination; legalization, or amnesty; and agricultural workers. Those subjects are discussed in various places throughout this book.—Ed.]

* * *

[d]—The Immigration Marriage Fraud Amendments of 1986

Reports of widespread frauds on the part of aliens seeking to obtain immigration benefits through marriage to American citizens and resident aliens have led to corrective action. The resulting legislation, designated as the Immigration Marriage Fraud Amendments of 1986, Pub.L. 99–639, 100

Stat. 3537 (November 10, 1986), made significant changes in the immigration laws * * * [to be discussed later.—Ed.]

* * *

[11]—The Immigration Act of 1990

* * *

* * * [T]he Immigration Act of 1990, unquestionably, was the most important immigration statute in many years. Most observers will agree that in many respects Congress rejected the suspicion and hostility which characterized the McCarran–Walter Act of 1952. In their place Congress adopted new measures that generally are more consonant with modern humanitarian concerns and enlightened national needs. But at the same time, many objected to some features of the statute which unjustifiably curtailed due process rights in deportation proceedings.

* * *

A striking and much publicized feature of the new law was the marked increase in the number of immigrants who will be admitted each year. This increase reflected the confidence of Congress in the future of the United States and its capacity for continuing to absorb new immigrants.

The 1990 law established an annual limit for worldwide immigration of 700,000 for three years, which would decrease to 675,000 thereafter [not counting overseas refugees, who at that time numbered approximately 125,000 per year]. * * *

———

As the authors of the above excerpt note, the 1990 law established a general overall ceiling of 675,000 immigrants per year, subject to the various exemptions already discussed. Within that annual allotment, a minimum of 480,000 visas were made available for family reunification, a slight increase over the previous admission levels. A minimum of 140,000 were set aside for "employment-based" immigrants—more than twice the previous ceiling. And 55,000 were allocated for "diversity" immigrants—nationals of countries from which relatively few people have immigrated to the United States in recent years. Details of each of these three programs appear in chapter 3 below.

The Immigration Act of 1990 made other fundamental changes as well. It codified "temporary protected status," a discretionary remedy designed for noncitizens who have fled war, natural disaster, or certain other dangers but who do not qualify for asylum. See chapter 11, section C, below. It made several, generally restrictive changes to the nonimmigrant provisions. See chapter 4 below. To reduce delays, it reformulated the naturalization process by transferring some of the procedural steps from the courts to the INS. See chapter 13 below.

The Act also revamped the exclusion grounds (now called grounds of "inadmissibility"). It repealed a provision that had been interpreted as excluding homosexuals, narrowed some of the ideological exclusion grounds, and added new exclusion grounds related to terrorism and to foreign policy. See chapter 5 below. It made miscellaneous changes to the deportation grounds. See chapter 7 below. It amended the conditional residence requirements for spouses and children by adding a specific waiver for certain battered spouses and children. See chapter 3, section B.2.b below. The Act generally toughened the substantive rules, and removed various procedural safeguards, for noncitizens deportable on crime-related grounds. See chapters 7, 8, and 9 below. It also created a Commission on Immigration Reform to study the impact of the present immigration law and to report periodically to Congress.

In 1994 the voters of California sent shock waves through immigrant and ethnic communities by passing Proposition 187. It prohibited public school districts from enrolling undocumented children and made all undocumented migrants ineligible for almost all public medical and health services. It also required school, health, and medical officials to make the necessary immigration status determinations. As discussed in chapter 12, the courts ultimately invalidated Proposition 187 on equal protection grounds. Still, the political mood it reflected and the fears it created persist.

In 1995 and 1996, anti-immigrant sentiments continued to escalate, fed in part by an interim report from Congress's Commission on Immigration Reform recommending reduced immigration levels. In response, various bills were introduced in Congress to cut legal immigration drastically. In the end, those efforts did not come to fruition. Other bills with substantial adverse impact on immigrants, however, did become law in 1996.

The Antiterrorism and Effective Death Penalty Act of 1996 (AEDPA), a comprehensive bill concerned generally with terrorism and other crime, contained numerous provisions relevant to immigration (many of which had nothing to do with either terrorism or crime). For noncitizens convicted of crimes, this legislation further expanded the deportation grounds and narrowed the provisions for discretionary relief. See chapters 7 and 8 below. It also eliminated some of the procedural safeguards for certain noncitizens found in the United States without having been inspected, and for asylum seekers who appear at ports of entry without proper documents. See chapters 9 and 11, respectively.

But the harshness of the 1996 reforms extended to LPRs as well. In that year Congress passed a welfare reform bill, the Personal Responsibility and Work Opportunity Reconciliation Act of 1996. Title IV of the Act deals specifically with noncitizens. With some exceptions, it makes even LPRs ineligible for most federal means-tested benefits, including food stamps and supplemental security income (SSI), and it authorizes states to adopt similar disqualifications with respect to state benefits. See chapter 13 below. The same legislation makes it harder for prospective immigrants to overcome the public charge exclusion through use of affidavits of support from American family members and other sponsors. See chapter 5 below.

AEDPA and welfare reform notwithstanding, the major event of the year—indeed one of the most sweeping immigration reform packages ever enacted—was the Illegal Immigration Reform and Immigrant Responsibility Act of 1996 (IIRIRA). As its name implies, most of its provisions focused on the apprehension and speedy removal of undocumented migrants. In the process, though, Congress fundamentally changed several other areas of immigration law. To immigrants and immigrant advocates, the changes were devastating. You will encounter most of them in other chapters. They expand the substantive criteria for removing noncitizens, further restrict discretionary relief, introduce a number of "expedited" procedures for noncitizens facing removal from the United States, impose additional restrictions on asylum seekers, and purport to immunize a range of federal immigration determinations from judicial review. Important court decisions discussed in chapter 9 restrict the sweep of those provisions. IIRIRA did not, however, significantly change the definitions of the qualifying categories for immigrants. See generally Juan P. Osuna, Understanding the 1996 Immigration Act (1997).

Since then, by far the most significant changes to the U.S. immigration laws have been the sweeping national security measures adopted in response to the terrorist attacks of September 11, 2001. The reorganization of the executive branch immigration functions, entailing the dissolution of the INS and the transfer of almost all its functions to various agencies within the new Department of Homeland Security, was described in the Overview chapter. The substantive and procedural changes are too far-reaching to be summarized here; they are considered in chapter 10 below.

What are the numbers? The following will summarize the changing ethnic composition of the U.S. immigrant stream:

IMMIGRATION FROM SELECTED COUNTRIES AND REGIONS[a]
FISCAL YEARS 1821–2003
(All figures are in thousands.)

	Mexico[b]	Canada	Caribbean	Central America	Northern Europe[c]	Southern Europe	Asia	Africa	Other	Worldwide
1821–30	5	2	4	0	96	3	0	0	33	143
1831–40	7	14	12	0	491	5	0	0	70	599
1841–50	3	42	14	0	1592	5	0	0	57	1713
1851–60	3	59	11	0	2433	20	42	0	30	2598
1861–70	2	154	9	0	2044	21	65	0	20	2315
1871–80	5	384	14	0	2197	75	124	0	13	2812
1881–90	2	393	29	0	4398	337	70	1	17	5247
1891–1900	1	3	33	1	2838	717	75	0	20	3688
1901–10	50	179	108	8	5693	2363	324	7	63	8795
1911–20	219	742	123	17	2855	1467	247	8	58	5736
1921–30	459	925	75	16	1869	594	112	6	51	4107
1931–40	22	109	16	6	255	93	17	2	8	528
1941–50	61	172	50	22	547	74	37	7	65	1035
1951–60	300	378	123	45	1056	270	153	14	176	2515
1961–70	454	413	470	101	679	444	428	29	304	3322
1971–80	640	170	741	135	394	406	1588	81	338	4493
1981–90	1656	157	872	468	545	216	2738	177	509	7338
1991–2000	2249	192	979	527	1112	247	2796	355	638	9095
2001–03	537	74	259	193	368	90	900	152	261	2834
Total[d] 1821–1998	6675	4562	3942	1539	31,462	7447	9716	839	2731	68,913

a.   Source: 2003 Yearbook of Immigration Statistics, Table 2, at 12–14 (Sept. 2004). Technical qualifications are set out in the original source.

b.   An ad hoc legalization program resulted in unusually high figures for Mexico for fiscal years 1990 and 1991. Since then, annual immigration has reverted to historical levels.

c.   For purposes of this chart, Southern Europe encompasses Greece, Italy, Portugal, Romania, Spain, and Yugoslavia. Northern Europe comprises all other European nations, including those lumped together in the Yearbook under the heading "Other Europe."

d.   The total for each column equals the sum of the entries. Because of rounding, these totals sometimes differ slightly from the ones that appear in the Yearbook.

The chart permits some useful generalizations. First, the overall immigration history of the United States has been heavily Northern European— 46% of the worldwide total from 1821 to 2003. When Northern Europeans and Canadians are combined, the figure rises to 52%.

Taken alone, however, those figures would be misleading. They conceal dramatic changes over time. From 1991 on, for example, Northern Europeans and Canadians together have comprised only 15% of all immigrants; the dominant regions have become Asia and Latin America. In order, the countries of birth of the greatest numbers of immigrants admitted to the United States in fiscal year 2003 were:

Country	Number Admitted (in thousands)
Mexico	116
India	50
Philippines	45
People's Republic of China	41
El Salvador	28
Dominican Republic	26
Vietnam	22
Colombia	15
Guatemala	14
Russia	14

Source: 2003 Yearbook of Immigration Statistics, Table B, at 8.

The historical table also illustrates radical changes in the immigration levels of two particular groups: Asians and Southern Europeans. You might have noticed that significant numbers of Asians began arriving in the 1850's (mainly to work on the inter-Continental railroad after the discovery of gold in California), and that those numbers increased in the 1860's and 1870's. During those years, virtually all the Asian immigrants were from China. The Chinese Exclusion Act, passed in 1882, diminished that migration. Soon afterwards, large numbers of immigrants began to arrive from Japan, particularly from 1900 until 1924. In that latter year, Congress barred the entry of most Japanese immigrants, thus producing the much lower figures that appear in the chart for Asian immigration in the 1930's and 1940's. The 1952 Act relaxed (but did not eliminate) the anti-Asian provisions, and from that point on the chart shows steadily increasing numbers. As you can see from the chart, Chinese immigration has enjoyed a resurgence, but modern Asian immigrants to the United States are much more likely to come from India and the Philippines than from Japan.

There are similar statutory explanations for the sudden changes in numbers of Southern Europeans. You can see from the historical chart that immigration from Southern Europe began to escalate in the 1870's, peaking from 1900 to 1920. The sharp drop in the 1920's was no coincidence. In 1921 Congress enacted temporary legislation, made permanent in 1924, which established the national origins quota system described earlier. Since the new scheme based each country's quota on the proportion of persons in the United States whose ancestry could be traced to that country, and since at that time only a small proportion of people in the United States had Southern European roots, the (fully intended) effect of the new quota system was to stem the influx of Southern Europeans. Notice how sharp the drop-off was. With the exception of some unusual post-war migration patterns, the low numbers of Southern European immigrants persisted until Congress abolished the national origins quota system in 1965. That action explains the increased levels of Southern European immigration during the 1960's and 1970's.

SECTION B.   THE MORAL DIMENSIONS OF IMMIGRATION CONTROL

Citizens of the United States are generally free to come and go as they please and to remain in the country as long as they wish. See, e.g., *Mathews v. Diaz*, 426 U.S. 67, 80, 96 S.Ct. 1883, 48 L.Ed.2d 478 (1976). In contrast, as you have already begun to discover, noncitizens are subject to a complex set of rules that restrict their admission and the duration and other terms of their stay. While many people dispute either the wisdom or the justice of particular provisions of the immigration laws, relatively few have questioned the underlying premise that a sovereign state has the moral power to enact restrictions. But is the moral basis for such a power really that clear? The following materials explore that question:

Roger Nett, The Civil Right We Are Not Ready For: The Right of Free Movement of People on the Face of the Earth

81 Ethics 212, at 216, 218–20, 225–27 (1971).

* * *

Whereas, in the past, civil rights were defined largely as devices by which people might escape from tyranny and direct abuse, *the right of people to equal opportunities is rather clearly the underlying theme of all civil rights today.* We still talk about free speech, religion, and the right to vote as though they were ends in themselves, and indeed they can be. But people have become conscious that their purpose in seeking or maintaining them is to equalize opportunities, to make possible a life that would otherwise be denied, and that it is in this sense that we are most likely to define justice today. The phrase "life, liberty, and the pursuit of happiness" in the American constitution, whether intentionally or not, implies an order of security in which opportunity rests on liberty, which in turn rests on the right to exist. People are looking more and more at the goal as they enunciate the means.

It is therefore correct to say that, commensurate with the times, we find ourselves discovering new rights, meaning new fundamental conditions which insure some amount of justice and equity among people. * * *

* * *

If the set of rights is not functionally complete, what needs to be added to the rights we now recognize in order to make a working set? What rights might we expect some future Magna Carta to include? We suggest that one other "right" relates directly to opportunity and would go a long way, virtually all the way, to close the existing set of rights and make it functionally much more viable. At some future point in world civilization, it may well be discovered that the right to free and open movement of people on the surface of the earth is fundamental to the structure of human opportunity and is therefore basic in the same sense as is free religion, speech, and the franchise. * * *

What is implied in the right to free movement as it relates to fair opportunity? One dimension is material, the right of people who are trapped in overcrowded areas or areas without sufficient resources to go where resources are not so taken up. The other, more purely political, is the right of people to move away from oppression, persecution, unfair restriction, or even disagreeable social environments and social orders. One involves the right to come; the other, the right to go.

I think people have always recognized this right de facto, and ancient as well as modern history is full of instances of migration to avoid persecution and in search of better opportunities. * * *

* * *

Do we have any knowledge of how an open system of world migration might work? We have limited cases. One might think of free movement of people within the British system. A clearer example, however, is within the United States of America, where people have, and have had, the right of free movement since slavery was abolished more than a century ago. Here we have a fair-sized experiment to see how free movement operates in one instance. It works surprisingly well on one subcontinent anyway. When there is a drought in one region, as in the dust-bowl days of the 1930s, people move to another region, and opportunities are somewhat equalized. When clumsy state officials or demagogues disrupt a school system, teachers move to another state. This has a corrective effect on state policies or, if it does not, enriches the states which have better policies or more to offer. Imagine what it would be like if everybody were kept within the boundaries of his own state, and you have a fair picture of most of the rest of the world today!

* * *

What disadvantages and what benefits would there be in a desegregated or even less segregated world? We begin by noting some of the advantages. Once certain benefit is that a system of open migration would further remove the unrealistic ideas that people have about others and enable their governments to focus more on real rather than imagined problems of human intention and welfare. Once the pain of giving up an "Old South" mentality subsided in the privileged nations, a number of beneficial effects could be expected to ensue. People in more ordinary circumstances would discover or rediscover that humans on the surface of the earth are indeed one species not too different from themselves. As generations with hardened attitudes died out, new generations would soon come to feel that the right to movement about the surface of the earth is normal and beneficial. The incentive for war could possibly be greatly lowered, as it is, say between California and New York, who now allow free cross-migration.

A second and highly related consideration of the utmost importance is that nationalism, the dominant and perhaps most effective institution of our time—certainly the most cherished—could continue ostensibly in its present form, although in a denatured, and to a few culture purists, debased form. Instead of doing away with her, the "sacred cow" of nationalism might only be dehorned. One would not have to tackle head-on the greater problem of uniting the world or to interfere unnecessarily with the diversity of cultures or cultural pluralism, although the latter would certainly be affected, again as the inclusion of the American Negro affects both Negro and white customs.

The main and most concrete advantage to all societies, however, is that a major type of social waste would begin to dry up. Adding open migration to the basic human rights would be a giant step, perhaps the biggest we could now seriously imagine, toward providing a functional basis for doing away with situational inopportunity *at relatively low world cost*. Any other social device for doing the same, including laissez faire, would probably cause much more dislocation and entail more effort. By eliminating one primal cause of poverty and involuntary subordination, it would allow individuals to rise by their individual energies and give hope of real betterment to untold numbers where little now exists. All of this might be done by changing only one key factor.

The social waste referred to is of two parts; one is the loss of contributions to overall human purposes—talent for science, production, higher humanistic efforts—from people who are so disadvantaged that they spend virtually all their time and energies just maintaining life. The other is the amount of concrete effort, including emotional energy, spent by those who try to contain the former. It is hardly possible to measure the costs of all the different kinds of reaction, which may well include undeclared and cold wars and more generally noncooperation, where cooperation could reasonably be hoped for.

Finally, and closely connected is that *such a right if properly deployed could solve another of our greatest problems, that of overpopulation.* Here we would argue that, at the moment, the earth is not necessarily overpopulated in terms of its resources. Rather, some parts of it are, and people are multiplying rapidly to fill up parts of it that are relatively vacant. Would it not be better to move the population over to the more open parts and at the same time, for the privilege, demand more responsible reproductive behavior? Are we not losing one of the world's great opportunities? To be sure, a way for doing this is yet to be worked out and the difficulties should not be under-rated.

The Costs of a System of Open Migration

What would be the principal liabilities to a system of free and open migration? What would be the problems of getting existing nations to agree to a more open system? Does the question really pertain to today's structure of power and politics?

Any extension of civil rights also increases disequilibrium and brings new stresses into a society or societies—at the present time into the world at large. It is quite possible that the world needs time to adjust to present levels of acculturation and to assimilate peoples already displaced. In addition to the practical problems, there is a psychological problem which must be mentioned first—the preoccupation with national systems has convinced most politicians that there is a futility or utopian unreality to any treatment of mankind as a single group and to giving international planning, especially world planning, its just due. There is thus an ideological problem that may inhibit consideration of the practical problems. Social scientists do not yet know how to measure this type of variable.

The right to free movement would present two sets of practical problems, one connected with the right to leave a country—brain drain, political use of information, loss of subjects (e.g., military draftees), and the implied rejection or loss of popularity of a country or its leaders when people have left it. The other set, connected with the right to be let into a country, involves problems of finding housing and employment, of graduating political participation in order to prevent the "swamping" of a social or cultural system, of extending educational, health, and other social facilities. Finally, there is a separate problem of limiting births to culturally acceptable levels so that people would not feel they were being displaced by raw Darwinian tactics. * * *

The problem of getting nations to agree to a system of open migration is harder to assess. Initially, one might have the impression that progress in that direction is now virtually impossible. There are a few indicators to the contrary. One is that the demands for opportunity are coming more and more from those who feel most offended by the world system—those in the poor countries. More privileged nations may increasingly be forced to react to demands which anticipate such a shape of the future. In this century, powerful nations as well as classes have already been seen to relinquish empires and privileges which they once thought were secure, sometimes reluctantly but often willingly as the costs became too great. It is no longer utopian to want to get rid of poverty and lack of opportunity; the question has rather become by what means, and there is now more willingness to look at solutions once considered unlikely. Individual nations do not always have control over social change, and a map of present conditions may indicate the likelihood or even inevitability of introducing new elements into the world system.

But suppose there were a rational choice. It could be described as one between the costs of maintaining many people whose chances are restricted by underprivilege as against the alternative providing for their assimilation into a new and less wasteful world system in which the potential of all could be realized—or, if the latter should prove too remote an ideal, at least to get the unhappy ones to quit throwing bricks at the rest of organized society. It is surely not unimaginable that responsible nations might deliberately strive for a relatively quick assimilation of the underprivileged as against the high cost of maintaining present restrictions. What seems radical in terms of past policies may come to seem more like common sense in a world situation with fewer alternatives. A policy of gradualism extending intermigration privileges between select nations would be one type of beginning. If some nations were to begin opening their boundaries, it would probably put others at a political disadvantage so that they could not stand still. A new geopolitics could begin on that basis, one with sufficient latitude for political realism.

NOTES AND QUESTIONS

1. Are moral considerations that reflect the individual interests of would-be immigrants even relevant, or should a nation's immigration policy be viewed simply as an instrument for promoting the welfare of its own citizens? See John A. Scanlan & O.T. Kent, *The Force of Moral Arguments for a Just Immigration Policy in a Hobbesian Universe: The Contemporary American Example*, in Mark Gibney (ed.), Open Borders? Closed Societies? The Ethical and Political Issues, at 61, 78–82 (1988) (moral considerations are not only relevant but are themselves part of national interest). See generally Warren F. Schwartz (ed.), Justice in Immigration (1995); Joseph H. Carens, *Aliens and Citizens: The Case for Open Borders*, 49 The Rev. of Politics 251 (1987); Howard F. Chang, *Immigration Policy, Liberal Principles, and the Republican Tradition*, 85 Georgetown L.J. 2105 (1997) (history of immigration restrictions generally, and discriminatory immigration restrictions in particular, are incompatible with liberal principles of political theory on which republic was based); Kevin R. Johnson, *Open Borders?*, 51 UCLA L. Rev. 193 (2003); R. George Wright, *Federal Immigration Law and the Case for Open Entry*, 27 Loyola L.A.L.Rev. 1265 (1994). Presenting

an historical case for open borders is Satvinder S. Juss, *Free Movement and the World Order*, 16 Internat'l J. Refugee L. 289 (2004).

2. Although Nett's prescriptions are rooted in human rights arguments, he also maintains that at any rate the actual benefits of open migration would outweigh the costs. In making that argument, is Nett comparing the global benefits and costs, or the benefits and costs to the receiving nation? Which type of utilitarianism—global or national—strikes you as more relevant to the question of open migration? See Timothy King, *Immigration from Developing Countries: Some Philosophical Issues*, 93 Ethics 525, 526–31 (1983).

3. Our society generally disdains social clubs that exclude prospective members because of race, ethnicity, gender or other disfavored criteria. In certain economic contexts—including employment, education, housing, and public accommodations—society's disapproval has even been codified into law. And, generally speaking, the Constitution prohibits the government itself from engaging in such discrimination unless there is an especially close connection between the classification used and a legitimate and sufficiently important goal.

The most disfavored forms of discrimination tend to be those based irrationally on circumstances of birth. To be sure, we often treat one another differently because of characteristics shaped at least partially by accident of birth. Intelligence and other personal traits influence decisions on university admissions, jobs, and other benefits when native ability is relevant to likely performance level. The laws of nature that endow some individuals with greater talents than others might be unfair, but society accepts selection criteria that reflect those disparities when the reasons for employing such criteria are strong enough. Moreover, our free enterprise system inevitably results in a resource distribution based partly on circumstances of birth. But we don't usually applaud that feature of the system. We accept it as an unfortunate side effect of an economic model that, in society's view, contains enough offsetting advantages to commend it.

Yet, one of the most crucial policy decisions the nation must make— who will be allowed to *be* here—is based on citizenship. As you will see in more detail in chapter 13, citizenship in turn is legally determined in the vast majority of cases by the circumstances of one's birth: Place of birth and identity of parents are usually dispositive. Unlike most of the other laws that in their practical operation permit important consequences to turn on accident of birth, the immigration laws expressly mandate such differential treatment. *By law, one's place of birth and one's parentage are relevant to, and often conclusive of, one's rights to enter and to remain.* See chapter 13, section A. If Nett is right to call ours a segregated world, then the segregation is de jure, not merely de facto.

Several writers see the power to restrict immigration as a basic freedom of a nation's existing members. In varying ways, they have depicted this freedom as akin to the freedom to choose the people with whom one will associate or contract. Immigration restrictions have also been portrayed as a vehicle to achieve the "communal independence" vital to fostering both a sense of belonging and a sense of commitment to the common good. See e.g., Kenneth L. Karst, *Equality and Community: Lessons from the Civil Rights Era*, 56 Notre Dame Lawyer 183, 183–84 (1980); David A. Martin, *Due Process and Membership in the National Community: Political Asylum and Beyond*, 44 Univ. Pittsburgh L.Rev. 165, 194–208 (1983); Peter H. Schuck, *The Transformation of Immigration Law*, 84 Columbia L.Rev. 1, 85–90 (1984); Michael Walzer, *The Distribution of Membership*, in Peter G. Brown & Henry Shue (Eds.), Boundaries—National Autonomy and Its Limits, at 1, 32 (1981).

All those rationales—freedom of association, freedom of contract, and the benefits of achieving a sense of community—can also be, and have been, invoked in debates over civil rights legislation. To prohibit private job discrimination based on race, for example, Congress had to restrict the freedom of the employer to choose the people with whom he or she would associate or contract. In the contexts with which the various civil rights laws are concerned, Congress decided that those freedoms were less compelling than the corresponding equality interests. Constitutional limitations on government-sponsored discrimination similarly reflect the triumph of equality interests over other concerns. The question here is whether immigration policy should be seen any differently. Is the government on any firmer a moral footing when it excludes individuals because of their place of birth or their parentage than either a private or governmental employer or university is when it rejects applicants because of their race? Why is it, exactly, that equality interests come out ahead in one context but not the other? Is a nation that acts in its sovereign capacity morally different from other groups of individuals? Alternatively, is discrimination based on citizenship morally different from discrimination based on other accidents of birth?

Consider also some of the following possible moral justifications for restricting immigration. For each, decide first whether you find the argument persuasive and, second, whether the argument applies with any more force to immigration than to any of the civil rights contexts in which society has condemned discrimination based on other accidents of birth.

a. We were here first.

b. Our parents contributed to this society and thus earned the right to pass on the fruits of their labor to us. Those fruits include the right to remain in the United States to enjoy the society they helped create.

c. Those of us who are already here have stronger ties to the national community in which we live than do those who wish to enter that community for the first time. If the nation's resources are not sufficient to accommodate everyone who wants to live here, excluding newcomers is therefore preferable to severing existing ties. See generally T. Alexander Aleinikoff, *Aliens, Due Process and "Community Ties": A Response to Martin*, 44 Univ. Pittsburgh L.Rev. 237 (1983).

d. It is true that immigration laws ultimately are based on accident of birth, but only because the particular accident of birth defines the person's *citizenship.* In a world composed of nation-states, citizenship has significance. For example, citizenship legally implies allegiance. It is right that a nation extend special protection to those who owe it allegiance. On this issue, see generally Stephen H. Legomsky, *Why Citizenship?*, 35 Virginia J. Internat'L. 279 (1994).

e. Our own citizens, having usually been born and raised in the United States, are more likely to have values compatible with those of the existing culture. And we have as much right to form a culturally homogeneous nation as a social club does to maintain a culturally homogeneous membership.

f. It is unlikely that all countries would agree to open migration, and one prosperous country could not go it alone. If it tried, it would receive more immigrants than it could absorb, and that would unfairly place the citizens of the receiving country at a disadvantage vis a vis those of other prosperous nations who continued to restrict immigration. (As a side point, do you think Nett's assessment of the chances of worldwide agreement on this subject is realistic?)

4. Professor Bruce Ackerman has argued that immigration can morally be restricted *only* to the extent necessary to preserve the liberal polity itself. Bruce A. Ackerman, Social Justice in the Liberal State 95 (1980). He defines a liberal polity as one in which anyone asserting power over another must provide a rational defense of his or her decision; for this purpose, rationality precludes assertions that the power-holder has morally superior interests. *Id.* at 93. Whether he is right or wrong to exclude other possible justifications, do you agree with him that admission restrictions are morally defensible even then? Such thoughts were expressed in the early days of the United States by those who feared the immigration of "monarchists" intent on destroying the fledgling democracy. See, e.g., Roy L. Garis, Immigration Restriction 25–26 (1927); Maldwyn A. Jones, American Immigration 80 (1960). In modern times, although commentators have not argued that open borders would literally topple the American liberal polity, some have suggested that too liberal an immigration policy could trigger a serious political backlash. See, e.g., Peter H. Schuck, *The Transformation of Immigration Law*, 84 Columbia L.Rev. 1, 81 (1984); Michael S. Teitelbaum, *Right versus Right: Immigration and Refugee Policy in the United States*, 59 Foreign Affairs 21, 51–52 (1980).

5. Is freedom of association an argument *for* or *against* open borders? Do you think freedom of association is more important at the small group level or at the national level? See Judith Lichtenberg, *National Boundaries and Moral Boundaries: A Cosmopolitan View*, in Peter G. Brown & Henry Shue (Eds.), Boundaries—National Autonomy and Its Limits, at 79, 96–97 (1981) (capacity for equal commitment to others affected by intimacy of contact).

6. Who has the burden of proof here—those who assert the morality of restricting immigration, or those who believe such restrictions are immoral? Is the admission of an immigrant an act of affirmative assistance,

or is exclusion an act of affirmative interference with personal freedom? Is the distinction merely semantic, or does it have moral significance?

You might recall from your study of either torts or criminal law that in the United States the legal system generally imposes no obligation to render affirmative assistance to others. See, e.g., Dan B. Dobbs, The Law of Torts, chap. 21 (2000). But the line that separates action from inaction is not always easy to draw. Moreover, the law has recognized exceptions to the no-duty-to-rescue rule. *Id.* One exception is that a person who even innocently created the peril to another has a duty to render reasonable assistance. *Id.* Does that principle have any applicability to the issue of open borders? Some have argued that a nation's exploitative economic policies, when responsible for modern day disparities in wealth, create an obligation to admit immigrants from third world countries. See, e.g., Developments in the Law, *Immigration Policy and the Rights of Aliens*, 96 Harv.L.Rev. 1286, 1465 n. 13 (1983).

Legalities aside, it has often been argued that one has a moral obligation to render reasonable assistance to those in distress. The principle of "mutual aid," posited by John Rawls in *A Theory of Justice*, at 114 (1971), holds that positive assistance is morally required when one person needs aid and another person is in a position to give it without "excessive risk or loss." Do you agree? If so, should this principle extend to the immigration policies of nation-states? See generally Michael Walzer, *The Distribution of Membership*, in Peter G. Brown & Henry Shue (Eds.), Boundaries—National Autonomy and Its Limits, at 1, 15–23 (1981).

7.   Although most of the analogies have been to families, or to clubs, or to neighborhoods, or to commercial transactions, it is possible also to analogize immigration law to property law. Would Nett recognize a human right to move onto another person's private property, as long as the move expanded the mover's opportunities for happiness without causing excessive harm to the original owner? If not, how would Nett distinguish migration across national boundaries? Should the citizens of a country be regarded as the "owners" of the nation's territory, possessed of a right to exclude unwanted visitors?

8.   No country today has open borders, but there are arrangements in which groups of two or more countries have agreed to virtually free migration within the group. The best known arrangement of that type is the European Union, which allows free movement of workers who are nationals of EU member states. In December 2003, the Southern Cone Common Market (MERCOSUR), a trade bloc composed of Argentina, Brazil, Paraguay, and Uruguay (with Chile and Bolivia as associate members), agreed to establish a migration system much like that of the European Union. The agreement obligates the member states to grant freedom of movement and freedom of employment to each other's nationals. The total population of the Mercosur countries is 230 million. The agreement hinges on the (expected) assent of each of the national parliaments. See Gonzalo Baeza, *Latin America nears broad immigration pact*, UPI Release (Nov. 27, 2002). Other regional arrangements providing for

either free or less restricted migration have been undertaken in West Africa, Central Africa, the Andean Pact (several South American countries), and the Nordic Community. See generally Richard Plender, International Migration Law, chs. 6, 8 (rev. 2d ed. 1988). New Zealand and Australia permit their nationals to travel freely between the two countries. See, e.g., (New Zealand) Immigration Regulations 1987, No. 301, 1st Sched., Part II.

In 1993 the governments of Mexico, the United States, and Canada signed the North American Free Trade Agreement [NAFTA]. Except for some provisions on nonimmigrants (see page 377 below), there was no attempt to address immigration.

Should there be some sort of North American free movement treaty? Two respected commentators have recently suggested both the wisdom and the long-term inevitability of the free movement of labor within North America. See T. Alexander Aleinikoff, *Legal Immigration Reform: Toward Rationality and Equity*, in Richard D. Lamm & Alan Simpson, Center for Immigration Studies, Blueprints for an Ideal Legal Immigration Policy, Center Paper 17 (March 2001), http://cis.org/articles/2001/blueprints/toc.html; Kevin R. Johnson, *Legal Immigration in the 21st Century*, in Lamm & Simpson, above.

9.   The broad question raised by this section has been whether, given the existing criteria for citizenship, the exclusion of noncitizens is morally defensible. In chapter 13 you will have the opportunity to consider what the criteria for citizenship ought to be and whether the law should even embody the concept of citizenship at all.

10.   A related question is the morality of *emigration* restrictions. For an effective criticism of national policies that prevent people from leaving, see Alan Dowty, Closed Borders—The Contemporary Assault on Freedom of Movement (1987). For a thoughtful analysis of both the conceptual and the political links between emigration and immigration, see Thomas Kleven, *Why International Law Favors Emigration over Immigration*, 33 U. Miami Inter–Amer. L. Rev. 69 (2002).

SECTION C.   IMMIGRATION, RACE, CULTURE, AND LANGUAGE

The immigration policies of any nation obviously affect its racial, cultural, and linguistic composition. Conversely, considerations of race, culture, and language influence immigration policies. Official government policy aside, public sentiments about immigration profoundly affect the daily lives of immigrants, the daily lives of those native-born ethnic minorities who are publicly perceived as associated with immigration, and the national community as a whole. In this book, the materials on the relationship of immigration policy to race, culture, and language are organized in the following way:

The present subsection considers questions broadly related to multiculturalism. Do we *want* a multicultural society? What does the term really mean? How much do we value assimilation? How much do we value cultural pluralism? Do the two values conflict? What does it mean to be a nation? How important is a common racial or cultural heritage? How important is a common language? Normative values aside, how do immigrants affect the racial, cultural, or linguistic life of the nation?

A separate but related subject is how public attitudes on race, culture, and language have actually shaped United States immigration policy, both historically and today. This book explores that subject in two ways. It is treated explicitly as part of the more general discussion, in section F below, of the politics of immigration. The subject is also considered pervasively, in connection with several specific historical and contemporary immigration developments—for example, the effects of anti-Asian sentiments on the early Asian exclusion laws (chapter 2); the relationship between race and such programs as the national origins quota system, per-country limits, and the admission of "diversity" immigrants (chapter 3); the abuse of Mexican guest workers under the Bracero program (chapter 4); the issues surrounding the profiling of Muslims, Arabs, and others in the context of immigration and national security (chapter 10); the racial underpinnings of the Haitian interdiction program (chapter 11); the racial issues that surfaced in California during the Proposition 187 campaign (chapter 12); the racial implications of employer sanctions (chapter 12); and the race discrimination remedies established by IRCA and by the Civil Rights Act of 1964 (chapter 12).

A third set of related issues concerns the impact of public attitudes and behavior on immigrants themselves and on those ethnic minorities whom many members of the public consciously or unconsciously treat as foreign. Native-born and naturalized United States citizens of Asian, Latino, or Arab descent are especially likely to experience such treatment, as the literature you will see illustrates. This subject is part of subsection H, which deals generally with immigrants' self-identities and the concept of "home."

With that introduction, we return to the theme of the present subsection—the link between immigration and multiculturalism. The writings excerpted below display the views of four commentators on the roles that race, culture, and language have played, and should play, in American immigration policy. Because several of those pieces refer to the 1965 immigration reforms, here is a one-paragraph refresher on what those reforms were:

Since 1921, United States law has limited the number of immigrants who could be admitted to the United States from any one country in any one year. Until 1965, those limits varied from country to country. United States law made each country's limit proportional to the number of Americans whose national origins could be traced to that country. The objective was to preserve the existing ethnic composition of the United States population and, in particular, to minimize the immigration of southern Europeans, eastern Europeans (particularly Jews), and Asians. But in 1965, in the anti-discriminatory spirit of the 1964 Civil Rights Act, Congress repealed these "national origins" quotas and substituted a uniform per-country limit of (then) 20,000 immigrants per year. The moment the national origins constraints were removed, both the absolute numbers and the percentages of immigrants who were from southern Europe, eastern Europe, and Asia all rapidly increased. Ever since, immigration commentators and public officials have vigorously debated the pros and cons of the 1965 reforms.

The first excerpt, from a book by Peter Schuck, provides some of the critical background on the subject of diversity. The second excerpt is from one of the most attention-getting of the recent anti-immigration writings. The author, Peter Brimelow, is himself an immigrant from England. Responses from Kevin Johnson and Juan Perea follow.

Peter H. Schuck, Diversity in America—Keeping Government at a Safe Distance

Pages 3–7 (2003).

America is probably the most diverse society on earth—certainly the most diverse industrial one. This is true regardless of how one thinks about or measures diversity or which kind of diversity is under discussion. * * *

This diversity is *itself* remarkably diverse—and dynamic. Like a blastula of cells undergoing mitosis, American society constantly proliferates new divisions and differentiations. * * *

Remarkably, this diversification is occurring amid social developments that commentators usually consider homogenizing. The national mass media, advertising, and popular culture penetrate every nook and cranny of our lives. Latinos, Asians, and other groups increasingly intermarry with whites and with each other. The federal government deploys much of its political, fiscal, and regulatory power in a quest for national uniformity. A steadily aging population buttresses familiar demographic patterns. Some pundits, eager to debunk Arthur Schlesinger's claim that diversity is unraveling the social fabric, even assert that "[w]hile ideologically 'all are different,' Americans in fact are remarkably 'all the same.'"

Yet diversity grows apace despite these homogenizing factors, and sometimes because of them. While the number of daily newspapers has declined, the number and variety of other mass media outlets—cable, radio, satellite, the Internet, films—have vastly increased. Advertising is more highly differentiated in order to reach diverse audiences, specialized interests, and niche markets. More diverse immigrants, religious sectarianism, linguistic enclaves, and ideological shifts make ethnic identity—a term hardly used before the 1950s—more salient. Women have entered and transformed previously all-male occupations. Congress has permitted states, localities, and private actors to go their own separate ways in many policy domains. Economic and medical advances for the elderly have multiplied their lifestyle choices. Fringe groups, free to purify their political ideologies, can appeal to narrow, discontented voter blocs. Suburbs, long derided by urban elites as the triumph of bland uniformity over piquant diversity, increasingly mimic the heterogeneous cities they surround. Corporate culture, traditionally conformist, now deploys the theory, practice, and rhetoric of diversity. Popular culture has become so transracial, according to one black commentator, that it spells "the end of white America."

The growing social acceptance of diversity is nowhere more striking than in the evolving views of openly gay relationships and lifestyles by a society that harshly repressed them—and to an extent still does. * * *

* * *

The traditional resistance to diversity should not surprise us. * * * [F]ew thinkers and fewer political or religious leaders in world history have considered diversity to be anything but a threat that should be suppressed or contained. Even today, most societies would view the claim that diversity is a social virtue as subversive, if not suicidal, nonsense. For them, toleration is but a survival tactic, a temporary expedient. * * *

One can easily understand, then, why Crèvecoeur, Tocqueville, James Bryce, Dickens, and many other visitors to America have been perplexed as well as intrigued by our diversity. So far as one can tell from their writings, none of these close observers of American diversity ever endorsed it for their own societies. Even those who most admired it seriously doubted whether the United States could sustain a strong civil society and a democracy built with such disparate social materials. Tocqueville, who uncannily prophesied the long Russo–U.S. struggle, also predicted that America's diversity would culminate in a race war. The notion that American democracy and civil society could coexist with a far greater diversity than they or anyone else could then imagine would have struck them as lunacy.

Yet this is precisely what happened in the decades following Appomattox. Despite (or perhaps because of) a succession of crises—industrialization, mass immigration, the Great Depression, wars, the McCarthy era, the civil rights and antiwar movements, new waves of even more diverse immigration, and now a war on terrorism waged in regions from which many Americans and new immigrants come—the American polity's enduring stability and unity remain the envy of the world. At the dawn of the twenty-first century, every other polyglot nation—India, Indonesia, Russia, Nigeria, Turkey, South Africa, Sri Lanka, and even Canada—is at serious risk of fragmenting into ethnic shards. (Australia and Switzerland stand, so far, as notable exceptions.) Indeed, even strong unitary states like the United Kingdom, Spain, France, and China, and religiously homogeneous states like Belgium, are being roiled by militant demands for devolution or even full independence. In sharp contrast, the United States has maintained its social and political cohesion, even achieving a kind of cultural coherence (though this is more debatable). Moreover, it has done so without sacrificing its economic, social, and cultural dynamism.

How has this singular feat been accomplished? That question is among the most compelling and complex issues facing diverse societies like ours. This book analyzes an important part of the answer: the role of law. It examines the different ways and policy contexts in which we have used law to protect, import, define, certify, subsidize, mandate, exploit—in a word, *manage*—diversity. "Manage" is a serviceable term to characterize how government self-consciously approaches diversity—so long as one bears in mind that "manage" includes both decisions to make diversity a subject of active legal intervention and decisions to leave diversity to informal unregulated choices.

Peter Brimelow, Alien Nation—Common Sense About America's Immigration Disaster

Pages 116–19, 123–26, 202–03, 206–09, 216–17, 264–65 (1995).

"So What?" In Perspective

Race! *RACE!!* As an immigrant, I was fascinated, once again, to watch the mere threat of an accusation of racism send the native born Americans scattering for cover like hightailing rabbits. * * *

Similarly, * * * an implicit accusation of racism is the common reaction of a vocal minority of Americans to news of their country's shifting ethnic balance: *"So what?"* And, given prevailing sensitivities, it is the most dangerous response to answer.

I say a vocal minority because I think the vast majority of Americans regard as just a matter of common sense that the composition of a country's population cannot, in fact, be changed without risking dramatic consequences. You can tell from the momentary perplexity that comes into their eyes when confronted with the "So What?" reflex.

But they lack the language to express their concerns. So they hesitate and fall silent. Time and again, the "So What?" reflex succeeds in effectively crippling all discussion of America's impeding ethnic revolution in particular—and, indeed, of immigration in general.

This happens although there are some extraordinary aspects of the impeding ethnic revolution that, by any standard, deserve discussion in a democracy:

- *It is unprecedented in history.* No sovereign state has ever undergone such a radical and rapid transformation.

- *It is wholly and entirely the result of government policy.* Immigration is causing both the shifting American ethnic balance and also the projected massive increase of overall population. Left to themselves, pre–1965 Americans would be stabilizing both their ethnic proportions and their overall numbers.

* * *

The entire question needs to be refocused as follows:

- The onus should not be on critics of current immigration policy to explain their motives. Instead, supporters of current policy must explain why they wish to transform the American nation as it had evolved by 1965.

In other words, the answer to the "So What?" reflex is "So why?" *Why does America have to be transformed? What have you got against it?*

There is a class of people in America who absolutely, positively (as it says in the Federal Express TV ads) do want to transform America. And they look to immigration to help them achieve this object. Their alienation from America as it currently exists is so powerful as to justify calling them "alienists"—the opposite of the much-denounced "nativists" whose attachment to America is so intense that they distrust anyone who might conceivably change it.

Alienists, therefore, do have answers to the question "So why?" One common alienist answer: *because American whites must be swamped by immigration to make it impossible for them to act on their racist impulses.*

[As evidence, Brimelow here quotes one Jewish advocate's opinion that, after World War II, the American Jewish community played a leadership role in repealing the national origins quotas—Ed.]

* * *

Well—*Do* Multiracial Societies Work?

Over three years after I first met Julian Simon [an advocate of increased immigration—Ed.], I was having dinner with him to debate our differences. We got on the question of whether multiethnic and multiracial societies can work.

"Yugoslavia . . .," I began, thinking of the Serb–Croatian–Bosnian war that had exploded into the headlines.

"Yes! Yugoslavia!" he interrupted gleefully. "That supports my case, doesn't it?"

I was so surprised that I felt my jaw drop—something that really happens, I find, and not just in cartoons. It took me several seconds to realize what he meant:

- The former Yugoslavs are fighting *despite* the fact that they are all the same race (white). Indeed, they are all members of the same general ethnic group (South Slav). Even the language spoken by the two major contestants (Serbs and Croats) is basically the same (although written, respectively, in Cyrillic and Roman script).

So—Simon is saying—you can't blame all civil conflict or the divisive results on nontraditional immigration. Homogeneity is no guarantee against strife.

All right, all right! For the record, let me admit (in fact, assert): you can't blame *everything* on immigration or on racial differences.

But who said you could? The fact remains that the Yugoslav spectacle can only be seen as chilling—and as a Horrid Warning about current U.S. immigration policy. The differences between the Yugoslavs are indeed relatively minor—certainly compared to the differences between the American nation of 1965 and the immigrants who are now arriving. *And that's the point.* Those minor differences were still enough to tear the country apart.

* * *

Multiracial Societies: The Evidence

Of course, our follow-up question, about whether multiracial societies work, is a fairly shocking one.

It's actually much more shocking than the original question—why do the immigration enthusiasts want to transform America? No one ever thinks to ask that. But asking about whether multiracial societies work is quite obviously a direct challenge to America's recently established religion. And, since America has been biracial since Colonial times, it appears to imply a pessimistic view of the prospects for black-white harmony—the greatest problem of American life (until the post–1965 immigration).

But there's a plain fact to be considered: the evidence that multiracial societies work is—what shall we say?—*not very encouraging*.

There have, of course, been multiracial societies (strictly speaking, usually multiethnic) in the past. Famous examples are the Roman Empire, or the Arab Caliphate, which briefly ruled from Spain to Samarkand in the name of Muhammad. But these were old-fashioned despotisms, not modern democracies. And, even so, ethnic divisions still kept surfacing. * * *

Heterogeneous empires that lasted, such as the Eastern Roman Empire of Byzantium, which survived until 1453, were generally based on a core ethnic-group—distinctly like our old friend the "racial hegemony of white Americans." In the case of Byzantium, for instance, this core group was Greek.

In modern times, there has been a lot of seductive murmuring about internationalism, united nations, new world orders, and so on. But, meanwhile, the role of ethnicity and race has proved to be elemental—absolute—fundamental. Look at the record, working back from the present:

[Here Brimelow cites examples of multi-ethnic countries that have eventually broken up. His list includes Czechoslovakia, the Soviet Union, Yugoslavia, Lebanon, Cyprus, Pakistan, and Malaysia.—Ed.]

And these are just the cases where ethnic and racial differences have actually succeeded in breaking a country up. Many other cases are not yet resolved, because of often-bloody repression.

* * *

Immigration Has Consequences: A Less Perfect Union

> *It is commonly said that America is more than a nation; it is an idea. My thesis today is the precise opposite: America is more than an idea; it is a nation.*

—John O'Sullivan,

Boston University, March 31, 1993

There is no room in this country for hyphenated American-
ism. . . . The one absolutely certain way of bringing this
nation to ruin, of preventing all possibility of its continu-
ing to be a nation at all, would be to permit it to become a
tangle of squabbling nationalities.

—Theodore Roosevelt,

speech before the Knights of Columbus, New York, October 12,
1915

* * *

Nation-State and Nation

Let's start with a definition. What is a "nation-state"? It is the
political expression of a nation. And what is a "nation"? It is an *ethnocul-*
tural community—an interlacing of ethnicity and culture. Invariably, it
speaks one language.

In recent years in the United States, there has been a tendency to
emphasize the cultural part of the equation. But this is to miss a critical
point. The word "nation" is derived from the Latin *nescare*, to be born. It
intrinsically implies a link by blood. A nation in a real sense is an extended
family. The merging process by which all nations are created is not merely
cultural, but to a considerable extent biological, through intermarriage.

* * *

Some American commentators, for various reasons, find the idea of a
nation's common ethnicity deeply distressing. They regularly denounce
references to the subject as "nativism" or "tribalism."

* * *

A Universal Nation?

* * * Ben Wattenberg is able to get away with talking about the
United States becoming a "Universal Nation."

On its face, this is a contradiction in terms. A nation cannot be
universal because it is, of its essence, specific—ethnically and culturally.
* * *

It's possible, as Wattenberg variously implies, that he means the
diverse immigrant groups will eventually intermarry, producing what he
calls, quoting the English poet John Masefield, a "wondrous race." Or that
they will at least be assimilated by American culture, which, while globally
dominant, is hardly "universal." But meanwhile there are hard questions:

What language is this "universal nation" going to speak? How is it
going to avoid ethnic strife? dual loyalties? collapsing like the
Tower of Babel?

Wattenberg is not asked to reconcile these contradictions, although he is aware of at least some of them, because the ideal of an American nation-state is in eclipse in the American political conversation.

Ironically, the same weaknesses were apparent in the rather similar concept of "cultural pluralism" which was invented by Horace M. Kallen at the height of the last great immigration debate, before the Quota Acts of the 1920s. * * *

* * *

America: Idea or Nation?

And Kallenism underlies another helpful remark that someone always makes in any discussion of U.S. immigration policy: *"America isn't a nation like the other nations—it's an idea."*

Once more, this American exceptionalism is really more a matter of degree than kind. Many other nations have some sort of ideational reinforcement. Quite often it is religious, such as Poland's Roman Catholicism; sometimes cultural, such as France's ineffable Frenchness. And occasionally it is political.

* * *

What is unusual in the current American immigration debate, however, is that Americans are now being urged to abandon the bonds of a common ethnicity so completely and to trust instead entirely to ideology to hold together their state (. . . polity).

This is an extraordinary experiment, like suddenly replacing all the blood in a patient's body. History suggests little reason to suppose it will succeed. * * *

* * *

Let's be clear about this: the American experience with immigration has been a triumphant success. It has so far transcended anything seen in Europe as to make the application of European lessons an exercise to be performed with care.

But there are very clear reasons why the American nation has been able to absorb and assimilate immigrants. In considering further immigration, its enthusiasts must ask themselves honestly: *do these reasons still apply?*

One reason America could assimilate immigrants, as we have seen, is that there were regular pauses for digestion. Another reason is that the American political elite *wanted the immigrants to assimilate*. And it did not hesitate to ensure that they did.

Over two hundred years of U.S. history, a number of tried-and-true, but undeniably tough, assimilation techniques had been perfected. But today, they have been substantially abandoned.

The economic culture of the United States has changed significantly—from classical liberalism to government-regulated welfare statism. Earlier immigrants were basically free to succeed or fail. And many failed: as we have seen, as many as 40 percent of the 1880–1920 immigrants went back home. But now, public policy interposes itself, with the usual debatable results.

* * *

And it's not just the American economic culture that has changed. So has the political culture. Almost a century ago, the last Great Wave of immigrants were met with the unflinching demand that they "Americanize." Now they are told that they should retain and reinforce their diversity.

Ethnically fueled "multiculturalism" taught in the public schools * * * inevitably raises the question: *Is there still an "American Idea"—and if so, what is it?*

[Here, Brimelow criticizes affirmative action and, in particular, its applicability to "Hispanics"—a group he argues is not defined by a common race, culture, or even language.—Ed.]

* * *

Immigration and the National Question

[This is] *The National Question:*

- **Is America still that interlacing of ethnicity and culture that we call a nation? Can the United States survive as a nation-state, the political expression of that nation?**

To begin at the most sensitive point:

The American nation of 1965, nearly 90 percent white, was explicitly promised that the new immigration policy would not shift the country's racial balance. But it did.

Race is destiny in American politics. Its importance has only been intensified by the supposedly color-blind civil rights legislation of the 1960s—which paradoxically has turned out to mean elaborate race-conscious affirmative action programs. Any change in the racial balance must obviously be fraught with consequences for the survival and success of the American nation.

It is simply common sense that Americans have a legitimate interest in their country's racial balance. It is common sense that they have a right to insist that their government stop shifting it. Indeed, it seems to me that they have a right to insist that it be shifted back.

This does not necessarily mean an absolute ban on any group. *"Numbers are of the essence,"* in the words of Enoch Powell, the prophetic critic of Britain's disastrous postimperial immigration policy. In small numbers, all kinds of immigrants can arrive in America and be assimilated. Culture is a substitute for ethnicity. But numbers so high that they shift the American demographic balance make this impossible.

One right that Americans certainly have is the right to insist that immigrants, whatever their race, become Americans. The full force of public policy should be placed behind another "Americanization" campaign, modeled on that during the last Great Wave of Immigration. All diversion of public funds to promote "diversity," "multiculturalism" and foreign-language retention must be struck down as subversive of this American ideal. Hyphenated identities must remain a private matter, as throughout most of American history. An English-language requirement for potential immigrants would make Americanization easier. The English-language requirement for citizenship should be enforced and the various recent exceptions, such as for spouses and the elderly, abolished—they were symbolic gestures anyway, and now the symbols are needed elsewhere. There must be a concerted legislative attack on bilingual manifestations, beginning with the U.S. Department of Education's promotion of "bilingual" education. (The Quebec government's defense of French through restrictions on English should be studied with care.) A Constitutional amendment making English the official language of the United States could be a decisive step.

* * *

Kevin R. Johnson, Fear of an "Alien Nation": Race, Immigration and Immigrants

7 Stanford Law & Policy Rev. 111, 111–17 (1996).

* * * Peter Brimelow's provocative book, Alien Nation: Common Sense About America's Immigration Disaster, has sparked considerable discussion and controversy. In synch with the move toward restrictionism, Brimelow attributes a wide array of political, economic, and social problems to immigration, immigrants, and "immigration enthusiasts." Proclaiming that his call for drastic overhaul of U.S. immigration laws is justified by the fact that "race and ethnicity are destiny in American politics," Brimelow strikingly illustrates recurrent political and racial features of the immigration debate in this country. In attacking affirmative action, multiculturalism, and bilingual education, he in effect blames immigrants for the dismal state of race-relations in the United States.

Reading between the lines of Alien Nation, one discerns Brimelow's special concern with "Hispanic" immigration. This is consistent with the observation that some anti-immigrant sentiment in the United States, though clearly not all, is animated by anti-Latino sentiment. Brimelow believes that all Latinos, born-and-bred citizens as well as immigrants from Latin America, damage the American fabric and threaten the nation. The anti-Latino tinge to Brimelow's restrictionist arguments reveals the underside of the immigration debate in the 1990s.

Besides exemplifying political and racial scapegoating, Alien Nation illustrates the deeply personal and volatile nature of the immigration debate in the United States, particularly during times of social crisis. Similar to other incendiary public policy issues, such as crime, affirmative action, and taxes, immigration impacts our communities in readily discernible ways. Despite attacking others for allowing personal concerns to color their views, Brimelow reveals how the threats he personally feels from immigration influence his restrictionist views. He pleads for the United States to admit more immigrants like him—white, English-speaking, educated, and from a Western culture—and repeatedly invokes fears about the future for his young son, whom he describes with pride as being white with blue eyes and blond hair.

* * *

I. THE CHANGING RACIAL AND ETHNIC DEMOGRAPHICS OF IMMIGRATION

To place the modern immigration debate in context, we must consider a few demographic trends over the last thirty years. In 1965, Congress repealed the national origin quota system, which favored immigration from nations in northwestern Europe. Since that change in the law, a much greater proportion of immigrants have been people of color from developing nations. For example, between 1955 and 1964, 7.7% of all immigrants to the United States came from Asia, compared to 39.6% in fiscal year 1993. The family reunification provisions of the immigration laws, which favor persons seeking to join family members in this country, have contributed to the demographic shift. More people of color have immigrated to this country since 1965 than in preceding years, and in a sort of chain migration they have been able to bring family members as well.

Immigration from Mexico has attracted particular public and academic attention. Mexico contributed more legal immigrants to the United States than any other country in fiscal year 1993. Mexican citizens constituted the vast majority of persons "legalized" under the Immigration Reform and Control Act of 1986. A significant portion of the undocumented persons in this country, though not as many as popularly believed, also come from Mexico. It is interesting that any increase in Mexican migration cannot be attributed to the 1965 law that eliminated the national origin quotas. Indeed, that law for the first time limited immigration from the Western Hemisphere; Congress sought to avoid increased immigration from Latin America. Consequently, the demise of the quota system can hardly be blamed, as Brimelow seems to do, for the increased levels of legal immigration from Mexico or from Latin America in general.

In a society in which race is a prominent dividing line, one would be surprised if the fact that many newcomers are people of color did not have a social impact. Nevertheless, in light of modern sensibilities, most in the mainstream do not state publicly that an excessive number of people of color immigrate to the United States. Although this indicates progress in our nation's racial sensitivities, it does not mean that race does not influence the immigration debate. Reliance upon facially neutral proxies for race and ethnicity may disguise invidious motivations. Objections to the language and culture of immigrants and their so-called refusal to assimilate, for example, may conceal more deeply-seated racial concerns. As Professor Bill Ong Hing has observed:

> While this culture-based argument studiously avoids race and ethnicity, the implications of the argument are distinctly race-based. Given the huge numbers of immigrants who enter this country from Asian and Latin American countries whose citizens are not white and who in most cases do not speak English, criticism of the inability to speak English coincides neatly with race.

* * *

In analyzing the negative reaction to today's immigrants, it is important to distinguish between two distinct forces at work: nativism and racism. Nativism, defined by John Higham as the "intense opposition to an internal minority on the grounds of its foreign (i.e., 'un-American') connections," has been historically directed at most waves of immigrants—white and non-white alike. Although many large immigrant groups have provoked nativist reactions, immigrants of color have been singled out for special disfavor. In general, the presence of non-white immigrants at any moment in this nation's history has heightened the intensity of anti-immigrant sentiment. For example, although German and Irish immigrants in the nineteenth century faced hostility, the anti-immigrant sentiment directed at them unquestionably did not compare to the racially-driven animus directed at Chinese immigrants during the same century.

* * *

II.   IMMIGRATION AND THE CREATION OF AN "ALIEN NATION"

Peter Brimelow and many who share his views object to current immigration laws on several counts. Brimelow opposes the current level of immigration, which as previously mentioned increased substantially in the early 1990s. He also voices concern about the alleged adverse economic impact of immigration, although ultimately conceding that immigrants neither help nor hurt the economy to any significant degree. These, however, are not Brimelow's primary concerns, nor the ones that make Alien Nation notable. Unlike many restrictionists, Brimelow does not shy away from the volatile issue of race. Indeed, the central thesis of Alien Nation is that the race and culture of many of today's immigrants pose a serious threat to the nation as we know it. Brimelow specifically expresses serious concern with the impact that the race of today's immigrants will have on the political process.

A dialogue on the racial demographics of immigration is well worth having. However, the seamier side of Brimelow's views on the subject make Alien Nation an unlikely starting point for constructive discussion. For example, he repeatedly comments on the physical differences of people of color. Brimelow laments that since 1965, "immigrants are overwhelmingly visible minorities from the Third World." One may question the special concern with "visible minorities." Brimelow's comparison of an Immigration and Naturalization Service office to a New York City subway is similarly thought-provoking: "You find yourself in an underworld that is not just teeming but is also almost entirely colored." Combining the "underworld," often used synonymously with crime, with the antiquated term "colored" is typical of the negative racial imagery used in Alien Nation when discussing immigrants of color.

Notwithstanding these statements, Brimelow denies that his objections to immigration from developing nations are purely based on skin color. Instead, he contends that immigrants of color are culturally deficient, placing great emphasis on the need to speak English (apparently as a native language). As discussed previously, such concerns may mask racial concerns and, at a minimum, coincide with race. Consider some of the so-called cultural problems allegedly posed by today's immigrants.

A. "THE NEED FOR HOMOGENEITY"

Brimelow proclaims that "by introducing diverse populations, [immigration] strikes at the nation-state's Achilles' heel: the need for homogeneity." Appealing to tradition, he declares that "the American nation has always had a specific ethnic core. And that core has been white." To avert the impending disaster attributable to increased diversity, Brimelow apparently endorses revival of the much-maligned national origin quotas of the pre–1965 immigration laws.

There is a critical piece missing from Brimelow's argument for cultural homogeneity. Except for a few references to this nation's unique diversity, and a suggestion or two that such diversity may ultimately produce a Bosnia or Lebanon in the United States, Brimelow fails to provide support for the need for homogeneity. Because the premise is so central to his conclusions, this missing element is a damning flaw. Even some conservatives strongly disagree with the prescription of national homogeneity. * * *

In contrast to those attempting to constructively analyze the issues posed by an increasingly heterogeneous society, Brimelow simplistically advocates a return to an idyllic past when homogeneity supposedly reigned. In so doing, he virtually ignores this nation's long history of diversity. African Americans and Latinos have lived in the United States for centuries, and a great variety of white ethnic immigrants have come to this nation.

Moreover, the practicality of a return to a homogeneous United States is far from clear. In light of the diversity of this nation's current population, it is highly doubtful that any colorable proposal—especially one that focuses exclusively on immigration—would result in the creation of a homogeneous Anglo Saxon nation. In Linda Chavez's words, the mere idea "seem[s] ridiculous today in a country in which 150 million persons are descended from people who did not come here from the British Isles."

B.   TOO MANY "HISPANICS"

Brimelow above all else faults excessive immigration from Latin America for many of society's problems, a recurring feature of the immigration debate in the twentieth century. He observes that the Hispanic population grew from 2.6% of the population in 1950 to 9% in 1990. He stretches the facts by suggesting that illegal immigration since 1986 has been "overwhelmingly Hispanic." The Immigration and Naturalization Service, however, estimates that the undocumented population in this country is diverse, including significant numbers of people from many different nations, including non-Hispanic nations such as Canada, Poland, and Italy, as well as from Latin American nations like Mexico, El Salvador, and Guatemala. Deeper political fears are reflected in the suggestion that Mexican immigrants are either co-conspirators with or simply unwitting dupes of Mexican–American radicals and the Mexican government. Offering little elaboration and no proof, Brimelow speculates that heavy Mexican immigration to the United States might result in a movement to reunite part of the Southwest with Mexico.

1.   "Hispanics," Immigrants, and Affirmative Action

A careful study of Alien Nation reveals that Brimelow's concerns with Latinos are not limited to immigrants. The book singles out "Hispanics," an all-encompassing referent that includes citizens as well as immigrants, as a minority group that deserves particular criticism. Rejecting the term "Hispanic," as do many who fall within the category, Brimelow gratuitously argues that the Bureau of the Census should abolish the term. He further proclaims that

> "Hispanics" are being treated by U.S. government agencies as an homogenous "protected class" essentially as a result of ethnic lobbying in Washington. They have been supplied with "leaders" financed in large part by the Ford Foundation. They are now much less encouraged to "Americanize" than anything seen in the previous Great Wave. Instead, they are being issued with a new, artificial "Hispanic" identity.

How this relates to immigration reform, the ostensible topic of the book, is uncertain. However, it reveals the scapegoating phenomenon so prevalent in U.S. immigration history: Latin American immigrants are blamed for such perceived problems as affirmative action, which has much more to do with U.S. citizens than immigrants.

As this attack illustrates, Brimelow lumps all Latinos in the United States together with Latin–American immigrants. This is understandable because, in Brimelow's view, all Latinos are foreign to this nation's "white" core. But not all Latinos in the United States are immigrants. Mexicans, for example, lived in the Southwest long before the region became part of this country. Moreover, the Latino community is far from monolithic and is especially heterogeneous with respect to citizenship and immigration status. This community includes citizens and noncitizens, both lawful permanent residents and undocumented immigrants. Though acknowledging diversity in the Latino community, Brimelow fails to make a fundamental distinction between Latino immigrants and Latino citizens.

* * *

2. Bilingualism

Brimelow also rails against "all forms of government-imposed 'bilingualism,'" a movement often associated with the Latino community. Bilingual education, however, is neither supported exclusively, nor perhaps even primarily, by immigrants; U.S. citizens who fear a loss of cultural identity also support protection of their languages. Indeed, Latinos born and raised in this country initially pressed for bilingual education and have the political power—power denied to noncitizens—to succeed in securing the creation of such programs. The demand for bilingual education cannot simply be marginalized as an "immigrant movement." Moreover, evidence shows that access to bilingual education does not prevent Latino immigrants and their children from learning English.

* * *

3. Assimilation

When confining his complaints to Latino immigrants, as opposed to all Latinos, Brimelow seems concerned with their alleged refusal to assimilate, a proposition with which some conservatives disagree. However, Alien Nation fails to advocate measures that would encourage assimilation, such as additional funding for English-as-a-Second–Language programs and streamlining the naturalization process to allow immigrants to become citizens more quickly. Brimelow instead offers a deceptively simple answer: bar the immigration of people of color so that we no longer have to worry about assimilation.

In stark contrast to Brimelow's approach, some commentators have tried to offer constructive proposals to foster immigrant assimilation. Though the concept of "assimilation" is open to many interpretations, it is difficult to argue that efforts should not be made to integrate immigrants into the political community. The same Latino activist groups that Brimelow derides, for example, have tried to integrate immigrants into the political community by encouraging naturalization.

* * *

C. VENTING PERSONAL FRUSTRATIONS

Besides its anti-Latino tilt, Alien Nation implicitly suggests why the immigration debate is so volatile. Immigration raises deeply personal and often emotional questions. Who will be permitted to join the American community? How do "they" fit in with "us"? How will "they" affect "my" life? Consequently, the immigration debate brings to the fore public concern with self-preservation and fear of change.

Despite Brimelow's principal focus on the race and culture of today's immigrants, immigration represents for Brimelow nothing more than a convenient soapbox from which to voice many political, social, and personal frustrations. In addition to concerns about affirmative action and bilingualism, Brimelow expresses dissatisfaction with developments as far-ranging as multiculturalism and sensitivity training in the workplace. * * *

* * *

Brimelow's personal motivations are strikingly illustrated on a much smaller scale by the book's discussion of the relative benefits of British and Zulu immigration. During his 1992 run for the presidency, Patrick Buchanan provoked controversy by contending that British immigration would cause fewer problems for the people of Virginia than Zulu immigration. A Wall Street Journal editorial disagreed on the ground that Zulu immigrants probably would work harder than English ones. Lashing back with great ferocity, Brimelow asserts that such a view "reveals an utter innocence about the reality of ethnic and cultural differences, let alone about little things like tradition and history." He gratuitously mentions that the founder of the Zulu Empire "among other exploits killed all his concubines' children, sometimes with his own hands, massacred some seven thousand of his own subjects to mark his mother's death, sliced open a hundred pregnant women to satisfy a fleeting interest in embryology, and ordered executions at whim daily until his assassination in 1828...." Although this inflammatory outburst allows Brimelow to vent steam about the apparent insult to his countrymen, it is woefully out of place in a serious discussion of modern immigration.

D.   NATIVISM PURE AND SIMPLE

In the end, one would be hard-pressed not to classify Brimelow, who readily offers to defend nativists, as a nativist who relies on race and culture to define what is "un-American" and "foreign." Indeed, Brimelow's racially-tinged arguments and alarmist tone are disturbingly reminiscent of past nativist appeals. Consistent with the self-perception of previous nativist groups, most notably the Know Nothings of the nineteenth century, Brimelow describes critics of current U.S. immigration policies as "Patriots."

Juan F. Perea, "Am I an American or Not?" Reflections on Citizenship, Americanization, and Race, in Noah M.J. Pickus (Ed.), Immigration and Citizenship in the Twenty–First Century

Pages 49, 60, 62–66, 68 (1998).

* * * During the 1990s we are witnessing a resurgence of nativism, anti-immigrant sentiment in many respects like the nativism of the 1920s. Interestingly, far from celebrating the relative race neutrality in our laws after 1965, some current advocates of immigration restriction *blame* these

same laws for what they perceive as a threatening and disunifying degree of racial and ethnic diversity in the country. Immigration restrictionists complain bitterly that the national origins quotas were abandoned in a deceptive way that deliberately understated the amount of immigrants from Latin America and Asia over the past thirty years. As Peter Brimelow has written in *Alien Nation*, "The current wave of immigration—and therefore America's shifting ethnic balance—is wholly and entirely the result of government policy. Specifically, it is the result of the Immigration Act of 1965, and the further legislation of 1986 and 1990." Brimelow laments the increasing number of people of color in the United States and argues for a return to its white racial roots: "The American nation has always had a specific ethnic core. And that core has been white." Brimelow's argument for a return to race-conscious immigration policies designed to restore white supremacy confirms the importance of race as a current variable in immigration debates and in the conception of American nationality. While there are many less objectionable, valid arguments for immigration restriction, and while Brimelow's may represent an extreme position, the popularity of his book suggests that he represents a significant current of thought among those opposed to immigration.

[Here, Perea criticizes a proposed constitutional amendment that would withhold United States citizenship from persons born in the United States to undocumented immigrant parents, and he marshals substantial evidence of a racial impetus for the proposal. He also argues that, at any rate, citizenship has often proven less valuable for citizens of color than for white citizens. He cites the treatment of Cherokee Indians, the abuse of Mexican–American citizens in the 1930s, and the internment of citizens of Japanese descent during World War II—Ed.]

The Proposed Revival of Americanization

If I am right that the value of citizenship varies by race, then I necessarily raise a question about the relation of race to Americanization, the process through which the country attempts to assimilate immigrants and make them citizens. I have argued earlier that assimilation, in the cases of the Cherokee and Japanese Americans, was of little avail when their civil rights interfered with the will of a majority of Americans. So I would argue that, like citizenship, Americanization has less value, in general, for people of color than for white immigrants. Indeed, some commentators have remarked on the extent to which Americanization has depended on adopting our existing racial hierarchies.

The Commission on Immigration Reform has reiterated "its call for the Americanization of new immigrants, that is, the cultivation of a shared commitment to the American values of liberty, democracy and equal opportunity." The commission envisions the core of American nationality as adherence to these principles: "Lawfully admitted newcomers of any ancestral nationality—without regard to race, ethnicity, or religion—truly become Americans when they give allegiance to these principles and values." The commission's 1997 report states several recommendations: for orienting and educating immigrants about our civic culture; for the acquisition of English; for testing the English-language competence of aspiring immigrants; and for federal and state support for these aspects of Americanization. The commission recognizes that immigration represents a *mutual and reciprocal* process and that "Americanization cannot be forced." The commission report states:

> Immigration presents mutual obligations. Immigrants must accept the obligations we impose—to obey our laws, to pay taxes, to respect other cultures and ethnic groups. At the same time, citizens incur obligations to provide an environment in which newcomers can become fully participating members of our society.

The commission also recommends education in our history and civic culture for all students, "immigrants and natives alike." The commission advocates a strong role for federal, state, and local governments and private institutions in the education of immigrants and aspiring citizens, regarding our civic culture, our democratic institutions, and English-language instruction.

The commission has altered its view of Americanization from the traditional view of one-way adaptation by immigrants to majoritarian norms to a reciprocal and more mutually respectful process. I believe this change is crucial, for Americans must learn to appreciate their new citizens and aspiring citizens and to treat them with less resentment, racism, and distrust. A reconceived Americanization, based on widespread education in the content and ideals of our civic culture, begins to counteract the massive anti-immigrant rhetoric that has swept the country in recent years, fomenting distrust and animosity towards legal and illegal immigrants alike.

The commission has written that Americanization involves "a shared commitment to the American values of liberty, democracy, and equal opportunity." These are core American values, and I believe this is the most important meaning of Americanization and U.S. nationality: Joining the nation must mean agreeing to abide by its enduring values and constitutional, democratic structures for political expression. In my view, the phrase "commitment to the American values of liberty, democracy, and equal opportunity" expresses well the essence of the civic culture that we ask aspiring immigrants to join.

Interestingly, the commission's current expression of the substance of our civic culture does not seem very different from much earlier understandings of American nationalism, including Kesler's exposition of the founding principles. As Philip Gleason has written, American nationalism was always based on ideology:

> A sense of distinctive peoplehood could be founded only on ideas ... because the great majority of Americans shared language, literature, religion, and other cultural traditions with the nation against which they had successfully rebelled ... The United States defined itself as a nation by commitment to the principles of liberty, equality, and government on the basis of consent, and the

nationality of its people derived from their identification with those principles.

However, the commission's current sense of equality as an essential component of our civic culture and ideology seems more well founded than ascribing that principle to the nation's Founders. Prior to the Fourteenth Amendment, "equality" was tautological and race-based: Only propertied white men considered themselves and each other equal. There was no notion of equality in the Constitution until 1868, with the adoption of the Equal Protection Clause of the Fourteenth Amendment. Even that equality-granting language was understood by its drafters to apply only to a formal legal equality—that is, equality in access to civil rights—and not to "social equality"—that is, full equality of stature and respect and full access to our public and private institutions. It was this very limited understanding of equality that made the separate-but-equal doctrine consistent with the equal protection clause.

It is not until much later, the period between the 1940s and the 1960s, that a commitment to equality in its present-day sense of full equal treatment can be considered part of American ideology and constitutive of American nationality. As a result of antidiscrimination efforts during and after World War II and the civil rights movement of the 1950s and 1960s, some national commitment to equality in all the spheres of life seems unquestionably to be part of our civic culture. However much we may debate the proper means of accomplishing equality, and the degree of its present accomplishment, equality as a constitutional and social goal seems firmly established today.

I think Americanization must be reframed, as the commission has, as a reciprocal and mutual process of accommodation, rather than a one-way process of assimilation by immigrants. Immigrants, aspiring Americans, have a relationship with current American citizens and with the country they wish to join. This relationship implies a mutuality of responsibility and obligation. As long as existing Americans do not fulfill the obligations of their civic culture, as long as we fail to honor the principles of liberty, democracy, and perhaps most importantly, equality, then we make Americanization an impossible dream. I suggest that, historically, problems of failed Americanization or assimilation are problems caused by the fear and racism of American citizens who feel little if any duty or obligation to ensure the success of aspiring immigrants, especially if those immigrants look different from them.

Existing Americans, therefore, are truly in need of Americanization. Americans must be educated about their civic culture, which includes those crucial ideals of equality, liberty, and democracy. Americans must accept the responsibility of making full membership possible to people of all races. Americans must accept that the American identity of the future, as well as the American identity of our past, has been multiracial, not solely a white, identity. They must bury, not resurrect, the Framers' conception of America as an all-white nation.

* * *

* * * Immigrants should and will learn English. The economic and social incentives to do so are overwhelming. Indeed, recent evidence suggests that recent immigrants, especially Latinos, are acquiring English at least as fast, if not faster than past generations of immigrants. But Americans should learn to respect the languages of immigrants. Americans should recognize that the United States has been a multilingual country from its beginning, when German, Dutch, French, and Indian languages could be heard in addition to English, until the present. The Articles of Confederation were ordered published by the Continental Congress in French and German, in addition to English. Indeed, several states were officially bilingual in different languages during the nineteenth century and, in the case of New Mexico, until 1952.

Our history cautions against restriction of the use of other languages as a way of supporting the use of English. Nativism has often sought expression through the restriction of foreign languages. The nativism of the World War I-era led to numerous state laws prohibiting the teaching and use of German. Today the Official English movement seeks legislation that would prohibit the federal government from acting in any language other than English, except in exceptional circumstances. * * *

* * *

The commission's renewed emphasis on Americanization, its attempt to "take the word back" and reclaim it with a different meaning than it came to have in the 1920s, raises the crucial issue of whether Americanization can be divorced from its history such that the term can have a different meaning today than it had during the time of its greatest excesses. I do not believe it is possible to uncouple this term from the history of its implementation. So the risk posed by renewed Americanization is that there will be nothing new about it. Despite the commission's apparently more balanced approach, the risk is that "Americanization" will mean the same coerced, one-way Anglocentric assimilation that it meant in the past. For these reasons, I believe it is a mistake to resurrect "Americanization." There is much less harm in simply offering to immigrants, without fanfare or "Americanization," instruction in the English language and in American ways of government and then letting them contribute to America as they will.

NOTES AND QUESTIONS

1. The last paragraph of the excerpt from Peter Schuck's "Diversity in America" reflects a central theme of his book—that the U.S. has managed diversity through a combination of affirmative governmental intervention and unregulated private action. As discussed in chapter 3, section D below (on the "diversity immigrant" program), Schuck praises diversity and acknowledges the legitimacy of government programs to protect diversity. Ultimately, however, he opposes government efforts to "create or promote any *particular* kind of diversity" (emphasis in original). Schuck at 123–31, 324.

2. Schuck also observes that diversity takes many forms. To what kinds of diversity do you think immigration contributes?

3. The U.S. Census Bureau reports that, as of March 2004, approximately 12% of the U.S. population was foreign-born. Of the foreign-born, 53% were born in Latin America (mainly Mexico and Central America), 25% in Asia, and 14% in Europe. U.S. Census Bureau, The Foreign–Born Population of the United States (Feb. 2005).

What sort of society has this combination of native-born Americans and immigrants actually built? Two competing metaphors are in common use. Under one vision, America is a melting pot; every ethnic group eventually "melts" into a unified community defined more by similarity than by difference. Under another vision, America is a patchwork quilt (or a mosaic); every piece maintains its own enclave and its distinctive culture, with the various communities coexisting side by side. One writing offers (as an ideal) an intermediate metaphor—a large bowl of granola. Under this vision, all the diverse ingredients retain their own distinctive flavors, no ingredient feels overwhelmed by the others, each ingredient brings out the best flavors of the others, the total useable protein is much greater than if all the ingredients were separated and eaten one at a time, and the resulting mix is zestier and more vibrant. See Stephen H. Legomsky, *Immigrants, Minorities, and Pluralism: What Kind of Society Do We Really Want?*, 6 Willamette J. Internat'l L. & Dispute Resolution 153, 160–61 (1998). Which of these visions do you think best describes present-day America?

4. What *should* the United States strive to be? Brimelow argues that, to succeed, the United States must be a "nation." He then defines "nation" as requiring a common ethnic core. Others (whom he cites) disagree; they maintain that common ethnicity is unnecessary if there is a common "idea" to which the nation's inhabitants subscribe. See Brimelow, above, at 203–11. Let us put aside the definitional question. Whatever the word "nation" signifies to different people, do you agree with Brimelow that ultimately the success of a sovereign state requires a homogeneous ethnic core? What, exactly, is wrong with a sovereign state—in this case the United States—deriving its sense of national identity from a common ideology rather than from a common ethnicity? Do you agree with Brimelow that such a strategy is doomed to fail?

5. Also at the heart of the debate are the 1965 reforms, summarized at the beginning of this subsection. Brimelow urges their repeal; if there must be immigration at all, he contends, the national origins quotas should be restored. Johnson and Perea both disagree. What is your view?

6. Frequently, the way a question is framed predetermines the answer. Brimelow complains that supporters of current United States immigration policy often respond to his observations about the emerging ethnic trends by asking "So what?". He objects to this response. He believes that critics of current policy should not be expected to "explain their motives." Rather, he argues, "supporters of current immigration policy must explain why they wish to transform the American nation as it had evolved by

1965." This is a crucial point for Brimelow. He argues that the case for the current policy hinges on an affirmative showing that the country would be better off with a higher nonwhite population percentage, and he challenges supporters of the current policy to make that showing. Has he framed the question properly?

7.　The reason Brimelow raises the burden of proof and motive issues is that, in his view, immigration supporters have a hidden agenda. He suggests that many of them "absolutely, positively . . . want to transform America . . . because American whites must be swamped by immigration to make it impossible for them to act on their racist impulses." Brimelow, above, at 119. Do you think this is what drives most (or many) supporters of the current policy?

8.　Kevin Johnson responds to Brimelow at several levels. One recurring theme in Johnson's work is the relation between nativism and racism. He argues that Americans who feel animosity toward people of color often transfer that animosity, consciously or unconsciously, to immigrants, a more socially acceptable target. See especially Kevin R. Johnson, *Race, The Immigration Laws, and Domestic Race Relations: A "Magic Mirror" into the Heart of Darkness*, 73 Indiana L.J. 1111, 1154–58 (1998). In the piece you just read, Johnson quotes Professor Bill Ong Hing, who makes an analogous point about the commentary and legislation on official English. In the present piece, Johnson also sees in the writings of Brimelow and in several recent political developments a systematic bias against immigrants of color, and especially against Latinos (whether native-born or immigrants). Do you agree?

9.　Perea's paper expresses concerns about recent proposals for the "Americanization" of immigrants. First, be sure you can distinguish the Americanization proposal of the Commission on Immigration Reform from the version advocated by Brimelow. Second, do you agree with Perea that, for people of color, even the Commission's brand of Americanization would bring only minor benefits and pose special risks?

10.　Do you agree with both Perea and the Commission on Immigration Reform that Americanization *should* be a two-way street? Or is it appropriate to view immigration as a sovereign prerogative and to place the exclusive onus on immigrants to adapt to the language and culture of their new country?

11.　Do you see any ironies in Brimelow's belief that naturalization should be made harder to obtain?

12.　There is some other fine commentary on the benefits and dangers of assimilation and on the relationship among assimilation, race, and identity. See, e.g., Enid Trucios–Haynes, *The Legacy of Racially Restrictive Immigration Laws and Policies and the Construction of the American National Identity*, 76 Oregon L. Rev. 369 (1997); Kevin R. Johnson, *"Melting Pot" or "Ring of Fire"?: Assimilation and the Mexican–American Experience*, 85 California L. Rev. 1259 (1997); George A. Martínez, *Latinos, Assimilation and the Law: A Philosophical Perspective*, 20 Chicano–Latino

L. Rev. 1 (1999). A useful demographic description of the new national diversity and of some positive initiatives to integrate immigrants appears in Bill Ong Hing, *Answering Challenges of the New Immigrant–Driven Diversity: Considering Integration Strategies*, 40 Univ. Louisville Brandeis L.J. 861 (2002).

13. The Brimelow book quickly generated strong responses. For a sampling of some other excellent (and highly critical) book reviews, see Daniel Kanstroom, *Dangerous Undertones of the New Nativism: Peter Brimelow and the Decline of the West*, in Juan F. Perea, Immigrants Out! The New Nativism and the Anti–Immigrant Impulse in the United States, at 300 et seq. (1997); Hiroshi Motomura, *Whose Alien Nation?: Two Models of Constitutional Immigration Law*, 94 Michigan L. Rev. 1927 (1996); Peter H. Schuck, *Alien Rumination*, 105 Yale L.J. 1963 (1996); Aristide Zolberg, Book Review, 21 Population & Development Rev. 659 (1995).

NOTE ON THE ENGLISH–ONLY MOVEMENT

Language, as we all know, is a touchy subject. Because it is a means of communication, language plays a vital functional role in the everyday life of every society. And because it is also a component of both personal and ethnic identity, language has emotional significance with both positive and negative overtones. Hence, its relevance to the present discussion of immigration, race, and culture.

Is language also a component of *national* identity? Should it be? Does the answer depend on how pluralist the particular nation otherwise is? Can a common language be imposed by force of law? If so, will such a law unify people or divide them?

These are some of the questions that arise from time to time in the United States and elsewhere, typically during periods of large-scale immigration, ethnic strife, economic dislocation, or other transformative events. Today, the English–Only Movement—which really comprises several sub-movements—has reemerged in American public discourse. While not formally a part of immigration law, the English–Only Movement obviously affects immigrants in special ways. Many would argue, moreover, that the movement is both motivated and sustained by anti-immigrant (and perhaps anti-Latino) sentiment. For both reasons, it is worth pausing briefly to think about what this movement is and about the direction in which it would take America.

First, the so-called "English–Only" Movement has taken several forms. Rooted in nineteenth century nativism and fortified by the anti-German hysteria that followed World War I, the ancestors of today's English–Only movements focused on the subject of foreign language instruction. See generally Leila Sadat Wexler, *Official English, Nationalism and Linguistic Terror: A French Lesson*, 71 Washington L.Rev. 285, 339–41 (1996) [hereafter cited as Sadat]. According to one study, shortly after World War I some 23 states restricted foreign language instruction; some of them singled out German. *Id*. at 340–41. In *Meyer v. Nebraska*, 262 U.S. 390, 43 S.Ct. 625,

67 L.Ed. 1042 (1923), the Supreme Court struck down on substantive due process grounds a Nebraska statute that (a) banned the teaching of any subject in a language other than English, in either public or private schools; and (b) banned the teaching of foreign language itself before ninth grade. Whether the Court's decision reflected tolerance for foreign languages or merely a hostility to government interference with parental rights is not clear. Barbara Bennett Woodhouse, *"Who Owns the Child?":* *Meyer and Pierce and the Child as Property*, 33 William & Mary L.Rev. 995, 1036–37 (1992). The contemporary debate over bilingual education raises some analogous issues, as illustrated in Irene Scharf, *Tired of Your Masses:* *A History of and Judicial Responses to Early 20th Century Anti–Immigrant Legislation*, 21 Univ. Hawaii L. Rev. 131 (1999).

A more modern strand of the English–Only Movement is "Official English." Its proponents seek to make English the sole language for conducting the business of government. At both the federal and the state levels, the main vehicles have been proposed legislation and proposed constitutional amendments. Some proposals are worded in general, symbolic terms, while others mandate the use of English in specific contexts. Those efforts have not (yet) prevailed at the federal level, but at least 22 states and many municipalities have enacted official English laws. See generally William Branigin, *Spread of Spanish Greeted by Some Unwelcome Signs: Businesses Facing Language Restrictions*, Washington Post, Feb. 6, 1999, at A4; Sadat, above, at 288 n.5, 351–68.

In 1988 the voters of Arizona narrowly passed a referendum amending the state constitution. The amendment declared English to be the official language of the state and required the state and its political subdivisions to "act in English and no other language" (with a few narrow exceptions). In *Yniguez v. Arizonans for Official English*, 69 F.3d 920 (9th Cir. en banc 1995), the court, by a vote of 6–5, struck down the Arizona provision on the ground that it violated the first amendment rights of both state employees and private individuals who sought information from state employees. The court rejected the state's arguments that the choice of language is conduct rather than speech and that employees' speech in the course of their employment is not entitled to first amendment protection. The United States Supreme Court vacated the decision on mootness grounds and thus did not reach the merits, *sub nom, Arizonans for Official English v. Arizona*, 520 U.S. 43, 117 S.Ct. 1055, 137 L.Ed.2d 170 (1997), but the Arizona Supreme Court ultimately invalidated the provision on both first amendment and equal protection grounds. *Ruiz v. Hull*, 191 Ariz. 441, 957 P.2d 984 (Ariz. 1998).

Analogous issues have arisen with respect to drivers' license exams. In *Alexander v. Sandoval*, 532 U.S. 275, 121 S.Ct. 1511, 149 L.Ed.2d 517 (2001), private plaintiffs challenged an Alabama Department of Public Safety policy that required driver's license examinations to be administered entirely in English. The Court of Appeals for the 11th Circuit struck down the policy as violative of Title 6 of the federal Civil Rights Act of 1964. That title prohibits discrimination—both intentional and unintentional—based on national origin in programs that receive federal funds. In a 5–4 decision, the Supreme Court reversed. It held that Title 6 does not authorize private causes of action based solely on disparate impact.

One writer has criticized the refusal of many courts to invalidate private employers' English-only policies as impermissible national origin discrimination. Christopher David Ruiz Cameron, *How the García Cousins Lost their Accents: Understanding the Language of Title 7 Decisions Approving English–Only Rules as the Product of Racial Dualism, Latino Invisibility, and Legal Indeterminacy*, 85 California L. Rev. 261 (1997). For a contrary decision, see *EEOC v. Premier Operator Services, Inc.*, 113 F.Supp.2d 1066 (N.D. Tex. 2000). In that case, the employer had hired thirteen Latino workers precisely for their abilities to speak Spanish with Spanish-speaking callers but then prohibited them from speaking Spanish at any other time, even during lunch and breaks. The policy was held to violate Title 7.

In 1999, the city of El Cenizo, Texas, situated about ten miles from Laredo, struck back. It passed an ordinance requiring all city meetings and functions to be conducted in Spanish. English translations are available if requested 48 hours in advance. An estimated 90% of the city's residents speak Spanish, though many of them speak English too. A few others, mostly young people, speak only English. See Madeline Baro Diaz, Assoc. Press, Aug. 20, 1999.

A third area of controversy has concerned restrictions on commercial speech. The town of Norcross, Georgia, for example, initially prohibited the posting of any commercial sign on which more than 25% of the words are in a language other than English:

> Consider Maria Cobarrubias, who has built her general store into a profitable fixture in the Atlanta suburb of Norcross by catering to a growing Hispanic community that is transforming many parts of the South.

> Cobarrubias was stunned to receive a visit recently from the local marshal, who fined her for having a sign with the store's name—Supermercado Jalisco—in Spanish. Supermercado is the Spanish word for supermarket, and Jalisco is the Mexican state where Cobarrubias was born. * * *

> She said she paid a $115 fine but is thinking about fighting back in court. Enforcement of the ordinance has outraged Mexican diplomats, and the American Civil Liberties Union said it may challenge the law as unconstitutional.

> * * *

> * * * Officially, the reason is to help police, fire and rescue personnel identify and locate businesses in emergencies. * * *

> At a nearby competing grocery called La Mexicana, manager Jaime Elizondo, 42, said he also paid a fine and had to change several words on the store's sign before it opened last spring.

> * * *

Sgt. H. Smith, the Norcross marshal, said he has also issued citations to several Korean churches and an "Oriental beauty shop." Some Spanish words are "acceptable," he said, while others, such as "supermercado," must be changed.

"The 'super' is English. But I don't know what 'mercado' means," he said. "If an American was out there driving by, he wouldn't know what that was."

* * *

Neighboring Doraville, also home to large numbers of Hispanic and Asian immigrants, has an ordinance like the one in Norcross but has chosen not to enforce it.

Branigan, above.

Query: In Norcross and Doraville, do you think a person would be criminally prosecuted for posting a restaurant sign with the name "Chez Louis"?

In response to a lawsuit brought by Cobarrubias, the city repealed its ordinance in May 1999. The next month, however, it substituted an ordinance that imposed other requirements on any on-premises commercial signs that display any non-English words. The business must file with the city a sworn affidavit that translates those words into English. The translation must be provided by a competent translator who is not the owner of the business. See Eric Gold, *Leyes del "Inglés Solamente" ("English–Only Laws")*, at 3–9 (unpublished seminar paper, 2003); see also Editorial, *Norcross, Businesses Can Show Signs of Cooperation*, Atlanta Journal & Constitution, May 10, 1999, at 10A (applauding repeal but putting charitable and diplomatic spin on City Council's motives); Editorial, *A Farce in Any Language*, Chicago Tribune, May 10, 1999, at 12 (adopting less charitable interpretation).

As others have shown, the fear that English is losing its dominance seems misplaced. Linguistic assimilation among immigrants and their children is the norm, not the exception. One recent study, surveying 2843 children of immigrants in South Florida, found that "1) knowledge of English is near universal; 2) preference for English is almost as high, even among children educated in bilingual schools; 3) preservation of parental languages varies inversely with length of U.S. residence and residential locations away from areas of ethnic concentration." Alejandro Portes & Richard Schauffler, *Language and the Second Generation: Bilingualism Yesterday and Today*, 28 International Migration Rev. 640 (1994). For some useful statistics, see Peter H. Schuck, Diversity in America 106–23 (2003); T. Alexander Aleinikoff & Ruben Rumbaut, *Terms of Belonging: Are Models of Membership Self–Fulfilling Prophecies?*, 13 Georgetown Immigration L.J. 1 (1998).

The United States, of course, is not alone in having large segments of its population speak differing first languages. Some nations, such as Canada, Switzerland, and South Africa, officially recognize more than one language. At the other end of the spectrum is France; French is not only the official language of government, but also the only language permitted in certain private transactions. Professor Sadat, in the article noted above, provides an interesting comparison of the national language movements in the United States and France. She argues that the French language restrictions have not served France well and cautions the United States not to follow the same path.

There has been some good scholarly commentary on various elements of the English-only movement. See, e.g., Bill Piatt, Only English? Law and Language Policy in the United States (1990); Juan F. Perea, *Demography and Distrust: An Essay on American Languages, Cultural Pluralism, and Official English*, 77 Minnesota L. Rev. 269 (1992); *cf.* Mari J. Matsuda, *Voices of America: Accent, Antidiscrimination Law, and a Jurisprudence for the Last Reconstruction,* 100 Yale L.J. 1329 (1991) (examining the legal treatment of accent discrimination and the role of accent in a plural society).

Should English be made the official language of the United States? What would such a change accomplish? What would be the costs? Ultimately, would an English Language Amendment be a legitimate way to foster communication, express an "English" cultural heritage, and unify the American populace? Or would it be more likely to convey belligerence, rationalize intolerance, and reinforce ethnic division? Which way do you come out?

SECTION D.   THE ECONOMIC IMPACT OF IMMIGRATION

In the United States the economic consequences of immigration have been fiercely debated since the nineteenth century. See, e.g., Act of Feb. 26, 1885, ch. 164, 23 Stat. 332 (excluding certain contract laborers). Some of the debate has centered on fiscal questions, such as the amounts immigrants contribute in taxes and the amounts they receive in public welfare benefits. See pages 1353–58 below. But the most animated debate has concerned the impact of immigrants on the labor market. Do they siphon jobs from Americans? Do they, by consuming goods and services and by sustaining otherwise marginal companies or industries, *create* jobs for Americans? Do they provide a source of cheap labor that on the one hand adversely affects the wages or working conditions of American workers but on the other hand benefits employers and consumers?

Most economists today recognize all of those (and other) positive and negative effects to some extent but hold vastly differing views about the magnitudes of those effects. In addition, of course, different people assign different values to the importance of worker protection, consumer benefits, employers' economic strength, etc. The labels and political coalitions familiar in most other immigration debates break down here. It is not unusual for "liberal" Democrats with ties to organized labor to urge restrictions on the admission of foreign workers, or for politically "conservative" free-market Republicans to urge higher ceilings on employment-based immigration.

For all those reasons, there is no bottom-line consensus either on the economically optimum level of immigration or on precisely which classes of immigrants would bring the greatest economic benefits. This subsection highlights most of the major competing arguments. For those interested in more sophisticated analyses of the economics of immigration, endless sources—including the books and articles from which the excerpts below have been drawn—are available. A somewhat dated but still useful bibliography is Bill Ong Hing, The Economic Impact of Immigration: A Brief Survey of the Literature 2–42 (1989).

George J. Borjas, Heaven's Door—Immigration Policy and the American Economy
Pages 62–67 (1999).

* * *

Do immigrants harm the employment opportunities of native workers? If so, how large is the loss in the economic well-being of natives? And are all native groups equally affected by immigration?

These questions have always been at the core of the immigration debate. In 1852, soon after the potato famine unleashed a new wave of Irish and British immigration, an observer described the connection between immigration and wages in a way that, with minor casting changes in the ethnic origin of the characters, could easily have been written a century and a half later:

> Great Britain is now pouring upon us in a full tide the surplus ... of her population. The ocean, which once separated us, steam has contracted to a span ... we are now virtually two contiguous countries ... To expect that, in two countries thus situated, without any special direction of public policy towards maintaining some barrier between them, the pressure of population, the profits of capital, and the wages of labor can long remain very unequal, would be as idle as to believe that, without the erection of a dam, water could be maintained at two different levels in the same pond. Throw down the little that remains of our protective system, and let the emigration from Great Britain and Ireland to our shores increase ... and within the lifetime of the present generation, the laborer's hire in our Atlantic states will be as low as it is in England. Our manufactures would flourish then, as those of Great Britain flourish now; cheap labor is the only requisite for placing them upon the same level.

Throughout the history of the immigration debate, therefore, immigration restrictions have been justified, at least publicly, by arguing that those restrictions improve the economic well-being of native workers. In fact, public opinion polls indicate that native workers disapprove of immigration (typically by very large margins) mainly because they perceive or fear that immigrants reduce wages or take away jobs.

It turns out, however, that this is one of those contentious issues where there is a wide gulf—actually more of a deep chasm—dividing public opinion and the findings from academic studies. Although many researchers have tried, it has proved surprisingly difficult to document that immigration has a sizable adverse effect on native workers. In a 1990 review of these studies, I concluded that "the methodological arsenal of modern econometrics cannot find a single shred of evidence that immigrants have a sizable adverse impact on the earnings and employment opportunities of natives in the United States." An academic survey published in 1995 states that "the effect of immigration on the labor market outcomes of natives is small." And the 1997 National Academy of Sciences report argued that "the weight of the empirical evidence suggests that the impact of immigration on the wages of competing native workers is small." This kind of consensus is rare indeed in social science, particularly when many workers keep insisting that immigrants harm their economic opportunities and when the commonsense intuition behind the economic laws of supply and demand suggests that an increase in the number of workers should reduce the wage.

This chapter presents a revisionist interpretation of the available evidence. I conclude that the native workers' apprehensions are not completely misguided, since many of them—particularly those at the bottom of the skill distribution—have much to fear from the entry of large numbers of less-skilled immigrants.

Put differently, I question the validity of much of the evidence that is typically marshaled by those who claim that immigrants do not affect native economic opportunities. Much of this evidence is based on comparisons of the labor market outcomes of native workers who reside in cities with large numbers of immigrants (such as Los Angeles and San Diego) with the outcomes of natives who reside in cities where few immigrants live (such as Atlanta and Pittsburgh). These "spatial correlations" often suggest that the average native wage is somewhat lower in labor markets where immigrants tend to cluster—but the wage differential between the markets may be so small that it is not worth worrying about.

But a weak spatial correlation does not necessarily prove that immigrants have a benign impact on the employment opportunities of native workers. Suppose, for example, that immigration into San Diego reduces the earnings of native workers there substantially. Native workers will probably react. Many will move out of the San Diego area to other cities, and workers who were considering moving to San Diego will move somewhere else instead. As natives respond to immigration by voting with their feet (creating what has been called "the new white flight"), the adverse impact of immigration on the San Diego labor market will be transmitted to the entire economy. In the end, all native workers will be worse off because of immigration, not just those who reside in the "immigrant cities."

In this chapter, I argue that the economic impact of immigration at the national level may be quite important. The 1980s witnessed a substantial increase in the wage gap between high school dropouts and workers with more education. The decade also witnessed the entry of large numbers of less-skilled immigrants. It turns out that almost half of the decline in the relative wage of high school dropouts may be attributed to immigration.

The dramatic increase in wage inequality that occurred in the 1980s and 1990s raises serious social, economic, and political concerns for the United States. And the fact that part of this increase can be linked to immigration raises equally serious concerns about immigration policy.

In an important sense, the United States pursues social policies that have conflicting goals. Presumably, the objective of many of the redistribution policies enshrined in liberal political ideology and implemented through the welfare state—from public assistance programs to the earned income tax credit—is to redistribute income to less-skilled workers and to improve their economic status.

At the same time, immigration policy has tacitly encouraged the admission of very large numbers of less-skilled workers—either by insisting that only family connections matter when awarding entry visas, or by looking the other way as millions of "unscreened" illegal aliens cross the border. This type of immigration policy probably aggravates the social and economic problems faced by workers at the bottom of the income distribution, and helps undo—and perhaps even unravel—many of the benefits that would have accrued from the redistributive policies aimed at improving their economic status.

IMMIGRATION AND LOCAL LABOR MARKETS

Immigrants in the United States tend to settle in a limited number of states and cities. And this clustering seems to have increased over time. In 1960, 60 percent of the immigrants lived in one of the six main immigrant-receiving states: California, New York, Texas, Florida, New Jersey, and Illinois. By 1998, about 72 percent of immigrants lived in those states, with 32 percent living in California alone. This extreme geographic concentration reflects both the immigrants' propensity to enter the United States through a limited number of gateway cities (such as Los Angeles and New York) and the fact that immigrants—unlike natives—do not seem to move much around the country. Once immigrants enter one of the gateway cities, they tend to stay there.

Much can be learned about the economic impact of immigration by paying particularly close attention to California, the state heaviest hit by the Second Great Migration. * * *

The geographic clustering of immigrants is even more remarkable when one looks at specific cities. In 1990, 42 percent of immigrants lived in just five metropolitan areas (Los Angeles, New York, Miami, Chicago, and Anaheim), but only 13 percent of natives lived in those localities. And, not surprisingly, California's cities were hit particularly hard by the influx.

Between 1980 and 1990, the foreign-born share rose from 25 to 40 percent in Los Angeles, 15 to 28 percent in Anaheim, and 14 to 22 percent in San Diego.

* * *

What happens when immigration increases the supply of workers in a particular labor market? The traditional approach to this question—the one that has greatly influenced the direction of the immigration debate—takes a myopic, short-run perspective. The entry of immigrants into the local labor market should lower the wage of competing workers (workers who have the same types of skills as immigrants) and perhaps increase the wage of complementary workers (workers whose skills become more valuable because of immigration). For example, an influx of foreign-born laborers reduces the economic opportunities for laborers who already live in the locality—all laborers now face stiffer competition in the labor market. At the same time, highly skilled natives may gain substantially. They pay less for the services that laborers provide, such as painting the house and mowing the lawn, and natives who hire these laborers can now specialize in producing the goods and services that better suit their skills.

This short-run perspective, however, can be very misleading. Over time, natives—both those who live in the city targeted by immigrants as well as those living in other cities—will likely respond to the entry of immigrants. It is not in the best interest of native-owned firms or native workers to sit still and watch immigrants change economic opportunities. All natives now have incentives to change their behavior in ways that take advantage of the altered economic landscape.

For example, native-owned firms see that cities flooded by less-skilled immigrants tend to pay lower wages to laborers. Employers who hire laborers will want to relocate to those cities, and entrepreneurs thinking about starting up new firms will find it more profitable to open them in immigrant areas. In other words, immigration increases the returns to capitalists in the affected cities, and capital will naturally flow to those areas where the returns are highest. The flow of jobs to the immigrant receiving hit areas helps cushion the adverse effect of immigration on the wage of competing workers in these localities.

* * *

The forces that tend to equalize employment opportunities across labor markets are reinforced by the fact that native workers will also respond. Laborers living in Michigan or Mississippi were perhaps thinking about moving to California before the immigrants entered that state. These laborers quickly learn that immigration has reduced their potential wages in California. As a result, many will decide to remain where they are or move elsewhere—and some Californians might actually find it worthwhile to incur the cost of leaving the state to search for better opportunities. The migration of native workers within the United States, in effect, accomplishes what the immigrant flow, with its tendency to cluster in a small number of gateway cities, could not—a "spreading out" of the additional workers over the entire nation, rather than in just a limited number of localities. * * *

Howard F. Chang, Migration as International Trade: The Economic Gains From the Liberalized Movement of Labor

3 UCLA Journal of Internat'l Law & Foreign Affairs 371, 371–73, 376–78 (1998).

Since multilateral trade negotiations produced the General Agreement on Tariffs and Trade (GATT) in Geneva in 1947, the world has made dramatic progress toward free trade in goods. Several subsequent rounds of negotiations under the GATT have steadily liberalized international trade, and numerous regional initiatives seek to deepen economic integration among countries prepared to go further. Standard economic theory prescribes free trade as the regime that maximizes global economic welfare. Economists also recommend trade liberalization as a policy that is likely to produce gains for each country.

The gains from trade arise from the fact that different countries will produce various goods at different costs. When countries restrict trade, the price of a good will be low in countries that can produce the good at low cost, but its price will be high in countries that can produce the good only at higher cost. Liberalized trade allows both countries to gain: the high-price country can import the good at a price less than what it would cost to produce the good at home; the low-price country can export the good and receive a higher price than it would otherwise fetch.

Precisely the same theory applied to trade in goods also applies to trade in services. The Uruguay Round of trade negotiations recognized this fact in 1994, extending the international regulation of trade to service markets through the General Agreement on Trade in Services (GATS). Free trade in all services, including labor services, would imply free movement of people across borders. To provide many services, workers must cross borders to where the work must be performed, either on a temporary basis or to accept permanent employment. Thus, the free movement of workers across borders promotes economic welfare by promoting free trade in the labor market. The European Union recognizes the importance of free mobility of labor as an element of a comprehensive free trade regime, enshrining this freedom in its constitution as one of the "four freedoms" that are the basic pillars of the European common market, "an area without internal frontiers in which the free movement of goods, persons, services, and capital is ensured." This "freedom of movement for workers" in turn entails "the abolition of any discrimination based on nationality between workers with respect to employment."

Immigration barriers interfere with the free flow of labor internationally and thereby cause wage rates for the same class of labor to diverge widely among different countries. For any given class of labor, residents of high-wage countries could gain by employing more immigrant labor, and residents of low-wage countries could gain by selling more of their labor to employers in high-wage countries. Economic efficiency in the global labor market would call for unrestricted migration, which would allow labor to move freely to the country where it earns the highest return. Market forces would thus direct labor to the market where its marginal product is highest. Given the large international differences in wages, it should be apparent that the potential gains from international trade in labor (and the costs we bear as a result of immigration barriers) are large.

Indeed, studies suggest that the gains to the world economy from removing immigration barriers could well be enormous and greatly exceed the gains from removing trade barriers. For example, Bob Hamilton and John Whalley provide estimates that suggest that the gains from free migration of labor would more than double worldwide real income, indicating that immigration controls "are one of the (and perhaps the) most important policy issues facing the global economy." Even their most conservative estimate suggests that the gains would be a significant fraction (over thirteen percent) of worldwide real income. Furthermore, their analysis indicates that the free migration of labor would also greatly improve the global distribution of income by raising real wages dramatically for the world's poorest workers.

* * *

* * * In evaluating the effects of immigration policies upon economic welfare, however, we must first address the question of whose welfare we are considering. Should we seek to maximize the welfare of natives (those born in the country of immigration) alone? Should we seek to maximize national economic welfare or global economic welfare? Once we decide whose welfare counts, we must also address whether our objective is merely to maximize their wealth (that is, to pursue economic efficiency with respect to their welfare) or our objectives also include an equitable distribution of wealth among them. If our objectives include distributive concerns, then our measure of social welfare must specify how much weight to give these concerns. Thus, the optimal policy will depend upon what measure of social welfare we choose to maximize.

I will not in this article set forth a philosophical defense of any particular welfare objective. Instead, my strategy will be to examine what policies the United States would pursue if its goal were simply to maximize the economic welfare of U.S. natives, not because I believe that immigration policy should be guided solely by considerations of economic self-interest, but because such concerns have in fact played a dominant role in the public debate over immigration policy. National governments, including the U.S. government, will probably continue to deem the promotion of the interests of natives as the paramount objective of immigration policies. * * *

This thought experiment reveals, however, that even from this narrow perspective, which "stacks the deck" against the immigrant, optimal policies would probably allow higher levels of employment-based and family-based immigration than current U.S. immigration laws permit. Even if we give zero weight to the welfare of aliens in our measure of social welfare, the optimal immigration policy would be more liberal than our current laws in most important respects. In particular, although the economic welfare of natives and distributive justice among natives are often advanced as reasons to reduce immigration, I will demonstrate that neither objective provides a sound justification for more restrictive laws regarding employment-based and family-based immigration.

* * *

Optimal immigration policy would instead take the form of a "tariff," that is, a tax imposed on immigrants. This tariff could take the form of an income tax that discriminates between citizens and aliens. Although some economists have previously suggested a tax on foreign workers, my comprehensive analysis builds on that suggestion by exploring the features of the optimal immigration tariff in detail. I find that the optimal tariff is positive for immigrants with low incomes but is likely to be negative for immigrants with sufficiently high incomes. These results suggest that skilled immigration should be permitted (indeed encouraged) without quantitative or other protectionist restrictions and that unskilled immigration should be permitted without quantitative restrictions but subject to less generous fiscal policies than those applied to natives.

In Part III, I introduce distributive justice among natives as an objective. Concern for the distribution of income among natives, however, does not imply that more restrictive immigration laws are in order. Instead, the appropriate response to distributive concerns is redistribution through progressive reforms of tax and transfer policies, not immigration restrictions. * * *

James P. Smith & Barry Edmonston (Eds.), National Research Council of the National Academy of Sciences, The New Americans—Economic, Demographic, and Fiscal Effects of Immigration

Pages 4–8, 220 (1997).

* * * Economic theory points to possible effects [of immigration] on the employment and wages of domestic workers, U.S. trade with other countries, the growth rate of the economy, and the prices people pay for goods and services. To address these issues, the panel relied both on theoretical insights on what the likely effects would be, and on empirical estimates of the magnitude of the actual effects.

Using a basic economic model, with plausible assumptions, we show that immigration produces net economic gains for domestic residents, for several reasons. At the most basic level, immigrants increase the supply of labor and help produce new goods and services. But since they are paid less than the total value of these new goods and services, domestic workers as a group must gain.

The gains to the domestic economy come from a number of sources. On the production side, immigration allows domestic workers to be used more productively, specializing in producing goods at which they are relatively more efficient. Specialization in consumption also yields a gain.

* * *

In our baseline analysis, we assume that the U.S. economy is characterized by constant returns to scale—that is, growth in the size and scale of the economy neither reduces nor increases the productivity of labor and capital. Existing research has not convincingly demonstrated that, in the aggregate, either decreasing returns due to fixed factors or congestion effects, or increasing returns, are more compelling alternatives. We caution, however, that we would not extrapolate far beyond current levels and say that immigration flows much larger tha[n] those considered in our demographic projections would always produce economic gains. With far larger flows, and over long periods of time, the uncertainty about increasing or decreasing returns to scale would have to be resolved with sound empirical evidence.

Even when the economy as a whole gains, however, there may be losers as well as gainers among different groups of U.S. residents. Along with immigrants themselves, the gainers are the owners of productive factors that are complementary with the labor of immigrants—that is, domestic, higher-skilled workers, and perhaps owners of capital—whose incomes will rise. Those who buy goods and services produced by immigrant labor also benefit. The losers may be the less-skilled domestic workers who compete with immigrants and whose wages will fall. To the extent that immigrants specialize in activities that otherwise would not have existed domestically, immigration can be beneficial for all domestic residents. In this case, there is little substitution of new immigrant workers for domestic workers, and domestic consumers gain from the lower prices of these services.

In the long run, assuming constant returns to scale, immigrants can affect rates of economic growth only to the extent that they differ from the native-born—if, for example, they arrive with a different mix of skills from those of native-born workers. To have an effect on growth rates, this difference between immigrants and natives must persist over each new generation. If the children of immigrants—or, if not the children, the grandchildren and great-grandchildren—come to be just like the native-born, then all that immigration does is augment the population and the scale of the economy; it does not change the rate of growth of income per capita.

Overall, in the massive and complex U.S. economy, immigration is unlikely to have a very large effect on relative earnings or on gross domestic product per capita. Among the legions of factors that affect the economy, many are far more critical than immigration, including savings and investment and the human capital of U.S. workers. Immigration over the 1980s increased the labor supply of all workers by about 4 percent. On the basis of evidence from the literature on labor demand, this increase could have reduced the wages of all competing native-born workers by about 1 or 2 percent. Meanwhile, noncompeting native-born workers would have seen their wages increase, and both competing and noncompeting workers may have benefitted as consumers.

Overall, barring sizable immigration-induced economies or diseconomies of scale, the most plausible magnitudes of the impacts of immigration on the economy are modest for those who benefit from immigration, for those who lose from immigration, and for total gross domestic product. The domestic gain may run on the order of $1 billion to $10 billion a year. Although this gain may be modest relative to the size of the U.S. economy, it remains a significant positive gain in absolute terms.

Potentially, immigration may have much larger effects on certain parts of the labor market—workers in geographic areas that receive large numbers of immigrants or those with low levels of education. However, comparisons of geographic areas with different levels of immigration show only a weak relationship between native wages and the number of immigrants in a city or state. Furthermore, in these studies the numerically weak relationship between native wages and immigration is observed across all types of native workers, skilled and unskilled, male and female, minority and nonminority. The one group that appears to suffer substantially from new waves of immigrants are immigrants from earlier waves, for whom the recent immigrants are close substitutes in the labor market.

While some have suspected that blacks suffer disproportionately from the inflow of low-skilled immigrants, none of the available evidence suggests that they have been particularly hard-hit on a national level. Some have lost their jobs, especially in places where immigrants are concentrated. But the majority of blacks live elsewhere, and their economic fortunes are tied largely to other factors.

There are a number of problems with studies based on local labor market analyses. If native workers and firms adapt to the entry of immigrants by moving to areas offering them better opportunities, then there is no reason to expect local-level correlation between the wages of natives and the presence of immigrants. The wages of all competing native workers would fall, not just the wages of natives working in the cities where immigrants cluster.

* * *

The evidence points to the conclusion that immigration has had a relatively small adverse impact on the wage and employment opportunities of competing native groups. This effect does not appear to be concentrated in the local areas where immigrants live, but instead is dispersed across the United States. This dispersal comes about in part because competing native workers migrate out of the areas to which immigrants move. Over the last two decades, immigration thus played some role in explaining the declining wages of high school dropouts, but little part in the expanding wage inequality for any other group of native workers.

* * *

Once in the United States, the foreign-born on average earn less than native workers. This gap between foreign-born and native workers has widened recently. Among both men and women, those who have arrived most recently and those who come from Latin America earn the lowest wages. Even though recent new arrivals are better educated than their earlier counterparts, the education of the native-born has improved even more, so that the gap in skills, and thus in wages, has widened. This relative decline in immigrant skills and wages can be attributed essentially to a single factor—the fact that those who have come most recently have come from poorer countries, where the average education and wage and skill levels are far below those in the United States.

Part of this growing wage gap may stem from the influx of illegal immigrants, who are generally more poorly educated, but it is not due exclusively to them. There is also evidence of widening in the gap among legal immigrants, brought about not only through shifts in their countries of origin, but also through changes in the composition of refugees and more severe limits on the entry of certain highly skilled immigrants (specifically, physicians). Over time, the wage gap closes for some—significantly for immigrants from Europe and Asia, and at least modestly for some others— but not at all for those from Mexico.

Employment rates of recent immigrants have also fallen relative to those of natives. However, immigrants catch up to natives relatively quickly, so that after some years in the United States their employment rates are quite similar to those of natives.

What jobs do immigrants do? A higher proportion of immigrants than of the native-born work in many jobs that call for high levels of education: they are college teachers of foreign languages, medical scientists, economists. But they are even more disproportionately represented in many of the lowest-paying jobs: as waiters and waitresses, agricultural graders and sorters, private household workers. Immigrants also account for a disproportionate number of workers in many occupations that require little education but much skill, such as tailors, dressmakers, and jewelers.

* * *

The weight of the empirical evidence suggests that the impact of immigration on the wages of competing native-born workers is small— possibly reducing them by only 1 or 2 percent. Why does this effect seem so small? One reason is that it is easy to exaggerate the importance of immigration. Although immigration touches some hot button issues, the American economy is extremely large and complex, running at $7.6 trillion a year. This economy is the end result of tens of thousands of factors, many of which are far more critical than the country's immigration policy. Such factors include the rate at which the country saves and invests and the human capital of its own workers. It is simply not plausible that immigration, even across a decade, by increasing the supply of workers by 4 percent could seriously impact such an economy. However, although it is easy to exaggerate the aggregate effects of immigration, they should not be minimized. As measured by changes in wages, the economic benefits of immigration run as much as $10 billion a year. In addition, the economic benefits of immigration that operate only through lower prices, without displacing or disadvantaging competitive domestic labor, add to the positive effects of immigration.

NOTES AND QUESTIONS

1.   It is often said that immigrants do not displace American workers because the jobs immigrants take tend to be those which native workers spurn. Borjas disagrees. He argues in effect that there is no such thing as a true labor shortage. In his view, when there is an apparent labor shortage, the true explanation is that the wages are simply too low to attract the necessary workers. Absent immigration, he contends, employers would be forced to bid up the prevailing wages to whatever levels would entice adequate numbers of native workers. Do you agree?

2.   Among the economists who take a dim view of immigration, Borjas is probably the leading figure today. Notice his language: California is the state "heaviest hit" by recent immigration. California's cities "were hit particularly hard by the influx." Wages drop in cities that are "flooded" by less-skilled immigrants. These are not neutral, scholarly terms. Yet, elsewhere in the same book, Borjas acknowledges that "On net, therefore, the country benefits [and he means economically] from immigration." George J. Borjas, Heaven's Door 87 (1999). He goes on to articulate several reasons. Are the negative references quoted above consistent with that acknowledgment? Argue both ways.

3.   While Borjas argues that immigration reduces the wages of native low-wage workers and thus increases the differential between high-wage and low-wage earners, Chang argues that immigration actually diminishes wage differentials. Can these seemingly opposite views be reconciled?

4.   It is not yet clear whether Borjas is right when he says that immigration tends to hurt low-wage native workers, especially high school dropouts. But suppose he is. What policy should follow?

5.   What do you think of Chang's proposed tariff system?

6.   Both Borjas and the National Academy of Sciences speak of the dispersal effect of immigration policy. They maintain that relatively unskilled workers migrate from high-immigration to low-immigration cities and regions to lessen the competition they face in applying for jobs. Conversely, they conclude, firms often relocate from low-immigration to high-immigration cities and regions to have access to a larger and cheaper labor supply. Suppose they are right. Are these conclusions a convincing argument for reducing immigration?

7. A subject of growing importance has been the impact of immigration on social security. The late Julian Simon, a pro-immigration economist, had this to say:

> The ongoing debate over Social Security is agonizing. Every proposed policy inflicts pain because it boils down either to a decrease in benefits to the elderly or an increase in taxes upon working persons. And so it must be, as long as the numbers of elderly and of workers remain unchanged.
>
> * * * There remains, then, only one condition that can lessen the tax burden upon working persons without reducing benefits—a larger number of young working persons. Having more children will help, but not until a couple of decades hence. Only immigration provides immediate help.
>
> As soon as the average immigrant begins working—which generally is quite soon after arriving in this country—the immigrant begins to contribute to the Social Security coffers. The immigrant's own eventual receipt of Social Security benefits, decades in the future, does not offset these immediate benefits to natives * * *.
>
> The benefit to natives stems from the difference in age composition between the population of present residents of the US, and that of each cohort of immigrants. * * * Moreover, even that small fraction of the immigrants who are elderly are not eligible to receive Social Security. Therefore each cohort of new immigrants contributes substantially to reduce the Social Security burden of natives, in proportion to its numbers.
>
> * * *
>
> As to whether US natives must pay the piper for this benefit from immigrants when the young immigrants get older and themselves receive Social Security—the answer is "no" * * *. First, the impact of this year's immigrants on Social Security say 30 years from now properly has little weight in the overall assessment, because a dollar to be received or paid out 30 years from now is worth much less now when discounted at even a modest rate. Second and more important * * * [b]y the time the immigrant workers retire and collect Social Security, they typically have raised children who are then contributing taxes to Social Security and thereby balancing out the parents' receipts, just as is the case with native families. In this way there is a one-time benefit to natives because the immigrants arrive without a generation of elderly parents who might receive Social Security.

Julian L. Simon, The Economic Consequences of Immigration 132–34 (2d ed. 1999).

What is your reaction?

8. The same Professor Simon was also a proponent of the United States simply selling its immigrant visas at a worldwide auction. He wrote:

* * * Individuals with the most to gain economically would offer the highest prices. Inevitably, these people have the most to contribute economically to us all.

* * * How would an auction system work? It would begin with a worldwide quota for the number of people to be admitted in a given year. For political convenience, the total might at first be the same size as it is today. (The United States would benefit from admitting many more immigrants than it does now—and far more than are conceivable under existing political arrangements.) Here is the most straightforward method: First, ask for written bids from all comers, anywhere in the world, perhaps twice a year; second, rank the bids from high to low; third, accept enough high bidders to fill the quota, plus enough to make up any shortfall arising from some high bidders changing their minds. (Under one variant, each person would pay the amount he or she bid; under another, each would pay the amount bid by the lowest winning bidder.) The chief virtue of an auction is that it would identify people who have an especially large capacity to produce goods of high economic value in this country. Charging an admission fee would also accentuate the tendency of immigrants to move when they are young and strong, because admission has higher (discounted) future lifetime value for younger than for older people.

Would an auction mean only the wealthiest could get in? One way to prevent this is to allow "buyers" to enter now and pay later together with income tax. Failure to pay might result in deportation. There is little reason to believe the very wealthy would want to move here. Tax havens such as Caribbean countries and Monaco are financially more attractive. Besides, the wealthy can come as tourists if they like life here.

The ambitious, for whom America is a large, rich market in which to make a lot of money, would have a special desire to immigrate. An immigrant who makes a lot of money would benefit the United States by providing jobs and paying taxes.

* * *

Present policy is discriminatory: It does not offer all potential immigrants the same opportunity to be admitted. * * * What is unfairest of all is that relatives of people in this country have a better chance of immigration than people who have no such connections.

An auction discriminates according to the standard of a market-oriented society: ability and willingness to pay. An auction would be fair in that it would allow anybody in any part of the world the same opportunity to buy a visa.

Julian L. Simon, *Auction the Right to Be an Immigrant,* New York Times, January 28, 1986, at A25.

On what philosophical premises was Simon's proposal based? Do you agree with him either that those "with the most to gain economically would offer the highest prices" or that an auction "would allow anybody in any part of the world the same opportunity to buy a visa"?

University of Chicago economist Gary Becker has also advocated the sale of immigrant visas. Unlike Simon, Becker proposes retaining the present admission system and simply adding a separate new track for immigrants who are willing to pay the fee. Also unlike Simon, Becker favors a flat fee rather than an auction. He suggests, apparently only for illustrative purposes, an amount of $50,000. He explains that this system would not exclude poor people because they could save or borrow the necessary funds, perhaps from prospective U.S. employers or commercial lenders (evidently without collateral) or possibly from the federal government. Gary Becker, *Why Not Let Immigrants Pay for Speedy Entry?,* Business Week, March 2, 1987, at 20.

9. Do immigrants pay their way? How do the amounts they pay in taxes compare to what they receive in government services? Do the answers vary by category of immigrant (LPRs, undocumented), by level of government (federal, state, and local), and by geographic region? Views on these questions differ. See pages 1195–96 (undocumented migrants) and 1353–58 (LPRs) below.

10. One study of the *children* of immigrants reveals some striking patterns:

> While the United States benefits from the entry of skilled foreign-born professionals and international students, research shows that the country gains even more from their children. An astounding 60 percent of the top science students in the United States and 65 percent of the top math students are the children of immigrants.

Stuart Anderson, *The Multiplier Effect,* Internat'l Educator 13, 15 (Summer 2004), citing findings of the National Foundation for American Policy, a nonpartisan research organization.

SECTION E. IMMIGRATION, POPULATION, AND THE ENVIRONMENT

United States environmentalists are deeply divided over immigration. Some fear that high levels of immigration, by increasing the population size and dispersal patterns, will exacerbate congestion, sprawl, pollution, and consumption of scarce resources. Other ecologists, for reasons discussed below, find the projections of environmental harm exaggerated, argue that any additional environmental negatives need to be weighed against both economic gains and social policies, and contend that at any rate the focus should be on the world environment rather than on the United States environment alone.

This subsection is a brief introduction to the environmental implications of United States immigration policy. It considers two subjects: (1) how immigration alters the size and characteristics of the United States population; and (2) in turn, how those population changes affect the environment.

James P. Smith & Barry Edmonston (Eds.), National Research Council of the National Academy of Sciences, The New Americans—Economic, Demographic, and Fiscal Effects of Immigration

Pages 1, 76–79, 94–96, 99 (1997).

* * * Congress in 1990 appointed a bipartisan Commission on Immigration Reform to review the nation's policies and laws and to recommend changes. In turn, the Commission in 1995 asked the National Research Council [of the National Academy of Sciences—Ed.] to convene a panel of experts to assess the demographic, economic, and fiscal consequences of immigration.

* * *

How will the population of the United States change on the way to the middle of the 21st century? How will immigration—current and future—contribute to that change? This chapter seeks to answer the second question, which in turn will help answer the first. It focuses on the characteristics of immigrants and their descendants and explores how they will change the demography of the United States over the next six decades.

Immigration is not the only force at work shaping the size and the structure of the United States in the coming years. It will interact with other demographic forces, already in place, that also play a large role in what the country will look like by the middle of the next century.

First, in the two decades following World War II, the baby boom greatly increased the annual rate of U.S. population growth and provided birth cohorts from 1946 to about 1963 that were much larger than those of either the decade before or after. The baby boom and the subsequent baby bust will have major ramifications over the next half century: the population will age as the baby-boom generations become older; when they eventually retire, the number of retirees will be much larger than this country has ever seen.

Second, the future level of mortality among the elderly will have fundamental implications for their numbers. These changes, in turn, will affect their demand for private and public pensions and for health services. Because the small baby-bust generations will be the workers at that time, a relatively few income-producing residents will be providing for the older generations.

* * *

* * * [N]ot every group of immigrants into the United States bears children at the same rate. Immigrant groups with persistently high fertility rates will grow over time, absolutely and in relation to other immigrant groups. Second, not every group of immigrants has the same life span—that is, their mortality rates differ; these, too, may change over time and thus shift in their relation to one another.

If immigrants have a higher fertility rate than does the resident population, the nation will grow younger on average. And if immigrants have a higher mortality rate—that is, if they die at an earlier age—that trend will be reinforced. Again, the differences among groups of immigrants also matter, and so do the shifts within groups and between groups as the generations unfold.

Previewing the U.S. population in 2050, then, calls for making assumptions about the numbers of people entering and leaving the country, about the numbers from various racial and ethnic groups within the totals, and about the fertility and mortality rates of individual groups. Moreover, it calls for assumptions about *exogamy* and *ethnic affiliation*—the degree to which groups intermarry and the way the descendants of intergroup marriages identify themselves.

* * *

The number and age structure of the population are determined by fertility, mortality, and migration. The last factor has attracted considerably less attention in formal models than the first two, which have been extensively examined by means of stable population models and their various extensions.

At the simplest level, that of total population numbers, only net migration appears in the demographic balancing equation: population change = births—deaths + net migration. * * *

The world population has been growing at a historically unprecedented rate for the past century and numbered an estimated 5.8 billion in 1996. In 1990, the U.S. population accounted for 4 percent of the world's population. Since 1950, the U.S. population has been declining as a proportion of the world's population, decreasing from 6 percent in 1950. * * *

Because we project that the United States will experience moderate population growth for the next six decades, its proportion of the world's population will remain constant at 4 percent. Some other regions, such as Europe, will account for a diminishing proportion of the world's population over the next six decades, and regions such as Africa are likely to increase their relative proportion.

* * *

Immigration can play a critical role in determining the future size of the U.S. population. Within the population balancing equation, population growth could rise substantially if fertility or net immigration rises or if mortality declines. The rate of fertility, which has been below the replacement level for almost 20 years, shows little evidence of reviving sufficiently to alter the course of population growth. Our mortality assumptions incorporate mortality declines over the projection period, which will lead to higher levels of natural increase and population growth. Population growth will be even higher if there is an even greater improvement in life expectancy.

That leaves immigration as the most likely factor acting to spur population growth in the coming decades. Apart from the additions its net numbers make to the population, immigration, because it alters the age and racial/ethnic composition of the population, influences the rates of fertility and mortality that are the basic components of population change.

* * *

Table 3.3 [omitted here—Ed.] lists our projections of the future size of the American population under five alternative immigration assumptions. It is important to remember that this country's population will continue to grow well into the next century, even if net immigration was immediately eliminated forever. Under the assumption of zero immigration, the population of the United States will grow slowly, reaching a peak of 311 million in about 2035. Thereafter, it will very slowly decline [to 307 million in 2050—Ed.], because, as the baby-boom cohorts age, deaths will outweigh births.

[The table] also demonstrates that population growth will be significantly higher under any of our scenarios of positive levels of immigration. According to our medium immigration assumption (under which current levels persist indefinitely into the future), the size of the population will be [387 million] * * * by the year 2050. * * * Allowing immigration to continue at its current levels for the next 55 years will produce a population that is 80 million people larger than it would have been if all net immigration ceased instantly. These additional people are the direct effect of the 45 million more immigrants over this period. Then come the dual indirect effects of the descendants of these immigrants (compounded by higher fertility rates among immigrants) and of their lower overall mortality rate due to the relative youth of immigrants.

Immigration, then, will obviously play the dominant role in our future population growth. Of the 124 million additional people living in 2050 under the medium immigration assumption, 80 million will be the direct or indirect consequence of immigration.

[The table] also displays what population growth would be under realistic ranges of alterations in immigration policy. For example, if, on one hand, net immigration were halved, to 410,000 per year, growth would be slower, but the population would still rise to 349 million by the middle of the next century. If, on the other hand, net immigration were to increase by half, to 1,230,000 a year, the population would rise to 426 million by

2050. In either policy scenario, the population will be different from that under the medium immigration assumption—and by more than the simple addition or subtraction of immigrants, since the descendants of these immigrants will also be part of the future nation.

* * *

However, it should be noted that immigration involves primarily a redistribution of the world's population, not an absolute increase. Indeed, since the fertility of immigrants tends to decline after they come to the United States, total world population will be slightly lower. The potential for negative environmental effects (congestion and the like) must then be primarily local. From a world perspective, (negative) environmental effects in the United States may be counterbalanced by possible (positive) effects in the sending countries that are losing population. Total consumption by immigrants will typically be higher in the United States than in the places they left (which, after all, is one reason they immigrated). But efforts to abate environmental effects at any given level of consumption may also be higher in the United States. A weighting of the factors should enter into an evaluation of the environmental effects of immigration.

Ellen Percy Kraly, Research Paper for the U.S. Commission on Immigration Reform, U.S. Immigration and the Environment: Scientific Research and Analytic Issues

Pages i–iv (1995).

* * * [R]emarkably little hard evidence exists about the environmental effects of alien migration on the United States. A great deal of speculation exists about the nature of the relationship and there is increasing popular commentary about the degree to which immigration is associated with environmental problems in local areas as well as in the nation as a whole. The direct or causal effects of U.S. immigration on the environment have not been established, however, through scientific study. Moreover, there are significant limitations in U.S. statistics on immigration and population for the study of environmental impacts.

* * *

The general model of environmental impact identifies three broad sets of factors influencing environmental change: *Environmental impact* [I] is conceptualized as a function of *population* characteristics [P], patterns of *consumption* [A, for affluence] and *technology* [T], the use and manipulation of energy and other natural resources. While this model has provided an organizing framework for much of the debate concerning population and the environment, it has also been criticized for incomplete conceptualization of the components and lack of grounding in social scientific theory. The degree to which the population concept is well specified or connected to theory is also contested: uses of the model focus primarily on the increase in population size without specification of the different sources of population growth, for example natural increase (births minus deaths) relative to net migration.

Theories on population and environment vary in assumptions about the relative importance and direction of the effect of each of the factors (P,A,T) as well as the significance of interrelationships among the factors. Neo–Malthusian perspectives emphasize the significant influence of population growth for environmental impact and conceptualize a negative relationship between population growth and the availability and, increasingly, the quality of environmental resources. In contrast, more "optimistic" perspectives emphasize the enhanced potential inherent in positive population growth for social, economic, and technological progress, and hence, the means to solve environmental problems. Primary importance is given to changes in technology and social and economic organization in mitigating the effects of the other two factors. A third approach conceptualizes population pressure and short-run negative effects as a stimulus to technological innovation and more effective use of resources.

Perspectives thus vary in the degree to which population is proportional to environmental change. According to the demographer Keyfitz:

> If all else is equal, action damaging the environment is directly proportional to the number of people. That at least seems the most appropriate initial hypothesis ... The burden of proof is on anyone who argues against the proportionality hypothesis in either way.

In thinking about the impact of alien immigration on the U.S. environment, relevant questions center on the degree to which the impact of alien migration is proportionally less than, greater than, or equal to the number of immigrants.

* * *

In addition to the need to specify more clearly the role of migration in theories of population and environment, several additional issues emerge from the review of theory. Both geographic level and temporal frame of analysis must be specified in theoretical models and ultimately in empirical research. The effects of immigration on environmental processes may be expected to be significantly different for metropolitan areas, rural communities, states, and in the short-term versus the long-term. A third issue is the importance of understanding linkages or connections among geographic areas, economic sectors, and through time. For example, the concentration of immigration in certain metropolitan areas in the United States may have environmental consequences for areas and natural resources geographically removed from the cities.

The most fundamental recommendation for theory development is to revise models of population and environment to break population growth into its component parts in order to consider more clearly the effects of migration. Of particular relevance for the United States, moreover, is the specification of effects for different types of international population movements, including permanent resettlement, refugee migration, temporary labor migration, and tourism, within theories of environmental impact.

NOTES AND QUESTIONS

1. In recent years, the national membership of the Sierra Club has been deeply divided over the environmental impact of immigration (as well as over how to balance the environmental impact against other social policies). In this connection, read carefully the last paragraph of the excerpt from the National Academy of Sciences study. It highlights the extremely important point that "immigration involves primarily a redistribution of the world's population, not an absolute increase." What follows from this observation? At first glance, one might assume that any negative environmental impact on the receiving country (here, the United States) is exactly offset by a positive impact on the sending countries. For the reasons given in the same paragraph, however, that assumption is not necessarily true. The very act of migrating affects the migrating group's fertility rates and consumption habits. Migration might also affect the pace of environmental technology.

Suppose, hypothetically, that the impact of migration on the United States environment is negative but that its net impact on the world environment is neutral or even positive. With which set of effects should a true environmentalist be more concerned?

2. Professor Kraly argues that we still lack adequate data to reach any meaningful conclusions about the impact of immigration on the United States environment. First, identify precisely what data Kraly believes are still missing. Second, which of those data do you think are realistically attainable? Would the combination of existing information and that which could readily be compiled permit a reasonably accurate picture of the impact of immigration on the environment of the United States?

3. The present subsection has considered the impact of immigration on the environment. The converse question is the impact of the environment on immigration. Increasingly, environmental catastrophe spurs flight from less developed countries to more developed ones. See Suzette Brooks Masters, *Environmentally Induced Migration: Beyond a Culture of Reaction*, 14 Georgetown Immigration L.J. 855 (2000).

SECTION F.   THE POLITICS OF IMMIGRATION

As you have seen, immigration policy is truly a constellation of sub-policies. The subjects include the ones featured in these readings—family, jobs, race, culture, language, security, economics, population, and the environment. They also include policy questions on refugee protection, a subject you will explore in chapter 11.

Like any other volatile public issue, immigration policy additionally reflects partisan and interest group politics. This short section attempts only to summarize some of the more salient forces.

Race, of course, has figured prominently in discussions of immigration history. See, e.g., Richard A. Boswell, *Racism and U.S. Immigration Law: Prospects for Reform after "9/11"?*, 7 J. Gender, Race & Justice 315 (2003); Charles J. Ogletree, Jr., *America's Schizophrenic Immigration Policy: Race, Class, and Reason*, 41 Boston College L. Rev. 755 (2000) (both arguing that racial animus has historically driven immigration politics); Patrick Weil, *Races at the Gate: A Century of Racial Distinctions in American Immigration Policy*, 15 Georgetown Immigration L.J. 625 (2001). The anti-Asian sentiments of the late 19th and early 20th centuries, described in the previous readings on Chinese exclusion, as well as later laws targeted at Japanese immigrants, were among the earlier, and most fully explicated, American examples of the direct impact of race on immigration policy. Professor Gilbert Carrasco, in examining the connection between immigration history and race, cites several episodes of abusive treatment of Mexican workers—ranging from the Bracero guestworker program initiated in World War II to "Operation Wetback" and other programs designed to repatriate Mexicans when their labor was no longer needed. Gilbert Paul Carrasco, *Latinos in the United States—Invitation and Exile*, in Juan F. Perea (ed.), Immigrants Out! The New Nativism and the Anti–Immigrant Impulse in the United States, at 190 et seq. (1997); see also Gerald P. Lopez, *Undocumented Mexican Migration: In Search of a Just Immigration Law and Policy*, 28 UCLA L.Rev. 615 (1981); Andrew Silverman, *An Historical and Legal Perspective of Mexican Migration*, 1988 Arizona J. Internat'l & Comp. L. 138. Many believe that a combination of racial attitudes and anti-immigrant feelings have historically influenced not only Congress and the executive, but also the courts. See generally Stephen H. Legomsky, *Immigration Law and the Principle of Plenary Congressional Power*, 1984 Supreme Ct. Rev. 255, 286–95; Irene Scharf, *Tired of Your Masses: A History of and Judicial Responses to Early Twentieth Century Anti–Immigrant Legislation*, 21 Univ. of Hawaii L. Rev. 131 (1999) (speaking specifically to court decisions that upheld various anti-Asian or anti-immigrant land laws, English language laws, and other laws with disproportionate adverse effects on immigrants or on particular ethnic groups).

Is this just history, or does race continue to influence the making of immigration policy? Certainly animus toward immigrants generally, and toward immigrants of color in particular, remains a serious problem in 21st-century America. See section H below. Many writers contend that race remains a major driving force behind a number of recent anti-immigration policy decisions. Some examples appear elsewhere in this book. See especially the discussions of the "diversity immigrant" program, in chapter 3, section D below; the Haitian interdiction program, in chapter 11; and California Proposition 187, in chapter 12. For some thoughtful explorations, see, e.g., Howard F. Chang, *Immigration Policy, Liberal Principles, and the Republican Tradition*, 85 Georgetown L. Rev. 2101, 2115–19 (1997); Bill Ong Hing, *No Place for Angels: In Reaction to Kevin Johnson,*

2000 Univ. Illinois L. Rev. 559, 583–601; John Scanlan, Book Review, *Something Happened: Descent into the Immigration Maelstrom*, 4 Indiana J. Global Legal Studies 239 (1996). The initiative process poses special concerns. See Kevin R. Johnson, *An Essay on Immigration Politics, Popular Democracy, and California's Proposition 187: The Political Relevance and Legal Irrelevance of Race*, 70 Washington L. Rev. 629 (1995).

Sometimes these forces are generic reactions to immigrants; at other times, they are reactions to ethnic subgroups. You have seen examples of specifically anti-Asian movements. Several writers have also commented on the particular political obstacles faced by Latino immigrants. In addition to the literature cited in sections C above and H below, see, e.g., Kevin R. Johnson, *Civil Rights and Immigration: Challenges for the Latino Community in the Twenty–First Century*, 8 La Raza L.J. 42 (1995).

Other scholars argue that recent immigration policy has reflected bias toward Arabs and Arab–Americans. Professor Susan Akram, for example, suggests that western stereotyping of Arabs and Muslims has driven both asylum policy and procedures for secret evidence hearings in cases of alleged terrorism. See, respectively, Susan Musarrat Akram, *Orientalism Revisited in Asylum and Refugee Claims*, 12 Internat'l J. of Refugee L. 7 (2000); Susan M. Akram, *Scheherezade Meets Kafka: Two Dozen Sordid Tales of Ideological Exclusion*, 14 Georgetown Immigration L.J. 51 (1999). Other writers find analogous anti-Arab stereotyping in a leading Supreme Court decision, *Reno v. American–Arab Anti–Discrimination Committee*, 525 U.S. 471, 119 S.Ct. 936, 142 L.Ed.2d 940 (1999). See Berta Esperanza Hernández-Truyol, *Nativism, Terrorism, and Human Rights: The Global Wrongs of Reno v. American–Arab Anti–Discrimination Committee*, 31 Columbia Human Rights L. Rev. 521 (2000); Adrien Katherine Wing, *Reno v. American–Arab Anti–Discrimination Committee: A Critical Race Perspective*, 31 Columbia Human Rights L. Rev. 561, especially at 571–87 (2000).

As the introduction to this section signaled, however, race is hardly the only factor that shapes United States immigration policy. Perhaps as a result, today's immigration debates defy traditional liberal/conservative lines. See generally Gary P. Freeman & Bob Birrell, *Divergent Paths of Immigration Politics in the United States and Australia*, 27 Population & Development Rev. 525 (2001) (arguing that restrictionist immigration policies have taken hold more easily in U.S. than in Australia and considering why); Kevin R. Johnson, *Los Olvidados: Images of the Immigrant, Political Power of Noncitizens, and Immigration Law and Enforcement*, 1993 Brigham Young Univ. L. Rev. 1139; Peter H. Schuck, *The Politics of Rapid Legal Change: Immigration Policy in the 1980's*, 6 Studies in Amer. Political Development 37 (1992); Peter H. Schuck, *The Emerging Political Consensus on Immigration Law*, 5 Georgetown Immigration L.J. 1 (1991); see also Jeanette Money, Fences and Neighbors: The Political Geography of Immigration Control (1999) (demonstrating that sometimes the geographic distribution of immigrants *within* a destination country can affect political calculations).

Professor Kevin Johnson, while acknowledging many proud moments in U.S. immigration history, Kevin R. Johnson, The "Huddled Masses" Myth–Immigration and Civil Rights at 1–2 (2004), sees a common and disturbing thread in the overall civil rights record of U.S. immigration policy. Citing the treatment of racial minorities, political pariahs, the poor, criminals, women, and gays and lesbians, he paints a picture of pervasive (and recurrent) civil rights abuses.

Yet, one of the more striking features of immigration politics is their volatility. This is not merely a modern trend. Public sentiments toward immigrants have always fluctuated. In recent years, the fluctuations have been especially rapid.

In the mid–1990s, anti-immigrant sentiment peaked. While some of the feeling bubbled below the surface, other signs were quite visible—the recommendations of Congress's Commission on Immigration Reform for radically lowering the ceilings on family-sponsored immigration; (unsuccessful) bills in Congress to implement those recommendations; the overwhelming passage in 1994 of California Proposition 187, which would have prohibited local school districts from enrolling undocumented noncitizen children (but which was permanently enjoined by a court order); the massive changes introduced by IIRIRA; a 1996 anti-terrorism law that contains numerous anti-immigrant provisions unrelated to terrorism; a 1996 welfare reform law that bars even legal immigrants from the main safety net programs; a serious movement to amend the Constitution to deny citizenship to children born in the United States to undocumented parents; a fast-moving official English movement; and strident 1996 presidential election-year rhetoric, particularly in California. These and other recent events are taken up in various chapters of this book. One might hold favorable or unfavorable views of any of these events, but together they paint an unmistakable picture of a political climate that did not bode well for immigrants.

Why did this happen? Almost certainly there were multiple causes, and consensus is lacking as to which factors were the most influential. With the caveat that different concerns drive different people, one might suggest that major contributing forces probably included pessimism and insecurity about America's economic future, perceptions that immigration causes unemployment or low wages, racial and ethnic animosity or at least discomfort, a fear of national balkanization, a fear of crime, the tendency for anger about illegal immigration to spill over unconsciously into a general antipathy toward immigrants, and the public's lack of knowledge about what the legal requirements for the admission of immigrants actually are. Stephen H. Legomsky, *E Pluribus Unum: Immigration, Race, and Other Deep Divides*, 21 Southern Illinois Univ. L.Rev. 101 (1996); see also Bill Ong Hing, *Immigration Policies: Messages of Exclusion to African Americans*, 37 Howard L.Rev. 237 (1994)(noting many African Americans' perceptions that they are losing jobs to immigrants); Romano L. Mazzoli & Enid Trucios–Haynes, *Public Sentiment and Congressional Response: 15*

Years of Immigration Policymaking, 73 IR 469 (Apr. 12, 1996) (stressing the dangers of linking legal and illegal immigration reform).

In a few short years, the playing field shifted dramatically. In 1993, some 65% of all Americans favored reducing or halting immigration. By the fall of 1997—only one year after the spate of 1996 federal anti-immigration legislation—that percentage had fallen to 46%, largely, one presumes, because of the booming economy. USA Today, Oct. 13, 1997, at 1, 11. By September 2000, the same percentage had fallen again, to 38%. Jeffrey M. Jones, Gallup Press Release, Sept. 22, 2000. Interestingly, the responses of Democrats and Republicans were almost identical. The one significant positive correlation was between level of education and favorable views of immigration. 46% of those respondents who had only a high school education or less wanted immigration reduced. Among those with advanced degrees, only 24% wanted immigration reduced.

A June 2001 survey showed that 41% of Americans wanted immigration reduced. The ethnicity of the respondents mattered. Only 25% of Latino respondents wanted to reduce immigration; the corresponding figures for blacks and for non-Latino whites were 31% and 45%, respectively. Jeffrey M. Jones, Gallup News Service, *Americans Have Mixed Opinions about Immigration* (July 18, 2001).

The post–1996 changes were felt in more concrete ways as well. In a period of just a few years, Congress grandparented certain classes of immigrants who were present at the time of the 1996 welfare reforms, passed special legislation to benefit certain Central American and Soviet bloc nationals, enacted additional special legislation on behalf of certain Haitian nationals, and eased some of the naturalization requirements and some of the requirements for citizenship by descent. The former INS— under pressure from Congress and with supplemental appropriations— allocated additional resources to sharply reduce the long processing backlogs for naturalization applications, LPR visa petitions, and other filings. The Supreme Court handed down several immigration-related decisions; while not all were favorable to immigrants, several were notable for their favorable rulings on the issues of indefinite detention, judicial review of expulsion decisions, and the non-retroactivity of restrictions on certain forms of discretionary relief. The various developments are covered in more detail throughout this book.

Then came the September 11, 2001 terrorist attacks on the United States. In a combined New York Times / CBS News poll taken in the immediate aftermath of the attacks (2–3 days later), the percentage of respondents who felt that the levels of immigration were too high jumped to 53%. Richard L. Berke & Janet Elder, *Poll Finds Majority Back Use of Military*, New York Times (Sept. 16, 2001). One year later, that figure was largely unchanged, with 54% in favor of decreasing immigration. USA Today (Sept. 6, 2002). By 2004, however, opinion had begun to soften; only 41% favored immigration reductions, NPR/Kaiser/Kennedy School Poll, *Immigration—Summary of Findings* at 1 (May 27—Aug. 2, 2004), and by February 2005, the figure had dropped to 39% (versus 37% in favor of maintaining current levels and 14% favoring immigration increases). Westhill Partners/Hotline Poll, The Hotline (Feb. 2005).

At this writing, the U.S. economy continues to sputter and America is still reeling from the terrorist attacks of September 11, 2001 and the daily reports on the war in Iraq. The polling results will surely change, but it is too early to predict by how much and in precisely which respects.

Public opinion aside, at least two factors account for the occasional surges in the political power of immigrants. One factor is the immigrants themselves. Although LPRs and other noncitizens may not vote, see David Weissbrodt & Laura Danielson, Immigration Law and Procedure in a Nutshell 520–21 (5th ed. 2005), those who eventually naturalize do become eligible to vote. And they do have memories. (Whether the voting patterns of naturalized citizens differ appreciably from those of native-born citizens is not yet clear.)

A second source of immigrants' political power is coalitions with other groups. Ethnic constituencies are among the relevant alliances. Professor Gerald Lopez has emphasized the growing numbers of Latinos in the United States and the growing clout that those numbers would be expected to bring. Gerald P. Lopez, *Learning about Latinos*, 19 Chicano–Latino L. Rev. 363 (1998). Both of the major political parties aggressively pursue Latino votes. The intensity of those efforts, as well as the intensity of efforts to woo other ethnic constituencies, vary by region and district.

Politics make strange bedfellows, and immigration politics seem to make unusually strange bedfellows. As noted earlier, it is not uncommon for free-market Republicans to team up with civil rights-oriented Democrats on behalf of immigration, or (at least in the past) for socially conservative Republicans to team up with labor union Democrats and (some) environmental advocates in opposition to immigration. But today, even those formerly predictable patterns often fail to hold. The AFL–CIO, anxious to boost its declining membership, was one of the early interest groups to call for an amnesty for undocumented immigrants. Manufacturing, agricultural, and other business interests frequently favor increasing or otherwise facilitating immigration, as readers of the Wall Street Journal will readily attest. And many African–Americans, concerned about job competition with immigrants, have had mixed feelings about liberalizing the immigration laws. See Bill Ong Hing, *Immigration Policies: Messages of Exclusion to African–Americans*, 37 Howard L.J. 237 (1994). Generalizations have become hazardous, and even those that seem momentarily safe are subject to new surprises.

Because coalitions hold so much potential for achieving reform, several scholars have begun to prioritize conscious bridgebuilding. Professor Berta Hernández-Truyol has written a series of three articles advocating Latino alliances with various others. See Berta Esperanza Hernández-Truyol, *Building Bridges–Latinas and Latinos at the Crossroads: Realities, Rhetoric and Replacement*, 25 Columbia Human Rights L. Rev. 369 (1994) (urging an alliance among all Latino/a subgroups); Berta Esperanza Hernández-Truyol, *Building Bridges: Bringing International Human Rights*

Home, 9 La Raza L.J. 69 (1996) (urging a global-local alliance that would promote both civil/political rights and social/economic rights); Berta Esperanza Hernández-Truyol, *Building Bridges III: Personal Narratives, Incoherent Paradigms, and Plural Citizens*, 19 Chicano–Latino L. Rev. 303 (1998) (urging alliances among communities of color); see also Kevin R. Johnson, *The Case for African American and Latina/o Cooperation in Challenging Racial Profiling in Law Enforcement*, 55 Florida L. Rev. 341 (2003); George A. Martínez, *African-Americans, Latinos, and the Construction of Race: Toward an Epistemic Coalition*, 19 Chicano–Latino L. Rev. 213 (1998) (calling for a coalition between Latinos and African–Americans); Victor C. Romero, *"Aren't You Latino?" Building Bridges upon Common Misperceptions*, 33 U.C. Davis L. Rev. 837 (2000) (urging oppressed minorities to join forces rather than compete against one another); Victor C. Romero, *On Elián and Aliens: A Political Solution to the Plenary Power Problem*, 4 NYU J. of Legislation & Public Policy 343, 362–63 (2000–01) (urging new citizens of Latino and Asian ethnicities to join forces in lobbying for immigration reform).

Throughout United States history, congressional and presidential commissions have also played influential roles in the design of the nation's immigration laws. During the mid-to-late 1990s, the Commission on Immigration Reform made a number of important recommendations. For a good before-and-after discussion of its work, see Carlos Ortiz Miranda, *United States Commission on Immigration Reform: The Interim and Final Reports*, 38 Santa Clara L. Rev. 645 (1998); Carlos O. Miranda, *An Agenda for the Commission on Immigration Reform*, 29 San Diego L. Rev. 701 (1992).

For a comparative view of the political processes by which immigration policies are constructed, see the highly interesting article by a principal architect of several other countries' immigration laws, James A.R. Nafziger, *A Comparison of Processes for Reforming Migration Laws in Transitional States: China, Kazakhstan, and Albania*, 70 Washington L. Rev. 757 (1995).

Finally, so much of the political theory that underlies the appropriate content of a nation's immigration policy, the process by which that policy should be formulated, and the determinations of who should participate in that process rests on fundamental notions of the meaning of citizenship. That subject is taken up in chapter 13, section C.

SECTION G.   IMMIGRATION AND NATIONAL SECURITY: AN INTRODUCTION

Within seconds of the September 11, 2001 terrorist attacks the media, government officials, and the public all zeroed in on the foreign nationalities of the perpetrators. It is no longer possible to talk about U.S. immigration policy without serious discussion of the national security implications, both real and perceived. The questions are fundamental: How does a nation dedicated to the principles of liberal democracy preserve basic individual freedoms and still protect its inhabitants from violent attack? And how does a nation of immigrants reconcile the civil and human rights of noncitizens with its legitimate national security needs?

These questions will be deferred until chapter 10, which considers in detail the panoply of national security measures taken by Congress and the executive branch in the wake of September 11. Generally, the initiatives have fallen into several rough categories—detention, intelligence-gathering, expanding the grounds on which noncitizens may be removed from the United States, contracting noncitizens' procedural rights, stricter visa and other overseas policies, and enhanced border enforcement. Among the other controversies that these policies have generated, they have disproportionately affected noncitizens who are either Muslim or of Arab descent (or both). Consequently, chapter 10 also takes up the hotly debated issue of ethnic and religious profiling.

SECTION H.   IMMIGRANTS, SELF-IDENTITY, AND HOME

In the following essay one immigrant relates his personal feelings about what it means to be an immigrant. Experiences differ widely, of course, and the achievements of this particular individual (who died in 2005) were unusual. Nonetheless, his thoughtful comments have struck responsive chords with many other immigrants who have sought to discover their own inner feelings about who they were and who they have become.

Henry Grunwald, Home is Where you are Happy

Time, July 8, 1985, pp. 100–01.

The author, Time Inc.'s editor in chief, came to America from Austria at the age of 17 with his family. His father was a noted Viennese librettist.

Every immigrant leads a double life. Every immigrant has a double identity and a double vision, being suspended between an old and a new home, an old and a new self.

The very notion of a new home, of course, is in a sense as impossible as the notion of new parents. Parents *are* who they are; home *is* what it is. Home is the wallpaper above the bed, the family dinner table, the church bells in the morning, the bruised shins of the playground, the small fears that come with dusk, the streets and squares and monuments and shops that constitute one's first universe. Home is one's birthplace, ratified by memory.

Yet home, like parentage, must be legitimized through love; otherwise, it is only a fact of geography or biology. Most immigrants to America found their love of their old homes betrayed. Whether Ireland starved them, or Nazi Germany persecuted them, or Viet Nam drove them into the sea, they did not really abandon their countries; their countries abandoned them. In

America, they found the possibility of a new love, the chance to nurture new selves.

Not uniformly, not without exceptions. Every generation has its Know–Nothing movement, its fear—often understandable—and hatred of alien invasion. That is as true today as it always was. In spite of all this, the American attitude remains unique. Throughout history, exile has been a calamity; America turned it into a triumph and placed its immigrants in the center of a national epic. It is still symbolized by that old copper-plated cliché, the Statue of Liberty, notwithstanding the condescension and the awful poetry of the famous Emma Lazarus lines ("the wretched refuse of your teeming shore").

The epic is possible because America is an idea as much as it is a country. America has nothing to do with allegiance to a dynasty and very little to do with allegiance to a particular place, but everything to do with allegiance to a set of principles. To immigrants, those principles are especially real because so often they were absent or violated in their native lands. It was no accident in the '60s and '70s, when alienation was in flower, that it often seemed to be "native" Americans who felt alienated, while aliens or the children of aliens upheld the native values. The immigrant's double vision results in a special, somewhat skewed perspective on America that can mislead but that can also find revelation in the things that to native Americans are obvious. Psychiatrist Robert Coles speaks of those "who straddle worlds and make of that very experience a new world."

It is not easy. Successive waves of immigration differ, of course, and a refugee from wartime Europe does not have the same experiences as a refugee from postwar Viet Nam 40 years later. But all immigrants have certain things in common, and all know the classic, opposite impulses: to draw together in protective enclaves where through churches, clubs, cafés, newspapers, the old culture is fiercely maintained; and on the other hand to rush headlong into the American mainstream, seeking to adopt indiscriminately new manners, clothes, technology and sometimes names.

Inevitably, the immigrant is a student, and his more or less permanent occupation is learning. That is a nervous business ("Have I got it right?"); depending on one's temperament, it is also a series of joyful discoveries. For younger immigrants, those discoveries begin in school, and the initial, most amazing one is the openness, the absence of the compulsion and petty tyranny that characterize the classroom almost everywhere else in the world. But if that openness is indeed joyful and liberating to young minds, the accompanying lack of discipline is also frightening and destructive: the heart of the perennial American conflict between freedom and order.

The immigrant's education continues everywhere. He must master not only a new history but a whole new imagination. The process goes on at various speeds, and odd gaps can appear. The immigrant carries different nursery rhymes in his head, different fairy tales. He may have just graduated from college Phi Beta Kappa but not know who Mary Poppins is. He may be taking the bar examination and be rather dim about Popeye. Prince Eugene of Savoy lodges stubbornly in the mind (song learned at the age of seven: "Prince Eugene, the noble knight . . ."), while Patrick Henry appears as a stranger, an image full of gaps, like an unfinished sketch.

A continuing part of the immigrant's education is the comparison between the anticipated or imagined America and the real country. The anticipation depends on time and place, but the reality is always startling. If the vision of America was formed by Ginger Rogers and Fred Astaire dancing atop glittering skyscrapers, how to accept the slums? If the vision was noise and materialist chaos, how to account for a Quaker meeting house or the daily, relentless idealism of legions of American do-gooders? If the vision was a childhood fantasy of the Wild West, how can one grasp the fact that Sitting Bull was a real man fighting a real Government and dying a real death?

A new language: nagging impediment to some, liberation to others. There is the constant struggle to achieve the proper accent, like trying to sing one's way into some strange and maddeningly elusive music. There is the pain and bother of trying as an adult or near adult to learn new words and meanings. But these words and meanings have a certain innocence, a certain freshness, free of the constraint, the boredom, the touches of shame that are imposed on one's native language in the classroom or the nursery.

English is illogical and headily free compared, for example, with the grammatical rigidities of French or German. Some newcomers are lost in this malleable structure; others fall upon English with an instinctive sense of recognition, as one might discover a hitherto unknown brother. Shake-speare and Melville gradually replace Goethe and Racine, though drilled-in passages never quite fade; the experience can begin as vague disloyalty and end in passion. Immigrants who know English as one of the great unifiers of America will never be reconciled to those others * * * who refuse to accept English fully, thus creating an ominous dual culture in many parts of the U.S. Language is life. For many immigrants, the true act of naturalization occurs when they start having dreams in English.

More puzzling and complicated than language is the American social syntax. The first impression is one of dazzling and rather unsettling informality, an indiscriminate camaraderie. But one learns that going to the opera in shirt-sleeves (an outrage, surely!) does not mean contempt for culture or even necessarily a lack of rules. Calling the boss by his first name, which takes some effort, does not mean that he and the office boy are equals. Indeed, equality is both the great illusion and the great reality of America. The immigrant is slow to understand that below the egalitarian surface there are hierarchies and tribes, proper and improper addresses, great names and lowly names, old money looking down on new money, older immigrants looking down on newer—a topography to which there are very few maps.

But after this discovery there gradually comes yet another insight that whipsaws the immigrant back toward the original perception: there really is no fixed social structure after all. There is above everything else that much vaunted mobility—from place to place, career to career, status to status—which turns so many native-born Americans into immigrants in their own country.

In philosophical terms, Europe (or Asia or Africa) is the world of being; America is the world of becoming. In Europe, one is what one is; in America, one is what one does. To the immigrant this is a discovery of high excitement and also of some anxiety. Opportunity is not just opportunity but an imperative and a reproach. If anyone can make it in America, why haven't you? If anyone can be what he wants to be, why aren't you more?

There follows the suspicion that making it is the only American morality. But no—it can't be that simple. The first tangible hint of American moral attitudes comes on the immigration form: the solemn requirement to swear that you are not a Communist, or not a prostitute, or whatever. To those coming from older and more cynical societies, this is the utmost sort of naiveté. For the immigrant, it foreshadows the American conviction that one can mandate, even legislate morality. That conviction represents an amalgam of Puritanism, with its belief in a permanently flawed human nature, and the Enlightenment tradition, with its belief in the perfectibility of man. Cotton Mather, meet Thomas Jefferson. This contradictory combination bespeaks the sheer and sometimes hopelessly unrealistic determination to overcome any evil that cannot be ignored, the refusal to accept the status quo in the universe.

The moral landscape the immigrant left behind was usually dominated by the spires of one church or perhaps of two churches living in uneasy peace after centuries of bloody contest. He is therefore overwhelmed by the dizzying variety of religion in America, by the churches, sects, subsects and cults that proliferate in a sort of spiritual shopping mall. But he learns to appreciate the fact that a country that can create God in so many images, no matter how eccentric, has never used fire and sword to impose a faith on its citizens.

The most awesome thing to learn about America is the land itself. No newcomer is ever prepared for its size: the vastness of a country that is a continent. The quintessential American landscape is not found in the mountains or on the shore but in the Great Plains. Space (terrestrial space, not space out there) is the true metaphor for the American condition. Speed can conquer it, but nothing built by man can dominate it. That is perhaps one reason why even the most imposing American skylines can look strangely impermanent and fragile. America does not build for the ages. There are no American palaces and no (convincing) American cathedrals.

But the beauty of America is not in its buildings, not in its artifacts or its arts. Its greatest beauty is in its ideas. Freedom is the ultimate value, whether aesthetic or political. * * *

                                    * * *

The hardest situation for the immigrant comes when the future seems in doubt and when America seems about to default on its promise. It happened during the Great Depression, and it happened again during Viet Nam. It happens today whenever one contemplates the dark and yet quite visible underside of American life: the New York City subway or the filth of a roadside service station, the American infernos of drugs and crime and sexual decadence, the dregs of the cities—"wretched refuse" indeed. At such moments it sometimes seems that many of the lands the immigrants left behind are actually doing better than America, that they have in a sense "won." Of course, it is not so. It would be dishonest and thus disloyal to ignore the dreadful scars and blemishes of America, but they are themselves to a large extent the result of freedom—sometimes an excess of freedom. For freedom can be dangerous. Yet freedom also holds within it the means to correct its defects, for it allows, indeed encourages, people to criticize their society, to tinker with it, to improve it.

Ultimately, the education of every immigrant is personal, individual. No immigrant can speak for all others. But a Viennese librettist, Alfred Grunwald, who came to America in 1940 and sought to continue practicing his art, wrote some lyrics that sum up much of the immigrant experience in America: "*Deine Heimat ist wo das Glück dich grüsst ... *" Roughly translated, "Home is where you are happy." Sentimental, perhaps, and certainly not conventionally patriotic, but appropriate for a country that wrote the pursuit of happiness into its founding document.

That pursuit continues for the immigrant in America, and it never stops. But it comes to rest at a certain moment. The moment is hard to pin down, but it occurs perhaps when the immigrant's double life and double vision converge toward a single state of mind. When the old life, the old home fade into a certain unreality: places one merely visits, in fact or in the mind, practicing the tourism of memory. It occurs when the immigrant learns his ultimate lesson: above all countries, America, if loved, returns love.

———

Grunwald's success story is exceptional; most people, whether native-born or immigrants, do not become editors-in-chief of Time Magazine. (Grunwald later became the U.S. Ambassador to Austria.) Immigrants of color are especially likely to report markedly different sorts of daily life experiences. As the following passages illustrate, many *United States citizens* of color also are sometimes consciously or unconsciously assumed to be "foreign," either literally or figuratively.

Berta Esperanza Hernández–Truyol, Natives, Newcomers and Nativism: A Human Rights Model for the Twenty–First Century

23 Fordham Urban L.J. 1075, 1075–76 (1996).

Saturday, October 7, 1995. 7:00 p.m. Friends and I meet at an art gallery and, after looking at some of the new work, amble down the street to a local restaurant. The place is small and, as usual, crowded. We wait outside, chatting, for fifteen minutes before being seated. The owner leads us to our table, a crowded four-top arranged at a diagonal against the wall and flanked by two-tops on either side. With my computer in tow over my right shoulder and a jean jacket over my left arm, I stand at the top of the diagonal trying to figure out how I can get in to take my seat. All of a sudden, and out of the blue, I hear "Excuse me, you're in America now, you say 'excuse me,' SAVAGE, ANIMAL." It appears that a sleeve of my jacket has brushed against the Angry Diner. I have no opportunity to apologize or even to realize what has happened. Angry Diner continues to mutter, unintelligibly, under his breath. One of my friends, Rosa, who has been walking right behind me, upon seeing my stunned expression simply says, "Forget it, let's just sit down." By the time Meika and Mercedes, our two other friends, join us, they are rather curious—wondering what mischief I have caused. After relaying the incident to my now equally stunned friends, we move on to have our nice dinner, or try, anyway. Angry Diner, Rosa tells me later, never stopped muttering things under his breath. Finally, I think peace is at hand when Angry Diner and his companion get up to leave. He moves their table toward ours so that she can negotiate a tight corner (on the other side of our table). As he passes our table, he turns around, stares at me, utters an obscenity, and shoves Meika's chair before rushing to make his final exit—this time with wait persons chasing after him. Again, we are stunned. The restaurant owner joins our table to find out what had taken place, and after hearing the whole sordid story she says, "This is America, eh? Sure it is, and he is not welcome here anymore." Her English, unlike mine, is foreign accented; her look, unlike mine, is not brown.

Imagine. It is 1996 and we are about to move into the twenty-first century. We live in a city that is known globally as *The* City. *The* City where, since the turn of the nineteenth century, Lady Liberty, the quintessential representation of freedom, has greeted foreign subjects. The poem gracing her impressive figure is a symbol of welcomeness, diversity, shelter:

> Give me your tired, your poor,
> Your huddled masses yearning to breathe free,
> The wretched refuse of your teeming shore.
> Send these, the homeless, the tempest-tost to me,
> I lift my lamp beside the golden door.

Unfortunately, this feeling of fellowship is anything but evident in our glorious city, across our nation, or even world-wide these days. This was made patently clear to *me* while trying to enjoy a quiet dinner with friends. [The author here cites several anti-immigrant measures that were then recently enacted or pending.] * * * Such developments make one wonder what has occurred to the apparent (but largely mythical) *esprit de corps* that welcomed foreigners in earlier days of our republic.

Michael A. Olivas, The Chronicles, My Grandfather's Stories, and Immigration Law: The Slave Traders Chronicle as Racial History

34 St. Louis Univ. L.J. 425, 425–27 (1990).

The funny thing about stories is that everyone has one. My grandfather had them, with plenty to spare. When I was very young, he would regale me with stories, usually about politics, baseball, and honor. These were his themes, the subject matter he carved out for himself and his grandchildren. As the oldest grandson and his first godchild, I held a special place of responsibility and affection. In Mexican families, this patrimony handed to young boys is one remnant of older times that is fading, like the use of Spanish in the home, posadas at Christmas, or the deference accorded all elders.

In Sabino Olivas' world, there were three verities, ones that he adhered to his entire life: political and personal loyalties are paramount; children should work hard and respect their elders; and people should conduct their lives with honor. Of course, each of these themes had a canon of stories designed, like parables, to illustrate the larger theme, and, like the Bible, to be interlocking, cross referenced, and synoptic. That is, they could be embellished in the retelling, but they had to conform to the general themes of loyalty, hard work, and honor.

* * *

His other favorite story, which included a strong admonition to me, was a story about how he and other Hispanics had been treated in Texas on their way to World War I. A trainload of soldiers from Arizona and northern New Mexico, predominantly of Mexican origin (both New Mexico and Arizona had only recently become states), were going by train to training camp in Ft. Hays, Kansas. Their train stopped in a town near Amarillo, Texas, and all the men poured out of the train to eat at a restaurant, one that catered to train travelers. But only to some. There was a sign prominently displayed, "No colored or Mexicans allowed," and word spread among them that this admissions policy was taken seriously.

My grandfather, who until this time had never been outside the Territory or the State of New Mexico (after 1912), was not used to this kind of indignity. After all, he was from a state where Hispanics and Indians constituted a majority of the population, especially in the North, and it was his first face-to-face encounter with racism, Texas style. Shamefacedly, the New Mexicans ate the food that Anglo soldiers bought and brought to the train, but he never forgot the humiliation and anger he felt that day. Sixty-five years later, when he told me this story, he remembered clearly how most of the men died in France or elsewhere in Europe, defending a country that never fully accorded them their rights.

Natsu Taylor Saito, Alien and Non–Alien Alike: Citizenship, "Foreignness," and Racial Hierarchy in American Law

76 Oregon L. Rev. 261, 262–64, 295–97, 301–02, 310–11 (1997).

[W]ithin the United States, if a person is racially identified as African American or white, that person is presumed to be legally a U.S. citizen and socially an American ... [but] these presumptions are not present for Asian Americans, Latinos, Arab Americans, and other non-Black racial minorities. Rather, there is the opposite presumption that these people are foreigners; or, if they are U.S. citizens, then their racial identity includes a foreign component.

[Neil Gotanda, *Asian American Rights and the "Miss Saigon Syndrome,"* in Hyung–Chan Kim (ed.), Asian Americans and the Supreme Court 1087, 1096 (1992).]

Why is it that, even after living in the United States for four or five generations, Asian Americans are still identified as foreign? * * * My thesis is that the "racing" of Asian Americans as foreign reinforces the American racial hierarchy in two ways. First, it creates a buffer zone between those identified as "black" and "white." Second, it constructs Asian Americans as instant outsiders, or "faux" citizens, against whom "real Americans" can unite in times of crisis.

* * *

From the ugly "Go back to where you came from" to the purportedly neutral "Where are you from?" or the intended-to-be-complimentary "You speak such good English," Asian Americans are confronted daily with the presumption that they are not really Americans. Where does this presumption come from? Why is it so pervasive and so apparently acceptable?

* * *

The attribution of foreignness takes on both ostensibly positive and negative forms. Positive portrayals generally include images of Asians as hardworking, industrious, thrifty, family-oriented and, for women, seductively mysterious and exotic. The negative images are almost invariably the same traits, simply portrayed with different connotations. * * * Hardworking and industrious becomes unfairly competitive; family-oriented becomes clannish; mysterious becomes dangerously inscrutable. Nonetheless, both the positive and negative forms of foreignness are portrayals of outsiders, of the "other."

Part of what allows for this fluidity, this right-before-your-eyes magical transformation from model minority to yellow peril and back to model minority again is the construct of foreignness. Each of the images has been painted with the brush of foreignness, and it is this tinting that provides the continuity behind the changing value-attribution. * * *

[Here, Saito suggests that attributing foreignness to Asians served the historical function of creating a pool of cheap labor.]

* * *

A second significant function served by the attribution of foreignness to Asian Americans is the ability to turn them into enemies on a moment's notice. This has been true both metaphorically, as enemies in trade wars, and in a literal sense. Asians have been identified as the enemy in the most significant armed conflicts involving the United States within the memory of most Americans–World War II, the Korean War, and the war in Vietnam, as well as the Cold War. Racial stereotypes of Asians have been used to make them appear evil and inhuman and perhaps, thus, easier to kill. * * *

* * * Those same stereotypes, because they are race-based, can then be turned against any of the other subgroups. This is illustrated by how easily the portrayal of Chinese as good and Japanese as evil during World War II was reversed during the Cold War.

* * *

Numerous incidents of reported violence against Asian Americans involve "foreigner" or "enemy" imagery. For example, in 1989 a Chinese American man was beaten to death in Raleigh, North Carolina by white men who attacked him "because they didn't like Vietnamese" and because "their brothers went over to Vietnam in the war and they never came back." In 1992, a Vietnamese student at the University of Miami was beaten to death by several white youths who called him "Chink" and "Viet Cong."

The 458 incidents reported to the national Asian Pacific American Legal Consortium in 1995 included a twenty-three-year-old Vietnamese American who died after an assault by three young men who taunted him with statements such as "[w]hat the f—k are you looking at, gook?" A twenty-three-year-old Chinese American was stabbed to death in the parking lot of a grocery store by an unemployed musician who stated that he had decided to "kill me a Chinaman" because Asians "got all the good jobs." A Pakistani taxi driver was beaten by a New York City police officer who said, "[y]ou immigrants think we're stupid. . . . This is my country, I'll teach you a lesson." A middle-aged Chinese American woman was beaten by people who yelled, "[f]—k you chink, go back to your country," and an East Indian woman's home was vandalized by neighbors who said, "[y]ou Hindu bitches, why did you have to move here?"

Victor C. Romero, Broadening Our World: Citizens and Immigrants of Color in America

27 Capital Univ. L. Rev. 13, 29–33 (1998).

* * *

* * * [P[rivately motivated violence against Asian–Americans has escalated dramatically in recent years. Indeed, the stereotype of the "Asian–American as foreigner" still remains today, as the following example from my own experience in rustic Carlisle, Pennsylvania demonstrates. * * *

Academic year 1995–96, my first year in law teaching, was an exceptionally good year. The fall of 1995 saw my wife's and my return to Pennsylvania after many years, where I was fortunate to be offered a job teaching at the Dickinson School of Law in Carlisle, just twenty minutes outside of Harrisburg, the state capital. Needless to say, we were both thrilled—Corie, because she would be closer to her family after having spent a good bit of time in California, and me, because I was thrilled to be offered the opportunity to teach law. Having had our fill of Los Angeles, we were both excited to be moving to peaceful, rural south central Pennsylvania; we gladly gave up our hour-long commutes in exchange for smog-free walks to the law school. And we settled into Carlisle nicely: on a handshake (our wonderful landlady did not believe in leases), we rented the ground floor of a lovely Victorian home in the historic district and looked forward to quickly assimilating into the culture of small-town life. * * * In a year's time, we have become small-town folk and have enjoyed the transformation along the way.

However, unlike probably ninety percent of Carlisle's married couples, we have an interracial marriage—Corie traces her Caucasian roots to Europe, specifically, Wales, the Netherlands, Germany, and Norway, while I came to the U.S. from the Philippines in 1984. And while ninety-nine percent of the time Corie and I are never reminded of this difference by others, when we are, it can sometimes be a painful and frightening experience. On a balmy May evening a couple of weeks before the Class of 96's graduation, Corie and I decided to take a walk around the neighborhood, something which we have enjoyed on many an afternoon. As we crossed Willow heading south on West Street, we noticed a pick-up truck whose occupants began to whistle wolf-calls and shout lewd remarks. * * * It soon became clear that we were the targets of these obscenities:

"Hey, you Japanese sonofabitch! Why don't you fuck her? I have!"

That said, the truck slowly turned the corner, more obscenities coming from within. * * * After several tense moments, we were relieved to see the truck pull away as it rounded the corner. As a last show of power, one of the occupants extended his white arm and thrust his fist into the night air while simultaneously letting out a taunting laugh.

As the truck left our view, Corie and I abandoned our walk and hurried home. Surprisingly, the primary emotion we felt was not anger, but hurt and sadness. Hurt, because we felt that it was unfair that we could no longer enjoy walking around our neighborhood at night; sadness, because here we were in 1996, in what was otherwise an idyllic community, and we had to endure the kind of racist remarks many people only read about in books. Indeed, Corie told me later that evening, "For the first time, I experienced what it is like to be a minority."

Almost two years since the incident, I realize how lucky Corie and I are that we were not hurt that evening. Vincent Chin was not so lucky. In 1982, Chin, a young Chinese–American engineer, was beaten to death with a baseball bat by two white auto workers who, thinking he was Japanese, blamed him for the recession of the American auto industry. Worse, the killer served no jail time. Sadly, the stereotype of the "Asian–American as foreigner" remains, and the consequences can sometimes be fatal.

Asian–Americans are not the only people of color who live within the border of perpetual foreignness. Latino–Americans, especially Mexican–Americans, also suffer this stigma. * * *

NOTES AND QUESTIONS

1.   Professor Kevin Johnson has touched thoughtfully on several sub-issues related to Latino identity. The son of an Anglo father and a Latino mother, Johnson has written a book sensitively describing the process of identity formation for children whose parents are of different ethnicities. See Kevin R. Johnson, How Did You Get to Be Mexican? (1999). He has also drawn a useful distinction between the formation of one's *personal* identity and the formation of one's *group* identity. Kevin R. Johnson, *Immigration and Latino Identity*, 19 Chicano–Latino L. Rev. 197, 197 (1998). With respect to the latter, Johnson distinguishes two kinds of potential conflicts—those between Latinos and non-Latinos, and intra-Latino conflicts between Mexican immigrants and United States citizens of Mexican descent. *Id.* at 199–206.

2.   The interaction of race and gender can complicate the identity question. See Berta Esperanza Hernandez–Truyol, *Borders (En)gendered: Normativities, Latinas, and the LatCrit Paradigm*, 72 NYU L. Rev. 882 (1997) (Latinas live a multidimensional existence that requires constant travel between worlds).

3.   Most of the news stories about racial profiling have concerned African–Americans, but profiling has been a part of the daily lives of people of color generally and has posed particular problems for Mexican–Americans. See generally Kevin R. Johnson, *The Case Against Race Profiling in Immigration Enforcement*, 78 Washington Univ. L.Q. 675 (2000); Victor C. Romero, *Racial Profiling: "Driving While Mexican" and Affirmative Action*, 6 Michigan J. Race & Law 195 (2000).

4.   In chapter 2, you will read about the historical attitudes toward Asians and the relationship of those attitudes to the immigration laws of the late 19th and early 20th centuries. The materials you have just read suggest that many of the same attitudes stubbornly persist. Professor Leti Volpp, after examining differing models of citizenship and considering them in the specific context of Asians and Asian Americans, reaches the following conclusion:

> That the political engagement of Asian Americans in the American republic will inevitably be accompanied by concerns about their loyalty, their trustworthiness, and their ability to prioritize national as opposed to foreign interests is a form of cultural racism. To be seen as primarily governed by group loyalty to one's country of origin suggests a limited capacity for agency, will, or rational thought. This is obviously dehumanizing, since our beliefs as to what is "human" rest on such capacities. The differentiation of who is allowed to be "human," through discourses about racial inferiority, has been fundamental to the creation of many modern democracies. The American rights-bearing subject was allowed to consolidate through the very exclusion of certain racialized subjects.

Leti Volpp, *'Obnoxious to their Very Nature': Asian Americans and Constitutional Citizenship*, 5 Citizenship Studies 57, 68 (2001).

There is now an abundance of literature on the treatment and identities of Asians and Asian–Americans. Some common themes emerge—that the historical suspicions towards Asian immigrants have profoundly influenced the development of United States immigration law, that vestiges of immigration law's anti-Asian genesis can still be found in today's law and practice, and that these suspicions extend beyond Asian immigrants to encompass even United States citizens of Asian descent. For a sampling of the more thoughtful writings, see Robert S. Chang, *Toward an Asian American Legal Scholarship: Critical Race Theory, Post–Structuralism, and Narrative Space*, 81 California L. Rev. 1241 (1993); Neil Gotanda, *"Other Non–Whites" in American Legal History: A Review of* Justice at War, 85 Columbia L. Rev. 1186 (1985); Kevin R. Johnson, *Racial Hierarchy, Asian Americans and Latinos as "Foreigners" and Social Change: Is Law the Way to Go?*, 76 Oregon L. Rev. 347 (1997); Estelle T. Lau, *Excavating the "Chinese Wall": Towards a Socio–Historical Perspective on the Development of United States Immigration Administration and Chinese Exclusion*, 92 Northwestern Univ. L. Rev. 1068 (1998) (book review of Salyer); Frank H. Wu, *Neither Black Nor White: Asian Americans and Affirmative Action*, 15 Boston College Third World L.J. 225 (1995). See also the books and articles by Gyory, Hing, Salyer, Takaki, Ting, and Cole & Chin cited in the discussion following the *Chinese Exclusion Case* in chapter 2, as well as those excerpted above. For a poignant and vivid account, written as fictional narrative but relating the agonizing by interned U.S. citizens of Japanese descent over whether to refuse induction into the U.S. armed forces, see Frank H. Wu, *Difficult Decisions During Wartime: A Letter from a Non–Alien in an Internment Camp to a Friend Back Home*, 54 Case Western Reserve L. Rev. 1301 (2004); see generally Eric K. Yamamoto et al, Race, Rights and Reparation: Law and the Japanese American Internment (2001).

5. Anti–Asian rhetoric was quite noticeable in 1996, amidst reports of contributions by noncitizen Asians to the Democratic National Committee. See Frank H. Wu & Francey Lim Youngberg, *People from China Crossing the River: Asian American Political Empowerment and Foreign Influence*, in Gordon H. Chang (ed.), Asian Americans and Politics, ch. 12 (2001).

6. Many anti-Asian land laws remain on the books today, but a law student project has succeeded in persuading several states to repeal them. The project was carried out by law students at the University of Cincinnati, led by Professor Gabriel J. Chin, with follow-up by law students at the University of New Mexico. See Elizabeth Mulcahy & Mary Schmidt–Nowara, *Law Students Work to Repeal Jim Crow–Era Anti–Asian Alien Land Laws*, 6 BIB 611 (June 15, 2001).

7. Is it better to be criticized or to be ignored? Several commentators believe that, in discussions of racial issues in the United States, Asians and Asian Americans tend to get forgotten. See Robert S. Chang, Disoriented: Asian Americans, Law, and the Nation–State (1999); Eric K. Yamamoto,

Interracial Justice: Conflict and Reconciliation in Post-/Civil Rights America (1999); Harvey Gee, *Asian Americans, the Law, and Illegal Immigration in Post–Civil Rights America: A Review of Three Books*, 77 Univ. Detroit Mercy L. Rev. 71 (1999).

8. Some of the writing has dealt specifically with the treatment or identity formations of immigrants from particular Asian countries (or citizens whose ethnicity traces to particular Asian countries). On Chinese immigrants, see Peter Kwong, Forbidden Workers: Illegal Chinese Immigrants and American Labor (1999); Bill Ong Hing, *No Place for Angels: In Reaction to Kevin Johnson*, 2000 Univ. of Illinois L. Rev. 559; Jan Ting, *"Other than a Chinaman": How U.S. Immigration Law Resulted from and Still Reflects a Policy of Excluding and Restricting Asian Immigration*, 4 Temple Political & Civil Rights L. Rev. 301 (1995). For a poignant, partly fictionalized, autobiographical novel by one Vietnamese boat person, see Lan Cao, Monkey Bridge (1997). The special cultural problems faced by two Southeast Asian refugee groups are described in Bill Ong Hing, *Refugee Policy and Cultural Identity: In the Voice of Hmong and Iu Mein Young Adults*, 1 Race & Poverty L.J. 111 (2003). For a description of the unusual public perceptions of Filipino immigrants, who often have Spanish surnames but Asian appearances, see Victor C. Romero, *"Aren't You Latino?": Building Bridges upon Common Misperceptions*, 33 U.C. Davis L. Rev. 837 (2000).

9. Since Latinos and Asians have constituted the largest numbers of immigrants in recent years, it is hardly surprising that they have featured the most frequently in the literature on immigration and race. Less often discussed, at least until very recently, has been the reception of Arab–Americans. The classic work is Edward W. Said, Orientalism (1978). For well documented arguments that Arab immigrants and Arab–Americans have too often been the victims of racial and religious stereotyping under the immigration laws, see Susan Mussarat Akram, *Orientalism Revisited in Asylum and Refugee Claims*, 12 Internat'l J. Refugee Law 7 (2000); Susan M. Akram, *Scheherezade Meets Kafka: Two Dozen Sordid Tales of Ideological Exclusion*, 14 Georgetown Immigration L.J. 51 (1999).

The public mood turned particularly ugly in the wake of the September 11, 2001 terrorist attacks on the World Trade Towers and the Pentagon. Numerous assaults against Arab–Americans, Muslims (whether or not of Arabic origin), and Muslim mosques were reported. See, e.g., Michael Conlon, *Attacks Against Arab–Americans Escalate in U.S.*, Reuters (Sept. 13, 2001); Bill Ong Hing, *Vigilante Racism: The De–Americanization of Immigrant America*, 7 Michigan J. Race & Law 441 (2002); Leti Volpp, *The Citizen and the Terrorist*, 49 UCLA L. Rev. 1575 (2002) (discussing hate crimes against new, post 9/11, consolidated group of people who appear Middle Eastern, Arab, or Muslim); *cf.* Muneer I. Ahmad, *A Rage Shared by Law: Post–September 11 Racial Violence as Crimes of Passion*, 92 California L. Rev. 1259, 1264 (2004) (discussing public tendency to aggregate "Muslim-looking people" such as Arabs, Muslims, and South Asians). In response, the Justice Department has condemned such hate crimes and the FBI has conducted 360 investigations with state and local law enforcement authorities, having brought criminal charges against approximately 100 individuals as of August 2002. See Final Rule (concerning NSEERS), 67 Fed. Reg. 52584, 52585 (Aug. 12, 2002). Sadly, similar racial episodes immediately spread throughout the world. See, e.g., Kelly Burke, *Muslim Women, Children Targeted*, Sydney Morning Herald, Sept. 14, 2001.

Professor Ahmad, above, adds this:

[A]lthough Americans have condemned the killings of Arabs, Muslims, and South Asians after September 11, these killings have been understood as the result of a displaced anger, one with which many Americans have sympathized and agreed. By this account, the perpetrators of hate crimes against Arabs, Muslims, and South Asians were not guilty of malicious intent or depraved indifference, but of expressing a socially appropriate emotion—overwhelming anger in the aftermath of the terrorist attacks—in socially inappropriate ways. Borrowing from criminal law, the hate crime killings before September 11 were understood as crimes of moral depravity, while the hate killings since September 11 have been understood as crimes of passion. Whereas crimes of moral depravity are devoid of any justification whatsoever, crimes of passion are treated as morally understandable though still illegal transgressions.

Ahmad, above, at 1264.

Along related lines, a recent national poll commissioned by Cornell University's Department of Communication revealed strong public sentiment for restricting the civil liberties of Muslim Americans. 27% of the respondents favored requiring all Muslim Americans to register their addresses with the federal government. 29% approved of undercover law enforcement agents infiltrating Muslim civic organizations. 22% said Muslim and Middle Eastern citizens should be profiled. In total, 44% felt it necessary to curtail the civil liberties of Muslim Americans. Cornell University, Press Release (Dec. 17, 2004).

10. For a thoughtful depiction of African–Americans as perpetual immigrants, see Lolita K. Buckner Innis, *Tricky Magic: Blacks as Immigrants and the Paradox of Foreignness*, 49 DePaul L. Rev. 85 (1999). On the related subject of the perception and treatment of immigrants of African descent, see the material on the Haitian interdiction program, pages 1112–35 below.

11. For some healthy criticisms of white legal academics' scant attention to the scholarship of minority authors in the field of immigration, see Kevin R. Johnson, *Race Matters: Immigration Law and Policy Scholarship, Law in the Ivory Tower, and the Legal Indifference of the Race Critique*, 2000 Univ. Illinois L. Rev. 525. For the responses to Johnson's article, see Joan Fitzpatrick, *Race, Immigration, and Legal Scholarship: A Response to Kevin Johnson*, 2000 Univ. Illinois L. Rev. 603 (qualifying Johnson's thesis); Hing, item 8 above (supplying additional examples of the centrality of race in U.S. immigration policy); George A. Martínez, *Race and Immigration Law: A Paradigm Shift*, 2000 Univ. Illinois L. Rev. 517 (arguing that the paradigm shift advocated by Johnson is in fact beginning to take

shape); Michael A. Olivas, *Immigration Law Teaching and Scholarship in the Ivory Tower: A Response to* Race Matters, 2000 Univ. Illinois 613 (agreeing with Johnson and adding analogous comments concerning teaching); John A. Scanlan, *Call and Response: The Particular and the General*, 2000 Univ. Illinois 639 (qualifying Johnson's thesis); see also Guadalupe T. Luna, *"Zoo Island:" Latcrit Theory, "Don Pepe" and Señora Peralta*, 19 Chicano–Latino L. Rev. 339 (1998) (arguing that the academy shortchanges both Latino scholars and relevant law).

12.   In a 2004 opinion poll, 61% of U.S. immigrants believed that "recent immigrants have been unfairly discriminated against." 30% said they themselves have experienced discrimination in housing, employment, and public services. And 39% of the immigrants surveyed believed the levels of discrimination have increased since September 11, 2001. NPR/Kaiser/Kennedy School Poll, *Immigration: Summary of Findings* at 5–6 (May 27–Aug. 2, 2004).

13.   Compare the Grunwald essay with the writings that follow it. Which of the impressions that Grunwald relates concerning the immigrant experience do you think are universal? Which do you think are more personal?

14.   Recall the debate, in section C above, on the merits of a multiethnic society. How might the accounts that you have just read affect the views of Brimelow? How might they affect the views of Johnson and Perea?

15.   The attribution of "foreignness" to members of some ethnic groups but not others is one of the most powerful themes in much of the writing on this subject. Test the thesis on yourself: When you encounter a person whom you do not know (and whom you have not heard speak), and the person has a Latino, Asian, or Arabic physical appearance, do you think you instinctively presume that he or she is "from somewhere else?" Suppose instead that the person is black. Or white. Would your instinctive presumption be the same? Does your answer depend on the geographic location, or on the person's clothing, demeanor, facial expression, or other cultural signal, or would your answer be the same even in the absence of additional evidence? Your own reaction aside, what do you think accounts for the widespread presumption of foreignness for Latinos, Asians, and Arabs, but not for African–Americans or whites?

16.   Most of the essays you just read rely at least partly on stories. Are these stories useful, either to members of the public or to policymakers?

17.   The last several writings suggest that racism remains a serious problem for both immigrants and citizens of color. If you share that view, where do the solutions lie?

18.   In 1993, one author offered this prediction: "In the United States, immigration policy will become *the* civil rights issue of the 21st century." Stephen H. Legomsky, *Immigration, Equality and Diversity*, 31 Columbia J. Transnat'l Law 319, 320 (1993) (emphasis in original); see also Stephen H. Legomsky, *Immigrants, Minorities, and Pluralism: What Kind of Society Do We Really Want?*, 6 Willamette J. Internat'l Law & Dispute Resolution 153, 157–60 (1998) (renewing prediction and elaborating on why). Do you think we are there yet?

CHAPTER 2

IMMIGRATION AND THE CONSTITUTION[1]

SECTION A. SOURCES OF THE FEDERAL IMMIGRATION POWER

The federal government has actively regulated immigration for more than a century. The current Immigration and Nationality Act, amended frequently since its enactment in 1952, is now hundreds of pages long. In minute detail, it specifies which noncitizens may enter the United States

---

1. A set of three writings by the author of this coursebook attempts to treat comprehensively the sources and the constitutional limits of Congress's powers to exclude and deport noncitizens, as well as the role of the courts in pronouncing those limits. See generally Stephen H. Legomsky, Immigration and the Judiciary—Law and Politics in Britain and America, chap. 3 (1987)(tracing and explaining the historical development of the plenary congressional power over immigration); *Immigration Law and the Principle of Plenary Congressional Power*, 1984 Supreme Ct. Rev. 255 (identifying and critiquing the doctrinal theories for judicial deference, suggesting external influences on judges' decisions in leading immigration cases, and describing the devices by which lower courts have softened some of the Supreme Court's more extreme holdings); and *Ten More Years of Plenary Power: Immigration, Congress, and the Courts*, 22 Hastings Const. L.Q. 925 (1995)(updating the two prior pieces); see also T. Alexander Aleinikoff, Semblances of Sovereignty—The Constitution, the State, and American Citizenship (2002); Gerald L. Neuman, Strangers to the Constitution—Immigrants, Borders, and Fundamental Law (1996); Linda Kelly, *Preserving the Fundamental Right to Family Unity: Championing Notions of Social Contract and Community Ties in the Battle of Plenary Power versus Aliens' Rights*, 41 Villanova L. Rev. 725 (1996); Robert Pauw, *Plenary Power: An Outmoded Doctrine that Should Not Limit IIRIRA Reform*, 51 Emory L.J. 1095 (2002); Vic-

tor C. Romero, Alienated–Immigrant Rights, the Constitution, and Equality in America (2005); Peter H. Schuck, *The Transformation of Immigration Law*, 84 Colum.L.Rev. 1 (1984); Frank H. Wu, *The Future of the American Mosaic: Issues in American Immigration Reform*, 7 Stan.L. & Policy Rev. 35 (1996). Some fine articles by other authors— Professors Aleinikoff, Hart, Henkin, Hesse, Johnson, Motomura, Nafziger, Neuman, Scanlan, and Scaperlanda—are cited in 22 Hastings Const.L.Q. at 927 n.9, 929–30 nn.26–31. They elaborate on specific aspects of the congressional power and the role of judicial review.

In addition to these writings, several commentators have examined the relationship between judicial review of what could be termed "pure immigration" laws (those that govern the admission and expulsion of noncitizens) and judicial review of other laws that treat citizens differently from noncitizens (for example, laws that regulate professional licenses, welfare, or medical coverage). Three excellent articles along those lines include Linda S. Bosniak, *Membership, Equality, and the Difference that Alienage Makes*, 69 N.Y.U.L.Rev. 1047 (1994); Michael Scaperlanda, *Partial Membership: Aliens and the Constitutional Community*, 81 Iowa L.Rev. 707 (1996); and Margaret H. Taylor, *Detained Aliens Challenging Conditions of Confinement and the Porous Borders of the Plenary Power Doctrine*, 22 Hastings Const.L.Q. 1087 (1995).

and which of those already here may stay. Its many provisions, together with hundreds of pages of administrative regulations, spell out the procedures by which those and other determinations are to be made.

But before we can examine the specific workings of the present statutory scheme, we need to solve a larger mystery. The problem is easy enough to state: The federal government of the United States generally possesses only those powers that are either enumerated in the Constitution or "necessary and proper" for executing the enumerated powers. And nowhere does the Constitution expressly authorize the federal government to regulate immigration. Does this mean our whole elaborate system of immigration control is unconstitutional? Is it possible that Congress has no power to exclude or to deport noncitizens?

Most people today would instinctively resist such conclusions. To accept them would require one to believe that the framers intended either (a) to mandate open borders or (b) to vest in the individual states the exclusive power to regulate immigration.[2]

If you are uneasy about concluding that all our immigration laws are unconstitutional, then the question becomes: Where, exactly, *does* the federal government get the power to regulate immigration? The Supreme Court has struggled with this problem since the mid-nineteenth century, and no single dispositive answer has ever emerged. There are, however, several arguable answers.

1.   THE ENUMERATED POWERS

a.   THE COMMERCE CLAUSE

Congress may "regulate commerce with foreign nations." U.S. Const. art. I, § 8, cl. 3. But is immigration really a regulation of commerce? Two distinct theories might be offered:

The traditional theory emerged in a series of nineteenth century Supreme Court decisions invalidating *state* attempts to regulate immigration. When New York and Massachusetts imposed head taxes on certain categories of arriving noncitizen passengers, the Court had to decide whether these state actions infringed any exclusively federal power. In the *Passenger Cases,* 48 U.S. (7 How.) 283, 12 L.Ed. 702 (1849), the Court voted 5–4 to strike down both statutes. No single rationale commanded a majority, but four Justices regarded these actions as usurpations of the federal power to regulate commerce with foreign nations.

Can people be objects of commerce? The four dissenters believed they could not. One of them was Justice Woodbury:

> [I]f to "regulate commerce" extends also to the regulation of mere navigation, and hence to the business of carrying passengers, in which it may be employed, it is confined to a forfeiture of the

---

2. As for option (b), see the informative article by Gerald L. Neuman, *The Lost Centu-* *ry of American Immigration Law (1776– 1875),* 93 Columbia L.Rev. 1833 (1993).

vessel, and does not legitimately involve a prohibition of persons, except when articles of commerce, like slaves.

48 U.S. (7 How.) at 541, 12 L.Ed. at 810. Similar reservations were expressed by Chief Justice Taney, *id.* at 481, 12 L.Ed. at 785, and by Justices Daniel, *id.* at 501–06, 12 L.Ed. at 793–95, and Nelson, *id.* at 518, 12 L.Ed. at 801 (agreeing with Taney, C.J.).

In *Henderson v. Mayor of New York,* 92 U.S. (2 Otto) 259, 23 L.Ed. 543 (1876), the Supreme Court struck down a state statute requiring the master of a vessel to choose between paying taxes on arriving noncitizen passengers or posting bonds. This time the Court was unanimous:

> * * * As was said in *United States v. Holliday,* "Commerce with foreign nations means commerce between citizens of the United States and citizens or subjects of foreign governments." It means trade, and it means intercourse. It means commercial intercourse between nations, and parts of nations, in all its branches. It includes navigation, as the principal means by which foreign intercourse is effected. To regulate this trade and intercourse is to prescribe the rules by which it shall be conducted. * * *

> * * * [T]he transportation of passengers from European ports to those of the United States has attained a magnitude and importance far beyond its proportion at that time to other branches of commerce. It has become a part of our commerce with foreign nations, of vast interest to this country, as well as to the immigrants who come among us to find a welcome and a home within our borders. In addition to the wealth which some of them bring, they bring still more largely the labor which we need to till our soil, build our railroads, and develop the latent resources of the country in its minerals, its manufacturers, and its agriculture. Is the regulation of this great system a regulation of commerce? Can it be doubted that a law which prescribes the terms on which vessels shall engage in it is a law regulating this branch of commerce?

Id. at 270–71, 23 L.Ed. at 548–49.

In the *Head Money Cases,* 112 U.S. 580, 5 S.Ct. 247, 28 L.Ed. 798 (1884), the Court for the first time considered the constitutionality of a *federal* statute that regulated immigration.[3] The Court unanimously upheld the statute as a valid exercise of the congressional power to regulate commerce with other nations. *Cf. Edwards v. California,* 314 U.S. 160, 172, 62 S.Ct. 164, 166, 86 L.Ed. 119, 124 (1941) (transportation of persons is commerce for purposes of *interstate* commerce clause).

---

3. That the Supreme Court had never before decided whether Congress could constitutionally regulate immigration might seem surprising at first. Except for the short-lived Alien Act of 1798, however, Congress left the borders open until 1875. See pp. 108–09 below.

Are you now persuaded that the movement of human beings across national boundaries is itself commerce? If not, here is a second theory for connecting immigration to the commerce clause: The Supreme Court has held that the *interstate* commerce clause permits Congress to regulate activities "substantially affecting" interstate commerce—even when the effects are "indirect." See, e.g., *Wickard v. Filburn,* 317 U.S. 111, 63 S.Ct. 82, 87 L.Ed. 122 (1942). Moreover, it is enough that the effects are substantial when combined with those of many other similar activities. *Id.* The economic effects of large-scale immigration on both interstate and international commerce are complex and controversial, but few today would deny they are substantial. For a useful bibliography, see Bill Ong Hing, The Economic Impact of Immigration—A Brief Survey of the Literature (1990).

From these observations, either of two sub-arguments for an "affecting commerce" theory could be advanced: Immigration affects *interstate* commerce; or the "affecting commerce" principle extends to the *international* branch of the commerce clause, and immigration affects international commerce.

b. THE MIGRATION OR IMPORTATION CLAUSE

Under Article I, § 9, cl. 1 of the Constitution,

The Migration or Importation of such Persons as any of the States now existing shall think proper to permit, shall not be prohibited by the Congress prior to the year one thousand eight hundred and eight. * * *

The implication appears to be that Congress *may* prohibit (and, a fortiori, restrict) migration and importation after 1808. But the Justices in the *Passenger Cases* differed over whether this power is even relevant to immigration. Historical sources make clear that the central concern was with the slave trade. Does that mean the provision is inapplicable to the migration of free persons? For sharply contrasting views of the historical data, compare the opinion of Justice McKinley, 48 U.S. (7 How.) at 452–54, 12 L.Ed. at 773–74, with those of Chief Justice Taney, *id.* at 474–78, 12 L.Ed. at 782–83, and Justices Daniel, *id.* at 511–14, 12 L.Ed. at 798–99, and Woodbury, *id.* at 540–41, 12 L.Ed. at 810–12. See also Walter Berns, *The Constitution and the Migration of Slaves,* 78 Yale L.J. 198 (1968).

c. THE NATURALIZATION CLAUSE

Article I, § 8, cl. 4 authorizes Congress "[t]o establish an uniform Rule of Naturalization." To be sure, admission and expulsion, which concern the physical movement of noncitizens into and out of the United States, differ from naturalization, which concerns membership in the nation's political community. Chapter 13 will examine the legal and political significance of citizenship; for now, it is enough to note that immigration and naturalization are not synonymous. They describe different processes and promote different policies. Still, could immigration control be brought within the naturalization clause, with a little help from the "necessary and proper" clause? Chief Justice Taney, dissenting in the *Passenger Cases,* raised and rejected this possibility:

> * * * [C]itizens of each State are entitled to the privileges and immunities of citizens in the several States * * * [A]s every citizen of a State is also a citizen of the United States, a single State, without [the naturalization clause], might have given to any number of foreigners it pleased the right to all the privileges of citizenship in commerce, trade, and navigation, although they did not even reside amongst us.
>
> The nature of our institutions under the Federal government made it a matter of absolute necessity that this power should be confided to the government of the Union, where all the States were represented, and where all had a voice. * * * The article has nothing to do with the admission or rejection of aliens, nor with immigration, but with the rights of citizenship. * * *

48 U.S. (7 How.) at 482–83, 12 L.Ed. at 786.

In exercising its power to prescribe "an uniform rule of naturalization," Congress made lawful admission as a permanent resident a prerequisite to naturalization. INA § 316. Having made that decision, may Congress go on to specify the conditions for admission of permanent residents as necessary and proper for prescribing naturalization requirements? How would Chief Justice Taney have answered that question?

d.   THE WAR CLAUSE

Congress has the power "[t]o declare war." U.S. Const. art. I, § 8, cl. 11. Justice Daniel, dissenting in the *Passenger Cases,* conceded that this provision authorizes Congress to regulate "alien *enemies*"—i.e., nationals of countries with which the United States is at war. But he doubted that the war clause could be stretched far enough to cover regulation of other noncitizens (known as "alien friends"). 48 U.S. (7 How.) at 509–10, 12 L.Ed. at 797. Do you agree? Is there any way in which regulating the immigration of "alien friends" could be justified as necessary and proper for deciding whether to declare war? Could the war power, for example, be interpreted as encompassing a power to *prevent* war? If it can, is regulation of immigration sufficiently connected to the prevention of war? For a detailed history of the Alien Act of 1798 and an argument that the Act was a constitutionally valid exercise of Congress's war powers (based on the undeclared war with France), see Gregory Fehlings, *Storm on the Constitution: The First Deportation Law,* 10 Tulsa J. Comp. & Internat'l L. 63 (2002).

2.   IMPLIED CONSTITUTIONAL POWERS

The previous subsection considered only those powers expressly enumerated in the Constitution (or necessary and proper for executing the enumerated powers). Might the Constitution be read, however, as creating a federal immigration power by general implication? To answer that question, we begin with the granddaddy of all immigration cases—an early decision that continues to influence the law today. To place that opinion in context, however, one must appreciate that it and several other important subsequent opinions were written during a period of intense racial turmoil on the West Coast:

> The conflict had been in the making since 1848 when the gold rush had begun. That rush was on in 1850 when California was admitted to the Union as a free state. That same year the Taiping Rebellion broke out in China—it raged for fourteen years. During this period California continued to grow in population and develop as an American community. Orchards needed to be pruned and the fruit picked. Farms needed to be worked. Mines had to be operated. Highways and railroads needed to be built. Clothes had to be washed. Furniture and shoes had to be made. A source of "inexpensive" labor was of the essence. The answer? The Chinese from a war-torn China.

> In 1869, * * * the great transcontinental railroad linking the eastern United States with the West Coast was finished. Now the whole of California began to be heavily populated with people from all over the United States—and a post-Civil War depression was beginning to creep with cat-feet upon the entire nation. Chinese labor became a glut on the California market. At least so said organized labor, which was by then beginning to flex its political muscle throughout the nation. By 1869 it was a foregone conclusion that the Chinese had to go. * * *

> Thirteen years later, in 1882, the conflict over Chinese immigration that had been building up on the West Coast since the end of the Civil War exploded into congressional action. The Chinese were abruptly excluded from immigrating into the United States. * * *

Frank F. Chuman, The Bamboo People 3–4 (1976). See also the literature on analogous modern attitudes toward both Asian immigrants and Asian-Americans, discussed on pages 94–100 above.

Chae Chan Ping v. United States (The Chinese Exclusion Case)

Supreme Court of the United States, 1889.
130 U.S. 581, 9 S.Ct. 623, 32 L.Ed. 1068.

■ MR. JUSTICE FIELD delivered the opinion of the court.

[Chae Chan Ping, a Chinese laborer, immigrated to the United States in 1875. As noted above, Congress in 1882 suspended all future immigration of Chinese laborers. The statute provided, however, that those who had been living in the United States since 1880 were free to leave and return. To implement the proviso, the statute authorized the issuance of certificates to departing Chinese laborers, evidencing their rights to return.

Chae Chan Ping obtained such a certificate and then left in 1887 for a visit to China. While he was on his return voyage in 1888, Congress passed a law that discontinued the certificate program and prohibited the return of even those Chinese laborers who had already received certificates. Chae Chan Ping arrived in the United States one week after passage of the statute and was excluded.

He attacked the validity of the 1888 Act on two grounds—that it violated an 1880 treaty between the United States and China, and that it violated the Constitution. The Court acknowledged that the statute conflicted with the treaty but held that statutes and treaties were on equal footing and that the statute, being later in time, would prevail. The Court then turned to the constitutional question:]

There being nothing in the treaties between China and the United States to impair the validity of the act of Congress of October 1, 1888, was it on any other ground beyond the competency of Congress to pass it? If so, it must be because it was not within the power of Congress to prohibit Chinese laborers who had at the time departed from the United States, or should subsequently depart, from returning to the United States. Those laborers are not citizens of the United States; they are aliens. That the government of the United States, through the action of the legislative department, can exclude aliens from its territory is a proposition which we do not think open to controversy. Jurisdiction over its own territory to that extent is an incident of every independent nation. It is a part of its independence. If it could not exclude aliens it would be to that extent subject to the control of another power. As said by this court in the case of *The Exchange,* 7 Cranch, 116, 136, speaking by Chief Justice Marshall: "The jurisdiction of the nation within its own territory is necessarily exclusive and absolute. It is susceptible of no limitation not imposed by itself. Any restriction upon it, deriving validity from an external source, would imply a diminution of its sovereignty to the extent of the restriction, and an investment of that sovereignty to the same extent in that power which could impose such restriction. All exceptions, therefore, to the full and complete power of a nation within its own territories, must be traced up to the consent of the nation itself. They can flow from no other legitimate source."

While under our Constitution and form of government the great mass of local matters is controlled by local authorities, the United States, in their relation to foreign countries and their subjects or citizens are one nation, invested with powers which belong to independent nations, the exercise of which can be invoked for the maintenance of its absolute independence and security throughout its entire territory. The powers to declare war, make treaties, suppress insurrection, repel invasion, regulate foreign commerce, secure republican governments to the States, and admit subjects of other nations to citizenship, are all sovereign powers, restricted in their exercise only by the Constitution itself and considerations of public policy and justice which control, more or less, the conduct of all civilized nations. As said by this court in the case of *Cohens v. Virginia,* speaking by the same great Chief Justice: "That the United States form, for many, and for most important purposes, a single nation, has not yet been denied. In war, we are one people. In making peace we are one people. In all commercial regulations, we are one and the same people. In many other respects, the American people are one; and the government which is alone capable of controlling and managing their interests in all these respects, is the government of the Union." * * *

* * *

To preserve its independence, and give security against foreign aggression and encroachment, is the highest duty of every nation, and to attain these ends nearly all other considerations are to be subordinated. It matters not in what form such aggression and encroachment come, whether from the foreign nation acting in its national character or from vast hordes of its people crowding in upon us. The government, possessing the powers which are to be exercised for protection and security, is clothed with authority to determine the occasion on which the powers shall be called forth; and its determination, so far as the subjects affected are concerned, are necessarily conclusive upon all its departments and officers. If, therefore, the government of the United States, through its legislative department, considers the presence of foreigners of a different race in this country, who will not assimilate with us, to be dangerous to its peace and security, their exclusion is not to be stayed because at the time there are no actual hostilities with the nation of which the foreigners are subjects. The existence of war would render the necessity of the proceeding only more obvious and pressing. The same necessity, in a less pressing degree, may arise when war does not exist, and the same authority which adjudges the necessity in one case must also determine it in the other. In both cases its determination is conclusive upon the judiciary. If the government of the country of which the foreigners excluded are subjects is dissatisfied with this action it can make complaint to the executive head of our government, or resort to any other measure which, in its judgment, its interests or dignity may demand; and there lies its only remedy.

The power of the government to exclude foreigners from the country whenever, in its judgment, the public interests require such exclusion, has been asserted in repeated instances, and never denied by the executive or legislative departments.

[The Court here cites letters from various United States Secretaries of State asserting the power of every sovereign nation to exclude aliens.]

* * *

The power of exclusion of foreigners being an incident of sovereignty belonging to the government of the United States, as a part of those sovereign powers delegated by the Constitution, the right to its exercise at any time when, in the judgment of the government, the interests of the country require it, cannot be granted away or restrained on behalf of any one. The powers of government are delegated in trust to the United States, and are incapable of transfer to any other parties. They cannot be abandoned or surrendered. Nor can their exercise be hampered, when needed for the public good, by any considerations of private interest. The exercise of these public trusts is not the subject of barter or contract. Whatever license, therefore, Chinese laborers may have obtained, previous to the act of October 1, 1888, to return to the United States after their departure, is held at the will of the government, revocable at any time, at its pleasure. Whether a proper consideration by our government of its previous laws, or a proper respect for the nation whose subjects are affected by its action, ought to have qualified its inhibition and made it applicable only to persons departing from the country after the passage of the act, are not questions for judicial determination. If there be any just ground of complaint on the part of China, it must be made to the political department of our government, which is alone competent to act upon the subject.

* * *

NOTES AND QUESTIONS

1.   Precisely what constitutional provision(s) does Chae Chan Ping say Congress has violated?

2.   The Court in the *Chinese Exclusion Case* sees the federal power to exclude noncitizens as inherent in the very notion of a sovereign State. "If *it* could not exclude aliens," the Court says in the first paragraph of the edited opinion, "*it* would be to that extent subject to the control of another power." Read that and the surrounding sentences carefully. What is the antecedent of the word "it"—the nation or the Congress? With that distinction in mind, how might Chae Chan Ping have responded?

3.   In any event, the inherent sovereign power that the Court discovers was assumed to be "delegated by the Constitution." (See the last reproduced paragraph of the Court's opinion.) Where does the Constitution delegate "sovereign" powers? Moreover, what makes the regulation of immigration "sovereign?"

4.   At several points in its opinion, the Court assumes that the Constitution delegates to the federal government a general power to regulate foreign affairs. Federal control of foreign relations seems sensible as a matter of policy, but the constitutional basis for a general federal foreign affairs power has proved illusory. It is of course possible to maintain that the Constitution as a whole reflects an intent to endow the federal government with those powers the exercise of which affects the nation as a whole, and then to argue that foreign policy decisions fit that description. It is more difficult to locate specific constitutional language that creates a general federal power over foreign relations. One commentator describes the dilemma:

> * * * [W]here foreign relations are concerned the Constitution seems a strange, laconic document: although it explicitly lodges important foreign affairs powers in one branch or another

of the federal government, and denies important powers to the States, many others are not mentioned.

* * *

Congress is given power to regulate commerce with foreign nations, to define offenses against the law of nations, to declare war, and the President the power to make treaties and send and receive ambassadors, but these hardly add up to the power to conduct foreign relations. Where is the power to recognize other states or governments, to maintain or break diplomatic relations, to open consulates elsewhere and permit them here, to acquire or cede territory, to give or withhold foreign aid, to proclaim a Monroe Doctrine or an Open–Door Policy, indeed to determine all the attitudes and carry out all the details in the myriads of relationships with other nations that are "the foreign policy" and "the foreign relations" of the United States? The power to make treaties is granted, but where is the power to break, denounce, or terminate them? The power to declare war is there, but where is the power to make peace, to proclaim neutrality in the wars of others, to recognize or deny rights to belligerents or insurgents? Congress can punish violations of international law but where is the power to assert rights or to carry out obligations under international law, to make new international law or to disregard or violate law? Congress can regulate foreign commerce but where is the power to make other laws relating to our foreign relations— to regulate immigration, or the status and rights of aliens, or activities of citizens at home or abroad affecting our foreign relations? These "missing" powers, and a host of others, were clearly intended for and have always been exercised by the federal government, but where does the Constitution say that it shall be so?

* * *

The attempt to build all the foreign affairs powers of the federal government with the few bricks provided by the Constitution has not been accepted as successful. It requires considerable stretching of language, much reading between lines, and bold extrapolation from "the Constitution as a whole," and that still does not plausibly add up to all the power which the federal government in fact exercises.

Louis Henkin, Foreign Affairs and the Constitution 16–18 (1972).

Do you agree with Professor Henkin's conclusion that the specific constitutional "bricks" do not add up to a general foreign affairs power? Could all peaceful overtures to foreign countries (recognizing them, maintaining diplomatic relations, opening and permitting consulates, etc.) be viewed as necessary and proper for conducting commerce? And could all belligerent actions (breaking diplomatic relations, proclaiming a Monroe Doctrine, etc.) be considered necessary and proper for deciding whether to declare war? Or does that constitute "stretching of language, much reading between lines, and bold extrapolation from 'the Constitution as a whole' "?

5.   If the federal government does possess a general power to conduct foreign policy, is it axiomatic that immigration decisions are inherently foreign policy? See Stephen H. Legomsky, Immigration and the Judiciary— Law and Politics in Britain and America 319–21 (1987) (arguing no); *accord,* Ibrahim J. Wani, *Truth, Strangers and Fiction: The Illegitimate Uses of Legal Fiction in Immigration Law,* 11 Cardozo L.Rev. 51, 78–82 (1989). Notice how the Court in the *Chinese Exclusion Case* connects immigration to foreign affairs: "It matters not in what form [foreign] aggression and encroachment come, whether from the foreign nation acting in its national character or from vast hordes of its people crowding in upon us."[4] What, exactly, are the links between immigration and foreign relations?

6.   Structural theories. A related set of theories can be used to extract a federal immigration power from the overall structure of the Constitution. In a sense, the foreign affairs theory already discussed could be described as structural: The structure of the Constitution arguably suggests a general power to conduct foreign affairs, and immigration is just one specific aspect of that power. But is it possible to infer a federal immigration power from the constitutional structure without having to rely on either the existence of a general federal power to make foreign policy or the characterization of immigration as a component of foreign policy?

Professors T. Alexander Aleinikoff and David Martin have offered two such theories: (a) The overall constitutional structure reveals an intent to place the federal government of the United States on an equal footing with the central governments of other nations, and the latter have the power to exclude noncitizens; and (b) The framers must have intended to authorize the federal government to define who we are as a people. See T. Alexander Aleinikoff & David A. Martin, Immigration: Process and Policy 16–18 (1st ed. 1985).

All of these arguments elicit structure from the fundamental purposes of the Constitution. Structure can also be distilled from the interaction of specific provisions. Justice Douglas, writing the opinion of the Court in *Griswold v. Connecticut,* 381 U.S. 479, 85 S.Ct. 1678, 14 L.Ed.2d 510 (1965), found in various constitutional clauses a purpose to protect individual privacy. This recurring pattern suggested to him a "penumbral" privacy right that went beyond the specific protections set forth in the constitutional text. Can an analogous argument be constructed for a federal power over immigration? Justice Field in the *Chinese Exclusion Case* listed "[t]he [federal] powers to declare war, make treaties, suppress insurrection, repel invasion, regulate foreign commerce, secure republican governments to the States, and admit subjects of other nations to citizenship" as

---

4. The links between immigration and foreign affairs are also relevant to the scope of judicial review in cases in which federal immigration statutes are challenged on individual rights grounds. We shall return briefly to that subject in section B below.

examples of "sovereign" powers. Does the pattern he has identified suggest a general federal power to perform "sovereign" functions? If so, how does one tell whether a given function or power is "sovereign?" Does regulating immigration qualify?

7. Obviousness theory. One last constitutional theory is that the framers declined to specify a federal power to exclude aliens because they believed such a power was too obvious to require mention. In evaluating this and the previous theories, consider the following discussion:

Stephen H. Legomsky, Immigration and the Judiciary: Law and Politics in Britain and America
Pages 187–90 (1987).

Both in colonial times and in the early years of the new republic, the general practice was to encourage immigration. There were wide open spaces that required development; labour was in short supply; and settlers were needed to defend the frontiers against hostile forces. The demand for immigrants was evidenced by numerous practices. In many cases, colonists would pay transportation costs in order to obtain indentured servants. Colonial legislatures offered a variety of inducements, including land grants, cash bounties to defray shipping fares, tax exemptions, immunity from actions for debt, and liberal naturalization rules. Demand was so great that it became common to kidnap English children and sell them into slavery in the colonies. The colonists' desire for new settlers was evidenced by the Declaration of Independence, which complained that the King had hampered immigration to the Colonies.

All this is not to imply that immigrants were unreservedly welcomed. Many of the early Americans had serious misgivings about immigration. Several colonial leaders, including Franklin and Jefferson, urged restrictions. A number of colonial legislatures passed laws to discourage specified classes of immigrants—commonly paupers, criminals, and members of unpopular religious sects.

It seems likely, therefore, that the framers did not intend to foreclose the possibility of restricting immigration. There remains, however, the question of whether they meant to vest such a power in the federal government or the states. On the one hand, as observed in the Supreme Court decisions discussed thus far, the need for uniformity is a strong policy reason for federal control. But contrary policy arguments have also been advanced. One nineteenth-century state immigration official conceded that the federal government is properly empowered to enter treaties governing passage of immigrants on the high seas, but argued that, once the immigrant lands, the matter is solely one of state concern. His position was that the disproportionate effects of immigration on certain states should entitle those states to make policy unilaterally.

A look at the actual positions taken by early legislatures and colonial leaders is equally inconclusive. The Alien Act of 1798, which permitted the

President to deport dangerous aliens, might be thought to evidence a contemporary view that the framers intended to create a federal power over immigration. For several reasons, however, that evidence is weak. The statute was an unusual act, passed because peace with England had not yet been fully achieved in all respects. The statute was highly unpopular, and thus was not renewed when it expired two years later. Several colonial leaders in fact believed the Act was unconstitutional as being outside the enumerated powers, but the courts were unable to address the question because no person was ever deported under this Act. Not until the Chinese Exclusion Act did Congress ever again even claim the power of deportation. For all those reasons the Alien Act of 1798 should be viewed as an aberration, providing little insight into the framers' views on federal immigration control.

There were, in fact, several indicators that immigration control was thought to be a matter for state legislatures. In 1787, Franklin urged the *states* to pass laws stemming the influx of European criminals. A year later, on the eve of Constitutional ratification, the Continental Congress passed a resolution urging the states to pass legislation excluding aliens convicted of crimes. This pre-Constitution evidence is reinforced by the positive responses of several states, in some cases after ratification of the Constitution. State laws containing these and other restrictions became especially common through the first half of the nineteenth century. * * *

Thus, early attitudes and actions concerning immigration reveal ambivalence. General immigration was encouraged, but certain specific classes of immigrants were discouraged. As to whether exclusion of the latter was intended to be a matter for the federal government or the states, the evidence is mixed. It seems unlikely, therefore, that the framers omitted an express federal power to exclude aliens out of a belief that the existence of such a power was too obvious to require mention. That four of the nine Supreme Court Justices in the *Passenger Cases* were unwilling to recognise a federal power to exclude aliens accentuates the difficulty of ascribing the omission to obviousness.

* * *

NOTE ON THE PUBLIC REACTION TO ASIAN IMMIGRATION

You might have found it striking that, in its opinion in the *Chinese Exclusion Case*, the Supreme Court so easily credited supposed justifications for Congress seeing danger in "the presence of foreigners of a different race." Before reading the opinion, you saw a capsule summary of the events that preceded the 1882 Act. The abuse of the Chinese took other forms as well. Chinese immigrants increasingly became the subjects of verbal and physical attacks. The hostility was not confined to the private sector. One leading author describes some of the discriminatory actions taken by the state government of California and the federal government of the United States:

* * * It is clear enough now that California did not permit the Chinese immigrant to become assimilated: he was denied citizenship through naturalization; he was held ineligible to testify in any case in a court of law for or against a white person; he was subject to special heavy taxes; he could not vote; he was excluded from schools. He was made the scapegoat for mining and real estate booms and slumps; for crime waves requiring vigilance committees; for corruption, extravagance, and profligacy in state and city government; and for land and railway monopoly.

In view of the facts as we know them today, how did it happen that Congress passed acts discriminating against the Chinese? The following reasons may be suggested:

(1) There were very few Chinese persons outside the West Coast; the country as a whole was ignorant of the ways in which Chinese immigrants behaved; and congressmen and citizens generally thought that the California propagandists told the truth.

(2) China was not a great power; she did not threaten or shake a big stick. Her deferential inquiries and mildly-worded protests were considered signs of weakness.

(3) In national elections California was frequently, if not always, an uncertain state, so that each political party made an effort to win its support. "All but one of some eight anti-Chinese measures passed by Congress were passed on the eve of national elections and for avowed political purposes."

(4) * * * After 1876 the Negro problem and the Chinese question were linked when it came to voting in Congress on anti-Chinese measures: "Without exception, these measures were passed by the vote of representatives from the Pacific Coast and the Deep South." The South, it has been said, "was quite willing to join with the Pacific Coast in fitting the Chinese into a caste system which, in many respects, closely resembled that which prevailed throughout the former slave belt."

Milton R. Konvitz, The Alien and the Asiatic in American Law 10–12 (1946).

What influence, if any, do you think these contemporary social and political forces had on the disposition of the *Chinese Exclusion Case?* Justice Stephen Field wrote the opinion of the Court. Professor Konvitz, discussing Justice Field, noted: "It has been said that [before becoming a Supreme Court Justice] he had more to do with the passage of restrictive legislation than any other man. He is said to have written the plank of the Democratic national convention urging upon Congress the suppression of Chinese labor immigration. Much of this activity was engaged in by Field with an eye on the presidency." Konvitz, above, at 10 n. 29. Excerpts from Justice Field's dissenting opinion in *Chew Heong v. United States,* 112 U.S.

536, 560–78, 5 S.Ct. 255, 267–77, 28 L.Ed. 770, 779–85 (1884), written only five years before the *Chinese Exclusion Case,* leave little doubt where he stood:

> But, notwithstanding * * * [our] opening the whole of our country to them * * *, they have remained among us a separate people, retaining their original peculiarities of dress, manners, habits, and modes of living, which are as marked as their complexion and language. They live by themselves; they constitute a distinct organization with the laws and customs which they brought from China. Our institutions have made no impression on them during the more than thirty years they have been in the country. * * * They do not and will not assimilate with our people; and their dying wish is that their bodies may be taken to China for burial.

Id. at 566–67, 5 S.Ct. at 270–71, 28 L.Ed. at 781. Justice Field concludes, in light of those and other factors, that

> * * * it is not surprising that there went up from the whole of the Pacific Coast an earnest appeal to Congress to restrain the further immigration of Chinese. * * * Thoughtful persons who were exempt from race prejudice saw * * * that * * * vast hordes would pour in upon us, overrunning our coast and controlling its institutions. A restriction was felt to be necessary to prevent the degradation of white labor, and to preserve to ourselves the inestimable benefits of our Christian civilization.

Id. at 568–69, 5 S.Ct. at 272, 28 L.Ed. at 781. See also the views of Justice Bradley, *id.* at 579, 5 S.Ct. at 277, 28 L.Ed. at 785 ("Chinese of the lower class have little respect for the solemnity of an oath."), and even those of Justice Brewer, whose later dissent in *Fong Yue Ting* (which you will see presently) conceded that the statutes had been "directed only at the obnoxious Chinese," whom he described as a "distasteful class."

Was Justice Field in *Chew Heong* purporting to express his own views about Chinese immigration or merely his perception of popular sentiments (or both)? Either way, consider whether the opinion in the *Chinese Exclusion Case* was the product not only of pure "legal" analysis but also of external influences. Immigration cases are not, of course, the only ones capable of raising politically volatile issues. But they do seem to do so with unusual frequency. Is it legitimate for Supreme Court Justices to permit either their own values or their readings of popular preferences to affect their analyses of constitutional questions? Can they entirely avoid it?

There is now a wealth of scholarly literature on the anti-Asian aspects of United States immigration history. In addition to the writings already cited, see, e.g., Andrew Gyory, Closing the Gate—Race, Politics, and the Chinese Exclusion Act (1998) (a political history of the Act); Bill Ong Hing, Making and Remaking Asian America through Immigration Policy, 1850–1990 (1993); Lucy Salyer, Laws Harsh as Tigers: Chinese Immigrants and the Shaping of Modern Immigration Law (1995); Ronald T. Takaki, Strangers from a Different Shore—A History of Asian Americans (1989), especially ch. 3; Jan C. Ting, *"Other than a Chinaman": How U.S. Immigration Law Resulted from and Still Reflects a Policy of Excluding and Restricting Asian Immigration*, 4 Temple Pol. & Civil Rights L. Rev. 301, 301–10 (1995); *cf.* Richard P. Cole & Gabriel J. Chin, *Emerging from the Margins of Historical Consciousness: Chinese Immigrants and the History of American Law*, 17 Law & History Rev. 325 (1999) (highlighting the impact of Chinese immigrants on the early development of United States public law). A thoughtful article on the tendency of immigration inspectors to exclude unmarried Chinese immigrant women as prostitutes during this same period is Kerry Abrams, *Polygamy, Prostitution, and the Federalization of Immigration Law*, 105 Columbia L. Rev. 641 (2005). For writings that focus more on the present-day effects of anti-Asian sentiment, see pages 94–100 above.

3.   BEYOND THE CONSTITUTION

Thus far, attention has focused on the Constitution as a potential source of federal power over immigration. Might there be sources beyond the Constitution? Justice Sutherland, writing the opinion of the Court in *United States v. Curtiss–Wright Export Corp.*, 299 U.S. 304, 315–18, 57 S.Ct. 216, 219–20, 81 L.Ed. 255, 260–62 (1936), located an extra-constitutional federal power to manage external affairs. His reasoning can be summarized by the following syllogism:

a.   During the colonial period, sovereignty rested with the British Crown.

b.   Upon the Declaration of Independence, sovereignty passed from the Crown to the states in their *collective* capacity—not to the states in their *individual* capacities.

c.   The only powers that the Constitution intended to reallocate were those that the states possessed in their individual capacities.

d.   Therefore, even after ratification of the Constitution, all sovereign powers remained with the states in their *collective* capacity—that is, with the federal government.

e.   Consequently, no federal sovereign power is dependent on an affirmative constitutional grant.

The *Curtiss–Wright* theory is controversial. Some have questioned the historical accuracy of assumptions b and c above. See, e.g., Raoul Berger, *The Presidential Monopoly of Foreign Relations*, 71 Mich.L.Rev. 1, 26–33 (1972); David M. Levitan, *The Foreign Relations Power: An Analysis of Mr. Justice Sutherland's Theory*, 55 Yale L.J. 467, 479–90 (1946). Professor Henkin has asked why, if the framers did not intend to reallocate "sovereign" powers, they expressly enumerated several powers clearly qualifying as "sovereign" (e.g., the powers to declare war and to make treaties) while declining to list others. Louis Henkin, Foreign Affairs and the Constitution 22–24 (1972).

Does *Curtiss–Wright* provide an extra-constitutional federal power to regulate immigration? How does one determine whether a given power is "sovereign?" Again, does immigration qualify?

4.   RESIDUAL STATE POWER

Once it is found that the federal government may regulate immigration, and once that power is actually exercised, the resulting legislation can preempt concurrent regulation by the states. Whether preemption will be found will depend on the scope of both the federal action and the state action. See *DeCanas v. Bica,* 424 U.S. 351, 96 S.Ct. 933, 47 L.Ed.2d 43 (1976) (upholding California statute prohibiting the employment of certain undocumented aliens).

But at the time of the *Passenger Cases* and *Henderson,* the federal government, whatever the breadth of its power, had not yet acted to regulate immigration. Why, then, could not the states do so? Two distinct reasons have been advanced. In *Henderson,* discussed earlier, the Court emphasized the need for uniform admission practices within the United States. It said: "The laws which govern the right to land passengers in the United States from other countries ought to be the same in New York, Boston, New Orleans, and San Francisco." 92 U.S. (2 Otto) at 273, 23 L.Ed. at 549. (Why?)

A second reason was supplied in *Chy Lung v. Freeman,* 92 U.S. (2 Otto) 275, 23 L.Ed. 550 (1876). If individual states could require masters of vessels to post bonds, then:

> a silly, an obstinate, or a wicked [state] commissioner may bring disgrace upon the whole country, the enmity of a powerful nation, or the loss of an equally powerful friend. * * *
>
> * * * The passage of laws which concern the admission of citizens and subjects of foreign nations to our shores belongs to Congress, and not to the States. * * * If it be otherwise, a single State can, at her pleasure, embroil us in disastrous quarrels with other nations.

92 U.S. (2 Otto) at 279–80, 23 L.Ed. at 552. Can you articulate differences between the uniformity argument and the embroilment argument? Do you agree with either? See generally Peter J. Spiro, *The States and Immigration in an Era of Demi–Sovereignties*, 35 Virginia J. Internat'l L. 121 (1994); Peter J. Spiro, *Learning to Live with Immigration Federalism*, 29 Connecticut L. Rev. 1627 (1997) (arguing "steam-valve" theory—allowing greater state control would confine effects of anti-immigrant sentiment to affected states, rather than spur national legislation).

Despite the sentiments reflected in the above quotations, the scope of the state power is extremely unclear. In each of the three cited cases the state action had been the imposition of either a bond or a tax on all arriving immigrants. In each case the state action had been struck down. Does this mean a state may not directly exclude those immigrants who possess specified undesirable characteristics? The above rhetoric would seem to imply that a state may not do so, but the dicta in these same opinions were surprisingly cautious on this point. In the *Passenger Cases,* at least two of the Justices who voted to invalidate the state statutes taxing arriving passengers suggested that a state could constitutionally exclude noncitizens who were found to be "lunatics, idiots, [etc.]" and who did not post security against becoming public charges. 48 U.S. (7 How.) at 410, 12 L.Ed. at 755 (McLean, J.), *id.* at 457, 12 L.Ed. at 775 (Grier, J). This power was said to be a matter of "self-defense." *Id.* And the unanimous opinions in *Henderson,* 92 U.S. (2 Otto) at 275, 23 L.Ed. at 550, and *Chy Lung,* 92 U.S. (2 Otto) at 280, 23 L.Ed. at 552, expressly left open whether, in the absence of federal legislation, a state could constitutionally exclude undesirable noncitizens. What is your reaction to these dicta?

Professor Huyen Pham has made a cogent argument that constitutional federal exclusivity in the immigration sphere (not just statutory preemption) prohibits state and local *enforcement* of the immigration laws (not just state lawmaking). See Huyen Pham, *The Inherent Flaws in the Inherent Authority Position: Why Inviting Local Enforcement of Immigration Laws Violates the Constitution,* 31 Florida State Univ. L. Rev. 965 (2004). This argument has important contemporary potential as the federal government enlists the cooperation of state officials in resisting both illegal immigration and terrorism, as discussed in chapter 12.

If the power to regulate "immigration" is exclusively federal, then it becomes critical to ascertain what constitutes immigration regulation, as distinguished from other regulation of noncitizens. One author argues effectively for a broad definition that would deny states the power to decide which noncitizens may receive state welfare assistance. See Michael J. Wishnie, *Laboratories of Bigotry? Devolution of the Immigration Power, Equal Protection, and Federalism,* 76 NYU L. Rev. 493 (2000).

We shall return to the subject of state regulation of noncitizens later. In chapter 12, the focus will be on states' attempts to regulate those noncitizens who have violated the immigration laws. Chapter 13 will consider state (and federal) actions that treat LPRs differently from United States citizens.

SECTION B.   LIMITS TO THE FEDERAL IMMIGRATION POWER

Despite continuing uncertainty about the precise source of the federal immigration power, it is settled law today that the power exists. But what are the constitutional limits to that congressional power? And how much power do courts have to pronounce those limits? Could Congress constitutionally exclude all noncitizens of Mexican ancestry? Could it exclude all noncitizens who are atheists? What about procedure? Could Congress authorize immigration officers to deny excluded noncitizens the opportunity to be heard? Do the answers to any of those questions change if, instead of exclusion, the context is deportation? And if any of these congressional actions would be unconstitutional, is it free from doubt that a court would have the power to say so? Think about these questions as you analyze the cases that follow.

Before you read the cases, though, an explanation of the terminology is necessary. From here on, you will sometimes encounter cases that draw sharp distinctions between "exclusion" and "deportation." Until 1996, the various immigration statutes recognized a similar distinction; the government might "exclude" a noncitizen who sought to enter, and might "deport" a noncitizen who had already entered and wished to remain. IIRIRA abolished that terminology. Since 1996, the name of the proceeding in which both kinds of determinations are made is a "removal" proceeding. There are still separate grounds of "inadmissibility" and "deportability" for those who seek admission and those who have already been admitted, respectively. The significance of these statutory distinctions will be explored in several future chapters.

At this writing, however, there is no reason to believe that the changes to the statutory terminology will alter the lines that the courts have drawn *for constitutional purposes*. If the Constitution allows Congress to do some things and not others, Congress's decision to change the terminology should not alter the constitutional parameters that the courts have established. For constitutional purposes, therefore, it will often be convenient in this book to use the words "exclusion" and "deportation" as the courts have used them—to distinguish the act of denying admission at a port of entry from the act of expelling individuals from the interior.

A brief word on organization: Immigration officials make a range of important decisions in individual cases. As you will see in chapter 9, IIRIRA contained several provisions that bar or restrict judicial review of many of these. Several courts, including now the United States Supreme Court in *INS v. St. Cyr*, 533 U.S. 289, 121 S.Ct. 2271, 150 L.Ed.2d 347 (2001), have considered both the meaning and the constitutionality of some of those provisions. Because of the difficult statutory interpretation issues, those provisions are covered in the judicial review section of chapter 9, rather than here.

1.   THE FOUNDATION CASES

The *Chinese Exclusion Case* appeared to address only the question whether Congress had the power to exclude noncitizens (or, possibly, the narrower question whether Congress had the power to exclude a particular class of noncitizens). The opinion did not consider the individual rights limitations that might attend the exercise of that power—due process, the First Amendment, etc. Yet the Court's language was quite sweeping. You should re-read now the last three printed paragraphs of the opinion. When you do, you will see statements that Congress's decisions are "conclusive upon the judiciary," or "not questions for judicial determination."

Read in context, what do these phrases mean? Was the Court saying only that this particular congressional decision was conclusive *because it was constitutional?* Or was the Court disclaiming the power *to decide* the constitutionality of the statute? As you will see in the readings that follow, the case has generally been cited for the latter proposition. If so interpreted, is the *Chinese Exclusion Case* consistent with *Marbury v. Madison,* 5 U.S. (1 Cranch) 137, 2 L.Ed. 60 (1803), where the Supreme Court asserted the power to review congressional Acts for constitutionality?

In answering these questions, you should read with particular care the last printed paragraph of the opinion in the *Chinese Exclusion Case.* It contains no fewer than three distinct theories for holding the congressional decision conclusive upon the judiciary. Can you find them? If you are having trouble, notice three key words or phrases: (1) "sovereign powers," (2) "license," and (3) "political department." Try to articulate the full theories, and then evaluate each. These and other arguments for judicial deference to Congress in immigration matters are precursors of themes that will recur throughout this section.

Ekiu v. United States

Supreme Court of the United States, 1892.
142 U.S. 651, 12 S.Ct. 336, 35 L.Ed. 1146.

■ MR. JUSTICE GRAY * * * delivered the opinion of the Court.

[Nishimura Ekiu, a citizen of Japan, arrived in the United States by steamship. She told the immigration inspector that her husband had been living in the United States for one year and that he would call for her at a prearranged hotel. She did not know his current address. She possessed $22 in cash. The immigration inspector, not believing her statements, excluded her on the statutory ground that she was likely to become a public charge.

Nishimura Ekiu applied for habeas corpus and offered evidence to meet the charge. The circuit court excluded her evidence and denied relief. In its view, the statute made the administrative findings of fact conclusive upon the judiciary. She had argued that, if so construed, the statute violated due process.]

It is an accepted maxim of international law, that every sovereign nation has the power, as inherent in sovereignty, and essential to self-preservation, to forbid the entrance of foreigners within its dominions, or to admit them only in such cases and upon such conditions as it may see fit to prescribe. In the United States this power is vested in the national government, to which the Constitution has committed the entire control of international relations, in peace as well as in war. It belongs to the political department of the government, and may be exercised either through treaties made by the President and Senate, or through statutes enacted by Congress, upon whom the Constitution has conferred power to regulate commerce with foreign nations, including the entrance of ships, the importation of goods and the bringing of persons into the ports of the United States; to establish a uniform rule of naturalization; to declare war, and to provide and maintain armies and navies; and to make all laws which may be necessary and proper for carrying into effect these powers and all other powers vested by the Constitution in the government of the United States or in any department or officer thereof. Constitution, art. 1, sec. 8; *Head Money Cases; Chae Chan Ping v. United States.*

The supervision of the admission of aliens into the United States may be entrusted by Congress either to the Department of State, having the general management of foreign relations, or to the Department of the Treasury, charged with the enforcement of the laws regulating foreign commerce; and Congress has often passed acts forbidding the immigration of particular classes of foreigners, and has committed the execution of these acts to the Secretary of the Treasury, to collectors of customs and to inspectors acting under their authority.

An alien immigrant, prevented from landing by any such officer claiming authority to do so under an act of Congress, and thereby restrained of his liberty, is doubtless entitled to a writ of *habeas corpus* to ascertain whether the restraint is lawful. And Congress may, if it sees fit, * * * authorize the courts to investigate and ascertain the facts on which the right to land depends. But, on the other hand, the final determination of those facts may be entrusted by Congress to executive officers; and in such a case, as in all others, in which a statute gives a discretionary power to an officer, to be exercised by him upon his own opinion of certain facts, he is made the sole and exclusive judge of the existence of those facts, and no other tribunal, unless expressly authorized by law to do so, is at liberty to reexamine or controvert the sufficiency of the evidence on which he acted. It is not within the province of the judiciary to order that foreigners who have never been naturalized, nor acquired any domicil or residence within the United States, nor even been admitted into the country pursuant to law, shall be permitted to enter, in opposition to the constitutional and lawful measures of the legislative and executive branches of the national government. As to such persons, the decisions of executive or administrative officers, acting within powers expressly conferred by Congress, are due process of law.

[The Court then interpreted the statute as entrusting the final fact-finding to the administrative officials.]

* * *

Order of the Circuit Court is affirmed.

■ MR. JUSTICE BREWER dissented.

QUESTIONS

1. In the first paragraph after the statement of facts, the Court sets out several propositions concerning governmental power to exclude noncitizens. Can you distinguish what the court says about (a) the power of a nation as a matter of international law, (b) the power of the United States federal government as a matter of domestic constitutional law, and (c) the distribution of power between the federal courts and the two "political" branches of the federal government, also as a matter of constitutional law?

2. For purposes of this section, the most important aspect of *Ekiu* is (c) above. According to the opinion, what is the job of the reviewing court when an excluded noncitizen attacks the statutory procedure on due process grounds? Suppose the statute had explicitly permitted the administrative officials to use whatever procedure they saw fit, and those officials, short on resources, had turned away all noncitizens who "looked destitute" without affording them any opportunity to be heard? Would the Court still have upheld the exclusion? To answer that question, you need to figure out how broad the Court intends its holding to be. Does the Court hold merely that Congress does not violate due process by entrusting the factfinding exclusively to administrative officials rather than judges? Or does the Court hold, more broadly, that Congress alone decides what process is constitutionally due in exclusion cases? As with any case in which the breadth of a court's holding is in doubt, examine both the literal language of the opinion and the court's reasoning. In this case, do they point in the same direction or in opposite directions? What was Ekiu's procedural grievance? Is there any point in the opinion at which the Court actually assesses the fairness of the prescribed procedure?

3. The Court says the power to exclude noncitizens "or to admit them only in such cases and upon such conditions as it may see fit to prescribe" belongs to "the political department" of the federal government. For that proposition the Court cites the *Head Money Cases* (described on page 105 above) and the *Chinese Exclusion Case*. Based on what you have now read, do you think those cases support that proposition, or does *Ekiu* go a step further? Consider the difference between the existence of a power and the limits to that power, and think especially about the specific constitutional objections that the immigrants in the *Chinese Exclusion Case* and *Ekiu* were raising.

Fong Yue Ting v. United States

Supreme Court of the United States, 1893.
149 U.S. 698, 13 S.Ct. 1016, 37 L.Ed. 905.

[The Act of May 5, 1892, ch. 60, § 6, provided:

SEC. 6. And it shall be the duty of all Chinese laborers, within the limits of the United States at the time of the passage of this act, and who are entitled to remain in the United States, to apply to the collector of internal revenue of their respective districts, within one year after the passage of this act, for a certificate of residence; and any Chinese laborer, within the limits of the United States, who shall neglect, fail or refuse to comply with the provisions of this act, or who, after one year from the passage hereof, shall be found within the jurisdiction of the United States without such certificate of residence, shall be deemed and adjudged to be unlawfully within the United States, and may be arrested by any United States customs official, collector of internal revenue or his deputies, United States marshal or his deputies, and taken before a United States judge, whose duty it shall be to order that he be deported from the United States as hereinbefore provided, unless he shall establish clearly, to the satisfaction of said judge, that by reason of accident, sickness, or other unavoidable cause, he has been unable to procure his certificate, and to the satisfaction of the court, and *by at least one credible white witness,* that he was a resident of the United States at the time of the passage of this act; and if upon the hearing it shall appear that he is so entitled to a certificate, it shall be granted, upon his paying the cost (emphasis added).

Three Chinese laborers were arrested for failure to possess the required certificates. All claimed to have been living in the United States at the time the statute had been enacted, but none was able to produce a white witness who could attest to his residence. They challenge the constitutionality of the white witness requirement.]

■ MR. JUSTICE GRAY, after stating the facts, delivered the opinion of the court.

In the recent case of *Nishimura Ekiu v. United States,* the court, in sustaining the action of the executive department, putting in force an act of Congress for the exclusion of aliens, said: "It is an accepted maxim of international law, that every sovereign nation has the power, as inherent in sovereignty, and essential to self-preservation, to forbid the entrance of foreigners within its dominions, or to admit them only in such cases and upon such conditions as it may see fit to prescribe. In the United States, this power is vested in the national government, to which the Constitution has committed the entire control of international relations, in peace as well as in war. It belongs to the political department of the government, and may be exercised either through treaties made by the President and Senate, or through statutes enacted by Congress."

* * *

The right of a nation to expel or deport foreigners, who have not been naturalized or taken any steps towards becoming citizens of the country, rests upon the same grounds, and is as absolute and unqualified as the right to prohibit and prevent their entrance into the country.

* * *

Vattel says: "Every nation has the right to refuse to admit a foreigner into the country, when he cannot enter without putting the nation in evident danger, or doing it a manifest injury. What it owes to itself, the care of its own safety, gives it this right; and in virtue of its natural liberty, it belongs to the nation to judge whether its circumstances will or will not justify the admission of the foreigner. Thus, also, it has a right to send them elsewhere, if it has just cause to fear that they will corrupt the manners of the citizens; that they will create religious disturbances, or occasion any other disorder, contrary to the public safety. * * * "

Ortolan says: "The government of each state has always the right to compel foreigners who are found within its territory to go away, by having them taken to the frontier. This right is based on the fact that, the foreigner not making part of the nation, his individual reception into the territory is matter of pure permission, of simple tolerance, and creates no obligation. * * * "

* * *

The right to exclude or to expel all aliens, or any class of aliens, absolutely or upon certain conditions, in war or in peace, being an inherent and inalienable right of every sovereign and independent nation, essential to its safety, its independence and its welfare, the question now before the court is whether the manner in which Congress has exercised this right in section [6] of the act of 1892 is consistent with the Constitution.

The United States are a sovereign and independent nation, and are vested by the Constitution with the entire control of international relations, and with all the powers of government necessary to maintain that control and to make it effective. The only government of this country, which other nations recognize or treat with, is the government of the Union; and the only American flag known throughout the world is the flag of the United States.

* * *

In exercising the great power which the people of the United States, by establishing a written Constitution as the supreme and paramount law, have vested in this court, of determining, whenever the question is properly brought before it, whether the acts of the legislature or of the executive are consistent with the Constitution, it behooves the court to be careful that it does not undertake to pass upon political questions, the final decision of which has been committed by the Constitution to the other departments of the government.

* * *

The power to exclude or to expel aliens, being a power affecting international relations, is vested in the political departments of the government, and is to be regulated by treaty or by act of Congress, and to be executed by the executive authority according to the regulations so established, except so far as the judicial department has been authorized by treaty or by statute, or is required by the paramount law of the Constitution, to intervene.

In *Nishimura Ekiu's* case, it was adjudged that, although Congress might, if it saw fit, authorize the courts to investigate and ascertain the facts upon which the alien's right to land was made by the statutes to depend, yet Congress might intrust the final determination of those facts to an executive officer, and that, if it did so, his order was due process of law, and no other tribunal, unless expressly authorized by law to do so, was at liberty to reexamine the evidence on which he acted, or to controvert its sufficiency.

The power to exclude aliens and the power to expel them rest upon one foundation, are derived from one source, are supported by the same reasons, and are in truth but parts of one and the same power.

The power of Congress, therefore, to expel, like the power to exclude aliens, or any specified class of aliens, from the country, may be exercised entirely through executive officers; or Congress may call in the aid of the judiciary to ascertain any contested facts on which an alien's right to be in the country has been made by Congress to depend.

Congress, having the right, as it may see fit, to expel aliens of a particular class, or to permit them to remain, has undoubtedly the right to provide a system of registration and identification of the members of that class within the country, and to take all proper means to carry out the system which it provides.

* * *

Chinese laborers, therefore, like all other aliens residing in the United States for a shorter or longer time, are entitled, so long as they are permitted by the government of the United States to remain in the country, to the safeguards of the Constitution, and to the protection of the laws, in regard to their rights of person and of property, and to their civil and criminal responsibility. But they continue to be aliens, having taken no steps towards becoming citizens, and incapable of becoming such under the naturalization laws; and therefore remain subject to the power of Congress to expel them, or to order them to be removed and deported from the country, whenever in its judgment their removal is necessary or expedient for the public interest.

* * *

For the reasons stated in the earlier part of this opinion, Congress, under the power to exclude or expel aliens, might have directed any Chinese laborer, found in the United States without a certificate of residence, to be removed out of the country by executive officers, without judicial trial or examination, just as it might have authorized such officers absolutely to prevent his entrance into the country. But Congress has not undertaken to do this.

The effect of the provisions of section 6 of the act of 1892 is that, if a Chinese laborer, after the opportunity afforded him to obtain a certificate of residence within a year, at a convenient place, and without cost, is found without such a certificate, he shall be so far presumed to be not entitled to remain within the United States, that an officer of the customs, or a collector of internal revenue, or a marshal, or a deputy of either, may arrest him, not with a view to imprisonment or punishment, or to his immediate deportation without further inquiry, but in order to take him before a judge, for the purpose of a judicial hearing and determination of the only facts which, under the act of Congress, can have a material bearing upon the question whether he shall be sent out of the country, or be permitted to remain.

* * *

The provision which puts the burden of proof upon him of rebutting the presumption arising from his having no certificate, as well as the requirement of proof, "by at least one credible white witness, that he was a resident of the United States at the time of the passage of this act," is within the acknowledged power of every legislature to prescribe the evidence which shall be received, and the effect of that evidence, in the courts of its own government. * * * The competency of all witnesses, without regard to their color, to testify in the courts of the United States, rests on acts of Congress, which Congress may at its discretion modify or repeal. The reason for requiring a Chinese alien, claiming the privilege of remaining in the United States, to prove the fact of his residence here, at the time of the passage of the act, "by at least one credible white witness," may have been the experience of Congress, as mentioned by Mr. Justice Field in *Chae Chan Ping's case,* that the enforcement of former acts, under which the testimony of Chinese persons was admitted to prove similar facts, "was attended with great embarrassment, from the suspicious nature, in many instances, of the testimony offered to establish the residence of the parties, arising from the loose notions entertained by the witnesses of the obligation of an oath." And this requirement, not allowing such a fact to be proved solely by the testimony of aliens in a like situation, or of the same race, is quite analogous to the provision, which has existed for seventy-seven years in the naturalization laws, by which aliens applying for naturalization must prove their residence within the limits and under the jurisdiction of the United States, for five years next preceding, "by the oath or affirmation of citizens of the United States."

The proceeding before a United States judge, as provided for in section 6 of the act of 1892, is in no proper sense a trial and sentence for a crime or offence. It is simply the ascertainment, by appropriate and lawful means, of the fact whether the conditions exist upon which Congress has enacted that an alien of this class may remain within the country. The order of deportation is not a punishment for crime. It is not a banishment, in the sense in which that word is often applied to the expulsion of a citizen from his country by way of punishment. It is but a method of enforcing the return to his own country of an alien who has not complied with the conditions upon the performance of which the government of the nation, acting within its constitutional authority and through the proper departments, has determined that his continuing to reside here shall depend. He has not, therefore, been deprived of life, liberty or property, without due process of law; and the provisions of the Constitution, securing the right of trial by jury, and prohibiting unreasonable searches and seizures, and cruel and unusual punishments, have no application.

The question whether, and upon what conditions, these aliens shall be permitted to remain within the United States being one to be determined by the political departments of the government, the judicial department cannot properly express an opinion upon the wisdom, the policy or the justice of the measures enacted by Congress in the exercise of the powers confided to it by the Constitution over this subject.

The three cases now before us do not differ from one another in any material particular.

[The lower court judgment ordering the immigrants deported is affirmed.]

* * *

■ MR. JUSTICE BREWER dissenting.

* * *

I rest my dissent on three propositions: First, that the persons against whom the penalties of section 6 of the act of 1892 are directed are persons lawfully residing within the United States secondly, that as such they are within the protection of the Constitution, and secured by its guarantees against oppression and wrong; and third, that section 6 deprives them of liberty and imposes punishment without due process of law, and in disregard of constitutional guarantees, especially those found in the Fourth, Fifth, Sixth, and Eighth Articles of the Amendments.

* * *

* * * We must take judicial notice of that which is disclosed by the census, and which is also a matter of common knowledge. There are 100,000 and more of these persons living in this country, making their homes here, and striving by their labor to earn a livelihood. They are not travellers, but resident aliens.

* * *

* * * They have lived in this country, respectively, since 1879, 1877, and 1874—almost as long a time as some of those who were members of the Congress that passed this act of punishment and expulsion.

That those who have become domiciled in a country are entitled to a more distinct and larger measure of protection than those who are simply passing through, or temporarily in it, has long been recognized by the law of nations. * * *

[It was once] said by Secretary Marcy: "This right to protect persons having a domicil, though not native-born or naturalized citizens, rests on the firm foundation of justice, and the claim to be protected is earned by considerations which the protecting power is not at liberty to disregard. Such domiciled citizen pays the same price for his protection as native-born or naturalized citizens pay for theirs. He is under the bonds of allegiance to the country of his residence, and if he breaks them incurs the same penalties; he owes the same obedience to the civil laws ... ; his property is in the same way and to the same extent as theirs liable to contribute to the support of the government.... In nearly all respects his and their condition as to the duties and burdens of government are undistinguishable."

* * *

It is said that the power here asserted is inherent in sovereignty. This doctrine of powers inherent in sovereignty is one both indefinite and dangerous. Where are the limits to such powers to be found, and by whom are they to be pronounced? Is it within legislative capacity to declare the limits? If so, then the mere assertion of an inherent power creates it, and despotism exists. May the courts establish the boundaries? Whence do they obtain the authority for this? Shall they look to the practices of other nations to ascertain the limits? The governments of other nations have elastic powers—ours is fixed and bounded by a written constitution. The expulsion of a race may be within the inherent powers of a despotism. History, before the adoption of this Constitution, was not destitute of examples of the exercise of such a power; and its framers were familiar with history, and wisely, as it seems to me, they gave to this government no general power to banish. Banishment may be resorted to as punishment for crime; but among the powers reserved to the people and not delegated to the government is that of determining whether whole classes in our midst shall, for no crime but that of their race and birthplace, be driven from our territory.

Whatever may be true as to exclusion, and as to that see *Chinese Exclusion Case* and *Nishimura Ekiu v. United States,* I deny that there is any arbitrary and unrestrained power to banish residents, even resident aliens. What, it may be asked, is the reason for any difference? The answer is obvious. The Constitution has no extraterritorial effect, and those who have not come lawfully within our territory cannot claim any protection from its provisions. And it may be that the national government, having full control of all matters relating to other nations, has the power to build, as it were, a Chinese wall around our borders and absolutely forbid aliens to enter. But the Constitution has potency everywhere within the limits of our territory, and the powers which the national government may exercise within such limits are those, and only those, given to it by that instrument. Now, the power to remove resident aliens is, confessedly, not expressed. Even if it be among the powers implied, yet still it can be exercised only in subordination to the limitations and restrictions imposed by the Constitution. In the case of *Monongahela Navigation Company v. United States,* it was said: "But like the other powers granted to Congress by the Constitution, the power to regulate commerce is subject to all the limitations imposed by such instrument, and among them is that of the Fifth Amendment we have heretofore quoted. Congress has supreme control over the regulation of commerce; but if, in exercising that supreme control, it deems it necessary to take private property, then it must proceed subject to the limitations imposed by this Fifth Amendment, and can take only on payment of just compensation." And if that be true of the powers expressly granted, it must as certainly be true of those that are only granted by implication.

* * *

In the case of *Yick Wo v. Hopkins,* it was said: "The Fourteenth Amendment to the Constitution is not confined to the protection of citizens. It says: 'Nor shall any State deprive any person of life, liberty, or property without due process of law; nor deny to any person within its jurisdiction the equal protection of the laws.' These provisions are universal in their application to all persons within the territorial jurisdiction, without regard to any differences of race, of color, or of nationality; and the equal protection of the laws is a pledge of the protection of equal laws." * * *

If the use of the word "person" in the Fourteenth Amendment protects all individuals lawfully within the State, the use of the same word "person" in the Fifth must be equally comprehensive, and secures to all persons lawfully within the territory of the United States the protection named therein; and a like conclusion must follow as to the Sixth.

I pass, therefore, to the consideration of my third proposition: Section 6 deprives of "life, liberty, and property without due process of law." It imposes punishment without a trial, and punishment cruel and severe. It places the liberty of one individual subject to the unrestrained control of another. Notice its provisions: It first commands all to register. He who does not register violates that law, and may be punished; and so the section goes on to say that one who has not complied with its requirements, and has no certificate of residence, "shall be deemed and adjudged to be unlawfully within the United States," and then it imposes as a penalty his deportation from the country. Deportation is punishment. It involves first an arrest, a deprival of liberty; and, second, a removal from home, from family, from business, from property. * * *

[It] needs no citation of authorities to support the proposition that deportation is punishment. Every one knows that to be forcibly taken away from home, and family, and friends, and business, and property, and sent across the ocean to a distant land, is punishment; and that often times most severe and cruel. Apt and just are the words of one of the framers of this Constitution, President Madison, when he says "If the banishment of an alien from a country into which he has been invited as the asylum most auspicious to his happiness—a country where he may have formed the most tender connections; where he may have invested his entire property, and acquired property of the real and permanent, as well as the movable and temporary kind; where he enjoys, under the laws, a greater share of the blessings of personal security and personal liberty than he can elsewhere hope for; ... if, moreover, in the execution of the sentence against him he is to be exposed, not only to the ordinary dangers of the sea, but to the peculiar casualties incident to a crisis of war and of unusual licentiousness on that element, and possibly to vindictive purposes, which his immigration itself may have provoked—if a banishment of this sort be not a punishment, and among the severest of punishments, it will be difficult to imagine a doom to which the name can be applied."

But punishment implies a trial: "No person shall be deprived of life, liberty, or property, without due process of law." Due process requires that a man be heard before he is condemned, and both heard and condemned in the due and orderly procedure of a trial as recognized by the common law from time immemorial. * * *

Again, it is absolutely within the discretion of the collector to give or refuse a certificate to one who applies therefor. Nowhere is it provided what evidence shall be furnished to the collector, and nowhere is it made mandatory upon him to grant a certificate on the production of such evidence. It cannot be due process of law to impose punishment on any person for failing to have that in his possession, the possession of which he can obtain only at the arbitrary and unregulated discretion of any official. It will not do to say that the presumption is that the official will act reasonably and not arbitrarily. When the right to liberty and residence is involved, some other protection than the mere discretion of any official is required. * * *

* * *

It is true this statute is directed only against the obnoxious Chinese; but if the power exists, who shall say it will not be exercised to-morrow against other classes and other people? If the guarantees of these amendments can be thus ignored in order to get rid of this distasteful class, what security have others that a like disregard of its provisions may not be resorted to? * * *

* * *

In view of this enactment of the highest legislative body of the foremost Christian nation, may not the thoughtful Chinese disciple of Confucius fairly ask, Why do they send missionaries here?

■ MR. JUSTICE FIELD, dissenting.

* * *

I had the honor to be the organ of the court in announcing [its opinion in the *Chinese Exclusion Case.*] I still adhere to the views there expressed in all particulars; but between legislation for the exclusion of Chinese persons—that is, to prevent them from entering the country—and legislation for the deportation of those who have acquired a residence in the country under a treaty with China, there is a wide and essential difference. The power of the government to exclude foreigners from this country, that is, to prevent them from entering it, whenever the public interests in its judgment require such exclusion, has been repeatedly asserted by the legislative and executive departments of our government and never denied; but its power to deport from the country persons lawfully domiciled therein by its consent, and engaged in the ordinary pursuits of life, has never been asserted by the legislative or executive departments except for crime, or as an act of war in view of existing or anticipated hostilities, unless the alien act of June 25, 1798, can be considered as recognizing that doctrine. That act vested in the President power to order all such aliens as he should adjudge dangerous to the peace and safety of the United States, or should have reasonable grounds to suspect were concerned in any treasonable or secret machinations against the government, to depart out of the territory of the United States within such time as should be expressed in his order. * * *

* * *

[Justice Field here describes the unpopular reception of the 1798 Act, contemporary doubts about its constitutionality, and Congress's refusal to renew the Act when it expired after two years.]

* * *

* * * Is it possible that Congress can, at its pleasure, in disregard of the guarantees of the Constitution, expel at any time the Irish, German, French, and English who may have taken up their residence here on the invitation of the government, while we are at peace with the countries from which they came, simply on the ground that they have not been naturalized?

* * *

[T]he only question for our consideration is the lawfulness of the procedure provided for its accomplishment, and this must be tested by the provisions of the Constitution and laws intended for the protection of all persons against encroachment upon their rights. Aliens from countries at peace with us, domiciled within our country by its consent, are entitled to all the guaranties for the protection of their persons and property which are secured to native-born citizens. The moment any human being from a country at peace with us comes within the jurisdiction of the United States, with their consent—and such consent will always be implied when not expressly withheld, and in the case of the Chinese laborers before us was in terms given by the treaty referred to—he becomes subject to all their laws, is amenable to their punishment and entitled to their protection. Arbitrary and despotic power can no more be exercised over them with reference to their persons and property, than over the persons and property of native-born citizens. They differ only from citizens in that they cannot vote or hold any public office. * * * If a foreigner who resides in the country by its consent commits a public offence, is he subject to be cut down, maltreated, imprisoned, or put to death by violence, without accusation made, trial had, and judgment of an established tribunal following the regular forms of judicial procedure? If any rule in the administration of justice is to be omitted or discarded in his case, what rule is it to be? If one rule may lawfully be laid aside in his case, another rule may also be laid aside, and all rules may be discarded. In such instances a rule of evidence may be set aside in one case, a rule of pleading in another; the testimony of eye-witnesses may be rejected and hearsay adopted, or no evidence at all may be received, but simply an inspection of the accused, as is often the case in tribunals of Asiatic countries where personal caprice and not settled rules prevail. That would be to establish a pure, simple, undisguised depotism and tyranny with respect to foreigners resident in the country by its consent, and such an exercise of power is not permissible under our Constitution. * * *

I utterly dissent from and reject the doctrine expressed in the opinion of the majority, that "Congress, under the power to exclude or expel aliens, might have directed any Chinese laborer found in the United States without a certificate of residence to be removed out of the country by executive officers, without judicial trial or examination, just as it might have authorized such officers absolutely to prevent his entrance into the country." An arrest in that way for that purpose would not be a reasonable seizure of the person within the meaning of the Fourth Article of the amendments to the Constitution. It would be brutal and oppressive. The existence of the power thus stated is only consistent with the admission that the government is one of unlimited and despotic power so far as aliens domiciled in the country are concerned. According to its theory, Congress might have ordered executive officers to take the Chinese laborers to the ocean and put them into a boat and set them adrift; or to take them to the borders of Mexico and turn them loose there; and in both cases without any means of support; indeed, it might have sanctioned towards these laborers the most shocking brutality conceivable. I utterly repudiate all such notions, and reply that brutality, inhumanity, and cruelty cannot be made elements in any procedure for the enforcement of the laws of the United States.

The majority of the court have, in their opinion, made numerous citations from the courts and the utterances of individuals upon the power of the government of an independent nation to exclude foreigners from entering its limits, but none, beyond a few loose observations, as to its power to expel and deport from the country those who are domiciled therein by its consent. * * * Deportation from the realm has not been exercised in England since Magna Charta, except in punishment for crime, or as a measure in view of existing or anticipated hostilities. But even if that power were exercised by every government of Europe, it would have no bearing in these cases. It may be admitted that the power has been exercised by the various governments of Europe. Spain expelled the Moors; England, in the reign of Edward I, banished fifteen thousand Jews; and Louis XIV, in 1685, by revoking the Edict of Nantes, which gave religious liberty to Protestants in France, drove out the Huguenots. Nor does such severity of European governments belong only to the distant past. Within three years Russia has banished many thousands of Jews, and apparently intends the expulsion of the whole race—an act of barbarity which has aroused the indignation of all Christendom. * * * Indeed, all the instances mentioned have been condemned for their barbarity and cruelty, and no power to perpetrate such barbarity is to be implied from the nature of our government, and certainly is not found in any delegated powers under the Constitution.

The government of the United States is one of limited and delegated powers. It takes nothing from the usages or the former action of European governments, nor does it take any power by any supposed inherent sovereignty. There is a great deal of confusion in the use of the word "sovereignty" by law writers. Sovereignty or supreme power is in this country vested in the people, and only in the people. By them certain sovereign powers have been delegated to the government of the United States and other sovereign powers reserved to the States or to themselves. This is not a matter of inference and argument, but is the express declaration of the Tenth Amendment to the Constitution, passed to avoid any misinterpretation of the powers of the general government. That amendment declares that "The powers not delegated to the United States by the Constitution, nor prohibited by it to the States, are reserved to the States, respectively, or to the people." When, therefore, power is exercised by Congress, authority for it must be found in express terms in the Constitution, or in the means necessary or proper for the execution of the power expressed. If it cannot be thus found, it does not exist.

* * *

The punishment is beyond all reason in its severity. It is out of all proportion to the alleged offence. It is cruel and unusual. As to its cruelty, nothing can exceed a forcible deportation from a country of one's residence, and the breaking up of all the relations of friendship, family, and business there contracted. The laborer may be seized at a distance from his home, his family and his business, and taken before the judge for his condemnation, without permission to visit his home, see his family, or complete any unfinished business. * * *

* * *

There are numerous other objections to the provisions of the act under consideration. Every step in the procedure provided, as truly said by counsel, tramples upon some constitutional right. Grossly it violates the Fourth Amendment, which declares that: "The right of the people to be secure in their persons, ... against unreasonable searches and seizures, shall not be violated, and no warrant shall issue but upon probable cause, supported by oath or affirmation, and particularly describing the ... persons ... to be seized."

* * *

I will not pursue the subject further. The decision of the court and the sanction it would give to legislation depriving resident aliens of the guaranties of the Constitution fills me with apprehensions. Those guaranties are of priceless value to every one resident in the country, whether citizen or alien. I cannot but regard the decision as a blow against constitutional liberty, when it declares that Congress has the right to disregard the guaranties of the Constitution intended for the protection of all men, domiciled in the country with the consent of the government, in their rights of person and property. How far will its legislation go? The unnaturalized resident feels it today, but if Congress can disregard the guaranties with respect to any one domiciled in this country with its consent, it may disregard the guaranties with respect to naturalized citizens. What assurance have we that it may not declare that naturalized citizens of a particular country cannot remain in the United States after a certain day, unless they have in their possession a certificate that they are of good moral character and attached to the principles of our Constitution, which certificate they must obtain from a collector of internal revenue upon the testimony of at least one competent witness of a class or nationality to be designated by the government?

What answer could the naturalized citizen in that case make to his arrest for deportation, which cannot be urged in behalf of the Chinese laborers of to-day?

I am of the opinion that the orders of the court below should be reversed, and the petitioners should be discharged.

■ MR. CHIEF JUSTICE FULLER dissenting.

* * *

If the protection of the Constitution extends to Chinese laborers who are lawfully within and entitled to remain in the United States under previous treaties and laws, then the question whether this act of Congress so far as it relates to them is in conflict with that instrument, is a judicial question, and its determination belongs to the judicial department.

* * *

The argument is that friendly aliens, who have lawfully acquired a domicil in this country, are entitled to avail themselves of the safeguards of the Constitution only while permitted to remain, and that the power to expel them and the manner of its exercise are unaffected by that instrument. It is difficult to see how this can be so in view of the operation of the power upon the existing rights of individuals; * * * Conceding that the exercise of the power to exclude is committed to the political department, and that the denial of entrance is not necessarily the subject of judicial cognizance, the exercise of the power to expel, the manner in which the right to remain may be terminated, rest on different ground, since limitations exist or are imposed upon the deprivation of that which has been lawfully acquired. * * * [T]he act directs the performance of a judicial function in a particular way, and inflicts punishment without a judicial trial. It is, in effect, a legislative sentence of banishment, and, as such, absolutely void. Moreover, it contains within it the germs of the assertion of an unlimited and arbitrary power, in general, incompatible with the immutable principles of justice, inconsistent with the nature of our government, and in conflict with the written Constitution by which that government was created and those principles secured.

NOTES AND QUESTIONS

In *Fong Yue Ting* the Court must decide whether the broad federal powers recognized in the *Chinese Exclusion Case* and in *Ekiu* are limited to the context of exclusion. The majority rejects that limitation, extrapolating to deportation the basic principles previously applied to exclusion: that the nation has the power in international law to exclude noncitizens, that in the United States this power is held by the federal government (not the states), and that within the federal government the power lies with the political branches (not the courts). The first three notes below consider how the Court extends these principles from exclusion to deportation.

1. For its conclusion on international law, the Court quotes passages from several treatises. Two of the quoted passages—those by Vattel and Ortolan—are reproduced in the above excerpt. How does the reasoning of those two writers differ?

Today it is accepted that international law permits nations both to exclude and to deport aliens. At the same time, however, it is clear that international law limits the exercise of those powers in various ways. See, e.g., T. Alexander Aleinikoff & Vincent Chetail (Eds.), Migration and International Legal Norms (2003); Guy S. Goodwin–Gill, International Law and the Movement of Persons Between States (1978); Richard Plender, International Migration Law (rev. 2d ed. 1988); James A.R. Nafziger, *A Commentary on American Legal Scholarship Concerning the Admission of Migrants,* 17 U.Mich.J.L.Reform 165 (1984). The international constraints are clearest in the context of refugees, as you will see in detail in chapter 11, especially section C.

2. To find a *federal* power to deport noncitizens, the Court observes that the federal government is "vested by the Constitution with the entire control of international relations, and with all the powers of government necessary to maintain that control and to make it effective." What, exactly, is the connection between deportation and foreign affairs? Recall the discussion in the *Chinese Exclusion Case* linking admission decisions to foreign policy. Does the same rationale apply to deportation? Can you articulate other ways in which decisions whom to deport could be a foreign policy tool? What is your reaction to the use of the deportation power as a weapon of foreign policy? Should it matter whether the deportees are "alien friends" or "alien enemies"? Should it matter whether they entered legally or illegally? If they entered legally, should it matter whether they are permanent residents or temporary visitors?

The Court gets from a federal exclusion power to a federal deportation power by identifying the rationales for the former and concluding that the same rationales apply to the latter. Could the Court have fortified its result by arguing that, regardless whether it was right or wrong to recognize the federal exclusion power, the very fact that it has done so makes it sensible to recognize a federal deportation power? Consider two possible arguments along those lines:

a.   If the federal government could exclude noncitizens but could not deport them, inadmissible noncitizens would simply enter surreptitiously. Once in, they would be safe forever. (Are there either enforcement techniques or legal consequences other than deportation that would deter such illegal entries? We shall examine this question in chapter 12.)

b.   Exclusion and deportation are logically inseparable. Deportation is just a way of correcting errors or lapses in the admissions process and enforcing the conditions attached to proper admissions.

(What *is* the function of deportation? Is it really just a check on the admissions process? You will see in chapter 7 that, although some deportation grounds can be related back to entry, others cover post-entry conduct.)

3.   Given a federal power to deport, how, if at all, does the Constitution limit the exercise of that power? And, again, what is the judicial role in pronouncing those limits? Those questions are at least partly addressed by the majority opinion. For what principle does the case actually stand?

Suppose Congress had authorized each immigration officer to deport any Chinese laborer whenever the officer suspected either that the person had no certificate of residence or that the certificate had been forged. If such a statute had provided no opportunity for the individual to be heard, would it have been upheld? To answer this question, try to determine whether the Court held (a) that due process simply does not apply in deportation cases, (b) that due process applies but that Congress, not the Court, decides what process is due, or (c) that due process applies and the Court decides what process is due, but that the white witness rule was a reasonable evidentiary decision meeting the requirements of due process. How would each of those readings affect the answer to the hypothetical?

4.   Whatever the precise scope of the Court's conclusions concerning the procedural limits to the deportation power, there is no doubt that the opinion reveals great deference to Congress. Why is the Court so deferential? At one point the Court suggests that the constitutionality of a congressional decision concerning deportation is a political question, presumably because it affects foreign affairs. Was the white witness requirement an attempt to promote good foreign relations? Or was Congress pursuing purely domestic aims, even at the *expense* of antagonizing another nation? Is this a question a court should decide, or should the Court treat every deportation provision as reflecting a foreign policy objective even when common sense makes a contrary conclusion obvious? *Can* a court make an informed judgment as to when judicial intervention would disrupt foreign policy? Can it afford not to? See Stephen H. Legomsky, *Immigration Law and the Principle of Plenary Congressional Power,* 1984 Supreme Ct.Rev. 255, 262–69.

Related to the theory that the foreign policy ramifications of deportation dictate judicial deference is another theme that recurs throughout the majority opinion—that the deportation power is sovereign in nature and that sovereign powers are subject to few, if any, constitutional constraints. Justice Field, dissenting, replies by rejecting the notion that the federal government "take[s] any power by any supposed inherent sovereignty." 149 U.S. at 757, 13 S.Ct. at 1039, 37 L.Ed. at 928. Re-read carefully, on page 135 above, the paragraph of Justice Field's dissent that begins with the phrase "The government of the United States."

Remembering that only four years earlier the same Justice Field had written the opinion of the Court in the *Chinese Exclusion Case,* and that that opinion had relied explicitly on a "sovereign" federal power to exclude noncitizens, how do you account for this paragraph? His two opinions can certainly be reconciled on the facts of the cases; Justice Field might have accepted a sovereign power to exclude noncitizens while rejecting a sovereign power to deport them. But that explanation alone would hardly explain the breadth and forcefulness of his language, which expressly repudiates sovereignty as the source of *any* federal power. Given his admitted adherence to the views expressed in the *Chinese Exclusion Case* "in all particulars," 149 U.S. at 746, 13 S.Ct. at 1035, 37 L.Ed. at 924, the question is whether his two opinions can be fully reconciled. More specifically, did Justice Field believe there was such a thing as a federal power inherent in sovereignty, or didn't he? In answering this question, recall also the distinction between a sovereign power implied by the Constitution and a sovereign power that rests on extraconstitutional sources. Does that distinction help to explain Justice Field's position?

For intriguing discussions of the contrasting ways in which the Supreme Court has treated sovereignty claims in the Indian and immigration contexts, see T. Alexander Aleinikoff, Semblances of Sovereignty: The Constitution, the State, and American Citizenship (2002); Sarah H. Cleveland, *Powers Inherent in Sovereignty: Indians, Aliens, Territories, and the Nineteenth–Century Origins of Plenary Power over Foreign Affairs,* 81 Texas L. Rev. 1 (2002); Sarah H. Cleveland, *The Plenary Power Background of Curtiss–Wright,* 70 Univ. Colorado L. Rev. 1127 (1999); Philip P. Frickey, *Domesticating Federal Indian Law,* 81 Minnesota L.Rev. 31 (1996); Natsu Taylor Saito, *Asserting Plenary Power over the "Other": Indians, Immigrants, Colonial Subjects, and Why U.S. Jurisprudence Needs to Incorporate International Law,* 20 Yale L. & Policy Rev. 427 (2002).

5. The plaintiffs in *Fong Yue Ting* challenged the *procedural* fairness of the white-witness requirement. Note, however, that the requirement itself was imposed only on Chinese laborers. Suppose the plaintiffs had argued that the statute was *substantively* unconstitutional because it was racially[5] discriminatory. Would the Court's reasoning similarly have dictated rejection of the substantive constitutional argument? Did the Supreme Court decide that issue *sub silentio* in the *Chinese Exclusion Case* and

---

5. The discrimination cannot be dismissed as based only on country of citizenship rather than on race. Other sections made clear that the statute extended to "Chinese persons and persons of Chinese descent." See Act of May 5, 1892, ch. 60, §§ 1, 2, 3, 4, 27 Stat. 25; see especially § 2 (removal of "Chinese person or person of Chinese descent" shall be to country of citizenship unless that country would impose a tax as a condition of accepting the person, in which case removal would be to China.)

Ekiu? Or does the distinction between exclusion and deportation prevent extrapolation even if these previous cases are read as upholding racially discriminatory exclusion provisions? If Congress had decreed that any noncitizen who criticizes the government of the United States shall be deported, would a First Amendment argument have met a similar fate? We shall return to the problem of substantive constitutional limitations in section B.2.c below.

6.   How far does Justice Brewer go in his dissent? Does he claim that Congress has no power to deport noncitizens? Would he, for example, recognize a federal power to deport those noncitizens who had evaded inspection or entered in some other unlawful way? Would he allow the deportation of a noncitizen who had been admitted lawfully as a temporary visitor but overstayed? Are there circumstances in which he would permit the deportation of even an LPR?

7.   *Fong Yue Ting* is still good law insofar as it holds that international law permits the deportation of even lawfully admitted immigrants and that United States constitutional law lodges that power in the federal government. The Court's great reluctance to review that congressional decision for compliance with the Bill of Rights is similarly consistent with current law. But in one important respect the modern law has left *Fong Yue Ting* behind. As you will see shortly, it is now clear that one particular constitutional right—procedural due process—applies in deportation cases (not as clear in exclusion cases).

Why should either the applicability or the content of due process hinge on the distinction between exclusion and deportation? The various opinions in *Fong Yue Ting* suggest several possible reasons:

a.   Justice Brewer emphasizes that deportation operates on those who are within the United States while exclusion operates only on persons who, in the eyes of the law, are outside the country. He attaches significance to that distinction because, in his view, the Constitution does not apply outside United States territory. If that is his belief, though, how could he have dissented in *Ekiu,* where the majority rejected the immigrant's constitutional challenge to her exclusion? (Justice Brewer himself provided no explanation for his dissent.)

Today, the statement that the Constitution is inapplicable outside the United States is not categorically true. To be sure, the Supreme Court has interpreted *certain* constitutional provisions as being inapplicable in *certain* extraterritorial contexts. See, e.g., *United States v. Verdugo–Urquidez,* 494 U.S. 259, 110 S.Ct. 1056, 108 L.Ed.2d 222 (1990); *Balzac v. People of Porto Rico,* 258 U.S. 298, 42 S.Ct. 343, 66 L.Ed. 627 (1922); *Downes v. Bidwell,* 182 U.S. 244, 21 S.Ct. 770, 45 L.Ed. 1088 (1901). But several cases have extended certain constitutional guarantees to United States citizens living abroad. See, e.g., *Reid v. Covert,* 354 U.S. 1, 77 S.Ct. 1222, 1 L.Ed.2d 1148 (1957), and its progeny. Occasionally a court will go a step further and apply constitutional restrictions to the actions of the United States government even when the aggrieved individuals are noncitizens living overseas. See, e.g., *Russian Volunteer Fleet v. United States,* 282 U.S. 481, 51 S.Ct.

229, 75 L.Ed. 473 (1931) (Fifth Amendment requires government to provide just compensation when seizing contractual rights of nonresident corporation); *United States v. Tiede,* 86 F.R.D. 227 (U.S.Ct. for Berlin, 1979) (Sixth Amendment requires government to offer jury trial to nonresident noncitizen criminally prosecuted by U.S. authorities in Berlin). *Cf. Rasul v. Bush,* ___ U.S. ___, 124 S.Ct. 2686, 159 L.Ed.2d 548 (2004) (construing habeas corpus *statute* as extending to Guantánamo). For a sophisticated discussion of the extraterritorial reach of the United States Constitution (including analysis of whether it should matter that the aggrieved individual is not a citizen), see Gerald L. Neuman, *Whose Constitution?,* 100 Yale L.J. 909 (1991).

Assuming, however, that the distinction between noncitizens outside the United States and those within it is constitutionally significant, in what sense is a noncitizen who faces exclusion outside the United States? Not in the physical sense. For a variety of practical reasons, the inspection and removal of arriving noncitizens almost invariably take place on the United States side of the border. Noncitizens who seek admission are outside the United States only because the law *deems* them to be. Should Congress, through the simple expedient of declaring that a noncitizen who is physically here is legally not, be able to render the Constitution inapplicable? Conversely, however, should any noncitizen, by taking a few steps into United States territory, be able to assert constitutional rights that he or she otherwise would not have possessed? From either perspective, should physical location determine whether a noncitizen may assert constitutional rights?

b. Chief Justice Fuller, also dissenting, takes a different tack. The significant point for him is that deportation takes away "that which has been lawfully acquired." Presumably he would not object to the deportation of a noncitizen who entered illegally. But how would he handle the *exclusion* of someone like Chae Chan Ping (in the *Chinese Exclusion Case*), who was seeking to resume his lawful permanent residence in the United States? Would he say that the government was attempting to take away a lawfully acquired residence? Or would he say that Chae Chan Ping had relinquished his residence already by voluntarily leaving the country, albeit only temporarily?

c. An additional difference between exclusion and deportation concerns the potential magnitudes of the individual interests at stake. Perhaps Chief Justice Fuller's emphasis on deportation as a deprivation of an existing legal right can be viewed as a factor that makes the interest of a person resisting deportation greater than the interest of a person seeking admission. Moreover, even when the initial entry was illegal, various ties to the community can form with the passage of time. Would those differences justify either (a) holding the due process clause applicable to deportation but not exclusion, or (b) applying the due process clause to both but holding that greater process is due in deportation proceedings than in exclusion proceedings?

In examining that question, ask yourself how accurate the exclusion/deportation distinction is as a barometer of the individual interest. Chae Chan Ping and Ekiu were challenging only exclusion orders, but Chae Chan Ping was a returning resident and Ekiu, though seeking only initial entry, claimed to be rejoining her United States citizen husband. Were their individual interests trivial?

If you agree that even excluded noncitizens can have important interests at stake, what should the law be? Should the inaccuracy of the exclusion/deportation distinction be tolerated on the theory that, although imperfect, it is at least a rough indicator of individual interest in most cases? Should exceptions be made for returning residents? For alleged family members of United States citizens?

d.   Justice Brewer's argument that deportation is punishment forms a fourth possible basis for distinguishing deportation from exclusion. Whether deportation is punishment is important because, if it is, then deportation proceedings arguably are subject to at least some of the many constitutional safeguards applicable in criminal proceedings. Those include the Fifth Amendment bar on double jeopardy, the Sixth Amendment rights to a speedy, public, jury trial and to counsel, the Eighth Amendment prohibitions on excessive bail and on cruel and unusual punishment, the ex post facto clause, and other provisions.

After concluding that deportation is not punishment, the Court in *Fong Yue Ting* says that the person "has not, *therefore*, been deprived of life, liberty or property, without due process of law." 149 U.S. at 730, 13 S.Ct. at 1029, 37 L.Ed. at 919 (emphasis added). Is the Court suggesting that the due process clause is another one of those constitutional provisions that restrict only the imposition of punishment? If so, the Court was on shaky ground; even by that time either the due process clause itself or the procedural fairness principles underlying it had been applied outside the context of punishment. See, e.g., *Windsor v. McVeigh,* 93 U.S. (3 Otto) 274, 277–78, 23 L.Ed. 914 (1876) (fair notice required for *in rem* jurisdiction); *Baldwin v. Hale,* 68 U.S. (1 Wall.) 223, 233, 17 L.Ed. 531, 534 (1863). Today it is clearer still that the due process clause is not restricted to punishment. See, e.g., *Mathews v. Eldridge,* 424 U.S. 319, 96 S.Ct. 893, 47 L.Ed.2d 18 (1976) (termination of social security disability benefits).

At any rate, is the Court convincing when it concludes that deportation is not punishment? The Court reasons that deportation is merely "a method of enforcing the return to his own country of an alien who has not complied with the conditions upon the performance of which the government of the nation, acting within its constitutional authority and through the proper departments, has determined that his continuing to reside here shall depend." 149 U.S. at 730, 13 S.Ct. at 1028, 37 L.Ed. at 919. Is it that simple? Could not an imprisonment pursuant to a federal criminal sentence (clearly punishment) be described as merely "a method of enforcing the transfer to a prison facility of a person who has not complied with the conditions upon the performance of which the government of the nation, acting within its constitutional authority and through the proper departments, has determined that his continuing to remain at large shall depend?"

Yet Justice Brewer's analysis seems equally unsatisfying. He says: "Every one knows that to be forcibly taken away from home, and family, and friends, and business, and property, and sent across the ocean to a distant land, is punishment." 149 U.S. at 740, 13 S.Ct. at 1032, 37 L.Ed. at 922. Notice that Justice Brewer focuses solely on the *consequences* of deportation.

It would be equally possible to consider the *purposes* of punishment and then to assess their applicability to deportation. Criminologists differ, but the more commonly held theories of punishment include retribution, deterrence (both general deterrence, which aims to discourage others from committing specified acts, and specific deterrence, which seeks to dissuade a particular offender from repeating deviant behavior), incapacitation (isolating the offender from society), and rehabilitation of the offender. See Wayne R. LaFave, Criminal Law, § 1.5 (4th ed. 2003). Do any of these goals of punishment coincide with the purposes of deportation? Think especially about whether the incapacitation goal has an analog in deportation policy.

We shall return to this theme in chapter 7, where the theories of deportation are considered more comprehensively.

8.   The due process clause states: "No person shall * * * be deprived of life, liberty, or property, without due process of law." U.S. Const. amend. V. Importantly, protection extends to any "person;" unlike certain other constitutional provisions,[6] coverage is not limited to the "citizen." Under modern due process analysis, however, that observation leaves two other questions: When will the interest of which a person has been deprived be regarded as a "life, liberty, or property" interest? And, when a person has been deprived of such an interest, what process is due?

Precisely when a life, liberty, or property interest will be found is not easy to say. In *Board of Regents v. Roth,* 408 U.S. 564, 92 S.Ct. 2701, 33 L.Ed.2d 548 (1972), the Court flatly rejected "the wooden distinction between rights and privileges that once seemed to govern the applicability of due process rights." *Id.* at 571, 92 S.Ct. at 2706, 33 L.Ed.2d at 557. It defined "liberty" broadly to extend beyond bodily restraint and to encompass "those privileges long recognized ... as essential to the orderly pursuit of happiness by free men." *Id.* at 572, 92 S.Ct. at 2707, 33 L.Ed.2d at 558 (quoting from prior decision). A "property" interest, in contrast, was more narrowly conceived. It was held to require "a legitimate claim of entitlement" (not just a "unilateral expectation"), and that entitlement has to have been created by some independent source of law (not by the Constitution itself.) *Id.* at 577, 92 S.Ct. at 2709, 33 L.Ed.2d at 561. The

---

6.   E.g., only a citizen may be a member of the House of Representatives, U.S. Const. art. I, § 2, cl. 2, or a Senator, art. I, § 3, cl. 3, or the President, art. II, § 5. The voting rights of *citizens* may not be abridged on account of race, amend. XIV, § 1, or sex, amend. XIX, § 1, or age, if over 18, amend. XXVI, § 1, or by a poll tax, amend. XXIV, § 1. And states may not abridge the privileges and immunities of citizens. *Id.* amend. XIV, § 1.

cases applying these requirements are complex, difficult to reconcile, and, fortunately, beyond the scope of a coursebook on immigration law. Whether a noncitizen's interest in admission rises to the level of a liberty or property interest is therefore not entirely clear. Do you think either liberty or property interests are implicated in deportation proceedings? Does it matter whether the person is in lawful immigration status? Whether the person is an immigrant or a nonimmigrant? These questions will recur throughout this chapter. See generally Rodney A. Smolla, *The Reemergence of the Right–Privilege Distinction in Constitutional Law: The Price of Protesting Too Much,* 35 Stanford L.Rev. 69 (1982); William W. Van Alstyne, *The Demise of the Right–Privilege Distinction in Constitutional Law,* 81 Harvard L.Rev. 1439 (1968).

Once a life, liberty, or property interest is held to be at stake, the next question is what process is due. The leading formula comes from *Mathews v. Eldridge,* 424 U.S. 319, 335, 96 S.Ct. 893, 903, 47 L.Ed.2d 18, 33 (1976). There the Court identified three factors to balance: "First, the private interest that will be affected by the official action; second, the risk of an erroneous deprivation of such interest through the procedures used, and the probable value, if any, of additional or substitute procedural safeguards; and finally, the Government's interest, including the function involved and the fiscal and administrative burdens that the additional or substitute procedural requirement would entail." Under the *Eldridge* test, is the white witness rule constitutional?

2.   MODERN DEVELOPMENTS

The *Chinese Exclusion Case, Ekiu,* and *Fong Yue Ting* can be viewed as the three basic building blocks of the "plenary" congressional power over immigration. The *Chinese Exclusion Case* recognized an inherent federal power to exclude noncitizens; *Ekiu* appeared to reject due process limits on the exercise of that power; and *Fong Yue Ting* extended the principles of both cases from exclusion to deportation. This subsection examines modern applications of those fundamental principles.

a.   PROCEDURAL DUE PROCESS IN EXCLUSION CASES

After *Ekiu,* the Court handed down a series of decisions rejecting the due process arguments of excluded immigrants. In those opinions, however, the Court's language tended to be more guarded. The opinions did not repeat the sweeping words of *Ekiu:* "As to [noncitizens seeking admission], the decisions of executive or administrative officers, acting within powers expressly conferred by Congress, *are* due process of law." 142 U.S. at 660 (emphasis added). Instead, the post-*Ekiu* decisions generally held only that due process does not require judicial factfinding. See, e.g., *Lee Lung v. Patterson,* 186 U.S. 168, 22 S.Ct. 795, 46 L.Ed. 1108 (1902); *Lem Moon Sing v. United States,* 158 U.S. 538, 15 S.Ct. 967, 39 L.Ed. 1082 (1895).

That more moderate pattern changed abruptly in *United States ex rel. Knauff v. Shaughnessy,* 338 U.S. 537, 70 S.Ct. 309, 94 L.Ed. 317 (1950).

Ellen Knauff was the noncitizen wife of a United States citizen. She was excluded without a hearing under an administrative regulation that permitted the Attorney General to bypass a hearing upon finding from confidential information that the person was inadmissible. Rejecting Knauff's due process challenge, the Court classified her admission as a privilege rather than a right and characterized the exclusion of a noncitizen as a fundamental sovereign act "inherent in the executive power to control the foreign affairs of the nation." *Id.* at 542, 70 S.Ct. at 312, 94 L.Ed. at 324. In words that every immigration scholar now knows by heart, the Court then announced: "Whatever the procedure authorized by Congress is, it is due process as far as an alien denied entry is concerned." *Id.* at 544, 70 S.Ct. at 312, 94 L.Ed. at 324.[7]

A reader of those chilling words might assume that *Knauff* represents the low water mark for noncitizens' rights. In fact, however, the Court was just getting warmed up. There were still two ingredients to add: What if the excluded person is a long-term LPR returning from a temporary visit abroad? And what if the practical consequence of exclusion is that the government will hold that LPR in captivity, possibly for life? Would the principle of plenary congressional power over immigration render due process constraints inapplicable even then? Or would these additional factors require at least some retreat from the rigidity of *Knauff*? Read on.

Shaughnessy v. United States ex rel. Mezei

Supreme Court of the United States, 1953.
345 U.S. 206, 73 S.Ct. 625, 97 L.Ed. 956.

■ MR. JUSTICE CLARK delivered the opinion of the Court.

This case concerns an alien immigrant permanently excluded from the United States on security grounds but stranded in his temporary haven on Ellis Island because other countries will not take him back. The issue is whether the Attorney General's continued exclusion of respondent without a hearing amounts to an unlawful detention, so that courts may admit him temporarily to the United States on bond until arrangements are made for his departure abroad. After a hearing on respondent's petition for a writ of habeas corpus, the District Court so held and authorized his temporary admission on $5,000 bond. The Court of Appeals affirmed that action, but directed reconsideration of the terms of the parole. Accordingly, the District Court entered a modified order reducing bond to $3,000 and permitting respondent to travel and reside in Buffalo, New York. Bond was posted and respondent released. Because of resultant serious problems in the enforcement of the immigration laws, we granted certiorari.

---

7. The Knauff story had a happy ending. The Justice Department eventually granted an evidentiary hearing. She did not prevail at that hearing, but on appeal to the Board of Immigration Appeals Knauff was found admissible. She later wrote a moving account of her ordeal. Ellen R. Knauff, The Ellen Knauff Story (1952); see also Charles D. Weisselberg, *The Exclusion and Detention of Aliens: Lessons from the Lives of Ellen Knauff and Ignatz Mezei*, 143 U.Pa.L.Rev. 933, 955–64 (1995).

Respondent's present dilemma springs from these circumstances: Though, as the District Court observed, "[t]here is a certain vagueness about [his] history," respondent seemingly was born in Gibraltar of Hungarian or Rumanian parents and lived in the United States from 1923 to 1948. In May of that year he sailed for Europe, apparently to visit his dying mother in Rumania. Denied entry there, he remained in Hungary for some 19 months, due to "difficulty in securing an exit permit." Finally, armed with a quota immigration visa issued by the American Consul in Budapest, he proceeded to France and boarded the *Ile de France* in Le Havre bound for New York. Upon arrival on February 9, 1950, he was temporarily excluded from the United States by an immigration inspector acting pursuant to the Passport Act as amended and regulations thereunder. Pending disposition of his case he was received at Ellis Island. After reviewing the evidence, the Attorney General on May 10, 1950, ordered the temporary exclusion to be made permanent without a hearing before a board of special inquiry, on the "basis of information of a confidential nature, the disclosure of which would be prejudicial to the public interest." That determination rested on a finding that respondent's entry would be prejudicial to the public interest for security reasons. But thus far all attempts to effect respondent's departure have failed: Twice he shipped out to return whence he came; France and Great Britain refused him permission to land. The State Department has unsuccessfully negotiated with Hungary for his readmission. Respondent personally applied for entry to about a dozen Latin–American countries but all turned him down. So in June 1951 respondent advised the Immigration and Naturalization Service that he would exert no further efforts to depart. In short, respondent sat on Ellis Island because this country shut him out and others were unwilling to take him in.

Asserting unlawful confinement on Ellis Island, he sought relief through a series of habeas corpus proceedings. After four unsuccessful efforts on respondent's part, the United States District Court for the Southern District of New York on November 9, 1951, sustained the writ. The District Judge, vexed by the problem of "an alien who has no place to go," did not question the validity of the exclusion order but deemed further "detention" after 21 months excessive and justifiable only by affirmative proof of respondent's danger to the public safety. When the Government declined to divulge such evidence, even *in camera*, the District Court directed respondent's conditional parole on bond. By a divided vote, the Court of Appeals affirmed. Postulating that the power to hold could never be broader than the power to remove or shut out and that to "continue an alien's confinement beyond that moment when deportation becomes patently impossible is to deprive him of his liberty," the court found respondent's "confinement" no longer justifiable as a means of removal elsewhere, thus not authorized by statute, and in violation of due process. Judge Learned Hand, dissenting, took a different view: The Attorney General's order was one of "exclusion" and not "deportation"; respondent's transfer from ship to shore on Ellis Island conferred no additional rights; in fact, no alien so situated "can force us to admit him at all."

Courts have long recognized the power to expel or exclude aliens as a fundamental sovereign attribute exercised by the Government's political departments largely immune from judicial control. *The Chinese Exclusion Case; Fong Yue Ting v. United States; Knauff v. Shaughnessy; Harisiades v. Shaughnessy.* In the exercise of these powers, Congress expressly authorized the President to impose additional restrictions on aliens entering or leaving the United States during periods of international tension and strife. That authorization, originally enacted in the Passport Act of 1918, continues in effect during the present emergency. Under it, the Attorney General, acting for the President, may shut out aliens whose "entry would be prejudicial to the interests of the United States." And he may exclude without a hearing when the exclusion is based on confidential information the disclosure of which may be prejudicial to the public interest [citing the Attorney General's regulations]. The Attorney General in this case proceeded in accord with these provisions; he made the necessary determinations and barred the alien from entering the United States.

It is true that aliens who have once passed through our gates, even illegally, may be expelled only after proceedings conforming to traditional standards of fairness encompassed in due process of law. But an alien on the threshold of initial entry stands on a different footing: "Whatever the procedure authorized by Congress is, it is due process as far as an alien denied entry is concerned." *Knauff v. Shaughnessy; Ekiu v. United States.* And because the action of the executive officer under such authority is final and conclusive, the Attorney General cannot be compelled to disclose the evidence underlying his determinations in an exclusion case; "it is not within the province of any court, unless expressly authorized by law, to review the determination of the political branch of the Government." * * *

Neither respondent's harborage on Ellis Island nor his prior residence here transforms this into something other than an exclusion proceeding. Concededly, his movements are restrained by authority of the United States, and he may by habeas corpus test the validity of his exclusion. But that is true whether he enjoys temporary refuge on land, *Ekiu v. United States,* or remains continuously aboard ship. In sum, harborage at Ellis Island is not an entry into the United States. For purposes of the immigration laws, moreover, the legal incidents of an alien's entry remain unaltered whether he has been here once before or not. He is an entering alien just the same, and may be excluded if unqualified for admission under existing immigration laws.

To be sure, a lawful resident alien may not captiously be deprived of his constitutional rights to procedural due process. Only the other day we held that under some circumstances temporary absence from our shores cannot constitutionally deprive a returning lawfully resident alien of his right to be heard. *Kwong Hai Chew v. Colding.* Chew, an alien seaman admitted by an Act of Congress to permanent residence in the United States, signed articles of maritime employment as chief steward on a vessel of American registry with home port in New York City. Though cleared by the Coast Guard for his voyage, on his return from four months at sea he was "excluded" without a hearing on security grounds. On the facts of that case, including reference to § 307(d)(2) of the Nationality Act of 1940, we felt justified in "assimilating" his status for constitutional purposes to that of continuously present alien residents entitled to hearings at least before an executive or administrative tribunal. Accordingly, to escape constitutional conflict we held the administrative regulations authorizing exclusion without hearing in certain security cases inapplicable to aliens so protected by the Fifth Amendment.

But respondent's history here drastically differs from that disclosed in Chew's case. Unlike Chew who with full security clearance and documentation pursued his vocation for four months aboard an American ship, respondent, apparently without authorization or reentry papers, simply left the United States and remained behind the Iron Curtain for 19 months. Moreover, while § 307 of the 1940 Nationality Act regards maritime service such as Chew's to be continuous residence for naturalization purposes, that section deems protracted absence such as respondent's a clear break in an alien's continuous residence here. In such circumstances, we have no difficulty in holding respondent an entrant alien or "assimilated to [that] status" for constitutional purposes. That being so, the Attorney General may lawfully exclude respondent without a hearing as authorized by the emergency regulations promulgated pursuant to the Passport Act. Nor need he disclose the evidence upon which that determination rests.

There remains the issue of respondent's continued exclusion on Ellis Island. Aliens seeking entry from contiguous lands obviously can be turned back at the border without more. While the Government might keep entrants by sea aboard the vessel pending determination of their admissibility, resulting hardships to the alien and inconvenience to the carrier persuaded Congress to adopt a more generous course. By statute it authorized, in cases such as this, aliens' temporary removal from ship to shore. But such temporary harborage, an act of legislative grace, bestows no additional rights. Congress meticulously specified that such shelter ashore "shall not be considered a landing" nor relieve the vessel of the duty to transport back the alien if ultimately excluded. And this Court has long considered such temporary arrangements as not affecting an alien's status; he is treated as if stopped at the border.

Thus we do not think that respondent's continued exclusion deprives him of any statutory or constitutional right. It is true that resident aliens temporarily detained pending expeditious consummation of deportation proceedings may be released on bond by the Attorney General whose discretion is subject to judicial review. By that procedure aliens uprooted from our midst may rejoin the community until the Government effects their leave. An exclusion proceeding grounded on danger to the national security, however, presents different considerations; neither the rationale nor the statutory authority for such release exists. Ordinarily to admit an alien barred from entry on security grounds nullifies the very purpose of the exclusion proceeding; Congress in 1950 declined to include such authority in the statute. That exclusion by the United States plus other nations' inhospitality results in present hardship cannot be ignored. But, the times being what they are, Congress may well have felt that other countries ought not shift the onus to us; that an alien in respondent's position is no more ours than theirs. Whatever our individual estimate of that policy and the fears on which it rests, respondent's right to enter the United States depends on the congressional will, and courts cannot substitute their judgment for the legislative mandate.

Reversed.

[The dissenting opinion of Justice BLACK is omitted.]

* * *

■ MR. JUSTICE JACKSON, whom MR. JUSTICE FRANKFURTER joins, dissenting.

Fortunately it still is startling, in this country, to find a person held indefinitely in executive custody without accusation of crime or judicial trial. Executive imprisonment has been considered oppressive and lawless since John, at Runnymede, pledged that no free man should be imprisoned, dispossessed, outlawed, or exiled save by the judgment of his peers or by the law of the land. The judges of England developed the writ of habeas corpus largely to preserve these immunities from executive restraint. Under the best tradition of Anglo–American law, courts will not deny hearing to an unconvicted prisoner just because he is an alien whose keep, in legal theory, is just outside our gates. Lord Mansfield, in the celebrated case holding that slavery was unknown to the common law of England, ran his writ of habeas corpus in favor of an alien, an African Negro slave, and against the master of a ship at anchor in the Thames.

I.

What is our case? In contemplation of law, I agree, it is that of an alien who asks admission to the country. Concretely, however, it is that of a lawful and law-abiding inhabitant of our country for a quarter of a century, long ago admitted for permanent residence, who seeks to return home. After a foreign visit to his aged and ailing mother that was prolonged by disturbed conditions of Eastern Europe, he obtained a visa for admission issued by our consul and returned to New York. There the Attorney General refused to honor his documents and turned him back as a menace to this Nation's security. This man, who seems to have led a life of unrelieved insignificance, must have been astonished to find himself suddenly putting the Government of the United States in such fear that it was afraid to tell him why it was afraid of him. He was shipped and reshipped to France, which twice refused him landing. Great Britain declined, and no other European country has been found willing to open its doors to him. Twelve countries of the American Hemisphere refused his applications. Since we proclaimed him a Samson who might pull down the pillars of our temple, we should not be surprised if people less prosperous, less strongly established and less stable feared to take him off our timorous hands. With something of a record as an unwanted man, neither his efforts nor those of the United States Government any longer promise to find him an abiding place. For nearly two years he was held in custody of the immigration authorities of the United States at Ellis Island, and if the Government has its way he seems likely to be detained indefinitely, perhaps for life, for a cause known only to the Attorney General.

Is respondent deprived of liberty? The Government answers that he was "transferred to Ellis Island on August 1, 1950, for safekeeping," and "is not being detained in the usual sense but is in custody solely to prevent him from gaining entry to the United States in violation of law. He is free to depart from the United States to any country of his own choice." Government counsel ingeniously argued that Ellis Island is his "refuge" whence he is free to take leave in any direction except west. That might mean freedom, if only he were an amphibian! Realistically, this man is incarcerated by a combination of forces which keep him as effectually as a prison, the dominant and proximate of these forces being the United States immigration authority. It overworks legal fiction to say that one is free in law when by the commonest of common sense he is bound. Despite the impeccable legal logic of the Government's argument on this point, it leads to an artificial and unreal conclusion. We must regard this alien as deprived of liberty, and the question is whether the deprivation is a denial of due process of law. *Procedural Due Process*

The Government on this point argues that "no alien has any constitutional right to entry into the United States"; that "the alien has only such rights as Congress sees fit to grant in exclusion proceedings"; that "the so-called detention is still merely a continuation of the exclusion which is specifically authorized by Congress"; that since "the restraint is not incidental to an order [of exclusion] but is, itself, the effectuation of the exclusion order, there is no limit to its continuance" other than statutory, which means no limit at all. The Government all but adopts the words of one of the officials responsible for the administration of this Act who testified before a congressional committee as to an alien applicant, that "He has no rights."

The interpretations of the Fifth Amendment's command that no person shall be deprived of life, liberty or property without due process of law, come about to this: reasonable general legislation reasonably applied to the individual. The question is whether the Government's detention of respondent is compatible with these tests of substance and procedure.

* * *

III. PROCEDURAL DUE PROCESS.

Procedural fairness, if not all that originally was meant by due process of law, is at least what it most uncompromisingly requires. Procedural due process is more elemental and less flexible than substantive due process. It yields less to the times, varies less with conditions, and defers much less to legislative judgment. Insofar as it is technical law, it must be a specialized responsibility within the competence of the judiciary on which they do not bend before political branches of the Government, as they should on matters of policy which comprise substantive law.

If it be conceded that in some way this alien could be confined, does it matter what the procedure is? Only the untaught layman or the charlatan lawyer can answer that procedures matter not. Procedural fairness and regularity are of the indispensable essence of liberty. Severe substantive laws can be endured if they are fairly and impartially applied. Indeed, if put to the choice, one might well prefer to live under Soviet substantive law applied in good faith by our common-law procedures than under our substantive law enforced by Soviet procedural practices. Let it not be overlooked that due process of law is not for the sole benefit of an accused. It is the best insurance for the Government itself against those blunders which leave lasting stains on a system of justice but which are bound to occur on *ex parte* consideration. *Cf. Knauff v. Shaughnessy,* which was a near miss, saved by further administrative and congressional hearings from perpetrating an injustice.

Our law may, and rightly does, place more restrictions on the alien than on the citizen. But basic fairness in hearing procedures does not vary with the status of the accused. If the procedures used to judge this alien are fair and just, no good reason can be given why they should not be extended to simplify the condemnation of citizens. If they would be unfair to citizens, we cannot defend the fairness of them when applied to the more helpless and handicapped alien. This is at the root of our holdings that the resident alien must be given a fair hearing to test an official claim that he is one of a deportable class.

* * *

Because the respondent has no right of entry, does it follow that he has no rights at all? Does the power to exclude mean that exclusion may be continued or effectuated by any means which happen to seem appropriate to the authorities? It would effectuate his exclusion to eject him bodily into the sea or to set him adrift in a rowboat. Would not such measures be condemned judicially as a deprivation of life without due process of law? Suppose the authorities decide to disable an alien from entry by confiscating his valuables and money. Would we not hold this a taking of property without due process of law? Here we have a case that lies between the taking of life and the taking of property; it is the taking of liberty. It seems to me that this, occurring within the United States or its territorial waters, may be done only by proceedings which meet the test of due process of law.

Exclusion of an alien without judicial hearing, of course, does not deny due process when it can be accomplished merely by turning him back on land or returning him by sea. But when indefinite confinement becomes the means of enforcing exclusion, it seems to me that due process requires that the alien be informed of its grounds and have a fair chance to overcome them. This is the more due him when he is entrapped into leaving the other shore by reliance on a visa which the Attorney General refuses to honor.

It is evident that confinement of respondent no longer can be justified as a step in the process of turning him back to the country whence he came. Confinement is no longer ancillary to exclusion; it can now be justified only as the alternative to normal exclusion. It is an end in itself.

The Communist conspiratorial technique of infiltration poses a problem which sorely tempts the Government to resort to confinement of suspects on secret information secretly judged. I have not been one to discount the Communist evil. But my apprehensions about the security of our form of government are about equally aroused by those who refuse to recognize the dangers of Communism and those who will not see danger in anything else.

Congress has ample power to determine whom we will admit to our shores and by what means it will effectuate its exclusion policy. The only limitation is that it may not do so by authorizing United States officers to take without due process of law the life, the liberty or the property of an alien who has come within our jurisdiction; and that means he must meet a fair hearing with fair notice of the charges.[9]

It is inconceivable to me that this measure of simple justice and fair dealing would menace the security of this country. No one can make me believe that we are that far gone.

GENERAL NOTES AND QUESTIONS

1. Just as Knauff ultimately received relief from the BIA, so too Mezei, after exceptional publicity and four years of detention on Ellis Island, was paroled into the United States. See Charles D. Weisselberg, *The Exclusion and Detention of Aliens: Lessons from the Lives of Ellen Knauff and Ignatz Mezei,* 143 Univ. Pennsylvania L.Rev. 933, 964–84 (1995). The fate of lesser known individuals excluded on security grounds without hearings is more difficult to discover.

2. How far did the Court go in *Mezei* ? Did it hold only that, in light of national security considerations peculiar to the case, the process afforded was all that was due? Or did it hold, more broadly, that a noncitizen facing exclusion may not invoke the due process clause at all? One recent decision so interpreted *Knauff* and *Mezei*, holding that a noncitizen who seeks initial entry has literally no due process rights concerning his or her admission or exclusion. *Pazcoguin v. Radcliffe,* 292 F.3d 1209, 1218 (9th Cir. 2002). Professor Henry Hart, in his classic dialogue, *The Power of Congress to Limit the Jurisdiction of the Federal Courts: An Exercise in Dialectic,* 66

---

9. The trial court sought to reconcile due process for the individual with claims of security by suggesting that the Attorney General disclose *in camera* enough to enable a judicial determination of the legality of the confinement. The Attorney General refused. I do not know just how an *in camera* proceeding would be handled in this kind of case. If respondent, with or without counsel, were present, disclosures to them might well result in disclosures by them. If they are not allowed to be present, it is hard to see how it would answer the purpose of testing the Government's case by cross-examination or counter-evidence, which is what a hearing is for. * * *

Harvard L.Rev. 1362, 1391–96 (1953), similarly read *Knauff* and *Mezei* as denying the very applicability of due process to excluded noncitizens. So construing them, he criticized these cases sharply. Subsequent commentary has been similarly critical. See, e.g., T. Alexander Aleinikoff, *Aliens, Due Process, and "Community Ties": A Response to Martin,* 44 Univ. Pittsburgh L.Rev. 237, 237–39, 258–60 (1983); Stephen H. Legomsky, Immigration and the Judiciary: Law and Politics in Britain and America 199–201 (1987); David A. Martin, *Due Process and Membership in the National Community: Political Asylum and Beyond,* 44 Univ. Pittsburgh L.Rev. 165, 173–80 (1983).

3.   Adjudication procedures for arriving noncitizens who are alleged to be threats to the national security pose difficult policy problems. Since 1996 the INA has prescribed a procedure similar to the one applied in *Mezei.* See INA § 235(c), discussed in chapter 6, section E.5.a below.

Apart from its teachings on the general applicability of procedural due process to excluded noncitizens, *Mezei* raises important issues concerning two more specific subjects: the exclusion of returning residents and the concomitant detention of inadmissible noncitizens.

NOTES AND QUESTIONS ON THE EXCLUSION OF RETURNING RESIDENTS: SOME CRACKS IN THE PLENARY CONGRESSIONAL POWER

1.   In dismissing Mezei's due process argument, the Court explicitly refuses to distinguish initial entrants from returning residents. Should that distinction matter? If so, should it go to the applicability of due process or to the content of the process that is due?

2.   Concerning the content of due process, would *in camera* disclosure of the confidential evidence be desirable? Justice Jackson finds that solution unacceptable. In footnote 9 of his dissent, he suggests that in camera revelations would be self-defeating if the noncitizen is present and unproductive otherwise. Do you agree? How do you come out if you apply the *Eldridge* factors, discussed in the Notes following *Fong Yue Ting*? Would an in camera procedure be sufficient? Would it be *too* intrusive? Just right? In 1996, Congress authorized (but at this writing the executive branch has yet to use) a special in camera procedure for determining the admissibility or the deportability of noncitizens suspected to be terrorists. INA §§ 501–07, discussed on pages 735–38 below; see also David A. Martin, *Graduated Application of Constitutional Protections for Aliens: The Real Meaning of* Zadvydas v. Davis, 2001 Supreme Ct. Rev. 47. Chapter 10 of this book examines how national security has affected, and how it should affect, this and other areas of immigration law.

3.   The Court distinguishes *Kwong Hai Chew v. Colding* on the facts. How persuasive do you find the distinctions? Can you articulate general principles that are compatible with the results of both cases?

4. The most significant post-*Mezei* development on the subject of due process for excluded noncitizens is *Landon v. Plasencia*, 459 U.S. 21, 103 S.Ct. 321, 74 L.Ed.2d 21 (1982). An LPR left the United States for a two-day visit to Tijuana, Mexico. Upon her attempted return she was ordered excluded. The charge was that she, knowingly and for gain, had assisted other noncitizens to enter the United States unlawfully. Plasencia argued that the statutory exclusion procedures violated due process. The Court said:

> * * * We agree with Plasencia that under the circumstances of this case, she can invoke the Due Process Clause on returning to this country, although we do not decide the contours of the process that is due or whether the process accorded Plasencia was insufficient.
>
> This Court has long held that an alien seeking initial admission to the United States requests a privilege and has no constitutional rights regarding his application, for the power to admit or exclude aliens is a sovereign prerogative. See, *e.g., United States ex rel. Knauff v. Shaughnessy; Nishimura Ekiu v. United States.* Our recent decisions confirm that view. [H]owever, once an alien gains admission to our country and begins to develop the ties that go with permanent residence, his constitutional status changes accordingly. Our cases have frequently suggested that a continuously present resident alien is entitled to a fair hearing when threatened with deportation * * * [More, shortly, on the applicability of due process to deportation proceedings—Ed.]
>
> * * *
>
> If the permanent resident alien's absence is extended, of course, he may lose his entitlement to "assimilat[ion of his] status," *Kwong Hai Chew v. Colding,* to that of an alien continuously residing and physically present in the United States. In *Shaughnessy v. United States ex rel. Mezei,* this Court rejected the argument of an alien who had left the country for some 20 months that he was entitled to due process in assessing his right to admission on his return. We did not suggest that no returning resident alien has a right to due process, for we explicitly reaffirmed *Chew.* We need not now decide the scope of *Mezei;* it does not govern this case, for Plasencia was absent from the country only a few days, and the United States has conceded that she has a right to due process.
>
> The constitutional sufficiency of procedures provided in any situation, of course, varies with the circumstances. In evaluating the procedures in any case, the courts must consider the interest at stake for the individual, the risk of an erroneous deprivation of the interest through the procedures used as well as the probable value of additional or different procedural safeguards, and the interest of the government in using the current procedures rather

than additional or different procedures. *Mathews v. Eldridge.* Plasencia's interest here is, without question, a weighty one. She stands to lose the right "to stay and live and work in this land of freedom." Further, she may lose the right to rejoin her immediate family, a right that ranks high among the interests of the individual. The Government's interest in efficient administration of the immigration laws at the border also is weighty. Further, it must weigh heavily in the balance that control over matters of immigration is a sovereign prerogative, largely within the control of the Executive and the Legislature. The role of the judiciary is limited to determining whether the procedures meet the essential standard of fairness under the Due Process Clause and does not extend to imposing procedures that merely displace congressional choices of policy. * * *

459 U.S. at 32–35, 103 S.Ct. at 329–30, 74 L.Ed.2d at 32–34.

The D.C. Circuit later reconciled *Mezei* with *Kwong Hai Chew* and *Plasencia* on the sole basis of duration of absence. Only when the trip was lengthy, the court held, would a returning resident be stripped of his or her due process rights; nefarious activities associated with the excursion would be irrelevant. *Rafeedie v. I.N.S.*, 880 F.2d 506, 519–24 (D.C.Cir.1989). Even the presence of national security factors, while relevant to what process is due, would not render the due process clause inoperative. *Id.* at 523.

5. Suppose the applicability of due process to returning residents in exclusion proceedings were a question of first impression. What principle would you lay down? Should *every* returning resident be accorded due process rights? Only certain ones? None?

For that matter, why stop with returning residents? Why not hold that every noncitizen applying for admission at the United States border is protected by the due process clause? Your immediate instinct might be that the U.S. lacks the resources to conduct full-scale evidentiary hearings for all of the literally millions of noncitizens who want to enter the country. Remember, however, that holding due process applicable does not mean requiring elaborate formal adjudication. As the Court observed in *Eldridge,* the process that is due reflects the financial and administrative costs to the government. Second and more important, recognizing procedural due process in no way relaxes the substantive criteria for admission. Perhaps even those who fail the substantive requirements will travel to the United States in the hope of being admitted by immigration officials despite their inadmissibility, but (apart from asylum cases, which generate special issues discussed in chapter 11, section B below) are they really going to do so solely because their inadmissibility will be ascertained only after a fair hearing? And even if people were willing to take that gamble, would commercial carriers, who are generally liable for the expenses resulting from the exclusion of undocumented passengers, see INA § 257, be willing to transport them?

If practicality does not explain the Court's refusal to hold due process generally applicable to arriving noncitizens, what does? Are we again back to the distinction between rights and privileges? Is it a belief that no liberty or property interests are at stake? Is it the notion, suggested by Justice Brewer in his *Fong Yue Ting* dissent, that the Constitution is simply inapplicable to those noncitizens who are deemed to be outside United States territory? Is it, as Justice Brewer also suggested, the interdependence of allegiance and protection? Is it the perceived sovereign source of the power to exclude? Is it the perceived connection between exclusion and foreign affairs?

NOTES AND QUESTIONS ON THE DETENTION OF EXCLUDED NONCITIZENS

1. Mezei faced more than exclusion; he faced the prospect of indefinite, possibly life-long, detention. Even one who believes that the noncitizen's interest in *admission* is not a liberty interest would surely concede that *detention* is a deprivation of liberty. Why, then, was due process inapplicable? What was the Court's point when it stated that the "harborage [the Court's term], an act of legislative grace, bestows no additional rights"? See generally Ibrahim J. Wani, *Truth, Strangers, and Fiction: The Illegitimate Use of Legal Fiction in Immigration Law*, 11 Cardozo L.Rev. 51, 97–100 (1989).

2. The indefinite detention of excluded noncitizens is not just a relic of the Cold War era. It has remained a vital issue in recent years. In 1980, the Cuban government sent approximately 125,000 of its nationals to the United States by boat. Most of these "Marielitos" (so-called because they had departed from the port of Mariel, Cuba) had relatives in the United States. Among the new arrivals, however, were 2746 whom the former INS identified as either having committed serious crimes or having mental illnesses that made them dangerous to society. The United States sought to return the 2746 to Cuba, but Cuba would not take them back. The United States government, citing public safety, was unwilling to release them from confinement. Yet the alternative—indefinite detention—seemed at least equally unacceptable. See generally Richard A. Boswell, *Rethinking Exclusion—the Rights of Cuban Refugees Facing Indefinite Detention in the United States*, 17 Vanderbilt J. Transnat'l L. 925 (1984); Paul W. Schmidt, *Detention of Aliens*, 24 San Diego L.Rev. 305, 324–29 (1987); see also Maryellen Fullerton, *Cuban Exceptionalism: Migration and Asylum in Spain and the United States*, 35 Inter–American L. Rev. 527 (2004).

As a partial response, the Justice Department began releasing on administrative "parole," an uncertain status that you will see in various contexts throughout this book, those Cuban detainees who were felt not to be dangerous. See INA § 212(d)(5); Note, *Legal Fictions Mask Human Suffering: The Detention of the Mariel Cubans—Constitutional, Statutory, International Law, and Human Considerations*, 62 Southern California L.Rev. 1733, 1736 (1989) [hereafter cited as Southern California Note]. In December 1984, after years of negotiation, the United States and Cuba reached an agreement. Cuba would take back, at the rate of 100 per month, the 2746 named individuals whom the former INS had originally separated out. See Press Statement, White House Office of the Press Secretary (Dec. 14, 1984), reproduced in 61 IR at 1080–85 (1984). The agreement was short-lived. Soon after the initial installments of prisoners had been delivered, President Reagan intensified the anti-Castro broadcasts of Radio Marti to the Caribbean. President Castro retaliated by suspending the agreement.

To complicate matters, several thousand of those who had been released on parole either committed crimes or otherwise violated the terms of their parole. The INS revoked parole in those cases and took the offenders back into custody. Southern California Note, above, at 1736–37. Many were housed at the Atlanta Penitentiary under grossly crowded conditions that a congressional subcommittee would later describe as "brutal and inhumane," and "intolerable." *Id.* at 1741. Others were detained at the Oakdale Federal Detention Center in Louisiana. *Id.* at 1739–40.

In 1987 the Justice Department (a) instituted a program for reviewing which of the remaining detainees on the list of 2746 should be repatriated to Cuba; and (b) started reviewing the cases of all non-repatriated detainees to determine whether release on parole was warranted. See 8 C.F.R. § 212.12 (2004). Somewhere between 94,000 and 100,000 of the original 125,000 Marielitos eventually received lawful permanent residence under special legislation discussed on pages 610–11 below.

During roughly the same time period, significant numbers of Haitians began fleeing to the United States by boat with the hope of receiving asylum. The position of the Reagan Administration was that these asylum claims were generally without merit. It believed that a policy of detaining the Haitians while their exclusion proceedings were pending would deter people from coming. The high volume of applications had, however, produced a heavy backlog of undecided cases. As a result, the Haitian asylum-seekers often had to wait several years for decisions, and in the meantime they languished in detention. The merits of their asylum claims and the procedures for adjudicating them are explored in chapter 11 below.

Haitian and Cuban detainees were differently situated. The Haitian government, unlike Cuba's, was prepared to take them back. The Haitian detainees, however, asserted fears of persecution if returned to Haiti. And, although their detention at least would not be permanent, the slowness of the asylum process meant they could be detained for many years.

In August 1994 a new exodus from Cuba suddenly began. Thousands of rafters were allowed to leave for the United States. Until then, Cubans who had made their way to the United States had generally been either admitted or paroled, and eventually allowed to adjust to permanent residence under the Cuban Adjustment Act of 1966. In a dramatic policy shift, the United States started interdicting Cuban vessels and transporting the occupants to Guantánamo. See generally 71 IR 1091–93 (Aug. 22, 1994).

In September 1994, the United States and Cuba entered into an agreement. Cuba agreed to "take effective measures in every way it can to prevent unsafe departures, using mainly persuasive methods." The United States agreed to continue to issue visas to qualifying immigrants at the United States Interests section in Havana, and to guarantee that at least 20,000 Cubans per year (plus the immediate relatives of US citizens) would be allowed to migrate to the United States. For the full text of the agreement, see 71 IR 1236–37 (Sept. 12, 1994). A good comprehensive discussion of the Cuban exodus is Joyce A. Hughes, *Flight from Cuba*, 36 California Western L. Rev. 39 (1999). At this writing a number of the original Cuban Marielitos remain indefinitely detained.

In recent years Haitian boat people have again resumed perilous passages to the United States by boat, despite U.S. policies of interdicting vessels and automatically detaining those Haitians who make it to U.S. shores. See generally pages 1112–35 below.

The detention issues that have arisen in all the cases discussed above— *Mezei, Plasencia, Kwong Hai Chew*, the Cuban cases, and the Haitian cases—have one element in common. The noncitizens who raised them were arriving passengers who faced exclusion, rather than individuals who had already entered the United States and faced deportation. The decisions in *Mezei* and most of the other cases, moreover, considered only the question of procedural due process. Thus, two detention-related questions remained: Does the procedural due process holding in *Mezei* extend to *deportable* detainees? And, due process aside, for either a deportable or an inadmissible noncitizen whom there is no realistic likelihood of expelling, does indefinite detention violate the INA? To what extent is the statutory interpretation affected by the constitutional questions that a permissive reading would generate? These questions are taken up in the discussion of the *Zadvydas* and *Martinez* decisions on pages 191–210 below.

3. Analogous issues have arisen in connection with the noncitizens captured by U.S. forces during the war in Afghanistan and detained at Guantánamo. In *Rasul v. Bush*, ___ U.S. ___, 124 S.Ct. 2686, 159 L.Ed.2d 548 (2004), the Supreme Court allowed Guantánamo prisoners (at least the plaintiffs before the Court, all of whom were third country nationals and thus not "enemy aliens") to use habeas corpus to test the legality of their detentions. The case and its implications, including questions as to its compatibility with *Mezei*, are discussed on pages 856–66 below.

b. PROCEDURAL DUE PROCESS IN DEPORTATION CASES: MORE CRACKS IN THE PLENARY CONGRESSIONAL POWER

As the preceding materials demonstrate, the line of cases that began with *Nishimura Ekiu* and culminated in *Knauff* and *Mezei* took an extremely hard stand. Those cases seemed to hold that excluded noncitizens simply could not invoke the due process clause at all—even when they were returning residents and even when the practical consequence of exclusion was indefinite detention. As you also saw, however, this principle of absolute congressional power to decide the procedure for excluding noncitizens began to develop cracks. The Supreme Court decisions in *Kwong Hai*

Chew and *Plasencia* (coming before and after *Mezei,* respectively) created exceptions for most returning residents.

But in the deportation context the principle of congressional omnipotence had already developed a much wider fissure. The leading case follows:

Yamataya v. Fisher
(The Japanese Immigrant Case)

Supreme Court of the United States, 1903.
189 U.S. 86, 23 S.Ct. 611, 47 L.Ed. 721.

■ MR. JUSTICE HARLAN * * * delivered the opinion of the Court.

[Four days after entering the United States, a citizen of Japan was deported on the ground that she had been inadmissible at the time of entry. The basis for the alleged inadmissibility was that she was a pauper and likely to become a public charge. She challenged her deportation order on grounds described in the opinion.—Ed.]

* * *

The constitutionality of the legislation in question, in its general aspects, is no longer open to discussion in this court. That Congress may exclude aliens of a particular race from the United States; prescribe the terms and conditions upon which certain classes of aliens may come to this country; establish regulations for sending out of the country such aliens as come here in violation of law; and commit the enforcement of such provisions, conditions and regulations exclusively to executive officers, without judicial intervention, are principles firmly established by the decisions of this court. *Nishimura Ekiu v. United States; Fong Yue Ting v. United States.*

* * *

It is contended, however, that in respect of an alien who has already landed it is consistent with the acts of Congress that he may be deported without previous notice of any purpose to deport him, and without any opportunity on his part to show by competent evidence before the executive officers charged with the execution of the acts of Congress, that he is not here in violation of law; that the deportation of an alien without provision for such a notice and for an opportunity to be heard was inconsistent with the due process of law required by the Fifth Amendment of the Constitution.

Leaving on one side the question whether an alien can rightfully invoke the due process clause of the Constitution who has entered the country clandestinely, and who has been here for too brief a period to have become, in any real sense, a part of our population, before his right to remain is disputed, we have to say that the rigid construction of the acts of Congress suggested by the appellant are not justified. Those acts do not necessarily exclude opportunity to the immigrant to be heard, when such opportunity is of right. * * * Now, it has been settled that the power to exclude or expel aliens belonged to the political department of the Government, and that the order of an executive officer, invested with the power to determine finally the facts upon which an alien's right to enter this country, or remain in it, depended, was "due process of law, and no other tribunal, unless expressly authorized by law to do so, was at liberty to reexamine the evidence on which he acted, or to controvert its sufficiency." *Fong Yue Ting v. United States; Ekiu v. United States.* But this court has never held, nor must we now be understood as holding, that administrative officers, when executing the provisions of a statute involving the liberty of persons, may disregard the fundamental principles that inhere in "due process of law" as understood at the time of the adoption of the Constitution. One of these principles is that no person shall be deprived of his liberty without opportunity, at some time, to be heard, before such officers, in respect of the matters upon which that liberty depends—not necessarily an opportunity upon a regular, set occasion, and according to the forms of judicial procedure, but one that will secure the prompt, vigorous action contemplated by Congress, and at the same time be appropriate to the nature of the case upon which such officers are required to act. Therefore, it is not competent for the Secretary of the Treasury or any executive officer, at any time within the year limited by the statute, arbitrarily to cause an alien, who has entered the country, and has become subject in all respects to its jurisdiction, and a part of its population, although alleged to be illegally here, to be taken into custody and deported without giving him all opportunity to be heard upon the questions involving his right to be and remain in the United States. No such arbitrary power can exist where the principles involved in due process of law are recognized.

This is the reasonable construction of the acts of Congress here in question, and they need not be otherwise interpreted. In the case of all acts of Congress, such interpretation ought to be adopted as, without doing violence to the import of the words used, will bring them into harmony with the Constitution. An act of Congress must be taken to be constitutional unless the contrary plainly and palpably appears. The words here used do not require an interpretation that would invest executive or administrative officers with the absolute, arbitrary power implied in the contention of the appellant. Besides, the record now before us shows that the appellant had notice, although not a formal one, of the investigation instituted for the purpose of ascertaining whether she was illegally in this country. The traverse to the return made by the Immigration Inspector shows upon its face that she was before that officer pending the investigation of her right to be in the United States, and made answers to questions propounded to her. It is true that she pleads a want of knowledge of our language; that she did not understand the nature and import of the questions propounded to her; that the investigation made was a "pretended" one; and that she did not, at the time, know that the investigation had reference to her being deported from the country. These considerations cannot justify the intervention of the courts. They could have been presented to the officer having primary control of such a case, as well as upon an appeal to the Secretary of the Treasury, who had power to order another investigation if that course was demanded by law or by the ends of justice. It is not to be assumed that either would have refused a second or fuller investigation, if a proper application and showing for one had been made by or for the appellant. Whether further investigation should have been ordered was for the officers, charged with the execution of the statutes, to determine. Their action in that regard is not subject to judicial review. Suffice it to say, it does not appear that appellant was denied an opportunity to be heard. And as no appeal was taken to the Secretary from the decision of the Immigration Inspector, that decision was final and conclusive. If the appellant's want of knowledge of the English language put her at some disadvantage in the investigation conducted by that officer, that was her misfortune, and constitutes no reason, under the acts of Congress, or under any rule of law, for the intervention of the court by *habeas corpus*. We perceive no ground for such intervention—none for the contention that due process of law was denied to appellant.

The judgment is *Affirmed.*

■ MR. JUSTICE BREWER and MR. JUSTICE PECKHAM dissented.

NOTES AND QUESTIONS

1. Yamataya argued that the statute denied her notice of the charges and the opportunity to be heard. She maintained that, as thus construed, the statute violated due process. The Court, however, reads the statute differently. And, to reach its statutory conclusion, the Court relies on its belief that due process does indeed attach in deportation proceedings. Be sure you understand how the Court's constitutional analysis shapes its interpretation of the statute. What maxim of statutory construction is the Court employing?

2. What if Congress, in prescribing the mechanics for deportation, had expressly eliminated the possibility of notice of charges and opportunity to be heard? Would the Court have struck down the statute, or was the holding in *Yamataya* meant only to limit *executive* action?

3. Is *Yamataya* consistent with *Fong Yue Ting?*

4. The Court leaves open whether a noncitizen who entered the country clandestinely and who has not been present long enough to be "in any real sense, a part of our population" may claim due process rights. The Court's statement also leaves unclear whether due process extends to the noncitizen who enters lawfully but has been in the country only a short time or, conversely, the noncitizen who entered clandestinely but has been here a long time.

Today the law is clear that all individuals who face expulsion are protected by due process, whether they entered the United States lawfully or clandestinely and whether they arrived long ago or recently. Recall the dictum in *Mezei*, page 147 above, that "aliens who have once passed through our gates, *even illegally*, may be expelled only after proceedings conforming to traditional standards of fairness encompassed in due process of law" [emphasis added]. As a result, most of the important due process battles in the deportation setting have concerned only the content of the process that is due.

5. As to content, consider how the Court in *Yamataya* applies the requirements of due process. The immigrant, who had not been represented by counsel, alleged that because of language difficulties she had been unable to understand the questions asked of her and had not understood even that deportation was at issue. Still, the Court held the due process requirements satisfied. What if the proceedings had been conducted in her absence?[8] Would the Court still have found the procedure adequate? Is there a meaningful difference between a hearing at which the person is absent and one that is conducted in a language she cannot understand? See *Tejeda–Mata v. INS,* 626 F.2d 721, 726–27 (9th Cir.1980) (implicitly holding absence of interpreter violative of due process, but affirming deportation order because error harmless); *El Rescate Legal Services, Inc. v. EOIR,* 941 F.2d 950 (9th Cir.1991) (interpretation of entire exclusion or deportation hearing is not necessary).

Modern conceptions of the process due in deportation proceedings are far more expansive. See, e.g., *Massieu v. Reno,* 915 F.Supp. 681 (D.N.J. 1996)(striking down, as impermissibly vague and therefore violative of due process, a deportation provision requiring "potentially serious adverse foreign policy consequences"), rev'd on other grounds, 91 F.3d 416 (3d Cir. 1996). For more detail on the procedural due process exception to the plenary power doctrine, see Stephen H. Legomsky, *Immigration Law and the Principle of Plenary Congressional Power,* 1984 Supreme Ct. Rev. 255, 298–99; accord, Hiroshi Motomura, *The Curious Evolution of Immigration Law: Procedural Surrogates for Substantive Constitutional Rights,* 92 Columbia L.Rev. 1625 (1992).

6. Does due process or any other constitutional safeguard mandate some opportunity for judicial review of administratively final deportation orders? Does it matter whether the alleged error is one of fact or one of law? If law, does it matter whether the underlying claim is that Congress (or the executive branch) has violated the Constitution? Several provisions of IIRIRA could be read to bar judicial review of Congress's own decisions and executive branch decisions in the field of immigration. This subject is discussed in chapter 9, section B.6(b).

7. *Yamataya* was decided before *Mezei.* Yet the Court in *Mezei* declined to extend due process guarantees to a returning LPR in exclusion proceedings. The Court's refusal produced no technical inconsistency; it relied on the distinction between exclusion and deportation. From a policy standpoint, however, do you agree that that distinction should be conclusive? In answering, consider again the individual interests at stake in the two proceedings. Do they differ appreciably? Or is that beside the point? Consider again the theories, discussed in the Notes following *Fong Yue*

---

8. The Immigration Act of 1990 expressly authorizes in absentia deportation hearings under certain circumstances. The issues are considered on pages 838–39 below.

Ting, for distinguishing exclusion from deportation. For purposes of the policies reflected in those theories, is the exclusion of a returning LPR more like exclusion of an initial entrant or more like deportation of one who has entered?

8. The openings that cases like *Kwong Hai Chew, Plasencia, Yamataya,* and others have left for procedural due process challenges have not gone unnoticed. One effect of those openings has been to encourage noncitizens to cast in procedural due process terms those constitutional attacks that could arguably be described as either substantive or procedural. That strategy succeeded several times in challenges to a statutory provision that prohibits the Attorney General from releasing certain categories of noncitizen criminal offenders on bail while their deportation proceedings are pending—until 2003, when the Supreme Court upheld mandatory detention in *Demore v. Hyung Joon Kim,* covered on pages 211–29 below. A similar strategy has occasionally worked in challenges to a (now toned down) provision that once precluded the granting of permanent residence on the basis of any marriage entered into during exclusion or deportation proceedings unless the subject had left the United States for at least two years after the marriage. Because you will better understand the significance of the labelling strategy once you have studied the substantive contours of the plenary power doctrine, these cases will be deferred until then.

c. SUBSTANTIVE APPLICATIONS OF THE PLENARY POWER DOCTRINE

You have now considered the applicability of procedural due process to noncitizens in the contexts of both exclusion and deportation. The pattern of judicial deference that you have observed is one of staunch absolutism in the early decisions, followed by exceptions and qualifications in the later decisions. This section moves from procedure to substance. As you work through the cases, watch for some of the same themes that have prompted such exceptional restraint in the procedural due process cases.

Harisiades v. Shaughnessy

Supreme Court of the United States, 1952.
342 U.S. 580, 72 S.Ct. 512, 96 L.Ed. 586.

[All three plaintiffs had been LPRs for several decades, since their arrival in the United States as teenagers. Two were now married to United States citizens and one to another LPR. All had United States citizen children.

The three plaintiffs joined the Communist Party at various times after entry. All three eventually left the Party; one quit voluntarily, and in the other two cases the Party discontinued membership for reasons that will appear in section III of the Court's opinion. After the party membership of all three plaintiffs had terminated, Congress enacted legislation that rendered deportable, among others, noncitizens who had ever been members of organizations that advocate the overthrow of the government by force and violence. In administrative proceedings, all three were found deportable on that ground. In each case there was an uncontested finding that the Communist Party advocates forceful overthrow of the Government.[9] Through various procedures, all three plaintiffs brought actions to challenge the constitutionality of the new law. In each case the lower court upheld the statute and entered judgment for the government.]

■ MR. JUSTICE JACKSON delivered the opinion of the Court.

* * *

* * * Admittedly, each of these deportations is authorized and required by the letter, spirit and intention of the statute. But the Act is assailed on three grounds: (1) that it deprives the aliens of liberty without due process of law in violation of the Fifth Amendment; (2) that it abridges their freedoms of speech and assembly in contravention of the First Amendment; and (3) that it is an *ex post facto* law which Congress is forbidden to pass by Art. I, § 9, cl. 3 of the Constitution.

* * *

I.

These aliens ask us to forbid their expulsion by a departure from the long-accepted application to such cases of the Fifth Amendment provision that no person shall be deprived of life, liberty or property without due process of law. Their basic contention is that admission for permanent residence confers a "vested right" on the alien, equal to that of the citizen, to remain within the country, and that the alien is entitled to constitutional protection in that matter to the same extent as the citizen. Their second line of defense is that if any power to deport domiciled aliens exists it is so dispersed that the judiciary must concur in the grounds for its exercise to the extent of finding them reasonable. The argument goes on to the contention that the grounds prescribed by the Act of 1940 bear no reasonable relation to protection of legitimate interests of the United States and concludes that the Act should be declared invalid. Admittedly these propositions are not founded in precedents of this Court.

For over thirty years each of these aliens has enjoyed such advantages as accrue from residence here without renouncing his foreign allegiance or formally acknowledging adherence to the Constitution he now invokes. Each was admitted to the United States, upon passing formidable exclusionary hurdles, in the hope that, after what may be called a probationary period, he would desire and be found desirable for citizenship. Each has been offered naturalization, with all of the rights and privileges of citizen-

---

9. Congress later amended the statute to make either present or past membership in the Communist Party a specific ground for deportation. See INA § 241(a)(6)(C), pre–1990 version. The amendment eliminated the need for findings, in individual cases, that the Communist Party advocates the forceful overthrow of the Government. In 1990 Congress largely eliminated this ground but replaced it with a provision that raises different issues. See pages 432–33, 567 below.

ship, conditioned only upon open and honest assumption of undivided allegiance to our Government. But acceptance was and is not compulsory. Each has been permitted to prolong his original nationality indefinitely.

So long as one thus perpetuates a dual status as an American inhabitant but foreign citizen, he may derive advantages from two sources of law—American and international. He may claim protection against our Government unavailable to the citizen. As an alien he retains a claim upon the state of his citizenship to diplomatic intervention on his behalf, a patronage often of considerable value. The state of origin of each of these aliens could presently enter diplomatic remonstrance against these deportations if they were inconsistent with international law, the prevailing custom among nations or their own practices.

The alien retains immunities from burdens which the citizen must shoulder. By withholding his allegiance from the United States, he leaves outstanding a foreign call on his loyalties which international law not only permits our Government to recognize but commands it to respect. In deference to it certain dispensations from conscription for any military service have been granted foreign nationals. They cannot, consistently with our international commitments, be compelled "to take part in the operations of war directed against their own country." In addition to such general immunities they may enjoy particular treaty privileges.

Under our law, the alien in several respects stands on an equal footing with citizens, but in others has never been conceded legal parity with the citizen. Most importantly, to protract this ambiguous status within the country is not his right but is a matter of permission and tolerance. The Government's power to terminate its hospitality has been asserted and sustained by this Court since the question first arose.

War, of course, is the most usual occasion for extensive resort to the power. Though the resident alien may be personally loyal to the United States, if his nation becomes our enemy his allegiance prevails over his personal preference and makes him also our enemy, liable to expulsion or internment, and his property becomes subject to seizure and perhaps confiscation. But it does not require war to bring the power of deportation into existence or to authorize its exercise. Congressional apprehension of foreign or internal dangers short of war may lead to its use. So long as the alien elects to continue the ambiguity of his allegiance his domicile here is held by a precarious tenure.

That aliens remain vulnerable to expulsion after long residence is a practice that bristles with severities. But it is a weapon of defense and reprisal confirmed by international law as a power inherent in every sovereign state. Such is the traditional power of the Nation over the alien and we leave the law on the subject as we find it.

This brings us to the alternative defense under the Due Process Clause—that, granting the power, it is so unreasonably and harshly exercised by this enactment that it should be held unconstitutional.

In historical context the Act before us stands out as an extreme application of the expulsion power. There is no denying that as world convulsions have driven us toward a closed society the expulsion power has been exercised with increasing severity, manifest in multiplication of grounds for deportation, in expanding the subject classes from illegal entrants to legal residents, and in greatly lengthening the period of residence after which one may be expelled. This is said to have reached a point where it is the duty of this Court to call a halt upon the political branches of the Government.

It is pertinent to observe that any policy toward aliens is vitally and intricately interwoven with contemporaneous policies in regard to the conduct of foreign relations, the war power, and the maintenance of a republican form of government. Such matters are so exclusively entrusted to the political branches of government as to be largely immune from judicial inquiry or interference.

These restraints upon the judiciary, occasioned by different events, do not control today's decision but they are pertinent. It is not necessary and probably not possible to delineate a fixed and precise line of separation in these matters between political and judicial power under the Constitution. Certainly, however, nothing in the structure of our Government or the text of our Constitution would warrant judicial review by standards which would require us to equate our political judgment with that of Congress.

Under the conditions which produced this Act, can we declare that congressional alarm about a coalition of Communist power without and Communist conspiracy within the United States is either a fantasy or a pretense? This Act was approved by President Roosevelt June 28, 1940, when a world war was threatening to involve us, as soon it did. Communists in the United States were exerting every effort to defeat and delay our preparations. Certainly no responsible American would say that there were then or are now no possible grounds on which Congress might believe that Communists in our midst are inimical to our security.

Congress received evidence that the Communist movement here has been heavily laden with aliens and that Soviet control of the American Communist Party has been largely through alien Communists. It would be easy for those of us who do not have security responsibility to say that those who do are taking Communism too seriously and overestimating its danger. But we have an Act of one Congress which, for a decade, subsequent Congresses have never repealed but have strengthened and extended. We, in our private opinions, need not concur in Congress' policies to hold its enactments constitutional. Judicially we must tolerate what personally we may regard as a legislative mistake.

We are urged, because the policy inflicts severe and undoubted hardship on affected individuals, to find a restraint in the Due Process Clause. But the Due Process Clause does not shield the citizen from conscription and the consequent calamity of being separated from family, friends, home and business while he is transported to foreign lands to stem the tide of Communism. If Communist aggression creates such hardships for loyal citizens, it is hard to find justification for holding that the Constitution requires that its hardships must be spared the Communist alien. When citizens raised the Constitution as a shield against expulsion from their homes and places of business, the Court refused to find hardship a cause for judicial intervention.

We think that, in the present state of the world, it would be rash and irresponsible to reinterpret our fundamental law to deny or qualify the Government's power of deportation. However desirable world-wide amelioration of the lot of aliens, we think it is peculiarly a subject for international diplomacy. It should not be initiated by judicial decision which can only deprive our own Government of a power of defense and reprisal without obtaining for American citizens abroad any reciprocal privileges or immunities. Reform in this field must be entrusted to the branches of the Government in control of our international relations and treaty-making powers.

We hold that the Act is not invalid under the Due Process Clause.
* * *

II.

The First Amendment is invoked as a barrier against this enactment. The claim is that in joining an organization advocating overthrow of government by force and violence the alien has merely exercised freedoms of speech, press and assembly which that Amendment guarantees to him.

The assumption is that the First Amendment allows Congress to make no distinction between advocating change in the existing order by lawful elective processes and advocating change by force and violence, that freedom for the one includes freedom for the other, and that when teaching of violence is denied so is freedom of speech.

Our Constitution sought to leave no excuse for violent attack on the status quo by providing a legal alternative—attack by ballot. To arm all men for orderly change, the Constitution put in their hands a right to influence the electorate by press, speech and assembly. This means freedom to advocate or promote Communism by means of the ballot box, but it does not include the practice or incitement of violence.

True, it often is difficult to determine whether ambiguous speech is advocacy of political methods or subtly shades into a methodical but prudent incitement to violence. Communist governments avoid the inquiry by suppressing everything distasteful. Some would have us avoid the difficulty by going to the opposite extreme of permitting incitement to violent overthrow at least unless it seems certain to succeed immediately. We apprehend that the Constitution enjoins upon us the duty, however difficult, of distinguishing between the two. Different formulae have been applied in different situations and the test applicable to the Communist Party has been stated too recently to make further discussion at this time profitable.[19] We think the First Amendment does not prevent the deportation of these aliens.

III.

The remaining claim is that this Act conflicts with Art. I, § 9, of the Constitution forbidding *ex post facto* enactments. An impression of retroactivity results from reading as a new and isolated enactment what is actually a continuation of prior legislation.

During all the years since 1920 Congress has maintained a standing admonition to aliens, on pain of deportation, not to become members of any organization that advocates overthrow of the United States Government by force and violence, a category repeatedly held to include the Communist Party. These aliens violated that prohibition and incurred liability to deportation. They were not caught unawares by a change of law. There can be no contention that they were not adequately forewarned both that their conduct was prohibited and of its consequences.

In 1939, this Court decided *Kessler v. Strecker*, in which it was held that Congress, in the statute as it then stood, had not clearly expressed an intent that Communist Party membership remained cause for deportation after it ceased. The Court concluded that in the absence of such expression only contemporaneous membership would authorize deportation.

The reaction of the Communist Party was to drop aliens from membership, at least in form, in order to immunize them from the consequences of their party membership.

The reaction of Congress was that the Court had misunderstood its legislation. In the Act here before us it supplied unmistakable language that past violators of its prohibitions continued to be deportable in spite of resignation or expulsion from the party. It regarded the fact that an alien defied our laws to join the Communist Party as an indication that he had developed little comprehension of the principles or practice of representative government or else was unwilling to abide by them.

However, even if the Act were found to be retroactive, to strike it down would require us to overrule the construction of the *ex post facto* provision which has been followed by this Court from earliest times. It always has been considered that that which it forbids is penal legislation which imposes or increases criminal punishment for conduct lawful previous to its enactment. Deportation, however severe its consequences, has been consistently classified as a civil rather than a criminal procedure. Both of these doctrines as original proposals might be debatable, but both have been considered closed for many years and a body of statute and decisional law has been built upon them. In *Bugajewitz v. Adams*, Mr. Justice Holmes, for the Court, said: " * * * [N]or is the deportation a punishment; it is simply

19. [*Dennis v. United States*, 341 U.S. 494, 71 S.Ct. 857, 95 L.Ed. 1137 (1951)].

a refusal by the Government to harbor persons whom it does not want.
* * * "

                                    * * *

Affirmed.

■ MR. JUSTICE CLARK took no part in the consideration or decision of these cases.

■ MR. JUSTICE FRANKFURTER, concurring.

It is not for this Court to reshape a world order based on politically sovereign States. In such an international ordering of the world a national State implies a special relationship of one body of people, *i.e.,* citizens of that State, whereby the citizens of each State are aliens in relation to every other State. Ever since national States have come into being, the right of people to enjoy the hospitality of a State of which they are not citizens has been a matter of political determination by each State. (I put to one side the oddities of dual citizenship.) Though as a matter of political outlook and economic need this country has traditionally welcomed aliens to come to its shores, it has done so exclusively as a matter of political outlook and national self-interest. This policy has been a political policy, belonging to the political branch of the Government wholly outside the concern and the competence of the Judiciary.

Accordingly, when this policy changed and the political and law-making branch of this Government, the Congress, decided to restrict the right of immigration about seventy years ago, this Court thereupon and ever since has recognized that the determination of a selective and exclusionary immigration policy was for the Congress and not for the Judiciary. The conditions for entry of every alien, the particular classes of aliens that shall be denied entry altogether, the basis for determining such classification, the right to terminate hospitality to aliens, the grounds on which such determination shall be based, have been recognized as matters solely for the responsibility of the Congress and wholly outside the power of this Court to control.

The Court's acknowledgment of the sole responsibility of Congress for these matters has been made possible by Justices whose cultural outlook, whose breadth of view and robust tolerance were not exceeded by those of Jefferson. In their personal views, libertarians like Mr. Justice Holmes and Mr. Justice Brandeis doubtless disapproved of some of these policies, departures as they were from the best traditions of this country and based as they have been in part on discredited racial theories or manipulation of figures in formulating what is known as the quota system. But whether immigration laws have been crude and cruel, whether they may have reflected xenophobia in general or anti-Semitism or anti-Catholicism, the responsibility belongs to Congress. Courts do enforce the requirements imposed by Congress upon officials in administering immigration laws, *e.g.,* *Kwock Jan Fat v. White,* and the requirement of Due Process may entail certain procedural observances. *E.g., Ng Fung Ho v. White.* But the underlying policies of what classes of aliens shall be allowed to enter and what classes of aliens shall be allowed to stay, are for Congress exclusively to determine even though such determination may be deemed to offend American traditions and may, as has been the case, jeopardize peace.

In recognizing this power and this responsibility of Congress, one does not in the remotest degree align oneself with fears unworthy of the American spirit or with hostility to the bracing air of the free spirit. One merely recognizes that the place to resist unwise or cruel legislation touching aliens is the Congress, not this Court.

I, therefore, join in the Court's opinion in these cases.

■ MR. JUSTICE DOUGLAS, with whom MR. JUSTICE BLACK concurs, dissenting.

There are two possible bases for sustaining this Act:

(1) A person who was once a Communist is tainted for all time and forever dangerous to our society; or

(2) Punishment through banishment from the country may be placed upon an alien not for what he did, but for what his political views once were.

Each of these is foreign to our philosophy. We repudiate our traditions of tolerance and our articles of faith based upon the Bill of Rights when we bow to them by sustaining an Act of Congress which has them as a foundation.

The view that the power of Congress to deport aliens is absolute and may be exercised for any reason which Congress deems appropriate rests on *Fong Yue Ting v. United States,* decided in 1893 by a six-to-three vote. That decision seems to me to be inconsistent with the philosophy of constitutional law which we have developed for the protection of resident aliens. We have long held that a resident alien is a "person" within the meaning of the Fifth and the Fourteenth Amendments. He therefore may not be deprived either by the National Government or by any state of life, liberty, or property without due process of law. Nor may he be denied the equal protection of the laws. A state was not allowed to exclude an alien from the laundry business because he was a Chinese, nor discharge him from employment because he was not a citizen, nor deprive him of the right to fish because he was a Japanese ineligible to citizenship. An alien's property (provided he is not an enemy alien), may not be taken without just compensation. He is entitled to habeas corpus to test the legality of his restraint, to the protection of the Fifth and Sixth Amendments in criminal trials, and to the right of free speech as guaranteed by the First Amendment.

An alien, who is assimilated in our society, is treated as a citizen so far as his property and his liberty are concerned. He can live and work here and raise a family, secure in the personal guarantees every resident has and safe from discriminations that might be leveled against him because he was born abroad. Those guarantees of liberty and livelihood are the essence of the freedom which this country from the beginning has offered the people of all lands. If those rights, great as they are, have constitutional protection, I think the more important one—the right to remain here—has a like dignity.

* * *

NOTES AND QUESTIONS

The opinion in *Harisiades* is the Supreme Court's most comprehensive and most detailed exposition of the arguments for exceptional judicial deference to Congress in immigration cases. This set of Notes considers separately the several constitutional attacks the Court considers.

1. Section I of the Court's opinion addresses the two due process arguments. The plaintiffs first maintain that admission to LPR status creates a vested right to remain. As a fallback position they contend that, if deportation of an LPR is ever constitutionally permissible, the deportation ground must at least be reasonable. It might not be obvious to you why the due process clause would be invoked to support an argument based on substantive "reasonableness." There are two related constitutional developments that you should note.

One is known generally as "substantive due process." Under this doctrine, the due process clause is seen as conferring not only a right to fair procedure, but also certain substantive protection, including freedom from substantively arbitrary governmental action. The degree of rationality that substantive due process requires has varied with the times and with the type of governmental regulation at issue. See generally Gerald Gunther & Kathleen M. Sullivan, Constitutional Law, ch. 8 (13th ed. 1997).

The other aspect of due process pertinent here concerns the permissibility of governmental distinctions between two or more groups. Section 1 of the fourteenth amendment prohibits each state from "deny[ing] to any person within its jurisdiction the equal protection of the laws." Nothing in the Constitution *expressly* puts analogous restrictions on the federal government, but fifth amendment due process has been held to prohibit unjustifiable federal discrimination. See, e.g., *Bolling v. Sharpe,* 347 U.S. 497, 74 S.Ct. 693, 98 L.Ed. 884 (1954).

2. After *Harisiades,* may a court review the substantive rationality of a distinction drawn by a federal immigration statute? Examine the Court's language: "[A]ny policy toward aliens is vitally and intricately interwoven with * * * foreign relations, the war power, and the maintenance of a republican form of government. Such matters are so exclusively entrusted to the political branches of government as to be largely immune from judicial inquiry or interference." What does the Court mean by "largely immune"? Would it take an enactment that is utterly baffling before a reviewing court would be permitted to strike down the legislation as unreasonable? Less than that? More than that?

Observe how the Court actually applies the principle it has announced to the particular provision in question. It asks whether "congressional alarm" about a "Communist conspiracy within the United States is either *a fantasy or a pretense"* (emphasis added). It rejects the conclusion "that there were then or are now *no possible* grounds on which Congress might believe that Communists in our midst are inimical to our security" (emphasis added). To what extent is the Court evaluating the importance of the congressional objective? To what extent does the Court consider the fit between that objective and the means used to promote it?

The manner in which a rationality test is phrased can be revealing. As the author of the majority opinion in *Harisiades,* Justice Jackson disparages the plaintiffs' fallback position as being "that if any power to deport domiciled aliens exists it is so dispersed that the judiciary must concur in the grounds for its exercise to the extent of finding them reasonable." Only a year later, the same Justice Jackson would dissent in *Mezei,* arguing that due process requires "reasonable general legislation reasonably applied to the individual." 345 U.S. at 222, 73 S.Ct. at 634, 97 L.Ed. at 968. Is his *Mezei* formulation any different, analytically, from the proposition he ridicules in *Harisiades?* Is it psychologically different?

Further, does the Court's description of the plaintiffs' argument in *Harisiades* suggest that it does *not* believe it should be reviewing even for reasonableness? Or does its analysis of why Congress has enacted the provision in question indicate a willingness to review for at least minimal rationality?

Justice Frankfurter's concurring opinion is lavishly sprinkled with phrases like "exclusively," "wholly," and "solely" congressional powers. Is he advocating even less judicial involvement than the majority is?

3. Why is the Court being so deferential to Congress? As you study section I of the opinion, see how many different reasons you can locate. Be sure to distinguish reasons for rejecting the vested rights argument from those for rejecting the reasonableness argument.

Many of the old themes that you have seen before resurface in *Harisiades:* the connection between immigration and foreign affairs and the attendant applicability of the political question doctrine; the sovereign nature of the power to deport; the distinction between rights and privileges; and the interdependence of allegiance and protection. In the process, however, the Court sounds some new themes:

a. These noncitizens have been here long enough to naturalize, and they have declined the opportunity. They should not complain now about being denied the rights of citizenship.

b. International law gives noncitizens certain remedies not available to citizens. Invoking the Constitution to insulate LPRs from deportation would therefore be unfair because they, unlike citizens, would then "derive advantages from two sources of law—American and international."

What is your reaction to argument (a)? In evaluating it, consider that in 1940 Congress prohibited the naturalization of noncitizens like Harisiades who had joined organizations found to advocate the forceful overthrow of the United States government. Nationality Act of 1940, ch. 876, § 305, 54 Stat. 1137, 1141. Assuming, however, that the Court's premise had been correct—that the plaintiffs had turned down the chance to become naturalized—do you find the argument persuasive?

What about argument (b)? How valuable do the two international law advantages cited by the Court (diplomatic intervention and the right to decline participation in a war against one's country of nationality) seem to you, in comparison with constitutional protection from deportation? Would immunity from deportation, combined with the advantages derived from international law, really give LPRs an unfair advantage over citizens? Which package of rights and obligations would you rather have? (Keep your answer tentative; in chapter 13 you will see in more detail some of the non-immigration disabilities that attend noncitizen status.)

There are other schools of thought as well. Some have attributed the unusual deference in immigration cases to a judicial assumption that noncitizens simply are not *members* of the political community; they are mere "guests" for whom admission and permission to remain are privileges rather than rights. See, e.g., T. Alexander Aleinikoff, *Citizens, Aliens, Membership and the Constitution*, 7 Constitutional Commentary 9 (1990); Stephen H. Legomsky, *Immigration Law and the Principle of Plenary Congressional Power*, 1984 Supreme Court Rev. 255, 269–70; Peter H. Schuck, *The Transformation of Immigration Law*, 84 Columbia L.Rev. 1 (1984). The subject of membership will be explored in some depth in chapter 13, section C, below.

Professor Kevin R. Johnson, in *Responding to the Litigation Explosion: The Plain Meaning of Executive Branch Primacy over Immigration*, 71 North Carolina L. Rev. 413 (1993), ascribes some of the deference to a judicial interest in speeding the disposition of cases and discouraging litigation. Professor Michael Scaperlanda believes that the plenary power doctrine partly reflects the emphasis of classical international law on state sovereignty (versus individual rights). He argues that the emergence of modern human rights law, which explicitly recognizes individual rights rooted in international law, renders the doctrine obsolete. See Michael Scaperlanda, *Polishing the Tarnished Golden Door*, 1993 Wisconsin L. Rev. 965; see also Kif Augustine–Adams, *The Plenary Power Doctrine After September 11*, 38 U.C. Davis L.Rev. 701 (2005) (linking the content of constitutional protection of noncitizens to international human rights law).

4. Whatever the independent merits of the arguments you have seen thus far, there is no doubt that *stare decisis* has also played an important role in perpetuating the special judicial restraint in immigration cases:

> * * * [M]uch could be said for the view, were we writing on a clean slate, that the Due Process Clause qualifies the scope of political discretion heretofore recognized as belonging to Congress in regulating the entry and deportation of aliens. * * *

> But the slate is not clean. * * * [T]hat the formulation of these policies is entrusted exclusively to Congress has become about as firmly imbedded in the legislative and judicial tissues of our body politic as any aspect of our government.

Galvan v. Press, 347 U.S. 522, 530–31, 74 S.Ct. 737, 742–43, 98 L.Ed. 911, 921–22 (1954) (opinion of Court, per Justice Frankfurter).

The principal values traditionally associated with *stare decisis* include (a) predictability in the law; (b) equal treatment of similarly situated litigants; and (c) judicial efficiency. When deciding whether to overrule a precedent, a court must balance these values against the perceived superiority of the new rule. How weighty do you find these values as applied to the question at hand? Should the principle of special judicial restraint in immigration cases be followed, abandoned, or modified?

5.   In the early cases you read at the start of this chapter, the plaintiffs were almost always Chinese or Japanese. As discussed earlier, it seems natural to explain the extreme results as the combined products of legal doctrine and external social and political influences. Is the same true of cases like *Knauff, Mezei, Harisiades, Galvan,* and other immigration decisions rendered during the Cold War and the McCarthy era? To what extent did the national preoccupation with Communism affect either the reasoning or the results of those cases? Consider especially the portion of the *Harisiades* opinion in which the Court implies it would be incongruous to spare the deportation of noncitizen Communists at a time when citizens were being drafted specifically to fight Communism. What is your reaction to that portion of the opinion?

6.   One of the more significant modern Supreme Court opinions on this subject is *Fiallo v. Bell,* 430 U.S. 787, 97 S.Ct. 1473, 52 L.Ed.2d 50 (1977). As you will see later, the Immigration and Nationality Act generally confers immigration benefits on both the parents and the children of United States citizens. At the time of *Fiallo,*[10] however, the statute did not recognize for this purpose the relationship between a father and his child born out of wedlock. Several pairs of fathers and their out-of-wedlock children argued that the discrimination violated the "equal protection" component of due process (see item 1 above).

When either the federal or a state government treats two groups of people differently, equal protection principles generally require a rational relationship between the particular distinction and some legitimate governmental interest. See generally Gerald Gunther & Kathleen M. Sullivan, Constitutional Law 635–62 (13th ed. 1997). Certain classifications, however, have been held to demand more—typically both a more substantial government interest ("ends" scrutiny) and a closer relationship between the challenged classification and that interest ("means" scrutiny). Gender and legitimacy are among such classifications, see generally *id.* at 681–720, 725–28, and *both* were present in *Fiallo.* Moreover, as the plaintiffs pointed out, the foreign policy factors on which the Court had purported to rely in the early cases were absent here. 430 U.S. at 796, 97 S.Ct. at 1480, 52 L.Ed.2d at 58. Yet once again, relying on the sovereign nature of the power

---

10.   INA § 101(b)(1)(D). In 1986 Congress amended this provision so as to recognize the relationship between a father and his out-of-wedlock child in cases where there is or has been "a bona fide parent-child relationship." IRCA § 315(a).

to exclude aliens and the force of *stare decisis,* the Court held the congressional power to be "largely immune from judicial control." *Id.* at 792, 97 S.Ct. at 1478, 52 L.Ed.2d at 56.

At the same time, the Court conceded in dictum what has proven to be a significant opening. The government had argued that "substantive policies regulating the admission of aliens [were] not an appropriate subject for judicial review." The Court responded:

> * * * Our cases [none cited] reflect acceptance of a limited judicial responsibility under the Constitution *even with respect to the power of Congress to regulate the admission and exclusion of aliens,* and there is no occasion to consider in this case whether there may be actions of the Congress with respect to aliens that are so essentially political in character as to be nonjusticiable [emphasis added].

Id. at 793 n. 5, 97 S.Ct. at 1478, 52 L.Ed.2d at 57. The clear implication is that substantive admission criteria will normally be subject to judicial review for constitutionality and that the only uncertainty is about whether there might be *some* exceptions that call for nonjusticiability. Still unclear, however, is what the "limited" judicial responsibility entails. In *Fiallo,* the Court observed that Congress might have singled out the relationship between fathers and their out-of-wedlock children because of the potential for fraudulent paternity claims. *Id.* at 799 n. 8, 97 S.Ct. at 1481, 52 L.Ed.2d at 60. The "limited judicial responsibility" to which the Court in *Fiallo* cryptically referred might thus amount to assuring rationality. As you will see later in this chapter, the lower courts now often make precisely that assumption when addressing substantive constitutional challenges to federal immigration statutes.

Do you think the assumptions that underlie the statutory distinctions in *Fiallo* reflect biological fact or gender stereotyping? This question loomed large in *Nguyen v. INS,* 533 U.S. 53, 121 S.Ct. 2053, 150 L.Ed.2d 115 (2001), where the Supreme Court upheld (by a vote of 5–4) the constitutionality of a statutory provision dealing with citizenship by descent. For children born out of wedlock, the statute made it harder to derive United States citizenship from their fathers than to derive it from their mothers. In *Nguyen* there was a question whether the plenary power doctrine carried over from admission and expulsion cases to citizenship cases. The majority avoided that difficult question by concluding that the statute survived even the intermediate level of enhanced scrutiny usually applicable in gender discrimination cases. To reach that conclusion, the majority offered two alternative rationales. The first one was the paternity fraud rationale that you encountered in *Fiallo.* Mindful that DNA and other technologies now diminish that concern, the Court in *Nguyen* reasoned alternatively that as a matter of "biological fact" only the mother could carry the unborn child and only the mother could be counted on to be present at the birth. Those biological facts, the Court said, increased the probability of a close bond between the mother and child and thus furnished a substantial link between the statutory gender distinction and an important governmental objective. Justice O'Connor, dissenting, doubted that the Court's scrutiny actually reached the level contemplated by intermediate gender scrutiny and suggested that in any event the second rationale amounted to gender stereotyping rather than biological fact. In a thoughtful pre-*Nguyen* article, Professor Linda Kelly prophetically distilled a general pattern of gender stereotyping in immigration law, with special attention to *Fiallo*. See Linda Kelly, *Republican Mothers, Bastards' Fathers and Good Victims: Discarding Citizens and Equal Protection through the Failures of Legal Images*, 51 Hastings L.J. 557 (2000).

7. Does the principle of special judicial deference in immigration extend to actions of the executive branch? The Eleventh Circuit thought so in *Jean v. Nelson*, 727 F.2d 957 (11th Cir.1984) (en banc); *cf. Kleindienst v. Mandel*, 408 U.S. 753, 92 S.Ct. 2576, 33 L.Ed.2d 683 (1972) (a First Amendment case discussed below). In *Jean*, noted earlier, the plaintiffs were Haitians who had been detained several years pending adjudication of the asylum claims they had filed in exclusion proceedings. They alleged that the Attorney General, in deciding whom to detain pending exclusion decisions, had unconstitutionally discriminated against Haitians. The en banc court disposed of this argument by concluding that noncitizens in exclusion proceedings simply have no constitutional rights that pertain to immigration, even as against executive officials and even when they are challenging their detention rather than their exclusion. 727 F.2d at 967–75.

8. The plaintiffs in *Harisiades* also make a First Amendment argument. Section II has been reproduced in full; what you read represents the Court's entire discussion of that issue. That section is interesting for what it does *not* do. Nowhere does it refer to the plenary power of Congress or to the exceptional judicial deference required in immigration cases. Instead, the Court's stated reason for rejecting the First Amendment claim rests solely on the distinction between the advocacy of lawful change and the advocacy of violent change. The court cites a non-immigration case, *Dennis v. United States*, as embodying "the test applicable to the Communist Party".

On its face, then, nothing in *Harisiades* contracts the scope of the First Amendment in the deportation context. In *American–Arab Anti–Discrimination Committee v. Meese*, 714 F.Supp. 1060 (C.D.Cal.1989) (*ADC*), rev'd on other grounds, 940 F.2d 445 (9th Cir.1991), a district court hinged its decision on that fact. The INS had brought removal proceedings against eight noncitizens. Two of them, both LPRs, were charged with supporting the Popular Front for the Liberation of Palestine, an organization alleged to advocate various terrorist acts. The other six were charged with overstaying their visas. All eight sought to enjoin the removal proceedings on the ground that the government had selectively targeted them because of their membership in the PFLP. They argued, among other things, that the selective prosecution violated their First Amendment rights to free speech and free association.

The district court in *ADC* held that, far from supporting the application of the plenary power doctrine to the First Amendment in deportation cases, *Harisiades* demonstrated that in such cases the usual First Amendment standards were to govern. In *Dennis,* which the Supreme Court had cited approvingly in *Harisiades,* the constitutional test was whether the restricted speech posed a "clear and present danger" of bringing about a sufficiently important evil. *Dennis v. United States,* 341 U.S. 494, 515, 71 S.Ct. 857, 870, 95 L.Ed. 1137, 1155 (1951). By the time of *ADC,* the Supreme Court had also decided *Brandenburg v. Ohio,* 395 U.S. 444, 89 S.Ct. 1827, 23 L.Ed.2d 430 (1969), in which it had held that advocacy of even lawless action cannot be proscribed unless the advocacy "is directed to inciting or producing imminent lawless action and is likely to incite or produce such action." *Id.* at 447, 89 S.Ct. at 1829, 23 L.Ed.2d at 434. Applying the *Brandenburg* test, the district court in *ADC* struck down various INA provisions that rendered noncitizens deportable for advocating Communism or opposition to organized government, for joining organizations that advocate those ideas, or for engaging in other specified forms of expression or association. *ADC,* 714 F.Supp. at 1083–84; accord, 70 F.3d 1045, 1064 (9th Cir. 1995)(related case of same name, addressing selective prosecution argument); *cf. Rafeedie v. INS,* 795 F.Supp. 13 (D.D.C. 1992)(striking down analogous exclusion grounds as overbroad).

It is certainly possible to construe *Harisiades* as the district court did in *ADC.* Having read the facts of *Harisiades,* however, and having now seen the *Dennis* test, do you think one can seriously maintain that the Court in *Harisiades* applied the then prevailing First Amendment standards? More specifically, was there any point in the *Harisiades* opinion at which the court considered whether the plaintiffs' advocacy or associations posed a "clear and present danger"?

Sensitive to that difficulty, the court in *ADC* acknowledged in a footnote that commentators had questioned whether the Court in *Harisiades* had correctly applied *Dennis.* 714 F.Supp. at 1077 n. 12. In the view of the *ADC* court, however, it did not matter whether the Court in *Harisiades* had applied the usual First Amendment principles correctly or incorrectly; the important point was that it had invoked those principles at all in the face of the government's argument that it should not do so. *Id.* Do you agree with the interpretation placed on *Harisiades* by the district court in *ADC?*

The Supreme Court granted certiorari in *ADC* to decide whether recent legislation eliminated the lower courts' power to hear the case before the issuance of final removal orders. In *Reno v. American–Arab Anti–Discrimination Committee,* 525 U.S. 471, 119 S.Ct. 936, 142 L.Ed.2d 940 (1999), the Court ultimately held jurisdiction was lacking. The jurisdictional issue is discussed in chapter 9. In the process of deciding the jurisdictional issue, however, the majority declared that "an alien unlawfully in this country has no constitutional right to assert selective enforcement as a defense against his deportation." 525 U.S. at 488. In a nearby footnote, the Court, possibly unintentionally, used even broader language. It said "Our holding generally deprives *deportable* aliens of the defense of selective prosecution [emphasis added]." *Id*. at 488 n.10. The latter language, if interpreted literally, would deny this defense even to LPRs.

The Court offered several reasons for barring selective prosecution claims in removal proceedings. It suggested that the delay caused by such claims would cause special problems in the removal context, both because noncitizens have an inherent incentive to delay removal hearings and because delay permits "a continuing violation of United States law." In addition, the Court said, disclosure of the government's reasons for prosecuting could expose sensitive foreign policy strategies. Finally, it was suggested, deportation is not punishment, and therefore the individual interest is less compelling than in a criminal case. 525 U.S. at 489–91.

Possible limitations on the Court's holding should be considered. The Court did not go so far as to bar all First Amendment claims in removal hearings. Most likely it did not mean to do so, since its rationales were specific to selective prosecution. Moreover, the Court expressly left open the possibility that a prosecution could reflect discrimination "so outrageous that the foregoing considerations can be overcome." 525 U.S. at 491. It concluded by saying "When an alien's continuing presence in this country is in violation of the immigration laws," selective prosecution based on membership of an organization that supports terrorist activity is permissible. *Id*. at 491–92. The repeated references to continuing presence might well mean that the Court did not intend to bar LPRs from asserting selective prosecution claims; their continuing presence would not violate the immigration laws. Justice Souter, dissenting, characterized the Court's conclusions about selective prosecution as dicta, since the Court ultimately found a lack of subject matter jurisdiction.

For a superb history and critique of the first amendment issues raised by the *ADC* litigation, see John A. Scanlan, *American-Arab—Getting the Balance Wrong–Again!*, 52 Administrative L. Rev. 347 (2000). Gerald Neuman argues that the Court's language in *ADC* concerning selective prosecution should be narrowly construed. Gerald L. Neuman, *Terrorism, Selective Deportation and the First Amendment after Reno v. AADC*, 14 Georgetown Immigration L.J. 313 (2000). In contrast, David A. Martin argues that the Court rightly intended a broad interpretation of the bar on selective prosecution defenses. David A. Martin, *On Counterintuitive Consequences and Choosing the Right Control Group: A Defense of Reno v. AADC*, 14 Georgetown Immigration L.J. 363 (2000).

A postscript on the *ADC* case: After the Supreme Court decision, the case was remanded to immigration judge Bruce Einhorn in Los Angeles. In 2001, Judge Einhorn dismissed the main deportability charges against the lead respondents, holding that the charged grounds were not meant to apply retroactively to acts (in this instance participating in demonstrations, distributing newspapers, and organizing fundraisers for humanitarian projects sponsored by a group that the United States government determined to be terrorist) committed before the deportability grounds were enacted. Press Release, Marc van der Hout & David Cole, *The LA8 Case* (June 26, 2001).

Two leading exclusion cases are also significant. In *United States ex rel. Turner v. Williams,* 194 U.S. 279, 24 S.Ct. 719, 48 L.Ed. 979 (1904), the Supreme Court upheld a federal statutory provision excluding "anarchists." The Court held that, even if construed to encompass anarchists who are merely "political philosophers, innocent of evil intent," the statute would survive the First Amendment. *Id.* at 294, 24 S.Ct. at 724, 48 L.Ed. at 985.

In *Kleindienst v. Mandel,* 408 U.S. 753, 92 S.Ct. 2576, 33 L.Ed.2d 683 (1972), a noncitizen was excluded under a statutory provision that barred the entry of those who advocate, or who publish works advocating, the "doctrines of world communism." INA § 212(a)(28)(D, G (v)), pre–1990 version. The Attorney General, who had the statutory discretion to waive the bar, *id.* § 212(d)(3), declined to do so. Several United States citizens brought suit, alleging a deprivation of *their* first amendment rights to receive the noncitizen's ideas. Rather than apply the *Brandenburg* test (which by then had become the generally applicable standard for restrictions on political speech), the Court held the Attorney General could constitutionally deny a waiver whenever there was a "facially legitimate and bona fide reason" for doing so. There would be no need to balance that reason against the first amendment interests of the citizen plaintiffs. The Court did not expressly address the constitutionality of the statutory exclusion ground, but it did ultimately uphold an exclusion order that had been based on that ground. Arguably, therefore, the Court upheld that provision sub silentio. See also Justice Marshall's dissent, 408 U.S. at 774–85, 92 S.Ct. at 2587–93, 33 L.Ed.2d at 698–705 (finding statutory exclusion ground unconstitutional at least when citizens' rights to receive ideas are involved). Unlike the First Amendment analysis in *Harisiades* and possibly *Turner,* the analysis in *Mandel* rested squarely on the plenary nature of Congress's power to regulate immigration. See *Turner,* 194 U.S. at 289–92, 24 S.Ct. at 722–23, 48 L.Ed. at 983–85 (discussion of plenary power doctrine seemingly limited to certain other constitutional objections); *Mandel,* 408 U.S. at 765–67, 769–70, 92 S.Ct. at 2583–85, 33 L.Ed.2d at 693–96.

Professor Adam Cox makes the innovative argument that the plenary power doctrine largely reflects the Court's assumption that noncitizens lack standing to invoke full judicial scrutiny of immigration legislation (in addition to reflecting the Court's views on judicial deference and its views on the narrowness of the limits to congressional power). He goes on to urge a broader conception of *citizens'* standing to challenge immigration laws—a strategy employed by the plaintiffs in *Kleindienst v. Mandel.* See Adam B. Cox, *Citizenship, Standing, and Immigration Law,* 92 California L. Rev. 373 (2004).

The commentary has been highly critical of the *Mandel* decision and of the ideological exclusion grounds themselves. For some especially cogent attacks, see John A. Scanlan, *Aliens in the Marketplace of Ideas: The Government, The Academy, and the McCarran–Walter Act,* 66 Texas L.Rev. 1481 (1988); Steven R. Shapiro, *Ideological Exclusions: Closing the Border to Political Dissidents,* 100 Harv.L.Rev. 930 (1987); Comment, *Ideological*

Exclusion, Plenary Power, and the PLO, 77 California L.Rev. 831 (1989). For a while, these and other criticisms bore fruit. Congress soon whittled away at the ideological bases for excluding and deporting noncitizens. Major reforms enacted in 1990 are examined on pp. 427–35 below (exclusion) and 567–68 below (deportation). As discussed in chapters 5 and 10, however, the counterterrorism laws that followed the attacks of September 11, 2001 have added new removal grounds based on associations and other generally protected activities.

The United States, incidentally, is not alone in threatening deportation as a sanction against unwelcome advocacy. In 2001, Venezuela's beleaguered President Hugo Chavez said in a public speech: "I have given instructions that from today onward, any foreigner who comes here and says anything offensive against the nation or the government or the president or the people will be expelled from Venezuela." New York Times (June 12, 2001) at A14.

9. In section III of the *Harisiades* opinion, the Court rejects an argument based on the *ex post facto* clause. First, the Court concludes that the legislation in question was not truly retroactive. On that point, which of two arguments is the Court making? (a) Even though no law in force while those plaintiffs were members made *past* membership a deportation ground, *present* membership had been a deportation ground all along; or (b) Even past membership had been a deportation ground all along; it's just that in *Kessler* the Court had not realized this, and it took the 1940 Act to set the record straight. If the Court meant (a), do you agree that the 1940 Act was not retroactive? If the Court meant (b), do you think the 1940 Act proves the *Kessler* Court was wrong to interpret the previous statute as it did? Was the 1940 Congress any better equipped than the 1939 Supreme Court to construe legislation enacted by a prior Congress?

The broader basis on which the Court rejected the plaintiffs' *ex post facto* argument was that the ex post facto clause restricts only penal legislation and that deportation is not penal. Both elements of that rule remain good law. See, e.g., *Perez v. Elwood,* 294 F.3d 552, 557 (3d Cir. 2002). Whether deportation *should* be viewed as penal was explored earlier in connection with *Fong Yue Ting.*

Apart from the *ex post facto* clause, Professor Nancy Morawetz has argued convincingly that substantive due process might bar retroactive deportation charges. See Nancy Morawetz, *Rethinking Retroactive Deportation Laws and the Due Process Clause,* 73 NYU L. Rev. 97 (1998).

10. With all this emphasis on *judicial* interpretation of the Constitution, keep in mind that every member of Congress is also "bound by oath or affirmation, to support [the] Constitution." U.S. Const. art. VI, § 3. For a cogent reminder of this obligation in the immigration context, see Michael Scaperlanda, *Who is My Neighbor? An Essay on Immigrants, Welfare Reform, and the Constitution,* 29 Conn. L. Rev. 1587 (1997).

SUBSTANTIVE CRACKS IN THE PLENARY CONGRESSIONAL POWER

As you have just read, the district court in the *ADC* case refused to apply the plenary power doctrine to a first amendment challenge to a deportation ground. Outside the first amendment context there have been other dents in a doctrine that once seemed impervious to attack. Recall *Fiallo,* where the Supreme Court in a footnote conceded that courts might strike down immigration provisions that lack at least a modicum of rationality. In the case below, a court seemed to anticipate that invitation:

Francis v. INS

United States Court of Appeals, Second Circuit, 1976.
532 F.2d 268.

[Ten years after his admission as an LPR, Francis was convicted of possession of marijuana. The INS instituted deportation proceedings on the basis of that conviction. He conceded he was deportable but applied for discretionary relief under former INA § 212(c) [later replaced by present INA § 240A(a)]. In relevant part, this provision then read:

> Aliens lawfully admitted for permanent residence who temporarily proceeded abroad voluntarily and not under an order of deportation, and who are returning to a lawful unrelinquished domicile of seven consecutive years, may be admitted in the discretion of the Attorney General without regard to [most of the exclusion grounds]. * * *

Although this provision then spoke explicitly only to admission, it had long been held applicable to deportation for reasons that will be discussed in chapter 8. In particular, the Board of Immigration Appeals had previously held that an LPR who commits a deportable act, then leaves the United States temporarily, and then returns to a lawful unrelinquished domicile of at least seven years in the United States is statutorily eligible for discretionary relief under this section. Francis's problem was that he had never departed. Consequently, the immigration judge denied his application and the Board of Immigration Appeals affirmed. Under the applicable statutory procedure, he petitioned the court of appeals for review. After examining the legislative history, the court concluded that the Board had correctly interpreted section 212(c) as inapplicable to a person who has never left the United States. It then continued:]

It is the petitioner's contention that if this statutory construction is applied to his case, then he is deprived of the equal protection of the laws as guaranteed by the fifth amendment.[5] He argues that the statute as so applied creates two classes of aliens identical in every respect except for the fact that members of one class have departed and returned to this country

---

5. "[I]f a classification would be invalid under the Equal Protection Clause of the Fourteenth Amendment, it is also inconsis- tent with the due process requirement of the Fifth Amendment."

at some point after they became deportable. Thus the distinction is not rationally related to any legitimate purpose of the statute.

The authority of Congress and the executive branch to regulate the admission and retention of aliens is virtually unrestricted. Enforcement of the immigration laws is often related to considerations both of foreign policy and the domestic economy. Nevertheless "[i]n the enforcement of these policies, the Executive Branch of the Government must respect the procedural safeguards of due process...."

It has long been held that the constitutional promise of equal protection of the laws applies to aliens as well as citizens. Recently, this court reaffirmed the applicability of the equal protection guarantee to deportation proceedings. [The court here cites cases applying the rational basis test and finding the challenged statutory distinctions rational.] * * *

Under the minimal scrutiny test, which we consider applicable in this case, distinctions between different classes of persons

> must be reasonable, not arbitrary, and must rest upon some ground of difference having a fair and substantial relation to the object of the legislation, so that all persons similarly circumstanced shall be treated alike.

In determining whether the Board's policy survives minimal scrutiny, the purpose of Section 212(c) must be examined. As the government notes in its brief, Congress was concerned that there be some degree of flexibility to permit worthy returning aliens to continue their relationships with family members in the United States despite a ground for exclusion. Realizing that these considerations apply with equal force to an alien who has already reentered, perhaps illegally, the Board chose to expand eligibility to that group. Thus an alien who had been convicted of two crimes involving moral turpitude and, therefore, was deportable, was eligible for Section 212(c) discretion because he was able to demonstrate that several months after his last conviction he left the country for a few hours to attend a funeral in Canada. The government has failed to suggest any reason why this petitioner's failure to travel abroad following his conviction should be a crucial factor in determining whether he may be permitted to remain in this country. Reason and fairness would suggest that an alien whose ties with this country are so strong that he has never departed after his initial entry should receive at least as much consideration as an individual who may leave and return from time to time.

* * *

Fundamental fairness dictates that permanent resident aliens who are in like circumstances, but for irrelevant and fortuitous factors, be treated in a like manner. We do not dispute the power of the Congress to create different standards of admission and deportation for different groups of aliens.[8] However, once those choices are made, individuals within a particu-

---

8. To that extent we agree with our brethren that "the validity of distinctions drawn by Congress with respect to deporta-bility is not a proper subject for judicial concern."

lar group may not be subjected to disparate treatment on criteria wholly unrelated to any legitimate governmental interest. We find that the Board's interpretation of Section 212(c) is unconstitutional as applied to this petitioner.

Accordingly, the petition is granted. The case is remanded to the Board so that the Attorney General's discretion under Section 212(c) may be exercised.

NOTES AND QUESTIONS

1. As interpreted by the Board, the statutory provision in question did indeed draw a distinction that defied explanation. A noncitizen who committed an act that was a ground for deportation, and who then left the country temporarily and returned, would be eligible for discretionary relief. Francis, similarly situated except that he stayed within the United States after commission of his act, was not. The distinction was surely irrational.

The question, though, is whether a court is permitted to strike down a federal deportation provision even if the provision *is* substantively irrational. Didn't you just read in *Harisiades* that federal immigration policy, being intimately connected with foreign affairs, is so exclusively entrusted to the political branches as to be "largely immune from judicial inquiry or interference"? And didn't the Supreme Court in *Galvan v. Press* then reject, as too wild a deviation from settled principles, the suggestion that in immigration cases the due process clause "qualifies the scope of political discretion heretofore recognized as belonging to Congress"? Perhaps some flexibility derives from the *Fiallo* footnote discussed above, but at the time of the *Francis* case *Fiallo* had not yet been decided.

The court appears to acknowledge the problem. In footnote 8 it concedes that "the validity of distinctions drawn by Congress with respect to deportability is not a proper subject for judicial concern." Yet isn't the court invalidating precisely "a distinction drawn by Congress with respect to deportability"?

Perhaps the court would say that the distinction it is actually invalidating is merely one drawn by the BIA, not one drawn by Congress. But the court admits to sharing the Board's conclusion that the statute is inapplicable to noncitizens like Francis; nor does the court question the Board's previous conclusion that the statute applies to noncitizens who leave and return after committing the deportable act. In those circumstances, it seems fair to read the court's opinion as proceeding on the assumption that the *statute* draws the distinction imputed to it by the Board.

The court's method of distinguishing the Supreme Court decisions appears in the next-to-last paragraph, which you should now re-read. Are you persuaded? Is there really a difference between statutes that "create different standards * * * for different groups'' and statutes that subject "individuals within a particular group * * * to disparate treatment''? The court seemingly accepts that the validity of the former distinctions "is not a proper subject for judicial concern'', but it assumes it may review the latter to see whether they constitute "criteria wholly unrelated to any legitimate governmental interest." Isn't that simply review for (minimal) rationality? If so, then under the court's formulation judges must determine whether a given instance of differential treatment is a distinction between groups or a distinction between individuals within a group. As a practical matter, cannot almost any statutory distinction be classified either way? If, as counsel for the INS, you had wanted to characterize the classification in *Francis* as a distinction between groups, and therefore presumably not susceptible to rationality review in light of the court's concession, how would you define the two groups?

2.   *Francis* was adopted by the Board of Immigration Appeals later that same year. *Matter of Silva,* 16 I. & N. Dec. 26 (1976). Several years later, *Francis* was also followed in *Tapia–Acuna v. INS,* 640 F.2d 223 (9th Cir.1981).

The Board's adoption of *Francis* raises interesting questions. The Board has always taken the view that it lacks the power to decide constitutional questions. See, e.g., *Matter of Cortez,* 16 I. & N. Dec. 289, 291 n. 2 (1977); *Matter of Lennon,* 15 I. & N. Dec. 9, 27 (1974). How, then, could it adopt *Francis,* in which the result had been based on constitutional grounds?

The opinion in *Silva* does not answer this question. Could the Board simply have been interpreting section 212(c) as extending to noncitizens in Francis's position? That course would seem precluded, at least in the Second and Ninth Circuits where the Board is bound by the contrary interpretation placed on the statute by both courts. Might the Board simply have considered itself bound by the constitutional determinations of the Second and Ninth Circuits within the territory covered by those two courts? Even that theory would not explain the Board's voluntary adherence to *Francis* nationwide.

3.   Apart from the specific issue presented in *Francis,* several other lower courts have applied the rational basis test to provisions of the Immigration and Nationality Act, though ultimately finding the distinctions rational. See, e.g., *De Leon–Reynoso v. Ashcroft,* 293 F.3d 633, 638 (3d Cir. 2002) (explicitly adopting rational basis scrutiny for immigration statutes but applying test very deferentially); *Newton v. INS,* 736 F.2d 336, 339–43 (6th Cir.1984); *Narenji v. Civiletti,* 617 F.2d 745, 747 (D.C.Cir. 1979). The Supreme Court has done the same. *Reno v. Flores,* 507 U.S. 292, 113 S.Ct. 1439, 123 L.Ed.2d 1 (1993). Occasionally a lower court will actually strike down a challenged immigration provision as irrational. In addition to *Francis* and *Tapia-Acuna,* see, e.g., *Dillingham v. INS,* 267 F.3d 996 (9th Cir. 2001); *Garberding v. INS,* 30 F.3d 1187 (9th Cir. 1994).

4.   The limits of the plenary power doctrine were similarly tested in a line of cases challenging a provision of the Immigration Marriage Fraud

Amendments of 1986 [IMFA]. As you will see in detail in chapter 3, marriage to a United States citizen or to an LPR is generally a basis for immigrating to the United States. Section 5 of IMFA, however, originally provided (it has since been softened) that a marriage entered into while exclusion or deportation proceedings were pending would not be a basis for immigration benefits unless and until the noncitizen beneficiary resided outside the United States for at least two years after the marriage. The theory behind IMFA § 5 was that marriages contracted during exclusion or deportation proceedings are especially likely to be fraudulent but that, if such a marriage could withstand two years of early separation, it was probably genuine. In a series of cases, noncitizens and their citizen sponsors attacked that limitation on a variety of constitutional grounds. As you will see on pages 277–80 below, most of those challenges failed.

But at least one court held IMFA § 5 unconstitutional. The decision in *Manwani v. United States Dept. of Justice*, 736 F.Supp. 1367 (W.D.N.C. 1990), illustrates well the importance of deciding whether to call a statutory provision substantive or procedural. The plaintiffs—a United States citizen and her noncitizen husband—had married while deportation proceedings were pending against the husband. All indications were that the marriage was in fact genuine, but under IMFA § 5 his immigration was barred nonetheless. The plaintiffs argued that the statute created a conclusive presumption that marriages contracted during exclusion or deportation proceedings were fraudulent unless the a noncitizen has resided outside the United States for two years after marrying. Characterizing marital unity as a fundamental right, the plaintiffs contended that the conclusive presumption violated procedural due process; they argued they were entitled to a reasonable opportunity to prove that their marriage was genuine.

The court read *Fiallo* as imposing only *substantive* limitations on noncitizens' constitutional rights and classified IMFA § 5 as *procedural*. For the latter conclusion, the court relied mainly on the two-year clause: All IMFA § 5 affected, the court reasoned, was the timing of the visa petition; adjudication of the petition would simply be deferred two years. *Id.* at 1377. Moreover, the court observed, the challenged provision was part of INA § 204, which is entitled *"Procedure* for Granting Immigrant Status"* (emphasis added). *Id.* Thus finding the provision procedural, the court applied the *Mathews v. Eldridge* formula described earlier, see page 144 above, ultimately holding the statutory procedure violative of due process. *Id.* at 1383–86. It would have been possible, of course, for the court to call the two-year foreign residence requirement substantive and invoke the plenary power doctrine, as the Supreme Court had done in *Fiallo*.

Interestingly, the court in *Manwani* alternatively found IMFA § 5 substantively defective on equal protection grounds. In the court's view, the statute discriminated against those citizens who marry during their spouses' immigration proceedings. The fundamental right at stake, the court held, triggered strict scrutiny. By singling out such marriages as fraudulent rather than attempting to identify individual cases of actual fraud, Congress had used an approach too loosely tailored to its goal to withstand strict scrutiny. *Id.* at 1388–89. Even if the Constitution required only a rational basis, the court added, IMFA § 5 would fail the test.

5. Until 2003, there was one other line of lower court cases in which noncitizens frequently overcame the plenary power doctrine. Various provisions of the INA make detention mandatory, while removal proceedings are pending, in certain defined situations (for example where noncitizens are charged with being removable on certain crime-related or national security-related grounds). The lower courts divided on the constitutionality of mandatory detention. Most of them held that due process (sometimes substantive, sometimes procedural) prohibits detention pending removal proceedings, absent a determination that the particular individual is likely either to abscond or to endanger the public safety. In *Demore v. Hyung Joon Kim*, 538 U.S. 510, 123 S.Ct. 1708, 155 L.Ed.2d 724 (2003), the Supreme Court upheld the constitutionality of mandatory detention. The case and its implications are discussed on pages 211–24 below.

d. STILL MORE CRACKS

INS v. Chadha

Supreme Court of the United States, 1983.
462 U.S. 919, 103 S.Ct. 2764, 77 L.Ed.2d 317.

■ CHIEF JUSTICE BURGER delivered the opinion of the Court.

* * *

I

Chadha is an East Indian who was born in Kenya and holds a British passport. He was lawfully admitted to the United States in 1966 on a nonimmigrant student visa. His visa expired on June 30, 1972. On October 11, 1973, the District Director of the Immigration and Naturalization Service ordered Chadha to show cause why he should not be deported for having "remained in the United States for a longer time than permitted." Pursuant to § 242(b) of the Immigration and Nationality Act (Act), a deportation hearing was held before an Immigration Judge on January 11, 1974. Chadha conceded that he was deportable for over-staying his visa and the hearing was adjourned to enable him to file an application for suspension of deportation under § 244(a)(1) of the Act.[a] Section 244(a)(1) at the time in question, provided:

"As hereinafter prescribed in this section, the Attorney General may, in his discretion, suspend deportation and adjust the status to that of an alien lawfully admitted for permanent residence, in the case of an alien who applies to the Attorney General for suspension of deportation and—

"(1) is deportable under any law of the United States except the provisions specified in paragraph (2) of this subsec-

a. Now replaced by INA § 240A(b)—
Ed.

tion; has been physically present in the United States for a continuous period of not less than seven years immediately preceding the date of such application, and proves that during all of such period he was and is a person of good moral character; and is a person whose deportation would, in the opinion of the Attorney General, result in extreme hardship to the alien or to his spouse, parent, or child, who is a citizen of the United States or an alien lawfully admitted for permanent residence.''

After Chadha submitted his application for suspension of deportation, the deportation hearing was resumed on February 7, 1974. On the basis of evidence adduced at the hearing, affidavits submitted with the application, and the results of a character investigation conducted by the INS, the Immigration Judge, on June 25, 1974, ordered that Chadha's deportation be suspended. The Immigration Judge found that Chadha met the requirements of § 244(a)(1): he had resided continuously in the United States for over seven years, was of good moral character, and would suffer ''extreme hardship'' if deported.

* * *

* * * Section 244(c)(2) provides:

''(2) In the case of an alien specified in paragraph (1) of subsection (a) of this subsection—

''if during the session of the Congress at which a case is reported, or prior to the close of the session of the Congress next following the session at which a case is reported, either the Senate or the House of Representatives passes a resolution stating in substance that it does not favor the suspension of such deportation, the Attorney General shall thereupon deport such alien or authorize the alien's voluntary departure at his own expense under the order of deportation in the manner provided by law. If, within the time above specified, neither the Senate nor the House of Representatives shall pass such a resolution, the Attorney General shall cancel deportation proceedings.''

* * *

On December 12, 1975, Representative Eilberg, Chairman of the Judiciary Subcommittee on Immigration, Citizenship, and International Law, introduced a resolution opposing ''the granting of permanent residence in the United States to [six] aliens,'' including Chadha. * * * The resolution was passed without debate or recorded vote. Since the House action was pursuant to § 244(c)(2), the resolution was not treated as an Art. I legislative act; it was not submitted to the Senate or presented to the President for his action.

After the House veto of the Attorney General's decision to allow Chadha to remain in the United States, the Immigration Judge reopened the deportation proceedings to implement the House order deporting Chadha. Chadha moved to terminate the proceedings on the ground that § 244(c)(2) is unconstitutional. The Immigration Judge held that he had no authority to rule on the constitutional validity of § 244(c)(2). On November 8, 1976, Chadha was ordered deported pursuant to the House action.

Chadha appealed the deportation order to the Board of Immigration Appeals, again contending that § 244(c)(2) is unconstitutional. The Board held that it had "no power to declare unconstitutional an act of Congress" and Chadha's appeal was dismissed.

* * * Chadha filed a petition for review of the deportation order in the United States Court of Appeals for the Ninth Circuit. The Immigration and Naturalization Service agreed with Chadha's position before the Court of Appeals and joined him in arguing that § 244(c)(2) is unconstitutional. In light of the importance of the question, the Court of Appeals invited both the Senate and the House of Representatives to file briefs *amici curiae*.

After full briefing and oral argument, the Court of Appeals held that the House was without constitutional authority to order Chadha's deportation; accordingly it directed the Attorney General "to cease and desist from taking any steps to deport this alien based upon the resolution enacted by the House of Representatives." The essence of its holding was that § 244(c)(2) violates the constitutional doctrine of separation of powers.

* * *

* * * [W]e now affirm.

II

Before we address the important question of the constitutionality of the one-House veto provision of § 244(c)(2), we first consider several challenges to the authority of this Court to resolve the issue raised.

* * *

G

Political Question

It is also argued that these cases present a nonjusticiable political question because Chadha is merely challenging Congress' authority under the Naturalization Clause, U.S. Const., Art. I, § 8, cl. 4, and the Necessary and Proper Clause, U.S. Const., Art. I, § 8, cl. 18. It is argued that Congress' Art. I power "To establish an uniform Rule of Naturalization," combined with the Necessary and Proper Clause, grants it unreviewable authority over the regulation of aliens. The plenary authority of Congress over aliens under Art. I, § 8, cl. 4, is not open to question, but what is challenged here is whether Congress has chosen a constitutionally permissible means of implementing that power. As we made clear in *Buckley v. Valeo,* "Congress has plenary authority in all cases in which it has substantive legislative jurisdiction, *McCulloch v. Maryland,* so long as the exercise of that authority does not offend some other constitutional restriction."

A brief review of those factors which may indicate the presence of a nonjusticiable political question satisfies us that our assertion of jurisdiction over these cases does no violence to the political question doctrine. As identified in *Baker v. Carr,* a political question may arise when any one of the following circumstances is present:

"(1) a textually demonstrable constitutional commitment of the issue to a coordinate political department; or (2) a lack of judicially discoverable and manageable standards for resolving it; or (3) the impossibility of deciding without an initial policy determination of a kind clearly for nonjudicial discretion; or (4) the impossibility of a court's undertaking independent resolution without expressing lack of the respect due coordinate branches of government; or (5) an unusual need for unquestioning adherence to a political decision already made; or (6) the potentiality of embarrassment from multifarious pronouncements by various departments on one question."

Congress apparently directs its assertion of nonjusticiability to the first of the *Baker* factors by asserting that Chadha's claim is "an assault on the legislative authority to enact Section 244(c)(2)." But if this turns the question into a political question virtually every challenge to the constitutionality of a statute would be a political question. Chadha indeed argues that one House of Congress cannot constitutionally veto the Attorney General's decision to allow him to remain in this country. No policy underlying the political question doctrine suggests that Congress or the Executive, or both acting in concert and in compliance with Art. I, can decide the constitutionality of a statute; that is a decision for the courts.

Other *Baker* factors are likewise inapplicable to this case. As we discuss more fully below, Art. I provides the "judicially discoverable and manageable standards" of *Baker* for resolving the question presented by this case. Those standards forestall reliance by this Court on nonjudicial "policy determinations" or any showing of disrespect for a coordinate branch. Similarly, if Chadha's arguments are accepted, § 244(c)(2) cannot stand, and, since the constitutionality of that statute is for this Court to resolve, there is no possibility of "multifarious pronouncements" on this question.

It is correct that this controversy may, in a sense, be termed "political." But the presence of constitutional issues with significant political overtones does not automatically invoke the political question doctrine. Resolution of litigation challenging the constitutional authority of one of the three branches cannot be evaded by courts because the issues have political implications in the sense urged by Congress. *Marbury v. Madison* was also a "political" case, involving as it did claims under a judicial commission alleged to have been duly signed by the President but not delivered. But "courts cannot reject as 'no law suit' a bona fide controversy as to whether some action denominated 'political' exceeds constitutional authority." *Baker v. Carr.*

[The Court proceeded to hold that § 244(c)(2) was unconstitutional because it permitted either House of Congress to "legislate" without following the requirements that the Constitution lays out for legislation: passage by both Houses of Congress, and either Presidential assent or a Congressional override of a Presidential veto.]

* * *

NOTES AND QUESTIONS

1. The issue on the merits—whether legislative vetoes comport with separation of powers principles—is both intriguing and immensely important in public law generally. One Senator counted some 295 legislative veto provisions enacted in the fifty-year period that preceded *Chadha*. James Abourezk, *The Congressional Veto: A Contemporary Response to Executive Encroachment on Legislative Prerogatives,* 52 Ind.L.Rev. 323, 324 (1977); see also Peter L. Strauss, *Was there a Baby in the Bathwater? A Comment on the Supreme Court's Legislative Veto Decision,* 1983 Duke L.J. 789. We shall leave to courses in constitutional law and administrative law the difficult questions raised on the merits.

2. More relevant here is that this case remains the only occasion to date on which the Supreme Court has struck down a federal statutory provision concerned with the admission or the expulsion of noncitizens. How could the Court even get to the merits of the constitutional issue? As you have seen, the Supreme Court, in case after case, for almost one hundred years, has been emphasizing Congress's "plenary" power to decide which classes of noncitizens to deport. The Court has reminded us repeatedly that this Congressional determination is "conclusive upon the Judiciary," to quote the early cases, or at least "largely immune from judicial scrutiny," to quote the more modern decisions. Yet in *Chadha* the Court makes clear that Congress's decision is *not* immune from judicial scrutiny. Congress attempted to deport certain noncitizens, subject to an exception that it defined to include the absence of a one-House veto. The Court scrutinizes the statute and finds it unconstitutional.

In explaining how it could review the exercise of a "plenary" congressional power, the Court says: "The plenary authority of Congress over aliens under Art. I, § 8, cl. 4 [the naturalization clause] is not open to question, but what is challenged here is whether Congress has chosen a constitutionally permissible means of implementing that power." In what sense, then, is the congressional power "plenary"? Does "plenary" simply mean full—i.e., extending to a broad range of related subjects? Very possibly it should, but is that really the sense in which previous cases used the term when they rejected arguments that particular exercises of the power had violated the Bill of Rights?

3. The Court's application of the political question criteria assembled in *Baker v. Carr* (decided in 1962) leads it to hold the constitutional issue justiciable. Its analysis of those factors seems straightforward. But what happened to the intimate connection between immigration and foreign policy that had so profoundly influenced the previous decisions? Was the statutory provision in *Chadha* any less reflective of foreign policy judg-

ments than were the provisions that had received such great judicial deference in the previous cases?

4. Although the House of Representatives cited in its brief all the familiar plenary power doctrine cases that you read earlier,[11] the opinion in *Chadha* does not acknowledge them. Have they been implicitly overruled? Or can they be distinguished? Does it matter that in the previous cases the constitutional issues on the merits involved individual rights while in *Chadha* the constitutional issue concerns separation of powers? Exactly why should that distinction be legally relevant to the issue of justiciability? Are we simply back to the procedural/substantive distinction and the implicit labelling of separation of powers as "procedural"? See Stephen H. Legomsky, *Immigration Law and the Principle of Plenary Congressional Power,* 1984 Supreme Ct.Rev. 255, 303.

By the same token, could not the technique employed in *Chadha*— examining the *Baker* factors and concluding that they do not dictate nonjusticiability—be invoked in most future cases in which noncitizens challenge the constitutionality of Congress's deportation decisions? Could the same reasoning be invoked even in exclusion cases? In short, where are we now?

5. For an interesting personal account of Jagdish Chadha and the political and legal battles that his case spawned (complete with photographs), see Barbara H. Craig, Chadha—The Story of an Epic Constitutional Struggle (1988). In 1984 Chadha became a naturalized citizen of the United States. *Id.* at 3–4.

Zadvydas v. Davis

Supreme Court of the United States, 2001.
533 U.S. 678, 121 S.Ct. 2491, 150 L.Ed.2d 653.

■ JUSTICE BREYER delivered the opinion of the Court.

When an alien has been found to be unlawfully present in the United States and a final order of removal has been entered, the Government ordinarily secures the alien's removal during a subsequent 90–day statutory "removal period," during which time the alien normally is held in custody.

A special statute authorizes further detention if the Government fails to remove the alien during those 90 days. It says:

"An alien ordered removed [1] who is inadmissible ..., [2] [who is deportable on certain crime-related and certain other grounds,] or [3] who has been determined by the Attorney General to be a risk to the community or unlikely to comply with the order of removal, may be detained beyond the removal period and, if released, shall be subject to [certain] terms of supervision...." *INA § 241*(a)(6).

11. See Second Supplemental Brief of House of Reps. at 10–22.

In these cases, we must decide whether this post-removal-period statute authorizes the Attorney General to detain a removable alien indefinitely beyond the removal period or only for a period reasonably necessary to secure the alien's removal. We deal here with aliens who were admitted to the United States but subsequently ordered removed. Aliens who have not yet gained initial admission to this country would present a very different question. Based on our conclusion that indefinite detention of aliens in the former category would raise serious constitutional concerns, we construe the statute to contain an implicit "reasonable time" limitation, the application of which is subject to federal court review.

I

A

* * *

Related Immigration and Naturalization Service (INS) regulations add that the INS District Director will initially review the alien's records to decide whether further detention or release under supervision is warranted after the 90–day removal period expires. If the decision is to detain, then an INS panel will review the matter further, at the expiration of a 3–month period or soon thereafter. And the panel will decide, on the basis of records and a possible personal interview, between still further detention or release under supervision. * * * To authorize release, the panel must find that the alien is not likely to be violent, to pose a threat to the community, to flee if released, or to violate the conditions of release. * * * If the panel decides against release, it must review the matter again within a year, and can review it earlier if conditions change.

B

1

We consider two separate instances of detention. The first concerns Kestutis Zadvydas, a resident alien who was born, apparently of Lithuanian parents, in a displaced persons camp in Germany in 1948. When he was eight years old, Zadvydas immigrated to the United States with his parents and other family members, and he has lived here ever since.

Zadvydas has a long criminal record, involving drug crimes, attempted robbery, attempted burglary, and theft. He has a history of flight, from both criminal and deportation proceedings. Most recently, he was convicted of possessing, with intent to distribute, cocaine; sentenced to 16 years' imprisonment; released on parole after two years; taken into INS custody; and, in 1994, ordered deported to Germany.

In 1994, Germany told the INS that it would not accept Zadvydas because he was not a German citizen. Shortly thereafter, Lithuania refused to accept Zadvydas because he was neither a Lithuanian citizen nor a permanent resident. In 1996, the INS asked the Dominican Republic (Zadvydas' wife's country) to accept him, but this effort proved unsuccessful. In 1998, Lithuania rejected, as inadequately documented, Zadvydas' effort to obtain Lithuanian citizenship based on his parents' citizenship; Zadvydas' reapplication is apparently still pending.

The INS kept Zadvydas in custody after expiration of the removal period. In September 1995, Zadvydas filed a petition for a writ of habeas corpus under *28 U.S.C. § 2241* challenging his continued detention. In October 1997, a Federal District Court granted that writ and ordered him released under supervision. In its view, the Government would never succeed in its efforts to remove Zadvydas from the United States, leading to his permanent confinement, contrary to the Constitution.

The Fifth Circuit reversed this decision. It concluded that Zadvydas' detention did not violate the Constitution because eventual deportation was not "impossible," good faith efforts to remove him from the United States continued, and his detention was subject to periodic administrative review.
* * *

2

The second case is that of Kim Ho Ma. Ma was born in Cambodia in 1977. When he was two, his family fled, taking him to refugee camps in Thailand and the Philippines and eventually to the United States, where he has lived as a resident alien since the age of seven. In 1995, at age 17, Ma was involved in a gang-related shooting, convicted of manslaughter, and sentenced to 38 months' imprisonment. He served two years, after which he was released into INS custody.

In light of his conviction of an "aggravated felony," Ma was ordered removed. The 90–day removal period expired in early 1999, but the INS continued to keep Ma in custody, because, in light of his former gang membership, the nature of his crime, and his planned participation in a prison hunger strike, it was "unable to conclude that Mr. Ma would remain nonviolent and not violate the conditions of release."

In 1999 Ma filed a petition for a writ of habeas corpus under *28 U.S.C. § 2241*. A panel of five judges in the Federal District Court for the Western District of Washington, considering Ma's and about 100 similar cases together, issued a joint order holding that the Constitution forbids post-removal-period detention unless there is "a realistic chance that [the] alien will be deported" (thereby permitting classification of the detention as "in aid of deportation"). The District Court then held an evidentiary hearing, decided that there was no "realistic chance" that Cambodia (which has no repatriation treaty with the United States) would accept Ma, and ordered Ma released.

The Ninth Circuit affirmed Ma's release. It concluded, based in part on constitutional concerns, that the statute did not authorize detention for more than a "reasonable time" beyond the 90–day period authorized for removal. And, given the lack of a repatriation agreement with Cambodia, that time had expired upon passage of the 90 days.

* * *

II

We note at the outset that the primary federal habeas corpus statute, *28 U.S.C. § 2241*, confers jurisdiction upon the federal courts to hear these cases. * * *

* * *

III

* * *

The Government argues that the statute means what it literally says. It sets no "limit on the length of time beyond the removal period that an alien who falls within one of the Section 241(a)(6) categories may be detained." Hence, "whether to continue to detain such an alien and, if so, in what circumstances and for how long" is up to the Attorney General, not up to the courts.

"It is a cardinal principle" of statutory interpretation, however, that when an Act of Congress raises "a serious doubt" as to its constitutionality, "this Court will first ascertain whether a construction of the statute is fairly possible by which the question may be avoided." * * * In our view, the statute, read in light of the Constitution's demands, limits an alien's post-removal-period detention to a period reasonably necessary to bring about that alien's removal from the United States. It does not permit indefinite detention.

A

A statute permitting indefinite detention of an alien would raise a serious constitutional problem. The Fifth Amendment's Due Process Clause forbids the Government to "deprive" any "person ... of ... liberty ... without due process of law." Freedom from imprisonment—from government custody, detention, or other forms of physical restraint—lies at the heart of the liberty that Clause protects. And this Court has said that government detention violates that Clause unless the detention is ordered in a criminal proceeding with adequate procedural protections or, in certain special and "narrow" non-punitive "circumstances," where a special justification, such as harm-threatening mental illness, outweighs the "individual's constitutionally protected interest in avoiding physical restraint." The proceedings at issue here are civil, not criminal, and we assume that they are nonpunitive in purpose and effect. There is no sufficiently strong special justification here for indefinite civil detention—at least as administered under this statute. The statute, says the Government, has two regulatory goals: "ensuring the appearance of aliens at future immigration proceedings" and "preventing danger to the community." But by definition the first justification—preventing flight—is weak or nonexistent where removal seems a remote possibility at best. As this Court said in *Jackson v. Indiana*, where detention's goal is no longer practically attainable, detention no longer "bears [a] reasonable relation to the purpose for which the individual [was] committed."

The second justification—protecting the community—does not necessarily diminish in force over time. But we have upheld preventive detention based on dangerousness only when limited to specially dangerous individuals and subject to strong procedural protections. * * *

The civil confinement here at issue is not limited, but potentially permanent. * * * The provision authorizing detention does not apply narrowly to "a small segment of particularly dangerous individuals," say suspected terrorists, but broadly to aliens ordered removed for many and various reasons, including tourist visa violations. * * *

Moreover, the sole procedural protections available to the alien are found in administrative proceedings, where the alien bears the burden of proving he is not dangerous, without (in the Government's view) significant later judicial review. This Court has suggested, however, that the Constitution may well preclude granting "an administrative body the unreviewable authority to make determinations implicating fundamental rights." * * *

The Government argues that, from a constitutional perspective, alien status itself can justify indefinite detention, and points to *Shaughnessy v. United States ex rel. Mezei* as support. That case involved a once lawfully admitted alien who left the United States, returned after a trip abroad, was refused admission, and was left on Ellis Island, indefinitely detained there because the Government could not find another country to accept him. The Court held that Mezei's detention did not violate the Constitution.

Although Mezei, like the present cases, involves indefinite detention, it differs from the present cases in a critical respect. As the Court emphasized, the alien's extended departure from the United States required him to seek entry into this country once again. His presence on Ellis Island did not count as entry into the United States. Hence, he was "treated," for constitutional purposes, "as if stopped at the border." And that made all the difference.

The distinction between an alien who has effected an entry into the United States and one who has never entered runs throughout immigration law. * * * It is well established that certain constitutional protections available to persons inside the United States are unavailable to aliens outside of our geographic borders. But once an alien enters the country, the legal circumstance changes, for the Due Process Clause applies to all "persons" within the United States, including aliens, whether their presence here is lawful, unlawful, temporary, or permanent. * * *

* * *

In light of this critical distinction between Mezei and the present cases, Mezei does not offer the Government significant support, and we need not consider the aliens' claim that subsequent developments have undermined Mezei's legal authority. Nor are we aware of any other authority that would support JUSTICE KENNEDY's limitation of due process protection for removable aliens to freedom from detention that is arbitrary or capricious.

The Government also looks for support to cases holding that Congress has "plenary power" to create immigration law, and that the judicial branch must defer to executive and legislative branch decisionmaking in that area. But that power is subject to important constitutional limitations. See *INS v. Chadha* (Congress must choose "a constitutionally permissible means of implementing" that power); *The Chinese Exclusion Case* (congressional authority limited "by the Constitution itself and considerations of public policy and justice which control, more or less, the conduct of all civilized nations"). In these cases, we focus upon those limitations. In doing so, we nowhere deny the right of Congress to remove aliens, to subject them to supervision with conditions when released from detention, or to incarcerate them where appropriate for violations of those conditions. * * *

Nor do the cases before us require us to consider the political branches' authority to control entry into the United States. Hence we leave no "unprotected spot in the Nation's armor." Neither do we consider terrorism or other special circumstances where special arguments might be made for forms of preventive detention and for heightened deference to the judgments of the political branches with respect to matters of national security. The sole foreign policy consideration the Government mentions here is the concern lest courts interfere with "sensitive" repatriation negotiations. But neither the Government nor the dissents explain how a habeas court's efforts to determine the likelihood of repatriation, if handled with appropriate sensitivity, could make a significant difference in this respect.

Finally, the Government argues that, whatever liberty interest the aliens possess, it is "greatly diminished" by their lack of a legal right to "live at large in this country." The choice, however, is not between imprisonment and the alien "living at large." It is between imprisonment and supervision under release conditions that may not be violated. And, for the reasons we have set forth, we believe that an alien's liberty interest is, at the least, strong enough to raise a serious question as to whether, irrespective of the procedures used, the Constitution permits detention that is indefinite and potentially permanent.

B

Despite this constitutional problem, if "Congress has made its intent" in the statute "clear, 'we must give effect to that intent.' " We cannot find here, however, any clear indication of congressional intent to grant the Attorney General the power to hold indefinitely in confinement an alien ordered removed. And that is so whether protecting the community from dangerous aliens is a primary or (as we believe) secondary statutory purpose. After all, the provision is part of a statute that has as its basic purpose effectuating an alien's removal. Why should we assume that Congress saw the alien's dangerousness as unrelated to this purpose?

The Government points to the statute's word "may." But while "may" suggests discretion, it does not necessarily suggest unlimited discretion. * * *

We have found nothing in the history of these statutes that clearly demonstrates a congressional intent to authorize indefinite, perhaps permanent, detention. Consequently, interpreting the statute to avoid a serious constitutional threat, we conclude that, once removal is no longer reasonably foreseeable, continued detention is no longer authorized by statute. * * *

IV

The Government seems to argue that, even under our interpretation of the statute, a federal habeas court would have to accept the Government's view about whether the implicit statutory limitation is satisfied in a particular case, conducting little or no independent review of the matter. In our view, that is not so. Whether a set of particular circumstances amounts to detention within, or beyond, a period reasonably necessary to secure removal is determinative of whether the detention is, or is not, pursuant to statutory authority. The basic federal habeas corpus statute grants the federal courts authority to answer that question. See *28 U.S.C. § 2241*(c)(3) (granting courts authority to determine whether detention is "in violation of the . . . laws . . . of the United States"). * * *

In answering that basic question, the habeas court must ask whether the detention in question exceeds a period reasonably necessary to secure removal. It should measure reasonableness primarily in terms of the statute's basic purpose, namely assuring the alien's presence at the moment of removal. Thus, if removal is not reasonably foreseeable, the court should hold continued detention unreasonable and no longer authorized by statute. In that case, of course, the alien's release may and should be conditioned on any of the various forms of supervised release that are appropriate in the circumstances, and the alien may no doubt be returned to custody upon a violation of those conditions. And if removal is reasonably foreseeable, the habeas court should consider the risk of the alien's committing further crimes as a factor potentially justifying confinement within that reasonable removal period.

We recognize, as the Government points out, that review must take appropriate account of the greater immigration-related expertise of the Executive Branch, of the serious administrative needs and concerns inherent in the necessarily extensive INS efforts to enforce this complex statute, and the Nation's need to "speak with one voice" in immigration matters. But we believe that courts can take appropriate account of such matters without abdicating their legal responsibility to review the lawfulness of an alien's continued detention.

Ordinary principles of judicial review in this area recognize primary Executive Branch responsibility. They counsel judges to give expert agencies decisionmaking leeway in matters that invoke their expertise. They recognize Executive Branch primacy in foreign policy matters. And they consequently require courts to listen with care when the Government's foreign policy judgments, including, for example, the status of repatriation negotiations, are at issue, and to grant the Government appropriate leeway when its judgments rest upon foreign policy expertise.

We realize that recognizing this necessary Executive leeway will often call for difficult judgments. In order to limit the occasions when courts will need to make them, we think it practically necessary to recognize some presumptively reasonable period of detention. * * *

While an argument can be made for confining any presumption to 90 days, we doubt that when Congress shortened the removal period to 90 days in 1996 it believed that all reasonably foreseeable removals could be accomplished in that time. We do have reason to believe, however, that Congress previously doubted the constitutionality of detention for more than six months. Consequently, for the sake of uniform administration in the federal courts, we recognize that period. After this 6–month period, once the alien provides good reason to believe that there is no significant likelihood of removal in the reasonably foreseeable future, the Government must respond with evidence sufficient to rebut that showing. And for detention to remain reasonable, as the period of prior post-removal confinement grows, what counts as the "reasonably foreseeable future" conversely would have to shrink. This 6–month presumption, of course, does not mean that every alien not removed must be released after six months. To the contrary, an alien may be held in confinement until it has been determined that there is no significant likelihood of removal in the reasonably foreseeable future.

* * *

■ JUSTICE SCALIA, with whom JUSTICE THOMAS joins, dissenting.

I join Part I of JUSTICE KENNEDY's dissent, which establishes the Attorney General's clear statutory authority to detain criminal aliens with no specified time limit. I write separately because I do not believe that, as JUSTICE KENNEDY suggests in Part II of his opinion, there may be some situations in which the courts can order release. * * * This claim can be repackaged as freedom from "physical restraint" or freedom from "indefinite detention," but it is at bottom a claimed right of release into this country by an individual who concededly has no legal right to be here. There is no such constitutional right.

Like a criminal alien under final order of removal, an inadmissible alien at the border has no right to be in the United States. *The Chinese Exclusion Case.* In *Mezei,* we upheld potentially indefinite detention of such an inadmissible alien whom the Government was unable to return anywhere else. * * * While four members of the Court thought that Mezei deserved greater procedural protections (the Attorney General had refused to divulge any information as to why Mezei was being detained), no Justice asserted that Mezei had a substantive constitutional right to release into this country. And Justice Jackson's dissent, joined by Justice Frankfurter, affirmatively asserted the opposite, with no contradiction from the Court: "Due process does not invest any alien with a right to enter the United States, nor confer on those admitted the right to remain against the national will. Nothing in the Constitution requires admission or sufferance of aliens hostile to our scheme of government." Insofar as a claimed legal right to release into this country is concerned, an alien under final order of removal stands on an equal footing with an inadmissible alien at the threshold of entry: He has no such right.

The Court expressly declines to apply or overrule Mezei but attempts to distinguish it—or, I should rather say, to obscure it in a legal fog. First, the Court claims that "the distinction between an alien who has effected an entry into the United States and one who has never entered runs throughout immigration law." True enough, but only where that distinction makes perfect sense: with regard to the question of what procedures are necessary to prevent entry, as opposed to what procedures are necessary to eject a person already in the United States. * * * The Court's citation of *Wong Wing* for the proposition that we have "held that the Due Process Clause protects an alien subject to a final order of deportation" is arguably relevant. That case at least involved aliens under final order of deportation. But all it held is that they could not be subjected to the punishment of hard labor without a judicial trial. I am sure they cannot be tortured, as well—but neither prohibition has anything to do with their right to be released into the United States. Nor does Wong Wing show that the rights of detained aliens subject to final order of deportation are different from the rights of aliens arrested and detained at the border—unless the Court believes that the detained alien in Mezei could have been set to hard labor.

Mezei thus stands unexplained and undistinguished by the Court's opinion. We are offered no justification why an alien under a valid and final order of removal—which has totally extinguished whatever right to presence in this country he possessed—has any greater due process right to be released into the country than an alien at the border seeking entry. Congress undoubtedly thought that both groups of aliens—inadmissible aliens at the threshold and criminal aliens under final order of removal—could be constitutionally detained on the same terms, since it provided the authority to detain both groups in the very same statutory provision. * * *

■ JUSTICE KENNEDY, with whom the CHIEF JUSTICE joins, and with whom JUSTICE SCALIA and JUSTICE THOMAS join as to Part I, dissenting.

The Court says its duty is to avoid a constitutional question. It deems the duty performed by interpreting a statute in obvious disregard of congressional intent; curing the resulting gap by writing a statutory amendment of its own; committing its own grave constitutional error by arrogating to the Judicial Branch the power to summon high officers of the Executive to assess their progress in conducting some of the Nation's most sensitive negotiations with foreign powers; and then likely releasing into our general population at least hundreds of removable or inadmissible aliens who have been found by fair procedures to be flight risks, dangers to the community, or both. Far from avoiding a constitutional question, the Court's ruling causes systemic dislocation in the balance of powers, thus raising serious constitutional concerns not just for the cases at hand but for the Court's own view of its proper authority. Any supposed respect the

Court seeks in not reaching the constitutional question is outweighed by the intrusive and erroneous exercise of its own powers. In the guise of judicial restraint the Court ought not to intrude upon the other branches. The constitutional question the statute presents, it must be acknowledged, may be a significant one in some later case; but it ought not to drive us to an incorrect interpretation of the statute. The Court having reached the wrong result for the wrong reason, this respectful dissent is required.

I

* * *

By this statute, Congress confers upon the Attorney General discretion to detain an alien ordered removed. It gives express authorization to detain "beyond the removal period." * * * The issue to be determined is whether the authorization to detain beyond the removal period is subject to the implied, nontextual limitation that the detention be no longer than reasonably necessary to effect removal to another country. The majority invokes the canon of constitutional doubt to read that implied term into the statute. One can accept the premise that a substantial constitutional question is presented by the prospect of lengthy, even unending, detention in some instances; but the statutory construction the Court adopts should be rejected in any event. The interpretation has no basis in the language or structure of the INA and in fact contradicts and defeats the purpose set forth in the express terms of the statutory text.

* * * [The Court's] analysis is not consistent with our precedents explaining the limits of the constitutional doubt rule. The rule allows courts to choose among constructions which are "fairly possible," not to " 'press statutory construction to the point of disingenuous evasion even to avoid a constitutional question' " Were a court to find two interpretations of equal plausibility, it should choose the construction that avoids confronting a constitutional question. The majority's reading of the statutory authorization to "detain beyond the removal period," however, is not plausible. * * *

Other provisions in § 241 itself do link the requirement of a reasonable time period to the removal process. * * * That Congress chose to impose the limitation in these sections and not in § 241(a)(6) is evidence of its intent to measure the detention period by other standards. * * *

The 6–month period invented by the Court, even when modified by its sliding standard of reasonableness for certain repatriation negotiations, makes the statutory purpose to protect the community ineffective. The risk to the community exists whether or not the repatriation negotiations have some end in sight; in fact, when the negotiations end, the risk may be greater. * * *

* * *

The majority's unanchored interpretation ignores another indication that the Attorney General's detention discretion was not limited to this truncated period. Section 241(a)(6) permits continued detention not only of removable aliens but also of inadmissible aliens, for instance those stopped at the border before entry. Congress provides for detention of both categories within the same statutory grant of authority. Accepting the majority's interpretation, then, there are two possibilities, neither of which is sustainable. On the one hand, it may be that the majority's rule applies to both categories of aliens, in which case we are asked to assume that Congress intended to restrict the discretion it could confer upon the Attorney General so that all inadmissible aliens must be allowed into our community within six months. On the other hand, the majority's logic might be that inadmissible and removable aliens can be treated differently. Yet it is not a plausible construction of § 241(a)(6) to imply a time limit as to one class but not to another. The text does not admit of this possibility. As a result, it is difficult to see why "aliens who have not yet gained initial admission to this country would present a very different question."

* * *

The majority's interpretation, moreover, defeats the very repatriation goal in which it professes such interest. The Court rushes to substitute a judicial judgment for the Executive's discretion and authority. As the Government represents to us, judicial orders requiring release of removable aliens, even on a temporary basis, have the potential to undermine the obvious necessity that the Nation speak with one voice on immigration and foreign affairs matters. The result of the Court's rule is that, by refusing to accept repatriation of their own nationals, other countries can effect the release of these individuals back into the American community. If their own nationals are now at large in the United States, the nation of origin may ignore or disclaim responsibility to accept their return. The interference with sensitive foreign relations becomes even more acute where hostility or tension characterizes the relationship, for other countries can use the fact of judicially mandated release to their strategic advantage, refusing the return of their nationals to force dangerous aliens upon us. One of the more alarming aspects of the Court's new venture into foreign affairs management is the suggestion that the district court can expand or contract the reasonable period of detention based on its own assessment of the course of negotiations with foreign powers. The Court says it will allow the Executive to perform its duties on its own for six months; after that, foreign relations go into judicially supervised receivership.

* * *

In addition to weakening the hand of our Government, court ordered release cannot help but encourage dilatory and obstructive tactics by aliens who, emboldened by the Court's new rule, have good reason not to cooperate by making their own repatriation or transfer seem foreseeable. An alien ordered deported also has less incentive to cooperate or to facilitate expeditious removal when he has been released, even on a supervised basis, than does an alien held at an Immigration and Naturalization Service (INS) detention facility. Neither the alien nor his family would find any urgency in assisting with a petition to other countries to accept the alien back if the alien could simply remain in the United States indefinitely.

* * *

The majority's rule is not limited to aliens once lawfully admitted. Today's result may well mandate the release of those aliens who first gained entry illegally or by fraud, and, indeed, is broad enough to require even that inadmissible and excludable aliens detained at the border be set free in our community. * * *

* * *

It is curious that the majority would approve of continued detention beyond the 90–day period, or, for that matter, during the 90–day period, where deportation is not reasonably foreseeable. If the INS cannot detain an alien because he is dangerous, it would seem irrelevant to the Constitution or to the majority's presumption that the INS has detained the alien for only a little while. The reason detention is permitted at all is that a removable alien does not have the same liberty interest as a citizen does. The Court cannot bring itself to acknowledge this established proposition. Likewise, it is far from evident under the majority's theory why the INS can condition and supervise the release of aliens who are not removable in the reasonably foreseeable future, or why "the alien may no doubt be returned to custody upon a violation of those conditions." It is true that threat of revocation of supervised release is necessary to make the supervised release itself effective, a fact even counsel for Zadvydas acknowledged. If that is so, however, the whole foundation for the Court's position collapses.

* * *

II

The aliens' claims are substantial; their plight is real. They face continued detention, perhaps for life, unless it is shown they no longer present a flight risk or a danger to the community. In a later case the specific circumstances of a detention may present a substantial constitutional question. That is not a reason, however, for framing a rule which ignores the law governing alien status.

As persons within our jurisdiction, the aliens are entitled to the protection of the Due Process Clause. * * *. No party to this proceeding contests the initial premise that the aliens have been determined to be removable after a fair hearing under lawful and proper procedures. * * *

* * *

* * * [I]t must be made clear these aliens are in a position far different from aliens with a lawful right to remain here. They are removable, and their rights must be defined in accordance with that status. * * *

* * *

* * * Neither Zadvydas nor Ma argues that the Attorney General has applied the procedures in an improper manner; they challenge only the Attorney General's authority to detain at all where removal is no longer foreseeable. The Government has conceded that habeas jurisdiction is available under *28 U.S.C. § 2241* to review an alien's challenge to detention following entry of a final order of deportation, although it does not detail what the nature of the habeas review would be. As a result, we need not decide today whether, and to what extent, a habeas court could review the Attorney General's determination that a detained alien continues to be dangerous or a flight risk. Given the undeniable deprivation of liberty caused by the detention, there might be substantial questions concerning the severity necessary for there to be a community risk; the adequacy of judicial review in specific cases where it is alleged there is no justification for concluding an alien is dangerous or a flight risk; and other issues. These matters are not presented to us here.

* * *

NOTES AND QUESTIONS

1. Until just before the decision in *Zadvydas,* the former INS was holding approximately 3000 persons in indefinite detention. 78 IR 397 (Feb. 26, 2001). The courts were divided concerning the constitutionality of indefinite detention. A good synthesis of the pre-*Zadvydas* decisions is Francesco Isgro, *Immigration Litigation Update: Constitutionality of Indefinite Detention,* 28 Migration World, issue 1–2, at 46–48 (2000).

2. As you will see repeatedly throughout this book, liberal statutory interpretation has been a time-honored judicial device for escaping some of the harsher applications of the plenary power doctrine. For a fuller treatment of the sharp contrast between the courts' restrictive readings of the Constitution and their liberal (and nonliteral) statutory interpretations in immigration cases, see Stephen H. Legomsky, Immigration and the Judiciary—Law and Politics in Britain and America at 155–70, 177–222 (1987).

3. On the statutory interpretation question here, Justice Kennedy's dissent argues that the majority's reading is not even "plausible." Do you agree? Is it clear that "beyond the removal period" means "forever?"

4. One of the Court's concerns is that the statute empowers administrative officials to make unreviewable determinations concerning fundamental rights. Suppose Congress were to amend the statute to transfer the detention decision from administrative officials to article III judges. Alternatively, suppose Congress were to leave such determinations in the hands of administrative officials but authorize judicial review of the reasonableness of those decisions. Would either amendment satisfy the Court's constitutional concerns?

5. In form, the decision in *Zadvydas* is one of statutory interpretation. But the rationale is that a contrary interpretation of the statute would raise "a serious constitutional problem." Still, positing a serious "problem" is not quite the same as concluding that indefinite detention would in fact

be unconstitutional. Suppose, therefore, Congress were now to amend the statute to say: "The Attorney General shall detain all noncitizens who have been ordered removed, until removal can be accomplished or until he concludes that the noncitizen is not likely to abscond or to threaten the public safety, whichever is earlier. This provision is specifically intended to authorize even indefinite and lifelong detention, regardless of the likelihood of eventual removal." Would the Court declare such a statute unconstitutional?

6.   Citing *Chadha*, the Court says that even the plenary power doctrine is "subject to important constitutional limitations." If that is so, then what does "plenary" mean and what is left of the doctrine? As was true after *Chadha*, it is not clear where this language leaves us. One possibility is that the plenary power doctrine no longer requires *any* special judicial deference to Congress in immigration matters—only a recognition that, for purposes of the exclusive federal power to regulate immigration, the term "immigration" is broadly defined. A second, more likely possibility is that plenary power still signifies special judicial deference but that that deference is only a matter of degree; the greater the deprivation of individual liberty, the more insistent the Court will be on a substantial explanation for the policy. A third possibility is that the Court in *Chadha* has in mind the line of authority recognizing procedural due process as an exception to the congressional plenary power in expulsion cases. See pages 158–63 above. That interpretation taken alone would not account for the result in *Zadvydas*, though, because the individual interest at stake was the substantive interest in being free of indefinite detention, not just the interest in a fair procedure. A fourth possibility is that the Court's incursion into plenary congressional power is detention-specific and that the doctrine remains intact with respect to decisions concerning whom to admit or expel. Section III.A of the Court's opinion does, after all, rest heavily on the exceptional liberty interests implicated by imprisonment. As to that, however, see *Demore v. Hyung Joon Kim*, excerpted below.

Professor Peter Spiro (writing before the decision in *Demore*, below), predicted that *Zadvydas* (and one other case, *Nguyen v. INS*, 533 U.S. 53, 121 S.Ct. 2053, 150 L.Ed.2d 115 (2001), discussed on pages 175–76 above), together augured the demise of the plenary power doctrine. Peter J. Spiro, *Explaining the End of Plenary Power*, 16 Georgetown Immigration L.J. 339 (2002). Others disagree. See, e.g., T. Alexander Aleinikoff, *Detaining Plenary Power: The Meaning and Impact of* Zadvydas v. Davis, 16 Georgetown Immigration L.J. 365 (2002); Michele R. Pistone, *A Times Sensitive Response to Professor Aleinikoff's* Detaining Plenary Power, 16 Georgetown Immigration L.J. 391 (2002).

7.   Justice Scalia, dissenting, says the plaintiffs claim a "constitutional right of supervised release into the United States." He then concludes that the plaintiffs have no more right to such release than do noncitizens who are on the threshold of initial entry. Do you agree with either his characterization of their claim or his conclusion?

8.   During oral argument, Justice Scalia posed an interesting question: If Congress can constitutionally prescribe life sentences for noncitizens who are convicted of designated crimes, why is indefinite detention (a lesser sanction, in his view) unconstitutional? First, had you been counsel for Mr. Zadvydas, how would you have responded? Second, now that this case has been decided, suppose Congress were to pass a law that makes indefinite detention a formal part of the criminal sentence for any noncitizen convicted of certain designated federal crimes? (Assume the new law defines indefinite detention as lasting until the earlier of the person's removal from the United States or the court's determination that the person is unlikely to abscond or threaten the public safety.) Would such a statute be constitutional?

9.   Justice Kennedy believes that the majority opinion impermissibly obstructs the executive branch in its dealings with foreign governments, particularly with respect to sensitive negotiations over the return of foreign nationals. Is he convincing?

10.   Justice Kennedy makes another interesting point. If the only acceptable reason for detaining noncitizens pending removal is to secure their eventual removal, then why, he asks, does the majority allow automatic detention even during the first 90 days (or, for that matter, the first six months)?

11.   On remand in *Ma*, the Ninth Circuit found there was "no reasonable likelihood that the INS will be able to accomplish Ma's removal in the reasonably foreseeable future." The court relied both on the absence of a repatriation agreement with Cambodia and on the slim chances of such an agreement being concluded. *Kim Ho Ma v. Ashcroft*, 257 F.3d 1095, 1099 (9th Cir. 2001).

12.   The terrorist attacks of September 11, 2001 occurred just two months after *Zadvydas*, while the Justice Department was drafting its formal plan for implementing the decision. The resulting regulations established procedures for determining whether a detainee's removal is likely in the reasonably foreseeable future. If removal is found likely, detention may continue, subject to review every six months. If removal is found not likely, the regulations generally require release but authorize appropriate conditions of supervision. Upon violation of those conditions, the person may be returned to custody until the next six-month review. 8 C.F.R. § 241.13(i) (2004).

Citing the Supreme Court's caveat that the *Zadvydas* case did not involve "particularly dangerous individuals, say suspected terrorists," see page 195 above, the regulation authorizes indefinite detention of certain noncitizens even when removal is found not to be likely in the reasonably foreseeable future. It lays out four such categories—highly contagious diseases, adverse foreign policy consequences, significant national security or terrorism risks, and other individuals found "specially dangerous" because of convictions of crimes of violence or mental conditions. 8 C.F.R. § 241.14(b, c, d, f) (2004). The procedures vary by category. One court of appeals has cast doubt on the validity of at least some of those exceptions.

In *Tuan Thai v. Ashcroft*, 366 F.3d 790 (9th Cir. 2004), the court held that the Supreme Court did not intend to permit an exception for the dangers posed by a mentally ill detainee—any more, the court said, than for the dangers of convicted criminals. The public is already safeguarded, the court observed, by state laws that authorize the involuntary civil commitment of dangerous mental patients.

Other Justice Department devices for circumventing *Zadvydas* have included imposing conditions of release that it knows the person cannot meet (e.g. setting a high bond) and taking released prisoners back into custody after alleging violations of the conditions of release. See Thomas Hutchins, *Detention of Aliens: An Overview of Current Law*, April 2003 Immigration Briefings, at 10.

In the meantime, Congress had already enacted the USA PATRIOT Act of 2001. Section 412 of that Act authorizes the Attorney General to "certify" any noncitizen, including an LPR, whom the Attorney General "has reasonable grounds to believe" is either inadmissible or deportable on certain terrorism or other national security grounds or "is engaged in any other activity that endangers the national security of the United States." INA § 236A(a)(3). Upon certification, the Act explicitly mandates detention until the person is either removed or found not to be removable, *id.* § 236A(a)(1, 2, 6), and explicitly authorizes *indefinite* detention in renewable six-month increments. *Id.* § 236A(a)(6). At this writing, the Attorney General has yet to invoke the certification authority, opting instead to use a number of other detention powers. See generally chapter 10, section A, below.

13.   The Australian High Court, contrary to *Zadvydas*, has upheld the indefinite detention of a stateless person whom no other country would take. See *Al-Kateb v. Godwin* [2004] HCA 37 (6 Aug. 2004). Since Australia does not have an entrenched bill of rights (its Constitution, while entrenched, deals almost exclusively with federalism and separation of powers), parliamentary enactments are legally unrestrained to that extent.

––––––––

In the light of *Zadvydas*, may the government detain *inadmissible* noncitizens indefinitely when removal cannot be effected? Attorney General John Ashcroft thought so. In his post-decision memorandum to the former INS, Ashcroft argued that nothing in the *Zadvydas* decision affects noncitizens who are "legally still at our borders." See Memorandum from John Ashcroft, Attorney General, to Acting Commissioner of the INS (July 19, 2001), reproduced in 6 BIB 798 et seq. (Aug. 1, 2001), at 799. The issue affects not only those who are physically at ports of entry, but also those who have been paroled into the United States under INA § 212(d)(5)—particularly the Cuban Marielitos (see pages 156–58 above). See generally David A. Martin, *Graduated Application of Constitutional Protections for Aliens: The Real Meaning of* Zadvydas v. Davis, 2001 Supreme Ct. Rev. 47

(arguing that content of due process should reflect hierarchy of differing noncitizen categories).

The lower courts quickly divided. Compare, e.g., *Rosales-Garcia v. Holland*, 322 F.3d 386 (6th Cir. 2003); *Lin Guo Xi v. INS*, 298 F.3d 832 (9th Cir. 2002) (both extending *Zadvydas* to inadmissible noncitizens) with *Sierra v. Romaine*, 347 F.3d 559 (3d Cir. 2003); *Borrero v. Aljets*, 325 F.3d 1003 (8th Cir. 2003) (both holding *Zadvydas* inapplicable to inadmissible noncitizens).

The decisions in *Rosales-Garcia* and *Lin Guo Xi* illustrate the risks that dissenting judges take when they make reductio ad absurdum arguments. Both of the dissenting opinions in *Zadvydas* (those of Justices Scalia and Kennedy) argue that Congress used the same language to govern the permissible duration of detention for *deportable* noncitizens who have been ordered removed and *inadmissible* noncitizens who have been ordered removed. (The premise that the dissenters had hoped the majority would adopt was that Congress would not have wanted to preclude indefinite detention in inadmissibility cases). Since the dissenters' position on deportable noncitizens did not prevail in *Zadvydas*, they ended up providing ammunition to inadmissible noncitizens who challenged their indefinite detentions in future cases—presumably the last thing the dissenters wanted to do. In both *Rosales-Garcia* and *Lin Guo Xi*, the courts ran with that ball. Noting the result in *Zadvydas* for deportable noncitizens who had been ordered removed, and observing (as Justices Scalia and Kennedy had done) that on this issue the statutory language treats inadmissible and deportable noncitizens alike, both courts, in 2–1 decisions, extended *Zadvydas* to the inadmissibility context. See *Rosales-Garcia*, 322 F.3d at 404–05; *Lin Guo Xi*, 298 F.3d at 835. Judge Heaney, dissenting in *Borrero*, made a similar argument, quoting the *Zadvydas* dissents of Justices Scalia and Kennedy. *Borrero*, 325 F.3d at 1009. One suspects this is not how Justices Scalia and Kennedy wanted to be remembered.

The strategic point is a more general one. Dissenting judges often face a tactical dilemma. On the one hand, they want their opinions to be as convincing as possible. To that end, they might be tempted to offer reductio ad absurdum arguments, demonstrating that the situation before the court is logically indistinguishable from a hypothetical case in which the same reasoning would later produce radical and undesirable results. On the other hand, once the decision in the present case is handed down, and the very hypothetical case the dissent had imagined now comes before the same court (or a lower court in the same jurisdiction), advocates of the more radical result are now armed with the words of the prior dissenters. The lesson? Reductio ad absurdum arguments are a gamble.

Just how great a gamble that was would soon become evident to Justices Scalia and Kennedy. The first time the Supreme Court had an opportunity to resolve the circuit split, it denied certiorari. See *Snyder v. Rosales–Garcia*, 539 U.S. 941, 123 S.Ct. 2607, 156 L.Ed.2d 627 (2003). But with so many Cuban Marielitos still in detention, the issue would not go away. In the case that follows, the Court extended *Zadvydas* to inadmissible noncitizens by a 7–2 vote.

The Justices who had dissented in *Zadvydas* found themselves caught between a rock and a hard place. Having approved indefinite detention for deportable noncitizens, they presumably would have felt even fewer compunctions about approving it for inadmissible noncitizens. But the question was whether there was a respectable escape from the argument they had pressed so forcefully in their *Zadvydas* dissents—that the statute must have the same meaning in both contexts. One of the *Zadvydas* dissenters, Justice Scalia, thought there was not. Swallowing hard, he ended up writing the majority opinion below, construing the statute to bar the indefinite detention of inadmissible noncitizens. Another of the *Zadvydas* dissenters, Justice Thomas, felt otherwise. He dissented again in the following case.

To give you a better sense of the dialogue between Justices Scalia and Thomas, the excerpts from their dueling opinions have been rearranged in point-counterpoint form:

Clark v. Martinez

Supreme Court of the United States, 2005.
___ U.S. ___, 125 S.Ct. 716, 160 L.Ed.2d 734.

Justice Scalia: The operative language of § 241(a)(6), "may be detained beyond the removal period," applies without differentiation to all three categories of aliens [those who are inadmissible, those who are deportable on certain specified grounds, and those considered a safety risk or flight risk—Ed.] that are its subject. To give these same words a different meaning for each category would be to invent a statute rather than interpret one. As the Court in *Zadvydas* recognized, the statute can be construed "literally" to authorize indefinite detention or (as the Court ultimately held) it can be read to "suggest [less than] unlimited discretion" to detain. It cannot, however, be interpreted to do both at the same time.

Justice Thomas: The majority concedes that *Zadvydas* explicitly reserved the question whether its statutory holding as to *admitted* aliens applied equally to *inadmissible* aliens. This reservation was front and center in *Zadvydas*. * * * The Court reserved this question because the *constitutional* questions raised by detaining inadmissible aliens are different from those raised by detaining admitted aliens. It stated that the detention period in § 241(a)(6) was limited because it "read [the statute] in light of the Constitution's demands."

Justice Scalia: The Government, joined by the dissent, argues that the statutory purpose and the constitutional concerns that influenced our statutory construction in *Zadvydas* are not present for aliens, such as Martinez and Benitez, who have not been admitted to the United States. Be that as it may, it cannot justify giving the *same* detention provision a different meaning when such aliens are involved. It is not at all unusual to give a statute's ambiguous language a limiting construction called for by one of the statute's applications, even though other of the statute's applications, standing alone, would not support the same limitation. The lowest common denominator, as it were, must govern.

Justice Thomas: [T]he Court's lowest common denominator principle allows a limiting construction of an ambiguous statute prompted by constitutional doubts to infect other applications of the statute—even if the statute raises no constitutional doubt as applied to the specific litigant in a given case and even if the constitutionally unproblematic application of the statute to the litigant is severable from the constitutionally dubious applications. The lowest common denominator principle thus allows an end run around black-letter constitutional doctrine governing facial and as-applied constitutional challenges to statutes: A litigant ordinarily cannot attack statutes as constitutionally invalid based on constitutional doubts concerning other litigants or factual circumstances.

Justice Scalia: This accusation misconceives—and fundamentally so—the role played by the canon of constitutional avoidance in statutory interpretation. The canon is not a method of adjudicating constitutional questions by other means. Indeed, one of the canon's chief justifications is that it allows courts to *avoid* the decision of constitutional questions. It is a tool for choosing between competing plausible interpretations of a statutory text, resting on the reasonable presumption that Congress did not intend the alternative which raises serious constitutional doubts. * * * [T]he novel interpretive approach advocated by the dissent * * * would render every statute a chameleon, its meaning subject to change depending on the presence or absence of constitutional concerns in each individual case.

Justice Thomas: The Court misses the point by answering that the canon of constitutional avoidance "is not a method of adjudicating constitutional questions by other means," and that the canon rests on a presumption that "Congress did not intend the alternative which raises serious constitutional doubts." That is true, but in deciding whether a plausible interpretation "raises serious constitutional doubts," a court must employ the usual rules of constitutional adjudication.

Justice Scalia: The dissent's contention that our reading of *Zadvydas* is "implausible" is hard to reconcile with the fact that it is the identical reading espoused by the *Zadvydas* dissenters, who included the author of today's dissent. Worse still, what the *Zadvydas* dissent *did* find "not . . . plausible" was precisely the reading adopted by today's dissent:

> The majority's logic might be that inadmissible and removable aliens can be treated differently. Yet it is not a plausible construction of § 241(a)(6) to imply a time limit as to one class but not to another. The text does not admit of this possibility. As a result, it is difficult to see why "aliens who have not yet gained initial admission to this country would present a very different question." *Zadvydas* (KENNEDY, J., dissenting).

The *Zadvydas* dissent later concluded that the release of "Mariel Cubans and other illegal, inadmissible aliens ... would seem *a necessary consequence of the majority's construction of the statute.*"

Justice Thomas: But the *Zadvydas* majority disagreed with that assumption and adopted a contrary interpretation of § 241(a)(6). For as the dissent recognized, *Zadvydas'* "logic might be that inadmissible and removable aliens might be treated differently." That was *Zadvydas'* logic precisely, as its repeated statements limiting its decision to inadmissible aliens show. To interpret *Zadvydas* properly, we must take its logic as given, not the logic of the *reductio ad absurdum* of *Zadvydas* that I joined in dissent.

Justice Scalia: This mistakes the reservation of a question with its answer. Neither the opinion of the Court nor the dissent in *Zadvydas* so much as hints that the Court adopted the novel interpretation of § 241(a)(6) proposed by today's dissent. * * * Despite the dissent's repeated claims that § 241(a)(6) could not be given a different reading for inadmissible aliens, the Court *refused to decide* that question—the question we answer today.

Justice Thomas: The Court is also mistaken in affording *Zadvydas stare decisis* effect. *Zadvydas* was wrong in both its statutory and its constitutional analysis for the reasons expressed well by the dissents in that case [and therefore should be overruled—Ed.].

————

In both *Zadvydas* and *Martinez* the Supreme Court grappled with the question of *indefinite* detention. The courts have also struggled with the constitutionality of *mandatory* detention for particular categories of noncitizens in removal proceedings. Until 1988, the INA gave the Attorney General the discretion either to detain a noncitizen pending removal proceedings or to release the person (on bond or on his or her own recognizance). The person would normally be released pending the hearing unless, after an individualized inquiry, it was determined that the person was likely either to abscond or to endanger the public. The Anti–Drug Abuse Act of 1988, Pub. L. 100–690, § 7343(a), 102 Stat. 4181, 4470, carved out an exception to the Attorney General's discretion. It expressly required detention, pending what were then called deportation proceedings, of any noncitizen who had been convicted of an "aggravated felony" (a term broadly defined in INA § 101(a)(43)). Subsequent amendments extended the reach of mandatory detention to a wide range of other categories. These include persons who are either inadmissible or deportable on almost any of the crime-related grounds (not just aggravated felonies), INA § 236(c)(1)(A, B, C); those who are inadmissible or deportable on terrorism-related grounds, INA § 236(c)(1)(D); persons who are subjected to a special accelerated procedure called "expedited removal," INA § 235(b)(1)(B)(iii)(IV); and persons who have been ordered removed, INA § 241(a)(2). A few additional categories of mandatory detention, assertedly related to national security, are discussed in chapter 10, section A.1.

Many noncitizens (including LPRs) who had finished serving their criminal sentences but who were detained pending their deportation or removal proceedings went to court to challenge some of these provisions on constitutional grounds. The most common argument was that, before a person may be detained for the often lengthy period that removal proceedings take, due process requires an individualized evaluation of whether the person is likely to abscond or to endanger the public; categorical assumptions are not sufficient. For many years the lower courts divided. The majority of them agreed that mandatory, categorical detention under such circumstances violates due process.

Zadvydas was decided just before the terrorist attacks of September 11, 2001. The mandatory detention issue reached the Supreme Court just nineteen months later but in a changed world:

Demore v. Hyung Joon Kim

Supreme Court of the United States, 2003.
538 U.S. 510, 123 S.Ct. 1708, 155 L.Ed.2d 724.

■ CHIEF JUSTICE REHNQUIST delivered the opinion of the Court.

Section 236(c) of the Immigration and Nationality Act provides that "the Attorney General shall take into custody any alien who" is removable from this country because he has been convicted of one of a specified set of crimes. Respondent is a citizen of the Republic of South Korea. He entered the United States in 1984, at the age of six, and became a lawful permanent resident of the United States two years later. In July 1996, he was convicted of first-degree burglary in state court in California and, in April 1997, he was convicted of a second crime, "petty theft with priors." The Immigration and Naturalization Service (INS) charged respondent with being deportable from the United States in light of these convictions, and detained him pending his removal hearing. We hold that Congress, justifiably concerned that deportable criminal aliens who are not detained continue to engage in crime and fail to appear for their removal hearings in large numbers, may require that persons such as respondent be detained for the brief period necessary for their removal proceedings.

Respondent does not dispute the validity of his prior convictions, which were obtained following the full procedural protections our criminal justice system offers. Respondent also did not dispute the INS' conclusion that he is subject to mandatory detention under § 236(c). In conceding that he was deportable, respondent forwent a hearing at which he would have been entitled to raise any nonfrivolous argument available to demonstrate that he was not properly included in a mandatory detention category. See 8 CFR § 3.19(h)(2)(ii) (2002); *In re Joseph*, 22 I. & N. Dec. 799 (1999).[3] Respon-

---

3. This "*Joseph* hearing" is immediately provided to a detainee who claims that he is not covered by § 236(c). At the hearing, the detainee may avoid mandatory detention by demonstrating that he is not an alien, was not convicted of the predicate crime, or that the INS is otherwise substantially unlikely to establish that he is in fact subject to manda-

dent instead filed a habeas corpus action pursuant to 28 U.S.C. § 2241 in the United States District Court for the Northern District of California challenging the constitutionality of § 236(c) itself. He argued that his detention under § 236(c) violated due process because the INS had made no determination that he posed either a danger to society or a flight risk.

The District Court agreed with respondent that § 236(c)'s requirement of mandatory detention for certain criminal aliens was unconstitutional. The District Court therefore granted respondent's petition subject to the INS' prompt undertaking of an individualized bond hearing to determine whether respondent posed either a flight risk or a danger to the community. Following that decision, the District Director of the INS released respondent on $5,000 bond.

The Court of Appeals for the Ninth Circuit affirmed. That court held that § 236(c) violates substantive due process as applied to respondent because he is a permanent resident alien. It noted that permanent resident aliens constitute the most favored category of aliens and that they have the right to reside permanently in the United States, to work here, and to apply for citizenship. The court recognized and rejected the Government's two principal justifications for mandatory detention under § 236(c): (1) ensuring the presence of criminal aliens at their removal proceedings; and (2) protecting the public from dangerous criminal aliens. The Court of Appeals discounted the first justification because it found that not all aliens detained pursuant to § 236(c) would ultimately be deported. And it discounted the second justification on the grounds that the aggravated felony classification triggering respondent's detention included crimes that the court did not consider "egregious" or otherwise sufficiently dangerous to the public to necessitate mandatory detention. Respondent's crimes of first-degree burglary (burglary of an inhabited dwelling) and petty theft, for instance, the Ninth Circuit dismissed as "rather ordinary crimes." Relying upon our recent decision in *Zadvydas* v. *Davis,* the Court of Appeals concluded that the INS had not provided a justification "for no-bail civil detention sufficient to overcome a lawful permanent resident alien's liberty interest."

Three other Courts of Appeals have reached the same conclusion. The Seventh Circuit, however, rejected a constitutional challenge to § 236(c) by a permanent resident alien. We granted certiorari to resolve this conflict and now reverse.

I

[In this section of the opinion the Court rejects a jurisdictional challenge. See chapter 9, § B.6.b below.]

* * *

tory detention. Because respondent conceded that he was deportable because of a conviction that triggers § 236(c) and thus sought no *Joseph* hearing, we have no occasion to review the adequacy of *Joseph* hearings gen-

erally in screening out those who are improperly detained pursuant to § 236(c). Such individualized review is available, however, and the dissent is mistaken if it means to suggest otherwise.

II

Having determined that the federal courts have jurisdiction to review a constitutional challenge to § 236(c), we proceed to review respondent's claim. Section 236(c) mandates detention during removal proceedings for a limited class of deportable aliens—including those convicted of an aggravated felony. Congress adopted this provision against a backdrop of wholesale failure by the INS to deal with increasing rates of criminal activity by aliens. Criminal aliens were the fastest growing segment of the federal prison population, already constituting roughly 25% of all federal prisoners, and they formed a rapidly rising share of state prison populations as well. Congress' investigations showed, however, that the INS could not even *identify* most deportable aliens, much less locate them and remove them from the country. One study showed that, at the then-current rate of deportation, it would take 23 years to remove every criminal alien already subject to deportation. Making matters worse, criminal aliens who were deported swiftly reentered the country illegally in great numbers.

The agency's near-total inability to remove deportable criminal aliens imposed more than a monetary cost on the Nation. First, as Congress explained, "aliens who enter or remain in the United States in violation of our law are effectively taking immigration opportunities that might otherwise be extended to others." Second, deportable criminal aliens who remained in the United States often committed more crimes before being removed. One 1986 study showed that, after criminal aliens were identified as deportable, 77% were arrested at least once more and 45%—nearly half—were arrested multiple times before their deportation proceedings even began.

Congress also had before it evidence that one of the major causes of the INS' failure to remove deportable criminal aliens was the agency's failure to detain those aliens during their deportation proceedings. The Attorney General at the time had broad discretion to conduct individualized bond hearings and to release criminal aliens from custody during their removal proceedings when those aliens were determined not to present an excessive flight risk or threat to society. Despite this discretion to conduct bond hearings, however, in practice the INS faced severe limitations on funding and detention space, which considerations affected its release determinations. "Release determinations are made by the INS in large part, according to the number of beds available in a particular region."

Once released, more than 20% of deportable criminal aliens failed to appear for their removal hearings. The dissent disputes that statistic but goes on to praise a subsequent study conducted by the Vera Institute of Justice that more than confirms it. As the dissent explains, the Vera study found that "77% of those [deportable criminal aliens] released on bond" showed up for their removal proceedings. * * * The Vera Institute study strongly supports Congress' concern that, even with individualized screening, releasing deportable criminal aliens on bond would lead to an unacceptable rate of flight.

* * *

* * * This Court has firmly and repeatedly endorsed the proposition that Congress may make rules as to aliens that would be unacceptable if applied to citizens. * * *

* * *

"It is well established that the Fifth Amendment entitles aliens to due process of law in deportation proceedings." At the same time, however, this Court has recognized detention during deportation proceedings as a constitutionally valid aspect of the deportation process. As we said more than a century ago, deportation proceedings "would be vain if those accused could not be held in custody pending the inquiry into their true character." * * *

* * *

Despite this Court's longstanding view that the Government may constitutionally detain deportable aliens during the limited period necessary for their removal proceedings, respondent argues that the narrow detention policy reflected in INA § 236(c) violates due process. Respondent, like the four Courts of Appeals that have held § 236(c) to be unconstitutional, relies heavily upon our recent opinion in *Zadvydas* v. *Davis*.

In *Zadvydas*, the Court considered a due process challenge to detention of aliens under INA § 241, which governs detention following a final order of removal. Section 241(a)(6) provides, among other things, that when an alien who has been ordered removed is not in fact removed during the 90–day statutory "removal period," that alien "may be detained beyond the removal period" in the discretion of the Attorney General. The Court in *Zadvydas* read § 241 to authorize continued detention of an alien following the 90–day removal period for only such time as is reasonably necessary to secure the alien's removal.

But *Zadvydas* is materially different from the present case in two respects.

First, in *Zadvydas*, the aliens challenging their detention following final orders of deportation were ones for whom removal was "no longer practically attainable." The Court thus held that the detention there did not serve its purported immigration purpose. In so holding, the Court rejected the Government's claim that, by detaining the aliens involved, it could prevent them from fleeing prior to their removal. The Court observed that where, as there, "detention's goal is no longer practically attainable, detention no longer bears a reasonable relation to the purpose for which the individual was committed."

In the present case, the statutory provision at issue governs detention of deportable criminal aliens *pending their removal proceedings*. Such detention necessarily serves the purpose of preventing deportable criminal aliens from fleeing prior to or during their removal proceedings, thus increasing the chance that, if ordered removed, the aliens will be successfully removed. Respondent disagrees, arguing that there is no evidence that mandatory detention is necessary because the Government has never shown that individualized bond hearings would be ineffective. But as discussed above, in adopting § 236(c), Congress had before it evidence suggesting that permitting discretionary release of aliens pending their removal hearings would lead to large numbers of deportable criminal aliens skipping their hearings and remaining at large in the United States unlawfully.

Respondent argues that these statistics are irrelevant and do not demonstrate that individualized bond hearings "are ineffective or burdensome." It is of course true that when Congress enacted § 236, individualized bail determinations had not been tested under optimal conditions, or tested in all their possible permutations. But when the Government deals with deportable aliens, the Due Process Clause does not require it to employ the least burdensome means to accomplish its goal. The evidence Congress had before it certainly supports the approach it selected even if other, hypothetical studies might have suggested different courses of action.

Zadvydas is materially different from the present case in a second respect as well. While the period of detention at issue in *Zadvydas* was "indefinite" and "potentially permanent," the detention here is of a much shorter duration.

Zadvydas distinguished the statutory provision it was there considering from § 236 on these very grounds, noting that "post-removal-period detention, *unlike detention pending a determination of removability* ..., has no obvious termination point." Under 236(c), not only does detention have a definite termination point, in the majority of cases it lasts for less than the 90 days we considered presumptively valid in *Zadvydas*. The Executive Office for Immigration Review has calculated that, in 85% of the cases in which aliens are detained pursuant to § 236(c), removal proceedings are completed in an average time of 47 days and a median of 30 days. In the remaining 15% of cases, in which the alien appeals the decision of the Immigration Judge to the Board of Immigration Appeals, appeal takes an average of four months, with a median time that is slightly shorter.

These statistics do not include the many cases in which removal proceedings are completed while the alien is still serving time for the underlying conviction. In those cases, the aliens involved are never subjected to mandatory detention at all. * * *

* * * The judgment of the Court of Appeals is reversed.

■ JUSTICE KENNEDY, concurring.

While the justification for INA § 236(c) is based upon the Government's concerns over the risks of flight and danger to the community, the ultimate purpose behind the detention is premised upon the alien's deportability. As a consequence, due process requires individualized procedures to ensure there is at least some merit to the Immigration and Naturalization Service's (INS) charge and, therefore, sufficient justification to detain a lawful permanent resident alien pending a more formal hearing. * * * If the Government cannot satisfy this minimal, threshold burden, then the permissibility of continued detention pending deportation proceedings turns solely upon the alien's ability to satisfy the ordinary bond procedures—namely, whether if released the alien would pose a risk of flight or a danger to the community.

As the Court notes, these procedures were apparently available to respondent in this case. Respondent was entitled to a hearing in which he could have "raised any nonfrivolous argument available to demonstrate that he was not properly included in a mandatory detention category." Had he prevailed in such a proceeding, the Immigration Judge then would have had to determine if respondent "could be considered . . . for release under the general bond provisions" of § 236(a). Respondent, however, did not seek relief under these procedures, and the Court had no occasion here to determine their adequacy.

For similar reasons, since the Due Process Clause prohibits arbitrary deprivations of liberty, a lawful permanent resident alien such as respondent could be entitled to an individualized determination as to his risk of flight and dangerousness if the continued detention became unreasonable or unjustified. Were there to be an unreasonable delay by the INS in pursuing and completing deportation proceedings, it could become necessary then to inquire whether the detention is not to facilitate deportation, or to protect against risk of flight or dangerousness, but to incarcerate for other reasons. That is not a proper inference, however, either from the statutory scheme itself or from the circumstances of this case. The Court's careful opinion is consistent with these premises, and I join it in full.

■ JUSTICE O'CONNOR, with whom JUSTICE SCALIA and JUSTICE THOMAS join, concurring in part and concurring in the judgment.

I join all but Part I of the Court's opinion because, a majority having determined there is jurisdiction, I agree with the Court's resolution of respondent's challenge on the merits. I cannot join Part I because I believe that INA § 236(e) unequivocally deprives federal courts of jurisdiction to set aside "any action or decision" by the Attorney General in detaining criminal aliens under § 236(c) while removal proceedings are ongoing. That is precisely the nature of the action before us.

* * *

■ JUSTICE SOUTER, with whom JUSTICE STEVENS and JUSTICE GINSBURG join, concurring in part and dissenting in part.

* * *

I join Part I of the Court's opinion, which upholds federal jurisdiction in this case, but I dissent from the Court's disposition on the merits. The Court's holding that the Constitution permits the Government to lock up a lawful permanent resident of this country when there is concededly no reason to do so forgets over a century of precedent acknowledging the rights of permanent residents, including the basic liberty from physical confinement lying at the heart of due process. The INS has never argued that detaining Kim is necessary to guarantee his appearance for removal proceedings or to protect anyone from danger in the meantime. Instead, shortly after the District Court issued its order in this case, the INS, *sua sponte* and without even holding a custody hearing, concluded that Kim "would not be considered a threat" and that any risk of flight could be met by a bond of $5,000. He was released soon thereafter, and there is no indication that he is not complying with the terms of his release.

The Court's approval of lengthy mandatory detention can therefore claim no justification in national emergency or any risk posed by Kim particularly. The Court's judgment is unjustified by past cases or current facts, and I respectfully dissent.

I

At the outset, there is the Court's mistaken suggestion that Kim "conceded" his removability. The Court cites no statement before any court conceding removability, and I can find none. At the first opportunity, Kim applied to the Immigration Court for withholding of removal [a remedy related to asylum and considered in chapter 11—Ed.], and he represents that he intends to assert that his criminal convictions are not for removable offenses and that he is independently eligible for statutory relief from removal. In his brief before the Ninth Circuit, Kim stated that his removability was "an open question," that he was "still fighting [his] removal administratively," and that the Immigration Court had yet to hold a merits hearing. At oral argument here, his counsel stated that Kim was challenging his removability.

The suggestion that Kim should have contested his removability in this habeas corpus petition misses the point that all he claims, or could now claim, is that his detention pending removal proceedings violates the Constitution. Challenges to removability itself, and applications for relief from removal, are usually submitted in the first instance to an immigration judge. The Immigration Judge had not yet held an initial hearing on the substantive issue of removability when Kim filed his habeas petition in the District Court, even though Kim had been detained for over three months under § 236(c). If Kim's habeas corpus petition had claimed "that he himself was not 'deportable,'" as the Court suggests it should have, the District Court would probably have dismissed the claim as unexhausted. Kim did not, therefore, "concede that he is deportable" by challenging removability before the Immigration Judge and challenging detention in a federal court.

* * *

II

A

It has been settled for over a century that all aliens within our territory are "persons" entitled to the protection of the Due Process Clause. * * *

The constitutional protection of an alien's person and property is particularly strong in the case of aliens lawfully admitted to permanent residence (LPRs). The immigration laws give LPRs the opportunity to establish a life permanently in this country by developing economic, familial, and social ties indistinguishable from those of a citizen. In fact, the law of the United States goes out of its way to encourage just such attachments by creating immigration preferences for those with a citizen as a close relation, and those with valuable professional skills or other assets promising benefits to the United States.

Once they are admitted to permanent residence, LPRs share in the economic freedom enjoyed by citizens: they may compete for most jobs in the private and public sectors without obtaining job-specific authorization, and apart from the franchise, jury duty, and certain forms of public assistance, their lives are generally indistinguishable from those of United States citizens. That goes for obligations as well as opportunities. Unlike temporary, nonimmigrant aliens, who are generally taxed only on income from domestic sources or connected with a domestic business, LPRs, like citizens, are taxed on their worldwide income. Male LPRs between the ages of 18 and 26 must register under the Selective Service Act of 1948. "Resident aliens, like citizens, pay taxes, support the economy, serve in the Armed Forces, and contribute in myriad other ways to our society." And if they choose, they may apply for full membership in the national polity through naturalization.

The attachments fostered through these legal mechanisms are all the more intense for LPRs brought to the United States as children. They grow up here as members of the society around them, probably without much touch with their country of citizenship, probably considering the United States as home just as much as a native-born, younger brother or sister entitled to United States citizenship. * * * Kim is an example. He moved to the United States at the age of six and was lawfully admitted to permanent residence when he was eight. His mother is a citizen, and his father and brother are LPRs. LPRs in Kim's situation have little or no reason to feel or to establish firm ties with any place besides the United States.

* * *

B

Kim's claim is a limited one: not that the Government may not detain LPRs to ensure their appearance at removal hearings, but that due process under the Fifth Amendment conditions a potentially lengthy detention on a hearing and an impartial decisionmaker's finding that detention is necessary to a governmental purpose. He thus invokes our repeated decisions that the claim of liberty protected by the Fifth Amendment is at its strongest when government seeks to detain an individual. THE CHIEF JUSTICE wrote in 1987 that "in our society liberty is the norm, and detention prior to trial or without trial is the carefully limited exception." * * *

Accordingly, the Fifth Amendment permits detention only where "heightened, substantive due process scrutiny" finds a " 'sufficiently compelling' " governmental need. In deciding in [*United States v. Salerno*, 481 U.S. 739 (1987)] that this principle did not categorically bar pretrial detention of criminal defendants without bail under the Bail Reform Act of 1984, it was crucial that the statute provided that, "in a full-blown adversary hearing, the Government must convince a neutral decisionmaker by clear and convincing evidence that no conditions of release can reasonably assure the safety of the community or any person." * * *

We have reviewed involuntary civil commitment statutes the same way. In *Addington* v. *Texas,* 441 U.S. 418, 60 L. Ed. 2d 323, 99 S. Ct. 1804 (1979), we held that a State could not civilly commit the mentally ill without showing by "clear and convincing evidence" that the person was dangerous to others. * * *

* * *

The substantive demands of due process necessarily go hand in hand with the procedural, and the cases insist at the least on an opportunity for a detainee to challenge the reason claimed for committing him. * * *

These cases yield a simple distillate that should govern the result here. Due process calls for an individual determination before someone is locked away. In none of the cases cited did we ever suggest that the government could avoid the Due Process Clause by doing what § 236(c) does, by selecting a class of people for confinement on a categorical basis and denying members of that class any chance to dispute the necessity of putting them away. The cases, of course, would mean nothing if citizens and comparable residents could be shorn of due process by this sort of categorical sleight of hand. Without any "full-blown adversary hearing" before detention, or heightened burden of proof, or other procedures to show the government's interest in committing an individual, procedural rights would amount to nothing but mechanisms for testing group membership. * * *

C

We held as much just two Terms ago in *Zadvydas* v. *Davis,* which stands for the proposition that detaining an alien requires more than the rationality of a general detention statute; any justification must go to the alien himself. *Zadvydas* considered detention of two aliens, Zadvydas and Ma, who had already been ordered removed and therefore enjoyed no lawful immigration status. Their cases arose because actual removal appeared unlikely owing to the refusal of their native countries to accept them, with the result that they had been detained not only for the standard 90-day removal period, during which time most removal orders are executed, but beyond that period because the INS considered them to be a " 'risk to the community' " and " 'unlikely to comply with the order of removal.' " * * *

The *Zadvydas* opinion opened by noting the clear applicability of general due process standards: physical detention requires both a "special justification" that "outweighs the 'individual's constitutionally protected interest in avoiding physical restraint' " and "adequate procedural protections." Nowhere did we suggest that the "constitutionally protected liberty interest" in avoiding physical confinement, even for aliens already ordered removed, was conceptually different from the liberty interest of citizens. * * *

Thus, we began by positing commonly accepted substantive standards and proceeded to enquire into any "special justification" that might outweigh the aliens' powerful interest in avoiding physical confinement "under [individually ordered] release conditions that may not be violated." We found nothing to justify the Government's position. * * * [W]e remanded the cases to the Courts of Appeals for a determination of the sufficiency of the Government's interests in Zadvydas's and Ma's individual detention.

Our individualized analysis and disposition in *Zadvydas* support Kim's claim for an individualized review of his challenge to the reasons that are supposed to justify confining him prior to any determination of removability. In fact, aliens in removal proceedings have an additional interest in avoiding confinement, beyond anything considered in *Zadvydas*: detention prior to entry of a removal order may well impede the alien's ability to develop and present his case on the very issue of removability. After all, our recognition that the serious penalty of removal must be justified on a heightened standard of proof will not mean all that much when the INS can detain, transfer, and isolate aliens away from their lawyers, witnesses, and evidence. Kim's right to defend against removal gives him an even stronger claim than the aliens in *Zadvydas* could raise.

* * *

Hence the *Zadvydas* dissent's focus on "whether there are adequate procedures" allowing "persons once subject to detention to show that through rehabilitation, new appreciation of their responsibilities, or under other standards, they no longer present special risks or danger if put at large." Indeed, there is further support for Kim's claim in the dissent's view that the process afforded to removable aliens like Zadvydas and Ma "[went] far toward the objective" of satisfying procedural due process; that process stands in stark contrast to the total absence of custody review available in response to Kim's claim that he is neither dangerous nor a flight risk.[12] * * * Every Court of Appeals to consider the detention of an LPR under § 236(c) after *Zadvydas* reached the same conclusion.

---

12. The hearing recognized in *Matter of Joseph*, 22 I. & N. Dec. 799 (BIA 1999), is no response to this deficiency. As the Court notes, the " '*Joseph* hearing' " only permits an alien to show that he does not meet the statutory criteria for mandatory detention under § 236(c). Kim argues that, even assuming that he fits under the statute, the statute's application to LPRs like him does not fit under the Due Process Clause.

JUSTICE KENNEDY recognizes that the Due Process Clause requires "an individ-ualized determination as to [an LPR's] risk of flight and dangerousness if the continued detention [becomes] unreasonable or unjustified." It is difficult to see how Kim's detention in this case is anything but unreasonable and unjustified, since the Government concedes that detention is not necessary to completion of his removal proceedings or to the community's protection. Certainly the fact that "there is at least some merit to the [INS's] charge" that Kim should be held to be removable does not establish a compelling

D

By these standards, Kim's case is an easy one. "Heightened, substantive due process scrutiny" uncovers serious infirmities in § 236(c). Detention is not limited to dangerous criminal aliens or those found likely to flee, but applies to all aliens claimed to be deportable for criminal convictions, even where the underlying offenses are minor. *E. g., Michel* v. *INS*, 206 F.3d 253, 256 (CA2 2000) (possession of stolen bus transfers); *Matter of Bart*, 20 I. & N. Dec. 436 (BIA 1992) (issuance of a bad check). Detention under § 236(c) is not limited by the kind of time limit imposed by the Speedy Trial Act, and while it lasts only as long as the removal proceedings, those proceedings have no deadline and may last over a year. Section 236(c) neither requires nor permits an official to determine whether Kim's detention was necessary to prevent flight or danger.

Kim's detention without particular justification in these respects, or the opportunity to enquire into it, violates both components of due process, and I would accordingly affirm the judgment of the Court of Appeals requiring the INS to hold a bail hearing to see whether detention is needed to avoid a risk of flight or a danger to the community. This is surely little enough, given the fact that 8 U.S.C. § 1536 gives an LPR charged with being a foreign terrorist the right to a release hearing pending a determination that he be removed.

III

* * *

A

* * *

First, the Court says that § 236(c) "serves the purpose of preventing deportable criminal aliens from fleeing prior to or during their removal proceedings." Yes it does, and the statute in *Zadvydas*, viewed outside the context of any individual alien's detention, served the purpose of preventing aliens ordered to be deported from fleeing prior to actual deportation. In each case, the fact that a statute serves its purpose in general fails to justify the detention of an individual in particular. Some individual aliens covered by § 236(c) have meritorious challenges to removability or claims for relief from removal. * * *

The Court appears to respond that Congress may require detention of removable aliens based on a general conclusion that detention is needed for effective removal of criminal aliens on a class-wide basis. But on that logic *Zadvydas* should have come out the other way, for detention of the entire class of aliens who have actually been ordered removed will in general "serve the purpose" of their effective removal. Yet neither the Court nor

reason for detention. The INS releases many noncriminal aliens on bond or on conditional parole under § 236(a)(2) pending removal proceedings, and the fact that Kim has been convicted of criminal offenses does not on its own justify his detention.

JUSTICE KENNEDY in dissent suggested that scrutiny under the Due Process Clause could be satisfied at such a general level. Rather, we remanded the individual cases of Zadvydas and Ma for determinations of the strength of the Government's reasons for detaining them in particular. We can insist on nothing less here, since the Government's justification for detaining individuals like Zadvydas and Ma, who had no right to remain in this country and were proven flight risks and dangers to society, is certainly stronger (and at least no weaker) than its interest in detaining a lawful permanent resident who has not been shown (or even claimed) to be either a flight risk or a threat to the community.

The Court's closest approach to a reason justifying class-wide detention without exception here is a Senate Report stating that over 20% of nondetained criminal aliens failed to appear for removal hearings. To begin with, the Senate Report's statistic treats all criminal aliens alike and does not distinguish between LPRs like Kim, who are likely to have developed strong ties within the United States, and temporary visitors or illegal entrants. Even more importantly, the statistic tells us nothing about flight risk at all because, as both the Court and the Senate Report recognize, the INS was making its custody determinations not on the ground of likelihood of flight or dangerousness, but "in large part, according to the number of beds available in a particular region." * * *

* * *

The Court nowhere addresses the Vera Institute's conclusion that criminal aliens released under supervisory conditions are overwhelmingly likely to attend their hearings. * * *

* * *

The Court's second effort [to distinguish *Zadvydas*] is its claim that mandatory detention under § 236(c) is generally of a "much shorter duration" than the incarceration at issue in *Zadvydas*. While it is true that removal proceedings are unlikely to prove "indefinite and potentially permanent," they are not formally limited to any period, and often extend beyond the time suggested by the Court, that is, "an average time of 47 days" or, for aliens who exercise their right of appeal, "an average of four months." * * *

In the first place, the average time from receipt of charging documents to decision obscures the fact that the alien may receive charging documents only after being detained for a substantial period. Kim, for example, was not charged until five weeks after the INS detained him.

Even more revealing is an explanation of the raw numbers that are averaged out. As the Solicitor General conceded, the length of the average detention period in great part reflects the fact that the vast majority of cases involve aliens who raise no challenge to removability at all. LPRs like Kim, however, will hardly fit that pattern. Unlike many illegal entrants and temporary nonimmigrants, LPRs are the aliens most likely to press substantial challenges to removability requiring lengthy proceedings. * * *

* * *

IV

This case is not about the National Government's undisputed power to detain aliens in order to avoid flight or prevent danger to the community. The issue is whether that power may be exercised by detaining a still lawful permanent resident alien when there is no reason for it and no way to challenge it. The Court's holding that the Due Process Clause allows this under a blanket rule is devoid of even ostensible justification in fact and at odds with the settled standard of liberty. I respectfully dissent.

■ JUSTICE BREYER, concurring in part and dissenting in part.

I agree with the majority that the courts have jurisdiction, and I join Part I of its opinion. If I believed (as the majority apparently believes) that Kim had conceded that he is deportable, then I would conclude that the Government could detain him without bail for the few weeks ordinarily necessary for formal entry of a removal order. Time limits of the kind set forth in *Zadvydas* v. *Davis* should govern these and longer periods of detention, for an alien's concession that he is deportable. * * *

This case, however, is not one in which an alien concedes deportability. As JUSTICE SOUTER points out, Kim argues to the contrary. Kim claims that his earlier convictions were neither for an " 'aggravated felony,' " nor for two crimes of " 'moral turpitude.' " And given shifting lower court views on such matters, I cannot say that his arguments are insubstantial or interposed solely for purposes of delay. * * *.

That being so—as long as Kim's legal arguments are neither insubstantial nor interposed solely for purposes of delay—then the immigration statutes, interpreted in light of the Constitution, permit Kim (if neither dangerous nor a flight risk) to obtain bail. For one thing, Kim's constitutional claims to bail in these circumstances are strong. * * *

* * *

Finally, bail standards drawn from the criminal justice system are available to fill this statutory gap. Federal law makes bail available to a criminal defendant after conviction and pending appeal provided (1) the appeal is "not for the purpose of delay," (2) the appeal "raises a substantial question of law or fact," and (3) the defendant shows by "clear and convincing evidence" that, if released, he "is not likely to flee or pose a danger to the safety" of the community. 18 U.S.C. § 3143(b). These standards give considerable weight to any special governmental interest in detention (*e.g.*, process-related concerns or class-related flight risks). The standards are more protective of a detained alien's liberty interest than those currently administered in the INS' *Joseph* hearings. And they have proved workable in practice in the criminal justice system. Nothing in the statute forbids their use when § 236(c) deportability is in doubt.

I would interpret the (silent) statute as imposing these bail standards. So interpreted, the statute would require the Government to permit a detained alien to seek an individualized assessment of flight risk and dangerousness as long as the alien's claim that he is not deportable is (1) not interposed solely for purposes of delay and (2) raises a question of "law or fact" that is not insubstantial. And that interpretation, in my view, is consistent with what the Constitution demands. I would remand this case to the Ninth Circuit to determine whether Kim has raised such a claim.

With respect, I dissent from the Court's contrary disposition.

———

In the case you just read, the various Justices' opinions frequently refer to "mandatory" detention, sometimes called "categorical" detention, as distinguished from "discretionary" or "individualized" or "case-by-case" detention determinations. Before proceeding further, consider carefully what those terms really mean.

In truth, those terms are flexible enough to describe almost any of the competing models that the various Justices discussed. Justice Kennedy's concurring opinion, for example, suggested that the rule being challenged here—that detention is mandatory if a noncitizen has been convicted of an aggravated felony—in fact provides for individualized inquiry. As he observed, the person has a right to a hearing (called a *Joseph* hearing after the BIA decision that authorized it) at which the detainee may argue that the criteria Congress has established for mandatory detention have not been met—for example, the respondent is a citizen, or he or she has not been convicted, or the crime does not constitute an aggravated felony. The majority opinion makes the same point in different language. The dissent, in contrast, argues that the individualized inquiry required by due process entails determinations of whether the person is likely to abscond or to endanger the public. But those are also categories; i.e., if the statute had said that all noncitizens who are likely to abscond or to endanger the public must be detained and that all others must be released on bond, the formulation could literally be described as just another kind of mandatory categorical approach. Under each model, there are general categories that determine whether the person must be detained, and the individual has an opportunity for a hearing to contest that he or she fits any of those categories.

Thus, the difference between mandatory categorical detention and individualized, case-by-case detention determinations is essentially one of degree. The more closely the *legal criteria* for detention resemble the *policy justifications* for it, the more intuitive it is to label the process an "individualized" one and the less intuitive it becomes to describe the detention as "mandatory." Under the dissent's model, the criteria and the justifications are congruent. The very reasons for detaining the person are to prevent him or her from absconding or endangering the public, and it is only when those reasons apply to the particular individual that detention is permitted.

In contrast, the majority opinion approves the use of proxies, or correlations. It does not dispute that assuring the person's appearance at the hearing and protecting the public safety are the justifications for detention, but it allows Congress to gauge those risks by use of a proxy—whether the person has been convicted of an "aggravated felony." The majority does not, in other words, insist that the rules be as closely tailored to the ultimate objectives.

With those thoughts in mind, consider the following arguments for and against mandatory, categorical detention:

Stephen H. Legomsky, The Detention of Aliens: Theories, Rules, and Discretion

30 Univ. Miami Inter–Amer. L. Rev. 531, 544–48 (1999).

[This article first examines the theories for detaining noncitizens in connection with removal proceedings and the costs of those detentions. On the benefit side, the article concludes that detention cannot be explained on punishment grounds, but that three other theories can be legitimately invoked in particular circumstances—preventing absconding, protecting public safety, and (subject to stringent limits) deterring immigration violations. The costs of detention include, first, the human costs—the deprivation of the detainee's liberty and the loss of opportunity to work, attend school, socialize, and interact with family and friends; the economic loss to the detainee and his or her dependents if the detainee is eligible to work (as well as the loss of income tax revenues for the federal and state governments in such cases); and serious practical obstacles to the detainees in the preparation of their removal cases (access to lawyers, witnesses, interpreters, documentary evidence, etc.) The article then goes on to compare the merits of mandatory categorical detention to those of individualized detention determinations.]

* * *

A. Theories of Mandatory Detention

1. Saving Money

The most obvious advantage of mandatory detention is that it avoids the expense of individual hearings. With scarce resources, that advantage cannot be dismissed casually. Still, the financial argument has several limitations.

First, out of deference to the liberty interests at stake, we willingly accept the cost of pretrial hearings before we detain people suspected of crimes. Why should we be any less willing to provide hearings before detaining people suspected to be removable?

To some, the inherent differences between citizens and noncitizens might be enough of an answer. Citizens, being widely regarded as possessing greater membership rights than noncitizens, might be assumed entitled to greater procedural safeguards before being detained. As relevant as the distinction is to one's interest in entering or remaining in the United States, however, fundamental liberty interests like freedom from pretrial detention should not hinge on one's citizenship status. Even in the criminal context, the law of pretrial detention does not distinguish based on the citizenship status of the suspect. Moreover, certain noncitizens—including lawfully admitted permanent residents and asylum claimants—have special interests at stake. Finally, as noted earlier, the detention of noncitizens can affect the family members and others as well, both economically and emotionally. These other affected individuals might be United States citizens.

* * *

2.   Avoiding False Negatives

No matter how thorough a case-by-case detention determination process is, and how talented and diligent the hearing officer is, errors are possible. Predictions about the likelihood that a given person will abscond or pose a threat to the public safety are inherently perilous. Not all the material evidence will always be discovered or presented. Not all the findings of primary fact will be accurate. Even if all the raw information is complete and accurate, not all predictions of future events will pan out. One theory of mandatory detention, therefore, is that it avoids what I shall call false negatives—i.e., cases in which the hearing officer predicts that the person will neither abscond nor threaten the public and consequently releases the person on bond, and the prediction proves wrong. Mandatory detention eliminates that risk.

That benefit, of course, comes at a price—a certain number of false positives. This problem is discussed below. Moreover, the question remains why false negatives are tolerated in the criminal context but not in the removal context. * * *

3.   Deterring Immigration Violations

Earlier discussion highlighted one of the most commonly invoked arguments for detention—deterring immigration violations in the first place. Arguably, making the detention mandatory makes the deterrent stronger. * * *

B.   Theories of Individualized Adjudication

1.   Avoiding False Positives

Mandatory detention inevitably generates a certain number of false positives—i.e., those people who are detained because they fall within one of the statutorily prescribed categories but who in fact would not have absconded or caused any harm to the community if released. In each of these cases, all the costs associated with detention are needlessly incurred. * * * [They] add up to great waste of both human and financial resources.

Conversely, many persons who do not fall within any of the categories predesignated for mandatory detention might well present real risks of absconding or real dangers to the public safety. Every time the INS is required to use a detention bed for a person who in fact poses no threat at all, it has one fewer bed available for a person who poses a threat and whom the INS would have had the discretion to detain. * * *

2. Cutting Corners on Humane Treatment

Stanley Mailman and Stephen Yale–Loehr make another strong argument against mandatory detention. By exacerbating the pressure on the INS to find adequate bed space, mandatory detention forces the INS to rely increasingly heavily on contracts with privately run facilities, where some of the least humane conditions prevail.

3. Deterring Enforcement of the Immigration Laws

Ironically, mandatory detention might have the effect of discouraging immigration officials from zealously enforcing the immigration laws. One INS district director, commenting on the space crunch at the local INS detention facility, stated he "would strongly consider not starting deportation proceedings against felons—especially if their offenses were minor or committed years ago."

4. Avoiding Detention Costs

* * *

* * * [A] certain proportion of those who receive individual bond hearings will prevail. The detention costs are saved in those cases. * * *

* * *

NOTES AND QUESTIONS

1. How would you have decided this case? First, based on everything you have now read, do you agree with the majority opinion that Congress's categorical approach adequately protects the liberty interests at stake? Second and more specifically, Justice Souter, at the beginning of his dissent, described the majority opinion as "holding that the Constitution permits the government to lock up a lawful permanent resident of this country when there is concededly no reason to do so." Was his characterization accurate?

2. Is the issue one of substantive due process or procedural due process? Justice Souter in dissent says the demands of the two doctrines "go hand in hand" and, later, that mandatory detention violates both. As applied to the issue of mandatory detention, what, exactly, is the relationship between the substantive due process and procedural due process arguments? Do you think it matters which of the two characterizations of the issue the Court adopts? Think about (a) precisely what factual issues the opposing sides say the person has a right to a hearing on; and (b) how the choice of characterization might affect the standard of review.

3.   Whichever strand of due process the Court thinks it is considering, what standard of review does it apply? How great must the government's interests be to justify detention during removal proceedings? How narrowly tailored must the criteria be to the achievement of those interests?

4.   Both the majority opinion and Justice Souter's dissent address the question whether *Zadvydas* compels the Court to hold mandatory detention unconstitutional. How is it possible for the two sides to answer that question differently? Which reading of *Zadvydas* do you find more convincing?

5.   Kim was an LPR, not a nonimmigrant or an undocumented migrant, for example. And he was facing expulsion from the United States, not, for example, removal at a port of entry. Therefore one would expect his interests to be at the top of the noncitizen hierarchy, and we can safely assume the majority would have reached the same result, a fortiori, had his situation been otherwise. But what about the dissent? Would it make sense for Justice Souter to prescribe the same results in the case of either (a) a noncitizen with a lesser immigration status; or (b) a noncitizen arriving at a port of entry?

6.   Both the majority opinion and the Souter dissent devote considerable space to the fact question whether Kim has conceded deportability. For Justice Breyer, in fact, the issue is outcome-determinative. As you will see in chapters 7 and 8, a typical removal proceeding (for a person who has been admitted to the United States and wants to remain) normally proceeds in two phases. In the first phase the government must prove the person is "deportable"—i.e., that he or she fits within one of the many grounds for expulsion. In most cases deportability is conceded and the hearing proceeds to the second phase. There the noncitizen applies for discretionary relief under one or more of the many affirmative relief provisions scattered throughout the INA. Mr. Kim apparently intended at his removal hearing to do both. He planned to argue that he was not deportable because the crimes of which he had been convicted did not meet the legal definition of "aggravated felony," a term you will study later. Alternatively, he planned to request a form of affirmative relief called "withholding of removal," a remedy related to asylum. Fact questions aside, should the permissibility of mandatory detention hinge on whether deportability has been conceded?

7.   Justice Souter in dissent analogizes to the rules for pre-trial detention in criminal cases and the rules for involuntary civil commitment of dangerous individuals. Are his analogies apt?

8.   Justice Breyer offers an interesting analogy of his own and reads the immigration statute as implicitly embodying it. He too draws from the bail standards in criminal cases, but, for reasons he does not explain, the criminal law standards he chooses to import are the ones that govern detention pending *appeals* from criminal convictions—not *pretrial* detention. A person who requests bail pending appeal, he says, must show not only that he or she is unlikely to flee or endanger public safety (and must show this by "clear and convincing evidence"), but also that the appeal is

not for delay purposes and, importantly, that the appeal "raises a substantial question of law or fact." What do you think of this analogy?

9. What does this case augur for the future of the plenary power doctrine? In particular, is the procedural due process exception to the doctrine still intact?

10. As noted earlier, *Zadvydas* was decided shortly before September 11, 2001. The present case was decided about nineteen months after September 11. The composition of the Court did not change in the interim. Do you think September 11 influenced the Court's decision in *Kim*? Are there future national security-related scenarios that the Court might have been anticipating? Don't spend too much time on this question now. In chapter 10 you will encounter the host of post-September 11 developments that relate to the interaction of national security and immigration (or at least to the interaction of national security and noncitizens). Section A of that chapter deals specifically with the numerous detention strategies implemented for reasons of national security.

11. For general commentary on mandatory detention, see Legomsky, above; Peter H. Schuck, *INS Detention and Removal: A "White Paper,"* 11 Georgetown Immigration L.J. 667 (1997); Margaret H. Taylor, *The 1996 Immigration Act: Detention and Related Issues*, 74 IR 209 (Feb. 3, 1997); Margaret H. Taylor, *Symbolic Detention*, 20 In Defense of the Alien 153 (1998); Vera Institute of Justice, The Appearance Assistance Program (1998). For some compelling accounts of life inside U.S. immigration detention facilities, see, e.g., Mark Dow, American Gulag—Inside U.S. Immigration Prisons (2004); Margaret H. Taylor, *Detained Aliens Challenging Conditions of Confinement and the Porous Border of the Plenary Power Doctrine*, 22 Hastings Constitutional L.Q. 1087 (1995); see also M. Isabel Medina, *Demore v. Kim—A Dance of Power and Human Rights*, 18 Georgetown Immigration L.J. 697 (2004).

e. WHERE ARE WE NOW?

Is there really such a thing as the "plenary power doctrine," or do the so-called plenary power cases merely reflect the more generally applicable contemporary norms of the eras in which they were decided? Professor Gabriel J. Chin argues that many of the most extreme plenary power decisions, despite the rhetoric of special deference to Congress on immigration matters, in fact reached results that would have been reached in analogous non-immigration cases under the accepted constitutional norms then prevailing. See Gabriel J. Chin, *Is There a Plenary Power Doctrine? A Tentative Apology and Prediction for Our Strange but Unexceptional Constitutional Immigration Law*, 14 Georgetown Immigration L.J. 257 (2000). Some other commentators disagree. See Kevin R. Johnson, *Race and Immigration Law and Enforcement: A Response to Is There a Plenary Power Doctrine?*, 14 Georgetown Immigration L.J. 289 (2000); Stephen H. Legomsky, *Immigration Exceptionalism: Commentary on Is There a Plenary Power Doctrine?*, 14 Georgetown Immigration L.J. 307 (2000).

Whether the doctrine is all rhetoric, all substance, or parts of each, there is still uncertainty about both its actual impact and its current status. As to its impact, the views of two respected scholars are especially relevant here:

Professor Margaret Taylor has argued that the plenary power doctrine has infected subject areas that go beyond pure "immigration" law, producing adverse results with respect to federal regulation of noncitizens on a range of matters other than admission or expulsion. At the same time, she notes and analyzes a line of cases in which courts have willingly reviewed the physical conditions of the facilities in which inadmissible and deportable noncitizens are confined. Margaret H. Taylor, *Detained Aliens Challenging Conditions of Confinement and the Porous Border of the Plenary Power Doctrine*, 22 Hastings Constitutional L.Q. 1087 (1995). In a later article she maintains that, within the Justice Department, policy development and litigation strategy tend to converge when plenary power issues are argued. See Margaret H. Taylor, *Behind the Scenes of St. Cyr and Zadvydas: Making Policy in the Midst of Litigation*, 16 Georgetown Immigration L.J. 271 (2002).

Professor Kevin Johnson argues that the plenary power doctrine has seeped into political soil, contributing to the public backlash against immigrants. Kevin R. Johnson, *The Antiterrorism Act, the Immigration Reform Act, and Ideological Regulation in the Immigration Laws: Important Lessons for Citizens and Noncitizens*, 28 St. Mary's L.J. 833 (1997).

At any rate, it is clear that the Supreme Court and the lower courts have moved beyond the absolutist conception of plenary power embraced by at least the language of some of the older Supreme Court opinions. Modern courts have fashioned a number of escape routes, exceptions, and limitations. You have now seen most of them. Here is a summary:

1.   As discussed in connection with *Zadvydas* and *Martinez,* courts will often **interpret immigration statutes** favorably to noncitizens in order to avoid not only the need to decide constitutional questions, but also the harsh results of the plenary power doctrine. See generally Stephen H. Legomsky, Immigration and the Judiciary—Law and Politics in Britain and America at 155–70, 177–222 (1987). For additional examples of the same phenomenon, see Hiroshi Motomura, *Immigration Law After a Century of Plenary Power: Phantom Constitutional Norms and Statutory Interpretation,* 100 Yale L.J. 545 (1990).

2.   As you will see in more detail in chapter 9, the Supreme Court's recent decisions in *Demore v. Hyung Joon Kim,* 538 U.S. 510, 123 S.Ct. 1708, 155 L.Ed.2d 724 (2003) and *INS v. St. Cyr,* 533 U.S. 289, 121 S.Ct. 2271, 150 L.Ed.2d 347 (2001), recognized noncitizens' rights to judicial review of removal orders by way of **habeas corpus**. Like *Zadvydas,* these decisions were nominally statutory interpretations but were influenced by the Court's desire to avoid assumed constitutional constraints. Outside the immigration setting you will later encounter similar Supreme Court recognition of habeas corpus as a vehicle for testing the legality of the Guantána-

mo noncitizen detentions in *Rasul v. Bush*, ___ U.S. ___, 124 S.Ct. 2686, 159 L.Ed.2d 548 (2004), excerpted and discussed on pages 854–66 below.

3. **Procedural due process** is clearly required in expulsion cases and in most cases involving the exclusion of returning LPRs. See the earlier materials on *Yamataya* and *Plasencia*, respectively. As discussed in the Notes and Questions following *Francis*, some constitutional arguments are capable of being framed as either procedural due process or substantive due process. Many lower courts have found ways to characterize challenges as procedural in order to avoid the problem of plenary congressional power. Contra, *Demore v. Hyung Joon Kim*, 538 U.S. 510, 123 S.Ct. 1708, 155 L.Ed.2d 724 (2003).

4. Even with respect to substantive due process or federal "equal protection," lower courts often translate the plenary power doctrine into a **"rational basis"** test. See generally Stephen H. Legomsky, *Immigration Law and the Principle of Plenary Congressional Power*, 1984 Supreme Ct. Rev. 255, 304. The *Francis* case is a leading example. In *Fiallo* (see pages 174–76 above), the Supreme Court seemed to follow suit.

5. There is at least some authority for the proposition that immigration statutes are subject to the same **first amendment** standards as other statutes. For the reasons considered earlier (see pages 176–80 above), the validity of that proposition is unclear.

6. The Supreme Court decision in *Chadha* suggests that **separation of powers** challenges (as distinguished from individual rights challenges) might be at least somewhat less vulnerable to the plenary power doctrine.

7. The recent Supreme Court decisions in *Zadvydas* and *Martinez* might signal a general weakening of the plenary power doctrine. At the very least, these cases evidence a willingness to consider constitutional limitations when **prolonged detention** is challenged, a lesson that can perhaps be distilled also from *Rasul v. Bush*, ___ U.S. ___, 124 S.Ct. 2686, 159 L.Ed.2d 548 (2004). But cf. *Demore v. Hyung Joon Kim*, 538 U.S. 510, 123 S.Ct. 1708, 155 L.Ed.2d 724 (2003), discussed on pages 211–29 above (upholding mandatory categorical detention for entire duration of removal proceedings, at least in certain circumstances).

———

The present author once predicted that the plenary power doctrine was unlikely to be formally and suddenly overruled, but that the Supreme Court would gradually whittle it down through a process of cumulative limitations and exceptions. Eventually, it was thought, the Court would confirm that even immigration statutes are subject to constitutional restraints, simply deny that a doctrine of special immigration deference ever really existed, and characterize the "doctrine" as merely a prudent reminder that immigration statutes often reflect sensitive policy judgments by the political branches. Under this scenario, like old soldiers, the plenary power doctrine never dies; it just fades away. The result, it was predicted, would be "PPD-lite." See Stephen H. Legomsky, *Ten More Years of Plenary Power: Immigration, Congress, and the Courts*, 22 Hastings Constitutional L.Q. 925, 934–37 (1995). Do you think that what we now have is PPD-lite, something more, or something less?

The following passages were excerpted from an article that won the 1998 Association of American Law Schools Scholarly Paper Competition. In it, Professor Gabriel Chin carefully investigates the explicit racial impetus for the Chinese Exclusion Act, for related legislation, and for the Supreme Court cases that invented the plenary power doctrine. Section I examines the history. In section II, Professor Chin draws on that history and subsequent developments to argue that the Supreme Court would not countenance similar racially discriminatory immigration legislation today. Most of section II focuses on domestic law developments within the United States; one specific argument made by Professor Chin is that, even if the Court today were to apply only a rational basis test to racial classifications in immigration law, those classifications would fail that test.

The portion reproduced below, however, draws reinforcement from modern conceptions of international law. In this enterprise, Professor Chin credits and builds on the contributions of other scholars who have urged United States legislators, executive officials, and judges to heed international law when dealing with immigration. See, e.g., Joan Fitzpatrick & William McKay Bennett, *A Lion in the Path? The Influence of International Law on the Immigration Policy of the United States*, 70 Washington L. Rev. 589 (1995); Berta Esperanza Hernández-Truyol, *Natives, Newcomers and Nativism: A Human Rights Model for the Twenty–First Century*, 23 Fordham Urban L.J. 1075 (1996); Berta Esperanza Hernández-Truyol & Kimberly A. Johns, *Global Rights, Local Wrongs and Legal Fixes: An International Human Rights Critique of Immigration and Welfare "Reform,"* 71 Southern California L. Rev. 547 (1998); James A.R. Nafziger, *The General Admission of Aliens Under International Law*, 77 Amer. J. Internat'l L. 804 (1983); Michael Scaperlanda, *Polishing the Tarnished Golden Door*, 1993 Wisconsin L. Rev. 965.

Gabriel J. Chin, Segregation's Last Stronghold: Race Discrimination and the Constitutional Law of Immigration

46 UCLA L. Rev. 1, 58–62 (1998).

* * *

B.   The International Law Foundation of the Plenary Power Doctrine

The Court derived the plenary power doctrine from its understanding of international law rather than any specific provision of the Constitution. In United States v. Curtiss–Wright Export Corp., the Court explained, "the power to expel undesirable aliens, which is [not] expressly affirmed by the Constitution, nevertheless exists as inherently inseparable from the conception of nationality. This the court recognized, and found the warrant for its conclusions not in the provisions of the Constitution, but in the law of nations." Similarly, in Nishimura Ekiu v. United States, the Court stated that "it is an accepted maxim of international law, that every sovereign nation has the power, as inherent in sovereignty, and essential to self-preservation, to forbid the entrance of foreigners within its dominions, or to admit them only in such cases as it may see fit to prescribe." Modern cases continue to locate the font of plenary power in international law.

In the last century, the law of nations may have imposed few limits on the acts of nations in this context. However, as Michael Scaperlanda has pointed out, "sovereignty is not a static concept." Of course, the Supreme Court has not been eager to rely on international law to limit the authority of Congress, but the argument is different in the plenary power context. By defining congressional power over immigration by reference to an external standard, the Court itself has provided for the possibility that domestic law will change as international law changes. As Professor Scaperlanda explains: "Where the international law of sovereignty provides the background norm for constitutional decisionmaking, as it does in [immigration] cases, the Court ought to look at the current norm with its recent limitations."

C. The Nondiscrimination Principle in International Law

If the Court meant to grant Congress an unlimited power over immigration by linking the immigration power to international law, it failed. As Professors Hernandez and Scaperlanda have written, international legal doctrine has changed dramatically since the Court created the plenary power doctrine. If international law ever permitted, or was neutral, on the issue of governmental racial discrimination, it is no longer; modern international law generally prohibits racial discrimination. Accordingly, the notion that an inherent part of national sovereignty is the power to discriminate against aliens on the basis of race is no longer a part of international law.

The International Convention on the Elimination of All Forms of Racial Discrimination is perhaps the broadest expression of the antidiscrimination principle in international law. Signatory nations, including the United States, commit "to engage in no act or practice of racial discrimination against persons, groups of persons or institutions and to ensure that all public authorities shall act in conformity with this obligation." The International Covenant on Civil and Political Rights, to which the United States is a party, also prohibits racial discrimination. Other international agreements [citing the United Nations Charter and the Universal Declaration of Human Rights—Ed.] also make the point that racial discrimination is disfavored.

The prohibition against racial discrimination applies to treatment of aliens as well as citizens. For example, the Protocol Relating to the Status of Refugees, which the United States has ratified, requires signers to offer benefits to refugees "without discrimination as to race, religion or country of origin." Similarly, the Geneva Convention Relative to the Treatment of Prisoners of War prohibits "any adverse distinction based on race, nationality, religious belief or political opinions, or any other distinction founded on similar criteria." Other treaties also make the point [citing multinational conventions that prohibit apartheid and genocide—Ed.].

The Restatement (Third) of the Foreign Relations Law of the United States recognizes the effect of this body of law, concluding that "systematic racial discrimination" now violates customary international law. Thus, while there is no doubt that international law permits nations to regulate and limit immigration, it does not authorize them to do so on the basis of race. Because an important support for the nation's right to discriminate on the basis of race in the immigration context has been removed, it seems logical that the right to do so should be as well.

SIMULATION EXERCISE

Before doing this exercise, consider the above excerpts from Professor Chin's article and review the other materials you have read in this chapter.

In the year 2012, race riots erupted in the Latino barrios of Los Angeles, Miami, and several other major United States cities. Congress responded by enacting the Immigration and Race Relations Improvement Act of 2012. The Conference Committee report preceding its passage stated that the Act "was generally aimed at easing racial tensions in the long run by reducing the Latino immigrant population." To that end, the Act included the following provisions:

> Section 201. Notwithstanding any other provision of law, no more than 10,000 aliens of Latino descent shall be admitted into the United States for permanent residence in any fiscal year.

> Section 202. Notwithstanding any other provision of federal law, no more than 10,000 aliens who are nationals of countries in which the principal spoken language is Spanish shall be admitted into the United States for permanent residence in any fiscal year.

> Section 301. Every immigration inspector at a border inspection station is hereby authorized to exclude from the United States any Latino alien who does not possess an entry document that appears to the inspector to be valid and authentic. This procedure shall not be construed to require that the alien be informed of the basis for the inspector's suspicion or given an opportunity to provide evidence. For purposes of this section, a Latino alien is an alien who is of Latino descent or who is a national of a country in which the principal spoken language is Spanish.

> Section 401. Any alien who at any time has participated in a demonstration organized principally to protest the condition of Latinos in the United States, and who is not the spouse, parent, or child of a United States citizen or of an alien lawfully admitted for permanent residence, shall be removed.

Many noncitizens who were removed from the United States because of the various provisions of the 2012 Act challenged its constitutionality in court. Four such cases eventually worked their way up to the Supreme Court, which consolidated them and granted certiorari to decide all the federal issues those cases raised.

Noncitizen #1 is Maria Boisin. Her mother's family history is entirely Argentine, and her father's family history is entirely French. Boisin is a national of France. Upon her arrival at a United States port of entry, she was excluded under section 201 because the quota of 10,000 was already fully subscribed.

Noncitizen #2 is Hans Melzer, whose German ancestry goes back several generations. Melzer was born in, and has always been a national of, Mexico. Upon his arrival at a United States port of entry, he was excluded from the United States pursuant to section 202 because the quota of 10,000 was already fully subscribed.

Noncitizen #3 is Alicia Avalos, a Guatemalan national of Guatemalan descent. Avalos was admitted to the United States as an LPR in 2009. In 2013, she visited her grandparents in Guatemala for eight months. Upon returning, Avalos presented to the immigration inspector the "green card" that DHS had given her as evidence of her lawful admission for permanent residence. The immigration inspector did not think the picture on the green card was a sufficient likeness. He questioned her further and concluded the document was not hers. The inspector rejected her offer to summon witnesses who she said would be able to verify her identity. She was excluded, without further investigation, pursuant to section 301.

Noncitizen #4 is Mahmud Ali, a national of Bangla Desh. Ali was admitted to the United States as an LPR in 2000. Active in the American Civil Liberties Union and other civil rights organizations, Ali in 2002 joined a peaceful demonstration at which he heard speakers denounce the poor economic status of American Latinos. He has no relatives in the United States. In 2013, Ali was found deportable and ordered removed under section 401.

(a) The Court has ordered the four cases consolidated for purposes of oral argument. Unless your instructor specifies otherwise, assume you could be called upon to represent either the noncitizen or ICE in any of the four cases. Prepare for oral argument by drafting an outline of the points you would make in each of those situations. In doing so, you should anticipate the arguments of your opponent and be ready to meet them. You may raise any plausible arguments for either *distinguishing* or *overruling* prior cases. Assume opposing counsel will do the same.

(b) Now you are one of the Supreme Court Justices hearing the cases. Jot down any questions or hypotheticals you might pose to either attorney at oral argument, and try to form tentative views on how you will vote.

CONCLUDING NOTE ON THE PLENARY POWER OVER IMMIGRATION: HISTORICAL PARALLELS FROM ACROSS THE ATLANTIC

At about the same time that the United States Supreme Court was discovering Congress's inherent and plenary power over immigration, remarkably similar theories were germinating in Great Britain. To understand them, one must be aware of some fundamental differences between the constitutional frameworks of the two countries.

The United Kingdom is often said to have an "unwritten" constitution. That term can be misleading, for British constitutional principles are certainly embodied in writing. It is just that the writing is not a single, comprehensive document as is the case in the United States and most other countries. Instead, British constitutional law is laid out in the Magna Carta, the Bill of Rights of 1689, certain other fundamental statutes, a rich body of case law, and customs and conventions described in a variety of documents. Today, too, the European Convention on Human Rights (discussed in chapter13, section C below) and the law of the European Union sometimes function like constitutional checks on domestic legislation.

Far more significant than form, therefore, is a substantive difference that concerns supremacy: In the United States the supreme law is the Constitution. Further (as in Australia, India, and a few other democracies), the courts may review Acts of the national legislature for constitutionality. In contrast, the ultimate authority in the United Kingdom is Parliament, which may alter the Constitution at any time. There is no judicial review of the constitutionality of British statutes because, by definition, what Parliament does *is* constitutional. Moreover, just as the powers of the United States Congress are generally confined to those affirmatively granted by the Constitution, so too the powers of the British Crown (the executive branch) are generally limited to those affirmatively bestowed by the supreme British authority—the Parliament.[12]

How does all this affect immigration? At the beginning of this chapter you saw a trilogy of United States Supreme Court cases decided between 1889 and 1893—the *Chinese Exclusion Case, Ekiu,* and *Fong Yue Ting.* In that sequence of cases, the Court began by invoking the international law maxim that nations may exclude and deport noncitizens. It relied on that principle in locating an inherent sovereign power of Congress as a matter of domestic constitutional law—notwithstanding the doctrine of enumerated powers. Finally, relying heavily on the inherent nature of the immigration power and its international law roots, the Court held the exercise of this congressional power to be virtually immune from judicial review for constitutionality.

From 1891 to 1906, the Privy Council and the highest Scottish court rendered their own trilogy of foundation cases. See *Attorney General for Canada v. Cain* [1906] A.C. 542 (Privy Council); *Poll v. Lord Advocate* [1899] 1 F. 823 (Ct. of Sessions, Scotland); *Musgrove v. Chun Teeong Toy* [1891] A.C. 272 (Privy Council). Those cases similarly began with the observation that international law empowers nations to exclude and to deport noncitizens. The cases appeared to suggest that that principle led to

---

12. Of course the origins of these principles are very different. The enumerated powers doctrine in the United States reflects federalism principles that have no counterparts in the unitary system of the United Kingdom.

a "prerogative" (inherent) power of the Crown to perform those functions—notwithstanding the doctrine that the Crown's powers are normally derived from Parliamentary grant.[13] Finally, because the source of the power was the royal prerogative (rather than a Parliamentary grant), at least the first two of these cases assumed no court could review the legality of the exercise of the power in an individual case. Thus, in each country the progression was from the nation's power in international law, to an inherent power possessed by an organ of government normally dependent on affirmative grants from the supreme authority, to immunization from judicial review.

The parallels have continued through the twentieth century. While later United States cases like *Knauff, Mezei, Harisiades,* and *Galvan* applied the harsh doctrine of the foundation cases, British courts were displaying analogous deference when asked to review the Crown's exercise of broadly worded statutory powers over immigration. See, e.g., *Schmidt v. Sec. of State for Home Affairs* [1969] 2 Ch. 149 (Ct. of App.); *R. v. Gov'r of Brixton Prison, ex parte Soblen* [1963] 2 Q.B. 243 (Ct. of App.); *R. v. Sec. of State for Home Affairs, ex parte Duke of Chateau Thierry* [1917] 1 K.B. 922 (C.A.). And, just as cracks are finally beginning to appear in the absolutism of the American immigration cases, British absolutism has begun to suffer similar erosion. See, e.g., *R. v. Imm. App. Trib., ex parte Khan* [1983] 2 All E.R. 420 (C.A.); *cf. Council of Civil Service Unions v. Minister for the Civil Service* [1984] 3 All E.R. 934, 948, 950–51, 956 (not an immigration case; majority holds prerogative acts reviewable).

In vivid contrast to the special judicial deference exhibited by American and British judges is the willingness of the German Federal Constitutional Court to review the constitutionality of federal immigration statutes. See Gerald L. Neuman, *Immigration and Judicial Review in the Federal Republic of Germany,* 23 N.Y.U. J.Int'l L. & Politics 35 (1990).

---

13. One distinguished British writer found this jump to be a nonsequitur. See Cedric H.R. Thornberry, *Dr. Soblen and the Alien Law of the United Kingdom,* 12 Internat'l & Comparative L.Q. 414, 424–28 (1963). Whether the Crown then had a prerogative immigration power is the subject of historical debate. Compare Thornberry, *supra* at 422–24 (prerogative power had atrophied from non-use) with Thomas W. Haycraft, *Alien Legislation and the Prerogative of the Crown,* 13 L.Q. Rev. 165, 175–84 (1897) (power alive and well).

CHAPTER 3

IMMIGRANT PRIORITIES

United States law classifies all noncitizens as immigrants or nonimmigrants. As you will see in the next chapter, a nonimmigrant who wants to enter the United States must prove that he or she fits one of the many statutory pigeonholes: students, tourists, business visitors, intra-company transferees, and so on. All the possible categories are laid out neatly in a single provision, INA § 101(a)(15). Most of the nonimmigrant categories require a temporary stay of fixed duration.

The same provision defines "immigrant" by process of elimination—any noncitizen who cannot establish that he or she meets the requirements for one of the enumerated nonimmigrant classes. Like a nonimmigrant, an intending immigrant must fit one of several qualifying categories laid out in the statute. The system of immigrant classifications, however, is less tidy; the INA establishes a complex set of preferred immigrant categories and numerical quotas that it takes several long sections of the statute to lay out.

Lawfully admitted immigrants are known by several names. The technical term is "aliens lawfully admitted for permanent residence." Sometimes you will see the phrases "permanent resident aliens" or "lawful permanent residents" ("LPR's," the abbreviation used in this book). Upon admission as an LPR, one receives documentary proof of status, 63 Fed. Reg. 70313 (Dec. 21, 1998), known familiarly as a "green card." Despite its name, this card actually has changed colors several times over the years. It is plastic and about the size of a credit card.

Upon admission, immigrants enjoy far greater benefits than nonimmigrants. Immigrants may remain in the United States permanently so long as they refrain from deportable misconduct. Unlike most categories of nonimmigrants, immigrants may work. Immigrants also qualify for some government-provided benefits not available to nonimmigrants, although welfare reform legislation enacted in 1996 has greatly limited even immigrants' eligibility for welfare. After an initial qualifying period, if certain conditions discussed in chapter 13 are met, immigrants may (but need not) become United States citizens. For all these reasons, the admission standards for immigrants are more rigorous than those prescribed for nonimmigrants. This and other chapters will examine those differences in some detail.

Although this chapter considers the criteria for *acquiring* LPR status, you should keep in mind that one can lose this status by leaving the United

States too often, for too long, or with the wrong intentions. The criteria and procedures are considered on pages 521–22 below.

SECTION A.   THE FUNDAMENTALS: QUOTAS AND PREFERENCES

The starting point in understanding United States immigration law is this: To qualify for admission, an immigrant must affirmatively fit within one of the various admission categories established by Congress. It is not enough, in other words, that the person has no criminal convictions, contagious diseases, or other blemishes. Only those with certain positive credentials are eligible.[1]

Most of the qualifying categories are subject to annual numerical limits. These limits are often called "quotas" even though they are ceilings rather than floors. Certain classes of immigrants, however, are exempt from the numerical restrictions:

1.   IMMIGRANTS EXEMPT FROM THE GENERAL QUOTAS

By far the most important exempt group consists of "immediate relatives." These are the spouses, parents, and children of United States citizens, except that in the case of a parent the citizen son or daughter must be at least 21 years of age. INA § 201(b)(2)(A)(i). To be a "child" for immigration purposes, one must be unmarried and under age 21. INA § 101(b)(1). There are additional requirements for stepchildren, adopted children, and children born out of wedlock; those will be taken up later.

Immediate relative admissions stayed fairly stable during the years leading up to 1996. For the eight fiscal years from 1988 to 1995, inclusive, annual immediate relative admissions ranged from 217,514 (1989) to 255,-059 (1993). INS 1995 Statistical Yearbook, Table 4. In 1996, however, many of the people who had benefitted from an earlier legalization program became naturalized United States citizens eligible to petition for their immediate relatives. For that and other reasons explored in chapter 13, section A below, immediate relative admissions later increased, averaging slightly more than 300,000 during fiscal years 1996 through 2000, inclusive. 2003 Yearbook of Immigration Statistics, Table 4, at 20 (Sept. 2004). After a large spike in fiscal years 2001 and 2002 (averaging 464,000 per year), immediate relative admissions reverted to 333,000 in fiscal year 2003. *Id.*

---

1. Before the Immigration Act of 1990, if any quota visas were left over after demand from the preferred groups of applicants had been satisfied, other "nonpreference" immigrants would become eligible. INA § 203(a)(7), pre–1990 version. In practice, though, the demand for preference visas was so great that nonpreference visas were never available after 1978. *Solis–Ramirez v. U.S.D.O.J.*, 758 F.2d 1426, 1429 (11th Cir. 1985).

Certain other groups are also numerically unrestricted. LPRs who are returning from temporary visits abroad are not counted against the quota; either they were exempt at the time of their original admission or they were already counted once before. See INA §§ 101(a)(27)(A), 201(b)(1)(A). Similarly exempt are certain former United States citizens, INA §§ 101(a)(27)(B), 201(b)(1)(A), children born to LPRs temporarily abroad, INA § 201(b)(2)(B), and persons who receive certain permanent forms of discretionary relief from removal that you will study in chapter 8, INA § 201(b)(1)(C, D, E). People fleeing persecution are also exempt from the general quota, INA § 201(b)(1)(B), but they are subject to special numerical restrictions of their own. Their situations are considered in depth in chapter 11.

"Parolees" are another group permitted into the United States without numerical restriction. Under INA § 212(d)(5), the Secretary of Homeland Security has the discretion to "parole" a noncitizen into the United States temporarily. Until 1980 the parole provision was often used to allow groups of refugees into the United States for indefinite periods, as you will see in some detail in chapter 11. The current provision generally prohibits that practice, see INA § 212(d)(5)(B), and today the provision is typically used either to enable noncitizens to come to the United States temporarily for urgent personal reasons or to allow applicants for admission to remain at large pending determinations of admissibility. Whatever the reason for allowing the particular person to come in, a grant of parole is *not* considered an admission. INA § 212(d)(5)(A). In the eyes of the law, the parolee is still outside the United States. Consequently, there is no need for a statutory provision expressly exempting parolees from the general quotas applicable to those who seek visas or "admission."

Apart from all these permanent statutory provisions that create classes of immigrants exempt from the general quota, Congress from time to time admits special groups ad hoc on a nonquota basis. Various legalization programs enacted in 1986 (which actually are now listed as specific exemptions in INA § 201(b)(1)(C)) are examples.[2] Congress at least three times in recent years has also authorized the issuance of a limited number of additional immigrant visas, each time on a one-shot basis, to nationals of countries that are regarded as underrepresented in terms of immigration to the United States. See, e.g., Immigration Act of 1990, §§ 132, 133; Pub.L. 100–658, §§ 2, 3, 102 Stat. 3908, 3908–09 (Nov. 15, 1988); Pub.L. 99–603 (IRCA), § 314, 100 Stat. 3359, 3439 (Nov. 6, 1986). Congress has also occasionally awarded lawful permanent residence on a nonquota basis to groups of people who arrive from selected countries as part of an unusual migration. In recent years, Cubans and Haitians have benefitted from such one-time-only statutes. See IRCA § 202. Finally, to relieve a serious and chronic shortage of nurses, Congress enacted temporary legislation to allow certain nurses already working in the United States on nonimmigrant visas to adjust to permanent residence without regard to the usual numerical

---

2. The general legalization program and the program for "special agricultural workers," see INA §§ 210, 245A, are discussed on pages 609–10 below.

constraints. Immigration Nursing Relief Act of 1989, Pub.L. 101–238, 103 Stat. 2099 (Dec. 18, 1989).

But most immigrant visa applicants are subject to annual numerical ceilings. In modern times the demand for those visas has vastly exceeded the statutory supply. What are the overall limits, and how do our immigration laws allocate the available slots?

2.   IMMIGRANTS SUBJECT TO THE GENERAL QUOTAS

The admission of "quota" immigrants to the United States is governed by a mathematically intricate system of ceilings and sub-ceilings. The INA lays out categories of immigrants who may be admitted. For each such category, the INA limits the number who may come in during any one fiscal year. In addition to these "worldwide" caps, some of the categories are subject to "per-country" limits that are discussed below.

Immigration law is about choices, and the quota system is especially about choices. When Congress divides applicants into groups, and assigns different numerical caps to the various groups, it is making the most fundamental policy decisions known to immigration law: Who should get preference over whom? In some instances, Congress has expressed those decisions in mathematical language. You will probably be pleased to know that most of the technical mathematical issues are beyond the scope of this book. But certain precepts are too central to be ignored. In the readings that follow, the goals are simply to acquaint you with the basic structure of the quota system and to get you thinking about the fundamental policy choices that the various rules and formulas reflect.

a.   PROGRAMS AND CEILINGS

At the most general level, there are three main programs for immigrants who are subject to the general quotas. These programs encompass "family-sponsored immigrants," "employment-based immigrants," and "diversity immigrants." (Overseas refugees could logically be viewed as a fourth category, but they are treated separately in chapter 11, section A below.)

Each of these three broad programs has its own worldwide ceiling. Two of the three ceilings change from year to year in accordance with statutory formulas.

Family-sponsored immigrants generally comprise immigrants who have certain family members in the United States. The specified relationships are not quite close enough to qualify the immigrants as immediate relatives (who, you will recall, are entirely exempt from the quota limitations) but are still close enough to warrant immigration preference. The qualifying categories are listed in INA § 203(a), which you will examine later in more detail. The total annual worldwide limit for family-sponsored immigrants is determined by the following formula: 480,000, minus the number of immediate relatives (and children born to LPRs temporarily abroad) who were admitted in the preceding fiscal year, plus any employment-based visas that were available in the preceding fiscal year but were not used. Certain grants of parole also slightly reduce the annual ceiling. INA § 201(c)(1)(A)(ii). There is one proviso: In any year in which that formula produces a number less than 226,000, the ceiling will be bumped up to 226,000. See INA § 201(c).

That formula was a product of the Immigration Act of 1990, and it reflects an important and controversial change. Immediate relatives are still exempt from the quota, but the number of visas they take are now deducted from the supply available during the next fiscal year to other family members of United States citizens and of LPRs. To address the fear that high immediate relative numbers could wipe out all or most of the visas allotted to other family members, Congress provided for the 226,000 minimum.

Employment-based immigrants include those with certain occupational skills, certain investors, and miscellaneous others. The specific criteria appear in INA § 203(b), which you will see later in more detail. For now, it is enough to know that the annual worldwide limit on employment-based immigrants is 140,000 plus any family-sponsored visas that were available in the preceding year but were not used.

Notice that the ceiling for *family-sponsored* visas includes any unused *employment-based* visas from the preceding year, and vice-versa. Why do you suppose Congress used this criss-cross approach (rather than give unused family-sponsored visas to the next year's family-sponsored immigrants and unused employment-based visas to the next year's employment-based immigrants)?

Diversity immigrants are those who are admitted because they were born in countries or regions from which the United States has received relatively little immigration in recent years. The program is described in INA § 203(c) and discussed in section D below. The basic annual ceiling is 55,000, see INA § 201(e), but that figure is now reduced to 50,000 to offset some of the Guatemalan and Salvadoran admissions authorized by special 1997 legislation (NACARA, discussed in chapter 8).

Those are the formulas for the annual *worldwide* ceilings for each of the main immigrant programs. These programs are also subject to *per-country* limits. For purposes of those limits, an immigrant is "charged" to the country or colony in which he or she was born, with some exceptions. INA § 202(b). Generally, in each fiscal year, the combined numbers of family-sponsored and employment-based immigrants from a single country may not exceed 7% of the combined worldwide limits for family-sponsored and employment-based immigrants. For the colony of a foreign country, the corresponding figure is 2%. INA § 202(a)(2). Immediate relatives and others who are exempt from the worldwide limitations are similarly exempt from the per-country limitations. As discussed below, one subgroup of family-sponsored immigrants (some of the so-called "2A's") are also exempt from per-country limitations. Under the diversity immigrant program, similarly, no more than 7% of the visas may go to natives of a single country in the same fiscal year.

Under section 104 of the American Competitiveness in the Twenty–First Century Act, Pub. L. 106–313, 114 Stat. 1251 (Oct. 17, 2000), employment-based immigrants are exempt from per-country limits during any calendar quarter in which the total worldwide ceiling for employment-based immigrants exceeds the worldwide number of qualified applicants. INA § 202(a)(5)(A).

PROBLEM 1

In fiscal year 1, the ceilings on family-sponsored and employment-based immigrants were 260,000 and 140,000, respectively. In the chart that follows, "qualified applicants" are those who meet the requirements of the designated category and do not fall within any of the exclusion grounds (such as criminality, disease, etc.). The figures given for qualified applicants include not only those who applied during the particular fiscal year, but also any who applied in past years and are still waiting. In this Problem, ignore the deductions for children born to LPRs temporarily abroad and for parolees.

Applying the statutory formulas laid out above, fill in the blank columns:

| | **Fiscal Year 1** | **Fiscal Year 2** | | **Fiscal Year 3** | |
| | | Qualified | | Qualified | |
	Visas Issued	Visa Applicants	Visas Issued	Visa Applicants	Visas Issued
Immediate relatives	230,000	275,000	_____	290,000	_____
Family-sponsored immigrants	260,000	330,000	_____	340,000	_____
Employment-based immigrants	135,000	130,000	_____	150,000	_____

b. PREFERENCE CATEGORIES AND SUB–CEILINGS

The family-sponsored program is subdivided into four "preference categories" laid out in INA § 203(a). These preference provisions serve two functions: They describe the different groups of people who qualify as family-sponsored immigrants, and they set annual numerical sub-ceilings for each of these four groups. The four family-sponsored preferences are

First preference: the unmarried sons and daughters of United States citizens.

Second preference: the spouses and the unmarried sons and daughters of LPRs.

Third preference: the married sons and daughters of United States citizens.

Fourth preference: the brothers and sisters of over-age–21 United States citizens.

Here are the numerical subceilings for each of the four family-sponsored preferences:

First preference: 23,400 plus any visas that the fourth preference applicants don't need.

Second preference: 114,200 plus any visas that the first preference applicants don't need, plus the amount, if any, by which the total worldwide family-sponsored ceiling exceeds 226,000.

Third preference: 23,400 plus any visas that the first and second preference applicants don't need.

Fourth preference: 65,000 plus any visas that the first, second, and third preference applicants don't need.

The second preference (spouses and unmarried sons and daughters of LPRs) requires additional comment. Before the Immigration Act of 1990, the second preference had become hopelessly backed up—several years generally and more than 10 years for Mexicans. See United States Dept. of State, Visa Bulletin at 2 (Nov. 1990). Congress recognized the hardship in separating nuclear families for that length of time and set out to reduce the waiting period. One action it took was to increase the annual base number from 70,200 to 114,200. In addition, Congress provided that, whenever the total ceiling for family-sponsored immigrants exceeded 226,000, the entire excess would go to the second preference. (See above.)

Congress also decided to split the second preference into two subgroups. The first one (usually called the "2A's") consists of spouses and "children" of LPRs. (Remember that "children" have to be under 21, see INA § 101(b)). The 2B's were all other second preference immigrants (i.e. the over-age–21 unmarried sons and daughters of LPRs). Believing that the admission of the 2A's should be a higher priority than the admission of the 2B's, Congress did two things. First, it required that at least 77% of the worldwide second preference visas be set aside for the 2A's. The resulting figure—i.e., 77% of the worldwide second preference ceiling—is called the "2A floor." INA § 203(a)(2). Second, Congress exempted 75% of the 2A floor from the per-country limits. INA § 202(a)(4). That combination of measures helped to shorten many of the waiting periods for the 2A's, but the waits are still several years long, as the Visa Bulletin chart on page 254 below illustrates.

For employment-based immigrants, the math is simpler but the descriptions of the various preference categories are much longer and more detailed. There are five employment-based preferences, several of them subdivided. They are laid out in INA § 203(b). You will encounter these preferences in more detail in section C. For now, the five categories and their ceilings can be summarized briefly:

The first preference is for "priority workers." This term includes three subgroups—persons with "extraordinary ability in the sciences, arts, education, business, or athletics;" "outstanding professors and researchers;" and certain "multinational executives and managers." These immigrants annually receive 28.6% of all the employment-based visas, plus any visas that the fourth and fifth preference applicants don't need.

The second preference is for "members of the professions holding advanced degrees" (usually meaning graduate degrees) and "aliens of exceptional ability." ("Exceptional" ability is not as exceptional as "extraordinary" ability). Second preference immigrants similarly get 28.6% of the employment-based visas, plus any visas that the first preference applicants don't need.

The third employment-based preference is for "skilled workers, professionals" [without advanced degrees], and other workers who can show their labor is needed in the United States. This category is also allocated 28.6% of the employment-based visas, plus any visas that the first and second preference applicants don't need. Of these, no more than 10,000 (minus an offset for some of the Guatemalans and Salvadorans benefitted by NACARA, see chapter 8) may go to the "other workers."

The fourth preference is for certain "special immigrants." This category includes, among others, certain religious workers and certain long-term foreign employees of the United States government. The allotment is 7.1% of the employment-based visas. There is no provision for adding the visas that other preference categories don't need.

The fifth employment-based preference is entitled "Employment creation." It covers entrepreneurs who invest at least $1,000,000 each (less in specified instances) in enterprises that employ at least ten Americans. These immigrants are admitted subject to certain future conditions considered in section C. They may receive up to 7.1% of the employment-based visas. Again there is no provision for adding visas that the other preference applicants don't need.

The program for "diversity immigrants" is not broken down into preference categories. It does, however, contain a series of fiendishly complicated formulas that you can look forward to seeing (or skipping) in section D.

Finally, under INA § 203(d), a "spouse or child" who is "accompanying, or following to join" an immigrant who is within any of the three broad preference categories—family, employment, or diversity—is entitled to the same preference status and to the same place in the queue as the principal immigrant. See also 22 C.F.R. § 42.53(c) (2004). Curiously, there has never been any comparable provision for the spouse or child accompanying or following to join *an immediate relative*. Importantly also, for section 203(d) to apply, the spouse or child must be acquired *before* the principal immigrant's admission as an LPR. 22 C.F.R. § 42.53(c) (2004). (Try to figure out why a contrary interpretation would render INA § 203(a)(2)(A) superfluous.) Interestingly, however, the regulations treat a child as having satisfied this condition if the child is the product of a marriage that took place before the principal immigrant's admission as an LPR. A spouse or child will be regarded as "accompanying" the principal immigrant until six months after the issuance of the principal immigrant's visa (or adjustment of status, a process considered in chapter 6). 22 C.F.R. § 40.1(a) (2004). There is no analogous time limit on a spouse or child who is "following to join." 9 F.A.M. § 40.1 n.7.1.

PROBLEM 2

In fiscal year x, 220,000 immediate relatives were admitted to the United States. 245,000 family-sponsored immigrant visas were available that year and 235,000 of them were used. Exactly 140,000 employment-based visas were available, and all were taken. First, calculate the total worldwide ceiling for *the following* fiscal year (x + 1), both (a) for family-sponsored immigrants and (b) for employment-based immigrants. For purposes of this Problem, assume there are no deductions for children born to LPRs temporarily abroad or for parolees.

Next, look at the chart below. The column headed "Statutory Quota" summarizes the formulas for computing the statutory ceilings for each of the four family-sponsored, and each of the five employment-based, preference categories. Refer to INA §§ 201(c, d) and 203(a, b) for more details if needed. The next column gives you the hypothetical number of qualified visa applicants in each preference category, *for year x + 1.* Complete the column headed "Visas Issued."

FISCAL YEAR X + 1

Preference	Statutory Quota	Qualified Visa Applicants	Visas Issued
Family 1st	23,400 plus unused 4ths	29,400	_____
Family 2nd	114,200 plus unused 1st's, plus any excess of total family-sponsored ceiling over 226,000	200,000	_____
Family 3rd	23,400 plus unused 1st's and 2d's	18,400	_____
Family 4th	65,000 plus unused 1st's, 2d's, and 3rd's	67,000	_____
Total Family–Sponsored		**314,800**	_____
Employment 1st	28.6% of E–B ceiling + unused 4th's and 5th's	12,900	_____
Employment 2d	28.6% of E–B ceiling + unused 1st's	22,900	_____
Employment 3rd	28.6% of E–B ceiling + unused 1st's and 2nd's	105,900	_____
Employment 4th	7.1% of E–B ceiling	5,650	_____
Employment 5th	7.1% of E–B ceiling	5,650	_____
Total Employment–Based		**153,000**	_____

c. SELECTING INDIVIDUAL APPLICANTS

All this leaves one last question: When the demand for visas for a particular preference category exceeds the statutory sub-ceiling, which applicants get the available visas? The general answer is easy: whoever applies first. For purposes of establishing one's place in line, the clock starts when the applicant files the first relevant document. For a good description, see Stanley Krieger, *Priority Dates—How to Get Them—How to Keep Them,* in AILA, 1990 (2) Immigration and Nationality Law at 284–96. What that document is varies from one preference category to another; you will study the procedural requirements in chapter 6.

The date on which the applicant files the relevant document is called his or her "priority date." It resembles the number you take when you enter a crowded delicatessen, except that the wait for visas, unlike that for rye bread or bagels, can last years rather than minutes. Immigrants at the front of the line are processed in monthly gulps; they advance in steps until their priority dates become "current."

The one major complication is the per-country limit. Suppose within a particular country 50,000 family-sponsored and employment-based applicants have priority dates that would be current if there were no per-country limits, but the per-country limit for that year is only 27,000. Which 27,000 applicants get in, and which ones have to wait until next year (or longer)?

The simplest method would be to award visas, within that group, in the order in which people applied. But that is not the method used. Before 1990 (when there was just one combined set of numbered preferences that covered both family relationships and occupational skills), visas would go to all of an oversubscribed country's qualified first preference applicants whose priority dates were within the worldwide limits, then to all the qualified second preference applicants within the worldwide limits, and so on, until the per-country limit (then 20,000) was reached. Without some adjustment, this system would have made life impossible for the bottom preferences. If year after year the demand from the top preferences was alone greater than 20,000—and in some countries it often was—the people in the bottom preferences would have waited in line literally forever.

To avoid that problem, the law contained a safety valve: Whenever a country used up its full allowance of 20,000 quota visas in a given fiscal year, the quota visas available for that country in the following year were "prorated" among the various preference categories in the same proportions as those applicable worldwide. See INA § 202(e), pre–1990 version; *Olivares v. INS,* 685 F.2d 1174 (9th Cir.1982); *Angco v. Haig,* 514 F.Supp. 1328 (E.D.Pa.1981).

The current law takes a slightly modified approach. Rather than delay the solution until the following fiscal year, the present version of section 202(e) requires proration in the very year in which the per-country limit is reached. Suppose, for example, that in a particular year the worldwide family-sponsored ceiling turns out to be twice as great as the worldwide employment-based ceiling. In that example, within a particular oversubscribed country family-sponsored applicants will receive twice as many visas as employment-based applicants do. INA § 202(e)(1). Similarly, *within* the family-sponsored program, the visas for an oversubscribed country are allocated among the four preference categories in the same proportions that apply worldwide for that year. INA § 202(e)(2). Thus, if the ceiling for family-sponsored third-preference immigrants worldwide turns out to be 10% of the total worldwide family-sponsored ceiling, then within a given oversubscribed country 10% of the family-sponsored visas would go to third-preference applicants. The same proration technique is used for the five employment-based preferences within a given oversubscribed country. INA § 202(e)(3). When prorating is used, adjustments are made to account for the fact that most of the 2A's are exempt from the per-country limitations. INA § 202(a)(4)(B, C).

All this means that the delicatessen analogy is incomplete. A typical deli doesn't have one queue for buying bagels, another for cream cheese, and so on. Usually there is one combined queue for all customers, and people are waited on in the order in which they establish their place in that queue.

In contrast is a type of queuing system in which different customers wait in different lines. Picture a typical supermarket. There is a separate queue for each cashier. Someone who gets in line after you do might be served before you if he or she was lucky enough to have picked a faster-moving line. Still, you had a free choice; you too could have chosen that person's line. Suppose, however, that rules beyond your control determine which queue you must wait in. Hospitals do not make patients who need emergency medical care wait in the same queue as those who are awaiting elective surgery. The hospital's rules reflect the differing personal needs of their patients.

The immigration laws follow the hospital model—different queues, and therefore different waiting times, for different categories of customers. One's preference category and one's country generally determine in which queue one must wait.

Before adopting that system, Congress had to make many policy decisions, some consciously and some unconsciously. Try to identify and evaluate those policy choices as you work through the following questions:

QUESTIONS

1. Should there even be a preference system at all, or would it better simply to admit qualified immigrants on a uniform first-come, first-served basis?

2. Should there be per-country limits? Some commentators have advocated repealing them. See, e.g., T. Alexander Aleinikoff, *Legal Immigration Reform: Toward Rationality and Equity*, in Richard D. Lamm & Alan Simpson (Eds.), Center for Immigration Studies, Blueprints for an Ideal Legal Immigration Policy (2001), http://cis.org/articles/2001/blueprints/toc.html; Bernard Trujillo, *Immigrant Visa Distribution: The Case of Mexico*, 2000 Wisconsin L. Rev. 713. (Keep your opinion tentative. The material on diversity immigrants in section D might affect your thinking.) If per-country limits are retained, should every country have the same limit?

3. Given the per-country limits, which immigrants *within an oversubscribed country* should receive visas? Options include (a) Within the family-sponsored program, admit all the qualified first preference applicants who are within the worldwide cutoff, then all the seconds, etc., until the per-country limit is reached; do the same for the employment-based program; (b) Pro-rate the visas among the various preference categories in proportion to the worldwide preference allocations; or (c) Admit qualified applicants who are within the worldwide cutoff, strictly in order by priority date, until the per-country limit is reached.

4. Given all you have now read, and thinking especially about the issues raised in question 3 above, are the preference categories in hierarchial order? E.g., are family-sponsored first preference immigrants better off than seconds, seconds better off than thirds, and so on?

5. In recent years, an increasingly serious practical problem has contaminated this elaborate statutory scheme. Quite apart from the backlogs that result from statutory quotas, *administrative processing* can add years to the waiting times. The sizes of the backlogs vary widely both from one category of case to another and from one geographic district or region to another. As you will see in chapter 6, the procedure for prospective immigrants usually involves some combination of visa processing by consular offices, Labor Department (and state employment agency) processing, and USCIS processing, depending on the category of case. The current waiting times can be viewed on the following websites: for consular visa wait times, http://travel.state.gov/visa/tempvisitors_wait.php; for the Labor Department, http://www.ows.doleta.gov/foreign/times.asp#reg; and for USCIS, http://egov.immigration.gov/cris/jsps/index.jsp.

As a result of a "Backlog Elimination Plan" initiated by USCIS Director Eduardo Aguirre in 2004, the agency has put a major dent in its multi-million-case backlog. According to USCIS statistics, the backlog decreased by 13% from October 2003 to August 2004. During that period, the administrative processing times for petitions to classify noncitizen relatives (usually the first step in the admission process) fell from 27 months to 12 months. The Director attributes the improvement to a combination of efficiency measures that he predicts will eliminate the backlog entirely, and reduce most processing times to six months, by the end of 2006. See USCIS, Backlog Elimination Plan–Fiscal Year 2004, 3rd Quarter Update (Nov. 5, 2004).

————

Now that you have examined the general structure of the immigrant selection system, it is time to focus more specifically on each of its three principal branches: family, employment, and diversity.

Section B.   Family Immigration[4]

1.   The Basics

As you might recall from chapter 1 (but probably don't), numerical immigration quotas debuted in 1921. The Immigration Act of 1924 exempted the wives, and the unmarried, under-age–18 children, of United States citizens from the quota. See ch. 190, § 4(a), 43 Stat. 153, 155 (May 26, 1924). The 1952 Act established the first comprehensive set of family-based preferences. Since then, one central value that United States immigration laws have long promoted, albeit to varying degrees, is family unity.[5]

Several permanent provisions of the present INA aid the reunification of the temporarily divided family. They include section 201(b)(2), which exempts from the quotas "immediate relatives" and children born to LPRs temporarily abroad; section 203(a), which bestows special preferences on certain immigrants with slightly less compelling family relationships to United States citizens or to LPRs; and section 203(d), which gives preference to spouses and children accompanying or following to join most (but not all) classes of immigrants. You should now review the cited provisions and the description, on pages 245–46 above, of "accompanying or following to join." You will need to be familiar with these concepts to do the Problems below.

One who consults an immigration lawyer to acquire permanent residence for himself or herself or for another person wants to know more than simply whether immigration will be possible. The client also wants to know how long it will take. If the prospective immigrant is exempt from the

4. See generally Sarah B. Ignatius & Elisabeth S. Stickney, Immigration Law and the Family (1995, continually updated); Sarah B. Ignatius, *Selected Recent Developments in Family Immigration Law*, Immigration Briefings (Oct. 1996); Hiroshi Motomura, *The Family and Immigration: A Roadmap for the Ruritanian Lawmaker*, 43 American J.Comp.L. 511 (1995).

5. But see Carol Sanger, *Immigration Reform and Control of the Undocumented Family*, 2 Georgetown Immigration L.J. 295 (1987) (arguing that the 1986 legalization program, by failing to provide for the nuclear families of legalized immigrants, deviated from that tradition).

quota, then the only delays are those needed for the applicant to gather up the necessary documents and for the relevant government agencies to process them. The waiting times vary, as just noted. If the immigrant is subject to the quota, however, the wait can be anywhere from very short to very long, depending on two basic variables. First, both the supply of visas and the demand for visas—and hence the length of the wait—vary from one preference category to another. Second, because there are per-country limits, and because the demand for a given preference can vary greatly from one country to another, the wait is affected by the country to which the visa will be "charged."

Immigration lawyers, prospective immigrants, their families and employers, the general public, and government officials all need some way to estimate the likely waiting time. To assist them, the State Department's Visa Office, in Washington, D.C., publishes a monthly "Visa Bulletin." Included in the Visa Bulletin is a chart that indicates, for every combination of country and preference category, how long ago the people who are now about to receive visas first applied. The chart does this by displaying the "priority date" (recall this is the date the first relevant document is filed) of the person who will be first in line for the next month. If there is no backlog at all for the particular preference/country combination, the class is said to be "current," and the letter C appears. If no visas will be available that month (because the annual numerical limits for the year have already been reached), the letter "U," for "Unavailable," appears. A copy of the chart for April 2005 appears on page 254 below.

The Visa Office Bulletin tells us only how long those who are *now* receiving visas had to wait. For example, the chart below shows that family-sponsored third-preference Mexicans who began the process on April 8, 1995 received visas in April 2005. They waited ten years. That doesn't necessarily tell us how long those who are initiating the process today will have to wait. On the demand side, perhaps an unusually high (or low) number of applications for a particular country/preference combination have been filed since the priority date displayed in the chart. And on the supply side, the various statutory formulas that you have already seen cause the numerical ceilings to change from year to year. Still, absent great fluctuations in the supply and demand variables, and absent cataclysmic statutory changes of the kind enacted in 1990, the data contained in successive monthly issues of the Visa Bulletins provide at least crude estimates of the likely future waiting times.

When you read the Visa Bulletin, you might be struck by the length of some of the waiting periods—many of them several years. The long delays have caused major problems. The most obvious problem is the hardship of lengthy separation, especially in the spousal and parent-child contexts. Another problem is "aging-out." It is not unusual for the applicant's immigration status to change for the worse while the application is pending, typically because the person attains age 21 or marries.

Congress's liberalization of the "2A" category for the unmarried sons and daughters of LPRs, discussed earlier, was one important response to the hardship problem. In 2000, as part of the Legal Immigration Family Equity Act [LIFE], Congress took another (very limited) step by creating "V-visas." Beneficiaries of 2A visa petitions that were filed on or before December 21, 2000 (the enactment date of LIFE) may enter the United States as nonimmigrants once their waiting times exceed three years, INA § 101(a)(15)(V), and may work, INA § 214(o)(1)(A). If the permanent application is ultimately denied, V-status terminates 30 days later. INA § 214(o)(1)(B). Since the statute specifies no other ending date, V-status otherwise continues until LPR status is attained.

The "aging out" problem is more complicated. As you will see in chapter 6, the process for obtaining an immigrant visa on family grounds typically begins with the United States citizen or LPR family member filing a "visa petition" with USCIS to establish the claimed relationship. Once USCIS approves the visa petition, it forwards the approval to the State Department, which sends it on to the relevant consulate overseas. (There is an alternative process called "adjustment of status" for certain intending immigrants who are already in the United States, but to keep this discussion manageable let us assume use of the visa process.) At some point the noncitizen "beneficiary" (i.e., the person attempting to immigrate) then files a "visa application" with the consulate. Eventually the beneficiary appears at a consulate for an interview and a decision on the visa is made.

All this takes time—not just time waiting for the person's priority date to come up (in the case of quota visas that are not current), but also administrative processing time by both USCIS and the consulate. What if the particular immigrant category requires that the beneficiary be a "child" and therefore under age 21, and the beneficiary is indeed under age 21 when the visa petition is filed, but he or she turns 21 before the process is completed?

Congress did not think it fair to count the *administrative processing* time against the applicants. To remedy that problem, Congress in 2002 passed the Child Status Protection Act, Pub. L. 107–208, 116 Stat. 927 (Aug. 6, 2002). Delays attributable to the *numerical ceilings* are a different story. Subject to one quirk noted below, the statute does not attempt to freeze the beneficiary's age while that person is waiting for his or her priority date to become current.

The most relevant provisions of the Child Status Protection Act are sections 2 and 3. They address the aging-out problems for the sons and daughters of United States citizens (section 2, which added section 201(f) to the INA) and the sons and daughters of LPRs (section 3, which added INA § 203(h)).

The upshot of section 2 is that for immediate relative purposes the beneficiary's age is frozen as of the date the visa petition was filed. The beneficiary will be treated as the "child" of a United States citizen, in other words, as long as he or she was under age 21 at the time the parent filed the petition with USCIS (and all other requirements are met). The same section makes appropriate adjustments for cases in which the beneficiary *becomes* an immediate relative while some other visa petition is otherwise pending—for example, where the parent is an LPR who has filed a family-sponsored 2A petition for the child, but the parent naturalizes while that petition is pending. See INA § 201(f) for details.

Section 3 does somewhat analogous things for the "children" of LPRs. The main preferences for children of LPRs are the 2A preference and section 203(d), for children "following or accompanying to join" their preference immigrant parents. Again, both categories refer specifically to the "child," which in turn means the person must be under age 21. For purposes of that requirement, section 3 lays out a formula for determining the age the child should be treated as having attained. Generally, the consulate is to go by the beneficiary's age at the time the visa becomes available (which happens when the priority date for the particular category becomes current and the visa petition has been approved), *but reduced by the amount of time the visa petition was pending.* INA § 203(h)(1). For this section to apply, there is a further requirement that the beneficiary file the necessary forms with the consulate within one year of the visa becoming available. *Id.* § 203(h)(1)(A).

The provision for reducing the beneficiary's age by the amount of time the visa petition was pending is, however, a bit odd. The obvious goal was to make sure processing time did not adversely affect the applicant's immigrant status, but it is not clear that that is all this provision does. Suppose an LPR files a family-sponsored 2A petition for his or her 17–year-old unmarried daughter. Assume that, solely because of quota backlogs, it takes five years for the 2A petition to become current. The daughter is now 22, seemingly ineligible for 2A status. But if it turns out that during that five-year waiting period USCIS took two years to approve the visa peti-tion—a delay that would not have seemed to matter because she had to wait five years anyway—then the daughter will be treated as if she were age 20. Thus, she will qualify for 2A status. In contrast, if USCIS had processed her visa petition in six months, then, when her priority date became current five years after the process was started, she would be treated as if she were 21 ½—too old to qualify for 2A status. It is one thing to assure that she not be disadvantaged by USCIS processing time. But in the former case, isn't she positively advantaged by a seemingly irrelevant delay? Much will turn on how the affected Departments and the courts interpret the formula provided by INA § 203(h)(1).

United States Department of State Bureau of Consular Affairs

VISA BULLETIN

April 2005

Priority Dates for Family–Sponsored Immigrant Visas

Family	All Chargeability Areas Except Those Listed	CHINA	INDIA	MEXICO	PHILIPPINES
1st	15MAR01	15MAR01	15MAR01	22OCT94	15DEC90
2A	08JAN01	08JAN01	08JAN01	15JAN98	08JAN01
2B	15OCT95	15OCT95	15OCT95	15MAR92	15OCT95
3rd	22JAN98	22JAN98	22JAN98	08APR95	01AUG90
4th	15MAY93	15MAY93	08SEP92	15MAY93	22NOV82

Priority Dates for Employment–Based Immigrant Visas

Employment	All Chargeability Areas Except Those Listed	CHINA	INDIA	MEXICO	PHILIPPINES
1st	C	C	C	C	C
2nd	C	C	C	C	C
3rd	C	C	01APR02	01APR02	C	01APR02
Other Workers	01JUL01	01JUL01	01JUL01	01JUL01	01JUL01
4th	C	C	C	C	C
5th	C	C	C	C	C

PROBLEMS 3–4

In doing the Problems in this set, assume it is now April 2005 and consider the immigrants' possible routes to permanent residence in the United States. To map out your strategy, you will need to consult the preceding Visa Bulletin chart. Keep in mind also that, after five years of LPR status (or three years "living in marital union" with a United States citizen after attainment of LPR status), one may apply for naturalization to United States citizenship. INA §§ 316(a), 319(a).

Problem 3. X, who was admitted as an LPR four years ago, has just married Y, a native and citizen of Costa Rica. Y wants to become an LPR as well. Y is very close to her sister Z, who is married and has two sons, ages 2 and 7. Z and her husband and sons are all Costa Rican citizens. X is in your office. He wants your help in securing LPR status for Y and, if possible, Z and her husband and sons. What advice would you give X? Would your advice change if all the intending immigrants were natives of the Philippines rather than Costa Rica?

Problem 4. A, who is a native and citizen of Denmark, telephones you from Europe. She is contemplating marriage to B, who is also a native and citizen of Denmark. A is six months shy of her twenty-first birthday. Her father is a citizen and resident of the United States. A wants to know whether she and her future husband will be eligible to immigrate to the United States and whether there is any reason for them to delay their marriage.

2. SPOUSES

a. SAME–SEX MARRIAGES

Adams v. Howerton

United States Court of Appeals, Ninth Circuit, 1982.
673 F.2d 1036.

■ WALLACE, CIRCUIT JUDGE:

Adams, a male American citizen, and Sullivan, a male alien, appeal from the district court's entry of summary judgment for Howerton, Acting District Director of the Immigration and Naturalization Service (INS). The district court held that their homosexual marriage did not qualify Sullivan as Adams's spouse pursuant to section 201(b) of the Immigration and Nationality Act of 1952. We affirm.

I

Following the expiration of Sullivan's visitor's visa, Adams and Sullivan obtained a marriage license from the county clerk in Boulder, Colorado, and were "married" by a minister. Adams then petitioned the INS for classification of Sullivan as an immediate relative of an American citizen, based upon Sullivan's alleged status as Adams's spouse. The petition was denied, and the denial was affirmed on appeal by the Board of Immigration Appeals. Adams and Sullivan then filed an action in district court challenging this final administrative decision on both statutory and constitutional grounds. * * * On cross-motions for summary judgment, the district court entered judgment for the INS. * * *

II

Two questions are presented in this appeal: first, whether a citizen's spouse within the meaning of section 201(b) of the Act must be an individual of the opposite sex; and second, whether the statute, if so interpreted, is constitutional.

* * * Section 201(b) defines "immediate relatives" to include the spouses of United States citizens. * * * Neither that section nor any subsequent amendments further define the term "spouse" directly.

Cases interpreting the Act indicate that a two-step analysis is necessary to determine whether a marriage will be recognized for immigration purposes. The first is whether the marriage is valid under state law. The second is whether that state-approved marriage qualifies under the Act. Both steps are required. * * *

* * *

It is not clear * * * whether Colorado would recognize a homosexual marriage. * * *

While we might well make an educated guess as to how the Colorado courts would decide this issue, it is unnecessary for us to do so. We decide this case solely upon construction of section 201(b), the second step in our two-step analysis.

III

Even if the Adams–Sullivan marriage were valid under Colorado law, the marriage might still be insufficient to confer spouse status for purposes of federal immigration law. So long as Congress acts within constitutional constraints, it may determine the conditions under which immigration visas are issued. Therefore, the intent of Congress governs the conferral of spouse status under section 201(b), and a valid marriage is determinative only if Congress so intends.

It is clear to us that Congress did not intend the mere validity of a marriage under state law to be controlling. Although the 1965 amendments do not define the term "spouse," the Act itself limits the persons who may be deemed spouses. Section 101(a)(35) of the Act specifically provides that the term "spouse" does not include

> a spouse, wife, or husband by reason of any marriage ceremony where the contracting parties thereto are not physically present in the presence of each other, unless the marriage shall have been consummated.

Furthermore, valid marriages entered into by parties not intending to live together as husband and wife are not recognized for immigration purposes. Therefore, even though two persons contract a marriage valid under state law and are recognized as spouses by that state, they are not necessarily spouses for purposes of section 201(b).

We thus turn to the question of whether Congress intended that homosexual marriages confer spouse status under section 201(b). Where a statute has been interpreted by the agency charged with its enforcement, we are ordinarily required to accord substantial deference to that construction, and should follow it "unless there are compelling indications that it is wrong." Thus, we must be mindful that the INS, in carrying out its broad responsibilities, has interpreted the term "spouse" to exclude a person entering a homosexual marriage.

While we do accord this construction proper weight, we base our decision primarily on the Act itself. Nothing in the Act, the 1965 amendments or the legislative history suggests that the reference to "spouse" in section 201(b) was intended to include a person of the same sex as the citizen in question. It is "a fundamental canon of statutory construction" that, "unless otherwise defined, words will be interpreted as taking their ordinary, contemporary, common meaning." The term "marriage" ordinarily contemplates a relationship between a man and a woman. *See* Webster's Third New International Dictionary 1384 (1971); Black's Law Dictionary 876 (5th ed. 1979). The term "spouse" commonly refers to one of the parties in a marital relationship so defined. Congress has not indicated an intent to enlarge the ordinary meaning of those words. In the absence of such a congressional directive, it would be inappropriate for us to expand the meaning of the term "spouse" for immigration purposes.
* * *

Our conclusion is supported by a further review of the 1965 amendments to the Act. These amendments not only added section 201(b) in its present form, but also amended the mandatory exclusion provisions of section 212(a) of the Act. Yet, both * * * the amendments and the accompanying Senate Report clearly express an intent to exclude homosexuals. As our duty is to ascertain and apply the intent of Congress, we strive to interpret language in one section of a statute consistently with the language of other sections and with the purposes of the entire statute considered as a whole. We think it unlikely that Congress intended to give homosexual spouses preferential admission treatment under section 201(b) of the Act when, in the very same amendments adding that section, it mandated their exclusion. Reading these provisions together, we can only conclude that Congress intended that only partners in heterosexual marriages be considered spouses under section 201(b).

IV

We next consider the constitutionality of the section 201(b) so interpreted. Adams and Sullivan contend that the law violates the equal protection clause because it discriminates against them on the bases of sex and homosexuality. They also argue that review of this claimed violation must be pursuant to a strict standard because the federal law abridges their fundamental right to marry. We need not and do not reach the question of the nature of the claimed right or whether such a right is implicated in this case. Even if it were, we would not apply a strict scrutiny standard of review to the statute. Congress has almost plenary power to admit or exclude aliens, and the decisions of Congress are subject only to limited judicial review.

* * *

We do know that where there is a rational basis for Congress's exercise of its power, whether articulated or not, the Court will uphold the immigration laws that Congress enacts. * * * [I]t is not clear what treatment a seemingly irrational statute should receive. * * *

We need not, however, delineate the exact outer boundaries of this limited judicial review. We hold that Congress's decision to confer spouse status under section 201(b) only upon the parties to heterosexual marriages has a rational basis and therefore comports with the due process clause and its equal protection requirements. There is no occasion to consider in this case whether some lesser standard of review should apply.

Congress manifested its concern for family integrity when it passed laws facilitating the immigration of the spouses of some valid heterosexual marriages. This distinction is one of many drawn by Congress pursuant to its determination to provide some—but not all—close relationships with relief from immigration restrictions that might otherwise hinder reunification in this country. In effect, Congress has determined that preferential status is not warranted for the spouses of homosexual marriages. Perhaps this is because homosexual marriages never produce offspring, because they are not recognized in most, if in any, of the states, or because they violate traditional and often prevailing societal mores. In any event, having found that Congress rationally intended to deny preferential status to the spouses of such marriages, we need not further "probe and test the justifications for the legislative decision."

We hold that section 201(b) of the Act is not unconstitutional because it denies spouses of homosexual marriages the preferences accorded to spouses of heterosexual marriages.

AFFIRMED.

NOTES AND QUESTIONS

1.   Decided in 1982, the *Adams* decision drew little public attention. Same-sex marriages simply were not a front page issue at the time. They certainly are today, as the developments traced in the discussion below illustrate.

First, as a general matter, should the federal immigration laws simply recognize every marriage that is legally valid in the jurisdiction in which it was celebrated? Argue both ways.

2.   The court refrains from deciding whether same-sex marriages are valid under Colorado law, holding that, even if they are, Congress intended not to recognize them for immigration purposes. How many different statutory interpretation techniques does the court use in arriving at that conclusion?

3.   In seeking to ascertain the intent of Congress, the court does not attempt to identify the purpose of the provision favoring spouses of United States citizens or the extent to which recognition of state-approved same-sex marriages would further that purpose. (The court considers possible purposes later when it addresses the constitutional issue, but only after it has decided the statutory interpretation issue). Why, exactly, did Congress give preference to spouses of United States citizens? Does the rationale you have just identified apply any less forcefully to same-sex marriages (assuming *arguendo*, as the court did, that they are valid under state law) than to heterosexual ones?

In general, if the language of a statute is not dispositive, and if a given interpretation advances the overall purpose of that statute, *must* a court choose that interpretation? Or might there be circumstances in which the court should reject that interpretation even then? Consider *United States v. Kirby*, 74 U.S. (7 Wall.) 482, 19 L.Ed. 278 (1869). A local sheriff arrested a mail carrier for murder. The sheriff was convicted of violating a federal statute that prohibited "knowingly and willfully obstruct[ing] or retard[ing] the passage of the mail, or of any driver * * * carrying the same." Under a literal interpretation, the sheriff was clearly guilty; he had knowingly and willfully obstructed the passage of the mail carrier. Moreover, one could say that the purpose of the statute was to assure the flow of the mail. Prohibiting law enforcement officers from arresting mail carriers presumably would further that purpose. Yet the Supreme Court, concluding such a result would be absurd, reversed the conviction. Although a conviction would have contributed to the congressional purpose broadly defined, countervailing considerations—the importance of enforcing other criminal laws—prevailed. Could similar reasoning explain the statutory interpretation conclusion in *Adams?* Was this a case in which the court believed that a literal interpretation—even if it advances the general congressional purpose—was offset by countervailing considerations?

4. The court observes that in 1952 Congress made homosexuality a ground for exclusion. The pre-*Adams* history of that provision is instructive. The original enactment, Act of June 27, 1952, § 212(a)(4), 66 Stat. 163, 182, barred noncitizens who were "afflicted with psychopathic personality, epilepsy, or a mental defect." Archaic as it sounds today, the legislative history reveals a strong likelihood that the 1952 Congress meant the term "psychopathic personality" to include homosexuality. See Jorge L. Carro, *From Constitutional Psychopathic Inferiority to AIDS: What Is in the Future for Homosexual Aliens?*, 7 Yale L. & Policy Rev. 201, 208–17 (1989); Note, *The Propriety of Denying Entry to Homosexual Aliens: Examining the Public Health Service's Authority over Medical Exclusions*, 17 Univ. Michigan J.L. Reform 331, 332–38 (1984). To remove some lingering doubt, however, Congress in 1965 amended section 212(a)(4) by adding the phrase "or sexual deviation" (and simultaneously deleting "epilepsy"). Pub.L. 89–236, § 15(b), 79 Stat. 911, 919 (Oct. 3, 1965). The Supreme Court in *Boutilier v. INS,* 387 U.S. 118, 120, 87 S.Ct. 1563, 1565, 18 L.Ed.2d 661, 664 (1967), later held that the phrase "psychopathic personality", and thus even the pre–1965 version of section 212(a)(4), was intended to encompass homosexuality. The Court then rejected Boutilier's argument that, as so construed, the statutory phrase was unconstitutionally vague.

But a difficult issue remained. The procedure for excluding noncitizens on any of the medical or psychological grounds required a certification by the Public Health Service (PHS) that the individual fit the definition of the particular exclusion ground. In 1979 the Surgeon General announced that, in light of modern medical knowledge, the PHS would no longer certify homosexuality as a "psychopathic personality" or a "sexual deviation." See *Matter of Longstaff,* 716 F.2d 1439, 1444 (5th Cir.1983). The question soon arose whether, in the absence of such a certification, the INS could exclude a self-declared homosexual.

At the time of the *Adams* case, that issue had not been adjudicated. (The post-*Adams* history will be noted presently). Should the Surgeon General's 1979 announcement have affected the court's analysis of whether a party to a state-approved same-sex marriage can be a "spouse"? Should either changes in medical norms as reflected by the PHS announcement, or changes in societal norms, influence that determination?

5. Apart from the merits of the case, why wouldn't the court's observation that homosexuality was then an exclusion ground moot the

issue of what "spouse" means? Even if the court had held Adams was a spouse, wouldn't he have been excluded?

6. Shortly after *Adams,* two courts considered whether the INS could exclude a self-declared homosexual without a PHS certification. On that issue the courts split. Compare *Hill v. INS,* 714 F.2d 1470 (9th Cir.1983) (no) with *Matter of Longstaff,* 716 F.2d 1439 (5th Cir.1983) (yes). The INS announced it would not follow *Hill* except in cases that arise within the Ninth Circuit. See 62 IR 166–67 (1985). (If you were then a gay or lesbian noncitizen who wished to move from your country of origin to a city located within the Fifth Circuit, might the decisions in *Hill* and *Longstaff* have affected your travel itinerary?)

Congress finally repealed the bar on homosexual noncitizens in 1990. See Immigration Act of 1990, § 601, amending INA § 212(a). That repeal made the issue in *Adams* more important because, if a court were to recognize same-sex marriages for immediate relative purposes, the beneficiary would no longer face exclusion on homosexuality grounds. Do you think the court in *Adams* would have reached a different result had it been deciding the case shortly after 1990?

7. The INS later brought deportation proceedings against Sullivan, the intending immigrant in the present case, on the ground he had overstayed his nonimmigrant visa. Sullivan sought discretionary relief under former INA § 244(a) [now replaced by INA § 240A(b), which you will study later]. That provision then required, among other elements, a showing that deportation would cause "extreme hardship" to the noncitizen or to any of certain specified relatives, including his or her "spouse." See chapter 8, § A.1.b below. The BIA found the hardship to Sullivan insufficient and dismissed as irrelevant the hardship to Adams, whom the BIA did not regard as a "spouse." The court of appeals affirmed. *Sullivan v. INS,* 772 F.2d 609 (9th Cir.1985).

8. The personal history of the gay couple who litigated *Adams v. Howerton* is recounted in Lesbian and Gay Immigration Rights Task Force, *Task Force Update,* at 1, 11 (Summer 1996) and 7 (Fall 1996). Richard Adams, a United States citizen, had filed a visa petition on behalf of his Australian partner, Tony Sullivan. The INS denied the petition. Its letter read:

> Upon consideration, it is ordered that your visa petition filed on April 28, 1975 for classification of Anthony Corbett Sullivan as the spouse of a United States citizen be denied for the following reasons:
>
> You have failed to establish that a bona fide marital relationship can exist between two faggots.
>
> November 24, 1975

Adams and Sullivan held a press conference to reveal the contents of the letter. After that, the INS withdrew the decision and issued another letter reaching the same conclusion but in less overtly bigoted language. Task Force Update, above, at 11. As to the constitutionality of deporting same-sex partners, see Victor C. Romero, *The Selective Deportation of Same–Gender Partners: In Search of the "Rara Avis,"* 56 Univ. Miami L. Rev. 537 (2002).

9. At the time *Adams v. Howerton* was decided, no United States jurisdiction was clearly on record as recognizing same-sex marriages, although there were several states (apparently including Colorado) whose laws were silent on the issue. Since *Adams*, the subject of same-sex marriages has heated up considerably.

In *Baehr v. Lewin*, 74 Haw. 530, 852 P.2d 44 (1993), the Hawaii Supreme Court held that a state statute which it interpreted as barring same-sex marriages violated the equal protection clause of the Hawaii State Constitution (which expressly prohibited sex discrimination), unless the marriage bar was necessary to a compelling state interest. On remand, a Hawaii trial court found that the state had no compelling interest in banning same-sex marriages, *Baehr v. Miike*, Civ. No. 91–1394, 1996 WL 694235 (Haw. Cir. Ct. 1996), and the Hawaii Supreme Court affirmed without a published opinion, 87 Haw. 34, 950 P.2d 1234 (Dec. 19, 1997). But the victory was short-lived. In 1998, Hawaii voters passed a state constitutional amendment that prohibited same-sex marriages. Sam Howe Verhovek, *The 1998 Elections: The States—Initiatives*, New York Times, Nov. 5, 1998, at B1. On the same day, Alaska voters took similar action. *Id.* By March 11, 1999, some 29 states had expressly banned same-sex marriages. Al Knight, *Same-Sex Marriage: Losing War*, Denver Post, Mar. 11, 1999, at B–7; see generally D.L. Hawley, *Gays, Lesbians and Immigration*, August 1999 Immigration Briefings.

The Hawaii Court had drawn an important distinction. The issue, it said, was not whether the legislature could prohibit *homosexual* marriages. It had purported to prohibit *same-sex* marriages. The distinction was crucial. The Hawaii constitution does not explicitly bar discrimination on the basis of sexual orientation, but it does expressly bar sex discrimination.

The prospect of Hawaii formally recognizing same-sex marriages triggered nationwide hysteria. Article IV, section 1 of the United States Constitution provides that "[f]ull faith and credit shall be given in each State to the public Acts, Records, and judicial Proceedings of every other State." Does the full faith and credit clause mean that all the states would be required to recognize same-sex marriages that were performed in, and recognized by, Hawaii? The answer is not yet clear.

Particularly relevant now, recognition of same-sex marriages by any state makes the issue in *Adams v. Howerton* even more pressing. The court in that case assumed only arguendo that state law permitted same-sex marriages. The court held that, even under such an assumption, the INA did not recognize same-sex marriages and the Constitution did not require Congress to do so. Actual state recognition makes the issue far more immediate.

10. Hawaii's then impending recognition of same-sex marriages led Congress to enact the Defense of Marriage Act, Pub.L. 104–199, 110 Stat.

2419 (Sept. 21, 1996) [DOMA]. The Act has two major provisions. Section 2 of DOMA provides that states need not give effect to acts, records, or judicial proceedings of other states allowing same-sex marriages. Whether section 2 is compatible with the full faith and credit clause will surely be tested.

Section 3 is of more immediate relevance here. It reads:

> In determining the meaning of any Act of Congress, or of any ruling, regulation, or interpretation of the various administrative bureaus and agencies of the United States, the word "marriage" means only a legal union between one man and one woman as husband and wife, and the word "spouse" refers only to a person of the opposite sex who is a husband or a wife.

Does section 3 of DOMA settle the issue in *Adams v. Howerton*? Statutory interpretation problems are not apparent. The INA makes "spouses" immediate relatives. INA § 201(b)(2)(A)(i). Is section 3 vulnerable to constitutional attack? The provision does regulate an area (marriage) traditionally regulated by the states, but as earlier discussion notes, Congress has often attached conditions to marriage for immigration purposes (such as not recognizing marriages that meet all the requirements of the states in which they were contracted but where the parties did not intend to establish a life together, see the next subsection). Is an equal protection challenge plausible? You have seen that Congress has plenary power to decide which noncitizens to admit, but you have also seen lower court decisions strike down federal immigration provisions found to lack a rational basis. Moreover, since same-sex marriages classify on the basis of gender (not just sexual orientation), is some form of heightened judicial scrutiny applicable?

Even without heightened scrutiny, is it rational to withhold recognition of same-sex marriages for immigration purposes? The court in *Adams* thought it was. Why, exactly, does the law do so? Precisely what societal attitudes toward homosexuality does the policy reflect? What position *should* Congress take? Before answering these questions, consider the materials below.

One commentator believes DOMA has special implications for the Asian Pacific community. See Victor C. Romero, *Asians, Gay Marriage, and Immigration: Family Unification at a Crossroads*, 15 Indiana Internat'l & Comp. L. Rev., issue #2 (forthcoming 2005).

11. DOMA, of course, has not ended the controversy. In 2003, the Massachusetts Supreme Judicial Court, relying on a combination of liberty and equality interests, held that the state constitution bars the Commonwealth of Massachusetts from rejecting same-sex marriages while recognizing opposite-sex marriages. *Goodridge v. Department of Mental Health*, 440 Mass. 309, 798 N.E.2d 941 (2003). The court found no rational basis for the difference in treatment. The effect of *Goodridge* was to enable same-sex couples to marry in Massachusetts.

Another nationwide panic—even more frenetic than the one that followed the Hawaii court's decision—immediately set in. Several states, including Massachusetts itself, began the process of amending their constitutions to bar same-sex marriages and constrain "activist judges." Several such ballot initiatives have already succeeded. Efforts to amend the U.S. Constitution to define marriage as a union of one man and one woman are similarly under way. The issue figured prominently in the 2004 Presidential campaigns and appears to have galvanized millions of voters.

12. Professor Isabel Medina, after examining the general role of constitutional amendments, the link between same-sex marriages and constitutionally protected rights, and the influence of animus, reaches the following conclusion:

> * * * It is unlikely that allowing same-sex couples to marry will materially affect the vast number of heterosexual marriages that are celebrated in this country. Moreover, recognizing same-sex marriage furthers values of community, autonomy, equality, stability, and intimacy. There appears to be no reason to discriminate against same-sex couples other than because traditionally marriage has been a heterosexual institution. But the traditional view of homosexuals and lesbians reflects substantial tolerance for rabid animus, expressed through legal norms and sometimes, through violent acts, towards gay and lesbian individuals and the sexual conduct that is at the heart of their status. * * *
>
> Nothing about the institution of marriage is peculiarly heterosexual—not caring for children, not privacy or intimacy, not support. Prohibiting persons who are homosexual or lesbian from enjoying the legal celebration of their marital union, and from enjoying the "[t]angible and intangible benefits" which flow from marriage, furthers no legitimate state goal and burdens one of the most basic of human rights—the right to establish and enjoy an intimate relationship—a family—with another adult.

M. Isabel Medina, *Of Constitutional Amendments, Human Rights, and Same–Sex Marriages*, 64 Louisiana L. Rev. 459, 474–75 (2004).

Do you agree with Professor Medina?

13. Meanwhile, several other countries have recently recognized same-sex marriages. The Netherlands on September 12, 2000 became the first to do so. See Note, *Queer Reasoning: Immigration Policy, Baker v. State of Vermont, and the (Non)Recognition of Same-Gender Relationships*, 10 Law & Sexuality 211, 214 (2001). Belgium quickly followed, allowing same-sex marriages as long as one of the partners lives in Belgium or visits regularly. See *Gay Expats Can Marry in Belgium*, Expatica News (Jan. 26, 2004). In 2005 Spain became the third nation to do so, and Canada is expected to become the fourth in July 2005. See AP, *Spain Legalizes Same-Sex Marriages*, New York Times (June 30, 2005); see also *Reference re Same-Sex Marriage*, 2004 SCC 79 (Canadian Supreme Court 2004) (render-

ing advisory opinion that national same-sex marriage law would violate neither federalism principles nor the constitutionally protected freedom of religion of those who object to the practice). If a United States citizen or LPR legally marries a noncitizen of the same sex in the Netherlands, Belgium, Spain, Canada, or Massachusetts, a literal reading of DOMA (item 10) would nonetheless bar immigration preference based on that marriage.

14.   Should the immigration laws recognize foreign *polygamous* marriages that are valid in the countries where they were celebrated, assuming all the parties are consenting adults? How do the arguments pro and con match up with those for and against recognition of *same-sex* marriages? See generally Kerry Abrams, *Polygamy, Prostitution, and the Federalization of Immigration Law*, 105 Columbia L. Rev. 641 (2005).

Note, An Argument for the Application of Equal Protection Heightened Scrutiny to Classifications Based on Homosexuality

57 So.Cal.L.Rev. 797, 817–24 (1984).

[The footnotes in the original article cite empirical authority to support the various factual assertions. Those citations have been edited out here.— Ed.]

* * *

Researchers have extensively studied the origins of sexual orientation, but still have no generally accepted explanation of its development. Although no consensus exists as to how or why a person turns out to be gay or straight, agreement does exist on some basic facts.

1.   *The Acquisition of Homosexuality is not Subject to Control*

Research indicates that neither individuals nor their parents can control whether the person turns out to be gay, bisexual, or heterosexual. Individuals do not choose their sexual orientation. Sexual orientation develops very early in life; most research indicates that it is determined by a person's fifth or sixth birthday. The most conservative estimate is that sexual orientation is firmly established by adolescence notwithstanding one's level of sexual activity.

* * *

2.   *Sexual Orientation is Immutable*

Sexual orientation is generally impervious to change. * * *

B.   GAYS ARE THE SUBJECT OF INCORRECT STEREOTYPES

The basis for most laws that disadvantage gays is usually one or more stereotypes with no or very little basis in fact. * * *

1. *Homosexuals as "Pied Pipers"*

One of the more common stereotypes of gays is that they proselytize children to homosexuality or present role models that make homosexuality appear so attractive that young people will embrace it as a lifestyle. This notion has no basis in fact. Gays do not try to convert children, nor will mere exposure to a gay person affect a child's sexual orientation. Sexual orientation is established very early in life and cannot be consciously acquired. A gay can no more "convert" heterosexual children than a heterosexual can "convert" homosexual children. Not even the seduction or molestation of a child by an older member of the same sex will affect the child's sexual orientation.

2. *Homosexuals as Child Molesters*

The most offensive stereotype is that homosexuals are somehow more likely or more willing to molest children than are heterosexuals. Officials use this misperception to justify sodomy statutes and employment discrimination. The average homosexual is neither likely to be a child molester, nor more likely than a heterosexual to be one. Indeed, with respect to physical sexual response alone, heterosexuals are more likely to be aroused by children than are homosexuals. Finally, the typical child molester is much more likely to be heterosexual than homosexual.

3. *Homosexuals as Mentally Ill Persons*

Another ground for some discriminatory governmental policies is the stereotype that gays are mentally ill. The premise of this stereotype is an idea that homosexuality is a mental disease and that therefore gays are inferior or unstable. The truth is that "homosexual adults who have come to terms with their homosexuality ... are no more distressed psychologically than are heterosexual men and women." Homosexuality is not an indicator of psychopathology. As early as 1935 Freud wrote that "[h]omosexuality is assuredly no advantage, but it is nothing to be ashamed of ..., it cannot be classified as an illness; we consider it to be a variation of the sexual function...." Official acceptance came much later, but the National Association for Mental Health, the American Psychiatric Association, and the Surgeon General now agree that homosexuality, in and of itself, is not a mental illness. * * *

NOTES AND QUESTIONS

1.   The empirical conclusions summarized in the preceding excerpts are fairly representative of those reached in the vast majority of scientific studies. There is as yet no clearly correct identification of the precise determinants of one's sexual orientation. But researchers almost universal-

ly agree that there is a multiplicity of factors, that a person does not and cannot "choose" his or her sexual orientation, that orientation is fixed by early childhood at the latest, and that homosexuality is as deeply ingrained in an individual as is heterosexuality. One leading author summarizes the evidence as follows:

> Perhaps the most important source of homophobic reactions * * * is the widespread ignorance that exists in the general public about what makes people homosexual. Many people tend to think of homosexuality either as a pattern that is freely chosen by a conscious act of will, or as something that is "caught" from others, either as a result of seduction or by an "infectious" imitation or "modeling" of oneself after homosexuals to whom one has been exposed. * * *

> Understandably, most parents in our culture have fears with regard to their children becoming homosexual. These fears are easily stimulated by ignorant or malicious assertions that children exposed to homosexual teachers (particularly if these teachers are popular and likeable) are in danger of modeling themselves after such teachers and thus becoming homosexual themselves. Yet there is not an iota of evidence for such assertions! As we have seen, the etiology of homosexuality is affected by many factors, some possibly genetic or constitutional, others dependent on early familial relationships, still others deriving from sociocultural elements. People do not "choose" to be homosexual any more than they "choose" to be heterosexual. In almost all instances, the basic factors that lead to a homosexual propensity are established before the age of six, well before the school years even begin. * * *

Judd Marmor, *Overview: The Multiple Roots of Homosexual Behavior,* in Judd Marmor (ed.), Homosexual Behavior—A Modern Reappraisal 19–20 (1980). See, e.g., Alan P. Bell, Martin S. Weinberg & Sue K. Hammersmith, Sexual Preference—Its Development in Men and Women 183–92, 212–20 (1981); John Money & Anke A. Ehrhardt, Man and Woman, Boy and Girl (1972); Ritch C. Savin–Williams, *Theoretical Perspectives Accounting for Adolescent Homosexuality,* 9 J. Adolescent Health Care 95 (1988); Carol Warren, *Homosexuality and Stigma,* in Judd Marmor, Homosexual Behavior—A Modern Reappraisal, at 123, 125–26 (1980). For more specific studies of either genetic or hormonal influences, see, e.g., Michael Ruse, Homosexuality—A Philosophical Inquiry, ch. 5 (1988) (hormones); Garfield Tourney, *Hormones and Homosexuality,* in Marmor, above, at 41–58; John Money, *Genetic and Chromosomal Aspects of Homosexual Etiology,* in Marmor, above, at 59–72. An exceptionally interesting long-term case study of heterosexual and homosexual males from childhood to adulthood is Richard Green, The "Sissy Boy Syndrome" and the Development of Homosexuality (1987). See generally David F. Greenberg, The Construction of Homosexuality (1988).

2. Homosexuality cuts across lines that separate widely varying cultures, time periods, and even species. See Marmor, item 1 above, at 6–7. Dr.

Marmor, distilling results from various studies, finds it "fair to conclude, conservatively, that the incidence of more or less exclusively homosexual behavior in Western culture ranges from 5 to 10 percent for adult males and from 3 to 5 percent for adult females. If bisexual behavior is included, the incidence may well be twice these figures." *Id.* at 7. Its range and its persistence through generations have raised for biologists the question whether homosexuality, contrary to popular assumption, might even serve a positive evolutionary function. See, e.g., Savin–Williams, item 1 above, at 95–96.

3.   In the United States, the social norms concerning homosexuality have changed markedly in modern times. Sodomy laws, while often facially neutral with respect to sexual orientation, historically and currently have been directed and enforced primarily against homosexuals. John D'Emilio, Sexual Politics, Sexual Communities—The Making of a Homosexual Minority in the United States 1940–1970, at 14 (1983); *Survey on the Constitutional Right to Privacy in the Context of Homosexual Activity,* 40 Univ. Miami L.Rev. 521, 525 (1986). The decline of these laws reflects the liberalized societal attitudes toward homosexuality. Until 1961, all fifty states punished consensual sodomy. Survey, above, at 526. In that year Illinois adopted the American Law Institute's Model Penal Code provision decriminalizing private sexual conduct between consenting adults, and since then the vast majority of the states have repealed their prohibitions of sodomy between consenting adults in private, at least absent commercial gain. See *Lawrence v. Texas*, 539 U.S. 558, 123 S.Ct. 2472, 156 L.Ed.2d 508 (2003); see also Jorge L. Carro, *From Constitutional Psychopathic Inferiority to AIDS: What is in the Future for Homosexual Aliens?*, 7 Yale L. & Policy Rev. 201, 202–03 & n. 8 (1989); Survey, above, at 524–27. (Many other western nations had already done so. Carro, above, at 205–06; Survey, above, at 526). In *Bowers v. Hardwick*, 478 U.S. 186, 106 S.Ct. 2841, 92 L.Ed.2d 140 (1986), the Supreme Court upheld the constitutionality of a state statute that barred consensual sodomy. The *Bowers* decision was overruled, however, in *Lawrence v. Texas*, above. Observing that in both the United States and Europe prohibitions on homosexual sodomy were now the exception rather than the norm, the Court could not find a moral consensus strong enough to outweigh the relevant liberty interests. For a detailed study that traces the history from ancient times, see Arno Karlen, *Homosexuality in History*, in Marmor, *above,* at 75–99. For lucid insights from both international law and comparative law on the subject, see Berta Hernández-Truyol, *Querying Lawrence*, 65 Ohio State L.J. 1151, 1173–1212 (2004).

4.   Although the 1990 repeal of the statutory provision excluding homosexual noncitizens was widely perceived as ending their discriminatory treatment under the immigration laws, the *Adams* case illustrates another component of the statutory discrimination: the granting of immigration preference based on opposite-sex marriages but not same-sex marriages (even if state-recognized). You now have enough information to think critically about why our immigration laws discriminate against gays and lesbians (and, in the present context, gender) and whether the possible

justifications hold up. The original exclusion clearly was not enacted for health reasons; as noted earlier, it had found its way into our law decades before anyone had ever heard of AIDS or associated it with homosexuality. Possibly the prohibition mirrored widely held fears that gays would molest or "convert" children. As the preceding literature makes clear, researchers now know these fears to be misguided.

So is there today a legitimate reason to treat homosexual noncitizens less favorably than heterosexual noncitizens? Putting aside for a moment the association between gay males and AIDS (this will be discussed in chapter 5, but for now you might note this correlation at any rate would not explain the non-recognition of lesbian marriages), it seems clear that, if there is a justification, it has its roots in some shared notion of morality. In examining the basis for that moral judgment, keep in mind that the pre–1990 exclusion provision, INA § 212(a)(4), defined the excludable class by reference to mental state, not just actions. Does that distinction have either moral or pragmatic significance? Can orientation be safely used as a proxy for likelihood of engaging in prohibited acts? The present discrimination (definition of spouse) turns on gender; a *male* noncitizen who marries a male citizen will not be a spouse, while an otherwise similarly situated *female* noncitizen who marries a male citizen will be. Is that statutory distinction justifiable?

More fundamentally, what is it about homosexual attractions and acts that lead some to view them as immoral? Some people argue simply that homosexuality is "unnatural." What does that mean? Surely, if a class of persons is to receive adverse treatment solely because a trait they have is "unnatural," that word must be defined to mean more than that the trait is possessed only by a minority. (Left-handed people are also a minority. Is left-handedness "unnatural"?) Does "unnatural," rather, mean counter-instinctive? Homosexuals themselves, by definition, do not regard same-sex attractions as counter-instinctive; again, we are back to a simple matter of majority versus minority preferences. Is homosexuality unnatural in the morphological sense that the body parts are not shaped to fit together in "that way"? (The shapes of the body parts do not seem to bother the participants. Why should heterosexuals care?) Or are homosexual acts unnatural because they do not serve a procreative function? If that is what is meant by "unnatural," then that term should apply as well to masturbation, use of birth control, or any other sex act not intended or likely to result in conception. Should immigrants who have engaged in those acts also be treated less favorably than others?

Perhaps the real explanation is a religious one. In western societies the historical origins of public antipathy toward homosexuals are deeply rooted in Judeo–Christian teachings. See *Karlen, above.* Is that fact alone enough to justify discriminating against parties to homosexual marriages? Would it violate constitutional principles of separation of church and state to base such discrimination solely on religious doctrine? Or is the government free to act on the basis of commonly held moral beliefs even though religion was the historical stimulus for those beliefs? (Analogous issues surround the relationship between Roman Catholic theology and abortion laws.)

Is the adverse treatment of homosexual immigrants, like any other law directed against homosexuals, justifiable as a means to promote "family" values? Judge Wallace, in *Adams*, seemed to imply as much. He said that, in confining the immigration preferences to heterosexual partners, "Congress manifested its concern for family integrity." What assumption was Judge Wallace making about the meaning of "family?" A paper commissioned by the HHS Secretary's Task Force on Youth Suicide found homosexual children two to three times as likely as heterosexual children to attempt suicide. The paper cited social stigma and discrimination as likely explanations. See Paul Gibson, *Gay Male and Lesbian Youth Suicide,* in 3 Report of the Secretary's Task Force on Youth Suicide 110 (Jan.1989). Dr. Louis Sullivan, then President Bush's Secretary of Health and Human Services, took public exception to those views on the ground they "run contrary * * * to advancing traditional family values." Letter from Hon. Louis W. Sullivan, M.D. to Hon. William Dannemeyer (Oct. 13, 1989). But in what sense are the partners to a homosexual marriage not "family"? If the notion is that they are unable to conceive children, as the court suggested in *Adams*, are gay couples distinguishable from those heterosexual couples who are physically unable to conceive? The former do indeed have additional difficulty in adopting children, but those roadblocks are themselves the products of either law or adoption agency policy.

Do not these and other laws directed against homosexuals really boil down to the notion that the heterosexual majority simply finds homosexual acts offputting? If that assumption about the majority reaction is factually correct, is it sound policy to codify that widely held instinct as law? Or, rather, should the law reflect the fact that, however repugnant many heterosexuals might find the concept of even consensual homosexual acts, the significant minority whose sexual orientation is different find the same concept perfectly natural and pleasurable? In short, how should a society draw the line between codifying broadly held moral beliefs and tolerating the moral beliefs of a minority? And if a majority—rationally or irrationally—regards a given practice as immoral, is that alone a good enough reason to bar noncitizens who engage in that practice? In the United States, where so many people believe in God and belong to one of the major established religions, should the immigration laws decline to recognize marriages between atheists?

Finally, would federal recognition of same-sex marriages be tantamount to affirmatively endorsing homosexuality? Or is there a real difference between endorsement and tolerance?

5. Same-sex and other nonmarital relationships are recognized for immigration purposes in several other countries, where the criteria for family-related preferences emphasize either financial dependence or the seriousness of the relationship, rather than formal marriage vows. See generally Denise C. Hammond, *Immigration and Sexual Orientation: Developing Standards, Options and Obstacles,* 77 IR 113, 118–20 (Jan. 24, 2000)

(list includes Australia, Belgium, Canada, Denmark, Finland, France, Iceland, Namibia, the Netherlands, New Zealand, Norway, South Africa, Sweden, and the United Kingdom); see also Internat'l Lesbian & Gay Association, *World Legal Survey*, http://www.ilga.org/Information/legal_survey/summary_information_by_subject.htm (adding Iceland and several of the German länder); Note, *Coming to America: The Immigration Obstacle Facing Binational Same–Sex Couples*, 73 Southern Calif. L. Rev. 811, 813 nn. 6 & 8, and 827–35 (2000).

6. For fuller accounts of the opposing views on whether the immigration laws should recognize same-sex marriages for purposes of family reunification programs, compare Note, *Coming to America*, item 5 above (arguing yes) with Michael A. Scaperlanda, *Kulturkampf in the Backwaters: Homosexuality and Immigration Law*, 11 Widener J. Pub. L. 475, 487–500 (2002) (arguing no).

b. FRAUDULENT MARRIAGES

You have seen several ways in which marriage to a United States citizen, or in some instances to an LPR, can improve one's chances of securing lawful permanent residence. Marriage can confer immediate relative or family-sponsored second preference status, or make the person a spouse "accompanying or following to join" a preference immigrant. As you will see later, one can also derive immigration benefits from accompanying or following to join a nonimmigrant or an asylee. Later chapters will illustrate still other immigration-related advantages of marriage in the contexts of admission, deportation, and naturalization. These benefits include both automatic exemption from, and discretionary waivers of, requirements or sanctions that would otherwise be imposed.

Given both the attraction permanent residence holds for so many people and the legal advantages of marriage in attaining residence, it can certainly be tempting for a noncitizen to marry for immigration benefits. As the court noted in *Adams,* however, to suffice for immigration purposes a marriage must be not only *legally* valid in the jurisdiction in which it was celebrated (parties of marriageable age, parties not already married to others, ceremony performed by authorized official, etc.), but also *factually* genuine. The standard test for the latter is whether, at the inception of the marriage, the parties intended to establish a life together. *Rodriguez v. INS*, 204 F.3d 25, 27 (1st Cir. 2000); *Bark v. INS*, 511 F.2d 1200, 1201, 1202 (9th Cir.1975); *Matter of Laureano,* 19 I. & N. Dec. 1, 2–3 (BIA 1983). (Is an intent to establish a life together necessarily inconsistent with the marriage being motivated solely by the prospect of immigration benefits? If a couple plans to live together permanently, but they would not have formalized their relationship through marriage had there been no immigration benefits, *should* they receive preference?)

Sham marriages are of two types. The most common are bilateral arrangements in which both "spouses" marry solely to facilitate immigration. In a bilateral sham marriage, the intending immigrant spouse (the "beneficiary") typically pays the citizen or LPR spouse (the "petitioner") to enter into the marriage. Other sham marriages, in contrast, are based on unilateral fraud; the beneficiary spouse deceives the petitioner spouse as to the beneficiary's feelings and intentions. See Joe A. Tucker, *Assimilation to the United States: A Study of the Adjustment of Status and the Immigration Marriage Fraud Statutes,* 7 Yale L. & Policy Rev. 20, 33–34 (1989).

Until 1986, the principal INS device for detecting a sham marriage was to interview the petitioner and, if present in the United States, the beneficiary, before approving the petition. One commentator describes some of the questions that the interviewers frequently asked:

> During the marriage fraud interview—part of the statutory "investigation of facts"—the INS may interrogate both spouses about many aspects of the relationship. Officials typically interview the husband and wife separately in order to check for discrepancies between their answers. The INS may, for example, ask questions about the couple's courtship, their wedding ceremony, the decor of their residence, the division of household chores, or what they had for breakfast on the morning of the interview. More important, although they are advised against doing so, INS officials often inquire into the most intimate aspects of the marital relationship. Probing questions about the method of birth control used, the consummation of the marriage, and the sexual conduct of the couple before and after marriage are not uncommon.

Note, *The Constitutionality of the INS Sham Marriage Investigation Policy,* 99 Harvard L.Rev. 1238, 1242–43 (1986).

Those pre-approval interviews and examination of pertinent documents together ferreted out a certain number of sham marriages. In addition, like other kinds of fraud, prior or current marriage fraud can be a ground for inadmissibility, discovered by consular officers abroad during the visa process or by INS inspectors at the border, see INA § 212(a)(6)(C), or a ground for deportability, see INA § 237(a)(1)(A, G).

The INS and others believed nonetheless that large-scale marriage fraud remained rampant. In 1985, then INS Commissioner Alan Nelson testified before the Senate immigration subcommittee in support of strong legislation to combat marriage fraud. The Commissioner announced that the INS had conducted a preliminary survey on marriage fraud, and he informed the subcommittee that, in the light of the admittedly preliminary survey results, "we believe as much as 30%, which is an extremely high figure, of the spouse relationships may be fraudulent." Fraudulent Marriage and Fiancé Arrangements to Obtain Permanent Resident Immigration Status, Hearing Before the Subcommittee on Immigration and Refugee Policy of the Senate Comm. on the Judiciary, S. Hrg. 99–325, 99th Cong., 1st Sess. 35 (July 26, 1985). Impressed by this testimony, see H.Rep. No. 99–906, 99th Cong., 2d Sess. 6 (Sept. 26, 1986), reproduced in 1986 U.S.Code Cong. & Admin.News 5978, the House Judiciary Committee recommended, and Congress passed, the Immigration Marriage Fraud Amendments of 1986, Act of Nov. 10, 1986, Pub.L. 99–639, 100 Stat. 3537 [IMFA]. This Act, aimed at reducing marriage fraud and achieving some other related goals, contained a number of controversial provisions—some since amended—that you will see shortly.

Soon, however, some disturbing revelations emerged. More than a year after the enactment of IMFA, the INS disclosed the basis for its "30%" conclusion. The survey the Commissioner had cited was a 1983–84 INS study in which INS investigators had reviewed *selected* spousal petitions. The limitations of the survey were significant. Certain categories of marriage petitions thought to contain a low incidence of fraud were automatically excluded from the sample. The remaining (high-risk) cases were reviewed "in as much depth as possible given the [one to two months] for completion of the survey;" sometimes the parties were interviewed and other times they were not. In each case the investigator was asked whether, based on this preliminary review, he or she *suspected* fraud—not whether actual fraud had been found. In 30% of what was already, therefore, a high-risk sample, the investigators reported their "suspicions" of fraud. 65 IR 25–26 (1988).

More information came to light in 1989 when ACLU attorney Lucas Guttentag, representing a noncitizen in a case challenging the constitutionality of one particular IMFA provision, deposed David Nachtsheim, the INS official who had written up the results of the survey. Mr. Nachtsheim, testifying under oath, revealed that he and others had known that, for all the reasons noted above, the survey "was statistically invalid and lacked any probative value regarding the actual incidence of marriage fraud." 66 IR 1011 (1989). Rather, Mr. Nachtsheim explained, the sole purpose of the study was to project future INS workloads (hence, the emphasis on incidence of suspected fraud rather than actual fraud). Lucas Guttentag & Judith Rabinovitz, Plaintiffs' trial brief (Sept. 1, 1989), at 9–10 n. 7, in *Manwani v. INS*, later reported at 736 F.Supp. 1367 (W.D.N.C.1990). Mr. Nachtsheim also testified that top INS officials had been aware of the flaws in the study, had ordered another one conducted, and, well before Commissioner Nelson's congressional testimony, had recommended that the study not be cited as probative of the incidence of fraud. 66 IR 1012 (1989). As discussed earlier, Commissioner Nelson cited the 30% figure anyway, and IMFA was enacted into law. See generally *Manwani*, 736 F.Supp. at 1372–73.

Skepticism about the actual levels of marriage fraud, combined with questions about the severity and the rationality of various IMFA provisions, led to many criticisms. Those criticisms surfaced in constitutional challenges to selected provisions and in legislative reform efforts. Both will be considered below. First, however, it is necessary to describe generally those marriage-related provisions of IMFA that affect the immigration preferences. Passed at the eleventh hour, the statute was replete with ambiguities. See generally 67 IR 334–46 (1990) (INS answers to 109 questions from the American Immigration Lawyers Association); Charles Gordon, *The Marriage Fraud Act of 1986*, 4 Georgetown Immigration L.J. 183 (1990); Harvey Kaplan, *Immigration Marriage Fraud Practice Advisory* (running column in AILA Monthly Mailings); Tucker, above; Charles

Wheeler, *Until INS Do Us Part: A Guide to IMFA,* Immigration Briefings (March 1990).

The central core of IMFA was section 2(a), which added a new section 216 to the INA. That provision introduced the concept of "conditional" permanent residence.[6] Whenever a noncitizen receives LPR status as an immediate relative, as a family-sponsored second preference immigrant, or as a fiancé of a United States citizen (see chapter 4, § D below), by virtue of a marriage that is less than two years old, the resulting permanent residence will be subject to certain conditions subsequent. INA §§ 216(a)(1), 216(g)(1). Note the provision does not apply to accompanying or following spouses under INA § 203(d). See INA § 216(g)(1).

The conditions subsequent are these: If, at any time during the individual's first two years of permanent residence, the "Attorney General" [now the Secretary of Homeland Security] finds that the marriage was entered into for the purpose of procuring immigrant status, or that the marriage has been judicially annulled or terminated (other than by the spouse's death), or that a fee (other than an attorney fee) was given for the filing of the petition, then permanent resident status is terminated. INA § 216(b)(1). The noncitizen may contest the finding at a removal hearing at which the government will have the burden of proof. INA § 216(b)(2).

Second, the conditional resident and his or her spouse have an affirmative duty to jointly petition for removal of the condition and to appear at an interview in connection with that petition. INA § 216(c). The petition must be filed during the ninety-day period immediately preceding the second anniversary of the person's admission for permanent residence. INA § 216(d)(2)(A). If the joint petition is not filed on time, or if without good cause either spouse fails to appear at the interview, then permanent residence is terminated. INA § 216(c)(2)(A). Through the petition and the interview the noncitizen seeks to establish that the marriage was legally valid, that it has not been judicially annulled or terminated (other than through the death of the noncitizen's spouse), that it was not entered into for immigration purposes, and that no fee (other than an attorney fee) was paid for the filing of the petition. INA §§ 216(c)(3)(A), 216(d)(1). If the decision is favorable, the condition is "removed." INA § 216(c)(3)(B). If the decision is unfavorable, permanent resident status is terminated. INA § 216(c)(3)(C). In the latter case, the noncitizen may contest the finding at a removal hearing, where, again, the government has the burden of proof. INA § 216(c)(3)(D).

An immigrant who is unable to meet the usual requirements for removing the conditions subsequent may apply for a waiver under INA § 216(c)(4). The former INS liberally construed the waiver authority as applying also to proceedings to terminate permanent resident status. Legal

---

6. An analogous concept had appeared in 1965. See Pub.L. 89–236, § 3, 79 Stat. 911, 913 (Oct. 3, 1965) (certain refugees condition- ally admitted). See also INA § 216A (conditional residence awarded to immigrant entrepreneurs).

Opinion of INS (then Acting) General Counsel William P. Cook (Jan. 9, 1990), reproduced in 67 IR 168–70 (1990).

One basis for a statutory waiver is a finding that removal would entail "extreme hardship." INA § 216(c)(4)(A). The statute does not say who must suffer the extreme hardship, but the former INS suggested that the person could be the conditional resident or his or her spouse or dependent child. See 67 IR at 341, Question 57 (1990). "Extreme hardship" is a term of art in immigration law; it is a difficult standard to meet, as you will discover in some detail in another context, former INA § 244(a) (suspension of deportation). See chapter 8, § A.1.b.ii below.

Until 1990 the only other available waiver provision required the conditional resident to show that he or she (a) entered into the marriage in good faith, (b) terminated the marriage for good cause, and (c) was not at fault in failing to meet the usual requirements. INA § 216(c)(4)(B), pre–1990 version. The middle requirement proved problematic. The actual wording was that the marriage had to have been "terminated * * * by the alien spouse for good cause." The "good cause" requirement was difficult to apply in the many jurisdictions that no longer require a showing of fault in divorce actions. In such cases, the only recourse of the noncitizen spouse was to litigate before the immigration authorities the kinds of issues that would have been litigated in the divorce action had the jurisdiction not adopted no-fault divorce.

A more significant problem was the requirement that the marriage be terminated "by the alien spouse." If the citizen spouse filed the actual divorce petition, could the noncitizen still be eligible for a waiver? Could the noncitizen be eligible if the two spouses co-petitioned for divorce? The INS answered no to the first question, yes to the second. See 67 IR at 340, Question 47 (1990). If a marriage was on the rocks and nearing the end of the two-year conditional period, what was the noncitizen spouse to do? Continue on, hoping that the citizen spouse would not file for divorce until after the conditions had been removed? Race to the courthouse to become the plaintiff, hoping the immigration authorities would later determine that he or she had "good cause" to terminate the marriage? That last dilemma would exist in any difficult marital situation subject to the two–year IMFA condition, but the hardship was greatest in spousal abuse cases, where noncitizen wives frequently endured dangerous physical abuse for two years rather than risk deportation. See generally Tucker, above, at 94; Wheeler, above, at 10–11.

Those sorts of problems led Congress, as part of the 1990 reform package, to liberalize the grounds for waivers. Section 701 of the Immigration Act of 1990 deleted from INA § 216(c)(4)(B) the requirement that the termination of the marriage be "by the alien spouse for good cause". The Act also added a third waiver addressed specifically to battered spouses and spouses otherwise subjected to "extreme cruelty." INA § 216(c)(4)(C). Read section 216(c)(4) and try to figure out whether paragraph (C) covers any situations not already covered by the amended version of (B). See generally Janet M. Calvo, *Spouse-Based Immigration Laws: The Legacies of Cover-*

ture, 28 San Diego L.Rev. 593 (1991) (commending the 1990 amendments but questioning whether they go far enough); Janet M. Calvo, *A Decade of Spouse–Based Immigration Laws: Coverture's Diminishment, But Not Its Demise*, 24 Northern Illinois Univ. L. Rev. 153 (2004) (arguing that the omissions persist).

Up to now, this discussion of the conditional residence concept has focused exclusively on spouses. IMFA goes a step further. The statute extends also to anyone who acquires permanent resident status "by virtue of being the son or daughter of an individual through a qualifying marriage." INA §§ 216(a)(1), 216(g)(2).

A related provision, also introduced by IMFA, is INA § 204(a)(2). This provision, which you should read now, places certain restrictions on the person who obtains LPR status by marrying a United States citizen or another LPR and then, after termination of that marriage, marries another noncitizen and seeks family-sponsored second preference status for the latter. What would you assume is the purpose of section 204(a)(2)? See also INA § 204(c) (prior marriage fraud precludes granting of present visa petition).

PROBLEMS 5–11

To do these Problems, you will have to consult the text of INA § 216. For Problems 10 and 11, you will also have to read INA § 204(a)(2).

Problem 5. A, a United States citizen living in Amsterdam, marries B, a noncitizen. Eighteen months later, having decided they would like to live in the United States, they begin the process by filing a "visa petition" with USCIS. Three months after that (i.e., 21 months after the wedding), B receives an immigrant visa. Under INA § 221(c), B has up to six months in which to use that visa to enter the United States. Do A and B need any advice at this point?

[handwritten marginalia: 216 only applies for marriages less than 2 years.]

Problem 6. C and D, having been married exactly one year, are simultaneously admitted to the United States as LPRs. C is admitted under one of the employment-based preferences and D is admitted as the accompanying husband. One year later, they divorce. D has heard of IMFA and wants to know whether the divorce will affect his immigration status. What would you tell him?

[handwritten marginalia: visa not marriage based. IMFA N/A.]

Problem 7. E entered the United States on an immediate relative visa as the wife of F, a naturalized U.S. citizen whom she had married a year and a half earlier. E and F are still happily married, but it is now 23 months since E's admission and F adamantly refuses to appear for their scheduled interview. E pleads with him to come, but F has traumatic memories of his own contacts with the former INS and simply will not set foot in a government immigration office. What should E do?

Problem 8. G, a citizen of Mexico, would like to immigrate to the United States to live with his father, an LPR who is now elderly and in need of both financial support and daily help. G knows that he could eventually come in under the family-sponsored 2B preference as the un-married son of an LPR, but in Mexico that queue is many years long and G feels his father needs him now. G therefore arranges a sham marriage to H, a United States citizen, enters the United States on an immediate relative visa a few months later, moves in with his father, and immediately divorces H. Twenty-one months after G's admission, his father is still alive and in much the same condition. G seeks advice as to what he should do now.

Problem 9. J is admitted to the United States as an LPR on the basis of her one-year-old marriage to K, a United States citizen. A year after her admission, the marriage breaks down irretrievably. J is a devout Roman Catholic whose personal religious convictions preclude her petitioning for divorce, and her vindictive husband will neither initiate divorce proceedings himself nor join in her future petition to remove the conditions on her resident status. What advice do you give J?[7]

Problem 10. L marries M, a United States citizen, and six months later attains conditional LPR status as an immediate relative based on that marriage. Two years after her admission, the conditions on L's status are removed. Six months after that, L and M divorce. A month later, L marries N, a noncitizen whom she had dated before meeting M. She then immedi-ately files a petition to classify N as a family-sponsored 2A immigrant. Should the petition be granted?

Problem 11. P marries Q, a United States citizen, and six months later attains conditional LPR status on the basis of that marriage. Two years after her admission, the conditions on P's status are removed. A year and a day after that, P moves out of the house and sues for divorce. The same day, P applies for naturalization, which an LPR who has lived in marital union with a citizen for three years (and satisfies other require-ments) may receive. P attains naturalization six months later. One month after that, P receives the final divorce decree. The very next day she marries R, a noncitizen whom she had dated before meeting Q, and files a petition to classify R as an immediate relative. Should the petition be granted?

NOTES AND QUESTIONS

1. What is your reaction to the IMFA conditions? When a person attains LPR status by virtue of marriage, *should* that status terminate if the marriage breaks down within two years?

2. If there is to be a condition subsequent, should the two-year probation period begin when the parties marry or when the noncitizen beneficiary receives LPR status?

3. The former INS took the position that, if the spouses were separat-ed and the marriage was "in the process of being dissolved," the petition to

[7]. The author thanks immigration at-torney James Acoba for the idea for this Problem.

remove the conditions should not be approved—even if the marriage was valid at its inception. 67 IR at 338, Question 32 (1990). That the marriage is "no longer viable," in other words, was thought to be a ground for denying the petition. *Id.* Eventually the INS retreated, acknowledging that "non-viability" is not a basis for refusing to remove the conditions on one's conditional status. See Opinion of the INS General Counsel, reproduced in 69 IR at 80–82 (Jan. 13, 1992). Which position is more compatible with the statutory text?

The former INS also argued that, even if there were no plans to divorce, a separation with no foreseeable reconciliation would make it "difficult to prove that the marriage was not entered into for immigration purposes," although still "possible * * * under the right set of circumstances." Id., Question 38. Do you agree?

4. INA § 216(g)(1)(B) expressly exempts from the conditional residence requirements spouses accompanying or following to join preference immigrants under section 203(d). Why?

———

Although the conditional residence program has always been the centerpiece of IMFA, another of its provisions once generated the most controversy. IMFA § 5, among other things, added section 204(h) [now 204(g)] to the INA. In its original 1986 form, this provision read:

> (h) * * * [A visa] petition may not be approved to grant an alien immediate relative status or preference status by reason of a marriage which was entered into during [removal proceedings], until the alien has resided outside the United States for a 2–year period beginning after the date of the marriage.

The premise of IMFA § 5 was that noncitizens who marry either United States citizens or LPRs during removal proceedings are especially likely to have married for immigration purposes. Congress's hope was that, by preventing the noncitizen from using the marriage even to initiate the immigration process until he or she has left the country for two years after the marriage, Congress would discourage fraudulent "eleventh hour" marriages. The United States citizen or LPR spouse might need to stay in the United States during that period for employment or other reasons, but if the marriage was strong enough to withstand two years of early separation, the thinking went, then it probably was not sham.

Many practitioners and commentators attacked IMFA § 5 as unnecessarily harsh, unduly rigid, and even irrational. See, e.g., Charles Gordon, *The Marriage Fraud Act of 1986,* 4 Georgetown Immigration L.J. 183 (1990); Tucker, above. Several lawsuits challenged its constitutionality. The arguments included equal protection (distinctions irrational), deprivation of a fundamental right to marry, procedural due process (no opportunity to demonstrate genuineness of marriage), and irrebuttable presumption (conclusively presumes marriage formed while deportation proceedings pending is sham). The leading litigator in these cases was Lucas Guttentag, on behalf of the ACLU. His and Judy Rabinovitz's successful trial brief in *Manwani v. INS,* 736 F.Supp. 1367 (W.D.N.C.1990), stressed the absence of evidence that the targeted marriages were particularly likely to be fraudulent and the ways (discussed below) in which IMFA § 5 rewarded the clever while punishing those who were innocent but less savvy.

The court in *Manwani* agreed. Despite the broad deference courts usually accord Congress in immigration cases, see chapter 2, the court found IMFA § 5 irrational in its actual operation and struck it down on both due process and equal protection grounds. Most of the other courts that have addressed the constitutionality of IMFA § 5 have upheld it because of Congress's plenary power over immigration. See, e.g., *Azizi v. Thornburgh,* 908 F.2d 1130 (2d Cir.1990); *Anetekhai v. INS,* 876 F.2d 1218 (5th Cir.1989); *Almario v. Attorney General,* 872 F.2d 147 (6th Cir.1989); *Minatsis v. Brown,* 713 F.Supp. 1056 (S.D.Ohio 1989); *Smith v. INS,* 684 F.Supp. 1113 (D.Mass.1988). As discussed on pp. 94–95 above, these disparate results frequently reflected differing views about the characterization of IMFA § 5 as substantive or procedural.

Constitutionality aside, the forceful criticisms of IMFA § 5 eventually bore fruit. Senator Paul Simon, the principal sponsor of IMFA, had conceded even before those court decisions that, in section 5,

> * * * we may have gone too far and are now infringing on the rights of those U.S. citizens and alien spouses who marry out of true love and respect for each other. * * *
>
> * * * [T]he American citizen should not be placed in the situation of having to choose between his or her country, career, and other family on the one hand and moving away to a foreign land where he or she may not know the language and customs or be able to work for a 2–year period on the other in order to live with the new spouse.

134 Cong.Rec. S1625 (daily ed. Feb. 29, 1988). He therefore urged the outright repeal of IMFA § 5. *Id.*

Congress was not willing to go that far, but in section 702 of the Immigration Act of 1990 Congress accepted a compromise that had been suggested in the Guttentag and Rabinovitz brief, at 72. Congress permitted the affected noncitizens to avoid the two-year foreign residence requirement by proving the genuineness of their marriages (and certain other facts) by "clear and convincing evidence." The present wording of INA § 204(g) reflects that change.

NOTES AND QUESTIONS ON MARRIAGES DURING REMOVAL PROCEEDINGS

1.   For those who can supply "clear and convincing evidence" that their marriages are genuine, the 1990 amendment solves the problem. But what about those who cannot, or those who are not confident that the

government will find their evidence "clear and convincing?" In their brief, Guttentag and Rabinovitz describe one vehicle for avoiding IMFA § 5: marrying outside the United States after removal proceedings are completed and then applying for LPR status on the basis of the marriage.[8] But what if the noncitizen marries during the pendency of removal proceedings and *then* learns of IMFA § 5? One of the ironic consequences of this provision has been that it has prompted happily married couples to divorce, remarry each other outside the United States after removal proceedings have been completed, and then seek LPR status on the basis of those latter marriages. Does that strategy work? The former INS said no, if the divorce was a "sham"—i.e., obtained solely for the purpose of evading IMFA § 5. If, in contrast, the divorce resulted from "genuine marital discord," then a bona fide remarriage will qualify. Legal Opinion of (then) INS General Counsel Raymond M. Momboisse, Jan. 31, 1989, reproduced in 66 IR at 637, 638–40 (1989). Ironically, the parties to a roller-coaster marriage might thus have an easier path to family unification than do the parties to a more stable marriage. See also Legal Opinion of (then) Acting General Counsel Paul W. Virtue, Nov. 10, 1990, reproduced in 66 IR at 1422–27 (1989) (same position concerning annulment); *cf. Matter of Aldecoaotalora,* 18 I. & N. Dec. 430 (BIA 1983) (divorce solely for purpose of making noncitizen "unmarried" son or daughter of LPR under second preference will not be recognized).

Immigration attorney Harvey Kaplan, who chaired the AILA Task Force on Marriage Fraud Amendments, argued (before the 1990 amendments were enacted) that in these cases the divorce or annulment might reflect the reality that "the marriage could not endure under the present circumstances" and thus should be seen as having been undertaken for reasons broader than simply obtaining immigration benefits. Harvey Kaplan, *Immigration Marriage Fraud Practice Advisory,* Feb. 1990 AILA Monthly Mailing 77, 78. First, do you agree with Kaplan? Second, even if a divorce or annulment *is* found to have been obtained solely for immigration purposes, does it follow that it should not be recognized for those purposes?

2. You will soon discover some of the ethical issues that arise when a client wants an attorney's help in attaining or extending *nonimmigrant* status and the attorney suspects, but is not sure, that the client fully intends to remain permanently. See chapter 4, § F.1 below. Many analogous issues surface when the attorney suspects marriage fraud. To what extent is the attorney expected to investigate the truth of the client's representations? What information should the attorney disclose to the government? How strong must the lawyer's suspicions be before it would be unethical to assist the client? When, in marriage fraud cases, does the immigration lawyer need to worry about either professional disciplinary

---

8. As you will see later, removal orders themselves bar readmission for varying numbers of years, although the bar is waivable. INA § 212(a)(6)(B). The noncitizen who contemplates future return therefore typically requests "voluntary departure," which the various immigration authorities have the discretion to grant in many cases in lieu of removal. INA § 240B.

sanctions or criminal liability for fraud? The answers unfortunately are not clear. You might wish to revisit these questions after you have examined the applicable ethics principles in chapter 4, § F.1 below. See generally Comment, *Ethical Problems in Representing Aliens Applying for Visas Based on Marriages to United States Citizens,* 28 Santa Clara L.Rev. 709 (1988).

3.   Given all the legal and ethical issues concerning the technical validity and factual genuineness of marriages, and given the stability of many unions not formalized by marriage, should the immigration laws simply repeal all references to "spouses" and replace them with references to intimate unions that are intended to be permanent?

4.   IMFA also made a fraudulent immigration marriage a criminal offense. For a strong argument against criminalizing selected marriages, see Maria Isabel Medina, *The Criminalization of Immigration Law: Employer Sanctions and Marriage Fraud,* 5 George Mason L. Rev. 669, 696–717 (1997).

3.   OTHER FAMILY MEMBERS

United States immigration law extends preferential treatment to several family members other than spouses. "Parents" and "children" of United States citizens are included in the "immediate relative" definition, INA § 201(b)(2)(A)(i), and a "child" who is accompanying or following to join a preference immigrant also receives preference, INA § 203(d). The various family-sponsored preference categories refer to "sons and daughters" and to "brothers and sisters." INA § 203(a). In later chapters you will also see ways in which certain family members of citizens or of LPRs are made eligible for special treatment in the contexts of removal and naturalization.

United States law accords no preference to relatives other than the family members just mentioned. Many other countries do. Canada, for example, provides preferences for grandparents, grandchildren, nieces, and nephews, and even allows the Canadian citizen who has no foreign relatives in that list to sponsor one more distant "relative." François Crépeau & Kinga Janik, Comparative Study on Immigration and Social Transformation—Canada 25–35 (2004); Donald Galloway, Immigration Law 142–52 (1997). British law allows the immigration of certain dependent grandparents, uncles, and aunts. Statement of Changes in Immigration Rules, 14 June 1989, paras. 56, 57.

The word "child," defined in INA § 101(b)(1), has presented particular difficulties for immigration practitioners. A "child" must be unmarried and under age 21. *Id.* Beyond those requirements, however, are a number of commonly applicable restrictions involving children born out of wedlock, stepchildren, and adopted children. As you will also see, the definition of "child" affects the classification of a person as a "son or daughter," a "parent," and, as the following case illustrates, a "brother or sister." Before reading *Mourillon,* study carefully INA § 101(b)(1).

Matter of Mourillon

Board of Immigration Appeals, 1981.
18 I. & N. Dec. 122.

This matter is before the Board on appeal from the District Director's decision of April 9, 1980, denying the petition to classify the beneficiary as the sister of a United States citizen under section 203(a)(5) [now 203(a)(4)—Ed.] of the Immigration and Nationality Act. The appeal will be sustained.

The petitioner is a 52–year–old citizen of the United States who was born out of wedlock in the British West Indies on December 16, 1928. His parents never married, and only a few months after his birth his mother left the household, never to return. The petitioner and his father subsequently immigrated to Curacao, Netherlands Antilles (Dutch West Indies). There, on July 22, 1942, his father married, and they all lived together as a family unit until the petitioner came to the United States in late 1954. In September 1953, the beneficiary was born in Curacao to the petitioner's father and stepmother. The petitioner and beneficiary have apparently continued to maintain their family ties, with the record reflecting that the beneficiary came to the United States in 1971 as a nonimmigrant student and was residing with the petitioner at the time the instant petition was filed on October 30, 1974.

The District Director correctly noted that in order to establish the existence of a sibling relationship the petitioner must show that he and the beneficiary are, or once were, "children" of a common "parent" within the meaning of section 101(b)(1) and (2) of the Act. The District Director then examined the relationship of the petitioner and beneficiary through their father, and concluded that they did not qualify as siblings under the Act because the petitioner was illegitimate and had not been legitimated by his father. Therefore, he denied the petition.

On appeal, the petitioner asserts that he was legitimated by his father according to the law of Curacao, Netherlands Antilles. He also argues that he and the beneficiary are qualified siblings by virtue of their relationship through their other common parent, their stepmother/mother.

The petitioner has now submitted for the record certain provisions of Title XII, Book I of the Civil Code of Curacao ("the Code") which pertain to paternity and filiation in Curacao, Netherlands Antilles. The petitioner contends that under either the legitimation provisions of Title XII, section 2, or the acknowledgment provisions of section 3 of that title, he qualifies as a legitimated child under section 101(b)(1)(C) of the Act. A careful examination of these provisions reveals that this argument is without merit.

Under section 2 of the Code, legitimation of a child born out of wedlock occurs only by the subsequent marriage of the natural parents together with a prior or contemporaneous acknowledgment of the child. Upon legitimation, the child acquires the same rights as if he were legitimate at birth. Thus, it is clear that because the petitioner's natural parents never married he has not been legitimated under the law of Curacao, Netherlands Antilles.

As for the petitioner's acknowledgment claim, we note preliminarily that the general rule outside of communist-bloc countries is that acknowledgment alone does not constitute legitimation; there must also be a subsequent marriage of the natural parents. A "legitimated" child is one placed "in all respects upon the same footing as if begotten and born in wedlock." Only where acknowledgment places the child in the same status as a legitimated child will acknowledgment be deemed the equivalent of legitimation. Such is not the case here. Acknowledgment under section 3 of the Code merely creates "civil rights" between the acknowledged child and his parents. While this term is apparently not defined, the acknowledgment provision, unlike the preceding legitimation provision, does *not* declare that an acknowledged child enjoys the same rights as if he were born legitimate. Therefore, it must be said that because the law of the Netherlands Antilles does not place an acknowledged child in the same status as a legitimated child, it does not make acknowledgment the equivalent of legitimation. This conclusion also finds support in the fact that because the law of the Netherlands Antilles specifically differentiates between acknowledgment and legitimation in the two statutory provisions it is reasonable to presume, absent an affirmative showing to the contrary, that the law does not create a distinction without a difference. ("[A] statute should not be construed in such a way as to render certain provisions superfluous or insignificant.")

In view of the foregoing, we find that the petitioner does not qualify as a legitimated child under section 101(b)(1)(C) of the Act. Therefore, he and the beneficiary do not qualify through their father as "brother" and "sister" * * *.

Turning next to the issue of the petitioner's relationship to the beneficiary through their stepmother/mother, it is clear that the beneficiary once qualified as the legitimate "child" of her mother under section 101(b)(1)(A) of the Act. As for the petitioner, section 101(b)(1)(B) defines the term "child" as an unmarried person under the age of 21 years who is a "stepchild, whether or not born out of wedlock, provided the child had not reached the age of eighteen years at the time the marriage creating the status of stepchild occurred." Here, the petitioner's natural father married when the petitioner was 13 years of age, thus giving rise to a valid stepmother/stepchild relationship under the Act. Therefore, * * * at the time of the beneficiary's birth she and the petitioner were qualified siblings as the "children" of a common "parent."

One further issue remains. Unlike consanguineous relationships, step-relationships can be terminated by the death or divorce of the parties whose marriage created the step-relationship. Thus, in the case of stepsiblings it is appropriate to determine not only whether the petitioner and beneficiary were once the "children" of a common "parent," but also whether the marriage which created the step-relationships still exists at the time the visa petition to accord the stepsibling classification is being considered. Where that marriage does still exist, the stepsibling relationship likewise continues to exist. Difficulties arise, however, where this is not the case.

In the context of stepparent and stepchild, we recently held that where the parties to the marriage which created that step-relationship have legally separated or where the marriage has been terminated by divorce or death, the appropriate inquiry is whether a family relationship has continued to exist as a matter of fact between the stepparent and stepchild. A similar inquiry is no less appropriate in the case of stepsiblings. Accordingly, we hold that in order to qualify as stepsiblings either (1) the marriage which created the step-relationships must continue to exist, or (2) where the parties to that marriage have legally separated or the marriage has been terminated by death or divorce, a family relationship must continue to exist as a matter of fact between the "stepsiblings." Whether the stepsiblings continue to maintain a family relationship is a question of fact which must be determined under the particular circumstances of each case.

Here, the record does not clearly show whether the petitioner's father and the beneficiary's mother are still alive and remain married. Nevertheless, as noted earlier, the record reflects that the petitioner and the beneficiary do continue to maintain their family relationship, including the fact that the beneficiary has lived with the petitioner during her stay in the United States as a nonimmigrant student. Therefore, it has been established that they were "children" of a common "parent" and that their relationship as stepbrother and stepsister continues to exist. Accordingly, the beneficiary qualifies as the petitioner's sister under section 203(a)(5) of the Act.

ORDER: The appeal is sustained and the petition is approved.

NOTES AND QUESTIONS

1. You might have been struck by the fact that the petitioner in *Mourillon* could not qualify as the child of his biological father, who raised him, even though, as soon as the father married another woman, the petitioner instantly became her child! That peculiar result flowed from a statutory provision, in effect until 1986, that disallowed petitions based on a father/child relationship when the child was born out of wedlock. As you saw in chapter 2, the Supreme Court rejected an equal protection challenge to that provision in *Fiallo v. Bell,* 430 U.S. 787, 97 S.Ct. 1473, 52 L.Ed.2d 50 (1977). In 1986, however, Congress amended the provision, INA § 101(b)(1)(D), to allow such a petition "if the father has or had a bona fide parent-child relationship with the person." Act of Nov. 6, 1986, Pub.L. 99–603, § 315(a), 100 Stat. 3359, 3439. For a discussion of the factors and the evidence relevant to whether a bona fide parent-child relationship exists, see *Matter of Pineda,* 20 I. & N.Dec. 70 (BIA 1989); *Matter of Vizcaino,* 19 I. & N.Dec. 644 (BIA 1988); 8 C.F.R. § 204.2(d)(2)(iii) (2004). The Supreme Court has recently upheld analogous gender-based distinctions in the

criteria for citizenship by descent. *Nguyen v. INS*, 533 U.S. 53, 121 S.Ct. 2053, 150 L.Ed.2d 115 (2001).

Why do you suppose the immigration laws attach restrictions to the father/out-of-wedlock child relationship but not to the mother/out-of-wedlock child relationship? Do you think that newer technologies such as (a) DNA testing and (b) gestational surrogacy affect the justifications for that distinction? As to the latter, see Bernard Friedland & Valerie Epps, *The Changing Family and the U.S. Immigration Laws: The Impact of Medical Reproductive Technology on the Immigration and Nationality Act's Definition of the Family*, 11 Georgetown Immigration L.J. 429 (1997).

2. How would *Mourillon* have come out if the present version of section 101(b)(1)(D) had then been in force? Also, suppose Mourillon's father had deserted him at birth and Mourillon had never met or communicated with his father or his father's wife. What result under the present law?

3. Even a person who was born out of wedlock will be recognized as a "child" for immigration purposes if he or she has been "legitimated" under the law of either the child's or the father's residence or domicile. The legitimation must take place before the child turns 18 and while the legitimating parent or parents have legal custody. INA § 101(b)(1)(C). See generally Paul W. Schmidt, *Immigration Benefits for Children Born Out of Wedlock and for their Natural Fathers: A Survey of the Law*, 16 San Diego L.Rev. 11, 20–28 (1978).

As noted in *Mourillon,* legitimation requires that the child be placed "in all respects upon the same footing as if begotten and born in wedlock." In *De Los Santos v. INS*, 690 F.2d 56 (2d Cir.1982), the law of the Dominican Republic allowed "natural filiation" by the father's acknowledgment of paternity or by court decision. Natural filiation created in the child the same rights as a legitimate child *except* that, if the parent died intestate, the "filiated" child would receive a lesser share of the estate than would a legitimate child. Because of that exception, the court held that a child "filiated" under Dominican law has not been legitimated for purposes of the United States immigration laws.

Why would the courts interpret "legitimation" to require legal parity with children born in wedlock? Think particularly about why Congress would restrict the recognition of children born out of wedlock at all and why it would exempt "legitimated" children from those restrictions.

4. The legacies of United States involvement in the Korean War and later in Vietnam included the "Amerasian" children fathered by American soldiers. In many cases the non-Asian lineage of the children was obvious from their facial features but the American fathers either could not be identified or were unwilling to accept custody. Even if the father was willing to bring the child to the United States and the mother was willing to accept that arrangement, the legitimacy restrictions on the definition of "child" often proved insurmountable. Feeling a special responsibility toward these children, Congress in 1982 enacted legislation to permit their

immigration and their placement in the homes of American sponsors. Act of Oct. 22, 1982, Pub.L. 97–359, 96 Stat. 1716. The precise requirements appear in INA § 204(f).

5. Having dismissed the legitimation claim, the Board in *Mourillon* turns to the alternative claim based on the step-relationship. Here the Board is willing to recognize a step-relationship even if the marriage that created it has since terminated, but only if the step-relationship continues "as a matter of fact." Conversely, in *Palmer v. Reddy,* 622 F.2d 463 (9th Cir.1980), the court held that, as long as the marriage had taken place before the child turned 18, and the marriage was still intact, a step-relationship would be found even if there was no parent-child relationship in fact. The BIA now accepts the holding in *Palmer.* See *Matter of McMillan,* 17 I. & N. Dec. 605 (BIA 1981).

6. In *Mourillon* the legitimation and stepchild issues were relevant because for immigration purposes two people will be considered siblings only if they were once "children" of a common parent. That rule is well settled. See, e.g., *Matter of May,* 18 I. & N. Dec. 381 (BIA 1983). Thus, if one of the alleged siblings was never a child of the claimed common parent because, for example, the claimed step-relationship rested on a marriage that took place after the "child" had turned 18, a sibling relationship does not exist. *Matter of Garner,* 15 I. & N. Dec. 215 (BIA 1975). If each of the two purported siblings can identify a time when he or she was the "child" of the common parent, however, the two will be siblings even though there was no point in time at which both siblings met the child definition simultaneously. *Matter of Gur,* 16 I. & N. Dec. 123 (BIA 1977). The BIA in *Mourillon* seems to have accepted this interpretation sub silentio; the petitioner turned 21 before the beneficiary was born, yet the Board ultimately found them to be siblings. You will see illustrations of those interpretations in the Problems below.

7. The "child" definition becomes relevant not only when a petition is filed on behalf of the child or the child's sibling, but in other cases as well. To be someone's "son or daughter," a noncitizen must at one time have been that person's "child." *Matter of Martinez,* 18 I. & N. Dec. 399, 400 (BIA 1983). Similarly, a noncitizen can qualify as a person's "parent" only if that person was at one time the noncitizen's "child." See INA § 101(b)(2); *Chiaramonte v. INS,* 626 F.2d 1093, 1100 (2d Cir.1980).

8. INA 101(a)(27)(J) confers "special immigrant" status on a noncitizen juvenile who has been "declared dependent on a juvenile court located in the United States" and has been committed to long-term foster care because of "abuse, neglect, or abandonment." The statute further requires a showing that "it would not be in the alien's best interest" to be returned to the home country, the consent of the Attorney General, and certain other conditions. Professor David Thronson observes that this provision is the *only* place where the INA currently adopts a "best interest of the child" standard. He makes a strong argument for extending that standard throughout immigration law and entrusting its implementation to persons with child welfare expertise rather than immigration law enforcement

Thronson !

officials. See David B. Thronson, *Kids Will Be Kids? Reconsidering Conceptions of Children's Rights Underlying Immigration Law*, 63 Ohio State L.J. 979 (2002).

PROBLEMS 12–15

For some of these Problems, you will again need to refer to the Visa Office chart on page 254 above.

Problem 12. A and her eighteen-year-old daughter B (from a prior marriage) are citizens of Turkey. A marries C, an LPR living in the United States. Can A and B immigrate?

Problem 13. D and her daughter E (who was born out of wedlock) are also citizens of Turkey. E's biological father, F, is a United States citizen. He deserted D before E's birth and has never communicated with D or E, although they know his whereabouts. When E was seventeen, D married G, who had just been admitted to the United States a few days earlier as an LPR. D and E delayed initiating the immigration process because D needed to stay in Turkey to care for her ailing father. D's father died one year later (at E's age 18), and D and E would now like to immigrate to the United States. What is their best strategy?

Problem 14. While H and J were married, H fathered a child by K, a single woman. All three adults were citizens and residents of Iceland. H and J remained married, and H avoided all contact with his and K's child, whom they named "L." Eventually L grew up, at age 25 married a United States citizen, and entered the United States as an immediate relative. At age 31 she became a naturalized citizen. H learned of this and now wonders whether L (if she is willing to help) might be his and his wife's ticket to LPR status in the United States. Is she? See *Matter of Fong,* 17 I. & N. Dec. 212 (BIA 1980).

Problem 15. N is the legitimate son of M. N's mother (M's wife) died during childbirth. P is the mother of Q, who was born out of wedlock. At a time when N was 22 and Q was 8, M and P married. N was later admitted to the United States as an LPR and eventually attained naturalization. Q is now 18 and would like to immigrate to the United States. M and P are still married. Q's only American "relative" is N. May Q immigrate? See *Matter of Gur,* 16 I. & N. Dec. 123 (BIA 1977).

NOTE ON FOREIGN ADOPTIONS

Those Americans who have sought to adopt children in recent years have experienced firsthand the anguish and frustration of long waits and near misses. The difficulties are rooted in the laws of supply and demand: The number of American couples (and singles) who would like to adopt healthy children far exceeds the number of children available. Renee Schoof, *More U.S. Couples Adopting Abroad* (A.P. release, Jan. 9, 1999).

For many, the solution has been foreign adoptions, particularly from third world countries in which families are often unable to support unwanted children, orphanages are poorly funded, and either economic realities or cultural taboos hinder domestic adoptions. In those cases, foreign adoptions serve the needs of both the children and the adoptive parents.

But the availability of foreign children is highly sensitive to international developments, a fact highlighted not too long ago by events in South Korea. For years, South Korea was regarded as the foreign adoption capital of the world. From 1960 to 1990, approximately 160,000 Korean children were adopted by foreigners, roughly half of whom were Americans. Washington Times, March 13, 1990 at A10. In fiscal years 1988 and 1989, Americans adopted 17,068 foreign children, about half of whom were Korean. 1988 INS Statistical Yearbook, Table 14, at 29; 1989 INS Statistical Yearbook, Table 14, at 29. In early 1990, however, South Korea announced its intention to phase out its foreign adoption program. Washington Times, March 13, 1990, at A10.

The 1988 Seoul Olympics, which focused world attention on South Korea, partly precipitated this change. Many Koreans were embarrassed by the image of a third world country that could not take adequate care of its own children. At the same time, declining birth rates, enhanced prosperity, and greater cultural acceptance of domestic adoptions reduced the need to place Korean children with foreigners. New York Times, Feb. 12, 1990, at B10; Christian Science Monitor, Feb. 28, 1990, at 13. Fears were also fanned by (unfounded) rumors that Americans were importing Korean children to obtain body organs for transplants. Washington Times, March 13, 1990, at A10.

When Korean adoptions dried up, Americans turned increasingly to India, Thailand, the Philippines, Brazil and Colombia. But changes in national outlooks made those and other sources volatile. A new wave of religious fundamentalism in India, for example, discouraged some social workers there from placing Indian children in American homes. New York Times, Feb. 12, 1990, at B10. For various reasons, Brazil reduced foreign adoptions of its children. Christian Science Monitor, May 22, 1990, at 11. Romanian orphanages overflowed with abandoned children because of Ceausescu's ban on contraception; the inadequate health care and nutrition left huge numbers of those orphaned babies diseased and close to death. In the post-Ceausescu era, the authorities nonetheless turned the spigot on and off at will. See Washington Post, July 15, 1990, at D1, D9.

In the early 1990's, China became the largest source country for international adoptions by American parents. Then China too tightened its rules, scrutinizing prospective parents more intensively and awarding healthy Chinese babies only to childless couples over age 35. Kristina Sauerwein, *Stricter Adoption Laws Benefit Children, Experts Say*, St. Louis Post–Dispatch, Dec. 8, 1996, at 7A.

Starting in the mid–1990s, however, international adoptions in the United States began to soar. In 1998 China loosened many of its restrictions, Schoof, above, and in fiscal year 2003 once again became the largest source country for the U.S. adoption of orphaned children, with 6638 adoptions (despite a temporary suspension of foreign adoptions that year because of SARS, see 80 IR 755 (May 23, 2003)). Of those, more than 95% were girls. See 2003 Yearbook of Immigration Statistics, Table 10 at 37–38 (Sept. 2004). The gender imbalance surely reflects the interaction of China's one-child policies with the Chinese public's cultural and economic preferences for sons.

After China, the five largest foreign source countries for U.S. adoption of orphaned children in 2003 were Russia (5134), Guatemala (2327), South Korea (1793), Kazakhstan (819), and Ukraine (691). *Id.* In more than 90% of these cases, the adopted children were ages 4 or under. *Id.*

The reasons for the recent increases in U.S. international adoptions are varied, and they augur continued growth. One expert points to the increasing scarcity of healthy white infants in the United States. (In the mid–1990s, "fewer than 2% of unwed white mothers gave their children up for adoption," compared to almost 20% in 1973. See Cheryl Wetzstein, *Foreign Adoptions Grow to Record Level*, Wash. Times (Dec. 6, 2002)). Secondly, U.S. adults are increasingly willing to adopt children of different races. *Id.* In addition, children available for international adoption tend to be younger than those available in the United States through the foster care system. *Id.* Still, the conditions that turn foreign children into orphans remain distressing. AIDS alone has produced almost 8 million African orphans, many of whom are themselves HIV-positive. See Schoof, above.

Apart from foreign restrictions, prospective adoptive parents in the United States must consider the requirements of the American immigration laws. Until 1957 this country's laws did not bestow immigration benefits on adopted children at all. See 3 Gordon, Mailman, & Yale–Loehr § 36.04[6][a]. The fear was that "sham" adoptions could be arranged to evade the immigrant quotas.

In 1957, Congress amended the "child" definition to include certain adopted children. Act of Sept. 11, 1957, Pub.L. 85–316, § 2, 71 Stat. 639. In 1961, Congress added a separate permanent provision for the admission of "orphan" children. Act of Sept. 26, 1961, Pub.L. 87–301, 75 Stat. 650.

Express restrictions aimed at preventing fraud remain. Under the adopted child provision (subsection E), the child has to have been adopted while under age 16, and has to have been in the legal custody of, and have resided with, the adopting parent for at least two years. Further, the biological parents may not thereafter receive any immigration benefits by virtue of such parentage. *Id.* Adoptive parents may be anyone eligible to petition generally for the immigration of their children—i.e., either United States citizens or LPRs.

In addition to the express statutory requirements, the BIA has read in a general requirement analogous to that used in marriage cases: The adoption must not have been entered into solely for immigration purposes. *Matter of Marquez*, 20 I. & N.Dec. 160 (BIA 1990). The BIA scrutinizes especially closely when the adopting parent is a close relative, particularly if a biological parent continues to live in the same household as the child and the adopting parent. See, e.g., *id.; Matter of Cuello*, 20 I. & N.Dec. 94 (BIA 1989).

Under the "orphan" provision (subsection F), certain United States citizens (not LPRs) may petition for the admission of children under age 16 who have experienced the death, disappearance, or abandonment of both parents or sometimes just one parent.

At least up to now, these provisions (as amended from time to time) have been the two primary vehicles for adopting foreign children and bringing them to the United States. The provisions are codified as INA §§ 101(b)(1)(E and F), respectively.

There is now a third, international method for overseas adoptions in the United States. In recent years, the international community has become increasingly concerned with child abduction, trafficking of kidnapped children, and other forms of abuse. After extensive negotiation, many of the world's leading source countries and destination countries for adopted children signed the Hague Convention on Protection of Children and Co–Operation in Respect of Intercountry Adoption, 32 I.L.M. 1134 (1993). The Convention requires certain minimum procedures designed to protect children, biological parents, and adoptive parents. Following ratification by the United States Senate, Congress in 2000 enacted the necessary implementation. Intercountry Adoption Act of 2000, Pub. L. 106–279, 114 Stat. 825 (Oct. 6, 2000). The new law assigns primary regulatory responsibility for foreign adoptions to the State Department and expands slightly the range of children whom United States citizen parents may bring to the United States from other states parties. For the details, see INA § 101(b)(1)(G).

A final, practical consideration: Foreign adoptions are not cheap. The adopting parents must be willing to pay the legal fees of foreign and American lawyers, adoption agency fees, and travel expenses. Typical costs range from $7,000 to $25,000 (in contrast to domestic adoptions through the foster care system, where the costs range from nominal to $2,500, or in contrast to private domestic adoptions, with costs of $4,000 to $30,000). Wetzstein, above.

One difficult issue has been when to permit the biological mother of a child born out of wedlock to release her child for foreign adoption without the consent of the biological father, if the mother is unable to provide proper care. On the one hand, the father might well have disappeared or otherwise become either unable or unwilling to consent; allowing unilateral release can therefore be essential. On the other hand, there will always be cases in which the father should be permitted to assert parental rights. For a helpful discussion of Congress's 1995 resolution of this problem, see Kathleen M. Sullivan, *Congress Streamlines Procedures for Certain Intercountry "Orphan" Adoptions*, 1 BIB #3 (1996).

For more detail on the immigration of adopted or orphaned children, see generally 2 Gordon, Mailman & Yale–Loehr § 36.04[6,7]; Kathleen M.

Sullivan, *Intercountry Adoption Act Becomes Law*, 5 BIB 977 (Dec. 1, 2000); Aarti Kohli & Kathleen M. Sullivan, *Intercountry Adoption: A Practitioner's Update*, July 2001 Immigration Briefings.

4.   FAMILY UNIFICATION POLICY IN PERSPECTIVE

NOTES AND QUESTIONS

1.   Is family-based immigration "nepotism," a word some immigration restriction organizations like to use? Or is it a legitimate basis for immigration preference?

2.   There has been much debate over the continuation and level of the sibling (family-sponsored fourth) preference. Some have criticized the sibling preference on the ground, among others, that it precipitates "chain" migration: An LPR naturalizes and brings in his or her sibling, who brings in his or her spouse and children, who in turn naturalize and bring in the spouse's parents and siblings, etc. See, e.g., Panel I, *Family–Sponsored Immigration,* 4 Georgetown Immigration L.J. 201, 206 (1990) (comments of Dan Stein). Others acknowledge that such chain migration is theoretically possible but cite studies that cast doubt on whether it actually occurs to any significant degree. See *id.* at 211–12 (comments of Cecilia Munoz); Robert Bach & Doris Meissner, America's Labor Market in the 1990's: What Role Should Immigration Play? 13–14 (1990). See generally Fred Arnold, *Unanswered Questions About the Immigration Multiplier,* 23 Internat'l Migration Rev. 889 (1989); Michael S. Teitelbaum, *Skeptical Noises about the Immigration Multiplier,* 23 Internat'l Migration Rev. 893 (1989).

Apart from the specific issue of chain migration, there has been a sometimes rancorous debate over the division of limited family visas between nuclear family members (principally immediate relatives and the first three family-sponsored preferences) and siblings. Along similar lines, some have argued that even the sons and daughters of United States citizens and of LPRs should be eliminated from the preference categories once those sons and daughters turn 21.

In 1995, the United States Commission on Immigration Reform (often called the Jordan Commission, after its late Chair, Hon. Barbara Jordan) recommended cutting immigration generally and family immigration in particular. As for the latter, the Commission recommended (with Commissioner Warren Leiden dissenting) the repeal of the family-sponsored 1st, 2B, 3rd, and 4th preferences. The only family members who would receive preference under the Commission proposal were those who correspond to immediate relatives and 2A's. See U.S. Comm'n on Immigration Reform, Legal Immigration: Setting Priorities 45–80 (June 1995). For criticisms, see Linda Kelly, *Family Planning: American Style,* 52 Alabama L. Rev. 943 (2001) (arguing that the immigration laws should reflect a broader social construction of family, more in keeping with the demise of the nuclear family and the modern realities of nontraditional arrangements); Enid Trucios–Haynes, *"Family Values" 1990s Style: U.S. Immigration Reform*

Proposals and the Abandonment of the Family, 36 Brandeis J. Family L. 241 (1997–98).

Would you eliminate the preferences for siblings or for adult sons and daughters?

3.   A source of longstanding frustration for many LPRs has been the lengthy waiting periods that their spouses and minor children must often endure before the family can be reunited. As of April 2005, the family-sponsored worldwide 2A backlog was more than four years. See the Visa Office Bulletin on page 254 above. Some have argued that, like the nuclear family members of United States citizens, this group should be classified as immediate relatives and admitted without numerical limit. Then Professor (later BIA member) John Guendelsberger, in *Implementing Family Unification Rights in American Immigration Law: Proposed Amendments,* 25 San Diego L.Rev. 253 (1988), argued that the courts should recognize a constitutional right of LPRs to family unity, absent compelling governmental interests to the contrary. He also urged Congress, whether constitutionally compelled or not, to make the spouses and minor children of LPRs immediate relatives. What arguments might you make for or against Professor Guendelsberger's latter proposal if you were testifying before a congressional subcommittee?

4.   For some interesting comparisons of family unification policies in the United States with those in France, Germany, and the Caribbean, respectively, see John Guendelsberger, *The Right to Family Reunification in French and United States Immigration Law,* 21 Cornell Internat'l L.J. 1 (1988); Hiroshi Motomura, *The Family and Immigration: A Roadmap for the Ruritanian Lawmaker,* 43 American J. Comp.L. 511 (1995); Leonard Storchevoy, *The Right to Family Reunification in the Immigration Law of the Commonwealth Caribbean and the United States: A Comparative Study,* 7 Touro Internat'l L. Rev. 177, 203–06 (1997); see generally Nora V. Demleitner, *How Much Do Western Democracies Value Family and Marriage?: Immigration Law's Conflicted Answers,* 32 Hofstra L. Rev. 273 (2003).

5.   Article 8 of the European Convention for the Protection of Human Rights and Fundamental Freedoms, 213 U.N.T.S. 222 (Nov. 4, 1950), reads as follows:

> 1.   Everyone has the right to respect for his private and family life, his home and his correspondence.

> 2.   There shall be no interference by a public authority with the exercise of this right except such as is in accordance with the law and is necessary in a democratic society in the interests of national security, public safety or the economic well-being of the country, for the prevention of disorder or crime, for the protection of health or morals, or for the protection of the rights and freedoms of others.

The case law of the European Court of Human Rights, binding on all member states of the Council of Europe, has relied on article 8 to limit both the exclusion and the expulsion of noncitizens with family members. For a good summary, see Hélène Lambert, *The European Court of Human Rights and the Right of Refugees and Other Persons in Need of Protection to Family Reunion*, 11 Internat'l J. Refugee L. 427 (1999).

Other sources of international law also constrain family separation in the exclusion and deportation contexts. See, e.g., *Baker v. Minister of Citizenship and Immigration*, [1999] 2 S.C.R. 817 (Supreme Court of Canada) (interpreting Convention on the Rights of the Child); *Winata & Li v. Australia*, UN Doc. CCPR/C/72/D/930/2000 (Human Rights Committee, 2001) (interpreting International Covenant on Civil and Political Rights). For an excellent summary of the international law constraints, with emphasis on refugees' families, see Kate Jastram & Kathleen Newland, *Family Unity and Refugee Protection*, in Erika Feller, Volker Türk & Frances Nicholson (Eds.), Refugee Protection in International Law at 555–603 (2003).

6. At the beginning of the twenty-first century, it is worth looking back to a time when the United States rules on family immigration were simpler:

> [A]ny admissible alien, or any alien heretofore or hereafter legally admitted, or any citizen of the United States, may bring in or send for his father or grandfather over fifty-five years of age, his wife, his mother, his grandmother, or his unmarried or widowed daughter, if otherwise admissible, whether such relative can read or not; and such relative shall be permitted to enter.

Immigration Act of 1917, ch. 29, § 3, para. 3, 39 Stat. 874, 877 (Feb. 5, 1917). Keep in mind that this provision predated numerical quotas; its main significance was that it exempted the named family members from the exclusion grounds, including the literacy requirement. The absence of numerical quotas also probably explains why relatives of citizens and relatives of LPRs enjoyed equal priority.

Note also the underlying assumptions about gender. Unmarried female relatives were assumed to be dependent upon their parents, children, or grandchildren; male relatives were not, unless they were elderly. Men could bring in their wives, but women could not bring in their husbands. Children of citizens (and of immigrants) were similarly classified by gender. Nor, in referring to "unmarried or widowed daughters," did Congress include divorced daughters. Perhaps divorce was still unusual enough that Congress did not spot the issue, or perhaps Congress assumed that divorced daughters would receive alimony from their ex-husbands and thus would have no financial need to immigrate.

SECTION C.   EMPLOYMENT–BASED IMMIGRATION

In this technological age, Congress has steadily expanded the programs for admitting immigrants on the basis of occupational credentials. The most fundamental of these changes were part of the Immigration Act of

1990. Generally, Congress more than doubled the overall ceiling on employment-based immigrants, expanded the number of qualifying categories, and assigned a higher priority to professional and other highly skilled workers. The same statute sharply reduced the admission of unskilled workers (more on that in a moment). Then, in 2000, Congress exempted most employment-based immigrants from the per-country limits. See page 243 above.

The five employment-based preference categories were summarized earlier on pages 244–45 above. As you have seen, the first three represent skills that Congress believes are needed in the United States. Each of those three preference categories is allocated approximately 40,000 visas—i.e., 120,000 in total—plus any visas not used by the fourth and fifth preference applicants.

The fourth preference is "employment-based" only in the sense that most of its many prongs relate somehow to the individual's past or present work. Those prongs are generally there to reward special equities, such as loyal long-term U.S. government employees and Hong Kong embassy employees, rather than to recognize particular skills as needed in the United States. The approximately 10,000 visas allotted to this category are for certain sub-groups of the "special immigrants" defined in INA § 101(a)(27).

The fifth preference is for up to approximately 10,000 entrepreneurs. This group is considered "employment-based" not because of its members' occupational skills, but because they are expected to create jobs for United States workers.

You should now skim subsections 1–3 of INA § 203(b).

1. THE FIRST THREE PREFERENCES: SUPERSTARS, STARS AND OTHERS

a. GENERAL ELIGIBILITY REQUIREMENTS

Unlike the four family-sponsored preferences, the first three employment-based preferences form a clear pecking order. The first preference is generally reserved for superstars. It includes immigrants with "extraordinary ability in the sciences, arts, education, business or athletics which has been demonstrated by sustained national or international acclaim;" and professors and researchers[9] who are "outstanding." (Apparently Congress thought "extraordinary" was an unrealistic standard for professors; they need only be "outstanding.") The one exception to the superstar characterization is a third prong for certain multinational executives and managers; they need not demonstrate any particular level of fame or success. See INA § 203(b)(1).

---

9. See generally George S. Newman, *Considerations in Recruitment of Foreign Scholars for Faculty Appointments,* in AILA, 1990 (2) Immigration and Nationality Law at 195–202.

The regulations define "extraordinary ability" as "a level of expertise indicating that the individual is one of that small percentage who have risen to the very top of the field of endeavor." 8 C.F.R. § 204.5(h)(2) (2004). The regulations then list numerous types of supporting evidence that the applicant may submit. *Id.* § 204.5(h)(3, 4).

Major league athletes sometimes apply for first preference status by asserting "extraordinary ability in ... athletics." Courts have held on the one hand that major league status does not per se establish extraordinary ability but that, on the other hand, an athlete doesn't have to be among the best in the league to qualify either. The location of the line is still not clear. See Herbert A. Weiss, *Employment-Based Immigrant Visa Petitions: An Update*, June 1996 Immigration Briefings. If you were the USCIS General Counsel, how would you apply the above regulation? Suppose the applicant is an American League outfielder who typically hits .290 to .300 with 10–12 home runs and is at about the league average in terms of defensive skills. Should he receive first preference status?

The second preference has two prongs: "members of the professions holding advanced degrees or their equivalent" and immigrants with "exceptional ability in the sciences, arts, or business." INA § 203(b)(2). Where the first preference uses the word "extraordinary," the latter prong of the second preference uses the word "exceptional." Moreover, the second prong does not expressly include ability in the fields of education or athletics, although the government interprets the "arts" to include athletics. See Weiss, above, at 10.

The second preference differs from the first preference in one other important respect; it generally requires the applicant to demonstrate a job offer from an American employer, INA § 203(b)(2)(A), and obtain a document called "labor certification" from the Department of Labor, INA § 212(a)(5)(A, C). The latter, discussed in detail in the next subsection, generally requires showings that able, willing, and qualified American workers are not available and that the applicant's employment will not adversely affect the wages and working conditions of similarly employed United States workers. *Id.*

For second preference applicants, however, the government has the discretion to waive the job offer requirement in the national interest. INA § 203(b)(2)(B). The regulations assume that a waiver of the job offer requirement also waives the requirement of labor certification. See 8 C.F.R. § 204.5(k)(4)(ii) (2004).

Through most of the 1990s, the former INS granted national interest waivers fairly liberally. See generally Enid Trucios–Haynes, *National Interest Waivers*, July 1995 Immigration Briefings; Wall Street Journal, Aug. 20, 1998, at 1. In 1998, however, the world of national interest waivers shrank dramatically with the decision of the INS Acting Associate Commissioner in *Matter of New York State Dept. of Transportation [NYSDOT]*, 22 I. & N. Dec. 215 (Aug. 7, 1998). The decision in *NYSDOT* restricted national interest waivers in several ways. The former INS held it is not enough that the applicant has a particular level of training or education. General arguments about the importance of a given field or the urgency of a given issue similarly do not suffice. Nor is it enough to show a shortage of qualified workers in a given field.

Instead, the INS held, an applicant for a national interest waiver must show (1) that the area of employment is one of "substantial intrinsic merit;" (2) that the person's employment will benefit the nation, not just the local area; and (3) that the particular applicant "will serve the national interest to a substantially greater degree than would an available U.S. worker having the same minimum qualifications [emphasis added]." 22 I. & N. Dec. at 217–18. To illustrate the second requirement, the INS said "[W]hile education is in the national interest, the impact of a single schoolteacher in one elementary school would not be in the national interest [for waiver purposes]." *Id.* at 217 n.3. For effective critiques of this position, see Stanley Mailman & Stephen Yale–Loehr, *The "National Interest" Waiver*, 4 BIB 271 (Apr. 1, 1999); Nathan A. Waxman, *New York State Department of Transportation: National Interest Waivers One Year Down the Road*, 76 IR 1641 (Nov. 15, 1999). For an illuminating summary of how the government has applied the third element to researchers, see Sean Koehler & Stephen Yale–Loehr, *National Interest Waiver Petitions for Researchers: Demonstrating a Measurable Impact on the Larger Field*, 9 BIB 1341 (Nov. 15, 2004).

The third preference contains three subprongs: immigrants capable of performing certain "skilled labor" for which qualified U.S. workers are not available; immigrants who have baccalaureate degrees and are members of the professions; and "other workers" who are capable of performing unskilled labor for which qualified U.S. workers are not available. INA § 203(b)(3). As with the second preference, labor certification is required, see INA §§ 203(b)(3)(C), 212(a)(5)(C); unlike the second preference, however, there is no provision for national interest waivers. Importantly also, the statute provides that no more than 10,000 of the third preference visas may be awarded to the "other workers" prong in a single fiscal year. INA § 203(b)(3)(B).

In the past few years, the first three preferences—especially the first two—have been perennially underutilized. See Weiss, above, at 3. The Commission on Immigration Reform, in fact, recommended substantially reducing the employment-based ceilings generally. See U.S. Commission on Immigration Reform, Legal Immigration: Setting Priorities 81–120 (June 1995). At this writing, the first and second employment-based preferences are current (i.e. no waiting period); the third preference is current except for natives of China, India, and the Philippines, and except for the "other workers" subcategory. See the April 2005 Visa Bulletin on page 254 above.

b. LABOR CERTIFICATION

Long considered a staple of the immigration lawyer's work, labor certification attained even greater importance with the enactment of the 1990 Act and the attendant expansion of employment-based immigration. The INA requires labor certification for those who apply under the second and third employment-based preferences, INA § 212(a)(5)(D), except, as mentioned earlier, that national interest waivers are sometimes possible for second preference applicants, INA § 203(b)(2)(B). The precise statutory criteria for a grant of labor certification, designed to assure that the immigrant's employment will neither displace nor otherwise disadvantage American workers, appear in INA § 212(a)(5)(A). That provision requires a certification by the Secretary of Labor that

> (i)(I) there are not sufficient workers who are able, willing, qualified (or equally qualified in the case of an alien described in clause (ii)) and available at the time of application for a visa and admission to the United States and at the place where the alien is to perform such skilled or unskilled labor, and

> (II) the employment of such alien will not adversely affect the wages and working conditions of workers in the United States similarly employed.

> (ii) Certain aliens subject to special rule

> For purposes of clause (i)(I), an alien described in this clause is an alien who—

> > (I) is a member of the teaching profession, or

> > (II) has exceptional ability in the sciences or the arts.

Although this chapter is generally confined to the substantive criteria for admission (procedure will be the subject of chapter 6), a brief digression on labor certification procedure should help you follow the cases in this subsection. For many years, the labor certification process has been plagued by complexity, great expense (for both the employer and the government), huge backlogs, and long delays. Apart from the impossible position for the employer who needs to fill the job, the long administrative delays have created hardship for the prospective immigrants. In recent years the Department of Labor has searched for ways to speed the administrative process. For an excellent description of the innovation known as "Reduction in Recruitment" [R.I.R.], see Linda Rose, *De-Mystifying Reduction in Recruitment*, 19 Immigration Law Today 205 (April 2000). Still, administrative backlogs grew so large that the combined waiting times for processing the labor certification application and the visa petition frequently totaled several years. The process involves both "state workforce agencies" (SWAs) and the U.S. Labor Department's Employment and Training Administration (ETA). Most of the delay occurred at the SWAs, where the waiting times varied considerably from state to state. For up-to-date estimates of the waiting times at both the state and federal levels, see the DOL website, http:www.ows.doleta.gov/foreign/times.asp#reg.

Amidst a general consensus that improved efficiency had become essential, the ETA in 2005 finalized a comprehensive overhaul known as "PERM" (Program Electronic Review Management). The new procedures took effect on March 28, 2005. The details are laid out in 69 Fed. Reg. 77325–77421 (Dec. 27, 2004), amending 8 C.F.R. § 656. Here is a summary:

You need to know initially that, when labor certification is required, it is merely the first step in the process. Once labor certification issues, a "visa petition" (standardized form I–140) is ordinarily filed with USCIS to classify the immigrant as one who fits within the claimed preference category. INA § 204(a)(1)(C, D). You will see more on visa petitions later.

How does the immigrant (or, more commonly, the immigrant's employer) obtain labor certification? One of the first steps is to check "Schedule A," published by the Labor Department in 20 C.F.R. § 656.5 (2005). Schedule A lists those occupations that the Labor Department has "pre-certified" as meeting the statutory requirements for labor certification. At this writing, the only listed occupations are physical therapists, nurses, and immigrants of "exceptional ability in the sciences or arts." If the employee fits one of those headings, labor certification is deemed to have been automatically granted. The immigrant or employer therefore bypasses the Labor Department entirely and files a petition with USCIS, which then decides whether the immigrant's job really does fall within one of the Schedule A occupations. *Id*. § 656.15. Until 2005, the Department also maintained a Schedule B, which listed occupations for which labor certification ordinarily would *not* be granted; for those occupations, the applicants had to apply for waivers and make special showings. See 20 C.F.R. §§ 656.11, 656.23 (2004). Since processing the waiver applications required the same resources as simply processing the labor certification applications directly, PERM omits any provision for Schedule B.

In the usual case, the occupation is not listed on Schedule A and therefore an individual application for labor certification must be filed. Under the old system, the application was submitted to the relevant "state employment security agency," or SESA, now known as a "state workforce agency," or SWA. The local SWA would then assist the employer in recruiting domestic workers and, eventually, forward the file to the ETA for decision. Under the new system, the application is filed directly with ETA, but before filing it the employer (a) must request the SWA to determine the prevailing wage for the particular job; and (b) must take certain specified recruiting steps to determine whether qualified U.S. workers are available. The application may be filed either electronically or by mail, and it need not include any documentation. It contains only attestations by the employer as to the essential facts. ETA screens the applications and selects a fraction of them for audits. Only if audited must an employer document the statements made in the application. See 8 C.F.R. § 656.17 (2005).

The application is decided by an ETA official known as a "certifying officer" (CO). By way of exception, the CO may refer the case to the "National Certifying Officer" at DOL headquarters if the application "presents a special or unique problem" or falls within a category of cases predesignated by the National Certifying Officer for referral. See generally 20 C.F.R. § 656.24(a)(2) (2004).

If the CO decides that the applicant meets all the requirements, labor certification is granted. 20 C.F.R. § 656.24(d) (2004). Otherwise the CO denies the application, stating the reasons for the denial (in writing) and advising the employer that review may be requested within 30 days. *Id.* § 656.24(e). Upon a timely request for review, the file is forwarded to the Labor Department's Board of Alien Labor Certification Appeals (BALCA). *Id.* § 656.26. BALCA sits in Washington, D.C. It may act in three-member panels, *id.* § 656.27(a), and customarily does. Occasionally, BALCA goes en banc. The regulations do not explicitly authorize BALCA to designate its decisions as precedents, but improved consistency was the reason for its creation, so in practice BALCA frequently cites its own prior decisions for support. 4 Gordon, Mailman & Yale–Loehr § 44.05[4]. BALCA's decisions in turn are subject to judicial review in federal district court. *Id.* § 44.09. BALCA's published decisions are available on the web at www.oalj.dol.gov/libina.htm.

An employer may also request review of the SWA prevailing wage determination. Review is performed by the CO, with the right of further review by BALCA. 8 C.F.R. § 656.41 (2005).

As you will see in chapter 6, many applicants for LPR status use a procedure known as adjustment of status, which permits certain otherwise qualified individuals who are already in the United States—typically as lawful temporary workers—to complete the LPR process without having to return home first. In 2000, Congress supplied a partial corrective to the labor certification delay problem, available only to adjustment of status applicants. Once such applicants have been waiting more than 180 days, they are now free to change to another employer or to another job "in the same or a similar occupational classification," without the need for USCIS or DOL approval. This development has major substantive implications for labor certification. See the American Competitiveness in the Twenty–First Century Act, Pub. L. 106–313, 114 Stat. 1251, 1254, § 106(c) (Oct. 17, 2000), adding INA §§ 204(j) and 212(a)(5)(A)(iv). For more detail, see Ronald Klasko, *American Competitiveness in the 21st Century: H–1Bs and Much More*, 77 IR 1689, 1694–95 (Dec. 11, 2000); Herbert A. Weiss, *Twenty-First Century Developments in Employment–Based (EB) Immigration Law*, May 2003 Immigration Briefings, at 8–14.

i. Displacing American Workers

Matter of Marion Graham

Board of Alien Labor Certification Appeals, Feb. 2, 1990.
No. 88–INA–102 (en banc).

This appeal arises from an application for labor certification pursuant to Section 212(a)(14) [now 212(a)(5)(A)—Ed.] of the Immigration and Nationality Act. The Certifying Officer (CO) of the United States Department of Labor denied the application, and Employer requested * * * review. * * *

* * * [A]n alien seeking to enter the United States for the purpose of performing skilled or unskilled labor is ineligible to receive a visa unless the Secretary of Labor (Secretary) has determined and certified to the

Secretary of State and to the [Secretary of Homeland Security] that: (1) there are not sufficient workers in the United States who are able, willing, qualified, and available at the time of application for a visa and admission into the United States and at the place where the alien is to perform such labor; and (2) the employment of the alien will not adversely affect the wages and working conditions of United States workers similarly employed.

Employers desiring to employ aliens on a permanent basis must apply for labor certification pursuant to 20 C.F.R. Part 656. These regulations require an employer to document that the job opportunity has been and is being described without unduly restrictive requirements. If the job requirements which an employer is requiring of U.S. workers are: (1) other than those normally required for the job in the United States; (2) exceed the requirements listed in the Dictionary of Occupational Titles (D.O.T.); (3) include a foreign language; (4) involve a combination of duties or (5) require the worker to live on employer's premises, they are presumptively unduly restrictive, and the employer must demonstrate by documentation that its requirements arise from a business necessity.

* * *

On December 26, 1986, an application for labor certification * * * was submitted by Marion Graham (Employer) on behalf of Gladys Yolanda Ulloa (Alien) for the position of "HOUSEWORKER GENERAL/CHILD MONITOR (Live–In)." The duties of the position were listed on ETA Form 750–A as follows:

Responsible for cleaning 2 story house of 3,000 square feet.

Cleans 3 bedrooms, 4 bathrooms, 2 living rooms, 1 dining room, 1 bar area, 1 kitchen area, also cleans garage area. Irons clothes. Polishes furniture and silverware and glassware. Waters plants. Changes linens. Answers phone and bell door. Feed 2 dogs. Cleans 8 glass windows, 9 glass doors and 3 big mirrors.

Full supervision and responsibility on absence of parent of 1 infant girl of 1 (one) years of age. Cooks meals and prepare formulas for her. Bathe, dress her. Supervise and participate in her play activities.

* * * As a condition of employment, Employer required that the person hired live in her home, have 3–months experience and be willing to work Monday through Friday, Saturdays and Sundays when requested, and 3 to 4 hours overtime daily. Employer also required that the employee not smoke or drink [alcoholic beverages] at the work site and that he or she have a legal right to work in the United States. No U.S. workers responded to Employer's advertisement.

On April 30, 1987, the CO issued a Notice of Findings (NOF) which proposed to deny certification on the basis of § 656.21(b)(2), which requires that the job opportunity be described without unduly restrictive requirements. In the NOF the CO challenged the requirement that the employee hired live in the employer's home as being unduly restrictive. The CO stated, however, that Employer could delete the live-in requirement and readvertise the position, or she could provide documentation that the live-in requirement arises from a business necessity.

In its letter of rebuttal, dated May 23, 1987, Employer attempted to demonstrate that the live-in requirement arises from a business necessity. Employer asserted that the work shift is divided so that 50–percent of the working hours pertain to the household cleaning and 50–percent child monitoring; the household is very busy; because Employer's husband is a Hospital President, on call 24 hours a day a live-in employee is needed to screen calls at night; Employer personally accompanies her husband at times on his business trips, and therefore a live-in is required to take full responsibility for the child and household; the cost of paying a housekeeper and a night care child monitor is very expensive; Employer has to run different types of personal errands every day, including helping to care for her sick mother. Employer also asserted that because the Alien has cared for the child since birth, she has confidence in her.

On July 15, 1987, the CO issued a Final Determination (FD) denying certification finding that Employer had failed to document the live-in requirement as arising from a business necessity. * * *

II. Applicability of [business necessity requirement]

* * * [A]n employer must document that the job opportunity has been described without unduly restrictive job requirements. In instances where the worker is required to live on the employer's premises, the requirement will be deemed unduly restrictive unless the employer adequately documents that the requirement arises from a business necessity.

* * *

III. "Business" to which [the business necessity requirement] applies

* * *

Considering the absence of guidance from the Act or the regulations as to the meaning of the term "business necessity", the fact that the federal district and circuit courts which have touched on the subject imply that many factors are relevant when determining business necessity in a live-in domestic situation, the fact that dictionary definitions of "business" do not exclude use of the term in non-commercial contexts, and the context of labor certification which does not direct the Secretary to make any sort of judgment on the value of the employment opportunity offered but only on availability of and impact on U.S. workers, we conclude that the relevant "business" is the "business" of running a household or managing one's personal affairs. To construe "business necessity" so as to require consideration to be limited to the employer's outside business interests in the context of labor certification of a domestic worker would infuse the Secretary with the discretion to decide what business needs and personal social and economic preferences are best for the country—a discretion that goes well beyond the responsibility imposed on the Secretary under the Act.

IV.   Application of business necessity test in live-in domestic context

To establish the business necessity for a live-on-the-premises require-ment for a domestic worker, the employer must demonstrate that the requirement is essential to perform, in a reasonable manner, the job duties as described by the employer. In the context of a domestic live-in worker, pertinent factors in determining whether the live-on-the-premises require-ment is essential for the performance of the job duties include the Employ-er's occupation or commercial activities outside the home, the circum-stances of the household itself, and any other extenuating circumstances. Those factors must be weighed on a case-by-case basis. The presence or absence of any one concern in a particular case may not be determinative.[5]

Although a judgment on the merits of the job opportunity as it relates to a private employer's lifestyle choice is not a relevant consideration,[6] a mere personal preference to have an employee live on the premises does not establish business necessity.

V.   Application of the test to Marion Graham, Employer

To meet the business necessity test, * * * Ms. Graham's evidence must establish that the live-on-the-premises requirement is essential for the Alien to perform, in a reasonable manner, the job duties of general household worker/child monitor.

Written assertions which are reasonably specific and indicate their sources or bases are to be considered documentation which must be given the weight it rationally deserves. When applying the business necessity test in a live-in domestic situation, a requisite degree of specificity for a written assertion generally should, at the very least, enable the Certifying Officer to determine whether there are cost-effective alternatives to a live-in requirement and whether the needs of the household for a live-in worker are genuine. For example, if one of the reasons proffered for the live-in requirement is absence of Employer from the home, the assertions should specify the length (e.g. overnight, days at a time, 18–hours per day, etc.) and frequency (e.g., three or four days a week, weekends, etc.) of the absences. The Board also notes that, as a general matter, documentation to bolster assertions of a need for a live-in requirement will go a long way in establishing the credibility of those assertions (e.g., travel vouchers; written

---

5. The fact that a particular Employer does not have an occupation outside the home, for example, would not preclude that Employer from obtaining labor certification for a domestic live-in worker if some other factor showing business necessity is docu-mented for the live-in requirement, such as the Employer being an invalid. On the other hand, the mere fact that an Employer is an invalid may not itself establish the business necessity for a live on the premises require-ment. Hence, if several United States work-ers could perform the work required, the fact that the Employer is an invalid who needs constant care may not justify the live-in re-quirement. It is noted, however, that employ-ment of an around-the-clock service may prove to be exorbitantly expensive and there-fore inappropriate.

6. For example, a Certifying Officer may not conclude that business necessity has not been shown simply because that Officer believes that live-in domestic service is a lux-ury reserved for the rich.

estimates of the costs of alternatives such as a phone answering service or babysitters).

The relevant evidence in this case consists entirely of written assertions made by Employer in her December 13, 1986 letter to the California Employment Development Office and her May 23, 1987 letter of rebuttal. The assertions show four factors purportedly making the live-on-the-premises requirement essential for the Alien to perform, in a reasonable manner, the job duties of general household worker/child monitor: (1) the need for a person to screen telephone calls since Employer's husband is a hospital president who is on call 24–hours per day; (2) the need for someone to attend the house and to monitor Employer's child while employer is away on business trips with her husband, running errands, or attending her sick mother; (3) the need for someone to be present when the Grahams return home in the evening; and (4) the lessened expense of hiring a live-in domestic as opposed to hiring both a housekeeper and a night child care monitor.

We conclude that Employer's statements herein do not constitute documentation: they are neither reasonably specific nor do they adequately indicate their sources or bases. The record fails to show the frequency of late-night telephone calls, or why a professional answering service could not perform the screening function Employer asserts is necessary. Neither does the record show the number of days per month Ms. Graham has been away from home overnight, or the likelihood of her future absences from home on business with her husband, performing errands, or caring for her sick mother. Further, the record does not show how much extra cost, if any, would be involved in hiring a child monitor and housekeeper for the particular nights that the Grahams anticipate being away from home. In short, the record established by Employer in this case consists solely of unsupported allegations which are insufficient to document business necessity for the live-on-the-premises requirement. Hence, the Certifying Officer's denial of labor certification must be affirmed.

* * *

[Three ALJ's, while accepting the majority's business necessity test and its application to domestic workers, dissented on the ground that the CO had never asked the employer for the detailed documentation the majority now requires.—Ed.].

NOTES AND QUESTIONS

1. In *Marion Graham* the Board summarized the Labor Department regulations that listed the various situations in which an employer will be required to demonstrate "business necessity." The same five categories exist today, but with the advent of PERM the language and organization of the regulations have changed slightly. A showing of "business necessity" is still required for the first three categories listed—job requirements "not normally required for the job," job requirements exceed those listed in the

Dictionary of Occupational Titles (now replaced by an electronic source known as O*NET and discussed below), and foreign language requirements. For purposes of those three categories, the regulations now codify the *Information Industries* test, changed slightly to read as follows:

> To establish a business necessity, an employer must demonstrate the job duties and requirements bear a reasonable relationship to the occupation in the context of the employer's business and are essential to perform the job in a reasonable manner.

8 C.F.R. § 656.17(h)(1) (2005). For the 4th and 5th categories—combination of duties (now combination of "occupations") and live-on-the-premises requirements—the new regulations do not expressly require "business necessity" but prescribe its functional equivalent. *Id.* §§ 656.17(h)(3), 656.17(j)(2).

Where does the Labor Department get the power to require business necessity or its equivalent in the first place? To what statutory requirement is business necessity relevant?

2. The meaning of "business necessity" has been perhaps the most contentious of all labor certification issues. Long before PERM, the Board decided the leading case of *Matter of Information Industries,* No. 88–INA–82 (BALCA, Feb. 9, 1989) (en banc). There the Board provided a two-part test:

> We hold that, to establish business necessity . . . an employer must demonstrate that the job requirements bear a reasonable relationship to the occupation in the context of the employer's business and are essential to perform, in a reasonable manner, the job duties as required by the employer.

Id. at 7.

First, study that definition carefully. Notice that each part limits only the job "requirements" (i.e., the credentials on which the employer is insisting); neither part purports to limit the job "duties" (i.e., the functions the employee will have to perform). The Board stressed that distinction in *Information Industries.* Yet the first part of the test uses the phrase "bears a reasonable relationship to," while the second part uses the seemingly more demanding phrase "are essential to." If both parts are restricting the job requirements, and if "essential" requires more than "reasonable," is the first part redundant? Or is it possible for a given set of job requirements to satisfy the second part of the test but fail the first?

More common is the reverse scenario, in which the Board finds that a requirement bears a reasonable relationship to the occupation but is not essential to the performance of the employee's duties. See, e.g., *Matter of Southeastern Capital Corp.,* No. 88–INA–198 (BALCA, Aug. 2, 1989) (80–word–per–minute typing requirement for secretary); *Matter of Golden Jade Restaurant,* No. 88–INA–342 (BALCA, July 28, 1989) (knowledge of ethnic Chinese dishes for waiter in Chinese restaurant) (2–1 decision), aff'd en banc (Feb. 7, 1990).

Second, in the commentary accompanying the final PERM rule, ETA claimed to be "incorporating the standard for business necessity adopted by BALCA in Information Industries," quoting the actual language of the *Information Industries* test above, and to be marking "a return to the status quo." 69 Fed. Reg. at 77351. But the language that it actually added to the regulations (reproduced in item 1 above) differs from that of the *Information Industries* test in subtle ways. Identify the differences and determine whether they substantially alter the meaning.

3.   As a normative matter, *should* the Labor Department insist that the job duties—not just the job requirements—be reasonable?

4.   In formulating the standard it did, the Board in *Information Industries* rejected two other proffered tests for business necessity—one more favorable to the employer and the immigrant, the other less favorable. In *Ratnayake v. Mack,* 499 F.2d 1207 (8th Cir.1974), the court held the employer's job requirements need only "be reasonable and tend to contribute to or enhance the efficiency and quality of the business." *Id.* at 1212. At the other end of the spectrum was a decision rendered in another context, *Diaz v. Pan American World Airways, Inc.,* 442 F.2d 385 (5th Cir.1971). There the question was how to interpret the business necessity exception to Title 7 of the Civil Rights Act of 1964, 42 U.S.C. § 2000e–2(e)(1). The court held that business necessity, a defense to certain forms of employment discrimination, applies only when the employer's actions were needed to avoid undermining "the essence of the business operation." *Id.* at 388. (The Pan Am policy of hiring only female flight attendants was held not to satisfy that standard). At one time, the Labor Department regulations applied the *Diaz* test to business necessity issues in the labor certification context. In *Information Industries,* however, both sides conceded that neither extreme was appropriate and the Board ended up enunciating the test that you read in item 2 above.

First, identify the competing economic interests that would explain a preference for either *Ratnayake* or *Diaz* in the labor certification context. Second, should the tests for business necessity be the same for labor certification cases as for Title 7 cases?

5.   For some time, a large number of labor certification applications have been for live-in housekeepers. See Lenni Benson and Roxana C. Bacon, *A Practitioner's Guide to Successful Alien Labor Certifications,* May 1988 Immigration Briefings at 7. In general, housekeepers are considered plentiful, but those who are willing to live on the premises are scarce. The Board in *Marion Graham* has the difficult task of applying the concept of "business necessity" to the operation of a person's home. Are you satisfied with the Board's resolution of that question? What practical alternatives did it have? See also *Pesikoff v. Secretary of Labor,* 501 F.2d 757 (D.C.Cir. 1974) (employer failed to prove his domestic needs required live-in maid).

The PERM rules for live-in housekeepers change somewhat the test announced in *Information Industries.* They do not refer to "business necessity" at all. Instead, they require the employer to demonstrate that "the [live-in] requirement is essential to perform, in a reasonable manner, the job duties as described by the employer and there are not cost-effective alternatives to a live-in household requirement." Would that formulation have changed the outcome in *Marion Graham*? (PERM also elaborates on the required documentation for live-in housekeeper applications. See 8 C.F.R. § 656.19 (2005)).

Professor Nora Demleitner, in a February 8, 1999 letter to the author, added another, highly important dimension. She wrote:

> It seemed to me that many of the issues surrounding labor certification for live-in housekeepers have to do with our perception of women and childcare, women's roles in the household, social class, and society's continued uneasiness about those issues. In addition, the decision [in *Marion Graham*] is also interesting insofar as it is focused on the issue of U.S. worker replacement without considering, for example, the child's interest. Might it not make more sense (emotionally, if not economically) to leave the child with the caretaker who has been in charge of her since birth?

There has been some poignant commentary about the "maid trade" and its conflicting social implications for women. On the one hand, the childcare services that foreign migrants provide have enabled young mothers in the destination states to enter the workforce. Consequently, the 1990 United States legislation that capped the third preference "other workers" at 10,000 per year has been criticized for its impact on women. Joan Fitzpatrick, *The Gender Dimension of U.S. Immigration Policy*, 9 Yale J. Law & Feminism 23, 34–37 (1997). On the other hand, the maids themselves—mainly women who have migrated from Asian countries to more developed Asian countries and to the Middle East—frequently endure exploitation and abuse. Joan Fitzpatrick & Katrina Kelly, *Gendered Aspects of Migration: Law and the Female Migrant*, 22 Hastings Internat'l & Comparative L. Rev. 47, 58–92 (1998).

6.   In another large chunk of the business necessity cases, the job requirements include proficiency in a particular foreign language. See, e.g., *Matter of Tel–Ko Electronics*, No. 88–INA–416 (BALCA, July 30, 1990) (en banc). Can you speculate as to why foreign language requirement cases are so frequent and why one might expect BALCA to be skeptical? In *Matter of Shamp Plumbing and Building*, No. 94–INA–530 (BALCA, Feb. 23, 1996), a plumbing company in western Montana asserted a need for a business manager who was fluent in both French and German because the region was becoming more international. The Board was not persuaded.

BALCA's panels have differed over whether business necessity will be found when the clients with whom the employee will be interacting speak a foreign language only out of preference. See *Tel-Ko Electronics*, above, at n.3. Under PERM, "business necessity for a foreign language requirement may be based upon the following: * * * The need to communicate with a large majority of the employer's customers, contractors, or employees who *can not* communicate effectively in English * * * " (emphasis added). Should business necessity be found in such a case? Should the owner of a Mexican restaurant that is located in a Mexican barrio of Los Angeles and patronized primarily by native Spanish-speakers be permitted to require that his or her servers speak Spanish?

A separate issue is whether a non-English-speaking *workforce*, as distinguished from a non-English-speaking clientele, can justify a foreign language requirement. In *Matter of Lucky Horse Fashion*, No. 97–INA–182 (BALCA, Aug. 22, 2000), the Board en banc held that the answer is usually no. The employer wanted to hire a sewing machine operator who could speak Chinese, because its entire workforce was Chinese and only 10% spoke English well enough to communicate machine problems. The employer also documented various inefficiencies that would result if translators were continually required. The Board denied labor certification for failure to satisfy the first element of the *Information Industries* test. Foreign language proficiency, the Board reasoned, is not reasonably related to the occupation of sewing machine repair, even in the context of this employer's business. It expressed additional concern that, if foreign language requirements were too easily justified on the basis of non-English-speaking workforces, employers would have little incentive to hire Americans. The dissent argued that non-English-speaking workforces are a sociological reality, especially in some geographic areas, and that employers in such areas might have genuine need to hire bilingual supervisors or other staff. The PERM rule just noted applies to communications with fellow employees as well as communications with customers.

7. What if the employer proposes to combine two functions in a single job? In *Matter of Robert L. Lippert Theatres*, No. 88–INA–433 (BALCA, May 30, 1990) (en banc), a theater owner wanted to hire a noncitizen to be both an accountant and a film projectionist. There were efficiency-related reasons for doing so. The Board first held that an employer who wished to combine duties must establish business necessity unless the employer normally combines the two functions in a single position or it is customary to do so. There being no such custom and no such practice by this employer, the Board insisted on a showing of business necessity. For that, the Board held the *Information Industries* test inapplicable (except that the *Information Industries* test would continue to govern whether the requirements for each individual function were unduly restrictive). Instead, the Board ruled, the employer must demonstrate that hiring two separate employees would be not just inefficient or costly, but so impractical as to be "infeasible." In a later decision, *Matter of Chinese Community Center*, 91–INA–99 (BALCA, June 4, 1991), the Board stated expressly that merely saving money or making the operation more efficient would not satisfy this standard. PERM codifies the *Lippert Theatres* test except that instead of saying the employer must demonstrate that it normally combines the functions, *or* that it is customary to do so, *or* that there is a business necessity, it replaces each "or" with a cryptic "and/or." 8 C.F.R. § 656.17(h)(3) (2005).

At any rate, what do you think it would take to meet the "infeasibility" test?

8.   Another recurring problem is the intending immigrant who owns or controls the company and wants to hire himself or herself or a close family member. BALCA has held that in such a case the employer must demonstrate that he or she would not be "unlikely to replace the alien" and that "there is a bona fide job opportunity clearly open to any qualified U.S. worker." *Matter of Lignomat USA,* No. 88–INA–276 (BALCA, Oct. 24, 1989) (en banc), reconsideration denied, Jan. 24, 1990; see also *Hall v. McLaughlin,* 864 F.2d 868, 873–80 (D.C.Cir.1989) (employer must show company not sham and corporation not so heavily dependent on immigrant beneficiary that real choice is unlikely). These tests are hard to meet, but they are not impossible. In *Matter of Paris Bakery Corp.,* No. 88–INA–337 (BALCA, Jan. 4, 1990) (en banc), for example, the President and sole stockholder of a bakery was granted labor certification to employ his brother as a French baker. Experienced U.S. workers were unavailable. In contrast, in *Matter of Cleanex House Cleaning Service, Inc.,* No. 2003–INA–208 (BALCA, Sept. 7, 2004), the Board denied labor certification to the brother of the company President, finding more experienced U.S. applicants available for the position of janitorial supervisor. And in *Bulk Farms, Inc. v. Martin,* 963 F.2d 1286 (9th Cir. 1992), the court upheld a Labor Department regulation that required the work be "by an employee for an employee other than himself." Finding the regulation reasonably related to the congressional goal of assuring good faith efforts to locate United States workers, the court affirmed the Department's denial of labor certification for the company's sole shareholder, President, and "chief cheesemaker." See also 8 C.F.R. § 656.17(*l*) (2005).

9.   INA § 212(a)(5)(A) requires the applicant for labor certification to demonstrate that no "able, willing, *qualified*" workers are available. With only two exceptions (teachers and those with exceptional ability in the sciences or the arts), it is not enough for the employer to show that no *equally* qualified workers are available. Thus, the employer ordinarily must hire a minimally qualified U.S. worker over a more qualified noncitizen (or hire no one at all). Is that good or bad?

10.   Fraudulent labor certification applications have long been of concern to the Labor Department. Some people have been known to set up bogus corporations solely for labor certification purposes. For a good description of one such scheme and the ensuing criminal conviction of an immigration lawyer, see 64 IR 1291 (1987).

But most will agree that such blatant frauds taint only a small proportion of the applications, and that, despite isolated anecdotes involving questionable practices, the ethics of today's immigration lawyers are high. See, e.g., Bruce Hake, *"Attorney Misconduct"—A Rebuttal,* 4 Georgetown Immigration L.J. 727, 728–35 (1990). Probably more common, and in most instances too dependent on subjective judgment to be labeled fraud, are those cases in which the job requirements are tailored so closely to the beneficiary's qualifications that, realistically, no one else will qualify. Writer Calvin Trillin says:

* * * The process of getting labor certification amounts to staging a sort of sham employment offer. The lawyer writes a job description that complies with the Department of Labor's standards, and the potential employer of the alien actually advertises such a job through the state employment commission. If someone shows up who is a citizen [or LPR—Ed.] and has the qualifications outlined in the ad and is willing to work for the stated wage, the labor certification is not granted—although the employer has no obligation to give the citizen a job. If the lawyer who wrote the job description has been skillful, there is a good chance that no qualified citizen will show up. Writing job descriptions that pass the Department of Labor but attract no other potential employees is what [immigration lawyer] Ed Prud'homme calls "one of the few art forms in the business," and Beaumont Martin [also an immigration lawyer—Ed.] is considered one of the artists. One of the Chinese students had managed to get a job in the accounting department of a small oil company, and, since the job required some computer expertise, Martin decided to write a job description that nudged her over a bit from accounting to computer analysis. ("There are a lot of people running around with accounting degrees.") When he had typed it up, he handed it to her:

SYSTEMS ANALYST 020.067–018

Conduct analyses of accounting, management, and operational problems and formulate mathematical models for solution by IBM computer system, using FORTRAN, COBOL, and PASCAL. Analyze problems in terms of management information. Write computer programs and devise and install accounting system and related procedures. Masters or equal in management information systems. $1667/month.

She read it over. "It's beautiful," she said.

* * *

When I was discussing labor certification with [immigration lawyer] Pete Williamson one afternoon, he mentioned a young woman he had seen that day who wanted to stay in the country but did not fall into any of the categories of family reunification. * * * Her only occupation was looking after the children of a neighbor.

I said that it didn't sound promising. A few days with immigration lawyers had greatly broadened my view of how the employment sections of the immigration law were actually used. I was no longer under the delusion that the law worked to bring to this country people who had rare skills or worked in fields where there were serious shortages of American workers. * * * Still, it seemed unlikely that being a mother's helper in Texas was a job "for which a shortage of employable and willing persons exists."

> There were two other important elements in the case, Williamson said. The young woman in question was a college graduate. Also, both she and the children she looked after were Muslims—all from Pakistan. Williamson intended to nudge her over from a nanny to a tutor—a tutor qualified to instruct children in their own culture and religion. He thought it unlikely that any citizen with similar qualifications would respond to the ad. * * *

Calvin Trillin, *Making Adjustments,* The New Yorker, May 28, 1984, at 50, 63–66.

It is not easy to draw a bright line that separates commendable zealous representation of the client's interests from fraud. The immigration lawyer who wants to observe competing sets of sometimes hard-to-reconcile obligations can be caught in a judgment bind. Do you agree with Trillin that the labor certification process "amounts to staging a sort of sham employment offer?" On which side of the line would you place his examples?

11.   The ethical temptations of labor certification work are the subject of an excellent article by Daniel F. Boyle, *Labor Certification Pitfalls*, 9 BIB 1354 (Nov. 15, 2004). He identifies the many "opportunities for misrepresentation, fraud and deceit" that the process presents. The most sobering part of his article is the finish:

> My license to practice law was suspended by the State of Colorado for two years based primarily on labor certification activities that were violations of Colorado Rule of Professional Conduct 8.4(c), that is, conduct involving fraud, deceit, dishonesty, and misrepresentation. * * * The examples that I have outlined in this paper demonstrate the need for attorneys to stay aboveboard at every step in the immigration process.

> Many of the shenanigans that I engaged in during the labor certification process were fraudulent, not merely exaggeration and puffery. They caused me extreme internal conflict and stress. Notwithstanding these feelings, I rationalized and minimized, and to some degree trivialized, the activities. This trivialization actually caused me additional internal turmoil and conflict. Therefore, when I finally stipulated to violations of [the Code], it afforded me a certain sense of relief. I had confessed to my wrongdoing, the first step in the path toward redemption.

> On another level, for many years after my suspension I continued to minimize or justify my activities. After all, the clients were nice people deserving of residency. Moreover, the labor certification and immigration system itself was full of odd and illogical bureaucratic red tape. Thus, to some extent, I had the unrepentant attitude that I had simply pushed the line in certain cases because of the nature of the system.

> During the past several years, however, I have come to realize that my activities were dishonest and wrong. It is not my place to

circumvent congressional or agency directives, even if I disagree with them. Rather, it is my job to zealously represent my clients within the bounds of the law. I now realize that I must take my clients with the cards that they are dealt and I cannot cheat by giving them a new hand. I must do everything within my power for my client, but only within the confines of honesty.

At the time I perpetrated the violations in the labor certification context, I had an otherwise good relationship with the local immigration judges and most of the government attorneys. I was known as a candid and honest lawyer. On the inside, however, I knew differently. I have often been asked how an attorney with an otherwise good reputation could participate in the activities as set forth in this paper. The primary reasons are:

1. **The lucrative nature of the cases and my enjoyment of the income they afforded.** In other words, I valued money more than my integrity.

2. **The fact that the clients were usually nice people, well deserving of residency, who often had no other way of gaining it and/or the business really needed the employee.** In other words, I put the cart of serving my clients in front of the horse of serving the law. The ends do not justify the means.

3. **The strange nature of the system itself.** In other words, I justified and rationalized to the point that I suppressed my cognitive understanding that my actions were wrong.

4. **My own shortcomings and lack of integrity.** In other words, I failed to live up to the standards for lawyers and [to] the standards I now have for myself as a husband, father, and member of society.

Id. at 1363. See generally John L. Pinnix (ed.), Ethics in a Brave New World (2004); David Weissbrodt & Laura Danielson, Immigration Law and Procedure in A Nutshell, chap. 15 (5th ed. 2005); William J. Flynn III & Dilip Patel, *Employers, Employees and Ethics*, in Alfonso Caprara, Rumi Engineer & Barbara Marcouiller (Eds.), AILA, Ethics and Your Immigration Practice: Have you Considered . . .?, at 31–50 (1998).

One other common ethical dilemma specific to labor certification is whom to consider the client—the employer, the employee, or both? The decision has practical implications for how to resolve conflicts, whether to give advice, and when to treat communications as confidential. For a careful analysis, see Bruce A. Hake, *Dual Representation in Immigration Practice: The Simple Solution is the Wrong Solution*, 5 Georgetown Immigration L.J. 581 (1991); Weissbrodt & Danielson, above, at 597–601.

12. An additional controversy has been simmering over the fact that a very high proportion of all labor certification applications are filed on behalf of existing employees. A leading treatise once estimated the figure at

80%. See 1 Austin T. Fragomen, Alfred J. Del Rey & Sam Bernsen, Immigration Law and Business at 4–5 (June 1994). This is not surprising. Even with reduced quota-related waits, the labor certification process can be quite lengthy. Few employers can afford to hold the positions open for the lengthy period that the procedure will take.

There are, however, two different subcategories of such cases. In some cases, the worker is employed illegally. This type of case is now rarer because the prospect of employer sanctions makes illegal employment less inviting to employers. Moreover, when an application for labor certification reveals illegal employment, the Labor Department makes the information available for use in employer sanctions prosecutions. See Fragomen, Del Rey & Bernsen, above, at 4–5; Ashley Dunn, *INS Arresting Nannies Who Seek Legal Status*, Los Angeles Times, Mar. 21, 1991, at A1. This policy has clearly dissuaded many employers from seeking labor certification on behalf of those whom they employ illegally. 70 IR at 291–92 (Mar. 8, 1993).

The more important subgroup are noncitizens who are working lawfully, on temporary work visas, for the employers who are applying for labor certification on their behalf. The Labor Department has criticized this practice, arguing that it amounts to employers hiring foreign workers on a tryout basis. See Stuart Anderson, *Widespread Abuse of H–1Bs and Employment-Based Immigration? The Evidence Says Otherwise*, 73 IR 637, 638 (May 13, 1996). As Anderson points out, however, Congress made a conscious decision to allow precisely such a practice, probably because Congress recognized the practical difficulties that employers would otherwise face in filling essential positions in reasonable amounts of time. See *id.* at 638. You will see more about the various types of temporary worker categories in chapter 4.

One specific issue that can arise in this context is what should happen when an employer requires a certain amount of experience and the noncitizen beneficiary attained that experience (either legally or illegally) on the very job for which labor certification is now being sought. Why might such an application be denied? What responses might the employer give? See 8 C.F.R. § 656.17(i)(3) (2005); Benson & Bacon, question 5 above, at 20–21.

13. There is no law that requires an immigrant who has been admitted on the basis of a labor certification to remain in the certified job for any specified length of time. Should there be? What are the competing policies?

In *Yui Sing Tse v. INS*, 596 F.2d 831 (9th Cir.1979), the immigrant received labor certification for a position as a Chinese cook. He entered the United States with the intention of working full-time in the certified job for the approximately four years that it would take him to finish dental school, after which he would work only as a dentist. In a 2–1 decision, the court held his admission proper. It ruled that an immigrant need only intend to perform the certified job for a time period that is reasonable when measured in the light of the competing policies. Which way would you have come out on those facts?

14. To avoid having to demonstrate business necessity, an employer must show, among other things, that the job requirements do "not exceed the Specific Vocational Preparation level assigned to the occupation as shown in the O*NET Job Zones." 20 C.F.R. § 656.17(h)(1) (2005) (added by PERM). This raises an obvious question: "WHAT?" Here is the explanation: The "O*NET" (the "Occupational Information Network Online"), posted and from time to time revised by ETA, is a comprehensive electronic listing of every known type of job in the United States and the duties typically associated with each job. Its URL is http://online.onetcenter.org. For every job listed, O*NET also includes something called a "Specific Vocational Preparation," or SVP. This is an index of the amount of education and experience customarily required. By prohibiting employers from setting job requirements above the SVP level for the particular occupation, the Labor Department hopes to prevent employers from rejecting qualified U.S. applicants.

The predecessor of O*NET was a hard copy publication called the Dictionary of Occupational Titles (D.O.T.) The Fourth Revised Edition of the D.O.T. (1991) was apparently the last. The Labor Department has announced it will no longer update or maintain the D.O.T., preferring to rely instead on O*NET. See 80 IR 1526 (Nov. 3, 2003). Recognition of O*NET by PERM, above, and by BALCA, see *Matter of David Razo Gardening Service*, 2002–INA–129 (Apr. 23, 2003), has now relegated D.O.T. to the archives.

Nonetheless, its rich flavor (most of which survives on the pages of O*NET) should come through in the following excerpts from this book review:

David Isaacson, We're All Entitled: The Literary and Cultural Significance of the Dictionary of Occupational Titles

27 Reference Quarterly 226 (1987).

* * *

The title of this volume probably doesn't whet most people's intellectual appetites: *Dictionary of Occupational Titles.* This work, now in its fourth edition (1977), is published by the Employment and Training Administration, a division of the U.S. Department of Labor. At first glance, this imposing 1,371–page volume, which lists, classifies, and defines over 20,000 jobs, is best described as a tool; one doesn't *read* such a book, one simply uses it to look up things. But besides being an eminently useful source, the *DOT* can offer hours of pleasurable, even enlightening reading; it can be admired as a model of precise expository prose; it can be studied profitably as a document in our cultural history; and, without intending to, this book is a fascinating tribute to our very American dream of an egalitarian society. * * *

The *DOT* was first published in 1939 to provide an organized job-classification system, making it easier to re-employ people during the Depression. That edition contained nearly 17,500 occupational definitions divided into 550 skilled, semi-skilled, or unskilled jobs. The second and third editions, published in 1949 and 1965, added new jobs and simplified the classification system. * * *

As a dictionary, the *DOT* rigorously and meticulously defines each of these jobs so it is difficult to mistake one job for another. But the *DOT* not only defines; it classifies these jobs by broad and then progressively narrower classes that are a delight to contemplate. The *DOT* does for jobs what Linnaeus did for plants, but what Melvil Dewey and the Library of Congress have not done for books: it has constructed a rational classification scheme that is flexible without being Procrustean. Part of the literary pleasure of the *DOT* comes from an appreciation of the way all the parts cohere into an intricately structured whole. Here, for example, is a typical definition:

686.686–010 Felt–Tipping Machine Tender (pen and pencil) tipping machine operator

Feeds machine that shapes felt tips for stencil marking pens: Fills hopper of machine with felt tips and presses switch to start machine that automatically shapes sides and bevels or rounds end of tips for making pens.

The first part of each occupational definition is the nine-digit code; each set of three digits has a specific meaning that uniquely identifies that occupation. * * *

* * *

Of course, the *DOT* includes jobs that are more intellectually demanding than felt-tipping machine tender. But the same objective standards of definition and classification apply. The *DOT* usually does as good a job in defining mental as physical tasks. Take, for example, the definition of the poet:

131.067–042 Poet

Writes narrative, dramatic or lyric poetry for magazines, books, and other publications: Chooses subject matter and suitable form to express personal feeling and individual experience or to narrate story or event. May write doggerel or other type verse.

This is certainly a concise, straightforward definition. It is deliberately prosaic. There is no unnecessary description, no embellishment of the social standing of this job, no "nonsense" like Shelley's notion that the poet is the unacknowledged legislator of mankind, or some kind of prophet. "You want to be a poet?" the *DOT* seems to say, "Well, go ahead, be one: here's what you'll be doing. It's one way of making a living, but no more elevated than thousands of others." * * *

* * *

The utilitarian purpose of the *DOT* is to facilitate the work of employment counselors, job analysts, and anyone seeking a job. The classification scheme (especially in its current computerized form) quickly allows the Employment Service of the Labor Department to categorize precisely job applicants and to match them with job openings. Any other government or private agency using this system, or some modification of it, can reap its benefits. Furthermore, because the numerical codes make statistical records relatively easy to compile and analyze, all sorts of employment patterns can be studied for trends, projections, and patterns. Analysts probably can tell us how many job openings there are for felt-tipping-machine tenders and perhaps even the likelihood of formal employment as a poet.

* * *

The *DOT* is also a cultural document because it is an illuminating compilation of colorful names. It is difficult, even in the somewhat jaded times we live in now, not to be moved, as you browse through this book, by a Whitmanesque celebration of the wondrously varied things people do for a living in this country. * * * [Consider] this selection of a few of the jobs listed in the *DOT:* acrobat, bead builder, contortionist, door patcher, expeditor, fatback trimmer, glass grinder, hot-car operator, impresario, jersey-knitter, knife changer, log marker, mail sorter, nodulizer, oak tanner, peanut blancher, quill changer, rounder, scrap wheeler, table tender, upper doubler, veneer clipper, warp coiler, x-ray technician, yarn examiner, zipper setter.

* * *

The *DOT* is a serious, sometimes even a solemn book, but it can also be a source of humor and whimsy, all the funnier because it does not intend to be. * * *

Some job titles resemble the German language in its penchant for numerous nouns strung together in a long phrase, the result of which can be quite a mouthful, as in: suction-dredge pipe-line placing supervisor, or line-fabric impregnating-range back tender, or manhole-and-underground-steam-line inspector.

Sometimes the position of adjectives and nouns in a job title creates rather unusual combinations. A continuous pillowcase cutter, for instance, does not continually cut pillowcases, but rather tends "a machine that cuts rolls of tubular cloth into pillowcase lengths." Nor is a self-propelled dredge operator a person whose propulsive abilities emanate from within himself, but he does operate, by himself, a hydraulic dredge to cultivate, transplant, and harvest marine life.

* * *

Some job titles strike an outsider like me as being unnecessarily specialized: bonbon creamer warmer, panama-hat smearer, armhole-and-shoulder off-presser, felt-hat-mellowing machine operator, remelt sugar cutter, and a matzo-forming machine operator. But these specialists may very well wonder, in turn, why there are so many different librarians listed in the *DOT*.

Besides the obvious titles of humorist and comedian, other jobs seem to require a sense of humor to perform: beeswax bleacher (tends vats and filter presses to bleach wax used in candlemaking); defective-cigarette slitter; pantyhose-crotch-closing machine operator; pickle pumper (tends machine that automatically injects meat with curing solution); egg smeller (smells broken eggs to detect spoiled ones and dumps them into waste container); Easter Bunny (one example, besides Santa Claus and The Three Little Pigs, of an impersonator); and a white-kid buffer (in leather manufacturing, a particular kind of buffing-machine operator).

There are also a number of occupations whose titles, if taken literally, suggest hitherto unrecognized ways of improving society: defect cutters are unfortunately only formally defined as operating saw machines to cut out defects in furnished woodstock. Diversion clerks are not employed to amuse their colleagues, but to reroute freight shipments. Lingo cleaners do not include language authorities like William Safire and Edwin Newman, but they do clean lingos, or metal weights attached to looms. A maturity checker, a position one might like to see widely distributed in our youth-worshipping culture, is restricted to tending a machine that crushes peas to ascertain their hardness (or maturity). A mother repairer is not a new kind of counselor, but someone who repairs the matrix of a metal phonograph record. A finger waver is not a scold, but one of many specialties available to cosmetologists. A gutter-mouth cutter is not interested in cleaner speech, but is a type of stonemason who works with ornamental and structural stone. A save-all operator is not a clergy member, but one who runs a machine salvaging suspended wood pulp. And a revival clerk does not assist an evangelist, but rather compiles data on lapsed insurance policies to determine eligibility for their automatic reinstatement.

* * *

Most job titles in the *DOT,* however, don't have ambiguous titles. Some, indeed, are exceedingly graphic: * * * Carcass splitter, aitchbone breaker, side splitter, head trimmer, snout puller, tongue cutter, offal separator, bung grader, casing puller, viscera washer, hog sticker, skin-peeling-machine operator, hide spreader, neck skewer, toe puller, and animal stunner are just a few of the titles that might cause a revival in vegetarianism.

What finally emerges after some period of time reading in the *DOT* is a broad appreciation of the variety of things people do for a living in this country. Far from being just another reference book, *DOT* is, in a special sense, a literary document. If one of the ends of literature is to help us understand and accept the variety of life, then it is not hyperbole to say the *DOT* serves this purpose. This book does not intend to be anything more than a utilitarian classification of jobs, but it also suggests, since every job has a formal title, that all jobs have at least verbal dignity. While each job is assigned an impersonal number, each job also has a distinct, precise name. In the strange ambience of this book, every job from the first named—abalone diver—to the last—zyglo inspector—seems to be equal, as a title, at least, to every other job. * * *

ii.   Adversely Affecting the Wages and Working Conditions of American Workers

Industrial Holographics, Inc. v. Donovan

United States Court of Appeals, Seventh Circuit, 1983.
722 F.2d 1362.

■ CUDAHY, CIRCUIT JUDGE.

* * *

I

Under section 212(a)(14) [now 212(a)(5)(A)—Ed.] of the Immigration and Nationality Act, the State Department may not issue an alien a visa for admission to the United States for purposes of employment unless the Secretary of Labor certifies that American workers are not "able, willing, qualified . . ., and available" for the work, and that the employment of the alien "will not adversely affect the wages and working conditions" of similarly employed Americans. The Secretary of Labor has promulgated regulations which establish standards and procedures for the certification of alien workers under section 212(a)(14). If an employer wishes to hire an alien for work in the United States, these regulations require the employer first to recruit among American workers offering the "prevailing wage" and "prevailing working conditions" to determine whether any American workers are "able, willing, qualified, and available" for the job. If an employer submits documentation showing it has been unable to recruit American workers on these terms, then the Secretary of Labor may certify the alien to enter the country and perform the work.

* * *

Plaintiff Industrial Holographics, Inc. (the "employer") manufactures and tests machinery used to make rubber tires. Plaintiff Roger K. Yu is an alien whom Industrial Holographics has sought to employ in Michigan as an export manager. The record indicates that Yu has never been in the United States. In June 1979, Industrial Holographics applied for labor certification on behalf of Yu. Industrial Holographics followed the various provisions in 20 C.F.R. § 656.21 (1980), requiring it to post the job for internal recruitment, to advertise the job in newspapers and to post the job with the state employment service. On August 24, 1979, the employer submitted to the certifying officer documentation showing that it had complied with the requirements of section 656.21.

The employer, however, had advertised that the salary for the job of export manager was $1,000 per month. Section 656.21 requires the employer to advertise and post the job at the "prevailing wage" and "prevailing working conditions" in order to obtain certification. The Michigan Employment Security Commission (the "MESC") was responsible for determining the prevailing wage in this case, and it determined that the prevailing wage for export managers in the area was $1,666 per month. Therefore, the certifying officer issued to the employer a Notice of Findings proposing to deny labor certification for Yu because the employer had failed to advertise the job at the prevailing wage.

After receiving the Notice of Findings, the employer agreed to repeat the advertising and recruiting process at the higher salary of $1,666 per month. The employer advertised the job at the higher salary, but it failed to comply with all of the requirements of section 656.21. Specifically, the employer did not show it had posted the job for internal recruitment at the higher salary * * *. Because the employer had failed to comply with the strict advertising requirements within the relevant time limits, the certifying officer denied the certification for Yu. On review within the Department of Labor, the administrative law judge[a] concluded that the employer had failed to comply with the regulations and that certification was properly denied.

Plaintiffs then sought review in the district court. Judge Moran granted summary judgment for the Department of Labor in an unpublished memorandum opinion. He held (1) that the Secretary of Labor had the statutory authority to issue the advertising regulations contained in section 656.21; * * * and (4) that the Department of Labor's use of the prevailing wage standard in the regulations was not arbitrary and capricious.

* * *

II

Appellants contend first that the Secretary of Labor exceeded his statutory authority by requiring the employer to advertise the position at the "prevailing wage." The applicable statutory language says that the Secretary shall certify the alien only if his or her employment "will not adversely affect the wages and working conditions" of similarly employed workers in the United States. INA § 212(a)(14)(B).

* * * [Appellants argue] that the regulations improperly equate the statute's standard of adverse effects with the payment of wages below "prevailing wages."

* * *

The regulations here assume, as a general proposition, that the employment of an alien at wages below the prevailing wage will tend to affect adversely the wages and working conditions of American workers. Appellants have provided no evidence to persuade us that this general assumption is arbitrary or capricious. While it may be possible to conceive of cases

---

a. At the time of this case, there was no BALCA. Appeals from the decisions of certifying officers went to individual administrative law judges.—Ed.

in which the prevailing wage standard would be inconsistent with the statute's purpose, that is not the case here.

Appellants argue that two federal decisions support their contention that the prevailing wage standard is contrary to the statute. *See Naporano Metal & Iron Co. v. Secretary of Labor,* 529 F.2d 537 (3d Cir.1976); *Ozbirman v. Regional Manpower Adm'r,* 335 F.Supp. 467 (S.D.N.Y.1971). Neither opinion persuades us that the Secretary's use of the prevailing wage standard was improper in this case.

* * *

[In *Ozbirman*] an alien was denied labor certification as an auto mechanic. The wage he was offered matched the union negotiated wage in the area, but the Secretary found the wage to be below the "prevailing wage" as required by the predecessor regulation of section 656.21. The district court remanded the matter to the Secretary. * * * The court discussed at length the complexity of a thorough determination of whether a particular package of wages and other benefits and working conditions would adversely affect American wages and working conditions. It concluded that the "prevailing wage" standard did not adequately take into account the other relevant variables. We agree with the *Ozbirman* court that a truly thorough analysis of adverse effects involves factors other than wages. However, we do not agree that the Secretary of Labor is without authority to issue regulations simplifying the inquiry so that decisions will be less arbitrary and more consistent.

We conclude that the Secretary acted reasonably in giving operational content to the language of section 212(a)(14) by applying the prevailing wage standard in this case. * * *

III

* * *

In this case the MESC contacted five Michigan employers to determine the salary each paid its export manager. From answers received from these inquiries, the MESC calculated that the average wage of export managers in Michigan was $1,666 per month.

Appellants argue that this calculation was improper because the MESC surveyed employers in industries other than the rubber tire machinery business. They contend that the export managers for the other employers are not "similarly employed" as the regulations require. However, we do not believe that the agency acted arbitrarily and capriciously in surveying the other five employers. The agency concluded that jobs with similar functions in other industries were sufficiently comparable for purposes of determining a prevailing wage. Appellants have provided no evidence showing that the other jobs are not comparable.

* * *

Affirmed.

NOTES AND QUESTIONS

1. The court in *Industrial Holographics* first has to assess the validity of a Labor Department regulation that equates a job offer below the prevailing wage with an adverse effect on the wages of American workers. In *Ozbirman,* on which the plaintiffs relied, the court said:

> [T]he Secretary of Labor has effectively failed to recognize or consider that all forms of compensation do not take the form of money. * * * [T]he interrelationship between one's pay rate and other fringe benefits indicates that such an adverse effect would not necessarily occur. * * * Shorter hours, unique vacation periods or working conditions, proximity to home and family, and exceptional fringe benefits are all factors which influence the labor market and have an effect on wages in this country.

335 F.Supp. at 472. The court in *Ozbirman* concluded that "the Secretary of Labor should determine which factors play a major role in affecting wage rates and consider such items as a package." *Id.* at 472 n. 5. Interpreting the same regulation, the Board in *Matter of Kids "R" Us,* No. 89–INA–311 et al (BALCA, Jan. 28, 1991), later held that, apart from wages controlled either by statute or by union contract, fringe benefits could be taken into account in ascertaining adverse effect.

Which approach do you find more convincing—*Industrial Holographics* or *Ozbirman?*

2. Even if both the wages and the fringe benefits are below the prevailing norms, does it necessarily follow that hiring the person would adversely affect the wages and working conditions of American workers? What economic assumptions underlie the assumed causal connection?

3. On the other hand, is it *enough* to insist that the employer offer the prevailing wage (and that no able, willing, and qualified United States workers are available)? Why might organized labor feel that the employment of noncitizens even at the prevailing wage could adversely affect the United States work force?

4. Once the prevailing wage standard is accepted, the question is how to determine it. Generally the "prevailing wage" is the average wage of workers "similarly employed in the area of intended employment" (with a 5% leeway). 20 C.F.R. § 656.40(a)(2)(i) (2004). It is clear that "area" refers to geography, not to occupational field, since the regulations define "area of intended employment" as "the area within normal commuting distance of the place (address) of intended employment." 20 C.F.R. § 656.3 (2004). Is that good policy? If the local prevailing wage is lower than the national prevailing wage, which rate should the employer be required to match? What if the local prevailing wage is higher than the national prevailing wage?

5. More difficult, perhaps, is the application of the term "similarly employed." The regulations define that phrase to mean "having substantially comparable jobs in the occupational category in the area of intended

employment." If there are no such jobs in the local area, then "similarly employed" means "having jobs requiring a substantially similar level of skills" within the local area, or, if no substantially comparable jobs exist locally, then outside that local area. 20 C.F.R. § 656.40(d) (2005).

In *Industrial Holographics* the employer argued that the Labor Department had erred in going outside the industry for data. Given the above regulation, was the court right or wrong to reject that argument?

6.   What if the particular employer can cite special circumstances? In *Matter of Tuskegee University*, No. 87–INA–561 (BALCA, Feb. 23, 1988), a small, private, predominantly African–American university in Alabama wanted to hire a noncitizen as an associate professor of physics. The Alabama Employment Service found a prevailing wage of $30,670, based on the average salaries of associate professors at three private colleges in the local area. The employer applying for labor certification was offering only $27,340. Its argument was that the CO, rather than look to associate professor salaries generally, should have looked to associate professor salaries at private *African-American* colleges, where fewer resources were available for faculty salaries. The employer submitted evidence showing that, within the groups of United Negro College Fund (UNCF) colleges, its offer was competitive. In a 4–3 decision, BALCA held that "similarly employed" refers not only to the job titles and duties, but also to "the nature of the business or institution where the jobs are located—for example, public or private, secular or religious, profit or nonprofit ..." It then ordered the CO to explain why he had rejected that argument. (Another issue the majority ordered the CO to reconsider on remand was whether he had been right to consider associate professor salaries in fields other than physics.)

The decision in *Tuskegee University* was short-lived. In *Matter of Hathaway Children's Services*, 91–INA–388 (BALCA, Feb. 4, 1994, en banc), a nonprofit treatment center for handicapped and emotionally disturbed children sought to pay a wage lower than that paid for otherwise similar services at for-profit institutions. The Board denied labor certification and expressly overruled *Tuskegee University*. The Board in *Hathaway* held "similarly employed" refers only to the skill and knowledge levels required for the job, not to the nature of the employing institution or the employer's ability to pay, and, in particular, not to whether the institution is for-profit or nonprofit. Accord, *Matter of Columbus Hospital*, 95–INA–282 (BALCA, Apr. 16, 1996)(small hospital with limited revenues must offer foreign workers same wages as larger hospitals with greater revenues).

The higher education community and numerous federal agencies that make use of foreign researchers reacted with alarm to the decision in *Hathaway*. They believed that requiring colleges and universities to pay researchers the same wages that prevail in industry would make it financially impossible for them to hire foreign researchers at all. Moreover, they argued, since they could not afford to pay their American researchers the wages offered by industry, the *Hathaway* rule would mean that colleges and universities would have to pay their foreign researchers more than they pay their American researchers—a consequence that would breed both unfairness and bad will.

Accepting these and other arguments, the Labor Department in 1998 amended its regulations to allow colleges, universities, and federal research centers to pay researchers the wages prevailing at similar institutions in the area of intended employment. See 63 Fed. Reg. 13756–67 (Mar. 20, 1998). Congress has since codified that rule as INA § 212(p)(1).

First, as a general matter, should "similarly employed" reflect the financial resources of the employer or just the job titles and job duties? Second, what do you think about the special rule for colleges, universities, and federal research centers? Third, and more specifically, what policy should be adopted for UNCF colleges like Tuskegee?

c. PERSPECTIVE ON EMPLOYMENT–BASED IMMIGRATION

Here are some excerpts from one of the more impressive, and more innovative, of the recent reform proposals:

Demetrios G. Papademetriou & Stephen Yale–Loehr, Balancing Interests: Rethinking U.S. Selection of Skilled Immigrants

Pages 15–34, 141–61 (1996).

When Congress developed many of today's economic immigration provisions in 1952, most of the nation was successfully completing the conversion to a peacetime economy by redirecting manufacturing industries toward the production of consumer goods and employing large numbers of discharged military personnel in its factories. Accordingly, manufacturing and agriculture dominated a domestically focused economy. As tensions between East and West intensified, a growing military-industrial complex created hundreds of thousands of additional jobs. Finally, the country was beginning to invest large amounts of public capital in physical infrastructure, supplying still more employment and the means to move the goods that U.S. workers were producing.

* * *

At the center of this postwar economic explosion, managing its growth and guaranteeing its stability, was the large U.S. corporation, which soon became the core of the nation's economic life. * * *

Corporations could play this central role largely because they were able to craft and maintain a "bargain" between the labor and management that guaranteed continued growth * * *.

In this bargain, U.S. workers essentially "relinquished" the option of seeking to exert influence over broad institutional policy issues in exchange for job security (virtually *de facto* lifetime employment), seniority-based advancement, adequate compensation to support a family, and access to generous benefits—i.e., the key ingredients for a middle-class existence. In return, the corporation expected production workers and middle managers to learn how to work within large and vertically integrated bureaucratic organizations, be reliable, work hard, and follow orders—and rarely sought their input on product development or process innovation.

* * *

New technologies and products—the key to an industry's success—were developed over long periods of time almost exclusively by research and development shops within the corporation itself or with allies in academia, not by eliciting worker input. * * *

* * *

Immigration played a relatively modest but nonetheless significant role in the spectacular postwar rise of the Untied States. * * *

As a result, the admission of economic-stream immigrants was pegged primarily to filling jobs for which no U.S. workers were available, while U.S. workers were presumed to be "protected" from declines in their wages and working conditions through the wage provisions of labor certification. The INA thus formalized the notion that immigration should essentially respond to surges in the demand for labor and its inevitable supply shortfalls.

The 1965 amendments to the INA reinforced that notion. With the emerging appreciation that technological advancement would assume a more important role in maintaining the rate of economic growth, the 1965 amendments sought to facilitate the admission of skilled and educated foreigners by acknowledging the emergence of a global economy.

Soon after the passage of the 1965 amendments to the Immigration and Nationality Act, the edifice of the postwar economic order—and the U.S. economy's dominant place in it—began to crumble. * * *

* * *

Globalization and the reality of full economic interdependence are, of course, inescapable facts. The figures are nothing less than astounding. During the period under discussion, U.S. exports grew from about $20 billion in 1959 (and just $27.5 billion in 1965) to more than $700 billion in 1994. Imports during the same period registered similar growth—from about $22 billion to more than $800 billion. The total value of international economic transactions (imports plus exports) grew from a little more than 8 percent of the GDP to more than 22 percent of GDP. By 1991, total international sales by U.S. multinationals (from exports, direct investments, or joint ventures) generated an estimated $1.2 trillion—accounting for nearly 30 percent of corporate revenue.

Even more telling, U.S.-owned firms are now competing with foreign-owned firms *not only abroad but also in the United States*. It has thus become as difficult—and in many respects much less useful—to distinguish

"American" from "foreign" firms as it is to separate "domestic" from "foreign" markets for one's products.

* * *

More important for this study, globalization has placed a premium on a better educated and trained workforce. A firm's productivity and competitiveness depend increasingly on its products' *knowledge content* (as distinct from its content of capital and other physical resources), on the innovativeness of its processes, on "first-to-market" corporate strategies, and on the ability to develop and exploit global connections by what Moss Kanter calls "managing the intersections" at the "crossroads of cultures." The constantly shifting need for specific (rather than generic) expertise means that firms can obtain the needed talent more easily, if not cheaply, from outside—in effect adopting a "just-in-time" approach to the composition of the workforce. Flexible staffing, as this is called, has lessened interest in investing in the training of one's workers.

* * *

Without a flexible and well-managed economic immigration selection mechanism, many of our most competitive firms with vast global operations may reconsider their investments in additional capacity. Firms whose products are primarily knowledge-based, such as software developers, can choose to expand wherever the main intangible asset they need—"knowledge workers"—is in ample supply. "Real-time" satellite communications that bridge distances instantly and lower labor costs, together with incentive packages from other countries, make the temptation to locate abroad ever more enticing.

* * *

In this chapter, we propose fundamental changes in the way we select most economic-stream immigrants and non-immigrants. The forty-year-old, shortage-anchored, case-by-case determination that underpins the current labor certification system may have been an appropriate job and wage protection mechanism for the unskilled and semi-skilled workers who dominated employment-based admissions in the 1950s and 1960s. However, as the analysis of the last two decades' economic and labor market changes in chapter 1 makes clear, the system no longer adequately meets U.S. needs or interests. Our proposed reforms would generally shift the selection system's focus to one that chooses immigrants on the basis of their promise for long-term contributions to our economy. Employers would continue to make all selection decisions, but they would select from pools of individuals who can pass a threshold of requirements that include a points test. Employers would also be required to attest to certain recruitment, wage, and employment conditions. Numerical limitations would continue to be imposed, but a year's ceilings would be based on the previous year's usage.

* * *

In the *non-permanent system*, most of the changes we propose focus on the H–1B category. * * *

* * *

The Goals of Economic–Stream Immigration

Within some numerical parameters (see below), the U.S. economy should be able to access key talent wherever it is available, with procedures that are fully transparent and have predictable outcomes. Moss Kanter's "thinkers," "traders," and in certain narrow instances, "makers" best represent the types of talented foreign-born workers that enhance the competitive positions of the firms that employ them and are most beneficial in the long run both to the broader economy and to their fellow employees. * * *

Conversely, in all but the most exceptional circumstances, there is no reason to admit unskilled or semi-skilled workers under our permanent economic-stream immigration system. * * *

* * *

We believe that the following general propositions should guide the reform effort:

General Proposition 1: Most economic-stream *immigrants* should continue to be selected by employers on the basis of their expected contributions to that employer. However, they should be selected from a pool of individuals who possess characteristics that enhance the prospects that they will also make substantial long-term contributions to the economic strength of the United States.

General Proposition 2: Most economic *non-immigrants* should be admitted: (a) to fill a specific labor need for a temporary period * * *

* * *

We propose dividing economic-stream immigration into three tiers. The top tier would be similar to the current EB–1 immigrant visa category. The second tier, where the bulk of our proposed changes apply, would include an employer sponsorship requirement, a work experience requirement, wage and other attestations, and several selection criteria against which candidates would be "tested." The third tier would be for investors.

* * *

The system we propose would replace the labor certification function currently used for admitting most immigrants in the employment-based second and third preference categories. We recommend abolishing this function because its emphasis on "shortages" is no longer an appropriate framework for the affirmative immigration policies that undergird successful global economies. Despite endless attempts at "correction," it continues to be unable to work as intended, is riddled with delays that make a mockery of its stated intentions and, as discussed at length [earlier], provides virtually no protection for U.S. workers.

In addition, the labor certification system focuses on only a short-term goal: the immediate needs of the labor market. Immigrants are *permanent* additions to the labor force. It makes little sense to admit them (using labor certification or any similar system) *solely* on the basis of a specific job opening that may quickly become redundant or for a function that may offer few long-term benefits for either the employer or the country. Instead, a key goal of the economic immigrant selection system should be to satisfy ourselves that those who are admitted into the United States as presumptive members of our society have a proper mix of skills and other attributes, such as experience, education, and language, that maximizes the probability of long-term success in the labor force. Even if it worked perfectly, the existing labor certification process would have no more than a haphazard relationship to that goal.

* * *

The top tier of the new economic immigrant visa system would be similar to the current EB–1 immigrant visa category for "priority workers." Foreign nationals with extraordinary ability presumptively enhance the economic strength of the United States. So do outstanding professors and researchers. And foreign executives and managers who currently meet the EB–1–3 subcategory's requirements clearly facilitate international trade with the United States.

The shortcomings of the current immigration system are clearest with regard to the second-tier economic-stream, and this is where we propose to make the most changes.

To qualify for our proposed second-tier economic-stream immigrant visa category, foreign nationals would have to satisfy three prerequisites. First, they must have a job offer from a U.S. employer. Second, they must have at least three years' work experience in the specific occupation for which they are being sponsored. Third, the sponsoring employer must make certain attestations, including a commitment to pay them the higher of (a) the actual wage the employer pays to other similarly qualified and employed individuals, or (b) the prevailing wage rate for the occupation in the area of employment. Individuals who satisfy these prerequisites would also need to qualify under a selection formula that awards value points for certain human capital attributes.

Employer Sponsorship Requirement. Requiring immigrants in the second tier to have a job offer before coming to the United States will ensure that a U.S. employer will be at the controls of both timetable and process, and that the selected immigrant will be working as soon as he or she enters the United States. This will give immigrants immediate access to economic opportunity, allowing them to make a more complete transition into U.S. society. A job offer is the best single assurance that an economic need is being met (an imperfect yet credible substitute for a demand-and-supply test) and that economic-stream immigration occurs in an orderly fashion.

Together with the selection criteria suggested below, employer sponsorship helps assure the immigrant's immediate contribution to the United States.

More important, requiring employer sponsorship adds another level of screening to a selection process that costs the government nothing. Before an immigrant qualifies under the second tier of our proposed system, an employer will have had to review and approve his or her credentials, interpersonal and communications skills, and likelihood of career success. Furthermore, by the time the employer begins the actual visa petitioning process, the firm will already have decided that the prospective immigrant is essential to its business and will have made a preliminary judgment that he or she will be able to meet the screening criteria for admission. The fact that the foreign worker meets the program's other selection criteria means that he or she will also have the tools to make a long-term contribution to the broader economy.

Experience Requirement. As a rule, experienced workers make a more immediate contribution to their employer and to the broader economy than do inexperienced workers. Furthermore, admitting inexperienced economic-stream immigrants to the United States could create unnecessary competition for U.S. workers vying for entry-level positions. Therefore, we propose that an individual must have at least three years of prior work experience in the specific field and subfield for which an employer is recruiting to be eligible for second-tier immigrant status.

Attestation Requirements. We propose that sponsoring employers fulfill a three-part attestation requirement for second-tier economic-stream immigrants: (a) a wage attestation; (b) a no strike or lockout attestation; and (c) a notice requirement.

Wage attestation. Employers sponsoring a second-tier immigrant would be required to attest that they will pay the foreign worker the higher of (a) the actual wage the employer pays other individuals who are similarly employed with similar qualifications or (b) the prevailing wage rate for the occupation in the area of employment. Our emphasis on an objective and reliable wage attestation requirement stems from our conviction that nothing in the permanent or non-permanent U.S. economic-stream selection system should encourage employers to "prefer" hiring foreign workers simply because they are cheaper. Doing so amounts to a governmental subsidy that hurts U.S. workers. * * *

* * *

As long as prevailing wage surveys follow generally accepted survey methodology standards, employers can rely on them to make sure they are paying the prevailing wage. In the event of a dispute, a rule of reason should apply—i.e., whether the source data are reasonable and consistent with industry standards.

No strike or lockout attestation: We also believe that employers should attest that there is no strike or lockout at the place of employment. * * *

* * *

Notice-of-filing attestation. Finally, we propose that employers should also attest that they have given their employees notice of the filing of the attestation, both by posting the attestation at the worksite and by giving notice to the union or professional association representative, if there is one. Such a notice requirement gives U.S. workers an opportunity to participate in the process, and to file a complaint if they believe the employer is violating the law.

Satisfying the attestation requirements. Employers would have two ways to satisfy our proposed attestation requirements: (a) prequalification or (b) case-by-case. To prequalify, employers would have to document that their recruitment, compensation, and employment policies are within a band of "acceptable" business norms, for example, in the way they advertise for, recruit, interview, and select employees. A company requesting attestation prequalification would have to show that it has a formal company-wide compensation and employment policy that is communicated to all employees and that covers such standard issues as salary increases, bonuses, benefits, and job classifications. The company's compensation system would have to rely on market data to set wage and benefit levels. Other factors that might be considered for the prequalification component include whether the company has a human resources or personnel department to administer its compensation system, has established documentation for job categories, and routinely relies on up-to-date national or area salary surveys to establish wage levels.

Companies that meet these eligibility requirements would be prequalified as meeting the attestation requirements for second-tier purposes for two years, renewable in two-year increments upon resubmitting relevant information. During this period, the employer would simply file second-tier immigrant visa petitions, with copies of the posted attestation and the blanket approval, with the INS. The employer would also send the DOL a copy of the attestation for audit and investigation purposes. We intend for prequalification to raise a rebuttable presumption that the employer is complying with the attestation requirements. The DOL should be able to investigate alleged violations by such employers only if it receives credible allegations of fraud or other serious violations.

* * *

Companies that do not meet the prequalification requirements for second-tier attestation purposes, or that do not want to use the prequalification alternative for any reason, would continue to file individual attestations. Such individual attestations would be filed with the INS rather than with the DOL, although a copy would be sent to the DOL for audit and investigation purposes. Evidence to show compliance with the prevailing wage attestation condition could consist of a copy of the survey or other reliable data on which the prevailing wage is based. Evidence of the actual wage could be documented by a copy of the job posting showing the salary offered and a summary of what other workers in the same position earn. Employers would not be required, however, to document their entire wage system.

Enforcing Compliance. We recognize that shifting to an attestation process to ensure compliance with our proposed system raises basic questions of enforceability. As a result, we recommend enhancing enforceability by requiring employers to maintain an adequate "paper trail" for audit and enforcement purposes should they later come under scrutiny or investigation. For instance, employers should be required to keep a record of their sources for prevailing wage information, adequate payroll records to determine the actual wage paid, records of what steps they took to recruit U.S. workers, copies of W–2s or other payroll information, etc. Considering that most of the firms that are likely to use our proposed second-tier immigrant system will be well-organized firms with clearly articulated personnel policies and well-staffed human resources departments, the requirements we recommend are far less intrusive and unusual—or costly—than one might think. The increasing reliance on electronic systems means that personnel files can easily be programmed to include the information required under our proposals.

Moreover, the attestations themselves should be kept by the INS and the DOL in a computer database, so that any interested person or entity could readily access non-proprietary data, properly protected for privacy, in a usable format. Complaints about any aspect of the attestation process should be received and acted upon on an anonymous basis. Our concept is to repose a greater degree of trust in the employer at the inception of the process, but not to let the employer off the hook. Those who betray that trust should pay a heavy price in terms of fines, debarment from immigration programs for specified periods, and even criminal prosecutions in appropriate cases.

Employer sponsorship, previous work experience, and attestations are the prerequisites that employers and prospective immigrants must meet if they are to be eligible to file an immigrant visa petition under our proposed second tier. To actually *obtain* a second-tier immigrant visa, however, the pre-selected immigrant must also have personal characteristics that are essential to making a sustained and substantial contribution to the United States. These characteristics are as follows:

- The language ability and communications skills necessary to interact effectively with colleagues and customers;

- An educational background that has instilled both specific knowledge or technical skills *and* a facility for abstract thinking;

- A demonstrated commitment to improving one's own human capital endowments;

- A familiarity with U.S. culture and economic institutions adequate to allow one to adapt to dramatic labor market changes over his or her career; and

 - An age that permits one to make a long-term substantial contribution to one's adopted country before retirement.

Table **4–2** outlines our proposal for selection criteria, with suggested numerical weights. However, considering the rate at which economic conditions change, we believe that it makes little sense to legislate these factors. Congress moves too slowly for it to enact detailed changes on immigration, particularly on the controversial and highly complex topic of economic-stream immigration. Just as we want the economic immigrants we choose to be able to adapt, so too we need flexibility in our selection system. Hence, immigration officials should be given authority to change both the criteria for selecting economic immigrants and the number of points needed to qualify periodically, as economic conditions change. Such flexibility is essential for our system's success. Moreover, Congress' need to stay engaged can be discharged relatively easily by requiring that proposed changes be vetted in advance with the two subcommittees charged with overseeing immigration.

4.2. Proposed Selection Criteria System (Second–Tier Immigrants and H–1 Non-immigrants Only)

Factor	Criteria	Points	Max
Education	High School	1	7
	Some College	2	
	Bachelor's Degree	4	
	Master's/MBA/JD	6	
	PhD/MD	7	
	Completion of Apprenticeship/Vocational Program, plus five years' post vocational program experience	5	
	Master Craftsperson/Teacher of Trainers	1	
Age	<25	1	3
	25–50	3	
	>50	1	
Language	Functional English	3	8
	Fluent English	5	
	Fluency in a third language other than English or native language	3	
Adaptability	Has previously worked or studied for a substantial period of time in the U.S. or another foreign country	2	5
	Has taken advantage of opportunities for personal or professional development, including language classes, or completed on-the-job or other training, as evidenced by a certificate of completion	1	
	Has taken a leadership role in teamwork arrangements, as evidenced by an affidavit from employer or supervisor	1	

	Has worked in a multi-country team setting before, as evidenced by an affidavit from employer or supervisor	1	
	Total Maximum Points:	23	
	Proposed Pass Mark Number for Second–Tier Immigrants:	15	
	Proposed Pass Mark Number for H–1 Non–Immigrants	12	

Our proposed selection criteria system is superior to the current system for a number of reasons. First, it better accords with the policy goal of maximizing the probability of long-term economic contributions and success in the labor force.

Second, it better satisfies the programmatic objective that the immigrant selection process should be efficient, timely, fair, and transparent for all parties. * * *

It is up to Congress to engage the appropriate actors in a dialogue about the precise number of points to be initially accorded to each factor, and the minimum number of points that should qualify an immigrant under the system. We believe, however, that the following factors are critical to making a sustained economic contribution to the United States, and therefore should be included in any selection criteria system. Our selection criteria scheme, based on the following factors, would have a maximum of 23 points and a pass mark of 15 points. As the INS accumulates experience with the system over time, it may want to consider a larger range to be able to make finer distinctions within factors or to change weights among factors.

Education. * * *

Education is the strongest predictor of economic success. * * * The DOL estimates that the number of jobs requiring at least a bachelor's degree will expand by about 40 percent by 2005, while jobs that do not require a college education will grow by only 17 percent during the same period.

Age. Other things being equal, younger workers will have more time to make a contribution to the U.S. economy than will older workers. However, young workers with little or no experience will make a smaller immediate contribution than more experienced workers, while also competing for entry-level positions with new or recent U.S. college graduates. * * *

* * *

Language. A person cannot succeed in today's labor market without being able to conceptualize and communicate in English effectively. Employers know this and would be unlikely to hire someone permanently who is unable to communicate effectively in English. * * *

* * *

We also propose awarding extra points to individuals who are fluent in a language other than their native language and English. Knowledge of three languages makes a person more likely to succeed in the labor force and to make a more significant contribution to the U.S. economy, especially in the growing international marketplace.

NOTES AND QUESTIONS

1. What do you think the economic goals of employment-based immigration should be? Compared to the present labor certification system, how well does the Papademetriou/Yale–Loehr proposal accommodate both the long-term and the short-term economic needs that you have just identified?

2. What *process* goals would you set for an employment-based immigration program? What qualities, in other words, do you think the ideal procedure should embody? Compared to the present labor certification system, how well does the Papademetriou/Yale–Loehr proposal serve those goals?

3. The authors' proposal contains several crucial ingredients. One of the most significant is the substitution of employer attestation for labor certification. (Note that PERM, by freeing employers from documentation obligations unless and until they are audited, brings the current process closer to what the authors have proposed.) As to that:

a. How might employers manipulate the proposed system? What safeguards do the authors recommend to thwart those efforts? Are the suggested safeguards sufficient? If an employer is intent on evading the requirement that foreign workers receive equal pay, are there ways to do so? (Consider especially the need to identify workers who are "similarly employed" and possess "similar qualifications." What is to prevent employers from defining comparability in such a way as to deflate the wage scales?)

b. What is your reaction to the two-year blanket attestation feature?

c. Under the proposed system, what should happen if the immigrant leaves his or her original job after a short time and takes a similar job with another employer? Should the new employer be required to pay him or her the greater of the prevailing wage and the new employer's actual wage for the same position? Or should the wage requirements lapse after the first job?

4. If the goal is to replace the current system's emphasis on short-term employer needs with criteria that augur the employee's long-term contributions, then why require a job offer?

5. The authors propose a requirement of three years work experience in the particular field (and subfield) for which the employer is recruiting. What are the pros and cons of a work experience requirement?

6. Interestingly, the proposed system does not require the employer even to attempt to recruit American workers before hiring a qualified noncitizen. Even if 50 qualified Americans apply for the job, the proposed policy would permit the employer to hire a qualified (even a less credentialed) noncitizen if all the other requirements are met. Argue for and against a recruitment requirement.

7. If all the other requirements are met, the applicant must tally a specified number of points. English language capability is one of the elements in the point total. Argue the pros and cons of assigning points for English language. (Consider especially the racial implications.)

8. The proposal for a points system raises some interesting "Who decides?" questions. Broad delegations of legislative authority to the executive branch are generally less common and more constrained in the United States than they are in the parliamentary democracies, a pattern that is evident in immigration as well as in other spheres of federal regulation. See generally Stephen H. Legomsky, *The Making of United States Refugee Policy: Separation of Powers in the Post–Cold War Era*, 70 Washington L. Rev. 675 (1995). Yet the proposed points system calls for the executive branch (with broad guidance from Congress) to decide (a) which attributes garner points; (b) how many points a given attribute receives; and (c) how many total points it takes to be admissible. In addition to formulating these general rules, the government would also determine how many points each applicant has earned. What are your reactions to the proposed decisionmaking apparatus?

9. Like the final report of the U.S. Commission on Immigration Reform, Legal Immigration: Setting Priorities 81–104 (1995), Papademetriou and Yale–Loehr advocate the elimination of employment-based visas for unskilled workers. Do you agree?

10. For another thoughtful analysis of United States employment-based immigration policy, see Susan Martin, B. Lindsay Lowell & Philip Martin, *U.S. Immigration Policy: Admission of High Skilled Workers*, 16 Georgetown Immigration L.J. 619 (2002).

11. For some good discussions of Australian and European programs for both temporary and permanent skills-based immigration, and some thoughtful comparative studies, see Mary E. Crock, *Contract or Compact: Skilled Migration and the Dictates of Politics and Ideology*, 16 Georgetown Immigration L.J. 133 (2001); Kay Hailbronner, *Labor Transfer Schemes— In Whose National Interest? Globalization and the Transfer of Labor—The European Experience*, 16 Georgetown Immigration L.J. 773 (2002); B. Lindsay Lowell & Susan Martin, *Transatlantic Roundtable on High Skilled Migration: A Report on the Proceedings*, 15 Georgetown Immigration L.J. 649 (2001); Ron McCallum, *Australian Labor Law, Migration and the Performance of Work*, 16 Georgetown Immigration L.J. 637 (2002); Stephen

Yale–Loehr & Christoph Hoashi–Erhardt, *A Comparative Look at Immigration and Human Capital Assessment*, 16 Georgetown Immigration L.J. 99 (2001).

12. Professor Bill Ong Hing suggests an entirely different direction. He argues that perceptions within the African–American community that immigrants are taking jobs from African–Americans are enough reason to reduce or even repeal skills-based immigration entirely and to expand job training programs for African–Americans. See Bill Ong Hing, *Immigration Policies: Messages of Exclusion to African Americans*, 37 Howard L.J. 237, 239, 262–81 (1994).

13. Professor Howard Chang, analogizing to principles of international trade, finds immigration to be a net economic benefit under any of several hypotheses. In sharp contrast to Professor Hing, he argues that that benefit would increase if Congress were to eliminate the ceiling on employment-based immigration, repeal the labor certification requirement, and tax immigration. See Howard F. Chang, *Liberalized Immigration as Free Trade: Economic Welfare and the Optimal Immigration Policy*, 145 Univ. Pennsylvania L. Rev. 1147 (1997), expanded and updated in Howard F. Chang, *Migration as International Trade: The Economic Gains from the Liberalized Movement of Labor*, 3 UCLA J. Law & Foreign Affairs 371 (1998). Excerpts from the latter article appear on pages 66–68 above. Chang further argues that the labor certification program is essentially government-mandated job discrimination against noncitizens. Howard F. Chang, *Immigration and the Workplace: Immigration Restrictions as Employment Discrimination*, 78 Chicago–Kent L. Rev. 291 (2003).

2.   THE FOURTH PREFERENCE: CERTAIN "SPECIAL IMMIGRANTS"

As noted earlier, the various prongs of the fourth employment-based preference, INA § 203(b)(4), are not generally aimed at redressing labor shortages. Rather, they serve a variety of other miscellaneous functions, mostly concerned with the special circumstances of the people they encompass. This preference covers every category of "special immigrant" described in INA § 101(a)(27), except those described in subsections (A) and (B). You might wish to skim section 101(a)(27) to get a sense of the types of categories included. For a good treatment of one of the main subgroups, see Enid Trucios–Haynes, *Religion and the Immigration and Nationality Act: Using Old Saws on New Bones*, 9 Georgetown Immigration L.J. 1 (1995). The religious workers subcategory has now been extended to October 1, 2008, at which time it will sunset unless it is either extended again or made permanent. See Pub. L. 108–99, 117 Stat. 1176 (Oct. 15, 2003).

As a result of section 421 of the USA PATRIOT Act, the fourth preference can now be used in one other type of case. Congress did not want the beneficiaries of family-sponsored, employment-based, and certain other visa petitions filed before September 11, 2001 to lose out because of the deaths of their citizen or LPR sponsors or because of the physical destruction of property essential to the businesses of their employer sponsors, occasioned by the terrorist attacks of that day. With some qualifications, therefore, section 421 granted special immigrant status to those individuals under INA § 101(a)(27), thus qualifying them for the employment-based fourth preference.

3. THE FIFTH PREFERENCE: IMMIGRANT INVESTORS

Until 1990, Congress had never made explicit provision for the admission of immigrants who wished to start commercial enterprises in the United States. Nonimmigrant investors could enter under INA § 101(a)(15)(E)(ii), as you will see in chapter 4. At one time an immigrant investor, if otherwise admissible, could enter on a nonpreference basis under the pre–1990 version of INA § 203(a)(7). INS regulations exempted from the labor certification requirement any immigrant who invested a specified minimum amount (which changed over the years) in a United States enterprise, would serve as the principal manager, and would employ at least one United States citizen or LPR other than the investor or his or her family. 8 C.F.R. § 212.8(b)(4) (1990). Such an immigrant was deemed not to be entering the United States to perform labor. Upon the evaporation of nonpreference slots in 1978, however, see *Solis–Ramirez v. U.S.D.O.J.*, 758 F.2d 1426, 1429 (11th Cir.1985), that regulation gathered dust. Some investors tried to start companies, obtain labor certification for themselves as "employees," and enter under an employment-based preference, but there were substantial barriers. See page 307 above.

Canada and Australia have long had formal programs for the permanent admission of immigrant investors. See generally Comment, *Immigration for Investors: A Comparative Analysis of U.S., Canadian, and Australian Policies,* 7 Boston College Internat'l & Comp. L. Rev. 113 (1984). Over the years many observers advocated a similar program for the United States, both to create jobs and to improve the country's balance of trade. See, e.g., Select Comm'n on Immigration and Refugee Policy, U.S. Immigration Policy and the National Interest (Final Report) 131–32 (1981); Austin T. Fragomen & Gwendolyn M. Robosson, *The Foreign Investor: Current Approaches Toward United States Immigration Law,* 18 Vanderbilt J. Transnat'l L. 335, 371–73 (1985).

Others have objected to the whole concept, viewing it as a means for the rich to "buy" their way into the United States. See, e.g., Select Comm'n on Immigration and Refugee Policy, above, at 336 (statement of Theodore M. Hesburgh, Chair of Comm'n); 129 Cong. Rec. S6738 (May 16, 1983) (Sen. Bumpers). One might also ask whether, as a matter of policy, the United States ought to be encouraging the flow of capital from third world countries. Just as INA § 212(e) seeks to avoid a "brain drain" by restricting the ability of exchange visitors to attain permanent residence, should the law similarly discourage a "capital drain" from less developed countries?

The Immigration Act of 1990, § 121(a), added a new provision for immigrant investors, INA § 203(b)(5). Under this program, approximately 10,000 visas per year are reserved for immigrants (and their spouses and children accompanying or following to join, see INA § 203(d)) who establish new commercial enterprises in the United States, invest at least $1,000,000 (subject to the discretion of the Secretary of Homeland Security to modify the minimum amount in specified ways), and employ at least ten Americans. A pilot program enacted in 1992 allows more flexible showings of indirect job creation when enterprises are concentrated in "regional centers." Pub. L. 102–395, 106 Stat. 1828, § 610 (Oct. 6, 1992). See generally Lincoln Stone, *Immigrant Investment in Local Clusters*, 80 IR 837 (June 16, 2003).

In 2002, Congress amended INA § 203(b)(5) in several places to eliminate the requirement that the applicant "establish" a commercial enterprise. It is now enough that the applicant "invest in" it. See Twenty–First Century Department of Justice Appropriations Authorization Act, Pub. L. 107–273, 116 Stat. 1758, § 11036 (Nov. 2, 2002).

What would prevent someone from starting a new company, investing the requisite capital, hiring ten or more Americans, acquiring LPR status, and then immediately shutting down the company, laying off the employees, and withdrawing his or her funds? To avoid that scenario, Congress attached conditions subsequent, parallel to the kinds of conditions subsequent that you saw earlier in connection with marriage-based immigration. INA § 216A empowers the Secretary to terminate the immigrant investor's status within two years upon finding that "the establishment of the commercial enterprise was intended solely as a means of evading the immigration laws" or that the various requirements for fifth preference status (commercial enterprise, minimum investment amount, etc.) are not being sustained. There is also an affirmative requirement, again analogous to that of the marriage fraud provision, that the immigrant investor, during the 90–day period immediately preceding the second anniversary of his or her admission as an LPR, petition for removal of the conditions.

Termination of the investor's permanent residence on the ground that "the establishment of the commercial enterprise was intended solely as a means of evading the immigration laws" is of course analogous to the IMFA provision that authorizes termination when "the qualifying marriage * * * was entered into for the purpose of procuring an alien's entry as an immigrant." INA § 216(b)(1)(A)(i). The latter provision reflects the view that one should not marry for immigration benefits. In investor cases, however, does an analogous policy really make sense? In contrast to marriage-based immigration, isn't the whole point of the investor preference to entice noncitizens to start up American enterprises? Is the person who accepts that invitation doing anything wrong? Or is there perhaps some difference between the person who establishes an enterprise "solely as a means of evading the immigration laws" (forbidden for investors) and the person who establishes it "for the purpose of procuring [his or her] entry as an immigrant" (the analogous test for marriage fraud under INA § 216(b)(1)(A)(i))? One possibility is that the evasion provision was meant merely to ensure that the investment involves actual risk, rather than a repurchase agreement more in the nature of a loan. On this issue there has been internal disagreement within the former INS. See *Matter of Izummi*, 22 I. & N. Dec. 169 (INS 1998). Alternatively, does the investor program have other purposes? Possibilities include (a) speeding the admission of those people who would have invested in the United States anyway, so that jobs for Americans can be created that much sooner; and (b) overcoming resistance to "foreigners buying up America" by *making* the foreigners Americans.

Investors need not pay the entire minimum amount up front; they need only be "actively in the process of investing" that amount. INA § 203(a)(5)(A)(ii). To meet that requirement, investors have used a variety of methods, including secured promissory notes, balloon payments, options to sell, and pooled investments. Many immigration investment consultants advertised that even a $125,000 investment under certain circumstances could meet the threshold requirement, and the INS in fact approved many such schemes. See Stanley Mailman & Stephen Yale–Loehr, *Controversy over Investor Category*, 3 BIB 491 (May 15, 1998). The program began to gather steam.

But the bubble burst in December 1997 when the INS General Counsel issued a 36–page legal opinion disapproving many of these arrangements. See Memorandum from the Office of General Counsel to Paul W. Virtue, HQCOU 70/6.1.8 & 70/9–P (Dec. 19, 1997), reproduced in 75 IR No. 9, App. I (Mar. 9, 1998). The opinion also made the change retroactive, resulting in the revocation of previously granted visa petitions. Mailman & Yale–Loehr, above, at 494–95. The former INS and the consular officers then proceeded to place 5th preference visa petitions and visa applications on hold. See David Hirson & Catherine I. Mayou, *The Sinking of the Titanic or the Rising of the Phoenix?—An Update on Immigrant Investor Visas*, September 1998 Immigration Briefings. In the following summer, the INS Associate Commissioner for Examinations issued a series of four published opinions that together take a strict view of qualifying investments. See *Matter of Ho*, 22 I. & N. Dec. 206 (INS 1998); *Matter of Hsiung*, 22 I. & N. Dec. 201 (INS 1998); *Matter of Izummi*, 22 I. & N. Dec. 169 (INS 1998); *Matter of Soffici*, 22 I. & N. Dec. 158 (INS 1998).

After much emotional torment and passionate debate, the investor preference has become a non-event. The annual ceiling is approximately 10,000, but from its inception through fiscal year 1998, annual admissions ranged from 59 to 1361. (And that counts accompanying spouses and children). See 1998 INS Statistical Yearbook, Table 4 at 28. Since 1997, annual admissions have dropped every year, plummeting to 65 in 2003. See 2003 Yearbook of Immigration Statistics, Table 4 at 20 (Sept. 2004). In contrast, by July 1999, Canada had attracted 16,417 immigrant investors (not counting family members). 76 IR 1027 (July 2, 1999). Canada's new Immigration and Refugee Protection Act, S.C. 2001, c.27, allows the admission of both "investors" and "entrepreneurs." See Benjamin A. Kranc, *The New Canadian Immigration and Refugee Protection Act*, 79 IR 1565, 1568 (Oct. 21, 2002).

Proponents of an investor program have attributed the lackluster response to several factors. One commentator emphasizes the former INS's long delay in issuing the necessary regulations; the $1,000,000 threshold investment amount, less favorable than the lower capital amounts required in Canada and Australia; certain other restrictions; the risks posed by the two-year conditional status; and the relative lack of efficiency and understanding exhibited by immigration officials when processing investor applications. Hirson, above, at 8. Papademetriou and Yale–Loehr agree that the $1,000,000 threshold and the two-year requirement might be putting off potential investors; they identify, as additional factors, the requirement that ten jobs be created and the agency requirement that the investor supply the last five years' personal income tax returns disclosing worldwide income. Demetrios G. Papademetriou & Stephen Yale–Loehr, Carnegie Endowment for International Peace, Rethinking U.S. Selection of Skilled Immigrants 164–66 (1996). The U.S. policy of taxing the worldwide income of LPRs (as well as that of U.S. citizens) might be a further deterrent. See Stone, above, at 838. In an attempt to make the program more attractive, USCIS has now established a new "Investor and Regional Center Unit" at USCIS headquarters to speed the processing of applications. See Stephen Yale–Loehr, *USCIS Vows to Improve EB–5 Immigrant Investor Programs*, 10 BIB 169 (Feb. 15, 2005); Stanley Mailman & Stephen Yale–Loehr, *Immigrant Investor Green Cards: Rise of the Phoenix*, 10 BIB 801 (May 15, 2005).

SECTION D.   DIVERSITY IMMIGRANTS

Almost from the inception of immigration controls, the United States laws have consciously influenced the distribution of immigrant admissions by national origin. As you saw in chapter 2, the early immigration laws imposed special restrictions on the Chinese and, shortly thereafter, on Asians generally. The national origins quota system, first inaugurated in 1921 and made permanent three years later, was a comprehensive effort to control the ethnicity of the immigrant stream. Under that system, the quota for immigrants from any given country was a fixed percentage of the number of Americans who could trace their ancestries to that country. See pages 16–17 above. In 1965 Congress finally repealed the national origins quota system but at the same time imposed per-country limitations (initially only on Eastern Hemisphere nations, extended to Western Hemisphere nations in 1976). See pages 19–20 above. For the political history of the diversity program, see Peter H. Schuck, Diversity in America–Keeping Government at a Safe Distance, chap. 4 (2003); Anna O. Law, *The Diversity Visa Lottery: A Cycle of Unintended Consequences in U.S. Immigration Policy*, 21 J. Amer. Ethnic History, issue no. 4, at 3 (2002).

Despite those conscious efforts either to favor some ethnic groups over others or simply to make the ethnic composition of the immigrant stream generally diverse, today's immigrants do not hail in equal numbers from all parts of the world. As you saw earlier, the vast majority of the legal immigrants in the 1970's, 1980's, and 1990's have come from Asia, Mexico and Latin America, and the Caribbean. There are several reasons, including geographic proximity (in the case of the Americas) and economic disparities, for these modern immigration patterns. Many people ascribe the patterns to the priority American immigration law has given to family preferences since 1952. As the number of immigrants from a given country increases, the opportunities for the future immigration of family members (typically from the same country) also increase. In this way, a high priority on family unity tends to make immigration patterns self-reinforcing.

In recent years Congress has taken several steps to diversify the admission of immigrants. The per-country limits are one such mechanism. Several temporary programs have also been enacted. The so-called NP–5 program, see Pub.L. 99–603 (IRCA), § 314, 100 Stat. 3359, 3439 (Nov. 6, 1986), authorized the admission of 5000 nonpreference immigrants (hence the name "NP–5") in each of fiscal years 1987 and 1988. They were to come from "foreign states the immigration of whose natives to the United States was adversely affected by" the 1965 law abolishing national origin quotas. Some 1.3 million people applied. As expected, Ireland captured by far the greatest number of the NP–5 visas. Canada and the U.K. ran second and third. See 64 IR 291 (1987). Within the group of "adversely affected" countries, applicants were selected in the order in which their applications arrived by mail, but their applications were not counted if they arrived *before* a specified date. See 52 Fed.Reg. 1447, 1450–51 (Jan. 14, 1987). The effect was to reward those applicants who best predicted the precise number of days the mail would take to get to the designated post office box in the United States. In 1988, Congress extended the program, authorizing 15,000 additional NP–5 visas in each of fiscal years 1989 and 1990. Immigration Amendments of 1988, Pub.L. 100–658, § 2, 102 Stat. 3908 (Nov. 15, 1988).

In the same statute that extended NP–5, Congress established what later became known as the OP–1 program. *Id.* § 3. Under OP–1, 10,000 additional immigrants could be admitted in each of fiscal years 1990 and 1991 from "underrepresented countries," defined to include any country that used less than 25% of its per-country limit in fiscal year 1988. Among those who applied during a designated one-month period, the winners were selected by lottery. *Id.* § 3(b).

The Immigration Act of 1990 continued this tradition in two ways. First, it established the "AA–1" program for nationals of countries that were "adversely affected" by the abolition of the national origins quota system. These individuals were allotted 40,000 visas in each of fiscal years 1992, 1993, and 1994. Imm. Act 1990, § 132. Selections were by lottery, except that each year at least 40% of the 40,000 visas (i.e., 16,000) were reserved for whichever country had received the greatest number of NP–5 visas (Ireland). *Id.* § 132(c), as amended by Pub.L. 102–232, § 302(b)(6)(D)(i), 105 Stat. 1733 (Dec. 12, 1991).

At the same time, Congress enacted the first permanent immigrant preference based on diversity. It admits up to 50,000 "diversity immigrants" each year. Imm. Act 1990, § 131. (The original ceiling was 55,000, but the practical effect of section 203(d) of a statute known as NACARA, discussed on pages 605–06 below, was to reduce the figure to 50,000 per year, starting in fiscal year 1999.) The selection of the 50,000 winners is based on a series of elaborate formulas laid out in INA § 203(c). You will eventually consider the arguments for and against this and the other diversity-driven enactments, but first you need to understand how section 203(c) actually works. To do the latter, you will need to study the statutory language. The following summary might help you to follow the mathematics more easily.

Each year USCIS performs certain statutory calculations. For each foreign state, USCIS tabulates the number of people who became LPRs during the preceding five-year period as immediate relatives, family-sponsored preference immigrants, or employment-based preference immigrants (or certain miscellaneous categories, all low-volume). Any foreign state for which that five-year number exceeds 50,000 is classified as a "high-admission state;" every other state is "low-admission." All of the 50,000 diversity visas are allocated to natives of low-admission states.

To determine which of those applicants receive the 50,000 visas, USCIS must do other calculations. For that purpose the statute divides the world into six "regions:" Africa; Asia; Europe; North America (other than Mexico); Oceania; and South America, Mexico, Central America, and the Caribbean (the last four constituting one region). Each year USCIS classifies each of the six regions as either high-admission or low admission. A region is high-admission if its natives accounted for more than one-sixth of the total LPR grants of the preceding five-year period. Every other region is "low-admission."

Next, USCIS computes, for each region, the total population of the low-admission states of that region.

Having compiled those data, USCIS now essentially divides up the 50,000 visas between two groups: the group of high-admission regions and the group of low-admission regions. To do this, USCIS first figures out what percentage of the last five years' immigrants were natives of high-admission regions. The *low*-admission regions together then receive that percentage of the 50,000 visas. The high-admission regions get the rest. For example, if 90% of the past five years' immigrants were from high-admission regions, then the low-admission regions would get 90% of the diversity visas as an offset.

Within the group of low-admission regions, the visas are allocated among the individual regions in proportion to the combined populations of the low-admission states in each of those regions. Similarly, within the group of high-admission regions, the visas are allocated among the regions in proportion to the combined populations of the low-admission states in those regions. If it appears that a region will not use its full allotment in a particular year, the unused visas are distributed among the other regions in proportion to the allotments they would otherwise have received.

Through this method, each region ends up with a prescribed share of the 50,000 diversity visas. Within each region, the individual winners are then selected "strictly in a random order established by the Secretary of

State"—i.e., by lottery. INA § 203(e)(2). There are a few qualifications: The individual must meet specified requirements concerning education level or work experience. Not more than 7% of the 50,000 visas (i.e., 3500) may go to natives of any single state in a given fiscal year. In addition, the "winners" must complete certain paperwork by the end of the relevant fiscal year. In practice, processing delays and other problems frequently prevent this. As a result, not all of the 50,000 authorized diversity visas are actually awarded. In fiscal year 2003, for example, only 46,347 of the congressionally authorized 50,000 diversity immigrants were actually admitted. See 2003 Yearbook of Immigration Statistics, Table 8 at 29 (Sept. 2004).

As is normally the case, Europe received the greatest number of diversity visas in 2003 and Africa was a close second. *Id.* The State Department's calculations for fiscal year 2006 show 15 countries as high-admission, and therefore ineligible for diversity visas: Canada, China (mainland-born), Colombia, the Dominican Republic, El Salvador, Haiti, India, Jamaica, Mexico, Pakistan, the Philippines, Russia, South Korea, the United Kingdom (except for Northern Ireland, which is treated separately), and Vietnam. U.S. Dept. of State, Instructions for the 2006 Diversity Immigrant Visa Program (2004). For that year's lottery, 6.3 million entries were received. 10 BIB 401 (Mar. 1, 2005).

PROBLEM 16

Before attempting this Problem, you should study the above description. Consult INA § 203(c) if you want more detail. You won't need a calculator.

Note that the data provided in this Problem are hypothetical, not actual. In most instances they are not far off from reality, but some liberties have been taken (for example, inflating the population of Oceania) in order to simplify the arithmetic.

As a USCIS attorney, you have been handed a copy of INA § 203(c) and asked to allocate the 50,000 diversity visas among the six regions. You have gathered, for the preceding five-year period, the data that appear in the table below. How many diversity visas will each region receive?

	Immigration Past Five Years	Population of Low-admission States in Region	Number of Diversity Visas
Africa	60,000	300,000,000	_____
Asia	1,200,000	900,000,000	_____
Europe	450,000	650,000,000	_____
North America (excluding Mexico)	60,000	–0–	_____
Oceania	30,000	50,000,000	_____
South America, Mexico, Central America, and the Caribbean	1,200,000	100,000,000	_____
TOTAL	**3,000,000**	**2,000,000,000**	**50,000**

ESSAY ON DIVERSITY IMMIGRANTS[10]

In the United States and elsewhere, debates about immigration policy often reflect sharply differing conceptions about life in a multi-racial society. Conservative political columnist (and former White House Press Secretary) Pat Buchanan has denounced in strong language the multi-ethnic direction in which he sees the United States heading. Fearing United States counterparts to the French separatist movement in Quebec, Buchanan stresses examples of the havoc he thinks members of various ethnic groups can wreak: "Moscow's Jewish Mafia got itself transplanted to Brighton Beach;" some of the Cuban Marielitos in 1980 were "psychotics and criminals;" some Mexican immigrants seek "prey" rather than "work." He quotes with approval another writer who asks rhetorically "What will it be like in the next century, when, as Time so cheerfully predicts, white people will be in the minority?" and who maintains that "[h]igh rates of *non-European* immigration * * * will swamp us" (emphasis added). Buchanan asserts (and thinks it important) that "black on white is the most common form of interracial crime," asks "Who speaks for the Euro–Americans, who founded the U.S.A.?" and pleads "Is it not time to take America back?" (From whom?) Patrick Buchanan, *What Lesson for the U.S. in Canada?*, Washington Times, June 27, 1990, at F–1. In chapter 1, you encountered the similar sentiments of Peter Brimelow.

Analogous rhetoric has flourished across the Atlantic. A 1988 debate in the British House of Commons included these comments from members of the then governing Conservative Party:

Ours is a society which * * * has had its identity threatened by a massive invasion of tribes and cultures. * * *

Hon. Tony Marlow

Many people * * * are exiles in their own country because of the way in which the character of our towns and cities has been altered.

Hon. Christopher Gill

The invaders * * * are indeed invaders * * *. Is [the Home Secretary] aware that one in three children born in Greater London is of ethnic extraction?

Hon. Jim Janman

10. This essay originally appeared in the first edition of this book (1992). For an updated and expanded version, see Stephen H. Legomsky, *Immigration, Equality, and Diversity*, 31 Columbia J. Transnat'l L. 319 (1993); see also Bill Ong Hing, *Beyond the Rhetoric of Assimilation and Cultural Pluralism: Addressing the Tension of Separatism and Conflict in an Immigration–Driven Mul-* *tiracial Society*, 81 California L. Rev. 863 (1993); *cf.* Daniel Kanstroom, *Wer Sind Wir Wieder? Laws of Asylum, Immigration, and Citizenship in the Struggle for the Soul of the New Germany*, 18 Yale J. Internat'l L. 155 (1993)(finding excessive Germany's emphasis on ethnic homogeneity in its citizenship and immigration laws).

Joint Council for the Welfare of Immigrants, 3 *Bulletin* No. 8 at 12 (Nov. 1988).

Buchanan and his British counterparts might be cruder than most other public figures in their objections to multi-ethnic societies, but there is no question that they speak for many others—both leaders and rank and file. It would be unrealistic to pretend that bigotry played no significant role in the political coalition that produced the "diversity" provisions, which bestowed special preference predominantly on natives of European countries.

At the same time, it would be unfair to dismiss supporters of the "diversity" programs as racists. Many proponents of those programs believe that United States immigration laws have unwittingly discriminated *against* Europeans, and in favor of Asians, Latinos, and selected other groups. Their argument is that current law, which assigns the highest priority to family unity, benefits disproportionately those who hail from countries that have sent the greatest numbers of recent immigrants to the United States. Natives of those countries, the argument runs, are much more likely to have relatives in the United States to petition for them. See, *e.g.,* Michael S. Teitelbaum, *Skeptical Noises About the Immigration Multiplier,* 23 Int'l Migration Rev. 893, 895–96 (1989). Europeans, in contrast, are said to have been "shut out" by laws that admit relatively few without family connections. See, e.g., Joan Biskupic, *Diversity Is One Principal Goal in Deciding Whom to Let In,* Cong. Q., Aug. 4, 1990, at 2519.

A related argument is that a diversity program "responds to the adverse impact of the 1965 law" [the law that abolished the national origins quota system]. *Id.,* quoting Rep. Morrison (then Chair of House immigration subcommittee). As you will recall, immigrants from countries whose natives had been "adversely affected" by the 1965 law benefitted from ad hoc legislation in the years leading up to the permanent diversity program.

Those arguments are more respectable than the not-so-subtle appeals to racial prejudice by Buchanan and others. To be sure, our laws do allocate the greatest number of immigrant visas to family members—even with the addition of the diversity program. Still, the argument is worth examining. What, precisely, does it mean to say that the emphasis on family unity "discriminates" against, for example, Europeans? Presumably the reference is to de facto discrimination, an inevitable result of the demographic reality that Europeans are today less likely than Asians or Latinos to have close American relatives. If one were to dip one giant hand into Sweden and another giant hand into Mexico, and pluck out one randomly selected individual from each country, it is therefore true that the Mexican would have a higher probability of qualifying for immigration than would the Swede.

But is that type of de facto discrimination unjust? Would it not be more probative to ask whether a randomly selected Swede would have as high a probability of being eligible as would a *similarly situated* Mexican? The emphasis on family unity reflects the shared value that separation entails hardship and a premium on alleviating that hardship. The Swede who has a United States citizen spouse is treated exactly the same as the Mexican with a United States citizen spouse. The Swede with an LPR spouse is in fact treated far *better* than the Mexican with an LPR spouse; the effect of the per-country limitation is that, even without the diversity program, the Swede may jump ahead of the Mexican in the queue.

A related point: Would anyone seriously suggest that our refugee policy unfairly discriminates against Norwegians because Norwegians are statistically less likely than many others to face persecution at home? To such an argument, the response would be simple: The refugee admission program is there, at least in part, to alleviate one particular form of suffering. Surely no one today would maintain that, with all else equal, favoring genuine refugees is unfairly discriminatory. Doesn't the same answer apply to family unity preferences?

The suggestion that a diversity program is a necessary offset to the "adverse effects" of the 1965 law is really a different point. The argument seems to be that the diversity program is just affirmative action for Europeans, a remedy to compensate for the disproportionate adverse impact of the 1965 law. One must remember, however, that the 1965 law did not discriminate against Europeans; it merely repealed the national origins quotas that had previously discriminated in their favor. Do Europeans deserve favoritism now to offset that "adverse effect"? While we're at it, should our laws create special privileges for Southern whites whose ancestors were "adversely affected" by the abolition of slavery?

But even if the kind of "diversity" that the 1990 Act seeks to attain is accepted as a valid goal, the machinery of both the permanent new program and the various temporary programs is difficult to fathom. The Irish citizen who has been waiting for several years to join her LPR husband in the United States might be forgiven for wondering why another Irish citizen, without any specific equities, will be able to skip ahead of her and immigrate immediately on the basis of a lottery. The explanation that "we want an ethnically diverse immigrant stream" will not dispel her confusion.

It is difficult to be against "diversity." The word conjures up positive images of a richness drawn from a wide range of interesting and valuable traditions. A diverse society can only be applauded. But the "diversity" to which section 203(c) refers is confined to the immigrant stream, not to the resulting society. Since many more Americans already trace their ancestry to Europe than to Asia or Latin America, the statutory "diversity" program is in truth an *"anti-diversity"* program; it causes the resulting population mix to be *less* diverse than it would otherwise be.

Perhaps this whole debate boils down to the way one conceptualizes immigrants. Should they be seen as individuals, to be treated equally when similarly situated, or should they be viewed as delegates of the countries in which they were born? This author accepts the former characterization and believes that the so-called "diversity" program unjustly permits Europeans and selected others to bypass similarly situated Latinos and Asians. Those who have been waiting patiently in the queue should be treated with equal, individualized respect.

This essay is solely the viewpoint of the author. What is your reaction?

————

Professor Peter Schuck, in addition to specifically criticizing the diversity visa program, takes a broader shot. While lauding the social benefits of diversity, and suggesting that the government should praise and protect diversity, he makes a sophisticated argument that nonetheless it should not be the role of government to "create or promote any *particular* kind of diversity" (emphasis in original). See Peter H. Schuck, Diversity in America–Keeping Government at a Safe Distance 123–31, 324 (2003). Professor Jan Ting, testifying before Congress, has similarly criticized the concept of diversity visas. See Jan Ting, Testimony to Subcomm. on Immigration, Border Security, and Claims, Comm. on the Judiciary, U.S. House of Reps. (Apr. 29, 2004).

For a well argued contrary view, see Andowah A. Newton, *Injecting Diversity into U.S. Immigration Policy: The Diversity Visa Program and the Missing Discourse on its Impact on African Immigration to the United States*, 38 Cornell Internat'l L.J. issue 3 (forthcoming 2005). Newton emphasizes that, whatever the congressional motives, the program has ended up providing one of the few opportunities realistically available for African immigrants. She further argues that the use of electronic filing and the requirement of a high school diploma adversely affect would-be African applicants disproportionately.

CHAPTER 4

Nonimmigrant Priorities

As you have seen in previous chapters, the United States immigration laws divide all non-U.S. citizens into two groups—immigrants and nonimmigrants. The former are admitted for permanent residence; the latter are admitted for specific purposes, such as study, temporary work, business, or pleasure, and ordinarily for only a temporary visit of fixed duration.

U.S. law first recognized nonimmigrants in 1819. See 2003 Yearbook of Immigration Statistics at 74. Despite that lineage, the academic literature on immigration has lavished almost exclusive attention on immigrants. The high stakes typically present in the immigrant cases make such emphasis understandable. As the practicing bar can attest, however, nonimmigrant cases also often raise difficult issues of great importance to the parties and to the public, and they typically make up a substantial proportion of the immigration lawyer's caseload. Moreover, nonimmigrants have numerical significance. In fiscal year 2003, there were an estimated 181 million nonimmigrant admissions (including multiple entries by the same individuals, the vast majority being Canadian and Mexican commuters), compared to only 706,000 immigrants. *Id.* at 74 (nonimmigrants), Table 2 at 14 (immigrants). That aside, nonimmigrants have been in the limelight in recent years, at first because of President Bush's proposed guest worker program and then because of sweeping new restrictions introduced in the wake of September 11. For the moment, it is enough to note that some of the policy responses to September 11 caused marked drops in nonimmigrant admissions.

Because of the restrictions that the law places on nonimmigrants' lengths of stay and permitted activities, their admission criteria are generally less demanding than those for immigrants. For one thing, most immigrant admissions are numerically restricted; most nonimmigrant admissions are not. For another, the substantive eligibility rules are generally more stringent for immigrants.

Subject to some exceptions, noncitizens seeking admission are *presumed* to be immigrants and therefore subject to the higher standards of immigrant selection; to rebut that presumption they must show they qualify as nonimmigrants. INA § 214(b). To do that, they have to fit within one of the many categories of nonimmigrant laid out in section 101(a)(15) of the Act. Skim that provision now to get a sense of the kinds of nonimmigrants the law recognizes and the requirements they must meet.

A word on terminology: Both the State Department in issuing visas and DHS in granting admission often refer to nonimmigrant classes by the letters and numbers of the applicable subsections of INA § 101(a)(15). For example, section 101(a)(15)(F)(i) authorizes the admission of students, and section 101(a)(15)(F)(ii) authorizes the admission of their families. Consequently, students are said to enter on "F–1" visas, their families on "F–2" visas. The following chart shows the various nonimmigrant categories, their visa symbols, and the number of people in each category who were admitted in fiscal year 2003:

UNITED STATES DEPARTMENT OF HOMELAND SECURITY
OFFICE OF IMMIGRATION STATISTICS
2003 YEARBOOK OF IMMIGRATION STATISTICS

TABLE 24
NONIMMIGRANTS ADMITTED BY CLASS OF ADMISSION

Class of Admission	Number Admitted
All classes	**27,849,443**[1]
Foreign government officials and families (A)	**138,496**
Temporary visitors	**24,358,623**
For business (B1)	4,215,714
Visa Waiver, business	1,970,364
For pleasure (B2)	20,142,909
Visa Waiver, pleasure	11,610,325
Transit aliens (C)	**554,559**
Treaty traders and investors and families	**168,508**
Treaty traders (E1)	44,090
Treaty investors (E2)	124,418
Students	**624,917**
Academic students (F1)	617,556
Vocational students (M1)	7,361
Spouses and children of students	**38,049**
Representatives (and families) to international organizations (G)	**98,389**
Temporary workers and trainees	**650,126**
Registered nurses (H1A)	924
Specialty occupations (H1B)	360,498
[Certain other registered nurses (H1C)]	48
Performing services unavailable in the United States (H2)	116,927

1. This figure includes only those admissions that were officially recorded. In fiscal year 2003 the vast majority of the estimated 181,000,000 total nonimmigrant admissions related to Canadian and Mexican commuters and were not recorded. See *id.* at 73–74.

Class of Admission	**Number Admitted**
Agricultural workers (H2A)	14,094
Nonagricultural workers (H2B)	102,833
Industrial trainees (H3)	2,370
Workers with extraordinary ability/achievement (O1)	25,541
Workers accompanying and assisting in performance of O1 workers (O2)	5,321
Internationally recognized athletes or entertainers (P1)	43,274
Artists or entertainers in reciprocal exchange programs (P2)	3,898
Artists or entertainers in culturally unique programs (P3)	8,869
Workers in international cultural exchange programs (Q1)	2,074
[Irish Peace Workers (Q2)]	664
Workers in religious occupations (R1)	20,272
[NAFTA professionals (TN)]	59,446
Spouses and children of temporary workers and trainees	148,369
Representatives (and families) of foreign information media (I1)	32,030
Exchange visitors (J1)	321,660
Spouses and children of exchange visitors (J2)	41,122
Fiancé(e)s of U.S. citizens (K1)	24,643
Children of fiancé(e)s of U.S. citizens (K2)	3,652
Intracompany transferees (L1)	298,054
Spouses and children of intracompany transferees (L2)	136,227
NATO officials and families (N1–7)	12,569
Parents or children of international organization special immigrants (N8–9)	68
[LIFE Act, for certain people whose immigrant processing has been long delayed (K3–4 and V1–3)]	80,794
Victims of Trafficking and Violence Protection Act (T1–4 and U1–4)	1,005
Unknown	117,583

———

A nonimmigrant who seeks admission must overcome two separate hurdles: fitting into one of the specific statutory pigeonholes and avoiding the various affirmative grounds of inadmissibility. Using the same organization that chapter 3 used for immigrants, this chapter addresses only the problem of categorical qualification for nonimmigrants; the exclusion grounds for both immigrants and nonimmigrants are explored in the next chapter.

Finally, admission procedure is the subject of chapter 6. To understand the cases that follow, it is enough to know that the usual process for entering the United States as a nonimmigrant comprises at least two steps: applying for a visa at the appropriate United States consulate abroad, and presenting the visa to the CBP immigration inspector at the port of entry. As you will see, some nonimmigrants are exempt from the visa requirement, and conversely some must follow additional procedures. Labor certification is required in certain cases, employer attestations in certain others. For some categories, a person or company in the United States (an employer, a fiancé(e), etc., depending on the type of nonimmigrant) must first file a visa petition with USCIS.

SECTION A. COMMERCIAL CATEGORIES OF NONIMMIGRANTS[2]

1. BUSINESS VISITORS

International Union of Bricklayers and Allied Craftsmen v. Meese

United States District Court, Northern District of California, 1985.
616 F.Supp. 1387.

■ LEGGE, DISTRICT JUDGE.

Plaintiff International Union of Bricklayers and Allied Craftsmen ("International Union") represents approximately 100,000 masonry craftsmen working in the construction industry in the United States. Plaintiff Local No. 7, California, International Union of Bricklayers and Allied Craftsmen ("Local 7") is affiliated with plaintiff International Union in Northern California, and represents masonry craftsmen working in Lake County, California.

Defendants Edwin Meese III ("Attorney General"), George P. Schultz ("Secretary of State"), and the Immigration and Naturalization Service ("INS") are charged with the administration and enforcement of the immigration laws in the United States. Defendant-intervenor Homestake Mining Company of California ("Homestake") is a California corporation, and the owner of the McLaughlin Gold Project in Lake County, California.

* * *

---

2. See generally Austin T. Fragomen, Alfred J. Del Rey & Sam Bernsen, Immigration Law and Business (1996)(2 vols.); 2 Gordon, Mailman & Yale–Loehr, chs. 12–29; Rodney A. Malpert & Amanda Petersen (Eds.), Business Immigration Law: Strategies for Employing Foreign Nationals (2000).

A
Temporary Visitors for Business

The first class of nonimmigrant aliens relevant here is the "temporary visitor for business" class. Section 101(a)(15)(B) of the Act defines a "temporary visitor for business" as:

> an alien (other than one coming for the purpose of study or of performing skilled or unskilled labor or as a representative of foreign press, radio, film, or other foreign information media coming to engage in such vocation) having a residence in a foreign country which he has no intention of abandoning and who is visiting the United States temporarily for business. . . .

An alien qualifying for this nonimmigrant status is entitled to receive a "B-1" visa.

Pursuant to his authority under the Act, the Secretary of State has promulgated a regulation defining the term "business" for purposes of the B-1 "temporary visitor for business" class:

> The term "business", as used in section 101(a)(15)(B) of the Act, refers to legitimate activities of a commercial or professional character. It does not include purely local employment or labor for hire. An alien seeking to enter as a nonimmigrant for employment or labor pursuant to a contract or other prearrangement shall be required to qualify under [the regulations that govern H-2 temporary workers, discussed below].

* * *

Among the criteria utilized to determine an alien's eligibility for B-1 "temporary visitor for business" status is INS Operations Instruction 214.2(b)(5), an INS internal agency guideline that is the subject of this dispute. The Operations Instruction provides:

> Each of the following may also be classified as a B-1 nonimmigrant if he/she is to receive no salary or other remuneration from a United States source (other than an expense allowance or other reimbursement for expenses incidental to the temporary stay):

* * *

> (5) An alien coming to install, service, or repair commercial or industrial equipment or machinery purchased from a company outside the U.S. or to train U.S. workers to perform such service, provided: the contract of sale specifically requires the seller to perform such services or training, the alien possesses specialized knowledge essential to the seller's contractual obligation to provide services or training, the alien will receive no remuneration from a U.S. source, and the trip is to take place within the first year following the purchase.

* * *

Pursuant to the Operations Instruction, B–1 visas have been issued to the foreign laborers who came to the United States to work on the project owned by Homestake, and to foreign laborers to do other work throughout the United States. The central issue in this case is whether the Operations Instruction violates the Act and the regulations promulgated under the Act.

B
Temporary Workers

The second class of nonimmigrant aliens involved here is the "temporary worker" class. Section 101(a)(15)(H)(ii) of the Act defines a "temporary worker" as:

> an alien having a residence in a foreign country which he has no intention of abandoning ... [and] who is coming temporarily to the United States to perform temporary services or labor, if unemployed persons capable of performing such service or labor cannot be found in this country. . . .

An alien qualifying for this nonimmigrant status is entitled to receive an "H–2" [now H–2B—Ed.] visa.

* * *

Pursuant to his authority under the Act, the Attorney General has promulgated a regulation which requires the petitioning employer for an H–2 "temporary worker" applicant to seek labor certification from the Secretary of Labor prior to approval of the applicant's petition. * * *

II
The Present Case

* * *

Homestake began construction in early 1984 on its McLaughlin Gold Project in order to open a new gold mine. Due to metallurgical problems in the Lake County region, Homestake concluded that it was necessary to employ technology not used previously in the gold mining industry. Davy McKee Corporation ("Davy McKee"), Homestake's construction manager, therefore conducted a search to locate the appropriate technology.

On behalf of Homestake, Davy McKee agreed to purchase a newly-designed gold ore processing system from Didier–Werke ("Didier"), a West German manufacturing company. Although the purchase agreement required Didier to supply an integrated processing system, it was not possible to premanufacture the entire system in West Germany. The purchase agreement was therefore made contingent upon Didier's West German employees completing the work on the system at the project site in Lake County.

In September 1984, Didier submitted B–1 "temporary visitor for business" visa petitions on behalf of ten of its West German employees to United States consular officers in Bonn, West Germany. Relying upon INS Operations Instruction 214.2(b)(5), consular officers approved the petitions and issued B–1 visas to the West Germans. In January 1985, the West Germans entered the United States to work on the processing system. The work involves the installation of the interior linings of the system's autoclaves, and requires certain technical bricklaying skills.

* * *

Plaintiffs allege that the federal defendants' practice of issuing B–1 "temporary visitor for business" visas under the authority of INS Operations Instruction 214.2(b)(5) violates two provisions of the Act. First, plaintiffs allege that the practice violates section 101(a)(15)(B) of the Act, because the issuance of B–1 visas to aliens coming to the United States to perform skilled or unskilled labor is expressly prohibited by section 101(a)(15)(B). Second, plaintiffs allege that the practice violates section 101(a)(15)(H)(ii) of the Act, because aliens have been permitted to bypass the labor certification requirements contained in the regulations under section 101(a)(15)(H)(ii).

Plaintiffs therefore ask this court to declare that INS Operations Instruction 214.2(b)(5) violates the Act; to permanently enjoin the federal defendants from issuing B–1 visas under the authority of the Operations Instruction; and to order the federal defendants to reclassify the visa status of all B–1 "temporary visitor for business" alien nonimmigrants who are currently performing skilled or unskilled labor in the United States.

* * *

[In section III the court holds that the plaintiff labor unions have standing to raise these issues on behalf of their members.]

IV
The Validity of the Operations Instruction Under the Act

* * *

In testing the Operations Instruction against the Act, the court's task is to interpret the Act in light of the purposes Congress sought to achieve in enacting it. The starting point must be the language employed by Congress. Absent a clearly expressed legislative intention to the contrary, the statutory language is to be regarded as conclusive.

A
The Language of the Act and the Operations Instruction

* * *

INS Operations Instruction 214.2(b)(5) provides that an alien may be classified as a "temporary visitor for business" nonimmigrant if:

> *he/she is* to receive no salary or other remuneration from a United States source (other than an expense allowance or other reimbursement for expenses incidental to the temporary stay) ... [and is] *coming to install, service, or repair commercial or industrial*

equipment or machinery purchased from a company outside the U.S. or to train U.S. workers to perform such service....

A comparison of the language of section 101(a)(15)(B) of the Act with the language of INS Operations Instruction 214.2(b)(5) demonstrates that the Operations Instruction contravenes that section of the Act. Section 101(a)(15)(B) unequivocally excludes from the B–1 "temporary visitor for business" classification an alien who is "coming for the purpose of ... performing skilled or unskilled labor." That exclusion is reinforced by the federal defendants' own regulations. In this regard, the Secretary of State has promulgated a regulation defining "business" for purposes of section 101(a)(15)(B): "The term 'business' ... refers to legitimate activities of a commercial or professional character. *It does not include purely local employment or labor for hire.*" 22 C.F.R. § 41.25(b) (1985) (emphasis added).

INS Operations Instruction 214.2(b)(5), however, does not contain an exclusion for an alien seeking to enter the United States to perform skilled or unskilled labor. The Operations Instruction provides that an alien may be classified as a "temporary visitor for business" if the alien is "coming to install, service, or repair commercial or industrial equipment or machinery." The effect of this language is to authorize the issuance of a B–1 visa to an alien coming to this country to perform skilled or unskilled labor. In the present case, for example, the West Germans undeniably are performing labor—whether it be deemed skilled or unskilled—in connection with the installation of the gold ore processing system at the McLaughlin Gold Project.

Similarly, a comparison of the language of section 101(a)(15)(H)(ii) of the Act with the language of INS Operations Instruction 214.2(b)(5) shows that the Operations Instruction also contravenes that section of the Act. Section 101(a)(15)(H)(ii) classifies an H–2 "temporary worker" as an alien "coming ... to perform temporary services or labor, if unemployed persons capable of performing such service or labor cannot be found in this country." Because the Act requires the Attorney General to consult other agencies of the government concerning "temporary worker" visas, *see* INA § 214(c), the Attorney General has established H–2 labor certification procedures. Thus, an H–2 visa petition cannot be approved unless the alien's employer obtains either *"[a] certification from the Secretary of Labor* ... stating *that qualified persons in the United States are not available and that the employment* of the beneficiary *will not adversely affect wages and working conditions of workers in the United States* similarly employed ... [or] notice that such certification *cannot* be made."

In contrast, INS Operations Instruction 214.2(b)(5) does not require an alien to seek labor certification prior to obtaining a nonimmigrant visa. More importantly, the Operations Instruction authorizes the issuance of a nonimmigrant visa to a person performing skilled or unskilled labor, though qualified Americans may be available to perform the work involved. The Operations Instruction therefore lacks the safeguards contained in section 101(a)(15)(H)(ii) of the Act and the regulation promulgated under that section. Again, the present case illustrates this point, because the parties have stipulated that neither the West Germans nor their employer was required to seek labor certification from the Secretary of Labor prior to the issuance of the visas to the West Germans.

* * *

B
The Intent of Congress

* * *

The current substantive versions of sections 101(a)(15)(B) and 101(a)(15)(H)(ii) of the Act were enacted in 1952. Congress, however, demonstrated its concern for the protection of American workers as early as 1885. In the Act of Feb. 26, 1885, Congress enacted legislation prohibiting the entry of contract laborers. Contract laborers generally were unskilled aliens who received minimal wages in return for passage to the United States. The importation of those laborers was intended "to oversupply the demand for labor so that the domestic laborers would be forced to work at reduced wages." * * *

* * *

Significant changes in the immigration laws were enacted by Congress in the Immigration and Nationality Act of 1952. Congress amended section 101(a)(15)(B) of the Act—the successor to section 3(2) of the 1924 Act—to include a specific provision *excluding* an alien from the B–1 "temporary visitor for business" class who comes to the United States "for the purpose of ... performing skilled or unskilled labor." Further, Congress enacted section 101(a)(15)(H)(ii) of the Act, thereby establishing the H–2 "temporary worker" class.

In taking these actions, Congress evidenced a continuing concern for the protection of American workers from unnecessary foreign competition. The House Report accompanying the 1952 Act explained that the purpose of section 101(a)(15)(H)(ii) was to:

> grant the Attorney General sufficient authority to admit *temporarily certain alien workers,* industrial, agricultural, or otherwise, *for the purpose of alleviating labor shortages as they exist or may develop* in certain areas or certain branches of American productive enterprises....

* * *

The foregoing legislative history demonstrates that one of Congress' central purposes in the Act was the protection of American labor. The legislative history also demonstrates that sections 101(a)(15)(B) and 101(a)(15)(H)(ii) of the Act were intended to restrict the influx of aliens seeking to perform skilled or unskilled labor in the United States. Thus, to the extent that INS Operations Instruction 214.2(b)(5) permits aliens to circumvent the restrictions enacted by Congress in those sections, the

Operations Instruction is inconsistent with both the language and the legislative intent of the Act.

C
Defendants' Arguments

Defendants contend that INS Operations Instruction 214.2(b)(5) should be upheld because it embodies a reasonable administrative interpretation of the Act.

Defendants' argument centers on the purposes Congress sought to achieve in sections 101(a)(15)(B) and 101(a)(15)(H)(ii) of the Act. Defendants contend that those sections evidence Congress' intent to foster multiple purposes. Although defendants acknowledge that one such purpose was the protection of American labor, they argue that another was the promotion of international commerce. Further, defendants assert that the language in sections 101(a)(15)(B) and 101(a)(15)(H)(ii) reveals a tension between American labor interests and international commerce interests; that the Operations Instruction seeks to minimize the tension; and that the Operations Instruction is therefore consistent with the multiple purposes in the Act.

Defendants rely primarily upon the decision of the Board of Immigration Appeals in *Matter of Hira,* 11 I. & N. Dec. 824 (BIA 1966). In *Hira,* an alien employed by a Hong Kong custom-made clothing manufacturer had entered the United States under the authority of a B–1 "temporary visitor for business" visa. While in this country, the alien took orders on behalf of his employer from prospective customers, and took the measurements of those customers. Prior to the expiration of the alien's visa, the INS commenced deportation proceedings against him. The INS concluded that the alien's activities involved the performance of skilled labor, and ordered that the alien be deported for failure to maintain his B–1 "temporary visitor for business" status. On appeal, the Board of Immigration Appeals focused its analysis on the term "business" within section 101(a)(15)(B) of the Act. Adopting the Supreme Court's definition from an earlier version of the Act, the Board held that "business," for purposes of section 101(a)(15)(B) of the Act, "contemplate[s] only 'intercourse of a commercial character.'" In support of that definition, the Board alluded to prior administrative cases in which aliens were found eligible for "temporary visitor for business" status because "there was involved international trade or commerce and the employment was a necessary incident thereto." The Board also elaborated upon the underlying requirements for eligibility as a "temporary visitor for business" nonimmigrant:

> The significant considerations to be stressed are that there is a clear intent on the part of the alien to continue the foreign residence and not to abandon the existing domicile; the principal place of business and the actual place of eventual accrual of profits, at least predominantly, remains in the foreign country; the business activity itself need not be temporary, and indeed may long continue; the various entries into the United States made in

the course thereof must be individually or separately of a plainly temporary nature in keeping with the existence of the two preceding considerations.

Applying those principles the Board in *Hira* concluded that the alien's business was intercourse of a commercial character, even though he took prospective customers' measurements in connection with the business. Thus, the Board held that the alien was entitled to B–1 "temporary visitor for business" status. The Attorney General subsequently affirmed the Board's decision, and certified it as controlling.

Defendants argue that *Hira* controls the result in this case, since the principles underlying INS Operations Instruction 214.2(b)(5) and *Hira* are nearly identical. Defendants focus on the portion of *Hira* that permits the issuance of B–1 "temporary visitor for business" visas to an alien coming to the United States to engage in "intercourse of a commercial character," or coming to work as a "necessary incident" to international trade or commerce. Defendants argue that here the West Germans came to this country only as a necessary incident to the purchase and sale of the gold-ore processing system, rather than as individuals hired expressly as laborers. Further, defendants contend that it must be presumed that Congress has acquiesced in the policies underlying the Operations Instruction, because Congress has been aware of those policies for many years but has failed to take action.

Defendants' arguments are answered primarily by the language of the Act. It is important to reemphasize that in matters of statutory interpretation, a court must interpret the statute in light of the purposes Congress sought to achieve in enacting it. And absent a clearly expressed legislative intention to the contrary, the statutory language is regarded as conclusive. Under those principles, the language of section 101(a)(15)(B) of the Act which *excludes* an alien "coming for the purpose of . . . performing skilled or unskilled labor," precludes defendants' purported distinction between business and labor in this case; so does the expressed congressional intent of protecting American labor.

Similarly, there is no indication that Congress has acquiesced in the policies underlying INS Operations Instruction 214.2(b)(5). The current substantive versions of sections 101(a)(15)(B) and 101(a)(15)(H)(ii) were enacted in 1952. The Operations Instruction was not promulgated until 1972. And there is no suggestion from legislative history that Congress considered either the specific holding of the Board of Immigration Appeals in *Hira* in 1966, or *Hira*'s impact on other types of foreign labor performed in the United States.

The interpretation of a federal statute by the officials responsible for its administration is entitled to deference. A court, however, must reject an administrative interpretation "that [is] inconsistent with the statutory mandate or that frustrate[s] the policy that Congress sought to implement." * * *

Chevron Deference

The court concludes * * * that INS Operations Instruction 214.2(b)(5) violates sections 101(a)(15)(B) and 101(a)(15)(H)(ii) of the Act.

* * *

NOTES AND QUESTIONS

1.   Consider the hierarchy of the various "laws" relevant to this case: statute, then agency regulations, then the agency's internal operations instructions. The agency regulations must conform to the statute (no one in *Bricklayers Union* is claiming they do not) and the INS (now DHS) Operations Instructions in turn must conform to the regulations. See *Flores v. Bowen,* 790 F.2d 740, 742 (9th Cir.1986). A fortiori, the Operations Instructions must conform to the statute; in *Bricklayers Union* the court holds they do not.

2.   How a court interprets statutes reveals a great deal about the court's conception of its role and, in particular, its view of the allocation of power between judges and legislators. Over the years, three principal philosophies of statutory interpretation have competed for dominance:

The "Literal Plain Meaning Rule," as its name implies, focuses on the literal language of the statute. When that language admits of only one meaning, the court must adopt that meaning even if doing so will produce absurd results. (The Literal Plain Meaning Rule has no application to the case in which the statutory language is ambiguous.)

The "Social Purpose Rule" is at the other end of the spectrum. The court seeks out the purposes of the legislation and adopts whichever interpretation will best advance those purposes. To ascertain the purposes, the court has recourse to numerous sources. The statutory language itself is just one of those sources.

The "Golden Rule" is an intermediate approach. The court gives the literal language its ordinary meaning, *unless* doing so would produce an absurd result.

Which of these three approaches is followed in *Bricklayers Union*? Would the result have been different if one of the other approaches had been adopted?

3.   The meaning of a statutory provision can sometimes be gleaned from its interaction with other provisions of the same statute. When that is done, the court's approach is often described as "contextual" or "systematic." How does the court in *Bricklayers Union* derive meaning from the interaction of INA §§ 101(a)(15)(B) and 101(a)(15)(H)(ii)?

4.   The defendants identified competing economic policies that would be affected by the possible interpretations of section 101(a)(15)(B). How does the court know which policy Congress wanted to see prevail?

5.   What point is the court making in its discussion of the legislative history of the provision restricting the admission of foreign laborers? Even if the history reveals the purpose underlying previous statutes, how does

the court know Congress did not change its mind when it passed a new law in 1952?

6. Courts commonly say that the interpretation placed on a statute by the agency charged with administering it is entitled to judicial deference. But the scope of that principle is not at all clear. Many courts have accepted agency interpretations as long as those interpretations were "reasonable." Other courts have substituted their own statutory interpretations for those of the agencies even when the language was ambiguous enough that reasonable minds could differ. Why should courts defer at all to agency interpretation? And how does the court in *Bricklayers Union* apply the principle of agency deference?

7. Litigants will sometimes argue that Congress's failure to enact legislation expressly altering an accepted construction evidences acquiescence in that construction. What counter-arguments might generally be made? How does the court in *Bricklayers Union* handle the acquiescence argument?

8. Is *Hira* disapproved or distinguished?

9. B–1 visitors are ordinarily admitted for up to one year, with the possibility of multiple extensions in six-month increments. See 8 C.F.R. § 214.2(b)(1) (2004). On a reciprocal basis, however, nationals of some designated countries may be admitted for indefinite durations. See 54 Fed.Reg. 27969 (July 3, 1989).

10. A firestorm of protest followed the district court's decision. U.S. companies feared that difficulties in securing repairs of highly complex machinery would not only cause the eventual deterioration of products already purchased, but also choke off companies' access to future state-of-the-art equipment. Foreign governments threatened reciprocal action. Ultimately, the United States government and the union agreed, with the court's consent, to a more limited injunction. See 51 Fed.Reg. 44266 (Dec. 9, 1986); Austin T. Fragomen, Alfred J. Del Rey & Sam Bernsen (law firm), *Proper Standards for Admission in the B–1 Category*, 1990 Immigration & Nationality L.Rev. 363, 372. The resulting regulation provides:

> *Construction workers not admissible.* Aliens seeking to enter the country to perform building or construction work, whether on-site or in-plant, are not eligible for classification or admission as B–1 nonimmigrants under section 101(a)(15)(B) of the Act. However, alien nonimmigrants otherwise qualified as B–1 nonimmigrants may be issued visas and may enter for the purpose of supervision or training of others engaged in building or construction work, but not for the purpose of actually performing any such building or construction work themselves.

8 C.F.R. § 214.2(b)(5) (2004). The State Department, following suit, added analogous language to its visa regulations. See 22 C.F.R. § 41.31(b)(1) (2004).

a. Why does the new regulation exempt individuals who supervise or train those engaged in building or construction work? Are the policy considerations any different from those applicable to the workers who actually do the building or construction?

b.   Now is *Hira* still good law?

c.   As the court points out, the BIA has said that manual work may be "business" (and thus the basis for a B–1 visa) rather than "labor" (for which labor certification and an H–2 visa would be necessary) if the work is "a necessary incident to international trade or commerce." See also *Matter of Cote,* 17 I. & N. Dec. 336, 338 (BIA 1980). The cases applying that criterion have had to struggle to draw the line. See generally 2 Gordon, Mailman & Yale–Loehr § 14.05. The linedrawing problems continue to plague the State Department, which has developed more specific guidance for consular officers. See 78 IR 937 (June 4, 2001).

11.   In *Greyhound Lines v. INS*, Civ. No. 95–1608(NHJ) (D.D.C. Oct. 23, 1995), a district court held that Canadian citizens who drove Greyhound buses from Montreal to New York City were not entitled to B–1 visas if, en route, they picked up passengers in the United States and discharged some of those passengers at other stops in the United States. The court found that the intra-United States journeys, which accounted for about 30% of the passengers on the Montreal-to-New York route, were not necessary incidents to international trade. The BIA had reached an analogous conclusion in the context of transportation of goods, and neither the BIA nor the court saw any reason to treat the transportation of passengers differently.

12.   Although the procedures for obtaining B–1 and other visas are the subject of chapter 6 below, note for the moment that B–1 visitors from certain countries are exempted from having to procure visas before arriving in the United States. This visa waiver program, discussed on page 462 below, has been made stricter since September 11, 2001. The recent restrictions are discussed in chapter 10 (Immigration and National Security), section E.5.

PROBLEMS 1–3

Problem 1. X, a citizen and resident of Guatemala, owns a truck. To earn extra money, he would occasionally like to transport the products of various Guatemalan manufacturers from Guatemala to the United States. Should he be granted a B–1 visa? Does your answer change if, in addition to transporting goods from Guatemala to the United States, X also picks up goods at points in the United States that are en route to his ultimate destination and drops them off at intermediate points that are also en route?

Problem 2. Suppose X, instead of being an owner-operator, is an employee of a large Guatemalan trucking company. He will regularly drive the company's trucks back and forth between Guatemala and the United States, delivering and picking up goods. Is he entitled to a B–1 visa?

Problem 3. Y, a citizen and resident of Belgium, wants to come to the United States for two months to paint pictures of the Grand Canyon, which she would then bring home for sale (the pictures, not the Canyon). Should she be granted a B–1 visa? What if she plans to sell her paintings in the United States?

2.   TREATY TRADERS AND INVESTORS

Closely related to the B–1 business visitor are the two groups of nonimmigrants described in INA § 101(a)(15)(E), which you should read now. Individuals admitted under prong (i) have "E–1" status and are known colloquially as "treaty traders." Those admitted under prong (ii) have "E–2" status and are called "treaty investors."

Since the person must be "entitled to enter the United States under and in pursuance of the provisions of a treaty," the eligibility of a given individual rests ultimately on the terms of the particular treaty. In practice, however, the various treaties tend to track the statutory language. Thus, the best guides to the meanings of the treaties are the statute itself and other sources interpreting it. The latter sources include the views of the former INS, embodied in its regulations and Operations Instructions, and the State Department views, embodied in its regulations and in volume 9 of its Foreign Affairs Manual. There is also a fair amount of case law.

As of September 2004, according to the State Department, the United States had formally entered into such treaties with 77 countries. Of those, 4 provided only for treaty traders and 28 provided only for treaty investors; the rest provided for both. U.S. Dept. of State, 9 Foreign Affairs Manual § 41.51 Exh. I (Sept. 2004). For periodic updates that include additional useful information, see Eugene Flynn, *Countries Which the U.S. Recognizes as Eligible (or soon to be eligible) for E–1 or E–2 Status*. As Professor Flynn points out, the breakups of the former Soviet Union and Yugoslavia have generated several new treaties.

Both categories of E-entrants are ordinarily admitted for up to two years initially, with an unlimited number of possible two-year extensions. 8 C.F.R. § 214.2(e)(19, 20) (2004). Neither the statutory definition nor the regulations expressly require an intent *to retain one's foreign residence*. (Compare, in this regard, the statutory requirements for the B-nonimmigrants discussed earlier and the H–2 nonimmigrants who will be discussed later.) The regulations, however, do require an intent *to depart* upon termination of E-status. 8 C.F.R. § 214.2(e)(5); 22 C.F.R. §§ 41.51(a)(2) (traders), 41.51(b)(3) (investors) (2004). How does an intent to depart differ in practical terms from an intent not to abandon one's foreign residence? Is the government justified to read in either requirement?

As you will see in section F.1 below, an additional complication is "dual intent"—i.e., an intent to leave the United States by the expiration of one's lawful stay, coupled with a hope of acquiring lawful permanent residence. For the consequences of dual intent in the specific context of E-visas, see

Liam Schwartz, *E-Visa Classification: The Case for a Single Policy on Dual Intent*, 21 Immigration L. Today 691 (Nov. 2002).

INA § 101(a)(15)(E) also authorizes the admission of the spouses and children who are following or accompanying to join either E–1 or E–2 visitors. In 2002, Congress added new INA § 214(e)(6), which grants the spouses permission to work. Pub. L. 107–124, 115 Stat. 2402 (Jan. 16, 2002).

Nice v. Turnage

United States Court of Appeals, Ninth Circuit, 1985.
752 F.2d 431.

■ PER CURIAM:

Nice's application for a change in visa status from a "B–1 Visitor for Business" to an "E–2 Treaty Investor," was denied on the ground, among others, that he failed to prove he was the "source of funds" used to make the investment. We affirm.

INA § 101(a)(15)(E)(ii) requires an applicant for nonimmigrant treaty investor status to show "*he* has invested ... a substantial amount of capital." (Emphasis added.) INS asked Nice to explain the source of the funds he invested in the car wash. Nice proffered a $25,000 check drawn on a foreign bank signed by Nice's wife and used by Nice to make the investment. The Regional Commissioner noted several irregularities surrounding the check, including absence of proof of the identity of the principal who issued the power of attorney under which Mrs. Nice claimed to have acted in signing the check. The Commissioner concluded that Nice had failed to prove the funds invested were his own risk capital, and that the record suggested that in fact the investment had been made by Nice's father-in-law.

Nice argues that an alien can be required to establish the source of invested funds only if necessary to show that a "sham investment" is not involved. He relies on a statement in the Report of the House Committee that the treaty investor provision "is intended to provide for the temporary admission of such aliens who will be engaged in developing or directing the operations of a real operating enterprise *and not a fictitious paper operation.*" We have characterized the legislative history as "of little assistance" in determining qualifications for treaty investor status. Certainly the passing reference in the House Report does not provide a reasonable basis for limiting the broad statutory requirement that the alien demonstrate that "*he* has invested" substantial capital in a local enterprise.

Nice claims he need only show the funds are in his "possession and control." He relies on a portion of a 1977 State Department Circular Instruction stating that if an alien "can satisfactorily establish that he possessed and exercised dominion over the money invested, the manner in which it was originally acquired would be irrelevant." On its face, the Circular addresses only * * * an unrelated regulation not at issue here.

Moreover, other portions of the Circular indicate that the INS is expected to investigate the source of funds to determine whether the alien placed his own funds at risk.

Nice's interpretation of § 101(a)(15)(E)(ii) would permit wholesale evasion of immigration quotas through the treaty investor provision. An alien could claim nonimmigrant treaty investor status merely by acting as a "front" for an investment in fact made by a third party.

We conclude the district court correctly held that INS could require proof that Nice was personally at risk and did not abuse its discretion in concluding that the proof offered by Nice was insufficient.

AFFIRMED.

NOTES AND QUESTIONS

1. The court rejects the application of the 1977 State Department Circular, concluding it is relevant only to another, unrelated, regulation. In doing so, is the court disputing the rule that, if an individual "possessed and exercised dominion over the money invested, the manner in which it was originally acquired would be irrelevant?" Or is the court simply saying that that rule doesn't help Nice? Suppose Nice had proved that his father-in-law had given him the money, no strings attached. Would the result have been different? Should it be different? What does the court mean when it says that Nice's interpretation would permit a noncitizen to act as a "front" for a third party investor?

2. What, precisely, is the likely purpose of the treaty investor provision? Would that purpose be impeded if a noncitizen came to the United States to direct and develop an enterprise in which some other noncitizen had invested? Would there be affirmative costs?

3. One exception to the requirement that the investor be personally at risk is that, with some qualifications, certain managerial or other skilled nonimmigrants may enter as the employees of eligible treaty investors. See generally 2 Gordon, Mailman & Yale–Loehr, § 17.04.

4. The statute requires that the person invest "a substantial amount of capital." If you were the government attorney in charge of drafting guidelines on substantiality, would you employ a bright line test, or would you simply identify factors that should inform the determination? If the former, what test would you select? If the latter, what factors would you identify? See generally *Matter of Walsh & Pollard*, 20 I. & N.Dec. 60 (BIA 1988); see also 8 C.F.R. § 214.2(e)(14) (2004) (investment amount must be "substantial" in relation to total cost of enterprise, sufficient to ensure the investor's financial commitment, and large enough that the investor is likely to direct and develop the enterprise). The regulations add that the enterprise may not be "marginal." 8 C.F.R. § 214.2(e)(15) (2004).

5. An employee who seeks E–1 status to conduct trade for his or her foreign employer must either be in an executive/supervisory position or

have skills that are essential to the company's U.S. operations. 9 F.A.M. § 41.51, nn. 1.1(6) (Dec. 2003), 14.2 (Sept. 2003).

6. The treaty trader provision also requires "substantial" trade. For that purpose, the regulations now provide that the arrangement must contemplate ongoing activity, not an isolated transaction. 8 C.F.R. § 214.2(e)(10) (2004).

7. As you have probably figured out already, there is considerable overlap between the B–1 and the E–1 requirements. Examining the statutory language and the cases and text you have now read, try to identify the tactical pros and cons of applying for E–1 status versus B–1 status.

3. TEMPORARY WORKERS

"Man hat Arbeitskräfte gerufen, und es kommen Menschen." [We sought *workers*, and *human beings* came.] Max Frisch, Überfremdung I, in Schweiz als Heimat?, at 219 (1990).

As this quotation from a celebrated Swiss author suggests, the subject of temporary workers, or guest workers as they are commonly known in Europe, touches several raw nerves. Even with a clear initial understanding that the stay is meant to be temporary, roots inevitably form and deepen. Fundamental questions arise: Will there be a realistic opportunity to acquire lawful permanent residence down the road? If not, will the workers stay on anyway, in irregular status? If so, what will be the consequences? Will they be exploited, relative to either the norms of their host country or the norms of their countries of origin, during either the period of temporary lawful admission or thereafter? Are they filling a need that cannot be met by domestic workers at acceptable costs? What impact will the program have on the jobs, wages, and working conditions of domestic workers? The materials that follow touch on some of these questions. As discussed below, the questions are coming from several quarters, but a guestworker proposal floated by President Bush in January 2004 has added immediacy to the debate.

a. "SPECIALTY OCCUPATIONS," ATHLETES, AND ENTERTAINERS: H–1B's, O's, AND P's

Three categories of temporary workers—H–1B's, O's, and P's—are best considered together. Before going any further, you should read subsections H(i)(b), O, and P of INA § 101(a)(15).

INA § 101(a)(15)(H)(i)(b) is the principal vehicle for the admission of temporary professional workers. But the provision does not refer to "professionals."[3] Instead, subsection H(i)(b) requires that the person be "in a

---

3. Until the Immigration Act of 1990, H–1B status required "distinguished merit and ability." The Justice Department regulations defined that term to encompass "one who is a member of the professions or one who is prominent in his or her field …" 8 C.F.R. § 214.2(h)(3)(ii)(A), as amended by 55 Fed.Reg. 2606, 2622 (Jan. 26, 1990). The Department's definition of "the professions," see *id.*, was virtually identical to the wording

specialty occupation."[4] A "specialty occupation" is one that requires "theoretical and practical application of a body of highly specialized knowledge" and that, in the United States, requires at least a bachelor's degree in the particular specialty or the "equivalent" of a bachelor's degree. INA § 214(i)(1). Many of the more difficult issues have concerned those kinds of equivalency determinations. Apart from the various requirements that the occupation must meet in order to be a "specialty" occupation, the statute spells out the credentials that the individual must possess in order to be "in" that occupation. INA § 214(i)(2).

The H–1B nonimmigrant must be "coming temporarily to the United States." He or she may be admitted for up to six years. INA § 214(g)(4). As a result of free trade agreements with Chile and Singapore, a new "H–1B1" category exempts nationals of those two countries from the six-year durational limit and eases some other H–1B requirements as well. See Daniel C. Horne, *Requests for Evidence*, 8 BIB 1626 (Oct. 15, 2003).

The durational limit does not, however, bar H–1Bs from entering with the hope of attaining LPR status at some future time. Often a noncitizen's skills are needed in the United States now, and the person qualifies substantively for employment-based immigrant preference, but the waiting period for LPR status is too long for the employer or the employee. In such cases, the relatively short processing times for H–1B visas enable the person to begin work in the interim. Congress in 1990 expressly declared that a noncitizen's seeking of permanent resident status is not "evidence of an intention to abandon a foreign residence for purposes of obtaining" an H–1B visa (or an L-visa, discussed below). Imm.Act 1990, § 205(b)(2), adding INA § 214(h).[5] The subject of preexisting intent to remain is taken up more generally in section F.1 below.

Since 1990, certain groups of nonimmigrants who formerly had been eligible for H–1B status are diverted into separate categories. Agricultural workers, athletes, and entertainers are now generally ineligible for H–1B visas. Instead, they must normally apply for H–2A, O, or P status, the requirements for which are discussed below. As you will see shortly, those requirements are both more demanding and less demanding than the requirements for H–1B status.

---

now used to define "specialty occupation," below.

To avoid the problem of the person's six-year maximum work authorization running out while waiting for a decision on his or her application for LPR status, Congress in 2002 permitted yearly extensions of H1–B status, beginning one year after the person files either an application for labor certification or a visa petition (described in chapter 6). See Twenty–First Century Department of Justice Appropriations Authorization Act, Pub. L. 107–273, 116 Stat. 1758, 1836–37, § 11030A (Nov. 2, 2002).

4. Besides members in specialty occupations, subsection H(i)(b) also includes fashion models "of distinguished merit and ability."

5. The wording of that provision of the 1990 Act is odd, since the same statute eliminated the requirement that an H–1B have "a residence in a foreign country which he has no intention of abandoning." Imm.Act 1990, § 205(e). Perhaps Congress meant to say that the seeking of permanent resident status does not destroy the requirement (which the 1990 Act retained) that the H–1B nonimmigrant be "coming temporarily." INA § 101(a)(15)(H)(i)(b).

In an H–1B case, the employer must file a "labor condition application" (LCA) with the Department of Labor. See INA §§ 101(a)(15)(H)(i)(b), 212(n). In the LCA the employer attests to several things, including (i) it is paying at least the prevailing wage level in the area of employment or the actual wage level at the place of employment, whichever is greater; (ii) the working conditions of similarly employed workers will not be adversely affected; (iii) there is not a strike or lockout; and (iv) the employer has notified its existing employees of the filing, in specified ways (so that they can object if they wish). See generally Carl M. Shusterman & David L. Neal, *Survey and Analysis of H–1B Labor Condition Application Decisions*, 72 IR 49 (Jan. 9, 1995).

Normally, the Labor Department's Employment and Training Administration (ETA) provides the necessary certification unless the LCA is "incomplete or obviously inaccurate." Complaints may be filed with the Department's Wage and Hour Division (WHD), which investigates those cases that it believes warrant investigation. WHD then issues a "determination" letter that states whether it has found a violation and, if so, the penalty. The penalty can include fines, back pay, and in certain cases an order making the employer ineligible to file LCA's, employment-based visa petitions, and certain nonimmigrant visa petitions for a prescribed time period. Any interested party may appeal the WHD's determination to an administrative law judge, then to the Secretary of Labor, and eventually to a federal court. See INA § 212(n); Ted J. Chiappari, *Survey of Labor Condition Application Enforcement Proceedings*, 73 IR 673 (May 20, 1996).

One of the more difficult and controversial LCA issues has been the method for computing the required wage. This problem is expertly analyzed in Margaret H. McCormick & David Stanton, *Finding the Correct Wage for LCAs: Recent Developments in H–1B Practice*, April 1995 Immigration Briefings, and in Ted J. Chiappari, *LCA Wage Regulations: A Can of Worms for the Employer to Open*, 72 IR 1437 (Oct. 23, 1995).

The best approach for the employer, of course, is meticulous compliance that will prevent violations at the outset. On that score, two knowledgeable observers recommend self-audits. For detailed suggestions as to the elements of such self-audits, see the two-part article by Angelo A. Paparelli & J. Ira Burkemper, *Skeletons in the Closet: LCA Audits in the Age of H–1B Uncertainty*, 73 IR 745 (June 3, 1996), 781 (June 10, 1996).

Over the years, the Labor Department, trade unions, and others have worried that H–1B petitions generally, and LCA's in particular, are being abused. Following a 1996 audit, the Inspector General of the Labor Department severely criticized the LCA program (and also the permanent labor certification program that you saw in chapter 3) as paper shuffles that do not adequately protect American workers. More specifically, the Inspector General concluded that many employers were abusing the process by not paying H–1B's the advertised prevailing wage. See generally 73 IR 653 (May 13, 1996). Others have taken strong issue with those findings, questioning the accuracy of the results, the auditors' motives, and their understanding of the congressional objectives. See, e.g., Stuart Anderson,

Widespread Abuse of H–1Bs and Employment–Based Immigration? The Evidence Says Otherwise, 73 IR 637 (May 13, 1996); see also Demetrios G. Papademetriou & Stephen Yale–Loehr, Balancing Interests: Rethinking U.S. Selection of Skilled Immigrants 175–79 (1996)(excerpted in chapter 3 above).

Until 1990 there were no numerical limits on any groups of nonimmigrants. In that year, Congress limited the annual admissions of H–1B nonimmigrants to 65,000 (not counting their spouses and children). INA § 214(g)(1, 2). In the late 1990s, however, an economic boom—particularly in the information technology sector—generated increasing demand for professional workers. To meet their needs, employers came to rely increasingly on foreign workers. The caps on H–1Bs were becoming a major source of frustration. In response, Congress passed the American Competitiveness and Workforce Improvement Act of 1998, Pub. L. 105–277, 112 Stat. 2681 (Oct. 21, 1998). Among other things, the Act provided temporary relief, increasing the H1–B caps to 115,000 in each of the fiscal years 1999 and 2000, and to 107,500 in fiscal year 2001. The caps were to revert to 65,000 starting in fiscal year 2002. *Id.*, Div. C, § 411, amending INA § 214(g)(1)(A). But in 2000, when even the increased caps proved insufficient to accommodate the demand for professional workers, Congress passed the American Competitiveness in the Twenty–First Century Act of 2000, Pub. L. 106–313, 114 Stat. 1251 (Oct. 17, 2000). This statute further amended INA § 214(g)(1)(A) by increasing the H1–B caps to 195,000 for each of the fiscal years 2001, 2002, and 2003 and exempting higher education institutions and nonprofit and governmental research institutions from the caps.

The ink was barely dry on the 2000 law when an economic slowdown produced large layoffs of professional workers generally and foreign workers in particular. Starting in fiscal year 2004, therefore, Congress allowed the annual ceiling for H–1B workers to revert to the original 65,000 cap. In fiscal year 2004 the cap was reached in less than five months, 81 IR 246 (Feb. 23, 2004), and in fiscal year 2005 it was reached on the very first day, USCIS Press Release (Oct. 1, 2004). (For fiscal year 2005 the cap was further reduced by 6800 visas that had been set aside for the new H–1B1 programs under the free trade agreements with Chile and Singapore noted above. Thus the actual cap was 58,200. *Id.*) The procedures by which those who were disqualified by the cap (and first-time applicants) may apply or re-apply for the next fiscal year are described in a USCIS Notice, 69 Fed. Reg. 68154 (Nov. 23, 2004). As partial relief, Congress in December 2004 authorized an additional 20,000 H–1B visas per year for noncitizens who hold masters' degrees or higher from U.S. institutions of higher learning, effective March 2005. See Consolidated Appropriations Act, Pub. L. 108–447, 118 Stat. 2809, 3356, Div. J, § 425(a) (Dec. 8, 2004), adding INA § 214(g)(5)(C); 70 Fed.Reg. 23375 (May 5, 2005) (interim implementing regulations). For some creative suggestions for living with the H–1B cap, see William A. Stock, *So, Now What? A Lighthearted Look at Strategies for Dealing with the H–1B Cap*, 10 BIB 471 (Mar. 15, 2005).

The strategies of the 1998 and 2000 statutes were to link the temporary numerical increases to more enduring reforms targeted at the root causes of the labor shortfall. Both laws followed heated debates over whether the increased numbers of foreign workers were really needed or were merely an industry device to intensify job competition and thereby reduce wages. The compromises included several new innovations. Congress imposed a $500 fee on employer H–1B petitions (again exempting higher education and nonprofit and government institutions) and subsequently increased the fee to $1000, the proceeds to be allocated mainly to job training programs for U.S. workers. See Pub. L. 106–311, 114 Stat. 1247 (Oct. 17, 2000). Firms adjudged to be "H–1B-dependent" under a formula that takes account of the total number of employees and the percentage who are H–1Bs are subjected to more rigorous requirements when filing their labor condition applications. And, to diminish the opportunity for employer exploitation, Congress added a "portability" provision that made it easier for H1–Bs to change jobs after their arrival. See INA § 214(n). For more detail, see H. Ronald Klasko, *American Competitiveness in the 21st Century: H1–Bs and Much More*, 77 IR 1689 (Dec. 11, 2000). Some commentators have urged the repeal of the H1–B cap. See, e.g., Suzette Brooks Masters & Ted Ruthizer, *The H1–B Straitjacket: Why Congress Should Repeal the Cap on Foreign–Born Highly Skilled Workers*, Immigration Briefings (May 2000); see also Enid Trucios–Haynes, *Temporary Workers and Future Immigration Policy Conflicts: Protecting U.S. Workers and Satisfying the Demand for Global Human Capital*, 40 Univ. Louisville Brandeis L.J. 967 (2002). Analogous issues in Australia and Germany are discussed, respectively, in Mary E. Crock, *Contract or Compact: Skilled Migration and the Dictates of Politics and Ideology*, 16 Georgetown Immigration L.J. 133 (2001); Kay Hailbronner, *Labour Transfer Schemes—In Whose National Interest? Globalisation and the Transfer of Labour—The European Experience*, 16 Georgetown Immigration L.J. 773 (2002).

As noted earlier, consideration of H–1B's must take into account several nonimmigrant categories created by the Immigration Act of 1990. One of them is INA § 101(a)(15)(O). The O-category covers athletes, entertainers, persons in the other arts, the sciences, education, and business. In any of those fields, the O-nonimmigrant must have "extraordinary ability * * * which has been demonstrated by sustained national or international acclaim"—the same standard used to judge immigrants under the employment-based first preference. The O-category also covers certain members of the principal nonimmigrant's support staff and certain family members of either the principal or the support staff. Initial admission under the O-category may be for a period of up to three years, with possible one-year extensions. See 8 C.F.R. §§ 214.2(*o*)(6)(iii), 214.2(*o*)(12)(ii) (2004).

The P-category covers, in its first subsection, internationally recognized (but not necessarily "extraordinary") athletes, and members of internationally recognized entertainment groups performing in specific events. Nonimmigrants in that first subsection are denominated P–1's. Other subsections take in artists and entertainers who enter under reciprocal exchange programs (the P–2's), or entertainers or artists who would provide programs that are "culturally unique" (the P–3's). Unlike H–1B's, neither O's nor P's are numerically limited. P–1 individual athletes may be admitted initially for up to five years, and extended for up to five additional years. 8 C.F.R. §§ 214.2(p)(8)(iii)(A), 214.2(p)(14)(ii)(A) (2004). For all other P-entrants (including athletic team members and entertainers), initial admission is for up to one year and extensions are in one-year increments. 8 C.F.R. §§ 214.2(p)(8)(iii), 214.2(p)(14)(ii)(B) (2004).

Finally, Congress from time to time has passed special legislation addressing periodic shortages of nurses. See, e.g., the Nursing Relief for Disadvantaged Areas Act of 1999, Pub. L. 106–95, 113 Stat. 1312 (Nov. 12, 1999); INA §§ 101(a)(15)(H)(i)(c), 212(m).

b. LESSER SKILLS AND LABOR SHORTAGES: H–2's

An "H–2" nonimmigrant comes to the United States "(a) * * * to perform agricultural labor or services * * * of a temporary or seasonal nature, or (b) * * * to perform other temporary service or labor if unemployed persons capable of performing such service or labor cannot be found in this country [except for foreign medical school graduates coming to perform professional medical services]." Under both prongs of H–2, the person must have "a residence in a foreign country which he has no intention of abandoning" and must be "coming temporarily to the United States."

Clause (a), pertaining to temporary agricultural laborers, was one of the major reforms enacted in 1986. But its roots are much deeper. As early as 1942, when U.S. labor was in short supply because of the war, the United States and Mexico began creating "bracero" programs to import temporary Mexican farmworkers. See, e.g., Michael A. Olivas, *The Chronicles, My Grandfather's Stories, and Immigration Law: The Slave Traders Chronicle as Racial History,* 34 St. Louis Univ. L.J. 425, 435–39 (1990); *cf.* Juan R. Garcia, Operation Wetback, The Mass Deportation of Mexican Undocumented Workers in 1954 (1980). In the aftermath of the Bracero programs, approximately one million persons of Mexican ancestry—including some United States citizens—were "repatriated" to Mexico. See generally Francisco E. Balderrama & Raymond Rodríguez, Decade of Betrayal: Mexican Repatriation in the 1930s (1995); Kevin R. Johnson, *International Human Rights Class Actions: New Frontiers for Group Litigation,* 2004 Michigan State L. Rev. 643, 661–70. Professor Gilbert Carrasco discusses the abuses inflicted on Braceros and the general historical patterns of treating Mexican workers as disposable. Gilbert Paul Carrasco, *Latinos in the United States—Invitation and Exile,* in Juan F. Perea (ed.), Immigrants Out! The New Nativism and the Anti–Immigrant Impulse in the United States, at 190 et seq. (1997).

Until 1986, the admission of temporary agricultural workers was governed by the general provision applicable to other temporary workers— the provision now designated as section 101(a)(15)(H)(ii)(b), discussed below. That provision was seldom used in agriculture. Growers argued that the procedure associated with this general provision was too time-consuming to permit the harvesting of perishable crops. In practice, therefore, foreign agricultural laborers tended overwhelmingly to be undocumented. The prospect of punishing employers of undocumented immigrants (see chapter 12, section B, below) raised fears among growers that this supply of foreign labor would dry up.

In 1986, therefore, Congress created a new "H–2A" status, INA § 101(a)(15)(H)(ii)(a), and streamlined the procedures, *id.* § 218. As was true before, the employer must still obtain from the Labor Department a certification that sufficient American workers cannot be found and that the nonimmigrant's employment will not "adversely affect the wages and working conditions" of American workers. *Id.* § 218(a). For the latter purpose the Labor Department annually publishes "adverse effect wage rates" (AEWR's) that vary from state to state. These are the minimum hourly rates that employers must pay H–2A farmworkers. The rates vary from state to state and are updated annually. For fiscal year 2005, the minimum required hourly wage ranged from $7.63 (Arizona and New Mexico) to $9.75 (Hawaii). 70 Fed. Reg. 10152 (Mar. 2, 2005).

Agricultural guest workers are controversial. They can supply needed farm labor at wages that enable growers to keep prices down for consumers. Moreover, whether or not their wages are low by American standards, they are generally higher than what the same individuals would receive in their countries of origin. The dangers, however, are considerable. They include exploitation of the guestworkers not only through low wages, but also through oppressive working conditions; the corresponding impact on the wages and working conditions of the domestic labor force; the potential for practical restrictions on guestworkers' economic freedom; and the likelihood of guestworkers staying on in unlawful status. For those reasons, and also because of a general skepticism about the growers' claims that domestic farm labor is in short supply, the U.S. Commission on Immigration Reform counseled caution. Legal Immigration: Setting Priorities 172–73 (1995); see also Philip Martin, *Does the U.S. Need a New Bracero Program?*, 9 J. Internat'l L. & Policy 127 (2003)(expressing additional concerns with recent guestworker proposals). For some good descriptions of the present program, see Guadalupe Luna, *"Agricultural Underdogs" and International Agreements: The Legal Context of Agricultural Workers within the Rural Economy*, 26 New Mexico L. Rev. 9 (1996) (proposing international agreements to protect farmworkers); Maurice A. Roberts & Stephen Yale–Loehr, Understanding the 1986 Immigration Law, ch. 4, §§ 1, 2 (1986); Stephen Yale–Loehr, *Foreign Farm Workers in the U.S.: The Impact of the Immigration Reform and Control Act of 1986*, 15 N.Y.U. Rev. of L. & Social Change 333, 335–46 (1986–87).

The exploitation issues are highlighted in the excerpt that follows:

David Bacon, Be Our Guests

The Nation (Sept. 27, 2004).
Pages 22–26.

Julio Cesar Guerrero came north from Mexico in the spring of 2001 as a temporary contract worker. Recruited by Manpower of the Americas, he was sent to North Carolina, where he began working on the tobacco farm of Anthony Smith. After a few weeks, his fingers started to hurt, and then, one by one, his fingernails began falling off. Although Smith told him he couldn't see a doctor, he went anyway. The doctor said his problem was possibly caused by working without gloves in fields sprayed with pesticides. So Guerrero, who was employed through the H2–A federal guest worker program, called Legal Aid of North Carolina. But Smith warned him not to talk with legal workers.

Guerrero returned to Mexico at the end of the season. The next year, when he tried to get another job, he found his name on a blacklist maintained by MOA and the North Carolina Growers Association (NCGA). Legal Aid protested, and as a result, Guerrero was sent to the United States again. That year, he worked for grower Rodney Jackson, who kept the workers' drinking water on a moving truck in the fields, forcing them to run after it with their mouths under the spigot. When Guerrero filed a complaint with the Occupational Safety and Health Administration, Jackson gave a warning notice and asked him to sign it. When Guerrero refused, Jackson fired him. A foreman took him to the bus station, telling him to go back to Mexico. Again Legal Aid intervened and got him assigned to another grower. Soon a growers' association representative gave Guerrero another warning notice, which he again refused to sign.

When the 2003 season began, Guerrero tried once more to sign up with MOA, but the recruiter told him that he'd already been given a second chance. Since he'd continued to make complaints, his name stayed on the blacklist.

Guerrero had had enough. In 2004 he became a plaintiff in a racketeering suit filed on April 13 in Wake County Superior Court, by Legal Aid of North Carolina, charging the NCGA with maintaining an illegal blacklist.

* * *

Andrew McGuffin, staff attorney for Legal Aid of North Carolina, cautions, "the problem isn't that we don't have worker protection laws. It's that with guest workers they're not enforced, and when workers try to use these laws, they're blacklisted."

The growers, through NCGA, and Legal Aid have been squaring off for years. The growers' handbook warns workers not to talk to Legal Aid staff, calling them "enemies of the H2–A program" who are "trying to eliminate your job." The handbook also warns workers that any effort to "deliberately restrict production" or to "work slowly" will result in discipline or termination. Strikes or slowdowns are prohibited.

Last September a foreman for grower Chester Pilson informed guest worker Juan Villarreal Abundiz that there was no more work for him because he'd talked with Legal Aid, and an NCGA rep told him he'd probably be denied a job the following season. Villarreal was brought to the association office in Vass, North Carolina—a huge barn with a balcony along one side. As 200 workers gathered below, a foreman named Santos and an NCGA employee addressed them from the balcony, instructing them to take Legal Aid's pink "know your rights" booklets out of their luggage and throw them in a trash can in the middle of the floor. According to Villarreal, NCGA head Stan Eury and his assistants gave him a paper he couldn't read and told him if he didn't sign it, he'd have to pay his own bus fare back to Mexico. Villarreal signed.

The blacklist is not secret. The handbook calls it a "record of eligibility [that] contains a list of workers, who because of violations of their contract, have been suspended from the program." Although the handbook says no one will be disciplined for reporting violations of their rights, in fact that happens all the time.

The US Department of Labor, which certifies employers for the H2–A program, has never taken action to end the practice. * * *

The 1997 list, called the "1997 NCGA Ineligible for Rehire Report," consists of 1,709 names. The reason for ineligibility is most often listed as abandoning a job or voluntary resignation. Legal Aid charges that when workers are fired for complaining, they're given a paper to sign saying they quit voluntarily. Among the hundreds of names are also many whose reason for ineligibility is given as "mother sick," "death in the family," "lazy," "slow," "work hours too long," "work too hot and hard" or "slowing up other workers." In 2003 the list for just one Mexican state, Durango, had 517 names.

Abuse of the H2–A program isn't limited to North Carolina. The most spectacular suppression of guest workers' rights came on November 21, 1986, when Caribbean cane cutters stopped work on the Fanjul family sugar plantation in south Florida. When the Fanjuls tried to pay a rate lower than what the workers considered fair, 384 cutters refused to leave their labor camp. The company called in the cops, who used guns, batons and dogs to force workers onto buses, some in their underwear. They were taken to Miami and repatriated.

* * *

Guest workers in Canada, who work under a program like H2–A, have had similar experiences. On April 25, 2001, Mexicans laboring in Mastron Enterprises' tomato greenhouses in Leamington, Ontario, stopped work over complaints of abuse by a foreman. The day following the protest, about twenty-four were repatriated.

Other workers told representatives of the United Farm Workers that they had been working twelve-hour days, six and a half days a week, without overtime pay, for $7 an hour. * * * "They think we're animals. The first threat that they always make is that if you don't like it, you can go back to Mexico." Chris Ramsaroop of Justicia for Migrant Workers observes, "To change their situation migrants must be guaranteed the right to form unions, the right to social and economic mobility in Canada, and most important, the right to regularization: Workers must have the right to apply for citizenship in Canada."

If Canadian guest workers can't get rights like these, in a country where labor rights are more vigilantly enforced, how likely is it that US guest workers will fare better?

According to the AFL–CIO, workers are routinely fired in 31 percent of all US union organizing drives. Most then face, in addition, disqualification from unemployment benefits as a result of the bogus claims that accompany such terminations. For guest workers, however, just being without a job violates the conditions for their visas, and makes them subject to immediate deportation.

In addition, they're strangers. It's much more difficult for them to find support from unions, legal aid workers or other community institutions. Jorge, a guest worker from Huehuetenango in Guatemala (who didn't want his real name used for fear of the blacklist), explained that when he was cheated on his wages "we didn't protest because we couldn't. We were far away from the company office," he said, "and maybe the next year they wouldn't give us the chance to go [to the US again]."

For Fernando Rodriguez Aguilar, even getting help from a priest was forbidden. Rodriguez was brought to North Carolina in 2002 to work for tobacco grower Jeffrey Lee in rural Johnston County. When he saw the crew leader selling alcoholic beverages in the fields, and cutting the hours of workers who wouldn't buy them, he complained to Father Tony Rojas. Then NCGA representative Jose Luis told him he shouldn't go to Father Tony's church. "If you keep going, you'll have problems," he threatened. Sure enough, the following season, MOA put Rodriguez on the blacklist.

––––––––

Outside the realm of agriculture, temporary workers receive what is now called "H–2B" status. H–2B's are initially admitted for up to a year; they may receive one-year extensions, up to a total stay of three years. 8 C.F.R. §§ 214.2(h)(9)(iii)(B), 214.2(h)(15)(ii)(C) (2004). Unlike the H–1's, the H–2B's until 2005 first had to apply for labor certification; after all, the whole point of section 101(a)(15)(H)(ii) is to enable employers to fill jobs for which labor is in short supply. Recall the *Bricklayers* litigation, in which the problem lay in determining whether the nonimmigrants in question were H–2's who had to apply for labor certification or business visitors (B–1's) who did not. In 2005, however, the Labor Department and USCIS issued proposed rules to replace H–2B labor certifications with the same kinds of labor attestations required for H–1Bs. The employer need not provide supporting documentation unless it is audited. For the details, see 70 Fed. Reg. 3984 (Jan. 27, 2005) (USCIS); 70 Fed. Reg. 3993 (Jan. 27, 2005) (ETA).

No more than 66,000 H–2B's may be admitted in any one fiscal year. INA § 214(g)(1)(B). Exempt from that ceiling are the worker's family members, INA § 214(g)(2), and, as a result of REAL ID Act § 402(a), anyone who was granted H–2B status in the preceding three years, INA § 214(g)(9)(A). No more than 33,000 of the 66,000 workers subject to the ceiling may be admitted during the first half of any fiscal year. INA § 214(g)(10), added by REAL ID Act, § 405.

In case you noticed the much higher figure in the nonimmigrant admissions chart on pages 346–47 above and are wondering how that can be, the answer is that that chart reflects the multiple admissions of many of the same individuals. In fact, the H–2B cap was reached about five months into fiscal year 2004, USCIS Public Notice (Dec. 13, 2004), and about three months into fiscal year 2005, 10 BIB 101 (Feb. 1, 2005).

Professor Howard Chang has identified the liberal paradox that policies on guest workers must somehow address. Americans receive the benefits of their cheap labor but, because there is no provision for eventually adjusting to LPR status, the American beneficiaries of that labor bear little or no cost for welfare expenditures. The potential for exploitation is therefore a concern. Yet, he suggests, guest workers might still be better off if allowed to come than if not allowed to come. Howard F. Chang, *Liberal Ideals and Political Feasibility: Guest–Worker Programs as Second–Best Policies*, 27 North Carolina J. Internat'l & Commercial Regulation 465 (2002). He ultimately advocates a cosmopolitan policy of liberal admission of guest workers combined with conferral of social benefits. See Howard F. Chang, *The Immigration Paradox: Poverty, Distributive Justice, and Liberal Egalitarianism*, 52 DePaul L. Rev. 759 (2003).

During the year 2000, the growing political strength of the United States Latino population, the popularity of Mexican President Vicente Fox, and support from American industry all combined to produce high-level negotiations aimed at linking a new temporary worker program for Mexican (and possibly other) nationals to a delayed legalization program. See Joint Statement of U.S.-Mexico High–Level Working Group on Migration (Apr. 4, 2001), digested in 78 IR at 642–43 (Apr. 9, 2001) (placing temporary worker program for Mexican nationals on agenda). The September 11, 2001 terrorist attacks brought the process to a temporary halt. In January 2004, however, President Bush announced he would propose an ambitious guest worker program, albeit without any provisions for eventual adjustment to permanent resident status. The details were not spelled out. The announcement has generated vigorous debate, but at this writing the future of the guest worker proposal is highly uncertain.

Under current law, the H2–B must be coming "to perform * * * temporary service or labor." The following case illustrates one of the more difficult problems:

Matter of Artee Corporation

Commissioner of the I.N.S., 1982.
18 I. & N. Dec. 366.

This case is before the Commissioner on certification of the Regional Commissioner's decision of June 2, 1982.

The petitioner is seeking to classify the beneficiaries under section 101(a)(15)(H)(ii) of the Act, as machinists. The petitioner provides temporary help to technically-oriented firms.

The sole issue in this case is the temporary need of the petitioner for the services of the beneficiary. * * * The petitioner in this case is a temporary help service and I agree with the Regional Commissioner that it qualifies as a petitioner and is the actual employer of the beneficiaries. The Regional Commissioner found that, because of the current wide-spread shortage of machinists in the United States, the nature of the employment offered must be viewed as permanent and not temporary. The decision examined the use of the beneficiaries' services by the customer of the help service in reaching this conclusion. I do not believe that this is the proper view of the employment situation involved. The test of the true nature of the temporary need for the position lies in examination of the temporary need of the temporary help service, not its customers.

Section 101(a)(15)(H)(ii) defines an H–2 temporary worker as an alien "who is coming temporarily to the United States to perform temporary services or labor, if unemployed persons capable of performing such services or labor cannot be found in this country ..." As noted in *Matter of Contopoulos,* 10 I. & N. Dec. 654, 657 (Acting R.C.1964), "... both the coming to the United States and the performance of service or labor must be *temporary,* the term 'temporary' being used twice." The nature of the duties to be performed were controlling, not the intent of the petitioner and the beneficiary concerning the time that the individual beneficiary would be employed in that position.

The Service now views this interpretation as incorrect. It is not the nature or the duties of the position which must be examined to determine the temporary need. It is the nature of the need for the duties to be performed which determines the temporariness of the position. Under this interpretation the key question in *Contopoulos* is: "Can the petitioner credibly establish that she has not employed a mother's helper in the past and that her need for a mother's helper will end in the near, definable future?" Likewise, in the instant case, the primary question becomes: "Can Artee establish that they have not employed machinists in the past and will not need the services of machinists in the near, definable future?" Here, as in *Contopoulos,* we are considering the second temporary requirement of the statute which concerns the position itself and not the first requirement which relates to the intent of the alien to enter for a temporary period. The function of a temporary help service is to provide for the fluctuating needs of other enterprises for specified services. In this case the petitioner provides technically-oriented personnel of a skilled nature to industries requiring such services. The customers of the petitioner do not have a steady need for a specific number of employees. Their business fluctuates and in so changing, their personnel needs change. To meet their needs, the customers of the petitioner turn to the petitioner to provide temporary help. While it is true that the temporary help may be needed for periods of

2 to 3 years, it is also true that shorter periods can be involved and that the need of the customer may not continue.

The situation of a temporary help service differs, however. The business of a temporary help service is to meet the temporary needs of its clients. To do this they must have a *permanent* cadre of employees available to refer to their customers for the jobs for which there is frequently or generally a demand. By the very nature of this arrangement, it is obvious that a temporary help service will maintain on its payroll, more or less continuously, the types of skilled employee most in demand. This does not mean that a temporary help service can never offer employment of a temporary nature. If there is no demand for a particular type of skill, the temporary help service does not have a continuing and permanent need. Thus a temporary help service may be able to demonstrate that in addition to its regularly employed workers and permanent staff needs it also hires workers for temporary positions. For a temporary help service company, temporary positions would include positions requiring skill for which the company has a non-recurring demand or infrequent demand.

There is currently a wide-spread shortage of skilled machinists in the United States. Because of this shortage, the petitioner, as a prudent business measure, has ensured that it can supply machinists to its customers. Its need to supply machinists to its customers is ongoing. Therefore, as long as this universal shortage of machinists exists, the nature of the need for the position with the petitioner is such that the duties are not temporary and will persist as long as the shortage.

* * *

ORDER: The petition is denied.

NOTES AND QUESTIONS

1. In the *Contopoulos* case that the Commissioner disapproves, an LPR who wished to work on a two-year research project needed day care and Greek language instruction for her children during that period. She petitioned the former INS to grant H–2 status to a particular noncitizen for that purpose. The INS did not dispute that both the petitioner and the noncitizen beneficiary intended that the beneficiary's employment would end after two years. The INS nonetheless denied the petition. It reasoned that the duties in question—the care and rearing of children—would continue to exist when the employment was over. The fact that in two years the mother would be performing those duties herself rather than employing someone else was held to be irrelevant.

The Commissioner in *Artee* rejects the *Contopoulos* distinction in favor of a different distinction. Together, the two formulations suggest three possible interpretations that *could* be placed on the phrase "perform temporary services or labor": the *Contopoulos* view, the *Artee* view, and the petitioner's view that was rejected in *Artee*. Before going further, make sure you can articulate all three possibilities.

2. How would Ms. Contopoulos have fared under the *Artee* test?

3. Is the literal statutory language "plain," or does it permit more than one of the competing interpretations?

4. The operative phrase is "perform temporary services or labor." Would it have made any difference if Congress had said "temporarily" instead of "temporary?"

5. Assume that the permanent business of the Artee Corporation is to hire foreign machinists under one-year, nonrenewable contracts, and to farm out those employees to various manufacturers during that year. Assume also that Artee has a track record of the employment actually ending after one year as agreed. Assume, finally, that there are not enough American machinists to fill this need.

On those assumptions, what policies would be furthered by the Commissioner's interpretation? What policies would be impeded?

6. The Commissioner concedes that "If there is no demand for a particular type of skill, the temporary help service does not have a continuing and permanent need." In such a situation, however, wouldn't the noncitizen lose for failure to prove that "unemployed persons capable of performing such service or labor cannot be found in this country?" The point extends beyond the specific context of temporary help companies: How can *anyone* acquire H–2B status in the light of *Artee*? If there are sufficient American workers, won't the person lose on that ground? And if the mere *absence* of sufficient American workers enables the government to conclude that the employer's needs are permanent, doesn't the person lose on that ground? The Commissioner, seemingly aware of that paradox, left open a narrow window: "positions requiring skill for which the company has a non-recurring demand or infrequent demand." Is that really all Congress meant to accomplish when it enacted this provision?

On the other hand, would a contrary interpretation—one requiring only that the employment of the particular noncitizen be temporary—render superfluous the phrase "coming temporarily to the United States?" (Probably not—but can you figure out why?)

7. Several courts have followed *Artee*. See, e.g., *Seven Star, Inc. v. United States*, 873 F.2d 225 (9th Cir.1989); *Sussex Engineering, Ltd. v. Montgomery*, 825 F.2d 1084 (6th Cir.1987) and cases cited *id.* at 1089 n.4. The regulations now codify *Artee*. They provide:

> Temporary services or labor under the H–2B classification refers to any job in which the petitioner's need for the duties to be performed by the employee(s) is temporary, whether or not the underlying job can be described as permanent or temporary.

8 C.F.R. § 214.2(h)(6)(ii)(A) (2004); see also U.S. Dept. of Labor, General Administration Letter No. G.A.L. 1–95, § II.A (Nov. 10, 1994), reproduced in 72 IR at 107–13 (Jan. 13, 1995).

The relevant agencies have identified four situations in which the employer's needs for the duties will be found to be temporary–one-time occurrences, seasonal needs, peakload needs, and intermittent needs. For more detail, see 8 C.F.R. § 214.2(h)(6)(ii)(B) (2004); G.A.L. No. 1–95, above, § II.B.

8.   As a result of 1970 legislation, the H–1 provision does *not* contain language analogous to the "perform temporary services or labor" requirement. The H–1 must be coming to the United States temporarily, but the services to be performed need not be temporary. *Matter of Ord,* 18 I. & N. Dec. 285 (Regional Comm'r 1982). If the beneficiaries in *Artee* had had college degrees, might they have been able to obtain admission?

c.   TRAINEES: H–3's

The H–3 must be a person who has "a residence in a foreign country which he has no intention of abandoning who is coming temporarily to the United States as a trainee." INA § 101(a)(15)(H)(iii). Graduate medical training is excluded, and the training program may not be one "designed primarily to provide productive employment." *Id.*

The H–3 program is tightly regulated to prevent its misuse as a vehicle for obtaining ordinary workers. See generally 8 C.F.R. § 214.2(h)(7) (2004). An H–3 trainee may generally be initially admitted for (or granted extensions of stay up to a total of) two years. See 8 C.F.R. §§ 214.2(h)(9)(iii)(C)(1), 214.2(h)(15)(ii)(D) (2004).

d.   MISCELLANEOUS OTHER TEMPORARY WORKERS

The statute recognizes a few other categories of occupational nonimmigrants—crew members of foreign vessels and aircrafts, INA § 101(a)(15)(D); foreign journalists, *id.* § 101(a)(15)(I); official representatives of foreign governments and international organizations, *id.* § 101(a)(15)(A, G); and religious workers, *id.* § 101(a)(15)(R); see generally Enid Trucios–Haynes, *Religion and the Immigration and Nationality Act: Using Old Saws on New Bones,* 9 Georgetown Immigration L.J. 1 (1995).

Another relatively new classification is INA § 101(a)(15)(Q), added by Imm. Act 1990, § 208. It is for the person who participates in

an international cultural exchange program approved by the Attorney General for the purpose of providing practical training, *employment,* and the sharing of the history, culture and traditions of the country of the alien's nationality (emphasis added).

There are some other requirements as well. INA § 101(a)(15)(Q). The authorized period of admission is limited to fifteen months. 8 C.F.R. § 214.2(q)(7)(iii) (2004).

This provision reflects the lobbying efforts of the Walt Disney organization, which envisioned the use of these Q-visas for foreign youth who might wish to come to the United States for short periods to work at Disneyland or Disney World. On Capitol Hill, the program was quickly dubbed the "Disney" provision. Since there is no requirement that qualified domestic workers be unavailable (an omission consistent with the congressional purpose of fostering cultural exchanges), since there is no quota on Q-visas, and since a wide range of programs would fit the broad statutory definition, the Q-category carries the potential for widespread use. To prevent its use as a back door for ordinary employment, the regulations say that the "work component must serve as the vehicle to achieve the objectives of the cultural component." 8 C.F.R. § 214.2(q)(3)(iii)(C) (2004).

On January 1, 1994 the North American Free Trade Agreement Between the Government of the United States of America, the Government of Canada and the Government of the United Mexican States [NAFTA] went into effect. See the North American Free Trade Agreement Implementation Act, Pub. L. 103–182, 107 Stat. 2057 (Dec. 8, 1993). Building on the Canada–United States Free Trade Agreement, NAFTA expanded the free trade zone to include Mexico, thus reducing tariffs and other trade barriers among the three signatories.

Chapter 16 of NAFTA modifies slightly, for nationals of Mexico and Canada, certain of the criteria and procedures for certain of the nonimmigrant categories (business visitors, treaty traders and investors, intracompany transferees, and temporary professional workers). It also creates a new nonimmigrant category for "NAFTA professionals." See NAFTA, ch. 16, Annex 1603, § C. The complexities of the NAFTA provisions on nonimmigrants are beyond the scope of this book, but some excellent descriptions are available. See, e.g., Janet H. Cheetham (ed.), Immigration Practice and Procedure under the North American Free Trade Agreement (1995); Harry J. Joe, *Temporary Entry of Business Persons to the United States under the North American Free Trade Agreement*, 8 Georgetown Immigration L.J. 391 (1994); Kevin R. Johnson, *Free Trade and Closed Borders: NAFTA and Mexican Immigration to the United States*, 27 U.C. Davis L.Rev. 937 (1994); James F. Smith, *NAFTA and Human Rights: A Necessary Linkage*, 27 U.C. Davis L.Rev. 793 (1994); Jorge A. Vargas, *NAFTA, the Chiapas Rebellion, and the Emergence of Mexican Ethnic Law*, 25 California Western Internat'l L.J. 1 (1994).

PROBLEMS 4–5

Problem 4. X, a United States citizen, owns a night club in Miami Beach. He ordinarily hires singers for one-week engagements. A number of the singers have become regulars who return for several stints per year. While on vacation in Mexico, X discovers "El Fantastico," a talented night club singer who is beginning to develop a popular following in and around Acapulco. X would like to bring "El Fantastico" back to the United States to perform in Miami Beach for a week. As X's lawyer, what possible avenues would you explore?

Problem 5. Y, a citizen of Argentina, is currently the tenth-ranked woman tennis player in her country. Last year she was ranked twelfth. She wants to come to the United States to compete in the U.S. Open. As her immigration lawyer, what should you do?

4.   INTRA-COMPANY TRANSFEREES

The last commercial category of nonimmigrant covered here is the L-category. Read INA § 101(a)(15)(L) before studying the case that follows.

Karmali v. INS

United States Court of Appeals, Ninth Circuit, 1983.
707 F.2d 408.

■ CHOY, CIRCUIT JUDGE:

* * *

I

Karmali was born in Tanzania. He subsequently emigrated to Canada and became a Canadian citizen. In November 1976, Karmali began employment with AF–CHIM, a Canadian corporation closely held by his brother-in-law, Sultan Nazerali Walji. Karmali was "to assist and to investigate new holdings in the management of AF–CHIM's holdings wherever these holdings were located."

In April 1977, Walji and his wife (Karmali's sister) advanced money to Karmali in order to allow Karmali to purchase the Lantern Motel, Cafe, and KOA campground at Bonners Ferry, Idaho. On July 20, 1977, the purchase transaction was completed and Karmali entered the United States with his wife to operate the business. Karmali remained in the United States and managed the Idaho property * * *

On December 9, 1977, AF–CHIM filed a petition with the Service's Spokane office for an intra-company transfer visa on behalf of Karmali. The District Director denied the petition. The District Director's decision was appealed to the Regional Commissioner, who affirmed the decision and also denied AF–CHIM's subsequent motion for reconsideration. On December 29, 1980, the appellants filed a complaint in the district court, * * * contending that the Service's denial of the petition "was arbitrary and capricious and without legal basis," and seeking "an order directing the [Service] to issue" the petition. The presiding magistrate concluded that the Regional Commissioner did not abuse his discretion in denying AF–CHIM's petition and granted the Service's motion for summary judgment. The instant appeal followed.

* * *

The Regional Commissioner interpreted the language "employed continuously for one year" in section 101(a)(15)(L) of the Act to mean one year of continuous employment *abroad* prior to seeking admission into this country as an intra-company transferee. Thus, the Regional Commissioner determined that Karmali does not qualify as an intra-company transferee because he entered the United States in July 1977, only eight months after he started working for AF–CHIM in Canada in November 1976, and remained and worked here until AF–CHIM filed the intra-company transferee petition for Karmali in December 1977. The appellants contend that the language "employed continuously for one year" means no more than what it says, and that neither section 101(a)(15)(L) nor its legislative history precludes a prospective intra-company transferee from spending part of the qualifying one-year employment period in the United States. Since Karmali's presence in this country constituted continuous employment for AF–CHIM, the appellants argue, Karmali had satisfied the requisite one-year employment period by the time AF–CHIM filed the petition in December 1977.

The Service's interpretation of the statutory language in question should be given deference. *Olivares v. Immigration and Naturalization Service,* 685 F.2d 1174, 1177 (9th Cir.1982) ("The interpretation of a statute by the agency or department charged with its administration is entitled to great deference and should be accepted unless demonstrably irrational or clearly contrary to the plain and sensible meaning of the statute."). Despite the appellants' bald assertion to the contrary, we find clear legislative support for the Service's position that the requisite one year of continuous employment by a prospective intra-company transferee take place abroad.

Section 101(a)(15)(L) of the Act states that an intra-company transferee is not merely one "who, immediately preceding the time of his application for admission into the United States, has been employed continuously for one year," but also one "who seeks to enter the United States temporarily." As the Service persuasively notes, the two requirements evince congressional intent that the requisite one year of continuous employment take place *abroad*. Such an interpretation is supported by the following analysis of the section prepared by the House Judiciary Committee:

> Consideration of the petition will involve verification of the prior employment of the individual for a continuous period of at least 1 year *abroad* by a company affiliated with the parent, subsidiary, or branch located in the United States and verification that the subject of the petition is in a managerial, executive, or specialized knowledge capacity and is the subject of a transfer to the United States (emphasis added by court).

While the Service's interpretation of section 101(a)(15)(L) as requiring one year of continuous employment abroad is plainly consistent with congressional intent, the appellants have not advanced any support for their assertion that part of the one-year employment period can be spent in the United States. We therefore conclude that the Service did not abuse its discretion. * * *

NOTES AND QUESTIONS

1. The Immigration Act of 1990, section 206(c), amended INA § 101(a)(15)(L) to permit the year of continuous employment to take place any time during the *three*-year period that preceded the application for

admission. At the same time, Congress changed the L–provision in other respects not pertaining to the prior employment requirement. See Imm. Act § 206(a, b) and items 6 and 7 below. How might one argue that the 1990 amendments *strengthen* the vitality of the decision in *Karmali?*

2. The court in *Karmali* rejects a literal interpretation; it chooses instead to read into the statute a requirement that the year of previous employment take place abroad. To reach that result, it uses at least three common techniques of statutory interpretation:

(a) *Deference to Administrative Agencies.* The court invokes the maxim that the interpretation of the responsible agency should be accepted unless it is "demonstrably irrational or clearly contrary to the plain and sensible meaning of the statute." (Actually, that is a relatively strong description of the standard that a party challenging the agency interpretation must meet.) Recall similar reasoning in *Bricklayers Union.* There, however, the court found affirmative evidence that Congress had wanted to delegate the interpretive function to the agency. Does the court purport to find such evidence here?

Judicial deference is sometimes also explained as reflecting respect for the agency's expertise. But shouldn't an agency that adopts an interpretation at odds with the literal language be expected to explain why it has done so? Did the INS do that in this case?

(b) *Use of Legislative History.* The court cites the House Committee Report, which uses the word "abroad." How might Karmali's counsel have argued that the use of that word was inadvertent?

(c) *Contextual Analysis.* The court says the requirement of continuous employment for one year should be read in the context of the additional requirement that the L-nonimmigrant seek to enter the United States temporarily. Does that context really shed any light on whether the statute requires that the previous employment take place abroad?

3. If the statutory language conflicts with the language of the Committee report, which should control? What are the dangers in relying on the language of Committee reports?

4. What do you suppose prompted Congress to create L–status in the first place? Would those policies be impeded if the one-year employment requirement could be satisfied in the United States? Would any other policies be hindered? Is the court right to find the agency interpretation rational?

5. Could any noncitizen who wants to work in the United States simply create a foreign corporation, make herself the President of the company, wait a year, hire an American lawyer to set up a U.S. subsidiary, and then, once the subsidiary has been formed, enter the United States on an L–1 visa to work for that subsidiary? Would such a course of action

frustrate the policy, reflected in the H–2 provision, of protecting American labor?

6. Note two other important statutory requirements for L visas: First, the U.S. office must be that of the foreign employer or its subsidiary or affiliate; it is for that reason that L's are called *"intra*-company transferees." Second, the employee must be "managerial" or "executive" or have "specialized knowledge." After periods of controversy, Congress in 1990 made clear that "managers" include not only those who manage people but also those who manage company functions. Imm. Act 1990, § 123, adding INA § 101(a)(44)(A)(ii). The change is an important one, particularly for those with high-level technical or financial responsibilities.

7. One who qualifies for L–status as a manager or executive may be admitted for up to seven years; one who qualifies on the basis of specialized knowledge may be admitted for up to five years. INA § 214(c)(2)(D).

8. INA § 101(a)(15)(L) also authorizes the admission of the spouses and children who are following or accompanying to join L-visitors. In 2002 Congress added new INA § 214(c)(2)(e), which grants the spouses permission to work. Pub. L. 107–125, 115 Stat. 2403 (Jan. 16, 2002).

9. Under certain conditions, employers may file "blanket" petitions to import multiple intra-company transferees. See INA § 214(c)(2)(A), as amended by Pub. L. 108–447, 118 Stat. 2809, Div. J, § 413 (Dec. 8, 2004).

10. A recent controversy has arisen over the use of L–1 visas by Indian companies to send information technology workers to the United States. The question is whether the U.S. affiliates have used these employees to displace more highly paid U.S. workers. Some have argued that professional workers should be admitted only as H–1Bs, so as to trigger the labor protections you saw earlier. The subject is expertly analyzed in A. James Vázquez-Aspiri & Daniel C. Horne, *The Impotence of Being Earnest: Revisiting the L–1 Controversy*, 8 BIB 1607 (Oct. 15, 2003).

5. COMPARING COMMERCIAL CATEGORIES

PROBLEMS 6–7

Problem 6. X, a citizen of the United Kingdom, attended Cal Tech for two years in his youth. While there, he studied mechanical engineering. Financially unable to finish his degree, he returned to the U.K. and began a long career at Irving, Ltd., a corporation that manufactures machine parts. During his first five years there, X served as an assistant to one of the company's engineers. His engineering work was outstanding, and he gradually moved up the corporate ladder into positions that combined technical and managerial responsibilities. For the past eight years he has been a second vice-president in the company's marketing division. He occasionally gives presentations at industry conferences in the U.K. and in that way has become reasonably well known. Irving, Ltd. would now like to send X to Cleveland for two to three years so that he can spend full time working with Boring–Is–Us, one of Irving's most important clients. If he can come, X's job would be to solve product design problems; he would be trying to adapt Irving's production methods to the needs of Boring–Is–Us.

You are a lawyer retained by Irving Ltd. For what types of nonimmigrant visas would you consider applying, and what problems would you foresee?

Problem 7. Y, a citizen of Italy, developed a love of chess early in life. She served as President of the Chess Club during her two years as an undergraduate at the University of Arizona back in the late 1970's, but she dropped out of college after her sophomore year so that she could devote full time to competing in chess tournaments throughout Europe. She was quite successful, winning a number of lesser competitions and finishing respectably in several major ones.

Thirteen years ago, after several years of competitions, Y set up an Italian corporation whose business was to manufacture and distribute elegant chess sets. She ran the business herself, individually handcrafting the pieces at first, and eventually preparing designs for machine production. Soon the company was a thriving enterprise. Within five years, its annual worldwide sales were the equivalent of 3,000,000 U.S. dollars. Y also found time to continue competing in national and local chess tournaments. The most recent ratings of the Italian Chess Federation ranked her 17th in Italy.

Y is now anxious to expand her geographic and career horizons. While lawfully on vacation in the United States on a B–2 visa, she consults you, an immigration lawyer, for advice. She plans to return home to Italy before her authorized stay expires and continue to run her chess set business. In about a year or so, however, she would like to come to the United States to establish a second corporation. The main function of that corporation, which she estimates would require an initial investment of $200,000 (an amount she has available), would be to set up and promote professional chess tournaments throughout the United States. Y would want to run the company herself for at least the first two or three years. After that, depending on how well the company is doing and how much she is enjoying life in the United States, she would like the flexibility to decide then whether to stay on for a longer but still temporary period (rather than return to Italy at that time and hire someone else to run the U.S. company). Either way, her intention is to remain in the United States no longer than five years at the most. She also sees this United States company as a high-volume buyer of the chess sets manufactured by her Italian company. While in the United States, she would occasionally compete for prize money in some of the tournaments herself.

Y would like to know what options she has under the United States immigration laws and, if there is more than one choice, the tactical pros and cons of applying for the various possible nonimmigrant visas.

What advice will you give her?

SECTION B. EDUCATIONAL CATEGORIES

1. STUDENTS

The events of September 11, 2001 have brought foreign students into public focus, and they have profoundly affected foreign students' decisions whether to come to the United States, as well as their lives while they are here. The main provision on foreign students is INA § 101(a)(15)(F), which you should now read carefully. This provision covers the "F–1" students (F–2 in the cases of spouses and children). Another, much smaller group of students come to the United States to attend vocational or other "nonacademic" institutions. INA § 101(a)(15)(M). A third related category that includes students as well as other educational visitors, INA § 101(a)(15)(J) (exchange visitors), is taken up in the next subsection.

In fiscal year 2003, some 617,556 F–1 students and an additional 7,361 M–1 students were admitted to the United States. 2003 Yearbook of Immigration Statistics, Table 24.

What do we know about them? The Institute of International Education, in its most recent comprehensive annual report, Open Doors–Report on International Educational Exchange (2004) [Open Doors], summarized the data for academic year 2003–04: The largest sending countries, in order, were India, China, Korea, Japan, and Canada. *Id.* at 8. Approximately 57% of all foreign students in the United States in AY 2003–04 were from Asia. *Id.* at 8–9. The University of Southern California (for the third straight year) led the nation in foreign student enrollment; rounding out the top ten, in order, were Columbia, Purdue (main campus), NYU, the University of Texas at Austin, the University of Illinois at Urbana–Champaign, the University of Michigan, Boston University, UCLA, and Ohio State. *Id.* at 12. In that academic year, foreign students comprised only 2.5% of the undergraduate students at U.S. colleges and universities, but 14.5% of the graduate students. *Id.* at 2. The most popular fields of study for foreign students that year were business and management (19%), engineering (17%), and mathematics and computer sciences (12%). *Id.* at 14–15.

The large numbers of foreign students clearly reflect foreign perceptions of the quality of U.S. universities, combined sometimes with hopes of living permanently in the United States after graduation. Jagdish Bhagwati & Milind Rao, *The U.S. Brain Gain—At the Expense of Blacks?*, 39 Challenge 50 (March 1996). Another major draw is the growing importance of English language proficiency in the globalized economy. Joyce Howard Price, *World speaks our language and attends our colleges*, Wash. Times, Dec. 29, 2004. There is evidence as well that the hands-on instructional methods practiced in many U.S. universities are becoming increasingly popular with foreign students. *Id.*

But in the 2003–04 academic year, while postgraduate foreign student enrollment actually increased by 2.4%, undergraduate foreign student enrollment dropped by 5%. The combined effect was a 2.4% drop in foreign student enrollments. *Id.* at 2–3.

This significant decrease is both unusual and worrisome, for the United States benefits enormously from foreign students. For quite some time, fewer and fewer U.S. students have been applying to graduate programs, partly because the college-age American population has been decreasing and partly because American college graduates have tended to opt for the work force rather than for long courses of further study. New York Times, Nov. 29, 1990, at 3. Consequently, U.S. colleges and universities have become ever more dependent on foreign students, particularly at the graduate level. In addition, foreign students now spend $13 billion per year in the United States, mainly on tuition, room, board, and other expenditures. Open Doors, above, at 4–5; see also Paul Desruisseaux, *Foreign Students Continue to Flock to the U.S.*, Chronicle of Higher Education, Dec. 10, 1999, at A57. More than 70% of these expenditures come from overseas sources, principally the students' families and governments. Open Doors, above, at 6–7. IIE President and CEO Allan Goodman puts it succinctly: "International students in U.S. classrooms widen the perspectives of their U.S. classmates, contribute to vital research activities, strengthen the local economies in which they live, and build lasting ties between their home countries and the United States." IIE Press Release, Nov. 15, 2004. As the 9/11 attacks sadly demonstrated, exposure to the United States does not guarantee good will; nonetheless, most observers agree that in the long run such exposure helps much more than it hurts.

Perhaps most importantly, the foreign graduate students who come to the United States tend to be the cream of the crop of their countries. In India, for example, only about 2% of the applicants are admitted to the Indian Institutes of Technology (modeled on M.I.T. and Cal. Tech.) A 1990 study found that the graduates of those "IIT's," as they are called, made up about 78% of all Indian PhD recipients in engineering in the United States. When PhDs of that caliber become permanent residents of the United States, as many do, they enhance the nation's scientific achievements and its competitive position in the world economy. Bhagwati & Rao, above.

Despite these mutual benefits, foreign students have not always been received with gracious hospitality. For at least two to three decades, signs of tension have become visible. Foreign students can be especially vulnerable during periods of political stress. During the Iranian hostage crisis of 1980, hostility toward Iranians in the United States was intense. President Carter ordered the Attorney General to require all Iranian students to report to INS offices so that they could be inspected for compliance with the conditions of their stay. 15 Weekly Compilation of Presidential Documents 2107 (1979). There followed a series of cases in which Iranian students were deported for highly technical violations of their student status, such as transferring schools before receiving INS approvals of the transfer requests. See, e.g., *Matter of Yazdani,* 17 I. & N. Dec. 626 (BIA 1981).

In the 1980s, politicians in several states called for state universities to charge their foreign students extra tuition. They argued that the extra charges would offset the subsidies reflected in the tuition rates for state residents and would eventually reduce the numbers of foreigners in American universities and later in the professional workforce. Baker, *Foreign Students Under Fire*, Newsweek (Oct. 19, 1987), at 73–74.

Resistance soon came from another quarter as well. One educator blamed foreign students for the low numbers of African–American PhDs. See Anthony DePalma, *Drop in Black Ph.D.'s Brings Debate on Aid for Foreigners*, New York Times, Apr. 21, 1992, at 1, quoting Frank Morris, then Dean of Graduate Studies at historically African–American Morgan State University. Others counter that the increasing numbers of foreign graduate students and the low number of African–American graduate students are unrelated. Bhagwati and Rao, above, for example, argue that the supply of slots in doctoral programs is highly elastic; that over the past two decades the number of Americans in Ph.D programs has remained roughly constant while the number of foreign doctoral students, and therefore total doctoral students, has risen; that foreign students are ineligible for affirmative action funding; and that the real explanation for the small number of African–American doctoral students in science and engineering has been the low number of African–Americans receiving bachelors' degrees in those fields. Bhagwati & Rao, above.

In the early to middle 1990s, the various concerns about foreign students merged into the more general anti-immigration fervor that by that time was sweeping the country. IIRIRA § 625 created INA § 214(m), which prohibits F–1 students from attending public elementary schools, INA § 214(m)(1)(A). The same provision prohibits F–1 students from attending public secondary schools unless they pay the full per-capita costs of their education, and it sets a maximum duration of twelve months. INA § 214(m)(1)(B). F–1 students may still attend private elementary and secondary schools. INA § 214(m)(2). Any student violating section 214 becomes not only deportable, see INA § 237(a)(1)(C)(i), but also inadmissible for five years after the date of the violation, INA § 212(a)(6)(G). In addition, IIRIRA § 641 required the Attorney General, in consultation with the Secretary of State and the Secretary of Education, to collect individualized information from colleges and universities on every foreign student they enroll. An institution that failed to provide the required information automatically lost its authority to accept foreign students. This system was the precursor of the SEVIS and US VISIT programs noted below.

But the most serious concerns about foreign students to date were those that set in after the terrorist attacks of September 11, 2001. Just nine days after the attacks, U.S. Senator Dianne Feinstein of California, upon learning that at least one of the hijackers had been admitted to the United States on a student visa to study English, proposed a six-month moratorium on all student visas. Diana Jean Schemo, *A Nation Challenged:*

Foreign Students, New York Times, Sept. 21, 2001. Cooler heads prevailed, but a number of the post 9/11 security measures taken by Congress and the executive branch did aim specifically at foreign students. Some of the strategies had the effect of making the visa process more complicated and more protracted, creating unexpected delays that caused students to miss registration deadlines. Other strategies involved collecting, maintaining, and liberalizing access to a wide range of student information that might otherwise have been protected by the Family Educational Rights and Privacy Act of 1974 [FERPA]. The SEVIS program for foreign students was an outgrowth of those strategies, as was the more generic data collection system now known as US VISIT. These are discussed generally in chapter 10, section B below. As for their applicability to students, see Victor C. Romero, *Noncitizen Students and Immigration Policy Post 9/11*, 17 Georgetown Immigration L.J. 357 (2003). The same section of chapter 10 also describes the resulting delays in the issuance of student (and other educational) visas and the practical problems those delays have engendered. Muslim and Arab nationals have been particularly affected, as discussed more fully in chapter 10, section F below. Finally, because several of the September 11 hijackers had taken flight training courses in the United States, Congress also specifically restricted the use of student visas to attend flight training schools. See Aviation and Transportation Security Act, Pub. L. 107-71, 115 Stat. 597 (Nov. 19, 2001), discussed in 78 IR at 1822 (Dec. 3, 2001).

How much of the dropoff in foreign student enrollment can be attributed to the post-September 11 security measures is hard to gauge, but many educators see at least some causal connection. The impact has been especially noticeable with respect to applicants from the Middle East, whose numbers dropped by 10% in 2002–03 and then another 9% in 2003–04. IIE Press Release, above. But other factors are also at play. Competition for foreign students from other English-speaking countries such as Canada, the UK, and Australia has become more aggressive, and bachelor's and master's degree programs in those other countries are often shorter and almost always much cheaper than in the United States. *Id*; Price, above. Whether political opposition to U.S. policy in Iraq has further contributed to the decline is difficult to say.

The United States is not, of course, the only country in which foreign students have encountered hostility. In the late 1980s in England, bogus colleges often duped overseas students into paying exorbitant tuition for inadequate educational services. The British Home Office responded with well-publicized raids that snared both college staff and student victims. 3 Bulletin of the Joint Council for the Welfare of Immigrants, No. 7 (August 1988) at 7. In China, relations between African students and Chinese students have frequently been tense. In December 1988, after a Saturday night brawl in Nanjing, thousands of Chinese students and University employees pelted the dormitories of the African students with rocks and shouted racial slurs for seven hours. These events were followed by several days of anti-African demonstrations. New York Times, Dec. 30, 1988, at A-3.

To receive a student visa, one must generally pursue a course of full-time study. By way of exception, the regulations now allow an F–1 student to take less than a full courseload, upon the advice of school officials, when there are "initial difficulties with the English language or reading requirements, unfamiliarity with U.S. teaching methods, or improper course level placement," and for certain other prescribed reasons. 8 C.F.R. § 214.2(f)(6)(iii) (2004). Usually the "reduced course load must consist of at least six semester or quarter hours, or half the clock hours required for a full course of study." *Id.*

At one time, F–1 students were admitted for fixed time periods. If they later discovered that they needed more time to complete their programs, the students could apply to the former INS for fixed-term extensions of stay. Today, however, foreign students are admitted for "duration of status." A "designated school official" estimates a reasonable "completion date" for the particular program. The student may remain in the United States until that date, assuming he or she remains a full-time student in good standing. If unable to complete his or her studies by this time, the student applies to the university (not to USCIS) for an extension. It will be granted only upon a showing of "compelling academic or medical reasons, such as changes of major or research topics, unexpected research problems, or documented illnesses." The university must then inform USCIS of the extension. 8 C.F.R. § 214.2(f)(7) (2004). For an extension of an F–1 stay, one must "agree to depart the United States at the expiration of his or her authorized period of ... extension ..." 8 C.F.R. § 214.1(a)(3) (2004).

An applicant for a student visa must also demonstrate sufficient funds. See generally INA § 212(a)(4). There are stringent restrictions on employment. Foreign students may work on campus, as part of their educational programs, up to 20 hours per week while school is in session and 40 hours per week during school vacations. Off-campus employment is generally allowed only when unforeseen circumstances arising after admission make employment after the first year economically necessary and USCIS grants permission. 8 C.F.R. § 214.2(f)(9) (2004). Foreign students may also engage in "optional practical training" [OPT]. As a result of the same regulation that implements SEVIS, 67 Fed. Reg. 76256 (Dec. 11, 2002), OPT may now be utilized after completion of each higher education level (for example, once after a bachelor's degree, again after a master's degree, and yet again after a doctorate). See 8 C.F.R. § 214.2(f)(10) (2004).

In the Border Student Commuter Act of 2002, Pub. L. 107–274, 116 Stat. 1923 (Nov. 2, 2002), Congress allowed Canadian and Mexican nationals who reside in their home countries to commute to United States schools for full-time *or part-time* studies. For this purpose, the statute created new F–3 and M–3 (the latter for vocational and other "non-academic" institutions) visa categories. See INA §§ 101(a)(15)(f)(3), 101(a)(15)(m)(3).

2. EXCHANGE VISITORS

"Exchange visitors" are part of a mutual exchange program in which students, teachers, scholars, and others enter the country temporarily to pursue various education-related goals. The purposes of the program are to provide training that will enable the visitors to benefit their countries of origin when they return, to foster intellectual and cultural interchange, and in the process to build positive foreign relations. The exchange visitors themselves obtain J–1 status; their noncitizen spouses and minor children, if accompanying or following them, acquire J–2 status. Admission is authorized by INA § 101(a)(15)(J), which you should read now. See generally Naomi Schorr & Stephen Yale–Loehr, *The Odyssey of the J–2: Forty–Three Years of Trying Not to Go Home Again,* 18 Georgetown Immigration L.J. 221 (2004).

The more closely the exchange visitor's program resembles what might be thought of as employment, the more controversial the program has been. For this reason, there has been much discussion about the use of exchange visitor visas by "au pairs." An au pair is a foreign national who comes to the United States for a year to live with a host family, provide child care, and (now) attend a post-secondary educational institution at least part time. When the program works as intended, everyone benefits. The au pair receives a culturally enriching experience, educational benefits, and the opportunity to spend a year overseas. The host family receives dependable child care and the chance to form a close relationship with a young person from a different country. But the program has not always worked as expected. There have been perennial concerns that au pairs are exploited, that the au pair program is less a cultural experience than a source of cheap child care, and that some au pairs have been irresponsible in their duties.

Until 1997, the au pair program was temporary. In that year Congress made the program permanent and the requirements more rigorous. See Pub. L. 105–48, 111 Stat. 1165 (Oct. 1, 1997). The State Department has similarly upgraded the program. Generally, an au pair must be over age 18, a secondary school graduate, and proficient in English, and he or she must pass a background check. While in the United States, the person must attend a postsecondary educational institution for at least six hours per week and is limited to 45 hours per week of child care. The duration of stay is one year. 22 C.F.R. § 62.31(c)(1) (2004). In 2001, the State Department added a new branch called "EduCare" to the au pair program; under this special provision, designed for households with only school-age children, the au pair attends postsecondary school for at least 12 hours per week (instead of 6) and may not perform more than 30 hours per week of childcare services (instead of 45). See 66 Fed. Reg. 43087 (Aug. 17, 2001), amending 22 C.F.R. § 62.31.

Even with these improvements, au pairs remain controversial. Professor Linda Kelly, examining the au pair program and other immigration policies in the light of society's "supermom" expectations, has proposed replacing the present program with one that insists on rigorous childrearing credentials and admits the qualifying applicants as skilled immigrants. Linda Kelly, *The Fantastic Adventure of Supermom and the Alien: Educat-*

ing Immigration Policy on the Facts of Life, 31 Connecticut L. Rev. 1045 (1999).

One of the most popular uses of J-visas has been for study in the United States. To a student, one advantage of a J–1 visa over an F–1 visa lies in the slightly more liberal employment rules governing J-visas (both for the principal nonimmigrant and for the spouse and children). Compare 22 C.F.R. §§ 62.16, 62.23(g) (2004) and 8 C.F.R. § 214.2(j)(1)(v) (2004) (J-visas) with 8 C.F.R. § 214.2(f)(9, 15) (2004) (F–visas). Moreover, many of the exchange visitor programs provide fellowships or other types of funding.

Maximum duration of stay for exchange visitors depends on the category (professor, student, etc.). For professors and researchers, recent regulations now allow five-year stays but with no extensions. See 70 Fed. Reg. 28815 (May 19, 2005), amending 22 C.F.R. § 62.20(i). J-students in degree programs may remain as long as they are pursuing full courses of study at the institutions for which they were approved and are "maintaining satisfactory advancement." 22 C.F.R. § 62.23(h)(1) (2004). Recall that students on F–1 visas similarly may remain for the duration of their student status. Thus, intended duration of stay is not usually a significant factor in choosing between F–1 and J–1 status.

Why, then, don't all noncitizens who wish to study in the United States request J-visas rather than F-visas? One reason is that the person might not qualify for J-status. The studies must be part of a specific program approved in advance by the State Department. In addition, the applicant must be sponsored by a U.S. government agency (including the State Department itself or the Agency for International Development), a recognized international agency, or one of various private agencies. See 22 C.F.R. §§ 62.1(b), 62.3 (2004).

But the biggest hitch of all for J-entrants is INA § 212(e). The following materials explore some of its intricacies. Before going any further, read section 212(e) closely.

Sheku–Kamara v. Karn

United States District Court, Eastern District of Pennsylvania, 1984.
581 F.Supp. 582.

■ BECHTLE, DISTRICT JUDGE.

* * *

On August 27, 1978, Benedict V. Sheku–Kamara, ("Mr. Sheku–Kamara"), a citizen and native of Sierra Leone, entered the United States as an exchange visitor pursuant to section 101(a)(15)(J) of the Immigration and Nationality Act * * * ("the Act"), to pursue a program of graduate studies sponsored by the United Nations at the University of Pennsylvania. Since this program was admittedly financed by the U.S. Government, Mr. Sheku–Kamara was subject to INA § 212(e), which, *inter alia,* imposes a two year foreign residence requirement on all persons who enter the United States pursuant to INA § 101(a)(15)(J) and participate in a program financed by the United States (known as a "J–1" visa). The two year foreign residence requirement requires that all subject persons return to and reside and be physically present in the country of their nationality or last residence for an aggregate of at least two years following departure from the United States before applying for * * * [permanent residence].

On January 16, 1981, the Immigration and Naturalization Service ("INS") completed a request by Mr. Sheku–Kamara for a change of program. The change, retroactive to October 9, 1979, transferred Mr. Sheku–Kamara's sponsorship from the United Nations program to a privately funded program sponsored by the University of Pennsylvania. Mr. Sheku–Kamara received no Government funding while in this privately funded program.

On August 18, 1979, Mr. Sheku–Kamara married plaintiff, Mrs. Sheku–Kamara, *nee* Josephine Kebbie, in London, England. On March 6, 1980, plaintiff Jawa Sheku–Kamara, the son of Mr. and Mrs. Sheku–Kamara, was born in England. On August 5, 1980, the United States Embassy in London, England, issued a visa to Mrs. Sheku–Kamara and Jawa Sheku–Kamara as the dependents of Mr. Sheku–Kamara (known as "J–2" visas). Shortly thereafter Mrs. Sheku–Kamara and her son entered the United States.

While in the United States, Mrs. Sheku–Kamara applied to the INS for adjustment of status from nonimmigrant to immigrant pursuant to section 245 of the Act. On September 7, 1983, the application for adjustment of status was denied by defendant. The denial was based on the determination that Mrs. Sheku–Kamara was not eligible to become a lawful permanent resident of the United States since she, along with her child and husband, was subject to the two year foreign residence requirement imposed by INA § 212(e).

Plaintiffs * * * seek a declaratory judgment that they are not subject to the two year foreign residence requirement.

II. DISCUSSION

While it is not disputed that Mr. Sheku–Kamara is subject to the two year residence requirement, plaintiffs argue that they are not subject to the requirement because they entered the United States after Mr. Sheku–Kamara stopped participating in a Government funded program. Having entered at such time, plaintiffs argue that they did not receive any benefit from any Government funding and therefore Mr. Sheku–Kamara's status should not be imputed to them. Plaintiffs' argument fails for a number of reasons.

Firstly, a regulation which governs this situation has been promulgated. The regulation as set forth in 8 C.F.R. § 212.7(c)(4) provides:

A spouse or child admitted to the United States or accorded status under section 101(a)(15)(J) of the act to accompany or follow to join an exchange visitor who is subject to the foreign residence requirement of section 212(e) of the Act is also subject to that requirement.

Plaintiffs argue that this regulation is inapplicable to the situation before the court.[8] Plaintiffs also argue that nothing in the Act, or in the relevant administrative history requires application of the foreign residence requirement to a spouse and child of an exchange visitor in a Government financed program where they, the spouse and child, enter the United States after the principal alien has left the Government financed program. Such an argument is incorrect since it ignores a plain reading of the regulation and is a narrow incorrect reading of the leading case on the subject.

In *Matter of Tabcum,* 14 I. & N. Dec. 113 (1972), a spouse of an exchange visitor was denied adjustment of her nonimmigrant status on the basis that she had entered the United States with her husband and therefore was subject to fulfilling the two year residence requirement prior to adjustment of status. The Regional Commissioner rejected the applicant's argument that the foreign residence requirement did not apply to spouses accompanying an exchange visitor. In so doing the Regional Commissioner noted that "to the extent she was permitted to enter and remain in the United States and was a beneficiary to the financial aspects of the principal alien's participation in the Government-sponsored program, she too derived benefits from such program."

Plaintiffs do not suggest that *Matter of Tabcum* is incorrect. Rather, they argue that *Matter of Tabcum* is supportive of their position that a spouse or child must in some way be a beneficiary of the financial aspects of a Government-sponsored program before they can be subject to the two year foreign residence requirement. While *Matter of Tabcum* does stand for the proposition that an exchange visitor's spouse [or child] who receives some benefit from the Government's funding of a program is subject to the two year requirement, the scope of the decision is broader. As the Regional Commissioner stated without qualification, "the two-year foreign residence requirement . . . applies to the spouse [and child] of an exchange visitor where the principal alien is subject to such provision." Additionally, the fact that plaintiffs have not derived any financial benefit from Mr. Sheku–Kamara's participation in a Government funded program is not dispositive where, as here, plaintiffs have received the more significant benefit of having been permitted to enter the United States solely because Mr. Sheku–Kamara has been and continues to be an exchange visitor.

Secondly, to decide that plaintiffs are not required to comply with the two year foreign residence requirement would create the anomalous result of putting plaintiffs, who derive their status solely through Mr. Sheku–Kamara, in a better position than Mr. Sheku–Kamara who remains subject to the two year requirement.

---

8. Plaintiffs do not argue that the regulation is invalid as against the statute but rather, only that the regulation is inapplicable to the circumstances of this case.

Thirdly, finding that plaintiffs are subject to the foreign residence requirement is consistent with one of the primary objectives of the Exchange Visitor Program which is to facilitate the impartation of live impressions of the United States and its culture to other societies. Even though this objective is directed primarily towards the principal alien, this court does not see why it cannot be equally applicable to a spouse and child of the principal alien thereby subjecting them to the foreign residence requirement.[10]

* * *

[The court grants summary judgment for the defendant.]

* * *

NOTES AND QUESTIONS

1. The plaintiffs in *Sheku–Kamara* seem to argue only that the regulation should be interpreted as inapplicable to the plaintiffs. Did they concede too much? Read the regulation carefully. Is it clear on its face? Now re-read section 212(e). Is it really clear from the statutory language whether *any* J–2's (even those who entered before the J–1 nonimmigrant had ceased receiving government funding) are subject to the two-year requirement?

2. The court concludes that Congress meant for the two-year requirement to apply to J–2's regardless whether they entered before or after the J–1 stopped receiving government funding. Evaluate the policy reasons the court gives in support of that conclusion.

3. Although the basis for subjecting Sheku–Kamara to section 212(e) was that his program had been government-financed, note that the home country's need for the J–1 nonimmigrant's skills is another common trigger for the two-year requirement. A third trigger affects certain graduate medical students. INA §§ 212(e)(iii), 214(*l*)(1).

Waivers aside, how do you feel about the two-year rule itself? In particular, *should* United States law impose such a constraint (a) in government funding cases and (b) in cases in which the home country needs the individual's skills? Argue both ways, keeping in mind not only the purposes of a foreign exchange program but also the reasons for limiting it.

4. Section 212(e) provides no fewer than four different waivers of the two-year rule—requests by "interested United States government agenc[ies];" cases of "exceptional hardship;" no-objection letters from the applicants' home countries; and persecution. Keep in mind too that even a person who is statutorily eligible for one of these waivers needs the

---

10. It should be further noted, as it was in *Matter of Tabcum,* that in cases such as this where both a J–2 spouse and child are involved, if the spouse and child are not subject to the foreign residence requirement, the principal alien could possibly gain a backdoor access to a waiver of the residence requirement on the basis of hardship grounds.

favorable exercise of discretion. In practice, discretion is rarely exercised favorably in the government funding cases. See Michael Maggio, *Interested Government Agency Exchange Visitor Waivers,* 12 Immigration J. 1, at 1 (July–Sept.1989).

5. The "interested United States Government agency" contemplated by the waiver provision is typically the federal agency (if any) that has hired or wishes to hire the J-entrant. Common federal sponsors include the National Science Foundation, the Department of Defense, the Department of Energy, the Department of Education, and the Department of Health and Human Services. See Maggio, item 1 above, at 50; Suzanne Seltzer, *Demystifying the HHS Waiver Process*, 9 BIB 1165 (Oct. 1, 2004).

6. A waiver request based on either exceptional hardship or persecution is initially submitted to USCIS; if the USCIS reaction is favorable, the request is then forwarded to the Waiver Review Division of the Office of Exchange Visitor Program Services, which is part of the State Department's Bureau of Consular Affairs. 22 C.F.R. § 41.63(b) (2004). In contrast, a waiver request from an interested government agency is submitted directly to the Waiver Review Division, and its recommendation is considered that of the Department of State. *Id.* § 41.63(c)(5). A no-objection letter from the individual's home country is directed to the Secretary of State through diplomatic channels spelled out in the regulations. *Id.* § 41.63(d)(1). The Chief of the Waiver Review Division of the Office of Exchange Visitor Program Services has the discretion to refer any of these cases to the (different and separate) Exchange Visitor Waiver Review Division, which then issues the required recommendation to USCIS. 22 C.F.R. § 41.63(g)(1, 4, 8) (2004).

PROBLEMS 8–9

Problem 8. X, a citizen of Ghana, has been awarded a Smithford Foundation grant to pursue a bachelors degree in chemistry for four years at NYU. Smithford is a private nonprofit organization that receives 75% of its funds from private contributions and 25% from the U.S. government. By its terms, the grant is contingent upon X obtaining a J–1 visa.

X is not now certain of his future, post-degree plans. Graduate education is one possibility. Perhaps he will want to return to Ghana, or perhaps he will want to find a way to remain in the United States.

X has the option of turning down the Smithford grant and instead borrowing money from his parents to study at NYU, in which case he would be eligible only for an F–1 visa. But he would eventually have to pay his parents back, and in addition the amount they can spare is less than the amount of the Smithford grant (though still adequate to support himself, his wife, and his three young children, all of whom would be coming with him).

X wants to know whether he would be better off with a J–1 visa and a Smithford fellowship, or an F–1 visa and borrowed funds. As his lawyer, what advice do you give him?

Problem 9. Y, a citizen of India, entered the United States on a J–1 visa four years ago. She has received no government funding at all, but she does possess skills that are needed by her home country. A few months ago she married a United States citizen and applied to USCIS to adjust her status to that of LPR. With her application she requested a waiver of section 212(e), asserting exceptional hardship. She has contracted a life-threatening (but noncontagious) disease for which medical treatment is available only in the United States. Living with her and her new husband is her seven-year-old daughter from a previous marriage. Her daughter, who is an LPR, speaks only English, knows only American culture, and thus will find life difficult if the family has to move to India. You are the relevant USCIS official. Should you recommend the waiver?

SECTION C.   TOURISTS

INA § 101(a)(15)(B) authorizes the admission of certain nonimmigrants who want to visit the United States temporarily either for business (the B–1's you studied earlier) or for pleasure (B–2's). As the chart at the beginning of this chapter shows, there were more than 20,000,000 B–2 visitors in fiscal year 2003—about 72% of all nonimmigrants admitted that year. Except for those who enter under a special visa waiver program, see INA § 217 and page 462 below, the authorized period of initial admission ranges from six months to one year, and extensions may be granted in six-month increments. 8 C.F.R. § 214.2(b)(1, 2) (2004).

The B–2 cases, though numerically significant, used to be relatively noncontroversial. When they were denied, it was usually because the consular officers believed the applicants intended to remain permanently. Try to imagine the fact situations likely to give rise to that belief.

In this post-September 11 world, all categories of noncitizens are now controversial. Increased scrutiny of almost all applicants for B–2 visas is now the norm, and those who seek to enter under the visa waiver program face a host of new restrictions, some concerning the applicants and some concerning the country of origin. See chapter 10, section E.5 below.

As the following case demonstrates, B–2's can encounter other admission problems as well.

Matter of Healy and Goodchild

Board of Immigration Appeals, 1979.
17 I. & N. Dec. 22.

* * *

[Two holders of B–2 visitor-for-pleasure visas arrived at U.S. ports of entry. Each one was carrying a letter of acceptance for admission to a nine-month program of the Clayton School for Continuing Education. The former INS had not approved the school for foreign students. The immigration judges and the BIA found both individuals inadmissible under old INA § 212(a)(6) (now 212(a)(7)(B)) as nonimmigrants who lacked valid nonimmigrant visas.]

The facts underlying the section 212(a)(26) charge present an issue common to both applicants, specifically, whether an alien seeking admission to the United States for the primary purpose of attending an educational institution that has not been approved by the Attorney General for attendance by alien students in accordance with section 101(a)(15)(F) of the Act, may be properly admitted as a nonimmigrant visitor for pleasure pursuant to section 101(a)(15)(B) of the Act.

Under section 101(a)(15) of the Act, every alien is considered to be an immigrant unless he is able to establish that he is entitled to nonimmigrant status under one of the specified classes of nonimmigrants designated by Congress in section 101(a)(15) * * *. Moreover, the burden is upon the alien to establish that he is entitled to the nonimmigrant classification and type of nonimmigrant visa for which he is an applicant.

The applicants conceded that they are not entitled to status as nonimmigrant students under section 101(a)(15)(F) inasmuch as the Claymont School has not been approved by the Attorney General or his delegate. Each applicant further acknowledged that the principal purpose of his visit was to participate in the basic course to which he was admitted at the Claymont School, that he had paid a deposit of $100 toward the $2,750 tuition for the course prior to seeking admission to the United States, and that he had been in attendance at the school since his parole into this country.

Counsel does not seriously contest the fact that the Claymont School is a school and that the applicants are students within the ordinary usage of those terms and we are satisfied that they are properly classifiable as such.[2] Counsel argues instead that section 101(a)(15)(F) is solely concerned with alien students destined for approved schools. Since the Claymont School has not been accredited by the Service, he insists that the applicants are

---

2. The purpose and program of the basic course at the Claymont School are described as follows in excerpts from the institution's 1977–78 catalog (Ex. 4A):

> The Claymont School for Continuous Education is founded on the principle that true education must include techniques of self-perfecting in mind, body, and spirit and must realize the potential latent in normal men and women.... The daily schedule normally begins at 6 a.m. All students and staff share in psychological and spiritual exercises until breakfast. After breakfast, 4–5 hours are devoted to practical activities involving the acquisition of a wide variety of skills such as cooking, breadmaking, carpentry, housepainting, plumbing and electrical work, gardening, logging, animal and vegetable husbandry, repairs and special crafts and skills such as spinning, woodworking and pottery to meet particular needs.... In the afternoon ... the two groups not on house duty attend classes, which include work at the Gurdjieff sacred gymnastics, psychology, cosmology, art, music, and theatre. There are also special classes, some conducted by the School staff, some by visiting tutors, on subjects such as health, ecology and intermediate technology....

not subject to the provisions of section 101(a)(15)(F) of the Act but are admissible as visitors for pleasure. We disagree.

It is clear that absent Service approval of the school to which an alien student is destined, he may not establish eligibility for a nonimmigrant student visa under section 101(a)(15)(F). It does not follow ipso facto, however, that an alien bound for the United States for the primary purpose of pursuing a course of study at an unapproved school is entitled to status as a nonimmigrant visitor for pleasure under section 101(a)(15)(B). That such alien is not entitled to status as a nonimmigrant visitor is evident from the express terms of section 101(a)(15)(B) which includes among those classifiable as nonimmigrants:

> an alien (*other than one coming for the purpose of study* or of performing skilled or unskilled labor or as a representative of foreign press, radio, film, or other foreign information media coming to engage in such vocation) having a residence in a foreign country which he has no intention of abandoning and who is visiting the United States temporarily for business or temporarily for pleasure; . . . (Emphasis added.)

While the statutory term "pleasure" is not defined in the Act, State Department regulation 22 C.F.R. § 41.25 provides the following definition:

> (c) The term "pleasure", as used in section 101(a)(15)(B) of the Act, refers to legitimate activities of a recreational character, including tourism, amusement, visits with friends or relatives and rest; medical treatment, or activities of a fraternal, social or service nature.

It is thus apparent from the explicit language of section 101(a)(15)(B), as supplemented by the foregoing regulation, that the B–2, or visitor for pleasure, nonimmigrant category was not intended to be a "catch-all" classification available to all who wish to come to the United States temporarily for whatever purpose. Instead, as is the case with the other nonimmigrant classes enumerated by Congress in section 101(a)(15), section 101(a)(15)(B) was designed to encompass a specific, defined class of aliens; by the express terms of the statute, that class does not include aliens coming for the purpose of study. To accept counsel's theory would not only disregard the explicit language of section 101(a)(15)(B) but would undermine the requirements for entitlement to student status under section 101(a)(15)(F) and the detailed regulations which have been promulgated to implement that section.[3]

We accordingly hold that an alien bound for the United States for the primary purpose of study is not admissible as a nonimmigrant visitor for pleasure as defined by section 101(a)(15)(B) but must instead establish his entitlement to nonimmigrant student status under section 101(a)(15)(F)

---

3. Section 101(a)(15)(F) and the correlative regulations manifestly have the dual purpose of protecting alien students by ensuring the legitimacy of the school to be attended and of facilitating the enforcement of the immigration laws with respect to those students.

and the pertinent regulations. We recognize that our decision in effect declares unapproved educational institutions such as the Claymont School to be unavailable to alien students. Our holding, however, is in keeping with the clear statutory scheme drawn by Congress which deems all aliens to be immigrants unless they can demonstrate that they qualify for status under one of the distinct nonimmigrant classes enumerated in section 101(a)(15). The dispositive fact is that Congress made no provision thereunder for aliens destined for the United States for the primary purpose of pursuing a course of study at an unapproved school.

* * *

NOTES AND QUESTIONS

1.   Although B–2's are often thought of as tourists, the BIA acknowledges that the provision also authorizes visits for other purposes—including medical treatment, seeing friends or relatives, and so forth. In 2001, the State Department informed all diplomatic and consular posts that "accompanying one's 'significant other' who is temporarily working or studying in the U.S. would be considered travel for pleasure" and that "this is true for both opposite and same-sex partners." See John McCaslin, Washington Times, July 12, 2001.

But one activity from which all B–2 nonimmigrants are absolutely foreclosed is employment. In that respect, B–2s are unusual. All other nonimmigrant visa[6] categories either specifically contemplate employment or at least give USCIS the discretion to authorize employment in individual cases. See 8 C.F.R. § 214.1(e) (2004). Why would the regulations single out the B–2 category as the only one for which the government has no discretion to authorize employment?

2.   Given the express parenthetical in section 101(a)(15)(B), the BIA in *Healy & Goodchild* probably had little choice but to interpret the provision as it did. As a policy matter, however, why *not* have a nonimmigrant catchall provision for individuals who fall between the holes (rather than the present statutory approach of seeking to identify all possible purposes of temporary entry)?

3.   What harm would result if Healy and Goodchild were admitted for nine months to complete their courses of study at an unapproved school?

SECTION D.   FIANCÉS AND FIANCÉES

As you saw in chapter 3, marriage to an American citizen is one of the more important routes to admission for *permanent* residence in the United States. If the couple has not yet married, and the noncitizen spouse is already in the United States, the marriage can take place here. Then,

---

6. Nonimmigrants admitted for transit purposes under INA § 101(a)(15)(C) *without* visas are also ineligible to work. 8 C.F.R. § 214.1(e) (2004).

depending on his or her immigration status, the noncitizen might or might not be able to acquire LPR status without leaving the country. See chapter 6, § F (adjustment of status) below.

But what if the couple have not yet married and the noncitizen is outside the United States? The citizen could, of course, travel to the noncitizen's home country, assuming that country permits it. That can be expensive and, if both parties plan to return to the United States to live, wasteful. In addition it will often be difficult for the U.S. family members to attend the wedding. Moreover, the noncitizen cannot apply for an immigrant visa until after the marriage, and the processing can take a few months. The newlyweds would therefore have to choose between temporarily separating or remaining outside the United States in the interim—a potentially difficult wait if the citizen spouse has a job in the United States.

To alleviate the problem, Congress enacted INA §§ 101(a)(15)(K) and 214(d), both of which you should read now. The noncitizen fiancé(e) receives K–1 status; any noncitizen minor children accompanying or following to join receive K–2 status.

Section 214(d) requires that the fiancé(e)s have met each other during the two-year period preceding the filing of the petition. That provision was added by IMFA § 3(a), and it was controversial. Can you figure out why the requirement was added and what problems it can create? To what extent should United States immigration laws respond to cultural norms different from our own?

As you have seen, spouses of United States citizens normally acquire immigrant status as immediate relatives. Because immediate relatives are not numerically restricted, admission in this manner is theoretically immediate. In practice, however, long processing delays have kept spouses separated for lengthy periods. To diminish the problem, Congress in 2000 added INA § 101(a)(15)(K)(ii), which permits the spouses of United States citizens to enter as K-nonimmigrants (and to work) while their immigrant visas are being processed. See LIFE Act, § 1103(a). The noncitizen spouses receive "K–3" visas; their children following or accompanying to join receive "K–4" visas. Of course, the K-process itself can take time; how much separation time the new provision will actually avoid is therefore unclear.

If all goes well, the noncitizen fiancé(e) receives a visa, enters the United States, and marries the petitioning citizen within the statutory three-month period. But what if the noncitizen enters on a K–1 visa and the marriage does *not* take place within three months? Is that the end of it? Read on.

Moss v. INS

United States Court of Appeals, Fifth Circuit, 1981.
651 F.2d 1091.

■ GARZA, CIRCUIT JUDGE:

Appellant, Juanita de los Santos Moss, is a native and citizen of the Philippines. On or about July 16, 1977, she was admitted into the United

States under a "K visa" as a nonimmigrant alien fiancee of a United States citizen as provided by [INA §] 101(a)(15)(K). * * *[2]

The record indicates that Mrs. Moss had lived with her fiance for a year while in the Philippines and it is undisputed that both parties intended to marry at the time of her entry into the United States. On October 18, 1977, (92 days after her entry)[a] she married the man whom she had planned to marry. There is no doubt that the marriage was bona fide and no allegation has been made that she entered the United States for marriage solely in order to obtain immigration benefits. A child was born of their marriage, however, two months prior to the child's birth Mrs. Moss' husband abandoned her.

On March 16, 1978, the Immigration and Naturalization Service (I.N.S.) issued to Mrs. Moss a show cause order in order to establish her deportability. At the show cause hearing Mrs. Moss admitted that she had married ninety two days after her arrival but contended she was not subject to deportation because she had substantially complied with § 214(d) of the Act. The Immigration Judge, however, interpreted § 214(d) as a rigid and mandatory time period which must be strictly adhered to and, therefore, refused to allow evidence regarding the reasons why the marriage did not occur within the ninety-day time period. Consequently, the Judge found Mrs. Moss deportable because she was not married within the ninety-day period authorized by her "K visa". The Board of Immigration Appeals upheld the decision of the Immigration Judge.

The testimony at the hearing is not clear as to the reason why the marriage ceremony was not conducted within ninety days of Mrs. Moss' arrival. However, the testimony and record on appeal indicate that illness or other factors beyond Mrs. Moss' control may have caused the wedding to be delayed past the ninety-day time period. On appeal Mrs. Moss contends that § 214(d) does not set forth a hard and fast rule requiring a marriage ceremony within ninety days, but instead allows the ninety-day period to be tolled to compensate for delays beyond the alien's control. She argues that she substantially complied with § 214(d) and requests that her case be remanded in order that she may show that the delay in her marriage was due to no fault of her own. We believe Mrs. Moss' argument has merit.

---

2. INA § 214(d) [then] provide[d]:

[The petition] * * * shall be approved only after satisfactory evidence is submitted by the petitioner to establish that the parties have a *bona fide intention* to marry and are legally able and actually willing to conclude a valid marriage in the United States *within a period of ninety days* after the alien's arrival. In the event the marriage with the petitioner does not occur within *three months* of entry of the said alien and minor children, they shall be required to depart from the United States and upon failure to do so shall be deported * * * (emphasis added).

a. October 18 is actually 94 days after entry. If she had really married after only 92 days, there would probably be no issue here, since 92 days after July 16 would be October 16, which is exactly three months after entry.—Ed.

In 1970 Congress added the "K visa" provision to § 101(a)(15) in order to allow an alien fiancee or fiance to enter the United States to marry a United States citizen. "The purpose behind § 214(d) is to facilitate formation of marital relationships. ...The relevant inquiry, enunciated in the statute, is whether the parties have a *bona fide intent* to marry after the alien enters." *Menezes v. I.N.S.,* 601 F.2d 1028 (9th Cir.1979) (emphasis added). As a prerequisite to approval and issuance of the "K visa," the Attorney General must be satisfied that the petitioner-citizen and alien have a bona fide intention to marry soon after the alien's arrival.

Although the fourth sentence of § 214(d) provides for deportation in the event the marriage is not completed within ninety days, it seems the purpose of the time limit is to qualify the intention of the alien to soon marry upon entrance into the United States rather than to place an absolute and mandatory period of time within which the marriage ceremony must occur. "Marriage within the time limit essentially confirms the intent to marry after entry was bona fide." *Menezes v. I.N.S., supra.*

In this case it is beyond dispute that the parties intended to be married within ninety days of Mrs. Moss' arrival and were, in fact, married. It would be incongruous indeed to hold that the very same statute which facilitates entry into the United States for purposes of marriage would require deportation because the ceremony occurs two days late due to circumstances beyond the control of the nonimmigrant alien. As stated in Board Member Appleman's dissenting opinion, Congress did not intend the ninety-day limit to be so rigidly applied that it could not be tolled when, due to circumstances beyond the aliens' control, it becomes impossible to formalize the marriage within ninety days.[4] We hold that Mrs. Moss should have been allowed to show why she could not formalize her marriage within the ninety-day time period and, if she can demonstrate the two-day delay was due to factors beyond her control, the ninety-day time period must be tolled accordingly. For these reasons the decision of the Board of Immigration Appeals is reversed and the case remanded to the Immigration Judge for a determination of cause for the delay of the marriage.

REVERSED and REMANDED.

NOTES AND QUESTIONS

1. What do you think of the "substantial compliance" rule? What factors might have prompted the court to adopt a flexible interpretation?

2. Suppose as a member of the BIA you now had to decide whether a person who had been admitted on a fiancé(e) visa, and whose marriage had

---

4. We also find it significant that § 214(d) uses both "ninety days" and "three months" to describe the time period contemplated by the statute. We take notice of the fact that, with the exception of February, any three month period of the year will always amount to more than ninety days. If Congress had intended, as I.N.S. suggests, that the time period of § 214(d) was of controlling importance, we believe Congress would have used greater precision in defining that time period.

not taken place until four months after entry, is deportable. What would you do?

3.   A person admitted under subsection K may not extend his or her stay, 8 C.F.R. § 214.1(c)(3)(iv) (2004), may not change to a different nonimmigrant status, 8 C.F.R. § 248.2(b) (2004), and may not adjust his or her status to that of permanent resident other than on the basis of the marriage to the citizen petitioner, INA § 245(d). The permanent residence that results from such adjustments of status will be conditional under IMFA. *Id.*

PROBLEM 10

X enters the United States on a valid K–1 visa. Two months later, her 10–year–old son from a prior marriage joins her by entering on a valid K–2 visa. Two months after that, X marries the citizen petitioner. Are she and her son deportable under INA § 214(d)?

SECTION E.   A FEW OTHER NONIMMIGRANT CATEGORIES

INA § 101(a)(27) creates nonimmigrant "S" visas (often called "snitch" visas) for individuals who are able to share "critical reliable information" about either ordinary criminal organizations or terrorist organizations. Shortly after September 11, 2001 Congress made the "S" visa program a permanent part of immigration law; previously, it had been a temporary pilot program. Pub. L. 107–45, 115 Stat. 258 (Oct. 1, 2001). At about the same time, then Attorney General Ashcroft made clear that he wanted Justice Department employees to use them more frequently. The details on S visas and their renewed popularity are recounted in chapter 10, section B.6.

Statutes enacted in 2000 added several new nonimmigrant categories to the list. The details appear in Stephen Yale–Loehr et al, *T, U and V Visas: More Alphabet Soup for Immigration Practitioners*, 6 BIB 113 (Feb. 1, 2001). Here is a brief summary:

International trafficking of women and girls has become endemic:

Annually, at least 700,000 people, most of whom are women and children, are trafficked within and across international borders. Approximately 50,000 of those people are trafficked into the United States. Much of the trafficking involves trapping victims in the international sex trade through force, fraud, or coercion. However, a growing sector of victims are forced into labor.

The victims of trafficking are primarily impoverished women and girls who are lured into trafficking networks through "false promises of decent working conditions at relatively good pay as nannies, maids, dancers, factory workers, restaurant workers, sales clerks or models." Other traffickers simply purchase "children from poor families and sell them into prostitution or into various types of forced or bonded labor."

Once within the trafficking networks, the victims are frequently transported away from their home communities. They are forced to "engage in sex acts and slavery-like labor" through physical violence such as rape, torture, starvation, imprisonment, threats, physical abuse, and coercion. The traffickers threaten them with physical harm to themselves and their families if they escape or even attempt to escape. The women and children are often further victimized because they are illegally present in the United States.

Yale–Loehr et al, above, at 113–14; see also David Kyle & Rey Koslowski (Eds.), Global Human Smuggling: Comparative Perspectives (2001); Nora Demleitner, *The Law at a Crossroads: The Construction of Migrant Women Trafficked into Prostitution*, in Kyle & Koslowski, above, at 257 et seq.

In response, the Trafficking Victims Protection Act of 2000 (part of the Victims of Trafficking and Violence Protection Act of 2000, Pub. L. 106–386, 114 Stat. 1464 (Oct. 28, 2000)), Div. A, § 107(e), created a new INA § 101(a)(15)(T). The T-visas are for victims of "a severe form of trafficking in persons" who are physically present in the United States or a port of entry as a result of that trafficking. If age 15 or over, the person must comply with any reasonable request for assistance in the investigation or prosecution of the trafficking. The person must also demonstrate "extreme hardship involving unusual and severe harm upon removal." The Secretary of Homeland Security may also grant T-status to designated family members who are accompanying or following to join. INA § 101(a)(15)(T). The principal T-nonimmigrant may work. INA § 101(i)(2). There is a limit of 5,000 T-visas per year, not counting the family members. INA § 214(o)(2). After three years the T-nonimmigrants may adjust to LPR status under prescribed conditions. INA § 245(l)(1)(A). See generally Lisa Raffonelli, *INS Final Rule to Assist Victims of Trafficking*, 23 Refugee Reports 1 (Apr. 2002) (commenting on T visas).

The Violence Against Women Act of 2000 (also part of the Victims of Trafficking and Violence Protection Act of 2000, above), Div. B, § 1513(b), created new INA § 101(a)(15)(U). The U-visas are for those who have "suffered substantial physical or mental abuse" as a result of any of several enumerated acts of violence. The list includes rape, torture, trafficking, incest, domestic violence, sexual assault, prostitution, female genital mutilation, involuntary servitude, abduction, felonious assault, and several other criminal acts. The person must possess information concerning that criminal activity and must help law enforcement officials to investigate or prosecute. Various family members may also be admitted if extreme hardship would otherwise ensue and the investigation or prosecution would be harmed without those family members' assistance. INA § 101(a)(15)(U). The annual numerical limit on U-visas is 10,000, not counting the family members. INA § 214(p)(2). U-nonimmigrants may work. INA

§ 214(p)(3)(B). After three years, U-nonimmigrants may adjust to LPR status under prescribed conditions. INA § 245(m)(1)(A).

Finally, the LIFE Act added new INA § 101(a)(15)(V) to provide limited relief to certain long-divided families. As discussed earlier, to remedy the problem of lengthy administrative processing times for immigrant visas for spouses of United States citizens, the LIFE Act expanded K (fiancé) visas to admit spouses of citizens as nonimmigrants. The same statute provided analogous, but much more limited, relief for the spouses and children of LPRs. The new V-category permits their admission as nonimmigrants while they wait for their priority dates to become current, but only if the petition was filed before December 21, 2000, the petition has since been approved (even though the State Department has not yet issued the visa), and only after the wait has exceeded three years. INA § 101(a)(15)(V). There are no numerical limits on V-visas. Employment is permitted, INA § 214(q)(1)(A), and adjustment of status to permanent residence is contemplated, INA § 214(q)(3).

SECTION F. GENERAL NONIMMIGRANT PROBLEMS

1. INTENT TO REMAIN PERMANENTLY

Most of the nonimmigrant categories you have studied require either that the person seek to enter the country "temporarily," e.g., INA § 101(a)(15)(B, H, J, L), or that the person have a foreign residence "which he has no intention of abandoning," e.g., INA § 101(a)(15)(B, F, J), or both. In any of those cases, the individual who unequivocally intends to remain permanently in the United States is obviously ineligible.

The problem can arise in several contexts. The person might be applying for one of the relevant nonimmigrant visas. The person might already have received the visa and be applying for admission at a designated port of entry. After admission, the person might be applying for extension of his or her stay or for a change to another nonimmigrant status that is similarly inconsistent with an intent to remain permanently. Moreover, if after admission ICE discovers that the person originally entered with the intent to remain permanently, he or she might be deportable as one who was inadmissible at entry, INA § 237(a)(1)(A), or as one who failed to maintain his or her nonimmigrant status, INA § 237(a)(1)(C)(i). A finding of preconceived intent to remain can also be a negative factor in various discretionary determinations. *Cubillos–Gonzalez v. INS,* 352 F.2d 782, 783–84 (9th Cir.1965).

But preconceived intent to remain does not preclude a genuine change of mind. Of course, if the change occurs very soon after the initial admission, the immigration authorities are more likely to suspect fraud. Ultimately, however, the question presented is one of fact.

Preconceived intent to remain also differs from what has been called "dual intent." A person might enter the United States with alternative plans in mind. The BIA and several courts have held that "a desire to remain in this country permanently in accordance with the law, should the opportunity to do so present itself, is not necessarily inconsistent with lawful nonimmigrant status." *Matter of Hosseinpour,* 15 I. & N. Dec. 191, 192 (BIA 1975)(citing court decisions); accord, *Lauvik v. INS,* 910 F.2d 658, 660–61 (9th Cir.1990). Thus, if a nonimmigrant enters with the intent to remain only temporarily, but with the hope of acquiring LPR status some day if the law permits it, there is no violation.

Intent to remain raises not only legal issues, but also ethical ones. Professors David Weissbrodt and Laura Danielson summarize three of the sources of ethical constraints on immigration lawyers:

> The Model Rules of Professional Conduct drafted by the American Bar Association (ABA) have now been adopted by more than three-fourths of the jurisdictions in the U.S., including Washington, D.C., either completely or with relatively minor changes. While the Model Rules constitute the predominant approach to legal ethics, there are other relevant standards. Immigration lawyers are subject to the ethical rules of practice before the Department of Homeland Security [and EOIR—Ed.]. Also, there are still some states (e.g., New York) that apply the Model Code of Professional Responsibility, which was the ABA-drafted predecessor of the Model Rules. * * *

> [There are] three sources of ethical constraint on the immigration lawyer. The first source is the Model Rules adopted by the ABA in 1983. The Model Rules include aspirational goals, rules of permissible conduct, and mandatory rules. In the Model Rules, the word "should" expresses an aspirational goal and the word "may" expresses other permissible conduct that lawyers are not necessarily required to follow. Almost all of the rules, however, mandate a minimum level of conduct for the lawyer. Should the attorney's conduct fall below this minimum level he or she may be subject to sanction. The Model Rules use the words "shall" and "shall not" to identify rules for which lawyers may be disciplined.

> The second source derives from the regulations governing the conduct of lawyers who appear before [DHS and EOIR]. The Code of Federal Regulations [now lists twelve] nonexclusive reasons for suspending or disbarring the immigration lawyer, some of which overlap the Model Rules and some of which are unique to immigration practice. [8 C.F.R. § 1003.103 (2004).] * * *

> The third source is the Model Code adopted by the ABA in 1969. The Model Code identifies ethical considerations that the lawyer strives to achieve. Should the lawyer fail to abide by ethical considerations, however, there are theoretically no sanctions in most states. The Model Code also contains disciplinary rules that mandate a minimum level of conduct for the lawyer. Should the attorney's conduct fall below this minimum level he or she may be subject to disbarment, suspension, or other sanction.

David Weissbrodt & Laura Danielson, Immigration Law and Procedure in a Nutshell 587–89 (5th ed. 2005).

Only in recent years has there been much writing on the ethical problems specific to immigration law. Here is an updated excerpt from one of the pioneering pieces:

David Weissbrodt and Laura Danielson, Should the Lawyer Tell the Client About a Fixed Intent to Immigrate?, in Immigration Law and Procedure in a Nutshell

pp. 593–96 (5th ed. 2005).

Different sorts of ethical problems are raised in advising the client regarding his or her fixed intent to immigrate to the United States. The problem arises when a client, otherwise eligible for a non-immigrant visa, for example an F–1 student visa, informs the lawyer that he or she wants to immigrate to the United States. The client would be ineligible for the F–1 visa and most other nonimmigrant visas, however, if he or she has a present intent to immigrate. What should the lawyer tell the client to do? If the lawyer tells the client not to form a present intent to immigrate, would the lawyer be assisting the client in perpetrating a fraud?

Both the Model Code and the Model Rules have sections dealing with client fraud and the lawyer's duty, none of which provide any clear-cut solutions to this problem. Rule 1.2(d) of the Model Rules refers most directly to this situation: "[a] lawyer shall not counsel to engage, or assist a client, in conduct that the lawyer knows is criminal or fraudulent ..." The Model Code contains similar prohibitions. According to DR 7–102(A) of the Model Code:

(A) a lawyer shall not: * * *

(6) Participate in the creation or preservation of evidence when he knows or it is obvious that the evidence is false.

(7) Counsel or assist his client in conduct that the lawyer knows to be illegal or fraudulent.

In addition, EC 7–6 of the Model Code discusses the lawyer's position in assisting the client in developing state of mind evidence. It provides:

[The lawyer] may properly assist his client in the development and preservation of evidence of existing motive, intent, or desire; obviously, he may not do anything furthering the creation or preservation of false evidence.

* * * Those provisions, however, do not resolve whether the client commits a fraud in declaring that he or she has no present intent to immigrate. It is not clear that the lawyer would assist the client in committing a fraud or in preserving false evidence by discussing the effect of the client's intent on his or her immigration status. The situation is made more complex because only the client knows his or her own intent. An attorney, however, can

advise the client as to the consequences of pursuing a specific course of conduct, which is separate from the question of the client's intent.

Other sections of the Model Rules and the Model Code imply that the lawyer has an obligation to discuss the probable consequences of alternate courses of action with the client. Rule 1.2 of the Model Rules prohibits the lawyer from assisting the client in fraudulent conduct, but "a lawyer may discuss the legal consequences of any proposed course of conduct with a client and may counsel or assist a client to make a good faith effort to determine the validity, scope, meaning or application of the law." Model Rule 1.2(d). EC 7–8 of the Model Code provides that "[a] lawyer should advise his client of the possible effect of each legal alternative." In this situation, the lawyer is not urging the client to adopt one course of action over another. Rather, he or she is merely discussing the client's two legal alternatives—to form a present intent to become an immigrant or a non-immigrant—and the legal effects of each. The lawyer explains the consequences and the client makes the decision about his or her present intent. Such advice does not appear to be the kind of fraud contemplated by the drafters of the Model Code and the Model Rules.

In addition, one might draw inferences from the drafting history of the Model Rules. In an earlier discussion draft of the Model Rules, Rule 2.3(a)(2) declared that a lawyer could not give advice that he or she "could reasonably foresee would . . . aid the client in contriving false testimony." No counterpart to this draft Rule 2.3 appears in the Model Rules adopted in 1983. From this omission one could infer (1) that the drafting committee did not consider this advice an ethical violation, (2) that in a criminal law context this draft provision would be inappropriate, or (3) possibly that Rule 1.2 already covered this situation. In any case, even if draft Rule 2.3(a)(2) had appeared in the final version, the lawyer's advice would be unethical only in the unlikely event that it aided the client in contriving false testimony. Hence, the immigration lawyer can probably ethically explain the consequences of the client's present intent to immigrate on his or her eligibility for a nonimmigrant visa without ethical violation, so long as the lawyer does not suggest which course of action the client should actually adopt.

———

See also Harry J. Joe, *Ethics in Immigration Law: Immigration Benefit Fraud and the Peril of Conscious Avoidance*, June 2002 Immigration Briefings ("wilful blindness," or the conscious avoidance of information that would confirm the lawyer's suspicion of fraud, can constitute knowledge for ethical purposes).

PROBLEMS 11–13

(Problems in Ethics)

In working out these problems, you need to know that Rule 1.3 of the ABA Model Rules of Professional Conduct requires the lawyer to "act with reasonable diligence and promptness in representing a client." The comment accompanying Rule 1.3 adds:

> * * * A lawyer should act with commitment and dedication to the interests of the client and with zeal in advocacy upon the client's behalf. However, a lawyer is not bound to press for every advantage that might be realized for a client. A lawyer has professional discretion in determining the means by which a matter should be pursued.

Consider also ABA Model Rule 1.6:

> (a) A lawyer shall not reveal information relating to representation of a client unless the client consents after consultation, except for disclosures that are impliedly authorized in order to carry out the representation, and except as stated in paragraph (b).

> (b) A lawyer may reveal such information to the extent the lawyer reasonably believes necessary:

> (1) to prevent the client from committing a criminal act that the lawyer believes is likely to result in imminent death or substantial bodily harm; OR

> (2) * * * [not applicable here].

Two final pieces of information: ABA Model Rule 1.6(b), which lists the exceptions to the confidentiality requirement, replaced Disciplinary Rule 4–101(C), subparagraph (3) of which had permitted a lawyer to reveal "the intention of his client to commit a crime and the information necessary to prevent the crime." In some states, versions of DR 4–101(C) are still in force.

The last datum is that the "Terminology" section introducing the ABA Model Rules provides in item [5]:

> "Knowingly," "Known," or "Knows" denotes actual knowledge of the fact in question. A person's knowledge may be inferred from circumstances.

Problem 11. Your client tells you she plans to apply for an extension of her F–1 visa. In the course of the conversation, however, she makes crystal clear that she intends to remain permanently in the United States whether she can do so lawfully or not. What, exactly, should you tell her?

Problem 12. After you give the client the advice you consider appropriate, she says she plans to file her application for an F–1 extension anyway. She tells you she is "willing to take the chance of getting caught." Should you report her to the government?

Problem 13. You now have a subtler client. The following exchange takes place:

Client: I'd like to get a green card. Is there any chance of that?

Lawyer (after exhausting all the possibilities): I'm afraid there's really no way.

Client: Then how about just extending my B–1? When it runs out, I'll stay on. The worst that can happen is they deport me.

Lawyer: Well, I have to tell you that if that's your intent you're not eligible for an extension. To qualify for a B–1 extension, you need an intent not to abandon your foreign residence.

Client: Well, why don't you just send it in for me anyway? I'll worry about my immigration problems when the time comes.

Lawyer: Sorry, that would violate my ethical obligations as an attorney.

Client (with knowing smile): OK, I understand the bind you're in. I just changed my mind. All I want to do is stay for another year. Then I plan to go home.

Lawyer: I appreciate your sensitivity, but obviously you're just saying this to insulate me. We both know you plan to stay on.

Client (still smiling): No, seriously, I really mean it. I'll leave in a year.

Lawyer: Sorry, I just can't do it.

Client (no longer smiling): OK, so you're an ethical lawyer. That's very nice. Fine. I'll agree not to commit a fraud. I truly will leave in a year. Honestly.

Lawyer: Well, I don't know . . .

Client: Hey, come on. Are you my lawyer or my judge?

You're still inclined not to believe him, but there is no way to be sure of your instincts. Should you fill out the application for him?

2. CHANGE OF NONIMMIGRANT STATUS

As the preceding materials demonstrate, intentions can change. A person who was admitted as a student might now wish to become a treaty trader. Someone who was admitted as a business visitor might want to switch to intra-company transferee. An individual admitted as a temporary worker might now wish to become an LPR.

For the nonimmigrant who would now prefer either another nonimmigrant category or permanent residence, and who qualifies substantively for the desired status, one procedural option is to go home and apply to the appropriate U.S. consulate for a new visa. But home might be far away, or home might be a country that cannot be counted on to allow the person to leave again or, for any of several other reasons, it might simply be more convenient to do the paperwork here.

Recognizing those needs, Congress has enacted two provisions. Under INA section 245, certain nonimmigrants (among others) can become permanent residents without leaving the United States. Under section 248, certain nonimmigrants can switch to different nonimmigrant categories without leaving the country. The usual terminology is that one *adjusts* to *permanent* resident status under section 245 but *changes* to another *nonimmigrant* status under section 248.

Section 245 will be explored fully in chapter 6. The emphasis here will be on section 248, which you should read now. Note one important structural similarity: To receive the benefit of either section, the person must not only satisfy several specific conditions of eligibility, but also obtain the favorable exercise of administrative discretion. Notice too that the person has to have been lawfully admitted as a nonimmigrant; that he or she must be "continuing to maintain that status;" and that certain categories of nonimmigrants are ineligible to change to certain other categories.[7] Noncitizens who are inadmissible for having been unlawfully present for more than six months, and certain other designated noncitizens, are also ineligible for change of status. See INA §§ 212(a)(9)(B)(i), 248.

Suppose, instead of wanting to change to a different nonimmigrant category, a nonimmigrant simply wants to extend his or her existing stay. Normally, it is not necessary to return home for a new visa. The person generally may apply to USCIS for an extension (assuming the substantive criteria for the particular nonimmigrant category are met). 8 C.F.R. § 214.1(c) (2004). Extensions are not available, however, to those who have overstayed or otherwise violated the terms of their existing stays, absent "extraordinary circumstances." *Id.* § 214.1(c)(4).

PROBLEM 14

X, an Australian law professor, is doing research at the American Bar Foundation under a grant provided by the Australian government. He is here on a J–1 visa, and his authorized stay will expire eight months from now. He would like to enroll in an LL.M. program at Boalt Hall. No extension of his J–1 visa is possible. What should he do with respect to his immigration status? (This is tricky; read INA §§ 248 *and* 212(e) carefully).

---

7. The regulations exclude additional combinations. An M–1 nonimmigrant (vocational student) may not use section 248 to obtain F–1 (academic student) status. 8 C.F.R. § 248.1(c) (2004). And no one can use section 248 to obtain K (fiancé) or C (transit) status. *Id.* § 248.1(a).

CHAPTER 5

EXCLUSION GROUNDS AND WAIVERS

As you saw in the two preceding chapters, every noncitizen who seeks admission to the United States must fit within one of the statutory categories of immigrant or nonimmigrant. Even then, however, there is another set of hurdles—the inadmissibility grounds (often called "exclusion grounds"). Under INA § 212(a), various classes of noncitizens are "ineligible to receive visas and ineligible to be admitted to the United States" unless they qualify for waivers under any of the specific statutory provisions that you will see throughout this chapter. The exclusion grounds cover a wide range of subject matter: communicable diseases, criminal activity, national security, poverty, protection of the work force, the functioning of the immigration system itself, and miscellaneous other concerns.

In addition to making noncitizens ineligible for visas and rendering them "inadmissible" at ports of entry, these provisions can affect noncitizens who are already present in the United States. Nonimmigrants can sometimes adjust to immigrant status without having to go abroad for new visas, but only if they are "admissible." INA § 245(a). Many years after entry a noncitizen can be removed if, at the time of entry or adjustment of status, he or she was in fact "inadmissible." INA § 237(a)(1)(A). The lawfulness of one's original admission can also be called into question if he or she eventually applies for naturalization to United States citizenship. INA § 316(a).

As a result of IIRIRA, the exclusion grounds directly affect one other large group of noncitizens even though they are already in the United States—those who entered without inspection. Until 1996, noncitizens who were outside the United States and seeking to "enter" were subject to the various "exclusion" grounds, while those who had already entered—legally or illegally—could not be removed unless they fell within a separate list of "deportation" grounds. "Entry," in other words, determined which set of grounds would govern a person's physical removal.

In 1996, following a suggestion advanced in T. Alexander Aleinikoff & David A. Martin, Immigration Process and Policy 342–47 (1st ed. 1985), Congress decided that the line should be drawn instead at "admission." In IIRIRA § 302(a), Congress amended INA § 235(a)(1) to say that "[a]n alien present in the United States who has not been admitted ... shall be deemed for purposes of this Act an applicant for admission." As an applicant for admission, such a person becomes inadmissible (with some exceptions) under INA § 212(a)(6)(A).

With so much turning on whether a noncitizen has been "admitted," careful definition becomes crucial. At the same time that Congress enacted the above change, it replaced the statutory definition of "entry" with a definition of "admission." The latter appears in INA § 101(a)(13) and raises some complex issues that will be deferred until chapter 7. See generally Linton Joaquin, *The 1996 Immigration Act: Grounds of Inadmissibility and Deportability and Available Waivers*, 73 IR 1641 (Nov. 25, 1996). For now, it is enough to know that the exclusion grounds apply not only to those who are outside the United States trying to come in, but also to those who are already here without having been admitted.

A further word on terminology: Before IIRIRA, noncitizens who were found to be "inadmissible," and who did not receive discretionary relief, were "excluded." Those who were found to be "deportable," and who did not receive discretionary relief, were "deported." IIRIRA changed the vocabulary. Now, noncitizens who are found either inadmissible or deportable, and who do not receive discretionary relief, are "removed." This might mean either turning them away at the border or evicting them from the interior. The proceedings themselves used to be called either "exclusion" or "deportation" proceedings, depending on whether the person was inadmissible or deportable; now, both are called "removal" proceedings.

From the inception of immigration control in 1875, the exclusion grounds have expanded steadily in response to the changing social concerns of succeeding eras. The pattern is easy to describe: Congress frequently added new grounds but rarely repealed old ones.[1] In a famous passage, one court characterized the growing list of exclusions as "a magic mirror, reflecting the fears and concerns of past Congresses." *Lennon v. INS,* 527 F.2d 187, 189 (2d Cir.1975).

The excerpt that follows will describe how and why the various exclusion grounds evolved. This account is of more than historical interest. Although recent amendments have been substantial, the vast majority of the older exclusion grounds remain intact. Moreover, immigration lawyers need at least a passing familiarity with even the repealed grounds. As noted earlier, a noncitizen's admissibility at the time of his or her original entry (or adjustment of status) often affects removal, naturalization, and other immigration-related proceedings many years down the road. For all these reasons, your study of the exclusion grounds needs to include their historical roots.

---

1. The Immigration Act of 1990 was a large exception. For the first (and, so far, only) time in United States history, Congress repealed or narrowed several exclusion grounds. For an excellent description of the exclusion grounds added or changed by IIRI- RA, see Enid Trucios–Haynes & Lois Gimpel Shaukat, *Grounds of Inadmissibility under the Illegal Immigration Reform and Immigrant Responsibility Act of 1996*, January & February 1998 Immigration Briefings (2 parts).

Committee on the Judiciary, United States House of Representatives, Grounds for Exclusion of Aliens Under the Immigration and Nationality Act

Serial No. 7, 1988.
Pp. 5–27.

* * *

The first Federal legislation designating excludable classes was enacted in 1875. During the period prior to 1875 there was a series of colonial and State enactments focusing primarily on the exclusion of paupers and convicts. The colony of Massachusetts enacted legislation prohibiting the entry of paupers as early as 1645, and a law enacted in 1700 excluded the infirm unless security was given that they would not become public charges. In colonial and subsequently State legislation, Massachusetts and New York adopted the practice of requiring security or bonds that would be forfeited if immigrants became public charges. * * *

During the earliest days of the colonial period, the British government adopted a policy of exporting convicts to the colonies. Concern about the exportation of convicts dates back to this period in our history. The colonies of Virginia and Pennsylvania adopted resolutions in the 17th century against the bringing in of "jail-bird" and "fellons" and Delaware enacted similar legislation in 1704. The States followed suit, with the encouragement of the Continental Congress which unanimously resolved on September 16, 1788: "That it be and it is thereby recommended to the several states to pass laws for preventing the transportation of convicted malefactors from foreign countries into the United States." Six States are reported to have "promptly adopted suitable laws."

Regulating the entry of aliens was considered the responsibility of the affected States well into the 19th century. At this point, the Federal Government began to take an increasing interest in regulating the admission of aliens. * * *

The Act of March 3, 1875 was the first Federal legislation designating excludable classes. The Act prohibited the entry of aliens convicted of certain crimes as well as the importation of women for the purpose of prostitution. With amendment, both exclusions remain in effect today.

* * *

[In 1882] Congress added mental defectives ("lunatic[s]" and "idiot[s]") and "any person unable to take care of himself or herself without becoming a public charge" to the excludable class * * *.

The 1882 legislation was enacted primarily in response to the U.S. Supreme Court's 1875 ruling that New York's attempts to regulate immigration by taxing or requiring bonds for incoming immigrants was unconstitutional. The Court held that the tax act was unconstitutional because it was a violation of the commerce clause, as were similar laws of Louisiana and California. This ended the State source of funds which had been used to assist the large numbers of immigrants entering through the immigrant depot of Castle Garden in New York, and gave rise to extensive lobbying for Federal control and financial support of immigration. * * *

* * *

[Historian John] Higham also observed, "Although the basic Chinese exclusion law was enacted in 1882, the year of the first general immigration law, the Congress that passed the two measures sensed no connection between them." The Chinese Exclusion Act of May 6, 1882 was enacted out of a concern for protecting domestic labor from foreign competition, combined with racial prejudice. It had more in common with subsequent racially-based numerical restrictions than with the qualitative grounds for exclusion. The Chinese exclusion laws were repealed by the Act of December 17, 1943.

* * *

The first of the alien contract labor laws was enacted on February 26, 1885, against a background of depression, strikes, and intense lobbying by the Knights of Labor. The Act prohibited the importation of contract foreign labor. Its purpose was to protect domestic labor, primarily by curtailing the practice of employers importing large numbers of foreign workers in order to force domestic workers to work at reduced wages. This was particularly prevalent in the coal fields. Certain exceptions to the prohibition were allowed, including skilled labor which could not be found in this country, and others were added and deleted by subsequent amendments. The contract labor provisions were the subject of considerable discussion and revision before their repeal in 1952. * * *

* * *

The 1891 Act increased the list of excludable aliens, adding insane persons, polygamists, and, in response to fear of epidemics in Europe, "persons suffering from a loathsome or a dangerous contagious disease." A medical examination of aliens before landing was required as part of the inspection process. * * * Regarding criminals, the 1891 Act made excludable "persons who have been convicted of a felony or other infamous crime or misdemeanor involving moral turpitude." This is the first use of the term "moral turpitude" in the immigration law, and it was adopted without comment in the accompanying reports.

* * *

Concern about the forced or assisted immigration of undesirables to the United States plays an essential role in the historical development of the exclusion laws, dating back to the colonial period. Involuntary immigration is not generally a concern today, although the experience with the criminals included among the Mariel entrants from Cuba in 1980 is a vivid example of what past legislators feared.

The debate on the 1891 legislation also marked the beginning of a shift from a dominant concern about control of the largely involuntary or contracted migration of undesirables to a desire for more general restriction of the numbers and quality of immigrants coming voluntarily. The chief instrument of this restriction, proposed repeatedly until its final enactment in 1917, was the literacy test barring the entry of aliens who were unable to read or write. * * *

The House report on the 1891 legislation specifically rejected an "educational examination." However, legislation including a literacy requirement passed both houses 6 years later in 1897, only to be vetoed by President Grover Cleveland in the first of four Presidential vetoes. Quoting from President Cleveland's veto message:

> A radical departure from our national policy relating to immigration is here presented. Heretofore we have welcomed all who came to us from other lands, except those whose moral or physical condition or history threatened danger to our national welfare and safety. * * *

> The ability to read and write as required in this bill, in and of itself, affords, in my opinion, a misleading test of contented industry and supplies unsatisfactory evidence of desirable citizenship or a proper apprehension of the benefits of our institutions.

* * *

The exclusion of anarchists had been recommended during the 19th century by, among others, the Ford Committee in 1889. The adoption of such a provision in 1903 followed the assassination of President William McKinley in 1901 by Leon Czolgosz, described by John Higham as "an anarchist of American birth but obviously foreign extraction." * * *

The 1903 Act provided in section 2 for the exclusion of "anarchists, or persons who believe in or advocate the overthrow by force or violence of the Government of the United States or of all governments or of all forms of law, or the assassination of public officials." Section 38 prohibited the entry of anarchists and their affiliates in even greater detail. This marked a significant change in the law. As John Higham notes, "By forbidding the admission and authorizing the deportation of foreign proponents of anarchism, the law penalized newcomers for their opinions for the first time since 1798," under the unpopular Alien and Sedition Acts.

* * *

In addition to "idiots" and "insane persons," the 1903 Act provided for the exclusion of "epileptics," and "persons who have been insane within five years previously" and "persons who have had two or more attacks of insanity at any time previously." According to the report of the House Committee on Immigration and Naturalization, these additions were included "at the solicitation of some of the States whose asylums for treatment of the insane have become overcrowded with aliens, who, after the expiration of one year from the date of arrival, can not be deported, and thus become permanent and onerous charges upon communities having their own burdens of this kind to bear."

The 1903 legislation also provided a limited waiver of excludability for persons afflicted with a loathsome or dangerous contagious disease, in the case of wives or children sent for by immigrants who have filed for citizenship.

* * *

In what was described in the House report as a "humane provision," the 1903 Act provided for the return with any rejected alien who was helpless because of "sickness, physical disability, or infancy" of any accompanying alien whose protection or guardianship was required by the rejected alien. * * *

Statistics were provided in the report of the Senate Committee on Immigration on aliens debarred by cause during the decade 1892–1901. Out of a total of 26,031 debarred aliens, the largest group were paupers or persons likely to become public charges (17,868). The next largest groups were contract laborers (6,119), and persons with loathsome or dangerous contagious diseases (1,487).

* * *

* * * More than a million aliens entered in fiscal year 1905 alone, which caused President Theodore Roosevelt to observe, "In other words, in the single year that has just elapsed there came to this country a greater number of people than came here during the one hundred and sixty-nine years of our colonial life which intervened between the first landing of Jamestown and the Declaration of Independence."

* * *

Exclusion of individual aliens on qualitative grounds continued to be the principal means of immigration control under the 1907 Act, which again enlarged the classes of excludable aliens. The Act's additions most notably did not include an educational or literacy test, which had been favored by immigration restrictionists and supported by President Roosevelt. * * *

* * *

Immigration legislation was vetoed three times [between 1911 and 1917], once by President William Taft and twice by President Woodrow Wilson. President Wilson's second veto was overridden, and the legislation was enacted as the Immigration Act of February 5, 1917. With amendments, the 1917 Act remained in effect until its recodification, revision, and repeal in 1952.

* * *

The focal point of the controversy over immigration legislation during the 20–year period beginning at the turn of the century, and particularly between 1911 and 1917, was the literacy requirement. Section 3 of the legislation enacted in 1917 provided for the exclusion of "all aliens over sixteen years of age, physically capable of reading, who can not read the

English language, or some other language or dialect, including Hebrew or Yiddish,'' with exemptions for specified relatives of immigrants and U.S. citizens and for aliens seeking entry to avoid religious persecution.

The literacy requirement was controversial because it marked a turning point in U.S. immigration policy. Although it related to individual qualifications, the literacy test was perceived as a means of restricting the number of aliens entering. This shift in policy was more obvious in the next decade, with the adoption of outright numerical limitations, but there was no question that this was also the intent of the literacy provision. * * *

Commenting on President Wilson's veto in 1915, Congressman Augustus Gardner of Massachusetts said:

> The President is entirely correct when he says in his veto message that the object of the literacy test in the immigration bill is restriction, not selection. The President believes that every able-bodied person not of questionable character ought to be admitted to this country. Now without doubt, that is our historic policy. . . .

> We restrictionists believe that altogether too many able-bodied persons are coming into this country, whether their characters are good, bad, or indifferent. We believe that immigrants are coming too fast to be assimilated, and we believe that the low wages which they are willing to accept are a menace to our high standard of living. Therefore we declare that the time has come for Congress to abandon the historic policy of letting in every able-bodied person whose character is not questionable, and in lieu of that policy we believe that we ought to adopt the policy of substantially cutting down the number of immigrants, even if in so doing we are forced to exclude many persons who might prove to be desirable citizens.

The Dillingham Commission [established by Congress in 1907 had] recommended the literacy provision as the best means of restricting what they defined as the less desirable "new immigration." In their view, the "old immigration" occurred prior to 1883 and was essentially a movement of permanent settlers from Northern and Western Europe. The "new immigration" came primarily from Eastern and Southern Europe, and was made up predominantly of single males rather than families, many of whom were coming temporarily to make money in the cities. The "new immigration" was generally characterized by the Dillingham Commission in much less-favorable terms than the "old immigration": more than 35 percent of the "new immigrants" were illiterate, they congregated together in groups rather than assimilating, and they were used to low wages and willing to accept them here, to the detriment of U.S. workers. * * *

The mathematical rationale behind the proposed literacy provision was explained as follows by Senator Dillingham on the Senate floor in 1916:

> We took the nations from which this immigration comes so largely, the eastern and southern nations of Europe, and ascertained what the literacy percentage was among the people of those

nations. We saw at once that if we adopted the educational test, it would substantially decrease the volume of that stream 30 percent, which was just about what we wanted to accomplish. On the other hand, the educational test would in no way affect England or Scotland or Ireland or the Scandinavian countries or Germany or France. The degree of illiteracy in those countries is negligible. . . .

Like the Commission he had chaired, Senator Dillingham urged Congress to adopt the literacy provision in lieu of any numerical formula as a means of restricting immigration.

* * *

As noted previously, legislation including the literacy requirement was first vetoed in 1897, by President Grover Cleveland. It was vetoed a second time on February 14, 1913 by President William Taft, who described the provision as violating "a principle that ought, in my opinion, to be upheld in immigration," and referred to the accompanying letter of his Secretary of Commerce and Labor. Secretary Charles Nagel outlined his opposition to the literacy provision in detail, in part as follows:

So far as the industrial conditions are concerned, I think the question has been superficially considered. We need labor in this country, and the natives are unwilling to do the work which the aliens come over to do. * * *

* * *

President Woodrow Wilson vetoed bills containing the literacy provision twice, in 1915 and 1917, the second time unsuccessfully. He argued basically against the concept of restriction, and against basing eligibility on opportunity rather than personal quality. * * *

* * *

The 1917 legislation added to the list of those excludable as mental or physical defectives, "persons of constitutional psychopathic inferiority; persons with chronic alcoholism," and persons afflicted with tuberculosis "in any form." The report of the House Committee on Immigration and Naturalization went into some detail about the new eugenic category of "persons of constitutional psychopathic inferiority," noting that while the term was unfamiliar to laymen, "with alienists, however, it has a well-defined meaning. One has defined it to be 'a congenital defect in the emotional or volitional fields of mental activity which results in inability to make proper adjustment to the environments.' " * * *

The 1917 Act also limited the provision excluding aliens with a defect which would prevent them from earning a living to those with physical, as opposed to mental, defects, as in current law. Quoting from the report of the Senate Committee on Immigration, "The reasons for excluding a physically defective alien are likelihood of his becoming a public charge and inability by his own exertions to care for himself and those dependent upon him, while the real object of excluding the mentally defective is to prevent the introduction into the country of strains of mental defect that may continue and multiply through succeeding generations, irrespective of the immediate effect thereof on earning capacity."

* * *

The 1917 Act also added to the list of excludable aliens "persons who have been deported under any of the provisions of this Act, and who may again seek admission within 1 year from the date of such deportation, unless [the Secretary of Labor consents to their reapplying.]" The Senate Committee on Immigration explained that the purpose of this provision was "to reach the quite extensive and very annoying practice of aliens expelled from the country or debarred at the ports thereof immediately reattempting to break past the barriers and enter."

* * *

* * * [In] the Act of June 5, 1920 * * * [t]he excludable classes were enlarged to cover saboteurs, aliens engaged in writing, publishing, etc., matter advocating proscribed activities and aliens who were members of associations involved in the circulation of such matter. * * *

* * *

The purpose of the Immigration Act of May 26, 1924 was clearly stated in the title, which designated it as, "An act to limit the immigration of aliens into the United States, and for other purposes." Like the temporary Act of May 19, 1921, it accomplished this purpose directly rather than indirectly, by means of numerical limitations eventually in the form of the national origins quota system. * * * From 1921 to the present time, immigration has been regulated quantitatively as well as qualitatively, by the increasing list of grounds for exclusion. Together with the 1917 Act, the 1924 Act constituted the basic immigration law until 1952.

The 1924 Act [excluded] most aliens who were ineligible for citizenship * * *. At the time, this provision served to totally exclude the Japanese, and was controversial. According to the House Committee on Immigration and Naturalization, naturalization then was limited "to 'free white persons and to aliens of African nativity and to persons of African descent'." The Committee wrote, "All must agree that nothing can be gained by permitting to be built up in the United States colonies of those who can not, under the law, become naturalized citizens, and must therefore owe allegiance to another government."

* * *

With the exception of legislation on the exclusion of subversives and related classes,[a] which is discussed separately below, only minor changes

***

a. Important statutes enacted at the peak of the Cold War are discussed on pages 17–19 above.—Ed.

were made in the grounds for exclusion during the period 1924–1952, which encompassed the depression and World War II. The 1917 Act remained the basic law on exclusion during this lengthy period.

Significant changes were made in the administration of the 1917 Act beginning in 1929, in response to pressure from the Congress to impose numerical limits on Mexico, a move strongly opposed by the State Department on foreign policy grounds. According to historian Robert Divine, the State Department in January 1929 issued instructions to American consuls in Mexico ordering them to apply the exclusion grounds more stringently, particularly the provisions relating to literacy, contract labor, and becoming a public charge. Quoting Divine, "When an applicant was asked about his financial status, if he replied he had a job waiting for him in the United States, he was ruled out on the contract labor provision, while if he answered that he had no job in sight, he was rejected as likely to become a public charge."

The change in policy was effective in reducing Mexican immigration to 12,703 in fiscal year 1930, compared to 40,154 in 1929. * * * The tactic was successful in heading off numerical limits on Mexico which, with the rest of the Western Hemisphere, remained subject only to qualitative restrictions until 1968.

* * *

The Displaced Persons Act [of 1948] * * * provided that, "any person who shall willfully make a misrepresentation for the purpose of gaining admission into the United States as an eligible displaced person shall thereafter not be admitted to the United States." * * *

* * *

The Immigration and Nationality Act of June 27, 1952, popularly known as the McCarran–Walter Act after its principal Senate and House sponsors, revised, codified, and repealed virtually all existing immigration law. President Harry Truman vetoed the bill, primarily because it carried forward the national origins quota system of numerical limitation. The bill was enacted over his veto and remains in effect today with substantial amendment, including the repeal of the national origins quota system in 1965. * * *

* * *

Among other things, the McCarran–Walter Act both lengthened and "strengthened" the list of excludable classes. Senator McCarran stated on the Senate floor, "our present laws are shot through with weaknesses and loopholes, and ... criminals, Communists, and subversives of all descriptions are even now gaining admission into this country like water through a sieve and we cannot under our present laws effectively exclude or deport them."

Based in large part on the recommendations of the Senate Judiciary Special Subcommittee's report, the McCarran–Walter Act retained most of the previously existing grounds for exclusion, with the notable exception of the contract labor provision for which it substituted the labor certification requirement. It revised some of the previously existing categories, generally in the direction of expanding their coverage. It also added a number of new categories, including narcotics law violators and addicts, aliens coming to engage in immoral sexual acts, aliens entering by means of false statements, and aliens aiding illegal immigration. * * *

* * *

———

The preceding excerpt takes you through enactment of the 1952 Act. From then until 1990, the exclusion grounds underwent relatively little change. There were some amendments to existing grounds and the addition of three new grounds—foreign medical graduates who had not passed prescribed tests, Nazi war criminals, and certain noncitizens who have claimed immunity from criminal prosecution. See INA § 212(a)(32–34), pre–1990 version.

The pre–1990 list of exclusion grounds struck many as archaic. The Select Commission on Immigration and Refugee Policy, while unwilling to take on the daunting task of rewriting a whole new list from scratch, recommended that Congress do so. See Final Report and Recommendations, U.S. Immigration Policy and the National Interest 282–83 (1981). Rep. Barney Frank (D–Mass) made several attempts, see, e.g., H.R. 1280 (1989), and Senator Alan Simpson (R–Wyoming) introduced such a bill as well, see S. 953 (1989). Eventually their efforts led to the inclusion of section 601 in the Immigration Act of 1990. That section revamped the list of exclusion grounds.

Only a few grounds changed significantly in content, but those few had been among the most controversial of the exclusions. The Act eliminated the exclusion of homosexuals; authorized the HHS Secretary to remove AIDS from the list of diseases that render noncitizens inadmissible; modernized and narrowed the exclusions relating to mental illness; repealed the exclusion grounds for illiteracy and mental retardation; and significantly narrowed various exclusion grounds based on political beliefs, statements, and associations. At the same time, Congress added an exclusion ground for anyone whose entry or activities in the United States might adversely affect United States foreign policy.

Since 1990, the former trend to expand the grounds for inadmissibility has reemerged. IIRIRA significantly lengthened the list. The more important changes will be noted in later sections of this chapter.

The exclusion grounds generally appear in INA § 212. That section also contains provisions—some automatic, others discretionary—for waiving certain exclusion grounds in certain circumstances. Most of the grounds for inadmissibility appear in subsection (a), but a few appear in other subsections.[2] See, e.g., INA § 212(e,f,j,m,n); see also INA § 211. The remaining subsections provide for waivers. Skim section 212(a) now to get a sense of its layout.

How frequently are the various exclusion grounds invoked? The Visa Office (VO), a component of the State Department's Bureau of Consular Affairs, reports annually on the number of visa denials by exclusion ground, broken down separately for immigrants and nonimmigrants. The figures are reproduced below for fiscal year 2002, which (surprisingly) are the most recent VO statistics available as of June 2005. When reading them, keep in mind that often a visa is denied because of inadequate paperwork or some other curable defect in the application. Moreover, some inadmissible applicants qualify for waivers. Consequently, VO also reports the number of cases in which initial findings of ineligibility were overcome.[3]

SELECTED VISA INELIGIBILITIES IN FISCAL YEAR 2002[4]

[Note: The only grounds displayed below are those in which at least one column was at least 1000.]

Exclusion Ground	Immigrants' Ineligibilities		Nonimmigrants' Ineligibilities	
	Found	Overcome	Found	Overcome
Crime involving moral turpitude	426	231	2,068	519
Controlled substance violators	251	32	1,611	295
Controlled substance traffickers	127	0	2,567	61
Public charge	17,511	17,825	2,472	300
Labor certification	9,368	173	N/A	N/A
Misrepresentation	5,961	773	13,569	403
Smugglers of aliens	285	30	2,729	32

2.   For some time, the statutory exclusion grounds have generally been assumed to be exhaustive. The State Department regulations have allowed consular officers to deny visas "only upon a ground specifically set out in the law or implementing regulations." 22 C.F.R. § 40.6 (2004). The latter are either interpretations of INA § 212 or documentary requirements for establishing conformity with INA § 212. Similarly, noncitizens may be excluded at ports of entry only on the basis of the statutory grounds. *Gegiow v. Uhl*, 239 U.S. 3, 36 S.Ct. 2, 60 L.Ed. 114 (1915). But see *Matter of O*, 8 I. & N. Dec. 291 (Ass't Comm'r & BIA, 1959) (noncitizen may be excluded if, upon admission, he or she would immediately be deportable). In 1990, Congress implied for the first time that immigration officers have no discretion to deny either admission or adjustment of status, and that consular officers similarly have no discretion to deny visas, on grounds not laid out in INA § 212. See Imm.Act 1990, § 601(b),

amending INA § 212(b) (requiring those officers to provide written notice of the specific exclusion grounds).

3.   Sometimes an applicant who is found ineligible during a given fiscal year overcomes that ineligibility in the following fiscal year. In the chart that follows, the columns for ineligibilities overcome represent the number of *overcomings* recorded in fiscal year 2002, not the number of overcomings attributable to *ineligibilities* found in 2002. Also, a given applicant can be found inadmissible on more than one ground, and on more than one occasion on the same ground, in a given fiscal year. In this chart, all figures refer to the number of times a given inadmissibility ground was found or overcome, not the number of applicants actually removed on such a ground.

4.   Source: Report of the Visa Office 2002, Table XX.

Nonimmigrant documentation requirement	N/A	N/A	1,121	705
Ordered removed upon arrival	440	255	1,092	26
Unlawfully present 365 or more days	2,259	3,162	2,142	127
Failure to establish entitlement to nonimmigrant status	N/A	N/A	1,890,995	51,846
Noncompliance with provisions of the INA or regulations issued pursuant thereto	183,862	142,744	676,022	388,671
Total	**223,218**	**166,031**	**2,600,367**	**443,282**

The remaining sections of this chapter will take you through some of the current exclusion grounds and waiver provisions. Coverage here will be highly selective.[5]

SECTION A. GROUNDS RELATED TO IMMIGRATION CONTROL

Most of the exclusion grounds reflect congressional judgments that certain classes of noncitizens would have an adverse impact on the nation's health and welfare. To implement this network of substantive exclusion grounds requires elaborate procedures. Not surprisingly, compliance with those procedures has also been made a condition of admittance. Many of the modern exclusion grounds are, in other words, simply instruments for making the immigration controls effective.

One group of exclusion grounds relating solely to immigration control concerns the integrity of documents. Thus, subsections 7(A) and 7(B) of INA § 212(a) exclude, respectively, immigrants and nonimmigrants who are not in possession of valid passports and visas (or sometimes alternative entry documents), subject to a discretionary waiver authority granted in section 212(k). Similarly, as you saw earlier, certain employment-based immigrants will be inadmissible under INA § 212(a)(5)(A) if they do not have "labor certification." Although not directly concerned with documents, a provision excluding stowaways, INA § 212(a)(6)(D), serves analogous functions.

Certain of these documents-related exclusion grounds deal specifically with fraud.[6] For example, noncitizens who have committed specified forms of document fraud are subject to administrative fines under INA § 274C; upon being formally ordered to pay such penalties, they become inadmissible, INA § 212(a)(6)(F), subject to discretionary waivers in certain family-related circumstances, INA § 212(d)(12). Noncitizens who procure visas,

5. Most of the inadmissibility grounds have counterpart deportability grounds, and many of the latter will be examined in chapter 7. One of the exclusion waivers, INA § 212(e) (for exchange visitors), was taken up on pages 389–94 above. The other waiver provisions are either statutorily limited to, or in some cases theoretically general but in

practice commonly sought in relation to, certain exclusion grounds. They are discussed along with the grounds to which they pertain.

6. For some good discussion of the kinds of fraud and misrepresentations that can lead to removal, see Kathleen M. Sullivan, *When Representations Cross the Line*, 1 BIB 16 (Oct. 1996).

admission, or certain other documents or benefits by fraud or misrepresentation become inadmissible for life. INA § 212(a)(6)(C)(i). False claims of citizenship, both oral and written, constitute independent grounds for inadmissibility. INA § 212(a)(6)(C)(ii).

Another set of immigration-control-related exclusion grounds relates to surreptitious entry. As noted in the introduction to this chapter, IIRIRA renders inadmissible those noncitizens who are present in the United States without having been admitted or paroled, as well as those who arrive other than at officially designated ports of entry. INA § 212(a)(6)(A). Assisting other noncitizens to enter unlawfully is also a ground for inadmissibility, subject to certain conditions and waivers. INA §§ 212(a)(6)(E), 212(d)(11).

Some of the exclusion grounds encompass noncitizens who are or were out of status. INA § 212(a)(9)(B), another product of IIRIRA, is especially important. It renders certain noncitizens who have been "unlawfully present" in the United States for 180 days or for one year inadmissible for three years or ten years, respectively. Please read INA § 212(a)(9)(B) carefully at this time.

INA § 212(a)(9)(B)(ii) defines a person as being "unlawfully present" if he or she "is present in the United States after the expiration of the period of stay authorized by the Attorney General or is present in the United States without being admitted or paroled." This definition has generated some difficult issues. For a good survey, see Stephen Yale–Loehr & Brian Palmer, *Unlawful Presence Update*, 6 BIB 507 (June 1, 2001).

One important interpretation source is a June 17, 1997 memorandum from then Acting INS Executive Associate Commissioner Paul Virtue, reproduced in July/August 1997 AILA Monthly Mailing at 635–38. The agency position was that section 212(a)(9)(B) contemplates *continuous* unlawful presence, not an *aggregate* of two or more separate stays. By way of example, Mr. Virtue said, a person with two separate four-month periods of unlawful presence would *not* be inadmissible under the 180–day provision. *Id.* Note that the two sub-prongs of section 212(a)(9)(B) are differently worded. The 3–year exclusion refers to unlawful presence for "*a period* of more than 180 days . . . (emphasis added)," while the 10–year exclusion refers simply to unlawful presence "for one year or more." Nonetheless, the memo made clear that its interpretation applied to both subprongs.

A subsequent memo from Mr. Virtue, dated September 19, 1997 and reproduced in 2 BIB at 842–45 (Oct. 15, 1997), furnished additional guidance, mostly on the question of when presence will be considered "unlawful." The first issue the memo addressed concerned a remedy called "voluntary departure," which you will study in chapter 8. It is common for either ICE or an immigration judge to allow a person under certain circumstances to depart voluntarily rather than be formally removed. Typically the person is given until a certain date to leave. The memo of the former INS, reversing an earlier interpretation, held that an individual who is granted the remedy of "voluntary departure" is not considered "unlawfully present" until the due date for his or her departure. *Id.* at 842–43.

What happens if a nonimmigrant violates the terms of his or her admittance other than by overstaying? Suppose, for example, a person admitted as an F–1 student drops out of school or works without authorization. Does his or her presence become "unlawful" at that point? The violation of the terms of admission makes the person deportable, INA § 237(a)(1)(C)(i), but the memo took the position that the *presence* does not thereby become unlawful, and thus the 180–day and one-year periods do not start to run, until the immigration judge hears the case and determines that the violation has occurred. 2 BIB at 843–44.

There has been little dispute concerning those issues. In contrast, there has been major controversy on another, immensely important issue. When ICE believes someone is deportable, it begins removal proceedings by filing a document called a "notice to appear." INA § 239(a)(1). Because of huge administrative backlogs, it can take months or sometimes even years to hold the removal hearing, and there is no authority to remove the person before the hearing has been held. Does the time from the notice to appear until the issuance of a removal order count as unlawful presence? The memo from the former INS said yes, unless the person ultimately is found not to be deportable. 2 BIB at 844. Justice Department regulations (issued before the INS memo) implied the same result. 8 C.F.R. § 239.3 (1997, but unchanged as of 2004). Further complications arise if the immigration judge finds the person deportable but grants any of several discretionary remedies that you will study in chapter 8.

But that is not necessarily the end of the story. The Executive Office for Immigration Review (which, you will recall, houses the immigration judges and the Board of Immigration Appeals, among others) apparently rejects the interpretation of the former INS. It believes that time spent in removal proceedings is not unlawful presence. Several years ago that disagreement was said to be one of the reasons that the Department of Justice had yet to issue final regulations implementing the "unlawful presence" provision. May 1999 AILA Monthly Mailing at 455. At this writing, comprehensive regulations defining "unlawful presence" still have not been issued.

One other "unlawful presence" issue requires attention. Nonimmigrants who have been admitted for fixed durations frequently apply to USCIS for either extensions of stay or changes of status to other nonimmigrant categories. Suppose a person files such an application before his or her original stay has expired, but USCIS does not decide the application for an extension or change until after the person's original stay has expired. In that situation, INA § 212(a)(9)(B)(iv) tolls the accumulation of unlawful presence time during the period from expiration of the original stay to the time USCIS decides the application, provided the application is "nonfrivolous" and the applicant has not worked without authorization. The tolling language applies only to the 3–year bar (not the 10–year bar), and even then the maximum tolling provided by the statute is 120 days. Under the literal language, therefore, any period of physical presence beyond the 120–day period constitutes unlawful presence, even if USCIS takes inordinate time to adjudicate the application. To remedy that consequence, the former INS in 2000 issued a memo that designates the entire period during which a timely filed, nonfrivolous application for either extension of stay or change of status is pending as "a period of stay authorized by the Attorney General" for purposes of section 212(a)(9), provided the person has not worked without authorization. Memorandum of Michael A. Pearson, INS Exec. Assoc. Comm'r for Field Operations (Mar. 3, 2000), digested in 77 IR at 300–01 (Mar. 13, 2000). The practical effect of the INS memo was to eliminate the 120–day limit and to extend the tolling to cover the 10–year bar as well as the 3–year bar.

The 9(b) provisions have had harsh effects. One respected scholar and former INS General Counsel has gone so far as to call for their outright repeal. See David A. Martin, *Waiting for Solutions: Extending the Period of Time for Migrants to Apply for Green Cards Doesn't Get at the Real Problem*, Legal Times (May 28, 2001), at 66.

The last category of immigration-control-related exclusion grounds concerns the removal process more directly. INA § 212(a)(6)(B) (the no-show provision) renders inadmissible for five years any noncitizen who, without reasonable cause, fails to attend his or her removal hearing. Under INA § 212(a)(9)(A), noncitizens who are ordered removed are generally inadmissible for either 5 years or 10 years, depending on whether they were removed upon or after arrival (20 years for second offenders, forever for "aggravated felons," a term that you will examine later). Under section 212(a)(9)(A)(iii), the Secretary of Homeland Security has the discretion to waive this ground of inadmissibility by consenting to the person applying for admission.

Finally, one who either was unlawfully present for "an aggregate period of more than one year" or was removed for any reason, and who then enters or attempts to enter "without being admitted," becomes inadmissible for at least ten years, after which time the Secretary of Homeland Security may grant permission to reapply for admission. INA § 212(a)(9)(C). Since the statute expressly uses the term "aggregate," the position of the former INS was that two or more separate periods may be aggregated for purposes of section 212(a)(9)(C). See Virtue memo of Sept. 19, 1997, in 2 BIB at 636, 637 (contrasting this interpretation with that of the slightly different language in section 212(a)(9)(B)).

An important and more general provision, INA § 212(d)(3), authorizes joint Secretary of Homeland Security / Secretary of State waivers, for nonimmigrants only, of all but a handful of the exclusion grounds. You will see more on the d(3) waivers later.

At this time, please read INA §§ 212(a)(6,7, and 9), 212(d)(3,11, and 12), and 212(i). You need to be familiar with them to do the Problems that follow. Note also that INA § 212(a)(9)(B)(i)(I) refers to the person having "voluntarily departed." This concept is fully explored in chapter 8. For now, all you need to know is that a person who leaves the United States after having been ordered removed is not considered to have "voluntarily departed."

PROBLEMS 1–5

Problem 1. X, a noncitizen, was born on July 1, 1985. On July 1, 2002, he made an unauthorized crossing into the United States and remained. On February 1, 2004, ICE apprehended X and initiated removal proceedings. One month later, while the removal proceedings were still pending, X left the United States on his own. It is now March 1, 2006. X meets the requirements for H–1B status, and there is no backlog for that category. Is he admissible?

Problem 2. Y (an adult) entered the United States on June 1, 2002 on a nonimmigrant visa that was valid for one year. On May 1, 2003, she applied for a one-year extension of stay. USCIS, believing that the request generated some difficult issues, considered her case until December 1, 2003, at which time it finally denied a renewal. Y stayed on nonetheless, and on March 1, 2004, Y gave birth, out of wedlock, to a baby girl (who is a United States citizen because of her birth in the United States). Y and her daughter remained in the United States until May 1, 2004. On that date, they returned to Y's country of origin. It is now May 1, 2006, and Y has a job offer in the United States that would qualify her for employment-based immigrant status if she is otherwise admissible. Y has also recently learned that her young daughter has a life-threatening disease for which the only successful treatment is in the United States. Is Y admissible?

Problem 3. Z, a noncitizen, entered the United States surreptitiously on January 1, 2003. On December 1, 2003, ICE apprehended him, initiated removal proceedings, and detained him pending a removal hearing on February 1, 2004. At the hearing, Z was ordered removed and was kept in continued detention until his actual removal on February 5, 2004. Now, six years later, Z meets the requirements for employment-based second preference status and would like to immigrate to the United States. Is he admissible?

Problem 4. A, the noncitizen beneficiary of a family-sponsored second preference visa petition on which the priority date was not yet current, tried to enter the United States in May 2006 at an undesignated point in the middle of the night. He was apprehended and removed from the United States under INA § 212(a)(6)(A) for arriving at a place not designated as a port of entry. In October 2006 his priority date became current and he formally applied to the United States consulate for an immigrant visa. At the interview, the consular officer asked A whether he had ever before tried to enter the United States. A said he had not. The consular officer then noticed in A's file a letter from ICE revealing the prior removal order. Should the consular officer issue the visa?

Problem 5. B, a noncitizen, entered the United States on June 1, 2005 on a one-year B–1 business visitor visa. On August 1, 2005, she tried unsuccessfully to obtain a counterfeit birth certificate that would have stated her place of birth as Waterbury, Connecticut. Had she succeeded, she planned to use that document to support an eventual United States citizenship claim. Unable to obtain the birth certificate, B left the United

States on October 1, 2005. It is now 2007, and B is back in her native country. She wants to return to the United States for a month's vacation. May the consular officer issue her a visitor for pleasure (B–2) visa?

SECTION B.   POLITICAL AND NATIONAL SECURITY GROUNDS

Americans are often surprised to learn that our immigration laws exclude individuals solely because of their political views. To many people, inhibiting the free flow of ideas in this way seems incompatible with the tenets of a liberal democracy. Yet ideological restrictions have been part of United States immigration law since the beginning of the century. In fact, with one important exception discussed below, they have steadily expanded.

As the Judiciary Committee print at the beginning of this chapter pointed out, President McKinley was assassinated in 1901 by an anarchist of American citizenship and birth but foreign ancestry. The aftermath included the first permanent[7] statutory provision barring noncitizens because of their political views. That statute, enacted in 1903, excluded anarchists and certain others who "believe in or advocate" the forceful overthrow of the United States government or all government. Act of March 3, 1903, ch. 1012, §§ 2, 38, 32 Stat. 1213, 1214, 1221.

From those humble origins, the list of politically related exclusion grounds grew long. Major amendments enacted after World War I broadened the original grounds to include, among others, people who wrote or published material advocating specified prohibited acts or who joined organizations that distributed such materials. Act of June 5, 1920, ch. 251, 41 Stat. 1008, 1009. In 1950, at the peak of the Cold War, Congress expressly made past or present membership in, or affiliation with, the Communist Party a specific ground for exclusion. See Internal Security Act of 1950, ch. 1024, Title I, § 22, 64 Stat. 987, 1006. By identifying the Communist Party by name, the 1950 Act eliminated the need for the government to prove in each case that the Communist Party advocated the forceful overthrow of the government. At the same time, section 22 of the 1950 Act added an exclusion ground for those who sought entry in order to engage in activities "prejudicial to the public interest."

Enacted in 1952, the INA contained three broad exclusion grounds pertaining to either national security or political expression. INA § 212(a)(27), a carryover from the 1950 Act, covered noncitizens believed to be entering the United States to engage in activities "prejudicial to the public interest." Section 212(a)(28), which was quite long, excluded anyone who had ever advocated, been members of or affiliated with any organization that advocated, or published or circulated writings advocating, any of certain political views, including communism, anarchy, or the propriety of

---

7. The Alien Act of 1798, see Act of June 25, 1798, 1 Stat. 570, had also penalized certain noncitizens for their political opinions, but this statute expired after two years. In the face of a highly unpopular reception, Congress declined to renew the law. See generally James M. Smith, Freedom's Fetters (1956).

overthrowing the United States government or all government. And section 212(a)(29) reached noncitizens believed likely to engage, after entry, in such activities as espionage, sabotage, or other subversion. The Immigration Act of 1990, § 601, added a related ground, now INA § 212(a)(3)(C), that covers certain individuals whose entries or activities might adversely affect U.S. foreign policy.

Of the various grounds, section 212(a)(28) always stood out as different in kind. For one thing, it was much longer than the others; Congress tried hard not to leave out any of the political viewpoints that it considered undesirable. In the postwar environments in which most of those exclusion grounds were conceived, a wide array of unpopular political philosophies incurred congressional disapproval.

More important, the various prongs of section 212(a)(28) covered beliefs, statements, advocacy, writings, publications, and associations— precisely the sorts of freedoms the First Amendment is generally designed to protect. Although the distinction should not be overstated, the other provisions covered activities generally not protected by the Constitution— either intended or expected future activities inimical to the national welfare. Section 212(a)(28) was thus typically regarded as being far less serious than the other "political" grounds.

That distinction is crucial to understanding the development of the present statutory exclusions and waivers. INA § 212(d)(3) authorizes the Secretary of Homeland Security, after a favorable recommendation by the Secretary of State or a consular officer, to admit a *nonimmigrant* who is inadmissible on any ground other than a specified few. Under the pre–1990 numbering scheme, grounds 27, 29 and 33 (the last relating to Nazi war criminals) were the only ones for which 212(d)(3) waivers were not permitted. Noncitizens who were excludable only under ground 28 thus qualified for 212(d)(3) waivers. Indeed, the vast majority of the individuals found excludable on political grounds were charged under paragraph 28; the bulk of those were nonimmigrants; and the vast majority of those succeeded in obtaining 212(d)(3) waivers. See Committee on the Judiciary, United States House of Representatives, Committee Print, Grounds for Exclusion of Aliens Under the Immigration and Nationality Act (Sept. 1988), Table II–1 at 30–31 (exclusions under 212(a)(27)), Tables II–2, II–3 at 54–55 (exclusions under, and waivers of, 212(a)(28)), Table II–4 at 63 (exclusions under 212(a)(29)), Table II–5 at 65–66 (exclusions under 212(a)(33)). The current list of nonwaivable grounds is discussed in item 9 of the Notes and Questions below.

Still, over the years, many prominent individuals were excluded on those various political grounds. Most were political figures, scholars, or other authors. The list includes Hortensia de Allende (widow of slain Chilean President Salvador Allende), General Nino Pasti (the former Italian Senator and NATO General who had criticized United States missile deployment in Europe), former Canadian Prime Minister Pierre Trudeau (for once having attended an economic conference in Moscow), PLO Chair Yasir Arafat, and United Kingdom MP's Ian Paisley and Bernadette Devlin (at opposite ends of the Northern Ireland political spectrum). Also excluded were a number of Nobel Prize-winning authors—Gabriel Marquez, Carlos Fuentes, and Csezlaw Milosz. Others included Argentinean author Julio Cortazar, Italian playwright Dario Fo, British novelist Graham Greene, Canadian naturalist and biologist Farley Mowat, and French actors Maurice Chevalier and Yves Montand. See Grounds for Exclusion of Aliens, above; Arthur C. Helton, *Reconciling the Power to Bar or Expel Aliens on Political Grounds with Fairness and the Freedoms of Speech and Association: An Analysis of Recent Legislative Proposals*, 11 Fordham Int'l L.J. 467 (1988); John A. Scanlan, *Aliens in the Marketplace of Ideas: The Government, The Academy, and the McCarran–Walter Act*, 66 Texas L.Rev. 1481, 1497 & n. 75 (1988); New York Times, Feb. 2, 1990, at A–1, A–4.

In 1975, the United States and 34 other nations signed the Final Act of the Conference on Security and Co–Operation in Europe (Helsinki, August 1, 1975) [commonly called the Helsinki Accords]. This historic agreement reflected a commitment to foster greater freedom of movement between signatory States and to encourage freer flows of information. See David Carliner, *United States Compliance with the Helsinki Final Act: The Treatment of Aliens*, 13 Vanderbilt J. Transnat'l L. 397 (1980). With the Helsinki Final Act prominently in mind, Congress in 1977 passed the so-called McGovern Amendment, codified as 22 U.S.C. § 2691 and itself amended in 1978 and again in 1979.[8] The McGovern amendment provided that, when a nonimmigrant was excludable solely "by reason of membership in or affiliation with a proscribed organization," the Secretary of State "should" recommend a waiver, unless the Secretary of State certifies to Congress that the individual's admission would be contrary to national security interests.

But the McGovern amendment did not halt the denial of visas on ideological grounds. It merely shifted the battleground. With its power to exclude people on the direct basis of their membership in proscribed organizations now curtailed, the government began to make greater use of then INA § 212(a)(27) (noncitizens who "seek to enter * * * to engage in activities which would be prejudicial to the public interest * * * "). The government's strategy was to allege inadmissibility under section 212(a)(27), reasoning that the person's membership in the proscribed organization would by itself make the entry "prejudicial to the national interest." In *Allende v. Shultz*, 845 F.2d 1111 (1st Cir. 1988), the court rejected such an effort, holding that the government's interpretation would effectively nullify the McGovern amendment.

As human rights have come to attract increased national and international attention, Congress has added a series of grounds excluding various classes of human rights violators. The first such ground, enacted in 1978, covered designated participants in Nazi war crimes before and during World War II. See Act of Oct. 30, 1978, Pub. L. 95–549, § 101, 92 Stat.

---

8. See Pub.L. 95–426, § 119, 92 Stat. 963, 970 (Oct. 7, 1978); Pub.L. 96–60, § 109, 93 Stat. 395, 397–98 (Aug. 15, 1979).

2065, at 2065, adding what is now INA § 212(a)(3)(E)(i). Over the ensuing years Congress added exclusion grounds for individuals who had engaged in genocide, INA § 212(a)(3)(E)(ii); foreign government officials who, within the preceding two years, were responsible for "particularly severe violations of religious freedom," INA § 212(a)(2)(G); and, as part of the Intelligence Reform and Terrorism Prevention Act of 2004, Pub. L. 108–458, § 5501(a)(2), 118 Stat. 3638 (Dec. 17, 2004), those who have participated in acts of torture or, if acting under color of foreign law, extrajudicial killings, INA § 212(a)(3)(E)(iii).

Today, the most vigorous debate over the proper scope of ideological and national security exclusions has centered around terrorism. Until the 1990's, foreign terrorism rarely occurred on United States soil—at least so it seemed. Security precautions were generally less stringent in the United States than in Europe and other places. The World Trade Center bombing, the Oklahoma City bombing (though not perpetrated by foreign nationals), and other events shocked Americans and brought terrorism into the public eye. One congressional response was AEDPA, a comprehensive anti-terrorism (and general immigrant-restriction) statute enacted in 1996. The terrorist attacks of September 11, 2001 triggered a variety of additional congressional (and executive branch) responses. Most relevant here is section 411 of the USA PATRIOT Act, which retroactively expanded the range of terrorism-related actions and associations that lead to inadmissibility under INA § 212(a)(3)(B). The REAL ID Act, § 103, lengthened the list further.

INA § 212(a)(3)(B), as amended by these and other statutes, contains those exclusion grounds that relate specifically to terrorism. This subsection is a long one, but it can be broken down into a few manageable parts, of which a few are the most important. First, subsection (i) lays out nine different terrorism-related exclusion grounds, some of which refer to those who "engage" (or have engaged or are "likely" to engage) in terrorism. Note that all of the grounds describe individuals who are associated in specified ways with either (a) terrorist *activity* or (b) terrorist *organizations*. Other important subsections (iii, iv, and vi) define the crucial terms "terrorist activity," "engage," and "terrorist organization," respectively. In defining "terrorist organization," subsection (vi) includes (among others) the specific organizations that the Secretary of State has officially designated as terrorist organizations under either INA § 212(a)(3)(B)(vi)(II) or INA § 219. The names of the designated organizations are published in the Federal Register. Since September 11, 2001, many groups have been added to the list. See 8 BIB 1237 (Oct. 15, 2002).

Please read INA § 212(a)(3)(B) in full at this time.

A few things might have struck you as you read this subsection. Note, first, how broadly the term "terrorist *activity*" is defined in subsection iii(V)(b). It includes the use of any "weapon or dangerous device (other than for mere personal monetary gain), with intent to endanger, directly or indirectly, the safety of one or more individuals or to cause substantial damage to property." Many terrorist acts would fit that definition, but so too would many garden variety crimes that have nothing to do with terrorism as that term is commonly understood. Professor David Cole uses the examples of an LPR who "brandished a kitchen knife in a domestic dispute with her abusive husband" or who "found himself in a barroom brawl, picked up a bottle, and threatened another person with it." David Cole, *Enemy Aliens*, 54 Stanford L. Rev. 953, 971 (2002). Indeed, some acts of youthful vandalism would meet the statutory definition if the damage is "substantial." Of course, if ICE elected to charge inadmissibility based upon such acts, the noncitizen might well attempt ejusdem generis arguments similar to those examined in question 1 below. Certain *associations* with terrorist organizations are also grounds for inadmissibility, with differing required levels of actual or imputed awareness that the organization engages in the proscribed activities. Note also INA § 212(a)(3)(B)(i)(VII), which was added by the REAL ID Act, § 103(a). It covers the noncitizen who "endorses or espouses terrorist activity."

A related exclusion ground arises out of EBSVERA § 306. It extends the concept of guilt by association with an organization one step further— to guilt by association with a country. This provision renders inadmissible any nonimmigrant who is "from" a country that the Secretary of State has designated as a "state sponsor of terrorism," unless after consultation with other Departments the Secretary of State finds that the particular individual "does not pose a threat to the safety or national security of the United States." The term "state sponsor of terrorism" is defined to mean a country that the Secretary of State determines has "repeatedly provided support for acts of international terrorism." *Id.* § 306(b).

You should now read INA § 212(a)(3) in its entirety.

NOTES AND QUESTIONS ON THE POLITICAL AND NATIONAL SECURITY GROUNDS

1.   The present law contains no real counterpart to the broad "prejudicial to the public interest" language of old subsection 27,[9] but current subsection 3(A) excludes individuals believed to be seeking entry to engage in specified unlawful activities, including espionage, sabotage, and the forceful overthrow of the government. Subsection 3(A)(ii) extends to the case in which the consular officer or the Secretary of Homeland Security has reason to believe that the person seeks to enter the United States to engage in "any other unlawful activity."

How broad do you think Congress meant that exclusion to be? Is a noncitizen who seeks to enter the United States to violate the littering laws really excludable? Criminal lawyers would regard such a violation as a civil offense (*malum prohibitum*) rather than a true crime (*malum in se*), but does that matter? The statute, after all, does not say "crime;" it says "unlawful activity."

---

9. But *cf.* INA § 212(f) (*President* may exclude noncitizen whose entry "would be   detrimental to the interests of the United States").

On the assumption that Congress nonetheless had no intention of excluding people for such trivial offenses, there remains the question whether even serious crimes are necessarily all included. If the consular officer had "reason to believe" that someone sought entry to commit a burglary, would exclusion under subsection 3(A)(ii) be appropriate? A literal interpretation would suggest that that person is indeed inadmissible, but courts commonly employ a maxim known as "ejusdem generis" (same class of things). Under that principle, when a list of specific words is followed by general words, the latter are often interpreted to apply only to things of the same class as the specific words. In *McBoyle v. United States,* 283 U.S. 25, 51 S.Ct. 340, 75 L.Ed. 816 (1931), for example, the Supreme Court had to decide whether the National Motor Vehicle Theft Act applied to airplanes. The statute defined "motor vehicle" as "an automobile, automobile truck, automobile wagon, motor cycle, or any other self-propelled vehicle not designed for running on rails." The Court observed that all the specific vehicles listed were land vehicles and thus concluded that the last phrase was not meant to extend to airplanes. Given that principle, what limitations, if any, would you expect a court to place on the phrase "other unlawful activity" in INA § 212(a)(3)(A)(ii)?

2.   Of particular interest is subsection 3(C), the foreign policy exclusion introduced by the Immigration Act of 1990. In response to fears that this provision might be used to exclude people on the basis of their beliefs, statements, or associations, Congress added the exceptions contained in subsections 3(C)(ii and iii). Do you think the exceptions sufficiently accommodate that concern? What is the difference between "potentially serious adverse foreign policy consequences" (the basic exclusion ground) and the compromising of "a compelling United States foreign policy interest" (the applicable standard when subsection 3(C)(iii) applies)?

3.   The language of both exceptions triggers another difficult question: What beliefs, statements, or associations *are* "lawful within the United States?" As for statements, the leading case is *Brandenburg v. Ohio,* 395 U.S. 444, 89 S.Ct. 1827, 23 L.Ed.2d 430 (1969), where the Supreme Court, reversing the criminal conviction of a Ku Klux Klan official, held that the first amendment protects the advocacy of even lawless action unless the advocacy is both intended to, and likely to, incite *imminent* lawless action. See generally Laurence H. Tribe, American Constitutional Law, § 12–9 (2d ed. 1988). As for associations, the present law is stated succinctly by Professor Tribe:

> * * * First, an association or organization cannot be made illegal * * * in the absence of a clear showing that the group is actively engaged in lawless conduct, or in such incitement to lawless action as would itself be punishable as a clear and present danger of harm that more speech could not avoid. And second, an individual cannot be punished for joining, associating with, or attending meetings of, an association or organization unless the association meets the first requirement and the individual is shown to have affiliated with it (a) with knowledge of its illegality,

and (b) with the specific intent of furthering its illegal aims by such affiliations.

Tribe, above, at 1015.

4. In 1996, Congress added another foreign policy-related exclusion. In response to Cuba's downing of private aircraft off its shores, Congress imposed broad sanctions against Cuba and certain others who trade with Cuba. One provision of that legislation excludes noncitizens who have confiscated the property of U.S. nationals in Cuba, or who traffic in such confiscated property (and the spouses and children of those noncitizens). Cuban Liberty and Democratic Solidarity Act of 1996, Pub.L. 104–114, § 401, 110 Stat. 785, 822–23 (Mar. 12, 1996)(Helms–Burton Act). For State Department guidelines, see 73 IR at 867–68 (July 1, 1996).

5. Notice that Communist Party membership or affiliation is no longer an exclusion ground for nonimmigrants and that, even for immigrants, it is now subject to some fairly broad exceptions. INA § 212(a)(3)(D). This provision does, however, raise questions as to the nature of the proscribed associations. The courts and the BIA interpreted its predecessor to require a "meaningful association." *Firestone v. Howerton,* 671 F.2d 317 (9th Cir.1982); *Berdo v. INS,* 432 F.2d 824 (6th Cir.1970); *Matter of Rusin,* 20 I. & N. Dec. 128 (BIA 1989). The Supreme Court had previously read the same limitation into the analogous deportation ground. See *Gastelum-Quinones v. Kennedy,* 374 U.S. 469, 471, 83 S.Ct. 1819, 1820, 10 L.Ed.2d 1013, 1015 (1963); *Rowoldt v. Perfetto,* 355 U.S. 115, 120, 78 S.Ct. 180, 183, 2 L.Ed.2d 140, 144 (1957). In *Rowoldt,* the noncitizen had joined the Communist Party voluntarily in the United States, paid dues, and attended meetings until his arrest for deportation proceedings, at which time he resigned. Even on those facts the association was held not to be meaningful. (In that case, though, the person had been an LPR for 43 years).

6. Are subsections 3(C) and 3(D) constitutional? There are two separate problems: First, do the excluded noncitizens have first amendment rights? Second, do their citizen sponsors have first amendment rights to receive the noncitizens' ideas? In chapter 2, you briefly encountered both questions. The answers given by the Supreme Court in *Kleindienst v. Mandel* seem to be: As to the first question, no. As to the second question, yes, but the rights are not violated as long as the government has a "facially legitimate and bona fide" reason for refusing the visa or admission. See pages 176–80 above.

7. Many of the people excluded under old subsection 212(a)(28) were scholars who had been invited to the United States to participate in academic conferences. Professor John Scanlan, in a thoughtful and interesting piece, has attacked the ideological exclusions of foreign academics in part by arguing that academic freedom occupies a special place in First Amendment law, such that the scope of the permitted discourse is given "the widest possible range * * * in the university setting." See John A. Scanlan, *Aliens in the Marketplace of Ideas: The Government, the Academy,*

and the McCarran–Walter Act, 66 Texas L.Rev. 1481, 1485 (1988). What is your gut reaction?

8.   To implement the national security exclusions, the government since 1904 has maintained a "lookout list" containing information on suspect individuals. The list, with names deleted but certain basic information about each entry retained, was finally divulged in 1990 as a result of a Freedom of Information Act request and the ensuing litigation. See *Lawyers Committee for Human Rights v. INS,* 721 F.Supp. 552 (S.D.N.Y.1989). The list was found to include more than 350,000 entries (some possibly duplicative) of people from 146 countries. See Lawyers Committee for Human Rights, The Alien Blacklist: A Dangerous Legacy of the McCarthy Era 4 (1990). About two-thirds of the names were entered during the 1980's. *Id.* at 6. Under Imm. Act 1990, § 601(c), the Attorney General [now the Secretary of Homeland Security] and the Secretary of State are required to update the lookout list and, in particular, to delete the name of every person who seeks a determination of admissibility and whose excludability is found to have been eliminated by the amendments to § 212. Since September 11, 2001, this and similar lists have been used primarily in the counterterrorism context. See generally chapter 10 below.

9.   Under the current law, the only inadmissibility grounds that may *not* be waived for nonimmigrants under INA § 212(d)(3) are those that cover individuals believed to be entering to engage in espionage, sabotage, forceful overthrow of the government, or "other unlawful activity," those relating to foreign policy, and those that relate to World War II-era Nazis and genocide. The terrorist exclusion, interestingly enough, remains waivable, even after the events of September 11. (In fact the REAL ID Act, § 104, gives the Secretary of State the "unreviewable discretion" to waive certain designated terrorism-related exclusion grounds for immigrants and nonimmigrants alike. See INA § 212(d)(3)(B)). Given the anti-terrorist political climate, why do you think Congress chose to make terrorism waivable?

10.   One commentator writes as follows:

> Every sovereign nation has the right to control its borders. But in a nation premised on the notion that sovereignty flows from the popular will and that the popular will is determined by political debate, ideological exclusions cannot be justified. They represent bad policy and bad law. If our government really believes that the decision to place American missiles in Western Europe cannot be sold to the American people if Nino Pasti is permitted to address a disarmament rally in the United States, then perhaps the decision should be reconsidered. The suppression of speech is surely not the answer in a constitutional democracy. * * *

Steven R. Shapiro, *Ideological Exclusions: Closing the Border to Political Dissidents,* 100 Harvard L. Rev. 930, 944–45 (1987). That statement was written before some of the recent liberalizations, but immigrants who are or were members of the Communist Party remain excludable on that basis alone, with some exceptions. Do you agree with Shapiro? Constitutional concerns aside, should INA § 212(a)(3)(D) be repealed entirely, modified, or left just as it is? See generally Kevin R. Johnson, *The Antiterrorism Act, the Immigration Reform Act, and Ideological Regulation in the Immigration Laws: Important Lessons for Citizens and Noncitizens*, 28 St. Mary's L.J. 833 (1997).

PROBLEMS 6-8

Problem 6. X is a British citizen and a lecturer in geology at Kings College, University of London. The University of Maryland has offered her a one-year visiting appointment, which X is keen to accept, mainly because she and the University are hopeful that the visit will lead to a permanent tenure-track appointment down the road. The only hitch is that X joined the British Communist Party a year ago and has been attending monthly meetings. You are the General Counsel for the University of Maryland. What advice will you give the geology Department?

Problem 7. Y and Z, both noncitizens, want to enter the United States for a two-week tour in which each would deliver a series of speeches critical of their government. Y is an opposition candidate for national office in his country. Z is a political ally of Y but is not herself a government official or candidate. Y and Z believe that their speeches will receive broader publicity if made in the United States than if made at home. The incumbent President of their country is extremely upset at the prospect of the United States giving Y and Z a "propaganda forum," as he calls it, and has threatened to recall his Ambassador if either of the two speakers is admitted. Are they admissible?

Problem 8. W, a citizen of Bulgaria, is a world-renowned scientist interested in immigrating to the United States to join his 30–year-old daughter, who has lived in San Diego as an LPR for eight years. W has a permanent job offer from a leading United States think tank whose personnel manager has consulted you for advice. There appears to be little difficulty in getting W classified as an employment-based first preference immigrant, and the first preference is current, but W has been a vigorous and long-term member of the Communist Party and is not willing to terminate his membership. Will it be possible for W to immigrate?

SECTION C.   CRIMINAL GROUNDS

Most of the crime-related exclusion grounds have deportation analogs that you will see later in much more detail. For now, read closely INA §§ 212(a)(2) and 212(h).

As you will see in chapter 7, one *deportability* ground is that the person has been convicted of an "aggravated felony," now defined expansively to cover a wide range of criminal offenses. (There is no analogous *inadmissibility* ground.) You might have noticed that relief under INA § 212(h) is unavailable to anyone who has been convicted of an aggravated felony *after having been admitted as an LPR*. In *Matter of Michel*, 21 I. & N. Dec. 1101 (BIA 1998), the Board interpreted this disqualification literally, holding it did not bar 212(h) relief to an otherwise eligible aggravated felon who had never been admitted to permanent residence. Despite the anomaly of treating former LPRs more harshly than those otherwise similarly situated (including undocumented immigrants), the Board felt bound by the plain language.

The same portion of section 212(h) also disqualifies anyone who has previously been admitted as an LPR and who, since that admission, has not lawfully resided continuously in the United States for at least seven years "immediately preceding the initiation of [removal] proceedings." (Keep this language in mind when you do Problem 12 below.) This strange provision was interpreted in *Matter of Ayala–Arevalo*, 22 I. & N. Dec. 398 (BIA 1998). Ayala was admitted as an LPR and did not subsequently reside in the United States for seven years. At the time of his admission, he in fact had been inadmissible (on fraud grounds). He thus argued that he had not been "lawfully" admitted for permanent residence and therefore did not fall within the disqualification. The BIA disagreed. To avoid an "arbitrary and capricious" result, *id*. at 401, it interpreted the disqualification as covering even those who had been "unlawfully" admitted to permanent residence. The decision prompted a strong dissent from Board member Lory Rosenberg. *Id*. at 403–07. Contrast the statutory interpretation approach in *Ayala-Arevalo* with that in *Michel*, where the Board had construed the statute literally even in the face of an anomaly.

Is it unconstitutionally discriminatory for Congress to treat LPRs less favorably than undocumented immigrants? At least one district court held the distinction violative of equal protection, concluding it "defies logic." *Young Hak Song v. INS*, 82 F. Supp.2d 1121 (C.D. Cal. 2000). But the courts of appeals, invoking the principle of special judicial deference to Congress in immigration cases and finding theoretical justifications for the apparent anomaly, have upheld the statutory distinction.

Those courts have accepted three possible rationales: First, Congress wanted to expedite the removal of aggravated felons and might have selected LPR aggravated felons as a "first step." Second, Congress might have reasoned that LPRs already have more rights than undocumented immigrants and thus should be held to a higher standard. And third, the fact that immigrants who enjoyed important rights were willing to jeopardize them by committing crimes might indicate that LPR aggravated felons will have higher recidivism rates than undocumented aggravated felons. See, e.g., *Latu v. Ashcroft*, 375 F.3d 1012, 1020–21 (10th Cir. 2004); *Finau v. INS*, 277 F.3d 1146 (9th Cir. 2002) (amended opinion); *De Leon–Reynoso v. Ashcroft*, 293 F.3d 633 (3d Cir. 2002); *Lukowski v. INS*, 279 F.3d 644 (8th Cir. 2002); *Moore v. Ashcroft*, 251 F.3d 919, 925 (11th Cir. 2001); *Lara-Ruiz v. INS*, 241 F.3d 934, 947–48 (7th Cir. 2001). Since the district court that had decided *Young Hak Song* is situated in the Ninth Circuit, its decision is now implicitly disapproved by *Finau*.

Using the provisions cited in this subsection (and, if necessary, any others you have already studied), work out answers to the following Problems:

PROBLEMS 9–12

Problem 9. W, a citizen of Canada, was born on April 1, 1983. On March 1, 2001 she was arrested for burglary, a crime held to involve moral turpitude and punishable by up to two years imprisonment. W pleaded guilty on May 1, 2001. On June 1, 2001, the trial judge imposed a one-year jail sentence, which she began serving that day. She was released early, for good behavior, on December 1, 2001.

It is now February 1, 2007. W has applied for an F–1 (student) visa to pursue a bachelor's degree at the University of Florida, where she has been accepted for admission. She has no United States relatives. You are the consular officer. What action should you take?

Problem 10. Assume the same facts as in Problem 9, except that this time W tells you about one additional brush she had with the law: A year ago she committed shoplifting (also a crime involving moral turpitude), was apprehended by the shopkeeper, and confessed to the police. She was not arrested, because the shopkeeper did not press charges. The maximum penalty for shoplifting in the Canadian province where her act took place was six months in jail. As a consular officer, what should you do?

Problem 11. Y and his wife, citizens of Spain, have a twenty-four-year-old United States citizen son. They decide they would like to immigrate to the United States. The problem is Y. In response to a question from the consular officer, Y admitted that twenty-five years ago, as a 22–year–old college senior, he had bought two marijuana cigarettes, had tried one of them, had not liked it, had sold the second one to a friend, and had never tried illicit drugs again. May Y be admitted?

Problem 12. Z, a citizen of Ghana, was admitted as an LPR in November 1992 under one of the employment preferences. In early 2003, ICE discovered that Z had fraudulently misstated her professional credentials. On April 1, 2003, Z was criminally convicted of defrauding the United States. (Assume this is a crime that involves moral turpitude, but not an "aggravated felony," a term you will explore more fully in chapter 7.) She was sentenced to a year in prison. Removal proceedings were convened in the prison facility, and she was ordered removed. On December 1, 2003, after serving eight months, she was released and the removal order was executed. It is now November 1, 2006. Z is back in Ghana. She has now entered into a bona fide marriage with a United States citizen. Z's new husband needs to return to the United States to be with his mother, who has leukemia and is expected not to survive more than a few years. Z would like to immigrate to the United States with her husband. Will she be admitted?

SECTION D.   ECONOMIC GROUNDS

As the historical summary in section A illustrated, Congress from time to time has enacted exclusion grounds that were either explicitly economic or at least partly driven by economic concerns. Some of the latter—including some of the medical exclusions and illiteracy—reflected fears that the classes of noncitizens they covered were likely to require public assistance.

The Immigration Act of 1990 repealed many of those grounds. Only two explicitly economic grounds were left: INA §§ 212(a)(5)(A) (labor certification), which you have already studied, and 212(a)(4) (public charge), which will be considered presently. The illiteracy ground has been repealed, and as discussed below the health-related exclusions have been narrowed.

In 1996, Congress added another "economic" exclusion. In recent years, many wealthy Americans have discovered that they could reduce their income tax liability by renouncing their United States citizenship and moving to other countries. That way, they would be neither United States citizens nor LPRs. See generally Alice G. Abreu, *Taxing Exits*, 29 U.C. Davis L.Rev. 1087 (1996). IIRIRA § 352 added a new exclusion ground for those who formally renounced their United States citizenship "for the purpose of avoiding taxation by the United States." INA § 212(a)(10)(E). You will see more on that in chapter 13.

The main economic exclusion ground is INA § 212(a)(4) (noncitizens "likely at any time to become public charges"). Emma Lazarus's inspiring words, "Give me your tired, your poor * * *," were inscribed in the Statue of Liberty in 1903, see John Higham, Send These to Me: Immigrants in Urban America 71–74 (rev. ed. 1984), but by 1882 Congress had already acted to exclude "any person unable to take care of himself or herself without becoming a public charge." Act of August 3, 1882, ch. 376, § 2, 22 Stat. 214.

The public charge provision raises two basic implementation questions: What does "public charge" mean? And what evidence will permit a prediction that a person is "likely" to become one?

As to the first question, the State Department Foreign Affairs Manual, amended in important ways in 1999, 76 IR 980 (June 28, 1999), clarifies that the mere receipt of public funds does not make a person a public charge. Rather, the State Department defines "public charge" to mean "primarily dependent on the U.S. Government for subsistence," as demonstrated by "the receipt of public cash assistance for income maintenance" or "institutionalization for long-term care at U.S. Government expense." 9 F.A.M. § 40.41 n.2a (2004). These include such programs as Supplemental Security Income (SSI), Temporary Assistance for Needy Families (TANF), and state general assistance. *Id.* n.2.1. Even programs for which qualifying requirements include income specifications do not necessarily constitute cash assistance "for income maintenance;" the State Department offers as examples of non-public-charge programs the Food Stamp Program, Medicaid (other than long-term institutional care), the Child Health Insurance Program (CHIP), emergency medical services, the nutritional program for women, infants, and children (WIC), Head Start, job training programs, provision of in-kind services such as soup kitchens or crisis counseling, and several others. *Id.* n.2.2. The question in all cases is whether the program is "intended to be a primary source of cash for income maintenance." Moreover, earned cash benefit programs like Social Security payments and veterans benefits are not considered public-charge programs. *Id.*

Trying to predict the likelihood that a given individual will become a public charge is more problematic. Often an applicant for an immigrant visa lines up a permanent job that will produce an adequate income. If not, however, the applicant can still avoid public charge problems by showing funds sufficient to provide support until a job is found. How much will be required depends, of course, on the needs of the applicant and his or her dependents and on the applicant's prospects for getting work. As a result of IIRIRA § 531(a), the public charge exclusion ground now lays out the factors that will affect public charge determinations. They include age, health, family status, financial status, education, skills, and "affidavits of support." INA § 212(a)(4)(B).

That last item has been controversial. Until 1996, a person who could not show sufficiently promising prospects of adequate employment was allowed to submit an "affidavit of support," in which a sponsor stated a willingness to come to the applicant's aid in the event aid is later needed. State courts were divided over whether such affidavits were legally binding on the affiant, see 9 F.A.M. § 40.41 n.6.4 (1993), but even in states where affidavits were held not to be binding, they were often accepted as strong evidence of future support. See, e.g., *Matter of Kohama*, 17 I. & N. Dec. 257 (INS Assoc. Comm'r 1978). The factors affecting the weight to be placed on affidavits of support included the motivation of the sponsor, his or her relationship to the applicant, and of course the sponsor's financial ability to provide the promised support. See 9 F.A.M. § 40.41 n.6.2 (1993).

In 1996, heightened public hostility toward both immigrants and welfare recipients culminated in long-anticipated welfare "reform." The Personal Responsibility and Work Opportunity Reconciliation Act of 1996, Pub. L. 104–193, 110 Stat. 2105 (Aug. 22, 1996) [hereafter the Welfare Act], restricted welfare in many ways and took special aim at immigrants, as discussed in chapter 13 below. Affidavits of support prompted particular concern, to which Congress responded in section 423 of the Welfare Act, adding new INA § 213A (amended a few weeks later by IIRIRA § 551(a)). The new section puts severe restrictions on affidavits of support.

The regulations spell out most of the details. See 8 C.F.R. § 213a (2004); 22 C.F.R. § 40.41 (2004); see also Beth Stickney, *Whither Family Unity? A Post–IIRIRA Update*, December 1998 Immigration Briefings; Charles Wheeler, *Affidavit of Support: A Year in Review*, 4 BIB at 97 (Feb.

1, 1999); Charles Wheeler, *The Affidavit of Support and Sponsorship Requirements: A Critical Analysis*, June 1998 Immigration Briefings.

The most important change was to make the affidavit a binding contract. It must be "legally enforceable against the sponsor by the sponsored immigrant, the Federal Government, any state (or any political subdivision of such state), or by any other entity that provides any means-tested public benefit." INA § 213A(a)(1)(B). The promise is binding for 40 qualifying quarter-years after the immigrant last receives benefits or until naturalization if sooner. INA § 213A(a)(2).

The sponsor must be a United States national or an LPR, over age 18, and domiciled in the United States. INA § 213A(f)(1)(A,B,C). The sponsor must be the person who is petitioning for the immigrant's admission. INA § 213A(f)(1)(D). If the petitioner lacks the required resources (see below), he or she may join with another person as a co-sponsor. INA § 213A(f)(5).

The combination of the foregoing requirements has significant effects independent of the public charge issue. Before 1996, a United States citizen could petition for the admission of an otherwise qualifying noncitizen family member even if the petitioner was living overseas. That is no longer possible. Since the petitioner must be a sponsor (either alone or jointly), and since a sponsor has to be domiciled in the United States, citizens domiciled overseas may no longer petition for the admission of their family members. See David A. Martin, (then) INS General Counsel, Legal Opinion 97–10 (July 8, 1997), reproduced in 75 IR at 380–83 (Mar. 16, 1998). Nor, according to the former INS, can a citizen domiciled overseas solve the problem by enlisting a co-sponsor domiciled in the United States; a co-sponsor will not suffice unless the petitioner is also eligible to be a sponsor. *Id.* The only opening in such cases is that the citizen petitioner, although physically overseas, might be able to prove that his or her foreign presence is temporary and that the plan is to return to the United States. *Id.*

The sponsor's income must be at least 125% of the poverty level. See INA §§ 213A(f)(1)(E), 213A(f)(6). Moreover, for immediate relative and family-sponsored petitions (except for certain widowed and certain abused family members), affidavits of support are mandatory, not optional. INA § 212(a)(4)(C).

Even before the 1996 reforms, the sponsor's assets and income were treated as if they belonged to the beneficiary for purposes of calculating the latter's eligibility for specified federal welfare programs, for varying periods of years after admission. Section 421 of the Welfare Act expanded these "deeming" provisions. Subject to some exceptions added by IIRIRA § 552, the Welfare Act extended deeming to all federal means-tested benefits and lengthened the time period during which deeming would operate (until naturalization or until the applicant has worked for 40 qualifying quarter-years, whichever comes sooner). Section 422 of the Welfare Act authorized states to take similar action with respect to state means-tested benefits.

The public charge ground may be waived upon the giving of what is usually called a "public charge" bond. INA § 213. The person who furnishes the bond promises to indemnify the United States or any state or local governmental unit in which the sponsored individual becomes a public charge. Security may be provided. In practice, the decision whether to accept such a bond is made in the local USCIS office after a request from a consular officer abroad. 8 C.F.R. § 213 (2004). Such requests are made "only in borderline cases." 9 F.A.M. § 40.41 n.4.6–4 (2004).

As noted above, sponsors must now demonstrate income equal to 125% of the federal poverty levels. For purposes of that requirement, the State Department uses the Poverty Income Guidelines prepared and revised annually by the Department of Health and Human Services. These guidelines are designed principally for use in administering federal welfare programs, awarding block grants, and compiling Census data.

For fiscal year 2005, the HHS Poverty Guideline was $9570 per year for a one-person household plus $3260 for each additional person (higher figures for Hawaii and Alaska). 70 Fed. Reg. 8373 (Feb. 18, 2005). The sponsor's annual income must therefore be 125% of that figure.

NOTES AND QUESTIONS

1. Which philosophy do you prefer—that of Emma Lazarus or that reflected in INA § 212(a)(4)? Do they necessarily conflict?

2. Should affidavits of support be legally binding on the sponsors? Argue both ways.

3. Why should an affidavit of support be mandatory? What if the beneficiary has an independent means of support, such as a job offer or savings?

4. Was Congress right to insist that the sponsor be the petitioner?

5. Was it wise for Congress to require the sponsor's income to be 125% of the poverty level (rather than 100%)? Should family unity be a luxury reserved for middle and upper income Americans?

6. The deeming provisions of the 1996 welfare reform legislation were highly contentious, mainly because they could result in low-income immigrants being denied welfare years later if they fall into distress. In theory immigrants may enforce the promises made by their sponsors, but with the passage of time not all sponsors will remain financially capable of providing the promised support. The question whether lawfully admitted immigrants should be disqualified from federal or state welfare benefits is taken up more generally in chapter 13.

7. For some insightful observations concerning the "chilling" effects of the 1996 reforms on immigrants in need of welfare, see Linton Joaquin & Braden Cancilla, *Protecting Immigrants and the Community: A New Approach to Public Charge Determinations*, 76 IR 885 (June 7, 1999).

SECTION E. PUBLIC HEALTH AND MORALS

Several exclusion grounds might be broadly characterized as concerned with either public health or safety or the congressional view of public morals. The health and safety grounds, see generally INA § 212(a)(1), describe various physical and mental disorders.[10] Until 1990, these included people who "are mentally retarded," "are insane," "have had one or more attacks of insanity," and, among others, those with disorders that might affect their abilities to earn livings. See INA § 212(a)(1–7), pre–1990 version. The Immigration Act of 1990 narrowed the list significantly. Now, neither a physical nor a mental disorder is generally a basis for exclusion unless the associated behavior poses one of several specified threats. See INA § 212(a)(1)(A)(iii). Even then, discretionary waivers are possible. INA § 212(g)(3). Drug addicts and drug abusers are specifically inadmissible. INA § 212(a)(1)(A)(iv).

But by far the most significant modern issue connected with the health exclusions has been how to handle AIDS and HIV. Since 1891, the immigration laws have barred the admission of noncitizens with various diseases. Act of March 3, 1891, ch. 551, § 1, 26 Stat. 1084. During the 1980's and early 1990's there was much wrangling over whether the law excluded, and whether the law should exclude, individuals infected with HIV, the virus that causes AIDS. The tortured history is summarized in the first edition of this coursebook at 351–53, and discussed in greater detail in Jorge L. Carro, *From Constitutional Psychopathic Inferiority to AIDS: What is in the Future for Homosexual Aliens?*, 7 Yale L. & Policy Rev. 201, 222–23 (1989); Juan P. Osuna, *The Exclusion from the United States of Aliens Infected with the AIDS Virus: Recent Developments and Prospects for the Future*, 16 Houston J. Internat'l L. 1, 7–12 (1993). Given the volatility of the debate on AIDS, neither Congresses nor Presidents have been anxious to take responsibility for policies that would facilitate the admission of noncitizens with HIV.

In 1993, however, Congress enacted the National Institutes of Health Revitalization Act, Pub.L. 103–43, 107 Stat. 122 (1993). Section 2007 of that statute amended INA § 212(a)(1)(A)(i) to expressly exclude noncitizens who are determined by the Department of Health and Human Services to have "a communicable disease of public health significance, which shall include infection with [HIV]." The Secretary of Homeland Security has the discretion to waive that exclusion ground for spouses and certain other close family members of United States citizens or LPRs. Gay males in permanent relationships with United States citizens have seldom benefitted from the waiver provision because, as you saw in chapter 3, § B.2.a above, United States immigration law does not recognize same-sex marriages. Even with the waiver provision, there are serious questions whether the United States policy comports with the international law restrictions on the treatment of people with HIV. See Joan Fitzpatrick & William McKay Bennett, *A Lion in the Path? The Influence of International Law on the Immigration Policy of the United States*, 70 Washington L. Rev. 589, 608–618 (1995).

---

10. See also INA § 212(a)(5)(B) (restricting admission of foreign physicians).

For opposing views on whether HIV should be a basis for exclusion, compare Carro, above, at 221–28 (immigrants testing positive for HIV should be excluded) with Lynn Acker Starr, *The Ineffectiveness and Impact of the Human Immunodeficiency Virus (HIV) Exclusion in U.S. Immigration Law,* 3 Georgetown Immigration L.J. 87 (1989) (HIV should not be ground for exclusion).

Quite apart from the subject of public health, some exclusion grounds are rooted in congressional perceptions of public morality. The Immigration Act of 1990 significantly trimmed that list. Gone are the exclusions of homosexuals, see chapter 3, § B.2.a above, and of noncitizens "coming to the United States to engage in any immoral sexual act," INA § 212(a)(13), pre–1990 version. The former exclusion of those who "*advocate* polygamy," INA § 212(a)(11), was cut back to cover only immigrants, and then only if they are "*coming to the United States to practice* polygamy," INA § 212(a)(9)(A) (emphasis added). There remains the exclusion of noncitizens involved in prostitution or other commercialized vice (even absent criminal convictions). INA § 212(a)(2)(D).

QUESTION

Should United States law exclude noncitizens with HIV? Is your answer the same for immigrants as for nonimmigrants?

CHAPTER 6

Admission Procedure

The procedures for admitting noncitizens to the United States have undergone dramatic change since September 11, 2001. Those changes that relate specifically to national security are collected in chapter 10, which takes up the question of national security more comprehensively. Within that chapter, the sections most relevant to admission procedure are the ones on intelligence-gathering (section B), visa policies (sections E.1 through E.4), border enhancement strategies (section F), and profiling practices (section G). To minimize repetition, most of the new admission-related national security precautions are mentioned only briefly in the present chapter.

Section A. The Early Days

During the first few decades of the twentieth century, immigrants typically arrived by boat at either of two main receiving points. Asians ordinarily came to Angel Island, in San Francisco Bay. Europeans usually arrived at Ellis Island, in New York Harbor.[1]

The passages that follow will give you the general flavor of life and process on Angel Island:

Him Mark Lai, Genny Lim & Judy Yung, Island—Poetry and History of Chinese Immigrants on Angel Island 1910–1940

Pp. 8, 42, 52, 54, 56, 60, 73, 109–11, 116, 118, 130 (2d ed. 1986).

Angel Island, now an idyllic state park out in San Francisco Bay not far from Alcatraz, was the point of entry for the majority of the approximately 175,000 Chinese immigrants who came to America between 1910 and 1940. Modeled after New York's Ellis Island, the site was used as the immigration detention headquarters for Chinese awaiting * * * the outcomes of medical examinations and immigration papers. It was also the holding ground for deportees awaiting transportation back to the motherland. The ordeal of immigration and detention left an indelible mark in the minds of many Chinese, a number of whom wrote poetry on the barrack

---

1. See generally Ann Novotny, Strangers at the Door: Ellis Island, Castle Garden, and the Great Migration to America (1971); Thomas M. Pitkin, Keepers of the Gate: A History of Ellis Island (1975).

walls, recording the impressions of their voyage to America, their longing for families back home, and their outrage and humiliation at the treatment America accorded them.

When the center's doors shut in 1940, one of the most bitter chapters in the history of Chinese immigration to America came to a close. The poems expressing the thoughts of the Chinese immigrants were locked behind those doors and soon forgotten. Those poems have been resurrected and preserved in this book. It was by accident that they have survived. The three of us, offspring of Angel Island inmates, plunged into the project of translation and historical documentation as a personal hobby which later evolved into this book. * * *

[The authors also interviewed immigrants who had been detained at Angel Island and immigration officials who had been stationed there. The following account of one detainee describes her arrival, lockup, and daily life on the island:]

* * *

"When we arrived, they locked us up like criminals in compartments like the cages at the zoo. They counted us and then took us upstairs to our rooms. There were two to three rooms in the women's section, all facing the shore. Each of the rooms could fit twenty or thirty persons. The spring beds could be folded up. The main door was locked, but we could go into the other rooms from the hallway. The hall was wide, with tables and chairs where you could play dominoes. You didn't have to stay in your room during the day. You could come out into the hall. There was also an office there. We could ask questions of the white woman who took care of us at the office. One kid who had stayed for two years could speak English. He called her Mama. He was eight or nine. He translated for us. The woman even gave haircuts to the three boys staying in the women's section then. There was a back yard that was fenced in so we couldn't get out. We could hang our wash out there. It wasn't too bad. It was just that you couldn't go out. The place was very clean. There were two bathrooms and three or four stalls inside of each. The toilet doors were cut off at the bottom so they could see your feet. Maybe it was because they were afraid of people committing suicide. There were wash basins and sinks, bathtubs, hot water, toilet paper, and soap for us to use. People chatted in the hallway or in their rooms, sang for pleasure, or read books. The old-timers were familiar with one another, but they left the newcomers pretty much alone. We were Sam Yup [a geographic region of China—Ed.] and didn't know them. When we arrived, we were kind of shy and distant, so there really wasn't much to say."

Mrs. Woo, age 23 in 1940

[Here are some varying impressions of the adjudication procedure in actual practice:]

"At that time, a new arrival was held for a hearing before a Board of Special Inquiry, as we called it. That consisted of two inspectors, a stenographer, and an interpreter. The inspector, to whom the case was assigned, was handed the file with any related files of that person's family. It was up to him to review the old file and start questioning the applicant about his birth and family home and in the course of the questioning and testimony, it would develop the applicant was either very much in accord with the old files or that there were rather serious discrepancies between him and the other family members. It was the only means we had, although it wasn't a very good method, because in a way, the Immigration Service built up a way for them to be coached and learn their testimony to get by. We just worked on the theory that this was the law and we had to carry it out. I felt each was entitled to a fair deal and I tried to give it to him as best as I could. In a way, it (laws discriminating against the Chinese) did touch me, and when the Exclusion Law was repealed, I thought that was a good thing.

* * *

"They (interrogation rooms) were bright, airy rooms. There would be the stenographer's desk and another desk or two. When the applicant was brought in, he would be given a seat where he could be at ease and talk as he wished and where the interpreter would communicate with him. Around 15 percent of the cases I handled were women. I don't remember any prostitutes, except one instance after World War II. There were many, many boys coming through—12, 14, 15 years old, a lot of them smart kids. They were very sure of themselves.

"The testimony was taken directly on the typewriter. He would be questioned about his birthday, his parents, his brothers and sisters, and about the village he lived in. That might be quite brief or it might drag out with some inspectors to forty or fifty pages of typed testimony. It took from one to three or four days for him and the witnesses altogether. There usually was a certain field to be covered, according to his claims and the old claims. Usually you would start with the immigrant himself and check his testimony against his relatives'. If the testimonies matched, we had to give them the benefit of the doubt. A minor discrepancy would not carry much weight. If it was something serious . . . I remember a case of a boy whose father was bringing him in. He said his mother was so-and-so, but his father said his mother was so-and-so. He wasn't landed.

"After the Board heard the testimony, they would be pretty much in accord as to what was right and what was not. Any disagreement would mean a denial for the person. If two voted to land him and one voted to deny him, the dissenting member could appeal the case. But if he didn't wish to appeal, the person was landed. If the testimony was in accord, the file would be sent to the detention quarters and the person ordered to land. If denied, the person was not notified until the testimony was all summarized, but he would be given that notice eventually. If the applicant wished to appeal, the copy of the testimony would be sent to the central office in Washington and the attorney handling the case would be given a copy from which he made his appeal. They (Washington) would probably make its decision based on the transcript alone. More than 75 percent passed the interrogation at Angel Island. There could have been indications of fraud in some of them, but nothing that would stand up in court to debar them. Of those that were denied here, there was always an appeal to Washington and probably only 5 percent of those denied were ever really deported. Some who were deported came back and tried again, and made it. They knew you knew they were here before. If we found they were using another name, they could be excluded. Those deported had photographs taken that were held here to be checked. I've known of families of four or five coming together. They would question one briefly, just to a certain point. Then they would call back the first one and just go a little bit further. So they couldn't get together and talk about what they had just said.

"The interpreters we had were pretty good on most of the dialects. They would use one interpreter with one applicant. Then when they had a witness, they would change interpreters. The inspector in charge had to rotate the interpreters so that the first interpreter would usually not be available when recalled for a second hearing with the same applicant. I one time asked one of our interpreters what percentage of cases were fraudulent. I asked if 90 percent were. He said probably. I was aware of it from the beginning. I remember one case I was very sorry about. The father had brought a boy in, although it really was a daughter that he had had. She later came and I forget how he brought it up that she was really his daughter, and she really was, but the boys that he had gotten paid for bringing in had spoiled things for her. She was deported, but she married a G.I. and later came back.

"There were few bribes offered. I know it did happen, but the cases were very rare. I don't think I ever had anything offered to me, but in a few cases, some of the others had. It was something that was hard to prove. I was aware that coaching papers were being sneaked in. They (the administration) tried to prevent it. I did hear of a capsule being put in a bowl of soup with a note inside. They got the capsule but nothing developed from it. I know the kitchen help used to give them a lot of help (*laughs*), but there was nothing we could do about it."

Immigration inspector #1, 1929–1940

* * *

"When it was my turn to be interrogated, they first made me wait in a small room. After awhile, they called me in and started asking me this and that, this and that, until I had a headache. After three or four hours of this, they confined me to a downstairs room where I stayed overnight. The next day, they questioned me again. They very seldom question you one day only and allow you to return upstairs. One strange question they asked me was: 'What is your living room floor made of?' I replied, 'Brick.' They said, 'Okay. What is the floor under your bed made of?' So I thought if the living room floor was brick, then the bedroom must also be brick. So I said, 'Brick!' They typed the answer down and didn't say anything. The next day, they asked the same question and I replied, 'Brick' again. They said my father had said it was dirt. What happened was that the floor was dirt at first, but later, after my father left for America, I changed the floor myself to brick. Where I really went wrong was in answering the question about who gave me the passage money. My father had written that he would send the money home to my mother to give me so that's what I said. But what happened was my father didn't really have the money and another relative loaned the money to my mother. So although I was a real son, I failed the interrogation. My deepest impression of Angel Island now was the rudeness of the white interrogators. They kept saying, 'Come on, answer, answer.' They kept rushing me to answer until I couldn't remember the answers anymore. And it wasn't just the whites. The Chinese interpreters did too."

Mr. Leung, age 24 in 1936

"During the interrogation, if the inspector pursued a point, the situation would become tense. They even asked me where the rice bin was kept. Can you imagine? If your father had said the left side and the son, the right side, that won't do. In our days, we didn't have electricity, just kerosene lamps. And you know, a kerosene lamp's a moveable object. So what was I supposed to say if they asked where was the lamp kept? My father might have said the middle of the table or the end of the table. I didn't know. I couldn't understand why they asked such questions. They asked about everything and anything. When I was serving as a witness for my brother, they asked me how far the *shameen*[33] was from the wharf. I said, 'Very close.' The next time I was interrogated, they asked me the same question and I replied the same, 'Very close.' They then said, 'Okay, come get your brother tomorrow.' They were trying to trap me. I was interrogated only once for several hours in one day. I knew that most people who were interrogated in the morning would be landed the next day. It was bad if no news came by then."

Mr. Poon, age 18 in 1927

* * *

"Prior to interrogation, you were not allowed to have any visitors. The guards said, 'Here they come, here they come!' but they never let you see them. When I went, the interrogators were very thoughtful. The white lady gave me some candy and by the time I had finished eating my candy, the interrogation was over. It took not more than ten minutes. They asked a few questions, nothing much: what is your father's name, what village are you from, how old are you, so forth. Maybe they asked less questions than usual because they had questioned my husband first. They questioned him, then me, then my son. After they finished the interrogation, two days later, I was able to get on the ship. I took the boat and my relatives met me in San Francisco."

---

33. Cantonese pronunciation of Shamian, an island on the Pearl River at Guangzhou, where the United States Consulate used to be located.

Mrs. Jew, age 33 in 1922

* * *

"If the guard came in and called out a name and said *'sai gaai,'*[27] it meant that that person was freed to land. If an applicant was to be deported, the guard would make motions as if he were crying."

Mr. Lee, age 20 in 1930

* * *

[The following poems were among those found inscribed on the prison walls:]

10

Poem by One Named Xu From Xiangshan
Encouraging the Traveler

Just talk about going to the land of the Flowery Flag and my countenance
   fills with happiness.

Not without hard work were 1,000 pieces of gold dug up and gathered
   together.

There were words of farewell to the parents, but the throat choked up first.

There were many feelings, many tears flowing face to face, when parting
   with the wife.

Waves big as mountains often astonished this traveller.

With laws harsh as tigers, I had a taste of all the barbarities.

Do not forget this day when you land ashore.

Push yourself ahead and do not be lazy or idle.

* * *

12

Today is the last day of winter,

Tomorrow morning is the vernal equinox.

One year's prospects have changed to another.

Sadness kills the person in the wooden building.

* * *

15

The insects chirp outside the four walls.

The inmates often sigh.

---

27. Probably a corruption of "Hou sai gaai," a colloquial term meaning "good fortune." At other times, guards apparently also shouted, "Seung ngon," or "go ashore."

Thinking of affairs back home,

Unconscious tears wet my lapel.

* * *

19

Living on Island away from home elicits a hundred feelings.

My chest is filled with a sadness and anger I cannot bear to explain.

Night and day, I sit passively and listlessly.

Fortunately, I have a novel as my companion.

* * *

24

I, a seven foot man, am ashamed I cannot extend myself.

Curled up in an enclosure, my movements are dictated by others.

Enduring a hundred humiliations, I can only cry in vain.

This person's tears fall, but what can the blue heavens do?

* * *

65

Bidding farewell to the wooden building, I return to Hong Kong.

From hence forward, I will arouse my country and flaunt my aspirations.

I'll tell my compatriots to inform their fellow villagers.

If they possess even a small surplus of food and clothing,

They should not drift across the ocean.

For fascinating transcripts of the immigration inspections of two other Chinese detainees at Angel Island, see the illuminating article by their son, Bill Ong Hing, *No Place for Angels: In Reaction to Kevin Johnson*, 2000 Univ. Illinois L. Rev. 559.

SECTION B.   MODERN PROCEDURE: PRELIMINARY COMMENTS

In some respects little has changed since the days of Angel Island. Certain categories of arriving noncitizens are still routinely detained while their admission decisions are pending. See pages 156–58 above. And the courts still hold, as you saw in chapter 2, that the Constitution provides little protection—substantive or procedural—to the noncitizen who seeks initial admission to the United States.

In other respects, however, we have come a long way. The Immigration and Nationality Act, the regulations of several administrative agencies, and other less formal agency action together provide a process far more intricate, and in most cases fairer, than the procedure of several decades ago. You will also see a massive exception. "Expedited removal" and other abbreviated procedures introduced in 1996 actually leave less procedural protection for certain large categories of arriving noncitizens than was the case at Angel Island.

The next few sections of this chapter will take you through these processes. Several federal Departments are involved: the Department of Homeland Security; the Department of Justice, mainly its Executive Office for Immigration Review [EOIR]; the Department of State; and the Department of Labor. In cases that involve medical exclusions, the Department of Health and Human Services also plays a role.

Although the procedure for admitting immigrants is generally more exacting than that for nonimmigrants, many of the steps you will study are common to both. You can think of the admission process as comprising up to four hurdles that the prospective entrant must clear:

The first hurdle applies only to individuals who seek certain statuses. Generally, immigrants applying under the second and the third employment-based preferences must first obtain labor certification. See INA § 212(a)(5)(A) and chapter 3, § C.1.b above. Employers of certain nonimmigrants must also apply for labor certification or, in some instances, file "labor condition applications" ("LCA's"). See chapter 4, § A.3 above.

The second hurdle, also limited to certain statuses, is the visa petition, which is filed with USCIS. Its purpose is to establish that the noncitizen beneficiary meets the definition of the particular status.

The third potential step is getting a visa. (Some noncitizens are exempt from this requirement, as you will see.) Once USCIS has approved a visa *petition* (if one is required), the beneficiary next ordinarily files a visa *application* with the appropriate United States consulate abroad. The beneficiary will need to persuade the consulate not only that he or she fits the definition of the applicable status, but also that none of the affirmative grounds for inadmissibility applies. The process involves paperwork and, in the case of certain statuses, a personal interview. The terrorist attacks of September 11, 2001 have clearly resulted in more resource-intensive background checks for greater numbers of visa applicants. (Under specified circumstances that you will study in section F, it is possible for certain noncitizens who are already in the United States, and who now meet the substantive requirements for admission as LPRs, to "adjust status" in the United States, thus avoiding the need to travel abroad for immigrant visas.)

The fourth hurdle is actual admission to the United States. Armed with a visa, the person appears at an authorized entry point and formally applies for admission. A visa is usually essential to admission, see INA § 212(a)(7), but it does not guarantee admission. Under a double-check system, the CBP immigration inspector may reexamine the noncitizen to assure that none of the statutory inadmissibility grounds applies. In practice, for travelers in possession of visas, the border inspection has normally been quite cursory, though less so since September 11, 2001.

Before proceeding further, figure out why the law would generally impose this multi-step process—visa petition, visa application, and inspection at port of entry (all preceded by labor certification in certain employment-related contexts). Would it be better to have a single agency make all the determinations on which admissibility hinges? Recent studies have now taken up this question. See generally United States Commission on Immigration Reform, Becoming an American: Immigration and Immigrant Policy 161–69 (recommending consolidation of all admission functions in State Department), 175–83 (recommending establishment of independent agency to review immigration-related administrative decisions) (Sept. 1997). An excellent critique by Professor Lenni Benson depicts much of the superfluous processing as "bureaucratic borders" superimposed upon physical borders. See Lenni B. Benson, *Breaking Bureaucratic Borders: A Necessary Step Toward Immigration Law Reform*, 54 Administrative L. Rev. 203 (2002).

The next several sections will cover all these procedural steps (except labor certification, which was addressed in chapter 3). Keep in mind that, with some exceptions, a noncitizen is subject to inspection and possible exclusion ("removal") every time he or she seeks admission. After initial admission, however, immigrants and certain categories of nonimmigrants who leave the United States for brief periods will ordinarily be readmitted upon presentation of certain documents at ports of entry. See 8 C.F.R. §§ 211.1(a)(2) (immigrants), 214.1(b) (certain nonimmigrants) (2004).

SECTION C. VISA PETITIONS

Here is some basic information about the mechanics and terminology associated with visa petitions: First, the petition itself is a standardized form. The party who files it is called the "petitioner;" the noncitizen on whose behalf the petition is filed is called the "beneficiary." Two particular forms are in such common use that their numbers have become part of the lingo: The visa petition filed with USCIS on behalf of immediate relatives and family-based preference immigrants is the I–130; for employment-based immigrants, it is the I–140.

Normally, in immediate relative and family preference cases, the United States citizen or LPR family member is the one who must file the visa petition. INA § 204(a)(1)(A, B). If that person declines to do so, the would-be immigrant is generally powerless to apply for LPR status. This means the United States spouse has enormous power over the noncitizen beneficiary. Until 1994, that source of power left noncitizen spouses exceptionally vulnerable to subtle or even explicit pressure not to complain about domestic violence or other abuse.

In 1994, as part of a comprehensive crime statute, Congress authorized certain abused immigrants to petition on their own behalf. See Pub. L. 103–322, § 40701, 108 Stat. 1796, 1953–55 (Sept. 13, 1994), amending INA § 204(a)(1). The provision applies to those who have been battered, or subjected to "extreme cruelty," by their United States citizen or LPR spouses. The 1994 law also required the self-petitioner to show good moral character, prior residence in the United States with the spouse, good faith in entering into the marriage, and extreme hardship to the petitioner or the petitioner's child. It established analogous protections for noncitizen children who have been battered, or subjected to extreme cruelty, by their citizen or LPR parents (or parents' spouses). See generally Janet M. Calvo, *A Decade of Spouse–Based Immigration Laws: Coverture's Diminishment, But Not Its Demise*, 24 Northern Illinois Univ. L. Rev. 153 (2004); Janet M. Calvo, *The Violence Against Women Act: An Opportunity for the Justice Department to Confront Domestic Violence*, 72 IR 485, 487–89 (Apr. 10, 1995); Linda Kelly, *Stories from the Front: Seeking Refuge for Battered Immigrants in the Violence against Women Act*, 92 Northwestern L. Rev. 665 (1998).

Still, the 1994 legislation left some difficult obstacles for battered self-petitioners. For one thing, while the law clearly contemplates self-petitions from people who are already present in the United States, nothing in the law exempts the self-petitioner from removal on the ground of presence without admission. Thus, the self-petitioner must take a calculated risk. Having brought her presence to the attention of ICE, she now risks removal if the petition is denied.[2] Professors Linda Kelly and Cecelia Espenoza have both discussed another difficult practical obstacle. If, as often happens, both parties to a physical dispute are charged with domestic violence, and convictions ensue, the battered woman might be unable to establish the "good moral character" required for self-petitions. See Linda Kelly, *Domestic Violence Survivors: Surviving the Beatings of 1996*, 11 Georgetown Immigration L.J. 303, 315 n.63 (1997); Cecelia M. Espenoza, *No Relief for the Weary: VAWA Relief Denied for Battered Immigrants Lost in the Intersections*, 83 Marquette L. Rev. 163 (1999) (urging repeal of the good moral character requirement because it can be triggered by the false claims of a violent spouse that the victim was also guilty of domestic abuse). Finally, extreme hardship can be quite difficult to prove.

The Victims of Trafficking and Violence Prevention Act of 2000, Pub. L. 106–386, § 1503, 114 Stat. 1464, 1518 (Oct. 28, 2000), addressed some of these concerns but not all of them. It repealed the extreme hardship requirement and provided a discretion to waive the good moral character requirement in certain instances in which the otherwise disqualifying behavior was connected to the original violence. Related statutory provisions authorize nonimmigrant U-visas for certain domestic violence victims who cooperate with the police (see chapter 4) and relax the requirements for the discretionary remedy known as cancellation of removal in the cases of certain victims of battery or other extreme cruelty (see chapter 8).

---

2. Thanks to Professor Victor Romero and his students for spotting this issue.

Linda Kelly, Stories From the Front: Seeking Refuge for Battered Immigrants in the Violence Against Women Act

92 Northwestern Univ. L. Rev. 665, at 665 (1998).

Sonya's Story:

We met at a vocational and technical education school. We began dating and fell in love. I was four months into my pregnancy when we got married. The abuse started when I became pregnant and gradually progressed in severity. The verbal insults turned into physical abuse. When I fought back he would beat me and then force me to have sex with him. He told me that because I was not willing to please him as a good wife should, I had become a mere servant in his home. He would hide food. He said that I could eat it off the floor since I was no more than a dog. When he hid my passport I hid one of his guns that he would keep on top of the television. The police only told him to be careful with Latin women because they had fiery tempers. He laughed as they left and told me that he would show me that he had the power because he was American and that no one would believe me. He would yell at me that I was nothing but an immigrant and that he, as a citizen, had all the power.

* * *

In a separate, unpublished writing, Professor Kelly posed the following two questions:

Question 1. What problems may a victim of domestic violence like Sonya encounter in documenting and proving the abuse? How does a domestic violence survivor's position as an undocumented immigrant compound this problem?

Question 2. What problems may a victim of domestic violence encounter in documenting and proving good faith marriage? How does a domestic violence survivor's position as an undocumented immigrant compound this problem?

———

Certain employment-based first preference immigrants (those with "extraordinary ability") may either petition for themselves or have others, such as their employers, petition for them. INA § 204(a)(1)(E). For most other employment-based preferences, the petitioner must be the employer. INA § 204(a)(1)(F).

USCIS comprises three geographic "regions"—the Eastern, the Central, and the Western—each of which in turn encompasses several local "districts." See 8 C.F.R. § 100.4(a) (2004). In the past, almost all interaction between individual applicants and the former INS occurred at the district level. Today, each of the three regions operates a "regional office" that adjudicates a wide variety of applications and petitions for which personal interviews are assumed to be generally unnecessary. They are currently located in Burlington, Vermont; Dallas, Texas; and Laguna Niguel, California. *Id.* Most visa petitions filed within the United States are mailed directly to those regional offices. Certain petitioners who live outside the United States may file in offices overseas. 8 C.F.R. § 204.1(e)(2) (2004). In addition, designated United States consulates may adjudicate certain visa petitions that are "clearly approvable." 8 C.F.R. § 204.1(e)(3) (2004). All visa petitions, wherever filed, must be supported by documents that establish the essential facts. 8 C.F.R. § 204.1(f, g, h) (2004).

Recall that immigrants who are subject to numerical quotas receive "priority dates" fixing their places in the queue. The priority date for a family-based preference immigrant is the date that the visa petition was filed. INA § 203(e)(1); 22 C.F.R. § 42.53(a) (2004). The priority date for an employment-based preference immigrant is similarly the date on which the petition was filed, INA § 203(e)(1), but for this purpose the regulations deem the visa petition filed on the date the request for labor certification was accepted for processing (assuming the particular preference category in fact requires labor certification). 8 C.F.R. § 204.5(d) (2004).[3]

USCIS has the discretion to require both the petitioner and the beneficiary to appear in person for an interview. 8 C.F.R. § 103.2(b)(9) (2004). In practice, that authority is seldom invoked. The only basis for denying a visa petition is that the petitioner has not shown the beneficiary has the claimed status, see *Matter of O,* 8 I. & N. Dec. 295, 297 (BIA 1959); that decision—unlike the later determination whether any of the exclusion grounds applies—can normally be made without a personal interview.

In some instances, it is the petitioner who wants the opportunity to be heard orally. The regulations provide no right to such a hearing. They do provide, however, that, before an adverse decision can be made on the basis of derogatory non-classified information of which the petitioner or beneficiary is unaware, he or she must be given that information and an opportunity to respond. 8 C.F.R. § 103.2(b)(16)(i) (2004). The procedure must also comport with the demands of due process, and for that purpose the balancing test set out in *Mathews v. Eldridge* (see page 144 above) applies. *Ali v. INS,* 661 F.Supp. 1234, 1249–51 (D.Mass.1986). In New York City, a consent decree approved in *Stokes v. United States INS,* 74 Civ. 1022 (S.D.N.Y.1976) (unpublished), required the former INS to follow a number of additional agreed-upon safeguards designed to remedy recurring problems in that district. See 4 Gordon, Mailman & Yale–Loehr, § 41.01[4][b]; *Matter of Pradieu,* 19 I. & N. Dec. 419 (BIA 1986).

When USCIS denies a visa petition it must state its reasons for doing so. 8 C.F.R. § 204.2(a)(3) (2004). That is important, because denials of visa petitions are subject to both administrative and judicial review. In the case of administrative review, the forum depends on the type of visa petition. Denials of most kinds of family-based petitions are appealable to the BIA. 8

3. If an individual labor certification is unnecessary because the immigrant's occupation is listed on the Labor Department's Schedule A, the priority date will be the date on which the visa petition is filed with US-CIS. 8 C.F.R. § 204.5(d) (2004).

C.F.R. § 1003.1(b)(5) (2004). Denials of employment-based petitions are normally appealable within USCIS to a unit called the Administrative Appeals Office (the AAO).[4] Until 1996, judicial review of the final administrative decision concerning either type of visa petition was explicitly made available in federal district court. INA § 279. As discussed in chapter 9, however, IIRIRA § 381 amended INA § 279; the amended version authorizes suits by the United States but not suits against it. Nonetheless, general federal question jurisdiction under 28 U.S.C. § 1331 might well be available. See pages 479–80 below.

Once USCIS approves an immigrant visa petition, it forwards the approval to the State Department's National Visa Center (NVC), in Portsmouth, New Hampshire. The NVC checks the petition for accuracy and completeness, creates a file, and sends the file to the appropriate United States consulate overseas. See generally 71 IR 714–16 (May 27, 1994). At that point, the visa application process—examined in the next section—begins.

In recent years serious backlogs have accumulated in the processing of visa petitions (among other forms), with the result that even those immigrants whom Congress has chosen to exempt from the numerical quotas (e.g., immediate relatives) have been routinely subjected to disturbing delays. In section 204(a) of the Immigration Services and Infrastructure Improvements Act of 2000, which is title II of the American Competitiveness in the Twenty–First Century Act of 2000, Pub. L. 106–313, 114 Stat. 1251 (Oct. 17, 2000), Congress mandated the Attorney General to take whatever measures were necessary to reduce the "backlog in the processing of immigration benefit applications, with the *objective*" of eliminating the backlog entirely within one year (i.e., by October 17, 2001). Funding was provided for that purpose. *Id.* The objective was not met, but when Congress passed the Homeland Security Act in 2002, it included a provision, section 458, which set a new target date of one year after enactment of the HSA, i.e., by November 25, 2003. Since then, USCIS Director Eduardo Aguirre has introduced a "Backlog Elimination Plan" that he hopes will reduce most processing times to six months by the end of 2006. See 82 IR 536 (Mar. 28, 2005). For the details, and for websites that display current waiting times, see item 5 at the end of section A of chapter 3 above.

One controversial INS solution to the backlog problem was to introduce, in 2001, a concept that it called "premium processing." Those employer petitioners who are willing to pay a fee of $1000 (in addition to the regular filing fee) could have their petitions processed within 15 days. The direct beneficiaries are the employers, who hope to recruit and hire

---

4. Former 8 C.F.R. § 103.1(f)(iii)(B) (2003) expressly authorized such appeals. DHS has now chosen not to codify that authority, see 68 Fed. Reg. 10923 (Mar. 6, 2003), but the current regulations still mention the Administrative Appeals "Unit" (its former name), 8 C.F.R. § 103.3(a)(1)(iv) (2004). On the allocation of administrative appellate authority between the BIA and the former AAU (now AAO), see Stephen H. Legomsky, *Forum Choices for the Review of Agency Adjudication: A Study of the Immigration Process,* 71 Iowa L.Rev. 1297 (1986).

foreign workers as quickly after a job becomes available as possible, and of course the noncitizen employees. The former INS pledged, however, to use the additional revenues to hire additional staff to reduce the processing times for other petitioners as well. See generally 66 Fed. Reg. 29682–86 (June 1, 2001); 78 IR 920 (June 4, 2001).

NOTES AND QUESTIONS

1.   As an immigration lawyer, what documents would you submit to prove the facts essential to successful visa petitions for each of the four family-sponsored preference categories? What sorts of complications can you envision? See generally 8 C.F.R. § 204 (2004).

2.   INA § 205 authorizes the Secretary of Homeland Security to revoke a previous approval of a visa petition "for what he deems to be good and sufficient cause." The regulations, 8 C.F.R. § 205.1 (2004), specify certain events that will trigger *automatic* revocation. Keeping in mind the substantive requirements for the various statuses, try to figure out what events should be included in that list.

3.   Apart from automatic revocation, USCIS may revoke a visa petition for any other "good and sufficient cause" in the particular case, including simply a change of heart. INA § 205. The beneficiary must receive notice of an intention to revoke and an opportunity to respond. See *Matter of Ho,* 19 I. & N. Dec. 582 (BIA 1988); *Matter of Estime,* 19 I. & N. Dec. 450 (BIA 1987).

4.   The approval of a visa petition may not be revoked once the beneficiary has begun his or her journey to the United States. INA § 205. Revocations are appealable to the BIA in family cases, 8 C.F.R. § 3.1(b)(5) (2004), and to the Administrative Appeals Office of USCIS in employment cases (procedure no longer codified).

Florida Bar v. Matus

Supreme Court of Florida, 1988.
528 So.2d 895.

■ BARKETT, JUSTICE.

This cause is before us upon The Florida Bar's petition to enjoin Dr. Francisco J. Matus d/b/a Latinoamericana De Inmigracion, Inc., from the unauthorized practice of law. * * *

* * *

The allegations indicate that the respondent is not a member of The Florida Bar and engaged in the following activities:

1.   On or about May 18, 1987, Florida Bar staff investigator Enrique T. Torres visited Respondent's offices * * *. Respondent's office displayed diplomas, degrees, presidential appointments and

presidential citations from Nicaragua, as well as a State of Florida Notary Public Appointment.

2. At the time of the May 18, 1987, visit, Torres obtained a business card from Respondent. The card, printed in Spanish, represented Respondent as a general immigration service, showing the corporate logo and the services offered, including, but not limited to, tourist visa extensions, student visas, political asylum, and residency. The business card lists Respondent, Dr. Francisco J. Matus, as president of Latinoamericana De Inmigracion, Inc. Respondent also advertises his availability to perform the above services in "La Estrella de Nicaragua", a Spanish publication circulated in Miami.

3. During the May 18, 1987, visit, Torres indicated to Respondent that he wished to obtain permanent residence status for his girlfriend who had entered the United States illegally from Peru in 1980. Respondent informed Torres that his girlfriend would need documentation and affidavits showing her residency in the United States from the date of her arrival. Respondent informed Torres that upon receiving the documents, Respondent would complete the documentation required by the new amnesty program for a fee of two hundred and fifty (250) dollars.

4. During the May 18, 1987, visit, Torres further asked Respondent whether he could assist Torres in obtaining an extension of his tourist visa. Respondent informed Torres that he had all of the forms in his office and would file the necessary extension with the Immigration Service for a fee of four hundred (400) dollars. Torres then' asked Respondent whether he could assist Torres in obtaining permanent residence status in the United States. Respondent informed Torres that for a fee of three thousand (3,000) to five thousand (5,000) dollars, he could arrange a marriage between Torres and an American citizen. After the marriage, Respondent would file the necessary documentation to obtain permanent residence status for Torres.

5. Respondent was not and is not authorized by Federal Law or the Immigration and Naturalization Service to perform the services outlined in paragraphs two (2) through four (4) above.

The preparation of forms to effect a change in immigration status requires legal training and familiarity with immigration laws, and failure to properly prepare the forms could result in great harm, including deportation. Holding oneself out to be an attorney when not so licensed itself constitutes the unauthorized practice of law.

Accepting the uncontested allegations in this petition as true, we hold that respondent held himself out as legally qualified to perform immigration services, which constitutes the unauthorized practice of law in Florida. We therefore permanently enjoin and restrain respondent from engaging in the acts complained of and from otherwise engaging in the practice of law in this state.

It is so ordered.

NOTES AND QUESTIONS

1.   In the present case the Florida State Bar sought merely to enjoin Matus from continuing to practice law. You should be aware, however, that the unauthorized practice of law is also a criminal offense and a growing problem in immigration. Increased numbers of notaries and other nonlawyers hold themselves out as qualified to take on immigration cases.

In addition to criminal and civil legislation and to the ethical constraints imposed by state disciplinary codes, attorneys (and others) who practice before USCIS or EOIR are subject to the disciplinary rules laid out in the DHS and DOJ regulations. Those rules, revamped in 2000, see 65 Fed. Reg. 39513 (June 27, 2000), appear in 8 C.F.R. § 1003.102 (2004). One provision disciplines anyone who "[k]nowingly or with reckless disregard makes a false or misleading communication about his or her qualifications or services." *Id.* § 1003.102(f).

2.   Can you identify all the things Matus did that the court considered wrongful?

3.   If you have taken a course in professional responsibility, you know that it is not easy to determine when particular services amount to the practice of law. In the specific context of immigration, the regulations provide some guidance. They define "practice" to include "the preparation or filing of any brief or other document, paper, application, or petition on behalf of another person ..." 8 C.F.R. § 1001.1(i) (2004). The word "preparation," in turn, is defined as "the study of the facts of a case and the applicable laws, coupled with the giving of advice and auxiliary activities, including the incidental preparation of papers, but does not include the lawful functions of a notary public or service consisting solely of assistance in the completion of blank spaces on printed Service forms by one whose remuneration, if any, is nominal and who does not hold himself out as qualified in legal matters or in immigration and naturalization procedure." 8 C.F.R. § 1001.1(k) (2004).

4.   In a 1992 legal opinion elaborating on those regulations, the then INS General Counsel, Grover Joseph Rees III, quoted approvingly from a case called *Unauthorized Practice Committee v. Cortez*, 692 S.W.2d 47 (Tex. 1985): "Although the act of recording a client's responses to the questions on the form I–130 probably does not require legal skill or knowledge, the act of determining whether the I–130 should be filed at all does require special legal skills." See 69 IR 823, 827 (July 6, 1992). See also Memorandum from Hon. Doris Meissner, Commissioner of the INS, to various INS officers (Jan. 18, 1995), reproduced in March 1995 AILA Monthly Mailing at 203, 205.

5.   Are the current regulations consistent with *Cortez* (and therefore with the former INS General Counsel's opinion citing *Cortez*?) The regula-

tions seem to allow a nonlawyer to help a client fill out a standardized form as long as remuneration is nominal and the nonlawyer does not hold himself or herself out as qualified in legal or procedural matters. Does *Cortez* allow that?

6. Apart from the unauthorized practice of law, those who help people fill out immigration forms or assemble documents need to worry about the consequences of either false or frivolous filings. IIRIRA created several new offenses and stiffened the penalties for some old ones:

a. INA § 274C(a)(5) makes it a civil offense, punishable by fines of $250 to $2000 for first offenders (higher for repeat offenders), "to prepare, file, or assist" the filing of any immigration-related application or document "with knowledge or reckless disregard of the fact that such application or document was falsely made."

b. A provision of the U.S. criminal code, 18 U.S.C. § 1546(a), para. 4, makes it a crime, punishable by up to ten years in prison, to "knowingly present any [application or document required by the immigration laws] which contains any ... false statement *or which fails to contain any reasonable basis in law or fact*" (emphasis added.)

c. Under INA § 274C(e), a person who "knowingly and willfully fails to disclose, conceals, or covers up the fact that they have, on behalf of any person and for a fee or other remuneration, prepared or assisted in preparing an application which was falsely made" is subject to a prison term of up to five years and barred from preparing future applications. The term "falsely made" is defined in section 274C(f).

PROBLEMS 1–3

Problem 1. Your friend, a United States citizen who has just married a noncitizen, knows that you are a law student and that you are enrolled in an immigration course. She cannot afford to hire an attorney, so she asks whether you would fill out her I–130 (visa petition) for her. The marriage is clearly genuine, and her case strikes you as straightforward. But you have just read the *Matus* decision and the information following it, and this has made you nervous about helping her. Should you do it?

Problem 2. Rule 5.5(b) of the ABA Model Rules of Professional Responsibility prohibits a lawyer from "assist[ing] a person who is not a member of the bar in the performance of activity that constitutes the unauthorized practice of law." The analogous provision in the old ABA Model Code (still followed in some states) was Disciplinary Rule 3–101: "A lawyer shall not aid a non-lawyer in the unauthorized practice of law."[5] That Disciplinary Rule was supplemented by Ethical Consideration 3–6, which provided:

5. Under the ABA Model Code, the Ethical Considerations (EC's) were the standards to which all attorneys were urged to aspire. The Disciplinary Rules (DR's) were the man-datory rules that were to give rise to disciplinary proceedings. The Model Rules abandoned that terminology.

EC 3–6. A lawyer often delegates tasks to clerks, secretaries, and other lay persons. Such delegation is proper if the lawyer maintains a direct relationship with his client, supervises the delegated work, and has complete professional responsibility for the work product. This delegation enables a lawyer to render legal service more economically and efficiently.

In 2000, the Justice Department added an analogous disciplinary ground for practice before the former INS, immigration judges, and the BIA. It punishes anyone who "[a]ssists any person, other than a practitioner [who is authorized to practice in those forums], in the performance of activity that constitutes the unauthorized practice of law." 8 C.F.R. § 3.102(m) (2004).

You are a third-year law student enrolled in your school's clinical program. You have been placed in an office that handles immigration cases for low-income clients. The office handles a high volume of cases, and your personal case load is a heavy one. One of your tasks is to interview the client, fill out an intake sheet, and then, while the client is waiting, bring the intake sheet to your supervisor, a licensed attorney who reads the sheet and discusses the case with you. If there are no unusual problems, and if the next step in the case is to prepare a form for the client to submit to USCIS, the office procedure is that you fill out the form, make copies for the office files and the client, mail the forms and supporting documentation to USCIS, and provide the client any other necessary instruction, including whether and when the client should return to your office. Are you engaged in the unauthorized practice of law? Is the supervising attorney complying with his or her ethical duties?

Problem 3. Your client, X, is a licensed attorney who has been charged with violating INA § 274C(e). The facts are uncontested. X is an immigration lawyer. He helped prepare an I–130 visa petition for his United States citizen client, Y. Y was petitioning for immediate relative status on behalf of her noncitizen daughter. Y's daughter in fact was 21 years old, but Y told X that Y's daughter was only 19 (which would have qualified her as an immediate relative). Y gave X a forged birth certificate showing her daughter's age as 19. X, unaware of the fraud, then filed the visa petition and the accompanying documents, including the forged birth certificate. Although the petition specifically asked for the name of the preparer, if any, X deliberately left that line blank. He told Y, "My name is mud right now with USCIS. I think you're better off if they don't know this is my case." USCIS detected the forged birth certificate, and now X faces criminal prosecution and possible imprisonment.

As X's attorney, what arguments might you make? Before answering, read carefully subsections (e) and (f) of INA § 274C.

SECTION D.   VISA APPLICATIONS

With only a few narrow exceptions, noncitizens need visas to enter the United States. INA §§ 211(a), 212(a)(7)(A) (immigrants), 212(a)(7)(B)(i)(II) (nonimmigrants). The authority for issuing visas and the basic information the applicants must furnish are described in INA §§ 221 and 222.

One major exception is the visa waiver program. Under INA § 217, the Secretary of Homeland Security and the Secretary of State have jointly implemented a program under which nationals of countries that have historically low rates of visa refusals may enter the United States as tourists or business visitors for up to 90 days without having to procure visas. There are several other requirements. For example, the country must be one that agrees to extend reciprocal privileges to United States citizens; the individual must present a return ticket and must not be a safety threat; and various responsibilities are placed on the commercial carriers that transport non-visa passengers. The designated countries are listed in 8 C.F.R. § 217.2(a) (2004). At this writing 27 countries are on the list; 22 of them are in Europe.

While some had worried about the security implications of the visa waiver program even before September 11, the worries intensified after the events of that day. As debate raged over whether the trade and tourism benefits of the program outweighed its security risks, Congress responded with a series of measures designed to keep the program intact but tighten security. Of immediate importance is USA PATRIOT Act § 417(c), amending INA § 217(a)(3) to require that, beginning October 1, 2003 (extended to June 26, 2005, see DHS & DOS Press Release of May 12, 2005), the passports of all visa waiver applicants be machine-readable. By October 26, 2005, the passports will also have to be tamper-resistant and incorporate biometric and document authentication identifiers that meet certain specified standards. EBSVERA § 303(c), as amended by Pub. L. 108–299, 118 Stat. 1100 (Aug. 9, 2004). For the details on these and other security precautions added to the visa waiver program, see chapter 10, section E.5 below.

This section of the chapter will examine the visa process in more detail. See also James A.R. Nafziger, *Review of Visa Denials by Consular Officers*, 66 Washington L.Rev. 1, § IV.B (1991). If the type of visa the person is seeking requires preliminary steps, such as labor certification or USCIS approval of a visa petition or both, then the following discussion assumes those steps have been completed.

1 Charles Gordon, Stanley Mailman & Stephen Yale–Loehr, Immigration Law and Procedure

§ 8.04 (2004).

[1]—Comparison Between Nonimmigrant and Immigrant Visas, In General

While the procedures for processing nonimmigrant visas (NIVs) and immigrant visas (IVs) are similar, there are also basic differences that set them apart. In both instances, they are designed to screen the applicants to determine whether they are eligible for the status they seek. And in both, visa issuance provides a document that permits the applicant to obtain transportation to the United States and which satisfies the requirement for admission, subject to the [CBP] second check at inspection. Again in respect of both, the applicant is subject to qualitative grounds of exclusion, although not all of these apply to nonimmigrants, and some of the waiver provisions are not available to immigrants. * * *

* * *

The major practical difference between IVs and NIVs stems from the disparity in importance usually attributed to the two. Nonimmigrant visas are used for usually short periods of stay, immigrant visas for permanent residence, which often leads to citizenship. This factor largely accounts for the more detailed attention ordinarily given to immigrant visa applications. It is reflected, for example, in the application forms: a single, short one for nonimmigrants; several detailed questionnaires for immigrants. Moreover, while both are subjected to a computer check, an immigrant visa applicant must also produce police certificates from abroad and is put through extensive FBI and security clearances. Moreover, on-site checks to verify employment letters are more common for IVs than NIVs.

* * *

Finally, the difference in sheer volume of business is dramatic. * * * The need to service the large and widespread demand for NIVs, and to do so promptly, is why there are many more consular posts with NIV jurisdiction than for IV issuance. And at large posts that handle both types of visas, there is a separate queue for each in different areas.

The regulations make no reference to the representation of applicants by lawyers. Under Visa Office policy, and ordinarily in practice, such representation is honored and posts will communicate with designated counsel. Allowing counsel to be present at interviews, however, is a matter of consular discretion, and practice varies.

* * *

[2]—Nonimmigrant (Temporary)

An application for a nonimmigrant visa is usually made at the consular post abroad where the alien resides. [As a result of the Intelligence Reform and Terrorism Prevention Act of 2004, Pub. L. 108–458, 188 Stat. 3638, § 5301 (Dec. 17, 2004), adding INA § 222(h), with only limited exceptions every applicant for a nonimmigrant visa between ages 14 and 79 now requires an in-person interview with a consular officer.—Ed.]

Application is made on Form DS–156,[a] an innocuous-looking short form that asks all the right questions surrounding the purpose of an

---

a. A copy of this form, completed by a fictional applicant for a student visa, appears on pages 822–23 below.—Ed.

applicant's trip. Photographs are also needed, and such documents as the consul requests.

B–2 (tourist) visas are usually issued without the need for supporting documents. An E–1 (treaty trader) or E–2 (treaty investor) application, on the other hand, will clearly require extensive documentation to show that the substantive requirements are met. Even here, documentation may be minimized if the treaty company has the basic documentation on file with the consulate. For some visas, official documents must also be presented: for example, for the student (F–1), the school's I–20 form; for the exchange visitor (J–1), the program sponsor's form DS–2019.

Still other visas require the prior approval of a visa petition by [USCIS]. These are the temporary worker (H), intracompany transferee (L), fiance(e) (K), alien of extraordinary ability in the sciences, arts, education, business or athletics (O), and athlete or performing artist (P). Under DHS regulations, consuls have a larger role in the issuance of certain L visas under blanket petition approvals by USCIS. It should be stressed that even in respect of applications based on individual petitions, approval by USCIS does not guarantee issuance of the visa by the consul, who must determine the applicant's personal eligibility. The burden of proving eligibility is always on the applicant.

The key question is usually whether the applicant is a bona fide nonimmigrant, namely, seeking to enter the United States temporarily for the purpose contemplated by the requested category. The application will also be denied if the alien is qualitatively ineligible, for example, has been convicted of certain crimes, unless the disqualification can be, and is, waived.

The nonimmigrant visa is to be endorsed or inserted on a page of the passport or equivalent document and includes the date and place of issuance, the visa classification, the limited number of entries for which it is valid or the word "multiple," and the period of validity. In the case of classifications requiring a petition, the validity of the visa may not exceed the period of the petition approval by INS.

Note: There is no necessary relationship between the validity of the visa and the length of time for which the alien will be admitted to the United States. The admission period is set by the CBP inspector at the time of admission and is ordinarily limited only by the regulations and by the validity of the petition, if a petition is required.

[3]—Immigrant (Permanent)

* * *

Applications for immigrant visas are ordinarily to be made at the consular post abroad that services the applicant's residence. An alien living temporarily in the United States is considered to be a resident of the consular district of his or her last residence abroad. While no personal appearance need ordinarily be made at the consulate during the processing, at the end the applicant must physically attend the scheduled interview with the consul to secure the visa. The residence rule, even with its exceptions, is extremely problematic in cases where it is a hardship for aliens to return to their home country.

The regulation requires a consulate to accept an application from a nonresident applicant who is physically within the consular district, and expects to remain long enough in another country to process the visa. Consuls may, in their discretion, and must, at the direction of the Department, accept the cases of aliens who are neither residents of the consular district nor physically there. Moreover, consulates are encouraged to exercise their discretion in accepting cases that clearly involve hardships, but most, under severe budget constraints, are reluctant to do so.

* * *

Visa processing consists of a succession of "packets" sent by the consular office, containing information and questionnaires to be completed and returned by the applicant. If the applicant is successful, the processing culminates in an interview with a consul at which a formal application, Form OF–230 Parts I and II, is signed, and the visa issued on Form OF–155.

* * * [I]mmigrant visa petitions approved by USCIS are sent to the National Visa Center (NVC) in Portsmouth, New Hampshire. That center transmits the approval to the appropriate consular office and so notifies the alien beneficiary and any attorney of record, or simply the attorney, if there is one and the beneficiary is in the United States. The notice is accompanied by the initial packet.

* * *

Visa processing also includes government agency clearances to determine whether the applicant is excludable on criminal or subversive grounds, and requires the applicant to submit police certificates relating to previous residences outside the United States.

It is not until all of the preliminary inquiries are completed and a visa number allocated, if one is needed, that a medical examination and formal interview are scheduled, and the consul either issues or refuses the visa. A visa, if issued, is annexed to a signed copy of the formal application, Form OF–230 Parts I and II, and a copy of each document requested by the consul, and given to the immigrant for presentation to the CBP inspector at entry.

* * *

NOTES AND QUESTIONS

1. Once issued, a visa will be valid only for a limited time. An immigrant visa must be used (i.e., presented to a CBP inspector at a United States port of entry) within six months. INA § 221(c). For nonimmigrant visas, the validity periods vary by nonimmigrant category and by country of

origin, according to State Department regulations. See 22 C.F.R. § 41.112(b) (2004).

2. Why doesn't the law permit noncitizens to apply for visas at any U.S. consulate they wish (assuming the particular consulate issues the type of visas they seek)?

3. Attorneys do not usually accompany applicants to their visa interviews, and consular officers are generally not enthusiastic about attorneys' involvement. The State Department's Foreign Affairs Manual says that, if "the consular officer is reasonably satisfied that an attorney-client relationship exists, correspondence between the post and the attorney *may* [emphasis added] be treated with the same courtesy provided to the visa applicant." 9 F.A.M. § 40.4 n.12 (2004). The F.A.M. then adds:

> Consular officers shall *not* [emphasis in original] advise applicants against employing attorneys * * *. However, if an alien makes a specific inquiry regarding the advisability of retaining an attorney, the consular officer shall advise the inquirer that the decision to retain an attorney is one to be made by the concerned party. *The consular officer, however, may inform the alien that representation by an attorney is not required to apply for a visa* [emphasis added].

Id. n.12.4

Why do you think the State Department is not excited about having attorneys present during the visa interviews?

4. As a practical matter, consular officers exercise a great deal of subjective discretion. See Michael Maggio, Larry S. Rifkin & Sheila T. Starkey, *Immigration Fundamentals for International Lawyers*, 13 Amer. Univ. Internat'l L. Rev. 857, 868–71 (1998).

A scandal at the United States consulate in Sao Paulo, Brazil exposed the dangers of those powers. The consulate engaged in explicit racial and economic stereotyping and fired an officer who refused to comply with the "profiles." The officer sued and won reinstatement. See *Olsen v. Albright*, 990 F.Supp. 31 (D.D.C. 1997).

According to the manual issued by the consulate, "Officers sometimes use abbreviations on the [visa application forms]: RK = Rich Kid, LP= Looks Poor, TP = Talks Poor, LR = Looks Rough, TC = Take Care." Some of the stated reasons for denying nonimmigrant visas included "Slimy looking[;] wears jacket on shoulders w/ earring," "bad appearance," "looks + talks poor." 990 F.Supp. at 33. The manual also contained a passage headed "KOREAN/CHINESE FRAUD," which said "Major fraud; hard to check. * * * Visas are rarely issued to these groups unless they have had previous visas and are older." *Id.* The manual then listed certain Brazilian cities "known for fraud"—most of them with predominantly black populations—and cautioned that "anyone born in these locations is suspect unless older, well-traveled, etc." *Id.* A separate memorandum distributed to all the U.S. consulates in Brazil instructed that "Arab and Chinese last names set off bells and whistles, regardless of what passport/nationality they may have. * * * Most Brazilians have no interest in [assuming a false identity], but Arabs and Chinese are two groups to worry about." *Id.* at 34.

Apart from the economic and racial stereotyping, the dismissed officer's superiors had told him "that he should spend approximately three minutes per interview *and that he should attempt to achieve a thirty percent refusal rate*. To achieve these goals, they said, Plaintiff should base his judgment on the profiles" [emphasis added]. *Id.* As the court noted, *id.* at 37, the law is otherwise: "[N]o person shall receive any preference or priority or be discriminated against in the issuance of an immigrant visa because of the person's race, sex, nationality, place of birth, or place of residence [except as specifically provided by the INA]." INA § 202(a)(1)(A).

5. The Sao Paolo affair pre-dated the September 11, 2001 terrorist attacks. Since September 11, the visa process has come under heavy criticism from a different direction. There is a widely held perception that the visa process, beset by large volumes and little time for scrutiny of each individual application, is a point of great vulnerability. How the process can be substantially improved when approximately 20,000,000 tourists alone enter the United States each year has been a major challenge for policymakers.

One move Congress made was to inject the new Department of Homeland Security into the visa process. While individual visa applications are still decided by the State Department's consular officers at posts overseas, HSA § 428 now charges the Secretary of Homeland Security with administering the visa issuance process, issuing regulations, and arranging for DHS officials to train consular officers and monitor their visa decisions for compliance with security needs. See 6 U.S.C. § 236(b)(1). In addition, personal interviews are now required in the vast majority of nonimmigrant cases (see above), new data gathering and data technologies are required (with particularly stringent requirements for student visas), and noncitizens from certain countries designated as harboring terrorists require scrutiny at higher levels of government. Further, when a visa is denied, the consular officer is now required to enter the relevant information into an electronic database. Later, if the same noncitizen files another visa application, the consular officer must review the information on the previous denial, document that he or she has reviewed that record, and, if inclined to grant the visa, explain why approval is now appropriate. HSA § 429, adding 6 U.S.C. § 237. For the details on these and other national security precautions imposed on the visa process, see chapter 10, sections E.1 through E.4 below.

————

What if the consular officer refuses to issue the visa? Does the applicant have any recourse?

At present, despite the magnitudes of the individual interests often at stake, there is no administrative appeal, and no judicial review, of a consular decision denying an application for either an immigrant or a nonimmigrant visa. Some limited safeguards do exist. The State Department regulations require the principal consular officer at the particular post to review all refusals. 22 C.F.R. §§ 41.121(c) (2004) (nonimmigrants), 42.81(c) (2004) (immigrants). And the Visa Office in Washington, D.C. (known as "VO") *may* issue an "advisory" opinion. *Id.* §§ 41.121(d) (nonimmigrants), 42.81(d) (immigrants). If it does, its opinion binds the consulate on "an interpretation of law." *Id.* On a question of fact or on "an application of the law to the facts," the VO opinion is purely advisory; the consulate may reject VO's advice as long as the consulate submits reasons to VO for doing so. *Id.*

An attorney who would like VO to issue an advisory opinion may request it directly, but a usually wiser strategy is to encourage the consular officer to make the request because a consular request is more likely to be granted. Even when VO is willing to issue an opinion, however, the participation of the applicant and his or her counsel is quite limited:

> The attorney may also submit a legal brief to the State Department accompanying the request for an advisory opinion, with a copy to the consular officer. Attorneys are officially denied access to either the wording of the advisory opinion request submitted by consular officers or the written advisory opinion itself. An attorney learns of the opinion by receiving a brief letter sent by the Department of State confirming that a decision has been rendered.

Robert A. Free, Angelo A. Paparelli & Jan M. Peterson, *Consular Processing,* in AILA, 1989(1) Immigration and Nationality Law at 225, 237; see also Robert A. Free, *The Lawyer's Role in Consular Visa Refusals,* Nov. 1990 Immigration Briefings.

Beyond the kinds of internal consular review and advisory opinions discussed above, the statute arguably forbids, and in any event clearly does not require, the Secretary of State to provide for *administrative* appeals of visa denials. INA § 104(a) charges the Secretary of State with the administration and enforcement of all immigration laws "relating to (1) the powers, duties and functions of diplomatic and consular officers of the United States, *except those powers, duties and functions conferred upon the consular officers relating to the granting or refusal of visas; * * * "* (emphasis added).[6] Further, under HSA § 428(b)(1), adding 6 U.S.C. § 236(a)(1), the Secretary of Homeland Security may not alter or reverse a consular officer's denial of a visa application (but may refuse a visa that the consular officer had approved). *Judicial* review, for more mysterious reasons that will be examined shortly, has also been held generally unavailable.

---

6. Professor Nafziger has suggested that a reason for insulating the Secretary of State from visa decisions might have been to enable the Secretary "to disclaim responsibility for a politically delicate exclusion" when complaints are registered by foreign officials. James A.R. Nafziger, *Review of Visa Denials by Consular Officers,* 66 Washington L.Rev. 1, 24 (1991).

Over the years, a steady chorus of scholarly commentary has denounced this notion of "consular absolutism." A sample includes Sam Bernsen, *Consular Absolutism in Visa Cases,* 63 IR 388 (1986); Charles Gordon, *Recent Developments in Judicial Review of Immigration Cases,* 15 San Diego L.Rev. 9, 16–17 (1977); Stephen H. Legomsky, Immigration and the Judiciary—Law and Politics in Britain and America 144–51 (1987); James A.R. Nafziger, *Review of Visa Denials by Consular Officers,* 66 Washington L.Rev. 1 (1991); Angelo A. Paparelli & Mitchell C. Tilner, *A Proposal for Legislation Establishing a System of Review of Visa Refusals in Selected Cases,* 65 IR 1027 (1988); Harry N. Rosenfield, *Consular Non-Reviewability: A Case Study in Administrative Absolutism,* 41 A.B.A.J. 1109 (1955); Leon Wildes, *Consular Nonreviewability—A Reexamination,* 64 IR 1012 (1987); Note, *Judicial Review of Visa Denials: Reexamining Consular Nonreviewability,* 52 N.Y.U. L.Rev. 1137 (1977); see also Commission on Immigration Reform, Becoming an American: Immigration and Immigrant Policy at 175–83 (Sept. 1997) (advocating administrative review of selected visa denials, as well as judicial review, *id.* at 82).

In a legal system in which far less important agency adjudication is routinely subjected to both administrative and judicial review, consular absolutism is a striking phenomenon. What is keeping this doctrine afloat? The most authoritative study of consular nonreviewability to date is the thoughtful 1990 report by Professor James Nafziger for the Administrative Conference of the United States. The following passages, excerpted from a revised version of that Report, identify and evaluate some of the practical concerns that underlie the nonreviewability principle:

James A.R. Nafziger, Review of Visa Denials by Consular Officers

66 Washington L.Rev. 1, 53–63 (1991).

* * *

The judiciary is understandably skeptical about the weight to be given practical considerations when "fundamental rights are involved." Although "[p]rocedure by presumption is always cheaper and easier than individualized determination," administrative convenience by itself is not a persuasive justification for cutting the corners of individual claims. Practical considerations are, however, highly influential in shaping legislative or administrative reform.

* * *

Consular officers are well trained, representing one of the most carefully selected, career-groomed corps of government, the Foreign Service. Consular officers possess high levels of competence and morale. Most officers have had special training in the visa process and are familiar with the characteristics and idiosyncracies of the local culture. They generally have an experienced eye for fraud and chutzpah by applicants.

On the other hand, to err is human and any exercise of discretion is potentially fallible. That is why the decisions of other agencies of government are subject to review despite their expertise. Consular interpretation of such terms as "public charges" and "reason to believe" are necessarily subjective, and guidelines are not always effective in promoting uniformity or consistency. To the extent that errors are avoidable, the prospect of review would also encourage accountability. It would encourage consular officers to maintain a high level of care and commitment to applying the law correctly. Few officers would relish reversal by an outsider.

More importantly, a belt-tightening budget restricts the scope and efficacy of consular expertise. Many consulates are so financially hardpressed that they cannot devote much time and expert judgment to a single applicant. "Batching" or group processing of applications in the same class may be necessary. On-line interviews of applicants for nonimmigrant visas average a minute or less because of severe budget constraints that spread on-line officers very thinly. Officers have little time to carefully investigate documents and employment letters and may rely heavily on income, property, and other guidelines without undertaking a more effective, case-by-case appraisal of applicants. Similarly, supervising officers often do not have enough time to review each visa denial thoroughly. Spot checks or random samplings of denials are often the only alternative. Binding decisions on interpretations of the law by the Visa Office, congressional inquiries, and other intra-departmental processes of review, though important, are too sporadic to substitute for careful review within the consulate. Thus, budget constraints lead to a need for outside review. Internal review procedures are deficient, not because the working relationship between consular and reviewing officers is too cozy to ensure an objective review, but because too little time and money is available for a thorough review of all denials.

* * *

Efficient and effective management of the visa process would seem to require speed and finality, insulation of *initial* policymaking from judicial review, and uniformity or consistency of decisions. These normal considerations of public administration might appear to be especially significant in the specific context of consular activity because of possible foreign policy implications of visa decisions. It is questionable, however, whether the foreign dimension of consular decisions should routinely set them apart from other types of administrative decisions, such as domestic decisions to locate state penitentiaries or nuclear power plants on the Canadian or Mexican border. In any event, review of consular determinations simply applying the INA to the facts in a particular case would not seem to involve "an initial policy determination of a kind clearly for nonjudicial discretion." Nor is the need for a quick decision necessarily strong enough to overcome the need for a more deliberate, potentially correct decision. Delay of a final visa denial to allow for review is not likely to cause the kind of problem that delay of a more truly political decision, such as whether to suspend trade and tariff concessions, is apt to entail.

The need for uniformity or consistency of decisions justifies either greater regulatory control over consular discretion or review of consular decisions. Of these, the former might help alleviate the need for the latter. * * *

* * *

The prospect of overburdening the State Department or clogging the courts has been cited as an important justification for non-reviewability. Today, perhaps, it is *the* major practical justification, and at least partially explains INA section 104's mysterious insulation of visa denials from supervision by the Secretary of State. It has been used to support an inference against judicial review drawn from that provision. The volume of appeals is, of course, a serious consideration. Consulates issue close to a million visa denials every year. It is difficult to estimate what percentage of denied applicants would take advantage of judicial review if it were available. At a time when the federal courts are already overburdened, authorizing judicial review of all visa denials would therefore be quite risky. On the other hand, barring all judicial review seems unnecessary to avoid court congestion. Any burden to the government could be controlled to a large extent by the standard of review selected.

Moreover, specialists have argued that the volume of appeals of visa denials would be small. Only a small proportion of denied applicants are likely to seek judicial review. Unlike deportation cases, where aliens already in the United States may have some incentive to file frivolous court actions to obtain delay, the visa applicant waiting to enter the United States has nothing to gain from delay. Further, financial costs are associated with judicial review, particularly when the alien must arrange for filing from abroad.

The likely demand for judicial review is reflected in the exclusion cases. In fiscal year 1984, for example, thousands of aliens were excluded at United States entry points. Yet, only twenty-seven aliens in that year exercised their statutory right to obtain judicial review of their exclusion orders, and only ten of these were non-asylum petitioners. Significantly, these petitioners had already traveled to the United States, often at great expense. Visa applicants would seem even less likely to have actions brought on their behalf in court.

If the burden on the judicial system were still deemed to be excessive, Congress might limit the categories of visas from whose denials appeal could be taken. Thus, only family reunification cases, national security cases, or cases where the applicant has a "real stake" or "high stake" in obtaining a visa might be reviewable. Gradual inclusion of nonimmigrant visa denials in a review process might begin with a pilot program involving a single class or two of visas, such as treaty trader and treaty investor visas. * * *

* * *

* * * A serious problem under present budgetary constraints is that the record available for either administrative or judicial appeal would be very limited. On-line consular officers must state reasons for visa denials, but often have too little time to record much more than a citation of authority for a denial, with perhaps a few scribbled words of factual explanation. Sometimes consular notations are scarcely legible. If the issue on appeal is whether an officer has applied the law to the facts, but that officer had too little time to write up the facts or to communicate them clearly and legibly, what can an administrative appeals board or court review? With more time and resources to create a clearer, more complete record for appeal, much of this problem would dissolve. Under present budgetary circumstances, it might be unfair to sustain an appeal on the basis of an inadequate record, and yet it also seems unfair to applicants to allow the characteristic inadequacy of a consular refusal sheet to inhibit a more adequate review process.

In evaluating the adequacy of the record of a visa denial, the credibility and demeanor of applicants are often determinative factors. Although administrative tribunals seldom defer to assessments of credibility by executive officials, such assessments play a particularly important role in the visa process; by definition, applicants are generally unable to appear in the United States. * * *

Voice recordings on cassette tape might substitute for the parsimonious and sometimes cryptic written records of consular adjudications. Such recordings, however, involve two problems. First, recording an adjudication could interfere with its integrity: the existence of the process itself might encourage both applicants and officers to rehearse and perform as they might not otherwise. Voice recordings do not, of course, convey live images, which are ordinarily critical in determinations of an applicant's credibility and demeanor. Videotapes would largely resolve this problem, but do not appear to be politically feasible at this time because of strong opposition by the consular corps.

* * *

The visa process necessarily relies on judgmental factors of an applicant's demeanor and credibility, as well as evolving circumstances in the local socio-economic environment. These factors argue for a relatively limited standard of review of consular discretion (as opposed to more objective issues of law and fact), such as whether a denial was "arbitrary, capricious, an abuse of discretion, or otherwise not in accordance with law."

* * *

Another type of cost is psychological, namely, the threat and perceived nuisance that review might present to already overburdened consular officers. Nobody likes to be overruled. Moreover, little love is lost between attorneys and consular officers. The aversion of some officers to further involvement of attorneys is understandable. Still, experienced foreign service officers have minimized the psychological cost and were open-minded about the possibility of a modest formalization of the review process. They acknowledged that the guidance and encouragement of greater uniformity that review could provide might make their work easier.

* * *

————

From time to time various members of Congress have proposed legislation that would create, within the State Department, an administrative review board to hear appeals from designated categories of visa denials. See, e.g., H.R. 3305 (1993) (per Rep. Frank); S. 3202, § 3 (1969) (per Sen. Kennedy); H.R. 1156 (1999) (per Rep. Frank). The following bill, introduced unsuccessfully in 1987, is illustrative:

H.R. 2567

Rep. Gonzalez, 1987

A BILL

To establish a Visa Review Board within the Department of State to review denials of certain visa applications.

Be it enacted by the Senate and House of Representatives of the United States of America in Congress assembled,

Section 1. Visa Review Board.

(a) AMENDMENT TO INA.—Chapter 3 of title II of the Immigration and Nationality Act is amended by adding after section 224 the following new section:

"VISA REVIEW BOARD

"SEC. 225.(a)(1) There is hereby established, within the Department of State, a Visa Review Board (hereinafter referred to as the 'Board') which shall be composed of regular and ad hoc members to be appointed by the Secretary of State. Regular members shall serve on a full-time basis. Ad hoc members may be designated from among senior officers of the Department of State or from persons not employed by the Department. Members shall be attorneys in good standing admitted to practice in any State, or in any territory or possession of the United States.

"(2) In considering any appeal, the Board shall act through a panel of 3 members, not more than 2 of whom may be ad hoc members, and not more than 1 of whom may be a current consular officer.

"(3) The Board shall have authority, as provided in this section, to review the case of aliens specified under paragraph (4) who have been denied visas.

"(4) An alien referred to in paragraph (3) is an alien described as follows:

"(A) a special immigrant (as defined in section 101(a)(27));

"(B) an immediate relative (as defined in section 201(b));

"(C) an immigrant having a preference status under section 203(a) [now 203(a, b)—Ed.];

"(D) a nonimmigrant described in sections 101(a)(15)(F), 101(a)(15)(J), or 101(a)(15)(M), who is seeking to reenter the United States; or

"(E) a nonimmigrant described in sections 101(a)(15)(E)(ii), 101(a)(15)(H), 101(a)(15)(K), or 101(a)(15)(L).

"(b)(1) Whenever a consular officer shall deny an immigrant or nonimmigrant visa to an alien described in subsection (a)(4), such consular officer shall inform such alien (and [the petitioner]) * * * of the provisions for review under this section.

"(2) The Board shall review each denial by a consular officer of an immigrant or nonimmigrant visa to an alien described in subsection (a)(4) upon the request of such alien, or of [the petitioner]. * * * Such request for review must be made in writing to the Board within 60 days after receipt of notice of the denial and may be accompanied by an affidavit, signed by such alien or by [the petitioner,] * * * setting forth any facts which have a bearing upon such alien's eligibility for a visa.

"(c)(1) Upon receipt of any request for review under subsection (b), the Board shall, within 15 days, notify the consular officer with respect to whose decision a review is sought, and, upon receipt of such notice, such officer shall promptly (but in no event greater than 30 days after such receipt) forward to the Board a concise statement of the material facts upon which the denial of a visa was based.

"(2) The Board may, at any time after receiving a request for review under subsection (b), obtain from any consular officer such information, together with certified copies of such documents, reports, records, and other data, which are available to or obtainable by such officer, as the Board may deem necessary to properly review the case of any alien.

"(3) In reviewing the decision of a consular officer denying a visa to an alien, the Board shall hear testimony and receive evidence from (A) any official of the Government requesting the privilege to be heard with respect to a matter pending before the Board, and (B) the attorney or other designated representative of the alien * * * whose case the Board is reviewing, or the attorney or other designated representative of the [petitioner.] * * *

"(d)(1) In reviewing the decision of any consular officer denying a visa to an alien, the Board shall consider all the information before it with respect to such alien, and shall give due consideration to the reasons set forth by such officer for denial of a visa. To be effective, the decision of the

Board must be concurred in by at least two members, and shall affirm, overrule, or remand, for further consideration, the decision of such officer.

"(2) If the Board overrules the decision of a consular officer with respect to the eligibility of an alien for a visa, such officer shall, upon notification by the Board, promptly cause the issuance of the visa to such alien which would have been issued to the alien if the visa had been approved.

"(e) Nothing contained in this section shall require the Board, or any officer or employee of the United States or any consular officer to make public disclosure of any confidential information the disclosure of which, in the opinion of the Board, such officer or employee, or such consular officer, as the case may be, would be prejudicial to the public interest, safety, or security."

(b) REGULATIONS.—Within 120 days after the date of the enactment of this Act, the Secretary of State shall establish rules and regulations implementing the authority of the Visa Review Board established under section 225 of the Immigration and Nationality Act (as added by subsection (a)).

* * *

SIMULATION EXERCISE

(1) Assume that the House Judiciary Committee has reported out H.R. 2567 favorably and that the bill is now being debated on the House floor. You are a member of the House of Representatives and a supporter of the bill. Outline the points you would make in your speech.

(2) Assume you are opposed. Outline the points you would now make in your speech.

———

On the subject of administrative appeal, the principal debate has been at the policy level: *Should* a formal administrative review mechanism be created and, if so, what properties should it possess? Analogous policy questions surround judicial review as well, but the central question there, in contrast, has been one of statutory interpretation: *Does* the current statute require, permit, or prohibit judicial review of visa refusals?

Hermina Sague v. United States

United States District Court, District of Puerto Rico, 1976.
416 F.Supp. 217.

■ TORRUELLA, DISTRICT JUDGE.

On September 18, 1971 in France, * * * Plaintiff Berger, a citizen of the Republic of France, married * * * Plaintiff Sague, a citizen of the United States of America. Thereafter, on November 9, 1973, Plaintiff

Berger applied for an immigration [sic] visa to the United States Consular Officer in France. His application was denied by said official pursuant to a decision that Plaintiff Berger was ineligible for a visa under INA § 212(a).

Plaintiffs contend that the denial of Plaintiff Berger's visa has deprived them of enjoying a family life together with Plaintiff Berger's relatives, who live within the territory of the United States, and has deprived both of them of rights, privileges and immunities guaranteed by the Constitution and Laws of the United States. Plaintiffs have thus filed an action pursuant to 42 U.S.C. § 1981 et seq., requesting that this Court declare unconstitutional the laws upon which Defendants relied to deny Plaintiff Berger's petition, and seek an order directing Defendants to grant a visa to Plaintiff Berger. Plaintiffs further claim monetary damages from Defendants.

Defendants have filed a Motion to Dismiss alleging that this Court lacks jurisdiction over the subject matter of this action in that the same is tantamount to a judicial review of the consular officer's decision to withhold the visa, a procedure which Defendants contend is not contemplated by any law.

We are forced to conclude that this contention is well taken.

The exclusion of aliens from within the territory of a nation is a fundamental act of sovereignty concomitant with the executive power to control the foreign affairs thereof. This exercise of executive power is promulgated exclusively through the representatives of said Branch of Government, without judicial intervention. *Kleindienst v. Mandel,* 408 U.S. 753, 92 S.Ct. 2576, 33 L.Ed.2d 683 (1972).

* * *

Congress has conferred upon consular officers the authority to issue visas to eligible immigrants under the provisions of the law, INA §§ 101(a)(9, 16), 221. It has been consistently held that the consular officer's decision to issue or withhold a visa is not subject, either to administrative or judicial review. *U.S. ex rel. Ulrich v. Kellogg,* 30 F.2d 984 (C.A.D.C., 1929), cert. den. 279 U.S. 868, 49 S.Ct. 482, 73 L.Ed. 1005 (1928); *Licea–Gomez v. Pilliod,* 193 F.Supp. 577, 582 (N.D.Ill., 1960); *Burrafato v. United States Department of State,* 523 F.2d 554 (C.A.2, 1975); *Loza–Bedoya v. Immigration and Naturalization Service,* 410 F.2d 343, 347 (9th Cir.1969); *Kleindienst v. Mandel,* supra.

Since 1929, in *United States ex rel. Ulrich v. Kellogg,* wherein a German citizen married to a United States citizen applied for a nonimmigrant visa to the United States consul in Berlin, it has been held that:

> We are not able to find any provision of the immigration laws which provides for an official review of the action of the consular officer in such cases by a cabinet officer or other authority.

In the case of *Licea–Gomez v. Pilliod,* the plaintiff asked the Court to clarify his status in applying for an immigrant visa. The Court held:

> To allow plaintiff a hearing and adjudication on his eligibility for citizenship would completely circumvent the provisions of the

Immigration and Nationality Act of 1952 granting exclusively to consuls the right to issue visas. Such a hearing would mean that everyone denied a visa by a consul could present himself at a border without a visa and get an adjudication on his status under any of the various exclusionary provisions of INA § 212. Then after such a declaration, if favorable, he could reapply to the consul. This is certainly not what Congress intended in the statute, and the Court cannot here undermine the statutory scheme and allow plaintiff by this proceeding, to review the consul's action.

In the case of *Loza–Bedoya v. Immigration and Naturalization Service,* cited by both parties, the petitioner asked for a visa in Mexico which was denied based upon erroneous information in his records. He sought to correct that information through a motion to reopen his deportation case. The Court did find the error in the records which excluded petitioner from obtaining the visa, but held:

> Though erroneous this Court is without jurisdiction to order an American consular official to issue a visa to any alien whether excludable or not.

* * *

Plaintiff Berger is not within the territory of the United States.

In *Brownell v. Thom* [sic—Tom] *We Shung,* the Supreme Court held that *exclusion orders* may be challenged either by habeas corpus or by declaratory judgment action. * * * Nevertheless, the Supreme Court noted:

> We do not suggest, of course, that an alien who has never presented himself at the borders of this country may avail himself of the declaratory judgment action by bringing the action from abroad.

The Court further cited Senate Report Number 1137, 82d Cong., 2d Sess., as follows:

> Exclusion procedures ... The omission of the language is not intended to grant any review of determinations made by consular officers ...

Additionally, in the legislative history of the Immigration and Nationality Act, we find further support for Defendant's contention:

> *Consular decisions.*—Although many suggestions were made to the committee with a view toward creating in the Department of State a semijudicial board, similar to the Board of Immigration Appeals, with jurisdiction to review consular decisions pertaining to the granting or refusal of visas, the committee does not feel that such body should be created by legislative enactment, nor that the power, duties and junctions [sic] conferred upon consular officers by the instant bill should be made subject to review by the Secretary of State.

(House Report No. 1365, 82nd Congress, 2d Session), 1952.

* * *

Plaintiff Sague contends that as a citizen of the United States, married to an alien to whom a visa has been denied, she has been deprived of her right to live within the territory of the United States with her husband and her family. However plausible this argument may seem, there is no constitutional right of a citizen spouse, who voluntarily chooses to marry an alien outside the jurisdiction of the United States, to have her alien spouse enter the United States. No citizen can, by the individual action of contracting matrimony in a foreign jurisdiction with an alien, deprive the United States of as fundamental an act of sovereignty as is the determination of what aliens may enter its territory.

* * *

In the case at bar, Plaintiff Berger, an alien, was denied a visa to enter the United States by the consular officer in France. He is not within the territorial jurisdiction of the United States. He has not been the subject of an exclusion or deportation proceeding. He seeks review of the consul's determination. As the Court of Appeals for the Second Circuit held in the case of *United States ex rel. London v. Phelps,* * * *

> Whether the consul has acted reasonably or unreasonably, is not for us to determine. Unjustifiable refusal to visé a passport may be ground for diplomatic complaint by the nation whose subject has been discriminated against ... It is beyond the jurisdiction of the court.

* * *

Therefore, this Court concludes that it lacks jurisdiction to entertain this petition.

* * *

NOTES AND QUESTIONS

1.   The doctrine that consular decisions denying visas are not subject to judicial review originated with a pair of appellate court decisions handed down in the 1920's: *United States ex rel. London v. Phelps,* 22 F.2d 288 (2d Cir.1927) and *United States ex rel. Ulrich v. Kellogg,* 30 F.2d 984 (D.C.Cir. 1929). Those two opinions together provided three rationales that form the basis for most of the modern decisions. The court in *London,* without elaborating, held it lacked "jurisdiction" to review the denial of a visa. *London,* 22 F.2d at 290. In *Ulrich,* the court actually addressed and rejected on the merits the plaintiff's argument that the consular officer had erred. *Ulrich,* 30 F.2d at 985–86. After doing so, however, the court made two observations that have found their way into the modern cases. Citing the Immigration Act of 1924, the court said "the authority to issue a visa is *committed* to 'consular' officers" (emphasis added). *Id.* at 986. (The actual wording of the cited provision was that a "consular officer * * * may

[under specified conditions] issue" a visa. Act of May 26, 1924, ch. 190, § 2(a), 43 Stat. 153). Second, the court said: "We are not able to find any provision of the immigration laws which provides for an official review of the action of the consular officers in such case by a cabinet officer or other authority." *Ulrich,* 30 F.2d at 986.

Thus, three themes—a lack of jurisdiction, the absence of a statutory provision that affirmatively authorizes review, and the "committing" of the visa-issuing authority to the consular officers—emerge from the early cases. Stephen H. Legomsky, Immigration and the Judiciary—Law and Politics in Britain and America 144–51 (1987). The notes that follow will explore those three themes and some miscellaneous others.

2.   The court in *Hermina Sague* accepts the government's argument that there is no "jurisdiction over the subject matter." Later in the opinion the court quotes with approval the language in *London* disclaiming "jurisdiction." Whatever merit that unexplained conclusion might have commanded in 1927, when *London* was decided, it was baffling at the time *Hermina Sague* was decided and it is baffling today. INA § 279, which was part of the original 1952 Act and thus was in force at the time of *Hermina Sague,* then read: "The district courts of the United States shall have jurisdiction of all causes, civil and criminal, arising under any of the provisions of this title" [title II]. The present issues arose under Title II. INA §§ 221 and 222 (both within title II) lay out the general procedures to be followed by visa applicants and consular officers. INA § 221(a) specifically authorizes the consular officer to issue visas, and INA § 221(g) forbids visa issuance to anyone who is ineligible under section 212(a) or other provisions of law. INA § 212(a), which you have already studied, is also within title II. It sets out the substantive grounds for denying visas. If there was an ambiguity in INA § 279, it is not apparent.

Today the analysis would change. In IIRIRA § 381, Congress restricted the use of INA § 279. It now applies only to suits brought by the government; private plaintiffs can no longer invoke section 279 as a basis for federal jurisdiction.

But a broader grant of federal jurisdiction still exists. Under 28 U.S.C. § 1331 (think back to your civil procedure course), the district courts "have original jurisdiction of all civil actions arising under the Constitution, laws, or treaties of the United States." At the time *Hermina Sague* was decided, this provision also required that the amount in controversy exceed $10,000. Given that limitation, INA § 279 was necessary if the courts were to have jurisdiction to review the myriad of immigration decisions that the statute and regulations authorized. For the same reason, outside the realm of immigration, Congress enacted statutes conferring federal jurisdiction over a range of cases presenting other specific issues of federal law. But in 1976, Congress eliminated the amount-in-controversy requirement for actions against the federal government, Pub.L. 94–574, § 2, 90 Stat. 2721 (Oct. 21, 1976), and in 1980 Congress abolished the requirement entirely, Pub.L. 96–486, § 2(a), 94 Stat. 2369 (Dec. 1, 1980). As a result, the federal courts obtained jurisdiction over all cases that present questions of federal law.

Statutory grants of jurisdiction over specific federal subject matter (like section 279) thus became superfluous.

To summarize: At the time of *Hermina Sague,* 28 U.S.C. § 1331 (general federal question jurisdiction), which then required a minimum amount in controversy, probably did not apply, but INA § 279 seemed right on point. Today, the reverse is true: Section 279 is now inapplicable because the plaintiffs are private parties, but general federal question jurisdiction, shorn of its amount-in-controversy requirement, seems directly on point. (There is, however, one other wrinkle, which you will see in question 3(e) below.)

Perhaps the court thought that the applicant's absence from the United States destroyed the court's jurisdiction. Yet courts have long asserted the jurisdiction to review orders excluding noncitizens at ports of entry, see pre–1996 version of INA § 106(b) and present INA § 242(a), even though, as you have seen, noncitizens at ports of entry are similarly regarded as being outside the United States. For purposes of territorial jurisdiction, should visa denials be treated differently?

3. One of the reasons given in *Ulrich* was that no statutory provision affirmatively authorized review of visa denials. The court in *Hermina Sague* quotes that rationale with approval. Since 1946, however, the Administrative Procedure Act (APA) has *presumed* reviewability: "[F]inal agency action for which there is no other adequate remedy in a court [is] subject to judicial review." 5 U.S.C. § 704. That provision applies "except to the extent that (1) statutes preclude judicial review; or (2) agency action is committed to agency discretion by law." *Id.* § 701(a). The Supreme Court has repeatedly interpreted that language as requiring judicial review unless there is "clear and convincing evidence" of a contrary congressional intent. See, e.g., *Abbott Laboratories v. Gardner,* 387 U.S. 136, 141, 87 S.Ct. 1507, 1511, 18 L.Ed.2d 681, 687 (1967).

In *Hermina Sague* was there clear and convincing evidence of a congressional intent to preclude judicial review of visa denials? On the one hand, INA § 279 (in the form in which it appeared at the time of *Hermina Sague*) and general federal question jurisdiction today, seem to provide affirmatively for such review. On the other hand:

a. For the proposition that visa denials are "not subject to either administrative *or judicial* review" (emphasis added), one court has cited INA § 221(a). See *Loza–Bedoya v. INS,* 410 F.2d 343, 347 (9th Cir.1969), where, as noted in *Hermina Sague,* the court acknowledged that the visa had been denied on legally erroneous grounds but disavowed any power to intervene. Does INA § 221(a) support that position?

b. In *Licea–Gomez v. Pilliod,* 193 F.Supp. 577 (N.D.Ill. 1960), the court similarly refused to review, saying "[A] consul's decision to withhold a visa is not reviewable, not even by the Secretary of State" (citing INA §§ 104(a) and 221, *Ulrich,* and one other case). "This is what Congress has provided," the court added. You have already reviewed section 221. Does section 104(a) support the court's position that there is no *judicial* review of visa denials?

c.   Some courts have cited legislative history that they have read as evidencing an intent to bar judicial review. The court in *Hermina Sague,* for example, quotes a passage from House Report No. 1365, prepared in connection with the 1952 Act. Does the quoted passage shed any light on Congress's intentions concerning judicial review?

d.   Unlike the preceding evidence, the excerpt the court cites from Senate Report No. 1137 needs to be taken seriously. The full passage is reproduced in *Tom We Shung,* 352 U.S. at 185 n. 6, 77 S.Ct. at 256 n. 6, 1 L.Ed.2d at 230 n. 6 (1956). Prior bills, which the Report cites, would have imposed various restrictions on the scope of judicial review of what were then called *exclusion* orders (*i.e.,* orders refusing admission at ports of entry). In contrast, the bill that Senate Report 1137 was accompanying (soon to become the INA) omitted those particular restrictions. The portion of the Report reproduced in *Hermina Sague* cautioned that the omissions were "not intended to grant any review of determinations made by consular officers * * *." Is this "clear and convincing" evidence of a congressional intent to preclude judicial review of visa denials?

e.   Could the government argue today that, by amending INA § 279 to make it unavailable to private plaintiffs (see item 2 above), Congress in 1996 implicitly precluded the use of general federal question jurisdiction to challenge immigration decisions? As the government attorney, what points might you make in support of that position? As the visa applicant's attorney, how would you respond? Before answering the latter question, you should (a) read INA § 279 in full; and (b) note the conference committee's explanation of its amendment to section 279. The explanation reads, in full:

> This section clarifies that the grant of jurisdiction under section 279 of the INA is to permit the Government to institute lawsuits for enforcement of provisions of the INA, not for private parties to sue the Government. This has no effect on other statutory or constitutional grounds for private suits against the Government.

Congressional Record at H–10901, § 381 (Sept. 24, 1996).

4.   There is some indication that the court in *Ulrich* was also influenced by the breadth of the consular officers' discretion in adjudicating visa applications. The power was, the court said, "committed" to consular officers. *Ulrich,* 30 F.2d at 986. Today the word "committed" has statutory significance. As noted in item 3 above, the APA exempts an agency decision from judicial review not only when a statute precludes review (already discussed), but also when the "agency action is committed to agency discretion by law." 5 U.S.C. § 701(a). The phrase "*committed* to agency discretion" clearly means more than that the decision is discretionary; otherwise, the APA provision permitting courts to set aside agency action found to be an "abuse of discretion," 5 U.S.C. § 706(2)(A), would be

meaningless. But precisely when action will be held "committed" to agency discretion is difficult to predict. In *Heckler v. Chaney,* 470 U.S. 821, 830, 105 S.Ct. 1649, 1655, 84 L.Ed.2d 714, 723 (1985), the Supreme Court interpreted that exception to apply when "a court would have no meaningful standard against which to judge the agency's exercise of discretion." The State Department regulations provide:

> A visa can be refused only upon a ground specifically set out in the law or implementing regulations. The term "reason to believe," as used in INA § 221(g), shall be considered to require a determination based upon facts or circumstances which would lead a reasonable person to conclude that the applicant is ineligible to receive a visa * * *.

22 C.F.R. § 40.6 (2004). Combining what you already knew about the statutory exclusion grounds with what you just read concerning the meaning of "committed to agency discretion by law" and the authority of consular officers to deny visas, do you think visa decisions are "committed" to agency discretion by law?

Note: As you will see in section B.6 of chapter 9 below, Congress in 1996 barred courts from reviewing certain administrative decisions that the statute specifies to be discretionary. INA § 242(a)(2)(B)(ii). The REAL ID Act of 2005, § 101(f)(2), clarifies that that bar is not limited to removal proceedings. Nonetheless, since visa decisions require findings of fact and interpretations of law (rather than the exercise of statutory discretion), section 242(a)(2)(B)(ii) seems inapplicable here.

5. 6 U.S.C. § 236(f) now provides that "[n]othing in this section [which deals generally with visa issuance] shall be construed to create or authorize a private right of action to challenge" a visa grant or denial. Does that provision bear on whether visa denials are judicially reviewable?

6. How do the explicit racial profiling and other improper criteria employed in Sao Paulo (see pages 466–67 above), together with at least the possibility of more subtle practices in other United States consulates, affect the present issue? Are these practices an argument for or against review of visa denials?

7. Apart from the basic themes traceable to *London* and *Ulrich,* some courts have cited the plenary congressional power over immigration as a basis for holding visa denials unreviewable. See, e.g., *Pena v. Kissinger,* 409 F.Supp. 1182 (S.D.N.Y.1976), followed in *Rivera De Gomez v. Kissinger,* 534 F.2d 518 (2d Cir.1976). In *Hermina Sague,* a complication was that the underlying substantive argument was a constitutional one. The plenary power doctrine that you studied in chapter 2 would probably have prevented the plaintiffs from succeeding even if the court had held visa denials otherwise reviewable. (In fact, despite its conclusion that visa denials are unreviewable, the court seems to reject the constitutional argument on the merits.) In most of the reported visa denial cases, however, the alleged errors have concerned either the interpretation of the statutory inadmissibility ground or the application of the statutory language to the facts. In

those cases, does the plenary power doctrine aid the analysis of whether visa denials are reviewable?

8. Another tricky problem in visa denial cases is "standing." It is sometimes said that a nonresident noncitizen outside the United States lacks standing to sue in a United States court. See, e.g., *Berlin Democratic Club v. Rumsfeld,* 410 F.Supp. 144, 152 (D.D.C.1976). That rule is not airtight, and in addition a court will sometimes recognize the standing of a United States citizen who is adversely affected by a decision concerning a noncitizen overseas. See generally Nafziger, above, at 60.

9. The principle of consular nonreviewability has become sufficiently entrenched that courts are frequently content simply to cite other court decisions that have declined to review, without seriously examining the source or legitimacy of the nonreviewability principle. See, e.g., *Burrafato v. United States Dept. of State,* 523 F.2d 554, 555–56 n. 2 (2d Cir.1975) (citing *London*). One commonly mis-cited case is *Kleindienst v. Mandel,* discussed for its constitutional significance on pages 179–80 above. The Supreme Court in that case arguably was not being asked to review the consular visa denial, but rather to review the Attorney General's refusal to grant a waiver that would eventually have permitted the consul to issue a visa. At any rate, as others have pointed out, see Nafziger, above, at 32–34, the Court in *Mandel* did actually review the challenged decision, however characterized; only the standard of review ("facially legitimate and bona fide reason") was deferential. And it remains unclear whether even that component of the Court's deference could be attributed to the fact that the challenged decision was (arguably) a visa denial, rather than to the fact that the particular challenge entailed a constitutional attack on the statute. *Id.*

10. In *Saavedra Bruno v. Albright,* 197 F.3d 1153 (D.C. Cir. 1999), the nation's leading court of appeals on matters of administrative law gathered up a combination of these arguments to uphold the principle of consular absolutism. The dominant themes were deeply imbedded precedent, the plenary power doctrine, the assumed absence of congressional authorization (the court did not explain why general federal question jurisdiction did not apply), and the need to protect national security. The court also added one new element. It noted that, starting in 1961, habeas corpus was the only vehicle for challenging an *exclusion* order (i.e., an order removing a noncitizen at a port of entry). Assuming that habeas would be unavailable in the absence of custody, the court concluded that exclusion orders were therefore unreviewable if the noncitizen was not in custody. Assuming further that Congress could not have meant to give noncitizens who had not yet even reached ports of entry (i.e., those who had been denied visas) greater review rights than those who were excluded at the border, the court concluded that Congress must therefore have intended to make visa denials unreviewable. The court was apparently unaware that in 1996 Congress had repealed the provision on which this argument rested. As you will see in chapter 9, Congress replaced habeas with the petition for review in the court of appeals as the vehicle for obtaining judicial review of

exclusion orders (now called removal orders). INA § 242(a)(1) (except for the special expedited removal procedure, discussed below). And petitions for review do not require custody. Thus, the anomaly that the court thought consular absolutism prevented had ceased to exist.

11.   Whatever one's opinion of the reasons courts have invoked for holding visa denials unreviewable, the fact is that the results have now been generally uniform over time. At this point, do you think Congress can be said to have acquiesced in those decisions?

12.   Notwithstanding what has been said up to this point, a handful of courts have found ways around the principle of consular nonreviewability in sympathetic cases. See, e.g., *Abourezk v. Reagan,* 785 F.2d 1043, 1050–52 & n. 6 (D.C.Cir.1986) (United States citizen plaintiffs had standing to obtain review of State Department officials'—not consular officers'—decisions to refuse visas), aff'd per curiam by 3–3 vote, 484 U.S. 1, 108 S.Ct. 252, 98 L.Ed.2d 1 (1987); *cf. Shimizu v. Dept. of State,* No. CV–89–2741–WMB (C.D.Cal.1990) (reviewing *revocation* of visa outside United States, and expressly distinguishing visa *denials*).

In *Legal Assistance for Vietnamese Asylum Seekers v. Department of State*, 45 F.3d 469 (D.C. Cir. 1995), the court by a 2–1 vote reviewed on the merits the policy of the U.S. embassy in Hong Kong not to process Vietnamese visa applications. The court went on to hold the policy violative of a statutory prohibition on nationality discrimination. IIRIRA § 633, however, then amended INA § 202(a)(1) to expand the authority of the Secretary of State to determine the procedures and locations for processing immigrant visa applications. The Supreme Court vacated the court of appeals decision and remanded for further consideration in the light of IIRIRA. 519 U.S. 1, 117 S.Ct. 378, 136 L.Ed.2d 1 (1996).

The decision in *Abourezk* is especially significant, since the Court of Appeals for the D.C. Circuit—without mentioning its prior decision in *Ulrich*—founded subject matter jurisdiction on both 28 U.S.C. § 1331 (general federal question) and INA § 279. See 785 F.2d at 1050; see generally Katherine L. Vaughns, *A Tale of Two Opinions: The Meaning of Statutes and the Nature of Judicial Decision–Making in the Administrative Context*, 1995 Brigham Young Univ. L. Rev. 139 (criticizing both the majority and dissenting opinions in *Abourezk* as too result-oriented).

13.   The European nations typically allow judicial review of visa denials. See Bryan Paul Christian, *Visa Policy, Inspection and Exit Controls: Transatlantic Perspectives on Migration Management*, 14 Georgetown Immigration L.J. 215, 222–23 (1999).

14.   As a policy matter, the pros and cons of judicial review of agency action generally resemble those you encountered earlier in connection with administrative review, though with a few important differences. See Stephen H. Legomsky, Immigration and the Judiciary—Law and Politics in Britain and America 273–98 (1987). The practical consequences of judicial review are difficult to predict. For a welcome and much needed empirical assessment of those effects, see Peter H. Schuck & E. Donald Elliott,

Studying Administrative Law: A Methodology for, and Report on, New Empirical Research, 42 Administrative L.Rev. 519 (1990).

SECTION E. ACTUAL ADMISSION

1. AT THE BORDER

Upon arriving at United States ports of entry,[7] travelers encounter CBP immigration inspectors. The job of the immigration inspector is to determine whether the traveler is a United States citizen and, if not, whether any of the inadmissibility grounds enumerated in INA § 212(a) appear to apply. In practice, as noted earlier, this border inspection is ordinarily superficial. The noncitizen passenger either has a visa, in which case he or she has already undergone rigorous screening at the Consulate, or lacks a visa, in which case he or she will generally be inadmissible on that ground alone. See INA § 212(a)(7).

New security precautions devised after September 11, however, make the process more rigorous than in former times. Starting January 1, 2004, *all* nonimmigrant visitors are fingerprinted and digitally photographed, and their travel documents are scanned. These and other new national security border initiatives are detailed in chapter 10, section B.3 below. Other border enhancement strategies, most of which are aimed at immigration enforcement generally rather than at national security specifically, are covered in chapter 12.

At a typical airport, seaport, or land border, travelers present their papers to immigration inspectors who perform "primary inspection"—for most people, a quick process that entails scanning the passport (and visa, if there is one) and possibly checking a "lookout" list on the computer. If there are doubts or complications, the person is referred to a "secondary inspections" area for more intensive scrutiny.

As a result of 1996 amendments, immigration officers at ports of entry may remove certain arriving noncitizens through a special process known as "expedited removal." This procedure is described in subsection E.4 below. When the regular process applies, however, the immigration officer decides whether the noncitizen is "clearly and beyond a doubt entitled to be admitted." If so, then the person is admitted; if not, then he or she "shall be detained" for a removal proceeding. INA § 235(b)(2)(A). The "shall be detained" language does not literally require detention in all cases; other statutory provisions give the Secretary of Homeland Security the discretion to "parole" a noncitizen into the United States temporarily for emergent reasons, subject to some constraints in the case of certain individuals who are removable on criminal or national security grounds. See INA §§ 212(d)(5), 236.

---

7. The inspection procedure described in this section ordinarily takes place on United States soil. Passengers departing from certain countries undergo "preinspection" at overseas airports. 8 C.F.R. § 235.5 (2004).

2.   HEARINGS BEFORE IMMIGRATION JUDGES[8]

At one time, the INA referred to "exclusion" hearings. IIRIRA re-named them "removal" hearings. Despite what you might have assumed, only a small proportion of those arriving passengers whom the immigration officers refuse to admit actually exercise their statutory right to a hearing. The vast majority simply give up and go home. Why? A large part of the answer is the new expedited removal procedure, described below. In addi-tion, many are unwilling to accept detention. Some, not being represented by counsel, might feel intimidated. And some might want to avoid a formal removal order, which would bar future admission for up to five years (longer for second removals and for aggravated felons). INA § 212(a)(9)(A). The Secretary of Homeland Security has the discretion to permit such noncitizens to withdraw their applications for admission and depart imme-diately. INA § 235(a)(4). This discretion is a mixed blessing. Immigration inspectors can use this power compassionately, to enable individuals to avoid the bar on future readmission, but at least one study suggests that immigration inspectors often pressure noncitizens to withdraw their appli-cations in order to fit the schedules of the relevant airlines and reduce the officers' paperwork. Janet A. Gilboy, *Implications of "Third–Party" In-volvement in Enforcement: The INS, Illegal Travelers, and International Airlines*, 31 L. & Society Rev. 505 (1997).

A removal proceeding formally begins when ICE serves on the nonciti-zen a document called a "Notice to Appear." It specifies the time and place of the hearing, the alleged facts and charged inadmissibility grounds, and the individual's procedural rights. INA § 239(a). To afford the person at least some opportunity to secure counsel, the hearing may not start until ten days after service of the Notice to Appear, unless the noncitizen requests an earlier date. INA § 239(b)(1). If he or she is unable to procure counsel within ten days, the hearing may proceed without counsel. INA § 239(b)(3).

In a removal proceeding the opposing parties are the noncitizen and ICE. The immigration judges, until 1983 employees of the former INS, are today formally independent of the immigration agencies. They are part of the Justice Department's Executive Office for Immigration Review. See 8 C.F.R. § 1003.10 (2004); see also INA § 101(b)(4).

The procedures followed in removal hearings are contained in INA § 240 and in the "Rules of Procedure for Immigration Judge Proceedings," which appear in 8 C.F.R. §§ 1003.12–1003.46 (2004). Although the formal rules of evidence do not apply, removal hearings are solemn affairs in which both parties are commonly represented by counsel. The hearings are recorded verbatim, and formal records are maintained. *Id.* §§ 1003.28, 1003.36.

---

8. The term is defined in INA § 101(b)(4). Before 1996, the INA used the title "special inquiry officers."

INA § 291 has always made clear that an arriving noncitizen bears the burden of proving admissibility. Before IIRIRA, however, the INA did not specify the *standard* of proof that the immigration judge was supposed to apply at the exclusion hearing. IIRIRA § 304, in creating new INA § 240, appears to address that issue. According to INA § 240(c)(2)(A), an applicant for admission must now prove he or she "is clearly and beyond doubt entitled to be admitted and is not inadmissible under section 212." If interpreted literally, that amendment is quite far-reaching. It is one thing to require an immigration officer to refer the person for a hearing upon finding that he or she is not "clearly and beyond doubt" entitled to be admitted. It is another to insist on such a showing as a requirement for prevailing at the hearing. This test, on its face, seems tantamount to a reverse "beyond a reasonable doubt" test. (Actually it seems even stronger, because not even a "reasonable" doubt is permitted.)

One possible ameliorating interpretation[9] arises from an ambiguity in the language quoted above. Does the phrase "clearly and beyond doubt" modify only the words "entitled to be admitted," or does it also modify the succeeding words "and is not inadmissible?" Note that the word "is" appears twice. Literally, the statute requires the noncitizen to prove that he or she (a) "is clearly and beyond doubt entitled to be admitted" and (b) "is not inadmissible." But what's the difference between "entitled to enter" and "not inadmissible," anyway? The latter refers explicitly to the inadmissibility grounds laid out in INA § 212. Perhaps the former phrase refers only to the person's need to qualify affirmatively under one of the quota-exempt or preference categories—family, employment, or diversity. Under that interpretation, the noncitizen would have to prove his or her affirmative credentials clearly and beyond doubt and would have to prove by some unspecified standard (as was true before IIRIRA) that none of the inadmissibility grounds applies.

You have seen that, as a result of IIRIRA, noncitizens who are alleged to be present in the United States without having been admitted (formerly described as entry without inspection) are regarded as applicants for admission. This means they must establish either that they are admissible or that they in fact have been lawfully admitted. Under INA § 240(c)(2)(B), the noncitizen must make the latter showing by "clear and convincing evidence."

Obtaining counsel for removal hearings is not always easy. Many noncitizens who seek admission cannot afford to pay for counsel. Some legal services organizations provide free representation to noncitizens, but those that receive funding from the Legal Services Corporation are prohibited from representing most categories of noncitizens. See pages 665–66 below. And, although the Equal Access to Justice Act (EAJA) has been interpreted as allowing attorney fee awards to the prevailing parties in certain kinds of immigration-related administrative proceedings, see page 667 below, removal proceedings are not among them. See *Matter of Saa,*

9. The author thanks Gerald Neuman for spotting this distinction.

No. A28 852 512 (BIA, May 12, 1989) and *Matter of Shaker,* No. A27 560 431 (BIA, May 12, 1989), both digested in 66 IR at 656 (1989).

3.   APPEALS FROM IMMIGRATION JUDGE DECISIONS

The regulations authorize either the noncitizen or ICE to appeal to the Board of Immigration Appeals (BIA) from an adverse decision of the immigration judge in removal proceedings. 8 C.F.R. § 1003.1(b)(1, 3) (2004). The BIA, as noted earlier, is part of the Attorney General's Executive Office for Immigration Review. You will see a more detailed description of BIA procedure in chapter 9, § B.4 below.

Until IIRIRA, the usual procedure for obtaining judicial review of an administratively final exclusion order was to apply for habeas corpus in federal district court. INA § 106(b) (pre-IIRIRA version). Now the general rule is that judicial review of a removal order—whether for inadmissibility or deportability—is by petition for review filed directly in the court of appeals. INA § 242(a)(1). There are, however, several exceptions to the reviewability of removal and removal-related decisions. These exceptions, and other details of the review process, are discussed in section E.4 and chapter 9 below.

4.   EXPEDITED REMOVAL

In March 1993, the television show "60 Minutes" reported that large numbers of noncitizens were arriving at New York's JFK Airport without documents and claiming asylum. Because there was not enough detention space to hold them pending the exclusion hearings to which they were then entitled, the documentary reported, these individuals were going underground. The media had a field day. See, e.g., David Cole, Legal Times, Dec. 27, 1993, at 26; David Crosland, Don't Fence in America, Wash. Post, Aug. 8, 1993 at C–7; San Diego Union–Tribune, May 22, 1993, at A–8; Atlanta J. & Const., Mar. 30, 1993, at 12.

Several bills were introduced in Congress to cure this problem through an abbreviated procedure known generically as "summary exclusion." Because the various summary exclusion provisions were typically included in more sweeping immigration reform bills that bogged down for other reasons, it took three years for summary exclusion to become law (by which time the former INS had essentially solved the JFK problem by expanding the detention facilities). Under the name "expedited removal," summary exclusion was resuscitated in 1996 by AEDPA § 422 and promptly amended by IIRIRA § 302(a). The amended version now appears as INA § 235(b)(1). It applies whenever the immigration officer at the border "determines" that an arriving noncitizen is inadmissible under either section 212(a)(6)(C) (fraud) or section 212(a)(7) (lack of proper documents). INA § 235(b)(1)(A)(i). One important qualification, considered in more detail in chapter 11, § B.7.b.iv below, is that noncitizens who indicate a fear of persecution or an intention to apply for asylum receive screening interviews. The purpose of those interviews is to determine whether their cases are strong enough to warrant providing the regular asylum procedures that you will study in chapter 11. INA § 235(b)(1)(A)(i, ii).

Except for asylum claimants, here is how the expedited removal procedure works: Once the immigration inspector concludes that an arriving noncitizen is inadmissible under either of the two listed grounds, the person is ordered removed without further hearing. INA § 235(b)(1)(A)(i). There is no administrative appeal, except for returning LPRs, admitted refugees, and people who have already received asylum. INA § 235(b)(1)(C). Subject to the same exceptions, there is no judicial review with respect to either admissibility or relief from removal. INA § 242(e)(5). The only permissible judicial review of expedited removals is on the issues of whether the person is a citizen, whether the person was in fact ordered removed, and whether the person comes within one of the above exceptions (LPRs, refugees, and asylees). INA § 242(e)(2). The statute even purports to bar constitutional challenges to the statute and accompanying regulations (beginning 60 days after the statute took effect). INA § 242(e)(3). Whether Congress can constitutionally bar judicial review of removal decisions, especially when the challenge is to the constitutionality of the statute itself, is not clear. See Chapter 9, § B.6.b. below.

Debates over both the effectiveness and the fairness of expedited removal are volatile, and the verdict is still out. Most observers agree there are both benefits and dangers, but there is much debate over which predominate and about ways to improve the process. Does expedited removal discourage illegal immigration? Does it save substantial administrative resources? On the other hand, do the lesser procedural safeguards lead to injustice or other harm to refugees or other applicants? These are the questions that will continue to require direct observation, empirical investigation, and anecdotal evidence from noncitizens and their representatives.

Because most of the controversy over expedited removal has related to its use in potential asylum cases, the subject will be revisited in that context. See chapter 11, § B.7.b.iv below.

5.   OTHER SPECIAL REMOVAL PROCEDURES

a.   NATIONAL SECURITY AND FOREIGN POLICY CASES

You saw in the *Mezei* case, pages 145–58 above, how the tension between fairness to the individual and protection of national security can generate difficult policy issues in the context of admission procedure. One especially hard question is how to provide adequate notice and opportunity to be heard without disclosing confidential information that would endanger public safety.

INA § 235(c) sets up a special procedure for cases that present such issues. "If an immigration officer or an immigration judge *suspects* that an arriving alien may be inadmissible under [INA §§ 212(a)(3)(A)(i or iii), (B), or (C)], the officer or judge shall order the alien removed (emphasis added)." INA § 235(c)(1). The designated exclusion grounds cover those who seek to enter the United States to engage in acts involving sabotage, espionage, violent overthrow of the government, etc; those involved in specified ways in terrorism; and certain individuals whose admission or activities in the United States would adversely affect the country's foreign policy.

The Secretary of Homeland Security automatically reviews these removal orders. If the Secretary concludes, based on confidential information the disclosure of which would be "prejudicial to the public interest," that a noncitizen is inadmissible on one of the specified grounds, then the Secretary may order the person removed without further hearing. Otherwise, the Secretary decides what further inquiry is to be conducted. INA § 235(c)(2). The noncitizen may submit a written statement and additional information for the Secretary to consider. INA § 235(c)(3).

b. TERRORISM CASES

Noncitizen terrorists, already covered by the special national security procedures just discussed, may also be removed through another expedited process. Unlike the INA § 235(c) procedure for national security cases, the special removal procedure for alleged terrorists applies to both inadmissible and deportable noncitizens. It is considered in chapter 10 below. As of this writing the special terrorist removal court has yet to be convened, but other measures, such as closed removal hearings and secret evidence removal hearings, have been used frequently and remain controversial. For detailed discussions of the latter procedures, see chapter 10, sections D.3 and D.4 below.

SECTION F.   ADJUSTMENT OF STATUS[10]

With few exceptions, the admission procedure outlined in the preceding sections requires a noncitizen to obtain a visa from a United States consulate abroad. Ordinarily, that process makes a good deal of sense. Before burning their bridges back home, and before incurring the expense and effort of travel to the United States, inadmissible individuals are usually (not always) weeded out at the visa stage. Moreover, from the government's point of view, rigorous consular screening permits a faster and easier border inspection.

But suppose the noncitizen, instead of being abroad when the process is initiated, is already in the United States, either lawfully or unlawfully? Assume further that he or she meets all the substantive requirements for admission as an immigrant and that the particular immigrant category is

---

10. See generally Stanley Mailman, *The New Adjustment of Status Law: Background and Analysis*, 71 IR 1505 (Nov. 14, 1994); David L. Neal, *The Changing Dynamics of Adjustment of Status*, Immigration Briefings (May and June 1996) (2–part article); Joe A. Tucker, *Assimilation to the United States: A Study of the Adjustment of Status and the Immigration Marriage Fraud Statutes*, 7 Yale L. & Policy Rev. 20 (1989).

current. Does it make sense to require the person to leave the United States, get an immigrant visa, and then come back?

Until 1952, that is precisely what Congress required. As one commentator has explained:

> * * * In effect, the alien was required to leave the country in order to return. This illogical requirement did not escape the notice of either the immigration bureaucracy or interested aliens. Not only did the practice cause monetary and emotional hardship for the alien and her family, but it generated unnecessary paper work and delay for the agencies involved. * * *

> Due to the problems caused by this requirement, the INS created the pre-examination program in the 1930s. This program permitted adjustment applicants to apply for the benefit in Canada rather than returning to their country of origin. [Essentially the same program would later be resurrected under the name "Stateside Criteria Program."—Ed.] * * *

Joe A. Tucker, *Assimilation to the United States: A Study of the Adjustment of Status and the Immigration Marriage Fraud Statutes*, 7 Yale L. & Policy Rev. 20, 42–43 (1989).

Allowing the immigrant to do the paperwork in Canada was better than requiring a trip to more remote countries, but the question remained why the processing could not be performed in the United States. In 1952, when Congress enacted the INA, it included for the first time a provision authorizing certain noncitizens already here to "adjust their status" to that of LPR without having to leave the country. INA § 245. Today, adjustment is not just a footnote; in fiscal years 2001, 2002, and 2003 combined, this procedure accounted for more than half of all legal immigration to the United States. 2003 Yearbook of Immigration Statistics, Table A at 7 (2004).

Adjustment in no way relaxes the substantive criteria for LPR status (except indirectly with respect to one particular inadmissibility ground, INA § 212(a)(9)(B)(i), discussed below). The adjustment applicant must be admissible as an immigrant, and the particular immigrant category must be current. INA § 245(a). In addition, one who applies for adjustment of status must meet extra requirements not imposed on those who seek LPR status through the traditional visa route.

These extra requirements have changed frequently over time. They have been part of what immigration lawyers know as the continuing saga of INA § 245(i). Until the Immigration Act of 1990, a person had to have been "inspected and admitted [essentially a nonimmigrant] or paroled" to qualify for adjustment of status to permanent residence. INA § 245(a). Those who had entered without inspection were therefore ineligible. There were several other disqualifications, collected in INA § 245(c). These included crew members, most people (other than immediate relatives and special immigrants) who have been out of status at any time after entry, and certain nonimmigrants admitted without visas.

All those restrictions (and some new ones) were at least temporarily softened in 1994, when Congress enacted temporary legislation to permit and affirmatively encourage adjustment of status. Section 506(b) of Pub. L. 103–317, 108 Stat. 1724, 1765–66 (Aug. 26, 1994), added a new subsection 245(i) to the INA. This amendment exempted certain noncitizens from the disqualifications created by their entries without inspection or by subsection 245(c). To qualify for a 245(i) exemption, however, the applicant had to pay an additional penalty fee of $1000. Former INA § 245(i)(1). (Some were excused from the penalty fee.) Congress passed this provision both to raise revenue and to encourage applicants for permanent residence to use adjustment of status rather than overburden U.S. consulates abroad.

These temporary provisions survived until January 14, 1998. Since then, there have been temporary, limited restorations of 245(i). Visa petitions or labor certification applications that were filed before January 14, 1998 may still be processed under section 245(i). Pub. L. 105–119, § 111(a), 111 Stat. 2440, 2458 (Nov. 26, 1997), amending INA § 245(i). The LIFE Act, in section 1502, allowed individuals who were present in the United States on December 21, 2000 to file 245(i) applications until April 30, 2001. Bills have been introduced in Congress to reinstate section 245(i) on a limited basis. Like many other proposed immigration reforms, however, extensions of section 245(i) face an uphill battle in the wake of the September 11, 2001 terrorist attacks.

At the same time that Congress in 1998 allowed 245(i) to lapse, it added a partly analogous provision solely for certain employment-based applicants. Under INA § 245(k), otherwise eligible applicants for the 1st, 2nd, 3rd, and some 4th preference employment-based slots could adjust their status, even if currently or formerly out of status, provided they had entered lawfully and were not out of status more than 180 days.

One of the reasons the former version of section 245(i) was so important was its interaction with another provision that you studied in chapter 5. INA § 212(a)(9)(B)(i)(I), you will recall, renders inadmissible for three years any noncitizen who has been unlawfully present more than 180 days but less than one year. But the inadmissibility attaches only upon the person's departure from the United States before the commencement of removal proceedings. Thus, if a person who has been out of status more than 180 days but who now meets all the substantive requirements for immigrant status leaves the United States to obtain his or her visa, the person becomes inadmissible, and therefore ineligible for a visa, for three years. The same point applies to section 212(a)(9)(B)(i)(II), the one-year unlawful presence/ ten-year bar. In contrast, if the person were allowed to apply for adjustment of status, he or she would not have to leave the country and thus would not be inadmissible, even though out of status. In this situation, therefore, there is much more at stake than the expense and inconvenience of traveling overseas to get the visa. One's very ability to become an LPR in the near future can hinge on the availability of section 245(i). With that point in mind, Professor David Martin has suggested simply repealing the unlawful presence exclusion grounds that lie at the heart of the 245(i) debate. David A. Martin, *Waiting for Solutions: Extending the Period of Time for Migrants to Apply for Green Cards Doesn't Get at the Real Problem*, Legal Times (May 28, 2001), at 66.

At this time, please read INA § 245(a, b, c, and k).

NOTES AND QUESTIONS

1.   INA § 245(a) says an immigrant visa must be "immediately available" at the time the application is filed. If the applicant is subject to a numerical quota, a visa will not be considered "immediately available" unless the latest Visa Office Bulletin shows either that the particular preference category is current in the applicant's country or that the person's priority date has been reached. See 8 C.F.R. § 245.1(g)(1) (2004). Obviously, this constraint is inapplicable to immediate relatives and anyone else exempt from numerical limitations. In addition, a visa will not be considered available until USCIS has approved the visa petition. 8 C.F.R. § 245.2(a)(2)(i)(B) (2004). For administrative convenience, however, USCIS generally permits the simultaneous submission of the visa petition and the adjustment of status application, provided approval of the visa petition would *make* the visa immediately available. *Id.* That would be the case, for example, when the applicant is an immediate relative or a preference immigrant whose country/preference combination is current. Note too that in recent years the administrative processing of adjustment applications has been badly backlogged. See Nadine K. Wettstein, *Wasted Days and Wasted Nights: INS Visa Processing Delays and How to Combat Them*, 76 IR 1441 (Sept. 30, 1999); see generally pages 456–57 above.

2.   What do you think of the disqualifications for entering without inspection or for otherwise being out of status? How do you feel about the concept of 245(i)?

3.   Should INA § 245 be discretionary? If a noncitizen now meets all the admission requirements for immigrants (both numerical and qualitative), then why give immigration officials the discretion to deny adjustment?

4.   Normally there is no administrative appeal from a USCIS decision denying an application for adjustment of status. 8 C.F.R. § 245.2(a)(5)(ii) (2004). The only administrative recourse for an applicant who believes USCIS wrongly denied adjustment is to wait for ICE to initiate removal proceedings (typically on the ground that by then the person's authorized stay will have expired) and then renew the adjustment application before the immigration judge. *Id.* (Of course, the applicant might then encounter a § 245(c)(2) problem).

Before IIRIRA, the courts were divided over whether the applicant could seek *judicial* review of an INS decision denying adjustment, instead of waiting for deportation proceedings and then renewing the application. But IIRIRA added INA § 242(a)(2)(B)(i), which bars review of "any judgment regarding the granting of relief under [various relief provisions, including section 245]." The REAL ID Act, § 101(f)(2), passed in 2005, amended that provision to clarify that it applies both in and outside of removal proceedings. It is now clear, therefore, that this jurisdictional bar applies to both USCIS and immigration judge denials of adjustment of status. Even still, the bar is not as sweeping as it first appears. The courts have generally construed it to preclude judicial review of only the *discretionary* components of the listed remedies. A determination that the applicant is statutorily ineligible for adjustment (for example, because the person is out of status, or is inadmissible because of a criminal conviction, etc.) appears to remain reviewable—at least when the challenge to the ineligibility determination raises a question of law, see REAL ID Act, § 106(a)(1)(A)(iii), adding INA § 242(a)(2)(D), and perhaps even when the challenge raises a question of fact. See generally chapter 9, § B.6.a.ii below.

5. Under certain conditions a grant of adjustment of status may be rescinded. See INA § 246 and chapter 9, § E.7 below.

PROBLEMS 4–7

To do the Problems that follow, you will need to consult INA § 245(a, c, and k) and review sections 212(a)(6)(A), 212(a)(9)(A), and 212(a)(9)(B).

Problem 4. You represent X, a 19–year-old noncitizen lawfully in the United States on a student (F–1) visa. She is authorized to remain for the duration of her student status, which is expected to last another two years. X would like to become an LPR, and at the moment she qualifies for family-sponsored 2A status as the unmarried daughter of an LPR, but the latest Visa Office Bulletin shows a 7–year wait for that category for her country. As her attorney, what would you advise her to do?

Problem 5. Y, a noncitizen, entered the United States without inspection or admission 15 months ago. Now married to a United States citizen, he would like to become an LPR. Will he be able to obtain either an immigrant visa at a U.S. consulate overseas or adjustment of status in the United States?

Problem 6. Z is a 46–year-old business executive from a country that severely restricts emigration. He entered the United States 14 months ago as a business visitor (B–1) and was authorized to remain one year. He has not applied for any extension of his nonimmigrant stay. Unbeknownst to his country's authorities, who would never have let him leave had they known, Z's mother is a citizen and resident of the United States. He thus qualifies for family-sponsored first preference status, which you should assume is current. Z is convinced, however, that if he were to return home to apply for an immigrant visa, his government would not permit him to leave again. Z now comes to you for legal advice. What should you tell him? See 22 C.F.R. § 42.61(a) (2004).

Problem 7. W, a citizen of Pakistan, entered the United States on a student visa and was admitted for the duration of his student status. He enrolled at Arizona State University to do a bachelor's degree in physics. In the fall of his junior year, a large manufacturing company offered him a permanent position that was to begin immediately after graduation. W, delighted, consulted you, an immigration lawyer, as soon as he received the offer. You helped the company apply for and receive labor certification, and in March of his junior year USCIS approved the required visa petition. His priority date became current in January of his senior year. You immediately filed an application for adjustment of status. On May 15, while the application was still pending, W graduated. On July 1, to your surprise, USCIS denied adjustment on the ground that W had once been convicted, in Pakistan, of a crime involving moral turpitude. Your research found no case precisely on point, but analogous cases suggested USCIS was probably wrong to classify the particular crime as one that involves moral turpitude. You informally reported your findings to the director of the local USCIS office, but you could not convince her. On July 15, your client's F-1 status expired. It is now August 1. ICE has not instituted any removal proceedings. W has not worked, and within a few months his savings will run out. What are his options?

CHAPTER 7

DEPORTABILITY GROUNDS

SECTION A. GENERAL CONSIDERATIONS

As you will recall, IIRIRA restructured much of what used to be called the "exclusion" and "deportation" processes. Now there is a single name for the proceeding at which a noncitizen's inadmissibility or deportability is decided—a "removal" proceeding. INA § 240.

Importantly, however, IIRIRA preserves the fundamental distinction between what used to be called exclusion and deportation. There is still a list of grounds on which noncitizens who seek admission to the United States will be found "inadmissible," see INA § 212(a), and a separate list of grounds on which noncitizens who have already been admitted to the United States will be found "deportable," see INA § 237(a). Moreover, the availability of discretionary relief for either "inadmissible" or "deportable" individuals still depends on which of the two sets of grounds applies, as you will see in chapter 8. Finally, there were only a few significant procedural differences between exclusion and deportation even before IIRIRA, and most of those were also preserved. As you will see in chapter 9, the burden of proof still varies depending on whether the charge is inadmissibility or deportability. So does the length of time that a person who has been found inadmissible or deportable must wait before returning. Nor does it seem likely that the distinction between noncitizens arriving at ports of entry and those who are already in the interior of the country will lose its constitutional significance—at least not because of IIRIRA.

In practice, therefore, the traditional line between exclusion and expulsion remains intact. But IIRIRA moved one important group of noncitizens from one side of the line to the other. Before IIRIRA, "entry" determined whether a noncitizen would be tested against the exclusion grounds or the deportation grounds; the former were for people who had not yet "entered;" the latter were for those who had. Following a suggestion first advanced by Professors T. Alexander Aleinikoff and David Martin in Immigration Process and Policy at 342–47 (1st ed. 1985), Congress decided to redraw the line at "admission." Noncitizens who have not yet been admitted must contend with the grounds for inadmissibility; those who have already been admitted contend with the grounds for deportability. The practical consequence is that noncitizens who have entered but have not been admitted—i.e., those people who entered without inspection—are now considered inadmissible rather than deportable. See INA §§ 212(a)(6)(A), 235(a)(1).

Because both the policy considerations and the legal consequences of expelling noncitizens who have reached the interior frequently differ from those concerning the removal of noncitizens arriving at ports of entry, it will sometimes be convenient to use the terms "exclusion" and "deportation" to refer, respectively, to the removal of arriving noncitizens and the removal of noncitizens from the interior. The reader should understand that such usages are now meant only as generic descriptions, not statutory terminology.

This chapter is the first of three on the removal of "deportable" noncitizens, a term used to describe those who fall within any of the deportability grounds listed in INA § 237(a). The present chapter examines those grounds and also the inadmissibility of noncitizens who are present without admission. Chapter 8 will consider various forms of discretionary relief available to deportable individuals. Chapter 9 will take up deportation procedure.

The chapter separation is not, however, as clean as might be ideal. A few of the affirmative defenses are confined to specified deportability grounds. Those defenses are convenient to discuss in this chapter, in conjunction with the particular grounds that they waive. Similarly, although procedure is treated in chapter 9, a few of the basic procedural elements are worth laying out now so that you can better follow the cases. For a more detailed overview of deportation procedure, see chapter 9, § A below.

In a removal proceeding the opposing parties are ICE and the noncitizen. ICE starts the formal process by serving on the noncitizen a document called a Notice to Appear (until 1996 an "Order to Show Cause"). INA § 239. That document alleges facts and specifies the statutory deportability (or inadmissibility) grounds that ICE is charging, in much the same way that a criminal indictment or information alleges facts and specific criminal offenses. A Justice Department official known as an immigration judge presides over the removal hearing. After considering the evidence and the arguments, he or she determines whether the person is a noncitizen and, if so, whether the person is "deportable"—i.e., whether the noncitizen fits within one or more of the alleged deportability grounds. If the person is found deportable, the immigration judge next decides whether the individual is eligible for, and deserving of, any affirmative discretionary relief for which he or she has applied.

If the immigration judge finds the person is not deportable, the proceedings are terminated. If the immigration judge finds the person deportable and denies discretionary relief, an order of removal is entered. And if the immigration judge finds the person deportable but grants discretionary relief, then, depending on the particular form of relief granted, the immigration judge either orders the proceedings terminated or grants "voluntary departure," a remedy discussed in the next chapter. Some forms of discretionary relief additionally result in the award of LPR status.

Either ICE or the noncitizen may appeal the immigration judge's order to the Board of Immigration Appeals. The noncitizen, but not ICE, can obtain judicial review of the BIA decision by filing a "petition for review" directly in the applicable United States court of appeals, INA § 242(a)(1), subject to some large exceptions that you will see in chapter 9. Most of the opinions you will read on the removal of deportable noncitizens, therefore, are decisions of the BIA, a court of appeals, or the Supreme Court.

1. HISTORICAL OVERVIEW OF AMERICAN DEPORTATION POLICY

As is plain from chapter 2, the Supreme Court has read the Constitution as giving Congress virtual carte blanche to decide which classes of noncitizens should be deported. How has Congress exercised that authority over the years?

3 Charles Gordon, Stanley Mailman, and Stephen Yale–Loehr, Immigration Law and Procedure

§ 71.01[2] (2003).

The measures adopted by Congress for the control of aliens and for the ejection of those deemed undesirable have occupied a constantly expanding orbit. The first deportation efforts were contained in the Alien and Sedition Acts of 1798, which authorized the President to deport: (1) resident aliens who were citizens of nations at war with the United States (alien enemies); and (2) aliens whom the President judged "dangerous to the peace and safety of the United States." The latter section apparently was never invoked, and was allowed to expire at the end of its two-year term. The Alien Enemy Act, however, remains on the statute books.

Almost 90 years elapsed before the appearance of any additional legislation dealing with deportation. In 1888 Congress sanctioned the deportation of alien contract laborers within 1 year after entry. This power of expulsion was extended in 1891 to all aliens who had entered in violation of law. The immigration statutes since then have included similar directives for the deportation of aliens entering in violation of law. The period of limitations for bringing such proceedings was steadily enlarged, and finally was eliminated in the Immigration and Nationality Act (INA) of 1952, making it possible to bring expulsion proceedings for any irregular entry, however remote.

In the early phase of this development, the deportation statutes were an adjunct to the process of exclusion. Barring the admission of undesirables and ejecting those who evaded the bar were regarded as different sides of the same coin. * * *

In 1910 Congress decreed that aliens identified with prostitution in the United States should be deported. This was an expansion in the horizon of the deportation statute, for it reached aliens who had entered properly, but who had misbehaved while residing in this country. In effect, deportation was imposed as a form of punishment for such misconduct. Thereafter,

Congress added constantly to the catalogue of misbehavior that subjects an alien to expulsion. [The resulting expulsion grounds enumerated in the present statute predominantly reflect post-entry conduct—Ed.]

2.   THE THEORY OF DEPORTATION

Although the word "deportation" no longer appears in the INA, it will be convenient to use it here to describe the removal of a noncitizen from the interior of the United States (as distinguished from removal at a port of entry). As the cases in these three chapters will demonstrate, deportation is a harsh sanction. Depending on one's personal circumstances and on the destination country, deportation can entail great economic hardship, restricted personal freedom, and fundamental and unwelcome lifestyle changes. If the person has established roots—family, friends, employers, or others—the separation can be particularly traumatic, both for the deported individual and for those who remain behind.

Apart from the suffering of the affected individuals, nagging questions persist. Of whose society is the noncitizen really a product? At what point, if any, should the country in which the noncitizen resides take responsibility for his or her behavior? Is a country that deports a long-term resident because of recent misconduct sloughing off to another nation an undesirable person for whom the sending nation should be responsible?

Those actual and potential negatives make it important to ask what purposes deportation serves. As you saw earlier, the courts have consistently denied that deportation is designed to punish. See, e.g., *Mahler v. Eby,* 264 U.S. 32, 39, 44 S.Ct. 283, 286, 68 L.Ed. 549, 554 (1924); *Bugajewitz v. Adams,* 228 U.S. 585, 591, 33 S.Ct. 607, 608, 57 L.Ed. 978, 980 (1913).

Commentators have questioned the dogma that deportation is not punishment. The present author addressed this issue in a pair of student Notes in 1976 and 1977. The first Note argued that both the consequences and the purposes of deportation at least arguably mirror those of punishment. Stephen H. Legomsky, Recent Development, *Deportation of an Alien for a Marihuana Conviction Can Constitute Cruel and Unusual Punishment,* 13 San Diego L. Rev. 454, 456–64 (1976). The second Note focused more specifically on the expulsion of noncitizen criminal offenders. It compared the purposes of deportation with those of traditional criminal punishment, argued that analytically the two sets of purposes are virtually indistinguishable, suggested that the only convincing rationale for the deportation of noncitizen criminal offenders was incapacitation, and concluded that to avoid double punishment such deportation decisions should be individualized rather than categorical. Stephen H. Legomsky, *The Alien Criminal Defendant,* 14 San Diego L. Rev. 105, 121–27 (1977).

More modern (and more sophisticated) commentary has explored those themes further. Javier Bleichmar, in *Deportation as Punishment: A Historical Analysis of the British Practice of Banishment and Its Impact on Modern Constitutional Law,* 14 Georgetown Immigration L.J. 115 (1999), traces the roots of deportation to the historical practices of banishment and transportation as punishments for crime. Daniel Kanstroom, in *Deportation, Social Control, and Punishment: Some Thoughts about Why Hard Cases Make Bad Laws*, 113 Harvard L. Rev. 1890 (2000), argues that the recent trend toward harsh deportation criteria for noncitizen criminal offenders strengthens the depiction of crime-related deportation as punishment and should trigger corresponding constitutional limitations. And Robert Pauw, in *A New Look at Deportation as Punishment: Why at Least Some of the Constitution's Criminal Procedure Provisions Must Apply*, 52 Administrative L. Rev. 305 (2000), argues that for constitutional purposes deportation *can* be punishment, either because of the particular ground or because of the facts of the particular case.

What, exactly, are the justifications for deportation? As the preceding excerpt from Gordon, Mailman & Yale–Loehr noted, the historical function of deportation was to serve as a check on the admission process. Deportation was originally conceived as a device for removing those noncitizens who should not have entered in the first place—either because they never were admitted or because they were admitted but shouldn't have been. In the latter instance, perhaps the contract between the noncitizen and the government can be thought of as having been void or at least voidable right from the start; deportation thus provides a remedy akin to rescission.

A related theory recognizes deportation as a means of expelling those noncitizens who were properly admitted but who, after entry, violated conditions that had been imposed on them at the time of entry. An example would be the noncitizen who is deported for having worked without authorization. See, e.g., Guy S. Goodwin–Gill, International Law and the Movement of Persons Between States 255, 262 (1978). Under that theory, deportation can be analogized to a remedy for breach of a valid contract.

As you will see in the next subsection, however, today's deportation grounds encompass a wide variety of post-entry behavior that cannot realistically be linked either to admissions errors or to violations of conditions imposed at entry. Instead, the thrust of our modern deportation policy is simply to remove from our midst those noncitizens whose continued presence Congress finds injurious to the public welfare. See, e.g., *Mahler v. Eby*, 264 U.S. 32, 39, 44 S.Ct. 283, 286, 68 L.Ed. 549, 554 (1924); *Bugajewitz v. Adams*, 228 U.S. 585, 591, 33 S.Ct. 607, 608, 57 L.Ed. 978, 980 (1913). In theory, even under this conception one would have to read into the contract an implied term that certain behavior (which might not have been a deportation ground at the time of entry or even at the time of the person's conduct) will be grounds for removal.

What is your opinion of these justifications? Can you think of others?

3.   CURRENT DEPORTABILITY GROUNDS

Section 237(a) of the Immigration and Nationality Act lays out the grounds for removing deportable noncitizens from the United States, as well as some of the provisions for waivers of, and exemptions from, those grounds. Additional waivers and exemptions appear in other sections of the

INA and will be taken up in this chapter or the next one. You should now skim section 237(a) to get a general sense of its layout and of the sorts of things that can make a person deportable.

In recent years the number of formal removals has steadily increased, reaching 186,181 in fiscal year 2003. Of those, approximately 97,000 were removals from the interior. A far greater number—that year, 887,115—left the United States under grants of "voluntary departure," a remedy explored in the next chapter. For now, note that, despite its name, voluntary departure does not mean the person had the option of staying; it means only that the forced departure is not regarded as a "removal" for purposes of various statutory penalties on removal that will be taken up later. See 2003 Yearbook of Immigration Statistics at 148–51 & Table 40. Almost half the formal removals were on crime-related grounds. *Id.*, Table 43 at 165.

4.   DEPORTATION AND STATUTORY INTERPRETATION

Courts often apply special statutory interpretation principles in deportation cases. One of the more important has long been associated with the following Supreme Court decision:

Fong Haw Tan v. Phelan

Supreme Court of the United States, 1948.
333 U.S. 6, 68 S.Ct. 374, 92 L.Ed. 433.

■ MR. JUSTICE DOUGLAS delivered the opinion of the Court.

An alien "who is sentenced more than once" to imprisonment for a term of one year or more because of conviction in this country of a crime involving moral turpitude committed after his entry shall, with exceptions not material here, be deported. It appears that petitioner, a native of China, was convicted of murder under each of two counts of an indictment, one count charging the murder of one Lai Quan, the other charging the murder on or about the same date of one Ong Kim. The jury fixed the punishment for each murder at life imprisonment. He was thereupon sentenced to prison for the period of his natural life by one judgment, construed by the Circuit Court of Appeals to impose that sentence on him for each of the convictions. Sometime thereafter a warrant for his deportation to China issued. Later he was paroled, released from prison, and taken into the custody of the Immigration Service. He then filed a petition for a writ of habeas corpus challenging the legality of his detention. The District Court denied the petition. * * * The Circuit Court of Appeals affirmed. The case is here on a petition for a writ of certiorari which we granted because of the contrariety of views among the circuits concerning the meaning of the statutory words "sentenced more than once."

The Ninth Circuit view is that a conviction and sentence for more than one offense, whether at the same or different times and whether carrying concurrent or consecutive sentences, satisfy the statute. * * * The Second Circuit holds that an alien who is given consecutive sentences is sentenced more than once, while an alien who is given concurrent sentences is not, even though the crimes are distinct. The Fourth Circuit takes the position that the statute is satisfied whether or not the sentences imposed run concurrently or consecutively provided that the two crimes which are committed and for which separate sentences are imposed arise out of separate transactions. The Fifth Circuit takes the view that an alien is "sentenced once when, after a conviction or plea of guilty, he is called before the bar and receives judgment, whether for one or several crimes, with one or several terms of imprisonment. He is sentenced more than once when that happens again." That view is an adaptation of the position taken earlier by a District Court in the same circuit that Congress by this provision aimed to deport "repeaters," viz. "persons who commit a crime and are sentenced, and then commit another and are sentenced again."

The latter is the reading we give the statute. There is a trace of that purpose found in its legislative history. Congressman Sabath who proposed the provision as an amendment said it was aimed at the alien "who is a criminal at heart, a man who is guilty of a second offense involving moral turpitude and for the second time is convicted." Congressman Burnett, who was in charge of the bill on the floor of the House, gave the same emphasis when he said that the amendment proposed "that those who committed a second crime involving moral turpitude showed then a criminal heart and a criminal tendency, and they should then be deported." The Committee Report in the Senate put the matter into sharper focus when it stated that the provision was "intended to reach the alien who after entry shows himself to be a criminal of the confirmed type." Perhaps the plainest "confirmed type" of criminal is the repeater. We give expression to that view by reading this provision of the statute to authorize deportation only where an alien having committed a crime involving moral turpitude and having been convicted and sentenced, once again commits a crime of that nature and is convicted and sentenced for it.

We resolve the doubts in favor of that construction because deportation is a drastic measure and at times the equivalent of banishment or exile. It is the forfeiture for misconduct of a residence in this country. Such a forfeiture is a penalty. To construe this statutory provision less generously to the alien might find support in logic. But since the stakes are considerable for the individual, we will not assume that Congress meant to trench on his freedom beyond that which is required by the narrowest of several possible meanings of the words used.

Reversed.

NOTES AND QUESTIONS

1. To interpret the phrase "sentenced more than once," the Court turns first to the legislative history. What principle does the Court distill from that history? Assuming that principle can be imputed to Congress, does the interpretation that the Court ultimately places on the disputed phrase follow? Finally, *should* the Court assume that the cited statements

represent the will of Congress? What are the pros and cons of reading significance into (a) comments like those of Representatives Sabath and Burnett, and (b) the Senate committee report?

2.   The last full paragraph of the Court's opinion is the part most frequently quoted. Do you agree that doubts in deportation statutes should be construed in favor of the noncitizen? This principle is still frequently invoked, though it is seldom clear whether it actually influences outcomes or serves merely as a makeweight or afterthought. See, e.g., *INS v. St. Cyr*, 533 U.S. 289, 320, 121 S.Ct. 2271, 150 L.Ed.2d 347 (2001); *Jobson v. Ashcroft*, 326 F.3d 367, 376 (2d Cir. 2003).

3.   In *Chevron USA v. NRDC*, 467 U.S. 837, 843–44, 104 S.Ct. 2778, 81 L.Ed.2d 694 (1984), the Supreme Court held that courts must defer to "reasonable" interpretations of federal statutes by the relevant administrative agencies. In the deportation context, *Chevron* deference can collide head-on with *Fong Haw Tan*. For a thoughtful analysis, see Brian G. Slocum, *The Immigration Rule of Lenity and Chevron Deference*, 17 Georgetown Immigration L.J. 515 (2003); *cf.* John W. Guendelsberger, *Judicial Deference to Agency Decisions in Removal Proceedings in Light of INS v. Ventura*, 18 Georgetown Immigration L.J. 605 (2005).

4.   In David R. Woodward & Ronald M. Levin, *In Defense of Deference: Judicial Review of Agency Action*, 31 Administrative L. Rev. 329 (1979) (written before *Chevron*), the authors focus their analysis of judicial deference on the benefits of the agency's accumulated specialized expertise. That expertise, they say, "is assumed to result not only from the frequency of an agency's contact with the statute, but also from its immersion in day-to-day administrative operations that reveal the practical consequences of one statutory interpretation as opposed to another." *Id.* at 132. If the authors are right about the sources of the relevant agency expertise, then (a) does their rationale favor judicial deference to the BIA in deportation cases? And (b) does the 2002 transfer of executive functions from the former INS (which was in the Justice Department, as is the BIA) to DHS affect the arguments for *Chevron* deference to BIA decisions?

5.   In chapter 2, you saw that in constitutional cases the Supreme Court has shown exceptional deference to Congress at the expense of the noncitizen. The *Fong Haw Tan* principle, applicable to statutory interpretation cases, stands in marked contrast. Why the difference? See generally Stephen H. Legomsky, Immigration and the Judiciary—Law and Politics in Britain and America 155–70, 177–222, 239–41 (1987) (comparing judicial approaches to statutory and constitutional interpretation).

6.   The Notes that follow the *Bricklayers Union* case in chapter 4 (see page 356 above) summarize the three principal schools of statutory interpretation—the Literal Plain Meaning Rule, the Golden Rule, and the Social Purpose Rule. Review them now. What result would each of them produce in the present case?

7.   The Court notes the Fourth Circuit view that the provision in question should be read to require two crimes arising out of separate

transactions. The present statute adopts that approach; the analogous current deportability ground covers any noncitizen who, after entry, "is convicted of two or more crimes involving moral turpitude, not arising out of a single scheme of criminal misconduct * * *." INA § 237(a)(2)(A)(ii).

SECTION B.   THE MEANING AND SIGNIFICANCE OF "ENTRY" AND "ADMISSION"

Until IIRIRA, one of the most important words in immigration law was "entry." First, as noted earlier, no deportation proceedings could be brought at all unless and until the noncitizen had made an entry. That might sound like a benefit to the noncitizen, but in most cases it was detrimental. When a noncitizen was found merely to be seeking entry, rather than to have achieved it, the government could institute exclusion proceedings instead. As you will see, the inadmissibility grounds are generally somewhat broader than the deportability grounds, the provisions for affirmative relief are narrower, and the procedural safeguards—both constitutional and statutory—are fewer.

Second, either the manner or the timing of the person's entry was an essential element of many of the specific deportation grounds enumerated in the pre-IIRIRA version of the INA. See, e.g., INA § 241(a) (pre-IIRIRA), grounds 1(A) (inadmissible at time of "entry"), 1(B) ("entered" without inspection or at an unauthorized place), 2(A)(i) (convicted of crime involving moral turpitude that was committed within five years after "entry").

Third, entry into the United States was an essential element of certain criminal offenses. See, e.g., INA §§ 275, 276, 277; see generally chapter 12 of this book.

IIRIRA has drained the word "entry" of much of its significance. Now, as you have seen, it is "admission," not "entry," that determines whether a noncitizen will be subject to the inadmissibility grounds or the deportability grounds. See INA § 240(e)(2). In addition, IIRIRA § 308(f) amended many of the specific inadmissibility and deportability grounds by replacing "entry" with "admission" and "enter" with "be admitted." In the contest for "most important word," admission has clearly surpassed entry.

For several reasons, however, entry is still a crucial concept in immigration law. *Some* of the inadmissibility grounds still use either the word "entry" or the word "enter." See, e.g., INA §§ 212(a)(3)(C)(i), 212(a)(5)(A)(i), 212(a)(6)(E), 212(a)(7)(A)(i)(I). The same is true of *some* of the deportability grounds. See, e.g., INA §§ 237(a)(1)(A) (inadmissibility at "entry"), 237(a)(1)(E) (smuggling noncitizens within five years of "entry"), 237(a)(5) (becoming a public charge within five years of "entry"). Congress's decision to change only selected grounds of inadmissibility and deportability, and to leave other grounds intact, was clearly deliberate. IIRIRA § 308(f) referred to designated grounds, and sometimes to only designated uses of the word "entry" in the same ground, when it could have directed that the substitution be made throughout all of INA sections 212 and 237.

In chapter 8, you will encounter a number of statutory relief provisions for deportable (and sometimes inadmissible) noncitizens. You might note here that several of these provisions similarly retain the word "entry" or "enter" in specifying which noncitizens qualify. See, e.g., INA §§ 245(c)(2), 245(i)(1) (adjustment of status), 249 (registry).

In the same vein, the criminal provisions mentioned above continue to make "entry" an essential element of various offenses.

"Entry" can also occasionally make a difference when it comes to procedure. Although arriving noncitizens and those who have effected entry without inspection are both required to prove admissibility, the standards of proof for the two classes of people vary slightly. See INA § 240(c)(2). Moreover, while arriving noncitizens whom immigration inspectors find inadmissible on document or fraud grounds are automatically subjected to the expedited removal procedure described in chapter 6, that procedure is inapplicable to noncitizens who have been present in the United States at least two years, and even its applicability to those present less than two years is at the discretion of the Attorney General. INA § 235(b)(1)(A). Arguably, "entry" determines presence. In addition, if a noncitizen who has been ordered removed (or who leaves under an alternative method known as "voluntary departure") subsequently "reenter[s]" the United States, the prior removal order is reinstated and the person can be ejected without a new removal hearing. INA § 241(a)(5).

Finally, even in those places where Congress replaced "entry" with "admission," the former remains important. That is because Congress's definition of "admission" itself refers to "entry." As a result of IIRIRA § 301(a):

> The terms "admission" and "admitted" mean, with respect to an alien, the lawful *entry* of the alien into the United States after inspection and authorization by an immigration officer. * * * [emphasis added].

INA § 101(a)(13). (This definition is subject to an important exception for returning residents that will be considered shortly.)

So "entry" retains importance, both because it is vital to understanding "admission" and for independent reasons. Unfortunately, the question whether someone has entered the United States is not as straightforward as you might assume, for not every physical crossing into United States territory constitutes an entry. Two main problems have arisen over the years. The following case illustrates one of them:

Matter of Ching and Chen

Board of Immigration Appeals, 1984.
19 I. & N. Dec. 203.

The immigration judge, in a decision rendered August 10, 1984, found that the applicants are amenable only to deportation proceedings and therefore he ordered these exclusion proceedings terminated. The Immigration and Naturalization Service appeals. The appeal will be dismissed.

The applicants are a 22–year–old female and an 18–year–old male, natives and citizens of the People's Republic of China * * *. They were among a group of five aliens traveling from Hong Kong to Guatemala via Tokyo and Los Angeles on a commercial airline. Upon arrival at Los Angeles International Airport on July 20, 1984, the carrier (airline) presented the group for inspection and admission under the transit without visa (TRWOV) privilege.[a] The examining immigration officer denied the five aliens entry as TRWOVs and issued to the carrier a Form I–259 (Notice to Detain, Deport, Remove, or Present Aliens), formally directing that they be detained by the carrier pending their removal on the carrier's next available return flight to Hong Kong. The aliens apparently made no attempt to obtain a further determination of their admissibility as TRWOVs at a continued or deferred inspection, or to pursue their applications for admission at an exclusion hearing before an immigration judge, but agreed to abide by the examining immigration officer's decision and return to Hong Kong. They then apparently were kept in isolation in a waiting area or lounge within the airport until their final removal by the carrier could be effected. While in this carrier custody, the instant two applicants surreptitiously left the detention lounge and the Los Angeles International Airport, abandoning their passports, airline tickets, and baggage. Two days later they were apprehended on board an eastbound commercial bus at the border patrol check point at Sierra Blanca, Texas. The Service served the applicants with Orders to Show Cause and held them in custody at a Service detention facility. The Service later cancelled the Orders to Show Cause and instead issued to each applicant a Form I–122 (Notice to Applicant for Admission Detained for Hearing Before Immigration Judge) placing them in these exclusion proceedings.

The applicants argued before the immigration judge that the exclusion proceedings should be terminated because they properly were subject only to deportation proceedings in that they had succeeded in entering the United States without inspection; they asserted this result is consistent with a factually analogous case, *Matter of A–*, 9 I. & N. Dec. 356 (BIA 1961), where an alien stowaway detained on board a vessel awaiting removal who subsequently escaped from the carrier's custody, landed on shore, and remained in the country undetected for 2 years was held to have effected an "entry" and so was amenable only to deportation proceedings. The Service countered that this matter is controlled by *Matter of Lin*, 18 I. & N. Dec. 219 (BIA 1982), where an alien who absconded from a Service detention facility while awaiting an exclusion hearing did not make an entry into the United States and was properly placed in exclusion proceedings. The immigration judge agreed with the applicants and terminated the exclusion proceedings. This appeal by the Service followed.

a. Certain noncitizens "proceeding in immediate and continuous transit through the United States" need not obtain visas. See INA §§ 101(a)(15)(C), 212(d)(4)(C).—Ed.

Resolution of this case turns upon whether the applicants actually "entered" the United States and so are subject only to deportation proceedings. Section 101(a)(13) of the Immigration and Nationality Act, generally defines "entry" as "any coming of an alien into the United States from a foreign port or place or from an outlying possession." In *Matter of Pierre*, 14 I. & N. Dec. 467 (BIA 1973), we examined prior case precedent involving the entry issue and synthesized a three-part analysis, concluding that an entry involves: (1) a crossing into the territorial limits of the United States, *i.e.*, physical presence; (2)(a) inspection and admission by an immigration officer or (b) actual and intentional evasion of inspection at the nearest inspection point; and (3) freedom from official restraint. Moreover, it is well settled that an alien's parole from Service custody into the United States does not constitute an entry and he is not entitled to deportation proceedings. Similarly, an alien detained by the Service, rather than granted parole, pending an exclusion hearing who escapes from custody does not enter the United States and remains subject to exclusion proceedings. *Matter of Lin.*

Under the facts herein, we conclude that the applicants' escape from carrier custody into the United States constituted an entry. The applicants arrived by aircraft at Los Angeles International Airport and remained in the custody of the carrier before, during, and after completion of the inspection process; when they sought admission under the TRWOV privilege and were refused such status by the examining immigration officer, the applicants simply remained in the carrier's custody pending their return to Hong Kong. The applicants did not seek to further test their admissibility as TRWOVs but ostensibly accepted the immigration officer's refusal of admission and agreed to return home. It is clear that the inspection process was not to be ongoing or held in abeyance but that the applicants' inspection was completed and the determination of the immigration officer was final. Thus, this case is readily distinguishable from *Matter of Lin,* where the alien absconded after being placed in exclusion proceedings and while awaiting a hearing before an immigration judge; Lin's processing for admission was not finalized but his application for admission was a continuing application throughout the exclusion proceedings. Here, by contrast, the applicants' inspection and application for admission were completed and they remained in the carrier's custody within the detention lounge without having actually "landed", *i.e.,* they were in a position legally equivalent to aliens "on the threshhold" [sic] and outside a United States land border. In summary, the critical distinction between this case and *Lin* is that Lin was already in exclusion proceedings (following service of a Form I–122) and awaiting a formal hearing when he escaped whereas here the applicants were not in exclusion proceedings pursuing a continuing application for admission but their application and inspection were completed, the determination was final, and they were merely awaiting return transportation. In effect, the applicants made two separate attempts to enter the United States: their first failed when they were rejected for admission as TRWOVs; their second succeeded when they slipped away from the detention lounge, evading detection by either carrier or Service authorities and fleeing into the country's interior. This successful second attempt which combined the applicants' physical presence with their actual and intentional evasion of inspection while free of official restraint satisfies the *Pierre* three-part test and so constitutes an entry.

We agree with the applicants that their situation is legally analogous to that in *Matter of A*. There, the alien had been discovered on board a commercial ocean vessel as a stowaway before it arrived in port in the United States. Upon arrival, the alien was inspected by an immigration officer who determined the alien was a stowaway and refused him entry. Accordingly, the carrier was ordered to detain the stowaway on board and remove him when the ship left port. *See* section 273(d) of the Act. Thus, formal disposition by the Service of the stowaway's application for admission was concluded. However, he later managed to escape from the ship and come ashore and was not apprehended in the United States until 2 years later. The Board held that the alien had entered without inspection and his removal could be enforced only through deportation proceedings. This is essentially what occurred in this case as well. Both here and in *Matter of A*, the aliens, although physically present within this country's territorial jurisdiction, did not actually "land" in the United States, their inspections and applications for admission were completed and a final determination was made refusing to admit them and ordering them removed, and they were detained by the carrier pending final removal during which time they escaped and made their way into the United States. Therefore, consistent with *Matter of A*, the instant applicants must be deemed to have entered the United States without inspection.

* * *

NOTES AND QUESTIONS

1.   On June 6, 1993, the freighter "Golden Venture," carrying 300 passengers, ran aground on a sand bar just 100—200 yards off the coast of New York. It turned out that the passengers were would-be Chinese immigrants who were being transported as part of a multi-million dollar immigrant smuggling ring. They would pay the large fees by agreeing to years of indentured servitude in the United States. *Matter of G*, 20 I. & N. Dec. 764, 766–68 (BIA 1993).

Seven passengers died. Some of the survivors remained on the ship and were eventually rescued. Some others swam to shore and were confined to the beach, in an area cordoned off by the former INS. Still others escaped into the interior; many of the latter were then apprehended after varying periods of time. *Id*. at 769.

The BIA concluded that those who had either stayed with the ship or made it no further than the cordoned off beach area had never become free of official restraint, the third element of the *Pierre* test. In contrast, those individuals who had reached the interior, only to be detected and apprehended later, were free of official restraint and therefore had "entered" the United States. The problem was that, amidst all the confusion and the urgency, the INS was not able to record which passengers had been rescued from the ship, which ones had swum safely to shore and remained there, and which ones had been apprehended in the interior. The BIA ruled that each individual would have the burden of proving "entry" and that anyone who did not sustain his or her burden could properly be placed in exclusion proceedings. *Id.* at 770–71. Subsequent judicial decisions reached similar conclusions. See, e.g., *Chen Zhou Chai v. Carroll*, 48 F.3d 1331, 1343 (4th Cir. 1995) (passenger rescued from ship had never become free of official restraint); *Xin-Chang Zhang v. Slattery*, 55 F.3d 732, 754–55 (2d Cir. 1995) (person who swam ashore but was always under surveillance was not free of official restraint).

With the enactment of IIRIRA, of course, there are no longer "exclusion" and "deportation" proceedings; there are only "removal" proceedings. Nor will the admissibility of noncitizens like Ching, Chen, and the Golden Venture passengers depend on whether they effected "entries." If they did, they will probably be inadmissible for being present without admission; if they didn't, they will be inadmissible for having arrived at places that were not designated ports of entry. Either way, they will be placed in removal proceedings and found inadmissible.

In this context, then, is "entry" now irrelevant? Not quite. Among the various consequences that "entry" now generally retains, at least two are specifically applicable here: (1) the difference between mandatory expedited removal and, for those who are apprehended quickly, discretionary expedited removal; and (2) for those who have previously been ordered removed, the loss of the right to a removal hearing if they illegally "reenter."

But aside from the relevance of "entry" to the specific facts of *Ching and Chen* and the Golden Venture episode, the earlier general discussion demonstrates the wide variety of contexts in which "entry" retains importance. For that reason, definitional issues remain alive. And since IIRIRA § 301(a) repealed the statutory definition of "entry," the question now is whether the cases interpreting the word "entry" are still good law. On the one hand, the legislation has not affirmatively superseded them. On the other hand, most of those cases (not all) were decided at a time when a statutory definition of "entry" was on the books; whether these cases will continue to inform the meaning of that term is a question that so far has received little judicial guidance.

2. Read carefully the language of INA § 275(a), which imposes criminal penalties on noncitizens who enter the United States in certain specified ways. Would knowledge of that provision have affected your strategy if you had been representing Ching and Chen in the exclusion case you just read?

3. The problem in *Ching and Chen* is a classic example of the question "Is this fact situation more like case X (*Matter of Lin*) or more like case Y (*Matter of A*)?" The difficulty here is that it is not obvious why *Matter of Lin* and *Matter of A* should have been decided differently in the first place. How does the Board distinguish them from each other? As a

matter of policy, does the articulated distinction explain why Lin had to face exclusion proceedings when A did not?

4.   Why should Lin be treated less favorably than the noncitizen who crosses the border surreptitiously, evades immigration personnel, makes her way inland, and then, like Ching and Chen, is apprehended two days later?

5.   Apply the elements of the *Pierre* test to the facts of *Ching and Chen*.

6.   If you were unable to come up with convincing explanations for the result combinations noted in questions 3 or 4 above, can you devise a better general formulation—one that would avoid those kinds of anomalies?

PROBLEMS 1–3

Problem 1. X, a noncitizen, arrived at a United States airport on a flight from Lisbon. She waited in line to pass through immigration control. When her turn came, the immigration inspector looked at her passport and her B–2 (visitor for pleasure) visa stamp, asked her a few questions, and then told her to go through, adding "Enjoy your stay." On the other side of the room, 35 feet in front of her, was a doorway that led to the baggage claim area and eventually to Customs. Just as she was about to pass through the doorway, another immigration inspector, who happened to be walking past her en route to his lunch break, noticed what looked like needle marks on her arm. He pulled her aside, questioned her further, and detained her pending a medical inspection. Has she made an "entry?" See generally *Correa v. Thornburgh*, 901 F.2d 1166, 1171–72 (2d Cir.1990); *Matter of Patel*, 20 I. & N. Dec. 368 (BIA 1991).

Problem 2. Y, a noncitizen, furtively crossed the border from Tijuana, Mexico to San Ysidro, California in the middle of the night at a point not designated for crossing. A Border Patrol officer standing 50 feet on the United States side of the border spotted Y while he was on the Mexican side. The officer kept Y under surveillance until he had proceeded about 100 yards into United States territory. At that point, the officer placed Y under arrest. Has he "entered?" (In *United States v. Ruiz–Lopez*, 234 F.3d 445 (9th Cir. 2000) (as amended), the court held that border surveillance constituted restraint, and thus there was no entry, for purposes of an analogous criminal statute.)

Problem 3. Suppose in the previous Problem the Border Patrol officer, instead of apprehending Y 100 yards inside United States territory, had tracked him until that point and then lost sight of him. Suppose further that Y escaped into the night, made his way north, and was picked up three days later in Los Angeles. Has he now "entered?" See *United States v. Hernandez–Herrera*, 273 F.3d 1213, 1218–20 (9th Cir. 2001) (holding person who was under surveillance but who then escaped it, even for just 50 yards, *not* to have made an "entry," for purposes of criminal prosecution for entry without inspection).

————

The second common type of entry problem arises when an LPR leaves the United States temporarily and then returns. Is the return an "entry?" The following landmark case, still highly controversial, discusses the problem:

Rosenberg v. Fleuti

Supreme Court of the United States, 1963.
374 U.S. 449, 83 S.Ct. 1804, 10 L.Ed.2d 1000.

■ Mr. Justice Goldberg delivered the opinion of the Court.

Respondent Fleuti is a Swiss national who was originally admitted to this country for permanent residence on October 9, 1952, and has been here continuously since except for a visit of "about a couple hours" duration to Ensenada, Mexico, in August 1956. The Immigration and Naturalization Service, of which petitioner Rosenberg is the Los Angeles District Director, sought in April 1959 to deport respondent on the ground that at the time of his return in 1956 he "was within one or more of the classes of aliens excludable by the law existing at the time of such entry," INA § 241(a)(1).[a] In particular, the Service alleged * * * that he had been excludable at the time of his 1956 return as an alien "afflicted with psychopathic personality," INA § 212(a)(4),[b] by reason of the fact that he was a homosexual. Deportation was ordered on this ground and Fleuti's appeal to the Board of Immigration Appeals was dismissed, whereupon he brought the present action for declaratory judgment and review of the administrative action. It was stipulated that among the issues to be litigated was the question whether § 212(a)(4) is "unconstitutional as being vague and ambiguous." The trial court rejected respondent's contentions in this regard and in general, and granted the Government's motion for summary judgment. On appeal, however, the United States Court of Appeals for the Ninth Circuit set aside the deportation order and enjoined its enforcement, holding that as applied to Fleuti § 212(a)(4) was unconstitutionally vague in that homosexuality was not sufficiently encompassed within the term "psychopathic personality."

The Government petitioned this Court for certiorari, which we granted in order to consider the constitutionality of § 212(a)(4) as applied to respondent Fleuti. Upon consideration of the case, however, and in accordance with the long-established principle that "we ought not to pass on questions of constitutionality * * * unless such adjudication is unavoidable," we have concluded that there is a threshold issue of statutory

a. Now INA § 237(a)(1)(A).—Ed.

b. Now repealed. See chapter 3, § B.2.a above.—Ed.

interpretation in the case, the existence of which obviates decision here as to whether § 212(a)(4) is constitutional as applied to respondent.

That issue is whether Fleuti's return to the United States from his afternoon trip to Ensenada, Mexico, in August 1956 constituted an "entry" within the meaning of § 101(a)(13) of the Immigration and Nationality Act of 1952, such that Fleuti was excludable for a condition existing at that time even though he had been permanently and continuously resident in this country for nearly four years prior thereto. Section 101(a)(13), which has never been directly construed by this Court in relation to the kind of brief absence from the country that characterizes the present case, reads as follows:

> The term "entry" means any coming of an alien into the United States, from a foreign port or place or from an outlying possession, whether voluntarily or otherwise, except that an alien having a lawful permanent residence in the United States shall not be regarded as making an entry into the United States for the purposes of the immigration laws if the alien proves to the satisfaction of the Attorney General that his departure to a foreign port or place or to an outlying possession was not intended or reasonably to be expected by him or his presence in a foreign port or place or in an outlying possession was not voluntary * * *:[c]

The question we must consider, more specifically, is whether Fleuti's short visit to Mexico can possibly be regarded as a "departure to a foreign port or place * * * [that] was not intended," within the meaning of the exception to the term "entry" created by the statute. Whether the 1956 return was within that exception is crucial, because Fleuti concededly was not excludable as a "psychopathic personality" at the time of his 1952 entry.[2]

The definition of "entry" as applied for various purposes in our immigration laws was evolved judicially, only becoming encased in statutory form with the inclusion of § 101(a)(13) in the 1952 Act. In the early cases there was developed a judicial definition of "entry" which had harsh consequences for aliens. This viewpoint was expressed most restrictively in United States ex rel. Volpe v. Smith, in which the Court, speaking through Mr. Justice McReynolds, upheld deportation of an alien who, after 24 years of residence in this country following a lawful entry, was held to be excludable on his return from "a brief visit to Cuba." The Court stated that "the word 'entry' * * * includes any coming of an alien from a foreign

---

c. IIRIRA § 301(a) replaced this "entry" definition with a definition of "admission." See items 10–14 of the Notes and Questions following this case.

2. The 1952 Act became effective on December 24, 1952, and Fleuti entered the country for permanent residence on October 9, 1952, a fact which is of significance because § 241(a)(1) of the Act only commands the deportation of aliens "excludable by the law existing at the time of such entry * * *." Hence, since respondent's homosexuality did not make him excludable by any law existing at the time of his 1952 entry, it is critical to determine whether his return from a few hours in Mexico in 1956 was an "entry" in the statutory sense. If it was not, the question whether § 212(a)(4) could constitutionally be applied to him need not be resolved.

country into the United States whether such coming be the first or any subsequent one." Although cases in the lower courts applying the strict re-entry doctrine to aliens who had left the country for brief visits to Canada or Mexico or elsewhere were numerous, many courts applied the doctrine in such instances with express reluctance and explicit recognition of its harsh consequences, and there were a few instances in which district judges refused to hold that aliens who had been absent from the country only briefly had made "entries" upon their return.

Reaction to the severe effects produced by adherence to the strict definition of "entry" resulted in a substantial inroad being made upon that definition in 1947 by a decision of the Second Circuit and a decision of this Court. The Second Circuit, in an opinion by Judge Learned Hand, refused to allow a deportation which depended on the alien's being regarded as having re-entered this country after having taken an overnight sleeper from Buffalo to Detroit on a route lying through Canada. Di Pasquale v. Karnuth. Judge Hand recognized that the alien "acquiesced in whatever route the railroad might choose to pull the car," but held that it would be too harsh to impute the carrier's intent to the alien, there being no showing that the alien knew he would be entering Canada. "Were it otherwise," Judge Hand went on, "the alien would be subjected without means of protecting himself to the forfeiture of privileges which may be, and often are, of the most grave importance to him." If there were a duty upon aliens to inquire about a carrier's route, it "would in practice become a trap, whose closing upon them would have no rational relation to anything they could foresee as significant. We cannot believe that Congress meant to subject those who had acquired a residence, to the sport of chance, when the interests at stake may be so momentous." Concluding, Judge Hand said that if the alien's return were held to be an "entry" under the circumstances, his "vested interest in his residence" would

> "be forfeited because of perfectly lawful conduct which he could not possibly have supposed would result in anything of the sort. Caprice in the incidence of punishment is one of the indicia of tyranny, and nothing can be more disingenuous than to say that deportation in these circumstances is not punishment. It is well that we should be free to rid ourselves of those who abuse our hospitality; but it is more important that the continued enjoyment of that hospitality once granted, shall not be subject to meaningless and irrational hazards."

Later the same year this Court, because of a conflict between Di Pasquale and [a Ninth Circuit decision], granted certiorari in the latter case and reversed a deportation order affecting an alien who, upon rescue after his intercoastal merchant ship was torpedoed in the Caribbean during World War II, had been taken to Cuba to recuperate for a week before returning to this country. Delgadillo v. Carmichael. The Court pointed out that it was "the exigencies of war, not his voluntary act," which put the alien on foreign soil, adding that "[w]e might as well hold that if he had been kidnapped and taken to Cuba, he made a statutory 'entry' on his voluntary return. Respect for law does not thrive on captious interpretations." Since "[t]he stakes are indeed high and momentous for the alien who has acquired his residence here," the Court held that

> "[w]e will not attribute to Congress a purpose to make his right to remain here dependent on circumstances so fortuitous and capricious as those upon which the Immigration Service has here seized. The hazards to which we are now asked to subject the alien are too irrational to square with the statutory scheme."

The increased protection of returning resident aliens which was brought about by the Delgadillo decision, both in its result and in its express approval of Di Pasquale, was reflected in at least two subsequent lower-court decisions prior to the enactment of § 101(a)(13). * * *

It was in light of all of these developments in the case law that § 101(a)(13) was included in the immigration laws with the 1952 revision. As the House and Senate Committee Reports, the relevant material from which is quoted in the margin,[8] make clear, the major congressional concern in codifying the definition of "entry" was with "the status of an alien who has previously entered the United States and resided therein * * *." This concern was in the direction of ameliorating the harsh results visited upon resident aliens by the rule of United States ex rel. Volpe v. Smith, supra, as is indicated by the recognition that "the courts have departed from the rigidity of [the earlier] rule," and the statement that "[t]he bill [gives] due recognition to the judicial precedents." It must be recognized, of course, that the only liberalizing decisions to which the

---

8. The House and Senate Committee Reports preceding enactment of the bill both contained the following relevant paragraph:

> "Section 101(a)(13) defines the term 'entry.' Frequent reference is made to the term 'entry' in the immigration laws, and many consequences relating to the entry and departure of aliens flow from its use, but the term is not precisely defined in the present law. Normally an entry occurs when the alien crosses the border of the United States and makes a physical entry, and the question of whether an entry has been made is susceptible of a precise determination. However, for the purposes of determining the effect of a subsequent entry upon the status of an alien who has previously entered the United States and resided therein, the preciseness of the term 'entry' has not been found to be as apparent. Earlier judicial constructions of the term in the immigration laws, as set forth in United States ex rel. Volpe v. Smith, generally held

that the term 'entry' included any coming of an alien from a foreign country to the United States whether such coming be the first or a subsequent one. More recently, the courts have departed from the rigidity of that rule and have recognized that an alien does not make an entry upon his return to the United States from a foreign country where he had no intent to leave the United States (Di Pasquale v. Karnuth), or did not leave the country voluntarily (Delgadillo v. Carmichael). The bill defines the term 'entry' as precisely as practicable, giving due recognition to the judicial precedents. Thus any coming of an alien from a foreign port or place or an outlying possession into the United States is to be considered an entry, whether voluntary or otherwise, unless the Attorney General is satisfied that the departure of the alien, other than a deportee, from this country was unintentional or was not voluntary."

Reports referred specifically were Di Pasquale and Delgadillo, and that there is no indication one way or the other in the legislative history of what Congress thought about the problem of resident aliens who leave the country for insignificantly short periods of time. Nevertheless, it requires but brief consideration of the policies underlying § 101(a)(13), and of certain other aspects of the rights of returning resident aliens, to conclude that Congress, in approving the judicial undermining of Volpe, supra, and the relief brought about by the Di Pasquale and Delgadillo decisions, could not have meant to limit the meaning of the exceptions it created in § 101(a)(13) to the facts of those two cases.

The most basic guide to congressional intent as to the reach of the exceptions is the eloquent language of Di Pasquale and Delgadillo themselves, beginning with the recognition that the "interests at stake" for the resident alien are "momentous," and that "[t]he stakes are indeed high and momentous for the alien who has acquired his residence here." This general premise of the two decisions impelled the more general conclusion that "it is * * * important that the continued enjoyment of [our] hospitality once granted, shall not be subject to meaningless and irrational hazards." See also Delgadillo, supra. Coupling these essential principles of the two decisions explicitly approved by Congress in enacting § 101(a)(13) with the more general observation, appearing in Delgadillo as well as elsewhere, that "[d]eportation can be the equivalent of banishment or exile," it is difficult to conceive that Congress meant its approval of the liberalization wrought by Di Pasquale and Delgadillo to be interpreted mechanistically to apply only to cases presenting factual situations identical to what was involved in those two decisions.

The idea that the exceptions to § 101(a)(13) should be read nonrestrictively is given additional credence by the way in which the immigration laws define what constitutes "continuous residence" for an alien wishing to be naturalized. Section 316 of the 1952 Act, which liberalized previous law in some respects, provides that an alien who wishes to seek naturalization does not begin to endanger the five years of "continuous residence" in this country which must precede his application until he remains outside the country for six months, and does not damage his position by cumulative temporary absences unless they total over half of the five years preceding the filing of his petition for naturalization. This enlightened concept of what constitutes a meaningful interruption of the continuous residence which must support a petition for naturalization, reflecting as it does a congressional judgment that an alien's status is not necessarily to be endangered by his absence from the country, strengthens the foundation underlying a belief that the exceptions to § 101(a)(13) should be read to protect resident aliens who are only briefly absent from the country. Of further, although less specific, effect in this regard is this Court's holding in Kwong Hai Chew v. Colding, that the returning resident alien is entitled as a matter of due process to a hearing on the charges underlying any attempt to exclude him, a holding which supports the general proposition that a resident alien who leaves this country is to be regarded as retaining certain basic rights.

Given that the congressional protection of returning resident aliens in § 101(a)(13) is not to be woodenly construed, we turn specifically to construction of the exceptions contained in that section as they relate to resident aliens who leave the country briefly. What we face here is another harsh consequence of the strict "entry" doctrine which, while not governed directly by Delgadillo, nevertheless calls into play the same considerations, which led to the results specifically approved in the Congressional Committee Reports. It would be as "fortuitous and capricious," and as "irrational to square with the statutory scheme," to hold that an alien may necessarily be deported because he falls into one of the classes enumerated in § 212(a) when he returns from "a couple hours" visit to Mexico as it would have been to uphold the order of deportation in Delgadillo. Certainly when an alien like Fleuti who has entered the country lawfully and has acquired a residence here steps across a border and, in effect, steps right back, subjecting him to exclusion for a condition, for which he could not have been deported had he remained in the country seems to be placing him at the mercy of the "sport of chance" and the "meaningless and irrational hazards" to which Judge Hand alluded. In making such a casual trip the alien would seldom be aware that he was possibly walking into a trap, for the insignificance of a brief trip to Mexico or Canada bears little rational relation to the punitive consequence of subsequent excludability. There are, of course, valid policy reasons for saying that an alien wishing to retain his classification as a permanent resident of this country imperils his status by interrupting his residence too frequently or for an overly long period of time, but we discern no rational policy supporting application of a re-entry limitation in all cases in which a resident alien crosses an international border for a short visit. Certainly if that trip is innocent, casual, and brief, it is consistent with all the discernible signs of congressional purpose to hold that the "departure * * * was not intended" within the meaning and ameliorative intent of the exception of § 101(a)(13). Congress unquestionably has the power to exclude all classes of undesirable aliens from this country, and the courts are charged with enforcing such exclusion when Congress has directed it, but we do not think Congress intended to exclude aliens long resident in this country after lawful entry who have merely stepped across an international border and returned in "about a couple hours." Such a holding would be inconsistent with the general purpose of Congress in enacting § 101(a)(13) to ameliorate the severe effects of the strict "entry" doctrine.

We conclude, then, that it effectuates congressional purpose to construe the intent exception to § 101(a)(13) as meaning an intent to depart in a manner which can be regarded as meaningfully interruptive of the alien's permanent residence. One major factor relevant to whether such intent can be inferred is, of course, the length of time the alien is absent. Another is the purpose of the visit, for if the purpose of leaving the country is to accomplish some object which is itself contrary to some policy reflected in our immigration laws, it would appear that the interruption of residence thereby occurring would properly be regarded as meaningful. Still another is whether the alien has to procure any travel documents in order to make his trip, since the need to obtain such items might well cause the alien to consider more fully the implications involved in his leaving the country. Although the operation of these and other possibly relevant factors remains to be developed "by the gradual process of judicial inclusion and exclusion," we declare today simply that an innocent, casual, and brief excursion by a resident alien outside this country's borders may not have been "intended" as a departure disruptive of his resident alien status and therefore may not subject him to the consequences of an "entry" into the country on his return. The more civilized application of our immigration laws given recognition by Congress in § 101(a)(13) and other provisions of the 1952 Act protects the resident alien from unsuspected risks and unintended consequences of such a wholly innocent action. Respondent here, so far as appears from the record, is among those to be protected. However, because attention was not previously focused upon the application of § 101(a)(13) to the case, the record contains no detailed description or characterization of his trip to Mexico in 1956, except for his testimony that he was gone "about a couple hours," and that he was "just visiting; taking a trip." That being the case, we deem it appropriate to remand the case for further consideration of the application of § 101(a)(13) to this case in light of our discussion herein. If it is determined that respondent did not "intend" to depart in the sense contemplated by § 101(a)(13), the deportation order will not stand and adjudication of the constitutional issue reached by the court below will be obviated. * * *

* * *

■ MR. JUSTICE CLARK, with whom MR. JUSTICE Harlan, Mr. Justice STEWART and MR. JUSTICE WHITE join, dissenting.

I dissent from the Court's judgment and opinion because "statutory construction" means to me that the Court can *construe* statutes but not that it can *construct* them. The latter function is reserved to the Congress, which clearly said what it meant and undoubtedly meant what it said when it defined "entry" for immigration purposes as follows: * * *. That this definition of "entry" includes the respondent's entry after his brief trip to Mexico in 1956 is a conclusion which seems to me inescapable. The conclusion is compelled by the plain meaning of the statute, its legislative history, and the consistent interpretation by the federal courts. Indeed, the respondent himself did not even question that his return to the United States was an "entry" within the meaning of § 101(a)(13). Nonetheless, the Court has rewritten the Act *sua sponte,* creating a definition of "entry" which was suggested by many organizations during the hearings prior to its enactment but which was rejected by the Congress. I believe the authorities discussed in the Court's opinion demonstrate that "entry" as defined in § 101(a)(13) cannot mean what the Court says it means, but I will add a few words of explanation.

The word "entry" had acquired a well-defined meaning for immigration purposes at the time the Immigration and Nationality Act was passed in 1952. * * *

* * *

These cases and others discussed by the Court establish the setting in which the Immigration and Nationality Act was passed in 1952. The House and Senate reports quoted by the Court show that the Congress recognized the courts' difficulty with the rule that "any coming" of an alien into the United States was an "entry," even when the departure from the country was unintentional or involuntary. The reports discuss the broad rule of the Volpe case and the specific limitations of the Di Pasquale and Delgadillo cases, citing those cases by name, and conclude with the following language:

[The dissent here quotes the language reproduced in the last two sentences of footnote 8 of the majority opinion.—Ed.]

* * *

Thus there is nothing in the legislative history or in the statute itself which would exempt the respondent's return from Mexico from the definition of "entry". Rather, the statute in retaining the definition expressed in Volpe seems clearly to cover respondent's entry, which occurred after he knowingly left the United States in order to travel to a city in Mexico. That the trip may have been "innocent, casual, and brief" does not alter the fact that, in the words of the Court in Delgadillo, the respondent "plainly expected or planned to enter a foreign port or place."

It is true that this application of the law to a resident alien may be harsh, but harshness is a far cry from the irrationality condemned in Delgadillo. There and in Di Pasquale contrary results would have meant that a resident alien, who was not deportable unless he left the country and reentered, could be deported as a result of circumstances either beyond his control or beyond his knowledge. Here, of course, there is no claim that respondent did not know he was leaving the country to enter Mexico and, since one is presumed to know the law, he knew that his brief trip and reentry would render him deportable. The Congress clearly has chosen so to apply the long-established definition, and this Court cannot alter that legislative determination in the guise of statutory construction. Had the Congress not wished the definition of "entry" to include a return after a brief but voluntary and intentional trip, it could have done so. The Court's discussion of § 316 of the Act shows that the Congress knows well how to temper rigidity when it wishes. Nor can it be said that the Congress was unaware of the breadth of its definition. Even aside from the evidence that it was aware of the judicial precedents, numerous organizations unsuccessfully urged that the definition be narrowed to accomplish what the Court does today. Thus, it was urged that the Act's definition of "entry" "should, we believe, be narrowed so that it will not be applicable to an alien returning from abroad, after a temporary absence, to an unrelinquished domicile here." Other groups complained also that "[t]he term 'entry' is defined to mean any coming of an alien into the United States. It is recommended that this be narrowed to provide that a return, after a temporary absence, to an unrelinquished domicile, shall not constitute a new entry." Despite such urging, however, the Congress made no change in the definition. Further, this Court in 1958 specifically recognized that the word "entry" retained its plain meaning, stating that "a resident alien who leaves the country for any period, however brief, does make a new entry on his return * * *."

All this to the contrary notwithstanding, the Court today decides that one does not really intend to leave the country unless he plans a long trip, or his journey is for an illegal purpose, or he needs travel documents in order to make the trip. This is clearly contrary to the definition in the Act and to any definition of "intent" that I was taught.

* * *

NOTES AND QUESTIONS

IIRIRA § 301(a) repealed the statutory "entry" definition that the Court in *Fleuti* was interpreting and replaced it with a definition of "admission." INA § 101(a)(13). Nonetheless, for reasons that will be taken up presently, the decision in *Fleuti* remains vital. In the Notes and Questions that follow, items 1 through 9 require you to analyze and critique this landmark decision, item 10 considers a related issue, and items 11–15 then explore the statutory changes.

1. What principle of judicial decisionmaking led the Court to address the "entry" issue rather than the "psychopathic personality" issue? What would you assume is the rationale for that principle?

2. The majority and dissenting opinions in *Fleuti* invoke several common statutory interpretation techniques. Consider first the literal language of the statutory "entry" definition. Precisely which word or phrase does the Court refuse to interpret literally? What interpretation does the Court place on that phrase?

3. The *Fleuti* Court's rejection of seemingly clear statutory language has angered some commentators. One student writer, criticizing the Court's refusal to give the statute its "obvious meaning," began his analysis of *Fleuti* by quoting a famous judicial passage:

[W]e are in the never-never land of the Immigration and Nationality Act, where plain words do not always mean what they say.

Yuen Sang Low v. Attorney General, 479 F.2d 820, 821 (9th Cir.1973), quoted in Comment, *Exclusion and Deportation of Resident Aliens: The Re-Entry Doctrine and the Need for Reform,* 13 San Diego L.Rev. 192, 197 (1975); see also *id.* at 198. The authors of the original edition of another casebook began the set of Notes following *Fleuti* by asking "Isn't *Fleuti* an embarrassment to the United States Supreme Court?" T. Alexander Aleinikoff & David A. Martin, Immigration Process and Policy 335 (1st ed. 1985).

It is not surprising that a decision like *Fleuti* would stir strong emotions. People have powerful convictions about the proper role of courts to begin with. In *Fleuti,* the Court deviated not only from the literal statutory language, but also from what some might see as compelling historical evidence of congressional intent (more on the latter in a moment).

But is it really so obvious that the Court exceeded proper bounds? Isn't this simply a case in which the Court rejected the Literal Plain Meaning Rule of statutory interpretation in favor of the Golden Rule? (See page 356 above.) Wouldn't a literal construction have produced an absurd result? If you think not, then answer this question: Why *would* Congress have wanted the deportation of an LPR to hinge on whether the person had once made an innocent, casual, and brief visit outside the United States? Alternatively, even if such a result does not rise to the level of the "absurd," might not the Court's analysis simply reflect its preference for the Social Purpose approach? See also Ibrahim J. Wani, *Truth, Strangers, and Fiction: The Illegitimate Uses of Legal Fiction in Immigration Law,* 11 Cardozo L.Rev. 51, 93–96 (1989) (criticizing the incongruous judicial responses that flow from *Fleuti*'s emphasis on intent).

4. To answer that last question, it is necessary of course to ascertain what the congressional purpose actually was. Several items of evidence are available. Both sides agree, for example, that section 101(a)(13) was intended to codify the decisions in *Di Pasquale* and *Delgadillo.* That being so, how can the two sides reach such differing conclusions about what the provision means?

5. The dissent finds more specific evidence of congressional intent. It observes that several organizations had urged in committee hearings that the proposed entry definition be amended to make clear that the exception encompasses the temporary absences of LPRs. The dissent reads significance into Congress's refusal to amend the bill as suggested. If you were Fleuti's counsel, how might you respond to that argument?

6. The preceding notes focus attention on the literal language of the disputed provision and on the legislative history, both as evidence of congressional intent. Related provisions can be additional sources of evidence. In *Fleuti,* both sides support their readings of section 101(a)(13) by citing another INA provision, section 316 (dealing with naturalization). What contrary inferences do the two sides draw from section 316? Can you generalize the opposing arguments into statutory interpretation principles that transcend the specific provisions at issue here?

7. The dissent argues that Fleuti, like anyone else, is presumed to know the law, and that he must therefore be treated as having realized that a temporary visit to Mexico would subject him to exclusion upon his return. How might Fleuti's counsel have responded to that argument (assuming the opportunity presented itself before the Supreme Court's decision)?

8. *Fleuti* has been applied in a long list of BIA and lower court decisions. Those decisions have made clear that even a trip much longer than the "couple hours" of Fleuti's visit can be non-meaningful. In some cases, absences of several months have qualified as non-meaningful. See, e.g., *Itzcovitz v. Selective Service Local Bd. No. 6,* 447 F.2d 888 (2d Cir.1971); *cf. Jubilado v. United States,* 819 F.2d 210 (9th Cir.1987) (departure not meaningful enough to permit exclusion proceedings rather than deportation proceedings); *Git Foo Wong v. INS,* 358 F.2d 151 (9th Cir.1966) (analogous determination whether foreign visit disturbed conti-

nuity of physical presence for purposes of provision affording affirmative relief from deportation).

9.   To this point, discussion has focused on whether an overseas trip by an LPR was meaningful enough that, upon return to the United States, he or she is subject to the legal consequences of an "entry" or an "admission." A different question is whether the trip was so meaningful that it exposes the returning LPR to a consequence even more severe—a finding that the person has relinquished, or abandoned, his or her LPR status.

For this purpose, INA § 101(a)(27)(A) defines a "special immigrant" as an LPR "returning from a temporary visit abroad." Abandonment turns on whether the visit is found to be "temporary." Temporariness, in turn, rests on the intent of the LPR. The intent required to make the visit temporary, however, is not an intent to retain one's LPR status; rather, as several cases have held, the LPR must have had, at the time of departure from the U.S., "the intent to return to the United States within a relatively short period." *Khodagholian v. Ashcroft*, 335 F.3d 1003, 1007 (9th Cir. 2003). More specifically,

> A permanent resident alien returns from a "temporary visit abroad" only when (a) the permanent resident's visit is for a period relatively short, fixed by some early event, or (b) the permanent resident's visit will terminate upon the occurrence of an event having a reasonable possibility of occurring within a relatively short period of time. [In the latter case], if the event does not occur within a relatively short period of time, the visit will be considered a "temporary visit abroad" only if the alien has a continuous, uninterrupted intention to return to the United States during the entirety of his visit.

Id. at 1006–07, quoting *Chavez–Ramirez v. INS*, 792 F.2d 932, 936–37 (9th Cir. 1986); accord, *Moin v. Ashcroft*, 335 F.3d 415, 419 (5th Cir. 2003); *Ahmed v. Ashcroft*, 286 F.3d 611, 613 (2d Cir. 2002). Evidence of the requisite intention can include (in addition to the actual length of the visit and the person's conduct overseas) family ties, property, and business affiliations in both the United States and the foreign country. *Khodagholian*, 335 F.3d at 1007.

Of course, even if the person substantively qualifies as a returning LPR, all the admissibility requirements, including the documentary requirements, remain in effect. By way of exception, if the absence does not exceed one year, the LPR may satisfy the documentary requirements simply by presenting his or her valid, unexpired "green card" (formally called a "permanent resident card" or form I–551). See 8 C.F.R. § 211.3 (2004). In addition, an LPR may apply in advance for a "reentry permit" for a trip of (usually) no more than two years. INA § 223; 8 C.F.R. § 223 (2004). If the LPR then presents the reentry permit upon return, his or her LPR status will be found to continue unless the government proves abandonment by "clear, unequivocal, and convincing evidence." *Moin*, 335 F.3d at 419; *cf. Khodagholian*, 335 F.3d at 1006 (burden of proof shifts to government when person has "colorable claim to returning resident status").

For some helpful commentary on the issue of abandonment of LPR status, see Gordon, Mailman & Yale–Loehr, § 35.02; Lory Diana Rosenberg, *Ask Lory—Clash of Intentions*, 8 BIB 1881 (Dec. 15, 2003); Stephen Yale–Loehr and Roni Reed, *Preserving Permanent Residency*, 1 BIB 14 (1996).

10.   In 1987, Rep. Romano Mazzoli, then chair of the House immigration subcommittee, introduced H.R. 2921. One of its provisions, section 101, would have amended INA § 101(a)(13) to read:

> The term "entry" means any coming of an alien (other than an alien having a lawful permanent residence in the United States) into the United States, from a foreign port or place or from an outlying possession, whether voluntarily or otherwise.

The bill did not pass. Had it become law, what would its practical consequences have been? Had you been a member of Congress, would you have supported it?

11.   As noted earlier, IIRIRA § 301(a) replaced the statutory "entry" definition with a definition of the words "admission" and "admitted." In doing so, Congress in effect modified and codified the *Fleuti* principle. The new provision reads:

> (A) The terms "admission" and "admitted" mean, with respect to an alien, the lawful entry of the alien into the United States after inspection and authorization by an immigration officer.

* * *

> (C) An alien lawfully admitted for permanent residence in the United States shall not be regarded as seeking an admission into the United States for purposes of the immigration laws unless the alien—
>
> (i) has abandoned or relinquished that status,
>
> (ii) has been absent from the United States for a continuous period in excess of 180 days,
>
> (iii) has engaged in illegal activity after having departed the United States,
>
> (iv) has departed from the United States while under legal process seeking removal of the alien from the United States, including removal proceedings under this Act and extradition proceedings,
>
> (v) has committed an offense identified in section 212(a)(2), unless since such offense the alien has been granted relief under section 212(h) or 240A(a), or

(vi) is attempting to enter at a time or place other than as designated by immigration officers or has not been admitted to the United States after inspection and authorization by an immigration officer.

INA § 101(a)(13).

The *Fleuti* decision, of course, remains essential to understanding how the law evolved to its present state. Moreover, as the preceding notes and questions illustrate, the opinion in *Fleuti* is a rich store of statutory interpretation techniques. Apart from its historical relevance and its contributions to legal process, though, is the *Fleuti* principle still a part of United States immigration law?

As a first step toward answering that question, identify the specific differences between the present statutory definition of "admission" and the principle announced in *Fleuti*.

12.   Notice the structure of new INA § 101(a)(13). It defines "admission" as "lawful *entry*" after inspection and authorization. Then it creates an exception; an LPR will not be regarded as seeking admission "*unless*" one of certain things is true—the person has relinquished permanent residence, or the absence has been greater than 180 days, or the person has committed a crime covered by section 212(a)(2), etc. Thus, if there has been a lawful entry, and a returning LPR does not fall within any of the listed categories, there will not be a new admission.

But what about the converse? The statute says an LPR will *not* be regarded as seeking admission *unless* one of several events has occurred. If one of the listed events has occurred, does the statute imply that an LPR who has made an entry *is* regarded as seeking an admission? Or does the statute simply not take a position either way on that issue? Suppose you say to someone, "I'm definitely going jogging tomorrow unless it rains." Do you necessarily mean that you won't jog if it does rain, or do you mean merely that you will jog if it doesn't rain and that you might or might not jog if it does?

In *Matter of Collado–Munoz*, 21 I. & N. Dec. 1061 (BIA 1998) (amended opinion), the Board held that a returning LPR who falls within one of the six subcategories listed in section 101(a)(13)(C) is to be regarded as seeking admission. In such circumstances, the Board held, *Fleuti* is irrelevant. Several court of appeals decisions quickly followed *Collado*, in varied contexts. See, e.g., *Tapia v. Ashcroft*, 351 F.3d 795 (7th Cir. 2003); *Tineo v. Ashcroft*, 350 F.3d 382 (3d Cir. 2003); *Rivera-Jiminez v. INS*, 214 F.3d 1213 (10th Cir. 2000). None of those decisions acknowledged any of the arguments made above.

In contrast, the dissent of BIA member Lory Rosenberg in *Collado* adopted the above reasoning. She observed that the word "unless" ordinarily does not imply the converse and illustrated the point with additional examples drawn mostly from other legal settings. 21 I. & N. Dec. at 1071–73. Later the same year a federal district court followed suit. It noted that returning LPRs who do not fit any of the six subcategories are not regarded as seeking admission. For those returning residents who fall within any of the six subcategories, the court then held, the *Fleuti* doctrine determines whether the departure meaningfully interrupted the person's permanent residence in the United States. *Richardson v. Reno*, 994 F.Supp. 1466 (S.D.Fla. 1998), rev'd on other grounds, 162 F.3d 1338 (11th Cir. 1998) (amended opinion). Thus, while the majority of courts have read an implied converse into the statute, opinion has not been unanimous. The current status of *Fleuti*, therefore, remains open.

Assume, however, that an implied converse is read into the statute, so that a returning LPR who has "entered" is automatically regarded as seeking admission if one of the enumerated events has occurred. Now suppose that a returning LPR has been away more than 180 days or has committed a crime listed in INA § 212(a)(2), or that the case falls within one of the other listed categories. Does this mean the person is regarded as seeking admission? The answer still would seem to depend on whether there has been an "entry." But what does "entry" mean? Does *Fleuti* still define that term? If so, then even a visit that exceeds 180 days might not result in an "entry" when the combination of *Fleuti* factors suggests the intent was not to depart in a manner meaningfully interruptive of permanent residence. The Board in *Collado–Munoz* did not explain how the word "entry," in the "admission" definition of section 101(a)(13), is to be defined. Argue both ways on the issue of whether *Fleuti* still governs the definition of "entry" in the (now fewer) contexts in which that term remains relevant.

13. Here is another situation where *Fleuti* arguably still applies: An LPR leaves the country for less than 180 days and the trip is perfectly innocent. Some time after returning, he or she is charged with being deportable for having been inadmissible at the time of "reentry." (Assume the person had been admissible at the time of the original admission.) To determine whether the return constituted an entry, should the court apply the *Fleuti* factors?

14. With respect to the unlawful activity factor, the literal language of the new definition is much farther reaching. The *Fleuti* Court spoke only about "the purpose of leaving the country" being "contrary to some policy reflected in our immigration laws." The new law, in INA § 101(a)(13)(C)(v), sweeps in anyone who "has committed" any of the offenses included in INA § 212(a)(2) (the crime-related inadmissibility grounds). Did Congress literally mean that, once an LPR commits such an offense, he or she is forever barred from invoking the returning LPR exception to the admission definition? Or did Congress have in mind only those offenses that are connected with the trip? Consider also section 101(a)(13)(C)(iii), which covers the person who "has engaged in illegal activity after having departed the United States." On its face this language is even broader than that of subsection C(v).

15. There are also two types of retroactive situations in which *Fleuti* might apply. First, IIRIRA § 309(a) makes clear that the definitional change effected by IIRIRA § 301(a) does not govern anyone whose removal

proceeding began before April 1, 1997 (subject to a limited exception at the discretion of the Attorney General, see IIRIRA § 309(c)). *Fleuti* is clearly applicable in those cases. Second, does *Fleuti* apply even to proceedings commenced after April 1, 1997, if the charges rest on alleged "entries" that occurred before that date? This is an important question. There is no statute of limitations on removal, so inadmissible LPRs who entered before April 1, 1997 can be found deportable decades later. If deportability is alleged in such a case, would *Fleuti* guide the entry determination (even if its use in situations like the one in item 13 above is otherwise rejected)?

PROBLEMS 4–6

Problem 4. Under INA § 237(a)(2)(A)(i)(I), which you will study later in this chapter, a noncitizen is deportable if he or she commits, within five years after "admission," a crime involving "moral turpitude" punishable by a year or more, and is subsequently convicted. A, admitted as an LPR six years earlier, goes abroad for seven months on an innocent trip. A few months after returning, he commits a crime involving moral turpitude that is punishable by more than a year. A is convicted. Is he deportable?

Problem 5. B, also admitted as an LPR six years ago, similarly commits a crime involving moral turpitude. She too is convicted. After serving her sentence, B goes abroad for one month on an innocent trip. Shortly after being readmitted, B is charged with being deportable for having been inadmissible at "entry." The alleged entry is her return from overseas, and the alleged ground of inadmissibility is INA § 212(a)(2)(A)(i)(I) (convicted of crime involving moral turpitude). Is B deportable?

Problem 6. Noncitizen C, lawfully present in the United States on an F–1 student visa, is studying at SUNY Buffalo. She and some of her American friends went to Toronto for a week over the spring break. When she returned at the end of her vacation, she presented her original documents to the immigration inspector and was allowed in. In case it ever affects her future status, does that return constitute an "admission?"

SECTION C.   DEPORTABILITY GROUNDS CONCERNED WITH IMMIGRATION CONTROL

Most of the deportability grounds listed in INA § 237(a) are aimed at those noncitizens whom Congress regards as substantively undesirable. These are people whom Congress perceives as threats to public health or safety, public morality, the economy, or national security.

Enforcing those restrictions and analogous ones contained in the exclusion grounds requires an elaborate system of immigration control. The efficacy of that system depends on rules. As this section demonstrates, violations of those rules are themselves grounds for removal.

1.   ENTRY WITHOUT INSPECTION

Until 1996, noncitizens who entered the United States without inspection were deportable. INA § 241(a)(1)(B), pre–1996 version. As you saw in chapter 5, that year Congress repealed entry without inspection as a deportability ground and instead made presence in the United States without admission a ground for inadmissibility. A noncitizen also commits a criminal offense by entering without inspection. See INA § 275. After a prior removal order, the offense can be a felony. INA § 276.

Presence without Admission v. EWI [handwritten marginal note]

In case you are wondering, it can be a criminal offense even for a United States citizen to enter the country surreptitiously. The customs laws require every "individual" who arrives "in the United States other than by vessel, vehicle, or aircraft" to enter at an authorized crossing point and immediately report his or her arrival to the customs officer. 19 U.S.C. § 1459(a). Offenders are subject to civil fines and, in the case of intentional violations, criminal penalties—including imprisonment for up to a year. *Id.* § 1459 (e, f, g). See also INA § 215(b) (unlawful for United States citizen "to depart from or enter, or attempt to depart from or enter, the United States" without valid passport, except as otherwise provided by President).

2.   ENTRY WHILE INADMISSIBLE AND RELATED ISSUES

One important deportability ground is INA § 237(a)(1)(A), which renders deportable "[a]ny alien who at the time of entry or adjustment of status was within one or more of the classes of aliens inadmissible by the law existing at such time." Of all the deportability grounds, inadmissibility at entry most clearly reflects the view of deportation as an instrument for correcting errors or lapses in the admission process. It is invoked in a wide variety of contexts.

One especially common use is where the person entered while inadmissible because of fraud. Ordinarily in those cases, inadmissibility is alleged under INA § 212(a)(6)(C)(i), which you should re-read now. In some such cases, however, ICE also alleges inadmissibility under INA § 212(a)(7)(A) (not in possession of valid entry documents), the theory being that the fraud rendered the entry documents invalid. In still others, ICE invokes the more specific provisions that make noncitizens either inadmissible or deportable for false claims of United States citizenship. See, respectively, INA §§ 212(a)(6)(C)(ii), 237(a)(3)(D).

False citizenship claims actually raise one other interesting issue, which Professor Gerald Neuman noted in an October 23, 1997 e-mail to the author. In *Reid v. INS*, 420 U.S. 619, 95 S.Ct. 1164, 43 L.Ed.2d 501 (1975), decided before IIRIRA, the Supreme Court held that a noncitizen who gains entry by falsely claiming to be a United States citizen has not been "inspected" and therefore is deportable for having entered without inspection. As noted earlier, IIRIRA eliminated entry without inspection from the list of deportability grounds but added presence without admission to the list of inadmissibility grounds. Professor Neuman wondered whether *Reid* survives IIRIRA. If entry via a false citizenship claim still results in no "inspection," then the person presumably has also not been "admitted," because the latter requires a lawful entry "after inspection." INA § 101(a)(13)(A). (At any rate there is probably no "lawful" entry.) Under that interpretation, a noncitizen who gains entry by falsely claiming United States citizenship is inadmissible for being present without admission.

In order to answer the Questions and Problems that follow, please review INA §§ 212(a)(6)(A)(i), 212(a)(6)(C)(i, ii), 212(a)(7)(A), and 237(a)(1)(A). Then read INA §§ 237(a)(3)(D) (false citizenship claim as deportability ground) and 237(a)(1)(H) (provision for waiving certain frauds).

NOTES AND QUESTIONS

1.   Explain why the last sentence of INA § 237(a)(1)(H) is necessary, when section 237(a)(1)(H)(i)(II) already covers people who are inadmissible under subsections 5(A) and 7(A) for reasons directly resulting from the fraud.

2.   Explain why, in section 237(a)(1)(H)(i)(II), it was necessary to include, in the list of exceptions to the "otherwise admissible" requirement, section 212(a)(7)(A). After all, if the noncitizen is "in possession of an immigrant visa or equivalent document," as the provision requires, then why would he or she need an exemption from section 212(a)(7)(A)?

3.   To obtain relief under INA § 237(a)(1)(H), the person also needs the favorable exercise of discretion. In *INS v. Yueh–Shaio Yang*, 519 U.S. 26, 117 S.Ct. 350, 136 L.Ed.2d 288 (1996), the Supreme Court held the BIA could lawfully consider the underlying fraud as a negative factor for purposes of the discretionary hurdle even though fraud is the misconduct that applicants for 237(a)(1)(H) relief will always be seeking to waive. Especially is this true, the Court said, when there has been a whole pattern of fraud.

PROBLEMS 7–13

Problem 7. X, a noncitizen, enters the United States in the middle of the night at a place not designated as an inspection facility, returns home on her own initiative after a month, and then, ten years later, marries a United States citizen, obtains an immigrant visa, and is admitted. A year later, ICE somehow learns of her earlier entry. Is there any ground on which she is deportable?

Note: In the pre-IIRIRA case of *Gunaydin v. INS*, 742 F.2d 776 (3d Cir.1984), two LPRs traveled to Mexico, returned without inspection, were charged with being deportable for entering without inspection, and then, while proceedings were pending, left again and returned through proper channels. The court held that a proper entry does not erase a prior entry without inspection and that accordingly they were deportable. The *Gunaydin* holding no longer applies directly, because entry without inspection is no longer a ground for deportability, but is there nonetheless another way for ICE to urge the same result? Consider INA § 237(a)(1)(A).

Problem 8. In Problem 7 above, should X have been admitted when she presented herself at a port of entry the second time? If the answer is yes (i.e., if you conclude that no apparent ground of inadmissibility applied to her at that time), should the immigration inspector have admitted her and then, the moment she entered, have told her that she is now deportable on the ground you discovered in Problem 7?

Problem 9. A, a 30–year–old married noncitizen male, has a United States citizen father. To obtain a family-sponsored first preference visa, A tells the consular officer that he has never been married. A receives his visa and is admitted to the United States as an LPR. A year later, ICE discovers the fraud. What deportability charges should it bring? Will A be eligible for relief under INA § 237(a)(1)(H)?

Problem 10. B was admitted for permanent residence as the wife of a United States citizen. One year later, ICE learns that, eighteen years before entry, at age 22, B had committed a burglary, had been convicted, and had received a two-year prison sentence. Yet B had answered "no" to a question on her visa application asking whether she had ever been convicted of a crime. ICE institutes removal proceedings.

To analyze this Problem, you will have to review INA § 212(h) and the description of it on pages 435–36 above. Since the present Problem involves deportability, you need to know that section 212(h) can be applied retroactively, in the following way: If a person is deportable for having entered while inadmissible, and the inadmissibility ground was one of the crime-related grounds that section 212(h) waives, then section 212(h) can waive that earlier inadmissibility—provided the person met all the requirements for 212(h) relief at that earlier time. *Matter of Millard*, 11 I. & N. Dec. 175 (BIA 1965). (Credit is due to Professor Virgil Wiebe and his students for identifying the retroactivity issue.)

With that information, do you think INA § 237(a)(1)(H) will be of any use to B?

Problem 11. Noncitizen C, age 17 and married, enters the United States lawfully on an F–1 student visa. She is authorized to remain for the duration of her student status. One year after admission, she obtains a final divorce decree and applies for adjustment of status as the child of a United States citizen (immediate relative). USCIS grants the application. A year after that, however, ICE receives information suggesting C originally entered with a preconceived intent to remain permanently (not permitted for F–1's). ICE brings removal proceedings. It alleges she is deportable under section 237(a)(1)(A) as having entered while inadmissible under sections 212(a)(6)(C)(i) (fraud) and 212(a)(7)(A) (not in possession of valid immigrant visa). Will section 237(a)(1)(H) be of use to her?

Problem 12. D, a noncitizen, marries a United States citizen. He obtains an immigrant visa and is admitted for conditional permanent residence on the basis of the marriage. Almost two years later, USCIS makes a finding pursuant to the Immigration Marriage Fraud Amendments that the marriage was genuine and still legally intact. Consequently, it removes the condition. A year after that, however, ICE is tipped off that the marriage has been a sham from its inception. It charges D with being deportable under INA § 237(a)(1)(A) for having entered while inadmissible under INA § 212(a)(6)(C)(i) (fraudulent visa and fraudulent admission). Will section 237(a)(1)(H) be useful to D?

Problem 13. Noncitizen E arrives at a United States port of entry and presents a counterfeit United States passport. She is admitted. A year later, she gives birth to a child in the United States. Two years after that, she is apprehended and the passport fraud is discovered. On what grounds will she be removable? Will she qualify for relief under INA § 237(a)(1)(H)?

3.   POST-ENTRY CONDUCT RELATED TO IMMIGRATION CONTROL

In this section on deportability grounds related to immigration control, the first two subsections dealt generally with defects in the noncitizen's entry. This third subsection concerns post-entry events.

One such ground is INA § 237(a)(1)(B), which describes any noncitizen who "is present in the United States in violation of this Act or any other law * * *." That language is sometimes invoked when a nonimmigrant violates the conditions of his or her stay—for example by overstaying or by working without authorization. Those kinds of violations simultaneously trigger INA § 237(a)(1)(C)(i) (failure to maintain, or to comply with the conditions of, one's nonimmigrant status.)

You will recall that, under IMFA, noncitizens admitted on the basis of certain marriages receive only conditional permanent residence for the first two years. INA § 216. The same is true under an analogous program for the conditional admittance of immigrant investors. INA § 216A. An immigrant whose conditional status was terminated under either program becomes deportable under INA § 237(a)(1)(D). This provision too can be thought of as reaching individuals who fail to comply with one particular condition on which they are admitted.

In the previous subsection, you saw that inadmissibility at the time of entry is a ground for deportability. INA § 237(a)(1)(A). The same provision makes deportable any noncitizen who was inadmissible at the time he or she received adjustment of status.

INA §§ 261–266 impose certain registration, address reporting, and other requirements on various classes of noncitizens present in the United States. See especially INA § 265(a) (noncitizens subject to registration requirement must report changes of address within ten days). Wilful violations of these requirements are criminal offenses, INA § 266, and can be grounds for deportability even without criminal convictions. INA § 266(b). As discussed more fully in chapter 10, section B.2, the government has rediscovered the registration provisions and is enforcing them far more vigorously in the wake of September 11.

Finally, INA § 237(a)(1)(E) covers certain cases of people-smuggling. A criminal conviction is not required. The Secretary of Homeland Security has the discretion to waive this ground for LPRs who assist only certain family members. INA § 237(a)(1)(E)(iii).

SECTION D.   CRIME-RELATED DEPORTABILITY GROUNDS

Criminal activity can affect a noncitizen's immigration status in various ways. It can constitute a ground for inadmissibility or a ground for deportability or both. It can destroy a person's statutory eligibility for various forms of affirmative relief from removal. It can determine whether a person will be detained while removal proceedings are pending. It can make a person ineligible for naturalization. And it can weigh against the favorable exercise of administrative discretion in a range of contexts.

The immigration consequences of criminal activity are complex, but there is a good deal of helpful literature. See especially Dan Kesselbrenner & Lory D. Rosenberg, National Lawyers Guild, Immigration Law and Crimes (originally published in 1984, updated periodically); Mary E. Kramer & Amy R. Novick (eds.), AILA, Immigration Consequences of Criminal Convictions in the Nineties: What Every Immigration and Criminal Lawyer Needs to Know (1995); Maryellen Fullerton & Noah Kinigstein, *Strategies for Ameliorating the Immigration Consequences of Criminal Convictions: A Guide for Defense Attorneys*, 23 American Criminal L.Rev. 425 (1986); Anna Marie Gallagher, *Immigration Consequences of Criminal Convictions: Protecting Your Client's Immigration Interests in Criminal Proceedings*, April 2001 Immigration Briefings; Lory Diana Rosenberg & Nelson Vargas–Padilla, *An Odyssey of Immigration Consequences of Crime: The BIA's 2001 Interpretations*, 78 IR 909 (June 4, 2001); Lory D. Rosenberg & Nelson Vargas–Padilla, *Immigration Consequences of Crimes on the Doorstep of the Twenty–First Century*, 77 IR 685 (May 26, 2000).

The link between immigration law and criminal law runs in two directions. Some scholars—most notably Professors Robert Pauw and Isabel Medina—have argued that criminal law has been increasingly invoked as a tool for enforcing immigration restrictions, see Maria Isabel Medina, *The Criminalization of Immigration Law: Employer Sanctions and Marriage Fraud*, 5 George Mason L. Rev. 669 (1997); Robert Pauw, *A New Look at Deportation as Punishment: Why at Least Some of the Constitution's Criminal Procedure Provisions Must Apply*, 52 Administrative L. Rev. 305 (2000). Conversely, Professor Nora Demleitner has called attention to the increasing use of immigration law as a tool for criminal law enforcement, see Nora V. Demleitner, *Immigration Threats and Rewards: Effective Law Enforcement Tools in the "War" on Terrorism*, 51 Emory L.J. 1059 (2002) (criticizing certain uses of immigration law as "adjunct" for criminal enforcement). For two careful analyses of how both these trends have come to characterize immigration "reform," see Teresa A. Miller, *Citizenship and Severity: Recent Immigration Reforms and the New Penology*, 17 Georgetown Immigration L.J. 611 (2003); Teresa A. Miller, *Blurring the*

Boundaries Between Immigration and Crime Control After September 11,
25 Boston College Third World L. Rev. 81 (2005).

Are immigrants prone to crime? A comprehensive study by the National Bureau of Economic Research suggests they are not. Because the vast bulk of criminal offenses are committed by young males, the study focused on men aged 18–40 in the United States. Within that group, the study found immigrants to be less likely, not more likely, to be institutionalized than the native-born "and much less likely to be institutionalized than native-born men with similar demographic characteristics." The same study found that recent immigrants are less likely than earlier immigrants to be institutionalized. Kristin F. Butcher & Anne Morrison Piehl, Recent Immigrants: Unexpected Implications for Crime and Incarceration, NBER Working Paper No. 6067, at i (June 1997).

Nonetheless, starting in the late 1980's, the subject of noncitizen criminals began to attract heightened public scrutiny and spur frenzied congressional activity. A stream of amendments has generally expanded the crime-related inadmissibility and deportability grounds, narrowed the availability of discretionary relief, added to the powers of law enforcement personnel, and abbreviated the procedures used in selected categories of crime-related removal cases. You will encounter most of those changes in this section and in the next two chapters. The various immigration authorities have responded in kind, redoubling their efforts to apprehend and remove noncitizens convicted of crimes. A record 79,395 noncitizens were removed on criminal grounds in 2003. See 2003 Yearbook of Immigration Statistics at 150.

Although the present concern is with the deportability *grounds* that hinge on criminal conduct, it will be convenient to include here the few affirmative defenses that are specific to the crime-related deportability grounds. The more generic affirmative defenses appear in the next chapter.

Before confronting some of the specific crime-related deportability grounds, you should now skim INA § 237(a)(2) to get a general sense of its coverage.

Have you ever wondered how ICE finds out that a noncitizen has been convicted of a crime? Sometimes the individual reveals the conviction when answering a specific question in an application form or in a personal interview. Sometimes an informant will provide a tip. In addition, ICE employs full-time investigators to ferret out noncitizens who have committed crimes. See generally Maryellen Fullerton & Noah Kinigstein, *Strategies for Ameliorating the Immigration Consequences of Criminal Convictions: A Guide for Defense Attorneys*, 23 American Criminal L. Rev. 425, 426–27 (1986) (now somewhat dated in its details). Moreover, under 42 U.S.C. § 3753(a)(11), any state that wants to receive federal drug control grants must agree to furnish to the immigration authorities, free of charge and within 30 days, certified records of conviction of all noncitizens who are convicted of crimes in that state. Still, despite the increased congressional attention, some commentators believe that the logistical barriers to removing high proportions of criminal noncitizens remain formidable. See generally Peter H. Schuck & John Williams, *Removing Criminal Aliens: The Pitfalls and Promises of Federalism*, 22 Harvard J. L. & Public Policy 367 (1999) (lamenting the slow pace of removal of noncitizen criminals, ascribing some of the obstacles to federalism, and urging greater use of state law enforcement personnel).

1.   WHAT IS A CONVICTION?

Common to several deportability grounds is a requirement that the person have been "convicted" of a crime. See, e.g., INA §§ 237(a)(2)(A)(i, ii, iii, iv), 237(a)(2)(B)(i), 237(a)(2)(C, D, E(1)), 237(a)(3)(B).

Defining "conviction" has been difficult, however, largely because in modern times both the federal government and the states have crafted various formulas for avoiding the harsh effects of criminal convictions— especially in cases of youthful offenders, first-time offenders, and lower-level crimes. In the immigration context, the BIA has frequently had to adapt its definition of "conviction" to the changes in federal and state criminal procedures. The history is summarized well in *Matter of Ozkok*, 19 I. & N. Dec. 546 (BIA 1988), and in *Matter of Punu*, 22 I. & N. Dec. 224 (BIA 1998) (Rosenberg dissent).

In 1996, Congress for the first time provided a statutory definition of "conviction" for purposes of the INA. It reads:

a formal judgment of guilt of the alien entered by a court or, if adjudication of guilt has been withheld, where

(i) a judge or jury has found the alien guilty or the alien has entered a plea of guilty or nolo contendere or has admitted sufficient facts to warrant a finding of guilt, and

(ii) the judge has ordered some form of punishment, penalty, or restraint on the alien's liberty to be imposed.

INA § 101(a)(48)(A), added by IIRIRA § 322(a)(1). For purposes of this definition, probation is punishment. *Matter of Punu*, 22 I. & N. Dec. 224, 228 (BIA 1998).

In many states, sentencing judges have the discretion to defer entry of final judgments of guilt in certain cases. Typically, the judge in such a case accepts a plea of guilty or nolo contendere or finds guilt, then orders the defendant to pay a fine and/or serve a period of probation, and, absent further problems, terminates the proceeding without ever entering a formal judgment of guilt. Before IIRIRA, many of those proceedings were held not to have resulted in "convictions." But after IIRIRA, the finding or admission of guilt, followed by an order of punishment, amounts to a conviction. See *Punu*, above.

The word "conviction" also implies a "crime." The so-called "civil offenses" do not qualify. In *Matter of Eslamizar*, 23 I. & N. Dec. 684 (BIA 2004), a noncitizen was found guilty of a "violation" under Oregon law. The Oregon procedure required proof only by a preponderance of the evidence, not beyond a reasonable doubt, and it provided no right to either counsel or a jury trial. The Board held that, to give rise to a conviction of a crime for immigration purposes, the procedure has to provide "the constitutional safeguards normally attendant upon a criminal conviction." The Oregon procedure for trying alleged "violations" did not meet that standard. In dictum, the Board exempted foreign convictions from that requirement; for them, the test is whether the foreign jurisdiction treats the proceeding as criminal.

Until IIRIRA, it was also clear that the immigration consequences of a conviction would not attach until the conviction was final. The leading case was *Pino v. Landon*, 349 U.S. 901, 75 S.Ct. 576, 99 L.Ed. 1239 (1955). The courts uniformly held that a conviction was not final while a direct appeal as of right was still pending. (Neither a discretionary appeal nor a collateral attack on the conviction precluded finality.) See, e.g., *Morales–Alvarado v. INS*, 655 F.2d 172, 175 (9th Cir. 1981). In *Punu*, however, over a strong dissent by Board Member Lory Rosenberg, the BIA interpreted IIRIRA as repealing the finality requirement. Consequently, the pendency of even a direct appeal as of right no longer relieves the defendant of the immigration consequences of a criminal conviction. See *Montenegro v. Ashcroft*, 355 F.3d 1035, 1037–38 (7th Cir. 2004); see generally Anna Marie Gallagher, *Immigration Consequences of Criminal Convictions: Protecting Your Client's Immigration Interests in Criminal Proceedings*, April 2001 Immigration Briefings 8–9.

Most of these issues can be lumped under the heading "Was there *ever* a conviction?" In many cases, however, the existence of a conviction is clear under any standard, and the question is whether subsequent events have erased that conviction for purposes of immigration.

While the validity of a criminal conviction may not be collaterally attacked *in removal proceedings*, see, e.g., *Zinnanti v. INS*, 651 F.2d 420, 421 (5th Cir.1981), there are post-conviction remedies that can be pursued *in the court that entered the conviction*. A full examination of those remedies is beyond the scope of this book, but a few are common enough in deportation cases to warrant consideration here. For a thorough treatment, see Dan Kesselbrenner & Lory D. Rosenberg, National Lawyers Guild, Immigration Law and Crimes (continually updated).

a.   WITHDRAWING GUILTY PLEAS

United States v. Parrino

United States Court of Appeals, Second Circuit, 1954.
212 F.2d 919.

■ HINCKS, CIRCUIT JUDGE.

* * * [The defendant] pleaded guilty to the second count of the indictment which charged a conspiracy to kidnap—an offense denounced by Section 1201(c) of the Code—whereupon the first count, charging commission of the substantive offense denounced by Section 1201(a), was dismissed with the consent of the United States Attorney. * * *

This motion, invoking Rule 32(d) of the Federal Rules of Criminal Procedure, seeks to vacate the judgment of conviction and to permit the defendant to withdraw his prior plea of guilty (on the strength of which a sentence of two years was imposed which now has been fully served) on the ground that he pleaded guilty only in reliance on the assurance of his counsel at the time that the plea would not have effect of subjecting him to deportation, and that now, notwithstanding that assurance, a deportation proceeding has been instituted against him, the validity of which depends upon the conviction which in turn depended solely upon his plea of guilty. Thus is presented the question whether on the underlying record it would constitute "manifest injustice" within the purview of Rule 32(d) to hold him to his plea and leave the judgment of conviction undisturbed.

Before proceeding to discuss this question we should state that the record on this appeal amply supports the finding below that in fact before changing his plea the defendant was indeed informed by the lawyer then representing him that a plea of guilty would not subject him to deportation. The pending motion is supported in that respect not only by affidavits of the defendant and his wife but also by the lawyer himself. And there is no dispute that this information, doubtless innocently made, was erroneous. Although there was no express finding by the court below that the defendant acted in reasonable reliance on this erroneous information, for purposes of this opinion we assume that that was so.

But even so, we think the order should be affirmed. Generally in criminal cases, the defendant's surprise as to the severity of sentence imposed after a plea of guilty, standing alone, is not such manifest injustice as to require vacation of the judgment and permission to withdraw a plea of guilty. True, when surprise stems from a misunderstanding, reasonably entertained, of remarks by the Judge himself, * * * or from assurances by the United States Attorney, it may be ground for post-conviction relief. But surprise, as in the instant case, which results from erroneous information received from the defendant's own attorney, at least without a clear showing of unprofessional conduct, is not enough.

Moreover, here the subject-matter of the claimed surprise was not the severity of the sentence directly flowing from the judgment but a collateral consequence thereof, namely, deportability. * * *

Doubtless there may frequently arise tax evasion cases in which after conviction on a plea of guilty the defendant is unpleasantly surprised when, confronted with a civil action for the recovery of the evaded taxes, he finds a defense foreclosed by his plea in the criminal cases. And after pleading guilty to an offense which, though of small dimensions, is classified as a felony, a defendant may be shocked to find that he has lost his civil rights,—or that, after his conviction has faded into the past, he is faced with loss of his employment because he can only answer in the affirmative some questionnaire demanding to know if he has ever been convicted of a felony. The writer of this opinion, during his tenure on the trial bench, was more than once consulted by young men, duly convicted on a plea of guilty to a comparatively small offense, who were distressed to find that a later consequence of their plea was ineligibility for enlistment in the armed services. We think it plainly unsound to hold, as now in principle we are urged to hold, that such defendants are subjected to manifest injustice, if held to their plea, merely because they did not understand or foresee such collateral consequences. * * *

* * *

Order affirmed.

■ FRANK, CIRCUIT JUDGE (dissenting).

* * *

The defendant before he pleaded guilty was primarily concerned, not with the length of the jail sentence that might be imposed, but with the question uppermost in his mind, whether as a consequence of being again sentenced, he could be deported. As previously noted, he addressed this question to his lawyer, a former Commissioner of Immigration, who unequivocally answered No. But for that answer, he would not have entered his plea of guilty which he now seeks to withdraw.

My colleagues say that to prevent "manifest injustice," such permission to withdraw a guilty plea must be granted if a defendant's surprise related to the length of his sentence and stemmed from defendant's reasonable misunderstanding of remarks made by the judge or by the prosecutor. But my colleagues hold (a) that surprise as to the grave consequences of a sentence—here deportation—does not have the same effect; and that, in any event, (b) it does not suffice that the surprise was induced by the advice of the defendant's own lawyer—even when, as here, that advice was so thoroughly wrong as, in itself, to disclose unmistakable glaring incompetence on the part of that lawyer. I disagree as to both (a) and (b). I shall discuss them in turn.

1. Deportation, while not literally constituting criminal punishment, may have far more dire effects on this defendant than his sentence of imprisonment for two years. For all practical purposes, the court sentenced him to serve (a) two years in jail and (b) the rest of his life in exile.[a] * * *

* * *

2. This is not a case of collateral attack on a judgment of conviction by way of habeas corpus or the like. In such cases, some (not all) courts have held there is no lack of due process because of defendant's counsel's gross incompetence, if his counsel was of defendant's choosing. But here the issue is not one of unconstitutionality. The issue is this: On a motion to vacate a conviction and withdraw a guilty plea, in order to permit defendant to go to trial, does the fact that the plea resulted from the grossly

a. At the time of this decision, a deportation order barred future readmission forever, unless the INS, in its discretion, granted permission to reapply for admission. The same result would occur today for Parrino, but only because his particular crime would qualify as an aggravated felony. INA § 212(a)(9)(A). Generally, the present statute prescribes a ten-year bar after removal from the interior. *Id.*—Ed.

erroneous advice to the defendant by his own lawyer render it "manifestly unjust" to leave the consequent conviction standing? Several courts have held that it does—and (contrary to my colleagues' suggestion) without any showing that the lawyer was guilty of what my colleagues call "unprofessional conduct" (which I assume means conduct justifying disbarment). * * *

In cases where a defendant on appeal from a conviction asks reversal on the ground that his lawyer made a mistake during the trial, many courts have denied relief unless the mistake was magnificent and clearly prejudiced defendant. Those courts in such cases seem to have felt (1) that what might seem to be a mistake, was part of the lawyer's deliberate tactics, or (2) that, in the heat of trial, some "errors of judgment" on the part of counsel, when under such pressure, are so likely often to occur that they should not invalidate a conviction. But here the lawyer's mistake did not occur during a trial; he was under no pressure whatever; there was no need for haste. And his error cannot conceivably be described as one involving merely "bad judgment."

The courts (as I have said) do reverse a conviction on appeal when defendant's counsel was hopelessly incompetent and the incompetence seriously prejudiced defendant. So, e.g., where counsel was unfamiliar with the rules of evidence, or did not know that "he could procure witnesses and have forcible process to obtain them in defendant's behalf."

That a lawyer who had served as a Commissioner of Immigration, even if he had been asked for a curbstone opinion only, should give advice flatly contrary to the deportation statute would be surprising enough. But when, with ample time to examine the statute, and a Supreme Court decision sustaining its validity, this lawyer did not do so and recklessly gave completely wrong advice, he was, beyond any possible doubt, egregiously derelict in the discharge of his duty to his client. Surely the courts have a considerable responsibility for the conduct of lawyers whom they admit to practice and whom they thereby invest with power to counsel laymen. To be sure, as my colleagues say, a court does not represent "that the members of its bar are infallible." But it does, I think, represent that they will not recklessly fail to read a statute before answering a single simple legal question. What is the sense of the constitutional requirement that defendant have counsel before pleading guilty, if the counsel be utterly without legal competence to guide his client? When a lawyer gives his client an erroneous opinion on a question the correct answer to which, by no stretch of the imagination, could be considered doubtful, and the client, relying on that opinion, enters a plea of guilty which will disastrously affect his future life, it is hard to understand how it can be maintained that "manifest injustice" has not occurred. If not, I wonder how manifest the injustice must be.

* * *

My colleagues, surprisingly, refer to cases in which a defendant who, *without any previous inquiry as to the consequences,* is convicted on a plea of guilty, later learns that, because of his conviction, he has lost his civil rights or is ineligible for enlistment in the armed services. What has any such case to do with this case where the defendant did inquire whether conviction could lead to a life of exile and received the answer that it could not, an answer given by his lawyer, who ought eminently to know how ridiculous that answer was?

We must not be gullible but must eye with due suspicion attempts to use the Rule to circumvent justice. But, as Cardinal de Retz observed, more men become dupes through fear of being taken in than through over-gullibility. As an earnest that this man is not playing a game with the court, not seeking by clever tricks to evade his just deserts, we have this striking fact: He has already served his two-year jail sentence. Yet he is willing to take the chance of a new trial, as a result of which, unless the jury acquits him, he will not be sent again to jail but to the death chair, so that the sentence he has served will count for nothing.

Sometimes a statute inescapably commands judges to conform to a legal ritual indifferent to justice. Then, regret it as we may, we judges must administer "injustice according to law." But we should regard such instances as exceptional, deplorable, and should not, generalizing from them, conclude that doing justice is not our role, that the "administration of justice" is an empty phrase not to be taken literally. When, therefore, a Rule tells us in the plainest words to avoid manifest injustice, I believe we should eagerly embrace the opportunity, not extend earlier decisions to escape it.

* * *

NOTES AND QUESTIONS

1. First, what do you think of the principle that, before accepting a guilty plea, the trial judge must advise the defendant of the direct consequences but not the collateral consequences? Second, what do you think of the rule that deportation is only a collateral consequence?

Today most courts subscribe to both propositions. See the long list of cases cited in *People v. Pozo*, 746 P.2d 523, 526 (Colo. 1987). For a potent attack on the collateral consequences rule (not just in the deportation context), see Gabriel J. Chin & Richard W. Holmes, *Effective Assistance of Counsel and the Consequences of Guilty Pleas*, 87 Cornell L. Rev. 697 (2002). For an analogous attack on the principle that deportation is a merely collateral consequence, see Lea McDermid, *Deportation is Different: Noncitizens and Ineffective Assistance of Counsel*, 89 California L. Rev. 741, 756–64 (2001).

2. As of 2003, somewhere between 18 and 21 states had passed laws that require either the sentencing judge or the defense attorney to advise the noncitizen defendant that a conviction might jeopardize his or her immigration status. See Attila Bogdan, *Guilty Pleas by Non–Citizens in Illinois: Immigration Consequences Reconsidered*, 53 DePaul L. Rev. 19, 49–50 (2003); John J. Francis, *Failure to Advise Non–Citizens of Immigra-*

tion Consequences of Criminal Convictions: Should This Be Grounds to Withdraw a Guilty Plea?, 36 Univ. Michigan J. L. Reform 691, 694 n.13 (2003); Christina LaBrie, *Lack of Uniformity in the Deportation of Criminal Aliens*, 25 NYU Rev. L. & Social Change 357, 373 n.93 (1999).

3.   A related theory for attacking convictions like those in *Parrino* is that the attorney's incompetence constituted ineffective assistance of counsel, in violation of the Sixth Amendment right to counsel in a criminal case. This subject is taken up separately chapter 9, § B.2.d below.

b. EXPUNGEMENTS

Under various federal and state statutes, it is sometimes possible to expunge criminal convictions. The statutes are diverse; some apply to youth offenders, others to first offenders, and still others to adults who have been sentenced to probation. Do such expungements erase the convictions for immigration purposes? A long line of cases has fashioned complex rules that hinge on whether the statute is state or federal, whether it is for adults or youth offenders, and whether the conviction is a crime involving moral turpitude, a drug offense, a firearms offense, or some other crime.

Much of the case law developed before 1996. In that year, Congress added to the INA a specific definition of "conviction," INA § 101(a)(48)(A), as you have seen. The definition for the most part tracked the language of the then most recent BIA decisions. In a dramatic shift, the BIA in 1999 interpreted the new statutory language to mean that expungement under a state rehabilitative statute never erases the conviction for immigration purposes. *Matter of Roldan*, 22 I. & N. Dec. 512 (BIA 1999). The Board based its decision on what it believed to be the plain language of the statutory conviction definition and on the congressional purpose of promoting uniform results from state to state. There were two strong dissents. For an effective criticism, see James A.R. Nafziger & Michael Yimesgen, *The Effect of Expungement on Removability of Non–Citizens*, 36 Univ. Michigan J. L. Reform 915 (2003). The BIA has since recognized one narrow exception, for expungements under state statutes that correspond to federal juvenile delinquency provisions. See *Matter of Devison*, 22 I. & N. Dec. 1362 (BIA 2000).

What happens if a final judgment of conviction is entered, but the judgment is reversed or vacated because of a flaw in the original proceeding? It might seem obvious that such a conviction does not suffice for removal purposes, and the Attorney General has so indicated. *Matter of Marroquin–Garcia*, 23 I. & N. Dec. 705, 713 (A.G. 2005) (statutory definition of "conviction" is "clearly not intended to encompass convictions that have been formally entered but subsequently reversed on appeal or in a collateral proceeding for reasons pertaining to the factual basis for, or procedural validity of, the underlying judgment"). To reconcile that result with the definition provided by INA § 101(a)(48)(A), the Attorney General concluded that in such a case there would simply be no formal adjudication of guilt. See also *Sandoval v. INS*, 240 F.3d 577 (7th Cir. 2001); *Matter of Pickering*, 23 I. & N. Dec. 621 (BIA 2003); *Matter of Rodriguez–Ruiz*, 22 I. & N. Dec. 1378 (BIA 2000); see generally Lory Diana Rosenberg, *Recogni-*

tion of Vacation of Conviction and Matter of Pickering: Comity or Tragedy?, 8 BIB 1103 (July 1, 2003).

In what can only be described as a caricature of judicial formalism, one court—the Fifth Circuit—has held otherwise. In *Discipio v. Ashcroft*, 369 F.3d 472 (5th Cir. 2004), the court held that even a conviction that is reversed because of flaws in the underlying original judgment survives for purposes of removal. The court acknowledged that that result defied both common sense and the statute itself, *id.* at 473, but felt bound to reach that conclusion because one of its prior decisions, *Renteria-Gonzalez v. INS*, 322 F.3d 804 (5th Cir. 2002), while admittedly presenting a different issue (whether vacating a conviction on equitable grounds for the apparent purpose of avoiding removal eliminates the conviction) had used broad language which, literally read, would extend to reversals on the merits. Under those circumstances, the *Discipio* panel said, it was powerless to distinguish *Renteria-Gonzalez* on the facts; only the full court sitting en banc or the Supreme Court could do that. It is hard to imagine that the *Discipio* ruling will last for long.

The federal First Offender Act (the FFOA) permits expungements of convictions of simple possession of narcotics by first-time offenders. Before IIRIRA, it was clear that federal first offender expungements eliminated the convictions for removal purposes. At least two courts have expressly declined to decide that issue. *Acosta v. Ashcroft*, 341 F.3d 218, 224 (3d Cir. 2003); *Gill v. Ashcroft*, 335 F.3d 574, 578–79 (7th Cir. 2003). On the assumption that the FFOA exception survives IIRIRA, the question has arisen whether the same is true of expungements under similar *state* statutes. The Ninth Circuit has held that it is, reasoning that to recognize federal expungements while withholding recognition from similar state expungements would be irrational and, therefore, violative of equal protection. *Lujan-Armendariz v. INS*, 222 F.3d 728 (9th Cir. 2000). The courts in *Acosta* and *Gill*, above, disagree, holding that under IIRIRA's statutory definition of conviction, a conviction survives the state equivalent of an FFOA expungement; *cf. Vasquez-Velezmoro v. USINS*, 281 F.3d 693 (8th Cir. 2002) (conviction survives at least in the case where the defendant's sentence exceeded the maximum that would have been allowable under the analogous federal law). The BIA also disagrees with the Ninth Circuit view and has announced it will not apply it except in Ninth Circuit cases. *Matter of Salazar–Regino*, 23 I. & N. Dec. 223 (BIA 2002).

The Attorney General has declined to decide the continued viability of either the FFOA exception or its state equivalents. *Matter of Marroquin–Garcia*, 23 I. & N. Dec. 705, 717 (A.G. 2005). He has now held, however, that, at least when a conviction does *not* involve first-time simple possession of narcotics, the federal definition "encompasses convictions ... that have been vacated or set aside under an expungement statute for reasons that do not go to the legal propriety of the original judgment, and that continue to impose some restraints or penalties upon the defendant's liberty." *Id.* at 705. The same now appears to be true in the Ninth Circuit, where the court declined to recognize an expungement entered pursuant to a general adult expungement statute. *Murillo-Espinoza v. INS*, 261 F.3d 771 (9th Cir. 2001).

Finally, in *Dillingham v. INS*, 267 F.3d 996 (9th Cir. 2001), the Ninth Circuit gave effect to a *foreign* expungement of a drug conviction, where the person would have qualified for expungement under the U.S. federal First Offenders Act had the violation been one of United States federal law. The court reached that result on equal protection grounds, finding no rational basis for recognizing United States federal and state expungements while refusing to recognize foreign expungements.

QUESTIONS

1.   As a policy matter, should expungements erase *any* criminal convictions, for purposes of deportability?

2.   How do the philosophical premises for recognizing at least certain expungements compare with the philosophical premises that underlie the definition of "conviction" in INA § 101(a)(48)(A)?

c.   EXECUTIVE PARDONS

Under INA § 237(a)(2)(A)(v), a Presidential or gubernatorial pardon eliminates deportability under § 237(a)(2)(A), which covers moral turpitude crimes, aggravated felonies, and convictions of high-speed flight from immigration checkpoints. There is no analogous provision for the other crime-related deportability grounds.

d.   MISCELLANEOUS COLLATERAL ATTACKS

Collateral attacks on criminal convictions can take a variety of other forms as well. See, e.g., Ira P. Robbins, *The Revitalization of the Common Law Civil Writ of Audita Querela as a Post–Conviction Remedy in Criminal Cases: The Immigration Context and Beyond*, 6 Georgetown Immigration L.J. 643, 672–87 (1992). The old writ of error "coram nobis" can sometimes be used to vacate a criminal conviction because of error at trial. See Julie M. Song, *In re L: Overcoming an Aggravated Felony Conviction through the Common Law Remedy of Coram Nobis*, 77 IR 993 (July 24, 2000).

2.   CRIMES INVOLVING MORAL TURPITUDE

INA §§ 237(a)(2)(A)(i and ii) cover certain noncitizens who have been convicted of one or more crimes involving "moral turpitude." The issues here are multitudinous; these materials provide only a sampling. Read both subsections now.

a.   THE MEANING OF "CRIME INVOLVING MORAL TURPITUDE"

Marciano v. INS

United States Court of Appeals, Eighth Circuit, 1971.
450 F.2d 1022.

■ VAN OOSTERHOUT, CIRCUIT JUDGE.

* * *

* * * Petitioner admits that he was convicted of statutory rape in violation of Minnesota Statutes Annot. § 609.295(4), that he was sentenced to three-years imprisonment and that his conviction was affirmed by the Supreme Court of Minnesota on April 3, 1969. He contends, however, that such conviction does not form a basis for deportation for the reasons hereinafter stated.

* * *

I.

Petitioner's first contention that the phrase "crime involving moral turpitude" as defined in the deportation statute lacks sufficient standards to justify deportation and is therefor [sic] unconstitutional for vagueness has been rejected by the Supreme Court in Jordan v. DeGeorge. We are foreclosed by that decision from considering the constitutional issue urged.

II.

We are satisfied that petitioner's second contention to the effect that the statutory rape offense of which he was convicted is not a crime involving moral turpitude lacks merit. Minnesota Statutes Annot. § 609.295(4), the criminal statute under which petitioner was convicted, reads:

"Whoever has sexual intercourse with a female child under the age of 18 years and not his spouse may be sentenced as follows:

* * *

(4) if the child is 16 years of age but under the age of 18 years and the offender is 21 years of age or older, by imprisonment for not more than three years."

* * *

The Minnesota Supreme Court * * * holds that criminal intent is not an element of an offense against a minor under the age of consent and that an honest belief of the accused that the victim had reached the age of consent when in fact she had not constitutes no defense. * * *

* * *

* * * Marciano was told by his victim that she was fifteen or sixteen years of age prior to the commission of the offense, that the petitioner had sexual intercourse with the victim on the date charged, and that petitioner was the aggressor. * * *

Federal courts [and the BIA—Ed.] have consistently held that statutory rape is a crime involving moral turpitude. * * *

* * *

The deportation order is affirmed.

■ GARNETT THOMAS EISELE, DISTRICT JUDGE (dissenting).

I must dissent from the opinion of the majority.[1] I feel that a proper reading of the phrase "crime involving moral turpitude", contained in INA § 241(a)(4), would require that the case be returned to the Board of Immigration Appeals to determine if the petitioner's criminal conduct here did or did not, factually, "involve moral turpitude." * * *

* * * What might be called the "traditional" rule of construction of this phrase was expressed well by Judge Learned Hand:

> "Neither the immigration officials, nor we, may consider the circumstances under which the crime was in fact committed. When by its definition it does not necessarily involve moral turpitude, the alien cannot be deported because in the particular instance his conduct was immoral."

Other decisions make it clear that the "definition" of the crime referred to in this statement of the rule includes the terms of the statute, any definitive construction of it by state courts, and the language of the indictment or information. The Service and reviewing courts, in following this approach, must determine whether *all* hypothetically possible criminal conduct, falling within those limits, *must necessarily* involve moral turpitude. If it does, the alien may be deported; if not, he may not be.[2] This rule is followed in the Second, Seventh, Ninth and District of Columbia Circuits, and probably in the Fifth Circuit as well.

* * * The reason stated for the rule, when a rationale is given, is one of practical administrative convenience. It is said, probably correctly, that it would be extremely difficult and time-consuming for the Immigration Service to examine into the factual context of every conviction sustained by an alien to see whether moral turpitude was, or was not, present in the circumstances of the particular crime as committed. In addition, examples are often given of conduct clearly criminal, but which would just as clearly not have involved moral turpitude. To relieve the Service of a heavy factfinding burden, and to prevent miscarriages of justice in instances where the conduct did not involve moral turpitude, five Circuits have said that the crime as charged must under all possible sets of circumstances necessarily involve moral turpitude before the alien can be deported. Under this rule, it does not matter how clear it is that the particular petitioner-

---

1. Petitioner also states in his brief that aliens are not being dealt with according to any uniform standards applicable generally across the country. This is true. For example, in the present case, the information charged that the girl was sixteen at the time of the violation of Minnesota's laws. The two could have engaged in the act of intercourse in any one of twenty-seven states without Marciano being subject to prosecution for "statutory rape". In any of those states, he would not have committed this crime, and thus Congress' requirements for deportation would not have been met. * * *

2. This rule could be supported by the grammatical structure of the statute, as could the one I advocate in this opinion. I do not believe that prior decisions have made an analysis of the grammar as such. Here "crime" in the phrase "crime involving moral turpitude" could be interpreted with reference to: (1) the statutory or common law statement; or (2) the facts alleged to constitute the violation. My view is that the statutory or common law statement cannot constitute a "crime". The crime must consist in the *acts* in violation of that legal statement.

alien did indeed engage in morally turpitudinous conduct. In fact, the Service and the courts, using this approach, are barred from inquiring into the facts of any individual case and can only look at the indictment, the language of the statute, and court decisions construing same.

More recently, however, the First Circuit has criticized the traditional rule and adopted a somewhat different one. That court, in Pino v. Nicolls, 215 F.2d 237 (1954), indicated its view that the accurate application of the older rule would practically emasculate § 241(a)(4):

> "[I]t is possible to conceive of circumstances under which almost any crime might be committed for the purest of motives, motives, however, which the law does not accept as a defense."

This criticism seems to me entirely valid, and I would add the additional observation that the criticized rule must certainly have resulted in the permitting of any number of aliens who had indeed committed crimes involving moral turpitude to remain in this country. I cannot believe that Congress intended for such persons to be allowed to remain simply because there might have been no moral turpitude in the commission by other individuals (real or hypothetical) of crimes described by the wording of the same statute under an identical indictment.

This Court, in its opinion today, appears to implicitly agree that the traditional rule is not the best one.[4] Certainly it has not followed it. Rather, it appears to adopt and follow the rationale stated in Pino v. Nicolls:

> "If the crime in its general nature is one which in common usage would be classified as a crime involving moral turpitude, neither the administrative officials in a deportation proceeding nor the courts on review of administrative action are under the oppressive burden of taking and considering evidence of the circumstances of a particular offense so as to determine whether there were extenuating circumstances which might relieve the offender of the stigma of moral obliquity."

The majority here takes the same approach, and this is the point at which my disagreement begins.

I cannot agree that Pino v. Nicolls adopted the best rule when it asked that the Service and the reviewing courts look only to the "general nature" of the crime and its classification in "common usage". Congress did not decree deportation where there was a conviction of a crime which "generally" or "commonly" involves moral turpitude. It said that deportation was the consequence when the crime involved moral turpitude, and I can only assume that it meant when moral turpitude was in fact involved.

There are many instances in which the application of the Pino v. Nicolls rule would itself result in a miscarriage of justice. There are the cases cited by Judge Anderson in his dissent in Tillinghast v. Edmead, 31

---

4. If the "traditional" rule were to be followed here, the decision of the Board of Immigration Appeals, in my opinion, would have to be reversed and Marciano discharged from the effect of the deportation order.

F.2d 81 (1st Cir.1929), of a mother stealing milk for her hungry child, of a "foolish college student" stealing a sign, and of a boy stealing an apple from an orchard; and there is the situation posed by Judge Learned Hand of a boy's forcing his way into a vacant building. There are, of course, literally hundreds of other examples that could be given. All of these hypothetical situations are crimes, involving criminal intent and criminal culpability. All of them could result in deportation under the rule of Pino v. Nicolls, and of the majority here, because such crimes as larceny, burglary, and breaking and entering "usually", "commonly" and "generally" involve moral turpitude. None of them can be said to involve moral turpitude, however; not, at least, without further examination into the factual context. It might be that today some crimes would be held to involve moral turpitude which judges writing in past years did not think contravened the moral standards of that time. The converse might be true with regard to other types of offenses. The point is that I do not believe Congress intended for all aliens in these, and many other hypothetical situations, [to] be deported. The statute says deportation shall follow *when the crime committed involves moral turpitude,* not when that type of crime "commonly" or "usually" does.

It seems obvious, therefore, that both the "traditional" rule and the Pino v. Nicolls rule produce results contrary to those intended by the plain language of the deportation statute. The Pino v. Nicolls rule, in addition, mandates the extremely severe consequence of deportation from this country in at least some instances which may admittedly (by its very hypothesis) result in gross miscarriages of justice. The rule I think preferable has, as far as I am aware, been stated at the appellate levels only in the dissent in Tillinghast v. Edmead, *supra.* Judge Anderson there quoted the lower court opinion and urged it upon his colleagues. I will do the same here:

> "Whether any particular conviction involves moral turpitude under this test may be a question of fact. Some crimes are of such character as necessarily to involve this element; others * * * do not; and still others might involve it or might not. As to this last class the circumstances must be regarded to determine whether moral turpitude was shown."

Perhaps the Pino v. Nicolls analysis ("it is possible to conceive of circumstances under which almost any crime might be committed for the purest of motives") is so universally applicable that it would completely eliminate the first of these three categories of crimes, but that for present purposes is immaterial. I think the three-classification approach is the most appropriate one, however nearly all-inclusive the "might or might not" class may be.

* * *

Since moral turpitude is different from criminality, the statute seems to require that that element be assessed separately. Undoubtedly it is difficult for the Service to make continual determinations of the nation's shifting and often indistinct moral standards. Nevertheless, it seems to me that such determinations are what the law requires. Considerations of administrative convenience should certainly be secondary to the determination and enforcement of the obvious legislative intent. It may or may not be wise to charge an administrative agency with this sort of duty, but Congress has done so and the Supreme Court has said that the standard provided is sufficiently definite that administrators will be able to apply it.

* * *

At the time of Marciano's original guilty plea, Minnesota law required only two elements to be shown to sustain a conviction under its statutory rape statute: an act of intercourse, and the statutorily prescribed age of the girl. Defenses such as the previous unchaste character of the girl, reasonable mistake as to age, a marriage which the parties thought they had contracted in the past but which was void for some technical defect,[6] all of which are available as defenses to at least some other states' "statutory rape" laws, were no bar in Minnesota to prosecution or conviction. Neither, of course, was the consent of the girl to the act. * * *

No one can reasonably say that every act warranting conviction under a statute such as Minnesota's would necessarily constitute a crime involving moral turpitude. I do not think, therefore, that this crime can be put into the first classification suggested by Ex parte Edmead, with Mr. Marciano consequently deported without a factual determination ever having been made as to the presence or absence of moral turpitude.

* * *

I must concede that the four judicial, and the one administrative, decisions cited by the majority, along with several others, are unanimous in holding "statutory rape" to be a crime involving moral turpitude without regard to the actual, factual context. I also concede, arguendo, that such crimes "usually" and "commonly" involve moral turpitude.[7] The particular decisions reveal very little about the nature of the offenses as defined by the separate states' laws or about the circumstances surrounding the crimes as committed by the particular individuals in those cases. With knowledge of such matters I might, or might not, have agreed with the results reached in those decisions. However, to the extent that they hold

---

6. This situation is clearly possible under the Minnesota statute. A man over twenty-one and a girl over sixteen, with the consent of her parents, may legally marry. If such a couple went through a marriage ceremony which they thought was valid, but which was not because, say, the person performing the ceremony was not licensed properly, the man might nevertheless be convicted under the Act if he had intercourse with his assumed "wife" on their assumed "honeymoon" because the girl would not be "his spouse" and thus excepted under the Act. See Minn.Statutes Anno. § 609.295(4).

7. Actually, the validity of such an assumption is doubtful at best. It would certainly be true if we were dealing with Delaware's statutory rape law, which sets the age of consent at seven years, or with the laws of a state setting it at ten, or twelve. Minnesota, however, is among the states with the highest ages of consent, and the proposition assumed above for argument's sake is extremely tenuous when speaking of a state statute that includes young women a few days short of their eighteenth birthday within its prohibition.

the factual context irrelevant, and to the extent that they hold that every hypothetically possible instance of intercourse with an underage female must of necessity involve moral turpitude, I must disagree with them. I might be inclined to a different view if fornication and adultery were held in all instances to involve moral turpitude, but such is not the case. I believe the appellation, the short title, of the crime (particularly the word "rape") has had a tendency to mislead courts in the past. I seriously doubt that in today's society an instance of consensual intercourse *necessarily* involves moral turpitude just because the state in which the act took place has raised the age of consent to eighteen years. * * *

In summary, the "traditional" rule would prevent the deportation of many persons who had committed crimes actually involving moral turpitude. On the other hand, under the rule of Pino v. Nicolls, now apparently followed by this Court, persons committing crimes *not* involving moral turpitude may be deported if such crimes are *generally* ones that, when committed, involve moral turpitude. It seems unlikely that Congress intended either result.

* * *

NOTES AND QUESTIONS

1. The court first dismisses, as precluded by the Supreme Court decision in *Jordan v. DeGeorge,* the argument that the statutory phrase "moral turpitude" is unconstitutionally vague. Surfacing most commonly in the criminal context, the doctrine that statutory language must not be unduly vague stems from fairness concerns that are part of procedural due process. See, e.g., *Palmer v. City of Euclid,* 402 U.S. 544, 91 S.Ct. 1563, 29 L.Ed.2d 98 (1971). Before leaving this portion of *Marciano,* try to figure out (a) precisely what it is about vague statutes that makes them unfair, and (b) whether those objections apply to the provision that makes conviction of a "moral turpitude" crime a deportability ground.

2. The dissenting opinion of Judge Eisele suggests three different views of what Congress meant by the requirement that the "crime" involve moral turpitude—the traditional view, the view of the majority opinion in *Marciano,* and the view of the dissent. Articulate all three views and then identify the pros and cons of each.

3. Is Judge Eisele correct to assume that the *Marciano* majority implicitly adopted the *Pino* formulation?

4. This issue has produced more than its share of confusion. In *Matter of R,* 6 I. & N. Dec. 444 (1954), where the BIA explicitly adopted the traditional view, this sentence appears: "If we find that violation of the law under any and all circumstances involves moral turpitude, then we *must* conclude that *all* convictions under that law involved moral turpitude although the 'particular acts evidence no immorality' " (emphasis in original). *Id.* at 448. Does the "although" clause make sense?

5. How does the *Pino* view, which the dissent ascribes to the *Marciano* majority, actually work? What is meant by "common usage?" Is this an appeal to the sense of the community? If so, what community? Is the court expected to seek out the gut instincts of the "reasonable person" whom you came to know and admire in torts? Is deportation ultimately to be decided by the rider on the Clapham omnibus?

6. In theory, the vast majority of courts today subscribe to the traditional rule. See, e.g., *Knapik v. Ashcroft*, 384 F.3d 84 (3d Cir. 2004). In practice, it is difficult to see how some of the crimes that have been held to involve moral turpitude (see especially the larceny hypotheticals cited in the dissent) could possibly be said to involve moral turpitude in *all* the fact situations that those crimes could conceivably embrace. Do the courts truly mean to suggest that the "mother stealing milk for her hungry child" has acted not only criminally but with moral turpitude as well?

7. The three views discussed up to this point go to the question of *what* must involve moral turpitude—the crime in the abstract, the actual conduct of the particular defendant, or something in between. Under any of those views, there remains the question of what "moral turpitude" means. The leading definition is "an act of baseness, vileness, or depravity in the private and social duties which a man owes to his fellow men, or to society in general, contrary to the accepted and customary rule of right and duty between man and man." *Marciano*, 450 F.2d at 1025. Apart from its archaic gendered language, the weakness in this definition lies in its probably unavoidable level of generality. How does a court determine whether an act is base, vile, or depraved? (Is the disjunctive to be taken literally? Can an act be vile and depraved without being base?) Does this formulation have religious connotations? Should a court ask whether a given act violates the Ten Commandments? Whether the sin is cardinal rather than venial? What, in other words, does this definition add to the phrase "moral turpitude?"

8. Along the same lines, by whose standards is moral turpitude to be judged? This question has several dimensions: Is it the court's moral standards or those of the community? If the latter, then which community—national, state, local, ethnic? And what is the pertinent time period for assessing social mores? Should a court go by the values prevailing at the time the phrase "moral turpitude" first appeared in an immigration statute? (The phrase first emerged in an exclusion provision. See Act of March 3, 1891, ch. 551, § 1, 26 Stat. 1084.) The last time the deportation provision was amended? The last time the INA was amended? The time of the conduct that gave rise to the crime? The time of the removal hearing? Which of these options would you select? The BIA position is that "contemporary moral standards" are the governing criteria. *Matter of Torres-Varela*, 23 I. & N. Dec. 78 (BIA 2001).

9. The accumulated case law now provides a fairly detailed catalog of crimes that do, and crimes that do not, involve moral turpitude. Certain patterns emerge: Crimes that involve fraud or intent to defraud are almost always classified as moral turpitude crimes. Simple assault generally does

not involve moral turpitude, but aggravated forms of assault (e.g. assault with a deadly weapon, assault with intent to kill, etc.) generally do. So do murder and voluntary manslaughter, but involuntary manslaughter ordinarily does not, unless the particular statute requires "reckless" conduct, *Franklin v. INS*, 72 F.3d 571 (8th Cir. 1995). If a crime does not involve moral turpitude, then repeated convictions of the same offense do not give rise to moral turpitude even if a statute makes a repeat performance an "aggravated" offense. *Matter of Torres–Varela*, 23 I. & N. Dec. 78 (BIA 2001) (aggravated driving under the influence). In contrast, aggravated driving under the influence can be a crime involving moral turpitude if defined to require knowledge that one's license has been suspended because of prior offenses. *Matter of Lopez–Meza*, 22 I. & N. Dec. 1188 (BIA 1999). For lists of which crimes have been held to involve moral turpitude and which have not, see 6 Gordon, Mailman & Yale–Loehr § 71.05[1][d][iii]; Norton Tooby, *Sourcelist of Cases Defining "Crimes of Moral Turpitude" under the Immigration and Nationality Act*, http://www.criminalandimmigrationlaw.com/cmt/cmt.html.

10.   A separate deportability ground is conviction of an "aggravated felony." INA § 237(a)(2)(A)(iii), discussed in § D.4 below. As you will see, courts use the same categorical approach when classifying crimes as aggravated felonies as they do when classifying crimes as involving moral turpitude.

PROBLEMS 14–16[1]

Which of the following individuals have been convicted of crimes involving moral turpitude? For each, apply all three of the views discussed by Judge Eisele.

Problem 14. A committed a mercy killing. She took the life of her father, who had been in the final weeks of a clearly fatal disease and who had been suffering intense physical pain. She was convicted of voluntary manslaughter.

Problem 15. A state statute makes it a crime to receive property if the person "knows or should have known that said property is stolen." B was charged with that offense. At trial, a prosecution witness testified she had overheard the defendant saying he had known all along the property had been stolen. The defendant denied having made that statement. The jury found him guilty, and a judgment of conviction was entered.

Problem 16. C, arrested after a brutal beating of his wife, was charged with assault with intent to kill. The jury found him guilty of a lesser charge, simple assault. At the removal hearing, the immigration judge made a finding that C in fact had harbored an intent to kill.

1. As discussed in § D.4 below, conviction of an "aggravated felony" is an independent ground for deportability; no showing of moral turpitude is required. INA § 237(a)(2)(A)(iii). The crimes committed in this set of Problems might or might not be aggravated felonies, depending on the sentencing. For purposes of this exercise, assume they are not. Under that assumption, the moral turpitude issues are not moot.

b. "COMMITTED WITHIN FIVE YEARS ... AFTER THE DATE OF ADMISSION"

Read INA § 237(a)(2)(A)(i) carefully before doing the following Problems:

PROBLEMS 17–18

Problem 17. X was admitted to the United States as an LPR in February 2001. In December 2005 he was arrested on charges of state income tax fraud (in the amount of $3,000), punishable in this jurisdiction by up to five years in state prison. At a jury trial in March 2006 he was found guilty and a judgment of conviction was entered. He was sentenced to six months in county jail. Assume this jurisdiction holds that this crime involves moral turpitude. Is X deportable?

Problem 18. Y was admitted to the United States as an LPR on November 16, 1999. In December 2004 he went to Bangladesh to visit his relatives and to start up a business that would export gift items to the United States. When he returned ten months later, in October 2005, he was greeted by the local sheriff and arrested on charges of petit larceny, a crime punishable in this jurisdiction by up to one year of confinement. The subsequent indictment alleged that the acts constituting the larceny had occurred "on or about November 15, 2004." In January 2006, Y was convicted of petit larceny and sentenced to six months in jail. Is he deportable?

c. SENTENCING REQUIREMENTS

One other requirement under section 237(a)(2)(A)(i) is that "a sentence of one year or longer *may* be imposed" (emphasis added). That language reflects a change introduced by AEDPA § 435 in 1996. Before then, only a person actually sentenced to a year or more would be deportable on this ground. INA § 241(a)(2)(A)(i)(II) (pre–1996 version). Now, *potential* punishment is what counts for this purpose.

d. TWO CRIMES INVOLVING MORAL TURPITUDE

A separate deportability ground, INA § 237(a)(2)(A)(ii), reaches noncitizens who after admission have been convicted of two crimes involving moral turpitude "not arising out of a single scheme of criminal misconduct," regardless of how many years after admission and regardless of the nature or length of the sentence. The quoted phrase is not defined in the statute, and the courts have essentially divided into two camps.

In *Pacheco v. INS*, 546 F.2d 448 (1st Cir.1976), the First Circuit held that, to constitute a single scheme, the crimes "must take place at one time; there must be no substantial interruption that would allow the participant to disassociate himself from his enterprise and reflect on what he has done." *Id.* at 451. Applying that test, the court in *Pacheco* found that two break-ins separated by two days did not arise out of a "single scheme." The BIA approved the *Pacheco* approach in *Matter of Adetiba*, 20 I. & N.Dec. 506 (BIA 1992), and several other circuits have followed suit. See *Adetiba*, 20 I. & N.Dec. at 508–12 and cases cited therein.

The Ninth Circuit rejects *Pacheco* and *Adetiba*. Emphasizing that the statute refers to a single *scheme* rather than to a single *act*, the court in *Gonzalez–Sandoval v. U.S. INS*, 910 F.2d 614 (9th Cir.1990), held it sufficient that the two crimes "were planned at the same time and executed in accordance with that plan." *Id.* at 616. The Second Circuit had earlier reached a similar conclusion in *Nason v. INS*, 394 F.2d 223, 227 (2d Cir. 1968). More recently, however, in *Michel v. INS*, 206 F.3d 253 (2d Cir. 2000), the Second Circuit expressly left open whether *Nason* has been superseded by *Chevron USA, Inc. v. NRDC, Inc.*, 467 U.S. 837, 843–44, 104 S.Ct. 2778, 81 L.Ed.2d 694 (1984), where the Supreme Court held that a court must defer to a "reasonable" interpretation of a statute by an administrative agency charged with implementing it. The majority opinion in *Michel* concluded that the two crimes it was considering would not be part of a "single scheme" under either of the competing formulations and thus decided not to reach the issue of which test should be adopted. Judge Cabranes, in a concurring opinion, would have taken on the issue and would have chosen the BIA's narrower view of "single scheme." *Michel*, 206 F.3d at 267.

Read INA § 237(a)(2)(A)(ii) and then do the following Problem:

PROBLEM 19

X, a noncitizen, was admitted to the United States as an LPR on June 14, 2000. On October 7, 2005, X was tried on two counts of bribing a public official, a crime punishable by up to ten years in prison. The evidence showed that X had given the head of the city licensing division $1000 in cash to secure a liquor license for one of X's two restaurants, and that later that same day X had returned to give the same official another $1000 to obtain a liquor license for the other restaurant. Several weeks later a secretary who had witnessed both exchanges came forward. She was able to testify at trial that the exchanges had taken place in June 2005, though she could not recall the exact date. X was convicted on both counts and, because of some unusually sympathetic circumstances, received concurrent sentences of only six months. Is X deportable?

e. JUDICIAL RECOMMENDATIONS AGAINST DEPORTATION

Until the Immigration Act of 1990, the law provided an important remedy known as the "judicial recommendation against deportation." Immigration lawyers generally used the acronym "JRAD" (pronounced "jay-rad"). It applied only to those noncitizens who were otherwise deportable under the predecessor of INA §§ 237(a)(2)(A)(i) (conviction of one crime involving moral turpitude) or 237(a)(2)(A)(ii) (two or more such crimes)—not, for example, to anyone deportable because of drug offenses (discussed below). Under former INA § 241(b)(2) the sentencing judge, at the time of sentencing or within thirty days thereafter, could make a "recommendation" that the person not be deported. Before deciding whether to issue the recommendation, the judge had to give the prosecution and the former INS "due notice" and an opportunity to be heard. Despite its name, a properly issued JRAD was more than just helpful advice; it *prohibited* the INS from deporting the person on the basis of the particular crime.

These timing and notice requirements were rigidly interpreted. In many cases, neither the criminal defense lawyer nor the judge had ever heard of JRADs, and it was only after the INS had initiated deportation proceedings and the noncitizen had engaged an immigration lawyer that the the criminal court learned of the existence of this remedy. By then, the 30–day time period had long since elapsed. Sentencing judges who believed that the facts of particular cases warranted clemency attempted to issue late JRADs, but the courts and the BIA were virtually unanimous in rejecting those attempts. See, e.g., *Velez–Lozano v. INS,* 463 F.2d 1305, 1308 (D.C.Cir.1972) ("troubled by a deportation that will now occur because of failings in the trial judge and petitioner's trial counsel," but feeling bound to invalidate the JRAD); *United States ex rel. Piperkoff v. Esperdy,* 267 F.2d 72 (2d Cir.1959) (sentencing judge may not avoid 30–day limit by vacating criminal conviction, entering new judgment, and then issuing JRAD within 30 days of new judgment); *Matter of M.G.,* 5 I. & N. Dec. 531 (BIA 1953) (criminal defense lawyer requested JRAD in time, but judge was on vacation and returned after 30–day period had expired; late JRAD held invalid). Occasionally, a sentencing judge would hold that the defense lawyer's failure to request a JRAD constituted ineffective assistance of counsel, vacate the sentence on that ground, pronounce a new sentence, and at the same time issue a JRAD. One court upheld a JRAD issued under those circumstances. *Janvier v. United States,* 793 F.2d 449 (2d Cir.1986).

The Immigration Act of 1990, § 505, repealed the JRAD provision. The repeal was retroactive to the extent that it prohibited courts from issuing future JRADs even in connection with pre–1990 *convictions. Id.* § 505(b). Under the interpretation of the former INS, however, the repeal provision does not destroy the validity of pre–1990 *JRADs.* See 8 C.F.R. §§ 240.10(d), 240.48(c) (2001); *Renteria-Gonzalez v. INS,* 322 F.3d 804, 811 n.5 (5th Cir. 2002) (amended opinion). Even today, therefore, the immigration lawyer needs to know what a JRAD is and what its consequences are.

JRADs raise a fundamental question about who should decide whether to remove a noncitizen who has been convicted of a crime. Congress can make the decision itself by enacting fixed rules, or it can delegate discretionary power to others. When it takes the latter course, it must decide who those others are and how much discretion they should have. Authorizing judges to issue binding JRADs thus shifts some measure of power from the immigration officials to the courts. What would be the pros and cons of restoring JRADs?

One alternative, more radical than the resurrection of JRADs, is also worth considering. Instead of *prescribing* removal unless the sentencing judge recommends *against* it, the statute could *bar* removal unless the sentencing judge recommends *in favor of* it. Such an approach would eliminate the problem of noncitizens being removed because of their attorneys', or judges', ignorance of immigration law. The idea might sound far-fetched, but it has in fact been adopted in the United Kingdom (which doesn't mean it isn't far-fetched). See Immigration Act 1971, § 3(6). What do you think of that approach?

More recently, Congress has authorized the sentencing judges to enter removal orders themselves in certain criminal cases. These "judicial deportations" will be taken up in chapter 9 below.

3.   DRUG OFFENSES

Narrow classes of noncitizen drug offenders have been deportable since 1922. See Act of May 26, 1922, ch. 202, 42 Stat. 596, 597. Over the years, Congress has expanded the range of drug offenses that would trigger deportation. The main drug-related deportability ground today is INA § 237(a)(2)(B), which you should now read carefully. Note that this ground refers to the federal statutory definition of "controlled substance" in 21 U.S.C. § 802. Subsection (6) of the latter provision, in turn, defines a "controlled substance" as any substance that appears in one of five schedules contained within 21 U.S.C. § 812. Under 21 U.S.C. § 811, the Attorney General has the authority to expand those schedules.

Since 1988, a noncitizen convicted of any offense that is considered "illicit trafficking in a controlled substance" has more to worry about than INA § 237(a)(2)(B). Such an offense is also classified as an "aggravated felony." INA § 101(a)(43)(B). Noncitizens convicted of aggravated felonies are subject to removal on an additional ground, INA § 237(a)(2)(A)(iii), and they are adversely affected in other ways that are explored in the next subsection.

PROBLEMS 20–21

For purposes of the next two Problems, ignore any issues concerning aggravated felonies.

Problem 20. A was admitted as an LPR at age 13. Eight years later, A was convicted of selling two marijuana joints to his college roommate. Is he deportable?

Problem 21. B, a noncitizen, pleads guilty, in state court, to one count of driving while under the influence of a controlled substance. The state's definition of "controlled substance" includes some drugs that do not appear in the federal definition. The record of conviction does not specify the particular drug that B used. Is she deportable?

You have seen in this subsection a number of respects in which the deportability provisions treat even the mildest drug offenses more severely than some of the more serious crimes involving moral turpitude: the five-years–after–entry requirement that is part of INA § 237(a)(2)(A)(i) but not part of section 237(a)(2)(B)(i); the one–year–sentence requirement for which the same is true; and the availability of executive pardons when deportability is based on § 237(a)(2)(A)(i) but not when it is based on section 237(a)(2)(B)(i). Earlier you saw a similar pattern in the inadmissibility grounds. See INA § 212(a)(2)(A)(ii) (containing exceptions to the inadmissibility of people convicted of crimes involving moral turpitude but not for those convicted of drug offenses). When the particular drug offenses also constitute aggravated felonies (see the next subsection), the treatment is harsher still. What do you think of this pattern? If you are not satisfied, in what general direction would you move the law? Liberalize the drug provisions? Toughen the provisions that govern crimes involving moral turpitude? Both? (Congress's approach has been to make more of the moral turpitude crimes aggravated felonies. For another approach, see Stephen H. Legomsky, *Reforming the Criteria for the Exclusion and the Deportation of Alien Criminal Offenders*, 12 In Defense of the Alien 64 (1990)).

4. AGGRAVATED FELONIES

In 1988, heightened concerns about drug abuse led Congress to add a new deportation ground that would soon expand far beyond the drug context. The Anti–Drug Abuse Act of 1988, Pub.L. 100–690, §§ 7341, 7344, 102 Stat. 4181, 4469–71 (Nov. 18, 1988), created a new concept called "aggravated felony" and rendered deportable any noncitizen who, after entry (now changed to "after admission"), has been convicted of an aggravated felony. INA § 237(a)(2)(A)(iii). Some good general summaries include Joseph Justin Rollin, *Humpty Dumpty Logic: Arguing against the "Aggravated Misdemeanor" in Immigration Law*, 6 BIB 445 (May 15, 2001); Lory Diana Rosenberg & Nelson Vargas–Padilla, *An Odyssey of Immigration Consequences of Crime: The BIA's 2001 Interpretations*, 78 IR 909, 911–12 (June 4, 2001); Lory D. Rosenberg & Nelson Vargas–Padilla, *Immigration Consequences of Crimes on the Doorstep of the Twenty–First Century*, 77 IR 685 (May 26, 2000).

The consequences of making a crime an aggravated felony are far-reaching. One major consequence is that, unlike the deportability ground for moral turpitude crimes, aggravated felonies don't have to be committed within five years after admission in order to give rise to deportability. An LPR who was first admitted as a small child and who commits an aggravated felony at age 60 becomes deportable. Also unlike the moral turpitude provision, an aggravated felony makes a person deportable without regard to the potential or actual sentence (although *some* crimes—not all—won't *be* "aggravated felonies" unless certain sentencing requirements are met.) As you will see later, calling a crime an aggravated felony also eliminates most discretionary relief possibilities (chapter 8), deletes certain procedural safeguards (chapter 9), triggers mandatory detention from the time removal proceedings begin until the time the person is removed, INA § 236(c)(1)(B), prevents the person after removal from ever returning to the United States without special permission from the Secretary of Homeland Security, see INA § 212(a)(9)(A)(ii), and subjects the person to a 20–year prison term if found in the United States unlawfully without that special permission, INA § 276(b)(2). In addition, under the United States Sentencing Guidelines, the sentence imposed in a federal criminal case can be increased dramatically if the person has previously been deported because of a conviction of an aggravated felony, see 18 U.S.C. App. § 2.L.1.2(b)(1)(A), though the recent Supreme Court decision in *United States v. Booker*, ___ U.S. ___, 125 S.Ct. 738, 160 L.Ed.2d 621 (2005), has made those guidelines advisory rather than mandatory. For that reason, the case law on criminal sentence enhancement has become a fertile source of the meaning of "aggravated felony."

All these otherwise sweeping consequences would be relatively unsurprising if the definition of aggravated felony were narrow enough. The original definition was, in fact, a modest one. It included murder, drug trafficking, and firearms trafficking (plus conspiracies and attempts to commit these crimes). See INA § 101(a)(43) (1988 version).

From its humble origins, however, the aggravated felony definition has grown into a colossus. A series of amendments have steadily expanded its reach, to the point where an "aggravated felony" need not be "aggravated" and, as explained below, need not be a felony. See, e.g., Imm. Act 1990, § 501(a)(3); Immigration and Nationality Technical Corrections Act of 1994, Pub.L. 103–416, § 222, 108 Stat. 4305, 4320–22 (Oct. 25, 1994); AEDPA § 440(e) (1996); IIRIRA § 321 (1996); see generally Nancy Morawetz, *Understanding the Impact of the 1996 Deportation Laws and the Limited Scope of Proposed Reforms*, 113 Harvard L. Rev. 1936, 1939 (2000).

Among the many prongs of the aggravated felony definition that you will soon see, some expressly require that the crime be a felony, not a misdemeanor. Most, however, do not say. A divided BIA had once held en banc that at least one of the prongs that was silent on the issue (sexual abuse of a minor) had to be a felony in order to be an "aggravated felony." *Matter of Crammond*, 23 I. & N. Dec. 9 (BIA 2001), vacated on unrelated jurisdictional grounds, 23 I. & N. Dec. 179 (BIA 2001). But shortly thereafter the BIA, in another divided en banc decision, reversed course. In *Matter of Small*, 23 I. & N. Dec. 48 (BIA 2002), the Board held that the "sexual abuse of a minor" prong of the aggravated felony definition does indeed cover misdemeanors. Rather than reexamine the issue on the merits, the BIA relied principally on the fact that, by then, three courts of appeals had interpreted the same provision to encompass misdemeanors. See *United States v. Gonzales–Vela*, 276 F.3d 763 (6th Cir. 2001); *United States v. Marin–Navarette*, 244 F.3d 1284 (11th Cir. 2001); *Guerrero-Perez v. INS*, 242 F.3d 727, pet'n for rehearing denied, 256 F.3d 546 (7th Cir. 2001).

One major complication has been retroactivity. As just noted, a series of statutes has expanded the aggravated felony definition. These various enactments have provided differing degrees of retroactivity. To understand the variations, remember that labelling a crime an aggravated felony has many consequences—not just deportability. It is necessary, therefore, to distinguish between the effective date of a change in the *definition* of "aggravated felony" and the effective dates of the provisions that assign various specific *consequences* to aggravated felony convictions.[2] The complexity has prompted two commentators to say, in reference to the retroactivity issue, "If you're not confused, you don't understand the situation." James P. Fleissner & James A. Shapiro, *Federal Sentences for Aliens Convicted of Illegal Reentry Following Deportation: Who Needs the Aggravation?*, 9 Georgetown Immigration L.J. 451 (1995); see also *Matter of Reyes*, 20 I. & N. Dec. 789 (BIA 1994); *Matter of A.A.*, 20 I. & N.Dec. 492, 495–500 (BIA 1992). For present purposes it is enough to note the retroactivity issues rather than try to resolve them.

One last observation: When you study the aggravated felony definition in INA § 101(a)(43), you might notice that some of the listed crimes require a "term of imprisonment" of a certain duration (e.g. subsections F, G, P, R, and S) while others require only that a certain sentence "may be imposed" or that the offense be "punishable" by a certain term (e.g., subsections J, Q, and T). When the phrase "term of imprisonment" is used, Congress means to refer to the sentence actually imposed (not the maximum possible sentence under the statute). INA § 101(a)(48)(B).

At this time, please read INA §§ 237(a)(2)(A)(iii), 101(a)(43), and 101(a)(48)(B).

One of the most important prongs of the aggravated felony definition is prong (F), which relates to "crimes of violence." The following Supreme Court opinion explores its limits:

Leocal v. Ashcroft

Supreme Court of the United States, 2004.
543 U.S. 1, 125 S.Ct. 377, 160 L.Ed.2d 271.

■ CHIEF JUSTICE REHNQUIST delivered the opinion of the Court.

Petitioner Josue Leocal, a Haitian citizen, * * * immigrated to the United States in 1980 and became a lawful permanent resident in 1987. In January 2000, he was charged with two counts of DUI causing serious bodily injury under Fla. Stat. § 316.193(3)(c)(2), after he caused an accident resulting in injury to two people. He pleaded guilty to both counts and was sentenced to two and a half years in prison.

In November 2000, while he was serving his sentence, the Immigration and Naturalization Service (INS) initiated removal proceedings against him pursuant to § 237(a)[(2)(A)(iii)] of the INA. Under that provision, "any alien who is convicted of an aggravated felony ... is deportable" and may

---

2. The author is indebted to Hon. Lory Rosenberg and Professor Daniel Kanstroom for articulating this distinction.

be removed upon an order of the Attorney General. Section 101(a)(43)[(F)] of the INA defines "aggravated felony" to include, inter alia, "a crime of violence (as defined in section 16 of title 18, but not including a purely political offense) for which the term of imprisonment [is] at least one year." Title 18 U.S.C. § 16, in turn, defines the term "crime of violence" to mean:

> (a) an offense that has as an element the use, attempted use, or threatened use of physical force against the person or property of another, or

> "(b) any other offense that is a felony and that, by its nature, involves a substantial risk that physical force against the person or property of another may be used in the course of committing the offense."

Here, the INS claimed that petitioner's DUI conviction was a "crime of violence" under § 16, and therefore an "aggravated felony" under the INA.

In October 2001, an Immigration Judge found petitioner removable, relying upon the Eleventh Circuit's decision in *Le v. United States Attorney General*, 196 F.3d 1352 (1999) (per curiam), which held that a conviction under the Florida DUI statute qualified as a crime of violence. The BIA affirmed. Petitioner completed his sentence and was removed to Haiti in November 2002. In June 2003, the Court of Appeals for the Eleventh Circuit dismissed petitioner's petition for review, relying on its previous ruling in *Le, supra*. We granted certiorari to resolve a conflict among the Courts of Appeals on the question whether state DUI offenses similar to the one in Florida, which either do not have a *mens rea* component or require only a showing of negligence in the operation of a vehicle, qualify as a crime of violence. * * * We now reverse the Eleventh Circuit.

Title 18 U.S.C. § 16 was enacted as part of the Comprehensive Crime Control Act of 1984, which broadly reformed the federal criminal code in such areas as sentencing, bail, and drug enforcement, and which added a variety of new violent and nonviolent offenses. Congress employed the term "crime of violence" in numerous places in the Act, such as for defining the elements of particular offenses, see, e.g., 18 U.S.C. § 1959 (prohibiting threats to commit crimes of violence in aid of racketeering activity), or for directing when a hearing is required before a charged individual can be released on bail, see § 3142(f) (requiring a pretrial detention hearing for those alleged to have committed a crime of violence). Congress therefore provided in § 16 a general definition of the term "crime of violence" to be used throughout the Act. Section 16 has since been incorporated into a variety of statutory provisions, both criminal and noncriminal.

Here, pursuant to § 237(a) of the INA, the Court of Appeals applied § 16 to find that petitioner's DUI conviction rendered him deportable. In determining whether petitioner's conviction falls within the ambit of § 16, the statute directs our focus to the "offense" of conviction. See § 16(a) (defining a crime of violence as *"an offense* that has *as an element* the use ... of physical force against the person or property of another"" (emphasis added)); § 16(b) (defining the term as *"any other offense* that is a felony and that, *by its nature*, involves a substantial risk that physical force against the person or property of another may be used in the course of committing the offense" (emphasis added)). This language requires us to look to the elements and the nature of the offense of conviction, rather than to the particular facts relating to petitioner's crime.

Florida Stat. § 316.193(3)(c)(2) makes it a third-degree felony for a person to operate a vehicle while under the influence and, "by reason of such operation, cause ... serious bodily injury to another." The Florida statute, while it requires proof of causation of injury, does not require proof of any particular mental state. * * * Many States have enacted similar statutes, criminalizing DUI causing serious bodily injury or death without requiring proof of any mental state or, in some States, appearing to require only proof that the person acted negligently in operating the vehicle. The question here is whether § 16 can be interpreted to include such offenses.

Our analysis begins with the language of the statute. See *Bailey v. United States*, 516 U.S. 137, 144, 133 L. Ed. 2d 472, 116 S. Ct. 501 (1995). The plain text of § 16(a) states that an offense, to qualify as a crime of violence, must have "as an element the use, attempted use, or threatened use of physical force against the person or property of another." We do not deal here with an *attempted* or *threatened* use of force. Petitioner contends that his conviction did not require the "use" of force against another person because the most common employment of the word "use" connotes the *intentional* availment of force, which is not required under the Florida DUI statute. The Government counters that the "use" of force does not incorporate any *mens rea* component, and that petitioner's DUI conviction necessarily includes the use of force. To support its position, the Government dissects the meaning of the word "use," employing dictionaries, legislation, and our own case law in contending that a use of force may be negligent or even inadvertent.

Whether or not the word "use" alone supplies a *mens rea* element, the parties' primary focus on that word is too narrow. Particularly when interpreting a statute that features as elastic a word as "use," we construe language in its context and in light of the terms surrounding it. The critical aspect of § 16(a) is that a crime of violence is one involving the "use ... of physical force *against the person or property of another*." (Emphasis added.) As we said in a similar context in *Bailey*, "use" requires active employment. While one may, in theory, actively employ *something* in an accidental manner, it is much less natural to say that a person actively employs physical force against another person by accident. Thus, a person would "use ... physical force against" another when pushing him; however, we would not ordinarily say a person "uses ... physical force against" another by stumbling and falling into him. When interpreting a statute, we must give words their "ordinary or natural" meaning. The key phrase in § 16(a)—the "use ... of physical force against the person or property of another"—most naturally suggests a higher degree of intent than negligent or merely accidental conduct. Petitioner's DUI offense therefore is not a crime of violence under § 16(a).

Neither is petitioner's DUI conviction a crime of violence under § 16(b). Section 16(b) sweeps more broadly than § 16(a), defining a crime of violence as including "any other offense that is a felony and that, by its nature, involves a substantial risk that physical force against the person or property of another may be used in the course of committing the offense." But § 16(b) does not thereby encompass all negligent misconduct, such as the negligent operation of a vehicle. It simply covers offenses that naturally involve a person acting in disregard of the risk that physical force might be used against another in committing an offense. The reckless disregard in § 16 relates *not* to the general conduct or to the possibility that harm will result from a person's conduct, but to the risk that the use of physical force against another might be required in committing a crime. The classic example is burglary. A burglary would be covered under § 16(b) *not* because the offense can be committed in a generally reckless way or because someone may be injured, but because burglary, by its nature, involves a substantial risk that the burglar will use force against a victim in completing the crime.

Thus, while § 16(b) is broader than § 16(a) in the sense that physical force need not actually be applied, it contains the same formulation we found to be determinative in § 16(a): the use of physical force against the person or property of another. Accordingly, we must give the language in § 16(b) an identical construction, requiring a higher *mens rea* than the merely accidental or negligent conduct involved in a DUI offense. This is particularly true in light of § 16(b)'s requirement that the "substantial risk" be a risk of using physical force against another person "in the course of committing the offense." In no "ordinary or natural" sense can it be said that a person risks having to "use" physical force against another person in the course of operating a vehicle while intoxicated and causing injury.

In construing both parts of § 16, we cannot forget that we ultimately are determining the meaning of the term "crime of violence." The ordinary meaning of this term, combined with § 16's emphasis on the use of physical force against another person (or the risk of having to use such force in committing a crime), suggests a category of violent, active crimes that cannot be said naturally to include DUI offenses. * * * Interpreting § 16 to encompass accidental or negligent conduct would blur the distinction between the "violent" crimes Congress sought to distinguish for heightened punishment and other crimes.

* * *

[Here the Court observes that, just nine months before incorporating crimes of violence into the aggravated felony definition, Congress enacted an unrelated provision that similarly distinguished crimes of violence from both DUI and reckless driving. See INA § 101(h).—Ed.]

This case does not present us with the question whether a state or federal offense that requires proof of the *reckless* use of force against a person or property of another qualifies as a crime of violence under 18 U.S.C. § 16. DUI statutes such as Florida's do not require any mental state with respect to the use of force against another person, thus reaching individuals who were negligent or less. Drunk driving is a nationwide problem, as evidenced by the efforts of legislatures to prohibit such conduct and impose appropriate penalties. But this fact does not warrant our shoehorning it into statutory sections where it does not fit. The judgment of the United States Court of Appeals for the Eleventh Circuit is therefore reversed, and the case is remanded for further proceedings consistent with this opinion.

NOTES AND QUESTIONS

1. Throughout this book you have encountered the principle that courts must defer to "reasonable" interpretations of federal statutes by the administrative agencies that are charged with administering them. *Chevron USA v. NRDC*, 467 U.S. 837, 843–44, 104 S.Ct. 2778, 81 L.Ed.2d 694 (1984). Yet deference to the BIA was noticeably absent in *Leocal*. Why do you suppose that was? Consider *Garcia-Lopez v. Ashcroft*, 334 F.3d 840 (9th Cir. 2003). There the court was reviewing a BIA determination that a particular California statute permitted a criminal sentence of greater than one year, for purposes of the petty offense exception to the moral turpitude deportability ground, INA § 212(a)(2)(A)(i). The court declined to give deference to the BIA interpretation of the California statute because it was not a statute that the BIA administered and therefore not a statute that the Board had any special expertise in interpreting. *Id*. at 843 & n.3. Could similar reasoning apply to the issue of whether a particular crime fits the definition of "aggravated felony?" On this issue, does the BIA have any comparative advantage over the federal courts? (Acknowledgments are due to Margaret Taylor, David Martin, and Debbie Smith for their e-mail contributions.)

Second, consider a related point. In *Leocal*, the *Chevron* deference principle combined in an odd way with two BIA practices—the practice of overruling its prior interpretations and the practice of considering itself bound by the law of the circuit in which a case arises. Originally, the BIA position was that DUI is a crime of violence. See, e.g., *Matter of Puente-Salazar*, 22 I. & N. Dec. 1006, 1012–13 (BIA 1999) (en banc). In *Le v. U.S. Attorney General*, 196 F.3d 1352, 1353–54 (11th Cir. 1999), the Court of Appeals for the Eleventh Circuit reached a similar result (albeit with respect to a slightly differently worded statute), and it did so by deferring to what it regarded as the BIA's "reasonable" interpretation. Then in *Matter of Ramos*, 23 I. & N. Dec. 336, 346 (BIA 2002) (en banc), the BIA overruled *Puente* and held that, in cases that arise in circuits that have not yet passed on the issue, DUI was not a crime of violence unless the particular statute required the reckless or intentional use of force against the person or property of another. If a case arises in a circuit that holds otherwise, the BIA said, it will follow the law of that circuit. *Id*. at 346–47. Since the present case (*Leocal*) arose in the Eleventh Circuit, the BIA felt bound by the Eleventh Circuit position that DUI is a crime of violence—

even though the Eleventh Circuit in turn had arrived at that position by deferring to the BIA's own prior, and since repudiated, stance!

Now that the Supreme Court has resolved this specific issue, of course, the new BIA position on DUI has become the law of the land. But the same combination of practices—judicial deference to the agency interpretation, corresponding agency deference to the court of appeals for the relevant circuit, and the power of an agency to overrule its prior interpretation—remains alive on all other questions of law that come before the BIA and the courts. What do you think are the reasons for *Chevron* deference in the first place? Given those reasons, does this combination of practices make sense?

2.   Like the BIA, the Supreme Court in *Leocal* adopted a categorical approach to determining whether an offense is a "crime of violence." Rather than ask whether Mr. Leocal used physical force on the person or property of another, or whether his particular actions posed a substantial risk of such force being used, the Court confined its inquiry to the elements of the statute. It asked whether the criminal statute in question *required*, as an element of guilt, that the defendant use physical force, or create a substantial risk of such force, on the person or property of another. Earlier you saw that the same categorical test governs whether a crime involves "moral turpitude" for purposes of INA § 237(a)(2)(A)(i)(I). (In each of those contexts, a modification is required when a statute has two or more prongs; in those cases, the court may consult the charging document to determine which of the two prongs triggered the conviction.) For a thoughtful analysis, see Andrew Moore, *Matter of Jacques Martin*, 7 BIB 1502 (Dec. 1, 2002).

First, as a matter of statutory interpretation, do you agree with the Supreme Court that 18 U.S.C. § 16 contemplates a categorical test for crimes of violence? Second, note that the lower courts have applied a categorical test for aggravated felonies generally, not just for crimes of violence. Under INA § 101(a)(43)(G), for example, a "theft" offense will be an aggravated felony if the term of imprisonment is at least one year. The courts have held that whether a particular offense qualifies as a "theft" offense is determined by comparing the elements of the statutory crime to the "generic" definition of "theft," not by looking at the facts of the individual case. See, e.g., *Martinez-Perez v. Ashcroft*, 393 F.3d 1018, 1021–22 (9th Cir. 2004). The same is true of "sexual abuse of a minor" for purposes of INA § 101(a)(43)(A). See *Espinoza-Franco v. Ashcroft*, 394 F.3d 461, 465 (7th Cir. 2005). As a policy matter, what do you think is the better way to decide whether a crime is an aggravated felony—a categorical test or a test that rests on the facts of the individual case?

3.   As the Supreme Court points out, the circuits had split on the question whether DUI is a crime of violence for aggravated felony purposes. Yet the Supreme Court, not noted for its unanimity in immigration cases (or, for that matter, in *any* controversial cases), reached a 9–0 decision in *Leocal*. Was the statutory interpretation a slam dunk? What do you think accounts for this rare display of unanimity?

4. Suppose a state statute makes it a felony to "possess a firearm after having been convicted of a felony." After *Leocal*, would the possession offense be a "crime of violence" for aggravated felony purposes?

5. In *Jobson v. Ashcroft*, 326 F.3d 367 (2d Cir. 2003), decided before *Leocal*, a noncitizen had been convicted of manslaughter under a state statute that prohibits "recklessly caus[ing] the death of another person." The BIA found the crime to be a prong (b) crime of violence. (The parties agreed prong (a) did not apply.) The court of appeals reversed, for two reasons. First, while the conduct that made the killing reckless entails a substantial risk of injury or death, it doesn't necessarily entail a substantial risk that *the defendant* will apply force against the victim. The court offered as an example the crime of reckless driving resulting in death. Second, even if the force could be attributed to the defendant, the court interpreted the word "use" in the crime of violence definition as requiring the intentional, and not merely the reckless, application of force to the person or property of another. Since the manslaughter statute could be violated by conduct that was reckless but not intentional, the court reasoned, the categorical approach meant this offense was not a crime of violence.

Is *Jobson* still good law after *Leocal*? As a policy matter, should the immigration laws treat the person convicted of an intentional battery more harshly than the person who is convicted of a reckless killing?

6. The courts of appeals are divided over whether vehicle burglaries are prong (b) crimes of violence. Compare *United States v. Guzman–Landeros*, 207 F.3d 1034 (8th Cir. 2000) and *Lopez-Elias v. Reno*, 209 F.3d 788 (5th Cir. 2000) (both holding yes) with *Ye v. INS*, 214 F.3d 1128, 1133–34 (9th Cir. 2000) (holding no). The Supreme Court in *Leocal* says in dictum that burglary is a crime of violence, since by its nature it involves a substantial risk that the burglar will use force against a victim. But there is no indication that the Court thought about vehicle burglary, a crime for which that risk might well be lower than for the traditional residential burglary. Under the categorical approach, a general burglary statute that encompasses vehicle burglary might thus be found not to be a crime of violence, notwithstanding the dictum in *Leocal*.

A complication here is that INA § 101(a)(43)(G) specifically makes burglary an aggravated felony, as long as the term of imprisonment is at least one year. In *Taylor v. United States*, 495 U.S. 575, 590–99, 110 S.Ct. 2143, 109 L.Ed.2d 607 (1990), however, the Supreme Court held that for sentence enhancement purposes the "burglary" prong of aggravated felony has a uniform, generic federal meaning, which the Court found requires the breaking and entering of a building or structure—not a vehicle. Following *Taylor*, the BIA and the courts now appear in agreement that the same is true for purposes of removal proceedings against aggravated felons; thus, a conviction of vehicle burglary does not satisfy prong (G) of the aggravated felony definition in removal proceedings. See, e.g., *Lopez-Elias v. Reno*, 209 F.3d 788 (5th Cir. 2000); *Solarzano-Patlan v. INS*, 207 F.3d 869, 873 (7th Cir. 2000); *Ye v. INS*, 214 F.3d 1128, 1132 (9th Cir. 2000); *Matter of Perez*, 22 I. & N. Dec. 1325 (BIA 2000).

7. One other prong of the aggravated felony definition that has attracted recent attention is INA § 101(a)(43)(B). This provision contains two sub-prongs—"illicit trafficking in a controlled substance" (as defined in 21 U.S.C. § 802) and "a drug trafficking crime" (as defined in 18 U.S.C. § 924(c)). Of course, a crime that falls within either of those sub-prongs will also normally render the person deportable under INA § 237(a)(2)(B), which covers convictions of "controlled substance" offenses. The aggravated felony provision remains critical nonetheless, because, as you have seen, aggravated felony convictions preclude most forms of discretionary relief and have a host of other adverse consequences as well.

The first sub-prong of section 101(a)(43)(B) has been generally noncontroversial, but the latter ("drug trafficking" crimes) has generated some important case law. Under 21 U.S.C. § 924(c)(2), a "drug trafficking crime" is defined as "any *felony* punishable under the Controlled Substance Act ... [emphasis added]." The key word is "felony." A federal conviction usually presents no significant issue. But suppose a person is convicted of a state drug offense, and the particular state classifies the offense as a felony, but the same conduct would have been only a misdemeanor under federal law. Conversely, suppose the person is convicted of a state misdemeanor drug offense but the federal law makes the same conduct a felony. These scenarios are especially common in cases of simple possession, particularly for first offenders. When they arise, which drug law—federal or state—determines whether the offense is a "felony?"

The BIA originally held that, to be a drug trafficking offense, a state drug law had to cover conduct that would have been a felony under federal law. See, e.g., *Matter of L–G–*, 21 I. & N. Dec. 89, 102 (BIA 1995). After the courts of appeals began to split on the same issue in an analogous context (criminal cases involving reentry after aggravated felony convictions), the BIA held that it would follow whatever rule appeared to be favored in the circuit in which the case arose. See *Matter of Yanez–Garcia*, 23 I. & N. Dec. 390 (BIA 2002). The problem in *Yanez* was that the Seventh Circuit had not yet decided the issue. The Board chose to follow what it regarded as the majority view—that the state "felony" determination would control. See *Yanez-Garcia v. Ashcroft*, 388 F.3d 280 (7th Cir. 2004) (lacking jurisdiction to review directly, but transferring case to district court for habeas corpus review). At this writing, the courts remain divided. For a good synthesis, see Lory Rosenberg, *Understanding Immigration Consequences: The Elusive Construction of Controlled Substance Possession Convictions*, 7 BIB 1295 (Nov. 1, 2002).

8. The expansions of the aggravated felony definition, having swept in many minor criminal offenses, have provoked severe criticisms from immigration commentators and journalists. In 2000, Pulitzer Prize-winning New York Times columnist Anthony Lewis brought the case of Mary Ann Gehris to the nation's attention. See Anthony Lewis, *This Has Got Me in Some Kind of Whirlwind*, N.Y. Times, Jan. 8, 2000, at A13; Anthony Lewis, *Measure of Justice*, N.Y. Times, June 23, 2000, at A13. Gehris had been adopted by U.S. citizen parents and brought to the United States at age 2.

Later in life she pleaded guilty to a misdemeanor battery charge for pulling the hair of a woman who had been with Gehris's boyfriend. Gehris received a one-year suspended sentence. The former INS sought to remove her as an "aggravated felon" on the ground that battery is a "crime of violence" for which she had been sentenced to "at least one year" (the suspension of sentence being irrelevant under section 101(a)(48)(B)). Had the removal succeeded, she would have been barred forever from returning to the United States, absent special permission from the Secretary of Homeland Security. Only the unusual national publicity prevented that result. The Georgia State Board of Pardons and Paroles granted her a pardon, thus erasing her conviction for removal purposes. See Joseph Justin Rollin, *Humpty Dumpty Logic: Arguing Against the "Aggravated Misdemeanor" in Immigration Law*, 6 BIB 445 (May 15, 2001).

Other relatively minor misdemeanors, such as petty larceny, can similarly give rise to "aggravated felony" removals, as long as the person receives at least a one-year sentence, suspended or otherwise. See, e.g., *United States v. Christopher*, 239 F.3d 1191 (11th Cir. 2001) (shoplifting); *United States v. Graham*, 169 F.3d 787 (3d Cir. 1999) (petit larceny).

9.   Some common criminal defense strategies have emerged in response to the aggravated felony provisions. Because many of the offenses listed in the aggravated felony definition require a term of imprisonment of "one year or more," defense attorneys now frequently ask sentencing judges who are otherwise inclined to impose one-year sentences to impose 364-day sentences instead. In addition, the BIA has held that, if a sentence of one year or more is imposed but then vacated to permit the judge to reduce the sentence to under one year, the new sentence is the one that counts. This strategy succeeded in *Matter of Min Song*, 23 I. & N. Dec. 173 (BIA 2001).

10.   Do you think the combination of an expanded "aggravated felony" definition and the broad consequences of an aggravated felony conviction have made the resulting law too harsh, or are the results appropriate?

PROBLEMS 22–24

In the following Problems, ignore any complications presented by the varying retroactivity of the several statutory amendments.

Problem 22. Six years after his admission as an LPR, X swindled someone out of several thousand dollars and was later convicted of "obtaining property by false pretenses." The crime is punishable by up to five years in prison, and X received a sentence of one year, of which six months were suspended. Is he deportable?

Problem 23. Six years after being admitted to the United States as an LPR, Y committed the misdemeanor of "breaking and entering the dwelling of another." Y was convicted and received the maximum sentence of one year, but she was released from confinement after four months for good behavior. Is she deportable?

Problem 24. You have just received a frantic phone call from your client, Z, whom you helped to obtain LPR status seven years ago. Z is in France, and is in some trouble. While on a three-month summer vacation in Paris, Z was involved in a fight with some locals and was arrested by the police. Claiming Z had a knife (he denies it), the prosecutor charged him with assault with a deadly weapon, a felony punishable by up to twenty years in prison. Because Z is a French national, the authorities allowed him to remain at large pending a preliminary hearing at which he was ordered to appear. Calling the charge "bogus," Z did not show up at the hearing, choosing instead to leave town and spend the rest of his summer in the French Riviera. The police put out a warrant for his arrest. After further investigation, however, the police became convinced that Z had not had a knife and that in fact he had been acting only in self-defense. Still, they were upset at his failure to appear, and when he was apprehended a few days later in the Riviera, he was arrested and charged with the crime of failure to appear before a court pursuant to a court order.

Pay the Fine

Z was brought before a French court and pleaded guilty to the charged offense. The judge has given him a choice between paying a fine equivalent to about US $1500 or spending 15 days in jail. Z wants to know whether confinement would jeopardize his immigration status. He has called you because his French criminal lawyer knows nothing about U.S. immigration law. What advice will you give him?

5.   Miscellaneous Criminal Grounds

The deportability grounds discussed in the preceding subsections are by far the most important of the grounds that are based on criminal convictions: crimes involving moral turpitude, drug offenses, and aggravated felonies. There are, however, a number of other crime-related deportability grounds. Several of these cover noncitizens who have been convicted under specified federal statutes. See, e.g., INA § 237(a), paragraphs 2(C) (certain firearms offenses), 2(D) (national security offenses), 2(E) (domestic violence), 3(B) (failure to register and document fraud). Unlike section 237(a)(2)(A)(i), none of these miscellaneous grounds requires either that a particular sentence be imposed or that the crime be committed within a certain number of years after admission.

There are, in addition, deportability grounds that do not require a criminal conviction at all, even though the conduct they describe often happens also to constitute a criminal offense. This category includes some of the immigration control provisions you saw earlier, such as smuggling noncitizens into the United States, INA § 237(a)(1)(E), marriage fraud, *id.* § 237(a)(1)(G), and breach of certain registration and reporting requirements, *id.* § 237(a)(3)(A). Other deportability grounds that describe what are also criminal acts include illegal voting, *id.* § 237(a)(6), certain of the grounds concerned with war crimes, affiliation with subversive groups, and national security, *id.* § 237(a)(4)(A, B, D). You will see this latter group in section E below.

One last crime-related deportability ground is worthy of mention. As you saw earlier, a nonimmigrant who fails to maintain his or her status or to comply with the conditions of that status is deportable under INA § 237(a)(1)(C)(i). Under INA § 214(a), the admission of nonimmigrants "shall be for such time and under such conditions as the [Secretary of Homeland Security] may by regulations prescribe * * *." The regulations declare that a condition of every nonimmigrant's stay is obedience to all federal or state laws prohibiting "the commission of crimes of violence * * * for which a sentence of more than one year imprisonment *may be imposed*." 8 C.F.R. § 214.1(g) (2004) [emphasis added]. Under that regulation, a conviction of such a crime makes the person deportable for having failed to maintain status. *Id.* Note that the language "may be imposed" is broader than the statutory "term of imprisonment" language in the corresponding portion of the aggravated felony definition, INA § 101(a)(43)(F). The latter refers to the sentence *actually* imposed. INA § 101(a)(48)(B).

Can they really do that? Doesn't this regulation effectively add a new deportability ground? If so, is that something Congress has authorized DHS to do? Is the policy of this regulation consistent with the limitations built into §§ 237(a)(2)(A)(i), 237(a)(2)(A)(iii), and related provisions?

What other conditions is DHS entitled to add? Could it declare, as a condition of every nonimmigrant's stay, that the person must refrain from violating any law punishable by confinement for any length of time or by a fine of at least, say, $100? Could it make compliance with *all* laws a condition of stay? For that matter, could DHS spell out behavior that is not against the law at all, but which DHS considers socially undesirable, and then deem that behavior a violation of a nonimmigrant's conditions of stay?

NOTE ON COMPARATIVE LAW, SEPARATION OF POWERS, AND THE MAKING OF IMMIGRATION POLICY

Apart from the issue of its legality, the DHS regulation just discussed raises interesting questions about who *should* define the grounds on which noncitizens may be removed. In the United States a common assumption has been that broad, sufficiently important national policy decisions—as distinguished from the application of those policies to individual cases—should be made by Congress. For the most part, the immigration laws reflect that assumption. The INA spells out in detail the qualifying categories for the admission of both nonimmigrants and immigrants; the numerical quotas on immigrants; the grounds for inadmissibility and for deportability; the fact situations in which the immigration officials are permitted to waive either inadmissibility or deportability; the basic elements of the procedures for admitting and removing noncitizens; and the substantive criteria and procedures governing both the acquisition and the loss of citizenship. To be sure, there are exceptions. As you will see in Chapter 11, the President has wide powers to decide which overseas refugees to admit and how many. ICE has wide latitude in its enforcement and prosecution priorities. And BIA precedent decisions (as well as judicial decisions) establish important policies. But there is no question that Congress makes the bulk of the crucial policy decisions in immigration law.

It is not that way in all other democracies. In most Parliamentary systems, for example, major national policy decisions—even when formally enshrined in Acts of Parliament—are normally driven by the views of the executive branch. See, e.g., Geoffrey W.R. Palmer, Unbridled Power—An Interpretation of New Zealand's Constitution and Government 8, 28–29, 38, 70–71 (2d ed. 1987). Moreover, Parliaments are far more likely than the United States Congress to expressly delegate broad policymaking authority to the executive branch. In the United Kingdom, for example, the Immigration Act 1971 provides only a few specific grounds for deportation: § 3(5)(b) (family member being deported); § 3(6) (convicted of offense punishable by conviction and recommended for deportation by court); and sched. 2, paras. 8, 9 ("removal" of "illegal entrants", defined in § 33(1) as those who enter in breach of the immigration laws, in breach of prior deportation orders, or by deception). Parliament has given the Home Secretary the residual authority to deport any non-British citizen whenever the Secretary "deems his deportation to be conducive to the public good." *Id.* § 3(5)(a). Would you favor a similar grant of power to the Secretary of Homeland Security in the United States? Cf. Mexico (not a parliamentary country), where the executive has broad discretion in deciding whom to "expel." See generally Carlos Narvaez–Hasfura, Immigration in Mexico and America: Constitutional Reciprocity within a Plenary Power, Part 2 (J.S.D. dissertation, Washington University School of Law, 1995).

6. THE MERITS OF REMOVING NONCITIZEN CRIMINAL OFFENDERS

In section A.2 of this chapter, you read a brief introduction to the theory of deportation. This is an appropriate point at which to consider a slightly more specific problem: Under what circumstances, if any, should noncitizens who have committed crimes be removed?

The first question to resolve is whether it is *ever* appropriate to remove noncitizens on the basis of criminal activity. Don't jump to conclusions here. Think about the purposes of removal and try to work out whether those purposes apply when the particular ground is a criminal conviction.

Assuming you are not prepared to rule out per se the removal of noncitizens who commit crimes, what should the criteria be? You have seen the crime-related deportability grounds up close, and have witnessed complications, ambiguities, and anomalies. If you have found yourself criticizing various elements of the statutory scheme, the exercise that follows will give you the chance to be constructive.

DRAFTING EXERCISE

You are the counsel to the House subcommittee responsible for immigration. The chair of the subcommittee is a reform-minded Representative who tends generally to be on the same ideological wavelength as you.

Knowing that you are familiar with the existing crime-related deportability grounds and that you are generally dissatisfied with them, she is giving you a crack at revising them. Draft a new set of provisions to govern the deportability of noncitizen criminal offenders. You are not obligated to retain the moral turpitude, aggravated felony, or any other provisions of existing law, though you are free to do so if you wish.

For two attempts at solution, see Stephen H. Legomsky, *Reforming the Criteria for the Exclusion and the Deportation of Alien Criminal Offenders*, 12 In Defense of the Alien 64 (1989) (proposing length of sentence as the principal determinant); Jacqueline P. Ulin, Note, *A Common Sense Reconstruction of the INA's Crime–Related Removal System: Eliminating the Caveats from the Statue of Liberty's Welcoming Words*, 78 Washington Univ. L.Q. 1549 (2000) (proposing presumption of deportability after felony conviction, and requiring felon to prove either absence of threat to public safety or personal stakes that outweigh threat).

SECTION E. POLITICAL AND NATIONAL SECURITY GROUNDS

In chapter 5, section B you saw the political and national security inadmissibility grounds in some detail. There is an analogous set of deportability grounds. They generally either track the language of the corresponding inadmissibility grounds or expressly incorporate them by reference. See generally INA § 237(a)(4).

One significant exception concerns the Communist Party. You saw in chapter 5, section B, that even after the statutory liberalizations in 1990 various affiliations with the Communist Party can render nonimmigrants (but not immigrants) inadmissible from the United States. In contrast, there is no longer any deportability ground based specifically on affiliation with the Communist Party.

Until 2005, the terrorism-related grounds were another exception. The pre-2005 deportability grounds for terrorism were substantially narrower than the corresponding inadmissibility grounds; only the latter, for example, covered the person who is "likely" to engage in terrorist activity or one who is a "representative" of a terrorist organization. Compare former INA §§ 212(a)(3)(B), 237(a)(4)(B). The REAL ID Act, § 105(a), expands the terrorism-related deportability grounds to cover all of the corresponding inadmissibility grounds. For a fuller discussion, see the coverage of this topic in chapter 5, section B, as well as the material in chapter 10, section C (on the national security measures that have affected both inadmissibility and deportability).

Finally, even when the deportability grounds are narrower than the corresponding inadmissibility grounds, the latter can come into play after arrival. As you saw earlier, INA § 237(a)(1)(A) renders deportable any noncitizen who was inadmissible at the time of either entry or adjustment of status.

SECTION F. OTHER DEPORTABILITY GROUNDS

Several other deportability grounds, not neatly classifiable under any of the preceding section headings, also deserve mention. Roughly speaking, these miscellaneous grounds reflect economic, moral, and health-related concerns. Most such grounds overlap at least two of those categories, and some indirectly implicate law enforcement concerns as well. See, e.g., INA § 237(a), subsections 1(C)(ii) (violating health-related conditions imposed at entry), 2(B)(ii) (past or present drug abuse or addiction).

Under INA § 237(a)(5), a noncitizen who becomes a "public charge" within five years after entry is deportable unless he or she can affirmatively show causes arising after entry. This provision needs to be considered in the context of related legal developments. As you saw in chapter 5, comprehensive welfare reform legislation enacted in 1996 (amended by IIRIRA) raised the barriers for intending immigrants, in part by conditioning admittance on binding affidavits of support. As you will see in chapter 11, that same legislation (with some exceptions) also disqualified even LPRs from most of the main public assistance programs. Together with existing barriers, these provisions greatly reduce the likelihood of LPRs being eligible for public assistance soon after entry. An immigrant who nonetheless meets the welfare eligibility requirements needs to consider section 237(a)(5) before deciding whether to apply.

SECTION G. TIME LIMITS

Most of the deportability grounds either explicitly require acts or events occurring "at the time of" or "after" entry or admission, e.g., INA § 237(a), subsections 1(A), 2(A, B, C), 4(A, B), and 5, or else require the kinds of events—such as violating the conditions of one's stay or getting convicted under a United States statute—that, practically speaking, invariably occur only after entry, e.g., subsections 1(C, D), 3(A, B), and 4(C). Although there are a few exceptions, e.g., subsections 1(E) (smuggling of noncitizens), 4(D) (various human rights violators), the basic pattern should not be particularly surprising. It is usually (not always) unnecessary for the deportation grounds to cover pre-entry conduct because, if conduct that occurs before entry is the kind that would have triggered removal had it occurred after entry, that pre-entry conduct will ordinarily be a ground for exclusion. In such a case, the person will ordinarily have been inadmissible at the time of entry, and therefore deportable under § 237(a)(1)(A).

Apart from those explicit or implicit requirements that acts or events take place at or after entry or admission, most of the deportability grounds operate without regard to time. Is that good? There are at least four different kinds of time limits to which deportability grounds *could* be made subject. The discussion that follows examines the degree to which the INA already does, and the degree to which it should, embody these various types of limitations.

What will here be called a category I time limit is the kind that confines the deportation ground to those acts or events that occur within a certain number of years after entry or admission. At present, only a few deportability grounds are subject to this kind of time limit. See, e.g., INA § 237(a), subsections 1(E) (smuggling of noncitizens), 2(A)(i) (crimes of moral turpitude), and 5 (public charge). What are the pros and cons of category I time limits?

A category II limitation would constrain the time interval between the act or event that makes the person deportable and the commencement of removal proceedings. This type of restriction is what lawyers in most areas of both civil and criminal practice call a "statute of limitations." In the United States, deportation provisions were once subject to such time limits. See, e.g., Act of March 3, 1903, ch. 1012, § 20, 32 Stat. 1213, 1218. In some countries they still are. In New Zealand, for example, when deportation is based on a criminal conviction, not only must deportation proceedings begin, but the actual deportation *order* must issue, no later than six months after the judgment of conviction (or six months after release from imprisonment). Immigration Act 1987, § 93. In the United States, however, the 1952 Act eliminated statutes of limitations on deportation, and at the time of this writing no deportability grounds contain them.

Interestingly, there are some analogous concepts elsewhere in our immigration laws. If a noncitizen receives adjustment of status at a time when he or she is in fact ineligible for it, the INS will have only five years to rescind the grant of adjustment. INA § 246. Recall also INA § 212(a)(2)(A)(ii)(I), which renders inadmissible any noncitizen convicted of a crime involving moral turpitude, but subject to an important exception: A person who committed only one such crime, and who committed it while under age 18, will not be denied a visa once five years have passed since the commission of the offense (or since his or her release from any resulting confinement).

Congress might have envisioned that last five-year rule as a limited analog of the five-year limit built into the corresponding deportability ground, section 237(a)(2)(A)(i). There is a certain symmetry. Under the exception to the exclusion ground, the person prevails if the visa issuance is more than five years after the crime. Under the deportability provision, the individual prevails if the crime is more than five years after admission.

But that mirror image relationship is deceiving. Think about why Congress would enact the five-year exception contained in section 212(a)(2)(A)(ii)(I). You will probably discover that the reasons are similar to those offered generally for category II limitations. (What would you assume those reasons are?) Now recall the reasons you came up with earlier for the (category I) five-year requirement that is part of section 237(a)(2)(A)(i). You will probably discover that, if Congress had wanted to build into section 237(a)(2)(A)(i) a time limit serving roughly the same purposes as the one it built into section 212(a)(2)(A)(ii)(I), it would have prohibited removal more than five years after *the criminal act*.

A category III limitation would combine the periods encompassed by categories I and II. It would require that any removal proceedings be started within a certain number of years after entry (or admission). By now you have probably figured out the dominant theme underlying category I: Roots develop with time. The deeper those roots, the more hardship removal is likely to cause. If that rationale—compassion for those who have acquired roots—is the principal function of category I limitations, wouldn't a category III limitation do a better job? Should an individual who has lived here thirty years be deportable on the basis of a crime that was committed four years after entry? How would you compare the relative advantages of category I and category III limitations?

A category IV limitation would require that the conduct on which removal is based occur after the enactment of the statutory provision that makes the conduct a deportability ground. This would be a bar on *ex post facto* legislation. As you saw in *Harisiades,* pages 168–69 above, the *ex post facto* clause of the United States Constitution has been held not to prohibit retroactive deportation laws. (The clause pertains only to punishment, and deportation technically is not punishment.) Until 1990, a few deportability grounds were expressly confined to acts or events that occur "hereafter" (meaning after enactment of the "hereafter" language). E.g., INA §§ 241(a)(3, 11, 17), pre–1990 version. After the 1990 Act the word "hereafter" no longer expressly qualifies any of the deportability grounds, though issues persist concerning the retroactivity of the specific deportability ground for aggravated felons. See section D.4 above; see also INA § 237(a)(1)(A) (entered while inadmissible "by the law existing at [the time of entry]"). Professor Nancy Morawetz has argued that retroactive deportation laws violate due process. See Nancy Morawetz, *Rethinking Retroactive Deportation Laws and the Due Process Clause*, 73 NYU L. Rev. 97 (1998).

What do you see as the pros and cons of category IV limitations?

The following Problems illustrate some of the time limits just discussed. To do them, reread the portions of INA §§ 212(a)(1)(A)(iv) and 237(a)(2)(B)(ii) that deal with drug addicts.

PROBLEMS 25–27

Problem 25. X, a noncitizen, entered the United States and then left. While away, she became addicted to heroin and then rehabilitated. Several years after her rehabilitation, Congress enacted what is now INA § 237(a)(2)(B)(ii). After that, she reentered the United States. Is she deportable?

Problem 26. After the enactment of INA § 237(a)(2)(B)(ii), noncitizen Y, in his native country, became addicted to heroin but rehabilitated. Then he entered the United States. Is he deportable?

Problem 27. After the enactment of INA § 237(a)(2)(B)(ii), noncitizen Z entered the United States. She then became addicted to heroin, but later she was rehabilitated. She then left the country. Now, two years later, she wants to come back. Is she admissible? If she is readmitted, will she be deportable?

CHAPTER 8

RELIEF FROM DEPORTABILITY

Noncitizens who fall within any of the grounds set out in INA § 237(a) are said to be "deportable." But the immigration laws do not require the removal of every deportable noncitizen. The statute authorizes several forms of relief. In part, these relief provisions reflect the realities that removal has potentially severe consequences and that, while many of the deportability grounds entail extreme misconduct, many others do not. The relief provisions also reflect the philosophy that even serious misconduct must be weighed against other factors, such as long-term residence, or an unusual degree of hardship, or the likelihood of persecution in a foreign country. Moreover, some of these provisions eliminate the need to hold formal removal proceedings, thus avoiding significant administrative costs. Indeed, one of the remedies you will study—voluntary departure—accounts for the vast majority of dispositions in cases where admittedly deportable noncitizens are apprehended.

A word about coverage: The relief provisions examined in this chapter can be thought of as affirmative defenses—i.e., defenses for which the noncitizen has the burden of proof. They do not include, therefore, the defense that an essential element of the particular deportability ground has not been made out. Also omitted are those few affirmative relief provisions that are specific to particular deportability grounds. Those were covered in the previous chapter—executive pardons, the section 237(a)(1)(H) fraud waiver, etc. For convenience, the persecution-related remedies are deferred to chapter 11.

Despite the title of this chapter, some of the remedies discussed here can waive inadmissibility as well as deportability. Because most of the major remedies discussed in this chapter require specified periods of prior presence or residence in the United States, however, the only arriving noncitizens whom those remedies would typically affect are returning residents. When a particular remedy also waives inadmissibility, that feature will be noted.

All the relief provisions have different requirements, and many have different consequences. Among the variables that distinguish the remedies covered in this chapter are (1) the deportability grounds to which the provision supplies a defense; (2) the prerequisites to obtaining relief; (3) whether, once those prerequisites are met, relief is automatic or subject to the exercise of someone's discretion; (4) how far-reaching the consequences are (permitting the person to remain permanently, or simply putting removal on temporary hold, or something lesser still); and (5) who decides whether to grant relief (the immigration judge and the BIA in removal proceedings, or USCIS outside removal proceedings).

As you study the various remedies, you will notice several recurring limitations. Here are a few to bear in mind:

First, individuals who are properly notified of their removal hearings and fail to appear, or who receive voluntary departure (discussed below) and fail to leave on time, become ineligible to apply for any of several specified remedies for ten years. See INA §§ 240(b)(7), 240B(d). The unavailable remedies include cancellation of removal, voluntary departure, and registry. All are considered below.

Second, aggravated felons (and in some cases other criminal offenders as well) are expressly disqualified from most of the major relief provisions, including cancellation of removal, INA §§ 240A(a)(3), 240A(b)(1)(C), voluntary departure, INA § 240B(a)(1), and registry, INA § 249. Moreover, a conviction of an aggravated felony precludes a showing of good moral character, INA § 101(f)(8), which is itself a required element of several of the relief provisions.

Third, anyone who is deportable on terrorist grounds (and in some cases other national security grounds) is also barred from several forms of discretionary relief. See, e.g., INA §§ 240A(c)(4) (cancellation of removal), 240B(a)(1), 240B(b)(1)(C) (voluntary departure), 249(d) (registry).

Fourth, as a result of regulations issued in 2005, DHS now requires anyone who applies for any form of relief that confers a right to reside in the United States (including, for example, cancellation of removal, adjustment of status, registry, and asylum) to provide certain biographical and biometric data. Using those data, DHS then performs elaborate identity, law enforcement, and national security background checks. Relief may not be granted until those checks are satisfactorily completed. DHS hopes to perform the checks promptly, ideally after a removal hearing has been scheduled but before it has actually taken place; at this writing it is uncertain whether that expectation is realistic. See generally 70 Fed. Reg. 4743 (Jan. 26, 2005), adding 8 C.F.R. § 1003.47 and amending 8 C.F.R. § 1208.4.

Finally, IIRIRA § 306(a)(2) severely curtailed judicial review of denials of discretionary relief. It amended INA § 242(a)(2)(B) to bar judicial review of "any judgment regarding the granting of relief under" certain provisions (which include cancellation of removal, voluntary departure, and adjustment of status). The same law bars review of almost every "other decision or action of the Attorney General the authority for which is specified under this title to be in the discretion of the Attorney General." But these provisions have been held not to bar all judicial review of orders denying discretionary relief. As you will see in chapter 9, § B.6.a.ii below, the courts have usually remained willing to review, for example, *some* agency determinations that applicants are statutorily ineligible for discretionary relief.

SECTION A. LASTING RELIEF

The most sweeping forms of relief are those that enable the person not only to avoid removal, but also to attain (or in some cases retain) LPR status. Here are a few such remedies:

1. CANCELLATION OF REMOVAL

The phrase "cancellation of removal" made its debut with the enactment of IIRIRA § 304(a)(3), which added section 240A to the INA. In IIRIRA, Congress scaled down two existing remedies and then gathered them under one umbrella.

The first prong of the cancellation provision, INA § 240A(a) [here called "cancellation of removal, part A"], describes a remedy that is available only to certain LPRs. Its most common use is in cases where the deportability charges stem from criminal convictions.

The second prong of cancellation of removal, INA § 240A(b), is here called "cancellation of removal, part B." The caption for part (b) refers to cancellation of removal for "certain nonpermanent residents," and indeed the remedy is most commonly requested by noncitizens who are out of status. But nothing in the actual text precludes the use of part (b) by those LPRs who do not meet all the requirements of part (a).

The cancellation provision also contains other subsections (c, d, and e), but these subsections do not create additional remedies. They set out various limitations and definitions that apply to both part (a) and part (b).

a. CANCELLATION OF REMOVAL: PART A

i. *General Applicability and Scope*

This remedy has had a tumultuous history. Its form, location, and content have all changed over the years. To understand the rationale, modern operation, and practical impact of cancellation of removal, part A (and because its immediate predecessor is still applicable in many situations, as discussed below), it is necessary to consider some of the crucial historical events that brought us to where we are today.[1]

---

1. Professor Elwin Griffith, in *The Road between the Section 212(c) Waiver and Cancellation of Removal under Section 240A of the Immigration and Nationality Act—The Impact of the 1996 Reform Legislation*, 12 Georgetown Immigration L.J. 65 (1997), comprehensively analyzes the issues that arose under former INA § 212(c) and the effect of substituting cancellation of removal. For some good descriptions of the pre-IIRIRA version of this remedy, see Lory D. Rosenberg & Denise Sabagh, *A Practitioner's Guide to INA § 212(c)*, Immigration Briefings (April 1993); Stephen Yale-Loehr, *An Overview of INA § 212(c)*, Immigration Briefings (Feb. 1995).

The origins of what is now cancellation part A can be found in the Immigration Act of 1917, ch. 29, § 3, 7th proviso, 39 Stat. 874, 878 (Feb. 5, 1917). The so-called 7th proviso read, in its entirety, as follows:

> [A]liens returning after a temporary absence to an unrelinquished United States domicile of seven consecutive years may be admitted in the discretion of the Secretary of Labor, and under such conditions as he may prescribe.

This seemingly simple provision and its successors have generated some immensely complicated case law, only a portion of which needs to be recounted here.

Notice first: All this original provision said was that certain returning residents may be *admitted*. What, you might be wondering, does any of that have to do with deportability?

The explanation lies in a trilogy of important cases. The first was *Matter of L.,* 1 I. & N. Dec. 1 (BIA), approved by A.G. (1940). A long-term LPR was convicted of a crime involving moral turpitude. As would be the case today, see INA § 237(a)(2)(A)(i), the crime did not render him deportable because it occurred more than five years after his initial admission. Fifteen years later, however, L left the United States for two months to settle a family matter and was readmitted upon his return. The former INS charged he was deportable for having entered the United States after having been convicted of a crime involving moral turpitude. The modern equivalent would be deportability under INA § 237(a)(1)(A) for having entered while inadmissible under section 212(a)(2)(A)(i)(I) because of conviction of a moral turpitude crime. Since there was no *Fleuti* doctrine at the time, L was clearly deportable. The only question was whether he qualified for relief under the 7th proviso.

The Attorney General acknowledged that the literal statutory language covered only exclusion cases. *Matter of L.,* 1 I. & N. Dec. at 5. But L would not have been deportable had he remained in the United States. Moreover, even having left, he would have qualified for relief had he applied for it at the border upon his return. Observing that "[n]o policy of Congress could possibly be served by such irrational result" [meaning the result that would be reached if relief were unavailable in deportation proceedings], *id.,* the Attorney General concluded that relief could be granted *nunc pro tunc,* thereby waiving the inadmissibility that had existed at the time of L's readmission. The effect of the waiver was to eliminate an essential element of the deportability charge.

The second case in the trilogy was *Matter of G.A.,* 7 I. & N. Dec. 274 (BIA 1956). By this time, INA § 212(c) had replaced the 7th proviso, but the content was substantially similar. Again a long-term LPR was convicted of a crime. This time, however, the offense involved marihuana. Unlike the moral turpitude offense of which L had been convicted, G.A.'s marihuana offense rendered him deportable under INA § 241(a)(11) [now 237(a)(2)(B)(i)] even though he had committed the crime more than five years after admission. Several years after the conviction, G.A., like L, departed and returned to the United States. His trip made him deportable on the additional ground, INA § 241(a)(1) [now 237(a)(1)(A)], that he had entered the United States while inadmissible under section 212(a)(23) [now 212(a)(2)(A)(i)(II)] because of his drug conviction. The BIA granted section 212(c) relief. Citing *Matter of L.,* the Board waived, *nunc pro tunc,* the inadmissibility that had existed at the time of G.A.'s return. The waiver eliminated the charge of inadmissibility at entry.

But there remained the more direct deportation charge under then section 241(a)(11). That charge did not rest on G.A.'s reentry; it resulted solely from the fact of the marihuana conviction. The BIA held nonetheless that, when section 212(c) is invoked to waive a ground of inadmissibility arising from a criminal conviction, the INS may not then base deportability on the same conviction. The effect of the decision was to extend section 212(c) to deportability even when the particular deportability ground did not hinge on inadmissibility at entry.

The opinion in G.A. avoided an anomaly: A decision to waive the inadmissibility resulting from a criminal conviction reflects a judgment that, all things considered, the person should be permitted to maintain his or her permanent residence in the United States. That discretionary judgment would be defeated if, after inadmissibility is waived, the person could be deported on the basis of the very misconduct that had just been forgiven.

In avoiding that anomaly, however, the opinion in *G.A.* left a troubling question: If G.A. had not left the United States after his conviction, would he still have been eligible for relief under section 212(c)? The provision appears to say no. That result, however, seems unfair and arbitrary. Why should someone lose out simply because, after a criminal conviction, he or she does not leave and return to the United States? Conversely, why should someone who is otherwise deportable gain an affirmative advantage simply by leaving the United States and then returning?

The third case in the trilogy addressed that dilemma. In *Francis v. INS,* 532 F.2d 268 (2d Cir.1976), which you read earlier for its teachings on the standard of constitutional review in deportation cases, see pages 181–86 above, the court recognized the anomaly. Finding that it would indeed be irrational to limit section 212(c) relief to those long-term LPRs who temporarily leave the United States after the events that render them deportable, the court held that such a distinction violated equal protection. The effect of *Francis* was to extend the reach of section 212(c) to otherwise eligible individuals who had never left the United States. The BIA quickly acceded to *Francis,* see *Matter of Silva,* 16 I. & N. Dec. 26 (1976), and several other circuits soon followed suit. See, e.g., *Cortes-Castillo v. INS,* 997 F.2d 1199 (7th Cir. 1993); *Tapia–Acuna v. INS,* 640 F.2d 223 (9th Cir.1981).

Through this trilogy of cases, relief was thus extended to deportable noncitizens, even those who had not made temporary overseas excursions. Taken individually, each of the expansions served a rational purpose; each one avoided an anomolous result. Taken together, though, these decisions moved 212(c) far beyond the literal statutory language.

And that proved to be the rub. In *Matter of Granados*, 16 I. & N. Dec. 726 (BIA 1979), the BIA abruptly halted the expansion. It held that 212(c) relief would not be a defense to deportability unless the particular deportability ground is also a ground of inadmissibility. In *Granados*, the deportability ground covered those who had been convicted of certain weapons offenses. Because there was no analogous inadmissibility ground at the time, the Board held Granados ineligible for relief.

Then, in *Matter of Hernandez–Casillas*, 20 I. & N. Dec. 262 (1990), the BIA overruled *Granados*. Hernandez was deportable for having entered without inspection, a charge for which there was no analogous exclusion ground. The Board observed that section 212(c), by its terms, made certain exclusion grounds nonwaivable. As long as the particular deportability ground was not analogous to one of these nonwaivable exclusion grounds, the Board held, section 212(c) would apply. It would not be necessary to link the deportability ground affirmatively to one of the waivable exclusion grounds. Either approach, the Board reasoned, would be "equally logical and bear equally little resemblance to the statute as written." *Id.* at 266.

But the battle was not over. Under 8 C.F.R. § 3.1(h)(1)(iii) (2001), the Commissioner of the former INS could request the Attorney General to review a decision of the BIA. The Commissioner made such a request in this case, arguing not merely that the Board had erred in declining to require an exclusion analog, but that 212(c) relief should be held entirely unavailable in deportation proceedings. In his letter to the Attorney General transmitting the administrative record, BIA chairperson David L. Milhollan called the INS request "unprecedented" in its scope:

> Rather than simply requesting review of the specific matters in issue in *Matter of Hernandez,* the Service is requesting consideration of some 50 years' of statutory construction dating to Attorney General Jackson's 1940 decision in *Matter of L.* * * * [As this request] is first made by the Service in this referral, this issue was neither briefed by the parties before the Board nor addressed in the Board decision now on review.

Letter from Hon. David L. Milhollan to Hon. Dick Thornburgh, April 6, 1990, at 1, reproduced in 67 IR 480 (1990). The letter went on to list several early and more recent official INS affirmations that section 212(c) may be applied in deportation proceedings. *Id.* For that and other reasons, the letter strongly urged the Attorney General to decline the INS invitation. Attached to the letter was a ten-page summary of the fifty-year evolution of the law on this subject. *Id.* at 481. The Attorney General agreed not to revisit *Francis* or the cases extending 212(c) to deportation.

He did, however, reverse the BIA and reinstate *Granados*. See 20 I. & N. Dec. at 28–93. Section 212(c), the Attorney General ruled, was meant to waive only those deportability grounds that are also grounds for exclusion.

That way, he reasoned, the application of section 212(c) would bear at least some relationship to the statutory language referring to admission.

From a policy standpoint, the Attorney General's decision led to some peculiar results. Some deportability grounds embrace conduct that gives rise not only to removal but also to future inadmissibility. Others embrace conduct (presumably thought by Congress to be *less* serious, not *more* serious) that triggers removal but not future exclusion. The effect of the Attorney General's interpretation is that relief will be available to noncitizens charged with the offenses Congress regarded as the most serious but not to those charged with the offenses Congress regarded as less serious. Would Congress really have wanted conduct that is not a basis for exclusion at all to be treated more harshly than conduct that is a basis for exclusion? Along the same lines, suppose Congress had *toughened* the immigration laws by adding a specific exclusion ground for noncitizens who had ever entered the United States without inspection. Under the Attorney General's ruling, the effect of Congress's new get-tough policy would have been just the opposite—to provide relief to such individuals.

Nor was it ever clear what the Board and the Attorney General meant when they referred to deportability grounds that are also exclusion grounds. One of the early Board decisions following *Granados* was *Matter of Wadud*, 19 I. & N. Dec. 182 (BIA 1984). The alleged deportability ground was conviction of violating 18 U.S.C. § 1546 (aiding and abetting another noncitizen to commit visa fraud). Wadud pointed out correctly that that crime involved moral turpitude and thus rendered him excludable under the provision for moral turpitude crimes. The Board held nonetheless that the deportability ground was not sufficiently analogous, because it also encompassed several other crimes, some of which did not involve moral turpitude. To accept Wadud's argument "would be to reward those guilty of a more egregious offense for their greater culpability"—a result the Board would not assume Congress intended. Had Congress broken up the deportability ground into several separate grounds, would those that involve moral turpitude then have qualified for 212(c) relief?

The Board's objection to affirmatively rewarding moral turpitude is understandable. But don't results like that become inevitable once the Board holds that the only deportability grounds for which discretionary relief will be possible are those that encompass conduct Congress found objectionable enough to render noncitizens inadmissible?

Perhaps the Board was actually concerned with the opposite problem— the deportability ground being narrower than the exclusion ground. The latter covered all crimes of moral turpitude, not just those concerned with visa fraud. But is there any policy reason to distinguish entire exclusion grounds from subcategories of exclusion grounds?[2]

---

2. In *Francis*, the noncitizen had been deportable under then INA § 241(a)(11) because he had been convicted of a drug offense. The court in *Francis* assumed that the corresponding exclusion ground was section 212(a)(23) [now 212(a)(2)(A)(i)(II)]. The latter, however, then covered not only people who had been convicted of drug offenses, but

Consider, finally, what happens when the BIA or the Attorney General concludes that a deportable noncitizen is ineligible for relief because of the absence of an analogous exclusion ground. Suppose, after his conviction but before the start of deportation proceedings, Wadud had left the United States (meaningfully interrupting his residence) and then had sought to return. Could he have been excluded? On what ground? Would he have been eligible for section 212(c)? If so, and if it had been granted, thus enabling him to reenter, and he had done so, could he then have been deported on the basis of the very criminal conviction that gave rise to the exclusion ground that had just been forgiven? (Recall *Matter of G.A.,* discussed above.) If the answer is no, doesn't the Attorney General's decision in *Hernandez–Casillas* produce a brand new *Francis* problem?

Despite all these difficulties, the Fifth Circuit affirmed the Attorney General in a memorandum decision, 983 F.2d 231 (BIA 1993), and the other courts of appeals almost uniformly affirmed subsequent BIA decisions applying the Attorney General's ruling. See, e.g., *Gjonaj v. INS*, 47 F.3d 824, 827 (6th Cir. 1995); *Rodriguez-Padron v. INS*, 13 F.3d 1455, 1459–60 (11th Cir. 1994); but cf. *Cato v. INS*, 84 F.3d 597 (2d Cir. 1996)(applying Attorney General's rule, but only in cases where enactment of analogous exclusion ground would have been logically possible).

IIRIRA codified many of the foregoing developments. It has effectively approved the original trilogy on which subsequent developments have been based. The new provision makes clear that relief will be available to both inadmissible and deportable noncitizens, even when the particular charge does not rest on entry or admission. It is equally clear under the new provision that a deportable noncitizen will not have to leave and return in order to qualify. The *Hernandez-Casillas* issue has also been resolved; the new provision does not require deportable noncitizens to identify a comparable inadmissibility ground, as the Attorney General had required under the old provision. IIRIRA also settled many of the timing issues described below.

At this time, read carefully INA § 240A(a).

ii. Timing

As you have just seen, INA § 240A(a) contains two separate timing requirements. The first is five years of LPR status. One issue is when LPR status ends. The INA doesn't say, but the regulations provide that LPR status "terminates upon entry of a final administrative order of exclusion, deportation, or removal." 8 C.F.R. § 1.1(p) (2004). For this and other purposes, the administrative order is deemed final when the BIA affirms it or the time for filing a BIA appeal lapses. INA § 101(a)(47)(B). Further, LPR status obtained by fraud will not be recognized at all for purposes of

also one other group—those whom consular officers or immigration officers had known or had had reason to believe were, or had been, drug traffickers. The fact that section 241(a)(11) corresponded only to a subcategory of section 212(a)(23) did not render section 212(c) inapplicable in *Francis*.

cancellation of removal, part A. *Matter of Koloamatangi*, 23 I. & N. Dec. 548 (BIA 2003).

Second, cancellation of removal, part A requires that the person "resided in the United States continuously for 7 years after having been admitted in any status." INA § 240A(a)(2). In *Matter of Blancas-Lara*, 23 I. & N. Dec. 458 (BIA 2002), the Board held that, for this purpose, nonimmigrant stays are fully counted. The former INS had argued in *Blancas* that most nonimmigrant categories are inconsistent with an intent to reside permanently and that counting such stays as residence would therefore reward those who wrongly intend to remain permanently. The BIA disagreed. It observed that a contrary interpretation—i.e., one requiring LPR status for seven years—would render the five-year LPR requirement superfluous.

Many other issues arise: When does continuous residence start? Does time spent in unlawful presence count? When does continuous residence end? When the person committed the act that triggered deportability? When the notice to appear is issued, or served? When deportability is conceded? When the immigration judge issues a removal order? When the BIA does so (or when the appeal time has lapsed)? Only when judicial review has been completed, or the time period for applying for it has lapsed?

For some of the answers, read carefully INA § 240A(d)(1).

iii.   Disqualifications

Certain noncitizens are statutorily disqualified from cancellation of removal, part A (and in some instances part B as well). Among the more important classes disqualified from part A are aggravated felons. INA § 240A(a)(3). See INA § 240A(c) for a list of other ineligible classes.

iv.   Discretion

In addition to establishing statutory eligibility, the applicant must show he or she merits the favorable exercise of discretion. As to the exercise of that discretion, see generally *Matter of C.V.T.*, 22 I. & N. Dec. 7 (BIA 1998).

QUESTIONS

1. Step back for a moment from all the technical distinctions that this relief provision has generated. What are the basic policy tradeoffs that cancellation of removal, part A, reflects?

2. Both the present provision and its predecessors have required determinations of when LPR status ends. Make a list of the various points in time that courts *could* use to mark the end of lawful permanent residence. Then articulate the pros and cons of the various possibilities, thinking about how they relate to what permanent residence really means and to what cancellation of removal, part A, is designed to achieve.

PROBLEMS 1–3

Problem 1. A was admitted to the United States as an LPR in June 1999. In June 2003, ICE issued a Notice to Appear for a removal hearing, alleging A had been convicted of a crime involving moral turpitude. The immigration judge terminated the removal hearing, ruling that the particular crime did not involve moral turpitude. In 2004, A took a 100–day summer vacation in Europe. In July 2006, he committed a drug offense (possession of cocaine), pleaded guilty, and was sentenced to probation. In August 2006, ICE issued a notice to appear for another removal hearing. This time, the immigration judge found A deportable for having been convicted of violating a law relating to a controlled substance. Is A eligible for cancellation of removal, part A? *Cf. Matter of Cisneros–Gonzalez*, 23 I. & N. Dec. 668 (BIA en banc, 2004) (holding, in the context of cancellation of removal, *part B*, that the term "notice to appear" in INA § 240A(d)(1) refers only to the notice filed in the current removal proceeding, not to any filed in prior proceedings). In that case, the person had been previously (and properly) deported, had returned without inspection, and had then accumulated ten new years of physical presence.

Problem 2. In April 1998, B was admitted to the United States for one year on a business visitor visa. She overstayed, but in April 2000 she adjusted her status to that of LPR on the basis of her marriage to a United States citizen. In May 2005, B was found in possession of illegal amphetamines and three months later was convicted of that crime. An immigration judge has found her deportable. Is B eligible for cancellation of removal, part A?

Problem 3. C was admitted to the United States on an L–1 intracompany transferee visa in 1996. In February 2000 he married a United States citizen. In August 2000, with his authorized stay not having expired, he obtained adjustment of status as an immediate relative. In April 2004, ICE discovered that his marriage had been a sham and issued a Notice to Appear for a removal hearing. ICE alleged that C was deportable for having been inadmissible (on fraud grounds) at the time of adjustment of status. See INA § 237(a)(1)(A). In June 2004, the immigration judge ordered C removed, and in June 2005 the BIA affirmed. In September 2005, C moved to reopen for the purpose of applying for cancellation of removal, part A, alleging that by then he had accrued the required 5 years of LPR status. Is C now eligible for cancellation?

b. CANCELLATION OF REMOVAL: PART B

INA § 240A(b) contains a modified version of a remedy that, until IIRIRA, was known as "suspension of deportation." For an excellent history and analysis of the practical effects of the changes, see Elwin Griffith, *The Transition Between Suspension of Deportation and Cancellation of Removal for Nonpermanent Residents under the Immigration and Nationality Act: The Impact of the 1996 Reform Legislation*, 48 Drake L. Rev. 79 (1999). Unlike cancellation of removal part A, which is available only to LPRs, cancellation part B can be invoked by anyone who otherwise meets its requirements. In practice, the principal beneficiaries of part B are undocumented migrants.

Now please read INA § 240A(b)(1).

A few initial observations: First, this remedy is available to both inadmissible and deportable noncitizens. Since one eligibility requirement is ten years of continuous physical presence in the United States, however, the usual type of inadmissibility that cancellation part B will waive is presence without admission. In addition, arriving noncitizens who return from temporary visits abroad after ten years of undocumented presence in the United States may also apply for cancellation part B.

Second, there are two separate branches of cancellation part B—a general branch, and a special branch for battered spouses and battered children. The special branch was added in 1994 by the Violence Against Women Act. See Pub.L. 103–322, § 40703, 108 Stat. 1796, 1955 (Sept. 13, 1994).

The two branches contain roughly parallel requirements—continuous physical presence, good moral character, and hardship. Both provisions are subject to various disqualifications. The general difference is that, for applicants who have been "battered or subjected to extreme cruelty" under specified circumstances, the requirements are loosened. The details appear in INA § 240A(b)(2). For a good analysis of the operation of this provision and the practical context in which it is set, see Janet M. Calvo, *The Violence Against Women Act: An Opportunity for the Justice Department to Confront Domestic Violence*, 72 IR 485 (Apr. 10, 1995). Professor Lee Teran has urged the elimination of the "extreme hardship" requirement for battered spouses and children. Lee J. Teran, *Barriers to Protection at Home and Abroad: Mexican Victims of Domestic Violence and the Violence Against Women Act,* 17 Boston Univ. Internat'l L.J. 1 (1999). Her suggestion was heeded for purposes of the self-petitioning procedure (see chapter 6), but as of this writing the special cancellation of removal provision still requires a showing of extreme hardship. INA § 240A(b)(2)(A)(v).

Third, as is true of cancellation part A, applicants for cancellation part B have two separate hurdles to clear. They must establish statutory eligibility, and then they must receive the favorable exercise of discretion.

Finally, note that under INA § 240A(e)(1) "the Attorney General may not cancel the removal and adjust the status under this section" (or under the former suspension of deportation provision) of more than 4000 individuals in any fiscal year. As this language indicates, this remedy accomplishes two things: It avoids removal, and it results in LPR status. The Justice Department's interim regulations regard the two parts of the remedy as inseparable and establish a queuing system analogous to the preference-based quota systems that you saw in chapter 3. Once relief has been granted to 4000 applicants in a given fiscal year, immigration judges and the BIA may not grant relief in any further cases that year, even conditionally. They may deny pending applications for cancellation on certain statutory eligibility grounds but will reserve decision on all other pending applications. These pending applications will be taken up in the order in which they were filed, as soon as the quota permits. See 8 C.F.R. § 240.21(c) (2004); see generally Nadine Wettstein, *The Peddler Sells His Caps: The EOIR and INS Issue a New Rule on the Suspension/Cancellation Ceiling*, 3 BIB 1083 (Nov. 1, 1998).

The Nicaraguan Adjustment and Central American Relief Act, Pub. L. 105–100, Title II, 111 Stat. 2160, 2193 (Nov. 19, 1997) [NACARA], among other things relaxed the substantive criteria for cancellation of removal part B for certain nationals of Guatemala, El Salvador, the Soviet Union and its successor republics, and most Eastern European nations. The details are discussed in subsection (iv) below. For now, it is enough to note that these NACARA adjustments are not counted against the 4000 limit. INA § 240A(e)(3)(A).

i. Continuous Physical Presence

When IIRIRA replaced suspension of deportation with cancellation of removal, part B, it made the continuous physical presence requirement more demanding. One change was an increase in the length of the period from 7 years to 10. See INA § 244(a)(1). IIRIRA also specified, for the first time, that service of a Notice to Appear automatically ends a person's continuous physical presence. INA § 240A(d)(1). As a result, it is impossible to reach the ten-year threshold while waiting for a removal hearing or an appellate proceeding. (Commission of any of several crimes will also terminate continuous physical presence, *id.*, but the subsequent conviction would have been an independent disqualifying event anyway. INA § 240A(b)(1)(C)).

The last major change that IIRIRA made to the continuous physical presence requirement concerns the meaning of "continuous." What happens if the person has made one or more temporary trips outside the United States? You will recall that the *Fleuti* doctrine, discussed on pages 511–25 above, has been used to relieve LPRs of the consequences of reentry when they return from temporary overseas visits that were not meant to be meaningfully interruptive of permanent residence. In *Wadman v. INS*, 329 F.2d 812 (9th Cir. 1964), the court applied the same principle to determine whether a temporary excursion destroyed the continuity of one's physical presence in the United States, for purposes of suspension of deportation.

After *Wadman*, and until 1984, the courts and the BIA applied the meaningful interruption test almost universally. See, e.g., *McColvin v. INS*, 648 F.2d 935, 938–39 (4th Cir.1981) (though departure held meaningfully interruptive); *Heitland v. INS*, 551 F.2d 495, 501–04 (2d Cir.1977) (same); *Matter of Wong*, 12 I. & N. Dec. 271 (BIA 1967) (applicable nationwide, *id.* at 276). But *cf. Fidalgo/Velez v. INS*, 697 F.2d 1026, 1029, 1030 (11th Cir.1983) (preferring literal interpretation, though ultimately holding only that "Petitioner's trip was meaningfully interruptive").

In 1984, however, the Supreme Court dropped a bombshell. The case was *INS v. Phinpathya,* 464 U.S. 183, 104 S.Ct. 584, 78 L.Ed.2d 401 (1984).

A noncitizen who had overstayed her nonimmigrant visa left the United States for three months and, while abroad, defrauded the United States consulate in order to obtain the new visa that she then used upon her return. The BIA found no continuous physical presence and denied suspension. The Court of Appeals for the Ninth Circuit remanded for reconsideration, holding that the BIA had failed to apply the proper formula.

In the Supreme Court, the former INS argued that this time the Ninth Circuit had gone too far. The INS granted that the continuous physical presence language requires a flexible interpretation, under which only meaningful absences destroy continuity, but contended that on these facts the absence was meaningful. Three Justices—Brennan, Marshall, and Stevens—accepted the INS argument. But a majority of the Justices went much further. They held that even a non-meaningful absence would preclude continuous physical presence. In so holding, they took on an issue that was not raised by the facts, that no one had argued or briefed, that required the disapproval of twenty years of virtually unbroken case law, that reached a result at odds with the BIA interpretation, and that produced law far more extreme than what even the INS had sought. Interpreting the continuous physical presence requirement literally, the Court held that any absence, no matter how insignificant, would disrupt the continuity of the person's physical presence and thus, if the absence occurred in the past seven years, preclude suspension. No matter how long the individual had resided in the United States, how commendably he or she had lived, or how severe the resulting hardship, the immigration judge and the BIA would have no power to suspend deportation if, within the past seven years, the person had gone shopping for the afternoon in Tijuana.

Congress was not pleased. Five months later the House voted 411–4 to supersede *Phinpathya*. The House bill would have amended the INA to provide expressly that only a meaningfully interruptive absence would disrupt continuous physical presence. 130 Cong.Rec. 16348–50 (June 14, 1984). The Senate did not act on the issue that year, but when Congress passed IRCA two years later it added a provision that read:

> An alien shall not be considered to have failed to maintain continuous physical presence * * * if the absence from the United States was brief, casual, and innocent and did not meaningfully interrupt the continuous physical presence.

INA § 244(b)(2) (pre-IIRIRA).

In IIRIRA, Congress preserved the practice of permitting temporary absences, but it replaced the flexible test (innocent, casual, brief, and no meaningful interruption) with two bright line rules. Under the new provision, INA § 240A(d)(2), a single departure of more than 90 days automatically destroys continuous physical presence, as do cumulative absences of more than 180 days. At least one court has held, however, that these were not the *only* absences capable of destroying the requisite continuity of physical presence; voluntary departure (discussed below) will also have that effect, but only if the noncitizen was informed that voluntary departure was actually being granted and accepted it. *Reyes-Vasquez v. Ashcroft*, 395 F.3d 903, 907–09 (8th Cir. 2005).

Finally, note that for certain noncitizens who have been battered or otherwise subjected to "extreme cruelty," the continuous physical presence requirement has been reduced to three years. INA § 240A(b)(2)(B).

QUESTIONS

1. What do you think are the rationales for (a) having such a remedy as cancellation of removal part B in the first place; (b) requiring a certain number of years of physical presence; (c) requiring that the physical presence be continuous; and (d) applying bright line rules, rather than weighing factors, to decide whether the continuity has been broken?

2. Is there a technical glitch in the drafting of section 240A? To qualify, the person has to have been physically present for ten years "immediately preceding the date of such application." INA § 240A(b)(1)(A). But the application is filed in removal proceedings, after service of the Notice to Appear has already terminated the person's continuous physical presence. INA § 240A(d)(1). Under the literal wording, then, how can *anyone* qualify for relief? How would you amend the statute to eliminate the problem?

PROBLEM 4

A, her husband, and their three young children were all admitted to the United States in October 1995 (A as the principal, on an H–1B visa, and the others as accompanying spouse and children on H–4 visas). In October 2001, all received adjustment of status to lawful permanent residence. Every summer, starting in 1996, the family has taken a three-week vacation overseas to visit relatives. In December 2005, ICE served all the family members with notices to appear, alleging all were deportable for having obtained adjustment of status while inadmissible, under INA § 237(a)(1)(A). All the family members would experience various unusually severe hardships if ordered removed. Will they be eligible for cancellation of removal?

ii. Hardship

Ever since suspension of deportation (the predecessor to cancellation of removal, part B) was introduced in 1940, eligibility has required a showing that deportation would cause some special brand or degree of hardship. Over the years, however, Congress has flip-flopped in its views of precisely how severe the hardship should have to be. The changes are well summarized by former BIA member Lory Rosenberg:

> [W]hen the first suspension provision was enacted in 1940, the required showing was only "serious economic detriment to a citizen or legally resident alien who is the spouse, parent, or minor

child of such deportable alien." In 1952, for a variety of reasons, the socio-political pendulum swung in the opposite direction and Congress enacted the far more restrictive standard of "exceptional and extremely unusual hardship." Ten years later, Congress retreated from this position, and while it retained "exceptional and extremely unusual" as the standard for relief under section 244(a)(2) of the Act [the prong for noncitizen criminal offenders and those who are deportable on certain other particularly serious grounds—Ed.], it required only "extreme hardship" for section 244(a)(1) [all other—Ed.] cases.

Matter of O.J.O., 21 I. & N. Dec. 381, 398 (BIA 1996) (en banc) (Rosenberg, concurring).

Three months after that description appeared, the pendulum swung again. In converting suspension of deportation to cancellation of removal, part B, Congress once again amended the hardship standard. The requirement of "exceptional and extremely unusual hardship," previously reserved for the most serious categories of deportable noncitizens, was made applicable to all applicants except those who have been battered or otherwise subjected to extreme cruelty. INA §§ 240A(b)(1)(D), 240A(b)(2)(E). In addition, for the person who applies under the general provision, even "exceptional and extremely unusual hardship" to the applicant is not enough; now, the requisite hardship must be suffered by the applicant's qualifying family member. In contrast, for the person who applies under the battered spouse or child provision, extreme hardship to the applicant will suffice. *Id*. The difference between "extreme hardship" and "exceptional and extremely unusual hardship" is one of degree and will be taken up shortly.

Whatever the exact formulation, the hardship requirement has typically been the most formidable hurdle to clear. Certainly this is the element that has spawned the most litigation.

The issue of when hardship is "exceptional and extremely unusual" can surface in either of two distinct settings that it is crucial to separate. The issue arises in its most direct form when a noncitizen in removal proceedings applies to the immigration judge for cancellation. The applicant has the burden of establishing the required hardship (along with all the other elements of removal). Since the immigration judge's decision whether to order removal is appealable to the BIA, the BIA frequently becomes enmeshed in hardship determinations as well. Before IIRIRA, when the courts could freely review denials of suspension of deportation, they too would make frequent contributions to the law on extreme hardship.

IIRIRA § 306(a)(2) curbs judicial involvement in these issues. It bars the courts from reviewing "any judgment regarding the granting of relief under section ... 240A." INA § 242(a)(2)(B)(i). As you will see in chapter 9, the courts have generally interpreted this provision as allowing judicial review of the non-discretionary prerequisites to cancellation of removal. The "exceptional and extremely unusual hardship" requirement has been held to be discretionary in nature, however, and therefore not directly reviewable. See *Romero–Torres v. Ashcroft*, 327 F.3d 887 (9th Cir. 2003); *Gonzalez–Oropeza v. U.S. Attorney General*, 321 F.3d 1331, 1332–33 (11th Cir. 2003).

But there is a second way in which the hardship issue arises. This one requires more explanation and will likely continue to keep the courts occupied with hardship issues. As you might recall, it is only while removal proceedings are pending before the immigration judge (or the BIA) that one may apply for cancellation at all. 8 C.F.R. §§ 1240.11(a), 1240.20(b) (2004). Suppose a person is ineligible for cancellation at the time of those administrative proceedings but, before actual removal from the United States, he or she becomes eligible.

That scenario used to be quite common. Removal proceedings can drag on, and in addition delays often occur between issuance of a final removal order and the person's physical departure. During that latter interval, the seventh year of continuous physical presence might have accrued. Today, that particular sequence can no longer occur, because, as noted earlier, service of the Notice to Appear terminates one's continuous physical presence. But other events can make noncitizens eligible. A new personal development, for example, might permit a showing of exceptional and extremely unusual hardship. Or new personal circumstances might enhance the general equities that influence the exercise of administrative discretion required for removal.

In any of those cases, as in any other case where previously unavailable evidence affects either deportability or eligibility for affirmative relief, the proper procedure is to move to reopen removal proceedings. 8 C.F.R. §§ 1003.2, 1003.23 (2004). If the BIA has already handed down a decision in the case, then the motion is filed with the BIA. *Id.* § 1003.2. Otherwise the motion is filed with the immigration judge. *Id.* § 1003.23. (The requirements for motions to reopen are taken up separately in chapter 9.)

The immigration judges and the BIA have the discretion to grant or deny a motion to reopen. If such a motion is granted, and if its purpose was to enable the person to apply for cancellation, he or she then files the cancellation application with the immigration judge at the reopened hearing. There the immigration judge will have to determine (a) whether the applicant meets the various statutory prerequisites for removal; and (b) if so, whether discretion should be favorably exercised. The decision of the immigration judge in this reopened proceeding is appealable to the BIA. 8 C.F.R. § 1003.1(b)(3) (2004). By the same token, if the immigration judge denies the motion to reopen, that denial is appealable to the BIA. *Id.*

Thus, a noncitizen who files a motion to reopen is virtually assured the opportunity to get his or her case before the BIA one way or the other. Although there is no automatic right to a stay of removal while a motion to reopen is pending, 8 C.F.R. § 1003.6(b) (2004), immigration judges and the BIA for obvious reasons are reluctant to allow removal to occur before they have had a chance to rule on the motions. Moreover, as you will see in chapter 9, a BIA decision denying reopening, and sometimes a BIA decision denying cancellation, are reviewable in the court of appeals. Nothing in

IIRIRA eliminates the courts' jurisdiction to review denials of motions to reopen removal proceedings.[3] Once that review process is initiated, the court has the discretion whether to stay removal. INA § 242(b)(3)(B).

The combination of these various procedural rules means that the filing of a motion to reopen will frequently delay removal whether the motion ultimately succeeds or not. For that reason, motions to reopen have been extremely controversial. ICE, and at times the BIA, have seen them as procedural devices calculated primarily to buy noncitizens additional time in the United States. The immigration bar sees them as legitimate and necessary vehicles for raising new considerations relevant to the decision whether to remove. See generally chapter 9, § B.5 below.

As you study the cases that follow, keep in mind that a substantive decision to grant *cancellation of removal* avoids removal and confers LPR status. In contrast, a decision to *reopen* entitles the person only to an evidentiary hearing at which he or she will have the opportunity to prove the facts necessary for cancellation (and possibly a temporary stay of removal). Because the consequences of the two decisions are so different, be sure you are clear which of them is actually being reviewed in a given case.

INS v. Jong Ha Wang

Supreme Court of the United States, 1981.
450 U.S. 139, 101 S.Ct. 1027, 67 L.Ed.2d 123.

■ PER CURIAM.

[This case was decided long before IIRIRA. The INA section numbers, the terminology, and several of the eligibility requirements have now changed, as discussed in the preceding text. But the essential issues raised in this opinion remain relevant today.—Ed.]

Section 244 of the Immigration and Nationality Act (Act), as amended, provides that the Attorney General in his discretion may suspend deportation and adjust the status of an otherwise deportable alien who (1) has been physically present in the United States for not less than seven years; (2) is a person of good moral character; and (3) is "a person whose deportation would, in the opinion of the Attorney General, result in extreme hardship to the alien or to his spouse, parent, or child, who is a citizen of the United States or an alien lawfully admitted for permanent residence." The Attorney General is authorized to delegate his powers under the Act, INA § 103, and his authority under § 244 has been delegated by regulation to specified authorities in the Immigration and Naturalization Service.

3. INA § 242(a)(2)(B)(ii) bars the courts from reviewing any "decision or action of the Attorney General the authority for which is specified *under this title* to be in the discretion of the Attorney General ..." (emphasis added). But the Attorney General's discretion to grant reopening arises by regulation (cited in the text), not by statute. Moreover, INA § 242(b)(6) affirmatively recognizes that courts will have occasion to review denials of motions to reopen. *Sarmadi v. INS*, 121 F.3d 1319, 1322 (9th Cir. 1997); *King Sang Chow v. INS*, 113 F.3d 659, 664 (7th Cir. 1997).

The § 244 issue usually arises in an alien's deportation hearing. It can arise, however, as it did in this case, on a motion to reopen after deportation has been duly ordered. The Act itself does not expressly provide for a motion to reopen, but regulations promulgated under the Act allow such a procedure. The regulations also provide that the motion to reopen shall "state the new fact to be proved at the reopened hearing and shall be supported by affidavits or other evidentiary material." Motions to reopen are thus permitted in those cases in which the events or circumstances occurring after the order of deportation would satisfy the extreme-hardship standard of § 244. Such motions will not be granted "when a prima facie case of eligibility for the relief sought has not been established."

Respondents, husband and wife, are natives and citizens of Korea who first entered the United States in January 1970 as nonimmigrant treaty traders. They were authorized to remain until January 10, 1972, but they remained beyond that date without permission and were found deportable after a hearing in November 1974. They were granted the privilege of voluntarily departing by February 1, 1975. They did not do so. Instead, they applied for adjustment of status under § 245 of the Act, but were found ineligible for this relief after a hearing on July 15, 1975. Their appeal from this ruling was dismissed by the Board of Immigration Appeals in October 1977. Respondents then filed a second motion to reopen their deportation proceedings in December 1977, this time claiming suspension under § 244 of the Act. Respondents by then had satisfied the 7–year– continuous-physical-presence requirement of that section. The motion alleged that deportation would result in extreme hardship to respondents' two American-born children because neither child spoke Korean and would thus lose "educational opportunities" if forced to leave this country. Respondents also claimed economic hardship to themselves and their children resulting from the forced liquidation of their assets at a possible loss. None of the allegations was sworn or otherwise supported by evidentiary materials, but it appeared that all of respondents' close relatives, aside from their children, resided in Korea and that respondents had purchased a dry-cleaning business in August 1977, some three years after they had been found deportable. The business was valued at $75,000 and provided an income of $650 per week. Respondents also owned a home purchased in 1974 and valued at $60,000. They had $24,000 in a savings account and some $20,000 in miscellaneous assets. Liabilities were approximately $81,000.

The Board of Immigration Appeals denied respondents' motion to reopen without a hearing, concluding that they had failed to demonstrate a prima facie case that deportation would result in extreme hardship to either themselves or their children so as to entitle them to discretionary relief under the Act. The Board noted that a mere showing of economic detriment is not sufficient to establish extreme hardship under the Act. This was particularly true since respondents had "significant financial resources and there [was] nothing to suggest that the college-educated male respondent could not find suitable employment in Korea." With respect to the claims involving the children, the Board ruled that the alleged loss of educational opportunities to the young children of relatively affluent, educated Korean parents did not constitute extreme hardship within the meaning of § 244.

The Court of Appeals for the Ninth Circuit, sitting en banc, reversed. Contrary to the Board's holding, the Court of Appeals found that respondents had alleged a sufficient prima facie case of extreme hardship to entitle them to a hearing. The court reasoned that the statute should be liberally construed to effectuate its ameliorative purpose. The combined effect of the allegation of harm to the minor children, which the court thought was hard to discern without a hearing, and the impact on respondents' economic interests was sufficient to constitute a prima facie case requiring a hearing where the Board would "consider the total potential effect of deportation on the alien and his family."

The Court of Appeals erred in two respects. First, the court ignored the regulation which requires the alien seeking suspension to allege and support by affidavit or other evidentiary material the particular facts claimed to constitute extreme hardship. Here, the allegations of hardship were in the main conclusory and unsupported by affidavit. By requiring a hearing on such a motion, the Court of Appeals circumvented this aspect of the regulation, which was obviously designed to permit the Board to select for hearing only those motions reliably indicating the specific recent events that would render deportation a matter of extreme hardship for the alien or his children.[5]

Secondly, and more fundamentally, the Court of Appeals improvidently encroached on the authority which the Act confers on the Attorney General and his delegates. The crucial question in this case is what constitutes "extreme hardship." These words are not self-explanatory, and reasonable men could easily differ as to their construction. But the Act commits their definition in the first instance to the Attorney General and his delegates, and their construction and application of this standard should not be overturned by a reviewing court simply because it may prefer another interpretation of the statute. Here, the Board considered the facts alleged and found that neither respondents nor their children would suffer extreme hardship. The Board considered it well settled that a mere showing of economic detriment was insufficient to satisfy the requirements of § 244

---

5. The present regulation is framed negatively; it directs the Board not to reopen unless certain showings are made. It does not affirmatively require the Board to reopen the proceedings under any particular condition. Thus, the regulations may be construed to provide the Board with discretion in determining under what circumstances proceedings should be reopened. See *Villena v. INS,* 622 F.2d 1352 (CA9 1980) (en banc) (Wallace, J., dissenting). In his dissent, Judge Wallace stated that INS had discretion beyond requiring proof of a prima facie case:

"If INS discretion is to mean anything, it must be that the INS has some latitude in deciding when to reopen a case. The INS should have the right to be restrictive. Granting such motions too freely will permit endless delay of deportation by aliens creative and fertile enough to continuously produce new and material facts sufficient to establish a prima facie case. It will also waste the time and efforts of immigration judges called upon to preside at hearings automatically required by the prima facie allegations."

and in any event noted that respondents had significant financial resources while finding nothing to suggest that Mr. Wang could not find suitable employment in Korea. It also followed that respondents' two children would not suffer serious economic deprivation if they returned to Korea. Finally, the Board could not believe that the two "young children of affluent, educated parents" would be subject to such educational deprivations in Korea as to amount to extreme hardship. In making these determinations, the Board was acting within its authority. As we see it, nothing in the allegations indicated that this is a particularly unusual case requiring the Board to reopen the deportation proceedings.

The Court of Appeals nevertheless ruled that the hardship requirement of § 244 is satisfied if an alien produces sufficient evidence to suggest that the "hardship from deportation would be different and more severe than that suffered by the ordinary alien who is deported." Also, as Judge Goodwin observed in dissent, the majority of the Court of Appeals also strongly indicated that respondents should prevail under such an understanding of the statute. * * *

The Attorney General and his delegates have the authority to construe "extreme hardship" narrowly should they deem it wise to do so. Such a narrow interpretation is consistent with the "extreme hardship" language, which itself indicates the exceptional nature of the suspension remedy. Moreover, the Government has a legitimate interest in creating official procedures for handling motions to reopen deportation proceedings so as readily to identify those cases raising new and meritorious considerations. Under the standard applied by the court below, many aliens could obtain a hearing based upon quite minimal showings. As stated in dissent below, "by using the majority opinion as a blueprint, any foreign visitor who has fertility, money, and the ability to stay out of trouble with the police for seven years can change his status from that of tourist or student to that of permanent resident without the inconvenience of immigration quotas. This strategy is not fair to those waiting for a quota." (Goodwin, J., dissenting). Judge Goodwin further observed that the relaxed standard of the majority opinion "is likely to shift the administration of hardship deportation cases from the Immigration and Naturalization Service to this court."

We are convinced that the Board did not exceed its authority and that the Court of Appeals erred in ordering that the case be reopened. Accordingly, the petition for certiorari is granted, and the judgment of the Court of Appeals is reversed.

So ordered.

■ BRENNAN, MARSHALL and BLACKMUN would grant the petition for certiorari and give the case plenary consideration.

NOTES AND QUESTIONS

1. It is hornbook administrative law that a reviewing court generally may not affirm the decision of an administrative agency "unless the

grounds upon which the agency acted in exercising its powers were those upon which its action can be sustained." *SEC v. Chenery Corp.,* 318 U.S. 80, 95, 63 S.Ct. 454, 462, 87 L.Ed. 626, 637 (1943). Put another way, a court will not ordinarily affirm an agency decision on a ground not invoked by the agency itself. Can you figure out the rationale for that principle?

What reason did the *BIA* give for its refusal to reopen deportation proceedings to permit an application for suspension? What two reasons does the *Supreme Court* give for upholding the BIA decision? Is the Supreme Court decision compatible with *Chenery?*

2. The Ninth Circuit had held in this case that (a) a BIA decision refusing to reopen deportation proceedings is reviewable only for abuse of discretion; but (b) if the purpose of the motion is to obtain the opportunity to apply for suspension, and the noncitizen makes out a "prima facie case" that he or she is eligible for suspension, it is an abuse of discretion not to reopen; and (c) the present applicants had made out such a prima facie case.

As Judge Sneed noted in his Ninth Circuit concurrence, see *Jong Ha Wang v. INS,* 622 F.2d 1341, 1350 n. 1 (9th Cir.1980), the BIA itself invented the "prima facie case" test in 1972. The Ninth Circuit in *Jong Ha Wang* (and in its previous decisions) adopted that test. At the time of *Jong Ha Wang,* however, neither the BIA nor the courts had ever explained what the term means. By analogy to other areas of law you have studied, can you surmise what must constitute a prima facie case of eligibility for suspension? Do you agree with the Ninth Circuit that the present allegations establish a prima facie case? See *Abudu v. INS,* 802 F.2d 1096, 1100 (9th Cir.1986), rev'd, *INS v. Abudu,* 485 U.S. 94, 108 S.Ct. 904, 99 L.Ed.2d 90 (1988).

3. *Should* allegations that establish a prima facie case of eligibility require the BIA to reopen, or should the BIA have the discretion to deny reopening even then? One instance in which that issue arises is where the Board concludes that, even if the person ultimately proves statutory eligibility, there are negatives that would persuade the Board to deny suspension (now cancellation) on discretionary grounds in any event. The Supreme Court held in *INS v. Rios–Pineda,* 471 U.S. 444, 105 S.Ct. 2098, 85 L.Ed.2d 452 (1985), that in such a case the BIA does not abuse its discretion by denying reopening. Accord, *INS v. Abudu,* 485 U.S. 94, 105, 108 S.Ct. 904, 912, 99 L.Ed.2d 90, 102 (1988) (dictum).

The same question arises when the BIA concludes that the allegations would establish extreme hardship if true, but the BIA finds the allegations outlandish on their face. Should a denial of reopening be held to constitute an abuse of discretion in that instance?

Assume, however, that the applicant alleges non-outlandish facts establishing a prima facie case of eligibility, and that there are no factors clearly requiring a negative exercise of discretion. What are the pros and cons of a rule that would require the Board to reopen under those circumstances?

Note, incidentally, that the Justice Department regulations now expressly say "The Board [of Immigration Appeals] has discretion to deny a motion to reopen even if the party moving has made out a *prima facie* case for relief." 8 C.F.R. § 1003.2(a) (2004).

4.   In his Ninth Circuit concurring opinion, Judge Sneed said:

* * * Were [the BIA's] refusal based solely on the belief that the facts as alleged are insufficient to constitute hardship under section 244(a)(1), the issue before us should be merely whether this conclusion reflects an abuse of discretion on the part of the Attorney General. A hearing should be unnecessary because the alien's version of the facts has been accepted by the INS [sic—he must mean the BIA]. A hearing to establish what is admitted serves no purpose * * *. Were this case in that posture I would conclude the Attorney General has not abused his discretion in refusing to open deportation proceedings.

On the other hand, were the refusal to reopen based wholly, or even in material part, on an assertion or belief that the facts are other than the alien asserts, it would be, I believe, an abuse of discretion not to reopen deportation proceedings for a hearing. As previously indicated it is not clear on what ground the refusal to reopen was based in this case [because it is not clear what the BIA means by the phrase "prima facie case."] Where facts are disputed a hearing is necessary to permit the Attorney General's discretion to be exercised wisely and on the basis of all the relevant facts.

622 F.2d at 1230.

Is Judge Sneed right to suggest that a hearing would be pointless under his first scenario? Suppose the moving papers contain the following allegations: The noncitizen parents, ordered removed to Thailand, have a ten-year-old, fifth grade, United States citizen child who has lived in the United States all her life and speaks only English. The child has two surviving grandparents. They live 50 miles away and see the child about once every two weeks on the average. The child has a sensitive nature and would be extremely sad to leave her grandparents and her friends. In addition, she would feel great isolation because both her inability to speak the Thai language and her striking cultural differences would make it difficult for her to make friends with the other children.

Let us assume those allegations are undisputed. Does it follow that the BIA can intelligently assess the degree of hardship without a hearing? Shouldn't it want to know *how* great the child's sense of linguistic and cultural isolation would be? Shouldn't it want to know *how* saddened the child would be by separation from her grandparents and her friends? These are questions of degree. Don't they depend on *how* sensitive this child really is, and on *how* meaningful a relationship she had with her grandparents? Is it really true that a hearing at which the immigration judge could question the child, her parents, and her grandparents "serves no purpose" because "the alien's version of the facts has been accepted by the [former]

INS"? When the "facts" are statements of degree, can they be neatly categorized as either accepted or disputed? Finally, is it really obvious that the BIA would not change its mind after a hearing?

5. Do you agree with Judge Goodwin, whom the Supreme Court quotes approvingly near the end of its opinion, that the Ninth Circuit decision would be a blueprint for unfairly jumping the queue and attaining LPR status?

6. At bottom, the litigation in *Jong Ha Wang* raises fundamental questions about the allocation, between the administrative authorities and the courts, of the power to decide what level of hardship qualifies as "extreme" (now "exceptional and extremely unusual"), or at least the power to decide what hardship qualifies as severe enough to justify a hearing on the issue. In one of the more frequently quoted sentences of this opinion, the Court states, "The Attorney General and his delegates have the authority to construe 'extreme hardship' narrowly should they deem it wise to do so." Do you agree? Can the statement be reconciled with the *Fong Haw Tan* principle that ambiguities in deportation statutes should be construed favorably to the noncitizens?

7. Would the Supreme Court have required the same judicial deference toward the BIA if the decision under review had been a denial of suspension on the merits (after a hearing) rather than a refusal to reopen?

8. What has the Supreme Court actually held here? Can you take anything concrete from this case?

9. The Ninth Circuit opinion in *Jong Ha Wang* had offered guidance concerning the factors that should influence extreme hardship determinations. Similar observations can be found in the decisions of other courts. They include the following:

a. Equities that arise while the person knows he or she is here illegally should generally be weighted less heavily than equities that arise during legal status, but even the former cannot be discounted entirely. 622 F.2d at 1346.

b. The applicant need only demonstrate extreme hardship to one of the persons listed in the statute: the applicant's citizen or LPR spouse, parent, or child. But the applicant may also prevail by showing that the "aggregate hardship to two or more of those persons * * * is extreme even if the hardship as to any one person would not be extreme viewed in isolation." *Id.* at 1347 & n.6.

c. Economic loss alone is not per se hardship, but it is an additional factor to be considered along with others, *id.* at 1348, and in some cases might be extreme enough to be independently sufficient, *id.* at 1348–49.

d. Other factors include medical problems, the ages of the children, the effects of removal on the children's education, separation from other relatives, and the difficulties in adjusting to life in a foreign country. *Id.* at 1348 n.7.

e. The evidence of hardship must be considered cumulatively. *Id.* at 1349; accord, *Watkins v. INS*, 63 F.3d 844 (9th Cir. 1995).

For more general guidance on the kinds of facts that might add up to "extreme hardship," see *Matter of O.J.O.*, 21 I. & N. Dec. 381, 389–96 (BIA en banc, 1996) (Holmes, concurring) (digesting prior BIA decisions on meaning of "extreme hardship"); *Matter of Anderson*, 16 I. & N. Dec. 596 (BIA 1978); Edith Z. Friedler, *From Extreme Hardship to Extreme Deference: United States Deportation of its Own Children*, 22 Hastings Constitutional L.Q. 491 (1995); cf. Michael G. Heyman, *Judicial Review of Discretionary Immigration Decisionmaking*, 31 San Diego L.Rev. 861, 888–95 (1994) (examining *Wang*).

10. As noted earlier, people applying under the general provision of cancellation of removal, Part B (i.e., not the special provision for battered spouses and children) must now establish "exceptional and extremely unusual hardship" rather than the "extreme hardship" that was required at the time of *Wang*. In the conference committee report accompanying IIRIRA, the committee said the change was meant to emphasize that the harm must be "substantially beyond that which ordinarily would be expected to result from the alien's deportation." Cong. Rec. at H10896 (Sept. 24, 1996).

The committee interpreted *Matter of O.J.O.*, 21 I. & N. Dec. 381 (BIA en banc 1996), as "holding that forced removal of an alien who has become 'acclimated' to the United States" would suffice for extreme hardship, and went on to make clear that mere acclimation would not satisfy the committee's proposed "exceptional and extremely unusual standard." Cong. Rec. at H10896 (Sept. 24, 1996). (The committee's interpretation of *O.J.O.* is debatable; the Board in that case actually examined a combination of factors.) The committee also made clear that a person could not satisfy the proposed standard merely by showing that his or her United States citizen child "would fare less well in the alien's country of nationality than in the United States." *Id*. Since decisions that have found "extreme hardship" based solely on acclimation to the United States or on a child doing "less well" are rare indeed (if they exist at all), it is not clear how much impact the amendment will have on the outcomes of actual cases.

But it is clearly having some impact. In *Matter of Monreal–Aguinaga*, 23 I. & N. Dec. 56 (BIA 2001), the Board suggested that even the new standard does not require a showing of "unconscionable" consequences, but, quoting the above language from the conference report, concluded that the new standard is still higher than the former "extreme hardship" test. Monreal–Aguinaga was a 34–year-old undocumented immigrant from Mexico. He had been in the United States since age 14 and lived with his two United States citizen children, ages 8 and 12. Also in the United States were his LPR parents, who spent time with their grandchildren, and seven LPR siblings. His wife and youngest child had returned to Mexico. He was the sole support of himself, his wife, and the three children. On those facts, the Board said that he might have prevailed under the "extreme hardship" standard but held that he could not satisfy the higher standard of "exceptional and extremely unusual hardship." *Id. at 59–64.* The Board's observation that the result might have been different under the former law appears to reflect a combination of two different changes—the heightened standard and the elimination of consideration of hardship to the applicant. Similarly, in *Matter of Andazola*, 23 I. & N. Dec. 319, at 322, 324 (BIA 2002), the Board found that the facts of the case did not meet the "exceptional and extremely unusual hardship" standard but twice suggested, as it had in *Monreal*, that the facts might well have satisfied the old "extreme hardship" standard.

11. The Ninth Circuit is without question the preeminent circuit on matters of immigration law, historically receiving as many immigration cases as all other circuits combined (though the Second Circuit immigration caseload is rising rapidly, as you will see in chapter 9, section B.6 below). The Ninth Circuit's expertise in this subject area is of course no reason for the Supreme Court to rubber-stamp its decisions, but one would expect the Supreme Court to study the issues carefully before reversing.

In *Jong Ha Wang,* there was further reason to treat the Ninth Circuit opinion with particular respect. The decision was not that of a three-judge panel, but that of a nine-judge limited en banc court. Because en banc decisionmaking is so labor-intensive, courts generally reserve that procedure for cases that are either unusually important or require the overruling of a prior three-judge panel decision. In *Jong Ha Wang,* the en banc court produced a comprehensive and detailed opinion intended to provide concrete guidance to all involved in extreme hardship cases. The nine judges who participated in the en banc decision were on the whole a generally conservative lot. (Seven of those nine, and three of the five who made up the majority, had been appointed by Republican Presidents.)

Thus presented with a comprehensive, en banc decision by a court possessing special expertise in the subject area, the Supreme Court, one might assume, would surely proceed cautiously before reversing. So when you reached the end of the majority opinion, and saw that three Justices "would grant the petition for certiorari and give the case plenary consideration," you might have wondered "Isn't that what the majority just did?" As it turns out, it is not. The Supreme Court in *Jong Ha Wang* employed a special summary procedure usually reserved for cases that either require emergency action or are extremely clear-cut. It reversed the en banc decision of the Ninth Circuit without allowing oral argument and without even waiting for briefs!

Why would the Supreme Court act so precipitously? Was it trying to do more than simply correct what it perceived as a legal error? Was it sending a more general signal? What might the message be? The fiery relationship between the Supreme Court and the Ninth Circuit during the early 1980's is explored again on pages 704–05 below. For commentary on the generally hostile tone of the Supreme Court in *Jong Ha Wang*, see Michael G. Heyman, *Immigration Law in the Supreme Court: The Flagging Spirit of the Law*, 28 J. of Legislation 113, 116–19 (2002).

12.   After the Supreme Court's decision in *Jong Ha Wang,* the question remains: When the BIA denies a motion to reopen to apply for suspension (now cancellation of removal, part B), and the basis for the denial is that the applicant did not establish sufficient hardship, what *is* the job of the reviewing court? To put the question another way, what effect has *Wang* actually had?

The reaction of one Ninth Circuit panel can be found in *Hee Yung Ahn v. INS.* This case required two separate decisions by the Ninth Circuit, both reproduced below. The first one you will see is a "memorandum" (i.e., unpublished) decision that the Ninth Circuit handed down after its en banc opinion in *Wang* but before the Supreme Court's reversal of *Wang.* After the Supreme Court decision, the same three-judge panel of the Ninth Circuit reheard *Hee Yung Ahn.* The second decision you will see is the product of that rehearing and is an "opinion" (i.e., a published disposition). It supersedes the first decision.[4]

Hee Yung Ahn v. INS

United States Court of Appeals for the Ninth Circuit, 1980.
Memorandum Decision, No. 79–7062.

■ Before: TRASK and SNEED, CIRCUIT JUDGES and EAST, DISTRICT JUDGE.

The decision of the Board of Immigration Appeals does not indicate whether the Board either considered all of the pertinent factors bearing on extreme hardship or weighed any of the factors cumulatively in affirming the immigration judge's denial of the Ahns' applications for suspension of deportation. We, therefore, vacate the decision of the Board denying suspension of deportation and remand for consideration of all of the evidence. The Board's subsequent ruling should contain a discussion of the reasons for its decision and an indication that all of the pertinent factors, individually and combined, were considered.

VACATED AND REMANDED.

Hee Yung Ahn v. INS

United States Court of Appeals for the Ninth Circuit, 1981.
651 F.2d 1285.

■ SNEED, CIRCUIT JUDGE:

The Ahns seek suspension of deportation under section 244(a)(1) of the Immigration and Nationality Act, arguing that they will suffer extreme hardship if deported. An immigration judge and the Board of Immigration Appeals considered their claim and concluded that they had not shown

---

4. Now that denials of what used to be called suspension of deportation are no longer directly reviewable in court, INA § 242(a)(2)(B)(i), cases like *Ahn* would be dismissed for lack of jurisdiction. But the substantive issues with which the *Ahn* court was dealing can continue to surface in the context of motions to reopen. For present purposes, therefore, the illustrative value of *Ahn* has not been diminished.

extreme hardship. The Ahns petitioned this court for review of the Board's order * * *. We decline to disturb the order denying suspension of deportation.

Mr. and Mrs. Ahn entered the United States from Korea as non-immigrants in 1967 and 1965 respectively. They have two children, both of whom were born in the United States. The Immigration and Naturalization Service instituted deportation proceedings against them in 1974. The Ahns conceded deportability but applied for suspension of deportation. Under section 244(a)(1) the Attorney General may suspend deportation of an alien who has been in the United States for seven years, is a person of good moral character, and shows that deportation would result in extreme hardship. Following a hearing, an immigration judge found that the Ahns had not established extreme hardship and the Board affirmed.

The Ahns' primary argument is that their son Shane's eye condition makes it extremely hard on them to return to Korea. * * * The immigration judge * * * directed the Ahns' counsel to present some medical evidence that Shane's condition would be adversely affected by deportation. None was presented at a hearing five months later.

The Ahns also argued that Mr. Ahn's political activity as a college student would make it difficult for him to get a job in Korea. A few minutes of the oral presentation to the immigration judge were devoted to this issue. Mr. Ahn does not claim that he would suffer persecution, a ground for withholding deportation under section 243(h) of the Act. He stated, rather, that a friend from his college days who was a member of his circle told him that he might have difficulty getting a job. In response to his attorney's questions, Mr. Ahn further stated that his friend had a job in Korea and that the government has not pressured his friend. Upon eliciting this testimony, Mr. Ahn's attorney dropped this line of questions.

The Board reconsidered these arguments, as well as the Ahns' claim that forcing them to leave this country would cause them to suffer extreme hardship because they are now accustomed to American ways of life. In its summary paragraph the Board concluded:

> Our review of the record leads us to conclude that the respondents have failed to demonstrate that "extreme hardship" will be incurred by them or their children if deported to Korea. The respondents are in their forties and in apparent good health. The prospect of "cultural shock," a lower standard of living, and diminished job opportunities are faced by nearly every alien who is forced to leave the United States. This type of detriment *alone* does not amount to "extreme hardship." The uprooting of their citizen children and the probable liquidation of their real estate holdings are additional factors to be considered but they are not conclusive. Finally, the evidence thus far presented concerning the son's eye ailment does not convince us that he will experience the degree of medical hardship that would warrant suspending deportation of his parents. [emphasis added by court].

The Board has broad discretion in determining what constitutes extreme hardship. In INS v. Wang, the Supreme Court summarily reversed an en banc decision of this court because we substituted our opinion of what constitutes extreme hardship for that of the Board. The Court stated:

> [T]he Court of Appeals improvidently encroached on the authority which the Act confers on the Attorney General and his delegates. The crucial question in this case is what constitutes "extreme hardship." These words are not self-explanatory, and reasonable men could easily differ as to their construction. But the Act commits their definition in the first instance to the Attorney General and his delegates, and their construction and application of this standard should not be overturned by a reviewing court simply because it may prefer another interpretation of the statute.

The Court went on to note that: "The Attorney General and his delegates have the authority to construe 'extreme hardship' narrowly should they deem it wise to do so. Such a narrow interpretation is consistent with the 'extreme hardship' language, which itself indicates the exceptional nature of the suspension remedy."

The petitioners claim that the Board made three different errors. They style their claims as arguments that the Board committed procedural errors in an attempt to evade *Wang*.[1] First, the petitioners claim that the Board failed to consider their long duration in this country, 11½ and 13 years. However, the Board in its decision, issued in 1978, noted that Mrs. Ahn was first admitted in 1965 and Mr. Ahn was first admitted in 1967. The

---

1. A number of petitioners have convinced panels of this court to endorse similar arguments since *Wang* was decided on March 2, 1981. For example, in *Sida v. INS,* 648 F.2d 638 (9th Cir.1981), the petitioners sought to reopen deportation proceedings because they claimed new evidence indicated that their son's health would be adversely affected by deportation. The court held that it was error for the Board to refuse to consider this second motion to reopen because the new evidence might establish extreme hardship. It reversed despite the finding of an immigration judge that the petitioners had not satisfied the seven years of continuous residency requirement of section 244(a)(1). Thus, even if the Board concludes on remand that the Sidas established extreme hardship, it would still lack discretion to suspend their deportation.

In *Santana–Figueroa v. INS,* 644 F.2d 1354 (9th Cir.1981), the court reversed a Board decision ordering the deportation of a sympathetic alien. The court noted that the petitioner was a 70–year–old, responsible, law-abiding, tax-paying, church-going Mexican maintenance man who, despite being uneducated and unskilled, used his meager earnings to support both his family in Mexico and himself without public assistance. The Board erred, the court held, in characterizing the petitioner's claim as one of mere economic detriment when in fact he would be completely unable to find employment if deported. This distinction was termed qualitative.

And in *Perez v. INS,* 643 F.2d 640 (9th Cir.1981), the court reversed the Board's denial of a motion to reopen. Although the Board's regulations prohibit reopening unless the new facts on which the motion is based are supported by "affidavits or other evidentiary material," 8 C.F.R. § 3.8 (1979), the court disregarded the petitioners' "unfortunate" failure to support their petition and reversed because it found the Board's record deficient.

Although *Sida, Santana–Figueroa,* and *Perez* indicate that this court will strain to find reasons to reverse the Board despite *Wang,* that is not the sort of precedent we are bound to follow.

extreme hardship issue cannot arise under section 244(a)(1) unless the deportable alien has been in the country for at least seven years. It is not clear why the additional time these petitioners have spent in this country should be entitled to any weight. While unhelpful to the Ahns, it is relevant to note that much of the additional time has been spent avoiding deportation. Mr. Ahn had only been in this country for eight years when the Immigration and Naturalization Service began their investigation in 1975. And, as the report of that investigation and the immigration judge both concluded, the Ahns had managed to stay that long only because they had deceived the Service.

Second, the petitioners pluck the word "alone" from the conclusion of the Board, printed above, and state that the Board erred by failing to consider the factors cumulatively rather than in isolation. This is not how we read the paragraph. The Board first noted that the Ahns are in good health. It then noted that if deported they would face a lower standard of living, a common situation that "alone" does not constitute extreme hardship. It then considered "additional factors," uprooting the children and liquidating their property. Finally, it noted that the evidence concerning Shane's eye condition was deficient. The language used admittedly does not show that the Board added these factors together rather than considering them separately, although it may be interpreted either way. The opinion read as a whole, however, makes clear that the Board found little substance to any of the arguments, considered separately or together. Sending the case back for further proceedings is unnecessary. The Board would not change its mind. More delay and additional useless hearings would be the only result.

Third, the petitioners claim that the Board overruled *Matter of Kojoory,* 12 I. & N. Dec. 215 (1967), because it failed to consider Mr. Ahn's claims that his political acts will cause him hardship. This is simply wrong. The Board has consistently held that political claims must be considered under section 243(h) rather than section 244(a)(1). * * * Furthermore, as the Supreme Court recently told us in *Wang,* the Board has broad discretion in defining extreme hardship. If it decides to define it narrowly so that political claims are considered under section 243(h) and not under section 244(a)(1), that is within its discretion.

We affirm the Board's decision.

■ EAST, SENIOR DISTRICT JUDGE, dissenting:

I respectfully dissent from the majority's opinion. I do not believe the record indicates the Board properly considered the factors of hardship, nor do I read the Board's prior cases to exclude consideration of economic hardship. Finally, I believe the majority is unduly influenced by the wash of the wake of *Wang.*

The Board must *cumulatively consider* the factors of economic hardship presented by an alien. My reading of the Board's concluding paragraph, quoted by the majority, does not convince me that the Board considered the hardship factors together. The decision notes that certain detriment "alone" is insufficient, and other hardships are "additional factors to be considered" but not conclusive. This does not assure me that the Board properly reviewed the Ahns' petition, nor can it assure the Ahns that they received the treatment they were legally entitled to.

The Board also improperly excluded from its consideration potential economic detriment rooted in political sources. I agree with the majority that the fact of political persecution itself should be considered in an application under section 243(h) and not section 244(a)(1). However, the Board has considered politically based sources of economic hardship in considering section 244(a)(1) applications. * * * To allow the Board to ignore the politically based economic hardship here is procedurally impermissible and pragmatically unfair to the Ahns.

Finally, I believe the majority embraces an over-restrictive reading of the Supreme Court's decision in *Wang*. As the majority rightly points out, that court disapproved what it perceived as the Court of Appeals substituting its judgment of extreme hardship for that of the Board. But to recognize and defer to the Board's discretion in its substantive judgments does not require this court to approve all aspects of the Board's decisions. We still must assure ourselves, by de novo review, that the Board's decision was reached consistently with the Constitution and all applicable laws and regulations. To retreat from a careful consideration of the Board's procedures would be to retreat from our judicial responsibility to review. I do not read *Wang* to lighten this obligation. Moreover, we should not decline to remand in the face of procedural defects because we may speculate that the "Board would not change its mind." If the Board can be allowed to circumvent the established process at its discretion, the essence of its fairness has been lost. I believe the Board in this case has utilized improper procedures tainting its ultimate exercise of discretion. I would remand for further consideration consistent with the applicable statutes, regulations, and rulings of this court.

NOTES AND QUESTIONS

1. The petitioners' three arguments can be boiled down to two: The BIA ignored certain relevant factors, and those it did consider were weighed individually rather than cumulatively. Before the Supreme Court decision in *Wang*, the panel in *Ahn* had accepted both arguments. On rehearing *Ahn* after *Wang*, the same panel rejected both arguments. Should *Wang* have affected the outcome in *Ahn?*

2. The petitioners also claimed error in the BIA's refusal to consider the adverse effect of their previous political activities on job opportunities in Korea. The BIA had held that, because political persecution is relevant to another form of statutory relief, it must be irrelevant to a hardship determination. The court accepts the BIA position. Was it right to do so? If Congress had never enacted INA § 243(h), would the Ahn's have been better off? Second, does Judge Sneed actually give any reasons in support of the BIA interpretation? If not, is he assuming that the BIA need not have a

reason—that a reviewing court must simply accept not only the Board's weighting of the various factors, but also the Board's conclusion about whether a factor is relevant at all? What do you think the reviewing court should do when the noncitizen and the BIA disagree about whether a particular factor should have been considered?

At any rate, subsequent decisions in the Ninth Circuit and elsewhere have held that political hardship, whether or not sufficient to establish asylum, is also relevant to hardship determinations. The same cases have made clear that even after *Wang* it is appropriate for a reviewing court to remand when the BIA failed to consider all relevant factors. See, e.g., *Ordonez v. INS*, 137 F.3d 1120 (9th Cir. 1998) (holding persecution relevant to extreme hardship even when the persecution would not satisfy the requirements for asylum); *Blanco v. INS*, 68 F.3d 642, 646 (2d Cir. 1995).

3. The petitioners also argued that the BIA had failed to consider the evidence cumulatively. As they saw it, the Board had concluded only that the cultural and economic factors alone were not extreme, that the uprooting was not alone extreme, and that the medical hardship alone was not extreme—rather than consider whether the sum of all those hardships qualified as extreme.

First, do you agree with the petitioners that the Board in fact evaluated each component of hardship in isolation? To answer this question, study the pertinent quoted paragraph from the Board's decision, and the debate between Judges Sneed and East on this point. Second, and more important, does the majority opinion accept the assumption that failure to consider the factors cumulatively would be a ground for reversal? (Later Ninth Circuit decisions have reversed BIA decisions for failure to consider the evidence cumulatively. See, e.g., *Watkins v. INS*, 63 F.3d 844 (9th Cir. 1995). The Seventh Circuit is in accord. See *Urban v. INS*, 123 F.3d 644, 650 (7th Cir. 1997)).

4. In footnote 1, Judge Sneed describes three post-*Wang* cases in which the Ninth Circuit reversed BIA decisions involving extreme hardship determinations. He dismisses them by saying "Although [these cases] indicate that this court will strain to find reasons to reverse the Board despite *Wang*, that is not the sort of precedent we are bound to follow." Why? Because he disagrees with those cases? Or because he finds them distinguishable? The words of the footnote strongly suggest disapproval. So, too, does the text to which the footnote corresponds. As Judge Sneed must surely have been aware, however, a regular court of appeals panel *is* bound by precedent decisions of the same court whether it agrees with them or not; only an en banc court may overrule a prior panel decision. See, e.g., *Linebery v. United States*, 512 F.2d 510, 510 (5th Cir.1975) and cases cited therein; *Ellis v. Carter*, 291 F.2d 270, 273 n. 3 (9th Cir.1961). Since he had no power to overrule those decisions, how might Judge Sneed have gone about distinguishing them?

In any event, the description of *Sida* is quite misleading. The immigration judge, finding a one-month absence meaningfully interruptive, had indeed concluded that the seven years of continuous physical presence were lacking. But the court of appeals expressly held the IJ had erred in that determination. See *Sida v. INS*, 665 F.2d 851, 855 (9th Cir.1981) (amended version of 648 F.2d 638). Moreover, by the time of the court of appeals decision, more than seven years had expired since the applicants' absence (and the court found that the BIA appeal and the petition for review had not been baseless). Nor, at that time, did the continuous physical presence period terminate with service of the Order to Show Cause (as it was then called). Thus, contrary to what Judge Sneed says about *Sida*, the Board did *not* lack discretion to grant suspension on remand.[5]

5. Judicial reactions to *Wang* have been mixed. Several cases reflect the kind of deference that you saw in *Ahn*. In some such cases, courts that had reversed BIA decisions before *Wang* ended up rehearing those cases after *Wang* and ultimately affirming the BIA. See, e.g., *Hamid v. INS*, 648 F.2d 635 (9th Cir.1981), replacing memorandum decision, 626 F.2d 866 (1980); *Ki Yun Cho v. INS*, 649 F.2d 867 (9th Cir.1981), replacing memorandum decision of Dec. 18, 1980.

Hamid is particularly illustrative. A noncitizen moved the BIA to reconsider its denial of his motion to reopen. He attached the affidavit of his United States citizen wife stating that when she married him she had had no idea he would be deported. The BIA found that statement "inherently unbelievable" and thus not warranting a hearing. Do you agree? Before taking immigration law, would you have known that the government deports the husbands of American citizens? Apart from that, note the Board's reason for refusing a hearing: that it doubted the truth—not the sufficiency—of the allegations in the moving papers. Did *Wang* compel the Ninth Circuit's turnaround on that point?

Hamid is instructive on another point as well. The applicant had attached a letter from his infant son's pediatrician. The letter stated the child "showed severe and unusual reactions to routine immunizations of diphtheria" and other diseases prevalent in Pakistan, the country to which Hamid would be deported. Administrative Record at 50. The child could not safely be vaccinated against those diseases and, consequently, risked serious illness or even death if the family were to accompany the deported father to Pakistan. *Id.* In its first decision the court found that evidence persuasive and held the BIA had abused its discretion in denying a hearing. After the Supreme Court decision in *Wang*, the court of appeals reheard the case and upheld the BIA, reasoning that there might be medical facilities in Pakistan that could treat the child if he were to contract one of the life-threatening diseases the doctor had listed. 648 F.2d at 637. Is that degree of substantive deference required by *Wang*?

The Fifth Circuit has also read the *Wang* edict broadly. Although ultimately reversing the BIA for failure to consider all the relevant factors,

---

5. The *Sida* case eventually came back to the Ninth Circuit twice more. 732 F.2d 164 (1984) and 783 F.2d 947 (1986).

the court in *Ramos v. INS,* 695 F.2d 181, 185 (5th Cir.1983), said that in light of *Wang* "we doubt that there remains much, *if any,* scope for judicial *substantive* review * * * of no 'extreme hardship' determinations" (emphasis added). Quoting that language approvingly, the court in *Hernandez–Cordero v. U.S. INS,* 819 F.2d 558 (5th Cir.1987), held that substantive abuse of discretion could be found "only in a case where the hardship is uniquely extreme, at or closely approaching the outer limits of the most severe hardship the alien could suffer * * *." *Id.* at 563 (again acknowledging the propriety of *procedural* review). This means, as the court says later, "virtually no substantive review." *Id.*

Many courts, however, have refused to throw in the towel. The cases cited by Judge Sneed in footnote 1 of his opinion in *Ahn* are examples. See especially *Santana–Figueroa,* where the review was substantive rather than procedural. For a long list of other examples, see Developments in the Law, *Immigration Policy and the Rights of Aliens,* 96 Harv.L.Rev. 1286, 1396–97 (1983). As that passage illustrates, though, most reversals are based on procedural grounds, of which three are particularly common: the failure to consider a relevant factor, the failure to weigh the various hardship components cumulatively, and the failure to give reasons for the decision. *Id.* Accord (on all three propositions), *Arrozal v. INS,* 159 F.3d 429 (9th Cir. 1998).

What some call undue judicial intrusion, others call responsible judicial review of agency action. What some call appropriate judicial deference, others call abdication of duty. A clear picture of the amount of leeway Congress intended to give an administrative agency can seldom be gleaned from the literal language of the statutory grant. Inevitably, that picture reflects the judge's personal conception of the respective roles of courts and agencies. Given *Wang,* where would *you* draw the line?

iii.   Other Hurdles: Good Moral Character, Disqualified Groups, Discretion, and Reporting to Congress

Although the physical presence and hardship requirements can be significant barriers to cancellation of removal, part B, there are other hurdles as well. As you saw earlier, for example, INA § 240A(b)(1)(B) requires good moral character for the entire ten years. INA § 101(f) lays out several classes of noncitizens who, as a matter of law, *lack* good moral character (not only for purposes of cancellation, but also for purposes of other provisions of the Act that contain that phrase). These preclusive categories include alcoholism, specified criminal activities, and "false testimony for the purpose of obtaining any benefits" under the INA. Keep in mind that the list is not exhaustive. That the person does not fall within any of the precluded categories does not compel a finding of good moral character. *Matter of Turcotte,* 12 I. & N. Dec. 206 (BIA 1967).

Certain noncitizens who meet the physical presence, hardship, and good moral character requirements are nonetheless disqualified from applying. These classes of individuals are described in INA § 240A(c). They include crew members, certain exchange visitors, and most people who are inadmissible or deportable on political or national security grounds. Recall too that cancellation is one of the remedies that noncitizens who fail to appear at their removal hearings or who fail to meet other specified obligations are ineligible to obtain for ten years. INA §§ 240(b)(7), 240B(d).

INA § 240A(b), like section 240A(a) (for LPRs) says the Attorney General (and therefore the immigration court, see 8 C.F.R. § 1240.20 (2004)) *may* cancel the removal of a noncitizen who satisfies the various statutory prerequisites discussed thus far. The word "may" implies the exercise of administrative discretion. This discretion should be distinguished from, and is broader than, the discretion inherent in the "exceptional and extremely unusual hardship" determination. It has not been the norm to deny cancellation of removal part B (or its predecessor, suspension of deportation) on discretionary grounds when the person has established statutory eligibility, but such denials do sometimes occur.

Former BIA Chairperson Maurice Roberts, concerned about the breadth of the administrative discretion, has suggested the issuance of guidelines that would at least articulate some of the relevant factors. See Maurice A. Roberts, *The Exercise of Administrative Discretion Under the Immigration Laws,* 13 San Diego L.Rev. 144, 158, 164–65 (1975). The late Judge Friendly expressed similar sentiments. See *Wong Wing Hang v. INS,* 360 F.2d 715, 718 (2d Cir.1966). Do you think such an enterprise would be (a) feasible and (b) beneficial?

Until 1983, an administratively final decision to grant suspension of deportation was subject to one last hurdle: congressional acquiescence. Former INA § 244(c) provided that suspension grants under section 244(a)(1) (then applicable to the less serious deportation grounds) required congressional inaction for a specified time, and that grants under section 244(a)(2) (then applicable to the more serious deportation grounds) required affirmative approval of both Houses of Congress. As you saw on pages 186–91 above, the Supreme Court explicitly struck down the first type of "legislative veto" in *INS v. Chadha,* 462 U.S. 919, 103 S.Ct. 2764, 77 L.Ed.2d 317 (1983). In 1988, Congress repealed both legislative veto provisions. Pub.L. 100–525, § 2(q), 102 Stat. 2609, 2614 (Oct. 24, 1988).

iv. NACARA

As a result of prolonged civil war in Nicaragua, Guatemala and El Salvador and some related legal and political developments in the United States, there have been hundreds of thousands of undocumented Central Americans living in uncertain status in the United States for many years. You will see more on this subject in chapter 11, in the context of asylum and related remedies.

In an attempt to alleviate at least part of the problem, Congress in 1997 passed the Nicaraguan Adjustment and Central American Relief Act, Pub. L. 105–100, Title II, 111 Stat. 2160, 2193 (Nov. 19, 1997), best known as NACARA. This statute granted special dispensations to nationals of certain named countries. The relief it provided is of two kinds.

The more generous relief, in the nature of an amnesty, is for certain nationals of Nicaragua and Cuba. It is discussed in the subsection on legalization, below. (A subsequent, more limited amnesty for certain Haitian nationals is simultaneously discussed.)

Certain nationals of selected other countries—Guatemala, El Salvador, the former USSR and its successor republics, and most Eastern European nations—received a lesser but still important form of relief that will be taken up here. They received the right to apply for cancellation of removal (and adjustment of status) under the less onerous substantive criteria embodied in the pre-IIRIRA suspension of deportation provision. This latter relief is usually referred to as "special rule" cancellation of removal. Moreover, if a person receives special rule cancellation, then his or her spouse, child, and (if here by October 1, 1990) adult son or daughter may receive special rule cancellation as well. NACARA § 203(a, b).

To qualify for the special rule, the person has to have entered before a specified date in 1990. (The date varies depending on the applicant's nationality.) One must affirmatively apply. As noted earlier, the substantive requirements are virtually the same as those formerly in place under the pre-IIRIRA version of suspension of deportation. The most important relaxations are the seven-year physical presence requirement (rather than the new requirement of ten years), the requirement of merely "extreme" hardship to oneself or one's family members (rather than the more demanding "exceptional and extremely unusual" hardship only to one's family members); and the inapplicability of the IIRIRA rule that continuous physical presence ends with the filing of a notice to appear or with the commission of a designated crime. Note, however, that under even those more liberal rules, the remedy is still discretionary. There is no judicial review of a decision by the immigration judge or the BIA denying special rule cancellation. NACARA § 203(a)(1).

Even though the adjustments of status that result from NACARA are exempt from the 4000 limit, some of those grants—namely, those to the Guatemalan and Salvadoran beneficiaries—are deducted from the quotas available in future years for two other programs that you studied earlier. Under the statutory formula, one-half of the Guatemalan and Salvadoran adjustments are subtracted from the annual ceilings for diversity immigrants, and the other one-half from the annual ceilings for the "other workers" prong of the employment-based third preference category. In no event, however, may the reduction to either quota exceed 5000 in any given fiscal year. NACARA § 203(d). Given the hundreds of thousands of NACARA beneficiaries, the maximum reductions of 5000 per year to the diversity and "other workers" programs will continue for many years.

For more detail on the substantive criteria and procedures under NACARA, see the statute, the regulations, and Mario M. Lovo, *Nicaraguan Adjustment and Central American Relief Act "NACARA"*, Nov. 1998 Immigration Briefings; Mark Silverman & Linton Joaquin, *NACARA for Guatemalans, Salvadorans and Former Soviet Bloc Nationals: An Update*, 76 IR 1141 (Aug. 2, 1999).

2. REGISTRY

Another remedy used principally by undocumented but long-term residents is INA § 249, which you should read now. Familiarly known as "registry," this provision confers a discretionary authority on the Attorney General to award LPR status to certain noncitizens who entered the United States before a specified date. From time to time, Congress has advanced that date. The most recent amendment, part of IRCA in 1986, advanced the cutoff date from June 30, 1948 to January 1, 1972. Many have criticized the practice of defining the required length of stay by reference to a fixed date. The leading immigration law treatise points out that that feature makes registry "a remedy of constantly decreasing utility" and suggests replacing the practice of periodic statutory amendments with a specific qualifying period (X years), as is done with cancellation of removal. 4 Gordon, Mailman & Yale–Loehr § 54.01. Do you agree?

Notice a few crucial features of section 249: The applicant may not fall within any of the more serious inadmissibility grounds; must have maintained continuous residence (not the more easily interrupted physical presence) since entry; and must be of good moral character. Finally, registry is one of the remedies made generally unavailable for ten years to individuals who have failed to appear at their removal hearings or failed to comply with their voluntary departure orders. INA §§ 240(b)(7), 240B(d).

Before removal proceedings, one applies to USCIS for registry. Once proceedings have begun, the application is filed with the immigration judge. See 8 C.F.R. § 249.2(a) (2004).

Try to formulate hypotheticals in which a person who is ineligible for cancellation of removal, part B is eligible for registry, and vice-versa.

3. LEGALIZATION

For a brief period before September 11, 2001, legalization was a hot topic. High-level talks between President Bush and Mexican President Vicente Fox, combined with a growing appreciation of the importance of Latino votes in the United States, appeared to make legalization politically viable. Even the AFL–CIO, a traditional foe of legalizing undocumented workers, urged a broad legalization program in 2000 and repeated that call in 2002. See 77 IR 237 (Feb. 28, 2000); 79 IR 39 (Jan. 7, 2002). Public opinion was sharply divided. Compare, e.g., *A New Compact on Immigration*, Chicago Tribune, Aug. 16, 2001 (editorial favoring amnesty) with Peter Skerry, *Why Amnesty is the Wrong Way to Go*, Washington Post, Aug. 12, 2001 at B1. September 11 undermined the prospects for legalization. Instead, talk has centered mainly on President Bush's proposal for a guest worker program that would provide a temporary reprieve. See page 372 above.

The most ambitious immigration amnesty in U.S. history came in 1986. The Immigration Reform and Control Act of 1986 (IRCA) embodied a wide-ranging set of strategies designed to reduce the undocumented immigrant population of the United States. One major component of that strategy was to impose sanctions on anyone who employs unauthorized workers. The rationale for sanctions was that drying up the job prospects for undocumented immigrants would remove the incentive for future unlawful entries (or overstays). This subject is explored in chapter 12.

But a second strategy for reducing the undocumented immigrant population focused on those who were already present in the United States. This strategy was legalization, known in the popular press as amnesty. It allowed certain noncitizens who had been residing unlawfully in the United States for several years to regularize their status. The program came about for several reasons—compassion for people who had become part of American society, a realistic appreciation that the millions of immigrants living underground would never be apprehended and removed, the social harms that inevitably flow from the existence of a huge underground subculture, and the political judgment that a coalition with legalization proponents was crucial to the enactment of employer sanctions.

In some ways the words legalization and amnesty are imprecise labels for the IRCA programs commonly called by those names. Other remedies—cancellation of removal part B and registry—are also analytically "legalization" or "amnesty" programs. Like IRCA, they legalize, or forgive, noncitizens who are here unlawfully, and like IRCA they provide a means to attain LPR status. Moreover, IRCA actually created not just one, but three different legalization programs—a general legalization plan, a special legalization program for agricultural workers, and a special program for Cubans and Haitians.

Although the three programs legalized millions of people and raised interesting and difficult questions of law and policy, detailed coverage is unnecessary[6] because all three programs were one-time-only opportunities for which the statutory application deadlines have long since passed. Several court decisions, however, invalidated former INS interpretations of the eligibility criteria and remedied the errors by permitting certain adversely affected noncitizens to apply late. After protracted litigation, final settlements now appear to have produced closure. See 9 BIB 89 (Feb. 1, 2004), 339 (Mar. 15, 2004).

In total, almost 2.7 million people acquired LPR status through IRCA's various legalization programs. Of those, approximately 1.6 million benefited from the general legalization program, 1.1 million from the program for agricultural workers, and about 38,000 from the special program for Haitians and Cubans. INS 1994 Statistical Yearbook, Table 4, at 32. Over 90% of the legalized immigrants completed the process by the end of fiscal year 1991; after that, the various programs ground almost to a halt. *Id.*

---

6. For more detail, see, e.g., Maurice A. Roberts & Stephen Yale–Loehr, Understanding the 1986 Immigration Law, chs. 3, 4 (1987); *The Simpson–Rodino Act Analyzed: Part II—Legalization*, 63 IR 1021–29 (1986). For a comparative perspective, see Francesco Isgro, *Italy Enacts Law to Protect Basic Human Rights of Foreign Workers*, 1 Georgetown Immigration L.J. 693, 698–99 (1986); David S. North, Alien Legalization and Naturalization: What the United States can Learn from Down Under (1984).

Over the course of the program, about 94% of all applications were eventually approved. INS, Immigration Reform and Control Act: Report on the Legalized Alien Population (1992), digested in 69 IR 844–45 (July 13, 1992). The INS Report provides some interesting profile information. 70% of the successful applicants were from Mexico. 55% settled in California; another 31% settled in Texas, Illinois, and New York. Some 84% lived in metropolitan areas. The median age was 30. About 58% were men. *Id.*

a. GENERAL LEGALIZATION IN 1986

The most important of the three IRCA legalization schemes is the general program laid out in INA § 245A. Under that provision, legalization proceeded in two phases. From May 5, 1987 to May 4, 1988, eligible individuals could apply to the former INS for "temporary resident alien" (TRA) status. INA § 245A(a)(1)(A). The principal eligibility requirement was "continuous unlawful residence" from January 1, 1982 until the filing of the application. INA § 245A(a)(2)(A). If the applicant established eligibility, the application had to be granted; there was no discretionary hurdle as in suspension or registry.

The second phase was governed by INA § 245A(b)(1)(A). A person who received temporary resident status had to apply for LPR status during the two-year period that began one and one-half years after he or she had attained TRA status. If the person did not apply in time, TRA status terminated. INA § 245A(b)(2)(C). Since the last date to apply for TRA status was May 4, 1988, and since the INS adjudicated most applications promptly, the last people to receive TRA status generally had to apply for LPR status between November 1989 and November 1991 (except for those cases in which appeals or other delays in final adjudication of TRA applications resulted in the receipt of TRA status appreciably later than May 1988). That is why the general legalization program wound down after fiscal year 1991.

The main eligibility requirements for LPR status were continuous residence since attainment of TRA status; admissibility as an immigrant (with roughly the same exceptions as for TRA eligibility); and, very importantly, demonstration of certain English language skills and knowledge of American history and government. INA § 245A(b)(1). As with TRA status, LPR status had to be granted once the applicant met the statutory requirements. INA § 245A(b)(1) ("Attorney General *shall* adjust …").

Those who attain permanent resident status under IRCA are treated like any other LPRs for most purposes. But there are a few important differences. First, they were not subject to, and were not charged against, the numerical quotas. INA §§ 201(b)(1)(C), 245A(d)(1).

Second, IRCA made no provision for the families of legalized immigrants. Upon attaining LPR status under IRCA, the individual could, like any other LPR, file a family-sponsored second preference visa petition for his or her spouse or children. As you saw in chapter 3, however, the queue for second preference visas is several years long. See generally Carol

Sanger, *Immigration Reform and Control of the Undocumented Family*, 2 Georgetown Immigration L.J. 295 (1987) (criticizing the failure to provide for spouses and children of legalized immigrants). An administrative measure taken by then INS Commissioner Gene McNary, followed soon by a provision in the Immigration Act of 1990, § 112, provided limited relief for some of the affected spouses and children.

b. LEGALIZATION OF AGRICULTURAL WORKERS IN 1986[7]

As discussed earlier, the debates over IRCA reflected growers' concerns that employer sanctions would deprive them of the seasonal labor they needed to harvest perishable crops. In IRCA Congress placated the growers in several ways: It liberalized the provisions for the admission of nonimmigrant agricultural workers (the H–2A's discussed in chapter 4); it established a legalization program for "special agricultural workers" (SAWs), with much more lenient requirements than those of the general legalization program; and it enacted a program to bring in "replenishment agricultural workers" (RAWs) during fiscal years 1990 through 1993.[8]

The SAW requirements are contained in INA § 210. Like the general legalization program, the SAW process had two phases: temporary resident status and permanent resident status. The main requirement for temporary resident status was that the person had "performed seasonal agricultural services in the United States for at least 90 man-days, during the 12–month period ending on May 1, 1986." INA § 210(a)(1)(B). For other requirements, see INA §§ 210(a)(1)(B)(i), 210(a)(1)(C), 210(c)(2). People had to apply for TRA status under the SAW program between June 1, 1987 and December 1, 1988. INA § 210(a)(1)(A). Converting to permanent resident status was also far easier for SAWs than it was for beneficiaries of the general legalization program. See generally INA § 210(a)(2). As with the general legalization program, SAW legalizations were not subject to the usual numerical immigrant quotas. INA §§ 201(b)(1)(C), 210(c)(1).

c. CUBANS AND HAITIANS IN 1986

Section 202 of IRCA (not codified), as amended by Pub.L. 100–525, § 2(i), 102 Stat. 2609, 2612 (Oct. 24, 1988), established a special legalization program for certain nationals of Cuba and Haiti. Unlike both the general legalization and SAW programs, this one (a) was discretionary; (b) allowed qualified applicants to obtain LPR status immediately (i.e., there was no TRA phase); and (c) the new status was effective retroactively to January 1, 1982. Applications had to be filed by November 7, 1988. See 65 IR 1172 (1988).

---

7. For an excellent summary, see Stephen Yale–Loehr, *Foreign Farm Workers in the U.S.: The Impact of the Immigration Reform and Control Act of 1986,* 15 N.Y.U. Review of L. & Soc. Change 333 (1986–87).

8. INA § 210A, repealed by Pub.L. 103–416, § 219(ee)(1), 108 Stat. 4319 (Oct. 25, 1994). No RAWs were ever admitted. They were to be admitted only if the Secretaries of Labor and Agriculture found shortages of seasonal agricultural labor. No such shortage was found during the operative years.

d.   NICARAGUANS AND CUBANS IN 1997

In addition to creating the "special rule" cancellation discussed earlier, NACARA in 1997 established an amnesty program for certain Nicaraguan and Cuban nationals continuously physically present in the United States since December 1, 1995. (Absences of 180 days or less did not destroy the continuity.) The person had to have been otherwise admissible, except that certain common inadmissibility grounds were made inapplicable. These included public charge, lack of labor certification, presence without admission, and inadequate documents. NACARA § 202(a,b). By virtue of a curative amendment, the inadmissibility grounds for those who have been out of status 180 days or one year, INA § 212(a)(9)(B), were also made inapplicable. Technical Corrections to the Nicaraguan Adjustment and Central American Relief Act, Pub. L. 105–139, §§ 1(a)(2)(B), 1(b)(2)(C), 111 Stat. 2644 (Dec. 2, 1997), amending NACARA §§ 202(a)(1)(B), 202(d)(1)(D). Unlike the discretionary special rule cancellation section of NACARA, this program was mandatory; the statute said the Attorney General "shall" adjust the status of those applicants who meet all the requirements. NACARA § 202(a)(1). Applications had to be filed by April 1, 2000. NACARA § 202(a)(1)(A). Approximately 150,000 Nicaraguans and 5,000 Cubans were expected to benefit. See Nadine Wettstein, *The Peddler Sells His Caps: The EOIR and INS Issue a New Rule on the Suspension/Cancellation Ceiling*, 3 BIB 1083 (Nov. 1, 1998).

e.   HAITIANS IN 1998

In granting amnesty to Nicaraguans and Cubans, and special rule cancellations of removal and adjustments of status to Guatemalans, Salvadorans, Soviets, and Eastern Europeans (see the earlier discussion), NACARA left a gaping hole. As you have seen, Haitian refugees have fled to the United States in significant numbers in recent years, and their plight seems every bit as desperate as that of the people covered by NACARA. After volatile public debate, Congress therefore enacted the Haitian Refugee Immigration Fairness Act of 1998, Pub. L. 105–277, Div. A, § 101(h), Title IX, 112 Stat. 2681 (Nov. 2, 1998). This statute provided legalization, culminating in adjustment of status, for certain Haitian nationals who had resided in the United States since December 31, 1995 and who had applied for asylum or had been paroled before that date. Applications were due by April 1, 2000.

QUESTIONS

1.   What are the general pros and cons of legalization?

2.   As you have seen, the final step in the 1986 general legalization program was the acquisition of permanent resident status. This required, among other things, a demonstration of English language proficiency and knowledge of American history and government. What are the pros and cons of imposing those requirements?

3. As noted above, the 1986 legalization programs contained no provisions for the family members of those who legalized. If there is another legalization, should it include the spouses and children (and/or other family members)? Argue both ways.

4. In 2005 Spain granted legalization to approximately 700,000 undocumented migrants, over the objections of other EU member states. See Katya Adler, *Spain Stands by Immigrant Amnesty* (BBC News, May 25, 2005).

4. Adjustment of Status

In chapter 6 you encountered INA § 245, which establishes a procedure known as "adjustment of status." In that chapter you saw adjustment simply as an alternative to the visa process. Noncitizens who originally entered the United States as nonimmigrants or parolees, but who now wish to become LPRs without having to return home for visas, may apply for adjustment if they meet various conditions.

In the deportability context, adjustment can serve a dual function—affirmative relief from removal and (as before) a means of attaining LPR status without leaving the United States. At this time you should re-read INA § 245 to refresh your recollection of its requirements and its consequences. Note particularly the requirement that the person be "admissible." As is true when one applies for permanent residence from abroad, the various provisions for waiving specified exclusion grounds can also be used by adjustment applicants to establish admissibility. See, e.g., *Matter of Parodi,* 17 I. & N. Dec. 608, 611 (BIA 1980).

As a result of a series of changes to section 245 over the past several years, complications now arise when noncitizens who are out of status apply for adjustment of status in removal proceedings. Consider, first, those who are deportable as overstayers. Before 1986, adjustment was an ideal remedy for nonimmigrants who had overstayed or otherwise violated the terms of their admission, had been found deportable, and had become substantively qualified to immigrate. As you learned in chapter 6, however, Congress in that year required adjustment applicants to have *continuous* lawful status. Not many people who have continuously maintained lawful status are deportable. Those whose deportability charges stem from criminal activity might have maintained status, but most of the crime-related deportability grounds are also exclusion grounds that make the individual not "admissible" and therefore ineligible for adjustment on that basis alone. So the main categories of deportable noncitizens who, immediately after 1986, could still benefit from adjustment are those whom Congress exempted from the continuous status requirement—immediate relatives, special immigrants, and those whose transgressions were "through no fault of [the noncitizen] or for technical reasons." INA § 245(c).

As discussed in more detail above, the temporary creation of INA § 245(i) in 1994 generally enabled otherwise eligible overstayers to qualify for adjustment by paying a penalty fee. The lapsing of section 245(i) in

January 1998 eliminated both possibilities. Except for a very limited extension provided by the LIFE Act in 2000, section 245(i) is now of little practical use to people who are in removal proceedings. See pages 491–93 above. By way of exception, those who are deportable for overstaying or otherwise violating the terms of their nonimmigrant visas, and who are exempt from the out-of-status bar because they are now either immediate relatives, INA § 245(c)(2), or employment-based preference immigrants who have not been out of status more than 180 days, INA § 245(k), can still qualify for adjustment of status.

Remember also that adjustment of status is one of the remedies that is now unavailable for ten years to those noncitizens who fail to appear at removal hearings or fail to comply with the terms of their voluntary departure orders (considered below). See INA §§ 240(b)(7), 240B(d).

Once removal proceedings have begun, the application for adjustment of status is filed with the immigration judge. 8 C.F.R. § 245.2(a)(1) (2004). The IJ's eventual decision on adjustment of status will be reflected in his or her ultimate decision whether to order removal; the latter decision, in turn, is appealable to the BIA in the usual way. 8 C.F.R. § 1003.1(b)(3) (2004). A decision of the BIA denying adjustment of status might not be subject to judicial review, INA § 242(a)(2)(B)(i), though again it is not clear whether the courts may at least review denials of adjustment based on BIA findings of statutory ineligibility, as they can for cancellation of removal, discussed above.

5. PRIVATE BILLS

One remedy of last resort is the "private bill"—legislation that provides LPR status for a specific individual when existing general provisions would not. Excellent summaries of the history of, and criteria and procedures for, private bills include Robert Hopper & Juan P. Osuna, *Remedies of Last Resort: Private Bills and Deferred Action*, June 1997 Immigration Briefings; Bernadette Maguire, Immigration: Public Legislation and Private Bills (1997); Ryan Quinn & Stephen Yale–Loehr, *Private Immigration Bills: An Overview*, 9 BIB 1147 (Oct. 1, 2004); David Weissbrodt & Laura Danielson, Immigration Law and Procedure in a Nutshell 99–104 (5th ed. 2005).

Private immigration bills were once quite common. For one stretch during the 1960's, they constituted about 50% of all bills introduced in Congress—several thousand each year. Hopper & Osuna, above, at 3. As a result of numerous scandals—including the ABSCAM affair, in which an FBI sting operation caught several members of Congress accepting bribes from foreign business persons in exchange for the introduction of private bills—both the number of such bills introduced and the number enacted have slowed to a trickle. In the two years of the 104th Congress (1995–96), only 27 private immigration bills were introduced and only two were enacted. INS, 1998 Statistical Yearbook of the Immigration and Naturalization Service, Table 75 at 237.

Several commentators predicted that IIRIRA, by severely curtailing other discretionary relief from removal, might prompt at least a modest resurgence of private immigration legislation. Hopper & Osuna, above, at 3; see also Weissbrodt & Danielson, above, at 96. It appears they were right. In the two Congresses that followed IIRIRA (105th and 106th, covering calendar years 1997–2000 inclusive), the number of bills introduced jumped from 27 to 67 and then to 121, and the number enacted increased from 2 to 9 and then to 18. (The figures receded in the 107th Congress, covering 2001–02, to 85 introduced and 1 enacted.) See Quinn & Yale–Loehr, above, at 1147.

One recent high-profile example is the bill introduced by Rep. Bill McCollum, a Florida Republican, on behalf of the son of a powerful Republican party official. After serving four years in prison for 13 felony convictions on theft and fraud counts, the son had been ordered deported to Canada, his country of nationality. As a result of IIRIRA's elimination of all other avenues of discretionary relief, existing law left him without a remedy. Having actively supported IIRIRA, McCollum drew criticism for seeking relief on behalf of the friend of a party official. McCollum denied any political motive for the bill. Syndicated columnist Anthony Lewis observed "Congressman McCollum may be moved by the human consequences of the 1996 law now that he sees them. It is easy to be for harsh measures in the abstract. It is not so easy when you see the result in shattered lives." See Anthony Lewis, *Abroad at Home: The Quality of Mercy*, New York Times, Feb. 27, 1999 at A15.

The first step in obtaining a private immigration bill is persuading a member of Congress to introduce it. Once such bills are introduced, they are ordinarily routed to the immigration subcommittees of the Judiciary Committees of the respective Houses. Both subcommittees now have formal rules that lay out the procedures for, and discuss generally the substantive criteria for granting, private immigration legislation. The latest versions of those rules are reproduced in 79 IR at 420–27 (Mar. 18, 2002). Examples of the kinds of hardships to which Congress has and has not been receptive appear in Quinn & Yale–Loehr, above, at 1149–51.

The rules do not provide for automatic stays of removal pending congressional consideration of private bills. In practice, however, the immigration agencies have stayed removal upon receiving congressional subcommittee chairs' requests for reports. Quinn & Yale–Loehr, above, at 1151–52.

Philosophically, what do you think of the concept of private immigration bills? What functions do they serve? What dangers do they present?

SECTION B.   LIMITED RELIEF

1.   DEFERRED ACTION

ICE does not bring removal proceedings against every noncitizen whom it suspects of being deportable. For one thing, it recognizes that, in some cases, extraordinary sympathetic factors would make removal unconscionable. For another, ICE could not remove all deportable individuals even if it wanted to. Removal proceedings require apprehension, investigation, processing, possibly detention, prosecution, adjudication, removal, and record-keeping. Like any other government agency, ICE has limited resources that it wants to deploy efficiently.

For some time, government policy (starting with the former INS) has been to refrain from initiating removal proceedings in certain unusually compassionate cases. That policy has been given different names over the years: "prosecutorial discretion," "nonpriority status," and, most commonly today, "deferred action." Whatever the name, the theory has been that the case is simply put on the back burner. Technically ICE remains free to proceed against the person in the future if its workload or its priorities change; realistically, since the actual reason for holding back is the presence of exceptionally sympathetic factors, relief will typically be permanent unless those factors change.

Not until John Lennon and Yoko Ono came to the United States in the early 1970's and retained attorney Leon Wildes to help them with an assortment of immigration problems did the details of the non-priority program, as it was then called, become public knowledge.[9] Mr. Wildes successfully used the Freedom of Information Act, 5 U.S.C. § 552, to pry from the former INS its unpublished description of the criteria for nonpriority status and the facts of cases in which nonpriority status had previously been granted. As a result of that litigation, the INS published an Operations Instruction describing the program. See Wildes, footnote 9 above, at 42–49. In general, that Operations Instruction prescribed nonpriority status for cases in which "humanitarian" factors would make deportation "unconscionable." *Id.* at 49–50. It was later amended, and at some point it simply disappeared from the INS Operations Instructions without any Federal Register notice or opportunity for public comment, but prosecutorial discretion remains. See 6 Gordon, Mailman & Yale–Loehr § 72.03[2][h] n.120.

The Ninth Circuit, finding that the deferred action program fell within the Administrative Procedure Act's "general statement of policy" exception to its usual notice-and-comment requirements, had previously upheld a similarly unpublished change to the deferred action program. See *Mada-Luna v. Fitzpatrick*, 813 F.2d 1006 (9th Cir. 1987). Whether the same principle would apply to a full rescission of the Operations Instruction has not been tested. Importantly, the Ninth Circuit made clear that its willingness to recognize the exemption from the notice and comment procedures rested on the content of the particular policy, not on the INS decision to call it an internal Operations Instruction rather than a regulation.

---

9. Lennon and Ono were in the United States to search for Ono's child by a prior marriage. Although Ono had been awarded custody, the father had absconded with the child. The former INS instituted deportation proceedings, and Lennon and Ono sought nonpriority status so that they could continue their search. Leon Wildes, *The Nonpriority Program of the Immigration and Naturalization Service Goes Public: The Litigative Use of the Freedom of Information Act,* 14 San Diego L. Rev. 42, 44–45 (1976).

On her last day in office (November 17, 2000), former INS Commissioner Doris Meissner sent a memorandum to all relevant INS personnel spelling out the INS policy on deferred action. The memo, reproduced in 77 IR at 1673–85 (Dec. 4, 2000), is widely believed to reflect the Commissioner's view that, in light of the harshness of the IIRIRA restrictions on formal discretionary relief, greater use of prosecutorial discretion in compassionate cases should be encouraged.

Commissioner Meissner's memo explained that the source of the agency's prosecutorial discretion, like that of other prosecutorial agencies, was its finite resources. Consequently, she said, the overriding criterion in the decision whether to institute removal proceedings was the relative importance of the applicable federal government interest. *Id.* at 1676. She provided a list of more specific factors. They include whether the person is an LPR, the duration of his or her residence, any criminal history, humanitarian concerns, whether there were past immigration violations, the likelihood of ultimate removal, the availability of alternative courses of action, how long a bar to future return removal would create, past cooperation with authorities, military service, the person's role in the community, and the availability of detention space. *Id.* At 1680. The overall tone of the memo is perhaps best captured in these two sentences: "[I]t is appropriate and expected that the INS will exercise this authority in appropriate cases. * * * Supervisory officials * * * should encourage their personnel to bring potentially suitable cases for the favorable exercise of discretion to their attention for appropriate resolution." *Id.* at 1682–83.

Near the end of the memo, however, there appears the following important paragraph:

> The principles set forth in this memorandum* * * are intended solely for the guidance of INS personnel in performing their duties. They are not intended to, do not, and may not be relied upon to create a right or benefit, substantive or procedural, enforceable at law by any individual or other party in removal proceedings, in litigation with the United States, or in any other form or manner.

Id. at 1685.

That last paragraph reflects the controversial history of deferred action. In 1979 the Ninth Circuit held that an INS decision denying deferred action was judicially reviewable for abuse of discretion. *Nicholas v. INS,* 590 F.2d 802 (9th Cir.1979). See Leon Wildes, *The Operations Instructions of the Immigration Service: Internal Guides or Binding Rules?*, 17 San Diego L. Rev. 99 (1979). The court based that result on its finding that the deferred action program existed as a benefit to the noncitizen in compassionate cases rather than as an internal guide to the efficient exercise of prosecutorial discretion.[10] (Had the purpose been the latter, then a decision to prosecute could have been set aside only upon a showing that race, religion, or other impermissible considerations had induced the

---

10. *Contra, Pasquini v. Morris,* 700 F.2d 658 (11th Cir.1983).

INS to depart from established norms. *Id.* at 805). At the time of *Nicholas,* the Operations Instructions prescribed deferred action whenever the District Director found deportation would be "unconscionable" because of "appealing humanitarian factors." See INS OI 103.1(a)(1)(ii) (1979). The INS response was to amend the Operations Instruction to emphasize the INS goal of structuring prosecutorial discretion. INS Operations Instruction 242.1(a)(22) (1993). The strategy worked. In *Siverts v. Craig,* 602 F.Supp. 50, 53 (D.Haw.1985), a district court within the Ninth Circuit held *Nicholas* inapplicable to the new version of the deferred action instruction. Today, as a result of IIRIRA § 306(b), the decision to commence removal proceedings is clearly unreviewable, see INA § 242(g) and *Botezatu v. INS,* 195 F.3d 311 (7th Cir. 1999), and as noted earlier the Operations Instruction no longer exists. Commissioner Meissner's cautionary paragraph was undoubtedly designed to preserve the insulation of denials of deferred action from judicial review. She might also have hoped to deflect arguments that deferred action unlawfully nullifies the limitations attached to the various statutory forms of discretionary relief.

NOTES AND QUESTIONS

1. INA § 237(a) provides that "[a]ny alien * * * in and admitted to the United States *shall*, upon the order of the [Secretary of Homeland Security], be removed if the alien is within one or more of the following classes of deportable aliens" (emphasis added). Given the mandatory word "shall," is deferred action legal? Apart from that particular barrier, from what source did the INS, and now ICE, derive the authority to provide relief from removal? Could ICE lawfully announce a policy not to remove any noncitizen who has displayed good moral character for the past three years?

2. Should the availability or scope of judicial review turn on whether the program was intended as a benefit to the noncitizen or as a device for administrative efficiency? What would be the practical pros and cons of allowing judicial review of ICE decisions denying deferred action?

3. Once ICE has filed a Notice to Appear with the immigration judge, the IJ acquires jurisdiction over the case. At that point ICE no longer has the discretion not to prosecute; it may file a motion to dismiss (without prejudice), but it is up to the IJ whether to grant the motion. *Matter of G–N–C–,* 22 I. & N. Dec. 281 (BIA 1998).

4. For the most current analyses of deferred action and some helpful practice pointers, see Robert Hopper & Juan P. Osuna, *Remedies of Last Resort: Private Bills and Deferred Action,* June 1997 Immigration Briefings at 9–12; Leon Wildes, *The Deferred Action Program of the Bureau of Citizenship and Immigration Services: A Possible Remedy for Impossible Immigration Cases,* 41 San Diego L. Rev. 819 (2004).

2. VOLUNTARY DEPARTURE

The person who receives and accepts a grant of voluntary departure under INA § 240B leaves the United States "voluntarily;" in exchange, no formal removal order issues. The practical consequences of that latter fact are discussed below. For now, you should note that there are actually two distinct types of voluntary departure, differentiated by timing.

Under subsection (a) of INA § 240B, the Secretary of Homeland Security may permit certain noncitizens to depart voluntarily, at their own expense, *either in lieu of removal proceedings or before removal proceedings have been completed.* (INA § 241(e)(3)(C) provides an exception to the "own expense" rule.) Aggravated felons, individuals who are inadmissible under the terrorism exclusion, and those who were previously removed but then returned while still inadmissible are all ineligible. INA §§ 240B(a)(1), 240B(c). The person "may" be required to post bond, INA § 240B(a)(3), and the voluntary departure period may be as long as 120 days, INA § 240B(a)(2).

Subsection (b) authorizes voluntary departure *at the conclusion of removal proceedings*, again at the individual's own expense. Under this subsection, the applicant is subject not only to the same disqualifications as those who apply under subsection (a), see INA §§ 240B(b)(1)(C), 240B(c), but also to several others that you will soon discover. See especially sections 240B(b)(1)(A) (one year of physical presence immediately preceding the notice to appear) and 240B(b)(1)(B) (good moral character for the five years immediately preceding the application). Bond for subsection (b) applicants is mandatory, not discretionary. INA § 240B(b)(3). If voluntary departure is granted under subsection (b), the maximum period allowed is 60 days. INA § 240B(b)(2).

The regulations empower both ICE and EOIR (immigration judges and the BIA) to grant voluntary departure, but in differing circumstances. ICE has authority to grant voluntary departure only under subsection (a) of section 240B, and only in lieu of removal proceedings. 8 C.F.R. § 240.25(a) (2004). If proceedings have not yet commenced (because no Notice to Appear has yet been filed), then ICE simply grants voluntary departure on its own. If proceedings have commenced (with the filing of the Notice to Appear), and ICE agrees to voluntary departure, then it has two options. One option is to join with the noncitizen in a motion to the immigration judge to dismiss the case. If the motion is granted, ICE may then grant voluntary departure. The other option is to join with the noncitizen in requesting the immigration judge to grant voluntary departure, which he or she may then do. *Id.* § 240.25(d).

At a certain point, however, even the immigration judge loses the power to grant voluntary departure under subsection (a) of section 240B. To explain what that point is, a brief detour is necessary.

Before holding a full removal hearing, an immigration judge normally schedules a shorter and less formal event called a "master calendar" hearing. The main purposes of the master calendar hearing are to complete certain preliminary tasks, get a sense of the complexity of the issues likely to arise, and to set a date and time for the full hearing. For more detail on master calendar hearings, see page 539 below.

Under the regulations, one who applies to an immigration judge for voluntary departure under subsection (a) must apply either before or during the master calendar hearing. Moreover, the immigration judge may grant subsection (a) voluntary departure only up to 30 days after the master calendar hearing, unless ICE stipulates to such a grant some time before the completion of removal proceedings. 8 C.F.R. § 1240.26(b) (2004). Thus, absent an ICE stipulation, the only brand of voluntary departure that an immigration judge has the power to grant more than 30 days after the master calendar hearing (and note that the actual removal hearing is almost always more than 30 days later) is subsection (b) voluntary departure. *Id.* § 1240.26(c). For that, the substantive requirements are more stringent and the maximum duration is shorter (60 days rather than 120 days). The practical effect of the regulation is to bar a subsection (a) voluntary departure application at a point long before "removal proceedings have been completed" (the deadline that the statute imposes in subsection (a)). See also *Matter of Arguelles–Campos*, 22 I. & N. Dec. 811, 820 (BIA 1999) (Grant, concurring) (noting this administrative interpretation).

The voluntary departure provision is inartfully drafted. Subsection (a) purports to operate "prior to the completion" of removal proceedings. Taken alone, that provision implies, and the regulations discussed above similarly assume, that subsection (a) voluntary departure may be granted either before proceedings begin or while they are going on. In contrast, the more difficult subsection (b) voluntary departure may be granted only "at the conclusion" of removal proceedings. The problem is that a grant of voluntary departure ends the removal proceeding; by definition, therefore, it is *always* at the conclusion of the proceeding (assuming a proceeding has commenced). Under the literal wording, therefore, the portion of subsection (a) that authorizes voluntary departure "prior to completion" is useless. If proceedings have commenced but not finished, voluntary departure ends the proceedings and therefore would seem to be governed by subsection (b). The regulations commendably take a nonliteral approach and allow the more lenient subsection (a) voluntary departure even after commencement of removal proceedings.

The timing distinctions drawn by the voluntary departure provisions are significant for another reason as well. Recall the "unlawful presence" exclusion that you studied in chapter 5. Under INA § 212(a)(9)(B)(i), one who was unlawfully present in the United States for more than 180 days but less than a year, and who "voluntarily departed ... *prior to the commencement* of [removal] proceedings [emphasis added]" is inadmissible to return for three years. Whether one departs before or after the filing of the Notice to Appear therefore has legal significance, as the Problems below illustrate.

The vast majority of the deportable noncitizens who are required to leave the United States do so by way of voluntary departure rather than removal. In fiscal year 2003, there were 887,115 voluntary departures, compared to about 97,000 removals of deportable noncitizens from the interior. See page 501 above. The bulk of the voluntary departures occur before proceedings have commenced.

As you might have gathered from those figures, pre-hearing voluntary departures are enormously beneficial to the government. To hold almost a million removal hearings per year would impose staggering costs. Post-hearing voluntary departures, while not avoiding the costs of the hearings, at least save the costs of transporting the individuals out of the country.

That the government benefits so significantly from voluntary departure is both good and bad. On the positive side, tremendous resources are saved. The danger, however, is that ICE can be tempted to pressure noncitizens who have arguably valid cases to accept voluntary departure. In *Orantes-Hernandez v. Meese*, 685 F.Supp. 1488 (C.D. Cal. 1988), aff'd, 919 F.2d 549 (9th Cir. 1990), a federal district court found and enjoined systematic INS efforts to coerce Salvadoran asylum claimants to forego their asylum claims and leave the country voluntarily. The court found that

> INS agents directed, intimidated, or otherwise coerced Salvadorans within their custody, who had not expressed a desire to return to El Salvador, to sign form I–274A for voluntary departure. INS agents used a variety of techniques to procure voluntary departure, ranging from subtle persuasion to outright threats and misrepresentations. Many class members were intimidated or coerced to accept voluntary departure even when they had unequivocally expressed a fear of returning to El Salvador.

685 F.Supp. at 1494. An especially difficult issue is how to deal with pressure exerted on noncitizen children to accept voluntary departure rather than request removal hearings. See Irene Scharf & Christine Hess, *What Process is Due? Unaccompanied Minors' Rights to Deportation Hearings*, 1988 Duke L.J. 114.

What is in it for the noncitizens? Absent coercion or deception, why would they ever agree to leave voluntarily? There are at least two important reasons: First, noncitizens who are formally ordered "removed" (other than upon arrival at a port of entry) are ineligible to return to the United States for at least ten years (twenty years for a second offense, forever if convicted of an "aggravated felony"), unless they can obtain permission from the Secretary of Homeland Security to reapply for admission sooner. INA § 212(a)(9)(A). If they return anyway, they face felony charges. INA § 276. In contrast, those who accept voluntary departure (and who pay their own way) are not subject to that particular bar, although as the Problems below illustrate, they are not home free either.

A second, often overlooked advantage of voluntary departure is more practical. Frequently there is little to gain by waiting for a removal hearing, and in the meantime the individual must either post bond or remain in detention. In contrast, one who departs voluntarily might simply try to reenter surreptitiously. See T. Alexander Aleinikoff & David A. Martin, Immigration Process and Policy 465 (1st ed.1985).

Both forms of voluntary departure are among the remedies now generally unavailable for ten years to noncitizens who have failed to appear at removal hearings after proper notice, or who have failed to honor the terms of a prior voluntary departure order. See INA §§ 240(b)(7), 240B(d).

INA § 240B(f) bars judicial review of an order denying voluntary departure under subsection (b). You might have assumed that Congress intended to preserve review of denials under subsection (a), but that is not the case. Another provision, INA § 242(a)(2)(B)(i), prohibits the courts from reviewing "any judgment regarding the granting of relief under section ... 240B." Even more drastic is INA § 240B(e), which empowers the Secretary of Homeland Security to "limit eligibility for voluntary departure." The provision places no explicit parameters on the Secretary's power to add further restrictions, and it purports to bar all judicial review of such regulations. *Id.*

In two leading 1935 cases, the Supreme Court struck down congressional attempts to delegate virtually unlimited regulatory discretion. See *A.L.A. Schechter Poultry Corp. v. United States,* 295 U.S. 495, 55 S.Ct. 837, 79 L.Ed. 1570 (1935); *Panama Refining Co. v. Ryan,* 293 U.S. 388, 55 S.Ct. 241, 79 L.Ed. 446 (1935). Since then, the "nondelegation doctrine" has fallen into disfavor. But the courts still profess to require that Congress, when delegating power, supply at least an "intelligible principle" for the delegated authority to apply. E.g., *Mistretta v. United States,* 488 U.S. 361, 372 (1989).

Does INA § 240B(e) cross the line? Has Congress given the Secretary of Homeland Security any "intelligible principle" to apply in deciding what substantive limits to attach to eligibility for voluntary departure? If not, does the nondelegation doctrine collide with the plenary power doctrine that you encountered in chapter 2? Given the bar on judicial review, would anyone even be able to test those arguments in court?

The former INS used to employ on occasion a device known as "extended voluntary departure" (EVD). The most significant modern use of EVD was as a blanket permission to remain in the United States, for nationals of a particular country in which either political or natural conditions would have made return exceptionally dangerous. Often such grants were limited to those who had entered the United States before a specified date. The Immigration Act of 1990, § 302, however, replaced EVD with a new program known as "temporary protected status" (TPS). The program is contained in INA § 244 and discussed in chapter 11, § C.2.a below.

Please read INA § 240B before approaching the Questions and Problems below.

QUESTIONS

1. How do the requirements for, and the consequences of, voluntary departure under subsection (a) differ from those under subsection (b)?

2. As you discovered when answering question 1, subsection (b) is both more demanding and generally less beneficial to the noncitizen once granted. First, why would Congress desire that result? Consider an analogy offered by Professor Nora Demleitner in a February 8, 1998 e-mail to the author. She compares the voluntary departure scheme to the federal criminal sentencing guidelines, which allow sentence reductions for defendants who plead guilty. The stated rationale for that guideline is that a person should be rewarded for "accepting responsibility" and for saving the time and expense of a trial. Second, what are the disadvantages of making subsection (b) a less generous provision than subsection (a)?

PROBLEMS 5–6

Before attempting these Problems, carefully review subsections 9(A) and 9(B) of INA § 212(a). Be prepared for some strange results.

Problem 5. X, a noncitizen, entered the United States without inspection. Eight months later he was apprehended. His wife, an LPR, had earlier filed a family-sponsored 2A petition on his behalf, and his priority date is likely to come up about two years from now. ICE has offered him voluntary departure in lieu of commencing removal proceedings. He calls you to ask whether he should accept the offer. What advice will you give him?

[handwritten margin note: Go into proceedings, then depart — 3-year bar won't apply.]

Problem 6. Now assume the same facts as in Problem 5, except that this time X was apprehended 14 months after entering. Would your advice change?

3. OBJECTIONS TO DESTINATION

Sometimes the place a noncitizen is sent is as important as the fact of removal. Yet, until 1950, the noncitizen had little say in the matter. He or she could introduce evidence on the issue, but the official who presided over the deportation hearing (as it was then called) had the ultimate say as to destination. See 6 Gordon, Mailman & Yale–Loehr, § 72.08[2][a]. After several changes over the years, see, e.g., Internal Security Act of 1950, § 23, 64 Stat. 987, 1010 (Sept. 23, 1950); *Matter of R.*, 5 I. & N. Dec. 29, 39–40 (BIA 1952), the immigration judge at the removal hearing now selects the removal country. That selection is structured, however, by INA § 241(b)(2), which you should now read carefully.[11]

As you have just seen, section 241(b)(2) sets up a multi-step approach to selecting the removal country. Step 1 is the noncitizen's designation of a preferred country. If ordered removed, the person must be removed to the designated country unless any of several exceptions applies, in which case the designation may be disregarded. INA § 241(b)(2)(A, B, C). In that event, step 2 kicks in, and the person must be removed to the country of which he or she is a "subject, national, or citizen," again with some

11. INA § 241(b)(1) contains analogous rules for noncitizens who are ordered removed upon arrival. As is evident, the latter individuals have far less freedom of destination.

exceptions. INA § 241(b)(2)(D). If one of the exceptions applies and the person is not removed to the step 2 country, then step 3 requires the immigration judge to choose from one of six other possibilities—the country from which the person was admitted to the United States, the person's country of birth, etc. INA § 241(b)(2)(E)(i–vi). (Of course, the various criteria will often refer to the same country.) Finally, if removal to those six countries is "impracticable, inadvisable, or impossible," then (in what the Supreme Court describes as a fourth step, see below), the immigration judge is free to designate "another country whose government will accept the alien into that country." INA § 241(b)(2)(E)(vii).

In recent years, a major country-of-removal problem has arisen with respect to Somalia, which has been without any functioning government. Removals to Somalia are physically possible, either by force or by the absence of resistance, but formal "acceptance" has not been possible. The Somalia problem precipitated a broader debate over which of the several steps involved in the selection of a destination country should be interpreted as being contingent on that country's affirmative acceptance. (There was a related debate over whether a country like Somalia, lacking a functioning government, can even be considered a "country" for purposes of section 241(b)(2)).

In January 2005, amid conflicting court decisions, DHS and DOJ jointly issued final regulations interpreting section 241(b). See 70 Fed. Reg. 661 (Jan. 5, 2005). The regulations take the position that section 241(b)(2)(E)(vii) (the Supreme Court's "fourth step") is the *only* step in which the country's affirmative acceptance is a prerequisite to removal. Under that view, the country's lack of acceptance does not preclude the immigration judge from ordering removal to a country that the noncitizen designated, or to the person's country of citizenship, or to any of the countries listed in subsections E(i) through E(vi). As for step 1, the government observed that the statute says only that the noncitizen's designation "may" be disregarded if the designated country does not accept; it does not say the designation must be disregarded. Step 2 is trickier. The statute says the Secretary of Homeland Security "shall" remove the person to the country of which he or she is a subject, national, or citizen "unless" the government of that country does not accept the person (in prescribed ways). The regulations construe that language as requiring the immigration judge to remove the person to that country if the country accepts, but, if the country doesn't accept, as giving the immigration judge the discretion whether to order removal to that country. As for step 3, the government's view is that, while section 241(b)(2)(E)(vii) ("another country whose government will accept the alien ...") explicitly requires acceptance, the other sections of 241(b)(2)(E) contain no similar wording. Thus, the government reasons, removal to the countries described in those other sections is not contingent upon their governments accepting the person. See the commentary in 70 Fed. Reg. at 665–68. The same commentary rejects the notion that a functioning government is a prerequisite to being a "country" for purposes of section 241(b). *Id.* at 663–65. The new interpretations are in 8 C.F.R. §§ 241.15 (DHS) and 1240.10(f) (DOJ).

Just one week after issuance of the final rules, the Supreme Court decided *Jama v. ICE*, ___ U.S. ___, 125 S.Ct. 694, 160 L.Ed.2d 708 (2005). Jama, both a native and a citizen of Somalia, was ordered removed. He had declined to designate a country, and the immigration judge did not invoke step 2 (country of citizenship), apparently interpreting that step as requiring acceptance by the receiving country. Instead Somalia was selected under step 3, as Jama's country of birth under section 241(b)(2)(E)(iv). Jama sought to prevent his removal there on the ground that step 3 requires acceptance, which Somalia, lacking a functioning government, could not provide. In a 5–4 decision, the Court interpreted step 3 (which it defined as consisting of subsections E(i) through E(vi)) as not requiring acceptance by the receiving country. Jama had pointed to the language in E(vii) "*another* country whose government will accept the alien" (emphasis added) and had argued that the word "another" implied that the preceding six choices similarly required acceptance. The Court disagreed, concluding that "another" modified only the word "country."

Jama had also argued that, since country of citizenship and country of birth were often (in fact usually) the same country, the Court's interpretation would now permit immigration judges in most cases to circumvent the acceptance condition in step 2 (country of citizenship) simply by ordering removal to the same country under step 3 (country of birth, under subsection E(iv)). The Court rejected that argument too, reasoning that citizenship and birth do not *always* coincide, and thus avoiding the question whether step 2 (country of citizenship) in fact requires the acceptance of the receiving country. *Jama*, 125 S.Ct. at 703 n.7, 160 L.Ed.2d at 719 n.7. The four dissenters would have held that step 2 requires acceptance and that the majority's interpretation does indeed permit immigration judges in most cases to evade that requirement by invoking step 3 instead.

Strikingly, the Court in *Jama* did not mention the then one-week-old regulations. The Court could have made its task easier by arguing that *Chevron* deference required only a finding that the agencies' interpretation was reasonable. Perhaps both the attorney from the Solicitor General's Office and the Justices themselves were simply unaware of the new regulations.

It is one thing for a court—even the Supreme Court of the United States—to hand down a decision. It is another thing for the executive branch to enforce it. Since Somalia has no functioning government, Jama had no way to obtain a Somali passport, without which the airlines would not let Jama board. At a hearing in federal district court in Minneapolis shortly after the Supreme Court decision, it emerged that ICE had been exploring some unorthodox ways to return Jama to Somalia. These included trying to obtain a false passport through "contacts in Egypt," "negotiating with mercenaries and warlords for permission to land a chartered plane that could drop Jama off," and bringing Jama to the border and then physically pushing him onto the Somali side, as Jama's lawyer attested U.S. officials had done in the past. The district judge called the ICE arguments "hogwash" and said the contemplated ICE actions "sound more than vaguely illegal." See Eric Black, The Star Tribune (Minneapolis), Mar. 25, 2005.

The case that follows illustrates another important contemporary setting in which the country of destination issue can arise—shifting borders. In the process the case raises fundamental questions about the contrasting objectives of deportation and extradition.

Linnas v. INS

United States Court of Appeals, Second Circuit, 1986.
790 F.2d 1024.

■ ALTIMARI, CIRCUIT JUDGE:

* * *

Karl Linnas was born in Estonia in 1919 and entered the United States in 1951 under the auspices of the Displaced Persons Act. In order to gain admittance to the United States as a displaced person, Linnas informed members of the Army Counter Intelligence Corps that he had been a university student during the years 1940 to 1943. In May 1951 Linnas signed an immigration form stating that he had "never advocated or assisted in the persecution of any person because of race, religion or national origin." Upon entering the United States some three months later, Linnas swore to the truth of that statement. The New York State Supreme Court (Suffolk County) admitted Linnas to citizenship in 1960.

[A federal district court ordered Linnas denaturalized upon finding he had procured naturalization by concealment and misrepresentation. See INA § 340(a) and chapter 13 below. The court here recounts the atrocities committed by Linnas during his tenure as Chief of the Nazi concentration camp in Tartu, Estonia.—Ed.]

* * *

Following Linnas' denaturalization, the government began deportation proceedings under section 242 of the INA. Immigration Judge Howard I. Cohen ruled on May 19, 1983 that Linnas was deportable. Linnas had designated "the free and independent Republic of Estonia" as the country to which he wished to be deported. The independent Republic of Estonia was forcibly incorporated into the Soviet Union following World War II. Linnas apparently intended his designation to mean the office building in New York currently housing the representatives of the independent Republic of Estonia. Immigration Judge Cohen, however, apparently took Linnas' designation to mean that geographic territory historically associated with the Republic of Estonia and currently incorporated in the Soviet Union. In attempting to comply with § 243 of the INA,[a] Immigration Judge Cohen ordered that Linnas be deported from the United States to Estonia, but that if Estonia was unwilling to accept Linnas he was to be deported to the Soviet Union. The Soviet Union, which had tried Linnas in absentia and

---

a.   Now INA § 241(b)(2)—Ed.

sentenced him to death for his war crimes, was the only country which had expressed a willingness to accept Linnas. * * *

Linnas filed a timely appeal to the BIA. On July 31, 1984 the BIA affirmed the decision of the immigration judge except as to the country of deportation. The BIA remanded the case to the immigration judge with instructions to consider the effect of the United States' non-recognition of the Soviet annexation of Estonia and to articulate a statutory basis for the designation of a country of deportation.

On remand, Immigration Judge Cohen reviewed the three step process delineated in § 243(a) of the INA for designation of a country of deportation. Step one, the designation of a country by the deportee, was ruled inapplicable because of Linnas' designation of an office building in New York. Step two, the designation of a country of which the deportee is a citizen, was also held inapplicable. Linnas claimed to be a citizen of the Republic of Estonia, but that country no longer exists as an independent geographic territory. Under step three, the immigration judge may designate deportation to any country which falls within one of seven categories. Immigration Judge Cohen, therefore, considered deportation: * * *

> (4) to the country in which the place of his birth is situated at the time he is ordered deported; * * * or
>
> (7) if deportation to any of the foregoing places or countries is impracticable, inadvisable, or impossible, then to any country which is willing to accept such alien into its territory.

INA § 243(a). On April 9, 1985, after considering a letter from the Legal Advisor of the Department of State to the effect that Linnas' deportation to the Soviet Union would not violate the nonrecognition policy, Immigration Judge Cohen held that Linnas should be deported to the Soviet Union under either category (4) or (7). Linnas once again appealed to the BIA, which, in a decision dated October 16, 1985, affirmed the immigration judge's decision based on § 243(a)(7).

* * *

Linnas claims that his deportation to the Soviet Union is in fact a disguised extradition. Linnas was convicted *in absentia* in the Soviet Union and sentenced to death for his war crimes. Linnas contends that the Soviet trial was a sham and that deporting him to the Soviet Union is in fact extradition in the absence of an extradition treaty. Linnas argues that to deport him under these circumstances will deprive him of his life without due process.

The irony of Karl Linnas objecting to execution without due process is not lost on this court. The right to due process is, of course, essential to the American system of ordered liberty, and must be extended to all persons in the United States. The fact that Linnas enjoys the right to due process has enabled him to remain in the United States until 1986 even though the government began the denaturalization process in 1979. The considerable length of time that Linnas has been able to remain in the United States after the discovery of his heinous past is a small price to pay for a system of law which separates our government from the government that Linnas served as Chief of the Tartu concentration camp. We now, therefore, examine the merits of the petitioner's due process claim.

* * * [N]o extradition has taken place in this case. Extradition may be applied to either a citizen or noncitizen, whereas deportation applies only to noncitizens such as Linnas. Extradition is initiated by a foreign state. While the Soviet Union may have an interest in the trial of Nazi war criminals, the impetus for the denaturalization and removal of Linnas appears to have come from the government of the United States. The legislative history of the Holtzman amendment indicates that the Congress intended to rid this nation of Nazi war criminals, not to court favor with nations having no extradition treaties with the United States. Ruling this procedure to be an extradition would greatly reduce the ability of this nation to deport those who have committed crimes of moral turpitude in their own countries.

In addition, Linnas was given the same opportunity given to any deportee to designate a country to which he wished to be sent. Linnas designated an office building in New York, thus wasting the opportunity to choose a proper place of deportation. The fact that such an opportunity was offered, however, strongly undercuts his contention that his deportation was a disguised attempt to extradite him to the Soviet Union. The record also indicates that the government made at least some attempt to find a country other than the Soviet Union which would accept Linnas. There is no support in the record for Linnas' claim that the government's efforts in this regard were a mere facade. Linnas' own failure to designate a country of deportation lends credence to the immigration judge's finding that no country other than the Soviet Union would accept him. Accordingly, there was no abuse of discretion in designating the Soviet Union as the country of deportation under INA § 243(a)(7). That designation did not transform the deportation of Linnas into an extradition.

* * *

We are not, however, deaf to Linnas' protestations concerning the fate which may await him in the Soviet Union. In *Gallina v. Fraser* this court permitted the extradition of a man convicted *in absentia* in a foreign country. The *Gallina* court hypothesized, however, that there could arise a situation in which the person to be removed from the United States would be subjected to "procedures or punishment so antipathetic to a federal court's sense of decency" as to require judicial intervention. This is not such a case.

The foundation of Linnas' due process argument is an appeal to the court's sense of decency and compassion. Noble words such as "decency" and "compassion" ring hollow when spoken by a man who ordered the extermination of innocent men, women and children kneeling at the edge of a mass grave. Karl Linnas' appeal to humanity, a humanity which he has grossly, callously and monstrously offended, truly offends this court's sense of decency.

* * *

The petition for review is denied.

NOTES AND QUESTIONS

1.   Postscript: In 1987 Linnas was deported to the former Soviet Union. Before the death sentence that had been imposed in absentia could be carried out, he died of natural causes.

2.   Estonia is now once again an independent country. Similar problems have arisen, however, with respect to Yugoslavia. In *Osmani v. INS*, 14 F.3d 13 (7th Cir. 1994), a native of Macedonia had been ordered deported to Yugoslavia before the breakup of the latter. After affirming the deportation order, the court urged the BIA to modify the order to specify Macedonia as the country of deportation. The court explicitly held that the fact the United States had not yet recognized Macedonia did not bar such an order. *Id.* at 15.

3.   The wording of present INA § 241(b)(2) differs from that of former section 243(a), but the substance is virtually identical.

4.   Should Congress amend INA § 241(b)(2) to allow the noncitizen to designate a second choice in the event he or she is rejected by the first country? Should there be opportunity for a third choice? As many choices as the person wishes?

5.   What do you think of Linnas's tactical decision to designate "the free and independent Republic of Estonia"? What *should* the immigration judge do when the noncitizen's designation is ambiguous?

6.   What would have happened if the Soviet Union had been unwilling to receive Linnas? Consider the other options provided by section 241(b)(2), and read also section 241(a)(1, 2, 3, 7).

7.   Suppose a citizen and resident of Canada has no interest in immigrating to the United States but would love a free South Pacific vacation. What prevents her from entering the United States surreptitiously, turning herself in, refusing voluntary departure, and designating Fiji?

8.   The crux of Linnas's argument was that the United States was using deportation as a ploy to extradite him to the Soviet Union. First, precisely how do the characteristics and purposes of deportation (now removal) differ from those of extradition? Second, given those differences, *would* it be bad policy to use deportation as an instrument for accomplishing the goals of extradition (assuming the elements of the deportability ground are all present)? In a case where the IJ has the discretion to select the destination country, would it be an abuse of discretion to take into account the fact that country X, to which the person resists being sent, affirmatively wants that person back?

9. What limitations does the court place on its holding? After *Linnas,* under what circumstances might a court invalidate, as a disguised extradition, a decision to remove a noncitizen to a particular country?

10. Assume that the noncitizen's designated country (W) says no; that the country of citizenship (X) no longer exists; that country Y requests his or her extradition; and that country Z, to which the person wants to go, says yes. Would the immigration judge abuse his or her discretion by ordering removal to country Y rather than Z?

A somewhat similar problem arose in a celebrated English case, *R. v. Governor of Brixton Prison, ex parte Soblen* [1963] 2 Q.B. 243 (Div.Ct. and Ct. of Appeal). Dr. Robert Soblen, an American citizen, had been convicted in the United States of conspiracy to commit espionage. He escaped to Israel, but the Israeli authorities placed him on a specially chartered plane to the United States. During the flight, Soblen deliberately cut his wrists. Upon a stopover in London, he was rushed to the hospital for emergency treatment. Once he was physically able to travel again, the British Home Secretary ordered him deported on the statutory ground that his removal would be "conducive to the public good." Although the pertinent extradition treaty did not cover espionage, the United States requested Soblen's return. Soblen requested deportation to Czechoslovakia, which had issued him an entry visa (and which was then still in existence). The Home Secretary, in his discretion, chose nonetheless to deport Soblen to the United States. (The U.K. did not have an automatic designation provision analogous to INA § 241(b)(2)). No reasons for the destination decision were given.

The English trial court and then the Court of Appeal affirmed the decision of the Home Secretary. The opinions of the various Court of Appeal judges reasoned that the United States, being the country of citizenship, was the only country required by international law to receive Soblen; that the Home Secretary might simply have been motivated by a legitimate desire to help an ally; or that perhaps the Home Secretary's purpose had been to deter the type of conduct by which Soblen had gained admission to England in the first place. (The story has a grim postscript; after exhausting his legal appeals, Dr. Soblen committed suicide.)

What is your reaction to the reasons given by the Court of Appeal for upholding the decision of the Home Secretary? See generally Stephen H. Legomsky, Immigration and the Judiciary—Law and Politics in Britain and America 39–40, 97–99 (1987).

11. Step aside for a moment from the legal analysis employed in *Linnas.* Do you detect in the court's opinion any external factors that might have played a part in the result?

12. Difficult issues of both international law and domestic United States law have arisen concerning American extradition of Nazi war criminals to Israel. For a useful account, see Steven Lubet & Jan S. Reed, *Extradition of Nazis from the United States to Israel: A Survey of Issues in Transnational Criminal Law,* 22 Stanford J. Internat'l L. 1 (1986).

13. Another provision, INA § 241(b)(3)(A), prohibits removal to any country in which the "alien's life or freedom would be threatened * * * because of the alien's race, religion, nationality, membership in a particular social group, or political opinion" (with some exceptions). That provision will be explored in depth in chapter 11.

PROBLEM 7

X, born in the Netherlands, immigrated from there to the United States, stopping for a week in Costa Rica en route. Several years later he became a naturalized United States citizen. To attain naturalization he had to take an oath renouncing his Dutch citizenship. See INA § 337(a)(2). (Naturalization is taken up in chapter 13, § A.2 below. Assume for now that the law of the Netherlands gives full effect to such renunciations.) Three years ago, upon finding that X had misrepresented material facts in his naturalization application, a federal district court revoked his naturalization under INA § 340(a). X has now been ordered removed on grounds that are not pertinent here. X designated Costa Rica as the country to which he wished to be removed, but Costa Rica has refused to accept him. The Dutch government has indicated it will receive X, but X would prefer to go to Canada, which is also willing to take him. Given section 241(b)(2), does the immigration judge have the discretion to order X removed to Canada?

4. STAYS OF REMOVAL

After an immigration judge or the BIA has issued a final removal order, ICE generally gives the person a certain amount of time to take care of any personal matters before leaving the United States. Sometimes, however, that time is not enough. In such a case the remedy is to request ICE, in its discretion, to grant a temporary stay under 8 C.F.R. § 241.6 (2004).

Stays are especially important in the context of motions to reopen removal proceedings. The mere filing of a motion to reopen does not automatically stay removal, 8 C.F.R. § 1003.6(b) (2004), and once removal occurs, the motion to reopen is deemed withdrawn, 8 C.F.R. § 1003.2(d) (2004). Thus, unless removal is stayed while the motion to reopen is pending, ICE could, by removing the person, prevent a decision on the motion to reopen. It is best, therefore, to couple a motion to reopen with a request for a stay to permit a decision on the motion. Try to figure out why the regulations would choose not to make stays pending motions to reopen automatic, and what might prompt the IJ or the BIA to deny a stay request that accompanies a motion to reopen.

SECTION C. MISCELLANEOUS DEFENSES

A number of other defenses to removal require brief mention. One is citizenship. Since only noncitizens may be removed, see, e.g., INA § 237(a)

("Any alien * * *"); *Ng Fung Ho v. White,* 259 U.S. 276, 42 S.Ct. 492, 66 L.Ed. 938 (1922), a person who can prove United States citizenship will have a complete defense to removal. Chapter 13 will acquaint you with the requirements and consequences of citizenship.

You saw in chapter 2 the difficulties faced by anyone who challenges an INA provision on any of the more common constitutional grounds—due process, equal protection, and the first amendment, to name a few. One frequent argument, thus far rejected by all the courts to which it has been addressed, has been made in cases where deportable parents have United States citizen children. The argument is that removing the parents results *de facto* in the unconstitutional removal of the citizen children. Rejecting that contention, courts have reasoned (a) that a citizen child cannot make a real choice about where to live and thus is dependent on the decision of his or her parents; (b) that the child's removal from the country is not inevitable because the parents might choose to leave the child with foster parents in the United States; and (c) that, upon attaining majority, the citizen child will be free to return to the United States. See *Newton v. INS,* 736 F.2d 336, 342–43 (6th Cir.1984), quoting *Acosta v. Gaffney,* 558 F.2d 1153, 1157–58 (3d Cir.1977). What is your reaction?

Other generally *unsuccessful* constitutional defenses include all of those that would have required the courts to characterize removal as punishment. You saw one early example in *Fong Yue Ting,* pages 124–44 above, where the Supreme Court rejected a procedural due process challenge that the Court believed rested on classifying deportation as punitive in nature. Similarly holding that deportation is not punishment, courts have turned away challenges based on the *ex post facto* clause, e.g., *Bugajewitz v. Adams,* 228 U.S. 585, 33 S.Ct. 607, 57 L.Ed. 978 (1913), and on the cruel and unusual punishment clause, *Lieggi v. U.S.I.N.S.,* memorandum decision noted at 529 F.2d 530 (7th Cir.1976), rev'g 389 F.Supp. 12 (N.D.Ill.1975).

Sometimes a person becomes deportable partly because a government official either acted wrongly or failed to take timely action. In those cases, noncitizens have sometimes argued that the government should be estopped from deporting them. Those efforts too have been unsuccessful. The leading case is *INS v. Miranda,* 459 U.S. 14, 103 S.Ct. 281, 74 L.Ed.2d 12 (1982), where the former INS had failed to act on an immediate relative petition for eighteen months. Eventually the marriage dissolved, the citizen spouse withdrew the petition, deportation proceedings were initiated, and the immigration judge denied the noncitizen's application for adjustment of status and ordered deportation. Summarily reversing the Court of Appeals for the Ninth Circuit, the Supreme Court refused to estop the INS from going forward with the deportation. The Court held that, if estopping the government is ever permissible (an issue it has still not decided as of this writing), it requires at a minimum a showing of "affirmative misconduct." On the facts of *Miranda,* such a showing was not made.

What constitutes affirmative misconduct is not so clear. You might have assumed that the word "affirmative" was meant to signify action rather than inaction, but evidently that word is not the key. In two of the cases cited approvingly in *Miranda,* affirmative misstatements by government officials were held not to constitute "affirmative misconduct." See *Schweiker v. Hansen,* 450 U.S. 785, 101 S.Ct. 1468, 67 L.Ed.2d 685 (1981); *Montana v. Kennedy,* 366 U.S. 308, 81 S.Ct. 1336, 6 L.Ed.2d 313 (1961). Rather, the Court in *Miranda* appeared to have in mind a degree of blameworthiness that surpassed the level of fault reflected in the particular governmental errors at issue in the cited cases. See generally Bill Ong Hing, *Estoppel in Immigration Proceedings—New Life from Akbarin and Miranda,* 20 San Diego L.Rev. 11 (1982).

SECTION D. A PERSPECTIVE ON RELIEF FROM DEPORTABILITY

In this chapter you have encountered the major forms of relief requested by deportable noncitizens. Most of them are in the form "If A, B, and C, then the Attorney General (or the Secretary of Homeland Security, as the case may be) *may* do X." Most of the provisions, in other words, restrict the relevant official's humanitarian discretion to the case in which certain statutory prerequisites have been met.

Contrast that system with New Zealand's Immigration Act 1987. Under that statute, the Minister of Immigration "*may* * * * order * * * deportation" in specified cases. *Id.* §§ 91(1), 92(2) (emphasis added). Under section 63 of the Act, any person who has been ordered removed may appeal to the Minister, who may cancel the removal order when "exceptional circumstances of a humanitarian nature [would make removal] unjust or unduly harsh" and "it would not in all the circumstances be contrary to the public interest to allow the appellant to remain." An advisory panel makes recommendations to the Minister on the exercise of the discretion conferred by that provision. *Id.* § 94.

The contrast highlights a perennial battle in administrative law—fixed rules versus administrative discretion. Professor Daniel Kanstroom makes a strong argument for *more* fixed rules and *less* delegated discretion in immigration cases. See Daniel Kanstroom, *Surrounding the Hole in the Doughnut: Discretion and Deference in U.S. Immigration Law,* 71 Tulane L. Rev. 703 (1997) (also arguing for other ways to structure discretion, including judicial review).

Should either (a) ICE or (b) immigration judges be granted a similar open-ended discretion not to remove deportable noncitizens? Compare the merits of the United States and New Zealand approaches.

CHAPTER 9

DEPORTATION PROCEDURE

The two preceding chapters introduced you to the grounds on which noncitizens may be found deportable and the affirmative relief provisions available to some deportable noncitizens. Here the focus shifts to procedure.

As you now know, IIRIRA abolished the terms "exclusion" proceedings and "deportation" proceedings, substituting the term "removal" proceedings for both. But there are still two classes of removable noncitizens—those who are "inadmissible" and those who are "deportable." You have seen that each class has its own set of substantive grounds and its own set of affirmative relief provisions.

In addition, despite the common name ("removal"), the procedures for these two classes of removable noncitizens continue to differ. The procedures for determining inadmissibility are part of the larger admission process, which you encountered in chapter 6. The procedures for removing deportable noncitizens are treated here. And since it is cumbersome to keep referring to "procedures for removing deportable noncitizens," this book will use the shorter term "deportation procedure" for that purpose. Recognize, however, that when used in this way "deportation" is a generic word, no longer a term of art.

A second complication is that, since 1996, presence without admission (formerly called entry without inspection) has been a ground for inadmissibility, not deportability. INA § 212(a)(6)(A). Nonetheless, certain of the procedural issues such cases present—especially issues relating to apprehension, detention, and burden of proof—fit more easily into a discussion of deportation procedure than into a discussion of admission procedure. Consequently, this chapter will also encompass the procedural problems arising from the removal of those who are present without admission.

We start with a general overview of the deportation process. Succeeding pages will explore in some detail a sampling of the more specific problems associated with deportation procedure. Remaining sections will provide a case study of the sequence of events in deportation proceedings, immerse you in a simulated removal hearing of your own, and examine some of the exceptions to the usual deportation process.

SECTION A. OVERVIEW

1. APPREHENSION

Removable noncitizens are apprehended in a variety of places—in border areas and in the interior; in vehicles and on foot; in factories, in agricultural fields, in restaurants, in other places of business, and occasionally in dwellings. Sometimes the discovery is by chance encounter; at other times apprehension is the product of investigation and planning. In most instances apprehensions are effected by employees of ICE or CBP. In many cases, however, other federal law enforcement officers or even state or local police arrest a person suspected of criminal activity and later report to ICE when they discover that the individual is not a United States citizen.[1] Where is the statutory authority for these various operations? And which government officials are clothed with these responsibilities?

The INA charges the Secretary of Homeland Security with "the administration and enforcement" of the immigration laws. INA § 103(a)(1). More specifically, it gives the Secretary both the power and the duty "to control and guard the boundaries and borders of the United States against the illegal entry of aliens." INA § 103(a)(5). Another provision, INA § 287(a), lists several specific powers that properly designated DHS employees may exercise *without a search or arrest warrant*. Those pertinent here include (1) the power to interrogate any person believed to be a noncitizen as to his or her right to be in the United States; (2) the power to arrest any noncitizen in the country if there is "reason to believe that the alien so arrested is in the United States in violation of [the immigration laws] and is likely to escape before [an arrest] warrant can be obtained;" (3) within a "reasonable distance[2] from any external boundary," the power to board any vessel within United States territorial waters and any train, aircraft, or other vehicle, for the purpose of searching for noncitizens; and (4) within twenty-five miles of any external boundary, the power to enter private lands other than dwellings for the purpose of patrolling the border. The Secretary has authorized every DHS employee who bears the title "immigration officer" to exercise one or more of those powers. 8 C.F.R. § 287.5(a) (2004). Immigration officers include all immigration inspectors at the border, all border patrol agents, all investigators, and many others. 8 C.F.R. § 103.1(b) (2004). The Secretary may also deputize properly trained state employees to perform investigation, apprehension, and detention functions. See INA § 287(g).

These various statutory powers—none of which requires a warrant—are quite sweeping. Not surprisingly, except at the border or its "functional equivalent," the courts have recognized various Fourth Amendment limita-

---

1. Conversely, DHS agents may arrest individuals suspected of crimes that are not related to immigration. INA § 287(a)(5).

2. With some exceptions, the regulations define "reasonable distance" as 100 miles. 8 C.F.R. § 287.1(a)(2) (2004).

tions. The details of those limitations are beyond the scope of this book, but you should note generally that in certain situations the immigration officer must have a "reasonable suspicion" that the subject is not a citizen; in others, there must be reasonable suspicion not only that the person is a noncitizen, but also that he or she is in the United States in violation of law; still other actions require "probable cause" (a higher standard than reasonable suspicion) to believe the person is a noncitizen who is here unlawfully. There are several variables. In general, more is demanded when the person is in the interior than when the person is at or near the border; more is demanded when mobile units engage in roving patrols than when DHS sets up stationary highway checkpoints through which all vehicles must pass; more is demanded for a search than for a mere stop/interrogation; and still more is required for an arrest. See generally David Carliner, Lucas Guttentag, Arthur C. Helton & Wade Henderson, The Rights of Aliens and Refugees 118–39 (2d ed. 1990). One issue of recently increased importance is whether ethnic profiling is ever a permissible practice in immigration apprehensions and arrests. This subject is taken up in chapter 10, § G below.

Until 1956, every deportation proceeding began with the person's arrest. See 8 C.F.R. § 242 (1952). In that year, the Justice Department amended its regulations to eliminate the requirement of an arrest; instead, proceedings were to begin when the former INS served on the subject a document then called an "order to show cause." 21 Fed.Reg. 98 (Jan. 6, 1956). But the power to arrest still exists. INA § 242(a).

2. BEFORE THE HEARING

Within 48 hours of the arrest (7 days for those certified as suspected terrorists under section 412(a) of the USA PATRIOT Act of 2001, see INA § 236A(a)(5)), unless DHS has granted voluntary departure, it must decide "whether there is prima facie evidence that the arrested alien is in the United States in violation of law." 8 C.F.R. § 287.3(b) (2004). If there is prima facie evidence, then DHS issues a Notice to Appear, serves it on the alleged noncitizen, and files it with the "immigration court." In deportability cases, Notices to Appear are usually issued by ICE, but a range of other DHS agencies and officials are also authorized to issue them. See 8 C.F.R. §§ 239.1, 1239.1 (2004). In some cities, one or more immigration judges are permanently based. In others (called "detail cities"), hearings are held by nearby immigration judges who visit periodically. The service of the Notice to Appear officially commences removal proceedings and vests jurisdiction in the immigration judge.

The Notice to Appear serves several useful functions. It explains the nature of the proceeding, specifies the deportability grounds charged, recites all the factual allegations necessary to establish those charges, states the time and place of the person's required appearance before the immigration judge, and instructs the person to keep the government apprised of his or her address and the consequences of failing to do so. INA § 239(a)(1). Those consequences now include the possibility of an in absentia removal hearing, a subject discussed separately in section E.3 below. Finally, the service of the Notice to Appear marks the start of a ten–day waiting period, designed to give the person a chance to secure counsel, before the removal hearing may be scheduled. INA § 239(b)(1).

During this same 48–hour period DHS must decide whether to detain the person pending a final removal decision. The detention decision is extremely important, because removal proceedings typically take at least several months, and sometimes several years, to complete. Detention entails not only a loss of liberty for the detainee, but also impaired access to counsel, potential economic and other hardships for the detainee's family members, and of course great expense for the government. Stephen H. Legomsky, *The Detention of Aliens: Theories, Rules, and Discretion*, 30 Univ. Miami Inter–American L. Rev. 531 (1999).

Today, detention is *mandatory* for certain categories of noncitizens. In 1988, Congress required detention for aggravated felons (a category then defined narrowly) while deportation proceedings were pending. Pub. L. 100–690, §§ 7341, 7343(a), 7344, 102 Stat. 4181, 4469–71 (Nov. 18, 1988). In 1996, AEDPA and IIRIRA combined to extend mandatory detention to several other major categories: (1) almost anyone who is inadmissible or deportable on crime-related grounds (not just aggravated felons); (2) those who are inadmissible or deportable on terrorism grounds (expanded by sections 411 and 412 of the USA PATRIOT Act of 2001, as noted earlier); (3) most arriving passengers (including those subject to expedited removal); and (4) individuals awaiting the execution of final removal orders. See INA §§ 235(b)(1)(B)(iii)(IV), 235(b)(2)(A), 236(c)(1)(A, B, C, D), 241(a)(1, 2, 3). In 2003, the Supreme Court in *Demore* (pages 211–24 above) upheld the constitutionality of mandatory detention, at least for noncitizens charged with crime-related deportability grounds.

In all other cases DHS has the discretion whether to detain the person without bond, release on cash bond of at least $1500, or release on "conditional parole." INA § 236(a). Release is permitted only if DHS is satisfied that the individual "would not pose a danger to property or persons and * * * is likely to appear for any future proceeding." 8 C.F.R. § 236.1(c)(8) (2004).

The rule that permits DHS to hold the people it apprehends for 48 hours (even if not suspected of terrorism) is a product of the September 11, 2001 terrorist attacks on the World Trade Center and the Pentagon. Until then, the maximum holding period, without a decision to issue a Notice to Appear, was 24 hours. Apart from expanding the period to 48 hours, the new rule allows "an additional reasonable period of time" when there is an "emergency or other extraordinary circumstance." 8 C.F.R. § 287.3(d) (2004).

While removal proceedings are pending the person is not permitted to work, unless he or she would have been eligible to work had removal proceedings not been brought. INA § 236(a)(3). Special problems arise in the case of juveniles. See *Reno v. Flores*, 507 U.S. 292, 113 S.Ct. 1439, 123 L.Ed.2d 1 (1993).

The regulations allow a person who is dissatisfied with the DHS custody decision to obtain a de novo bond redetermination hearing before an immigration judge. 8 C.F.R. § 1003.19 (2004). The redetermination hearing, which is entirely separate from the removal hearing, is prompt, informal, and often (in "detail cities," usually) telephonic. See 8 C.F.R. § 1003.19(b) (2004). Either the noncitizen or DHS may appeal the immigration judge's custody decision to the BIA. 8 C.F.R. §§ 1003.19(f), 1003.38 (2004). In any case in which DHS ordered the person detained or set the bond amount at $10,000 or more, a release order by the IJ is automatically stayed if DHS within one day files a notice of an intent to appeal and within ten days files an actual notice of appeal. The automatic stay lasts until the BIA decides the case. 8 C.F.R. § 1003.19(i)(2) (2004).

A fascinating two-part study by Dr. Janet Gilboy provides insights into the dynamics of the bond redetermination process. Her data (now somewhat dated) reveal that in the Chicago district, from October 1981 through December 1984, IJ's decreased the bond amounts in 95% of the cases studied and increased them in none. Janet A. Gilboy, *Setting Bail in Deportation Cases: The Role of Immigration Judges,* 24 San Diego L.Rev. 347, 369 (1987). On average, the IJ's reduced the bonds to about one-third of the amounts set by the former INS. *Id.* at 370–71. The result is a circular game in which the immigration enforcement authorities set higher than necessary amounts because they know the amounts they set will be reduced by immigration judges. The IJ's in turn reduce the amounts because they know that the enforcement officials set artificially high bonds in the expectation that the IJ's will reduce them. Janet A. Gilboy, *Administrative Review in a System of Conflicting Values,* 13 L. & Social Inquiry 515, 538 (1988). As you will see in chapter 10, sections A.1 and A.2, the government has been far more prone to oppose release on bond, and far more likely to appeal bond decisions to the BIA, since September 11, 2001.

With all the powers to stop, interrogate, arrest, and detain, the question arises whether DHS is required to advise the suspects of their various procedural rights. In *Miranda v. Arizona,* 384 U.S. 436, 86 S.Ct. 1602, 16 L.Ed.2d 694 (1966), the Supreme Court held that statements made during custodial interrogations may not be used in *criminal* proceedings unless the statements were preceded by warnings that the person has the right to remain silent, that any statement he or she chooses to make may be admitted into evidence, and that there is a right to have a lawyer present. The lower courts have held the *Miranda* rule inapplicable to deportation proceedings. See, e.g., *Bustos–Torres v. INS,* 898 F.2d 1053, 1056 (5th Cir.1990); *Nai Cheng Chen v. INS,* 537 F.2d 566, 568 (1st Cir.1976) (but immigration officers sometimes gives *Miranda* warnings anyway to preserve option of bringing criminal prosecution).

Although the Constitution does not require *Miranda* warnings in removal proceedings, the regulations require certain more limited advice at various stages. When DHS decides to institute removal proceedings against a person whom it already has in custody, it must advise that any statements the person makes can be used against him or her, must advise of the right to counsel at the person's own expense, and must provide a list of any free legal services programs available in the locale. 8 C.F.R. § 287.3(c) (2004). The enumerated advisals include no mention of the right to remain silent. As you will see momentarily, the IJ must also advise of certain rights, at the removal hearing.

But you should notice one important limitation common to all those provisions: Each of them comes into play only at some point after DHS has made the decision to institute formal proceedings. By delaying that decision, therefore, DHS can extract valuable information before the person learns of his or her rights. It was not always that way. As the leading immigration treatise observes:

> For almost 15 years * * * the questioning of prospective deportees who were in custody or otherwise meaningfully deprived of their freedom of action customarily was preceded by a warning of their right to silence and to the assistance of counsel. This practice was ended in 1980, and the regulations now require such a warning only after deportation or removal proceedings are started.

6 Gordon, Mailman & Yale–Loehr, § 72.02[2][f]. Why would DHS make that change? Is it justifiable?

Under the Vienna Convention on Consular Relations, art. 5(i), 21 U.S.T. 77, 84, 596 U.N.T.S. 261, 268 (Apr. 24, 1963), consulates have the right to represent their own nationals before the tribunals of the host state. Because of a Memorandum of Understanding on Consular Protection of Mexican and United States Nationals (May 7, 1996) and an earlier settlement agreement in United States domestic litigation, U.S. immigration officials who believe an arrestee is unlawfully in the United States must notify the person of his or her right to communicate with the relevant consulate. For a good discussion, see Jorge A. Vargas, *Consular Protection to Illegal Migratory Workers and Mexican Undocumented Minors: Two Sensitive Issues Addressed by the Thirteenth Annual Meeting of the United States–Mexico Binational Commission*, 6 Florida State Univ. J. Transnat'l L. & Policy 143 (1996).

Soon after DHS has filed the Notice to Appear with the immigration court, the noncitizen or his or her counsel appears at a master calendar hearing. Sometimes, especially in detail cities, the master calendar hearing is telephonic. At this hearing, the noncitizen might plead to the allegations and deportability charges contained in the Notice to Appear and might designate the country to which he or she would prefer to be sent in the event removal is ordered. Simple cases and uncontested cases are sometimes finally decided at this stage. In other cases, however, the IJ uses the master calendar hearing to identify the issues and set a schedule for the filing of any motions or applications for relief. The IJ then estimates the amount of time the removal hearing is likely to take and schedules a hearing date accordingly.

During the interval between the master calendar hearing and the actual removal hearing, various procedural events can occur. Either party may request a continuance, which the IJ has the discretion to grant "for good cause shown." 8 C.F.R. § 1003.29 (2004). Either party may move to change venue, *id.* § 1003.20(b), to remand to DHS for consideration of an application that would moot removal proceedings, or to suppress evidence. (As you will see later, the grounds for suppressing evidence as illegally obtained are quite narrow.) Limited discovery is possible; in particular, the regulations expressly authorize depositions, *id.* § 1003.35, and Freedom of Information Act requests, *id.* §§ 103.8 et seq. The IJ also has the discretion, exercised occasionally, to hold a pre-hearing conference "to narrow issues, to attain stipulations between the parties, to exchange information voluntarily, and otherwise to simplify and organize the proceeding." *Id.* § 1003.21(a).

Certain of these procedural devices will be unrealistic when the parties are not represented by counsel. In every case in which removability is contested, and in certain other situations, ICE must be represented by a lawyer known as a "trial attorney." See 8 C.F.R. §§ 1240.2(b), 1240.10(d) (2004). The noncitizen has a statutory right to be represented by counsel, but only at his or her own expense; unlike indigent criminal defendants, indigent noncitizens in removal proceedings generally have no right to appointed counsel. INA § 240(b)(4)(A). Section B.2 below will examine the devices by which indigent noncitizens can sometimes secure representation.

3. THE REMOVAL HEARING

The Administrative Procedure Act (APA), 5 U.S.C. § 556, prescribes various procedures generally applicable to federal administrative agencies engaged in formal adjudication. As you will see later, the Supreme Court has interpreted the INA as exempting deportation [now removal] hearings from those procedures. In most respects, however, the conduct of removal hearings is functionally equivalent to that of the hearings subject to the APA. Some differences do exist and they will be explored below.

The opposing parties at a removal hearing are ICE and the noncitizen. An immigration judge presides over the hearing. The hearing is normally held at an EOIR "immigration court," although in recent years video conferencing has been used increasingly. See 81 IR 1495–96 (Oct. 25, 2004); Lory Rosenberg, *Arrests, Jails, and Video Hearings*, 9 BIB 1233 (Oct. 15, 2004).

As you saw earlier, the immigration judges are subject to the general supervision of the Chief Immigration Judge, who in turn is part of the Executive Office for Immigration Review (EOIR). EOIR was created by the Attorney General in 1983, see 48 Fed.Reg. 8039 (Feb. 25, 1983); 8 C.F.R. §§ 1003.0, 1003.9, 1003.10 (2004), and remains part of the Department of Justice. The IJ's are not article III judges, but they clearly perform judicial functions and many of the physical trappings are similar to those of the general article III courts—judicial robes, a raised dais, separate tables for the two sides, sometimes a witness box, etc.

In deportability cases, removal hearings are open to the public, except that the IJ has the discretion to limit the number in attendance to accommodate the physical facilities and may close the hearing entirely to protect witnesses, abused spouses or children, other parties, or the public interest. 8 C.F.R. § 1003.27 (2004). The dramatically increased use of closed removal hearings and secret evidence removal hearings in cases that raise issues of national security is taken up in chapter 10, sections D.3 and D.4.

The IJ turns on a tape recorder at the start of the hearing. It remains on throughout the hearing unless the IJ wishes to go off the record. 8 C.F.R. §§ 1003.28, 1003.36, 1240.9 (2004). The IJ then announces for the record that he or she is holding a removal hearing and states the noncitizen's name and "A-number" (an identification number assigned by DHS), the time and place of the hearing, and the presence of the parties, their counsel, and any interpreters. If the individual is not already represented, the IJ advises of the right to counsel at no expense to the government and makes sure the person has received a list of any free legal services programs locally available. *Id.* § 1240.10(a). The IJ verifies that the Notice to Appear has been served on the noncitizen and then enters it into the record as an exhibit. The IJ reads various other rights and explains the contents of the Notice to Appear in nontechnical terms unless, as is common when the person is represented by counsel, these explanations are waived. After that, the IJ places the person under oath. *Id.*

If the person has not already pleaded to the allegations in the Notice to Appear, the IJ takes the pleading at this time. The noncitizen (or counsel) must either admit or deny each of the factual allegations and then concede or deny deportability. *Id.* § 1240.10(c). The IJ also permits the person to designate the country to which he or she wishes to be sent in the event removal is ordered. INA § 241(b)(2).

At the removal hearing, ICE first has the burden of proving by clear and convincing evidence that the subject of the hearing is a noncitizen. Only then, see, e.g., *Murphy v. INS*, 54 F.3d 605 (9th Cir. 1995), does the burden shift to the noncitizen to prove by clear and convincing evidence that he or she is lawfully present pursuant to a prior admission. INA § 240(b)(2)(B). If the noncitizen does so, the burden shifts back to ICE to prove the alleged deportability grounds by clear and convincing evidence. INA § 240(c)(3)(A). One may be ordered removed only on the grounds formally charged, but at any time during the proceeding ICE may lodge additional charges. 8 C.F.R. § 1003.30 (2004). In that event the noncitizen may receive a reasonable continuance to prepare to meet the new charges. *Id.* The noncitizen has the burden of establishing eligibility and deservedness for any affirmative relief for which he or she applies at the hearing. INA § 240(c)(4)(A).

If deportability is contested, ICE presents its case first. When it finishes, the noncitizen presents his or her case. The ICE case may consist of documents, live testimony, or both. When ICE calls a witness, the ICE trial attorney conducts direct examination and the noncitizen then has the opportunity to cross-examine. ICE may re-examine the witness if it wishes. If it does so, then the noncitizen may re-cross. During the noncitizen's case-in-chief, the same process applies in reverse; the noncitizen examines the witness, ICE cross-examines, and so forth. During either side's case, the IJ is free to interject additional questions. Some IJ's ask only a few questions; others play a more dominant role.

If the IJ finds the person deportable, the hearing may enter a second phase in which the noncitizen applies for one or more forms of affirmative relief (voluntary departure, cancellation of removal, adjustment, asylum, etc.). In this phase the noncitizen proceeds first, attempting to establish all the elements required for the relief sought. ICE then has the opportunity to put on any evidence relevant to that relief.

The testimony of all witnesses is under oath or affirmation. 8 C.F.R. §§ 1003.34, 1240.7(b) (2004). Formal rules of evidence, however, do not apply in removal proceedings. *Bustos–Torres v. INS*, 898 F.2d 1053, 1055 (5th Cir.1990). The regulations allow the admission of any relevant evidence, 8 C.F.R. § 1240.7(a) (2004), but as discussed in subsection B.3 below, the courts have added a fundamental fairness test for hearsay evidence. The "exclusionary rule" applicable in criminal proceedings is generally inapplicable in removal proceedings. See pages 686–704 below.

If the noncitizen lacks an adequate command of the English language, EOIR will supply an interpreter to interpret the noncitizen's own testimony (but not the testimony of other witnesses or the exchanges between the IJ and counsel). See *El Rescate Legal Services, Inc. v. EOIR*, 959 F.2d 742 (9th Cir. 1991) (amended opinion). Some interpreters are EOIR employees; others (especially those who interpret the less common foreign languages) work for EOIR on a contract basis as needed. See generally William R. Robie, *The Purpose and Effect of the Proposed Rules of Procedure for Proceedings Before Immigration Judges*, 1 Georgetown Immigration L.J. 269, 279 (1986). Deficiencies in the quality of the interpretation have been a longstanding problem in removal proceedings. If severe enough, these deficiencies can violate due process or undermine the factual basis for an immigration judge's non-credibility finding. See, e.g., *He v. Ashcroft*, 328 F.3d 593 (9th Cir. 2003). Foreign language documents require certified English translations. 8 C.F.R. § 1003.33 (2004).

After all the evidence is in, the IJ renders a decision. The decision may be an oral one announced in the presence of the parties, or it may be rendered in written form and served on the parties later. 8 C.F.R. §§ 1003.37(a), 1240.13 (2004). Either way (unless deportability was conceded), the decision must contain the IJ's findings as to deportability and the IJ's reasons. *Id.* § 1240.12(a) (2004). The decision must also contain a formal order directing removal to a specified country, terminating proceedings, or otherwise disposing of the case (for example, by granting voluntary departure within a specified time period). *Id.* § 1240.12(c).

4. ADMINISTRATIVE REVIEW

Each of the opposing parties (the noncitizen and ICE) has the right to appeal the decision of the IJ to the Board of Immigration Appeals (BIA). 8

C.F.R. § 1003.1(b)(3) (2004). The BIA, like the IJs, is part of EOIR. Unlike the IJ's, who are scattered in various cities throughout the United States and ride circuit to other cities, the BIA sits in a fixed location (Falls Church, Virginia). It now has eleven members, appointed by the Attorney General. *Id.* § 1003.1(a)(1).

As a result of highly controversial reforms inaugurated in 2002 and 2003 by Attorney General Ashcroft, the Board now decides most of its cases by single-member "affirmances without opinion" (AWOs). The remaining cases are usually decided by three-member panels and are typically accompanied by reasoned opinions. See generally section B.4 below. Some of the latter opinions are designated for publication and become binding precedents for DHS officials and IJs. 8 C.F.R. § 1003.1(g) (2004). Occasionally the Board decides cases en banc. The Attorney General has reserved the power to review the decisions of the BIA, *id.* § 1003.1(h), but typically exercises this power only when a case raises exceptionally important questions of law or policy.

The process begins when the noncitizen or ICE files a notice of appeal. It must be filed within thirty days after service of the IJ's decision. See 8 C.F.R. § 1003.38(b) (2004). The filing of that notice automatically stays execution of the IJ's decision. *Id.* § 1003.6(a). There are very specific time deadlines for preparing and reviewing the transcripts, filing briefs, and rendering decisions. See *id.* §§ 1003.1(e)(8), 1003.3(c), 1003.5. The BIA reviews the immigration judge's legal conclusions and exercises of discretion de novo, but as a result of the 2002 reforms the BIA may not reverse findings of fact, including credibility determinations, unless they are "clearly erroneous." *Id.* § 1003.1(d)(3).

One of the most controversial elements of the 2002 reforms was the reduction in the authorized size of the BIA from 23 members to 11 and the Attorney General's accompanying selection of particular Board members for removal. The dramatically expanded use of single-member affirmances without opinion ("AWOs") has been equally controversial. These and other issues concerning the BIA are taken up in more detail in subsection B.4 below.

5.   JUDICIAL REVIEW

The law that governs judicial review of removal orders is a technical minefield; you will encounter some of the details in section B.6 below. A few basic principles are worth understanding at this juncture.

Ordinarily, the exclusive procedure for obtaining judicial review of a removal order is to file a petition for review in the United States Court of Appeals for the circuit in which the removal hearing was held. INA § 242(b)(2). To be reviewable, the removal order must be administratively final. INA § 242(a)(1).

Sweeping provisions of IIRIRA appeared to immunize some of the most important removal orders from judicial review. These include orders of expedited removal, most removal orders based on crime-related deportability grounds, and almost all denials of discretionary relief. It similarly appeared that most of the alternatives to the petition for review—including habeas corpus, class actions, and suits for injunctive relief—had been eliminated or severely curtailed. But in several decisions the Supreme Court has interpreted the IIRIRA restrictions narrowly. Many noncitizens who are blocked from filing petitions for review in the courts of appeals may now test the legality of their removal orders by filing habeas corpus applications in the district courts. And even within the realm of petitions for review, both the Supreme Court and the lower courts have construed the statute as still permitting review of *some* elements of the removal orders—even with respect to the crime-related deportability grounds and even with respect to denials of discretionary relief. These decisions and the state of the current limitations on judicial review are explored in subsection B.6 below.

There are several conditions to filing petitions for review. Generally, the petitioner must first exhaust all administrative remedies, INA § 242(d)(1), including appeal to the BIA. The petition must be filed within thirty days of the administratively final removal order. INA § 242(b)(1).

At one time the service of the petition for review automatically stayed removal pending the court's decision. It no longer has that effect; the government remains free to remove the noncitizen before the court has decided the petition for review unless the court has affirmatively granted a request for a stay. INA § 242(b)(3)(B). On a petition for review, the court may review not only the finding of deportability, but also denials of motions to reopen. INA § 242(b)(6). The reviewing court decides the case on the basis of the administrative record, not by taking new evidence of its own. *Id.* § 242(b)(4)(A).

A word on terminology: During administrative proceedings before the IJ or the BIA, the person whom the government seeks to remove is called the "respondent." Once the person petitions for review in the court of appeals, he or she becomes the "petitioner" and the government becomes the "respondent."

6.   THE EXECUTION OF THE REMOVAL ORDER

IIRIRA tightened the rules for executing final orders of removal. Congress directed that noncitizens be removed within 90 days of the dates their orders become administratively final (with adjustments in cases where there has been judicial review or confinement). INA § 241(a)(1). Congress also provided, in INA § 241(a)(2), that the Attorney General [now the Secretary of Homeland Security] "shall detain the alien" during the removal period. It is not clear whether the word "shall" is to be taken literally, because the same provision goes on to say that "[u]nder no circumstances during the removal period shall the Attorney General release" certain of those removable noncitizens—namely, those whose removability rests on almost any of the crime-related grounds. INA § 241(a)(2). The latter prescription seems inexplicable if the former is meant to be construed literally. Finally, if the person is in prison because of a conviction for a nonviolent offense, the Secretary may execute the removal order even before the criminal sentence has been completed (with the state's permission in the case of state prisoners). INA § 241(a)(4)(B).

One event that can delay removal is a stay granted in connection with a motion to reopen or reconsider. In general, a motion to reopen is appropriate when one of the parties discovers previously unavailable evidence that might alter the decision; in contrast, a motion to reconsider typically challenges the correctness of the decision at the time it was rendered. See 8 C.F.R. §§ 1003.2 (motions to BIA), 1003.23(b) (motions to IJ), 103.5 (motions to DHS) (2004). These motions are controversial because of the delays they can entail. The filing of a motion to reopen or reconsider does not automatically stay the challenged decision, but the body to whom the motion is made has the discretion to stay execution while the motion is pending. See *id.* §§ 1003.2(f), 1003.23(b)(1)(v), 103.5(a)(1)(iv) (2004). As discussed in section B.5 below, however, both EOIR and Congress have recently imposed severe restrictions on the filing of motions to reopen or reconsider.

If no stays or other formal barriers remain, DHS prepares to execute the removal order. The noncitizen's cooperation in securing the necessary travel documents is important,[3] and IIRIRA may impose civil fines on any noncitizen who "fails to make timely application in good faith" for the necessary travel documents, willfully fails to depart, or otherwise hampers departure. INA § 274D. Under INA § 241(a)(2) detention is possibly mandatory (there is some ambiguity) for noncitizens who have been ordered removed. If for some reason the person is not in DHS detention, DHS serves a formal notice to report for removal at a specified time and place. This letter is known in the vernacular as a "bag and baggage" letter, though some people have been heard to call it a "run" letter.

In 1993, the former INS used a less conventional approach. To induce 600 noncitizens under deportation orders to appear for deportation, the INS San Diego District Office sent out letters promising them amnesty pursuant to the terms of a fictional new law. The INS deliberately refrained from sending copies of the letters to these noncitizens' lawyers for fear that "the lawyers would alert their clients to the sting." After much negative publicity, the Acting Commissioner of the INS disapproved the operation. For a thorough description and effective critique of this tactic, see Lenni B. Benson, *By Hook or by Crook: Exploring the Legality of an INS Sting Operation*, 31 San Diego L.Rev. 813 (1994).

At the latest, the government will have custody over the person from the time the person reports for removal until it escorts him or her onto the plane or other vehicle (or to the border if removal is to a contiguous

---

3. The travel document need not be a passport. Often it is simply a letter issued by the foreign country's U.S. consulate verifying that the person is a national of that country. For this and some of the other information on the mechanics of executing removal orders, the author thanks Chester Moyer, Officer in Charge, St. Louis Suboffice, former INS.

country.)[4] Subject to various restrictions that you saw in chapter 8, § B.3 above, deportable noncitizens who are ordered removed are usually sent to the countries that they designated at their removal hearings.

SECTION B.   A SAMPLING OF SPECIFIC PROCEDURAL INGREDIENTS

1.   THE HEARING PROCESS: HISTORY, THE APA, AND SEPARATION OF FUNCTIONS

Sidney B. Rawitz, From Wong Yang Sung to Black Robes

65 IR 453–59 (1988).

* * *

Few will dispute that immigration judges wield great power in making decisions that profoundly affect individual lives. Their judicial attire lending verisimilitude, they bring dignity and authority to the hearings over which they preside. But it was not always thus. Their predecessors as INS hearing officers labored in an uncertain and unrewarding environment. They possessed none of the independence guaranteed today's immigration judges; by and large, they did not command respect; and they were poorly compensated for their efforts.

* * *

In 1950, I was one of the Examiners assigned to the Hearing Review Unit of the Adjudications Division in the INS Central Office. Our principal duties were to review deportation and exclusion hearing records and prepare decisions for the signature of the Assistant Commissioner. The Central Office, after a war-time exile to Philadelphia, had been brought back to Washington in 1948 and relocated in a ramshackle two-story building known as Tempo X, across from the D.C. Armory and a stone's throw from where RFK stadium now stands.

I recall well that wintry afternoon of February 20, 1950, when a colleague, visibly excited, burst into my Tempo X office to tell me: "You can stop whatever you're working on. The Court has just decided the *Sung* case." Wong Yang Sung was the name of the deserting Chinese crewman who rocked—and nearly capsized—the boat of the Immigration Service.[2]

---

4. If the person is dangerous to others (e.g., because of serious criminal activity or mental illness), the airline might require a DHS officer to accompany him or her all the way to the final destination. And if the person must change planes en route, DHS normally makes "meet and greet" arrangements in which law enforcement officers from the relevant DHS districts escort removed noncitizens to their connecting flights.

2. *Wong Yang Sung v. McGrath,* 339 U.S. 33, 70 S.Ct. 445, 94 L.Ed. 616 (1950).

Let me briefly describe the procedures the U.S. Supreme Court invalidated on that memorable day. Expulsion (or deportation) proceedings were carried out under the authority of the Immigration Act of February 5, 1917, which stipulated in § 19 that certain designated aliens "shall upon the warrant of the Attorney General be taken into custody and deported." This meager statutory language constituted the authority for the deportation process. To initiate the deportation proceeding, the alien was served with a warrant of arrest which informed him in summary language of the section(s) of law and ground(s) upon which his deportation was being sought. No recitation of factual allegations was served on the alien then or at any time in the proceedings.

Hearings were conducted by an immigrant inspector whose duties also included investigating like cases of deportable aliens. When performing the hearing officer function, the immigrant inspector was referred to as the "Presiding Inspector," but he was not permitted to hear a case in which he had been the investigating officer unless the alien consented.

In the more complex and lengthy hearings, an "examining officer" might be assigned to represent the government. Before the days of the feminist movement, these hearings were known as "two-man" hearings. Mostly there were "one-man" hearings. The presiding inspector, an employee under the supervision and control of the District Director, presented the government's evidence, interrogated the alien and all witnesses, and prepared a recommended decision. The presiding inspector was graded by the U.S. Civil Service Commission in an immigrant inspector classification series, in the equivalent range between a GS–7 and GS–9.[6]

The deportation hearing typically commenced with a series of threshold questions put to the alien by the presiding inspector:

What is your full, true, and correct name?

Have you ever been known by any other name?

What was your father's name?

What was your mother's name?

When and where were you born?

Of what country are you a citizen?

When and where did you last enter the United States?

By what means of transportation did you arrive in the United States?

The questions went on. The alien's testimony was extracted bit by bit, in both relevant and nonrelevant detail, consuming needless time and resulting in multiple pages of transcript even when the basis of deportability might rest on a simple "remained longer" or "entry without inspection" charge. An alien's application for discretionary relief would elicit similar detailed interrogation by the presiding inspector.

---

6. Only a small number of the 90–120 presiding inspectors were burdened with college education.

The presiding inspector was required to set forth formal Findings of Fact and Conclusions of Law as to deportability, which could easily consume an entire typewritten page. Not infrequently, the presiding inspector elected to set forth Findings of Fact and Conclusions of Law on issues of discretionary relief such as an application for suspension of deportation.

The hearings were recorded by live stenographers—today almost an extinct species. The stenographer attending the hearing was responsible for preparing the transcript and certifying in writing to the accuracy of the record.

When an immigrant inspector was assigned to conduct a hearing, he was handed the alien's entire file to review. The file was the repository of all information concerning the particular alien and might contain hearsay, "spite" letters, classified information, or other prejudicial material.

After the presiding inspector's recommended decision was served on the alien, the entire case file, including the hearing transcript, was forwarded to the Central Office. Following action by an Examiner in the Hearing Review Unit, as previously described, the case went to the O.A.R.—Office of Adjudications Review—for further scrutiny. If the proposed decision appeared satisfactory, the O.A.R. Examiner initialed and sent the case to the Assistant Commissioner for signature. An adverse decision was appealable without fee to the Board of Immigration Appeals (BIA).

As can be seen, there was no paucity of review. But, again, bear in mind that the presiding inspector combined functions of prosecutor and judge and at each level the entire file, regardless of the contaminating nature of its contents, was in the hands of the reviewing authority.

* * *

The Administrative Procedure Act (APA) was enacted in 1946 in the wake of a strong demand for reform of federal agency administrative and hearing procedures. In regard to the conduct of hearings, the APA sought not only to assure the independence and impartiality of the hearing examiner but, as its fundamental purpose, to curtail or invalidate the frequent practice of embodying in one person or agency the duties of prosecutor and judge.

Faced with the reality of the APA, the INS General Counsel and the Office of the Solicitor General of the Department of Justice pooled their wisdom and concluded that deportation proceedings were exempted from the statute's reach. Their confidence was bolstered as they saw their views prevail in the U.S. District Court and the Court of Appeals over Wong Yang Sung's contention that the deportation order entered in his case was invalid because the proceedings had not conformed to the APA. But, as so often has happened, the Supreme Court confounded the government's experts. In its 6–1 decision in the *Sung* case, the Court held that the APA was indeed applicable to deportation hearings.

* * *

[The pertinent provision of the APA, 5 U.S.C. § 554, prescribes certain procedural safeguards, including the separation of the adjudication function from both prosecution and investigation functions, whenever adjudication is "required by statute to be determined on the record after an opportunity for an agency hearing." At the time of *Wong Yang Sung,* no statute required such a hearing in deportation cases. The Court interpreted the phrase "required by statute," however, to include hearings that were required by due process, and it further held that in deportation cases due process required hearings on the record. The Court bolstered its textual reasoning by observing that the APA had been enacted primarily to curtail precisely the kinds of commingling of functions that then characterized deportation hearings.—Ed.]

The torpedo delivered by the 1950 *Sung* decision caught the Service totally unprepared to deal with its consequences. All pending deportation proceedings and unexecuted deportation orders in which the hearings had been conducted subsequent to the enactment of the APA in 1946 were necessarily invalid for failure to comply with the statute's requirements. There were thousands of such cases which would now have to be reopened for *de novo* APA hearings. Adding to the dismay, the Service had no hearing examiners who had been selected and appointed in conformity with section 11 of the APA.

With disaster close at hand, INS prevailed upon the Civil Service Commission to grant it authority to make temporary appointments of APA Hearing Examiners. Most of the incumbent presiding inspectors received such appointments. Hearings resumed under APA strictures and, of course, an examining/prosecuting officer appeared in behalf of INS in every case.

This revolutionary state of affairs enjoyed a short life. Congress responded to supplications by INS for an exemption from APA coverage. INS argued that the volume of deportation proceedings made adherence to that statute both too costly and too cumbersome. The Act of September 27, 1950, an appropriations bill, contained a rider giving the Service its exemption. Thus, the Supreme Court's edict conforming deportation hearing procedures to the APA lost its vitality after a mere seven months. However, it had unleashed forces which were to have a more profound effect.

For about the next two years, from September 1950 until December 24, 1952, the effective date of the Immigration and Nationality Act (INA), the Service substantially reverted to its former hearing procedures, albeit with greater awareness of the need to measure up to prevailing concepts of fairness and administrative due process. The officers conducting deportation hearings during this period were allowed to continue using the title of Hearing Examiner, thereby giving the final burial to the title of Presiding Inspector.

Presumably aware of this history in writing the INA, Congress made changes and some improvements in the INS hearing systems, but eschewed the opportunity to initiate fundamental reforms. One of the more notable improvements was the designation of special inquiry officers to conduct hearings and make decisions in both exclusion and expulsion proceedings.

Special Inquiry Officers (SIO's) were defined as immigration officers whom "the Attorney General deemed specially qualified to conduct specified classes of proceedings." But therein reposed a problem. With the effective date of the 1952 Act close at hand, the agency had taken no steps to make the determination of who was "specially qualified." Caught short once more, INS asked the Civil Service Commission for authority to appoint temporary SIO's. The authority was granted with the understanding that an examination process would be developed looking toward the selection and appointment of permanent SIO's at the then elevated grade of GS–11.

For the officers who had been conducting deportation hearings, these had been years of upheaval and uncertainty. With no assurance of eventual retention as SIO's, a number concluded that it was time to redirect their careers through transfers to positions in more stable activities.

This brings us to the SIO selection process. It was decided at the outset that it would not be feasible to determine who was "specially qualified" for the SIO position without an oral interview of each candidate. It was further decided, in another breakthrough, that naturalization examiners, of whom a substantial number were attorneys, would be deemed to meet a specialized experience requirement, notwithstanding their general lack of immigration hearing experience. Finally, agreement was reached to award extra points in the rating scale to holders of college and law degrees. This may seem unexceptional today, but it was another 90–degree turn by an agency which in shaping its personnel policies had generally viewed border patrol experience more positively than higher education.

* * *

The appointment of "specially qualified" SIO's to conduct exclusion and deportation hearings pursuant to procedures deliberately mandated by Congress in the INA failed to still the critics who had seen the *Sung* decision as their finest hour. Law professors and immigration attorneys renewed their attacks on what they perceived to be a continuing lack of overall fairness in the hearing process and specifically on the INS failure to ensure both separation of functions and the independence of the SIO's. It would take another two to three years before INS, prodded by the Justice Department, would undertake extensive internal reforms from which would emerge the progenitor of today's corps of immigration judges.

It was in 1956 that truly radical changes were made in the INS hearing structure:

- SIO's were removed from operational supervision by District Directors and placed organizationally under a Chief Special Inquiry Officer acting through four Regional Special Inquiry Officers. The positions of Chief SIO and Regional SIO were newly created. The Chief SIO was made responsible solely to the Commissioner.

- The Order to Show Cause (OSC), a major innovation, replaced the warrant of arrest as the instrument for initiating a deportation proceeding. The pleading process was introduced at the same time.

- To avoid commingling of functions, an examining/prosecuting officer was made mandatory in every case in which deportability was contested.

- The novel concept of creating a "Record File" for the SIO's use was put into practice as a means of insulating him from prejudicial material that might be contained in the alien's general file.

* * *

Concurrently with these changes, a plan was approved to phase out all non-attorneys from the SIO position as soon as feasible. This would not turn out to be a major problem, for by this time nearly four out of five SIO's were members of the bar. Attrition, transfers, and reduction in force would play their part in reaching the goal of an all-attorney corps of SIO's.

Between 1956 and 1962 the SIO's were upgraded twice to reach the GS–13 level. Their next two promotions to GS–14 and GS–15 (their current grade) would come at a somewhat slower pace.

In 1973, having mounted their own vigorous campaign, the SIO's were authorized to use the working title of Immigration Judge and to wear the traditional robes of the judiciary in their "courtrooms." Finally, in 1983, they achieved a long-sought objective when they were granted a divorce *a vinculo matrimonii* from INS and positioned within the Executive Office for Immigration Review, a newly created entity within the Department of Justice.

* * *

NOTES AND QUESTIONS

1. Footnote 21 of the Rawitz article (not reproduced above) reads:

In 1955 the Supreme Court ruled that the procedural provisions of the APA, including those relating to the appointment and selection of examiners and separation of functions, were inapplicable to deportation hearings conducted under the INA. *Marcello v. Bonds,* 349 U.S. 302, 75 S.Ct. 757, 99 L.Ed. 1107 (1955).

The *Marcello* decision makes clear that, at least since the enactment of the INA in 1952, the APA has not governed the conduct of deportation (now removal) hearings. In most respects, however, INA § 240(b) and the various agency regulations together provide roughly the same procedure that the APA would require if it applied.

2. The main procedural ingredient of APA procedure that is commonly cited as missing from removal hearings is separation of functions. When formal APA procedure applies (i.e., when a hearing on the record is "required by statute" within the meaning of *Wong Yang Sung*), the presiding officer at the hearing must not have been "engaged in the

performance of investigative or prosecuting functions for an agency * * * in that or a factually related case." 5 U.S.C. § 554(d). Moreover, he or she must not "be responsible to or subject to the supervision or direction of an employee or agent engaged in the performance of investigative or prosecuting functions for an agency." *Id.* § 554(d)(2).

Be sure to distinguish at least four types of "separation of functions" problems: (1) The adjudicator has been an investigator in the same case or in a factually related case; (2) The adjudicator, when not adjudicating cases, investigates or prosecutes other unrelated cases; (3) The adjudicator, at the hearing, is empowered to perform prosecutor-type functions such as presenting evidence and examining witnesses; and (4) The adjudicator's supervisor has investigation or prosecution responsibilities. Which of those arrangements characterize removal proceedings? Which ones would violate the APA if the APA applied to removal? What are the dangers in each? Should the APA be made applicable to removal hearings?

3.   From 1983, when immigration judges were first removed from the former INS, until 2001, there was rarely any reason to doubt the decisional independence of the immigration judges. In April 2001, however, the INS telephoned the Office of the Chief Immigration Judge, *ex parte,* to complain about a ruling of immigration judge William Van Wyke. Chief Immigration Judge Michael J. Creppy intervened, granting an INS request that the immigration judge had denied. Judge Van Wyke then recused himself from the case. Excerpts from Judge Van Wyke's opinion follow:

> On April 16, 2001 the court ordered this case administratively (i.e. temporarily) closed over INS objection because no non-frivolous reason was shown for keeping it open at the time. * * * The court had waited over 90 days for the INS to adjudicate a visa petition that serves as a predicate for the next likely step—a hearing on an application for adjustment of status. The INS trial attorney had failed or refused to inquire of his client when the necessary work would be completed, obstructing the meaningful calendaring of the case for any particular date. In similar cases the INS has stalled half a year to a year in adjudicating such petitions while the potential beneficiaries lingered in jail and removal proceedings stood still. * * *

* * *

> * * * If the court ordered a respondent's lawyer to submit an application on a client's behalf by a certain date and the attorney offered similar excuses for inaction, immediate and grave consequences would follow for his client. The asymmetry of ordering one party, but asking, begging, pleading and cajoling the other party hearing after hearing without effect, can only diminish the court's stature as an authoritative and independent arbiter in the public's eyes. To recalendar this case for no other reason than to offer a forum for still further demonstrations of the court's impotence and the INS's intransigence serves no useful purpose.

* * * [T]he [INS] motion to recalendar shall be and is hereby DENIED.

The court's decision on this motion will not be given practical effect, however, because the Office of the Chief Immigration Judge (OCIJ) has intervened in this case and recalendared it on its own motion, or in response to the INS motion, over the IJ's objection. This was done following a telephone call by INS district counsel to the OCIJ on or about April 19, 2001, complaining about the IJ's April 16 decision, and a commitment by the Office of the Chief Immigration Judge to "look into it." On April 23 the OCIJ directed this IJ to vacate his April 16 decision and place the case back on the active docket, because the decision was supposedly contrary to BIA precedent due to the lack of INS consent to the closing, and because it conflicted with administrative goals of the OCIJ. On April 24 this IJ asked the OCIJ to reconsider its order. The Chief Immigration Judge is an administrative and policy officer without appellate or other legal authority to overrule the immigration judge's procedural decisions in the case, see 8 CFR 3.9, 3.1(b), and ethical rules require the Chief Immigration Judge as well as immigration judges to refrain from taking action in a specific case following an ex parte communication about the case by one of the parties. ABA Model Code of Judicial Conduct, Canon 3.B.7. The OCIJ decided to bypass the immigration judge on April 27 and issued its own order to the court clerk to return the case to the court's active docket. * * *

The court's decision to close the case temporarily was not a mere "administrative" one subject to OCIJ's general direction. The existence of three BIA precedents in contested appeals is ample demonstration that a decision to administratively close is of a legal nature affecting the rights of the parties, and not a mere administrative one that has no particular meaning or impact. * * * As an administrative office which does not hear specific cases, the OCIJ may obviously receive and investigate complaints about a judge from any source without any ethical violation. But once a complaint about a specific case is either communicated to the IJ in charge of the "pending or impending case" or the OCIJ itself takes action in such a case, without giving the opposing party an opportunity to be heard, Canon 3.B.7 is apparently violated. * * *

* * * OCIJ's intervention has undermined the court's efforts by protecting the INS from having to defend its position legally before the BIA. This gives a procedural tactical advantage to the INS by demonstrating to respondent, rightly or wrongly, that an INS call to the Office of the Chief Immigration Judge may be enough to undo what the immigration judge does in open court, while encouraging the INS to continue to seek results from the

OCIJ privately that it might not be able to get from the BIA publicly.

* * * If permitted to exercise his independent legal judgment now or on the day the OCIJ has rescheduled this case, and all else being equal, this IJ would ignore the OCIJ's intervention and would administratively close the case again. * * * If the court were permitted to so rule, the INS would have the opportunity to argue before the BIA that the OCIJ's order is correct and should take precedence over the IJ's order, if it should wish to do so.

Lacking, however, the authority to make that decision (and the OCIJ's recalendaring of this case over the judge's objection demonstrates he *does* lack that authority), and in the absence of a withdrawal by OCIJ of its order, this judge can do nothing to remove the appearance of impropriety with which district counsel's ex parte communication and OCIJ's intervention have tainted this case. Only the OCIJ, which went beyond mere administrative generalities to direct a particular course of action in this case, is in a position to cure the appearance of impropriety its intervention has produced.

* * *

Unable to "establish" or "enforce" the standards of conduct that he believes must apply to these circumstances, this judge will recuse himself from further consideration of this case. The court will refer the case back to the Chief Immigration Judge for whatever action he may deem fit and appropriate.

Matter of R.M. (Immigration Court, York County Prison, Penn., May 21, 2001).

Somewhat different threats to the independence of the administrative appellate tribunals have emerged in the United States with the selective dismissals of BIA members, and in Australia with the threats (carried out) to nonrenew the appointments of members of the Refugee Review Tribunal. See the discussion of those developments in section B.4 below.

Do any of these actions implicate either independence or the appearance of independence? *Should* administrative tribunals that decide immigration cases be independent?

2.   REPRESENTATION

Several empirical studies and other statistical compilations now make clear that representation by counsel is one of the key correlates of success for noncitizens in removal proceedings. A recent CLINIC (Catholic Legal Immigration Network, Inc.) compilation of figures released by EOIR for fiscal year 2003 breaks down the success rates of represented and unrepresented respondents in removal proceedings by type of case (for example, asylum, adjustment of status, cancellation of removal, etc.) and by whether the person was detained. Respondents who were represented (either by attorneys or by qualified non-attorneys, as discussed below) fared substantially better in almost all categories. Most striking were the figures for EOIR asylum cases. Among non-detained applicants in fiscal year 2003 (and considering only cases decided on the merits, not those dismissed for procedural reasons), the approval rates were 39% and 14% for represented and unrepresented applicants, respectively. Among detained applicants, the corresponding approval rates were 18% and 3%. See Donald Kerwin, *Charitable Legal Programs for Immigrants: What They Do, Why They Matter and How They Can Be Expanded*, June 2004 Immigration Briefings. Over the years, other studies have consistently shown similar results. For some impressive data, see Andrew I. Schoenholtz & Jonathan Jacobs, *The State of Asylum Representation: Ideas for Change*, 16 Georgetown Immigration L.J. 739, especially at 741–46 and 765–72 (2002); see also United States General Accounting Office, *Asylum Approval Rates for Selected Applicants* (1987); Lisa Getter, *Few Applicants Succeed in Immigration Courts*, L.A. Times, Apr. 15, 2001, at A–20.

Correlations, of course, do not prove causation. Those individuals who were able to obtain counsel—especially pro bono counsel—might well have succeeded in doing so precisely because their cases were stronger on the merits. The higher approval rates in those cases therefore do not necessarily confirm the effects of representation. Still, few involved in the removal process would seriously doubt the value of competent counsel, particularly in asylum cases, where success frequently requires meticulous documentation of the applicant's personal history and the conditions in his or her country of origin.

So how hard is it to get counsel? As the following materials will show, it can be extremely hard for those noncitizens who are indigent, and many of those who need counsel the most go lacking. See Kerwin, above. An increasingly difficult problem has been securing representation for the thousands of undocumented children detained in refugee camps in South Texas and elsewhere. For some constructive proposals, see Michael A. Olivas, *Unaccompanied Refugee Children: Detention, Due Process, and Disgrace,* 2 Stanford L. & Policy Rev. 159 (1990).

In part because the number of people in need of qualified counsel so vastly exceeds the supply, noncitizens can be highly vulnerable to the predatory practices of unqualified immigration "consultants" who often describe themselves as "notarios." Some notarios pose as immigration attorneys and target Latino communities, where confusion can arise because in some Latin American countries a "notario" is a type of lawyer. The American Immigration Lawyers Association [AILA] has long campaigned for federal legislation that would effectively shut down the notarios, but there have been practical obstacles. See, e.g., Feb. 2005 AILA Dispatch at 6.

In removal proceedings one has "the privilege of being represented at no expense to the Government, by counsel of the alien's choosing who is authorized to practice in [removal] proceedings." INA § 240(b)(4)(A), repeated in INA § 292. The discussion that follows will explore four related problems: Who *is* authorized to practice in removal proceedings? What practical options are available to the indigent? What are the special ethical criteria for immigration practitioners and what procedures are in place for those charged with violating them? Finally, what are the elements of, and the remedies for, ineffective assistance of counsel?

a. AUTHORIZATION TO PRACTICE

8 C.F.R. §§ 292.1, 292.2 (2004)

[duplicated in 8 C.F.R. §§ 1292.1, 1292.2 (2004)].

§ 292.1   Representation of others.

(a) A person entitled to representation may be represented by any of the following:

(1) *Attorneys in the United States.* * * *

(2) *Law students and law graduates not yet admitted to the bar.* A law student who is enrolled in an accredited law school, or a law graduate who is not yet admitted to the bar, provided that:

(i) He or she is appearing at the request of the person entitled to representation;

(ii) In the case of a law student, he or she has filed a statement that he or she is participating, under the direct supervision of a faculty member, licensed attorney, or accredited representative, in a legal aid program or clinic conducted by a law school or non-profit organization, and that he or she is appearing without direct or indirect remuneration from the alien he or she represents;

(iii) In the case of a law graduate, he or she has filed a statement that he or she is appearing under the supervision of a licensed attorney or accredited representative and that he or she is appearing without direct or indirect remuneration from the alien he or she represents; and

(iv) The law student's or law graduate's appearance is permitted by the official before whom he or she wishes to appear * * *. The official or officials may require that a law student be accompanied by the supervising faculty member, attorney, or accredited representative.

(3) *Reputable individuals.* Any reputable individual of good moral character, provided that:

(i) He is appearing on an individual case basis, at the request of the person entitled to representation;

(ii) He is appearing without direct or indirect remuneration and files a written declaration to that effect;

(iii) He has a pre-existing relationship or connection with the person entitled to representation (e.g., as a relative, neighbor, clergyman, business associate or personal friend), provided that such requirement may be waived, as a matter of administrative discretion, in cases where adequate representation would not otherwise be available; and

(iv) His appearance is permitted by the official before whom he wished to appear * * *, provided that such permission shall not be granted with respect to any individual who regularly engages in immigration and naturalization practice or preparation, or holds himself out to the public as qualified to do so.

(4) *Accredited representatives.* A person representing an organization described in § 292.2 of this chapter who has been accredited by the [BIA].

[Paragraphs 5 and 6 cover foreign officials and foreign attorneys.—Ed.]

* * *

(e) Except as set forth in this section, no other person or persons shall represent others in any case.

§ 292.2   Organizations qualified for recognition; requests for recognition; withdrawal of recognition; accreditation of representatives; roster.

(a) *Qualifications of organizations.* A non-profit religious, charitable, social service, or similar organization established in the United States and recognized as such by the Board may designate a representative or representatives to practice before the Service [now USCIS] alone or the Service and the Board (including practice before the Immigration Court). Such organization must establish to the satisfaction of the Board that:

(1) It makes only nominal charges and assesses no excessive membership dues for persons given assistance; and

(2) It has at its disposal adequate knowledge, information and experience.

* * *

(d) *Accreditation of representatives.* An organization recognized by the Board under paragraph (b) of this section may apply for accreditation of persons of good moral character as its representatives. An organization may apply to have a representative accredited to practice before the Service alone or the Service and the Board (including practice before immigration judges). An application for accreditation shall fully set forth the nature and extent of the proposed representative's experience and knowledge of immigration and naturalization law and procedure and the category of accreditation sought. * * *

NOTES AND QUESTIONS

1. Should the categories of eligible representatives be broadened? Should they be narrowed?

2. Until 1975 there was no provision specifically authorizing law students or law school graduates not yet admitted to the bar to provide

representation in Justice Department proceedings. To appear, they had to qualify under either the "reputable individuals" or "accredited representatives" categories. See 8 C.F.R. § 292.1(b, c) (1975). In that year, however, the Department created a new category for *final-year* law students and law graduates. 40 Fed. Reg. 23271 (May 29, 1975). In 1990 the final-year limitation was removed. 55 Fed. Reg. 49250 (Nov. 27, 1990). What would be the pros and cons of limiting law student representation to either (a) those in their final year or (b) upperclass students?

3.   Section 292.1(a)(2) of the regulations that you just read reflects some changes that were finalized in 1997. See 62 Fed. Reg. 23634 (May 1, 1997). Those amendments relaxed the requirements for law student and law graduate representation. One change was to eliminate the requirement that a law student be working in a law school program; now, any nonprofit organization may provide the required supervision. A second change added accredited representatives to the list of people who could supervise law students.

A third change concerned remuneration. Before the amendments, neither law students nor law school graduates not yet admitted to the Bar could receive any direct or indirect remuneration. The amendments permit both categories to receive remuneration as long as it doesn't come from the person represented; the employer, for example, may pay the student's, or law graduate's, salary (provided, presumably, that the employer does not then charge the noncitizen for it).

First, why should remuneration play *any* role in determining whether law students and law graduates not yet admitted to the Bar may represent noncitizens in immigration cases? Second, why should it matter whether the remuneration comes from the represented person or the organization?

4.   The accredited individuals mentioned in section 292.1(a)(4) must represent *recognized* organizations. For general guidance as to the requirements for recognition of an organization, see *Matter of Lutheran Ministries of Florida,* 20 I. & N.Dec. 185 (BIA 1990). One requirement is that the organization make "only nominal charges" to persons receiving assistance. 8 C.F.R. § 292.2(a)(1) (2004) (reproduced above). The current funding crisis faced by charitable organizations has prompted recent efforts to persuade the Justice Department to delete the prohibition of more than nominal charges. As of this writing, the movement has not met with success. See Donald M. Kerwin, *Don't Give Me Your Tired, Your Poor or Your Huddled Masses: The Impact of Pending Legislation,* 73 IR 181, 186–87 (Feb. 12, 1996); Donald M. Kerwin, *Charitable Legal Immigration Programs: Can They Survive?,* 74 IR 813 (May 19, 1997).

b.   FINDING LAWYERS FOR THE INDIGENT

As others have observed, indigent noncitizens have long had serious problems obtaining representation in deportation cases. See, e.g., Note, *INS Transfer Policy: Interference with Detained Aliens' Due Process Right to Retain Counsel,* 100 Harvard L. Rev. 2001, 2005–06 (1987). The Erlenborn

Commission, created for the purpose of studying the restrictions on representation by offices that receive Legal Services Corporation funds (more on that in subsection ii below), summed up the problem as follows:

> Private attorneys are unlikely to undertake the representation of alien agricultural worker clients. Four chief reasons are: (i) the mobility of the client population, (ii) language barriers involved in serving a non-English speaking population, (iii) the high costs incurred in cases involving aliens, and (iv) the lack of any potential for large fee awards.

Legal Services Corporation, *The Erlenborn Commission Report*, 15 Georgetown Immigration L.J. 99, 131 (2001). The Commission found these barriers particularly formidable for migrant farmworkers. *Id*. at 132–34.

You probably noticed earlier that the statutory provisions creating the privilege of counsel in removal proceedings emphasize that such counsel will be "at no expense to the Government." INA §§ 240(b)(4)(A), 292. One option, of course, is for the indigent person to go unrepresented. Another frequently available option is to secure the services of a knowledgeable nonlawyer. As you have seen, the regulations authorize representation by various categories of law students, law school graduates, accredited representatives, and other reputable individuals.

But what about those people whose cases are complex enough and meritorious enough to require a lawyer? The material that follows explores the main options.

i. A Constitutional Right to Counsel?

Aguilera–Enriquez v. INS

United States Court of Appeals, Sixth Circuit, 1975.
516 F.2d 565.

■ CELEBREZZE, CIRCUIT JUDGE.

* * *

A thirty-nine-year-old native and citizen of Mexico, Petitioner has resided in the United States since December 18, 1967, when he was admitted for permanent residence. He is a married farm worker, living with his wife and three daughters in Saginaw, Michigan.

In December 1971, Petitioner traveled to Mexico for a vacation. An officer of the Saginaw, Michigan Police Department notified federal customs officers at the Mexican border that he had reason to believe that Petitioner would be returning with a quantity of heroin. When Petitioner crossed the border on his return, he was subjected to a search which produced no heroin but did reveal two grams of cocaine.

On April 12, 1972, Petitioner pleaded guilty in the United States District Court for the Western District of Texas, on one count of knowingly possessing a quantity of cocaine, a Schedule II controlled substance, in violation of 21 U.S.C. § 844(a) (1970). Petitioner received a suspended one-year sentence, was placed on probation for five years, and was fined $3,000, to be paid in fifty-dollar monthly installments over the five-year probationary period. Neither Petitioner's appointed counsel nor the District Court informed him that a narcotics conviction would almost certainly lead to his deportation.

On December 7, 1972, the Immigration and Naturalization Service issued an Order to Show Cause and Notice of Hearing, charging that because of his narcotics conviction, Petitioner should be deported under section 241(a)(11)[a] of the Immigration and Nationality Act.

On February 6, 1973 Petitioner appeared before the Immigration Judge and requested appointed counsel. The Immigration Judge refused this request. After a hearing Petitioner was ordered deported and was not afforded the option of voluntary departure.

Shortly after the Immigration Judge's ruling, Petitioner engaged as counsel a Michigan legal assistance attorney, who in turn secured the services of a Texas attorney.

On February 14, 1973, Petitioner filed an appeal to the Board of Immigration Appeals, stating that the validity of the Texas conviction was being challenged.

On May 23, 1973, Petitioner's Texas counsel filed a motion to withdraw his guilty plea under Rule 32(d), F.R.Crim.P. The motion asserted that the District Court had not followed Rule 11 in accepting the plea because it had not properly determined that there was a factual basis for the plea and that the plea was made with a full understanding of the probable consequences.

On February 1, 1974, after full briefing and oral argument by counsel for Petitioner and the Government, the Board of Immigration Appeals dismissed Petitioner's appeal. A petition for review was timely filed in this Court.

The issue Petitioner raises here is whether an indigent alien has the right to appointed counsel in a deportation proceeding. He attacks the constitutional validity of INA § 242(b)(2),[b] which gives an alien facing deportation proceedings "the privilege of being represented (at no expense to the Government) by such counsel, authorized to practice in such proceedings, as he shall choose." The Immigration Judge held that this section prevented appointment of counsel at Government expense. Since he could not afford to hire a lawyer, he did not have one before the Immigration Judge.

* * *

[The court here observes that noncitizens in deportation proceedings are protected by procedural due process—Ed.]

---

a. Now INA § 237(a)(2)(B)(i).—Ed.   **b.** Now INA § 240(b)(4)(A)—Ed.

The test for whether due process requires the appointment of counsel for an indigent alien is whether, in a given case, the assistance of counsel would be necessary to provide "fundamental fairness—the touchstone of due process." Gagnon v. Scarpelli, 411 U.S. 778, 790, 93 S.Ct. 1756, 1763, 36 L.Ed.2d 656 (1973).[3]

In Petitioner's case the absence of counsel at his hearing before the Immigration Judge did not deprive his deportation proceeding of fundamental fairness.

Petitioner was held to be deportable under section 241(a)(11) of the Immigration and Nationality Act, which states in relevant part:

(a) Any alien in the United States . . . shall, upon the order of the Attorney General, be deported who—. . .

(11) . . . at any time has been convicted of a violation of . . . any law or regulation relating to the illicit possession of or traffic in narcotic drugs . . .

Before the Immigration Judge, Petitioner raised no defense to the charge that he had been convicted in April 1972 of a violation of 21 U.S.C. § 844(a). Thus, he was clearly within the purview of section 241(a)(11) of the Act, and no defense for which a lawyer would have helped the argument was presented to the Immigration Judge for consideration. After the decision of the Immigration Judge, Petitioner moved to withdraw his guilty plea in the Texas District Court under Rule 32(d), F.R.Crim.P. He then urged before the Board of Immigration Appeals that this motion took him outside the reach of section 241(a)(11), because the likelihood of success on that motion meant that he had not been "convicted" of a narcotics offense. He was effectively represented by counsel before the Board, and his argument was considered upon briefing and oral argument. The lack of counsel before the Immigration Judge did not prevent full administrative consideration of his argument. Counsel could have obtained no different administrative result. "Fundamental fairness," therefore, was not abridged during the administrative proceedings, and the order of deportation is not subject to constitutional attack for a lack of due process.
* * *

* * *

The petition for review is denied.

---

3. The Supreme Court's holdings in Gagnon, Morrissey v. Brewer, 408 U.S. 471, 92 S.Ct. 2593, 33 L.Ed.2d 484 (1972), and In re Gault, 387 U.S. 1, 87 S.Ct. 1428, 18 L.Ed.2d 527 (1967), have undermined the position that counsel must be provided to indigents only in criminal proceedings. Decisions * * * which contain dictum appearing to set forth a *per se* rule against providing counsel to indigent aliens facing deportation, rested largely on the outmoded distinction between criminal cases (where the Sixth Amendment guarantees indigents appointed counsel) and civil proceedings (where the Fifth Amendment applies). Where an unrepresented indigent alien would require counsel to present his position adequately to an immigration judge, he must be provided with a lawyer at the Government's expense. Otherwise, "fundamental fairness" would be violated.

■ DeMascio, District Judge (dissenting).

A deportation proceeding so jeopardizes a resident alien's basic and fundamental right to personal liberty that I cannot agree due process is guaranteed by a "fundamental fairness" analysis on a case-by-case basis. Gagnon v. Scarpelli, 411 U.S. 778, 93 S.Ct. 1756, 36 L.Ed.2d 656 (1973). I think a resident alien has an unqualified right to the appointment of counsel. When the government, with plenary power to exclude, agrees to allow an alien lawful residence, it is unconscionable for the government to unilaterally terminate that agreement without affording an indigent resident alien assistance of appointed counsel. Expulsion is such lasting punishment that meaningful due process can require no less. Assuredly, it inflicts punishment as grave as the institutionalization which may follow an In re Gault finding of delinquency. A resident alien's right to due process should not be tempered by a classification of the deportation proceeding as "civil," "criminal," or "administrative." No matter the classification, deportation is punishment, pure and simple.

In *Gagnon,* the Supreme Court acknowledged that it was affording parolees and probationers less due process than it afforded juveniles in In re Gault. It reached this result because a parolee or probationer is in that position solely because he was previously convicted of a crime. The court reasoned that parolees and probationers should be required to demonstrate that an attorney would serve a useful purpose prior to compelling the government to provide counsel at government expense. But, in a deportation proceeding, the respondent need not necessarily be before the immigration judge because of a prior conviction.[1] The fact of conviction is only one of numerous grounds for deportation outlined in the statute. Similar to the juvenile, an alien may only stand accused of an offense.

As noted in *Gagnon,* the function of the probation or parole officer is not to "compel conformance to a strict code of behavior" but to "supervise a course of rehabilitation." Insertion of counsel into such a "predictive and discretionary" proceeding could inadvertently circumscribe the officer's flexibility. However, no such justification for the exclusion of counsel exists in deportation proceedings where the sole duty of the immigration law judge is to determine whether a deportable offense has occurred.

Further, a probation revocation hearing is a non-adversary proceeding. The government is not represented by a prosecutor. There are no procedural rights which may be lost as in a criminal trial. A deportation hearing on the other hand is always an adversary proceeding. *Gagnon* does not go so far as to hold that in adversary proceedings due process may be afforded on a case-by-case basis by retrospective determination that the hearing was characterized by "fundamental fairness."

---

1. If the court wishes to extend *Gagnon,* perhaps a better approach is to limit the case-by-case appointment of counsel to proceedings where respondent is being deported because he has a previous conviction and is, therefore, entitled to less due process. In all other instances, counsel should be appointed as a matter of right under the due process clause. * * *

The court today has fashioned a test to resolve whether a resident alien's due-process right requires appointment of counsel. That test is whether "... in a given case, the assistance of counsel would be necessary to provide 'fundamental fairness—the touchstone of due process.' " *Gagnon*. The majority concludes that lack of counsel before the immigration judge did not prevent full consideration of petitioner's sole argument and no different result would have been obtained had counsel been appointed. Accordingly, the court holds the hearing was fundamentally fair. These conclusions are reached by second guessing the record—a record made without petitioner's meaningful participation.

In my view, the absence of counsel at respondent's hearing before the immigration judge inherently denied him fundamental fairness. Moreover, I do not believe that we should make the initial determination that counsel is unnecessary; or that lack of counsel did not prevent full administrative consideration of petitioner's argument; or that counsel could not have obtained a different administrative result. We should not speculate at this stage what contentions appointed counsel could have raised before the immigration judge. For example, a lawyer may well have contended that § 241(a)(11) is an unconstitutional deprivation of the equal protection of the laws by arguing that alienage was the sole basis for the infliction of punishment, additional to that imposed by criminal law; that since the government elected to rely upon the criminal law sanctions, it may not now additionally exile petitioner without demonstrating a compelling governmental interest.

I do not intend to imply such a contention has validity. I cite this only to emphasize the danger of attempting to speculate at this stage whether counsel could have obtained a different result and to show that it is possible that the immigration judge did not fully consider all of petitioner's arguments.

Because the consequences of a deportation proceeding parallel punishment for crime, only a per se rule requiring appointment of counsel will assure a resident alien due process of law. In this case, the respondent, a resident alien for seven years, committed a criminal offense. Our laws require that he be punished and he was. Now, he must face additional punishment in the form of banishment. He will be deprived of the life, liberty, and pursuit of happiness he enjoyed by governmental consent.[6] It may be proper that he be compelled to face the consequences of such a proceeding. But, when he does, he should have a lawyer at his side and one at government expense, if necessary. When the government consents to grant an alien residency, it cannot constitutionally expel unless and until it affords that alien due process. Our country's constitutional dedication to freedom is thwarted by a watered-down version of due process on a case-by-case basis.

I would reverse and remand for the appointment of counsel before the immigration judge.

6. Of course, what I have said applies only to a resident alien. * * *

NOTES AND QUESTIONS

1. In the landmark case of *Gideon v. Wainwright*, 372 U.S. 335, 83 S.Ct. 792, 9 L.Ed.2d 799 (1963), the Supreme Court held that the Constitution requires the states to provide counsel to indigent defendants in all criminal cases (not just capital cases, as had previously been held). The Sixth Amendment right to counsel had earlier been interpreted to require appointed counsel for all indigent *federal* criminal defendants, but in *Gideon* the Court, overruling a prior decision, extended this obligation to the states by incorporating the Sixth Amendment right to counsel into Fourteenth Amendment due process.

Since the Sixth Amendment right to counsel covers only criminal proceedings, however, it has no applicability to removal, which as you have seen is classified as a "civil" proceeding. See, e.g., *United States v. Campos–Asencio*, 822 F.2d 506, 509 (5th Cir.1987). On the other hand, all noncitizens whom the government seeks to expel—even those who have not been lawfully admitted—are protected by fifth amendment due process. See generally Developments in the Law, *Immigration Policy and the Rights of Aliens*, 96 Harvard L.Rev. 1286, 1384–95 (1983). The question on which the majority and dissent in *Aguilera–Enriquez* differ concerns the *content* of due process. In deportation (now removal) cases, does due process *always* require the provision of assigned counsel to indigent noncitizens (or at least those who are LPRs), or does the need for assigned counsel depend on the facts of the individual case? On that issue, the majority opinion in *Aguilera–Enriquez* accords with the decisions of other courts. See, e.g., *Magallanes–Damian v. INS*, 783 F.2d 931, 933 (9th Cir.1986); *United States ex rel. Castro–Louzan v. Zimmerman*, 94 F.Supp. 22, 25–26 (E.D.Pa.1950).

2. You earlier encountered *Mathews v. Eldridge*, 424 U.S. 319, 96 S.Ct. 893, 47 L.Ed.2d 18 (1976), in which the Supreme Court identified three factors to be weighed in determining whether due process requires a given procedural element—the private interest at stake, the probable value of the particular procedural element in reducing the risk of an erroneous deprivation of the private interest, and the government's interest in dispensing with the procedural element in question. *Id.* at 335. See page 144 above. The nature and magnitude of the private interests at stake in removal proceedings range widely. What variables do you think a court that adopts either a case-by-case approach or a categorical approach should take into account when evaluating the importance of the private interests in the removal context?

3. The government's interest in not providing assigned counsel is also difficult to quantify. The principal benefit is obviously the economic savings, and that amount is not easy to gauge. In his dissent, Judge DeMascio observes that the Supreme Court in *Gagnon* had focused on an additional concern: "Insertion of counsel into * * * a 'predictive and discretionary' [probation or parole revocation] proceeding could inadvertently circumscribe the officer's flexibility." Judge DeMascio then concludes that no analogous justification for excluding counsel exists in deportation proceedings, "where the sole duty of the immigration law judge [sic] is to

determine whether a deportable offense has occurred." First, do you agree with the Supreme Court in *Gagnon* that introducing counsel into a "predictive and discretionary" proceeding could circumscribe the flexibility of the decisionmaker? Second, now that you have studied chapters 7 and 8, do you accept Judge DeMascio's characterization of the IJ's function in removal proceedings? Can probation revocation proceedings really be distinguished from removal proceedings on the basis of their discretionary components?

4.   The *Eldridge* factor that seems to provoke the greatest difference of opinion in *Aguilera–Enriquez* is the value of counsel in helping to avoid erroneous results. What, precisely, can counsel accomplish in removal cases?

5.   As is evident from the two opinions in this case, the Supreme Court has held that in certain types of civil proceedings due process automatically requires the provision of assigned counsel to indigent parties, e.g., *Gault* (juvenile delinquency proceedings), whereas in certain other types of civil proceedings the constitutional necessity to assign counsel is ascertained on a case-by-case basis, e.g., *Gagnon* (revocation of probation); *Morrissey v. Brewer* (footnote 3) (revocation of parole). What factors should determine on which side of the line a given type of civil proceeding belongs?

6.   Commentators have generally supported a requirement of assigned counsel in at least certain deportation cases, though they have differed as to where and how the line should be drawn. The most exhaustive treatment of the subject is Robert N. Black, *Due Process and Deportation—Is there a Right to Assigned Counsel?*, 8 U.C. Davis L.Rev. 289 (1975); see also Irving A. Appleman, *Right to Counsel in Deportation Proceedings,* 14 San Diego L.Rev. 130 (1976) (former BIA member makes effective argument for case-by-case approach); Comment, *An Opportunity to be Heard: The Right to Counsel in a Deportation Hearing,* 63 Washington L.Rev. 1019 (1988).

7.   Judge DeMascio, objecting to the majority's case-by-case approach, questions whether a reviewing court can ever accurately determine what the record would have contained had there been counsel. Note, however, that Aguilera–Enriquez in fact had counsel at the BIA stage and the judicial review stage. By the time of the court's decision, couldn't counsel have done whatever factual investigation and legal research he or she would have done before or during the original hearing? If counsel even now has neither unearthed relevant evidence nor discovered legal authority that might have altered the decision below, then what would be the point of reversing for lack of counsel? To put the question another way, what is wrong with a prejudice requirement? (In answering this question, think also about the dual function of an appellate opinion—correcting errors of law that affect the parties to the litigation, and providing guidance for the future.)

8.   Apart from the question of appointed counsel, courts have invalidated deportation orders when noncitizens' waivers of their statutory right to counsel (not at government expense) were not knowing and voluntary. See, e.g., *Castro–O'Ryan v. U.S. INS,* 847 F.2d 1307 (9th Cir.1987) (revers-

ing on statutory grounds); *Reyes–Palacios v. U.S. INS*, 836 F.2d 1154 (9th Cir.1988) (reversing on due process grounds).

ii. Legal Aid

As noted earlier, the immigration judge must "advise the respondent of the availability of free legal services * * *." 8 C.F.R. § 1240.10(a)(2) (2004). The usefulness of that advice was curtailed in 1982. In that year Congress included in the Legal Services Corporation (LSC) appropriations bill a provision that prohibited LSC grantees (legal aid organizations) from using LSC funds to provide legal assistance to most categories of noncitizens. The only noncitizens eligible for legal assistance under that 1982 legislation (assuming they met the financial guidelines) were (a) LPRs; (b) those who possess specified relationships to United States citizens, have already applied for adjustment of status, and have not yet been rejected; (c) those who have already been granted refugee or asylum status; Pub.L. 97–377, 96 Stat. 1830, 1874–75 (Dec. 21, 1982); and, now, certain battered spouses and children, 45 C.F.R. § 1626.4 (2004). See generally Robert L. Bach, *Building Community among Diversity: Legal Services for Impoverished Immigrants*, 27 Univ. Michigan J. Law Reform 639, 641–45 (1994) (describing immigrants' access to legal services). Exceptionally, since 1986, LSC funds have been available to H–2A nonimmigrants (see chapter 4, § A.3.b above), but only for certain housing, transportation, and employment matters, not for immigration matters. Pub.L. 99–603 (IRCA), § 305, 100 Stat. 3359, 3434 (Nov. 6, 1986); 45 C.F.R. § 1626.11 (2004). See generally Legal Services Corporation, *The Erlenborn Commission Report*, 15 Georgetown Immigration L.J. 99 (2001).

Until 1996, organizations that received LSC funds could at least represent otherwise ineligible noncitizens as long as "all costs of such representation, including staff time, are funded from non-Corporation [i.e. non-LSC] sources." 45 C.F.R. § 1626.3(b)(iii) (1996). In 1996, Congress eliminated even that possibility. The Omnibus Consolidated Rescissions and Appropriations Act of 1996, Pub.L. 104–134, 110 Stat. 1321, § 504(a), prohibited the grant of LSC funds "to any person or entity ... (11) that provides legal assistance for on behalf of any alien, unless the alien is present in the United States" and is within one of the eligible categories described above (LPR, etc.). See generally 45 C.F.R. §§ 1626.3, 1626.5 (2004). The practical effect is to prevent LSC grantees from representing almost all noncitizens in removal proceedings, even if they use funding that private donors specifically earmarked for that purpose.

Because the overwhelming majority of noncitizens in removal hearings are within the ineligible categories, the combined impact of the various statutory restrictions is huge. There are, however, some outs. At least some noncitizens in removal proceedings are within the exempted categories. Some of those who are not might be able to secure assistance from community service organizations that receive no LSC funding. And some agencies that formerly used independent funds to represent indigent noncitizens have split off their immigration units into separate legal entities that do not receive LSC funds.

iii. Pro Bono Legal Services

Bar Associations often maintain referral services that provide the names of attorneys who have volunteered to take removal cases pro bono. One of the most impressive pro bono projects has been ProBAR, a joint effort of the American Bar Association, the State Bar of Texas, and the American Immigration Lawyers Association. ProBAR relies on lawyers and law students who donate time to represent indigent noncitizens in South Texas. See also Barbara Frey & Deepika Udagama, *Assisting Indigent Political Asylum Seekers in the United States: A Model for Volunteer Legal Assistance,* 13 Hamline L.Rev. 661 (1990) (describing Pro Bono Asylum Project of the Minnesota Lawyers International Human Rights Committee).

In recent years, however, pro bono representation has become more elusive for noncitizens in removal proceedings. DHS now relies more heavily on large detention centers generally located in remote areas where local attorneys are few in number. In theory attorneys from other locations could travel to the detention centers to assist pro bono, and in fact some do. Realistically, however, the time costs are prohibitive for even the most public-spirited members of the Bar. The problems are particularly acute in asylum cases and are well described in Margaret H. Taylor, *Promoting Legal Representation for Detained Aliens: Litigation and Administrative Reform*, 29 Connecticut L. Rev. 1647 (1997). EOIR is trying to encourage broader pro bono representation of detainees. See Christina DeConcini & Molly McKenna, *BIA Pro Bono Project: Representing Detained Migrants Before the BIA and Uncovering Government Obstacles to Pro Se Detainees Appealing their Cases,* 6 BIB 809 (Aug. 15, 2001).

The Anti–Drug Abuse Act of 1988 mandated special procedures to expedite the removal of noncitizens who have been convicted of "aggravated felonies." These procedures have since been extended to other crime-related deportability grounds. See section E.2 below. One method for speeding removal in these cases is to hold removal hearings at prison facilities, while the subjects are still serving their criminal sentences. The Office of the Chief Immigration Judge has encouraged immigration lawyers to assist the prisoners on a pro bono basis, but the prisons at which the hearings are held lie in such remote areas that, again, the costs to the best intentioned lawyers are often prohibitive.

One innovative response, pioneered by the Florence Immigrant Rights Project in Arizona with the cooperation of both the former INS and the EOIR, is to go into the prisons and give group presentations in advance of the removal hearings. See Christopher Nugent, *Strengthening Access to Justice: Prehearing Rights Presentations for Detained Respondents*, 76 IR 1077 (July 19, 1999).

iv.   Equal Access to Justice Act

The Equal Access to Justice Act (EAJA), 5 U.S.C. § 504 and 28 U.S.C. § 2412, allows the prevailing parties in certain adversarial proceedings to recover attorney fees from the Government. Does this provision cover noncitizens in removal hearings? The relevant statutory language reads as follows: "[A]n agency that conducts an adversary adjudication shall award, to a prevailing party other than the United States, fees and other expenses incurred by that party in connection with that proceeding, unless the adjudicative officer of the agency finds that the position of the agency was substantially justified or that special circumstances make an award unjust." 5 U.S.C. § 504(a)(1).

In *Ardestani v. INS*, 502 U.S. 129, 112 S.Ct. 515, 116 L.Ed.2d 496 (1991), the Supreme Court held that this definition did not apply to removal (then deportation) proceedings. The statutory analysis is intricate. (For excerpts of the opinion and detailed analysis of the various statutory interpretation arguments, see the 3rd edition of this book, at 667–81.)

NOTES AND QUESTIONS

1.   Statutory interpretation aside, is it good policy to award attorney fees to noncitizens who prevail in removal proceedings, assuming the government's position was not "substantially justified?" Argue both sides.

2.   The provision interpreted in *Ardestani* provided attorney fees in connection with the *administrative agency* phase of the adversary adjudication. A separate part of EAJA provides:

> Except as otherwise specifically provided by statute, a court shall award to a prevailing party other than the United States fees and other expenses ... incurred by that party in any civil action (other than cases sounding in tort), including proceedings for judicial review of agency action ... unless the court finds that the position of the United States was substantially justified or that special circumstances make an award unjust.

28 U.S.C. § 2412(d)(1)(A). Under this provision, it is the judicial review phase for which attorney fees are awarded, and the limiting language "adversary adjudication" is absent.

The Court in *Ardestani* did not decide whether attorney fees may be awarded in connection with the judicial review phase of deportation (now removal) proceedings. The Ninth Circuit had answered that question in the affirmative, in *Escobar Ruiz v. INS*, 838 F.2d 1020 (9th Cir. en banc 1988), which, as the Supreme Court noted in *Ardestani*, was the one lower court case that had also held EAJA applicable to the administrative phase of deportation proceedings.

3.   For a thoughtful analysis of *Ardestani*, see Kevin R. Johnson, *Responding to the Litigation Explosion: The Plain Meaning of Executive Branch Primacy over Immigration*, 71 North Carolina L. Rev. 413, 479–87 (1993).

c. DISCIPLINE OF IMMIGRATION PRACTITIONERS

Attorneys who practice in immigration proceedings are of course subject to all the usual ethical and disciplinary rules established by the jurisdictions in which they are licensed to practice. In addition, all who practice before either DHS or EOIR (including the immigration judges and the BIA) are subject to special rules, many of which overlap with the ABA Model Rules. These rules apply to all "practitioners," 8 C.F.R. § 1003.101(b) (2004), defined in *id.* § 1001.1(f, j) to encompass all of the categories of people authorized by section 1292.1 to practice in immigration proceedings—not just attorneys, but also representatives.

The sanctions for violating the disciplinary rules include permanent expulsion from practice before EOIR, DHS, or both; temporary suspension; public or private censure; or "such other disciplinary sanctions as the adjudicating official or the Board deems appropriate." *Id.* § 1003.101(a).

The procedures for disciplining the practitioners who represent the noncitizens are laid out in 8 C.F.R. §§ 1003.101–108 (2004). Any person may file a complaint against a practitioner who is believed to have violated the disciplinary rules. The complaint is filed with the Office of General Counsel of either EOIR or DHS. The Office of General Counsel will conduct the necessary investigation and, if it thinks there is a prima facie case, will issue a "Notice of Intent to Discipline" containing specific allegations. The practitioner has the opportunity to file an answer admitting or denying each allegation and providing any additional information or argument. There will then be a hearing before an immigration judge. Either the government or the practitioner may appeal the decision to the BIA. For further details, see 8 C.F.R. §§ 1003.101–108 (2004).

Note that this procedure applies only to complaints that are filed against practitioners. Complaints against Justice Department attorneys (including immigration judges and BIA members) are filed with the Department's Office of Professional Responsibility and processed under an entirely separate procedure. See *id.* § 1003.109.

Here are the substantive grounds for the discipline of immigration practitioners:

8 C.F.R. § 1003.102 (2004)

It is deemed to be in the public interest for an adjudicating official or the Board to impose disciplinary sanctions against any practitioner who falls within one or more of the categories enumerated in this section, but these categories do not constitute the exclusive grounds for which the disciplinary sanctions may be imposed in the public interest. Nothing in this regulation should be read to denigrate the practitioners's duty to represent zealously his or her client within the bounds of the law. A practitioner who falls within one of the following categories shall be subject to disciplinary sanctions in the public interest if he or she:

(a) Charges or receives, either directly or indirectly:

(1) In the case of an attorney, any fee or compensation for specific services rendered for any person that shall be deemed to be grossly excessive. * * *

(2) In the case of an accredited representative * * *, any fee or compensation for specific services rendered for any person, except that an accredited representative may be regularly compensated by the organization of which he or she is an accredited representative, or

(3) In the case of a law student or law graduate * * *, any fee or compensation for specific services rendered for any person, except that a law student or law graduate may be regularly compensated by the organization or firm with which he or she is associated as long as he or she is appearing without direct or indirect remuneration from the client he or she represents;

(b) Bribes, attempts to bribe, coerces, or attempts to coerce, by any means whatsoever, any person * * * to commit an act or to refrain from performing any act in connection with any case;

(c) Knowingly or with reckless disregard makes a false statement of material fact or law, or willfully misleads, misinforms, threatens, or deceives any person * * * concerning any material and relevant matter relating to a case * * *;

(d) Solicits professional employment through in-person or live telephone contact or through the use of runners, from a prospective client with whom the practitioner has no family or prior professional relationship, when a significant motive for the practitioner's doing so is the practitioner's pecuniary gain * * *;

(e) Is subject to a final order of disbarment or suspension, or has resigned with an admission of misconduct * * *.

(f) Knowingly or with reckless disregard makes a false or misleading communication about his or her qualifications or services. * * * A practitioner shall not state or imply that he or she has been recognized or certified as a specialist in immigration and/or nationality law unless such certification is granted by the appropriate state regulatory authority or by an organization that has been approved by the appropriate state regulatory authority to grant such certification;

(g) Engages in contumelious or otherwise obnoxious conduct, in regard to a case in which he or she acts in a representative capacity, which would constitute contempt of court in a judicial proceeding;

(h) Has been found guilty of, or pleaded guilty or *nolo contendere* to, a serious crime [defined];

(i) Knowingly or with reckless disregard falsely certifies a copy of a document as being a true and complete copy of an original;

(j) Engages in frivolous behavior in a proceeding before an Immigration Court, the Board, or any other administrative appellate body under title II of the Immigration and Nationality Act, provided:

(1) A practitioner engages in frivolous behavior when he or she knows or reasonably should have known that his or her actions lack an arguable basis in law or in fact, or are taken for an improper purpose, such as to harass or to cause unnecessary delay. Actions that, if taken improperly, may be subject to disciplinary sanctions include, but are not limited to, the making of an argument on any factual or legal question, the submission of an application for discretionary relief, the filing of a motion, or the filing of an appeal. The signature of a practitioner on any filing, application, motion, appeal, brief, or other document constitutes certification by the signer that the signer has read the filing, application, motion, appeal, brief, or other document and that, to the best of the signer's knowledge, information, and belief, formed after inquiry reasonable under the circumstances, the document is well grounded in fact, is warranted by existing law or by a good faith argument for the extension, modification, or reversal of existing law or the establishment of new law, and is not interposed for any improper purpose. * * *.

(k) Engages in conduct that constitutes ineffective assistance of counsel, as previously determined in a finding by the Board or an Immigration Judge in an immigration proceeding, and a disciplinary complaint is filed within one year of the finding;

(*l*) Repeatedly fails to appear for scheduled hearings in a timely manner without good cause; or

(m) Assists any person, other than a practitioner * * *, in the performance of activity that constitutes the unauthorized practice of law.

NOTES AND QUESTIONS

1. Paragraph (j) defines "frivolous behavior" and makes it a ground for discipline. Would you change this provision?

2. Although paragraph (j) penalizes the making of frivolous arguments, until 2000 no provision addressed the opposite problem—the practitioner who failed to provide zealous representation. What if the practitioner fails to show up at the removal hearing, or never gets around to filing the appropriate applications for discretionary relief or files them late, or neglects to file a notice of appeal to the BIA on time? What if the practitioner doesn't take the time to do reasonable research, or to raise reasonable issues, or to make reasonable arguments? Should those failings similarly be grounds for discipline?

Paragraph (k) now addresses this issue. It disciplines any practitioner who "[e]ngages in conduct that constitutes ineffective assistance of counsel, as previously determined in a finding by the Board or an Immigration Judge in an immigration proceeding," provided the complaint is filed within one year of the finding of ineffective assistance. The Department's expressed concern about the prior absence of such a disciplinary ground was that a noncitizen could move to reopen removal proceedings on the basis of ineffective assistance of counsel, and the counsel in question could then admit having been ineffective without incurring any consequences. 63 Fed. Reg. 2901, 2902 (Jan. 20, 1998) (proposed rules). The objective of the amendment was to discourage the filing of motions to reopen based on alleged ineffective assistance, rather than to deter or sanction ineffective representation. First, why do you suppose that until 2000 the Justice Department punished frivolous arguments but not ineffective assistance? Second, do you see any dangers in disciplining immigration practitioners for ineffective assistance?

3.   As you will see in the next subsection, ineffective assistance of counsel will not usually be a basis for withdrawing a guilty plea in criminal proceedings or for reopening a removal proceeding unless the ineffectiveness prejudiced the client. In a disciplinary proceeding against a practitioner for alleged ineffective assistance of counsel, should the government similarly be required to prove prejudice?

4.   During the notice and comment period, the ABA objected to the entire structure of the proposed rules. As you will recall, it is the ABA whose Model Code or Model Rules are in place in the 50 states. The ABA position is that, since lawyers are already subject to state ethical rules, additional Justice Department rules are unnecessary, except for nonlawyer representatives. Instead, the ABA argues, complaints about lawyer misconduct in immigration cases should simply be referred to the appropriate state authorities. In particular, the ABA objects that the same federal agency that is lodging the complaint would be investigating the lawyer who is opposing it—a recipe for unfair prosecution. At any rate, the ABA feels, the procedures for government lawyers should be the same as those for private lawyers. See letter from ABA President Robert D. Evans to Ms. Margaret M. Philbin, EOIR General Counsel (Mar. 23, 1998).

What is your reaction to the whole concept of adding a separate set of disciplinary rules just for immigration practitioners? Do you agree with the Justice Department that the additional rules are useful, or do you agree with the ABA that they are unnecessary and even undesirable?

5.   For more thorough descriptions of the various sources of ethical duties owed by lawyers in immigration cases, see David Weissbrodt & Laura Danielson, Immigration Law and Procedure in a Nutshell, ch. 15 (5th ed. 2005) (concerned principally with ABA Model Code and Model Rules); Bruce A. Hake, *"Attorney Misconduct"—A Rebuttal*, 4 Georgetown Immigration L.J. 727 (1990). A good analysis of the 2000 amendments is Bruce A. Hake, *A Great Wind: The New INS/EOIR Attorney Discipline Regime*, 5 BIB 885 (Nov. 1, 2000).

d.   INEFFECTIVE ASSISTANCE OF COUNSEL

You now have a sense of who is allowed to represent noncitizens in removal proceedings, the special challenges for the indigent in obtaining the services of eligible practitioners, and the relevant ethical constraints. Access to authorized counsel is of little use, however, when counsel is ineffective. Ineffectiveness of counsel is a ground for discipline, as you have seen, and hopefully the disciplinary rules have a beneficial deterrent effect, but they don't help the client once he or she has already been harmed. Other law is necessary to do that. In immigration, as in other fields, a body of rules has developed to define what constitutes ineffective assistance of counsel and to formulate remedies and procedures.

There are two common ways in which the ineffectiveness issue arises in removal cases. In one setting, the removal charge hinges on the person's criminal conviction and the person seeks to vacate the underlying conviction on the ground that his or her counsel was ineffective during those criminal proceedings. In the other common setting, the claim is that counsel was ineffective in the removal proceeding itself.

People v. Pozo

Supreme Court of Colorado, 1987.
746 P.2d 523.

■ KIRSHBAUM, JUSTICE.

* * *

I

Pozo, an alien legally residing in the United States, came to this country from Cuba in April 1980. In October 1982, pursuant to a plea agreement, Pozo entered pleas of guilty to second degree sexual assault and to escape. Pozo received a sentence to the Department of Corrections of two years for the escape conviction and a consecutive sentence of two years and six months for the sexual assault conviction. In May 1983, after a detainer was filed against him by the Immigration and Naturalization Service, Pozo filed motions to vacate the judgments of conviction under Crim.P. 35(c). He asserted * * * that he did not receive effective assistance of counsel because his trial counsel did not advise him of the possible deportation consequences of his guilty pleas.

A hearing on these motions was held in June 1983. Pozo testified through an interpreter that in October 1982 he had not been aware of any possible deportation consequences of his guilty pleas and that he would not have entered such pleas had he been aware of those consequences. An affidavit signed by Pozo's trial counsel, stating that he had not discussed the possible deportation consequences of the guilty pleas with Pozo, was introduced into evidence. The trial court found that prior to entering the guilty pleas Pozo had not discussed deportation consequences with his trial counsel or any other counsel and was not aware of such consequences. However, the trial court concluded that Pozo had been represented by competent and effective counsel. The Court of Appeals concluded that Pozo had been denied effective assistance of counsel, reversed the trial court's ruling and remanded the case to the trial court with directions to reinstate the original charges and allow Pozo to plead anew.

II

* * *

In *Hill v. Lockhart,* the Supreme Court applied the two-part test of *Strickland v. Washington* to a sixth amendment claim of ineffective assistance of counsel in connection with the entry of a guilty plea. Under *Strickland,* a defendant claiming a violation of the constitutional right to representation by competent counsel must show that his attorney's performance fell below an objective standard of reasonableness and that the deficient performance resulted in prejudice to the defendant. * * *

It is well settled that a trial court is not required to advise a defendant *sua sponte* of potential federal deportation consequences of a plea of guilty to a felony charge when accepting such plea. This rule is grounded in the notion that in accepting a plea of guilty a trial court is not required to ascertain the defendant's knowledge or understanding of collateral consequences of the conviction. The trial court is required to advise the defendant only of the direct consequences of the conviction to satisfy the due process concerns that a plea be made knowingly and with full understanding of the consequences thereof.

Sixth amendment constitutional standards requiring effective assistance of counsel involve examination of quite different considerations, however. One who relies on the advice of a legally trained representative when answering criminal charges is entitled to assume that the attorney will provide sufficiently accurate advice to enable the defendant to fully understand and assess the serious legal proceedings in which he is involved. * * * The duty of counsel is, in essence, the duty to act as any reasonable attorney would act in the same circumstances. Thus, questions regarding the type of conduct or communication required of an attorney representing a client can rarely be answered by abstract concepts. From this perspective, it is not surprising that courts considering the issue of whether defense counsel has a duty to advise alien clients of potential deportation consequences have reached conflicting results. * * *

We are not prepared to state in absolute terms, as did the Court of Appeals, that an attorney has a duty to advise an alien client of the possible deportation consequences of a guilty plea. Nor can we conclude, as the trial court did, that an attorney has no such duty. The general issue framed by Pozo's Crim.P. 35(c) motions was whether he was denied effective assistance of counsel. Whether counsel adequately represented Pozo in view of the lack of advice concerning possible deportation consequences depends initially on whether counsel had a duty to apprise himself of this aspect of immigration law. If no such duty existed, counsel of course had no responsibility to discuss deportation consequences with Pozo. In essence, then, this case presents the question of whether an attorney's failure to research and investigate a particular body of law while representing a client rendered the attorney's assistance constitutionally ineffective. In cases alleging ineffective assistance of counsel, the trial court must judge the reasonableness of the attorney's conduct on the basis of all of the factual circumstances of the particular case, viewed in light of the prevailing standards of minimally acceptable professional conduct as of the time of the challenged conduct. Such inquiry must include an initial determination of whether the body of law was relevant to the circumstances of the client and the matters for which the attorney was retained. The inquiry must also include a determination of whether the attorney had reason to believe that the area of law in question was relevant to the client and the client's legal problems.

[The court here discusses various ways in which the strategy of the criminal defense lawyer can affect the immigration status of the noncitizen client.—Ed.]

* * *

In view of these factors, we conclude that the potential deportation consequences of guilty pleas in criminal proceedings brought against alien defendants are material to critical phases of such proceedings. The determination of whether the failure to investigate those consequences constitutes ineffective assistance of counsel turns to a significant degree upon whether the attorney had sufficient information to form a reasonable belief that the client was in fact an alien. When defense counsel in a criminal case is aware that his client is an alien, he may reasonably be required to investigate relevant immigration law. This duty stems not from a duty to advise specifically of deportation consequences, but rather from the more fundamental principle that attorneys must inform themselves of material legal principles that may significantly impact the particular circumstances of their clients. In cases involving alien criminal defendants, for example, thorough knowledge of fundamental principles of deportation law may have significant impact on a client's decisions concerning plea negotiations and defense strategies.

The record in this case does not establish whether Pozo's counsel had reason to know before the plea was entered that Pozo was an alien. * * * Furthermore, as *Strickland* indicates, a finding that defense counsel had reason to know of Pozo's alien status and failed to conduct appropriate research would not render the attorney's performance inadequate in the absence of a finding that such conduct resulted in prejudice to Pozo. The trial court made no specific findings concerning the question of prejudice— and again, the trial court is in the best position to evaluate the evidence and the credibility of witnesses with regard to this portion of the *Strickland* test.[8]

Because critical determinations remain to be made before a conclusion concerning Pozo's claim of ineffective assistance of counsel can be made,

---

8. In considering whether a defendant who challenges a previously entered guilty plea on the basis of ineffective assistance of counsel has suffered prejudice, trial courts must focus upon whether counsel's conduct affected the outcome of the plea process. *Hill v. Lockhart*, 474 U.S. 52, 106 S.Ct. 366, 88 L.Ed.2d 203 (1985). In *Hill* the Supreme Court observed that, "in order to satisfy the [*Strickland*] prejudice requirement, the defendant must show that there is some reasonable probability that but for counsel's errors, he would not have pleaded guilty and would have insisted on going to trial."

the judgment of the Court of Appeals must be reversed and the case must be returned to the trial court for further proceedings.

* * *

■ ROVIRA, JUSTICE, dissenting:

I respectfully dissent.

The majority holds today that an attorney's failure to inform his client of the possible deportation consequences of a guilty plea may constitute ineffective assistance of counsel and thus render the plea involuntary. By casting its analysis in terms of the effectiveness of counsel and focusing on the severity of a collateral consequence of a guilty plea, the majority loses sight of the nature of the right at issue. I believe that the defendant's guilty pleas are not constitutionally infirm and would reverse the holding of the court of appeals and affirm the trial court's order.

* * *

There is no contention by Pozo that he did not understand the direct consequences of his plea or that his plea was invalid because of any threat, misrepresentation, or other impropriety. Therefore, he is left with his "but/for argument," *i.e.,* but/for the failure of my lawyer in not advising me that I might be deported if I pleaded guilty, I would not have pleaded guilty.

* * *

Our inquiry should be directed, then, solely to determine whether he understood the direct consequences of his plea. Clearly, as the majority acknowledges, deportation is a collateral consequence of conviction and not a direct consequence.

I agree with the substantial majority of courts that have utilized the collateral/direct consequence distinction to reject the claim that a defendant's ignorance of deportation consequences reflects ineffective assistance of counsel and renders his plea involuntary.

The collateral/direct consequence distinction reflects the nature of the rights a defendant has in pleading guilty. The Supreme Court identified the bases for those rights in the following words:

> A defendant who enters such a [guilty] plea simultaneously waives several constitutional rights, including his privilege against compulsory self-incrimination, his right to trial by jury, and his right to confront his accusers. For this waiver to be valid under the Due Process Clause, it must be "an intentional relinquishment of a known right or privilege." Consequently, if a defendant's guilty plea is not equally voluntary and knowing, it has been obtained in violation of due process and is therefore void. Moreover, because a guilty plea is an admission of all the elements of a formal criminal charge, it cannot be truly voluntary unless the defendant possesses an understanding of the law in relation to the facts.

In addition, a defendant must understand the penalty the legislature has fixed for the criminal conduct to which he is pleading guilty. Absent such an understanding, the defendant may plead guilty under a misguided expectation—however induced—that his plea will result in some measure of sentencing leniency.

None of those reasons supports the rule the majority adopts today. It cannot be disputed that a defendant may attach substantial importance to some collateral consequences of a guilty plea. We have never before held, however, that the potential importance of a particular collateral consequence may give rise to a constitutional right to be apprised of that consequence by defense counsel. The loss of one's right to vote, exclusion from military service, or other disabilities attached to a felony conviction may be just as harsh a consequence to a citizen defendant as deportation may be to an alien, yet courts have consistently denied that defendants have a constitutional right to be informed of the former collateral consequences.[1] The majority opinion focuses on the potential deportation consequences of guilty pleas in criminal proceedings, and thereby opens the door to innumerable challenges to pleas based on the defendant's ignorance of other serious collateral consequences.

* * *

The defendant has never claimed that he did not commit the crimes that he pleaded guilty to. Nothing has been brought to my attention which gives me reason to question the reliability of defendant's guilty plea as establishing his actual commission of the crimes charged.

An additional problem with the majority opinion is the burden it places on the trial courts to determine whether an attorney whose client is an alien has reasonably investigated relevant immigration law. The majority opinion states that "an examination of the relevant statutes and governing

---

1. Although deportation has an undeniable impact on a defendant's life, so do other collateral consequences which often flow from a guilty plea. Failure to inform the defendant of the following consequences of his guilty plea has been held not to render the plea invalid. *Wright v. United States,* 624 F.2d 557, 561 (5th Cir.1980) (a plea's possible enhancing effects on a subsequent sentence); *Moore v. Hinton,* 513 F.2d 781 (5th Cir.1975) (suspension of auto license); *United States v. Crowley,* 529 F.2d 1066, 1072 (3rd Cir.), *cert. denied,* 425 U.S. 995, 96 S.Ct. 2209, 48 L.Ed.2d 820 (1976) (loss of civil service job as result of felony conviction); *Cuthrell v. Director,* 475 F.2d 1364, 1366 (4th Cir.), *cert. denied,* 414 U.S. 1005, 94 S.Ct. 362, 38 L.Ed.2d 241 (1973) (institution of separate civil proceedings against defendant for commitment to a mental health facility); *Hutchi-* son v. United States, 450 F.2d 930, 931 (10th Cir.1971) (loss of good time credit); *Waddy v. Davis,* 445 F.2d 1 (5th Cir.1971) (disenfranchisement); *United States v. Vermeulen,* 436 F.2d 72, 75 (2d Cir.1970), *cert. denied,* 402 U.S. 911, 91 S.Ct. 1390, 28 L.Ed.2d 653 (1971) (possibility of imposition of consecutive sentences); *Meaton v. United States,* 328 F.2d 379 (5th Cir.1964), *cert. denied,* 380 U.S. 916, 85 S.Ct. 902, 13 L.Ed.2d 801 (1965) (deprivation of rights to vote and to travel abroad); *United States v. Cariola,* 323 F.2d 180 (3d Cir.1963) (deprivation of right to vote in some jurisdictions); *Redwine v. Zuckert,* 317 F.2d 336 (D.C.Cir.1963) (possibility of undesirable discharge from the armed forces); *State v. Riggins,* 466 A.2d 981 (N.J.Super.Ct.App.Div.1983) (loss of employment).

law" is necessary to determine "whether the performance of Pozo's counsel fell below an objective standard of reasonable conduct." * * *

A cursory review of the United States immigration law and the applicable regulations suggests that the trial court will be required to hold an extensive evidentiary hearing in order to determine whether an attorney's performance was "reasonable."

United States immigration law is complex and the regulations and judicial decisions interpreting the law represent a body of knowledge to which some attorneys devote their full time and attention. A public defender or attorney in private practice who represents defendants in criminal cases should not be found to be "ineffective" for failing to advise his client about a body of civil law which is not directly related to the issues involved in a Crim.P. 11 hearing. The majority, by opening the Pandora's box of collateral consequences, has further burdened an overtaxed judicial system. It has also provided defendants who have knowingly, intelligently, and voluntarily entered pleas of guilty an opportunity to withdraw those pleas, sometimes years after witnesses and evidence have been lost, on the ground that "but/for" their attorney's failure to advise of collateral consequences they would not have entered such a plea.

Finally, although the majority acknowledges the unanimous rule that the trial court need not advise the defendant sua sponte of his possible deportation following conviction, that rule is shorn of meaning by the majority's decision today. The majority holds, in effect, that an alien defendant has a constitutional right to know the possible deportation consequences of his guilty plea. To say that it is the duty of defendant's counsel—and not of the trial court—to inform the defendant of those consequences is of little practical effect; a judge who diligently follows the requirements of Crim.P. 11 but does not inquire into the defendant's alienage and knowledge of deportation consequences no longer ensures that the guilty plea he accepts is being made voluntarily. * * *

* * *

I am authorized to say that ERICKSON and VOLLACK, JJ., join in this dissent.

NOTES AND QUESTIONS

1. Recall *United States v. Parrino*, excerpted and discussed on pages 533–38 above. There, an LPR pleaded guilty to conspiracy to kidnap. Before entering the plea, he had asked his criminal defense attorney, a former INS commissioner, whether a conviction might lead to deportation. Without researching the issue, the attorney had told him it would not—an answer that was clearly wrong. After the conviction, deportation proceedings were instituted and Parrino moved to withdraw his guilty plea. Despite the seemingly glaring incompetence of counsel at the plea stage, Parrino did not ground his motion in a constitutional claim of ineffective assistance of counsel; rather, he argued that *the trial judge* should have advised him of

the deportation consequences before accepting his guilty plea. The court denied his motion, reasoning that deportation is merely a collateral consequence of his plea, not a direct one (such as the criminal sentence), and that the trial judge need inform the defendant only of the direct consequences. As you also saw, several states now have statutes that expressly require sentencing judges to advise noncitizen defendants of the potential deportation consequences of their guilty pleas.

2.   The court in *Pozo* follows the lead of *Hill v. Lockhart.* There the Supreme Court applied to guilty pleas the two-part test more generally prescribed by *Strickland v. Washington* for claims based on ineffective assistance of counsel: The attorney's performance must fall below an objective reasonableness standard, and the defendant must be prejudiced as a result. Consider first the reasonableness requirement. Should it matter whether the facts are (a) the attorney and the defendant simply did not discuss the possible deportation consequences, or (b) the attorney affirmatively misinformed the defendant that a guilty plea would not lead to deportation? The latter cases, sometimes inelegantly called the "misadvice" cases, have historically generated greater judicial sympathy. A well argued student Note has observed that, with the dramatically expanded aggravated felony definition ushered in by IIRIRA and AEDPA, courts are much more frequently finding ineffective assistance of counsel in the misadvice cases. The same Note argues that that development, while welcome, does not go far enough; the Note urges the courts to hold that the failure to advise the noncitizen defendant of the removal consequences of a guilty plea is ineffective assistance of counsel whether the defendant initiated the inquiry or not. See Rob A. Justman, *The Effects of AEDPA and IIRIRA on Ineffective Assistance of Counsel Claims for Failure to Advise Alien Defendants of Deportation Consequences of Pleading Guilty to an Aggravated Felony*, 2004 Utah L. Rev. 701, reprinted, 10 BIB 73 (Feb. 1, 2005). What significance, if any, do you think the law should attach to this distinction?

3.   What extra *ethical* obligations, if any, do you think a criminal defense lawyer has when his or her client is a noncitizen? In particular, do you feel that a criminal defense attorney should be expected to know about or discover applicable removal grounds? In answering that question, imagine yourself as a criminal defense lawyer who has never taken a course in immigration law. (Most attorneys have not). Assume you have reason to believe your client is a noncitizen. (The client says so, or the client has difficulty with English or has a foreign accent, etc.) Do you think it would occur to you that a criminal conviction might adversely affect your client's immigration status? Once that thought crossed your mind, what would you do? Forget the whole thing? Refer your client to an immigration specialist? Consult one yourself? Do preliminary immigration research of your own? If you decided to plunge into it yourself, where would you start? Would the research steps you have just identified be likely to lead you to the applicable deportation grounds? See Franco Capriotti, Linda Friedman Ramirez, Leslie Norikay & Rachel Unger, *Small-Time Crime, Big–Time Trouble: The New Immigration Laws*, 13 Crim. Justice #2 (1998) (cautioning criminal defense lawyers that, if the client is a noncitizen, even a seemingly minor

crime can jeopardize his or her immigration status); Susan L. Pilcher, *Justice without a Blindfold: Criminal Proceedings and the Alien Defendant*, 50 Arkansas L. Rev. 269, 328–32 (1997) (taking a broad view of the responsibilities of both defense counsel and prosecutor).

This problem raises a broader question. At one time immigration law was regarded as an esoteric specialty area of legal practice. Today both general practitioners and attorneys who specialize in areas other than immigration—criminal law, family law, labor law, corporate planning, tax— are becoming increasingly conscious that immigration law will often affect their clients' cases.

Does this mean that general practitioners, as well as practitioners in some of the specialty areas other than immigration, have an ethical obligation to familiarize themselves with at least the basic principles of immigration law? Conversely, are immigration specialists ethically bound to learn the fundamentals of related subject areas? On the one hand, when a specialized body of law is extended to new contexts, it is likely to affect previously unaffected individuals. The attendant justification for expecting those individuals' attorneys to inform themselves about that specialty strengthens. On the other hand, that is more easily said than done. It is precisely when a body of law expands that the heightened complexity makes it more difficult and more time-consuming for outsiders to develop the necessary knowledge. In this age of increasing specialization the problem clearly is not limited to immigration. In thinking about this, review Rule 1.3 of the ABA Model Rules of Professional Conduct and the accompanying Comment, on page 303 above. See also Stephen H. Legomsky, Specialized Justice—Courts, Administrative Tribunals, and a Cross–National Theory of Specialization (1990).

4.   Suppose you are a criminal defense lawyer representing client X, a noncitizen, in a drug case. You advise X to plead guilty. You don't think about, and therefore don't mention to X, the likelihood that a drug conviction would lead to removal. Relying on your advice, X pleads guilty, is convicted, and fully serves his sentence. Two years later, X calls and tells you that DHS is now seeking to remove him on the basis of the conviction. Regardless what you should have done earlier, what do you think are your ethical duties now (a) if X wants you to represent him in some capacity and (b) if X, understandably, wants to hire a different attorney?

5.   The second element of the *Strickland* test for an ineffective assistance of counsel claim is a showing of prejudice. How, exactly, would that requirement be applied in the context of a guilty plea that led to removal? Complete this sentence: The defendant has been prejudiced if, but for the attorney's deficient advice, _____.

6.   As the court in *Pozo* points out, modern cases go both ways on the question whether an attorney's failure to advise his or her client that a guilty plea might lead to removal constitutes ineffective assistance of counsel and, therefore, a basis for withdrawing the guilty plea. The courts are more likely to find ineffective assistance in cases of affirmative misinformation than in cases where the attorney and the client did not discuss

the issue at all. See, e.g., *United States v. Del Rosario*, 902 F.2d 55, 59 n. 2 (D.C.Cir.1990). In *Matter of Resendiz*, 25 Cal.4th 230, 19 P.3d 1171, 105 Cal.Rptr.2d 431 (2001), where the trial judge had read to the defendant the statutorily required warning that a conviction could lead to deportation, the California Supreme Court in a 4–3 decision nonetheless found ineffective assistance of counsel for wrongly advising the defendant that a guilty plea would *not* lead to removal. Withdrawal of the guilty plea was denied, however, because the evidence showed that knowledge of that possibility would not have altered the defendant's plea.

7.   Apart from both the criminal and the immigration consequences for the client, and apart from the ethical and disciplinary ramifications for the attorney, do you think either Parrino or Pozo would have a civil cause of action against his attorney for negligence? If so, what would be the remedy?

8.   Just as the criminal defense attorneys in these and other cases can be faulted for having failed to take important immigration consequences into account, an immigration lawyer would be derelict if he or she moved to withdraw a noncitizen client's guilty plea without considering and disclosing to the client the possible criminal consequences. Withdrawing a plea carries obvious risks. If the court permits withdrawal, the plea bargain is rescinded and, unless a new agreement is struck, a trial might result. The person might be convicted of the same or even a more serious crime and in either event might receive a more severe sentence. As noted in the dissent, Parrino would have faced a possible death sentence had the court allowed him to withdraw his guilty plea. He was apparently willing to take that chance rather than accept deportation.

9.   In both *Parrino* and *Pozo*, the defense attorneys failed to advise their clients about the potential deportation consequences of pleading guilty. But what about the opposite problem? Suppose, as part of the plea agreement, the federal *prosecutor* promises the noncitizen defendant that the government will not initiate removal proceedings. Is DHS bound by that agreement?

On that issue too, the courts are divided. In several recent cases, federal prosecutors are alleged to have promised not to remove noncitizen defendants, in exchange for the defendants pleading guilty to specified charges (and in some cases agreeing also to aid the government's prosecution of other defendants). In *San Pedro v. United States*, 79 F.3d 1065 (11th Cir. 1996), the noncitizen defendant sought specific performance of the plea agreement (not rescission of the agreement, which would presumably have led to withdrawal of the guilty plea). Assuming arguendo that the government had made the disputed promise, the court held that prosecutors are bound only by those promises that they have the actual authority, express or implied, to make. In private agency law, apparent authority is generally enough, but in the case of government promises, the court held, actual authority is required. The court went on to hold that neither the statute nor any administrative actions of the executive branch had given prosecutors the power to promise non-deportation. Some other courts, in contrast, have held the prosecutors had such an implied power and, consequently, that such promises are binding. See *Margalli–Olvera v. INS*, 43 F.3d 345 (8th Cir. 1994); *Thomas v. INS*, 35 F.3d 1332 (9th Cir. 1994). For a strong defense of the latter view, see Victor C. Romero, *Expanding the Circle of Membership by Reconstructing the "Alien": Lessons from Social Psychology and the "Promise Enforcement" Cases*, 32 Univ. Mich. Journal of Law Reform 1, 20–34 (1998).

After these decisions, the Justice Department issued a regulation specifying that the INS (then still in existence) would not be bound by plea agreements unless the government agent who made the promise had first secured a written authorization from the INS. 28 C.F.R. § 0.197 (2001). Despite the transfer of INS functions to DHS, that regulation remains on the books as of this writing. Presumably, if even the former INS was not bound by the promises of attorneys operating within the same Department of government, DHS similarly will be found not to be bound. So, suppose a federal prosecutor, contrary to the regulation, enters into a plea agreement promising a noncitizen defendant that the government will not bring deportation or other removal proceedings, and the defendant doesn't know that the prosecutor lacks the authority to make that promise. If you were the judge, would you enforce the promise?

Matter of Lozada

Board of Immigration Appeals, 1988.
19 I. & N. Dec. 637, aff'd, 857 F.2d 10 (1st Cir. 1988).

[Lozada, an LPR, was found deportable for having been convicted of a crime involving moral turpitude. At his deportation hearing he applied for relief under former INA § 212(c) (the predecessor to cancellation of removal, part A) and, alternatively, for voluntary departure. The IJ denied 212(c) relief in the exercise of discretion and held Lozada statutorily ineligible for voluntary departure because of his criminal conviction. Lozada appealed to the BIA, which ordered summary dismissal, finding that his counsel had inadequately specified the grounds for appeal in the notice of appeal and then had failed to file a promised brief. Lozada petitioned the court of appeals for review. While the petition was pending, he moved the BIA to reopen his removal proceeding, alleging ineffective assistance of counsel. The opinion below is the BIA's disposition of that motion.—Ed.]

* * *

Any right a respondent in deportation proceedings may have to counsel is grounded in the fifth amendment guarantee of due process. Ineffective assistance of counsel in a deportation proceeding is a denial of due process only if the proceeding was so fundamentally unfair that the alien was prevented from reasonably presenting his case. * * * One must show, moreover, that he was prejudiced by his representative's performance.

The Government maintains that the fact that prior counsel did not submit a brief does not in itself amount to deprivation of due process. We agree.

Failure to specify reasons for an appeal is grounds for summary dismissal under 8 C.F.R. § 3.1(d)(1–a)(i) (1988). It would be anomalous to hold that the same action or, more accurately, inaction that gives rise to a summary dismissal of an appeal could, without more, serve as the basis of a motion to reopen. To allow such anomaly would permit an alien to circumvent at will the appeals process, with its regulatory time constraints, by the simple expedient of failing to properly pursue his appeal rights, then claiming ineffective assistance of counsel. Litigants are generally bound by the conduct of their attorneys, absent egregious circumstances. No such egregious circumstances have been established in this case.

A motion based upon a claim of ineffective assistance of counsel should be supported by an affidavit of the allegedly aggrieved respondent attesting to the relevant facts. In the case before us, that affidavit should include a statement that sets forth in detail the agreement that was entered into with former counsel with respect to the actions to be taken on appeal and what counsel did or did not represent to the respondent in this regard. Furthermore, before allegations of ineffective assistance of former counsel are presented to the Board, former counsel must be informed of the allegations and allowed the opportunity to respond. Any subsequent response from counsel, or report of counsel's failure or refusal to respond, should be submitted with the motion. Finally, if it is asserted that prior counsel's handling of the case involved a violation of ethical or legal responsibilities, the motion should reflect whether a complaint has been filed with appropriate disciplinary authorities regarding such representation, and if not, why not.

The high standard announced here is necessary if we are to have a basis for assessing the substantial number of claims of ineffective assistance of counsel that come before the Board. Where essential information is lacking, it is impossible to evaluate the substance of such claim. In the instant case, for example, the respondent has not alleged, let alone established, that former counsel ever agreed to prepare a brief on appeal or was engaged to undertake the task. Then, too, the potential for abuse is apparent where no mechanism exists for allowing former counsel, whose integrity or competence is being impugned, to present his version of events if he so chooses, thereby discouraging baseless allegations. The requirement that disciplinary authorities be notified of breaches of professional conduct not only serves to deter meritless claims of ineffective representation but also highlights the standards which should be expected of attorneys who represent persons in immigration proceedings, the outcome of which may, and often does, have enormous significance for the person.

The respondent's motion is wholly insufficient in light of the foregoing guidelines. We note, moreover, that no prejudice was shown to have resulted from prior counsel's failure to or decision not to file a brief in support of the appeal. The respondent received a full and fair hearing at which he was given every opportunity to present his case. We do not find, and the respondent does not allege, any inadequacy in the quality of prior counsel's representation at the hearing. The immigration judge considered and properly evaluated all the evidence presented, and his conclusions that the respondent did not merit a grant of section 212(c) relief as a matter of discretion and that he was ineligible for voluntary departure as a matter of law are supported by the record.

The allegations of error ascribed to the immigration judge in the respondent's motion are unfounded. Contrary to present counsel's contention, it is clear from the transcript of hearing and the immigration judge's decision that the immigration judge was well aware that the respondent committed the offense of obtaining money under false pretenses several years prior to his conviction of that offense. And contrary to counsel's contention, the immigration judge correctly determined that the respondent was not eligible for a grant of voluntary departure. * * *

* * *

ORDER: The motion is denied.

NOTES AND QUESTIONS

1. *Lozada* has been described as "the leading administrative decision governing ineffective assistance of counsel claims." 77 IR at 624 (May 15, 2000). But in *Matter of Assaad*, 23 I. & N. Dec. 553 (BIA 2003), the INS strenuously urged the Board to overrule *Lozada* and hold that there simply is no right to the effective assistance of counsel in removal cases. The INS based its argument on Supreme Court decisions denying such a right in connection with discretionary appeals from state criminal convictions. In those cases the Court had reasoned that, in situations where the Constitution provides no right to *appointed* counsel for indigents, there can be no right to the *effective* assistance of counsel, even if counsel was retained rather than appointed. Since there is no Sixth Amendment right to appointed counsel in removal cases, the INS argument continued, there should be no right to the effective assistance of even retained counsel in removal cases. Relying heavily on accumulated lower court decisions, the BIA disagreed. It held that due process requires a fundamentally fair proceeding and that the ineffective assistance of counsel can make a hearing unfair.

Still, *Lozada* substantially limits ineffective assistance claims by setting what it acknowledges to be "high standards." Note especially the Board's insistence on an affidavit, a statement of the attorney-client agreement and the attorney's representations, submission of the allegations to the attorney and a summary of the attorney's response, and the filing of a formal disciplinary complaint against the attorney or an explanation of why no such complaint was filed.

In practice, as former BIA member Lory Rosenberg has pointed out, the BIA has generally refused to entertain ineffective assistance claims on the merits unless, among other things, the noncitizen files a formal bar complaint about his or her attorney. As she notes, however, a number of courts have required the reopening of removal proceedings based on ineffective assistance of counsel without applying all the criteria laid out in *Lozada*. See generally Lory Diana Rosenberg, *It's Alive: A Noncitizen's Right to Competent Counsel Before the EOIR and BCIS After Matter of Assaad*, 8 BIB 943 (June 1, 2003); see also *Rodriguez-Lariz v. INS*, 282 F.3d 1218 (9th Cir. 2002) (finding ineffective assistance where counsel had failed to file forms for suspension of deportation despite repeated phone-calls from client; court made clear that the *Lozada* requirements are not essential when ineffective assistance is clear).

In *Escobar–Ramos v. INS,* 927 F.2d 482 (9th Cir.1991), one court held that it was not fair to punish noncitizens for the sins of their lawyers. In that case the BIA ordered summary dismissal because, as in *Lozada*, the noncitizens' lawyer had not specified the grounds for the appeal in the notice of appeal and had breached a promise to file a brief. In addition, the BIA found the appeal frivolous, in part because the repeated practice of the particular attorney had been to file generally worded notices of appeal and then to renege on the promised briefs.

In the court of appeals the noncitizens in *Escobar-Ramos* asserted that the immigration court had mailed thirty different hearing transcripts to their lawyer during a two-month period and that consequently their lawyer had been unable to file their brief on time. (They also stated, and the court considered, that water damage to their lawyer's office had contributed to the delay. The relevance of that damage is questionable, since it did not occur until about four months after their lawyer had received the transcript in their case, and three months after the deadline for filing their brief had passed.) The court held summary dismissal improper, ruling it "is not an appropriate way of dealing with an improper course of conduct by the party's attorney." *Id*. at 483–84. The court also found no indication that the Board had reviewed the record before finding the appeal "frivolous" (then an alternative ground for summary dismissal). *Id*. at 484. The court relied heavily on the unusual events asserted as justifications for the missed deadline. *Id*. at 485–86.

2.   The BIA says that a noncitizen who moves to reopen on the ground of ineffective counsel should submit an affidavit containing several elements. One omission on which the BIA decision relied was that "the respondent has not alleged, let alone established, that former counsel ever agreed to prepare a brief on appeal or was engaged to undertake the task." What is your reaction? If the issues are such that competent counsel would have filed a brief, should counsel be forgiven because he or she had not "agreed" to submit one? Is that the kind of matter a lay client should be expected to initiate?

3.   The BIA also concludes that counsel's shortcomings caused no prejudice. It points out that the IJ's discretionary denial of Lozada's 212(c) application was "supported by the record" and that there were no errors in

other respects. Do you see any problems with that analysis? Remember that the BIA reviews discretionary determinations de novo.

4. In the *Assaad* case (reaffirming *Lozada*), the Board ultimately denied the motion to reopen, finding the movant had failed to demonstrate that he had been prejudiced by the ineffective assistance. There, counsel had failed to file a timely appeal to the BIA. Lory Rosenberg responds: "By broadly construing harmless error to find that Assaad received a fair and complete hearing before the immigration judge and failed to establish a valid marriage, the BIA essentially decided the appeal without the transcript, without briefing, and without allowing the appellate process to take its course." Lory Diana Rosenberg, *It's Alive: A Noncitizen's Right to Competent Counsel Before the EOIR and BCIS After Matter of Assaad*, 8 BIB 943, 951 (June 1, 2003).

In contrast to *Assaad*, see *Mohammed v. Gonzales*, 400 F.3d 785 (9th Cir. 2005). There, the noncitizen asylum claimant alleged ineffective assistance based on counsel's failure to argue that the female genital mutilation which she had been forced to undergo as a child constituted past persecution. The court agreed. In that case, ineffectiveness was admitted, and the court interpreted the prejudice element to require only that the argument counsel should have made "may" have affected, or that it was "plausible" that it affected, the outcome.

3.   EVIDENCE AND PROOF

a.   ADMISSIBILITY OF EVIDENCE

There are few specific rules to guide immigration judges in deciding what evidence is admissible in removal hearings. The formal rules of evidence do not apply. See, e.g., *Felzcerek v. INS*, 75 F.3d 112, 116 (2d Cir. 1996); *Baliza v. INS,* 709 F.2d 1231, 1233 (9th Cir.1983). All testimony is under oath or affirmation, 8 C.F.R. §§ 1003.34, 1240.7(b) (2004), and by statute the noncitizen has the right to cross-examine the government's witnesses, INA § 240(b)(4)(B). Under 8 C.F.R. § 1240.7(a) (2004), any written or oral statements are perfectly admissible in removal proceedings, even though hearsay evidence would be generally inadmissible under Rule 802 of the Federal Rules of Evidence. Court decisions have subjected hearsay evidence to the additional requirement that its admission be fundamentally fair. *Abreu-Reyes v. INS*, 292 F.3d 1029, 1032 (9th Cir. 2002); *Felzcerek*, 75 F.3d at 115; *Bustos–Torres v. INS*, 898 F.2d 1053, 1055 (5th Cir.1990).

Can the government, by introducing hearsay statements rather than live testimony, effectively deprive the person of his or her right to cross-examine? To prevent this, the courts have held that fundamental fairness requires the government to make a reasonable effort to produce the witness at the hearing before resorting to hearsay. Courts have found the government's unsuccessful efforts adequate in some cases, e.g., *Trias–Hernandez v. INS*, 528 F.2d 366, 369 (9th Cir.1975), and inadequate in others, e.g., *Hernandez-Guadarrama v. Ashcroft*, 394 F.3d 674, 679–83 (9th Cir. 2005);

Cunanan v. INS, 856 F.2d 1373, 1375 (9th Cir.1988). In *Hernandez-Guadarrama,* the sole probative evidence against the noncitizen was a hearsay statement that he had smuggled other noncitizens into the United States. Since the declarant had avoided a felony prosecution by providing the statement, and since the government had made no reasonable effort to produce the declarant to testify, the court held the admission of the evidence fundamentally unfair. In *Cunanan,* the INS sought to introduce an affidavit executed by the noncitizen's wife. The affidavit asserted that the marriage had been a sham, a fact the noncitizen adamantly denied. The INS made no effort to produce the wife as a witness, and until the hearing date the noncitizen was unaware of his wife's statement. On those facts the court held the admission of the evidence fundamentally unfair.

One particular evidentiary problem is worth considering in some detail: If the government obtains evidence illegally, may that evidence nonetheless be introduced in removal hearings?

INS v. Lopez–Mendoza

Supreme Court of the United States, 1984.
468 U.S. 1032, 104 S.Ct. 3479, 82 L.Ed.2d 778.

■ JUSTICE O'CONNOR announced the judgment of the Court and delivered the opinion of the Court with respect to Parts I, II, III, and IV, and an opinion with respect to Part V, in which JUSTICE BLACKMUN, JUSTICE POWELL, and JUSTICE REHNQUIST joined.**

This litigation requires us to decide whether an admission of unlawful presence in this country made subsequent to an allegedly unlawful arrest must be excluded as evidence in a civil deportation hearing. We hold that the exclusionary rule need not be applied in such a proceeding.

I

Respondents Adan Lopez–Mendoza and Elias Sandoval–Sanchez, both citizens of Mexico, were summoned to separate deportation proceedings in California and Washington, and both were ordered deported. They challenged the regularity of those proceedings on grounds related to the lawfulness of their respective arrests by officials of the Immigration and Naturalization Service (INS). On administrative appeal the Board of Immigration Appeals (BIA), an agency of the Department of Justice, affirmed the deportation orders.

The Court of Appeals for the Ninth Circuit, sitting en banc, reversed Sandoval–Sanchez' deportation order and vacated and remanded Lopez–Mendoza's deportation order. It ruled that Sandoval–Sanchez' admission of his illegal presence in this country was the fruit of an unlawful arrest, and that the exclusionary rule applied in a deportation proceeding. Lopez–Mendoza's deportation order was vacated and his case remanded to the BIA

_____

** THE CHIEF JUSTICE joins all but
Part V of this opinion.

to determine whether the Fourth Amendment had been violated in the course of his arrest. We granted certiorari.

A

Respondent Lopez–Mendoza was arrested in 1976 by INS agents at his place of employment, a transmission repair shop in San Mateo, Cal. Responding to a tip, INS investigators arrived at the shop shortly before 8 a.m. The agents had not sought a warrant to search the premises or to arrest any of its occupants. The proprietor of the shop firmly refused to allow the agents to interview his employees during working hours. Nevertheless, while one agent engaged the proprietor in conversation another entered the shop and approached Lopez–Mendoza. In response to the agent's questioning, Lopez–Mendoza gave his name and indicated that he was from Mexico with no close family ties in the United States. The agent then placed him under arrest. Lopez–Mendoza underwent further questioning at INS offices, where he admitted he was born in Mexico, was still a citizen of Mexico, and had entered this country without inspection by immigration authorities. Based on his answers, the agents prepared a "Record of Deportable Alien" (Form I–213), and an affidavit which Lopez–Mendoza executed, admitting his Mexican nationality and his illegal entry into this country.

A hearing was held before an Immigration Judge. Lopez–Mendoza's counsel moved to terminate the proceeding on the ground that Lopez–Mendoza had been arrested illegally. The judge ruled that the legality of the arrest was not relevant to the deportation proceeding and therefore declined to rule on the legality of Lopez–Mendoza's arrest. The Form I–213 and the affidavit executed by Lopez–Mendoza were received into evidence without objection from Lopez–Mendoza. On the basis of this evidence the Immigration Judge found Lopez–Mendoza deportable. Lopez–Mendoza was granted the option of voluntary departure.

The BIA dismissed Lopez–Mendoza's appeal. It noted that "[t]he mere fact of an illegal arrest has no bearing on a subsequent deportation proceeding," and observed that Lopez–Mendoza had not objected to the admission into evidence of Form I–213 and the affidavit he had executed. The BIA also noted that the exclusionary rule is not applied to redress the injury to the privacy of the search victim, and that the BIA had previously concluded that application of the rule in deportation proceedings to deter unlawful INS conduct was inappropriate. *Matter of Sandoval,* 17 I. & N. Dec. 70 (BIA 1979).

The Court of Appeals vacated the order of deportation and remanded for a determination whether Lopez–Mendoza's Fourth Amendment rights had been violated when he was arrested.

B

Respondent Sandoval–Sanchez (who is not the same individual who was involved in *Matter of Sandoval, supra*) was arrested in 1977 at his place of employment, a potato processing plant in Pasco, Wash. INS Agent

Bower and other officers went to the plant, with the permission of its personnel manager, to check for illegal aliens. During a change in shift, officers stationed themselves at the exits while Bower and a uniformed Border Patrol agent entered the plant. They went to the lunchroom and identified themselves as immigration officers. Many people in the room rose and headed for the exits or milled around; others in the plant left their equipment and started running; still others who were entering the plant turned around and started walking back out. The two officers eventually stationed themselves at the main entrance to the plant and looked for passing employees who averted their heads, avoided eye contact, or tried to hide themselves in a group. Those individuals were addressed with innocuous questions in English. Any who could not respond in English and who otherwise aroused Agent Bower's suspicions were questioned in Spanish as to their right to be in the United States.

Respondent Sandoval–Sanchez was in a line of workers entering the plant. Sandoval–Sanchez testified that he did not realize that immigration officers were checking people entering the plant, but that he did see standing at the plant entrance a man in uniform who appeared to be a police officer. Agent Bower testified that it was probable that he, not his partner, had questioned Sandoval–Sanchez at the plant, but that he could not be absolutely positive. The employee he thought he remembered as Sandoval–Sanchez had been "very evasive," had averted his head, turned around, and walked away when he saw Agent Bower. Bower was certain that no one was questioned about his status unless his actions had given the agents reason to believe that he was an undocumented alien.

Thirty-seven employees, including Sandoval–Sanchez, were briefly detained at the plant and then taken to the county jail. About one-third immediately availed themselves of the option of voluntary departure and were put on a bus to Mexico. Sandoval–Sanchez exercised his right to a deportation hearing. Sandoval–Sanchez was then questioned further, and Agent Bower recorded Sandoval–Sanchez' admission of unlawful entry. Sandoval–Sanchez contends he was not aware that he had a right to remain silent.

At his deportation hearing Sandoval–Sanchez contended that the evidence offered by the INS should be suppressed as the fruit of an unlawful arrest. The Immigration Judge considered and rejected Sandoval–Sanchez' claim that he had been illegally arrested, but ruled in the alternative that the legality of the arrest was not relevant to the deportation hearing. Based on the written record of Sandoval–Sanchez' admissions the Immigration Judge found him deportable and granted him voluntary departure. The BIA dismissed Sandoval–Sanchez' appeal. It concluded that the circumstances of the arrest had not affected the voluntariness of his recorded admission, and again declined to invoke the exclusionary rule, relying on its earlier decision in *Matter of Sandoval*.

On appeal the Court of Appeals concluded that Sandoval–Sanchez' detention by the immigration officers violated the Fourth Amendment, that the statements he made were a product of that detention, and that the exclusionary rule barred their use in a deportation hearing. The deportation order against Sandoval–Sanchez was accordingly reversed.

II

A deportation proceeding is a purely civil action to determine eligibility to remain in this country, not to punish an unlawful entry, though entering or remaining unlawfully in this country is itself a crime. INA §§ 262, 266, 275.[a] The deportation hearing looks prospectively to the respondent's right to remain in this country in the future. Past conduct is relevant only insofar as it may shed light on the respondent's right to remain.

* * * Consistent with the civil nature of the proceeding, various protections that apply in the context of a criminal trial do not apply in a deportation hearing. The respondent must be given "a reasonable opportunity to be present at [the] proceeding," but if the respondent fails to avail himself of that opportunity the hearing may proceed in his absence. INA § 242(b).[b] In many deportation cases the INS must show only identity and alienage; the burden then shifts to the respondent to prove the time, place, and manner of his entry. See INA § 291. A decision of deportability need be based only on "reasonable, substantial, and probative evidence." INA § 242(b)(4).[c] The BIA for its part has required only "clear, unequivocal and convincing" evidence of the respondent's deportability, not proof beyond a reasonable doubt. The Courts of Appeals have held, for example that the absence of *Miranda* warnings does not render an otherwise voluntary statement by the respondent inadmissible in a deportation case. * * *

III

The "body" or identity of a defendant or respondent in a criminal or civil proceeding is never itself suppressible as a fruit of an unlawful arrest, even if it is conceded that an unlawful arrest, search, or interrogation occurred. * * *

On this basis alone the Court of Appeals' decision as to respondent Lopez–Mendoza must be reversed. At his deportation hearing Lopez–Mendoza objected only to the fact that he had been summoned to a deportation hearing following an unlawful arrest; he entered no objection to the evidence offered against him. The BIA correctly ruled that "[t]he mere fact of an illegal arrest has no bearing on a subsequent deportation proceeding."

IV

Respondent Sandoval–Sanchez has a more substantial claim. He objected not to his compelled presence at a deportation proceeding, but to

---

a. The Court's reference to "remaining unlawfully" is too broad. Remaining without obeying certain registration requirements, see INA §§ 262, 266, is a crime, but no provision makes overstaying a nonimmigrant visa (the most common type of prohibited stay) a criminal offense.—Ed.

b. The consequences of failing to appear at a removal hearing are now described in INA § 240(b)(5).—Ed.

c. Now INA § 240(c)(3).—Ed.

evidence offered at that proceeding. The general rule in a criminal proceeding is that statements and other evidence obtained as a result of an unlawful, warrantless arrest are suppressible if the link between the evidence and the unlawful conduct is not too attenuated. The reach of the exclusionary rule beyond the context of a criminal prosecution, however, is less clear. Although this Court has once stated in dictum that "[i]t may be assumed that evidence obtained by the [Labor] Department through an illegal search and seizure cannot be made the basis of a finding in deportation proceedings," the Court has never squarely addressed the question before. Lower court decisions dealing with this question are sparse.

In *United States v. Janis,* 428 U.S. 433, 96 S.Ct. 3021, 49 L.Ed.2d 1046 (1976), this Court set forth a framework for deciding in what types of proceeding application of the exclusionary rule is appropriate. Imprecise as the exercise may be, the Court recognized in *Janis* that there is no choice but to weigh the likely social benefits of excluding unlawfully seized evidence against the likely costs. On the benefit side of the balance "the 'prime purpose' of the [exclusionary] rule, if not the sole one, 'is to deter future unlawful police conduct.' " On the cost side there is the loss of often probative evidence and all of the secondary costs that flow from the less accurate or more cumbersome adjudication that therefore occurs.

At stake in *Janis* was application of the exclusionary rule in a federal civil tax assessment proceeding following the unlawful seizure of evidence by state, not federal, officials. The Court noted at the outset that "[i]n the complex and turbulent history of the rule, the Court never has applied it to exclude evidence from a civil proceeding, federal or state." Two factors in *Janis* suggested that the deterrence value of the exclusionary rule in the context of that case was slight. First, the state law enforcement officials were already "punished" by the exclusion of the evidence in the state criminal trial as a result of the same conduct. Second, the evidence was also excludable in any federal criminal trial that might be held. Both factors suggested that further application of the exclusionary rule in the federal civil proceeding would contribute little more to the deterrence of unlawful conduct by state officials. On the cost side of the balance, *Janis* focused simply on the loss of "concededly relevant and reliable evidence." The Court concluded that, on balance, this cost outweighed the likely social benefits achievable through application of the exclusionary rule in the federal civil proceeding.

While it seems likely that the deterrence value of applying the exclusionary rule in deportation proceedings would be higher than it was in *Janis,* it is also quite clear that the social costs would be very much greater as well. Applying the *Janis* balancing test to the benefits and costs of excluding concededly reliable evidence from a deportation proceeding, we therefore reach the same conclusion as in *Janis.*

The likely deterrence value of the exclusionary rule in deportation proceedings is difficult to assess. On the one hand, a civil deportation proceeding is a civil complement to a possible criminal prosecution, and to this extent it resembles the civil proceeding under review in *Janis*. The INS does not suggest that the exclusionary rule should not continue to apply in criminal proceedings against an alien who unlawfully enters or remains in this country, and the prospect of losing evidence that might otherwise be used in a criminal prosecution undoubtedly supplies some residual deterrent to unlawful conduct by INS officials. But it must be acknowledged that only a very small percentage of arrests of aliens are intended or expected to lead to criminal prosecutions. Thus the arresting officer's primary objective, in practice, will be to use evidence in the civil deportation proceeding. Moreover, here, in contrast to *Janis,* the agency officials who effect the unlawful arrest are the same officials who subsequently bring the deportation action. As recognized in *Janis,* the exclusionary rule is likely to be most effective when applied to such "intrasovereign" violations.

Nonetheless, several other factors significantly reduce the likely deterrent value of the exclusionary rule in a civil deportation proceeding. First, regardless of how the arrest is effected, deportation will still be possible when evidence not derived directly from the arrest is sufficient to support deportation. As the BIA has recognized, in many deportation proceedings "the sole matters necessary for the Government to establish are the respondent's identity and alienage—at which point the burden shifts to the respondent to prove the time, place and manner of entry." Since the person and identity of the respondent are not themselves suppressible, the INS must prove only alienage, and that will sometimes be possible using evidence gathered independently of, or sufficiently attenuated from, the original arrest. The INS's task is simplified in this regard by the civil nature of the proceeding. As Justice Brandeis stated: "Silence is often evidence of the most persuasive character.... [T]here is no rule of law which prohibits officers charged with the administration of the immigration law from drawing an inference from the silence of one who is called upon to speak.... A person arrested on the preliminary warrant is not protected by a presumption of citizenship comparable to the presumption of innocence in a criminal case. There is no provision which forbids drawing an adverse inference from the fact of standing mute."

The second factor is a practical one. In the course of a year the average INS agent arrests almost 500 illegal aliens. Over 97.5% apparently agree to voluntary deportation [sic] without a formal hearing. Among the remainder who do request a formal hearing (apparently a dozen or so in all, per officer, per year) very few challenge the circumstances of their arrests. As noted by the Court of Appeals, "the BIA was able to find only two reported immigration cases since 1899 in which the [exclusionary] rule was applied to bar unlawfully seized evidence, only one other case in which the rule's application was specifically addressed, and fewer than fifty BIA proceedings since 1952 in which a Fourth Amendment challenge to the introduction of evidence was even raised." Every INS agent knows, therefore, that it is highly unlikely that any particular arrestee will end up challenging the lawfulness of his arrest in a formal deportation proceeding. When an occasional challenge is brought, the consequences from the point of view of the officer's overall arrest and deportation record will be trivial. In these circumstances, the arresting officer is most unlikely to shape his conduct in anticipation of the exclusion of evidence at a formal deportation hearing.

Third, and perhaps most important, the INS has its own comprehensive scheme for deterring Fourth Amendment violations by its officers. Most arrests of illegal aliens away from the border occur during farm, factory, or other workplace surveys. Large numbers of illegal aliens are often arrested at one time, and conditions are understandably chaotic. To safeguard the rights of those who are lawfully present at inspected workplaces the INS has developed rules restricting stop, interrogation, and arrest practices. These regulations require that no one be detained without reasonable suspicion of illegal alienage, and that no one be arrested unless there is an admission of illegal alienage or other strong evidence thereof. New immigration officers receive instruction and examination in Fourth Amendment law, and others receive periodic refresher courses in law. Evidence seized through intentionally unlawful conduct is excluded by Department of Justice policy from the proceeding for which it was obtained. The INS also has in place a procedure for investigating and punishing immigration officers who commit Fourth Amendment violations. The INS's attention to Fourth Amendment interests cannot guarantee that constitutional violations will not occur, but it does reduce the likely deterrent value of the exclusionary rule. Deterrence must be measured at the margin.

Finally, the deterrent value of the exclusionary rule in deportation proceedings is undermined by the availability of alternative remedies for institutional practices by the INS that might violate Fourth Amendment rights. The INS is a single agency, under central federal control, and engaged in operations of broad scope but highly repetitive character. The possibility of declaratory relief against the agency thus offers a means for challenging the validity of INS practices, when standing requirements for bringing such an action can be met.

Respondents contend that retention of the exclusionary rule is necessary to safeguard the Fourth Amendment rights of ethnic Americans, particularly the Hispanic–Americans lawfully in this country. We recognize that respondents raise here legitimate and important concerns. But application of the exclusionary rule to civil deportation proceedings can be justified only if the rule is likely to add significant protection to these Fourth Amendment rights. The exclusionary rule provides no remedy for completed wrongs; those lawfully in this country can be interested in its application only insofar as it may serve as an effective deterrent to future INS misconduct. For the reasons we have discussed we conclude that application of the rule in INS civil deportation proceedings, as in the circumstances discussed in *Janis,* "is unlikely to provide significant, much less substantial, additional deterrence." Important as it is to protect the Fourth Amendment rights of all persons, there is no convincing indication that application of the exclusionary rule in civil deportation proceedings will contribute materially to that end.

On the other side of the scale, the social costs of applying the exclusionary rule in deportation proceedings are both unusual and significant. The first cost is one that is unique to continuing violations of the law. Applying the exclusionary rule in proceedings that are intended not to punish past transgressions but to prevent their continuance or renewal would require the courts to close their eyes to ongoing violations of the law. This Court has never before accepted costs of this character in applying the exclusionary rule.

Presumably no one would argue that the exclusionary rule should be invoked to prevent an agency from ordering corrective action at a leaking hazardous waste dump if the evidence underlying the order had been improperly obtained, or to compel police to return contraband explosives or drugs to their owner if the contraband had been unlawfully seized. On the rare occasions that it has considered costs of this type the Court has firmly indicated that the exclusionary rule does not extend this far. * * * Precisely the same can be said here. Sandoval–Sanchez is a person whose unregistered presence in this country, without more, constitutes a crime.[3] His release within our borders would immediately subject him to criminal penalties. His release would clearly frustrate the express public policy against an alien's unregistered presence in this country. Even the objective of deterring Fourth Amendment violations should not require such a result. The constable's blunder may allow the criminal to go free, but we have never suggested that it allows the criminal to continue in the commission of an ongoing crime. When the crime in question involves unlawful presence in this country, the criminal may go free, but he should not go free within our borders.

Other factors also weigh against applying the exclusionary rule in deportation proceedings. The INS currently operates a deliberately simple deportation hearing system, streamlined to permit the quick resolution of very large numbers of deportation actions, and it is against this backdrop that the costs of the exclusionary rule must be assessed. The costs of applying the exclusionary rule, like the benefits, must be measured at the margin.

The average immigration judge handles about six deportation hearings per day. Neither the hearing officers nor the attorneys participating in those hearings are likely to be well versed in the intricacies of Fourth Amendment law. The prospect of even occasional invocation of the exclu-

---

3. Sandoval–Sanchez was arrested on June 23, 1977. His deportation hearing was held on October 7, 1977. By that time he was under a duty to apply for registration as an alien. A failure to do so plainly constituted a continuing crime. INA §§ 262, 266. Sandoval–Sanchez was not, of course, prosecuted for this crime, and we do not know whether or not he did make the required application. But it is safe to assume that the exclusionary rule would never be at issue in a deportation proceeding brought against an alien who entered the country unlawfully and then voluntarily admitted to his unlawful presence in an application for registration.

Sandoval–Sanchez was also not prosecuted for his initial illegal entry into this country, an independent crime under INA § 275. We need not decide whether or not remaining in this country following an illegal entry is a continuing or a completed crime under § 275. The question is academic, of course, since in either event the unlawful entry remains both punishable and continuing grounds for deportation.

sionary rule might significantly change and complicate the character of these proceedings. The BIA has described the practical problems as follows:

"Absent the applicability of the exclusionary rule, questions relating to deportability routinely involve simple factual allegations and matters of proof. When Fourth Amendment issues are raised at deportation hearings, the result is a diversion of attention from the main issues which those proceedings were created to resolve, both in terms of the expertise of the administrative decision makers and of the structure of the forum to accommodate inquiries into search and seizure questions. The result frequently seems to be a long, confused record in which the issues are not clearly defined and in which there is voluminous testimony.... The ensuing delays and inordinate amount of time spent on such cases at all levels has an adverse impact on the effective administration of the immigration laws.... This is particularly true in a proceeding where delay may be the only 'defense' available and where problems already exist with the use of dilatory tactics."

This sober assessment of the exclusionary rule's likely costs, by the agency that would have to administer the rule in at least the administrative tiers of its application, cannot be brushed off lightly.

The BIA's concerns are reinforced by the staggering dimension of the problem that the INS confronts. Immigration officers apprehend over one million deportable aliens in this country every year. A single agent may arrest many illegal aliens every day. Although the investigatory burden does not justify the commission of constitutional violations, the officers cannot be expected to compile elaborate, contemporaneous, written reports detailing the circumstances of every arrest. At present an officer simply completes a "Record of Deportable Alien" that is introduced to prove the INS's case at the deportation hearing; the officer rarely must attend the hearing. Fourth Amendment suppression hearings would undoubtedly require considerably more, and the likely burden on the administration of the immigration laws would be correspondingly severe.

Finally, the INS advances the credible argument that applying the exclusionary rule to deportation proceedings might well result in the suppression of large amounts of information that had been obtained entirely lawfully. INS arrests occur in crowded and confused circumstances. Though the INS agents are instructed to follow procedures that adequately protect Fourth Amendment interests, agents will usually be able to testify only to the fact that they followed INS rules. The demand for a precise account of exactly what happened in each particular arrest would plainly preclude mass arrests, even when the INS is confronted, as it often is, with massed numbers of ascertainably illegal aliens, and even when the arrests can be and are conducted in full compliance with all Fourth Amendment requirements.

In these circumstances we are persuaded that the *Janis* balance between costs and benefits comes out against applying the exclusionary rule in civil deportation hearings held by the INS. By all appearances the

INS has already taken sensible and reasonable steps to deter Fourth Amendment violations by its officers, and this makes the likely additional deterrent value of the exclusionary rule small. The costs of applying the exclusionary rule in the context of civil deportation hearings are high. * * *

V

We do not condone any violations of the Fourth Amendment that may have occurred in the arrests of respondents Lopez–Mendoza or Sandoval–Sanchez. Moreover, no challenge is raised here to the INS's own internal regulations. Our conclusions concerning the exclusionary rule's value might change, if there developed good reason to believe that Fourth Amendment violations by INS officers were widespread. Finally, we do not deal here with egregious violations of Fourth Amendment or other liberties that might transgress notions of fundamental fairness and undermine the probative value of the evidence obtained.[5] At issue here is the exclusion of credible evidence gathered in connection with peaceful arrests by INS officers. We hold that evidence derived from such arrests need not be suppressed in an INS civil deportation hearing.

The judgment of the Court of Appeals is therefore

Reversed.

■ JUSTICE BRENNAN, dissenting.

I fully agree with JUSTICE WHITE that under the analysis developed by the Court in such cases as *United States v. Janis,* the exclusionary rule must apply in civil deportation proceedings. However, * * * I believe the basis for the exclusionary rule does not derive from its effectiveness as a deterrent, but is instead found in the requirements of the Fourth Amendment itself. My view of the exclusionary rule would, of course, require affirmance of the Court of Appeals. In this case, federal law enforcement officers arrested respondents Sandoval–Sanchez and Lopez–Mendoza in violation of their Fourth Amendment rights. The subsequent admission of any evidence secured pursuant to these unlawful arrests in civil deportation proceedings would, in my view, also infringe those rights. The Government of the United States bears an obligation to obey the Fourth Amendment; that obligation is not lifted simply because the law enforcement officers were agents of the Immigration and Naturalization Service, nor because the evidence obtained by those officers was to be used in civil deportation proceedings.

---

5. We note that subsequent to its decision in *Matter of Sandoval,* 17 I. & N.Dec. 70 (1979), the BIA held that evidence will be excluded if the circumstances surrounding a particular arrest and interrogation would render use of the evidence obtained thereby "fundamentally unfair" and in violation of due process requirements of the Fifth Amendment. *Matter of Toro,* 17 I. & N. Dec. 340, 343 (1980). See also *Matter of Garcia,* 17 I. & N. Dec. 319, 321 (BIA 1980) (suppression of admission of alienage obtained after request for counsel had been repeatedly refused) * * *.

■ JUSTICE WHITE, dissenting.

The Court today holds that the exclusionary rule does not apply in civil deportation proceedings. Because I believe that the conclusion of the majority is based upon an incorrect assessment of the costs and benefits of applying the rule in such proceedings, I respectfully dissent.

The paradigmatic case in which the exclusionary rule is applied is when the prosecutor seeks to use evidence illegally obtained by law enforcement officials in his case-in-chief in a criminal trial. In other classes of cases, the rule is applicable only when the likelihood of deterring the unwanted conduct outweighs the societal costs imposed by exclusion of relevant evidence. *United States v. Janis.* Thus, the Court has, in a number of situations, refused to extend the exclusionary rule to proceedings other than the criminal trial itself. For example, in *Stone v. Powell,* the Court held that the deterrent effect of the rule would not be reduced by refusing to allow a state prisoner to litigate a Fourth Amendment claim in federal habeas corpus proceedings if he was afforded a full and fair opportunity to litigate it in state court. Similarly, in *United States v. Calandra,* we concluded that "[a]ny incremental deterrent effect which might be achieved by extending the rule to grand jury proceedings is uncertain at best." And in *United States v. Janis,* we declined to extend the exclusionary rule to bar the introduction in a federal civil proceeding of evidence unconstitutionally seized by a state law enforcement officer. In all of these cases it was unquestioned that the illegally seized evidence would not be admissible in the case-in-chief of the proceeding for which the evidence was gathered; only its collateral use was permitted.

Civil deportation proceedings are in no sense "collateral." The majority correctly acknowledges that the "primary objective" of the INS agent is "to use evidence in the civil deportation proceeding" and that "the agency officials who effect the unlawful arrest are the same officials who subsequently bring the deportation action." The Immigration and Naturalization Service likewise concedes that INS agents are "in the business of conducting searches for and seizures of illegal aliens for the purpose of bringing about their deportation." Thus, unlike the situation in *Janis,* the conduct challenged here falls within "the offending officer's zone of primary interest." The majority nonetheless concludes that application of the rule in such proceedings is unlikely to provide significant deterrence. Because INS agents are law enforcement officials whose mission is closely analogous to that of police officers and because civil deportation proceedings are to INS agents what criminal trials are to police officers, I cannot agree with that assessment.

The exclusionary rule rests on the Court's belief that exclusion has a sufficient deterrent effect to justify its imposition, and the Court has not abandoned the rule. As long as that is the case, there is no principled basis for distinguishing between the deterrent effect of the rule in criminal cases and in civil deportation proceedings. The majority attempts to justify the distinction by asserting that deportation will still be possible when evidence not derived from the illegal search or seizure is independently sufficient. However, that is no less true in criminal cases. The suppression of some evidence does not bar prosecution for the crime, and in many cases even though some evidence is suppressed a conviction will nonetheless be obtained.

The majority also suggests that the fact that most aliens elect voluntary departure dilutes the deterrent effect of the exclusionary rule, because the infrequency of challenges to admission of evidence will mean that "the consequences from the point of view of the officer's overall arrest and deportation record will be trivial." It is true that a majority of apprehended aliens elect voluntary departure, while a lesser number go through civil deportation proceedings and a still smaller number are criminally prosecuted. However, that fact no more diminishes the importance of the exclusionary sanction than the fact that many criminal defendants plead guilty dilutes the rule's deterrent effect in criminal cases. The possibility of exclusion of evidence quite obviously plays a part in the decision whether to contest either civil deportation or criminal prosecution. Moreover, in concentrating on the incentives under which the individual agent operates to the exclusion of the incentives under which the agency as a whole operates neglects the "systemic" deterrent effect that may lead the agency to adopt policies and procedures that conform to Fourth Amendment standards.

The majority believes "perhaps most important" the fact that the INS has a "comprehensive scheme" in place for deterring Fourth Amendment violations by punishing agents who commit such violations, but it points to not a single instance in which that scheme has been invoked.[2] Also, immigration officers are instructed and examined in Fourth Amendment law, and it is suggested that this education is another reason why the exclusionary rule is unnecessary. A contrary lesson could be discerned from the existence of these programs, however, when it is recalled that they were instituted during "a legal regime in which the cases and commentators uniformly sanctioned the invocation of the rule in deportation proceedings." Thus, rather than supporting a conclusion that the exclusionary rule is unnecessary, the existence of these programs instead suggests that the exclusionary rule has created incentives for the agency to ensure that its officers follow the dictates of the Constitution. Since the deterrent function of the rule is furthered if it alters either "the behavior of individual law enforcement officers or the policies of their departments," it seems likely that it was the rule's deterrent effect that led to the programs to which the Court now points for its assertion that the rule would have no deterrent effect.

The suggestion that alternative remedies, such as civil suits, provide adequate protection is unrealistic. Contrary to the situation in criminal cases, once the Government has improperly obtained evidence against an illegal alien, he is removed from the country and is therefore in no position

---

2. The INS suggests that its disciplinary rules are "not mere paper procedures" and that over a period of four years 20 officers were suspended or terminated for misconduct toward aliens. The INS does not assert, however, that any of these officers were disciplined for Fourth Amendment violations, and it appears that the 11 officers who were terminated were terminated for rape or assault.

to file civil actions in federal courts. Moreover, those who are legally in the country but are nonetheless subjected to illegal searches and seizures are likely to be poor and uneducated, and many will not speak English. It is doubtful that the threat of civil suits by these persons will strike fear into the hearts of those who enforce the Nation's immigration laws.

It is also my belief that the majority exaggerates the costs associated with applying the exclusionary rule in this context. Evidence obtained through violation of the Fourth Amendment is not automatically suppressed, and any inquiry into the burdens associated with application of the exclusionary rule must take that fact into account. In *United States v. Leon,* we have held that the exclusionary rule is not applicable when officers are acting in objective good faith. Thus, if the agents neither knew nor should have known that they were acting contrary to the dictates of the Fourth Amendment, evidence will not be suppressed even if it is held that their conduct was illegal.

As is noted, the BIA has already held that evidence will be suppressed if it results from egregious violations of constitutional standards. Thus, the mechanism for dealing with suppression motions exists and is utilized, significantly decreasing the force of the majority's predictions of dire consequences flowing from "even occasional invocation of the exclusionary rule." Although the standard currently utilized by the BIA may not be precisely coextensive with the good-faith exception, any incremental increase in the amount of evidence that is suppressed through application of *Leon* is unlikely to be significant. Likewise, any difference that may exist between the two standards is unlikely to increase significantly the number of suppression motions filed.

Contrary to the view of the majority, it is not the case that Sandoval–Sanchez' "unregistered presence in this country, without more, constitutes a crime." Section 275 of the Immigration and Nationality Act makes it a crime to enter the United States illegally. The first offense constitutes a misdemeanor, and subsequent offenses constitute felonies. Those few cases that have construed this statute have held that a violation takes place at the time of entry and that the statute does not describe a continuing offense. Although this Court has not construed the statute, it has suggested in dictum that this interpretation is correct, and it is relatively clear that such an interpretation is most consistent with the statutory language. Therefore, it is simply not the case that suppressing evidence in deportation proceedings will "allo[w] the criminal to continue in the commission of an ongoing crime." It is true that some courts have construed § 276 of the Act, which applies to aliens previously deported who enter or are found in the United States, to describe a continuing offense. In such cases, however, the Government will have a record of the prior deportation and will have little need for any evidence that might be suppressed through application of the exclusionary rule. * * *

Although the majority relies on the registration provisions of INA §§ 262 and 266 for its "continuing crime" argument, those provisions provide little support for the general rule laid down that the exclusionary rule does not apply in civil deportation proceedings. First, § 262 requires that aliens register within 30 days of entry into the country. Thus, for the first 30 days failure to register is not a crime. Second, § 266 provides that only *willful* failure to register is a misdemeanor. Therefore, "unregistered presence in this country, without more," does not constitute a crime; rather, unregistered presence plus willfulness must be shown. There is no finding that Sandoval–Sanchez willfully failed to register, which is a necessary predicate to the conclusion that he is engaged in a continuing crime. Third, only aliens 14 years of age or older are required to register; those under 14 years of age are to be registered by their parents or guardian. By the majority's reasoning, therefore, perhaps the exclusionary rule should apply in proceedings to deport children under 14, since their failure to register does not constitute a crime.

Application of the rule, we are told, will also seriously interfere with the "streamlined" nature of deportation hearings because "[n]either the hearing officers nor the attorneys participating in those hearings are likely to be well versed in the intricacies of Fourth Amendment law." Yet the majority deprecates the deterrent benefit of the exclusionary rule in part on the ground that immigration officers receive a thorough education in Fourth Amendment law. The implication that hearing officers should defer to law enforcement officers' superior understanding of constitutional principles is startling indeed.

Prior to the decision of the Board of Immigration Appeals in *Matter of Sandoval,* neither the Board nor any court had held that the exclusionary rule did not apply in civil deportation proceedings. The Board in *Sandoval* noted that there were "fewer than fifty" BIA proceedings since 1952 in which motions had been made to suppress evidence on Fourth Amendment grounds. This is so despite the fact that "immigration law practitioners have been informed by the major treatise in their field that the exclusionary rule was available to clients facing deportation. See 1A C. Gordon and H. Rosenfield, Immigration Law and Procedure § 5.2c at 5–31 (rev. ed. 1980)." The suggestion that "[t]he prospect of even occasional invocation of the exclusionary rule might significantly change and complicate the character of these proceedings," is thus difficult to credit. The simple fact is that prior to 1979 the exclusionary rule was available in civil deportation proceedings, and there is no indication that it significantly interfered with the ability of the INS to function.

Finally, the majority suggests that application of the exclusionary rule might well result in the suppression of large amounts of information legally obtained because of the "crowded and confused circumstances" surrounding mass arrests. The result would be that INS agents would have to keep a "precise account of exactly what happened in each particular arrest," which would be impractical considering the "massed numbers of ascertainably illegal aliens." Rather than constituting a rejection of the application of the exclusionary rule in civil deportation proceedings, however, this argument amounts to a rejection of the application of the Fourth Amendment to the activities of INS agents. If the pandemonium attending immigration arrests is so great that violations of the Fourth Amendment cannot be ascertained for the purpose of applying the exclusionary rule, there is no reason to think that such violations can be ascertained for purposes of civil suits or internal disciplinary proceedings, both of which are proceedings that the majority suggests provide adequate deterrence against Fourth Amendment violations. The Court may be willing to throw up its hands in dismay because it is administratively inconvenient to determine whether constitutional rights have been violated, but we neglect our duty when we subordinate constitutional rights to expediency in such a manner. Particularly is this so when, as here, there is but a weak showing that administrative efficiency will be seriously compromised.

In sum, I believe that the costs and benefits of applying the exclusionary rule in civil deportation proceedings do not differ in any significant way from the costs and benefits of applying the rule in ordinary criminal proceedings. Unless the exclusionary rule is to be wholly done away with and the Court's belief that it has deterrent effects abandoned, it should be applied in deportation proceedings when evidence has been obtained by deliberate violations of the Fourth Amendment or by conduct a reasonably competent officer would know is contrary to the Constitution. Accordingly, I dissent.

■ JUSTICE MARSHALL, dissenting.

I agree with Justice WHITE that application to this case of the mode of analysis embodied in the decisions of the Court in *United States v. Janis and United States v. Calandra* compels the conclusion that the exclusionary rule should apply in civil deportation proceedings. However, I continue to believe that that mode of analysis fails to reflect the constitutionally mandated character of the exclusionary rule. In my view, a sufficient reason for excluding from civil deportation proceedings evidence obtained in violation of the Fourth Amendment is that there is no other way to achieve "the twin goals of enabling the judiciary to avoid the taint of partnership in official lawlessness and of assuring the people—all potential victims of unlawful government conduct—that the government would not profit from its lawless behavior, thus minimizing the risk of seriously undermining popular trust in government."

■ JUSTICE STEVENS, dissenting.

Because the Court has not yet held that the rule of *United States v. Leon* has any application to warrantless searches, I do not join the portion of JUSTICE WHITE's opinion that relies on that case. I do, however, agree with the remainder of his dissenting opinion.

NOTES AND QUESTIONS

1.   Compare the constitutional objections raised by the two individuals in *Lopez–Mendoza*. Why was the Court able to reject Lopez–Mendoza's objection more easily than that of Sandoval–Sanchez?

2. The question whether to extend the exclusionary rule to deportation proceedings arose partly because of the courts' uniform depiction of deportation as "civil" rather than "criminal." As you saw in *Fong Yue Ting*, pages 124–44 above, this characterization has colored the courts' analyses of various procedural issues in deportation cases. Now that you have studied the subject in greater depth, you should reevaluate the extent, if any, to which the goals of deportation really deviate from those of criminal punishment. See also Victor C. Romero, *The Domestic Fourth Amendment Rights of Undocumented Immigrants: On Gutierrez and the Tort Law / Immigration Law Parallel,* 35 Harvard Civil Rights—Civil Liberties L. Rev. 57 (2000); Ibrahim J. Wani, *Truth, Strangers, and Fiction: The Illegitimate Uses of Legal Fiction in Immigration Law,* 11 Cardozo L.Rev. 51, 100–06 (1989).

3. Unlike the approaches of Justices Brennan and Marshall, those of the majority and Justice White require the balancing of competing interests. Yet the latter two opinions differ from each other not merely in the weights they assign the various benefits and costs, but also in the starting points of their analyses. In order to determine whether the exclusionary rule should apply in deportation proceedings, what fundamentally different *questions* do the majority and Justice White attempt to answer?

4. To the extent possible, match up each of the majority's arguments with the corresponding responses of Justice White. Which do you find more persuasive? Are there any other arguments you would add?

5. Section V of the Court's opinion sets out some important qualifiers. The Court says, for example: "[W]e do not deal here with egregious violations of Fourth Amendment or other liberties that might transgress notions of fundamental fairness *and undermine the probative value of the evidence obtained*" (emphasis added).

That dictum is especially relevant in the context of the modern debate over racial profiling. What if an immigration officer stops only those cars whose drivers "look Latino" (or Arabic, or Muslim)? In *United States v. Brignoni–Ponce,* 422 U.S. 873, 885–87, 95 S.Ct. 2574, 2582–83, 45 L.Ed.2d 607, 619–20 (1975), the Supreme Court held that ethnic appearance alone cannot support a finding of reasonable suspicion for a Border Patrol stop. In dictum, however, the Court suggested that Border Patrol officers could legally consider Latino appearance as one factor that, combined with others, could give rise to reasonable suspicion. In *United States v. Montero–Camargo,* 208 F.3d 1122 (9th Cir. 2000) (en banc), the Ninth Circuit rejected that dictum. The court reasoned that (a) the much higher Latino percentage of the local population now makes demographic links between Latino ethnicity and unlawful status unreliable; and (b) racial profiling unfairly stigmatizes.

Suppose, then, a vehicle is stopped either solely or partly because the driver was of Latino appearance. On the assumption that the stop was unlawful, is the resulting evidence suppressible in a removal proceeding? The Ninth Circuit in *Arguelles–Vasquez v. INS,* 786 F.2d 1433 (9th Cir. 1986), held such conduct "egregious" for *Lopez–Mendoza* purposes and ordered the evidence suppressed. Accord, *Gonzalez-Rivera v. INS*, 22 F.3d 1441 (9th Cir. 1994), where the court expressly concluded that violations can be "egregious" for *Lopez-Mendoza* purposes even when the evidence is probative. And in *Orhorhaghe v. INS*, 38 F.3d 488 (9th Cir. 1994), the court held that the INS's investigation of an individual based solely on his or her "foreign-sounding" name is also egregious, and that the resulting evidence would be suppressed even though it was probative. At a time of increased selective investigation of Arab–Americans and Muslims, these issues command ever greater significance. See the ethnic profiling discussion in chapter 10, section G.

Is the Ninth Circuit right? Do the cases described in footnote 5 of *Lopez-Mendoza* (accompanying the text quoted above) shed any light on whether the Supreme Court thinks probative evidence is ever suppressible on egregiousness grounds in removal proceedings? If it is, would the Supreme Court regard racial profiling as "egregious"?

OTHER ILLEGALLY OBTAINED STATEMENTS

In *Lopez-Mendoza* the constitutional provision that the INS officers had been accused of violating was the Fourth Amendment ban on unreasonable searches and seizures. The Court leaves open whether "egregious violations of Fourth Amendment *or other liberties*" (emphasis added) might compel contrary results.

The type of illegally obtained statement in which the argument for suppression is strongest is the statement that has been illegally coerced. The law is clear that fifth amendment due process makes such a statement suppressible in deportation proceedings. E.g., *Bustos–Torres v. INS*, 898 F.2d 1053, 1057 (5th Cir.1990); *Matter of Garcia*, 17 I. & N. Dec. 319, 321 (BIA 1980). In such a case, quite apart from the benefit of deterring official lawlessness, the statement will be suppressed simply because its probative value is dubious.

The fifth amendment privilege against self-incrimination can be asserted in any type of proceeding to refuse disclosure of "incriminating" information—i.e., that which either could be used in a subsequent criminal proceeding or could lead to other evidence that might be used in a criminal proceeding. *In re Gault*, 387 U.S. 1, 47–48, 87 S.Ct. 1428, 1454, 18 L.Ed.2d 527, 557 (1967). The privilege applies in removal cases, therefore, as long as the particular statement would be incriminating. See, e.g., *United States v. Alderete–Deras*, 743 F.2d 645 (9th Cir.1984); *Wall v. INS*, 722 F.2d 1442, 1443 (9th Cir.1984). Most removal cases involving deportability entail conduct that constitutes a crime or at least some of the essential elements of a crime, e.g., INA §§ 266(a), 266(b), 275, 276 (registration and entry-related crimes), although one common deportability ground—overstaying a nonimmigrant visa—does not. See *Matter of Santos*, 19 I. & N. Dec. 105, 109–10 n. 2 (BIA 1984).

An interesting problem arises under INA § 235(a)(5). This provision says: "An applicant for admission may be required to state under oath any information sought by an immigration officer regarding ... whether the applicant is inadmissible." Recall that under INA § 235(a)(1) "an alien present in the United States who has not been admitted" is deemed to be "an applicant for admission." The combination suggests that an immigration officer may require a noncitizen who is present without having been admitted to state under oath any information regarding admissibility.

Several issues follow. First, is a noncitizen who is apprehended in the interior of the United States required to provide the information described in section 235(a)(5)? Or could the person refuse, on the ground that one is not deemed to be an applicant for admission unless he or she is present without admission, and the government has not yet established the latter?

Second, section 235(a)(1) refers to "an alien" who is present without admission. Assume an immigration officer encounters, in the interior of the United States, a person whom the officer reasonably suspects to be an "alien." Before that person will be deemed to be an applicant for admission, and therefore subject to the requirement in section 235(a)(5) to provide information, must DHS prove that he or she is in fact a noncitizen?[5] The Justice Department regulations say yes. 8 C.F.R. § 1240.8(c) (2004). We shall return to the more general problem of burden of proof in section B.3.b below.

Third, to the extent that section 235(a) is construed to require the involuntary revelation of adverse information, does the statute violate the fifth amendment privilege against self-incrimination? The answer depends on what the information is. If the information would tend to incriminate, then, as discussed above, the fifth amendment appears to prohibit the government from compelling the person to provide it. In the case of a person who is present without admission, information as to the means of entry would almost surely be incriminating, for INA § 275 makes entry without inspection a criminal offense. And since INA § 275 also makes it a crime to *attempt* to enter without inspection, even a noncitizen arriving at a port of entry might be able to invoke a valid fifth amendment privilege against self-incrimination. The issue would probably turn not on the meaning of the fifth amendment, but on the scope of the plenary congressional power over immigration.

Apart from the specific context of section 235(a), suppose one who admits to being (or who has been proved to be) a noncitizen validly asserts his or her privilege against self-incrimination, and the government nonetheless requires the person to answer. In such a case the resulting statement will be suppressible in removal proceedings. *Tashnizi v. INS*, 585 F.2d 781, 782 (5th Cir.1978); *Matter of Carillo*, 17 I. & N.Dec. 30, 32–33 (BIA 1979).

The converse question arises when the person remains silent. In contrast to criminal proceedings, where the law clearly prohibits the

5. The author thanks Dan Kanstroom for spotting the connection between section 235(a)(5) and the burden of proof issue.

government from compelling the defendant to testify, it is unclear whether an immigration judge in deportability proceedings may compel the respondent to testify. Professor Daniel Kanstroom makes a strong argument that the IJ lacks the power to compel the person to answer even non-incriminating questions. See Daniel Kanstroom, *Hello Darkness: Involuntary Testimony and Silence as Evidence in Deportation Proceedings,* 4 Georgetown Immigration L.J. 599, 611–18 (1990). We shall return to that problem, and to the related question of whether silence will support adverse inferences, on pages 715–17 below.

Things change when the problematic government conduct occurs overseas. In *United States v. Verdugo–Urquidez,* 494 U.S. 259, 110 S.Ct. 1056, 108 L.Ed.2d 222 (1990), the Supreme Court held that the Fourth Amendment does not apply to overseas searches and seizures, by United States officials, of the property of noncitizens who reside outside the United States. Professor Victor Romero sees a common thread in this case and *Lopez-Mendoza.* See Victor C. Romero, *Whatever Happened to the Fourth Amendment? Undocumented Immigrants' Rights after INS v. Lopez–Mendoza and United States v. Verdugo–Urquidez,* 65 Southern California L. Rev. 999 (1992). In *United States v. Alvarez–Machain,* 504 U.S. 655, 112 S.Ct. 2188, 119 L.Ed.2d 441 (1992), the Court went a step further. It held that the U.S. government's forcible abduction of a Mexican national from Mexico did not violate the United States–Mexico extradition treaty and did not destroy the criminal jurisdiction of the United States court. The Supreme Court has also ruled that the Fifth Amendment privilege against self-incrimination does not protect against the threat of *foreign* prosecution. See *United States v. Balsys,* 524 U.S. 666, 118 S.Ct. 2218, 141 L.Ed.2d 575 (1998); Irene Scharf, *Commentary on United States v. Balsys,* 3 BIB 886 (Sept. 1, 1998).

Finally, article 36 of the Vienna Convention on Consular Relations, 21 U.S.T. 77 (Apr. 24, 1963), requires law enforcement officials to advise any arrested foreign nationals of their right to communicate with their consulates. At least two courts have held, however, that the government's violation of this rule does not make the arrestee's subsequent statement suppressible. *United States v. Lombera–Camorlinga,* 206 F.3d 882 (9th Cir. 2000) (en banc); *United States v. Li,* 206 F.3d 56 (1st Cir. 2000).

NOTE ON JUDICIAL POLITICS

INS v. Lopez–Mendoza is an excellent illustration of the political dynamics that sometimes characterize the relationship between courts. In the early 1980's the Ninth Circuit and the Supreme Court tangled hard and often. A greater ideological gulf between two federal courts would be difficult to imagine. The 1978 enactment of the Omnibus Judge Act, Pub.L. 95–486, 92 Stat. 1629, combined with natural attrition, had enabled President Carter to appoint 15 of the 26 Ninth Circuit judges. In the space of a few years a Republican-dominated court had been transformed into a court dominated by Democrats.[6] The Supreme Court had a far more conservative membership than the Ninth Circuit even then.

During those years, the Supreme Court reversed the Ninth Circuit again and again. The battles encompassed a wide range of subject matter, see Hager, *9th Circuit is "0 for 22" in High Court Reviews,* Los Angeles Times (June 25, 1984), at 1, 16, but nowhere was the ideological rift wider than in immigration. Since the Ninth Circuit then handled the lion's share of the nation's immigration cases, those skirmishes took on more than the usual importance.

You have already seen many of the clashes. In *Jong Ha Wang,* pages 588–97 above, decided in 1981, the Supreme Court ordered a summary reversal (no briefs, no oral argument) of the Ninth Circuit's en banc decision on the subjects of motions to reopen and extreme hardship. In 1982 the Supreme Court in *INS v. Miranda,* 459 U.S. 14, 103 S.Ct. 281, 74 L.Ed.2d 12 (1982), again by summary reversal, overturned a Ninth Circuit decision applying the doctrine of equitable estoppel against the INS. A week later, in *Landon v. Plasencia,* 459 U.S. 21, 103 S.Ct. 321, 74 L.Ed.2d 21 (1982), the Supreme Court reversed a Ninth Circuit decision requiring that *Fleuti* determinations be made in deportation proceedings (rather than exclusion proceedings). The Court's decision in *INS v. Phinpathya,* noted on pages 583–84 above, rendered in 1984, reversed the Ninth Circuit and, in the process, disapproved a twenty-year-old line of Ninth Circuit decisions that had flexibly interpreted the continuous physical presence requirement for suspension of deportation (the predecessor to cancellation of removal, part B). The 1984 *Lopez–Mendoza* decision that you just read was also a reversal of the Ninth Circuit. See also *INS v. Abudu,* page 726 below (reversing Ninth Circuit decision liberalizing standard of review of refusals to reopen). See generally Sana Loue, *Alien Rights and Government Authority: An Examination of the Conflicting Views of the Ninth Circuit Court of Appeals and the United States Supreme Court,* 22 San Diego L.Rev. 1021 (1985).

Immigration, as you no doubt have discovered by now, is intensely ideological. Strongly held views about sovereignty, law enforcement, and national security inevitably collide with equally strong views on human rights, civil liberties, and compassion. Apart from those and a wide range of other naturally conflicting substantive values, the immigration cases frequently raise questions that implicate the role of the courts vis-a-vis both a democratically elected Congress and an administrative bureaucracy to which Congress has delegated important policymaking authority.

b. BURDEN OF PROOF AND SUFFICIENCY OF THE EVIDENCE

Woodby v. INS

Supreme Court of the United States, 1966.
385 U.S. 276, 87 S.Ct. 483, 17 L.Ed.2d 362.

■ MR. JUSTICE STEWART delivered the opinion of the Court.

The question presented by these cases is what burden of proof the Government must sustain in deportation proceedings. We have concluded

---

6. Successive presidents have further transformed the Ninth Circuit.

that it is incumbent upon the Government in such proceedings to establish the facts supporting deportability by clear, unequivocal, and convincing evidence.

In *Sherman* (No. 80), the petitioner is a resident alien who entered this country from Poland in 1920 as a 14–year–old boy. In 1963 the Immigration and Naturalization Service instituted proceedings to deport him upon the ground that he had re-entered the United States in 1938, following a trip abroad, without inspection as an alien. After a hearing before a special inquiry officer, the petitioner was ordered to be deported, and the Board of Immigration Appeals dismissed his appeal.

The Government's evidence showed that the petitioner had obtained a passport in 1937 under the name of Samuel Levine, representing himself as a United States citizen. Someone using this passport sailed to France in June 1937, proceeded to Spain, returned to the United States in December 1938, aboard the S.S. *Ausonia,* and was admitted without being examined as an alien. To establish that it was the petitioner who had traveled under this passport, the Government introduced the testimony of Edward Morrow, an American citizen who had fought in the Spanish Civil War. Morrow was at first unable to remember the name Samuel Levine or identify the petitioner, but eventually stated that he thought he had known the petitioner as "Sam Levine," had seen him while fighting for the Loyalists in Spain during 1937 and 1938, and had returned with him to the United States aboard the S.S. *Ausonia* in December 1938. Morrow conceded that his recollection of events occurring 27 years earlier was imperfect, and admitted that his identification of the petitioner might be mistaken.

It is not clear what standard of proof the special inquiry officer and the Board of Immigration Appeals on *de novo* review applied in determining that it was the petitioner who had traveled to Spain and re-entered the United States under the Samuel Levine passport. * * *

Upon petition for review, the Court of Appeals for the Second Circuit originally set aside the deportation order, upon the ground that the Government has the burden of proving the facts supporting deportability beyond a reasonable doubt. The court reversed itself, however, upon a rehearing *en banc,* holding that the Government need only prove its case with "reasonable, substantial, and probative evidence." We granted certiorari.

* * *

[*Sherman* was consolidated with *Woodby v. INS*, where the immigration judge and the BIA had found an LPR deportable on grounds stemming from prostitution. There had been questions of fact concerning whether the prostitution had been the product of duress. The Sixth Circuit affirmed. Neither the administrative authorities nor the court of appeals specified the governing standard of proof.—Ed.]

In the prevailing opinion in the *Sherman* case, the Court of Appeals for the Second Circuit stated that "[i]f the slate were clean," it "might well agree that the standard of persuasion for deportation should be similar to that in denaturalization, where the Supreme Court has insisted that the evidence must be 'clear, unequivocal, and convincing' and that the Government needs 'more than a bare preponderance of the evidence' to prevail. * * * But here," the court thought, "Congress has spoken * * *." This view was based upon two provisions of the Immigration and Nationality Act which use the language "reasonable, substantial, and probative evidence" in connection with deportation orders. The provisions in question are § 106(a)(4) of the Act which states that a deportation order, "if supported by reasonable, substantial, and probative evidence on the record considered as a whole, shall be conclusive," and § 242(b)(4) of the Act which provides *inter alia* that "no decision of deportability shall be valid unless it is based upon reasonable, substantial, and probative evidence."[a]

It seems clear, however, that these two statutory provisions are addressed not to the degree of proof required at the administrative level in deportation proceedings, but to quite a different subject—the scope of judicial review. The elementary but crucial difference between burden of proof and scope of review is, of course, a commonplace in the law. The difference is most graphically illustrated in a criminal case. There the prosecution is generally required to prove the elements of the offense beyond a reasonable doubt. But if the correct burden of proof was imposed at the trial, judicial review is generally limited to ascertaining whether the evidence relied upon by the trier of fact was of sufficient quality and substantiality to support the rationality of the judgment. In other words, an appellate court in a criminal case ordinarily does not ask itself whether it believes that the evidence at the trial established guilt beyond a reasonable doubt, but whether the judgment is supported by substantial evidence.

That § 106(a)(4) relates exclusively to judicial review is made abundantly clear by its language, its context, and its legislative history. Section 106 was added to the Act in 1961 in order "to create a single, separate, statutory form of judicial review of administrative orders for the deportation and exclusion of aliens from the United States." The section is entitled "Judicial Review of Orders of Deportation and Exclusion," and by its terms provides "the sole and exclusive procedure for" the "judicial review of all final orders of deportation." Subsection 106(a)(4) is a specific directive to the courts in which petitions for review are filed.

It is hardly less clear that the other provision upon which the Court of Appeals for the Second Circuit relied, § 242(b)(4) of the Act, is also addressed to reviewing courts, and, insofar as it represents a yardstick for the administrative factfinder, goes, not to the burden of proof, but rather to the quality and nature of the evidence upon which a deportation order

---

a. Former INA § 106(a)(4) has been replaced by section 242(b)(4)(B), which makes the administrative findings of fact "conclusive unless any reasonable adjudicator would be compelled to conclude to the contrary." Former INA § 242(b)(4) now appears, word for word, in INA § 240(c)(3).—Ed.

must be based. The provision declares that "reasonable, substantial, and probative evidence" shall be the measure of whether a deportability decision is "valid"—a word that implies scrutiny by a reviewing tribunal of a decision already reached by the trier of the facts. The location of this provision in a section containing provisions dealing with procedures before the special inquiry officer has little significance when it is remembered that the original 1952 Act did not itself contain a framework for judicial review—although such review was, of course, available by habeas corpus or otherwise. And whatever ambiguity might be thought to lie in the location of this section is resolved by its legislative history. The Senate Report explained § 242(b)(4) as follows: "The requirement that the decision of the special inquiry officer shall be based on reasonable, substantial and probative evidence means that, where the decision rests upon evidence of such a nature that it cannot be said that a reasonable person might not have reached the conclusion which was reached, the case may not be reversed because the judgment of the appellate body differs from that of the administrative body."

We conclude, therefore, that Congress has not addressed itself to the question of what degree of proof is required in deportation proceedings. It is the kind of question which has traditionally been left to the judiciary to resolve, and its resolution is necessary in the interest of the evenhanded administration of the Immigration and Nationality Act.

The petitioners urge that the appropriate burden of proof in deportation proceedings should be that which the law imposes in criminal cases— the duty of proving the essential facts beyond a reasonable doubt. The Government, on the other hand, points out that a deportation proceeding is not a criminal case, and that the appropriate burden of proof should consequently be the one generally imposed in civil cases and administrative proceedings—the duty of prevailing by a mere preponderance of the evidence.

To be sure, a deportation proceeding is not a criminal prosecution. But it does not syllogistically follow that a person may be banished from this country upon no higher degree of proof than applies in a negligence case. This Court has not closed its eyes to the drastic deprivations that may follow when a resident of this country is compelled by our Government to forsake all the bonds formed here and go to a foreign land where he often has no contemporary identification. * * *

In denaturalization cases the Court has required the Government to establish its allegations by clear, unequivocal, and convincing evidence. The same burden has been imposed in expatriation cases.[17] That standard of proof is no stranger to the civil law.

---

17. [Expatriation cases are those in which the government seeks to prove that a person has voluntarily relinquished his or her citizenship. Since *Woodby,* the standard of proof in these cases has been reduced from "clear, unequivocal, and convincing evidence" to the preponderance of the evidence standard familiar in other civil cases. See pp. 1336–50 below.—Ed.]

No less a burden of proof is appropriate in deportation proceedings. The immediate hardship of deportation is often greater than that inflicted by denaturalization, which does not, immediately at least, result in expulsion from our shores. And many resident aliens have lived in this country longer and established stronger family, social, and economic ties here than some who have become naturalized citizens.

We hold that no deportation order may be entered unless it is found by clear, unequivocal, and convincing evidence that the facts alleged as grounds for deportation are true. Accordingly, in each of the cases before us, the judgment of the Court of Appeals is set aside, and the case is remanded with directions to remand to the Immigration and Naturalization Service for such further proceedings as, consistent with this opinion, may be deemed appropriate.

* * *

■ MR. JUSTICE CLARK, whom MR. JUSTICE HARLAN joins, dissenting.

The Court, by placing a higher standard of proof on the Government, in deportation cases, has usurped the legislative function of the Congress and has in one fell swoop repealed the long-established "reasonable, substantial, and probative" burden of proof placed on the Government by specific Act of the Congress, and substituted its own "clear, unequivocal, and convincing" standard. This is but another case in a long line in which the Court has tightened the noose around the Government's neck in immigration cases.

I.

I agree that § 106(a)(4), the 1961 amendment to the Immigration and Nationality Act of 1952, relates to judicial review of administrative orders of the Immigration Service but, with due deference, I cannot see how "It is hardly less clear" that § 242(b)(4) of the Act, as the Court says, likewise applies exclusively to judicial review. Indeed, on the contrary, the latter section was specifically enacted as the only standard of proof to be applied in deportation cases.

* * *

In essence that section, § 242(b), provides for notice and a hearing before a "special inquiry officer" of the Immigration Service; * * * The section also specifically provides that the regulations shall include requirements that "no decision of deportability shall be valid unless it is based upon reasonable, substantial, and probative evidence" and that this standard shall be the "sole and exclusive procedure for determining the deportability of an alien under this section." This was the first time in our history that Congress had expressly placed a specific standard of proof on the Government in deportation cases. And the language Congress used made it clear that this standard related to the "burden of proof" as well as "the quality and nature of the evidence." The requirement of "reasonable" evidence cannot be meant merely to exclude "unreasonable" or "irrational" evidence but carries the obvious connotation from history and tradition of sufficiency to sustain a conclusion by a preponderance of the evidence.[1] Congress in overruling *Wong Yang Sung,* supra, carved deportation proceedings from the judicial overtones of the Administrative Procedure Act and established a *built-in* administrative procedure.

This is made crystal clear by the reports of both Houses of Congress on § 242(b). The Committee Reports state in simple understandable language that:

> "The requirement that the decision of the special inquiry officer shall be based on reasonable, substantial, and probative evidence means that, where the decision rests upon evidence of such a nature that it cannot be said that a reasonable person might not have reached the conclusion which was reached, the case may not be reversed because the judgment of the appellate body differs from that below." * * *

The Court, however, in Shaughnessy v. Pedreiro, once again extended the Administrative Procedure Act's provision respecting judicial review to deportation cases. The reaction of the Congress was identical to that of 1952 when it overruled *Wong Yang Sung,* supra. It enacted, in 1961, § 106(a)(4) of the Act. Just as § 242(b) was the first statutory standard of proof, § 106(a)(4) was the first express statutory standard of judicial review. It provided:

> " * * * the petition [for review] shall be determined solely upon the administrative record upon which the deportation order is based and the Attorney General's findings of fact, if supported by reasonable, substantial, and probative evidence on the record considered as a whole, shall be conclusive."

Why Congress passed § 106(a)(4) if judicial review, as the Court holds, was already exclusively covered by § 242(b) is beyond my comprehension—unless it was engaged in shadow boxing. I cannot believe that it was.

* * *

The Court now extends the standard of Schneiderman v. United States, in denaturalization cases, i.e., "clear, unequivocal, and convincing evidence," to deportation cases. But denaturalization and expatriation are much more oppressive cases than deportation. They deprive one of citizenship which the United States had previously conferred. The *Schneiderman* rule only follows the principle that vested rights can be canceled only upon clear, unequivocal, and convincing proof; it gives stability and finality to a most precious right—citizenship. An alien, however, does not enjoy citizenship but only a conditional privilege extended to him by the Congress as a

---

1. Thus the judicial review provision of the Administrative Procedure Act, 5 U.S.C. § 1009(e)(5), limits the scope of review to a determination of support by "substantial evidence," and 5 U.S.C. § 1006 limits the agencies to acting on "reliable, probative, and substantial evidence." This pattern has traditionally been held satisfied when the agency decides on the preponderance of the evidence.

matter of grace. Both petitioners, the record shows, knew this, yet they remained in this country for years—46 in the case of Sherman and 10 in that of Woodby. Still, neither made any effort to obtain citizenship.

* * *

NOTES AND QUESTIONS

1. In interpreting former INA § 106(a)(4), the Court in *Woodby* employs what is sometimes called a "contextual" approach to statutory interpretation: It looks to the overall context of a statutory scheme to gain insight into the meaning of a particular provision. Section 106, of which section 106(a)(4) is a part, was enacted to provide a comprehensive set of rules governing judicial review of deportation and exclusion orders. Both the title of that section and its introductory words made clear that the focus was on judicial review. In contrast, section 242(b), of which section 242(b)(4) was a part, dealt generally with the conduct of the deportation hearing itself. Why, then, did the Court not employ an analogous contextual approach to section 242(b)(4) and hold that that provision sets forth the standard of proof at the deportation hearing, rather than the standard of judicial review? In answering this question, keep in mind that section 242 was part of the original INA enacted in 1952 and that section 106 was added in 1961.

2. Even if the placement of section 242(b)(4) provides no clue as to its meaning, Justice Clark in dissent asks a fair question: Why *would* Congress have added section 106(a)(4) in 1961 if, as the majority concludes, section 242(b)(4) already specified the standard of judicial review? (You will study the successor to section 106 in more detail later. See section B.6 below.) For now, you should note that former section 242 had many subsections that laid out not only the standard of review, but also various other features, including the proper court, the geographic venue, the timing, the parties, the procedure, and the requirement of prior exhaustion of administrative remedies.

3. Section 242(b)(4) required the Attorney General *to issue regulations* specifying that a finding of deportability will not be valid unless based on reasonable, substantial, and probative evidence. (Its successor provision, present INA § 240(c)(3), imposes this standard directly rather than require the Attorney General to announce it by regulation.) If you had been the INS counsel at the time, what inference might you have asked the court to draw from the fact that Congress, rather than simply stating the standard directly, instructed the Attorney General to embody it in the administrative regulations?

4. It is generally assumed that "reasonable, substantial, and probative evidence" is no different from the familiar "substantial evidence" standard normally used to review administrative agency factfinding in formal adjudication. The adjective "reasonable" presumably adds nothing, since even "substantial evidence" has been held to incorporate a reasonableness requirement. See, e.g., *Consolo v. Federal Maritime Com'n,* 383

U.S. 607, 619–20, 86 S.Ct. 1018, 1026, 16 L.Ed.2d 131, 140 (1966). The word "probative" seems equally superfluous, since it is difficult to imagine non-probative evidence that would meet the substantiality requirement of either test.[7]

Is it even conceivable, then, that Congress would declare "reasonable, substantial, and probative evidence" to be the standard of *proof* in deportation cases? Would Congress really require the immigration judge to find the noncitizen deportable whenever, on the record as a whole, there is evidence from which a reasonable person *could* find deportability? Such a rule would be tantamount to a reverse "beyond a reasonable doubt" standard: the noncitizen would be deportable unless no reasonable person could find otherwise. How does Justice Clark handle this problem in his dissent? Do you find his explanation convincing?

5. The dissent accepts that section 106(a)(4) makes "reasonable, substantial, and probative evidence" the standard of judicial review. It concludes, however, that section 242(b)(4) makes "reasonable, substantial, and probative evidence" the standard of proof at the original deportation hearing. If the dissent is right, has Congress required the administrative authorities and the reviewing court to apply the same standard?

6. Both the majority and dissenting opinions quote approvingly from the Senate committee report's explanation of section 242(b)(4) and the identically worded passage in the House report. Whose position do you think the quoted passage supports?

7. The preceding notes raised questions as to the interpretation of section 242(b). From this point on, let us assume the majority was right to interpret sections 106(a)(4) and 242(b)(4) as prescribing only standards of review. On that assumption, the INA does not specify the standard of proof and the Court is free to adopt whatever course seems wisest. As a policy matter, how should it decide? The classic formulation of the consequences of selecting the standard of proof is this perceptive statement by Justice Harlan:

> * * * [T]he trier of fact will sometimes, despite his best efforts, be wrong in his factual conclusions. In a lawsuit between two parties, a factual error can make a difference in one of two ways. First, it can result in a judgment in favor of the plaintiff when the true facts warrant a judgment for the defendant. The analogue in a criminal case would be the conviction of an innocent man. On the other hand, an erroneous factual determination can result in a judgment for the defendant when the true facts justify a judgment in plaintiff's favor. The criminal analogue would be the acquittal of a guilty man.

7. Professor Gerald Neuman has demonstrated that the "substantial evidence" test is more expansive than the "some evidence" test. Gerald L. Neuman, *The Constitutional Requirement of "Some Evidence,"* 25 San Diego L. Rev. 631, 661–63 (1988). The latter test was used during the early stages of immigration law (and in other contexts) to review findings of fact in exclusion cases. *Id.* at 637–41.

The standard of proof influences the relative frequency of these two types of erroneous outcomes. If, for example, the standard of proof for a criminal trial were a preponderance of the evidence rather than proof beyond a reasonable doubt, there would be a smaller risk of factual errors that result in freeing guilty persons, but a far greater risk of factual errors that result in convicting the innocent. Because the standard of proof affects the comparative frequency of these two types of erroneous outcomes, the choice of the standard to be applied in a particular kind of litigation should, in a rational world, reflect an assessment of the comparative social disutility of each.

In re Winship, 397 U.S. 358, 370–71, 90 S.Ct. 1068, 1076, 25 L.Ed.2d 368, 379 (1970) (Harlan, J., concurring).

The majority opinion in *Woodby* considers the enormous potential stakes for the noncitizen. Given the observations of Justice Harlan in *Winship,* what else should the majority opinion have taken into account, and how should it have completed its analysis?

8. After *Woodby,* the Justice Department regulations codified the "clear, unequivocal, and convincing evidence" standard of proof for deportation proceedings. Cf. the present version, 8 C.F.R. § 1240.8(a) (2004) ("clear and convincing"). What does this standard mean? From the analysis in *Woodby* it is clear that the standard falls somewhere between "preponderance of the evidence" and "beyond a reasonable doubt." The BIA explicitly confirmed that assumption in *Matter of Patel,* 19 I. & N. Dec. 774, 783 (BIA 1988). The Board in *Patel* had to apply the "clear and convincing evidence" standard set out in INA § 204(a)(2) (remarriage of immigrant who had attained her LPR status by marriage). The Board said: "The clear and convincing standard imposes a lower burden than the clear, unequivocal, and convincing standard applied in deportation and denaturalization proceedings because it does not require that the evidence be unequivocal *or of such a quality as to dispel all doubt.*" *Id.* (emphasis added). Was the Board assuming that the "clear, unequivocal, and convincing evidence" standard, in contrast, does require that the evidence "dispel all doubt?" Would even the "beyond a reasonable doubt" standard require that?

9. In 1996, Congress codified *Woodby,* but with some modifications. If a noncitizen has previously been admitted to the United States, ICE must now prove deportability by "clear and convincing evidence." INA § 240(c)(3)(A). The word "unequivocal" has been dropped.

Observe also, however, that this rule operates only in the case of noncitizens who have previously been admitted. As noted in subsection A.3 above, in every removal proceeding ICE first has the burden of proving that the subject of the proceeding is a noncitizen. Once it does so, the burden is on the noncitizen to prove either "(A) if the alien is an applicant for admission, that the alien is clearly and beyond doubt entitled to be admitted and is not inadmissible under section 212; or (B) by clear and convincing evidence, that the alien is lawfully present in the United States pursuant to a prior admission." INA § 240(c)(2). For purposes of prong (A), a noncitizen who is present without admission is "deemed ... an applicant for admission," INA § 235(a)(1), and moreover is inadmissible under INA § 212(a)(6)(A)(i). Under prong (B), once the noncitizen proves lawful presence pursuant to a prior admission, ICE will then have the burden of proving an alleged deportability ground by clear and convincing evidence. INA § 240(c)(3)(A). (If ICE does so, the noncitizen will then have the opportunity to apply for discretionary relief; if any such applications are filed, the noncitizen will have the burden of establishing his or her statutory eligibility and deservedness. See INA § 240(c)(4)).

As you try to digest these provisions, be sure to distinguish *burden* of proof (which party must persuade the finder of fact) from *standard* of proof (how convinced the factfinder must be in order for the burden to be considered discharged). With that distinction in mind, consider the following questions:

(a) What general criteria should legislatures (and courts, when legislatures have not spoken) use in deciding which of two opposing parties should have the burden of proof on a given issue? In particular, although the Harlan formulation was crafted with an eye on standard of proof, would it be helpful also with respect to burden of proof? What other criteria would make sense?

(b) Using the general criteria you have just identified, who ought to bear the burden of proof when the issue is whether a given noncitizen is present without admission?

(c) The majority opinion in *Woodby* points out that the government has the burden of proof in denaturalization proceedings (just as in deportation). In contrast, the noncitizen has the burden of proof in what were formerly called exclusion cases (now, determinations of inadmissibility), INA § 240(c)(2), and also in naturalization cases, INA §§ 312, 316(e), 318. What patterns can you distill?

10.   INA § 291 creates an exception to the government's burden of proof in deportability cases: A person against whom proceedings are brought has the burden of proving "the time, place, and manner" of his or her entry into the United States. If that burden is not sustained, the person is (rebuttably) presumed to be in the United States in violation of law, *id.,* and thus deportable under INA § 237(a)(1)(B). Although section 291 refers to any "person," courts have assumed that the government must establish "alienage" before the burden of proving time, place and manner of entry will shift. See e.g., *Corona–Palomera v. INS,* 661 F.2d 814, 818 (9th Cir.1981); *Iran v. INS,* 656 F.2d 469, 471 (9th Cir.1981). In discharging that burden, ICE is aided by a judicially created rebuttable presumption that a person born abroad is a noncitizen. E.g., *Corona–Palomera,* 661 F.2d at 818; *Matter of Benitez,* 19 I. & N. Dec. 173, 176 (BIA 1984).

Before IIRIRA, the former INS had ample occasion to use section 291. If a noncitizen was believed to have entered without inspection or to have overstayed a temporary visa, but the noncitizen chose to remain mute, he or she would be found to have failed to discharge the burden of proving the time, place, and manner of entry. Accordingly, he or she would be presumed to be in the United States in violation of law. By continuing to remain mute, the person would have failed to rebut that presumption and therefore would have been deportable under what is now section 237(a)(1)(B).

IIRIRA did not repeal section 291, but it made other changes that have rendered section 291 largely superfluous. As noted earlier, every noncitizen in removal proceedings has the burden of proving either admissibility or lawful presence pursuant to a prior admission. A noncitizen who chooses to remain mute or otherwise fails to sustain that burden of proof will thus be found to be either present without admission, which is now an inadmissibility ground, INA § 212(a)(6)(A)(i), or otherwise inadmissible.

11.   But there is one rub. The preceding analysis assumes that the person is a noncitizen. As noted, the pre-IIRIRA courts held that the INS had the burden of proving "alienage." Nothing in IIRIRA expressly superseded these holdings. Accord, 8 C.F.R. § 1240.8(c) (2004) (for those present without having been admitted); *Lopez–Chavez v. INS*, 259 F.3d 1176 (9th Cir. 2001) (applying "clear and convincing evidence" standard of proof); *Murphy v. INS*, 54 F.3d 605 (9th Cir. 1995).

How can ICE prove that somebody is not a citizen? Usually the apprehending officer asks the suspect about his or her citizenship, and the person reflexively provides that information or discloses his or her country of birth. The officer then records the person's statement on a standardized form that the ICE trial attorney will later be able to introduce into evidence at the removal hearing. If properly authenticated, those forms are admissible and can constitute "clear and convincing evidence" that the person is not a citizen. *Lopez–Chavez*, 259 F.3d at 1181.

But what if the person refuses to disclose his or her citizenship to the apprehending officer and continues to remain mute at the removal hearing? In 1985, Immigration Judge Watkins proposed a new strategy: The Justice Department could grant a limited immunity that would prevent the use, in subsequent criminal proceedings, of statements the person makes during the deportation hearing. The conferral of the immunity would make his or her testimony non-incriminating. Thus, Judge Watkins reasoned, the individual could either answer or suffer the drawing of adverse inferences from his or her silence. Henry G. Watkins, *Streamlining Deportation Proceedings: Self–Incrimination, Immunity from Prosecution, and the Duty to Testify in a Deportation Context*, 22 San Diego L.Rev. 1075 (1985).

The former INS took up that suggestion a few years later. In 1988, in "Operation Homestretch," 40 INS agents combined forces with 46 Massachusetts state troopers to raid the Suffolk Downs race track. A number of suspects were arrested and placed in deportation proceedings on charges of entry without inspection. See generally Daniel Kanstroom, *Hello Darkness: Involuntary Testimony and Silence as Evidence in Deportation Proceedings*, 4 Georgetown Immigration L.J. 599, at 599–600 (1990).[8] To defeat the

---

8.   A similar grant of immunity had met with at least temporary success in a Texas case discussed in Kanstroom, at 601 n.12, 607–08. Operation Homestretch, however,

suspects' strategy of remaining mute, the INS then issued "agency orders" purporting to immunize the suspects from the future use, in criminal proceedings, of any testimony they give in their deportation hearings.

One of those cases was *Matter of Guevara*, 20 I. & N.Dec. 238 (BIA 1990, reconsideration denied 1991). Although given such an "agency order," Guevara refused to testify. He maintained that the INS attempt to grant immunity was invalid (as to that, see Kanstroom, above, at 606–11) and that, even if it were valid, the immigration judge could not force him to testify. The immigration judge disagreed and inferred from Guevara's silence that he was not a United States citizen. The effect was to trigger INA § 291, thus requiring Guevara to prove the time, place, and manner of his entry. Since Guevara did not do so, the IJ found him deportable.

The Supreme Court has held that in a criminal case it is impermissible to draw adverse inferences from the defendant's decision to remain silent. *Griffin v. California*, 380 U.S. 609, 614–15, 85 S.Ct. 1229, 14 L.Ed.2d 106 (1965). Such inferences are permissible, however, in deportation (removal) cases. *United States v. Solano–Godines*, 120 F.3d 957, 962 (9th Cir. 1997); *Cabral–Avila v. INS*, 589 F.2d 957, 959 (9th Cir. 1978). Still, do such inferences standing alone satisfy the then applicable *Woodby* standard of "clear, unequivocal, and convincing evidence?" Professor Kanstroom, above, at 623–33,[9] argued strenuously that they do not, even if the silence is unprivileged. The BIA ultimately agreed. It acknowledged that an IJ may draw negative inferences from unprivileged silence and that those inferences, *when combined with other evidence,* could meet the *Woodby* standard. But silence alone, the Board held, would not be enough. Accord, *Matter of Perez–Gonzales*, A73 128 867 (BIA, April 28, 2000) (unpublished decision).

12. Some especially difficult burden of proof (and other) problems arise when the subject of the proceedings is a minor. See Dan Kesselbrenner, *Contesting Deportability: A Strategy for Minor Respondents,* 67 IR 1 (1990).

PROBLEM 1

Immigration officers in Boston raid a restaurant at which undocumented immigrants are known to be employed. Officer Gehler spots a dishwasher and asks him whether he is a United States citizen. The dishwasher answers no. Gehler then asks him to produce his immigration papers. The dishwasher refuses to speak another word. Gehler places him under arrest. Assume that neither Officer Gehler nor any other govern-

---

raised some additional issues concerning the legality of the searches and seizures. *Id.* at 599–600.

9. One alternative that Kanstroom offered, at 621–23, was for the government to seek a court order holding the person in contempt for refusing to testify. That technique, Kanstroom argued, would not only have produced a federal court decision on whether the IJ had the power to compel testimony, but also have permitted a full hearing on the circumstances of the arrest.

ment employee has done anything unlawful. ICE wishes to institute removal proceedings. First, what inadmissibility or deportability grounds should it allege? Second, will ICE be able to meet the statutory standard of proof? Third, suppose the dishwasher had refused to answer the question about citizenship. Would ICE still be able to prove its case?

4. ADMINISTRATIVE REVIEW: THE BOARD OF IMMIGRATION APPEALS

Either the noncitizen or ICE may appeal the decision of the IJ, as of right, to the Board of Immigration Appeals (BIA). 8 C.F.R. § 1003.1(b)(3) (2004). Created by the Attorney General in 1940, 5 Fed. Reg. 3503 (Sept. 4, 1940), the BIA, like the immigration judges, is now part of EOIR. Unlike the IJ's, who are spread throughout the United States, the BIA sits in a fixed location (Falls Church, Virginia). The Attorney General appoints its members, 8 C.F.R. § 1003.1(a)(1) (2004), of whom there were originally five. See Anna Gallagher, *Practice and Procedure Before the Board of Immigration Appeals: An Update,* Feb. 2003 Immigration Briefings at 3. Various attorneys general gradually expanded its membership to 23 to keep pace with a caseload that has multiplied dramatically. 66 Fed. Reg. 47379 (Sept. 12, 2001). There are now only 11 permanent members, as discussed below. The Director of EOIR may designate IJ's to serve as temporary additional members. *Id.* A sizeable legal support staff assists the BIA members in their work.

Because the BIA is a creature of the Attorney General, it lacks the power to declare any of the Attorney General's regulations *ultra vires* the INA (i.e., exceeding the power conferred by the INA). *E.g., Matter of Bilbao–Bastida,* 11 I. & N. Dec. 615, 616, 617 (BIA 1966); *Matter of Tzimas,* 10 I. & N. Dec. 101, 102 (BIA 1962). It similarly lacks the power to consider the constitutionality of the INA. *E.g., Dastmalchi v. INS,* 660 F.2d 880, 886 (3d Cir. 1981); *Matter of Cortez,* 16 I. & N. Dec. 289, 291 n.2 (BIA 1977).

At one time, although three-member panels of the BIA would hear oral argument, all of the then five members would participate in every decision. After extensive study, the Administrative Conference of the United States recommended in 1985 that the BIA decide cases by three-member panels. 1 C.F.R. § 305.85–4, Rec. B.1 (1985). The arguments for a panel system are set out in the consultant's report, which appears in revised form as Stephen H. Legomsky, *Forum Choices for the Review of Agency Adjudication: A Study of the Immigration Process,* 71 Iowa L. Rev. 1297, 1370–74 (1986). Throughout the study, the Justice Department had vigorously resisted the proposed change. *Id.* at 1373–74. Three years later, however, persuaded by the increased BIA caseload and the inefficiency in deciding all cases en banc, the Department adopted a panel system. 53 Fed. Reg. 15660 (May 3, 1988).

From then until 1999, almost all cases were decided by three-member panels (except for some en banc decisions). In that year, a mounting backlog prompted Attorney General Janet Reno to issue regulations that authorized the Chair of the BIA to designate particular categories of cases for one-member review. See 64 Fed. Reg. 56135 (Oct. 18, 1999). From 1999 to 2001, several such categories were designated. See Dorsey & Whitney LLP, Study Conducted for the American Bar Association Commission on Immigration Policy, Practice and Pro Bono, Re Board of Immigration Appeals: Procedural Reforms to Improve Case Management (July 22, 2003) [Dorsey & Whitney], § III. These developments reflected the Justice Department's concern that the often long duration of the BIA process, combined with the automatic stay of removal while the appeal is pending (see below), can create incentives for some noncitizens to file frivolous appeals solely to delay their removal. Whatever the impact on the accuracy of the decisions, there was no doubt that the new procedures noticeably improved the Board's productivity. *Id.*

Despite the success of these procedures in reducing the backlog, Attorney General John Ashcroft in 2002 issued a highly controversial rule similarly aimed at the backlog. 67 Fed. Reg. 54878 (Aug. 26, 2002). The new rule has fundamentally altered the size, the character, the day-to-day operations, and the ultimate decisions of the BIA. It has several components. The rule introduced a new "case management screening system." 67 Fed. Reg. at 54903–04, amending 8 C.F.R. § 1003.1(e). The new system substantially expanded the use of both one-member decisions and affirmances without reasoned opinions. The rule also narrowed the scope of BIA review of IJ findings of fact, speeded up the timetable for briefing and transcript preparation, and (notwithstanding the Department's stated concerns about the backlog) reduced the membership of the Board from 23 authorized positions to 11. Each of these elements is discussed below. For some excellent data compilation and commentary concerning the 2002 reforms, see generally ABA Commission on Immigration Policy, Practice & Pro Bono, Seeking Meaningful Review: Findings and Recommendations in Response to Dorsey & Whitney Study of Board of Immigration Appeals Procedural Reforms (Oct. 2003); Dorsey & Whitney, above; Gallagher, above; Peter J. Levinson, *The Facade of Quasi–Judicial Independence in Immigration Appellate Adjudications*, 9 BIB 1154 (Oct. 1, 2004); Stephen Yale–Loehr, AILA, *Statement on the Operations of the Executive Office for Immigration Review (EOIR) Before the House Committee on the Judiciary Subcommittee on Immigration and Claims* (Feb. 6, 2002); cf. Philip G. Schrag, *The Summary Affirmance Proposal of the Board of Immigration Appeals*, 12 Georgetown Immigration L.J. 531 (1998) (strenuously objecting to the 1999 affirmance without opinion proposal).

The process now works like this: The appellant (who is usually the noncitizen but could be ICE) files a notice of appeal with the IJ no later than thirty days after service of the IJ's decision. 8 C.F.R. § 1003.38(b) (2004). The filing of that notice automatically stays execution of the IJ's decision. *Id.* § 1003.6(a). Under the new system every appeal is initially referred to one of the Board members whom the Chair of the Board has designated for that purpose. 8 C.F.R. § 1003.1(e)(1) (2004). The Board member who screens the case has the power to enter a "summary dismissal" if he or she concludes that any of several conditions are met. Among the bases for summary dismissal are (1) the notice of appeal fails to specify the reasons for appeal; (2) the appeal was "filed for an improper purpose, such as to cause unnecessary delay, or . . . the appeal lacks an arguable basis in fact or in law;" (3) the appellant indicates an intention to file a brief but fails to do so or to explain why; (4) "the appeal does not fall within the Board's jurisdiction;" (5) the appeal is untimely; and other miscellaneous reasons. *Id.* § 1003.1(d)(2) (2004). In those instances, that member dismisses the appeal, normally even before briefs have been filed or a transcript of the removal hearing has been prepared.

Absent summary dismissal, arrangements are made to prepare a transcript of the removal hearing and a briefing schedule is set up. Once that record has been compiled and received, the single member then decides whether to act alone or to forward the case to a three-member panel. In contrast to the 1999 reforms, under which single member decisions were confined to certain cases that were believed not to raise significant factual or legal issues, 64 Fed. Reg. 46135–42 (Oct. 18, 1999), the new rule makes single member decisions the norm. The single member *must* act alone unless he or she finds that the case falls within one of six enumerated situations—inconsistent rulings among immigration judges, a need for a precedential decision, a decision "not in conformity with the law," a "major national impact," a finding of fact that was "clearly erroneous," or the need to reverse the decision. 8 C.F.R. § 1003.1(e)(6) (2004). If the single member decides that the case falls within one of those exceptions, he or she refers the case to a three-member panel.

In the past, the norm was to write an opinion, similar to that of a court, explaining the reasons for the decision. Under the new rule, whenever a single member acts alone (now the norm), he or she must affirm the appealed decision and is *prohibited* from writing an opinion, if the member believes that the result is correct, that any errors are either harmless or non-material, and that either (A) the issues are squarely controlled by existing precedent; or (B) the issues are "not so substantial" as to warrant a written opinion. *Id.* § 1003.1(e)(4)(i). Each of these so-called single-member "AWOs" (affirmances without opinion) culminates in an order that must read, in its entirety, as follows: "The Board affirms, without opinion, the result of the decision below. The decision below is, therefore, the final agency determination. See 8 C.F.R. [100]3.1(e)(4)." *Id.* § 1003.1(e)(4)(ii). The regulation goes on to say that such an order "shall not include further explanation or reasoning." *Id.* In certain narrowly defined situations, the single member is authorized instead to "issue a brief order affirming, modifying, or remanding the decision under review." *Id.* § 1003.1(e)(5).

In those cases that do go to 3–member panels, a panel may still opt for summary dismissal if it finds one of the relevant criteria has been met. 8 C.F.R. § 1003.1(d)(2) (2004). Otherwise the panel has the discretion to hold oral argument, *id.* § 1003.1(e)(7), though in practice oral argument today is the exception rather than the norm.

In unusually important cases, the Board still occasionally proceeds en banc. For that purpose a majority of the permanent members of the Board constitute a quorum. 8 C.F.R. § 1003.1(a)(5) (2004).

The Attorney General has reserved the power to review the decisions of the BIA. 8 C.F.R. § 1003.1(h) (2004). This power is typically exercised only when a case raises exceptionally important questions of law or policy. The power survives the transfer of most immigration functions from the INS to the DHS. See HSA § 1102(3), adding INA § 103(g)(1).

The BIA process culminates in a written decision (with or without reasons) that is served on the parties. 8 C.F.R. § 1003.1(f) (2004). The BIA decision (or that of the Attorney General if he or she exercises the review power noted above) is binding on all IJ's and on all DHS officers and employees in the particular case. *Id.* § 1003.1(g). If designated as precedential, it is binding in similar cases as well. *Id.*

The one-member AWOs have been the target of particular attack. A Los Angeles Times investigation discovered that more than half of the Board's dispositions in October 2002 were affirmances without opinion (AWOs). The investigation also revealed that some BIA members acknowledge deciding up to 50 cases in a day. See Lisa Getter & Jonathan Peterson, L.A. Times (Jan. 5, 2003).

For that and other reasons, some have expressed serious doubts about the quality of the resulting appellate decisionmaking. In one case, the Ninth Circuit excoriated the IJ for writing an "indecipherable" and "literally incomprehensible" opinion, one that was "extreme in its lack of a coherent explanation" (a deficiency that it acknowledged might have reflected the unrealistic caseloads of the IJs). The court then implicitly faulted the BIA for affirming such a decision without opinion. The Court said "When the agency's only explanation of its final action is incoherent, we may not substantively review it without violating basic principles of judicial review." *Recinos De Leon v. Gonzales,* 400 F.3d 1185, 1187 (9th Cir. 2005). The Seventh Circuit, a longstanding critic of the quality of BIA opinions, fired this recent volley:

> We close by noting six disturbing features of the handling of this case that bulk large in the immigration cases that we are seeing: * * * [a]ffirmances by the Board of Immigration Appeals either with no opinion or with a very short, unhelpful, boilerplate opinion, even when, as in this case, the immigration judge's opinion contains manifest errors of fact and logic.

Zhen Li Iao v. Gonzales, 400 F.3d 530, 533–35 (7th Cir. 2005). The court speculated that the problems might reflect "caseload pressures" and "resource constraints," lamenting that "it is possible that nothing better can realistically be expected than what we are seeing in this and like cases." *Id.* at 535.

The L.A. Times study also noted that the increase in one-member decisions has coincided with an increase in the rate at which the Board ultimately rejects appeals on the merits. In October 2002, the Board rejected 86% of the appeals, compared with 59% the previous October. An even more dramatic dropoff in the percentage of cases in which the noncitizen prevailed was empirically confirmed in Dorsey & Whitney, above.

At any rate, several federal courts of appeals are reporting spectacular increases in the number of petitions for review of BIA decisions. See pages 729–31 below. Whether the sharp increase in judicial filings reflects increased dissatisfaction with the BIA appellate process, or whether it can be ascribed entirely to other factors, is not known with certainty, but a sophisticated empirical study in progress at the time of this writing strongly suggests the former. See John R.B. Palmer, Stephen W. Yale Loehr & Elizabeth Cronin, *Why Are So Many People Challenging Board of Immigration Appeals Decisions in Federal Court? An Empirical Analysis of the Recent Surge in Petitions for Review* (unpublished manuscript 2005).

The new rule also restricts the scope of the Board's review. Under the prior regulations, the Board reviewed de novo, substituting its collective judgment for that of the immigration judges on all components of the decision—findings of fact, conclusions of law, and the exercise of discretion. The new rule retains de novo review of legal and discretionary determinations but prohibits the Board from reversing an IJ's findings of fact unless they are "clearly erroneous." 8 C.F.R. § 1003.1(d)(3) (2004). Among such findings of fact are the IJ's credibility determinations (particularly crucial in asylum cases). *Id*; see generally Lory Rosenberg, *Credibility Determinations in Asylum Cases: Evidentiary Factors and Regulatory Limits Under the Clearly Erroneous Standard*, 8 BIB 573 (Apr. 1, 2003); see also Yale–Loehr Statement, above, at 7–8 (arguing that the reduced BIA scope of review will increase both the use of judicial review and the number of judicial remands to the BIA).

The new rule also speeds up the process by setting deadlines for some of the specific steps. The deadlines for filing briefs, for example, are now somewhat more rigorous for cases in which the noncitizens are detained than for other cases. There are also strict deadlines for preparing the hearing transcript, for IJ review of the hearing transcript, and for the BIA to decide the case. The details are in 8 C.F.R. §§ 1003.1(e)(8), 1003.3(c), 1003.5 (2004).

Finally, the new rule provided that, within six months of the implementation of the "case management" system, the authorized size of the Board would be reduced from 23 members to 11. See 67 Fed. Reg. at 54901, amending what is now 8 C.F.R. § 1003.1(a)(1) (2004). The contraction of the Board has also been highly controversial. First, many have questioned whether such a small number of people will have the time to provide meaningful review in the thousands of cases, many of them highly complex, that the Board decides each year.

Second, both the process and the result have raised serious doubts about the continued independence of the BIA. Neither the rule itself nor any other announcement specified concrete criteria for determining which Board members would be removed. That omission was problematic for two reasons. For one thing, when the axe finally fell, it fell almost entirely on those Board members whose decisions had most frequently favored the noncitizens; credentials and seniority clearly played little if any role, as former House Judiciary Committee attorney Peter Levinson has demonstrated empirically. See Levinson, above; accord, ABA Commission, above at 4 ("It is undisputed that the Board members ultimately reassigned to other positions within the government were those with a history of being more favorable to noncitizens' claims than those who remain on the Board.")

Moreover, since the Attorney General announced many months in advance that the Board membership would be cut, and since he provided no criteria for selecting the fired members (such as credentials or seniority), there followed a long period in which Board members could not avoid wondering how the outcomes of the cases they were about to decide might affect their job security. As Levinson confirmed by studying outcomes in en banc cases, several Board members' percentages of rulings in favor of noncitizens dropped sharply in the months that followed the Attorney General's announcement. Several other Board members who had formerly tended to rule in favor of noncitizens continued to do so after the announcement. When the purge came, only one of the latter survived. *Id.*

The independence issue is a serious one. Since the creation of the BIA in 1940, the United States attorneys general have been an ideologically diverse group with widely divergent views on immigration. Yet no attorney general had ever dismissed a member of the BIA. Although Board members have never enjoyed the formal job security of article III judges, the assumption had always been that they were free to render the decisions they felt were required by the evidence presented and their interpretations of the applicable law, without fear of losing their jobs if they displeased the Attorney General. Obviously that can no longer be safely assumed.

Unprecedented as the Attorney General's "purge of the liberals" was in the United States, somewhat analogous (and, at the time, equally unprecedented) developments had taken place in Australia in 1996–97. After a pair of decisions by Australia's Refugee Review Tribunal had reversed asylum denials by the government, the Minister of Immigration, Mr. Philip Ruddock, made a series of public statements denouncing the individuals who had handed down the decisions. The same statements threatened not to renew the appointments of members who ruled in similar ways. He carried out that threat as soon as the appointments came up for renewal several months later, non-renewing 16 out of 35 and substituting new members of his own choosing. During the month in which the Minister's department interviewed the members in connection with their possible reappointments, the proportion of appeals in which the tribunal set aside the Minister's decisions plummeted from more than 15% to less than 3%. See Stephen H. Legomsky, *Refugees, Administrative Tribunals, and Real Independence: Dangers Ahead for Australia*, 76 Washington Univ. L.Q. 243, 248–54 (1998). As the cited article asks, "Would any readers of this article want their cases to be decided by people who had been told in

no uncertain terms that they could lose their jobs by ruling in your favor?''
Id. at 251.

In the wake of the BIA downsizing, calls for restoring independence to
the process have come from several quarters. See, e.g., ABA Commission,
above, at 6; American Immigration Lawyers Association, Press Release,
AILA Renews Call for an Independent Immigration Court (May 27, 2003);
Dorsey & Whitney, above; Stephen H. Legomsky, *The Deportation Process,
the War on Independence, and Reverse Darwinism: Why We Need Habeas
Corpus More than Ever*, 91 Cornell L. Rev., issue #2 (forthcoming 2006);
Levinson, above; Yale–Loehr Statement, above.

NOTES AND QUESTIONS

1.   Given the dramatically increased BIA caseloads, backlogs, and
delays, one would be hard pressed to fault the Justice Department for
seeking ways to enhance the Board's efficiency. The challenge is to reconcile the efficiency goals with the sometimes competing justice interests of
fairness, accuracy, consistency, and public acceptability. In that vein, compare two of the BIA efficiency measures described in these materials—
summary dismissals and single-member affirmances without opinion
(AWOs). First, review the criteria for both. Note especially that one of the
most common reasons for summary dismissal is that the notice of appeal
failed to identify the alleged errors with enough specificity. With that in
mind, and remembering that summary dismissal usually occurs before
transcripts are prepared or briefs are filed, how do you suppose its policy
objectives differ from those of single-member AWOs? Are there any policy
objectives that the two provisions share? (Countervailing policy problems
are considered below.)

2.   As just noted, one of the most common reasons for summary
dismissal is the appellant's failure to meaningfully specify the grounds for
appeal. First, exactly what does the appellant lose when the BIA orders
summary dismissal on that ground (as opposed to letting the case progress
through the normal process)? That is, if the BIA orders summary dismissal,
can't one safely assume that the BIA would have affirmed anyway? (In
addressing this question, consider that the BIA reviews the IJ's legal and
discretionary determinations de novo, though findings of fact are now
reviewed only under the "clearly erroneous" standard. 8 C.F.R.
§ 1003.1(d)(3)(i) (2004)). Second, when the BIA receives notices of appeal
that fail to meaningfully identify the grounds for appeal, might there have
been policy alternatives to summary dismissal?

3.   If the faulty notice of appeal was filed by a lawyer, it is sometimes
possible to argue ineffective assistance of counsel, a subject taken up in
section B.2.d above. The leading case is *Lozada v. INS*, 857 F.2d 10 (1st
Cir. 1988), excerpted on pages 681–83 above. The lawyer filed a notice of
appeal that simply said the decision of the IJ was "against the weight of
the evidence," "against the law controlling the case," and "arbitrary and
capricious." The court upheld the use of summary dismissal (and ultimate-

ly rejected the ineffective assistance of counsel claim). But how specific, exactly, does the appellant really have to be at the notice of appeal stage? The current regulations read:

> The statement [in the Notice of Appeal] must specifically identify the findings of fact, the conclusions of law, or both, that are being challenged. If a question of law is presented, supporting authority must be cited. If the dispute is over the findings of fact, the specific facts contested must be identified. Where the appeal concerns discretionary relief, the appellant must state whether the alleged error relates to statutory grounds of eligibility or to the exercise of discretion and must identify the specific factual and legal finding or findings that are being challenged.

8 C.F.R. § 1003.3(b) (2004).

This regulation makes clear that the *notice of appeal* must meaningfully identify the claimed errors; clarifying the issues in a subsequent brief is not enough. First, consider the logistics. The notice of appeal must be filed within thirty days of the IJ's decision, 8 C.F.R. § 1003.38(b) (2004), well before the hearing transcript is available. The brief, in contrast, will not be due until some time after the hearing transcript. *Id.* § 1003.3(c)(1). Given that reality, do you think the degree of specificity required for the notice of appeal is reasonable? Second, what is gained by insisting on specificity at the notice of appeal stage, rather than letting it wait until the briefing stage?

4.   In *Padilla–Agustin v. INS*, 21 F.3d 970 (9th Cir. 1994), overruled on other grounds, *Stone v. INS*, 514 U.S. 386, 115 S.Ct. 1537, 131 L.Ed.2d 465 (1995), the Ninth Circuit observed that the standardized notice of appeal form provided only a small space in which to state the reasons for the appeal (though the form specifies that the appellant is permitted to attach additional sheets). Concerned that the small space allowed on the form could mislead an appellant as to the expected degree of detail, and noting that the government could easily furnish clearer explanations, the court applied the *Eldridge* factors discussed on page 144 above and found a violation of procedural due process. Eight years after *Padilla–Agustin*, the same court found the same dissonance between the standardized notice of appeal form that the noncitizen had to fill out and the actual requirements for avoiding summary dismissal. *Vargas–Garcia v. INS*, 287 F.3d 882 (9th Cir. 2002).

5.   What do you see as the down sides of (a) single-member BIA decisions rather than decisions by three-member panels; and (b) decisions not accompanied by opinions? (The hoped-for benefits were considered in question 1 above.)

6.   The legality of AWOs has been challenged on due process grounds (and occasionally on separation of powers grounds, the theory being that the Attorney General, who is part of the executive branch, is dictating the procedure to adjudicators). The courts have uniformly rejected these arguments; it is sufficient, they have said, that the IJ opinion that the BIA was

reviewing was specific enough to permit meaningful review. See, e.g., *Reyes–Vasquez v. Ashcroft*, 395 F.3d 903, 905–06 (8th Cir. 2005); *Disu v. Ashcroft*, 338 F.3d 13 (1st Cir. 2003); *Falcon–Carriche v. Ashcroft*, 335 F.3d 1009 (9th Cir. 2003).

7.   The courts have divided, however, over whether they may reverse an AWO on the ground that the particular case did not fall within the AWO criteria laid out in the regulations. Courts reviewed such decisions in *Smriko v. Ashcroft*, 387 F.3d 279 (3d Cir. 2004), and *Chong Shin Chen v. Ashcroft*, 378 F.3d 1081 (9th Cir. 2004). Contra, *Tsegay v. Ashcroft*, 386 F.3d 1347 (10th Cir. 2004); *Ngure v. Ashcroft*, 367 F.3d 975, 981–88 (8th Cir. 2004) (holding decision "committed to agency discretion by law," for purposes of the Administrative Procedure Act, 5 U.S.C. § 701(a)(2)).

8.   As you have read, many commentators and organizations have decried the practical impact of the 2002 BIA reforms on the independence of the Board members. First, why, exactly, is it important for those who adjudicate cases to enjoy decisional independence? Second, does decisional independence have policy *costs*? See generally Stephen H. Legomsky, *The Deportation Process, the War on Independence, and Reverse Darwinism: Why We Need Habeas Corpus More than Ever*, 91 Cornell L. Rev., issue #2 (forthcoming 2006).

5.   MOTIONS TO REOPEN OR RECONSIDER

Under various circumstances either ICE or the noncitizen may file a motion either to reopen or to reconsider a removal proceeding. The motion is filed with the BIA if it has already rendered a decision in the case; otherwise the motion is filed with the immigration judge. 8 C.F.R. §§ 1003.2(a), 1003.23(b) (2004). A motion to *reopen* is the vehicle used to present material new facts that were "not available and could not have been discovered or presented at the former hearing." *Id*. § 1003.2(c)(1). In contrast, a motion to *reconsider* is filed for the purpose of calling attention to "errors of fact or law in the prior Board decision" and, therefore, must "be supported by pertinent authority." *Id*. § 1003.2(b)(1).

Earlier you encountered motions to reopen in the specific context of the predecessor to cancellation of removal. See pages 587–97 above. As you will recall from that discussion, these motions have stirred controversies: Are they a legitimate vehicle for presenting new evidence, or a ruse to delay removal, or both? How should the power to decide them be allocated between courts and administrative tribunals? This is a good time to review those pages. Here, with the focus on deportation procedure generally, a few additional comments are necessary.

Even with the substantial restrictions that Congress placed on judicial review of removal orders in 1996, see subsection 6 below, it appears clear that administratively final orders denying motions to reopen removal proceedings are still judicially reviewable. See INA § 242(b)(6) (requiring that judicial review of such orders be consolidated with any judicial review of the underlying removal orders). As discussed in connection with the court-stripping provision for certain discretionary decisions, INA § 242(a)(2)(B)(ii), see page 737 below, several courts have explicitly so held. As the same discussion shows, however, the broad reasoning used by at least two other circuits in a different context (motions for continuances) could have implications for the reviewability of denials of motions to reopen in those circuits. At any rate, the scope of the court's review is the narrow "abuse of discretion" standard. See *Jong Ha Wang,* discussed on pages 588–91 above.

In *INS v. Abudu,* 485 U.S. 94, 108 S.Ct. 904, 99 L.Ed.2d 90 (1988), the Supreme Court provided additional general guidance. The Court summarized three of the grounds on which the BIA may deny motions to reopen: "that the movant has not established a prima facie case for the underlying substantive relief sought; * * * that the movant has not introduced previously unavailable, material evidence; * * * [and] in cases in which the ultimate grant of relief is discretionary * * *, [that] the movant would not be entitled to the discretionary grant of relief." 485 U.S. at 104–05. The Court concluded that denials on the latter two grounds are reviewable only for abuse of discretion. It did not have occasion to address the standard of review for denials based on the first ground (lack of prima facie case), but at least one court has held that those denials too are reviewable only for abuse of discretion. See *M.A. v. U.S. INS,* 899 F.2d 304, 307–10 (4th Cir. en banc, 1990) (6–5 vote).

But there are now additional grounds for denying both motions to reopen and motions to reconsider. In recent years a series of measures—the Immigration Act of 1990, IIRIRA, and administrative regulations—have imposed major procedural restrictions on the filing of motions to reopen or reconsider. The noncitizen may file only one motion to *reconsider* a removal order, and it must be filed within 30 days of the final administrative decision. The noncitizen may also file one (and only one) motion to *reopen* a removal order, and it must be filed within 90 days of the final administrative decision. See INA §§ 240(c)(6)(A, B), 240(c)(7)(A), 240(c)(7)(C)(i). Certain asylum cases are exempt from the 90–day time limit. INA § 240(c)(7)(C)(ii). One court has held that ineffective assistance of counsel can equitably toll the 90–day time limit if the person has exercised due diligence. *Iavorski v. INS,* 232 F.3d 124 (2d Cir. 2000). There are also special provisions for entering removal orders in absentia, subject to reopening within 180 days. See section E.3 below.

Even apart from those exceptions, there is some flexibility. The BIA can always choose to reopen or reconsider on its own motion. 8 C.F.R. § 1003.2(a) (2004). In addition, any motion to reopen that is jointly filed by all the parties is exempt from both the one-motion rule and the time limit. *Id.* § 1003.23(b)(4)(iv). The practical consequence is that, if the noncitizen can persuade either ICE or the BIA that the special facts of the case warrant another look, a mechanism to reopen is available. In practice, neither ICE nor the BIA has been inclined to exercise that authority in the absence of unusual circumstances.

QUESTION

What do you think is driving Congress and the Justice Department to limit the time and number of motions to reopen or reconsider? Are such limitations a good idea?

6. JUDICIAL REVIEW OF REMOVAL ORDERS[10]

In chapter 2, you met up with the principle of plenary congressional power. Harsh as that doctrine might be, it has for the most part been reserved for challenges to the constitutionality of *congressional* action; only occasionally—until recently—have courts held the immigration decisions of *administrative officials* immune from judicial review. The one glaring exception has been the longstanding refusal of the courts to review the decisions of consular officers denying visas. And that one exception—the doctrine of consular absolutism—seems so striking precisely because it is so exceptional. When administrative officials make decisions that have great impact on the lives of individuals—even in the field of immigration—one has come to expect that the legality of those decisions will be subject to judicial review.

For the most part, until 1996, they were. But the subject of judicial review has always aroused political passions, especially in the field of immigration. In 1996 those passions erupted into all-out war. That year, with the enactment of AEDPA and IIRIRA, Congress attempted to strip the courts of jurisdiction over a broad range of important cases related to the removal of noncitizens. Since then, the law of judicial review—always complex and always controversial—has become both a technical and an ideological minefield. On one side are those who perceive the judiciary as an obstructive, anti-democratic institution that delays the removal of deportable noncitizens and displays undue sympathy toward undeserving violators of our laws.[11] On the other side are those who perceive the judiciary as a principled and dispassionate dispenser of justice and a bulwark against unlawful government action, particularly important when the litigants (noncitizens) are distinctively exposed to volatile and often hostile political sentiments. There is middle ground, of course, but the loud clash of opposing forces continues to leave this subject mired in controversy and uncertainty.

---

10. See generally 8 Gordon, Mailman & Yale–Loehr, chap. 104; Stephen H. Legomsky, *Fear and Loathing in Congress and the Courts: Immigration and Judicial Review*, 78 Texas L. Rev. 1615 (2000); David W. Leopold & Karen Grisez, *The Nuts and Bolts of Federal Court Litigation*, in AILA, Immigration and Nationality Law Handbook 384–96 (2000–01); Gerald L. Neuman, *Jurisdiction and the Rule of Law After the 1996 Immigration Act*, 113 Harvard L. Rev. 1963 (2000); Gerald L. Neuman, *Federal Courts Issues in Immigration Law*, 78 Texas L. Rev. 1661 (2000).

11. Actually, from 1990 to 2000, the government prevailed in approximately 83% of all immigration cases filed in the courts of appeals. U.S. Dept. of Justice, 4 Immigration Litigation Bulletin 2 (Sept. 29, 2000). (The reported figures are for cases argued by the Department's Office of Immigration Litigation. They do not include Second Circuit cases, which are argued by U.S. attorneys.)

With the passage of the REAL ID Act in 2005, Congress has once again entered the fray. The materials that follow will describe the key developments, piece together the current picture, and explore the remaining uncertainties.

The longstanding general rule, now subject to gaping exceptions that you will study in this section, remains easy to state: Once all the relevant administrative authorities have passed on a case, the noncitizen has a right to judicial review of an order of removal. At first, absent any explicit statutory provision for judicial review, the district courts reviewed deportation cases by way of habeas corpus. See generally Henry Hart, *The Power of Congress to Limit the Jurisdiction of the Federal Courts: An Exercise in Dialectic,* 66 Harvard L.Rev. 1362, 1389–96 (1953). But habeas carried some baggage, the most significant being that the person could not seek habeas until he or she was in "custody." And custody was initially assumed to require physical restraint, which often did not occur until the very end of the process. The INA was enacted in 1952, however, and in 1955 the Supreme Court construed the INA to mean that noncitizens ordered deported could obtain judicial review by seeking declaratory judgments or injunctions under the Administrative Procedure Act, 5 U.S.C. § 703. See *Shaughnessy v. Pedreiro,* 349 U.S. 48, 75 S.Ct. 591, 99 L.Ed. 868 (1955).

Tales of long delays in executing administratively final deportation orders began to circulate. The most famous and most frequently invoked example was the extraordinary story of alleged mobster Carlos Marcello, whose deportation case literally dragged on for decades. See Mark A. Mancini, *The Carlos Marcello Case,* 1990(2) Immigration and Nationality Law at 2–10. The magnitude of the delay in his case was hardly typical, and at any rate the bulk of that delay resulted from other countries' refusals to receive him rather than from defects in the United States review system. *Id.* Nonetheless, his and other cases led Congress in 1961 to create a specific statutory provision for judicial review, former INA § 106(a). Under that procedure, which is similar to the procedure used in a variety of other administrative agency settings, the noncitizen bypasses the district court and files a "petition for review" in the court of appeals.

In 1996, IIRIRA repealed INA § 106 and substituted a new provision, INA § 242. Under the new law, the petition for review in the court of appeals is still, generally, the exclusive vehicle for obtaining judicial review of an administratively final removal order—more explicitly so in the light of the REAL ID Act, as discussed below. As just noted, however, IIRIRA carved out several broad exceptions to the right of judicial review. These provisions purport to bar judicial review of whole categories of removal orders, prohibit review of most denials of discretionary relief, make several forms of action and other judicial remedies unavailable, and erect several other barriers to judicial review of administrative decisions in removal cases. As you will see, not all of Congress's attempts have succeeded. Some of the statutory language has been subjected to a combination of non-literal statutory construction and constitutional scrutiny.

Ironically, despite all the statutory restrictions on judicial review, the past few years have witnessed a stunning rise in the number of immigration cases filed in federal court. For that reason, at this writing judicial review of BIA removal orders is a hotter issue than ever. Since 2002, when Attorney General Ashcroft implemented the BIA reforms discussed in subsection 4 above, appeals from BIA removal orders to the federal courts have skyrocketed. As noted below, no one disputes the causal connection between the BIA reforms and the surge in federal filings, but there are differing views about why that causal link has occurred and what it tells us. Nor does the phenomenon appear to be short-term.

The numbers are dramatic. During the first twelve months following implementation of the BIA reforms (i.e. the year ending March 2003), the number of BIA removal orders for which review was sought in federal court increased by 379% from the prior year, to 8,446 filings. Administrative Office of the U.S. Courts, 35 Newsletter of the Federal Courts No. 9 (Sept. 2003) [hereafter AO Newsletter]. In 2002, just before the BIA reforms, only 5% of the BIA decisions were being appealed to the federal courts; by November 2004 that figure was 25%. Tom Perrotta, *Immigration Appeals Surge in Second Circuit*, New York L.J., Nov. 4, 2004. Conversely, in 2001 immigration cases accounted for approximately 3% of the combined dockets of the U.S. courts of appeals; by 2003, that figure had leaped to 15%. Stanley Mailman & Stephen Yale–Loehr, *Immigration Appeals Overwhelm Federal Courts*, 10 BIB 45, at 45 (Jan. 15, 2005). Moreover, the crush of petitions for review has prevented the BIA from promptly preparing and transmitting to the courts the usually bulky certified records of proceedings that the courts need just to start the briefing process, thus exacerbating the judicial backlogs. AO Newsletter.

Two circuits—the Ninth (based in San Francisco) and the Second (based in New York)—have borne the brunt of the impact. In the Ninth Circuit, in calendar year 2001 (just before the BIA reforms), 896 immigration cases were filed. In 2002, with the BIA reforms in place, the number of filings soared to 3578. In 2003, they increased again, to 3966. E-mail from Cathy Catterson, Clerk of the U.S. Court of Appeals for the Ninth Circuit, to author (Dec. 6, 2004). As of August 31, 2004, filings for 2004 were already up to 3126, *id.*, which would translate to an annual rate of 4689. The huge bump in 2002, in other words, has been followed by additional steady increases in each subsequent year, so that, as of November 2004, immigration cases made up an astounding 43% of the entire Ninth Circuit docket. Perrotta, above.

In the Second Circuit, the change has been even more stunning. From February 2002 to February 2003 (the first year of the BIA reforms), Second Circuit immigration filings increased by 781%. AO Newsletter. In the twelve-month period that ended in June 2004, immigration cases comprised 44% of the Second Circuit's total docket, compared to 9% in 2002. Perrotta, above; see also Comm. on Federal Courts, The Surge of Immigration Appeals and Its Impact on the Second Circuit Court of Appeals (2004).

The vastly increased caseloads are overtaxing not only the resources of the judiciary, but also the resources of the executive branch. For one thing, since so many noncitizens are now detained while their federal cases are pending, the increase in federal filings has driven up the total detention costs. For another, someone has to represent the government in each of these cases. The Justice Department has redeployed several hundred additional lawyers from other fields for this purpose. Mailman & Yale–Loehr, above. Government attorneys in the Second Circuit are unusually affected, because the Second Circuit is the only one in which attorneys from the U.S. Attorney's Office (the Southern District of New York) represent the government in immigration cases; in all other circuits, the Justice Department's Office of Immigration Litigation (OIL) provides the representation. Perrotta, above. Before the BIA reforms, 9 attorneys from the local U.S. Attorney's Office did the work in the Second Circuit; now the Office has had to enlist all 53 attorneys in its Civil Division, plus some in its Criminal Division, plus some from other judicial districts. *Id.*

So the situation is serious. Part of the increase in court filings reflects the fact that the BIA reforms have boosted the number of total BIA dispositions per year. Thus, even a constant rate of appeal to the federal courts would have increased the absolute number of filings. But even the Justice Department acknowledges that that factor accounts for no more than 20% of the increase in court filings. The other 80% results from the huge increase (from 5% to 25%, noted above) in the rate of appeal. EOIR, Fact Sheet (Sept. 15, 2004).

Why, exactly, would the BIA reforms cause the rate of appeal from its decisions to increase? That is the question on which views tend to differ. Most analysts attribute the surge to the sharply reduced quality of the BIA opinions. The combination of deciding so many more cases per day and not having to justify the affirmances with written explanation are thought to have produced more poorly reasoned decisions and to have left noncitizens and their attorneys with the feeling that review has been inadequate. See generally the sources cited in subsection 4 above.

The Justice Department disagrees. It says, "There is no evidence that the affirmance and reversal/remand rates of BIA decisions [by the reviewing courts] has [sic] changed significantly in the wake of the restructuring regulation. This indicates that the quality of the Board's jurisprudence has remained consistent and unaffected by" the BIA reforms. EOIR Fact Sheet, above. (That statement is misleading. EOIR does not claim to have evidence that the reversal rates have *not* changed; it simply does not cite evidence in either direction.)

If EOIR is right to claim that the BIA reforms have not diminished the quality of its decisions, then why has the rate of appeal from its decisions surged? EOIR offers the following hypothesis:

A factor which may be contributing to the rise in the rate of appeals is the reduced time involved in completing cases appealed to the Board. Thus, for those aliens who wish to postpone deportation, filing an appeal to the circuit courts may be a much more

> attractive option than in the past. To the extent that the courts
> are routinely granting stays of deportation pending their review,
> the incentive to file an appeal and to request a stay will be high.

Id. Does that sound right? Certainly many noncitizens have a real incentive
to buy additional time in the United States by seeking judicial review in
federal court. But was that incentive really *lower* for people in the past
because they had *already* been in the U.S. for the longer period that BIA
appeals were then taking? If anything, wouldn't one expect that, all else
equal, a person who had spent a lengthy period in the United States would
have deeper roots and therefore a *greater* incentive to prolong his or her
future stay?

Before proceeding further, skim INA § 242 to get a general sense of its
layout, its content, and its scope.

a. PETITIONS FOR REVIEW

INA § 242(a)(1) says that "[j]udicial review of a final order of removal
. . . is governed only by chapter 158 of title 28 of the United States Code."
The reference is to a law known as the Hobbs Act, which applies to a wide
range of administrative contexts, not just immigration. Under the Hobbs
Act, one files a "petition for review" in the court of appeals.

Direct review in the court of appeals avoids the duplication that arises
when a district court reviews an agency action and the district court
decision is then appealed to the court of appeals. Why, then, do you suppose
Congress doesn't simply channel *all* judicial review of agency action directly
to the courts of appeals? As a matter of judicial efficiency, consider (a) court
of appeals decisions normally require three-judge panels; (b) not all district
court judgments are appealed; and (c) district courts and courts of appeals
are generally expert at different things. With those and any other relevant
factors in mind, how would you analyze when it is better to assign a given
class of reviewable administrative agency decisions to the district courts
(with a right of appeal to the courts of appeals), and when it is better to
assign cases directly to the courts of appeals? See generally David P. Currie
& Frank I. Goodman, *Judicial Review of Federal Administrative Action:
Quest for the Optimum Forum,* 75 Columbia L.Rev. 1 (1975); Stephen H.
Legomsky, *Forum Choices for the Review of Agency Adjudication: A Study
of the Immigration Process,* 71 Iowa L.Rev. 1297, 1312–34 (1986).

The petition for review is filed in the circuit in which the removal
hearing was held. INA § 242(b)(2). The petition itself must be filed no later
than 30 days after the (administratively) final removal order. INA
§ 242(b)(1). A motion to reopen or reconsider does not toll the clock. *Stone
v. INS,* 514 U.S. 386, 115 S.Ct. 1537, 131 L.Ed.2d 465 (1995). The statute
requires the noncitizen to file a brief within 40 days after the administrative record "is available;" otherwise, the court must dismiss the case
"unless a manifest injustice would result." INA § 242(b)(3)(C). In contrast,
there is no statutory time limit on the filing of the government brief. *Id.*
The latter would be governed by any relevant nonstatutory rules of court.

Until 1996, service of the petition for review automatically stayed the person's deportation pending the court's decision, unless the court directed otherwise (a rare event) or the person had been convicted of an aggravated felony. If, nonetheless, the person departed from the United States while the petition for review was pending, the petition would be dismissed and the deportation order would become final. Former INA § 106(c). IIRIRA changed both rules. There is no longer any automatic stay of removal; the person must move the court to grant it. INA § 242(b)(3)(B). Conversely, however, the person's departure no longer bars judicial review; the case proceeds in the person's absence. Under the version of the REAL ID Act passed by the House of Representatives, courts of appeals would have been *prohibited* from staying removal pending their decisions! That provision was not passed by the Senate, however, and it was not included in the conference committee bill that finally became law.

As a result, it is now routine practice for noncitizens to couple their petitions for review with motions for stays of removal pending decision. These motions pose difficult questions of judicial administration. Should the court invest time studying the merits before deciding the motion for a stay, and then, if the stay is granted, pick up the case later and study the merits again? Or, to save time, should the court either (a) deny the stay without examining the merits, thus allowing DHS to remove the petitioner from the country before the court can decide whether the petition is meritorious; or (b) grant the stay without examining the merits, thus permitting the person to buy time in the United States by filing a nonmeritorious petition? Which of these options do you think will be the most popular with busy appellate judges?

The Ninth Circuit has taken the position that, upon the filing of a motion for a stay in conjunction with a petition for review, removal will automatically be stayed until the court can rule on *the motion*. DHS has seven days from the time the motion is served on it to decide whether to oppose the motion. After DHS decides whether to oppose, a motions panel will decide whether to extend the stay until the petition for review is decided. See *De Leon v. INS*, 115 F.3d 643 (9th Cir. 1997).

As for the substantive standard for determining whether to stay removal pending the court's final disposition, a near-consensus appears to be emerging. The Ninth Circuit applies the same standard that it uses generally for preliminary injunctions—"either (1) a probability of success on the merits and the possibility of irreparable injury, or (2) that serious legal questions are raised and the balance of hardships tips sharply in the petitioner's favor." *Andreiu v. Ashcroft*, 253 F.3d 477, 483 (9th Cir. 2001) (en banc). At this writing, all but one of the other circuits that have passed on the issue have applied roughly similar standards. For a comprehensive survey and analysis, see *Tesfamichael v. Gonzales*, No. 04–61180 (5th Cir., May 24, 2005). The only circuit to reject that view is the Eleventh. That court requires "clear and convincing evidence" that the BIA decision was "prohibited as a matter of law," the standard provided by INA § 242(f)(1) to "enjoin or restrain" a removal order. *Weng v. U.S. Attorney General*, 287

F.3d 1335 (11th Cir. 2002). Note that under the Eleventh Circuit approach, it takes more to temporarily stay a removal order pending the final decision than to obtain a full reversal of the removal order on the merits.

Several other limitations on petitions for review are carryovers from prior law. One must first exhaust all administrative remedies that are available as of right. INA § 242(d)(1). Res judicata and collateral estoppel are fully applicable; thus, with limited exceptions, another court cannot have previously decided the validity of the removal order. INA § 242(d)(2).

If the petition for review survives all the barriers discussed above and all those to be discussed below, the reviewing court decides the merits solely on the basis of the administrative record. INA § 242(b)(4)(A). Normally, that record will contain the charging document, the transcript of the removal hearing, any documentary evidence that was submitted, the decision of the immigration judge, and the papers connected with the BIA proceeding (including the opposing briefs to, and the decision by, the BIA). For a sample of the administrative record in an actual case, see the case file provided in section C of this chapter.

The statute contains an odd provision concerning the scope of the court's review. According to INA § 242(b)(4)(B), "the administrative findings of fact are conclusive unless any reasonable adjudicator would be compelled to conclude to the contrary." Earlier, however, you encountered INA § 240(c)(3), which says, among other things: "No decision on deportability shall be valid unless it is based upon reasonable, substantial, and probative evidence."

Do those two provisions conflict?[12] The "reasonable, substantial, and probative evidence" test is probably indistinguishable from the simpler-sounding "substantial evidence" test more commonly used to review formal agency factfinding. And the latter, in turn, has generally been construed to require only that the evidence in the record enable a reasonable adjudicator to make the challenged finding. See item 4 of the Notes and Questions following the *Woodby* case, above. Perhaps, then, section 242(b)(4)(B), which makes the findings of fact conclusive "unless any reasonable adjudicator would be compelled to conclude to the contrary," is merely the functional equivalent of the traditional "substantial evidence" test. Under that interpretation, sections 242(b)(4)(B) and 240(c)(3) are reconcilable.

At several points, the discussion below refers to changes wrought by the REAL ID Act. Those changes took effect immediately upon the enactment date of May 11, 2005, regardless of when the administratively final removal orders were issued. District courts were required to transfer, to the relevant courts of appeals, all then pending habeas claims challenging removal orders. See REAL ID Act, § 106(b, c).

---

12. It is clear that the phrase "reasonable, substantial, and probative evidence," even though included in a section dealing generally with the conduct of the removal hearing rather than with judicial review, describes the standard of *review*, not the standard of *proof*. The standard of proof, "clear and convincing evidence," is laid out in the immediately preceding sentence.

Those are the general parameters. As the introduction to this section noted, Congress has carved out some large exceptions to the availability of petitions for review. Here are the major ones:

i.   Crime–Related Removal Orders

Under INA § 242(a)(2)(C), "no court shall have jurisdiction to review" a removal order if the person "is removable" on almost any of the crime-related grounds. The deportability grounds that fall within that bar cover aggravated felonies, controlled substance offenses, firearms offenses, other miscellaneous crimes, and two moral turpitude crimes punishable by sentences of at least one year each. *Id.* In *St. Cyr*, below, the Supreme Court interpreted this language as *not* barring review by district courts under the general federal habeas corpus statute, 28 U.S.C. § 2241. In the REAL ID Act of 2005, Congress responded to *St. Cyr* by amending section 242(a)(2)(C) (and all of the other similarly worded court-stripping provisions in the INA) to state, explicitly, that the bar on judicial review supersedes all other provisions of law, statutory or nonstatutory, including specifically 28 U.S.C. § 2241 and other habeas corpus provisions.

Still, this preclusion remains narrower than might first appear. As a compromise, Congress added new INA § 242(a)(2)(D). This provision specifies that the various limitations on judicial review do not preclude "review of constitutional claims or questions of law raised upon a petition for review ..." Rather, as the conference committee report explains, Congress's goal was simply to channel all judicial review into a uniform process that avoids the delays occasioned by the sequence of district court review followed by appeal to the court of appeals. Report 109–72 (109th Cong., 1st Sess.) (May 3, 2005), at 172–75.

Before the REAL ID Act, the courts had effectively recognized at least two situations in which noncitizens who had been ordered removed on crime-related grounds might nonetheless obtain judicial review of their removal orders on questions of law. First, the literal language bars judicial review only when the person "is removable." Because courts always have jurisdiction to determine their own jurisdiction, they have consistently interpreted section 242(a)(2)(C) as *not* barring review of whether the person is, in fact, removable.

Thus, for example, if the deportability ground is conviction of an aggravated felony, the determination of whether the crime in question constitutes an aggravated felony remains reviewable. See, e.g., *Dalton v. Ashcroft*, 257 F.3d 200, 203 (2d Cir. 2001); *Drakes v. Zimski*, 240 F.3d 246 (3d Cir. 2001); *Lewis v. INS*, 194 F.3d 539 (4th Cir. 1999); *Nehme v. INS*, 252 F.3d 415 (5th Cir. 2001); *Guerrero-Perez v. INS*, 242 F.3d 727 (7th Cir. 2001); *Penuliar v. Ashcroft*, 395 F.3d 1037, 1040 (9th Cir. 2005); *contra, Berehe v. INS*, 114 F.3d 159 (10th Cir. 1997). In the face of what was becoming a judicial consensus, the government conceded the point, see *Calcano-Martinez v. INS*, 533 U.S. 348, 350 n.2, 121 S.Ct. 2268, 150 L.Ed.2d 392 (2001), and the Supreme Court in *Leocal v. Ashcroft*, 543 U.S. ___, 125 S.Ct. 377, 160 L.Ed.2d 271 (2004), seems to have agreed sub silentio. The same principle is applied for crimes involving moral turpitude. See, e.g., *Carty v. Ashcroft*, 395 F.3d 1081, 1082–83 (9th Cir. 2005). Both before and after the REAL ID Act, therefore, the main practical impact of section 242(a)(2)(C) has been in the many cases in which noncitizens conceded deportability, applied for discretionary relief, and were denied. (In those situations, judicial review is additionally constrained by the separate bar on review of most exercises of discretion, as discussed below.)

Second, apart from their roles in interpreting and applying the statutory limitations on jurisdiction, pre-REAL ID Act court decisions suggested that section 242(a)(2)(C) did not prevent courts from reviewing claims that raised "substantial constitutional questions." See, e.g., *Calcano-Martinez v. INS*, 533 U.S. 348, 350 n.2, 121 S.Ct. 2268, 150 L.Ed.2d 347 (2001) (noting government's concession that "the courts of appeals retain jurisdiction to review 'substantial constitutional challenges' raised by aliens who come within the strictures of" section 242(a)(2)(C)); James Feroli, *Habeas Corpus Subject Matter Jurisdiction over Final Orders of Removal Pursuant to 28 U.S.C.A. § 2241*, Sept. 2004 Immigration Briefings.

Since both these exemptions from the limitations on petitions for review discussed above (interpretation of statutory jurisdictional limitations and substantial constitutional questions) are questions of law, new section 241(a)(2)(D) effectively codifies both exceptions. Indeed, it extends the exceptions to cover *all* "constitutional claims or questions of law." (Since constitutional questions *are* questions of law, the former reference is probably superfluous anyway.) As for questions of law, therefore, the main effects of these changes would seem to be (1) to expand judicial review in crime-related removal cases to cover all questions of law; and (2) to assure they are reviewed only by courts of appeals rather than allow some cases to originate in the district courts.

Still not entirely clear is the meaning of "questions of law." Does this phrase cover the question whether the administrative authorities correctly applied the law to the facts, or whether as a matter of law the evidence sufficiently supports the findings of fact, or whether as a matter of law the administrative authorities either failed to exercise, or abused, their discretion? Determining whether such claims are now reviewable will entail both interpretation of INA § 242 and, to the extent section 242 is construed to bar their review, determinations of the constitutional constraints on Congress's power to bar habeas review. This subject will be taken up in the Notes and Questions that follow *St. Cyr*, below.

ii.   Denials of Discretionary Relief

Regardless of the ground for deportability, INA § 242(a)(2)(B) strips the courts of jurisdiction to review two groups of discretionary decisions. Like section 242(a)(2)(C) above, this provision does not preclude judicial review of "constitutional claims or questions of law." INA § 242(a)(2)(D), added by REAL ID Act, § 106(a)(1). See generally Daniel Kanstroom, *Surrounding the Hole in the Doughnut: Discretion and Deference in U.S. Immigration Law*, 71 Tulane L. Rev. 703 (1997).

The first prong (B(i)) bars review of "any judgment regarding the granting of relief under" any of several specifically enumerated provisions of the INA. The list includes most of the major affirmative relief provisions available in removal proceedings—cancellation of removal (both part A and part B), voluntary departure, adjustment of status, and waivers of inadmissibility under sections 212(h) (relief from certain crime-related grounds) and 212(i) (relief from inadmissibility based on fraud).[13]

It now seems settled, however, that the bar on review is limited to the discretionary *components* of the named remedies. Recall that the typical affirmative relief provision is in the form "If A, B, and C, then the Attorney General has the discretion to do X." *Legal* issues concerning the applicant's statutory eligibility for discretionary relief are now expressly reviewable. INA § 242(a)(2)(D). As for review of agency factfinding, several courts construed the pre-REAL ID Act version of section 242(a)(2)(B)(i) as not barring judicial review of administrative findings of fact concerning eligibility for affirmative relief. See, e.g. *Reyes-Vasquez v. Ashcroft*, 395 F.3d 903, 907–09 (8th Cir. 2005) (holding BIA finding of no "continuous physical presence" for cancellation of removal purposes non-discretionary and therefore reviewable); *Morales-Morales v. Ashcroft*, 384 F.3d 418, 421–23 (7th Cir. 2004) (same); *Mireles-Valdez v. Ashcroft*, 349 F.3d 213 (5th Cir. 2003) (same); *Gomez-Lopez v. Ashcroft*, 391 F.3d 1109, 1111 (9th Cir. 2004) (holding finding of no "good moral character," for cancellation of removal purposes, non-discretionary and therefore reviewable). *Cf. Romero-Torres v. Ashcroft*, 327 F.3d 887, 889–92 (9th Cir. 2003) (holding that determination concerning "exceptional and extremely unusual hardship," for cancellation of removal purposes, is discretionary and therefore unreviewable, but that legal definition of "child" for purposes of same hardship requirement is discretionary). Nothing in the REAL ID Act purports to supersede those results.

The second prong, INA § 242(a)(2)(B)(ii), covers "any other decision or action of the Attorney General the authority for which is specified under this title to be in the discretion of the Attorney General" [except asylum]. This provision has sweeping consequences, but it too is probably less absolute than it first appears. Thus far it has attracted only a moderate amount of case law. It seems destined to give rise to several issues.

First, the provision does not make all the Attorney General's discretionary decisions unreviewable—only those that are authorized by "this title," which is Title II of the INA. Not covered, therefore, are Attorney General (now Secretary of Homeland Security) decisions under other titles of the INA (for example, those relating to citizenship, in title III) and Attorney General decisions under other statutes (including any immigration-related decisions contained in statutes or statutory provisions that did not amend the INA).

---

13. A separate provision, INA § 212(a)(9)(B)(v), allows discretionary waivers of inadmissibility for certain immigrants who were unlawfully present in the United States but whose citizen or LPR family members would suffer extreme hardship. It then goes on to bar judicial review of denials of such waivers.

Thus, this provision appears to cover discretionary decisions under INA §§ 205 (revocation of visa petition); 207 (refugee admissions); 209 (adjustment of status of refugees); 236 (detention pending removal of arriving noncitizens); 248 (change of nonimmigrant status); and 249 (registry). In each of those cases, title II of the INA expressly bestows a discretionary power on the Attorney General (or the Secretary of Homeland Security).

Other provisions of title II, in contrast, are worded in mandatory terms. See, e.g., INA §§ 204(b) (denial of visa petition); 241(b) (removal to country designated by noncitizen); 241(b)(3) (no removal to country of persecution); 245A (legalization); and 246 (rescission of adjustment of status). In those cases, the courts retain the power to reverse administrative decisions in which findings of fact are not sufficiently supported by the evidence or interpretations of law are held to be erroneous.

Second, it is not clear whether B(ii) reaches those Attorney General decisions that are authorized by regulation rather than by statute. (How might one argue that it does?) A few courts have now weighed in on that issue, and they have split. Several courts have expressly invoked the statute/regulation distinction to conclude that denials of motions to reopen, which are authorized by administrative regulation, are reviewable (for abuse of discretion). See *Yu Zhao v. Gonzales*, 404 F.3d 295 (5th Cir. 2005); *Singh v. Gonzales*, 404 F.3d 1024, 1026–27 (7th Cir. 2005); *Medina–Morales v. Ashcroft*, 362 F.3d 1263 (9th Cir. 2004). (The court in *Singh* also cited INA § 242(b)(6), which requires that judicial review of denials of motions to reopen be consolidated with judicial review of the underlying removal orders. That requirement would make no sense if denials of motions to reopen were not reviewable.) See also *Barker v. Ashcroft*, 382 F.3d 313, 315 (3d Cir. 2003) (holding denials of motion to reopen reviewable, but not addressing the distinction between discretionary authority conferred by statute and that conferred by regulation). Two other courts have held that section 242(a)(2)(B)(ii) bars review of discretionary decisions that are made under powers conferred by *regulations* implementing title II of the statute. See *Yerkovich v. Ashcroft*, 381 F.3d 990 (10th Cir. 2004); *Onyinkwa v. Ashcroft*, 376 F.3d 797, 799 (8th Cir. 2004). In both the latter cases the petitioners had challenged decisions by immigration judges denying continuances.

Third, even when a provision within title II makes relief contingent on the favorable exercise of administrative discretion, it is not clear that all judicial review is barred. As noted with respect to B(i), many denials of discretionary relief are based not on discretionary grounds but on an administrative conclusion that the applicant is statutorily ineligible. The applicant's challenge to the correctness of that determination might be either legal or factual. Again, challenges to the legal conclusions are now expressly exempt from this jurisdictional bar. INA § 242(a)(2)(D). But what if the applicant believes the administrative findings of fact were not supported by the evidence? Suppose, for example, the BIA denies an application for registry under INA § 249 because it does not believe that the applicant entered the United States before 1972. May a court reverse the BIA on the ground that the evidence does not reasonably support that finding? Does INA § 242(a)(2)(B)(ii) preclude judicial review of the eligibility determination? Or was Congress restricting review only of the discretionary component of the decision?

In answering this question, consider first the literal language of section 242(a)(2)(B)(ii). Congress has immunized the "decision or action" that is specified to be in the discretion of the Attorney General. What decision, exactly, is in the Attorney General's discretion? Is it the decision whether to grant relief to a person who is statutorily eligible? Is it the decision whether to find the person eligible in the first place? Both?

Consider also another statutory interpretation technique that you have seen several times already. When Congress uses different phraseology in analogous provisions of the same statute, courts generally find the contrasts deliberate. In that vein, compare section 242(a)(2)(B)(ii) with some of the other INA provisions (especially those amended by IIRIRA) that preclude judicial review. See, e.g., INA §§ 242(a)(2)(B)(i) ("judgment regarding the granting of relief under" specific provisions); 212(d)(12)(A) (no jurisdiction "to review a decision of the Attorney General to grant or deny a waiver under this paragraph"). When Congress wanted to preclude review of the entire decision, and not just the discretionary portion of it, Congress arguably knew how to say so.

Along similar lines, the court in *Nakamoto v. Ashcroft*, 363 F.3d 874, 879 (9th Cir. 2004), construed B(ii) as limited to pure discretionary decisions. A statutory provision that required the Attorney General to decide the bona fides of a marriage used phrases like "in the opinion of the Attorney General" and "it appears to the satisfaction of the Attorney General." Rejecting the government's argument that that language rendered the decision discretionary, the court held the determination reviewable.

Before the REAL ID Act, a related question was whether the limitations imposed by section 242(a)(2)(B)(ii) were confined to removal orders, or whether Congress meant to bar judicial review of INS (now USCIS) decisions even outside the context of removal proceedings. The question is important, because USCIS makes a host of discretionary decisions either before removal proceedings or in contexts unrelated to removal—for example, denials of change of nonimmigrant status, extensions of stay, requests to transfer schools, etc. The REAL ID Act, § 101(f)(2), amended INA § 242(a)(2)(B) to clarify that the jurisdictional bar extends to all the discretionary decisions otherwise covered, regardless of whether they were made in removal proceedings.

Whichever decisions INA § 242(a)(2)(B) insulates from petitions for review, the REAL ID Act reveals Congress's intent to insulate those same claims from habeas corpus. We return to that subject in subsection (b) below.

iii. Expedited Removal Orders

On another front, recall INA § 235(b)(1), which authorizes "expedited removal" of arriving noncitizens whom immigration inspectors believe to be inadmissible on documentary or fraud grounds. The Attorney General has the discretion to extend the expedited removal procedure to those who are present in the United States and unable to prove two years continuous physical presence, INA § 235(b)(1)(A)(iii), and has exercised that authority on several occasions, see section E.1 below. Under INA § 242(a)(2)(A), courts lack the jurisdiction to review, on the merits, either kind of expedited removal order. (A court may use habeas corpus to review a claim that the person is a citizen, or that the person was not in fact the subject of an expedited removal order, or that the expedited removal procedure should not have been used because the person was a returning LPR. See INA § 242(e)(2). But review of the merits is otherwise barred.)

Also with respect to expedited removal, IIRIRA introduced statutory limitations on the power of courts to entertain challenges to the legality of administrative policies and even the constitutionality of the statute itself. Under INA § 242(e)(3)(A), the District Court for the District of Columbia has jurisdiction to decide whether section 235(b)(1) or any implementing regulations are constitutional, as well as jurisdiction to decide whether the Attorney General's regulations or other written policy statements comply with the statute and other laws. But INA § 242(e)(3)(B) says that "[a]ny action instituted under this paragraph must be filed no later than 60 days after [implementation of the challenged rule]".

The REAL ID Act made clear that these provisions too are meant to be habeas-proof. See, e.g., REAL ID Act § 106(a), amending INA §§ 242(a)(2)(A), 242(a)(5). Can Congress constitutionally preclude judicial review of constitutional challenges? (Note that the new exception that allows judicial review for "constitutional claims and questions of law," INA § 242(a)(2)(D), applies only to subsections B and C of section 242(a)(2)— not to the bar on judicial review of expedited removal orders.) For that matter, are there even some nonconstitutional challenges that Congress cannot constitutionally insulate from judicial review? See the habeas corpus discussion below.

iv. Voluntary Departure Regulations

Somewhat analogous problems arise out of INA § 240B(e). Under that subsection, the Attorney General "may by regulation limit eligibility for voluntary departure ..." There are no express statutory constraints on what extra conditions the Attorney General may add. Consequently, as you saw on page 621 above, unless statutory constraints are read in, possible nondelegation questions arise. More pertinent here, the same subsection goes on to bar judicial review of any such regulation. If the courts sanction such an open-ended delegation of power to the executive branch, how are they likely to treat the provision barring judicial review of the executive decision? Will the combination of congressional and judicial absence from the process trouble the courts? Or will the breadth of the executive power, if anything, counsel in favor of judicial abstention, on the ground that, within the meaning of the Administrative Procedure Act, Congress has "committed" the question to agency discretion? Recall the analogous discussion of visa denials, on pages 481–82 above.

v. Prosecutorial Discretion

Yet another court-stripping provision is INA § 242(g). It bars judicial review of such decisions as whether to commence removal proceedings (a matter of generally unreviewable prosecutorial discretion) and whether to execute a removal order (rather than temporarily stay removal). See *Reno v. American–Arab Anti–Discrimination Committee*, 525 U.S. 471, 119 S.Ct. 936, 142 L.Ed.2d 940 (1999); *Botezatu v. INS*, 195 F.3d 311, 313 (7th Cir. 1999); Nancy Morawetz, *Predicting the Meaning of INA § 242(b)(9)*, 14 Georgetown Immigration L.J. 453 (2000); Hiroshi Motomura, *Judicial Review in Immigration Cases after AADC: Lessons from Civil Procedure*, 14 Georgetown Immigration L.J. 385 (2000); Leti Volpp, *Court-Stripping and Class–Wide Relief: A Response to Judicial Review in Immigration Cases after AADC*, 14 Georgetown Immigration L.J. 463 (2000).

vi. Detention Decisions

Another court-stripping provision relates to detention. While removal proceedings are pending, various administrative officials have the discretion whether to detain the noncitizen, release him or her on bond, or grant parole without requiring bond. INA § 236(a). By way of exception, detention is mandatory for people who are deportable under most of the criminal provisions or the terrorist provisions. INA § 236(c). As you saw earlier (pages 211–24 above), the Supreme Court upheld the constitutionality of this mandatory detention provision in *Demore v. Kim*, 538 U.S. 510, 123 S.Ct. 1708, 155 L.Ed.2d 724 (2003).

Under INA § 236(e), "[n]o court may set aside any action or decision of the Attorney General under this section regarding the detention or release of any alien or the grant, revocation, or denial of bond or parole." While section 236(e) literally bars review of the Attorney General's decisions implementing section 236, the Court in *Demore* read the provision as not barring the use of habeas corpus to challenge the constitutionality of section 236 itself. Does this mean a court may also review the Attorney General's future decision to apply section 236 in a particular case? On the one hand, the Court in *Demore* emphasized that the challenge before it was to the constitutionality of the statute, rather than to the Attorney General's application of it to the facts of the case. On the other hand, the Court also relied heavily on the fact that Congress had not expressly precluded habeas corpus, a rationale equally applicable to challenges to the application of the statute. The REAL ID Act did not change INA § 236(e), and the conference committee report stated that the Act "would not preclude habeas review over challenges to detention that are independent of challenges to removal orders." Report 109–72 accompanying H.R. 1268 (109th Cong., 1st Sess.) (May 3, 2005), at 175.

b.   HABEAS CORPUS[14]

As noted in the introduction to this subsection, habeas corpus was the usual method for obtaining judicial review of deportation orders, long before Congress in 1961 expressly authorized petitions for review of deportation orders in the courts of appeals. Even after 1961, when the general rule was that petitions for review were the *exclusive* means for reviewing deportation orders, Congress carved out an express exception for habeas corpus. Former INA § 106(a)(10) (pre–1996) read: "Any alien held in custody pursuant to an order of deportation may obtain judicial review thereof by habeas corpus proceedings."

In 1996, in AEDPA § 401(e)(3), Congress repealed INA § 106(a)(10). With one minor exception the INA no longer recognizes habeas as an alternative to the petition for review. Under 28 U.S.C. § 2241, the general federal habeas statute, "[w]rits of habeas corpus may be granted by the Supreme Court, any justice thereof, the district courts and any circuit judge within their respective jurisdictions." As you have seen, the REAL ID Act now expressly forecloses the use of 28 U.S.C. § 2241 in removal proceedings.

Keep in mind, however, that habeas corpus is grounded in the United States Constitution. Article I, § 9, clause 2 says: "The Privilege of the Writ of Habeas Corpus shall not be suspended, unless when in Cases of Rebellion or Invasion the public Safety may require it." This provision not only directly constrains Congress's power to suspend the writ of habeas corpus, but also influences courts' interpretations of statutory provisions that might otherwise be read to suspend the writ. The suspension clause aside, the constitutionality of the 1996 court-stripping provisions has been questioned on both procedural due process grounds (fundamental fairness requires an opportunity for judicial review of administrative or even

---

14. There has been some fine recent commentary on the use of habeas corpus in removal cases after AEDPA and IIRIRA (but before the REAL ID Act of 2005). For a sampling, see Lenni Benson, *The New World of Judicial Review of Removal Orders*, 12 Georgetown Immigration L.J. 233 (1998); Lenni Benson, *Back to the Future: Congress Attacks the Right to Judicial Review of Immigration Proceedings*, 29 Connecticut L. Rev. 1411 (1997); David Cole, *Jurisdiction and Liberty: Habeas Corpus and Due Process as Limits on Congress's Control of Federal Jurisdiction*, 86 Georgetown L.J. 2481 (1998); Richard H. Fallon, *Applying the Suspension Clause to Immigration Cases*, 98 Columbia L. Rev. 1068 (1998); M. Isabel Medina, *Judicial Review—A Nice Thing? Article III, Separa-* *tion of Powers and the Illegal Immigration Reform and Immigrant Responsibility Act of 1996*, 29 Connecticut L. Rev. 1525 (1997); Gerald L. Neuman, *The Habeas Corpus Suspension Clause After INS v. St. Cyr*, 33 Columbia Human Rights L. Rev. 555 (2002); Gerald L. Neuman, *Habeas Corpus, Executive Detention, and the Removal of Aliens*, 98 Columbia L. Rev. 961 (1998); Kathleen M. Sullivan, *Commentary on Reno v. American–Arab Anti–Discrimination Committee*, 4 BIB 249 (Mar. 15, 1999); see also Stephen H. Legomsky, *The Deportation Process, the War on Independence, and Reverse Darwinism: Why We Need Habeas Corpus More than Ever*, 91 Cornell L. Rev., issue #2 (forthcoming 2006); see generally Larry W. Yackle, Federal Courts–Habeas Corpus (2003).

congressional decisions) and separation of powers grounds (it is the job of the judiciary to interpret the law).

As you will discover presently, the Supreme Court in 2001 interpreted the pre-REAL ID Act version of one of the 1996 provisions as not foreclosing habeas corpus. It did so in order to avoid "serious constitutional questions" concerning the suspension clause. That opinion (*St. Cyr*) is reproduced below. But first, read the following excerpt from one of the classic discussions of this subject. The author focuses specifically on habeas corpus, but elements of his reasoning apply to court-stripping provisions generally.

Henry M. Hart, Jr., The Power of Congress to Limit the Jurisdiction of Federal Courts: An Exercise in Dialectic
66 Harvard L.Rev. 1362, 1386–96 (1953).

Q: * * * What happens if the Government is hurting people and not simply refusing to help them? Suppose Congress authorizes a program of direct action by government officials against private persons or private property. Suppose, further, that it not only dispenses with judicial enforcement but either limits the jurisdiction of the federal courts to inquire into what the officials do or denies it altogether.

A.   Relief Under General Jurisdiction

A.   * * * Obviously, the answer is that the validity of the jurisdictional limitation depends on the validity of the program itself, or the particular part of it in question. If the court finds that what is being done is invalid, its duty is simply to declare the jurisdictional limitation invalid also, and then proceed under the general grant of jurisdiction.

Q.   That can't be as easy as you make it sound. Is that what the federal courts actually do?

A.   That's what they've often done.

Take the clearest case—an attempt by Congress to authorize the administrative imposition of infamous punishment. That, substantially, is *Wong Wing v. United States,* one of the bulwarks of the Constitution. There Congress had directed that any Chinese person adjudged in a summary proceeding by any judge or United States commissioner to be in the country unlawfully should first be imprisoned at hard labor for not more than a year and then deported. In the exercise of its general jurisdiction in habeas corpus, the Court ordered the prisoners discharged from such imprisonment—without prejudice of course to their detention according to law for deportation.

In *Lipke v. Lederer,* the Court found that a payment required by the tax laws was actually a penalty enforceable only by the process of the criminal law. It exercised general federal question jurisdiction to enjoin summary collection, in spite of the statute prohibiting injunctions against federal taxes.

Q.   In those cases the whole extra-judicial procedure was found unconstitutional. That's an unusual situation. What if the party simply says that the executive officers are proceeding erroneously in his particular case?

A.   If he has a constitutional right to have that question examined in court, and the court has general jurisdiction, it can disregard any special jurisdictional limitation and go ahead and examine it.

That's what the Court did, for example, in *Ng Fung Ho v. White*. That case involved an administrative order to deport an asserted alien who claimed to be a citizen. On habeas corpus the court held that the Due Process Clause entitled the claimant to a trial *de novo* and an independent judicial judgment on the issue of citizenship; and it directed the district court to give it to him. * * *

* * *

Q.   But even admitted[a] aliens have access to the courts on habeas corpus on the question of their right to enter or remain in the country, don't they?

A.   Yes, although the scope of review, of course, falls short of trial *de novo*. Indeed, judicial review in exclusion and deportation cases is one of the most impressive examples of the general point I am making, and currently provides a testing crucible of basic principle.

The structure of review has been developed by the courts in the face of a statutory plan of administrative control which looked neither to their help nor interference. For years the statutes have provided that orders of the Secretary of Labor (now of the Attorney General) in these matters shall be "final."

Q.   How then can aliens have any rights to assert in habeas corpus? I thought they came and stayed only at the pleasure of Congress.

A.   The Supreme Court seemed to think so, too, at first. In its earliest decisions the Court started with the premise of plenary legislative power and on that basis seemed to be prepared to take the word "final" in the statutes literally and to decline any review whatever, even in deportation cases.

Before long, however, it began to see that the premise needed to be qualified—that a power to lay down general rules, even if it were plenary, did not necessarily include a power to be arbitrary or to authorize administrative officials to be arbitrary. It saw that, on the contrary, the very existence of a jurisdiction in habeas corpus, coupled with the constitutional guarantee of due process, implied a regime of law. It saw that in such a regime the courts had a responsibility to see that statutory authority was not transgressed, that a reasonable procedure was used in exercising the authority, and—seemingly also—that human beings were not unreasonably

---

a. By "admitted aliens," Professor Hart did not mean those who have been admitted into the United States. He was referring to people who admit they are "aliens," as opposed to people like Ng Fung Ho who claim to be citizens.—Ed.

subjected, even by direction of Congress, to an uncontrolled official discretion.

Under the benign influence of these ideas, the law grew and flourished, like Egypt under the rule of Joseph. Thousands of cases were decided whose presence in the courts cannot be explained on any other basis.[86] But what the status of many of these cases is now is not altogether clear.

Q. Why?

A. There arose up new justices in Washington which knew not Joseph. Citing only the harsh precepts of the very earliest decisions, they began to decide cases accordingly, as if nothing had happened in the years between.

In the *Knauff* case, Justice Minton said that, "Whatever the rule may be concerning deportation of persons who have gained entry into the United States, it is not within the province of any court, unless expressly authorized by law, to review the determination of the political branch of the Government to exclude a given alien." Since Congress has never expressly authorized any court to review an exclusion order, this statement either ignores or renders obsolete every habeas corpus case in the books involving an exclusion proceeding.

On the procedural side, Justice Minton went so far as to say that, "Whatever the procedure authorized by Congress is, it is due process as far as an alien denied entry is concerned," a patently preposterous proposition.

Justice Clark repeated and applied both statements in the *Mezei* case.

Q. Then we're back where we started half a century ago?

A. Oh no. The aberrations have been largely confined to admission cases. In deportations, for the most part, the Court has adhered to the sound and humane philosophy of the middle period. In some respects it has even extended its applications.

What is happening is what so often happens when there has been a development in the law of which the judges are incompletely aware. Some decisions follow the earlier precedents and some the later, until the conflict of principle becomes intolerable, and it gets ironed out.

Q. Do you mean to say that you don't think there are any material differences between the case of an alien trying to get into the country and the case of one whom the Government is trying to put out?

A. No. Of course there are differences in these alien cases—not only those simple ones but many others. But such differences are material only in determining the content of due process in the particular situation. What process is due always depends upon the circumstances, and the Due Process Clause is always flexible enough to take the circumstances into account.

---

86. See the hundreds of pages of decisions on the writ of habeas corpus in both admission and deportation cases listed under the heading *Aliens* in 3 Fed. Dig. 137–457 (1940).

The distinctions the Court has been drawing recently, however, are of a different order. They are distinctions between when the Constitution applies and when it does not apply at all. Any such distinction as that produces a conflict of basic principle, and is inadmissible.

Q.   What basic principle?

A.   The great and generating principle of this whole body of law—that the Constitution always applies when a court is sitting with jurisdiction in habeas corpus. For then the court has always to inquire, not only whether the statutes have been observed, but whether the petitioner before it has been "deprived of life, liberty, or property, without due process of law," or injured in any other way in violation of the fundamental law.

That is the premise of the deportation cases,[93] and it applies in exactly the same way in admission cases. The harsh early decisions announcing a contrary premise applied such a contrary premise without distinction in both deportations and admissions. Indeed, Justice Minton cited early admission and deportation precedents indiscriminately in *Knauff*, without noticing that the principle which had compelled repudiation of the deportation precedents required repudiation also of the others.

That principle forbids a constitutional court with jurisdiction in habeas corpus from ever accepting as an adequate return to the writ the mere statement that what has been done is authorized by act of Congress. The inquiry remains, if *Marbury v. Madison* still stands, whether the act of Congress is consistent with the fundamental law. Only upon such a principle could the court reject, as it surely would, a return to the writ which informed it that the applicant for admission lay stretched upon a rack with pins driven in behind his finger nails pursuant to authority duly conferred by statute in order to secure the information necessary to determine his admissibility. The same principle which would justify rejection of this return imposes responsibility to inquire into the adequacy of other returns.

Granting that the requirements of due process must vary with the circumstances, and allowing them all the flexibility that can conceivably be claimed, it still remains true that the court is obliged, by the presuppositions of its whole jurisdiction in this area, to decide whether what has been done is consistent with due process—and not simply pass back the buck to an assertedly all-powerful and unimpeachable Congress.

* * *

93. See * * * Heikkila v. Barber, 345 U.S. 229 (1953). Speaking for the Court, Justice Clark there held squarely that judicial review in deportation cases is "required by the Constitution." He said that "regardless of whether or not the scope of inquiry on habeas corpus has been expanded, the function of the courts has always been limited to the enforcement of due process requirements." *Id.* at 236.

It is to be observed that since the courts in habeas corpus have always enforced statutory requirements, too, Justice Clark must here be understood as saying that the Constitution gives the alien a right, among others, to have the statutes observed. The statement seems to apply equally to admission cases. * * *

Q. But that is what the Court has held. And so I guess that's that.

A. No, it isn't.

The deepest assumptions of the legal order require that the decisions of the highest court in the land be accepted as settling the rights and wrongs of the particular matter immediately in controversy. But the judges who sit for the time being on the court have no authority to remake by fiat alone the fabric of principle by which future cases are to be decided. They are only the custodians of the law and not the owners of it. The law belongs to the people of the country, and to the hundreds of thousands of lawyers and judges who through the years have struggled, in their behalf, to make it coherent and intelligible and responsive to the people's sense of justice.

And so, when justices of the Supreme Court sit down and write opinions in behalf of the Court which ignore the painful forward steps of a whole half century of adjudication, making no effort to relate what then is being done to what the Court has done before, they write without authority for the future. The appeal to principle is still open and, so long as courts of the United States sit with general jurisdiction in habeas corpus, that means an appeal to them and their successors.

* * *

QUESTION

Based on what you saw in chapter 2 concerning the plenary congressional power over immigration, and after reading the excerpts from Professor Hart's dialogue, do you think the Constitution requires judicial review of administratively final orders removing deportable noncitizens? You should revisit this question after reading the case that follows.

INS v. St. Cyr

Supreme Court of the United States, 2001.
533 U.S. 289, 121 S.Ct. 2271, 150 L.Ed.2d 347.

STEVENS, J., delivered the opinion of the Court, in which KENNEDY, SOUTER, GINSBURG, and BREYER, JJ., joined. O'CONNOR, J., filed a dissenting opinion. SCALIA, J., filed a dissenting opinion, in which REHNQUIST, C. J., and THOMAS, J., joined, and in which O'CONNOR, J., joined, as to Parts I and III.

■ JUSTICE STEVENS delivered the opinion of the Court.

Both the Antiterrorism and Effective Death Penalty Act of 1996 (AEDPA), enacted on April 24, 1996, and the Illegal Immigration Reform and Immigrant Responsibility Act of 1996 (IIRIRA), enacted on September 30, 1996, contain comprehensive amendments to the Immigration and Nationality Act (INA). This case raises two important questions about the impact of those amendments. The first question is a procedural one, concerning the effect of those amendments on the availability of habeas corpus jurisdiction under 28 U.S.C. § 2241. The second question is a substantive one, concerning the impact of the amendments on conduct that occurred before their enactment and on the availability of discretionary relief from deportation.

Respondent, Enrico St. Cyr, is a citizen of Haiti who was admitted to the United States as a lawful permanent resident in 1986. Ten years later, on March 8, 1996 [just before both AEDPA and IIRIRA—Ed.], he pled guilty in a state court to a charge of selling a controlled substance in violation of Connecticut law. That conviction made him deportable. * * *

[Before AEDPA, the relief for which St. Cyr would have been eligible was former INA § 212(c). AEDPA and IIRIRA together replaced section 212(c) with cancellation of removal, part A, for which "aggravated felons" (a category that covers St. Cyr) are ineligible. See pages 574–81 above.— Ed.]

In his habeas corpus petition, respondent has alleged that the restrictions on discretionary relief from deportation contained in the 1996 statutes do not apply to removal proceedings brought against an alien who pled guilty to a deportable crime before their enactment. The District Court accepted jurisdiction of his application and agreed with his submission. In accord with the decisions of four other Circuits, the Court of Appeals for the Second Circuit affirmed. The importance of both questions warranted our grant of certiorari.

* * *

In the Attorney General's opinion, these amendments have entirely withdrawn his § 212(c) authority to waive deportation for aliens previously convicted of aggravated felonies. Moreover, as a result of other amendments adopted in AEDPA and IIRIRA, the Attorney General also maintains that there is no judicial forum available to decide whether these statutes did, in fact, deprive him of the power to grant such relief. As we shall explain below, we disagree on both points. In our view, a federal court does have jurisdiction to decide the merits of the legal question, and the District Court and the Court of Appeals decided that question correctly in this case.

II

The first question we must consider is whether the District Court retains jurisdiction under the general habeas corpus statute, 28 U.S.C. § 2241, to entertain St. Cyr's challenge. His application for a writ raises a pure question of law. He does not dispute any of the facts that establish his deportability or the conclusion that he is deportable. Nor does he contend that he would have any right to have an unfavorable exercise of the Attorney General's discretion reviewed in a judicial forum. Rather, he contests the Attorney General's conclusion that, as a matter of statutory interpretation, he is not eligible for discretionary relief.

The District Court held, and the Court of Appeals agreed, that it had jurisdiction to answer that question in a habeas corpus proceeding. The INS argues, however, that four sections of the 1996 statutes—specifically, § 401(e) of AEDPA and three sections of IIRIRA (INA §§ 242(a)(1),

242(a)(2)(C), and 242(b)(9))—stripped the courts of jurisdiction to decide the question of law presented by respondent's habeas corpus application.

For the INS to prevail it must overcome both the strong presumption in favor of judicial review of administrative action and the longstanding rule requiring a clear statement of congressional intent to repeal habeas jurisdiction. * * * Implications from statutory text or legislative history are not sufficient to repeal habeas jurisdiction; instead, Congress must articulate specific and unambiguous statutory directives to effect a repeal. * * *

In this case, the plain statement rule draws additional reinforcement from other canons of statutory construction. First, as a general matter, when a particular interpretation of a statute invokes the outer limits of Congress' power, we expect a clear indication that Congress intended that result. * * * Second, if an otherwise acceptable construction of a statute would raise serious constitutional problems, and where an alternative interpretation of the statute is "fairly possible," we are obligated to construe the statute to avoid such problems.

A construction of the amendments at issue that would entirely preclude review of a pure question of law by any court would give rise to substantial constitutional questions. Article I, § 9, cl. 2, of the Constitution provides: "The Privilege of the Writ of Habeas Corpus shall not be suspended, unless when in Cases of Rebellion or Invasion the public Safety may require it." Because of that Clause, some "judicial intervention in deportation cases" is unquestionably "required by the Constitution."

Unlike the provisions of AEDPA that we construed in Felker v. Turpin (1996), this case involves an alien subject to a federal removal order rather than a person confined pursuant to a state-court conviction. Accordingly, regardless of whether the protection of the Suspension Clause encompasses all cases covered by the 1867 Amendment extending the protection of the writ to state prisoners, or by subsequent legal developments, at the absolute minimum, the Suspension Clause protects the writ "as it existed in 1789."

At its historical core, the writ of habeas corpus has served as a means of reviewing the legality of executive detention, and it is in that context that its protections have been strongest. * * *

Notwithstanding the historical use of habeas corpus to remedy unlawful executive action, the INS argues that this case falls outside the traditional scope of the writ at common law. It acknowledges that the writ protected an individual who was held without legal authority, but argues that the writ would not issue where "an official had statutory authorization to detain the individual but ... the official was not properly exercising his discretionary power to determine whether the individual should be released." In this case, the INS points out, there is no dispute that the INS had authority in law to hold St. Cyr, as he is eligible for removal. St. Cyr counters that there is historical evidence of the writ issuing to redress the improper exercise of official discretion.

St. Cyr's constitutional position also finds some support in our prior immigration cases. In Heikkila v. Barber, the Court observed that the then-existing statutory immigration scheme "had the effect of precluding judicial intervention in deportation cases except insofar as it was required by the Constitution"—and that scheme, as discussed below, did allow for review on habeas of questions of law concerning an alien's eligibility for discretionary relief. Therefore, while the INS' historical arguments are not insubstantial, the ambiguities in the scope of the exercise of the writ at common law identified by St. Cyr, and the suggestions in this Court's prior decisions as to the extent to which habeas review could be limited consistent with the Constitution, convince us that the Suspension Clause questions that would be presented by the INS' reading of the immigration statutes before us are difficult and significant.

In sum, even assuming that the Suspension Clause protects only the writ as it existed in 1789, there is substantial evidence to support the proposition that pure questions of law like the one raised by the respondent in this case could have been answered in 1789 by a common law judge with power to issue the writ of habeas corpus. It necessarily follows that a serious Suspension Clause issue would be presented if we were to accept the INS's submission that the 1996 statutes have withdrawn that power from federal judges and provided no adequate substitute for its exercise. See Hart, The Power of Congress to Limit the Jurisdiction of Federal Courts: An Exercise in Dialectic, 66 Harv. L. Rev. 1362, 1395–1397 (1953). The necessity of resolving such a serious and difficult constitutional issue—and the desirability of avoiding that necessity—simply reinforce the reasons for requiring a clear and unambiguous statement of constitutional intent.

Moreover, to conclude that the writ is no longer available in this context would represent a departure from historical practice in immigration law. The writ of habeas corpus has always been available to review the legality of executive detention. Federal courts have been authorized to issue writs of habeas corpus since the enactment of the Judiciary Act of 1789, and § 2241 of the Judicial Code provides that federal judges may grant the writ of habeas corpus on the application of a prisoner held "in custody in violation of the Constitution or laws or treaties of the United States." 28 U.S.C. § 2241. Before and after the enactment in 1875 of the first statute regulating immigration, that jurisdiction was regularly invoked on behalf of noncitizens, particularly in the immigration context.

Until the enactment of the 1952 Immigration and Nationality Act, the sole means by which an alien could test the legality of his or her deportation order was by bringing a habeas corpus action in district court. In such cases, other than the question whether there was some evidence to support the order,[27] the courts generally did not review factual determinations made by the Executive. However, they did review the Executive's legal determinations. * * * In case after case, courts answered questions of law

---

27. See, e.g., United States ex rel. Vajtauer v. Commissioner of Immigration (Supreme Court, 1927) (holding that deportation "on charges unsupported by any evidence is a denial of due process which may be corrected on habeas corpus").

in habeas corpus proceedings brought by aliens challenging Executive interpretations of the immigration laws.

Habeas courts also regularly answered questions of law that arose in the context of discretionary relief.[30] Traditionally, courts recognized a distinction between eligibility for discretionary relief, on the one hand, and the favorable exercise of discretion, on the other hand. See Neuman, 113 Harv. L. Rev., at 1991 (noting the "strong tradition in habeas corpus law . . . that subjects the legally erroneous failure to exercise discretion, unlike a substantively unwise exercise of discretion, to inquiry on the writ"). Eligibility that was "governed by specific statutory standards" provided "a right to a ruling on an applicant's eligibility," even though the actual granting of relief was "not a matter of right under any circumstances, but rather is in all cases a matter of grace." Thus, even though the actual suspension of deportation authorized by § 19(c) of the Immigration Act of 1917 was a matter of grace, in United States ex rel. Accardi v. Shaughnessy (1954), we held that a deportable alien had a right to challenge the Executive's failure to exercise the discretion authorized by the law. The exercise of the District Court's habeas corpus jurisdiction to answer a pure question of law in this case is entirely consistent with the exercise of such jurisdiction in Accardi.

Thus, under the pre–1996 statutory scheme—and consistent with its common-law antecedents—it is clear that St. Cyr could have brought his challenge to the Board of Immigration Appeals' legal determination in a habeas corpus petition under 28 U.S.C. § 2241. The INS argues, however, that AEDPA and IIRIRA contain four provisions that express a clear and unambiguous statement of Congress' intent to bar petitions brought under § 2241, despite the fact that none of them mention that section. * * * [Here the Court concludes that none of the cited provisions clearly eliminated habeas review under section 2241—Ed.]

* * *

If it were clear that the question of law could be answered in another judicial forum, it might be permissible to accept the INS' reading of § 242. But the absence of such a forum, coupled with the lack of a clear, unambiguous, and express statement of congressional intent to preclude judicial consideration on habeas of such an important question of law, strongly counsels against adopting a construction that would raise serious constitutional questions.[38] Accordingly, we conclude that habeas jurisdiction under § 2241 was not repealed by AEDPA and IIRIRA.

---

30. Indeed, under the pre–1952 regime which provided only what Heikkila termed the constitutional minimum of review, on habeas lower federal courts routinely reviewed decisions under the Seventh Proviso, the statutory predecessor to § 212(c), to ensure the lawful exercise of discretion. During the same period, habeas was also used to review legal questions that arose in the context of the Government's exercise of other forms of discretionary relief under the 1917 Act.

38. The dissent argues that our decision will afford more rights to criminal aliens than to noncriminal aliens. However, as we have noted, the scope of review on habeas is considerably more limited than on APA-style

III

[Having found jurisdiction, the Court in this section of the opinion addresses the merits.—Ed.]

* * *

* * * We therefore hold that § 212(c) relief remains available for aliens, like respondent, whose convictions were obtained through plea agreements and who, notwithstanding those convictions, would have been eligible for § 212(c) relief at the time of their plea under the law then in effect.

The judgment is affirmed.

It is so ordered.

■ JUSTICE O'CONNOR, dissenting.

I join Parts I and III of JUSTICE SCALIA's dissenting opinion in this case. I do not join Part II because I believe that, assuming, arguendo, that the Suspension Clause guarantees some minimum extent of habeas review, the right asserted by the alien in this case falls outside the scope of that review for the reasons explained by JUSTICE SCALIA in Part II–B of his dissenting opinion. The question whether the Suspension Clause assures habeas jurisdiction in this particular case properly is resolved on this ground alone, and there is no need to say more.

■ JUSTICE SCALIA, with whom the CHIEF JUSTICE and JUSTICE THOMAS join, and with whom JUSTICE O'CONNOR joins as to Parts I and III, dissenting.

The Court today finds ambiguity in the utterly clear language of a statute that forbids the district court (and all other courts) to entertain the claims of aliens such as respondent St. Cyr, who have been found deportable by reason of their criminal acts. It fabricates a superclear statement, "magic words" requirement for the congressional expression of such an intent, unjustified in law and unparalleled in any other area of our jurisprudence. And as the fruit of its labors, it brings forth a version of the statute that affords criminal aliens more opportunities for delay-inducing judicial review than are afforded to non-criminal aliens, or even than were afforded to criminal aliens prior to this legislation concededly designed to expedite their removal. Because it is clear that the law deprives us of jurisdiction to entertain this suit, I respectfully dissent.

I

In categorical terms that admit of no exception, [IIRIRA] unambiguously repeals the application of 28 U.S.C. § 2241 (the general habeas corpus provision), and of all other provisions for judicial review, to deportation challenges brought by certain kinds of criminal aliens. [Here Justice

review. Moreover, this case raises only a pure question of law as to respondent's statutory eligibility for discretionary relief, not, as the dissent suggests, an objection to the manner in which discretion was exercised. As to the question of timing and congruent means of review, we note that Congress could, without raising any constitutional questions, provide an adequate substitute through the courts of appeals. * * *

Scalia explains why he feels the then existing statute clearly prohibited habeas review even though it did not refer specifically to habeas corpus or to 28 U.S.C. § 2241—Ed.]

* * *

It has happened before—too frequently, alas—that courts have distorted plain statutory text in order to produce a "more sensible" result. The unique accomplishment of today's opinion is that the result it produces is as far removed from what is sensible as its statutory construction is from the language of the text. One would have to study our statute books for a long time to come up with a more unlikely disposition. By authorizing § 2241 habeas review in the district court but foreclosing review in the court of appeals, the Court's interpretation routes all legal challenges to removal orders brought by criminal aliens to the district court, to be adjudicated under that court's § 2241 habeas authority, which specifies no time limits. After review by that court, criminal aliens will presumably have an appeal as of right to the court of appeals, and can then petition this Court for a writ of certiorari. In contrast, noncriminal aliens seeking to challenge their removal orders—for example, those charged with having been inadmissible at the time of entry, with having failed to maintain their nonimmigrant status, with having procured a visa through a marriage that was not bona fide, or with having become, within five years after the date of entry, a public charge—will still presumably be required to proceed directly to the court of appeals by way of petition for review, under the restrictive modified Hobbs Act review provisions set forth in § 242(a)(1), including the 30–day filing deadline, see § 242(b)(1). In fact, prior to the enactment of IIRIRA, criminal aliens also had to follow this procedure for immediate modified Hobbs Act review in the court of appeals. The Court has therefore succeeded in perverting a statutory scheme designed to expedite the removal of criminal aliens into one that now affords them more opportunities for (and layers of) judicial review (and hence more opportunities for delay) than are afforded non-criminal aliens—and more than were afforded criminal aliens prior to the enactment of IIRIRA. This outcome speaks for itself; no Congress ever imagined it.

To excuse the violence it does to the statutory text, the Court invokes the doctrine of constitutional doubt, which it asserts is raised by the Suspension Clause, U.S. Const., Art. I, § 9, cl. 2. This uses one distortion to justify another, transmogrifying a doctrine designed to maintain "a just respect for the legislature," into a means of thwarting the clearly expressed intent of the legislature. The doctrine of constitutional doubt is * * * a device for interpreting what the statute says—not for ignoring what the statute says in order to avoid the trouble of determining whether what it says is unconstitutional. * * *

In the remainder of this opinion I address the question the Court should have addressed: Whether these provisions of IIRIRA are unconstitutional.

II

A. The Suspension Clause of the Constitution, Art. I, § 9, cl. 2, provides as follows:

"The Privilege of the Writ of Habeas Corpus shall not be suspended, unless when in Cases of Rebellion or Invasion the public Safety may require it."

A straightforward reading of this text discloses that it does not guarantee any content to (or even the existence of) the writ of habeas corpus, but merely provides that the writ shall not (except in case of rebellion or invasion) be suspended. * * *

To "suspend" the writ was not to fail to enact it, much less to refuse to accord it particular content. * * * This was a distinct abuse of majority power, and one that had manifested itself often in the Framers' experience: temporarily but entirely eliminating the "Privilege of the Writ" for a certain geographic area or areas, or for a certain class or classes of individuals. * * *

In the present case, of course, Congress has not temporarily withheld operation of the writ, but has permanently altered its content. That is, to be sure, an act subject to majoritarian abuse, as is Congress's framing (or its determination not to frame) a habeas statute in the first place. But that is not the majoritarian abuse against which the Suspension Clause was directed. It is no more irrational to guard against the common and well known "suspension" abuse, without guaranteeing any particular habeas right that enjoys immunity from suspension, than it is, in the Equal Protection Clause, to guard against unequal application of the laws, without guaranteeing any particular law which enjoys that protection. * * *

The Court cites many cases which it says establish that it is a "serious and difficult constitutional issue" whether the Suspension Clause prohibits the elimination of habeas jurisdiction effected by IIRIRA. Every one of those cases, however, pertains not to the meaning of the Suspension Clause, but to the content of the habeas corpus provision of the United States Code, which is quite a different matter. * * *

* * *

B. Even if one were to assume that the Suspension Clause, despite its text and the Marshall Court's understanding, guarantees some constitutional minimum of habeas relief, that minimum would assuredly not embrace the rarified right asserted here: the right to judicial compulsion of the exercise of Executive discretion (which may be exercised favorably or unfavorably) regarding a prisoner's release. If one reads the Suspension Clause as a guarantee of habeas relief, the obvious question presented is: What habeas relief? There are only two alternatives, the first of which is too absurd to be seriously entertained. It could be contended that Congress "suspends" the writ whenever it eliminates any prior ground for the writ that it adopted. Thus, if Congress should ever (in the view of this Court) have authorized immediate habeas corpus—without the need to exhaust administrative remedies—for a person arrested as an illegal alien, Congress would never be able (in the light of sad experience) to revise that disposition. The Suspension Clause, in other words, would be a one-way ratchet that enshrines in the Constitution every grant of habeas jurisdiction. This is, as I say, too absurd to be contemplated, and I shall contemplate it no further.

The other alternative is that the Suspension Clause guarantees the common-law right of habeas corpus, as it was understood when the Constitution was ratified. There is no doubt whatever that this did not include the right to obtain discretionary release. The Court notes with apparent credulity respondent's contention "that there is historical evidence of the writ issuing to redress the improper exercise of official discretion". The only Framing-era or earlier cases it alludes to in support of that contention establish no such thing. * * *

* * *

III

Given the insubstantiality of the due process and Article III arguments against barring judicial review of respondent's claim (the Court does not even bother to mention them, and the Court of Appeals barely acknowledges them), I will address them only briefly.

The Due Process Clause does not "requir[e] judicial determination of" respondent's claim. Respondent has no legal entitlement to suspension of deportation, no matter how appealing his case. "The Attorney General's suspension of deportation [is] 'an act of grace' which is accorded pursuant to her 'unfettered discretion,' and [can be likened, as Judge Learned Hand observed] to 'a judge's power to suspend the execution of a sentence, or the President's to pardon a convict.' " * * *

Article III, § 1's investment of the "judicial Power of the United States" in the federal courts does not prevent Congress from committing the adjudication of respondent's legal claim wholly to "non-Article III federal adjudicative bodies". The notion that Article III requires every Executive determination, on a question of law or of fact, to be subject to judicial review has no support in our jurisprudence. * * *

The Court has created a version of IIRIRA that is not only unrecognizable to its framers (or to anyone who can read) but gives the statutory scheme precisely the opposite of its intended effect, affording criminal aliens more opportunities for delay-inducing judicial review than others have, or even than criminal aliens had prior to the enactment of this legislation. Because § 2241's exclusion of judicial review is unmistakably clear, and unquestionably constitutional, both this Court and the courts below were without power to entertain respondent's claims. I would set aside the judgment of the court below and remand with instructions to have the District Court dismiss for want of jurisdiction. I respectfully dissent from the judgment of the Court.

NOTES AND QUESTIONS

1.   As you have seen, the specific statutory language that the Supreme Court interpreted in *St. Cyr* has now been amended. The REAL ID Act makes clear that statutory habeas corpus is no longer available to review final administrative orders of removal. But the opinion in *St. Cyr* remains essential reading. First, the case illustrates the time-honored judicial technique of reading deportation (and other) statutes in such a way as to avoid serious constitutional problems. See *Zadvydas* and *Kim Ho Ma*, discussed on pages 191–208 above. Second, and of more direct relevance here, the amendments made by the REAL ID Act will now require the courts to confront directly the constitutional questions discussed by both the majority and the dissent in *St. Cyr*.

2.   Consider the statutory strategy first. Why, exactly, are implied repeals of habeas corpus disfavored? Justice Scalia assumes that the underlying premise for this principle of statutory construction is that it helps the court divine the congressional intent. Does the principle do so? And is that its only rationale?

3.   At several points in its opinion the Court stresses that the question raised on the merits (whether the amendments to former INA § 212(c) were meant to be retroactive) was one of "pure law." Suppose, instead, that a noncitizen challenges a crime-related removal order on the ground that the BIA had erred in its application of broad statutory language like "exceptional and extremely unusual hardship" or "good moral character" to specific facts. Given the current version of INA § 242, do you think the Supreme Court would permit a federal court to review the BIA decision? First, would it interpret the statute itself as allowing judicial review by way of either (a) a petition for review in the court of appeals; or (b) a habeas application under 28 U.S.C. § 2241 in the district court? Second, if the Court were to interpret the statute as barring all judicial review of that claim, would it recognize constitutional habeas under the suspension clause?

4.   Now that *St. Cyr* has been decided and the REAL ID Act has been passed, may a court reverse a crime-related removal order on the ground that the agency findings of fact are not supported by substantial evidence? Suppose, for example, that a noncitizen is ordered removed under INA § 237(a)(2)(A)(i)(I) (crime involving moral turpitude committed within fiver years after admission). Suppose further that the noncitizen admits the crime but argues there was insufficient evidence that the crime was committed within five years after admission. May a court review that claim? See the Court's brief reference to the *Vajtauer* case, in footnote 27 and the accompanying text. For an enlightening (pre-*St. Cyr*) discussion, see Gerald A. Neuman, *The Constitutional Requirement of "Some Evidence,"* 25 San Diego L. Rev. 631 (1988).

5.   Justice Scalia makes the interesting argument that the majority's interpretation leaves those noncitizens who are deportable on criminal grounds better off than other deportable noncitizens. The former, he

observes, are freed from the 30–day filing deadline for petitions for review and, moreover, can obtain two layers of review—in district court and, if unsuccessful there, in the court of appeals. Since Congress especially wanted to expedite the removal of noncitizen criminal offenders, and since Congress regarded the crime-related deportability grounds as being among the most serious, treating them more favorably than other deportable noncitizens is anomalous. First, is it clear, as Justice Scalia assumes, that the holding in *St. Cyr* reaches only those noncitizens who are deportable on criminal grounds? Second, if that is indeed the result, are there any special reasons to make habeas available to noncitizens deportable for crimes but not for other deportable noncitizens? (Consider especially any role that detention should play.) Third, is two-tiered review necessarily an advantage for the noncitizen in terms of either (a) a longer stay in the United States; or (b) a second bite at the apple? Argue both ways.

6. Is Justice Scalia right to say that the majority is taking a "magic words" approach?

7. Apart from the use of habeas corpus to challenge the legality of removal orders, the Supreme Court has also recognized the use of habeas by noncitizens to challenge the legality of their detentions. See the discussions of *Zadvydas* and *Clark v. Martinez* in chapter 2 (detention in connection with removal proceedings) and the discussion of *Rasul* in chapter 10 (detention of noncitizen prisoners captured in combat). As noted earlier, the conference committee report on the REAL ID Act, Rpt. 109–172 (May 3, 2005), at 175, assumes the continued availability of habeas to review the lawfulness of detention, independently of challenges to the associated removal orders. See also *Demore v. Hyung Joon Kim*, 538 U.S. 510, 123 S.Ct. 1708, 155 L.Ed.2d 724 (2003) (asserting habeas jurisdiction to hear constitutional challenge to mandatory detention provision).

8. The previous edition of this book asked what would happen if Congress were to amend each of the relevant provisions by adding language like "Notwithstanding 28 U.S.C. § 2241 or any other grant of habeas corpus ..." The REAL ID Act has made that hypothetical a reality, but with the important addition of INA § 242(a)(2)(D), which exempts questions of law from the bar on judicial review. Given that exemption, do you think the present statute satisfies the constitutional concerns discussed in *St. Cyr*?

9. Justice Scalia sees no reason that Congress could not constitutionally abolish the writ of habeas corpus entirely. All the Constitution says, he argues, is that the writ cannot be temporarily suspended. Does that sound right? Argue both ways.

10. What lesson do you derive from the Henry Hart dialogue that preceded this case? How do you think Justice Scalia would respond? Can Hart's and Scalia's constitutional positions be reconciled? For an excellent historical account of habeas corpus as it relates to the issues in *St. Cyr*, see James Oldham & Michael J. Wishnie, *The Historical Scope of Habeas Corpus and INS v. St. Cyr*, 16 Georgetown Immigration L.J. 485 (2002).

11. Can *St. Cyr* coexist peacefully with the plenary power doctrine? The cases you read in chapter 2 suggest that in the field of immigration Congress has especially wide power (literally unreviewable power, according to some of the cases) to do things that would be constitutionally unacceptable in other spheres. Yet the Court in *St. Cyr* finds at least a serious question whether Congress can constitutionally bar judicial review of deportation orders. Where, then, does this case leave the plenary power doctrine?

c. OTHER STRATEGIES

Beyond petitions for review and applications for habeas corpus, are there other sources of jurisdiction, forms of action, or remedies for noncitizens who wish to gain access to court to challenge administrative decisions that relate to removal?

i. *General Federal Question Jurisdiction*

28 U.S.C. § 1331 grants the district courts subject matter jurisdiction over cases that present issues of federal law. In INA § 279, Congress had once granted a more specific jurisdiction over causes arising under Title II of the INA (which covers almost everything related to removal). IIRIRA limited section 279 to actions brought by the government. Whether that amendment had any effect on general federal question jurisdiction was not clear. See pages 479–80 above. The sweeping language now added by the REAL ID Act to each of the provisions of INA § 242(a)(2) most likely ends that debate; it seems clear that Congress meant to eliminate *all* statutory review (and even nonstatutory review, whatever that phrase is meant to encompass) other than via petitions for review.

As you have seen, however, in addition to amending INA § 279, Congress added several other court-stripping provisions. Even before the REAL ID Act, at least one court held that section 242(a)(2)(C) (which eliminates "jurisdiction to review" most crime-related removal orders) forecloses not only petitions for review but also general federal question jurisdiction. *Miranda v. Reno*, 238 F.3d 1156 (9th Cir. 2001).

ii. *Injunctions and Class Actions*

In most instances the petition for review works well as a device for judicial review of final removal orders. For that reason, the exclusivity of section 242 is innocuous in the ordinary case. Sometimes, however, there are tactical or logistical advantages to using an alternative vehicle. Suppose, for example, a large class of noncitizens objects to a widespread DHS practice. Is it necessary for each affected individual to submit to that practice, and, if unsuccessful, wait for removal proceedings and then challenge the underlying procedures by filing in the court of appeals a petition for review of the resulting removal order? Or may plaintiffs band together and bring a class action seeking injunctive or declaratory relief? See generally Leti Volpp, *Court–Stripping and Class–Wide Relief: A Re-*

sponse to Judicial Review in Immigration Cases after AADC, 14 Georgetown Immigration L.J. 463 (2000).

The Supreme Court has not addressed directly whether the exclusivity of the petition for review would bar that procedure. In a landmark 1991 decision, however, the Court interpreted an analogous exclusivity provision concerned with the legalization of agricultural workers. *McNary v. Haitian Refugee Center,* 498 U.S. 479, 111 S.Ct. 888, 112 L.Ed.2d 1005 (1991). By a 7–2 vote, the Supreme Court held that the district court had jurisdiction to hear the case as a class action. The Court emphasized that postponing adjudication until individual deportation orders were entered and reviewed "would foster the very delay and procedural redundancy that Congress sought to eliminate in passing [the petition for review provision]." 498 U.S. at 490, 111 S.Ct. at 895, 112 L.Ed.2d at 1016 (quoting court of appeals). Importantly, the majority opinion also observed that relegating the plaintiffs to petitions for review would be functionally equivalent to withholding judicial review entirely, since a person would have to submit voluntarily to removal proceedings in order to receive review of the legalization denial. Professor Daniel Kanstroom offered a powerful analogy:

> You can play outside today if you do all your chores. Your older brother will decide if you've done them properly. If you think your brother has decided unfairly, and you want me to decide, you must confess something serious that you did wrong that I do not know about. If I decide your brother was wrong, I will let you play outside and forgive the other thing. But if I decide your brother was right, you cannot play outside and you will be punished further for the other thing.
>
> There is something fundamentally troubling about conditioning justice upon risk.

Daniel Kanstroom, *Judicial Review of Amnesty Denials: Must Aliens Bet Their Lives to Get into Court?,* 25 Harvard Civil Rights—Civil Liberties L.Rev. 53, 97 (1990).

Since *McNary v. Haitian Refugee Center,* there have been further Supreme Court and lower court opinions refining the scope of the pattern and practice exception to the exclusivity of petitions for review. See generally Robert Pauw, *Judicial Review of "Pattern and Practice" Cases: What to Do When the INS Acts Unlawfully,* 70 Washington L.Rev. 779 (1995); 72 IR 1453 (Oct. 23, 1995). Nothing in the REAL ID Act appears to amend the law on "pattern and practice" litigation.

While declaratory and injunctive relief are still available remedies, and class actions remain viable in immigration, IIRIRA narrowed their use considerably, at least in the context of arriving noncitizens. INA § 235(b) governs the inspection, examination, and removal of arriving noncitizens and of those who are present without admission. INA § 242(e)(3) prohibits actions to challenge the legality (including the constitutionality) of INA section 235(b) or of any regulations or other written policies issued to implement section 235(b), more than 60 days after the challenged section is implemented. During the 60–day period in which such challenges may be brought, only the District Court for the District of Columbia has jurisdiction, *id.*, and no such challenge may be brought by class action. INA § 242(e)(1)(B).

Under INA § 242(f)(1), no court (other than the Supreme Court) may enjoin the operation of any provision of chapter 4 of title II (which deals generally with removal), except with respect to an individual noncitizen (i.e., not a class). In such a case, the court may not enjoin removal unless the person proves by clear and convincing evidence that the challenged order is "prohibited as a matter of law." INA § 242(f)(2).

iii. Collateral Attack in Criminal Proceedings

INA § 276 makes it a felony for any noncitizen who has previously been excluded, deported, or removed, to enter, attempt to enter, or be found in, the United States without permission from the Attorney General. In the past, individuals charged under that provision frequently defended by asserting defects in their prior removal orders. Faced with a conflict among the circuits, the Supreme Court in *United States v. Mendoza–Lopez,* 481 U.S. 828, 107 S.Ct. 2148, 95 L.Ed.2d 772 (1987), held that the validity of the underlying removal order may not be collaterally attacked in subsequent criminal proceedings unless the defendant had not earlier been given a meaningful opportunity to seek direct judicial review of the deportation order. On the facts of *Mendoza–Lopez,* the Court concluded that the lack of advice as to the possibility of judicial review had effectively deprived the defendants of such an opportunity. The Court therefore permitted collateral attack.

AEDPA codified (and perhaps toughened) the holding of *Mendoza-Lopez.* It added new language to the end of INA § 276 barring collateral attack unless the person had exhausted all administrative remedies with respect to the underlying removal order, he or she had been improperly deprived of the opportunity for judicial review, and the removal order had been "fundamentally unfair." IIRIRA § 302(a) also prohibited collateral attacks on orders of "expedited removal."

iv. Claims of United States Nationality

In *Ng Fung Ho v. White,* 259 U.S. 276, 42 S.Ct. 492, 66 L.Ed. 938 (1922), the Supreme Court held (at least) that a person who makes a nonfrivolous claim of United States citizenship has a due process right not to be deported without a judicial trial on the issue of citizenship. INA § 242(b)(5), which you can consult for further detail, codifies that principle with some modifications.

d. CONSOLIDATING REVIEWABLE CLAIMS

DHS, the immigration judges, and the BIA all issue a variety of orders related in one way or another to removal. You have seen many of them— decisions on the various forms of discretionary relief; destination of removal; motions to reopen or reconsider; requests by nonimmigrants for extensions of stay, change of status, permission to work, or permission to transfer schools; etc. A question that occasionally arises is which of these orders the courts of appeals have exclusive jurisdiction to review under INA § 242.

In a series of cases decided before 1996, the Supreme Court and the lower courts developed some general criteria for answering that question. See especially *INS v. Chadha*, 462 U.S. 919, 103 S.Ct. 2764, 77 L.Ed.2d 317 (1983); *Cheng Fan Kwok v. INS*, 392 U.S. 206, 88 S.Ct. 1970, 20 L.Ed.2d 1037 (1968) (and cases cited therein). In those judicial decisions, however, the courts were interpreting the then applicable statutory language. IIRIRA §§ 306(a)(2) and 306(b) replaced the prior judicial review provision with INA § 242, the provision that you have been studying here. How much of the pre-IIRIRA case law can still be salvaged is not clear.

Since IIRIRA, the key provision on this subject is INA § 242(b)(9), which provides: "Judicial review of all questions of law and fact . . . *arising from* any action taken or proceeding brought to remove an alien from the United States under this title shall be available only in judicial review of a final order under this section" [emphasis added]. This provision has two potential consequences. First, it appears to define certain decisions, other than the removal order itself, that can be reviewed only by way of petition for review. Second, as to those decisions, all must be heard together, not brought piecemeal. Congress's intention was to require consolidation of various removal-related decisions in the same forum, rather than have them strung out one at a time in various fora.

But precisely which ancillary orders fall within the consolidation mandate? The answer is far from clear, mainly because the meaning of "arising from" is far from clear. Is Congress requiring consolidation of all decisions that are made during, and incident to, removal proceedings—for example, decisions as to destination of removal, or decisions denying discretionary relief from removal (to the extent reviewable)? Or is Congress perhaps referring to all decisions upon which removal is contingent—for example a USCIS decision to deny an extension of stay that would have avoided deportability in the first place?

INA § 242(b)(6) is more specific. It requires that any judicial review of an order denying a motion to reopen or reconsider a removal order be consolidated with any judicial review of the original removal order.

e. THE THEORY AND THE CONSEQUENCES OF JUDICIAL REVIEW

Two highly useful empirical studies have examined the actual impact of judicial review of administrative agency decisions. The first one analyzed judicial decisions in a wide range of administrative contexts (including immigration). Peter H. Schuck & E. Donald Elliott, *Studying Administrative Law: A Methodology for, and Report on, New Empirical Research*, 42 Administrative L.Rev.519 (1990). The other focused specifically on immigration. See Peter H. Schuck & Theodore H. Wang, *Continuity and Change:*

Patterns of Immigration Litigation in the Courts, 1979–1990, 45 Stanford L.Rev. 115 (1992). One portion of the latter article studied the actual outcomes of judicial review of immigration-related agency decisions (mostly deportation cases). The study showed differences in outcomes by year, by court, and by type of substantive claim.

QUESTION

What are the benefits of judicial review of immigration decisions? What are the costs? For more detail, see Stephen H. Legomsky, *Political Asylum and the Theory of Judicial Review*, 73 Minnesota L.Rev. 1205, 1209–16 (1989).

SECTION C.   A CASE FILE: FROM INITIAL NOTICE TO JUDICIAL REVIEW[15]

Like the cases you have read in your other courses, those that appear in this book are mostly appellate opinions. In immigration law, most of those decisions are rendered by federal courts or the BIA. Each appellate opinion discusses the legal issues raised by the "facts" of the case. But where do these facts come from?

In the present section you will see how a written record is created, developed, and then used by opposing counsel, the BIA, and the reviewing court to pin down the facts and to frame the issues on appeal. In the process, you will get some of the flavor of a modern-day removal proceeding as it progresses from the Notice to Appear through the different levels of the administrative and judicial processes. The materials have been extracted from actual removal proceedings in the matter of Mr. Feliciano Flores–Palomino, a citizen of Mexico.

To avoid confusion, keep in mind that during the administrative phase of the removal proceedings, the noncitizen is referred to as the "respondent." Once the petition for review is filed, however, the noncitizen becomes the "petitioner" and the United States becomes the "respondent."

The following (edited) documents will appear in chronological order:

(1) Notice to Appear (Aug. 26, 1998);

(2) INS custody determination (Aug. 26, 1998);

(3) Transcript of beginning of removal hearing (Sept. 10, 1998);

(4) Immigration judge's custody determination (Sept. 10, 1998);

---

15. The author is grateful to Stacie Powderly for her outstanding research assistance in connection with this case file, and to Michael Gans, Clerk of the Court of Appeals for the Eighth Circuit, for his extremely generous help. Because this case began before 2002, the prosecuting agency was the INS rather than ICE. The substantive issues and the essential procedures, however, are otherwise current. Throughout these materials, electronic signatures have been substituted for the original ones.

(5) Letter to immigration judge from respondent's attorney (Sept. 14, 1998);

(6) Transcript of continuation of removal hearing (Jan. 26 and Feb. 23, 1999);

(7) Application for cancellation of removal (Feb. 23, 1999);

(8) Continuation of removal hearing (Apr. 20, 1999);

(9) Respondent's trial brief (July 25, 1999);

(10) Continuation of removal hearing (Aug. 24, 1999);

(11) Oral decision of immigration judge (Aug. 24, 1999);

(12) Notice of appeal to BIA (Sept. 14, 1999);

(13) First BIA decision (Apr. 29, 2002);

(14) Second BIA decision (Nov. 7, 2002);

(15) Petition for Review (Dec. 4, 2002);

(16) Memorandum in support of motion for stay of removal (Dec. 4, 2002);

(17) Government's motion in opposition to motion for stay (Dec. 23, 2002);

(18) Court's order denying motion for stay of removal (Jan. 8, 2003);

(19) Brief for Petitioner (Jan. 13, 2003);

(20) AILF motion to file brief as amicus curiae (served Jan. 21, 2003);

(21) Court order granting AILF motion to file amicus brief (Feb. 7, 2003);

(22) Brief for Respondent (U.S.) (Mar. 24, 2003);

(23) Court decision denying petition for review (Jan. 15, 2004).

NB: The typographical errors that you will encounter in these materials are in the original documents; because they are numerous, the word "sic" has generally been omitted.

U.S. Department of Justice

Immigration and Naturalization Service   **Notice to Appear**

In removal proceedings under section 240 of the Immigration and Nationality Act

                                                                    File No: <u>A76 407 515</u>

In the Matter of:

Respondent: <u>Feliciano</u>   <u>FLORES-Palomino</u>

C/O USINS, 2901 Metro Drive, Suite 100
<u>Bloomington</u>   <u>MN</u>   <u>55524</u>
                    (Number, street, city, state and ZIP code)   (Area code and phone number)

☐ 1. You are an arriving alien.
■ 2. You are an alien present in the United States who has not been admitted or paroled.
☐ 3. You have been admitted to the United States, but are deportable for the reasons stated below.

The Service alleges that you:

1. Are not a native or citizen of the United States;
2. Are a native of Mexico and a citizen of Mexico;
3. Entered the United States at or near San Ysidro, California on or about June 15, 1997;
4. Were not then admitted or paroled after inspection by an Immigration Officer.

On the basis of the forgoing, it is charged that you are subject to removal from the United States pursuant to the following provision(s) of law:

212(a)(6)(A)(i) of the Immigration and Nationality Act (ACT), as amended, in that you are an alien present in the United States without being admitted or paroled, or who arrived in the United States at any time or place other than as designated by the Attorney General.

☐ This notice is being issued after an asylum offer has found that the respondent has demonstrated a credible fear of persecution.
☐ Section 235(b)(1) order was vacated pursuant to: ☐ 8 CFR 208.30(f)(2)   ☐ 8 CFR 235.3(b)(5)(iv)

YOU ARE ORDERED to appear before an immigration judge of the United States Department of Justice at:
<u>7850 Metro Parkway, Suite 320, Bloomington, Minnesota 55425</u>
                    (Complete Address of Immigration Court, Including Room Number, if any)

on ____<u>to be set</u>____ at ____<u>to be set</u>____ to show why you should not be removed from the United States based on the
          (Date)   (Time)
charge(s) set forth above.

                                        Mark S. Cargein
                                        Assistant District Director, Investigations

Date: ___<u>8/26/98</u>___   <u>Bloomington, MN</u>
                    See reverse for important information

                                        Form I-862- (Rev. 4-1-97)

Warning: Any statement you make may be used against you in removal proceedings.

Alien Registration: This copy of the Notice to Appear served upon you is evidence of your alien registration while you are under removal proceedings. You are required to carry it with you at all times.

Representation: If you so choose, you may be represented in this proceeding, at no expense to the Government, by an attorney or other individual authorized and qualified to represent persons before the Executive Office for Immigration Review, pursuant to 8 CFR 3.16. Unless you so request, no hearing will be scheduled earlier than ten days from the date of this notice, to allow you sufficient time to secure counsel. A list of qualified attorneys and organizations who may be available to represent you at no cost will be provided with this Notice.

Conduct of the hearing: At the time of your hearing, you should bring with you any affidavits or other documents which you desire to have considered in connection with your case. If any document is in a foreign language, you must bring the original and a certified English translation of the document. If you wish to have the testimony of any witnesses considered, you should arrange to have such witnesses present at the hearing.

At your hearing you will be given the opportunity to admit or deny any or all of the allegations in the Notice to Appear and that you are inadmissible or deportable on the charges contained in the Notice to Appear. You will have an opportunity to present evidence on your own behalf, to examine any evidence presented by the Government, to object, on proper legal grounds, to the receipt of evidence and to cross examine any witnesses presented by the Government.

You will be advised by the immigration judge before whom you appear, of any relief from removal for which you may appear eligible including the privilege of departing voluntarily. You will be given a reasonable opportunity to make any such application to the immigration judge.

Failure to appear: You are required to provide the INS, in writing, with your full mailing address and telephone number. You must notify the Immigration Court immediately by using Form EOIR-33 whenever you change your address or telephone number during the course of this proceeding. You will be provided with a copy of this form. Notices of hearing will be mailed to this address. If you do not submit Form EOIR-33 and do not other\vise provide an address at which you may be reached during proceedings,.then the Government shall not be required to provide you with written notice of your hearing. If you fail to attend the hearing at the time and place designated on this notice, or any date and time later directed by the Immigration Court, a removal order may be made by the immigration judge in your absence, and you may be arrested and detained by the INS.

Request for Prompt Hearing

To expedite a determination in my case, I request an immediate hearing. I waive my right to have a 10-day period prior to appearing before an immigration judge.

Feliciano Flores
(Signature of Respondent)

Before:

_____*Immigration Agent*_____   Date: ___8/28/98___
(Signature and Title of INS Officer)

Certificate of Service

This Notice to Appear was served on the respondent by me on   8/26/98   , in the following manner and in compliance with section 239(a)(1)(F) of the Act:

- ■ in person   ☐ by certified mail, return receipt requested   ☐ by regular mail

- ■ Attached is a list of organizations and attorneys which provide free legal services.

- ■ The alien was provided oral notice in the   English   language of the time and place of his or her hearing and of the consequences of failure to appear as provided in section 240(b)(7) of the Act.

_____*Feliciano Flores*_____   *Jeff Field* Jeff Field, Immigration Agent
(Signature of Respondent if Personally Served)   (Signature and Title of Officer)

U.S. Department of Justice
Immigration and Naturalization Service   **Notice of Custody Determination**

File No: <u>A76 407 515</u>
Date: <u>8/26/98</u>

Feliciano
Flores- Palomino
C/O USINS, 2901 Metro Drive, Suite 100
Bloomington   MN   55425

Pursuant to the authority contained in section 236 of the Immigration and Nationality Act and part 236 of title 8, Code of Federal Regulations, I have determined that pending a final determination by the Immigration Judge in your case, and in the event you are ordered removed from the United States, until you are taken into custody for removal, you shall be:

☐ detained in the custody of this Service.
■ released under bond in the amount of $ <u>5,000.00</u>   .
☐ released on your own recognizance.

■ You may request a review of this determination by an Immigration Judge.
☐ You may not request a review of this determination by an Immigration Judge because the Immigration and Nationality Act prohibits your release from custody.

<u>   Mark S. Cargein   </u>
(Signature of authorized officer)
<u>   Assistant District Director, Investigations   </u>
<u>   Bloomington, MN   </u>
(INS office location)

■ do request a redetermination of this custody decision by an Immigration Judge.
■ I acknowledge receipt of this notification.

<u>   Feliciano Flores   </u>   <u>   8/26/98   </u>
(Signature of respondent)   (Date)

Result of Custody Redetermination

On _____ , custody status/conditions for release were reconsidered by:

☐ Immigration Judge   ☐ District Director   ☐ Board of Immigration Appeals

The results of the redetermination/reconsideration are:
☐ No change - Original determination upheld.   ☐ Release - Order of Recognizance.
☐ Detained in custody of this Service.   ☐ Release - Personal Recognizance
☐ Bond amount reset to _____   ☐ Other: _____

<u>   </u>
(Signature of office)

Form I-286 (Rev. 40-1-97) N

U.S. DEPARTMENT OF JUSTICE
Executive Office for Immigration Review
Immigration Court

Matter of	File No.: A 76 407 515
FELICIANO FLORES–PALOMINO,)	IN REMOVAL PROCEEDINGS
)	
Respondent)	Transcript of Hearing

Before JOSEPH R. DIERKES, Immigration Judge

Date: September 10, 1998   Place: Bloomington, Minnesota

Transcribed by DEPOSITION SERVICES, INC.   At Rockville, Maryland

Official Interpreter: Arthur Suvarte

Language: Spanish

Appearances:

For the Immigration and   For the Respondent:
Naturalization Service:

Kristin Olmanson, Esquire   Christopher Gerard, Esquire

JUDGE FOR THE RECORD

This is Immigration Judge Joseph Dierkes, sitting in Bloomington, Minnesota, in the EOIR courtroom, or, rather, the detained space court-room, today's date September 10, 1998. This is an initial removal hearing regarding Feliciano Flores Palomino. F–E–L–I–C–I–A–N–O, Flores, F–L–O–R–E–S–Palomino, P–A–L–O–M–I–N–O, 76 407 515. The interpreter in Spanish is Arthur Suvarte.

JUDGE TO MR. SUVARTE

Q. Do you swear the interpretations you will give today in English and Spanish will be true and accurate to the best of your ability?

A. Yes.

JUDGE TO MR. FLORES

Q. Okay, to the respondent, sir, state your full name.

A. Feliciano Flores–Palomino

JUDGE TO MR. FLORES

Q. Seated next to you is Mr. Gerarrd (phonetic sp.). Will he be your attorney today?

A. Yes.

JUDGE TO MR. GERARD

Q. Okay. Identify yourself counsel?

A. Christopher Gerard, Western Minnesota Legal Services for the respondent.

JUDGE TO MS. OLMANSON

Q. Okay, for the Service?

A. Kristin Olmanson for the Government.

JUDGE TO MR. GERARD

Q. A Notice to Appear was issued August 26, 1998. Mr. Gerard, do you acknowledge your client has a copy of that?

A. Yes, we do, Your Honor.

Q. We'll mark that Exhibit 1. Before we went on the record, you stated that you would be requesting a continuance of the case for preparation purposes.

A. That is correct, Your Honor.

Q. Okay.

JUDGE TO MS. OLMANSON

Q. Any objection of one continuance, Ms. Olmanson?

A. No, Your Honor.

Q. Let's do this. We'll, mark—I have a Service exhibit which was marked bond Exhibit A. Do you want that included as a removal exhibit, Ms. Olmanson?

A. Yes, your honor.

Q. Mark that Exhibit 2.

JUDGE TO MR. GERARD

Q. Mr. Gerard, you filed a bond Exhibit which I marked exhibit B in the bond hearing. Do you want that included, as well?

A. Yes, your honor.

Q. We'll mark that as removal Exhibit 3. Okay. We'll continue this case to September 22nd at 1 o'clock, 09/22/98 at 1 o'clock. If your client bonds out before then, Mr. Gerard, you need to advise me and request that this matter be transferred to the non-detained docket. If he is still in custody at that time, we'll need to come back and complete his hearing on the 22nd.

A. Very good, Your Honor.

JUDGE TO MR. FLORES

Q. To the respondent, sir, we're going to continue your case to September 22, 1998 at 1 o'clock. Unless you hear otherwise from Mr. Gerard, you need to be in court at that time. If you bond out of custody, he may request an extension of your hearing date. But whenever your case is set for court again, you need to show up because, if you don't show up, you can be ordered deported in absentia. So far, you have not actually been deported from the United States. You've always been given the opportunity to leave voluntarily, so you want to show up, so you don't get an order of deportation. Okay.

JUDGE TO COUNSEL

Q. Anything else for me to sign?

A. (Mr. Gerard) Nothing, your honor.

A. (Ms. Olmanson) No, your honor.

Q. Okay. I'll serve a written notice of the new hearing date on both sides.

JUDGE FOR THE RECORD

This matter is continued, as stated.

HEARING CONTINUED

U.S. DEPARTMENT OF JUSTICE
Executive Office for Immigration Review
Office of the Immigration Judge

In the Matter of: Case No.: A _____76–407–515_____

___FLORES–PALOMINO, FELICIANO___   Docket: __BLOOMINGTON, MN__

RESPONDENT   IN REMOVAL PROCEEDINGS

ORDER OF THE IMMIGRATION JUDGE

Request having been made for a change in the custody status of the respondent pursuant to 8 C.F.R. 236 and having considered the representations of the Immigration and Naturalization Service and the respondent, it is HEREBY ORDERED that:

■ The request for a change in the custody status of the respondent be denied.

☐ The request for a change in the custody status of the respondent be granted and that the respondent be:

   (1) ☐ released from custody on respondent's own recognizance; or,

        ☐ released from custody upon posting a bond of $_____ : and

   (2) the conditions of the bond:

        ☐ remain unchanged; or,

        ☐ are changed as follows: _____

☐ Other _____

_____

_____

Appeal due by 10/13/98.   _Joseph R. Dierkes_

Immigration Judge

Date: _9/10/98_

Appeal: RESERVED A   Form EOIR–1
                                                          Rev. June 93

Deputy Director	**WESTERN MINNESOTA LEGAL SERVICES**	**LEGAL ASSISTANTS**
J. Richard Stemer	**OLDER AMERICANS LAW PROJECT**	**Kathy J. Holen**
	CHICANO AND LATINO ADVOCACY PROJECT	**Bonita A. Kallestad**
Attorneys	**MINNESOTA FAMILY FARM LAW PROJECT**	**Paul Mahoney**
John H. Burns	**620 Litchfield Avenue, SW, Suite 101**	**Mary Vrieze**
Christopher D. Gerrard	**P.O. Box 1866**	
	Wilmar, Minnesota 56201–1866	**LEGAL SECRETARY**
SUPERVISING ATTORNEY	**(320) 235–980**	**Margaret Lauinger**
Linda Grathwohl 1–888–360–3666 Toll Free (320) 235–9602 V/TDD (320) 235–1030		

BILINGUAL INTAKE WORKER
María Patiño

September 14, 1998

Honorable Joseph R. Dierkes
Executive Office for Immigration Review
Office of Immigration Judge
7850 Metro Parkway, Suite 320
Bloomington, MN 55425

RE: Feliciano Flores–Palomino

A876 407 515

Payment Bond

Dear Judge Dierkes:

Western Minnesota Legal Services represents Feliciano Flores–Palomino.
On Thursday, September 10, 1998. Mr. Flores came before you on a bond
redetermination hearing. At that hearing you denied his request for a
reduction of his bond from $5,000.00 to $3,000.00. You additionally set his
Master Calendar Hearing for September 22, 1998, at 1:00 p.m. You stated
that if Mr. Flores bonded out you would take his name off of the detention
calendar and reset his Master Calendar Hearing for a later date.

Please note that Martha Velazquez, Mr. Flores' wife, paid his bond on
Friday, September 11. 1998. Mr. Flores is now at home with his wife at 610
Rice Avenue SW, Willmar, Minnesota 56201. We therefore request on Mr.
Flores' behalf that his name now be removed from the detention calendar
and that a Master Calendar Hearing be set for a later date.

Please note additionally that we do not intend to appeal your denial of Mr. Flores' request to reduce his bond to $3,000.00. Please do not hesitate to contact us if you have any additional questions or concerns regarding this matter.

Sincerely,

WESTERN MINNESOTA LEGAL
SERVICES

Attorney at Law
Christopher D. Gerrard
Christopher D. Gerrard
Attorney at Law

CDG/ml

WMLS is a part of Mid–Minnesota Legal Assistance, Inc.

————

U.S. DEPARTMENT OF JUSTICE
Executive Office for Immigration Review
Immigration Court

Matter of	File No.: A 76 407 515

FELICIANO FLORES–PALOMINO	)	IN REMOVAL PROCEEDINGS
respondent	)	Transcript of Hearing

Before JOSEPH R. DIERKES, Immigration Judge

Date: January 26, 1999	Place: Bloomington, Minnesota

* * *

JUDGE FOR THE RECORD

This is Immigration Judge Joseph Dierkes sitting at Bloomington, Minnesota, in the EOIR courtroom on today's date, January 26, 1999. This is a continued removal hearing for Feliciano Flores–Palomino, File A 76 407 515. The interpreter in the Spanish language is Amy Johnson.

JUDGE TO MR. FLORES

Q.   To the respondent, sir, state your full name.

A.   Feliciano Flores–Palomino.

Q.   Okay. And, sir, what is your current address?

A.   610 Rice (phonetic sp.) Avenue, Southwest, Willmar, Minnesota.

JUDGE TO MS. TOEWS

Q.   Okay. And for the Government?

A.   Annette Toews, T–O–E–W–S.

JUDGE TO MR. FLORES

Sir, at a prior hearing, you were represented by attorney Christopher Gerrard.

A. Yes.

Q. Is he still your attorney?

A. No. No, it's this lady.

Q. Well, that's not your attorney. That is someone from your attorney's office.

A. No, she's here because he's not.

Q. All right.

JUDGE TO MS. OLSEN

Q. Would you identify yourself, ma'am?

A. Kristy Olsen.

Q. Okay. And you're from the office of attorney?

A. Steven Thal.

Q. Okay. And where is he today?

A. Today he is in Mexico. His plane was cancelled twice last night.

Q. Okay. So he's been unable to get back.

A. That's correct.

JUDGE TO MS. TOEWS

Q. And there was a call to our office about this yesterday, Ms. Toews, requesting a continuance on Mr. Thal's cases. Do you have any objection to the continuance?

A. No objection, your honor.

Q. I'm concerned that we're showing a different attorney of record here. I want to set this case over to February 23rd at 11:30. This case has been pending on the docket since back in September, so I want to move it forward. And Ms. Olsen, you're going to need to tell Mr. Thal if he's going to be representing this respondent, he needs to get his entry of appearance filed when he gets back in the country.

JUDGE TO MR. FLORES

Q. All right. Sir, the next hearing in your case will be February 23rd at 11:30. Okay, you need to be back in court at that time. If you fail to appear, you could be ordered deported in absentia and you would become ineligible to seek relief from removal for 10 years. Okay. We'll give you a written notice with the new hearing date and of the consequences of failing to appear. Okay. Have you understood everything that's gone on here today?

A. Yes.

Q. Okay.

JUDGE FOR THE RECORD

This matter is continued, as stated.

HEARING CONTINUED

———

Date: February 23, 1999   Place: Bloomington, Minnesota

* * *

JUDGE TO MR. FLORES

Q.   To the respondent, sir, state your full name.

A.   Feliciano Flores–Palomino.

Q.   Is Mr. Thal your attorney today?

A.   Yes.

JUDGE TO MR. THAL

Q.   Identify yourself counsel.

A.   Yes, Steven Thal representing Mr. Flores–Palomino

JUDGE TO MR. SOLI

Q.   And for the Service?

A.   Richard Soli, District Counsel.

Q.   Okay. The Notice to Appear was marked as Exhibit 1 back on September 10, 1998, and I'll note that Exhibit 2 was a Service submission that included an I–213 and some other records of the Service.

* * *

And then a copy of a drunk driving charge. That's all Exhibit 2. Exhibit 3 is a letter submitted regarding the respondent and that's all I really have as exhibits right now.

JUDGE TO MR. THAL

Q.   Your client understands the nature and purpose of these proceedings?

A.   Yes, your honor.

Q.   Did you waive formal reading of the Notice to Appear and of his rights?

A.   Yes, we'd waive that.

Q.   How do you plead to the four factual allegations?

A.   We would admit those.

Q.   Concede the charge?

A.   Yes.

Q.   Designate Mexico?

A.   Yes.

Q. What relief is he seeking?

A. We would seek cancellation of removal.

* * *

JUDGE TO MR. SOLI

Q. Anything from the Service today, Mr. Soli?

A. Yes.

MR. SOLI TO MR. THAL

Q. The service would like to know, perhaps, just from looking over at 213, who the qualifying relative is in this case?

A. His permanent resident wife, who's here in the courtroom.

Q. Okay. And do you have her file number?

A. Yes. A 043 035 377.

Q. Thank you.

JUDGE TO MR. SOLI

Q. Anything else?

A. No, Judge.

JUDGE TO MR. FLORES

Q. Okay, sir, the next hearing of your case will be April 20th at 11:00. The purpose of that hearing is for you to file your application for cancellation of removal. You need to be here in court on that day with your application. If you fail to file your application on that day, I could consider that you are abandoning the application. And if you fail to appear on that day, you could be ordered deported in absentia and you would become ineligible to seek other relief from removal for 10 years. Okay. You'll get a written notice of the new hearing date and of the consequences of failing to appear.

MR. SOLI TO MR. THAL

Q. The Service requests welfare and employment releases, as well as tax returns for the last 10 years.

JUDGE TO MR. FLORES

Q. Sir, have you understood everything that's gone on here today?

A. Yes.

Q. Okay.

JUDGE FOR THE RECORD

This is matter is continued, as stated.

HEARING CONTINUED

U.S. Department of Justice   OMB #1125-001
Executive Office for Immigration Review   Application for Cancellation of Removal and
                                   Adjustment of Status for Certain Nonpermanent Residents

PLEASE READ ADVICE AND INSTRUCTIONS BEFORE FILLING IN FORM	Fee Stamp
PLEASE TYPE OR PRINT	FP 3707652 SOM9913700013 Feb 23 1999

PART I - INFORMATION ABOUT YOURSELF

1) My present true name is: *(Last, First, Middle)* FLORES-PALOMINO Feliciano	2) Alien Registration Number: A76 407 515
3) My name given at birth was *(Last, First, Middle)* Same	4) Birth Place: *(City, Country)*

5) Date of Birth: *(Month, Day, Year)* 6/9/54	6) Gender: ■ Male ☐ Female	7) Height: 5'5"	8) Hair Color: BRO	9) Eye Color: BRO

10) Current Nationality & Citizenship: Mexican	11) Social Security Number:	12) Home Phone Number: (320) 231-3554	13) Work Phone Number: ( )

14) I currently reside at: *Apt. Number and/or in care of* 610 Rice Ave. SW *Number and Street* Willamr MN 56201 *City or Town State ZIP Code*	15) I have been known by these additional name(s): Pedro Flores-Palomino

16) I have resided in the following location in the United States: (List PRESENT ADDRESS FIRST, and work back in time for at least 10 years).

Street and Number - Apt. or Room # - City or Town - State - ZIP Code	Resided From: *(Month, Day, Year)*	Resided To: *(Month, Day, Year)*
Please see attachment		Present

PART 2 - INFORMATION ABOUT THIS APPLICATION

17) I, the undersigned, hereby request that my removal be cancelled under the provisions of section 240A(b) of the Immigration and Nationality Act (INA). I believe that I am eligible for cancellation of removal because: (check all that apply)

■ My removal would result in exceptional and extremely unusual hardship to my: *(Place a USC in the space if the family member is a citizen of the United States, an **L** If the family member is a lawful permanent resident of the United States, an **X** if the family member is neither and leave **BLANK** if not applicable.)*

_____ **Husband** ___L___ **Wife** _____ **Father** _____ **Mother** _____ **Child or Children.**

With the exception of absences described in question #25, I have resided in the United States since:

(Month, Day, Year) ___1/13/87___

☐ I, or my child, have been battered or subjected to extreme cruelty by a United States citizen or lawful permanent resident spouse or parent.

With the exception of absences described in question #25, I have resided in the United States since:
(Month, Day, Year) _____

Please use a separate sheet for additional entries.

(1)

Form EOIR-42B
4/97

PART 3 - INFORMATION ABOUT YOUR PRESENCE IN THE UNITED STATES

18) I first arrived in the United States under the name of: *(Last, First, Middle)* Feliciano Flores	19) I first arrived in the United States on: *(Month, Day, Year)* 1/13/87

20) Place or port of first arrival: *(Place or Port, City, and State)*
San Ysidro, CA

21) I arrived: ☐ as a lawful permanent resident, ☐ as a Visitor, ☐ as a student, ■ without inspection, or ☐ Other (Place an X in the correct box, if Other is selected please explain):

22) If admitted as a nonimmigrant, period for which admitted: *(Month, Day, Year)*N/A to	23) My last extension of stay in the United States expired on: *(Month, Day, Year)* N/A

24) If not inspected or if arrival occurred at other than a regular port, describe the circumstances as accurately as possible:
      I walked across the border.

25) Since the date of my first arrival I departed from and returned to the United States at the following places and on the following dates: (Please list all departures regardless of how briefly you were absent from the United States)

If you have never departed from the United States since your original date of arrival, please mark an X in the box: □

	Port of Departure / Port of Return	Departure Date / Return Date	Purpose of Travel / Manner of Return	Destination / Inspected & Admitted?
1	Port of Departure: (Place or Port, City and State) **Laredo, TX** Port of Return: (Place or Port, City and State) **San Ysidro, CA**	Departure Date (Month, Day, Year) **4/97** _Return Date (Month, Day, Year) **2 weeks later**	Purpose of Travel **Voluntary departure** Manner of Return **EWI**	Destination **Mexico** _Inspected & Admitted? □ Yes ■ No
2	Port of Departure: (Place or Port, City and State) **San Ysidro, CA** Port of Return: (Place or Port, City and State) **San Ysidro, CA**	Departure Date (Month, Day, Year) **9/96** Return Date (Month, Day, Year) **3 weeks later**	Purpose of Travel **My brother died** _Manner of Return **EWI**	Destination **Mexico** _Inspected & Admitted? □ Yes ■ No

26) Have you ever departed the United States:

         a) under an order of deportation, exclusion or removal? □ Yes ■ No

         b) pursuant to a grant of voluntary departure? -----■ Yes □ No

PART 4 - INFORMATION ABOUT YOUR MARITAL STATUS AND SPOUSE
(Continued on page 3)

27) I am not married: □ I am married: ■	28) If married, the name of my spouse is: (Last, First, Middle) **VELAZQUEZ Martha**	29) Date of marriage: *(Month, Day, Year)* **8/16/96**

30) The marriage took place in: *(City and Country)* Willmar, MN	31) Birth place of spouse: *(City and Country)* Mexico City, Mexico
32) My spouse currently resides at: *Apt. Number and/or in care of* **610 Rice Avenue SW** *Number and Street* **Willmar, MN 56201** *City or Town State/Country ZIP Code*	33) Birth date of spouse: *(Month, Day, Year)* **4/25/44** 34) My spouse is a citizen of: *(Country)* Mexico

35) If your spouse is other than a native born United States citizen, answer the following:

He/she arrived in the United States at: *(City, and State)*   Santa Monica, CA

He/she arrived in the United States on: *(Month, Day, Year)*   February, 1960

His/her alien registration number is: A#   A43 035 377

He/she was naturalized on (Month, Day, Year) N/A   at

(City and State)

36) My spouse ☐ - is ■ - is not employed. If employed, please give salary and the name and address of the place(s) of employment.

Full Name and Address of Employer	Earnings Per Week *(Approximately)*
	$
	$
	$

Please use a separate sheet for additional entries.
(20)

Form EOIR -42B
4/97

* * *

Date: April 20, 1999   Place: Bloomington, Minnesota

* * *

JUDGE FOR THE RECORD

A.   Let's ID all the exhibits. One is the Notice to Appear. Two is the Service exhibit that includes the I–213, the Ident records, a copy of a court record on a alcohol-related driving charge, an old I–213. That's all Exhibit 2. Exhibit 3 will be a filing, I believe this is the respondent's filing, it includes materials from a correctional officer in California, letter from respondent's wife, a letter from a Rodolfo Velazquez, V–E–L–A–Z–Q–U–E–Z, a letter from Willmar Chiropractic Clinic, from a Dr. Ault, A–U–L–T. Here's some other medical information. That's all Exhibit 3. Exhibit 4 will be respondent's application for cancellation of removal for non-permanent residents with attachments. * * *

JUDGE TO MR. THAL

Q.   And you have copies of all those, Mr. Thal?

A.   Yes, I do, your honor.

JUDGE TO COUNSEL

Q.   Any objections from either of you to any of these exhibits?

A.   (Mr. Soli) No, Judge.

A.   (Mr. Thai) No.

Q.   * * * The charge on the Notice to Appear, the allegations all were admitted, the charges conceded.

* * *

[After the proceedings had started, the INS lodged an additional deportability charge, INA § 237(a)(2)(A)(i) (crime involving moral turpitude), based on Flores's DUI conviction. The IJ ultimately ruled that DUI is not a crime involving moral turpitude. That discussion is omitted here.—Ed.]

JUDGE TO MR. SOLI

Q.   The Service is arguing that his voluntary returns break his continuous physical presence, right. Right?

A.   Yes, Judge.

Q.   These cases you've submitted today go to that issue?

A.   Yes, sir.

* * *

JUDGE TO MR. THAL

* * *

Q.   And what I'd want from you is * * * a response to the Service case law on the break in physical presence. * * *

* * *

JUDGE FOR THE RECORD

If there's nothing else for me to decide, this matter is continued, as stated.

HEARING CONTINUED

———

[The INS filed a trial brief in which it argued that Flores's DUI conviction rendered him additionally deportable under the lodged charge of conviction of a moral turpitude crime. That brief is not reproduced here—Ed.]

UNITED STATES DEPARTMENT OF JUSTICE
EXECUTIVE OFFICE FOR IMMIGRATION REVIEW
IMMIGRATION COURT
BLOOMINGTON, MINNESOTA

IN THE MATTER OF:)
)
Feliciano Flores–Palomino,   )
          Respondent   )
)
INS File No: A76 407 515   )
)
In Removal Proceedings   )

RESPONDENT'S TRIAL BRIEF

Steven C. Thal
11650 Wayzata Boulevard
Minnetonka, MN 55305
Tel. No: (612) 541–1090

I. Issues

A. Whether Respondent's departures from the U.S., none of which exceed 3 weeks in length, and which accumulatively do not exceed 6 weeks in length, render him ineligible for cancellation of removal.

B. Whether Respondent remains eligible for cancellation of removal notwithstanding a DWI conviction under Minnesota Statute § 169.121, Subd. 1(f) and 3(d)(1).

II. Facts

Mr. Feliciano Flores–Palomino is a nonpermanent resident applying for cancellation of removal under INA § 240A(b)(1) (1999). The facts are not in dispute. Mr. Flores–Palomino disclosed the DWI Conviction in his application and attached to it copies of the records relating to that offense.

Apparently the INS concedes (or at least it does not argue to the contrary) that Mr. Fores–Palomino remains eligible for cancellation of removal notwithstanding the brief absences from the U.S. Although this was raised as an issue at the Master Calendar Hearing on April 20, 1999, the Service never addressed it in its Memorandum to the Court. In any event, Mr. Fores–Palomino disclosed three departures from the United States: April, 1997, for two weeks under voluntary departure; September, 1996, for three weeks; and February, 1992, for one week. The longest of these trips was for three weeks and cumulatively, they would total six weeks.

III. Analysis

A. <u>Mr. Flores–Palomino remains eligible for cancellation of removal in that he has never had an absence for more than 90 days or any cumulative total exceeding 180 days.</u>

The requirements for cancellation of removal are set out in Section 240A of the Immigration Nationality Act. Section 240A(b)(1) provides in relevant part that: the Attorney General may cancel removal of and adjust to the status of an alien lawfully admitted for permanent residence, an alien who is inadmissible or deportable from the United States if the alien—

A. Has been physically present in the United States for a continuous period of not less than 10 years immediately preceding the date of such application;

The INS has not challenged the application date of Mr. Flores–Palomino, therefore, it is assumed he has met the ten year rule for dates immediately preceding the date of such application.

The statute further provides for treatment of certain breaks in presence. Section 240A(b)(2) provides that:

An alien shall be considered to have failed to maintain continuous physical presence in the United States under Subsections (b)(1) and (b)(2) of the section if the alien has departed from the United States for any period in excess of 90 days or for any periods in the aggregate exceeding 180 days.

As previously stated, none of the absences of Mr. Flores–Palomino from the United States has exceeded 90 days. Furthermore, the cumulative total of all absences does not exceed 42 days. Consequently, he remains statutorily eligible to pursue his cancellation of removal in that there has never been a break in his continuous physical presence for purposes of applying for cancellation of removal.

* * *

Respectfully submitted,

Dated: 7/25/99

By: Steven C. Thal

Steven C. Thal

Steven C. Thal (#141021)
Attorney for Respondent
11650 Wayzata Boulevard
Minnetonka, MN 55305
Tel. No: (612) 541–1090

––––––

Date: August 24, 1999   Place: Bloomington, Minnesota

* * *

JUDGE TO MR. THAL

    Q.   Identify yourself, counsel.

    A.   Yes, Steven Thal representing the respondent.

JUDGE TO MS. TOEWS

    Q.   Service.

    A.   Annette Toews, T–O–E–W–S.

JUDGE TO MR. THAL

    Q.   Okay, this is the fourth court appearance here. * * *

* * *

JUDGE FOR THE RECORD

Let me review the exhibits here. One is the Notice to Appear, two is Service exhibit that includes the 1–213, the INS past records. Maybe that's not the right term. I'll call them the record, showing respondent's prior encounters with the Service and a copy of the conviction record on the enhanced gross misdemeanor DWI.

Exhibit 3 is respondent's submission, materials from the California— Estevan Velazquez, a relative of the respondent's wife who is in California writing from—I guess he sent this under his employment. He works at the correctional institution, and other letters on behalf of the respondent, a letter from a chiropractor, from a doctor. Exhibit 4 is the Form EOIR 42B with attachments. * * *

JUDGE TO MR. THAL

Q. Correct, Mr. Thal?

A. Correct.

JUDGE FOR THE RECORD

Exhibit 6 is the Service brief, in this case. Exhibit 7 is respondent's brief. Okay. Now, at the last hearing, I had requested briefs on two issue— on one issue, really, on the remaining charge.

JUDGE TO MS. TOEWS

Q. Is the Service still taking the position that respondent is ineligible for cancellation because of his voluntary return?

A. Yes, your honor.

Q. Okay.

* * *

JUDGE TO MS. TOEWS

Q. Go ahead, Ms. Toews.

A. Judge the Service, at this point, would only just like to briefly respond to the respondent's memorandum submitted to the court, inasmuch as the Immigration Service understood that the court had requested briefs only on the issue of the charge and not on the issue of the cancellation—

Q. I think that's what I had said—

A. Of removal.

Q. I went back and listened to the tape.

A. So at this point, the Service would just like to say that it is well established that a departure pursuant to voluntary departure granted by the Service or by an Immigration Judge, meaningfully interrupts physical presence and I would like to cite to the Court *Matter of Barraqan*, 13 I. & N. Dec. 759 and *Hernandez-Luis v. INS*, 869 F.2d 496 (9th Cir. 1989).

Q. Well, we have a copy of that Federal Reporter case here. Okay.

JUDGE TO MR. THAL

Q.   Anything else from you, Mr. Thal?

A.   Yes, your honor. If I can, at least, address from what the 1996 Immigration Legislation Handbook from Westgroup says, with respect to the break in physical presence issue, basically, it says much case law had developed interpreting brief, casual, and innocent absences. The Board and the courts had applied the Supreme Court's test established in *Rosenberg v. Fleuti* in the citations given. It goes on to say that new Section 240A(b)(1) renders this case law moot by specifying the length of absences that break physical presence for cancellation of removal purposes. That's really our argument that Congress set out the statutory scheme. It's a new statutory scheme. The legislation that was enacted was subsequent to the case law cited by counsel and we would assert that we meet the test because we do meet the statutory requirements.

Q.   Is that just commentary from the West Publishing Company there?

A.   Commentary from the West Publishing Company and the author of that would be Austin Fragamen (phonetic sp.), Steven Bell (phonetic sp.) and Thomas Moseley (phonetic sp.), all recognized authorities.

Q.   Okay. Well, that's their view is what it is. Okay. I mean, they're not signing any legislative history or anything like that.

A.   No. But that's—

Q.   Okay.

A.   That's the analysis from West law.

Q.   Okay.

JUDGE TO COUNSEL

Q.   Anything else from either side?

A.   (Mr. Thal) Nothing else, your honor.

A.   (Ms. Toews) No, other than we believe that the prior case law is fully applicable to cancellation of removal.

Q.   Okay. Well, it's going to take me a while to actually render this. I'll tell you want I'm going to do, I'm not going to find the charge, but I am going to find that that is a break in the presence here. So I want to dictate a decision on that. That'll probably take 15, 20 minutes. I don't want to have everybody else sit around and wait for that, so let me put your case down to the end of the docket and I'll—I'll dictate a decision. Is that all right? Okay.

JUDGE FOR THE RECORD

We'll go off the record briefly here.

(OFF THE RECORD)

(ON THE RECORD)

JUDGE FOR THE RECORD

Back on the record here.

JUDGE TO MR. THAL

Q. Mr. Thal, you had something you wanted to include in the record, before I enter my decision?

A. Yes, your honor. During the recess, I was able to take again a second look at the selected legislative history of the Illegal Immigration Reform and Immigrant Responsibility Act of 1996 and specifically taking a look at the Conference Report on IIRAIRA of the 104th Congress, Second Session Report HR 104–828 September 24, 1996. At page 213 of the Conference Report, it does state, and I'm quoting, "new Section 240(A) establishes revised rules for the type of relief that is currently available to excludable and deportable aliens under Section 212(c) and 244 (a) through (d), Senate Amendment Section 150 recedes to these House provisions with modifications," end of quote.

It goes on to discuss the basic statutory scheme and then on Page 214 of the Conference Report, specifically with respect to the issue of continuous physical presence, the Conference Report provides, as follows, and I'm quoting, "Section 240a(b) provides that the period of continuous residence or a physical presence ends when an alien is served a Notice to Appear, under Section 239(a) for the commencement of removal proceedings under Section 240 or when the alien is convicted of an offense that renders the alien deportable from the United States, whichever is earliest. Period of continuous physical presence, under Section 240a(b) is broken if the alien has departed from the United States for any period of 90 days or for any periods in the aggregate exceeding 180 days. The continuous physical presence requirement does not apply to an alien who has served 24 months in active duty status in the United States Armed Forces, was in the United States at the time of enlistment or induction and was honorably discharged," end of quote.

The rest of the Conference Report, to my knowledge, is silent as to trying to go back to include old rules or old law, under the brief, casual, innocent standards that previously applied under the old line of cases that were with respect to the 7–year suspension of deportation claims, which are the exact kind of cases which the INS has raised as their argument to break the continuous physical presence.

In addition, in the Ira Curtspan (phonetic sp.) [Kurzban—ed.] Immigration Law Source Book of 1998 and '99, Sixth Edition, in Chapter 8 where it discussed relief from removal and, specifically, under Paragraph 5 where it talking about changes from the 7 and 10–year suspension provision under former INA Section 244(a) (1) & (2), paragraph D, reads the brief, casual, and innocent standard for determining when there has been a break in the physical presence requirement is replaced by a rule that terminates physical presence if a person is out of the U.S. for a 90 days or 180 days in the aggregate during the 10–year period, citing INA Section 240A(d)(2).

So, in addition to what I have read of the legislative history and, again, another source, Ira Curtspan with his authoritative interpretation of that section, again, it's still our position that we're under a new statutory scheme which was not meant to bring us back into the issues that we previously faced with the 7–year rule and the issues of the brief, casual, and innocent departure where we were now to have a bright line standard where you specifically count the number of days and avoid those types of issues, which is our position.

Q.   Well, my main concern with your approach here is, in theory, a person could be deported from the—if you apply your approach to it, a person could be deported 179 times from the United States within the la-year period and, as long as they came back on the same day they were deported, they would still be eligible to seek cancellation. I mean, if you completely disregard the deportations, voluntary returns, a person could be deported, well, 179 might be a stretch, but they could be deported 10 times, if they immediately re-violated the law and returned to the United States within that period, under your interpretation, they would still be eligible for cancellation, right?

A.   No, I don't believe so, because there would a difference between a re-entry after a deportation where you have a bar, for 5 or 10 years, of re-entry. You don't have that from a voluntary departure, so I would see that as a distinction.

Q.   A voluntary departure or a voluntary return at Government expense. What exactly did we have in this respondent's case? He had a voluntary return at government expense, if I recall. Is that right?

A.   To be honest, I'd have to look. I'm not—I'm not sure what that was.

Q.   Under the same theory, a person could get a dozen voluntary departures after being placed in proceedings, coming right back to the U.S. and still be eligible for cancellation, right?

A.   I guess, in theory, but as a practical matter, I can't see that the Service would ever stipulate to 11 voluntary departures, following the first.

Q.   I wouldn't be surprised how many people get multiple voluntary departures or voluntary returns, you know. But under your theory, you could have an awfully large number of enforced removals, whether through voluntary departure or possibly through deportation, as well, that would just be meaningless in the overall scheme of statutory eligibility for cancellation.

A.   Again, I would draw a distinction between voluntary departures and deportation because I think the consequences that render from the deportation would be different from those with respect to the voluntary departure, but you're correct in the sense that, yes, in theory, but I think it would be highly speculative and very highly unlikely that you would ever see a case where you have someone coming back 12 times and even with those 12 times, if that were to ever happen which, again, I submit would be very unlikely, you would still have to look at the accumulated number of days of absences, as well to count not only towards the aggregate but for any absence of 90 days or more.

MS. TOEWS TO JUDGE

Q. I don't know whether they were at Government expense or not, your honor. However, the INS position is that irrelevant.

Q. Okay.

A. It's irrelevant. The fact that Congress did say that certain things would be a bright line break does not preclude other things from also being a break. For instance, would—when talking about physical presence or residence then, are we also—I'm going to take back that thought. It was an unformulated thought and I think I started speaking before I should have, but it's basically irrelevant. A voluntary departure, a voluntary return, a deportation, when an alien is not supposed to be in the United States, has been encountered by the Government and has, pursuant to permission from the Government or an order from the Government, left the United States, that breaks physical presence and Congress certainly did not mean to grant those people relief when they then enter illegally after the government has seen to their departure.

Q. Okay.

JUDGE TO MR. THAL

Q. Anything you want to add, Mr. Thal or you?

A. Well, the only thought on that is that's not entirely correct in that, at the time IIRAIRA, the very legislation that we're talking about was passed, Congress extended at that time, Section 245(i), which left open those who had re-entered without inspection and ultimately before that legislation sunsetted in January 14, 1998, there were certainly people that had re-entered the United States without inspection who were still eligible to apply for relief, why, because Congress wanted to avoid the harsh results at that time and it certainly extended other relief that would allow for re-entry, even without permission, to be able to seek relief such as under 245(i).

MS. TOEWS TO JUDGE

Q. May I comment, your honor?

A. Yes.

Q. 245(i) is not—it is a form of relief in these proceedings but, keep in mind, it is not relief in and of itself, it is a vehicle through which somebody who's separately and independently is eligible, is an immediately relative or has—is eligible for an immigrant visa to merely stay here and process, rather than go abroad and process, but it's not, in and of itself, a whole new way, in and of itself, of gaining status in the United States; cancellation of removal is. It doesn't list status as only the vehicle through which somebody gets the immigrant visa that they are independently otherwise entitled to.

A. Well, 245(i) also included the imposition of a increasingly expensive penalty against people who were seeking that relief, too. I don't think it was, in *any* way, an endorsement of—or no-strings-attached amelioration

here, because it's now up to $1,000 penalty for seeking to adjust in the United States after falling under those provisions. Interesting issue.

JUDGE FOR THE RECORD

Okay. Off the record.

(OFF THE RECORD)

(ON THE RECORD)

JUDGE TO COUNSEL

Q.   One other thing to both counsel here, for purposes of this hearing, are you both in agreement that we will consider the respondent's application for a voluntary departure as being an application for voluntary departure at the conclusion of the removal proceedings, as noted in 8 C.F.R 240.26(c)?

A.   (Mr. Thal) Yes, your honor.

A.   (Ms. Toews) What was your exact citation in the beginning?

Q.   240.26(c) of the regs.

A.   (Ms. Toews) Yes.

A.   (Mr. Thal) Yes.

Q.   Yes.

A.   Yes, I had said yes already.

Q.   I'm sorry, I didn't hear you. Both sides are stipulated to that, Okay. Now is there anything else that—I'm going to make a finding that the respondent is not eligible to seek cancellation and removal, based on the guidance we have received, even though the suspension cap is in place at this time, pursuant to 8 C.F.R. 240.21(c)(1), I believe I am allowed to deny without reserving a decision or, in fact, I am pretermitting the application in which an applicant, in my view, has failed to establish statutory eligibility for relief. So do either of you have any opinion or view to the contrary that would indicate that I would be required to reserve decision at this time, in light of what I'm telling you I'm going to do with the case here today?

A.   (Ms. Toews) No, your honor.

A.   (Mr. Thal) I have no further information on that charge.

Q.   Okay.

JUDGE RENDERS ORAL DECISION

JUDGE TO MR. FLORES

Q.   Sir, I may have overlooked it before, but I want to get it clear in the record. Sir, do you have the funds to pay your way to leave the United States voluntarily, *if* that should become necessary?

A. Well, not right now, but my wife, she is ill and I have to, you know, be, you know, taking care of her at all times and she doesn't work either.

JUDGE FOR THE RECORD

Off the record

(OFF THE RECORD)

(ON THE RECORD)

JUDGE FOR THE RECORD

Back on the record here.

JUDGE TO MR. THAL

Q. Mr. Thal, did you have an opportunity to discuss my question with your client?

A. Right. I think he understands it more fully now, too, Judge. And, yes, he is working, so he would have sufficient funds, but he can again state that to the Court, as well.

Q. He's had employment authorization for quite a while.

A. He's got employment authorization and he also owns a car and he's able to come up with funds to be able to leave the United States if that should become necessary.

Q. So, sir, you would have the money available to just purchase a ticket to leave the United States, if necessary?

A. Yes.

Q. Okay.

––––––

U.S. DEPARTMENT OF JUSTICE
EXECUTIVE OFFICE FOR IMMIGRATION REVIEW
IMMIGRATION COURT
Bloomington, Minnesota

File No.: A 76 407 515   August 24, 1999

In the Matter of

FELICIANO FLORES–PALOMINO	)	IN REMOVAL PROCEEDINGS
	)	
Respondent	)	

CHARGE: Section 212(a)(6)(A)(i) of the Immigration and Nationality Act, as an alien present in the United States without being admitted or paroled. Lodged Section 212(a)(2)(A)(i)(I) of the I. & N. Act, as an alien who has been convicted of a crime involving moral turpitude.

APPLICATIONS: 1) Section 240A(b) of the I. & N. Act—Cancellation of removal and adjustment of status for certain non-permanent residents.

2) Section 240B of the I. & N. Act—Voluntary departure.

ON BEHALF OF RESPONDENT: ON BEHALF OF SERVICE:
Steven C. Thal   Annette Toews
Attorney At–Law   Assistant District Counsel

ORAL DECISION OF THE IMMIGRATION JUDGE

The respondent is a 45–year-old married male, who is a native and citizen of Mexico. The respondent last entered the United States on June 15, 1997, near San Ysidro, California. At the time of that entry, the respondent was not admitted or paroled after inspection by an Immigration officer. The respondent asserts that he initially entered the United States on January 13, 1987. His arrival at that time was also without inspection.

Removal proceedings were commenced on September 2, 1998, by the filing with the Immigration Court of a Notice to Appear, which is marked Exhibit 1. Subsequently, on April 19, 1999, the Immigration Service filed an additional charging document, which as been marked Exhibit 5. In that Form I–261, the Service charged the respondent had been convicted of enhanced gross misdemeanor driving with an alcohol concentration of 2.0 [sic] in violation of Minnesota law. The Service charged the respondent was inadmissible to the United States as an alien who had been convicted of a crime involving moral turpitude, relative to his alcohol-related traffic conviction.

At prior master calendar hearings in this case, respondent admitted all factual allegations and the charge contained in the Notice to Appear. Respondent was found removable as charged in the Notice to Appear. Respondent admitted factual allegation 5 contained in the form I–261, but denied the charge of removability. Based on respondent's admission of the charge in the Notice to Appear, the Court found that removability had been established by evidence that was clear, convincing, and unequivocal. The respondent designated Mexico as the country for removal.

Regarding relief from removal, the respondent is seeking cancellation of removal under Section 240A(b) of the Immigration and Nationality Act. The Immigration Service opposes cancellation for the respondent, noting that within the 10–year period, to qualify for cancellation and removal, the respondent had been encountered by the Immigration Service and had left the United States, apparently under an order of voluntary departure. The Service states that this enforced departure of the respondent from the United States, in effect, is a break in the respondent's continuous physical presence in the United States, as required in Section 240A(b)(1)(A) of the Act. Respondent does not dispute that he had been encountered by the Immigration Service and required to depart the United States during the qualifying period.

* * *

Also included in Exhibit 2 are other documents relating to the respondent from the Immigration Service. On page 12 of this exhibit is the Form I–213 noting that in April of 1997, respondent was arrested by the Immigration Service near Willmar, Minnesota. The record reflects that the respondent had last entered the United States at that time as of August 10, 1996, entering the United States near San Ysidro without being inspected. This record reflects the respondent was given a voluntary return under safeguards to Mexico at that time. At page 1 of the exhibit, an I–213 issued on August 26, 1998, reflects the respondent had been given three previous VRs from the United States. In the following pages, there are records reflecting respondent's prior apprehensions by the Immigration Service.

Exhibit 4 includes respondent's application for cancellation of removal. In this document, respondent at question 25 states that in April 1997 he was given voluntary departure from the United States. He returned illegally two weeks after that voluntary departure.

<u>Number 2 Analysis</u>

Removability on the charge contained in the Notice to Appear is not in dispute in this case. The respondent is clearly removable from the United States as a alien who is present in the United States without being admitted or paroled. * * * [Here the IJ rejects the lodged charge arising out of the DUI conviction—Ed.]

Turning to relief from removal, the Court notes that there is a long history of case law that reflects, that it is well established, that the voluntary departure of an alien after apprehension by the Service, whether granted administratively or by order of an Immigration Judge, has interrupted the period of continuous physical presence required for suspension of deportation under the prior 244(a) of the Act.

Respondent has emphasized that the new relief of cancellation of removal contains somewhat different language from that of the prior suspension of deportation statute.

Specifically, respondent cites Section 240A(d)(2) of the Act, discussing certain breaks in presence as reflecting a failure to maintain continuous physical presence. The statutory provision states that if an alien has departed from the United States for any period in excess of 90 days or for any periods in the aggregate exceeding 180 days, the alien shall be considered to have failed to maintain such continuous physical presence. There is no specific mention in that statutory section one way or the other relating to the departures being enforced by the Immigration Service.

The court believes that a departure from the United States after an enforcement action by the Immigration Service still should be considered to be an interruption in continuous physical presence. If the Court were to accept respondent's argument in this case an alien could be granted voluntary departure numerous times during the qualifying period, and continuously re-enter the United States shortly after departure, and then claim eligibility for cancellation. The court does not feel that this is an appropriate situation. The intervention of Government enforcement activity is a qualitatively different situation from an alien who briefly departs the United States without government compulsion, and who then returns at a later point. To allow an alien who has been the subject of an enforcement action, to re-enter the United States and seek cancellation relief without any penalty whatsoever for the enforced departure, makes no sense.

Simply put, the Court believes that this respondent's prior voluntary departure from the United States within the 10–year period does interrupt his continuous physical presence and bars him from the relief of cancellation and removal. It is the court's belief that Congress, by setting the 90 and 180 days top limits on absences from the United States or cancellation eligibility, did not thereby intend to abolish all lesser departures, as a result of government enforcement actions, from being considered interruptions of continuous physical presence. The Court will make a finding that respondent is not statutorily eligible for cancellation of removal, because he has failed to establish that he has been physically present in the United States for a continuous period of not less than 10 years immediately proceeding the date of his application.

Regarding voluntary departure, the Court would simply note that respondent is seeking voluntary departure at the close of removal proceedings. He has been physically present in the United States for at least one year proceeding the date of the Notice to Appear. The Court has made a finding that respondent's alcohol-related conviction is not a crime involving moral turpitude. The Court will find that respondent has been a person of good moral character for five years immediately proceeding his application for voluntary departure. He has not been convicted of a crime that would be classified as an aggravated felony. The court believes the respondent does have the means to depart the United States.

The following orders will be entered in this case:

1. Respondent was found to be removable from the United States as charged in the Notice to Appear.

2. Respondent is not found to be removable from the United States under the charge set forth in the Form I–261.

3. Respondent's application for cancellation of removal under Section 240A(b) of the Immigration and Nationality Act is pretermitted and denied, based on respondent's not having established that he has been physically present in the United States for a continuous period of not less than 10 years immediately preceding his application.

4. IT IS HEREBY ORDERED that the respondent be granted voluntary departure in lieu of removal, without expense to the Government on or before October 25, 1999. Since that is the maximum period allowed by law, no mention of extensions by the District Director will be made. As a condition of this grant of voluntary departure, a voluntary departure bond of $500 shall be required.

5. IT IS FURTHER ORDERED that if the respondent fails to depart, as required, the above order shall be withdrawn without further notice or proceedings and the following order should thereupon become immediately

effective: Respondent should be removed to Mexico on the charge in the Notice to Appear.

Joseph R. Dierkes

JOSEPH R. DIERKES
Immigration Judge

————

JUDGE TO COUNSEL

Q.   All right. You've both heard my decision. Do you both wish to reserve appeal?

A.   (Ms. Toews) Yes, your honor.

Q.   The due date for the appeal would be September 23, 1999. Is there anything else that either side wishes to include in the record at this time?

A.   (Mr. Thal) Nothing else, your honor.

MS. TOEWS TO JUDGE

Q.   No, your honor, other than the fact that, off the record, I don't think it made it on the record the Service had previously stated its opposition to voluntary departure in this case, as well as cancellation.

A.   And your—well, you've reserved appeal, you can—

Q.   And I've reserved appeal, but I just wanted to make it clear that the Service had not conceded eligibility for a voluntary departure, that the Service was opposing it.

A.   You're arguing statutory ineligibility for voluntary departure.

Q.   Statutory indiscretion, yes.

JUDGE TO COUNSEL

A.   All right. Okay.

Q.   Well, let me put it this way, did both of you have an opportunity to get everything in the record you want to today?

A.   (Mr. Thal) Yes, your honor.

A.   (Ms. Toews) I believe so, your honor.

Q.   Okay.

JUDGE TO MR. FLORES

Q.   To the respondent, sir, your attorney and the government's attorney have both reserved the right to appeal my decision. If you are going to appeal my decision, that appeal should be filed within 30 days. So make sure you work with the attorney to see that the appeal is filed in a timely manner, if that is what you wish to do. You understand that?

A. Yes.

Q. Okay.

JUDGE FOR THE RECORD

If there is nothing else from either side, I'll serve the order. This hearing is concluded.

———

U.S. Department of Justice
Executive Office for Immigration Review
Board of Immigration Appeals

OMB # 1105-0065
Notice of Appeal to the Board of Immigration
Appeals of Decision of Immigration Judge

1	List Name(s) and "A" Number(s) of all Applicant(s)/Respondent(s): FLORES-PALOMINO Feliciano A76 407 515	**For Official Use Only**
	! WARNING TO ALL APPLICANT(S)/RESPONDENT(S): Names and "A" Numbers of everyone appealing the order must be written in Item #1.	

2.   **Applicant/Respondent is currently**   ☐ **DETAINED**   ■ **NOT DETAINED**

3.   **Appeal from the Immigration Judge's decision dated**   _August 24, 1999_

4	State in detail the reason(s) for this appeal. You are not limited to the space provided below; use more sheets of paper if necessary. Write your name(s) and "A" number(s) on every sheet. **! WARNING:** The failure to specify the factual or legal basis for the appeal may lead to summary dismissal without further notice, unless you give specific details in a timely separate written brief or statement filed with the Board.
	Whether the Immigration Judge erred by denying Mr. Flore's application for cancellation of removal under Section 240A(b) where Mr. Flores was never absent from the U.S. for any period in exess of 90 days nor for 180 days in the aggregate in the 10 years immediately preceding the application for cancellation of removal? Whether the Immigration Judge erred by applying pre-cancellation of removal case law from the old suspension of deportation law in denying Mr. Flore's application for cancellation of removal? (Attach more sheets if necessary)

Form EOIR - 26
Revised April 1996

5.   I   ■ do
         ☐ do not   desire oral argument before the Board of Immigration Appeals.

6.   I   ■ will
         ☐ will not   file a separate written brief or statement in addition to the "Reason(s) for Appeal" written above or accompanying this form.

! WARNING: Your appeal may be summarily dismissed if you indicate in Item #6 that you will file a separate written brief or statement and, within the time set for filing, you fail to file the brief or statement and do not reasonably explain such failure.

✍ SIGN HERE →	7. **X** _Feliciano P. Flores_ Signature of Person Appealing	_09/14/99_ Date

8	Mailing Address of Applicant(s)/Respondent(s)	9	Mailing Address of Applicant(s)/Respondent(s)
	Feliciano FLORES-PALOMINO		
	(Name)		(Name)
	610 Rice Ave. SW		
	(Street Address)		(Street Address)
	(Apartment or Room Number)		(Apartment or Room Number)
	Willmar, MN 56201		
	(City, State, Zip Code)		(City, State, Zip Code)

! WARNING: An attorney or representative will not be recognized as counsel on appeal and will not receive documents or correspondence in connection with the appeal, unless he/she submits a completed Form EOIR-27.

CERTIFICATE OF SERVICE
(Must Be Completed)

10.

I   Steven C. Thal   mailed or delivered a copy of this notice of appeal

on   9/15/99   to   Mr. Richard Soli, INS District Counsel
    (Date)   (Opposing Party)

at   P.O. Box 11898, St. Paul, Minnesota 55111   .
        (Address of Opposing Party)

✍ SIGN
HERE ➜

X   _Richard Soli_
    Signature of Person Appealing
    (or attorney or representative)

Have You?

■ Read all of the General Instructions
■ Provided all of the requested information
■ Completed this form in English
■ Provided a certified English translation
   for all non-English attachments

■ Signed the form
■ Served a copy of this form and all
   attachments on the opposing party
■ Completed and signed the Certificate of Service
■ Attached the required fee or fee waiver request

U.S. Department of Justice   Decision of the Board of Immigration Appeals

U.S. Department of Justice
Decision of the Board of Immigration Appeals
Executive Office for Immigration Review

Falls Church, Virginia 22041

File: A76–407–515   Date: April 29, 2002

In re: FLORES–PALOMINO, FELICIANO

IN REMOVAL PROCEEDINGS

APPEAL

ON BEHALF OF RESPONDENT: Thal, Steven C., Esquire

ON BEHALF OF SERVICE: Toews, Annette M.

ORDER:

PER CURIAM. The Board affirms, without opinion, the results of the decision below ... The decision below is, therefore, the final agency determination. *See* 8 C.F.R. § 3.1(a)(7).

FURTHER ORDER: Pursuant to the Immigration Judge's order and conditioned upon compliance with conditions set forth by the Immigration Judge and the statute, the alien is "permitted to voluntarily depart from the United States, without expense to the Government, within 30 days from the date of this order or any extension beyond that time as may be granted by the district director." *See* section 240B(b) of the Immigration and Nationality Act; 8 *C.F.R.* §§ 240.26(c), (f). In the event the alien fails to so depart, the alien shall be removed as provided in the Immigration Judge's order.

NOTICE: If the alien fails to depart the United States within the time period specified, or any extensions granted by the district director, the alien shall be subject to a civil penalty of not less than $1,000 and not more than $5,000, and shall be ineligible for a period of 10 years for any further relief under section 240B and sections 240A, 245, 248, and 249 of the Immigration and Nationality Act. *See* section 240B(d) of the Act.

Frederick D. Hess
FOR THE BOARD

––––––––

U.S. Department of Justice
Decision of the Board of Immigration Appeals
Executive Office for Immigration Review
Falls Church, Virginia 22041

File: A76407 515—Bloomington   Date: NOV 07 2002

In re: FELICIANO FLORES–PALOMINO

IN REMOVAL PROCEEDINGS

APPEAL

ON BEHALF OF RESPONDENT: Steven C. Thal, Esquire

ON BEHALF OF SERVICE: Terry M. Louie
                        Assistant District Counsel

The Board issued a decision on April 29, 2002, which dismissed the respondent's appeal of the Immigration Judge's decision, and granted the respondent a period of 30 days to voluntarily depart the Unite4 States. The record indicates, however, that the decision was mailed to the respondent's attorney at an incorrect address. The Respondent, therefore, was never served with a copy of the order and, in fact, was unaware that the Board had rendered a decision in his case.

Respondent, through counsel, has now filed a motion to reopen, requesting removal proceedings be reopened so that the Board's April 29, 2002, decision be reissued. Though respondent's motion to reopen is untimely filed the Board will consider the motion sua sponte. *See Matter of J–J–*, 21 I. & N. Dec. 976 (BIA 1997). We note that the Service concurs with the respondent's request that the Board reissue the decision.

Accordingly, the motion to reopen will be granted, and our order of April 29, 2002, will be reissued with the current date.

ORDER: The motion to reopen is granted.

FURTHER ORDER: The Board's order dated April 29, 2002, is hereby reissued and shall be treated as entered as of today's date.

FURTHER ORDER: Respondent is granted 30 days within which to voluntarily depart the United States pursuant to the Board's order (reissued this date and attached hereto) dismissing his appeal.

Frederick D. Hess
FOR THE BOARD

————

UNITED STATES COURT OF APPEALS
FOR THE EIGHTH CIRCUIT

Feliciano FLORES PALOMINO,	)	
	)	
Petitioner,	)	No. _____
	)	
v.		
	)	INS File No. A76 407 515
United States Department of Justice,	)	
Immigration and Naturalization Service,	)	
And John Ashcroft, Attorney General	)	
	)	
Respondent,	)	
	)	

PETITION FOR REVIEW

Pursuant to Rule 15 of the Federal Rules of Appellate Procedure (FRAP), Petitioner, Feliciano Flores Palomino, hereby petitions this Court for the review of a final Order and Decision of the Board of Immigration Appeals, dated November 7, 2002, summarily denying Petitioner's application for cancellation of removal, without opinion. A copy of the Board's affirmance without opinion is attached hereto as *Exhibit A.*

The validity of the Board's Order has not been the subject of any other judicial proceedings.

To the extent the Board's summary decision and Order adopts, refers to, or incorporates the Immigration Judge's oral decision of August 24, 1999 (the "IJ's Order"), Petitioner also seeks review of the IJ's Order. A copy of the IJ's Order is attached hereto as *Exhibit B.*

The administrative proceedings which led to the Board's order were conducted within the territorial jurisdiction of this Court. This Court has jurisdiction over this matter pursuant to 8 U.S.C. §§ 1252(a) and (b).

Dated: December 4, 2002

> Respectfully submitted,
> *Steven C. Thal*
> Steven C. Thal, P.A.
> 11650 Wayzata Blvd
> Minnetonka, MN 55305
> Phone: 952–541–1090
> Attorney for Petitioner

UNITED STATES COURT OF APPEALS
FOR THE EIGHTH CIRCUIT

Feliciano FLORES PALOMINO,	)
	)
Petitioner,	) No.
	)
	)
v.	) INS File No. A76 407 515
	)
United States Department of Justice,	)
Immigration and Naturalization Service,	)
And John Ashcroft, Attorney General	)
	)
Respondent.	)
	)

MOTION FOR STAY OF REMOVAL

Petitioner, Feliciano Flores Palomino, through and by his counsel, hereby moves the Court for an Order staying his physical removal from the United States until such time as the Court has issued a final decision on Petitioner's Petition for Review as concurrently filed herewith. In support of such Motion, Petitioner states as follows:

1. Petitioner's administrative application for cancellation of removal under §§ 240A, of the Immigration and Nationality Act, 8 U.S.C. §§ 1229b was denied by the Board of Immigration Appeals on November 7, 2002.

2. The Petitioner is subject to immediate removal regardless of his judicial appeal because he has no more administrative appeals currently pending on the merits.

3. Petitioner contends that the Immigration Judge's finding of deportability and denial of relief from deportation and the Board's summary dismissal of his appeal was contrary to statute, regulations, and case law.

4. Petitioner will suffer irreparable harm if he is not granted a stay of deportation pending the decision on his Petition for Review. A denial of this stay will allow the INS to act to remove Petitioner and render moot his Petition for Review. It will foreclose a meaningful review of his case if he is forced to return to Mexico.

5. Petitioner is not in the custody of the Immigration and Naturalization Service (INS) and he poses no danger to the community.

6. No relief has been sought in the District Court because the Court of Appeals is the proper Court in which to seek this Stay.

7. On December 4, 2002, Petitioner submitted a request for Stay of Removal to the Immigration and Naturalization Service (INS) seeking administrative action by the INS to allow petitioner to remain in the United States while his Petition for Review is considered. As of the date of this Motion, however, the INS has failed to take or communicate any action in furtherance of Petitioner's request. Therefore, because the Petitioner has been ordered to depart voluntarily from the United States by December 6, 2002, the prompt action of this Court on this Petitioner's motion is necessary to preserve his continued presence in this Country pending resolution of his Petition for Review on the merits.

8. For the foregoing reasons, and as further articulated in Petitioner's memorandum in support hereof, Petitioner seeks the protection of this Court and respectfully requests that the Court issue an immediate Order granting a stay of removal pending the Court's decision on the Petition for Review.

Dated: December 4, 2002

Respectfully submitted,
Steven C. Thal

Steven C. Thal
Steven C. Thal, P.A.
11650 Wayzata Blvd
Minnetonka, MN 55305
Phone: 952–541–1090
Attorney for Petitioner

UNITED STATES COURT OF APPEALS
FOR THE EIGHTH CIRCUIT

Feliciano FLORES PALOMINO,   )
)
Petitioner,   ) No.
)
)
v.   ) INS File No. A76 407 515
)
) MEMORANDUM
United States Department of Justice,) IN SUPPORT OF
Immigration and Naturalization Service,) MOTION FOR STAY
And John Ashcroft, Attorney General) OF REMOVAL
)
Respondent.   )
)

* * *

Standard of Review Governing Motions for Stays of Removal

Prior to the enactment of the Illegal Immigration Reform and Immigrant Responsibility Act of 1996 ("IIRIRA"), Pub. L. 104–28, 100 Stat. 3009 (1996), an alien ordered deported generally received an automatic stay of deportation upon petitioning for review in federal court. *See* 8 U.S.C. § 1105(a)(3) (1994). This automatic stay provision was eliminated by IIRIRA however, and the federal circuits are currently split regarding the proper standard of review governing motions for a stay of removal. *Compare Andreiu v. Ashcroft,* 253 F.3d 477 (9th Cir. 2001) (applying traditional standard for discretionary stays and preliminary injunctions), *with Weng v. United States Attorney General,* 287 F.3d 1335 (11th Cir. 2002) (holding IIRIRA to require clear and convincing evidence that removal order is prohibited as a matter of law). Although the Eighth Circuit has not yet ruled on this issue, the Court should take this opportunity to adopt the majority *Andreiu* rule. * * *

* * *

The IIRIRA states that "[s]ervice of the petition [for review] on the officer or employee does not stay the removal of an alien pending the court's decision on the petition, *unless the court orders otherwise"* 8 U.S.C. § 1252(b)(3)(B) (emphasis added). * * * In *Andreiu v. Ashcroft,* the INS argued that 8 U.S.C. § 1252(f)(2) provided the standard for granting a stay of deportation. Section 1252(f)(2) states, in relevant part that: * * *

> (2) Particular cases. Notwithstanding any other provision of law, no court shall enjoin the removal of any alien pursuant to a final order under this section unless the alien shows by clear and convincing evidence that the entry or execution of such order is prohibited as a matter of law.

But the Ninth Circuit disagreed however, noting that the IIRIRA used the terms "enjoin" "restrain" and "stay" in different provisions, and therefore, each of these terms should be given some operative effect. The

Court concluded that "enjoin" meant to "legally prohibit or restrain by injunction," while a "stay" is a temporary halt to legal proceedings. Injunctions operate against parties; stays operate against courts and judgments. *See Andreiu,* 253 F.3d at 483.

The court also pointed out that interpreting the IIRIRA to require the petitioner to demonstrate by "clear and convincing evidence" that the removal order is "prohibited as a matter of law" would produce absurd results, because it would effectively require a more substantial showing for a stay of removal than it would for a reversal on the merits. *Id.* at 482. Furthermore, the clear and convincing evidence standard

> would require full-scale briefing at the beginning of the appellate process, often before the petitioner has even received a copy of the administrative record. In those cases in which a motions panel grants the stay on the basis that the INS's order is clearly prohibited as a matter of law, the issue before the merits panel would be the same issue that a motions panel had previously resolved in favor of the petitioner. None of these results are at all sensible as a matter of judicial administration or of the detailed structure the statute establishes for review of BIA decisions.

Id. at 482.

Consequently, because 8 U.S.C. § 1252(f)(2) is inapplicable to temporary stays of deportation, and in the absence of a specific statutory provision governing the standard for granting stays of removal, the Ninth Circuit applied the standard generally used for discretionary stays and preliminary injunctions in that circuit. * * * *Bejjani v. Ashcroft,* 271 F.3d 670, 688 (6th Cir. 2001) (same); *Sofinet v. INS,* 188 F.3d 703, 706 (7th Cir. 1999) (same). Indeed, only the Eleventh Circuit has imposed a different standard, finding a new "clear and convincing" standard applies to motions for stays of deportation under 8 U.S.C. § 1252(f)(2). *Weng v. United States Attorney General,* 287 F.3d 1335 (11th Cir. 2002) (failing to find meaningful distinction between "stay" and "enjoin"). * * * This Court should find *Andreiu's* reasoning persuasive and hold that the standard typically employed in this circuit for discretionary stays or preliminary injunctions applies to motions to stay deportation.

Argument

Under Eighth Circuit law, this Court considers four factors in determining whether to issue a preliminary injunction or temporary stay: (1) the threat of irreparable harm to the movant; (2) the state of the balance between this harm and the injury that granting the injunction will inflict on other parties; (3) the probability that the movant will succeed on the merits; and (4) the public interest. *See Dataphase Systems, Inc. v. C L Systems, Inc.,* 640 F.2d 109, 113 (8th Cir. 1981). Courts applying this standard in the context of a stay of removal of an alien pending appeal have noted that "the gravity of the injury to the alien if a stay is denied, compared to the lesser 'injury' to the Government if one alien is permitted to remain while an appeal is decided, suggests that the degree of likelihood of success on appeal need not be set too high."

Pursuant to section 240A(b) of the Immigration and Nationality Act ("INA"), 8 U.S.C. § 1229(b), the Attorney General, acting through the INS, may cancel removal of an alien to their home country if they have been physically present in the United States for a continuous period of not less than ten years immediately preceding the date of such application, have been a person of good moral character during such period, have not been convicted of certain offenses, and established that removal would result in exceptional and extremely unusual hardship to the alien's spouse, parent, or child who is a citizen of the United States or an alien lawfully admitted for permanent residence.

In this case, Mr. Flores–Palomino never got to present any of the evidence in support of his application of Cancellation of Removal because the Immigration Judge pretermited and denied the application prior to the taking of any testimony. The Immigration Judged ruled as a matter of law that any voluntary returns to Mexico during the ten years preceding the date of application broke Mr. Flores–Palomino's continuous physical presence in the United States. However, Mr. Flores–Palomino contends that was not the intent of Congress when it enacted changes in 1996 under the Illegal Immigration Reform and Immigrant Responsibility Act of 1996. Respondent contends that under the statute as enacted the period of continuous physical presence under § 240(b) is broken if the alien has departed from the United States for any period of 90 days or for any periods in the aggregate exceeding 180 days. Mr. Flores–Palomino contends that the Immigration Judge erred by applying pre IIRIRA case law, rather than applying the new standard of the 90 day or 180 day rule. The Board of Immigration Appeals failed in its entirety to even address this issue affirming the decision of the Immigration Judge without opinion. Mr. Flores–Palomino further contends that the Board erred in not providing any analysis of its decision and has effectively failed to review the decision of the Immigration Judge. Because Mr. Flores–Palomino has established that he is both likely to succeed on the merits of his petition for review and that he would suffer hardship if he were returned to Mexico while his appeal is pending, this Court should grant a Stay of Removal.

* * *

Date: December 4, 2002

Respectfully Submitted,
Steven C. Thal

Steven C. Thal, P.A.
Steven C. Thal
11650 Wayzata Blvd
Minnetonka, MN 55305
Phone: 952–541–1090
Attorney for Petitioner

No. 02–3961

IN THE UNITED STATES COURT OF APPEALS
FOR THE EIGHTH CIRCUIT

FELICIANO FLORES PALOMINO,
Petitioner,
v.
JOHN ASHCROFT,
United States Attorney General,
Respondent.

RESPONDENT'S MOTION INSTANTER IN OPPOSITION TO MO-
TION FOR STAY OF REMOVAL
A76 407 515

INTRODUCTION

* * * Respondent, John Ashcroft, United States Attorney General, hereby opposes petitioner's request for a stay of removal because Palomino has failed to meet his burden for a stay, and because the Board of Immigration Appeals has squarely addressed the only legal issue he raises: whether an alien's departure from the United States under a threat of removal interrupts the time he may have been accruing towards his ten-year physical presence requirement to qualify for cancellation of removal. *See Matter of Hilario Romalez–Alcaide*, 23 I. & N. Dec. 423, 428–29 (BIA 2002).

* * *

* * * Petitioner asserted that the INA permitted him to leave the United States (relying on section 240A(d)(2) of the INA, 8 U.S.C. l229b(d)(2) for a period of up to 90 days. [Exhibit A] at 6. However, the Immigration Judge noted that the statute did not apply to petitioner's voluntary departures and illegal reentries because "[t]he intervention of Government enforcement activity is a qualitatively different situation from an alien who briefly departs the United States without Government compulsion, and who then returns at a later point." *Id.* at 7. The Immigration Judge reasoned, "To allow an alien who has been the subject of an enforcement action, to reenter the United States and seek cancellation relief without any penalty whatsoever for the enforced departure, makes no sense. *Id.*; *C.f.* 8 U.S.C. § l229b(d)(1) (continuous period terminates upon service of charging document). Accordingly, the Immigration Judge pretermitted petitioner's application for cancellation of removal, but granted him the privilege of voluntary departure. *Id.* at 8–9.

On April 29, 2002, the Board affirmed, without opinion, the decision of the Immigration Judge. *See* Exhibit B (April 29, 2002 Decision of the Board). Because the Board's decision was mailed to an incorrect address, the Board re-opened the case, dismissed the appeal, and served petitioner again on November 7, 2002. Petitioner filed a timely Petition for Review and a Motion for Stay of Removal in this Court.

ARGUMENT

THIS COURT SHOULD DENY PETITIONER'S REQUEST FOR A STAY OF REMOVAL BECAUSE PETITIONER HAS NOT MET HIS BURDEN FOR A STAY.

This Court should deny petitioner's request for a stay because it is wholly without any legal or factual support. Courts treat a request for a stay of deportation as a request for a preliminary injunction. *See e.g.*, *Zardui–Quintana v. Richard*, 768 F.2d 1213, 1215 n.7 (11th Cir. 1985); *Jenkins v. INS*, 32 F.3d 11 14 (2d Cir. 1994); *Ignacio v. INS*, 955 F.2d 295, 299 (5th Cir. 1992). Congress has amended the test for injunctive relief by enacting section 242(f)(2) of the INA, which provides: "Notwithstanding any other provision of law, no court shall enjoin the removal of any alien pursuant to a final order under this section unless the alien shows by clear and convincing evidence that the entry or execution of such order is prohibited as a matter of law." 8 U.S.C. § 1252(f)(2) (2000). Therefore, aliens whose immigration proceedings are governed by IIRIRA's permanent rules, such as petitioner's, are subject to the heightened requirement of establishing "clear and convincing evidence" that their removal is "prohibited as a matter of law" in order to receive a stay of removal. *See Weng v. U.S. Attorney General*, 287 F.3d 1335, 1337–40 (11th Cir. 2002); *but see Bejjani*, 271 F.3d 670, 687–88 (6th Cir. 2001) (concluding that 8 U.S.C. § 1252(f) does not encompass stay orders); *Andreiu v. Ashcroft*, 253 F.3d 477, 480 (9th Cir. 2001) (same).

Petitioner has failed to provide clear and convincing evidence that his removal is prohibited as a matter of law as discussed below. Even under the traditional test for injunctive relief, however, Petitioners stay request would fail. * * *

Petitioner's motion fails because his removal is not prohibited as a matter of law. *See* 8 U.S.C. § 1252(f)(2). His only argument is that under the cancellation of removal statute, Congress did not intend that, as the Immigration Judge found, "voluntary" returns to an illegal alien's native country under a threat of INS enforcement action (in the form of removal proceedings) interrupt the alien's accrual of physical presence. Pet. Mem. at *8–9. He cites not a single statute, regulation, or case in support of his theory. Indeed, he ignores completely the fact that the Board has addressed the very issue he raises. *Romalez–Alcaide*, 23 I. & N. Dec. at 428–29.

The Board has recently held that an alien's "departures under threat of deportation [interrupt] his continuous physical presence in this country. Consequently, he cannot meet the 10 year continuous presence requirement for cancellation of removal." *Id.*; *see also* Section 240A(b)(1)(A) of the

INA, 8 U.S.C. § 1229b(b)(1)(A). The Board noted that its holding comports with the literal language of the cancellation of removal statute. *Romalez–Alcaide*, 23 I. & N. Dec. at 429. Moreover, its holding "is also supported by the statutory purpose behind enforcement actions": to deter illegal immigration into the United States by reducing the incentive for aliens to extend their stays in this country and prolong their cases in order to gain immigration benefits. *See id.* at 427–29 (citing H.R. Rep. No. 104–828 (1996), 1996 WL 563320). * * *

* * *

Finally, amendments to the INA reflect a strong public interest in removing illegal aliens as expeditiously as possible from the United States. *See* Sen. Jud. Comm-Rep. No. 104–249 at 7 ("Aliens who violate U.S. immigration law should be removed from this country *as soon as possible*. Exceptions should be provided only in *extraordinary cases* specified in the statute and approved by the Attorney General.") (emphasis added). * * *

CONCLUSION

For all the foregoing reasons, the Court should deny the petitioner's motion to stay removal.

Respectfully submitted,

ROBERT D. McCALLUM, JR.
Assistant Attorney General
EMILY ANNE RADFORD
Assistant Director

Joshua E. Braustein

JOSHUA E. BRAUNSTEIN
Attorney
Office of Immigration Litigation
Civil Division
U.S. Department of Justice
P.O. Box 878, Ben Franklin Station
Washington, D.C. 20044
(202) 305–0194

Dated: December 23, 2002   Attorneys for Respondent

UNITED STATES COURT OF APPEALS
FOR THE EIGHTH CIRCUIT

No.   02–3961

FELICIANO FLORES PALOMINO,)	
)	
Petitioner)	
)	Petition for Review of a Decision
v.)	of the Board of Immigration
)	Appeals
JOHN ASHCROFT,)	
Respondent)	

ORDER

Petitioner's motion for stay of removal pending review has been considered by the court and is denied.

January 8, 2003

Order Entered at the Direction of the Court:

Michael E. Gans

Clerk, U.S. Court of Appeals, Eighth Circuit

———

No. 02–3961

IN THE UNITED STATES COURT OF APPEALS
FOR THE EIGHTH CIRCUIT

FELICIANO FLORES PALOMINO,
Petitioner,
v.
JOHN ASHCROFT,
United States Attorney General
Respondent.

ON APPEAL FROM THE BOARD OF IMMIGRATION
APPEALS DECISION OF NOVEMBER 7, 2002

PETITIONER'S BRIEF

STEVEN C. THAL, P.A.
Steven C. Thal
Attorney I.D. #141021
Attorney for Petitioner
11650 Wayzata Boulevard
Minnetonka, MN 55305
Attorney for Petitioner

SUMMARY AND REQUEST FOR ORAL ARGUMENT

This is an appeal from the Board of Immigration Appeals' decision of November 7, 2002, which denied Petitioner/Appellant, Feliciano Flores–Palomino's application for cancellation of removal under INA § 240A(b)(1). Mr. Flores–Palomino appeared for his final hearing on this matter on August 24, 1999, before the Honorable Joseph Dierkes, Immigration Judge, in Bloomington, Minnesota. The Immigration Judge reached an oral decision on August 24, 1999 whereby he ordered the Appellant deported from the United States, but granted voluntary departure and pretermitted his application for cancellation of removal. Mr. Flores–Palomino appealed to the Board of Immigration Appeals (BIA) on September 15, 1999. He asked the BIA to reverse the decision of the Immigration Judge on the legal issue of whether his voluntary departures from the U.S. within the 10 year statutory period rendered him ineligible for cancellation of removal. The BIA issued an affirmance of the Immigration Judge's decision without opinion on November 7, 2002. Mr. Flores–Palomino now seeks review of the denial of that relief in this court. The BIA decision of *Matter of Romalez–Alcaide*, 23 I. & N. Dec. 423 (BIA 2002) has not been reviewed by this Court and involves important issues of statutory construction regarding the intent of Congress in replacing old suspension of deportation law with new rules for cancellation of removal. Appellant requests 15 minutes of oral argument to present his case to this court.

TABLE OF CONTENTS

SUMMARY AND REQUEST FOR ORAL ARGUMENT i

TABLE OF AUTHORITIES iv

JURISDICTIONAL STATEMENT 1

    I.   Board of Immigration Appeals Jurisdiction 1

    II.   Basis for Court of Appeals Jurisdiction 1

    III. Filing Dates Establishing Timelines of Petition for Review 2

    IV. Appeal from a Final Order 2

STATEMENT OF ISSUE FOR REVIEW 2

I.   Whether the Board of Immigration Appeals Erred in Affirming the Immigration Judge's Decision of pretermitting Mr. Flores–Palomino's application for cancellation of removal where his voluntary departures from the U.S. during the 10 year period of eligibility did not exceed 90 days nor 180 days cumulatively? 2

STATEMENT OF THE CASE 3

SUMMARY OF THE FACTS AND CASE 3

STANDARD OF REVIEW OF ISSUES BEFORE THE 8th CIRCUIT COURT OF APPEALS 4

SUMMARY OF ARGUMENT 5

I.   Mr. Flores–Palomino is eligible for cancellation of removal under Section 240A(b)(1) of the Immigration and Nationality Act in that he meets the statutory criteria of not having been absent from the U.S. for more than 90 days nor any cumulative total exceeding 180 days 5

II. The Legislative History Supports Mr. Flores–Palomino's Position 7

III. The BIA erred by affirming the Immigration Judge's Application of Suspension of Deportation Case Law to a Cancellation of Removal Case 9

CONCLUSION 20

ADDENDUM 22

* * *

[Here the appellant elaborates on the legal arguments that he presented during the administrative proceedings—Ed.]

CONCLUSION

The Court of Appeals should reverse the Board of Immigration Appeals Decision of November 7, 2002, and remand the matter for further proceedings to allow Mr. Flores–Palomino to proceed to a final hearing on his application for cancellation of removal.

Dated: ___1–13___, 2003

Respectfully Submitted,
STEVEN C. THAL, P.A.
By ___Steven C. Thal___
Steven C. Thal (#141021)
Attorney for Petitioner
11650 Wayzata Boulevard
Minnetonka, MN 55305
Telephone: (612) 541–1090

UNITED STATES COURT OF APPEALS
FOR THE EIGHTH CIRCUIT

Feliciano FLORES–PALOMINO,	)
	)
Petitioner	)
	)
v.	) No 02–3961
	)
John ASHCROFT,	)
Respondent	)
	)

MOTION TO FILE BRIEF AS AMICUS CURIAE

Pursuant to Rule 29 of the Federal Rules of Appellate Procedure, American Immigration Law Foundation ("AILF") moves the Court to grant this Motion to File Brief as Amicus Curiae for the Petitioner. AILF is submitting the proposed brief with this motion.

Petitioner consents to AILF's appearing as Amicus Curiae in this case. Undersigned Counsel telephoned Joshua Braunstein, of the Office of Immigration Litigation, attorney for Respondent, to determine if Respondent takes a position on this motion, but Mr. Braunstein was out of town and unavailable.

AILF is a non-profit organization established to increase public understanding of immigration law and policy and to advance fundamental fairness, due process, and constitutional and human rights in immigration law and administration. AILF has a direct interest in ensuring that the due process rights of noncitizens are protected in administrative removal proceedings and the federal courts.

Amicus Curiae's interest in this case arises from our serious concern and objection to the Board of Immigration Appeal's ("BIA" or "Board") use of the summary affirmance without opinion procedure. This procedure violates both administrative law and due process and could affect scores of people within this Circuit and others. First, under the controlling regulation, the BIA is authorized to use the summary affirmance procedure only in those cases that satisfy specified criteria. However, because the regulation prohibits the single Board Member from explaining his or her use of the procedure, the Court is deprived of the ability to determine whether the Board Member has adhered to the regulation. Second, the prohibition on any explanation of the reasons for the Board Member's decision violates fundamental rules of administrative law. It is impermissible for a Board Member to make an independent determination of a case and fail to either explicitly adopt the reasoning of the II or explain his or her own independent reasons for affirming the results of the II decision. Third, the opaque nature of the process, which discourages a meaningful, individualized administrative review of each case and insulates the Board Member's decision from any federal court review, violates due process.

To AILF's knowledge, the validity of this procedure has not been decided by this Court or any other court in a published decision.

Dated: December 20, 2002   Respectfully submitted,

_____*Nadine K. Wettstein*_____
Nadine K. Wettstein
Mary A. Kenney
Beth Werlin
Attorneys for Amicus Curiae
American Immigration Law Foundation
918 F Street, NW
Washington, DC 20004
(202) 742–5611
(202) 783–7857 (fax)

[Served on all counsel Jan. 21, 2003. AILF's 31–page brief is omitted here.—Ed.]

UNITED STATES COURT OF APPEALS
FOR THE EIGHTH CIRCUIT

No. 02–3961;

Feliciano Flores Palomino,	)	
	)	
Petitioner,	)	
	)	Petition for Review
v.	)	
	)	
	)	
John Ashcroft,	)	
	)	
Respondent.	)	

The motion of the American Immigration Law Foundation for leave to file an amicus brief on behalf of the Petitioner is granted. The clerk is directed to file the brief tendered with the motion. (5208–010199)

February 7, 2003

Order Entered Under Rule 27B(a):

Michael E. Gans
Clerk, U.S. Court of Appeals,
Eighth Circuit

No. 02–3961

IN THE UNITED STATES COURT OF APPEALS
FOR THE EIGHTH CIRCUIT

FELICIANO FLORES PALOMINO,
Petitioner,

v.

JOHN ASHCROFT,
Attorney General of the United States,
Respondent.

PETITION FOR REVIEW OF AN ORDER OF THE BOARD OF
IMMIGRATION APPEALS
INS No. A 76 407 515

BRIEF FOR RESPONDENT

ROBERT D. MCCALLUM, JR.
Assistant Attorney General
Civil Division

ERNESTO H. MOLINA, JR.
Senior Litigation Counsel

ERIC W. MARSTELLER
Law Intern
Office of Immigration Litigation
Civil Division
United States Department of Justice
P.O. Box 878, Ben Franklin Station
Washington, D.C. 20044
(202) 616–9344
Attorneys for Respondent

* * *

TABLE OF CONTENTS

STATEMENT OF JURISDICTION 1

COUNTER–STATEMENT OF THE ISSUE 3

COUNTER–STATEMENT OF THE CASE 3

STATEMENT OF THE FACTS 5

I. Background Facts 5

II. The Immigration Judge's Decision 5

III. Board of Immigration Appeals' Decision 7

SUMMARY OF ARGUMENT 8

ARGUMENT 9

I. THE IMMIGRATION JUDGE REASONABLY DETERMINED THAT FLORES DID NOT MAINTAIN TEN YEARS OF CONTINUOUS PHYSICAL PRESENCE AND IS THEREFORE INELIGIBLE FOR CANCELLATION OF REMOVAL 9

    A. Standard of Review 9

    B. Governing Statute 11

    C. Congress Has Spoken Clearly In Providing That INA § 240A(d)(2) Is Not The Exclusive Means By Which Continuous Physical Presence Is Broken 13

    D. The Court Should Defer To The Immigration Judge's Reasonable Interpretation That An Alien's Voluntary Departure Under A Threat Of Deportation Proceedings Interrupts Continuous Physical Presence 16

        1. The immigration judge properly concluded that prior case law for suspension of deportation held that voluntary departure under threat of enforcement was a break in the continuous physical presence of aliens . . . 16

        2. The Court should defer to the immigration judge's reasonable conclusion that § 240A(d)(2) does not preclude the termination of continuous physical presence where the alien voluntarily departed in lieu of enforcement proceedings 20

        3. The immigration judge's conclusion conforms with IIRIRA's legislative history 23

II. AMICUS CANNOT RAISE ISSUES NOT RAISED BY FLORES HIMSELF 24

CONCLUSION 27

COUNTER–STATEMENT OF THE ISSUE

Whether the immigration judge's determination that Flores' 1997 voluntary departure under threat of removal proceedings interrupted his "continuous physical presence" for purposes of Cancellation of Removal was reasonable. * * *

* * *

SUMMARY OF ARGUMENT

The Court should defer to the immigration judge's reasonable conclusion, as affirmed without opinion by the Board, that an alien's voluntary departure under threat of deportation proceedings breaks an alien's continuous physical presence for purposes of Cancellation of Removal. *INS v. Aguirre–Aguirre,* 526 U.S. 415, 424, 119 S.Ct. 1439, 143 L.Ed.2d 590 (1999). Congress was clear in providing that INA § 240A(d)(2), 8 U.S.C. § 1229b(d)(2) (2000), does not represent the exclusive means by which an alien's continuous physical presence is broken. INA § 240A(d)(2) specifies that it constitutes only a "special rule" applying to "certain breaks" in continuous physical presence and the text of the statute does not specify how shorter breaks must be treated.

The immigration judge's interpretation was reasonable. The immigration judge correctly determined that a departure from the United States after an enforcement action by the INS is still considered an interruption in continuous physical presence, despite the fact that the statutory language does not directly address the issue. Pet. App. 124. Congress, by setting the *90*– and 180–day limits on absences from the United States for eligibility for Cancellation, did not thereby intend to remove shorter, government-enforced departures from being considered interruptions of continuous physical presence. Moreover, the immigration judge's reliance on precedent holding that the voluntary departure of an alien after apprehension by the INS interrupts the period of continuous physical presence required for suspension of deportation under prior INA § 244(a) was appropriate.

* * *

[Here the government elaborates on the various legal arguments reproduced above—Ed.]

II.   AMICUS CANNOT RAISE ISSUES NOT RAISED BY FLORES HIMSELF

The American Immigration Law Foundation ("AILF") has filed a brief as amicus curiae for the petitioner challenging the Board's streamlining procedures. AILF Brf.; *see* 8 C.F.R. § 3.1(a)(7) (2002) ["streamlining procedures"]. Flores, by not raising any challenge to the streamlining procedures in his opening brief, waived the issue on appeal. *See, e.g., Oden v. N. Marianas Coll.,* 284 F.3d 1058, 1060 (9th Cir. 2002) (declining to consider issues not raised in appellant's opening brief).

Amicus AILF cannot raise issues not raised by the alien in his opening brief. [Citations omitted.] Accordingly, Amicus' effort to challenge the summary affirmance procedures of the Board is improper.

CONCLUSION

For the foregoing reasons, the Court should affirm the Board's decision and deny the petition for review.

Respectfully submitted,
ROBERT D. MCCALLUM, JR.
Assistant Attorney General
Civil Division

Ernesto H. Molina, Jr.

ERNESTO H. MOLINA, JR.
Senior Litigation Counsel
ERIC W. MARSTELLER
Law Intern
Office of Immigration Litigation
Civil Division
United States Department of Justice
P.O. Box 878, Ben Franklin Station
Washington, D.C. 20044
(202) 616–9344

Attorneys for Respondent

Dated: March 24, 2003

UNITED STATES COURT OF APPEALS
FOR THE EIGHTH CIRCUIT

No. 02–3961
[354 F.3d 942]

Feliciano Flores Palomino, Petitioner,	))))
v.	))
John Ashcroft, Attorney General of the United States,	)))
Respondent.	) Appeal from the Board of) Immigration Appeals.
_____	))
American Immigration Law Foundation,	)))
Amicus on Behalf of Petitioner.	))

Submitted: November 21, 2003
Filed: January 15, 2004

■ Before MURPHY, LAY, and BRIGHT, CIRCUIT JUDGES.

■ MURPHY, CIRCUIT JUDGE.

Feliciano Flores Palomino, a native and citizen of Mexico, seeks cancellation of removal from the United States under 8 U.S.C. § 1229b(b)(1). An immigration judge found Flores Palomino removable as an alien entering without inspection and denied his cancellation of removal application because he had previously voluntarily departed from this country under threat of deportation. The Board of Immigration Appeals (BIA) summarily affirmed, and Flores Palomino appeals. We affirm.

Flores Palomino first entered the United States without inspection in January 1987. He encountered Immigration and Naturalization Service (INS) officials after he reentered the United States without inspection in April 1997 near San Ysidro, California. The INS gave him the option of voluntarily departing or facing formal administrative deportation proceedings. Flores Palomino chose to depart voluntarily and left the United States in April 1997, but he returned a few weeks later without having been admitted or paroled into the country.

The INS commenced removal proceedings against Flores Palomino by sending him a notice to appear on September 2, 1998. The notice to appear alleged that Flores Palomino was removable because he had entered the country without inspection. * * * Flores Palomino admitted all the factual allegations and charges contained in the notice to appear, but * * * applied for cancellation of removal.

At a hearing on August 24, 1999, an immigration judge found Flores Palomino to be removable as an alien who was present in the United States without having been admitted or paroled and denied his application for cancellation of removal. The judge * * * rejected Flores Palomino's argument that under § 1229b(d)(2) he was entitled to cancellation of removal because he had not been outside the country for more than 90 days at one time or for a total of 180 days. The judge ruled that Flores Palomino could not meet the continuous physical presence requirement for cancellation of removal because his earlier voluntarily departure from the United States under threat of deportation had ended his period of continuous physical presence in this country. Flores Palomino was again granted voluntary departure to Mexico and appealed the denial of his application for cancellation of removal. The BIA summarily affirmed, and Flores Palomino appeals.

When the board summarily affirms an immigration judge's decision, we review the judge's findings as though they had been made by the BIA. *Dominguez v. Ashcroft*, 336 F.3d 678, 679 n.1 (8th Cir. 2003). Our standard of review for legal determinations is de novo, *INS v. Aguirre–Aguirre*, 526

U.S. 415, 424, 119 S.Ct. 1439, 143 L.Ed.2d 590 (1999), but some deference is appropriate in the immigration context because sensitive political decisions with important diplomatic repercussions may be involved. *Id.* at 425.

Cancellation of removal is discretionary relief which may be granted by the Attorney General under 8 U.S.C. § 1229b(b)(1). Eligibility for such relief requires that the nonpermanent resident alien have been physically present in the United States for a continuous period of not less than 10 years immediately preceding the date of application; have had good moral character during the preceding 10 years; have not been convicted of an offense under §§ 1182(a)(2), 1227(a)(2), or 1227(a)(3) (unless the Attorney General has granted a waiver); and have established that removal would result in exceptional and extremely unusual hardship to a spouse, parent, or child who is a citizen of the United States or a lawfully admitted permanent resident. *See* 8 U.S.C. § 1229b(b)(1) (2003). An alien cannot show continuous physical presence if he has committed certain crimes in this country, has received a notice to appear for deportation hearings, or has departed "from the United States for any period in excess of 90 days or for any periods in the aggregate exceeding 180 days." *Id.* at § 1229b(d)(2).

Flores Palomino claims that the immigration judge erred in denying his application for cancellation of removal by relying on *In re Romalez-Alcaide*, 23 I. & N. Dec. 423 (2002), and that the BIA has misinterpreted [IIRIRA]. He argues that the IIRIRA does not explicitly state that voluntary departure under threat of deportation interrupts continuous physical presence and argues that § 1229b(d)(2) should be read to make an alien ineligible for cancellation of removal only if he has departed from the United States for more than 90 days at one time or for a total of 180 days.

In its 2002 decision in *Romalez-Alcaide*, the BIA noted that departure for either a single interval of 90 days or an aggregate of 180 days is only one statutory ground for ineligibility for cancellation of removal. It held that continuous physical presence comes to an end when an alien voluntarily departs under threat of deportation. ("The objective command that departures of certain lengths 'shall' break continuous physical presence implies that shorter departures are acceptable, but it does not specifically exempt all such shorter departures.") 23 I. & N. Dec. at 426. The BIA also pointed out that its interpretation was consistent with preIIRIRA law under which voluntary departure under threat of forced removal interrupted an alien's continuous physical presence. *See INS v. Rios–Pineda*, 471 U.S. 444, 451 (1985).

Although the question before this court is not explicitly answered in the governing statute, the 90/180 day limit contained in § 1229b(d)(2) is by no means the exclusive definition of a break in continuous physical presence. Such a presence may be ended in other ways as well, such as when a notice to appear is served or when an alien is convicted of certain offenses. *Id.* at § 1229b(d)(1). The Attorney General has interpreted the statute to mean that the time provision in § 1229b(d)(2) is not the only way in which continuous physical presence may be interrupted, and we conclude that his interpretation is reasonable and consistent with the statute. *See Romalez–Alcaide*, 23 I. & N. Dec. at 423.

* * *

We agree with the Fifth and Ninth Circuits that the 1996 IIRIRA amendments gave the Attorney General substantial discretion in granting cancellation of removal and his reasonable conclusion that voluntary departure in the circumstances of this case interrupted the alien's continuous physical presence in this country is within his discretion.

For these reasons, the decision of the BIA is affirmed.

[In *Reyes-Vasquez v. Ashcroft*, 395 F.3d 903, 907–09 (8th Cir. 2005), the same court later limited the reach of its decision in this case. The court held that a voluntary departure would break the continuity of the person's physical presence for cancellation of removal purposes only if the person is informed that voluntary departure is being granted and accepts it. That was the case in *Flores–Palomino*, but not in *Reyes–Vasquez*, where the person was casually turned away at the border by an immigration inspector.—Ed.]

UNITED STATES COURT OF APPEALS
FOR THE EIGHTH CIRCUIT

No. 02–3961

Feliciano Flores Palomino,	)
	)
Petitioner,	)
	) Petition for Review of an
vs.	) Order of the Board of
	) Immigration Appeals
John Ashcroft, Attorney General	)
of the United States,	)
	)
Respondent.	)
	)
	)
American Immigration Law	)
Foundation,	)
	)
Amicus on Behalf of	)
Petitioner.	)

JUDGMENT

This cause was submitted on a Petition for Review of an order of the Board of Immigration Appeals, on the administrative record, briefs of the parties and was argued by counsel.

After consideration, it is hereby ordered and adjudged that the order of the Board of Immigration Appeals is affirmed in accordance with the opinion of this Court. (5272–010199)

January 15, 2004

Order Entered in Accordance with Opinion:

Michael E. Gans
Clerk, U.S. Court of Appeals,
Eighth Circuit.

SECTION D.   A SIMULATED REMOVAL HEARING*

You are about to begin a mock removal hearing. The subject of the hearing is a fictional character named Arnaud Godasse, a Swiss citizen. Your instructor will assign one or more students to be Godasse's counsel and one or more students to be ICE trial attorneys. The exercise will involve other players as well, including two additional witnesses, the immigration judge, and possibly an interpreter.

You will need to glean the relevant facts from a few documents that follow this introduction. The next few paragraphs describe those documents. To familiarize yourself with the facts, please proceed in the following order: Read the paragraphs that describe Document A, then Document A itself, then the paragraph that describes Document B, then Document B itself, etc. After you have finished the last document, read the "Ground Rules and Suggestions" that follow it.

The first document in the file, Document A, is Godasse's written signed statement taken by the ICE arresting officer. Normally the officer fills out a standardized form entitled "Record of Deportable / Inadmissible Alien," based on his or her own observations and the noncitizen's statements. In the present case, because Godasse provided so much detail, the officer typed up a separate sheet of paper embodying Godasse's story. Godasse voluntarily signed the statement, and the officer attached it to the standardized form. For this exercise you will not need a copy of the standardized form; the attached signed statement by Godasse is sufficient. Assume that all of Godasse's statements were uncoerced.

Godasse's statement contains some information about the terms of his admission to the United States. It will be easier to understand his story if you first review the following information about student visas. This passage appeared earlier on page 387 above:

At one time, F–1 students were admitted for fixed time periods. If they later discovered that they needed more time to complete their programs, the students could apply to the former INS for fixed-term extensions of

---

* The author is grateful to Locky Nimick for his exceptional assistance with this exercise.

stay. Today, however, foreign students are admitted for "duration of status." A "designated school official" estimates a reasonable "completion date" for the particular program. The student may remain in the United States until that date, assuming he or she remains a full-time student in good standing. If unable to complete his or her studies by this time, the student applies to the university (not to USCIS) for an extension. It will be granted only upon a showing of "compelling academic or medical reasons, such as changes of major or research topics, unexpected research problems, or documented illnesses." The university must then inform USCIS of the extension. 8 C.F.R. § 214.2(f)(7) (2004). For an extension of an F–1 stay, one must "agree to depart the United States at the expiration of his or her authorized period of . . . extension . . ." 8 C.F.R. § 214.1(a)(3) (2004).

Now you can read Document A.

Document B is the "Notice to Appear." ICE serves this document on the noncitizen and files a copy with the immigration court. Service of the Notice to Appear formally initiates the removal proceeding. The Notice to Appear contains the allegations that establish deportability. In this case Godasse will contest deportability and, in the alternative, apply for discretionary relief. (You might notice that the letterhead refers to the Department of Justice and the former INS. Now DHS is the relevant Department, but as of this writing the old form has not been revised.)

Document C is a copy of Godasse's completed application for his student visa. This was the application that he originally submitted to the visa section of the United States embassy in Berne, Switzerland. (The form, OF–156, is the one that was in use in 1996, when Godasse applied. In September 2001 the State Department substituted a slightly different form, DS–156.)

Documents D and E together constitute Godasse's application for cancellation of removal, part B, under INA § 240A(b). Document D is the required standardized form for requesting cancellation; it refers to certain supporting documents that for purposes of this exercise have been omitted. Document E, which Godasse will attach to the application form, is an affidavit that he executed for the purpose of establishing the "exceptional and extremely unusual hardship" required for cancellation. This affidavit is signed by Godasse, but in real life his lawyer would have drafted it before the removal hearing.

Here, then, are Documents A through E:

DOCUMENT A
STATEMENT OF ARNAUD GODASSE
ATTACHMENT TO RECORD OF
DEPORTABLE/INADMISSIBLE ALIEN

My name is Arnaud Marie Godasse. I am a citizen of Switzerland, born August 6, 1966 in Geneva. I am a doctoral candidate at the University of Texas. My address is 1402 Paseo Drive, Austin, Texas 78705.

I entered the United States on August 4, 1996 with an F–1 student visa. I didn't apply for an immigrant visa when I first came here from Switzerland, because urgent personal problems required me to leave Switzerland immediately and I was aware that I would have had to wait much longer for an immigrant visa than for an F–1 visa. I had also heard that I could keep renewing my F–1 visa for as long as I was a full-time student. Also, I had a bachelor's degree from the University of Geneva in history and was interested in going back to university to study American literature.

I first came here to do a bachelor's degree in American history at the University of Texas. The INS told me I could remain here until I was finished. I received my degree on May 30, 2000 and later that month was accepted into the University's Ph.D program. The people at the university estimated that it would take me 4 more years to complete the Ph.D, so they extended my F–1 status until May 30, 2004.

I finished the required coursework in three years, but my dissertation was taking me a little longer than expected, mostly because I was hitting unexpected conceptual problems and needed to modify my research topic. So on May 15, 2004, I asked the school officials for another two years, which they granted. That extended my authorized stay to May 30, 2006.

By early 2006, I had made a lot of progress on my dissertation, but it was becoming clear that I would never be able to finish by May 30. So on May 15, 2006 I applied to the school for one more two-year extension, which they granted. That made my expected completion date May 30, 2008.

A few weeks before I requested that last extension, a cultural organization called the Alliance Francaise approached me and said they might be interested in hiring me for a permanent position as a teacher of French language and culture. French is my native language. I said I might consider it but made no commitments. On May 19, 2006, Alliance Francaise applied for labor certification on my behalf. Their application apparently is still pending.

This evening I was celebrating my 40th birthday at Jason's Bar and Grill with friends. After a few drinks, while making a toast, I got a little careless with my words. I said, "I've managed to keep my F–1 alive for 10 years so far, and I'll keep extending it until they throw me out! Hooray for the USA! Here's to the geniuses at ICE!" Of course I hadn't realized there was an ICE agent at the next table taking a coffee break.

The ICE agent started questioning me. I explained that I was just being boisterous and having some fun on my birthday. All I had meant was that I was happy to be in the U.S. because it's a great country and because my son and I would encounter terrible personal problems if we had to go back to Switzerland. The ICE agent apparently thought I was saying that my plan was to stay forever and that I was mocking ICE by sarcastically calling them geniuses. But I was completely serious about that. There are some highly intelligent people at ICE. That was all I meant by that comment.

/s/ Arnaud Godasse

August 6, 2006

DOCUMENT B

Form I-862 Notice to appear

U.S. Department of Justice

Immigration and Naturalization Service

Notice to Appear

In removal proceedings under section 240 of the Immigration and Nationality Act

In the Matter of

Respondent: ____
at:

In the Matter of

File No: A45 365 902

Respondent: _____ Arnaud Marie Godasse _____ currently residing
at:

1402 Paseo Drive, Austin, TX 78705   (512) 475-2663
(Number, street, city, state and ZIP code)   (Area code and phone number)

☐ 1. You are an arriving alien.
☐ 2. You are an alien present in the United States who has not been admitted or paroled.
☒ 3. You have been admitted to the United States, but are deportable for the reasons stated below.

The Service alleges that you:

1. Are not a citizen or national of the United States.
2. Are a native of Switzerland and a citizen of Switzerland.
3. Entered the United States at Dallas, Texas on or about August 4, 1996.
4. On August 2, 1996, obtained an F-1 student visa by fraudulently concealing your intent to remain in the U.S. permanently.
5. On August 4, 1996, gained admission to the U.S. by fraudulently concealing your intent to remain in the U.S. permanently.
6. On May 21, 2006, obtained an extension of stay as an F-1 student.
7. Were ineligible for said extension because, at the time you received it, you intended to remain in the U.S. permanently.
8. Your last valid extension of stay expired May 30, 2006.

On the basis of the foregoing, it is charged that you are subject to removal from the United States pursuant to the following provision(s) of law:

Section 237(a)(1)(A) of the Immigration and Nationality Act (the Act) in that, at the time of your entry on or about August 4, 1996, you were inadmissible under section 212(a)(6)(C)(i) of the Act as an alien who, by fraudulently concealing your intent, had procured a visa, and as an alien who, by fraudulently concealing your intent, procured admission into the United States;

Section 237(a)(1)(B) of the Act, in that your last valid extension of stay expired May 30, 2006, and you are therefore in the United States in violation of law.

☐ This notice is being issued after an asylum officer has found that the respondent has demonstrated a credible fear of persecution.
☐ Section 235(b)(1) order was vacated pursuant to ☐ 8 CFR 208.30(f)(2) ☐ 8 CFR 208.30(b)(5)(iv)

YOU ARE ORDERED to appear before an immigration judge of the United States Department of Justice at:

2800 South I-35, Room 209, Austin, Texas
(Complete Address of Immigration Court, Including Room Number, if any)

On September 15, 2006 at 10:00 a.m. to show why you should not be removed from the United States based on the charge(s) set forth above.

/s/Roger R. Sax, Officer in Charge
(Signature and Title of Issuing Officer)

Date: August 7, 2006   Austin, Texas
(City and State)

Form I-862 (Rev. 4-1-97)

DOCUMENT C

NONIMMIGRANT VISA APPLICATION

PLEASE TYPE OR PRINT YOUR ANSWERS IN THE SPACE PROVIDED BELOW EACH ITEM

1. SURNAMES OR FAMILY NAMES *(Exactly as in Passport)* GODASSE	**DO NOT WRITE IN THIS SPACE** B-1/8-2 MAX B-1 MAX 8-2 MAX
2. FIRST NAME AND MIDDLE NAME *(Exactly as in Passport)* ARNAUD MARIE	OTHER _____ F-1 _____ MAX Visa Classification MULT OR _____ 1 Number Applications
3. OTHER NAMES *(Maiden, Religious, Professional, Aliases)*	

4. DATE OF BIRTH *(mm-dd-yy)* August 6, 1966	8. PASSPORT NUMBER F2359H	MONTHS _____ 6 Validity
5. PLACE OF BIRTH City, Province Geneva	Country Switzerland	DATE PASSPORT ISSUED *(mm-dd-yy)* March 11, 1994	L.O. CHECKED ON _____ BY _____

6. NATIONALITY Switzerland	7. SEX ☒ Male ☐ Female	DATE PASSPORT EXPIRES *(mm-dd-yy)* March 11, 2009	ISSUED/REFUSED ISSUED ON 8-2-96 BY RHL

9. HOME ADDRESS *(Include apartment no., street, city, province, and postal zone)* 31 Route des Morillons CH-1211 Geneva, Switzerland	UNDER SEC. 214(b) 221(g) OTHER: _____ INA
10. NAME AND STREET ADDRESS OF PRESENT EMPLOYER OR SCHOOL *(Postal box number unacceptable)* Self employed	REFUSAL REVIEWED BY _____

11. HOME TELEPHONE NO. 41-22-367-9111	12. BUSINESS TELEPHONE NO. Same

13. MARITAL STATUS
☐ Married ☒ Single ☐ Widowed ☐ Divorced ☐ Separated
If married, give name and nationality of spouse

14. NAMES AND RELATIONSHIPS OF PERSONS TRAVELING WITH YOU
(NOTE: *A separate application must be made for a visa for each traveler, regardless of age.*)

None

15. HAVE YOU EVER APPLIED FOR A U.S. NONIMMIGRANT VISA? ☒ NO ☐ YES HAVE YOU EVER APPLIED FOR A U.S. IMMIGRANT VISA? ☒ NO ☐ YES WHERE? _____ WHEN? VISA WAS ISSUED ☐ VISA WAS REFUSED ☐	19. PRESENT OCCUPATION *(If retired, state past occupation)* Author
16. HAS YOUR U.S. VISA EVER BEEN CANCELED? ☒ NO ☐ YES WHERE? _____ WHEN? _____ BY WHOM? _____	20. WHO WILL FURNISH FINANCIAL SUPPORT, INCLUDING TICKETS? Myself
	21. AT WHAT ADDRESS WILL YOU STAY IN THE U.S.A.? Austin, TX
	22. WHAT IS THE PURPOSE OF YOUR TRIP? To study
17. Bearers of visitor visas may generally not work or study in the U.S. DO YOU INTEND TO WORK IN THE U.S.? ☒ NO ☐ YES *If YES, explain.*	23. WHEN DO YOU INTEND TO ARRIVE IN THE U.S.A.? 8.4.96
	24. HOW LONG DO YOU PLAN TO STAY IN THE U.S.A.? 4 Years
18. DO YOU INTEND TO STUDY IN THE U.S.? ☐ NO ☒ YES *If YES, write name and address of school as it appears on Form I-20.* University of Texas, Austin	25. HAVE YOU EVER BEEN IN THE U.S.A.? ☒ NO ☐ YES WHEN? _____ FOR HOW LONG? _____

NONIMMIGRANT VISA APPLICATION	**COMPLETE ALL QUESTIONS ON REVERSE OF FORM**

26. HAVE YOU OR ANYONE ACTING FOR YOU EVER INDICATED TO A U.S. CONSULAR OR IMMIGRATION EMPLOYEE A DESIRE TO IMMIGRATE TO THE U.S. OR HAVE YOU EVER ENTERED A U.S. VISA LOTTERY?
☒ NO ☐ YES
HAS ANYONE EVER FILED AN IMMIGRANT VISA PETITION ON YOUR BEHALF?
☒ NO ☐ YES
HAS A LABOR CERTIFICATION FOR EMPLOYMENT IN THE U.S. EVER BEEN REQUESTED BY YOU OR ON YOUR BEHALF?
☒ NO ☐ YES

27. ARE ANY OF THE FOLLOWING IN THE U.S., RESIDE IN THE U.S., OR HAVE U.S. LEGAL PERMANENT RESIDENCE?
(Circle YES or NO and indicate that person's status in the U.S., i.e., studying, working, permanent resident, U.S. citizen, etc.)

YES NO	Husband/Wife	NO	YES NO	Fiance/Fiancee	NO	YES NO	Brother/Sister	NO
YES NO	Father/Mother	NO	YES NO	Son/Daughter	NO			

28. WHERE HAVE YOU LIVED FOR THE PAST FIVE YEARS? DO NOT INCLUDE PLACES YOU HAVE VISITED FOR PERIODS OF SIX MONTHS OR LESS.

Countries	Cities	Approximate Dates (mm-dd-yy)
Switzerland	Geneva	5-5-85 to present

29. IMPORTANT: ALL APPLICANTS MUST READ AND CHECK THE APPROPRIATE BOX FOR EACH ITEM.

A visa may not be issued to persons who are within specific categories defined by law as inadmissible to the United States (except when a waiver is obtained in advance). Are any of the following applicable to you?

- Have you ever been afflicted with a communicable disease of public health significance, a dangerous physical or mental disorder, or been a drug abuser or addict? (212(a)(1))   ☐ YES ☒ NO

- Have you ever been arrested or convicted for any offense or crime, even though subject of a pardon, amnesty or other similar legal action? Have you ever unlawfully distributed or sold a controlled substance (drug), or been a prostitute or procurer for prostitutes? (212(a)(2))   ☐ YES ☒ NO

- Do you seek to enter the United States to engage in export control violations, subversive or terrorist activities, or any other unlawful purpose? Are you a member or representative of a terrorist organization as currently designated by the U.S. Secretary of State? Have you ever participated in persecutions directed by the Nazi government of Germany; or have you ever participated in genocide? (212(a)(3))   ☐ YES ☒ NO

- Have you ever been refused admission to the U.S., or the subject of a deportation hearing, or sought to obtain or assist others to obtain a visa, entry into the U.S., or sought to obtain a visa or any U.S. Immigration benefit by fraud or willful misrepresentation? Have you attended a U.S. public elementary school on student (F) status, or a public secondary school without reimbursing the school after November 30, 1996? (212(a)(6))   ☐ YES ☒ NO

- Have you ever departed or remained outside the United States to avoid military service? (212(a)(8))   ☐ YES ☒ NO

- Have you ever violated the terms of a U.S. visa, or been unlawfully present in, or deported from, the United States? (212(a)(9))   ☐ YES ☒ NO

- Have you ever withheld custody of a U.S. citizen child outside the United States from a person granted legal custody by a U.S. court, voted in the United States in violation of any law or regulation, or renounced U.S. citizenship for the purpose of avoiding taxation? (212(a)(10))   ☐ YES ☒ NO

A YES answer does not automatically signify ineligibility for a visa, but if you answered YES to any of the above, or if you have any question in this regard, a personal appearance at this office is recommended. If an appearance is not possible at this time, attach a statement of facts in your case to this application.

30. I certify that I have read and understood all the questions set forth in this application and the answers I have furnished on this form are true and correct to the best of my knowledge and belief. I understand that any false or misleading statement may result in the permanent refusal of a visa or denial of entry into the United States. I understand that possession of a visa does not entitle the bearer to enter the United States of America upon arrival at port of entry if he or she is found inadmissible.

DATE OF APPLICATION (mm-dd-yy) ____ August 1, 1996 _____

APPLICANT'S SIGNATURE _____ /s/ Arnaud Marie Godasse _____

If this application has been prepared by a travel agency or another person on your behalf, the agent should indicate name and address of agency or person with appropriate signature of individual preparing form.

SIGNATURE OF PERSON PREPARING FORM
(If other than applicant)

DO NOT WRITE IN THIS SPACE

OPTIONAL FORM 156   PAGE 2
10-2000
U.S. Department of State

DOCUMENT D

U.S. Department of Justice
Executive Office for Immigration Review

OMB #1125-0001

**Application for Cancellation of Removal and
Adjustment of Status for Certain Nonpermanent Residents**

**PLEASE READ ADVICE AND INSTRUCTIONS
BEFORE FILLING IN FORM**

PLEASE TYPE OR PRINT

Fee Stamp

PART 1 INFORMATION ABOUT YOURSELF

1) My present true name is: *(Last, First, Middle)* Godasse, Arnaud Marie	2) Alien Registration Number: A45 365 902
3) My name given at birth was: *(Last, First, Middle)* Godasse, Arnaud Marie	4) Birth Place: *(City, Country)* Geneva, Switzerland

5) Date of Birth: *(Month, Day, Year)* August 6, 1966	6) Gender: ☒ Male ☐ Female	7) Height: 5' 10"	8) Hair Color: Brown	9) Eye Color: Green

10) Current Nationality & Citizenship: Switzerland	11) Social Security Number:	12) Home Phone Number: (512) 475-2663	13) Work Phone Number ( ) None

14) I currently reside at:	15) I have been known by these additional name(s): None
Apt. number and/or in care of 1402 Paseo Drive *Number and Street* Austin Texas 78705 *City or Town State ZIP Code*	

16) I have resided in the following locations in the United States: (List PRESENT ADDRESS FIRST, and work back in time for at least 10 years).

Street and Number - Apt. or Room # - City or Town - State - ZIP Code	Resided From: *(Month, Day, Year)*	Resided To: *(Month, Day, Year)*
1402 Paseo Drive Austin Texas 78705	Aug. 4, 1996	Present

PART 2 - INFORMATION ABOUT THIS APPLICATION

17) I, the undersigned, hereby request that my removal be cancelled under the provisions of section 240A(b) of the Immigration and Nationality Act (INA). I believe that I am eligible for cancellation of removal because: (check all that apply)

☒ My removal would result in exceptional and extremely unusual hardship to my: *(Place a USC in the space if the family member is a citizen of the United States, an L if the family member is a lawful permanent resident of the United States, an X if the family member is neither and leave BLANK if not applicable.)*

_____ **Husband** _____ **Wife** _____ **Father** _____ **Mother** __USC__ **Child or Children**

With the exception of absences described in question #25, I have resided in the United States since:
(Month, Day, Year) _____ August 4, 1996 _____

☐ I, or my child, have been battered or subjected to extreme cruelty by a United States citizen or lawful permanent resident spouse or parent.

With the exception of absences described in question #25, I have resided in the United States since:
(Month, Day, Year) _____

(Internet Version)   Please use a separate sheet for additional entries.   Form EOIR-42B
                                                        (1)   4/97

PART 3 - INFORMATION ABOUT YOUR PRESENCE IN THE UNITED STATES

18) I first arrived in the United States under the name of: *(Last, First, Middle)*
Godasse, Arnaud Marie

19) I first arrived in the United States on: *(Month, Day, Year)*
August 4, 1996

20) Place or port of first arrival: *(Place or Port, City and State)*
Dallas, Texas

21) I arrived: ☐ as a lawful permanent resident, ☐ as a Visitor, ☒ as a Student, ☐ without inspection, or ☐ Other *(Place an X in the correct box, if Other is selected please explain):*

22) If admitted as a nonimmigrant, period for which admitted: *(Month, Day, Year)* 8.4.96   to   5.30.00

23) My last extension of stay in the United States expired on: *(Month, Day, Year)*
May 30, 2008

24) If not inspected or if arrival occurred at other than a regular port, describe the circumstances as accurately as possible:

25) Since the date of my first arrival I departed from and returned to the United States at the following places and on the following dates:
(Please list all departures regardless of how briefly you were absent from the United States)
If you have never departed from the United States since your original date of arrival, please mark an X in the box: ☒

1	Port of Departure *(Place or Port, City and State)*	Departure Date *(Month, Day, Year)*	Purpose of Travel	Destination
	Port of Return *(Place or Port, City and State)*	Return Date *(Month, Day, Year)*	Manner of Return	Inspected & Admitted? ☐ Yes ☐ No
2	Port of Departure *(Place or Port, City and State)*	Departure Date *(Month, Day, Year)*	Purpose of Travel	Destination
	Port of Return *(Place or Port, City and State)*	Return Date *(Month, Day, Year)*	Manner of Return	Inspected & Admitted? ☐ Yes ☐ No

26) Have you ever departed the United States: a) under an order of deportation, exclusion or removal? ----------- ☐ Yes ☒ No
b) pursuant to a grant of voluntary departure? ---------------------- ☐ Yes ☒ No

PART 4 - INFORMATION ABOUT YOUR MARITAL STATUS AND SPOUSE *(Continued from page 3)*

27) I am not married: ☒
I am married: ☐

28) If married, the name of my spouse is: *(Last, First, Middle)*

29) Date of marriage: *(Month, Day, Year)*

30) The marriage took place in: *(City and Country)*

31) Birth place of spouse: *(City and Country)*

32) My spouse currently resides at:

Apt. number and/or care of

Number and Street

City or Town   State/Country   ZIP Code

33) Birth date of spouse: *(Month, Day, Year)*

34) My spouse is a citizen of: *(Country)*

35) If your spouse is other than a native born United States citizen, answer the following:
He/she arrived in the United States at: *(City and State)*
He/she arrived in the United States on: *(Month, Day, Year)*
His/her alien registration number is A#
He/she was naturalized on *(Month, Day, Year)* _____ at _____
(City and State)

36) My spouse ☐ - is ☐ - is not employed. If employed, please give salary and the name and address of the place(s) of employment.

Full Name and Address of Employer	Earnings Per Week *(Approximate)*
	$
	$
	$

(Internet Version)   *Please use a separate sheet for additional entries*   Form EOIR-42B
(2)   4/97

PART 4 - INFORMATION ABOUT YOUR MARITAL STATUS AND SPOUSE *(Continued)*

37) I ☐ - have ☒ - have not been previously married: *(If previously married, list the name of each prior spouse, the dates on which each marriage began and ended, the place where the marriage terminated, and describe how each marriage ended.)*

Name of prior spouse: *(Last, First, Middle)*	Date marriage began: Date marriage ended:	Place marriage ended: *(City and Country)*	Description or manner of how marriage was terminated or ended:

38) My present spouse ☐ - has ☐ - has not been previously married: *(If previously married, list the name of each prior spouse, the dates on which the marriage began and ended, the place where the marriage terminated, and describe how each marriage ended.)*

Name of prior spouse: *(Last, First, Middle)*	Date marriage began: Date marriage ended:	Place marriage ended: *(City and Country)*	Description or manner of how marriage was terminated or ended:

39) Have you been ordered by any court, or are otherwise under any legal obligation, to provide child support and/or spousal maintenance as a result of a separation and/or divorce?   ☐ Yes   ☒ No

PART 5 - INFORMATION ABOUT YOUR EMPLOYMENT AND FINANCIAL STATUS

40) Since my arrival into the United States, I have been employed by the following - named persons or firms: *(Please begin with present employment and work back in time. Any periods of unemployment or school attendance should be specified.)*

Full Name and Address of Employer	Earnings Per Week *(Approximate)*	Type of Work Performed	Employment From: *(Month, Day, Year)*	Employed to: *(Month, Day, Year)*
	$			
	$			
	$			

41) If self-employed, describe the nature of the business, the name of the business, its address, and net income derived therefrom:

42) My assets (and if married, my spouse's assets) in the United States and other countries, not including clothing and household necessities, are:

Self		**Jointly Owned with Spouse**	
Cash, Stocks, and Bonds -	$ 43,000	Cash, Stocks, and Bonds - - - - - - - - - - - - - - - - - - -	$
Real Estate -	$	Real Estate -	$
Automobile (value minus amount owed) - - - - - - - - -	$	Automobile (value minus amount owed) - - - - - - - -	$
Other (describe on line below) - - - - - - - - - - - - - - -	$	Other (describe on line below) - - - - - - - - - - - - - -	$
_____ **TOTAL**	$ 43,000	_____ **TOTAL**	$

43) I ☐ - have ☒ - have not received public or private relief or assistance (e.g., Welfare, Unemployment Benefits, Medicaid, ADC, etc.). If you have, please give full details including the type of relief or assistance received, date for which relief or assistance was received, place, and amount received during this time:

44) Please list each of the years in which you have filed an income tax return with the Internal Revenue Service:

PART 6 - INFORMATION ABOUT YOUR FAMILY *(Continued on page 5)*

45) I have _____1_____ *(Number of)* children. Please list information for each child below, include assets and earnings information for children over the age of sixteen who have separate incomes:

Name of Child: *(Last, First, Middle)* Child's Alien Registration Number:	Citizen of What Country: Birth Date: *(Month, Day, Year)*	Now Residing At: *(City and Country)* Birth Place: *(City and Country)*	Immigration Status of Child?
Paul Godasse A#:	USA October 12, 2004	Austin, Texas Austin, Texas	USC
Estimated Total of Assets: $_____ Estimated Average Weekly Earnings: $_____			
A#:			
Estimated Total of Assets: $_____ Estimated Average Weekly Earnings: $_____			
A#:			
Estimated Total of Assets: $_____ Estimated Average Weekly Earnings: $_____			

46) If your application is denied, would your spouse and all of your children accompany you to your:

Country of Birth -   ☒ Yes   ☐ No

Country of Nationality -   ☒ Yes   ☐ No

Country of Last Residence -   ☒ Yes   ☐ No

If you answered "NO" to any of the responses, please explain: _____

_____

_____

_____

47) Members of my family, including my spouse and/or child(ren) ☐ - have ☒ - have not received public or private relief or assistance (e.g., Unemployment Benefits, Welfare, Medicaid, ADC, etc.). If any member of your immediate family has received such relief or assistance, please give full details including identity of person(s) receiving relief or assistance, dates for which relief or assistance was received, place, and amount received during this time: _____

_____

_____

48) Please give the requested information about your parents, brothers, sisters, aunts, uncles, and grandparents. As to residence, show street address, city, and state, if in the United States; otherwise show only country:

Name: *(Last, First, Middle)* Alien Registration Number:	Citizen of What Country: Birth Date: *(Month, Day, Year)*	Relationship to Me: Birth Place: *(City and Country)*	Immigration Status of Listed Relative
Godasse, Henri A#:	Switzerland 9 / 10 / 29	Father Berne, Switzerland	
Complete Address of Current Residence: _____ Deceased _____			
Sermont, Marie A#:	Switzerland 5 / 8 / 31	Mother Berne, Switzerland	
Complete Address of Current Residence: _____ Deceased _____			

PART 6 - INFORMATION ABOUT YOUR FAMILY *(Continued)*

IF THIS APPLICATION IS BASED ON HARDSHIP TO A PARENT OR PARENTS, QUESTIONS 49 TO 52 MUST BE ANSWERED.

49) As to such parent who is not a citizen of the United States, give the date and place of arrival in the United States including full details as to the date, manner, and terms of admission into the United States.

50) My father ☐ - is ☐ -is not employed. If employed, please give salary and the name and address of the place(s) of employment.

Full Name and Address of Employer	Earnings Per Week *(Approximate)*
	$

51) My mother ☐ - is ☐ -is not employed. If employed, please give salary and the name and address of the place(s) of employment.

Full Name and Address of Employer	Earnings Per Week *(Approximate)*
	$

52) My parent's assets in the United States and other countries not including clothing and household necessities are:

Assets of father consist of the following:
Cash, Stocks, and Bonds - $_____
Real Estate - $_____
Automobile (value minus amount owed) - - - - - - - - - $_____
Other (describe on line below) - - - - - - - - - - - - - - - - $_____
                  TOTAL $_____

Assets of mother consist of the following:
Cash, Stocks, and Bonds - $_____
Real Estate - $_____
Automobile (value minus amount owed) - - - - - - - - - $_____
Other (describe on line below) - - - - - - - - - - - - - - - - $_____
                  TOTAL $_____

PART 7 - MISCELLANEOUS INFORMATION *(Continued on page 6)*

53) I ☐ - have ☒ - have not entered the United States as a crewman after June 30, 1964.

54) I ☐ - have ☒ - have not been admitted as, or after arrival in the United States acquired the status of, an exchange alien.

55) I ☒ - have ☐ - have not submitted address reports as required by section 265 of the Immigration and Nationality Act.

56) I ☐ - have ☒ - have never (either in the United States or in any foreign country) been arrested, summoned into court as a defendant, convicted, fined, imprisoned, placed on probation, or forfeited collateral for an act involving a felony, misdemeanor, or breach of any public law or ordinance (including, but not limited to, traffic violations or driving incidents involving alcohol). *(If answer is in the affirmative, please give a brief description of each offense including the name and location of the offense, date of conviction, any penalty imposed, any sentence imposed, and the time actually served).*

57) Have you ever served in the Armed Forces of the United States? ☐ - Yes ☒ - No. If "Yes", please state branch *(Army, Navy, etc.)* and service number. _____ .
Place of entry on duty: *(Place, City and State)* _____
Date of entry on duty: *(Month, Day, Year)* _____ .   Date of discharge: *(Month, Day, Year)* _____ .
Type of discharge *(Honorable, Dishonorable, etc.)*: _____
I served in active duty status from: *(Month, Day, Year)* _____ to   *(Month, Day, Year)* _____ .

58) Have you ever left the United States or the jurisdiction of the district where you registered for the draft to avoid being drafted into the military or naval forces of the United States?
            ☐ Yes ☒ No.

PART 7 - MISCELLANEOUS INFORMATION *(Continued)*

59) Have you ever deserted from the military or naval forces of the United States while the United States was at war? ☐ Yes ☒ No

60) If male, did you register under the Selective Service (Draft) law of 1917, 1918, 1948, 1951, or later Draft Laws? ☐ Yes ☒ No
If "Yes," please give date, Selective Service number, local draft board number, and your last draft classification: _____

61) Were you ever exempted from service because of conscientious objection, alienage, or any other reason? ☐ Yes ☒ No

62) Please list your present or past membership in or affiliation with every political organization, association, fund, foundation, party, club, society, or similar group in the United States or any other place since your 16th birthday. Include any foreign military service in this part. If none, write "NONE." Include the name of the organization, location, nature of the organization, and the dates of membership.

Name of Organization	Location of Organization	Nature of Organization	Member From: *(Month, Day, Year)*	Member to: *(Month, Day, Year)*
Alliance Francaise	Austin, Texas	Cultural organization	September 1998	Present

63) Have you ever:

☐ Yes ☒ No been ordered deported or removed?
☐ Yes ☒ No overstayed a grant of voluntary departure from an Immigration Judge or the Immigration and Naturalization Service (INS)?
☐ Yes ☒ No failed to appear for removal or deportation?

64) Have you ever been:

☐ Yes ☒ No a habitual drinker?
☐ Yes ☒ No one whose income is derived principally from illegal gambling?
☐ Yes ☒ No one who has given false testimony for the purpose of obtaining immigration benefits?
☐ Yes ☒ No engaged in prostitution or unlawful commercialized vice?
☐ Yes ☒ No involved in a serious criminal offense and asserted immunity from prosecution?
☐ Yes ☒ No a polygamist?
☐ Yes ☒ No one who aided and/or abetted another to enter the United States illegally?
☐ Yes ☒ No a trafficker of a controlled substance, or a knowing assister, abettor, conspirator, or colluder with others in any such controlled substance offense (not including a single offense of simple possession of 30 grams or less of marijuana?
☐ Yes ☒ No inadmissible or deportable on security-related grounds under section 212(a)(3) or 237(a)(4) of the INA?
☐ Yes ☒ No one who has ordered, incited, assisted, or otherwise participated in the persecution of an individual on account of his or her race, religion, nationality, membership in a particular social group, or political opinion?
☐ Yes ☒ No a person previously granted relief under sections 212(c) or 244(a) of the INA or whose removal has previously been cancelled under section 240A of the INA?

64) Are you: ☐ Yes ☒ No the beneficiary of an approved visa petition?
If yes, can you: ☐ Yes ☐ No arrange a trip outside the United States to obtain an immigrant visa. If no, please explain:

_____
_____
_____

PART 7 - MISCELLANEOUS INFORMATION *(Continued)*

65) The following certificates or other supporting documents are attached hereto as part of this application: *(Refer to the Instruction Sheet for documents which **should be attached**).*

Re physical presence:
    Letter from landlord
Re physical presence and moral character:
    Letter from University of Texas
Re moral character
    Police records
    Affidavits from 2 witnesses
Re hardship:
    My own affidavit

APPLICATION NOT TO BE SIGNED BELOW UNTIL APPLICANT APPEARS BEFORE AN IMMIGRATION JUDGE

I do swear (affirm) that the contents of the above application, including the documents attached hereto, are true to the best of my knowledge, and that this application is now signed by me with my full, true name.

(Complete and true signature of applicant or parent or guardian)

Subscribed and sworn to before me by the above-named applicant at _____

Immigration Judge

Date: (Month, Day Year)

CERTIFICATE OF SERVICE

I hereby certify that a copy of the foregoing was: ☐ - delivered in person,   ☐ - mailed first class, postage prepaid on

_____ *(Month, Day, Year)*   to _____
    (INS District Counsel and Address)

Signature of Applicant (or attorney or representative)

DOCUMENT E

In re: ARNAUD MARIE GODASSE

File No.: A45 365 902

AFFIDAVIT

COMES NOW Arnaud Marie Godasse, who deposes and says:

I am a national and citizen of Switzerland. I have been in the United States since August 4, 1996. In February 1996 I began dating a woman named Monique DesChamps, who lives in Geneva and is also a Swiss citizen. Some time in April 1996, she became pregnant. I do not know the identity of the father, but I am certain it was not I because Monique and I have never had sexual intercourse.

Though she never accused me or attempted to force me to acknowledge the child, I became the scapegoat in everyone else's eyes. A rumor that I was responsible for Monique's condition reached her father in July 1996. He "went ballistic," as you Americans say, and looked for me at my apartment. I strenuously maintained my innocence, but he refused to listen and insisted that I marry her. When I refused, he flew into a rage and tried to kill me. I bear a scar on my right arm that required 25 stitches as a result of his assault, and I narrowly escaped with my life. Shortly after this incident, Monique telephoned to warn me that her father had enlisted several of his friends to help him murder me.

About three years ago, I started dating a wonderful American woman and fell in love. We conceived a child together, and he was born here in Austin in October 2004. The mother died during childbirth. We had planned to get married but never did. My son's name is Paul. I have raised him myself.

If I were sent back to Switzerland, my life would be in jeopardy, my peace of mind would be shattered, and so would Paul's. We could not possibly be safe in Geneva and so would be forced to hide in a strange city, barred from contact with any of my friends for fear of news of my return spreading. Even then, we would be constantly fearful of being recognized. Switzerland is a small country, so even outside Geneva I would never be safe. Nor would I have any automatic right to resettle in any of the EU member states, because Switzerland is not a member of the EU. If I were killed or severely injured, there would be no one to take care of Paul.

Signed this 10th day of October, 2006.

/s/ Arnaud Marie Godasse

GROUND RULES AND SUGGESTIONS

Before attacking this exercise, *review section A.3 of this chapter;* it describes the sequence of events at a removal hearing, including the order in which the two sides present their cases. Remember that the formal rules of evidence do not apply in removal proceedings. When offering evidence, be guided by common sense: Make sure the documents you offer and the questions you ask of the witnesses are relevant to facts that the substantive law makes material. Keep your questions clear, simple, and precise. Do not lead the witnesses unnecessarily. Remain civil, even if you find a witness evasive, opposing counsel unreasonable, or an adverse ruling of the immigration judge disagreeable. You should not object solely on the ground that your opponents' offers of evidence do not meet the requirements of the Federal Rules of Evidence. In particular, since this is not a jury proceeding, you should not argue that the prejudicial impact of the evidence outweighs its probative value, unless the prejudice is extreme.

At the beginning of the hearing, the immigration judge will ask Godasse's counsel either to admit or to deny each of the 8 allegations in the Notice to Appear. In this exercise, counsel is required to admit allegations 1, 2, 3, and 6. Counsel should deny all the other allegations. After asking about each individual allegation, the immigration judge will ask Godasse's counsel either to concede or to deny deportability. In this exercise, counsel is required to deny deportability.

A suggestion on organizing your case and preparing for the hearing: After familiarizing yourself with the materials, make a systematic list of all the facts your side will have the burden of proving. If you are the ICE trial attorney, your list will include all the facts that establish deportability under the various charges. If you are Godasse's counsel, you will need to (a) decide which forms of discretionary relief to apply for (for this exercise you must include cancellation of removal); and (b) identify all the facts that establish your client's statutory eligibility for each of those remedies and the reasons your client deserves the favorable exercise of discretion. For each side, the next step is to go through your lists, item by item, and figure out precisely what evidence (testimony or documents) you will offer to prove each essential fact.

You will also need to anticipate your opponent's case. Think about the list of essential facts he or she will prepare and the evidence he or she will offer. Consider whether there are any objections you might raise to the introduction of particular evidence and whether there is contrary evidence you might introduce even though your opponent has the burden of proof.

In this exercise, the ICE trial attorney is required to offer Documents A and C into evidence during the deportability phase. (The immigration judge will already have received Document B, the Notice to Appear.) In the affirmative relief phase, Godasse's counsel is required to submit Godasse's application for cancellation of removal (Documents D and E). Both sides must come to the hearing with photocopies of the documents they plan to introduce. For present purposes, assume that photocopies of all the documents that appear in the file are as admissible as the originals.

As for witnesses: In the deportability phase, ICE *must* call immigration officer Leslie Kinney. ICE *may* additionally call Godasse, who must testify if called. Godasse's counsel *must* call Godasse if ICE doesn't. If ICE calls Godasse, then Godasse's counsel *may* call him back.

In the affirmative relief phase, Godasse's counsel *must* call Godasse, and *must* also call Elizabeth DesChamps, the sister of Monique Des-Champs. Elizabeth lives in Austin and will be willing to testify. She will confirm Godasse's story about the ferocity of her and Monique's father and will further testify that the situation has not improved in the ensuing years. She will also testify, however, that she does not believe Godasse's denial that he is the father of Monique's child. She is angry with Godasse for not sending Monique any child support payments, which Godasse will say Monique at any rate has never requested.

Your instructor will decide whether Elizabeth DesChamps is to testify in English or in French. If the latter, then your instructor will arrange for an interpreter to appear at the hearing.

Since this is a classroom exercise rather than a real case, certain liberties have been taken. In a real case, Godasse and his lawyer would have conversed at length before the hearing. So, too, would Godasse's lawyer and the witness, Elizabeth DesChamps. The opposing lawyers might have performed further factual investigation and possibly legal research. (You should not do either unless your instructor asks you to.) The opposing lawyers would not usually have had access to the same information, as they do here. Noncitizens in removal proceedings are rarely able to recite their immigration histories with the precision present in Godasse's statement. The noncitizen or his or her counsel or both would have appeared already at a "master calendar" hearing, where the noncitizen would have pleaded to the allegations in the Notice to Appear, the IJ would have developed the issues, and the date and time of the removal hearing would have been scheduled. A bond for Godasse's release pending the hearing might have been set. Limited discovery and/or informal negotiation might have taken place. There might even have been a pre-hearing conference. The record in a real case would contain certain documents beyond those reproduced here, including the ones mentioned in the application for cancellation of removal, the employer's labor certification application, and a standardized form on which counsel formally enters an appearance. Finally, in a real case Document E (respondent's affidavit) would not ordinarily have to be introduced into evidence, since the respondent can testify directly to all the stated facts.

The Notice to Appear (Document B) originally ordered Godasse to appear for a master calendar hearing on September 15, 2006. Assume that the date of the actual removal hearing is October 10, 2006. Assume also that the Labor Department denied labor certification on September 24, 2006.

END OF EXERCISE

SECTION E.   EXCEPTIONS TO USUAL REMOVAL PROCEDURES

1.   EXPEDITED REMOVAL

As you saw in chapter 6, AEDPA § 422(a) and IIRIRA § 302(a) created a new, abbreviated procedure officially known as "expedited removal." INA

§ 235(b)(1). The procedure entails various procedural short-cuts, which you have already seen, whenever an immigration inspector believes that an arriving noncitizen is inadmissible on either documentary or fraud grounds. You will encounter this procedure again in chapter 11 because it has special significance and special features in the context of asylum.

Expedited removal is primarily a border procedure for arriving noncitizens. But the Attorney General has the unreviewable discretion to extend it to noncitizens who are present in the United States without having been admitted, provided they are unable to prove continuous physical presence in the United States for the immediately preceding two years. INA § 235(b)(1)(A)(iii). For that group, the 1996 legislation made a double procedural change—subjecting them to grounds of inadmissibility rather than to grounds of deportability, and allowing the Attorney General to use the special summary procedure to adjudicate inadmissibility.

In 1999 the Attorney General announced a pilot program for extending expedited removal to noncitizens who had been convicted of the criminal offense of entry without inspection, INA § 275, were serving their sentences in any of three correctional facilities in Texas, and had been present in the United States for less than two years. See 64 Fed. Reg. 51338 (Sept. 22, 1999), discussed in 76 IR at 1416–17 (Sept. 27, 1999).

In 2002 the Attorney General extended expedited removal to another group of noncitizens who were physically present in the United States—those who had arrived by sea without having been admitted or paroled, and who have not been physically present in the United States for at least two continuous years. See 67 Fed. Reg. 68924 (Nov. 13, 2002). Individuals who are processed under this policy are detained automatically throughout the removal proceedings. With Haitian boat people principally in mind, the government's stated justifications were to deter illegal migration by sea and thereby to prevent loss of life. *Id.* For a strong argument that this extension violates the 1951 UN Refugee Convention, see Lory Diana Rosenberg, *The Courts and Interception: The United States' Interdiction Experience and Its Impact on Refugees and Asylum Seekers*, 17 Georgetown Immigration L.J. 199 (2003).

A third extension came in 2004. It authorized DHS to use the expedited removal procedure whenever a noncitizen who is present without admission is encountered by an immigration officer in any of certain designated border sectors, within 100 air miles of a land border, unless the person can establish that he or she has been continuously physically present in the United States for the past 14 days. DHS says it plans not to use this authority against Cuban nationals "because removals to Cuba cannot presently be assured and for other [unspecified] U.S. policy reasons." 69 Fed. Reg. 48877, 48879 (Aug. 11, 2004).

2. CRIMINAL CASES

a. PRISON HEARINGS

In the mid 1980's, Congress began to prioritize the removal of noncitizen criminal offenders. IRCA, enacted in 1986, contained a provision, section 701, requiring that deportation proceedings based on criminal convictions be started "as expeditiously as possible after the date of the conviction." To implement that requirement, EOIR established an "institutional hearing program" in which deportation (now removal) hearings for incarcerated noncitizens are held in designated state or federal prison facilities. See United States General Accounting Office, Criminal Aliens—Prison Deportation Hearings Include Opportunities to Contest Deportation, Report No. GAO/GGD–90–79 at 5 (1990).

Two years later Congress passed the Anti–Drug Abuse Act of 1988, Pub.L. 100–690, 102 Stat. 4181 (Nov. 18, 1988). That statute created the concept of the "aggravated felony." *Id.* § 7342, adding INA § 101(a)(43). Earlier chapters considered the recent expansions of that definition and the substantive significance of a conviction of an aggravated felony. The procedural effects are at least equally critical. Since 1988, the law has instructed the Attorney General to hold deportation (now removal) hearings for aggravated felons before they complete their criminal sentences. INA § 242A(a) (pre–1996). In 1996, Congress expanded the list of crime-related deportability grounds that are subject to that requirement. AEDPA § 440(g)(1)(A); IIRIRA § 306(d). The list now includes drug and firearm offenses, two crimes of moral turpitude (under certain circumstances), and other miscellaneous crimes. For more detail, see INA § 238(a)(1).

The goal is to complete all the administrative steps, including any BIA appeal, before the person's release from incarceration. INA §§ 238(a)(1), 238(b)(3)(A). If everything goes according to plan, then upon completion of the sentence DHS can take the individual directly from the prison and remove him or her from the United States without additional detention.

Sometimes, however, things don't go as planned, and the removal proceedings have not been completed by the time of the prisoner's scheduled release. INA § 241(a)(2) *requires* the Secretary of Homeland Security to detain most noncitizen criminal offenders as soon as they are released from criminal incarceration. As you saw earlier, the Supreme Court in *Demore* upheld the constitutionality of mandatory detention.

Conducting removal hearings at correctional facilities might well get the person out of the country sooner, but there are large costs. The physical remoteness of those federal and state penitentiaries that have been designated for removal hearings makes it exceedingly difficult for the noncitizen to obtain witnesses and, more important, counsel. This is particularly so when, as is often the case, the prisoner is indigent and therefore dependent on pro bono or other free representation. Congress has acknowledged the problem. INA § 242A(b) requires the Secretary, when selecting those prison sites at which removal hearings will be held, to "make reasonable efforts to ensure that the alien's access to counsel and right to counsel * * * are not impaired." Does this provision go far enough? If a given prisoner has no realistic opportunity to obtain counsel, does the fact that the government made a "reasonable" effort to ensure access to counsel when it chose the sites satisfy the demands of due process?

A congressionally mandated GAO report, see INA § 238(a)(4)(B), studied the extent to which holding removal hearings at prison facilities "may adversely affect the ability of such aliens to contest deportation effectively." United States General Accounting Office, Criminal Aliens—Prison Deportation Hearings Include Opportunities to Contest Deportation, Report No. GAO/GGD–90–79 (1990). Investigators attended 171 prison deportation hearings. The results were inconclusive. On the one hand, the investigators found the immigration judges had informed the prisoners of their procedural rights, including their rights to counsel. *Id.* at 3. On the other hand, the drafters of the report acknowledged they had made no attempt to find out how many of the prisoners eventually succeeded in obtaining representation. In the 171 hearings attended, 72 individuals were represented (five of them by telephone) and 36 others received continuances to obtain counsel. *Id.* at 6. As required by regulations, the immigration judges distributed lists of individuals and organizations that provide free or low-cost representation, but four of the five lists that the GAO investigators inspected were either "inaccurate or outdated." *Id.* at 7.

As noted earlier, the purpose of completing the removal hearings of imprisoned noncitizens before their release is to permit DHS to remove them from the United States at the moment of release. A related procedure sets a more ambitious goal—removing the person even *before* the prison term would otherwise have expired. Normally, early release for purposes of removal is not permitted. INA § 241(a)(4)(A). As a result of 1996 legislation, however, the Secretary now has the discretion to remove many categories of nonviolent offenders before completion of their federal sentences (or state sentences, upon the request of the state authorities). INA § 241(a)(4)(B).

b. ADMINISTRATIVE REMOVAL

In 1994, Congress further expedited the removal of aggravated felons. As part of a comprehensive crime bill, see Pub. L. 103–322, § 130004, 108 Stat. 1796, 2026–28 (Sept. 13, 1994), amended by Pub. L. 103–416, § 223(a)(1), 108 Stat. 4305, 4322 (Oct. 25, 1994), Congress established what came to be called "administrative deportation" and now "administrative removal." With the recent expansions in the definition of "aggravated felony," see page 554 above, administrative removal is in the process of becoming commonplace.

Most of the statutory framework now appears in INA § 238(b). The original statute required the Attorney General to issue regulations establishing abbreviated procedures for removing non-LPR aggravated felons. AEDPA § 442(a)(1) extended administrative removal to aggravated felons who were conditional permanent residents. See INA § 238(b)(2)(B).

The statute puts few constraints on the procedures that the regulations may prescribe. The noncitizen must receive reasonable notice of the charges and of the opportunity to be heard, may be represented by counsel (not at government expense), and must have a reasonable opportunity to inspect and to rebut the evidence; a record must be maintained; and the adjudicator may not be the person who issued the charges. INA § 238(b)(4). The removal order must be stayed for at least 14 days to give the person time to seek (extremely limited) judicial review. INA § 238(b)(3).

The regulations appear in 8 C.F.R. §§ 238, 1238 (2004). The procedure they require replaces the usual removal procedure (an evidentiary hearing before an immigration judge and a right of appeal to the BIA), with an administratively final decision by a DHS enforcement official. *Id.* Normally the entire proceeding is done on paper, without opportunity for an evidentiary hearing or even an informal interview. *Id.* For a good description of the procedure and a critical policy analysis, see Lory D. Rosenberg, *Administrative Deportation Proceedings: Accomplishment or Abomination?*, 72 IR 721 (May 25, 1996).

c. JUDICIAL REMOVAL

In subsection B.6 of this chapter, you studied the principal judicial function in removal cases—reviewing decisions reached by an administrative agency. When noncitizens are deportable because of criminal convictions, however, the sentencing courts can play a more direct role—deciding on their own whether the defendants ought to be removed from the United States.

There are now several different ways in which courts may do the latter. The pattern that these various mechanisms reveal is that sentencing judges have ample power to require removal but almost no power to prohibit it.

Thus, while courts once had the power to issue binding "judicial recommendations against deportation" (JRAD's) in certain criminal cases, that power disappeared with the Immigration Act of 1990. See pages 550–52 above. Today, therefore, sentencing judges have no power to enter *nonremoval* orders in contested cases.

In contrast, under INA § 238(c),[16] federal sentencing judges may enter *removal* orders as part of the criminal sentences. This provision had its origins in the Immigration and Nationality Technical Amendments Act of 1994, Pub. L. 103–416, § 224, 108 Stat. 4305, 4322–24 (Oct. 25, 1994), adding then INA § 242A(d), now INA § 238(c). Under the original 1994 version of this provision, federal sentencing judges could issue deportation orders against those noncitizens who were deportable because of convictions of moral turpitude crimes or aggravated felonies. IIRIRA § 374 extended this power to all cases in which criminal defendants are deportable. The power exists only if the prosecutor requests a removal order and DHS concurs in that request; then the sentencing judge has the discretion whether to exercise this jurisdiction. INA § 238(c)(1). Before deciding whether to order removal, the judge must hold what amounts to a mini-removal hearing on the issues of both deportability and affirmative relief. INA § 238(c)(2).

---

16. A technical glitch in IIRIRA § 671(b)(13) left the INA with two provisions denominated as § 238(c). The cited provision is the one entitled "Judicial Removal."

Either the defendant or DHS may appeal the district court's decision to the court of appeals. INA § 238(c)(3)(A). If the sentencing judge holds a hearing and decides against ordering removal (because the judge either finds the person not deportable or is willing to grant affirmative relief), DHS gets a second shot; it may initiate conventional removal proceedings de novo. (There is no analogous provision giving the defendant a second shot in conventional removal proceedings after the sentencing court has ordered him or her removed.)

The powers just described enable courts to order removal against the will of the defendant. Removal may also be ordered pursuant to negotiated plea bargains. INA § 238(c)(5) specifically authorizes United States Attorneys, with the concurrence of DHS, to enter into plea bargains with noncitizen criminal defendants stipulating to removal from the United States. The same provision empowers sentencing judges to enter judgments enforcing those stipulations.

What about a plea bargain in which the federal prosecutor agrees that the defendant will *not* be removed? As you saw on pages 680–81 above, U.S. Attorneys normally are not empowered to promise nonremoval; if they do so anyway, some courts are willing to enforce the promise while other courts are not. As you also saw, however, a Justice Department regulation now provides that DHS will not be bound by federal prosecutors' promises of nonremoval unless the prosecutor has first secured written authorization from DHS. See 28 C.F.R. § 0.197 (2004). The "unless" clause makes the analysis parallel to that in the 238(c)(5) cases above: Plea bargains may stipulate to either removal or nonremoval, but either way, the stipulation will be ineffective unless DHS concurs.

Professors Margaret Taylor and Ronald Wright have floated an intriguing proposal for more fully merging the criminal justice system with the removal system. They would entrust sentencing judges with nearly exclusive jurisdiction to determine whether noncitizens convicted of crimes are to be ordered removed. See Margaret H. Taylor & Ronald F. Wright, *The Sentencing Judge as Immigration Judge*, 51 Emory L.J. 1131 (2002).

3.   IN ABSENTIA REMOVAL HEARINGS

As the materials you have read to this point illustrate, there has been much recent emphasis on speeding the removal process and eliminating vehicles for delay. This emphasis has led inevitably to concern about noncitizens who do not show up for their removal hearings. Former INA § 242(b) (pre–1990) provided that, if the person "has been given a reasonable opportunity to be present at a [deportation] proceeding * * *, and without reasonable cause" fails to appear, the hearing may proceed in the person's absence. The Immigration Act of 1990, § 545(a), however, added some controversial new provisions to deal more specifically and more harshly with those who do not show up at their removal hearings.

The Notice to Appear, which is the document that officially marks the commencement of removal proceedings, advises the respondent of his or her duties and of the consequences of failing to discharge those duties. Among other things, it instructs the person to provide his or her address and telephone number and to inform DHS of any changes of address or telephone number. INA § 239(a)(1)(F)(i, ii). It also spells out the consequences of failing to do so. See INA § 239(a)(1)(F)(iii).

What are those consequences? If the required notice has been provided, or the notice was sent to the person's most recent known address but he or she had failed to notify DHS of an address or telephone change and as a result did not receive the notice, and the person does not appear, a removal hearing will be held in absentia. INA § 240(b)(5)(A, B). At that hearing ICE must prove by clear, unequivocal, and convincing evidence that the required notice was provided (or couldn't be provided because the respondent had not notified DHS of an address or telephone change) and that the person is deportable. *Id.* To get the removal order rescinded, the person must either (a) move to reopen within 180 days, showing "exceptional circumstances;" or (b) move to reopen at any time, showing he or she either did not receive the required notice, or was in custody and was not at fault in failing to appear. INA § 240(b)(4)(C). "Exceptional circumstances" means "serious illness of the alien or death of an immediate relative of the alien" or something else no "less compelling," and must be beyond the person's control. INA § 240(e)(1). One court has held that the 180–day deadline for moving to reopen will be equitably tolled if the person was defrauded by his or her own counsel. *Lopez v. INS*, 184 F.3d 1097 (9th Cir. 1999).

Judicial review of an in absentia removal order is available but is very limited in scope. The only issues the court has the jurisdiction to address are the adequacy of the notice, the reasons for the person's absence, and deportability. INA § 240(b)(5)(D). Not subject to litigation, for example, is eligibility for discretionary relief, which is probably the most common issue presented in petitions for review.

Noncitizens who are ordered removed in absentia suffer adverse consequences beyond the removal order itself. A person who receives oral notice of the hearing and still fails to appear (and doesn't demonstrate "exceptional circumstances") becomes ineligible for various discretionary remedies until ten years after the removal order. See INA § 240(b)(7). In addition, the failure to appear renders the person inadmissible to the United States for five years following his or her eventual departure. INA § 212(a)(6)(B).

What is your reaction to this procedure? Is it fair? If so, is it appropriately harsh or unduly so? See generally Iris Gomez, *The Consequences of Nonappearance: Interpreting New Section 242B of the Immigration and Nationality Act*, 30 San Diego L.Rev. 75 (1993).

4. NONCITIZENS REENTERING AFTER PRIOR REMOVALS

INA § 241(a)(5) expedites the removal of noncitizens who were previously removed or who voluntarily departed, but who then reentered unlawfully. ICE could of course institute new removal proceedings, typically on the ground that the person entered while inadmissible, INA § 237(a)(1)(A), or is "present in the United States in violation of [the INA]." INA § 237(a)(1)(B). As you now know, that process can be quite time-consuming. In such cases, therefore, once it is found that the individual has reentered unlawfully after a prior removal order, the prior order is reinstated and the person may be removed without further proceedings.

But questions as to the procedural machinery remain. The administrative regulations purport to entrust the decisionmaking authority to DHS immigration officers rather than to immigration judges. See 8 C.F.R. §§ 241.8, 1241.8 (2004). In *Morales-Izquierdo v. Ashcroft*, 388 F.3d 1299 (9th Cir. 2004), a unanimous panel struck down the regulations on the ground that they violate INA § 240(a)(1), which says that "an immigration judge shall conduct all proceedings for deciding the inadmissibility or deportability of an alien." The court noted that the previous regulations had allowed the noncitizen a hearing before an immigration judge on the issues of identity, the existence of a prior removal order, and a subsequent illegal reentry, as well as the opportunity to apply for discretionary relief and to appeal to the BIA. Whether other courts will follow the Ninth Circuit and whether DHS will change the regulations are not known as of this writing.

5.   CREW MEMBERS

A noncitizen who serves on board a vessel or aircraft is typically allowed to remain in the United States for a specified period of up to 29 days. See INA §§ 101(a)(10), 101(a)(15)(D), 252(a). The entry document is called a "conditional permit." INA § 252(a). Any immigration officer, upon determining that the noncitizen "is not a bona fide crewman, or does not intend to depart on the vessel or aircraft which brought him," has the discretion to revoke the conditional permit, take the person into custody, and require the captain to detain him or her on board the vessel or aircraft if practicable. INA § 252(b). DHS then removes the person at the expense of the carrier, and no removal proceedings ever take place. *Id.*

6.   TERRORIST REMOVAL PROCEEDINGS

Soon after (domestic) terrorists carried out the devastating 1995 bombing of the federal building in Oklahoma City, Congress enacted AEDPA. One provision, section 401, established a special new removal court for noncitizen terrorists. The procedure is laid out in INA §§ 501–507 and summarized in chapter 10, § D.2 below. At this writing the Court has yet to be convened; the government has preferred to deploy other, generally less formal alternatives that are also discussed in chapter 10 below.

7.   RESCISSION OF ADJUSTMENT OF STATUS

Under INA § 246, a grant of adjustment of status may be rescinded within five years if the person was in fact ineligible for adjustment at the time it was granted. The advantage of rescission to ICE is that, with the person's LPR status having terminated, ICE may be able to initiate removal proceedings on the ground that the person has now overstayed his or her original nonimmigrant visa.

In 1990, Congress expanded the deportability ground for noncitizens who were inadmissible at the time of *entry* to include also those who were inadmissible at the time of *adjustment of status*. Imm. Act 1990, § 602(d), amending INA § 237(a)(1)(A). That change sucked much of the significance from the rescission provision. Now, when the government believes that a person obtained adjustment of status while inadmissible, it can simply charge deportability based on inadmissibility at the time of adjustment of status; it doesn't have to bring proceedings to rescind status on that ground and then charge deportability based on the person now having overstayed his or her original nonimmigrant visa. Can you figure out why rescission remains useful nonetheless in some situations?

ICE must *initiate* rescission proceedings within five years of adjustment; the proceedings need not be concluded within that period. *Matter of Onal,* 18 I. & N. Dec. 147, 149 (BIA 1981). The mechanics are laid out in 8 C.F.R. §§ 246, 1246 (2004). The procedure resembles that of a removal hearing. ICE serves on the LPR a Notice of Intent to Rescind. *Id.* § 246.1. The LPR has the right to an evidentiary hearing before an immigration judge. *Id.* § 246.5. ICE must prove its case by "clear, unequivocal, and convincing evidence," *Waziri v. INS,* 392 F.2d 55, 57–58 (9th Cir.1968), just as in removal cases. Either party may appeal to the BIA, 8 C.F.R. §§ 246.7, 1003.1(b)(8) (2004), and the noncitizen presumably can obtain judicial review in federal district court under 28 U.S.C. § 1331 (general federal question jurisdiction) or in the court of appeals as part of a petition for review of the ensuing removal order.

NOTES AND QUESTIONS

1. As noted, rescission under section 246 requires only a finding that "the person was not in fact eligible for such adjustment of status." There is no requirement of fraud or deliberate concealment. Should there be? Argue both ways. In analyzing this issue, consider that, despite the mandatory-sounding wording of section 246 (Attorney General *shall* rescind adjustment), the provision has been interpreted as conferring merely a *discretion* to rescind when the terms of the provision are otherwise met. *Matter of Quan,* 12 I. & N. Dec. 487, 488 (Deputy Assoc. Comm'r 1967) (no authority cited). In *Quan,* the former INS had brought rescission proceedings against an individual who had adjusted her status on the basis of her marriage to a man who had falsely claimed to be a United States citizen. She had been unaware of the falsity and in the meantime had had two United States citizen children. The Deputy Associate Commissioner (who then heard appeals from rescission orders) made the discretionary decision not to rescind. See also *Matter of Saunders,* 16 I. & N. Dec. 326, 332 (BIA 1977) (Board Member Appleman, concurring, suggests possibility of reading in a requirement of fraud). But see *Matter of Tayabji,* 19 I. & N. Dec. 264 (BIA

1985) (affirming rescission even though person had been unaware of fact making him ineligible for adjustment).

2. Suppose A adjusts her status to permanent residence and then marries B. B then adjusts status to permanent residence under the family-sponsored second preference on the basis of the marriage. A's adjustment of status is then rescinded. Should that lead to rescission of B's adjustment? In *Matter of Valiyee,* 14 I. & N. Dec. 710 (IJ and BIA, 1974), the answer given was yes. Based on the language of section 246, would you have reached the same result?

3. It has been argued that the statutory five-year limitation on *rescission* should be interpreted as also limiting the initiation of *removal* proceedings against adjusted LPRs. Those arguments, however, have been rejected. For some detailed discussion, see *Oloteo v. INS,* 643 F.2d 679 (9th Cir. 1981); *Matter of Belenzo,* 17 I. & N. Dec. 374 (BIA & A.G. 1980–81).

CHAPTER 10

IMMIGRATION AND NATIONAL SECURITY

Let us be clear: *Immigration law does not revolve around national security or terrorism.* As you will see, national security is merely one of many policy ingredients in the mix. Moreover, only the most minute proportion of actual immigration cases present any national security issues at all. Conversely, while many of the policy responses to September 11 have been immigration-specific, most have not.

A full chapter devoted solely to immigration and national security runs the risk, therefore, of lending that subject undue prominence. This must be acknowledged. For two reasons, separate treatment of this material is useful nonetheless. First, in the aftermath of September 11, the inevitable preoccupation with terrorism and war has utterly dominated the public discourse on immigration. Welcome or not, that reality cannot be ignored. Second, Congress and the executive branch have responded with an array of counterterrorism initiatives. Many of them specifically target either noncitizens or particular classes of noncitizens. Synthesizing these measures makes it easier to describe, digest, and evaluate them in context.

A few organizational notes: Some of the programs discussed in this chapter—for example, those that deal with students, asylum seekers, detention, visa issuance, and border enforcement—relate fundamentally to the subjects of other chapters. These will be included here but at least cross-referenced elsewhere. Further, although the events of September 11 have affected areas of immigration law beyond those that relate to national security—for example, the diminished enthusiasm for guest worker, legalization, and other immigration reforms that had been on the Bush–Fox agenda[1]—this chapter will be confined to issues of national security. Finally, while the transfer of immigration functions from the INS to the DHS was clearly driven by national security objectives, the details of that reorganization appeared in the Overview chapter of this book and need not be repeated here.

Since the founding of the Republic, anxieties about national security have frequently found their way into United States immigration law. The Alien Act of 1798 authorized the President to deport any noncitizen he deemed "dangerous." Act of June 25, 1798, 1 Stat. 570. This unpopular statute was not renewed when it lapsed after two years, see Frank F.

---

1. See, e.g., Kevin R. Johnson, *September 11 and Mexican Immigrants: Collateral* *Damage Comes Home*, 52 DePaul L. Rev. 849, 866–67 (2003).

Chuman, The Bamboo People 53 (1976), but more than a century later, following the assassination of President McKinley, Congress passed a law that excluded noncitizen anarchists and certain others whose views were deemed subversive. Act of March 3, 1903, ch. 1012, §§ 2, 38, 32 Stat. 1213, 1214, 1221. These exclusions were broadened over the years and extended to deportation, as you saw in chapters 5 and 7. In 1996, mainly in response to the bombing of the federal building in Oklahoma City, Congress passed AEDPA, a comprehensive statute that added several anti-terrorism (and other immigration-related) programs.

But there is no question that the most devastating terrorist acts in the United States, and those that have prompted the most sweeping responses both generally and with specific respect to immigration, were the attacks of September 11, 2001. Among the congressional responses have been the USA PATRIOT Act, EBSVERA, the HSA, the Intelligence Reform and Terrorism Prevention Act of 2004, 108 Pub. L. 458, 118 Stat. 3638 (Dec. 17, 2004), and the REAL ID Act of 2005. A number of important executive branch actions have followed. These developments, together with relevant pre-September 11 programs, are highlighted here and throughout the book.

Generally, the national security strategies that are targeted specifically at noncitizens fall into the following seven areas: detention, intelligence-gathering, expansion of the grounds for removing noncitizens from the country, contracting noncitizens' procedural rights, visa and other overseas policies, enhanced border enforcement, and profiling.

SECTION A.   THE DETENTION OF NONCITIZENS[2]

One of the most publicized components of the post-September 11 national security strategy in the United States has been the vastly increased resort to preventive detention. Several detention programs should be distinguished:

1.   DETENTION IN CONNECTION WITH REMOVAL PROCEEDINGS

Removal proceedings can take months or even years. As a general rule, various governmental officials have the discretion whether to detain or release noncitizens while removal proceedings are pending. INA § 236(a). Release requires a finding that the noncitizen will not endanger persons or

---

2. See generally David Cole, Enemy Aliens–Double Standards and Constitutional Freedoms in the War on Terrorism (2003); David Cole, *Enemy Aliens*, 54 Stanford L. Rev. 953 (2002); David Cole, *In Aid of Removal: Due Process Limits on Immigration Detention*, 51 Emory L. Rev. 1003 (2002); Stephen H. Legomsky, *The Detention of Aliens: Theories, Rules, and Discretion*, 30 Univ. of Miami Inter–American L. Rev. 531 (1999); Natsu Taylor Saito, *Will Force Trump Legality After September 11? American Jurisprudence Confronts the Rule of Law*, 17 Georgetown Immigration L.J. 1 (2002); Peter H. Schuck, *INS Detention and Removal: A "White Paper,"* 11 Georgetown Immigration L.J. 667 (1997); Charles D. Weisselberg, *The Detention and Treatment of Aliens Three Years After September 11: A New New World?*, 38 U.C. Davis L.Rev. 815 (2005).

property and is likely to appear for the removal proceeding. 8 C.F.R. §§ 236.1(c)(8), 1236.1(c)(8) (2004).

By way of exception, however, detention has been made mandatory in certain categories of cases. Because mandatory detention gives rise to difficult constitutional issues, the subject was covered more comprehensively in chapter 2 (*Demore v. Kim*). At least three categories of mandatory detention relate specifically to national security and thus require brief mention here.

First, Congress in 1996 mandated the detention, pending removal proceedings, of any noncitizen who is alleged to be inadmissible or deportable on the basis of terrorist activities. INA § 236(c)(1)(D). The relevant inadmissibility and deportability grounds were described in chapters 5 and 7, respectively. See also INA § 236A (certification program, discussed below).

A second type of mandatory detention policy briefly affected certain asylum seekers. As you will see in chapter 11, one may apply for asylum either at a port of entry or in the interior of the United States. When a person applies for asylum at a port of entry, the immigration officials usually have the discretion either to detain the individual until the application is decided or permit him or her to remain at large. In March 2003, however, Homeland Security Secretary Tom Ridge announced an initiative called "Operation Liberty Shield." The initiative was accompanied by an administration list of some 34 countries designated as harboring terrorists. The list consisted almost entirely of countries that are predominantly Arab or Muslim or both. Under one key provision of Operation Liberty Shield, if a national of one of those 34 countries applied for asylum at a United States port of entry, and the person lacked valid entry documents (usually the case with asylum seekers at ports of entry), detention was mandatory until the person either received asylum or was removed. See U.S. Comm. for Refugees, March/April 2003 Refugee Reports, at 5. That policy was controversial at both legal and policy levels and was terminated after one month. See David Cole, Alien Enemies 51, 249 n.23 (2003).

A third type of mandatory detention can result from appeals in bond cases. When an immigration judge finds that a noncitizen in removal proceedings is not a threat to abscond or to endanger the public and therefore grants release on bond, ICE may appeal the decision to the BIA. The appeal, however, can take several months or longer. Until shortly after September 11, the rule was that the prosecuting agency (then the INS) could request the BIA to stay the person's release during this period, but the INS had to show that its appeal was likely to succeed and that the person's release would cause irreparable harm—roughly the same standard as for preliminary injunctions. A regulation issued by Attorney General Ashcroft in late 2001 eliminated those requirements. Whenever the prosecuting agency (now ICE) has determined that the person should not be released, the immigration judge's decision ordering release now *must* be stayed, and the noncitizen detained, for as long as the appeal takes. 8 C.F.R. § 1003.19(i)(2) (2004). ICE need not demonstrate, or even allege, any reasons for doubting the immigration judge's decision to release. As a result, simply by filing an appeal to the BIA, ICE can unilaterally effect the person's confinement for a period of months or even years. See generally David Cole, *In Aid of Removal: Due Process Limits on Immigration Detention*, 51 Emory L.J. 1003, 1030–31 (2002).

Two recent federal district court decisions cast doubt on the continued viability of the mandatory stays of release pending appeal. In *Tarango v. Ridge*, No. CV 03–1738–PA (D. Oreg., Jan. 9, 2004), the court held the regulation violated both substantive and procedural due process. In *Zavala v. Ridge*, 310 F. Supp. 2d 1071 (N.D. Cal. 2004), the court reached the same conclusion and held alternatively that the regulation conflicted with the statutory discretion conferred on immigration judges. Either more case law or a change in the regulation seems inevitable.

Apart from these examples of formally mandatory detention, national security considerations have recently influenced discretionary detention decisions as well. They have done so in at least two ways.

First, as you will see in more detail in the next subsection, the FBI arrested and interviewed hundreds of noncitizens in the months following the September 11 attacks. Many of the arrested individuals were believed to have violated the immigration laws. In those cases, the former INS instituted removal proceedings, and the FBI routinely sent memoranda to EOIR opposing discretionary release on bond pending the removal decisions. The memoranda contained the following boilerplate language: "The FBI is gathering and culling information that may corroborate or diminish our current suspicions of the individuals who have been detained. * * * [T]he FBI has been unable to rule out the possibility that respondent is somehow linked to, or possesses knowledge of, the terrorist attacks." See AILA, *Boiling the Frog Slowly: Executive Branch Actions Since September 11, 2001*, 7 BIB 1236, at 1236 (Oct. 15, 2002).

A second and more specific national security constraint on the discretion to release has recently arisen in the context of Haitian boat people. As you will see in chapter 11, for many years Haitians fleeing horrific conditions at home have attempted to reach United States shores by boat. In *Matter of D–J–*, 23 I. & N. Dec. 572 (A.G. 2003), a boat carrying 216 undocumented Haitians and Dominicans sailed into Biscayne Bay, Florida. One of the passengers, D–J–, was apprehended onshore and placed in removal proceedings. He applied for asylum and, while the claim was pending, for release on bond. Over the objections of the former INS, the immigration judge granted bond and the BIA affirmed. They found that D–J– was not likely to abscond or to endanger the community. Attorney General Ashcroft reversed the decision of the BIA. He reasoned that, in exercising their discretion whether to release or detain a noncitizen pending removal proceedings, the immigration authorities are additionally required to weigh any national security considerations that executive branch sources with relevant expertise bring to their attention.

That holding might seem innocuous on its face. After all, if a person is found to be a threat to national security, who could deny that that danger is relevant to the discretionary decision whether to release on bond? The impact of the Attorney General's decision lies, rather, in the way he applied that principle to the facts of the case. First, in response to the argument that due process requires individualized consideration of the particular applicant, the Attorney General held that the national security considerations may be applied categorically—in this case, to (at least) all the undocumented Haitians who were apprehended onshore, without regard to the circumstances of individual applicants. Second, to conclude that national security was at stake, the Attorney General had to define national security in broad terms. He credited two separate arguments advanced by the INS. One argument was that the release of undocumented Haitian boat people would encourage other Haitians to follow suit. This in turn would require the Coast Guard and others to respond, thereby straining "national and homeland security resources." 23 I. & N. Dec. at 577, 578–79. Second, and more generally, the INS argued, and the Attorney General agreed, that the September 11 terrorist attacks made it increasingly important to prevent undocumented migrants from avoiding the immigration inspections process. *Id.* at 577. This concern was heightened here, the argument ran, because the State Department had observed "an increase in third country nationals (Pakistanis, Palestinians, etc.) using Haiti as a staging point for attempted migration to the United States." *Id.* at 579. Since the same considerations will arise in virtually any case that involves Haitian vessels (and arguably in a range of other cases as well), the practical effect of the Attorney General's decision is to make detention mandatory in whole categories of cases.

Apart from the constitutional claim that due process requires case-by-case assessment (since rejected by the Supreme Court in *Demore v. Kim*, as you saw in chapter 2), D–J– made several arguments rooted in international law. Those arguments can be understood only in the context of the special rules applicable to asylum seekers and thus are deferred to chapter 11.

Professor Lee Hall has written a series of innovative articles that link the post–9/11 mandatory detention policies to the commercial profits gained by the operators of state and private detention facilities. She suggests there can be political rewards for legislators and officials who facilitate government contracts with private detention centers. See Lee Hall, *Nomads under the Tent of Blue: Migrants Fuel the U.S. Prison Industry*, 6 Rutgers Race & L.Rev., issue #2 (2003); Lee Hall, *Shackles and Shareholders: Developments in the Business of Immigration Detentions*, 9 BIB 394 (Apr. 1, 2004); Lee Hall, *Update to "Shackles and Shareholders: Developments in the Business of Immigration Detentions,"* 9 BIB 565 (May 1, 2004).

2. THE PENTTBOM INVESTIGATION

Immediately after the September 11 attacks, the FBI in cooperation with several other law enforcement agencies launched the Pentagon/Twin Towers Bombing Investigation (PENTTBOM). The investigation continues as of this writing. The general strategy is to question and in many cases detain individuals possibly involved in the September 11 attacks or other terrorist activities, as well as anyone else who might have useful information. In addition, when undocumented immigrants were encountered fortuitously during the course of the investigation, they too were arrested, turned over to the INS (now DHS), and detained. See U.S. Dept. of Justice, Office of the Inspector General, The September 11 Detainees: A Review of the Treatment of Aliens Held on Immigration Charges in Connection with the Investigation of the September 11 Attacks (April 2003) [hereafter cited as the OIG Report], at 69–70. Overall, the overwhelming majority of the questioned individuals have been noncitizens.

After initial interviews, the FBI and the former INS (now DHS) have detained three groups of people. One group, the so-called "immigration detainees," are noncitizens whom DHS believes to be in violation of their immigration statuses, typically because they are present without admission or have overstayed their temporary visas. In most cases, the initial questioning gave no reason to suspect these individuals of connections to September 11 or to any other terrorist activities, but because of their immigration violations they were placed in removal proceedings. In the approximately eleven months following September 11, the former INS detained 738 such individuals (762 counting another 24 arrested before the attacks). See OIG Report at 2.

Approximately 134 other noncitizens were held on terrorist-related criminal charges, and an additional, undisclosed number were held as material witnesses under 18 U.S.C. § 3144. See Center for National Security Studies v. U.S. Dept. of Justice, 331 F.3d 918 (D.C. Cir. 2003).

The focus here is on the immigration detainees. The overwhelming majority have been males, between ages 26 and 40, from Arab or Muslim countries. About one-third are from Pakistan. More than half were arrested in the State of New York. See OIG Report, above, at 20–23.

The immigration detainees have been held in a combination of federal, state, and private detention facilities while the FBI investigates them for possible terrorist connections. Following media allegations of mistreatment of the prisoners, the Justice Department's (independent) Office of the Inspector General investigated. The Office examined two detention facilities—the Metropolitan Detention Center in Brooklyn, New York (operated by the federal Bureau of Prisons) and the Passaic County Jail in Paterson, New Jersey. It chose those two facilities because together they then housed the majority of the immigration detainees and because they had attracted many complaints. OIG Report, above, at 2–3. The Office ultimately submitted a 198–page report that acknowledged the vital national security interests at stake and the difficulties under which the law enforcement agencies were operating but found, even in the light of those circumstances, that the government had acted inappropriately in significant ways (summarized below.)

The process works like this: After a preliminary interview, both the FBI and DHS decide whether to keep the individual in detention. Detention continues automatically if the FBI either finds the person to be "of interest" or has not yet decided whether he or she is of interest. Alternatively, detention automatically continues if DHS believes the person has committed an immigration violation. Unless the FBI clears the individual at the time of the initial interview, its investigation continues while the person is in detention.

The OIG Report ultimately expressed a number of serious criticisms. It chastised the FBI for making little attempt "to distinguish between aliens who it actually suspected of having a connection to terrorism from those aliens, who, while possibly guilty of violating federal immigration law, had no connection to terrorism but simply were encountered in connection with a PENTTBOM lead." OIG Report at 70, 196. The OIG Report also criticized the needlessly long duration of the detention; the practice of the former INS to oppose bond automatically in removal proceedings, without regard to the facts of the cases; and, even after removal orders had been entered, the INS practice of keeping the noncitizens in detention while awaiting FBI "clearance," for far longer than the 90–day statutory maximum.

Increasingly troubled by the threat of litigation, the Justice Department rescinded the "hold until cleared" policy in February 2002. Under the new policy, ICE keeps the FBI apprised of the results of removal proceedings so that the FBI can prioritize the investigations of those in whom it has interest, but ICE is now free to execute removal orders without waiting for FBI clearance. OIG Report at 104. By June 13, 2002, only 74 of the September 11 immigration detainees remained in custody. *Center for National Security Studies v. U.S. DOJ*, 331 F.3d 918, 921 (D.C. Cir. 2003).

The other major problems noted in the OIG Report concerned the conditions of confinement. OIG found "significant" problems in the treatment of the September 11 detainees. OIG Report at 195. These ranged from making too little effort to decide which of the prisoners really needed the highly restrictive confinement conditions and which ones did not; prison officials routinely telling detainees' family members and attorneys that the individuals were not there when in fact they were; making telephone access needlessly difficult; patterns of physical and verbal abuse (at the main facility); harsh living conditions, including 24–hour cell illumination; and inadequate INS visits to monitor these conditions. *Id.* at 195–97.

The Justice Department did not refute any of the findings or even respond to any of the specific criticisms. Instead, the Deputy Attorney General issued a tersely worded two-page memo that emphasized the crisis atmosphere, the novelty of the issues, and the monumental workload of the Department's employees. Under those circumstances, he said, "it is unfair to criticize the conduct of members of my staff during this period." Memo from Larry D. Thompson, Deputy Attorney General, to Glenn A. Fine, Inspector General (Apr. 4, 2003). In contrast, FBI Director Robert Mueller, speaking to the ACLU in June 2003, took a conciliatory tone. He acknowledged the failings identified by the Inspector General, agreed the FBI can do a better job, and committed himself to improving the process so as better to accommodate the sometimes conflicting demands of law enforcement and civil liberties.

Several other controversies, though not addressed in the OIG report, have arisen out of the continuing September 11 investigation. One is the issue of "profiling"—the practice of targeting individuals who fit preformulated demographic patterns. In the case of the September 11 investigation, law enforcement authorities are widely perceived to be profiling suspects based on ethnicity, religion, country of nationality, age, and gender. Because the profiling issue is also raised by many of the other national security initiatives discussed in this chapter (not just detention), it is taken up separately in section G below.

Two other issues are worth noting here:

a.   DISCLOSURE OF INFORMATION

One controversy has concerned the government's policies on the disclosure of information about the detainees. Professor Natsu Taylor Saito describes the early practices:

> In the weeks following September 11, 2001, the Justice Department * * * periodically announced a running total of the hundreds of people it was detaining in connection with the attacks. It did not, however, reveal who was in custody; what, if anything, they were charged with; or where they were being held. The media began reporting stories of the families of the "disappeared"—wives and children who came home to discover that their husbands or fathers had vanished; frantic inquiries to local and federal authorities which yielded no information; occasional phone calls from the men who reported that they were being moved from state to state, often held in maximum security prisons, questioned but not told why they were being held. Justice Department officials stated that the detainees had access to lawyers, but detainees have reported being denied access and lawyers that they were unable to find their clients.

> On October 29 [2001] a coalition of civil liberties and human rights organizations filed a request under the Freedom of Information Act ("FOIA") demanding the names, citizenship status and location of those arrested, the charges on which they were being held, and the names of their lawyers. Shortly thereafter, on November 5, the Justice Department announced that it would no longer release even the numbers of those detained, which, by then, was 1,147. Eighteen organizations * * * then joined in a lawsuit demanding the release of basic information on the detainees.

Natsu Taylor Saito, *Will Force Trump Legality After September 11? American Jurisprudence Confronts the Rule of Law*, 17 Georgetown Immigration L.J. 1, 6–7 (2002).

On April 22, 2002, the Justice Department issued an interim regulation, 67 Fed. Reg. 19508, made final on January 29, 2003, see 68 Fed. Reg.

4364–67, adding 8 C.F.R. § 236.6. The interim regulation prohibits non-federal detention facilities from releasing any information relating to their immigration detainees. The INS (now DHS) exclusively controls the release of such information to the public.

The FOIA request to which Professor Saito referred was denied by the Justice Department. The Department invoked various FOIA exemptions for information that is "compiled for law enforcement purposes" and which would reasonably interfere with enforcement proceedings, invade personal privacy, or endanger someone's life or physical safety. 5 U.S.C. § 552(b)(7)(A, C, F). The government emphasized the "mosaic" nature of intelligence operations. Information on an individual detainee is but a piece of a larger puzzle; whoever has access to all the pieces can more easily distill patterns. In these cases the government asserted that, if the full list of names were revealed, Al Qaeda operatives would have a "roadmap about the course and progress of an investigation," would be able to learn which of their agents remained at large and which ones were in imminent danger of apprehension, might be able to figure out who the confidential informants were, and could intimidate or endanger detainees and their families to deter them from cooperating. Moreover, the government argued, withholding the information would protect the privacy of the detainees. They, and their lawyers and families, remained free to decide which information they wished to reveal to the public. See *Center for National Security Studies v. U.S. DOJ*, 331 F.3d 918, 923 (D.C. Cir.2003); 67 Fed. Reg. at 19509.

The district court reached a compromise decision. It ordered the Department to disclose the names of the detainees and their lawyers but approved the Department's refusal to disclose the detainees' locations and release dates. 331 F.3d at 923–25. On appeal, the D.C. Circuit in a 2–1 decision handed the Department a more complete victory, holding that the government had the right to withhold all of the information. The majority opinion emphasized the importance of judicial deference to the government in matters of national security. The dissent found the government's national security justifications vague and felt, at any rate, that the majority opinion had given insufficient weight to the competing interest of the public in having a way to assure itself that the government was respecting the detainees' constitutional rights. *Id.* at 937–52 (Tatel, J, dissenting).

b.   MONITORING OF ATTORNEY–CLIENT CONVERSATIONS

Since many of the noncitizens who are detained pending removal proceedings are in facilities operated by the federal Bureau of Prisons, a Bureau of Prisons regulation rooted in the PENTTBOM investigation is of particular interest. About seven weeks after the September 11 attacks, the Bureau announced the following interim rule (still in force as of this writing, see 28 C.F.R. § 501.3 (2004)):

> In any case where the Attorney General specifically so orders, based on information from the head of a federal law enforcement or intelligence agency that reasonable suspicion exists to believe

that a particular inmate may use communications with attorneys or their agents to further or facilitate acts of terrorism, the Director, Bureau of prisons, shall * * * provide appropriate procedures for the monitoring or review of communications between that inmate and attorneys or attorneys' agents who are traditionally covered by the attorney-client privilege, for the purpose of deterring future acts that could result in death or serious bodily injury to person, or substantial damage to property that would entail the risk of death or serious bodily injury to persons.

66 Fed. Reg. 55062, 55066 (Oct. 31, 2001), amending 28 C.F.R. § 501.3(d).

Some safeguards are built in. As the above passage indicates, the information must come from the head of a qualifying agency and he or she must have "reasonable suspicion" that the attorney-client communications are meant to further terrorist acts. Another provision requires advance notice to the inmate and the attorney, except (a significant "except") with prior court authorization. *Id.* § 501.3(d)(2) (2004). Since the attorney-client privilege does not protect communications that are designed to facilitate criminal acts, the assumption appears to be that a court would give prior authorization only in such cases. Finally, the regulation establishes a "privilege team" whose members are to be separated from the investigation by a firewall, and the procedures must "minimize the intrusion into privileged material or conversations." *Id.* § 501(d)(3). Except when the head of the privilege team believes that violent or terrorist acts are "imminent," the privilege team is barred from disclosing any information without advance approval by a federal judge. *Id.* The regulation concludes by granting various Justice Department officials the same powers that it confers on the Director of the Bureau of Prisons. *Id.* § 501.3(f).

The American Bar Association reacted swiftly. "Deeply troubled" by what it regarded as an unwarranted intrusion into the sanctity of attorney-client communications, the ABA made the point that the government can always ask a judge to approve the monitoring of a conversation between a prisoner and his or her attorney in an appropriate case. To satisfy constitutional demands, however, the government would have to have "probable cause" to believe that a criminal act is being planned. The new regulation, the ABA observes, not only eliminates the requirement of prior court approval, but also replaces the "probable cause" standard with the lesser "reasonable suspicion" standard. 78 IR at 1743–44. For a contrary view, see Jan C. Ting, *Unobjectionable But Insufficient–Federal Initiatives in Response to the September 11 Terrorist Attacks*, 34 Connecticut L. Rev. 1145, 1151–52 (2002) (arguing that preventing the deaths of thousands of innocent people would justify monitoring the conversations of terrorists). On April 9, 2002, Attorney General Ashcroft announced the first invocation of the new rule, in the case of previously convicted terrorist Sheik Omar Abdel Rahman and his attorney, Lynne Stewart. *Id.* at 1152 n.46.

3. THE CERTIFICATION PROGRAM

The USA PATRIOT ACT, enacted on October 26, 2001, established the authority for a potentially wide-ranging noncitizen detention program.

Section 412 of the Act added a new section 236A to the INA. That section authorizes the Attorney General to "certify" any noncitizen whenever there are "reasonable grounds to believe" that the person is either inadmissible or deportable on certain national security-related grounds. INA § 236A(a)(3). Once the person is certified, detention becomes mandatory until he or she is removed from the country or removal proceedings are terminated. *Id.* § 236A(a)(1, 2, 6). Within seven days of the commencement of detention (as opposed to 48 hours in other cases), the government must decide whether to commence removal proceedings. *Id.* § 236A(a)(5).

Unlike the general detention powers discussed in the preceding subsections, this one expressly allows *indefinite* detention as long as the case is reviewed at least once every six months. *Id.* § 236A(a)(6). As discussed earlier, the Supreme Court in *Zadvydas*, just two months before the September 11 attacks, had casually noted that its decision prohibiting indefinite detention did not involve "particularly dangerous individuals, say suspected terrorists." See page 195 above. Whether the USA PATRIOT Act provision for indefinite detention comports with *Zadvydas* remains to be determined.

Professor David Cole has criticized the certification program on several grounds. If one condition for certifying someone in the first place is that the government has a reasonable basis for believing the person is inadmissible or deportable on specified grounds, then why, Cole asks, does the government need the power to hold the person for seven days without filing charges? The only practical consequence of the seven-day hold would be to prevent an immigration judge from reviewing the legality of the detention during that period. Moreover, Cole observes, the Supreme Court interprets the Fourth Amendment to require that arrested individuals be brought promptly, and presumptively within 48 hours, before a judge for a probable cause hearing. He doubts that the seven-day hold comports with that interpretation. Cole also raises difficult questions about the scope and the adequacy of the courts' powers to review the certification decision by way of habeas corpus. David Cole, *In Aid of Removal: Due Process Limits on Immigration Detention*, 51 Emory L.J. 1003, 1026–28 (2002).

As of March 26, 2003, the certification provision had yet to be invoked. See OIG Report at 27–28 n.28. Presumably, the Justice Department has found it easier simply to detain noncitizens suspected of terrorism either through the PENTTBOM program or through its ordinary power to detain noncitizens during the course of removal proceedings. See generally Margaret H. Taylor, *Dangerous by Decree: Detention Without Bond in Immigration Proceedings*, 50 Loyola L. Rev. 149 (2004).

NOTES AND QUESTIONS

1. You have now read about several different detention programs directed at noncitizens. All have been established for the stated purpose of protecting the national security of the United States. What do you see as (a) the potential benefits and (b) the potential costs of the general strategy

of detaining noncitizens on national security grounds? See generally Stephen H. Legomsky, *The Detention of Aliens: Theories, Rules, and Discretion*, 30 Univ. of Miami Inter–Amer. L. Rev. 531, 536–41 (1999).

2. One form of mandatory (i.e., automatic) detention, discussed in section A.1 above, occurs when an immigration judge orders the noncitizen released on bond during the removal proceedings but the INS (now DHS) appeals the release order to the BIA. As you saw, the appeal automatically stays the release order until the removal proceedings are concluded. The practical effect is to keep the noncitizen in detention for the several months or years that the removal proceedings take. What do you think of that strategy? Are there special arguments that can be made either pro or con, beyond those that can generally be made for or against mandatory detention generally?

3. In section A.2 you read about the Justice Department's "hold-until-cleared" policy (now rescinded). That policy required the INS to delay the removal of those PENTTBOM immigration detainees who had been ordered removed until the FBI had affirmatively cleared them of suspicion. What do you think of that policy? Argue both ways.

4. What is your reaction to the Bureau of Prisons rule that permits the monitoring of conversations between inmates and their attorneys? (See section A.2.b above.) Do the safeguards built into the rule adequately accommodate the concerns about invading the attorney-client privilege?

4.   DETENTION OF "UNLAWFUL COMBATANTS"

Approximately two months after the September 11, 2001 attacks, President Bush issued his controversial Military Order, aimed mainly at Al Qaeda and various other groups. Military Order of Nov. 13, 2001, 66 Fed. Reg. 57833. Asserting his authority "as President and as Commander in Chief of the Armed Forces of the United States," President Bush ordered the detention of specified categories of noncitizens and decreed that any criminal trials of the particular individuals be held in specially created military commissions rather than in military courts martial or the ordinary civilian courts. This subsection covers only the detention consequences of the Military Order; the provisions for criminal trials are discussed in subsection D.5 below.

The Military Order applies to noncitizens who the President has "reason to believe" (a) are members of Al Qaeda; (b) are involved in specified ways in present or potential future activities with "adverse effects on the United States, its citizens, national security, foreign policy, or economy;" or (c) have knowingly harbored any of the former individuals. Military Order, § 2(a). The Order requires that all such persons be detained at locations designated by the Secretary of Defense, either within or outside the United States. *Id.* §§ 2(b), 3(a). These detentions need not be linked to criminal, removal, or any other legal proceedings. Indeed, the Order puts no time limits on the detention.

The main use of the Military Order thus far has been for Taliban and Al Qaeda fighters captured in Afghanistan (but also elsewhere) and flown to the U.S. Naval Station at Guantánamo Bay, Cuba starting January 10, 2002. Within two weeks the 158 prisoners filled the base's capacity, but plans to expand the capacity to 2,000 were in place. See Agora, *Military Commissions*, 96 Amer. J. Internat'l L. 320, 320–21 (2002). Professor Saito describes the scene:

> Several hundred persons captured in Afghanistan have been brought to the U.S. naval base in Guantánamo Bay, Cuba, where they are being held indefinitely in hastily constructed outdoor cages and are apparently being interrogated by some combination of U.S. military and civilian intelligence agencies. They were brought in cargo planes, blindfolded, shackled, and in some cases drugged, and have been held for months in chain link cages where they sleep on mats, exposed to the elements. They have been allowed virtually no contact with the outside world, and the U.S. government has rebuffed efforts of American lawyers to visit them. The U.S. government's position has been that these men are "unlawful combatants" and therefore need not be accorded prisoner of war status. Reluctantly, the administration has allowed Red Cross inspections and has announced that the prisoners will be accorded most of the rights protected by the Geneva Conventions, but it has not conceded that such compliance is actually required by law.

Natsu Taylor Saito, *Will Force Trump Legality after September 11? American Jurisprudence Confronts the Rule of Law*, 17 Georgetown Immigration L.J. 1, 10–11 (2002).

The Military Order requires that the prisoners be treated "humanely, without any adverse distinction based on race, color, religion, gender, birth, wealth, or any similar criteria." Military Order, § 3(b). It also requires that they receive adequate food and amenities and that they be allowed "the free exercise of religion consistent with the requirements of such detention." *Id.* § 3(c,d). As the above excerpt indicates, however, the United States takes the position that the detainees are "unlawful combatants" and not "prisoners of war." The distinction is important, because the Third Geneva Convention on the Law of War (to which the U.S. is a party) entitles prisoners of war (POWs) to numerous protections. There are, for example, constraints on the information they may be required to divulge. See (Geneva) Convention (No. III) Relative to the Treatment of Prisoners of War, 75 U.N.T.S. 135 (done at Geneva, Aug. 12, 1949), art. 17. Importantly too, POWs must be released "without delay after the cessation of active hostilities." *Id.* art. 118. Both provisions could prove problematic if the true purpose of detaining these prisoners is to extract information that will help the government infiltrate Al Qaeda.

Whether the U.S. is correct in refusing to classify the detainees as POWs has been the subject of rancorous debate. There is general agreement that not all captured combatants in an international war qualify as

POWs. Those who are members of the armed forces of a state that is a party to the conflict explicitly qualify. *Id*. art. 4.A(1). Since the Taliban fighters were members of the armed forces of Afghanistan, it seems clear that they have the right to POW status. As for Al Qaeda fighters who are not part of the Taliban, the issues are murkier. The details are left to a course in international humanitarian law.

International law aside, does U.S. domestic law entitle the Guantánamo detainees to judicial determinations of the legality of their detention? The following landmark opinion addresses that question:

Rasul v. Bush

Supreme Court of the United States, 2004.
__ U.S. __, 124 S.Ct. 2686, 159 L.Ed.2d 548.

■ JUSTICE STEVENS delivered the opinion of the Court.

These two cases present the narrow but important question whether United States courts lack jurisdiction to consider challenges to the legality of the detention of foreign nationals captured abroad in connection with hostilities and incarcerated at the Guantanamo Bay Naval Base, Cuba.

I

On September 11, 2001, agents of the al Qaeda terrorist network hijacked four commercial airliners and used them as missiles to attack American targets. While one of the four attacks was foiled by the heroism of the plane's passengers, the other three killed approximately 3,000 innocent civilians, destroyed hundreds of millions of dollars of property, and severely damaged the U.S. economy. In response to the attacks, Congress passed a joint resolution authorizing the President to use "all necessary and appropriate force against those nations, organizations, or persons he determines planned, authorized, committed, or aided the terrorist attacks . . . or harbored such organizations or persons." Acting pursuant to that authorization, the President sent U.S. Armed Forces into Afghanistan to wage a military campaign against al Qaeda and the Taliban regime that had supported it.

Petitioners in these cases are 2 Australian citizens and 12 Kuwaiti citizens who were captured abroad during hostilities between the United States and the Taliban. Since early 2002, the U.S. military has held them—along with, according to the Government's estimate, approximately 640 other non-Americans captured abroad—at the Naval Base at Guantanamo Bay. The United States occupies the Base, which comprises 45 square miles of land and water along the southeast coast of Cuba, pursuant to a 1903 Lease Agreement executed with the newly independent Republic of Cuba in the aftermath of the Spanish–American War. Under the Agreement, "the United States recognizes the continuance of the ultimate sovereignty of the Republic of Cuba over the [leased areas]," while "the Republic of Cuba consents that during the period of the occupation by the United States . . . the United States shall exercise complete jurisdiction and control over and within said areas." In 1934, the parties entered into a treaty providing that, absent an agreement to modify or abrogate the lease, the lease would remain in effect "[s]o long as the United States of America shall not abandon the . . . naval station of Guantanamo."

In 2002, petitioners, through relatives acting as their next friends, filed various actions in the U.S. District Court for the District of Columbia challenging the legality of their detention at the Base. All alleged that none of the petitioners has ever been a combatant against the United States or has ever engaged in any terrorist acts.[4] They also alleged that none has been charged with any wrongdoing, permitted to consult with counsel, or provided access to the courts or any other tribunal.

* * *

Construing all three actions as petitions for writs of habeas corpus, the District Court dismissed them for want of jurisdiction. The court held, in reliance on our opinion in Johnson v. Eisentrager, 339 U.S. 763 (1950), that "aliens detained outside the sovereign territory of the United States [may not] invok[e] a petition for a writ of habeas corpus." The Court of Appeals affirmed. Reading Eisentrager to hold that " 'the privilege of litigation' does not extend to aliens in military custody who have no presence in 'any territory over which the United States is sovereign,' " it held that the District Court lacked jurisdiction over petitioners' habeas actions, as well as their remaining federal statutory claims that do not sound in habeas. We granted certiorari and now reverse.

* * *

Congress has granted federal district courts, "within their respective jurisdictions," the authority to hear applications for habeas corpus by any person who claims to be held "in custody in violation of the Constitution or laws or treaties of the United States." 28 U.S.C. §§ 2241(a), (c)(3). * * *

Habeas corpus is, however, "a writ antecedent to statute, . . . throwing its root deep into the genius of our common law." The writ appeared in English law several centuries ago, became "an integral part of our common-law heritage" by the time the Colonies achieved independence, and received explicit recognition in the Constitution, which forbids suspension of "[t]he Privilege of the Writ of Habeas Corpus . . . unless when in Cases of Rebellion or Invasion the public Safety may require it," Art. I, § 9, cl. 2.

As it has evolved over the past two centuries, the habeas statute clearly has expanded habeas corpus "beyond the limits that obtained during the 17th and 18th centuries." But "[a]t its historical core, the writ of habeas corpus has served as a means of reviewing the legality of Executive detention, and it is in that context that its protections have been strongest." * * *

---

4. Relatives of the Kuwaiti detainees allege that the detainees were taken captive "by local villagers seeking promised bounties or other financial rewards" while they were providing humanitarian aid in Afghanistan and Pakistan, and were subsequently turned over to U.S. custody.

Consistent with the historic purpose of the writ, this Court has recognized the federal courts' power to review applications for habeas relief in a wide variety of cases involving Executive detention, in wartime as well as in times of peace. The Court has, for example, entertained the habeas petitions of an American citizen who plotted an attack on military installations during the Civil War, Ex parte Milligan, 4 Wall. 2 (1866), and of admitted enemy aliens convicted of war crimes during a declared war and held in the United States, Ex parte Quirin, 317 U.S. 1 (1942), and its insular possessions, In re Yamashita, 327 U.S. 1 (1946). The question now before us is whether the habeas statute confers a right to judicial review of the legality of Executive detention of aliens in a territory over which the United States exercises plenary and exclusive jurisdiction, but not "ultimate sovereignty."

III

Respondents' primary submission is that the answer to the jurisdictional question is controlled by our decision in Eisentrager. In that case, we held that a Federal District Court lacked authority to issue a writ of habeas corpus to 21 German citizens who had been captured by U.S. forces in China, tried and convicted of war crimes by an American military commission headquartered in Nanking, and incarcerated in the Landsberg Prison in occupied Germany. * * *

Petitioners in these cases differ from the Eisentrager detainees in important respects: They are not nationals of countries at war with the United States, and they deny that they have engaged in or plotted acts of aggression against the United States; they have never been afforded access to any tribunal, much less charged with and convicted of wrongdoing; and for more than two years they have been imprisoned in territory over which the United States exercises exclusive jurisdiction and control.

Not only are petitioners differently situated from the Eisentrager detainees, but the Court in Eisentrager made quite clear that all * * * the facts critical to its disposition were relevant only to the question of the prisoners' *constitutional* entitlement to habeas corpus. The Court had far less to say on the question of the petitioners' *statutory* entitlement to habeas review. * * *

* * *

* * * In Braden v. 30th Judicial Circuit Court of Ky., 410 U.S. 484, 495 (1973), this Court held * * * that the prisoner's presence within the territorial jurisdiction of the district court is not "an invariable prerequisite" to the exercise of district court jurisdiction under the federal habeas statute. Rather, because "the writ of habeas corpus does not act upon the prisoner who seeks relief, but upon the person who holds him in what is alleged to be unlawful custody," a district court acts "within [its] respective jurisdiction" within the meaning of § 2241 as long as "the custodian can be reached by service of process." * * *

* * *

IV

Putting Eisentrager and Ahrens to one side, respondents contend that we can discern a limit on § 2241 through application of the "longstanding principle of American law" that congressional legislation is presumed not to have extraterritorial application unless such intent is clearly manifested. Whatever traction the presumption against extraterritoriality might have in other contexts, it certainly has no application to the operation of the habeas statute with respect to persons detained within "the territorial jurisdiction" of the United States. By the express terms of its agreements with Cuba, the United States exercises "complete jurisdiction and control" over the Guantanamo Bay Naval Base, and may continue to exercise such control permanently if it so chooses. Respondents themselves concede that the habeas statute would create federal court jurisdiction over the claims of an American citizen held at the base. Considering that the statute draws no distinction between Americans and aliens held in federal custody, there is little reason to think that Congress intended the geographical coverage of the statute to vary depending on the detainee's citizenship. Aliens held at the base, no less than American citizens, are entitled to invoke the federal courts' authority under § 2241.

* * *

In the end, the answer to the question presented is clear. Petitioners contend that they are being held in federal custody in violation of the laws of the United States. No party questions the District Court's jurisdiction over petitioners' custodians. Section 2241, by its terms, requires nothing more. We therefore hold that § 2241 confers on the District Court jurisdiction to hear petitioners' habeas corpus challenges to the legality of their detention at the Guantanamo Bay Naval Base.

* * *

VI

Whether and what further proceedings may become necessary after respondents make their response to the merits of petitioners' claims are matters that we need not address now. What is presently at stake is only whether the federal courts have jurisdiction to determine the legality of the Executive's potentially indefinite detention of individuals who claim to be wholly innocent of wrongdoing. Answering that question in the affirmative, we reverse the judgment of the Court of Appeals and remand for the District Court to consider in the first instance the merits of petitioners' claims.

■ JUSTICE KENNEDY, concurring in the judgment.

* * *

■ JUSTICE SCALIA, with whom THE CHIEF JUSTICE and JUSTICE THOMAS join, dissenting.

The Court today holds that the habeas statute, 28 U.S.C. § 2241, extends to aliens detained by the United States military oversees, outside the sovereign borders of the United States and beyond the territorial jurisdictions of all its courts. This is not only a novel holding; it contradicts a half-century-old precedent on which the military undoubtedly relied, Johnson v. Eisentrager. * * *

* * *

I

As we have repeatedly said: "Federal courts are courts of limited jurisdiction. They possess only that power authorized by Constitution and statute, which is not to be expanded by judicial decree. * * * " The petitioners do not argue that the Constitution independently requires jurisdiction here. Accordingly, this case turns on the words of § 2241, a text the Court today largely ignores. Even a cursory reading of the habeas statute shows that it presupposes a federal district court with territorial jurisdiction over the detainee. Section 2241(a) states:

> Writs of habeas corpus may be granted by the Supreme Court, any justice thereof, the district courts and any circuit judge *within their respective jurisdictions.*" (Emphasis added [by Justice Scalia]).

It further requires that "[t]he order of a circuit judge shall be entered in the records of the district court of *the district wherein the restraint complained of is had.*" * * * No matter to whom the writ is directed, custodian or detainee, the statute could not be clearer that a necessary requirement for issuing the writ is that some federal district court have territorial jurisdiction over the detainee. Here, as the Court allows, the Guantanamo Bay detainees are not located within the territorial jurisdiction of any federal district court. One would think that is the end of this case.

* * *

* * * Normally, we consider the interests of those who have relied on our decisions. Today, the Court springs a trap on the Executive, subjecting Guantanamo Bay to the oversight of the federal courts even though it has never before been thought to be within their jurisdiction—and thus making it a foolish place to have housed alien wartime detainees.

II

In abandoning the venerable statutory line drawn in Eisentrager, the Court boldly extends the scope of the habeas statute to the four corners of the earth. Part III of its opinion asserts * * * that "a district court acts 'within [its] respective jurisdiction' within the meaning of § 2241 as long as 'the custodian can be reached by service of process.' " Endorsement of that proposition is repeated in Part IV ("Section 2241, by its terms, requires nothing more [than the District Court's jurisdiction over petitioners' custodians]").

The consequence of this holding, as applied to aliens outside the country, is breathtaking. It permits an alien captured in a foreign theater of active combat to bring a § 2241 petition against the Secretary of Defense. Over the course of the last century, the United States has held millions of alien prisoners abroad. A great many of these prisoners would no doubt have complained about the circumstances of their capture and the terms of their confinement. The military is currently detaining over 600 prisoners at Guantanamo Bay alone; each detainee undoubtedly has complaints—real or contrived—about those terms and circumstances. The Court's unheralded expansion of federal court jurisdiction is not even mitigated by a comforting assurance that the legion of ensuing claims will be easily resolved on the merits. To the contrary, the Court says that the "[p]etitioners' allegations . . . unquestionably describe 'custody in violation of the Constitution or laws or treaties of the United States.' " From this point forward, federal courts will entertain petitions from these prisoners, and others like them around the world, challenging actions and events far away, and forcing the courts to oversee one aspect of the Executive's conduct of a foreign war.

Today's carefree Court disregards, without a word of acknowledgment, the dire warning of a more circumspect Court in Eisentrager:

> To grant the writ to these prisoners might mean that our army must transport them across the seas for hearing. This would require allocation for shipping space, guarding personnel, billeting and rations. It might also require transportation for whatever witnesses the prisoners desired to call as well as transportation for those necessary to defend legality of the sentence. The writ, since it is held to be a matter of right, would be equally available to enemies during active hostilities as in the present twilight between war and peace. Such trials would hamper the war effort and bring aid and comfort to the enemy. They would diminish the prestige of our commanders, not only with enemies but with wavering neutrals. It would be difficult to devise more effective fettering of a field commander than to allow the very enemies he is ordered to reduce to submission to call him to account in his own civil courts and divert his efforts and attention from the military offensive abroad to the legal defensive at home. Nor is it unlikely that the result of such enemy litigiousness would be conflict between judicial and military opinion highly comforting to enemies of the United States.

These results should not be brought about lightly, and certainly not without a textual basis in the statute * * *.

III

Part IV of the Court's opinion, dealing with the status of Guantanamo Bay, is a puzzlement. The Court might have made an effort (a vain one, as I shall discuss) to distinguish Eisentrager on the basis of a difference between the status of Landsberg Prison in Germany and Guantanamo Bay

Naval Base. But Part III flatly rejected such an approach, holding that the place of detention of an alien has no bearing on the statutory availability of habeas relief, but "is strictly relevant only to the question of the appropriate forum." That rejection is repeated at the end of Part IV: "In the end, the answer to the question presented is clear. . . . No party questions the District Court's jurisdiction over petitioners' custodians. . . . Section 2241, by its terms, requires nothing more." Once that has been said, the status of Guantanamo Bay is entirely irrelevant to the issue here. The habeas statute is (according to the Court) being applied domestically, to "petitioners' custodians," and the doctrine that statutes are presumed to have no extraterritorial effect simply has no application.

* * *

The Court does not explain how "complete jurisdiction and control" without sovereignty causes an enclave to be part of the United States for purposes of its domestic laws. Since "jurisdiction and control" obtained through a lease is no different in effect from "jurisdiction and control" acquired by lawful force of arms, parts of Afghanistan and Iraq should logically be regarded as subject to our domestic laws. Indeed, if "jurisdiction and control" rather than sovereignty were the test, so should the Landsberg Prison in Germany, where the United States held the Eisentrager detainees.

* * *

* * * For this Court to create such a monstrous scheme in time of war, and in frustration of our military commanders' reliance upon clearly stated prior law, is judicial adventurism of the worst sort. I dissent.

NOTES AND QUESTIONS

1. Recall the *Mezei* case, on pages 145–58 above. There, a returning LPR was confined indefinitely on Ellis Island and denied entry into the United States on unspecified national security grounds. He sought a hearing on his admissibility. The Supreme Court upheld the Attorney General's decision not to provide a hearing, declaring "Whatever the procedure authorized by Congress, it is due process as far as an alien denied entry is concerned." First, after reviewing that opinion, try to articulate the similarities between *Mezei* and *Rasul*. Second, are the results consistent?

2. The plaintiffs in *Rasul* were all citizens of countries friendly to the United States. Suppose instead they had been citizens of Afghanistan and therefore "enemy aliens." First, do you think the Court would have reached the same result? Second, *should* that fact matter?

3. On the same day that the Court decided *Rasul*, it also handed down a decision in *Hamdi v. Rumsfeld*, ___ U.S. ___, 124 S.Ct. 2633, 159 L.Ed.2d 578 (2004). Unlike the plaintiffs in *Rasul*, Hamdi was a United States citizen (as well as a citizen of Saudi Arabia). Hamdi was captured in

Afghanistan, allegedly for taking up arms with the Taliban and against the United States, and detained at a U.S. Navy brig in Charleston, South Carolina as an alleged "enemy combatant." He was not charged with a crime. Hamdi denied being an enemy combatant and applied for habeas corpus in federal district court. (No one disputed that a United States citizen detained in the United States could apply for habeas corpus.) A federal statute, 18 U.S.C. § 4001(a), prohibits the detention of a United States citizen "except pursuant to an Act of Congress," but a majority of the Court construed a post-September 11 congressional resolution as authorizing the detention of enemy combatants during the period of active combat, even if they are U.S. citizens. A different majority held, however, that such detainees had a due process right to contest their enemy combatant classifications at fair hearings.

The hardest question was what process was constitutionally due. The government argued that blanket determinations by military authorities, rather than individualized inquiries, would suffice. That position was quickly rejected. The Court held that "a citizen-detainee seeking to challenge his classification as an enemy combatant must receive notice of the factual basis for his classification, and a fair opportunity to rebut the Government's factual assertions before a neutral decisionmaker." The Court allowed, however, that neither a rebuttable presumption of enemy combatant status (thus shifting the burden of proof to the detainee) nor the use of hearsay evidence would violate due process. The Court also offered "the possibility" that "an appropriately authorized and properly constituted military tribunal" would be permissible.

Some three months after the Supreme Court decision, the Justice Department and Hamdi entered into an agreement. The government released him from custody and returned him to Saudi Arabia. Hamdi agreed that upon arriving in Saudi Arabia he would renounce his United States citizenship and comply with certain travel restrictions. Although the U.S. had maintained that it was too dangerous to release him or even to allow him access to court, the agreement did not require Hamdi's detention in Saudi Arabia.

4. Unlike in *Hamdi*, the Court in *Rasul* said nothing about the nature of the determinations that would have to be made. It specified neither the substantive criteria for detention (presumably whether the person is an "enemy combatant," but the meaning of that term is not obvious) nor the minimum procedures that the relevant legal sources demand. Should the district court on remand simply accept at face value the government's assertion that the detainee is an enemy combatant? If not, what procedures should it require? Should it simply incorporate the procedural guidance provided in *Hamdi*? (Recall that even in *Hamdi*, where the plaintiff was a U.S. citizen detained in the United States, the Court raised at least the possibility that properly authorized and constituted military tribunals would suffice.) See generally David A. Martin, *Offshore Detainees and the Role of Courts after Rasul v. Bush: The Underappreciated Virtues of Differentiated Review*, 25 Boston College Third World L. Rev. 125

(2005) (favoring resolution of claims by military tribunals, with "narrow and deferential federal habeas review").

At this writing, the answers to these questions are beginning to emerge. Nine days after the Supreme Court announced its decision in *Rasul*, the Defense Department created the Combatant Status Review Tribunal. Its charge was to decide, on a case-by-case basis, whether each Guantánamo detainee was indeed an "enemy combatant." The same Order defined "enemy combatant" as follows:

> The term "enemy combatant" shall mean an individual who was part of or supporting Taliban or al Qaeda forces, or associated forces that are engaged in hostilities against the United States or its coalition partners. This includes any person who has committed a belligerent act or has directly supported hostilities in aid of enemy armed forces.

Matter of Guantanámo Detainee Cases, 355 F.Supp.2d 443, text accompanying footnote 9 (D.D.C. 2005).

In January 2005, the United States District Court for the District of Columbia handed down two conflicting decisions. In each case, several of the detainees petitioned for habeas corpus, alleging violations of procedural due process and asserting other claims under both domestic United States and international law. In *Khalid v. Bush*, 355 F.Supp.2d 311 (D.D.C. 2005), Judge Richard Leon dismissed all the petitions. He ruled that the detainees, being nonresident noncitizens outside the country, were beyond the reach of the U.S. Constitution. Judge Leon also held they had failed to state any other claims. Later that month, however, Judge Joyce Hens Green, who had been charged with overseeing the Guantánamo detainee cases in that court, see *Rasul v. Bush*, No. 02–CV–0299 (CKK) (D.D.C. Aug. 17, 2004), disagreed. In *Matter of Guantanámo Detainee Cases*, above, she held that the plaintiffs are protected by due process; that the military procedures to confirm enemy combatant status violated due process; and that some of the plaintiffs had stated additional valid claims under the Geneva Convention. Judge Green actually issued two opinions. One contained classified information and was delivered only to the Defense Department, for it to share with the attorneys who possessed the appropriate security clearances and with the court of appeals in the event of appeal. The other, with the classified information redacted, was the version released to the public.

Among the specific rights that Judge Green held the military tribunal procedure had illegally denied were notice of the specific facts supporting the allegation of enemy combatant status, a fair opportunity to rebut the charges, and a neutral adjudicator. She also faulted the military for denying the plaintiffs access to the evidence and barring the use of counsel. The government may presume enemy combatant status, she held, but only after the government has introduced "credible evidence" and then only if the detainee has a fair chance to rebut it.

5. Cases like *Rasul* and *Hamdi* require courts to decide what their roles should be when they are called upon to protect civil liberties in times of national emergency. Writing before these decisions were handed down, David Cole argued that, contrary to common perceptions, courts have played an instrumental role even during such times. See David Cole, *Judging the Next Emergency: Judicial Review and Individual Rights in Times of Crisis*, 101 Michigan L. Rev. 2565 (2003). Still, what future impact do you expect *Rasul* to have? Is the holding Guantánamo-specific or, as Justice Scalia asserts in section II of his dissent, does this decision permit any "alien captured in a foreign theater of active combat to bring a [habeas] petition against the Secretary of Defense?" Review the Court's language carefully before answering. See also Gerald L. Neuman, *Closing the Guantánamo Loophole*, 50 Loyola L. Rev. 1 (2004) (carefully analyzing the constitutional limitations specific to Guantánamo).

6. Earlier discussion (see pages 207–08) illustrated the hazards that dissenting judges face when they make reductio ad absurdum arguments. By interpreting the majority opinion as broadly as he does (see item 5 above), Justice Scalia (already having given advocates and judges ammunition to use in connection with the extension of *Zadvydas* to inadmissible noncitizens) has provided potential ammunition to future soldiers captured by the U.S. and detained overseas. If such a case arises, it will be interesting to see whether Justice Scalia disavows that language.

7. In *Rumsfeld v. Padilla*, ___ U.S. ___, 124 S.Ct. 2711, 159 L.Ed.2d 513 (2004), a U.S. citizen suspected of planning to detonate a "dirty bomb" in Chicago was detained indefinitely in a military facility without criminal charges. The Supreme Court held that a U.S. citizen detained on suspicion of a criminal terrorist act could bring a habeas claim only in the particular judicial district in which he or she is detained. Decided on the same day as *Rasul* and *Hamdi*, this third case has received far less attention. But Professor Nancy Morawetz, in *Detention Decisions and Access to Habeas Corpus for Immigrants Facing Deportation*, 25 Boston College Third World L. Rev. 13 (2005), warns the case could have major implications for immigration law if the ruling is extended to noncitizens detained in connection with removal proceedings. The government could effectively invoke whatever case law most favors its position simply by choosing the detention site accordingly. As she notes, the largest such government detention facility is in Oakdale, Louisiana. The relevant district court is the Western District of Louisiana, in which the policy is to deny all motions for stays of removal pending habeas review. Thus, habeas petitioners in that district are removed from the United States before the court can review the legality of their removal orders. Moreover, the Fifth Circuit, in which that district is located, has held, see *Zalawadia v. Ashcroft*, 371 F.3d 292 (5th Cir. 2004), that even if counsel presses on after the person has been removed, and the court ultimately finds the removal order to be illegal, the only remedy is a declaration to that effect. The court will not order the person's readmission or even order the BIA to consider any underlying discretionary relief that it had wrongly refused to consider. The practical

effect would be to leave noncitizens who are wrongly ordered removed with no meaningful remedy.

SECTION B.   INTELLIGENCE-GATHERING

If nothing else, the events of September 11 exposed deep fault lines in the gathering, sharing, and use of intelligence data. But even some of the basic questions remain controversial. Precisely what information should the government have, and how should it get it?

Some of the intelligence-gathering—for example, the interrogations of the Guantánamo prisoners and the monitoring of inmate-attorney conversations—occurs in conjunction with the detention strategies that you have just read about. You have also seen that the government now performs elaborate security checks on applicants for some of the more common discretionary immigration benefits. See page 573 above. In chapter 12, you will see related material on the debates over national identity cards and the issuance of drivers' licenses to undocumented migrants; these issues too have intelligence consequences.

But most of the intelligence-gathering that relates to noncitizens takes place in other settings. As these materials will illustrate, national security and public safety objectives often clash with less tangible individual interests such as privacy, autonomy, and equality, as well as with more mundane interests like practical convenience (how many of us like long airport security lines?) and minimizing government spending.

Three parallel initiatives—one driven chiefly by immigration enforcement concerns, one by national security objectives, and one by both—are now in the process of being folded into a comprehensive intelligence operation called US VISIT. The first three subsections of this section will describe them. The next subsection elaborates on the current status of the combined system. The remaining subsections discuss other miscellaneous national security-related intelligence operations that relate specifically to noncitizens.

1.   THE AUTOMATED ENTRY-EXIT SYSTEM

For many years, numerous observers bemoaned the fact that the United States government did not keep systematic records of all entries and departures of noncitizens. The concerns were rarely based on national security; rather, the notion was that without such records it was impossible to effectively identify, apprehend, and remove overstayers.

In 1996, Congress gave the Attorney General two years to "develop an automated entry and exit control system" that would require the recording of every noncitizen's entry into the United States, the recording of every noncitizen's departure, and a matching of the two in order to identify all cases of overstay. IIRIRA § 110(a). There were strong and immediate objections that recording the hundreds of millions of annual border crossings would entail horrific congestion at border points and would jeopardize trade. See, e.g., Stanley Mailman & Stephen Yale–Loehr, *The Price of Tracking Overstays*, 3 BIB 179 (Mar. 1, 1998). Congress at least twice thereafter enacted laws that relaxed the time deadlines, exempted certain ports of entry, and/or reduced the data that had to be collected. See Omnibus Consolidated and Emergency Supplemental Appropriations Act of 1999, Pub. L. 105–277, 112 Stat. 2681, § 101(b), Title 1, § 116 (Oct. 21, 1998); Immigration and Naturalization Service Data Management Improvement Act of 2000, Pub. L. 106–215, 114 Stat. 337 (June 15, 2000).

The urgency levels picked up again, however, with the September 11 attacks. Section 414 of the USA PATRIOT Act, passed in October 2001, expressed the sense of the Congress that IIRIRA section 110, as amended by subsequent legislation, should be implemented as quickly as possible. The following year, Congress enacted EBSVERA, sections 302 and 303 of which set October 26, 2004 as the deadline for the administration to implement an integrated entry and exit data system. The same sections specified the technology standards, including use of biometric identifiers, that Congress expected the system to incorporate. The system is now up and running. CBP has reported that in fiscal year 2004 it processed 428 million people, 262 million of them noncitizens, seeking entry at U.S. ports of entry. 82 IR 370 (Feb. 21, 2005). See also subsection F and chapter 12 below (discussing the use of technology for national security-related border enforcement and more general immigration enforcement, respectively).

2. NSEERS

For decades, United States law has required almost all noncitizens who are ages 14 or over and who remain in the country 30 days or more to register with designated authorities and to be fingerprinted. INA § 262. Wilful violation is punishable by a fine and by imprisonment of up to six months. INA § 266(a). The same individuals are also required to report any change of address to the immigration authorities within ten days. INA § 265(a). Failure to do so is punishable by a fine and up to 30 days imprisonment, INA § 266(b), and, unless "reasonably excusable" and "not wilful," is also a basis for removal. INA § 237(a)(3)(A).

Before September 11, however, the registration requirements were rarely enforced. Few noncitizens were aware of the requirements, and the government made little attempt to publicize or enforce them. It was widely felt that the practical benefits of the information were outweighed by the administrative burdens and costs.

After September 11, of course, the government's desire to keep tabs on foreign nationals intensified. On June 5, 2002, Attorney General John Ashcroft announced the National Security Entry–Exit Registration System (NSEERS). See 67 Fed. Reg. 40581 (June 13, 2002) (notice of proposed rule); 67 Fed. Reg. 52584 (Aug. 12, 2002) (final rule), amending 8 C.F.R. § 264.1(f). Unlike at least the original version of the entry-exit system, which was (a) aimed mainly at overstays; (b) meant to record only arrival and departure information; and (c) generic (i.e., applicable to nationals of all foreign countries), NSEERS was (a) aimed at national security objectives, especially counter-terrorism; (b) designed to record a whole range of information concerning the individuals' activities in the United States, not just arrivals and departures; and (c) limited to nationals of selected countries that were suspected of harboring terrorists (and other individuals of whom the government was independently suspicious).

Under NSEERS, nearly all male nonimmigrants who were at least sixteen years of age and who were nationals of any of (by the end) 25 countries (24 Arab or predominantly Muslim countries plus North Korea) were fingerprinted and photographed at ports of entry. If they remained longer than 30 days, they were further required to report periodically to DHS. Upon departure, they had to appear at one of several specially designated ports so that their departures could be recorded. See generally 8 C.F.R. § 264 (2004); Howard W. Gordon & Nancy H. Morawetz, *Special Registration: A Nightmare for Foreign Visitors*, Immigration Law Today (Mar/Apr 2003), at 42, 44.

As of June 7, 2003, approximately 13,000 of the 82,000 males required to register (16 per cent) had been subjected to removal proceedings, in almost all cases because of immigration status violations. Many of the latter were individuals awaiting priority dates for family reunification; often they had mistakenly assumed that their cooperation in appearing for registration would not precipitate removal proceedings. See Rachel L. Swarns, The New York Times, *More than 13,000 May Face Deportation* (June 7, 2003). The annual registration component of the system was suspended in December 2003. See Shaun Waterman, *Special screening at ports will end*, UPI (June 14, 2004).

DHS now plans to end the concept of *special* registration by the end of 2005, at which time the same kinds of information will be collected from nearly all nonimmigrant visitors under the US VISIT program described below. Apart from addressing the issue of discrimination, the expansion responds to al Qaeda's strategy of recruiting terrorists from the countries of nationality that were not on the NSEERS list. Waterman, above.

3. SEVIS AND OTHER STUDENT-RELATED PROGRAMS[3]

In chapter 4, § B above, you read about the special attention that foreign students have received in the United States, even before September 11, 2001. Since September 11, that scrutiny has intensified. Upon learning that some of the nineteen hijackers had attended flight schools in the United States, Senator Diane Feinstein proposed a six-month moratorium on the admission of *all* foreign students (not just those attending flight schools). Cooler heads prevailed, but a concern that the student visa

---

3. See generally Susan N. Burgess, *SEVIS: Is It Academic?*, Feb. 2004 Immigration Briefings; Michael A. Olivas, *The War on Terrorism Touches the Ivory Tower—Colleges and Universities After September 11*, 30 J. College & University L. 233 (2004); Victor C. Romero, *Noncitizen Students and Immigration Policy Post–9/11*, 17 Georgetown Immigration L.J. 357 (2003).

program was capable of being abused by terrorists led to tighter regulation of foreign students. Probably the most significant of the responses is the "Student and Exchange Visitor Information System" (SEVIS) and its post September 11 expansion.

SEVIS had its roots in IIRIRA, enacted in 1996. Section 641 of IIRIRA required the Attorney General, in consultation with the Secretary of State, to collect individualized information from colleges and universities on every foreign student they enroll. An institution that failed to provide the required information would be barred from enrolling foreign students.

Originally, the required information included identity, address, dates of any changes in immigration status, whether the student is maintaining full-time student status, and any disciplinary action the institution has taken as a result of a criminal conviction. The student's privacy rights under the Family Educational Rights and Privacy Act of 1974 [FERPA] were expressly eliminated to the extent necessary to comply with IIRIRA. Ultimately, the Attorney General was to analyze the information and file a report with Congress.

The strong concerns of universities and colleges had left full implementation of this project uncertain, but the terrorist attacks of September 11, 2001 prompted renewed calls for close monitoring of foreign students. Section 416 of the USA PATRIOT Act of 2001 required full implementation of IIRIRA § 641 and expanded its reach from institutions of higher education to all approved educational institutions (defined to include flight training schools, language schools, and vocational schools).

At the same time, section 507 of the USA PATRIOT Act of 2001 created an exception to FERPA by allowing schools to disclose individual student records to designated government officials pursuant to an ex parte court order issued on suspicion of terrorism. Schools complying with such requests are insulated from the liability they would otherwise incur. Immediately after September 11, the FBI began asking schools for information on their foreign students. The schools typically complied, even without the court orders required by section 507. Professor Victor Romero suggests that in those circumstances the schools might well face liability under FERPA for the disclosure of protected information. Romero, note 3 above. Time will tell.

The next major step was the enactment of EBSVERA in May 2002. Section 501 added important new elements to the required student information system. Most significantly, the system must now provide an electronic means to verify key events, including the school's acceptance of every noncitizen applicant for admission; the transmittal of that acceptance to the State Department for use in its visa processing; the issuance of the visa and the student's admission; the government's notification to the relevant school that the person has been admitted; the student's enrollment and registration at the school; and other relevant actions, such as transfer to another school or termination of studies.

Two of the September 11 hijackers had entered on student visas but had failed to show up at school to register. Even more embarrassing for the former INS, it was not until several months after September 11 that the INS sent notices to the relevant schools that the two students had been admitted to the United States. After this, Congress wanted to be sure that a noncitizen student's failure to show up at school would be flagged. Section 501 also provided, therefore, that within 30 days after the school registration deadline, the school must notify the immigration authorities if the person has not enrolled. The same section of EBSVERA also added enrollment date, degree program, field of study, and the date and reasons for termination of enrollment to the list of data that the system must record. In addition, it requires noncitizen applicants for student visas (under the F, J, and M categories for academic students, exchange visitors, and vocational students, respectively) to supply further information when they apply for visas—address in the country of origin, names and addresses of specified family members, names of contacts at home who can verify the applicant's information, and previous work history.

Section 502 of EBSVERA requires periodic review of the performance of institutions authorized to enroll foreign students. An institution's "material failure" to comply with its recordkeeping and reporting obligations will lead to suspension for at least one year, or termination, of its authority to enroll foreign students.

SEVIS is the name of the electronic system designed by the government to meet these various statutory requirements. Internet-based, it stores the statutorily required student data and permits the transmission of those data, both among the relevant government agencies and between the agencies and the schools. After several transition phases, SEVIS became fully operational in 2003. See 68 Fed. Reg. 28129 (May 23, 2003) (interim rule); 70 Fed. Reg. 7853 (Feb. 16, 2005) (final rule). At least in its early stages, SEVIS has been plagued by technical glitches; users have identified major errors in the operation of the new system and have lamented the rush to implement the new system before it could be properly debugged. 8 BIB 696–701, 718–19 (Apr. 15, 2003).

4.   US VISIT

In 2003, Homeland Security Secretary Tom Ridge announced a new initiative called the U.S. Visitor and Immigration Status Indication Technology System (U.S. VISIT). When complete, the program will integrate entry-exit, NSEERS, and SEVIS into a single comprehensive electronic data system designed to keep track of nonimmigrants as they enter and leave the United States and as they interact with USCIS and other government agencies in between.

US VISIT is being implemented in phases. As of February 2005, the system is fully operational for *arrivals* at all airport and seaport admission points and at the 50 busiest land border ports of entry. By December 31, 2005 it must be operational for arrivals at all ports of entry. See Immigration and Naturalization Service Data Management Improvement Act of

2000, Pub. L. 106–215, 114 Stat. 337, § 2(a), amending IIRIRA § 110(d)(3); see generally United States DHS, Office of Inspector General, Implementation of the United States Visitor and Immigrant Status Indicator Technology Program at Land Border Ports of Entry, No. OIG–05–11 (Feb. 2005) [OIG US VISIT Report]; 69 Fed. Reg. 53318 (Aug. 31, 2004) (interim rule); www.dhs.gov/us-visit. For departing passengers, there is no estimated time for implementing the system at land ports of entry. OIG US VISIT Report at 20.

The program applies to all passengers who are between the ages of 14 and 79 and who arrive in the United States on nonimmigrant visas; at airports and seaports the program also applies to those nonimmigrants who travel under the visa waiver program (for tourists and business visitors from low visa refusal countries, described in § E.5 below). At the time of entry, the immigration inspector takes electronic prints of both of the visitor's index fingers and a digital photograph of the visitor's face. The person's travel documents are scanned. When the visitor leaves the United States, data are collected again. *Id.*

The goal is to collect these and, in the future, other biometric identifiers to create an electronic database that can be used for multiple purposes. Immigration inspectors at ports of entry use the data in the system to verify the match between the person described in the entry document and the person presenting it, and they also use it to flag any potential criminal, security, or other issues that require additional screening. It is hoped that, by tracking both entries and exits, the system will also aid in identifying visa violators. In addition it will be used when nonimmigrants apply to USCIS to extend their stays or change their status.

The information that U.S. VISIT expects eventually to collect includes the dates of arrival and departure; nationality; whether the person is an immigrant or a nonimmigrant; full name; date of birth; sex; passport number and country of issuance; country of residence; number, date, and place of issuance of United States visa; alien registration number; and complete address in the United States. The information is made available to CBP inspectors at ports of entry, special agents in ICE, adjudications staff at USCIS offices, U.S. consulates, and other law enforcement agencies. U.S. Dept. of Homeland Security, Press Release, *Fact Sheet: U.S.-VISIT Program* (May 19, 2003), reproduced in 8 BIB at 984–86 (June 1, 2003).

The challenge is staggering. As noted earlier (see subsection 1 above), over 262 million noncitizen entries (including LPRs and miscellaneous others who are exempt from US VISIT, and counting multiple entries of the same individuals) occurred in fiscal year 2004. As of January 24, 2005, some 18 million entries had been processed by US VISIT. The system revealed 1046 people with criminal records and another 1244 immigration violators. OIG US VISIT Report, above, at 7. The Report did not indicate whether any suspected terrorists were discovered.

As with some of the other immigration-related national security programs, U.S. VISIT has generated mixed reactions. Proponents hope it will help to identify potential terrorists, other criminals, and past or would-be immigration violators. Critics question its likely effectiveness and worry that it will merely encourage increased resort to smugglers and other methods of surreptitious entry, thus exacerbating the already high rates of border death. Tyche Hendricks, *U.S. Border Posts to Use New Entry–Exit System*, San Francisco Chronicle (May 30, 2003). (You will see more on the latter subject in chapter 12.) The American Immigration Lawyers Association (AILA) fears that, especially if implementation is rushed, there will be mistakes that cause problems for innocent noncitizens. AILA asks, for example, whether the system will be reliable enough to pick up visa extensions granted by USCIS, so that a person whose visa has been legally extended will not be erroneously detained or excluded on a subsequent visit because the immigration inspector thinks the person previously overstayed. There are additional concerns about airport congestion and delays of incoming international flights. See AILA, Press Release, *AILA Enumerates Concerns with the New "U.S. VISIT" Entry–Exit System* (May 21, 2003). The OIG US VISIT Report expresses similar concerns about delays, mainly at land ports of entry. Unlike at airports and seaports, where the immigration inspectors receive passenger manifests that they can process before the passengers arrive, the inspectors at land ports of entry must do all their screening while each passenger waits. To exacerbate the problem, OIG notes that inspectors must still check multiple databases; not all the relevant information has yet been consolidated. For OIG, these factors raise concerns about both the delays and the thoroughness of the inspections at the land ports of entry. OIG is additionally concerned about the exemptions—mainly the large number of Mexican and Canadian land border passengers who are permitted to enter without visas. See OIG US VISIT Report at 7–8, 16–19.

In fairness to both Congress and the relevant agencies, US VISIT is still in its infancy. It is far too early to predict whether the long-term benefits will outweigh the costs and the dangers.

5.   VOLUNTARY INTERVIEWS OF NONCITIZENS

One other response to the events of September 11, 2001 was a massive Justice Department project to interview thousands of noncitizens who might have information on potential terrorist activities. The idea was to talk with people whose demographics and immigration statuses resembled those of the nineteen hijackers. The interviews were to be voluntary, and the interviewees were to be regarded as potential sources of information, not as suspects. The project was coordinated by the Justice Department's Executive Office for United States Attorneys (EOUSA).

There were two rounds of interviews. The interviewees were a cross-section of male nonimmigrants, generally between ages 17 and 47, who had entered the United States between January 1, 2000 and February 27, 2002 and were nationals of any of 26 countries where Al Qaeda was thought to have a strong presence. Approximately 3200 were interviewed. See U.S. General Accounting Office, Report to Congressional Committees, Homeland Security–Justice Department's Project to Interview Aliens after September 11, 2001, No. GAO–03–459 (April 2003) [hereafter cited as GAO Report], at

7–8, 13; 7 BIB at 1240 (Oct. 15, 2002); 79 IR at 1360 (Nov. 9, 2002). The questions were preformulated and are reproduced in the GAO Report as Appendix I, at 21–27. Some of the questions elicited personal information about the interviewee (e.g., employment, education level, whether the person has ever visited Afghanistan, etc.), while others focused on whether the interviewee had knowledge of suspicious persons or activities. *Id.* There seems to be consensus that the interviews were conducted respectfully and professionally. *Id.* at 8.

Still, the interview program has been controversial. Views about its effectiveness differ. As of March 2003, senior EOUSA officials had not analyzed the aggregate data and had no plans to do so. Nonetheless, Justice Department officials say publicly that the program "netted intelligence information and had a disruptive effect on terrorists," adding that the program "led to meaningful investigative leads." *Id.* at 15–16. Of the 3200 interviewees, 20 were arrested, mainly on immigration violations. Three others were criminally charged, none in connection with terrorism. *Id.* at 13.

While there is no indication that anyone was coerced to participate, the interviewees did not always perceive the conversations to be truly voluntary. They "feared there could be [immigration-related] repercussions to them for declining to participate." *Id.* at 8–9. The Department did not report the number of people who declined. *Id.* at 13 n.10.

Finally, there were mixed reports on the impact of the program on government relations with the Arab–American community. Since the overwhelming majority of the interviewees were Muslim or of Arab origin or both, interviewees "felt they were being singled out and investigated because of their ethnicity or religious beliefs," according to immigration advocates or attorneys who sat in on interviews. That perception, combined with interviewees' doubts that participation was genuinely voluntary, had what many saw as a chilling effect on relations between law enforcement officials and the Arab community. *Id.* at 16–17. On the other hand, some law enforcement officials perceived beneficial effects on community relations. They say it gave them a chance "to present a friendly law enforcement presence, obtain information (including on potential hate crimes directed against the interviewees), and leave a business card so the interviewee could contact them." Some interviewees volunteered to interpret or to help out in other ways. *Id.* at 16.

A separate interviewing program occurred a year later. In March 2003, in connection with the then impending Iraq War, the FBI interviewed approximately 2000 Iraqi nationals living in the United States. Some of the same issues arose. For a discussion of that program, see 80 IR at 693–94 (May 12, 2003).

6. "SNITCH" VISAS AND THE "RESPONSIBLE COOPERATOR" PROGRAM

INA § 101(a)(15)(S) authorizes nonimmigrant visas for certain individuals who are willing to share or have shared "critical reliable information" about either a general criminal organization (so-called S–5s) or a "terrorist organization" (so-called S–6s). Certain family members accompanying or following to join may be included. The maximum duration of stay is three years. INA § 214(k)(2). No more than 200 persons per year may receive S–5 visas, and no more than 50 per year may receive S–6 visas. INA § 214(k)(1). Although the S-category had been a temporary program and had expired just two days after the September 11 attacks, Congress soon thereafter passed legislation to make the program permanent. Pub. L. 107–45, 115 Stat. 258 (Oct. 1, 2001).

On November 29, 2001, Attorney General Ashcroft wrote a memo launching the "Responsible Cooperators Program," in which he officially encouraged various Justice Department personnel to make liberal use of S-visas in "appropriate cases." In those instances in which a person who is willing to share important terrorism-related information is ineligible for an S-visa, the Attorney General urged the officials to consider parole or deferred action as an incentive for cooperation. See 78 IR at 1816–17 (Dec. 3, 2001).

The American–Arab Anti–Discrimination Committee (ADC) has expressed concern about the Ashcroft memo. It fears that the program could lead to "fraud and abuse," as people provide false information in order to gain immigration benefits. The ADC also suggests that in Arab communities the word "cooperator" has "an extremely negative connotation" that is likely to discourage participation. *Id.* at 1817.

NOTES AND QUESTIONS

1. The NSEERS program discussed in section B.2 above is now officially completed, but many of its more controversial features remain part of the new U.S. VISIT program. A major complaint about NSEERS, as you read, was that thousands of the nonimmigrants who cooperated by appearing for registration were arrested and detained and are being processed for removal on the ground that they were never admitted or that they have overstayed their visas. As a policy matter, what is your reaction to that practice? Argue both ways.

2. You might have sensed, as you were reading the material on SEVIS and other student-related programs, that Congress and government officials seem more worried about terrorists posing as students than about terrorists posing as other nonimmigrants. The commercial categories of nonimmigrants—the B–1 business visitors, the E–1 treaty traders, the E–2 treaty investors, the H–1 and H–2 temporary workers, the L–1 intracompany transferees, for example—are not subjected to the ambitious monitoring that foreign students endure. For that matter, even B–2 tourists, who may remain in the United States for months at a time, are not monitored to anywhere near the same degree as students. Why? Are there special reasons, or special evidence, to link students with terrorism?

SECTION C. EXPANSION OF REMOVAL GROUNDS

As you saw in chapter 5, the INA now devotes several pages to describing the categories of noncitizens who are inadmissible for reasons that relate to terrorism, specific terrorist activities, or associations with terrorist organizations. INA §§ 212(a)(3)(B), 219. See those INA sections and the discussion in chapter 5, section B above. The analogous deportability grounds, noted in chapter 7, incorporate most of those inadmissibility grounds by reference. The same materials also pointed out that in various ways both the 1996 legislation and some of the post-September 11, 2001 enactments have expanded the range of terrorism-related activities that trigger inadmissibility or deportability.

Recall that certain of these removal grounds require a connection to a "terrorist organization." Most of the relevant grounds also prescribe some kind of knowledge requirement that makes it fair to hold the person accountable for the actions of the group. But some of the grounds dispense with a knowledge requirement if the particular organization has been officially "designated" by the Secretary of State as a "foreign terrorist organization" under INA § 219. The point to add here is that, in the aftermath of September 11, many new organizations have been officially so designated. See generally 8 BIB 1237 (Oct. 15, 2002).

SECTION D. SHRINKING PROCEDURAL RIGHTS

Several provisions of United States law, some of them predating September 11, permit executive officials to bypass the usual procedural safeguards in certain cases involving national security. In some of those instances the stated justification has been the need to protect confidential government evidence. Those instances reflect the flip side of the government's information management strategies. Unlike the devices you saw in section B above by which the government has sought to *acquire* information, these strategies typically entail government attempts to *suppress* information. Some of the programs you will encounter (particularly the military tribunals discussed in subsection 5 below), however, reflect additional national security objectives.

1. ARRIVING NONCITIZENS

In the *Knauff* and *Mezei* decisions that you encountered in chapter 2, the Attorney General had invoked an administrative regulation that allowed him to withhold a hearing when, based on confidential information, he regarded an arriving noncitizen as a security threat. A similar provision now appears in the statute. Under INA § 235(c), an immigration officer or immigration judge who suspects that an arriving noncitizen is inadmissible on any of several specified national security-related grounds (including terrorism) is required to order the person removed and report the removal to the Secretary of Homeland Security. If the Secretary concludes from confidential information that the person is inadmissible on any of the designated grounds, and that disclosure of that information "would be prejudicial to the public interest, safety, or security," then the noncitizen may be removed without a hearing.

2. THE TERRORIST REMOVAL COURT

On April 15, 1995, a powerful blast gutted the Murrah Federal Building in Oklahoma City and killed 168 people. See Jo Thomas, *Starting Date Set for Trial on Oklahoma Bombing*, New York Times, Nov. 16, 1996, at 9. Coming on the heels of the bombing of the World Trade Center and other highly visible terrorist acts, the destruction in Oklahoma City brought home to Americans that they are as vulnerable to terrorism as anyone else is. It would be another six years before the devastating September 11, 2001 terrorist attacks on the World Trade Center and the Pentagon.

In April 1996, a year after Oklahoma City, Congress enacted AEDPA, a comprehensive legislative package designed to combat both domestic and international terrorism. Title IV of AEDPA dealt specifically with noncitizens suspected of terrorism. In particular, AEDPA § 401 created an elaborate new procedure for adjudicating either the inadmissibility or the deportability of suspected terrorists. See INA §§ 501–07. For a thoughtful analysis praising this new procedure as a reasonable compromise, see Michael Scaperlanda, *Are We That Far Gone?: Due Process and Secret Deportation Proceedings*, 7 Stanford L. & Policy Rev. 23 (1996). Later the same year, IIRIRA § 354 refined several of these provisions.

The statutory definition of "alien terrorist" requires several cross-references to decipher. INA § 501(1) refers the reader to section 237(a)(4)(B), which in turn refers to section 212(a)(3)(B)(iii), which in turn uses the phrase "terrorist activity," which in turn is defined in section 212(a)(3)(B)(ii). The upshot is that an "alien terrorist" is a noncitizen who is linked in any of several specified ways (expanded by section 411 of the USA PATRIOT Act of 2001) to terrorist organizations or any of several designated unlawful acts. The list of acts includes hijacking, sabotage, hostage taking, assassination, other miscellaneous crimes, and a "threat, attempt, or conspiracy" to commit any of the enumerated acts.

INA § 502(a) requires the Chief Justice of the United States to appoint five federal district judges to a "removal court." Each judge serves a five-year renewable term. INA § 502(b). The removal court then designates a panel of "special attorneys" whose security clearance affords them access to classified information. INA § 502(e)(1). Their role will be noted presently.

If the Secretary of Homeland Security does not need to rely on classified information, then this special removal court will not be used. In theory—but not always in practice, as noted in a moment—ICE would then proceed in the usual way, with a removal hearing before an immigration judge, followed by a BIA appeal and the usual opportunity for judicial review. The special procedure kicks in only if "the [Secretary] has classified information that an alien is an alien terrorist." In those cases the statutory procedure is as follows:

First, the Secretary may file an application with the removal court, stating the relevant facts. INA § 503(a). The application is ex parte (i.e. the noncitizen is not represented) and in camera (in chambers rather than in open court). INA § 503(a)(2). A single judge considers the information provided by the Secretary and any other available relevant information. INA § 503(c)(1).

If the judge finds probable cause to believe that the person is an "alien terrorist," that the person is present in the United States, and that a removal hearing under the general INA procedures would pose a risk to the national security, then the judge grants the application. INA § 503(c)(2). Otherwise the judge denies it, stating the reasons in writing but without disclosing any classified information. INA § 503(c)(3).

Granting an application does not mean the person is removed. It means only that the court will conduct a removal hearing, which will be open to the public. INA § 504(a). The noncitizen is entitled to reasonable notice of the charges, "including a general account of the basis for the charges." INA § 504(b)(1). He or she has the right to be present at the hearing, to be represented by counsel, and, if indigent, to have counsel appointed. INA § 504(c)(1). The person may introduce evidence and may examine any nonclassified evidence. INA §§ 504(c)(2, 3), 504(e). Constraints on the government's use of evidence that would be suppressible in other contexts are greatly relaxed. INA § 504(e)(1).

If the Secretary believes that publicly divulging a given piece of evidence would pose a risk to the national security because it is classified, the judge examines the evidence ex parte and in camera. INA § 504(e)(3)(A). The government must submit an unclassified summary of that evidence. If the court concludes that the summary is adequate to permit the person to prepare a defense, the judge gives the person a copy. Otherwise the court disapproves the summary and orders the Secretary to correct the deficiencies and submit a revised version.

The problem occurs if the judge concludes that even the revised summary is not adequate to permit a defense. The statute provides that in that case the judge must terminate the proceedings (thus allowing the individual to go free) unless the judge finds that both the person's continued presence and the alternative of releasing the summary "would likely cause serious and irreparable harm to the national security or death or serious bodily injury to any person." INA § 504(e)(3)(B, C, D). If the judge makes the latter findings, the court will hold a removal hearing in which the individual will have to proceed without the benefit of the summary. INA § 504(e)(3)(D)(i, ii). The Federal Rules of Evidence do not apply, and the government has the burden of proving by a preponderance of the evidence (not the usual clear and convincing evidence test) that the person is an "alien terrorist." INA § 504(g, h). The judge may not grant asylum, nonrefoulement (discussed in chapter 11), cancellation of removal, voluntary departure, adjustment of status, or registry. INA § 504(k).

If an LPR is required to proceed without a summary of the classified evidence, a limited safeguard is provided. The judge designates one of the special attorneys to represent him or her. The special attorney (who, you will recall, has obtained security clearance) reviews the classified information and may challenge its veracity in camera. The special attorney is subject to lengthy imprisonment if he or she discloses the information to the noncitizen or the noncitizen's attorney. INA § 504(e)(3)(F).

The government may appeal most of the preliminary decisions described above, and either side may appeal the final order of the removal court. Appeals are to be decided expeditiously by the United States Court of Appeals for the D.C. Circuit. Classified information remains sealed. If the person is an LPR and was denied a written summary, the special attorney continues to provide representation with respect to any issue concerning classified information. See INA § 505. There are broad provisions for detaining noncitizens while proceedings before either the removal court or the court of appeals are pending, as well as during the interval between final court review and actual removal. INA §§ 506, 507.

Now that you have slogged through this statutory procedure, here is the kicker: To date, the special terrorist court procedure just described has never been used. See 78 IR at 363 (Feb. 12, 2001) (noting the intention of the House Subcommittee on Immigration and Claims to investigate why). Instead, in cases where ICE suspects terrorism, the strategy has been to institute removal proceedings in the usual way (when there is an independent deportability ground) and invoke various secret evidence provisions to defeat otherwise applicable defenses. INA § 240(b)(4)(B), for example, gives the noncitizen in removal proceedings "a reasonable opportunity" to examine the adverse evidence, but adds that "these rights shall not entitle the alien to examine such national security information as the government may proffer *in opposition to the alien's admission to the United States or to an application by the alien for discretionary relief under this Act*" (emphasis added). Thus, although ICE must divulge the evidence needed to establish deportability, it can use this provision to offer evidence in camera to eliminate either statutory eligibility for discretionary relief or the favorable exercise of discretion. See also INA § 235(c) (special national security provisions in cases of inadmissibility). Today, in the wake of September 11, 2001, the government has stepped up its use of secret evidence proceedings and has supplemented them with removal hearings that are closed to the public and the press. Those procedures are examined in sections D.3 and D.4 below.

Professor (and former INS General Counsel) David Martin perceptively traces the non-use of the special terrorist removal court procedure to one of its jurisdictional limitations. Under INA § 503(a)(1)(D)(iii), a requirement for invoking the court's jurisdiction is a statement by the Secretary that "removal under title II would pose a risk to the national security of the United States." Title II encompasses the regular removal procedures and the modifications described in the preceding paragraph. In the case of a person arriving at a port of entry, those procedures include section 235(c), the special national security provision discussed above; in those cases, therefore, the special terrorist court procedure is not necessary. In the case of someone who either entered without inspection or entered as a nonimmigrant, it is usually easier for the government to charge presence without admission or overstay. And even in the case of an LPR, a secret evidence procedure will be available for purposes of any application for discretionary relief. Thus, the only cases in which the government could honestly claim that a title II proceeding would pose a national security risk are those in which the subject is either an LPR or a nonimmigrant with substantial time remaining, and the alleged terrorist activity is the only deportability ground available. Martin suggests those cases are simply very rare. E-mail from David A. Martin to IMMPROF, Nov. 14, 2004.

QUESTION

As is obvious from this summary, Congress recognized the inherent tension between personal freedom and public safety. Suppose it were your job to devise an adjudicative procedure for deciding whether to remove noncitizens suspected to be terrorists. Would your system differ from the one Congress has created? In particular, what should happen when the government asserts that the disclosure of evidence vital to its case would jeopardize public safety?

3. CLOSED REMOVAL HEARINGS

In the days following the September 11 attacks, the Justice Department identified a number of noncitizens who, it believed, either were connected to terrorist activities or had information useful to the government investigation of terrorism. These were designated "special interest" cases. On September 21, 2001, Chief Immigration Judge Michael Creppy sent a memorandum to all the immigration judges concerning those special interest cases in which removal hearings were to be held. The immigration judges were instructed to close the hearings to the public—"no visitors, no family, and no press." The directive also ordered the immigration judges not to discuss the cases or disclose any information about them to anyone outside the immigration courts. It barred the IJs even from "confirming or denying whether such a case is on the docket or scheduled for a hearing." *North Jersey Media Group v. Ashcroft*, 308 F.3d 198, 202–03 (3d Cir. 2002). As of May 8, 2003, closed removal hearings had been conducted in 641 cases; future closed hearings were not planned. Testimony of Kevin Rooney, Director of EOIR, before Subcomm. on Immigration, Border Security, and Claims, Comm. on the Judiciary, U.S. House of Reps. (May 8, 2003), summarized in 80 IR at 692–93 (May 12, 2003).

Questions about the constitutionality of closed removal hearings quickly surfaced. As Professor Jan Ting points out, not all the constitutional procedural safeguards that apply in criminal proceedings apply to noncitizens in removal proceedings. See Jan C. Ting, *Unobjectionable But Insuffi-cient–Federal Initiatives in Response to the September 11 Terrorist Attacks*, 34 Connecticut L. Rev. 1145, 1156 (2002). In this context, however, the constitutional challenges have been rooted in the right of the public and the press to have access to the proceeding, not in the procedural rights of the noncitizen. For that reason, attention has centered on the Supreme Court's decision in *Richmond Newspapers v. Virginia*, 448 U.S. 555, 100 S.Ct. 2814, 65 L.Ed.2d 973 (1980). There the Court had held that the First Amend-ment freedom of the press prohibits the closure of a criminal proceeding. It relied both on the history of openness of criminal proceedings and on the benefits that openness brings. The question presented is whether the same result is required in an administrative proceeding to remove a noncitizen from the United States, when national security concerns have been raised.

To date, two courts of appeals have addressed that issue. In each case, the government asserted two different interests to justify the closures. First, the government argued, closure prevents sophisticated terrorist or-ganizations like Al Qaeda from learning about the government's ongoing terrorism investigation, including, in particular, what information the government has and what information it lacks on specific terrorist cells. The organization could then decide which cells to activate. Second, the government asserted, closure was necessary to protect the identities and the privacy of the individual noncitizens; they could voluntarily disclose their identities to others, but the government would not make that decision for them. The ACLU, which argued both cases, emphasized the interest of the public and the press in knowing how (and how fairly) the government is proceeding when it deports people. It also stressed the tradition against secret proceedings in cases in which individual liberties are at issue.

The two courts of appeals divided. In *Detroit Free Press v. Ashcroft*, 303 F.3d 681 (6th Cir. 2002), the court held the Creppy directive violated freedom of the press. The court saw no reason for the government to impose a blanket rule. In the court's view, case-by-case determinations of the need for closure would have sufficed and would have been more narrowly tailored to the government's security objectives. In *North Jersey Media Group v. Ashcroft*, 308 F.3d 198 (3d Cir. 2002), by a vote of 2–1, the court rejected *Detroit Free Press*. It held that the *Richmond Newspapers* rule does not apply in removal proceedings, at least when the government asserts significant national security concerns.

For some cogent criticisms of closed removal hearings, see Lauren Gilbert, *When Democracy Dies Behind Closed Doors: The First Amendment and "Special Interest" Hearings*, 55 Rutgers L. Rev. 741 (2003); Mary–Rose Papandrea, *Under Attack: The Public's Right to Know and the War on Terror*, 25 Boston College Third World L. Rev. 35 (2005).

4.   SECRET EVIDENCE HEARINGS

As Professor Niels Frenzen has noted, secret evidence has been used for more than fifty years in proceedings to exclude or deport noncitizens. Niels W. Frenzen, *National Security and Procedural Fairness: Secret Evi-*

dence and the Immigration Laws, 76 IR 1677, at 1677 (Nov. 22, 1999). In subsection 1 above, you read about INA § 235(b), which permits secret evidence under certain circumstances in proceedings to remove *arriving* noncitizens. INA § 240(b)(4)(B) goes further, allowing the government to use secret "national security" information either in opposition to the person's admission to the United States (thus overlapping with section 235(b)) or, more importantly, in opposition to the person's application for discretionary relief (even in the deportation setting).

Professor David Martin nicely illustrates some of the problems that secret evidence can pose for the noncitizen:

> * * * Although the government typically provides an unclassified summary of the evidence in [secret evidence] cases, often such a summary is as brief and unhelpful as a one-sentence statement that the evidence concerns the respondent's "association ... with the Palestinian Islamic Jihad." It is logical to assume that the hidden evidence would contain dates and places of the individual's alleged contacts with persons believed to be associated with the terrorist organization. With such details, the individual could mount a focused defense, perhaps demonstrating presence elsewhere at the times indicated, or offering an innocent explanation for the contacts. Lacking such details, the defendant may be reduced to providing general character witnesses, completely failing to engage what might prove to be the crucial factual allegations underlying the government's case.

> * * * There is also the wholly legitimate concern that secrecy permits government abuse and sloppiness—allowing the government to rely too much on unfounded conjecture or on information that might derive only from deliberate falsehood planted by someone with a personal grudge [for example an estranged ex-spouse in two cited cases].

David A. Martin, *Graduated Application of Constitutional Protections for Aliens: The Real Meaning of Zadvydas v. Davis*, 2002 Supreme Ct. Rev. 47, 127–28.

Professor Frenzen identifies some additional problems:

> Lacking an unclassified summary, the affected individual is forced blindly to guess the contents of the secret evidence. There may be a circumstance where one has a suspicion or a hunch as to the contents of the secret evidence. This then presents a tactical question of whether one wants to present a rebuttal case based purely on guesswork; what if the guess is wrong? Will the presentation of such a blind rebuttal case simply make matters worse? Or will not making any effort to present a rebuttal case be worse? If forced to present a truly blind rebuttal case, does the individual affirmatively bare his or her soul and present a comprehensive case detailing each and every conceivable incident in the past that could somehow have been misconstrued or misunderstood? Ironi-

> cally, in the case of the individual who truly has done nothing wrong, in presenting an aggressive rebuttal case he or she may simply make unfounded allegations seem more plausible to the fact-finder through the act of responding to rumors of which he or she may also be aware.

Frenzen, above, at 1683. In addition, Professor Frenzen observes, secret evidence creates hearsay problems. The individual against whom the evidence is offered is prevented from learning not only the content of the accusation, but also its source. There is no way, therefore, to expose problems with the credibility of the source. Moreover, he notes, secret evidence might be the product of simple error, a point he illustrates with a real-life example involving an interpreter's mistake. Finally, he argues, the secret evidence procedure is capable of, and in fact has been, applied discriminatorily to Muslims and to individuals of Arab descent or appearance. *Id.* at 1683–85; see also Susan M. Akram, *Scheherezade Meets Kafka: Two Dozen Sordid Tales of Ideological Exclusion*, 14 Georgetown Immigration L.J. 51 (1999).

Again, the government's concerns are not trivial. As Professor Martin explains, above at 128–29:

> * * * Much of such classified information comes from confidential informants, and such sources are likely to become more important in the future. A prominent theme of the reaction to the September 11 bombings, even from civil liberties groups, has been the need to rely more fully on human intelligence—that is, on operatives who can work their way into a terrorist organization and provide information on its operations. This is an extremely dangerous business, and those who undertake it need the strongest possible assurance that their identities will be shielded. * * * [E]ven the minor detail of the date of an alleged meeting could reveal that a government informant was present at that moment. Associates still at large could work back from that information to root out or kill the informant.

Even before September 11 several courts had struck down, on due process grounds, the use of secret evidence in removal cases involving alleged terrorists. See Frenzen, above, at 1682–83; Martin, above, at 127 n.202. In a post-September 11 decision, *Harpal Singh v. INS*, 328 F.3d 1205 (9th Cir. 2003), an immigration judge had denied a noncitizen's applications for asylum and related remedies and had ordered the person removed, all on the basis of what the IJ herself had described as "factual inferences from the classified evidence." In judging the credibility of the noncitizen, the IJ had similarly relied on classified information. The BIA affirmed, and the noncitizen petitioned for review. The Court of Appeals for the Ninth Circuit ordered the former INS to produce "unexpurgated copies of the Immigration Judge's classified decision and all classified materials presented to the Immigration Judge." Without those materials, the court reasoned, it could not discharge its statutory duty to review the petition. The court did not require the administrative authorities to share the classified information with the noncitizen, at either the administrative stage or the judicial stage. But the court's order does insist that the government turn over the classified evidence to the judges, at least in camera. Since the court rested its decision on an interpretation of the statutory provision that authorizes judicial review, it also had no occasion to decide what the Constitution demands.

Of course, the constitutional requirements do not have to be cast in all-or-nothing terms. Professor Martin, in the above article, urges a "graduated" approach, in which different classes of noncitizens enjoy different bundles of due process protections. (The hierarchy he advocates would start with noncitizens who are applying for admission at ports of entry and move up the ranks to parolees, then to those who enter without inspection, then to admitted nonimmigrants, and finally to LPRs.) Applying that hierarchy to the secret evidence issue, he suggests that different classes of noncitizens might have different rights with respect to secret evidence. For some classes, for example, it might be that the government may shield the evidence from the noncitizen but be required to share it in camera with the adjudicator. See Martin, above, at 92–101 (hierarchy of noncitizens), 132–36 (application to secret evidence issue).

5. MILITARY TRIBUNALS

In subsection A.4 you read about President Bush's Military Order of November 13, 2001, reproduced in 66 Fed. Reg. at 57833. As discussed earlier, the Order applies to those noncitizens whom the President has reason to believe are members of Al Qaeda, are involved in specified ways in certain detrimental activities (broadly defined), or knowingly harbor any such individuals. Acting under the Military Order, the U.S. armed forces on January 10, 2002 began to fly captured Taliban and Al Qaeda fighters from Afghanistan, as well as suspected terrorists found in other countries, to the United States naval base at Guantánamo Bay, Cuba for detention.

Though not concerned specifically with either immigration-related misconduct or immigration-related consequences of other misconduct, the Military Order is worth mentioning here because it applies only to noncitizens and because it contracts noncitizens' procedural rights. Earlier discussion covered the detention aspects of the Military Order. The present subsection summarizes its provisions on possible criminal trials of the detainees.

The key provision is section 4(a). It requires that any individual subject to the Order, if tried for a criminal offense, be tried by a special "military commission" rather than by either the ordinary civilian courts or a military court martial. That requirement is important, because the procedural rights available in military commissions are narrower than those afforded in either civilian courts or even military courts martial. In a military commission, for example, there is no right to a jury trial. In addition, section 4(c)(3) of the Military Order specifies that all probative evidence shall be admissible. Thus, the exclusionary rule available in civilian criminal trials will not apply. Further, a 2/3 vote of the members of the commission suffices both to convict and to agree on a particular sentence; a unanimous verdict is not required. *Id.* § 4(c)(6,7). The death penalty is permissible, *id.* § 4(a), again by a 2/3 vote, in contrast with the unanimity requirement for the death penalty in military courts martial, see 78 IR at 1776 (Nov. 19, 2001).

Section 4(C) of the Military Order authorizes the Secretary of Defense to issue further orders supplying procedural details. The Secretary responded with Military Commission Order No. 1 (Mar. 21, 2002). See http://www.defenselink.mil/news/Mar2002/d20020321ord.pdf. Among the notable features of the latter are sections 4(A)(2) (each commission must have between 3 and 7 members), 4(A)(3) (all members must be commissioned military officers), 4(B and C) (qualifications of prosecutors and defense counsel), 5(B and C) (presumption of innocence and requirement of proof beyond reasonable doubt), and 6(H)(3, 4, 5, 6) (review of verdict by Secretary of Defense upon recommendation of review panel, with possible further review by President). Section 7(b)(2) of the President's Military Order expressly precludes any remedy in any United States federal or state court, foreign court, or international tribunal.

The Defense Department has also issued a separate set of eight "Instructions," one of which, Military Commission Instruction No. 2 (Apr. 30, 2003), elaborates the "Crimes and Elements for Trials by Military Commission." See http://www.defenselink.mil/news/May2003/b05022003_bt 297–03.html and 71 USLW at 2478 (May 27, 2003). This Instruction lays out eighteen different war crimes, eight other offenses, and seven other kinds of liability (complicity, conspiracy, etc.).

There has been much discussion, beyond the realm of a survey course in immigration law, of the wisdom of the Military Order, its constitutionality, and its compatibility with international law, including both humanitarian law (the international law of war) and human rights law. For an excellent and ideologically diverse set of analyses, see AGORA, *Military Commissions*, 96 Amer. J. Internat'l L. 320 (2002).

NOTES AND QUESTIONS

1.   The government has offered two justifications for closing "special interest" removal hearings to the public and the press. First, it has argued, information revealed at the hearing would otherwise help terrorist organizations learn about the course of the government's investigation. Since the alleged terrorist who is the subject of that hearing will be present to hear the evidence, and since after the hearing that individual will still be able to communicate with the outside world, does closure really advance the government's asserted objective?

2.   The government's second justification for closing removal hearings in special interest cases is protection of the respondent's privacy. Why might the privacy interest be greater in special interest cases than in other removal cases?

3. Compare closed hearings (subsection D.3 above) with secret evidence hearings (subsections D.1 and D.4 above). In each procedure the government has had to balance national security needs against other important interests. Which type of procedure do you think entails greater sacrifice of individual liberties?

SECTION E. VISAS AND OTHER OVERSEAS POLICIES

Every year nonimmigrants make hundreds of millions of entries into the United States, most with visas but many as either business visitors or tourists under the visa waiver program. After the events of September 11, many Americans heaped partial blame on the visa system. There were holes in the system, to be sure. But how can the United States square its critical national security requirements with the need for openness to tourists, students, exchange visitors, business visitors, intracompany transferees, temporary workers, journalists, diplomats, athletes, entertainers, treater traders, treaty investors, and other visitors who apply for visas and enter U.S. territory in such staggering numbers each year?

In the post-September 11 political climate, tradeoffs have been made and compromises reached. Some of the solutions target the visa system. Old-fashioned strategies like increased funding and more intense scrutiny per case have been combined with newer ones like greater use of electronic storage and transmission of data, greater insistence on inter-agency cooperation, and expedited development and installation of biometric identifiers. Like the strategies explored earlier in this chapter, the visa-oriented strategies additionally make heavy use of profiling, in ways noted below.

1. COUNTRY-SPECIFIC STRATEGIES

Section 306(a) of EBSVERA, enacted in May 2002, prohibited the issuance of any nonimmigrant visa to any noncitizen who is "from a country that is a state sponsor of international terrorism unless the Secretary of State determines, in consultation with the Attorney General and the heads of other appropriate United States agencies, that such alien does not pose a threat to the safety or national security of the United States." For purposes of this requirement, "state sponsor of international terrorism" refers to any country whose government has already been so classified for other purposes under any of several existing laws. *Id.* § 306(b).

As of May 2003, the State Department had designated seven countries as state sponsors of international terrorism—North Korea, Cuba, Syria, Sudan, Iran, Iraq, and Libya. See Victor C. Romero, *Decoupling "Terrorist" from "Immigrant:" An Enhanced Role for the Federal Courts Post 9/11*, 7 Univ. of Iowa J. of Gender, Race & Justice 201, 202 n.3 (2003); Liam Schwartz & Michelle L. Lazerow, *The Consul and the Visas Condor–Closely Scrutinizing*, Immigration Law Today (May/June 2003) 24, at 24. Applicants from the designated countries must complete substantial additional paperwork and must receive a "Visas Condor" clearance before the consular officer is permitted to issue the visa. That phrase refers to an intense security check performed by federal intelligence agencies. *Id.* According to one senior visa officer at an overseas consular post, the delays attributable to Visas Condor average three to four weeks, but "many others * * * can run into months." *Id.* at 26. The same officer explained that the statutory phrase *"from* a country ..." (emphasis added) has been interpreted to cover anyone born in that country, whether or not still a national of that country.

2.   INJECTING DHS INTO THE VISA PROCESS

Until 2002, the visa process was entirely under the control of the State Department. The State Department's consular officers still normally decide individual visa applications, but section 428 of the HSA, passed in November 2002, now gives DHS a major role in the issuance of visas. Under that section, codified in 6 U.S.C. § 236(b)(1), the Secretary of Homeland Security now has the authority to administer, and to issue regulations governing, the visa work of the consular officers. The Secretary of Homeland Security may also prevent a visa issuance but may not reverse a consular officer's refusal to issue a visa. *Id.* In addition, the Secretary may station DHS employees at the consulates to review individual visa applications, to perform investigations, and to advise and train consular officers on issues of national security. *Id.* § 236(e). DHS has been criticized by its Inspector General for failing to meet its statutory obligation to consolidate the terrorist watch lists compiled by the various federal agencies. See United States DHS, Office of the Inspector General, DHS Challenges in Consolidating Terrorist Watch List Information, No. OIG–04–31 (Aug. 2004).

3.   HEIGHTENED SCRUTINY AND DELAY

The delays from the elevated security precautions have been controversial. Worldwide (i.e. aside from the special scrutiny reserved for visitors from selected countries), probably the most heavily affected of the nonimmigrant categories have been students and other educational visitors. They are required to gather and furnish additional information when applying for visas. See EBSVERA § 501(b). More significantly, more cases are now "referred to the State Department and other federal agencies for additional screening and security approval, and the increased case load has resulted in prolonged processing time for nearly all student visa applications." Testimony of Shirley M. Tilghman, President, Princeton University, before Comm. on Science, U.S. House of Reps. (Mar. 26, 2003), digested in 8 BIB at 715 (Apr. 15, 2003). Moreover, foreign students and faculty who are already at their universities in the United States, but who leave the country for a few days to attend international conferences, often experience long delays in receiving the visas necessary to return to the United States to resume their classwork, teaching, or research. *Id.* at 717. The problems became significant enough that a group of 32 members of Congress wrote a letter to the Secretary of State to request that the problem be prioritized.

See Letter of Mar. 24, 2003, reproduced *id.* at 741. Similar problems have arisen with respect to H–1B temporary workers, particularly those involved in the sciences. *Id.* at 717.

Along the same lines, the State Department has issued an interim regulation that dramatically expands the number of cases in which applicants for nonimmigrant visas will need to appear for personal interviews with consular officers. INA § 222(e) gives the Department the discretion whether to require a personal appearance before the consular officer. Until August 1, 2003, waivers of the personal appearance requirement were liberally granted for most B–2 tourist visa applicants and certain other visa categories. Effective on that date, however, a State Department interim regulation now requires such interviews for *all* nonimmigrants except those who fall within any of six narrowly defined categories—(1) children under age 16; (2) persons age 60 or older; (3) applicants for specified visa categories (transit visitors and certain representatives of other countries or of international organizations); (4) certain other diplomats; (5) anyone who previously received a nonimmigrant visa and who is now applying, at the consular post of the person's usual residence, for the same category of visa less than a year after the previous visa expired, provided there is no indication of visa ineligibility or noncompliance with U.S. immigration laws; and (6) any case where either the consular officer or the Deputy Assistant Secretary of State for Visa Services in Washington determines that the national interest or "unusual circumstances" warrant a waiver of personal appearance. For those six categories, waiver of personal appearance is discretionary. 68 Fed. Reg. 40127 (July 7, 2003), amending 22 C.F.R. § 41.102. Time will tell how long the added delays will be and how effective the new regulation will be in identifying (or deterring) individuals who threaten the national security. Notwithstanding the new DHS role in administering the visa process, this interim regulation also confirms the continuing authority of the State Department "to set interview policies centrally." 68 Fed. Reg. at 40127.

4. TECHNOLOGICAL INNOVATION

Other parts of this chapter have noted instances in which post-September 11 legislation has mandated the use of new technologies for safeguarding the immigration process, including specifically the visa process. One such feature relevant here appears in EBSVERA § 303(b)(1). Since October 26, 2004, this provision has required that all visas issued by the United States be machine-readable, tamper-resistant, and coded with biometric identifiers. As you will see in section F below, EBSVERA § 303(b)(2) then requires that all U.S. ports of entry be equipped to read biometric data and to authenticate all U.S. visas and passports.

5. RESTRICTIONS ON THE VISA WAIVER PROGRAM

As discussed on page 462 above, INA § 217 permits the Secretary of Homeland Security, in consultation with the Secretary of State, to designate certain countries whose nationals may enter the United States for up to 90 days, as either B–1 business visitors or B–2 visitors for pleasure, without first having to obtain visas. There are several prerequisites to designation. The country has to have had low visa refusal rates and low rates of abuse of the visa waiver program during the preceding one or two years. (There are statutory formulas for this purpose.) INA §§ 217(c)(2)(A), 217(c)(3). The country must be one that extends reciprocal privileges to nationals of the United States. INA § 217(a)(2)(A). In addition to these country qualifications, the particular individual must not be a safety threat, must not have violated the terms of the visa waiver program in the past, and must have a return ticket. INA § 217(a)(6, 7, 8). The person's identity and possible inadmissibility must also have been checked against an electronic database. INA § 217(a)(9).

Even before September 11, 2001, some had questioned the national security implications of the visa waiver program. The Justice Department's Inspector General, Michael R. Bromwich, addressed that subject in U.S. Dept. of Justice, Office of the Inspector General, Inspection Report, The Potential for Fraud and INS's Efforts to Reduce the Risks of the Visa Waiver Pilot Program, Rpt. No. I–99–10 (Mar. 1999), digested in 76 IR 1117 (July 26, 1999). Soon after that, Congress made the visa waiver program permanent. (It had originally been only a pilot program.) Visa Waiver Permanent Program Act, Pub. L. 106–396, 114 Stat. 1637 (Oct. 30, 2000).

After the September 11 attacks, calls to reexamine the visa waiver program intensified. Congress responded with additional safeguards. Section 417(c) of the USA PATRIOT Act, amending INA § 217(a)(3), required that visa waiver applicants present "machine-readable" passports. After a discretionary extension authorized by the statute, that requirement was to become effective October 26, 2004, U.S. Dept. of State, Press Statement, Extension of Requirement for Biometric Passport Issuance by Visa Waiver Program Countries (Oct. 10, 2004), but was extended again, to June 26, 2005, see DHS & DOS Press Release of May 12, 2005. EBSVERA § 303(c), enacted in May 2002, added a further requirement. By October 26, 2004, the visa waiver countries were to certify that they have programs to issue their nationals passports which (in addition to being machine-readable) "are tamper-resistant and incorporate biometric and document authentication identifiers that comply with" specified modern standards. Congress recently extended that latter deadline by one year, to October 26, 2005. See Pub. L. 108–299, 118 Stat. 1100 (Aug. 9, 2004).

The relevant European Commissioner, Franco Frattini, wrote to House Judiciary Committee Chair James Sensenbrenner in March 2005 to inform him that only six of the EU member states would be able to meet the October 26, 2005 deadline and to request a further extension. Both the UK and Japan, by far the two leading tourist sending countries to the United States, are among the nations unable to produce the required biometric passports by the due date. An estimated 2 million travelers could be affected. (Far more travelers enter under the visa waiver program, as noted below, but during the transition period only those with recently issued passports are subject to the biometric requirements.) The travel industry fears that, unless the deadline is extended, many will elect not to come. And if 2,000,000 additional foreign visitors do apply for visas, it would seem an almost impossible task for the consulates to accommodate them. (There is the additional possibility that, during any period in which the U.S. requires visas of tourists from the current visa-waiver countries, those countries would retaliate by imposing similar requirements on U.S. tourists.) Still, as of April 2005, Mr. Sensenbrenner was insisting that a second extension is unlikely. He blames the delay on the decision of the EU to pursue unnecessarily sophisticated technology. See Shaun Waterman, *EU frets that U.S. will enforce visa pledge*, UPI (Apr. 11, 2005). Since neither the prospect of the U.S. consulates processing an additional 2,000,000 visas nor the prospect of excluding European and Japanese tourists for lack of visas is politically plausible, it seems likely that by the time this book is published an accommodation will have been found.

Another provision of EBSVERA requires the designated countries to file timely reports to the United States of the theft of any of their blank passports; in addition, the United States government must reevaluate all existing designations every two years (instead of every five years under prior law). See EBSVERA § 307(a), amending INA §§ 217(c)(2), 217(c)(5)(A)(i). A recent report by the DHS Inspector General criticized the Department for failing to perform the biennial country evaluations and suggested that lost and stolen passports represent the greatest security threat posed by the visa waiver program. United States DHS, Office of the Inspector General, An Evaluation of the Security Implications of the Visa Waiver Program, No. OIG–04–26, at 16–25 (Apr. 2004).

As of this writing, 27 countries participate in the visa waiver program. Twenty-two of them are in Europe; the other 5 are Australia, Brunei, Japan, New Zealand, and Singapore. 8 C.F.R. § 217.2(a) (2004). In fiscal year 2003, approximately 12 million B–2 visitors for pleasure and another 2 million B–1 visitors–almost 14 million in all—entered the United States under the visa waiver program. These accounted for about half the total admissions of B–1 and B–2 visitors that year. 2003 Yearbook of Immigration Statistics, Table 24 at 101. Well over half the visa waiver visitors came from two countries—the United Kingdom and Japan. *Id.*, Table F at 77.

In the light of ongoing national security concerns, some continue to call for repealing the visa waiver program entirely. One of the most prominent advocates of repeal is Professor Jan Ting. He argues that repeal would help block the entry into the United States of foreign terrorists, especially those who enter from western Europe on false passports. See Jan C. Ting, *Unobjectionable but Insufficient–Federal Initiatives in Response to the September 11 Terrorist Attacks*, 34 Conn. L. Rev. 1145, 1157–60 (2002).

In 2002, however, the General Accounting Office studied the visa waiver program and examined the implications of repeal. Its conclusions are summarized in the following excerpt:

* * * The U.S. government has not systematically collected data on how frequently potential terrorists and other criminals have entered the United States under the program. Anecdotal information indicates that such persons have entered the United States under the Visa Waiver Program as well as with valid U.S. visas. As a result, U.S. government officials expressed different opinions about the effect of the program on U.S. national security. They agreed that the visa screening process could serve as an additional tool to screen out terrorists but only to the extent that State had the necessary overseas resources, including relevant timely information on potential terrorists and sufficient staff and facilities to interview all or most visa applicants. They said that if current visa waiver travelers were required to apply for visas and States's current resource levels were not increased, consular officers would be inundated with paperwork for routine and low-risk cases and would become less effective and alert in dealing with cases needing additional scrutiny. The decision to eliminate the program could negatively affect U.S. relations with participating countries, could discourage some business and tourism in the United States, and would increase the need for State Department resources.

United States General Accounting Office, Border Security–Implications of Eliminating the Visa Waiver Program, No. GAO–03–38, at 3–4 (Nov. 2002); see also *id*. at 16–28 (detailed analysis). The Report added: "If the United States decides to eliminate visa waiver status for participating countries, those countries' governments could begin requiring Americans to obtain visas before visiting their countries." *Id*. at 20 (discussing the European Union countries as the leading example).

6. SLOWDOWNS IN THE ADMISSION OF OVERSEAS REFUGEES

As you will see in more detail in the next chapter, INA § 207 authorizes the President to announce, each year, the maximum number of overseas refugees who will be admitted to the United States that year. Since September 11, 2001, the number of overseas refugee applications actually processed and approved has plummeted. That subject is taken up in chapter 11, section A below. The official explanation for the huge drop was that the extra time required by special security checks had caused a backlog. 79 IR at 1467; see also Ricardo Alonso–Zaldivar, *Refugees on Hold and at Risk*, L.A. Times (July 7, 2003).

SECTION F. ENHANCED BORDER ENFORCEMENT

The preceding subsection focused on *overseas* enforcement initiatives prompted by national security concerns. Those measures complement various programs instituted at the ports of entry—the land borders, airports, and seaports through which noncitizens enter the United States. As a practical matter, most of the border enforcement strategies are designed not around the specific danger of terrorism, but around more general law enforcement issues, including illegal immigration. They are therefore discussed in more detail in chapter 12, which deals with undocumented migrants and immigration law enforcement. Nonetheless, September 11 lent added impetus and urgency to those efforts. A few of the newer resulting measures are thus worth noting here.

Part of the post-September 11 response has simply involved increased funding for additional immigration inspectors and investigators and their support staffs, for improved training, and for new technologies. See, e.g., USA PATRIOT Act §§ 402, 403 (tripling border patrol deployment along Canadian border); EBSVERA § 101. In addition, commercial airlines and sea transport companies must furnish immigration inspectors with "passenger manifests" that contain certain prescribed details about each arriving passenger and crew member (electronically as of January 1, 2003). EBSVERA § 402. As noted earlier, all United States ports of entry must now be equipped to read biometric identifiers. *Id.* § 303(b)(2). To make sure immigration inspectors have enough time to perform thorough searches, EBSVERA § 403(a) repeals the requirement that border inspections be completed within 45 minutes. Under section 403(b), however, DHS staffing levels at ports of entry must reflect the *goal* of performing inspections in less than 45 minutes. EBSVERA § 404 authorizes joint United States—Canadian inspection operations along the common border. Finally, the REAL ID Act, §§ 301–303, requires various studies and pilot programs to take maximum advantage of border security technology.

Section G. Profiling

Many of the programs you have read about in this chapter involve "profiling." Broadly defined, that term is used here to encompass a range of law enforcement strategies that focus special attention on individuals who have particular attributes believed to correlate positively with the targeted misconduct. Customs officials, for example, have long used profiles to identify travelers whose appearances and habits might give reason to suspect drug smuggling. Profiles of serial killers and serial rapists have been used by police in the course of their investigations. So defined, there is nothing inherently objectionable about profiling. As long as law enforcement resources are finite and police experts have reason to believe that certain appearances and behaviors tend to be disproportionately present in a given class of suspects, then profiling seems rational. It is simply a matter of relying on credible statistics and probabilities so that scarce law enforcement resources can be deployed as effectively as possible.

Issues arise, however, when the particular attributes of the profile are the person's race, religion, gender, or other commonly proscribed bases of discrimination. The issues arise for at least two reasons. First, there can be questions whether the profiles are truly accurate predictors of criminal conduct or merely the product of irrational prejudice. Those questions go to the very premise for profiling—its rationality. Second, even if the assumed correlation between the attributes and the criminal conduct is based on solid empirical evidence, the government's interest in thorough and efficient enforcement has to be balanced against the harms associated with government-sponsored discrimination. "Rational," in other words, does not necessarily mean "justified." See Stephen H. Legomsky, *The Ethnic and Religious Profiling of Noncitizens: National Security and International Human Rights*, 25 Boston College Third World L.J. 161 (2005).

In recent years, racial profiling became a major public issue as exposés uncovered systematic practices of local police stopping African–American motorists with unusual frequency. The term "driving while black" made its way into our vocabulary. Some have written revealing essays on analogous practices directed at Latino/as. See, e.g., Kevin R. Johnson, *The Case Against Race Profiling in Immigration Enforcement*, 78 Washington Univ. L.Q. 675 (2000); Victor C. Romero, *Racial Profiling: "Driving While Mexican" and Affirmative Action*, 6 Michigan J. Race & Law 195 (2000).

Since September 11, the issue has reemerged, as police agencies, engaged in both terrorism investigations and immigration enforcement, target individuals who are "from" Arab or Muslim countries, or who are of Arab descent, or who are Muslims, or who are thought to be any of the above. We have gone from "driving while black" to "flying while Arab." See David Cole, Enemy Aliens–Double Standards and Constitutional Freedoms in the War on Terrorism (2003); Susan Akram & Kevin Johnson, *Race, Civil Rights, and Immigration Law After September 11, 2001: The Targeting of Arabs and Muslims*, 58 NYU Ann. Survey Amer. L. 295 (2003); Susan M. Akram & Maritza Karmely, *Immigration and Constitutional Consequences of Post-9/11 Policies Involving Arabs and Muslims in the United States: Is Alienage a Distinction Without a DIfference?*, 38 U.C. Davis L.Rev. 609 (2005); David Cole, *Enemy Aliens*, 54 Stanford L. Rev. 953 (2002); Kevin R. Johnson, *September 11 and Mexican Immigrants: Collateral Damage Comes Home*, 52 DePaul L. Rev. 849, 867–70 (2003); Victor C. Romero, *Critical Race Theory in Three Acts: Racial Profiling, Affirmative Action, and the Diversity Visa Lottery*, 66 Albany L. Rev. 375 (2003); Victor C. Romero, *Proxies for Loyalty in Constitutional Immigration Law: Citizenship and Race After September 11*, 52 DePaul L. Rev. 871 (2003); Jan C. Ting, *Unobjectionable But Insufficient–Federal Initiatives in Response to the September 11 Terrorist Attacks*, 34 Connecticut L. Rev. 1145, 1152–54 (2002).

Professor Muneer Ahmad has synthesized some data that illustrate how dramatic some of the targeting has been. In the year that followed September 11, 2001, the numbers of deportable noncitizens apprehended rose 228% for Pakistanis, 239% for Saudis, 224% for Algerians, 83% for Egyptians, and 76% for Moroccans. The increases in actual removals for these same countries were similarly striking: 129% for Pakistanis, 113% for Saudis, 111% for Algerians, 199% for Egyptians, and 229% for Moroccans. Muneer I. Ahmad, *A Rage Shared by Law: Post–September 11 Racial Violence as Crimes of Passion*, 92 California L. Rev. 1259, 1276 (2004).

There are several kinds of profiling to distinguish here. The two that come most quickly to mind are ethnic profiling and religious profiling. These can be conscious and explicit, as where officials deliberately target people who appear to be of Arab descent or Muslim. Or the same results can occur indirectly, as the by-products of profiling on the basis of a third attribute—for example, policies that target individuals who are *nationals*, or possibly *natives*, of countries that the government designates as harboring terrorists. In addition, some of the programs that you just read about entail two other profiling attributes—gender and age. The program might, for example, target only those who are nationals of any of several enumerated countries and who are males within a specified age range. Almost all the post-September 11 strategies discussed in the preceding sections of this chapter involve profiling on the basis of one or more of these attributes.

Peter H. Schuck, A Case for Profiling

The American Lawyer, January 2002, pages 59–61.

The furor about racial profiling is easy to understand. "Driving while black" and "flying while Arab" are emblems of the indignities that law enforcement officials are said to inflict on minorities on the basis of demeaning stereotypes and racial prejudice. This is no laughing matter. Respect for the rule of law means that people must not be singled out for enforcement scrutiny simply because of their race or ethnicity.

Or does it? Much turns on the meaning of "simply" in the last sentence. Profiling is not only inevitable but sensible public policy under certain conditions and with appropriate safeguards against abuse. * * *

A fruitful debate on profiling properly begins with our values as a society. The most important of these, of course, is self-defense, without which no other values can be realized. But we should be wary of claims that we must sacrifice our ideals in the name of national security; this means that other ideals remain central to the inquiry. The one most threatened by profiling is the principle that all individuals are equal before the law by reason of their membership in a political community committed to formal equality. * * * Differential treatment must meet a burden of justification— in the case of racial classifications, a very high one.

This ideal has a corollary: Government may not treat individuals arbitrarily. To put this principle another way, it must base its action on information that is reliable enough to justify its exercise of power over free individuals. How good must the information be? The law's answer is that it depends. Criminal punishment requires proof beyond a reasonable doubt, while a tort judgment demands only the preponderance of the evidence. Health agencies can often act with little more than a rational suspicion that a substance might be dangerous. A consular official can deny a visa if in her "opinion" the applicant is likely to become a public charge and unlike the previous examples, courts may not review this decision. Information good enough for one kind of decision, then, is not nearly good enough for others. Context is everything.

This brings us to profiling by law enforcement officials. Consider the context in which an FBI agent must search for the September 11 terrorists, or a security officer at a railroad and airline terminal must screen for new ones. Vast numbers of individuals pass through the officer's line of vision, and they do so only fleetingly, for a few seconds at most. As a result, the official must make a decision about each of them within those few seconds, unless she is prepared to hold all of them up for the time it will take to interrogate each, one by one. She knows absolutely nothing about these individuals, other than the physical characteristics that she can immediately observe, and learning more about them through interrogation will take a lot of time. The time this would take is costly to her task; each question she stops to ask will either allow others to pass by unnoticed or prolong the wait of those in the already long, steadily lengthening line. The time is even more costly to those waiting in line; for them, more than for her, time is money and opportunity. Politicians know how their constituents hate lines and constantly press her along with customs, immigration, and toll officials to shorten them.

At the same time, her risks of being wrong are dramatically asymmetrical. If she stops everyone, she will cause all of the problems just described and all of the people (except one, perhaps) will turn out to be perfectly innocent. On the other hand, if she fails to stop the one person among them who is in fact a terrorist, she causes a social calamity of incalculable proportions (not to mention losing her job). In choosing, as she must, between these competing risks, her self-interest and the social interest will drive her in the direction of avoiding calamity. The fact that society also tells her to be evenhanded only adds to her dilemma, while providing no useful guidance as to what to do, given these incentives.

So what should she do? We can get at this question by asking what we would do were we in her place. To answer this question, we need not engage in moral speculation but can look to our own daily experiences. Each day, we all face choices that are very similar in structure, albeit far less consequential. We must make decisions very rapidly about things that matter to us. We know that our information is inadequate to the choice, but we also know that we cannot in the time available get information that is sufficiently better to improve our decision significantly. We consider our risks of error, which are often asymmetrical. Because we must momentarily integrate all this uncertainty into a concrete choice, we resort to shortcuts to decision-making. (Psychologists call these "heuristics.")

The most important and universal of these tactical shortcuts is the stereotype. The advantage of stereotypes is that they economize on information, enabling us to choose quickly when our information is inadequate. This is a great, indeed indispensable virtue, precisely because this problem is ubiquitous in daily life, so ubiquitous that we scarcely notice it; nor do we notice how often we use stereotypes to solve it. Indeed, we could not live without stereotypes. We use them * * * when we offer help to disabled people (though some of them find this presumptuous). We use them when we take safety precautions when a large, unkempt, angry-looking man approaches us on a dark street (though he may simply be asking directions). * * *

Stereotypes, of course, have an obvious downside: They are sometimes wrong, almost by definition. After all, if they were wrong all the time, no rational person would use them, and if they were never wrong, they would be indisputable facts, not stereotypes. Stereotypes fall somewhere in between these extremes, but it is hard to know precisely where, because we seldom know precisely how accurate they are. Although all stereotypes are over-broad, most are probably correct much more often than they are wrong; that is why they are useful. But when a stereotype is wrong, those who are exceptions to it naturally feel that they have not been treated equally as individuals, and they are right. Their uniqueness is being overlooked so that others can use stereotypes for the much larger universe of cases where the stereotypes are true and valuable. In this way, the palpable claims of discrete individuals are sacrificed to a disembodied social interest. * * *

This is where the law comes in. When we view these stereotype-based injustices as sufficiently grave, we prohibit them. Even then, however, we do so only in a qualified way that expresses our ambivalence. Civil rights law, for example, proscribes racial, gender, disability, and age stereotyping. At the same time, it allows government, employers, and others to adduce a public interest or business reason strong enough to justify using them. * * *

* * *

* * * A wise policy will insist that the justice of profiling depends on a number of variables. How serious is the crime risk? How do we feel about the relative costs of false positives and false negatives? How accurate is the stereotype? How practicable is it to pursue the facts through an individualized inquiry rather than through stereotypes? If stereotypes must be used, are there some that rely on less incendiary and objectionable factors?

A sensible profiling policy will also recognize that safeguards become more essential as the enforcement process progresses. Stereotypes that are reasonable at the stage of deciding whom to screen for questioning may be unacceptable at the later stages of arrest and prosecution, when official decisions should be based on more individualized information and when lawyers and other procedural safeguards can be made available. Screening officials can be taught about the many exceptions to even serviceable stereotypes, to recognize them when they appear, and to behave in ways that encourage those being screened not to take it personally.

* * *

NOTES AND QUESTIONS

1. Many of the themes in the excerpts from Peter Schuck's essay will be explored in the questions below. First, though, consider the question of scope. Almost all the examples he gives take place in settings where rapid,

spontaneous decisions are required and more nuanced data are not reasonably accessible. Many of the government programs that you read about in this chapter, in contrast, involve conscious, deliberate policymaking at the management level. Do you think Professor Schuck's analysis of racial profiling is limited to the former kinds of settings, or would his logic, if not his specific examples, apply to the latter as well?

2. One of the leading critics of government programs that target the Arab and Muslim communities (and the leading litigator in challenging some of those practices) is Professor David Cole. Putting aside for the moment the question of the harms associated with discrimination, some commentators have questioned whether the recent spate of profile-based counterterrorism initiatives are even effective. Professor Cole argues that effective law enforcement requires the cooperation of local communities. Better to work constructively with those communities, he submits, than to alienate them by treating their members as suspect solely because of their ethnicity. The same principle holds, he maintains, at the international level; the United States sorely needs the cooperation of the very nations whom the ethnic profiling policies are antagonizing. See Cole, above, 54 Stanford L. Rev. at 958–59.

But Professor Cole goes on to question the effectiveness of ethnic profiling in another way. Arguing that the profiling programs are not sufficiently tailored to their national security objectives to withstand constitutional scrutiny, he says this:

> First, the vast majority of persons who appear Arab and Muslim—probably well over 99.9 percent—have no involvement with terrorism. Arab and Muslim appearance, in other words, is a terribly inaccurate proxy. * * *

> Second, the use of ethnic stereotypes, far from being "necessary" for effective law enforcement, is likely to be ineffective. When one treats a whole group of people as presumptively suspicious, it means that agents are more likely to miss dangerous persons who do not fit the profile, such as Richard Reid, the British citizen who boarded a plane in Paris headed for Miami with a bomb in his shoe. In addition, the fact that the vast majority of those targeted on the basis of their Arab or Muslim appearance will prove to be innocent will inevitably cause agents to let their guard down. Overbroad ethnic generalizations, in other words, are not only not narrowly tailored to furthering effective law enforcement, but may actually undermine effectiveness.

Id. at 976–77. As a government attorney, what counterarguments might you offer?

3. The preceding question focuses on the perceived *benefits* of profiling. In the context of the programs discussed in this chapter, what, exactly, are the *costs* of profiling? What harms result from government-sponsored discrimination?

4. As many writers have pointed out, public attitudes toward racial profiling shifted dramatically after September 11, 2001. Before that fateful day, opinion polls made clear that the American public strongly disapproved of police practices that singled out African–American motorists. After September 11, the public was far more accepting of racial profiling as an instrument for preventing terrorism. See, e.g., Cole, above, 54 Stanford L. Rev. at 974–75; Victor C. Romero, *Proxies for Loyalty in Constitutional Immigration Law: Citizenship and Race After September 11*, 52 DePaul L. Rev. 871, 874–76 (2003). Is it inconsistent for a person to oppose the racial profiling of African–American motorists but approve the racial profiling of Arabs and Arab–Americans in the present national security context? Or can the two positions be reconciled?

5. Forget about immigration law for a moment (and only for a moment). Suppose there were credible empirical evidence that 2/3 of the members of a particular ethnic subcategory of *United States citizens* were involved in terrorist activities. And suppose further that members of that ethnic group could be easily and conclusively identified (i.e. there were no ambiguities as to who was a member of the group and who was not). As a policy matter—not as a constitutional matter—would you favor having the police subject each of them to involuntary questioning based solely on their ethnicity? Would your answer change if the percentage were much lower than 2/3—say, 2 per cent—but if the corresponding percentage for the entire U.S. population were much lower still—say, only 0.01 per cent?

6. Assume the same facts as in the preceding question, except this time assume the involuntary questioning is confined to *noncitizens* of the same ethnic group. Does your answer change?

7. Suppose now that the targeted group of noncitizens is defined not by ethnicity, but by country of nationality, as indeed is the case with many of the actual profiling strategies considered in this chapter. More specifically, suppose the government targets those noncitizens whose countries of nationality have been designated by the President as harboring terrorists. Is that appropriate? Is it any different from other country-specific immigration programs (for example the visa waiver program, the special border-crossing privileges for certain Canadian and Mexican nationals, the special treatment of Cuban nationals, the per-country ceilings on the admission of LPRs, etc.)? Does the fact that almost all the designated countries are predominantly Arab or Muslim affect your answer?

8. What if the profiling is based on appearances rather than on more objective criteria? Suppose, for example, that the government decides to question all those who "appear" to be either Muslim or of Arab descent, on the assumption that in each of those subgroups the number of terrorists is higher than in the general population. For this purpose the police are instructed to take into account individuals' physical features, clothing, accent, name (if known), neighborhood, place of worship, and any other correlates of ethnicity or religion that they can observe. Is that practice any more or less objectionable than any of the others already discussed?

9.   Does your answer to the preceding question change if, instead of basing the selection of interviewees *solely* on ethnic or religious appearance, the police were instructed to consider such appearance only as one factor, to be weighed along with any other factors that give reason to be suspicious? (Again, assume some demonstrated correlation between the targeted group and terrorist activities.)

10.   A different variable is what is actually done to the targeted group. Do your answers change if, instead of the government merely interviewing members of the targeted group (voluntarily or involuntarily), the government were to detain them, or deport them, or require them to register, or keep permanent information on them, or put more stringent visa or other immigration limitations on them?

11.   What statistical evidence, if any, would be useful in evaluating the propriety of any kind of profiling that has ethnic implications? Suppose, for example, that reliable empirical evidence demonstrated that, among those noncitizens who are Muslim or of Arab descent or both, only one in a thousand had any involvement in terrorist activities. Conversely, however, suppose the same study demonstrated that, of those noncitizens who are found to have been involved in terrorist activities that endangered civilians in the United States, 75% were Muslim or of Arab descent or both. (These numbers are purely hypothetical. They are made up solely to raise an issue.) Would it then be rational to profile noncitizens who are Muslim or of Arab descent or both?

12.   On February 27, 2001, President Bush told Congress that racial profiling is "wrong and we will end it in America." Following up two years later, the Civil Rights Division of the Department of Justice issued a memo entitled "Guidance Regarding the Use of Race by Federal Law Enforcement Agencies" (June 2003). The memo condemned racial profiling as "not merely wrong, but also ineffective" and as having "a terrible cost." *Id.* at 1. It prohibits consideration of race and ethnicity by federal law enforcement officers (with some exceptions, such as descriptions of specific suspects), *"even where the use of race or ethnicity might otherwise be lawful"* (emphasis added). *Id.* at 1–2.

But the memo then adds a sweeping caveat:

> The above standards do not affect current Federal policy with respect to law enforcement activities and other efforts to defend and safeguard against threats to national security or the integrity of the Nation's borders. * * * In investigating or preventing threats to national security or other catastrophic events (including the performance of duties related to air transportation security), or in enforcing laws protecting the integrity of the Nation's borders, Federal law enforcement officers may not consider race or ethnicity *except to the extent permitted by the Constitution and laws of the United States"* (emphasis added).

Id. at 2, 8. Note the contrast. Generally, federal law enforcement officers are instructed to avoid even legal racial profiling (except in describing specific suspects), but in the national security context legal racial profiling is expressly approved. The memo offers the example of U.S. intelligence reports that members of a particular ethnic group plan to hijack commercial jets next week, at an airport in California, and use them as weapons. The memo says, "[b]efore allowing men of that ethnic group to board commercial airplanes in California airports during the next week, [security personnel] may subject them to heightened scrutiny." *Id*. at 9.

For some thoughtful commentary on the Civil Rights Division guidelines, see Kevin R. Johnson, *Racial Profiling After September 11: The Department of Justice's 2003 Guidelines*, 50 Loyola L. Rev. 67 (2004).

13. The United States is a party to the International Convention on the Elimination of all Forms of Racial Discrimination, 660 U.N.T.S. 195 (done at New York, Mar. 7, 1966, entered into force, Jan. 4, 1969), usually known as the "Race Convention." It was ratified by the United States Senate on Oct. 21, 1994, albeit with several reservations, understandings, and declarations, and it entered into force for the United States on Nov. 20, 1994. Are the profiling features in the various U.S. national security strategies that you studied in this chapter compatible with U.S. obligations under the Race Convention?

Several provisions of the Convention prohibit "racial discrimination," a term defined in article 1 as

> any distinction, exclusion, restriction or preference based on race, colour, descent, or *national or ethnic origin* which has the *purpose or effect* of nullifying or impairing the recognition, enjoyment or exercise, on an equal footing, of *human rights and fundamental freedoms* in the political, economic, social, cultural or any other field of public life. [Emphasis added.]

Whether any of the U.S. programs amount to "racial discrimination" under that definition turns out to be a complicated question. Several theories are arguable, and the case law of the Committee Against Racial Discrimination, the supervisory body established by the Convention, is instructive. The issues are examined in Stephen H. Legomsky, *The Ethnic and Religious Profiling of Noncitizens: National Security and International Human Rights*, 25 Boston College Third World L.J. 161, 186–96 (2005). The cited pages analyze two broad sets of issues: "First, do the actions of the United States truly embody distinctions based on 'national or ethnic origin?' Second, do they—and, to be covered by the Convention, must they—implicate 'human rights and fundamental freedoms?' " *Id*. at 188.

SIMULATION EXERCISE

As the above discussion suggests, profiling—broadly defined for present purposes—is not *inherently* offensive. There are, however, many variables that might affect one's view as to whether *a given instance* of profiling is offensive. They include the rationality or effectiveness of profiling the particular group, as well as the magnitude of the harm that the profiling seeks to prevent. Another variable is the classification used for the profile—is it race, religion, country of nationality, age, gender? Arguably relevant also is the degree of intrusion involved. Is it voluntary questioning? Involuntary questioning? Detention? If detention, for how long and under what conditions? Registration? Keeping information on the person? Removal from the country? Criminal prosecution? Another variable is whether the policy operates on both citizens and noncitizens, or only on the latter. Still another might be whether the attributes are objectively identifiable or, instead, inferrable only from rough indicators like physical appearance, accent, name, etc. Perhaps some would find relevant whether the profiling is based *solely* on a disfavored attribute or whether that attribute is but one of many factors that the profiler is allowed to weigh and balance.

Again, some might find all of these variables relevant, some might find none of them relevant, and some might find some of the factors relevant and others not. After thinking about them, assume the following (hypothetical) bill has been introduced in Congress:

> No law enforcement officer of the United States or of any state or territory of the United States shall make any decision to allocate law enforcement resources toward a particular individual or group, or direct any question or investigation toward a particular individual or group, if the individual or group is defined, wholly or partly, on the basis of race, ethnicity, religion, country of citizenship or of nationality or of birth, gender, or age.

You are a member of the United States House of Representatives. The above bill has cleared the relevant committees and is about to be debated on the House floor. Your choices are to vote yes, vote no, or move to amend the bill. Decide which option you prefer, and prepare a speech to defend your position.

SECTION H.   IMMIGRATION AND NATIONAL SECURITY IN PERSPECTIVE

Mark Krikorian, Keeping Terror Out—Immigration Policy and Asymmetric Warfare

The National Interest, Spring 2004.

Supporters of open immigration have tried to de-link 9/11 from security concerns. "There's no relationship between immigration and terrorism," said a spokeswoman for the National Council of the advocacy group La Raza. "I don't think [9/11] can be attributed to the failure of our immigration laws," claimed the head of the immigration lawyers' guild a week after the attacks.

President Bush has not gone that far, but in his January 7 speech proposing an illegal alien amnesty and guest worker program, he claimed the federal government is now fulfilling its responsibility to control immigration, thus justifying a vast increase in the flow of newcomers to America. * * *

* * *

* * * As Deputy Secretary of Defense Paul Wolfowitz said in October 2002,

> Fifty years ago, when we said, "home front," we were referring to citizens back home doing their part to support the war front. Since last September, however, the home front has become a battlefront every bit as real as any we've known before.

> Nor is this an aberration, unique to Al–Qaeda or to Islamists generally. No enemy has any hope of defeating our armies in the field and must therefore resort to asymmetric means. And though there are many facets to asymmetric or "Fourth–Generation" warfare * * * [t]he Holy Grail of such a strategy is mass-casualty attacks on America.

> The military has responded to this new threat with the Northern Command. * * * [T]his front is different from other fronts; the goal is defensive, blocking and disrupting the enemy's ability to carry out attacks on our territory. This will then allow offensive forces to find, pin, and kill the enemy overseas.

> Because of the asymmetric nature of the threat, the burden of homeland defense is not borne mainly by our armed forces but by agencies formerly seen as civilian entities—mainly the Department of Homeland Security (DHS). And of DHS's expansive portfolio, immigration control is central. The reason is elementary: no matter the weapon or delivery system—hijacked airliners, shipping containers, suitcase nukes, anthrax spores—operatives are required to carry out the attacks. Those operatives have to enter and work in the United States. In a very real sense, the primary weapons of our enemies are not inanimate objects at all, but rather the terrorists themselves—especially in the case of suicide attackers. Thus keeping the terrorists out or apprehending them after they get in is indispensable to victory. As President Bush said recently, "Our country is a battlefield in the first war of the 21st century."

* * *

Our enemies have repeatedly exercised this option of inserting terrorists by exploiting weaknesses in our immigration system. A Center for Immigration Studies analysis of the immigration histories of the 48 foreign-born Al–Qaeda operatives who committed crimes in the United States from 1993 to 2001 (including the 9/11 hijackers) found that nearly every element of the immigration system has been penetrated by the enemy. Of the 48, one-third were here on various temporary visas, another third were legal residents or naturalized citizens, one-fourth were illegal aliens, and the remainder had pending asylum applications. Nearly half of the total had, at some point or another, violated existing immigration laws.

Supporters of loose borders deny that inadequate immigration control is a problem, usually pointing to flawed intelligence as the most important shortcoming that needs to be addressed. Mary Ryan, for example, former head of the State Department's Bureau of Consular Affairs (which issues visas), testified in January 2004 before the 9/11 Commission that

> Even under the best immigration controls, most of the September 11 terrorists would still be admitted to the United States today … because they had no criminal records, or known terrorist connections, and had not been identified by intelligence methods for special scrutiny.

But this turns out to be untrue, both for the hijackers and for earlier Al–Qaeda operatives in the United States. A normal level of visa scrutiny, for instance, would have excluded almost all the hijackers. Investigative reporter Joel Mowbray acquired copies of 15 of the 19 hijackers' visa applications (the other four were destroyed—yes, destroyed—by the State Department), and every one of the half-dozen current and former consular officers he consulted said every application should have been rejected on its face. Every application was incomplete or contained patently inadequate or absurd answers.

Even if the applications had been properly prepared, many of the hijackers, including Mohammed Atta and several others, were young, single, and had little income—precisely the kind of person likely to overstay his visa and become an illegal alien, and thus the kind of applicant who should be rejected. And, conveniently, those *least* likely to overstay their visas—older people with close family, property, and other commitments in their home countries—are also the very people least likely to commit suicide attacks.

9/11 was not the only terrorist plot to benefit from lax enforcement of ordinary immigration controls—every major Al–Qaeda attack or conspiracy in the United States has involved at least one terrorist who violated immigration law. Gazi Ibrahim Abu Mezer, for example, who was part of the plot to bomb the Brooklyn subway, was actually caught three times by the Border Patrol trying to sneak in from Canada. The third time the Canadians would not take him back. What did we do? Because of a lack of detention space, he was simply released into the country and told to show up for his deportation hearing. After all, with so many millions of illegal aliens here already, how much harm could one more do?

Another example is Mohammed Salameh, who rented the truck in the first World Trade Center bombing. He should never have been granted a visa in the first place. When he applied for a tourist visa he was young, single, and had no income and, in the event, did indeed end up remaining illegally. And when his application for a green card under the 1986 illegal-alien amnesty was rejected, there was (and remains today) no way to detain and remove rejected green-card applicants, so he simply remained living and working in the United States, none the worse for wear. The same was true of Hesham Mohamed Hadayet, who murdered two people at the El Al counter at Los Angeles International Airport on July 4, 2002—he was a visa overstayer whose asylum claim was rejected. Yet with no mechanism to remove him, he remained and, with his wife, continued to apply for the visa lottery until she won and procured green cards for both of them.

Ordinary immigration enforcement actually *has* kept out several terrorists that we know of. A vigilant inspector in Washington State stopped Ahmed Ressam because of nervous behavior, and a search of his car uncovered a trunk full of explosives, apparently intended for an attack on Los Angeles International Airport. Ramzi Binalshibh, one of the candidates for the label of "20th hijacker," was rejected four times for a visa, not because of concerns about terrorism but rather, according to a U.S. embassy source, "for the most ordinary of reasons, the same reasons most people are refused." That is, he was thought likely to overstay his visa and become an illegal alien. And Mohamed Al–Qahtani, another one of the "20th hijacker" candidates, was turned away by an airport inspector in Orlando because he had no return ticket and no hotel reservations, and he refused to identify the friend who was supposed to help him on his trip.

Prior to the growth of militant Islam, the only foreign threat to our population and territory in recent history has been the specter of nuclear attack by the Soviet Union. To continue that analogy, since the terrorists are themselves the weapons, immigration control is to asymmetric warfare what missile defense is to strategic warfare. There are other weapons we must use against an enemy employing asymmetric means—more effective international coordination, improved intelligence gathering and distribution, special military operations—but in the end, the lack of effective immigration control leaves us naked in the face of the enemy. This lack of defensive capability may have made sense with regard to the strategic nuclear threat under the doctrine of Mutually Assured Destruction, but it makes no sense with regard to the asymmetric threats we face today and in the future.

Unfortunately, our immigration response to the wake-up call delivered by the 9/11 attacks has been piecemeal and poorly coordinated. Specific initiatives that should have been set in motion years ago have finally begun to be enacted, but there is an *ad hoc* feel to our response, a sense that bureaucrats in the Justice and Homeland Security departments are searching for ways to tighten up immigration controls that will not alienate one or another of a bevy of special interest groups.

Rather than having federal employees cast about for whatever enforcement measures they feel they can get away with politically, we need a strategic assessment of what an effective immigration-control system would look like.

Homeland Security Begins Abroad

To extend the missile defense analogy, there are three layers of immigration control, comparable to the three phases of a ballistic missile's flight: boost, midcourse, and terminal. In immigration the layers are overseas, at the borders, and inside the country. But unlike existing missile defense systems, the redundancy built into our immigration control system permits us repeated opportunities to exclude or apprehend enemy operatives.

Entry to America by foreigners is not a right but a privilege, granted exclusively at the discretion of the American people. The first agency that exercises that discretion is the State Department's Bureau of Consular Affairs, whose officers make the all-important decisions about who gets a visa. Consular Affairs is, in effect, America's other Border Patrol. * * *

The visa filter is especially important because the closer an alien comes to the United States the more difficult it is to exclude him. There is relatively little problem, practically or politically, in rejecting a foreign visa applicant living abroad. Once a person presents himself at a port of entry, it becomes more difficult to turn him back, although the immigration inspector theoretically has a free hand to do so. Most difficult of all is finding and removing people who have actually been admitted; not only is there no specific chokepoint in which aliens can be controlled, but even the most superficial connections with American citizens or institutions can lead to vocal protests against enforcement of the law.

Even before 9/11, some improvements had been made to the first layer of immigration security: visas were made machine-readable and more difficult to forge than in the past, and the "watch list" of people who should not be granted visas was computerized, replacing the old microfiche-based system in place until just a few years ago.

Since the attacks, further improvements have taken place. The State Department has instituted the Biometric Visa Program at several consular posts and is preparing to meet a statutory deadline later this year for all visas to have biometric data, in the form of fingerprints and photographs. What's more, under a memorandum of understanding signed last fall, DHS assumed oversight and veto authority over the issuance of visas, and now has personnel overseeing visa officers in a number of consular posts overseas, including in Saudi Arabia, Egypt, Indonesia, Morocco, Pakistan, and the UAE.

Despite improvements, the most important flaw in the visa filter still exists: the State Department remains in charge of issuing visas. State has a corporate culture of diplomacy, geared toward currying favor with foreign governments. In the context of visa issuance, this has fostered a "customer-service" approach, which sees the foreign visa applicant as the customer who needs to be satisfied. The attitude in management is summed up by the catchphrase of the former U.S. consul general in Saudi Arabia: "People gotta have their visas!" Such an approach views high visa-refusal rates as a political problem, rather than an indicator of proper vigilance.

Nor will oversight of visa officers by DHS officials be an adequate antidote. As long as the decisions about raises, promotions, and future assignments for visa officers are made by the State Department, the culture of diplomacy will win out over the culture of law enforcement. In the end, the only remedy may be to remove the visa function from the State Department altogether.

Order at the Border

The next layer of immigration security is the border, which has two elements: "ports of entry," which are the points where people traveling by land, sea, or air enter the United States; and the stretches between those entry points. The first are staffed by inspectors working for DHS's Bureau of Customs and Border Protection, the second monitored by the Border Patrol and the Coast Guard, both now also part of DHS.

This is another important chokepoint, as almost all of the 48 Al–Qaeda operatives who committed terrorist acts through 2001 had had contact with immigration inspectors. But here, too, the system failed to do its job. For instance, Mohammed Atta was permitted to re-enter the country in January 2001 even though he had overstayed his visa the last time. Also, before 9/11 hijacker Khalid Al–Midhar's second trip to the United States, the CIA learned that he had been involved in the bombing of the U.S.S. Cole—but it took months for his name to be placed on the watch list used by airport inspectors, and by then he had already entered the country. * * *.

Political considerations fostered a dangerous culture of permissiveness in airport inspections. Bowing to complaints from airlines and the travel industry, Congress in 1990 required that incoming planes be cleared within 45 minutes, reinforcing the notion that the border was a nuisance to be evaded rather than a vital security tool. And the Orlando immigration inspector who turned back a Saudi national—Al–Qahtani, now believed to have been a part of the 9/11 plot—was well aware that he was taking a career risk, since Saudis were supposed to be treated even more permissively than other foreign nationals seeking entry.

There were also failures *between* the ports of entry. Abdelghani Meskini and Abdel Hakim Tizegha, both part of the Millennium Plot that included Ahmed Ressam, first entered the country as stowaways on ships that docked at U.S. ports. * * *

And finally, perhaps the biggest defect in this layer of security is the lack of effective tracking of departures. Without exit controls, there is no way to know who has overstayed his visa. This is especially important because most illegal alien terrorists have been overstayers. The opportunities for failure are numerous and the system is so dysfunctional that the INS's own statistics division declared that it was no longer possible to estimate the number of people who have overstayed their visas.

Certainly, there have been real improvements since 9/11. The US–VISIT system has begun to be implemented, with arriving visa-holders being digitally photographed and having their index fingerprints scanned; this will eventually grow into a "check in/check out" system to track them and other foreign visitors. Also, the 45–minute maximum for clearing foreign travelers has been repealed. Lastly, all foreign carriers are now required to forward their passenger manifests to immigration before the plane arrives.

But despite these and other improvements in the mechanics of border management, the same underlying problem exists here as in the visa process: lack of political seriousness about the security importance of immigration control. The Coast Guard, for instance, still considers the interdiction of illegal aliens a "nonsecurity" mission. More importantly, pressure to expedite entry at the expense of security persists; a DHS memo leaked in January outlined how the US–VISIT system would be suspended if lines at airports grew too long. And, to avoid complaints from businesses in Detroit, Buffalo, and elsewhere, most Canadian visitors have been exempted from the requirements of the US–VISIT system.

Also, there is continued resistance to using the military to back up the Border Patrol—resistance that predates the concern for overstretch caused by the occupation of Iraq. But controlling the Mexican border, apart from the other benefits it would produce, is an important security objective; at least two major rings have been uncovered which smuggled Middle Easterners into the United States via Mexico, with help from corrupt Mexican government employees. * * *

Safety Through Redundancy

The third layer of immigration security—the terminal phase, in missile defense jargon—is interior enforcement. Here, again, ordinary immigration control can be a powerful security tool. Of the 48 Al–Qaeda operatives, nearly half were either illegal aliens at the time of their crimes or had violated immigration laws at some point prior to their terrorist acts.

Many of these terrorists lived, worked, opened bank accounts, and received driver's licenses with little or no difficulty. Because such a large percentage of terrorists violated immigration laws, enforcing the law would be extremely helpful in disrupting and preventing terrorist attacks.

But interior enforcement is also the most politically difficult part of immigration control. While there is at least nominal agreement on the need for improvements to the mechanics of visas and border monitoring, there is no elite consensus regarding interior enforcement. This is especially dangerous given that interior enforcement is the last fallback for immigration control, the final link in a chain of redundancy that starts with the visa application overseas.

There are two elements to interior enforcement: first, conventional measures such as arrest, detention, and deportation; and second, verification of legal status when conducting important activities. The latter element is important because its goal is to disrupt the lives of illegal aliens so that many will return home on their own (and, in a security context, to disrupt the planning and execution of terrorist attacks).

Inadequacies in the first element of interior enforcement have clearly helped terrorists in the past. Because there is no way of determining which visitors have overstayed their visas, much less a mechanism for apprehending them, this has been a common means of remaining in the United States—of the 12 (out of 48) Al–Qaeda operatives who were illegal aliens when they took part in terrorism, seven were visa overstayers.

Among terrorists who were actually detained for one reason or another, several were released to go about their business inside America because of inadequate detention space. This lack of space means that most aliens in deportation proceedings are not detained, so that when ordered deported, they receive what is commonly known as a "run letter" instructing them to appear for deportation—and 94 percent of aliens from terrorist-sponsoring states disappear instead.

Lack of coordination between state and local police and federal immigration authorities is another major shortcoming. * * *

Perhaps the most outrageous phenomenon in this area of conventional immigration enforcement is the adoption of "sanctuary" policies by cities across the country. Such policies prohibit city employees—including police—from reporting immigration violations to federal authorities or even inquiring as to a suspect's immigration status. * * *

The second element of interior enforcement has been, if anything, even more neglected. The creation of "virtual chokepoints," where an alien's legal status would be verified, is an important tool of immigration control, making it difficult for illegals to engage in the activities necessary for modern life.

The most important chokepoint is employment. Unfortunately, enforcement of the prohibition against hiring illegal aliens, passed in 1986, has all but stopped. This might seem to be of little importance to security, but in fact holding a job can be important to terrorists for a number of reasons. By giving them a means of support, it helps them blend into society. Neighbors might well become suspicious of young men who do not work, but seem able to pay their bills. Moreover, supporting themselves by working would enable terrorists to avoid the scrutiny that might attend the transfer of money from abroad. Of course, terrorists who do not work can still arrive with large sums of cash, but this too creates risks of detection.

That said, the ban on employment by illegal aliens is one of the most widely violated immigration laws by terrorists. * * *

Other chokepoints include obtaining a driver's license and opening a bank account, two things that most of the 9/11 hijackers had done. * * *

As for bank accounts, the trend is toward making it easier for illegal aliens to open them. The governments of Mexico and several other countries have joined with several major banks to promote the use of consular identification cards (for illegals who can't get other ID) as a valid form of identification, something the U.S. Department of the Treasury explicitly sanctioned in an October 2002 report.

* * *

Former INS Commissioner James Ziglar expressed the general resistance to linking immigration law with homeland security when he said a month after the 9/11 attacks that "We're not talking about immigration, we're talking about evil." It is as if the terrorists were summoned from a magic lamp, rather than moving through our extensive but neglected immigration control system, by applying for visas, being admitted by inspectors, and violating laws with impunity inside America.

* * *

Mark Krikorian is executive director of the Center for Immigration Studies. [CIS is a research organization that lobbies against immigration.— Ed.]

Muzaffar A. Chishti, Doris Meissner, Demetrios G. Papademetriou, Jay Peterzell, Michael J. Wishnie & Stephen W. Yale–Loehr, Migration Policy Institute, America's Challenge: Domestic Security, Civil Liberties, and National Unity After September 11 (2003)

Pages 5–7.

On September 11, 2001, al Qaeda dealt the United States a catastrophic blow. The possibility of similar attacks with more lethal weapons poses an existential threat to the nation.

* * *

Since all 19 terrorists were foreign visitors who entered the country on valid visas, the government also responded with new immigration measures. Many of these measures single out for special scrutiny visitors and immigrants from Muslim countries.

Under the circumstances, a renewed focus on immigration controls was inevitable. But investigation and enforcement based on nationality discomfort America's sense of justice. September 11 challenged our country in many ways. None is more fundamental than the need to improve security while protecting civil liberties.

For most Americans, the new security measures are at most an inconvenience. Catching a flight may no longer be as simple as catching a bus, but that is a small price to pay for preventing future attacks.

Other individuals and communities in the United States are paying a far higher price. Indeed, the U.S. government has imposed some immigration measures that are more commonly associated with totalitarian regimes, measures that violate the fundamental freedoms defining America's identity. As this report details, there have been too many instances of longtime U.S. residents being detained by the government and held without charge, denied effective access to legal counsel, or having their immigration hearings held in secret.

Are these measures necessary to prevent another September 11?

It is too easy to say that if we abandon our civil liberties the terrorists win. It is just as easy to say that without security there will be little room for liberty. What is hard is to take both arguments with equal seriousness and to integrate them within a single framework.

As we worked on this report, we became convinced that it is not just security and civil liberties—that is, the rights of individuals—that are at stake. There is a third element: the character of the nation. On our humblest coin, the penny, are the words *e pluribus unum*, or "from many, one." The phrase goes to the heart of our identity as a nation and to the strength we derive from diversity. We believe that an effort to include Muslim communities in a more positive way in the fight against terrorism would not only serve this American value but help break the impasse between security and liberty, strengthening both.

* * *

Al Qaeda's hijackers were chosen to avoid detection: all but two were educated young men from middle-class families with no criminal record and no known connection to terrorism. Despite improvements in security, operatives of this sort would get into the country again today.

That does not mean that immigration controls are not useful. It means they are only as useful as the information provided by intelligence and law enforcement agencies. What immigration measures are able to do is bar terrorists about whom the government already has information from entering the country, and set up gateways and tracking systems so that someone already here can be found if intelligence agencies identify him as a suspect.

* * *

Chapter Two examines the recent national security measures in terms of their constitutionality and accordance with fundamental American legal tenets. We find that many of these measures violate core constitutional principles, including the right to due process, protection from detention without charge, the right to legal counsel, and the public's right to be informed about the actions of their government.

More than 1,200 people—the government refuses to say how many, who they are, or what has happened to all of them—have been detained. Many of them have suffered civil rights violations. Despite the government's determined efforts to shroud these actions in secrecy, as part of our research we were able to obtain information about 406 noncitizens detained after September 11. The appendix to this report contains these summaries, as well as a statistical analysis.

We found that the majority of the detainees had significant ties to the United States and roots in their communities. Of those for whom relevant information was available, over 46 percent had been in the United States at least six years, and almost half had spouses, children, or other family ties in the United States.

Most important, we found that the government's major successes in apprehending terrorists have not come from post-September 11 detentions but from other efforts such as international intelligence initiatives, law enforcement cooperation, and information provided by arrests made abroad. A few noncitizens detained through immigration initiatives after September 11 have been characterized as terrorists, but the charges brought against them were actually for routine immigration violations or unrelated crimes.

The negative impact of the government's actions and policies discussed in this report have principally affected recently arrived Arab and/or Muslim immigrants. Rather than concentrating its efforts on investigation, surveillance and law enforcement based on individualized suspicion, the government has essentially used national origin as a proxy for evidence of dangerousness. By the discriminatory action of targeting specific ethnic groups with its new measures, the government has violated a core principle of American justice.

* * *

We found that the new government security programs have put these communities under siege. Arabs and Muslims in America feel isolated and stigmatized. They feel they have been victimized twice: once by the terrorists and once by the reaction to terrorism. As one Arab–American community leader put it, "We, as Americans, were attacked. And at the same time, our fellow Americans are blaming us for something we didn't do."

But community leaders also point out a paradoxical effect: this period of trauma has spurred Muslim communities to begin to assert their rights and engage in the political process in ways that are classically American.

September 11 and its aftermath have ushered in what could be called the "Muslim moment": a period of rising Muslim self-consciousness, new alliances outside their own communities, and generational change. The sense of siege has strengthened some Muslim- and Arab–American political organizations and has led them to a greater focus on civil rights, social services, and economic development. The notion of a distinct "American Muslim" identity has gained new currency. It is an identity that seeks to assert its independence from forces abroad, one that combines the essential elements of Islam and the values of American constitutional democracy.

Meanwhile, applications for naturalization in Muslim- and Arab–American communities—driven in part by the increasing civil liberties risks faced by non-citizens—increased by 61 percent in the first three months after September 11. The image of newly minted Americans of Arab and Muslim descent waving flags at naturalization ceremonies is not what bin Laden had in mind when he ordered the September 11 attacks.

David Cole, The Priority of Morality: The Emergency Constitution's Blind Spot

113 Yale L.J. 1753, 1753–55 (2004).

In the wake of the terrorist attacks of September 11, Attorney General John Ashcroft announced a campaign of aggressive preventive detention. Invoking Robert Kennedy, the Attorney General announced that just as

Kennedy would arrest a mobster for "spitting on the sidewalk," so he, Ashcroft, would use every law in his power, including the immigration laws, to apprehend "suspected terrorists," lock them up, and prevent the next terrorist attack. As of January 2004, the government had detained more than 5000 foreign nationals through its antiterrorism efforts.[2] By any measure, the program has been spectacularly unsuccessful. None of these detainees has been determined to be involved with al Qaeda or the September 11 conspiracy. Only three have been charged with any terrorism-related crime, and two of those three were acquitted of the terrorism charges. The lone conviction—for conspiring to support some unspecified terrorist activity in the unspecified future—has been called into question by the revelation that the prosecution failed to disclose evidence that its principal witness had lied on the stand.

In June 2003, the Justice Department's own Inspector General issued a sharply critical report on the preventive detention campaign, finding, among other things, that people were detained and treated as "of interest" to the September 11 investigation on such information as an anonymous tip that there were "too many" Middle Eastern men working in a convenience store. Many were initially arrested without charges at all; over seven hundred of the arrests remain secret to this day; and more than six hundred detainees charged with immigration violations were tried in secret, without any showing that any information involved in their immigration hearings was classified. The vast majority were not only not charged with a terrorist crime, but were affirmatively cleared of any connection to terrorism by the FBI. Virtually all of the detainees were from predominantly Arab countries.

Prior mass preventive detention campaigns have been similarly unsuccessful and constitutionally suspect. In 1919, after terrorist bombs exploded virtually simultaneously in eight different cities across the United States, the Justice Department rounded up several thousand foreign nationals in what are now known as the Palmer Raids. They were herded into bullpens, interrogated without lawyers, and charged with technical immigration violations and association with various communist parties. Hundreds were eventually deported. Not one was found to have been involved with the bombings. And in the most infamous preventive detention campaign in American history, 110,000 persons—U.S. citizens and foreign nationals alike—were rounded up and interned during World War II simply because of their Japanese ancestry. None was found to have engaged in sabotage or espionage, the stated justifications for the internment.

2. In the first seven weeks of the campaign, the government admitted to detaining 1182 suspected terrorists, and virtually every time Ashcroft made a public statement he would give an update on the number of "suspected terrorists" detained. When people began to question why none of the 1182 persons had been charged with a terrorism-related crime, the Justice Department shifted gears and announced that it was too difficult to maintain a running total of detainees, so it would offer no further cumulative totals. Since then, however, the government has admitted to subjecting another 3900 people, virtually all foreign nationals, to preventive detention in antiterrorism initiatives in the United States, totaling more than 5000 in all.

Thus, the three principal preventive detention experiences in the United States over the last century all resulted in the mass incarceration of people who turned out *not* to pose the national security threat that purportedly justified their detention in the first place. Moreover, each campaign was characterized by widespread constitutional abuse. Freed of the ordinary requirement that they demonstrate objective, individualized evidence of dangerousness or flight risk in order to detain suspects, law enforcement officials resorted instead to political association, racial and ethnic identity, and religion as proxies for suspicion. The Palmer Raids and the Japanese internment are widely acknowledged as two of the most shameful moments in American history; the detention of thousands of Arabs and Muslims after September 11 deserves a place in that dubious pantheon.

These examples are not selectively chosen; there are *no* mass preventive detention success stories in our history. * * * While individual instances of preventive detention, predicated on objective showings of danger or flight risk, undoubtedly serve an important security function, there is no reason to believe that *suspicionless* preventive detention serves any legitimate purpose. * * *

NOTES AND QUESTIONS

1. Former Assistant Secretary of State for Consular Affairs Mary Ryan is quoted in Mark Krikorian's article as saying that even the best immigration controls would not have kept out most of the September 11 hijackers. Mr. Krikorian disagrees. Re-read Ryan's explanation and Krikorian's response. Which do you find more persuasive?

2. Krikorian calls the State Department "the most important flaw in the visa filter." He paints a picture of consular officers feeling pressures to grant visas to marginal applicants to avoid offending their countries of nationality. Having studied the visa process (and particularly the episode of the U.S. consulate in Brazil, which had employed racial stereotypes and recommended minimum refusal rates to keep down the number of visa approvals, see chapter 6, section D above), does Krikorian's premise seem realistic? In the wake of September 11, when a consular officer has even a nagging concern about the possibility of a given visa applicant being a terrorist, do you think the officer has a greater incentive to grant the visa or to deny it?

3. A recurring theme in many of Krikorian's positions is that several suspected terrorists had violated the terms of their immigration status. He reasons that measures to combat illegal immigration, apart from serving other goals, are therefore essential to fighting terrorism. The assumption is that *violation* of one's immigration status is a useful proxy for identifying which foreign nationals are likely to be terrorists. Absent empirical data (which Krikorian does not claim to have), does such a correlation seem instinctive? Would you expect an intelligent terrorist to be more likely, or less likely, to violate the terms of his or her visa?

4. Let us assume, for the sake of discussion, that the premise in item 3 above is true—i.e., that, among foreign nationals present in the United States, those who have violated their immigration status are statistically the most likely to be terrorists. Still, what policy prescriptions would logically follow? Should everyone who is ever found to have overstayed a visa be detained during removal proceedings, in case he or she is a terrorist? Should anyone who has ever violated the terms of his or her admission be removed and, after removal, barred permanently from the United States, regardless whether the violation was a year or a day and regardless of the family or other equities, in case he or she turns out to be a terrorist? More generally, what specific immigration control mechanisms would put a serious dent in terrorist capabilities at acceptable social and economic costs?

5. Continuing to assume *arguendo* that visa violators and other noncitizens who are out of status are disproportionately likely to be terrorists, Krikorian advocates laws that would require verification of immigration status during certain everyday transactions such as opening bank accounts, getting drivers' licenses, applying for jobs, and so forth. Now that you are well into this immigration law course, how easy do you think it would be for bank employees, Department of Motor Vehicles employees, and others to ascertain (a) which customers are U.S. citizens and which are not; and (b) which of the latter are out of status? Is that something that could be done reliably with a reasonable amount of training?

6. If all the measures Krikorian advocates for detecting, apprehending, and removing out-of-status noncitizens were actually adopted, what would you expect terrorists in the United States to do?

7. In the end, what do you think is going on here? Do proponents of restrictive immigration policies (with respect to legal immigration, illegal immigration, or both) truly see those restrictions as a way to combat terrorism? Or do they see terrorism as a way to mobilize public support for restrictive immigration policies?

8. The next two writings—one by the Migration Policy Institute and one by Professor Cole—both emphasize that non-U.S. citizens in the United States are paying a higher civil liberties price for U.S. national security than U.S. citizens are. Your reaction?

9. The MPI publication argues that, while national security and civil liberties both represent vital national interests, there is a third interest that sometimes gets lost in the shuffle—the character of the nation, as exemplified by the motto *"E pluribus unum."* In making that point, the authors have in mind the set of national security strategies that have involved targeting ethnic and religious groups. Philosophy aside, they make an instrumental argument—that in the long run it would be more effective to enlist the Muslim and Arab communities as partners in the battle against terrorism than to alienate them through ethnic and religious profiling practices. Do you agree? See also the discussion of this subject in section G above.

10. Take one last glance at all three of the preceding writings. To what extent does each of them meaningfully acknowledge and take into account countervailing interests?

11. There has been some fine general writing on the relationship between immigration control and national security. In addition to the writings excerpted above, see, e.g., United States Congressional Research Service, 9/11 Commission: Implications for U.S. Immigration Law and Policy (Sept. 30, 2004); David Cole, Enemy Aliens–Double Standards and Constitutional Freedoms in the War on Terrorism (2003); Raquel Aldana–Pindell, *The 9/11 "National Security" Cases: Three Principles Guiding Judges' Decision–Making*, 81 Oregon L. Rev. 985 (2002); Berta E. Hernández–Truyol, *Glocalizing Terror*, 81 Oreg. L. Rev. 941 (2002); Donald Kerwin, *Counterterrorism and Immigrant Rights Two Years Later*, 80 IR 1401 (Oct. 13, 2003); Peter Margulies, *Uncertain Arrivals: Immigration, Terror, and Democracy After September 11*, 2002 Utah L. Rev. 481 (2002) (offering thoughtful suggestions for integrating demands of democracy and security). Professor Natsu Taylor Saito has prepared a detailed and highly critical historical account that roots the post–9/11 counter-terrorism measures in the practices and desires of the FBI and other law enforcement agencies over the past several decades. See Natsu Taylor Saito, *Whose Liberty? Whose Security? The USA PATRIOT Act in the Context of COINTELPRO and the Unlawful Suppression of Political Dissent*, 81 Oregon L. Rev. 1051 (2002).

Although the EU and its member states have similarly taken serious steps to combat terrorism since 9/11 (including many steps that specifically target noncitizens), those measures have generally entailed less drastic human rights sacrifices than in the United States. For two informative analyses, see Sophie Robin–Olivier, *Citizens and Noncitizens in Europe: European Union Measures Against Terrorism After September 11*, 25 Boston College Third World L. Rev. 197 (2005); Kim Lane Scheppele, *Other People's PATRIOT Acts: Europe's Response to September 11*, 50 Loyola L. Rev. 67 (2004). In contrast, the harsh anti-terror measures adopted in India are described by Chris Gagné, *POTA: Lessons Learned from India's Anti–Terror Act*, 25 Boston College Third World L. Rev. 261 (2005).

CHAPTER 11

REFUGEES

You saw earlier some of the debate over the social and economic impact of immigrants. The prodigious contributions of immigrants to the American economy and culture have generally enabled policymakers to serve humanitarian ideals and national self-interest simultaneously. But many discount the link between compassion and self-interest, and in no area of migration law is the perceived clash more dramatic than in refugee and asylum policy. The problems have become the subject of a sprawling international[1] and interdisciplinary literature. The pages that follow provide a small sampling of the debate.

A few basic themes recur. On the one hand, it is difficult to imagine a class of people who deserve a humanitarian response more so than genuine refugees. Persecuted, generally homeless, and by definition unable to turn to their own governments for protection, refugees are utterly dependent on the good will of the people and the governments of foreign lands.

Much good will clearly exists, but it collides with several economic and political realities that you will encounter often in this chapter. One is the sheer scale of the world refugee crisis. As of January 1, 2004, there were approximately 13.7 million "refugees" in the world. UNHCR, 2003 Global Refugee Trends (15 June 2004), at 2 & n.1 (including the 4 million Palestinians who are the responsibility of a separate UN agency). And that figure does not count the approximately 22 million (as of January 1, 2003) "internally displaced persons," or "IDPs," who have been driven from

---

1. The leading treatises on international refugee law are Guy S. Goodwin Gill, The Refugee in International Law (2d ed. 1996); Atle Grahl–Madsen, The Status of Refugees in International Law (2 vols., 1966 and 1972); and James C. Hathaway, The Law of Refugee Status (1991). An excellent law school coursebook on the subject is Karen Musalo, Jennifer Moore & Richard A. Boswell, Refugee Law and Policy: A Comparative and International Approach (2d ed. 2002); see also the web site of the United Nations High Commissioner for Refugees, http://www.unhcr.ch; Edward Newman & Joanne van Selm (eds.), Refugees and Forced Displacement (2003).

Authoritative treatments of United States asylum law include Deborah E. Anker, Law of Asylum in the United States (3d ed. 1999) [hereafter Anker] and 3 Gordon, Mail-man & Yale–Loehr, chs. 33, 34; see also Ira J. Kurzban, Kurzban's Immigration Law Sourcebook—A Comprehensive Outline and Reference Tool, ch. 4 (9th ed. 2004); David A. Martin, Asylum Case Law Sourcebook (4th ed. 2003); Elwin Griffith, Problems of Interpretation in Asylum and Withholding of Deportation Proceedings under the Immigration and Nationality Act, 18 Loyola L.A. Internat'l & Comp. L.J. 255 (1996). For general commentary on the definition of "refugee," see Daniel J. Steinbock, Interpreting the Refugee Definition, 45 UCLA L. Rev. 733 (1998); Dirk Vanheule, A Comparison of the Judicial Interpretations of the Notion of Refugee, in Jean–Yves Carlier & Dirk Vanheule (eds.), Europe and Refugees: A Challenge?, chap. 5 (1997) (a comparison of the refugee definitions in 15 countries).

their homes but are still within their countries of origin. U.S. Committee for Refugees, World Refugee Survey 2003 (May 2003). The political will to accept either the ethnic diversity or the economic costs of resettlement often withers even as the need for greater compassion increases. Indeed, the international authorities typically have great difficulty raising the funds needed merely to sustain the refugees in temporary overseas camps pending resettlement.

A second prominent theme is the proper function of refugee policy. Should it be a humanitarian project, designed to relieve the suffering of those who have been forced to leave their home countries? Should refugee policies rest on human rights considerations, aiming to deter human rights violations or at least to repair some of the damage after the fact? Should refugee policy simply reflect national self-interest, pursued in the name of sovereignty? For a cynical view of the interests that have historically driven international refugee policy, see James C. Hathaway, *A Reconsideration of the Underlying Premise of Refugee Law,* 31 Harvard Internat'l L.J. 129 (1990); see also Arthur C. Helton, The Price of Indifference—Refugees and Humanitarian Action in the New Century (2002).

One specific aspect of the tension between national self-interest and either a humanitarian or a human rights-based vision of refugee policy is selection criteria. Since not all refugees can be absorbed by any one country, policymakers need criteria for deciding which ones to take. In the United States, that subject has produced angry debate. As the readings in this chapter will demonstrate, the overwhelming majority of those people whose refugee status the United States recognized in the past were people fleeing Communist regimes. Historically, those who have fled countries friendly to the United States—El Salvador, Guatemala, Haiti, and others—have had strikingly little success, as noted in more detail below. Critics of American refugee and asylum policy charge foreign policy bias. Defenders argue that those from countries allied to the United States tend to be "economic migrants" fleeing poverty, not true refugees fleeing persecution. Professor Daniel Steinbock carefully examines the sometimes competing missions of refugee policy and ultimately urges selection priorities that reflect a combination of national interest, the interests of the refugees themselves, and the interests of their countries of origin. See Daniel J. Steinbock, *The Qualities of Mercy: Maximizing the Impact of U.S. Refugee Resettlement*, 36 Univ. Michigan J. L. Reform 951 (2003).

Especially volatile—not only in the United States but throughout the refugee-receiving world—is the debate over whether asylum programs are being abused. Some believe that large numbers of individuals who do not meet the applicable definition of "refugee" are filing unfounded asylum claims, partly to buy time in the host countries while their claims are being processed. The large volumes noted earlier mean that the adjudication periods can be lengthy. Proponents of that view generally urge either abbreviated adjudication procedures or other deterrents to false claims, such as detention or refusal of work authorization. Others dispute that a high proportion of asylum claims are without foundation and add that some of the "cures" cause genuine refugees to be turned back.

Refugees are often distinguished from immigrants. The former are said to be forcibly displaced, while the latter are thought of as willing migrants. The line that separates voluntary and involuntary is not always easy to draw, however, and in fact the two groups of migrants have several common attributes. Among other things, both groups are at the epicenter of tumultuous arguments about economic, social, and cultural contributions and costs.

Under United States law, those and other recurring themes are played out in two different theaters. In one category are those refugees who are outside United States territory. In some receiving states, such individuals are called "offshore" refugees. Some within this group have fled their countries of origin and made their way to temporary refugee camps in countries of "first asylum;" others are still within their home countries. Either way, they are overseas and in need of transportation to, and usually permanent resettlement in, the United States or other refugee-receiving nations.

In the other category are those who have already managed to reach United States shores on their own. They are sometimes called "onshore" refugees. They seek to remain in the United States or at least to avoid being sent back to the country in which they fear persecution. Within this group, some are at ports of entry while others have already effected entry, legally or illegally. Of those who have already entered, some seek relief during removal proceedings while others affirmatively apply to USCIS for relief before removal proceedings are brought. The substantive criteria for relief for these various groups differ somewhat, but the most important differences are procedural.

The organization of this chapter reflects the fundamental distinction between overseas applicants and those who have arrived in the United States. Analytically, the admission of overseas refugees can be thought of as simply one element of legal (albeit involuntary) migration—analogous to immigration based on family, or employment, or diversity. This subject matter could logically have been covered in chapter 3. In contrast, when people reach United States territory and seek relief at the frontier or in the interior, the requested remedies resemble waivers of inadmissibility or deportability, respectively. Those remedies could logically have been included in chapters 5 and 8. Because these two refugee contexts generate so many common issues, however, and because those common issues differ in many respects from those encountered in the more general materials, it is convenient to treat refugees in a single chapter.

The terminology is often inconsistent. Probably the most common approach is to describe the first group as "refugees" or "overseas refugees," and the second group as "asylum-seekers." Those usages, however, produce at least two sources of confusion. First, the United States statutory definition of "refugee," INA § 101(a)(42), does not require that the person be outside the United States; in fact, one of the statutory requirements for asylum under United States law is that the person satisfy the statutory definition of "refugee." See INA § 208. Thus, even though many people use the word "refugee" to mean "overseas refugee" (as distinguished from those who have already reached United States territory), the legal terminology in the United States is different; under the statutory definition, every asylee is also a refugee. Second, just as the common usage of "refugee" differs from its statutory meaning, so too is there an ambiguity in the word "asylum." As noted above, some use this term to describe any persecution-related relief sought by any noncitizen who reaches United States shores. Under United States law, however, asylum actually refers only to one particular remedy for persecution—permission to remain at least temporarily, and usually permanently, in the United States, see INA §§ 208, 209(b), as distinguished from the narrower remedy of not being removed to the country of persecution, see INA § 241(b)(3).

So clear definitions are crucial. In this book, as in most, noncitizens who have not yet reached United States shores and who qualify for refugee status will be called "overseas refugees." They are the subject of section A. Those who have reached United States territory and who request relief from persecution will be discussed in section B. The relief available to the latter group under INA § 208 (permission to remain at least temporarily, and usually permanently, in the United States) will be called "asylum." The more limited form of relief—avoiding removal to the country of persecution but not necessarily to other countries—will be called either "nonrefoulement" (the French term used by international lawyers) or "withholding of removal" (the United States statutory term). In the United States, withholding of removal is authorized by INA § 241(b)(3).

As you will also see, the "refugee" definition used for both overseas refugee admissions and asylum is a narrow one. It covers only "persecution," and then only in certain prescribed situations. Many other individuals require refuge as well, and they are considered in section C. Among the protection mechanisms explored in section C are the Convention Against Torture, United States and international devices for temporary protection, and subsidiary protection under regional or global human rights conventions.

SECTION A.   OVERSEAS REFUGEES

As long as there have been governments, there have been refugees. The excerpt that follows discusses some of the root causes of past refugee flows and the likelihood of their future recurrence.

Astri Suhrke, Global Refugee Movements and Strategies of Response in Mary M. Kritz (Ed.), U.S. Immigration and Refugee Policy

Pages 163–65 (1983).

* * *

A * * * meaningful approach would be to examine the causes of major refugee flows in the past, and ask whether or not these are structurally embedded in contemporary societies. Three preliminary attempts in this direction have all concluded on a pessimistic note. One study notes a series of tension-building factors: "population growth continues . . . ; stakes in the worldwide competition for land and resources continue to escalate . . . ; unequal distribution of wealth is a source of increasing friction . . . ; mechanisms to resolve [international] disputes . . . are still too weak to keep the peace." Hence, it is claimed, "the underlying forces that contribute to the formation of refugee crises are, if anything, gathering strength." Another study is slightly less pessimistic about likely future trends in the Third World, but includes the possibility of huge numbers of refugees resulting from nuclear war and a high probability of large outflows from Eastern Europe. A third study postulates that structural weaknesses of many Third World nations will give rise to substantial refugee flows.

A more optimistic scenario can also be sketched. Considering only the Third World, it is evident that wars of independence have been a major cause of refugee movements in the past. This era is now drawing to a close; only southern Africa remains. Internal ethnic rivalries have caused some major outflows, but certainly not as frequently as the pervasive pattern of ethnic tension in African and Asian states might lead one to believe. Separatist conflicts stemming from artificial state boundaries have produced some notable refugee flows in Africa, but these conflicts typically were connected with the struggle for power in the immediate postindependence period. Moreover, African states seek to contain and moderate such conflicts. Internal conflict associated with the gap between elites and masses and an inequitable distribution of wealth is another common feature of many Third World countries. However, only in a few cases has this led to protracted violence or revolutionary wars, which in turn have caused major outflows. Some observers predict a future pattern of continued alienation but powerlessness on the part of the masses, rather than explosive class conflicts.

The main difference between a pessimistic and an optimistic scenario is that the former looks at sources of instability, while the latter focuses on actual conflicts and consequent refugee flows. Both agree that there are severe and widespread sources of instability, but the optimist notes that only in some cases have these led to conflicts that caused refugee flows. Obviously, some key intervening variables account for this variation. These have yet to be identified and systematically studied.

It is also important to note differences in outflows. Some types of conflicts (protracted warfare, international wars, and certain kinds of ethnic tension) seem to produce major outflows; other conflicts (typically elite rivalry, coups d'etat, governmental suppression of critics) tend to produce a trickle of a few, highly politicized individuals. Each movement presents different problems for receiving countries in terms of relief assistance or final settlement.

The impact of outflows on the sending country rarely has been included in studies of refugee movements; yet, this is a major factor that determines whether the government will facilitate or discourage outflows. Various considerations may be relevant: fears that refugees will spearhead revanchist movements, concern that skilled people are leaving, a desire to be rid of troublesome or undesirable groups, and more.

An analysis of causes of refugee movements also should include pull factors, that is, the prospect for assistance and conditions in recipient countries. Previous studies of refugee movements have generally excluded pull factors because it was assumed that refugees moved in response to push factors. If not, they were migrants. The issue was settled by definitional fiat, but this is not very satisfactory.

A refugee program may, in itself, be a significant pull factor. Refugee programs, once established, probably tend to attract a variety of people who seek to benefit. Two recent major flows—the Cubans and the Indochinese—are cases in point. Let us assume that for some persons the expectation of benefiting from a refugee program is a major factor in the decision to leave, as well as where and when to go, and call them quasi refugees. We can then approach the question are quasi refugees becoming an increasingly common phenomenon, growing pari passu with the international relief apparatus? The quasi refugees may not necessarily be less needy than other refugees. To accommodate them may be a recognition and not the creation of demand. The point here is, rather, the need to consider how existing programs can influence flows.

* * *

———

Although refugees have existed since ancient times, a body of international refugee law did not really begin to form until 1921. In that year the League of Nations appointed Norway's Arctic explorer Dr. Fridtjof Nansen to serve as High Commissioner for Russian Refugees. The so-called "Nansen passport" was the first travel document specially designed to facilitate the migration of refugees. See Paul Weis, *The Development of Refugee Law*, 1982 Mich. Yearbook Int'l Legal Studies 27, 28.

In October 1932, during a Presidential campaign speech, Herbert Hoover displayed his prophetic powers:

> With the growth of democracy in foreign countries political persecution has largely ceased. There is no longer a necessity for the United States to provide an asylum for those persecuted because of conscience.

9 IR 260, 261 (1932). Several months later, the rise of Adolph Hitler and the grisly persecution of Jews and others triggered the beginnings of what would become a mass exodus. The immediate question in the United States and other nations was whether to provide a safe haven to some of these refugees.

American public opinion was strongly opposed to doing so. Even by the summer of 1938, five years into the exodus from Germany, 67% of the Americans polled were opposed to the admission of refugees. See Robert A. Divine, American Immigration Policy, 1924–1952, at 96 (1957). By April 1939, after the gravity of the Nazi persecutions had become public knowledge, the proportion of Americans opposed to the admission of the Jewish refugees had risen to 83%. *Id.* at 98–99. Despite a hard-fought campaign by various humanitarian groups, Congress was unwilling even to enact legislation that would have enabled 20,000 refugee children to enter the United States. *Id.* at 99–102.

One of the most infamous episodes was that of the SS St. Louis. Professor Bill Ong Hing relates the details:

> The plight of European Jews fleeing Nazi Germany aboard the ship SS St. Louis in 1939 is a horrific example of how restrictionist views were manifested toward refugees at the time. In a diabolical propaganda ploy in the spring of 1939, the Nazis had allowed this ship carrying destitute European Jewish refugees to leave Hamburg bound for Cuba but had arranged for corrupt Cuban officials to deny them entry even after they had been granted visas. The German propaganda machine sought to demonstrate that no country wanted the Jews, and the world obliged. The St. Louis was not allowed to discharge its passengers and was ordered out of Havana harbor. As it sailed north, it neared U.S. territorial waters, yet the U.S. Coast Guard warned it away. President Franklin D. Roosevelt had said that the United States could not accept any more European refugees because of immigration quotas, as untold thousands had already fled Nazi terror in Central Europe, and many had come to the Depression-racked United States.
>
> Nearly two months after leaving Hamburg and due to the efforts of U.S. Jewish refugee assistance groups, the ship was allowed to land in Holland. Four nations agreed to accept the refugees—Great Britain, Holland, Belgium, and France. Two months later, the Nazis invaded Poland, and the Second World War began. Over 600 of the 937 passengers on the St. Louis were killed by the Nazis before the war was over. When the United States refused the S. Louis permission to land, many Americans were embarrassed; when the country discovered after the war what happened to the refugees, there was shame.

Bill Ong Hing, *No Place for Angels: In Reaction to Kevin Johnson*, 2000 Univ. Illinois L. Rev. 559, 590–91.

The reasons for the relentless restrictionism of the 1930's were varied and not always easy to decipher. A clear contributor was the Depression. With millions of Americans out of work, many were unwilling to admit those who with whom they would be competing for jobs. Other Americans feared that the refugee population contained subversive elements who would poison the United States with their radical views and their activities.

Anti-semitism was clearly an additional factor, though historians differ as to its magnitude and its impact. See Divine, above, ch. 5.

From a legal standpoint, the major obstacle to the admission of refugees was that the law contained no special provision exempting them from the restrictions generally applicable to immigrants. Restrictionists often argued that the existing laws were adequate and that refugees could come in, just like anyone else, whenever they met United States immigration standards. As a practical matter, of course, refugees ordinarily could not satisfy the general requirements. Most were destitute and thus inadmissible as likely to become public charges. Even those who could somehow clear that hurdle were subject to backlogged quotas that kept out all but a tiny proportion. The Roosevelt administration bowed to public opinion and refrained from asking Congress to liberalize the immigration laws, but the Administration did take some limited executive measures to admit a few thousand refugees during the pre-war period. Divine, above, at 102–03. Those measures were greatly expanded once the United States entered World War II. From 1941 to 1945, various administrative acts resulted in the admission of approximately 250,000 European refugees. *Id.* at 104.

The war itself produced millions of additional refugees, as the following excerpt explains:

Robert A. Divine, American Immigration Policy, 1924–1952

Pp. 110–12 (1957).

* * *

The displaced persons problem was a direct outgrowth of the war. When the Allies surveyed the population of the liberated enemy territory in the summer of 1945, they found eight million people in Germany, Austria, and Italy who had been displaced from their homes in other parts of Europe. The Nazi policy of importing vast numbers of forced laborers from conquered territory to fill the manpower needs of the German industrial system accounted for the great bulk of these uprooted peoples. The Germans had drawn upon all areas of Europe for involuntary workers, but the majority had come from central Europe, particularly Poland and the Baltic states. A second source of displaced persons was the large number of people who had fled before the Russian advance across Poland and into Germany in 1944 and 1945. Some had retreated into Germany out of fear or hatred of Communism, others simply to escape the zone of combat between the opposing armies. The Jewish victims of Nazi persecution who survived the mass exterminations in the concentration camps formed a third and much smaller category of displaced persons. In addition to these people who were in the occupied zones in 1945, there was a continuing stream of refugees which flowed into Germany and Austria from eastern Europe after the war's end. At first largely composed of Jews fleeing from anti-Semitic outbursts in Poland, the movement developed into an exodus by people of all faiths from the Communist nations of eastern and central Europe.

The first attempt to cope with the problem came at the Yalta Conference, where the Allied governments agreed on procedures for the repatriation of displaced persons. In the summer and fall of 1948 seven million people returned to their native countries under this agreement. However, the establishment of Communist regimes in the countries of eastern Europe prevented the easy consummation of the repatriation process. Approximately one million displaced natives of eastern Europe refused to go back to their countries of origin because they feared persecution by the newly instituted Communist governments. The Russians demanded their forcible repatriation, but the American, British, and French governments took a firm stand against involuntary return. This decision in effect committed the three governments to the custodianship of the one million displaced persons in their zones of Germany, Austria, and Italy. Having made the commitment, the democratic nations were faced with the difficult problem of how to dispose of the refugees, and while they groped for a final answer, they supported the homeless in temporary camps, with 600,000 under American care.

The presence of more than four million *Volksdeutsche* or German expellees in Western Germany further complicated the problem. At the Potsdam conference the democratic nations agreed to a Russian proposal for the transfer of all people of German ethnic origin from Czechoslovakia, Poland, and Hungary to Germany. This entailed not only the movement of Germans living in territory ceded to Poland and Czechoslovakia at the end of the war, but also the transfer of people of German descent who had lived in eastern Europe for centuries. A total of about twelve million people was involved in this gigantic transfer, which resulted in a critical population surplus in Germany. In view of this situation, the American, British, and French governments could not solve the displaced persons problem by disbanding the camps and forcing the displaced persons onto the already overburdened German economy.

By 1947 it had become apparent that the only feasible solution to the problem was to resettle the displaced persons outside of Germany. In order to carry out a resettlement program, the United Nations established the International Refugee Organization (IRO) supported by the United States, Canada, Australia, and the free countries of western Europe. The IRO provided the vehicle for resettlement, but it could be successful only if each of the member nations agreed to accept a portion of the group for permanent residence. * * *

* * *

––––––

As the preceding excerpt notes, the success of the international effort hinged ultimately on the responses of individual nations. In the United

States, the path to ameliorative legislation was a tortured one. All the objections that had surfaced during the 1930's resurfaced after the war: Refugees would compete with Americans for jobs. Refugees might harbor subversive sympathies. Refugees should remain in Europe to help out with reconstruction. The admission of refugees would upset the national origins quota system then in place.

In 1948 the United States finally enacted displaced persons legislation. See Act of June 25, 1948, ch. 647, 62 Stat. 1009. Some members of Congress cited moral and compassionate reasons. Others felt that relieving the population pressures on the western European nations would make those countries stronger bulwarks against Communism. See Divine, above, ch. 6.

To gain the votes of the restrictionists, however, the refugee advocates had to make significant concessions:

> First, the bill limited the number to 100,000 over a two-year period, only one-fourth the total in the Stratton bill, on the grounds that a greater number would be harmful to the American economy. In the second place, the subcommittee limited the program to those people who were registered as displaced persons on December 22, 1945, the date of President Truman's directive. This early cut-off date excluded some 100,000 people, mainly Jews, who had entered the camps in 1946 and early 1947. The subcommittee justified this provision on the grounds that help should be extended only to those people who had been directly displaced by the war.

Divine, above, at 120. President Truman and others denounced those restrictions as numerically insufficient and reflective of anti-semitism and, to a lesser extent, anti-Catholicism. After protracted battles, and despite the staunch opposition of Senate Judiciary Committee chair Pat McCarran (co-author of the 1952 Immigration and Nationality Act now in force) to any liberalization of the refugee laws, public opinion gradually softened. In 1950 Congress amended the 1948 Act. The 1950 legislation paved the way for the admission of more than 400,000 refugees and extended eligibility to those who had been displaced before January 1, 1949. The Act thus ended the exclusion of those Jewish refugees who had fled anti-semitism at the end of the war. See Divine, above, ch. 7.

At about the same time, the international community recognized the need for a permanent successor to the now defunct International Refugee Organization. The United Nations responded in 1950 by establishing the Office of the United Nations High Commissioner for Refugees (UNHCR). Professor Guy Goodwin–Gill, a former legal advisor in UNHCR, describes its charge and its current activities:

Guy S. Goodwin–Gill, The Refugee in International Law

Pages 129–31 (1983).

At its 1950 session, the General Assembly formally adopted the Statute of UNHCR as an annexe to Resolution 428(V), in which it also called upon governments to co-operate with the Office. The functions of UNHCR encompass "providing international protection" and "seeking permanent solutions" to the problems of refugees by way of voluntary repatriation or assimilation in new national communities. The Statute expressly provides that "the work of the High Commissioner shall be of an entirely non-political character; it shall be humanitarian and social and shall relate, as a rule, to groups and categories of refugees." Of the two functions, the provision of international protection is of primary importance, for without protection, such as intervention by the Office to secure admission of refugees, there can be no possibility of finding lasting solutions. Besides defining refugees the UNHCR Statute prescribes the relationship of the High Commissioner with the General Assembly and the Economic and Social Council (ECOSOC), makes provision for organization and finance, and identifies ways in which the High Commissioner is to provide for protection. These develop the functions engaged in by predecessor organizations and include: (i) promoting the conclusion of international conventions for the protection of refugees, supervising their application and proposing amendments thereto; (ii) promoting through special agreements with governments the execution of any measures calculated to improve the situation of refugees and to reduce the number requiring protection; and (iii) promoting the admission of refugees.

Notwithstanding the statutory injunction that the work of the Office shall relate, as a rule, to groups and categories of refugees, a major part of UNHCR's protection work is concerned with individual cases, as was that of its predecessor organizations. No state has objected to UNHCR taking up individual cases as such, although states may, and do, question whether an individual is indeed a refugee. Nevertheless, the individual dimension to the protection function is a natural corollary to the declared task of supervising the application of international conventions. Such instruments define refugees in essentially individualistic terms and provide rights on behalf of refugees which can only be understood in the sense of the particular. The acquiescence of states in the individual protection function of UNHCR, however, significantly delineates both the competence of the Office and the status of the individual refugee in international law.

———

The UNHCR cooperates with private agencies, national authorities, other U.N. organizations, and the International Organization for Migration (IOM), an important association of refugee-receiving nations that coordinates much of the resettlement work. See James L. Carlin, *Significant Refugee Crises since World War II and the Response of the International Community*, 1982 Michigan Yearbook Internat'l Legal Studies 3, 7–9.

A year after the creation of UNHCR, the United Nations took another major step. It adopted the 1951 Convention Relating to the Status of Refugees, 189 U.N.T.S. 137, accepted by United Nations Conference of Plenipotentiaries on the Status of Refugees and Stateless Persons, signed at Geneva, July 28, 1951 [hereafter cited as 1951 Convention]. Most members of the United Nations, including most of the western European nations and Canada, signed the Convention, but the United States held off until 1968, when it became a party indirectly by acceding to the 1967 Protocol discussed below. As of January 10, 2005, some 139 nations had signed both the 1951 Convention and the 1967 Protocol, and another 6 had signed one or the other. 24 Refugee Survey Q. #1 at 165 (2005).

Article I of the 1951 Convention defines the term "refugee" (more on that in a moment), and articles 3 through 34 require each signatory to accord certain protections to those refugees physically within its territory. With some qualifications, the protections include non-discrimination, religious freedom, access to court, work permits, education, welfare, labor laws, and free movement within the country. See arts. 3, 4, 16, 17, 22–24, 26–28. As you will see in the next section, article 33 of the Convention codifies the principle of nonrefoulement. Importantly, however, nothing in the 1951 Convention (or in the 1967 Protocol discussed below) requires any nation to admit overseas refugees in the first place. Moreover, the Convention and Protocol allow parties to exclude certain categories of people from protection—mainly those firmly resettled elsewhere, those guilty of certain major international crimes, and certain other criminal offenders. Some exclusions nullify only the protection against refoulement, while others render the entire Convention (and therefore all the protections afforded refugees) inoperative. See subsection B.5 below.

UNHCR is charged with supervising the implementation of the 1951 Convention, and the states parties have explicitly agreed to cooperate with UNHCR in the performance of that function. 1951 Convention, art. 35.1. In practice, its protection role also incorporates assistance to refugees and delivery of services. But neither the Convention nor any source of international law gives UNHCR powers to issue binding interpretations of the Convention or otherwise compel compliance. Professor James Hathaway has advocated the creation of an international entity that would play a broader oversight role. See James C. Hathaway, *Who Should Watch Over Refugee Law?*, 14 Forced Migration Rev. 23 (2002); see also Susan F. Martin, *Forced Migration and Professionalism*, 35 Internat'l Migration Rev. 226 (2001) (urging greater professionalization in training of international refugee workers).

In the United States, meanwhile, no statute generally authorized the admission of refugees. During the 1950's and 1960's, Congress occasionally passed ad hoc legislation to deal with specific crises. See United States Congressional Research Service, Review of U.S. Refugee Resettlement Programs and Policies 7–11 (Comm. Print, Senate Comm. on the Judiciary, 1980). In addition, various Attorneys General often used their powers under INA § 212(d)(5) to parole groups of refugees into the United States. Notable examples include Hungarians who fled their country after the Soviet Union had crushed the 1956 revolution and Cubans who left their country after Castro had seized power. *Id;* see also Carlin, above.

In retrospect, it seems extraordinary that the parole power, which had been intended principally as a device for according temporary relief to individuals, would become a numerically significant component of the nation's legal immigration system. Relying on parole for that purpose proved unsatisfying. From the standpoint of the parolee, there were no meaningful criteria for qualifying and there was virtually no procedural protection when a request for parole was turned down. Moreover, since even a person who receives parole has not technically been "admitted" (see chapter 7, section A), a parolee can be removed from the country at any time and for almost any reason. From Congress's viewpoint, the executive practice of mass parole precluded legislative input into national policy decisions that had sweeping domestic and international effects.

In 1965 Congress revamped the entire system of quotas and preferences. The change most pertinent here was the creation of a "seventh preference" for those who feared persecution and were fleeing either a "Communist-dominated" country or a country "within the general area of the Middle East." Pub.L. 89–236, § 3, 79 Stat. 911, 913 (Oct. 3, 1965), amending INA § 203(a)(7). The same preference category covered anyone who had been "uprooted by catastrophic natural calamity." *Id.*

This solution was, however, very limited. Apart from its ideological and geographic limitations, the new law reserved for the seventh preference only 6% of the total numerically restricted immigrant visas. Moreover, the seventh preference resulted only in "conditional" status, though one could then apply for adjustment of status to permanent residence after two years. *Id.*, adding INA § 203(g) (now repealed).

In 1967 the United Nations adopted the Protocol Relating to the Status of Refugees, 606 U.N.T.S. 267, 19 U.S.T. 6223, T.I.A.S. No. 6577, done at New York, January 31, 1967 [hereafter cited as the 1967 Protocol]. The 1951 Convention had limited the definition of "refugee" to those who had fled as a result of the specific events occurring in Europe before January 1, 1951. See 1951 Convention, art. 1. The 1967 Protocol removed that limitation, thus leaving the international community with a more generic refugee agreement. In 1968 the United States acceded to the 1967 Protocol; by that action it accepted the 1951 Convention as modified. 19 U.S.T. 6223, 6257 (1968).

The 1960's and 1970's saw further refugee flows. Czechs fled the Soviet invasion of 1968. Various events in Ethiopia induced well over a million people to flee to Somalia and the Sudan during the late 1960's and 1970's. The Indian–Pakistani war of 1971 resulted in a migration of millions from Pakistan to India. President Idi Amin of Uganda in 1972 expelled thousands of Asians. Several hundred thousand fled former Portuguese colonies in Africa in the mid–1970's. Soviet Jews began receiving exit permits in large numbers. About 250,000 people fled Rhodesia (now Zimbabwe) in the late 1970's, at the peak of the military actions that preceded independence. Since the end of the Vietnam War in 1975, hundreds of thousands have fled that country, by boat and by land. See generally Carlin, above, at 5–21. Professor Susan Akram examines the unique legal status of the Palestinian refugees and the corresponding protection gaps in the present international framework. See Susan M. Akram, *Palestinian Refugees and Their Legal Status: Rights, Politics, and Implications for a Just Solution*, 31/3 J. Palestine Studies No. 123, at 36 et seq. (2002).

In the United States, the seventh preference conditional entry program had become painfully inadequate. For one thing, the annual ceiling (17,400) was unrealistically low relative to the staggering size of the world refugee population. Of particular concern were the huge numbers of refugees from Indochina during the 1970's. Not surprisingly, Presidents largely bypassed the seventh preference conditional entry program and continued instead to use the parole power to admit large groups of refugees. Hundreds of thousands of Cubans, hundreds of thousands from Indochina, and several thousand Soviet and Eastern European refugees were paroled into the United States after 1965; other groups benefitted from ad hoc legislation. See United States Cong. Research Service, Report to Comm. on the Judiciary, United States Senate, Comm. Print, 96th Cong., 2d Sess. (1980) at 12–15; Deborah E. Anker & Michael H. Posner, *The Forty Year Crisis: A Legislative History of the Refugee Act of 1980,* 19 San Diego L.Rev. 9, 12–20 (1981). The central objective of the 1965 refugee reforms—to replace the use of the parole power with a more structured regime for admitting refugees—simply had not been attained.

The 1965 conditional entry program was inadequate for another more fundamental reason: It covered only those who were fleeing Communist-dominated countries or Middle East countries. Those who were fleeing repressive non-Communist governments (outside the Middle East) received no protection.

Aside from those deficiencies in the seventh preference provision, the continued use of the parole program left Congress with the same frustrations that had prompted it to enact the seventh preference in the first place—the unlimited executive discretion, the absence of a meaningful congressional role, and the uncertain consequences of parole for the individual.

These and other problems that will be discussed later led Congress to enact the first comprehensive refugee legislation in U.S. history. The Refugee Act of 1980, Pub.L. 96–212, 94 Stat. 102 (March 17, 1980), added several new provisions to the Immigration and Nationality Act and amended many others. It is now the principal domestic statutory law governing both overseas refugees and, as you will see in section B, noncitizens who have reached United States territory and seek either asylum or nonrefoulement.

The 1980 Act provided the first United States statutory definition of "refugee." The definition, which appears in INA § 101(a)(42), is modeled upon that of the 1951 Convention, as amended by the 1967 Protocol.[2] The

---

2. The Convention definition, however, extends only to those who are outside their countries of nationality. See 1951 Conven-

tion, art. I. The United States statutory definition, INA § 101(a)(42), omits that limitation.

statutory definition requires "persecution or a well-founded fear of persecution on account of race, religion, nationality, membership in a particular social group, or political opinion." By deleting all ideological and geographic limitations, the new definition addressed a crucial failing of the old seventh preference program. Because the refugee definition is also relevant to asylees, the various interpretation problems raised by section 101(a)(42) will be deferred to section B.

Under INA § 207(a), also added by the Refugee Act of 1980, the President makes an annual determination of how many refugees may be admitted in the upcoming fiscal year. The same Presidential Determination specifies how that total is to be allocated among refugees fleeing various countries and regions of the world. There are no upper or lower limits on the numbers the President may choose. Recognizing the sudden and unpredictable nature of refugee flows, Congress also authorized the President to provide additional slots if an "unforeseen emergency refugee situation" arises that cannot be accommodated by the originally announced quota. INA § 207(b). Not until 1999, when the world responded to the bloodshed in Kosovo, was the latter power ever exercised.

Before making any of those determinations the President must engage in "appropriate consultation" with Congress. INA §§ 207(a)(1,2,3), 207(b). The consultation requirement reflects Congress's dissatisfaction with its negligible role in many of the previous refugee admission programs and is spelled out in detail in INA § 207(d,e).

Subject to the Presidential Determinations of total worldwide ceilings and geographic distribution, the Secretary of Homeland Security may admit any refugee who is not "firmly resettled in any foreign country," is of "special humanitarian concern to the United States," and is "admissible" (with some exemptions from the admissibility requirement). INA § 207(c)(1). You will see more in section B on the meaning of "firmly resettled." As for admissibility, refugees are automatically exempted from certain exclusion grounds (labor certification, public charge, and required documents), and the Secretary has the discretion to waive most others. INA § 207(c)(3). Spouses and children accompanying or following to join qualifying refugees are admitted under the same criteria. INA § 207(c)(2). The Secretary may later terminate the refugee status of either the principal refugee or the spouse or child upon a determination that the principal refugee did not in fact meet the refugee definition at the time of admission. INA § 207(c)(4). Under INA § 209(a), a refugee whose status has not been terminated, and who is still admissible (with the help of the exemptions and waivers noted earlier) receives LPR status after one year. INA § 209(a).

Given the comprehensive nature of the process you have just read about, Congress wanted to make sure that process would actually be used. Consequently, it prohibited the Attorney General (now the Secretary) from *paroling* a refugee into the United States, absent "compelling reasons in the public interest with respect to that particular alien." INA § 212(d)(5)(B). Since the refugee definition does not encompass anyone fleeing only war or natural catastrophe, the prohibition does not affect the use of the parole power on behalf of those groups. But see section C below (temporary protected status).

The 1980 Act also established the Office of Refugee Resettlement, within the Department of HHS, and charged it with funding and administering various federal programs relating to resettlement. INA § 411. Within the State Department, the unit responsible for coordinating refugee policy is the Bureau of Population, Refugees, and Migration (PRM). The efforts of the federal government are supplemented by those of state and local governments and private voluntary agencies. See generally INA § 412.

You should now read INA §§ 101(a)(42), 207, 209(a,c), and 212(d)(5)(B).

———

The preceding passages outline the critical overseas refugee provisions of the 1980 Act. How has this program worked in practice? The chart below shows the Presidential authorizations for total refugee admissions for each fiscal year under the Refugee Act of 1980:

Fiscal Year	Presidential Authorizations[3]
1980	231,700
1981	217,000
1982	140,000
1983	90,000
1984	72,000
1985	70,000
1986	67,000
1987	70,000
1988	87,500
1989	116,500
1990	125,000
1991	131,000
1992	142,000
1993	132,000
1994	121,500
1995	112,000
1996	90,000
1997	78,000
1998	83,000
1999	91,000
2000	90,000
2001	80,000
2002	70,000
2003	70,000
2004	70,000
2005	70,000

3. For the 1980 and 1981 Presidential authorizations, see INS 1987 Statistical Yearbook, Table 25. For years 1982–87, see INS 1989 Statistical Yearbook, Table 26. For years 1988 through 1998, see U.S. Comm. for Refugees, Dec. 2000 Refugee Reports at 9. For fiscal years 1999 through 2003, see 2003 Yearbook of Immigration Statistics, Table 14 at 53. For fiscal year 2004, see 68 Fed. Reg. 63979 (Nov. 10, 2003). For fiscal year 2005, see 69 Fed. Reg. 60943 (Oct. 14, 2004). All

In scanning these figures, keep in mind that they are the *maximum* admissions authorized by the President. The Secretary of Homeland Security may approve any number up to those ceilings. Until September 11, 2001, the vast majority of the authorized numbers were actually assigned. But after the events of that day, the Bush Administration slowed the admission of overseas refugees to a trickle. As a result, only 18,652 of the 70,000 authorized for fiscal year 2002 were processed and approved for admission. 2003 Yearbook of Immigration Statistics, Table 14 at 53. In the following year, refugee advocates urged the President to ease the resulting backlog of refugee applicants by increasing the authorization for fiscal year 2003. Rejecting those pleas, the President authorized an even smaller number— 50,000—for fiscal year 2003 (not counting unallocated reserve, for which there is no federal funding), and of that number only 25,329 were approved for admission. *Id.* As the above chart shows, the Presidential authorizations remained at 70,000 for fiscal years 2004 and 2005 (again, including the 20,000 unallocated reserve), but in 2004 actual admissions increased to 52,875. U.S. Dept. of State, Press Statement 2004/1067 (Oct. 4, 2004). (Actual admissions include some refugees whose admissions were approved in prior years.)

To the extent that the Refugee Act of 1980 was meant to be the exclusive vehicle for admitting refugees, it has achieved only partial success. The Act was signed into law on March 17, 1980. Within weeks, the Mariel boatlift (see pages 156–58 above) was under way and more than 100,000 Cubans arrived at United States shores. During roughly the same time period, Haitians were fleeing to the United States in large numbers. Despite the express prohibition on paroling refugees, President Carter (after consulting with Congress) paroled the Cubans and the Haitians into the country. See 3 Gordon, Mailman & Yale–Loehr, § 33.01[4]. Special legislation eventually enabled them to become LPRs. IRCA § 202. The consultation with Congress in some ways might have made the President's action functionally equivalent to invoking the "unforeseen emergency" procedure of section 207(b), but the grant of parole rather than refugee status seems contrary to both the language and the spirit of the 1980 Act.

The so-called Lautenberg amendment to a 1990 foreign assistance appropriations bill eased the refugee status requirements for Soviet Jews, Soviet Evangelical Christians, and most Indochinese. Those individuals, if claiming persecution, need show only a "credible basis for concern about the possibility of such persecution." Pub. L. 101–167, §§ 599D, 599E, 103 Stat. 1195, 1261–64 (Nov. 21, 1989). That provision, now called the Spec-

---

figures represent the combined authorizations under INA §§ 207(a) (initial) with any mid-year adjustments, plus 207(b) (unforeseen emergencies). But NB: In fiscal years 2004 and 2005, the 70,000 authorizations each included a 20,000 "unallocated reserve" (i.e., an unfunded authorization not allocated to any specific country or region).

ter–Lautenberg amendment, has been renewed annually. At this writing its most recent version is the Consolidated Appropriations Act 2005, Pub. L. 108–447, 118 Stat. 2809, 3140–41, Div. F, § 213 (Dec. 8, 2004), which extends the provision to October 1, 2005 and adds persecuted Iranian religious minorities to the list of specially protected groups.

The larger goal of the 1980 Act—the elimination of foreign policy bias—is another story. In 1985, former United States Senator (and former U.S. Coordinator for Refugee Affairs) Dick Clark once estimated that "[n]o doubt close to 99 per cent of all the refugees who settled in the United States since World War II were persons fleeing communist governments." Foreword to Elizabeth Hull, Without Justice For All—The Constitutional Rights of Aliens ix (1985) (contrasting the admission of 40,000 Hungarians and, by that time, 750,000 Indochinese and 700,000 Cubans, with the refusal to allocate refugee slots to Chileans fleeing General Pinochet, or refugees from Haiti, El Salvador, or Guatemala). Many scholars have catalogued the vivid contrast between the generous admission of those fleeing Communism and the steadfast refusal to admit significant numbers of any other refugees. See, e.g., Hull, above, ch. 5; Gil Loescher & John A. Scanlan, Calculated Kindness—Refugees and America's Half–Open Door 1945–Present (1986). As you will see in section B, similar patterns dominated the adjudication of asylum claims during that period.

The Refugee Act of 1980 did not immediately alter these patterns. In every year from its adoption until the end of the Cold War, Presidents allocated almost the entire refugee quota to those who were fleeing communist countries (or occasionally other United States adversaries, such as Iran). The authorization for fiscal year 1991 was representative:

Africa	4,900
East Asia	52,000
Soviet Union	50,000
Eastern Europe	5,000
Near East/South Asia	6,000
Latin America/Caribbean	3,100
Not Designated (privately funded)	10,000
TOTAL (including 15,000 Amerasians)	131,000

55 Fed.Reg. 41979–80 (Oct. 17, 1991). The pattern might not be obvious on its face, but in 1989 virtually all the African refugees selected were from Ethiopia; almost all the East Asians were from Vietnam, Laos, and Kampuchea (formerly Cambodia); "Near East/South Asia" was reserved principally for Afghanistan and Iran; and the "Latin America/Caribbean" category was allotted almost entirely to Cuba and, until the recent change of government, Nicaragua. See INS 1989 Statistical Yearbook, Table 26. The stated legal basis for that pattern has been INA § 207(a)(3), which dictates that the admission of overseas refugees "be allocated among refugees *of special humanitarian concern to the United States*" (emphasis added).

After the almost complete collapse of Communism in 1989 and 1990, the numbers began to change, but not immediately. For several years the above patterns persisted. Gradually, however, the improved relations between the United States and both Communist and formerly Communist nations began to produce far lower allocations for the former Communist countries. But because United States refugee policy has been driven so strongly by Cold War politics, the net effect of the geopolitical changes was a decline in total United States refugee admissions, rather than a redistribution. As the chart above illustrates, total overseas refugee authorizations steadily dropped from 142,000 in 1992 to 78,000 in 1997. They have remained just below or just above that level ever since. For a thoughtful comment on the reactions of refugee-receiving states to the end of the Cold War, see Julie Mertus, *The State and the Post–Cold War Refugee Regime: New Models, New Questions*, 20 Michigan J. Int'l L. 59 (1998).

Many commentators have criticized the heavy influence of foreign policy on United States refugee selections. See, e.g., Joan Fitzpatrick & Robert Pauw, *Foreign Policy, Asylum, and Discretion*, 28 Willamette L.Rev. 751 (1992); Joyce A. Hughes, *Flight from Cuba*, 36 Calif. Western L. Rev. 39 (1999) (calling for foreign-policy-neutral refugee laws and an end to favoritism for Cubans); Hull, above; Stephen H. Legomsky, *The Making of United States Refugee Policy: Separation of Powers in the Post–Cold War Era*, 70 Washington L. Rev. 675 (1995); Loescher & Scanlan, above; see also Maryellen Fullerton, *Hungary, Refugees, and the Law of Return*, 8 Internat'l J. Refugee L. 499 (1996) (criticizing Hungary for using refugee program mainly as "law of return").

Once the President announces the total refugee quota and the regional or country breakdowns, the processing of individual applications takes place overseas. For this purpose the State Department and USCIS have developed, and periodically revise, a system of refugee priorities. For fiscal year 2005, priority 1 includes those refugees who are referred to the program by UNHCR, a U.S. embassy, or one of several designated NGOs because of "compelling" needs. Priority 2, assessed on a group basis, is for refugees of "special humanitarian concern" to the United States. These currently include certain groups of refugees processed in their countries of origin (the former Soviet Union, Cuba, and Vietnam), as well as miscellaneous other groups. And priority 3 is for nationals of designated countries who possess specified family relationships to previously admitted refugees. Once all priority 1 applicants have been processed, any remaining refugee authorizations are used for priority 2 applicants and then, to the extent available, for priority 3 applicants.

The processing is performed by specialized USCIS refugee adjudicators, see INA § 207(f), with help from UNHCR, the International Organization for Migration, various NGOs, the State Department, and the Dept. of Health and Human Services. For details on both the substantive priorities and the procedures for screening, admitting, and resettling overseas refugees in the United States, see United States Dept. of State, Dept. of Homeland Security, and Dept. of Health & Human Services, Proposed Refugee Admissions for Fiscal Year 2005, Report to the Congress (2004).

NOTES AND QUESTIONS

1.   Professor Suhrke thought wars of independence were essentially a thing of the past. Writing in 1983, she did not anticipate the upheavals in the former Soviet Union or Yugoslavia (or, perhaps, the ethnic bloodshed in Rwanda or the Sudan, or the independence movements in Kosovo, Chechnya, or East Timor). At this point, though, having read Professor Suhrke's analysis of the events that tend to stimulate refugee flows, would you predict an increase or a decrease in the world's refugee population in the coming years?

2.   After-the-fact responses to the problem of refugees in overseas camps have tended to fall into three categories: encouraging voluntary repatriation to the country from which the refugee fled; permanent stay in the refugee camp or elsewhere within the country in which that camp is located—i.e., "local integration" in the country of "first asylum;" and permanent resettlement in a third country. See also James C. Hathaway, *The Right of States to Repatriate Former Refugees*, 20 Ohio State J. Dispute Resolution 175 (2005) (criticizing UNHCR for failing to consider *mandatory* repatriation upon cessation of refugee status). First, are there practical mechanisms available to the world community or to individual nations to attack the root causes of refugee flows? Second, once a large refugee flow occurs, what practical considerations would you assume affect the selection among those options?

3.   Several leading commentators, finding the existing world refugee system inadequate on multiple fronts, have recently advocated multinational forms of protection, commonly known as "burden-sharing" or "responsibility-sharing." Peter Schuck, for example, argues for regional arrangements whereby states agree on refugee allocation criteria, delegate to an international agency the task of assigning quotas to the various signatories based on those criteria, try to recruit additional signatories, and freely trade quotas for money or other concessions. See Peter H. Schuck, *Refugee Burden–Sharing: A Modest Proposal*, 22 Yale J. Internat'l L. 243 (1997). James Hathaway and R. Alexander Neve argue that the leading causes of nations' increasing reluctance to admit refugees have been the perception that refugee programs can become back doors for voluntary migrants and a belief that the burdens have been unequal. Their blueprint calls not only for regional agreements, but also for other "interest-convergence group" initiatives. James C. Hathaway & R. Alexander Neve, *Making International Refugee Law Relevant Again: A Proposal for Collectivized and Solution-Oriented Protection*, 10 Harvard Human Rights J. 115 (1997). Both approaches are summarized, and then criticized for accepting cultural discrimination by states, in Satvinder Juss, *Toward a Morally Legitimate Form of Refugee Law: The Uses of Cultural Jurisprudence*, 11 Harvard Human Rights J. 311 (1998). For an innovative game theory approach to responsibility-sharing, see Gregor Noll, *Risky Games? A Theoretical Approach to Burden–Sharing in the Asylum Field*, 16 Internat'l J. Refugee L. 236 (2003).

Other prominent commentators agree that national procedures have impeded protection but reject both the premise that individualized adjudication is the culprit and the proffered solutions. See Deborah Anker, Joan Fitzpatrick & Andrew Shacknove, *Crisis and Cure: A Reply to Hathaway/Neve and Schuck*, 11 Harvard Human Rights J. 295 (1998). The U.S. Commission on Immigration Reform and many others have also urged the formation of regional "burden-sharing" schemes in which nations collectively provide temporary protection for non-Convention refugees. See U.S. Commission on Immigration Reform, U.S. Refugee Policy: Taking Leadership 20–25 (June 1997); Forced Migration Project, Open Society Institute, A Proposal to Establish a Temporary Refuge Scheme in the Caribbean Region for Refugee and Migration Emergencies (1995); Susan Martin, Andy Schoenholtz & Deborah Waller Meyers, *Temporary Protection: Towards a New Regional and Domestic Framework*, 12 Georgetown Immigration L.J. 543, 559–66 (1998). The subject is important enough that the Executive Committee of UNHCR (EXCOM) made it the 1998 annual theme. See 17 Refugee Survey Quarterly No. 4 at 1–221 (1998).

The UNHCR Director of International Protection lays out her three-pronged vision of the future shape of refugee protection in Erika Feller, *The Evolution of the International Refugee Protection Regime*, 5 Washington Univ. J. of L. & Policy 129 (2001). She urges reaffirmation of the 1951 Convention; a revisiting of some of the more restrictive interpretations that states have placed on it; and affirmative efforts to fill critical gaps that the Convention, even when liberally interpreted, leaves for the protection of highly endangered individuals and groups.

4.   The readings in this section reveal the powerful influence of ideology and foreign relations in United States refugee policy. Is there actually anything wrong with allowing such considerations to play a significant role? Argue both sides.

5.   Along similar lines, you have seen examples of ad hoc, country-specific refugee legislation (and executive parole) in response to particular refugee flows. What are the relative merits of generic and country-specific policies?

6.   How do you feel about the basic process of annual executive/legislative consultation followed by a Presidential determination of the numbers and categories of refugees to be admitted? Should the President's decision be subject to either one-house or two-house confirmation? Should the proportions of executive and legislative say in the final decision be altered in any other way? For an argument that an independent agency should make refugee selection policy decisions, see Stephen H. Legomsky, *The Making of United States Refugee Policy: Separation of Powers in the Post–Cold War Era*, 70 Wash.L.Rev. 675 (1995).

7.   The whole subject of refugee policy raises a fundamental question that, while worth noting now, will be deferred to section C of this chapter: Why confine the refugee definition to those who flee persecution when there are many other events—famine, natural catastrophe, and armed conflict—that also spur massive flights across national boundaries?

8.   One of the most wrenching of the world's refugee problems is the plight of "unaccompanied minors"—children who are fleeing either persecution or some event that does not qualify them for refugee status, and who are either orphaned or otherwise separated from their parents. Several commentators have provided thoughtful and sensitive treatments of this subject. See Jacqueline Bhabha, *Lone Travelers: Rights, Criminalization, and the Transnational Migration of Unaccompanied Children*, 7 Univ. Chicago L. School Roundtable 269 (2000); Michael A. Olivas, *"Breaking the Law" on Principle: An Essay on Lawyers' Dilemmas, Unpopular Causes, and Legal Regimes*, 52 Univ. Pittsburgh. L. Rev. 815, 820–35 (1991)(discussing lawyers' ethical responses to governments' treatment of unaccompanied refugee children); Michael A. Olivas, *Unaccompanied Refugee Children: Detention, Due Process, and Disgrace*, 2 Stanford L. & Policy Rev. 159 (1990); Daniel J. Steinbock, *The Admission of Unaccompanied Children into the United States*, 7 Yale L. & Policy Rev. 137 (1989); see generally Everett M. Ressler, Neil Boothby & Daniel J. Steinbock, Unaccompanied Children: Care and Protection in Wars, Natural Disasters, and Refugee Movements (1988). Children also face several forms of child-specific persecution and special problems in demonstrating even adult-style persecution. See Jacqueline Bhabha & Wendy A. Young, *Through a Child's Eyes: Protecting the Most Vulnerable Asylum Seekers*, 75 IR 757 (June 1, 1998).

9.   Refugees are generally eligible for adjustment of status to permanent residence after one year. Adjustment is an important rite of passage; it signifies an acceptance by both the refugee and the United States that resettlement here is now assumed to be permanent, not just a temporary haven pending improvement of conditions in the country of origin. How do you feel about the one-year waiting period? Would it be better simply to admit refugees as permanent residents right from the start? Or, if anything, should the waiting period be longer? See U.S. Commission on Immigration Reform, U.S. Refugee Policy: Taking Leadership 35–37 (June 1997) (urging elimination of one-year waiting period and immediate grant of permanent resident status); accord, David A. Martin, The United States Refugee Admission Program: Reforms for a New Era of Refugee Resettlement, § VII.E (2003) (report to DOS).

10.   The converse question is when refugee status should end. See Joan Fitzpatrick, *The End of Protection: Legal Standards for Cessation of Refugee Status*, 13 Georgetown Immigration L.J. 343 (1999).

11.   For a useful history of the European and African responses to refugee flows, see Isabelle R. Gunning, *Expanding the International Definition of Refugee: A Multicultural View*, 13 Fordham Int'l L.J. 35, 40–48 (1989–90).

12.   As noted earlier, the United States statutory definition of "refugee," unlike the definition in the 1951 Convention, extends to those who are still within their countries of origin. INA § 101(a)(42). In international law, those who otherwise meet the U.N. Convention definition of refugee except that they have not yet crossed an international border are usually called "internally displaced persons," or IDPs. Today, there are approxi-

mately 20–25 million IDPs in the world. See http://www.unhcr.org (under "Basic Facts"). Their problems can be just as serious as those faced by Convention refugees. For a lucid account by the Representative of the U.N. Secretary General for Internally Displaced Persons, see Francis Mading Deng, *The Global Challenge of Internal Displacement*, 5 Washington Univ. J. of L. & Policy 141 (2001). For additional helpful commentary, see Maryellen Fullerton & James A.R. Nafziger, *Draft Declaration on Internally Displaced Persons*, in Immigration Law Conference, Scholarship Panels Works in Progress 187–95 (1996) (members of, and reporting on, proposed declaration drafted by International Law Association's Committee on Internally Displaced Persons); International Law Association, Report of the Sixty–Ninth Conference at 791–832 (2000); Arthur C. Helton, *The CIS Migration Conference: A Chance to Prevent and Ameliorate Forced Movements of People in the Former Soviet Union*, 8 Internat'l J. Refugee L. 169 (1996); UNHCR Centre for Documentation & Research, *Internal Displacement in Africa*, 18 Refugee Survey Q., issue #1 (entire issue) (1999).

13. An excellent history of United States laws and policies governing Vietnamese refugees can be found in Bill Ong Hing, Making and Remaking Asian America Through Immigration Policy, 1850–1990, at 121–38 (1993). Professor Hing also describes the deportation, on criminal grounds, of Cambodian refugees who had been brought to the United States as young children. See Bill Ong Hing, *Detention to Deportation—Rethinking the Removal of Cambodian Refugees*, 38 U.C. Davis L. Rev. 891 (2005).

14. A modern problem of epic proportions is that of "secondary" refugee movements. Refugees today rarely proceed directly from their countries of origin to the countries where they seek permanent resettlement. When in danger, they are far more prone to seek the first port in a storm—typically a neighboring, third world country—and then, when circumstances permit, move on in search of more durable protection. The latter movements are usually called secondary movements, and permanent resettlement countries frequently look for ways to return the refugees to the "third countries" in which they enjoyed temporary refuge. The problem has become a prime subject of international debate. See generally Stephen H. Legomsky, *Secondary Refugee Movements and the Return of Asylum Seekers to Third Countries: The Meaning of Effective Protection*, 15 Internat'l J. Refugee L. 567 (2003) (consultant's report to UNHCR).

15. Another modern problem—exacerbated by September 11—is how to reconcile refugee admission and processing with national security (and the security of the refugees themselves). See generally Volker Türk, *Forced Migration and Security*, 15 Internat'l J. Refugee L. 113 (2003).

Section B. Asylum and Nonrefoulement

You have now read about refugees who are physically outside the United States. Here we consider those who have already reached United

States territory—either the border area or the interior—and who seek protection from persecution.

As pointed out at the beginning of this chapter, two entirely different remedies are potentially available to members of this latter group—asylum under INA § 208, which permits the person to remain in the United States at least temporarily and in most cases permanently, and nonrefoulement, a narrower remedy that prohibits forcible return to the country of persecution but not to third countries. In the United States, the statutory term for nonrefoulement is "withholding of removal." INA § 241(b)(3). The legal terminology is often inconsistent, however. The Justice Department regulations expressly use the word "asylum" in a generic sense to encompass both remedies (as well as a third remedy under the Convention Against Torture, discussed separately in section C.1 below). 8 C.F.R. § 208.1(a) (2004). The subsections that follow will contain detailed coverage of the substantive requirements and adjudication procedures for both asylum and withholding. Note now, however, that the application procedures for the two remedies are exactly the same. In fact, an application for asylum under section 208 is automatically treated as an application for withholding of removal under section 241(b)(3) in the event relief under section 208 is denied. 8 C.F.R. § 208.3(b) (2004).

Some basic background information: It is easiest to start with withholding of removal.[4] The concept first appeared in United States immigration law in 1950, when Congress prohibited the deportation "to any country in which the Attorney General shall find that such alien would be subjected to physical persecution." Internal Security Act of 1950, ch. 1024, § 23, 64 Stat. 987, 1010 (Sept. 23, 1950) (amending 1917 Act). When the Immigration and Nationality Act was passed in 1952, that provision was made discretionary rather than mandatory. Pub.L. 414, chap. 477, § 243(h), 66 Stat. 163, 214 (June 27, 1952). In 1965 Congress replaced the requirement of physical persecution, which had been interpreted by at least one court to require "confinement, torture, or death," see *Blazina v. Bouchard,* 286 F.2d 507, 511 (3d Cir.1961), with a requirement that the person "would be subject to persecution on account of race, religion, or political opinion." Pub.L. 89–236, § 11(f), 79 Stat. 911, 918 (Oct. 3, 1965).

In 1968 the United States acceded to the 1967 U.N. Protocol Relating to the Status of Refugees. By doing so, it became bound by the 1951 Convention. See 1967 Protocol, art. 1. Article 33.1 of the Convention, which is subject to certain exceptions, provides:

> 1. No Contracting State shall expel or return ("refouler") a refugee in any manner whatsoever to the frontiers of territories where his life or freedom would be threatened on account of his race, religion, nationality, membership of a particular social group or political opinion * * *.

4. For a succinct historical account of withholding of removal, see Elwin Griffith, *Deportation and the Refugee,* 1982 Michigan Yearbook Internat'l Legal Studies 125, 126–31. A more general description is Guy S. Goodwin–Gill, *Non–Refoulement and the New Asylum Seekers,* 26 Virginia J. Internat'l L. 899 (1986).

The United States provision, former INA § 243(h), was then less protective than the Convention. For one thing, section 243(h) applied only in deportation proceedings, not in exclusion proceedings. See *Leng May Ma v. Barber,* 357 U.S. 185, 78 S.Ct. 1072, 2 L.Ed.2d 1246 (1958); see also Ian Mackler & James K. Weeks, *The Fleeing Political Refugee's Final Hurdle—the Immigration and Nationality Act,* 5 No. Kentucky L. Rev. 9 (1978) (criticizing limitation to deportation proceedings). In addition, the list of persecution grounds omitted nationality and social group. Moreover, even when an applicant met the eligibility requirements, the Attorney General retained the discretion to deny relief.

These and other gaps led eventually to some important amendments. Twelve years after the United States agreed to follow the Convention provision on nonfoulement, the Refugee Act of 1980 brought United States statutory law into conformity with the Convention. IIRIRA § 305(a) changed the wording of the withholding provision slightly and moved it to INA § 241(b)(3). Subject to some significant exceptions that will be considered in section B.5 of this chapter, the withholding provision now reads:

> [The Secretary of Homeland Security] may not remove an alien to a country if the [Secretary] decides that the alien's life or freedom would be threatened in that country because of the alien's race, religion, nationality, membership in a particular social group, or political opinion.

INA § 241(b)(3).

Asylum, as noted previously, is further-reaching than withholding; it results in permission to remain, not just non-return to the country of persecution. Nothing in the 1951 Convention or 1967 Protocol obligates any nation to grant asylum, and until 1974 no United States statute or regulation expressly authorized it. The Attorney General sometimes used the parole power to accomplish what is now thought of as asylum. See Deborah E. Anker, *Discretionary Asylum: A Protection Remedy for Refugees Under the Refugee Act of 1980,* 28 Virginia J. Internat'l L. 1, 33 n.163 (1987); see also Elwin Griffith, *Asylum and Withholding of Deportation— Challenges to the Alien After the Refugee Act of 1980,* 12 Loyola L.A. Internat'l & Comp. L.J. 515, 518–19 (1990). In 1974 the Justice Department issued regulations providing asylum criteria and procedures, 39 Fed.Reg. 28439 (Aug. 1, 1974), but not until 1980 did asylum receive statutory recognition. INA § 208, added by the Refugee Act of 1980, Pub. L. 96–212, § 201(b), 94 Stat. 102, 103, 105 (Mar. 17, 1980), now authorizes the Secretary of Homeland Security, in his or her discretion, to grant asylum to any "refugee" who is "physically present in the United States or arrives in the United States," with some exceptions.

At this time you should read INA §§ 208 and 209(b, c). You might wish also to re-read the refugee definition in INA § 101(a)(42).

Subject again to some exceptions, the statute does not specify the procedure by which the Secretary is to adjudicate claims of asylum or withholding. The DHS and DOJ regulations perform that function. They provide two different procedures, depending on the timing of the application.

If DHS has already initiated removal proceedings, the application is filed with the immigration judge. 8 C.F.R. § 208.4(b)(3) (2004). The resulting decision whether to order removal is appealable to the BIA, *id.* § 1003.1(b)(3), and, if the applicant wishes, reviewable in court, INA § 242.

If removal proceedings have not yet been instituted, one may take the initiative and apply to USCIS (not to EOIR). 8 C.F.R. § 208.4(b)(1) (2004). These claims are commonly called "affirmative" applications, or "walk-ins." They are adjudicated by geographically dispersed USCIS "asylum officers," who have received specialized training in international law and country conditions. *Id.* § 208.1(b).

Except in "expedited removal" cases (discussed below), the applicant receives a "nonadversarial" interview. The applicant has the right to counsel and may submit affidavits of witnesses and other documents. 8 C.F.R. § 208.9(b) (2004). The asylum officer either grants asylum or refers the case to an immigration judge for removal proceedings (with some exceptions). *Id.* § 208.14(b,c). In the latter event, the person may renew the application de novo before the immigration judge. *Id.* § 208.14(a). The decision of the immigration judge is subject to both a BIA appeal and judicial review under the usual rules.

As earlier readings noted, the 1951 Convention recognized more than the right not to be refouled to one's persecutors. The states parties also promised to respect a whole range of other refugee rights. You should skim the Convention now to get a sense of the subjects they cover.

When the United States ratified the 1967 Protocol, it became derivatively bound by the 1951 Convention. Thus, international law obligates the United States to respect all the refugee rights that the Convention recognizes.

But how the United States internally allocates the responsibility for implementing those international legal obligations is a matter of domestic United States law. Domestic United States law, in turn, distinguishes those international agreements that are "self-executing" from those that are not. A self-executing agreement is one that creates binding *internal* law without the need for any subsequent implementing legislation. A treaty that is not self-executing still creates binding *international* legal obligations for all the states parties, but those obligations will not be enforceable in United States courts until Congress enacts the necessary implementing legislation. Even then, the resulting legal obligations normally flow from that statute, not from the treaty. To determine whether a treaty is self-executing, United States courts have considered the intentions of the states parties, executive branch statements made in connection with the United States treaty ratification process, and other factors. See generally Thomas Buergenthal & Sean D. Murphy, Public International Law in a Nutshell 190–93 (3d ed. 2002).

The United States courts have typically viewed the 1967 Protocol as being *non*-self-executing. See generally Stanley Mailman & Stephen Yale–Loehr, *Detaining and Criminalizing Asylum Seekers*, 8 BIB 764, 765–66 (May 1, 2003). And in *Matter of D–J-*, 23 I. & N. Dec. 572 (A.G. 2003), a case involving the selective detention of Haitian asylum seekers, the Attorney General recently fended off arguments rooted in the 1967 Protocol by declaring the Protocol non-self-executing (and refraining from discussion of whether U.S. policy comported with the Protocol). *Id.* at 584–85 n.8. Although a non-self-executing treaty cannot be enforced *in a U.S. domestic court*, it is not clear why the executive branch would not feel bound by U.S. treaty obligations on the *international* plane (and, therefore, why it would think that calling the treaty non-self-executing ends the inquiry).

This issue—the extent to which obligations created by the 1951 Convention and 1967 Protocol are enforceable in United States courts—has taken on new importance in recent years. While the Refugee Act of 1980 addresses the nonrefoulement obligation embodied in article 33 of the Convention, it does not attempt to implement any of the other Convention rights. Arguments that U.S. policy falls short of various Convention obligations have been advanced in several contexts other than nonrefoulement. (Some would argue that even the U.S. domestic law on nonrefoulement is deficient. See especially the difficult issues on standards of proof, discussed in connection with the *Stevic* decision on pages 1050–54 below, and on the interpretations of the exceptions to eligibility, pages 1067–77.) Aside from nonrefoulement, issues have arisen concerning (a) whether United States practices on the detention of asylum seekers comport with article 26 (freedom of movement) and article 31 (which prohibits penalties for illegal entry under certain circumstances); and (b) whether the criminal prosecutions of asylum seekers for entering the United States with false documents comport with article 31. These issues are taken up on pages 1106–10 below.

The pages that follow explore in greater depth some of the many controversial issues that asylum and withholding have generated. This material is difficult to compartmentalize, both because the various requirements for asylum under INA § 208 overlap with each other, and also because some of these elements have counterparts in INA § 241(b)(3) (withholding). Nonetheless, to keep the discussion manageable, this section will be organized around certain key elements of asylum or withholding or both. You should use these elements to separate the issues while keeping in mind that the compartments are not airtight.

1. PERSECUTION OR FEAR OF PERSECUTION

Matter of Acosta

Board of Immigration Appeals, 1985.
19 I. & N. Dec. 211.

* * *

The respondent is a 36–year-old male native and citizen of El Salvador. In a deportation hearing held before an immigration judge over the course of 2 days in July and August 1983, the respondent conceded his deportability for entering the United States without inspection and accordingly was found deportable as charged. The respondent sought relief from deportation by applying for a discretionary grant of asylum pursuant to section 208 of the Act, and for mandatory withholding of deportation to El Salvador pursuant to section 243(h) of the Act.[a] In an oral decision, the immigration judge denied the respondent's applications for these two forms of relief finding that he had failed to meet his burden of proof for such relief. It is this finding that the respondent has challenged on appeal.

* * *

In order to prove the facts underlying his applications for asylum and withholding of deportation, the respondent testified, and attested in an affidavit attached to his asylum application, to the following facts. In 1976 he, along with several other taxi drivers, founded COTAXI, a cooperative organization of taxi drivers of about 150 members. COTAXI was designed to enable its members to contribute the money they earned toward the purchase of their taxis. It was one of five taxi cooperatives in the city of San Salvador and one of many taxi cooperatives throughout the country of El Salvador. Between 1978 and 1981, the respondent held three management positions with COTAXI, the duties of which he described in detail, and his last position with the cooperative was that of general manager. He held that position from 1979 through February or March of 1981. During the time he was the general manager of COTAXI, the respondent continued on the weekends to work as a taxi driver.

Starting around 1978, COTAXI and its drivers began receiving phone calls and notes requesting them to participate in work stoppages. The requests were anonymous but the respondent and the other members of COTAXI believed them to be from anti-government guerrillas who had targeted small businesses in the transportation industry for work stoppages, in hopes of damaging El Salvador's economy. COTAXI's board of directors refused to comply with the requests because its members wished to keep working, and as a result COTAXI received threats of retaliation. Over the course of several years, COTAXI was threatened about 15 times. The other taxi cooperatives in the city also received similar threats.

Beginning in about 1979, taxis were seized and burned, or used as barricades, and COTAXI drivers were assaulted or killed. Ultimately, five members of COTAXI were killed in their taxis by unknown persons. Three of the COTAXI drivers who were killed were friends of the respondent and, like him, had been founders and officers of COTAXI. Each was killed after receiving an anonymous note threatening his life. One of these drivers, who died from injuries he sustained when he crashed his cab in order to avoid being shot by his passengers, told his friends before he died that three men

---

a. Now INA § 241(b)(3) and called "withholding of *removal*."—Ed.

identifying themselves as guerrillas had jumped into his taxi, demanded possession of his car, and announced they were going to kill him.

During January and February 1981, the respondent received three anonymous notes threatening his life. The first note, which was slipped through the window of his taxi and was addressed to the manager of COTAXI, stated: "Your turn has come, because you are a traitor." The second note, which was also put on the respondent's car, was directed to "the driver of Taxi No. 95," which was the car owned by the respondent, and warned: "You are on the black list." The third note was placed on the respondent's car in front of his home, was addressed to the manager of COTAXI, and stated: "We are going to execute you as a traitor." In February 1981, the respondent was beaten in his cab by three men who then warned him not to call the police and took his taxi. The respondent is of the opinion that the men who threatened his life and assaulted him were guerrillas who were seeking to disrupt transportation services in the city of San Salvador. He also has the impression, however, that COTAXI was not favored by some government officials because they viewed the cooperative as being too socialistic.

After being assaulted and receiving the three threatening notes, the respondent left El Salvador because he feared for his life. He declared at the hearing that he would not work as a taxi driver if he returned to El Salvador because he understands that there is little work for taxi drivers now. He explained that the people are too poor to call taxis. Additionally, he stated that the terrorists are no longer active.

* * *

* * * [W]e find the respondent's testimony, which was corroborated by other objective evidence in the record, to be worthy of belief. It remains to be determined, however, whether the respondent's facts are sufficient to meet the statutory standards of eligibility for asylum and withholding of deportation.

THE STATUTORY STANDARD FOR ASYLUM

A grant of asylum is a matter of discretion. However, an alien is eligible for a favorable exercise of discretion only if he qualifies as a "refugee" under section 101(a)(42)(A) of the Act. * * * The pertinent portion of section 101(a)(42) provides as follows:

> The term "refugee" means (A) any person who is outside any country of such person's nationality or, in the case of a person having no nationality, is outside any country in which such person last habitually resided, and who is unable or unwilling to return to, and is unable or unwilling to avail himself or herself of the protection of, that country because of persecution or a well-founded fear of persecution on account of race, religion, nationality, membership in a particular social group, or political opinion.
> * * *

This section creates four separate elements that must be satisfied before an alien qualifies as a refugee: (1) the alien must have a "fear" of "persecution"; (2) the fear must be "well-founded"; (3) the persecution feared must be "on account of race, religion, nationality, membership in a particular social group, or political opinion"; and (4) the alien must be unable or unwilling to return to his country of nationality or to the country in which he last habitually resided because of persecution or his well-founded fear of persecution.

(1) *The alien must have a "fear" of "persecution."*

Initially, we note that Congress added the elements in the definition of a refugee to our law by means of the Refugee Act of 1980. In so doing Congress intended to conform the Immigration and Nationality Act to the United Nations Protocol Relating to the Status of Refugees, Jan. 31, 1967 ("the Protocol"), to which the United States had acceded in 1968. Article 1.2 of the Protocol defines a refugee as one who:

> owing to well-founded fear of being persecuted for reasons of race, religion, nationality, membership of a particular social group or political opinion, is outside the country of his nationality and is unable or, owing to such fear, is unwilling to avail himself of the protection of that country; or who, not having a nationality and being outside the country of his former habitual residence, is unable or, owing to such fear, is unwilling to return to it.

Since Congress intended the definition of a refugee in section 101(a)(42)(A) of the Act to conform to the Protocol, it is appropriate for us to consider various international interpretations of that agreement. However, these interpretations are not binding upon us in construing the elements created by section 101(a)(42)(A) of the Act, for the determination of who should be considered a refugee is ultimately left by the Protocol to each state in whose territory a refugee finds himself.

In adding the definition of a refugee to the Act, Congress did not identify what one must show in order to establish a "fear of persecution." The phrase "fear of persecution" is not new to the Act. Prior to 1980, it appeared in former section 203(a)(7), which provided for the conditional admission to the United States of certain aliens if they fled a country because of persecution or "fear of persecution." Former section 203(a)(7) was applied by Service officers in allocating visas to immigrants abroad and by district directors in determining eligibility for adjustment of status under section 245 of the Act. Immigration judges and the Board were without authority to decide applications brought under former section 203(a)(7) and accordingly the meaning of the phrase "fear of persecution" was never directly at issue, or construed, in proceedings before the Board.

"Fear" is a subjective condition, an emotion characterized by the anticipation or awareness of danger. *Webster's Third New International Dictionary* 831 (16th ed. 1971). The Office of the United Nations High Commissioner for Refugees (UNHCR) has suggested in the *Handbook* that the definition of a refugee found in the Protocol requires fear to be a person's primary motivation for seeking refugee status. *See Handbook, supra,* at 11–12. While we do not consider the UNHCR's position in the *Handbook* to be controlling, the *Handbook* nevertheless is a useful tool to the extent that it provides us with one internationally recognized interpretation of the Protocol.

Given the prominence of the word "fear" in the definition of a refugee created by Congress, and given the *Handbook's* persuasive assessment in this instance that "fear" should be a refugee's primary motivation, we conclude that an alien seeking to qualify under section 101(a)(42)(A) of the Act must demonstrate that his primary motivation for requesting refuge in the United States is "fear," *i.e.,* a genuine apprehension or awareness of danger in another country. No other motivation, such as dissent or disagreement with the conditions in another country or a desire to experience greater economic advantage or personal freedom in the United States, satisfies the definition of a refugee created in the Act.

Prior to 1980, "persecution" was construed to mean either a threat to the life or freedom of, or the infliction of suffering or harm upon, those who differ in a way regarded as offensive. The harm or suffering inflicted could consist of confinement or torture. It also could consist of economic deprivation or restrictions so severe that they constitute a threat to an individual's life or freedom. Generally harsh conditions shared by many other persons did not amount to persecution. Prosecution for violating travel restrictions and laws of general applicability did not constitute persecution, unless the punishment was imposed for invidious reasons.

* * * [H]arm or suffering had to be inflicted either by the government of a country or by persons or an organization that the government was unable or unwilling to control.

* * *

As was the case prior to enactment of the Refugee Act, "persecution" as used in section 101(a)(42)(A) clearly contemplates that harm or suffering must be inflicted upon an individual in order to punish him for possessing a belief or characteristic a persecutor seeks to overcome. The word does not embrace harm arising out of civil strife or anarchy. In fact, Congress specifically rejected a definition of a refugee that would have included "displaced persons," *i.e.,* those who flee harm generated by military or civil disturbances. This construction is consistent with the international interpretation of "refugee" under the Protocol, for that term does not include persons who are displaced by civil or military strife in their countries of origin.

In the case before us, we find that the respondent has adequately established that his primary motivation for seeking asylum is fear of persecution. We must now consider whether it has been demonstrated that this fear is well founded and whether the other elements necessary to establish eligibility for asylum have been satisfied.

(2) *The fear of persecution must be "well-founded."*

[This subsection, which discusses the phrase "well-founded fear" and compares it to the showing required under former INA § 243(h), now 241(b)(3) (withholding of removal), is omitted because it has been superseded by the developments taken up on pages 899–920 below.—Ed.]

* * *

In the case before us, the respondent claims he fears persecution at the hands of two groups: the government and the guerrillas. * * * This means that he must demonstrate that (1) he possesses characteristics the government or the guerrillas seek to overcome by means of punishment of some sort; (2) the government or the guerrillas are aware or could easily[b] become aware that he possesses these characteristics; (3) the government or the guerrillas have the capability of punishing him; and (4) the government and the guerrillas have the inclination to punish him.

The respondent's fear of persecution by the government has no basis whatsoever in either his personal experiences or in other external events. To the contrary, by the respondent's own admission, this fear is based solely on his impression that some officials in the government may have viewed COTAXI as being too socialistic. This purely subjective impression is not sufficient to show a well-founded fear of persecution by the government.

In addition, whatever the facts may have been prior to the respondent's departure from El Salvador, those facts have changed significantly since 1981. Most importantly, the respondent admitted that he does not intend to work as a taxi driver upon his return to El Salvador. The respondent's facts do not show that the persecution of taxi drivers continued even after they stopped working as drivers. Furthermore, the respondent testified that the guerrillas' strength has diminished significantly in El Salvador since 1981. For these reasons, the respondent has not shown that at the present time he possesses characteristics the guerrillas seek to overcome or that the guerrillas have the inclination to punish him. Thus, * * * his fear of persecution upon deportation has not been shown to be "well-founded."

(3) *The persecution feared must be "on account of race, religion, nationality, membership in a particular social group, or political opinion."*

[In this section of its opinion the BIA holds that, even if Acosta had a well-founded fear of persecution, it would not be on account of either political opinion or membership in a particular social group. This subject is taken up in chapter 11, §§ B.2(b, c) below.—Ed.]

* * *

(4) *The alien must be unable or unwilling to return to his country of nationality or to the country in which he last habitually resided because of persecution or his well-founded fear of persecution.*

---

b. In *Matter of Mogharrabi,* 19 I. & N. Dec. 439 (BIA 1987), the Board amended this description by deleting the word "easily."— Ed.

Traditionally, a refugee has been an individual in whose case the bonds of trust, loyalty, protection, and assistance existing between a citizen and his country have been broken and have been replaced by the relation of an oppressor to a victim. Thus, inherent in refugee status is the concept that an individual requires international protection because his country of origin or of habitual residence is no longer safe for him. We consider this concept to be expressed, in part, by the requirement in the Act and the Protocol that a refugee must be unable or unwilling to return to a particular "country." *See* section 101(a)(42)(A) of the Act. We construe this requirement to mean that an alien seeking to meet the definition of a refugee must do more than show a well-founded fear of persecution in a particular place or abode within a country—he must show that the threat of persecution exists for him country-wide.

In the respondent's case, the facts show that taxi drivers in the city of San Salvador were threatened with persecution by the leftist guerrillas. However, the facts do not show that this threat existed in other cities in El Salvador. It may be the respondent could have avoided persecution by moving to another city in that country.[14] In any event, the respondent's facts did not demonstrate that the guerrillas' persecution of taxi drivers occurred throughout the country of El Salvador. Accordingly, the respondent did not meet this element of the standard for asylum.

In summary, the respondent's facts fail to show that (1) his present fear of persecution by the government and the guerrillas is "well-founded"; (2) the persecution he fears is on account of one of the five grounds specified in the Act; and (3) he is unable to return to the country of El Salvador, as opposed to a particular place in that country, because of persecution. Thus, he has not met three of the four elements in the statutory definition of a refugee created by section 101(a)(42)(A) of the Act. Accordingly, the respondent has not shown he is eligible for a grant of asylum.

[For similar reasons the Board holds Acosta ineligible for withholding.—Ed.]

* * *

NOTES AND QUESTIONS

1. The "refugee" definition contained in INA § 101(a)(42) requires "persecution *or* a well-founded fear of persecution" (emphasis added). There is one common situation in which the disjunctive takes on particular importance. A person who has already suffered persecution in a given country, and who as a result is unwilling to return to that country, qualifies as a refugee even if a change in conditions has eliminated any well-founded fear of future persecution. *Matter of Chen,* 20 I. & N.Dec. 16

---

14. It is unfortunate when persons may be obliged to give up their jobs and leave their homes as a result of fear. But that is not the issue here. The issue is, once that decision is made, does an individual have the right to come to the United States rather than to move elsewhere in his home country.

(BIA 1989); accord, *Desir v. Ilchert,* 840 F.2d 723, 729 (9th Cir.1988). See also 1951 Convention, art. 1(C)(5), as interpreted by UNHCR Handbook, para. 136. That does not mean relief will ultimately be granted; additional barriers to claims based solely on past persecution are considered on pages 1055–56 below.

More typical, though, is a claim like that in *Acosta,* based on a "fear" of future persecution. The BIA cites pages 11–12 of the UNHCR Handbook for the proposition that the fear must be "a person's primary motivation for seeking refugee status."

There actually is nothing relevant on page 11 of the Handbook, but paragraph 41, on page 12, deals with ways to assess the applicant's credibility and requires the factfinder to consider "everything that may serve to indicate that the predominant motive * * * is fear." Paragraph 39, at 12, however, states expressly that all reasons for escape other than persecution are simply "irrelevant" to the refugee definition. It adds that victims of other fates are ruled out "unless they *also*" fear persecution (emphasis in original). This language does not require that they fear persecution *more* than they fear anything else. The UNHCR Handbook, the sole source on which the BIA bases its conclusion, is thus ambiguous at best on this point.

In contrast to *Acosta,* see *Osorio v. INS,* 18 F.3d 1017 (2d Cir. 1994). There the court held that a person who has a well-founded fear of persecution on account of political opinion does not become ineligible for asylum just because the person additionally fears economic hardship.

As a matter of policy, why insist that the fear be the "primary" motivation? Is that interpretation dictated by (or consistent with) the literal statutory wording? What if an applicant is equally fearful of persecution and starvation? Or suppose an applicant believes that, if returned home, she would stand a 60% chance of being persecuted and a 90% chance of starving to death because of widespread famine. Could the "primary" motivation for this person's fear be said to be persecution? If not, is she really *less* worthy of relief than, say, one who believes there would be a 60% chance of persecution and *no* significant chance of starvation?

2.   A recent gathering of refugee experts at the University of Michigan Law School has concluded that the phrase "well-founded fear," while clearly requiring an objective showing, does not require actual *subjective* fear. The applicant need not prove, in other words, that he or she actually fears persecution; it is enough that, based on objective evaluation of the risk, there is reason to expect persecution. The analysis, based both on the text of the 1951 Convention and the policies underlying it, appears in Third Colloquium on Challenges in International Refugee Law, *The Michigan Guidelines on Well–Founded Fear*, 26 Michigan J. Internat'l L. 492 (2005) and James C. Hathaway & William S. Hicks, *Is There a Subjective Element in the Refugee Convention's Requirement of "Well–Founded Fear?,"* 26 Michigan J. Internat'l L. 505 (2005).

3.   A much more common problem is the meaning of the word "persecution." This is, as one of the foremost refugee authorities has put it, "the most substantial barrier to eligibility for many refugee claimants." Arthur C. Helton, *Persecution on Account of Membership in a Social Group as a Basis for Refugee Status,* 15 Columbia Human Rights L. Rev. 39, 56 (1983). The term "persecution" is not defined in the 1951 Convention or in the United States statute.

In the excerpt that you read, the Board in *Acosta* relies on an understanding expressed in the congressional committee reports that accompanied the Refugee Act of 1980. The committee assumed, as the Board does in *Acosta*, that "persecution" requires "either a threat to the life or freedom of, or the infliction of suffering or harm upon, those who differ in a way regarded as offensive." The Board adds that the term "clearly contemplates that harm or suffering must be inflicted upon an individual in order to punish him for possessing a belief or characteristic a persecutor seeks to overcome." (The punishment issue is discussed further in item 7 below.)

Other authorities have suggested different definitions. The Justice Department's proposed asylum regulations would define "persecution" as "the infliction of objectively serious harm or suffering that is subjectively experienced as serious harm or suffering by the applicant, regardless of whether the persecutor intends to cause harm." 65 Fed Reg. 76588, 76597 (Dec. 7, 2000). The proposed provision then adds that the home government must be either the party that is inflicting the harm or unwilling or unable to control a private actor who is inflicting it. The problem of the non-state actor has particular importance in the context of gender-based persecution and is explored more fully on pages 1025–37 below.

Professor Ryan Goodman was one of the first to propose linking the substantive content of "persecution" to international human rights norms. Writing while a student, and drawing insightfully on both historical evidence and contemporary policy norms, Goodman argued that violation of international human rights law should be a sufficient, though not a necessary, condition for characterizing behavior as persecution for purposes of refugee claims. See Ryan Goodman, Note, *The Incorporation of International Human Rights Standards into Sexual Orientation Asylum Claims: Cases of Involuntary "Medical" Intervention,* 105 Yale L.J. 255 (1995); see especially *id.* at 263 n.47. The Goodman model has particular potential for sexual orientation persecution claims, especially those that involve "medical" intervention to "cure" the victim's homosexuality. For discussion of those issues, see page 994 below.

Professor James Hathaway has offered a refinement of that approach. He has suggested linking the definition of "persecution" only to violations of "core" human rights. See James C. Hathaway, *The Relationship Between Human Rights and Refugee Law: What Refugee Law Judges Can Contribute,* 8 Human Rights & Refugee L. 80 (1998); see also James C. Hathaway, The Law of Refugee Status 104–05 (1991); Joan Fitzpatrick, *Human Rights and Forced Displacement: Converging Standards,* in Anne F. Bayefsky & Joan Fitzpatrick, Human Rights and Forced Displacement, 4 Refugees &

Human Rights 3 (2000). Generally accepting a human rights-based definition, but inclined to confine the human rights core more narrowly than Hathaway does, is David A. Martin, Book Review, *The Law of Refugee Status*, 87 Amer. J. Internat'l L. 348, 349–50 (1993).

You will see these formulations again as you consider some of the more specific issues raised by the "persecution" definition in the discussion below. See also the thoughtful exposition of this issue by T. Alexander Aleinikoff, *The Meaning of "Persecution" in United States Asylum Law*, 3 Internat'l J. Refugee L. 5 (1991).

4.   How individualized does an act have to be in order to constitute persecution? The BIA in *Acosta* says: "Generally harsh conditions shared by many other persons did not amount to persecution." (The Board is speaking in the past tense, but it holds later that this pre–1980 interpretation still stands.) Many courts have similarly emphasized the need for some sort of individual targeting. See, e.g., *Sayaxing v. INS*, 179 F.3d 515, 519, 520 (7th Cir. 1999); see also the cases discussed in Maureen Graves, *From Definition to Exploration: Social Groups and Political Asylum Eligibility*, 20 San Diego L.Rev. 740, 806–15 (1989).

Sometimes a court that expresses a singling-out requirement means nothing more than that exposure to the general dangers of war or other strife is not persecution. When that is all that is meant, the notion is probably innocuous as a statutory interpretation matter. If the only danger is that the person might get caught in the cross-fire, then he or she would be ineligible for asylum in any event because the consequence could not be said to occur on account of the victim's race, religion, etc. You will see more on that in section C.

Some courts, however, have made clear that they had in mind a more significant limitation. Some denied asylum even to applicants who had received personalized threats, on the ground that the threatened harm was too commonplace in the particular country. See Graves, above, at 806–08 (citing several examples). In *Bolanos–Hernandez v. INS*, 767 F.2d 1277 (9th Cir.1984), a former Salvadoran soldier and police officer claimed asylum on the basis that the guerrillas had threatened to kill him if he did not join their forces or leave the country. The guerrillas had already killed five of the claimant's friends and had similarly threatened and possibly killed the claimant's brother. The BIA nonetheless denied asylum on the ground that the applicant had not adequately "distinguished his situation from that of other Salvadorans." *Id.* at 1280. The BIA found the threat merely "representative of the general conditions in El Salvador." *Id.* at 1284. The Ninth Circuit reversed, holding that general evidence of violence, while not in itself sufficient to establish persecution, does not *negate* persecution when the applicant has also received an individualized threat; if anything, the court pointed out, general violence makes the specific threat more credible. *Id.* at 1284–85. Accord, *Hernandez–Ortiz v. INS*, 777 F.2d 509, 515 (9th Cir.1985). The leading treatise on United States asylum law concludes that the approach of rejecting a claim solely because many others face similar threats has now been "firmly rejected." See Anker at 69–72.

Should "persecution" be interpreted to require a threat appreciably distinct from that faced by a large segment of the particular country's population? See Graves, above, at 806–15.

5. A different, albeit related, issue is how to prove a (well-founded) fear of persecution in cases where an entire identifiable group is persecuted in a given country. The Justice Department regulations provide:

> In evaluating whether the applicant has sustained the burden of proving that he or she has a well-founded fear of persecution, the asylum officer or immigration judge shall not require the applicant to provide evidence that there is a real possibility he or she would be singled out individually for persecution if (A) The applicant establishes that there is a pattern or practice in his or her country of nationality or, if stateless, his or her last habitual residence, of persecution of a group of persons similarly situated to the applicant on account of race, religion, nationality, membership in a particular social group, or political opinion; and (B) The applicant establishes his or her own inclusion in, and identification with, such group of persons such that his or her fear of persecution upon return is reasonable.

8 C.F.R. § 208.13(b)(2)(iii) (2004); see also *id.* § 208.16(b)(2) (analogous provision for withholding). Under these provisions, does it matter how broad a segment of the population the particular group comprises? Does it matter whether there are other classes, of which the applicant is not a member, who suffer similar persecution?

6. Sometimes a facially neutral law or policy has a disproportionate adverse impact on a particular group. A military draft that contains no exemption for conscientious objectors poses particular problems for members of certain religions, such as Quakers or Jehovah's Witnesses. Dress requirements for women in some Muslim countries, with severe penalties for violators, disproportionately affect those Muslim women whose religious beliefs do not require the prescribed dress. Should those practices be held to constitute persecution? See *Martirosyan v. INS*, 229 F.3d 903, 909 (9th Cir. 2000); *Canas–Segovia v. INS,* 970 F.2d 599 (9th Cir.1992), on remand from *INS v. Canas–Segovia,* 502 U.S. 1086, 112 S.Ct. 1152, 117 L.Ed.2d 401 (1992). These issues are thoughtfully discussed in Karen Musalo, *Swords into Ploughshares: Why the United States Should Provide Refuge To Young Men Who Refuse to Bear Arms for Reasons of Conscience,* 26 San Diego L. Rev. 849 (1989).

7. In defining "persecution," the BIA in *Acosta* says that the "harm or suffering must be inflicted upon an individual *in order to punish him* . . . " [emphasis added]. The Ninth Circuit expressly rejected that view in *Pitcherskaia v. INS,* 118 F.3d 641 (9th Cir.1997). There, the Russian government purportedly attempted to "cure" homosexuality by forcible institutionalization, electroshock treatments, and drug injections. The court held this to be persecution. The plaintiff was not required to prove that the Russian government wished to harm or punish her. See Goodman, item 3 above, and the further discussion of *Pitcherskaia* and Professor

Goodman's approach, on page 994 below. The same holding can be inferred from *Matter of Kasinga*, 21 I. & N. Dec. 357 (BIA en banc 1996) (female genital mutilation held to be persecution even though it is not meant to be "punishment"), discussed in the social group materials below. Because military conscription ordinarily is not designed to be punishment, a further illustration is the line of cases that regard conscription into a military force whose conduct is condemned by the international community as persecution. See the *Izatula* case, reproduced below. The persecution definition contained in the proposed regulations would make explicit that persecution does not require an intent to harm or punish. See 65 Fed. Reg. 76588, 76590 (commentary), 76597 (Dec. 7, 2000).

8.   The word "persecution" usually conjures up images of execution, torture, confinement, threats, or perhaps a steady though less definable harassment. But do the consequences the applicant faces have to reach any particular level of severity in order to constitute persecution? One can hypothesize relatively minor deprivations aimed selectively at particular religious groups or nationalities. Suppose a government imposes on members of a particular religion a tax that is 1% higher than that applicable to the rest of the population, just to "make a point." Should this otherwise minor discriminatory practice be viewed as persecution on the basis of religion? If members of a private organization that the government is unable to control (*Acosta* points out such organizations can be the source of persecution) are systematically rude to racial minorities in shops and other public places, should a member of a minority group in that country receive asylum in the United States? See, e.g., *Sharif v. INS*, 87 F.3d 932, 935 (7th Cir. 1996) (persecution requires "death, imprisonment, or the infliction of substantial harm or suffering"); *Kovac v. INS*, 407 F.2d 102, 107 (9th Cir.1969) ("minor disadvantage or trivial inconvenience" not enough, but "substantial economic disadvantage" imposed on account of race, etc., can suffice). In *Guinac v. INS*, 179 F.3d 1156 (9th Cir. 1999), an indigenous Guatemalan man had been routinely beaten, and threatened with death, by his military superiors, because of his race. The BIA denied asylum, characterizing the beatings and threats as mere "discrimination" rather than "persecution." The Ninth Circuit reversed.

It is generally assumed that some threshold level of seriousness is needed for harm to constitute "persecution." One issue, however, is "serious from whose standpoint?" The victim's? The persecutor's? Society's? The proposed regulations would require "objectively serious harm or suffering that is subjectively experienced as serious harm or suffering by the applicant." 65 Fed. Reg. 76588, 76597 (Dec. 7, 2000). The proposed rule therefore requires both that the applicant regard the harm as serious and that an objective observer would share that view.

Consider the following:

Palestinians in Saudi Arabia are relegated to officially sanctioned second-class status incorporated into the legal and social structure of Saudi Arabia. * * * [Although Ahmed's] parents have lived in Saudi Arabia for 50 years and Ahmed was born in the country, neither he nor his parents have been able to obtain Saudi citizenship because Saudi Arabia reserves citizenship for people of Saudi descent. To remain in the country, Palestinians must renew their residence permits every two years for a fee of 2,000 Riyals (about $530). Palestinians must also be "sponsored" by a Saudi Arabian citizen to own real property, work, or own a business. To illustrate the harsh effects of this requirement, Ahmed related that his father had successfully operated and expanded a grocery store for 15 years, only to see his Saudi sponsor—the *de jure* owner of the store—take the business away once it became profitable. Each time a Palestinian wishes to change jobs, he must change sponsors for a fee of 6, 000 Riyals (about $1,600).

Ahmed * * * was barred from certain activities during high school and initially was not allowed to attend a university because he was an alien. Although he was able to gain admission to King Saud University in Riyadh because of his talent for soccer and the connections of a family friend, he was forced to study political and administrative science at the university because aliens could not choose their own topic of study. After graduating from the university and searching for a job for more than a year, Ahmed was hired in 1993 to sell cars. He testified that he was paid one-third as much as his Saudi counterparts and had to work significantly longer hours.

Ahmed v. Ashcroft, 341 F.3d 214, 215–16 (3d Cir. 2003). The BIA acknowledged that Ahmed had experienced "discrimination" but held that neither statelessness nor this type of economic disadvantage rose to the level of "persecution." The court affirmed.

9. Throughout this entire discussion, the assumption has been that "persecution" is legally relevant. When the relief sought is asylum under INA § 208, that assumption is clearly correct; asylum requires "refugee" status, and the refugee definition contained in INA § 101(a)(42) in turn expressly refers to "persecution." For similar reasons, persecution is critical to determinations made in the overseas refugee program. See INA § 207. But the relevance of "persecution" to withholding under INA § 241(b)(3) is not as obvious from the statutory text. That provision does not mention the word "persecution." It requires instead that the person's "life or freedom would be threatened." Despite that wording, both the BIA and the courts freely discuss the likelihood of "persecution" even when they are considering relief under section 241(b)(3). The assumption seems to be that the phrase "life or freedom," for purposes of withholding, is broad enough to cover the same deprivations that would constitute "persecution" for purposes of the refugee definition and, therefore, section 208. For a good discussion, see Carolyn P. Blum, *The Ninth Circuit and the Protection of Asylum Seekers Since the Passage of the Refugee Act of 1980*, 23 San Diego L.Rev. 327, 343–44 (1986). Be careful here: This issue is different from the *standard of proof* questions generated by the contrast

between the phrases "well-founded fear" and "would be threatened." Those latter questions are explored on pages 1050–54 below.

10. Now that you have studied the meaning of the "persecution" requirement, do you think, as a policy matter, that a well-founded fear of persecution should be enough to establish refugee status? Or is there good reason to impose the additional requirement that the persecution be linked to one of the five Convention (and U.S. statutory) grounds (race, religion, nationality, membership in a social group or political opinion)?

PERSECUTION VERSUS PROSECUTION

Matter of Izatula

Board of Immigration Appeals, 1990.
20 I. & N.Dec. 149.

* * *

The applicant is a 23–year–old native and citizen of Afghanistan. The applicant is married, but his wife and son are residing in Afghanistan. The applicant arrived in the United States on January 14, 1989. * * *

[In exclusion proceedings, the immigration judge denied asylum and withholding. The applicant appeals.—Ed.]

* * *

The applicant testified that he avoided the representatives of the Soviet-supported Afghan Army and the KHAD secret police when he was in Afghanistan, because he did not want to be conscripted and forced to fight against his own countrymen. The applicant testified further that between 1985 and 1988, he assisted the mujahedin [Afghan rebels—Ed.] by providing them with clothes, groceries, and other supplies. He stated that during this period he let his younger brother run the store. The applicant would obtain a list from the mujahedin indicating the items which they needed, and he would then obtain these supplies with the assistance of his brother. The applicant stated that his brother was able to travel freely around Kandahar because he was not old enough for the Army to be interested in conscripting him. The applicant also stated that he himself would deliver supplies to the mujahedin at night, so that he could avoid being seen by members of the Army or other security forces.

The applicant testified further that his brother was arrested by KHAD secret police in October 1988. He stated that someone informed the KHAD police that he and his brother were assisting the mujahedin. According to the applicant, the KHAD agents then came to the store and arrested his brother. The applicant learned from Ijim Mohammad, a man who lived next to the store, that the KHAD agents had asked for the applicant too when they arrested his brother. The applicant stated that he never saw or heard from his brother after the arrest, but he believed that his brother had been imprisoned.

The applicant stated that he hid at home for the 2 days following his brother's arrest. According to the applicant, on the second day that he was in hiding, a KHAD agent came to the house looking for him. The applicant's father told the KHAD agent that he did not know where the applicant was, and the agent "beat ... up" the applicant's father. The applicant stated that after the KHAD agent had left his home, he went to a village named Arghandab which is approximately 2 kilometers from Kandahar. The applicant's father moved with him to Arghandab, which was an area under mujahedin control. The applicant also stated that his uncle informed him that KHAD agents continued to look for him at his house in Kandahar after he had fled to Arghandab.

The applicant remained in Arghandab for 1 and 1/2 months. He fled Arghandab because of the "constant bombardment" there, and because his father was injured during an air raid near the house where the applicant and his father were living. The applicant travelled to Pakistan along with nine or ten members of the mujahedin. After he had arrived in Pakistan, the applicant stayed in Chaman for 3 days. He subsequently travelled to Karachi, where he remained for 20 days. In Karachi, the applicant paid a fee to an agent who provided him with a passport and a boarding pass. The applicant testified that he made arrangements to leave Pakistan because he had no family ties there, and because he could not afford to continue to pay for the hotel where he was staying in Karachi.

* * *

The immigration judge based his denial of the applicant's asylum request on two separate grounds. He found first that the applicant's fear of being conscripted by the pro-Soviet Afghan Army was no longer a valid basis for a persecution claim, due to the Soviet forces having withdrawn from Afghanistan in February 1989. Concerning the applicant's active support of the mujahedin, the immigration judge found that the applicant's fear of harm from the Afghan Government relates to "an act of prosecution rather than act of persecution for aiding groups in opposition in an attempt to overthrow the defacto [sic] government of Afghanistan."

We concur with the immigration judge's reasoning that the applicant is not eligible for asylum based on an unwillingness to perform military service in Afghanistan. Since the Soviet forces have withdrawn from Afghanistan, an asylum claim based on a refusal to serve in the Afghan military is no different than any other alien's claim that he will be punished because he did not serve in his country's armed forces.

We do not agree, however, with the immigration judge's rationale that the applicant would be subject to prosecution in Afghanistan due to the assistance which he rendered on behalf of the mujahedin. The applicant established through his testimony that his brother was arrested, and not heard from again, because of his support for the mujahedin. He further established that the authorities sought him out too because he had assisted the mujahedin.

The * * * Department of State's 1988 Country Reports on Human Rights Practices [hereinafter "Country Reports"] * * * provide the following concerning the Afghan Government's treatment of suspected political opponents:

> Regime authorities frequently employ torture to punish or to extract information or confessions. The policy is widespread, indicating that it has official sanction. Victims often claim that Soviet officials monitor and indirectly control the torture sessions. Torture techniques include both physical and psychological abuse. Use of electric shock to sensitive parts of the body, immersion in water, and beatings are common forms of physical abuse reported by victims and witnesses. Threats of abuse against family members and prolonged sleep deprivation are typical forms of psychological abuse. Persistent reports describe cases of mental disturbances induced by torture in regime prisons. Political prisoners are usually not segregated from criminal or mentally ill prisoners. Medical care is commonly described as minimal at Pol-e-Charkhi, where prisoners are generally required to wait at least a month before being allowed access to medical personnel. According to reliable reports, many prisoners died in 1988 as a result of inadequate diet, corporal punishment, and torture.

Furthermore, the Country Reports estimate that there are "at least several thousand" political prisoners being held in Afghanistan. The Immigration and Naturalization Service has submitted no evidence to rebut the information in the Country Reports concerning human rights conditions in Afghanistan. Thus, we find that the applicant has demonstrated that he is at risk of imprisonment, at a minimum, in Afghanistan because of his political activity there.

Moreover, we find no basis in the record to conclude, as the immigration judge did, that any punishment which the Afghan Government might impose on the applicant on account of his support for the mujahedin would be an example of a legitimate and internationally recognized government taking action to defend itself from an armed rebellion. The Country Reports explain that in Afghanistan, "[c]itizens have neither the right nor the ability peacefully to change their government. Afghanistan is a totalitarian state under the control of the [People's Democratic Party of Afghanistan], which is kept in power by the Soviet Union." We accordingly find the existing political situation in Afghanistan to be different from that of countries where citizens have an opportunity to seek change in the political structure of the government via peaceful processes. See Dwomoh v. Sava, 696 F.Supp. 970, 979 (S.D.N.Y.1988) ("general rule [that] prosecution for an attempt to overthrow a lawfully constituted government does not constitute persecution ... [is not] applicable in countries where a coup is the only means through which a change in the political regime can be effected"). Therefore, because we find that the applicant has established that he is at risk of being punished for his political activities in Afghanistan, and because there is no basis in the record to conclude that any punishment imposed by the Afghan Government would be a legitimate exercise of sovereign authority, we conclude that the applicant has established a well-founded fear of persecution in Afghanistan. * * *

* * *

[Exercising its discretion favorably, the Board grants asylum.—Ed.]

CONCURRING OPINION: Fred W. Vacca, Board Member

* * *

[Mr. Vacca agrees with the majority that in view of the Soviet withdrawal the Afghan government's conscription policies do not constitute persecution.—Ed.]

Where I disagree pertains to the applicant's contention that he would be persecuted because of his assistance to mujahedin rebels when he resided in Afghanistan. Specifically, the majority takes issue with the immigration judge's finding that the applicant's assistance to the mujahedin may result in his prosecution for criminal violations if he were to be returned to Afghanistan. The majority reasons that the assistance in furnishing supplies to the mujahedin was a political activity, that the applicant's brother was imprisoned by the Government for the same activity, and that in view of the thousands of Afghans who are imprisoned for political activity, the applicant "is at risk of imprisonment at a minimum." The majority rationalizes that "there is no basis in the record to conclude that any punishment imposed by the Afghan Government would be a legitimate exercise of sovereign authority...." In effect, the majority finds that the Afghan Government is illegitimate and therefore incapable of imposing a lawful punishment. This finding is based upon the notion that any government that does not provide for political change through democratic and peaceful processes cannot defend itself against armed rebellion, insurrection, and coup d'etat without engaging in persecution.

In its broadest ramifications, the majority wades in dangerous waters when it presumes to make judgments as to the legitimacy of sovereign nations by scrutinizing their political systems. Clearly, the President of the United States has constitutional authority to formulate and conduct foreign policy and does so through the Secretary of State and the Department of State. The Board, however, as a delegate of the Attorney General, has no authority to make pronouncements concerning the legitimacy of sovereign nations. Just as treason, insurrection, and providing aid and comfort to the enemy are punishable crimes under the political system of the United States, these acts are most probably punishable crimes in Ghana, El Salvador, Afghanistan, and almost all countries of the world. To hold that some governments may create laws affecting crimes, adjudicate criminal cases, and impose punishments upon offending citizens and other governments may not depending upon the nature of their political systems is patently absurd. The right of all nations to recruit soldiers and maintain armies to protect themselves from enemies within or without their borders is recognized as fundamental in international law. This sovereign right is not limited to countries whose internal political structures are democratic. If a totalitarian government prevents violent overthrow of its government, then the perpetrators of the failed coup are subject to the criminal laws of that government notwithstanding the fact that due process as we know it may not exist in that country.

* * *

* * * As pointed out in the [UNHCR Handbook], persons fleeing from prosecution are not normally refugees. However, prosecution for an offense may be a pretext for punishing an individual for his political opinion. Therefore such factors as the nature of the crime and the severity of the punishment vis-a-vis the crime committed should be considered. * * *

* * * In Afghanistan prisons and detention camps, political prisoners are routinely tortured, deprived of adequate food and medical care, and suffer corporal punishment. I find it reasonable to conclude that if the applicant were convicted for his crime and incarcerated he would suffer punishment disproportionate to his crime. Under these circumstances, his punishment would be in the nature of persecution. * * *

NOTES AND QUESTIONS

1. In *Acosta*, the BIA provided general guidance on the meaning of persecution. In *Izatula*, the BIA takes on a more specific issue: When does criminal punishment amount to persecution? See generally Anker at 199–209.

After rejecting the argument that the applicant would be persecuted for resisting the draft, both the majority opinion and that of Board Member Vacca address the applicant's fear of punishment for aiding the rebels. As Mr. Vacca points out, prosecuting a criminal violation is not ordinarily considered persecution, and intentionally assisting armed insurrection is surely a violation of the criminal law. The majority, however, recognizes an exception based on the totalitarian nature of the Afghan government. The majority seems to regard armed rebellion against a totalitarian government as serving a function akin to voting in a democracy—i.e., as the legitimate avenue for effecting change. Mr. Vacca disagrees. Who has the better of the argument? Would BIA and judicial evaluations of the legitimacy of foreign governments impinge on the President's authority to formulate foreign policy? Are adjudicative bodies competent to assess legitimacy? When the Third Reich executed members of the resistance during World War II, was it "persecuting" them?

2. Board Member Vacca also ends up finding a well-founded fear of persecution, but through a very different route. Paragraphs 85 and 86 of the UNHCR Handbook, which he cites, say:

> 85. Whether a political offender can also be considered a refugee will depend upon various other factors. Prosecution for an offence may, depending upon the circumstances, be a pretext for punishing the offender for his political opinions or the expression thereof.

Again, there may be reason to believe that a political offender would be exposed to excessive or arbitrary punishment for the alleged offence. Such excessive or arbitrary punishment will amount to persecution.

86.   In determining whether a political offender can be considered a refugee, regard should also be had to the following elements: personality of the applicant, his political opinion, the motive behind the act, the nature of the act committed, the nature of the prosecution and its motives; finally, also, the nature of the law on which the prosecution is based. * * *

Think especially about the second and third sentences of paragraph 85. Do you see any relationship between them? Do you find either of these two exceptions applicable to Izatula? How does Board Member Vacca apply them? How do you suppose he would have applied them if the punishment had simply been execution—after a fair trial and without torture?

3.   The UNHCR Handbook, in paragraphs 167–74, speaks specifically to the issue of draft evasion. Its interpretation is that punishment for refusing to be drafted may constitute persecution if either (a) the international community condemns the acts of the particular country's military forces or (b) the punishment is disproportionately severe on account of one of the five Convention/statutory grounds. Accord, *Selgeka v. Carroll*, 184 F.3d 337, 340 (4th Cir. 1999); *Matter of A.G.*, 19 I. & N. Dec. 502, 506 (BIA 1987). For an unusually strict reading of the first prong, see *M.A. v. U.S. I.N.S.*, 899 F.2d 304, 312–14 (4th Cir. en banc, 1990); see also *id.* at 321–24 (Winter, J., dissenting). The UNHCR Handbook, in paras. 170–72, discusses the effect of conscientious objection but leaves unclear whether "genuine political, religious or moral convictions" are an independent basis for a persecution claim or merely an essential element of a claim based on prong (a) above.

4.   Both the majority and Mr. Vacca reject Izatula's first argument. They hold that the Soviet troop withdrawal precludes classifying the government's punishment of draft evaders as persecution. Yet both opinions accept his second argument—that punishing him for aiding the rebels *is* persecution (and based on political opinion). Are the dispositions of his two claims reconcilable? Does either the majority's rationale (the government is totalitarian) or Mr. Vacca's rationale (the punishment is excessive) apply with any less force to Izatula's first claim? If anything, do not both rationales apply with even greater force to the first claim?

COERCIVE POPULATION CONTROLS AS PERSECUTION

In *Matter of Chang*, 20 I. & N.Dec. 38 (BIA 1989), a Chinese national objected to his country's "one-couple, one-child" policy. Chinese law provides a package of economic carrots and sticks designed to discourage couples from having more than one child. The applicant alleged that, although the law does not authorize anyone to *compel* abortion or sterilization, it is not unusual for local officials to do so unlawfully. See U.S. Dept.

of Justice, Office of Immigration Litigation, *China's One Baby Policy and the Definition of "Refugee,"* Immigration Litigation Bull. at 3–6 (Sept. 30, 2004). The BIA found as fact that Chang and his wife were unlikely to incur anything but economic sanctions if, as they desired, they were to have three children. The Board added, however, that in China even forcible sterilization would not constitute persecution. The Board saw such a measure as a reasonable response to China's extraordinary population problems; in addition, the Board observed that the Changs were not being treated differently from any other Chinese couple and that there was no evidence the government's policy was a pretext to accomplish any hidden goal. Do you agree with the Board's decision? What if the Changs were Roman Catholics whose religious convictions precluded abortion, sterilization, and most other forms of birth control?

All this has now changed. One month after the decision in *Chang*, Chinese government troops massacred members of the pro-democracy movement in Tiananmen Square. A few months later the U.S. Attorney General responded with interim regulations that superseded the specific result in *Chang*. Under the interim regulations, a well-founded fear of coerced abortion or sterilization automatically made a person eligible for asylum and withholding. See 55 Fed.Reg. 2803–05 (Jan. 29, 1990). After seven years of further administrative developments, Congress in 1996 amended the definition of "refugee" to supersede the BIA decision in *Chang*. Under the amended definition, any forced abortion or sterilization, or persecution for failure or refusal to submit to abortion or sterilization, constitutes persecution on account of political opinion. INA § 101(a)(42), as amended by IIRIRA § 601. It is no longer necessary, therefore, to prove a singling out because of race, religion, political opinion, or other impermissible reasons. In *Matter of X.P.T.*, 21 I. & N. Dec. 634 (BIA 1996), the Board interpreted the 1996 amendment as extending to withholding of removal.

While the 1996 amendment will help certain asylum claimants qualify as refugees, establishing refugee status does not guarantee asylum. As you will see in more detail in subsection B.6 below, an asylum claimant also needs the favorable exercise of discretion. When refugee status is based only on past persecution, rather than on a well-founded fear of future persecution, the favorable exercise of discretion is more tenuous, whether the persecution relates to coercive population control or anything else.

In *Matter of C–Y–Z–*, 21 I. & N. Dec. 915 (BIA 1997), the Board granted withholding of removal under this provision to an applicant whom the Chinese authorities had sterilized, even though there obviously was no fear of future sterilization. As you will also see later, past persecution triggers a presumption of future persecution which, under the then existing regulations, the government could have rebutted only by showing changed country conditions. 8 C.F.R. § 208.16(b)(2)(2004). A 2000 amendment now allows ICE to rebut the presumption through any evidence of changed circumstances (not just changed country conditions) that shows the absence of the required well-founded fear. 8 C.F.R. §§ 1208.13(b)(i)(A), 1208.16(b)(1)(A) (2004). Conversely, the discretion to grant asylum is often denied when a "fundamental" change of circumstances eliminates the fear of future persecution. *Id.* § 1208.13(b)(1)(i)(A). Nonetheless, the fact that forced sterilization cannot be repeated does not constitute the kind of changed circumstances that would dictate a discretionary denial. To the contrary, the BIA has said, forced sterilization is a "continuing" persecution. Moreover, it can be invoked by the spouse of the person who was sterilized. *Matter of Y–T–L-,* 23 I. & N. Dec. 601 (BIA 2003); accord, *Qu v. Gonzales,* 399 F.3d 1195 (9th Cir. 2005).

Until 2005, the statute limited the use of the 1996 amendment to 1,000 persons per year. See former INA § 207(a)(5). To accommodate the excess demand, EOIR developed a practice of "conditional" grants of asylum based on coercive population controls. In chronological order, the conditional grants eventually became outright grants. But huge backlogs accumulated, reaching approximately 9000 by February 1, 2005. See 10 BIB 100 (Feb. 1, 2005). At a rate of 1000 per year, it would have taken nine years for those applicants to receive asylum. In 2005, The REAL ID Act, § 101(g)(2), repealed the annual 1,000 cap.

The special treatment of claims based on coercive population controls does not spell automatic success for Chinese couples who allege fear of compulsory sterilization or abortion. The major hurdle is demonstrating that the fear is well-founded. In *Yong Hao Chen v. INS,* 195 F.3d 198 (4th Cir. 1999), the court noted the State Department's opinion that forced sterilizations and abortions have become less frequent in China, that they occur mainly in the rural areas, and that they are especially unlikely to affect people (like the couple in question) who bear children while attending university in the United States and then return home. *Id.* at 200, 204. Consequently, the court held, the burden is on the applicant to demonstrate either that the State Department is wrong or that he or she has particular reason to fear coerced sterilization or abortion. *Id.*

See generally Katherine L. Vaughns, *Retooling the "Refugee" Definition: The New Immigration Reform Law's Impact on United States Domestic Asylum Policy,* 1 Rutgers Race & L. Rev. 41 (1998) (questioning wisdom of special legislation to benefit particular group for ideological reasons); Mary Crock, *Apart from Us or a Part of Us? Immigrants' Rights, Public Opinion and the Rule of Law,* 10 Internat'l J. Refugee L. 49 (1998) (detailing responses of Australian courts to Chinese asylum claims based on fear of coerced sterilization and abortion).

QUESTION

Which view is more in keeping with what you have learned so far about the difference between prosecution and persecution—the BIA's position in *Chang* or Congress's position in IIRIRA?

————

Once the Board in *Izatula* found a well-founded fear of persecution (rather than prosecution), it held Izatula eligible for asylum. In doing so, however, it skipped over an important question: Was the persecution he feared on account of political opinion? Had he been a mercenary, acting solely for economic reasons rather than political ones, do you think the government would have punished him any less severely? If the answer is no, is the government really persecuting him because of his political opinions, or simply because it wants to deter people, whatever their views, from attempting to overthrow the government? Hold off on your answer; the next subsection will examine what it means for persecution to be "on account of" one of the five Convention/statutory grounds.

2. "ON ACCOUNT OF RACE, RELIGION, NATIONALITY, MEMBERSHIP IN A PARTICULAR SOCIAL GROUP, OR POLITICAL OPINION"

a. RACE, RELIGION, NATIONALITY

The vast majority of the asylum claimants in the United States have alleged persecution based on political opinion or social group. But claims based on race, religion, and nationality have been increasing.

The UNHCR Handbook, para. 68, defines race "in its widest sense to include all kinds of ethnic groups that are referred to as 'races' in common usage." With similar breadth, paragraph 74 defines "nationality" to include not only citizenship status, but also "membership of an ethnic or linguistic group." Naturally, these bases frequently overlap—with each other and with the social group and political opinion prongs considered below.

Race and nationality asylum claims have been relatively infrequent. See, e.g., *Matter of Tan,* 12 I. & N. Dec. 564 (BIA 1967) (Indonesian citizen of Chinese descent failed to show he would be singled out); *Matter of Rodriguez,* 10 I. & N. Dec. 488 (BIA 1964) (evidence insufficient to show East Indian mobs in British Guiana would persecute black asylum claimant because of race). In recent years, however, they have begun to increase. See Anker at 407–13; Stephen Yale–Loehr & Brian Palmer, Asylum Law Update, 5 BIB 633, at 633 (July 15, 2000). There have been claims by Fijians of Indian descent, *id.*, racially motivated rapes, e.g. *Shoafera v. INS,* 228 F.3d 1070 (9th Cir. 2000), and claims by Jews from the former Soviet Union, e.g. *Matter of O.Z. & I.Z.,* 22 I. & N. Dec. 23 (BIA 1998) (nationality).

Religion has played an important role in the United States overseas admission program, particularly with respect to Soviet Jews, Soviet evangelical Christians, and persecuted religious minorities in Iran. See section A. Until recently, however, *asylum* claims based on religion had been few and far between. That seems to be changing. See generally Karen Musalo, *Claims for Protection Based on Religion or Belief,* 16 Internat'l J. Refugee L. 165 (2004). Asylum claims by Soviet Jews and secular Muslims have become more common. See Yale–Loehr & Palmer, above, at 633–35; see also Anker at 398–407. The UNHCR Handbook does not define "religion," though paragraphs 71–73 furnish some examples of forms of persecution often incurred by religious groups.

Conscientious objector claims have also raised questions about religious persecution. See *Canas–Segovia v. INS*, 970 F.2d 599 (9th Cir.1992), on remand from *INS v. Canas–Segovia*, 502 U.S. 1086, 112 S.Ct. 1152, 117 L.Ed.2d 401 (1992), analyzed in Karen Musalo, *Swords into Ploughshares: Why the United States Should Provide Refuge for Young Men Who Refuse to Bear Arms for Reasons of Conscience*, 26 San Diego L.Rev. 849 (1989); see also *Barraza Rivera v. INS*, 913 F.2d 1443 (9th Cir.1990) (Salvadoran who deserted army because threatened with death if he did not betray own conscience by helping to murder two others had shown well-founded fear of persecution on account of "religion"). And the religion prong of the refugee definition might well prove useful in gender-based claims. See, e.g., *Matter of S.A.*, 22 I. & N. Dec. 1328 (BIA 2000) (fundamentalist father abused daughter for failing to obey his religious dictates), discussed below in the context of gender-based claims.

The International Religious Freedom Act of 1998, Pub. L. 105–292, 112 Stat. 2787 (Oct. 27, 1998) [IRFA], has potential ramifications for religion-based asylum claims. The Act creates, in the State Department, a new Office on International Religious Freedom, charged with monitoring religious persecution around the world. The Office will also assist the Secretary of State in preparing its annual Human Rights Reports and a separate "Annual Report on International Religious Freedom." IRFA §§ 101, 102. The latter is to be used by all who adjudicate asylum cases. *Id*. § 601. IRFA also established the United States Commission on International Religious Freedom, which reported annually for four years on the state of religious freedom overseas. *Id*. §§ 201–06. In February 2005 the Commission also published a comprehensive study on asylum seekers in the expedited removal system, discussed in section B.7 below. In addition, the statute requires training for all Justice Department and State Department personnel involved in refugee adjudication. See *id*. §§ 602(a)(adding INA § 207(f) for Justice Department adjudicators) and 602(b) (for foreign service officers). Professor Craig Mousin, analyzing IRFA, urges greater importation of international human rights standards into asylum claims based on denial of religious freedom. See Craig B. Mousin, *Standing with the Persecuted: Adjudicating Religious Asylum Claims after the Enactment of the International Religious Freedom Act of 1998*, 2003 BYU L. Rev. 541. The Hebrew Immigrant Aid Society (HIAS) has published a report cataloguing instances in which individuals with seemingly valid religious-based asylum claims were denied by the BIA for reasons that courts ultimately found flawed. See HIAS, Faithful but Forsaken: Real ID Act Harms Victims of Religious Persecution (Jan. 24, 2005) (including examples of Armenian Pentecostals, Eastern Orthodox Serbs, Bulgarian Protestants, Chinese Falun Gong and Yi Guan Do practitioners, Chinese Christians, Egyptian Coptic Christians, Eritrean and Ethiopian Jehovah's Witnesses, Fijians of mixed religions,

Indonesian Christians, Romanian Baptists, Russian Evangelicals, and Turkmenaian Jews).

b. POLITICAL OPINION[5]

INS v. Elias–Zacarias

Supreme Court of the United States, 1992.
502 U.S. 478, 112 S.Ct. 812, 117 L.Ed.2d 38.

■ Justice Scalia DELIVERED THE OPINION OF THE COURT.

The principal question presented by this case is whether a guerrilla organization's attempt to coerce a person into performing military service necessarily constitutes "persecution on account of . . . political opinion" under § 101(a)(42) of the Immigration and Nationality Act.

I

Respondent Elias–Zacarias, a native of Guatemala, was apprehended in July 1987 for entering the United States without inspection. In deportation proceedings brought by petitioner Immigration and Naturalization Service (INS), Elias–Zacarias conceded his deportability but requested asylum and withholding of deportation.

The Immigration Judge summarized Elias–Zacarias' testimony as follows:

"[A]round the end of January in 1987 [when Elias–Zacarias was 18], two armed, uniformed guerrillas with handkerchiefs covering part of their faces came to his home. Only he and his parents were there.... The guerrillas asked his parents and himself to join with them, but they all refused. The guerrillas asked them why and told them that they would be back, and that they should think it over about joining them.

"[Elias–Zacarias] did not want to join the guerrillas because the guerrillas are against the government and he was afraid that the government would retaliate against him and his family if he did join the guerrillas. He left Guatemala at the end of March [1987] . . . because he was afraid that the guerrillas would return."

The Immigration Judge understood from this testimony that Elias–Zacarias' request for asylum and for withholding of deportation was "based on this one attempted recruitment by the guerrillas." She concluded that Elias–Zacarias had failed to demonstrate persecution or a well-founded fear of persecution on account of race, religion, nationality, membership in a particular social group, or political opinion, and was not eligible for asylum. She further concluded that he did not qualify for withholding of deportation.

The Board of Immigration Appeals (BIA) summarily dismissed Elias–Zacarias' appeal on procedural grounds. Elias–Zacarias then moved the BIA to reopen his deportation hearing so that he could submit new evidence

---

5. See generally Anker at 290–376.

that, following his departure from Guatemala, the guerrillas had twice returned to his family's home in continued efforts to recruit him. The BIA denied reopening on the ground that even with this new evidence Elias–Zacarias had failed to make a prima facie showing of eligibility for asylum and had failed to show that the results of his deportation hearing would be changed.

The Court of Appeals for the Ninth Circuit, treating the BIA's denial of the motion to reopen as an affirmance on the merits of the Immigration Judge's ruling, reversed. The court ruled that acts of conscription by a nongovernmental group constitute persecution on account of political opinion, and determined that Elias–Zacarias had a "well-founded fear" of such conscription. We granted certiorari.

II

Section 208(a) of the Immigration and Nationality Act authorizes the Attorney General, in his discretion, to grant asylum to an alien who is a "refugee" as defined in the Act, i. e., an alien who is unable or unwilling to return to his home country "because of persecution or a well-founded fear of persecution on account of race, religion, nationality, membership in a particular social group, or political opinion." INA § 101(a)(42)(A). The BIA's determination that Elias–Zacarias was not eligible for asylum must be upheld if "supported by reasonable, substantial, and probative evidence on the record considered as a whole." INA § 106(a)(4). It can be reversed only if the evidence presented by Elias–Zacarias was such that a reasonable factfinder would have to conclude that the requisite fear of persecution existed.

The Court of Appeals found reversal warranted. In its view, a guerrilla organization's attempt to conscript a person into its military forces necessarily constitutes "persecution on account of . . . political opinion," because "the person resisting forced recruitment is expressing a political opinion hostile to the persecutor and because the persecutors' motive in carrying out the kidnapping is political." The first half of this seems to us untrue, and the second half irrelevant.

Even a person who supports a guerrilla movement might resist recruitment for a variety of reasons—fear of combat, a desire to remain with one's family and friends, a desire to earn a better living in civilian life, to mention only a few. The record in the present case not only failed to show a political motive on Elias–Zacarias' part; it showed the opposite. He testified that he refused to join the guerrillas because he was afraid that the government would retaliate against him and his family if he did so. Nor is there any indication (assuming, arguendo, it would suffice) that the guerrillas erroneously believed that Elias–Zacarias' refusal was politically based.

As for the Court of Appeals' conclusion that the guerrillas' "motive in carrying out the kidnapping is political": It apparently meant by this that the guerrillas seek to fill their ranks in order to carry on their war against the government and pursue their political goals. But that does not render the forced recruitment "persecution on account of . . . political opinion."

* * * The ordinary meaning of the phrase "persecution on account of . . . political opinion" in § 101(a)(42) is persecution on account of the *victim's* political opinion, not the persecutor's. If a Nazi regime persecutes Jews, it is not, within the ordinary meaning of language, engaging in persecution on account of political opinion; and if a fundamentalist Moslem regime persecutes democrats, it is not engaging in persecution on account of religion. Thus, the mere existence of a generalized "political" motive underlying the guerrillas' forced recruitment is inadequate to establish (and, indeed, goes far to refute) the proposition that Elias–Zacarias fears persecution *on account of* political opinion, as § 101(a)(42) requires.

Elias–Zacarias appears to argue that not taking sides with any political faction is itself the affirmative expression of a political opinion. That seems to us not ordinarily so, since we do not agree with the dissent that only a "narrow, grudging construction of the concept of 'political opinion' " would distinguish it from such quite different concepts as indifference, indecisiveness and risk-averseness. But we need not decide whether the evidence compels the conclusion that Elias–Zacarias held a political opinion. Even if it does, Elias–Zacarias still has to establish that the record also compels the conclusion that he has a "well-founded fear" that the guerrillas will persecute him because of that political opinion, rather than because of his refusal to fight with them. He has not done so with the degree of clarity necessary to permit reversal of a BIA finding to the contrary; indeed, he has not done so at all.

Elias–Zacarias objects that he cannot be expected to provide direct proof of his persecutors' motives. We do not require that. But since the statute makes motive critical, he must provide some evidence of it, direct or circumstantial. And if he seeks to obtain judicial reversal of the BIA's determination, he must show that the evidence he presented was so compelling that no reasonable factfinder could fail to find the requisite fear of persecution. That he has not done.

The BIA's determination should therefore have been upheld in all respects, and we reverse the Court of Appeals' judgment to the contrary.

It is so ordered.

■ JUSTICE STEVENS, with whom JUSTICE BLACKMUN and JUSTICE O'CONNOR join, dissenting.

* * *

It is undisputed that respondent has a well-founded fear that he will be harmed, if not killed, if he returns to Guatemala. It is also undisputed that the cause of that harm, if it should occur, is the guerrilla organization's displeasure with his refusal to join them in their armed insurrection against the government. The question of law that the case presents is whether respondent's well-founded fear is a "fear of persecution on account of . . . political opinion" within the meaning of § 101(a)(42) of the Immigration and Naturalization [sic] Act.

* * *

Today the Court holds that respondent's fear of persecution is not "on account of ... political opinion" for two reasons. First, he failed to prove that his refusal to join the guerrillas was politically motivated; indeed, he testified that he was at least in part motivated by a fear that government forces would retaliate against him or his family if he joined the guerrillas. Second, he failed to prove that his persecutors' motives were political. In particular, the Court holds that the persecutors' implicit threat to retaliate against respondent "because of his refusal to fight with them" is not persecution on account of political opinion. I disagree with both parts of the Court's reasoning.

I

A political opinion can be expressed negatively as well as affirmatively. A refusal to support a cause—by staying home on election day, by refusing to take an oath of allegiance, or by refusing to step forward at an induction center—can express a political opinion as effectively as an affirmative statement or affirmative conduct. Even if the refusal is motivated by nothing more than a simple desire to continue living an ordinary life with one's family, it is the kind of political expression that the asylum provisions of the statute were intended to protect.

As the Court of Appeals explained in *Bolanos-Hernandez v. INS*, 767 F. 2d 1277 (CA9 1985): "Choosing to remain neutral is no less a political decision than is choosing to affiliate with a particular political faction. * * *"

* * *

It follows as night follows day that the guerrillas' implied threat to "take" him or to "kill" him if he did not change his position constituted threatened persecution "on account of" that political opinion. As the Court of Appeals explained in *Bolanos-Hernandez, supra*:

"It does not matter to the persecutors what the individual's motivation is. The guerrillas in El Salvador do not inquire into the reasoning process of those who insist on remaining neutral and refuse to join their cause. They are concerned only with an act that constitutes an overt manifestation of a political opinion. Persecution because of that overt manifestation is persecution because of a political opinion."[6]

---

6. The Government has argued that respondent's statement is analogous to that of a person who leaves a country to avoid being drafted into military service. The INS has long recognized, however, that the normal enforcement of selective service laws is not "persecution" within the meaning of the statute even if the draftee's motive is political. Thus, while holding that an Afghan soldier who refused to fight under Soviet command qualified as a political refugee, *Matter of Salim*, the INS has adhered "to the long-accepted position that it is not persecution for a country to require military service of its citizens." *Matter of A_G_*; cf. United Nations High Commissioner for Refugees, Handbook on Procedures and Criteria for Determining Refugee Status, para. 167 (1979) ("Fear of prosecution and punishment for desertion or draft-evasion does not in itself constitute well-founded fear of persecution under the [1967 Protocol Relating to the Status of Refugees]").

* * * Because respondent expressed a political opinion by refusing to join the guerrillas, and they responded by threatening to "take" or to "kill" him if he did not change his mind, his fear that the guerrillas will persecute him on account of his political opinion is well founded.[7]

Accordingly, I would affirm the judgment of the Court of Appeals.

NOTES AND QUESTIONS

1. The majority opinion in *Elias-Zacarias* addresses two questions: whether the applicant has expressed a political opinion and, if so, whether the persecution he fears is on account of that political opinion. In discussing the first issue, the Court touches on several subissues: Can neutrality be political opinion? Can one express a political opinion through inaction? Should a person's reason for refusing to join a guerrilla army—self-preservation versus opposition to the guerrillas' goals—determine whether the refusal constitutes the expression of a political opinion? These questions are taken up below in a separate Note entitled "Neutrality as Political Opinion."

2. From this point on, assume that Elias–Zacarias's refusal to join the guerrillas was motivated by his political opinion. The question then becomes whether the feared persecution can be characterized as being on account of his political opinion. As to that, the Court makes clear that the persecution must be on account of *the victim's* political opinion; it is not enough that the persecution promoted the political objectives of *the persecutors*. The Justice Department has now made that principle a part of its proposed asylum regulations. 65 Fed. Reg. at 76592 (Dec. 7, 2000) (reaffirming political opinion portion of *Matter of R.A.*, 22 I. & N. Dec. 906 (BIA 1999, vacated by A.G. 2001)). Statutory interpretation aside, is such a rule good policy?

3. Put another way, the Court appears to say that the guerrillas will persecute Elias–Zacarias because he refuses to join them, not because they disapprove of his political opinions. The assumption is that the guerrillas won't care what political views, if any, motivated him to refuse their demands; all they will care about is that he refused. First, suppose a government persecutes union leaders in order to discourage strikes. If the government didn't care whether the union leaders were acting out of political conviction or self-aggrandizement, would an asylum claim fail for lack of a link between the persecution and the union leader's political opinion? Second, would *Izatula* have been decided differently had the Supreme Court already handed down its decision in *Elias-Zacarias*? Third,

---

7. In response to this dissent, the Court suggests that respondent and I have exaggerated the "well-foundedness" of his fear. The Court's legal analysis, however, would produce precisely the same result no matter how unambiguous the guerrillas' threatened retaliation might have been. Moreover, any doubts concerning the sinister character of a suggestion to "think it over" delivered by two uniformed masked men carrying machine guns should be resolved in respondent's favor.

can you hypothesize *any* asylum case based on political opinion that would satisfy the requirements imposed in *Elias-Zacarias*?

The issue of when a political *act* should be treated as a legitimate expression of political *opinion* has analogs in extradition treaties, which typically prohibit extradition for "political" offenses. See generally Comment, *The Turning Point Approaches: The Political Offense Exception to Extradition,* 24 San Diego L. Rev. 549 (1987). For some interesting analyses of the applicability of extradition principles to the question at hand, see Arthur C. Helton, *Harmonizing Political Asylum and International Extradition: Avoiding Analytical Cacophony,* 1 Georgetown Immigration L.J. 457, 460–80 (1986); *Matter of Maldonado–Cruz,* 19 I. & N. Dec. 509, 518–32 (BIA 1988) (Heilman, concurring).

4. The Court in *Elias-Zacarias* affirms a decision of the BIA. Why would the BIA hold Elias–Zacarias ineligible for asylum when it had previously granted asylum in *Izatula*? Could one argue that, if anything, Elias–Zacarias's claim was the stronger of the two?

5. The majority opinion in *Elias-Zacarias* makes only cursory reference to a doctrine known as imputed political opinion. Under that doctrine, as long as the persecutor *believes* the applicant holds a particular view and intends to persecute the person because of it, it does not matter that the belief is wrong. See, e.g., *Ramirez Rivas v. INS,* 899 F.2d 864, 867 (9th Cir.1990). Should imputed political opinion suffice? Argue both ways.

6. After suggesting that Elias–Zacarias's refusal to join the guerrillas was not politically based, the Court said: "Nor is there any indication (assuming, arguendo, it would suffice) that the guerrillas erroneously believed that Elias–Zacarias' refusal was politically based." [Emphasis in original.] For a while, that dictum left some uncertainty about the continued viability of imputed political opinion. See, e.g., Bruce J. Einhorn, *Political Asylum in the Ninth Circuit and the Case of Elias–Zacarias,* 29 San Diego L. Rev. 597 (1992). The doctrine now appears settled. It has been accepted by the General Council for the former INS, the BIA, the courts, and now the proposed Justice Department regulations. See Legal Opinion of then INS General Counsel Grover Joseph Rees III (Jan. 19, 1993, amended Mar. 4, 1993), reproduced in 70 IR 498–512 (April 12, 1993); *Matter of S.P.,* 21 I. & N. Dec. 486 (BIA en banc, 1996); *Shirazi-Parsa v. INS,* 14 F.3d 1424, 1430 (9th Cir. 1994); *Ravindran v. INS,* 976 F.2d 754, 760 (1st Cir. 1992); *Canas-Segovia v. INS,* 970 F.2d 599, 601–02 (9th Cir. 1992)(on remand from Supreme Court); 65 Fed. Reg. at 76597–98 (Dec. 7, 2000) (proposed regulations) (enough that persecutor would act "on account of what the persecutor *perceives* to be the applicant's ... political opinion") [emphasis added]. Canadian law similarly recognizes imputed political opinion. See *Re Attorney–General of Canada and Ward,* 103 D.L.R.4th 1 (Supreme Court of Canada, 1993); see generally Anker at 325–48.

7. In *Lazo-Majano v. INS,* 813 F.2d 1432 (9th Cir. 1987), one court of appeals took the imputed political opinion doctrine another step. A Salvadoran army sergeant had been holding Lazo–Majano in a state of virtual

bondage, savagely and repeatedly beating and raping her. He threatened to falsely accuse her of subversion if she were to leave or tell the police. The court held she made out a claim of persecution based on imputed political opinion. Since the persecutor was well aware that the victim was not a subversive, the court's conclusion required a holding that even falsely, or cynically, imputed political opinion could suffice. Accord, *Desir v. Ilchert*, 840 F.2d 723 (9th Cir. 1988). The German Constitutional Court similarly has recognized cynically imputed political opinion. See 5 Internat'l J. Refugee L. 474–75 (1993).

In *Matter of R.A.*, 22 I. & N. Dec. 906 (BIA 1999), the asylum applicant was a Guatemalan woman whose husband had subjected her to extreme, prolonged physical and mental abuse. The police would not protect her. She argued, among other things, that her husband was harming her in order to overcome her resistance to his male domination. The claim was one of imputed political opinion.

The Board found her testimony credible and found she had a well-founded fear of persecution. But the Board also concluded that there was no nexus between the persecution she feared and any political opinion her husband might impute to her. There was no evidence, the Board said, that he cared what her political opinions were.

Because the case arose in the Ninth Circuit, the Board had to distinguish *Lazo-Majano*. To do so, it read *Lazo-Majano* as standing only for the proposition that cynically imputed political opinion can suffice. Here, the Board believed, the persecution could not be linked to any imputed political opinion, cynical or otherwise.

In *Lazo-Majano*, however, the court had provided two other, independent rationales for the result. The court had treated the persecutor as seeking to overcome Lazo–Majano's actual political opinion that men should not be permitted to dominate women. In addition, the court had reasoned, Lazo–Majano's flight from persecution was itself an expression of political opinion, for which her tormentor would now persecute her if she were to return. But the Board declined to recognize those holdings, on the theory that they were inconsistent with *Elias-Zacarias*. There were, the Board said, no post-*Elias-Zacarias* cases in the Ninth Circuit confirming that those aspects of *Lazo-Majano* were still good law.

On January 19, 2001, on her last full day in office, Attorney General Janet Reno vacated the decision in *R.A.* (for reasons related to the Board's analysis of a "social group" issue explored in the next section) and ordered the Board to stay reconsideration until the proposed Justice Department regulations are made final. *Matter of R.A.*, 22 I. & N. Dec. at 906. These and subsequent developments in the case are discussed below in the context of R.A.'s social group claim.

Should cynically imputed political opinion qualify a person for asylum? Argue both ways.

8. For general critiques of *Elias-Zacarias*, see Deborah E. Anker, Carolyn P. Blum, & Kevin R. Johnson, *The Supreme Court's Decision in*

INS v. Elias–Zacarias: Is There any "There" There?, 69 IR 285 (Mar. 9, 1992); Arthur C. Helton, *Resistance to Military Conscription or Forced Recruitment by Insurgents as a Basis for Refugee Protection: A Comparative Perspective*, 29 San Diego L. Rev. 581 (1992). Several others have criticized the decision for failing to consider international interpretations of "persecution on account of political opinion." See Carolyn Patty Blum, *A Question of Values: Continuing Divergences Between U.S. and International Refugee Norms*, 15 Berkeley J. Internat'l L. 1, 38, 41–42 (1997); Jennifer Moore, *Restoring the Humanitarian Character of U.S. Refugee Law Lessons from the International Community*, 15 Berkeley J. Internat'l L. 51, 59–61 (1997).

NEUTRALITY AS POLITICAL OPINION[6]

In international wars, few citizens of the warring nations feel neutral, and even fewer openly express neutrality. Today, however, the vast majority of the wars raging at any given time are civil conflicts, contained within national borders. During the period 1989–92, 79 of the 82 wars were civil wars. Michael S. Teitelbaum & Myron Weiner (eds.), Introduction, Threatened Peoples, Threatened Borders 32 (1995).

During any civil war—unlike most international wars—there will be many who sympathize with neither of the opposing factions. Those people often fear recrimination. Some manage to flee to refugee-receiving nations. An emerging issue of considerable importance, therefore, is whether neutrality should be regarded as political opinion. Here are two opposing views:

> The government concedes that Bolanos has consciously chosen not to join either of the contending forces in El Salvador because he wishes to remain neutral, yet it argues that any persecution Bolanos might suffer would not be because of his political opinion. We find it somewhat difficult to follow the government's argument. The government contends that Bolanos' decision to remain politically neutral is not a political choice. There is nothing in the record to support this contention. Presumably the government is suggesting either that neutrality is always apolitical or that an individual who chooses neutrality must establish that the choice was made for political reasons. We disagree with both of these contentions.
>
> Choosing to remain neutral is no less a political decision than is choosing to affiliate with a particular political faction. Just as a nation's decision to remain neutral is a political one, so is an individual's. When a person is aware of contending political forces and affirmatively chooses not to join any faction, that choice is a political one. A rule that one must identify with one of two dominant warring political factions in order to possess a political opinion, when many persons may, in fact, be opposed to the views

6. See generally Mark R. von Sternberg, *Emerging Bases of "Persecution" in American Refugee Law: Political Opinion and* *the Dilemma of Neutrality,* 13 Suffolk Transnat'l L.J. 1 (1989).

and policies of both, would frustrate one of the basic objectives of the Refugee Act of 1980—to provide protection to all victims of persecution regardless of ideology. Moreover, construing "political opinion" in so short-sighted and grudging a manner could result in limiting the benefits under the ameliorative provisions of our immigration laws to those who join one political extreme or another; moderates who choose to sit out a battle would not qualify.

The government's second suggestion is equally unconvincing. The motive underlying any political choice may, if examined closely, prove to be, in whole or in part, non-political. Certainly a political affiliation may be undertaken for non-political, as well as political, reasons. A decision to join a particular political party may, for example, be made to curry favor, gain social acceptability, advance one's career, or obtain access to money or positions of power. Similarly, a decision to remain neutral may be made, in whole or in part, for non-political reasons. However, the reasons underlying an individual's political choice are of no significance for purposes of sections 243(h) [now 241(b)(3)] and 208(a) and the government may not inquire into them. Whatever the motivation, an individual's choice, once made, constitutes, for better or for worse, a manifestation of political opinion.

We have several reasons for reaching the conclusion that the government may not look behind the manifestation of an alien's political opinion and seek to determine why he made a particular political choice. First, it is simply improper for the government to inquire into the motives underlying an individual's political decisions. Second, the motives frequently will be both complex and difficult to ascertain; it may not be possible to separate the political from the non-political aspects. What standards would we use, for example, to determine whether a choice was sufficiently based on political principles or whether economic self-interest was the determinative factor? Third, and perhaps most important, it is irrelevant why the individual made his choice. It does not matter to the persecutors what the individual's motivation is. The guerrillas in El Salvador do not inquire into the reasoning process of those who insist on remaining neutral and refuse to join their cause. They are concerned only with an act that constitutes an overt manifestation of a political opinion. Persecution because of that overt manifestation is persecution because of a political opinion.

Here, Bolanos was quite aware of the political situation. He had severed his ties to the right-wing organizations with which he had been affiliated. However, he subsequently refused to join the guerrillas despite their threats to his life. By choosing neutrality and refusing to join a particular political faction, Bolanos expressed his opinion and took a political stance. That conduct is as much an affirmative expression of a political opinion as is joining a side, or speaking out for or against a side.[18]

Bolanos–Hernandez v. INS, 767 F.2d 1277, 1286–87 (9th Cir.1984) (opinion by Reinhardt J.).

We also differ from other circuits on the crucial question of what constitutes "persecution ... on account of ... political opinion." The Ninth Circuit has held that political neutrality is a political opinion for purposes of INA § 243(h). *See, e.g., Maldona-do–Cruz v. INS,* 883 F.2d 788, 791 (9th Cir.1989). This holding eviscerates the political opinion requirement of the statute. It means that a politically inactive alien, and perhaps most illegal aliens are, may now gain the protection of asylum. * * *

As a concept of international law, political asylum developed in response to the need to protect persons from persecution by their government because they had performed political acts or held political opinions in defiance of the state. Authorities interpreting the [1951] Convention * * *, for example, hold two different views regarding the nature of political opinion necessary to qualify for refugee status. Neither encompasses political neutrality. According to S. Prakash Sinha, an international authority on asylum:

Where the nature of the offense is mixed, one point of view maintains that the Convention applies only to those cases where the political opinion of the individual involved is decisive of the nature and severity of his punishment, while another viewpoint holds that it is sufficient that he has committed the offense because of his political opinion.

S. Prakash Sinha, *Asylum and International Law* 103 (1971).

This core idea of political activism underlies the concept of "refugee" status. As Sinha notes, the key element of political opinion involves the "ruptur[ing] of the refugee's normal relationship between him and his state." In turn, this rupture results from a political controversy, which "may arise from his non-submission to a new government for various political reasons, or from acts of political persecution by the government of his state, or from his own political offenses." We distort the meaning of an important requirement for refugee status when we permit political aloofness

---

18. We recognize that, unlike the act of joining a side, a lack of political involvement may in some instances not represent a political choice. We need not decide, however, whether a mere failure to join any side, absent a conscious choice, represents a political decision. In this case it is clear that Bolanos has not simply failed to join either political side; he has made a deliberate and considered decision not to do so. Nor need we decide here whether the mere refusal to join a *particular* side, absent more, constitutes the expression of a political opinion. Here, Bolanos made a choice of an affirmative political stance—neutrality. We leave to another time the question whether a purely negative choice—a simple rejection of a particular political group—necessarily reflects a "political opinion."

to serve as an active "political opinion," that endangers its holder. It also demeans the true martyr for whom asylum was intended.

It is not likely this concurring opinion will alter either the statutory or case law with which it is concerned. Nonetheless, from time-to-time sightings should be taken to establish one's position. Our ship appears to be at some distance from the main fleet but no reefs or shoals appear dead ahead. As a passenger, I shall go below and hope for the best.

Mendoza Perez v. INS, 902 F.2d 760, 767–68 (9th Cir.1990) (Sneed J., concurring specially). (The majority had held as a matter of law that the applicant was eligible for both asylum and withholding of removal. Judge Sneed accepted that result but wished to express his concern about several perceived differences between Ninth Circuit asylum law and that of other circuits.)

NOTES AND QUESTIONS

1. Judge Reinhardt in *Bolanos–Hernandez* notes the government's view that "Bolanos's decision to remain politically neutral is not a political choice." Interpreting that argument, he says: "Presumably the government is suggesting either that neutrality is always apolitical or that an individual who chooses neutrality must establish that the choice was made for political reasons." Now having read both this opinion and the concurring opinion of Judge Sneed in *Mendoza Perez,* can you come up with any other plausible interpretations of the government's position?

2. Does Judge Reinhardt adequately come to grips with the government's practical concern that, in a civil war setting, too broad a definition of political opinion could make the vast bulk of the populace refugees?

3. Do you agree with Judge Reinhardt that one's motives for expressing neutrality are irrelevant? Suppose a person proclaims a neutral position not because she rejects the views of both sides, but because she fears recrimination from each side if she supports the other side. Suppose further that the strategy backfires, resulting in fear that both sides will now attempt to kill her for withholding support. Is she being persecuted for her political *opinion* or for her political *strategy?* Should it matter?

4. Judge Reinhardt argues that holding neutrality not to be political opinion "could result in limiting [asylum] to those who join one political extreme or another; moderates who choose to sit out a battle would not qualify." Is he right?

5. Judge Sneed's concurring opinion in *Mendoza Perez* rests on some assumptions that are worth questioning. He expresses understandable concern that, without limits, recognizing neutrality as political opinion could allow a "politically inactive alien" to receive asylum. He repeats this concern when he refers to "political aloofness." Judge Sneed was perhaps unaware, however, that the Ninth Circuit had previously required, as a condition for recognizing neutrality as political opinion, that the person

have "made a conscious and deliberate choice" to remain neutral; a mere "fail[ure] to take any position" does not suffice. *Lopez v. INS,* 775 F.2d 1015, 1016–17 (9th Cir.1985) (resolving the issue left open in footnote 18 of *Bolanos–Hernandez*); accord, *Diaz–Escobar v. INS,* 782 F.2d 1488, 1494 (9th Cir.1986). In *Lopez,* the court denied relief to a Salvadoran national who had exhibited only "apathy, saying he does not oppose the government nor support the rebels and has no opinion on how the country should be governed." *Lopez,* 775 F.2d at 1017.

Do you think knowledge of that limitation would have eased Judge Sneed's reservations? Or is it practically infeasible for the BIA or a court to distinguish neutrality from apathy? How was Bolanos–Hernandez able to demonstrate that his neutrality reflected a "conscious and deliberate choice?"

6. Judge Sneed's opinion might have led you to view the Ninth Circuit as a renegade court. On some immigration issues that court is indeed in the minority, but on the issue of whether neutrality can be political opinion, there was actually almost no contrary case law. The BIA in *Matter of Maldonado–Cruz,* 19 I. & N. Dec. 509 (BIA 1988), rev'd on other grounds, 883 F.2d 788 (9th Cir.1989), declined to apply the Ninth Circuit view to a case arising in the Fifth Circuit because "no Fifth Circuit case * * * agrees with" the Ninth Circuit view. 19 I. & N. Dec. at 516. But there was also no Fifth Circuit case *disagreeing;* the issue simply had not arisen in that court. The BIA in any event did not decide the issue either; it held *Bolanos–Hernandez* inapplicable because it found that Maldonado–Cruz had not "establish[ed] a principled position of neutrality" and that the evidence suggested he would be persecuted for his desertion of the guerrillas rather than for his opinions. *Id.* Even *Perlera–Escobar v. Executive Office for Immigration,* 894 F.2d 1292 (11th Cir.1990), the one judicial decision that Judge Sneed cites as repudiating the Ninth Circuit view, see 902 F.2d at 767, said only that it found the BIA opinion in *Maldonado–Cruz* persuasive (the BIA opinion is consistent, on this issue, with the Ninth Circuit view expressed in *Lopez*); that the 11th Circuit has not adopted the Ninth Circuit view (actually it had not rejected it either); and that in any event the court would not consider the issue because there was no evidence that the person would be persecuted because of his neutrality. 894 F.2d at 1297 n.4, 1298.

7. Judge Sneed quotes a sentence from a 1971 text on asylum (Sinha). Although the opinion does not identify the context, the actual text reveals that Sinha was commenting on the specific issue of political crimes. As you saw in *Izatula* and the notes following it, courts have struggled with the problem of the person who fears punishment for aiding armed rebellion or for engaging in other criminal *acts* that were politically motivated. In such cases, the question arises whether the claimed persecution is on account of political opinion or on account of criminal activity. With that background information, re-read the quoted sentence to get a sense of the point Sinha was making. Does the quoted passage help prove Judge Sneed's point? What enables him to conclude that neither of the two views mentioned by

Sinha "encompasses political neutrality?" Are Sinha and Judge Sneed even speaking to the same issue?

8. Does the Supreme Court in *Elias-Zacarias* foreclose neutrality as political opinion? (At least the Ninth Circuit doesn't think so. See *Sangha v. INS*, 103 F.3d 1482, 1486–90 (9th Cir. 1997); see generally Anker at 316– 25.)

REFUGEES SUR PLACE

Neither the refugee definition contained in article 1 of the 1951 Convention (as modified by article 1 of the 1967 Protocol) nor any of the relevant United States statutory provisions (INA §§ 101(a)(42), 208, 241(b)(3)) are restricted to refugees who *fled* persecution. All that is necessary is that the person *now* meet the various statutory requirements. Accord, UNHCR Handbook, para. 94. Applicants who were not refugees when they left home, but who become refugees while abroad, are called "refugees sur place." *Id.*

Some refugees sur place attained that status because conditions at home changed while they were away. There might have been a coup, a new political movement, or a suspension of civil liberties. The UNHCR Handbook, para. 95, recognizes such people as refugees if they otherwise qualify, and that view is generally noncontroversial. This type of claim need not be limited to persecution based on political opinion; persecution based on any of the other statutory bases is just as plausible.

More often, however, asylum claims by refugees sur place arise because of the refugee's own actions or words rather than because of changes in the country of origin. In theory this type of refugee sur place similarly could assert any of the five statutory bases of persecution, but in practice these claims tend almost always to be based on political opinion. Because the threat of persecution is in one sense self-induced, and because a person might be tempted to assert an unpopular opinion for the very purpose of creating eligibility for asylum, these claims are often received more skeptically. The UNHCR Handbook, para. 96, recognizes such refugee claims but urges "a careful examination of the circumstances," with particular regard to whether the authorities in the country of origin are likely to know of the person's activities and how they are likely to view them. In the United States the courts have been less inclined to find a well-founded fear of persecution based on political opinion when the fear arises because of post-departure activities, but reliable general principles are difficult to locate. See Note, *Basing Asylum Claims on a Fear of Persecution Arising from a Prior Asylum Claim*, 56 Notre Dame Lawyer 719, 724–29 (1981) [hereafter cited as *Basing Asylum Claims*].

Among those asylum claims based on persecution resulting from post-departure activities, several common fact situations stand out:

(1) The applicant's departure, or failure to return within a specified time, violated the emigration laws of the country of origin. This is a specific example of the persecution/prosecution problem that you

saw earlier. See *Basing Asylum Claims,* above, at 727–30; see also UNHCR Handbook, para. 61. In *Rodriguez-Roman v. INS*, 98 F.3d 416 (9th Cir. 1996), an anti-Castro Cuban fled Cuba, in violation of Cuba's prohibition on unauthorized departures. If returned, he would have faced a 15–20 year prison term or possibly even death. The immigration judge and the BIA denied asylum on the ground that he faced only criminal prosecution, not persecution. The Ninth Circuit reversed. Citing the UNHCR Handbook, the court held that severe punishment for unauthorized emigration can be persecution if the departure was politically motivated. The court acknowledged *Elias-Zacarias* but held that the punishment was being meted out because of the political opinion that the government imputed to emigrés. See especially the impassioned concurrence of Judge Kozinski, in which the other panel members joined, stressing the fundamental importance of judicial review of asylum claims.

(2) After leaving the country of origin, the applicant began expressing political views or engaging in political associations that might lead to persecution upon his or her return. See *Basing Asylum Claims,* above, at 725–27.

(3) The applicant applied for asylum, was turned down, and now fears that the very act of having applied for asylum will prompt the government of the country of origin to brand him or her as a subversive or even a traitor. A New Zealand case illustrates the problem. An Iranian applied for asylum in New Zealand, claiming falsely that he had bought "The Satanic Verses" and that he would be persecuted in Iran as a result. After his claim was denied, he reapplied, arguing that he would now be persecuted for having applied for asylum and for having said he had bought the book. The New Zealand Refugee Status Appeals Authority again denied asylum, in part because of his prior deceit. See 7 Internat'l J. Refugee L. at 332–53 (1995).

During the Cold War, one especially common group of refugees sur place was defectors. Often these were celebrated athletes, entertainers, or artists who came to the United States as part of a cultural exchange. Cuban baseball players are the modern paradigm. Because of their prominence, their defections are particularly likely to attract the attention of their governments. They might fall within any of the above categories.

Which of these classes of refugees sur place do you feel should be held eligible for asylum? See generally Anker at 35–40.

c. "PARTICULAR SOCIAL GROUP"

Perhaps more so than any other categories of asylum claims, those based on social group raise the fundamental philosophical questions of why governments grant asylum and why they limit it. The term "particular social group" is vague enough that recourse to the basic objectives of asylum is essential to any serious discussion of its meaning and its applicability. The social group prong has also proved critical in most claims based on gender-related persecution, as you will see in subsection c(iii) below. See generally Anker at 376–98. The following materials present four different views—those of the BIA, a court, the Justice Department, and a leading commentator—on the meaning of the term "particular social group."

i.   *General Definition of "Social Group"*

Matter of Acosta

Board of Immigration Appeals, 1985.
19 I. & N. Dec. 211.

* * *

The respondent has argued that the persecution he fears at the hands of the guerrillas is on account of his membership in a particular social group comprised of COTAXI drivers and persons engaged in the transportation industry of El Salvador and is also on account of his political opinion.

* * *

We find the well-established doctrine of ejusdem generis, meaning literally, "of the same kind," to be most helpful in construing the phrase "membership in a particular social group." That doctrine holds that general words used in an enumeration with specific words should be construed in a manner consistent with the specific words. The other grounds of persecution in the Act and the Protocol listed in association with "membership in a particular social group" are persecution on account of "race," "religion," "nationality," and "political opinion." Each of these grounds describes persecution aimed at an immutable characteristic: a characteristic that either is beyond the power of an individual to change or is so fundamental to individual identity or conscience that it ought not be required to be changed. Thus, the other four grounds of persecution enumerated in the Act and the Protocol restrict refugee status to individuals who are either unable by their own actions, or as a matter of conscience should not be required, to avoid persecution.

Applying the doctrine of ejusdem generis, we interpret the phrase "persecution on account of membership in a particular social group" to mean persecution that is directed toward an individual who is a member of a group of persons all of whom share a common, immutable characteristic. The shared characteristic might be an innate one such as sex, color, or kinship ties, or in some circumstances it might be a shared past experience such as former military leadership or land ownership. The particular kind of group characteristic that will qualify under this construction remains to be determined on a case-by-case basis. However, whatever the common characteristic that defines the group, it must be one that the members of the group either cannot change, or should not be required to change because it is fundamental to their individual identities or consciences. * * *

In the respondent's case, the facts demonstrate that the guerrillas sought to harm the members of COTAXI, along with members of other taxi cooperatives in the city of San Salvador, because they refused to participate in work stoppages in that city. The characteristics defining the group of which the respondent was a member and subjecting that group to punishment were being a taxi driver in San Salvador and refusing to participate in guerrilla-sponsored work stoppages. Neither of these characteristics is immutable because the members of the group could avoid the threats of the guerrillas either by changing jobs or by cooperating in work stoppages. It may be unfortunate that the respondent either would have had to change his means of earning a living or cooperate with the guerrillas in order to avoid their threats. However, the internationally accepted concept of a refugee simply does not guarantee an individual a right to work in the job of his choice. * * *

* * *

Sanchez–Trujillo v. INS

United States Court of Appeals, Ninth Circuit, 1986.
801 F.2d 1571.

■ BEEZER, CIRCUIT JUDGE:

* * *

The threshold question is whether the petitioners' class of young, urban, [Salvadoran] working class males constitutes that type of "particular social group," membership in which should be regarded as indicative of refugee status under the applicable immigration statutes.

* * *

* * * We may agree that the "social group" category is a flexible one which extends broadly to encompass many groups who do not otherwise fall within the other categories of race, nationality, religion, or political opinion. Still, the scope of the term cannot be without some outer limit.

The statutory words "particular" and "social", which modify "group," indicate that the term does not encompass every broadly defined segment of a population, even if a certain demographic division does have some statistical relevance. Instead, the phrase *"particular social* group" implies a collection of people closely affiliated with each other, who are actuated by some common impulse or interest. Of central concern is the existence of a voluntary associational relationship among the purported members, which imparts some common characteristic that is fundamental to their identity as a member of that discrete social group.

Perhaps a prototypical example of a "particular social group" would consist of the immediate members of a certain family, the family being a focus of fundamental affiliational concerns and common interests for most people. In *Hernandez–Ortiz,* we regarded evidence of persecution directed against a family unit as relevant in determining refugee status, noting that a family was "a small, readily identifiable group." As a contrasting example, a statistical group of males taller than six feet would not constitute a "particular social group" under any reasonable construction of the statutory term, even if individuals with such characteristics could be shown to be at greater risk of persecution than the general population.

Likewise, the class of young, working class, urban males of military age does not exemplify the type of "social group" for which the immigration laws provide protection from persecution. Individuals falling within the parameters of this sweeping demographic division naturally manifest a plethora of different lifestyles, varying interests, diverse cultures, and contrary political leanings. * * *

In sum, such an all-encompassing grouping as the petitioners identify simply is not that type of cohesive, homogeneous group to which we believe the term "particular social group" was intended to apply. Major segments of the population of an embattled nation, even though undoubtedly at some risk from general political violence, will rarely, if ever, constitute a distinct "social group" for the purposes of establishing refugee status. To hold otherwise would be tantamount to extending refugee status to every alien displaced by general conditions of unrest or violence in his or her home country. * * *

* * *

———

In *Hernandez-Montiel v. INS*, 225 F.3d 1084, 1093 (9th Cir. 2000), the Ninth Circuit interpreted *Sanchez-Trujillo* as providing an *additional* way to establish social group, not as a rejection of the *Acosta* test. The court said:

> We thus hold that a "particular social group" is one united by a voluntary association, including a former association, *or* by an innate characteristic that is so fundamental to the identities or consciences of its members that members either cannot or should not be required to change it [emphasis in original].

United States Department of Justice, Proposed Rule

65 Fed. Reg. 76588, 76593–95, 76598 (Dec. 7, 2000).

* * *

The key Board decision on the meaning of "a particular social group" requires that members of the group share a "common, immutable" trait. Matter of Acosta. This rule codifies this basic approach at § 208.15(C)(1), by providing that "[a] particular social group is composed of members who share a common, immutable characteristic, such as sex, color, kinship ties, or past experience, that a member either cannot change or that is so fundamental to the identity or conscience of the member that he or she should not be required to change it." * * * Gender is clearly such an immutable trait, is listed as such in Matter of Acosta, and is incorporated in this rule. * * *

This rule also includes the principle that the particular social group in which an applicant claims membership cannot be defined by the harm which the applicant claims as persecution. It is well-established in the [United States] case law that this type of circular reasoning does not suffice to articulate a particular social group. * * * It is also supported by Convention-based understandings of the definition of membership in a particular social group. See, e.g., Islam v. Secretary of State for the Home Department [U.K. House of Lords, 1999] (" * * * [T]here is a general principle that there can only be a 'particular social group' if the group exists independently of the persecution") (Lord Steyn).

Proposed § 208.15(c)(2) provides that, "[w]hen past experience defines a particular social group, the past experience must be an experience that, at the time it occurred, the member either could not have changed or was so fundamental to his or her identity or conscience that he or she should not have been required to change it." This is consistent with current case law that recognizes that past experiences can be the basis for membership in a particular social group. The regulatory language preserves the key require-ment from Matter of Acosta, supra, that the trait defining a particular social group must be a fundamental one, which an individual should not be required to change. In reality, of course, no past experience can be changed, as it has already occurred. But not all past experiences should qualify as traits which, if shared by others, can define a particular social group for asylum and withholding purposes. The experience of joining a violent gang in the past, for example, cannot be changed. At that point in the past, however, that experience could have been avoided or changed. In other words, the individual could have refrained from joining the group. Certain-ly, it is reasonable for any society to require its members to refrain from certain forms of illegal activity. Thus, for example, under this language, persons who share the past experience of having joined a gang would not constitute a particular social group on the basis of a past experience.

* * *

Finally, the proposed language in § 208.15(C)(3) provides a non-exclu-sive list of additional factors that may be considered in determining whether a particular social group exists. These factors are drawn from existing administrative and judicial precedent on the meaning of the "particular social group" ground. These precedents have been subject to conflicting interpretations, however, and this provision resolves those ambi-guities by providing that, while these factors may be relevant in some cases, they are not requirements for the existence of a particular social group.

The first three factors in this section are drawn from the Ninth Circuit's decision in Sanchez–Trujillo v. INS. In that case, the Ninth Circuit stated that "the phrase 'particular social group' implies a collection of people closely affiliated with each other, who are actuated by some common impulse or interest," and that "[o]f central concern is the existence of a voluntary associational relationship among the purported members." These factors have often been interpreted as prerequisites for the existence of a particular social group in the Ninth Circuit. The Ninth Circuit clarified the significance of these factors in the recent case of Hernandez–Montiel v. INS. The court held that its decision in Sanchez–Trujillo should be interpreted as consistent with the Board's decision in Matter of Acosta and that the voluntary associational test is an alternative basis for establishing membership in a particular social group. Other circuits have not applied this factor, and, instead have simply relied on the Board's determination that the group must share a "common, immutable" characteristic. In cases arising outside the Ninth Circuit, the Board has decided that a particular social group may exist without reference to these factors. * * * To ensure uniform and fair administrative adjudications of particular social group asylum claims, this rule clarifies that the Department views the Sanchez–Trujillo factors as considerations that may be relevant in some cases, but not as requirements for a particular social group.

Similarly, the next three factors in this proposed section are drawn from the Board's decision in In re R.A. * * * [In *R.A.*, the Board held that the *Acosta* immutability test sets forth only a necessary condition for a social group, not a sufficient condition; that, once group membership is found to be immutable, several other factors must be weighed and balanced; and that Guatemalan women who are abused by their partners do not constitute a social group. As noted earlier, the Attorney General vacated the decision and stayed the Board's reconsideration pending the outcome of the proposed regulations excerpted here. The three factors referenced here appear below as proposed 8 C.F.R. § 208.15(c)(3)(iv, v, and vi).—Ed.] The Board did not characterize these elements as requirements, however. This rule incorporates them as factors, but confirms that they are considerations, which, while they may be relevant in some cases, are not determinative of the question of whether a particular social group exists.

* * *

Section 208.15 [of 8 C.F.R.] is revised to read as follows:

* * *

(c) Membership in a particular social group.

* * *

(3) Factors that may be considered in addition to the required factors set forth in * * * this section, but are not necessarily determinative, in deciding whether a particular social group exists include whether:

(i) The members of the group are closely affiliated with each other;

(ii) The members are driven by a common motive or interest;

(iii) A voluntary associational relationship exists among the members;

(iv) The group is recognized to be a societal faction or is otherwise a recognized segment of the population in the country in question;

(v) Members view themselves as members of the group; and

(vi) The society in which the group exists distinguishes members of the group for different treatment or status than is accorded to other members of the society.

* * *

Arthur C. Helton, Persecution on Account of Membership in a Social Group as a Basis for Refugee Status

15 Columbia Human Rights L. Rev. 39, 40–47, 51–52 (1983).

* * *

The term "social group" in the Refugee Act of 1980 is derived from the corresponding language in the United Nations Convention on refugees ("Refugee Convention"), from which the Protocol and Act were taken. The definition of "refugee" in the U.N. Convention was derived from the Constitution of the International Refugee Organization ("IRO"). * * *

Subsequent interpretations of the refugee definition in the IRO Constitution did not always comport with the framers' liberal intent. At the Conference of Plenipotentiaries, during which the United Nations Convention on refugees was written, several delegations pressed for "an ampler definition [of refugee] ... than the one figuring in the IRO's Constitution...." The Swedish representative introduced an amendment to include a catch-all "social group" category that had not been included in the IRO definition, because "experience had shown that certain refugees had been persecuted because they belonged to particular social groups." The delegates intended to guarantee security from persecution to all refugees, without invidious or unnecessary distinctions.[16] The "social group" category, designed to reaffirm this commitment, was adopted in the U.N. Convention without dissent, extending the protection of refugees far beyond what had previously been the norm.

* * *

[Here the author argues that the contrast between the phrase "social group" and narrower phrases used in other United Nations documents suggests a deliberate intention to define "social group" expansively.—Ed.]

C. *Recognition of Social Groups by the United Nations*

The United Nations has demonstrated a commitment to protecting many groups from persecution. This commitment takes two distinct forms.

---

16. * * * [T]he enumerated categories—race, religion, nationality, membership in a particular social group, and political opinion—are more properly seen as illustrative of the meaning of "persecution" than as restrictions upon the right of asylum.

First, there are conventions and resolutions condemning and proscribing certain governmental activities. Second, there are provisions for the protection of those individuals persecuted. The Genocide Convention falls into the first category. The Refugee Convention falls into the second category. The two forms of protection are complementary. Presumably, where the U.N. sees fit to outlaw persecution aimed at a particular group, it would also wish to provide sanctuary for those who suffer at the hands of transgressor states.

Examples of persecuted groups which are covered by implication in the "social group" category in the Refugee Convention are legion. The U.N. has addressed itself to persecution and discrimination against women, children, the elderly, the young, the adopted, the illegitimate, the disabled, the family, the worker, the unemployed, the trade unionist, the migrant worker, the slave, the illiterate, and many other groups.

* * * The "social group" category was meant to be a catch-all which could include all the bases for and types of persecution which an imaginative despot might conjure up. Thus, the framers' general intent is illustrated by the subsequent recognition of the many types of invidious persecution prevalent in the world today.

However, it can hardly be argued that the U.N. has addressed every conceivable form of persecution in its resolutions. The long list noted above is merely indicative of the broad scope of the term "social group" as it has already been applied. One observation that can be made about the list is that each group has very little in common with the other groups, except for the fact that each is an aggregation of people who suffer from arbitrary and capricious persecution.

* * * Until otherwise shown, * * * the presumption must be that it was intended that all victims of capricious persecution (as opposed to justifiable prosecution or differentiation) be included in the "social group" category. This is the implication of the Swedish representative's reference, noted above, to the lessons of "experience."

* * *

NOTES AND QUESTIONS

1.   Before proceeding further, you should map out the broad conclusions that each of these four readings reaches as to the meaning of the term "particular social group."

2.   Professor Maryellen Fullerton has uncovered some useful German cases interpreting the phrase "particular social group." During the 1980's the German courts handed down thirteen such decisions, which she summarizes in Maryellen Fullerton, *Persecution Due to Membership in a Particular Social Group: Jurisprudence in the Federal Republic of Germany,* 4 Georgetown Immigration L.J. 381 (1990). The claimed social groups and the courts' responses included entrepreneurs in Poland (yes), homosexuals in Iran (yes), corrupt former government officials in Ghana (no), and

tattooed people in Iran (no). *Id.* at 396–437. The Ghanain case adopted reasoning similar to that in *Sanchez–Trujillo,* suggesting that "social group" status requires "both a certain degree of homogeneity and some degree of inner structure." *Id.* at 417. In the Iranian homosexual case, in contrast, a different German court held it "irrelevant if group members knew each other or are members of an organization." *Id.* at 409. Instead, the court offered a test that differs from all four of the American viewpoints you have seen: "whether the general population views this collection of people as an unacceptable group." *Id.* Along similar lines, Professor Michael Heyman makes a thoughtful argument for rooting the "social group" definition in the "social perception" of the group by the applicant's home society. See Michael G. Heyman, *Asylum, Social Group Membership and the Non–State Actor: The Challenge of Domestic Violence,* 36 Univ. Michigan J. L. Reform 767 (2003). Fullerton agrees that such a group should qualify but argues that other groups, such as those that are "envied and resented," should also qualify. 4 Georgetown Immigration L.J. at 440.

For some other foreign and comparative discussions of social group, see Maryellen Fullerton, *A Comparative Look at Refugee Status Based on Persecution Due to Membership in a Particular Social Group,* 26 Cornell Internat'l L.J. 505 (1993) (comparing German, Canadian, and United States approaches); Penelope Mathew, *The High Court and "Particular Social Groups": Lessons for the Future,* 21 Melbourne Univ. L. Rev. 277 (1997) (Australian High Court's approach to social groups); *Meyers v. Canada,* 97 D.L.R. 4th 729 (1992) (defining social group as sharing similar social status and similar interests not held by their governments).

3. In 2002 UNHCR issued Guidelines on this subject. See UNHCR, Guidelines on International Protection: "Membership of a particular social group" within the context of article IA(2) of the 1951 Convention and/or its 1967 Protocol relating to the Status of Refugees, U.N. Doc. HCR/GIP/02/02 (May 7, 2002), reproduced, 81 IR 571 (Apr. 26, 2004) [hereafter UNCHR Guidelines on Social Group]. Drawing from several of the approaches that you have just read—particularly the *Acosta* immutability approach and the societal perception approach discussed in item 2 above—UNHCR offered the following two-pronged "single standard:"

> [A] particular social group is a group of persons who share a common characteristic other than their risk of being persecuted, or who are perceived as a group by society. The characteristic will *often* be one which is innate, unchangeable, or which is otherwise fundamental to identity, conscience or the exercise of one's human rights.

UNHCR Guidelines, para. II.B.11 (emphasis added).

The qualifier "other than their risk of being persecuted" is considered in item 13 below. Apart from that, is there *any* group that would not satisfy the UNHCR definition? In answering this question, note that the "common characteristic" required by the first prong is not qualified by the word "immutable," although this paragraph later observes that the common characteristic in fact will "often" be immutable (in the *Acosta* sense).

4.   The BIA in *Acosta* requires "immutable" characteristics, meaning not only traits that members cannot change, but also traits so fundamental to individual identity that members should not be required to change them. Statutory interpretation aside, what policy is served by making immutability the test for "social group?" What are the disadvantages of doing so?

5.   The U.S. Courts of Appeals have generally embraced the *Acosta* immutability test. See, e.g., *Gebremichael v. INS*, 10 F.3d 28, 36 (1st Cir. 1993); *Fatin v. INS*, 12 F.3d 1233 (3d Cir. 1993); *Ontunez-Tursios v. Ashcroft*, 303 F.3d 341, 352 (5th Cir. 2002); *Castellano-Chacon v. INS*, 341 F.3d 533, 546–47 (6th Cir. 2003); *Lwin v. INS*, 144 F.3d 505, 511–12 (7th Cir. 1998). As noted earlier, even the Ninth Circuit has resuscitated *Acosta*, finding a way to reconcile it with *Sanchez-Trujillo*. The highest courts of Canada and the United Kingdom have also rejected *Sanchez-Trujillo* in favor of *Acosta*. See *Matter of Attorney General and Ward*, 103 D.L.R.4th 1, 24–38 (Canadian S.Ct, 1993); *Islam (A.P.) v. Secretary of State for the Home Dept.* [1999] 2 A.C. 629, [1999] 2 All E.R. 545, [1999] 2 W.L.R. 1015 (U.K. House of Lords 1999).

No other United States courts of appeals have expressly adopted the *Sanchez-Trujillo* test. The Second Circuit cited the case with apparent approval but went on to follow a third approach. In *Gomez v. INS*, 947 F.2d 660, 664 (2d Cir. 1991), the court held that "social group" requires a common fundamental characteristic that is recognizable to its persecutors and to the outside world. Accord, *Saleh v. USDOJ*, 962 F.2d 234, 240 (2d Cir. 1992).

For some effective criticisms of the limitations announced in both *Acosta* and *Sanchez-Trujillo*, see Maureen Graves, *From Definition to Exploration: Social Groups and Political Asylum Eligibility*, 26 San Diego L.Rev. 740 (1989).

6.   Courts applying the *Acosta* immutability test have had little difficulty finding women to be a social group, since gender is obviously immutable in the *Acosta* sense. See, e.g., *Mohammed v. Gonzales*, 400 F.3d 785 (9th Cir. 2005) (female genital mutilation); *Fatin v. INS*, 12 F.3d 1233 (3d Cir. 1993) (religious dress code). The UNHCR Guidelines on Social Group, para. II.B.12, expressly recognize women as a social group; accord, UNHCR, Guidelines on International Protection: Gender–Related Persecution within the context of Article 1A(2) of the 1951 Convention and/or its 1967 Protocol relating to the Status of Refugees, U.N. Doc. HCR/GIP// 02/01, para. 30 (May 7, 2002), reproduced, 81 IR 561 (Apr. 26, 2004). Gender-related asylum claims are specifically considered in section B.2.c.iii below.

7.   The Justice Department's proposed regulations say that past experience can define a social group, but only when the past experience was one that "*at the time it occurred*, the member either could not have changed or was so fundamental to his or her identity or conscience that he or she should not have been required to change it [emphasis added]." Do you agree? Suppose the applicant is a convicted sex offender who has fully served his sentence and fears returning home because, in his country, the

local population persecutes released sex offenders and the government willingly stands back. Assume the court concludes that the actor could have refrained from committing the charged offense without altering anything fundamental to his identity or conscience. Is this a case of persecution on account of social group?

8. Consider first the position of the Ninth Circuit in *Sanchez–Trujillo*. Why require the element of "voluntary association," or "cohesion?" Why should it matter to what degree the group members socialize or otherwise mingle with each other? In fact, how might one argue that *lack* of cohesion should be a factor that favors protecting the group? (The UNHCR Guidelines on Social Group, item 3 above, para. II.B.15, expressly reject any requirement that the group be "cohesive" and add that the group members do not have to "know each other or associate with each other.")

9. What does the court in *Sanchez–Trujillo* mean when it says a social group must be "homogeneous?" Obviously the court is not requiring that the group members be clones. At the other extreme, the court must mean more than that there exists *some* attribute which every group member shares (and which distinguishes non-members). Otherwise every group capable of being described would qualify; the very act of defining the group would identify the shared characteristics. Thus, if the court really means to insist on homogeneity, it must have some middle ground in mind. But what is it?

The homogeneity requirement has possibly made a graceful exit. In *Hernandez-Montiel*, discussed after *Sanchez-Trujillo*, the court does not even mention the reference to "homogeneous;" the only part of *Sanchez-Trujillo* that the court includes in its holding is the requirement of a voluntary association. Similarly, the Justice Department proposed regulations, while listing factors that the regulations attribute to *Sanchez-Trujillo*, omit any mention of homogeneity. (The only factor that seems close is factor ii ("common motive or interest")).

10. There are two lines of family-related cases in which the choice between the *Acosta* test and the *Sanchez-Trujillo* test has been outcome-determinative. In one line of cases, the applicant has alleged that his or her own family constitutes a social group. After the Ninth Circuit decided *Sanchez-Trujillo* but, importantly, before it adopted *Acosta* as an alternative test in *Hernandez-Montiel*, the court decided *Estrada–Posadas v. INS*, 924 F.2d 916 (9th Cir.1991). In that case the applicant alleged she would be persecuted because of a vendetta against her family, which she argued constituted a social group. The court's entire response read:

> * * * [S]he cites to no case that extends the concept of persecution of a social group to the persecution of a family, and we hold it does not. If Congress had intended to grant refugee status on account of "family membership," it would have said so. Thus, Estrada has not shown that any persecution would be on account of her membership in any social group.

Id. at 919. First, does the second quoted sentence make any sense? Second, should Estrada–Posadas have prevailed even under the *Sanchez-Trujillo* test?

In *Jie Lin v. Ashcroft*, 377 F.3d 1014, 1028–29 (9th Cir. 2004), decided after *Hernandez-Montiel*, the Ninth Circuit changed course, expressly holding family to be a social group. And in *Thomas v. Gonzales*, 409 F.3d 1177 (9th Cir. 2005), the Ninth Circuit en banc ended the intra-circuit conflict by formally overruling *Estrada–Posadas*. Accord, *Gebremichael v. INS*, 10 F.3d 28, 36 (1st Cir. 1993) (also applying *Acosta* test).

A different question is whether the family members *of similarly situated others* can comprise a social group. Again the Ninth Circuit, applying *Sanchez-Trujillo*, held they could not. In *De Valle v. INS*, 901 F.2d 787 (9th Cir.1990), the alleged social group consisted of family members of army deserters, whom the applicant had asserted were in danger in El Salvador. Quoting the "voluntary association" language of *Sanchez–Trujillo*, the court held the class members were not "closely affiliated" and therefore not a social group. It also said "the differences between such families far outweigh the similarities," a consideration that would seem to go to the requirement of homogeneity. In contrast, the court in *Lwin v. INS*, 144 F.3d 505, 511–12 (7th Cir. 1998), applied the *Acosta* immutability test, concluding that the parents of Burmese dissidents constituted a social group.

11.   The INS has occasionally granted asylum to applicants who have claimed persecution because of HIV. William Branigin, *Gays' Cases Help to Expand Immigration Rights*, Wash. Post, Dec. 17, 1996, at 1. Immigration Judge John Gossart (Baltimore), applying *Acosta*, granted asylum to an HIV-positive woman who had established that in India she would be persecuted for her illness. The relevant social group was defined as "married women in India who have contracted HIV, who fear that their family or their in-laws will disown them or force them to obtain a divorce, and who wish to be, or need to be, employed." *Id.* at 17. *Matter of Rao*, A77 249 526 (IJ, Dec. 20, 2000). What results do you think both *Sanchez-Trujillo* and *Acosta* would produce? Should U.S. law allow asylum in such cases?

12.   The *Acosta* test is usually assumed to be more liberal than that of *Sanchez–Trujillo*. But is it clear that the members of COTAXI, unsuccessful in *Acosta*, would have failed the *Sanchez–Trujillo* test? Conversely, how would the young, working class, urban, Salvadoran males who lost in *Sanchez–Trujillo* have fared under the test announced in *Acosta?*

13.   There is an emerging consensus that a social group cannot be defined by the persecution itself; otherwise, the courts have said, circular reasoning could permit an applicant to define any group as a social group. In a domestic violence case, for example, one is unlikely to prevail with the argument that the social group consists of victims of domestic violence. *Id.* (Related theories that hold out greater promise are discussed in the materials on gender-related asylum claims, below.) See especially the Justice Department's proposed regulations excerpted above, as well as the various judgments in the *Islam* decision, reproduced on pages 1042–46

below. The UNHCR Guidelines on Social Group, item 3 above, are in accord, *id*. para. II.B.14, but they add that the persecution of a group might itself cause society to perceive the individuals as comprising a group, in which case the second prong of the UNHCR social group definition might well apply.

14. The Justice Department proposal also provides, in proposed 8 C.F.R. § 208.15(c)(3), a list of "factors" that "may be considered in addition to the required factors" but which "are not necessarily determinative, in deciding whether a particular social group exists." What does this mean? What, exactly, is the intended relevance of the various "factors?" Possible interpretations include (1) It's a both-and test; the traits that define the group must be immutable, *and* the enumerated factors must militate toward finding the group to be a social group (doubtful, because the commentary twice emphasizes that these factors are not "requirements," though that could mean merely that no single factor is a requirement); (2) It's an either-or test; the group will be a social group if either (a) the traits that define the group are immutable *or* (b) the enumerated factors militate toward finding the group to be a social group; and (3) the sole criterion is immutability, but the "factors" might help determine whether the group traits are immutable (doubtful also, because several of the specific listed factors seem irrelevant to immutability).

15. In the excerpt you read, the late Arthur Helton argued that "social group," like the other four bases, was meant only to illustrate—not to restrict—the types of fact situations that could constitute persecution. If he was right, then (a) what was the point of adding the adjective "social," and (b) how might the drafters have made their intentions clearer?

The UNHCR Guidelines on Social Group, discussed in item 3 above, say the social group prong "cannot be interpreted as a 'catch all' that applies to all persons fleeing persecution." Otherwise, UNHCR implies, it would "render the other four Convention grounds superfluous." *Id*. para. I.2. If the UNHCR definition of social group reproduced in item 3 above is interpreted literally, so that every group (except a group defined solely by reference to the persecution itself) qualifies as a social group, would the UNHCR definition render the other four Convention grounds superfluous, or would those grounds retain significance even then?

16. What, if anything, do you think would be a sensible definition of "social group?"

ii. Sexual Orientation and "Social Group"

Matter of Toboso–Alfonso

Board of Immigration Appeals, 1990.
20 I. & N.Dec. 819.[a]

* * *

[In exclusion proceedings, Toboso–Alfonso applied for asylum and withholding. The immigration judge denied asylum in the exercise of

a. When the BIA decided this case in 1990, it issued an unpublished, nonprecedent opinion. In 1994 the Attorney General or-dered the decision published as precedent. Attorney General Order No. 1895–94 (June 19, 1994).—Ed.

discretion (because of a conviction of possession of cocaine) but granted withholding. The former INS appealed from the latter decision.]

In the instant case, the applicant asserts that he is a homosexual who has been persecuted in Cuba and would be persecuted again on account of that status should he return to his homeland. He submits that homosexuals form a particular social group in Cuba and suffer persecution by the government as a result of that status.

The applicant testified that there is a municipal office within the Cuban Government which registers and maintains files on all homosexuals. He stated that his file was opened in 1967, and every 2 or 3 months for 13 years he received a notice to appear for a hearing. The notice, the applicant explained, was a sheet of paper, "it says Fidel Armando Toboso, homosexual and the date I have to appear." Each hearing consisted of a physical examination followed by questions concerning the applicant's sex life and sexual partners. While he indicated the "examination" was "primarily a health examination," he stated that on many occasions he would be detained in the police station for 3 or 4 days without being charged, and for no apparent reason. He testified that it was a criminal offense in Cuba simply to be a homosexual. The government's actions against him were not in response to specific conduct on his part (e.g., for engaging in homosexual acts); rather, they resulted simply from his status as a homosexual. He further testified that on one occasion when he had missed work, he was sent to a forced labor camp for 60 days as punishment because he was a homosexual (i.e., had he not been a homosexual he would not have been so punished).

The applicant stated that at the time of the Mariel boat lift, the Union of Communist Youth received permission to hold a demonstration against homosexuals at the factory where he worked. Several of the members got on top of a table and screamed that all homosexuals should leave—should go to the United States. He testified that on that same day there was a sheet of paper tacked to the door of his home which stated that he should report to "the public order." The applicant presented himself at the police station in the town of "Guines" where he was informed by the chief of police that he could spend 4 years in the penitentiary for being a homosexual, or leave Cuba for the United States. He was given a week to decide and decided to leave rather than be jailed.

The applicant further testified that the day he left his town, the neighbors threw eggs and tomatoes at him. He claims that the situation was so grave that the authorities were forced to reschedule his departure time from the afternoon to 2:00 a.m., in order to quell the protesting residents.

In addition to the applicant's testimony, he supplemented the record with the following information: several articles describing "Improper Conduct," a film which centers on the testimony of 28 Cuban refugees and recounts the human rights violations, including incarceration in forced labor camps known as "Military Units to Aid Production," suffered by Cubans whom the Government considers to be dissidents or "antisocial," particularly male homosexuals; a newspaper article entitled, "Gay Cubans Survive Torture and Imprisonment," in which Cuban homosexuals in the United States, most of whom were part of the Mariel boat lift, describe their treatment by the Cuban Government, including repeated detentions, incarcerations, and physical beatings; and, Amnesty International's Report for 1985 which describes the political situation in Cuba.

The immigration judge found the "applicant's testimony to be credible and worthy of belief, and, if anything, perceive[d] that he was restrained in his testimony as to the difficulty of his life during the years that he lived in Cuba." The immigration judge further concluded that the applicant had been persecuted in Cuba and that he has a well-founded fear of continued persecution in that country. He found that this persecution resulted from the applicant's membership in a particular social group, namely homosexuals. The immigration judge denied the applicant's asylum application in the exercise of discretion because of the nature of the applicant's criminal record in the United States. However, as the immigration judge found that the applicant's crimes did not bring him within the scope of section 243(h)(2)(B), he granted his application for withholding of deportation to Cuba.

The Immigration and Naturalization Service appeals from the grant of withholding of deportation to Cuba to the applicant, arguing that homosexuals were not a particular social group contemplated under the Act, that the applicant has not presented adequate evidence to show either a well-founded fear or a clear probability of persecution, and that the applicant is ineligible for [withholding of removal] because of his conviction for possession of cocaine.

We do not find that the Service has presented persuasive arguments on which to reverse the immigration judge's finding that the applicant established his membership in a particular social group in Cuba. The Service argues that "socially deviated behavior, i.e. homosexual activity is not a basis for finding a social group within the contemplation of the Act" and that such a conclusion "would be tantamount to awarding discretionary relief to those involved in behavior that is not only socially deviant in nature, but in violation of the laws or regulations of the country as well." The applicant's testimony and evidence, however, do not reflect that it was specific activity that resulted in the governmental actions against him in Cuba, it was his having the status of being a homosexual. Further, the immigration judge's initial finding that a particular social group existed in Cuba was not "tantamount to awarding discretionary relief" to that group. Individuals in a particular social group are not eligible for relief based on that fact alone, among other showings they must establish facts demonstrating that members of the group are persecuted, have a well-founded fear of persecution, or that their life or freedom would be threatened because of that status.

We principally note regarding this issue, however, that the Service has not challenged the immigration judge's finding that homosexuality is an "immutable" characteristic. Nor is there any evidence or argument that, once registered by the Cuban government as a homosexual, that that characterization is subject to change. This being the case, we do not find the Service's challenge to the immigration judge's finding that this applicant was a member of a particular social group in Cuba adequately supported by the arguments set forth on appeal.

The next issue is whether the immigration judge erred in finding that the applicant had established that his life or freedom would be threatened in Cuba. The immigration judge not only found the applicant's testimony regarding the events in Cuba credible, but concluded that, if anything, he was "restrained in his testimony as to the difficulty of his life during the years that he lived in Cuba." In this regard, he noted that the applicant simply took as a matter of course that he "would be frequently detained for days [by government officials] while being subjected to verbal and physical abusive treatment." The applicant's testimony that simply because of his status as a homosexual he was advised by his government to leave the country or face incarceration for a period of 4 years is not contested. There is no evidence or allegation that this "choice" he was given resulted from any specific acts on his part or that the government did not intend to jail him if he failed to leave. The record indicates that rather than a penalty for misconduct, this action resulted from the government's desire that all homosexuals be forced to leave their homeland. This is not simply a case involving the enforcement of laws against particular homosexual acts, nor is this simply a case of assertion of "gay rights." Particularly in view of the final governmental threat that precipitated the applicant's departure from Cuba, we agree with the immigration judge's finding that the applicant's freedom was and is threatened within the contemplation of [withholding of removal].

* * *

ORDER: The Service's appeal is dismissed.

[Board member Vacca writes a dissenting opinion joined by Board member Morris. The dissent argues that the evidence does not show a high enough probability of serious harm to Toboso–Alfonso in Cuba. The dissenters do not question the finding that homosexuality is immutable or the holding that homosexuals constitute a social group.—Ed.]

NOTES AND QUESTIONS

1. The opinion in *Toboso-Alfonso* describes specific forms of persecution of gays and lesbians in Cuba. The persecutors include both government officials (periodic detention and interrogation and a threat to impri-

son Toboso for four years if he did not leave the country) and the private sector (the youth demonstration and the mob actions of the neighbors). The plight of gays and lesbians in several other countries is well described in the following excerpt:

> Ciprian Cucu says he was jailed as a teenager in his native Romania and repeatedly raped. Jose Zambrano, by his account, was disowned by his parents, raped by a soldier at 13, assaulted by paramilitary thugs and threatened with death in El Salvador. Sergey Fedetov recounts being harassed, beaten and repeatedly interrogated by police in Russia.

* * *

> * * * "Membership in a particular social group is being defined by liberal judges and government bureaucrats in a way that was never intended by Congress, and certainly not by the American people." [quoting K.C. McAlpin, deputy director of the Federation for American Immigration Reform, an immigration restriction organization]

* * *

> * * * [A] Russian lesbian, Alla Pitcherskaia, 34, * * * says she faces forced psychiatric institutionalization, including electroshock therapy, to "cure" her of her sexual orientation if forced to return to her homeland. The Justice Department is contesting her [asylum] claim.

* * *

> [Two gay partners] were arrested under a Romanian law that criminalizes all homosexual acts. Turned in by his own family and incriminated by his diary, Cucu was thrown into a cell with up to 16 other men. There he was immediately raped by a "supervising inmate," who also forced him to have sex with other prisoners during his two-month incarceration, the affidavit said. At one point, Cucu said, he was beaten by the warden for complaining about the rapes in court. He said his lover later told him that he also had been beaten and repeatedly raped. Last year, he said, his lover committed suicide.

* * *

> In El Salvador, Zambrano suffered the first of a series of brutal sexual assaults when he was raped at the age of 13 by a soldier in his home town. "From an early age, I was effeminate," he wrote in an affidavit. The result was "a horrible childhood" filled with abuse by his parents, teachers and classmates.
>
> Describing his experiences in graphic detail, Zambrano said his mother tried to "make me a man" by dispatching him to a local brothel when he was 15. In San Salvador, where his parents subsequently sent him, he was sexually assaulted by police, sol-

diers and members of a "death squad" on several occasions, he wrote.

* * *

"In El Salvador, being a homosexual is the lowest thing in society," Zambrano said.

William Branigan, *Gays' Cases Help to Expand Immigrants' Rights*, Washington Post, Dec. 17, 1996 at A1.

Pitcherskaia, the Russian lesbian described in the above excerpt, eventually overcame a major hurdle. The BIA had denied her claim on the basis that the Russian authorities did not seek to "harm" her; rather, they sought to "cure" her homosexuality through psychiatric means. The Ninth Circuit, holding that persecution does not require an intent to harm, reversed and remanded to the BIA for further consideration. *Pitcherskaia v. INS*, 118 F.3d 641 (9th Cir. 1997). Professor Ryan Goodman, in a 1995 student Note written after the BIA decision in *Pitcherskaia* but before the Ninth Circuit decision, argued strongly in favor of defining "persecution" by reference to international human rights norms. He specifically advocated such an approach for "medical" intervention cases like *Pitcherskaia*. See Ryan Goodman, Note, *The Incorporation of International Human Rights Standards into Sexual Orientation Asylum Claims: Cases of Involuntary "Medical" Intervention*, 105 Yale L.J. 255 (1995). Although the Ninth Circuit ultimately rested its reversal on a finding that prior cases imposed no requirement of a subjective intent to punish, the last sentence of its analysis would find a comfortable home in Goodman's model: "Human rights laws cannot be sidestepped by simply couching actions that torture mentally or physically in benevolent terms such as 'curing' or 'treating' the victims." 118 F.3d at 648.

2. Toboso established that he would be persecuted solely for *being homosexual*, as distinguished from engaging in homosexual acts. Now that this case has been decided, how do you think the BIA would come out in a case in which an asylum claimant established only that he or she would be persecuted because of homosexual activities? Does the distinction between status and acts affect either (a) whether the consequences will be termed "persecution" or (b) whether the persecution is on account of membership in a "particular social group?" On this point, see Michael A. Scaperlanda, *Kulturkampf in the Backwaters: Homosexuality and Immigration Law*, 11 Widener J. Pub. L. 475, 501–12 (2002) (arguing against asylum in cases where claimed persecution is based on conduct rather than status).

3. Did the BIA hold in this case that gays and lesbians constitute a "particular social group?" If so, what remaining barriers do gay and lesbian asylum claimants face? In *Cornejo-Merida v. Ashcroft*, 116 Fed. Appx. 900, 903 (9th Cir. 2004) (unpublished memorandum), the court acknowledged "overt discrimination against gays" in the country of origin (Peru) but affirmed the BIA's denial of asylum because the applicant had not shown "that he would be targeted for persecution or that the persecution of gays in Peru is so rampant and severe that his mere membership in the group of

homosexual men sufficed to establish an objective well-founded fear of future persecution." In *Karouni v. Gonzales*, 399 F.3d 1163 (9th Cir. 2005), a Lebanese gay male presented detailed and corroborated evidence of threats directed personally to him and violence and executions of his gay friends. The immigration judge nonetheless found his fear of persecution not to be well-founded, and the BIA affirmed without opinion. The court held the evidence insufficient to support the BIA finding of no well-founded fear. Based on these decisions, can you generalize about the remaining challenges for asylum claims based on sexual orientation?

4. As a policy matter, do you believe that persecution on account of sexual orientation should suffice for asylum?

5. Under 8 C.F.R. § 3.1(g) (2001), BIA decisions are binding on the INS and on the immigration judges. In response to concerns raised by Rep. Barney Frank, INS General Counsel David Martin sent a memo to all INS attorneys reminding them that *Toboso-Alfonso* is binding precedent, that the INS now regards homosexuals as a social group, and that INS attorneys should not argue to the contrary. The memo, dated April 4, 1996, is reprinted in Lesbian and Gay Immigration Rights Task Force, Task Force Update 9 (Fall 1996). Tribunals in Canada and Germany have reached similar conclusions, see New York Times, Jan. 14, 1992, at A5, as has the United Kingdom's Immigration Appeal Tribunal, 5 Joint Council for the Welfare of Immigrants Bulletin, #8, at 8 (spring 1995).

6. For additional discussion of the legal effects of sexual orientation on noncitizens, see chapter 3, § B.2.a above.

iii. Gender and "Social Group"[7]

The treatment of gender-related refugee and asylum claims is probably the single most pressing refugee issue in the world today, as the following excerpt illustrates:

7. There has been a wealth of excellent recent literature on gender-related refugee and asylum claims. In addition to the writings excerpted below, see, e.g., Anker at 252–66; Deborah E. Anker, *Women Refugees: Forgotten No Longer?*, 32 San Diego L.Rev. 771 (1995) (applauding INS Gender Guidelines and other favorable developments for women refugees); Jacqueline Bhabha, *Embodied Rights: Gender Persecution, State Sovereignty, and Refugees*, 9 Public Culture 3 (1996); Linda Cipriani, *Gender and Persecution: Protecting Women under International Refugee Law*, 7 Georgetown Immigration L.J. 511 (1993); Heaven Crawley, Refugees and Gender–Law and Process (2001); Isabelle Daoust & Kristina Folkelius, *UNHCR Symposium on Gender–Based Persecution*, 8 Internat'l J. Refugee L. 180 (1996); Pamela Goldberg, *Women and Refugee Status: A Review Essay*, 7 Internat'l J. Refugee L. 756 (1995); Pamela Goldberg, *Anyplace but Home: Asylum in the United States for Women Fleeing Intimate Violence*, 26 Cornell Internat'l L.J. 565 (1993); Nancy Kelly & Deborah E. Anker (directing eds.), Refugee Law Center, 1 Gender Asylum Law in Different Countries–Decisions and Guidelines (1999); Nancy Kelly, *Gender-Related Persecution: Assessing the Asylum Claims of Women*, 26 Cornell Internat'l L.J. 625 (1993); Peter Margulies, *Asylum, Intersectionality, and AIDS: Women with HIV as a Persecuted Social Group*, 8 Georgetown Immigration L.J. 521 (1994); Susan Forbes Martin, Refugee Women (2d ed. 2004); Karen Musalo, *Gender-Based Asylum: An Analysis of Recent Trends*, 77 IR 1533 (Oct. 30, 2000). See also the literature concerned more specifically with female genital mutilation, and the readings on non-state actors, each discussed separately below.

In countries torn by war, armed conflict and political resistance, it is the women and children who frequently seek safety away from home. Their husbands and their fathers may be fighting or dead. * * *

* * *

Gradually women refugees are being counted. Ninety per cent of the Ethiopian refugees in Somalia are women and children under 15. Eighty per cent of the Kampuchean households along the Thai–Kampuchean borders are headed by women, as are over half of Palestinian households in Lebanon. Over 80 per cent of the Salvadorean refugees in Nicaragua are women and children. Most of the 11,000 people from Guatemala, who have sought asylum in Mexico, are women, children and old people. And while for centuries the warrior tribesmen of Afghanistan crossed the mountains of Central Asia to the plains of the Indian sub-continent, today the arduous trek is undertaken by refugee women and their children.

* * *

* * * [I]nternational law * * * ignores the persecution that girls and women endure, even die under, for stepping out of the closed circle of social norms; choosing a husband in place of accepting an arranged marriage; undergoing an abortion where it is illegal; becoming politically active in a woman's movement. Women are also abandoned or persecuted for being rape victims, bearing illegitimate children or marrying men of different races. It ignores women's specific needs; in policy terms it is gender-blind. There is no recognition that * * * they need legal *protection and refugee status both as individuals in their own right and as women.* * * *

Whose criteria define legitimate fear for purposes of recognising refugees? The decision that persecution on grounds of race or religion may lead to "a well-grounded fear" [sic] is recognised. Yet women who may be stoned or burnt to death for not bringing enough dowry—itself an outlawed institution—or for choosing their own husband, which according to the Universal Declaration of Human Rights they may, have no rights or protection. Why is a girl who is threatened by violence and who attempts to escape by fleeing from her country, and from her family who may even be her persecutors, not part of UNHCR's responsibility? * * *

Lucy Bonnerjea, Shaming the World—The Needs of Women Refugees 5–6 (1985). A later section of Bonnerjea's study details the gruesome deaths that await many young women who disgrace their families by becoming pregnant before marriage ("crimes of honor"), the killings of women whose families had provided insufficient dowries, and the practice of selling girls and women into prostitution. *Id.* at 19–20.

Reporting on an actual asylum case, two attorneys provided this account:

> Extensive documentation [showed] the high number of honor killings ("Thaer") of Jordanian women from traditional tribal backgrounds suspected of pre-marital or extramarital relationships with "non-original" [in this case Palestinian] Jordanian men. (At least 25–30 of these killings are officially reported each year but the actual number is estimated to be much higher.) The documentary evidence further showed the on-going history of lenient government treatment of the perpetrators (jail sentences are usually less than a year without any sanction against family members who are accomplices to the killings.) * * * [I]t was also shown that "original" Jordanian men can buy protection for any "dishonor" caused by their relationship with "original" Jordanian women through payment to the offended families of a negotiated amount.

Michael D. Gragert & Kathleen Harvey, *Asylum Granted in "Honor Killing" Case*, 7 BIB 513, at 513 (May 1, 2002).

———

Despite, or perhaps because of, the potential volume of gender-related instances of persecution, neither the United Nations Convention nor United States statutory law includes gender in the list of persecution grounds that will make a person a refugee. Should gender be added to the list? Or are the social group category and the other existing categories adequate? Here is one view:

Jacqueline Greatbatch, The Gender Difference: Feminist Critiques of Refugee Discourse

1 Internat'l J. Refugee L. 518 (1989).

* * *

The Geneva Convention definition of refugee has recently come under fire from feminists for its "neglect of gender as a critical consideration" in refugee determination. By portraying as universal that which is in fact a male paradigm, it is argued, women refugees face rejection of their claims because their experiences of persecution go unrecognized. Doreen Indra cites the omission of "gender" from the enumerated grounds of persecution as an illustration of "the depth of gender delegitimation in refugee contexts."

The absence of gender as an enumerated basis for fear of persecution in the Convention definition is an omission which ideally requires amelioration. However, feminist complaints go far beyond the language of the definition, to the root of what gender-based claims to persecution would look like, were it possible to make them.

Indra and others call for a redefinition of persecution which acknowledges the feminist theory of social bifurcation: that society is divided into public and private spheres of activity; that the public sphere is male-dominated and women are relegated to the private sphere. Radical feminist theorists such as Catherine MacKinnon and Margaret Thornton propound a distinct "women's experience" of the private sphere which, it is claimed, is the site of gender oppression. Law, history and epistemology are dismissed as "phallocentrism masquerading as universalism." The experience of women's oppression is viewed as trans-historical and trans-cultural. Objectivity is rejected as a method of enquiry and theory is derived instead from "women's experiences."

This theory of women's oppression is reflected in the views of feminist critics of the refugee convention, as exemplified by Indra's thesis that women's experiences of persecution are ignored because,

> the key criteria for being a refugee are drawn primarily from the realm of public sphere activities dominated by men. With regard to private sphere activities where women's presence is more strongly felt, there is primarily silence—silence compounded by an unconscious calculus that assigns the critical quality "political" to many public activities but few private ones. Thus, state oppression of a religious minority is political, while gender oppression at home is not.

In Indra's view, the addition of "gender" as a basis upon which to found a claim to refugee status would do little to improve the position of refugee women without a redefinition of "persecution" to give credibility to women's private-sphere experiences. * * *

* * *

[Using Iran and Chile as examples, Greatbatch describes common ways in which women suffer political persecution even in the public sphere. She then argues that the word "persecution" is elastic enough to cover at least those kinds of gender-specific oppression that can be linked to the State. As for non-state actors, see the separate subsection below.]

Certainly many claims to Convention refugee status by women can be framed upon one of the existing grounds: race, religion, nationality, membership of a particular social group or political opinion. It must be acknowledged, however, that in many cases women face a barrier to protection, even though their claims to a well-founded fear of persecution are comparable in every other way to those of members of the delineated groups.

In response to feminist critics, the European Parliament, followed by the UNHCR, has urged the recognition as a particular social group of "women who face harsh and inhuman treatment because they are considered to have transgressed the social mores of their society." This formulation capitalizes on the elasticity of the definition of persecution by incorporating the phrase "harsh and inhuman treatment." Further, it imbues political qualities to individual acts of resistance. In short, it goes a considerable way to address the concerns of critics such as Indra and Meijer.

Innovative use of the under-utilized social group category promises some amelioration for the absence of gender as a specified ground, but there are at least two stumbling blocks to it providing a complete solution: the problematic nature of claims to persecution of an economic or social nature; and the trend in third-country resettlement States to restrict entry into their domestic determination systems.

* * *

As the cases of Iran and Chile illustrate, women are among the first victims of economic and social repression. However, the proclivity of States of all political stripes to the oppression of women, coupled with the vagueness with which economic and social rights are proclaimed in international law, suggests that successful use of the "particular social group" category for claims to persecution of an economic or social nature will be minimal.

Finally, as States which traditionally offer permanent resettlement to refugees tighten controls on entry into their domestic determination systems, bearing the additional burden of establishing the existence of a particular social group is an unenviable prospect. * * *

The answer to adequate protection for women refugees then lies not merely in creating a separate "female paradigm" for gender-based claims to persecution. A human rights based approach to defining persecution, the recognition of women as a particular social group, documentation of discriminatory and repressive measures aimed at or particularly affecting women, access to full and fair determination procedures, and a liberal reading of the Convention definition, would provide the basis for the development of a profile of gender-based refugee claims, and for recognition of the difference gender makes.

NOTES AND QUESTIONS

1. As of this writing, women in the United States have had only mixed success with gender-based asylum claims. The materials below will elaborate. As the previous subsection noted, UNHCR now explicitly regards women as a social group. Accord, David L. Neal, *Women as a Social Group: Sex–Based Persecution as Grounds for Asylum,* 20 Columbia Human Rights L.Rev. 203 (1988). Professor Susan Kneebone, however, has criticized the tendency to pigeonhole women's claims into the social group category rather than the political opinion category; she argues that doing so constructs women culturally as the objects or victims of a power imbalance. Susan Kneebone, *Women Within the Refugee Construct: "Exclusionary Inclusion" in Policy and Practice—The Australian Experience,* 17 Internat'l J. Refugee L. 7 (2005). The problems of women refugees are also sometimes lumped in with the problems of child refugees. As to the dangers of doing

so, see Jacqueline Bhabha, *Demography and Rights: Women, Children and Access to Asylum*, 16 Internat'l J. Refugee L. 227 (2004).

2.   Why do you suppose the States that have signed the 1951 Convention don't just amend it to add gender to the "on account of" list? Why do you suppose the United States Congress doesn't make analogous amendments to the asylum and withholding provisions?

Fatin v. INS

United States Court of Appeals for the Third Circuit, 1993.
12 F.3d 1233.

■ ALITO, CIRCUIT JUDGE:

* * *

[An Iranian woman applied for asylum. The former INS denied her application, which she renewed in deportation proceedings.—Ed.]

When her attorney asked her why she feared going back to Iran, she responded: "Because of the government that is ruling the country. It is a strange government to me. It has different rules and regulations than I have been used to." She stated that "anybody who [had] been a Moslem" was required "to practice that religion" or "be punished in public or be jailed," and she added that she had been "raised in a way that you don't have to practice if you don't want to." Id. She subsequently stated that she would be required "to do things that [she] never had to do," such as wear a veil. When asked by her attorney whether she would wear a veil, she replied:

A.   I would have to, sir.

Q.   And if you didn't?

A.   I would be jailed or punished in public. Public mean by whipped or thrown stones and I would be going back to barbaric years.

Later, when the immigration judge asked her whether she would wear a veil or submit to arrest and punishment, she stated:

If I go back, I would try personally to avoid it as much as I could do. . . . I will start trying to avoid it as much as I could.

The petitioner also testified that she considered herself a "feminist" and explained:

As a feminist I mean that I believe in equal rights for women. I believe a woman as a human being can do and should be able to do what they want to do. And over there in . . . Iran at the time being a woman is a second class citizen, doesn't have any right to herself.

After the hearing, the immigration judge denied the petitioner's applications for withholding of deportation, asylum, and suspension of deportation. Addressing her request for withholding of deportation, the immigration judge stated that, although she would be subject to the same discriminatory treatment as all other women in Iran, there was "no indication that there is a likelihood that the Iranian government would be particularly interested in this individual and that they would persecute her." Similarly with respect to her renewed request for asylum, the judge stated:

> Respondent has offered no objective indicia which would lead the Court to believe that there is a possibility that she would be persecuted upon return to Iran. Respondent has not been politically active in the United States nor openly opposed to the Khomeni Government. It would appear that her fear of return to Iran while indeed understandable is based upon uncertainty and the unknown. In addition, it would appear that the respondent's fear upon return to Iran is her apparent dislike for the system and her belief that she as a woman would be subject to the severe restrictions presently imparted on Iranians in that country. Respondent therefore contends that her beliefs as a "feminist" would be compromised. While the Court is very much sympathetic to the respondent's desire not to return to Iran, nonetheless, in applying the law to include case law, the Court is compelled to find that the respondent has failed to sustain her burden of proof necessary to be accorded asylum in the United States. * * *

Petitioner then appealed to the Board of Immigration Appeals. In her brief, she argued that she feared persecution "on account of her membership of a particular social group, and on the basis of her political opinion." Her brief identified her "particular social group" as "the social group of the upper class of Iranian women who supported the Shah of Iran, a group of educated Westernized free-thinking individuals." Her brief also stated that she had a "deeply rooted belief in feminism" and in "equal rights for women, and the right to free choice of any expression and development of abilities, in the fields of education, work, home and family, and all other arenas of development." In addition, her brief observed that she would be forced upon return to Iran "to practice the Moslem religion." Her brief stated that "she would try to avoid practicing a religion as much as she could." Her brief added that she had "the personal desire to avoid as much practice as she could," but that she feared that "through religious ignorance and inexperience she would be unable to play the role of a religious Shi'ite woman." Id. Her brief contained one passage concerning the requirement that women in Iran wear a veil in public:

> In April 1983, the government adopted a law imposing one year's imprisonment on any women caught in public without the traditional Islamic veil, the Chador. However, from reports, it is clear that in many instances the revolutionary guards ... take the law into their own hands and abuse the transgressing women....

Her brief did not discuss the question whether she would comply with the law regarding the wearing of a chador. Nor did her brief explain what effect submitting to that requirement would have upon her.

* * *

The Board of Immigration Appeals dismissed the petitioner's appeal. The Board noted that she had argued that she was entitled to relief "as a member of the social group composed of upper-class Iranian women" and as a person who "was educated in the western tradition." Rejecting this argument, the Board stated that there was no evidence that she would be "singled out" for persecution. Instead, the Board observed that she would be "subject to the same restrictions and requirements" as the rest of the population. * * *

* * *

B.   Both courts and commentators have struggled to define "particular social group." Read in its broadest literal sense, the phrase is almost completely open-ended. Virtually any set including more than one person could be described as a "particular social group." Thus, the statutory language standing alone is not very instructive.

* * *

[Here the court adopts the immutability test from *Acosta*—Ed.]

With this understanding of the phrase "particular social group" in mind, we turn to the elements that an alien must establish in order to qualify for withholding of deportation or asylum based on membership in such a group. We believe that there are three such elements. The alien must (1) identify a group that constitutes a "particular social group" within the interpretation just discussed, (2) establish that he or she is a member of that group, and (3) show that he or she would be persecuted or has a well-founded fear of persecution based on that membership.

[In *Acosta*] the Board specifically mentioned "sex" as an innate characteristic that could link the members of a "particular social group." Thus, to the extent that the petitioner in this case suggests that she would be persecuted or has a well-founded fear that she would be persecuted in Iran simply because she is a woman, she has satisfied the first of the three elements that we have noted. She has not, however, satisfied the third element; that is, she has not shown that she would suffer or that she has a well-founded fear of suffering "persecution" based solely on her gender.

In Acosta, the BIA discussed the meaning of the term "persecution," concluding that "the pre-Refugee Act construction" of that term should still be followed. Heeding this construction, the BIA interpreted "persecution" to include threats to life, confinement, torture, and economic restrictions so severe that they constitute a threat to life or freedom. By contrast, the BIA suggested that "generally harsh conditions shared by many other persons" do not amount to persecution. Among the pre-Refugee Act cases on which the BIA relied was Blazina v. Bouchard (1961), where our court noted that the mere "repugnance of . . . a governmental policy to our own concepts of . . . freedom" was not sufficient to justify labelling that policy as persecution. Thus, we interpret Acosta as recognizing that the concept of persecution does not encompass all treatment that our society regards as unfair, unjust, or even unlawful or unconstitutional. If persecution were defined that expansively, a significant percentage of the world's population would qualify for asylum in this country—and it seems most unlikely that Congress intended such a result.

In this case, the evidence in the administrative record regarding the way in which women in Iran are generally treated is quite sparse. We certainly cannot say that "a reasonable factfinder would have to conclude," based on that record, that the petitioner, if returned to Iran, would face treatment amounting to "persecution" simply because she is a woman. While the amici supporting the petitioner have called to our attention articles describing the harsh restrictions placed on all women in Iran, the facts asserted in these articles are not part of the administrative record.
* * *

The petitioner's primary argument, in any event, is not that she faces persecution simply because she is a woman. Rather, she maintains that she faces persecution because she is a member of "a very visible and specific subgroup: Iranian women who refuse to conform to the government's gender-specific laws and social norms." This definition merits close consideration. It does not include all Iranian women who hold feminist views. Nor does it include all Iranian women who find the Iranian government's "gender-specific laws and repressive social norms" objectionable or offensive. Instead, it is limited to those Iranian women who find those laws so abhorrent that they "refuse to conform"—even though, according to the petitioner's brief, "the routine penalty" for noncompliance is "74 lashes, a year's imprisonment, and in many cases brutal rapes and death."

Limited in this way, the "particular social group" identified by the petitioner may well satisfy the BIA's definition of that concept, for if a woman's opposition to the Iranian laws in question is so profound that she would choose to suffer the severe consequences of noncompliance, her beliefs may well be characterized as "so fundamental to [her] identity or conscience that [they] ought not be required to be changed." The petitioner's difficulty, however, is that the administrative record does not establish that she is a member of this tightly defined group, for there is no evidence in that record showing that her opposition to the Iranian laws at issue is of the depth and importance required.

The Iranian restriction discussed most prominently in the petitioner's testimony was the requirement that women wear the chador or traditional veil, but the most that the petitioner's testimony showed was that she would find that requirement objectionable and would seek to avoid compliance if possible. When asked whether she would prefer to comply with that law or suffer the consequences of noncompliance, she stated only that she "would try to avoid" wearing a chador as much as she could. Similarly, her brief to the BIA stated only that she would seek to avoid Islamic practices "as much as she could." She never testified that she would refuse to comply with the law regarding the chador or any of the other gender-specific laws or social norms. Nor did she testify that wearing the chador or complying with any of the other restrictions was so deeply abhorrent to her that it would be tantamount to persecution. Instead, the most that emerges from her testimony is that she would find these requirements objectionable and would not observe them if she could avoid doing so. This testimony does not bring her within the particular social group that she has defined—Iranian women who refuse to conform with those requirements even if the consequences may be severe.

The "particular social group" that her testimony places her within is, instead, the presumably larger group consisting of Iranian women who find their country's gender-specific laws offensive and do not wish to comply with them. But if the petitioner's "particular social group" is defined in this way, she cannot prevail because the administrative record does not satisfy the third element described above, i.e., it does not show that the consequences that would befall her as a member of that group would constitute "persecution." According to the petitioner, she would have two options if she returned to Iran: comply with the Iranian laws or suffer severe consequences. Thus, while we agree with the petitioner that the indicated consequences of noncompliance would constitute persecution, we must still inquire whether her other option—compliance—would also constitute persecution.

In considering whether the petitioner established that this option would constitute persecution, we will assume for the sake of argument that the concept of persecution is broad enough to include governmental measures that compel an individual to engage in conduct that is not physically painful or harmful but is abhorrent to that individual's deepest beliefs. An example of such conduct might be requiring a person to renounce his or her religious beliefs or to desecrate an object of religious importance. Such conduct might be regarded as a form of "torture" and thus as falling within the Board's description of persecution in Acosta. Such a requirement could constitute "torture" or persecution, however, only if directed against a person who actually possessed the religious beliefs or attached religious importance to the object in question. Requiring an adherent of an entirely different religion or a non-believer to engage in the same conduct would not constitute persecution.[10]

Here, while we assume for the sake of argument that requiring some women to wear chadors may be so abhorrent to them that it would be tantamount to persecution, this requirement clearly does not constitute persecution for all women. Presumably, there are devout Shi'ite women in Iran who find this requirement entirely appropriate. Presumably, there are other women in Iran who find it either inconvenient, irritating, mildly objectionable, or highly offensive, but for whom it falls short of constituting persecution. As we have previously noted, the petitioner's testimony in this case simply does not show that for her the requirement of wearing the chador or complying with Iran's other gender-specific laws would be so profoundly abhorrent that it could aptly be called persecution. Accordingly,

---

10. We do not suggest that an alien could establish that he or she would be persecuted or has a well-founded fear of persecution based solely on his or her subjective reactions. Presumably, conduct could not constitute persecution or "torture" within Acosta unless an objective requirement is also satisfied.

we cannot hold that she is entitled to withholding of deportation or asylum based on her membership in a "particular social group."

[The court next rejects a parallel argument based on political opinion.—Ed.]

* * *

NOTES AND QUESTIONS

1. The court considers three possible "social groups:" (a) all women; (b) women who find it offensive to be forced to wear the chador (also described at one point as women who are westernized and freethinking); and (c) women who find it so offensive to be forced to wear the chador that they would refuse to do so, despite the severe penalties. To each of these possible social groups, the court applies a three-part test. Before proceeding further, make sure you are clear how the court's three-part test is applied to each of the three possible social group claims.

2. Focus first on social group #1—all women. The good news for women seeking asylum is that with this decision the Third Circuit became the first United States court to hold explicitly that women are a social group. That conclusion became inevitable once the court decided to adopt *Acosta*, since gender is an immutable characteristic. Accord, *Mohammed v. Gonzales*, 400 F.3d 785 (9th Cir. 2005); UNHCR, Guidelines on International Protection: "Membership of a particular social group" within the context of article IA(2) of the 1951 Convention and/or its 1967 Protocol relating to the Status of Refugees, U.N. Doc. HCR/GIP/02/02 (May 7, 2002), para. II.B.12, reproduced, 81 IR 571 (Apr. 26, 2004); UNHCR, Guidelines on International Protection: Gender–Related Persecution within the context of Article 1A(2) of the 1951 Convention and/or its 1967 Protocol relating to the Status of Refugees, U.N. Doc. HCR/GIP//02/01, para. 30 (May 7, 2002), reproduced, 81 IR 561 (Apr. 26, 2004).

But notice the way the court implicitly interprets the requirement that the persecution be "on account of" membership in a particular social group. In the court's view, the problem here is that Fatin "has not shown she would suffer ... 'persecution' based *solely* on her gender" (emphasis added). Does she really have to show that? The statutory definition of "refugee" doesn't use the word "solely." If, for example, a government persecutes a subcategory of one particular race (and no one else), is asylum really to be denied because the persecution is not "solely" on account of race? Or should "on account of" be read to mean "but for?" Under the latter interpretation, Fatin would prevail as long as she can show that the persecution of which she has a well founded fear would not occur but for her membership in the particular social group—in this case, but for her gender.

A but-for test would not have altered the result in this case, because Fatin's problem was that the court simply did not regard forced adherence to the Iranian dress code as persecution (at least not for her). Therefore, although the court says that the problem is that Fatin failed to prove a well founded fear of persecution based solely on gender, the real problem, in the court's eyes, is that Fatin hasn't proved a well founded fear of persecution, period. Had the court concluded that her forced compliance with the dress code rose to the level of persecution, would there have been any reason to deny asylum?

The meaning of "on account of" is taken up separately in section B.2.d below.

3. Now focus on social group #2—women who find the dress code offensive. Here we have a difficult line-drawing problem. The court acknowledges that, if a woman's convictions are so strong that she would defy the law and accept the consequences rather than wear the chador, then the practice rises to the level of persecution. In the last full paragraph of the opinion, the court also assumes *"for the sake of argument* that requiring some women to wear chadors may be so abhorrent to them that it would be tantamount to persecution" [emphasis added], even if they are not willing to defy the law. This question, which the court did not feel it needed to reach on its reading of the evidence, is a difficult one. What is your view? *Should* being forced to do something one finds abhorrent be held to constitute persecution, or should a court require a showing that the person finds the practice so abhorrent that she would defy the law and accept the consequences, whatever they might be? Should a woman have to risk being stoned to death for her convictions before a court will find that those convictions are fundamental to her personal identity? Or would most people sacrifice even things that are fundamental to their identities if they had to do so to save their lives? (The author thanks Professor Muneer Ahmad for his insightful help on this issue.)

4. Focus, finally, on social group #3—women whose convictions are so intense that they would defy the dress code, even knowing how dangerous defiance would be. As just noted, the court acknowledges that such women might well meet the refugee definition. Are there arguments that the government could make against granting asylum even to this group? Should the test be subjective (this particular woman would disobey the law), or objective (a reasonable person similarly situated would disobey the law), or both?

5. *Fatin* was decided in 1993. In May 1995, the former INS released an important memorandum providing guidance to INS asylum officers on the handling of gender-related asylum claims. Memorandum from Phyllis Coven, INS Office of International Affairs, to All INS Asylum Office/rs and HQASM Coordinators, May 26, 1995, reproduced in 72 IR at 781–90 (June 5, 1995) [hereafter cited as INS Gender Guidelines].

The INS Gender Guidelines were inspired by UNHCR gender guidelines issued in 1991, by comprehensive guidelines issued by Canada's Immigration and Refugee Board in 1993, and by proposed guidelines prepared by Harvard Law School's Women Refugees Project in 1994. See INS Gender Guidelines at 1. In addition to the United States and Canada, Australia has issued Gender Guidelines. For a thoughtful comparison of the three sets of guidelines, see Audrey Macklin, *Cross-Border Shopping for*

Ideas: A Critical Review of United States, Canadian, and Australian Approaches to Gender–Related Asylum Claims, 13 Georgetown Immigration L.J. 25 (1998).

The INS Gender Guidelines review various relevant international human rights instruments. They then admonish asylum officers to display sensitivity both in interviewing claimants who present gender-related claims and in assessing such claims. The Guidelines also analyze some of the legal issues that gender-based claims commonly generate. Most significantly, the Guidelines confirm that sexual violence can constitute persecution and that such persecution can be on account of political opinion (actual or imputed), social group, or possibly other protected grounds. The main goal was to emphasize to asylum adjudicators that gender-related asylum claims are to be taken seriously.

UNHCR has now issued a set of gender guidelines designed to provide interpretive guidance to governments and others. See item 2 above.

6. The degree of influence of the INS Gender Guidelines on the outcomes of cases has varied. In *Fisher v. INS*, 79 F.3d 955 (9th Cir. en banc 1996) (amended opinion), a divided court reached a result similar to that in *Fatin* (except that in *Fisher* the claimant had argued persecution only on the bases of religion and political opinion, not social group). Like the Third Circuit, the Ninth Circuit was not willing to hold the dress code to be persecution. Since the alleged persecution consisted of punishment for violation of law, the court asked only whether the punishment was selective, disproportionate, or pretextual. Concluding it was none of those, the court rejected the claim. Since the BIA decision that the court was reviewing had been rendered before the INS Guidelines, Judge Noonan, dissenting, urged a remand to the BIA for reconsideration in the light of those Guidelines. Significantly, a majority of the en banc court declined to do so.

Deborah Anker and Nancy Kelly, both instrumental in helping to shape the Guidelines, have noted many positive consequences. See 72 IR at 771–72 (June 5, 1995); see also Deborah Anker, Nancy Kelly, & John Willshire–Carrera, *Rape in the Community as a Basis for Asylum: The Treatment of Women Refugees' Claims to Protection in Canada and the United States–Part 2*, 2 BIB 608 (Aug. 1, 1997) (identifying numerous favorable concrete consequences, particularly in cases of ethnically motivated rape, but regretting inadequate implementation).

The decision in *Fisher* is interesting for another reason. The majority used language that might have been interpreted to mean that a government does not persecute when it treats all women the same—even if it treats women less favorably than men. Judge Canby's separate concurring opinion forcefully disavowed that notion. He stressed that the court was *not* foreclosing the possibility of asylum in a case where the government persecuted women because of their gender.

7.   Should forcing a person to practice a religion in which he or she does not believe be considered persecution? Is this different from denying a person the freedom to practice a religion in which he or she does believe?

8.   In two groundbreaking cases, Immigration Judge John Gossart (Baltimore) granted asylum to women who had asserted compelling gender-related persecution. In one case, the woman had been tortured and imprisoned by the Taliban in Afghanistan for working outside the home and for walking outside the home (to work). He found she had been persecuted solely for being a woman. See 77 IR 1166 (Aug. 14, 2000). In another case he granted asylum to an Indian woman who had been beaten and threatened with death if she failed to meet her mother-in-law's continuing dowry demands. In the latter case Judge Gossart found persecution on account of membership in a particular social group and defined the social group in very specific terms. See *Matter of Patel*, A74 974 011 at 10 (IJ Gossart, sitting at York, Pa., May 23, 1997).

9.   At the heart of this issue is the tension between two competing philosophies—cultural relativism, which emphasizes respect for the cultural norms of the country of origin, and universalism, which stresses the universality of internationally recognized human rights. For a sensitive discussion of the dangers of cultural relativism in the context of gender, see Jacqueline Bhabha, *Embodied Rights: Gender Persecution, State Sovereignty, and Refugees*, 9 Public Culture 3 (1996). We shall return to the subject of cultural relativism in the context of female genital mutilation, discussed below. For now, try to decide on which side of the line you would place the Iranian dress code. Does it transgress a fundamental human right? Or is it a justifiable expression of another country's cultural norms?

10.   Domestic violence has become one of the more common contexts in which gender-related persecution issues arise. Domestic violence cases, in turn, often raise difficult issues concerning how to analyze persecution by private actors. Both subjects—non-state actors and domestic violence claims—are taken up in a separate section below.

11.   The mass rapes in the former Yugoslavia focused renewed attention on how to treat asylum claims filed by rape victims. But the problem was soon exposed as a worldwide one. In *Matter of D.V.*, 21 I. & N. Dec. 77 (BIA 1993), a politically active woman was gang-raped and severely beaten by Haitian soldiers in retaliation for her support of President Aristide. Finding a well founded fear of persecution on account of both political opinion and religion (she did not argue social group), the Board granted asylum. As the case illustrates, rape-related asylum claims do not have to be based on social group. They may constitute persecution based on any of the protected grounds. See generally Anker, Kelly & Willshire–Carrera, item 6 above.

Matter of Kasinga

Board of Immigration Appeals, June 13, 1996.
21 I. & N. Dec. 357.

■ SCHMIDT, CHAIRMAN:

This is a timely appeal by the applicant from a decision of an Immigration Judge dated August 25, 1995. The Immigration Judge found the applicant excludable as an intending immigrant, denied her applications for asylum and withholding of deportation, and ordered her excluded and deported from the United States. Upon reviewing the appellate record anew ("de novo review"), we will sustain the applicant's appeal, grant asylum, and order her admitted to the United States as an asylee.

A fundamental issue before us is whether the practice of female genital mutilation ("FGM") can be the basis for a grant of asylum under section 208 of the Immigration and Nationality Act. On appeal, the parties agree that FGM can be the basis for a grant of asylum. We find that FGM can be a basis for asylum.

Nevertheless, the parties disagree about 1) the parameters of FGM as a ground for asylum in future cases, and 2) whether the applicant is entitled to asylum on the basis of the record before us. In deciding this case, we decline to speculate on, or establish rules for, cases that are not before us.

We make seven major findings in the applicant's case. Those findings are summarized below.

First, the record before us reflects that the applicant is a credible witness. Second, FGM, as practiced by the Tchamba–Kunsuntu Tribe of Togo and documented in the record, constitutes persecution. Third, the applicant is a member of a social group consisting of young women of the Tchamba–Kunsuntu Tribe who have not had FGM, as practiced by that tribe, and who oppose the practice. Fourth, the applicant has a well-founded fear of persecution. Fifth, the persecution the applicant fears is "on account of" her social group. Sixth, the applicant's fear of persecution is country-wide. Seventh, and finally, the applicant is eligible for and should be granted asylum in the exercise of discretion. Each finding is explained below.

I.   CREDIBILITY

A.   The Applicant's Testimony

The applicant is a 19–year-old native and citizen of Togo. She attended 2 years of high school. She is a member of the Tchamba–Kunsuntu Tribe of northern Togo. She testified that young women of her tribe normally undergo FGM at age 15. However, she did not because she initially was protected from FGM by her influential, but now deceased, father.

The applicant stated that upon her father's death in 1993, under tribal custom her aunt, her father's sister, became the primary authority figure in the family. The applicant's mother was driven from the family home, left Togo, and went to live with her family in Benin. The applicant testified that she does not currently know her mother's exact whereabouts.

The applicant further testified that her aunt forced her into a polygamous marriage in October 1994, when she was 17. The husband selected by her aunt was 45 years old and had three other wives at the time of marriage. The applicant testified that, under tribal custom, her aunt and her husband planned to force her to submit to FGM before the marriage was consummated.

The applicant testified that she feared imminent mutilation. With the help of her older sister, she fled Togo for Ghana. However, she was afraid that her aunt and her husband would locate her there. Consequently, using money from her mother, the applicant embarked for Germany by airplane.

Upon arrival in Germany, the applicant testified that she was somewhat disoriented and spent several hours wandering around the airport looking for fellow Africans who might help her. Finally, she struck up a conversation, in English, with a German woman.

After hearing the applicant's story, the woman offered to give the applicant temporary shelter in her home until the applicant decided what to do next. For the next 2 months, the applicant slept in the woman's living room, while performing cooking and cleaning duties.

The applicant further stated that in December 1994, while on her way to a shopping center, she met a young Nigerian man. He was the first person from Africa she had spoken to since arriving in Germany. They struck up a conversation, during which the applicant told the man about her situation. He offered to sell the applicant his sister's British passport so that she could seek asylum in the United States, where she has an aunt, an uncle, and a cousin. The applicant followed the man's suggestion, purchasing the passport and the ticket with money given to her by her sister.

The applicant did not attempt a fraudulent entry into the United States. Rather, upon arrival at Newark International Airport on December 17, 1994, she immediately requested asylum. She remained in detention by the Immigration and Naturalization Service ("INS") until April 1996.

The applicant testified that the Togolese police and the Government of Togo were aware of FGM and would take no steps to protect her from the practice. She further testified that her aunt had reported her to the Togolese police. Upon return, she would be taken back to her husband by the police and forced to undergo FGM. She testified at several points that there would be nobody to protect her from FGM in Togo.

* * *

The applicant testified that she could not find protection anywhere in Togo. She stated that Togo is a very small country and her husband and aunt, with the help of the police, could locate her anywhere she went. She also stated that her husband is well known in Togo and is a friend of the police. On cross-examination she stated that it would not be possible for her to live with another tribe in Togo.

The applicant also testified that the Togolese police could locate her in Ghana. She indicated that she did not seek asylum in Germany because she could not speak German and therefore could not continue her education there. She stated that she did not have relatives in Germany as she does in the United States.

[Here the Board summarizes the extensive testimony and documentary evidence establishing the preceding facts.—Ed.]

* * *

4. Description of FGM

According to the applicant's testimony, the FGM practiced by her tribe, the Tchamba–Kunsuntu, is of an extreme type involving cutting the genitalia with knives, extensive bleeding, and a 40–day recovery period. The background materials confirm that the FGM practiced in some African countries, such as Togo, is of an extreme nature causing permanent damage, and not just a minor form of genital ritual.

The record material establishes that FGM in its extreme forms is a practice in which portions of the female genitalia are cut away. In some cases, the vagina is sutured partially closed. This practice clearly inflicts harm or suffering upon the girl or woman who undergoes it.

FGM is extremely painful and at least temporarily incapacitating. It permanently disfigures the female genitalia. FGM exposes the girl or woman to the risk of serious, potentially life-threatening complications. These include, among others, bleeding, infection, urine retention, stress, shock, psychological trauma, and damage to the urethra and anus. It can result in permanent loss of genital sensation and can adversely affect sexual and erotic functions.

The FGM Alert, compiled and distributed by the INS Resource Information Center, notes that "few African countries have officially condemned female genital mutilation and still fewer have enacted legislation against the practice." Further, according to the FGM Alert, even in those few African countries where legislative efforts have been made, they are usually ineffective to protect women against FGM. The FGM Alert notes that "it remains practically true that [African] women have little legal recourse and may face threats to their freedom, threats or acts of physical violence, or social ostracization for refusing to undergo this harmful traditional practice for attempting to protect their female children." Id. at 6–7. Togo is not listed in the FGM Alert as among the African countries that have made even minimal efforts to protect women from FGM.

* * * [The INS Gender Guidelines] state that "rape . . ., sexual abuse and domestic violence, infanticide and genital mutilation are forms of mistreatment primarily directed at girls and women and they may serve as evidence of past persecution on account of one or more of the five grounds."

* * *

* * * [O]n the basis of the record before us, we find the applicant to be a credible witness.

II. FGM AS PERSECUTION

For the purposes of this case, we adopt the [above] description of FGM * * *. We agree with the parties that this level of harm can constitute "persecution" within the meaning of section 101(a)(42)(A) of the Act.

While a number of descriptions of persecution have been formulated in our past decisions, we have recognized that persecution can consist of the infliction of harm or suffering by a government, or persons a government is unwilling or unable to control, to overcome a characteristic of the victim. The "seeking to overcome" formulation has its antecedents in concepts of persecution that predate the Refugee Act of 1980.

As observed by the INS, many of our past cases involved actors who had a subjective intent to punish their victims. However, this subjective "punitive" or "malignant" intent is not required for harm to constitute persecution.

Our characterization of FGM as persecution is consistent with our past definitions of that term. We therefore reach the conclusion that FGM can be persecution without passing on the INS's proposed "shocks the conscience" test. * * *

III.   SOCIAL GROUP

* * *

In the context of this case, we find the particular social group to be the following: young women of the Tchamba–Kunsuntu Tribe who have not had FGM, as practiced by that tribe, and who oppose the practice. This is very similar to the formulations suggested by the parties.

The defined social group meets the test we set forth in Matter of Acosta. It also is consistent with the law of the United States Court of Appeals for the Third Circuit, where this case arose. Fatin v. INS, 12 F.3d 1233, 1241 (3d Cir. 1993) (stating that Iranian women who refuse to conform to the Iranian Government's gender-specific laws and social norms may well satisfy the Acosta definition).

In accordance with Acosta, the particular social group is defined by common characteristics that members of the group either cannot change, or should not be required to change because such characteristics are fundamental to their individual identities. The characteristics of being a "young woman" and a "member of the Tchamba–Kunsuntu Tribe" cannot be changed. The characteristic of having intact genitalia is one that is so fundamental to the individual identity of a young woman that she should not be required to change it.

IV.   WELL–FOUNDED FEAR

The burden of proof is upon an applicant for asylum to establish that a "reasonable person" in her circumstances would fear persecution upon return to Togo. The applicant has met this burden through a combination of her credible testimony and the introduction of documentary evidence and background information that supports her claim.

V.   "ON ACCOUNT OF"

To be eligible for asylum, the applicant must establish that her well-founded fear of persecution is "on account of" one of the five grounds specified in the Act, here, her membership in a "particular social group."

See, e.g., Matter of H——, supra (holding that harm or abuse because of clan membership constitutes persecution on account of social group).

Both parties have advanced, and the background materials support, the proposition that there is no legitimate reason for FGM. Group Exhibit 4 contains materials showing that the practice has been condemned by such groups as the United Nations, the International Federation of Gynecology and Obstetrics, the Council on Scientific Affairs, the World Health Organization, the International Medical Association, and the American Medical Association.

Record materials state that FGM "has been used to control woman's sexuality". It also is characterized as a form of "sexual oppression" that is "based on the manipulation of women's sexuality in order to assure male dominance and exploitation." During oral argument before us, the INS General Counsel agreed with the latter characterization. He also stated that the practice is a "severe bodily invasion" that should be regarded as meeting the asylum standard even if done with "subjectively benign intent".

We agree with the parties that, as described and documented in this record, FGM is practiced, at least in some significant part, to overcome sexual characteristics of young women of the tribe who have not been, and do not wish to be, subjected to FGM. We therefore find that the persecution the applicant fears in Togo is "on account of" her status as a member of the defined social group.

* * *

* * * [W]e find that this record adequately supports the applicant's claim that she has a country-wide fear of persecution in Togo.

VII. DISCRETION

* * *

We have weighed the favorable and adverse factors and are satisfied that discretion should be exercised in favor of the applicant. Therefore, we will grant asylum to the applicant.

* * *

CONCURRING OPINION: Lauri Steven Filppu, Board Member, joined by Michael J. Heilman, Board Member.

I respectfully concur. I write separately in part to respond more completely to several arguments advanced by the Immigration and Naturalization Service.

* * *

B. The Persecution Issues

The parties offer different theories for why FGM can amount to persecution, with the Service offering a novel "shocks the conscience" theory as part of its analysis. For purposes of this case, it is sufficient to observe that the level of suffering associated with FGM, as practiced by the applicant's tribe, would be more than enough to constitute persecution if inflicted exclusively on a religious or political minority.

The "on account of" and "particular social group" requirements of the statute are not in dispute here, except to the extent that the applicant's proposed "social group" definition includes an element of personal opposition by the victim which is not included in the Service's proposal. It is not essential to choose between these offerings. In view of the positions taken by the parties, the applicant would qualify for relief under either proffered social group.

* * *

III. THE SERVICE'S FRAMEWORK

Despite the absence of any major dispute between the parties in this case, the Service requests that we adopt its broad "framework of analysis" for claims of this type. Its suggestion candidly is aimed at addressing issues it sees arising in relation to claims that may be made by women from other "parts of the world where FGM is practiced" and by those "who have been subjected to it in the past."

The Board engages in case adjudication. It decides those issues that lead to the resolution of the cases before it. Our published rulings act as precedent under the regulations and can affect many related cases. But the Board is not well positioned, in the context of a single disposition of a novel issue, to establish comprehensive rules or guidelines for the adjudication of all cases presenting variations on the case at hand. Yet, it is the cases that are not before us that seem to draw much of the Service's attention in its brief.

The Service points out that it is "estimated that over eighty million females have been subjected to FGM." It further notes that there is "no indication" that "Congress considered application of [the asylum laws] to broad cultural practices of the type involved here." The Service proceeds to argue that "the underlying purposes of the asylum system . . . are unavoidably in tension" in both providing protection for those seriously in jeopardy and in maintaining broad overall governmental control over immigration. The Service further argues that "the Board's interpretation in this case must assure protection for those most at risk of the harms covered by the statute, but it cannot simply grant asylum to all who might be subjected to a practice deemed objectionable or a violation of a person's human rights." It is from these underpinnings that the Service argues that the class of FGM victims who may be eligible for asylum "does not consist of all women who come from the parts of the world where FGM is practiced, nor of all who have been subjected to it in the past."

The Service then offers its "framework of analysis." That framework includes a new "shocks the conscience" test for persecution.[a] The advan-

---

a. The INS was actually suggesting a two-pronged test. It argued that, to consti- tute "persecution," the particular harm must be either inflicted with "malignant or puni-

tages seen by the Service of this test evidently include: 1) the ability to define FGM as "persecution" notwithstanding any lack of intent to "punish" FGM victims on the part of the victims' parents or tribe members who may well "believe that they are simply performing an important cultural rite that bonds the individual to the society"; 2) the ability to exclude other cultural practices, such as "body scarring," from the definition of persecution as these do not shock the conscience; and 3) the ability to exclude past victims of FGM from asylum eligibility if "they consented" to it or "at least acquiesced," as in the case of a woman who experienced FGM as "a small child," since FGM would not shock the conscience unless inflicted on "an unconsenting or resisting individual."

With respect to the past persecution question, the Service references 8 C.F.R. § 208.13(b)(1) (1995), and notes "that a woman once circumcised cannot ordinarily be subjected to FGM a second time." The regulation cited by the Service provides in part for a presumption of future persecution that arises from past persecution, and allows only one way of overcoming the presumption, namely, a change in country conditions. As conditions in countries where FGM is practiced may not have changed, it may be anomalous to have a binding presumption of future persecution where the act of persecution will never again take place for the individual past victim.

The Service's broad framework of analysis also seems to have led it to offer a social group definition that in one respect fits the test set forth in Matter of Acosta, yet is also defined largely by the harm sought to be included in the concept of persecution. For example, we simply do not know from this record whether the similar social groups proposed by the parties are recognized as groupings for any other purposes within Togolese society aside from the serious personal harm at issue here. The record does not disclose whether this group is seen as a distinct body within Togo or within the tribe both before and after the infliction of FGM on its members, or whether it is a group that exists exclusively in relation to the particular offensive practice at issue here. Because the social group definition has not been a real source of dispute between the parties, we are also not well informed as to the degree of affiliation between or the homogeneity among its members. See Sanchez–Trujillo v. INS, 801 F.2d 1571 (9th Cir. 1986).[3]

tive intent" or "so extreme as to shock the conscience of the society from which asylum is sought." The INS argued that FGM is rarely inflicted with evil intent and thus will normally qualify as persecution only if it shocks the conscience. For that to happen, the INS argued, the harm must be "extreme," it must be inflicted on an unconsenting individual, and the person must actually suffer that harm rather than the harm that accompanies refusal. For purposes of that test, acquiescence—even by a small child— would prevent a person from showing past persecution. See Karen Musalo, *In re Kasinga: A Big Step Forward for Gender–Based*

Asylum Claims, 73 IR 853, 856 (July 1, 1996), quoting from the INS Brief.—Ed.

3. But for the concession of the Service on this point, I would be inclined to remand this case for further development on the "social group" question. The meaning of the phrase "membership in a particular social group" has not been completely explained by our case law. Nevertheless, it is questionable whether the statute was meant to encompass groups that are defined principally in relation to the harm feared by the asylum applicant. The record here sheds little light on this question.

The Service does not offer its new framework of analysis for our consideration as part of an effort to harmonize a line of past rulings, or otherwise to put some order into a series of decisions that have addressed FGM questions in a variety of contexts. Instead, the Service offers its new analysis in the context of a case of first impression for the Board. * * *

* * *

The Board certainly is not oblivious to immigration policy considerations in the disposition of cases falling within our jurisdiction. But we are not fundamentally a policy-making body. There may be some unsettling or unsatisfying aspects to the slower and less predictable development of legal guidelines that inures in the Board's case adjudication system. But there are alternatives if resort to the Board's issuance of precedent is not satisfactory in a particular context. The Service can seek to have the Attorney General issue regulations that comprehensively address competing concerns, or it can work within the Administration for appropriate legislative action by Congress.

CONCURRING OPINION: Lory D. Rosenberg, Board Member

Today, in the specific case before us, this Board decides that a young woman of a particular tribe in Togo, who opposes being subjected to female genital mutilation as practiced by that tribe, is a member of a particular social group, and that on account of that membership, a reasonable person could fear persecution as defined in the Immigration and Nationality Act. I join the majority decision in its entirety.

* * * [T]here are three important points with regard to our decision today that I believe require further elaboration.

First, this case involves the respondent's reasonable fear that she faces the possibility of harm or abuse, rising to the level of persecution, inflicted on account of her membership in a particular social group.

* * * [U]nlike the Service, which urges us to consider a new standard and a new framework which exceeds the bounds of this case, the applicant contends that we should draw on traditional principles of asylum jurisprudence to adopt a framework that is consistent and appropriate with the Refugee Act and international law. I agree.

In my view, there are three essential elements inherent in our definition of persecution, which, if established, constitute the basis for a discretionary grant of asylum, or a mandatory grant of withholding of deportation, or both. One is the factor of the applicant's genuine, subjective fear of persecution, which must be accompanied by objective evidence rendering the fear reasonable. The next is the factor of harm, abuse, or ill-treatment which rises to the level of, or amounts to, persecution and includes consideration of the applicant's attitude towards such treatment. The last is the reason for, or cause of, the infliction of persecution. This is known as the "on account of" factor, which includes consideration of the motives of the agent of persecution and requires a nexus between the infliction of harm which constitutes persecution and one of the five protected grounds or statuses, such as social group membership, set forth by the Act. In Fatin v. INS, 12 F.3d 1233, 1240 (3d Cir. 1993), the United States Court of Appeals for the Third Circuit held that to prevail, an applicant claiming social group persecution must identify a cognizable social group, establish her membership in it, and show that persecution is based on that membership.

In this case, I conclude that the applicant's fear is of imminent female genital mutilation, related to being forced to enter an arranged marriage, documented in the record as constituting a mandatory tribal custom. The harm or abuse amounting to persecution is the genital mutilation opposed by the applicant. The reason the persecution would be inflicted, the "on account of" element, is because of the persecutor's intent to overcome her state of being non-mutilated and accordingly, free from male-dominated tribal control, including an arranged marriage.

I see no reason to depart from our existing jurisprudence in order to determine the claim set forth here. In my view, this issue is controlled by our precedent decisions * * *.

* * *

Second, a social group definition that takes into account and differentiates the other component elements of the definition of persecution which warrant protection under United States law is critical.

There is nothing about a social group definition based upon gender that requires us to treat it as either an aberration, or as an unanticipated development requiring a new standard. While this is the first time that this Board has addressed the particular type of harm or abuse feared by the respondent—female genital mutilation—it is not the first time that the Board has addressed the "particular social group category". * * *

The social group category within the refugee definition incorporated into the Act has been recognized as having deliberately been included as a "catch-all" for individuals not falling into the first four specifically enumerated categories of political opinion, race, religion, or ethnicity. As Professor [Pamela] Goldberg discusses, the scope of the social group category has been addressed by preeminent international law scholars. For example, Atle Grahl–Madsen considers it to be broader than the other categories and to have been added to the Convention precisely to protect against persecution that would arise from unforeseeable circumstances. In addition, Guy Goodwin Gill asserts that the category allows states to expand it to various classes susceptible to persecution. In her article, Professor Goldberg proposes one definition of a gender-identified social group which would include a group of women characterized by circumstances or similar treatment, not unlike the definition we propose here.

Unlike requests for asylum premised upon political opinion, social group claims, like those involving race, ethnicity, or religion, are status based and do not necessarily require a showing of the presence of an individual's opinions or activities which spurs the persecutor's wrath or otherwise motivates the harm or persecution. Rather, such requests involve a determination of whether the shared characteristics are those which motivate an agent of persecution to seek to overcome or otherwise harm the individual. Consequently, while not inaccurate, it is surplusage to define the social group in this case by including as an element the applicant's opposition to the practice of female genital mutilation.

* * * As I have stated, the applicant's political or social views—her attitude or intent—is not relevant to our definition of the social group to which she belongs, but rather to whether the harm or abuse she faces constitutes persecution.

In Matter of H——, supra, this Board found, without difficulty or the need to qualify, that a man who was a member of a tribe in Somalia whose members were being systematically attacked by other tribes in retribution for the corruption and brutality of former ruler and tribe member, Siad Barre, had established persecution based on his clan membership alone. That his father and brother were killed and that he himself was brutally treated during detention was found to be persecution on account of his membership in a subclan in Somalia, a particular social group. His attitude towards that persecution was neither examined nor relevant.

The only distinguishing characteristic about this case that I can perceive to set it apart from others we already have decided is that it involves a woman. Reliance upon such a distinction to support a separate category for treatment of women's asylum claims, to my mind, would be impermissible. Here, the applicant is a member of a group: girls and women of a given tribe, some perhaps of marriageable age, whose members are routinely subjected to the harm which the majority finds to constitute persecution. The applicant's opposition (which happens to be present in this case) or the lack of it, is neither determinative, nor necessary to define the social group in accordance with the statutory language.

Third, it is the role of this Board to interpret and apply the statute in individual cases coming before us for the purpose of establishing a consistent framework for adjudication.

* * *

In an endorsement of the viability of the present statutory structure, the Service itself saw fit to develop gender guidelines to assist in the adjudication of asylum claims brought by women. Curiously, the position of the Service in this case makes no reference to its published guidance in that regard. However, it is notable that the guidelines recognize the importance of considering gender-based claims in light of international human rights instruments and the framework they provide. Indeed, the Service itself recognizes that gender-based asylum claims are "developments in refugee protection" and that its guidelines are a natural and multifaceted outgrowth of a set of gender guidelines issued by the UNHCR in 1991, the 1993 Canadian gender guidelines and other sources of expertise including the Women's Refugee Project of the Harvard Immigration and Refugee Program.

* * *

DISSENTING OPINION: Fred W. Vacca, Board Member

I respectfully dissent without opinion.

NOTES AND QUESTIONS

1. The *Kasinga* case was a media event. Professor Karen Musalo, the lead counsel for Kasinga, understood at an early stage the strategic importance of bringing the issue of female genital mutilation to the attention of the public. Through a highly successful grassroots organizing campaign, the legal team was able to generate crucial publicity about Kasinga's case and about some immigration judge decisions in similar cases. For a sampling of the articles, see Karen Musalo, *In re Kasinga: A Big Step Forward for Gender–Based Asylum Claims*, 73 IR 853, 861 (July 1, 1996); see also Fauziya Kassindya & Layli Miller Bashir, Do They Hear You When You Cry? (1999).

As the BIA notes with some concern, the former INS detained Kasinga for 16 months, despite repeated requests for parole pending the disposition of her case. Nine days after a front page New York Times article triggered widespread criticism of the INS, the agency released Kasinga from detention. In Musalo's words: "Although the INS denies that it paroled Ms. Kasinga due to media attention and public opinion, it appears more than coincidental that all previous efforts to secure Ms. Kasinga's release had been rebuffed, but the INS just happened to reconsider and release her nine days after the first New York Times article appeared." *Id.* at 861; Hope Lewis & Isabelle R. Gunning, *Cleaning Our Own House: "Exotic" and Familial Human Rights Violations*, 4 Buffalo Human Rights L. Rev. 123, 130–31 (1998) (describing the brutal conditions of Kasinga's detention).

By the time the case reached the BIA, the INS and Kasinga's counsel had reached agreement on what the BIA rightly called the "fundamental issue" in the case—whether FGM can be the basis for a grant of asylum. Both agreed that it could. With that stipulation, the real question was what the general principle would be for determining whether a given FGM claim qualifies. Immigration and refugee professionals waited anxiously for the answer to that question. Some even hoped that the BIA in *Kasinga* would clarify the meanings of the crucial phrases "persecution," "social group," and "on account of."

Asylum advocates cheered the positive outcome for Kasinga, but those who had hoped for coherent guidance on future cases came away disappointed. The BIA not only declined to clarify the general meanings of the critical statutory phrases, but also refrained from setting out even vague general principles for determining when FGM will constitute persecution or when that persecution will be regarded as being on account of membership in a social group. Instead, the BIA appears to have held that sometimes FGM will be a basis for asylum, sometimes it won't, and on these specific facts (this woman, this tribe, this particular surgical method) FGM is persecution on account of membership in a social group. After *Kasinga*, the government, the immigration judges, and the immigration bar remain uncertain what test is to be applied. See Jacqueline Bhabha, *Embodied Rights: Gender Persecution, State Sovereignty, and Refugees*, 9 Public Culture 3, 30 (1996) (describing BIA decision as "narrow ruling"); Arthur C. Helton & Alison Nicoll, *Female Genital Mutilation as Ground for Asylum in the United States: The Recent Case of In re Fauziya Kasinga and Prospects for More Gender Sensitive Approaches*, 28 Columbia Human Rights L. Rev. 375 (1997) (applauding specific result in *Kasinga* but lamenting lack of guidance for future cases).

Subsequent court decisions, however, have had little difficulty recognizing FGM as persecution. See, e.g., *Mohammed v. Gonzales*, 400 F.3d 785 (9th Cir. 2005); *Abay v. Ashcroft*, 368 F.3d 634 (6th Cir. 2004); *Abankwah v. INS*, 185 F.3d 18 (2d Cir. 1999).

While the opinion in *Kasinga* might be short on analytical value, the various opinions do expose some of the complexities. The discussion that follows examines some of the subissues.

2.   The various opinions in *Kasinga* struggled with the definition of the applicant's social group. The majority opinion defined her social group as consisting of "young women of the Tchamba–Kunsuntu Tribe who have not had FGM, as practiced by that tribe, and who oppose the practice." The Board had little difficulty finding that this group satisfied the *Acosta* immutability test, since Kasinga could not change her gender or her tribe, and "having intact genitalia is [a characteristic] that is so fundamental to the individual identity of a young woman that she should not be required to change it."

The Board's rationale raises more questions than it answers. First, why does the Board need to add the qualifiers concerning her membership in this particular tribe and the particular way in which this tribe practices FGM? If the idea is that having intact genitalia is fundamental to the identities of all young women, then wouldn't that rationale hold regardless of which tribe it is or which type of mutilation that tribe practices? Perhaps the method of FGM affects whether the practice constitutes persecution (a point taken up below), but if so, isn't it redundant to make it part of the social group definition?

Second, because this case arises in the Third Circuit, the Board is bound by *Fatin*, which it cites in support of its application of the social group definition. It is difficult, however, to figure out what aspect of *Fatin* the Board thinks it is following. In that case, as you might recall, the court considered several different possible social groups. The only one it specifically *rejected* was the one analogous to the definition that the majority opinion adopts in *Kasinga*—i.e., a definition that rests on the applicant being "opposed" to the particular practice. The court in *Fatin* had held that merely being opposed to the practice (in that case, requiring women to wear the chador) was not enough; only if a woman is so opposed that she will defy the law and suffer the consequences (or, possibly, so opposed that she would find the practice "abhorrent"), the court held, will persecution be found. Absent some explanation, it is unclear why the Board thought *Fatin* was consistent with its position. After the fact, however, can you come up with a principled argument for reconciling the two cases?

Third, the court in *Fatin* had also made clear that women—without any qualifiers—constitute a social group. Once the Board held that the FGM that was practiced in this case was persecution, could it not have held that the particular social group was simply all women (or all women and girls)?

3.   The concurring opinion of Board Member Filppu questions the propriety of defining the particular social group "principally in relation to the harm feared by the particular applicant." Presumably he has in mind the reference to those "who oppose the practice." Read carefully footnote 3 of the Filppu concurrence and the accompanying text. First, is Member Filppu attacking a straw person, or has the majority really defined the social group "principally in relation to the harm feared?" Second, does Member Filppu accept *Acosta*?

4.   Board Member Rosenberg is the only one who seems to have noticed that it is "surplusage" to include the applicant's opposition to FGM in the social group definition. As she points out, Kasinga's opposition to the practice is already taken into account in deciding whether the harm constitutes persecution. (Board Member Filppu questions the same qualification, see above, but on the ground that it is insufficient, not on the ground that it is duplicative.) Yet even Board Member Rosenberg does not question some of the other qualifiers that the majority opinion adds, such as membership in the particular tribe and the particular method by which this tribe performs FGM. To the extent those factors are thought relevant at all, don't they go merely to whether the feared harm constitutes persecution and to whether Kasinga has a well-founded fear that that harm will occur?

5.   The common thread in the approaches that the various Board members in this case take to the definition of social group is that every one of the formulations contains one or more elements that duplicate other requirements of a prima facie case of asylum. As a result, the determination of whether the hypothesized group meets the definition of a social group becomes much more complicated than it needs to be.

Wouldn't it have been a lot cleaner for the Board simply to hold that women are a social group, period? And isn't that what the Board's own decision in *Acosta* (social group is defined by immutable characteristics) and the court decision in *Fatin* (binding authority in this case) require? Had the Board done that, the main legal issue would have been whether the harm that Kasinga fears constitutes persecution, and the main fact question would have been whether she has a well-founded fear that the claimed harm will occur. (If you think that defining the social group as consisting of all females would have made it difficult for Kasinga to satisfy the "on account of" requirement, hold off on that point until you get to item 11 below.)

6.   Once the Board gets over the social group hurdle, it is in a position to address what should be the central legal issue in the case—whether FGM is "persecution." What possible answers could the BIA or a court give to that question? Consider here both bright-line rules and more elastic formulas.

7.   Probably the single most significant aspect of the *Kasinga* case was what the Board *didn't* do. It did not accept the invitation of the former INS to add new constraints to the general definition of persecution. Review the formula that INS General Counsel David Martin asked the Board to adopt. It is summarized in editor's footnote (a) to Member Filppu's concurring opinion. What is your reaction to the proposed test?

8.   Suppose the applicant is a young girl whose parents file an asylum claim on her behalf. They allege that she will be subjected to FGM against their will if she is returned. Should the child receive asylum? *Cf. Matter of Oluloro*, No. A72 147 491 (IJ Carter, Portland, Oregon, Mar. 23, 1994) (granting suspension of deportation after finding that United States citizen children were likely to be subjected to FGM if their mother were deported to Nigeria and she took them with her).

A separate question is whether the *parent* should receive asylum based on the FGM that the child would incur if the parent were removed and the child were to accompany the parent. On that question, the courts are divided. Compare, e.g., *Abay v. Ashcroft*, 368 F.3d 634 (6th Cir. 2004) (holding mother eligible for asylum) with *Olowo v. Ashcroft*, 368 F.3d 692 (7th Cir. 2004) (holding mother ineligible on ground she could choose to leave her LPR child behind in the United States). Which way would you come out? See generally Marcelle Rice, *Protecting Parents: Why Mothers and Fathers Who Oppose Female Genital Cutting Qualify for Asylum*, Nov. 2004 Immigration Briefings.

9.   Now that *Kasinga* has been decided, should circumcision of male infants be a basis for asylum? Or is that different?

10.   A few months after the former INS issued its Gender Guidelines, and of course before *Kasinga*, two immigration judges gave opposite answers to the question whether involuntary FGM constitutes persecution. On August 9, 1995, Immigration Judge Paul Nejelski (Arlington) granted asylum, declaring the practice to be "an atrocious form of persecution." Washington Post, Sept. 11, 1995, at D1; 72 IR at 1265 (Sept. 18, 1995). At about the same time, Immigration Judge John Gossart (Baltimore) denied the claim of a woman who had already been subjected to FGM and who feared that her daughters would suffer a similar fate. The claimant had also alleged that she and her daughters would be ostracized if they resisted FGM. The claimant herself had characterized FGM as an "important ritual" that "binds the tribe." *Matter of Johnson*, No. A72 370 565 (IJ Gossart, Apr. 28, 1995), at 3. Judge Gossart added an important observa-

tion: "[W]hile some cultures view FGM as abhorrent and/or even barbaric, others do not." *Id.* at 12.

Significantly, the INS opposed both asylum claims and appealed Judge Nejelski's ruling to the BIA. As you have seen, the INS also chose to oppose Kasinga's asylum claim before the IJ, to contest her appeal before the BIA, and to insist on keeping her detained. The INS positions in these cases have worried refugee and human rights advocates, who question whether the INS stance comports with the spirit of the recently issued Gender Guidelines. Washington Post, Sept. 11, 1995, at D1. Board Member Rosenberg gently raised the same concern in *Kasinga*.

The conclusions reached by Judges Nejelski and Gossart highlight a broader battle between cultural relativism and universalism. Judge Nejelski emphasizes the impact of the practice on the individual, finding FGM "atrocious." Judge Gossart emphasizes the foreign cultural norms that keep this practice afloat and the importance of tolerating and respecting those norms. The issue has particularly divided feminists. Those who see FGM as a cultural norm that the United States should tolerate object to the word "mutilation," preferring to call it female genital "surgery." For some sensitive discussion of the tension between responding to FGM and respecting the norms of other cultures, see Bhabha, item 1 above; Isabelle R. Gunning, *Arrogant Perception, World–Travelling and Multicultural Feminism: The Case of Female Genital Surgeries*, 23 Columbia Human Rights L.Rev. 189 (1992); Hope Lewis, *Between Irua and "Female Genital Mutilation": Feminist Human Rights Discourse and the Cultural Divide*, 8 Harvard Human Rights J. 1 (1995).

Keep in mind, too, that cultural relativism and universalism do not always diverge. Sometimes, in particular, the practice being condemned prevails in the host country as well, in a different form. Professor Isabelle Gunning, for example, has argued that the United States position, which criminalizes FGM and declares it to be persecution, reflects a hypocritical refusal to apply the same standards to analogous domestic practices. Isabelle R. Gunning, *Global Feminism at the Local Level: Criminal and Asylum Laws Regarding Female Genital Surgeries*, 3 J. Gender, Race & Justice 45 (1999). Professor Leti Volpp makes a similar point, focusing particularly on domestic violence. See Leti Volpp, *Blaming Culture for Bad Behavior*, 12 Yale J. L. & Humanities 89 (2000). More broadly, she maintains that violent incidents involving minorities or people from third world countries are depicted as cultural while similar incidents occurring in the United States are casually dismissed as anecdotal. Hence, she concludes, the oft-cited gulf between feminism and multiculturalism might be more apparent than real. Leti Volpp, *Feminism versus Multiculturalism*, 101 Columbia L. Rev. 1181 (2001).

What is your take on the characterization of FGM as persecution? If the applicant had been a male, and the tribal practice in question had been forcible castration, do you think the issue would have been analyzed differently?

11.   None of the opinions in *Kasinga* shed much light on what "on account of" means. (Board Member Rosenberg argues that the standard by which the applicant must prove it is one of reasonableness, but she has no occasion here to address its substantive meaning.) All presumably will agree that it represents some type of link between the persecution and the reason for the persecution. But what, precisely, is that link?

The issue is vital, because it influences the way a court or the BIA may choose to define the social group in the first place. Earlier it was suggested that the cleanest way to approach the *Kasinga* case would have been to define the social group as consisting of women and girls. Kasinga can easily demonstrate that she would not have been subjected to involuntary genital mutilation had she been a male. The custom is reserved for women and girls. Does that mean that the persecution (if FGM is held to be persecution) is "on account of" her membership in the social group of females? If "on account of" is interpreted to mean "because of," or "but for," then Kasinga is alleging she will be subjected to FGM on account of her gender, an immutable characteristic that makes females a social group. Under that formulation, the only serious legal issue is whether FGM is persecution. If, however, "on account of" is interpreted to mean something more than "but for," then the description of the social group becomes more complex and possibly indeterminate. At this point you needn't try to resolve the issue. Wait for the more general discussion of "on account of," in section B.2.d below.

12.   As then INS General Counsel David Martin pointed out in this case, about 80,000,000 women and girls have already been subjected to FGM. Would they be eligible for asylum on the basis of past persecution? In section B.4.a.ii below, you will see how past persecution is relevant to asylum claims. For now, it is enough to note that FGM presents special considerations, stemming from the fact that the procedure would not normally be performed twice on the same individual. Unlike the typical asylum claim, where a showing of past persecution often facilitates proof that the fear of future persecution is well-founded, a woman or girl who has already experienced FGM will not be able to prove that the procedure will be administered a second time. But in *Mohammed v. Gonzales*, 400 F.3d 785 (9th Cir. 2005), the court held an applicant who had already been subjected involuntarily to FGM eligible for asylum. Following a recent precedent involving a sterilization that similarly had already taken place, the court reasoned that the harm was "continuing" and that, therefore, the applicant had a well-founded fear of future persecution. As you will also see, past persecution can sometimes independently support an asylum claim, even without regard to what the past events say about the likelihood of future persecution.

13.   How much guidance should the BIA give, beyond the facts of the particular case? In *Kasinga*, the Board understandably declined to provide a comprehensive guide that would answer virtually all future FGM questions—especially since this was its first FGM case. But did the Board go to the other extreme? If the Board decides to hold, in a decision that it

chooses to designate as precedent, that sometimes FGM is persecution and sometimes it isn't, should it not discuss, at least in general terms, what its characterization depends on? Should it not at least reveal what it was about the particular facts in *Kasinga* that enabled the Board to find persecution?

14. Similarly, shouldn't Board Member Vacca have explained his dissent? As the only member of the Board who voted to deny asylum in this high-visibility, en banc, precedent case, should he not have offered at least a word of explanation? What, exactly, are the purposes of a dissenting opinion? To what audiences is a dissent addressed?

15. A growing issue has been the practice of FGM within the United States, by immigrants who come from cultures in which FGM is an accepted ritual. In IIRIRA § 645, Congress made FGM a federal criminal offense, punishable by up to five years in prison. At the same time, in section 644, Congress required the INS (now DHS) and the State Department to provide, at or before entry, to both immigrants and nonimmigrants who come from countries in which FGM is commonly practiced, information about the harm that FGM can cause and about possible criminal penalties.

But enforcement will be a challenge. Many immigrants regard FGM as a religious dictate and plan to have the procedure performed abroad on their daughters if necessary. Physicians are reluctant to report suspected cases of FGM to the child abuse authorities because they do not want well-meaning parents to go to prison. See Celia W. Dugger, *Tug of Taboos: African Genital Rite v. U.S. Law*, New York Times, Dec. 28, 1996, at 1,8.

16. The World Health Organization has condemned FGM, and UNHCR has officially declared it a human rights violation. UNHCR, finding the practice "causes severe pain as well as permanent physical harm," and relying on both the World Health Organization and the Convention on the Rights of the Child, considers FGM a basis for asylum. See UNHCR Position on Female Genital Mutilation (May 10, 1994) (unpublished memorandum), reproduced in Frank Newman & David Weissbrodt, International Human Rights: Law, Policy, and Process 668–69 (2d ed. 1996).

DOMESTIC VIOLENCE AND THE PROBLEM OF THE NON–STATE ACTOR

Does it matter who the persecutor is? One perplexing problem is the non-state actor—the private individual or group that threatens the asylum applicant in the event of return. The issue can arise in any number of contexts, including persecution by armed guerrilla forces. But the reason for situating the issue in this section is that it arises particularly often when women file gender-related asylum claims—with respect to FGM, dress codes, and, perhaps most importantly, domestic violence. Typically the immediate source of the feared violence is the claimant's male partner, not her government. Yet the government might be guilty of failing to make reasonable efforts to halt the violence, or it might be unable to do so.

Either the private actor or the government might be motivated by one of the Convention grounds or by some other ground. In any of those cases, the applicant cannot turn to her government for protection and the question is whether she qualifies as a refugee.

There is now a sophisticated literature on non-state actors, most of it in the context of domestic violence claims. In addition to the articles by Professors Jennifer Moore and Deborah Anker, excerpted below, see, e.g., Walter Kälin, *Non-State Agents of Persecution and the Inability of the State to Protect*, 15 Georgetown Immigration L.J. 415 (2001); Susan Kneebone, *Moving Beyond the State: Refugees, Accountability and Protection*, in Susan Kneebone (ed.), The Refugee Convention 50 Years On: Globalisation and International Law, ch. 11, at 281 et seq. (2003); Catherine Phuong, *Persecution by Non–State Agents: Comparative Judicial Interpretations of the 1951 Refugee Convention*, 4 Euro. J. Migration & L. 521 (2003); Volker Türk, *Non-State Agents of Persecution*, in V. Chetail & Vera Gowlland–Debbas (eds.), Switzerland and the International Protection of Refugees, at 95 et seq. (2002).

In the United States, the most controversial case has been *Matter of R.A.*, 22 I. & N. Dec. 906 (BIA 1999). R.A. had fled Guatemala to escape the prolonged and savage physical beatings and mental abuse inflicted on her by her husband. The graphic details are recounted in the opinion. She claimed asylum, alleging persecution on the alternative grounds of imputed political opinion (her husband interpreted her resistance as a political opinion that denied his right to dominate her, and he punished her for it) and particular social group (Guatemalan women involved intimately with Guatemalan men who believe in male domination of females). The immigration judge granted asylum on both grounds, but the former INS appealed and the BIA, in a 10–5 en banc decision, reversed.

The BIA had no trouble agreeing that the past events constituted persecution. Ultimately, however, it concluded that the persecution could not be linked to either her political opinion or any "particular social group." As for the social group claim, the BIA invoked the *Sanchez-Trujillo* test (because the case arose within the Ninth Circuit) and found that the claimed social group failed for lack of a "voluntary associational relationship" among the group members. *Id.* at 917–18. The Board could have stopped there. But it went on at some length to add that it would reject this social group even if it were not bound by *Sanchez-Trujillo*. The Board acknowledged that the group satisfied the *Acosta* immutability test, but it held that *Acosta* was merely a necessary, not a sufficient, condition for social group. The Board implied that the applicant had to make an additional "showing of how the characteristic is understood in the alien's society;" i.e., "whether anyone in Guatemala perceives this group to exist in any form whatsoever," or whether the group is a "recognized segment of the population." *Id.* at 918.

"The respondent's showing fails in another respect," the Board added: "[S]he has not shown that women are expected by society to be abused, or that there are any adverse societal consequences to women or their husbands if the women are not abused." *Id.* at 919. (Should such an extraordinary showing really be expected?) The Board hastened to add that these additional considerations are not "prerequisites" to a social group claim; they are just "appropriate, in our judgment, for consideration." *Id.* at 919–20. As the earlier discussion of the Justice Department's proposed asylum regulations noted, see pages 908–83 above, the legal significance of these factors remains unclear.

On January 19, 2001, her last day in office, Attorney General Janet Reno vacated the Board's decision in *R.A.*, and ordered the Board to reconsider the case in the light of the then pending asylum regulations once they were finalized. Until then, reconsideration was to be stayed. *Id.* at 906.

On February 21, 2003, still not having issued the final asylum regulations, Attorney General John Ashcroft "recertified" the case to himself for a decision. Amidst widespread rumors that Ashcroft planned to deny her claim, the Department of Homeland Security filed a brief with the Attorney General, urging him to grant R.A.'s request for asylum. See Lori A. Nessel, *"Willful Blindness" to Gender–Based Violence Abroad: United States' Implementation of Article Three of the United Nations Convention Against Torture*, 89 Minnesota L. Rev. 71, 110–11 (2004); see also 81 IR 245 (Feb. 23, 2004). In the end, Ashcroft decided not to decide, opting instead to remand the case to the BIA yet again for reconsideration following issuance of the final asylum regulations. *Matter of R.A.*, 23 I. & N. Dec. 694 (Jan. 19, 2005). At this writing, the final regulations have yet to appear and the case is still pending before the BIA.

There has also been much helpful commentary on the more general subject of domestic violence as a basis for asylum, much of it prompted by the developments in *R.A.* See, e.g., Deborah Anker, Lauren Gilbert & Nancy Kelly, *Women Whose Governments are Unable or Unwilling to Provide Reasonable Protection from Domestic Violence May Qualify as Refugees under United States Asylum Law*, 11 Georgetown Immigration L.J. 709 (1997); Pamela Goldberg, *Anyplace But Home: Asylum in the United States for Women Fleeing Intimate Violence*, 26 Cornell Internat'l L.J. 565 (1993); Pamela Goldberg & Bernadette Pasade Cissé, *Gender Issues in Asylum Law after Matter of R.A.*, Feb. 2000 Immigration Briefings; Karen Musalo, *Matter of R.A.: An Analysis of the Decision and Its Implications*, 76 IR 1177 (Aug. 9, 1999).

For some time the subject of non-state actors divided the world's receiving states. The United States, Canada, Australia, New Zealand, and most western European states recognized asylum claims based on persecution by private actors early on; accord UNHCR Handbook, para. 65; UNHCR, Guidelines on International Protection: "Membership of a particular social group" within the context of article IA(2) of the 1951 Convention and/or its 1967 Protocol relating to the Status of Refugees, U.N. Doc. HCR/GIP/02/02 (May 7, 2002), reproduced, 81 IR 571 (Apr. 26, 2004), para. II.B.20. Until recently, Germany and France were among the holdouts, with slight differences between them. See generally Moore, below, at 106–08. In the U.K., the House of Lords has held France and Germany not to be safe countries because of their practices of returning asylum claimants to states in which they would be in danger of persecution by non-State actors. See *R. v. Secretary of State for the Home Dept., ex parte Adan and Aitseguer* [2001] 2 W.L.R. 143 (U.K. House of Lords), reproduced in 13 Internat'l J. Refugee L. 202 (2001). The European Court of Human Rights has also examined the problems that resulted from a combination of the German practice of rejecting such claims and the Dublin Convention rules that governed which European country should decide asylum claims. See *T.I. v. United Kingdom*, Decision as to Admissibility of App. No. 43844/98 (Euro. Ct. Human Rts., Third Section, 2000), reproduced in 12 Internat'l J. Refugee L. 244 (2000). The case is excerpted and analyzed in section C.3 below.

Because of the adverse effects of differential refugee policies among the member states of the European Union, the EU has been working toward common standards on many refugee issues, including the substantive content of the refugee definition. See Commission of the European Communities, Proposal for a Council Directive on minimum standards for the qualification and status of third country nationals and stateless persons as refugees or as persons who otherwise need international protection, COM(2001), 510 final, 2001/0207 (CNS) (Dec. 9, 2001). Largely because of that initiative, Germany has now passed legislation, effective January 1, 2005, that officially recognizes non-state actor persecution claims. See Deutsche Welle, www.dw-world.de; see also Phuong, above, at 530. France is expected to recede as well.

Jennifer Moore, From Nation State to Failed State: International Protection From Human Rights Abuses by Non–State Agents

31 Columbia Human Rights L. Rev. 81, 102–05 (1999).

* * *

Given the emphasis in Article 1 [of the 1951 Convention] on the failure of state protection, it would appear significant that the conventional refugee definition does not identify the state as the necessary author or agent of the persecution feared. In fact, the text of Article 1 does not speak to the character of the persecution at all: the state is notable for its powerlessness in stopping persecution, rather than its status as persecutor per se. Moreover, in interpreting the silence of the treaty on the issue of agency, Paragraph 65 of the UNHCR Handbook reads Article 1 to encompass non-state agents of persecution. The text states explicitly that "offensive acts ... committed by the local populace ... can be considered as persecution ... if the authorities refuse, or prove unable, to offer effective protection." Paragraph 65 of the UNHCR Handbook has been widely cited and utilized by states.

Paragraph 65 has inspired a common sense approach to understanding a government's fundamental failure to provide effective protection from persecution by non-state agents which may underlie a claim to surrogate protection. Its language encompasses situations in which effective protection from unofficial abuses is lacking for one of two reasons: either the authorities will not or they cannot protect the individual with the well-founded fear. Situations in which the state "will not" provide protection generally involve complicity in, or at least tolerance of, human rights violations by a functional state, and fall within the outer ring of the conceptual framework established in the introductory section of this Article. In contrast, situations in which the state is "unable" to protect are often associated with internal armed conflict in which the state is either compromised or dysfunctional. These latter situations correspond to the intermediate ring or the central core of that framework, respectively.

Thus, under the UNHCR Handbook approach, the individual who fears persecution by non-state agents for an enumerated reason is entitled to refugee status, regardless of whether the national government "refuse[s]" or is "unable" to offer effective protection, and regardless of where along the radius of concentric circles—from order to conflict to failed state status—the government finds itself.

Scholarly analysis of the agency of persecution reinforces the UNHCR Handbook's approach, and confirms that refugee status is available to individuals fearing persecution by non-state as well as state agents. Prominent international jurists Atle Grahl–Madsen and Guy S. Goodwin–Gill attest that a central purpose of the Refugee Convention was to respond to the plight of refugees who flee situations in which there is no de facto protection, for whatever reason. Refugee status is triggered when "the government has the best of wills to prevent atrocities on the part of the public ... but for some reason or other is unable to do this," or "where protection is in fact unavailable."

On the issue of agency in general, Goodwin–Gill is most adamant in stating that "it does not follow that the concept [of persecution] is limited to the actions of governments or their agents." He further clarifies that "the issue of state responsibility for persecution ... is not part of the refugee definition." Goodwin–Gill is particularly eloquent in his condemnation of the exclusion from international protection of refugees who flee failed state situations. He cautions that "there is no basis in the 1951 Convention, or in general international law, for requiring the existence of effective operating institutions of government as a pre-condition to a successful claim to refugee status."

It is this basic concern for effective national protection—and the refugee's claim to surrogate international protection when such protection is lacking—that lies at the heart of the refugee definition. International protection is required in the absence of effective municipal protection—whether the state persecutes, or non-state agents persecute in a legal vacuum created by the state's refusal or incapacity to act. The concept of effective protection requires that the international community recognize persecution by non-state agents as a basis for refugee status, if the refugee protection regime is to be logically consistent and true to its underlying values and goals.

* * *

Deborah Anker, Refugee Status and Violence Against Women in the "Domestic" Sphere: The Non–State Actor Question

15 Georgetown Immigration L.J. 391, 392–98, 400–02 (2001).

[This paper was presented at the October 2000 conference of the International Association of Refugee Law Judges at Berne, Switzerland.—Ed.]

* * *

* * * [The non-state actor issue] is especially salient for women asylum seekers, since many face serious harms from "private" actors including tribal authorities in cases such as forced female genital mutilation, and members of their families or communities in cases such as bride burning and forced marriages. As Audrey Macklin has noted, a "paradigmatic example" of gender specific abuse committed by private actors is "domestic violence"—violations of women's core human rights, such as the right to physical integrity and protection from cruel, inhuman and degrading treatment or punishment by their husbands or domestic partners. * * * [I]n cases of violence by husbands and male domestic partners, the question of state protection is especially complex due to different levels of interweaving responsibility and enabling of the "private" harm by the state. In many countries where protection is not available, "it is the very inattention and inaction by the state in relation to battering that tacitly condones and sustains it as a systematic practice. In other words, the fact that [a] state does not adequately protect women from domestic and sexual violence is both an institutional manifestation of the degraded social status of women and a cause of its perpetuation."

Although women's claims raise challenging issues, their appropriate analysis fits within traditional refugee law. Gender is not a special or different category of refugee law. * * * Over the course of the past year and a half, an exceptional group of opinions has been issued in cases involving women applicants fleeing violence by their husbands. Taken together, these cases articulate a framework grounded in accepted refugee law doctrine for analyzing the relationship between private harm and state protection, with implications not only for women's claims.

The first of these is, again, the historic judgment of the House of Lords in *Shah* [aka *Islam*, considered on pages 1042–49 below], with the core analysis applied and elaborated in the Federal Court of Australia's decision in *Minister for Immigration and Multicultural Affairs v. Khawar* and in the notable recent opinion of Chairperson Rodger Haines of New Zealand's Refugee Status Appeals Authority (RSAA), *Refugee Appeal No. 71427/99*.

The evolution in this area of law and transmutation across the borders of signatory states will no doubt continue; indeed it is now extending to the United States. There the Attorney General vacated the Board of Immigration Appeal's decision, *In re R.A.*, denying status and protection to a Guatemalan woman fleeing her husband's severe physical and other violence, from which the State provided no protection. Pending regulations propose a more general framework that recognizes "domestic violence" as a basis for refugee status in some cases.

The Canadian Supreme Court's decision in *Ward* laid out the general principles for acceptance of claims by non-state actors. Most states parties recognize that nothing in the Convention requires that the agent of persecution be the state:

> The rationale upon which international refugee law rests is not simply the need to give shelter to those persecuted by the state, but, more widely, to provide refuge to those whose home state cannot or does not afford them protection from persecution. The former is, of course, comprised in the latter, but the drafters of the Convention had the latter, wider purpose in mind. The state's inability to protect the individual from persecution founded on one of the enumerated grounds constitutes failure of local protection.
>
> Persecution under the Convention includes situations where the state is not in strictness an accomplice to the persecution, but it is simply unable to protect its citizens.

The agent of persecution need not be the state, but there must be a failure of state protection and, in the language of the treaty, the persecution must be "for reasons of" one of the grounds listed in the Convention. What is the analysis of "persecution" in non-state actor cases; more particularly, what is the necessary relationship between the harms perpetrated by the non-state actor and the state? What level of state involvement is required? What is the standard for assessing state protection in such cases? How can causation or the nexus to a Convention ground be established? If the ground is a gender-defined particular social group, to what entity must the gender-related reason be attributable: the state, the non-state actor, or both? If the non-state actor violence is deemed personal, can the linkage be made if the failure of state protection is, in intent or effect, discriminatory on the basis of gender? These are among the issues addressed in the recent series of decisions from the UK, New Zealand and Australia.

Shah: The Meaning of Persecution

Shah involved the conjoined appeal of refugee claims of two Pakistani women, who came to the United Kingdom after fleeing their violent husbands. Both women feared continued assaults and violence by their husbands, and denunciation by them for adultery, with resulting criminal prosecutions and severe sanctions under Pakistani law. The House of Lords found that women in Pakistan suffer severe discrimination. Although the [Pakistani] constitution prohibits discrimination on grounds of sex, in law and practice married women are treated as subordinate to the will of their husbands and protection from abuse is effectively unavailable.

The central issue addressed in *Shah* was the particular social group ground, and a majority of their Lordships found that, especially in light of state-sanctioned and tolerated discrimination against women, Pakistani women constituted a particular social group. However, the determination of the Convention ground is not sufficient to establish refugee status. What comprised the persecution and how could the link or nexus be made between the feared persecution and the particular social group ground?

The only two opinions to address this question were those of Lords Steyn and Hoffman. These opinions analyzed persecution as constituted by both a serious harm and a failure of state protection. This is the formula, put forth by the Refugee Women's Legal Group and specifically referred to by Lord Hoffman, i.e. "Persecution = serious harm + failure of state protection." Both Lords found that even if the serious harm were committed by a non-state actor for personal, non-Convention reasons, the claims could be recognized where the failure of state protection was for a Convention reason, in this case, a gender-defined particular social group. The evidence of state tolerated or sanctioned discrimination established the link, since state inaction was as much the reason for the harm feared as the direct violence and threats of denunciation by the husbands. In the words of Lord Steyn, "given the central feature of state-tolerated and state-sanctioned gender discrimination, the argument that the appellants fear persecution not because of membership of a social group but because of the hostility of their husbands is unrealistic." Lord Hoffman made the failure of state protection/causation analysis even more explicit:

> What is the reason for the persecution which the appellants fear? Here it is important to notice that it is made up of two elements. First, there is the threat of violence to Mrs. Islam by her husband and his political friends and to Mrs. Shah by her husband. This is a personal affair, directed against them as individuals. Secondly, there is the inability or unwillingness of the state to do anything to protect them. There is nothing personal about this. The evidence was that the state would not assist them because they were women. It denied them a protection against violence which it would have given to men. These two elements have to be combined to constitute persecution within the meaning of the convention.

As noted, the non-state actor/nexus analysis of *Shah* has now been applied in two important decisions issuing from the Refugee Status Appeals Authority of New Zealand and the Federal Court of Australia. In elaborating on *Shah*, each raises new issues: in the New Zealand case, the standard for assessing state protection where the non-state actor is the agent of persecution * * *.

The Standard for Assessing State Protection: Refugee Appeal No. 71427/99 (Refugee Status Appeals Authority of New Zealand)

In the New Zealand case, * * * an Iranian woman [was] fleeing her violent first husband, in this case in the context of a custody battle over their son. As in *Shah*, there was overwhelming evidence that the state, in this case Iran, condoned, if not encouraged, the "private" violence from which the applicant fled. Especially with respect to the custody battle, the RSAA concluded that the state had established "the very legislative framework which to a large measure is the source of the harm" faced by the applicant. The RSAA readily found the Convention grounds of religion, political opinion, and particular social group applied; with respect to the latter, it described as "indisputable" that gender can be the defining characteristic of a social group and that "women" may constitute a particular social group.

On the critical question of nexus, Chairperson Haines restated the *Shah* conclusion and removed any ambiguity from its formulation or implications: persecution consists of a serious harm *and* a failure of state protection.

> This means that if a refugee claimant is at real risk of serious harm at the hands of a non-state agent (e.g. husband, partner or other non-state agent) for reasons unrelated to any of the Convention grounds, but the failure of state protection is for reason of a Convention ground, the nexus requirement is satisfied. Conversely, if the risk of harm by the non-state agent is Convention related, but the failure of state protection is not, the nexus requirement is still satisfied. In either case the persecution is for reason of the admitted Convention ground.

* * *

Addressing the standard for assessing state protection in such cases, Haines concluded that the state fails to protect when it does not bring the level of risk of harm from the non-state actor to below a well-founded fear. He rejected the reasoning of the House of Lords in *Horvath v. Secretary of State for the Home Office*, in which their Lordships, using various tests, concluded that the standard of state protection should be analyzed separately either from the concept of persecution or a well-founded fear. If the state has in place a system for the protection of the citizen and a reasonable willingness to operate it, then state protection is available, even if the person faces a well-founded fear of the persecution upon her return. Haines rejected this formulation in favor of a holistic understanding of refugee status and protection. "The purpose of refugee law is to identify those who have a well-founded fear for a Convention reason. If the net result of a state's 'reasonable willingness' to operate a system for the protection of the citizen is that it is incapable of preventing a real chance of persecution of a particular individual, refugee status cannot be denied that individual."

It should be emphasized that application of the New Zealand holistic formulation—recognizing refugee status where the applicant establishes a well-founded fear of persecution, the latter understood to include both the serious harm *and* the failure of state protection—will certainly not result in the granting of all "domestic violence" cases. In some instances, the harms by the husband will not be sufficiently serious to meet the first part of the persecution test. In others, there will not be a particularized failure of state protection: as Lord Hoffman stated in *Shah*, it is not the non-state actor/husbands' actions but, in the specific context, the availability of state protection that varies among countries. In some, systems of protection are in place which although not eliminating all risk, reduce the risk for the particular applicant to below the well-founded fear threshold. A woman who has never been abused and cannot articulate specific grounds for fearing that she will be battered in the future will be unable to establish an objective basis for her claim. A woman who was battered in the past, but successfully left the relationship and has lived openly and safely since then, will have difficulty establishing that any fear she has is "well-founded."

A woman may have access to protection if her husband is an ordinary citizen, but not if he is influential with government officials. In some countries, a female victim of such violations may be able to obtain state protection if she has the support of her family of origin in seeking it; in other cases, her access to such protection may be more limited without such support. The refugee status inquiry is always individual; it is always particularized.

* * *

Conclusion

One note of criticism about these decisions suggests where the "next stage" in development of the law may be headed. It should not be assumed that the reason for the violence by husbands against wives is "private" or personal. Domestic violence is purposeful behavior intended to control and dominate an intimate female partner. It serves a "historical, culturally sanctioned purpose, which was and is for men to keep their wives 'in their place.'" Studies of batterers have observed that "the typical batterer" uses violence "to meet needs for power and control over others. Their actions are often fueled by stereotypical sex-role expectations for 'their' women." It is no coincidence that "the strongest risk factor for being a victim of partner violence is being female."

This may suggest the relevance of the political opinion ground; it also suggests that the linkage to a Convention reason, be it to "women" as a particular social group or political opinion, can be the non-state actor husband, not (or as alluded to in *Khawar*, not *just*) the enabling state. It may be, therefore, that the requirements of the Convention's refugee definition can be met where the evidence available supports only a finding that the state is "unable" rather than in some sense "unwilling" to control the violations. In such cases, and assuming the bifurcated nature of the concept of persecution, the nexus between the Convention reason and the persecution can be provided by the "serious harm limb." These are what Lord Hoffman suggests may be the more difficult cases (although why more conceptually difficult, is not clear): where there is no evidence of a state discriminatory policy but evidence exists that the non-state actor is inflicting the harm on a discriminatory basis. This distinction may be important in "domestic violence" cases, especially where problems of lack of available evidence make it difficult to prove that the state's failure to protect is in some sense deliberate or discriminatory.

NOTES AND QUESTIONS

1. As a policy matter, why should it be necessary to link the persecution to the state at all? If the applicant has a well-founded fear that he or she will be persecuted by a private actor because of one of the protected grounds, why should that not be enough for asylum? Moreover, if private acts of persecution occur within a given country, won't it always be true that the state was either "unable" or "unwilling" to prevent them? In other words, don't those two possibilities together exhaust the universe of explanations? Finally, how would you expect Greatbatch or other feminist scholars to analyze this question?

2. If some link to the state is required, what should the required link be? Articulate and critique the two competing positions that Anker identifies (the New Zealand approach of Chairperson Rodger Haines and the British court's approach in *Horvath*). Professor Laura Adams makes the innovative argument that in domestic violence cases the social group should be defined as family membership and the emphasis should be on the state's policy of not intervening in intra-family matters. See Laura S. Adams, *Fleeing the Family: A Domestic Violence Victim's Particular Social Group*, 49 Loyola L. Rev. 287 (2003).

3. The applicant must also show that the persecution of which he or she has a well-founded fear is on one of the protected grounds. Do you agree with Chairperson Haines in the New Zealand case that, for this purpose, it should be enough to demonstrate that *either* the private actor or the state in failing to control the actor was motivated by one of the five protected grounds? (UNHCR shares this interpretation. See UNHCR, Guidelines on International Protection: "Membership of a particular social group" within the context of article IA(2) of the 1951 Convention and/or its 1967 Protocol relating to the Status of Refugees, U.N. Doc. HCR/GIP/02/02 (May 7, 2002), reproduced, 81 IR 571 (Apr. 26, 2004), paras. 21–23.

4. Anker takes the analysis of the British House of Lords in *Islam* another step. Suppose, she asks in effect, the applicant in a domestic violence case can offer no specific evidence of what is motivating either the private actor or the state. What empirical premise does she suggest should guide such a case? Do you agree with the premise? If the premise is accepted, what rule of law should flow from it?

5. The "unable or unwilling" standard has been explicitly embraced by UNHCR:

> There is no requirement that the persecutor be a State actor. Where serious discriminatory or other offensive acts are committed by the local populace, they can be considered as persecution if

they are knowingly tolerated by the authorities, or if the authorities refuse, or prove unable, to offer effective protection.

UNHCR, Guidelines on International Protection: "Membership of a particular social group" within the context of article IA(2) of the 1951 Convention and/or its 1967 Protocol relating to the Status of Refugees, U.N. Doc. HCR/GIP/02/02 (May 7, 2002), reproduced, 81 IR 571 (Apr. 26, 2004), para. II.B.20. Accord, *Thomas v. Gonzales*, 409 F.3d 1177 (9th Cir. en banc 2005) (holding private action sufficient when government is "unable or unwilling to control" it).

6. Consider the approach taken by the Justice Department's proposed rules on the issue of state action:

> * * * Inherent in the meaning of the term "persecution" is that the serious harm or suffering that an applicant experienced or fears must be inflicted by the government of the country of persecution or by a person or group that government is unwilling or unable to control. In evaluating whether a government is unwilling or unable to control the infliction of harm or suffering, the immigration judge or asylum officer should consider whether the government takes reasonable steps to control the infliction of harm or suffering and whether the applicant has reasonable access to the state protection that exists. Evidence of the following are pertinent and may be considered: Government complicity with respect to the infliction of harm or suffering at issue; attempts by the applicant, if any, to obtain protection from government officials and the government's response to these attempts; official action that is perfunctory; a pattern of government unresponsiveness; general country conditions and the government's denial of services; the nature of the government's policies with respect to the harm or suffering at issue; and any steps the government has taken to prevent infliction of such harm or suffering.

65 Fed. Reg. at 76597 (Dec. 7, 2000), proposing to amend 8 C.F.R. § 208.15(a).

The proposed regulation acknowledges that either "unwilling" or "unable" is sufficient. But look carefully at the list of factors the Department offers for determining "whether a government is unwilling or unable to control the infliction of harm or suffering." Are these factors relevant to "unable" or only to "unwilling?" What if a well-intentioned government takes all reasonable measures to prevent domestic violence, but contrary social norms are so entrenched that domestic violence is still rampant? Under the proposed regulation, does the applicant qualify for asylum or not? Does "unable" really mean only "unwilling to exert a reasonable effort?"

7. The non-state actor issue also surfaces frequently in claims based on the Convention Against Torture, particularly in the domestic violence context. See pages 1155–56 below.

d. "ON ACCOUNT OF": THE NEXUS REQUIREMENT

The U.S. statutory definition of "refugee" requires that the relevant persecution be "on account of" race, religion, etc. INA § 101(a)(42)(A,B). The 1951 Convention, in article IA(2), expresses the same concept with the phrase "for reasons of." That element of the refugee definition is often referred to as the "nexus" requirement, since it connects the persecution with one of the protected grounds. But what does it mean? The following represents the author's suggested answer. Decide whether you agree or disagree:

The refugee definition is inherently indeterminate. Application of terms like "persecution," "political opinion," and "social group" will always require a certain amount of judgment. Results will therefore be uncertain and, to some unavoidable extent, inconsistent. Judgment aside, however, perhaps the single greatest source of *logical* confusion has been the phrase "on account of." All the cases agree that those words require some sort of nexus between the alleged persecution and one of the five protected grounds. With the arguable exception of *Elias-Zacarias*, no United States court has seriously explored what this nexus is.

Yet these three simple words have proved to be of fundamental, albeit indirect, importance, particularly in cases of gender-related persecution. In *Fatin*, where a woman alleged persecution on account of gender, the court acknowledged that women form a social group but denied relief (under that theory) because the woman could not show she was being persecuted "solely" on account of her gender. The implication was that one who persecutes only a subcategory of a particular race, or religion, or social group has not engaged in persecution "on account of" race, or religion, or social group. Similarly, in *Kasinga*, the majority opinion reflected palpable confusion over how to define the social group in a way that would enable the Board to link it with the persecution. Should the group definition be confined to those women and girls who were members of Kasinga's tribe? To those who would be subjected to the particular FGM method that her tribe used? To those who are opposed to FGM? To those who are so opposed to it that they would refuse it and take the consequences? Since the Board's own case law (*Acosta*), the law of the circuit in which the case was decided (*Fatin*), and the UNHCR formulation discussed earlier all make it easy to hold that women are a social group (period), the only possible reason for the Board in *Kasinga* to flail around in search of all those qualifiers is its unstated assumption that, without such qualifiers, "on account of" would have been an obstacle to relief.

All of this confusion seems unnecessary. "On account of" should be interpreted according to its common sense, standard English, meaning— i.e., "because of." Congress apparently shares that view. In IIRIRA § 305(a), Congress for independent reasons amended the wording of the withholding provision. In the course of the rewriting, Congress changed "on account of" to "because of." See INA § 241(b)(3). The change was considered so innocuous that it was not even noted in the conference committee report and, to the best of the author's knowledge, has not been discussed by commentators. The explanation for the silence, presumably, is that the normal, accepted meaning of "on account of" is "because of." (Congress had no occasion to rewrite the "refugee" definition on which asylum depends.) Article 33(1) of the 1951 Convention similarly prohibits return when "life or freedom would be threatened on account of ...," while the "refugee" definition in article 1A(2) of the Convention refers to "fear of being persecuted *for reasons of* ..." [emphasis added].

Once the courts acknowledge explicitly that "on account of" simply means "because of"—and the Supreme Court in *Elias-Zacarias* came close to explicitness on that point—then there is a library full of case law in other subject areas to guide further development. In tort law and criminal law, causation principles are particularly well developed. In torts, the usual test for judging factual causation is the but-for test. A negligent act is ordinarily considered to have "caused" a given consequence if the consequence would not have occurred but for the negligent act. See generally Dan B. Dobbs, The Law of Torts, chaps. 9, 10 (2000).

There are two major qualifications. First, causation is sometimes found even when the consequence would have occurred anyway, as long as the negligent act was at least a "substantial factor" in producing the claimed consequence. This issue can arise in an either/or situation—i.e., where either negligent act A or some other event B would have been sufficient to produce consequence X. When that is the case, the but-for test fails, since it cannot be said that X would not have occurred but for A, but factual causation can be found nonetheless if act A was at least a "substantial" factor in producing consequence X. See Dobbs, above, § 171.

Second, factual causation in tort law (whether found through the but-for test or through the substantial factor test) is constrained by the doctrine of "proximate cause." Policy considerations dictate denying recovery if the causal link between the negligent act and the consequence is too attenuated. Proximate cause problems typically arise when either the consequences were unforeseeable or the intervening forces were too numerous, too unforeseeable, or too independent of the negligent act. *Id.* chap. 10.

In tort law as in refugee law, a common source of confusion has been the handling of cases in which two or more facts both had to exist in order for a given consequence to have occurred. A driver negligently sideswipes a car that is parked in a lawful space. The only reason the car was parked there in the first place is that the driver had a flat tire and had to pull over. The flat tire was clearly a cause of the accident in the but-for sense. But for the flat tire, the car would not have been parked in that place and therefore would not have been hit. Does that mean the negligent driver escapes liability? Of course not. The damage also would not have occurred but for the defendant's negligent driving. Both events—the negligent driving and the flat tire—were necessary predicates for the damage. The key is that there can be, and frequently are, two or more but-for causes of the same consequence.

The same is true in refugee law. A despot singles out university students of Asian ancestry for persecution. The victims are not being persecuted *solely* on account of race; only the subset of Asians who are university students are being targeted. Does this mean the victims are not being persecuted on account of race? Of course not. The persecution would not have occurred but for their status as university students, but it also would not have occurred but for their race. There can be, and typically are, two or more elements that jointly define the persecuted group. If "on account of" is interpreted to mean "but for," then this case is just as easy as the negligent driving case. There is persecution on account of race.

This approach would certainly have simplified the analysis in *Kasinga*. The BIA could simply have reasoned as follows: Gender is immutable. Under *Acosta*, an immutable characteristic defines a social group. Therefore, women are a social group. Kasinga would not be subjected to FGM if she were not a woman. Therefore, any persecution she fears will be on account of membership in a social group. Under that approach, there are really only two serious issues in the case: Has Kasinga proved a well-founded fear that she will be subjected to FGM? And, if so, is the FGM that she fears "persecution?"

But this approach has more than linguistics, logic, and simplicity to commend it. It makes practical common sense from a policy standpoint as well. In deciding on whom to confer refugee status, the drafters of the 1951 Convention and the drafters of the corresponding United States legislation distinguished among victims of persecution. While all victims of persecution would benefit from protection, the resources of the receiving countries are finite. Only those who have been persecuted on account of one of the five familiar grounds—race, religion, nationality, social group, or political opinion—will be protected as refugees. Like the drafters of the 1951 Convention, Congress presumably selected those categories because it believed that persecution, while inherently bad, is even worse when it discriminates on the basis of one of the named classifications or otherwise impedes the free flow of ideas. If a person or group persecutes someone on precisely that basis, the fact that the persecutor is additionally discriminating on some other basis doesn't *lessen* the harm or diminish the victim's need for protection. As long as the persecution would not have occurred but for the victim's race, religion, nationality, political opinion, or social group, then the person should be held to meet the statutory definition of "refugee."

Will this approach open the doors too wide? Not at all. Even if a person can show adverse treatment that would not have occurred but for his or her race, religion, etc., the key is that there must be a well-founded fear of persecution. That means two things. First, as a legal matter, the harm that the person claims to fear must rise to the level of persecution. That requirement is the principal screening device for separating minor hardship from serious persecution. Second, as a factual matter, the applicant must show that his or her fear of the harm occurring is well-founded, a requirement taken up in subsection B.3 below. And even if there is a well-founded fear of persecution, and even if the persecution would not have occurred but for a Convention motive, the proximate cause qualification discussed below will prevent the finding of nexus based on de minimis connections.

Thus, explicitly holding that "but-for" causation satisfies the "on account of" requirement will not convert trivial events into grants of asylum. Fatin, for example, would still have lost under a "but-for" test; the court simply did not regard forced adherence to the Islamic dress code as "persecution" (at least not for her). The proposed test would, however, simplify the analysis, honor the everyday English understanding of the words Congress used, and conform the results to the policies that underlay both Congress's decision to allow asylum and Congress's decision to limit it. Most important, the proposed test would eliminate one arbitrary obstacle to asylum in those cases in which both the literal statutory language and the broad legislative purpose point toward granting relief.

The but-for test that I am proposing for the nexus requirement in refugee law is subject to the same two modifications that apply in tort law. First, I emphasize that I offer it as a *sufficient* condition for nexus (subject to the second qualifier, below), not as a *necessary* condition. In refugee law, as in tort law, there might be instances in which either of two motives— one of the five Convention grounds and one other ground not recognized by the Convention—would alone have been enough to prompt the persecution. In that case, the but-for test would fail, because by hypothesis the persecution would have occurred even without the Convention ground. If the Convention motive was at least a *substantial* factor in the persecution, however, my view is that the nexus requirement has been met.

Conceptually, the but-for test can be envisioned as simply one specific application of the substantial factor test. If a particular motive is so important that without it the persecution would not have occurred, it seems difficult to deny that the motive was at least a "substantial" factor in the persecution. In practical terms, however, hypotheticals in which a refugee claimant would be able to satisfy the substantial factor test but not the but-for test do not come readily to mind. Since the but-for test seems adequate for the vast majority of cases in which nexus is the only element of the refugee definition that is in dispute, and since the but-for test provides a more tangible criterion than one that rests on degrees of substantiality, it seems more efficient to begin with the but-for test and, in the rare case in which it fails because there exists some other motive that would independently have triggered the persecution, fall back on the substantial factor test.

Second, there might be situations, most likely rare, in which persecution technically would not have occurred but for a Convention ground, but where the link between the Convention ground and the persecution is so remote that as a policy matter the nexus requirement should be held not to have been met. The analogy is to proximate cause in tort law.

Nexus has now been the subject of a very thoughtful study organized by James Hathaway and culminating in what the contributors entitled "the Michigan Guidelines on Nexus to a Convention Ground." See James C. Hathaway, *The Causal Nexus in International Refugee Law*, 23 Michigan J. Internat'l L. 207 (2002); *The Michigan Guidelines on Nexus to a Convention Ground*, 23 Michigan J. Internat'l L. 210 (2002); see also James C.

Hathaway & Michelle Foster, *The Causal Connection ("Nexus") to a Convention Ground*, 15 Internat'l J. Refugee L. 461, 472 (2003). The authors of that study dismiss the "but-for" test advocated here. Their explanation for doing so reads as follows: "Because refugee status determination is both protection-oriented and forward-looking, it is unlikely that pertinent guidance can be gleaned from standards of causation shaped by considerations relevant to the assessment of civil or criminal liability, or which are directed solely to the analysis of past events." Rec. 11, *id.* at 215, 217. It is certainly true that the purposes of both tort law and criminal law differ from those of refugee law, in the ways that sentence notes and in other ways as well. It follows that the causation tests used in tort law and criminal law cannot be *assumed* appropriate for refugee law. It hardly follows, however, that they should be assumed *not* to be of use. As the discussion above suggests, there are numerous arguments—based on text, logic, policy results, and practical workability—to use the but-for test, notwithstanding that its origins lie elsewhere.

At any rate, unlike the present discussion, the Michigan Guidelines mainly address a slightly different question—what, exactly, must be linked to one of the five Convention grounds? Or, to put the question a bit differently, *what* must be on account of (or because of) the person's race, religion, etc.? They suggest that the nexus requirement is met if the applicant's "predicament" arises on account of (or because of) one of the five grounds; predicament, in turn, might be evidenced by the reason for the persecutor threatening the harm or by the failure of the government of the country of origin to provide protection. See recs. 6–8, *id.* at 215.

The different question—the one with which the present discussion is concerned—is the nature of the link itself; i.e., what does "on account of" (or "because of") mean? The position taken here is that the but-for test should be a sufficient (and the usual) means of meeting the "on account of" (or "because of") test. Just as in torts or criminal law, however, the causal nexus should be held established even in some situations in which the but-for test breaks down because the fear of being persecuted would have existed even if the applicant had not been of the particular race, religion, etc. When the but-for test is not satisfied, nexus should be found nonetheless if the Convention ground was a "substantial factor" in causing the fear of persecution. At the same time, even if the but-for test is met, nexus should not be found if the link between the Convention motive and the persecution is simply too far-fetched.

The original version of this formulation (2nd edition, 1997) did not highlight the two qualifications described here, except in a footnote. The analysis in the Michigan Guidelines has persuaded me that both qualifications deserve greater emphasis. In the end, I now think the Michigan Guidelines, as elaborated on in the subsequent article by Hathaway and Foster, are consistent with the framework I have been suggesting. They require that one of the Convention grounds "*contribute* to the applicant's exposure to the risk of being persecuted" (emphasis added), Recs. 10, 13, *id.* at 215, 217, but they acknowledge an exception for contributions that are "remote to the point of irrelevance." That is, in essence, the substantial factor test. Conversely, Hathaway and Foster, in the article cited below, offer an example of a British case in which a person who witnesses a crime while on his way to church is threatened with persecution if he tells the police. The person would not have been threatened had he not gone to church that day; thus, the but-for connection to religion is *arguably* satisfied. (My own view is that the but-for test has not been met; it is the persecutor's motive, not the victim's actions, that must be linked to the persecution.) But even if one assumes that the but-for test has been met, the link between religion and persecution would be far too trivial to establish nexus. They assert a common sense limitation that would be very much at home in traditional tort analyses of proximate cause.

Some of the elements of this approach—a but-for test, with the two qualifications to avoid extreme and counterinstinctive results—have since been discussed by the British House of Lords in the following case. Consider the excerpts below and then decide whether you agree with a but-for approach.

Islam v. Secretary of State for the Home Department

[1999] 2 AC 629, [1999] 2 All ER 545, [1999] 2 W.L.R. 1015 (U.K. House of Lords).

[Two Pakistani women were driven from their homes by their husbands, who threatened to falsely accuse them of adultery. The evidence showed that in Pakistan such accusations were likely to lead to criminal proceedings for sexual immorality and severe punishment. Both women applied for asylum in the United Kingdom, alleging they would be persecuted because of their membership in a social group (defined in various ways). The administrative officials denied their applications. All five of their Lordships rejected the *Sanchez-Trujillo* test for social group, in favor of the *Acosta* test, at least in situations where, as here, the country of origin practiced discrimination in matters of fundamental human rights. Four of their Lordships proceeded to hold the applicants eligible for asylum. Lord Millett dissented.]

* * *

LORD HOFFMANN. My Lords, in Pakistan there is widespread discrimination against women. Despite the fact that the constitution prohibits discrimination on grounds of sex, an investigation by Amnesty International at the end of 1995 reported that government attempts to improve the position of women had made little headway against strongly entrenched cultural and religious attitudes. Women who were victims of rape or domestic violence often found it difficult to obtain protection from the police or a fair hearing in the courts. In matters of sexual conduct, laws which discriminated against women and carried severe penalties remained upon the statute book. The International Bar Association reported in December 1998 that its mission to Pakistan earlier in the year "heard and saw much evidence that women in Pakistan are discriminated against and have particular problems in gaining access to justice."

These appeals concern two women who became victims of domestic violence in Pakistan, came to the United Kingdom and claimed asylum as refugees. Shahanna Islam is a graduate school teacher from Karachi. In 1990 she became involved in a playground dispute between rival gangs of politically motivated boys. Those supporting the Mohaijur Quami Movement or "MQM" told her husband, who belonged to the same party, that she had been unfaithful to him. As a result he gave her severe beatings which eventually drove her out of the house. The other woman, Syeda Shah is simple and uneducated. She was frequently beaten by her husband and eventually, when pregnant, turned out of the house. She too came to the United Kingdom, where her child was born.

* * *

I turn, therefore, to the question of causation. What is the reason for the persecution which the appellants fear? Here it is important to notice that it is made up of two elements. First, there is the threat of violence to Mrs Islam by her husband and his political friends and to Mrs Shah by her husband. This is a personal affair, directed against them as individuals. Secondly, there is the inability or unwillingness of the state to do anything to protect them. There is nothing personal about this. The evidence was that the state would not assist them because they were women. It denied them a protection against violence which it would have given to men. These two elements have to be combined to constitute persecution within the meaning of the convention. * * *

* * * Suppose oneself in Germany in 1935. There is discrimination against Jews in general, but not all Jews are persecuted. Those who conform to the discriminatory laws, wear yellow stars out of doors and so forth can go about their ordinary business. But those who contravene the racial laws are persecuted. Are they being persecuted on grounds of race? In my opinion, they plainly are. It is therefore a fallacy to say that because not all members of a class are being persecuted, it follows that persecution of a few cannot be on grounds of membership of that class. Or to come nearer to the facts of the present case, suppose that the Nazi government in those early days did not actively organise violence against Jews, but pursued a policy of not giving any protection to Jews subjected to violence by neighbours. A Jewish shopkeeper is attacked by a gang organised by an Aryan competitor who smash his shop, beat him up and threaten to do it again if he remains in business. The competitor and his gang are motivated by business rivalry and a desire to settle old personal scores, but they would not have done what they did unless they knew that the authorities would allow them to act with impunity. And the ground upon which they enjoyed impunity was that the victim was a Jew. Is he being persecuted on grounds of race? Again, in my opinion, he is. An essential element in the persecution, the failure of the authorities to provide protection, is based upon race. It is true that one answer to the question "why was he attacked?" would be "because a competitor wanted to drive him out of business''. But another answer, and in my view the right answer in the context of the convention, would be ''he was attacked by a competitor who knew that he would receive no protection because he was a Jew''.

In the case of Mrs Islam, the legal and social conditions which according to the evidence existed in Pakistan and which left her unprotected against violence by men were discriminatory against women. For the purposes of the convention, this discrimination was the critical element in the persecution. In my opinion, this means that she feared persecution because she was a woman. There was no need to construct a more restricted social group simply for the purpose of satisfying the causal connection which the convention requires.

Mr Blake [counsel for the applicants], in supporting this argument, suggested that the requirement of causation could be satisfied by applying a ''but for'' test. If they would not have feared persecution but for the fact that they were women, then they feared persecution for reason of being women. I think that this goes from overcomplication to oversimplification. Once one has established the context in which a causal question is being asked, the answer involves the application of common sense notions rather than mechanical rules. I can think of cases in which a ''but for'' test would be satisfied but common sense would reject the conclusion that the persecution was for reasons of sex. Assume that during a time of civil unrest, women are particularly vulnerable to attack by marauding men, because the attacks are sexually motivated or because they are thought weaker and less able to defend themselves. The government is unable to protect them, not because of any discrimination but simply because its writ does not run in that part of the country. It is unable to protect men either. It may be true to say women would not fear attack but for the fact that they were women. But I do not think that they would be regarded as subject to persecution within the meaning of the convention. The necessary element of discrimination is lacking.

* * *

■ LORD MILLETT [dissenting].

* * *

* * * I turn to consider the social group to which the present appellants claim to belong and for membership of which they fear persecution. As formulated by the appellants it consists of women in Pakistan who have been or who are liable to be accused of adultery or other conduct transgressing social norms and who are unprotected by their husbands or other male relatives. It is a subset of the set ''women'' (and of the subset ''married women''). The third qualifying condition can be disposed of at once. The fact that the appellants have no one to protect them helps to show that their fear of persecution is well founded. But it does not help to define the social group to which they belong. I am content to assume that the appellants would not be persecuted if they had someone to protect them from attack. But they are not persecuted because they have no one to protect them; that is not the ground of persecution. The ''but for'' test of causation, which is always necessary but rarely sufficient, is beguilingly misleading in this context.

This qualifying condition was no doubt included because of an erroneous belief that all the members of the group must be equally liable to persecution. That is not the case. It is no answer to a claim for asylum that some members of the group may be able to escape persecution, either because they have powerful protectors or for geographical or other reasons. Such factors do not narrow the membership of the group, but go to the question whether the applicant's fear of persecution is well founded. Thus I would accept that homosexuals form a distinct social group. In a society which subjected practising homosexuals but not non-practising homosexuals to persecution the relevant social group would still consist of homosexuals, not of the sub-set practising homosexuals. A non-practising homosexual would have no difficulty in establishing that he was a member of a persecuted group. His only difficulty would be in establishing that his fear of persecution was well founded, having regard to the fact that he was not a practising homosexual. This would be a matter of evidence, but given the hostility encountered by all homosexuals in such a society and the obvious problems the applicant would have in satisfying his tormentors of his own sexual abstinence, I doubt that the difficulty would be a real one.

Whether the social group is taken to be that contended for by the appellants, however, or the wider one of Pakistani women who are perceived to have transgressed social norms, the result is the same. No cognisable social group exists independently of the social conditions on which the persecution is founded. The social group which the appellants identify is defined by the persecution, or more accurately (but just as fatally) by the discrimination which founds the persecution. It is an artificial construct called into being to meet the exigencies of the case.

The appellants contended for the subset because they recognised that the head set of "women" or "married women" would not do. Officially, I understand, Sharia law regards women as "separate but equal", a description which, I observe, was also applied, with scant regard for the truth, to apartheid in South Africa. The evidence clearly establishes that women in Pakistan are treated as inferior to men and subordinate to their husbands and that, by international standards, they are subject to serious and quite unacceptable discrimination on account of their sex. But persecution is not merely an aggravated form of discrimination; and even if women (or married women) constitute a particular social group it is not accurate to say that those women in Pakistan who are persecuted are persecuted because they are members of it. They are persecuted because they are thought to have transgressed social norms, not because they are women. There is no evidence that men who transgress the different social norms which apply to them are treated more favourably.

In the course of argument an illuminating instance was put forward. Suppose, in the early years of the Third Reich, Jews in Nazi Germany were required to wear a yellow star on pain of being sent to a concentration camp and murdered if they did not. Would they have failed to qualify as refugees on the ground that they were not liable to persecution on racial·grounds, but because they were defying the law? Of course we know now that they should not have failed to qualify, because the law was not merely discriminatory but a necessary part of the intended persecution. Jews were required to wear a distinguishing badge in order to mark them out for persecution. At the time this would have been a matter of evidence; but given the absence of any other rational explanation for the law, the virulence of the state-inspired racial propaganda which formed the background against which it was enacted, and the wholly disproportionate penalty for disobedience, there should have been no difficulty in satisfying the requirements of the convention even in the absence of other evidence of persecution (of which there was an abundance). I find the example instructive precisely because of the differences between it and the present case rather than the similarities.

I am accordingly not willing to accept, as a general proposition, the submission that those who are persecuted because they refuse to conform to discriminatory laws to which, as members of a particular social group, they are subject, thereby qualify for refugee status. Such persons are discriminated against because they are members of the social group in question; but they are persecuted because they refuse to conform, not because they are members of the social group. * * *

* * *

* * * The evidence in the present case is that the widespread discrimination against women in Pakistan is based on religious law, and the persecution of those who refuse to conform to social and religious norms, while in no sense required by religious law, is sanctioned or at least tolerated by the authorities. But these norms are not a pretext for persecution nor have they been recently imposed. They are deeply embedded in the society in which the appellants have been brought up and in which they live. Women who are perceived to have transgressed them are treated badly, particularly by their husbands, and the authorities do little to protect them. But this is not because they are women. They are persecuted as individuals for what each of them has done or is thought to have done. They are not jointly condemned as females or persecuted for what they are. The appellants need to establish that the reason that they are left unprotected by the authorities and are liable to be persecuted by their husbands is that they are women. In my opinion they have not done so.

* * *

NOTES AND QUESTIONS

1. Despite the suggestion in *Fatin* that the persecution must be "solely" because of one of the protected grounds, the authorities generally agree on one thing: An asylum applicant need not show that every member of the protected group (for example every woman, every member of a particular religion, etc.) is in danger of being persecuted. The fact that only a subset of the protected group is targeted is no barrier to asylum. Lords

Hoffmann and Millett (as well as Lord Steyn, whose judgment is not reproduced) in the *Islam* case are explicit on this point, as are the Justice Department's proposed regulations, 65 Fed. Reg. 76592–93, 76598 (Dec. 7, 2000), proposing to amend 8 C.F.R. § 208.15(b)(last sentence). See also *Garcia-Martinez v. Ashcroft*, 371 F.3d 1066, 1073 (9th Cir. 2004) (expressly rejecting notion that persecution must be "solely" on account of one of the five protected grounds); *Jahed v. INS*, 356 F.3d 991, 998 (9th Cir. 2004) (same).

But when the persecutor has multiple motives, there remains the question of precisely what "on account of" means, as the Notes and Questions below illustrate.

2. Both Lord Hoffmann and Lord Millett analyse the Nazi require-ment that Jews wear the yellow Star of David as an identifying badge. Suppose, they ask, the only Jews who were in danger of persecution were those who violated this rule. Could it still be said that the latter group was being persecuted because of race? (Assume for purposes of this hypothetical that Jews constitute a race, not only a religion.) First, be sure you understand the analyses of this hypothetical by Lords Hoffman and Millett. Second, what does Lord Hoffmann say this hypothetical has to do with the present case? Third, does Lord Millett convincingly distinguish the Jewish hypothetical from the present case?

3. Consider also the second hypothetical involving Jewish persecution in Nazi Germany. Shopkeepers attack Jewish competitors for commercial gain, not because they hate Jews, but because they know that the German government's refusal to protect Jews will enable the shopkeepers to get away with the attacks. The question is whether the persecution can be said to be on account of race. What are the similarities between this hypotheti-cal and the present case?

4. Counsel for the asylum claimants argued for a "but-for" test, the same test advocated in the essay that precedes the case. If the applicants can show that they would not be in danger of persecution but for the fact that they are women, he argues, then the persecution should be found to be on account of gender. See, e.g., *Li v. Ashcroft*, 356 F.3d 1153, 1160 (9th Cir. en banc 2004) (applying but-for test).

Lord Hoffmann rejects the "but-for" test. He calls it an "oversimplifi-cation." To explain why, he says "I can think of cases in which a 'but for' test would be satisfied but common sense would reject the conclusion that the persecution was for reasons of sex." He offers one such hypothetical case: "During a time of civil unrest, women are particularly vulnerable to attack by marauding men, because the attacks are sexually motivated or because they are thought weaker and less able to defend themselves. The government is unable to protect them, not because of any discrimination but simply because its writ does not run in that part of the country." His position is that in such a case it is "common sense" that the persecution is not on account of gender. What is your reaction to this reasoning? First, is he right that this applicant would fail to qualify for asylum? Second, if there is indeed a problem with granting asylum in this case, is it really because of a defect in the "but-for" test or because of the absence of a government role in the persecution?

5.   Lord Millett would dismiss the social group claim entirely. In his view, if the social group is defined as Pakistani women suspected of adultery, the claim fails because the adultery accusations are the very persecution being alleged, and the social group must be defined independently of the persecution. More relevant here, if the social group is defined more broadly to include all Pakistani women, then in his view the claim fails for "on account of" reasons. He suggests that the applicants fear persecution not because they are women, but because they are thought to have transgressed social norms. First, can one agree that the applicants are persecuted for being thought to have violated social norms yet believe that they are *also* persecuted because of their gender? Second, consider Lord Millett's additional observation on this issue. For all we know, he says, men who transgress social norms are persecuted too; at least there is no evidence to the contrary. Suppose men are indeed persecuted when they violate social norms. Does it follow that women who are persecuted for violating social norms are not being persecuted on account of gender? Does it matter whether the social norms for men differ from those for women? Is it possible, in other words, for a given country to persecute *both* men and women on account of gender? Consider the Taliban prohibitions on women working or attending university, the simultaneous prohibitions on men cutting their beards, and the severe consequences for both violations.

6.   Problems can arise in cases where the persecutor had "mixed motives." Citing several cases, the Justice Department's commentary to its proposed asylum regulations acknowledges that "[u]nder long-standing principles of U.S. refugee law, it is not necessary for an applicant to show that his or her possession of a protected characteristic is the *sole* reason that the persecutor seeks to harm him or her." 65 Fed. Reg. at 76591 [emphasis added]. But the commentary goes on to say "Consistent with current law, this language [allows asylum in mixed motives cases but] does, however, require that the victim's protected characteristic be *central* to the persecutor's decision to act against the victim. For example, under this definition, it clearly would not be sufficient if the protected characteristic was *incidental or tangential* to the persecutor's motivation" [emphasis added]. *Id.* at 76592; see also *id.* at 76598, proposing to amend 8 C.F.R. § 208.15(b). Professor Deborah Anker has vigorously criticized the proposed centrality requirement. She argues that under existing case law (which the commentary to the proposed regulations acknowledges, 65 Fed. Reg. at 76591) it is enough that the persecutor acts "at least in part" because of a protected characteristic. See Deborah E. Anker, *Gender and Social Group: Comments to Proposed Regulations*, 6 BIB 185, 191–94 (Feb. 15, 2001). First, do you think that the centrality requirement proposed by the Justice Department is consistent with the "at least in part" language that it cites and that Professor Anker advocates codifying? Second, would a but-for test solve this problem too?

The REAL ID Act, § 101(a)(3), now provides a statutory answer. It requires proof that one of the five protected grounds "was or will be at least one central reason for persecuting the applicant." INA § 208(b)(1)(B)(i). The precise meaning of that requirement will surely be the subject of litigation.

7.   For some helpful critiques of the *Islam* case, see Deborah E. Anker, Nancy Kelly & John Willshire–Carrerra, *Defining "Particular Social Group" in Terms of Gender: The Shah Decision and U.S. Law*, 76 IR 1005 (July 2, 1999); Guy S. Goodwin–Gill, *Judicial Reasoning and Social Group after Islam and Shah*, 11 Internat'l J. Refugee L. 537 (1999); Karen Musalo, *Revisiting Social Group and Nexus in Gender Asylum Claims: A Unifying Rationale for Evolving Jurisprudence*, 52 DePaul L. Rev. 777, 787–91 (2003); Mavelyn Vidal, *Membership of a "Particular Social Group" and the Effect of Islam and Shah*, 11 Internat'l J. Refugee L. 528 (1999).

e.   PROBLEMS

PROBLEMS 1–5

Discuss whether each of the following applicants is eligible for asylum:

Problem 1. Fanatical army officers staged a successful coup, overthrowing a democratically elected government. The new leaders, eager to purge the country of western influences, have begun a ruthless "relocation" campaign in which professionals are forcibly moved from the cities to rural areas to perform agricultural labor at subsistence wages. Lawyers have been particularly hard hit, since the new government sees them as the bulwark of the old capitalist establishment and also as a symbol of the rule of law. Your client, a lawyer, escaped and managed eventually to make her way to the United States border, where she applied for admission. She tells you that if she is sent back she will be forcibly relocated and required to do agricultural labor even though she is 55 years old, unaccustomed to such work, and suffering from a heart condition that would be life-threatening if she over-exerts. She also tells you, consistently with human rights reports, that those who resist relocation are taken away and never heard from again.

Problem 2. The government of a foreign country (a democracy) has lately been denouncing homosexuals, accusing them of immorality and of spreading AIDS. Spurred on by that rhetoric, private citizens have frequently attacked and looted homosexual business establishments throughout the country and have occasionally assaulted individuals who "seem gay." Your client tells you he lived and worked in an area of the capital that is widely known to be a gay neighborhood. He ran a bookstore that specialized in gay and lesbian books. Two doors down the street from his store a coffee shop with a gay clientele had been firebombed and several patrons killed. The next day, there had appeared on the door of your client's bookstore a note warning him to expect the same. He called the police. The officer with whom he spoke told him there was nothing the police could do. The officer added that sodomy was a criminal offense punishable by up to ten years in prison, that the government was vigorous-ly enforcing that law, and that your client "had better think about that." As a matter of principle, your client will not disclose his sexual orientation.[8]

Problem 3. A woman asserts that in the culture of her country women are expected to be homemakers. Most people are generally hostile to the few women who work outside the home or attend college. She would like to attend college, but she cannot afford the tuition on her own and women are legally ineligible for the government education grants routinely awarded to qualified men.

Problem 4. A Protestant couple from a predominantly Roman Catho-lic country object to a law that prohibits the sale or possession of any artificial birth control device. Violations of the law are punishable by up to a year in prison. The couple has made a firm decision not to have children.

Problem 5. A twenty-year-old woman left her country, which is ruled by a despot whose armed forces routinely round up and execute anyone who speaks out in opposition. She has testified that she is consumed by hatred of her country's ruler, that because of the consequences of dissi-dence she forced herself to remain silent, and that she finally left the country because she knew that if she remained she would be unable to restrain herself any longer. She says her feelings have grown so intense that if she were sent back she knows she would have to speak her mind.

3.   "WELL–FOUNDED" FEAR AND "WOULD BE THREATENED": THE STANDARDS OF PROOF

You have now seen that an applicant for asylum under INA § 208 must establish "refugee" status, which in turn requires a fear of persecu-tion on account of one of the five protected grounds. INA § 101(a)(42). The applicant must also prove, however, that that fear is "well-founded." *Id.* The analogous requirement for withholding of removal under section 241(b)(3) is that the applicant's life or freedom "would be threatened." What do these requirements mean? For the fear to be "well-founded," as section 208 requires, how likely must it be that the claimed persecution will actually occur? For an adjudicator to find life or freedom "would be threatened," as section 241(b)(3) requires, how likely must it be that the threatened harm will actually materialize? And, importantly, are the an-swers to these last two questions the same or different?

The law governing the standard of proof for withholding of removal developed first. For many years the courts interpreted former section 243(h) [the predecessor of present section 241(b)(3)] to require a "clear probability of persecution." See the cases cited in *Matter of Dunar*, 14 I. & N. Dec. 310, 318–19 (BIA 1973). When the United States in 1968 acceded to the 1967 Protocol, it became derivatively bound by the 1951 Convention. Article 33.1 of the Convention sets out the principle of nonrefoulement (the international analog to the United States statutory term "withholding of

---

8. The author thanks Locky Nimick for his thoughtful contributions to this Problem.

removal"). The question arose whether article 33.1 altered the "clear probability" standard previously applied to then section 243(h). In *Dunar,* above, the BIA held it did not. But questions persisted, and when Congress in the Refugee Act of 1980 amended section 243(h) in several respects, there arose the analogous question whether the "clear probability" standard governed the new version of section 243(h).

In a landmark decision, *INS v. Stevic,* 467 U.S. 407, 104 S.Ct. 2489, 81 L.Ed.2d 321 (1984), the Supreme Court held that a person seeking withholding of removal under what is now INA § 241(b)(3) must still establish a "clear probability" that his or her life or freedom would be threatened on account of one of the five statutory grounds. The Court held also that for this purpose "clear probability" means "more likely than not." 467 U.S. at 424, 104 S.Ct. at 2498, 81 L.Ed.2d at 334.

Three years later, in *INS v. Cardoza–Fonseca,* 480 U.S. 421, 107 S.Ct. 1207, 94 L.Ed.2d 434 (1987), the Supreme Court interpreted the phrase "well-founded fear," which is an element of the "refugee" definition, INA § 101(a)(42), and therefore a requirement for asylum under section 208. In *Cardoza-Fonseca* the former INS argued that "well-founded fear" similarly embodies a "more likely than not" standard. The Court disagreed, construing it to require something less but declining to spell out the precise standard. The BIA and the lower courts subsequently held that a fear is "well-founded" if "a reasonable person in [the applicant's] circumstances would fear persecution." See, e.g., *Matter of Mogharrabi,* 19 I. & N. Dec. 439, 445 (BIA 1987); *Zamora–Morel v. INS,* 905 F.2d 833, 837 (5th Cir.1990); *De Valle v. INS,* 901 F.2d 787, 790 (9th Cir.1990). The regulations now essentially codify those holdings. See 8 C.F.R. §§ 208.13(b)(2)(B), 1208.13(b)(2)(B) (2004) ("reasonable possibility of suffering such persecution"). A "reasonable" possibility is clearly less than a 50% chance. In *Montecino v. INS,* 915 F.2d 518, 520 (9th Cir.1990), the court suggested that a well-founded fear is made out when an applicant, "on the basis of objective circumstances personally known to him, believes that he has at least a one in ten chance of being killed by the guerrillas." The Ninth Circuit has more recently reaffirmed that statement. *Knezevic v. Ashcroft,* 367 F.3d 1206, 1212 (9th Cir. 2004). For a useful synthesis of the Second Circuit's applications of the relevant standards of proof in the context of gender-related claims, see Pamela Goldberg, *Analytical Approaches in Search of Consistent Application: A Comparative Analysis of the Second Circuit Decisions Addressing Gender in the Asylum Law Context,* 66 Brooklyn L. Rev. 309 (2000).

NOTES AND QUESTIONS

1. In *Cardoza-Fonseca* one of the government's arguments was that Congress must have intended "well-founded fear" to be at least as stringent as "clear probability." Otherwise, the government observed, the applicant would have to prove more just to receive withholding of removal than to receive asylum, which is a *more* desirable remedy. This, the

government argued, is a result Congress could not possibly have intended. Had you been writing the majority opinion, how would you have answered that argument? (In fact, the Court provided an answer. 480 U.S. at 443–45.)

2. As a policy matter, *should* the law permit the involuntary return of a person who has a well-founded fear of persecution as long as the probability of such persecution actually occurring is not greater than 50%?

3. Can a fear of persecution be well-founded if one can avoid persecution by moving to another part of the same country? The BIA in *Acosta* (see page 947 above) in effect gave a "no" answer to that question. It observed that the danger of non-governmental persecution must be countrywide; if there is an internal flight alternative, then the fear is not well-founded. The asylum regulations now make this principle explicit; persecution is not well-founded if it is "reasonable to expect the applicant" to relocate internally. 8 C.F.R. §§ 208.13(b)(2)(C)(ii), 1208.13(b)(2)(C)(ii) (2004). A nonexclusive list of factors relevant to reasonableness includes "whether the applicant would face other serious harm in the place of suggested relocation; any ongoing civil strife within the country; administrative, economic or judicial infrastructure; geographical limitations; and social and cultural constraints, such as age, gender, health, and social and familial ties." *Id*. §§ 208.13(b)(3), 1208.13(b)(3). By way of exception, if the government is either the perpetrator or the sponsor of the persecution (or the applicant has demonstrated past persecution), there is a rebuttable presumption that relocation is not a reasonable alternative. *Id*. §§ 208.13(b)(3)(ii), 1208.13(b)(3)(ii). See also James C. Hathaway, *International Refugee Law: The Michigan Guidelines on the Internal Protection Alternative*, 21 Michigan J. Internat'l L. 131 (1999) (colloquium participants urging that denial on internal flight alternative grounds be permitted only when relocation alternative is "meaningful," specifically requiring real protection from persecution, protection from other serious risks such as famine or armed conflict, and compliance with other international refugee law norms, including procedural fairness); see generally Anker at 55–67.

Thus, an applicant who is able to retreat safely to another location within his or her country is ineligible for asylum. As you might recall from previous courses, American law is generally disinclined to deny otherwise valid defenses solely because a retreat option is available. In both criminal law and torts, for example, most states permit people to use even deadly force in self-defense rather than accept a safe retreat. And virtually all jurisdictions reach that result when retreat would entail fleeing one's home. See Wayne R. LaFave, Criminal Law § 10.4(f) (4th ed. 2003); Dan B. Dobbs, The Law of Torts, § 71 (2000). Yet in immigration law, retreat from one's home is held preferable to asylum. Why do you think that is? How does this issue differ from its criminal law and torts analogs?

4. Nationals of the European Union member states enjoy almost unrestricted freedom of movement within the Union. By analogy to the principle that one must show country-wide persecution in order to qualify for asylum, should nationals of EU countries have to prove Union-wide

persecution? Or does that question present different policy tradeoffs? The issue could command increasing importance with the recent enlargement of the EU to include Eastern European countries.[9]

5.   Special problems arise when conditions in the country of origin improve as a result of democratic change. Professor Peter Margulies argues that unrealistic assumptions about the speed of change often result in asylum being denied even when the fear of persecution is still well-founded. See Peter Margulies, *Democratic Transitions and the Future of Asylum Law*, 71 Univ. Colorado L. Rev. 3, 14–15 (2000); see also *Matter of N.M.A.*, 22 I. & N. Dec. 312 (BIA 1998). A reviewing court must give the BIA an opportunity to decide a changed circumstances issue rather than decide the issue itself. *INS v. Ventura*, 537 U.S. 12, 123 S.Ct. 353, 154 L.Ed.2d 272 (2002).

6.   Keep prominently in mind that, aside from nonrefoulement, establishing "refugee" status entitles the person to a whole range of rights spelled out in articles 3–34 of the 1951 Convention. These provisions deal with such subjects as nondiscrimination, freedom of religion, property rights, freedom of association, access to court, housing, employment, and welfare, among other things. In *Cardoza-Fonseca*, the Court said: "[T]hose who can only show a well-founded fear of persecution are not entitled to *anything*, but are eligible for the discretionary relief of asylum" [emphasis added]. 480 U.S. at 444. Two commentators have criticized this dictum, interpreting it to mean that, without a clear probability of persecution, refugees are not entitled to any of the refugee rights enumerated in the Convention. James C. Hathaway & Anne K. Cusick, *Refugee Rights Are Not Negotiable*, 14 Georgetown Immigration L.J. 481, 514–16 (2000). Query whether the Court, focused as it was on the specific question of standard of proof under article 33, literally meant to convey such a radical intention. See also Andrew Schoenholtz, *Beyond the Supreme Court: A Modest Plea to Improve Our Asylum System*, 14 Georgetown Immigration L.J. 541, 541–42 (2000) (arguing the standard of proof issues in *Stevic* and *Cardoza-Fonseca* have proven to be of little importance, since well-founded fear almost always translates into asylum).

PROBLEM 6

As the immigration judge in a particular case, you have reached the following conclusions: The applicant has a well-founded fear of persecution; it is slightly less likely than not that he will be persecuted if returned home; there is a third country (not the one designated by the applicant under INA § 241(b)(2)) that might be willing to take him, but at the time of your decision you cannot be sure whether it will do so; and there are some negative factors that leave you uneasy about granting asylum, but those negatives are not so strong that you would want to send him back to

9. Credit is due to Werner Dillmann, then an LL.M student from Austria, for spot-   ting this issue.

the country in which he fears persecution if you can help it. Realistically, what would you probably do?

4. METHODS OF PROOF

Preceding sections have examined the substantive elements that the applicant for either asylum or withholding of removal must establish, including the requisite likelihood of persecution. As a practical matter, how does the applicant go about proving that his or her fear of persecution is well-founded, or that a return to a particular country is more likely than not to threaten the applicant's life or freedom? In general, any probative evidence is admissible for these purposes, but certain specific strategies are common enough to warrant special mention. Two problems should be distinguished: First, what commonly occurring *facts* are material to the likelihood of persecution? Second, what *evidence* is relevant to (and sufficient to establish) those facts or any other facts affecting the likelihood of persecution?

a. MATERIAL FACTS

i. *Membership in a Persecuted Group*

In the *Acosta* materials you saw the notion, accepted by different courts with different degrees of conviction, that "persecution" implies a "singling out" of the particular individual. Yet it is well known that governments all too often persecute entire identifiable groups; Jews in Nazi Germany are the classic example. In such cases two questions arise. First, as a substantive matter, would such group persecution satisfy the "singling out" requirement? That question was considered earlier. Second, and more pertinent here, even when the group consequences can be termed "persecution," does membership in the persecuted group establish that the particular applicant is sufficiently likely to incur those consequences?

In thinking about this question, consider that the persecution must be on account of "race, religion, nationality, membership in a particular social group, or political opinion." The first four categories expressly contemplate persecution based on group membership. That does not mean, however, that group membership, with nothing more, creates a high enough probability that the particular applicant would actually suffer the feared persecution. See UNHCR Handbook, paras. 70, 73, 74, 79. Absent "special circumstances," more will generally be required. *Id.* Now that you have studied the "well-founded fear" standard, take another look at 8 C.F.R. §§ 208.13(b)(2)(iii), 1208.13(b)(2)(iii) (2004), reproduced on page 951 above. These provisions permit the applicant to establish a well-founded fear of persecution by showing a pattern or practice of the country persecuting a group of people and the applicant's inclusion in that group, but add the qualifier "such that [the applicant's] fear of persecution upon return is reasonable." See also *id.* §§ 208.16(b)(2), 1208.16(b)(2) (analogous provisions for withholding of removal, adjusted to reflect higher standard of proof).

ii.   Past Persecution

Persecution that a person suffered in the past can be material to asylum eligibility in two ways. First, evidence of past persecution can help the applicant establish a well-founded fear of future persecution. Second, the refugee definition in INA § 101(a)(42) makes past persecution an independent basis for refugee status—i.e., even when there is no threat of future persecution. As discussed below, both concepts are subject to limitations. See generally Anker at 40–55.

Following *Matter of Chen,* 20 I. & N. Dec. 16 (BIA 1989), the regulations provide a rebuttable presumption that one who has suffered past persecution has a well-founded fear of future persecution. 8 C.F.R. §§ 208.13(b)(1), 1208.13(b)(1) (2004). Until 2000, the only way the government could rebut that presumption was to prove that the conditions in the country of origin had sufficiently improved. See *Matter of C.Y.Z.,* 21 I. & N. Dec. 915 (BIA 1997), review denied, I.D. 3503 (A.G. Dec. 1, 2004). Many felt that restricting the government's proof in that way made little sense in those cases where the very nature of the past persecution made repeat persecution unlikely or even impossible. Female genital mutilation was offered as an example; an applicant who has already undergone FGM will not be subjected to the procedure a second time, yet in the absence of changed country conditions the holding in *C.Y.Z.* would require a counterinstinctive finding that the applicant fears future persecution. See generally Timothy P. McIlmail, *Toward a More Reasonably Rebutted Presumption: A Proposal to Amend the "Past Persecution" Asylum Regulation—8 C.F.R. § 208.13(b)(1),* 12 Georgetown Immigration L.J. 265 (1998) (urging regulatory change to create other rebuttal avenues).

In 2000, the Justice Department amended its regulations to permit the government to rebut the presumption of well-founded fear of future persecution either (a) by showing any "fundamental change in circumstances" that eliminates the required well-founded fear on one of the protected grounds (i.e., changes in personal circumstances as well as country conditions); or (b) by showing that "[t]he applicant could avoid future persecution by relocating to another part of the applicant's country ... and under all the circumstances, it would be reasonable to expect the applicant to do so." 65 Fed. Reg. 76133, amending 8 C.F.R. § 208.13 (b)(1)(i) [and now § 1208.13(b)(1)(i)]. The cited provisions govern asylum; the rules for withholding of removal are similar. 8 C.F.R. §§ 208.16(b)(1), 1208.16(b)(1) (2004). As you saw earlier, however, both the BIA and the courts have occasionally been willing to find a well-founded fear of future persecution, based on a presumption of past persecution, even when there was no danger that the previous act would be repeated. They have done so in the contexts of sterilization, see *Qu v. Gonzales,* 399 F.3d 1195 (9th Cir. 2005); *Matter of Y–T–L–,* 23 I. & N. Dec. 601 (BIA 2003), and female genital mutilation, *Mohammed v. Gonzales,* 400 F.3d 785 (9th Cir. 2005). In each setting the reasoning has been that the past persecution was of such a nature as to constitute a "continuing" harm.

But if past persecution is an independent ground for refugee status, as the Board in *Chen* had earlier acknowledged, 20 I. & N.Dec. at 18, why would it matter whether past persecution also helps the applicant establish the alternative ground of a well-founded fear of future persecution? The answer lies mainly in the discretionary component of asylum. Suppose the adjudicator finds past persecution but, even with the aid of the presumption, cannot find a well-founded fear of future persecution. By what standard should the discretionary decision be made?

In such cases, the regulations, reflecting the same 2000 amendments, now structure the exercise of asylum officers' and immigration judges' discretion. If a person is found to be a refugee solely on the basis of past persecution, then asylum must be denied on discretionary grounds unless the person has demonstrated either (a) "compelling" reasons for being unable or unwilling to return; or (b) "a reasonable possibility that he or she may suffer other serious harm upon removal to that country." 8 C.F.R. §§ 208.13(b)(1)(i, iii), 1208.13(b)(1)(i,iii) (2004).

The discretionary hurdle in INA § 208 is one reason for asserting past persecution as an indicator of future persecution even though the former is itself a basis for refugee status. There is another reason. Although the refugee definition incorporated in section 208 expressly encompasses actual (past) persecution, withholding of removal under section 241(b)(3) does not embody the refugee definition. Nor does that section otherwise make actual past persecution a basis for eligibility. Section 241(b)(3) requires that the applicant's life or freedom "would be threatened," a phrase that you now know has been interpreted to require that future persecution be more likely than not. Thus, an applicant who has suffered past persecution but who lacks the "compelling reasons" or "reasonable possibility" of "serious harm" critical to the favorable exercise of discretion will want to assert the past persecution as a way of establishing a future threat to life or freedom.

b. RELEVANT EVIDENCE

i. *The Applicant's Own Testimony*

Courts and the BIA have recognized that "[a]uthentic refugees rarely are able to offer direct corroboration of specific threats or specific incidents of persecution." *Turcios v. INS,* 821 F.2d 1396, 1402 (9th Cir.1987); accord, *Matter of Mogharrabi,* 19 I. & N. Dec. 439, 445 (BIA 1987). As Stephen Yale–Loehr and John Palmer put it:

> Genuine asylum seekers often have great difficulty obtaining evidence to support their claims. They usually have neither the foresight, the time, nor the ability to collect corroborating evidence before fleeing their homes. The documents they do bring along may be destroyed or stolen during flight. Once they have departed, asylum applicants may have difficulties in obtaining evidence from their countries of origin. Long distances and unreliable mail may present logistical problems; friends and family members may be unwilling to provide statements or even assist in obtaining docu-

ments due to fear of reprisal. The fact that applicants are often held in detention while preparing their cases only compounds these difficulties. Moreover, corroborating evidence may simply not be available, given the often clandestine practices of regimes responsible for persecution.

Stephen Yale–Loehr & John R.B. Palmer, *Evidentiary Issues in Asylum Cases*, 6 BIB 595, at 595 (June 15, 2001); see also UNHCR Handbook, para. 196.

Consequently, asylum claimants often must rely solely on their own testimony to establish the specific events that leave them vulnerable to persecution. For those reasons, the credibility of the applicant is an especially critical issue in asylum cases. Two kinds of issues arise frequently. One is how to assess the credibility of the applicant. The other is what should happen when the applicant's testimony is found credible. Will credible testimony alone establish eligibility for asylum, or is corroborating evidence necessary? See generally Anker at 150–69; Yale–Loehr & Palmer, above. In the REAL ID Act, Congress addressed both questions.

As to the first issue: Testimony that establishes eligibility for asylum will obviously serve the applicant's own interests, but that fact does not mean the testimony is false. See *Dawood–Haio v. INS*, 800 F.2d 90, 96 (6th Cir.1986). How, then, can an asylum officer or an immigration judge decide whether the applicant's testimony is credible? And by what standards should the BIA and the courts review the credibility assessments of the immigration judge? For a comprehensive analysis by an immigration judge, see Henry G. Watkins, *Credibility Findings in Deportation Proceedings: "Bear[ing] Witness Unto the Truth"*, 2 Georgetown Immigration L.J. 231 (1987); see also Elwin Griffith, *Asylum and Withholding of Deportation— Challenges to the Alien after the Refugee Act of 1980*, 12 Loyola of L.A. Int'l & Comp. L.J. 515, 529–32 (1990).

The REAL ID Act, § 101(a)(3), added section 208(b)(1)(B)(iii) to the INA. It enumerates some of the factors relevant to credibility:

the demeanor, candor, or responsiveness of the applicant or witness, the inherent plausibility of the applicant's or witness's account, the consistency between the applicant's or witness's written and oral statements (whenever made and whether or not under oath, and considering the circumstances under which the statements were made), the internal consistency of each such statement, the consistency of such statements with other evidence of record (including the reports of the Department of State on country conditions), and any inaccuracies or falsehoods in such statements, without regard to whether an inconsistency, inaccuracy, or falsehood goes to the heart of the applicant's claim, or any other relevant factor.

In the past several years, the second issue—whether credible testimony by the applicant is enough to sustain his or her burden of proof without corroboration—has heated up. The BIA has seemed increasingly inclined to allow immigration judges to deny asylum claims on grounds of lack of corroborating evidence, even as reviewing courts remind the Board of the obstacles faced by persecution victims in procuring supporting documents. See, e.g, *Senathirajah v. INS*, 157 F.3d 210, 215–16 (3d Cir. 1998). More generally, the Board has steadily increased its deference to adverse credibility determinations by immigration judges. For useful summaries and critiques of this trend, see Eleanor Acer & Beth Lyon, *And the Boat Is Still Rocking: Asylum Practice Update in the Midst of Shifting Regulations and Caselaw: Part Two*, March 1999 Immigration Briefings at 8; Harvey Kaplan & Maureen O'Sullivan, *The Role of the BIA in Reviewing Negative Credibility Findings: Circumventing the Well–Founded Fear Standard*, 75 IR 1181 (Aug. 31, 1998); Thomas K. Ragland, *Presumed Incredible: A View from the Dissent*, 75 IR 1541 (Nov. 9, 1998); Margaret Kuehne Taylor, *The Mogharrabi Rule in 1998: A Review of Recent BIA Asylum Decisions*, 75 IR 901 (July 6, 1998). Most of those decisions have prompted strong dissents, some suggesting that the Board's decisions on this subject have implicitly imported a legal presumption that an asylum claimant's testimony is fraudulent. See, e.g., *Matter of A–S–*, 21 I. & N. Dec. 1106, 1124–25 (BIA en banc 1998) (Rosenberg, dissenting). The courts of appeals have adopted varying approaches. Compare, e.g., *Diallo v. INS*, 232 F.3d 279, 286 (2d Cir. 2000) (approving BIA rule that even credible applicant must offer corroborating evidence or explain why he or she did not, whenever such evidence is "reasonable to expect") with *Ladha v. INS*, 215 F.3d 889, 901 (9th Cir. 2000) (holding credible testimony that is unrefuted, direct, and specific renders corroboration unnecessary).

Professor Ilene Durst has advocated a formal presumption that the applicant is credible, one that could be rebutted only by "clear and convincing evidence of material misrepresentations or other material distortion of the facts." See Ilene Durst, *Lost in Translation: Why Due Process Demands Deference to the Refugee's Narrative*, 53 Rutgers L. Rev. 127, 128 (2000).

In an attempt to forge a uniform standard, the REAL ID Act, § 101(a)(3), added section 208(b)(1)(B)(ii) to the INA. This provision confirms that the applicant's testimony may suffice without corroboration, "but only if the applicant satisfies the trier of fact that the applicant's testimony is credible, is persuasive, and refers to specific facts sufficient to demonstrate that the applicant is a refugee." The same provision goes on to say that, if the trier of fact requests corroboration of credible testimony, "such evidence must be provided unless the applicant does not have the evidence and cannot reasonably obtain the evidence." INA § 208(b)(1)(B)(iii) then expressly rejects any "presumption of credibility" for the trier of fact, "but if no adverse credibility determination is explicitly made, the applicant or witness shall have a rebuttable presumption of credibility on appeal." *Id.*

The provisions discussed up to this point relate specifically to asylum claims under INA § 208. Another provision of the REAL ID Act, § 101(c), adding INA § 241(b)(3)(C), extends the same principles to withholding of removal under INA § 241(b)(3).

Damaize–Job v. INS

United States Court of Appeals, Ninth Circuit, 1986.
787 F.2d 1332.

■ FLETCHER, CIRCUIT JUDGE:

Alberto Damaize–Job appeals from the Board of Immigration Appeals's (BIA's) denial of his application for withholding of deportation under section 243(h)[a] of the Immigration and Nationality Act, and for political asylum under section 208(a) of the Refugee Act of 1980. We find that the BIA's decision is not supported by substantial evidence, and that Damaize satisfies both the "clear probability of persecution" standard of section 243(h) and the "well-founded fear of persecution" standard of section 208(a). We therefore reverse the BIA on Damaize's section 243(h) claim and reverse and remand on his section 208(a) claim so that the Attorney General can exercise his discretion and determine whether to grant Damaize asylum.

* * *

[After considering the applicant's claim and the evidence, the Board concludes] that Damaize's allegations, if true, are sufficient to satisfy the clear probability of persecution standard of section 243(h) and would entitle him to withholding of deportation under section 243(h).

3.   *The Credibility Findings of the IJ*

The IJ questioned Damaize's credibility for three specific reasons: (1) the discrepancies in certain dates provided in his asylum application and oral testimony; (2) his failure to marry the mother of his two children; and (3) his failure to apply for asylum in the other countries which he visited or in which he worked prior to coming to the United States. We conclude that none of these is a valid ground upon which to base a finding that an asylum applicant is not credible.

First, minor discrepancies in dates that are attributable to the applicant's language problems or typographical errors and cannot be viewed as attempts by the applicant to enhance his claims of persecution have no bearing on credibility. Damaize stated in his oral testimony that his daughter was born in 1968 and in his asylum application that she was born in 1967; his asylum application indicated that his other child was born nine months after Damaize himself was born, which was clearly a mistake. The IJ nowhere explained how these inaccuracies reflected on the credibility of his persecution claims or for what possible reason Damaize would intentionally have provided incorrect information on such trivial points. These trivial errors merely provided an excuse upon which to predicate a finding of no credibility.

---

a.   Now INA § 241(b)(3)—Ed.

Second, to the extent that the IJ questioned Damaize's credibility based upon his failure to marry the mother of his children, this was clearly impermissible. The personal choices that an asylum applicant has made concerning marriage, children, and living arrangements should not be used to evaluate the applicant's credibility concerning his claims of persecution, unless they reflect some inconsistency in a relevant portion of the applicant's testimony.

Finally, Damaize's failure to apply for asylum in any of the countries through which he passed or in which he worked prior to his arrival in the United States does not provide a valid basis for questioning the credibility of his persecution claims. The IJ appears to have assumed that an individual who truly fears persecution in his homeland will automatically seek asylum in the first country in which he arrives. However, there is no basis for this assumption. Damaize's claims of persecution are no less credible because once he left Nicaragua, he was not satisfied with "any port in a storm." It is quite reasonable for an individual like Damaize, who has experienced persecution in Nicaragua, to seek a new homeland that is insulated from the instability of Central America and that offers more promising economic opportunities. Moreover, to qualify for relief under sections 243(h) and 208(a), Damaize must demonstrate only that he may be "subject to persecution *in [his] homeland*" [citing legislative history]. Thus, it was perfectly consistent for Damaize, once he was out of Nicaragua and thus out of immediate danger, not to seek asylum in the first place where he arrived. Damaize's failure to contact United States embassies in Central America and Mexico may simply indicate a lack of awareness about this procedure, a fear of authority or rejection, or both.

In short, the information relied upon by the IJ to question Damaize's credibility reveals nothing about whether or not Damaize is an honest individual, or whether or not he feared for his safety in Nicaragua. The IJ had no legitimate, articulable basis to question Damaize's credibility, nor did he offer "a specific, cogent reason for [his] disbelief."

In the present case, the record has been thoroughly developed. Damaize testified in detail concerning his activities since 1979 and his basis for believing that he likely will be persecuted if he returns to Nicaragua. Damaize vividly described his incarceration, his torture, the threats to his life, and his fears of persecution as a Miskito. The IJ had a full opportunity to cross-examine Damaize and to expose any internal inconsistencies and improbabilities in his story. Yet other than the impermissible or insignificant reasons given by the IJ for questioning Damaize's testimony, there is a "total absence of contradictory evidence" in the record as a whole that potentially undermines Damaize's credibility. Nor is there "any inherent improbability [or inconsistency] in [Damaize's] testimony" itself.

We presume that if the IJ had any additional reasons to doubt Damaize's credibility, the IJ would have stated so in the decision below. Because the IJ expressed no further concerns, and the only explicitly articulated reasons rested on impermissible factors, then we conclude from the IJ's opinion that Damaize was an otherwise credible witness. * * *

* * *

■ BURNS, J., respectfully dissents.

NOTES AND QUESTIONS

1. Historically, reviewing courts have generally accorded great deference to the credibility determinations of the immigration judge, who "views the witness as the testimony is given." *Canjura–Flores v. INS*, 784 F.2d 885, 888 (9th Cir.1985). The BIA now reviews IJ findings of fact under a "clearly erroneous" standard, see 8 C.F.R. § 1003.1(d)(3) (2004), but even when it used to review findings of fact de novo, it typically deferred to the IJ's credibility assessments, again because he or she had the opportunity to observe the applicant's demeanor. *Matter of Kulle*, 19 I. & N. Dec. 318, 331 (BIA 1985); see also Susan Kneebone, *The Refugee Review Tribunal and the Assessment of Credibility: An Inquisitorial Role?*, 5 Australian J. Administrative L. 78 (1998).

Still, as the court in Damaize–Job indicates, an immigration judge who disbelieves the applicant's testimony must give specific reasons for doing so. Accord, *Osorio v. INS*, 99 F.3d 928, 931 (9th Cir. 1996) (IJ must have "legitimate articulable basis" to question credibility and "must offer a specific, cogent reason"). As noted earlier, INA § 208(b)(1)(B)(iii) now provides a (non-exclusive) list of factors relevant to credibility.

2. Among the factors listed in section 208(b)(1)(B)(iii) are internal inconsistencies (between the applicants' statements, written or oral, or within a single statement). The court in *Damaize–Job* makes clear that minor inconsistencies will not support an adverse credibility assessment. Accord, *Osorio*, 99 F.3d at 931; *Blanco–Comarribas v. INS*, 830 F.2d 1039, 1043 (9th Cir.1987). In *Aguilera–Cota v. USINS*, 914 F.2d 1375 (9th Cir.1990), the court held the immigration judge may not base an adverse credibility determination solely on the fact that the applicant's written application did not recite all the facts to which he or she later testified.

With the advent of expedited removal, immigration judges now often have access to the handwritten notes of the interview conducted by the CBP officer at the airport. In *Balasubramanrim v. INS*, 143 F.3d 157 (3d Cir. 1998), the court held that the immigration judge had relied far too heavily on apparent disparities between the airport notes and the applicant's hearing testimony. The court recited countless deficiencies in the airport notes that made their content unreliable and reversed the BIA's affirmance of the immigration judge.

In *Damaize–Job*, the IJ relied in part on the applicant's inconsistent statements concerning the birth years of his children. If INA § 208(b)(1)(B)(iii) had then been in force, would the IJ's reliance on those inconsistencies have been appropriate? As a normative matter, how *should* an IJ decide whether discrepancies—either positive misstatements or omissions—are significant enough to warrant adverse credibility determinations? Should it matter whether the applicant had a motive to misrepresent?

3. Character evidence can sometimes be damning. Note the reliance the immigration judge in *Damaize–Job* placed on the applicant's failure to marry the mother of his children. At one point, the immigration judge said that the failure to marry the mother "raises some questions about [the applicant's] morality," 787 F.2d at 1334 n. 4, a factor that the court believes affected the judge's credibility assessment. The reviewing court rejects that reasoning. Was it right to do so? Is there anything in INA § 208(b)(1)(B)(iii) that would have altered the analysis of this issue today?

4. Actual deliberate lies about other matters can obviously undermine any witness's credibility. See, e.g., *Sarvia–Quintanilla v. U.S. INS*, 767 F.2d 1387, 1393 (9th Cir.1985). But even a lie to which the applicant confesses will not always support an adverse credibility finding. In *Turcios v. INS*, 821 F.2d 1396 (9th Cir.1987), a Salvadoran asylum claimant admitted that, when apprehended by the former INS, he had told them he was Mexican so that he would not be deported to El Salvador. The court rejected the finding of no credibility, reasoning that, far from diminishing the person's claim of feared persecution, the lie actually supported it. The lie demonstrated the lengths to which the applicant was willing to go (even risking deportation to Mexico) rather than risk being returned to El Salvador. *Id.* at 1400–01. How might the government respond to that argument?

5. Vague or evasive statements can also detract from credibility. See, e.g., *Estrada v. INS*, 775 F.2d 1018, 1021 (9th Cir.1985).

6. The immigration judge may certainly reject testimony as inherently unbelievable, though that was not the case in *Damaize–Job*. Suppose the applicant testifies to having been persecuted by government officials because of her race, she delivers her testimony with what looks and sounds like great conviction, there are no internal discrepancies, the testimony is not contradicted, the statements are clear and detailed, and there is no evidence of character flaws, but the country is a democracy with a good human rights record. Under INA § 208(b)(1)(B)(iii), should the immigration judge find the testimony credible? *Cf. Matter of Dass*, 20 I.& N. Dec. 120 (BIA 1989) (pre-REAL ID Act).

7. Now assume that the facts to which the applicant testifies, if true, would establish eligibility for asylum. Assume also that there is no articulable reason to doubt the person's credibility. The issue, then, is whether that testimony is alone sufficient to establish eligibility for asylum.

The fact remains that an asylum claimant can have a motive to misrepresent. Suppose, therefore, that the immigration judge concludes there is no way to know whether the person testified as he or she did because (a) the stated facts are true or (b) the testimony would increase the chances of receiving asylum. If there is no other evidence, should the immigration judge find, or be permitted to find, that the person has not met his or her burden of proof? Should there be, as Professor Durst argued, see above, a rebuttable presumption that a witness is telling the truth, even when there is a motive to misrepresent? Alternatively, given the stakes, should the asylum claimant at least receive the benefit of the doubt? See UNHCR Handbook, paras. 203, 204 (yes, provided "all available evidence has been obtained and checked," the adjudicator is satisfied that the applicant is generally credible, and the statements are coherent, plausible, and not contrary to generally known facts).

ii. *State Department Opinions*

In recent years, one of the most controversial aspects of the asylum process has been the role of the State Department, which provides two kinds of information that asylum adjudicators can consult. By statute, see 22 U.S.C. § 2151n(d), the State Department must compile annual reports that describe the status of human rights in most of the world's countries. These "Country Reports" are now on line, at http://www.state.gov/g/drl/hr/c1470.htm. Their original purpose was to make promotion of human rights an element of our foreign assistance program, see 22 U.S.C. § 2151n(a), but in practice the Reports often are considered also by those involved in the asylum adjudication process. See David A. Martin, *Reforming Asylum Adjudication: On Navigating the Coast of Bohemia,* 138 U.Pa.L.Rev. 1247, 1310 (1990).

Human rights organizations have been highly critical of the Country Reports. A joint publication of two such organizations, before commenting on individual countries, offers this general critique:

The State Department's *Country Reports on Human Rights Practices for 1987* reflects the continuing influence of policy considerations on what should be an objective exercise. In certain countries—such as Chile, the Soviet Union, Peru, Czechoslovakia and Panama—the country reports are models of thoroughness and even-handed analysis. * * *

Unfortunately, a number of the reports depart from straightforward reporting to serve an advocacy function. In countries such as El Salvador, Guatemala, Haiti, Turkey, the Philippines and the People's Republic of China—countries where the Administration strongly identifies with the government or perceives important U.S. interests to be served by harmonious relations—the State Department fails adequately to portray human rights violations. Reports on those countries suffer from understatement and the glossing over of real abuses. Similarly, in some countries that the Administration perceives as ideological adversaries, such as Cuba, Nicaragua and Vietnam, the State Department tends to distort its reporting by discounting positive human rights developments and by emphasizing unverified or speculative allegations of abuses.

The State Department uses a variety of techniques to soften reports of violations by perceived allies, mainly by shading the presentation of violations in a way that blunts their impact. * * *

* * *

What emerges is that, despite repeated criticism on this score, foreign policy considerations continue to taint the State Department's human rights reporting. In condemning this politicizing of certain country reports, we are not suggesting that human rights should be the sole consideration in U.S. foreign policy. * * * We believe strongly, however, that competing foreign policy concerns should not affect the State Department's human rights reporting to Congress and the public. Despite inevitable differences over the precise foreign policy balance to be pursued, the facts about human rights practices should not be distorted. * * *

Human Rights Watch and Lawyers Committee for Human Rights, Critique—Review of the Department of State's Country Reports on Human Rights Practices for 1987, at 1–3 (1988).

In addition to the Country Reports, the State Department's Bureau of Human Rights and Humanitarian Affairs (BHRHA) may supply "advisory opinions" in individual asylum cases. At one time the practice was to furnish such opinions in all asylum cases and to include in each one the Department's bottom line conclusion as to whether the applicant had a well-founded fear of persecution. The adjudicator would then assign this evidence whatever weight he or she felt it deserved. In reality, most such letters were standard forms containing boilerplate language that reflected the findings of the relevant Country Report. See generally Martin, above, at 1310–11. In October 1987, responding to large increases in the volume of cases,[10] the State Department announced a new procedure, which it made official a few months later. See 65 IR 159 (1988); 53 Fed.Reg. 2893–94 (Feb. 2, 1988). Under the new policy, the State Department provided individualized letters only in a small fraction of cases. In other cases it either attached to the file a sticker referring the adjudicator to the State Department's Country Reports or sent supplementary information about either the country or the persecuted group.

Under the current regulations, the State Department is still notified of the case and given an opportunity to comment. 8 C.F.R. §§ 208.11, 1208.11 (2004). The former INS announced, however, that its asylum officers would be influenced only by those advisory opinions that contain information the asylum officers do not already have. See 67 IR 861 (1990). In particular, that meant "sticker" opinions would not be considered. *Id.*

---

10. In an article written shortly after enactment of the 1980 Act, two commentators proved prophetic: "It is unrealistic to think BHRHA will have sufficient staff to consider carefully every application for asylum in the country." Deborah E. Anker & Michael H. Posner, *The Forty-year Crisis: A Legislative History of the Refugee Act of 1980*, 19 San Diego L.Rev. 9, 76 (1981).

State Department participation in the asylum adjudication process has given rise to two different sorts of concerns. There is, as noted earlier, the problem of accuracy. One court, finding "the competency of State Department letters in matters of this kind * * * highly questionable," added:

> Such letters from the State Department do not carry the guarantees of reliability which the law demands of admissible evidence. A frank, but official, discussion of the political shortcomings of a friendly nation is not always compatible with the high duty to maintain advantageous diplomatic relations with nations throughout the world. * * * No hearing officer or court has the means to know the diplomatic necessities of the moment, in the light of which the statements must be weighed.

Kasravi v. INS, 400 F.2d 675, 677 n. 1 (9th Cir.1968); see also T. Alexander Aleinikoff, *Political Asylum in the Federal Republic of Germany and the Republic of France: Lessons for the United States,* 17 Univ. Michigan J. L. Reform 183, 194–95 (1984) (suggesting at least an *appearance* of political distortion).

A second and related concern is procedural fairness. Since there is no opportunity to cross-examine the writer of the letter to learn the basis for his or her opinion, it is often difficult to determine whether the opinion reflects only factors relevant to the likelihood of persecution or whether it was shaped also by foreign policy considerations. The regulations now require that State Department comments, unless classified, be made a part of the record and that the applicant have an opportunity to respond to them—but not by cross-examining the commenter. 8 C.F.R. §§ 208.11(d), 1208.11(d) (2004). In addressing the problem, Judge Friendly has invoked Professor Kenneth Culp Davis's classic distinction between "adjudicative facts" about the particular parties and "legislative facts" about more general events and conditions. Facts concerning the general attitudes of a government are, Judge Friendly said, properly classified as "legislative facts" on which the factfinder needs the best available information and for which cross-examination is unnecessary. In contrast, Judge Friendly reasoned, State Department assessments of the probability that the particular individual would be persecuted are "adjudicative" facts that should not be received into evidence without the safeguard of cross-examination. *Zamora v. INS,* 534 F.2d 1055, 1061 & nn. 4–5 (2d Cir.1976); see also Aleinikoff, above, at 194 (observing that applicant has no opportunity to question DOS); Arthur C. Helton, *Political Asylum under the 1980 Refugee Act: An Unfulfilled Promise,* 17 Univ. Michigan J. L. Reform 243, 263 (1984) (arguing DOS should not express opinion as to ultimate question in individual case; information on general conditions in country acceptable with proper disclosure).

Do you agree with Judge Friendly either (a) that DOS opinions concerning country conditions *should* be admissible even if cross-examination is not permitted or (b) that DOS opinions concerning the likelihood of persecution of the particular applicant *should not* be admitted? (As noted below, there are now alternative sources of country information available to adjudicators in asylum cases.)

iii.   Advice from UNHCR

When the United Nations formally laid out the responsibilities of the UNHCR, it entrusted it with two basic functions—"providing international protection" and "seeking permanent solutions" to the refugee problem. The U.N. called upon all its members to cooperate with UNHCR in the performance of those functions. See Guy S. Goodwin–Gill, *The Obligations of States and the Protection Function of the Office of the United Nations High Commissioner for Refugees,* 1982 Michigan Yearbook Internat'l Legal Studies 291, 292. Such cooperation has taken many forms:

> The role of the UNHCR in the determination of refugee status varies from country to country. In Belgium, the Minister of Foreign Affairs has delegated the determination of refugee status to the UNHCR, while in Italy, Somalia, and Tunisia, the UNHCR is one of the decision makers in the process. In seven other countries, the UNHCR is represented on an advisory commission that interviews applicants and makes recommendations to the final decision maker. In Spain, the UNHCR is consulted before a decision on refugee status is made, and in Austria the UNHCR may express its views prior to a decision.
>
> Other countries facilitate UNHCR oversight of the refugee determination process by various methods. For example, the UNHCR is informed of all applications for refugee status in Austria, Greece, and New Zealand, while in West Germany, a UNHCR representative may attend applicant interviews with the federal official who decides on applications. * * *

Arthur C. Helton, *Political Asylum Under the 1980 Refugee Act: An Unfulfilled Promise,* 17 Univ. Michigan J. of L. Reform 243, 263–64 (1984).

United States law makes no formal provision for UNHCR participation in the adjudication of asylum cases, although for a brief period during the late 1970's the State Department consulted UNHCR in the Haitian cases. See David A. Martin, *Reforming Asylum Adjudication: On Navigating the Coast of Bohemia,* 138 Univ. Pennsylvania L. Rev. 1247, 1319–20 (1990). Still, attorneys for asylum claimants frequently ask UNHCR for expressions of its views about the particular cases, and when UNHCR is able to accommodate the request the resulting letters are admissible as evidence. *Id.* at 1320. See also 8 C.F.R. §§ 208.12(a), 1208.12(a) (2004) (asylum officers may rely on such "credible sources" as "international organizations"). Many commentators have called for a more direct UNHCR role in the United States asylum (and withholding of removal) process. See, e.g., T. Alexander Aleinikoff, *Political Asylum in the Federal Republic of Germany and the Republic of France: Lessons for the United States,* 17 Univ. Michigan J. of L. Reform 183, 236 (1984); Deborah E. Anker & Michael H. Posner, *The Forty Year Crisis: A Legislative History of the Refugee Act of*

1980, 19 San Diego L. Rev. 9, 77–79 (1981); Helton, above, at 263–64. What role, if any, do you think UNHCR ought to play in individual asylum cases?

iv. Other Sources of Information

An important reform introduced in 1990 was the establishment, within the former INS (and now DHS), of "a documentation center with information on human rights conditions." 8 C.F.R. §§ 208.1(b), 1208.1(b) (2004). The regulations also authorize reliance on other "credible sources, such as international organizations, private voluntary agencies, news organizations, or academic institutions." *Id.* §§ 208.12(a), 1208.12(a).[11] Together with the training that the specialized asylum officers now receive, these various sources help to reduce dependence on State Department opinions.

One large development in recent years has been the BIA's practice of taking "administrative notice" of country conditions generally and changed country conditions in particular. Administrative notice is the government agency equivalent of judicial notice. It involves accepting certain facts as true without the taking of evidence. There are obvious fairness issues to be resolved. Deborah Anker provides this succinct summary of the guiding principles that limit its use:

> First, the noticed facts cannot be controverted, but must be generally accepted and "commonly acknowledged." Second, noticed facts must not be used in such a way as to deny the applicant an individualized adjudication. Third, the applicant must have a meaningful opportunity to submit rebuttal evidence.

Anker at 114. She observes that the Board has been inclined to disregard the third limitation in many cases, and she discusses the significance of that failure. See generally Anker at 112–50; see also *Kowalczyk v. INS,* 245 F.3d 1143 (10th Cir. 2001) (holding that asylum denial based on administrative notice of changed conditions in Poland, without affording applicant chance to rebut noticed facts, violated due process.)

5. EXCEPTIONS TO ELIGIBILITY

The preceding subsections have introduced you to the elements that applicants for asylum or withholding of removal must affirmatively prove. Both the 1951 Convention and United States domestic law disqualify certain people from both remedies. For excellent and more detailed discussions of the exceptions, see Anker at 415–64; Chaloka Beyani, Joan Fitzpatrick, Walter Kälin & Monette Zard (eds.), *Exclusion from Protection,* 12 Internat'l J. Refugee L. (special supp. issue, 2000).

---

11. Reports of human rights organizations were admissible under the pre–1990 regulations as well, but one empirical study raised doubts that immigration judges were actually assigning those reports significant weight. Deborah E. Anker, *Determining Asylum Claims in the United States—Summary Report of an Empirical Study of the Adjudication of Asylum Claims Before the Immigration Court,* 2 Internat'l J. Refugee L. 252, 257 (1990).

The 1951 Convention has two important provisions that exclude certain classes of applicants from protection. Under article 1(F), the entire Convention (including articles 3–34, which otherwise recognize certain basic rights of refugees) is inapplicable to certain international criminal offenders, those who have committed "serious nonpolitical crimes" before entering the host state, and those "guilty of acts contrary to the purposes and principles of the United Nations." Article 33.2 provides exceptions to the principle of nonrefoulement for those who are thought to be national security threats or who have been convicted of "particularly serious" crimes and constitute dangers to their communities.

The domestic law of the United States contains some rough parallels discussed in the pages that follow:

a.   FIRM RESETTLEMENT

When you studied the overseas refugee admission program in section A of this chapter, you might have noticed the statutory disqualification of those refugees who are "firmly resettled" in third countries. See INA § 207(c)(1). The statute imposes a similar disqualification on asylum claimants. INA § 208(b)(2)(A)(vi). For obvious reasons, there is no analogous limitation to withholding of removal; the fact that someone is firmly resettled in country A would be no reason to send him or her to country B, where life or freedom would be threatened.

Under the Justice Department regulations, a person will be considered "firmly resettled" in another country if, before arriving in the United States, the person received an offer to resettle permanently in that country. 8 C.F.R. §§ 208.15, 1208.15 (2004); *Abdille v. Ashcroft*, 242 F.3d 477 (3d Cir. 2001). By way of exception, firm resettlement will not be found if the person's entry into the third country was "a necessary consequence of his flight from persecution," he or she "remained in that country only as long as was necessary to arrange onward travel," and "significant ties" were not established. *Id.* §§ 208.15(a), 1208.15(a). Moreover, the conditions attached to residence can be "so substantially and consciously restricted" that in fact the person was not resettled. *Id.* §§ 208.15(b), 1208.15(b). Professor Anker persuasively criticizes, on human rights grounds, cases that appear to find firm resettlement in a country where the person was denied permission to work. Anker at 451. For the international analog of firm resettlement, see 1951 Convention, art. 1.E; UNHCR Handbook, paras. 144–46.

As a policy matter, suppose a refugee has received an offer of permanent resettlement from a country that he or she passed through en route to the United States; the conditions of residence in that country were not restrictive; and the person has no significant ties to *either* that country or the United States. Should he or she be eligible for asylum?

The issue of firm resettlement is related to, but different from, the concept of "safe third country," also known as "safe country of asylum." As a result of IIRIRA § 604(a), United States law now permits DHS to remove asylum applicants even to third countries in which they are not firmly resettled. There must be a bilateral or multilateral agreement, and certain minimum safeguards have to be present. INA § 208(a)(2). This issue is considered in section B.7.b.iii below.

b. PAST WRONGDOING[12]

The exception you just studied exists because an applicant's firm resettlement in a third country is considered relevant to his or her *need* for asylum. The exceptions you will see in this subsection are different in kind; they go to an applicant's *desirability as a member of society*. To understand the discussion that follows, first read INA §§ 208(b)(2)(A)(i to v), 208(b)(2)(B)(i), and 241(b)(3)(B).

As you have just seen, claimants who have participated in the persecution of others on account of race, religion, etc. are statutorily ineligible for both asylum and withholding of removal. INA §§ 208(b)(2)(A)(i), 241(b)(3)(B)(1). (The former is actually duplicative, because only a "refugee" may receive asylum, and the refugee definition already disqualifies the same group.) This exception does not appear to violate the nonrefoulement rules of the 1951 Convention, for the Convention contains a generally analogous proviso, art. 1.F(a, c). That proviso reflected a desire to disqualify war criminals, whose trials were a recent memory at the time the Convention was drafted. See UNHCR Handbook, para. 148.

One of the more interesting cases applying the persecution exception is *Matter of McMullen*, 19 I. & N. Dec. 90 (BIA 1984), aff'd on other grounds, 788 F.2d 591 (9th Cir.1986). McMullen was a former member of the Provisional Irish Republican Army (PIRA), an anti-British terrorist organization operating in Northern Ireland and Great Britain. Having left PIRA and then having refused PIRA's request to assist it in a kidnapping, McMullen feared reprisals from PIRA in the event he were returned to the British Isles. The Board held that the feared persecution would not be on account of political opinion because his rejection of PIRA's request had been prompted by safety concerns rather than political motives. Further, because McMullen had previously played an indirect support role in PIRA's assassinations of individuals who expressed anti-PIRA opinions, he was ineligible for both asylum and withholding for the additional reason that he had assisted in the persecution of others on account of political opinion. The combination of the two conclusions—that the persecution he had helped PIRA inflict on others was on account of political opinion while the persecution he feared PIRA would inflict on him was not—reveals the thin line that the BIA was willing to walk in that case. As you might also have figured out, a broad reading of the persecution exclusion is not necessarily bad news for asylum claimants, since the precedential value of such a reading will also influence future determinations of applicants' own well-founded fears of persecution on account of race, religion, etc.

---

12. See generally Anker at 415–64; James C. Hathaway & Colin J. Harvey, *Framing Refugee Protection in the New* *World Disorder*, 34 Cornell Internat'l L.J. 257 (2001).

Both asylum and withholding of removal are also unavailable when the Attorney General finds "reasonable grounds" for believing the person is "a danger to the security of the United States." INA §§ 208(b)(2)(A)(iv), 241(b)(3)(B)(iv). Terrorists are made specifically ineligible, although the terms vary slightly as between asylum and withholding of removal. Compare INA § 208(b)(2)(A)(5) with INA § 241(b)(3)(B) (last sentence).

The other exceptions discussed in this subsection entail criminal conduct. The crime-related disqualifications for asylum are the same as for withholding of removal, with one important caveat noted in item 4 of the Notes and Questions below. See INA §§ 208(b)(2)(A)(ii,iii), 241(b)(3)(B)(ii,iii). In the following case the BIA addresses a commonly recurring issue that arises under one of those exceptions:

Matter of Carballe

Board of Immigration Appeals, 1986.
19 I. & N. Dec. 357.

* * *

The applicant is a 22–year–old native and citizen of Cuba. After departing Cuba and arriving at Key West, Florida, in April 1980 as part of the Mariel boatlift, the applicant was paroled into the United States.

On February 18, 1983, in the Circuit Court for Dade County, Florida, the applicant was convicted, on his plea of guilty, of (1) robbery with a firearm, to wit, a pistol (two counts), (2) attempted robbery with a firearm, to wit, a pistol (two counts), (3) grand theft second degree, and (4) accessory after the fact, in violation of sections 812.13, 812.014, and 777.03 of the Florida Statutes. The applicant was sentenced to terms of 15 years each on the robbery and attempted robbery counts with the sentences to run concurrently. He also was sentenced to terms of 5 years each on the grand theft and accessory counts with the sentences to run concurrently with the robbery counts. He was incarcerated at the time of the exclusion hearing.

At his hearing, the applicant, through counsel, conceded [inadmissibility for both lack of valid entry documents and conviction of a crime involving moral turpitude]. He requested asylum and withholding of deportation. The applicant submitted that he would be imprisoned and singled out for disparate treatment by Cuban authorities because he was one of the first Cubans to enter the Peruvian Embassy in Havana in 1980. The record includes a "Safe Conduct Definitive," issued by the Cuban Government, which essentially authorized the applicant's safe conduct from the Peruvian Embassy to any country that offered him a visa. Also, the applicant stated that he would be persecuted in Cuba because of his robbery convictions in the United States.

The immigration judge denied the applicant's applications for asylum and withholding of deportation without reaching the merits of the claim or submitting any documents to the State Department for an advisory opinion. In view of the nature of the offenses that had been committed, the immigration judge found that the applicant was ineligible for relief under section 243(h) of the Act[a] as one who had been convicted of a particularly serious crime and constituted a danger to the community of the United States. For the same reason, the immigration judge denied asylum.

In pertinent part, section 243(h)(2)(B) of the Act[b] provides that withholding of deportation "shall not apply to any alien if the Attorney General determines that the alien, having been convicted by a final judgment of a particularly serious crime, constitutes a danger to the community of the United States."

On appeal, the applicant contends that the immigration judge erred in his interpretation of section 243(h)(2)(B) of the Act. Through counsel, he submits that section 243(h)(2)(B) requires two separate factual findings. First, it must be determined that an applicant has committed a particularly serious crime. Then, there must be a second, distinct finding that the applicant constitutes a danger to the community of the United States. The applicant submits that "the use of the present tense verb 'constitutes' in section 243(h)(2)(B) indicates that this second question should be appraised in light of present circumstances and the record should therefore be carefully scrutinized for evidence of rehabilitation or other factors indicating that [the] applicant may not now be a danger to the community."

The Service, however, argues that both the language of section 243(h)(2)(B) of the Act and its legislative history make clear that only one test is required. It is submitted that section 243(h)(2)(B) "establishes a cause and effect relationship between the two clauses." If Congress had "intended to establish two separate criteria," the Service argues, "it could have easily done so by its use of the conjunction 'and.' Instead, the grammatical structure shows that a conviction for a particularly serious crime is the sole factor which Congress has made determinative of whether the alien constitutes a danger to the community."

The Service contends that the legislative history of this statutory provision supports the contention that only one finding is required. The present provisions of section 243(h) of the Act were enacted as part of the Refugee Act of 1980. The House Judiciary Committee Report, in reviewing the provisions of section 243(h), noted that an exception to eligibility for such relief included "aliens ... who have been convicted of particularly serious crimes *which* make them a danger to the community of the United States." (Emphasis added [by BIA]). The Service submits that this language reflects the congressional understanding of how section 243(h)(2)(B) is properly read. The phrase "danger to the community" is an aid to defining a "particularly serious crime," not a mandate that administrative agencies or the courts determine whether an alien will become a recidivist.

We find section 243(h)(2)(B) of the Act does not require that two separate and distinct factual findings be made in order to render an alien

---

a. Now INA § 241(b)(3)—Ed.   **b.** Now INA § 241(b)(3)(B)(ii)—Ed.

ineligible for withholding of deportation. It must be determined that an applicant for relief constitutes a danger to the community of the United States to come within the purview of section 243(h)(2)(B). However, the statute provides the key for determining whether an alien constitutes such a danger. That is, those aliens who have been finally convicted of particularly serious crimes are presumptively dangers to this country's community. The clauses of section 243(h)(2)(B), nevertheless, are inextricably related. We have noted that the phrase "particularly serious crime" is not defined in the statute. In determining whether a conviction is for such a crime, the essential key is whether the nature of the crime is one which indicates that the alien poses a danger to the community. * * * [S]ome crimes * * * are inherently "particularly serious" while others clearly are not. There will be cases, however, where the seriousness of a crime will have to be judged by considering the nature of the conviction, the circumstances and underlying facts of the conviction, the sentence imposed, and whether the type and circumstances of the crime indicate the alien will be a danger to the community. The focus here is on the crime that was committed. If it is determined that the crime was a "particularly serious" one, the question of whether the alien is a danger to the community of the United States is answered in the affirmative. We do not find that there is a statutory requirement for a separate determination of dangerousness focusing on the likelihood of future serious misconduct on the part of the alien.

Has this applicant been convicted of a particularly serious crime? In addition to two other offenses, the applicant was convicted * * * of two counts of armed robbery and two counts of attempted armed robbery. The offenses involved the use of a firearm. They were felonies, as well as offenses against individuals. On their face, they were dangerous.

Robbery is a grave, serious, aggravated, infamous, and heinous crime. We have previously found a California conviction for armed robbery to be a crime rendering an alien statutorily ineligible for withholding of deportation. We have little difficulty concluding that the applicant herein has been convicted of a particularly serious crime and, therefore, constitutes a danger to the community of the United States within the meaning of section 243(h)(2)(B) of the Act. Moreover, the same reasons that lead us to conclude this applicant has been finally convicted of such a crime satisfy us that his request for asylum properly warrants denial in the exercise of discretion.[c]

The applicant complains that the immigration judge erred by refusing to admit background information, including the circumstances of the armed robberies, into evidence. We conclude that there has been no error on the part of the immigration judge as the crimes at issue in this case are inherently "particularly serious."

* * *

c. Today this exception destroys *eligibility* for asylum, not just the favorable exercise of discretion. INA § 208(b)(2)(A)(ii).

NOTES AND QUESTIONS

1. The courts have deferred to the Board's conclusion that the "particularly serious crime" exception does not require an independent finding of danger to the community. See, e.g., *Ahmetovic v. INS*, 62 F.3d 48, 52–53 (2d Cir. 1995); *Arauz v. Rivkind*, 845 F.2d 271, 275 (11th Cir.1988); *Ramirez–Ramos v. INS*, 814 F.2d 1394, 1396–97 (9th Cir.1987) (BIA interpretation accepted as "reasonable"). First, as a practical matter, what really turns on this issue? Second, do you agree with the Board's conclusion? Argue both sides, based (a) on the literal statutory language; (b) on the legislative history discussed in *Carballe;* and (c) on policy. As a matter of policy, should a 65–year-old person whose life or freedom would be threatened if she were sent home be made ineligible for withholding of removal because, at age 18, she had been convicted of a "particularly serious crime?" See generally Evangeline G. Abriel, *Presumed Ineligible: The Effect of Criminal Convictions on Applications for Asylum and Withholding of Deportation Under Section 515 of the Immigration Act of 1990*, 6 Georgetown Immigration L.J. 27 (1992).

2. A related question is how to tell whether a crime is "particularly serious." This disqualification is expressly permitted by article 33.2 of the 1951 Convention but, unlike the "serious nonpolitical crime" exception discussed below, is not interpreted in the UNHCR Handbook. The BIA in a previous case made clear that a crime may not be classified as "particularly serious" just because it is a crime "involving moral turpitude." *Matter of Frentescu*, 18 I. & N. Dec. 244, 246 n.7 (BIA 1982). The Board then offered more general guidance:

> [A] "particularly serious crime" is more serious than a "serious nonpolitical crime," although many crimes may be classified [as] both. * * * While there are crimes which, on their face, are "particularly serious crimes" or clearly are not "particularly serious crimes," the record in most proceedings will have to be analyzed on a case-by-case basis. In judging the seriousness of a crime, we look to such factors as the nature of the conviction, the circumstances and underlying facts of the conviction, the type of sentence imposed, and, most importantly, whether the type and circumstances of the crime indicate that the alien will be a danger to the community. Crimes against persons are more likely to be categorized as "particularly serious crimes." Nevertheless, we recognize that there may be instances where crimes * * * against property will be considered as such crimes.
>
> * * * On the record before us, we do not find that the applicant has been convicted of a "particularly serious crime." We do not condone his crime, in essence, burglary with intent to commit theft. However, considering the totality of the circumstances before us concerning this crime, we do not find it to be of such a particularly serious nature to preclude relief. The crime was an offense against property, rather than against a person. Although the applicant did enter a dwelling, there is no indication

that the dwelling was occupied or that the applicant was armed; nor is there any indication of an aggravating circumstance. Further, the applicant received a suspended sentence after spending a relatively short period of time in prison (3 months). Such sentence as viewed by the state circuit court judge, reflects upon the seriousness of the applicant's danger to the community.

Id. at 247. See also *Matter of Garcia–Garrocho,* 19 I. & N. Dec. 423, 425 (BIA 1986) (whether crime is "particularly serious" turns on whether actor represents danger to community).

In *Beltran–Zavala v. INS,* 912 F.2d 1027 (9th Cir.1990), the court expressly approved the holding in *Frentescu* that the determination whether a crime is "particularly serious" requires inquiry into the individual facts. *Id.* at 1031–32; accord, *Matter of L.S.,* 22 I. & N. Dec. 645 (BIA 1999). The court remanded to the BIA for a finding on whether the facts of this person's crime—sale of $10 worth of marijuana—made the offense "particularly serious." Contrast that willingness to examine the circumstances of the individual case with the approach the BIA and most courts use when deciding whether crimes involve "moral turpitude" for purposes of the removal grounds that contain that term. Recall that under the majority view "moral turpitude" determinations rest solely on the crime in the abstract, not on the evidence in the individual case. The same categorical approach is used in classifying crimes as "aggravated felonies." See pages 540–49, 560 above. Which approach is more favorable to the noncitizen?

3. As the BIA implied in *Frentescu,* item 2 above, some crimes are *inherently* "particularly serious;" for those crimes, the individual facts need not be examined. See, e.g., *Matter of Garcia–Garrocho,* 19 I. & N. Dec. 423 (BIA 1986) (burglary of a dwelling, with aggravating factors). See also *Arauz v. Rivkind,* 845 F.2d 271, 275 (11th Cir.1988); *Matter of Gonzalez,* 19 I. & N. Dec. 682 (BIA 1988) (both decisions holding drug trafficking offenses "particularly serious," seemingly *per se*).

4. An aggravated felony is automatically considered a "particularly serious crime" for purposes of asylum, see INA § 208(b)(2)(B)(i), and an aggravated felony for which the person has been sentenced to at least five years in prison is automatically considered a "particularly serious crime" for purposes of withholding of removal, see INA § 241(b)(3)(B). (The latter provision does not mean that an aggravated felony for which the person is sentenced to less than five years is not a particularly serious crime. *Id.*) Since the courts have accepted the holding in *Carballe* that a particularly serious crime automatically makes the person a danger to the community, the bottom line is that an aggravated felony conviction alone precludes asylum, and an aggravated felony conviction with a five-year sentence imposed bars even withholding of removal. See, e.g., *Kofa v. INS,* 60 F.3d 1084 (4th Cir. en banc 1995); *Al-Salehi v. INS,* 47 F.3d 390 (10th Cir. 1995); *Feroz v. INS,* 22 F.3d 225 (9th Cir. 1994). Coupled with the sweeping expansions of the aggravated felony definition in recent years, these holdings make asylum and withholding of removal unattainable for people

convicted of a wide range of crimes. Whether that result comports with the intent of the criminal exclusions in the 1951 Convention is not clear.

For criticisms of automatic criminal bars, see U.S. Commission on Immigration Reform, U.S. Refugee Policy: Taking Leadership 33–34 (June 1997); Evangeline G. Abriel, *The Effect of Criminal Conduct upon Refugee and Asylum Status*, 3 Southwestern J. L. & Trade in the Americas 359, 369–71 (1996). Note, however, that for purposes of withholding, when a person has been convicted of an aggravated felony but not sentenced to five or more years of confinement, a finding of "particularly serious crime" is not automatic. In that situation, the seriousness of the crime is assessed with reference to the facts of the individual case. *Matter of L–S–*, 22 I. & N. Dec. 645 (BIA 1999) (armed robbery of occupied home was "particularly serious"); *Matter of S–S–*, 22 I. & N. Dec. 458 (BIA 1999) (importation of undocumented migrant not "particularly serious"). In making that assessment, however, the adjudicator must now presume that a drug trafficking conviction is "particularly serious." Reversing the BIA, the Attorney General has held that only "extraordinary and compelling" circumstances can rebut that presumption. *Matter of Y–L–*, 23 I. & N. Dec. 270 (A.G. 2002).

5. Compare subsections ii and iii of INA § 241(b)(3)(B), element by element. Is (ii) just a subcategory of (iii), or does (ii) snare some people that (iii) misses?

6. The "serious nonpolitical crime" exception is taken from article 1.F(b) of the 1951 Convention. Paragraphs 151–61 of the UNHCR Handbook provide some useful guidance. Paragraph 156 requires the decision-maker to balance "the nature of the offence" against "the degree of persecution feared." The more severe the persecution that the applicant fears, the graver the crime must be before it can be considered "serious." The BIA, however, has explicitly rejected such a balancing approach, both for the "serious nonpolitical crime" exception and for the "particularly serious crime" exception, holding instead that the level of seriousness depends solely on the nature of the crime. *Matter of Garcia–Garrocho*, 19 I. & N. Dec. 423 (BIA 1986); *Matter of Rodriguez–Coto*, 19 I. & N.Dec. 208, 209–10 (BIA 1985). The Supreme Court has now resolved this issue. In *INS v. Aguirre–Aguirre*, 526 U.S. 415, 119 S.Ct. 1439, 143 L.Ed.2d 590 (1999), the Court held that the BIA interpretation of the "serious nonpolitical offense" exception was entitled to deference, was "reasonable," and therefore would be upheld. *Id.* at 1445–46. The contrary position of the UNHCR handbook, the Court said, was "useful" but not "binding." *Id.* at 1446–47. The case is thoughtfully analyzed in Andy Schoenholtz, *Supreme Court Orders Ninth Circuit to Defer to the BIA in Refugee Cases*, 4 BIB 615 (June 15, 1999).

Which approach seems sounder to you? Should the terms "serious" and "particularly serious" be treated as absolute, or as relative to the degree of persecution?

7. A more troublesome problem has been the meaning of the word "nonpolitical." Paragraph 153 of the UNHCR Handbook says:

In determining whether an offence is "non-political" or is, on the contrary, a "political" crime, regard should be given in the first place to its nature and purpose, i.e., whether it has been committed out of genuine political motives and not merely for personal reasons or gain. There should also be a close and direct causal link between the crime committed and its alleged political purpose and object. The political element of the offence should also outweigh its common-law character. This would not be the case if the acts committed are grossly out of proportion to the alleged objective. The political nature of the offence is also more difficult to accept if it involves acts of an atrocious nature.

Accord, *McMullen v. INS*, 788 F.2d 591, 596–97 (9th Cir.1986).

"Political offenses" are also commonly excepted from extradition treaties. Under the traditional test, acts that are "incident to or in furtherance of" an insurrection or rebellion are generally regarded as political for extradition purposes. *McMullen*, 788 F.2d at 596. The applicant in that case urged the court to apply the same formula to withholding of removal. The court declined, opting instead to apply the balancing test outlined in the UNHCR Handbook. The court rejected the analogy to extradition, in part because it saw deportation (unlike extradition) strictly as a matter between the United States and the individual. In deportation, the court said, the United States is seeking only to rid itself of an undesirable person; "[n]o other sovereign is involved," and "we are not 'interfering with any *internal* struggle' " (emphasis in original). *Id.* First, does this analysis take adequate account of the fact that the relief for which the crime disqualifies the applicant is withholding of removal, not asylum? Second, does the court's characterization of deportation as a purely domestic matter between the United States and the individual square with the courts' tendency to emphasize the foreign relations effects of immigration policy when they are asked to review statutory deportation provisions for constitutionality? Recall chapter 2.

The analogy to extradition is complex and beyond the scope of this book. For some thoughtful analyses, see Valerie Epps, *The Validity of the Political Offender Exception in Extradition Treaties in Anglo–American Jurisprudence*, 20 Harvard Internat'l L.J. 61 (1979) (advocating that political offense exception be replaced by increased reliance on other, more limited mechanisms); Steven Lubet, *Extradition Reform: Executive Discretion and Judicial Participation in the Extradition of Political Terrorists*, 15 Cornell Internat'l L.J. 247 (1982) (urging restrictions on political offense exception).

8. Compare the exceptions listed in section 241(b)(3)(B) to those listed in articles 1.F and 33.2 of the 1951 Convention. Does the United States law conform to its treaty obligations?

9. There has been surprisingly little study of what actually happens to genuine refugees who are returned to their countries of origin because of the criminal exceptions. For a provocative treatment, see Joan Fitzpatrick,

The Post–Exclusion Phase: Extradition, Prosecution and Expulsion, 12 Internat'l J. Refugee L. (special issue) at 272 (2000).

6. DISCRETION IN ASYLUM CASES

Sections B.1 through B.5 have taken you through the statutory eligibility requirements for INA §§ 208 and 241(b)(3). Asylum under INA § 208 additionally entails discretion, as you saw in the specific context of past persecution. Here, the subject of discretion under section 208 is addressed in a more general vein.[13]

At first, the BIA took a broad view of its discretionary power to deny asylum to applicants who had established a well-founded fear of persecution. In *Matter of Salim*, 18 I. & N. Dec. 311 (BIA 1982), an Afghan rebel fled to the United States and attempted to enter by displaying another person's passport. Finding that Salim had established "the requisite probability of persecution in Afghanistan," the Board granted withholding of removal. But the Board denied asylum on discretionary grounds. It said: "This Board finds that the fraudulent avoidance of the orderly refugee procedures that this country has established is an extremely adverse factor which can only be overcome with the most unusual showing of countervailing equities." *Id.* at 316.

The Board's rationale actually emphasized two different, though related, problems: (1) fraud and (2) the bypassing of the more orderly procedure for the admission of overseas refugees. This last factor—jumping the queue—was especially prominent in a later decision, *Matter of Gharadaghi*, 19 I. & N. Dec. 311 (BIA 1985), where even the fact that the rest of the applicant's immediate family was in the United States was not enough to offset the applicant's circumvention of the overseas refugee admission process.

Decisions like *Salim* and *Gharadaghi* provoked forceful criticism from prominent asylum scholars. Arthur Helton stressed the conflict between denying relief on grounds related to the manner of entry and the humanitarian objectives of asylum. Arthur C. Helton, *The Proper Role of Discretion in Political Asylum Determinations*, 22 San Diego L. Rev. 999, 1010–11 (1985). Further, given the small proportion of the world's refugees who are accepted for admission overseas, Helton questioned how realistic an alternative asylum claimants actually have. *Id.* at 1011. Finally, he pointed out, those who are refused asylum on discretionary grounds can all too often become "refugees in orbit." The metaphor refers to the unseemly scenario in which the asylum-denying nation deports the refugee to a third country, which refuses admission and sends the refugee right back to the asylum-denying country. Sometimes the person is shuttled back and forth more than once, and sometimes the third country returns the refugee to the country of persecution. *Id.* at 1018–19.

---

13. See generally Elwin Griffith, *Asylum and Withholding of Deportation—Challenges to the Alien after the Refugee Act of* 1980, 12 Loyola of L.A. Internat'l & Comp. L.J. 515, 563–69 (1990).

To these concerns Deborah Anker has added others. See Deborah E. Anker, *Discretionary Asylum: A Protection Remedy for Refugees Under the Refugee Act of 1980,* 28 Virginia J. Internat'l L. 1 (1987). To the extent the emphasis on fraud is intended to be a "moral screening" device, she observes, the *Salim* approach is even harsher than that ordinarily applied when *non-refugees* are excluded for fraud; the latter exclusions at least require that the misrepresentations be material. *Id.* at 20–22. Moreover, even though refugees' entry fraud is more likely to be compelled by circumstances beyond their control, *id.* at 18, the *Salim* approach to asylum is less forgiving than the discretionary practices in waiving fraud in non-refugee cases, *id.* at 22–23. As for the Board's emphasis on circumventing the overseas refugee process, Anker points out, the overwhelming majority of asylum-seekers have either entered surreptitiously or knowingly overstayed their nonimmigrant visas.[14] *Id.* at 29–30. Is entry by means of a false document morally worse, or are surreptitious entrants and overstayers also to be rejected, in the absence of "most unusual * * * countervailing equities?" If the latter, then for whom is asylum intended?

Anker concludes:

> [M]oral screening primarily should focus on those who are morally unfit in the sense that they present a serious danger and, secondarily, on those who prior to seeking asylum in the United States, had secured refuge elsewhere. A legitimate moral screening role is one which exposes individuals to the possibility of persecution only if they represent a substantial threat to the national community. * * * [T]he only coherent approach to discretion is one centered upon the existence of a viable safehaven.

Id. at 50–51. See also *Hernandez–Ortiz v. INS,* 777 F.2d 509, 519 (9th Cir.1985). Do you agree?

In *Matter of Pula,* 19 I. & N.Dec. 467 (BIA 1987), the Board abruptly changed course:

> We turn now to the issue of whether the applicant merits asylum in the exercise of discretion. In *Matter of Salim,* we * * * found the fraudulent avoidance of orderly refugee procedures to be an extremely adverse factor which could only be overcome with the most unusual showing of countervailing equities.

> * * *

> Yet while we find that an alien's manner of entry or attempted entry is a proper and relevant discretionary factor to consider in adjudicating asylum applications, we agree with the applicant that *Matter of Salim* places too much emphasis on the circumvention of

14. An asylum applicant must be "physically present in the United States or at a land border or port of entry, irrespective of such alien's status." INA § 208(a). The only significant categories of asylum-seekers who have complied with all United States immigration laws would be those who apply for asylum at a port of entry without having attempted to enter surreptitiously and nonimmigrant affirmative asylum applicants whose stays have not expired.

orderly refugee procedures. This circumvention can be a serious adverse factor, but it should not be considered in such a way that the practical effect is to deny relief in virtually all cases. This factor is only one of a number of factors which should be balanced in exercising discretion, and the weight accorded to this factor may vary depending on the facts of a particular case. We therefore withdraw from *Matter of Salim* insofar as it suggests that the circumvention of orderly refugee procedures alone is sufficient to require the most unusual showing of countervailing equities.

Instead of focusing only on the circumvention of orderly refugee procedures, the totality of the circumstances and actions of an alien in his flight from the country where he fears persecution should be examined in determining whether a favorable exercise of discretion is warranted. Among those factors which should be considered are whether the alien passed through any other countries or arrived in the United States directly from his country, whether orderly refugee procedures were in fact available to help him in any country he passed through, and whether he made any attempts to seek asylum before coming to the United States. In addition, the length of time the alien remained in a third country, and his living conditions, safety, and potential for long-term residency there are also relevant. For example, an alien who is forced to remain in hiding to elude persecutors, or who faces imminent deportation back to the country where he fears persecution, may not have found a safe haven even though he has escaped to another country. Further, whether the alien has relatives legally in the United States or other personal ties to this country which motivated him to seek asylum here rather than elsewhere is another factor to consider. In this regard, the extent of the alien's ties to any other countries where he does not fear persecution should also be examined. Moreover, if the alien engaged in fraud to circumvent orderly refugee procedures, the seriousness of the fraud should be considered. The use of fraudulent documents to escape the country of persecution itself is not a significant adverse factor while, at the other extreme, entry under the assumed identity of a United States citizen with a United States passport, which was fraudulently obtained by the alien from the United States Government, is very serious fraud.

In addition to the circumstances and actions of the alien in his flight from the country where he fears persecution, general humanitarian considerations, such as an alien's tender age or poor health, may also be relevant in a discretionary determination. A situation of particular concern involves an alien who has established his statutory eligibility for asylum but cannot meet the higher burden required for [withholding of removal]. Deportation to a country where the alien may be persecuted thus becomes a strong possibility. In such a case, the discretionary factors should be carefully evaluated in light of the unusually harsh consequences which may befall an alien who has established a well-founded fear of persecution; the danger of persecution should generally outweigh all but the most egregious of adverse factors.

Each of the factors mentioned above will not, of course, be found in every case. An applicant for asylum has the burden of establishing that the favorable exercise of discretion is warranted. Therefore, the alien should present evidence on any relevant factors which he believes support the favorable exercise of discretion in his case. In the absence of any adverse factors, however, asylum should be granted in the exercise of discretion.

Id. at 472–74.

The last two paragraphs of the above excerpt from *Pula* raise some interesting possibilities. The last sentence counsels the favorable exercise of discretion whenever there are no adverse factors, but it says nothing about how strong the positive equities must be when there are adverse factors. In the preceding paragraph, however, the Board suggests that one who demonstrates a well-founded fear of persecution but not the clear probability required for withholding of removal should receive asylum unless the adverse factors are "most egregious." Accord, *Matter of Rivera–Rioseco,* 19 I. & N. Dec. 833, 836 (BIA 1988). Suppose applicant A establishes a well-founded fear of persecution but not a clear probability, applicant B establishes a clear probability, neither applicant has any ties to the United States or other positive equities, and in both cases there exist factors that are "adverse" but not "egregious." Under the *Pula* formulation, what will happen to each person? Does that combination of results make sense?

The *Pula* decision came down just as the Anker article was going to press. In a postscript, Anker welcomed the Board's reduced emphasis on fraudulent entries but criticized the Board for not going far enough. In her view, the Board should simply have "reject[ed] manner of entry as a significant consideration." Anker, 28 Virginia J. Internat'l L. at 71. Her concern was timely; about a year later the Board in an unpublished decision granted withholding of removal but denied asylum on discretionary grounds because the person had been criminally convicted of entering the United States on a fraudulent passport. Distinguishing *Pula,* the Board found the crime outweighed the applicant's positive equities. *Matter of Bhupinder Sigh Kamboj,* A27 887 288, AILA Monthly Mailing (Feb.1989) at 100. Do you agree with Anker that manner of entry should not be a significant factor in exercising discretion for asylum purposes?

A still unsettled question is whether foreign policy is a proper subject of the discretion involved in asylum cases. The Supreme Court once granted certiorari to decide that and other issues but ultimately disposed of the case on other grounds. *INS v. Doherty,* 502 U.S. 314, 112 S.Ct. 719, 116 L.Ed.2d 823 (1992). For a convincing analysis, see Joan Fitzpatrick & Robert Pauw, *Foreign Policy, Asylum and Discretion,* 28 Willamette L. Rev. 751, 769–71 (1992).

Although decisions like *Pula* diminish the significance of the discretionary element as a barrier to asylum, anecdotal evidence suggests the issue is beginning to reemerge. Practitioners now report a growing practice among some immigration judges (either sua sponte or upon requests by some ICE trial attorneys) to promote the functional equivalent of a plea bargain. They offer the applicant withholding of removal under INA § 241(b)(3) in exchange for a withdrawal of the application for asylum under section 208.

Those kinds of offers can force some difficult personal decisions. The applicant who accepts such an offer will receive protection from persecution but will not become an LPR (a year later) and will have no basis for bringing in his or her spouse or minor children. But if the applicant turns down the offer, there is a risk that the IJ will deny both asylum and withholding and return the applicant to his or her persecutors. In theory, that risk should not exist. That the offer was made should mean the IJ has found the applicant eligible for withholding (which is a nondiscretionary remedy). And if that is the case, and the applicant turns down the offer in the hope that the IJ will grant asylum, the IJ should be required to grant at least withholding (assuming circumstances don't change in the interim). But the applicant can never be certain that the practice will follow the theory. Thus, on the one hand, the applicant has to choose between gambling with his or her life or freedom and parting with his or her family, possibly forever—a cruel choice. On the other hand, can one rationally argue against having the option of accepting withholding? How can it be worse than not having the option? (One possibility is that some applicants will accept the offers because they perceive, rightly or wrongly, that to do otherwise would antagonize their judges and provoke denials of all relief.)

7.   PROCEDURE

The procedures for adjudicating asylum and withholding of removal claims have developed over the years in response to changing refugee flows, political climates, and congressional commands. For a useful history, see David A. Martin, *Reforming Asylum Adjudication: On Navigating the Coast of Bohemia,* 138 Univ. Pennsylvania L. Rev. 1247, 1294–98 (1990) [hereafter cited in this subsection as Martin, *Reforming Asylum*].

A clear, detailed, and comprehensive description of the current United States asylum process appears in Anker at 523–74; see also Philip Schrag, A Well–Founded Fear—The Congressional Battle to Save Asylum in America (2000) (a fascinating insider's account of the political process of asylum reform); Stephen H. Legomsky, *An Asylum Seeker's Bill of Rights for a Non–Utopian World,* 14 Georgetown Immigration L.J. 619 (2000) (formulating minimum procedural rights in asylum cases). For some good comparative studies of asylum procedure, see Randall Hansen, Susan Martin, Andrew Schoenholtz & Patrick Weil, *Report on the Workshop on Refugee and Asylum Policy in Practice in Europe and North America,* 14 Georgetown Immigration L.J. 801 (2000); Susan F. Martin & Andrew I. Schoenholtz, *Asylum in Practice: Successes, Failures, and the Challenges Ahead,* 14 Georgetown Immigration L.J. 589 (2000).

a.   GENERAL PRINCIPLES OF UNITED STATES ASYLUM PROCEDURE

The first thing to understand about United States asylum procedure is that two separate adjudication systems are in place. One system is administered by USCIS. The other is administered by the EOIR—more specifically, by immigration judges and the BIA. In each system, the application procedure for asylum under section 208 is essentially the same as the procedure for withholding of removal under section 241(b)(3). In fact, as noted earlier, an asylum application is automatically treated as an application for withholding of removal in the event asylum is denied. 8 C.F.R. § 208.3(b) (2004).

A person who is already in removal proceedings applies for asylum and/or withholding of removal by filing an application with the immigration judge. 8 C.F.R. § 208.4(b)(3) (2004). The decision of the immigration judge is appealable to the BIA, *id.* § 3.1(b)(3), and reviewable in court under INA § 242(a)(1). See also INA § 242(a)(2)(B)(ii) (exempting asylum from the general preclusion of judicial review of discretionary decisions).

A person who is not yet the subject of removal proceedings may take the initiative and apply to USCIS for asylum and/or withholding of removal. 8 C.F.R. § 208.4(b)(2) (2004). These claims are usually called "affirmative" applications, as distinguished from the "defensive" applications filed in removal proceedings. The details of the USCIS asylum procedure are laid out in United States CIS, Affirmative Asylum Procedures Manual (rev. Feb. 2003).

Until 1990, affirmative applications were filed with the local INS district office and processed by all-purpose immigration officials. Important reforms inaugurated that year, see 55 Fed.Reg. 30674–87 (July 27, 1990), created a new corps of INS (now USCIS) "asylum officers," specially trained in international law, country conditions, and asylum law. 8 C.F.R. § 208.1(b) (2004). The asylum officers are based in several major cities throughout the United States. After receiving the application, an asylum officer conducts a nonadversarial interview at which the claimant may be represented by counsel and may submit documentary evidence. 8 C.F.R. § 208.9(b) (2004).

After the interview, the asylum officer makes a decision. The 1994 reforms changed the nature of that decision. Under the pre–1994 regulations, the asylum officer either granted or denied the application. 8 C.F.R. §§ 208.14(a), 208.16, 208.17 (1994). If the asylum officer denied the application, and if (as was usually the case) the applicant did not otherwise have a lawful immigration status, the former INS was free to initiate deportation proceedings. If it did so, the claimant could then renew his or her application before the immigration judge. 8 C.F.R. § 208.18(b) (1994). At that point, the procedure described above for defensive applications—a formal evidentiary hearing, followed by a right of appeal to the BIA, followed by possible judicial review—was triggered.

As discussed in more detail below, both Congress and the Justice Department were concerned about mounting backlogs, long delays in disposing of cases, and a hit-and-miss pattern of removing deportable applicants whose asylum claims were finally denied. There was also a perception (right or wrong) that many claims were legally frivolous. The 1994 changes to the Justice Department regulations were aimed at those problems. See 59 Fed.Reg. 62284–303 (Dec. 5, 1994). Under the new regulations, with some exceptions, the asylum officer no longer "denies" an application for asylum or withholding of removal. Instead, after a more abbreviated procedure, the officer either grants the application or refers the case to an immigration judge for the initiation of removal proceedings. 8 C.F.R. § 208.14(b,c) (2004). In the latter event, the regular EOIR procedure—a removal hearing before the immigration judge, a right of appeal to the BIA, and a right of judicial review—kicks in.[15]

Congress took a more radical step in 1996. AEDPA created a new procedure called "expedited removal," which IIRIRA amended later the same year. Under the new procedure, certain arriving noncitizens—generally those without documents and those whom immigration inspectors suspect of fraud—are relegated to a more summary process that is detailed in section B.7.b.iv below.

Before asylum may be granted in any of these contexts, the statute requires a check of the applicant's identity against various government databases that are designed to reveal possible grounds of inadmissibility, deportability, or other ineligibility for asylum. INA § 208(d)(5)(A)(i). That requirement took on additional importance effective April 1, 2005, with the issuance of a regulation that made completion of a DHS identity, law enforcement, and security check a prerequisite to the granting of any relief that enables a noncitizen to reside in the United States (including asylum). See 70 Fed. Reg. 4743 (Jan. 26, 2005), adding 8 C.F.R. § 1003.47 and amending 8 C.F.R. § 1208.4. To initiate the check, the noncitizen must supply certain biographical data and biometric identifiers, usually by reporting to a DHS office. The DHS goal, expressed in the Federal Register notice, is to do the processing while the applicant is waiting for the hearing on the merits of the claim. There are concerns, however, that in practice the security checks will generate backlogs that delay grants of relief for substantial periods.

Finally, under INA § 209(b), individuals who have received asylum and thereafter remained in the United States for one year may adjust to permanent residence. Until 2005, the statute limited the number of adjustments of status available to asylees to 10,000 per year. That cap proved

---

15. For an interesting account of the political dynamics of the 1994 reforms, see David A. Martin, *Making Asylum Policy: The 1994 Reforms*, 70 Washington L. Rev. 725 (1995). For a helpful description of the effects on immigration practitioners, see Jeanne A. Butterfield, *The New Asylum Regulations: A Practitioner's Guide*, Immigration Briefings (Jan. 1995).

highly problematic. By March 1, 2004, the backlog of asylee adjustment applications had reached approximately 160,000. See 81 IR 583 (Apr. 26, 2004). A person granted asylum at that time would thus have had to wait 16 years to attain LPR status. During the waiting period, an asylee may travel overseas (after obtaining a "refugee travel document" from USCIS) and may work. INA § 208(c)(1)(B, C). Not being an LPR, however, an asylee does not qualify as a family-sponsored second preference petitioner and thus has no mechanism for uniting with an after-acquired spouse or child. (Under INA § 208(b)(3), a spouse or child accompanying or following to join the asylee may be admitted, but recall that 'accompanying or following to join" status is limited to preexisting spouses and children.) Not being an LPR, an asylee is also ineligible for naturalization. The REAL ID Act, § 101(g)(1), amended INA § 209(b) to remove the annual 10,000 cap.

Despite, and in some cases because of, these changes, certain features of the present adjudication process have been the subjects of wide-ranging debate. Among the problems that have received the most attention are these:

(1) *Political Bias.* As you saw earlier, admissions under the overseas refugee program have historically been tilted dramatically toward those refugees fleeing regimes unfriendly to the United States. For many years critics have similarly charged that the various officials who decide asylum cases improperly emphasize political factors. In part, the critics argue, this pattern reflects the foreign relations agenda of the State Department, whose advisory opinions used to influence both affirmative and defensive asylum adjudications. A small sampling of the many writers who have voiced those objections includes Elizabeth Hull, Without Justice for All— The Constitutional Rights of Aliens, ch. 5 (1985); Gil Loescher & John A. Scanlan, Calculated Kindness—Refugees and America's Half–Open Door 1945–Present, chs. 9–11 (1986); Norman L. Zucker & Naomi F. Zucker, The Guarded Gate—The Reality of American Refugee Policy, ch. 4 (1987); T. Alexander Aleinikoff, *Political Asylum in the Federal Republic of Germany and the Republic of France: Lessons for the United States,* 17 Univ. Michigan J. L. Reform 183, 193–95 (1984); Deborah E. Anker, *A Case Study on the Implementation of Legal Norms in an Unstructured Adjudicatory Environment,* 19 NYU Rev. L. & Social Change 433 (1992); *cf.* Ira J. Kurzban, *A Critical Analysis of Refugee Law,* 36 Univ. Miami L. Rev. 865, 876–78 (1982) (refugees from noncommunist countries effectively omitted from overseas refugee program and relegated to asylum program in which standards more demanding). See also *M.A. v. U.S. INS,* 899 F.2d 304, 320–21 (4th Cir.1990) (Winter, J., dissenting) (BIA interpretation should be accorded less deference than usual because Board has not respected congressional mandate to apply Refugee Act neutrally); Miami Herald, March 29, 1990, at 8 (Amnesty International charges United States with foreign policy bias in applying asylum criteria).

Past statistics certainly support historical accusations of political bias. For applications filed with the former INS from June 1983 to September 1988, the approval rates for applicants fleeing communist countries and other countries that the United States regarded as adversaries were dramatically higher than for applicants fleeing friendly countries whose human rights records were generally perceived as being at least equally bad. See Martin, *Reforming Asylum,* at 1305, Table II. The ten highest country approval rates, ranging from 30.0% to 61.7%, were for applicants from Iran, Syria, and eight communist countries. *Id.* The rate for Nicaragua was 27.9%; in contrast, the rates for El Salvador, Guatemala, and Haiti—all United States allies—were 2.7%, 2.1% and 2.0%, respectively. *Id.* Analogous figures for the immigration judges also showed a large disparity between the approval rate for Nicaraguans (37.4%) and that for Salvadorans (12%), though the difference was not as severe as the corresponding disparity for INS adjudications. *Id.* at 1309 n.160.

In 1985, those patterns prompted a class action by Salvadoran and Guatemalan asylum claimants against the former INS, EOIR, and the State Department. The complaint alleged a pattern and practice of widespread discrimination against nationals of El Salvador and Guatemala in the adjudication of asylum claims. In 1990 the parties signed, and in 1991 the district court for the Northern District of California approved, a settlement agreement destined to have monumental effects on the asylum process. *American Baptist Churches v. Thornburgh,* 760 F.Supp. 796 (N.D.Cal.1991) [the *ABC* Case]. Subject to some exceptions, the agreement permitted Salvadorans who had arrived in the United States by September 19, 1990 and Guatemalans who had arrived by October 1, 1990, and whose asylum claims had been turned down, to reapply under the revised procedures that had been inaugurated earlier that year. While those renewed claims were pending, the applicants could remain in the United States and could work. Similar stays of deportation and grants of work authorization were extended to those Salvadorans and Guatemalans who had arrived by the specified dates but who had not previously applied for asylum. The agreement affected hundreds of thousands of individuals and took many years to implement fully. See Washington Post, Dec. 20, 1990, at 1. See generally Debbie Smith & ABC Legal Team, *The ABC Settlement: A Guide for Class Members and Advocates*, 72 IR 1497 (Nov.6, 1995).

By the early 1990's, the end of the Cold War and a series of other world developments had combined to alter these patterns. There are now far fewer Communist countries in the world, and therefore fewer Communist countries in the high asylum approval group. But there is always a lag time between formal changes in international relations and formal responses. Thus, refugees from former Communist countries, as well as from the remaining Communist countries and other United States adversaries, remained disproportionately represented in favorable asylum decisions for several years. Still, such ideological patterns are not obvious today. See generally 2003 Yearbook of Immigration Statistics, Table 18, which lists the approval percentages by country of origin.

One fairly clear exception to the near elimination of anti-Communist bias in asylum cases is Cuba. In fiscal year 2003 the approval rate for

Cuban asylum applications was 50%, compared to an aggregate approval rate of 29%. *Id*. Does the difference reflect higher rates of actual persecution in Cuba than in most other totalitarian states, ideological preference, or both? Suggesting political explanations, Professor Joyce Hughes calls for foreign-policy-neutral refugee laws and an end to favoritism for Cubans. See Joyce A. Hughes, *Flight from Cuba*, 36 Calif. Western L. Rev. 39 (1999).

(2) *Long delays*. All sides agree that the huge volumes of asylum applications have placed pressure on the available adjudicative resources. The problem is not uniquely American; it is felt in most western democracies. In the United States, through the early 1990's, the INS asylum officers could handle only a fraction of the applications filed. The backlog kept growing. See 73 IR 45, 46 (Jan. 10, 1996). The 1994 amendments to the asylum regulations, discussed below, caused asylum applications to drop rapidly while dispositions rose. In fiscal year 1995, some 147,000 affirmative asylum applications were filed; 2003 Yearbook of Immigration Statistics, Table 16. As soon as the amendments went into effect in 1995, applications dropped dramatically and have stayed far below the 1995 figure ever since. (In fiscal year 2003, the number was 46,000. *Id*.)

The delays, which have clearly diminished, occur for many reasons: Administrative resources, though increased, are limited. Immigration judges' hearing calendars are backed up. Applicants sometimes need considerable time to obtain pro bono counsel. Martin, *Reforming Asylum,* at 1327–28. If either side appeals to the BIA, it can take months just to transcribe the recording of the removal hearing. In the small proportion of cases that go to court, judicial backlogs add further delay.

Delays are harmful for various reasons. As Professor Martin has pointed out, *id*. at 1293, they prolong the uncertainty for genuine refugees who need security and peace of mind. Moreover, as discussed below, the very act of applying for asylum can bring concrete interim benefits. See, e.g., Michael S. Teitelbaum, *Political Asylum in Theory and Practice,* 76 Pub. Interest 74 (1984). Thus, critics charge, long delays enlarge the incentives for ineligible applicants to file asylum claims, which in turn make the delays even longer, which in turn further increases the incentive for other ineligible applicants to file claims, etc. Somewhere, the argument runs, the cycle must be broken. As discussed below, the challenge is to find ways of reducing the delays without unduly sacrificing procedural fairness and accuracy.

(3) *Unfounded claims*. No one seriously disputes that some asylum applications lack reasonable foundation, but there has always been much difference of opinion as to how great that number is. See Ira J. Kurzban, *Restructuring the Asylum Process,* 19 San Diego L. Rev. 91, 96 (1981). There exist at least two incentives to file an unfounded asylum claim. The most obvious is the hope that the application will erroneously be granted. See Martin, *Reforming Asylum, id*. at 1287–88. The other is that certain interim benefits typically attach while the claim is pending. *Id*. at 1288–89. Perhaps the most significant interim benefit is permission to work, but the

1994 regulations have greatly restricted the employment authorization rules, as discussed in section B.7.b.vii below.

(4) *Fiscal Costs.* The present process is expensive and, in the minds of some, wasteful. Many have criticized as unnecessary, for example, the feature that permits "two bites at the apple"—an application to USCIS, followed by a renewal of the application before the immigration judge in removal proceedings. See, e.g., Martin, *Reforming Asylum,* at 1322–24; Ira J. Kurzban, *Restructuring the Asylum Process,* 19 San Diego L. Rev. 91, 111–12 (1981); see also 53 Fed.Reg. 32552 (Aug. 28, 1987) (proposed Justice Department regulations that would have eliminated opportunity to apply to immigration judge; not adopted). The additional costs associated with detention and other aspects of the asylum process are also considerable. See Martin, above, at 1379–80.

(5) *Procedural Fairness.* Many have questioned whether the current asylum process adequately safeguards the claimants' procedural needs. Access to counsel has been a major sticking point. As you saw in chapter 9, section B.2.b above, noncitizens in removal proceedings often face practical obstacles to securing counsel. The problem is of particular importance to asylum claimants, since their cases tend to present more than the usual complexities and thorough documentation is essential. As discussed earlier, represented asylum claimants fare far better than unrepresented claimants, though causation is not possible to gauge scientifically because lawyers are more likely to take strong cases than weaker ones. See pages 653–54 above.

Other elements of the hearing process have also been criticized. Some have questioned the adequacy of the government's foreign language interpreters in immigration judge proceedings. See, e.g., Deborah E. Anker, *Determining Asylum Claims in the United States—Summary Report of an Empirical Study of the Adjudication of Asylum Claims Before the Immigration Court,* 2 Internat'l J. Refugee L. 252, 257 (1990); see also *El Rescate Legal Services, Inc. v. EOIR,* 959 F.2d 742 (9th Cir.1991) (amended version) (reversing ruling that had required interpretation of entire exclusion or deportation hearing—not just respondent's own testimony—when respondent needs interpreter). See generally Angela McCaffrey, *Don't Get Lost in Translation: Teaching Law Students to Work with Language Interpreters,* 6 Clinical L. Rev. 347 (2000).

The asylum process for children has become a major issue in recent years. In 2003, approximately 50,000 children who had been separated from their families applied for asylum in Europe, and another 5,000 were detained in the United States. See Jacqueline Bhabha, *"More than Their Share of Sorrows": International Migration Law and the Rights of Children,* 22 St. Louis Univ. Public L. Rev. 253, 254–55 (2003); see also Jacqueline Bhabha, *Minors or Aliens? Inconsistent State Intervention and Separated Child Asylum–Seekers,* 3 Euro. J. Migration & L. 283 (2001); Daniel J. Steinbock, *Separated Children in Mass Migration: Causes and Cures,* 22 St. Louis Univ. Public L. Rev. 297 (2003). The fairness of the procedures in child asylum cases has also been questioned. See, e.g., Michael A. Olivas, *Unaccompanied Refugee Children: Detention, Due Pro-*

cess, and Disgrace, 2 Stanford L. & Policy Rev. 159 (1990). See generally Convention on the Rights of the Child, 1577 U.N.T.S. 3 (done at New York, Nov. 20, 1989), especially art. 22 (but not ratified by the United States); the various UNHCR Executive Committee Conclusions, reproduced in 23 Refugee Survey Q. #2 at 334–60; the (former) INS Guidelines for Children's Asylum Claims (Dec. 10, 1998), reproduced in 76 IR 5 (Jan. 4, 1999).

The most famous child asylum claimant was little Elián González, the 6–year-old boy who was rescued at sea clinging to an inner tube. His parents had divorced in Cuba, and his mother then tried to bring him to the U.S. without the knowledge of his father. His mother and several other adults drowned in the attempted escape from Cuba to the United States. Elián's great uncle in Miami filed an asylum claim on the child's behalf. Elián's father refused to consent to the claim and came to the United States to bring his son back to Cuba. Ultimately, the former INS, in its discretion, recognized the father's decision and declined to adjudicate the application. The stridently anti-Castro Cuban community in Miami lined up solidly on the side of Elián's great uncle. Amidst a passionate firestorm, intense domestic politics on all sides, the personal efforts of Fidel Castro to secure Elián's return, and a relentless media circus, the final decision fell to the courts. Eventually, the Eleventh Circuit upheld the discretionary power of the INS to decide who speaks for the child in an asylum case. Taking into account the young age of the child, the obviously close relationship between father and child, and the absence of evidence of likely persecution or other harm to Elián, the court further held that the INS had not abused its discretion. González v. Reno, 212 F.3d 1338 (11th Cir. 2000). There was extra drama at the end. While the litigation was pending, Elián was staying with his Miami relatives. When the relatives refused to release him to the INS so that he and his father could return to Cuba, the INS, after prolonged negotiations, seized him by force in a controversial surprise raid.

The Elián case, however, was more than melodrama. It highlighted a serious and difficult issue of law and policy: What *should* happen when a child applies for asylum against the wishes of his or her sole surviving parent or parents? Many observers had mixed feelings about the case. While few experts believed that 6–year-old Elián—a hero in Cuba—had a well-founded fear of persecution at the hands of his government (much less persecution because of his political opinions!), there was some queasiness about the precedent that the case could possibly set. Some provocative commentary has resulted. Thoughtful reactions include David Abraham, International Decisions, *González ex rel. González v. Reno, 212 F.3d 1338 (11th Cir. 2000),* 95 Amer. J. Internat'l L. 204 (2001); Hiroshi Motomura, *The Year is 2020: Looking Back on the Elian Gonzalez Case (A Fantasy),* 77 IR 853 (2000); Victor C. Romero, *On Elián and Aliens: A Political Solution to the Plenary Power Problem,* 4 NYU J. Legislation & Public Policy 343 (2000–01). Professor Peter Margulies brings family law to bear on the case. He identifies three common situations in which parents might object to their child's asylum claims—"(1) the parent as persecutor; (2) the parent in denial; and (3) the parent as true believer." See Peter Margulies, *Children,*

Parents, and Asylum, 15 Georgetown Immigration L.J. 289, 293 (2001). Professor Berta Esperanza Hernández-Truyol discusses the effects that the differing personal histories of Cuban-born law professors tend to have on their views of the Elian case. See Berta Esperanza Hernández-Truyol, *On Becoming the Other: Cubans, Castro, and Elian—A LatCritical Analysis*, 78 Denver Univ. L. Rev. 687 (2001).

Like most other components of post-September 11 U.S. immigration policy, the asylum process has been scrutinized for possible national security vulnerabilities. The conference committee report accompanying the REAL ID Act charged that terrorists have been able to exploit loopholes in the asylum procedure to enter, remain, and operate in the United States. See Rpt. 109–72 (109th Cong., 1st Sess.) (May 3, 2005), at 160–61, 164–65. The report cites examples of terrorists who entered the United States through the asylum system, though in most of the cited examples (not all), the terrorists entered either before September 11, 2001 or through procedures that have since been changed in the wake of September 11.

More general criticisms of the asylum process have begun to accumulate in recent years. See, e.g., Anker, above; Katherine L. Vaughns, *Taming the Asylum Adjudication Process: An Agenda for the Twenty–First Century*, 30 San Diego L. Rev. 1 (1993). In one case, a unanimous three-judge panel of the Ninth Circuit was unusually acerbic:

> The legal quality of the decisions in the case were substandard. * * * [In footnote: The State Department, whose relevant bureau enjoys a name that indicates a human and humanitarian purpose, instead of providing relevant data within its knowledge of the state of affairs in El Salvador, responded with the kind of perfunctory form letter that might be used by a department store dismissing a customer's mistaken complaint of an overcharge.] [Immigration] Judge Nail was unfamiliar with the statutory difference between the statutes on withholding deportation and granting asylum. The Board invented a new standard that was not responsive to the United States Supreme Court. The Board failed to address one of the two principal claims made by the petitioner. The whole record is one of a shoddy process. Courts of appeals spend countless hours of consideration on capital cases arising in this country. Here where Congress has provided that a helpless alien does not have to be sent back to face death if he is eligible for asylum, the process as it is revealed in this case is one of haste, carelessness and ineptitude. The State Department, the Board, and the Immigration Service need to improve their standards.

Montecino v. INS, 915 F.2d 518, 521 (9th Cir.1990).

Since the implementation of the grant-or-refer system, the asylum officers have been able to process far more cases per year, not only because there are more asylum officers, but also because the number of dispositions per officer has increased. Many, however, have questioned whether the price for that increased productivity has been sloppier decisionmaking. In 1996 the U.S. Committee for Refugees reported:

[A New York attorney lamented that asylum officers] "don't have time to conduct the interviews. If they can't get the full story in one hour, they blame the applicants for not telling their stories well, and refer the case. It is easier to refer than to grant."

Other practitioners complain that INS asylum officers come into the interviews unprepared, not having read the applications and supporting documents ahead of time.

"I consider myself lucky if the asylum officer has read the application form and declaration before the interview," said an attorney in Los Angeles. "You can't have a solid interview if the asylum officer is reviewing the file for the first time while the client is sitting there."

* * *

"Some denials—I can't bring myself to call them referrals—make your jaw drop," said a practitioner in Chicago. "We recommend that no one file affirmatively any more unless they have a very strong case."

"Before," said the Chicago practitioner, "asylum officers would take as long as they needed, two-to-three hours; they would call people back for another interview. Now, they're under pressure to crank them out."

Some practitioners noted that the performance rating system for AOs used in the INS's Arlington office is based on a point system that awards points for completing a case in a single day.
* * *

U.S. Comm. for Refugees, Refugee Reports at 3, 5 (June 30, 1996). Without minimizing the problems that these commentators have described, one should not assume that affirmative asylum applications are a waste of time. To the contrary, statistics for fiscal year 2003 show an approval rate by USCIS asylum officers of 29% for asylum claimants from all countries combined. The rates vary considerably, of course, by source country. See 2003 Yearbook of Immigration Statistics, Table 16.

IIRIRA imposed statutory time constraints on various steps in the adjudication process. With narrow exceptions, an asylum application may not be filed more than one year after the applicant's arrival in the United States. INA § 208(a)(2)(B,D). The concept of a time limit on filing asylum claims is considered separately in section B.7.b.i below. The hearing or interview must begin within 45 days of the filing, and the asylum officer or immigration judge must decide the case no later than 180 days after the filing. INA § 208(d)(5)(A)(ii,iii). Any administrative appeal must be filed within 30 days of the initial decision. INA § 208(d)(5)(A)(iv). These constraints might well speed up adjudication even further. Whether they exacerbate some of the problems noted above remains to be determined.

NOTES AND QUESTIONS

1. Not all observers agree about either the existence or the scale of all those problems. But each is seen as a significant problem by a significant number of people. Varying solutions, reflecting different substantive ideologies and procedural preferences, have been advanced over the years. One of the most comprehensive analyses of the United States asylum adjudication procedure is David Martin, *Reforming Asylum Adjudication: On Navigating the Coast of Bohemia*, 138 Univ. Pennsylvania L. Rev. 1247 (1990) (consultant's report to the Administrative Conference of the United States, a now defunct federal government agency that was charged with monitoring and improving the administrative process). Among Professor Martin's recommendations were (1) establish a corps of properly trained specialized asylum adjudicators (the INS, now USCIS, Asylum Office did not then exist); (2) locate that corps in a new department of EOIR; (3) substitute these asylum officers for the combination of INS (now USCIS) and immigration judge asylum decisionmaking, thus eliminating the "two bites at the apple" feature; (4) select adjudicators who were interested in international affairs and sensitive to cultural differences; (5) require they be lawyers; (6) create an official documentation center that would make reliance on State Department expertise unnecessary; (7) adopt a nonadversarial, interview-style procedure in which the specialized asylum adjudicator develops the factual record; and (8) proceed without counsel in the event the applicant cannot secure counsel within a reasonable time. The Administrative Conference of the United States substantially endorsed these recommendations. See 1 C.F.R. § 305.89(4) (1996). As the preceding discussion showed, most of the proposed reforms have made their way into the present asylum adjudication system, though some (most notably 2 and 3 above) have not.

2. Other commentators (as Martin acknowledges, *Reforming Asylum*, at 1338 n. 250), had also urged the use of specialized asylum adjudicators. See, e.g., Deborah E. Anker & Michael H. Posner, *The Forty–Year Crisis: A Legislative History of the Refugee Act of 1980*, 19 San Diego L. Rev. 9, 74–75 (1981); see also Cristopher Avery, *Refugee Status Decision–Making: The Systems of Ten Countries*, 19 Stanford J. Internat'l L. 235 (1983). What arguments can you make both for and against reliance on asylum specialists? For a general analysis of the benefits and costs of specialized adjudication, methods of identifying case types for which the benefits outweigh the costs, and the varying forms that specialized adjudication can take, see Stephen H. Legomsky, Specialized Justice—Courts, Administrative Tribunals, and a Cross–National Theory of Specialization, chaps. 1–3 (1990).

3. A more specific issue concerns the proper *degree* of specialization. Most people would regard immigration law as a highly specialized field and, thus, immigration judges as already performing highly specialized work. Asylum, being a subcategory of immigration law, is more specialized yet. Martin in fact raises, though he rejects as impractical for a country as large in area as the United States, the possibility of even greater specialization— the cases of asylum-seekers from particular countries or regions of the

world. One leading writer, emphasizing the dangers of cross-cultural mis-understandings, has argued that an asylum adjudicator should "deal with asylum-seekers from only one or a few culturally similar countries." Walter Kälin, *Troubled Communication: Cross–Cultural Misunderstandings in the Asylum–Hearing,* 20 Internat'l Migration Rev. 230, 239 (1986); see generally Angela McCaffrey, *Don't Get Lost in Translation: Teaching Law Students to Work with Language Interpreters,* 6 Clinical L. Rev. 347 (2000) (discussing both linguistic and cultural barriers to communication). What do you see as the optimal level of specialization in this context?

4.   Should all asylum adjudicators be lawyers?

5.   Before the 1994 amendments to the regulations, an asylum officer who was about to deny a claim would give the applicant a "Notice of Intent to Deny" [NOID], which stated the reasons for the proposed denial. The applicant would then have an opportunity to meet the deficiency by producing additional information. The 1994 amendments deleted NOIDs. 59 Fed.Reg. 62284, 62293–94, 62300 (1994). What do you see as the pros and cons of NOIDs?

6.   Martin argues against "two bites at the apple"—i.e., a non-adversarial interview with a (then) INS official and then a renewal of the application to an immigration judge at an adversarial hearing. Others similarly advocated eliminating the INS from the asylum process. See, e.g., Ira J. Kurzban, *Restructuring the Asylum Process,* 19 San Diego L. Rev. 91, 111–12 (1981); Michael P. Brady, *Asylum Adjudication: No Place for the INS,* 20 Columbia Human Rights L. Rev. 129 (1988). Are there any *advantages* to the present system? What about the possibility that a second round decreases the chance of error? Martin rejects that argument on the ground that there is no reason to think the pictures inside the head of the second adjudicator will be any more accurate than those inside the head of the first. Is he right about that? Either way, are there other advantages to the two-bite system?

7.   If one of the bites is to be eliminated, which one should it be? Initial adjudication (as distinguished from appeal or review) could be assigned solely to the immigration agency officials, as the INS once proposed, 52 Fed.Reg. 32552, 32554 (August 28, 1987), solely to immigration judges, or, as Martin proposes, solely to some third type of decisionmaker. If the last option is chosen, a further question is whether the adjudicators should remain within the Justice Department, be placed within some other Department, or be part of a new independent agency. Other variables affecting the degree of independence include whether the adjudicators are subject to removal by, and whether their decisions are reviewable by, political officials. For commentary advocating the independent agency approach, see T. Alexander Aleinikoff, *Political Asylum in the Federal Republic of Germany and the Republic of France: Lessons for the United States,* 17 Univ. Michigan J. L. Reform 183, 235–36 (1984) (would avoid public perception of political bias).

In answering these questions, think about what it is the adjudicators should be independent *of.* Is it control by political officials? Control by officials whose first priority is foreign policy? Control by officials who perform law enforcement functions? *Should* an individual persecution claim be seen as an "adjudicative" decision that reflects only an assessment of the law and the facts of the case, or should it be seen as a "policy" decision shaped also by assessments of the likely domestic and foreign affairs consequences? Is your analysis of this question the same for asylum as it is for withholding of removal?

8.   Martin favors non-adversarial proceedings, in which the adjudicator has the principal responsibility for identifying the issues and extracting the relevant facts and legal arguments. An adversarial system, in contrast, would rely more heavily on the efforts of the parties and their counsel. Which do you favor for asylum cases?

9.   A key element of Martin's nonadversarial system is that the hearing would proceed without counsel if counsel cannot be obtained quickly. That scenario would probably occur often since, as you saw earlier, affordable lawyers are frequently unavailable. The question, therefore, is how important it is for asylum claimants to be represented. Under the present system, obtaining counsel markedly improves the chances of approval, as you have seen. A good illustration is *Castro–O'Ryan v. United States Dept. of Immigration and Naturalization* [sic], 847 F.2d 1307 (9th Cir.1987), where the court reversed an asylum denial on the ground that the applicant's waiver of his right to counsel had not been intelligent and voluntary. The court noted a clear legal error by Immigration Judge Nail (the same IJ criticized in *Montecino*, pages 956–57 above) that competent counsel would have prevented. *Id.* at 1313. The court also observed a striking contrast between the vivid story related by the applicant and the immigration judge's summation of the evidence:

> In support of his request for asylum Castro prepared an affidavit in February 1985 which, written in his own hand, was filed with the Immigration Judge. It, in relevant part, reads:

> * * *

> * * * On the night of October 21st, 1975 (about 8:00 P.M.), as I left the student's residence, where I lived, in Santiago, during the school season, I was detained and escorted to a waiting Army truck, by two soldiers.

> I was ordered to lay face down on the truck's bed and to pull my trousers down to my knees. There were other two civilian detainees with me, in the same position. In the canvas' covered bed of the truck were about 10 soldiers. The ones closer to the tail, closed the tail gate and pulled down the tail canvas.

> The Army truck rode for about one hour before coming to a final stop.

> We (all three detainees) were order out, to what seemed to be an isolated country estate.

I never saw again the other two detainees.

I was order to remove all my cloth, and locked in a cell, without light, in the basement of the building.

After about two hours, two civilians came for me. I was taken nude to another room on the floor above. It was a walk in freezer, illuminated by very deem lighting. I was order to sat down on a metal chair. I was hand and leg strapped into the metal chair. The two civilians left.

About an hour later the two civilians came back. By this time I was getting close to be frozen in the freezer.

One of the civilians introduced himself as an Army Intelligence Officer.

He was the one that conducted the interrogation. I was asked about my participation in the movement, our plans, the names of other members of the movement. I denied any knowledge of the movement (if I had accepted any of their allegations, they would have had bases for my prosecution; if found guilty, I would have faced at least a long prison sentence, if not death). After about half an hour of interrogation, it became obvious to me that the Army Intelligence new more about the movement than I did myself. That only meant that they had infiltrated the movement.

After one hour of interrogation, the two civilians left. By this time I was in pain because of the cold, inside the freezer.

Half an hour later, my interrogator, with two soldiers came back. They hose me with high pressure water; unstrapped me, and took me out of the freezer. On my way back to the basement cell, the officer in civil cloth told me to leave the country.

I was given back my cloth and put back on the same cell. After about 4 to 5 hours, two soldiers come for me. I was brought back to the Army truck. Order to lay face down on the floor of the bed of the truck and to pull my trousers down to my knees. This time only two soldiers were on the back of the truck. I was the only civilian.

After half an hour of ride, the truck stopped and I was order out of it. I was left in the southwest suburbs of Santiago. It was 6:30 A.M., October 22nd, 1975. It had been over 10 hours since I was taken into custody.

* * *

* * * Judge Nail's [entire] description of the main incident described by Castro in his affidavit was as follows:

The Respondent stated that about October of 1975, that he was taken into custody by individuals of the Government and

> that he was held overnight and during the time that he was
> held he was questioned and he was mistreated.

Id. at 1310–12.

Under Martin's proposal, of course, the asylum adjudicators would receive specialized training and, through their caseloads, accumulate specialized expertise. There would also be, and indeed there now is, a documentation center capable of providing further support. Do you think those innovations, combined with the more assertive roles proposed for the adjudicators, would adequately compensate for lack of counsel?

10. IIRIRA all but eliminated judicial review in those asylum cases that are subject to the new expedited removal procedure. See the expedited removal discussion (item 3) below; Kevin R. Johnson, *A "Hard Look" at the Executive Branch's Asylum Decisions*, 1991 Utah L. Rev. 279 (urging more assertive judicial review of asylum denials).

What, exactly, does judicial review of asylum decisions accomplish? What are the costs of allowing such review? See generally Stephen H. Legomsky, *Political Asylum and the Theory of Judicial Review*, 73 Minnesota L. Rev. 1205, 1207 (1989).

11. Based on what you now know about the asylum process, is a competent terrorist very likely to apply for asylum rather than pursue other means of entering and remaining?

b. BARRING OR DISCOURAGING ACCESS TO THE ASYLUM PROCESS

The case management strategies that you have encountered up to this point are designed primarily to make the disposition of asylum claims speedier and more efficient. In contrast are a package of other asylum reforms adopted or considered in the United States in recent years. These latter reforms are generally meant to cut off access to the asylum system entirely or, in some instances, at least discourage potential asylum applicants from filing claims. They are described in this subsection. For more detail, see Stephen H. Legomsky, *The New Techniques for Managing High–Volume Asylum Systems*, 81 Iowa L. Rev. 671, 675–704 (1996).

To put the United States initiatives in perspective, you should note that similar actions have been taken or proposed in western Europe. See, e.g., Elspeth Guild, *The Impetus to Harmonize: Asylum Policy in the European Union*, in Frances Nicholson & Patrick Twomey (eds.), Refugee Rights and Realities (1999), at 313 et seq.; Kay Hailbronner, *New Techniques for Rendering Asylum Manageable*, in 4 Kay Hailbronner, David A. Martin & Hiroshi Motomura (eds.), Immigration Controls (1998), at 59 et seq.; Reinhard Marx & Katharina Lumpp, *The German Constitutional Court's Decision of 14 May 1996 on the Concept of "Safe Third Countries"—A Basis for Burden–Sharing in Europe*, 8 Internatl'l J. Refugee L. 419 (1996); Peter J. van Krieken (ed.), The Asylum Acquis Handbook (2000).

i. Filing Deadlines

IIRIRA § 604(a) imposed a new requirement for asylum (not for withholding of removal). The asylum claimant must prove by "clear and convincing evidence" that the application is being filed within one year of the applicant's arrival in the United States. INA § 208(a)(2)(B). There are two exceptions—"changed circumstances which materially affect the applicant's eligibility for asylum or extraordinary circumstances relating to the delay in filing." INA § 208(a)(2)(D). The regulations define "extraordinary circumstances" as "events or factors directly related to the failure to meet the 1–year deadline." 8 C.F.R. §§ 208.4(a)(5), 1208.4(a)(5) (2004). A non-exhaustive list of possible "extraordinary circumstances" includes physical, mental, and legal disabilities, and ineffective assistance of counsel (provided very rigorous conditions are met). *Id.* Once the administrative officials find an absence of clear and convincing evidence that the applicant arrived during the past year, and also find that neither of the exceptions applies, the asylum denials are final; no judicial review is permitted. INA § 208(a)(3).

Asylum professionals vigorously resisted the introduction of filing deadlines. The leading advocates were Professors Philip Schrag and Michele Pistone, who explained many of the practical reasons that asylum applicants often do not file their claims soon after arrival. The immediate priorities of most refugees are to locate United States relatives, friends, or others, who will help them find food and lodging. Genuine refugees are frequently still traumatized by the persecution they are fleeing. Many cannot speak English when they arrive and do not have a clue how to go about applying for asylum. Most important, it is immensely difficult to file an asylum application without help from a lawyer or other professional who specializes in asylum. Unfortunately, most refugees lack the resources to retain such professionals, and the supply of pro bono services falls far short of the demand. Even when a suitable lawyer is willing to take the case, gathering documentary support and otherwise preparing serious asylum applications are enormously labor-intensive. See Philip G. Schrag, *Don't Gut Political Asylum*, Wash. Post, Nov. 12, 1995, at C7, reproduced in 10 Georgetown Immigration L.J. at 93–94 (1996);[16] Michele R. Pistone, *Asylum Filing Deadlines: Unfair and Unnecessary*, 10 Georgetown Immigration L.J. 95 (1996); Philip G. Schrag & Michele R. Pistone, *The 1996 Immigration Act: Asylum Application Deadlines and Expedited Removal— What the INS Should Do*, 73 IR 1565 (Nov. 11, 1996).

ii. Safe Countries of Origin

In some European asylum systems, government officials have compiled lists of "safe" countries. These are usually defined as countries that neither practice the kinds of persecution with which the 1951 Convention is

---

16. At the time that article was written, pending legislation would have imposed an even shorter deadline. Most of Schrag's arguments, however, addressed the general concept of time limits.

concerned, nor return refugees to countries that will persecute them. Two different uses have been made of such lists.

One kind of safe country provision is the so-called"safe third country" restriction; it is described in the next subsection. The other is the "safe country of origin" constraint. Under this approach, which is in place in some European countries, asylum claimants from countries that are on the safe list are presumed ineligible. The presumption might lead to actual denial or it might merely trigger a more summary procedure. The two sides of the debate are superbly represented by Rosemary Byrne & Andrew Shacknove, *The Safe Country Notion in European Asylum Law*, 9 Harvard Human Rights J. 185 (1996) (critical of the safe country of origin concept); and Kay Hailbronner, *The Concept of "Safe Country" and Expeditious Asylum Procedures: A Western European Perspective*, 5 Internat'l J. Refugee L. 31, 49–58 (1993) (supportive of it). The United States has not adopted or even seriously contemplated such a constraint.

iii. *Returning Asylum–Seekers to Third Countries*

Refugees today seldom take direct routes from their countries of origin to the countries in which they intend to request asylum. For a variety of reasons, refugees are usually forced to travel circuitous routes to their ultimate intended destinations. The movement from the country of origin to one of the intermediate ("third") countries is often called a "primary" movement. The subsequent movement from a third country to the country in which asylum is sought is usually called a "secondary" movement.

Earlier, you saw that a person who is found to have been "firmly resettled" in a third country is generally ineligible for asylum in the United States. The idea is that a person does not need, and therefore should not receive, asylum if he or she is already firmly (and safely) resettled elsewhere. The firm resettlement exception can be thought of as one subcategory of a broader notion sometimes referred to as "first country of asylum."

A related, but different, practice prevalent in many countries is the "safe third country" restriction. Under certain circumstances, if a person travels through one or more "safe" third countries before arriving in the country where the asylum application is filed, the latter country will refuse to decide the asylum claim on the merits and, instead, return him or her to that safe third country. The theory is not that the person in fact had been granted refuge in that third country; it is that the person *could*, and *should*, at least have requested it there.

In Europe, both sorts of third country limitations—first country of asylum restrictions and "safe third country" restrictions—are now common. Typically, they entail regional agreements whereby states accept common rules for determining which of them should adjudicate the asylum claims of individuals whose flights have taken them through several signatory states. Those agreements normally contain language that purports to assure that asylum applicants are sent only to "safe" countries for adjudication of their claims. But there is disagreement over the very concept of a "safe third country" limitation, over the definition of "safe," and over how the definition is applied in practice. There is some excellent European literature on this subject. See, e.g., Jacqueline Bhabha, *European Harmonisation of Asylum Policy: A Flawed Process*, 35 Virginia J. Internat'l L. 101 (1994) (dealing more generally with the notion of uniform immigration laws within Europe); Rosemary Byrne & Andrew Shacknove, *The Safe Country Notion in European Asylum Law*, 9 Harvard Human Rights J. 185 (1996); Rosemary Byrne, Gregor Noll & Jens Vested–Hansen (eds.), New Asylum Countries? Migration Control and Refugee Protection in an Enlarged European Union (2002); Maryellen Fullerton, *Failing the Test: Germany Leads Europe in Dismantling Refugee Protection*, 36 Texas Internat'l L.J. 231, 243–50 (2001); Kay Hailbronner, *The Concept of "Safe" Country and Expeditious Asylum Procedures: A Western European Perspective*, 5 Internat'l J. Refugee L. 31 (1993); Agnes Hurwitz, *The Dublin Convention: A Comprehensive Assessment*, 11 Internat'l J. Refugee L. 646 (1999); Reinhard Marx & Katharina Lumpp, *The German Constitutional Court's Decision of 14 May 1996 on the Concept of "Safe Third Countries"—A Basis for Burden–Sharing in Europe?*, 8 Internat'l J. Refugee L. 419 (1996); Gregor Noll, *Formalism vs. Empiricism: Some Reflections on the Dublin Convention on the Occasion of Recent European Case Law* (unpublished paper, 2001).

Third country restrictions raise fundamental legal and policy questions. Precisely how much legal freedom should a person have to choose the country in which he or she will request asylum? From the standpoints of countries of origin, third countries, ultimate destination countries, and the world community, how should the responsibility for protecting refugees be allocated?

Depending on the way they are applied, third country restrictions can serve a useful and legitimate role. But they have also engendered major problems, both for the asylum seekers themselves and for the third countries to which the applicants are returned:

There is, first, the problem of "orbit"—refugees who have escaped from persecution or from other trauma, only to be shuttled consecutively from one country to another. There is the more serious problem of "chain" refoulement, in which the third country in turn refoules the person to his or her persecutors in the country of origin. The third country might not have a fair refugee status determination procedure in place. The third country might not be a party to the 1951 Refugee Convention. The third country might not provide formal refugee or other lawful status or might not provide the kind of documentation that the person needs to procure the necessities of life or to travel. The protection afforded by the third country might not be durable. The third country might be unable to protect the person from discrimination, or persecution, or other human rights violations; indeed, the government of the third country might engage in those practices itself. There might be threats to the applicant's physical security or basic subsistence. The third country might practice indiscriminate or long-term detention or might otherwise inhibit essential freedom of movement. One recurring problem has been the return of asylum seekers to third countries to which they have no links or connections. There might be serious deficiencies in the procedures by which the *destination country* itself decides whether return is appropriate in a particular case. Finally, some of the more common destination state practices have the effect of distributing the responsibility for refugee protection inequitably, so that the obligations fall disproportionately on developing countries and on countries whose frontiers are geographically the most accessible.

Stephen H. Legomsky, *Secondary Refugee Movements and the Return of Asylum Seekers to Third Countries: The Meaning of Effective Protection*, 15 Internat'l J. Refugee L. 567, 572 (2003) (consultant's report to UNHCR).

These persistent problems prompted UNHCR to take up the entire question of "secondary" refugee movements as part of its Agenda for Protection. It has long been assumed that international law prohibits the return of asylum seekers to third countries unless those third countries will provide "effective protection." But the content of "effective protection" remains elusive. To determine precisely what elements constitute the international legal minima and what additional protections are recommended, UNHCR commissioned the consultant's report cited above. The report concluded with the following recommendations concerning the minimum legal requirements, and the best practice criteria, for the return of asylum seekers to third countries:

1. Minimum legal requirements

Under certain circumstances, a destination country (i.e., a country in which an asylum application has been lodged) may decline to determine the application in substance and instead return the applicant to a third country (i.e. a country other than the destination country or the country of origin). Such returns are permissible, however, only if all of the following conditions, collectively referred to as effective protection, are met:

1. The third country has explicitly agreed (a) to readmit the particular individual; and (b) to accord him or her either a fair refugee status determination or effective protection without such a determination. To protect the applicant's privacy interests, however, the assurance described in part (b) is not required, and should not be requested by the destination country, without the applicant's authorization.

2. The applicant has no well-founded fear of being persecuted, in the third country, on any of the 1951 Convention grounds.

3. The applicant has no well-founded fear of being refouled by the third country, directly or indirectly, to a territory where his or her life or freedom would be threatened on any of the 1951 Refugee Convention grounds. * * * If the third country is not a

party to the 1951 Refugee Convention or the 1967 Refugee Proto-col, that fact must be considered in determining whether this and the other minimum legal requirements for return have been met.

4.   The destination country may not knowingly return the appli-cant to a third country that will violate any of the applicant's rights under the 1951 Refugee Convention (apart from nonrefoule-ment, which is treated separately in criterion 3 above). The degree of certainty required by the word "knowingly" should vary in-versely with the importance of the particular right. With respect to those Convention rights that are contingent upon the refugee "lawfully staying" in the third country, the destination country is not required to speculate that lawful stay will be granted. * * *

5.   The destination country may not knowingly return the appli-cant to a third country that will breach any of the applicant's rights under any human rights agreement to which the destination country is a party. The degree of certainty required by the word "knowingly" should vary inversely with the importance of the particular right. For purposes of this criterion, these violations encompass both harms that occur in the third country and harms that might result from the third country sending the applicant elsewhere. Depending on the circumstances of the case, knowingly sending the applicant to a third country where he or she will lack either physical security or basic subsistence can be "cruel, inhu-man or degrading treatment" for purposes of the various human rights agreements that use that term.

6.   The third country will either provide a fair refugee status determination or provide effective protection without such a deter-mination. * * * Many first countries of asylum provide no formal refugee status determination but nonetheless provide some form of de facto protection. Such arrangements are not adequate substi-tutes for refugee status determinations, unless in the particular case the lack of formal status or documentation does not impair the other requirements of effective protection enumerated here. A fair refugee status determination also requires respect for the privacy interests of the applicant and his or her family, as well as consideration of any special vulnerabilities of the applicant. Spe-cially vulnerable groups include, but are not limited to, torture victims, women, subcategories of women (for example victims of rape or other sexual violence, pregnant women, and women who are single heads of households), children (especially unaccompa-nied children), the elderly, the physically or mentally disabled, and stateless persons.

7.   The third country is willing and able to provide effective protection for as long as the person remains a refugee or until another source of durable effective protection can be found.

8.   Even when the third country will otherwise provide effective protection, return is prohibited if, in the light of the applicant's

comparative family ties to the destination country and the third country, return would violate the applicant's internationally recognized right to family unity.

9. The destination country must apply each of the above criteria on an individual, case-by-case basis. The applicant may not be returned involuntarily to the third country until this procedure, including appeal, has been completed.

2. Best practice criteria

In addition to the above conditions, which constitute the minimum requirements of international law, the following safeguards are recommended as best practice criteria:

1. The applicant should not be returned to a third country with which he or she lacks meaningful links, even if that third country is otherwise willing and able to provide effective protection. Mere transit or other momentary physical presence in the third country should not be deemed sufficient. Examples of meaningful links include family connections, cultural ties, knowledge of the language, the possession of a residence permit, the applicant's previous period of residence in the other State, and any other connections that would expedite or enhance the prospects of integration. Among the cited examples, family unity is especially critical and is treated separately in the list of minimum legal requirements. The applicant's links to the third country should not be evaluated in isolation; rather, the test should be whether the applicant's links to the destination country are greater than his or her links to the third country. Finally, while not controlling, the applicant's preference—as distinguished from links—is a relevant factor that the destination country should take into account in deciding whether to divert the application to a third country.

* * *

6. Normally, an asylum applicant should not be returned to a third country that is not bound by the 1951 Refugee Convention and the 1967 Refugee Protocol.

7. * * * It is further recommended that states avoid relying on preformulated lists of "safe" countries, even though such lists are not barred when individuals are given the opportunity to rebut the presumption of safety.

Legomsky, above, at 673–76. For the "Summary Conclusions" from the Lisbon UNHCR Expert Round Table on the report, see www.unhcr.ch, Protecting Refugees, Legal and Protection Policy Research Series, Expert Meetings, Effective Protection (Lisbon, Dec. 2002), Summary Conclusions from the Round Table.

While the firm resettlement restriction has not had major consequences in the United States, recent developments portend larger significance for the concept of safe third country. In 1996 Congress disqualified from asylum any person whom the Secretary of DHS finds "may be removed, pursuant to a bilateral or multilateral agreement," to a third country in which the person's life or freedom would not be threatened on account of race, religion, etc., and where the person "would have access to a full and fair procedure for determining a claim to asylum or equivalent temporary protection" (unless the Secretary finds that granting asylum would be in the public interest). IIRIRA § 604(a), amending INA § 208(a)(2)(A). The Secretary's decision under that provision is not subject to judicial review. INA § 208(a)(3).

By its terms, that provision was not to become operative until the United States entered into a safe third country agreement with one or more other nations. That has now happened. After several years of negotiation that had foundered over concerns about the adequacy of United States protection, see Bill Frelick, *Who's on First? The Canada–U.S. Memorandum of Agreement on Asylum*, 73 IR 217 (Feb. 26, 1996), the United States and Canada in December 2002 entered into an agreement to allocate responsibility for deciding asylum claims. Agreement Between the Government of Canada and the Government of the United States of America Regarding Asylum Claims Made at Land Borders (Dec. 15, 2002) [hereafter cited as Canada–U.S. Agreement], text reproduced in advance in 79 IR at 1446 et seq. (Sept. 23, 2002). The agreement spells out the two countries' respective responsibilities for those asylum seekers who travel through the territory of one of the two countries before applying for asylum at a land border port of entry in the other.

The agreement defines the term "country of last presence" to mean either Canada or the United States when the person was physically present in that country immediately before claiming refugee status at a land border port of entry. Canada–United States Agreement, art. 1.1(a). (Note the agreement does not apply to asylum applications filed at airports or seaports or to applications filed by those who enter at unauthorized points.) The agreement goes on to say that the country of last presence is generally responsible for deciding the asylum claim. *Id*. art. 4.1. Exceptions relate to family unity, transit passengers, arriving passengers with non-transit visas, and certain individuals who are permitted to enter without visas. *Id*. arts. 4.2, 5. Either state may voluntarily accept an asylum application even if the agreement does not obligate it to do so. *Id*. art.6. Importantly, once one of the two states returns a person to the other, the latter must decide the asylum application itself; it cannot simply return the person to yet another country for an asylum decision. *Id*. art. 3. For the final implementing rules on the U.S. side (by DHS and EOIR), see 69 Fed. Reg. 69479 (Nov. 29, 2004).

For various reasons—some relating to geography and others relating to the two countries' differing refugee policies—far more people travel through the United States to apply for asylum in Canada than vice versa. The agreement will therefore result in Canada returning more asylum seekers to the United States than vice versa. That fact is of concern to refugee advocates, because of U.S. detention practices (discussed below) and other less favorable U.S. refugee policies. See generally Bill Frelick, *North America Considers Agreement to Deflect Asylum Seekers*, 7 BIB 1404 (Nov. 15, 2002); Audrey Macklin, *Disappearing Refugees: Reflections on the Canada–U.S. Safe Third Country Agreement*, 36 Columbia Human Rights L. Rev. 101 (2005). The willingness of the United States to enter into the agreement apparently reflected an unrelated quid pro quo of greater Canadian cooperation in national security matters.

iv. Expedited Removal

Amid mounting concerns over both high levels of illegal immigration and large numbers of asylum applicants, western nations are increasingly prone to prescribe various summary procedures for the admission and exclusion of noncitizens. The new procedures are designed to deter fraudulent entries, reduce the number of asylum applications, and dispose cheaply and speedily of those asylum applications that are filed. The United States established such a system in 1996. In that year AEDPA created, and IIRIRA amended, the expedited removal procedure that you encountered earlier. As you might recall, expedited removal kicks in when an immigration officer "determines" that an arriving noncitizen is inadmissible for lack of documents or for fraud. INA § 235(b)(1)(A)(i).

If an immigration officer invokes the expedited removal provision, and the person either requests asylum or otherwise indicates a fear of persecution, then an asylum officer interviews the person and performs a preliminary screening to decide whether there is a "credible fear of persecution." INA § 235(b)(1)(B)(i,ii). For this purpose, "credible fear" requires a "significant possibility ... that the alien could establish eligibility for asylum." INA § 235(b)(1)(B)(v). If the asylum officer finds a credible fear, the person is detained for "further consideration of the application for asylum." INA § 235(b)(1)(B)(ii). The statute does not say what form such further consideration will take, but the Justice Department regulations clarify that one who demonstrates "credible fear" is placed in regular removal proceedings for "full consideration of the asylum and withholding of removal claim in [regular removal] proceedings." 8 C.F.R. § 208.30(f) (2001).

Upon finding no credible fear, the asylum officer orders the person removed and writes up a report summarizing the facts and the reasons for the finding. INA § 235(b)(1)(B)(iii)(I, II). Upon the individual's request, an immigration judge will "promptly" review the finding of no credible fear, either in person or by telephone or video, within 24 hours if practicable, and "in no case later than 7 days after the date of the determination." INA § 235(b)(1)(B)(iii)(III). There is no other administrative review unless the person attests under penalty of perjury that he or she has already been admitted as an LPR, a refugee, or an asylee. INA § 235(b)(1)(C). Nor, with very limited exceptions, is there any judicial review. INA §§ 242(a)(2)(A), 242(e).

Information on the actual experience with expedited removal has proved difficult to obtain. The first important study was the Expedited Removal Study, a project based at the University of California at Hastings and led by Professor Karen Musalo. For several years the former INS, citing concerns of personal privacy, declined to release statistical data or files or to permit observation of the process by either the Expedited Removal Study or other NGOs. In 2000, however, after negotiations conducted during litigation over the Study's Freedom of Information Act request, the former INS released much of the requested data, though not all. See Karen Musalo, Lauren Gibson, Stephen Knight & J. Edward Taylor, The Expedited Removal Study, Report on the First Three Years of Implementation of Expedited Removal (May 2000).

The released data covered the years 1997 through 1999. One surprising finding was that, in each of the three years studied, between 80% and 89% of all the expedited removals were on grounds of suspected fraud rather than on grounds of invalid documentation. That fact is extremely important, because, as you saw in chapter 5, immigration fraud usually makes the person inadmissible for life. INA § 212(a)(6)(C). In contrast, those removed only because of invalid documentation under section 212(a)(7) become inadmissible only for five years. Id. § 212(a)(9)(A)(i). A frequent basis for a finding of fraud is that the person states an intention to return home upon the expiration of his or her temporary visa and the immigration inspector believes the true intention is to remain permanently. In other cases it is clear that the person has misstated a fact but there is uncertainty whether the misstatement was deliberate or inadvertent. Both a determination that a fact has been misstated and the determination that the misstatement was intentional require judgment.

Because the consequences of removal—both the five-year or lifetime ban on readmission and the possibility of erroneous return to persecution—are so serious, and because of other process concerns, Congress requested the General Accounting Office to study four questions (discussed below). See United States General Accounting Office, Illegal Aliens: Opportunities to Improve the Expedited Removal Process (Sept. 2000). The GAO found itself unable to answer the questions directly, citing a lack of expertise in legal matters, inadequate resources, and the lack of an acceptable methodology. It compiled some additional data and studied the then existing INS management controls, id., but little conclusive information emerged and the study was later exposed to serious criticisms. See Karen Musalo, Lauren Gibson, Stephen Knight & J. Edward Taylor, The Expedited Removal Study, Evaluation of the General Accounting Office's Second Report on Expedited Removal (Oct. 2000).

Congress turned next to the U.S. Commission on International Religious Freedom, a bipartisan Commission established by the International Religious Freedom Act of 1998, Pub. L. 105–292, 112 Stat. 2787 (Oct. 27, 1998) [IRFA], to monitor religious freedom worldwide. Section 605 of IRFA specifically authorized the Commission to study expedited removal (not just with respect to religious-based asylum claims) and to address the same four questions that had been directed to the GAO. The Commission's voluminous study, United States Commission on International Religious Freedom,

Report on Asylum Seekers in Expedited Removal (Feb. 2005), included the following findings, which it synthesized in the Executive Summary at 5–8:

The first question was whether immigration inspectors were inappropriately encouraging people to withdraw their applications for admission rather than face expedited removal (with its consequent bar on future admission). In cases in which there is little chance of admission, withdrawal is generally a sensible option, but the concern is whether significant numbers of people who might otherwise have been admitted felt pressured to withdraw. The Commission did not find a common practice of immigration inspectors pressuring arriving noncitizens to return voluntarily, but it found such cases on occasion and emphasized the gravity of the harm that can result.

The second area of congressional concern related to those noncitizens who did not voluntarily withdraw their applications. The question was whether immigration inspectors were wrongly failing to refer them for credible fear interviews. Here, the Commission found a more serious problem. Although immigration inspectors are required to refer applicants for credible fear interviews when the latter indicate fears of persecution, the Commission discovered that 15% of the applicants whom it observed expressing specific fears of persecution were returned without credible fear interviews.

A third congressional inquiry was whether asylum seekers were being wrongly returned to places where they feared persecution. One specific finding of the Commission was that in only 1% of the cases did the asylum officers find a lack of credible fear. In the remaining cases, the immigration judges who decided the asylum claims approved 25% of those in which the applicants were represented by counsel but only 2% of the others.

The fourth congressional concern was detention. If the asylum officer finds no credible fear of persecution, and the applicant requests that an immigration judge review that decision, then the applicant "shall be detained pending a final determination of credible fear of persecution and, if found not to have such a fear, until removed." INA § 235(b)(1)(B)(iii)(IV). The literal statutory language appears to contemplate detention even after an asylum officer finds a credible fear of persecution, INA § 235(b)(1)(B)(ii), but this provision has been assumed not to supersede the parole power of the Secretary of DHS. In actual practice, the Commission discovered, the release rates of those who are found to have credible fear, pending their merits determinations, varied dramatically from one location to another—from 98% in Harlengen, Texas to 0.5% in New Orleans.

A related congressional detention question—relevant not only to expedited removal but to detention—concerned the conditions of confinement. DHS uses a combination of its own detention facilities, private facilities, and local jails. The Commission expressed deep concern that asylum seekers are consistently detained in jails or jail-like facilities, often together with criminal offenders.

In the light of all this, there remains considerable difference of opinion concerning the benefits and dangers of expedited removal and concerning possible improvements. Some observers continue to feel that expedited removal discourages illegal immigration, disposes quickly and cheaply of those cases that present no substantial factual or legal issues, and saves administrative resources for the cases in which significant risks of persecution are truly presented. See David A. Martin, *Two Cheers for Expedited Removal in the New Immigration Laws*, 40 Virginia J. Internat'l L. 673 (2000). Other observers concede the legitimacy of those goals but contend that expedited removal—because of either the law itself or its implementation—sacrifices accuracy and procedural fairness to an unacceptable degree. In addition to the sources already cited, see, e.g., Lawyer's Committee for Human Rights, Slamming "The Golden Door": A Year of Expedited Removal (1998); Anthony Lewis, *A Bad Time for Civil Liberties*, 5 Annual Survey Internat'l & Comp. L. 1 (1999) (powerful attack, replete with concrete examples); Philip G. Schrag & Michele R. Pistone, *The New Asylum Rule: Not Yet a Model of Fair Procedure*, 11 Georgetown Immigration L.J. 267, 283–86 (1997); U.S. Commission on Immigration Reform, U.S. Refugee Policy: Taking Leadership 30–31 (June 1997) (expedited removal should not apply to asylum claimants).

For other helpful commentary describing the workings of expedited removal, see Bo Cooper, *Procedures for Expedited Removal and Asylum Screening under the Illegal Immigration Reform and Immigrant Responsibility Act of 1996*, 29 Connecticut L. Rev. 1501 (1997); Juan P. Osuna & Patricia Mariani, *Expedited Removal: Authorities, Implementation, and Ongoing Policy and Practice Issues*, Nov. 1997 Immigration Briefings.

v. *Detention*

Earlier you saw that certain noncitizens are detained while their admissibility or deportability is being decided. Special considerations come into play, however, when the person is an asylum applicant.

Congress and the executive branch increasingly detain asylum seekers pending decisions on their claims. There is no provision for detaining those who file affirmative applications, but those who apply for asylum in removal proceedings are ordinarily subject to the same detention rules as anyone else in those proceedings. Generally, they may be held without bond, released on bond, or paroled without bond. INA § 236(a).

In at least three situations asylum seekers in the United States encounter special detention rules. First, as you saw earlier, in expedited removal cases detention is the norm at least until there has been a finding of credible fear. Second, Haitian boat people are routinely detained, partly in an attempt to deter mass migrations by sea. Third, for a brief period under a program called Operation Liberty Shield, noncitizens from any of 34 countries that the government designated as sponsors of terrorism were automatically detained when they applied for asylum at U.S. ports of entry.

Both the Haitian detention program and Operation Liberty Shield were discussed in some detail in chapter 9, section A.1. As that discussion explained, national security has been the stated justification for both programs. In the case of the Haitian program, the national security argument is somewhat attenuated. The Attorney General's principal rationale has been that detention will deter mass migrations of boat people; deterring them, in turn, avoids having to divert enforcement resources that could be used to combat terrorism. Moreover, the Attorney General argued, potential terrorists from other countries might be on board Haitian vessels. See chapter 10, section A.1 below for the details.

Whether these various detention programs are compatible with United States obligations under the 1951 Convention has been the subject of recent debate. Article 26 of the Convention reads: "Each Contracting State shall accord to refugees lawfully within its territory the right to choose their place of residence and to move freely within its territory, subject to any regulations applicable to aliens generally in the same circumstances." (For present purposes, let us assume (1) that asylum applicants at ports of entry are "within [the] territory" of the state; and (2) that one who presents himself or herself at the frontier is lawfully exercising a right recognized in international law, as well as U.S. law, and is therefore "lawfully" within the state's territory.) Article 31 of the 1951 Convention, also relevant here, prohibits "penalties, on account of their illegal entry or presence, on refugees who, coming directly from a territory where their life or freedom was threatened ..., enter or are present in their territory without authorization, provided they present themselves without delay to the authorities and show good cause for their illegal entry or presence." Article 3 requires the contracting states to "apply the provisions of this Convention to refugees without discrimination as to race, religion *or country of origin*" (emphasis added). Finally, consider article 14 of the Universal Declaration of Human Rights, which recognizes a "right to seek and to enjoy in other countries asylum from persecution."

Do any of the U.S. detention programs for asylum-seekers violate any of these provisions? Based mainly on article 31, UNHCR has roundly condemned the detention of asylum seekers, absent exceptional circumstances found after individualized determinations (as distinguished from the use of mandatory detention categories). See UNHCR Revised Guidelines on Applicable Criteria and Standards Relating to the Detention of Asylum–Seekers (Feb. 1999), confirming UNHCR Executive Committee, Ex. Com. Conclusion 44, *Detention of Refugees and Asylum–Seekers*, No. 44 (XXXVII) (1986). Under the UNHCR Ex. Com. Conclusion and subsequent 1999 Guidelines, an asylum seeker may be detained only if it is "necessary" to accomplish one of four things—verify the person's identity; determine the elements on which the person's claim is based; respond to the destruction of travel or identity documents or the use of fraudulent documents to mislead the authorities of the state in which the person applies for asylum; and "to protect national security and public order." The last objective, like all the others, may be invoked only when the facts pertaining to the particular individual so require; there must be "evidence to show that the asylum-seeker has criminal antecedents and/or affiliations which are likely to pose a risk to public order or national security . . ." See 1999 Guidelines, Guideline 3. Even then, detention is subject to a number of other conditions. *Id.*, Guidelines 4–10.

UNHCR has responded more specifically to the selective detention of Haitians. An April 15, 2002 advisory opinion by the UNHCR regional representative, reproduced in 79 IR at 630 et seq. (Apr. 29, 2002), reiterated that "there must be an individualized analysis of the need to detain a particular individual." *Id.* at 635. Deterrence, it said, "is an inappropriate goal and insufficient reason for detention." *Id.* Finally, the opinion added, "[t]he detention of asylum seekers based on their national origin" is discriminatory and therefore violates article 3. *Id.* at 636.

These UNHCR authorities suggest that not only the Haitian detention policy, but also Operation Liberty Shield and the detention of those asylum seekers who are subjected to expedited removal, run afoul of United States obligations under the Convention. In both the latter programs, decisions are categorical rather than individualized, and in the case of Operation Liberty Shield the other UNHCR objections—deterrence as an insufficient reason to detain and discrimination based on country of origin—equally apply.

The Attorney General might well have legal arguments in opposition to those advanced by UNHCR, but as noted earlier in this chapter he has chosen, rather, to dismiss the UNHCR objections on the ground that the Convention and Protocol are not self-executing. See *Matter of D–J-*, 23 I. & N. Dec. 572, 584–85 n.8 (A.G. 2003). Again, while a non-self-executing treaty cannot be enforced *in a domestic court*, it is not clear why the executive branch assumes it would not be bound by U.S. treaty obligations on the *international* plane.

The U.S. Commission on Immigration Reform similarly criticized detention in expedited removal cases, at least once credible fear has been found. U.S. Commission on Immigration Reform, U.S. Refugee Policy: Taking Leadership 32–33 (June 1997). While ICE frequently asserted that 85% of noncitizens in ICE custody fail to appear (aggregating noncitizens in pending removal proceedings with those who have been finally ordered removed), the Commission, using data provided by EOIR, found that among the relevant population—asylum claimants who had demonstrated credible fear and who had been released pending their removal hearings—the nonappearance rate was only 22%. See Bill Frelick, *U.S. Detention of Asylum Seekers: What's the Problem? What's the Solution?*, 10 BIB 159 (Apr. 1, 2005).

The commentary has been highly critical of recent U.S. detention policy for asylum claimants. In addition to the writings noted on pages 229 and 636–37 above, see, e.g., Amnesty International, United States of America: Lost in the Labyrinth: Detention of Asylum–Seekers, Rpt. AMR51/51/99 (Sept. 1999); Human Rights First, In Liberty's Shadow–U.S. Detention of Asylum Seekers in the Era of Homeland Security (2004); Michele R. Pistone, *Justice Delayed is Justice Denied: A Proposal for*

Ending the Unnecessary Detention of Asylum Seekers, 12 Harvard Human Rights J. 197 (1999) (arguing for rules modeled on those for pre-trial detention in criminal cases); Nicholas J. Rizza, *INS Detention: The Impact on Asylum Seekers*, 17 Refugee Reports No. 8, at 2 (Aug. 30, 1996) (describing the severe conditions). Others, while similarly deploring the conditions in which asylum claimants are confined, have additionally argued that detention tends to be ordered too often and for too long. See, e.g., Women's Commission for Refugee Women and Children, Liberty Denied: Women Seeking Asylum Imprisoned in the United States (April 1997); Women's Commission for Refugee Women and Children, An Uncertain Future, A Cruel Present: Women in INS Detention (1996), reviewed in 73 IR at 371 (Mar. 25, 1996).

vi. Criminal Prosecutions of Asylum–Seekers for Illegal Entry

In a departure from past practice, United States federal prosecutors are increasingly bringing criminal prosecutions against asylum seekers for entering the country with false documents. The practice came to light in South Florida, where "local attorneys report that some asylum seekers are arrested upon arrival at Miami International Airport while others have been charged after months of immigration detention." Tanya Weinberg, *Asylum Seekers Face U.S. Charges: Prosecutors Say Dozens Entered Country Illegally*, Sun–Sentinel (Ft. Lauderdale), Apr. 16, 2003. From fall 2003 through April 2004, the U.S. Attorney's Office in Miami obtained 75–80 such federal indictments. See Kathleen Sullivan, *The Year in Detention Law and Policy: Immigration Detention Developments May 2003–April 2004*, 9 BIB 851 (July 15, 2004). Some similar prosecutions were initiated in the United Kingdom until a court declared the practice violates article 31 of the 1951 Convention (the penalty provision discussed in subsection v above). See *R. v. Uxbridge Magistrates' Court, ex parte Adimi* [2001] Q.B. 667.

These practices raise serious issues. Eleanor Acer, the asylum program director for the Lawyers Committee for Human Rights, commented: "There's longstanding recognition that sometimes refugees are forced to flee from their persecutors with false documents.... That's why Raoul Wallenberg is seen as a hero, for giving false passports to Jews fleeing the Holocaust." Weinberg, above.

With those practicalities in mind, the drafters of the 1951 Convention included article 31, which you saw in the preceding subsections. The prohibition on penalizing refugees for illegal entry (including the use of false documents) is, however, subject to several conditions. Some of those conditions are highly indeterminate. When will refugees be found to have come "directly" from their countries of origin? Given the circuitous routes that refugees are often forced to take, this issue is critical. And what will constitute "good cause for their illegal entry or presence?" The British court in *Adimi*, above, took a broad view of the drafters' desire to immunize asylum seekers from being penalized for false documents. For a thorough and thoughtful treatment of article 31, see Guy S. Goodwin–Gill,

Article 31 of the 1951 Convention Relating to the Status of Refugees: Non-penalization, Detention and Protection, in Erika Feller, Volker Türk & Frances Nicholson (eds.), Refugee Protection in International Law: UNHCR's Global Consultations on International Protection, at 185–252 (2003).

One especially difficult problem is the interpretation of the "without delay" language of article 31. When a person applies for asylum immediately upon arrival at a port of entry, there is obviously no delay issue. (There might be a "coming directly" problem, depending on how long it took the person to reach the port of entry and by what route.) Similarly, the court in *Adimi* had no difficulty applying article 31 to individuals who had applied for asylum within a few days after their arrival in the U.K. But suppose a person who entered on false documents (or who evaded inspection) is apprehended months later and criminally prosecuted for the irregular entry. If the person then applies for asylum, must prosecution cease? If the asylum claim is ultimately denied, may prosecution then resume? The policy questions are difficult. On the one hand, a liberal interpretation of article 31 assures that valid claims are not chilled by the prospect of criminal prosecution. On the other hand, the Convention drafters surely did not intend to give everyone charged with illegal entry the power to stave off criminal charges simply by filing an asylum application. How and where the line should be drawn remains an unsettled issue.

vii. Denying Employment Authorization

Until 1995, it was relatively easy for an asylum claimant to obtain permission to work while the claim was pending. The claimant would apply for asylum and work authorization at the same time, and the latter would be granted within 90 days unless the application was found "frivolous." 8 C.F.R. § 208.7(a) (1995). As a result of the 1994 amendments to the Justice Department regulations (effective January 4, 1995), now effectively codified by INA § 208(d)(2), USCIS is barred from granting employment authorization until 180 days after the filing of the asylum application. Upon receiving asylum, the person automatically acquires the right to work. INA § 208(c)(1)(B). The goal was to discourage the filing of unfounded asylum claims.

In fact, asylum applications did drop markedly once the 1994 amendments to the regulations went into effect. Former INS Commissioner Doris Meissner attributed much of the decline to the new restrictions on employment authorization, stating that "INS has removed the primary incentive for baseless asylum claims." 73 IR at 46 (Jan. 10, 1996).

Measuring the causal connection between the more restrictive work authorization rules and the drop in filings is difficult. More difficult, perhaps, is measuring the human costs of those restrictions. With no welfare benefits and no right to work, how do asylum claimants—genuine refugees, noncitizens who file manifestly unfounded applications, and all those in between—survive? The answer that most private social service providers give is "not very well". See especially 17 Refugee Rpts. No. 6 at

6–7 (June 30, 1996) (more homelessness, psychological deterioration, stress, illegal work, exploitation, and begging). Other high-volume asylum countries, in contrast, either allow asylum claimants to work while their claims are pending or provide welfare. *Id.*

viii. Sanctioning Frivolous Applications

Earlier, you saw that attorneys and accredited representatives who engage in "frivolous behavior" in various immigration settings are subject to a range of disciplinary sanctions. Since the sanctions specifically govern behavior that takes place in proceedings before immigration judges or the BIA, they are fully applicable to asylum claims.

In addition to potential sanctions on the attorneys and representatives, IIRIRA § 604(a) imposed sanctions on the applicants themselves. Under INA § 208(d)(4)(A), the Secretary of Homeland Security must warn every asylum applicant of the consequences of filing a frivolous application for asylum. INA § 208(d)(6) then renders any noncitizen who "has knowingly made a frivolous application for asylum" and who has received the required notice "permanently ineligible for any benefits" under the INA. That sanction requires a specific finding of frivolousness by an immigration judge or the BIA. 8 C.F.R. § 208.20 (2004).

ix. Application Fees

Should the government charge an application fee for asylum or withholding of removal, or for permission to work while an asylum claim is pending? At present it does not do so, 8 C.F.R. § 103.7(b) (2004), although there is a fee for renewing or replacing a work authorization, *id.* § 274a.13(a)(2). The Justice Department in 1994 proposed charging $130 to apply for asylum and another $60 to apply for initial work authorization. 59 Fed.Reg. 14779, 14781, 14784 (Dec. 5, 1994). The former INS promoted the proposal mainly as a revenue measure and as an equitable "user-pays" device, 59 Fed.Reg. at 14781, but the proposal is included in the present discussion because its purpose and its effect could also be to discourage the filing of baseless asylum claims.

Commenters raised vigorous objections, both philosophical and practical. One practical obstacle proved fatal. The Department recognized that many genuine refugees would be unable to afford the proposed filing fees. It would therefore be necessary to waive the fees for indigent applicants. But indigence would have to be proved, and proof requires procedure. Since the stated purpose of the proposed application fees was to raise revenue, an expensive new system just to adjudicate requests for fee waivers would have been self-defeating. Consequently, the proposal was dropped. 59 Fed.Reg. at 62286–87, 62291 (Dec. 5, 1994). In IIRIRA § 604(a), Congress added a new INA § 208(d)(3) expressly authorizing the Attorney General (now the Secretary of Homeland Security) to charge filing fees for asylum and certain related applications, but at this writing the government has shown no interest in resurrecting the fee proposal. See 62 Fed.Reg. 444, 448 (Jan. 3, 1997).

x. Preinspection

Normally, the inspection of a noncitizen who seeks admission to the United States takes place at an authorized U.S. port of entry. For many years, however, the former INS—sometimes in conjunction with the former Customs Service—operated inspections stations at foreign airports. That practice continues; today, there are "pre-flight inspection" stations in 12 airports in Canada, the Bahamas, Bermuda, Aruba, and Ireland, as well as seaports in Vancouver and Victoria, Canada. 69 Fed. Reg. 51695 (Aug. 20, 2004). The idea is that passengers can be inspected before they make journeys to the United States, and, if found inadmissible, will not face voyages home. Of course, those travelers also do not have recourse to the adjudicative system available to most other arriving noncitizens—an evidentiary hearing before an immigration judge, appeal to the BIA, and a right of judicial review. INA § 235A requires the establishment of additional pre-inspection stations in foreign airports. They must be located in countries that observe the 1951 Convention or the 1967 Protocol. INA § 235A(a)(5)(C).

Many concerns have been expressed. They include the difficulties of successful negotiation with the host countries, the financial costs, the practical problems for returning residents who lose their green cards, and the fear that asylum claimants will be too casually screened out and unable to secure review. 73 IR at 1533–34 (Nov. 4, 1996).

xi. Visas and Carrier Sanctions

The combination of two other devices operates as a practical bar to the asylum system for many potential applicants. Under United States law, like that of most other major asylum countries, asylum requires that the person be "physically present in the United States" or arriving at a port of entry. INA § 208(a)(1). If the person cannot get to the port of entry, asylum is impossible.

A noncitizen normally requires a visa to gain admission to the United States. INA § 212(a)(7)(A)(i)(I). And commercial carriers are subject to heavy fines when they transport noncitizens to ports of entry without the required visas. INA § 273. For that reason, airlines and shipping lines will not board passengers who lack required visas. If the person is a refugee, the practical consequence is that he or she never gets the chance even to apply for asylum unless a false document convincing enough to fool the carrier can be procured.

xii. Interdiction of Vessels on the High Seas

One last device for preventing potential asylum claimants from gaining access to the asylum adjudication system requires a more extended discussion. The modern phenomenon of "boat-people" has been met, by some nations, with a strategy known as "interdiction," or "pushbacks." The intended asylum nation intercepts vessels suspected of carrying would-be entrants and either turns the vessels away before they reach the nation's shores or destroys the vessels and returns the passengers to their home countries. An estimated 4,000 boat people drown at sea each year, approximately half of them in the Mediterranean while crossing from northern Africa to southern Europe. See Owen Bowcott, *4000 Refugees Believed Drowned at Sea Every Year*, The Guardian (Oct. 9, 2004).

The most massive of the early pushback operations took place in Southeast Asia, see generally U.S. Comm. for Refugees, 11 Refugee Reports No. 5 at 1–8 (May 18, 1990), but boat-people from Haiti began fleeing ruthless regimes in significant numbers in the 1970's and have generally been interdicted by the United States, as discussed below. There have also been intermittent interceptions of Albanian boat people by Italian authorities, as well as highly controversial and longstanding interdictions of all suspected refugee vessels by Australia, see, e.g., Penelope Mathew, *Address–Legal Issues Concerning Interdiction*, 17 Georgetown Immigration L.J. 221 (2003). Recently the U.S. has been intercepting vessels off the coast of Ecuador and asserting the U.S. right to board and destroy vessels on the High Seas anywhere on the world. See Bruce Finley, *U.S. Takes Border War on the Road*, Denver Post (Feb. 23, 2005).

The initial response of the United States to the Haitian exodus was the Haitian Migrant Interdiction Program, designed to head off the Haitians before they could reach United States territory and acquire the right to formal hearings on their asylum claims. The history and mechanics of the program, as well as the problems with it, are well described in a detailed study by the Lawyers Committee for Human Rights, Refugee Refoulement: The Forced Return of Haitians Under the U.S.–Haitian Interdiction Agreement (Feb.1990). The following, which draws heavily on the Lawyers Committee report, summarizes the program and its results (with editorial commentary):

> During his first year in office, President Reagan, concerned about these numbers, entered into a co-operative agreement with the government of Haiti. The agreement authorized United States officials to board Haitian flag vessels on the high seas and to question the crew and passengers about "the registry, condition and destination of the vessel, and the status of those on board the vessel." If as a result of that questioning the U.S. officials find that a violation of either U.S. or Haitian law "has been or is being committed," then the U.S. officials are authorized to return the vessel to Haiti. At the same time, however, the United States pledged not to return to Haiti any migrant who is found to qualify as a refugee. To this end, the official INS programme guidelines provide:

> "If the interview suggests that a legitimate claim to refugee status exists, the person involved shall be removed from the

interdicted vessel, and his or her passage to the United States shall be arranged."

To implement the co-operative agreement, United States Coast Guard cutters with INS officials on board patrol the Windward Passage, the body of water that separates Haiti from Cuba and through which most ocean travel from Haiti to the United States customarily passes. In the event the Haitian vessel escapes through the Windward Passage undetected, another United States Coast Guard cutter patrols the coast of Miami. These naval operations are reinforced by aerial surveillance. If an aircraft picks up what looks like a suspicious vessel, it transmits the information to a central command centre, which in turn relays the information to the nearest Coast Guard cutter. The cutter then intercepts the vessel, and INS officials on board the cutter supervise the transfer of the passengers and crew from the Haitian vessel to the Coast Guard cutter, where the interviews take place. Although the INS programme guidelines require that the interviews be conducted out of the hearing of others, the interviews in fact are frequently held within eyesight, and sometimes (according to the Haitians) within hearing, of other passengers.

* * *

The reality is that it is almost unheard of for a Haitian who has been intercepted on the high seas ultimately to receive asylum in the United States. The Lawyers Committee Report compiled telling statistics. From the inception of the programme in 1981 until the time of the report (February 1990), the United States interdicted 364 vessels on the high seas and returned more than 21,000 Haitians. Out of that total, six Haitians were transported to the United States to apply for asylum.

The government takes great pride in those figures. It sees the high number of apprehensions as evidence that the interdiction programme is working. It points out that, but for this programme, up to 21,000 additional Haitians might have entered United States territory illegally. As for the low success rate on the asylum claims, the government sees this as confirmation of its long-held view that aliens fleeing Haiti are almost invariably economic migrants rather than political refugees.

I am unable to share the government's pride in those statistics. Respected human rights organizations have consistently documented the high incidence of grotesque human rights violations in Haiti. Given those reports, one can be forgiven for asking whether the low success rate has less to do with the merits of the claims than with the adequacy of the procedures.

Stephen H. Legomsky, *The Haitian Interdiction Programme, Human Rights, and the Role of Judicial Protection,* Int'l J. Refugee L. at 182–83 (special ed.1990); see also Lory Diana Rosenberg, *The Courts and Intercep-*

tion: The United States' Interdiction Experience and Its Impact on Refugees and Asylum Seekers, 17 Georgetown Immigration L.J. 199 (2003).

Some positive developments for the Haitian boat people were to follow. After the election of President Jean–Bertrand Aristide in December 1990, the number of Haitians fleeing the country dropped off dramatically. Miami Herald, March 20, 1991, at 1A. The Haitians anticipated substantial political reform. That emigration dropped off so suddenly without a corresponding change in the poverty levels vindicated the long held view of refugee advocates that large numbers of Haitians had been leaving out of genuine fear of political persecution rather than for purely economic reasons. *Id*; see also Kathleen Newland, *The Impact of U.S. Refugee Policies on U.S. Foreign Policy: A Case of the Tail Wagging the Dog?*, in Michael S. Teitelbaum & Myron Weiner (eds.), Threatened Peoples, Threatened Borders, ch. 5, at 199 (1995) (boat traffic dropped suddenly upon election of Aristide and then soared immediately upon his overthrow).

As the following case reveals, however, the Haitians' troubles were just beginning and the full implications of interdiction as a core element of United States refugee policy were just emerging:

Sale v. Haitian Centers Council

Supreme Court of the United States, 1993.
509 U.S. 155, 113 S.Ct. 2549, 125 L.Ed.2d 128.

■ JUSTICE STEVENS delivered the opinion of the Court.

The President has directed the Coast Guard to intercept vessels illegally transporting passengers from Haiti to the United States and to return those passengers to Haiti without first determining whether they may qualify as refugees. The question presented in this case is whether such forced repatriation, "authorized to be undertaken only beyond the territorial sea of the United States," violates § 243(h)(1) [now 241(b)(3)—Ed.] of the Immigration and Nationality Act of 1952 (INA or Act). We hold that neither § 243(h) nor Article 33 of the United Nations Protocol Relating to the Status of Refugees applies to action taken by the Coast Guard on the high seas.

I

* * * The INA offers [asylum and withholding of removal] only to aliens who reside in or have arrived at the border of the United States. For 12 years, in one form or another, the interdiction program challenged here has prevented Haitians such as respondents from reaching our shores and invoking those protections.

On September 23, 1981, the United States and the Republic of Haiti entered into an agreement authorizing the United States Coast Guard to intercept vessels engaged in the illegal transportation of undocumented aliens to our shores. While the parties agreed to prosecute "illegal traffickers," the Haitian Government also guaranteed that its repatriated citizens would not be punished for their illegal departure. The agreement also established that the United States Government would not return any passengers "whom the United States authorities determined to qualify for refugee status."

On September 29, 1981, President Reagan * * * suspended the entry of undocumented aliens from the high seas and ordered the Coast Guard to intercept vessels carrying such aliens and to return them to their point of origin. His executive order expressly "provided, however, that no person who is a refugee will be returned without his consent."

In the ensuing decade, the Coast Guard interdicted approximately 25,000 Haitian migrants. After interviews conducted on board Coast Guard cutters, aliens who were identified as economic migrants were "screened out" and promptly repatriated. Those who made a credible showing of political refugee status were "screened in" and transported to the United States to file formal applications for asylum.

On September 30, 1991, a group of military leaders displaced the government of Jean Bertrand Aristide, the first democratically elected president in Haitian history. As the District Court stated in an uncontested finding of fact, since the military coup "hundreds of Haitians have been killed, tortured, detained without a warrant, or subjected to violence and the destruction of their property because of their political beliefs. Thousands have been forced into hiding." Following the coup the Coast Guard suspended repatriations for a period of several weeks, and the United States imposed economic sanctions on Haiti.

On November 18, 1991, the Coast Guard announced that it would resume the program of interdiction and forced repatriation. * * *

In the meantime the Haitian exodus expanded dramatically. During the six months after October 1991, the Coast Guard interdicted over 34,000 Haitians. Because so many interdicted Haitians could not be safely processed on Coast Guard cutters, the Department of Defense established temporary facilities at the United States Naval Base in Guantanamo, Cuba, to accommodate them during the screening process. Those temporary facilities, however, had a capacity of only about 12,500 persons. In the first three weeks of May 1992, the Coast Guard intercepted 127 vessels (many of which were considered unseaworthy, overcrowded, and unsafe); those vessels carried 10,497 undocumented aliens. On May 22, 1992, the United States Navy determined that no additional migrants could safely be accommodated at Guantanamo.

With both the facilities at Guantanamo and available Coast Guard cutters saturated, and with the number of Haitian emigrants in unseaworthy craft increasing (many had drowned as they attempted the trip to Florida), the Government could no longer both protect our borders and offer the Haitians even a modified screening process. It had to choose between allowing Haitians into the United States for the screening process or repatriating them without giving them any opportunity to establish their qualifications as refugees. In the judgment of the President's advisors, the first choice not only would have defeated the original purpose of the program (controlling illegal immigration), but also would have impeded diplomatic efforts to restore democratic government in Haiti and would have posed a life-threatening danger to thousands of persons embarking on long voyages in dangerous craft. The second choice would have advanced those policies but deprived the fleeing Haitians of any screening process at a time when a significant minority of them were being screened in.

On May 23, 1992, President Bush adopted the second choice. After assuming office, President Clinton decided not to modify that order; it remains in effect today. The wisdom of the policy choices made by Presidents Reagan, Bush, and Clinton is not a matter for our consideration. We must decide only whether Executive Order No. 12807, which reflects and implements those choices, is consistent with § 243(h) of the INA.

II

Respondents filed this lawsuit * * * before the promulgation of Executive Order No. 12807. The plaintiffs include organizations that represent interdicted Haitians as well as Haitians who were then being detained at Guantanamo. They sued the Commissioner of the Immigration and Naturalization Service, the Attorney General, the Secretary of State, the Commandant of the Coast Guard, and the Commander of the Guantanamo Naval Base, complaining that the screening procedures provided on Coast Guard cutters and at Guantanamo did not adequately protect their statutory and treaty rights to apply for refugee status and avoid repatriation to Haiti.

They alleged that the September 1991 coup had "triggered a continuing widely publicized reign of terror in Haiti"; that over 1,500 Haitians were believed to "have been killed or subjected to violence and destruction of their property because of their political beliefs and affiliations"; and that thousands of Haitian refugees "have set out in small boats that are often overloaded, unseaworthy, lacking basic safety equipment, and operated by inexperienced persons, braving the hazards of a prolonged journey over high seas in search of safety and freedom."

In April, the District Court granted the plaintiffs a preliminary injunction requiring defendants to give Haitians on Guantanamo access to counsel for the screening process. We stayed that order on April 22, 1992, and, while the defendants' appeal from it was pending, the President issued the Executive Order now under attack. Plaintiffs then applied for a temporary restraining order to enjoin implementation of the Executive Order. They contended that it violated § 243(h) of the Act and Article 33 of the United Nations Protocol Relating to the Status of Refugees. The District Court denied the application because it concluded that § 243(h) is "unavailable as a source of relief for Haitian aliens in international waters," and that such a statutory provision was necessary because the Protocol's provisions are not "self-executing."

The Court of Appeals reversed. * * * [T]he Court held that § 243(h)(1) does not apply only to aliens within the United States. * * *

* * *

The Second Circuit's decision conflicted with the Eleventh Circuit's decision in Haitian Refugee Center v. Baker, 953 F.2d 1498 (1992). * * * Because of the manifest importance of the issue, we granted certiorari.

III

Both parties argue that the plain language of § 243(h)(1) is dispositive. It reads as follows:

> "The Attorney General shall not deport or return any alien * * * to a country if the Attorney General determines that such alien's life or freedom would be threatened in such country on account of race, religion, nationality, membership in a particular social group, or political opinion."[a]

Respondents emphasize the words "any alien" and "return"; neither term is limited to aliens within the United States. Respondents also contend that the 1980 amendment deleting the words "within the United States" from the prior text of § 243(h) obviously gave the statute an extraterritorial effect. This change, they further argue, was required in order to conform the statute to the text of Article 33.1 of the Convention, which they find as unambiguous as the present statutory text. Petitioners' response is that a fair reading of the INA as a whole demonstrates that § 243(h) does not apply to actions taken by the President or Coast Guard outside the United States; that the legislative history of the 1980 amendment supports their reading; and that both the text and the negotiating history of Article 33 of the Convention indicate that it was not intended to have any extraterritorial effect.

* * *

A.   The Text and Structure of the INA

Although § 243(h)(1) refers only to the Attorney General, the Court of Appeals found it "difficult to believe that the proscription of § 243(h)(1)—returning an alien to his persecutors—was forbidden if done by the Attorney General but permitted if done by some other arm of the executive branch." Congress "understood" that the Attorney General is the "President's agent for dealing with immigration matters," and would intend any reference to her to restrict similar actions of any government official. As evidence of this understanding, the court cited 8 U.S.C. § 1103(a). That section, however, conveys to us a different message. It provides, in part:

> "The Attorney General shall be charged with the administration and enforcement of this chapter and all other laws relating to the immigration

---

a. IIRIRA modified that wording. See   this case.—Ed.
item 12 in the Notes and Questions following

and naturalization of aliens, *except insofar as this chapter or such laws relate to the powers, functions, and duties conferred upon the President, the Secretary of State, the officers of the Department of State, or diplomatic or consular officers....*" (Emphasis added) [by the Court].

Other provisions of the Act expressly confer certain responsibilities on the Secretary of State, the President, and, indeed, on certain other officers as well. The 1981 and 1992 Executive Orders expressly relied on statutory provisions that confer authority on the President to suspend the entry of "any class of aliens" or to "impose on the entry of aliens any restrictions he may deem to be appropriate." We cannot say that the interdiction program created by the President, which the Coast Guard was ordered to enforce, usurped authority that Congress had delegated to, or implicated responsibilities that it had imposed on, the Attorney General alone.

The reference to the Attorney General in the statutory text is significant not only because that term cannot reasonably be construed to describe either the President or the Coast Guard, but also because it suggests that it applies only to the Attorney General's normal responsibilities under the INA. The most relevant of those responsibilities for our purposes are her conduct of the deportation and exclusion hearings in which requests for asylum or for withholding of deportation under § 243(h) are ordinarily advanced. Since there is no provision in the statute for the conduct of such proceedings outside the United States, and since Part V and other provisions of the INA obviously contemplate that such proceedings would be held in the country, we cannot reasonably construe § 243(h) to limit the Attorney General's actions in geographic areas where she has not been authorized to conduct such proceedings. Part V of the INA contains no reference to a possible extraterritorial application.

Even if Part V of the Act were not limited to strictly domestic procedures, the presumption that Acts of Congress do not ordinarily apply outside our borders would support an interpretation of § 243(h) as applying only within United States territory. * * * The Court of Appeals held that the presumption against extraterritoriality had "no relevance in the present context" because there was no risk that § 243(h), which can be enforced only in United States courts against the United States Attorney General, would conflict with the laws of other nations. We have recently held, however, that the presumption has a foundation broader than the desire to avoid conflict with the laws of other nations. *Smith v. United States*, 113 S.Ct. 1178, 1183 (1993).

Respondents' expansive interpretation of the word "return" raises another problem: it would make the word "deport" redundant. If "return" referred solely to the destination to which the alien is to be removed, it alone would have been sufficient to encompass aliens involved in both deportation and exclusion proceedings. And if Congress had meant to refer to all aliens who might be sent back to potential oppressors, regardless of their location, the word "deport" would have been unnecessary. By using both words, the statute implies an exclusively territorial application, in the context of both kinds of domestic immigration proceedings. The use of both words reflects the traditional division between the two kinds of aliens and the two kinds of hearings. We can reasonably conclude that Congress used the two words "deport or return" only to make § 243(h)'s protection available in both deportation and exclusion proceedings. Indeed, the history of the 1980 amendment confirms that conclusion.

B.   The History of the Refugee Act of 1980

As enacted in 1952, § 243(h) authorized the Attorney General to withhold deportation of aliens "within the United States." Six years later we considered the question whether it applied to an alien who had been paroled into the country while her admissibility was being determined. We held that even though she was physically present within our borders, she was not "within the United States" as those words were used in § 243(h). *Leng May Ma v. Barber*, 357 U.S. 185, 186 (1958). We explained the important distinction between "deportation" or "expulsion," on the one hand, and "exclusion," on the other.

* * *

Under the INA, both then and now, those seeking "admission" and trying to avoid "exclusion" were already within our territory (or at its border), but the law treated them as though they had never entered the United States at all; they were within United States territory but not "within the United States." Those who had been admitted (or found their way in) but sought to avoid "expulsion" had the added benefit of "deportation proceedings"; they were both within United States territory and "within the United States." Although the phrase "within the United States" presumed the alien's actual presence in the United States, it had more to do with an alien's legal status than with his location.

The 1980 amendment erased the long-maintained distinction between deportable and excludable aliens for purposes of § 243(h). By adding the word "return" and removing the words "within the United States" from § 243(h), Congress extended the statute's protection to both types of aliens, but it did nothing to change the presumption that both types of aliens would continue to be found only within United States territory. The removal of the phrase "within the United States" cured the most obvious drawback of § 243(h): as interpreted in *Leng May Ma*, its protection was available only to aliens subject to deportation proceedings.

Of course, in addition to this most obvious purpose, it is possible that the 1980 amendment also removed any territorial limitation of the statute, and Congress might have intended a double-barreled result. That possibility, however, is not a substitute for the affirmative evidence of intended extraterritorial application that our cases require. * * *

The addition of the phrase "or return" and the deletion of the phrase "within the United States" are the only relevant changes made by the 1980 amendment to § 243(h)(1), and they are fully explained by the intent to apply § 243(h) to exclusion as well as to deportation proceedings. That

intent is plainly identified in the legislative history of the amendment.
* * *

In sum, all available evidence about the meaning of § 243(h)—the government official at whom it is directed, its location in the Act, its failure to suggest any extraterritorial application, the 1980 amendment that gave it a dual reference to "deport or return," and the relevance of that dual structure to immigration law in general—leads unerringly to the conclusion that it applies in only one context: the domestic procedures by which the Attorney General determines whether deportable and excludable aliens may remain in the United States.

IV

* * * [B]ecause the history of the 1980 Act does disclose a general intent to conform our law to Article 33 of the Convention, it might be argued that the extraterritorial obligations imposed by Article 33 were so clear that Congress, in acceding to the Protocol, and then in amending the statute to harmonize the two, meant to give the latter a correspondingly extraterritorial effect. Or, just as the statute might have imposed an extraterritorial obligation that the Convention does not (the argument we have just rejected), the Convention might have established an extraterritorial obligation which the statute does not; under the Supremacy Clause, that broader treaty obligation might then provide the controlling rule of law. With those possibilities in mind we shall consider both the text and negotiating history of the Convention itself.

Like the text and the history of § 243(h), the text and negotiating history of Article 33 of the United Nations Convention are both completely silent with respect to the Article's possible application to actions taken by a country outside its own borders. Respondents argue that the Protocol's broad remedial goals require that a nation be prevented from repatriating refugees to their potential oppressors whether or not the refugees are within that nation's borders. In spite of the moral weight of that argument, both the text and negotiating history of Article 33 affirmatively indicate that it was not intended to have extraterritorial effect.

A.   The Text of the Convention

* * *

The full text of Article 33 reads as follows:

"Article 33.—Prohibition of expulsion or return ('refoulement')

"1. No Contracting State shall expel or return (*'refouler'*) a refugee in any manner whatsoever to the frontiers of territories where his life or freedom would be threatened on account of his race, religion, nationality, membership of a particular social group or political opinion.

"2. The benefit of the present provision may not, however, be claimed by a refugee whom there are reasonable grounds for regarding as a danger to the security of *the country in which he is,* or who, having been convicted by a final judgment of a particularly serious crime, constitutes a danger to the community of that country." Convention Relating to the Status of Refugees, July 28, 1951 [emphasis added by the Court].

Under the second paragraph of Article 33 an alien may not claim the benefit of the first paragraph if he poses a danger to the country in which he is located. If the first paragraph did apply on the high seas, no nation could invoke the second paragraph's exception with respect to an alien there: an alien intercepted on the high seas is in no country at all. If Article 33.1 applied extraterritorially, therefore, Article 33.2 would create an absurd anomaly: dangerous aliens on the high seas would be entitled to the benefits of 33.1 while those residing in the country that sought to expel them would not. It is more reasonable to assume that the coverage of 33.2 was limited to those already in the country because it was understood that 33.1 obligated the signatory state only with respect to aliens within its territory.

Article 33.1 uses the words "expel or return ('refouler')" as an obvious parallel to the words "deport or return" in § 243(h)(1). There is no dispute that "expel" has the same meaning as "deport"; it refers to the deportation or expulsion of an alien who is already present in the host country. The dual reference identified and explained in our opinion in *Leng May Ma v. Barber*, suggests that the term "return ('refouler')" refers to the exclusion of aliens who are merely "on the threshold of initial entry."

This suggestion—that "return" has a legal meaning narrower than its common meaning—is reinforced by the parenthetical reference to *"refouler"*, a French word that is not an exact synonym for the English word "return." Indeed, neither of two respected English–French Dictionaries mentions *"refouler"* as one of many possible French translations of "return."[37] Conversely, the English translations of *"refouler"* do not include the word "return." They do, however, include words like "repulse," "repel," "drive back," and even "expel." To the extent that they are relevant, these translations imply that "return" means a defensive act of resistance or exclusion at a border rather than an act of transporting someone to a particular destination. In the context of the Convention, to "return" means to "repulse" rather than to "reinstate."

* * *

The drafters of the Convention and the parties to the Protocol—like the drafters of § 243(h)—may not have contemplated that any nation would gather fleeing refugees and return them to the one country they had desperately sought to escape; such actions may even violate the spirit of Article 33; but a treaty cannot impose uncontemplated extraterritorial

---

37. The New Cassell's French Dictionary 440 (1973), gives this translation: "return (I) v.i. Revenir (to come back); retourner (to go back); rentrer (to come in again); repondre, repliquer (to answer). To return to the subject, revenir au sujet, (fam.) revenir ses moutons.—v.t. Rendre (to give back); ren-voyer (to send back); rembourser (to repay); * * *

Although there are additional translations in the Larousse Modern French–English Dictionary 545 (1978), 'refouler' is not among them."

obligations on those who ratify it through no more than its general humanitarian intent. Because the text of Article 33 cannot reasonably be read to say anything at all about a nation's actions toward aliens outside its own territory, it does not prohibit such actions.

B. The Negotiating History of the Convention

In early drafts of the Convention, what finally emerged as Article 33 was numbered 28. At a negotiating conference of plenipotentiaries held in Geneva, Switzerland on July 11, 1951, the Swiss delegate explained his understanding that the words "expel" and "return" covered only refugees who had entered the host country. He stated:

"Mr. ZUTTER (Switzerland) said that the Swiss Federal Government saw no reason why article 28 should not be adopted as it stood; for the article was a necessary one. He thought, however, that its wording left room for various interpretations, particularly as to the meaning to be attached to the words 'expel' and 'return'. In the Swiss Government's view, the term 'expulsion' applied to a refugee who had already been admitted to the territory of a country. The term *'refoulement'*, on the other hand, had a vaguer meaning; *it could not, however, be applied to a refugee who had not yet entered the territory of a country.* The word 'return', used in the English text, gave that idea exactly. Yet article 28 implied the existence of two categories of refugee: refugees who were liable to be expelled, and those who were liable to be returned. In any case, the States represented at the Conference should take a definite position with regard to the meaning to be attached to the word 'return'. The Swiss Government considered that in the present instance *the word applied solely to refugees who had already entered a country, but were not yet resident there.* According to that interpretation, States were not compelled to allow large groups of persons claiming refugee status to cross its frontiers. He would be glad to know whether the States represented at the Conference accepted his interpretations of the two terms in question. If they did, Switzerland would be willing to accept article 28, which was one of the articles in respect of which States could not, under article 36 of the draft Convention, enter a reservation." [Emphases added by the Court].

No one expressed disagreement with the position of the Swiss delegate on that day or at the session two weeks later when Article 28 was again discussed. At that session, the delegate of the Netherlands recalled the Swiss delegate's earlier position:

"Baron van BOETZELAER (Netherlands) recalled that at the first reading the Swiss representative had expressed the opinion that the word 'expulsion' related to a refugee already admitted into a country, whereas the word 'return' (*'refoulement'*) related to a refugee *already within the territory but not yet resident there.* According to that interpretation, article 28 would not have involved any obligations in the possible case of mass migrations across frontiers or of attempted mass migrations.

"He wished to revert to that point, because the Netherlands Government attached very great importance to the scope of the provision now contained in article 33. The Netherlands could not accept any legal obligations in respect of large groups of refugees seeking access to its territory.

"At the first reading the representatives of Belgium, the Federal Republic of Germany, Italy, the Netherlands and Sweden had supported the Swiss interpretation. From conversations he had since had with other representatives, he had gathered that the general consensus of opinion was in favour of the Swiss interpretation.

* * *

"There being no objection, the PRESIDENT *ruled* that the interpretation given by the Netherlands representative should be placed on record."

* * *

Although the significance of the President's comment that the remarks should be "placed on record" is not entirely clear, this much cannot be denied: at one time there was a "general consensus," and in July of 1951 several delegates understood the right of non-refoulement to apply only to aliens physically present in the host country. * * *

* * * The negotiating history, which suggests that the Convention's limited reach resulted from a deliberate bargain, is not dispositive, but it solidly supports our reluctance to interpret Article 33 to impose obligations on the contracting parties that are broader than the text commands. We do not read that text to apply to aliens interdicted on the high seas.

* * *

The judgment of the Court of Appeals is reversed.

* * *

■ JUSTICE BLACKMUN, dissenting.

When, in 1968, the United States acceded to the United Nations Protocol Relating to the Status of Refugees, it pledged not to "return ('*refouler*') a refugee in any manner whatsoever" to a place where he would face political persecution. In 1980, Congress amended our immigration law to reflect the Protocol's directives. Today's majority nevertheless decides that the forced repatriation of the Haitian refugees is perfectly legal, because the word "return" does not mean return, because the opposite of "within the United States" is not outside the United States, and because the official charged with controlling immigration has no role in enforcing an order to control immigration.

I believe that the duty of withholding of removal expressed in both the Protocol and the statute is clear. The majority finds it "extraordinary" that Congress would have intended the ban on returning "any alien" to apply to aliens at sea. That Congress would have meant what it said is not remarkable. What is extraordinary in this case is that the Executive, in disregard of the law, would take to the seas to intercept fleeing refugees and force them back to their persecutors—and that the Court would strain to sanction that conduct.

I

I begin with the Convention, for it is undisputed that the Refugee Act of 1980 was passed to conform our law to Article 33, and that "the nondiscretionary duty imposed by § 243(h) parallels the United States' mandatory *nonrefoulement* obligations under Article 33.1...." * * *

A

Article 33.1 of the Convention states categorically and without geographical limitation:

"No Contracting State shall expel or return (*'refouler'*) a refugee in any manner whatsoever to the frontiers of territories where his life or freedom would be threatened on account of his race, religion, nationality, membership of a particular social group or political opinion."

The terms are unambiguous. Vulnerable refugees shall not be returned. The language is clear, and the command is straightforward; that should be the end of the inquiry. Indeed, until litigation ensued, the Government consistently acknowledged that the Convention applied on the high seas.

The majority, however, has difficulty with the Treaty's use of the term "return (*'refouler'*)." "Return," it claims, does not mean return, but instead has a distinctive legal meaning. For this proposition the Court relies almost entirely on the fact that *American* law makes a general distinction between *deportation* and *exclusion*. Without explanation, the majority asserts that in light of this distinction the word "return" as used in the Treaty somehow must refer only to "the exclusion of aliens who are ... 'on the threshold of initial entry' ".

Setting aside for the moment the fact that respondents in this case seem very much "on the threshold of initial entry"—at least in the eyes of the Government that has ordered them seized for "attempting to come to the United States by sea without necessary documentation"—I find this tortured reading unsupported and unnecessary. The text of the Convention does not ban the "exclusion" of aliens who have reached some indeterminate "threshold"; it bans their "return." It is well settled that a treaty must first be construed according to its "ordinary meaning." Article 31.1 of the Vienna Convention on the Law of Treaties. The ordinary meaning of "return" is "to bring, send, or put (a person or thing) back to or in a former position." Webster's Third New International Dictionary 1941 (1986). That describes precisely what petitioners are doing to the Haitians. By dispensing with ordinary meaning at the outset, and by taking instead as its starting point the assumption that "return," as used in the Treaty, "has a legal meaning narrower than its common meaning," the majority leads itself astray.

The straightforward interpretation of the duty of withholding of removal is strongly reinforced by the Convention's use of the French term *"refouler."* The ordinary meaning of *"refouler,"* as the majority concedes, is "[t]o repulse, ...; to drive back, to repel." Thus construed, Article 33.1 of the Convention reads: "No contracting state shall expel or [repulse, drive back, or repel] a refugee in any manner whatsoever to the frontiers of territories where his life or freedom would be threatened...." That, of course, is exactly what the Government is doing. It thus is no surprise that when the French press has described the very policy challenged here, the term it has used is *"refouler."* See, e. g., *Le bourbier hatien*, Le Monde, May 31–June 1, 1992 ("[L]es États–Unis ont decidé de *refouler* directement les refugiés recueillis par la garde cotire." (The United States has decided [de refouler] directly the refugees picked up by the Coast Guard)).

And yet the majority insists that what has occurred is not, in fact, *"refoulement."* It reaches this conclusion in a peculiar fashion. After acknowledging that the ordinary meaning of *"refouler"* is "repulse," "repel," and "drive back," the majority without elaboration declares: "To the extent that they are relevant, these translations imply that 'return' means a defensive act of resistance or exclusion at a border...." I am at a loss to find the narrow notion of "exclusion at a border" in broad terms like "repulse," "repel," and "drive back." Gage was repulsed (initially) at Bunker Hill. Lee was repelled at Gettysburg. Rommel was driven back across North Africa. The majority's puzzling progression (*"refouler"* means repel or drive back; therefore "return" means only exclude at a border; therefore the treaty does not apply) hardly justifies a departure from the path of ordinary meaning. The text of Article 33.1 is clear, and whether the operative term is "return" or *"refouler,"* it prohibits the Government's actions.

Article 33.1 is clear not only in what it says, but also in what it does not say: it does not include any geographical limitation. It limits only where a refugee may be sent "to", not where he may be sent from. This is not surprising, given that the aim of the provision is to protect refugees against persecution.

Article 33.2, by contrast, *does* contain a geographical reference, and the majority seizes upon this as evidence that the section as a whole applies only within a signatory's borders. That inference is flawed. Article 33.2 states that the benefit of Article 33.1 "may not ... be claimed by a refugee whom there are reasonable grounds for regarding as a danger to the security of the country in which he is, or who, having been convicted by a final judgment of a particularly serious crime, constitutes a danger to the community of that country."

The signatories' understandable decision to allow nations to deport criminal aliens who have entered their territory hardly suggests an intent to permit the apprehension and return of noncriminal aliens who have not entered their territory, and who may have no desire ever to enter it. One wonders what the majority would make of an exception that removed from the Article's protection all refugees who "constitute a danger to their families." By the majority's logic, the inclusion of such an exception presumably would render Article 33.1 applicable only to refugees with families.

* * *

B

The majority further relies on a remark by Baron van Boetzelaer, the Netherlands' delegate at the Convention's negotiating conference, to support its contention that Article 33 does not apply extraterritorially. This reliance, for two reasons, is misplaced. First, the isolated statement of a delegate to the Convention cannot alter the plain meaning of the Treaty itself. Second, placed in its proper context, van Boetzelaer's comment does not support the majority's position.

It is axiomatic that a treaty's plain language must control absent "extraordinarily strong contrary evidence." Reliance on a treaty's negotiating history (*travaux préparatoires*) is a disfavored alternative of last resort, appropriate only where the terms of the document are obscure or lead to "manifestly absurd or unreasonable" results. See Vienna Convention on the Law of Treaties, Art. 32. Moreover, even the general rule of treaty construction allowing limited resort to *travaux préparatoires* "has no application to oral statements made by those engaged in negotiating the treaty which were not embodied in any writing and were not communicated to the government of the negotiator or to its ratifying body." There is no evidence that the comment on which the majority relies was ever communicated to the United States' Government or to the Senate in connection with the ratification of the Convention.

The pitfalls of relying on the negotiating record are underscored by the fact that Baron van Boetzelaer's remarks almost certainly represent, in the words of the United Nations High Commissioner for Refugees, a mere "parliamentary gesture by a delegate whose views did *not* prevail upon the negotiating conference as a whole" (emphasis in original). The Baron, like the Swiss delegate whose sentiments he restated, expressed a desire to reserve the right to *close borders to large groups* of refugees. "According to [the Swiss delegate's] interpretation, States were not compelled to allow large groups of persons claiming refugee status to cross [their] frontiers." * * * Yet no one seriously contends that the Treaty's protections depend on the number of refugees who are fleeing persecution. * * *

There is strong evidence as well that the Conference rejected the right to close land borders where to do so would trap refugees in the persecutors' territory. Indeed, the majority agrees that the Convention does apply to refugees who have reached the border. The majority thus cannot maintain that van Boetzelaer's interpretation prevailed.

That it did not is evidenced by the fact that Baron van Boetzelaer's interpretation was merely "placed on record," unlike formal amendments to the Convention which were "agreed to" or "adopted." It should not be assumed that other delegates agreed with the comment simply because they did not object to their colleague's request to memorialize it, and the majority's statement that "this much cannot be denied: at one time there was a 'general consensus' " is wrong. * * *

In any event, even if van Boetzelaer's statement *had* been "agreed to" as reflecting the dominant view, this is not a case about the right of a nation to close its borders. This is a case in which a Nation has gone forth to *seize* aliens who are not at its borders and *return* them to persecution.[8]

In sum, the fragments of negotiating history upon which the majority relies are not entitled to deference, were never voted on or adopted, probably represent a minority view, and in any event do not address the issue in this case. It goes without saying, therefore, that they do not provide the "extraordinarily strong contrary evidence" required to overcome the Convention's plain statement: "No Contracting State shall expel or return (*'refouler'*) a refugee in any manner whatsoever to the frontiers of territories where his life or freedom would be threatened...."

II

A

Like the Treaty whose dictates it embodies, § 243(h) is unambiguous. * * * "With regard to this very statutory scheme, we have considered ourselves bound to assume that the legislative purpose is expressed by the ordinary meaning of the words used." Ordinary, but not literal. The statement that "the Attorney General shall not deport or return any alien" obviously does not mean simply that the person who is the Attorney General at the moment is forbidden personally to deport or return any alien, but rather that her agents may not do so. In the present case the Coast Guard without question is acting as the agent of the Attorney General. "The officers of the Coast Guard insofar as they are engaged ... in enforcing any law of the United States shall ... be deemed to be acting as agents of the particular executive department ... charged with the administration of the particular law ... and ... be subject to all the rules and regulations promulgated by such Department ... with respect to the enforcement of that law." 14 U.S.C. § 89(b). The Coast Guard is engaged in enforcing the immigration laws. * * *

* * * Accordingly, there is no merit to the argument that the concomitant legal restrictions placed on the Attorney General by Congress do not apply with full force in this case.

B

Comparison with the pre–1980 version of § 243(h) confirms that the statute means what it says. Before 1980, § 243(h) provided:

"The Attorney General is authorized to *withhold deportation* of any alien ... *within the United States* to any country in which in his opinion the alien would be subject to persecution on account of race, religion, or

---

8. The majority also cites secondary sources that, it claims, share its reading of the Convention. Not one of these authorities suggests that any signatory nation sought to reserve the right to seize refugees outside its territory and forcibly return them to their persecutors. * * * These sources emphasize instead that nations need not *admit* refugees or grant them *asylum*—questions not at issue here. * * *

political opinion and for such period of time as he deems to be necessary for such reason" (emphasis added)[by the Court].

The Refugee Act of 1980 explicitly amended this provision in three critical respects. Congress (1) deleted the words "within the United States"; (2) barred the Government from "return[ing]," as well as "deport[ing]," alien refugees; and (3) made the prohibition against return mandatory, thereby eliminating the discretion of the Attorney General over such decisions.

The import of these changes is clear. Whether "within the United States" or not, a refugee may not be returned to his persecutors. To read into § 243(h)'s mandate a territorial restriction is to restore the very language that Congress removed. * * * Moreover, as all parties to this case acknowledge, the 1980 changes were made in order to conform our law to the United Nations Protocol. As has been shown above, that Treaty's absolute ban on *refoulement* is similarly devoid of territorial restrictions.

The problems with the majority's *Leng May Ma* theory run deeper, however. * * * The Refugee Act revised the immigration code to establish a comprehensive, tripartite system for the protection of refugees fleeing persecution. Section 207 governs overseas refugee processing. Section 208, in turn, governs asylum claims by aliens "physically present in the United States, or at a land border or entry port." Unlike these sections, however, which explicitly apply to persons present in specific locations, the amended § 243(h) includes no such limiting language. The basic prohibition against forced return to persecution applies simply to "any alien." The design of all three sections is instructive, and it undermines the majority's assertion that § 243(h) was meant to apply only to aliens physically present in the United States or at one of its borders. When Congress wanted a provision to apply only to aliens "physically present in the United States, or at a land border or port of entry," it said so. See § 208(a). * * *

C

That the clarity of the text and the implausibility of its theories do not give the majority more pause is due, I think, to the majority's heavy reliance on the presumption against extraterritoriality. The presumption runs throughout the majority's opinion, and it stacks the deck by requiring the Haitians to produce "affirmative evidence" that when Congress prohibited the return of "any" alien, it indeed meant to prohibit the interception and return of aliens at sea.

The judicially created canon of statutory construction against extraterritorial application of United States law has no role here, however. It applies only where congressional intent is "unexpressed." Here there is no room for doubt: a territorial restriction has been deliberately deleted from the statute.

* * *

In this case we deal with a statute that regulates a distinctively international subject matter: immigration, nationalities, and refugees. Whatever force the presumption may have with regard to a primarily domestic statute evaporates in this context. There is no danger that the Congress that enacted the Refugee Act was blind to the fact that the laws it was crafting had implications beyond this Nation's borders. * * *

* * *

III

The Convention that the Refugee Act embodies was enacted largely in response to the experience of Jewish refugees in Europe during the period of World War II. The tragic consequences of the world's indifference at that time are well known. The resulting ban on *refoulement*, as broad as the humanitarian purpose that inspired it, is easily applicable here, the Court's protestations of impotence and regret notwithstanding.

The refugees attempting to escape from Haiti do not claim a right of admission to this country. They do not even argue that the Government has no right to intercept their boats. They demand only that the United States, land of refugees and guardian of freedom, cease forcibly driving them back to detention, abuse, and death. That is a modest plea, vindicated by the Treaty and the statute. We should not close our ears to it.

I dissent.

NOTES AND QUESTIONS

1.   What was the original point of the interdiction policy? Why do you think the government didn't simply wait to see who arrived at United States shores and then use the regular asylum system to process any claims that the arriving Haitians filed? Were any other options available?

2.   Several commentators have suggested that, from the start, the Haitian interdiction program has been racially motivated. See, e.g., Joyce A. Hughes & Linda P. Crane, *Haitians: Seeking Refuge in the United States*, 7 Georgetown Immigration L.J. 747 (1993); Janice D. Villiers, *Closed Borders, Closed Ports: The Plight of Haitians Seeking Political Asylum in the United States*, 60 Brooklyn L. Rev. 841 (1994). Others see historical parallels in analogous mass movements of refugees to the United States. For a particularly poignant historical comparison, see Peter Margulies, *Difference and Distrust in Asylum Law: Haitian and Holocaust Refugee Narratives*, 6 St. Thomas L.Rev. 135 (1993); see also Michael J. Churgin, *Mass Exoduses: The Response of the United States*, 30 Internat'l Migration Rev. 310 (1996) (arguing United States has typically acted unilaterally in dealing with mass movements of refugees except in cases where international agreement would facilitate government action).

Professor Kevin Johnson offers another thoughtful view of the political forces that might have precipitated the policy challenged in *Sale*. He argues that the general judicial deference to the executive branch in immigration cases might have signaled President Bush that the courts would uphold his policy. See Kevin R. Johnson, *Judicial Acquiescence to the Executive Branch's Pursuit of Foreign Policy and Domestic Agendas in Immigration Matters: The Case of the Haitian Asylum–Seekers*, 7 Georgetown Immigration L.J. 1 (1993).

3. As for Haiti, much has happened since *Sale*. The Clinton Administration first tried to topple the military regime in Haiti through trade and other economic sanctions, but those efforts proved fruitless. In July 1993, on Governors Island in New York, the coup leaders agreed to step aside and allow President Aristide to return to power by October 30. That deadline was not honored, and in the meantime Aristide supporters continued to be rounded up and murdered in Haiti. A United States warship retreated from Haiti in the face of a mob. The United States then led a multinational blockade of Haiti. See Harold Hongju Koh, *The "Haiti Paradigm" in United States Human Rights Policy*, 103 Yale L.J. 2391, 2397–98 (1994).

In May 1994, President Clinton ended the automatic repatriation policy challenged in *Sale*. Instead, he announced, the government would interview interdicted Haitians to determine their eligibility for refugee status. In June 1994, Jamaica agreed to allow the United States to bring intercepted Haitians to Kingston Harbor, where they could be interviewed on board the U.S. ships. 71 IR at 743–44 (June 6, 1994). The United Kingdom, which administers the Turks and Caicos Islands just north of Haiti, allowed the asylum processing of the captured Haitians on land. *Id.* Unlike the preliminary screening previously performed at sea and at Guantánamo, these interviews were determinations on the merits. 71 IR at 885–86 (July 11, 1994). Also unlike the previous shipboard interviews, these were monitored and reviewed by UNHCR, and private agencies were permitted to assist the Haitians. *Id.* at 886. Initial approval rates were at about 30%. *Id.*

But a longer-term solution did not come until September 19, 1994, when an international military force led by the United States landed in Haiti to remove the coup leaders and restore President Aristide. See Rick Bragg, *Mission to Haiti: The Haitians*, New York Times, Sept. 20, 1994, at A–11. The coup leaders chose to leave peacefully, and on October 15, 1994, Aristide returned home and resumed his Presidency. John Kifner, *Mission to Haiti: The Homecoming*, New York Times, Oct. 16, 1994, at 1. These events were followed by the involuntary repatriation of those Haitians who had been housed at Guantánamo, amidst warnings by many that their safety could not yet be taken for granted. See 72 IR 129 (Jan. 23, 1995).

With the return of President Aristide, boat traffic from Haiti virtually stopped. See Kathleen Newland, *The Impact of U.S. Refugee Policies on U.S. Foreign Policy: A Case of the Tail Wagging the Dog?*, ch. 5 in Michael S. Teitelbaum & Myron Weiner (eds.), Threatened Peoples, Threatened Borders at 199 (1995). An independent expert retained by the UN Commission on Human Rights found that the human rights situation in Haiti had improved dramatically with the return of Aristide, but that significant human rights abuses still existed (mostly by the Haitian police), and that weaknesses in the judicial system persisted. See Adama Dieng, U.N. ECO-SOC Doc. No. E/CN.4/1996/94 (24 Jan. 1996). For comprehensive descriptions of events and prospects as seen during the mid 1990s, see Irwin P. Stotzky, Silencing the Guns in Haiti (1997); Patrick Costello, *Haiti: Prospects for Democracy*, 15 Ref. Survey Q. 1 (1996); Carlos Ortiz Miranda, *Haiti and the United States During the 1980s and 1990s, Refugees, Immigration, and Foreign Policy*, 32 San Diego L.Rev. 673 (1995).

NACARA, passed in 1997, addressed some of the immigration problems of designated Central Americans, Soviets, and Eastern Europeans—but not Haitians. See the earlier discussion in chapter 8. Believing Haitians to be equally deserving of special dispensation, President Clinton in January 1998 ordered temporary relief in the form of "deferred enforced departure" for Haitians who had been paroled, or had applied for asylum, before December 1, 1995. See 75 IR 2 (Jan. 5, 1998). The Haitian Refugee Immigration Fairness Act of 1998, Pub. L. 105–277, Div. A, § 101(h), Title IX, 112 Stat. 2681 (Nov. 2, 1998), eventually codified President Clinton's order.

President Aristide was ousted again in 2002. The United Nations dispatched a "Stabilization Mission" to Haiti to safeguard security, prepare for democratic elections, and protect human rights. A recent report, however, paints a discouraging picture of the human rights situation in Haiti and criticizes the UN Stabilization Mission for what the authors regard as a lackluster performance. See Harvard Law Student Advocates for Human Rights & Centro de Justico Global, Keeping the Peace in Haiti? (Mar. 2005).

4.   Whether INA § 243(h) [now section 241(b)(3)] was meant to apply outside United States territory is a difficult question of statutory interpretation. First, articulate both parties' plain meaning arguments.

5.   In construing narrowly the *limitation* on returning refugees, the Supreme Court in *Sale* relies heavily on a presumption against extraterritorial application of statutory language. With surprising ease, however, and notwithstanding the presumption against extraterritoriality, the Ninth Circuit subsequently held that the statutory enforcement powers of the former INS *did* apply on the high seas. *United States v. Chen*, 2 F.3d 330 (9th Cir. 1993) (approving an INS sting operation on the high seas).

What are the rationales for this presumption? Do those rationales apply to interdiction?

6.   The key word in *Sale* is "return." First, articulate what each of the opposing parties says that word means. Second, explain why the Court believes that the Haitians' interpretation of "return" would render the word "deport" redundant. As the Haitians' counsel, how would you respond to that argument? Third, although not discussed in the opinion, all the other INA provisions that you have studied then used the word "exclude" [but see item 12 below] to describe the act of turning away a noncitizen who is physically at a United States port of entry. What

argument might the Haitians' counsel have been able to make on the basis of that observation? What counter-arguments would you expect?

7. How, exactly, is the U.N. Convention legally relevant to the Haitians' arguments? If the Supreme Court had held that article 33 was meant to have extraterritorial reach, what legal consequences would that holding have had in this case?

8. As to the interpretation of article 33, the Court examines several factors. It suggests that, under the Haitians' construction, article 33.2 would lead to anomalous results. Why? How could the Haitians respond?

9. In your contracts course you saw how ambiguous an agreement can be even when both parties speak the same language. When multiple languages are involved, as they are in the typical multilateral convention, the problems are exacerbated. Here, the issue revolves around the English word "return" and the French word "refouler." To solve the problem, the Court dusts off its English–French dictionary. First, what does the Court learn from this dictionary? Second, looking at the list of French words that correspond to the English word "return," which one do you think would most closely have captured the Haitians' interpretation? Third, if your answer to the previous question was not "refouler," how might the Haitians have been able to salvage their interpretation?

10. Consider also the Court's use of the negotiating history of the Convention. First, what lesson does the Court distill from that history? Second, thinking about the geography of Switzerland, do you find the Court's interpretation of the Swiss representative's comments realistic? What point do you think the quoted participants were making?

11. The interdictions that the plaintiffs were challenging in *Sale* occurred in what were indisputably international waters. The Justice Department's Office of Legal Counsel later took the position that the result would be the same even in United States territorial waters. U.S. Comm. for Refugees, Refugee Reports (Aug. 19, 1994), at 11.

12. IIRIRA § 305(a) amended the withholding of removal provision and renumbered it INA § 241(b)(3). The changes are largely in the nature of housekeeping, to conform the language of the provision to other new terminology that IIRIRA introduced. In particular, Congress changed "deport or return" to "remove," which is the same word that Congress substituted for both "deport" and "exclude" throughout virtually the entire INA. It seems likely, therefore, that the amendment reflected congressional satisfaction with the decision in *Sale*. Of course, IIRIRA reveals nothing about the intended meaning of article 33, the wording of which has not changed. At any rate, just two years later, Congress in a comprehensive appropriations bill expressly forbade the use of the appropriated funds to effect the involuntary return of any person to a country in which he or she had a well-founded fear of persecution on account of any of the 1951 Convention's protected grounds. Pub. L. 105–277, § 2241(a), 112 Stat. 2681 at 2681–821 (Oct. 21, 1998). Then, several times in 1999, the Coast Guard interdicted Chinese vessels in U.S. territorial waters near the Northern Mariana Islands and forcibly returned the passengers to China. 76 IR 1490 (Oct. 11, 1999).

13.   Shortly after the Supreme Court decision in *Sale*, the Executive Committee of UNHCR issued a statement disagreeing with the decision, based on the language, structure, and purposes of the 1951 Convention. UNHCR strenuously maintains that article 33 of the Convention applies on the High Seas. Its statement chastised the Supreme Court:

UNHCR considers the Court's decision a setback to modern international refugee law which has been developing for more than forty years, since the end of World War II. It renders the work of the Office of the High Commissioner in its global refugee protection role more difficult and sets a very unfortunate example.

UN High Commissioner for Refugees Responds to U.S. Supreme Court Decision in Sale v. Haitian Centers Council, 32 I.L.M. 1215 (1993); accord, Daniel J. Steinbock, *Interpreting the Refugee Definition*, 45 UCLA L. Rev. 733, 755–56 (1998); *cf.* Andrew I. Schoenholtz, *Aiding and Abetting Persecutors: The Seizure and Return of Haitian Refugees in Violation of the U.N. Refugee Convention and Protocol*, 7 Georgetown Immigration L.J. 67 (1993) (arguing for the UNHCR position even before the decision in *Sale*).

The Inter–American Commission on Human Rights has expressed similar sentiments and has also suggested that the decision in *Sale* violated the American Declaration of the Rights and Duties of Man. See Louis Henkin, Gerald L. Neuman, Diane F. Orentlicher & David W. Leebron, Human Rights 426 (1999).

Some other international law issues related to the interdiction program have also been discussed. For an argument that article 33 is self-executing, see Carlos M. Vazquez, *The "Self–Executing" Character of the Refugee Protocol's Nonrefoulement Obligation*, 7 Georgetown Immigration L.J. 39 (1993). For a discussion of the international law of the sea limitations on interdiction, see Jon L. Jacobson, *At-Sea Interception of Alien Migrants: International Law Issues*, 28 Willamette L. Rev. 811 (1992). For the view that intercepting refugees on the high seas and returning them to their persecutors might violate both the Torture Convention and the International Covenant on Civil and Political Rights, see Gerald L. Neuman, *Extraterritorial Violations of Human Rights by the United States*, in Amer. Univ. J. Internat'l L. & Policy and Loyola L.A. Internat'l & Comp. L.J. (eds.), Immigration Law: International Perspectives on Asylum and Refugee Status at 213 (1994).

14.   The plaintiffs in *Sale* received pro bono representation from the Yale Law School's Lowenstein Human Rights Clinic. Under the supervision of Professor Harold Hongju Koh, some 100 law students teamed up to research the case and construct the arguments. Several other distinguished co-counsel chipped in. The lawyers and law students involved have written several articles that furnish fascinating glimpses into the legal strategies, logistical hurdles, emotional impact, and future implications of the experience and the result. See, e.g., Harold Hongju Koh, *Reflections on Refoulement and Haitian Centers Council*, 35 Harvard Internat'l L.J. 1 (1994); Harold Hongju Koh, *The "Haiti Paradigm" in United States Human Rights Policy*, 103 Yale L.J. 2391 (1994); Harold Hongju Koh, *The Human Face of the Haitian Interdiction Program*, 33 Virginia J. Internat'l L. 483

(1993); Essay, *Litigating as Law Students: An Inside Look at Haitian Centers Council*, 103 Yale L.J. 2337 (1994). Although the plaintiffs did not prevail in the *Sale* case, they did enjoy partial success in related litigation, winning the release of about 300 HIV-positive Haitians who had been confined at Guantánamo despite having been found to possess credible asylum claims. Essay, above, 103 Yale L.J. at 2342–45.

8. A SIMULATED ATTORNEY-CLIENT ASYLUM INTERVIEW[17]

You are an immigration lawyer about to interview a new client. You have not previously met. All you know at this stage is that your client is from Oquito, a tiny Spanish-speaking country in Central America, and that he or she wants to apply for asylum in the United States.

Your instructor will tell you how many minutes you have for this interview. Your instructor will also tell you whether the client speaks English. If not, a Spanish–English interpreter will be provided.

At the interview you will need to do several things: Naturally, you should try to gather as complete a picture of the facts as you can, while being sensitive to the special traumas faced by refugees. You should then make a preliminary judgment whether an asylum application is advisable, and you should share your initial impressions with the client. If you recommend applying for asylum, then you should explain to the client what he or she will need to establish and, generally, what the process will entail. At the end of the interview, be sure you and the client are clear as to what will happen next. (If this were a real-life initial consultation, you would also discuss your fees; for this exercise you can skip that discussion.)

To prepare for your part, you should (1) review what you have learned thus far concerning the substantive criteria and the procedures for asylum and withholding of removal, and jot down the essential elements of an asylum claim; (2) read the (fictional) U.S. State Department Country Report on Oquito (below); and (3) read the excerpts from "Interviewing a Client," immediately following the Country Report. Your instructor will supply the logistical details.

United States Department of State
Country Report on Human Rights Practices

Report for 2005.
Oquito.

I. Background

Oquito is a multiparty democracy with a constitution that provides for a strong executive, a bicameral legislature, and a tenured (until age 70)

17. Thanks are due to Stacie Powderly for her exceptional contributions to this exercise. I am also indebted to Pamela Goldberg, Isabel Medina, Michele Pistone, Bernard Trujillo, and Virgil Wiebe for their generous and detailed feedback on earlier drafts of this simulation. Philip Schrag deserves special mention for going well beyond the call of duty.

judiciary. Approved by referendum in 1990 and amended in 1994, the Constitution was written under the former military government of Roberto Gonzalez and retains certain institutional limits on popular rule. On June 30, 2005, Hector Caleros, of the Socialist Party, rose to power via military coup.

In elections held just one month after the coup, Caleros's Socialist Party won 55 of the 100 seats in the lower house. The Senate was divided 24–24 between the Socialist Party and Gonzalez supporters. The Supreme Judicial Court currently is comprised of seven judges. Five of the judges were appointed by Gonzalez, the others by Caleros. Although independent in theory, there is some uncertainty about the actual influence of the political branches and the military over individual judges.

The armed forces are constitutionally subordinate to the President through an appointed civilian Minister of Defense but enjoy a large degree of legal autonomy. Most notably, the President must have the concurrence of the National Security Council, which consists of military and civilian officials, to remove military chiefs. While the Minister of Defense generally maintains effective control of the military forces, a considerable number of soldiers commit human rights abuses.

Vestiges of the Gonzalez regime remain in the central government. Most notably, the Minister of Defense and the highest ranking general in the Oquito army under Gonzalez have been absorbed into the Caleros government. In addition, many soldiers and local police remain loyal to Gonzalez.

II. Human Rights

General Background: Since the departure of Gonzalez, the human rights situation in Oquito has improved. The Caleros government generally respects its citizens' human rights, though problems remain in some key areas noted below.

Respect for the Integrity of the Person:

Arbitrary or Unlawful Deprivation of Life: There were no confirmed reports of political killings this year, but it is widely believed that members of the federal and state police, as well as military personnel, committed extra-judicial killings during the year. Most of these extra-judicial killings resulted from excessive use of force or mistreatment of prisoners.

Disappearances: The Constitution prohibits forced disappearance. It also requires individuals to disobey orders to commit such crimes and prescribes criminal prosecution of the intellectual authors of the crimes. This year there were two credible reports of politically motivated disappearances. Neither of these disappearances has been linked to state actors.

Torture and Other Cruel, Inhuman or Degrading Treatment or Punishment: The Constitution prohibits torture. While torture is rare, there were five credible reports of torture by Oquito police and military officers this year. The abuse most commonly consisted of beatings during arrest or interrogation. The Caleros government has instituted independent investigations of all the allegations. A civilian minister oversees the investigations and has placed all of the accused on administrative leave pending the outcome of the investigations.

Arbitrary Interference with Privacy, Family, and Home: Constitutional provisions prohibit arbitrary interference with privacy, family, and home; however, the police and military continued to infringe on citizens' privacy rights by conducting searches of homes without warrants, especially during anticrime sweeps in poor neighborhoods. Reports of illegal wiretapping and invasion of privacy by the police and military forces increased during the year. In October and November, the Government released recordings of conversations it alleged occurred among opposition leaders. The Government did not divulge how it obtained the recordings.

Freedom of Speech:

The Oquito Constitution guarantees freedom of speech. Under the Gonzalez regime, however, freedom of speech was not respected. The Government regularly threatened or physically harmed those who spoke out against it. The Caleros government appears to have rejected any formal policy of targeting political dissidents.

Freedom of speech remains restricted. In several instances, Government authorities confiscated opposition newspapers and pamphlets and withheld television and radio air time from the opposition. Human rights groups also cite instances where the Caleros government has illegally imprisoned people for expressing anti-government opinions. The majority of those imprisoned were released promptly, since no formal law had been broken. The human rights groups acknowledge that physical violence against prisoners in custody is rare.

In several reported recent incidents, pro-Gonzalez loyalists within the military and local police forces have threatened or assaulted those who have criticized the Gonzalez regime. The families of the targeted individuals have also been threatened, imprisoned, and sometimes physically assaulted. As of this report, little has been done to control the Gonzalez loyalists who commit these abuses.

INTERVIEWING A CLIENT, ASYLUM LAW MANUAL, CENTER FOR APPLIED LEGAL STUDIES OF GEORGETOWN UNIVERSITY LAW CENTER (2005 edition)*

I. General Purposes of Initial Interview

An initial interview has several general purposes. They usually include (among others):

—explaining to the client who you are, * * * how the asylum process works, any possible non-asylum immigration alternatives, and (especially in an affirmative case) any risks involved in pursuing an asylum claim;

—enabling you and your client to decide whether to enter into an attorney-client relationship, and, if so, signing a retainer and other forms;

—creating a sound and trusting working relationship between you and your client;

—obtaining the information needed for further development of the case;

—[and] counseling the client about decisions he or she must make, and actions he or she can take (e.g., obtaining documents) to make success more likely * * *.

* * *

III.   Preparation

* * *

A.   Pre–Interview Study

* * *

* * * [L]earn something about the country from which your client has come, and particularly about its recent political and human rights history. * * * We suggest that before the interview you read at least (a) the U.S. State Department's most recent published information about the country and its human rights record, and (b) one independently published human rights report about the country (e.g., by Amnesty International or Human Rights Watch). * * *

* * *

C.   Interpersonal Relationships

* * *

[T]o what extent do you (and your partner) want to direct the interview (e.g., decide the order of topics, decide when to change topics, determine when it is appropriate for the interviewers to ask questions and when the interviewee should ask questions, decide what issues are "extraneous" and should not be discussed at length, etc.)? In the traditional model of legal interviewing, the lawyer is very much in charge. The idea, perhaps, is that while the client is the expert on the subject of the client's problem, the lawyer is the expert on the subject of how to conduct an interview. But in the last 25 years, some authorities have challenged this model, claiming that it reproduces the hierarchy that clients, particularly low-income clients, experience all too often in their lives. It puts the lawyer, who already has more social status than most clients, in a position of even more power. Thus, for a client who is used to standing in lines and answering bureaucrats' questions to obtain licenses, public benefits, or other services, the lawyer becomes still another bureaucrat who processes the client's claim—perhaps not the best start for a truly trusting relationship. Some of the critics of the traditional model suggest that the lawyer empower the client by putting the client in charge of the interview * * * or at least that they negotiate with clients, at the outset, about who should direct the interview or how control over the interview should be shared. Empowerment of relatively unempowered clients, they suggest, is both an important end in itself (and it may be a goal for some clients) and a facilitator of a positive lawyer-client relationship.

The traditional model has not withered away as a result of this criticism. Its proponents sometimes suggest that client-directed interviews can be exceedingly lengthy, inefficient, and frustrating, precisely because many clients lack the organizational skills necessary to cover all relevant topics thoroughly within a limited period of time. They note that because they do not know the law, clients cannot be expected even to know what aspects of their stories are relevant to the representation. It can also be argued that an excessively chaotic initial meeting of lawyer and client is less likely to instill a sense of trust than one organized by the lawyer, and that a client who comes to the interview expecting a lawyer to behave in the "traditional" way will be frustrated and disappointed if the lawyer asks the client to take charge.

There is no "right answer" to the question of control. But it is an important issue deserving of some of your time as you prepare for your first interviews.

Related issues involve how distant or friendly you should be, and how formal or informal you want the relationship to be. Whether or not they decide to control the interviewing process, some lawyers believe that they should maintain "professional distance" from the client, not only in the sense of exercising independent judgment about the case, but also in terms of the human dimensions of the relationship. Some methods of maintaining distance might include using last names, keeping a table between the lawyer and the client during interviews, not going to the client's residence, discouraging the client from talking about family matters unrelated to representation, etc. However, other lawyers think that a professional relationship cannot be fulfilling on either side if it is not a relationship between "whole people." Such lawyers might at least avoid creating what they would regard as barriers between themselves and their clients, and some think it a very positive development when lawyer-client relationships evolve into friendships. Some people have even concluded that a more "informal" relationship is not only more enjoyable, but also more successful; it builds a rapport that results in the client disclosing more details and cooperating more fully.

Still another related question involves empathy. Most lawyers would say that they want to maintain a considerable degree of intellectual detachment from their clients' cases, so that they can exercise independent professional judgment about the likely outcome and thereby counsel their clients more effectively. Emotional detachment is a more complex question. Asylum cases often involve strong emotional content, and discussing them may bring up feelings associated with separation from family and country, loss of community, and the disappearance or death of friends or relatives. Suppose that, during your interview, your client experiences or expresses strong feelings. Should you discourage the expression of those emotions, because they may restrict the flow of information? Should you try to feel your client's feelings with him or her? Should you encourage your client to express emotion but try to remain at an emotional as well as an intellectual distance from the case? If you feel emotions along with your client, should you express those emotions to him or her? What should you do if you experience emotion, but your emotions are quite different from those of your client? If you have experienced some of the same things your client has experienced, should you reveal that?

* * *

IV.   The Interview

* * * If your initial interview is fairly typical, it will include each of the following features: (a) you will tell the client something about yourself, your institution, the lawyer-client relationship, the nature and risks of the asylum process, and the bases for possible collateral routes to immigration, (b) you will gather information about your client's experiences and other facts relevant to the case, (c) you will have to deal with inter-cultural factors, and perhaps problems involving interpretation to and from English, that could interfere with communication during the interview, (d) you may have to answer questions or give advice, (e) you and your client will discuss and possibly sign a retainer agreement and other documents, and (f) you will bring the interview to a close, and if the client has decided to retain you, you will deal with such other matters as scheduling a next meeting and agreeing on tasks to be undertaken in the interim.

A.   Disclosures

* * *

1.   The confidential nature of the relationship. Clients should understand that they may provide information to you in confidence, and that neither you nor any interpreter with whom you work will share with people outside of the clinic any information they tell you in confidence that could reveal their identities. (You need not explain this detail unless asked, but even if a client ultimately decides not to retain you, your initial discussions are protected by the attorney-client privilege and the ethical duty to keep confidences).

* * *

4.   The process. * * * Absent unusual circumstances, before clients retain you to initiate or participate in a legal process, they should be educated about the basics of that process. If the client has no lawful immigration status and is initiating an asylum application, it is very

important that he or she be advised that the failure to obtain asylum at any level of the process could result in removal. If the client has other possible means for remaining in the United States (such as a family petition), these should be explored. * * *

* * *

8.   FOIA. * * *

—* * * [Y]ou should send a FOIA request to the Department of Homeland Security (with a copy to the Court) immediately after your first interview. You can have the client sign the G–639 Form at the first interview or at another early interview.

—If you see that a FOIA request was filed, but there has been no response, you should file a second request. Mark it as a second request, mark it urgent, and note the hearing date.

—As a last resort, contact the FOIA officer to follow up or contact the trial attorney to request a copy of the file or to prod the FOIA officer.

—If pages were withheld from the FOIA response, as a policy, we file an appeal with the FOIA/PA Appeals Office. * * *

* * *

B.   Information Gathering

* * *

2.   The funnel sequence. * * * [T]he interviewer starts an area of questioning with a broad question (e.g., tell me about any trouble you have had with the police) and only very gradually works down to specific questions (e.g., what did the officer say when he came to arrest you?). The image is that of a narrowing funnel, and the purpose of the technique is to permit the client to talk, and to provide leads for specific follow-up questions. By contrast, if the lawyer mainly asks specific questions, he or she might miss large areas of a case that the client might reveal if given a more open-ended opportunity to talk.

3.   Attention to vocabulary. Even when clients speak English fluently, lawyers must attend to vocabulary, taking pains neither to speak over their clients' heads nor to talk down to them. Lawyers are used to using jargon, and it is especially important to avoid or explain technical terms. Language barriers only compound the difficulty, and some interpreters may not even be able to translate legal terminology.

4.   Major issues. * * * These include, among others,

—your client's personal and family history;

—what happened to your client in his or her country;

—how your client got to the United States;

—your client's current immigration status;

—any prior legal representation or contact with [DHS];

—any relevant witnesses or documents;

—possible or actual criminal convictions;

—and time spent in a third country.

5. Details. It is very important to know the details of your client's experience, because details prove cases and make testimony credible. * * *

6. Corroborating evidence. * * * [C]orroborating evidence can be crucial to the success of a case. Therefore, it is important that your client fully understand that you will need his or her assistance in discovering how the case might be corroborated. Your client may immediately be aware of the availability of, for example, a death certificate which would corroborate the murder of a family member. Such a document might take weeks to produce. Accordingly, making your client aware of this important task at the first interview is a step not to be overlooked.

7. Contradictions. It is very common for asylum applicants not to tell the entire story at the first interview, or to tell a series of contradictory stories. Although the lapses and contradictions may well result from forgetfulness or trauma, they may be interpreted by adjudicators (or even by the applicants' lawyers) as lying. It is important to work with clients to develop accurate and stable facts, even though this may take several interviews. Steven Forester's article, "Haitian Asylum Advocacy: Questions to Ask Applicants and Notes on Interviewing and Representation, Part II," 20 Immigration Newsletter, no 2, p. 1 (1991) offers a series of suggestions in this regard. The article can also be found at 10 N.Y.L. Sch. J. Hum. Rts. 381 (1993), available on Westlaw. Some excerpts are noted here (not because we necessarily endorse these suggestions, but because they are worthy of your consideration):

> You can't expect your client to "open up" immediately. He or she may not do so for hours or until your third or fourth interview. . . . You may exasperate the client by asking so many questions, by investigating, cross-examining, triple-checking, taking pains. But you must: anything less is sloppy, disrespectful, and damning to the claim.
>
> You must often repeat a question in different ways. . . . Probe and follow up to confirm. * * * Don't take assertions at face value. Triple-check facts, numbers, specifics. Mix things up. If your client identifies a committee's president as Joseph Maxy and its vice-president as Sonia Gilbert, switch the names around: "So you said Sonia Gilbert was president?" Your client should correct you.
>
> Be demonstrative and vivid. . . . Soldiers stomped on your client's left leg, rebreaking it, while he was lying on the floor on his right side in the "djak" torture position. Ask him to demonstrate. If he is reluctant or slow, get on the floor on your right side in the djak position to check with him if that is how it was, or have someone else do so. Don't hesitate out of decorum or shyness. . . . Describe gore, rape, outrage explicitly, factually, and in detail. . . .

But ... tell the client <u>never to exaggerate</u> anything, or he or she loses; the truth suffices.

An additional threat to credible testimony arises when lawyers demand of clients that they speak with a false precision. If a client is unsure about certain facts, efforts to eliminate ambiguity may result in a story that changes at awkward moments and a client who feels s/he must lie to win asylum. You must decide when to push the client to give a clear account of facts and when to accept uncertainty.

C. Differences

* * * In your client's culture, for example, lawyers may be regarded with even greater suspicion than in the United States, or issues touching on sexual relations or sexuality may be taboo. * * * [B]e alert to the fact that an interview with a person from another culture is quite different from other interviews with which you may have experience (e.g., job interviews). Furthermore, you cannot always rely on an interpreter to give you or your client a precise interpretation. The interpreter may begin to paraphrase to save time, or because he or she thinks it is helpful. If you have any clue that you are not getting phrase-by-phrase interpretation, you may want to interrupt the interview to address the issue. The interpreter should not be paraphrasing your words, nor those of the client. Neither should the interpreter be inserting his or her own opinions or knowledge into the translation.

1. Torture Victims

Some * * * clients have been tortured. Interviewing victims of torture requires (1) special sensitivity to the experiences they have suffered, (2) attention to ways in which the effects of torture may impair their ability to tell you all the facts (particularly during the initial meetings with you), (3) awareness of the barriers that may make it difficult for them to communicate the facts to the asylum officer or judge, and (4) understanding of techniques that experts have developed for helping torture victims to tell sympathetic interviewers about what happened to them.

* * * [Here the Manual recommends] Chapter III, "General Interview Considerations," of the Manual "Examining Asylum Seekers" published by Physicians for Human Rights. The URL is http://www.phrusa.org/campaigns/pdf/asylum_pdf/03.pdf.

* * *

D. Counseling

It is not unusual for a client to ask lawyers for advice, even during the first interview. What should you do if a client asks you what to do, and you aren't sure you know enough to respond? A lawyer who seems to be withholding counseling, or who admits that he or she lacks enough knowledge to be able to provide advice, may cause the client to doubt his or her competence. On the other hand, poor advice may lead the client to make bad, even irrevocable decisions, and poor advice based on an undisclosed lack of knowledge could constitute malpractice. Similar issues may arise when a client asks for assurance that if he or she retains you, asylum will be granted. It is surely appropriate to say, if true, that you will do your best for a client, but a lawyer who promises a successful outcome risks disaster.

Another aspect of counseling is educating clients about the law of their case. Lawyers have various opinions about whether, when, and how this should be done. Some worry that early explanations about the applicable law may cause clients to tilt their stories and distort the facts to fit within the summaries of the law that their representatives offer them. Other lawyers believe early counseling along these lines to be very useful, precisely because it enables clients to organize their thoughts in a way that is useful to representatives.

* * *

F.   Closing

An interview should be concluded in an orderly, professional manner. The client should know what will happen next (it may be a second interview) and when it will happen. He or she should understand what you will do and what he or she will do during the week or two following the interview.

Before you close, be certain that you know how to get in touch with your client (and a suitable interpreter, if need be) on short notice. In addition to ascertaining all of your client's addresses and telephone numbers, try to obtain the telephone number of at least one friend or relative, residing at a different address, who will know how to reach your client if your client moves before the proceeding is over. Also be certain that your client knows that he or she can contact you * * *.

SECTION C.   BEYOND PERSECUTION: PROTECTION AGAINST OTHER DANGERS

The first two sections of this chapter deal, respectively, with offshore and onshore refugees. They consider protections afforded by both United States and international law, and they have one vital element in common– protection from certain categories of *persecution*.

But what if a person is fleeing from armed conflict, or the chaos of a failed state, or natural disaster, or mass starvation, or any other danger that does not qualify as "persecution?" Moreover, what happens if the person is fleeing persecution but does not qualify as a Convention refugee because (a) he or she is internally displaced; or (b) the persecution is not on account of one of the five protected grounds; or (c) the person falls within one of the criminal or other exclusions; or (d) procedural obstacles bar access to the host state's asylum determination system? And what if the person qualifies for nonrefoulement under the 1951 Convention, and the host state is willing to honor that principle but is not willing to grant asylum?

The materials in this section briefly survey a variety of other protection mechanisms to supplement, or in some cases substitute for, relief under the 1951 Convention. Some of the mechanisms discussed here have actually been adopted and applied by the United States, other states, regional associations, or the larger international community. Others have been merely proposed or discussed.

Three subjects are considered—the Convention Against Torture, Temporary Protection (TP), and Other Subsidiary Protection under International Law. As you read these materials, keep in mind that the three concepts overlap considerably, with each other and with the 1951 Convention. Torture, for example, is a form of persecution but not necessarily persecution on account of race, religion, nationality, etc. Temporary protection, as Professor Joan Fitzpatrick argues in her excerpted article, might be embraced by destination states in lieu of asylum rather than in addition to it, especially during times of mass influx. Human rights agreements that trigger nonrefoulement (for example, regional conventions and the Convention Against Torture) might require only temporary protection.

1. THE CONVENTION AGAINST TORTURE

On December 10, 1984 the United Nations General Assembly adopted the Convention Against Torture and Other Cruel, Inhuman or Degrading Treatment or Punishment. U.N.G.A. Res. 39/46, 39 U.N. GAOR Supp. (No. 51) at 197, U.N. Doc. A/39/51 (1984), reproduced in 23 Internat'l Legal Materials 1027 (1984), modifications in 24 Internat'l Legal Materials 535 (1985) [hereafter cited as CAT]. The United States Senate ratified CAT in 1990, see 136 Cong. Rec. S17491–92 (Oct. 27, 1990), albeit with a long list of reservations, understandings, and declarations that are examined below.

Until 1999, United States lawyers made scant use of CAT, principally because until then the domestic legal machinery for implementing CAT had not been established. In 1998, however, Congress passed the necessary implementing legislation, see Foreign Affairs Reform and Restructuring Act of 1998, Pub. L. 105–277, 112 Stat. 2681, Div. G, § 2242 (Oct. 21, 1998), and in 1999 the Justice Department issued interim regulations establishing the administrative machinery for the filing of CAT claims. 64 Fed. Reg. 8478 (Feb. 19, 1999). Since then, CAT claims have become a standard weapon in every refugee advocate's strategic arsenal. For helpful commentary, see, e.g., Anker at 465–522; Francisco Isgro, *Seeking Relief Under the Convention Against Torture*, 27 Migration World #3 at 44 (1999); Kristen B. Rosati, *Article 3 of the United Nations Convention Against Torture: A Powerful Tool to Prevent Removal Just Became More Powerful*, 4 BIB 137 (Feb. 15, 1999); Morton Sklar, *New Convention Against Torture Procedures and Standards*, July 1999 Immigration Briefings.

CAT is the first worldwide convention targeted specifically at torture and related cruelties. It requires the participating states to prevent torture within their own territories, to cooperate with other states by prosecuting or extraditing alleged perpetrators, and to do various things to protect actual or potential victims of torture. In addition CAT establishes a body called the "Committee against Torture," which has jurisdiction to investigate and adjudicate certain complaints of violations brought by individuals or states parties. As explained below, however, the Committee will play only a minor role in disputes that involve the United States.

Most relevant here is CAT article 3.1. It says: "No State Party shall expel, return (refouler) or extradite a person to another State where there are substantial grounds for believing that he would be in danger of being subjected to torture." Note the parallels to article 33 of the 1951 U.N. Refugee Convention.

Article 3.1 promises hope for some people who for various reasons are unable to procure nonrefoulement under the 1951 Convention. Some are individuals who cannot satisfy the substantive criteria for asylum because the harm they fear is not persecution or because the persecution is not on account of any of the five protected grounds. Personal grudges and police torture to extract confessions or other information are examples. Certain gender-related cruelties for which asylum is denied could possibly qualify under CAT. See, e.g., Lori Nessel, *"Wilful Blindness" to Gender–Based Violence Abroad: United States' Implementation of Article III of the United Nations Convention Against Torture*, 89 Minnesota L. Rev. 71 (2004) (arguing that CAT could, and should, be useful in domestic violence cases). In other instances, CAT claims can possibly avoid some of the procedural obstacles associated with relief under the 1951 Convention. Conversely, as you will also see, there are situations in which a persecution-based claim will lie even though a CAT claim will not.

Because of various modifications introduced by the Senate during the ratification process, and because of some disputes concerning the precise effects of CAT, a brief detour on the law of treaties is necessary. Treaty law consists of both international law and municipal law. As for international law, the most important source is the Convention on the Law of Treaties, U.N. Doc. A/CONF.39/27 (1969), 1155 U.N.T.S. 336 (signed at Vienna, May 23, 1969), commonly called the Vienna Convention or sometimes the Treaty on Treaties. The United States is not a party to the Vienna Convention, but the State Department nonetheless treats it as "the authoritative guide to current treaty law and practice." See Mark W. Janis, An Introduction to International Law 17 (4th ed. 2003).

Treaties are negotiated in different ways, ranging from informal discussions among executive branch officials to formal conferences that often precede major multinational conventions. Some treaties, including both the 1951 Convention and CAT, were officially sponsored by the United Nations.

Importantly, the fact that a state has "signed" a treaty does not ordinarily make the treaty legally binding on that state. Signing typically indicates only that the text of the document is accurate. Janis, above, at 20. The treaty itself normally specifies what a state has to do to become a party; usually the state must communicate its ratification in a specified manner. In the case of CAT, a state becomes a party by depositing the instrument of ratification with the Secretary–General of the United Nations. CAT art. 25.2.

States also have their own constraints, imposed by municipal law. In the United States, the President presents a proposed treaty to the Senate, which may ratify it by a two-thirds vote. U.S. Const. art. II, § 2, cl. 2. Treaties that are ratified in this way become part of the "Law of the Land." U.S. Const. art. VI, cl. 2. But what effect do they have in a United States domestic court?

The answer is "it depends." As discussed earlier, the internal allocation of the United States machinery for implementing its international legal obligations is a matter of domestic United States law. Those agreements that are "self-executing" create binding *internal* law and judicially enforceable obligations. Otherwise the treaty requires implementing legislation before an aggrieved individual will have a right of action in court—and then the action will be under the statute, not under the treaty. Whether a treaty is self-executing normally depends on the intentions of the states parties, but some courts will also consider executive branch statements made in connection with the United States treaty ratification process. See Thomas Buergenthal & Sean D. Murphy, Public International Law in a Nutshell 190–193 (3d ed. 2002).

Complications arise when the ratifying body—in the United States, the Senate—attaches conditions to ratification. These conditions take different forms. The most common condition is a "reservation;" the state purports to ratify the treaty but with modifications. Vienna Convention, art. 2(1)(d). This is permissible unless the treaty prohibits the reservation, or the treaty allows "only specified reservations, which do not include the reservation in question," or the reservation is "incompatible with the object and purpose of the treaty." Vienna Convention, art. 19. Depending on the treaty, a reservation might require affirmative acceptance by one or more of the other parties, or acceptance might be the default option. In any event, the reservation alters the obligations of the reserving state only as against those states that accept the reservation; furthermore, the alteration is reciprocal. See Janis, above, at 24.

When a state prefers not to make reciprocal modifications, it sometimes stops short of offering formal reservations and instead articulates its "understandings" or "declarations" of what particular provisions mean. Although it is the courts' job to interpret the law, they commonly defer to these pronouncements. See Barry E. Carter & Phillip R. Trimble, International Law 198 (2d ed. 1995).

With that background, the sequence of events that have made CAT a live option in the United States can be described. As noted earlier, the U.N. General Assembly passed a resolution adopting the Convention in 1984. The United States signed it in 1988, the Senate ratified it (with reservations, understandings, and declarations that you will soon see) in 1990, and the President deposited the ratification instrument with the U.N. Secretary–General in 1994. See Rosati, above, at 184. Only at that point did the

United States become a party. As noted above, the implementing legislation was passed in 1998 and the interim regulations in 1999.

The Senate declared that CAT is not self-executing, 136 Cong. Rec. S17492 (Oct. 27, 1990), Dec. #1, and the BIA (before Congress passed implementing legislation) accepted the Senate's conclusion. See *Matter of H–M–V-*, 22 I. & N. Dec. 256, 259–60 (BIA en banc 1998). At least one commentator vigorously disagrees. See Kristen B. Rosati, *The United Nations Convention Against Torture: A Self–Executing Treaty that Prevents the Removal of Persons Ineligible for Asylum and Withholding of Removal*, 26 Denver J. Internat'l L. 533 (1998). Since Congress has passed implementing legislation anyway, you might be wondering, why does it matter whether CAT is self-executing? The answer is that there are several respects in which the implementing statute, which reflects the Senate's reservations, understandings, and declarations, arguably falls short of meeting the United States obligations under CAT. If that turns out to be the case, nonrefoulement applicants will want to invoke the Convention directly; whether CAT is self-executing will thus become highly important.

Convention Against Torture and Other Cruel, Inhuman or Degrading Treatment or Punishment

U.N. General Assembly Res. 39/46, 39 U.N. GAOR Supp. (No. 51) at 197, U.N. Doc. A/39/51 (adopted Dec. 10, 1984).

Part I

Article 1

1. For the purposes of this Convention, torture means any act by which severe pain or suffering, whether physical or mental, is intentionally inflicted on a person for such purposes as obtaining from him or a third person information or a confession, punishing him for an act he or a third person has committed or is suspected of having committed, or intimidating or coercing him or a third person, or for any reason based on discrimination of any kind, when such pain or suffering is inflicted by or at the instigation of or with the consent or acquiescence of a public official or other person acting in an official capacity. It does not include pain or suffering arising only from, inherent in or incidental to lawful sanctions.

2. This article is without prejudice to any international instrument or national legislation which does or may contain provisions of wider application.

Article 2

1. Each State Party shall take effective legislative, administrative, judicial or other measures to prevent acts of torture in any territory under its jurisdiction.

2.   No exceptional circumstances whatsoever, whether a state of war or a threat of war, internal political instability or any other public emergency, may be invoked as a justification of torture.

3.   An order from a superior officer or a public authority may not be invoked as a justification of torture.

Article 3

1.   No State Party shall expel, return ("refouler") or extradite a person to another State where there are substantial grounds for believing that he would be in danger of being subjected to torture.

2.   For the purpose of determining whether there are such grounds, the competent authorities shall take into account all relevant considerations including, where applicable, the existence in the State concerned of a consistent pattern of gross, flagrant or mass violations of human rights.

* * *

Article 12

Each State Party shall ensure that its competent authorities proceed to a prompt and impartial investigation, wherever there is reasonable ground to believe that an act of torture has been committed in any territory under its jurisdiction.

Article 13

Each State Party shall ensure that any individual who alleges he has been subjected to torture in any territory under its jurisdiction has the right to complain to and to have his case promptly and impartially examined by its competent authorities. Steps shall be taken to insure that the complainant and witnesses are protected against all ill-treatment or intimidation as a consequence of his complaint or any evidence given.

* * *

Part II

Article 17

1.   There shall be established a Committee against Torture (hereinafter referred to as the Committee) which shall carry out the functions hereinafter provided. The Committee shall consist of 10 experts of high moral standing and recognized competence in the field of human rights, who shall serve in their personal capacity. The experts shall be elected by the States Parties, consideration being given to equitable geographical distribution and to the usefulness of the participation of some persons having legal experience.

* * *

Article 20

1. If the Committee receives reliable information which appears to it to contain well-founded indications that torture is being systematically practiced in the territory of a State Party, the Committee shall invite that State Party to co-operate in the examination of the information and to this end to submit observations with regard to the information concerned.

* * *

5. * * * [T]he Committee may, after consultations with the State Party concerned, decide to include a summary account of the results of the proceedings in its annual report * * *.

Article 21

1. A State Party to this Convention may at any time declare under this article that it recognizes the competence of the Committee to receive and consider communications to the effect that a State Party claims that another State Party is not fulfilling its obligations under this Convention. Such communications may be received and considered according to the procedures laid down in this article only if submitted by a State Party which has made a declaration recognizing in regard to itself the competence of the Committee. No communication shall be dealt with by the Committee under this article if it concerns a State Party which has not made such a declaration. * * *

* * *

(c) The Committee shall deal with a matter referred to it under this article only after it has ascertained that all domestic remedies have been invoked and exhausted in the matter, in conformity with the generally recognized principles of international law. This shall not be the rule where the application of the remedies is unreasonably prolonged or is unlikely to bring effective relief to the person who is the victim of the violation of this Convention.

* * *

Article 22

1. A State Party to this Convention may at any time declare under this article that it recognizes the competence of the Committee to receive and consider communications from or on behalf of individuals subject to its jurisdiction who claim to be victims of a violation by a State Party of the provisions of the Convention. No communication shall be received by the Committee if it concerns a State Party to the Convention which has not made such a declaration.

* * *

5. The Committee shall not consider any communications from an individual under this article unless it has ascertained that

(a) The same matter has not been, and is not being, examined under another procedure of international investigation or settlement;

(b) The individual has exhausted all available domestic remedies; this shall not be the rule where the application of the remedies is unreasonably prolonged or is unlikely to bring effective relief to the person who is the victim of the violation of this Convention.

* * *

Part III

Article 25

1.   This Convention is open for signature by all States.

2.   This Convention is subject to ratification. Instruments of ratification shall be deposited with the Secretary–General of the United Nations.

* * *

Article 28

1.   Each State may, at the time of signature or ratification of this Convention or accession thereto, declare that it does not recognize the competence of the Committee provided for in article 20.

2.   Any State Party having made a reservation in accordance with paragraph 1 of this article may, at any time, withdraw this reservation by notification to the Secretary–General of the United Nations.

* * *

Resolution of the United States Senate Ratifying the Convention Against Torture

101st Cong. 2nd Sess.
136 Cong. Rec. S17491–92.
October 27, 1990.

RESOLVED (TWO–THIRDS OF THE SENATORS PRESENT CONCURRING THEREIN), That the Senate advise and consent to the ratification of the Convention Against Torture and Other Cruel, Inhuman or Degrading Treatment or Punishment, adopted by unanimous agreement of the United Nations General Assembly on December 10, 1984, and signed by the United States on April 18, 1988: PROVIDED, That:

I.   The Senate's advice and consent is subject to the following reservations:

* * *

II.   The Senate's advice and consent is subject to the following understandings, which shall apply to the obligations of the United States under this Convention:

(1)(a) That with reference to Article 1, the United States understands that, in order to constitute torture, an act must be specifically intended to inflict severe physical or mental pain or suffering and that mental pain or suffering refers to prolonged mental harm caused by or resulting from: (1) the intentional infliction or threatened infliction of severe physical pain or suffering; (2) the administration or application, or threatened administration or application, of mind altering substances or other procedures calculated to disrupt profoundly the senses or the personality; (3) the threat of imminent death; or (4) the threat that another person will imminently be subjected to death, severe physical pain or suffering, or the administration or application of mind altering substances or other procedures calculated to disrupt profoundly the senses or personality.

(b) That the United States understands that the definition of torture in Article 1 is intended to apply only to acts directed against persons in the offender's custody or physical control.

(c) That with reference to Article 1 of the Convention, the United States understands that "sanctions" includes judicially imposed sanctions and other enforcement actions authorized by United States law or by judicial interpretation of such law. Nonetheless, the United States understands that a State Party could not through its domestic sanctions defeat the object and purpose of the Convention to prohibit torture.

(d) That with reference to Article 1 of the Convention, the United States understands that the term "acquiescence" requires that the public official, prior to the activity constituting torture, have awareness of such activity and thereafter breach his legal responsibility to intervene to prevent such activity.

(e) That with reference to Article 1 of the Convention, the United States understands that noncompliance with applicable legal procedural standards does not per se constitute torture.

(2) That the United States understands the phrase, "where there are substantial grounds for believing that he would be in danger of being subjected to torture," as used in Article 3 of the Convention, to mean "if it is more likely than not that he would be tortured."

* * *

III. The Senate's advice and consent is subject to the following declarations:

(1) That the United States declares that the provisions of Articles 1 through 16 of the Convention are not self-executing.

(2) That the United States declares, pursuant to Article 21, paragraph 1, of the Convention, that it recognizes the competence of the Committee against Torture to receive and consider communications to the effect that a State Party claims that another State Party is not fulfilling its obligations under the Convention. It is the understanding of the United States that, pursuant to the above mentioned article, such communications shall be

accepted and processed only if they come from a State Party which has made a similar declaration.

* * *

Foreign Affairs Reform and Restructuring Act of 1998

Pub. L. 105–277, Div. G, 112 Stat. 2681.
October 21, 1998.

SECTION 2242.   UNITED STATES POLICY WITH RESPECT TO THE INVOLUNTARY RETURN OF PERSONS IN DANGER OF SUBJECTION TO TORTURE.

(a) Policy.—It shall be the policy of the United States not to expel, extradite, or otherwise effect the involuntary return of any person to a country in which there are substantial grounds for believing the person would be in danger of being subjected to torture, regardless of whether the person is physically present in the United States.

(b) Regulations.—Not later than 120 days after the date of enactment of this Act, the heads of the appropriate agencies shall prescribe regulations to implement the obligations of the United States under Article 3 of the United Nations Convention Against Torture and Other Forms of Cruel, Inhuman or Degrading Treatment or Punishment, subject to any reservations, understandings, declarations, and provisos contained in the United States Senate resolution of ratification of the Convention.

(c) Exclusion of Certain Aliens.—To the maximum extent consistent with the obligations of the United States under the Convention, subject to any reservations, understandings, declarations, and provisos contained in the United States Senate resolution of ratification of the Convention, the regulations described in subsection (b) shall exclude from the protection of such regulations aliens described in [INA § 241(b)(3)(B)].

(d) Review and Construction.—Notwithstanding any other provision of law, and except as provided in the regulations described in subsection (b), no court shall have jurisdiction to review the regulations adopted to implement this section, and nothing in this section shall be construed as providing any court jurisdiction to consider or review claims raised under the Convention or this section, or any other determination made with respect to the application of the policy set forth in subsection (a), except as part of the review of a final order of removal pursuant to [INA § 242].

[The REAL ID Act, § 106(a)(1)(B), without altering the language of the above provision, added new INA § 242(a)(4), which further governs judicial review of CAT claims. Please read INA § 242(a)(4) now—ed.]

(e) Authority to Detain.—Nothing in this section shall be construed as limiting the authority of the Attorney General to detain any person under any provision of law, including, but not limited to, any provision of the Immigration and Nationality Act.

(f) Definitions.—

(1) Convention defined.—In this section, the term "Convention" means the United Nations Convention Against Torture and Other Forms of Cruel, Inhuman or Degrading Treatment or Punishment, done at New York on December 10, 1984.

(2) Same terms as in the convention.—Except as otherwise provided, the terms used in this section have the meanings given those terms in the Convention, subject to any reservations, understandings, declarations, and provisos contained in the United States Senate resolution of ratification of the Convention.

NOTES AND QUESTIONS

1. As the title of the Convention suggests, the drafters regard "torture" as a subset of "cruel, inhuman or degrading treatment or punishment." As the body of the Convention suggests, torture is seen as an especially virulent subset. The measures that CAT requires states to take with respect to torture are more stringent than those required with respect to "other cruel, inhuman or degrading treatment or punishment."

By way of example, states must take specific affirmative measures to prevent acts of torture within their respective territories, CAT art. 2.1, including criminalizing such acts, CAT art. 4. When torture is alleged, the state must either extradite or submit the case for prosecution. CAT art. 7. States must ensure procedures for torture victims to obtain compensation. CAT art. 14. Most important for present purposes, the nonrefoulement obligations imposed by article 3 apply only to torture.

The obligation to prevent and redress other cruel, inhuman or degrading treatment or punishment is narrower. CAT article 16.1 requires states to "undertake to prevent" such acts (by public officials) within their own territories, and it specifically makes articles 10–13 applicable to all cruel, inhuman or degrading treatment or punishment, not just torture. But those articles merely require states to include certain information in the education and training of law enforcement officials, investigate alleged misconduct, and provide a forum for complaints.

The phrase "cruel, inhuman or degrading treatment or punishment," or a very close variant, appears in other international human rights conventions as well. See, e.g, Universal Declaration of Human Rights, U.N.G.A. Res. 217A(III), U.N. Doc. A/810 at 71, art. 5 (1948); International Covenant on Civil and Political Rights, U.N.G.A. Res. 2200A(XXI), 21 U.N. GAOR Supp. (No. 16) at 52, U.N. Doc. A/6316, 999 U.N.T.S. 171, art. 7 (adopted Dec. 19, 1966); African [Banjul] Charter on Human and Peoples' Rights, OAU Doc. CAB/LEG/67/3 rev. 5, art. 5 (adopted June 27, 1981); American Convention on Human Rights, O.A.S. Treaty Series No. 36, at 1, OEA/Ser. L.V/II.23 doc. rev. 2, art. 5 (Nov. 22, 1969); [European] Convention for the Protection of Human Rights and Fundamental Freedoms, 213 U.N.T.S. 222, art. 3 (signed Nov. 4, 1950).

The present concern is with the nonrefoulement prohibition of article 3. Since that article by its terms covers only "torture," the discussion from this point on will cover only torture, not "other cruel, inhuman or degrading treatment or punishment."

2.   There are only two "reservations" to the Senate's ratification of CAT, and neither one is crucial to nonrefoulement. In contrast, Understandings 1(a), 1(b), 1(c), 1(d), 1(e), and 2, as well as Declaration 1, are highly significant here. In a moment you will have a chance to decide whether they are consistent with CAT. First, though, do you think it matters? Suppose the BIA, relying on one of the cited understandings and the declaration, denies a CAT claim. Assume the claim otherwise would have been granted. In a case that is properly brought, what should the court do (a) if the court finds that CAT is self-executing; and (b) if the court finds that it isn't? Before answering, consider not only CAT and the Senate ratification resolution, but also the subsequent implementing statute.

3.   Read carefully the Senate's Understanding #1(a), relating to mental suffering as a form of torture. Do you think this definition fulfills U.S. obligations under CAT? If initially it seems to fall short, does the second prong cure the defect? That prong covers "the administration or application, or threatened administration or application, of mind altering substances *or other procedures* calculated to disrupt profoundly the senses or the personality" [emphasis added].

4.   The torture definition in CAT article 1.1 lists several purposes for which torture might be inflicted—obtaining information or a confession, punishment, intimidation or coercion, and discrimination. Since the listed purposes are prefaced by the phrase "such purposes as," they seem merely illustrative, not exhaustive. The Senate committee that recommended ratification shares that view. See Comm. on Foreign Relations, United States Senate, Exec. Report 101–30, Convention Against Torture and Other Cruel, Inhuman or Degrading Treatment or Punishment at 14 (Aug. 30, 1990) [hereafter cited as Senate Foreign Relations Committee Report].

5.   The torture that CAT article 1.1 recognizes must be "inflicted by or at the instigation of or with the consent or acquiescence of a public official or other person acting in an official capacity." Compare this requirement to the non-state actor rule that you encountered earlier in connection with persecution-based asylum and nonrefoulement claims. That latter standard requires a government "unwilling or unable" to control the private actor.

What if a private individual or group inflicts torture and one or more government officials fail to intervene? Is this "acquiescence?" Senate Understanding 1(d) defines "acquiescence" to require "awareness" by the public official and a breach of "his legal responsibility."

The Senate Foreign Relations Committee Report, above at 9, says that the "awareness" requirement was added in order to clarify that even "wilful blindness" will suffice. Accord, *Ontunez-Tursios v. Ashcroft*, 303

F.3d 341, 354 (5th Cir. 2002). (Does adding an "awareness" requirement really clarify that wilful blindness establishes such awareness?)

As for the "legal responsibility" requirement, at least one commentator argues, and the General Counsel's Office of the former INS agreed, that "legal" includes international law and that the enforcement responsibilities created by CAT itself should therefore suffice. See Kristen Rosati, *Article 3 of the United Nations Convention Against Torture: A Powerful Tool to Prevent Removal Just Became More Powerful*, 4 BIB 137, 140–41 (Feb. 15, 1999).

A potentially more serious constraint is Understanding 1(b), which limits torture to "acts directed against persons in *the offender's* custody or physical control" [emphasis added]. In cases of government acquiescence in private acts, to which "offender" is the Senate referring? If it is the private actor, does the claim fail because he or she is not a public official? If it is the public official who offends by acquiescing, will Understanding 1(b) bar recovery, since the official does not have custody or control over the victim?

The early United States cases have been inconclusive. In *Matter of S.V.*, 22 I. & N. Dec. 1306 (BIA en banc 2000), the Board held that acts by rebel guerrillas would not constitute torture because the government could not be said to acquiesce in those acts. And in *Ali v. Reno*, 237 F.3d 591 (6th Cir. 2001), the court reached a similar conclusion with respect to violent acts committed against the applicant by her siblings. But in *Reyes-Reyes v. Ashcroft*, 384 F.3d 782 (9th Cir. 2004), the court majority held that the government need not *knowingly* acquiesce. *Id.* at 787. The concurring judge disagreed, relying on the language in the regulations, 8 C.F.R. § 208.18(a)(7) (2004) (drawn from Senate Understanding 1(d) above) to require that "the public official, prior to the activity constituting torture, have awareness of such activity and thereafter breach his or her legal responsibility to intervene to prevent such activity." 384 F.3d at 789–90. As in the persecution-based asylum and nonrefoulement cases, the issue is likely to assume particular significance in domestic violence cases. See Problem 9 below.

6. Note the second sentence of CAT article 1.1 (torture does not include suffering from "lawful sanctions"). The Senate Foreign Relations Committee Report, at 30, recommended the following Understanding:

> * * * [T]he United States understands that "sanctions" includes judicially imposed sanctions and other enforcement actions authorized by United States law or by judicial interpretations of such law provided that such sanctions or actions are not clearly prohibited under international law.

On the floor of the Senate, however, this recommended language was amended. The amended version eventually became Senate Understanding 1(c), which you should now review.

(a) Identify precisely how the recommended language differs from the language ultimately adopted.

(b) What practical significance do you think the amendment has?

(c) Do you see any circular logic problems in the 2nd sentence of Understanding 1(c) (the sentence that begins "Nonetheless")? Consider especially the qualifying phrase "to prohibit *torture*" [emphasis added].

7. Section B of this chapter dealt with asylum and withholding of removal in the context of persecution. Recall that asylum under INA § 208 requires the person to meet the "refugee" definition of INA § 101(a)(42), under which either past persecution or a well-founded fear of future persecution will suffice. Under the withholding of removal provision for persecution, INA § 241(b)(3), and under article 33 of the 1951 U.N. Refugee Convention, only a future threat to one's life or freedom suffices; past persecution is not a basis for 241(b)(3) relief.

In this respect the nonrefoulement remedy established by CAT article 3 is analogous to nonrefoulement in the persecution context. Both protect only against threats of future torture; past torture is not a basis for relief.

8. CAT article 3 prohibits refoulement "where there are substantial grounds for believing that he would be in danger of being subjected to torture." Senate Understanding #2 interprets this language to mean that torture must be "more likely than not." So far, that interpretation has held up. See, e.g., *Lukwago v. Ashcroft*, 329 F.3d 157, 182–83 (3rd Cir. 2003); *Matter of M–B–A-*, 23 I. & N. Dec. 474 (BIA 2002). The stated explanation was that, as you might recall, the United States uses a "more likely than not" test for nonrefoulement in persecution cases. Senate Foreign Relations Committee Report, above at 10. Does Senate Understanding #2 accurately interpret CAT article 3? If a physician told you there was a one-third chance that your disease would prove fatal, would you really doubt that there were "substantial" grounds to feel that you were at least "in danger?"

9. As you saw earlier, article 33.1 of the 1951 Convention prohibits refoulement in the persecution context, but article 33.2 expressly allows states to make exceptions on certain criminal and national security grounds. Exceptions along these lines (though arguably broader than what the 1951 Convention authorizes) also appear in the United States implementing legislation. INA § 241(b)(3)(B). These were discussed in section B.5 above.

CAT article 3, in sharp contrast to article 33 of the 1951 Convention, makes the prohibition on refoulement absolute. It allows no exceptions. The BIA appears to share that view, see *Matter of H–M–V*, 22 I. & N. Dec. 256, 258 (BIA en banc 1998) (dictum), as did the former INS. 64 Fed. Reg. 8478, 8481 (Feb. 19, 1999). International law, including decisions of the Committee Against Torture, takes a similar view. See Rosati, above, at 143–44. Even the Senate ratification resolution, which weakens the Convention in so many ways that you have already seen, makes no attempt to engraft criminal or national security exceptions onto article 3.

The implementing statute, however, raises the issue. Section 2242(b) requires "the appropriate agencies" to issue regulations implementing U.S. obligations under CAT. Section 2242(c) then says:

To the maximum extent consistent with the obligations of the United States under the Convention, * * * the regulations described in subsection (b) shall exclude from the protection of such regulations aliens described in [INA § 241(b)(3)(B)].

Since the Convention doesn't permit *any* exceptions to the bar on refoulement, the qualifying opening phrase would seem to render subsection 2242(c) a nullity. This provision thus posed a dilemma for the Justice Department. If its regulations truly excluded the 241(b)(3)(B) individuals from protection, the regulations would surely violate United States obligations under CAT. For the same reason, they would exceed the authority conferred by section 2242(c) above, given the opening qualifier. But if the regulations made no special provision at all for the 241(b)(3)(B) individuals, the Department would risk the political ire of Congress.

The solution was to issue interim regulations that distinguished "withholding of removal" (the usual remedy) from "deferral of removal" (a more limited remedy for 241(b)(3)(B) individuals). Both remedies prohibit refoulement for as long as there are substantial grounds to believe the person is in danger of torture, but the latter makes it procedurally less cumbersome to refoule the person once the danger subsides. The procedures are discussed more fully in item 13 below.

If the regulations were to change, and the Justice Department were to begin returning 241(b)(3)(B) individuals in circumstances in which CAT prohibits refoulement, the regulations would be vulnerable to challenge under the opening phrase of section 2242(c). In such an event, some difficult issues of judicial power would arise. These are discussed in item 14 below.

10.   In *Sale v. Haitian Centers Council*, reproduced and discussed on pages 922–38 above, the Supreme Court interpreted the nonrefoulement provisions of both the 1951 Convention and the United States statute [now INA § 241(b)(3)] as being inapplicable to anyone intercepted on the high seas. Compare the language of INA § 241(b)(3) with that of the CAT implementing statute, in particular section 2242(a). Do you think *Sale* will be held to apply to CAT claims if the issue arises?

11.   Based on what you have read so far, what do you see as the practical significance of CAT article 3 for noncitizens in the United States? Invent one or more hypotheticals in which a 241(b)(3) claim might fail while a CAT nonrefoulement claim might succeed.

12.   Conversely, is it possible for a CAT claim to fail when a persecution-based claim would succeed?

13.   The procedures for filing and adjudicating CAT claims are laid out in the regulations. Except as discussed in the next paragraph, they are essentially the same as the procedures for persecution-based claims. 8 C.F.R. § 208.16 (2004); see also *id.* § 208.30. Even the same application form—the familiar I–589—is prescribed for CAT claims, so that persecution-based claims and CAT requests can be made and decided together. The persecution-related nonrefoulement provisions of the expedited removal

process, which were discussed in section B.7.b.iv above, also apply equally to CAT claims, except that "credible fear of persecution" becomes "credible fear of torture." *Id.* § 235.3(b)(4). Note that nonrefoulement claims, whether based on persecution or torture, are not subject to the one-year (or any other) filing deadline applicable to asylum.

The one major procedural difference between CAT claims and persecution-based claims stems from the statutory constraint discussed in item 9 above. The CAT implementing statute, in section 2242(c), commands the administration to deny protection to anyone described in INA § 241(b)(3)(B) (individuals ineligible for persecution-based nonrefoulement because of crime, persecution, or national security concerns), "to the maximum extent consistent with the obligations of the United States under the Convention." Since the nonrefoulement obligations under CAT are not subject to any exceptions, the government recognized it could not deny all protection, even to 241(b)(3)(B) individuals. It therefore distinguished two protective remedies—"withholding of removal" and a slightly less favorable remedy called "deferral of removal." The former is for applicants who satisfy all the requirements of CAT and do not fall within any of the 241(b)(3)(B) disqualifications. The latter is for those who meet the CAT requirements but fall within one of the 241(b)(3)(B) disqualifications. See 8 C.F.R. § 208.17 (2004).

Both remedies bar the person's return to the country in which torture is feared but, like the persecution-related form of nonrefoulement that you studied earlier, neither remedy prevents the government from returning the person to a safe third country. The rules that govern detention and employment authorization pending proceedings to determine persecution-based asylum or nonrefoulement apply here as well.

The main difference between withholding and deferral concerns the ease of termination. To terminate withholding of removal, the government must move to reopen, produce new evidence that was previously unavailable, and sustain the burden of proving by a preponderance of the evidence that the person will not be tortured. 8 C.F.R. § 208.24(f) (2004). In contrast, to terminate deferral of removal, government need only move for a hearing and produce relevant evidence not previously considered. The immigration judge will then hold an expedited hearing at which the applicant will have the burden of proof. *Id.* § 208.17(d)(1,3,4). An order terminating either withholding or deferral is appealable to the BIA. *Id.* § 208.17(d)(4).

14.   The implementing statute, in section 2242(d), addresses the subject of judicial review. Please review that paragraph carefully at this time. Dissected, the provision consists of a "notwithstanding" clause, then an "except" clause, then a clause that speaks to the reviewability of the regulations themselves, then a pair of clauses dealing with the reviewability of the denials of individual claims, and finally another "except" clause—all in one breathtaking sentence. See some insightful parsing in Kristen Rosati's article, cited in item 5 above, at 145–46.

a.   Taken alone, section 2242(d) might have left some uncertainty whether the "notwithstanding" clause was meant to be subject to an implied habeas corpus exception. Recall the materials in chapter 9, section B.6.b above. But in 2005, the REAL ID Act, § 106(a)(1)(B), added new INA § 242(a)(4), which makes clear that the petition for review procedure is the exclusive means of challenging administratively final denials of Torture Convention claims; even habeas corpus is expressly excluded. If for some reason a petition for review is not possible in a given case (for example, because the time for filing the petition has lapsed), it is not clear whether the Constitution would require the availability of habeas. See generally the *St. Cyr* decision and the accompanying discussion in chapter 9, section B.6.b above. Also unclear is whether a total bar on judicial review of a CAT claim denial in a given case would violate the Convention itself.

b.   Suppose the BIA denies a CAT claim on the basis of something contained in the regulations, and the applicant files a petition for review of the resulting removal order. Suppose further that the court believes that the regulations exceeded the authority conferred by the statute. May the court reverse the BIA decision on the ground that the regulations on which it was based were invalid? (Watch the statutory punctuation.)

c.   The first "except" clause, near the beginning of the provision, purports to empower the Attorney General to decide, in the regulations, whether a court will have jurisdiction to review those regulations. In turn, the regulations say only that, pursuant to the statute, "there shall be no judicial appeal or review of any action, decision, or claim raised under the Convention or [section 2242(d], except as part of the review of a final order of removal [under INA § 242] ..." 8 C.F.R. § 208.18(e) (2004). What do you think of the first "except" clause in section 2242(d)?

15.   The procedures you have been considering are provided by United States municipal law. CAT also establishes some international remedies in torture cases, but as you will soon discover they will be of little use to CAT claimants in the United States, at least in the nonrefoulement context. To see why this is so, review CAT articles 20, 21, and 22 (which deal with three different powers of the Committee Against Torture), then CAT article 28, and then Declaration #2 of the Senate ratification resolution. Exactly which competencies of the Committee Against Torture does the United States accept?

16.   CAT Article 30.1 creates another international dispute resolution mechanism. If states parties disagree about the interpretation or application of CAT and cannot resolve the dispute through negotiation, any one of them may submit the case to arbitration. If after six months the parties cannot agree on the organization of the arbitration, then any of them may refer the case to the International Court of Justice (ICJ) in the Hague. Article 30.2, however, allows any State Party to opt out of article 30.1. In Reservation #2 of the Senate ratification resolution, the United States did so. The Senate Foreign Relations Committee Report, at 28, explained that this decision was in keeping with the Reagan Administration's 1985 with-

drawal from the compulsory jurisdiction of the ICJ (in the midst of Nicaragua's suit against the U.S.).

17. As is probably obvious from the long list of reservations, understandings, and declarations in the Senate ratification resolution, the final product reflected compromises among Senators with vastly different views about human rights, United States sovereignty, and the whole concept of an international legal order. Some Senators wanted CAT to have real teeth, even if that meant that the United States, like every other State Party, could be held accountable to an international body. Other Senators staunchly opposed ratification and as a fallback position sought to make CAT as ineffectual as possible. Contrast the following speeches on the Senate floor during the ratification debate:

Senator Nancy Kassebaum (R–Kansas):

Mr. President, I rise today to express my strong support for ratification of [CAT]. * * *

Last July, Amnesty International released its 1990 report documenting the incidence of torture of thousands of individuals in more than 100 countries. Though we do live with the reality of state-sanctioned torture in some countries, as well as its random occurrence, amnesty's statistics were nothing less than shocking.

Our ratification of the Convention Against Torture will, in itself, lead us closer to the goal it represents. The convention makes legitimate the right of nations to be concerned and to intercede regarding the behavior of another country toward its citizens. * * *

* * *

Critics of this convention also say it may give other countries opportunity to make charges against the United States. I do not agree with this because I believe we have nothing to fear about our compliance with the terms of this treaty. Torture is simply not accepted in this country, and never will be.

* * *

Mr. President, I would note that the United States is the only permanent member of the U.N. Security Council which has not ratified the convention. * * *

The Torture Convention * * * would send a powerful signal to torturers around the world that the United States will not tolerate its practice. As we near the end of the 20th century, let us take this step to help bring the world closer to ending practices which deny individuals basic human dignity.

136 Cong. Rec. at S17491 (Oct. 27, 1990).

Senator Jesse Helms (R–N.C.), Chairman, Senate Foreign Relations Committee:

* * * [Here Senator Helms is speaking in support of a contentious "sovereignty" reservation that would have made CAT subject to the U.S. Constitution insofar as it is enforced against the United States.] [O]ne only has to look at the current membership of the Committee on Torture, which includes a representative from the Soviet Union and a representative from Bulgaria.

The Soviet Union and Bulgaria have their own particular expertise in the matters of torture. This Convention's Committee on Torture is a farce, and it may be a dangerous farce. One could well say in this case that the lunatics are indeed running the asylum. I do not want those folks poking their noses into the operation of the U.S. legal system. They have plenty to do with the notorious injustice exemplified by the two countries I have just mentioned.

* * *

However, since this Convention is primarily symbolic, it is not necessary to engage in a superfluous debate. * * *

* * *

* * * [I]nternational law is a mere subordinate agent to the U.S. Constitution. * * * A treaty is a contract between two independent parties; but unlike domestic contracts which are subordinate to the U.S. Constitution and customary law, a treaty is without sanctions other than the good faith, prestige and power of the contracting parties.

* * * International law is merely a combination of codification and basic international customary practice leading to expectations of action by a nation state, but it can in no way be determinative of any such act.

* * *

The Torture Convention is by and large a rhetorical gesture, expressing the revulsion which every decent nation has against torture. * * *

But if the convention is meant in itself to be anything more than a rhetorical gesture, or to lay the basis to go beyond a rhetorical gesture, then it may present a clear and present danger to U.S. sovereignty and to the people of the United States. When even nations notorious in the annals of torture such as the Soviet Union and Bulgaria, piously sign such a treaty, it cheapens the consensus.

136 Cong. Rec. S17487–89 (Oct. 27, 1990).

18.   The Torture Victims Relief Act of 1998, Pub. L. 105–320, 112 Stat. 3016 (Oct. 30, 1998), is also relevant here. Sections 4 and 5 of this statute award grants to overseas and United States treatment centers for torture victims. Section 7 requires the Secretary of State to provide special

training for foreign service officers on the subject of torture, including gender-specific training for dealing with victims of sexual violence.

PROBLEMS 7–9

Problem 7. Police detectives in a totalitarian country have taken A into custody. Although they have no evidence that he has committed any crime, they think he knows the whereabouts of a prominent criminal fugitive. A denies knowing anything about the fugitive, but his captors do not believe him. After several hours of fruitless interrogation, his captors tell him that if he doesn't cooperate they will confine him permanently, and then one night in the next year they will kill him in his sleep. "Try thinking about that for a while," they tell him. They also tell him (falsely) that they have already killed his family. It has now been eight months, and A is still in detention. Has he been tortured (a) according to CAT; and (b) according to the U.S. Senate?

Problem 8. The secret police of another totalitarian country, acting on the direct orders of the President, apprehend and arrest B, one of the leaders of a peaceful democratic resistance movement. They detain him in a 4' by 4' jail cell. Every night the guards awaken him two or three times, beat him, and administer excruciating electrical shocks. He is given only enough food and water to stay alive and is never allowed to leave his cell. They tell him this treatment will continue until he signs a statement publicly denouncing the resistance movement and discrediting the other leaders by accusing them of fabricated crimes. B refuses. After three years in detention under those conditions, the President instructs the police to release him if he agrees to leave the country.

Emaciated, dangerously weak, and psychologically defeated, B agrees. Upon his release he obtains funds from the resistance, makes his way to the United States, and enters surreptitiously with the help of a smuggler. One week later ICE apprehends B and initiates removal proceedings. B applies for asylum under INA § 208 and for relief under CAT. While proceedings are pending, B, desperate for cash, commits an armed robbery of a gas station. He is convicted and sentenced to five years in prison. (Note his offense is an aggravated felony under INA § 101(a)(43)(F)). In the meantime, the democratic resistance movement that B helped to lead has toppled the totalitarian regime and now leads a democratic government. Nonetheless the haunting memories of his imprisonment and torture at the hands of the secret police are overwhelming, and B wishes never to return. B is still serving his criminal sentence and the removal hearing is about to begin. Is there any relief for which B is eligible? Before answering, review INA §§ 208(b)(2)(A,B) and 241(b)(3)(B).

Problem 9. C, who lives in a rural region of a third-world country, has been relentlessly abused by her husband for the duration of their two-year-old marriage. The abuse has included dangerous physical beatings and violent sexual assaults, occurring several times per month. Her husband repeatedly threatens to make the assaults even more brutal if she ever tells anyone or tries to escape. In any event, he assures her, he knows enough people that he could easily hunt her down anywhere in the country. Her screams and her conspicuous bruises make her situation obvious to all observers, including the police, but spousal violence is commonplace in her village and is routinely overlooked.

C escapes to the United States and applies for both asylum under INA § 208 and relief under CAT. Will she succeed?

2. TEMPORARY PROTECTION

a. UNITED STATES DOMESTIC LAW: TEMPORARY PROTECTED STATUS AND ITS PREDECESSORS

You have seen that the applicant for either asylum or withholding of removal must prove an individualized danger based on his or her race, religion, nationality, membership in a social group, or political opinion. The person who simply fears being caught in the crossfire of an armed conflict, or who is targeted because of some personal feud, or who is fleeing economic or natural catastrophe does not qualify. On this, if little else, the case law is clear. See, e.g., *Martinez–Romero v. INS,* 692 F.2d 595 (9th Cir.1982); *Matter of Mogharrabi,* 19 I. & N. Dec. 439 (BIA 1987).

Yet most will agree that those whose lives would be endangered at home present compelling humanitarian claims for protection even if they do not meet the Convention definition of refugee or the other Convention requirements for withholding of removal. Of particular importance, because of their vast numbers, are those who seek to escape armed conflict or natural disaster. As you will see in this section, many have advocated reforms designed to provide at least temporary, and under some proposals permanent, relief.

In the United States, two vehicles have historically supplied that relief on an ad hoc basis. As you saw earlier, noncitizens who have not yet entered the United States may, in the discretion of the Attorney General, be "paroled" in. INA § 212(d)(5).[18] Both before and after the Refugee Act of 1980, various Attorneys General invoked that authority on a blanket basis to aid groups of people fleeing armed conflict in particular countries. See Congressional Research Service, Review of U.S. Refugee Resettlement Programs and Policies 7–11 (Comm. Print, Senate Comm. on the Judiciary, 1980). That is no longer possible today, because IIRIRA § 602(a) amended INA § 212(d)(5) so as to confine it to case-by-case, rather than blanket, application. As a result, the executive branch today has no clearly available statutory authority to bring into the United States a group of people who face dangers other than persecution.

As for those who have already entered the United States, either unlawfully or as lawful nonimmigrants, the statute until 1990 provided no

---

18. "Refugees" have been ineligible for parole since 1980 in the absence of "compelling reasons in the public-interest," INA § 212(d)(5)(B), but we are concerned here with those do *not* meet the statutory definition of "refugee."

obvious form of relief. The executive branch had to be inventive. It responded by devising a remedy known as "extended voluntary departure" (EVD). As its name implies, EVD was technically an exercise of the Attorney General's power to grant voluntary departure in lieu of deportation. But EVD differed from the usual type of voluntary departure in several respects: First, EVD was granted on a blanket basis, typically to nationals of a particular war-torn country, though often limited to those who had already entered the United States by the date of the EVD announcement or some other date. In contrast, as you might recall, the usual voluntary departure is granted on a case-by-case basis. Second, unlike the usual voluntary departure, EVD was generally granted for a lengthy duration. The grant would typically be renewed if the danger had not sufficiently subsided by the initial expiration date; in some instances, Congress eventually enacted special legislation to allow adjustment of status to permanent residence. See 64 IR 1093 (1987). Third, while local officials and immigration judges routinely grant voluntary departure on a case-by-case basis under INA § 240B, only the Attorney General, acting nationwide and often upon the advice of the State Department, could then grant EVD. See Wire to INS Field Offices, Feb. 6, 1984, reproduced in 61 IR 103–04 (1984).

Here is a list of the known grants of EVD from 1960 on:

Country of Nationality	Year EVD Granted
Cuba	1960
Dominican Republic	1966
Czechoslovakia	1968
Chile	1971
Cambodia	1975
Vietnam	1975
Laos	1975
Lebanon	1976
Ethiopia	1977
Hungary	1977
Romania	1977
Uganda	1978
Iran	1979
Nicaragua	1979
Afghanistan	1980
Poland	1981

64 IR 1093 (1987) (also showing expiration dates and any subsequent legislation authorizing adjustment of status).

Ad hoc responses to specific crises had the advantage of flexibility. But they had clear disadvantages as well. As one commentator pointed out, "EVD is essentially ungoverned by any legally enacted standards." Michael G. Heyman, *Redefining Refugee: A Proposal for Relief for the Victims of Civil Strife*, 24 San Diego L.Rev. 449, 451 (1987). Consequently, the decision whether to grant EVD was subject to the same sorts of political biases that critics had imputed to the overseas refugee admission program and to asylum adjudication. A glance at the above list of countries whose nationals received EVD illustrates that the issue of foreign policy bias was a serious one. Almost all the countries on the list were adversaries of the United States at the pertinent times. The steadfast refusal of the executive branch to grant EVD to Salvadorans stood in marked contrast and during the 1980's was a continual focal point of the debates on EVD.

Also like parole, a decision not to grant EVD triggered few if any procedural rights, Heyman, above, and even a grant of EVD left the recipient with a highly uncertain, and therefore insecure, status. Apart from those considerations, there was a nagging question whether the decision to grant EVD should have been congressional, executive, or both.

For all those reasons, many suggested expanding and structuring the forms of relief available to individuals who flee civil strife. Professor Michael Heyman, in the article just mentioned, proposed amending the statutory refugee definition to embrace such people (and making corresponding changes to withholding of removal). See *id.* at 479–83. His approach was modeled on one adopted by the Organization for African Unity, whose position is discussed further below. The effect would have been to make asylum (as well as relief under the overseas admission program, which under INA § 207 applies to "refugees") available to those endangered by armed conflict.

Others advocated legislation establishing a special program, separate and apart from asylum and withholding of removal, for granting temporary refuge to those who flee generalized armed conflict or other enumerated dangers. See, e.g., the 1983 testimony of Professor T. Alexander Aleinikoff before the House Subcommittee on Immigration, Refugees and International Law, reproduced in T. Aleinikoff & D. Martin, Immigration Process and Policy 739–43 (1st ed. 1985). The generic terms for such relief are "safe haven" or "temporary protection." In the late 1980s a number of safe haven bills were introduced in Congress. Some would have set out general criteria applicable worldwide, e.g., H.R. 2922 (1987); some would have provided temporary safe haven to nationals of specific countries, e.g., S. 458 (1989) (El Salvador and Nicaragua); H.R. 2712 (1989) (China); and still others would have done both, e.g., H.R. 2929 (1989) (generic relief coupled with specific relief for Chinese nationals); H.R. 45 (1989) (generic, plus specific relief for nationals of El Salvador, Nicaragua, and China).

In 1990 those efforts bore fruit. The Immigration Act of 1990, § 302, created a new program to grant "temporary protected status" (TPS) to certain individuals who could not safely return home. The program is a modified version of Representative Romano Mazzoli's earlier bill, H.R. 2922 (1987). For a good summary of the TPS criteria and procedures, see Linton Joaquin, Mark Silverman & Lisa Klapal, Temporary Protected Status (National Immigration Law Center, May 1999). The TPS provision appears in INA § 244, which you should skim now.

Notice the following key elements of the statute and the implementing regulations: The Secretary of Homeland Security, after consulting with "appropriate" government agencies, may designate a foreign state or part of a foreign state under any of three circumstances: (A) There is an ongoing armed conflict that would pose a serious threat to the personal safety of the state's nationals if they were returned there; (B) An environmental disaster has substantially but temporarily disrupted living conditions, and the state has requested designation because it cannot adequately handle the return of its nationals; or (C) "[E]xtraordinary and temporary conditions" prevent safe return, and permitting the state's nationals to remain temporarily in the United States would not be contrary to the national interest. INA § 244(b)(1). The Secretary specifies the time period during which the designation will remain in force; that period must be somewhere between six and eighteen months. INA § 244(b)(2). Other paragraphs provide for periodic review of the conditions in the designated countries, premature terminations of those designations, and extensions. INA § 244(b)(3). There is no judicial review of the Secretary's decision whether to designate a particular state or whether to terminate or extend a designation. INA § 244(b)(5)(A).

Nationals of a designated country then apply individually for TPS. The Secretary's regulations generally require the person to apply to USCIS, even if removal proceedings have already begun by the time the Secretary designates the person's country. 8 C.F.R. § 244.7(a,d) (2004). Eligibility requirements include continuous physical presence in the United States since the effective date of the designation, continuous residence since a date specified by the Secretary, admissibility as an immigrant (with some exclusion grounds automatically excepted and some others waivable in the exercise of discretion), registration with USCIS within a specified time, and the absence of certain criminal and other disqualifications. INA § 244(c)(2).

The statute says the Secretary "may" grant TPS to an eligible national of a designated country. INA § 244(a)(1)(A). The Secretary has expressly delegated to the local USCIS directors not only the authority to decide eligibility, but also the discretion whether to grant TPS once eligibility is found. 8 C.F.R. § 244.10(b) (2004).

The statute also requires the Secretary to provide for administrative review of TPS denials and specifies that a national of a designated country may also claim TPS in removal proceedings. INA § 244(b)(5)(B). To implement that provision, the regulations authorize appeal of the local USCIS director's decision to the Administrative Appeals Unit (AAU), 8 C.F.R. § 244.10(c) (2004), unless the basis for the denial was a fact that also makes the applicant removable. In that latter event, the director must issue a charging document and the applicant will have the right to a de novo TPS determination in the ensuing removal hearing. *Id.* § 244.10(c).

The statute does not discuss judicial review of TPS denials. In the case where the TPS application is denied in removal proceedings, the removal order itself will be reviewable in the court of appeals under INA § 242, but the denial of TPS is another matter. A denial of TPS on discretionary grounds appears to be unreviewable. INA § 242(a)(2)(B)(ii). Whether eligibility determinations may be reviewed in court is not clear. Whether AAU denials will be subject to judicial review is also unclear. General federal question jurisdiction under 28 U.S.C. § 1331 might be asserted, but the same issue of whether INA § 242(a)(2)(B)(ii) precludes judicial review of the eligibility determination arises.

TPS can also be withdrawn. The statute requires withdrawal when the Secretary finds that the recipient was ineligible for TPS at the time it was granted, or has not remained continuously physically present since receiving TPS (with some exceptions), or the recipient, without good cause, fails to register annually with USCIS. See INA § 244(c)(3).

The main benefits of TPS are twofold: While TPS is in effect, the beneficiary may not be removed and may work. INA § 244(a)(1). Moreover, he or she is regarded as being in lawful nonimmigrant status for purposes of INA §§ 245 and 248 (adjustment of status to permanent residence and change of status from one nonimmigrant category to another, respectively), both of which require that the applicant be in lawful status. See INA § 244(f)(4). TPS beneficiaries may not travel abroad, however, without the Secretary's prior consent. *Id.* § 244(f)(3). The statute also provides that TPS–time does not count toward the continuous physical presence required for cancellation of removal, but then adds, mysteriously, "unless the Secretary of Homeland Security determines that extreme hardship exists." INA § 244(e). The effect of that provision is unclear, because if the Secretary *doesn't* find extreme hardship (and now, the more demanding "exceptional and extremely unusual hardship"), the individual will be ineligible for cancellation of removal anyway.

Importantly, section 244(g) makes TPS the "exclusive authority" of the Secretary of Homeland Security to allow parolees or deportable noncitizens to remain in the United States temporarily on the basis of country or region. The objective of that provision was to eliminate EVD.

As noted earlier, much of the debate over safe haven in the 1980's swirled around Salvadorans, whose asylum approval rates were unusually low. Congress included in the Immigration Act of 1990 a provision, section 303, specifically designating El Salvador as a TPS country.

As of March 2004, the U.S. has designated 15 different TPS countries (Angola, Bosnia–Herzegovina, Burundi, El Salvador, Guinea–Bissau, Honduras, Kuwait, Lebanon, Liberia, Montserrat, Nicaragua, Rwanda, Sierra Leone, Somalia, and Sudan) and one breakaway republic of Yugoslavia (Kosovo). In many cases the grants were renewed. Relief has typically been limited to people who arrived in the United States before the designation date. See 3 Gordon, Mailman & Yale–Loehr § 33.08[2]. Montserrat, in 1997, was the first state to be designated for TPS for environmental reasons. See 62 Fed. Reg. 45685–86 (Aug. 28, 1997). Soon after that, however, the devastation wrought by Hurricane Mitch prompted the Attorney General to designate Honduras and Nicaragua as TPS states. 64 Fed. Reg. 524, 526 (Jan. 5, 1999). Two authors have recently urged a grant of TPS status to Palestinians. See Susan M. Akram & Terry Rempel, *Temporary Protection as an Instrument for Implementing the Right of Return for Palestinian Refugees*, 22 Boston Univ. Internat'l L.J. 1 (2004).

Hot on the heels of TPS was the important court settlement announced in *American Baptist Churches v. Thornburgh,* 760 F.Supp. 796 (N.D.Cal.1991) (agreed upon by parties Dec. 19, 1990, approved by court Jan. 31, 1991) [the *ABC* case]. In *ABC,* a class action, Salvadoran and Guatemalan nationals in the United States alleged a pattern of discrimination by the various government agencies involved in the asylum adjudication process—the former INS, EOIR, and the State Department. The government acknowledged that foreign policy, law enforcement, and whether the government agrees or disagrees with the applicant's ideology are not relevant to whether the person has a well-founded fear of persecution. Under the terms of the settlement, Salvadorans and Guatemalans who had arrived in the United States by certain dates in 1990, and who were not aggravated felons, received various rights. To qualify, beneficiaries had to register during designated periods in 1991. Salvadorans applying for TPS were treated as having applied also for relief under *ABC.*

NOTES AND QUESTIONS

1.   Even with the enactment of TPS, United States law treats people who fear persecution differently from those who fear civil strife. Why do you think the law draws that distinction? *Should* it? Should national economic collapse be a basis for either asylum or TPS?

2.   Contrast the Heyman proposal to expand the statutory refugee definition with the TPS program that was eventually enacted. How do the two approaches differ in their practical effects? Accepting the goal of granting protection to individuals who would face generalized dangers at home, which solution do you prefer?

3.   Within the TPS program, identify the differences between the treatment of those who would face armed conflict and the treatment of those who would face environmental catastrophe. Should those two groups be treated differently?

4.   One of Professor Heyman's concerns about having to rely on EVD was that it was "essentially ungoverned by any legally enacted standards." Does TPS adequately address that concern? In answering, first identify the various sources of executive discretion built into the TPS program. They fall generally into two categories:

   a.   Some concern the decision as to country designations.

   b.   Others concern the adjudication of individual applications. One aspect of the latter discretion is INA § 244(a)(1)(A), which says the Secretary *may* grant TPS to an eligible national of a designated state. What other discretion does the Secretary or his or her delegates have in adjudicating individual cases?

   Do you approve of the various discretionary elements you have just identified?

5.   In contrast to the discretion not to *grant* TPS, there is no discretion not to *withdraw* TPS if any of the three grounds for withdrawal is

found. INA § 244(c)(3). One such ground is the beneficiary's failure, without good cause, to comply with the registration requirements (timing, form, and manner). *Id.* § 244(c)(3)(C). To put this in practical terms, a TPS beneficiary who registers a day late and does not have a good enough excuse *shall* be sent back to a country that the Secretary of Homeland Security has just characterized as too dangerous to return to. The Secretary is given no discretion to avoid that consequence, even in the most compelling case. Is the penalty proportionate to the transgression?

6. As its name implies, TPS is supposed to be "temporary." Relief is to last until it becomes safe for the person to return home. Some opponents of TPS were skeptical that the beneficiaries, after tasting prosperity and security and after developing deeper ties to people and institutions here, would really leave when their time was up. Many also believed that, once TPS had been granted for an extended period of time, Congress would be tempted to avoid hardship by passing special legislation granting permanent resident status to TPS beneficiaries. The compromise appears in INA § 244(h). TPS would be enacted, but Congress would not later pass the kind of permanent residence provision just described unless there was especially strong support for doing so. What effect will section 244(h) have if, at some future time, a simple majority in each House wishes to bestow permanent residence on TPS recipients from a particular country?

7. Another point of controversy during the years in which TPS was debated was the proper role of country-specific legislation. You have seen that section 302 of the Immigration Act of 1990 created generic criteria and procedures for TPS at the same time that section 303 was conferring TPS on nationals of one particular country, El Salvador. What do you see as the pros and cons of country-specific legislation in the context of TPS, either with or without corresponding generic legislation?

b. GLOBAL AND REGIONAL APPROACHES TO TEMPORARY PROTECTION

One of the first commentators to chide American immigration scholars for inadequate attention to international law was James A.R. Nafziger, *A Commentary on American Legal Scholarship Concerning the Admission of Migrants,* 17 Univ. Michigan J. L. Reform 165, 173–77 (1984). In that article Professor Nafziger advocated expanding the international definition of refugee to include a broader set of dangers; accord, Isabelle R. Gunning, *Expanding the International Definition of Refugee: A Multicultural View,* 13 Fordham Internat'l L.J. 35 (1989–90).

This call for a broader vision appears to have borne fruit, as abundant international refugee law scholarship soon blossomed in the United States. See, e.g., T. Alexander Aleinikoff & Vincent Chetail (eds.), Migration and International Legal Norms (2003); Anker at 9–11, 465–522; Gunning, above; Isabelle R. Gunning, *Modernizing Customary International Law and the Challenge of Human Rights,* 31 Virginia J. Internat'l L. 301 (1991); Richard B. Lillich, The Human Rights of Aliens in Contemporary International Law (1984); David A. Martin, *Effects of International Law on*

Migration Policy and Practice: The Uses of Hypocrisy, 23 Internat'l Migration Rev. 547 (1989); Deborah Perluss & Joan F. Hartman [subsequently Fitzpatrick], *Temporary Refuge: Emergence of a Customary Norm,* 26 Virginia J. Internat'l L. 551 (1986) [hereafter cited as Perluss & Fitzpatrick]; David Weissbrodt & Laura Danielson, Immigration Law and Procedure in a Nutshell, ch. 11 (5th ed. 2005); see also James A.R. Nafziger, *The General Admission of Aliens under International Law,* 77 Amer. J. Internat'l L. 804 (1983). For a long time overseas scholars have analyzed carefully the limitations that international law places on national sovereignty in the context of immigration. E.g., Guy S. Goodwin–Gill, The Refugee in International Law (2d ed. 1996); Guy S. Goodwin–Gill, International Law and the Movement of Persons Between States (1978); Atle Grahl–Madsen, The Status of Refugees in International Law (2 vols., 1966 and 1972); James C. Hathaway, The Law of Refugee Status (1991); Richard Plender, International Migration Law (rev. 2d ed.1988). But it remains true that the immigration literature has not fully tapped the rich resources of international law. And in no area of immigration is the potential relevance of international law greater than in the context of refugees, asylees, and other displaced persons.

The literature on temporary protection has reflected similar philosophical trends. The conventional wisdom has been that temporary protection of non-Convention refugees, while less advantageous to the beneficiary than asylum is, nonetheless provides an important safety valve for the affected individuals. Professor Joan Fitzpatrick in 1994 questioned that conventional wisdom. She argued that in actual practice the nations of the world frequently use temporary safe haven less as a supplement to the protections afforded by asylum than as an excuse for restricting grants of asylum. See Joan Fitzpatrick, *Flight from Asylum: Trends Toward Temporary "Refuge" and Local Responses to Forced Migrations,* 35 Virginia J. Internat'l L. 13 (1994). Her concern proved prophetic. There is now a lively debate about whether refugee advocates should favor increased reliance on temporary refuge as a strategy for persuading the world's receiving states to welcome larger numbers of refugees. See, e.g., Davor Sopf, *Temporary Protection in Europe after 1990: The "Right to Remain" of Genuine Convention Refugees,* 6 Washington Univ. J. L. & Policy 109 (2001).

In the article that follows, Professor Fitzpatrick develops that theme further. She considers not only the benefits and dangers of temporary protection regimes, but also whether temporary protection ought to be made the subject of an international agreement rather than left entirely to the discretion of individual states.

Joan Fitzpatrick, Temporary Protection of Refugees: Elements of a Formalized Regime

94 Amer. J. Internat'l L. 279, 279–80, 285–91, 296, 299–300, 303–04 (2000).

Temporary protection of refugees (TP) gained surprising prominence during the 1990s as a response to forced migration, at times seeming poised to displace the regime based on the 1951 Convention Relating to the Status of Refugees and its 1967 Protocol. The unprecedented Humanitarian Evacuation Programme to airlift Kosovar refugees to temporary safety in European and more distant states exemplifies TP's appeal and adaptability. The Kosovo experience, by restoring faith that some mass influxes are genuinely temporary, may reinvigorate enthusiasm for TP, which had flagged during the endgame to the Bosnian refugee crisis.

Temporary protection is not a new concept. Various versions of it were codified in a 1969 African refugee convention, promoted during mass flows from Southeast Asia two decades ago, and vigorously debated in the context of flight from Central American civil wars in the 1980s. Yet steps toward comprehensive codification of TP at the international level have been notably modest and slow. * * * The issue explored here is whether formalization of temporary protection, at the universal or regional level, is either likely or advisable.

* * *

Temporary protection is like a magic gift, assuming the desired form of its enthusiasts' policy objectives. Simultaneously, it serves as a magic mirror of its observers' fears. For refugee advocates, TP expands the protection of forced migrants who cannot satisfy the criteria under the 1951 Convention and it promises group-based protection when the determination of an individual's status proves impossible. At the same time, refugee rights organizations fear that informal and discretionary TP may dislodge refugee protection from the realm of enforceable human rights. For refugee agencies such as the United Nations High Commissioner for Refugees, TP serves as a short-term strategy to secure the immediate physical safety of refugees and a way station to more durable protection. But where TP is offered as a diluted substitute protection for Convention refugees, it represents a threat to the 1951 refugee regime. Moreover, regionalization of temporary protection could erode the UNHCR's influence. States, especially those under pressure from domestic constituencies preoccupied with migration, hope that TP will help them save costs on status determination, reduce social and economic benefits to asylum seekers, resist full integration of those who are granted asylum, and prioritize their rapid repatriation. TP may assist democratic states in mediating competing public demands that asylum not be a back door to immigration but that humanitarian ideals be sustained. Yet states also remain skeptical about formalizing temporary protection, since international TP obligations might expand the numbers of forced migrants eligible for legal protection against repatriation and pledges of international solidarity may create unpredictable and politically costly future burdens.

* * *

The establishment of a separate group-based status determination process through temporary protected status in the United States * * * [suggested] that TP's beneficiaries differ significantly from Convention refugees. First, TPS beneficiaries are assumed to be persons facing generalized danger rather than an individualized peril. Individual beneficiaries are approved through a streamlined process that focuses on nationality, rather than personal histories of harm and risk.

Second, leave to remain is limited in time, in contrast to open-ended grants of asylum, which by design often facilitate the rapid acquisition of permanent resident status. TPS preserves administrative discretion and avoids durable ties to beneficiaries. Although the statute sets forth general criteria for the grant, extension, and termination of TPS, the Attorney General's application of these criteria is not transparent or subject to external review. As a result, the duration of TPS is susceptible to significant political influence and is not necessarily tied to the severity of the danger prevailing in the state of origin. TPS thus contrasts markedly with *non-refoulement* under the 1951 Convention, which must be non-discriminatory on nationality grounds and is tied to the persistence of danger rather than artificial time constraints.

Third, TPS does not function as an admissions program but protects only those who happen to be in the United States at the time the Attorney General recognizes the crisis. Thus, TPS is not a strategy for responding to mass influx. In such crises the United States responds variably by establishing external safe havens or admitting the migrants as refugees.

The pressures of rapidly increasing asylum caseloads during the late 1980s and early 1990s in northern states attracted policymakers to temporary protection as a strategy to circumvent the highly contested arena of refugee status determination. Lesser-regulated and lower-visibility measures of protection could assuage demands for a humanitarian response to forced migrants, without committing the states of Western Europe to a durable solution or the full range of social and economic benefits extended to successful applicants for asylum.

In the early 1990s, European states found themselves in an unwanted frontline position with respect to forced migrants from the former Yugoslavia. They responded by favoring temporary protection and avoiding grants of durable asylum; additional interim measures of protection were introduced in national law and practice. Administrative costs could be saved by diverting TP beneficiaries from the process of refugee status determination. Because this sudden enthusiasm for temporary protection coincided with a substantial raising of barriers to entry by migrants from the former Yugoslavia, such as visa requirements and a general tightening of asylum procedures, the UNHCR acquiesced in the TP strategy as likely to contribute to an overall enhancement in safety. The European practice of temporary protection for these migrants was restrictive, however, and tended to favor those with strong claims to the status of Convention refugee. * * *

* * *

An additional factor animating resort to temporary protection in response to both the Bosnian and the Kosovo crises was the nature of the displacement. Ethnically based armed conflict is largely aimed at driving out disfavored populations. Offering durable asylum to the victims of "ethnic cleansing" poses a moral and political dilemma to receiving states, which wish to avoid complicity in genocide and to resist the persecutor's fait accompli. The Kosovo experience suggests that concerted intervention, accompanied by temporary protection in regional and more distant states, can reverse ethnic cleansing. However, Kosovo also demonstrates that rapid repatriation, even when voluntary, may precipitate new population displacement if conditions are insecure.

II.   THE WHY—OBJECTIVES AND MOTIVATIONS

At least four motivations influence the participants in the debate over TP. First, some are dissatisfied because the 1951 Convention does not encompass all forced migrants generally acknowledged to be in need of international protection. Formalization of temporary protection could fill this perceived gap in international legal standards, and provide a comprehensive framework to substitute for the current patchwork of national TP laws and practices.

Second, temporary protection serves as an interim response to mass influx, providing safety while a durable solution is sought. For developed states burdened with heavy asylum caseloads and social tensions over levels of immigration, temporary protection is an attractive option precisely because it seems to impose no enduring obligation and because in certain formulations regional solutions are prioritized. Since most refugees are located in the South, regional TP could advantage the North. There is obvious tension between the first objective to expand legal obligations to forced migrants and the second impulse toward discretion, flexibility, and avoidance of direct protection for endangered persons from distant regions.

Third, temporary protection is often associated with effective responsibility sharing, possibly involving the physical transfer of asylum seekers and structured schemes for financial assistance for states of refuge. This objective may be resisted by states seeking to avoid legal commitment and by refugee advocates who fear the commodification of refugee protection.

Fourth, states weary of their obligations under refugee law may look upon a TP regime as a strategy to shift refugee protection from the realm of law to that of politics and voluntary humanitarian assistance. The flat repudiation of the 1951 Convention without some substitute multilateral framework is unlikely, especially as the *non-refoulement* norm in general human rights law is strengthening, but TP can be presented as an adaptation to the contemporary realities of forced displacement. This possible ulterior state motivation dampens the enthusiasm of many refugee advocates for a formalized TP regime.

* * *

There are at least two drawbacks to a strategy of seeking to broaden the definition of refugee through the formalization of temporary protection. First, the dangers provoking the flight of non-Convention refugees (such as internal armed conflict) are not inherently more temporary than the risk of persecution. A system of protection rigidly designed to provide only short-term refuge for expanded categories of refugees would be counterproductive if premature and unsafe repatriation emerged as the likely endgame. Second, it may be misleading to associate non-Convention refugees with mass influx. Recent experience with forced migrants from Bosnia and Kosovo suggests that severe religious and political persecution, well within the 1951 definition, may trigger the flight of large groups of persons. The invocation of temporary protection in all circumstances of mass influx and the association of TP by policymakers and publics with non-Convention refugees could dilute existing legal guarantees under the 1951 Convention for persons who flee *en masse* from persecutory harm.

Concerns like these appear to have induced nongovernmental organizations such as the European Council on Refugees and Exiles to urge, and the European Commission to accept, a two-track approach to broadening the definition of refugee and formalizing temporary protection. ECRE argues that the humanitarian practices of many European states, in granting leave to remain to persons unable to satisfy national interpretations of the definition in the 1951 Convention, could usefully be harmonized and incorporated in a binding regional legal instrument. However, ECRE urges that this important task not be consigned to the process of constructing a regional system of temporary protection. The latter should be limited to situations of mass influx that genuinely overwhelm the system for determining refugee status, where temporary protection could serve as an interim solution until an appropriate long-term response could be collectively devised.

* * *

Temporary Protection and Mass Influx

Temporary protection is often linked to mass influx, but whether TP should be so restricted is not clearly agreed. Admission to safety and protection against unsafe forced return are commonly assumed to be the guarantees most vital to mass arrivals, while other aspects of their treatment may have to be compromised, at least in the short term, to avoid placing an unrealistic burden on the state of refuge.

Even when the causes of flight are not ephemeral, a time-limited form of protection may be desirable if large-scale arrivals overwhelm the system for determining refugee status or no such system even exists. TP, however, is not the only acceptable response to mass influx. Group-based status determination is also an alternative. Protection for such refugees may cease pursuant to the cessation clauses of the 1951 Convention or as a result of the availability of a durable solution that does not necessarily involve local settlement.

If a mass influx occurs in a state party to the 1951 Convention, a leap toward temporary protection may be questionable. When the causes of flight are likely to endure and the migrants have no concrete prospect of resettlement in third states, instituting a TP regime may involve a significant dilution in the standards of treatment under the 1951 Convention. A mass influx may include many persons who are fleeing persecution. Experience with the flight from Bosnia suggests that states may engage in wishful thinking with respect to the prospects for rapid and safe repatriation, and may implement TP when ordinary refugee status determination remains feasible.

Promoting Responsibility Sharing through Formalization of TP

The 1951 Convention has been criticized for setting universal obligations that are implemented in a highly decentralized manner. Where the dimensions of refugee flows are modest, this individuated system of protection may be robust and effective. However, the fortuitous aspect of being on the receiving end of a mass influx tends to stimulate demands for international solidarity. Responsibility sharing has long been noted as a vital aspect of refugee protection and proposals for construction of such regimes have aroused intense interest. While the barriers to creating sustainable and concrete responsibility sharing remain high, the prospect of mutual insurance against heavy and unpredictable risk attracts states to participate in discussions of TP formalization.

Responsibility sharing may involve a variety of supportive measures. Even under the current individuated system, wealthier states give financial support to international humanitarian agencies and heavily burdened states of refuge. Third states may also offer to resettle selected refugees. Further, third states may intervene to reduce conflict or rebuild shattered institutions in states of origin so as to facilitate safe and dignified return. While the UNHCR often plays a vital coordinating role, these responses are generally not considered obligatory, nor are they precisely defined.

* * *

Responsibility sharing might include the organized transfer of TP beneficiaries between participating states (separate from grants of durable resettlement) and access by states of refuge to a central fund. The European Union's resolution and decision on burden sharing in the context of mass influx tentatively address these aims.

This type of responsibility-sharing discussion creates unease. Financial transfers may appear to be a questionable substitute for the core obligation to provide direct physical protection to refugees, especially where such transfers take place between highly developed and lesser-developed states and resemble "burden shifting." Even where states at similar levels of development engage in responsibility sharing, commodifying refugee protection and overriding the locational preferences of TP beneficiaries are displeasing to some.

Moreover, placing responsibility-sharing obligations at the center of the formalization of TP risks undermining the absolute nature of the obligations of admission to safety and *non-refoulement*. If responsibility-sharing commitments are not met, participants in a TP regime may consider themselves released from their legal commitments to the displaced.

Nevertheless, strong state support for formalizing TP is difficult to envision without substantial advancement on the responsibility-sharing front. Thus, the decision in the Treaty of Amsterdam to set a firm five-year timetable for the harmonization of temporary protection while keeping the responsibility-sharing negotiations open-ended is likely to impede the attainment of a coherent and comprehensive agreement.

* * *

The UNHCR's insistence on admission to safety as a minimum response to mass influx contradicts the notion that mass influx inherently releases states from refugee law obligations. The most important function served by TP may be inducement of governments to provide physical safety—however tenuous, brief, and harsh—to forced migrants while a lasting solution is sought on their behalf. This feature was again illustrated during the 1990s, when temporary protection served to moderate barriers to admission that impeded flight from the Balkans.

Not all forms of temporary protection, however, include a right of admission. TPS in the United States does not function as an admissions program. Fearful of a magnet effect, TPS administrators consciously designate required dates of entry to ensure that the availability of TPS will not stimulate new movements toward the United States.

Especially where temporary protection displaces refugee status determination for flows that include Convention refugees, nonrejection at the frontier is required by existing treaty standards. As noted during informal consultations organized by the UNHCR:

> Temporary protection requires admission to safety without discrimination and guarantees protection against *refoulement* for the duration of the crisis which has generated the mass influx. Beneficiaries of temporary protection should be provided with a positive legal status which allows them to remain and from which definite legal rights derive. Persons from the country of origin concerned, who were already in the host country before the outbreak of the crisis that generated the mass influx, should be allowed to remain, without prejudice to a more favourable legal status which they may enjoy.

Nonrejection at the frontier implicates fundamental sovereignty interests. Where TP serves as an interim solution, the intrusion upon sovereignty may be lessened. But where formalized TP protects a broadened category of forced migrants from nonrejection at the frontier, it may be difficult to convince states to agree without offering them offsetting guarantees of physical or financial responsibility sharing.

[Here Professor Fitzpatrick discusses the regional focus of many TP programs.—Ed.]

* * *

Duration

Temporary protection should last until a durable solution is found, which may involve repatriation after the crisis has ceased. The same is logically true under the 1951 Convention, whose cessation clauses, definition of refugee, and provision on *non-refoulement* all suggest that international protection may be temporary. Political asylum may constitute a relatively brief interlude in a refugee's existence. Thus, the fact that the duration of TP is linked to the continuation of risk does not set it apart from the existing refugee regime.

Whether nonpersecutory causes of flight are inherently more ephemeral than persecution is disputable. While some data suggest that internal armed conflicts in the latter half of the twentieth century are generally brief (e.g., lasting five years), many conflicts persist for decades. Repatriation to postconflict societies poses severe challenges, owing to damaged infrastructure, pervasive violence, lack of economic opportunity, and distrust or lingering hatred between communities.

At the same time, victims of forced displacement often strongly desire to return and may self-repatriate before conditions are safe or settled. TP regimes may be consciously structured to cultivate this natural desire for repatriation and to encourage the recipients to conceive of exile as limited in time. TP recipients may be repatriated more commonly than successful asylum applicants.

States have adopted a variety of approaches to limit the duration of TP. These have included (1) the eventual restructuring of protection toward in-country processing (for example, the institution of orderly-departure programs for Vietnamese asylum seekers and the shift in U.S. policy toward Cubans from offshore refuge to processing in Havana); (2) deadlines for the distant resettlement of TP beneficiaries housed in camps; (3) the transition of TP beneficiaries into a more durable status following the passage of a set period; (4) termination of group-based TP in light of changed conditions in the state of origin, with the simultaneous opening of access to individualized procedures for refugee status determination; (5) periodic extensions or terminations of TP on the basis of assessments of conditions in the state of origin; and (6) repatriation under pressure of refugees on the basis of claimed changed circumstances.

Cessation of TP has a dual aspect. First, TP *may* be terminated, and its beneficiaries repatriated, when conditions in the state of origin permit return in safety and with dignity. Second, TP *should* be terminated, and a solution not involving involuntary repatriation provided, when danger persists in the state of origin and TP beneficiaries can no longer tolerably be maintained in uncertainty or under standards of treatment that fall substantially short of the 1951 Convention.

* * *

Standards of Treatment

TP programs instituted in various states encompass a striking variety of standards of treatment. Diverse approaches are taken to such matters as employment, education, housing, social benefits, and family unity. In some cases, TP beneficiaries receive treatment similar to that offered to recognized refugees. In others, states of refuge make conscious efforts to retard assimilative tendencies, or to limit the economic impact by such measures as restrictions on access to the labor market.

Harmonization of standards of treatment is a significant animating influence for EU action on TP. Disparity in standards of treatment not only can prompt secondary movements, but also implicates concerns about equity, consistency with basic human rights norms, and responsibility sharing. * * *

* * *

Family unity is a crucial issue. While the European Commission's draft limits family reunification to spouses and minor or dependent children, this guarantee is actually more generous than the practice of some European states during the crisis in the former Yugoslavia. * * *

When TP is withdrawn, beneficiaries should be given access to the system for determining refugee status prior to their removal. Where cessation of refugee protection is ordered on a class basis, recognized refugees are generally permitted to establish that a general change in conditions has not eliminated their individual well-founded fear. Since a mass influx may have included persons fleeing persecution, and access to status determination may have been delayed during the period of temporary protection, belated consideration of individual claims will ensure that no one is returned in violation of the 1951 Convention. The savings enjoyed by states substituting TP for Convention status may thereby be diminished, unless conditions have changed so dramatically that most TP beneficiaries embrace the opportunity for voluntary repatriation.

* * *

NOTES AND QUESTIONS

1. As this article makes abundantly clear, refugee advocates and governments of states of refuge tend to view TP in markedly different ways. Explain (a) precisely what attracts refugee advocates to TP and what concerns them; and (b) what attracts governments of destination states to TP and what concerns them.

2. What do you think are the effects of TP on the countries of origin? Among other things, consider Professor Fitzpatrick's discussion of ethnic cleansing.

3. After reading this article, do you think that either a regional or a universal convention specifying minimum standards for TP is desirable, or is the subject best left to each state?

4. Professor Fitzpatrick refers to a "formalized" regime of temporary protection. What does she mean by this, and how does it differ from what she calls "responsibility-sharing?"

5.   One crucial question raised by this article is what the substantive criteria for TP ought to be. Should TP be granted only in cases of mass influx? Only to non-Convention refugees? Only when there are *both* mass influx and non-Convention refugees? Only when there is *either* mass influx *or* non-Convention refugees?

6.   Should TP be an onshore program (i.e., for people who have already made their way to the territory of the destination state), an offshore program (for people who are still in their countries of origin or temporarily in third countries), or both?

7.   Earlier you saw that much has been written on "burden-sharing," another term for "responsibility-sharing." See item 3 in the Notes and Questions at the end of section A of this chapter. What criteria would an ideal responsibility-sharing agreement employ for determining how many people, and which ones, a signatory state should accept? In particular, should geographic region be a factor? See the thoughtful essay by Matthew J. Gibney, *Asylum and the Principle of Proximity*, 3 Ethics, Race & Environment 313 (2000).

8.   Considering both ideal goals and political realities, what package of rights should TP beneficiaries have? Consider here whether there should be a right to permanent resident status in the event safe repatriation proves impossible for a prescribed number of years, as well as social and economic rights. Should the rights of TP beneficiaries resemble those of LPRs? Of asylees? Of nonimmigrants? None of these?

9.   In 2001 the Council of the European Union issued Council Directive 2001/55/EC on Minimum Standards for giving protection in the event of a mass influx of displaced persons and on measures promoting a balance of efforts between Member States in receiving such persons and bearing the consequences thereof (20 July 2001) (binding on all Member States). For the full text, see http://www.ecre.org/eu_developments/tpdir.pdf.

10.   The International Law Association (ILA), a private nonprofit association of scholars, practitioners, and judges interested in international law, does most of its work through an elaborate network of committees. After several years of work on the subject of TP, the Committee on Refugee Procedures of the ILA released an interim report that included a draft declaration proposed for ILA adoption. The report was prepared by Professor Walter Kälin of the University of Berne. The internationally and ideologically diverse committee members reached consensus on some things but not others. Here is a summary excerpt:

> * * * There seems to be a consensus that temporary protection should be provided in situations where large numbers of persons arrive because they have to flee generalized violence or civil war and other forms of armed conflict. There is also agreement that temporary protection should make it possible for States to protect such persons without having to go into full-fledged status determination procedures by suspending asylum proceed-

ings for some time; at the same time, it is considered necessary to examine and accommodate, at some point, the claims of those who turn out to be genuine refugees in the sense of 1951 Convention Relating to the Status of Refugees (CSR51). Finally, the members of the Committee agree that temporary protection is a return-oriented concept although, in certain circumstances, it might turn out that return would not become a viable option for prolonged periods of time. There is also agreement that any temporary protection regime has to be framed in a way that is compatible with the [1951 Convention].

A certain disagreement exists regarding the rights that should be granted to those receiving temporary protection. Should these rights gradually improve and finally be assimilated to those of refugees under [the 1951 Convention] or should they be reduced to a minimum as to make it easier for receiving States to grant temporary protection? There is also a certain disagreement among the members of the Committee as to whether temporary protection should be limited in time.

Finally, some members of the Committee stressed the need to address the issue of burden-sharing among States.

Walter Kälin, Committee on Refugee Procedures, International Law Association, *Third Interim Report on Temporary Protection*, in International Law Association, Report of the Sixty–Ninth Conference at 902 et seq. (2000).

11. Several other international law sources have been invoked to support a right to temporary protection. Here are three:

a. In 1969 the Organization of African Unity (OAU) adopted a convention that defines "refugee" to include not only those who fall within the 1951 Convention definition, but also "every person who, owing to external aggression, occupation, foreign domination or events seriously disturbing public order in either part or the whole of his country of origin or nationality, is compelled to leave his place of habitual residence in order to seek refuge." Organization of African Unity Convention on Refugee Problems in Africa, 1001 U.N.T.S. 45, art. I, para. 2 (Sept. 10, 1969). The 1984 Cartagena Declaration, by several Latin American countries, incorporates a similar principle. UNHCR, 2 Collection of International Instruments and Other Legal Texts Concerning Refugees and Displaced Persons 206 (1995). One commentator has gone a step further, arguing for international protection of those who flee specified forms of *economic* deprivation. See Francis A. Gabor, *Reflections on the Freedom of Movement in Light of the Dismantled "Iron Curtain,"* 65 Tulane L. Rev. 849, 863–66 (1991); Francis A. Gabor, *The Immigration Reform and Control Act of 1986: An Analysis in the Light of Contemporary International Law*, 23 Internat'l Lawyer 485, 492–99 (1989).

b. A second source that some have argued provides a right not to be returned to a country in which armed conflict would threaten one's life is the Geneva Convention Relative to the Protection of Civilian Persons in

Time of War, Geneva Convention No. IV, 6 U.S.T. 3516, T.I.A.S. No. 3365, 75 U.N.T.S. 287 (Aug. 12, 1949, entered into force for United States Feb. 2, 1956) [the Fourth Geneva Convention]. As its name implies, that convention bestows various protections on civilians endangered by war. In *Matter of Medina*, 19 I. & N. Dec. 734 (BIA 1988), a Salvadoran national argued that the Fourth Geneva Convention prohibited the United States from deporting her to El Salvador while civil war was raging. The Board rejected her claim. It held that the Convention creates no right not to be returned to countries beset by civil war. The Board observed that all the provisions of that Convention except one were expressly limited to international, rather than civil, conflicts. The one exception, article 3, requires each "Party" to a civil conflict to treat non-combatants humanely. Since the United States was not a party to the conflict, the Board reasoned, article 3 was inapplicable. Accord, *Echeverria–Hernandez v. U.S. INS*, 923 F.2d 688, 693 (9th Cir.1991).

c. A third possibility is customary international law. In *The Paquete Habana*, 175 U.S. 677, 20 S.Ct. 290, 44 L.Ed. 320 (1900), the Supreme Court said:

> International law is part of our law, and must be ascertained and administered by the courts of justice of appropriate jurisdiction as often as questions of right depending upon it are presented for their determination. For this purpose, where there is no treaty and no controlling executive or legislative act or judicial decision, resort must be had to *the customs and usages of civilized nations.*

175 U.S. at 700, 20 S.Ct. at 299, 44 L.Ed. at 328–29 (emphasis added). To establish a customary norm of international law, one must ordinarily demonstrate (a) that states generally follow a particular practice and (b) that they do so out of a sense that the practice is legally obligatory. Perluss & Fitzpatrick, above, at 555–56. The latter requirement is captured by the shorthand term "opinio juris." *Id.* at 556.

Is there a customary norm of international law that prohibits states from forcibly returning individuals to countries in which their lives are threatened by armed conflict? Arguing yes are Perluss & Fitzpatrick, above; *cf.* Gunning [*Modernizing Customary International Law*], above (arguing that practices of trans-national and nongovernmental organizations should also be considered relevant evidence of international custom and that, if they are, there is a customary norm prohibiting forcible return to dangerous wartime conditions); see generally Guy S. Goodwin–Gill, *Non–Refoulement and the New Asylum Seekers,* 26 Virginia J. Internat'l L. 897 (1986). More skeptical, particularly about the application of *opinio juris,* is Kay Hailbronner, *Non–Refoulement and "Humanitarian" Refugees: Customary International Law or Wishful Legal Thinking?,* 26 Virginia J. Internat'l L. 857 (1986).

The BIA and at least one court have rejected arguments based on customary international law, finding the evidence inadequate to demonstrate *opinio juris. Matter of Medina*, 19 I. & N. Dec. 734, 744 (BIA 1988); *Echeverria–Hernandez v. U.S. INS*, 923 F.2d 688, 693 (9th Cir.1991). The

BIA in *Medina* further doubted that either immigration judges or the BIA would have the statutory authority to grant relief on the basis of customary international law even if a norm could be established. Observing that the *Paquete Habana* formulation assumes the absence of preemptive domestic legislation or executive action, the Board found the detailed provisions of the Refugee Act of 1980 and the accompanying regulations preemptive. *Id.* at 745–46. The enactment of TPS in 1990 seemingly strengthens that conclusion.

Immigration Judge Paul Nejelski, in *Matter of Santos–Gomez,* No. A29 564 781 (unpub'd decision, Aug. 24, 1990), reached a contrary conclusion. He held that the existence of a customary norm of international law was a question of fact. After taking detailed expert testimony and reviewing documentary evidence, he found a norm prohibiting forcible return to dangerous conditions of armed conflict. Judge Nejelski read *Medina* as resting narrowly on its readings of the various Geneva Conventions rather than on application of general "humanitarian law." The former INS appealed to the BIA, but the respondents were Salvadorans who later became eligible for statutory TPS; administrative closure of the case thus prevented a BIA decision on the merits.

3.   OTHER INTERNATIONAL LAW PROTECTION MECHANISMS

The Council of Europe is an association of (at this writing) 41 European states. It is the sponsor of one of the world's most effective human rights regimes, the European Convention for the Protection of Human Rights and Fundamental Freedoms, 213 U.N.T.S. 222, European T.S. No. 5 (signed at Rome, Nov. 4, 1950), as reconfigured by Protocol No. 11, European T.S. No. 155 (entered into force Nov. 1, 1998). Article 3 of the Convention reads: "No one shall be subjected to torture or to inhuman or degrading treatment or punishment."

Articles 19–51 of the Convention establish a permanent European Court of Human Rights. Under article 46, the signatory states agree to be bound by the Court's judgments in any cases in which they are parties. In the following case, the Court interprets and applies article 3 (and other articles not discussed here) in the context of an unsuccessful asylum claim.

T.I. v. United Kingdom

European Ct. of Human Rights, 2000.
Decision as to the Admissibility of Application No. 43844/98.

[T.I., a Sri Lankan man, applied for asylum in Germany. There he testified in detail about his imprisonment and repeated torture first by Tamil terrorists and later by government soldiers. Two German courts denied asylum, in the first instance because the court would not recognize persecution by non-State actors and did not regard the soldiers' actions as those of the state, and in the second instance because his story was not believed. He fled Germany and made his way to the United Kingdom, where he again applied for asylum. Under the Dublin Convention, signatory States in Europe had agreed on rules for determining which state is responsible for deciding asylum cases when the applicants have traveled through more than one state. (A regulation of the Council of the European Union has now superseded the Dublin regime. See Council Reg. (EC) No. 343/2003, establishing the criteria and mechanisms for determining the Member State responsible for examining an asylum application lodged in one of the Member States by a third-country national (18 Feb. 2003)). The U.K. and Germany agreed that the present case was Germany's responsibility. Consequently, the U.K. ordered T.I. removed to Germany. T.I. sought review of that decision in the U.K. courts, mainly on the ground that Germany was not a safe country because its laws permitted refoulement to non-State persecutors. [NB: German law has since been amended. As of January 1, 2005, it recognizes persecution by non-State actors. See page 1028 above.] While his request for judicial review was pending, T.I. gathered expert medical evidence concluding that his many physical scars and psychological symptoms show "very little doubt" that his injuries had been caused in the way he described. The U.K. domestic courts ultimately denied relief and approved the removal order to Germany. He then applied to the European Court of Human Rights, alleging, among other things, a violation of article 3 of the European Convention.—Ed.]

* * *

3.   United Kingdom case-law

The domestic courts' approach under Section 2 of the Asylum and Immigration Act 1996 prior to July 1999 was summarised as:

(i) The Secretary of State cannot simply rely upon the fact that the third country is a signatory to the Geneva Convention [meaning the 1951 U.N. Refugee Convention—Ed.]; he must be satisfied that in practice it complies with its obligations.

(ii) The issue is whether the third country adopts an approach within the range of responses of a Contracting State acting in good faith to implement its obligations under the Geneva Convention.

(iii) The Secretary of State must be satisfied that there is no real risk that the third country would send the applicant elsewhere in breach of the Geneva Convention.

In its judgment of 23 July 1999 in the case of *R. v. Secretary of State for the Home Department ex parte Adan, Subaskaran and Aitsegeur*, the Court of Appeal examined as a question of general importance whether the Secretary of State was entitled to return asylum seekers to France and Germany under section 2(2)(c) of the Asylum and Immigration Act 1996, as being countries which did not recognise as refugees those who feared persecution from non-State agents. Adan was a citizen of Somalia who had been refused asylum in Germany prior to her arrival in the United Kingdom; Subaskaran was a Sri Lankan national who claimed asylum in the United Kingdom on account of his ill-treatment by both the LTTE [the Tamil guerrillas—Ed.] and the Sri Lankan army but whose claims had been rejected by the German authorities; and Aitsegeur was a citizen of Algeria whose asylum application had been rejected by French authorities. The Court of Appeal held that the Geneva Convention extended protection to persons who feared persecution by non-State agents, where, for whatever cause, the State was unwilling or unable to offer protection itself. As the German and French authorities subscribed to the 'accountability theory'— i.e. refugee status was limited to those who feared persecution emanating from State or quasi-State authorities or persecution from non-State agents where it was shown that it was tolerated or encouraged by the State, or at least the State was unwilling to offer protection—the Secretary of State could not as a matter of law certify the claimants for return to these countries as safe third countries because these countries did not give effect to the Convention's core values:

'If a party to the Geneva Convention were to take a position which was at a variance with the Convention's true interpretation, and act upon it, it could not be regarded as a safe third country; not merely because the "real risk" test is not breached (though certainly it would be) but because in the particular case the Convention was not being applied at all.'

[The House of Lords has since affirmed the decision of the Court of Appeal. See *R. v. Secretary of State for the Home Department ex parte Adan and Aitseguer* [2001] 2 W.L.R. 143 (U.K. House of Lords)—Ed.]

* * *

4. German law concerning asylum-seekers and persons claiming protection

* * *

According to the constant case-law of the German Constitutional Court, recognition as a political refugee requires a risk of persecution emanating from a State or quasi-State like authority. Persecution by private organisations or persons qualifies only if it can be attributed to the State in that the State supports or passively tolerates the persecution by private groups or exceptionally if the State does not provide adequate protection due to its inability to act as a consequence of existing political or social structures. This does not cover situations where a State has factually lost control of parts of its territory.

* * *

If an asylum claim for protection against political persecution does not meet the necessary requirements under [German law], the Federal Office is obliged to examine whether an applicant faces a serious risk of treatment contrary to Article 3 of the [European Convention on Human Rights] if he were returned. [German law] prohibits expulsion in such circumstances.

* * *

If the preconditions for the application of section 53(4) [of Germany's Aliens Act] are not met, protection may be granted under section 53(6) of the Aliens Act, which grants a discretion to the authorities to suspend deportation in case of a substantial danger for life, personal integrity or liberty of an alien. This applies to concrete individual danger resulting from either State or private action. It does not require an intentional act, intervention or State measure and covers risks for life resulting from adverse living conditions, lack of necessary medical treatment, etc. This provision has also been applied to civil war or war situations where the threat derived from a non-State source. Persons afforded protection under this provision are granted temporary permission to remain for periods of three months, renewable by the authorities.

In the first six months of 1999, section 53(6) was applied to 24 Sri Lankan nationals in respect of serious individual risks of ill-treatment which could not be attributed to the Sri Lankan State. This included the case of a Tamil whose scars placed him in real danger of being apprehended by the security forces and submitted to renewed torture as a person suspected of LTTE involvement.

* * *

Concerning article 3 of the Convention

The applicant complains his expulsion to Germany by the United Kingdom would be in breach of Article 3 of the Convention, which provides that:

> "No one shall be subjected to torture or to inhuman or degrading treatment or punishment."

* * *

The United Kingdom Government submit that the substance of the applicant's asylum claim should be assessed in Germany, where his allegations that he risks ill-treatment if returned to Sri Lanka would be assessed by the competent authorities in accordance with their obligations under the 1951 Geneva Convention and article 3 of the [European Convention]. * * *

They submit that there is no real risk that the applicant would suffer treatment contrary to Article 3 if he was removed to Germany. They point out that the substance of his asylum claim has already been assessed by the German authorities in support of his claim. They reject the applicant's arguments that German law does not provide proper protection against removal, pointing out that, even if the authorities apply a different approach to non-State agent risks or the actions of rogue officers, the applicant would be entitled to remain in Germany under section 53(6) of the Aliens Law if he could show a serious risk of torture or inhuman treatment in Sri Lanka from whatever source. They refer to the large number of individuals granted protection under this provision and to the lack of any complaints before the court as to the alleged gap in protection in German law.

They further argue that this Court should be slow to find that the removal of a person from one Contracting State to another would infringe Article 3 of the Convention, as in this case, the applicant would be protected by the rule of law in Germany and would have recourse, if any problems arose, to this Court, including the possibility of applying for a Rule 39 indication to suspend his deportation. * * *

* * *

The applicant rejects the assertion that this position is remedied by the section 53(6) provision. He submits that this is an entirely discretionary and temporary measure and that there are no known cases of failed asylum seekers being afforded protection under this provision. In these circumstances, the United Kingdom Government cannot escape their obligations under Article 3 by relying on Germany's status as a Contracting State and the theoretical possibility that the applicant could apply to the Court from Germany to prevent a real risk of removal from Germany to Sri Lanka.

* * *

The German Government, which made written and oral submissions at the request of the Court, submitted that German law and practice fully complied with the Convention. They emphasise that, while the Federal Administrative Court has interpreted Article 3 somewhat differently from this Court, this did not result in any "protection gap", as risks for life and personal integrity were covered under section 53(6). * * * Even though section 53(6) was framed in discretionary terms, the case-law of the German courts made it clear that an applicant would be entitled to protection if he was facing a grave danger involving a serious risk to life and personal integrity. * * * If the applicant was not satisfied with the review by the courts, he could file a complaint with this Court. * * *

* * *

The Court * * * notes that the right to political asylum is not contained in either the Convention or its Protocols. It is however well-established in its case-law that the fundamentally important prohibition against torture and inhuman and degrading treatment under Article 3, read in conjunction with Article 1 of the Convention to "secure to everyone within their jurisdiction the rights and freedoms defined in [the] Convention", imposes an obligation on Contracting States not to expel a person to a country where substantial grounds have been shown for believing that he would face a real risk of being subjected to treatment contrary to Article 3.

The Court's case-law further indicates that the existence of this obligation is not dependent on whether the source of the risk of the treatment stems from factors which involve the responsibility, direct or indirect, of the authorities of the receiving country. Having regard to the absolute character of the right guaranteed, Article 3 may extend to situations where the danger emanates from persons or groups of persons who are not public officials, or from the consequences to health from the effects of serious illness. * * *

In the present case, the applicant is threatened with removal to Germany, where a deportation order was previously issued to remove him to Sri Lanka. It is accepted by all parties that the applicant is not, as such, threatened with any treatment contrary to Article 3 in Germany. His removal to Germany is however one link in a possible chain of events which might result in his return to Sri Lanka where it is alleged that he would face the real risk of such treatment.

The Court finds that the indirect removal in this case to an intermediary country, which is also a Contracting State, does not affect the responsibility of the United Kingdom to ensure that the applicant is not, as a result of its decision to expel, exposed to treatment contrary to Article 3 of the Convention. Nor can the United Kingdom rely automatically in that context on the arrangements made in the Dublin Convention concerning the attribution of responsibility between European countries for deciding asylum claims. Where States establish international organisations, or *mutatis mutandis* international agreements, to pursue co-operation in certain fields of activities, there may be implications for the protection of fundamental rights. It would be incompatible with the purpose and object of the Convention if Contracting States were thereby absolved from their responsibility under the Convention in relation to the field of activity covered by such attribution. The Court notes the comments of the UNHCR that, while the Dublin Convention may pursue laudable objectives, its effectiveness may be undermined in practice by the differing approaches adopted by Contracting States to the scope of protection offered. * * *

* * *

Before the Court, the applicant has provided two medical reports which strongly support his claims that he was tortured. He has also provided photographs of scars of his injuries on his arm, leg and head. These materials were not before the German authorities and it is not apparent that the German authorities gave any consideration to this aspect of the case. The applicant has also given further clarifications of events in Sri Lanka which explain to some extent the difficulties which the Bavarian Administrative Court found in his account.

The Court has also given consideration to the reports concerning Sri Lanka published by Amnesty International, the United Nations Special Rapporteur and the United States Department of State. This shows that torture and ill-treatment by the LTTE and government forces is a serious problem. Tamils, particularly young men, are at serious risk of detention and ill-treatment by security forces looking for Tamil Tigers. Young men, who bear scars, are at particular risk of being suspected of being involved with the Tamil Tigers.

* * *

Nonetheless, the Court notes that the apparent gap in protection resulting from the German approach to non-State agent risk is met, to at least some extent, by the application by the German authorities of section 53(6). It appears that this provision has been applied to give protection to persons facing risk to life and limb from non-State agents, including groups acting in opposition to the Government, in addition to persons threatened by more general health and environmental risks. It has also been applied to a number of Tamils, including a young male Tamil at risk of ill-treatment from security forces due to the presence of scars on his body. The applicant has emphasised the discretionary nature of this provision. The German Government, while accepting that it is phrased in discretionary terms, submit that the courts' interpretation makes it clear that there is an obligation to apply its protection to persons who have shown that they are in grave danger. This submission is supported by the case-law materials referred to. * * *

* * *

In these circumstances, the Court finds that it is not established that there is a real risk that Germany would expel the applicant to Sri Lanka in breach of Article 3 of the Convention. Consequently, the United Kingdom have not failed in their obligations under this provision by taking the decision to remove the applicant to Germany. * * *

* * *

NOTES AND QUESTIONS

1. More detailed discussion of the application of article 33 of the 1951 Convention (nonrefoulement) to non-State actors can be found in the materials on pages 1025–37 above. As noted there, Germany now recognizes non-State persecutors. For present purposes, though, recall the language of article 33.1 of the 1951 Convention:

> No contracting State shall expel or return ("*refouler*") a refugee in any manner whatsoever to the frontiers of territories where his life or freedom would be threatened on account of his race, religion, nationality, membership of a particular social group or political opinion.

Now compare the language of article 3 of the European Convention:

> No one shall be subjected to torture or to inhuman or degrading treatment or punishment.

Do any of the textual differences in these provisions explain how Germany and France could interpret article 3 as applicable to non-State actors but article 33 as inapplicable?

2. Jennifer Moore has examined some of the implications of divergent practices by European states on the non-State actor issue. See generally Jennifer Moore, *Whither the Accountability Theory: Second–Class Status for Third–Party Refugees as a Threat to International Refugee Protection*, 13 Internat'l J. Refugee L. 32 (2001). Do you think the decisions in *Adan* and *T.I.* will have any practical effects on the success of the Dublin Convention and its successor regime? Will the decisions influence the strategic decisions of future asylum claimants in Europe?

3. In *T.I.*, the applicant pointed out that section 53(6) of Germany's Aliens Act is discretionary. Thus, even if the German courts ultimately accepted that he was telling the truth and that he would again be tortured

in Sri Lanka, there was no guarantee that section 53(6) would prevent his return. The Court permitted the U.K. to remove him to Germany nonetheless, finding that for various reasons there was no "real risk" of Germany's returning him to Sri Lanka under those circumstances. Professor Moore, in the article cited in item 2 above, objected to that result. What is your reaction? Should the Court have held that the European Convention prohibits states parties from sending asylum claimants who allege persecution by non-State actors to any state whose law permits refoulement to non-State persecutors?

4.   Suppose T.I. had been able to demonstrate empirically that, apart from the non-State actor issue, the German government and courts have been disproportionately prone to dismiss Sri Lankan claims on credibility grounds. Should article 3 of the European Convention bar his removal to Germany?

5.   On July 1, 1994 the Parliamentary Assembly of the Council of Europe, citing article 3 of the European Convention, requested that all its member states refrain from returning Yugoslav deserters and draft resisters. See Press Release, Directorate of Information, Council of Europe (June 28—July 1, 1994), at 6.

6.   Subject to several limitations, article 8 of the European Convention guarantees "the right to respect for private and family life ..." This provision has been read to limit the power of states parties to exclude or deport noncitizens in some situations where family relationships are at stake. See generally Hélène Lambert, *The European Court of Human Rights and the Right of Refugees and Other Persons in Need of Protection to Family Reunion*, 11 Internat'l J. Refugee L. 427 (1999).

7.   The European Union has been increasingly active on the refugee and asylum front. You have already seen reference to the proposed EU directive on the subject of temporary protection. As a preliminary to abolishing internal frontiers (i.e., border controls between member states), the EU has also been keen to harmonize the external immigration criteria for third-country nationals.

8.   The Organization of American States (OAS) has also assembled a body of case law on the general subject of human rights. The United States is a member state and, as such, is bound by the OAS Charter, 119 U.N.T.S. 3 (signed Apr. 30, 1948). The OAS has adopted the American Declaration of the Rights and Duties of Man, OAS Res. XXX, adopted in 1948 by the 9th International Conference of American States, Bogotá, OEA/Ser.L/V/I.4 Rev (1965), as well as the American Convention on Human Rights, O.A.S. Treaty Series No. 36 at 1, O.A.S. Off. Rec. OEA.Ser.L/V/II.23 doc.rev.2 (signed Nov. 22, 1969). All OAS states are bound by the Charter, and there is some authority for the proposition that all OAS states are similarly bound by the American Declaration. See Louis Henkin, Gerald L. Neuman, Diane F. Orentlicher & David W. Leebron, Human Rights 343 (1999). In contrast, only some of the OAS states (and not the United States) are parties to the American Convention. *Id*. at 342–44, 523–51. Thus far, none of the OAS organs have had major impact on United States immigration or

refugee law, although as noted earlier the Inter–American Commission on Human Rights—an OAS organ—has suggested that the United States Supreme Court decision in *Sale* (the interdiction case explored on pages 1115–35 above) violated the American Declaration. See Henkin et al, *id.* at 426.

9.   The Organisation of African Unity in 1969 adopted the Convention Governing the Specific Aspects of Refugee Problems in Africa. The Convention was a response to the huge refugee flows spurred by a combination of decolonization and South African apartheid. This convention remains the foundation of the various regimes for protecting refugees and other displaced persons in Africa. See generally UNHCR, 20 Refugee Survey Q., issue #1 (2001).

10.   In addition to UNHCR, to which you have seen repeated references in this chapter, the United Nations has an extensive network of organs and instruments devoted generally to the promotion of human rights. The leading work is Philip Alston (ed.), The United Nations and Human Rights—A Critical Appraisal (1992); see also Institute for Global Legal Studies, The UN and the Protection of Human Rights, 5 Washington Univ. J. Law & Policy (2001).

11.   For a provocative argument that the statelessness of the Palestinian refugees should trigger the combined protections of statelessness conventions and other international treaties, see Susan M. Akram, *Reinterpreting Palestinian Refugee Rights Under International Law*, in Naseer Aruri (ed.), Palestinian Refugees—The Right of Return, ch. 10 (2001).

12.   For a fuller treatment of the international human rights mechanisms available to refugees, see Joan Fitzpatrick (ed.), Human Rights Protection for Refugees, Asylum–Seekers, and Internally Displaced Persons—A Guide to International Mechanisms and Procedures (2002).

13.   Amidst the growing enthusiasm for international law solutions, some commentators caution against overemphasizing international human rights law as the source of noncitizens' rights. See, e.g., Laura S. Adams, *Divergence and the Dynamic Relationship Between Domestic Immigration Law and International Human Rights*, 51 Emory L.J. 983 (2002); Hiroshi Motomura, *Federalism, International Human Rights, and Immigration Exceptionalism*, 70 Univ. Colorado L. Rev. 1361, 1375–92 (1999).

UNDOCUMENTED MIGRANTS AND LAW ENFORCEMENT

You have now explored the *legal* criteria and procedures that govern whether noncitizens may enter, and whether they may remain in, the United States. That material is the stuff of traditional immigration law, the core of this book, and the thrust of most law school courses on immigration.

As you have seen, however, the immigration laws are not always obeyed. Each year a certain number of individuals (no one knows precisely how many, as noted below) enter the United States unlawfully, overstay their nonimmigrant visas, or otherwise violate either the specific terms of their admission or some more general provision of the immigration laws.

The Terminology

One hears constantly of "illegal aliens." Whatever one's reaction to the word "alien," the term "illegal alien" is an unfortunate one. From a lawyer's point of view, it is both ambiguous and otherwise imprecise. Some people use the term to describe those noncitizens who have entered the country surreptitiously. Others mean to encompass also those who entered lawfully but then overstayed. Still others have in mind all deportable individuals, whether the deportability grounds stem from unlawful entry, overstay, or any other events. Even if the context makes the intended meaning clear, calling a *person* illegal because he or she has broken a law is surely imprecise and more surely dehumanizing, notwithstanding that the particular violation accounts for the person's very presence in the United States. Moreover, culpability should not be prejudged. Just as we do not declare someone "guilty" of a crime before the entry of a valid final conviction, so too we should not brand a person's conduct "illegal" until removal or other applicable proceedings have run their course. This last point has practical modern significance because even people who concede deportability often have valid claims to asylum or other legal remedies.

Even when the phrase "illegal aliens" is used in the abstract to refer to those individuals who in actual fact are both deportable and ineligible for asylum and all other discretionary relief, and even if both the imprecision and the syntactical problems are overlooked, the choice of terminology has social and political connotations of which you should be aware. As discussed in the Overview chapter of this book, many people find the statutory word "alien" a disturbing way to describe human beings who are not United States nationals. See, e.g., Kevin R. Johnson, *"Aliens" and the U.S.*

Immigration Laws: The Social and Legal Construction of Nonpersons, 28 Univ. Miami Inter–Amer. L. Rev. 263 (1996–97); Gerald L. Neuman, *Aliens as Outlaws: Government Services, Proposition 187, and the Structure of Equal Protection Doctrine*, 42 UCLA L. Rev. 1425, 1428 (1995); Victor C. Romero, *The Congruence Principle Applied: Rethinking Equal Protection Review of Federal Alienage Classifications after Adarand Constructors, Inc. v. Pena*, 76 Oregon L. Rev. 425, 426 n.4 (1997). Still, from a legal standpoint, the word "alien" at least is not technically incorrect. The same cannot be said of the phrase *"illegal* alien," which has no statutory or other legal warrant. More important, many feel, the phrase *"illegal* aliens" produces an image far more sinister than is warranted either by the degree of culpability or by the degree of social harm involved. For a thoughtful portrayal of the human face of this population, see James F. Smith, *United States Immigration Law As We Know It: El Clandestino, The American Gulag, Rounding Up the Usual Suspects*, 38 U.C. Davis L.Rev. 747 (2005). That is particularly true with respect to Mexicans, the argument runs, if one takes into account the general history of Mexican migration to the United States and the range of personal circumstances that tend to drive that migration.

Those who hold these views prefer the term "undocumented migrants," a reference to the lack of valid immigration documents. Others dismiss "undocumented migrants" as a euphemism. They object that the term wrongly implies that the transgression was merely a technical, documentary omission rather than a substantive wrong. Anti-immigrant lobbying organizations take this view and in their advocacy materials routinely refer to "illegal aliens" or "illegals," even when referring to asylum claimants. In this book, the term "undocumented migrants" will be used to describe any non-U.S. citizens who are present in the United States without valid documentation of lawful immigration status.

The Origins

One leading demographer describes the historical origins of today's undocumented migrant population:

> The roots of contemporary illegal immigration to the United States can be found in the "Bracero Program" which brought several million Mexican men to the United States as temporary farmworkers in southwestern states from 1942 until 1965. Although the Bracero Program served its purpose of providing growers with a substantial and inexpensive labor force, its lasting impact came from the access to U.S. labor markets it afforded Mexican laborers. The braceros gained familiarity with U.S. labor markets, made contacts with employers, and acquired U.S.-specific work skills (e.g., a small, working knowledge of English). The end of the official program was supposed to mean a shift by growers to a native labor force and more mechanized agriculture. However, the easy access to former braceros meant that growers substituted illegal labor for the formerly legal bracero labor.

Immigration between Mexico and the United States, especially illegal migration, then followed a pattern, still evident today for Mexican and other flows. The migration starts with "pioneer" immigrants, usually young males, often working in agriculture or other low-wage, low-skill jobs. Over time, these pioneers make multiple trips and accumulate experience in the U.S. labor force and knowledge of the new country. With this experience, more of these illegal *migrants* settle in the United States and become illegal *immigrants*.

After the pioneer males settle in the United States, family unification proceeds as they bring wives, children, and more distant relatives to the United States. The maturation of the migrant stream also opens it to friends and acquaintances as the benefits of migration become apparent to a larger circle in the migrants' home cities and towns. Some of the migration is legal, some illegal; but for many, illegal entry is simply a prelude to *legal* migration.

Jeffrey S. Passel, Recent Efforts to Control Illegal Immigration to the United States 3 (unpublished paper, presented to OECD Working Party on Migration, Paris, June 13–14, 1996).

The literature on undocumented migrants is vast, and there are important social, economic, and demographic issues on which consensus is lacking. There are, first, differences in emphasis over the root causes of unauthorized migration. Some stress the so-called "push" factors—i.e., those factors that impel people to leave their homelands. These include poverty, persecution, armed conflict, family separation, and a host of other hardships. Others stress the "pull factors"—i.e., positive attractions of the receiving country. These include economic opportunity, political freedom, personal safety, and family unification. As the excerpt from Passel illustrates, the Bracero program also encouraged the flow of labor from Mexico to the United States. See also Congressional Research Service, Illegal Aliens: Analysis and Background, U.S. House Comm. on the Judiciary, 95th Cong., 1st Sess. (1977); David W. Haines & Karen E. Rosenblum (eds.), Illegal Immigration in America—A Reference Handbook (1999).

The Scale

A precise count of the undocumented population in the United States is impossible, of course, but demographers have come up with ways to arrive at reasonable estimates. See generally U.S. General Accounting Office, Illegal Aliens—Despite Data Limitations, Current Methods Provide Better Population Estimates, GAO/PEMD–93–25 (Aug. 1993); Jeffrey S. Passel, Estimates of the Size and Characteristics of the Undocumented Population (Mar. 21, 2005) (using various sources to estimate the total foreign born U.S. population and the total number of legal residents, the difference being the undocumented population).

The 2005 Passel study, above, contains useful data. By his estimate, the number of undocumented migrants in the United States as of March 2005 was just under 11 million. This represents a jump from 8.4 million five years earlier. The average annual increase in the undocumented population during that period was about 485,000 per year (with very little variance from year to year). That figure reflects the annual number of new arrivals (700,000 to 800,000), minus those who leave the country, die, or achieve lawful status. Undocumented migrants make up about 29% of the foreign born residents of the United States. Passel, above; see also Regina Germain, *Perspectives on the Bush Administration's New Immigrant Guest-worker Proposal*, 32 Denver J. Internat'l L. & Policy 747, 748 n.9 (2004).

The same study reveals several characteristics of the undocumented population. Approximately 57% are from Mexico (a figure that has also remained relatively constant over the past ten years), 24% from other Latin American countries, 9% from Asia, 6% from Europe and Canada, and 4% from other regions. As for geographic dispersal within the United States, 68% of all undocumented migrants live in 8 states. California houses by far the largest number (24% of the total), followed by Texas, Florida, New York, Arizona, Illinois, New Jersey, and North Carolina. These figures reflect increasing dispersal. From 1990 to 2004, the proportion of undocumented migrants who reside in the top 6 states dropped from 88% to 61%. One-sixth of the undocumented residents of the United States are children. As of 2002, about 70% were workers; they made up approximately 5% of the U.S. labor force. Passel, above.

The Impact

Particularly elusive is the economic impact of undocumented migrants. On the negative side, to what extent, if any, do undocumented migrants either displace American workers or adversely affect the wages or working conditions of American workers? To what extent are the migrants themselves victims of exploitation, and how does the level of exploitation they suffer compare to the alternatives they would have faced at home? To what extent do undocumented migrants use government-provided services—public assistance, highways, schools, hospitals?

On the positive side, how much do undocumented migrants contribute in federal, state, and local taxes, both directly and indirectly? How do these revenues compare to what undocumented migrants receive in services? To what extent do undocumented migrants *create* jobs, by consuming goods and services and by sustaining marginal enterprises that also employ Americans? How many of the jobs that undocumented migrants take are ones that Americans simply would not accept in adequate numbers? Do undocumented migrants, by supplying needed labor, help keep down consumer costs? Professor Lenni Benson argues that the contributions of undocumented workers tend to go unnoticed, both because the workers themselves try not to be noticed and because native observers tend not to see the workers in nuanced ways. See Lenni Benson, *The Invisible Worker*, 27 North Carolina J. Internat'l L. & Commercial Regulation 483 (2002).

According to one credible estimate, undocumented migrants generate a net deficit (government expenditures less tax revenues), for federal, state, and local budgets combined, of about $2 billion per year. Jeffrey S. Passel &

Rebecca L. Clark, How Much Do Immigrants Really Cost? A Reappraisal of Huddle's "The Cost of Immigrants" (Feb. 1994). This comes out to approximately $8 per year per American. For summaries of the economic literature on these and other controversial questions concerning undocumented migrants, see Bill Ong Hing, The Economic Impact of Immigration: A Brief Survey of the Literature (1989); Peter H. Schuck, *The Emerging Political Consensus on Immigration Law,* 5 Georgetown Immigration L.J. 1, 13–18 (1991); Julian L. Simon, The Economic Consequences of Immigration, chap. 15 (2d ed. 1999).

The impact of illegal immigration is not, of course, solely economic. Undocumented migrants are, with distressingly increased frequency, easy prey for violent criminals in the border regions, as discussed below. A certain number of undocumented migrants will themselves turn to crime in the United States, though at present there is no evidence that undocumented immigrants are any more disposed to crime than analogous age-sex cohorts in the native population. See the studies cited by Simon, above, at 109–10. There is the increasingly serious issue of trafficking, considered in section A.1 below. Some speculate that large scale evasion of immigration restrictions fosters a more general climate of disrespect for law and for national sovereignty. And the underground subculture in which many undocumented migrants live out their daily lives can produce serious civil rights problems that some fear will grow worse with time.

Those factors account for much of the negative public reaction to undocumented migrants, but undoubtedly other factors are also at work. Various commentators have emphasized racism and xenophobia, Ronald Takaki, Strangers from a Different Shore: A History of Asian Americans (1989); Kevin R. Johnson, *Public Benefits and Immigration: The Intersection of Immigration Status, Ethnicity, Gender, and Class,* 42 UCLA L. Rev. 1509, 1544–49 (1995), general economic insecurity, see Richard A. Boswell, *Restrictions on Noncitizens' Access to Public Benefits: Flawed Premise, Unnecessary Response,* 42 UCLA L. Rev. 1475, 1477 (1995), and environmental concerns, Peter L. Reich, *Environmental Metaphor in the Alien Benefits Debate,* 42 UCLA L. Rev. 1577 (1995).

The Responses

If there is fundamental ambivalence about the impact of illegal immigration, there is even sharper disagreement about the solutions. See generally Evangeline G. Abriel, *Ending the Welcome: Changes in the United States Treatment of Undocumented Aliens (1986 to 1996),* 1 Rutgers Race & L. Rev. 41 (1998) (describing shifts in enforcement strategy). Congress has devised an assortment of antidotes. You have already seen one of the principal devices for combating violations of the immigration laws—removal proceedings. You have also seen that certain violations can destroy a noncitizen's eligibility for discretionary relief from removal, e.g., INA §§ 208(d)(6), 240(b)(7), 240B(c), or for future readmission, see INA § 212(a)(9)(B).

In recent years criminal and civil sanctions have taken on an increased role in immigration enforcement strategy. Congress has created more and more immigration-related criminal and civil offenses and has generally increased the penalties for existing offenses. The details are in sections A and B below. Civil forfeitures of vehicles and other property used in the commission of immigration offenses are another weapon in the government's arsenal, and they are controversial too. See Robert Pauw & Greg Boos, *Conveyance Seizures and Forfeitures: Constitutional Limits on Agency Decision–Making*, Immigration Briefings (Apr. 1996); Robert Pauw, *Gete v. INS: Vehicle Seizure Class Action*, 4 BIB 844 (Aug. 15, 1999).

In the past several years a higher priority has also been placed on immigration law enforcement resources. There has been a particular focus on the border with Mexico. Even before IIRIRA, the former INS began transferring enforcement personnel from the interior to the border. See generally 73 IR 101 (Jan. 22, 1996). "Linewatch" hours (total person-hours at the border) steadily rose from 1993 to 1995. Jeffrey S. Passel, Recent Efforts to Control Illegal Immigration to the United States (unpublished paper, presented to OECD Working Party on Migration, Paris, June 13–14, 1996), at 13. At the two busiest ports of entry from Mexico—El Paso and San Diego—the INS launched two ambitious initiatives. In El Paso, instead of concentrating resources at places where undocumented migrants tended to congregate after entering, the INS in 1993 undertook Operation "Hold the Line." Border Patrol officers saturated the border in an attempt to deter people from entering clandestinely in the first place. A year later, in San Diego, the INS began "Operation Gatekeeper," a multi-faceted approach that emphasized more formidable physical barriers—higher fences, high-intensity lights, etc. Whether these efforts actually reduced total illegal entries or simply diverted the entries to other border points is not yet clear. See *id.* at 14–17. It is also possible that the increased difficulty of entering has caused a rise in smuggler fees, with the result that people who succeed in entering unlawfully stay longer rather than go back and forth. *Id.* The verdict is not yet in.

IIRIRA endorsed the strategy of heightened border enforcement (as well as other strategies). IIRIRA § 101 increased the size of the Border Patrol, and section 102 required the building of a triple fence in the San Diego area. A new border initiative in Brownsville, Texas, called "Operation Rio Grande," is discussed in U.S. Comm. for Refugees, 19 Refugee Reports #7 (July 1998). The former INS summoned then new biometric technology in aid of border enforcement. See Daniel M. Kowalski, *The $99 Border Guard*, 4 BIB 579 (June 1, 1999). In response to the terrorist attacks of September 11, 2001, Congress in the USA PATRIOT Act of 2001, §§ 402 and 403, tripled the Border Patrol resources along the Canadian border and facilitated intelligence-sharing among the relevant federal agencies. Subsequent statutes continued to bolster the number of Border Patrol officers, other law enforcement personnel, technology, and other physical resources. See, e.g., Intelligence and Terrorism Prevention Act of 2004, Pub. L. 108–458, 118 Stat. 3638 (Dec. 17, 2004), especially Title V and §§ 7206–15. The latest enactment (at this writing) is the REAL ID Act, which authorizes the Secretary of Homeland Security to waive "all legal requirements such Secretary, in such Secretary's sole discretion, determines necessary to ensure expeditious construction of the barriers and roads" required by IIRIRA. REAL ID Act, § 102. The same provision bars all judicial review of the Secretary's decision except for constitutional claims. *Id.*

Drownings and other accidental deaths are a common fate for individuals who attempt to cross the Rio Grande, see 24 Migration World Magazine No. 3 at 10 (1996), and there is rising concern that Operation Gatekeeper has exacerbated the tragedy. By deliberately rerouting undocumented migrants to crossing points that are more difficult "due to harsh terrain and weather conditions," critics say, the Border Patrol has drastically increased the number of deaths. During the first five years of Operation Gatekeeper (1994–99), border deaths rose 600%, to an average of over 100 per year. Report, U.S.-Mexico Border Project, American Friends Service Committee (Nov. 1999). The operation prompted a 1999 border visit by UN High Commissioner for Human Rights Mary Robinson. *Id.* In the past ten years, more than 2600 deaths have occurred along the U.S.-Mexican border—"ten times more lives than the Berlin Wall claimed during its 28–year existence." Wayne A. Cornelius, *Evaluating Enhanced U.S. Border Enforcement*, 9 BIB 654 (May 15, 2004); see also Bill Ong Hing, *The Dark Side of Operation Gatekeeper*, 7 U.C. Davis J. Internat'l L. & Policy 121 (2001); Jorge A. Vargas, *U.S. Border Patrol Abuses, Undocumented Mexican Workers, and International Human Rights*, 2 San Diego Internat'l L.J. 1 (2001). In addition to the deaths along the land border, of course, are those that occur at sea, discussed in chapter 11, section B.7.b.12 above.

Border deaths of undocumented migrants are not unique to the United States. In 2004, some 289 North Africans and others trying to cross the Mediterranean in small boats bound for Spain died en route. Asociación pro Derechos Humanos de Andalucía, www.apdha.org. In Greece, 74 migrants have been killed by land mines near the Turkish border since 1994. (Greece mined the border after Turkey's 1974 invasion of northern Cyprus.) Agence France Presse, *Greece pledges to accelerate mine clearing along Turkish border* (Apr. 15, 2005).

Accidental deaths are not the only risks of clandestine entry. Violent criminals in the border area often find undocumented migrants to be easy prey. They are often helpless and in no position to summon the authorities.

Of additional concern are continuing allegations of the abuse of undocumented immigrants by Border Patrol officials. See generally 73 IR 368 (Mar. 25, 1996). In a highly publicized incident reminiscent of the Rodney King beating, a television helicopter crew videotaped sheriff's deputies from Riverside County, California repeatedly beating two suspected undocumented migrants from Mexico after a high-speed chase on April 1, 1996. See Los Angeles Times, Apr. 3, 1996, at 1. For some useful discussion of the former INS's citizen advisory panel on border violence, and the issues that have arisen with respect to complaint procedures, see Bill Ong Hing, *Border Patrol Abuse: Evaluating Complaint Procedures Available to Vic-*

tims, 9 Georgetown Immigration L.J. 757 (1995); Lee J. Teran, *Obtaining Remedies for INS Misconduct*, Immigration Briefings (May 1996).

In 1997, the Border Patrol and the local police of Chandler, Arizona (a suburb of Phoenix) joined forces in a massive five-day community sweep. 430 residents, all Latino, were arrested and removed from the United States. The Attorney General of Arizona wrote a highly critical report of the tactics, which included arrests based on nothing more than "skin color or Mexican appearance or use of the Spanish language." See Nadine Wettstein, *The Chandler Raids: Wake–Up Call or Harbinger of Local Police Enforcement of the INA?*, 3 BIB 101 (Feb. 1, 1998). Professor Kevin Johnson argues that more stringent limits on law enforcement powers, particularly with respect to drug and immigration-related border enforcement, would reduce over-reliance on racial profiling and at the same time enhance effectiveness. Kevin R. Johnson, *U.S. Border Enforcement: Drugs, Migrants, and the Rule of Law*, 47 Villanova L. Rev. 897 (2002).

More controversial still was the "Minuteman" project, a private initiative begun in April 2005. The goal was to organize a volunteer corps of hundreds of private citizens, armed with weapons, to patrol the border and either capture suspected undocumented migrants or report them to the Border Patrol. Criticized by President Bush and others as "vigilantes," they called for 1000 volunteers to appear in Arizona along the border in early April 2005. Although only an estimated 200 "Minutemen" actually materialized, the Border Patrol deployed an extra 500 agents in the area to prevent violence, and the Minutemen succeeded in attracting 200 journalists to cover the story. See David Kelly, *Border Watchers Capture Their Prey—the Media*, Los Angeles Times (Apr. 5, 2005), at A1; Editorial, *Amateurs on the Border*, Chicago Tribune (Apr. 5, 2005), at C22.

Border enforcement, whatever its impact on the number and nature of clandestine entries, cannot address the problem of overstayers. To apprehend overstayers, and also to apprehend those who managed to enter surreptitiously despite border controls, Congress and DHS have bolstered their enforcement efforts in the interior. IIRIRA § 132 increased the number of authorized overstay investigators. Section 131 bolstered the ranks of employer sanctions investigators (more on that in a moment). Section 204 increased the number of federal prosecuting attorneys to enforce immigration-related criminal laws.

The September 11 attacks have given rise to a new set of strategies aimed specifically at particular classes of noncitizens. Unlike the traditional strategies, the central target of which has been illegal immigration, some of the new programs are focused principally on national security, with particular attention to counter-terrorism. The two objectives are hard to separate, since many of the new programs have multiple rationales and multiple consequences.

Of the post-September 11 enforcement initiatives, those most relevant here are the increased reliance on preventive detention of noncitizens, the various intelligence-gathering operations, and the addition of vast new resources, technologies, and personnel to enhance border enforcement operations. See chapter 10 above.

One source of friction has been the issue of federal-state cooperation in responding to illegal immigration. In 1996, through IIRIRA § 133, Congress added section 287(g) to the INA. This provision authorized cooperative arrangements between the Attorney General (now the Secretary of DHS) and either states or their political subdivisions. Under these arrangements, state or local employees whom the Secretary regards as qualified are authorized to investigate, apprehend, or arrest people suspected of federal immigration violations. Several states have now entered into such agreements with DHS. See 9 BIB 641 (May 15, 2004). Professor Huyen Pham argues that *constitutional* federal exclusivity in the immigration sphere (not just congressional preemption) prohibits these arrangements. See Huyen Pham, *The Inherent Flaws in the Inherent Authority Position: Why Inviting Local Enforcement of the Immigration Laws Violates the Constitution*, 31 Florida State Univ. L. Rev. 965 (2004).

In addition to authorizing agreements for state and local employees to investigate, apprehend, and detain suspected immigration violators, IIRIRA prohibited any federal, state, or local entity or official from restricting the exchange of information with the former INS concerning an individual's immigration status. *Id.* § 642. This provision was a response to efforts by local municipalities to bar local police from releasing information on suspected immigration violators to the federal government. The motivations for the state and local restrictions usually included protecting privacy, preventing race discrimination by the police, encouraging people to apply for benefits to which they are legally entitled, and reserving finite enforcement resources for higher local priorities.

In New York City, for example, an executive order prohibited city employees from voluntarily giving information to federal officials about individuals' immigration status, with some exceptions. The policy clearly violated IIRIRA § 642, but the City argued that section 642 violated the 10th amendment. In *City of New York v. United States*, 179 F.3d 29 (2d Cir. 1999), the court of appeals upheld the constitutionality of section 642. In 2003 New York City Mayor Michael Bloomberg responded with Executive Order No. 41, City–Wide Privacy Policy and Amendment of Executive Order No. 34 Relating to City Policy Concerning Immigrant Access to City Services (Sept. 17, 2003). The new Executive Order declares that its goal is to encourage use of city services by promoting an expectation of confidentiality. *Id.*, Preamble. The Order prohibits the disclosure of "confidential information" (which includes information concerning immigration status) by City officers and employees except in certain situations. The exceptions include the case in which disclosure is "required by law," *id.* § 2(b), and, with respect to information relating to immigration status, the case in which the person is suspected of "engaging in illegal activity, *other than mere status as an undocumented alien*" or in investigations of potential terrorist activity [emphasis added], *id.* § 2(e). With some narrow exceptions, the Executive Order also prohibits City employees (including police officers) from inquiring about a person's immigration status. *Id.* § 4. See also Craig B. Mousin, *A Clear View from the Prairie: Harold Washington and the People of Illinois Respond to Federal Encroachment of Human Rights,* 29 Southern Illinois Univ. L. Rev. 285 (2005) (analyzing analogous Chicago restrictions).

Secure documentation is an additional ingredient of immigration enforcement strategy. IIRIRA §§ 656 and 657 took steps to make birth certificates and social security cards, respectively, more counterfeit-resistant. In addition, the development of several comprehensive databases, most of them currently in the process of being folded into US VISIT, is well under way as of this writing. They have been spurred on by September 11 and are discussed in chapter 10, section B above.

Some urge, as a further deterrent, a constitutional amendment that would deny birthright citizenship to children born in the United States of undocumented parents. You will see more on this in chapter 13. Statutes passed in 1996 further restricted the (already very narrow) range of public benefits available to undocumented migrants. They are considered in section C below, along with the related strategy of barring undocumented children from public schools. The same section takes up the issue of undocumented migrants and drivers' licenses.

Other strategies emphasize the positive. Many believe that, as long as the Mexican economy remains desperate, no fortification of law enforcement capabilities within economically and politically plausible limits—and no attempt to enforce employer sanctions—will appreciably diminish the flow. Those who hold that last view generally emphasize the kind of deterrent that would reduce the *need* for illegal immigration by supporting measures that would stimulate the Mexican economy and create jobs. Free trade between the United States and Mexico has long been seen by many as an essential component of that strategy. See, e.g., Rpt. of the Comm'n for the Study of Int'l Migration and Cooperative Economic Development, Unauthorized Migration: An Economic Development Response (July 1990).

As you saw earlier, NAFTA went into force in 1994. Most observers predicted that reduced farm subsidies in Mexico would cause economic dislocations that, in turn, would spur higher rates of illegal migration to the United States in the *short-term*. Since the reductions in agricultural subsidies were phased in slowly, that effect was expected to be small. Now that substantial time has elapsed, it remains impossible to isolate cause and effect. In the *long term*, NAFTA was expected to reduce illegal migration, principally by stimulating the Mexican economy, thereby creating jobs, raising wages, and lessening the incentive to migrate north. 70 IR 1472, 1473 (Nov. 8, 1993). Former INS Commissioner Doris Meissner added that NAFTA might well have been essential to Mexico's continued cooperation with United States border enforcement efforts. *Id.* at 1474; see also Kevin R. Johnson, *Free Trade and Closed Borders: NAFTA and Mexican Immigration to the United States,* 27 U.C. Davis L. Rev. 937 (1994).

Another tack, taken in 1986 as you have seen, is to acknowledge the practical impossibility of apprehending and removing those undocumented migrants who are already in the United States and to provide for legalization, or amnesty. See chapter 8, § A.3 above. As noted, the September 11, 2001 terrorist attacks brought the then thriving legalization drive to a screeching halt, partly because the national trauma aggravated public fear of foreigners and partly because the dominant priority became terrorism and the resulting war effort.

The labor laws are yet another bone of contention. Professor Peter Margulies argued early on that extending labor law protection to undocumented migrants would deter employers from luring them here. Peter Margulies, *Stranger and Afraid: Undocumented Workers and Federal Employment Law*, 38 DePaul L. Rev. 553 (1989). Other forceful pleas for protecting undocumented workers from unfair labor practices include Ruben J. Garcia, *Ghost Workers in an Interconnected World: Going Beyond the Dichotomies of Domestic Immigration and Labor Laws*, 36 Univ. Michigan J. L. Reform 737 (2003); Lori A. Nessel, *Undocumented Immigrants in the Workplace: The Fallacy of Labor Protection and the Need for Reform*, 36 Harvard Civil Rights—Civil Liberties L. Rev. 345 (2001); Maria L. Ontiveros, *Immigrant Workers' Rights in a Post–Hoffman World–Organizing Around the Thirteenth Amendment*, 18 Georgetown Immigration L.J. 651 (2005). The AFL–CIO similarly endorses workplace protection for undocumented employees. See 79 IR 39 (Jan. 7, 2002). And Professor Michael Wishnie, drawing on constitutional history, argues that many of the practices that now discourage undocumented workers from reporting labor abuses violate the first amendment right "to petition the Government for a redress of grievances." See Michael J. Wishnie, *Immigrants and the Right to Petition*, 78 NYU L. Rev. 667 (2003).

Professor Jennifer Gordon describes a seldom noted trend—the increasing migration of undocumented workers to the suburbs, where exploitation can be just as rampant as in the cities. As she writes:

> While this country's manufacturing base has withered, calls have increased for lawns to be mowed, bedrooms to be cleaned, pools and homes to be built, and office park floors to be swabbed. * * * Long Island, New York, mother of all suburbs, typifies the trend. Today it is home to over 300,000 Latino immigrants.

Jennifer Gordon, Suburban Sweatshops—The Fight for Immigrant Rights at 1 (2005). As Professor Gordon has also proved, however, immigrant groups can successfully organize and bargain for rights, even if many in their ranks are undocumented. She herself led a remarkable and highly successful effort to do precisely that. *Id.*, especially chs. 2–5 (describing the Workplace Project, in Hempstead, New York).

In *Sure-Tan, Inc. v. NLRB*, 467 U.S. 583, 104 S.Ct. 2803, 81 L.Ed.2d 732 (1984) (decided before IRCA prohibited employers from knowingly hiring unauthorized workers, as discussed in section B.1 below), the Supreme Court made clear that the NLRA prohibits employers from contacting the immigration authorities in retaliation for an employee's union organizing activities. And in *Hoffman Plastic Compounds v. NLRB*, 535 U.S. 137, 122 S.Ct. 1275, 152 L.Ed.2d 271 (2002), the Supreme Court appears to have confirmed that this rule survives IIRIRA. The real problem is remedy. In *Hoffman Plastic Compounds* the Court went on to hold, by a vote of 5–4, that undocumented workers who are wrongly discharged in retaliation for their union activities may not be awarded back pay for the period after their discharge, at least if they had obtained their employment by fraudulently tendering false documents. Left open are whether the remedy may include unpaid wages for work actually performed and whether back pay may be awarded, even for the period after discharge, when the employer knowingly employs an unauthorized worker. See Michael J. Wishnie, *Emerging Issues for Undocumented Workers*, 6 Univ. Pennsylvania J. Labor & Employment L. 497 (2004), reproduced in 9 BIB 1289, 1296–98 (Nov. 1, 2004). Professor Wishnie suggests that threatening deportation in retaliation for union organizing might even constitute the criminal offense of inducing involuntary servitude. 9 BIB at 1293 (quoting the majority opinion of Justice O'Connor in *United States v. Kozminski*, 487 U.S. 931, 948, 108 S.Ct. 2751, 101 L.Ed.2d 788 (1988)).

Professor Wishnie also contends that many of these labor practices violate international legal standards. He suggests use of both the domestic Alien Tort Claims Act and the North American Agreement for Labor Cooperation (a side agreement to NAFTA) as strategies to expose and redress the violations. See Michael J. Wishnie, *Immigrant Workers and the Domestic Enforcement of International Labor Rights*, 4 Univ. Pennsylvania J. Labor & Employment L. 529 (2002). On September 25, 2003, the Inter–American Court of Human Rights, at the request of Mexico, issued a nonbinding opinion disapproving of the *Hoffman Plastic* rule. See *Ruling backs rights of migrant workers*, The Associated Press (Sept. 26, 2003).

On March 14, 2003 the Convention on the Protection of the Rights of all Migrant Workers and Members of their Families, adopted by U.N. General Assembly resolution in 1990, see UNGA A/Res/45/158 annex, 45 UN GAOR Supp. (No. 49A) at 262 (Dec. 18, 1990), gathered enough ratifications to enter into force. The Convention lays out a variety of labor rights for migrant workers, including those workers who are undocumented. To date, however, neither the United States nor any of the other major immigrant-receiving nations have become parties to the Convention. At any rate, the protections it affords are highly qualified. Professor Linda Bosniak, writing after the Convention had been adopted but before it had gone into force, criticized the international community for elevating state sovereignty above the humane treatment of undocumented workers. See Linda S. Bosniak, *Human Rights, State Sovereignty and the Protection of Undocumented Migrants under the International Migrant Workers Convention*, 25 Internat'l Migration Rev. 737 (1991); see also Guadalupe T. Luna, *"Agricultural Underdogs" and International Agreements: The Legal Context of Agricultural Workers within the Rural Economy*, 26 New Mexico L. Rev. 9 (1996).

The remainder of this chapter examines, in more detail, a few of the more significant current programs that affect either undocumented migrants or criminal enforcement of the immigration laws, or both. Section A will consider the range of immigration-related conduct that is prohibited by law. Section B will examine one especially important set of offenses—employer sanctions—and an accompanying program that prohibits certain forms of job discrimination. Section C will explore the statutory restrictions on undocumented migrants' eligibility for various public benefits and the constitutionality of those constraints.

Section A.   Immigration Offenses[1]

In addition to making specified immigration-related misconduct a basis for removal or a barrier to discretionary relief, Congress has directly prohibited some such acts. In some instances Congress has made the conduct a crime. In others, Congress has chosen instead to make the conduct a civil offense and attach generally milder penalties. In considering those criminal and civil offenses, this chapter aims only to alert you to the existence of some of the more common immigration offenses and to sketch briefly the basic parameters of two specific classes of offenses created in 1986 by IRCA—the employer sanctions and the nondiscrimination provisions.

The following chart, published by DHS, gives you a rough idea of the various immigration and nationality *crimes* (not *civil* offenses) and the frequency of convictions. The figures shown are for fiscal year 2003. Total convictions have stayed virtually constant for several years. *Id.*

Offense	Number of Convictions
All violations	**22,478**
Immigration violations	**21,820**
Illegal Entries	14,199
Illegal Reentries by Deported Aliens	4,938
Bringing in, transporting, harboring, and inducing illegal entry	1,612
Fraud, and false statements for immigration benefits	270
Fraud, forgery, misuse of visas, registration offenses	253
Fraud, forgery, misuse of ID documents	390
Conspiracy to defraud United States	6
Employing unauthorized noncitizens, peonage, false employment attestations	72
Other immigration violations	80
Nationality violations	**137**
False representations as U.S. citizens	101
Fraud, misuse of citizenship papers	6
Fraud, forgery, misuse of U.S. passports	30

2003 Yearbook of Immigration Statistics, Table 49 at 180.

---

1. See generally David Weissbrodt & Laura Danielson, Immigration Law and Procedure in a Nutshell, ch. 14 (5th ed. 2005).

You know presence without admission as a ground for removal, but as the chart indicates, entry without authorization is also a criminal offense. Indeed, it is by far the most common immigration-related basis for criminal convictions. INA § 275(a) forbids several types of entries and attempted entries—those that occur at undesignated places, those in which the person eludes inspection, and those that are accomplished by fraud. As a result of IIRIRA § 105, additional civil penalties are now also possible. INA § 275(b). The crime is generally a misdemeanor, but any person who has once been removed, and who then reenters or attempts to reenter or is found in the United States without the consent of the Secretary of Homeland Security is guilty of a felony. INA § 276.[2] In *United States v. Mendoza–Lopez*, 481 U.S. 828, 107 S.Ct. 2148, 95 L.Ed.2d 772 (1987), the Supreme Court held that a person could not constitutionally be convicted under section 276 without having had, at some point, a meaningful opportunity to contest the validity of the underlying removal order. See also INA § 266 (criminal penalties for failing to register and for related offenses).

Another group of offenses, overlapping those just discussed, deals with fraud. The broadest provision in this group is 18 U.S.C. § 1001, which generally makes it a felony to defraud the United States government. Other provisions of the United States Criminal Code specifically cover frauds and related offenses concerned with citizenship, 18 U.S.C. §§ 1421–1429, passports, 18 U.S.C. §§ 1541–1545, and other immigration documents, 18 U.S.C. § 1546. The last-cited provision is supplemented by INA § 274C, which expands the range of document-related violations and prescribes civil penalties to be imposed after administrative proceedings. See generally Linton Joaquin & Charles Wheeler, *Document Fraud Enforcement the Second Time Around: Will the Right Lessons Be Learned?*, 78 IR 473 (Mar. 12, 2001). There are also provisions that specifically prohibit certain forms of marriage fraud and entrepreneurship fraud. INA § 275(c,d).

Of modern significance is the group of offenses defined by INA § 274(a)(1). That subsection prohibits various means of facilitating illegal immigration. Section 274(a)(1)(A, B, C, and D) generally cover, respectively, bringing noncitizens to the United States other than at designated ports of entry; transporting, within the United States, noncitizens who are present in violation of law (the transportation must be "in furtherance of such violation"); harboring such persons; and inducing illegal entry. The various subsections impose differing mens rea requirements. See also INA §§ 277 (importing noncitizen criminals), 278 (importing noncitizen prostitutes).

---

2. What if the reentry occurs after the period during which INA § 212(a)(6)(B) requires a grant of permission from the Secretary of Homeland Security to reapply for admission? Does section 276 still apply? See *United States v. Idowu*, 105 F.3d 728 (D.C. Cir. 1997); Eric H. Singer, *United States v. Idowu: Inadmissibility and Unlawful Reentry After Deportation—Still Confused After All These Years*, 29 Southwestern Univ. L. Rev. 301 (2000).

None of the preceding provisions expressly bars the *employment* of undocumented migrants. In fact, from the 1952 enactment of the INA until the passage of IRCA in 1986, section 274(a) concluded with this language:

> *Provided, however,* That for the purpose of this section, employment (including the usual and normal practices incident to employment) shall not be deemed to constitute harboring.

(Emphasis in original.) That wording, known as the Texas Proviso after the state then most prominently associated with its enactment, was repealed by IRCA § 112(a), amending INA § 274(a). Even without the Texas Proviso it is unclear whether employment alone could constitute harboring. The interpretation of the former INS was that it does not. See 52 Fed.Reg. 16216, 16217 (May 1, 1987); 63 IR 1181 (1986) (no intent to prosecute employers under harboring provision). IRCA did, however, enact a new program specifically prohibiting the employment of any noncitizens who are not authorized to work. The details of that program are the subject of section B of this chapter. As you will see, the IRCA penalties for employment are generally much less severe than the section 274 penalties for harboring; the harboring-as-employment issue, therefore, is not moot.

Probably the most important modern phenomenon arising out of section 274 has been the sanctuary movement. In chapter 11 you read about United States asylum laws and the widespread belief that Salvadorans, Guatemalans, and other individuals fleeing governments strongly allied with the United States were wrongly denied asylum during the 1980s. Many churches, other private institutions, and even some state and local governments responded by declaring themselves "sanctuaries" in which undocumented migrants who asserted eligibility for asylum would be free to remain. See Jorge L. Carro, *Municipal and State Sanctuary Declarations: Innocuous Symbolism or Improper Dictates?*, 16 Pepperdine L. Rev. 297 (1989).

Using INA § 274, the government prosecuted members of the sanctuary movement. Some interesting case law resulted. Among the defenses asserted were (a) the shielded individuals were in fact eligible for asylum, even though it was being wrongly denied, and thus were not here in violation of law; (b) the defendants believed, rightly or wrongly, that the individuals were eligible for asylum, and thus the defendants lacked the necessary mens rea; (c) the defendants were acting out of necessity, with the lives of others at stake; (d) the government's conduct—particularly the planting of informants in church congregations—impermissibly obstructed the free exercise of religion; (e) the government was selectively prosecuting those defendants who were politically prominent; and (f) the defendants' actions were consistent with U.S. treaty obligations. Those arguments generally failed to produce dismissals, see, e.g., *United States v. Aguilar,* 883 F.2d 662 (9th Cir.1989); *United States v. Merkt,* 764 F.2d 266 (5th Cir.1985); *United States v. Elder,* 601 F.Supp. 1574 (S.D.Tex.1985), although in some cases juries ultimately acquitted particular defendants. See JoAnne C. Adlerstein, *Immigration Crimes: A Practitioner's Guide,* January 1989 Immigration Briefings at 5.

A great deal of thoughtful and sometimes passionate commentary has focused on the sanctuary movement. See, e.g., Ignatius Bau, This Ground is Holy—Church Sanctuary and Central American Refugees (1985); Carro, above; Jorge L. Carro, *Sanctuary: The Resurgence of an Age–Old Right or a Dangerous Misinterpretation of an Abandoned Ancient Privilege?*, 54 Univ. Cincinnati L. Rev. 747 (1986); Barnaby W. Zall, *Asylum and Sanctuary— the American Dilemma*, 72 A.B.A.J. 66 (Aug. 1, 1986). Since the overwhelming proportion of those who received sanctuary were Salvadorans and Guatemalans, and since both groups came within the *ABC* settlement (and Salvadorans within the Temporary Protected Status program as well, see page 1168 above), the significance of the sanctuary movement diminished in the 1990's. The turmoil in Colombia triggered a brief resurgence. See Hernan Rozemberg, *Sanctuary Ready to Help*, The Arizona Republic (Mar. 26, 2002).

Perhaps the darkest side of illegal immigration is the growing trade in young girls and women, an adjunct of the increased use of professional smugglers and traffickers. The emerging trend has been one of international cooperation in addressing the related problems of "human smuggling" and "human trafficking." The latter term generally signifies an element of coercion or at least exploitation, frequently involving prostitution, slavery, or indentured servitude. For thoughtful studies, see David Kyle & Rey Koslowski (eds.), Global Human Smuggling: Comparative Perspectives (2001); Nora V. Demleitner, *The Law at a Crossroads: The Construction of Migrant Women Trafficked into Prostitution*, in Kyle & Koslowski, above, ch.10; Dina Francesca Haynes, *Used, Arrested and Deported: Extending Immigration Benefits to Protect the Victims of Trafficking and to Secure the Prosecution of Traffickers*, 26 Human Rights Q. 221 (2004); Institute for the Study of International Migration of Georgetown University & European Forum for Migration Studies of Univ. of Bamberg, *Transatlantic Workshop on Human Smuggling*, 15 Georgetown Immigration L.J. 167 (2001); Lisa Raffonelli, *INS Final Rule to Assist Victims of Trafficking*, 23 Refugee Reports 1 (Apr. 2002); United States Dept. of State, Trafficking in Persons Report (June 14, 2004), digested in 81 IR at 910 (July 12, 2004), followed by congressional hearings, 81 IR 931 (July 19, 2004).

Recent years have witnessed several international agreements to combat various forms of slavery and trafficking. The most important agreement is the so-called Palermo Protocol, officially the "Protocol to Prevent, Suppress and Punish Trafficking in Persons, Especially Women and Children, Supplementing the United Nations Convention against Transnational Organized Crime," adopted by U.N.G.A. Res. A/RES/55/25 (Nov. 15, 2000, entered into force 2003). It requires states to take a number of enforcement, educational, and other cooperative measures, but most of the requirements are worded flexibly enough to be more precatory than binding. A subsequent report of the UN High Commissioner for Human Rights to the UN Economic and Social Council, U.N. Doc. E/2002/68/Add.1 (distributed May 20, 2002), recommends a number of ways to concretize the prescriptions of the Palermo Protocol and otherwise resist trafficking. The United States signed the Palermo Protocol on December 13, 2000 but has not yet ratified it. See http://www1.umn.edu/humanrts/research/ratification-USA.html. The United States Congress has, however, passed the Trafficking Victims Protection Act of 2000, described more fully in chapter 4, section E above (allowing limited numbers of nonimmigrant "T" and "U" visas for trafficking victims). Like other countries, the United States sees the problem as not only a humanitarian issue, but also one of crime and border control.

One last kind of immigration penalty relevant here is imposed on commercial carriers. If you have flown internationally, you have probably noticed that the airline ticketing agent at the departure airport always asks to see your passport and any required visa. In case you were wondering what business it is of theirs, the answer is that the immigration laws of most countries require common carriers (airlines, shipping lines, railroads, bus companies, etc.) to check for the necessary entry documents. If the arriving passenger somehow shows up at the port of entry without them, the carrier will generally be liable to civil fines and responsible for transporting the person back at its own expense. See, e.g., INA §§ 271–73; see generally Robert J. Jarvis, *Rusting in Drydock: Stowaways, Shipowners and the Administrative Penalty Provision of INA Section 273(d)*, 13 Tulane Maritime L.J. 25 (1988). There are, in addition, provisions authorizing the civil forfeiture of vehicles used to assist the commission of specified immigration offenses. INA § 274(b). For a comprehensive account, see David Rubman, *Seizure and Forfeiture of Conveyances Under the INA*, February 1990 Immigration Briefings.

In recent years the trend in Congress has been to expand the use of criminal and civil penalties for immigration-related misconduct. Comprehensive crime legislation enacted in 1994 added several new immigration crimes. See 71 IR 1177 (Sept. 1, 1994). IIRIRA continued that trend, adding, for example, new criminal penalties for false citizenship claims, IIRIRA § 215, amending 18 U.S.C. § 1015, new civil penalties for destroying one's travel documents on board a common carrier to the United States, IIRIRA § 212(a), adding INA § 274C(a)(6), and civil penalties for failing to cooperate in arranging one's departure after a removal order, IIRIRA § 380, adding new INA § 274D. For some excellent writings on the increasing "criminalization" of immigration law, see, e.g., Nora V. Demleitner, *Immigration Threats and Rewards: Effective Law Enforcement Tools in the "War" on Terrorism*, 51 Emory L.J. 1059 (2002); Daniel Kanstroom, *Criminalizing the Undocumented: Ironic Boundaries of the Post–September 11th "Pale of Law,"* 29 North Carolina J. Internat'l L. & Commercial Regulation 639 (2004); Daniel Kanstroom, *Deportation, Social Control and Punishment: Some Thoughts About Why Hard Laws Make Bad Cases*, 113 Harvard L. Rev. 1889 (2000); Maria Isabel Medina, *The Criminalization of Immigration Law: Employer Sanctions and Marriage Fraud*, 5 George Mason L. Rev. 669 (1997); Teresa A. Miller, *Citizenship and Severity: Recent Immigration Reforms and the New Penology*, 17 Georgetown Immigration L.J. 611 (2003).

SECTION B.   EMPLOYER MISCONDUCT

1.   EMPLOYER SANCTIONS

After many years of debate, Congress in 1986 enacted the Immigration Reform and Control Act, Pub.L. 99–603, 100 Stat. 3359 (IRCA). The central target of IRCA was illegal immigration, which the statute attacked on several fronts. You have already encountered the legalization programs— general, agricultural, and Cuban/Haitian. See chapter 8, § A.3. These programs reduced the undocumented population by permitting several million to become documented. At the same time, Congress sought to shrink the incentive for future unlawful migration by drying up the job opportunities that it saw as the principal magnet. To that end, Congress added a new section 274A to the INA. That section imposes civil fines, and in certain instances criminal punishment, on those who knowingly hire anyone not authorized to work (or who do certain other things described below). The same section also requires employees and certain others to take specified affirmative steps to verify work authorization.

Employer sanctions became permanently etched in the American con- sciousness in early 1993, when it was reported that President Clinton's choice for Attorney General, Zoe Baird, had been employing an undocu- mented couple as domestic workers. The resulting uproar doomed her nomination. See Michael Kelly, *Settling In: The President's Day; Clinton Cancels Baird Nomination for Justice Dept.*, New York Times, Jan. 22, 1993, at A1. After it became known that the new President's second choice, Judge Kimba Wood, had also employed an undocumented migrant, the political climate persuaded Judge Wood to withdraw from consideration— even though her actions (unlike Baird's) had been entirely legal under the then existing law. New York Times, Feb. 6, 1993, at A–2. That the Attorney General was then responsible for enforcing the immigration laws served only to heighten the sensitivity of the issue. Still, the controversy renewed a broader discussion of what kinds of conduct ought to disqualify people from public office, as well as a debate about child care, gender, and double standards.

The pre–IRCA debates reflected sharp differences of opinion about the wisdom of employer sanctions. Proponents emphasized the problems associ- ated with undocumented migrants and portrayed employer sanctions as a promising way to deter both surreptitious entries and overstays. They also argued that no plausible alternative was apparent. Opponents expressed doubts that employer sanctions would achieve their stated goal, concerns about the administrative burdens on employers, and fears that employer sanctions would lead to various forms of job discrimination. To mitigate that last concern, Congress added INA § 274B, which prohibits certain discriminatory acts. How well employer sanctions have worked and what the negatives have been are discussed below. For now, it is enough to note that this package of employer sanctions, prohibitions on discrimination, and legalization was able to command majorities in both Houses of Congress and to become law. For a clear and thorough analysis of the statute as a whole, see Maurice A. Roberts & Stephen Yale–Loehr, Understanding the 1986 Immigration Law (1987).

The employer sanctions provision, INA § 274A, proscribes several acts. Subsection a(1)(A) makes it unlawful "to hire, or to recruit or refer for a fee, for employment in the United States an alien knowing the alien is an unauthorized alien ..." Under subsection a(2), it is unlawful "to continue to employ [an] alien in the United States knowing the alien is (or has become) an unauthorized alien ..." To be authorized to work, a noncitizen must be an LPR, or fall within one of the other categories of noncitizens for whom the INA automatically authorizes employment, or be a person who has received individual work authorization from USCIS. INA § 274A(h)(3). See generally Michael W. Straus, *Employment of Aliens: A Guideline for Employers and Employees,* 20 Univ. West L.A. L. Rev. 133 (1988–89). Importantly, IRCA § 101(a)(3) provided:

(3) GRANDFATHER FOR CURRENT EMPLOYEES.

(A) Section 274A(a)(1) of the Immigration and Nationality Act shall not apply to the hiring, or recruiting or referring of an individual for employment which has occurred before the date of the enactment of this Act.

(B) Section 274A(a)(2) of the Immigration and Nationality Act shall not apply to continuing employment of an alien who was hired before the date of the enactment of this Act.

There has been some concern about the applicability of IRCA to casual domestic employment. The literal statutory language contains no exemption for innocuous employment, but the regulations define employment *not* to include "casual employment by individuals who provide domestic service in a private home that is sporadic, irregular, or intermittent." 8 C.F.R. § 274a.1(h) (2004).

What "knowing" means has been the subject of some controversy. The issue arises most commonly when ICE does a routine check of an employer's records, discovers that the identification number that appeared on the green card that the person displayed to the employer either does not exist in the DHS computer database or belongs to someone else, and consequently notifies the employer that it suspects the employee is not authorized to work. If the employer does nothing, is it guilty of continuing to employ, "knowing" that the person is not authorized to work?

In *Mester Manufacturing Co. v. INS,* 879 F.2d 561 (9th Cir.1989), the court held, first, that "constructive" knowledge was enough. The court meant only that *"deliberate* failure to investigate suspicious circumstances imputes knowledge." *Id.* at 567 (emphasis added). Accord, *New El Rey Sausage Co. v. United States INS,* 925 F.2d 1153, 1157–58 (9th Cir.1991).

In *Collins Foods International, Inc. v. INS,* 948 F.2d 549 (9th Cir. 1991), the Chief Administrative Law Judge (see the procedural description below) had found an employer guilty of knowingly hiring an unauthorized migrant. Unbeknownst to the personnel officer, the social security card that the employee presented to establish work authorization was counterfeit. The ALJ found "constructive" knowledge because the personnel officer, after examining the document, had not compared the back of it to a sample social security card illustrated in a manual of the former INS.[3] The court reversed, observing that the statute requires only that the employer verify that the document on its face appear genuine; comparison with samples displayed in a government manual is not necessary.

Importantly, the court cited *Mester* and *New El Rey* as the only two federal cases finding constructive knowledge; the court emphasized that in both cases the employer had retained the employees *after being notified by the INS that the employees' green card numbers were false*. The court in *Collins Foods* then observed that both those cases had relied on *United States v. Jewell*, 532 F.2d 697, 704 (9th Cir. 1976), where constructive knowledge of a particular fact had been interpreted (in a different context) to require awareness that the fact was highly probable and a conscious decision to "avoid enlightenment"—in other words, wilful blindness.

Nonetheless, the regulations interpret "knowing" to include "knowledge which may fairly be inferred through notice of certain facts and circumstances which would lead a person, through the exercise of reasonable care, to know about a certain condition." 8 C.F.R. § 274a.l(1) (2004). That formulation goes beyond wilful blindness; it appears also to encompass what tort lawyers sometimes call "reason to know."

There still remains the question of when the employer's inaction in the face of such notice amounts to "continu[ing] to employ." In both *Mester Manufacturing* and *New El Rey Sausage Co.,* the Ninth Circuit made clear that the employer could not be found guilty for failing to fire or suspend an employee immediately upon receiving notice of the government's suspicion. Rather, the court said, the government "must provide an employer with a reasonable amount of time for compliance after the employer acquires knowledge that an employee is unauthorized." *New El Rey Sausage Co.,* 925 F.2d at 1156.

The subsections discussed up to this point define substantive prohibitions. In contrast, subsection a(1)(B) creates a separate, procedural offense. It imposes on the employer an affirmative obligation to perform certain paperwork before hiring *any* individual—whether a citizen or not. The specific requirements, which are designed to verify that the employee may lawfully be hired, are all laid out in subsection (b). A good faith *attempt* to comply with the verification procedures will excuse "a technical or proce-

---

3. The ALJ had also relied on the fact that the personnel officer had made the initial job offer over the phone (because the employee had been working for an affiliated company in another city), without examining the employee's documents. As the court pointed out, it is perfectly proper to make the offer by phone as long as the employer inspects the documents at or before the hiring. INA § 274A(a)(1)(B). Hiring, in turn, is defined as the "actual commencement of employment." 8 C.F.R. § 274a.1(c) (2004). Since the employer performed all the required tasks before the employee started work, there was no violation.

dural" failure. INA § 274A(b)(6). And *actual* good faith compliance with those requirements is also an automatic defense to the charge of violating the substantive provisions. INA § 274A(a)(3).

The verification system described in subsection (b) consists of several steps. First, the employer must examine certain documents furnished by the prospective employee. The statute lists examples of three categories of documents—those that simultaneously establish the employee's identity and his or her employment authorization, those that establish only the latter, and those that establish only the former. See subsections b(1)(B, C, and D) respectively. The employer must examine either a document listed in (B) or two separate documents—one listed in (C) and one listed in (D)—and assure that the documentation "reasonably appears on its face to be genuine." INA § 274A(b)(1)(A).

After examining the relevant documents, the employer must attest under penalty of perjury, on a standardized form, that it has performed the required verification. *Id.* On the same form the employee must then attest that he or she is either a United States citizen or otherwise authorized to work. INA § 274A(b)(2). The employer must retain the form for a specified time period, during which certain enforcement officials have the right to inspect it. INA § 274A(b)(3). Nothing in the statute requires the employer to keep copies of the inspected documents, but many employers do so anyway to prove that they performed the required inspection.

The Secretary of Homeland Security (originally the Attorney General) is the official charged with investigating and prosecuting suspected violations of the employer sanctions provisions. INA § 274A(e). A variety of enforcement techniques are applied toward that end. An early one, which has come under criticism, has been to arrange for the Labor Department to forward to the immigration officials copies of labor certification applications that appear to reveal past or ongoing employment of the undocumented beneficiaries. The information on those application forms is sometimes used to initiate sanctions proceedings against the employer and/or removal proceedings against the employee. Consider the pros and cons of that policy. See 70 IR 291–92 (Mar. 8, 1993).

Any person with knowledge of a potential violation of section 274A may file a complaint with ICE. 8 C.F.R. § 274a.9(a) (2004). ICE may investigate the complaint or investigate a suspected violation on its own initiative. If ICE finds a violation, it serves on the alleged violator either a Notice of Intent to Fine or a Warning Notice. *Id.* § 274a.9(b). The party then has the right to request a formal hearing before an administrative law judge (ALJ). INA § 274A(d)(ii)(C). The regulations spell out the details. See 28 C.F.R. § 68 (2004). In particular, they establish within the Executive Office for Immigration Review (the same agency that houses the immigration judges and the BIA) a separate Office of the Chief Administrative Hearing Officer (OCAHO). The ALJ's are situated within OCAHO. *Id.* § 68.2. ICE must prove its case by a preponderance of the evidence. INA § 274A(e)(3)(C). If it does, the ALJ imposes civil fines, which are higher for substantive violations than for paperwork violations. INA § 274A(e)(4, 5).

Criminal proceedings, in which the sentence can include imprisonment for up to six months, are possible when there has been a "pattern or practice" of violating the substantive provisions. INA § 274A(f)(1). The sentence can be as long as five years if, within a twelve-month period, the employer hired ten or more unauthorized workers with actual knowledge of their status. INA § 274(a)(3).

Under the Justice Department's regulations, the Chief Administrative Hearing Officer has the discretion to review the decision of the ALJ. 28 C.F.R. § 68.54(a) (2004); see also INA § 274A(e)(7). Judicial review of the final administrative decision is available by petition for review in the court of appeals. INA § 274A(e)(8).

The OCAHO decisions in these cases (and also in the anti-discrimination cases discussed in the next subsection) are sometimes accompanied by full opinions. Selected opinions of ALJ's and of the Chief Administrative Hearing Officer are now published in Administrative Decisions under the Employer Sanctions and Unfair Immigration–Related Employment Practices Laws. They can also be accessed through the EOIR website. Visit http://www.usdoj.gov/eoir and click on "Virtual Law Library" and then "OCAHO."

The verdict is still out on employer sanctions. Have they deterred illegal migration? Have the burdens imposed on business been within the range of acceptability? Have employer sanctions, despite the simultaneous enactment of prohibitions on certain discriminatory practices (more on those in subsection 2), in fact caused significant levels of discrimination? Should the employer sanctions provisions be retained as is, modified, or repealed? If they are either retained or modified, what changes in administration and enforcement, if any, would be beneficial?

Opinion on those questions is divided. For a good sampling, see Robert L. Bach & Doris Meissner, Employment and Immigration Reform: Employer Sanctions Four Years Later [hereafter Bach & Meissner] 4–5 (1990); Howard F. Chang, *Immigration and the Workplace: Immigration Restrictions as Employment Discrimination*, 78 Chicago–Kent L. Rev. 291 (2003) (characterizing employer sanctions as government-mandated employment discrimination against noncitizens); Cecelia M. Espenoza, *The Illusory Provisions of Sanctions: The Immigration Reform and Control Act of 1986*, 8 Georgetown Immigration L.J. 343 (1994); Michael Fix & Paul T. Hill, Enforcing Employer Sanctions: Challenges and Strategies [hereafter Fix & Hill] 11–15 (1990); Stephen H. Legomsky, *Employer Sanctions: Past and Future*, in Peter Duignan & Lewis H. Gann (eds.), The Debate in the United States over Immigration, chap. 6 (1998) (identifying benefits and costs of employer sanctions); Stanley Mailman, *The Employer as Immigration Inspector*, 1 BIB #8 at 20–25 (July 1996); M. Isabel Medina, *The Criminalization of Immigration Law: Employer Sanctions and Marriage Fraud*, 5 George Mason L. Rev. 669, 678–96 (1997); United States Commission on Immigration Reform, U.S. Immigration Policy: Restoring Credibility [hereafter CIR] 50–76 (Sept. 1994). The AFL–CIO has urged a full repeal of employer sanctions. See 79 IR 39 (Jan. 7, 2002).

Recognizing the need for evaluation, Congress included in IRCA a provision that requires the Comptroller General (who heads the General Accountability [formerly Accounting] Office) to prepare a series of three annual reports, beginning one year after enactment, reviewing the implementation of IRCA. Congress asked the GAO to determine whether

(A) [the employer sanctions] provisions have been carried out satisfactorily;

(B) a pattern of discrimination has resulted against citizens or nationals of the United States or against eligible workers seeking employment; and

(C) an unnecessary regulatory burden has been created for employers hiring such workers.

INA § 274A(j)(1). The statute also created an inter-agency task force that, in the event the GAO found a pattern of national origin discrimination, would be charged with recommending remedies. INA § 274A(k). Importantly, the Act provides that, if the GAO reports "a widespread pattern of discrimination has resulted * * * solely from the implementation of" employer sanctions, expedited procedures would be permitted in both the House and the Senate to decide whether employer sanctions should be repealed. INA § 274A(*l*)(1); see also *id.* § 274A(m,n).

The third and final GAO report, a detailed 162–page document, made a number of specific findings. The following excerpts are taken from the Executive Summary:

United States General Accounting Office, Immigration Reform—Employer Sanctions and the Question of Discrimination

Pp. 3–8 (March 1990).

Congress has mandated that GAO determine whether widespread discrimination has resulted solely from the law. This is difficult to prove or disprove. First, there is an absence of a sensitive pre-IRCA measure of discrimination. Further, there was no comparison group not subject to IRCA. Recognizing these limitations, GAO used the best available evidence to meet its congressional mandate.

IRCA also provides an option for Congress to repeal its antidiscrimination section if GAO determines that the section has been a vehicle for frivolous complaints against employers.

For this third report, GAO (1) reviewed federal agency implementation of IRCA, (2) reviewed discrimination complaints filed with federal agencies and data from groups representing aliens, and (3) used additional methods to obtain data on IRCA's effects. These methodologies included a statistically valid survey of over 9,400 of the Nation's employers, which projects to a universe of about 4.6 million employers. In collaboration with the Urban Institute, GAO also did a "hiring audit" in which pairs of persons matched closely on job qualifications applied for jobs with 360 employers in two cities. One member of each pair was a "foreign-appearing, foreign-sounding" Hispanic and the other was an Anglo with no foreign accent.

Results in Brief

GAO found that the law

- has apparently reduced illegal immigration and is not an unnecessary burden on employers,

- has generally been carried out satisfactorily by INS and Labor, and

- has not been used as a vehicle to launch frivolous complaints against employers.

GAO also found that there was widespread discrimination. But was there discrimination as a result of IRCA? That is the key question Congress directed GAO to answer. GAO's answer is yes.

Making such a link is exceedingly difficult. GAO used various techniques and approaches to try to measure the discrimination and determine the link. None of these techniques or approaches was or could be ideal. Some may disagree with GAO's conclusion. But, on the basis of employers' responses to key questions GAO asked about their hiring behavior and how it related to provisions of IRCA, GAO's judgment is that a substantial amount of the discrimination did occur as a result of IRCA.

The decision Congress must now make is difficult because of IRCA's mixed results. There has been discrimination. An estimated 461,000 employers, or 10 percent of all those surveyed, reported national origin discrimination as a result of the law, but 90 percent did not; thus, IRCA-related discrimination is serious but not pervasive. And the sanctions provision at this time appears to have slowed illegal immigration to the United States.

GAO believes many employers discriminated because the law's verification system does not provide a simple or reliable method to verify job applicants' eligibility to work. Thus, it is likely that the widespread pattern of discrimination GAO found could be reduced if employers were provided with more education on the law's requirements and a simpler and more reliable verification system.

In the final analysis, GAO sees three options for Congress: (1) leaving IRCA as is for the present, (2) repealing the sanctions and antidiscrimination provisions, or (3) amending IRCA's verification system to reduce the law's discriminatory effects.

Principal Findings

Illegal Immigration Being Reduced; Law Not an Unnecessary Burden

GAO's criteria in determining if the implementation of the sanctions section has caused an "unnecessary" regulatory burden on employers was based on whether the law's objectives were realized. GAO found that the burden of applying the law's verification requirements was not "unnecessary" because the law has apparently reduced illegal immigration and employment, as Congress envisioned. While not conclusive, nearly all available data suggests the law's objectives have been at least partially realized. For example,

- a statistical study by the Urban Institute concluded that the law had slowed illegal immigration,

- two surveys in Mexico found that people believe it is now harder to find work in the United States, and

- about 16 percent of aliens apprehended during employer sanctions investigations during August and September 1989 reported difficulty finding a job because of the law's verification system.

INS and Labor Have Met Their Minimum Responsibilities Under the Law

GAO decided that the sanctions section would have been carried out "satisfactorily" if the government developed plans and policies and implemented procedures that could reasonably be expected to (1) educate employers about their requirements under the law and (2) identify and fine violators. GAO found that INS and Labor have generally fulfilled their responsibilities under this definition of "satisfactorily." However, GAO also found that INS could improve its methods for determining employer compliance with the law's requirements.

As of September 1989, INS had issued notices of intent to fine employers for about 3,500 violations for knowingly hiring or continuing to employ unauthorized aliens. There were also about 36,000 violations for not completing the verification forms. The total fines assessed were about $17 million. GAO's review of about 300 randomly selected employer sanctions case files showed that INS field offices had correctly carried out the Commissioner's policy on employer fines. Between September 1987 and September 1989, Labor officials completed over 77,000 inspections of employers' verification forms.

Following the government's extensive efforts to educate employers, including direct contact with over 2 million employers, GAO estimates that 3.8 million (83 percent) of the 4.6 million employers in the survey population were aware of the law. Of the 2.4 million employers who were aware of the law and hired at least one employee during 1988, GAO estimates that 1.6 million (65 percent) reported being in full compliance with the verification requirement.

No Evidence of Frivolous Complaints

GAO's review of the Office of Special Counsel and the Equal Employment Opportunity Commission's discrimination data found no evidence of frivolous IRCA discrimination complaints to harass employers.

Employers Reported Discriminatory Practices Resulting From the Law

GAO's survey results indicate that national origin discrimination resulting from IRCA, while not pervasive, does exist at levels that amount to more than "just a few isolated cases" and constitutes "a serious pattern of discrimination." GAO estimates that 461,000 (or 10 percent) of the 4.6 million employers in the survey population nationwide began one or more practices that represent national origin discrimination. The survey responses do not reveal whether the persons affected by the discrimination were eligible to work. However, given that these employers hired an estimated 2.9 million employees in 1988, GAO believes it is reasonable to assume that many eligible workers were affected.

An estimated 227,000 employers reported that they began a practice, as a result of IRCA, not to hire job applicants whose foreign appearance or accent led them to suspect that they might be unauthorized aliens. Also, contrary to IRCA, an estimated 346,000 employers said that they applied IRCA's verification system only to persons who had a "foreign" appearance or accent. Some employers began both practices.

Employers reported that they engaged in practices which under the law would be classified as discriminatory verification and hiring practices. They were in a variety of industries and areas of the Nation and included firms of various sizes. The levels of discrimination ranged by geographical location from 3 to 16 percent and were higher in areas having high Hispanic and Asian populations.

These employer responses specifically related the discriminatory hiring and verification practices to IRCA. Therefore, they represent "new" national origin discrimination that would not have occurred without IRCA. There is no evidence that would lead GAO to believe that employers who said they discriminated as a result of IRCA did not. But even if some employers did not report accurately, the remaining group would be substantial.

Since these data meet the criteria in the law and its legislative history, GAO concluded that the national origin discriminatory practices reported do establish a widespread pattern of discrimination. On the basis of the information GAO has, GAO determined that it is more reasonable to conclude that a substantial amount of these discriminatory practices resulted from IRCA rather than not.

Finally, GAO's hiring audit of 360 employers in Chicago, Illinois, and San Diego, California, showed that the "foreign-appearing, foreign-sounding" Hispanic member of the matched pairs was three times more likely to encounter unfavorable treatment than the Anglo non-foreign-appearing member of the pairs. For example, the Anglo members received 52 percent more job offers than the Hispanics. These results, taken together with the survey responses, show a serious problem of national origin discrimination that GAO believes IRCA exacerbated.

Employers Reported Other Forms of Discriminatory Practices

While GAO's statutory determination is limited to national origin discrimination that can be linked directly to IRCA's sanctions section, GAO's survey results indicate that the law also resulted in citizenship discrimination.

GAO estimates that an additional 430,000 employers (9 percent) said that because of the law they began hiring only persons born in the United States or not hiring persons with temporary work eligibility documents. These practices are illegal and can harm people, particularly those of Hispanic and Asian origin.

Adding these employers to those who began national origin discrimination, GAO estimates that 891,000 (19 percent) of the 4.6 million employers in the survey population nationwide began one or more discriminatory practices as a result of the law.

Employers Want Improved Verification System

About 78 percent of employers said they wanted a simpler or better verification system. The portion of employers who wanted these changes was 16 to 19 percent greater among those who reported discriminatory practices than among those who did not report discriminatory practices. GAO believes the responses tend to reflect employers' confusion and uncertainty about the law's verification system and that a simpler system that relies on fewer documents could reduce discrimination.

Contributing to the uncertainty that arises from the variety of documents in use is the prevalence of counterfeit documents. INS apprehensions of unauthorized aliens show they commonly have counterfeit or fraudulently obtained documents—Social Security cards or one of the various INS alien work eligibility cards.

By the mid–1990s, INS plans to (1) reduce from 10 to 2 the number of work eligibility cards it issues and to make these 2 cards more difficult to counterfeit and (2) replace over 20 million old INS cards with the new ones. However, this schedule depends on additional funding and personnel. Unless this process is expedited, little will be accomplished in the near term to reduce employer confusion and uncertainty about aliens' work eligibility status.

Improved Verification System Needed If Sanctions Are Retained

GAO identified three possible reasons why employers discriminated: (1) lack of understanding of the law's major provisions, (2) confusion and uncertainty about how to determine eligibility, and (3) the prevalence of counterfeit and fraudulent documents that contributed to employer uncertainty over how to verify eligibility.

GAO's work suggests that the widespread pattern of discrimination it found could be effectively reduced by (1) increasing employer understanding through effective education efforts, (2) reducing the number of work eligibility documents, (3) making the documents harder to counterfeit, thereby reducing document fraud, and (4) applying the new documents to all members of the workforce.

* * *

Not all the GAO's conclusions are universally shared. One study viewed the reduced number of border apprehensions as "consistent with the possibility that some dampening effect on illegal crossings may have occurred" but cautioned that legalization might be responsible for that decrease and added that in any event more information is needed. Frank D. Bean, George Vernez & Charles B. Keely, Rand Corp. & Urban Institute, Opening and Closing the Doors—Evaluating Immigration Reform and Control 109 (1989). See generally *id.*, chaps. 5, 6. Since then, as you saw earlier, the undocumented population in the U.S. has grown steadily. That, of course, does not prove employer sanctions have been ineffective, since no one knows how large the increases would have been without employer sanctions. Another empirical study found widespread violations of IRCA, argued that Congress saw illegal immigration as economically beneficial and thus did not really wish to deter it, suggested that Congress enacted employer sanctions only because it felt pressure to satisfy the public, and concluded that Congress had known the law it passed would be easy to circumvent with fraudulent documents. Kitty Calavita, *Employer Sanctions Violations: Toward a Dialectical Model of White–Collar Crime*, 24 L. & Society Rev. 1041 (1990).

As you have just read, the GAO found that both the former INS and the Labor Department had satisfactorily performed their education and enforcement missions. Another study added that "[t]he INS has averted significant complaints about unfair or overzealous employer sanctions enforcement" and "has generally stayed within the bounds of administrative law." Michael Fix & Paul T. Hill, Enforcing Employer Sanctions: Challenges and Strategies iii (1990); see also *id.* at 104–05. The GAO also found that the burden on employers had not been unreasonable, GAO Report, ch. 6, and the study by Fix and Hill observed that the national business community had not mobilized any major opposition, Fix and Hill, above, at 104. Still, there remains a difficult line for employers to walk between observing the employer sanctions provisions and avoiding the kinds of discrimination that section 274B, examined below, prohibits. For a good discussion, see Maurice A. Roberts & Stephen Yale–Loehr, *Employers as Junior Immigration Inspectors: The Impact of the 1986 Immigration Reform and Control Act*, 21 Internat'l Lawyer 1013 (1987).

The most volatile of the GAO's conclusions was its finding that employer sanctions had caused widespread discrimination, both in hiring decisions and in decisions whether to demand documentation. Prior studies had reached similar results. See, e.g., U.S. Comm'n on Civil Rights, The Immigration Reform and Control Act: Assessing the Evaluation Process iv (Sept. 1989) (finding "no doubt that the employer sanctions have caused many employers to implement discriminatory hiring practices"); New York State Inter–Agency Task Force on Immigration Affairs, Workplace Discrimination Under the Immigration Reform and Control Act of 1986: A Study of Impacts on New Yorkers 10 (Nov. 4, 1988) (" 'widespread pattern of discrimination' has been documented in New York"); Martha F. Davis, Lucas Guttentag & Allan H. Wernick, *Report of the Committee on Immigration and Nationality Law of the Association of the Bar of the City of New*

York: An Analysis of Discrimination Resulting from Employer Sanctions and a Call for Repeal, 26 San Diego L. Rev. 711, 717–23 (1989).

But some have questioned that finding. An internal GAO memo from its chief methodologist stated that the data did not conclusively trace the "widespread" discrimination to employer sanctions. See Robert L. Bach & Doris Meissner, Employment and Immigration Reform: Employer Sanctions Four Years Later 16 & 44 n. 19 (Sept. 1990). Senator Alan Simpson, who led the congressional fight for sanctions, denounced the GAO report, arguing that the statute did not require expedited congressional action on a repeal resolution unless the GAO found the widespread pattern of discrimination resulted *"solely"* from the implementation of employer sanctions. See INA § 274A(*l*)(1)(A); Bach & Meissner, above, at 16. (If the statute is interpreted literally, could such a fact *ever* be found? See Davis, Guttentag & Wernick, above, at 733–35.)

To reduce discrimination, the GAO report that you just read suggested enhanced efforts to educate employers and the development of a more effective document system. Some other researchers agree, but at the same time call for more strenuous enforcement of the employer sanctions provisions. Bach & Meissner, above, at 34–39; Fix & Hill, above, at iii–iv, 107–09. And in 1991 the former INS consciously began shifting resources from education to enforcement. See 68 IR 429–31 (1991). Congress has taken some limited measures on the education front, such as mandating the dissemination of information on the anti-discrimination provisions, discussed in subsection 2 below. See INA § 274B(*l*). The GAO findings encouraged several members of Congress to introduce resolutions and bills that would have repealed sanctions entirely. For a list, see Bach & Meissner, above, at 41 nn. 2, 3. None of the resolutions or bills passed.

Of all the problems that have beset employer sanctions, however, the one that has garnered by far the most attention has been the proliferation of counterfeit and fraudulently obtained documents. Especially common have been false social security cards and false immigration documents. Of particular concern have been the so-called "breeder" documents, like birth certificates, that in turn are used to procure drivers' licenses, social security cards, and passports. See generally United States Comm'n on Immigration Reform, U.S. Immigration Policy: Restoring Credibility 54 (Sept. 1994) [hereafter CIR].

In response to the problem of document fraud, the CIR proposed, on a pilot basis, a national computerized registry of authorized workers and telephonic employer access. The idea was to create a centralized data bank with the name and social security number of every authorized worker in the United States—citizen and noncitizen alike. The employer would phone the data bank to verify that a job applicant's social security number is valid. The system would then either confirm that the named individual has that number or inform the employer that the name and the number do not match. See CIR, above, at 60–62.

In IIRIRA § 401, Congress obliged, creating a "Basic Pilot Program" along those lines (as well as two other pilot programs no longer in operation). The program has since been extended through November 30, 2008. Basic Pilot Program Extension and Expansion Act of 2003, Pub. L. No. 108–156, 117 Stat. 1944 (Dec. 3, 2003). The program originally existed only for employers in a few designated states, but, effective December 1, 2004, USCIS has extended it to all 50 states and the District of Columbia. 69 Fed. Reg. 75997 (Dec. 20, 2004). Now web-based rather than dial-in, the program enables participating employers to obtain confirmation of a job applicant's work authorization, usually "within seconds." *Id.* The CIR and Congress hope these programs will eliminate both document fraud and IRCA-related discrimination (the latter because employers could simply punch in a name and number rather than have to distinguish citizens from noncitizens).

Andrew Strojny, the former Acting Special Counsel for Immigration–Related Unfair Employment Practices (the person in charge of investigating and prosecuting claims arising under IRCA's antidiscrimination provisions) is not so sanguine. He fears that the practical implementation of a national computerized registry would lead to unacceptably frequent errors, improper use of information by government officials, and a loss of personal privacy. Andrew M. Strojny, *Papers, Papers . . . Please: A National ID or an Electronic Tattoo*, 72 IR 617 (May 8, 1995); see also Juan P. Osuna, *The 1996 Immigration Act: Employer Sanctions, Antidiscrimination and Work Verification*, 73 IR 1749 (Dec. 20, 1996). Professor Daniel Steinbock suggests that a national identity card system compatible with the Fourth Amendment, the self-incrimination clause, and other constitutional guarantees could be designed, but that the Constitution would significantly limit the uses to which the system could be put. See Daniel J. Steinbock, *National Identity Cards: Fourth and Fifth Amendment Issues*, 56 Florida L. Rev. 697 (2004).

What do you think? Precisely how might a national registry make employer sanctions more effective and/or reduce job discrimination? Precisely how might it bring about the harms described by Strojny? (The CIR report and the Strojny article provide much more detail.)

Employer sanctions laws have been enacted in several western countries. For some interesting comparative studies, see United States GAO, Illegal Aliens—Information on Selected Countries' Employment Prohibition Laws, No. GAO/GGD-86-17BR (Oct. 1985); M. Isabel Medina, *Employer Sanctions in the United States, Canada and Mexico: Exploring the Criminalization of Immigration Law*, 3 Southwestern J. L. & Trade in the Americas 333 (1996) (finding employer sanctions counterproductive); Mark J. Miller, Employer Sanctions in Western Europe (1987); Francesco Isgro, *Italy Enacts Law to Protect Basic Human Rights of Foreign Workers*, 1 Georgetown Immigration L.J. 693 (1986). In New Zealand, in fact, the law punishes not only one who employs unauthorized migrants, see Immigration Act 1987, § 39, but also anyone who provides education to them, *id.* § 40.

PROBLEMS 1–7

To do these Problems, you will need to consult the actual text of INA § 274A. Assume all hirings occurred after the enactment of IRCA (November 1986) unless specified otherwise.

Problem 1. A hired a noncitizen student who was authorized to work off campus up to 20 hours per week. A was aware of that limitation and initially respected it. As things got busier in the office, however, A occasionally asked the student to put in 30–hour weeks. The student obliged. Has A violated INA § 274A?

Problem 2. B, about to hire a noncitizen applicant, asks to see the documents required by IRCA. The applicant displays identification and says that he has a green card, but adds apologetically that he absentmindedly left it at home and would be glad to bring it in the next day. B believes the applicant and allows him to start work but tells him to be sure to remember to bring the green card. In fact the applicant is undocumented. B forgets that he has not verified the person's work authorization, and the employee continues on the job. What charges might be brought against B?

Problem 3. A B–1 business visitor with no employment authorization applies to C for a job. She displays proper identification and a document that shows she has been admitted as a business visitor. The document says nothing either way about employment. C's personnel officer, mistakenly believing that business visitors are allowed to work, attests to having examined the appropriate documents. What charges might be brought against C?

Problem 4. D, a homeowner, knows she will be out of town for the summer. She therefore hires Ken, a high school student who lives next door, to mow D's lawn throughout the summer. Ken, a United States citizen, agrees. He ends up mowing the lawn five times, for which D pays him $100 upon her return. D has known Ken since Ken was born and does not ask him to display any documents. Has D violated section 274A?

Problem 5. Benito was admitted to the United States in 1984 (before IRCA) on what was then an H–1 ("distinguished merit and ability") nonimmigrant visa, which permits employment. E hired him that year. Although Benito's authorized stay finally expired in 1990 (as E knew), he remained in the United States longer than that, all the time working for E. In January 1991 Benito left the United States for a three-month visit with family. He returned to the United States without inspection in April 1991, at which time he resumed the work he had been doing for E. He has remained on the job ever since. What charges might be brought against E?

Problem 6. F, the President of a small company, and Helen, a noncitizen employee, together consult you for legal advice. When Helen first applied to the company for a job, she showed the personnel officer a driver's license and a social security card. The latter bore a special message to the effect that it did not authorize employment. As Helen had hoped, the personnel officer did not notice that message. After three years on the job Helen has become a highly valued and respected employee. Two days ago she confessed to F that she was a noncitizen without work authorization and asked whether he would help her "become legal" by applying for labor certification. F would like to keep her on his staff, and your opinion is that her occupational skills would probably qualify her for labor certification. Having studied the material in this section, what advice would you give? In framing your answer, consider the substantive law, the practical consequences for all concerned, and the applicable ethical constraints.

Problem 7. G, a small company, hires John, a United States citizen, in 1985. In 1995, John formally and effectively renounces his United States citizenship. (That makes him a noncitizen. And since he has not been granted LPR status or permission to work, it also leaves him without authorization to work.) The manager of the company knows all this but keeps John as an employee because John is extremely good at what he does. It is now 2006. Is G subject to employer sanctions?

2.   PROHIBITIONS ON DISCRIMINATION[4]

As the preceding section shows, concerns that employer sanctions would trigger discrimination against "foreign-looking" workers played a prominent part in the debates leading up to IRCA. The greatest fear was that employers would reject Latinos, Asians, and others in order to reduce the risk of inadvertently hiring an unauthorized worker. To break the stalemate, Representative Barney Frank offered a compromise. Employer sanctions would be coupled with provisions that expressly prohibited designated forms of job discrimination and established new administrative machinery for enforcing those prohibitions. The anti-discrimination program was enacted as IRCA § 102, which added a new section 274B to the INA.

Section 274B was itself controversial. The Administration and some others disputed, first, that employer sanctions would lead to discrimination. They argued that employers would have no motive to discriminate, since, to avoid sanctions, they would need only to do the required paperwork and to refrain from knowingly hiring unauthorized workers. Opponents of employer sanctions responded that that position requires an unrealistic assumption that employers will know enough about the immigration laws to *realize* they can avoid liability without discriminating (and, presumably, an assumption that employers will have enough confidence in their knowledge of the law to be willing to act on the basis of it.)

The Administration's reaction was that, even if employer sanctions increase job discrimination, a new anti-discrimination program was unnecessary because existing civil rights laws already prohibited national origin discrimination. A new program, therefore, would simply add one more layer of bureaucracy.

---

4. Unlike the other programs explored in this chapter, the anti-discrimination provisions of IRCA are inapplicable to undocumented migrants. They appear in this chapter because they are immigration offenses and because they are a necessary adjunct to the employer sanctions provisions, which directly concern undocumented migrants.

Proponents of the anti-discrimination provisions responded by identifying various gaps in existing coverage. Title 7 of the Civil Rights Act of 1964, for example, prohibits employment discrimination on the basis of "race, color, religion, sex, or national origin." 42 U.S.C. § 2000e–2(a)(1). But that prohibition extends only to those who employ at least fifteen people, *id.* § 2000e(b), and even then it does not bar discrimination in favor of United States citizens against LPRs. See *Espinoza v. Farah Manufacturing Co.,* 414 U.S. 86, 94 S.Ct. 334, 38 L.Ed.2d 287 (1973). Post–Civil War legislation, 42 U.S.C. § 1981, provides that "[a]ll persons within the jurisdiction of the United States shall have the same right in every State and Territory to make and enforce contracts * * * as is enjoyed by white citizens * * *." That provision bars private discrimination based on race, see *Patterson v. McLean Credit Union,* 491 U.S. 164, 109 S.Ct. 2363, 105 L.Ed.2d 132 (1989), but at this writing the courts are divided over whether section 1981 bars private "alienage" discrimination. The Fifth Circuit held en banc, by a vote of 7–6, that section 1981 does *not* bar private "alienage" discrimination. *Bhandari v. First National Bank,* 829 F.2d 1343 (5th Cir.1987), cert. granted and case remanded for reconsideration in the light of *Patterson,* June 26, 1989, reaffirmed on remand, 887 F.2d 609 (5th Cir.1989). The Second Circuit later disagreed, finding in section 1981 a cause of action for private "alienage" discrimination. *Anderson v. Conboy,* 156 F.3d 167 (2d Cir. 1998). For a good analysis, see Irene Scharf, *Commentary by Irene Scharf on Anderson v. Conboy,* 3 BIB 1102 (Nov. 1, 1998).

The discussion that follows will describe INA § 274B as it now stands. The present version reflects a series of amendments made mostly by the Immigration Act of 1990. Most of those changes were designed to strengthen the program, both substantively and procedurally, so that it could combat more effectively the widespread discrimination identified by the final GAO report. One commentator has called for broader legal prohibitions on discrimination against actual or perceived immigrants. See Ruben J. Garcia, *Across the Borders: Immigrant Status and Identity in Law and LatCrit Theory,* 55 Fla. L. Rev. 511 (2003).

The core of INA § 274B is subsection a(1), which reads:

It is an unfair immigration-related employment practice for a person or other entity to discriminate against any individual [other than an alien not authorized to work] with respect to the hiring, or recruitment or referral for a fee, of the individual for employment or the discharging of the individual from employment

(A) because of such individual's national origin, or

(B) in the case of a protected individual * * *, because of such individual's citizenship status.

Section 534 of the Immigration Act of 1990 added certain forms of retaliation and intimidation to the list of prohibited conduct. And section 535 of the 1990 Act, adding INA § 274B(a)(6), clarified that asking for more or different documents than are required for compliance with the employer sanctions provisions, or scrutinizing them more carefully, can also amount to discrimination. IIRIRA § 421 later restricted the latter provision to cases in which the complainant can prove purposeful or intentional discrimination. Some believe that the new requirement will be almost impossible to meet. See Juan P. Osuna, *The 1996 Immigration Act: Employer Sanctions, Antidiscrimination and Work Verification*, 73 IR 1749, 1752 (Dec. 20, 1996).

Section 274B(a)(2) creates three exemptions. One of them, subsection a(2)(A), exempts entirely those who employ fewer than four persons. Another clause, INA § 274B(a)(2)(B), bars national origin discrimination claims that are already covered by 42 U.S.C. § 2000e–2, which is the analogous provision of the Civil Rights Act of 1964. And the third provision authorizes citizenship status discrimination whenever the law requires citizenship either as a condition of employment or as a condition of the employer contracting with federal, state, or local governments. INA § 274B(a)(2)(C).

As section 274B(a)(1) makes clear, only a "protected individual" may claim citizenship status discrimination. That term is defined to include United States citizens or nationals, LPRs, legalization beneficiaries (including certain agricultural workers), and refugees and asylees. INA § 274B(a)(3). The definition excludes, however, any LPR who did not apply for naturalization within six months after becoming eligible (or within six months after the November 1986 enactment of IRCA if later), or who did not complete the naturalization process promptly enough. *Id.* Moreover, an employer may choose a United States citizen or national over an *equally* qualified noncitizen. INA § 274B(a)(4).

Violations of section 274B are punishable by civil fines that, like those for employer sanctions, are graduated to reflect the number of prior offenses. Until 1990 the ranges of possible fines under section 274B were systematically lower than those under section 274A. The Immigration Act of 1990, § 536, responded by raising the penalty ranges under section 274B to match those under section 274A. See INA §§ 274A(e)(4)(A), 274B(g)(2)(B)(iii)(I, II, III). One exception is that the provision prohibiting unnecessary zealousness in document-checking establishes lesser fines. INA § 274B(g)(2)(B)(iii)(IV). Another exception is that, unlike section 274A, section 274B contains no criminal penalties for pattern and practice violations.

To implement section 274B, Congress established, within the Justice Department, the Office of the Special Counsel for Immigration–Related Unfair Employment Practices (OSC). That office investigates and prosecutes charges that arise under section 274B. See INA § 274B(c)(1, 2). The Special Counsel is appointed by the President and confirmed by the Senate "to serve for a term of four years." INA § 274B(c)(1). In his written statement accompanying his signing of IRCA, President Reagan, an outspoken opponent of the anti-discrimination provisions, announced:

> I understand this subsection to provide that the Special Counsel shall serve at the pleasure and with the policy guidance of the President, but for no longer than for a four-year term (subject to

reappointment by the President with the advice and consent of the Senate).

Statement on Signing S. 1200 into Law, 22 Weekly Comp. Pres. Doc. 1534, 1535 (Nov. 6, 1986). Do you agree with President Reagan that "to serve for a term of four years" means "to serve at the pleasure of the President for a term not to exceed four years?" Do you agree with him that the Special Counsel is to serve "with the policy guidance of the President?" The interpretation issues will not be definitively resolved unless either dismissal or Presidential influence in decisionmaking actually occurs or at least is threatened. Still, it takes little imagination to foresee that such a pronouncement could chill the Special Counsel's exercise of independent judgment. Is independence beneficial in this context?

The process begins when the party who alleges discrimination—the direct victim, another person "adversely affected," or an ICE officer—files a "charge" with the Office of the Special Counsel (OSC). See INA § 274B(b)(1). One may not file a charge *both* with the Special Counsel under IRCA and with the Equal Employment Opportunity Commission under Title 7 of the Civil Rights of 1964 based on the same facts unless one of those agencies has dismissed the charge as outside the scope of the applicable statute. INA § 274B(b)(2). The 274B charge must be filed within 180 days of the discriminatory act. INA § 274B(d)(3). The same time period governs Title 7 claims. 42 U.S.C. § 2000e–5(e). The EEOC and the OSC have entered into a memorandum of understanding that makes each agency an agent of the other "for the sole purpose of allowing charging parties to file charges to satisfy the statutory time limits." The memorandum also permits the agencies to refer charges to each other when appropriate. 63 Fed. Reg. 5518, 5519 (Feb. 3, 1998).

Once a 274B charge is filed, the OSC notifies the alleged violator and investigates the case. *Id.* The Special Counsel is supposed to decide, within 120 days after receiving the charge, whether "there is reasonable cause to believe the charge is true." If there is, the OSC may file a "complaint" with an ALJ who has received special training in the subject of employment discrimination. INA §§ 274B(d)(1), 274B(e)(2). If the charges allege "knowing and intentional discriminatory activity or a pattern or practice of discriminatory activity," the OSC must either file a complaint with an ALJ within 120 days after the filing of the charge or notify the charging party of its decision not to file a complaint during that period. In the latter event, the charging party may initiate a "private action" by filing his or her own complaint with the ALJ within 90 days after receiving the notice. INA § 274B(d)(2).

Once the complaint has been properly filed, the ALJ conducts a recorded evidentiary hearing. INA § 274B(e, f). If at the conclusion of the hearing the ALJ finds by a preponderance of the evidence that the charged party has violated section 274B, the ALJ orders that party to cease the violation and to pay a civil fine within the applicable statutory range. The ALJ has the discretion to order certain additional sanctions. See INA

§ 274B(g)(2). If the ALJ does not find a violation, the complaint is dismissed. INA § 274B(g)(3).

There is no administrative review, but either side may obtain judicial review in the court of appeals. INA § 274B(i). Strictly speaking, an unappealed decision of the ALJ is not directly enforceable; either the charging party or the OSC, however, may petition a federal district court to order the charged party to comply, presumably under penalty of contempt. INA § 274B(j)(1). The statute specifies that in such a proceeding the ALJ's order "shall not be subject to review," INA § 274B(j)(2), which leaves the question of whether the district judge has any actual decision to make. If yes, what? If no, why not make the ALJ order directly enforceable? (Perhaps Congress simply felt more comfortable vesting the contempt power, with its attendant broad discretion, in the courts rather than in the ALJ's.) In all three types of proceedings—the administrative hearing, court of appeals review, or district court enforcement action—a prevailing party other than the government may recover attorney fees from the losing party if the latter's arguments were "without reasonable foundation in law and fact." INA §§ 274B(h), 274B(j)(4).

Civil rights law distinguishes "disparate treatment" from "disparate impact." In the former, the complainant is alleging that the employer has intentionally treated members of one race, religion, etc., more favorably than others. See generally *McDonnell Douglas Corp. v. Green,* 411 U.S. 792, 93 S.Ct. 1817, 36 L.Ed.2d 668 (1973). In the latter, the complainant is alleging that, even if the employer lacks the intent to discriminate, and even if the challenged policy is facially neutral, the policy has a substantial disproportionate impact upon members of a particular race, religion, etc. See generally *Griggs v. Duke Power Co.,* 401 U.S. 424, 91 S.Ct. 849, 28 L.Ed.2d 158 (1971). Title 7 of the Civil Rights Act of 1964 covers both types of claims. In cases in which the plaintiff has established disparate impact, the employer may defend by producing evidence of a "business necessity" for the challenged policy. *Wards Cove Packing Co. v. Atonio,* 490 U.S. 642, 109 S.Ct. 2115, 104 L.Ed.2d 733 (1989).

Whether IRCA similarly authorizes "disparate impact" claims has been hotly debated. President Reagan argued in his signing statement that it does not. He asserted, first, that the language of INA § 274B(a)(1) (unlawful to "discriminate * * * because of such individual's national origin") parallels the phrase in Title 7 of the Civil Rights Act that has served as the basis for disparate treatment claims, 42 U.S.C. § 2000e–2(a)(1). In contrast, the Civil Rights Act language on which disparate impact claims are generally based, 42 U.S.C. § 2000e–2(a)(2) (unlawful to "adversely affect [an employee's status] because of such individual's race, * * * "), lacks a counterpart in IRCA.

Second, the President observed, INA § 274B(d)(2) authorizes private actions only by those who allege "knowing and intentional discriminatory activity" (which expressly requires intent) or "a pattern or practice of discriminatory activity" (a phrase the President argued had been taken from the Supreme Court's disparate treatment cases). Statement on Signing S. 1200 Into Law, 22 Weekly Comp.Pres.Doc. 1534, 1535 (Nov. 6, 1986). Accordingly, the President said, an employer might impose an English language requirement even if English was not needed to perform the job. Indeed, the President added, "unless the plaintiff presents evidence that the employer has intentionally discriminated on proscribed grounds, the employer need not offer *any* explanation for his employee selection procedures." *Id.* (emphasis in original). English-only employment cases have been rising sharply in the last several years; the EEOC and reported court decisions have generally found them violative of Title 7 in the absence of valid job-related reasons. See 77 IR 1551–52 (Oct. 30, 2000). Whether they also violate IRCA is not yet clear.

Representative Frank, the author of the provision, reacted angrily to the President's statement, calling it not just wrong, but "intellectually dishonest, mean-spirited." See 63 IR 1049, 1055 (1986). The language quoted by President Reagan in subsection d(2), it might be noted, is expressly limited to private actions; it does not extend to complaints filed by the Special Counsel. Congress might plausibly have drawn that distinction in order to discourage frivolous claims; the Special Counsel's stamp of approval reduces the chance that the claim is frivolous. Even for private actions, it is not clear that the phrase "pattern or practice of discriminatory activity" requires an intent to discriminate. Besides, if that phrase is interpreted to require such an intent, it is not clear what ground the resulting provision would cover that is not already covered by the phrase "knowing and intentional discriminatory activity."

At any rate, rightly or wrongly, dicta from ALJ decisions have consistently deferred to President Reagan's interpretation. In *United States v. Marcel Watch Corp.*, 1 OCAHO 988 (ALJ Morse, 1990), the ALJ stated that liability under IRCA's antidiscrimination provisions "is proven by a showing of deliberate discriminatory intent." For this proposition, the sole explanation was a citation to President Reagan's signing statement. *Id.* at 1001. The ALJ then said: "The complainant must establish intentional discrimination by a preponderance of the evidence, i.e., 'knowing and intentional discrimination,'" citing only INA § 274B(d)(2). The latter citation is puzzling, since it refers only to private actions filed after the Special Counsel decides not to file a complaint. (In *Marcel Watch*, the Special Counsel had found reasonable cause and therefore had filed the complaint!) The complainant prevailed anyway, since the ALJ ultimately found intentional discrimination based on citizenship status. (The interviewer had insisted that the applicant produce a green card even though the applicant had acquired United States citizenship by virtue of birth in Puerto Rico, and even though the interviewer's supervisor had explained to the interviewer that people born in Puerto Rico are U.S. citizens.)

Later OCAHO cases then relied on *Marcel Watch*, on subsequent cases that in turn had relied on *Marcel Watch*, and on President Reagan's signing statement, for the proposition that all IRCA discrimination claims require a showing of intentional discrimination. See, e.g., *Wije v. Barton Springs/Edward Aquifer Conservation District*, 5 OCAHO No. 785 at 21 (ALJ McGuire,

July 21, 1995); *Yefremov v. NYC Dept. of Transportation*, 3 OCAHO No. 562 at 22 (ALJ Morse, Sept. 21, 1993).

Recall that IIRIRA § 421 amended INA § 274B(a)(6) (the provision that bars employers from insisting on more documentation than is necessary) to require a showing of purposeful or intentional discrimination. Does the amendment provide any clues on the issue of whether IRCA generally requires a showing of intentional discrimination? Should a court read significance into the contrast between (a) an express requirement of intentional discrimination both for document discrimination claims and for private claims under section 274B(d)(2) versus (b) congressional silence with respect to the other IRCA discrimination claims?

Given what you now know about Congress's reasons for enacting section 274B, which interpretation makes more sense as a policy matter?

PROBLEMS 8–12

To do this Problem set, you will need to consult the actual text of INA § 274B. Assume all events occurred after enactment (November 1986) unless specified otherwise. Assume also that every employer has more than three workers.

Problem 8. Employer A, who has ten employees, has a firm policy of hiring only United States citizens of Italian extraction—citizens because he wants to do his part to encourage naturalization, ethnic Italians because he is of Italian ancestry himself and enjoys the cultural bonds that he shares with his employees. A acknowledges that neither requirement has anything to do with the employee's ability to perform the job.

X (who happens to be of Italian descent) was lawfully admitted as an LPR in 1998. She became eligible for naturalization in 2003 and formally applied in December 2005. In January 2006, while her naturalization application was pending, she applied to A for a job and was turned down because she was not a citizen. Y, a United States citizen, applied at the same time and was rejected because he was not of Italian descent. Z, a United States citizen of Italian descent, got the job.

Does either X or Y have a claim under INA § 274B? As a policy matter, what is your reaction to the results?

Problem 9. Employer B, who has also adopted a citizens-only policy, fires W because W is an LPR. Unbeknownst to B, W had just applied for naturalization, a few days after becoming eligible. W tells B about his pending application, but B says "I wish you had told me that earlier. I would have hired you back immediately, but now I can't because I've just given your job to someone else." Does W have a claim against B?

Problem 10. Employer C has a workforce of ten employees and a personnel manager who will hire only those who can show either proof of United States citizenship or a green card (possessed by LPRs). V, a nonimmigrant with work authorization, is rejected because of that policy. Does she have a claim under INA § 274B?

Problem 11. An applicant of Latino appearance, qualified for the job, displays his green card to the personnel officer of employer D. The officer thinks the card looks a little bit odd but can't quite put her finger on what is bothering her about it. What should she do?

Problem 12. Employer E rejects job applicant T because T does not meet E's minimum height requirements. T can see no particular job-related reason for the height policy and believes it is a pretext for rejecting Latino applicants, whose average height is less than that of Anglo workers. Four months later T learns that both Title 7 of the Civil Rights Act and IRCA prohibit national origin discrimination. To complicate matters, T believes E had a workforce of somewhere between 13 and 17 employees at the time of the alleged discrimination, but T is not sure of the precise number. What advice would you give T?

SECTION C.   UNDOCUMENTED MIGRANTS AND PUBLIC BENEFITS

Noncitizens' eligibility for public benefits has always been a contentious subject. See generally David Carliner, Lucas Guttentag, Arthur C. Helton & Wade Henderson, The Rights of Aliens and Refugees (2d ed. 1990); A. Peter Mutharika, The Alien under American Law (2 vols. 1980, 1981, with 1985 Supplement). The issue came to a head during the 1996 Presidential election campaigns. Through a combination of welfare reform legislation and IIRIRA, Congress imposed sweeping new restrictions on public benefits for LPRs (discussed in chapter 13) and additional restrictions on the few public benefits available to undocumented migrants (discussed in this section).

1.   THE LEGAL AND SOCIAL IDENTITIES OF UNDOCUMENTED MIGRANTS

What place do undocumented migrants occupy in the public mind, and what, exactly, are their rights? The following commentary speaks to those issues:

Linda S. Bosniak, Exclusion and Membership: The Dual Identity of the Undocumented Worker Under United States Law

1988 Wisconsin L. Rev. 955, 977–87.

* * *

Much of the identity and experience of the undocumented person in this country derives from her status as boundary violator, as physically present outsider. But the relationship between the undocumented immigrant and the state is not fully described by reference to government immigration regulation and its constraints. The undocumented immigrant has a second legal identity, often ignored by theoretical and policy literature on clandestine immigration: she inhabits a sphere of circumscribed, but real, civil and social membership. In certain formal and practical spheres, the undocumented alien functions as an acknowledged member of the national community.

State and federal courts, for instance, have held that undocumented aliens may sue in tort and contract. * * * Undocumented aliens' access to the courts has been interpreted to include the right to divorce, to bring suits on employment contracts to recover lost wages, and to sue for workmen's compensation. In one workmen's compensation case, the court emphasized that violation of immigration law did not make illegal the employment contract on which the workmen's compensation claim was based. The appropriate penalty for an immigration offense was deportation, not loss of employment benefits.

The individual states have also acknowledged that aliens have certain rights. Many states affirmatively empower any alien to serve as trustee for fiduciary trusts. Most states permit undocumented aliens to own real property, and "[t]here are almost no restrictions on the alien's right, regardless of his status under the immigration laws, to acquire and convey personal property." Moreover, prior to the passage of IRCA, an undocumented alien and her employer were free to enter into an employment relationship.

In short, until the implementation of employer sanctions, immigration law directly regulated border and entry only; the "private" relationships that the undocumented person might form with any other social member once she has entered the country were not the object of exclusionary regulation. Indeed, the undocumented alien was usually permitted to avail herself of the courts in order to enforce her bargains.

Certain constitutional rights beyond the immigration regulatory context have also attached to the undocumented alien by virtue of her personhood alone. In 1886, the Supreme Court established that all aliens are "persons" within the meaning of the fourteenth amendment. Ten years later, the Court declared that any person within the territorial jurisdiction of the United States was entitled to due process under the fifth and fourteenth amendments and that the fourteenth amendment's equal protection clause was universal in its application. Since then, the Court has required fourth, fifth, and sixth amendment rights for undocumented aliens in criminal proceedings. * * *

Courts have used equal protection analysis to strike down certain state laws or regulations depriving undocumented aliens of access to state services or benefits. In the most famous and far-reaching of these cases, Plyler v. Doe, the Supreme Court held that states cannot deny the provision of public education to undocumented children. * * * [That case is taken up below.—Ed.]

Since Plyler, many states have extended the protections of state programs to undocumented aliens. For instance, in response to a class action suit in 1985, California rescinded a policy that excluded the severely handicapped and medically needy children of undocumented immigrants from certain health services. Also in 1985, a California court held that the state attorney general's policy of precluding undocumented aliens from eligibility for resident tuition status at the state's universities was unconstitutional.

* * *

Finally, courts have held that undocumented workers are covered by the terms of federal labor protection statutes. In a 1984 opinion, the Supreme Court held that undocumented workers are "employees" within the meaning of the National Labor Relations Act, and thus protected under its provisions. * * * Coverage by the NLRA means, among other things, that undocumented workers may vote in union elections and may file unfair labor practice complaints. [NB: This article was written before *Hoffman Plastic*, discussed in section A above—Ed.]

Courts and administrative law judges have similarly held that undocumented workers are protected under the Fair Labor Standards Act. * * *

The law's protection and recognition of undocumented immigrants in certain contexts demonstrates that these immigrants have a legal identity distinct from that of alien—distinct, that is, from that defined by the nation's exclusionary project. This identity derives from their personhood and their territorial presence, and it demarcates a certain sphere of formally protected activity accorded to acknowledged community members. It is within this protected sphere that large numbers of undocumented workers have constructed lives that are often extensively integrated into the United States at both the economic and community levels. It is also within this sphere that the "equities," including "community ties," are established—equities that are required for eligibility for certain forms of discretionary relief from deportation.

While it is important to recognize the existence of this sphere of protected membership for undocumented aliens, the denial to them of a broad range of other membership rights and their subjection to the state's exclusionary project directly and indirectly nullify many of the protections they formally enjoy. Although undocumented aliens may be persons within the protection of the due process and equal protection clauses, courts have permitted the federal and state governments to discriminate against all aliens for some purposes and to distinguish between permanent resident aliens and undocumented aliens for others. * * * The undocumented are deprived of a range of services and benefits in many states which could not be legally denied to legally present aliens.

* * *

Finally, even where formal rights exist, the ability of the undocumented to exercise these rights in practice is limited. Undocumented aliens often fear exposing themselves to the exclusionary powers of the state and will often forego the exercise of membership rights in order to avoid such an eventuality. Undocumented immigrants commonly decline to report private or official abuse and are frequently unwilling to pursue civil claims in court or to step forward to receive benefits to which they are entitled. The undocumented are also part of a larger group of Americans whose lack of access to power in the form of money and information severely constrains their ability to obtain the protections and benefits to which they are formally entitled.

This analysis of the undocumented immigrant's status in the United States creates a more complex picture than many observers allow. The undocumented immigrant is not the unmitigated victim of government exclusionary policies. She is directly protected from aspects of the the state's exclusionary powers and is granted certain independent membership rights. At the same time, the incidents of membership she enjoys are severely circumscribed by her status as outsider, constrained directly and indirectly by the state's exclusionary powers. The experience and identity of the undocumented worker are thus defined along two matrices, exclusion and membership. It is this duality that has characterized her existence in United States society.

* * *

NOTES

1. At present, for purposes of legislative apportionment, undocumented migrants are included in the United States Census count. See U.S. Const. art. I, § 2, cl. 3, as amended by Amend. XIV., § 2 (referring to number of "persons," unlike other constitutional provisions that refer to "citizens"); U.S. Bureau of the Census, *Enumeration and Residence Rules for the 1990 Census*, 1990 Decennial Census Policy Memorandum No. 12 (1987). The Counsel to the Senate immigration subcommittee has argued that this should not be the case. Charles Wood, *Losing Control of America's Future—The Census, Birthright Citizenship, and Illegal Aliens*, 22 Harvard J. L. & Pub. Policy 465 (1999).

It is usually assumed, however, that undocumented migrants, being necessarily less visible, are systematically undercounted. The use of sampling techniques to supplement actual head counts, particularly for individuals who do not respond to initial surveys, would clearly enhance the accuracy of the count. But in a 5–4 decision that will have major implications for states with large undocumented populations, the Supreme Court has now construed the applicable statute as barring the use of even supplemental sampling for purposes of congressional apportionment. The Court's reading of the statute mooted the analogous constitutional question. *Department of Commerce v. United States House of Representatives*, 525 U.S. 316, 119 S.Ct. 765, 142 L.Ed.2d 797 (1999).

2.   For a thorough and thoughtful account of Australia's treatment of undocumented migrants, see Mary Crock, Immigration and Refugee Law in Australia, chs. 9, 10 (1998).

2.   UNDOCUMENTED MIGRANTS AND PUBLIC ASSISTANCE

As noted earlier, a pair of 1996 enactments altered the eligibility of noncitizens for public benefits. The comprehensive welfare reform bill known as the Personal Responsibility and Work Opportunity Reconciliation Act of 1996, Pub.L. 104–193, 110 Stat. 2105 (Aug. 22, 1996) [hereafter the Welfare Act], contained one part (Title IV) dealing specifically with noncitizens. Comprehensive immigration reform, IIRIRA, contained one part (Title V) dealing specifically with public benefits. While LPRs bore the brunt of the impact, undocumented migrants were also affected.

Undocumented migrants are now ineligible for all "federal public benefits," a term defined broadly to include any contracts, loans, professional or commercial licenses, retirement benefits, welfare, health or disability benefits, food assistance, housing, post-secondary education, or any other "similar" benefits provided by the federal government. Welfare Act, § 401(a, c). Limited exceptions include emergency medical care; short-term, non-cash emergency disaster relief; and certain treatment for communicable diseases. *Id.* § 401(b). Undocumented migrants are also ineligible to receive social security payments, regardless of how much they have contributed. IIRIRA § 503.

Undocumented migrants are further ineligible for state or local public benefits (defined by, and subject to exceptions similar to, the provision governing federal benefits), unless the state passes post-Welfare Act legislation to the contrary. Welfare Act, § 411. States are authorized to restrict or prohibit payment of general cash public assistance to noncitizens, as long as the restrictions are not broader than those imposed in any analogous federal programs. IIRIRA § 553. An excellent account of noncitizens' access to health care is Janet M. Calvo, Immigrant Status and Legal Access to Health Care (1993).

Commentators have generally favored welfare eligibility for immigrants. See, e.g., Peter L. Reich, *Jurisprudential Tradition and Undocumented Alien Entitlements*, 6 Georgetown Immigration L.J. 1 (1992); Peter L. Reich, *Public Benefits for Undocumented Aliens: State Law into the Breach Once More*, 21 New Mexico L. Rev. 219 (1991); see also Stephen H. Legomsky, *Immigration, Federalism, and the Welfare State*, 42 UCLA L.Rev. 1453 (1995).

3.   UNDOCUMENTED MIGRANTS AND PUBLIC EDUCATION

Probably the most volatile issue concerning state resources for undocumented migrants in recent years has been eligibility for free public elementary and secondary education. Proposition 187, passed by the voters of California in 1994, among other things barred all public school districts from enrolling undocumented children. Policy aside, is Proposition 187 constitutional? There are two separate but related constitutional constraints to consider—the equal protection clause and the doctrine of federal preemption.

Ordinarily, under equal protection law, either the federal government or a state may treat two groups of people differently as long as there is some rational basis for the distinction. Over the years, however, the Supreme Court has reviewed more intensively when there is something about either the particular classification or the particular individual interest at stake that demands a tougher standard. Certain classifications are said to be "suspect." They give rise to "strict scrutiny," under which the Court insists that the distinction be "necessary" to a "compelling" governmental interest. Race is the paradigm suspect classification. Certain other classifications, such as gender and legitimacy, have generated an intermediate level of scrutiny that requires something more than rationality but less than strict scrutiny—e.g., an "important" governmental interest and a "substantial" relationship between that interest and the means used to achieve it. Finally, the court will insist on more than mere rationality when a "fundamental" individual interest is at stake. See generally Gerald Gunther & Kathleen M. Sullivan, Constitutional Law 840–916 (13th ed. 1997).

In a line of cases that you will explore in chapter 13, the Court has held that state action discriminating against noncitizens (but not analogous federal action) will similarly trigger strict scrutiny, with some exceptions not pertinent here. In all those cases, however, the individuals in question were LPRs. What if a state discriminates against undocumented migrants? The following landmark case addresses that question:

Plyler v. Doe

Supreme Court of the United States, 1982.
457 U.S. 202, 102 S.Ct. 2382, 72 L.Ed.2d 786.

■ JUSTICE BRENNAN delivered the opinion of the Court.

The question presented by these cases is whether, consistent with the Equal Protection Clause of the Fourteenth Amendment, Texas may deny to undocumented school-age children the free public education that it provides to children who are citizens of the United States or legally admitted aliens.

Issue

I

Since the late 19th century, the United States has restricted immigration into this country. Unsanctioned entry into the United States is a crime, and those who have entered unlawfully are subject to deportation. But despite the existence of these legal restrictions, a substantial number of persons have succeeded in unlawfully entering the United States, and now live within various States, including the State of Texas.

In May 1975, the Texas Legislature revised its education laws to withhold from local school districts any state funds for the education of children who were not "legally admitted" into the United States. The 1975 revision also authorized local school districts to deny enrollment in their public schools to children not "legally admitted" to the country. Tex. Educ. Code Ann. § 21.031 (Vernon Supp. 1981). These cases involve constitutional challenges to those provisions.

Plyler v. Doe

This is a class action, filed in the United States District Court for the Eastern District of Texas in September 1977, on behalf of certain school-age children of Mexican origin residing in Smith County, Tex., who could not establish that they had been legally admitted into the United States. The action complained of the exclusion of plaintiff children from the public schools of the Tyler Independent School District. The Superintendent and members of the Board of Trustees of the School District were named as defendants; the State of Texas intervened as a party-defendant. After certifying a class consisting of all undocumented school-age children of Mexican origin residing within the School District, the District Court preliminarily enjoined defendants from denying a free education to members of the plaintiff class. In December 1977, the court conducted an extensive hearing on plaintiffs' motion for permanent injunctive relief.

In considering this motion, the District Court made extensive findings of fact. The court found that neither § 21.031 nor the School District policy implementing it had "either the purpose or effect of keeping illegal aliens out of the State of Texas." Respecting defendants' further claim that § 21.031 was simply a financial measure designed to avoid a drain on the State's fisc, the court recognized that the increases in population resulting from the immigration of Mexican nationals into the United States had created problems for the public schools of the State, and that these problems were exacerbated by the special educational needs of immigrant Mexican children. The court noted, however, that the increase in school enrollment was primarily attributable to the admission of children who were legal residents. It also found that while the "exclusion of all undocumented children from the public schools in Texas would eventually result in economies at some level," funding from both the State and Federal Governments was based primarily on the number of children enrolled. In net effect then, barring undocumented children from the schools would save money, but it would "not necessarily" improve "the quality of education." The court further observed that the impact of § 21.031 was borne primarily by a very small subclass of illegal aliens, "entire families who have migrated illegally and—for all practical purposes—permanently to the United States." Finally, the court noted that under current laws and practices "the illegal alien of today may well be the legal alien of tomorrow," and that without an education, these undocumented children, "[already] disadvantaged as a result of poverty, lack of English-speaking ability, and undeniable racial prejudices, . . . will become permanently locked into the lowest socio-economic class."

The District Court held that illegal aliens were entitled to the protection of the Equal Protection Clause of the Fourteenth Amendment, and that § 21.031 violated that Clause. Suggesting that "the state's exclusion of undocumented children from its public schools ... may well be the type of invidiously motivated state action for which the suspect classification doctrine was designed," the court held that it was unnecessary to decide whether the statute would survive a "strict scrutiny" analysis because, in any event, the discrimination embodied in the statute was not supported by a rational basis. * * *

Lower Court Ruling

The Court of Appeals for the Fifth Circuit upheld the District Court's injunction. The Court of Appeals held that the District Court had erred in finding the Texas statute pre-empted by federal law. With respect to equal protection, however, the Court of Appeals affirmed in all essential respects the analysis of the District Court, concluding that § 21.031 was "constitutionally infirm regardless of whether it was tested using the mere rational basis standard or some more stringent test". We noted probable jurisdiction.

[Here the Court describes similar litigation with which *Plyler* has been consolidated.—Ed.][8]

* * *

II

The Fourteenth Amendment provides that "[no] State shall ... deprive any person of life, liberty, or property, without due process of law; nor deny to any person within its jurisdiction the equal protection of the laws." Appellants argue at the outset that undocumented aliens, because of their immigration status, are not "persons within the jurisdiction" of the State of Texas, and that they therefore have no right to the equal protection of Texas law. We reject this argument. Whatever his status under the immigration laws, an alien is surely a "person" in any ordinary sense of that term. Aliens, even aliens whose presence in this country is unlawful, have long been recognized as "persons" guaranteed due process of law by the Fifth and Fourteenth Amendments. Indeed, we have clearly held that the Fifth Amendment protects aliens whose presence in this country is unlawful from invidious discrimination by the Federal Government. Mathews v. Diaz, 426 U.S. 67, 77 (1976).

Appellants seek to distinguish our prior cases, emphasizing that the Equal Protection Clause directs a State to afford its protection to persons within its jurisdiction while the Due Process Clauses of the Fifth and Fourteenth Amendments contain no such assertedly limiting phrase. In appellants' view, persons who have entered the United States illegally are not "within the jurisdiction" of a State even if they are present within a State's boundaries and subject to its laws. Neither our cases nor the logic of

---

8. Appellees in both cases continue to press the argument that § 21.031 is pre-empted by federal law and policy. In light of our disposition of the Fourteenth Amendment issue, we have no occasion to reach this claim.

the Fourteenth Amendment supports that constricting construction of the phrase "within its jurisdiction." * * *

* * *

Our conclusion that the illegal aliens who are plaintiffs in these cases may claim the benefit of the Fourteenth Amendment's guarantee of equal protection only begins the inquiry. The more difficult question is whether the Equal Protection Clause has been violated by the refusal of the State of Texas to reimburse local school boards for the education of children who cannot demonstrate that their presence within the United States is lawful, or by the imposition by those school boards of the burden of tuition on those children. It is to this question that we now turn.

III

* * * In applying the Equal Protection Clause to most forms of state action, we thus seek only the assurance that the classification at issue bears some fair relationship to a legitimate public purpose.

But we would not be faithful to our obligations under the Fourteenth Amendment if we applied so deferential a standard to every classification. The Equal Protection Clause was intended as a restriction on state legislative action inconsistent with elemental constitutional premises. Thus we have treated as presumptively invidious those classifications that disadvantage a "suspect class,"[14] or that impinge upon the exercise of a "fundamental right." With respect to such classifications, it is appropriate to enforce the mandate of equal protection by requiring the State to demonstrate that its classification has been precisely tailored to serve a compelling governmental interest. In addition, we have recognized that certain forms of legislative classification, while not facially invidious, nonetheless give rise to recurring constitutional difficulties; in these limited circumstances we have sought the assurance that the classification reflects a reasoned judgment consistent with the ideal of equal protection by inquiring whether it may fairly be viewed as furthering a substantial interest of the State. We turn to a consideration of the standard appropriate for the evaluation of § 21.031.

---

14. Several formulations might explain our treatment of certain classifications as "suspect." Some classifications are more likely than others to reflect deep-seated prejudice rather than legislative rationality in pursuit of some legitimate objective. Legislation predicated on such prejudice is easily recognized as incompatible with the constitutional understanding that each person is to be judged individually and is entitled to equal justice under the law. Classifications treated as suspect tend to be irrelevant to any proper legislative goal. Finally, certain groups, indeed largely the same groups, have historically been "relegated to such a position of political powerlessness as to command extraordinary protection from the majoritarian political process." The experience of our Nation has shown that prejudice may manifest itself in the treatment of some groups. Our response to that experience is reflected in the Equal Protection Clause of the Fourteenth Amendment. Legislation imposing special disabilities upon groups disfavored by virtue of circumstances beyond their control suggests the kind of "class or caste" treatment that the Fourteenth Amendment was designed to abolish.

A

Sheer incapability or lax enforcement of the laws barring entry into this country, coupled with the failure to establish an effective bar to the employment of undocumented aliens, has resulted in the creation of a substantial "shadow population" of illegal migrants—numbering in the millions—within our borders. This situation raises the specter of a permanent caste of undocumented resident aliens, encouraged by some to remain here as a source of cheap labor, but nevertheless denied the benefits that our society makes available to citizens and lawful residents. The existence of such an underclass presents most difficult problems for a Nation that prides itself on adherence to principles of equality under law.[19]

The children who are plaintiffs in these cases are special members of this underclass. Persuasive arguments support the view that a State may withhold its beneficence from those whose very presence within the United States is the product of their own unlawful conduct. These arguments do not apply with the same force to classifications imposing disabilities on the minor children of such illegal entrants. At the least, those who elect to enter our territory by stealth and in violation of our law should be prepared to bear the consequences, including, but not limited to, deportation. But the children of those illegal entrants are not comparably situated. Their "parents have the ability to conform their conduct to societal norms," and presumably the ability to remove themselves from the State's jurisdiction; but the children who are plaintiffs in these cases "can affect neither their parents' conduct nor their own status." Even if the State found it expedient to control the conduct of adults by acting against their children, legislation directing the onus of a parent's misconduct against his children does not comport with fundamental conceptions of justice. * * *

Of course, undocumented status is not irrelevant to any proper legislative goal. Nor is undocumented status an absolutely immutable characteristic since it is the product of conscious, indeed unlawful, action. But § 21.031 is directed against children, and imposes its discriminatory burden on the basis of a legal characteristic over which children can have little control. It is thus difficult to conceive of a rational justification for penalizing these children for their presence within the United States. Yet that appears to be precisely the effect of § 21.031.

19. We reject the claim that "illegal aliens" are a "suspect class." No case in which we have attempted to define a suspect class has addressed the status of persons unlawfully in our country. Unlike most of the classifications that we have recognized as suspect, entry into this class, by virtue of entry into this country, is the product of voluntary action. Indeed, entry into the class is itself a crime. In addition, it could hardly be suggested that undocumented status is a "constitutional irrelevancy." With respect to the actions of the Federal Government, alien-age classifications may be intimately related to the conduct of foreign policy, to the federal prerogative to control access to the United States, and to the plenary federal power to determine who has sufficiently manifested his allegiance to become a citizen of the Nation. No State may independently exercise a like power. But if the Federal Government has by uniform rule prescribed what it believes to be appropriate standards for the treatment of an alien subclass, the States may, of course, follow the federal direction. See De Canas v. Bica, 424 U.S. 351 (1976).

Public education is not a "right" granted to individuals by the Constitution. But neither is it merely some governmental "benefit" indistinguishable from other forms of social welfare legislation. Both the importance of education in maintaining our basic institutions, and the lasting impact of its deprivation on the life of the child, mark the distinction. * * * "[As] . . . pointed out early in our history, . . . some degree of education is necessary to prepare citizens to participate effectively and intelligently in our open political system if we are to preserve freedom and independence." * * * In sum, education has a fundamental role in maintaining the fabric of our society. We cannot ignore the significant social costs borne by our Nation when select groups are denied the means to absorb the values and skills upon which our social order rests.

In addition to the pivotal role of education in sustaining our political and cultural heritage, denial of education to some isolated group of children poses an affront to one of the goals of the Equal Protection Clause: the abolition of governmental barriers presenting unreasonable obstacles to advancement on the basis of individual merit. Paradoxically, by depriving the children of any disfavored group of an education, we foreclose the means by which that group might raise the level of esteem in which it is held by the majority. But more directly, "education prepares individuals to be self-reliant and self-sufficient participants in society." Illiteracy is an enduring disability. The inability to read and write will handicap the individual deprived of a basic education each and every day of his life. The inestimable toll of that deprivation on the social, economic, intellectual, and psychological well-being of the individual, and the obstacle it poses to individual achievement, make it most difficult to reconcile the cost or the principle of a status-based denial of basic education with the framework of equality embodied in the Equal Protection Clause. * * *

B

These well-settled principles allow us to determine the proper level of deference to be afforded § 21.031. Undocumented aliens cannot be treated as a suspect class because their presence in this country in violation of federal law is not a "constitutional irrelevancy." Nor is education a fundamental right; a State need not justify by compelling necessity every variation in the manner in which education is provided to its population. But more is involved in these cases than the abstract question whether § 21.031 discriminates against a suspect class, or whether education is a fundamental right. Section 21.031 imposes a lifetime hardship on a discrete class of children not accountable for their disabling status. The stigma of illiteracy will mark them for the rest of their lives. By denying these children a basic education, we deny them the ability to live within the structure of our civic institutions, and foreclose any realistic possibility that they will contribute in even the smallest way to the progress of our Nation. In determining the rationality of § 21.031, we may appropriately take into account its costs to the Nation and to the innocent children who are its victims. In light of these countervailing costs, the discrimination contained in § 21.031 can hardly be considered rational unless it furthers some substantial goal of the State.

IV

It is the State's principal argument, and apparently the view of the dissenting Justices, that the undocumented status of these children vel non establishes a sufficient rational basis for denying them benefits that a State might choose to afford other residents. The State notes that while other aliens are admitted "on an equality of legal privileges with all citizens under non-discriminatory laws," the asserted right of these children to an education can claim no implicit congressional imprimatur. Indeed, in the State's view, Congress' apparent disapproval of the presence of these children within the United States, and the evasion of the federal regulatory program that is the mark of undocumented status, provides authority for its decision to impose upon them special disabilities. Faced with an equal protection challenge respecting the treatment of aliens, we agree that the courts must be attentive to congressional policy; the exercise of congressional power might well affect the State's prerogatives to afford differential treatment to a particular class of aliens. But we are unable to find in the congressional immigration scheme any statement of policy that might weigh significantly in arriving at an equal protection balance concerning the State's authority to deprive these children of an education.

The Constitution grants Congress the power to "establish an uniform Rule of Naturalization." Drawing upon this power, upon its plenary authority with respect to foreign relations and international commerce, and upon the inherent power of a sovereign to close its borders, Congress has developed a complex scheme governing admission to our Nation and status within our borders. The obvious need for delicate policy judgments has counseled the Judicial Branch to avoid intrusion into this field. But this traditional caution does not persuade us that unusual deference must be shown the classification embodied in § 21.031. The States enjoy no power with respect to the classification of aliens. This power is "committed to the political branches of the Federal Government." Although it is "a routine and normally legitimate part" of the business of the Federal Government to classify on the basis of alien status, and to "take into account the character of the relationship between the alien and this country," only rarely are such matters relevant to legislation by a State.

As we recognized in De Canas v. Bica, 424 U.S. 351 (1976), the States do have some authority to act with respect to illegal aliens, at least where such action mirrors federal objectives and furthers a legitimate state goal. In De Canas, the State's program reflected Congress' intention to bar from employment all aliens except those possessing a grant of permission to work in this country. In contrast, there is no indication that the disability imposed by § 21.031 corresponds to any identifiable congressional policy. The State does not claim that the conservation of state educational resources was ever a congressional concern in restricting immigration. More importantly, the classification reflected in § 21.031 does not operate harmoniously within the federal program.

To be sure, like all persons who have entered the United States unlawfully, these children are subject to deportation. But there is no assurance that a child subject to deportation will ever be deported. An illegal entrant might be granted federal permission to continue to reside in this country, or even to become a citizen. In light of the discretionary federal power to grant relief from deportation, a State cannot realistically determine that any particular undocumented child will in fact be deported until after deportation proceedings have been completed. It would of course be most difficult for the State to justify a denial of education to a child enjoying an inchoate federal permission to remain.

We are reluctant to impute to Congress the intention to withhold from these children, for so long as they are present in this country through no fault of their own, access to a basic education. In other contexts, undocumented status, coupled with some articulable federal policy, might enhance state authority with respect to the treatment of undocumented aliens. But in the area of special constitutional sensitivity presented by these cases, and in the absence of any contrary indication fairly discernible in the present legislative record, we perceive no national policy that supports the State in denying these children an elementary education. The State may borrow the federal classification. But to justify its use as a criterion for its own discriminatory policy, the State must demonstrate that the classification is reasonably adapted to "the purposes for which the state desires to use it." We therefore turn to the state objectives that are said to support § 21.031.

V

Appellants argue that the classification at issue furthers an interest in the "preservation of the state's limited resources for the education of its lawful residents."[22] Of course, a concern for the preservation of resources standing alone can hardly justify the classification used in allocating those resources. * * * [W]e discern three colorable state interests that might support § 21.031.

First, appellants appear to suggest that the State may seek to protect itself from an influx of illegal immigrants. While a State might have an

---

22. Appellant School District sought at oral argument to characterize the alienage classification contained in § 21.031 as simply a test of residence. We are unable to uphold § 21.031 on that basis. Appellants conceded that if, for example, a Virginian or a legally admitted Mexican citizen entered Tyler with his school-age children, intending to remain only six months, those children would be viewed as residents entitled to attend Tyler schools. It is thus clear that Tyler's residence argument amounts to nothing more than the assertion that illegal entry, without more, prevents a person from becoming a resident for purposes of enrolling his children in the public schools. A State may not, however, accomplish what would otherwise be prohibited by the Equal Protection Clause, merely by defining a disfavored group as nonresident. And illegal entry into the country would not, under traditional criteria, bar a person from obtaining domicile within a State. * * *

interest in mitigating the potentially harsh economic effects of sudden shifts in population, § 21.031 hardly offers an effective method of dealing with an urgent demographic or economic problem. There is no evidence in the record suggesting that illegal entrants impose any significant burden on the State's economy. To the contrary, the available evidence suggests that illegal aliens underutilize public services, while contributing their labor to the local economy and tax money to the state fisc. The dominant incentive for illegal entry into the State of Texas is the availability of employment; few if any illegal immigrants come to this country, or presumably to the State of Texas, in order to avail themselves of a free education. Thus, even making the doubtful assumption that the net impact of illegal aliens on the economy of the State is negative, we think it clear that "[charging] tuition to undocumented children constitutes a ludicrously ineffectual attempt to stem the tide of illegal immigration," at least when compared with the alternative of prohibiting the employment of illegal aliens.

Second, while it is apparent that a State may "not . . . reduce expenditures for education by barring [some arbitrarily chosen class of] children from its schools," appellants suggest that undocumented children are appropriately singled out for exclusion because of the special burdens they impose on the State's ability to provide high-quality public education. But the record in no way supports the claim that exclusion of undocumented children is likely to improve the overall quality of education in the State. As the District Court in No. 80–1934 noted, the State failed to offer any "credible supporting evidence that a proportionately small diminution of the funds spent on each child [which might result from devoting some state funds to the education of the excluded group] will have a grave impact on the quality of education." * * * Of course, even if improvement in the quality of education were a likely result of barring some number of children from the schools of the State, the State must support its selection of this group as the appropriate target for exclusion. In terms of educational cost and need, however, undocumented children are "basically indistinguishable" from legally resident alien children.

Finally, appellants suggest that undocumented children are appropriately singled out because their unlawful presence within the United States renders them less likely than other children to remain within the boundaries of the State, and to put their education to productive social or political use within the State. Even assuming that such an interest is legitimate, it is an interest that is most difficult to quantify. The State has no assurance that any child, citizen or not, will employ the education provided by the State within the confines of the State's borders. In any event, the record is clear that many of the undocumented children disabled by this classification will remain in this country indefinitely, and that some will become lawful residents or citizens of the United States. It is difficult to understand precisely what the State hopes to achieve by promoting the creation and perpetuation of a subclass of illiterates within our boundaries, surely adding to the problems and costs of unemployment, welfare, and crime. It is thus clear that whatever savings might be achieved by denying these children an education, they are wholly insubstantial in light of the costs involved to these children, the State, and the Nation.

VI

If the State is to deny a discrete group of innocent children the free public education that it offers to other children residing within its borders, that denial must be justified by a showing that it furthers some substantial state interest. No such showing was made here. Accordingly, the judgment of the Court of Appeals in each of these cases is

Affirmed.

* * *

■ JUSTICE BLACKMUN, concurring.

* * *

In my view, when the State provides an education to some and denies it to others, it immediately and inevitably creates class distinctions of a type fundamentally inconsistent with those purposes, mentioned above, of the Equal Protection Clause. Children denied an education are placed at a permanent and insurmountable competitive disadvantage, for an uneducated child is denied even the opportunity to achieve. And when those children are members of an identifiable group, that group—through the State's action—will have been converted into a discrete underclass. Other benefits provided by the State, such as housing and public assistance, are of course important; to an individual in immediate need, they may be more desirable than the right to be educated. But classifications involving the complete denial of education are in a sense unique, for they strike at the heart of equal protection values by involving the State in the creation of permanent class distinctions. In a sense, then, denial of an education is the analogue of denial of the right to vote: the former relegates the individual to second-class social status; the latter places him at a permanent political disadvantage.

* * *

■ CHIEF JUSTICE BURGER, with whom JUSTICE WHITE, JUSTICE REHNQUIST, and JUSTICE O'CONNOR join, dissenting.

Were it our business to set the Nation's social policy, I would agree without hesitation that it is senseless for an enlightened society to deprive any children—including illegal aliens—of an elementary education. I fully agree that it would be folly—and wrong—to tolerate creation of a segment of society made up of illiterate persons, many having a limited or no command of our language.[1] However, the Constitution does not constitute

---

1. It does not follow, however, that a state should bear the costs of educating children whose illegal presence in this country results from the default of the political branches of the Federal Government. A state has no power to prevent unlawful immigration, and no power to deport illegal aliens; those powers are reserved exclusively to Congress and the Executive. If the Federal Government, properly chargeable with deporting

us as "Platonic Guardians" nor does it vest in this Court the authority to strike down laws because they do not meet our standards of desirable social policy, "wisdom," or "common sense." We trespass on the assigned function of the political branches under our structure of limited and separated powers when we assume a policymaking role as the Court does today.

* * *

The Court's holding today manifests the justly criticized judicial tendency to attempt speedy and wholesale formulation of "remedies" for the failures—or simply the laggard pace—of the political processes of our system of government. The Court employs, and in my view abuses, the Fourteenth Amendment in an effort to become an omnipotent and omniscient problem solver. That the motives for doing so are noble and compassionate does not alter the fact that the Court distorts our constitutional function to make amends for the defaults of others.

I

In a sense, the Court's opinion rests on such a unique confluence of theories and rationales that it will likely stand for little beyond the results in these particular cases. Yet the extent to which the Court departs from principled constitutional adjudication is nonetheless disturbing.

I have no quarrel with the conclusion that the Equal Protection Clause of the Fourteenth Amendment applies to aliens who, after their illegal entry into this country, are indeed physically "within the jurisdiction" of a state. However, as the Court concedes, this "only begins the inquiry." The Equal Protection Clause does not mandate identical treatment of different categories of persons.

The dispositive issue in these cases, simply put, is whether, for purposes of allocating its finite resources, a state has a legitimate reason to differentiate between persons who are lawfully within the state and those who are unlawfully there. The distinction the State of Texas has drawn—based not only upon its own legitimate interests but on classifications established by the Federal Government in its immigration laws and policies—is not unconstitutional.

A

The Court acknowledges that, except in those cases when state classifications disadvantage a "suspect class" or impinge upon a "fundamental right," the Equal Protection Clause permits a state "substantial latitude" in distinguishing between different groups of persons. Moreover, the Court expressly—and correctly—rejects any suggestion that illegal aliens are a suspect class, or that education is a fundamental right. Yet by patching together bits and pieces of what might be termed quasi-suspect-class and

illegal aliens, fails to do so, it should bear the burdens of their presence here. Surely if illegal alien children can be identified for purposes of this litigation, their parents can be identified for purposes of prompt deportation.

quasi-fundamental-rights analysis, the Court spins out a theory custom-tailored to the facts of these cases.

In the end, we are told little more than that the level of scrutiny employed to strike down the Texas law applies only when illegal alien children are deprived of a public education. If ever a court was guilty of an unabashedly result-oriented approach, this case is a prime example.

(1)

The Court first suggests that these illegal alien children, although not a suspect class, are entitled to special solicitude under the Equal Protection Clause because they lack "control" over or "responsibility" for their unlawful entry into this country. Similarly, the Court appears to take the position that § 21.031 is presumptively "irrational" because it has the effect of imposing "penalties" on "innocent" children.[4] However, the Equal Protection Clause does not preclude legislators from classifying among persons on the basis of factors and characteristics over which individuals may be said to lack "control." Indeed, in some circumstances persons generally, and children in particular, may have little control over or responsibility for such things as their ill health, need for public assistance, or place of residence. Yet a state legislature is not barred from considering, for example, relevant differences between the mentally healthy and the mentally ill, or between the residents of different counties, simply because these may be factors unrelated to individual choice or to any "wrongdoing." The Equal Protection Clause protects against arbitrary and irrational classifications, and against invidious discrimination stemming from prejudice and hostility; it is not an all-encompassing "equalizer" designed to eradicate every distinction for which persons are not "responsible."

The Court does not presume to suggest that appellees' purported lack of culpability for their illegal status prevents them from being deported or otherwise "penalized" under federal law. Yet would deportation be any less a "penalty" than denial of privileges provided to legal residents? Illegality of presence in the United States does not—and need not—depend on some amorphous concept of "guilt" or "innocence" concerning an alien's entry. Similarly, a state's use of federal immigration status as a basis for legislative classification is not necessarily rendered suspect for its failure to take such factors into account.

* * *

The second strand of the Court's analysis rests on the premise that, although public education is not a constitutionally guaranteed right, "neither is it merely some governmental 'benefit' indistinguishable from other

---

4. Both the opinion of the Court and JUSTICE POWELL's concurrence imply that appellees are being "penalized" because their parents are illegal entrants. However, Texas has classified appellees on the basis of their own illegal status, not that of their parents. Children born in this country to illegal alien parents, including some of appellees' siblings, are not excluded from the Texas schools. Nor does Texas discriminate against appellees because of their Mexican origin or citizenship. Texas provides a free public education to countless thousands of Mexican immigrants who are lawfully in this country.

forms of social welfare legislation." Whatever meaning or relevance this opaque observation might have in some other context, it simply has no bearing on the issues at hand. Indeed, it is never made clear what the Court's opinion means on this score.

The importance of education is beyond dispute. Yet we have held repeatedly that the importance of a governmental service does not elevate it to the status of a "fundamental right" for purposes of equal protection analysis. In San Antonio Independent School Dist., JUSTICE POWELL, speaking for the Court, expressly rejected the proposition that state laws dealing with public education are subject to special scrutiny under the Equal Protection Clause. Moreover, the Court points to no meaningful way to distinguish between education and other governmental benefits in this context. Is the Court suggesting that education is more "fundamental" than food, shelter, or medical care?

The Equal Protection Clause guarantees similar treatment of similarly situated persons, but it does not mandate a constitutional hierarchy of governmental services. JUSTICE POWELL, speaking for the Court in San Antonio Independent School Dist., put it well in stating that to the extent this Court raises or lowers the degree of "judicial scrutiny" in equal protection cases according to a transient Court majority's view of the societal importance of the interest affected, we "[assume] a legislative role and one for which the Court lacks both authority and competence." Yet that is precisely what the Court does today.

The central question in these cases, as in every equal protection case not involving truly fundamental rights "explicitly or implicitly guaranteed by the Constitution," is whether there is some legitimate basis for a legislative distinction between different classes of persons. The fact that the distinction is drawn in legislation affecting access to public education—as opposed to legislation allocating other important governmental benefits, such as public assistance, health care, or housing—cannot make a difference in the level of scrutiny applied.

B

Once it is conceded—as the Court does—that illegal aliens are not a suspect class, and that education is not a fundamental right, our inquiry should focus on and be limited to whether the legislative classification at issue bears a rational relationship to a legitimate state purpose.

The State contends primarily that § 21.031 serves to prevent undue depletion of its limited revenues available for education, and to preserve the fiscal integrity of the State's school-financing system against an ever-increasing flood of illegal aliens—aliens over whose entry or continued presence it has no control. Of course such fiscal concerns alone could not justify discrimination against a suspect class or an arbitrary and irrational denial of benefits to a particular group of persons. Yet I assume no Member of this Court would argue that prudent conservation of finite state revenues is per se an illegitimate goal. Indeed, the numerous classifications this Court has sustained in social welfare legislation were invariably related to the limited amount of revenues available to spend on any given program or set of programs. The significant question here is whether the requirement of tuition from illegal aliens who attend the public schools—as well as from residents of other states, for example—is a rational and reasonable means of furthering the State's legitimate fiscal ends.

Without laboring what will undoubtedly seem obvious to many, it simply is not "irrational" for a state to conclude that it does not have the same responsibility to provide benefits for persons whose very presence in the state and this country is illegal as it does to provide for persons lawfully present. By definition, illegal aliens have no right whatever to be here, and the state may reasonably, and constitutionally, elect not to provide them with governmental services at the expense of those who are lawfully in the state. In De Canas v. Bica, we held that a State may protect its "fiscal interests and lawfully resident labor force from the deleterious effects on its economy resulting from the employment of illegal aliens." And only recently this Court made clear that a State has a legitimate interest in protecting and preserving the quality of its schools and "the right of its own bona fide residents to attend such institutions on a preferential tuition basis." The Court has failed to offer even a plausible explanation why illegality of residence in this country is not a factor that may legitimately bear upon the bona fides of state residence and entitlement to the benefits of lawful residence.[12]

It is significant that the Federal Government has seen fit to exclude illegal aliens from numerous social welfare programs, such as the food stamp program, the old-age assistance, aid to families with dependent children, aid to the blind, aid to the permanently and totally disabled, and supplemental security income programs, the Medicare hospital insurance benefits program, and the Medicaid hospital insurance benefits for the aged and disabled program. Although these exclusions do not conclusively demonstrate the constitutionality of the State's use of the same classification for comparable purposes, at the very least they tend to support the rationality of excluding illegal alien residents of a state from such programs so as to preserve the state's finite revenues for the benefit of lawful residents.

The Court maintains—as if this were the issue—that "barring undocumented children from local schools would not necessarily improve the quality of education provided in those schools." However, the legitimacy of barring illegal aliens from programs such as Medicare or Medicaid does not depend on a showing that the barrier would "improve the quality" of medical care given to persons lawfully entitled to participate in such programs. Modern education, like medical care, is enormously expensive, and there can be no doubt that very large added costs will fall on the State or its local school districts as a result of the inclusion of illegal aliens in the

12.   * * * [T]he analogies to Virginians or legally admitted Mexican citizens entering Texas are spurious. A Virginian's right to migrate to Texas, without penalty, is protect-ed by the Constitution, and a lawfully admitted alien's right to enter the State is likewise protected by federal law.

tuition-free public schools. The State may, in its discretion, use any savings resulting from its tuition requirement to "improve the quality of education" in the public school system, or to enhance the funds available for other social programs, or to reduce the tax burden placed on its residents; each of these ends is "legitimate." The State need not show, as the Court implies, that the incremental cost of educating illegal aliens will send it into bankruptcy, or have a " 'grave impact on the quality of education;' " that is not dispositive under a "rational basis" scrutiny. In the absence of a constitutional imperative to provide for the education of illegal aliens, the State may "rationally" choose to take advantage of whatever savings will accrue from limiting access to the tuition-free public schools to its own lawful residents, excluding even citizens of neighboring States.

Denying a free education to illegal alien children is not a choice I would make were I a legislator. Apart from compassionate considerations, the long-range costs of excluding any children from the public schools may well outweigh the costs of educating them. But that is not the issue; the fact that there are sound policy arguments against the Texas Legislature's choice does not render that choice an unconstitutional one.

* * *

NOTES AND QUESTIONS

1. Perhaps the single most important decision the Court had to make in this case was what standard of review to select. Both the majority and the dissent purport to apply a rationality test, but they differ over what it should take to satisfy that test. The majority ends up invoking an intermediate level of scrutiny, requiring that the legislation "further some substantial goal of the State." (See the last sentence of section III of the Court's opinion.) The dissent argues that to adopt that level of scrutiny "only when illegal alien children are deprived of a public education" is "an unabashedly result-oriented approach." Do you agree with that characterization? And what do you make of the Chief Justice's dissent? He acknowledges that the policy in question is "senseless" and "folly" but ultimately finds it "rational." Are his two conclusions compatible?

2. More generally, what level of scrutiny *should* a Court employ when state legislation discriminates against undocumented migrants? See especially footnotes 14 and 19 of the majority opinion.

3. Consider now the various interests asserted by the State of Texas to justify the exclusion of undocumented children from public schools. First, the State argued that undocumented migrants have an adverse economic impact on the State and that the statute in question would dissuade some from coming. The Court rejects both premises. It finds no evidence in the record to suggest that the net economic impact of undocumented migrants on Texas is negative. (In fact, the evidence suggested the opposite). At any rate, the Court found, undocumented migrants generally come for employment, not for education; thus, the statute would not provide the hoped-for deterrence anyway. As counsel for the State of Texas,

how would you respond to both arguments? If the facts change (or if the empirical evidence of those facts changes), would *Plyler v. Doe* become inapplicable? (This is not an academic question, as you will see when you examine California Proposition 187 and accompanying materials, below).

4. The Court also rejects the State's argument that the cost of educating undocumented children was diminishing the quality of education the State could afford to provide for lawfully resident children. Was the Court right to reject that argument?

5. What legitimate *state* interest could Texas assert to justify treating those of its residents who are undocumented differently from those of its residents who are either (a) LPRs or (b) United States citizens who came to Texas from other states? Why, in other words, should *the State of Texas* care which of its residents lack a valid *federal* immigration status?

6. After *Plyler v. Doe*, can a state constitutionally treat its undocumented residents differently from its other residents? For example, is it constitutional for a state to disqualify undocumented migrants from welfare (food benefits, cash assistance, medical services, etc.)? In analyzing these questions, decide (a) whether the reasons given in *Plyler* for intermediate scrutiny would extend to welfare; (b) whether the specific rationales offered by the State of Texas to explain the statutory classification would still apply; and, if so, (c) whether the Court would have as much reason to reject those rationales in the welfare context as in the education context.

7. Would the Supreme Court strike down a *federal* law that prohibited the free public elementary and secondary education of all undocumented children? Before answering, think about the plenary power doctrine that you studied in chapter 2, and read footnote 19 of the Court's opinion. Consider also whether the degree of judicial deference should vary depending on whether the particular federal law is an "immigration" law or some other federal regulation of noncitizens. On that last point, see Linda S. Bosniak, *Membership, Equality, and the Difference that Alienage Makes*, 69 NYU L. Rev. 1047 (1994); Michael Scaperlanda, *Partial Membership: Aliens and the Constitutional Community*, 81 Iowa L. Rev. 707 (1996); Margaret H. Taylor, *Detained Aliens Challenging Conditions of Confinement and the Porous Border of the Plenary Power Doctrine*, 22 Hastings Constitutional L.Q. 1087 (1995).

8. The House version of the bill that eventually became IIRIRA contained a controversial amendment introduced by Rep. Elton Gallegly (R–Cal.). The Gallegly amendment would have authorized states to deny free public education to undocumented children. The House and Senate conferees agreed to drop the amendment when it became clear that it was jeopardizing the passage of IIRIRA. See 73 IR at 1281–82 (Sept. 30, 1996). Future efforts to enact the substance of the Gallegly amendment are always possible. Given *Plyler v. Doe*, would the Gallegly amendment or any state legislation enacted pursuant to it be constitutional?

9. In *Plyler v. Doe* the only constitutional challenge that the Court had to adjudicate was the one based on equal protection. The Court did not

have to decide whether the Texas statute unconstitutionally intruded into federally preempted subject matter. The two types of challenges turn on some common issues and will be considered below in the context of California Proposition 187.

10. Does *Plyler v. Doe* reveal the Supreme Court's view of what constitutes membership in the national community, or is the meaning of this case less profound? See Peter H. Schuck, *The Transformation of Immigration Law*, 84 Columbia L. Rev. 1, 58 (1984), and consider again the excerpts, reproduced above, from Linda S. Bosniak, *Exclusion and Membership: The Dual Identity of the Undocumented Worker under United States Law*, 1988 Wisconsin L. Rev. 955, 977–87. For some thoughtful contemporary responses to *Plyler v. Doe*, see Tom Gerety, *Children in the Labyrinth: The Complexities of Plyler v. Doe*, 44 Univ. Pittsburgh L. Rev. 379 (1983); Michael A. Olivas, *Plyler v. Doe, Toll v. Moreno, and Postsecondary Admissions: Undocumented Aliens and Enduring Disability*, 15 J.L. & Education 19 (1986).

PROPOSITION 187

On November 8, 1994 the voters of California passed Proposition 187.[5] Although litigation and a settlement permanently enjoined enforcement of most of its provisions, this initiative remains a point of national debate on the subject of the states' roles in responding to illegal migration.

Proposition 187 has been intensely controversial. Its best known provision is section 7, which would have prohibited every public elementary and secondary school in the state from allowing any undocumented child to attend school. By January 1, 1996, each school was to have verified the immigration status of every student and the parents or guardians of every student. In addition to expelling those students whom they found not to be in lawful status, the schools would have been required to report to the former INS the identities of any students, parents, or guardians suspected of being out of status. The practical consequence of the parent or guardian provision was that even U.S. citizen children would have been unable to attend school if their parents were undocumented, unless the children were willing to have their parents turned in to the INS.

Other sections of Proposition 187 prohibited publicly funded health facilities from serving undocumented migrants except in medical emergencies, and similarly prohibited public social services from serving undocumented migrants. These agencies were required to assess the immigration status of each patient or applicant and report to the INS the identities of those suspected to be out of status.

Immediately after its passage, opponents of Proposition 187 filed both federal and state lawsuits challenging its legality and seeking injunctive relief. A combination of federal and state preliminary injunctions promptly

---

5. The full text is reproduced in *League of United Latin American Citizens v. Wilson,* 908 F.Supp. 755, 787–91 (App. A) (C.D.Cal. 1995).

issued. The complaints alleged several constitutional deficiencies, including equal protection and federal preemption.

In 1995, federal district judge Mariana Pfaelzer temporarily enjoined enforcement of most of the central provisions of Proposition 187. *League of United Latin American Citizens v. Wilson*, 908 F.Supp. 755 (C.D.Cal. 1995) [hereafter cited as *LULAC*]. Citing *Plyler v. Doe*, the court invalidated the bar on undocumented children attending public elementary and secondary schools. Judge Pfaelzer also invalidated, on grounds of federal preemption, all the provisions that required state and local employees to investigate the immigration statuses of their patients, clients, or students, to instruct suspected undocumented migrants to leave the country, and to report their names to the INS.

While the preliminary injunction was in force, Congress in 1996 passed the Welfare Act. In its opinion rendering final judgment, 997 F.Supp. 1244 (C.D. Cal. 1997), the court held that the Welfare Act reflects "the intention of Congress to occupy the field of regulation of government benefits to aliens." *Id.* at 1253. Accordingly, it entered a final summary judgment invalidating almost all of Proposition 187. Only sections 2 and 3, which penalize specified forms of document fraud, and section 10, a "severability" clause that allows some sections to withstand the invalidation of others, survived.

Then things got interesting. The State of California appealed to the Ninth Circuit. While the appeal was pending, Governor Pete Wilson, one of the chief proponents of Proposition 187, completed his term of office. His successor, Gray Davis, had opposed Proposition 187. Everyone wondered: Would Governor Davis drop the appeal? To do so, he feared, would be a breach of his gubernatorial duty to uphold California law. To do otherwise, though, would jeopardize the educations of hundreds of thousands of schoolchildren in ways that he (and the district court) believed were unconstitutional.

Governor Davis's solution was to request the court of appeals to invoke its special mediation procedure, in which the opposing parties attempt to negotiate a settlement. That request was itself controversial. Backers of Proposition 187 objected that the two "opposing" parties in fact were of the same mind on Proposition 187—that it should be invalidated. They suggested that true negotiation was impossible. Opponents of Proposition 187 were also taken aback. They wanted Governor Davis simply to drop the appeal. In April 1999, the court granted the Governor's request for mediation. See Bob Egelko, *Court to Mediate California Proposition*, Assoc. Press (April 26, 1999); Dave Lesher, Los Angeles Times (May 21, 1999). And in July 1999, as expected, a settlement that accepted the district court's judgment was announced. Patrick J. McDonnell, *Davis Won't Appeal Prop. 187 Ruling, Ending Court Battles*, L.A. Times (July 29, 1999).

Preemption arguments of the kind advanced in *LULAC* have both constitutional and statutory components. The plaintiffs were arguing that, by enacting comprehensive immigration legislation, Congress had intended to preempt the states from regulating immigration. Ultimately, therefore, the issue is one of statutory interpretation. Once a court agrees that Congress, acting pursuant to a constitutionally enumerated power, intended to preempt state action, then state action within the preempted field violates the supremacy clause. U.S. Const. art. VI, cl. 2.

Distinguish a preemption argument, which requires a showing of preemptive congressional intent, from the federal exclusivity argument that you saw in *Henderson*, *Chy Lung*, and other early cases (chapter 2, § A.4 above). In those cases, you might recall, state action in the field of immigration was held unconstitutional even though Congress had not acted. The Constitution itself—not an Act of Congress—prohibited state regulation of immigration.

Exactly which issues either the Constitution or the Congress bars the states from deciding is difficult to say. States commonly regulate noncitizens, as you will see in chapter 13. Only when it thinks "immigration" is involved has the Supreme Court struck down state legislation on the ground that the Constitution mandated federal exclusivity. But how does a court draw the line between immigration legislation and other regulation of noncitizens? That question is thoughtfully presented in Linda S. Bosniak, *Immigrants, Preemption and Equality*, 35 Virginia J. Internat'l L. 179 (1994), and in Hiroshi Motomura, *Immigration and Alienage, Federalism and Proposition 187*, 35 Virginia J. Internat'l L. 201 (1994).

The *LULAC* case illustrates the problem. Is Proposition 187 just a regulation of noncitizens, and thus constitutionally permissible as long as Congress has not preempted the field (and subject to equal protection or any other affirmative constitutional restraint)? Or is Proposition 187 an immigration regulation that Congress could not delegate to the states even if it wanted to?

Professor Peter Spiro has argued that, in an age where the fifty states frequently do things that affect foreign relations, states should have far greater latitude to regulate noncitizens. See Peter J. Spiro, *The States and Immigration in an Era of Demi–Sovereignties*, 35 Virginia J. Internat'l L. 121 (1994); see also Peter J. Spiro, *Learning to Live with Immigration Federalism*, 29 Connecticut L. Rev. 1627 (1997). For several responses, see the Bosniak and Motomura articles cited above and Michael A. Olivas, *Preempting Preemption: Foreign Affairs, State Rights and Alienage Classifications*, 35 Virginia J. Internat'l L. 217 (1994).

NOTES AND QUESTIONS

1. As a policy matter, what do you think of Proposition 187?

2. The Supreme Court cases discussed in chapter 2, § A.4 above offered two distinct reasons for interpreting the Constitution to bar state regulation of immigration. In *Henderson*, the Court emphasized the importance of uniform immigration restrictions. In *Chy Lung*, the Court sought to prevent one state from taking action that could antagonize other nations and thus create foreign relations problems for the United States. Do those

rationales apply to Proposition 187? As for uniformity, what would happen if some states passed (and could enforce) 187–style legislation, and other states did not? As for embroilment, could Proposition 187 have foreign policy repercussions?

3.   As for preemption (as opposed to constitutional exclusivity), two different themes emerged from the plaintiffs' arguments in *LULAC*. One objection concerned procedure. To determine that particular individuals were undocumented, various state employees—school officials, welfare officials, and social workers—would have to interpret and apply principles of federal immigration law. First, is that good policy? Second, do you think that, as the state argued, Congress meant to leave open the possibility of state officials determining people's immigration statuses?

4.   The preemption issue concerns substantive decisionmaking as well. Who should decide which noncitizens are entitled to free public education—the federal government, or the state and local governments?

5.   Suppose California had argued in *LULAC* that one of the goals of the challenged legislation was to divert to neighboring states a portion of the undocumented population that California was disproportionately absorbing. Would that be a valid goal?

6.   The House of Representatives passed the Gallegly amendment noted earlier (authorizing states not to provide free public education to undocumented children), but Congress ultimately decided not to enact it. Yet the same Congress did specifically authorize states to withhold various welfare benefits from undocumented migrants, as discussed earlier. As counsel for plaintiffs in *LULAC*, how might you argue that the contrast between those two developments vindicates your position?

7.   By now you have probably noticed that, when the subject matter involves noncitizens, the equal protection argument that you saw in *Plyler* and the preemption argument that you saw in *LULAC* tend to overlap. For the state to defeat an equal protection argument, it has to identify some legitimate *state* interest to which the challenged classification is (at least) rationally related. If the only interests it can come up with to justify the challenged discrimination are interests that either the Constitution or the Congress has reserved for federal regulation, then the equal protection challenge will succeed.

8.   Having read *Plyler*, do you think the education provisions of Proposition 187 would have survived Supreme Court review? If you were representing the State of California in *LULAC*, what arguments might you make to the Supreme Court? Is Proposition 187 different from the Texas statute? Have any other relevant circumstances changed since *Plyler*?

9.   Several states have sued the federal government to recover costs they allege they have incurred as a result of the federal government's failure to adequately enforce the immigration laws. All such suits have been dismissed for lack of a justiciable issue—i.e., an issue suitable for judicial, rather than legislative, resolution. See, e.g., *New Jersey v. United*

States, 91 F.3d 463 (3d Cir. 1996); *Padavan v. United States*, 82 F.3d 23 (2d Cir. 1996); *Chiles v. United States*, 69 F.3d 1094 (11th Cir. 1995).

Nonetheless, Congress in recent years has taken limited measures to reimburse states for at least a portion of the cost associated with undocumented migrants. In IRCA § 204, Congress in 1986 authorized the award of "state legalization impact-assistance grants" to selected states to help offset any costs the states might incur as a result of the federal decision to legalize millions of undocumented migrants. Crime legislation enacted in 1994, the Violent Crime Control and Law Enforcement Act of 1994, Pub.L. 103–322, § 20301, 108 Stat. 1796, 1823 (Sept. 13, 1994), authorized federal reimbursement to states for the costs of incarcerating undocumented migrants who commit state crimes. And state public health facilities that provide free emergency medical care to indigent undocumented migrants can be reimbursed by the federal government if—and it's a big "if"— Congress appropriates sufficient funds. IIRIRA § 562.

Suppose a state can convincingly demonstrate that, as a result of a particular federal policy, it has suffered a disproportionate adverse impact that can be roughly quantified. Should the federal government reimburse the state for the amount lost? If California can show such an effect from illegal immigration, should the federal government pick up part (or all) of the tab?

10. Support for 187–style initiatives is building in several other states. Those initiatives raise a broad array of questions—legal, political, economic, sociological, and ethical. See especially Peter H. Schuck, *The Message of Proposition 187*, 26 Pacific L.J. 989 (1995) (criticizing 187 on policy grounds, examining likelihood of Supreme Court invalidating it, and blaming both restrictionists and expansionists for the climate that made it possible). For other helpful articles, see, e.g., Linda S. Bosniak, *Opposing Prop. 187: Undocumented Immigrants and the National Imagination*, 28 Connecticut L. Rev. 555 (1996); Kevin R. Johnson, *Something Old, Something New, Something Borrowed, Something Blue*, in Juan F. Perea (ed.), Immigrants Out! The New Nativism and the Anti–Immigrant Impulse in the United States at 165 et seq., 177–80 (1997); Kevin R. Johnson, *An Essay on Immigration Politics, Popular Democracy, and California's Proposition 187: The Political Relevance and Legal Irrelevance of Race*, 70 Washington L. Rev. 629 (1995) (discussing the dangers of initiatives); Stanley Mailman, *California's Proposition 187 and Its Lessons*, New York L.J. 3–7 (Jan. 3, 1995); see also the UCLA symposium containing several articles on noncitizens' eligibility for public benefits generally and Proposition 187 in particular: Evangeline G. Abriel, *Rethinking Preemption for Purposes of Aliens and Public Benefits*, 42 UCLA L. Rev. 1597 (1995); Richard A. Boswell, *Restrictions on Non–Citizens' Access to Public Benefits: Flawed Premise, Unnecessary Response*, 42 UCLA 1475 (1995); Lolita K. Buckner Inniss, *California's Proposition 187—Does It Mean What It Says? Does It Say What It Means? A Textual and Constitutional Analysis*, 10 Georgetown Immigration L.J. 577 (1996); Kevin R. Johnson, *Public Benefits and Immigration: The Intersection of Immigration Status, Ethnicity,*

Gender, and Class, 42 UCLA L. Rev. 1509 (1995); Stephen H. Legomsky, *Immigration, Federalism, and the Welfare State,* 42 UCLA L. Rev. 1453 (1995); Gerald L. Neuman, *Aliens as Outlaws: Government Services, Proposition 187, and the Structure of Equal Protection Doctrine,* 42 UCLA L. Rev. 1425 (1995); Peter L. Reich, *Environmental Metaphor in the Alien Benefits Debate,* 42 UCLA L. Rev. 1577 (1995).

11.   German law supplies an interesting twist. In Germany, the children (including lawfully resident children) of foreigners are *required* to attend public schools, rather than private schools. The stated purposes of the law are to prevent parallel societies from developing and to prepare the children for life in a German cultural environment. See *Foreigners' children told to attend public schools,* F.A.Z. Weekly (Germany) (Oct. 8, 2004).

POST–SECONDARY EDUCATION

Although the debate over California Proposition 187 focused almost entirely on elementary and secondary education, a lesser known provision, section 8, would similarly have barred undocumented students from enrolling in any public college, university, or other post-secondary educational institution in the State of California. But even when undocumented migrants are not statutorily barred from attending state colleges and universities, they frequently face insurmountable financial barriers. Given the combination of skyrocketing college tuition, legal ineligibility for most governmental grant, loan, and work assistance programs, see 20 U.S.C. § 1091(a)(5), and laws that declare undocumented migrants not to be state residents for purposes of in-state tuition rates (discussed below), these high school students—no matter how talented—ponder uncertain futures. For some sensitive portrayals of the problems, see Michael A. Olivas, *Storytelling Out of School: Undocumented College Residency, Race, and Reaction,* 22 Hastings Const. L.Q. 1019 (1995); Victor C. Romero, *Noncitizen Students and Immigration Policy Post–9/11,* 17 Georgetown Immigration L.J. 357 (2003), § IV; Victor C. Romero, *Postsecondary School Education Benefits for Undocumented Immigrants: Promises and Pitfalls,* 27 North Carolina J. Internat'l L. & Commercial Regulation 393 (2002); Andrew Stevenson, *DREAMing of an Equal Future for Immigrant Children: Federal and State Initiatives to Improve Undocumented Students' Access to Postsecondary Education,* 46 Arizona L. Rev. 551 (2004); Laura S. Yates, *Plyler v. Doe and the Rights of Undocumented Immigrants to Higher Education: Should Undocumented Students Be Eligible for In–State College Tuition Rates?,* 82 Washington Univ. L.Q. 585 (2004).

IIRIRA § 505(a) provides:

Notwithstanding any other provision of law, an alien who is not lawfully present in the United States shall not be eligible on the basis of residence within a State (or a political subdivision) for any postsecondary education benefit unless a citizen or national of the United States is eligible for such a benefit (in no less an amount, duration, and scope) without regard to whether the citizen or national is such a resident.

Despite IIRIRA § 505, many states have enacted legislation to accomplish the same end. For a compilation of the relevant state statutes and their descriptions, see James A. Ferg–Cadima, MALDEF, *Survey of Recent State Law and Legislation during the 2003–04 Legislative Term Aimed at Facilitating Undocumented Student Access to State Universities* (May 18, 2003). The most common strategy is to allow undocumented students to qualify for in-state resident tuition rates if they meet several conditions. Common conditions include graduation from a high school in the particular state; a certain number of years of attendance at a high school in the state; the signing of an affidavit pledging to apply for lawful permanent residence at the earliest opportunity; and sometimes residence in the state for a prescribed period. *Id.*

Professor Michael Olivas has led the charge for many years. In Michael A. Olivas, *A Rebuttal to FAIR: States Can Enact Residency Statutes for the Undocumented*, 7 BIB 652 (June 1, 2002), he argued that these state laws are compatible with IIRIRA § 505. Among his arguments were the following: (1) In-state residency determinations are a matter for the states, not the federal government. (2) The terms of IIRIRA § 505 restrict, at most, the granting of "postsecondary education *benefits*" (emphasis added); based on other provisions of IIRIRA, it appears Congress intended the word "benefits" to mean monetary benefits, not a state decision to classify a person as a resident. (3) Consistently with IIRIRA § 505, the state laws do not treat undocumented residents more favorably than U.S. citizens who are not residents of the state; to the contrary, the former are subjected to additional restrictions. To these arguments, one might add another: IIRIRA § 505 says only that an undocumented student may not, under certain circumstances, "be eligible *on the basis of residence* within a State" [emphasis added]. By hinging eligibility not on residence but on other criteria (for example, graduation from a high school in the state, attendance at a high school in the state for a specified duration, the signing of an affidavit), the state laws therefore respect the limitations in IIRIRA § 505.

But apart from the question of how best to interpret IIRIRA § 505, recent years have witnessed a flurry of advocacy and proposed bills to repeal IIRIRA § 505. Some of the bills would also allow certain undocumented students to adjust to lawful permanent residence, require states to classify certain undocumented students as state residents for purposes of in-state college tuition (as a condition to the state continuing to receive federal educational funding), or some combination. The best known of these bills is the DREAM Act. See generally Michael A. Olivas, *IIRIRA, the DREAM Act, and Undocumented College Student Residency*, 30 J. College & University L. 435 (2004).

NOTES AND QUESTIONS

1.   As a policy matter, *should* undocumented residents of a state qualify for in-state resident tuition rates at public colleges and universities?

2.   IIRIRA § 505 above disqualifies undocumented students from post-secondary education benefits based on residence, but only if U.S. citizens from other states are similarly ineligible. What do you think of that linkage?

3.   In *Plyler v. Doe*, the Court was considering a Texas law that allowed local school districts to bar undocumented students from public elementary and secondary schools. Suppose the Texas law had extended that bar to state colleges and universities (as California Proposition 187 did). In the absence of federal legislation on the subject (this was pre-IIRIRA), does either the language or the logic of the Court's opinion suggest what the Court would have done?

4.   UNDOCUMENTED MIGRANTS AND DRIVERS' LICENSES

Since September 11, 2001, drivers' licenses have been the subject of fervent debate. Several of the 9/11 hijackers, it is frequently noted, used state drivers' licenses to board the airplanes on that fateful day. (Those who offer that observation do not always candidly acknowledge that, had drivers' licenses been unavailable, the same terrorists could easily have boarded by displaying their passports.)

At the center of the debate are philosophical differences over the very purposes of drivers' licenses. Are they primarily a road safety device, a way of assuring that drivers achieve a minimal level of knowledge and proficiency before taking to the highways? Or have they also become de facto ID cards, for use by government and private actors in verifying the bearer's identity? Should they be designed to perform a third function—immigration enforcement?

The REAL ID Act clearly reflects the latter two philosophies. The law was passed in 2005 without any committee hearings or other debates. (The House of Representatives attached it to must-pass appropriations legislation for troops support and Tsunami relief, the Senate rejected it, and a conference committee accepted it with some modifications.) With respect to drivers' licenses, the Act goes into force three years after enactment (which will be May 11, 2008). It does two sorts of things.

First, it provides that no federal agency may accept a state-issued driver's license or identification card as identification unless the state has implemented a number of prescribed reliability measures. REAL ID Act, § 202(a)(1). The Secretary of Homeland Security must periodically determine whether each state is meeting those requirements. *Id.* § 202(a)(2).

Some of the requirements relate to the document itself. For example, the document must include a digital photograph, must be machine-readable, and must contain features designed to prevent tampering, counterfeiting, and duplication. *Id.* § 202(b). Other provisions require the state to take several precautions before issuing the driver's license or identification card. For example, the state must require every applicant to present four documents—a photo ID (or a document that shows the person's full legal name and date of birth); a document that shows the person's date of birth;

proof of the applicant's social security number (or proof of ineligibility for it); and documentation of the applicant's name and principal address. *Id.* § 202(c)(1). For this purpose, the only acceptable foreign document is a passport. *Id.* § 202(c)(3)(B). The state must then "verify, with the issuing agency, the issuance, validity, and completeness of" each of these documents. *Id.* § 202(c)(3)(A). On the first occasion that a given individual seeks a driver's license or identification card after the Act goes into force, this process will normally require the state DMV to check with the Social Security Administration, the local entity that issued the person's birth certificate, and local officials who can confirm the person's address. For applications to renew drivers' licenses or identification cards that are originally issued after the Act goes into force, the process is not yet clear; the statute says only that the state's procedure must be "effective," *id.* § 202(d)(4), though it appears the state may rely on paper copies of the documents it originally accepted (and which it is required to store for seven years, *id.* § 202(d)(2)). One who already has a driver's license issued by another state must supply proof that the previous license was or is being terminated. *Id.* § 202(d)(6). The state must also take specified steps to secure the physical facilities where the licenses are produced and the materials used to produce them, and it must subject all the relevant employees to security checks. *Id.* § 202(d)(7, 8). Finally, the state must establish and maintain an electronic database that contains all the information on each person's driver's license or identification card, as well as information on each person's driving history, and it must share that database with each of the other states. *Id.* § 202(d)(12, 13).

Those provisions apply to citizens and noncitizens alike. A separate question, of more relevance here, is whether noncitizens should have to be in lawful immigration status in order to receive a state-issued driver's license or identification card. On that subject, debate has raged for several years. The topic has been especially volatile in California, and particularly for Latinos, even influencing gubernatorial elections. See, e.g., Kevin R. Johnson, *Driver's Licenses and Undocumented Immigrants: The Future of Civil Rights Law?*, 5 Nevada L.J. 213, 232–35 (2004). Even before the REAL ID Act, a majority of states made undocumented migrants ineligible for drivers' licenses. *Id.* at 217.

Under the REAL ID Act, § 202(c)(2)(B), a state may not issue a driver's license or identification card without proof that the applicant is a United States citizen or national; a noncitizen with some type of valid immigration status; a person with a pending application for asylum, temporary protected status, or adjustment of status; or a person for whom deferred action has been approved. If the applicant falls within one of the above temporary categories, then the state may issue only a temporary driver's license or identification card, good only until the expiry of the person's authorized stay or, if the authorized stay does not have a definite ending time, one year. To renew the document, the person must demonstrate that his or her status has been extended. *Id.* § 202(c)(2)(C). To determine the applicant's immigration status, each state is required to use the Department of Homeland Security's electronic database (known as the

"Systematic Alien Verification for Entitlements," or "SAVE"). *Id.* § 202(c)(3)(C). In theory, a state may issue drivers' licenses and identification cards that do not comply with all these requirements. If it does, however, then any such documents may not be used, and must clearly indicate that they may not be used, for any federal identification purposes—including boarding a commercial aircraft. *Id.* §§ 201(3), 202(a)(1), 202(d)(11)(A). As a practical matter this means that, unless a state is willing to disable its residents from boarding commercial aircraft in the United States (or willing to require all its residents to obtain and carry passports when they fly), no state will be able to opt out.

What is the rationale for prohibiting each state from issuing drivers' licenses or identification cards to those of its residents who are out of status? Proponents appear to argue that drivers' licenses make it easier for terrorists to function in society and to get access to resources and places. Thus, by denying drivers' licenses and other identification to at least those terrorists who are undocumented, a federal ban is hoped to make terrorism more difficult to perpetrate.

But many arguments have been arrayed against such prohibitions. The most common arguments have been based on safety. The assumption is that undocumented residents of the United States will continue to drive out of practical necessity, with or without licenses. Therefore, it is argued, all the prohibition will do is put millions of untested, unlicensed, and uninsured drivers on the roads. See, e.g., Johnson, above, at 220–22. Professor Johnson's main concern, however, is with the civil rights implications. After reviewing the historical link in California between racial politics and the subject of drivers' licenses for undocumented migrants, and emphasizing the disparate impact that the drivers' licenses restrictions have had on people of Mexican ancestry, he cautions that the law must be vigilant "to ensure that it does not serve as a proxy for race." *Id.* at 215. Because thousands of DMV employees nationwide will now have access to each state's electronic database, and because those shared databases will now contain a great detail of personal information, there is the additional fear of identity theft. The fiscal costs and logistical problems for the state DMVs have also been a major concern. Some states are contemplating legal challenges to the drivers' licenses provisions (or even civil disobedience) on the ground that they constitute an unlawful unfunded mandate. See, e.g., Suzanne Gamboa, *States May Disobey Driver's License Rules*, Assoc. Press (May 10, 2005); Al Swanson, *Analysis: "Real ID Act" Scrutinized*, United Press Internat'l (May 10, 2005). Some of the security precautions also pose special difficulties for military personnel stationed abroad. See Margaret D. Stock, *The "REAL ID" Act—A Real Nightmare for DoD*, The Officer (Apr. 2005), at 12–13. For a survey of pre-REAL ID Act state practices and a thoughtful analysis of the constitutional and moral questions, see María Pabón López, *More than a License to Drive: State Restrictions on the Use of Driver's Licenses by Noncitizens*, 29 Southern Illinois Univ. L.J. 91 (2004).

These concerns aside, the REAL ID Act has some interesting implications for law enforcement and national security. The following article, written (shortly before enactment) by law professor Margaret Stock of the U.S. Military Academy at West Point, takes up that question.

Margaret D. Stock, Driver Licenses and National Security: Myths and Reality

10 Bender's Immigration Bulletin 422 (March 1, 2005).

* * *

The collective DMV databases are the largest law enforcement databases in the country, with records on more individual adults than any other law enforcement databases. The collective DMV databases are the only comprehensive internal security database. * * * Even DHS admits that its own databases are inferior to the DMV databases: When DHS wants to find someone, the primary government database it relies upon is the driver license database.

When a person appears at a state DMV and applies for a driver license, that person voluntarily provides the DMV with a variety of valuable personal information—including a key identifier, the digital photo.[4] DMV databases thus contain biometric information, and a wealth of other valuable information that is updated on a regular basis, voluntarily, by the individual who has the license. It is easy to see how valuable this data is by comparing the data available in a DMV database to other available government databases. The state birth certificate databases, for example, contain information only on those born or adopted in the United States, usually have no usable biometric information, and rarely have updated information, since most people do not notify vital statistics bureaus when they move. The federal Social Security databases contain records only on those persons who have Social Security numbers, have no biometric information, and may or may not have current address information; furthermore, their usefulness in providing information on the adult population is dropping rapidly as Social Security has tightened rules regarding the issuance of numbers. Internal Revenue Service databases contain information only on those persons who pay taxes; these databases have no biometric information at all, and no updated information unless the person files a tax return. The State Department's passport database contains biometric record, but only on US citizens and nationals who have applied for passports.

* * *

Those who are opposed to illegal immigration view the granting of driver licenses to illegal immigrants as a sort of reward and acknowledgment of complicity in their violation of the law. In fact, their opposition to granting licenses (and identification documents) to illegal immigrants is

---

4. American Ass'n of Motor Vehicle Administrators, Access to Drivers License & Identification Card Data by Law Enforcement, October 2003 ("Typically, the digital images (signature and photograph) are reliable, of good quality and in most cases provide the most recent image of a criminal suspect.") * * *

quite puzzling if one views the matter from a law enforcement and security perspective. * * * If those who oppose granting driver licenses and state identification documents to illegal immigrants have their way, only US citizens and legal aliens will be in the largest law enforcement database in the country. Thus, when a law enforcement official needs to find someone who happens to be an illegal immigrant, she will have no government database in which to look. Such a policy is likely to make it harder to enforce laws, not easier.

* * *

What happens when people can't get US driver licenses or state identification cards? If they are illegal migrants, they do not go home. They stay in the United States. They take public transportation; they walk; they hitch a ride. They use fake licenses; they use foreign licenses; they pay money to corrupt DMV employees to get real licenses when they are not legally entitled to them.[8] Sometimes they steal someone else's identity in order to obtain a license; this corrupts the existing database information, but also makes it difficult to locate them and prosecute them. They give their data to private entrepreneurs who sell them so-called "international drivers licenses;" when they purchase such nongovernmental identification, their data does not end up in the government's DMV database system, and cannot be accessed by US law enforcement officials.

Anyone even slightly familiar with US immigration law knows how complicated it is * * *. It is not possible today for a state or local law enforcement official to pick up the telephone and find out immediately if a given person is "legal;" it can take hours or even days to figure this out, and often the immediate information provided by DHS about a person's status can be wrong. Because state DMV officials are not immigration experts, when they cannot issue a license or identification document without confirming someone's status, they will inevitably issue some licenses to people who should not have them, and deny licenses to others who are entitled to them. In addition to harming security by making it harder for law enforcement to find and identify people, such a policy will inevitably lead to an increase in lawsuits brought by people who are entitled to have a license but are wrongfully denied one. Given the level of misinformation in some immigrant communities, it is also highly likely that fewer migrants will apply for a license, even if they are legally entitled to them.

A policy of denying licenses and state identification documents to illegal migrants will inevitably hurt law enforcement. A multitude of state, local, and federal law enforcement agencies access this data on a daily basis to investigate crimes, track down suspects, and prove crimes.[11] Immigration

---

8. In states that have instituted policies to bar licenses to illegal immigrants, the incidence of DMV employees selling licenses to unauthorized persons has increased significantly. * * *

11. Law enforcement agencies that rely on DMV databases daily include the US Department of State; the US Department of Justice; the US Department of Homeland Security; the Postal Inspection Service; the Department of Defense; the US Secret Service;

enforcement authorities rely on this data heavily. For example, driver license data is frequently used to prosecute illegal immigrants for such things as criminal reentry after deportation. DMV data is also used to confirm aliens' eligibility for government benefits, as when an alien must prove that he was present in the United States at a particular point in time. * * *

Here are five myths about driver licenses and security:

Myth #1: Terrorists can't get on airplanes if they don't have drivers licenses.

Reality: A potential terrorist could get on an airplane today using a wide variety of government-issued identification documents, including a US or foreign passport.

Myth #2: The 9/11 terrorists were able to obtain a total of 63 drivers licenses between them.

Reality: According to a Staff Report of the 9/11Commission, the 19 hijackers had 13 driver licenses. * * * One hijacker had neither a state ID nor a drivers license, and he boarded his target airplane with his foreign passport. It is important to note that information from the driver license records of the hijackers was invaluable after 9/11 in tracking where the terrorists had been in the United States and with whom they had associated. This information was also used to prosecute many individuals who would not have been discovered otherwise.

Myth #3: Our illegal immigrant problem will be solved if we just deny driver licenses to people who can't prove that they are lawfully in the United States.

Reality: Illegal immigrants do not leave the United States because they cannot get a driver license.

Myth #4: It's easy for state DMVs to determine whether someone is legal or illegal.

Reality: It's difficult even for DHS to tell whether someone is legal or illegal at any given moment. Immigration law is extremely complicated, and immigration status is a moving target. A person can be legal one day and illegal the next; illegal one day and legal the next. DHS often tries to deport US citizens under the mistaken belief that these US citizens are illegal immigrants. If DHS can't figure out whether someone is a citizen or an alien, or whether someone is legal or illegal, how is a state DMV employee going to do so?

Myth #5: Denying driver licenses to illegal immigrants will improve our national security.

the Department of the Army; the US Coast Guard; the National Center for Missing and Exploited Children; the Department of the Interior; the Veterans Administration; the National Insurance Crime Bureau; the Federal Protective Service; the Royal Canadian Mounted Police; Amtrak; and many others. * * *

Reality: Denying drivers licenses to illegal immigrants will hurt our national security by depriving law enforcement officials of critical information on substantial numbers of adults who are physically present in the United States. Law enforcement officials will be less able to find persons who may be security threats, and will have less information with which to prevent and solve crimes. When a terrorist incident happens, it will be harder afterwards to determine what happened, and when.

* * *

QUESTIONS

1. As discussed above, one provision of the REAL ID Act, section 202(d)(11), allows states to issue drivers' licenses or identification cards that do not comply with the requirements in the Act, but only if the documents are specially color-coded and display warnings that they may not be used for federal identification purposes. If a state offers that option, do you think its undocumented residents are likely to apply for such documents? What would be the strategic considerations for the applicants?

2. How would you expect this law to affect noncitizen terrorists (a) if they are in valid immigration status; and (b) if they are not?

3. Now that you have studied the various immigrant and nonimmigrant statuses, how easy do you think it will be for state DMV employees to decide which drivers' license applicants are in lawful immigration status and, for those who are, the durations of their authorized stays?

CHAPTER 13

CITIZENSHIP

You probably haven't thought much about citizenship since taking civics and social studies in grade school. After all these years, it might feel strange to come to law school and spend class time on "what citizenship means to me." But the law of citizenship, in addition to being a crucial part of the immigration lawyer's work, is at the heart of modern debates about personal autonomy, nationhood, membership, pluralism, and the nature of individual and collective responsibility.

Canadian Nobel Laureate Gerhard Herzberg once said, "A citizen is nothing more than an immigrant with seniority." Inscription on the Pier 21 Tribute to Immigrants, Halifax, Nova Scotia. U.S. President Franklin Delano Roosevelt, speaking at a meeting of the Daughters of the American Revolution, expressed a similar sentiment when he greeted his audience with the words "My fellow immigrants."

Here is what an even more authoritative source has to say on the subject:

> And if a stranger sojourn with thee in your land, ye shall not vex him.
>
> *But the stranger that dwelleth with you shall be unto you as one born among you,* and thou shalt love him as thyself; for ye were strangers in the land of Egypt: I am the Lord your God.

The Holy Bible, Leviticus, ch. 19, verses 33–34 (authorized King James version) (emphasis added).

Despite the italicized words, the laws of the United States—like those of other countries—do not treat the "stranger" who lives among us the same as the native-born citizen. As you have seen throughout this book, immigration restrictions apply only to noncitizens. To be sure, those laws can profoundly affect the lives of citizens, both individually and collectively. And certain provisions, including many of the offenses examined in chapter 12, regulate citizens directly. But the immigration laws do not, and constitutionally cannot, restrict the movement of citizens. See *Mathews v. Diaz*, 426 U.S. 67, 80, 96 S.Ct. 1883, 48 L.Ed.2d 478 (1976).

Nor are the legal distinctions between citizens and noncitizens confined to migration. Both the federal and state governments regulate the lives of noncitizens while they remain in the United States. As you will see presently, noncitizens are subject to various legal disabilities not imposed on citizens.

Should our law treat noncitizens who reside among us as well as it treats citizens? Or is the Biblical view outdated?

Before taking on that ponderous question, you should be aware of one technical point. In addition to citizens and "aliens," United States law recognizes a third category of persons—noncitizen nationals. Neither "citizens" nor "aliens," see INA § 101(a)(3),[1] this small group today consists mainly of those born in American Samoa and Swains Island. See INA §§ 308(1) (persons born in "outlying possessions" of United States), 101(a)(29) (defining "outlying possessions" as American Samoa and Swains Island). Except for their more limited capacity to help transmit United States citizenship to their children, compare INA §§ 301, 308, noncitizen nationals now have virtually the same rights as citizens. The inadmissibility and deportability grounds, for example, refer only to "aliens," see INA §§ 212(a), 237(a); thus, noncitizen nationals are free from immigration controls. Because so few nationals are noncitizens, and because at any rate the rights of noncitizen nationals differ so slightly from those of citizens, it is common for courts and commentators to use the terms "citizen" and "national" as if they were interchangeable. For the same reasons, this chapter will say nothing more about noncitizen nationals and will confine its remaining focus to the differences between citizens and "aliens."

In doing so, this chapter will address two broad subjects—the rules for attaining (and keeping) citizenship and the importance of citizenship. From a normative standpoint, these subjects raise mutually dependent issues. Whether important legal rights and obligations should turn on citizenship depends on what one has to do to *be* a citizen. Conversely, what the rules for becoming and remaining a citizen ought to be depends on the consequences of citizenship. There is no obvious escape from this chicken-and-egg problem, but we have to start somewhere. Thus the first two sections will examine, both descriptively and normatively, the substantive criteria and procedures for acquiring citizenship (section A) and for losing it (section B). Section C will then describe the existing legal consequences of citizenship and explore whether citizenship *ought* to have significant legal effects.

SECTION A. ACQUIRING CITIZENSHIP[2]

Long before the enactment of permanent federal laws restricting immigration, Congress passed the nation's first citizenship statute. Act of March 26, 1790, ch. 3, 1 Stat. 103. Today numerous paths to United States citizenship are available. They can be organized under two headings, differentiated solely by timing—citizenship acquired at birth and citizenship acquired at some later time.

---

1. This provision defines the word "alien" as "any person not a citizen or national of the United States." The reference to "citizen" is redundant because, under INA § 101(a)(22), citizens are a subset of nationals.

2. See generally 7 Gordon, Mailman & Yale–Loehr, chs. 91–98.

1. CITIZENSHIP ACQUIRED AT BIRTH

Throughout the world, two venerable principles have accorded citizenship at the moment of birth. As proof that these principles are venerable, they have Latin names. One is *jus soli,* literally "right of the land." Traditionally associated with the English common law and historically rooted in feudalism, the *jus soli* principle generally confers a nation's citizenship on persons born within that nation's territory. The other principle is *jus sanguinis.* This means "right of the blood." Long associated with European and other civil law systems, *jus sanguinis* generally bestows a nation's citizenship on the children of its existing citizens, regardless of where the children were born. Sometimes *jus sanguinis* is called "citizenship by descent." Today, as is true in most countries, see 7 Gordon, Mailman & Yale–Loehr, § 91.02[2], United States law combines both basic principles.

a. JUS SOLI

Until the Declaration of Independence the residents of the original thirteen colonies were British subjects. When independence was declared, each inhabitant who did not affirmatively choose to retain British nationality became a citizen of the particular state in which he or she lived. Upon the ratification of the Constitution, the citizens of the individual states all became citizens of the United States. As new states were admitted, the pertinent enactments generally made similar provision for designated inhabitants. See generally 7 Gordon, Mailman & Yale–Loehr, § 92.02.

But what about those who would later be born in the United States? Neither the original Constitution nor the 1790 Act said whether they would become citizens at birth. The Constitution did attach several consequences to citizenship and did require also that the President be not merely a citizen but a "natural born citizen." Nowhere, however, did the original Constitution say who the citizens are,[3] and nowhere does even the amended Constitution explain what "natural born" means. See Charles Gordon, *Who Can Be President of the United States: The Unresolved Enigma,* 28 Maryland L. Rev. 1 (1968). The term "natural born" clearly includes those born in the United States and clearly excludes those who acquired their citizenship by naturalization, but the status of those who were born overseas and inherited U.S. citizenship from their parents is not clear. *Id.* (In recent years there has been talk, fueled largely by the possible future presidential candidacy of Arnold Schwarzenneger, of amending the Constitution to delete the "natural-born" requirement.)

Perhaps these omissions by the framers were deliberate attempts to avoid such controversial issues as the status of the slaves and the relation between state citizenship and federal citizenship. See *Rogers v. Bellei,* 401 U.S. 815, 829, 91 S.Ct. 1060, 1068, 28 L.Ed.2d 499, 508 (1971); Charles

---

3. But see U.S. Const. art. 1, § 8, cl. 4 (Congress may establish "uniform Rule of Naturalization").

Gordon, *The Citizen and the State: Power of Congress to Expatriate American Citizens,* 53 Georgetown L. Rev. 315, 318 (1965). Whatever the explanation, it was widely assumed, consistently with the English common law principle of *jus soli,* that persons born in the United States would generally acquire citizenship at birth. 7 Gordon, Mailman & Yale–Loehr, § 92.03[1][b].

The citizenship of the slaves could not be put off forever. Dred Scott, a slave, sued in federal court for his freedom. Federal jurisdiction hinged on whether Scott was a "citizen" of the State of Missouri. The Supreme Court, in *Scott v. Sandford,* 60 U.S. (19 How.) 393, 15 L.Ed. 691 (1856), held that neither slaves nor the free descendants of slaves were "citizens" within the framers' understanding of that term.

The aftermath of the Civil War included three constitutional amendments intended in principal part to foster racial equality. The Thirteenth Amendment abolished slavery. The Fifteenth Amendment prohibited the denial of the vote on racial grounds. The Fourteenth Amendment did a number of things. Section 1, which includes both the due process clause and the equal protection clause, also responded specifically to the holding of *Dred Scott:*

> All persons born or naturalized in the United States, and subject to the jurisdiction thereof, are citizens of the United States and of the State wherein they reside.

That constitutional command has been codified into the statutory law. See INA § 301(a).

There was no doubt that the Fourteenth Amendment enabled African–Americans born in the United States to acquire citizenship at birth. The applicability of the Fourteenth Amendment to certain other groups was not so clear. The ambiguity lay in the qualifying phrase "subject to the jurisdiction thereof." In *Elk v. Wilkins,* 112 U.S. 94, 5 S.Ct. 41, 28 L.Ed. 643 (1884), the Supreme Court held that an Indian born in the United States but within tribal authority was not born "subject to the jurisdiction" of the United States and thus did not acquire United States citizenship at birth. (Nor would such a person attain citizenship later by leaving Indian territory and severing all relations with the tribe, although his or her children, if born in the United States outside Indian territory, presumably would acquire United States citizenship at birth.) By subsequent *statute,* "a person born in the United States to a member of an Indian, Eskimo, Aleutian, or other aboriginal tribe" now becomes a United States citizen at the moment of birth, INA § 301(b), but under *Elk* that statutory grant is not constitutionally compelled.

The last several decades of the nineteenth century saw significant immigration from China. As described earlier, see pages 115–18 above, both federal and state action discriminating against the Chinese, and eventually against Asians generally, became commonplace. Among those efforts were various statutes that generally made non-whites (interpreted to include Asians) ineligible for naturalization. You will see more on that subject shortly. One specific issue was whether a person born in the United States would become a citizen if his or her parents were LPRs who were themselves racially ineligible for naturalization. In *United States v. Wong Kim Ark*, 169 U.S. 649, 18 S.Ct. 456, 42 L.Ed. 890 (1898), the Supreme Court answered that question in the affirmative. More broadly, the Court added in dictum that the real purpose of the phrase "subject to the jurisdiction thereof" was

> to exclude * * * [besides Indians] the two classes of cases,— children born of alien enemies in hostile occupation, and children of diplomatic representatives of a foreign state—both of which * * * had been recognized exceptions to the fundamental rule of citizenship by birth within the country.

169 U.S. at 682, 18 S.Ct. at 469, 42 L.Ed. at 902.

As the years passed, that narrow reading of "subject to the jurisdiction thereof" became generally noncontroversial. It remained so until the publication of Peter H. Schuck & Rogers M. Smith, Citizenship Without Consent—Illegal Aliens in the American Polity (1985), in which the authors argued that the phrase should be reinterpreted to permit Congress to withhold citizenship from the United States-born children of noncitizens who were not LPRs. In the early 1990's, a serious movement to amend the Constitution to eliminate birthright citizenship for the children of undocumented migrants began to build. That subject is taken up on pages 1309–10 below.

One technical point on *jus soli:* The Fourteenth Amendment does not define the phrase "United States," and issues have sometimes arisen concerning birth in territorial possessions. The current statute makes clear that persons born in Puerto Rico, Guam, and the United States Virgin Islands are United States citizens. INA § 101(a)(38). The only territorial possessions in which birth does not confer United States citizenship are American Samoa and Swains Island; as mentioned earlier, persons born there become noncitizen nationals. INA §§ 101(a)(29), 308(1).

b.   JUS SANGUINIS

The Constitution has never mandated citizenship by descent, but the concept has been part of United States statutory law since 1790. See Act of March 26, 1790, ch. 3, 1 Stat. 103–04. The precise requirements have changed frequently over the years.

As you will soon see, citizenship by descent requires that one or both parents be citizens at the time of the child's birth. The law does not differentiate according to the method by which the parent(s) acquired citizenship. Consequently, one who acquires citizenship by descent can in turn pass such citizenship to his or her child, who can then pass it on to his or her child, and so on. If there were no restrictions, United States citizenship could thus be transmitted to successive generations in perpetuity, even if none of the recent descendants had ever set foot in the United States.

To prevent those results, Congress has attached two kinds of limits. First, it has generally insisted that the citizen parent(s) meet some specified residence or physical presence requirement in the United States before the child's birth. Second, at various times Congress has imposed conditions subsequent, also known as "retention requirements," decreeing that citizenship by descent terminates automatically if the child does not come to the United States and remain for a certain number of years between certain specified ages. In 1978 Congress abolished the retention requirement, but not retroactively; thus, people who had already lost citizenship by descent for failure to reside in the United States for the applicable periods did not benefit from the change. Act of Oct. 10, 1978, Pub.L. 95–432, § 1, 92 Stat. 1046. In 1994, however, Congress enacted legislation permitting anyone who had lost his or her citizenship because of the retention requirement (except for certain people ineligible on ideological grounds, see INA § 313) to regain citizenship simply by taking an oath of allegiance to the United States. See INA § 324(d), added by Pub.L. 103–416, § 103(a), 108 Stat. 4305, 4307–08 (Oct. 25, 1994).

The current provisions contain requirements concerning the parent's residence or physical presence but no longer impose any condition subsequent on the child. The two main provisions are INA §§ 301(c) and 301(g). The former subsection sets out the required elements of citizenship by descent when the child was born abroad to two United States citizen parents; the latter applies when the child was born abroad to one citizen parent and one noncitizen parent. You should now read both subsections in full.

Probably the greatest source of complexity in the descent laws is that the various statutory amendments have been given little retroactive effect. The descent law that was in force at the time of one's birth ordinarily determines whether one acquired citizenship by descent. Under that law, in turn, the claim often hinges on whether the claimant's *parent* was a citizen at the time of the claimant's birth. Unless the parent's citizenship changed, therefore, the claimant's citizenship might hinge on the law that had been in effect at the time of that *parent's* birth. Thus, the lawyer who seeks to ascertain a client's citizenship must sometimes consult laws that were repealed several decades ago.

One immigration attorney, Robert Mautino, has written a useful article describing how repealed citizenship laws continue to affect modern-day clients. Robert A. Mautino, *Acquisition of Citizenship*, Immigration Briefings (April 1990). After summarizing in tabular form the requirements for citizenship by descent for children born in wedlock during various time periods,[4] Mr. Mautino presents a series of fact Problems based on actual cases he has handled. Some of those Problems are reproduced below in the forms in which they appear in Mautino's article, with occasional modifications noted. Refer to his chart as you work through the Problems. In doing

---

4. An analogous table summarizes the statutory changes affecting children born out of wedlock. See *id.*, Chart 2, at 6.

so, assume you are the immigration lawyer and look for ways to establish the client's United States citizenship. Failing that, see whether anyone else's United States citizenship might be a basis for the client's admission as an LPR on family grounds.

Robert A. Mautino, **Acquisition of Citizenship**

Immigration Briefings (April 1990), pp. 5, 8, 12–13.

* * *

Date of Birth of Child	Residence Required of Parent(s) to Transmit Citizenship	Residence Required of Child to Retain Citizenship
Before 5/24/34	[Parent] is citizen who resided in U.S. before birth.	None
On or after 5/24/34 and before 1/13/41	a. Both parents are citizens, one with prior residence.	None
	b. One parent is citizen with prior residence.	Same as immediately below
On or after 1/13/41 and before 12/24/52	a. One parent is citizen with 10 years of prior residence in U.S., at least 5 of which were after age 16.	2 years continuous presence in U.S. between ages 14-28, except no retention requirement if born on or after 10/10/52.
	b. Both parents are citizens, one with prior residence in U.S.	None
On or after 12/24/52	a. Both parents are citizens, one with prior residence in U.S.	None
	b. One citizen parent with 10 years of prior physical presence in U.S., at least 5 of which were after age 14 (for births 12/24/52 to 11/13/86) or One citizen parent with 5 years of prior physical presence in U.S., at least 2 of which were after age 14 (for births on or after 11/14/86).	None. The retention requirement was abolished effective 10/10/78. Persons still citizens on that date have no retention requirements.

[In this chart, all references to "prior" residence or physical presence mean residence or physical presence prior to the birth of the citizenship claimant.—Ed.]

PROBLEMS 1–3[5]

Problem 1. Frank Alvarez and his sister Maria have just come to your office on a passport matter. Frank was denied a passport by the State Department's Passport Agency in Los Angeles, and he does not understand why—he has always considered himself a U.S. citizen. * * * You question Frank and Maria about their ancestry and learn the following facts. Frank was born in Mexico on May 3, 1941. Maria was born in Mexico on June 25, 1934. Their mother was born in the U.S. in 1917, and she is still a U.S. citizen. The mother went to Mexico in 1933 where she married their father and where she resided until 1942. At that time, she separated from the father and took the children to the U.S. where [Frank has] since resided. [Maria returned to Mexico on December 20, 1949 to stay with her father. She came back to the United States on December 20, 1960 and has lived here ever since.][a] The father was born in Mexico in 1913. However, his father (their paternal grandfather) was born in [the United States][b] in 1867. He moved to Mexico in 1875 and resided there for the rest of his life. The paternal grandmother was born in [the United States] in 1870 and moved to Mexico in 1876. * * *

[First, is either Frank or Maria a United States citizen? Second, try to figure out what assumptions the Passport Office probably made and why those assumptions might have prompted it to deny a passport to Frank. Third, on those same assumptions, do you think the Passport Office would have issued a passport to Maria?]

* * *

Problem 2. Guillermo Schmidt, a Mexican citizen, was referred by a lawyer who was handling his business arrangements. Guillermo wanted to open a business in the communications field in the Los Angeles area. Included in his plans was the possible purchase of a Spanish-language radio station plus other similar investments. Guillermo came to us to see how he could arrange his immigration status to accomplish his business objectives. He was ready to present us with a pound or two of business and financial documents, but we first asked him questions about his ancestors. We learned the following.

Guillermo was born in Mexico in 1937. He had been in the U.S. on countless occasions, but apart from two years when he attended high school in Michigan he never lived in the U.S. His father was born in northwestern Mexico in 1901, and his mother was born in central Mexico. His paternal grandfather was born in New York in 1850, but he lived most of his youth in Sacramento and San Francisco, California. When the paternal grandfa-

---

5. Problems 1–3 are modifications of Mautino's Problems 1, 9, and 10, respectively.

a. The bracketed sentences were added by the editor and are fictitious.—Ed.

b. The original Problem, as it appears in *Immigration Briefings,* states that the pa-

ternal grandfather was born in New Mexico. That fact has been deleted here in order to eliminate complications concerning the effect of birth in a place that had not yet achieved, but soon would achieve, statehood.—Ed.

ther married a Mexican national in 1890, his family disavowed him, and he moved with his wife to northern Mexico where he worked in the mining business. The paternal grandfather died suddenly in 1905, leaving his wife with five small children and one on the way. The wife then moved to the town of Nogales, Arizona, where she raised her children. She lived in Nogales the rest of her life, and died there in 1940.

* * *

Problem 3.[c] In 1988 David contacted our office. * * * [H]e wanted to apply for permanent residence. [He and his wife, Mary, had spent their entire lives in Canada. Mary is there now, and David is here in the United States on a temporary work visa. Mary's paternal great-grandfather was born in Pennsylvania in 1842 and moved to Canada as a small child. His son (Mary's paternal grandfather) was born in Canada, where he remained his entire life except for a three-year stay in the United States from 1889 to 1892. In 1930 Mary's father was born, also in Canada. Mary was born in Canada in 1953. In 1975, Mary's parents left Canada for the first time ever and moved permanently to the United States, where they continue to reside. What advice would you give David?]

JUS SANGUINIS AND THE CONSTITUTION

As noted earlier, nothing in the Constitution mandates citizenship by descent. That doesn't mean that Congress is constitutionally free to subject citizenship by descent to any conditions it wishes. But what are the limits?

These questions arose in *Rogers v. Bellei,* 401 U.S. 815, 91 S.Ct. 1060, 28 L.Ed.2d 499 (1971). Bellei, born abroad, had acquired United States citizenship at birth by virtue of having one United States citizen parent who had resided for a specified period in the United States before Bellei's birth. The applicable statute, however, provided that Bellei would eventually lose his citizenship if he himself did not reside continuously in the United States for certain lengths of time between certain ages. Having failed to meet that condition subsequent, he argued it violated, among other provisions, both fifth amendment due process and the constitutional dictate that "[a]ll persons born or naturalized in the United States, and subject to the jurisdiction thereof, are citizens of the United States * * *." U.S. Const. amend. XIV, § 1.

The Supreme Court upheld the statute by a 5–4 vote. The Court assumed, first, that Congress's power to confer citizenship by descent was part of its constitutionally delegated power to "establish an uniform Rule of Naturalization." U.S. Const. art. I, § 8, cl. 4. To support that assumption, the Court observed that "[t]he very first Congress * * * implement[ed] its power [under the naturalization clause], by producing the [1790] Act," which included a grant of citizenship by descent. 401 U.S. at 823, 91 S.Ct. at 1065, 28 L.Ed.2d at 505. (Note this interpretation of "naturalization" is

c. This Problem has been both substantively modified and paraphrased.—Ed.

broader than the present statutory definition, which is limited to nationality conferred "after birth." INA § 101(a)(23)).

Still, the Court held, Bellei was naturalized abroad, not "in the United States" as the Fourteenth Amendment citizenship clause requires. 401 U.S. at 827, 91 S.Ct. at 1067, 28 L.Ed.2d at 507. Thus, nothing in that clause required Congress to make his citizenship permanent. The dissenters argued that "born or naturalized in the United States" means "born in the United States or naturalized by the laws thereof," citing an earlier draft of the citizenship clause. 401 U.S. at 843, 91 S.Ct. at 1075, 28 L.Ed.2d at 516–17.

Having generally approved the use of statutory conditions subsequent, the Court had to assess "the constitutionality" of this particular condition subsequent. 401 U.S. at 831, 91 S.Ct. at 1069, 28 L.Ed.2d at 510. (The Court did not specify which constitutional limitation it was interpreting, but substantive due process is a good bet.) The Court assumed without explanation that the constitutional test was whether the condition was "unreasonable, arbitrary or unlawful." *Id.* Citing Congress's concern with the problems of dual citizenship (see section A.3 below), the Court then held that the subsequent residence condition met the constitutional test.

Several cases have raised questions concerning the constitutionality of gender-based classifications in provisions that confer citizenship by descent. By statute, individuals who were born outside the United States before 1934 could derive citizenship from their citizen fathers but not from their citizen mothers. See generally 7 Gordon, Mailman & Yale–Loehr, § 93.02[4]. In *Villanueva–Jurado v. INS,* 482 F.2d 886 (5th Cir.1973), the government brought deportation proceedings against a person who had been born abroad, before 1934, to a United States citizen mother and a noncitizen father. The respondent claimed citizenship, arguing the statutory distinction was "invidious" and therefore unconstitutional, presumably based on the fifth amendment due process equivalent of equal protection. Citing *Bellei,* the respondent argued that the court should at least inquire whether the distinction was "unreasonable, arbitrary, or unlawful." The court refused. It observed that an "alien has no constitutional right to citizenship which is a privilege conferred as a matter of grace by Congress * * *." *Id.* at 887. It added that "Congress has a completely free hand in defining citizenship as it relates to persons born abroad." *Id.* The court distinguished *Bellei* as concerned solely with conditions subsequent rather than conditions precedent. *Id.* at 887–88.

In *Elias v. United States Dept. of State,* 721 F.Supp. 243 (N.D.Cal. 1989), a district court took the opposite view. The plaintiff, also born abroad before 1934 to a citizen mother and a noncitizen father, applied for a United States passport. The State Department denied it on the ground that under the applicable statute she was not a United States citizen. She made two distinct equal protection arguments—that the gender classification violated her own right to equal protection, and that it violated her mother's right to equal protection by allowing men but not women to transmit citizenship to their children.

The court declined to address the plaintiff's first argument. It acknowledged that constitutional review of "immigration" legislation was limited but suggested that even under a narrow standard of review the plaintiff's first argument was "plausible" and that a court might disapprove the rationale of *Villanueva–Jurado.* The court preferred, however, to rest its decision on the plaintiff's second argument. After concluding she had standing to assert the equal protection rights of her deceased mother, the court turned to the merits. The government argued that the statute was essentially unreviewable, emphasizing first that there exists no constitutional right to transmit citizenship to one's children. The court pointed out that that fact does not avoid the need to obey the commands of equal protection when the government elects to permit the transmission of citizenship. *Id.* at 247–48.

The government then argued that the principle of plenary congressional power over immigration, which you studied in chapter 2, prohibited "judicial reevaluation" of this statute. *Id.* at 247. Citing *Kleindienst v. Mandel,* 408 U.S. 753, 92 S.Ct. 2576, 33 L.Ed.2d 683 (1972) (discussed on pages 179–80 above), the court held that, when *United States citizens* are affected by "immigration legislation," the government must show "at least a facially legitimate and bona fide reason for its action." 721 F.Supp. at 248.

Applying that test, the court in *Elias* noted the government had offered "no rationale at all" to support the statutory distinction. *Id.* at 249. Emphasizing also the "suspect" nature of the class (actually gender classifications have generally been held to trigger only intermediate scrutiny rather than the strict scrutiny applicable to suspect classes) and the important individual interest in family living arrangements, the court held the statutory discrimination against women unconstitutional.

Despite the decision, the State Department, quite concerned to establish that passport issuance is solely a Department prerogative, announced it would continue to deny passports in *Elias*-type fact situations and eventually to litigate the issue in another court. See Gary Endelman, *Mother Knows Best: A New Look at an Old Law,* 13 Immigration J. 29, 30 (Apr.–June 1990). Ultimately, the Department did not get its way. After another court followed *Elias,* see *Wauchope v. USDOS,* 985 F.2d 1407 (9th Cir. 1993), Congress in 1994 granted citizenship to people who had been born before 1934 to United States citizen mothers. See INA § 301(h).

Even in *Elias,* the court characterized the *jus sanguinis* provision as "immigration legislation" and therefore subject to exceptionally limited review for constitutionality. And the availability of even that limited review seemed to rest on the court's conclusion that the rights of *United States citizens* (there, the plaintiff's mother) were adversely affected. That the classification was disfavored might also have contributed to the result. Do you think the arguments for exceptional deference to Congress on matters concerning admission and expulsion apply with equal force to matters that concern citizenship? In framing your answer, consider the various theories of special deference that you encountered in chapter 2. See also *Price v.*

INS, 962 F.2d 836 (9th Cir.1991) (amended opinion) (displaying similar deference).

Gender discrimination in citizenship by descent has triggered other equal protection issues in recent years. INA § 309(a) has been especially difficult. It grants citizenship by descent to children born out of wedlock to United States citizen mothers, but not to children born out of wedlock to United States citizen fathers unless additional hurdles are cleared. The additional requirements in the father cases include a showing of biological parentage by "clear and convincing evidence" and further requirements concerning, among other things, parental financial responsibility. In numerous cases either the children or the fathers have challenged this statutory classification on equal protection grounds, observing that none of these requirements are imposed when an out-of-wedlock child claims citizenship through his or her mother. In *Miller v. Albright,* 523 U.S. 420, 118 S.Ct. 1428, 140 L.Ed.2d 575 (1998), a fractured Supreme Court was unable to forge a majority position. For a thoughtful critique, see Linda Kelly, *The Alienation of Fathers,* 6 Michigan J. Race & L. 181 (2000). Three years later, however, in *Nguyen v. INS,* 533 U.S. 53, 121 S.Ct. 2053, 150 L.Ed.2d 115 (2001), the Supreme Court upheld the constitutionality of section 309(a) by a vote of 5–4. As discussed on pages 175–76 above, the majority in *Nguyen* concluded that the statute withstood even the intermediate level of scrutiny generally applicable to gender-based classifications. Thus, the Court said, it was unnecessary to decide whether citizenship provisions warrant the exceptional deference to Congress that the plenary power doctrine prescribes for immigration statutes. See M. Isabel Medina, *Real Differences and Stereotypes—Two Visions of Gender, Citizenship, and International Law,* 7 N.Y. City L.Rev. 315 (2004).

2. CITIZENSHIP ACQUIRED AFTER BIRTH

The United States Constitution authorizes Congress to "establish an uniform Rule of Naturalization." U.S. Const. art. I, § 8, cl. 4.[6] The word "naturalization" usually conjures up heartwarming images of courtroom scenes in which judges confer citizenship on proud and thankful immigrants. That type of naturalization, which until 1990 required the applicant to complete an administrative agency process and then to appear in court, has been by far both the most common and the most familiar form of naturalization. In everyday parlance the word "naturalization" is typically used to describe that particular process.

For two reasons, however, that depiction is not entirely accurate. First, the Immigration Act of 1990, § 401, amending INA § 310(a), transferred from the courts to the Attorney General (now the Secretary of Homeland Security, delegated to USCIS) the authority to grant naturalization. The

---

6. The word "uniform" was inserted to prohibit the kinds of state-by-state variations that had been in force before ratification of the Constitution—not to prohibit other distinctions Congress might wish to draw. See generally 7 Gordon, Mailman & Yale–Loehr, § 94.01[1].

judicial role has not been entirely eliminated, however, since the applicant may elect, and in many cases may be required, to take the final oath in court. In addition, the courts have jurisdiction to review naturalization denials de novo. See INA §§ 310(b, c). The procedures are discussed in section A.2.a.ii below in more detail.

Second, the technical meaning of "naturalization" is nationality conferred after birth. See INA § 101(a)(23). Several miscellaneous laws that award nationality (which normally includes citizenship) after birth, therefore, are also forms of naturalization. To make the distinction, the immigration literature used to use the phrase "judicial naturalization" to describe the familiar type of naturalization discussed above. In the light of the 1990 amendments, a more appropriate name is "administrative naturalization," see Imm. Act 1990, § 401, and that term will be used here. The bulk of the coverage in this section will address the substantive criteria and procedures for receiving administrative naturalization. The other miscellaneous processes will be mentioned briefly below.

a. ADMINISTRATIVE NATURALIZATION

Congress wasted little time in enacting a naturalization statute. The Act of March 26, 1790, ch. 3, 1 Stat. 103–04, made eligible any applicant who was free, white (amended after the Civil War to add African–Americans), resident at least two years in the United States and at least one year in the state in which he or she applied, and of good moral character. The person had only to apply to "any common law court of record," prove the necessary facts, and take an oath of allegiance to the United States. *Id.* Since then the substantive requirements have frequently been either tightened or loosened in response to changing national attitudes toward immigration generally. At the same time, the corresponding procedures became steadily more elaborate, at least until the 1990 reforms.

After a three-year period of rapid rise (roughly five years after the large number of legalizations to LPR status in 1990 and 1991 as a result of IRCA), naturalizations have reverted to pre–1995 levels. The chart below demonstrates how quickly the numbers can change:

Year	Petitions Filed	Persons Naturalized
1991	206,668	308,058
1992	342,269	240,252
1993	522,298	314,681
1994	543,353	434,107
1995	959,963	488,088
1996	1,277,403	1,044,689
1997	1,412,712	598,225
1998	932,957	463,060
1999	764,346	839,944
2000	460,916	888,788
2001	501,646	608,205
2002	700,649	573,708
2003	523,408	463,204

2003 Yearbook of Immigration Statistics, Table 31 at 137. (The differences between filings and naturalizations do not represent denials. USCIS cannot complete all applications in the fiscal years in which they are filed; thus, naturalizations include approvals of applications that were filed in prior years.)

Of concern to many is the fact that immigrants from different countries have markedly different inclinations to naturalize. Inclinations are complex to assess because there are long gaps between admission for permanent residence and naturalization—generally a five-year minimum under current law, see INA § 316(a), considered shortly. Among those people who were admitted as immigrants in 1977, about 41.5% had naturalized by September 30, 1993. Within that 1977 cohort, the naturalization percentages varied considerably by country of nationality. Immigrants and refugees from the Soviet Union and Asia were by far the most likely to have naturalized. Mexicans and Canadians were among the least likely, but Mexican naturalization rates have increased significantly since 1993, for reasons you will encounter in a moment. Here are some selected naturalization *rates* from the 1977 cohort:

Country of Nationality	Percentage Naturalized
Soviet Union	63.3
Philippines	62.0
China	60.9
Korea	55.8
India	53.7
Cuba	39.8
Haiti	38.2
United Kingdom	19.3
Mexico	17.6
Italy	16.7
Germany	14.7
Canada	14.5

INS 1994 Statistical Yearbook, Table K.

By 2001, the naturalization rate for Mexicans had risen to 34% (again, for reasons considered below), and the corresponding rates for those born in other Latin American countries ranged from 40% to 58%. Michael Fix, Jeffrey S. Passel, & Kenneth Sucher, *Trends in Naturalization*, 80 IR 1473, 1475 (Oct. 27, 2003). In 2003, Mexico was the leading country of birth among persons naturalizing, but the leading region of birth was Asia, with 42% of the total. 2003 Yearbook of Immigration Statistics at 134.

CITIZENSHIP USA

Jana Mason, U.S. Committee for Refugees, Citizenship Under Attack: Congress Investigates Motives Behind INS Initiative

17 Refugee Reports, No. 11, at 1–4 (Nov./Dec. 1996).

Motherhood, apple pie, and citizenship. It used to be that these three were invoked together, as unassailable symbols of what it meant to be American. Until recently, immigration and refugee advocates believed that no matter how much immigration came under attack * * * the effort to naturalize new Americans would be held harmless. After all, what could there be to criticize about the process by which persons who come to this country for reasons of family, work, or freedom become fully participating members of society? In an election year, advocates found out, there can be much to criticize.

* * *

The reasons for th[e] dramatic increase [in naturalization petitions] are several-fold.[a] Perhaps the most important is the large number of immigrants who legalized their status under a 1986 law and have thus become eligible for citizenship. In addition, many advocates believe that the recently enacted welfare and immigration reform laws are providing an extra incentive for persons to change their status from "permanent resident" to U.S. citizen. * * * [See section C of this chapter for more detail on the welfare reform legislation.—Ed.]

* * *

While the conventional wisdom is that the specific impact of these laws is spurring permanent residents to become citizens, some observers also say that many immigrants are reacting to an increasingly hostile anti-immigrant mood in general. * * *

The rush to naturalize, however, did not start with the passage of these bills. The 1986 law, refugee admissions,and other factors had led to steady increases in the number of citizenship applications filed during the past several years and created large backlogs in processing as well as delays in swearing in those approved. In many cities, applicants often waited for a year or longer for an INS interview and then, once approved, had to wait again to be sworn in as citizens. * * *

* * *

a. Observers generally share the views expressed in the excerpted article concerning the causes of the upsurge. In addition to those causes, however, one researcher suggests others—economic and political instability in Mexico, an INS program requiring LPRs to replace their green cards if they wish to remain, and community-based naturalization drives. Rob Paral, *Naturalization: New Demands and New Directions at the INS*, 72 IR 937, 937–39 (July 17, 1995).—Ed.

In an effort to respond to both the backlogs and the growing criticism by advocates who contended that the naturalization process was unnecessarily confusing and intimidating, INS in August 1995 initiated Citizenship USA, an effort to reduce the naturalization waiting periods significantly by increasing staff, enhancing technology, streamlining procedures, and using community-based organizations to assist applicants with each stage of the process. INS also began exploring additional changes such as a standardized oral interview.

Initially concentrating on the five cities that account for 75 percent of all citizenship applications, Citizenship USA resulted in unprecedented increases in the numbers of immigrants processed for citizenship and became viewed by some observers as one of the much-criticized agency's most successful initiatives. * * *

Congress Probes Initiative, Calls for Independent Counsel. As Citizenship USA progressed and as the election neared, several members of Congress expressed concerns that the effort to naturalize large numbers of immigrants was a Clinton Administration strategy to increase the number of registered Democrats going to the polls. At the same time, allegations began to surface about two aspects of the initiative that would become the subject of Congressional hearings.

First, the use of community-based agencies as testing centers for the citizenship exam came under attack. * * * Although each applicant must be interviewed by an INS examiner, at which time spoken English ability is assessed, the knowledge of written English and history/civics is demonstrated through a written test that can be taken either at an INS office or at an approved test center location. Many advocates believe that the ability to take the written test outside of INS offices reduces the anxiety of many immigrants. * * *

In early July, the television show 20/20 aired a story about a testing company that helped immigrants pass the naturalization exam through fraud. In particular, proctors were accused of giving immigrants the answers to questions. In response, Rep. Zeliff and other members of Congress charged that a number of test centers were likely responsible for fraud or at least lax security. * * * (Although the vast majority of test centers are nonprofit agencies, a few are not.)

The second and more explosive allegation was the charge that INS had naturalized persons without completing the process of FBI fingerprint checks, which reveals whether the immigrant is in the FBI database and may have been convicted of an offense that makes the immigrant ineligible to naturalize. (A database match does not necessarily mean a conviction, however, because anyone who has ever been fingerprinted and whose prints have been sent to the FBI would be in the database.)

These allegations, particularly those related to the fingerprint checks, led some members of Congress and groups such as the Federation for American Immigration Reform (FAIR), which wants immigration reduced, to charge that the INS, under direct orders from the White House, was intentionally rushing the naturalization process to get as many new immigrants as possible through the process before the election. Although reliable data on the voting preferences of new immigrants is unavailable, some observers had speculated that welfare reform and the general anti-immigrant mood would cause new citizen voters to "punish" those responsible.

These concerns were aired and defended at Capitol Hill hearings held by [Rep. Bill Zeliff (R–N.H.), Senator Alan Simpson (R–Wyoming)], and House immigration subcommittee Chair Lamar Smith (R–Tex.). * * *

* * * The results of the investigation have since yielded little hard data, with naturalization proponents and critics debating both the numbers and the significance of the FBI records. Zeliff wrote to the governors of six states with large immigrant populations, saying the FBI records confirmed his worst fears and including examples of "the most egregious" cases of criminal aliens. Immigration officials have countered that only a small number of immigrants with felony convictions have slipped through the cracks, and that not all technical felonies are "egregious." In her own letter to all 50 governors, INS Commissioner Doris Meissner said, "INS deports criminal aliens; we do not naturalize them."

* * *

On November 1, Zeliff and four fellow committee Republicans wrote to the Attorney General requesting the appointment of an independent counsel to investigate "criminal fraud and abuse" in Citizenship USA. The letter charged that the program was "corrupted by a reckless drive for political gain" in the upcoming elections.

* * * A month later, on December 4, Attorney General Reno denied the request for an independent counsel. In a letter addressed to Zeliff, the Justice Department said there is "no specific and credible evidence" that senior Administration officials covered by the Independent Counsel Act participated in criminal activity related to Citizenship USA. "To the extent that there are allegations of wrongdoing that may warrant criminal investigation," said the letter, "at this time they relate only to low-ranking officials and private companies" and do not present a conflict of interest for the Justice Department in investigating and prosecuting them. The letter noted that one prosecution has already occurred.

On the same day, the Justice Department and INS publicly announced new initiatives, some of which had already begun, to improve the naturalization process. * * *

* * *

———

The former INS, with quality assurance review by the EOIR, later studied the granted cases in which criminal issues were present. The GAO then reviewed both studies and reported its (minor) recommendations. See U.S. General Accounting Office, Naturalized Aliens: Efforts to Determine If

INS Improperly Naturalized Some Aliens, GAO/GGD–98–62 (March 1998). A subsequent investigation by the Justice Department's Inspector General found flaws in the naturalization process but no political motivations. The report is digested in 77 IR at 1198 (Aug. 21, 2000).

Post-election surveys revealed an irony. Republicans were accusing Democrats of seeking to naturalize people liberally and speedily out of a belief that naturalized voters were disproportionately likely to vote for President Clinton. Yet Republican Candidate Bob Dole ended up doing better among foreign-born voters (receiving 46%) than he did among native-born voters (receiving 42%). AILA, Immigration Policy Report No. 26 (1997) (citing CNN/Time exit poll). That study, of course, does not reveal how the candidates fared among *recently* naturalized voters.

One interesting recent study sought to learn more about what motivates people to apply for naturalization and what obstacles they encountered. The authors interviewed 526 LPRs living in Texas who had at least taken preliminary steps toward naturalization. The study found the most important motivations to be "perceptions of the life chances they, their children, and extended family members will have in the U.S. as compared to the country of origin or to those available to them as non-citizen permanent residents." Susan González-Baker, Luis F.B. Plascenia, Gary P. Freeman & Manuel Orozco, Tomás Rivera Institute, *The Making of Americans—Results of the Texas Naturalization Survey*, Policy Brief (Aug. 2000). Other considerations, such as welfare benefits and dissatisfaction with their home governments, were found to be only "minor" motivating factors. *Id.* Few obstacles were reported; the most significant was the English language requirement, *id*, discussed below.

i.   Substantive Criteria

As already noted, only a "free white person" could qualify for naturalization under the 1790 Act. Over time, statutes created limited exceptions to the racial disqualification. African–Americans were made eligible after the Civil War. Act of July 14, 1870, ch. 254, § 7, 16 Stat. 254, 256.

In the 1920's the Supreme Court rendered a series of decisions holding various groups to be nonwhite. See *Takao Ozawa v. United States,* 260 U.S. 178, 43 S.Ct. 65, 67 L.Ed. 199 (1922) (Japanese); *United States v. Thind,* 261 U.S. 204, 43 S.Ct. 338, 67 L.Ed. 616 (1923) (Hindus); *Toyota v. United States,* 268 U.S. 402, 410, 45 S.Ct. 563, 565, 69 L.Ed. 1016, 1019 (1925) (Filipinos). To express support for a World War II ally, Congress exempted the Chinese. Act of December 17, 1943, ch. 344, § 3, 57 Stat. 600, 601. The INA, enacted in 1952, finally abolished all racial restrictions on naturalization. INA § 311.

At one time women faced analogous statutory discrimination. On the theory that a husband and wife were one person (namely, the husband), and that they should therefore share the husband's nationality, women married to noncitizens were ineligible for naturalization. The Act of Sept.

22, 1922, ch. 411, § 1, 42 Stat. 1021–22, removed that bar, and the present statute expressly prohibits sex discrimination in naturalization. INA § 311.

Although detailed examination of all the current naturalization criteria is not possible here,[7] a sketch of the basic requirements is worthwhile:

(1) *Lawful permanent residence.* To become eligible for naturalization, one must first be "lawfully admitted to the United States for permanent residence in accordance with all applicable provisions of [the INA]." INA § 318. Obviously, this language disqualifies those who have been admitted only as nonimmigrants and those who have not been admitted at all. Perhaps less obviously, the word "lawfully" leaves out those who were admitted as LPRs on the basis of fraudulent documents or while otherwise inadmissible. See generally 7 Gordon, Mailman & Yale–Loehr, § 95.02[2][a]. INA § 318 also specifies that naturalization may not be conferred while removal proceedings are pending or while a final finding of deportability is outstanding.

(2) *Residence and Physical Presence.* The applicant must "reside" continuously in the United States during the five-year period immediately preceding the filing of the application, all *after* admission as an LPR; must be "physically present" in the United States for at least half that period; and must "reside" continuously in the United States from the filing of the application to the grant of naturalization. INA § 316(a).[8] Both five-year requirements become three-year requirements if the petitioner "has been living in marital union" with a United States citizen during the applicable three-year period. INA § 319(a). Other relaxations of these and other substantive requirements apply to children of United States citizens, INA § 322, and to certain applicants who have served in the United States military, INA § 328. The general residence and physical presence requirements raise some interesting issues that will be explored below.

(3) *Good Moral Character.* During all the periods for which residence and physical presence are required, the petitioner must demonstrate good moral character. INA § 316(a)(3). The meaning of the phrase "good moral character" was explored earlier in a different context. See page 604 above. As you might recall, the statute lists specific characteristics that automatically preclude a showing of good moral character but cautions that those preclusions are not exhaustive. INA § 101(f); see generally 7 Gordon, Mailman & Yale–Loehr, § 95.04[1].

(4) *Age.* Only those age 18 and older may apply for *administrative* naturalization. INA § 334(b). Children are often eligible for *derivative* naturalization, discussed below.

(5) *English Language.* The petitioner must generally demonstrate "an understanding of the English language, including an ability to read, write, and speak words in ordinary usage." INA § 312(a)(1). There are exceptions based on physical disability and on combinations of age and long-term

---

7. See generally 7 Gordon, Mailman & Yale–Loehr, ch. 95.

8. Periods of conditional residence under INA § 216 (applicable to certain immi-grants who achieve permanent residence through marriage) count as continuous resi-dence. INA § 216(e).

United States residence. *Id.* Do you approve of the English language requirement? What if the applicant intends to reside permanently in Puerto Rico? Professor Peter Spiro has advocated repealing this requirement. See Peter J. Spiro, *Questioning Barriers to Naturalization*, 13 Georgetown Immigration L.J. 479 (1999).

(6) *Knowledge of Civics.* Also required is "a knowledge and understanding of the fundamentals of the history, and of the principles and form of government, of the United States." INA § 312(a)(2). Professor Spiro similarly urged repealing this requirement. See Spiro, item 5 above.

(7) *Political Requirements.* In previous chapters you encountered the wide range of political beliefs, statements, and associations that render noncitizens inadmissible and, until 1990, deportable. See chapter 5, § B above (exclusion) and chapter 7, § E above (deportation). The 1990 reforms do not extend to naturalization. INA § 313 disqualifies all applicants who, either during the ten-year period immediately preceding the filing of the application or during the interval between the filing and the taking of the final oath of citizenship, fell within any of the several related classes. The ineligible classes include advocates of opposition to organized government, members of the Communist Party, see INA § 313(a)(1, 2), and several others.

In addition to the absence of political disqualifications, the petitioner must affirmatively demonstrate an attachment to the principles of the United States Constitution. INA § 316(a). Along the same lines, the petitioner must swear under oath that he or she supports the Constitution, renounces all foreign allegiances, will defend all federal laws against all enemies, will bear true allegiance to those laws, and, subject to certain conscientious objector exceptions, will bear arms for the United States if required by law. INA § 337(a); see generally 7 Gordon, Mailman & Yale–Loehr, § 95.04[2]. The words of the required oath are laid out in 8 C.F.R. § 337.1(a) (2004). As noted in the discussion of dual citizenship, section A.3 below, not all countries give effect to the renunciation portions of such oaths.

The citizenship oath contains some archaic language (e.g., references to foreign princes and potentates). In 2003 USCIS floated a proposal (not published in the Federal Register) for modernizing the language and for expressly recognizing the multiple options of promising to defend the Constitution by "military, noncombatant or civilian service." The proposal encountered fierce resistance from traditionalists and was quietly shelved. See Shweta Govindarajan, *Criticism Puts Citizenship Oath Revision on Hold*, L.A. Times (Sept. 18, 2003), at A13.

In Re Petition for Naturalization of Vafaei–Makhsoos

United States District Court, District of Minnesota, 1984.
597 F.Supp. 499.

■ MacLaughlin, District Judge.

* * *

The facts in this case are undisputed. Petitioner, a resident of Burnsville, Minnesota, was born in Iran on May 14, 1946 and is a citizen of that country. His last permanent address prior to coming to the United States was in Teheran, Iran. Petitioner entered the United States in June 1968 as a student. Petitioner's status was adjusted to that of lawful permanent resident alien, pursuant to INA § 245, on December 22, 1977.

Petitioner left the United States in July, 1978 and remained outside the country until May of 1979. He left the United States again on or about June 26, 1979 in order to attend his mother's funeral in Iran and to take care of related family matters. Petitioner was accompanied by his wife, a citizen of Iran, and their child, a United States citizen. The American Embassy in Teheran was taken over by pro-revolutionary students in November of 1979, and the Iranian government banned all travel to the United States during the ensuing hostage crisis. Petitioner was therefore unable to return to the United States until June 1, 1981, at which time the Iranian government had lifted the travel ban.

When the petitioner attempted to reenter the United States, the immigration inspector refused to admit him as a lawful permanent resident because his reentry permit had expired. Petitioner was admitted to the country under "parole status," which meant that he could physically enter the United States despite his failure to comply with the legal requirements for entry. INS subsequently began deportation proceedings against him. A hearing was held before an immigration judge on January 20, 1982 and July 21, 1982. The issue at this hearing was whether the petitioner had abandoned his lawful permanent resident status due to his absence. The immigration judge held that petitioner had not abandoned this status, and allowed petitioner to remain in the United States as a lawful permanent resident.

Petitioner filed the instant petition for naturalization on June 9, 1983.
* * *

The INS has recommended that the instant petition be denied because it is barred by section 316(b) of the Immigration and Nationality Act of 1952, as amended. That section provides, in pertinent part, that:

> Absence from the United States for a continuous period of one year or more during the period for which continuous residence is required for admission to citizenship (whether preceding or subsequent to the filing of the petition for naturalization) shall break the continuity of such residence. . . .

The period of continuous residence that is required for naturalization is five years; the petitioner must be physically present in the country for periods totaling at least half of that time. *Id.* § 316(a). The statutory bar in section 316(b) for those persons absent for more than one year provides exceptions only for individuals employed by the United States government, by an American corporation engaged in foreign trade, by a public international organization, or by an American research institution recognized by the Attorney General.

The petitioner in the instant case clearly falls within the language of section 316(b). Petitioner was outside of the United States for almost two years during the five year period preceding his naturalization petition. Moreover, he does not fall within one of the specific narrow exceptions to section 316(b). The issue raised by the instant petition is whether petitioner's involuntary absence constitutes "absence" within the meaning of section 316(b). The statutory language itself draws no distinction between voluntary and involuntary absences. Moreover, the INS correctly cites two decisions which have held that a voluntary departure from the United States, followed by an involuntary absence of more than one year, precludes naturalization. * * * There is no authority to the contrary.[2]

While the strict interpretation * * * yields a harsh result, the reasoning of these cases is persuasive. The statute provides for several specific exceptions to the one year absence rule; the involuntary character of the petitioner's absence is not included within these exceptions. The conclusion that Congress meant to erect an absolute bar in cases of absences greater than one year is strengthened by the fact that the statute specifically allows petitioners the opportunity to demonstrate that they did not abandon their United States residence in cases of shorter absences (from six months to one year). INA § 316(b). Finally, the * * * purpose of the five year continuous residence requirement * * * was presumably to ensure that petitioners for citizenship have been considerably exposed to American institutions. An exception for involuntary absences would undercut this purpose.

Petitioner's argument is essentially that since the immigration judge has found that petitioner did not abandon his lawful permanent residence status due to the time he spent in Iran, this period should not be considered as an absence for the purposes of naturalization. This argument is without merit. The issues before the immigration judge at petitioner's deportation hearing are entirely distinct from the issue presently before the Court in connection with the instant petition for naturalization. At the deportation hearing, the critical issues were whether petitioner intended to abandon his permanent resident status when he left for Iran and whether he had a valid excuse for his failure to secure valid reentry documents. The immigration judge accepted petitioner's arguments that he did not intend to abandon his status because he planned only a temporary visit, and that the takeover of the United States Embassy constituted sufficient justification for his lack of reentry documents. The above determinations, which are highly relevant to the question of deportability, simply have nothing to do with whether petitioner has met the statutory requirements for naturalized citizenship.

2. In *In re Yarina*, 73 F. Supp. 688 (N.D. Ohio 1947), the district court granted a petition for naturalization filed by an individual whose absence for greater than a year was the result of his capture by the Japanese during World War II. The instant case is clearly distinguishable, since the petitioner voluntarily departed from the United States. The court in *In re Yarina* acknowledged that it might have reached a different result if the petitioner's initial departure had been voluntary.

Accordingly, the Court must deny the petition for naturalization at this time since the petitioner was continuously absent from the United States for a period of more than one year during the five year period prior to the date on which his petition was filed. The Court notes that petitioner will be allowed to remain in this country as a lawful permanent resident, and that he will be eligible to become a naturalized citizen in June of 1985.

* * *

NOTES AND QUESTIONS

1.   INA § 316(a), which you should read now, actually imposes three different residence requirements and one physical presence requirement. Be sure you can spot them. Although in other areas of the law residence usually requires an intent to remain permanently, the immigration law defines it as a person's "principal, actual dwelling place in fact, without regard to intent." INA § 101(a)(33). The former INS acknowledged that statutory definition but maintained that a naturalization petitioner nonetheless must establish the "continuing intention to reside permanently in the United States, following a lawful admission for such purpose." INS Interp. 316.1(b)(2)(iii). Is the interpretation of the former INS consistent with the statute?

2.   Consider the requirement of five years continuous residence. The court construes section 316(b) to mean that even an involuntary absence (of a year or more) breaks the continuity of one's residence. At least five considerations lead the court to that interpretation:

a.   The literal language of section 316(b) refers simply to "absence;" it makes no distinction between voluntary and involuntary absences. (How, then, could the court in *In re Yarina,* cited in footnote 2, have permitted an exception for involuntary *departures*?)

b.   The court points out that the pertinent paragraph of section 316(b) contrasts sharply with the preceding paragraph, which permits a person who was absent more than six months but less than a year to establish continuity by showing "he did not in fact abandon his residence." In the court's view, the contrast was deliberate and evidences a congressional intent "to erect an absolute bar in cases of absences greater than one year." This technique, which enables a court to infer the meaning of one statutory provision by contrasting it with others, is common and often quite useful. As counsel for the petitioner, however, how might you respond?

c.   The court observes that Congress went to the trouble of laying out several specific exceptions to the one-year rule, yet did not list involuntary absences among them. The inference is that involuntary absences were not intended to be exceptions. This interpretation technique is common enough to have its own name: *"Expressio unius est exclusio alterius."* (The expression of one thing implies the exclusion of another.) See generally Edgar Bodenheimer, John B. Oakley & Jean C. Love, An Introduction to the

Anglo–American Legal System 145–47 (2d ed. 1988). How might petitioner's counsel respond?

d. The court notes that its interpretation coincides with the only other reported decisions on point.

e. The court asserts that its interpretation gives effect to the congressional purpose of ensuring that naturalization petitioners "have been considerably exposed to American institutions." The former INS identified two other purposes. One of them, related to but slightly different from the purpose posited by the court, was that residence enables the petitioner to learn English and United States history and government. INS Interp. 316.1(b). In addition, the INS pointed out, residence affords a test of the petitioner's ability to obey the law. *Id.*

All these purposes seem rational enough, but they generate some difficult questions. First, can any of those rationales support Congress's decision to require *residence* rather than just *physical presence?* (The latter concept will be considered shortly.) Second, can any of those rationales support the distinction between involuntary *departures,* which do not destroy continuity, and involuntary *absences,* which do?

3. The immigration judge's conclusion that Vafaei–Makhsoos did not abandon his permanent residence does not, in the court's view, mean that he had not destroyed the continuity of his residence for naturalization purposes. As a policy matter, why would Congress make the rules that define abandonment of residence for purposes of readmission and expulsion more lenient than the rules that govern continuous residence for purposes of naturalization?

4. The court observes that Vafaei–Makhsoos would become eligible for naturalization in June 1985. From the facts given, explain how the court came up with that date. Accord, INS Interp. 316.1(b)(4).

5. What would you assume is the consequence of an absence of six months or less?

6. Why would Congress require three months residence in the state or the USCIS district in which the naturalization petition is filed? See *Petition for Naturalization of Castrinakis,* 179 F.Supp. 444, 445 (D.Md. 1959), where the court held that the state residence requirement, like the other requirements of INA § 316(a)(1), applies to the period immediately preceding the filing of the application. (Before the 1990 Act, the statute required six months of state residence. See INA § 316(a)(pre–1990 version)).

7. The court at one point states that the "[p]etitioner was outside of the United States for *almost two years* during the five-year period preceding his naturalization petition" (emphasis added). From the facts given, is the court's statement correct? Is this some kind of new math, or did the court simply forget about the first trip? After answering that question, look again at the physical presence requirement of section 316(a). Is that requirement satisfied? Isn't the whole continuous residence issue in this case moot?

8. Like the requirements for citizenship by descent, the requirements for naturalization raise some constitutional questions. Given what you have read about the scope of the congressional powers to admit and expel noncitizens, and set citizenship criteria, which of the following *naturalization* requirements do you think would be upheld today?

a. The former racial limitations?

b. Limitations based on country of nationality?

c. The present disqualification of past members of the Communist Party?[9]

9. One leading citizenship scholar has written a thoughtful article examining how one should evaluate naturalization criteria. As he demonstrates, the assessment of any particular requirement depends on one's more general view of what the criteria for selecting citizens should strive to accomplish. He considers four normative models, which he calls unilateral liberalism, bilateral liberalism, thin republicanism, and thick communitarianism, and he then tries those models out on three different naturalization requirements—the ideological requirements, knowledge of the English language, and renunciation of foreign allegiance. See Gerald L. Neuman, *Justifying U.S. Naturalization Policies*, 35 Virginia J. Internat'l L. 237 (1994). For a response that considers the possible purposes that citizenship itself is meant to serve, see Stephen H. Legomsky, *Why Citizenship?*, 35 Virginia J. Internat'l L. 279 (1994).

ii. *Procedure*

What used to be called "judicial" naturalization proceeded in two phases. There was first an administrative phase in which the former INS made "recommendations" to a court. In practice those recommendations were seldom rejected. Second, there was a judicial phase in which a court formally granted or denied naturalization.

In the late 1980's, large backlogs began to form in some judicial districts, including the New Jersey district of Rep. Peter Rodino, then chair of the House Judiciary Committee (the parent of the immigration subcommittee). See Robert A. Mautino, *Naturalization Changes Effected by Immigration Act of 1990,* in AILA, Understanding the Immigration Act of 1990, at 277, 278 (1991). These delays were serious, since, as you saw earlier, several legal consequences flow from citizenship—including the opportunity to begin the process of sponsoring the immigration of a family member. Reform finally came in section 401(a) of the Immigration Act of 1990, amending INA § 310(a). That section gave the Attorney General "the sole authority to naturalize persons." Under that provision, most cases were expected to proceed without any judicial involvement. The former INS was to do virtually everything. The applicant could elect to wait for a judicial ceremony, and the district courts at any rate retained the jurisdiction to

---

9. The author thanks Professor Gerald Neuman for raising these constitutional questions as well as some others that have found their way into this chapter.

review INS denials of naturalization de novo. INA § 310(c). Still, the assumption was that the typical applicant would never see a courtroom.

But nostalgia set in. Many people expressed sadness over the elimination of mandatory judicial ceremonies. The judicial ritual can be both meaningful and moving, a poignant reminder of the enormous step the new citizens have taken. Even though every successful applicant had the option to experience that ritual, some believed that it should have remained a required event. See, e.g., Ronald A. Taylor, *Citizenship Process Loses Luster*, Washington Times, Mar. 14, 1991, at A3.

That sentiment largely prevailed in Congress a year later. Persuaded that the judicial ceremony supplies dignity and solemnity, but still intent on eliminating long delays, Congress compromised. It allowed the federal district courts and most state courts of general jurisdiction to notify the Attorney General that they will assert exclusive authority to administer oaths of allegiance in naturalization cases. Pub.L. 102–232, § 102(a), 105 Stat. 1733 (Dec. 12, 1991), amending INA § 310(b). That exclusive jurisdiction, however, expired 45 days after the Attorney General certified that the applicant is eligible for naturalization. (The applicant could still elect to wait longer for a judicially administered oath.) Note that the 1991 amendment did not alter INA § 310(a), which gave the Attorney General the "sole authority to naturalize." Only the ceremonial function of administering the oath of allegiance was affected. With the enactment of the HSA in 2002, the functions of the Attorney General and the former INS are now performed by the Secretary of Homeland Security and USCIS, respectively.

The current regulations offer one other option. An applicant who is not subject to the judicial exclusivity rule (either because the court declines to assert exclusive jurisdiction or because the 45–day period has expired) may elect to have the oath administered by an immigration judge. For the details, see 8 C.F.R. § 337.2 (2004).

The process officially begins when the person files an application for naturalization with USCIS. INA § 334(a); 8 C.F.R. § 334.1 (2004). A USCIS examiner interviews the applicant and conducts whatever further investigation he or she thinks necessary. INA § 335(a). The questioning, which is under oath or affirmation, includes examination of the applicant's English language skills. 8 C.F.R. § 335.2(c) (2004). USCIS asks the relevant law enforcement agencies for a criminal background check, *id.* §§ 335.1, 335.2(b), but as a result of Citizenship USA, the thoroughness of those investigations has recently become an issue. See pages 1279–82 above. The record of the interview may be stenographic, mechanical, electronic, videotaped, or contained in an affidavit executed by the examiner. *Id.* § 335.2(c).

Eventually, the examiner either grants or denies the application; before doing so, he or she may grant a continuance to give the applicant a chance to cure possible deficiencies. 8 C.F.R. § 335.3 (2004). If the examiner does not announce his or her decision within 120 days, the applicant may request a hearing in the district court. INA § 336(b). In that event, the court may either decide the case itself or remand it to USCIS "with appropriate instructions.'' *Id*. If the determination is favorable, the applicant takes an oath of allegiance to the United States.

If the USCIS examiner denies the application, the applicant may request an evidentiary hearing before an ''immigration officer.'' INA § 336(a, c). If that hearing results in a denial, the applicant may seek review in the district court for the district in which he or she resides. INA § 310(c). The court makes its own independent findings of fact and conclusions of law and, at the applicant's request, conducts a de novo trial. *Id.*

In recent years backlogs have accumulated and crippling delays have ensued. At one point (in 1998) the average time from application to naturalization reached 28 months. The then INS Commissioner, Doris Meissner, prioritized naturalization petitions and announced in November 1999 that the processing times had been reduced to an average of 12 months with the goal of reducing them further, to six months, by September 2000. See 4 BIB 1079 (Nov. 15, 1999).

For a fine report recommending a range of procedural reforms to improve both the accuracy and the efficiency of the naturalization process, see Arnold Rochvarg, *Report to the Administrative Conference—Reforming the Administrative Naturalization Process: Reducing Delays While Increasing Fairness*, 9 Georgetown Immigration L.J. 397 (1995). An excellent account of the practicalities and flavor of the pre–1990 naturalization process is David S. North, The Long Gray Welcome; A Study of the American Naturalization Program (1985), especially ch. 1 (the process as seen by the applicant). For two comparative studies of naturalization procedure, see North, above, ch. 5 (Canada); David S. North, Alien Legalization and Naturalization: What the United States Can Learn from Down Under (1984), chs. 3,4 (Australia and New Zealand).

What procedural changes, if any, would *you* make?

b.   THE CHILD CITIZENSHIP ACT AND OTHER MISCELLANEOUS FORMS OF NATURALIZATION

The process you have just read about is, as noted earlier, the usual way in which a person acquires United States citizenship after birth. There are a number of other miscellaneous ways. While the details are beyond the scope of this book,[10] you should be aware that such alternatives exist and that, unlike administrative naturalization, they mostly occur by operation of law rather than by individual initiative. Through ad hoc legislation, Congress from time to time has also naturalized the inhabitants of newly acquired territories. That process is called ''collective naturalization.'' See 7 Gordon, Mailman & Yale–Loehr, § 98.04. Private bills to naturalize named individuals have also occasionally passed, but they are far less common than private immigration bills.[11]

---

10. See generally 7 Gordon, Mailman & Yale–Loehr, ch. 98.

11. See *id*. § 98.06. President Grant's daughter, who had lost her citizenship by marrying a noncitizen, regained it by special Act of Congress. *Id*.

The most important of these other post-birth citizenship mechanisms are two measures included in the Child Citizenship Act of 2000, Pub. L. 106–395, 114 Stat. 1631 (Oct. 30, 2000); see generally Daniel Levy, *The Child Citizenship Act of 2000*, 6 BIB 293 (Mar. 15, 2001); see also Victor C. Romero, *The Child Citizenship Act and the Family Reunification Act: Valuing the Citizen Child as Well as the Citizen Parent*, 55 Fla. L. Rev. 489 (2003) (applauding the Child Citizenship Act but urging additional steps to assure family reunification).

The first of the two measures automatically confers United States citizenship on any child who (a) has a United States citizen parent; (b) is under age 18; and (c) resides in the United States as an LPR, in the legal and physical custody of the citizen parent. INA § 320. As soon as there is any point in time at which all these conditions are met, citizenship attaches by operation of law; there is no need to apply for it. (It is prudent, however, to obtain a passport or some other government-issued documentation confirming one's citizenship.) The provision applies to both biological and adopted children. *Id*. By way of example, any child who is admitted to the United States as an immediate relative while under age 18, and in the legal and physical custody of his or her citizen parent, becomes a United States citizen immediately upon admission. Similarly, if an LPR naturalizes while his or her LPR child is under age 18, the child will automatically acquire citizenship as well (assuming legal and physical custody). This provision is not retroactive; individuals who attained age 18 before the enactment date of October 30, 2000 therefore do not benefit. See *Matter of Rodriguez–Tejedor*, 23 I. & N. Dec. 153 (BIA 2001); Levy, above, at 293.

For children who do not qualify for automatic citizenship under section 320, the Child Citizenship Act contains a second measure that permits a United States citizen parent to apply affirmatively for citizenship on behalf of the child, when certain conditions are met. This provision amends INA § 322. To understand it, recall first that a child born overseas, today, automatically acquires citizenship by descent if he or she has one citizen parent who before the child's birth was physically present in the United States for five years, at least two of which were after the parent was age 14. INA § 301(g). The amendment to section 322 benefits children born abroad who do not satisfy the requirements for automatic acquisition of citizenship under either section 301(g) (citizenship at birth) or section 320 (citizenship after birth but before age 18). Under section 322, the child may be naturalized as long as (1) he or she has one United States citizen parent (who must file the application); (2) either the citizen parent *or* the citizen parent's citizen parent (i.e., the child's grandparent) has been physically present in the United States for at least five years, at least two of which were after that parent's or grandparent's age 14; (3) the child is under age 18; and (4) the child resides outside the United States in the legal and physical custody of the citizen parent but is temporarily present in the United States after a lawful admission. Note two things about the five year

/ two year requirement. First, unlike section 301(g) (the provision for automatic citizenship by descent at birth), section 322 allows either the citizen parent or citizen parent's citizen parent to meet the requirement. Second, again unlike section 301(g), section 322 requires only that the five years / two years requirement be satisfied before the child turns 18; it is not necessary to satisfy these requirements before the child's birth. Section 322 makes clear that the parent must file the application before the child turns 18; though less clear, it appears that in addition the entire process must be completed before the child turns 18. See Levy, above, at 297.

c. A SWISS PERSPECTIVE

You saw in chapter 3 that the United States imposes stringent requirements for admission as an LPR. You have now seen, however, that once a person clears those hurdles the requirements for subsequent naturalization are quite liberal.

At the other end of the naturalization spectrum is Switzerland. Swiss law requires naturalization applicants to clear three levels of obstacles— national law, canton law (Switzerland is a federation composed of cantons), and local law. At the national level, the main requirement is 12 years of residence in Switzerland. At the cantonal and local levels, the requirements vary widely. The canton of Zermatt until recently required 30 years residence. Many cantons impose exorbitant fees, some as high as 6,000 U.S. dollars. See Fiona Fleck, *Swiss Under Fire for Ballot on Citizenship*, Sunday Telegraph (London), Mar. 19, 2000.

But the most controversial element of Swiss naturalization law is the requirement of local approval. The municipality of Emmen, a suburb of Lucerne, requires a town referendum on each individual applicant. In 2000, Emmen made news by voting to reject the applications of 48 of the 56 long-term residents recommended for naturalization by the local authority. Each voter in Emmen had received from the local authority a 100–page brochure that contained each applicant's photograph and information on each applicant's age, nationality, education, work, hobbies, taxable income, and assets. The Sunday Telegraph article, above, featured one of the rejected applicants, a Hungarian refugee who had lived and worked in Switzerland for 43 years and who felt particularly stung by the repudiation of his neighbors.

The larger story, though, was the likely influence of race on the Emmen vote. The rejected applicants tended to be eastern Europeans, including many Yugoslavs. The far-Right People's Party, growing rapidly in Switzerland and compared by many to Jörg Haider's party in Austria, has been campaigning for similar local referendum procedures throughout Switzerland. Councillor Urs Ischi, a People's Party member in Emmen and the initiator of the Emmen referendum, defended the result by saying, "Voters feel the mentality of people from western Europe suits our mentality, while that of people from eastern Europe does not." *Id.*

3. DUAL NATIONALITY[12]

Although no one has been able to estimate the number of dual nationals in the world, a combination of anecdotal evidence and theories based on other known trends leaves no doubt that that number has soared in recent years. Dual nationality is the product of three fundamental principles. Principle #1, which is subject to some (expanding) exceptions described below, is that every sovereign state decides who its own nationals are. Hague Convention on Certain Questions Relating to the Conflict of Nationality Laws, 179 L.N.T.S. 101, arts. 1, 2 (done at the Hague, April 12, 1930). Principle #2 is that the typical law provides alternative, multiple routes to nationality. For examples, see the website of the Defense Security Agency, a component of the United States Department of Defense, < http://www.dss.mil/training/adr/forpref/forprefF.htm >, and click on "Citizenship of 206 Foreign Countries." These alternative paths frequently confer nationality by virtue of birth in the state's territory ("jus soli"), by descent from one or both of one's parents ("jus sanguinis"), and by naturalization. Principle #3 is that in actual practice the rules vary from state to state. *Id.*

Thus, a person born in *jus soli* country X to a mother of citizenship Y and a father of citizenship Z might well acquire all three citizenships at birth if countries Y and Z recognize *jus sanguinis*. (Contrary to public perception, nothing in United States law requires a person born abroad to United States citizen parents to "elect" one of the citizenships later in life. See generally H. Ansgar Kelly, *Dual Nationality, the Myth of Election, and a Kinder, Gentler State Department*, 23 Univ. Miami Inter–American L.Rev. 421 (1991–92)).

Because of principle #1, it is possible, and today quite common, for dual nationality to result also from naturalization. Even though United States law requires naturalization applicants to take an oath swearing to renounce all former allegiances, INA § 337(a)(2), only the country whose nationality the applicant purports to renounce can ultimately decide whether to give effect to that renunciation. On that issue, actual practices of the world's nations vary. For a good description, see Eugene Goldstein & Victoria Piazza, *Naturalization, Dual Citizenship and Retention of Foreign Citizenship*, 75 IR 1613 & App. I at 1629–32 (Nov. 23, 1998).

Conversely, a United States citizen who applies for naturalization in another country might not be required to take an oath renouncing United States citizenship, because not all countries require such oaths. And even if such an oath is required and taken, the person will not lose his or her United States citizenship unless it is found that he or she subjectively intended to relinquish it, INA § 349(a)(1), an intent that the State Department has become increasingly hesitant to find. You will see more on that issue in section B.2 below.

---

12. The simultaneous retention of more than one nationality should probably be called "multiple" nationality rather than "dual," since one can hold more than two nationalities. But the term "dual nationality" is in common usage and will be employed here to mean two or more simultaneous nationalities.

Dual nationality has skyrocketed in recent years, particularly in the immigrant-receiving countries of North America and Western Europe. See Tomas Hammar, Democracy and the Nation State, chs. 5–7 (1990); Tomas Hammar, *State, Nation, and Dual Citizenship,* in William R. Brubaker (ed.), Immigration and the Politics of Citizenship in Europe and North America, at 81 et seq. (1989). There are several reasons for the increase: Greater migration means increases in the number of LPRs who bear children; liberalizations in citizenship laws (for example, allowing citizenship by descent through the maternal line) have increased the number of people who acquire the citizenship of their parents at birth; international marriages (and, thus, opportunities for the acquisition of dual citizenship by the offspring) have been on the increase; and, finally, many States are easing their legal restrictions on dual citizenship, especially in the naturalization context. Hammar, in Brubaker above, at 81–83.

Today there is a wealth of excellent literature on dual nationality. In addition to the Hammar and Kelly writings noted above, see Nissim Bar-Yaacov, Dual Nationality (1961); Randall Hansen & Patrick Weil, Dual Nationality, Social Rights and Federal Citizenship in the U.S. and Europe (2002); David A. Martin & Kay Hailbronner (eds.), Rights and Duties of Dual Nationals: Evolution and Prospects (2003); Linda Bosniak, *Multiple Nationality and the Postnational Transformation of Citizenship,* 42 Virginia J. Internat'l L. 979 (2002); Peter J. Spiro, Embracing Dual Nationality, Occasional Paper No. 1, Internat'l Migration Policy Program, Carnegie Endowment for International Peace (1998); T. Alexander Aleinikoff, Between Principles and Politics: The Direction of U.S. Citizenship Policy 25–40 (1998); Thomas M. Franck, *Clan and Superclan: Loyalty, Identity and Community in Law and Practice,* 90 Amer. J. Internat'l L. 359 (1996); Tomas Hammar, *Basic Civil Rights and Dual Citizenship* (unpublished paper at International Conference on Citizenship, State and Identity in a Globalizing World, Bilkent Univ., Ankara, Turkey, June 1–3, 2000); Rey Koslowski, *Changing Norms on Dual Nationality and Military Service* (unpublished draft prepared for German American Summer Institute on Immigration, Incorporation and Citizenship in Advanced Industrialized Democracies, Berlin, July 1997); David A. Martin, *New Rules on Dual Nationality for a Democratizing Globe: Between Rejection and Embrace,* 14 Georgetown Immigration L.J. 1 (1999); Kim Rubenstein & Daniel Adler, *International Citizenship: The Future of Nationality in a Globalized World,* 7 Indiana J. Global Legal Studies 519 (2000); Peter H. Schuck, *Plural Citizenships,* in Peter H. Schuck, Citizens, Strangers, and In–Betweens: Essays on Immigration and Citizenship, ch. 10 (1998); Peter J. Spiro, *Dual Nationality and the Meaning of Citizenship,* 46 Emory L.J. 1411 (1997); Jorge Vargas, *Dual Nationality for Mexicans,* 35 San Diego L. Rev. 823 (1998); cf. Linda Bosniak, *Citizenship Denationalized,* 7 Indiana J. Global Legal Studies 447 (2000) (examining range of possible citizenship links to entities broader than a single state).

Until very recently, the nearly unbroken scholarly tradition has been to tolerate dual citizenship but not to applaud it. See generally Nissim Bar-Yaacov, Dual Nationality (1961). The literature cited above recounts the concerns that have been expressed about dual nationality. Three themes seem to recur. One theme emphasizes the problem of divided loyalty. Dual nationality is analogized to bigamy; having two countries is compared to having two spouses. A second set of concerns appears to rest on a belief that the dual national is unjustly enriched, receiving legal benefits from a state to which he or she feels no meaningful personal attachment and to which he or she owes no significant binding obligations. The objection to allowing double voting might fall within this category. The objection to allowing otherwise unaffiliated individuals to "buy" citizenship in Dominica or other tax havens is another illustration. A third set of concerns focuses on the practical problems associated with dual nationality. These include double taxation, difficulties in diplomatic and consular intervention, greater physical maneuverability for those engaged in transnational crime, and complications in delineating military service eligibility and obligations. See generally Stephen H. Legomsky, *Dual Nationality and Military Service: Strategy Number Two*, in Martin & Hailbronner, above, at 79–126. For an extreme example of the conflict to which a dual national can be exposed, see *Kawakita v. United States,* 343 U.S. 717, 72 S.Ct. 950, 96 L.Ed. 1249 (1952) (dual United States and Japanese national in Japan during World War II, charged with committing treason against United States). Barriers to extradition of a country's own nationals have also been problematic. See Yaffa Zilbershats, *Extraditing Israeli Citizens to the United States—Extradition and Citizenship Dilemmas*, 21 Michigan J. Internat'l L. 297 (2000).

Most modern analysts, however, have counseled calm, concluding that the problems associated with dual nationality are small ones. Swedish Professor Tomas Hammar believes the problems have been exaggerated and that, if anything, the restrictions on dual citizenship should be eased in order to encourage long-term LPRs to naturalize. Hammar, in Brubaker above, at 83–95. At least one commentator, Peter Spiro, has explicitly embraced dual nationality as a positive good. By eliminating the need to give up one's original nationality, he argues, states can encourage LPRs to naturalize and, hence, assimilate. He also argues dual nationality can afford beneficial legal protections to the individual and expedite international travel. Peter J. Spiro, *Dual Nationality and the Meaning of Citizenship*, 46 Emory L.J. 1411 (1997); see also the thoughtful analysis of Gerald L. Neuman, *Justifying U.S. Naturalization Policies*, 35 Virginia J. Internat'l L. 237, 268–77 (1994) (exploring consequences of renunciation requirement from multiple philosophical perspectives). Thomas Franck, above, suggests that the increased tolerance of dual nationality is in keeping with a more general embrace of multiple allegiances in international law and in daily life.

There have been three major international conventions on dual nationality and a multitude of bilateral treaties. These conventions mirror the academic trend. The first one, open to all nations of the world, was adopted in 1930. The Convention on Certain Questions Relating to the Conflict of Nationality Laws, 179 League of Nations Treaty Series 101 (done at the Hague, Apr. 12, 1930), viewed dual nationality as highly problematic and sought ways to reduce it. The second one, a regional agreement open only to European states, was the 1963 Convention on the Reduction of Cases of Multiple Nationality and on Military Obligations in Cases of Multiple Nationality, European Treaty Series No. 043 (done at Strasbourg, June 5, 1963). As its name implies, it too reflected a desire to curb dual nationality. By the time the third major multinational agreement was adopted, the 1997 European Convention on Nationality, European Treaty Series No. 166 (done at Strasbourg, Nov. 6, 1997), attitudes had changed markedly, and the result was a consensus that dual nationality could be tolerated easily in most situations. The bilateral treaties take a wide variety of approaches that reflect not only shifting reactions to dual nationality, but also variations in the relationships among states. See Legomsky, in Martin & Hailbronner, above.

What is your reaction to dual nationality?

4.   STATELESSNESS

The same principles that give rise to dual nationality can give rise to the opposite problem of statelessness. The combination of each state deciding who its own nationals are and state practices actually varying can cause some unfortunate individuals to fall through the gaps. For example, a person born in *jus sanguinis* country X to parents who are both citizens of *jus soli* country Y could end up with no nationality at all. It is more common, however, for statelessness to develop later—perhaps because of expulsion or flight, perhaps because of international developments that affect the sovereignty of one's country of birth, or perhaps because of voluntary renunciation of citizenship. See 7 Gordon, Mailman & Yale–Loehr, § 91.01[3][e]. Statelessness is a more pressing concern than dual nationality because the stateless person lacks a sovereign government from whom he or she can expect protection if maltreated. International conferences and agreements have sought to address the issue, see, e.g., Convention Relating to the Status of Stateless Persons, U.N.T.S., No. 5158 (done at New York, Sept. 28, 1954); Convention Relating to the Status of Stateless Persons (entered into force June 6, 1960); and Convention on the Reduction of Statelessness (in force Dec. 13, 1975), 17 Refugee Survey Q. 101, 103 (1998), but the problem remains serious. *Id.* A good treatment of the current deficiencies is Carol A. Batchelor, *Stateless Persons: Some Gaps in International Protection*, 7 Internat'l J. Refugee L. 232 (1995).

Is there an international human right to have at least one citizenship? For a thoughtful analysis and a description of the current international regulation of statelessness, see Yaffa Zilbershats, The Human Right to Citizenship (2002).

5.   WHO SHOULD BE A UNITED STATES CITIZEN?

Peter H. Schuck & Rogers M. Smith, Citizenship Without Consent—Illegal Aliens in the American Polity

Pages 4–5, 116–21, 128–37 (1985).

* * *

* * * [T]his book will elaborate an important but previously neglected dichotomy between two radically different conceptions of political community, which we call the "ascriptive" and the "consensual." In its purest form, the principle of *ascription* holds that one's political membership is entirely and irrevocably determined by some objective circumstance—in this case, birth within a particular sovereign's allegiance or jurisdiction. According to this conception, human preferences do not affect political membership; only the natural, immutable circumstances of one's birth are considered relevant.

The principle of *consent* advances radically different premises. It holds that political membership can result only from free individual choices. In the consensualist view, the circumstances of one's origins may of course influence one's preferences for political affiliation, but they need not do so and in any event are not determinative.

In light of these contrasts, this book will propose and defend an essentially consensual ideal of citizenship. Such a citizenship, we shall argue, would be more legitimate in theory, more flexible in meeting practical policy problems, and more likely to generate a genuine sense of community among all citizens than the existing scheme, while protecting the established human rights of aliens. To those ends, we shall advocate a combination of measures to render American citizenship law more consensual than it has previously been and to ameliorate what is the greatest contemporary threat to a consensually based political community—the massive presence of illegal aliens. * * *

* * *

Three basic steps are required to achieve a law of citizenship at birth that is theoretically consistent, practical for addressing current policy problems, and consonant with the nation's fundamental claim that its government rests on the consent of the governed. The first step requires a reinterpretation of the Citizenship Clause of the Fourteenth Amendment. Its guarantee of citizenship to those born "subject to the jurisdiction" of the United States should be read to embody the public law's conception of consensual membership, and therefore to refer only to children of those legally admitted to permanent residence in the American community—that is, citizens and legal resident aliens.

* * *

On our consensualist reading, those born "subject to the jurisdiction" of the United States would be citizens at birth provisionally, in the sense that they would have the opportunity upon attaining majority to renounce that citizenship if they so desired. At no time, however, would they be vulnerable to any denial of consent to their membership on the part of the state. Their parents would be understood to have obtained for the children, as a condition of the parents' own consent to citizenship, the guarantee that their children would enjoy all the rights of citizenship during their minority (with the usual age restrictions) and would possess an absolute right to assume full citizenship at their majority if they wished. While it is obviously a fiction to assign parents any conscious decision to insist on citizenship for their children as a condition of their own membership, it is much more improbable to suppose that parents would wish things to be otherwise should the choice be presented to them. And since children are as yet incapable of consent, reliance on the parent's preferences until a child reaches maturity is the only way that citizenship can plausibly be said to rest on actual personal volition.

Native-born children of legal resident aliens would also be provisional citizens at birth and during their minority and would enjoy the same right to expatriation. As we have seen, the public-law tradition was admittedly divided on whether resident aliens should be treated as having obtained a guarantee of citizenship for their children upon entry, or as having received merely the promise of their own resident alien status for them. The abstract principle of consent alone, moreover, yields no obvious answer to this question. But in light of America's long-standing grant of citizenship to resident alien children, its historic tradition of openness, and the likelihood that the vast majority of such alien children could eventually acquire citizenship in other ways, we propose (following Burlamaqui but not Vattel) to treat the children of resident aliens equally with those of citizens in this regard.

In this view, however, citizenship at birth would not be guaranteed to the native-born children of those persons—illegal aliens and "nonimmigrant" aliens—who have never received the nation's consent to their permanent residence within it. The nation cannot plausibly be said to have guaranteed to such persons citizenship for their children even tacitly, as a condition of the parents' entry into the polity. It either did not approve their entry at all (in the case of illegal aliens), or it did so on the understanding that they and their dependents would depart at some set time (in the case of nonimmigrants). In this connection, it is of some interest that even the citizenship law of the United Kingdom, from whose antecedents our common law of citizenship was originally derived, and which continues to adhere to the birthright citizenship principle, does not extend it to the native-born children of either illegal aliens or temporary resident aliens. The same is true of other Western European countries.

* * *

In any event, Congress bears the ultimate responsibility for fashioning the structure of our immigration policy, and the role of birthright citizenship for the children of illegal and nonimmigrant aliens—the decision either to grant or withhold it—is obviously only a small piece of that structure. Congress must carefully weigh the moral claims of these children to membership relative to the claims of other groups, assessing the likely effects on illegal immigration of eliminating their present guarantee of citizenship, and considering how such a change should relate to the more comprehensive, systematic measures for reducing illegal immigration that we and others have proposed, including employer sanctions, enhanced border enforcement, and enlarged legal admissions quotas. Then, and only then, can Congress responsibly resolve the birthright citizenship question.

In the current state of knowledge, it is not at all obvious what the outcome of such a policy assessment would be. * * *

* * *

Our emphasis upon congressional power to define the contours of birthright citizenship is important. To insist on an automatic inclusiveness (in reality, *over*inclusiveness) by perpetuating the ascriptive principle in the Constitution, instead of by fully exposing immigration policies to public choice, is to betray a lack of confidence in the justice of consensual political self-definition that we believe is unwarranted today. It is doubtless true that if Americans gain full power to decide through normal democratic processes which aliens should be admitted to the national community, public debate over the issue will ventilate some of the mean-spirited nativistic sentiments that have always blighted American life. But we believe that after the issues are fully explored, contemporary Americans will decide generously, and that those so admitted and naturalized will be treated as full and equal citizens.

* * *

In general, * * * we believe that the nation's policy should be to make citizenship an option guaranteed to all children of an American parent, whether born in or out of the United States. Admittedly, it may seem incongruous to guarantee citizenship to someone who lives his entire life outside the United States, while denying it to someone who resides for the same period of time within it, albeit illegally. That incongruity, however, is only apparent; the consent principle permits, even if it does not require, differential treatment of these two situations. Thus, a concern to implement the community's choice to exclude some groups is perfectly consistent with a consensual decision to accept the children of all existing members, whether or not those children subsequently decide to remain abroad. Under our proposal, moreover, any remaining incongruity would result only if the current American community chose it. Congress would have the power, if it wished, to require positive affirmations of membership on the part of those born to American parents residing overseas. Their continued citizenship would then be no more incongruous than allowing continued citizenship for native-born Americans who live abroad without renouncing their nationality. Finally, as we have emphasized, Congress would also have the right to admit all those living in the United States illegally or without citizenship to full political membership. The relevant point, once again, is that the consensualist interpretation and policies that we propose would make the boundaries of the political community, for better or for worse, matters of self-conscious public choice.

Several plausible objections to our proposal for a more consensual citizenship law may be anticipated and deserve responses. Although there is something to be said for each of them, none seems decisive.

The first objection is textual in nature. It argues that the words of the Citizenship Clause of the Fourteenth Amendment literally preclude denying birthright citizenship to any individual who was "born in the United

States" and is subject to its "jurisdiction." In this view, the clause's words are clear and comprehensive; they represent a deliberate constitutional decision to bestow citizenship on all who are native-born; they say nothing explicit about the parents' legal status or congressional consent, and they should not be interpreted as if they did.

This broad reading of the clause is not obviously incorrect or illegitimate; indeed, the Supreme Court seems to have endorsed this reading in its recent *Plyler* decision. Yet a number of considerations undermine this objection, and we think that they must be decisive in the end. First, it is simply wrong to assert that there has ever been a conscious deliberate decision, by the framers of the Fourteenth Amendment or its judicial interpreters, to accord birthright citizenship under the clause to children of illegal aliens. We saw [earlier] * * * that the issue was not before the original framers of the Citizenship Clause; that the phrase "subject to the jurisdiction thereof," while ambiguous at best, suggests that they intended to grant the clause a scope narrower than universal citizenship for mere birth within the geographic United States; and that this phrase gave the clause a political and consensual meaning, not simply a legal and geographical one, that excluded several categories of individuals whom a purely geographic reading would have covered. Subsequently, as we saw in chapter 4, no Supreme Court decision—*Wong Kim Ark*[a] and *Plyler*[b] included—has ever faced the precise question posed by our proposal to limit birthright citizenship. Any claim that the nation has chosen to limit its consensual authority over political membership by constitutionally guaranteeing universal birthright citizenship must therefore proceed not from an appeal to the text, from explicit aims of the framers, or from authoritative judicial decisions, but rather from the hazier notion of "tacit consent."

This suggests a second line of criticism. It would accept the primacy of the consent principle in American political life but would argue that the long-standing acceptance of a broad birthright citizenship rule, coupled with the manifest ineffectiveness of current immigration enforcement efforts, should be understood as the political community's *tacit* consent to membership for the children born here of illegal alien parents. That tacit consent, it might be argued, creates a moral obligation to continue a policy of universal birthright citizenship today.

We believe, however, that any argument from tacit consent should be viewed with skepticism, and that this application of that argument is especially unconvincing. First, the inadequacy of immigration enforcement is not an unambiguous datum; it can only be properly evaluated in context. That context includes the inherent difficulty of the task (given the number of aliens who come and the ease of entering without detection) and the

a. In *United States v. Wong Kim Ark,* 169 U.S. 649, 18 S.Ct. 456, 42 L.Ed. 890 (1898), the Court held that children born in the United States to LPR parents acquire citizenship at birth.—Ed.

b. In *Plyler v. Doe,* 457 U.S. 202, 102 S.Ct. 2382, 72 L.Ed.2d 786 (1982), the Court struck down on equal protection grounds a state statute that denied undocumented children a free public education. See pages 1235–51 above.—Ed.

recent substantial increases in the INS's enforcement budget and in its apprehensions along the southern border. *All* law enforcement is ineffective in that it is neither designed nor funded to bring each and every offender to justice. But that certainly does not mean—except in the most trivial sense—that society tacitly consents to those offenses that are not detected or prosecuted.

A second, more important defect in the argument from tacit consent is that it amounts to a reflexive acceptance and legitimation of the status quo. * * * Instead of a consent defined by hypothesis and tautology, a democratic society should insist upon a consent exemplified by deliberate, self-conscious political choice. * * *

A third objection might invoke the special character of constitutionally protected rights. It would insist that even if the nation, in adopting the Fourteenth Amendment, did not consciously or tacitly limit its future choices concerning citizenship, the definition of political membership remains so crucial to the nature of any polity that it should nevertheless be treated as an issue of constitutional dimension, one not subject to the whims and prejudices of transient majorities. Sustaining birthright citizenship for all native-born as a constitutional guarantee might be seen as a way to safeguard basic national values against temporary aberrations, as is done for free speech and other basic rights.

The weakness in this argument is that it ignores the basic difference between a right that a community decides to safeguard for members and nonmembers against popular majorities, and a claimed right to *become* a member. The latter claim, if recognized, would limit a nation's very power to determine what it will be—and also to determine who will decide that question—in the future. The current dilemma created by the influx of illegal aliens suggests that if these choices cannot be made on a flexible, ongoing basis, they cannot be made at all.

Furthermore, insofar as the Constitution does explicitly indicate how questions of membership are to be decided, it does so by granting Congress power over immigration, naturalization, and expatriation. These powers establishing congressional authority over which individuals may enter the United States can best be understood as expressing the framers' concern to ensure that all individuals "born in the United States" will be born to parents who are present with the consent of the nation. These powers therefore imply an open-ended, consensual process permitting the redefinition of the nation's membership. Because our constitutional system thus generally remits questions of admission to membership to majoritarian processes, and because this course is most consistent with the nation's fundamental commitment to consent, we believe that the Citizenship Clause should be read in that spirit.

* * *

Fifth, it may be argued that the proposal is not as inclusive as the current rule, and that inclusiveness, like administrative simplicity, is a great advantage in a citizenship test. There can be no doubt that inclusiveness is especially important for a society that prides itself on its openness to immigrants and its liberality of spirit toward all those in need. We share that pride and are strongly committed to a genuinely inclusive political community. Again, we recognize that, over and above the formalities of consent, those who have been born and grown up within the United States often become in fact part of the actual, organic community that is produced by shared experiences, so that refusing them membership in the only community they really know may seem objectionable on grounds of liberal humanitarianism or territoriality. That is why we have proposed admission for all those who have been born in the United States under the current interpretation of the Citizenship Clause, and why we call for Congress to assess the value of such a change to an effective immigration policy.

We are convinced, however, that not even the most ardent advocates of a liberal immigration policy favor *universal* inclusiveness; few would dispute that the citizens of a nation have some right to shape their collective futures by controlling admissions. The real question, therefore, is what the appropriate principle of inclusion (or exclusion) ought to be, recognizing that a less-than-universal principle of inclusion must inevitably also exclude, and that exclusion must inevitably nullify some individuals' choices for membership. By confining citizenship at birth to children of citizens or legal permanent residents, levels of illegal immigration might be reduced, thereby lessening the problem of what to do about those who have long been in the midst of the community, albeit illegally. This reduction in illegal migration seems particularly likely if our birthright citizenship proposal were part of a broader program to discourage illegal immigration. If the nation adopted these measures but found that they did not diminish the number of children born of illegal alien parents who had spent most of their lives here and had acquired humanitarian claims to membership, Congress would retain the power to extend a generous amnesty or naturalization policy toward them.

That residual power, of course, would not guarantee as inclusive a policy as the existing birthright citizenship rule does. But the current rule achieves an inclusiveness that is both spurious and uncontrolled. It is spurious because it is based upon a purely geographical coincidence— literally an accident of birth—rather than upon a principle, such as consent, that can legitimate citizenship by making it conform to the moral and political presuppositions of the national community. Birthright citizenship's inclusiveness of membership is also uncontrolled because it abdicates what is perhaps the most fundamental question of our political life—who shall constitute "we the people"? Rather than squarely addressing that question as one that should be decided deliberately on moral and policy grounds by the national community, it leaves it to the self-interested decisions of those over whom we have no effective control.

Our proposal, in contrast, promises a more genuine inclusiveness. Being grounded in actual, explicit consent, the inclusiveness would be more legitimate, more truly reflective of national sentiment, than the current rule. It would be as generous (or as niggardly) as Americans self-consciously decided to make it. As suggested earlier, an immigration and citizenship policy that is widely perceived as being under the nation's direction and rooted in its consent seems far more likely to be generously inclusive than a policy, like the present one, that is viewed as abdicating control and violating national will. * * *

Sixth, it may be argued, in a somewhat similar vein, that the proposal does little to address the problem of the influx and status of illegal aliens. Indeed, by eliminating birthright citizenship for their native-born children, the proposal could (depending upon the magnitude of its countervailing disincentives to illegal migration) actually increase the number of individuals in illegal status. In this view, the current birthright citizenship rule has at least one virtue that our proposal lacks. It recognizes that in fact (due largely to ineffective immigration enforcement) many native-born children of illegal aliens, along with their parents, will successfully elude detection or avoid deportation and remain here indefinitely. Denying birthright citizenship to those children would add one more obstacle and disadvantage, one more source of stigma and discrimination, to those they must endure as they continue living in American society, as many will be able to do. This dilemma is compounded by the fact that these children's life prospects would be clouded by the action of others over whom they have no control—in this case, the illegal entry of their parents. Better (so defenders of the current rule might argue) to eliminate their cruel disability at the moment of birth than to maintain it thereafter.

Although superficially appealing, this argument from life prospects is ultimately unpersuasive. Our proposal to make one's national status turn, at least provisionally, on the national status of one's parents seems more morally acceptable and less determinative of one's life prospects than many other contingent factors—such as inherited wealth, upbringing, or genetic endowment—that are far more likely to shape those prospects in fundamental ways. Indeed, our proposal seems less arbitrary in terms of life prospects than the fundamental concept of birthright citizenship itself, which bases national status wholly upon the accident of geographical location at birth. And even if the innocence of the child and allied concern for his life prospects are accepted as morally or legally relevant, it does not follow that *citizenship,* as distinguished from mere nondiscrimination, should be the prize for that innocence. Nondiscrimination does not necessarily imply the same rights and benefits that citizenship or legal residence status confers. These children and their parents, by being denied birthright citizenship, would not be treated as the *Dred Scott* decision treated blacks; they would not be denied the law's protection. They would merely be required to choose among continuing to live in illegal status, with more limited equal protection and due process rights; seeking to obtain legal status; or returning to their home countries.

* * *

Gerald L. Neuman, Book Review [of Schuck and Smith], Back to Dred Scott?

24 San Diego L. Rev. 485, 489–500 (1987).

* * *

I regard the authors' recommendation as resting upon a tragic moral misjudgment, but I do not intend to address the proposal as a simple matter of public policy. To do so would concede their argument more ground than it deserves. Before they can balance the claims of undocumented children against the interests of the nation, Schuck & Smith must demonstrate that the Constitution leaves the issue open to the ordinary political process. They have failed to do this.

* * *

The authors' argument for a "consensual" interpretation of the citizenship clause rests on a feat of legerdemain. * * * They observe that in the course of the Senate debates, the amendment's framers sought to exclude from its scope a few groups (identifiable as not *subject to the jurisdiction* of the United States) whom they did not regard as part of their society. Based on the Senate debates the authors conclude that the framers subscribed to a consensual approach to citizenship, and that jurisdiction for citizenship clause purposes can be equated with "a more or less complete, direct power by government over the individual, and a reciprocal relationship between them at the time of birth, in which the government consented to the individual's presence and status and offered him complete protection." They conclude that the phrase "subject to the jurisdiction thereof" authorizes further specification of groups whose children can be denied citizenship. Ultimately, the authors describe Congress as having continuing authority to decide which native-born persons, other than those born to citizens or to permanent resident aliens, shall be eligible for citizenship.

This reliance on the legislative history of the citizenship clause is crucial to Schuck & Smith's argument. The word "jurisdiction" has various meanings in American law, but it has never been defined in terms remotely resembling the elaborate construct that Schuck & Smith have fashioned. * * *

The gap spanned by this interpretive trick is a wide one. True, the drafters of the citizenship clause understood that they were free to decide who would receive citizenship. It was, after all, a constitution they were amending. But once one accepts that citizenship can be defined by positive law, there is an inherent ambiguity in the notion of a "consensual" approach to citizenship. *Any* freely adopted rule of citizenship expresses the consent of the society that adopts it. That consent can be embodied in a constitution as easily as in a statute, and it may define the relevant classes by using traditional "ascriptive" categories as well as those that Schuck & Smith would approve as "consensual." A constitution that identifies the category of persons who are citizens need not confer on a court or legislature discretion to reject citizens on the basis of its own views regarding the appropriate objects of consent.

* * * Schuck & Smith * * * argue that it is inappropriate to treat the qualifications for birthright citizenship as an issue of constitutional dimension. The framers of the fourteenth amendment had strong reason to believe otherwise. They had just overthrown a system founded on denial of full membership to an alien race. Furthermore, the citizenship clause was designed to forestall future controversies, not only to stabilize the resolution of the African slavery question. For example, Senator Cowan, a vehement opponent of both the Civil Rights Act and the fourteenth amendment, predicted increasing difficulty over the Chinese on the Pacific coast. In response the supporters of the citizenship clause expressly confirmed their intent to recognize the American citizenship of children born there to Chinese parents. They refused the invitation to create an hereditary caste of voteless denizens, vulnerable to expulsion and exploitation. While Schuck & Smith appear to view this danger as exaggerated, others do not, and it is at least defensible as a matter of political theory to guard against such a possibility by constitutionally requiring citizenship for all children born within the community.

The legislative history and the received judicial construction of the citizenship clause confirm that the framers of the fourteenth amendment did deny constitutionally mandated citizenship to a few categories of children, whom they regarded as not "subject to the jurisdiction" of the United States. These were the common law exceptions for aliens closely associated with a foreign government, and an American addition—Indians living under tribal quasi-sovereignty. The common law exceptions concern children born on foreign public vessels or to ambassadors of foreign nations, both situations in which comity principles of international law restrain the state's exercise of lawmaking power, and children born to parents accompanying an invading army, which was not physically subject to the power of the state at all. Denial of citizenship to Indians living within their own self-governing quasi-sovereign societies reflects the framers' view that such Indians were not fully subject to the legislative power of the United States, as evidenced by the practice of negotiating treaties with Indian tribes as sovereign powers. The effective independence of many Indian tribes from state or federal governance made the notion of Indian tribes as separate, though domestic, nations more realistic in 1866 than it subsequently became. Thus, "jurisdiction" can be given a natural reading as actual subjection to the lawmaking power of the state; this interpretation fulfills the framers' intentions and echoes the common law notion of the king's "protection."

* * *

Schuck & Smith shrug off *Wong Kim Ark* as an "[e]xpansive, but not universal," use of ascriptive citizenship in the fourteenth amendment, and would limit it to children of lawfully admitted permanent resident aliens. This compromise ignores the havoc that *Wong Kim Ark* wreaks upon their theory of citizenship. The Court's courageous recognition of citizenship for Americans of Chinese descent was an extreme illustration of the irrelevance of "consent;" not only were affirmative manifestations of consent outside the citizenship clause itself unnecessary, but the Court overrode strong indications of unwillingness to admit the Chinese to the American polity. The United States had wanted Chinese labor, and had not yet perfected the technique of importing temporary workers. It denied the immigrants any opportunity for citizenship, then attempted to prevent more laborers from arriving, forbade their reentry if they left the country, and began expelling those who had not secured certificates demonstrating the legality of their presence. If the phrase "subject to the jurisdiction" left Congress any flexibility for consent-based restrictions at all, surely the Court could have read it as leaving aliens whose reception was so chilly still "subject to the jurisdiction" of their native land, and not of the United States. The result, not just the reasoning, of *Wong Kim Ark* is incompatible with the authors' "consensual" interpretation.

Nor could *Wong Kim Ark* have turned on some supposedly fundamental distinction between permanent residents and temporary residents. The modern status of "alien lawfully admitted for permanent residence" did not even exist at the time of the fourteenth amendment or of *Wong Kim Ark*. Until the twentieth century, federal immigration statutes did not distinguish between admission of aliens for temporary residence and admission as permanent residents. Aliens were either admitted or not. * * *

* * *

Failure to address the details of nineteenth century immigration law undermines the authors' argument in other respects as well. Schuck & Smith claim that the framers of the fourteenth amendment could not have contemplated conferring citizenship on children of illegal aliens "for the simple reason that no illegal aliens existed at that time, or indeed for some time thereafter". They paint a picture of an era of wholly unrestricted immigration, with the attendant implication that the fourteenth amendment could have nothing relevant to say about the children of aliens whose entry into the country was unlawful. The authors have the facts wrong.

First of all, the authors dismiss too quickly the regulation of immigration by the states. Several states with international seaports imposed inspection, taxation, and bond-posting schemes, targeted at paupers and other aliens who were likely to prove unable to support themselves. * * *

More importantly, Schuck & Smith overlook the problem of the citizenship of children of illegally imported African slaves. Although Congress had promptly exercised its constitutional power to forbid all further importation of slaves as of 1808, the shameful traffic continued. Congress was forced to legislate repeatedly for its suppression up through the time of the Civil War. But the borders of the United States proved as hard to patrol then as they are said to be today. * * *

Here, then, was a notorious category of "illegal aliens" whose presence in the United States was without the federal government's consent. If, as Schuck & Smith insist, "consent" does not extend to children of parents not lawfully admitted to the United States, then the fourteenth amendment did not constitutionally mandate American citizenship for the children of illegally imported slaves. Yet there can be no doubt how a court in 1868 should have resolved any attack on the citizenship of former slaves whose parents or grandparents had been illegally imported. Illegally imported slaves are not mentioned in the debates, but the framers made it clear that guaranteeing citizenship to *all* native-born blacks was their central purpose. * * *

* * *

The campaign for "control of our borders" is partly a struggle over the future racial, linguistic and cultural development of American society. Our nation has faced such a struggle before, and has concluded that it should not be waged through the high-stakes weapon of manipulating the citizenship of the native-born. Under provocation, the author of the citizenship clause expressed its purpose as "to put this question of citizenship and the rights of citizens and freedmen under the civil rights bill beyond the legislative power of such gentlemen as the Senator from Wisconsin." Before we throw off that wise restraint and even consider sacrificing the undocumented children, greater justification will have to be shown than the complaint of "Citizenship Without Consent."

———

One of the co-authors of Citizenship Without Consent, Professor Rogers Smith, wrote a letter to Professor Neuman responding to some of Neuman's criticisms. The letter focused on the history of the fourteenth amendment citizenship clause. Here are some excerpts:

> The heart of our argument centers on [the views of the framers of the 14th Amendment concerning] the status of Indians, and I do not think you really come to grips with that argument. You say "jurisdiction" should be read as "actual subjection to the lawmaking power of the state," but all the tribes WERE ultimately subject to U.S. lawmaking power, both in legal theory and actual practice. On your interpretation the tribes' members should all be constitutional citizens. But they weren't then, and as you note in a footnote, they aren't now; they are citizens only by congressional statute.

> How do we explain this? We argue they relied not on the common law understanding of membership, but the public law, more consensual understanding developed by Vattel and Burlamaqui, whom the Court explicitly cited in its Indian cases. The tribes had the Vattelian status of dependent nations—ultimately subject to U.S. law, but having retained by mutual consent a measure of sovereignty, which included the assignment to the tribe of the (alterable) nationality provided at birth to children born to their tribal members. * * *

> You next mention state regulation of immigration, but understandably make little of it, since those laws did not result in persons residing in the U.S. in violation of U.S. law. You do stress the status of children born to slaves imported illegally after 1808, and it's an interesting point. But again I believe it is settled in our favor if you look closely at the versions of consensual theory we

claim the framers were employing, Vattel and Burlamaqui. They call us to consider the status of the parent. What is that status? I think Vattel and Burlamaqui would classify the slaves as conquered subjects of American citizens. It is true that this conquest was wholly unjust, and if Americans had followed Locke on the subject of conquest, that conquest would have no bearing on their legal status. But Vattel and Burlamaqui, whom we suggest the framers followed, were less idealistic: they held international law should recognize that the nationality of persons subject to enduring conquest had been changed, even if that conquest was originally unjust and they were now subject to their conquering peoples. Marshall's Indian decisions, which set American law, follow Vattel's views of rights of conquest, not Locke's. Therefore, the nationality of the * * * conquered subjects of U.S. citizens was viewed *on Vattellian and Burlamaquian grounds* to be American, "subject to the jurisdiction thereof", and the children follow suit.

I certainly do not view this position as the fullest realization of consensually-based citizenship, which should refuse to give any recognition to unjust conquest. But we do not claim the 14th Amendment embodies the fullest such realization; only a move in that direction, away from common law ascription to the public law position of Vattel and Burlamaqui. This reading is consistent with that claim, which also takes into account the status of Indians and Wong Kim Ark. Your reading does not account for the status of Indians or the sources relied on in discussing them in American courts.

Children of contemporary illegal aliens are obviously not children of conquered subjects of U.S. citizens. Their parents are still recognized by municipal and international law as members of their original nations (if they are not, we urge their admission to the U.S. and its citizenship). Thus while your analogy is interesting, I do not think it is in point.

Finally, let me observe that while our book has inspired (inflamed!) some people to think again about the basis of citizenship, a fact of which I'm proud, there appears to be no prospect that Congress will try to adopt a policy of denying citizenship to children of illegal aliens. That fact makes me even happier than I expect it does you.

* * *

Letter from Prof. Rogers M. Smith to Prof. Gerald L. Neuman, July 9, 1987 (on file with author).

NOTES AND QUESTIONS

1. The issue on which Schuck and Smith differ from Neuman is not an academic one. In the past several years, there has been a growing

movement to withhold citizenship from children born in the United States to undocumented parents (and sometimes even documented but non-LPR parents). In the 104th Congress, both proposed constitutional amendments and proposed legislation were introduced, albeit unsuccessfully. See generally 73 IR 97–99 (Jan. 22, 1996). The 1996 Republican Party Platform stated: "We support a constitutional amendment or constitutionally valid legislation declaring that children born in the Unted States of parents who are not legally present in the United States or who are not long-term residents are not automatically citizens." http://www.convention96.rnc.org/platform.htm, at 14. (Query what the phrase "or who are not long-term residents" means.)

2.   Articulate what Schuck and Smith, on the one hand, and Neuman, on the other hand, say "subject to the jurisdiction thereof" means. Both agree that the Fourteenth Amendment mandated citizenship for the United States-born children of illegally imported African slaves, but not for American Indians born within tribal authority. Based on what you have seen of their debate, does the general formulation of Schuck and Smith produce those two results and the conclusion that the Constitution does *not* require citizenship for the United States-born children of undocumented aliens? Does Neuman's general formulation produce those first two results and the conclusion that the Constitution *does* require citizenship for the United States-born children of undocumented parents?

3.   In explaining why the consent principle permits the automatic grant of citizenship to those children who are born in the United States to citizen parents, Schuck and Smith invoke what they acknowledge is a legal fiction—that the parents, upon accepting their own citizenship, insisted on citizenship for their children (present and future). They defend the use of that fiction by observing that parents would not wish otherwise if given the choice. Do you find that explanation convincing?

4.   Going a step further, Schuck and Smith argue that the consent principle permits a similar result when the parents of the United States-born children are LPRs rather than citizens. They cite as reasons "America's long-standing grant of citizenship to resident alien children, its historic tradition of openness, and the likelihood that the vast majority of such alien children could eventually acquire citizenship in other ways." To what extent would those arguments really be any less forceful if applied to the United States-born children of *undocumented* parents?

5.   The authors also support citizenship by descent, for children born abroad to United States citizens. They acknowledge that "it may seem incongruous to guarantee citizenship to someone who lives his entire life outside the United States, while denying it to someone who resides for the same period of time within it, *albeit illegally*" (emphasis added). Is the italicized phrase, which qualifies their concession, accurate? If not, is the inaccuracy peripheral or central to their refutation of this apparent anomaly?

6.   An important element of the disagreement is captured by the third objection that Schuck and Smith anticipate and answer. The objection is

that decisions concerning political membership are fundamental enough to dictate constitutionalizing them rather than subjecting them to shifting political winds. The analogy is to free speech and other basic rights.

Arguably, Schuck and Smith should not have described the basic choice as being between "ascription" and "consent." The consent that they read the Fourteenth Amendment to require is a *congressional* decision to confer citizenship (and the individual's decision to accept it). So defined, the consent principle would be satisfied, for example, by a congressional decision to bestow citizenship on all children of United States citizens. Yet, if citizenship were based solely on parentage, citizenship would then be "entirely and irrevocably determined by some objective circumstance;" "only the natural, immutable circumstances of one's birth [would be] considered relevant." And that, you might recall, is the authors' definition of "ascription." The actual choice of constitutional interpretations, then, might more easily be expressed as simply an automatic constitutional rule versus a statutory rule; a rule of either stature could be either ascriptive or non-ascriptive.

However phrased, the basic question is whether, as a matter of constitutional interpretation, birthright citizenship for (almost) all who are born in the United States *should* be held automatic. Responding to the third objection, Schuck and Smith emphasize the distinction between rights that the community assures for its members (and nonmembers) against the majority, and the "claimed right to *become* a member" (emphasis in original). They maintain that recognition of the latter "would limit a nation's very power to determine what it will be—and also to determine who would decide that question—in the future." First, do you agree such recognition would limit *the nation's* power to decide those questions? Second, do you agree that limiting the nation's power in that way (not eliminating the power entirely) would be undesirable?

7.   In responding to the fifth objection—that inclusiveness is a positive quality when it comes to membership decisions—Schuck and Smith say that under the current rule the inclusiveness is "spurious because it is based upon a purely geographical coincidence—literally an accident of birth," rather than a principle legitimated by conformity to the prevailing national philosophy. Is that criticism consistent with their clear approval of statutory citizenship by descent?

8.   The sixth objection that Schuck and Smith anticipate includes concern for the welfare of the affected children and the injustice of maltreating them because of the sins of their parents. They respond by arguing that, in terms of its actual impact on one's life prospects, inherited citizenship is at least as morally acceptable as "inherited wealth, upbringing, or genetic endowment;" that *"citizenship,* as distinguished from mere nondiscrimination," need not be "the prize for [the children's] innocence" (emphasis in original); and that the children, rather than being denied all legal protection, would merely have to make some difficult choices. How would you expect Neuman to respond to each of those arguments?

9. Suppose a terrorist group blows up a U.S. embassy overseas, killing 100 United States citizens and other members of the embassy staff in the process. Suppose further that U.S. agents capture the ringleader and bring her to the United States, and she gives birth to a child while awaiting her criminal trial. Is the child a United States citizen? *Should* the child receive U.S. citizenship? (Thanks to Peter Schuck for formulating this issue.)

10. The existing wording of the Fourteenth Amendment obviously places *some* limits on Congress's power to withhold citizenship; the debate here goes only to what those limits are. Yet the authors do not propose a constitutional amendment deleting the citizenship clause entirely. Given their preference for consensual citizenship (by which they mean citizenship that the people's representatives in Congress consent to confer), why *don't* they propose such an amendment? Why would they want even those children who are born in the United States to United States citizen parents to receive citizenship without congressional approval?

11. The book by Schuck and Smith has stimulated some intriguing debate. In addition to Neuman's critique, which focuses on the constitutional interpretation issue, see David A. Martin, *Membership and Consent: Abstract or Organic?*, 11 Yale J. Internat'l L. 278 (1985), which emphasizes the philosophical basis and policy consequences of consensual citizenship. See also Peter H. Schuck & Rogers M. Smith, *Membership and Consent: Actual or Mythic?*, 11 Yale J. Internat'l L. 545 (1986), in which the authors clarify that their book called only for the recognition of a congressional power rather than for a congressional decision to exercise that power in a particular way. See especially Peter H. Schuck & Rogers M. Smith, Citizenship Without Consent—Illegal Aliens in the American Polity 119–20 (1985) (not obvious what decision Congress should reach); Peter H. Schuck, *Whose Membership Is It, Anyway? Comments on Gerald Neuman*, 35 Virginia J. Internat'l L. 321, 323 (1994) (stressing that he and Smith, while requiring consent of polity to citizenship criteria, recognize liberalism as limit on kinds of conditions polity may impose). See generally Christopher L. Eisgruber, *Birthright Citizenship and the Constitution*, 72 NYU L. Rev. 54 (1997) (arguing government should be responsive to, and thus 14th Amendment citizenship clause should be construed to cover, all people over whom government exercises jurisdiction); John W. Guendelsberger, *Access to Citizenship for Children Born within the State to Foreign Parents*, 40 Amer. J. Comparative L. 379 (1992) (favoring retention of jus soli); Dan Stein & John Bauer, *Interpreting the 14th Amendment: Automatic Citizenship for Children of Illegal Immigrants?*, 7 Stanford L. & Policy Rev. #2 at 127–31 (1996) (favoring either constitutional amendment or legislation to withhold jus soli from children of undocumented parents).

SECTION B.   LOSING CITIZENSHIP

With the repeal of conditions subsequent (also known as retention requirements) for derivative citizens, see page 1270 above, there are today only two ways in which United States citizenship can be lost. The first is revocation of naturalization, more commonly known as "denaturalization." As its name suggests, that consequence can befall only those who acquired their citizenship by naturalization. It arises when certain defects in the original naturalization process later come to light. It can now occur through either of two procedural routes discussed in subsection 1 below. The second way to lose citizenship, known as expatriation, applies to naturalized citizens and other citizens alike. As you will see in subsection 2, expatriation today requires a showing of voluntary renunciation.

1. REVOCATION OF NATURALIZATION

INA § 340(a) requires the revocation of any naturalization order that was "illegally procured or * * * procured by concealment of a material fact or by willful misrepresentation." The procedure is a court action that may be brought only by the United States attorneys. *Id.* The Supreme Court, recognizing the enormity of the individual interests at stake in denaturalization cases, held in *Schneiderman v. United States,* 320 U.S. 118, 63 S.Ct. 1333, 87 L.Ed. 1796 (1943), that the government must prove the statutory grounds by "clear, unequivocal, and convincing" evidence (rather than by a mere preponderance of the evidence). 320 U.S. at 125, 63 S.Ct. at 1336–37, 87 L.Ed.2d at 1802. This type of "judicial" denaturalization is the more traditional variety.

A second and more controversial method of revoking naturalization has recently emerged. INA § 340(h) used to allow a court to reopen proceedings in which it had granted naturalization and decide the case anew. Typically this would occur on motion of the former INS after discovery of fraud, mistake, or new and previously unavailable evidence. As you will recall, the Imm. Act 1990, § 401, transferred the sole power to naturalize from the courts to the Attorney General (now the Secretary of Homeland Security). INA § 310(a). In a conforming amendment, Imm. Act 1990, § 407(d)(18), Congress transferred from the courts to the Attorney General (again, now the Secretary of Homeland Security) the power "to correct, reopen, alter, modify, or vacate an order naturalizing the person." INA § 340(h). In this book, that type of revocation will be called "administrative denaturalization," to distinguish it from the more usual "judicial denaturalization" discussed above.

To implement its new statutory power, the former INS in 1996 issued a final rule. 61 Fed.Reg. 55550–55 (Oct. 28, 1996). That regulation, which can be found at 8 C.F.R. § 340.1 (2001), purports to authorize the INS (now USCIS) to reopen naturalization proceedings itself (rather than seek a court order), and revoke naturalization, under certain circumstances. According to the regulation, USCIS must have

> clear, convincing, and unequivocal evidence which: (1) Shows that [USCIS] granted the application by mistake; or (2) Was not known to the [USCIS] Officer during the original naturalization proceeding; and—(i) Would have had a material effect on the outcome of the original naturalization; and (ii) Would have proven that: (A) The applicant's application was based on fraud or misrepresenta-

tion or concealment of a material fact; or (B) The applicant was not, in fact, eligible for naturalization.

8 C.F.R. § 340.1(a) (2004). The regulation also provides that USCIS may exercise this power only by serving a "notice of intent to reopen naturalization proceedings" within two years of the effective date of the naturalization order. *Id.* § 340.1(b)(2).

The regulations give the "applicant" (as they call the person whose naturalization they seek to revoke) the right to a hearing before an immigration officer and, if unsuccessful, an appeal to the USCIS Administrative Appeals Unit. 8 C.F.R. §§ 340.1(b)(3)(ii), 340.1(e) (2004). Under INA § 310(c), an original denial of naturalization is reviewable in the district court, which conducts a hearing de novo. The regulations interpret INA § 310(c) as also covering decisions revoking naturalization after reopening. 8 C.F.R. § 340.1(f) (2004). That interpretation is not surprising, since the underlying rationale for allowing USCIS to bypass the usual judicial procedures is that USCIS is merely readjudicating the original application.

In *Gorbach v. Reno*, 219 F.3d 1087 (9th Cir. en banc 2000), the court affirmed a preliminary injunction restraining enforcement of 8 C.F.R. § 340(a). The court concluded that only the courts have the statutory power to revoke a person's citizenship. It declined to decide whether Congress could constitutionally authorize an administrative agency to revoke naturalization orders that the agency had granted. The district court subsequently made the injunction permanent. *Gorbach v. Reno*, 2001 WL 34145464 (W.D. Wash. 2001), digested in 77 IR at 442 (Mar. 5, 2001).

The substantive meanings of the various criteria for denaturalization have been the subjects of a long-running debate within the Supreme Court. In form, the debate has been about highly technical issues of statutory interpretation. Beneath those differences, however, lurk fundamentally differing conceptions of the theory for revoking naturalization. The following decision is the Court's most recent *attempt* to dispel the confusion:

Kungys v. United States

Supreme Court of the United States, 1988.
485 U.S. 759, 108 S.Ct. 1537, 99 L.Ed.2d 839.

■ JUSTICE SCALIA announced the judgment of the Court and delivered the opinion of the Court as to Parts I, II–A, and III–A, and an opinion as to Parts II–B and III–B in which the CHIEF JUSTICE and JUSTICE BRENNAN joined and in Parts III–B of which JUSTICE O'CONNOR joined.

Juozas Kungys seeks our review of a judgment and opinion of the Third Circuit remanding his case for the completion of denaturalization proceedings. The issues presented are: first, whether certain misrepresentations or concealments made by Kungys in connection with his naturalization proceeding were material within the meaning of INA § 340(a) and *Chaunt v. United States*, 364 US 350, 5 LEd2d 120, 81 SCt 147 (1960); and second, whether those misrepresentations, made under oath and in the form of forged documents, rendered Kungys' citizenship "illegally procured" under INA §§ 101(f)(b), 316(a)(3), and 340(a), because they established that he lacked the requisite good moral character when he was naturalized 34 years ago.

I

Petitioner applied for an immigration visa in Stuttgart, Germany, in 1947. In 1948, the visa was issued, and he came to the United States; he was naturalized as a citizen in 1954. In 1982, the United States, acting through the Office of Special Investigations of the Department of Justice, filed a complaint pursuant to INA § 340(a) to denaturalize him. The United States advanced three grounds. First, it attempted to show that Kungys had participated in executing over 2,000 Lithuanian civilians, most of them Jewish, in Kedainiai, Lithuania, between July and August 1941. As proof of this claim, the United States offered in evidence three videotaped depositions taken for use in this case in the Soviet Union. After determining that for numerous reasons the Soviet—source depositions were inherently unreliable, the District Court admitted them only for the limited purpose of showing that the atrocities actually occurred. The District Court then held that the admissible evidence was insufficient to sustain the charges that Kungys had participated in the Kedainiai atrocities.

Second, the United States attempted to show that, in applying for his visa and in his naturalization petition, Kungys had made false statements with respect to his date and place of birth, wartime occupations, and wartime residence. The District Court found that these misrepresentations had been made but held them not to be material within the meaning of INA § 340(a), as illuminated by language in Chaunt v. United States, supra.

Third, the United States argued that Kungys' citizenship had been "illegally procured" under § 340(a) because when he was naturalized he lacked the good moral character required of applicants for citizenship by INA § 316(a). In support of this theory, the United States asserted that Kungys' false representations, whether or not material, were sufficient to show that he had given false testimony to obtain immigration or naturalization benefits, which INA § 101(f)(6) makes determinative of lack of good moral character. The District Court ruled that the false statements at issue were not covered by § 101(f)(6) because they were not material.

Having rejected each of the three asserted grounds for denaturalization, the District Court entered judgment for Kungys. The United States appealed. The Third Circuit declined to pass on the United States' submission that the first asserted ground (participation in the Kedainiai atrocities) was wrongfully rejected because of error in failing to admit unqualifiedly the Soviet—source depositions. It reversed, however, the District Court's rejection of the second ground, concluding that Kungys' willful misrepresentation of the date and place of his birth in connection with his applications for visa and naturalization (which was no longer disputed), was material for purposes of the "concealment or misrepresentation" provision of § 340(a). Finally, the Third Circuit upheld the District Court's rejection of the third asserted ground for denaturalization agreeing that in order to establish "illegal procurement" under § 340(a) on account of lack of good moral character under § 101(f)(6), false testimony must be shown to have been material.

* * *

II

A

As noted above, INA § 340(a) provides for the denaturalization of citizens whose citizenship orders and certificates of naturalization "were procured by concealment of a material fact or by willful misrepresentation. ..." This Court has previously suggested, and the parties do not dispute, that this requires misrepresentations or concealments that are both willful and material. See Fedorenko v. United States, 449 US 490, 507–508, n 28, 66 LEd2d 686, 101 SCt 737 (1981). So understood, the provision plainly contains four independent requirements: the naturalized citizen must have misrepresented or concealed some fact, the misrepresentation or concealment must have been willful, the fact must have been material, and the naturalized citizen must have procured citizenship as a result of the misrepresentation or concealment. It is no longer in dispute that the first two of these requirements were met here, since petitioner now concedes that he willfully misrepresented the date and place of his birth in his naturalization proceeding in 1954 as well as in applying for his visa in 1947.[5]

* * * In Chaunt v United States, we held that a naturalized citizen who had willfully and falsely stated during the naturalization process that he had never been arrested could nevertheless not be denaturalized pursuant to § 340. A year later, in Costello v United States, we held that a naturalized citizen who had willfully and falsely stated during the naturalization process that his occupation was "real estate," when in fact it would more accurately have been described as "bootlegging," could be denaturalized pursuant to § 340. In neither case did the Court's opinion purport to

---

5. The Government asserted that the purpose of the misrepresentations was to distance Kungys from Kedainiai, where atrocities had occurred, and to make it more difficult to identify him as one of the perpetrators. Kungys contended that even greater atrocities had occurred in the city he falsely listed as his birthplace; and that the age difference (two years) was of little consequence for identification purposes. Kungys asserted that he had lied concerning his date and place of birth in obtaining identity documents from the Nazis to go from Lithuania to Germany—the purpose of the dissembling at that time being to place him above the age of conscription and to avoid the risk of persecution for his participation in the Lithuanian resistance movement. (Vydaudas Vidiekunas, a leader of the resistance movement, validated Kungys' account of his participation.) Kungys asserted that in applying for his visa he simply repeated the information contained on his identity documents, believing the falsities inconsequential for United States immigration purposes; and that with similar belief he conformed his naturalization petition to his visa application.

announce a conclusive judicial test to guide the determination whether a given misrepresentation or concealment was "material" and whether it "procured" a naturalization certificate. Indeed, in neither case did the opinion clearly differentiate between these two separate requirements. Nevertheless, it has been thought that a test for materiality can profitably be derived from certain language in Chaunt. That language comes at the end of the opinion, where the Court, in summarizing its holding, states that "the Government has failed to show by 'clear, unequivocal, and convincing' evidence either (1) that facts were suppressed which, if known, would have warranted denial of citizenship or (2) that their disclosure might have been useful in an investigation possibly leading to the discovery of other facts warranting denial of citizenship." The efforts to make this formulation the test for materiality have not met with notable success. Not only have the Courts of Appeals failed to arrive at a single interpretation, but our one attempt to dispel their confusion, Fedorenko, seemingly produced at least three variants on this Court.

With the wisdom of experience, we now conclude that the attempts to construct a standard from the Chaunt dicta have been both unnecessary and unfortunate. The term "material" in § 340(a) is not a hapax legomenon.[a] Its use in the context of false statements to public officials goes back as far as Lord Coke, who defined the crime of perjury [to require a "material" statement.] * * *

* * * Given these common-law antecedents, it is unsurprising that a number of federal statutes criminalizing false statements to public officials use the term "material." * * * The federal courts have long displayed a quite uniform understanding of the "materiality" concept as embodied in such statutes. The most common formulation of that understanding is that a concealment or misrepresentation is material if it "has a natural tendency to influence, or was capable of influencing, the decision of" the decision-making body to which it was addressed. While we have before us here a statute revoking citizenship rather than imposing criminal fine or imprisonment, neither the evident objective sought to be achieved by the materiality requirement, nor the gravity of the consequences that follow from its being met, is so different as to justify adoption of a different standard. "Where Congress uses terms that have accumulated settled meaning under either equity or the common law, a court must infer, unless the statute otherwise dictates, that Congress means to incorporate the established meaning of these terms."

One might perhaps view the Chaunt test as not a repudiation of the established meaning of "material," but as an attempt to craft a more precise test for what constitutes "a natural tendency to influence" a naturalization decision. Surely, however, there is no less need for precision in the criminal context than in the denaturalization context. The more general formulation is preferable there, as we think it is here, because the judgment in question does not lend itself to mechanical resolution. The

---

a. No relation to editor.—Ed.

disagreement between the District Court and the Court of Appeals in Fedorenko turned on whether the Chaunt test required that, had the truth been told, an investigation *would* have resulted which *would* have disclosed disqualifying facts, or rather that an investigation *would* have resulted which *might* have disclosed disqualifying facts. But if the ultimate question is "natural tendency to influence," it would seem to make little difference whether the probabilities of investigation and resulting disclosure, respectively, are 100%–20%, 20%–100%, 51%–51%, or even 30%–30%. It has never been the test of materiality that the misrepresentation or concealment would *more likely than not* have produced an erroneous decision, or even that it would *more likely than not* have triggered an investigation. Thus, while the Chaunt formulation may be an adequate explanation of why the misrepresentation in that case was judged not to have had a natural tendency to influence the decision, it does not necessarily facilitate judgment in the infinite variety of other factual patterns that may emerge—which is perhaps why we did not employ it in Costello a year later. We think it safer in the naturalization context, as elsewhere, to fix as our guide the central object of the inquiry: whether the misrepresentation or concealment was predictably capable of affecting, i.e., had a natural tendency to affect, the official decision. The official decision in question, of course, is whether the applicant meets the requirements for citizenship, so that the test more specifically is whether the misrepresentation or concealment had a natural tendency to produce the conclusion that the applicant was qualified. This test must be met, of course, by evidence that is clear, unequivocal, and convincing. See, e.g., Schneiderman v. United States, 320 US 118, 158, 87 LEd 1796, 63 SCt 1333 (1943). Though this formulation may seem less verbally precise than Chaunt, in application it may well produce greater uniformity, since judges are accustomed to using it, and can consult a large body of case precedent.

[The Court next concludes that the question whether a fact is material is one of law.—Ed.]

* * *

B

We turn, then, to whether the one misrepresentation on which the trial court's finding was considered and upheld by the Third Circuit—misrepresentation of the date and place of Kungys' birth—was material under the foregoing test. As discussed earlier, Kungys made that misrepresentation in both the 1947 visa proceeding and the 1954 naturalization proceeding. But insofar as application of the "concealment or misrepresentation" clause of § 340(a) is concerned, we find it improper to address the 1947 episode. Unlike § 101(f)(6), which covers false testimony "for the purpose of obtaining *any* benefits" under the immigration and naturalization laws, the "concealment or misrepresentation" clause of § 340(a) applies only where the "*order and certificate of naturalization* . . . were procured by concealment of a material fact or by willful misrepresentation." Procurement of other benefits, including visas, is not covered. Especially in light of this contrast with § 101(f)(6), we are unpersuaded by the Government's argument that a misrepresentation in the visa proceeding "procures" the naturalization because it obtains United States residence, which in turn is a prerequisite to naturalization. The same argument could be made with respect to a misrepresentation that effects free enrollment in a reading course, which produces the prerequisite of English literacy.[7] Such analysis stretches the "concealment or misrepresentation" clause of § 340(a) beyond its intent, which we think is limited to falsehoods or deceptions in the naturalization proceeding.[8]

Looking, therefore, solely to the question whether Kungys' misrepresentation of the date and place of his birth in his naturalization petition was material within the meaning of § 340(a), we conclude that it was not. There has been no suggestion that those facts were themselves relevant to his qualifications for citizenship. Even though they were not, the misrepresentation of them would have a natural tendency to influence the citizenship determination, and thus be a misrepresentation of material facts, if the true date and place of birth would predictably have disclosed other facts relevant to his qualifications.[9] But not even that has been found here. The Third Circuit merely held:

> [H]ad [Kungys] told the truth at the time he applied for his citizenship, the discrepancies between the truth and his visa materials would have resulted in either a field investigation or an outright denial of the petition. * * *

* * * [But section 340(a)] imposes denaturalization for "concealment *of a material fact*" *(emphasis added);* and the materiality requirement implicit in the misrepresentation provision likewise relates to misrepresentation *of a material fact.* Thus, for purposes of determining the natural tendency of a misrepresentation to affect a decision under § 340(a), what is relevant is what would have ensued from official knowledge of the misrepresented fact (in this case, Kungys' true date and place of birth), not what

---

7. JUSTICE WHITE considers the prospect of such coverage "foolish." As a policy matter it assuredly is, which is precisely why we use it as an example. JUSTICE WHITE fails to establish, however, how language requiring that the "order and certificate of naturalization [be] ... procured by ... misrepresentation" can conceivably be interpreted to exclude this example while yet including the misrepresentation at the visa stage which (we concede) would not as a policy matter be foolish. It is not our function to construct prudent policy except within the confines of the statutory text.

8. It is a quite different question, not argued here, whether, under the statutes governing the issuance of visas in 1947, Kungys' misrepresentations or concealments at that time *rendered his visa invalid,* thus

causing his United States residence to be unlawful, and (since lawful residence is a requirement of naturalization) his naturalization to be "illegally procured" under that separate provision of § 316(a).

9. JUSTICE STEVENS minimizes the substance of what we require by describing it as no more than a showing "by clear and convincing evidence that the true facts would have led to further investigation." But further investigation would not occur—and its predictability could assuredly not be clear and convincing—if the facts at issue were not such as gave cause to believe that the applicant was not qualified. We are not talking about investigations by detective hobbyists, but by public officials seeking only evidence concerning citizenship qualifications.

would have ensued from official knowledge of inconsistency between a posited assertion of the truth and an earlier assertion of falsehood. On the basis of the Third Circuit's reasoning, a misrepresentation that, in and of itself, is utterly immaterial *both* in the visa proceeding *and* in the naturalization proceeding, becomes material simply because it is repeated in both. That is not what the statute intends. What must have a natural tendency to influence the official decision is the misrepresentation itself, not the failure to create an inconsistency with an earlier misrepresentation; the failure to state the truth, not the failure to state what had been stated earlier. The Government has failed to establish clearly, unequivocally, and convincingly that Kungys' misrepresentation of the date and place of his birth had this natural tendency.

We leave it to the Third Circuit on remand to determine whether the other misrepresentations or concealments that the District Court found to have been made in 1954 were supported by the evidence and material to the naturalization decision under the standard we have described—bearing in mind the unusually high burden of proof in denaturalization cases. If so, it will have to reach the fourth § 340(a) issue described in our earlier analysis: whether Kungys "procured" his citizenship by means of those misrepresentations or concealments. That requirement demands, first of all, that citizenship be obtained as a result of the application process in which the misrepresentations or concealments were made. The difficult question, and that on which we part company with Justice Stevens' opinion concurring in the judgment, is what it demands beyond that. We do not agree with petitioner's contention that it requires the Government to establish that naturalization would not have been granted if the misrepresentations or concealments had not occurred. If such a "but for" causation requirement existed in § 340(a), it is most unlikely that a materiality requirement would have been added as well—requiring, in addition to distortion of the decision, a natural tendency to distort the decision. Moreover, the difficulty of establishing "but for" causality, by clear, unequivocal, and convincing evidence many years after the fact, is so great that we cannot conceive that Congress intended such a burden to be met before a material misrepresentation could be sanctioned. We do think, however, that the "procured by" language can and should be given some effect beyond the mere requirement that the misrepresentation have been made in the application proceeding. Proof of materiality can sometimes be regarded as establishing a rebuttable presumption. Though the "procured by" language of the present statute cannot be read to *require* proof of disqualification, we think it can be read to express the notion that one who obtained his citizenship in a proceeding where he made material misrepresentations was *presumably* disqualified. The importance of the rights at issue leads us to conclude that the naturalized citizen should be able to refute that presumption, and avoid the consequence of denaturalization, by showing, through a preponderance of the evidence, that the statutory requirement as to which the misrepresentation *had a natural tendency* to produce a favorable decision was in fact met. Such a construction gives ample meaning to both the "materiality" and "procured by" requirements.

■ JUSTICE STEVENS' concurrence would adopt a requirement of "but for" causality, emphasizing the necessity that the Government establish, at least, that the misrepresenting applicant was in fact not qualified to be naturalized. This emphasis highlights another difficulty with "but for" causality: that requirement is simply not a conceivable construction of the "procured by misrepresentation" provision of § 340(a) if one adheres, as JUSTICE STEVENS' concurrence purports to do, to our holding in Fedorenko that even without any misrepresentation the applicant's failure to meet a statutory requirement for naturalization subjects him to denaturalization under the "illegally procured" provision of § 340(a). Thus, JUSTICE STEVENS' concurrence's construction violates the cardinal rule of statutory interpretation that no provision should be construed to be entirely redundant. It makes nonsense of the statute to say that its misrepresentation provision can only be the basis of denaturalization if the Government establishes *in addition* a factor that is itself, without misrepresentation, a basis for denaturalization anyway. On JUSTICE STEVENS' concurrence's reading, the law says, in effect: Citizenship you obtain by lying may be revoked, but only for a reason other than lying. This is likely to have the congressionally desired deterrent effect upon only the most dim-witted of prevaricators. But worse than making an enigma of the statute, JUSTICE STEVENS' concurrence's position makes a scandal of the results the statute achieves: Proof that an applicant lied when he said he was not an SS officer at Dachau would not suffice for denaturalization without clear, unequivocal, and convincing proof—after 40 years of disappearing evidence—that he was guilty of war crimes.

III

A

The United States argues, as an alternative basis for affirming the Third Circuit's upholding of denaturalization, that Kungys' misrepresentations, made under oath and in the form of forged documents, rendered his citizenship "illegally procured" under INA §§ 101(f)(6), 316(a)(3), and 340(a). As discussed earlier, the alleged ground of "illegal procurement" is that Kungys lacked the requisite good moral character in 1954, at the time of his naturalization, because he had given false testimony for the purpose of obtaining benefits in both the visa and naturalization proceedings, in violation of § 101(f)(6). In connection with this aspect of the judgment, we address only the issue considered (and resolved in the affirmative) by the Third Circuit: whether § 101(f)(6) contains a materiality requirement for false testimony. We hold that it does not.

Under INA § 101(f)(6), a person shall be deemed not to be of good moral character if he "has given false testimony for the purpose of obtaining" immigration or naturalization benefits. On its face, § 101(f)(6) does not distinguish between material and immaterial misrepresentations. Literally read, it denominates a person to be of bad moral character on account of having given false testimony if he has told even the most immaterial of lies with the subjective intent of obtaining immigration or naturalization benefits. We think it means precisely what it says.

The absence of a materiality requirement in § 101(f)(6) can be explained by the fact that its primary purpose is not (like § 340(a)) to prevent false pertinent data from being introduced into the naturalization process (and to correct the result of the proceedings where that has occurred), but to identify lack of good moral character. The latter appears to some degree whenever there is a subjective intent to deceive, no matter how immaterial the deception. A literal reading of the statute does not produce draconian results, for several reasons. First, "testimony" is limited to oral statements made under oath. The United States concedes that it does not include "other types of misrepresentations or concealments, such as falsified documents or statements not made under oath." Second, § 101(f)(6) applies to only those misrepresentations made with the subjective intent of obtaining immigration benefits. As the Government acknowledges:

> It is only dishonesty accompanied by this precise intent that Congress found morally unacceptable. Willful misrepresentations made for other reasons, such as embarrassment, fear, or a desire for privacy, were not deemed sufficiently culpable to brand the applicant as someone who lacks good moral character.

Obviously, it will be relatively rare that the Government will be able to prove that a misrepresentation that does not have the natural tendency to influence the decision regarding immigration or naturalization benefits was nonetheless made with the subjective intent of obtaining those benefits. This is especially so since the invalidating intent, like all other factual matters necessary to support denaturalization, must be proved by " 'clear, unequivocal, and convincing' evidence which does not leave 'the issue in doubt.' " Third, unlike the misrepresentation clause of § 340(a), the false testimony provisions of § 101(f)(6) do not apply to "concealments." With all these built-in limitations, and given the evident purpose of the provision, we see no reason for straining to avoid its natural meaning.

* * *

B

Accordingly, it is clear that the Third Circuit erred in importing a materiality requirement into § 101(f)(6). Nevertheless, we cannot affirm denaturalization under that section because the question whether any misrepresentation made by Kungys constituted "false testimony for the purpose of obtaining" immigration or naturalization benefits cannot be answered without resolving an additional question of law and an additional question of fact. The former, which we choose not to resolve ourselves, since the case must be remanded in any event, is whether Kungys' misrepresentations constituted "testimony." The latter, which must be resolved by the trier of fact, is whether in making the misrepresentations Kungys possessed the subjective intent of thereby obtaining immigration or naturalization benefits. * * *

For the reasons stated, the judgment of the Third Circuit is reversed, and the case remanded for further proceedings consistent with this opinion.

* * *

■ JUSTICE KENNEDY took no part in the consideration or decision of this case.

■ JUSTICE BRENNAN, concurring.

I join the Court's opinion. I write separately, however, to spell out in more detail the showing I believe the Government must make to raise a presumption of ineligibility. * * *

* * * [In] my view a presumption of ineligibility does not arise unless the Government produces evidence sufficient to raise a fair inference that a statutory disqualifying fact actually existed. It is this fair inference of ineligibility, coupled with the fact that the citizen's misrepresentation necessarily frustrated the Government's investigative efforts, that in my mind justifies the burden-shifting presumption the Court employs. * * *

Because nothing in the Court's opinion is inconsistent with this standard, I join it.

■ JUSTICE STEVENS, with whom JUSTICE MARSHALL and JUSTICE BLACKMUN join, concurring in the judgment.

* * *

In this case the Government maintains that petitioner is subject to denaturalization because it has proved that he made certain misrepresentations in his 1947 Application for Immigration Visa (Quota), which he repeated in his October 23, 1953, Petition for Naturalization. He stated that his date of birth was October 4, 1913, when it in fact was September 21, 1915; he stated that his place of birth was Kaunas, Lithuania, when it was in fact Reistru. He asserted that he resided in Kedainiai, Lithuania, only through July 1941, when in fact he did not leave Kedainiai until October 1941. He failed to disclose that he had been a bookkeeper-clerk in a Kaunas brush and broom establishment during the war. The Government failed in its efforts to prove that petitioner would have been denied a visa if he had disclosed the true facts in his application. It also failed to prove that truthful responses would have led to a more complete investigation of petitioner's background before granting him a visa or that an investigation would have revealed any fact that would have disqualified petitioner from obtaining a visa. Indeed, the Government failed to prove the existence of any fact that, if known, would have led to the denial of petitioner's visa application or disqualified him from later becoming an American citizen.

In support of its position that petitioner's false statements in 1947 and 1953 justify his denaturalization the Government makes two separate legal arguments. First, it argues that the misrepresentations were "material" within the meaning of § 340(a) and that they procured petitioner's citizenship. Second, the Government urges that petitioner's citizenship was "illegally procured," because his misrepresentations—even if not material—

demonstrate that he lacked the requisite good moral character at the time of his application for citizenship. Neither argument is tenable.

I

Over a quarter of a century ago, in Chaunt v. United States, the Court considered a case in which the District Court found that petitioner had concealed his membership in the Communist Party as well as three arrests that, had they been disclosed, would have led to further investigation by the Immigration and Naturalization Service. Although the dissenting Justices thought that Chaunt's failure to tell the truth about his arrest record was sufficient reason to revoke his citizenship, the majority came to the contrary conclusion. It held that the Government had failed to prove "either (1) that facts were suppressed which, if known, would have warranted denial of citizenship or (2) that their disclosure might have been useful in an investigation possibly leading to the discovery of other facts warranting denial of citizenship." Thus we announced a test for whether citizenship was procured by a material misrepresentation that required the Government to prove the existence of a disqualifying fact. This result was compelled both by the statute's requirement that the misrepresentation be material and by the requirement that it procure citizenship. * * *

"Material" means "having real importance" or "great consequences." Webster's Ninth New Collegiate Dictionary 733 (1983). The adjective "material" is widely used to distinguish false statements that are actionable at law from those that are not. * * *

In all of these contexts, the use of the word "material" serves to distinguish the trivial from the substantive, drawing the line between statements that appear to be capable of influencing an outcome and those that do not. It is reasonable to assume that the term serves the same role in the denaturalization statute. It guarantees that trivial misstatements do not result in the loss of citizenship by making actionable only those that are capable of influencing the decision whether to confer citizenship. This principle may be stated more specifically. Unlike the decision to enter a contract or to do some act in detrimental reliance on the assertion of another, the decision whether to grant citizenship is an objective one. The applicant either does or does not possess the requisite qualifications. The process relies on facts, not hunches or intuitions. Thus, in the denaturalization context, the only statements that are capable of influencing the outcome are those that conceal disqualifying facts or that prevent or hinder the discovery of disqualifying facts. Our statement in Chaunt was not a rejection of the traditional definition of materiality, it was merely an acknowledgment of the realistic consequences of that term's use in the context of an objective decisionmaking process.

Our holding in Chaunt is also supported by the statutory requirement that there must be a causal connection between the misrepresentation and the award of citizenship. Section 340(a) provides that the Government must demonstrate that the misrepresentation "procured" citizenship. That is, the statute requires that the Government demonstrate that it relied on the misrepresentation in deciding whether to allow the applicant to become a citizen. * * *

* * *

Thus the Government cannot prevail in a denaturalization action based on a false statement in an application for a naturalization certificate unless it can prove by clear, unequivocal, and convincing evidence the existence of a disqualifying fact. To prove that a misrepresentation was material, the Government must prove that the statement concealed a disqualifying fact or hindered the discovery of a disqualifying fact. Further, the existence of a disqualifying fact is a necessary element of the Government's proof of reliance. Unless a disqualifying fact existed, it cannot be said that a misrepresentation "procured" citizenship. * * *

* * *

In my opinion, the wisdom of experience has provided firm support for Chaunt's holding. Our construction of the denaturalization statute must be animated by our longstanding recognition of the severity of the sanction being sought. I firmly believe that denaturalization is far too heavy a sanction to impose on an otherwise innocent citizen for making false statements in 1948 and 1953. Without evidence of any wrongdoing before he came to the United States in 1948 or after he acquired his citizenship in 1954, the revocation of petitioner's citizenship—a punishment that is tantamount to exile or banishment—is patently excessive.

* * *

Virtually ignoring the foregoing settled law, today the Court announces a new burden-shifting presumption that lowers the standard of proof required for the Government to prevail in a denaturalization proceeding. Under the Court's test, a misrepresentation or concealment is material if it concerned a fact that was relevant to the naturalization decision or if the true facts "would predictably have disclosed other facts relevant to [the citizen's] qualifications." A fact may be relevant if it would have led to an investigation. Thus the Government becomes entitled to the presumption that the citizen was not qualified to become a citizen, that is, to the presumption that citizenship was "procured by" the misrepresentation, if it shows by clear and convincing evidence that the true facts would have led to further investigation. The citizen then bears the burden of "showing, through a preponderance of the evidence, that the statutory requirement as to which the misrepresentation *had a natural tendency* to produce a favorable decision was in fact met." Since under the Court's test the Government is never required to identify a specific disqualifying fact, apparently the citizen must refute the existence of every disqualifying fact that might have been revealed by an investigation. The Government need not introduce any proof whatsoever suggesting the existence of a disqualifying fact.

Though joining the Court's opinion, Justice Brennan would require more. He would not allow the Government the benefit of the presumption unless it first produced "evidence sufficient to raise a fair inference that a statutory disqualifying fact actually existed." Although Justice Brennan imposes a burden of production on the Government, he agrees with the majority that the burden of ultimate persuasion rests with the defendant. Under Justice Brennan's approach, however, the defendant at least has the benefit of knowing specifically what disqualifying fact must be rebutted. Both approaches require the defendant to rebut the existence of the presumed disqualifying fact—even demonstrating that there is a completely innocent explanation for the misrepresentation would not be sufficient to rebut the presumption.

Neither the majority's nor Justice Brennan's formulation of shifting burdens is faithful to our previous recognition of the special burden the Government must bear when it seeks to denaturalize an American citizen or to our previous rejection of default judgments in denaturalization proceedings. * * * The use of burden-shifting presumptions to reduce the Government's burden of proof in criminal cases has been consistently rejected by this Court without regard to whether the presumptions were rebuttable. Such presumptions are equally objectionable in the denaturalization context.

II

The reasons why the Court has required the Government to carry a heavy burden of proof in denaturalization cases apply equally to the argument that petitioner is subject to denaturalization because his false statements demonstrate that he lacked good moral character in 1953.

As amended in 1961, § 340(a) allows the Government to revoke the citizenship of anyone whose citizenship was "illegally procured." In Fedorenko, we held that citizenship had been illegally procured because the petitioner, a former armed concentration camp guard, was ineligible for the visa he had been issued under the Displaced Persons Act of 1948 (DPA). Because the naturalization statutes required applicants to be lawfully admitted to the United States for permanent residence, petitioner had failed to "satisfy a statutory requirement which Congress has imposed as a prerequisite to the acquisition of citizenship by naturalization." One prerequisite to naturalization is that the applicant be of "good moral character." INA § 316(a). Certain minimum standards for being deemed in possession of good moral character are set out in INA § 101(f). Subsection 6 of § 101(f) provides that no person shall be deemed to be of good moral character if he or she "has given false testimony for the purpose of obtaining any benefits under this chapter." The Government contends that it is not necessary for it to establish that petitioner's false statements were material to denaturalize him under this provision. Under the Government's theory, the mere fact that the statements were false is sufficient to compel petitioner's denaturalization if they were made under oath and with the subjective intention of obtaining a benefit—any benefit, no matter how trivial[8]—under the naturalization laws. Because I am convinced that a materiality requirement is implicit in § 101(f)(6), I reject this contention.

* * *

It is obvious that there is some overlap between the scope of the misrepresentation and illegally-procured clauses of § 340(a).[11] That the

8. At oral argument, the Counsel for Government made the following remarks in response to questioning by a Member of the Court:

"QUESTION: You know, there are a lot of people that came to this country who were given different names at Ellis Island. The immigration officer couldn't pronounce the name, and they said, well, Sam, is that okay? Yeah, that's my name Sam. Now his name wasn't Sam.

"Did he give that name to procure the visa, or to procure admission to the United States, falsely to procure?

"MR. KLONOFF [Assistant to the Solicitor General]: That's a factual question in each case, we would submit.

"QUESTION: He just wants to facilitate the thing. The guy will never learn how to spell Salvator, or whatever the name is, and the officer—it's happened very often.

"MR. KLONOFF: It has to be a question of fact. If the person had adopted a false I.D. many, many years earlier for a totally different purpose—

"QUESTION: No, no, there is no evil purpose except to facilitate getting in. I don't want to be here, you know, trying to straighten out what the proper spelling of my name is. He says Sam, what do I care; Sam is fine.

"MR. KLONOFF: If he adopted a false identity to facilitate getting in and jumped ahead of the pack—

"QUESTION: Do you consider that facilitating getting in?

"MR. KLONOFF: We would.

"QUESTION: Just to facilitate—to make it quicker so the fellow doesn't have to figure out how to spell Salvator.

"MR. KLONOFF: That would be our position. That's consistent with the statutory—

"QUESTION: Wow, that's a tough position, and I think there are probably a lot of people that are excludable."

The observation that a lot of people would be excludable (and a lot of Americans put at risk of losing their citizenship) under the Government's interpretation is, of course, correct. The example instructs that misrepresentations as to matters that are immaterial to the decisions being made by immigration officials simply do not reflect the lack of good moral character § 101(f)(6) seeks to identify.

11. * * * Although the illegally-procured provision may reach some of the conduct encompassed within the material misrepresentation provision, the illegally-procured provision has an independent and broader reach.

Further, the material misrepresentation provision reaches some conduct not assailable under the illegally-procured provision. The Government contends that construing the material misrepresentation provision to require proof of a disqualifying fact renders that provision meaningless since the Government could always seek denaturalization under the illegally-procured provision if it could prove a disqualifying fact. The Government apparently construes our holding on the facts in Fedorenko that citizenship may be considered illegally procured if it is discovered that the applicant failed at the time citizenship was conferred to meet a statutory prerequisite of citizenship as warranting the conclusion that every newly discovered noncompliance, no matter how insignificant, would warrant a subsequent finding that citizenship had been illegally procured. Thus, for example, an innocent miscalculation of the applicant's period of physical presence within the United States or residence within a particular State would place a naturalized citizen's status in permanent jeopardy. I disagree. I do not construe the illegally-procured provision to reach such trivialities despite the reality that an individual who submitted an application for citizenship one day before fulfilling the residency requirements would technically

Government may in some cases be able to choose one of two available paths for denaturalizing a citizen for essentially the same conduct, however, does not suggest that either of the paths should be made more lenient than Congress intended.

* * *

■ JUSTICE O'CONNOR, concurring in part and dissenting in part.

I join Parts I, II–A, and III of Justice Scalia's opinion in this case. For the reasons given in Part II of Justice White's opinion, however, I dissent from Part II–B of Justice Scalia's opinion. In my view, when the correct standard of materiality is applied to the facts of this case, the misrepresentations made by petitioner are properly viewed as material.

■ JUSTICE WHITE, dissenting.

* * *

* * * Although I agree with Parts I, II–A, and III–A of the Court's opinion, I disagree with other parts and with the result it reaches. I therefore dissent.

I

I would affirm the judgment below and grant the Government's petition for denaturalization. The Court holds, and I agree, that there was error in the holding below that petitioner's misrepresentations must be material in order to constitute sufficient grounds for finding that petitioner lacks "good moral character" under § 101(f)(6). * * *

* * * [W]e must bear in mind the necessity of striking an appropriate balance between the serious consequences that attend loss of citizenship and the need for "strict compliance with all the congressionally imposed prerequisites to the acquisition of citizenship." We need not decide in this case whether § 101(f)(6) would bar naturalization of an individual who offered a single piece of false testimony in only one instance or who later offered a reasonable explanation for why misstatements were made; we also need not decide whether such a construction of the statute would be inconsistent with a proper balancing of the two important but opposing considerations set out above. There may well be cases in which a single willful but immaterial misrepresentation would be insufficient to establish lack of good character, but would constitute grounds for denaturalization if it were material. Similarly, there are cases like this one in which repeated and numerous willful misrepresentations justify a finding of lack of good moral character notwithstanding that the misrepresentations may not involve material facts.

have failed to "satisfy a statutory requirement which Congress has imposed as a prerequisite to the acquisition of citizenship by naturalization." However, if the Government could establish that a naturalized citizen had willfully misrepresented his or her time of residence and that he or she would have been denied citizenship if the true duration of residency had been known, that person would be subject to denaturalization under § 340(a).

Here, petitioner's false testimony was not confined to one occasion, nor did it concern only a single piece of evidence. And at no time before or during the naturalization process did petitioner voluntarily step forward and attempt to explain the reasons for his various misrepresentations. To the contrary, the facts as found by the District Court demonstrate clearly, unequivocally, and convincingly that petitioner engaged in a pattern of repeated misrepresentations and nondisclosures at both the visa application stage and during his naturalization proceedings. * * * The congressional mandate expressed in § 101(f)(6) speaks clearly to such a pattern of falsehoods, and that statute would have precluded a determination in 1954 that petitioner possessed "good moral character." Accordingly, petitioner lacked an essential prerequisite to becoming a naturalized citizen, and he is now subject to denaturalization for having "illegally procured" his citizenship.

Despite its recognition that materiality is not required by § 101(f)(6), the Court declines to uphold the judgment below, and remands the case for further consideration of one point of law and one point of fact. Neither point is at all substantial. The point of law is whether petitioner's misrepresentations constituted "testimony" within the meaning of the statute. As the Court notes, the term "testimony" in § 101(f)(6) has been construed as referring only to oral evidence, and thus as excluding the written documents submitted by petitioner in his naturalization petition. Yet petitioner in this case did make oral misrepresentations: he testified falsely when he swore under oath before a naturalization examiner that the contents of his naturalization forms were true. Furthermore, he had testified falsely in order to obtain his visa into this country.

The point of fact is whether petitioner made these misrepresentations "for the purpose of obtaining any benefits" under the immigration and naturalization laws. There is no difficulty about this point either. The willful misrepresentations at issue here were made in the context of petitioner's naturalization petition and were made earlier at the visa stage. The fact that the misrepresentations were willful, coupled with the fact that they were made during proceedings and on documents required for immigration and naturalization purposes—indeed, the very proceedings and documents that petitioner was required to complete in order to "obtai[n]" the "benefits" he sought of gaining naturalization—satisfies the elements of § 101(f)(6). The District Court itself found that petitioner's naturalization petition was false *in particular* because it "stated that defendant had not previously given false testimony to obtain benefits under the immigration and naturalization laws." In light of this specific finding by the District Court, there is no justification for remanding this issue to be resolved *again* by the trier of fact.

II

Because the Court declines to affirm the decision below on the basis of § 101(f)(6), it finds it necessary to revisit the definition of the term "material" as it is used in § 340(a). The Court today holds that the proper test of materiality is whether the misrepresentations "had a natural tendency to influence the decisions of the Immigration and Naturalization Service." I do not disagree with this definition, but the Court's application of the definition in this case is flawed.

To begin with, the Court finds it proper under § 340(a) to consider only the misrepresentations petitioner made in his naturalization proceedings but not those made in his earlier visa proceedings. The view of the United States is much more persuasive: the misrepresentations made by petitioner at the visa stage were instrumental to his procuring naturalization, for by obtaining the visa petitioner obtained lawful admission to residence in this country, which is one requirement for naturalization under § 318. The Court responds that by that logic, *any* misrepresentation that helps an individual to obtain *any* prerequisite to naturalization, such as English literacy, would be considered material. These two things, however, are not the same, and the Court's supposed extension of its logic is merely foolish. The visa proceedings and the naturalization proceedings are intimately related not only because they both are proceedings governed by the same provisions of the immigration and naturalization laws, but also because the visa and the certificate of naturalization are obtained as part of the same process for obtaining citizenship, and both must be *lawfully* procured. For example, it is not mere residence in this country that is a prerequisite to naturalization, but residence after being "lawfully admitted." § 318. It makes no sense, on the other hand, to speak of proceedings to attain "lawful" literacy skills or a "lawful" understanding of American history and government, as required under § 312, and the statute does not speak in these terms but instead manifests complete and understandable indifference as to how the individual came by those proficiencies. Thus the visa proceedings can accurately be regarded as one crucial stage in the naturalization proceedings themselves, yet the time spent acquiring literacy skills or an understanding of American history and government obviously cannot be regarded as a stage in those proceedings.

Even if I were to accept the proposition that we should consider only the materiality of the misrepresentations that petitioner made in the naturalization proceedings, those misrepresentations surely had a natural tendency to influence the decisions of the INS. As an initial matter, there is no requirement that the Court focus only on petitioner's misrepresentations about his date and place of his birth and leave aside his other potentially more significant misrepresentations that were also identified by the District Court.[4] But even limiting the focus as the Court does, I would find these statements to be material. In reaching this conclusion I would ask not only whether these misrepresentations of fact would have a natural tendency to influence the decisions of the INS, but also whether the fact of these misrepresentations *itself* would have had such a tendency. In other words, the proper inquiry is not only whether the true date and place of

---

4. The District Court found as a matter of fact that petitioner also misrepresented his residence and employment during the time in which the atrocities occurred at Kedainiai. The correctness of those factual findings has not been challenged. * * *

birth, in isolation, would have aroused suspicion, but also whether an investigation would have ensued had petitioner revealed the true facts and thereby disclosed the discrepancy between them and the false statements in his supporting documents. * * *

* * *

NOTES AND QUESTIONS

1. Before going any further, map out the points on which the Justices agree and those on which they differ. Be sure you understand to which of the three denaturalization grounds each point is relevant.

2. Consider first the charge that Kungys's naturalization was "illegally procured." The Court accepts the *Fedorenko* view that naturalization was illegally procured whenever the applicant was in fact ineligible for it. Here the main problem is whether, at the time of his naturalization, Kungys was ineligible for lack of "good moral character." INA § 316(a)(3). Good moral character is precluded by INA § 101(f)(6) if Kungys gave "false testimony for the purpose of obtaining any benefits under" the INA. As to that, the principal issue is whether section 101(f)(6) should be read to require testimony that is *materially* false. Justice Scalia clearly says no. Justice Stevens clearly says yes. But what, exactly, is Justice White saying? He begins section I of his opinion by agreeing with Justice Scalia that misrepresentations need not be material "to constitute sufficient grounds for finding that petitioner lacks 'good moral character' under § 101(f)(6)." Later, however, he urges that the serious consequences of denaturalization for the individual be balanced against the need to assure compliance with the requirements for obtaining naturalization. Applying that philosophy, he says:

> There may well be cases in which a single willful but immaterial misrepresentation would be insufficient to establish lack of good moral character, but would constitute grounds for denaturalization if it were material.

Is Justice White's position internally consistent? Is his a valid interpretation of section 101(f)(6)?

3. Apart from "illegally procured" naturalization, INA § 340(a) prescribes two other grounds for denaturalization: Naturalization was procured by (a) "concealment of a material fact" or (b) "willful misrepresentation." Without much discussion, the Court reads a willfulness requirement into (a) and a materiality requirement into (b). Neither requirement appears in the literal language. Moreover, one might have expected Justice Scalia to cite the contrast between these two adjacent and related phrases as evidence of a clear congressional intent to treat affirmative misrepresentations differently from concealments. He employed precisely such reasoning later in his opinion when he interpreted the language "*order and certificate of naturalization * * * were procured by * * * *"* (emphasis in original) not to extend to procurement of visas or other benefits. He relied on the contrast between that phrase and the broader statutory language of

INA § 101(f)(6) (false testimony "for the purpose of obtaining *any* [INA] benefits") (emphasis in original).

Selective usage of statutory interpretation techniques is nothing unusual. In this case, though, why would Justice Scalia want to read the additional requirements into the phrase "concealment of a material fact or * * * willful misrepresentation?"

4. Probably the most important issue the Court addresses in *Kungys* is what "material" means. Justice Stevens believes the Court already answered that question in *Chaunt*. There the Court suggested a misrepresentation would be material if the true facts either (a) would themselves have warranted a denial of naturalization or (b) might, if known, "have been useful in an investigation possibly leading to the discovery of other facts warranting denial" of naturalization. Justice Scalia does not read *Chaunt* as prescribing a fixed test. Writing for a majority on this issue in *Kungys,* he holds that a misrepresentation was material if it "had a natural tendency to produce the conclusion that the applicant was qualified." What does "natural tendency" mean, and how significant is the difference between the two formulations? How *can* a misrepresentation have a natural tendency to produce a favorable decision unless the true facts either would have constituted grounds for denial or at least might have triggered an investigation that might have led to other facts warranting denial? Can you devise a hypothetical in which the two tests would produce different outcomes?

5. Justices Scalia and White both accept the "natural tendency" test, but they apply it in different ways and reach different results on the facts of *Kungys*. Whose application of that test do you find more persuasive?

6. Assuming a misrepresentation was material, was naturalization "procured by" it? Justice Stevens would require the government to prove that the applicant would not have received naturalization but for the misrepresentation. Justice Scalia rejects that interpretation, arguing it would render the misrepresentation prong superfluous. First, explain why he believes that is so. Second, what do you think of Justice Stevens's explanation, contained in footnote 11 of his concurring opinion, of why his interpretation would not make the misrepresentation prong redundant? Third, what is your reaction to the whole idea of attaching such weight to the avoidance of redundancy? Are there other responses that Justice Stevens could have offered?

7. The divergent opinions in *Kungys* do illustrate the Justices' differing uses of statutory construction principles, but they seem to reflect deeper policy differences as well. At the most general level, it might be that the Justices simply vary in the priorities they would assign to the competing goals of protecting the individual interest in secure citizenship and preserving the integrity of the naturalization process. At a more specific level, while all the Justices appear to recognize actual ineligibility for naturalization as a basis for denaturalization, they display different degrees of enthusiasm for recognizing dishonesty as an independent ground. Justice White seems to stress the dishonesty factor the most, Justice Stevens the

least. Justice Scalia is somewhere in between. That theme figures in the debates over whether section 101(f)(6) requires materially false testimony, what makes a willful misrepresentation material, and what it means for naturalization to be "procured by" misrepresentation. See also Michael G. Heyman, *Language and Silence: The Supreme Court's Search for the Meaning of American Denaturalization Law*, 5 Georgetown Immigration L.J. 409, 425–29 (1991) (identifying a different kind of values differential).

As a policy matter, what *should* the grounds for denaturalization be? Should they differ from the grounds for denying naturalization? Cf. Heyman, above, at 429–31 (arguing that the lenient standards for granting naturalization should have influenced the standard for revoking it).

8.   The remand in *Kungys* culminated in a consent decree. Kungys accepted denaturalization in exchange for the government's promise not to institute deportation proceedings. The government defended its decision to settle by asserting that, even if Kungys were found deportable, he would be eligible for discretionary relief. 66 IR 1287–88 (1988). The editors of Interpreter Releases rightly questioned, however, whether Kungys would have been eligible for *any* relief if found deportable as a Nazi persecutor and whether, even if eligible, Kungys would have received the favorable exercise of discretion. *Id.* at 1288.

2.   EXPATRIATION

The previous subsection described the criteria and procedures for revoking naturalization orders. United States law now recognizes only one other way to lose one's citizenship—expatriation. Unlike denaturalization, expatriation applies without regard to the circumstances under which citizenship was originally acquired; it does not matter, in other words, whether the individual acquired citizenship by birth in the United States, by descent, or by naturalization. Also unlike denaturalization, expatriation today requires the consent of the individual, manifest in ways that will be examined below. It is that feature which distinguishes expatriation from a concept known in international law as "denationalization." The latter is usually defined to mean "the deprivation of nationality[13] by unilateral fiat of the State." See, e.g., Marjorie M. Whiteman, 8 Digest of Internat'l L. at 98 (1967).

At common law, allegiance to a country was perpetual. One could not renounce citizenship without the consent of the sovereign. See *Shanks v. Dupont*, 28 U.S. (3 Pet.) 242, 246, 7 L.Ed. 666 (1830). Thus, when British subjects became naturalized United States citizens and purported to renounce their British nationality in the process, the British government refused to recognize such renunciation. And when the British government enforced that view by seizing British-born, naturalized United States

---

13.   INA § 349 refers to loss of "nationality," rather than to loss of citizenship. Since citizenship is a subcategory of nationality, however, INA § 101(a)(22), loss of United States nationality will always entail loss of citizenship. In this section, the terms "nationality" and "citizenship" are used interchangeably. See page 1266 above.

citizens on the high seas and impressing them into military service, their actions hastened the War of 1812. See Charles Gordon, *The Citizen and the State: Power of Congress to Expatriate American Citizens,* 53 Georgetown L.Rev. 315, 319 (1965).

After the Civil War, other events began to shape the direction of citizenship law in the United States and elsewhere. The Fourteenth Amendment, section 1 of which confers citizenship on all who were "born or naturalized in the United States, and subject to the jurisdiction thereof," was approved in 1868. To avoid the perceived problems of dual citizenship, the United States in that same year began entering into reciprocal treaties with a number of other nations. Known as the Bancroft Treaties, these agreements recognized an individual right to renounce citizenship upon naturalization in a foreign country.[14] Finally, in response to British arrests of politically active naturalized Americans in Ireland, Congress passed the Expatriation Act of 1868, Act of July 27, 1868, ch. 249, 15 Stat. 223. In the Preamble to that Act, Congress proclaimed for the first time that "the right of expatriation is a natural and inherent right of all people." See generally Gordon, above, at 322–23.

The 1868 Act did not, however, spell out the manner in which United States citizenship could be renounced. Congress took that step when it passed the Act of March 2, 1907, Pub.L. 193, ch. 2534, 34 Stat. 1228. But the 1907 Act went further than recognizing the *right* to renounce one's citizenship; it also enumerated several courses of conduct that would result in a loss of citizenship whether the individual intended to renounce or not. See *id.* §§ 2, 3. In one fell swoop, Congress had established specific grounds not only for expatriation but also for denationalization.

One provision of the 1907 Act, section 3, automatically denationalized any American woman who, by the act of marrying a noncitizen, acquired a foreign nationality. One victim of that provision challenged its constitutionality, arguing that Congress had no power to take away United States citizenship against one's will. In *MacKenzie v. Hare,* 239 U.S. 299, 36 S.Ct. 106, 60 L.Ed. 297 (1915), the Supreme Court upheld the statute. The Court found an implied congressional power, related to the regulation of foreign affairs, to withdraw citizenship in response to *voluntary transactions* (such as marriage) even when the individual had not intended to *renounce citizenship.*

The Nationality Act of 1940, Act of Oct. 14, 1940, ch. 876, §§ 401–10, 54 Stat. 1137, 1168–71, expanded the list of activities that would result in loss of citizenship. The INA added further to the list. See Act of June 27, 1952, Pub.L. 414, ch. 477, §§ 349–57, 66 Stat. 163, 267–72. Not until 1958, however, did any of the denationalization grounds meet any serious constitutional resistance.

---

14. "Even Great Britain, the arch exponent of the principle of indissoluble allegiance, joined this movement and executed such a treaty with the United States in 1870." Gordon, above, at 322.

Suddenly, in one day, the Supreme Court handed down three landmark decisions. In *Perez v. Brownell,* 356 U.S. 44, 78 S.Ct. 568, 2 L.Ed.2d 603 (1958), the Court upheld by a 5–4 vote a provision that denationalized any American citizen who voted in a foreign political election. For the majority, it was enough that the conduct (voting in a foreign election) was voluntary and that Congress could reasonably perceive a nexus between that conduct and a potential embarrassment to United States foreign policy.

The second case in the trilogy was *Trop v. Dulles,* 356 U.S. 86, 78 S.Ct. 590, 2 L.Ed.2d 630 (1958). The challenged provision purported to denationalize anyone convicted of deserting the military in time of war. The same four Justices who had dissented in *Perez* joined in a plurality opinion. They believed not only that Congress had no power to take away one's citizenship involuntarily, but also that this particular denationalization ground was punitive and, in the light of the consequences of loss of citizenship, "cruel and unusual" and therefore violative of the Eighth Amendment. Justice Brennan, who had voted with the majority in *Perez,* continued to believe that Congress had the power to denationalize but found this particular provision lacked a rational relation to the war power. By a 5–4 vote, therefore, the provision was struck down.

The third decision announced that day was *Nishikawa v. Dulles,* 356 U.S. 129, 78 S.Ct. 612, 2 L.Ed.2d 659 (1958). The Court decided no constitutional issues in that case, but it did interpret the statute as imposing on the government the burden of proving the expatriating acts by clear, unequivocal, and convincing evidence. (We shall return to the proof issues presently.)

Later cases struck down other provisions that had purported to remove the citizenship of those who engaged in specified activities. See, e.g., *Kennedy v. Mendoza–Martinez,* 372 U.S. 144, 83 S.Ct. 554, 9 L.Ed.2d 644 (1963) (invalidating, as punishment imposed without procedural safeguards required for criminal proceedings, provision that divests citizenship of one who leaves or remains outside United States during wartime to evade military service) (5–4 vote); *Schneider v. Rusk,* 377 U.S. 163, 84 S.Ct. 1187, 12 L.Ed.2d 218 (1964) (invalidating, on equal protection grounds, provision that *naturalized* citizens, but not other citizens, lose citizenship by returning to native country and living there three years) (5–3 vote).

In none of those cases, however, did a majority go so far as to hold that citizenship cannot constitutionally be taken away without the individual's assent. The Court took that plunge, albeit by a 5–4 vote, in *Afroyim v. Rusk,* 387 U.S. 253, 87 S.Ct. 1660, 18 L.Ed.2d 757 (1967). As in *Perez,* the challenge was to the provision that denationalized anyone voting in a foreign political election. Expressly overruling *Perez* and striking down the statutory provision, the Court interpreted section 1 of the Fourteenth Amendment as giving every citizen "a constitutional right to remain a citizen * * * unless he voluntarily relinquishes that citizenship." 387 U.S. at 268, 87 S.Ct. at 1668, 18 L.Ed.2d at 767.[15]

---

15. Four years after *Afroyim,* the Court decided *Rogers v. Bellei,* 401 U.S. 815, 91 S.Ct. 1060, 28 L.Ed.2d 499 (1971), which you have already encountered. Despite *Afroyim,*

As the preceding summary illustrates, the United States law on loss of nationality has traveled a long road: from perpetual allegiance, to a combination of denationalization and expatriation, to expatriation alone.[16] In *Afroyim* the Court insisted on individual consent. But what kind of consent did it have in mind? The case that follows explores that issue and some related questions of proof.

Vance v. Terrazas

Supreme Court of the United States, 1980.
444 U.S. 252, 100 S.Ct. 540, 62 L.Ed.2d 461.

■ MR. JUSTICE WHITE delivered the opinion of the Court.

Section 349(a)(2) of the Immigration and Nationality Act provides that "a person who is a national of the United States whether by birth or naturalization, shall lose his nationality by . . . taking an oath or making an affirmation or other formal declaration of allegiance to a foreign state or a political subdivision thereof." The Act also provides that the party claiming that such loss of citizenship occurred must "establish such claim by a preponderance of the evidence" and that the voluntariness of the expatriating conduct is rebuttably presumed. § 349(c).[a] The issues in this case are whether, in establishing loss of citizenship under § 349(a)(2), a party must prove an intent to surrender United States citizenship and whether the United States Constitution permits Congress to legislate with respect to expatriation proceedings by providing the standard of proof and the statutory presumption contained in § 349(c).

I

Appellee, Laurence J. Terrazas, was born in this country, the son of a Mexican citizen. He thus acquired at birth both United States and Mexican citizenship. In the fall of 1970, while a student in Monterrey, Mexico, and at the age of 22, appellee executed an application for a certificate of Mexican nationality, swearing "adherence, obedience, and submission to

---

the Court in *Bellei* upheld the withdrawal of citizenship from one who had acquired citizenship by descent but who had then failed to satisfy the statutory conditions for retaining residence in the United States. The Court limited *Afroyim* to Fourteenth Amendment, section 1 citizens, held that citizens by descent do not come within that description because they were not born or naturalized "in the United States," and proceeded to find the particular conditions reasonable.

16. That progression has spawned some fine commentary that includes more detailed descriptions and analyses of how the modern law evolved. For a small sampling, see T.

Alexander Aleinikoff, *Theories of Loss of Citizenship,* 84 Michigan L. Rev. 1471, 1475–84 (1986); Donald K. Duvall, *Expatriation Under United States Law,* Perez to Afroyim: *The Search for a Philosophy of American Citizenship,* 56 Virginia L. Rev. 408, 411–30 (1970); Gary Endelman, *Saying Goodbye to Uncle Sam: Formal Renunciation of U.S. Citizenship,* 73 IR 709 (May 24, 1996); Charles Gordon, *The Citizen and the State: Power of Congress to Expatriate American Citizens,* 53 Georgetown L.J. 315, 317–33 (1965); Elwin Griffith, *Expatriation and the American Citizen,* 31 Howard L.J. 453, 455–78 (1988).

a. Now INA § 349(b).—Ed.

the laws and authorities of the Mexican Republic" and "expressly re-nounc[ing] United States citizenship, as well as any submission, obedience, and loyalty to any foreign government, especially to that of the United States of America, ..." The certificate, which issued upon this application on April 3, 1971, recited that Terrazas had sworn adherence to the United Mexican States and that he "has expressly renounced all rights inherent to any other nationality, as well as all submission, obedience, and loyalty to any foreign government, especially to those which have recognized him as that national." Terrazas read and understood the certificate upon receipt.

A few months later, following a discussion with an officer of the United States Consulate in Monterrey, proceedings were instituted to determine whether appellee had lost his United States citizenship by obtaining the certificate of Mexican nationality. Appellee denied that he had, but in December 1971 the Department of State issued a certificate of loss of nationality. The Board of Appellate Review of the Department of State, after a full hearing, affirmed that appellee had voluntarily renounced his United States citizenship. As permitted by § 360(a) of the Act, appellee then brought this suit against the Secretary of State for a declaration of his United States nationality. Trial was *de novo*.

* * * The District Court concluded that the United States had "proved by a preponderance of the evidence that Laurence J. Terrazas knowingly, understandingly and voluntarily took an oath of allegiance to Mexico, and concurrently renounced allegiance to the United States," and that he had therefore "voluntarily relinquished United States citizenship pursuant to § 349(a)(2) of the ... Act."

In its opinion accompanying its findings and conclusions, the District Court observed that appellee had acted "voluntarily in swearing allegiance to Mexico and renouncing allegiance to the United States," and that appellee "knew he was repudiating allegiance to the United States through his actions." The court also said * * * that "the declaration of allegiance to a foreign state in conjunction with the renunciatory language of United States citizenship 'would leave no room for ambiguity as to the intent of the applicant.' "

The Court of Appeals reversed. As the Court of Appeals understood the law—and there appears to have been no dispute on these basic require-ments in the Courts of Appeals—the United States had not only to prove the taking of an oath to a foreign state, but also to demonstrate an intent on appellee's part to renounce his United States citizenship. The District Court had found these basic elements to have been proved by a preponder-ance of the evidence; and the Court of Appeals observed that, "[a]ssuming that the proper [evidentiary] standards were applied, we are convinced that the record fully supports the court's findings." The Court of Appeals ruled, however, that under *Afroyim v. Rusk,* Congress had no power to legislate the evidentiary standard contained in § 349(c) and that the Constitution required that proof be not merely by a preponderance of the evidence, but by "clear, convincing and unequivocal evidence." The case was remanded to the District Court for further proceedings.

* * *

II

* * *

In *Afroyim v. Rusk,* the Court held that § 401(e) of the Nationality Act of 1940, which provided that an American citizen "shall lose his nationality by . . . [v]oting in a political election in a foreign state," contravened the Citizenship Clause of the Fourteenth Amendment. Afroyim was a naturalized American citizen who lived in Israel for 10 years. While in that nation, Afroyim voted in a political election. He in consequence was stripped of his United States citizenship. Consistently with *Perez v. Brownell,* which had sustained § 401(e), the District Court affirmed the power of Congress to expatriate for such conduct regardless of the citizen's intent to renounce his citizenship. This Court, however, in overruling *Perez,* "reject[ed] the idea . . . that, aside from the Fourteenth Amendment, Congress has any general power, express or implied, to take away an American citizen's citizenship without his assent." The *Afroyim* opinion continued: § 1 of the Fourteenth Amendment is "most reasonably . . . read as defining a citizenship which a citizen keeps unless he voluntarily relinquishes it."

The Secretary argues that *Afroyim* does not stand for the proposition that a specific intent to renounce must be shown before citizenship is relinquished. It is enough, he urges, to establish one of the expatriating acts specified in § 349(a) because Congress has declared each of those acts to be inherently inconsistent with the retention of citizenship. But *Afroyim* emphasized that loss of citizenship requires the individual's "assent," in addition to his voluntary commission of the expatriating act. It is difficult to understand that "assent" to loss of citizenship would mean anything less than an intent to relinquish citizenship, whether the intent is expressed in words or is found as a fair inference from proved conduct. *Perez* had sustained congressional power to expatriate without regard to the intent of the citizen to surrender his citizenship. *Afroyim* overturned this proposition. It may be, as the Secretary maintains, that a requirement of intent to relinquish citizenship poses substantial difficulties for the Government in performance of its essential task of determining who is a citizen. Nevertheless, the intent of the Fourteenth Amendment, among other things, was to define citizenship; and as interpreted in *Afroyim,* that definition cannot coexist with a congressional power to specify acts that work a renunciation of citizenship even absent an intent to renounce. In the last analysis, expatriation depends on the will of the citizen rather than on the will of Congress and its assessment of his conduct.

* * *

In any event, we are confident that it would be inconsistent with *Afroyim* to treat the expatriating acts specified in § 349(a) as the equiva-

lent of or as conclusive evidence of the indispensable voluntary assent of
the citizen. * * *

* * *

* * * [I]n the case now before us, the Board of Appellate Review of the
State Department found that appellee not only swore allegiance to Mexico,
but also intended to abandon his United States citizenship: "In consideration of the complete record, we view appellant's declaration of allegiance
to Mexico and his concurrent repudiation of any and all submission,
obedience, and loyalty to the United States as compelling evidence of a
specific intent to relinquish his United States citizenship." * * *

As we have said, *Afroyim* requires that the record support a finding
that the expatriating act was accompanied by an intent to terminate United
States citizenship. The submission of the United States is inconsistent with
this holding, and we are unprepared to reconsider it.

III

With respect to the principal issues before it, the Court of Appeals held
that Congress was without constitutional authority to prescribe the standard of proof in expatriation proceedings and that the proof in such cases
must be by clear and convincing evidence rather than by the preponderance
standard prescribed in § 349(c). We are in fundamental disagreement with
these conclusions.

In *Nishikawa v. Dulles,* an American-born citizen, temporarily in
Japan, was drafted into the Japanese Army. The Government later claimed
that, under § 401(c) of the Nationality Act of 1940, he had expatriated
himself by serving in the armed forces of a foreign nation. The Government
agreed that expatriation had not occurred if Nishikawa's army service had
been involuntary. Nishikawa contended that the Government had to prove
that his service was voluntary, while the Government urged that duress
was an affirmative defense that Nishikawa had the burden to prove by
overcoming the usual presumption of voluntariness. This Court held the
presumption unavailable to the Government and required proof of a
voluntary expatriating act by clear and convincing evidence.

Section 349(c) soon followed; its evident aim was to supplant the
evidentiary standards prescribed by *Nishikawa.* * * *

We see no basis for invalidating the evidentiary prescriptions contained
in § 349(c). *Nishikawa* was not rooted in the Constitution. The Court
noted, moreover, that it was acting in the absence of legislative guidance.
Nor do we agree with the Court of Appeals that, because under *Afroyim*
Congress is constitutionally devoid of power to impose expatriation on a
citizen, it is also without power to prescribe the evidentiary standards to
govern expatriation proceedings. Although § 349(c) had been law since
1961, *Afroyim* did not address or advert to that section; surely the Court
would have said so had it intended to construe the Constitution to exclude
expatriation proceedings from the traditional powers of Congress to prescribe rules of evidence and standards of proof in the federal courts. This

power, rooted in the authority of Congress conferred by Art. 1, § 8, cl. 9, of the Constitution to create inferior federal courts, is undoubted and has been frequently noted and sustained.

* * *

We are unable to conclude that the specific evidentiary standard provided by Congress in § 349(c) is invalid under either the Citizenship Clause or the Due Process Clause of the Fifth Amendment. It is true that in criminal and involuntary commitment contexts we have held that the Due Process Clause imposes requirements of proof beyond a preponderance of the evidence. This Court has also stressed the importance of citizenship and evinced a decided preference for requiring clear and convincing evidence to prove expatriation. But expatriation proceedings are civil in nature and do not threaten a loss of liberty. Moreover, as we have noted, *Nishikawa* did not purport to be [a] constitutional ruling, and the same is true of similar rulings in related areas. *Woodby v. INS* (deportation); *Schneiderman v. United States* (denaturalization). None of these cases involved a congressional judgment, such as that present here, that the preponderance standard of proof provides sufficient protection for the interest of the individual in retaining his citizenship. Contrary to the Secretary's position, we have held that expatriation requires the ultimate finding that the citizen has committed the expatriating act with the intent to renounce his citizenship. This in itself is a heavy burden, and we cannot hold that Congress has exceeded its powers by requiring proof of an intentional expatriating act by a preponderance of evidence.

IV

* * * We also conclude that the presumption of voluntariness provided in § 349(c) is not otherwise constitutionally infirm.

Section 349(c) provides in relevant part that "any person who commits or performs, or who has committed or performed, any act of expatriation under the provisions of this chapter or any other Act shall be presumed to have done so voluntarily, but such presumption may be rebutted upon a showing, by a preponderance of the evidence, that the act or acts committed or performed were not done voluntarily." In enacting § 349(c), Congress did not dispute the holding of *Nishikawa* that the alleged expatriating act—there, service in a foreign army—must be performed voluntarily, but it did insist that the Government have the benefit of the usual presumption of voluntariness and that one claiming that his act was involuntary make out his claim of duress by a preponderance of the evidence.

It is important at this juncture to note the scope of the statutory presumption. Section 349(c) provides that any of the statutory expatriating acts, if proved, are presumed to have been committed voluntarily. It does not also direct a presumption that the act has been performed with the intent to relinquish United States citizenship. That matter remains the burden of the party claiming expatriation to prove by a preponderance of the evidence. As so understood, we cannot invalidate the provision.

The majority opinion in *Nishikawa* referred to the "ordinary rule that duress is a matter of affirmative defense" to be proved by the party claiming the duress. Justices Frankfurter and Burton, concurring in the result, also referred to the "ordinarily controlling principles of evidence [that] would suggest that the individual, who is peculiarly equipped to clarify an ambiguity in the meaning of outward events should have the burden of proving what his state of mind was." * * * Yet the Court in *Nishikawa*, because it decided that "the consequences of denationalization are so drastic" and because it found nothing indicating a contrary result in the legislative history of the Nationality Act of 1940, held that the Government must carry the burden of proving that the expatriating act was performed voluntarily.

Section 349(c), which was enacted subsequently, and its legislative history make clear that Congress preferred the ordinary rule that voluntariness is presumed and that duress is an affirmative defense to be proved by the party asserting it. * * * The rationality of the procedural rule with respect to claims of involuntariness in ordinary civil cases cannot be doubted. To invalidate the rule here would be to disagree flatly with Congress on the balance to be struck between the interest in citizenship and the burden the Government must assume in demonstrating expatriating conduct. It would also constitutionalize that disagreement and give the Citizenship Clause of the Fourteenth Amendment far more scope in this context than the relevant circumstances that brought the Amendment into being would suggest appropriate. Thus we conclude that the presumption of voluntariness included in § 349(c) has continuing vitality.

V

In sum, we hold that in proving expatriation, an expatriating act and an intent to relinquish citizenship must be proved by a preponderance of the evidence. We also hold that when one of the statutory expatriating acts is proved, it is constitutional to presume it to have been a voluntary act until and unless proved otherwise by the actor. If he succeeds, there can be no expatriation. If he fails, the question remains whether on all the evidence the Government has satisfied its burden of proof that the expatriating act was performed with the necessary intent to relinquish citizenship.

The judgment of the Court of Appeals is reversed, and the case is remanded for further proceedings consistent with this opinion.

So ordered.

■ Mr. Justice Stewart dissents for the reasons stated in Part II of Mr. Justice Brennan's dissenting opinion, which he joins.

■ Mr. Justice Marshall, concurring in part and dissenting in part.

I agree with the Court's holding that a citizen of the United States may not lose his citizenship in the absence of a finding that he specifically intended to renounce it. I also concur in the adoption of a saving construction of INA § 349(a)(2) to require that the statutorily designated expatriating acts be done with a specific intent to relinquish citizenship.

I cannot, however, accept the majority's conclusion that a person may be found to have relinquished his American citizenship upon a preponderance of the evidence that he intended to do so. The Court's discussion of congressional power to "prescribe rules of evidence and standards of proof in the federal courts" is the beginning, not the end, of the inquiry. It remains the task of this Court to determine when those rules and standards impinge on constitutional rights. As my Brother Stevens indicates, the Court's casual dismissal of the importance of American citizenship cannot withstand scrutiny. And the mere fact that one who has been expatriated is not locked up in a prison does not dispose of the constitutional inquiry. As Mr. Chief Justice Warren stated over 20 years ago:

> "[T]he expatriate has lost the right to have rights.
>
> "This punishment is offensive to cardinal principles for which the Constitution stands. It subjects the individual to a fate of ever-increasing fear and distress. He knows not what discriminations may be established against him, what proscriptions may be directed against him, and when and for what cause his existence in his native land may be terminated. He may be subject to banishment, a fate universally decried by civilized people. He is stateless, a condition deplored in the international community of democracies. It is no answer to suggest that all the disastrous consequences of this fate may not be brought to bear on a stateless person. The threat makes the punishment obnoxious." *Trop v. Dulles* (plurality opinion).

For these reasons I cannot understand, much less accept, the Court's suggestion that "expatriation proceedings ... do not threaten a loss of liberty." Recognizing that a standard of proof ultimately " 'reflects the value society places' " on the interest at stake, I would hold that a citizen may not lose his citizenship in the absence of clear and convincing evidence that he intended to do so.

■ MR. JUSTICE STEVENS, concurring in part and dissenting in part.

The Court today unanimously reiterates the principle set forth in *Afroyim v. Rusk* that Congress may not deprive an American of his citizenship against his will, but may only effectuate the citizen's own intention to renounce his citizenship. I agree with the Court that Congress may establish certain standards for determining whether such a renunciation has occurred. It may, for example, provide that expatriation can be proved by evidence that a person has performed an act that is normally inconsistent with continued citizenship and that the person thereby specifically intended to relinquish his American citizenship.

I do not agree, however, with the conclusion that Congress has established a permissible standard in INA § 349(a)(2). Since we accept dual citizenship, taking an oath of allegiance to a foreign government is not necessarily inconsistent with an intent to remain an American citizen. Moreover, as now written, the statute cannot fairly be read to require a finding of specific intent to relinquish citizenship. * * *

I also disagree with the holding that a person may be deprived of his citizenship upon a showing by a mere preponderance of the evidence that he intended to relinquish it. The Court reasons that because the proceedings in question are civil in nature and do not result in any loss of physical liberty, no greater burden of proof is required than in the ordinary civil case. Such reasoning construes the constitutional concept of "liberty" too narrowly.

* * * In my judgment a person's interest in retaining his American citizenship is surely an aspect of "liberty" of which he cannot be deprived without due process of law. Because the interest at stake is comparable to that involved in *Addington v. Texas,* essentially for the reasons stated in THE CHIEF JUSTICE's opinion for a unanimous Court in that case, I believe that due process requires that a clear and convincing standard of proof be met in this case as well before the deprivation may occur.

■ Mr. Justice Brennan, with whom Mr. Justice Stewart joins as to Part II, dissenting.

* * * Because I would hold that one who acquires United States citizenship by virtue of being born in the United States, U.S. Const., Amdt. 14, § 1, can lose that citizenship only by formally renouncing it, and because I would hold that the act of which appellee is accused in this case cannot be an expatriating act, I dissent.

I

This case is governed by *Afroyim v. Rusk. Afroyim,* emphasizing the crucial importance of the right of citizenship, held unequivocally that a citizen has "a constitutional right to remain a citizen ... unless he voluntarily relinquishes that citizenship." * * *

* * * Congress has provided for a procedure by which one may formally renounce citizenship. In this case the appellant concedes that appellee has not renounced his citizenship under that procedure. Because one can lose citizenship only by voluntarily renouncing it and because appellee has not formally renounced his, I would hold that he remains a citizen. Accordingly, I would remand the case with orders that appellee be given a declaration of United States nationality.

II

I reach the same result by another, independent line of reasoning. Appellee was born a dual national. He is a citizen of the United States because he was born here and a citizen of Mexico because his father was Mexican. The only expatriating act of which appellee stands accused is having sworn an oath of allegiance to Mexico. If dual citizenship, *per se,* can be consistent with United States citizenship, then I cannot see why an oath of allegiance to the other country of which one is already a citizen should create inconsistency. One owes allegiance to any country of which one is a citizen, especially when one is living in that country. The formal oath adds nothing to the existing foreign citizenship and, therefore, cannot affect his United States citizenship.

LATER DEVELOPMENTS

INA § 349(a), which you should read now, lists the acts that can result in loss of nationality. The present version reflects some 1986 amendments intended to codify the holding in *Terrazas*. See Act of Nov. 14, 1986, Pub.L. 99–653, § 18, 100 Stat. 3655, 3658. Note in particular the explicit statutory requirements that the person (a) "voluntarily" perform one of the enumerated acts and (b) do so "with the intention of relinquishing United States nationality."

The State Department, which decides the vast bulk of all loss of nationality cases (more on that in a moment), made a dramatic announcement in 1990. It declared that individuals will be *presumed* to "intend to retain United States citizenship when they obtain naturalization in a foreign state, subscribe to routine declarations of allegiance to a foreign state, or accept non-policy level employment with a foreign government." State Dept. Cable to Diplomatic and Consular Posts (April 16, 1990), reproduced in 67 IR 1092, at 1093 (Oct. 1, 1990). In cases to which the presumption applies, the Department will find there was no intent to relinquish nationality unless the person affirmatively asserts, in a questionnaire provided by a consular officer, that he or she intended to relinquish citizenship. *Id.* See now 22 C.F.R. § 50.50 (2004). The Department cautions that the presumption is inapplicable in certain cases, including any in which the statutory expatriating act is "accompanied by conduct which is so inconsistent with retention of U.S. citizenship that it compels a conclusion that the individual intended to relinquish U.S. citizenship." 67 IR at 1093. The Statement adds, however, that the latter cases "are very rare." *Id.*

For the individual who *wants* to surrender his or her U.S. citizenship, this announcement means it will be necessary either to affirm that intention in writing to a U.S. consular officer or to formally renounce under INA § 349(a)(5). See 67 IR at 1094. For some helpful detail on the effectiveness of foreign renunciation oaths, see Gary Endelman, *Saying Goodbye to Uncle Sam: Formal Renunciation of U.S. Citizenship*, 73 IR 709 (May 24, 1996).

Importantly, the State Department announcement is retroactive; those who previously lost their U.S. citizenship may request reconsideration by writing to the nearest consulate or to the State Department in Washington, D.C. See 67 IR at 1094; see also H. Ansgar Kelly, *Dual Nationality, The Myth of Election, and a Kinder, Gentler State Department*, 23 Univ. Miami Inter–American L.Rev. 421, 442–48 (1991–92).

The new policy is expected to eliminate most loss of nationality cases. According to the State Department, in a typical year before the new policy approximately 800 people would be found to have lost their nationality. Only about 200 of those cases were based on express renunciations. For the vast majority of the rest, determinations of loss of nationality are now expected to be few. 67 IR at 1094–95. Especially affected by the retroactivity provision will be some 282,000 U.S.-born, naturalized Canadian citizens, including many draft-age males who moved to Canada during the Vietnam War. 67 IR 799, 800 (July 23, 1990).

The State Department's 1990 announcement reflects the government's general discomfort with renunciations of United States citizenship—especially, but not only, in cases where renunciation would result in statelessness. In 1995, Secretary of State Warren Christopher announced that the Department would go a step farther, proposing legislation to repeal all the expatriation grounds except the taking of a formal renunciation oath in a U.S. consulate. Endelman, above, at 715. To date, however, no such legislation has been enacted.

NOTES AND QUESTIONS

1. Loss of nationality issues can surface in various settings. Any time a legal benefit or sanction turns on a person's nationality, and there is an issue whether nationality has been lost, the official responsible for adjudicating the benefit or sanction generally must make a nationality decision in order to dispose of the case. See, e.g., *MacKenzie v. Hare*, 239 U.S. 299, 36 S.Ct. 106, 60 L.Ed. 297 (1915) (upholding local election officials' refusal of voter registration upon finding of expatriation).

More commonly, though, an administrative finding that an individual has lost nationality is made by DHS, the Justice Department, or the State Department. The Justice Department (EOIR) becomes involved, for example, when the subject of removal proceedings claims citizenship in removal proceedings and ICE responds that expatriation has occurred. As you have seen, BIA decisions are generally subject to judicial review. Similar issues can arise when USCIS denies a visa petition on the ground that the petitioner has lost his or her United States citizenship. See Gary Endelman, *How to Prevent Loss of Citizenship: Part I,* Immigration Briefings (Nov. 1989) at 4.

Most other loss of nationality cases come up through the State Department. The Secretary of State is responsible for making loss of nationality decisions when either the person is outside the United States, INA § 104(a)(3), or there is reason to believe the person lost his or her nationality while outside the United States, INA § 358. Both such situations are common. As you read the list of expatriating acts in INA § 349(a), you might have noticed that most are the sorts of acts that would normally occur in foreign countries. When they do, State Department officials (ordinarily diplomatic or consular officers) make the relevant findings. Passport officials also make decisions as to loss of nationality. See generally Endelman, above, at 4–7. Since 1967 (one year after *Afroyim*), these various State Department decisions have been appealable to a non-statutory tribunal called the Board of Appellate Review (BAR). Created by the State Department and located within the Department's Office of the Legal Adviser, the BAR reviews the relevant record and may take additional evidence; the precise standard of review is unclear. See generally 22 C.F.R. § 7 (2004); Alan G. James, *The Board of Appellate Review of the Depart-*

ment of State: The Right to Appellate Review of Administrative Determina-tions of Loss of Nationality, 23 San Diego L. Rev. 261 (1986). BAR and other agency decisions finding a loss of nationality are generally subject to judicial review. INA § 360 spells out various forms that the review can take.

2.   The Court in *Terrazas* makes clear that in expatriation cases the government must prove a specific intent to renounce citizenship. In a helpful article, Professor Aleinikoff considers four different theories for deciding who should possess citizenship and concludes that none of them supports the *Terrazas* principle. T. Alexander Aleinikoff, *Theories of Loss of Citizenship,* 84 Michigan L. Rev. 1471, 1484–98 (1986). The four are (a) the "Rights Perspective" (citizenship is a constitutional right); (b) the "Consent Perspective" (citizenship is the product of mutual consent between the individual and the nation); (c) the "Contractarian Perspective" (citizenship is part of the social contract among the individuals who created the nation); and (d) the "Communitarian perspective" (citizenship reflects the psycho-logical and social bonds that inevitably form between an individual and the society in which he or she is raised or is living).

Consider each of those theories and decide whether you agree with Aleinikoff that they do not lead to the conclusion reached in *Terrazas.* For some of them, you might need to take into account that the *Terrazas* doctrine is asymmetrical; that is, the individual may unilaterally end the relationship but the government may not.

3.   Having concluded that none of the four citizenship perspectives explains the prohibition on denationalization, Aleinikoff argues that the Court should shift its focus from consent to allegiance. More specifically, Aleinikoff proposes that the government be permitted to denationalize when it can prove the commission of "specific acts that demonstrate lapsed, transferred, or divided allegiance." *Id.* at 1500. For more detail, see *id.* at 1500–03. What dangers do you see in such an approach? Are there ways to minimize those dangers? What activities would you include in the list? What would be the benefits of his proposed change?

4.   To illustrate the contrast between an intent-based approach and an allegiance-based approach, Aleinikoff discusses the case of Rabbi Meir Kahane. Kahane, a United States citizen and the founder of the Jewish Defense League, immigrated to Israel. By doing so, he automatically acquired Israeli citizenship under Israel's Law of Return, which bestows citizenship upon any Jew who settles in that country. He was then elected to the Knesset (the Israeli Parliament). The State Department charged he had lost his United States nationality under INA § 349(a)(4)(A), by the combination of having served in a foreign government and having acquired foreign nationality. All along, however, Kahane had insisted to the State Department that he intended to retain his United States citizenship, which he pointed out he had a motive to preserve—it facilitated his travel to and from the United States. The State Department nonetheless found an intent to renounce, and the BAR affirmed. The Board observed that "actions

speak louder than words" and cited also Kahane's admission that his "primary loyalty is to Israel." See Aleinikoff, above, at 1471–72.

Aleinikoff criticizes the Board's analysis. While conceding that words are not conclusive, he notes the absence of *any* evidence of an intent to renounce and indeed the presence of an affirmative motive to retain United States citizenship. He suggests, convincingly, that the Board in fact based its result solely upon a finding that Kahane had transferred his allegiance—not, as the Board states, upon a finding that Kahane had intended to relinquish his United States citizenship. *Id.* at 1472–73. A federal district court ultimately reversed the BAR decision, holding that the evidence required a finding of intent to preserve United States citizenship. *Kahane v. Shultz,* 653 F.Supp. 1486 (E.D.N.Y.1987).

Kahane's victory proved hollow. The following year the Knesset enacted legislation forbidding its members to be citizens of any country but Israel. Kahane responded by appearing before a United States consulate, where, after receiving an explanation of the consequences of losing citizenship, he took a formal oath of renunciation. Because of some technical defects in the form of the oath, he returned to the consulate a month later and executed the renunciation a second time. The State Department issued a Certificate of Loss of Nationality (CLN). About one month later, the Israeli Supreme Court barred Kahane's political party (the Kach Party, which he had founded) from running in the 1988 Parliamentary elections. His Parliamentary career at least temporarily derailed, Kahane then attempted to withdraw his renunciation on the ground it was involuntary. The State Department refused his request. He brought an action to enjoin the State Department from enforcing his CLN and, as part of that action, moved for a preliminary injunction. The district court denied the motion, finding too little likelihood that he would prevail on the merits of the voluntariness issue. *Kahane v. Secretary of State,* 700 F.Supp. 1162 (D.D.C. 1988).

On November 5, 1990, while giving a speech in the United States, Rabbi Kahane was assassinated. New York Times, Nov. 6, 1990, at A1.

More generally, *should* acts that clearly demonstrate a lack of allegiance to the United States be ground for expatriation, or should a specific intent to renounce citizenship be required? What if a United States citizen is convicted of perpetrating a large-scale terrorist act, and it is proved that the act was done for the specific purpose of harming the United States? Should the person be stripped of his or her citizenship, either as part of the criminal punishment or in addition to it?

5. The Restatement II of Torts, § 8A, defines an "inten[ded]" consequence as one that the actor either "*desires*" to cause or "*believes is substantially certain to result* from his or her act" (emphasis added). The criminal law has traditionally adopted a similar view. See Wayne R. Lafave, Criminal Law § 5.2 (4th ed.2003). What would you think of an approach that adopts the *Terrazas* requirement of an intent to relinquish citizenship, but defines intent as tort lawyers and criminal lawyers do? Would that approach solve the theoretical problems? Would it be good policy? If a

person likes having United States citizenship but is willing to give it up when doing so will help achieve some other objective, why not recognize that choice?

6. Among the common responses to State Department allegations of intent to relinquish citizenship are (a) "I was unaware I had ever *acquired* United States citizenship in the first place" and (b) "I did not understand that I was giving it up." See generally Gary Endelman, *How to Prevent Loss of Citizenship: Part II,* December 1989 Immigration Briefings at 12–15.

7. The preceding notes concerned the requirement of an intent to relinquish citizenship. The Court in *Terrazas,* and now INA § 349(a) itself, make clear that expatriation also requires the *voluntary* commission of one of the specific acts enumerated in the statute. Justice Brennan believes that these acts, even if performed voluntarily and coupled with an intent to relinquish citizenship, do not suffice; rather, he would hold, one may surrender citizenship only by taking a formal oath of renunciation. That view, as you saw earlier, was also expressed by former Secretary of State Warren Christopher. Do you agree? That question aside, do you agree with Justice Brennan that Terrazas did nothing inconsistent with retention of United States citizenship?

8. You might have noticed from the list of expatriating acts in section 349(a) that it is nearly impossible for a person to give up his or her United States citizenship during peacetime without either leaving the United States or committing a serious crime. Subsection (6) permits renunciation in the United States in time of war, and subsection (7) permits renunciation by treason or other related crimes, but the other subsections encompass conduct that would normally occur abroad (foreign naturalization, oath of allegiance to foreign state, certain foreign military service, certain foreign government employment, renunciation before consular officer). Why do you suppose the law does not allow people to surrender their United States citizenship simply by taking an oath of renunciation before designated officials in the United States? Professors Peter Schuck and Rogers Smith, consistently with their consent-based view of citizenship, have proposed a procedure by which every United States citizen, upon attaining age 18, would receive a form on which the person could make a decision to renounce citizenship. Under their proposal, the form would contain information stressing the implications of that choice, and the default option would be retention. Peter H. Schuck & Rogers M. Smith, Citizenship Without Consent—Illegal Aliens in the American Polity 122–26 (1985). For a strong criticism of that proposal, see David A. Martin, *Membership and Consent: Abstract or Organic?,* 11 Yale J. Internat'l L. 278, 288–90 (1985).

How do you feel (a) about allowing surrender of citizenship by oath of renunciation in the United States; and (b) about the proposal to furnish renunciation forms at age 18?

9. One of the most common issues in expatriation cases is whether the expatriating act was committed under duress. Economic duress is

frequently asserted ("I had to acquire Canadian nationality in order to get work") but seldom successful. See Alan G. James, *The Board of Appellate Review of the Department of State: The Right to Appellate Review of Administrative Determinations of Loss of Nationality*, 23 San Diego L.Rev. 261, 291–93 (1986). But see the 3–2 decision finding economic duress in the case of controversial writer Margaret Randall, File No. A11 644 708 (BIA, July 27, 1989, unpublished), discussed in 66 IR at 843–44 (1989).

10. The flip side of the economic duress cases are those in which wealthy Americans formally renounce their United States citizenship and move overseas in order to reduce their United States income taxes. Recently this phenomenon has been occurring often, gathering publicity, and generating anger. In 1996, Congress responded with both barrels. It enacted various changes to the tax laws, see Alice G. Abreu, *Taxing Exits*, 29 U.C. Davis L. Rev. 1087 (1996), and it added an inadmissibility ground for former citizens who, after enactment, renounce their citizenship "for the purpose of avoiding taxation by the United States," see IIRIRA § 352(a), adding INA § 212(a)(10). Not all, however, find this expatriation practice objectionable. See, e.g., Alice G. Abreu, *The Difference Between Expatriates and Mrs. Gregory—Citizenship Can Matter*, 10 Tax Notes Internat'l 1612 (May 8, 1995) (arguing that U.S. tax laws should respect person's choice to relinquish citizenship, since the person is also giving up many non-tax benefits of citizenship). For a highly useful analysis, see David M. Hudson, *Tax Problems for Departing Aliens*, March 1997 Immigration Briefings.

Other sanctions for tax expatriates are also possible. The Internal Revenue Code now prescribes the posting of the names of citizenship renouncers in the Federal Register. 26 U.S.C. § 6039G(e). For a sample, see 64 Fed. Reg. 3339 (Jan. 21, 1999). Another approach is offered in Jeffrey M. Colon, *Changing U.S. Tax Jurisdiction: Expatriates, Immigrants, and the Need for a Coherent Tax Policy*, 34 San Diego L. Rev. 1 (1997) (advocating "mark-to-market" approach that would tax expatriates on accrued gains and losses).

11. Obtaining naturalization in a foreign state is one of the more important statutory expatriating acts. INA § 349(a)(1). Some foreign nations, like the United States, make oaths of renunciation of all other nationalities a prerequisite to naturalization. Others do not. For examples, see James, item 9 above, at 302–03. The liberalizations announced by the State Department in 1990 will eliminate many problems even for those who obtain naturalization in countries that require renunciation oaths.

12. The Court in *Terrazas* also addresses two proof problems, both arising under former INA § 349(c) [now 349(b)]. The Court first upholds the "preponderance of the evidence" standard. Refer back, on pages 712–13 above, to Justice Harlan's prescription for determining the appropriate standard of proof. If you apply it to expatriation, how do you personally come out?

13. Do you agree with the Court's decision to uphold the statutory rebuttable presumption that, if the individual committed one of the expatriating acts, the commission was voluntary?

SECTION C.   THE SIGNIFICANCE OF CITIZENSHIP

In emotional terms, citizenship means different things to different people. For many, citizenship is an element of personal identity, a link either between self and nation or between self and other individuals. The strength and meanings of those bonds vary with the values and experiences of the individual and with the history and culture of the particular nation. For some, citizenship represents a heritage that is as fundamental to personal identity as are family and ethnicity; for others, the meaning of citizenship is less profound.

From a legal standpoint, citizenship is a source of several specific rights. But the differences between citizens' rights and noncitizens' rights typically do not generate serious discussion unless the particular noncitizens are LPRs. Most people accept the legitimacy of treating either undocumented migrants or temporary visitors differently from citizens. LPRs have a stronger claim to community membership. Thus, when people talk about whether a particular legal right should be reserved for citizens, the hardest policy, and sometimes constitutional, questions usually concern the eligibility of LPRs.

In the United States, the most practically significant legal consequence of citizenship is freedom from the immigration laws. Without the right to *be* in the United States, most of the other rights provided by American law would be meaningless or at least far less important. As you have also seen, citizenship further enables one to petition for the admission of certain family members as immigrants. LPRs may also petition on behalf of certain family members, but both the range of qualifying relatives and the numerical quotas (and therefore the waiting periods) are much more restrictive than when citizens file analogous petitions.

One much overlooked benefit of citizenship is the (qualified) statutory right to pass it on to one's children. Transmission can occur in various ways that you encountered in section A.

International law has long emphasized the interdependence of allegiance and protection. A citizen is said to owe permanent allegiance to the country of citizenship, which in consequence may protect that individual when he or she is threatened with harm by a foreign nation. See generally Richard B. Lillich, The Human Rights of Aliens in Contemporary International Law 5–17 (1984). Nations have no analogous power to intervene on behalf of their LPRs.

Allegations of illegal foreign contributions to President Clinton's 1996 presidential campaign triggered proposals to ban all noncitizens—including LPRs—from contributing to federal election campaigns. One such bill, H.R. 34 (1998), passed the House of Representatives in 1998 but did not become law. See 144 Cong. Rec. H1764 (Mar. 30, 1998). For a comprehensive summary, see Covington & Burling and National Asian Pacific American Legal Consortium, *Protecting the Rights of Legal Permanent Residents: A*

First Amendment Analysis of Proposals to Prohibit Campaign Contributions and Expenditures by Legal Permanent Residents, 3 BIB 16 (Jan. 1, 1998). The issue is still alive.

In the United States, federal and state laws impose a host of other, miscellaneous disabilities on noncitizens. Even LPRs still sometimes find themselves ineligible for certain state professional licenses. See Luis F.B. Plascencia, Gary P. Freeman & Mark Setzler, Tomás Rivera Policy Institute, *Restricting Immigrant Access to Employment: An Examination of Regulations in Five States*, Policy Brief (Aug. 1999). Other common disabilities include ineligibility for government employment, public benefits, property ownership, and political participation. The laws of many countries (not the United States) also insulate their own citizens from extradition. See Yaffa Zilbershats, *Extraditing Israeli Citizens to the United States—Extradition and Citizenship Dilemmas*, 21 Michigan J. Internat'l L. 297 (2000). Some disabilities extend to all noncitizens, while others disadvantage only some—those who are not LPRs, or those who have lived in the United States for less than a prescribed time, etc. See generally David Carliner, Lucas Guttentag, Arthur C. Helton & Wade Henderson, The Rights of Aliens and Refugees—The Basic ACLU Guide to Alien and Refugee Rights (2d ed. 1990); A. Peter Mutharika, The Alien Under American Law (rev.ed. 1984); David Weissbrodt & Laura Danielson, Immigration Law and Procedure in a Nutshell, ch. 13 (5th ed. 2005).

Recent years have seen an explosion of interest in foreign, comparative, and international citizenship law. See, e.g., United States Office of Personnel Management, Investigations Service, Citizenship Laws of the World, http://www.opm.gov/extra/investigate/IS–01.pdf; T. Alexander Aleinikoff & Douglas Klusmeyer (eds.), Citizenship Today: Global Perspectives and Practices (2001); T. Alexander Aleinikoff & Douglas Klusmeyer (eds.), From Migrants to Citizens (2000); Lowell W. Barrington, *The Making of Citizenship Policy in the Baltic States*, 13 Georgetown Immigration L.J. 159 (1999); J. Donald Galloway, *The Dilemmas of Canadian Citizenship Law*, 13 Georgetown Immigration L.J. 201 (1999); John Guendelsberger, *Equal Protection and Resident Alien Access to Public Benefits in France and the United States*, 67 Tulane L. Rev. 669 (1993); Atsushi Kondo (ed.), Citizenship in a Global World–Comparing Citizenship Rights for Aliens (2001); Kim Rubenstein, *Citizenship in Australia: Unscrambling Its Meaning*, 20 Melbourne L. Rev. 503 (1995); Ayelet Shachar, *Whose Republic?: Citizenship and Membership in the Israeli Polity*, 13 Georgetown Immigration L.J. 233 (1999); Gianni Zappalà & Stephen Castles, *Citizenship and Immigration in Australia*, 13 Georgetown Immigration L.J. 273 (1999).

Government action that favors citizens over noncitizens can raise some difficult constitutional issues. In chapter 12, you saw some of the issues that can arise from governmental constraints on undocumented migrants (mainly actions of state governments). Laws that discriminate against LPRs require a different analysis.

Generally, congressional action that discriminates against noncitizens—even LPRs—has been upheld, in part because of Congress's plenary power to regulate immigration and the assumed similarity between immigration laws and other regulation of noncitizens. See, e.g., *Mathews v. Diaz,* 426 U.S. 67, 96 S.Ct. 1883, 48 L.Ed.2d 478 (1976); *Flemming v. Nestor,* 363 U.S. 603, 80 S.Ct. 1367, 4 L.Ed.2d 1435 (1960). But *cf. Hampton v. Mow Sun Wong,* 426 U.S. 88, 96 S.Ct. 1895, 48 L.Ed.2d 495 (1976) (*Civil Service Commission* lacked authority to disqualify all noncitizens from federal employment). Should federal regulation of noncitizens outside the contexts of admission and expulsion be subjected to the same special judicial deference as federal immigration laws are? If not, how does a court tell the difference between "immigration laws" and "other" citizenship regulation? You saw analogous issues in the context of preemption challenges to state regulatory action. For some thoughtful discussion, see Linda S. Bosniak, *Membership, Equality, and the Difference that Alienage Makes,* 69 NYU L. Rev. 1047 (1994); Victor C. Romero, *The Congruence Principle Applied: Rethinking Equal Protection Review of Federal Alienage Classifications after Adarand Constructors, Inc. v. Pena,* 76 Oregon L. Rev. 425 (1997) (urging courts to apply to federal citizenship classifications the same strict scrutiny that analogous state regulation would receive); Michael Scaperlanda, *Partial Membership: Aliens and the Constitutional Community,* 81 Iowa L. Rev. 707 (1996); Margaret H. Taylor, *Detained Aliens Challenging Conditions of Confinement and the Porous Border of the Plenary Power Doctrine,* 22 Hastings Constitutional L.Q. 1087 (1995).

State laws are another story. Given the wide sweep of the INA, some state laws have been struck down on the ground that federal law preempts them. E.g., *Toll v. Moreno,* 458 U.S. 1, 102 S.Ct. 2977, 73 L.Ed.2d 563 (1982); *Plyler v. Doe,* 457 U.S. 202, 102 S.Ct. 2382, 72 L.Ed.2d 786 (1982); but see *DeCanas v. Bica,* 424 U.S. 351, 96 S.Ct. 933, 47 L.Ed.2d 43 (1976) (approving state penalties on employers of undocumented workers).

More common have been challenges based on equal protection. Generally, state action that discriminates against LPRs has been held "suspect," a characterization that for equal protection purposes triggers strict scrutiny and as a practical matter almost certain invalidation. The list of Supreme Court decisions striking down state attempts to disqualify noncitizens from government employment, professional licenses, or welfare benefits is long. See, e.g., *Bernal v. Fainter,* 467 U.S. 216, 104 S.Ct. 2312, 81 L.Ed.2d 175 (1984) (notary public); *Nyquist v. Mauclet,* 432 U.S. 1, 97 S.Ct. 2120, 53 L.Ed.2d 63 (1977) (educational assistance funds); *Examining Board of Engineers, Architects and Surveyors v. Flores de Otero,* 426 U.S. 572, 96 S.Ct. 2264, 49 L.Ed.2d 65 (1976) (engineers); *In re Griffiths,* 413 U.S. 717, 93 S.Ct. 2851, 37 L.Ed.2d 910 (1973) (lawyers); *Sugarman v. Dougall,* 413 U.S. 634, 93 S.Ct. 2842, 37 L.Ed.2d 853 (1973) (state civil service employment); *Graham v. Richardson,* 403 U.S. 365, 91 S.Ct. 1848, 29 L.Ed.2d 534 (1971) (welfare benefits).

There is, however, an important exception to the otherwise near prohibition of state discrimination against noncitizens. It is an exception that goes to the heart of modern conceptions of citizenship. The Supreme Court has held that states may favor United States citizens—even over

LPRs—when the benefit in question sufficiently implicates the "political function" of the state. The paradigm example is the franchise. Although they did not always do so, all fifty states now limit the vote to United States citizens. David Weissbrodt & Laura Danielson, Immigration Law and Procedure in a Nutshell 520 (5th ed. 2005). The constitutionality of that limitation has been upheld. See *Skafte v. Rorex,* 191 Colo. 399, 553 P.2d 830 (1976), appeal dism'd, 430 U.S. 961, 97 S.Ct. 1638, 52 L.Ed.2d 352 (1977). But see Gerald M. Rosberg, *Aliens and Equal Protection: Why Not the Right to Vote?,* 75 Michigan L. Rev. 1092 (1977) (arguing for allowing LPRs to vote); see also Nora V. Demleitner, *The Fallacy of Social "Citizenship," or the Threat of Exclusion*, 12 Georgetown Immigration L.J. 35, 56–64 (1997) (advocating at least *local* voting rights for LPRs); *contra,* Christopher Goddard, *Valuing Citizenship: The Case for Retaining a Citizenship-Based Electorate* (unpublished student seminar paper, 2005). Also, as then Justice Rehnquist pointed out, several constitutional provisions expressly require citizenship for designated political office. See *Sugarman v. Dougall,* 413 U.S. 634, 651–52, 93 S.Ct. 2842, 2862, 37 L.Ed.2d 853, 865–66 (1973) (Rehnquist, J., dissenting), citing, among other provisions, U.S. Const. art. I, § 2, cl. 2 (U.S. Representatives); *id.* § 3, cl. 3 (Senators); *id.* art. II, § 1, cl. 5 (President must be "natural born citizen").

In recent years the political function exception has broadened to permit state-decreed citizenship restrictions that are not so clearly tied to political self-definition. Thus, the Supreme Court has upheld state action requiring citizenship for state troopers, *Foley v. Connelie,* 435 U.S. 291, 98 S.Ct. 1067, 55 L.Ed.2d 287 (1978), for public school teachers, *Ambach v. Norwick,* 441 U.S. 68, 99 S.Ct. 1589, 60 L.Ed.2d 49 (1979), and for probation officers, *Cabell v. Chavez–Salido,* 454 U.S. 432, 102 S.Ct. 735, 70 L.Ed.2d 677 (1982). In those cases the Court emphasized the power of the state to confine important sovereign functions to those who make up the political community. The Court rejected arguments that had stressed the absence of significant policymaking responsibilities in the regulated positions.

CITIZENSHIP AND WELFARE REFORM

The eligibility of immigrants for welfare has been a contentious issue. As you saw in chapter 12, undocumented migrants—with some narrow exceptions—have always been disqualified from almost all federal and state welfare programs. Until 1996, however, LPRs were generally eligible for the major welfare programs, though not always on exactly the same terms as United States citizens.

The Personal Responsibility and Work Opportunity Reconciliation Act of 1996, Pub.L. 104–193, 110 Stat. 2105 (Aug. 22, 1996) [hereafter the Welfare Act], changed all that. In this sweeping legislation, Congress made fundamental changes to the law governing public assistance—slashing it generally, eliminating longstanding safety nets, and shifting much of the responsibility for supporting the needy to the states.

Title IV of the Act deals specifically with noncitizens. It classifies all noncitizens as "qualified" or "unqualified." The "qualified" category includes LPRs, noncitizens who have been admitted under the overseas refugee program or granted asylum or nonreturn, and certain parolees. Welfare Act, § 431(b).

You saw in chapter 12 that anyone classified as "unqualified" (mainly undocumented migrants and nonimmigrants) are ineligible for almost all public assistance. Benefits for the "qualified" are more favorable, but they too are now quite limited.

"Qualified" noncitizens are ineligible for what are now the two major federal welfare programs—Supplemental Security Income (SSI) and food stamps. The main exceptions are (a) during the first five years after one is admitted as a refugee or granted asylum or withholding of removal; (b) LPRs who have worked for 40 Social Security Act-qualifying quarter-years without having received any federal means-tested public benefits; and (c) people on active duty in the United States Armed Forces, honorably discharged veterans, and certain of their dependents. Welfare Act, § 402(a)(1,2). The Farm Security and Rural Investment Act of 2002, Pub. L. 107–171, 116 Stat. 134 (May 13, 2002), § 4401, now adds another exception; certain "qualified" noncitizens are now eligible for the Food Stamp program if they have resided in the United States at least five years since becoming "qualified" or they are children or disabled. The eligibility of "qualified" noncitizens for state benefits, including temporary assistance for needy families (the successor to Aid to Families with Dependent Children) and Medicaid, is now a matter for the individual states to decide, subject to some federal statutory constraints. Welfare Act, §§ 402(b), 412. For a good and more detailed description of the Welfare Act, see Charles Wheeler, *The New Alien Restrictions on Public Benefits: The Full Impact Remains Uncertain*, 73 IR 1245 (Sept. 23, 1996).

Even for a person who fits the "qualified" category, welfare is now a dicey proposition. As you saw in chapter 5, section D, most intending immigrants are now required to submit affidavits of support from the petitioners who sponsor them, and those petitioners must demonstrate the financial ability to keep their promises. As you also saw, the assets and the income of the sponsor are "deemed" available to the immigrant, for purposes of determining the immigrant's financial eligibility for the particular welfare program. As a result, the immigrant's assets or incomes are likely to be treated as being too great to qualify for welfare. Moreover, an immigrant who does manage to obtain welfare benefits within five years after entry will become deportable unless he or she can affirmatively prove that the circumstances necessitating the welfare arose after entry.

There are, of course, two sides to this debate. The most succinct statement of the arguments in favor of the new restrictions is the one Congress itself provided, in the preamble to Title IV of the Welfare Act:

The Congress makes the following statements concerning national policy with respect to welfare and immigration:

(1) Self-sufficiency has been a basic principle of United States immigration law since this country's earliest immigration statutes.

(2) It continues to be the immigration policy of the United States that

(A) aliens within the nation's borders not depend on public resources to meet their needs, but rather rely on their own capabilities and the resources of their families, their sponsors, and private organizations, and

(B) the availability of public benefits not constitute an incentive for immigration to the United States.

(3) Despite the principle of self-sufficiency, aliens have been applying for and receiving public benefits from Federal, State, and local governments at increasing rates.

(4) Current eligibility rules for public assistance and unenforceable financial support agreements have proved wholly incapable of assuring that individual aliens not burden the public benefits system.

(5) It is a compelling government interest to enact new rules for eligibility and sponsorship agreements in order to assure that aliens be self-reliant in accordance with national immigration policy.

(6) It is a compelling government interest to remove the incentive for illegal immigration provided by the availability of public benefits.

* * *

The other side of the argument generally focuses on the hardship that the restrictions will cause, the unfairness of denying benefits to people whose tax contributions help fund the programs, and doubts about the need for restrictions. Since the passage of the Welfare Act, there has been particular concern for the survival of elderly immigrants who lack adequate income for food, shelter, and clothing. One critic, writing after President Clinton announced he would sign the bill, did not mince words:

They should have included, in this charade called welfare reform, instructions on how you actually get these useless elderly people out of their dwellings—these blind people, and the men and women addled by Alzheimer's, and the ones disabled by strokes or cancer or heart disease. I'm talking about the elderly disabled immigrants who, by the grace of our President and a rabid Congress, are soon to be suddenly destitute. Paying rent will be out of the question, so they will have to be evicted. Do you get stretchers and carry them out of their homes and leave them at the curb, or do you wheel them out, or do you just drag them out?

* * *

Meyer Shumyatsky is 96 years old and lives alone in a small apartment in Menorah Park, a complex for senior citizens and disabled people in San Francisco. Mr. Shumyatsky came to the U.S. from the Soviet Union in 1978. He was a store manager for several years. His wife died 10 years ago. Mr. Shumyatsky is legally blind, has severe hearing loss and a slight mobility problem. He spends most days sitting and talking with neighbors in a courtyard and listening to the radio. His monthly S.S.I. check is his sole income.

* * * Mr. Shumyatsky is in the U.S. legally but is not a citizen. Thus, his S.S.I. checks will cease when the welfare bill becomes law. He will have no money at all. Perhaps he will set up light housekeeping in a park. Maybe he'll curl up on a grate. Maybe he'll do the politicians a favor and just die.

* * *

The catastrophes will come by the hundreds of thousands, from all over the country, and they will come soon. Nursing homes are working on plans to toss out immigrants when the Federal money ends. Even food stamps will be cut off for nearly a million legal immigrants.

Bob Herbert, *In America; Throw Them Out*, New York Times, Aug. 2, 1996, at A27.

Sadly, those prophecies of doom often proved accurate. After receiving letters informing them that their SSI benefits would soon end, many people committed suicide:

In the fertile farmland of central California, Ignacio Muñoz told friends he would rather die than volunteer names of employers who had hired him when he was young and illegal. On March 17, the 75–year-old Mexican field hand descended a lonely gulch where he shot himself in the head.

In a small Wisconsin town, Chue Tou Vang considered the notice just another betrayal by the nation he fought for in Southeast Asia. On April 3, the 83–year-old Hmong refugee from Laos walked out to his barn and hanged himself.

And in a panorama of grief stretching coast to coast, at least seven elderly immigrants are known to have killed themselves in panic or depression over lost welfare benefits. Many more have attempted suicide, and social workers around the country say they are overwhelmed trying to cope with despondent immigrants contemplating suicide.

* * *

In March, a 75–year-old man in Stockton shot himself in the head and died three weeks after his notification that he might lose his SSI. Yang said his family has heard stories about a man in

Yuba City who killed himself because he failed the citizenship test. And stories about another man in Oroville who drank cleaning fluid and an elderly woman elsewhere in Northern California who starved herself to death.

Nancy Weaver Teichert, *Son's Love Leads Dad to Citizenship*, Sacramento Bee, May 14, 1997, at B1, reproduced in Bill Ong Hing, *The Emma Lazarus Effect: A Case Study in Philanthropic Revitalization of the Immigrant Rights Community*, 15 Georgetown Immigration L.J. 47, 50 (2001); see also Audrey Singer (ed.), *Immigrants, Their Families, and Their Communities in the Aftermath of Welfare Reform*, Research Perspectives in Migration (Carnegie Endowment for International Peace 2001).

Humanitarian considerations aside, many have questioned the necessity for the 1996 reforms. With just two significant exceptions, LPRs before 1996 received welfare at about the same rate that United States citizens did. The exceptions were refugees (particularly in their first few years) and the elderly, both of whom used welfare more frequently than United States citizens did. See Michael Fix & Wendy Zimmermann, *Patterns of Welfare Use Among Immigrants*, 23 Migration World, No. 5, at 15–17 (1995). Among the elderly, the higher than average welfare use is almost entirely attributable to SSI, a means-tested federal cash assistance program for the elderly, the blind, and the disabled. (Since many LPRs have not been in the United States long enough to qualify for social security old age payments, elderly immigrants made heavier than usual use of SSI.) *Id*; see also 73 IR at 1145–46 (Aug. 26, 1996). Still, there are some indications that, relative to citizens, immigrants generally are slightly heavier welfare users today than they were in former times. See George J. Borjas, Heaven's Door—Immigration Policy and the American Economy, ch. 6 (1999).

The Commission on Immigration Reform opposed the exclusion of lawful LPRs from welfare benefits. United States Commission on Immigration Reform, Becoming an American: Immigration and Immigrant Policy 73–75 (Sept. 1997). The scholarly commentary has generally expressed the same opinion. See, e.g., the UCLA Law Review symposium issue on immigrants and public benefits, which contains articles by Professors Abriel, Boswell, Johnson, Legomsky, Neuman, and Reich. 42 UCLA L. Rev. #6 (1995). (Citations to the individual articles appear on pages 1255–56 above.) See also Nora V. Demleitner, *Power, Perceptions, and the Politics of Immigration and Welfare*, 14 Industrial Development & Social Fabric 9 (1998) (exploring link between immigrants' political power and their rights in welfare state); Berta Esperanza Hernandez–Truyol & Kimberly A. Johns, *Global Rights, Local Wrongs, and Legal Fixes: An International Human Rights Critique of Immigration and Welfare "Reform,"* 71 Southern California L. Rev. 547 (1998) (raising human rights objections to 1996 restrictions on public assistance for noncitizens). For a statement of the arguments for and against extending public assistance to immigrants, see Stephen H. Legomsky, *Immigration, Federalism, and the Welfare State*, 42 UCLA L. Rev. 1453, 1462–70 (1995).

Congress quickly receded slightly from some of the 1996 welfare disqualifications for immigrants, mainly by restoring SSI and Food Stamps to certain immigrants who were already living in the United States on August 22, 1996 (the date the Welfare Act was enacted). See Balanced Budget Act of 1997, Pub. L. 105–33, 111 Stat. 251, §§ 5301–08 (Aug. 5, 1997); Agricultural Research Act of 1998, Pub. L. 105–185, 112 Stat. 523, §§ 503–10 (June 23, 1998). President Clinton proposed going much further, repealing some of the restrictions for future LPRs as well. See Esther Schrader, *GOP's Muted Response to Welfare Plan is a Telling Sign of the Times*, Los Angeles Times (Feb. 8, 1999). Except for the limited grandparenting in 1997 and 1998, however, the 1996 restrictions remain in force at this writing.

QUESTIONS

1.   If you had been a member of Congress in 1996, would you have voted for or against the restrictions that the Welfare Act imposed on LPRs?

2.   Can Congress constitutionally authorize the states to discriminate against LPRs? Can Congress help its case by declaring in advance that any actions the states take within the area of the delegated discretion will be considered necessary to a compelling governmental interest? In the Welfare Act, Congress did exactly that. Section 400(7) says:

> With respect to the State authority to make determinations concerning the eligibility of qualified aliens for public benefits in this title, a State that chooses to follow the Federal classification in determining the eligibility of such aliens for public assistance shall be considered to have chosen the least restrictive means available for achieving the compelling governmental interest of assuring that aliens be self-reliant in accordance with national immigration policy.

Based on the case law that you have just read about, do you think the Supreme Court would uphold state legislation that restricts welfare benefits for LPRs in ways that track the language of the Welfare Act? Would the Supreme Court regard the case as more like *Graham v. Richardson* or more like *Mathews v. Diaz* (both cited on page 1352 above)?

As for the constitutionality of section 400(7) itself (and any other federal laws that authorize states to disqualify noncitizens from state benefits), commentators differ. Doubting the constitutionality of such federal efforts are Gilbert Paul Carrasco, *Congressional Arrogation of Power: Alien Constellation in the Galaxy of Equal Protection*, 74 Boston Univ. L. Rev. 591 (1994); Michael J. Wishnie, *Laboratories of Bigotry? Devolution of the Immigration Power, Equal Protection, and Federalism*, 76 NYU L. Rev. 493 (2001). Howard Chang finds it hard to square that conclusion with the policy rationales of *Diaz* and *Graham*. See Howard F. Chang, *Public Benefits and Federal Authorization for Alienage Discrimination by the States*, 58 NYU Ann. Survey Amer. L. 357 (2002).

These and other comparisons between the respective rights of citizens and noncitizens have produced discussion of (a) whether under existing law citizenship in fact has important consequences and (b) whether citizenship *should* be important. Few deny that significant differences do, and should, separate citizens from undocumented migrants or even from lawful nonimmigrants. The most serious issues have involved the differences between citizens and LPRs. Here are the views of two respected commentators:

Peter H. Schuck, Membership in the Liberal Polity: The Devaluation of American Citizenship, in William R. Brubaker (Ed.), Immigration and the Politics of Citizenship in Europe and North America

Pp. 51, 60–65 (1989).
[reprinted in 3 Georgetown Immigration L.J. 1 (1989)].

[The author first argues that United States citizenship has been relatively easy for LPRs to acquire and hard to lose; that the legal and economic advantages of citizenship over LPR status are few; and that a large number of those who are eligible for naturalization either never apply for it or apply long after becoming eligible.]

* * *

But the devaluation of citizenship only serves to raise a further question: so what? Should we be concerned that American citizenship has manifestly little appeal for many aliens, or should we instead view this development with indifference or even satisfaction?

There are at least four dangers lurking in a devalued citizenship. The first is *political:* a concern for the quality of both the governmental process and the policy outcomes that it generates. Sound governance demands that those who are affected by the business of government participate in its decisions. The consent that invigorates liberal democracy must be as broad as the society that is coerced and governed in its name. But if millions of adult individuals subject to the exercise of governmental power are noncitizens who are legally disabled from voting, politicians have little incentive to learn about and respond to their claims. Under those conditions, the gap between power and accountability widens and the potential for exploiting noncitizens grows. When vitally affected interests remain voteless and (to that extent) voiceless, policy decisions are seriously deformed.

A second danger of a devalued citizenship is *cultural* in nature. An effective society—one that can accomplish its common goals, facilitate the private ends of its members, and nourish its system of values—requires that newcomers achieve at least a modest degree of assimilation into its culture. At a minimum, this must involve attaining competence in the common language in which that culture expresses and changes itself, but it also demands some comprehension of the nation's institutions and traditions. If newcomers do not value citizenship, if they fail to acquire the mastery of language and social knowledge that citizenship requires, they jeopardize their own well-being and (if they are sufficiently numerous) that of their adopted society. They create practical obstacles to the success of their own projects, while encouraging others to view them as strangers rather than as collaborators, as outsiders rather than as integrated members of the community.

The third danger created by the devaluation of citizenship is *spiritual* in nature. Democracy is more than a mechanism for governmental decisions, more than a technology for getting the public's work done well. It is also a normative order, an ethos that legitimates certain process values and nourishes particular ways of thinking about the means and ends of politics. Its success depends upon the discipline of self-restraint; a willingness to sacrifice advantages and share burdens; a concern for the public interest; the capacity to inspire and accept leadership; a reverence for law; and pride in one's political community.

A polity that devalues citizenship may discourage the development and diffusion of these civic virtues. Although citizenship cannot guarantee any of these virtues, it seems to be a necessary or at least instrumental condition for most of them. If noncitizens can claim the same benefits that citizens enjoy without having to bear the obligations of full membership, they may acquire an "entitlement mentality" that can erode those virtues. Most noncitizens are manifestly law-abiding and socially productive; they are presumably no less altruistic than other people. But by withholding their participation in and commitment to our civic life, they decline to be public-spirited in the fullest sense. To that extent, they may impoverish the democratic spirit of their communities.

A final danger concerns the *emotional* consequences of devalued citizenship. Fred Schauer has noted that citizenship serves as an especially important bond among individuals in a polyglot society like ours in which there are relatively few other effective linkages or commonalities. The ethnic, wealth, gender, religious, and lingual differences that divide us, Schauer points out, are inherently difficult for individuals to control or change. Citizenship, in contrast, is a status that can enable us to transcend these more enduring differences and achieve some common ground. If citizenship is to perform this special office, it must be accessible to all. But if it becomes too readily accessible, it may lose much of its capacity to bind us together in a meaningful, emotionally satisfying community.

Schauer's observation is really a point about how national communities are constituted and kept cohesive. Michael Walzer has hinted at an underlying emotional dynamic of such communities in his assertion that "Neighborhoods can be open only if countries are at least potentially closed." This suggestion, if true, has an important implication for citizenship. If we need the warmth and immediacy of parochial attachments to feel truly human, if there are spatial limits to our capacity for communal spirit, then citizenship may be a way to crystallize those attachments and define their outer boundaries. A liberal society committed to the equality and due process principles seeks to rationalize and bureaucratize relationships among individuals and with the state by appealing to universal, abstract standards. At the same time, its members commonly feel a heightened need for some refuge from that universalizing impulse, some enclave in which they can define themselves and their allegiances more locally and emotionally.

National citizenship is certainly not the only haven from universality, and it has never been the most satisfying one; for most people, that succor is more fully provided by family, friendships, neighborhoods, ethnicity, religion, and other less cosmopolitan attachments. But if, as Bickel showed, citizenship has not been particularly important in American law, it has surely affected how Americans feel about and define themselves and others. As citizenship's value and significance decline, therefore, we should expect that people's more parochial loyalties may loom correspondingly larger and may be asserted with greater intensity. Such a shift may yield neighborly pride, ethnic solidarity, and other emotional satisfactions. But it may also encourage a retreat from civic commitment toward some darker feelings that are never wholly absent from American life: xenophobia, petty localism, intolerance, and privatistic self-absorption.

The existence of these dangers reinforces a point that is often obscured by the liberal, minimalist conception of citizenship celebrated by Bickel and dominant in American law: society's interest in the value of citizenship transcends the valuation that the individuals in that society place upon it. Even if aliens' decisions to forego naturalization were truly voluntary and fully informed—indeed, even if those choices did not expose them to political exploitation or injustice at the hands of citizens—society might be justified in concluding that in the aggregate those choices debase, perhaps even imperil, the quality of its political life. Put another way, the level of political, and hence social, assimilation that aliens find perfectly congenial may seem inadequate from society's point of view.

But there is another side to this ledger. As we have seen, the devaluation of citizenship has been accomplished in part through the medium of the equality and due process principles, which have significantly reduced the differences between the rights of citizens and resident aliens. If this devaluation represents a loss to the distinctiveness of the citizenship status and involves some dangers, it also represents an immense gain for the liberal values of inclusiveness and equal treatment. These values, no less than the civic virtues described earlier, enhance the quality of political life.

* * *

It must also be conceded that the dangers of which I have written are for the most part still theoretical rather than imminent. Only the cultural danger—the risk posed by the failure of many Hispanics to master English and thus to gain the access to the society that only competency in the common language affords—arguably threatens the stability and well-being of American society. The others remain speculative and their potential magnitudes are difficult to assess. Moreover, while a devalued citizenship may plausibly be linked to these dangers, the actual strength of these relationships is not at all clear. The incentive structure that the equality and due process principles have altered is surely relevant to aliens' decisions about whether or not to naturalize (or migrate in the hope of conferring birthright citizenship on their children). But it would be foolish to think that decisions of that kind turn entirely upon these sorts of incentives or even that those decisions are wholly rational ones.

The question, then, of whether and to what extent the devaluation of citizenship constitutes a serious problem has no simple answer. But although there are substantial arguments on both sides, these arguments are not in equipoise. In fact, there are reasons to believe that the devaluation of citizenship is not—on balance—a cause for great concern. As we have just seen, most of the dangers seem remote. And even if these dangers were more proximate than they appear to be, it is not obvious either that altering our citizenship policy would forestall them or that we would know which particular alterations would be effective.

In addition, the devaluation of citizenship is probably irreversible, and necessity here should be seen as a virtue. The constitutional jurisprudence through which the equality and due process principles have helped to devalue citizenship cannot properly be viewed as either a doctrinal sport or a temporary ideological compromise. Rather, that jurisprudence reflects some fundamental dynamics in domestic law and international relations— the growing integration of the United States into the world economy, the emergence of group rights, the invigoration of judicial review—that are reshaping immigration law. These structural changes appear to have widespread support and are likely to be permanent.

Finally, and perhaps most fundamentally, the conception of membership that drives political institutions has steadily grown more fluid, functional, and context-dependent and seems likely to become even more so in the future. Before the rise of the modern nation-state, political membership was usually based upon kinship and ethnic ties. Today, at least in a liberal polity like the United States, membership is a far more complex, variegated, multipurpose idea. For certain purposes, such as voting, citizenship is the crucial status, but for others, such as the attribution of most constitutional rights, mere territorial presence suffices. For still other purposes, such as participation in an economic common market, membership is constituted by supranational groupings such as the recently established United States–Canada free trade zone or the still-evolving European Community.

We live in an increasingly integrated world. Transnational economic relationships are ubiquitous, international travel has become inexpensive, migratory pressures are already enormous and are steadily increasing, environmental problems are global, scientific and cultural exchange are highly valued, and political cooperation among nations is more essential than ever before. Even *within* our borders, citizenship represents an increasingly hollow ideal. It neither confers a distinctively advantageous status nor demands much of the individuals who possess it.

It would be premature, nonetheless, to conclude that national citizenship today is anachronistic. I have suggested that it provides a focus of political allegiance and emotional energy on a scale capable of satisfying deep human longings for solidarity, symbolic identification, and community. Such a focus may be especially important in a liberal ethos whose centrifugal, cosmopolitan aspirations for global principles and universal human rights must somehow be balanced against the more parochial imperatives of organizing societies dominated by more limited commitments to family, locality, region, and nation.

If the political and emotional aspects of citizenship remain significant, we nevertheless seem resolved as a society that little else of consequence should be allowed to turn upon it. But within that general understanding and social consensus, the precise role that citizenship should play and the special rights and obligations that ought to attach to it are emphatically open, contingent questions. As to these questions, only one proposition seems certain: today's conception of citizenship may not be adequate to meet tomorrow's needs.

––––––––

In the piece you just read, Professor Schuck outlined the respects in which citizenship had been devalued but cautioned that "[i]t would be premature, nonetheless, to conclude that national citizenship today is anachronistic." That careful qualification proved prescient. Seven years later Congress enacted the sweeping welfare reforms that you read about earlier. Those reforms and other intervening events prompted Schuck to revise his description; citizenship had made a comeback. In his words, "In a radically altered political environment, the question of citizenship is now both salient and divisive." Peter H. Schuck, *The Re–Evaluation of American Citizenship*, 12 Georgetown Immigration L.J. 1, 10 (1997). In the following excerpts, Schuck offers theories as to why citizenship has re-emerged as a hot button issue:

> * * * This re-evaluation has been prompted by deep concerns about the unity and coherence of the civic culture in the United States, concerns that flow from five developments in the post–1965 era. * * *

Multicultural Pressures

> With the enactment of the 1965 immigration law, the composition of the immigration stream to the United States changed radically. Of the top source countries, only the Philippines and India sent large numbers of English-speaking immigrants. Bilingual education thus became a major issue in public education * * *. With the growing politicization of ethnicity and widespread attacks on the traditional assimilative ideal, anxieties about linguistic and cultural fragmentation increased. * * *

> Meanwhile, as genuine racial integration proved elusive, the civil rights movement took a turn towards separatism. Blacks, already severely disadvantaged, were increasingly obliged to cede political and economic influence to more recently arrived Hispanic and Asian voters. * * * Certain economic sectors came to depend

almost entirely upon immigrant workers, legal and illegal. Relatively parochial immigrant enclaves grew larger. These multicultural pressures caused many Americans to feel more and more like strangers in their own country.

Loss of Unifying Ideology

The end of the Cold War deprived the United States of an ideology, anti-communism, that had served for many decades as a unifying, coherent force in American political culture and as an obsessive preoccupation and goal in U.S. foreign policy. No alternative ideology has yet emerged to replace it. Only constitutionalism, our civic religion, seems potentially capable of performing the function of binding together a nation of diverse peoples.

Technological Change

Rapid changes in transportation and communication technologies have transformed a world of sovereign nations into a global web of multinational enterprises and interdependent societies. Migration has become less expensive. Immigrants no longer need to make an irrevocable commitment to their new society; they can more easily retain emotional and other ties to their countries and cultures of origin. On the other hand, there is growing concern that television tends to assimilate second-generation immigrant youths into an underclass culture rather than into the mainstream American culture.

Welfare State Expansion

* * * With [the rapid growth of the welfare state], the behavior, values, and economic progress of immigrants became matters of great fiscal significance and public policy concern. In contrast to the historical pattern, immigration no longer ebbed and flowed with the business cycle—presumably because of the growth of the social safety-net. Immigration increasingly pitted citizens and aliens against one another as they competed for scarce public resources. The perennial debate over how the polity should conceive of community, affinity, and mutual obligation took on a new significance as the stakes in the outcome grew larger. Demands that Americans' obsession with legal rights be balanced by an equal concern for their social and civic responsibilities were increasingly heard in the land.

In August 1996, this long-simmering debate culminated in the radical restructuring of [the major public assistance programs]. * * *

Devaluation of Citizenship

The egalitarian thrust of the welfare state, its nourishing of entitlement as an ideal, and the repeal of the military draft led to a progressive erosion of citizenship as a distinctive status bearing special privileges and demanding special commitments and obligations. The rights of LPRs converged with those of citizens until there was little to separate them but the franchise, citizens' greater immigration sponsorship privileges, and their eligibility for the federal civil service. Americans began to feel that U.S. citizenship had lost much of its value and that it should somehow count for more.

These concerns, which have parallels in other countries, have prompted calls for a revitalization of citizenship. * * *

* * *

Id. at 17–19.

T. Alexander Aleinikoff, Citizens, Aliens, Membership and the Constitution
7 Constitutional Commentary 9, 23–24, 27–32 (1990).

* * *

[In chapter 2 you read about the exceptional deference the courts have accorded Congress when federal immigration statutes are attacked on constitutional grounds. In this article the author maintains that much of this deference can be ascribed to a tendency to think of citizens—and only citizens—as "members" of the national community. Although the author later argues that immigration laws should not be thought of solely in membership terms, he also believes that, *if* the standard of constitutional review is to rest on membership, LPRs should be considered members too. In making that latter argument, he first demonstrates that the constitutional text does not require the equation of citizenship with membership. He then continues:]

Citizenship-as-membership is also simply out of touch with the current reality of the immigration process. If citizenship constitutes full membership, then the theory should predict a naturalization process that carefully screens candidates acceding to the inner circle. (Consider how much more seriously many faculties and law firms take tenure and partnership decisions in comparison to initial hiring.) In actual practice, however, the immigration system makes its most careful membership decision at the time of entry, not at naturalization. Gaining admission to the United States is extraordinarily difficult. Numerical quotas and detailed grounds of exclusion disqualify the vast majority of the world's population from entering the United States. But for aliens who attain admission and seek citizenship, naturalization is usually a matter of course.

Furthermore, permanently residing aliens live and function much as citizens. They hold jobs, attend churches, send their children to school, and pay taxes. Children they give birth to here are United States citizens. From this perspective, the fact that aliens are not required by law to apply for citizenship is not surprising; in day-to-day terms, permanently residing aliens and citizens are already virtually indistinguishable.

Thus, both immigration practice and the daily lives of resident aliens suggest that true "membership" in the life of the nation begins at the point of admission for permanent residence. And the Court, in its better moments, seems to recognize this.

In *Graham v. [Richardson]* * * * the Court struck down statutes that excluded permanent resident aliens from state welfare programs. Justice Blackmun's majority opinion found the state laws doubly bad. By effectively denying aliens "entrance and abode," the state laws conflicted with federal immigration policy. This holding is at home in membership theory: the states cannot upset the terms of the federal government's invitation. The second ground of decision, however, ran quite counter to citizenship-as-membership. Justice Blackmun, with virtually no analysis, designated aliens "a discrete and insular minority," thereby triggering strict scrutiny of laws that discriminate against them. Labelling aliens "discrete and insular" is an effective way, under prevailing equal protection analysis, to invalidate unfriendly laws. But Justice Blackmun's invocation of the phrase glides too readily past serious analytical difficulties.

The last paragraph of his discussion of the equal protection claim, however, seems to take a different turn, one that seems to recognize admission for permanent residence as establishing membership:

> We agree with the three-judge court ... that the "justification of limiting expenses is particularly inappropriate and unreasonable when the discriminated class consists of aliens. Aliens like citizens pay taxes and may be called into the armed forces.... [A]liens may live within a state for many years, work in the state and contribute to the economic growth of the state." There can be no "special public interest" [justifying exclusion of aliens from state programs] in tax revenues to which aliens have contributed on an equal basis with the residents [*sic.*] of the State.

Although Blackmun does not appear to recognize the tension this paragraph creates for his opinion, in these lines he actually flips the justification for invalidating discriminatory state laws. The statutes in *Graham* should be invalidated not because aliens are a defenseless group needing judicial protection, but rather because—at least from the state's perspective—they are indistinguishable from other residents of the state. State laws excluding aliens from opportunities should be seen as no more legitimate than laws excluding redheads. Both would be invalid, not because such groups are downtrodden but because the state can offer no legitimate reason for singling them out.

* * *

What can be said against this broader theory of membership? The Court's concern seems to be that if we slide the membership line we will sap citizenship of any significance. The Court has justified exclusion of aliens from state political positions in part on the ground that it is important that we not " 'obliterate all the distinctions between citizens and aliens, and thus deprecate the historic value of citizenship.' " This justification may reflect deeply held intuitions. Consider the following comment taken from a student exam of several years ago: "Ever since reading *Plyler v. Doe* I have felt that there was something attractive about the argument that states should be able to deny benefits to aliens.... [Otherwise], what is the significance of citizenship?"

As an initial matter, there is something distasteful—if not unconstitutional—about inflicting harm solely to make the non-afflicted feel special. More important, the desire to retain *legal* disabilities in order to preserve citizenship as a meaningful concept shows the bias of the lawyer. Citizenship, particularly for native-born citizens, is an aspect of identity. Identification with one's homeland is organic, much as one's identification with one's ethnicity or religion. Few of us choose our citizenship, yet for most of us it is an important part of how we define ourselves in the world. Extending constitutional membership will not threaten this difference between citizens and aliens. It is unlikely that a person born a U.S. citizen will feel any less an "American" because a Honduran in the United States is entitled to similar benefits and opportunities, nor is the Honduran likely to feel any less Honduran. Indeed, it is not inconceivable that someday we will understand citizenship as we do ethnicity and religion today—that is, as an important aspect of one's identity but not a characteristic that the government may normally take into account in exercising power over the individual.

A second common defense of citizenship-as-membership is that it is important to emphasize and affirm a "national community" of, and for, Americans. Such a community may be valued for its fostering of a common culture and political system. Seeing aliens as outsiders reaffirms (and helps define) what is inside. It also helps prevent a watering down of commonalities that might occur if membership is defined broadly.

These kinds of claims have been pressed by scholars across the political spectrum. To conservatives, the project is one of assimilation: molding immigrants to the true American identity in order to preserve American traditions and institutions. To liberals, a "national community" is a liberating concept because it overcomes the irrational, tyrannical, constricting aspects of "tribal" loyalties. "Citizenship," representing membership in the national community, is the ticket to universalism and equality; it rejects (or downplays) group identifications and allegiances that cut individuals off from the full range of opportunities in society.

In recent years, the idea of a "national community" has appealed to scholars critical of the liberal tradition. Liberalism has seemed inadequate on both descriptive and normative grounds. The "new communitarianism" rejects liberalism's description of human beings as "unencumbered" selves. "Most of us," writes David Martin, "were simply born into our most basic affiliations—family, religion, nation. Those ties are not only objects of choice; to a significant extent they are constitutive of one's basic identity, anterior to choice." By stressing the social and historical bonds that connect members of a society, communitarianism makes a normative claim that institutions should nurture feelings of attachment that transcend personal self-interest. Pursuit of community goals will promote that which makes us most human (association with others) and will help overcome the anomie and alienation symptomatic of modern life.

Recognizing that we cannot return to a lost golden age of small town life, communitarianism—like the conservative and liberal perspectives—sees great promise in the concept of a "national community." It allows us to imagine an association of human beings who feel special obligations to one another. Once communitarianism reaches the national level, it readily turns to citizenship to demarcate the community. It seems to assume that, in a world of nation-states, citizenship is the appropriate category for the fostering of "ties that bind."

Despite the powerful attractions of the communitarian vision (a vision I share), the new communitarians get off track when they begin to talk about "citizenship as membership in a national community." It is too little noted that the phrase "national community" is either an oxymoron or requires a substantial shift in our usual understanding of the term "community." "A community," writes Thomas Bender, "involves a limited number of people in a somewhat restricted social space or network held together by shared understandings and a sense of obligation. Relationships are close, often intimate, and usually face to face." This conception of "community" poorly describes the United States whose spaciousness and diversity are matters of national pride. It is just wishful thinking to suggest that most Americans feel the kinds of obligations to other Americans that we usually associate with "community." * * *

A communitarian might respond as follows. No one is suggesting that we can replicate at the national level intimate feelings of community. What is wrong, however, with suggesting that members of a state ought to be urged to put the interests of their fellow citizens and the nation ahead of the pursuit of their personal private interests? Did John Kennedy's "ask not . . ." set too high a goal for a civilized polity?

Certainly these are noble goals. But it is never explained why *citizenship* is the appropriate category for the development of a communitarian ethos. Why wouldn't we seek the formation of a sense of reciprocal obligations among all persons living and working within the territory of the United States? We know, as an empirical matter, that strong bonds between citizens and resident aliens exist. These ties, based on familial relationship, ethnicity, religion, race, or location may be far more powerful than those that can be fostered among citizens who share nothing but American nationality.

* * * More importantly, it is quite doubtful that "citizenship" is a useful category for sorting those who do and do not share an "American Creed." What makes America attractive to immigrants are precisely those values that Americans celebrate: liberty, equality, opportunity, government under law. Indeed, those who have chosen to join us—and to give up a less

happy existence elsewhere—may well feel more committed to these values than those of us who happen to have been born here.

Finally, the concept of a national community, by defining who belongs, also defines who does not belong and what one must be in order to belong. In a nation as diverse as the United States, the risk is great that a "national community" will not be all-inviting or all-embracing. Rather, it will reflect the norms and culture of dominant groups. Placing emphasis on membership, in such a world, becomes a basis for excluding outsiders and compelling conformity from insiders. * * *

* * *

NOTES AND QUESTIONS

1. Although intervening events prompted Professor Schuck to revise both his descriptive account of the role citizenship actually plays and his normative conclusions, his analyses of the dangers and benefits of devaluing citizenship retain their value. He categorizes the dangers of devaluation as political, cultural, spiritual, and emotional. How do you suppose he would respond to each of the following objections?

a. *Political danger.* If those "who are affected by the business of government" are *willing* to sacrifice their participation in the political process as the price for retaining their original citizenship, then what's the problem?

b. *Cultural danger.*

i. It is true that in the United States naturalization requires some minimum mastery of the English language and understanding of American institutions and traditions. See INA § 312. But the converse is not true; one need not naturalize in order to attain such knowledge.

ii. It is easy to see how newcomers who do not acquire English language skill and a knowledge of American traditions and institutions disadvantage themselves, but how, exactly, do they "jeopardize * * * [the] well-being * * * of their adopted society?"

c. *Spiritual danger.*

i. Your argument states that "[i]f noncitizens can claim the same benefits that citizens enjoy without having to bear the obligations of full membership, they may require an 'entitlement mentality' that can erode [various] virtues" (emphasis added). But United States law imposes no significant obligations on citizens that are not also imposed on LPRs (the only noncitizens generally eligible for naturalization). For both reasons, refusing citizenship should not be seen as a way to avoid citizens' obligations without giving up any rights.

ii. Citizenship is not an accurate proxy for gauging a person's willingness to share communal burdens. Such willingness is far more likely to depend on one's personal values and on personal relationships to others in the community.

d. *Emotional danger.*

i. There is no empirical evidence that citizenship, if made more difficult to acquire, would provide a realistic basis for emotionally meaningful ties. As you acknowledge, other personal bonds already serve this function.

ii. Nor is there empirical evidence that citizenship affects one's definition of self. It seems at least as likely that one's self-image as an "American" stems from exposure to, and experience living in, American society, rather than from the legal abstraction we call "citizenship."

2. Professor David Abraham's thoughtful article argues that both the United States and Germany have in fact devalued their citizenships over the past two generations, in part by expanding the legal rights of LPRs. David Abraham, *The Good of Banality? The Emergence of Cost–Benefit Analysis and Proportionality in the Treatment of Aliens in the United States and Germany*, 4 Citizenship Studies 237 (2000).

3. Professor Aleinikoff believes that the distinction between citizens and LPRs should be accorded *less* significance than it now has. In *Harisiades v. Shaughnessy*, 342 U.S. 580, 72 S.Ct. 512, 96 L.Ed. 586 (1952), however, one argument the Supreme Court gave for weighing that distinction heavily was that, "[s]o long as the alien elects to continue the ambiguity of his allegiance, his domicile here is held by a precarious tenure." *Id.* at 587, 72 S.Ct. at 518, 96 L.Ed. at 597. What's wrong with reading significance into an LPR's decision not to pursue naturalization (at least after the five-year eligibility period, INA § 316, and the other requirements you have studied have been satisfied)? Isn't that decision an indicator of the person's investment in the nation? How do you suppose Aleinikoff would respond?

4. Aleinikoff makes some interesting observations about the opinion of Justice Blackmun in *Sugarman v. Dougall*. On the one hand, Aleinikoff points out, Justice Blackmun stresses the *differences* between citizens and LPRs and argues that those differences make LPRs a "discrete and insular minority" and therefore justify strict judicial scrutiny. On the other hand, in condemning the discrimination reflected in the statute, Justice Blackmun stresses the *similarities* between citizens and LPRs. To Aleinikoff, the two arguments are in "tension."

Does such a tension really exist? The particular similarities Justice Blackmun identifies relate to legal obligations (tax and draft) and economic contributions to society. Those similarities between citizens and LPRs, Justice Blackmun believes, are among the factors that make discrimination irrational. The differences he identifies concern the history of discrimination against noncitizens and their relative lack of political power. Those latter factors, in Justice Blackmun's view, should raise at least a suspicion that the legislation reflects unacceptable discriminatory motives. Is there anything contradictory about finding similar obligations and contributions while finding different histories of treatment and different degrees of political power? Is there really any contradiction in concluding both that there is reason to be suspicious of discriminatory state action and that a given statutory distinction is in fact irrational?

5. Chief Justice Earl Warren once wrote that citizenship "is nothing less than the right to have rights." *Perez v. Brownell,* 356 U.S. 44, 64, 78 S.Ct. 568, 579, 2 L.Ed.2d 603, 617 (1958). Given what you have read up to this point, was he correct?

6. Aleinikoff makes the specific argument that the concept of membership is broad enough to include LPRs. A larger question is the more general one: How broad should membership be? How are we to tell whether some other class of individuals should be regarded as members? At one point, while discussing the applicability of communitarian theory, Aleinikoff asks why "all persons living *and working* within the territory of the United States" should not be seen as part of the national community (emphasis added). Why would he add the qualifier "and working?" Is it one's contributions to the economy that create a claim to membership? What about those nonimmigrants who remain lawfully for several years? Should attachments be relevant? Lifestyle? What, in other words, is Aleinikoff's underlying premise as to the factors that should determine membership? What formulation would you favor?

7. Aleinikoff attacks the exceptional judicial reluctance to protect the constitutional rights of noncitizens. He ascribes that reluctance to a sometimes unspoken assumption that citizenship equals membership. He argues in the portion you read that, if membership is to be the test, LPRs should be considered members. In a later portion of the article, see 7 Constitutional Commentary at 32–34, he argues alternatively that at any rate membership should not be the test. For both reasons, he asserts, citizenship should not be conclusive of the standard of constitutional review.

All this suggests a more fundamental question: *Should the law even recognize such a concept as citizenship at all?* The value of citizenship is probably most evident in the international context, although even there its value is not obvious. One who accepts the inevitability of a world order based on sovereign states might argue that, as long as people travel across national boundaries, citizenship will be a prerequisite to receiving a passport or other travel document. The nations of the world could, however, create a United Nations or other intergovernmental agency to issue "world" passports without regard to country of citizenship. So is there some other essential international function that citizenship serves? The most compelling answer might be diplomatic protection. As long as nations violate the human rights of foreign nationals, the latter will need protection from someone. National intervention to protect citizens from foreign governments is one form of protection.

But even if one accepts citizenship or nationality as a useful construct in international law, does citizenship play a necessary, or even a desirable, role in a nation's domestic law? One domestic function of citizenship is to provide a convenient shorthand for describing the classes of people who are singled out in a wide variety of state and federal statutes concerned with voting, jury service, immigration, government employment, government benefits, etc. By laying out who is a citizen, Congress has enabled the drafters of all these other laws to incorporate the relevant criteria by reference, rather than reinvent the wheel each time they wish to define eligibility for important rights.

Is that good? The statutes in question determine who may vote, who is subject to immigration control, who may petition for the immigration of close family members, who may work for the government, who is eligible for welfare, who may serve on juries, who is subject to federal income tax liability, who may be drafted, who may own land, etc. The list is endless. Each of these decisions requires the accommodation of competing interests, and those sets of interests vary from one issue to the next. Do we really need—indeed, is it even beneficial to have—a single requirement common to all those rights and obligations? Why not abolish the citizenship concept entirely and redefine, by reference to ultimate facts rather than to a legal abstraction, the criteria on which each of those very different determinations is to be based?

One defense of citizenship appears in another section of the Aleinikoff article:

> * * * In a monarchy, sovereignty * * * is external to the subject and the alien alike. In a sense, every alien and every citizen faces the sovereign on a one-to-one basis. But in a democracy, sovereignty is something shared by citizens and citizens alone. Without a notion of citizenship, sovereignty has no home. * * *

Aleinikoff, 7 Constitutional Commentary at 14.

But that argument merely shifts the battleground. Instead of asking why we need a *citizenship* concept, we now must ask why, for purposes of domestic law, we need a *sovereignty* concept. The notion of *State* sovereignty helps explain international rules that govern the powers of nations over their respective territories, but why must the domestic law take any position about which *individuals* will be considered part of the "sovereign?" Cities, counties, and sewer districts get along fine without "citizens." Why do countries need them?

The temptation is to answer this question by observing that in a democracy there must be some law defining the people who will select the nation's leaders. Those individuals, however, need not be called "citizens;" they could simply be called "voters." The distinction is not merely semantical. The point is that the criteria for voting eligibility need not be the same as those for determining the myriad other rights that under current domestic law turn on citizenship.

For purposes of domestic law, do you think "citizenship" should be abolished? For a more detailed account of the theory and limitations of citizenship, see Stephen H. Legomsky, *Why Citizenship?*, 35 Virginia J. Internat'l L. 279 (1994).

8. The question whether citizenship should have important legal consequences has received increased attention in recent years. Emphasizing

the communal bonding aspects of citizenship are Frederick Schauer, *Community, Citizenship, and the Search for National Identity,* 84 Michigan L. Rev. 1504, 1513–17 (1986), and Michael Walzer, *The Distribution of Membership,* in Peter G. Brown & Henry Shue (eds.), Boundaries—National Autonomy and Its Limits, at 1–35 (1981). Applauding devalued citizenship is Alexander M. Bickel, The Morality of Consent 53–54 (1975) ("gratifying * * * that we live under a Constitution to which the concept of citizenship matters very little"); see also Arnold H. Leibowitz, A Time for Decision: Citizenship at the Millennium (Office of Refugee Resettlement, Nov. 1998) (arguing citizenship rightly holds only a modest place in U.S. history and culture); Judith Lichtenberg, *National Boundaries and Moral Boundaries: A Cosmopolitan View,* in Boundaries, above, at 79–100.

Rogers Smith suggests that United States citizenship law has historically reflected exclusionary impulses. He believes these impulses have had both positive and negative effects, enhancing cohesion but running counter to the civic myths on which the nation was founded. Rogers M. Smith, Civic Ideals: Conflicting Visions of Citizenship in U.S. History (1997). Reviewing the Smith book, Peter Spiro calls this the "citizenship dilemma." Since return to the days of exclusion seems unacceptable, he argues, the nation-state seems destined to become a less important source of associative identity. Peter J. Spiro, *The Citizenship Dilemma,* 51 Stanford L. Rev. 597 (1999).

9. Several analysts have tackled the provocative question of what it is, exactly, that a person is a citizen *of*. The usual assumption has been that one is, or should be, a citizen of a sovereign state. Professor Linda Bosniak, among others, questions that premise. She argues that one might be a citizen of the world (or a citizen of some sub-national entity, as noted below). See Linda Bosniak, *Citizenship Denationalized,* 7 Indiana J. Global Legal Studies 447 (2000). The growing significance of the European Community has required examination of whether one might be a citizen of an entity smaller than the world but still larger than the nation state. See, e.g., Randall Hansen & Patrick Weil (eds.), Towards a European Nationality—Citizenship, Immigration and Nationality Law in the EU (2001). And for a captivating discussion of the meaning and significance of citizenship at the sub-national level, see Peter H. Schuck, *Citizenship in Federal Systems*, 48 American J. Comparative L. 195 (2000). Similarly ranging beyond both the statist model that looks to individual states as the main source of law, and the cosmopolitan model that looks to one's obligations to all of humankind, two authors have specifically explored the notion of allegiance to one's diaspora. See, e.g., Anupam Chander, *Diaspora Bonds*, 76 NYU L. Rev. 1005 (2001); Spiro, item 8 above, at 621–25. Under any of these models, of course, the question arises: Whose interests should determine the citizenship criteria—only the existing members' interests or also those of the individuals who would be excluded from the status? Arguing the latter is J. Donald Galloway, *The Dilemmas of Canadian Citizenship Law*, 13 Georgetown Immigration L.J. 201, at 201 (1999).

*

INDEX

References are to Pages

ACTS
Legislation, this index

ADJUSTMENT OF STATUS
Admission procedure, 490–495
Asylum, persons who have received, 1083–1084
Deportability, relief from, 612–613
Rescission of adjustment, 840–841

ADMINISTRATIVE AGENCIES
Generally, 2–8
Deference to, 380
Organization chart, 6

ADMINISTRATIVE PROCEDURE ACT
Deportation proceedings, applicability, 639
Hearing process, 645–653

ADMINISTRATIVE REVIEW
Board of Immigration Appeals, 717–725
Executive Office for Immigration Review, 4
Exhaustion of administrative remedies, 642–643, 733

ADMISSION PROCEDURE
Generally, 444–495
Actual admission
    Generally, 485–490
    Appeals from immigration judge decisions, 488
    At the border, 485
    Burden of proving admissibility, 487
    Expedited removal of arriving passengers, 485, 488–489
    Fingerprinting and photographing, 485
    Foreign policy cases, special removal procedures, 489–490
    Hearing before immigration judge, below
    National security, special removal procedures, 489–490
    Standard of proof, 487
Adjustment of status, 490–495
Automated entry–exit system, 866–867
Hearing before immigration judge
    Generally, 486–488
    Appeals, 488
    Burden of proving admissibility, 487
    Notice to appear, 486
    Standard of proof, 487

ADMISSION PROCEDURE—Cont'd
Historical background, 444–450
Modern procedure generally, 450–452
Special removal procedures, national security and foreign policy cases, 489–490
Visas, this index

ADOPTION
Foreign adoptions, 286–290

AFFIDAVITS OF SUPPORT
Generally, 439–440

AFFIRMANCE WITHOUT OPINION
Appeals, this index

AGGRAVATED FELONIES
Asylum, exception to eligibility, 1074
Deportation, 553–564

AGRICULTURAL LABORERS
Legalization in 1986, 610
Temporary workers, 367–368

AIDS AND HIV
Asylum based on HIV, 988
Exclusion grounds, 442–443

AIR CARRIERS
Crews
    Removal of crew member, 840
    Temporary workers, 376
Sanctions, transporting persons without visas, 1112, 1208

AMERICANIZATION
Revival of, 51–54

AMNESTY
Generally, 607–612

ANTI–IMMIGRANT SENTIMENT
Generally, 84 et seq.

APPEALS
Administrative Review, this index
Affirmances without opinion (AWOs)
    Generally, 642, 720
    Challenge on due process grounds, 724–725
    Sample affirmance, 795
Arriving passengers, appeals from immigration judge decisions, 488

APPEALS—Cont'd
Deportation, this index
Judicial Review, this index
Notice of appeal, 642, 724

APPLICATIONS
Administrative naturalization, application, 1290
Asylum, sanctioning frivolous applications, 1111
Employment
Existing employees, applications on behalf of, 310–311
Fraudulent applications, 307 et seq.
Temporary workers, labor condition applications, 364
Visas, 461–485

ARAB–AMERICANS
Post–September 11, 100–101

ARREST WARRANTS
Homeland Security, Dept. of, exercise of powers without, 634

ASIAN IMMIGRANTS
Identity formations, 100
Land laws, 99
Public reaction to Asian immigration, 115–118

ASSIMILATION
Generally, 49

ASYLUM
Generally, 937 et seq.
Access to process, barring or discouraging, 1095–1135
Adjudicators, 1091
Adjustment to permanent residence, 1083–1084
Administrative notice of country conditions, 1067
Air carrier sanctions, transporting persons without visas, 1112
Application fees, 1111–1112
Attorney–client asylum interview, simulated, 1135–1144
Barring access to process, 1095–1135
Causal nexus requirement
Generally, 1037–1049
But for test, 1038 et seq.
Michigan Guidelines, 1041
Multiple motives, 1047–1048
On account of, defined, 1037–1038
Subset of protected group as target, 1046–1047
Character evidence, 1062
Children, fairness of process, 1087–1088
Clear probability standard of proof, 1051
Conscientious objectors, 963
Costs, 1087
Country conditions, administrative notice, 1067
Credibility of applicant's testimony, 1056–1063

ASYLUM—Cont'd
Criminal activity. Exceptions to eligibility, below
Criminal prosecution for illegal entry, 1109–1110
Delays, 1086
Detention
Generally, 1106–1109
At port of entry, 845
Discretion in asylum cases, 1077–1081
Domestic violence and problem of non–state actor, 1025–1036
Dress code, defying, 1006–1007
Employment authorization, denying, 1110–1111
European Court of Human Rights, 1183–1191
Evasive statements, 1062
Evidence
Character evidence, 1062
Methods of proof, below
Exceptions to eligibility
Generally, 1067–1077
Firm resettlement, 1068–1069
Past wrongdoing
Generally, 1069–1077
Particularly serious crimes, 1073 et seq.
Political offenses, 1076
Expedited removal, 1103–1106
Extended voluntary departure, 1165–1166
Fairness, procedural, 1087–1090
Fear of persecution. Persecution, below
Fees, 1111–1112
Filing deadlines, 1096
Firm resettlement, exception to eligibility, 1068–1069
Fiscal costs, 1087
Foreign policy as proper subject of discretion, 1080
Frivolous applications, sanctioning, 1111
Gender and social group
Generally, 935–1036
Domestic violence and problem of non-state actor, 1025–1036
Dress code, defying, 1006–1007
Genital mutilation, 1019 et seq.
Rape victims, 1008
Genital mutilation, 1019 et seq.
Global and regional approaches to temporary protection, 1170–1183
Grant–or–refer system, 1083, 1089–1090
Haitians, selective detention, 1108
Illegal entry, criminal prosecution, 1109–1110
Imputed political opinion doctrine, 969–970
Inconsistencies between statements, 1061
Inspection, pre–flight, 1112
Interdiction of vessels on high seas, 1112–1135
Internal flight alternative, 1052
Lies told by asylum–seeker, 1062
Mass influx and temporary protection, 1175 et seq.
Material facts. Methods of proof, below

ASYLUM—Cont'd
Membership in persecuted group, proof, 1054–1056
Methods of proof
    Generally, 1054–1067
    Administrative notice of country conditions, 1067
    Advice from UNHCR, 1066–1067
    Applicant's own testimony, 1056–1063
    Material facts
        Generally, 1054–1056
        Membership in persecuted group, 1054
        Past persecution, 1055–1056
    Relevant evidence
        Generally, 1056–1067
        Administrative notice of country conditions, 1067
        Advice from UNHCR, 1066–1067
        Applicant's own testimony, 1056–1063
        State Dept. opinions, 1063–1066
    State Dept. opinions, 1063–1066
Neutrality as political opinion, 971–976
Nonadversarial proposals, 1093–1095
Nonrefoulement
    Generally, 937–1144
    Withholding of removal, below
Non–state actor and domestic violence, 1025–1036
On account of. Causal nexus requirement, above
Other dangers, protection against
    Generally, 1144–1191
    European Court of Human Rights, 1183–1191
    Global and regional approaches, 1170–1183
    Temporary protection
        Generally, 1164–1183
        Global and regional approaches, 1170–1183
        U.S. domestic law, 1164–1170
    Torture, convention against (CAT), 1145–1164
Particular social group
    Generally, 977–1036
    Family–related cases, 987–989
    Gender and social group, above
    HIV, persons who have contracted, 988
    Homogeneity requirement, 987
    Immutability test, 986
    Justice Dept. factors, 989
    Sexual orientation and social group, 989–995
    Social group defined, 978–989
    UNHCR Guidelines, 985, 989
Past persecution, 1055–1056
Past wrongdoing. Exceptions to eligibility, above
Persecution or fear of persecution
    Generally, 941–962
    Draft evasion, 959
    Facially neutral law or policy, 951
    Identifiable group, persecution of, 951
    Other dangers, protection against, above

ASYLUM—Cont'd
Persecution or fear of persecution—Cont'd
    Personalized threats, 950
    Population controls, coercive, 959–961
    Prosecution distinguished, 954–959
    Singling–out, 950
    Well–founded fear, 948
Political bias, 1084–1086
Political opinion
    Generally, 964–977
    Imputed political opinion doctrine, 969–970
    Neutrality as political opinion, 971–976
Population controls, coercive, 959–961
Pre–flight inspection, 1112
Procedure
    Generally, 1081–1135
    Affirmative applications, 1082
    Barring or discouraging access to process, 1095–1135
    Criminal prosecution for illegal entry, 1109–1110
    Defensive applications filed in removal proceedings, 1082
    Delays, 1086
    Detention, 1106–1109
    Employment authorization, denying, 1110–1111
    Expedited removal, 1103–1106
    Fairness, 1087–1090
    Fees, 1111–1112
    Filing deadlines, 1096
    Frivolous applications, sanctioning, 1111
    General principles, 1082–1095
    Grant–or–refer system, 1083, 1089–1090
    Nonadversarial proposals, 1093–1095
    Pre–flight inspection, 1112
    Security checks, 1083
    Third countries, returning asylum–seekers to, 1097–1103
    Time constraints, 1090
    Vessels, interdiction on high seas, 1112–1135
    Visas and carrier sanctions, 1112
Proof. Methods of proof, above
Prosecution distinguished from persecution, 954–959
Race, religion, nationality, 962–964
Rape victims, 1008
Rebuttable presumptions
    Past persecution, 1055
    Relocation as reasonable alternative, 1052
Refugees, this index
Relocation internally, 1052
Removal. Withholding of removal, below
Removal proceedings, defensive applications filed in, 1082
Safe countries of origin, 1096–1097
Safe third country restriction, 1097–1103
Sanctions
    Air carriers transporting persons without visas, 1112
    Frivolous applications, 1111
Security checks, 1083

ASYLUM—Cont'd
Sexual orientation and social group, 989–995
Social group
  Gender and social group, above
  Particular social group, above
Standards of proof, 1050–1054
State Dept. opinions, 1063–1066
Temporary protected status, 1166 et seq.
Testimony of applicant, credibility, 1056–1063
Third countries, returning asylum–seekers to, 1097–1103
Time constraints, 1090
Torture, convention against (CAT), 1145–1164
Unfounded claims, 1086–1087
UNHCR
  Advice from, 1066–1067
  Haitians, selective detention, 1108
  Return of asylum seekers to third countries, 1099–1101
Vague statements, 1062
Vessels, interdiction on high seas, 1112–1135
Well–founded fear, 1050–1054
Withholding of removal
    Generally, 938 et seq.
    Causal nexus requirement, above
    Exceptions to eligibility, above
    Methods of proof, above
    Nonadversarial interview, 940
    On account of. Causal nexus requirement, above
    Particular social group, above
    Persecution or fear of persecution, above
    Political opinion, above
    Procedure, above
    Race, religion, nationality, 962–964
    Refugees sur place, 976–977
    Standards of proof, 1050–1054
    Statutory provision, 939
    Well–founded fear, 1050–1054
    Would be threatened, 1050–1054
Women. Gender and social group, above
Would be threatened, 1050–1054

ATHLETES
Employment–based immigration, 294
Temporary workers, admission as, 362–367

ATTORNEYS
Attorney–client relationship
  Asylum interview, simulated, 1135–1144
  Monitoring attorney–client conversations, 851–852
Discipline of immigration practitioners, 668–671
Frivolous behavior, 668–670
Ineffective assistance of counsel, 671–685
Representation in removal proceedings. Deportation, this index
Unauthorized practice of law, 459–460

ATTORNEY'S FEES
Equal Access to Justice Act, 667

AU PAIR PROGRAM
Generally, 388–389

BATTERED PERSONS
Domestic Violence, this index
Self–petitioners, 453
Spouses, 274

BILINGUALISM
Generally, 49
English–only movement, 57–61

BIRTH
Citizenship, this index

BOARD OF IMMIGRATION APPEALS
Generally, 717–725
Appeals, this index
Deportation, this index

BONDS
Conditional parole pending deportation hearing, 636
De novo bond redetermination hearing, 637
Detention, this index
Public charge bond, 440–441

BORDER ENFORCEMENT
Enhanced, 890–891, 1197 et seq.

BRIEFS
Court of Appeals review, 805 et seq.
Respondent's trial brief, sample, 778–780

BURDEN OF PROOF
Admission, 487
Deportation proceedings, 640, 705–717

BURGLARY
As crime of violence, 561

BUSINESS VISITORS
Generally, 348–359
U.S. Visitor and Immigration Status Indication Technology System (US VISIT), 870–872

CANCELLATION OF REMOVAL
Deportation, this index

CENSUS
Undocumented migrants, inclusion, 1233

CENTRAL AMERICA
Nicaraguan Adjustment and Central American Relief Act (NACARA), 605–606

CHARACTER
Asylum–seeker, character evidence, 1062
Cancellation of removal, good moral character, 604–605
Citizenship, good moral character, 1283

CHILDREN
Asylum, fairness of process, 1087–1088
Child Citizenship Act, 1291–1293
Child Status Protection Act, 252–53
Defined, 280, 285
Foreign adoptions, 286–290
Out–of–wedlock, 284–285
Refugees, 936
Special immigrant status, 285–286

CHINA
Coercive population controls as persecution, 959–961

CITIZENSHIP
Generally, 1265–1373
Acquiring citizenship
  Generally, 1266–1312
  Administrative naturalization, below
  Birth, below
  Post–birth, below
Administrative naturalization
  Generally, 1277–1291
  Age, 1283
  Application, 1290
  Backlogs and delays, 1291
  Civics, knowledge of, 1284
  Continuances, 1290
  English language, 1283–1284
  Evidentiary hearing on denial of application, 1291
  Five years' continuous residence, 1287–1288
  Good moral character, 1283
  Judicial ceremony, 1290
  Lawful permanent residence, 1283
  Political requirements, 1284
  Procedure, 1289–1291
  Rates of naturalization by country, 1278
  Residence and physical presence, 1283
  Substantive criteria, 1282–1289
Birth, citizenship acquired at
  Generally, 1267–1276
  Jus sanguinis, 1269–1276
  Jus soli, 1267–1269
Ceremony, 1290
Child Citizenship Act, 1291–1293
Consent principle, 1310–1311
Constitution and jus sanguinis, 1273–1276
Deportation, defense to
  Generally, 630–631
  Judicial review, 759
Descent, citizenship by, 1269–1276, 1310
Disabilities on noncitizens, 1351
Dual nationality, 1294–1297
Expatriation
  Generally, 1333–1349
  Consent of individual, 1333
  Historical background, 1333–1336
  Intent–based vs. allegiance–based approach, 1346 et seq.
  Obtaining naturalization in foreign state, 1349
  Presumption of no intent to relinquish nationality, 1344
  Specific intent to renounce, 1346 et seq.
  Tax expatriates, 1349
False citizenship claims, 526–527
Five years' continuous residence, 1287–1288
Foreign state, obtaining naturalization in, 1349
Jus sanguinis, 1269–1276
Jus soli, 1267–1269
Losing citizenship

CITIZENSHIP—Cont'd
Losing citizenship—Cont'd
  Generally, 1312–1349
  Expatriation, above
  Revocation of naturalization, below
Nationality, loss of. Expatriation, above
Naturalization
  Administrative naturalization, above
  Revocation of naturalization, below
Post–birth acquisition
  Generally, 1276–1293
  Administrative naturalization, below
  Child Naturalization Act, 1291–1293
  Swiss perspective, 1293
Revocation of naturalization
  Generally, 1313–1333
  Administrative vs. judicial denaturalization, 1313
  Illegally procured naturalization, 1331
  Material fact, concealment of, 1331–1332
  Natural tendency test, 1332
Significance of citizenship, 1350–1373
  Generally, 1350–1373
  Disabilities on noncitizens, 1351
  Voting rights, 1353
  Welfare reform, 1353–1359
Statelessness, 1297
Voting rights, 1353
Welfare reform, 1353–1359
Who should be a U.S. citizen, 1297–1312

CLASS ACTIONS
Deportation, 757–759

CLEAR AND CONVINCING EVIDENCE
Deportation proceedings, 640

COLLATERAL ATTACK
Removal order, collaterally attacking in criminal proceedings, 759

COMMERCE CLAUSE
Source of federal immigration power, 104–106

COMMERCIAL NONIMMIGRANTS
Nonimmigrants, this index

COMMERCIAL SPEECH
English–only movement, 59–60

COMMUNIST PARTY
Membership, 163–81, 427–35

CONDITIONAL PERMANENT RESIDENCE
Generally, 273 et seq.

CONSCIENTIOUS OBJECTORS
Asylum claims, 963

CONSTITUTIONAL LAW
Commerce clause, 104–106
Counsel, right to, 658–665
Due Process, this index
Equal Protection, this index
Ex post facto clause, 180

CONSTITUTIONAL LAW—Cont'd
Extra–constitutional federal power to manage
    external affairs, 118–119
Federal power. Sources of federal immigra-
    tion power, below
Immigration and the constitution
        Generally, 103–237
    Sources of federal immigration power, be-
        low
Implied powers, 107–118
Jus sanguinis and the Constitution,
    1273–1276
Limits to federal immigration power, 120–237
Migration or importation clause, 106
Naturalization clause, 106–107
Plenary power doctrine
        Generally, 229 et seq.
    Constitutional limitations, 204
    Deportation cases, 158–163
    Exclusion of returning residents, 153–156
    Historical parallels, 235–237
    Judicial review, 190–191
    Rational basis test, 231
    Statutory interpretation, 203–204
    Substantive applications, 163–186
Sources of federal immigration power
        Generally, 103–120
    Commerce clause, 104–106
    Deportation of noncitizens, 137 et seq.
    Extra–constitutional federal power to
        manage external affairs, 118–119
    Implied powers, 107–118
    Migration or importation clause, 106
    Naturalization clause, 106–107
    Structural theories, 113
    War clause, 107
Stare decisis, 173–174
War clause, 107

CONSTRUCTION OF STATUTES
Statutory Interpretation, this index

CONSTRUCTION WORKERS
Admission as nonimmigrants, 357–358

CONTINUANCES
Administrative naturalization, 1290
Deportation proceedings, 639, 640

CONTROLLED SUBSTANCES
Deportation, 552–553
Exclusion, 435–38
Illicit trafficking, 562

CONVENTIONS
European Convention for Protection of Hu-
    man Rights and Fundamental Free-
    doms, 1183 et seq.
Refugee Convention, 915–1191
Torture, Convention against (CAT),
    1145–1164
Vienna Convention on Consular Relations,
    this index

COUNSEL
Attorneys, this index
Deportation, this index

COURTS
Judicial Review, this index
Political dynamics, relationship between
    courts, 704–705

CRIMINAL CONVICTIONS
Asylum, past wrongdoing as exception to eli-
    gibility, 1069–1077
Conviction, what constitutes, 532–540
Deportation, grounds for
        Generally, 530–567
    Aggravated felonies, 553–564
    Conviction, what constitutes, 532–540
    Drug offenses, 552–553
    Judicial review, 734–735
    Merits of removing noncitizen criminal of-
        fenders, 566–567
    Moral turpitude, crimes involving, below
    Time limits, 568–571
Drug offenses, 552–553
Exclusion, grounds for, 435–437
Expungements, 538–540
First Offender Act, 539–540
Guilty plea, withdrawing, 533–538
Moral turpitude, crimes involving
        Generally, 540–552
    Five years after date of admission, com-
        mission within, 549
    Judicial recommendations against depor-
        tation (JRAD), 550–552
    Meaning of terms, 540–548
    Sentencing requirements, 549
    Two convictions not arising out of single
        scheme, 549–550
Violent crimes, 555 et seq.

CRIMINAL ORGANIZATIONS
Snitch visas, 401, 873–874

CUBA
Cuban Liberty and Democratic Solidarity Act
    of 1996, 433
Legalization program, 610–611

CULTURAL EXCHANGES
Temporary workers, 376–377

DECLARATORY RELIEF
Deportation, 758

DEMOGRAPHICS
Changing racial and ethnic demographics,
    45–46
Economic, demographic, and fiscal effects of
    immigration, 68–72

**DEPARTMENT OF HOMELAND SECU-
RITY**
Homeland Security, Dept. of, this index

DEPORTATION
        Generally, 11–12, 496–504
Acceptance by destination country, 623
Accredited individuals, representation by,
    655–657
Additional charges, lodging, 640

DEPORTATION—Cont'd

Adjustment of status, rescission, 840–841

Administrative Procedure Act, applicability, 639

Administrative removal, 836–837

Administrative review

Generally, 641–642, 717–725

Board of Immigration Appeals, below

Admission, meaning and significance, 504–525

Advice as to rights, 637–638

Affirmances without opinion (AWOs). Appeals, this index

Aggravated felonies, 553–564

Appeals

Board of Immigration Appeals, below

Judicial review, below

Apprehension, 634–635

Asylum, defensive applications filed in removal proceedings, 1082

Attorneys. Representation, below

Board of Immigration Appeals

Generally, 641–642, 717–725

Case management screening system, 718

Clearly erroneous standard, 721

Custody decision, 637

Independence of board, 721–722

Members, appointment by Attorney General, 717

Motions to reopen or reconsider, 725–727

Notice of appeal

Sample form, 793–794

Specification of grounds, 723–724

One–member review, 718–719

Scope of review, 721

Three–member panels, 719

Bond redetermination hearing, 636

Burden of proof, 640, 705–717

Cancellation of removal, part A

Generally, 574–579

Discretion, 581

Disqualifications, 580

Timing, 579–580

Cancellation of removal, part B

Generally, 581–606

Administrative discretion, 605

Continuous physical presence requirement, 583–585

Disqualified groups, 604–605

Good moral character, 604–605

Hardship requirement

Generally, 585–604

Factors, 594–595

Nicaraguan Adjustment and Central American Relief Act (NACARA), 605–606

Case file, sample, 761–817

Citizenship as defense, 630–631

Class actions, 757–759

Clear and convincing evidence, 640

Collateral attack in criminal proceedings, 759

Conditional parole, release pending hearing, 636

Consolidating reviewable claims, 759–760

DEPORTATION—Cont'd

Counsel. Representation, below

Crew members, 840

Criminal Convictions, this index

Criminal grounds not requiring conviction, 564–566

Custody decision, appeal to BIA, 637

Custody determination, sample form, 765

De novo bond redetermination hearing, 636

Decision of immigration judge

Generally, 641

Oral decision, 787 et seq.

Declaratory relief, 758

Deferred action, 614–617

Destination, objections to, 622–630

Detention pending hearing

Generally, 636–367

National security cases, mandatory detention, 844–847

Discipline of immigration practitioners, 668–671

Discovery, 639

Discretionary detention pending hearing, 636

Document samples, 761–817

Drug offenses, 552–553

Due process rights, Fifth Amendment, 663

Entry, meaning and significance

Generally, 504–525

Returnees from temporary visits abroad, 511 et seq.

Entry while inadmissible, 526–527

Entry without inspection, 526

Estoppel based on governmental misconduct, 631

Evidence

Admissibility, 685–705

Clear, unequivocal, and convincing evidence, 713, 716

Clear and convincing evidence, 640

Exclusionary rule, 701

Hearsay evidence, 641, 685

Illegally obtained evidence, 686 et seq.

Overseas searches and seizures, 704

Privilege against self–incrimination, 702–704

Silence, drawing inferences from, 716

Standard of proof, 713 et seq.

Substantial evidence rule, 711–712

Sufficiency of evidence, 705–717

Exclusion distinguished, 140 et seq.

Execution of removal order, 643–645

Exhaustion of administrative remedies, 643, 733

Extended voluntary departure, 621, 1165–1166

False citizenship claims, 526–527

Federal power to deport noncitizens, 137 et seq.

Fraud, 526–527

Grounds

Generally, 496–504

Aggravated felonies, 553–564

Criminal Convictions, this index

DEPORTATION—Cont'd
Grounds—Cont'd
Criminal grounds not requiring conviction, 564–566
Current grounds, 500–501
Drug offenses, 552–553
Economic, moral, and health–related concerns, 568
Entry and admission, significance of, 504–525
Entry while inadmissible, 526–527
Entry without inspection, 526
Immigration control, 525–530
Political and national security grounds, 567–568
Public charge, noncitizens who become, 568
Time limits, 568–571
Violating conditions of stay, 529–530
Habeas corpus, 230, 741–757
Hearings
Generally, 639–641
Failure to attend removal hearing, 423–425
History, the APA, and separation of functions, 645–653
In absentia removal hearings, 838–839
Prison hearings, 834–836
Simulated removal hearing, 817–833
Transcript, sample, 766 et seq.
Hearsay evidence, use of, 641, 685
Historical overview, 498–499
Immunity, limited, grant of, 715
In absentia removal hearings, 838–839
Inadmissibility distinguished, 496
Ineffective assistance of counsel, 671–685
Injunctions, 757–759
Interpreters, use of, 641
Judicial politics, 704–705
Judicial recommendations against deportation (JRAD), 550–552
Judicial removal, 837–838
Judicial review
Generally, 642–643, 727–761
Briefs, 805 et seq.
Claims of U.S. citizenship, 759
Class actions, 757–759
Collateral attack in criminal proceedings, 759
Consolidating reviewable claims, 759–760
Crime–related removal orders, 734–735
Declaratory relief, 758
Detention decisions, 740–741
Discretionary relief, denial of, 735–738
Expedited removal orders, 739
General federal question jurisdiction, 757
Habeas corpus, 741–757
In absentia removal order, 839
Increased caseloads, 729–730
Injunctions, 757–759
Opinion and judgment, 813 et seq.
Petitions for review
Generally, 731–741
Sample, 796–797

DEPORTATION—Cont'd
Judicial review—Cont'd
Prosecutorial discretion, 740
Scope of review, 733
Statutory restrictions, 728–729
Stay pending disposition, 732
Theory and consequences, 760–761
Voluntary departure regulations, 739–740
Justifications, 500
Law students and law graduates, representation by, 655–657
Legalization. Relief from deportability, below
Mandatory detention pending hearing, 636
Marriage during removal proceedings, 278–280
Master calendar hearings, 638
Motion to reopen or reconsider, 644, 725–727
Noncitizens reentering after prior removal, 839–840
Notice to Appear, 635, 763–764
Objections to destination, 622–630
Order, execution of, 643–645
Parents whose children are U.S. citizens, 631
Plea agreements, 680–681
Political dynamics, relationship between courts, 704–705
Pre–hearing conference, 639
Pre–hearing procedure, 635–639
Prison hearings, 834–836
Privilege against self–incrimination, 702–704
Procedural due process, 158–163
Procedural limits, 138
Procedural rights, advice as to, 637–638
Procedure
Generally, 633–842
Administrative Procedure Act, applicability, 639
Administrative review, 641–642, 717–725
Apprehension, 634–635
Burden of proof, 640, 705–717
Clear and convincing evidence, 640
Continuances, 639, 640
Custody decision, appeal to BIA, 637
De novo bond redetermination hearing, 636
Decision of immigration judge, 641
Detention pending hearing, 636–637
Discovery, 639
Evidence, above
Execution of removal order, 643–645
Exhaustion of administrative remedies, 643, 733
Hearing and hearing process, above
Hearsay evidence, use of, 641
Interpreters, use of, 641
Judicial review, 642–643, 727–61
Master calendar hearings, 638
Motion to reopen or reconsider, 644, 725–727
Notice to Appear, 635, 763–764
Pre–hearing conference, 639
Pre–hearing procedure, 635–639
Procedural rights, advice as to, 637–638
Release on conditional parole, 636

DEPORTATION—Cont'd
Procedure—Cont'd
Representation, below
Stays, below
Witnesses, 640–641
Prosecutorial discretion
Generally, 614–617
Judicial review, 740
Public, hearings open to, 640
Reentry of noncitizens after prior removal, 839–840
Registration and reporting violations, 529–530
Relief from deportability
Generally, 572–632
Adjustment of status, 612–613
Amnesty, 607–612
Cancellation of removal, above
Deferred action, 614–617
Legalization
Generally, 607–612
Agricultural workers, 610
Cubans and Haitians, 610–611
General legalization in 1986, 609–610
Nicaraguans, 611
Miscellaneous defenses, 630–632
Objections to destination, 622–630
Perspective, 632
Private bills, 613–614
Registry, 607
Voluntary departure, 617–622
Representation
Generally, 653–685
Authorization to practice, 655–657
Constitutional right to counsel, 658–665
Discipline of immigration practitioners, 668–671
Equal Access to Justice Act, 666
Frivolous behavior, 668–670
Indigent persons, finding lawyers for, 657–667
Ineffective assistance of counsel, 671–685
Law students, law graduates and accredited individuals, 655–657
Legal aid, 665–666
Misadvice cases, 678
Plea agreements, 680–681
Pro bono legal services, 666
Selective prosecution claims, 178
Separation of functions, 650–651
Silence, drawing inferences from, 716
Special Inquiry Officers, 649–650
Statutory interpretation, 501–504
Stays
Motion for stay with supporting and opposing papers, samples, 797 et seq.
Motion to reopen or reconsider, 644
Notice of appeal, stay of IJ's decision, 642
Petitions for review, 732
Release pending hearing, stay pending appeal, 637
Removal, stay of, 630
Terrorist removal proceedings, 840, 876–879
Theory of deportation, 499–500

DEPORTATION—Cont'd
Time limits, 568–571
Vienna Convention on Consular Relations, this index
Violating conditions of stay, 529–530
Voluntary departure
Generally, 617–622
Judicial review, 739–740
Witnesses, 640–641

DESCENT
Citizenship by descent, 1269–1276

DETENTION
Asylum–seekers, 845, 1106–1109
Deportation hearing, detention pending, 636–637
Excluded noncitizens, 156–158
Habeas corpus review, 756
Indefinite detention, 210–211
Judicial review, 740–741
Mandatory detention, 210–211, 224 et seq.
National Security, this index
Removal period, detention during, 634

DISCOVERY
Deportation proceedings, 639

DIVERSITY IMMIGRANTS
Quotas and preferences, 242, 245, 337–344
Statutory calculations, 339

DOCUMENTS
Exclusion on documents–related grounds, 422–423

DOMESTIC EMPLOYEES
Housekeepers, employment–based immigration, 302–304

DOMESTIC VIOLENCE
Asylum, domestic violence and problem of non–state actor, 1025–1036
Spouses, battered, 274
Violence against Women Act of 2000, 402

DRAFT EVASION
Persecution or fear of persecution, 959

DRIVERS' LICENSES
Exams, English–only movement, 58–59
Undocumented migrants, 1258–1264

DRIVING UNDER THE INFLUENCE
As crime of violence, 555 et seq.

DRUGS AND NARCOTICS
Deportation, drug offenses, 552–553
Exclusion grounds and waivers, 442
Trafficking in controlled substances, 562

DUAL NATIONALITY
Generally, 1294–1297

DUE PROCESS
Generally, 143–144
Affirmances without opinion (AWOs), challenge on due process grounds, 724–725

DUE PROCESS—Cont'd
Deportation proceedings, 663
National security detainees, 863 et seq.
Procedural due process
    Generally, 231
    Deportation cases, 158–163
    Exclusion cases, 143–144
Rationality test, 172
Substantive due process, 171

ECONOMIC IMPACT
    Generally, 61–75
Economic, demographic, and fiscal effects of
    immigration, 68–72
Liberalized movement of labor, economic
    gains, 66–68
Public Charge, this index
Undocumented migrants, 1195–96

ECONOMIC STREAM IMMIGRATION
Generally, 323 et seq.

EDUCATION
Au pair program, 388–389
Exchange visitors, 387–394
Foreign students, 383–387
Public education. Undocumented Migrants
    and Law Enforcement (this index)
SEVIS, 868

EL SALVADOR
Nicaraguan Adjustment and Central Ameri-
    can Relief Act (NACARA), 605–606

EMPLOYMENT
Advanced degree holders, 245
American workers, displacing, 298–316
Asylum–seekers, denying employment au-
    thorization, 1110–1111
Athletes, 294
Business necessity and job requirements,
    302–304
Economic stream immigration, 323 et seq.
Employer misconduct. Undocumented Mi-
    grants and Law Enforcement, this in-
    dex
Employment–based immigration
    Generally, 242, 292–337
    Advanced degree holders, 245, 294
    Athletes, 294
    Business necessity and job requirements,
        302–304
    Displacing American workers, 298–316
    Economic stream immigration, 323 et seq.
    Entrepreneurs, 245, 334–337
    Existing employees, applications on behalf
        of, 310–311
    Extraordinary ability, persons possessing,
        293–294
    Foreign language proficiency, 305–306
    Fraudulent applications, 307 et seq.
    Housekeepers, live–in, 302–304
    Labor certification, 295–321
    National interest waivers, 294–295
    Occupational Information Network Online
        (ONET), 312

EMPLOYMENT—Cont'd
Employment–based immigration—Cont'd
    Preference categories and subceilings,
        244–245
    Prevailing wage standard, 319–321
    Priority workers, 244–245
    Program Electronic Review Management,
        296–297
    Reform proposals, 321–333
    Skilled workers, professionals, 245, 295
    Special immigrants, 245, 333–334
    Specific Vocational Preparation (SVP) in-
        dex, 312
    Wages and working conditions of Ameri-
        can workers, adversely affecting,
        316–321
English–only policies, 59, 1228
Entrepreneurs, 245
Extraordinary ability, persons possessing,
    293–294
Foreign language proficiency, 305–306
Fraudulent applications, 307 et seq.
Housekeepers, live–in, 302–304
Intra–company transferees, 378–381
Labor certification, 295–321
National interest waivers, 294–295
Occupational Information Network Online
    (ONET), 312
PERM, 296–97
Preference categories and subceilings,
    244–245
Prevailing wage standard, 319–321
Priority workers, 244–245
Program Electronic Review Management,
    296–297
Reform proposals, 321–333
Skilled workers, professionals, 245
Special immigrants, 245, 333–334
Specific Vocational Preparation (SVP) index,
    312
Temporary workers
    Generally, 362–378
    Temporary Workers, this index
Undocumented Migrants and Law Enforce-
    ment, this index
Wages
    American workers, adversely affecting
        wages and working conditions,
        316–321
    Prevailing wage standard, 319–321

ENGLISH LANGUAGE
Citizenship, 1283–1284
English–only movement, 57–61

ENTERTAINERS
Temporary workers, admission as, 362–367

ENTREPRENEURS
Preference category, 245, 334–337

ENVIRONMENT
Immigration, population, and the environ-
    ment
    Generally, 75–81

ENVIRONMENT—Cont'd
Immigration—Cont'd
  Scientific research and analytic issues, 79–81

EQUAL ACCESS TO JUSTICE ACT
Attorney's fees, 667

EQUAL PROTECTION
Lawful permanent residents, discriminatory state action, 1352
Undocumented migrants and public education, 1235 et seq.

ESTOPPEL
Deportation, estoppel based on governmental misconduct, 631

ETHICAL ISSUES
Discipline of Immigration Practitioners, 668–71
Ineffective Assistance of Counsel, 671–85
Intent to Remain, 404–08
Labor Certification, 307–10
Unauthorized Practice of Law, 459–60

ETHNICITY
Changing racial and ethnic demographics, 45–46
Multiculturalism, 34 et seq.
Politics of immigration, 81–87

EUROPE
European Convention for Protection of Human Rights and Fundamental Freedoms, 1183 et seq.
European Union, free movement, 33

EVIDENCE
Deportation, this index
Secret evidence hearings, 880–883

EX POST FACTO CLAUSE
Generally, 180

EXCHANGE VISITORS
Generally, 387–394

EXCLUSION
Admission Procedure, this index
Deportation distinguished, 140 et seq., 496
Detention of excluded noncitizens, 156–158
Grounds. Exclusion Grounds and Waivers, this index
In camera disclosure of confidential evidence, 153
Procedural due process, 144–158
Returning residents, exclusion of, 153–156

EXCLUSION GROUNDS AND WAIVERS
Generally, 410–443
AIDS and HIV, 442–443
Changes made by Immigration Act of 1990, 420
Community Party membership, 433
Criminal grounds, 435–437
Cuba, trading with, 433
Documents–related exclusion grounds, 422–423
Economic grounds, 438–441
Human rights violators, 429–430
Immigration control, grounds related to, 422–427

EXCLUSION GROUNDS AND WAIVERS
—Cont'd
Lookout list, 434
Out–of–status noncitizens, 423
Political and national security grounds, 427–435
Public charge, likelihood to become, 438 et seq.
Public health and morals, 441–443
Removal hearing, failure to attend, 423–425
State sponsors of terrorism, persons from such countries, 431
Surreptitious entry, 423
Terminology, 411
Terrorist activity, 430–431
Tolling accumulation of unlawful presence time, 423–425
Unlawfully present persons, 423–425
Visa ineligibilities table, 421

EXCLUSIONARY RULE
Deportation proceedings, 701

EXEMPTIONS
Quotas and Preferences, this index

EXPATRIATION
Citizenship, this index

EXPEDITED REMOVAL
Generally, 842–843
Arriving passengers, 485, 488–489
Asylum–seekers, 1103–1106
Judicial review, 739

EXPUNGEMENTS
Criminal convictions, 538–540

FAMILIES
Family immigration
  Generally, 250–292
  Aging out, 251–253
  Chain migration, 290
  Child Status Protection Act, 252–253
  Conditional permanent residence, 273 et seq.
  Estimating waiting times, 251 et seq.
  Foreign adoption, 286–290
  Other family members, 280–290
  Out–of–wedlock children, 284–285
  Spouses
    Generally, 254–280
    Battered spouses, 274
    Conditions subsequent, 273–275
    Fraudulent marriages, 270–280
    Same–sex marriages, 254–270
  Unification policy, 290–292
Family–sponsored immigrants
  Generally, 241–242
  Citizens domiciled overseas as sponsors, 440
  Income requirements, sponsor's, 440–441
  Preference categories and subceilings, 243–244
Immediate relatives, exemption from quotas, 239

FAMILIES—Cont'd
Long–divided, admission of spouses and children as nonimmigrants, 403
Nonimmigrants, admission as (LIFE Act), 403
Unification policy, 290–292

FEDERAL AGENCIES
Generally, 2–8
Organization chart, 6

FEDERAL POWER
Constitutional Law, this index

FIANCES AND FIANCEES
Marriage in U.S., 397–401

FIFTH AMENDMENT
Due process rights, 663
Privilege against self–incrimination, 702–704
Silence, drawing inferences from, 716

FIRST OFFENDER ACT
Expungement of conviction, 539–540

FOREIGN POLICY
Adversely affecting, grounds for exclusion, 428
Asylum, foreign policy as proper subject of discretion, 1080
Special removal procedures, arriving passengers, 489–490

FORMS
Sample case file, 761–817

FRAUD
Deportation, 526–527
Labor certification, fraudulent applications, 307 et seq.
Marriages, fraudulent
Generally, 270–280
Marriage, this index
Undocumented migrants, 1205

FREEDOM OF INFORMATION ACT
Disclosure of information about detainees, 850–851

GENITAL MUTILATION
Asylum claims, 1019 et seq.

GUANTANAMO
Detention of unlawful combatants, 854–866

GUATEMALA
Nicaraguan Adjustment and Central American Relief Act (NACARA), 605–606

GUILTY PLEA
Withdrawing
Generally, 533–538
Ineffective assistance of counsel, 679–680

HABEAS CORPUS
Deportation, 741–757
Judicial review of removal orders, 230
REAL ID Act, 755

HAITIANS
Boat people, detention on national security grounds, 846–847
Interdiction program, 1113 et seq.
Legalization program, 610–611
Selective detention of asylum–seekers, 1108

HARDSHIP
Cancellation of removal, 585–604

HEARINGS
Arriving noncitizens
Hearing before immigration judge
Generally, 486–488
Admission Procedure, this index
Removal without hearing on national security grounds, 875–876
Closed removal hearings, 879–880
Deportation, this index
Military tribunals, 883–885
Prison hearings, 834–836
Sample transcript, 766 et seq.
Secret evidence hearings, 880–883
Simulated removal hearing, 817–833

HEARSAY EVIDENCE
Deportation proceedings, 641, 685

HELSINKI ACCORDS
McGovern amendment, 429

HISPANICS
Affirmative action, 48

HISTORICAL BACKGROUND
Generally, 14–25
Admission procedure, 444–450
Deportation, 498–499
Expatriation, 1333–1336
Federal controls, institution of, 15–16
Open frontier, 14–15
Restrictive policies, solidification, 16–17
Statistical table, 23

HIV
AIDS and HIV, this index

HOMELAND SECURITY, DEPT. OF
Refugees, secretary's authority to admit, 929
Reorganization of federal agencies, 2–8
Visa responsibilities, 5, 467, 886
Warrant, exercise of powers without, 634

HOMOSEXUALITY
Exclusion of, 442–43
Same–sex marriages, 254–270

HOMOSEXUALITY—Cont'd
Sexual orientation and social group for asylum purposes, 989–995

HOUSEKEEPERS
Employment–based immigration, 302–304

HUMAN RIGHTS
European Convention for Protection of Human Rights and Fundamental Freedoms, 1183 et seq.
Exclusion of human rights violators, 429–430

ILLEGITIMATE CHILDREN
Generally, 284–285

IMMEDIATE RELATIVES
Exemption from quotas, 239

IMMIGRANTS
See LAWFUL PERMANENT RESIDENTS, this index

IMMIGRATION ACTS
Legislation, this index

IMMUNITY
Limited immunity, grant of, 715

INDIGENT PERSONS
Finding lawyers for, 657–667
Public Charge, this index
Welfare Reform, this index

INJUNCTIONS
Deportation, 757–759

INTELLIGENCE GATHERING
National Security, this index

INTERNATIONAL ORGANIZATIONS
Representatives as temporary workers, 376

INTERPRETERS
Deportation proceedings, 641

INTERVIEWS
Asylum interview, simulated, 1135–1144
Intelligence gathering, voluntary interviews with noncitizens, 872–873
Visas, personal interviews with consular officers, 887

INVESTORS
Preference category, 245, 334–337
Treaty investors, 359–36wr2

JOURNALISTS
Temporary workers, 376

JUDICIAL REVIEW
Deportation, this index
Detention decisions, 740–741
Employer discrimination, 1227
Exhaustion of administrative remedies, 642–643, 733
REAL ID Act, 755–756
Removal orders. Deportation, this index
Visas, 475 et seq.
Voluntary departure, order denying, 621

LABOR AND LABOR MARKET
Employment, this index
Impact on, 61–75
Liberalized movement of labor, economic gains, 66–68
Local markets, 64–65

LAW STUDENTS AND LAW GRADUATES
Representation by, 655–657

LAWFUL PERMANENT RESIDENTS
Generally, 9–11, 238–239
Disabilities on noncitizens, 1351
Employment immigration. Employment, this index
Equal protection challenges, discriminatory state action, 1352
Family immigration. Families, this index
Quotas and Preferences, this index
Returnees from temporary visits abroad, 240, 511 et seq.
Welfare reform, 1353–1359

LEGAL AID
Deportation proceedings, 665–666

LEGISLATION
Amendments
1961 amendments, 19
1965 amendments, 19–20
Marriage Fraud Amendments of 1986, 20–21
Antiterrorism and Effective Death Penalty Act of 1996, 22
Child Status Protection Act, 252–253
Construction. Statutory Interpretation, this index
Cuban Liberty and Democratic Solidarity Act of 1996, 433
Defense of Marriage Act, 261–262
Equal Access to Justice Act, 667
First Offender Act, 539–540
Illegal Immigration Reform and Immigrant Responsibility Act of 1996, 23
Immigration Act of 1990, 21 et seq.
Immigration Acts of 1917 and 1924, 17
Immigration and Nationality Act of 1952, 17–18
Interpretation. Statutory Interpretation, this index
LIFE Act, 403
Marriage Fraud Amendments of 1986, 20–21
Personal Responsibility and Work Opportunity Reconciliation Act of 1996, 22
Post–1952 legislative activity, 18
Private bills, relief from deportability, 613–614
Proposition 187, 22
REAL ID Act
Asylum applicant's testimony, 1057–1058
Drivers' licenses, 1258–64
Judicial review, 755–756
Refugee Act of 1980, 20, 931–932
Trafficking Victims Protection Act of 2000, 401, 453
Violence Against Women Act of 2000, 402

MANSLAUGHTER
As crime of violence, 561

MARRIAGE
Conditional permanent residence, 273 et seq.
Defense of Marriage Act, 261–262
Fiances and fiancees, 397–401
Fraudulent marriages
    Generally, 270–280
    Conditions subsequent, 273–275
    Factually genuine test, 270
    Termination of marriage for good cause, 274
    Unilateral vs. bilateral fraud, 270
Immigration Marriage Fraud Amendments of 1986, 20–21
Polygamous marriages, 264
Removal proceedings, marriage during, 278–280
Same–sex marriages, 254–270
Termination of marriage for good cause, 274

MASTER CALENDAR HEARINGS
Deportation proceedings, 638
Voluntary departure applications, 618–619

MIGRATION OR IMPORTATION CLAUSE
Generally, 106

MORAL DIMENSIONS OF IMMIGRATION CONTROL
    Generally, 25–34
Justifications for restrictions, 31–32

MORALS
Exclusion grounds, 441–443
Moral turpitude. Criminal Convictions, this index

MULTICULTURALISM
    Generally, 34 et seq.

NAFTA
Illegal migration, effect on, 1201
Nonimmigrant category for NAFTA professionals, 377

NATIONAL SECURITY
    Generally, 843–914
Arriving noncitizens, removal without hearing, 875–876
Attorney–client conversations, monitoring, 851–852
Automated entry–exit system, 866–867
Border enforcement, enhanced, 890–891
Certification program, 852–854
Closed removal hearings, 879–880
Deportation, grounds for, 567–568
Detention of noncitizens
    Generally, 844–866
    Disclosure of information about detainees, 850–851

NATIONAL SECURITY—Cont'd
Detention of noncitizens—Cont'd
    Indefinite detention, certification program, 853
    Monitoring attorney–client conversations, 851–852
    PENTTBOM investigation, 847–852
    Removal proceedings, detention in connection with, 844–847
    Unlawful combatants, 854–866
Disclosure of information about detainees, 850–851
Exclusion, grounds for, 427–435
Immigration and, 87–88, 843–915
Intelligence gathering
    Generally, 866–874
    Automated entry–exit system, 866–867
    National Security Entry–Exit Registration System (NSEERS), 867–868
    SEVIS and other student–related programs, 868–870
    Snitch visas and responsible cooperators, 401, 873–874
    U.S. Visitor and Immigration Status Indication Technology System (US VISIT), 870–872
    Voluntary interviews with noncitizens, 872–873
Military Order, 854–855
Military tribunals, 883–885
National Security Entry–Exit Registration System (NSEERS), 867–868
Perspective on immigration and national security, 900–914
Profiling, 891–900
Removal grounds, expansion of, 870
Responsible cooperators, 873–874
Secret evidence hearings, 880–883
SEVIS and other student–related programs, 868–870
Snitch visas, 401, 873–874
Special removal procedures, arriving passengers, 489–490
Terrorist removal court, 876–879
Unlawful combatants, detention of, 854–866
U.S. Visitor and Immigration Status Indication Technology System (US VISIT), 870–872
Visas, this index
Voluntary interviews with noncitizens, 872–873

NATIONALITY
    Generally, 8–9
Citizenship, this index
Dual nationality, 1294–1297

NATURALIZATION
Citizenship, this index
Clause, 106–107

NICARAGUA
Legalization program, 611

NICARAGUA—Cont'd
Nicaraguan Adjustment and Central American Relief Act (NACARA), 605–606

NONIMMIGRANTS
Generally, 9–11, 345–409
Business visitors, 348–359
Change of nonimmigrant status, 408–409
Commercial categories
Generally, 348–382
Business visitors, 348–359
Comparing commercial categories, 381–382
Construction workers, 357–358
Intra–company transferees, 378–381
Temporary workers
Generally, 362–378
Temporary Workers, this index
Treaty traders and investors, 359–362
Domestic violence victims, 401–402
Dual intent, 403–404
Educational categories
Generally, 383–394
Au pair program, 388–389
Exchange visitors, 387–394
Students, 383–387
Fiances and fiancees, 397–401
Intent to remain permanently, 403–408
Intra–company transferees, 378–381
NAFTA professionals, 377
Snitch visas, 401, 873–874
Spouses and children in long–divided families, 403
Statistical table of admissions, 346–347
Temporary workers
Generally, 362–378
Temporary Workers, this index
Tourists, 394–397
Trafficking victims, women and girls, 401–402
Treaty traders and investors, 359–362

NONREFOULEMENT
Asylum, this index

NOTICE OF APPEAL
Generally, 642
Board of Immigration Appeals. Deportation, this index

NOTICE TO APPEAR
Hearing before immigration judge
Deportation of noncitizen, 497, 635
Exclusion of new arrival, 486
Sample form, 763–764

NSEERS
National Security Entry–Exit Registration System, 867–868

NURSES
Exemption from quotas, 240

OATH OR AFFIRMATION
Witnesses at deportation hearing, 641

OCCUPATIONAL INFORMATION NETWORK ONLINE (ONET)
Generally, 312

OMBUDSMAN
Generally, 4

OPEN MIGRATION
Generally, 26 et seq.

PARENT AND CHILD
Deportation, parents whose children are U.S. citizens, 631

PAROLE
Administrative parole, release on, 156–158
Parolees, exemption from quotas, 240

PERSECUTION
Asylum, this index

PETITIONS
Court of Appeals, petition for review
Generally, 731–741
Sample, 796–797
Visa petitions, 452–461

PLEA AGREEMENTS
Effective assistance of counsel, 680–681

PLENARY POWER DOCTRINE
Constitutional Law, this index

POLICY DEBATE
Anti–immigrant sentiment, 84 et seq.
Economic impact, 65–71
English–only movement, 57–61
Family reunification, 290–292
Historical background, 14–25
Immigration, population, and the environment, 75–81
Moral dimensions of immigration control, 25–34
Multiculturalism, 34 et seq.
National Security, this index
Politics of immigration, 81–87
Race, culture, and language
Generally, 34–61
Changing racial and ethnic demographics, 45–46

POLITICS AND POLITICAL VIEWS
Asylum claims, 964–977
Citizenship, 1284
Deportation, grounds for, 567–568
Exclusion, grounds for, 427–435
Political power of immigrants, 86–87
Politics of immigration, 81–87

POPULATION
Coercive population controls as persecution, 959–961
Immigration, population, and the environment, 75–81

POPULATION—Cont'd
Migration, 13

PRACTICE OF LAW
Attorneys, this index
Unauthorized, 459–460

PREFERENCE CATEGORIES AND SUBCEILINGS
Quotas and Preferences, this index

PRIORITY DATE
Generally, 247

PRISONS
Removal hearings, 834–836

PRIVATE BILLS
Relief from deportability, 613–614

PRIVILEGE AGAINST SELF–INCRIMI-NATION
Generally, 702–704

PRO BONO LEGAL SERVICES
Deportation proceedings, 666

PROCEDURAL DUE PROCESS
Due Process, this index

PROFILING
Ethnic profiling, 891–900
Racial profiling, 701–702

PROPOSITION 187
Generally, 22, 1251–1256

PUBLIC BENEFITS
Undocumented Migrants and Law Enforce-ment, this index

PUBLIC CHARGE
Deportation of noncitizens who become, 568
Exclusion of person likely to become
    Generally, 438 et seq.
      Bond, furnishing, 440–441

PUBLIC HEALTH
Exclusion grounds, 441–443

QUOTAS AND PREFERENCES
    Generally, 10–11, 239–250
Diversity immigrants, 242, 245, 337–344
Employment–based immigration
    Generally, 242, 292–337
    Employment, this index
Entrepreneurs, preference category, 245, 334–337
Exemptions
    Generally, 239–241
    Former U.S. citizens, 240
    Immediate relatives, 239
    Nurses, 240–241
    Parolees, 240
    Special groups admitted on ad hoc basis, 240
Family–sponsored immigrants
    Generally, 241–242

QUOTAS AND PREFERENCES—Cont'd
Family–sponsored immigrants—Cont'd
    Preference categories and subceilings, 243–244
General quotas, immigrants subject to
    Generally, 241–250
    Diversity immigrants, 242, 245, 337–344
    Employment–based immigrants, 242
    Family–sponsored immigrants, 241–242
    Preference categories and sub–ceilings, 243–247
    Programs and ceilings, 241–243
Per country limits, 247–248
Preference categories and subceilings
    Generally, 243–247
    Entrepreneurs, 245, 334–337
    Special immigrants, 245, 333–334
    Spouse or child accompanying or following to join, 245
Priority date, 247
Selecting individual applicants, 247–250
Special immigrants, 245, 333–334
Worldwide ceilings, 242

RACE
Policy Debate, this index
Profiling, 701–702

RAPE VICTIMS
Asylum, 1008

REAL ID ACT
Asylum applicant's testimony, 1057–1058
Drivers' licenses, 1258–1261
Habeas corpus review, 755–756

REFUGEES
    Generally, 915–1191
Adjustment of status to permanent residence, 936
Asylum, this index
Burden sharing, 934
Children separated from parents, 936
Congressional consultation, 929
Defined, 928–929, 936
Foreign policy influence, 932–933
Homeland Security, Secretary's authority, 929
Internally displaced persons, 936–937
Orphans, 936
Overseas refugees, 918–937
Persecution. Asylum, this index
Political opinions. Asylum, this index
Presidential authorizations, 929–931
Refugee Act of 1980, 20, 931–932
Refugees sur place, 976–977
Responsibility sharing, 934
Secondary refugee movements, 937
Seventh preference conditional entry pro-gram, 927–928
Slowdowns in admission, 890
Spector–Lautenberg amendment, 931–932
Unaccompanied minors, 936
UNHCR
    Generally, 925–926

REFUGEES—Cont'd
UNHCR—Cont'd
Membership in particular social group, 985, 989

REGISTRATION
Deportation, violations as grounds for, 529–530

REGISTRY
Relief from deportability, 607

REGULATORY AGENCIES
Generally, 2–8
Organization chart, 6

RELATIVES
Family immigration. Families, this index
Family–sponsored immigrants. Families, this index
Immediate relatives, exemption from quotas, 239

RELIGIOUS PERSECUTION
Asylum claims, 962–964

RELIGIOUS WORKERS
Temporary workers, 376

REMOVAL
Deportation, this index
Withholding of removal. Asylum, this index

RETROACTIVITY
Aggravated felony definition, 554–555

SANCTIONS
Asylum, this index
Undocumented migrants, employer misconduct, 1209–1223

SANCTUARY MOVEMENT
Generally, 1206–1207

SEARCH AND SEIZURE
Homeland Security, Dept. of, exercise of powers without search warrant, 634
Overseas searches and seizures, 704

SECURITY
National Security, this index

SELF–IDENTITY
Immigrants, self–identity, and home, 88–102

SEPTEMBER 11
Anti–immigrant sentiment, 85 et seq.
Arab–Americans, 100–101
Fingerprinting and photographing, nonimmigrant visitors, 485
National Security, this index
PENTTBOM investigation, 847–852
Terrorism, this index
Undocumented migrants, post–September 11 initiatives, 1199 et seq.
Visas, post–September 11 procedures, 467

SEVIS
Student and Exchange Visitor Information System, 868–870

SHIPS AND VESSELS
Crews
Removal of crew member, 840
Temporary workers, 376
Interdiction on high seas, 1112–1135

SILENCE
Drawing inferences from, 716

SNITCH VISAS
Generally, 401, 873–874

SOCIAL GROUP
Asylum, this index

SOMALIA
Deportation, objections to destination, 623 et seq.

SOUTHERN CONE COMMON MARKET (MERCOSUR)
Open borders, 33–34

SPECTOR–LAUTENBERG AMENDMENT
Religious minorities, protection of, 931–932

SPOUSES
Battered spouses, 274
Family immigration. Families, this index

STANDARD OF PROOF
Actual admission, 487
Deportation proceedings, 713 et seq.

STANDING
Visa denial, standing to challenge, 483

STARE DECISIS
Generally, 173–174

STATE DEPARTMENT
Asylum proceedings, State Dept. opinions, 1063–1066

STATE POWER
Residual state power, 119–120

STATELESSNESS
Generally, 1297

STATUTES
Legislation, this index

STATUTORY INTERPRETATION
Generally, 203–204, 230
Administrative agencies, deference to, 380, 503
Contextual analysis, 380, 711
Deportation, 501–504
Golden rule, 356, 520
Legislative history, use of, 380, 502

STATUTORY   INTERPRETATION
—Cont'd
Literal plain meaning rule, 356, 520
Social purpose rule, 356

STAYS
Deportation, this index

STUDENTS
Electronic verification of key events, 869
Foreign students, 383–387
Student and Exchange Visitor Information
    System (SEVIS), 868–870

SURREPTITIOUS ENTRY
Grounds for exclusion, 423

TAX EXPATRIATES
Generally, 1349

TEMPORARY WORKERS
Generally, 362–378
Agricultural laborers, 367–368
Athletes and entertainers, 362–367
Cultural exchange programs, 376–377
Foreign vessel and aircraft crews, 376
International organizations, representatives
    of, 376
Journalists, 376
Labor condition applications, 364
Lesser skills and labor shortages, 367–376
Numerical limits, 365–367, 371–372
Religious workers, 376
Specialty occupations, 362–367
Trainees, 376

TERMINOLOGY
Generally, 1–2

TERRORISM
Antiterrorism and Effective Death Penalty
    Act of 1996, 22
Exclusion, grounds for, terrorist activity,
    430–431
Lookout list, 434
National Security, this index
Removal proceedings, 840
Snitch visas, 401, 873–874
Special removal procedures, 490
State sponsors of terrorism, persons from
    such countries, 431
Terrorist removal court, 876–879
Waiver of exclusion, 434

TORTURE
Convention against (CAT), 1145–1164

TOURISTS
Generally, 394–397
Fingerprinting and photographing, 485
U.S. Visitor and Immigration Status Indica-
    tion Technology System (US VISIT),
    870–872

TRAFFICKING
Adjunct to illegal immigration, 1207
Controlled substances, 562

TRAFFICKING—Cont'd
Victims Protection Act of 2000, 401, 453

TRAINEES
Temporary workers, 376

TRANSCRIPTS
Sample transcript, 766 et seq.

TREATY TRADERS AND INVESTORS
Admission as nonimmigrants, 359–362

**UNDOCUMENTED   MIGRANTS   AND
    LAW ENFORCEMENT**
Generally, 1192–1264
Abuse of immigrants, 1198
Border enforcement, heightened, 1197 et seq.
Census, inclusion in, 1233
Citizen patrols, 1199
Deaths, accidental, 1198
Domestic employment, 1210
Drivers' licenses, 1258–1264
Drownings, 1198
Economic impact, 1195–1196
Employer misconduct
    Generally, 1209–1230
    Charge, filing and hearing, 1226–1227
    Constructive knowledge, 1210–1211
    Disparate treatment vs. disparate impact,
        1227
    Domestic employment, 1210
    Exemptions, 1225
    GAO report, 1214 et seq.
    Harboring, employment as, 1206
    Hearings before ALJ, 1212–1213
    Investigations, 1212
    Judicial review, 1227
    Prohibitions on discrimination, 1223–1230
    Retaliation and intimidation, 1224–1225
    Sanctions, 1209–1223
    Verification system, 1211–1212
Facilitating illegal entry, 1205–1206
Federal–state cooperation, 1200–1201
Fraud and related offenses, 1205
Free trade agreements (NAFTA), 1201
Harboring, 1206
Human trafficking, 1207
Immigration offenses
    Generally, 1204–1208
    Entry without authorization, 1205
    Facilitating illegal entry, 1205–1206
    Fraud, 1205
    Harboring, 1206
    Human trafficking, 1207
    Texas Proviso, 1206
Immigration Reform and Control Act, 1209 et
    seq.
Labor laws, 1202–1203
Numerical estimates, 1194–1195
Origins of migrant population, 1193–1194
Post–September 11 initiatives, 1199 et seq.
Proposition 187, 1251–1256
Public benefits
    Generally, 1230–1264
    Drivers' licenses, 1258–1264

UNDOCUMENTED MIGRANTS AND LAW ENFORCEMENT—Cont'd
Public benefits—Cont'd
    Legal and social identities, 1230–1234
    Public assistance, 1234
    Public education, 1234–1258
Public education
        Generally, 1234–1258
        Equal protection claims, 1235 et seq.
        Post–secondary education, 1256–1258
        Proposition 187, 1251–1256
Responses, 1196–1204
Sanctions, employer misconduct, 1209–1223
Sanctuary movement, 1206–1207
Secure documentation, 1201
Texas Proviso, 1206

UNHCR
Asylum, this index
Refugees, this index

UNIVERSITIES AND COLLEGES
Undocumented students, 1256–1258

UNLAWFUL COMBATANTS
Citizen–detainees, 863
Detention of, 854–866

UNLAWFUL PRESENCE
Exclusion grounds, 423–425

VESSELS
Ships and vessels, this index

VIENNA CONVENTION ON CONSULAR RELATIONS
Advice of rights, 704
Representation of nationals, 638

VIOLENCE
Crimes of violence, 555 et seq.
Violence Against Women Act of 2000, 402

VISAS
Advisory opinions, 468
Air carrier sanctions, transporting persons without visas, 1112, 1208
Applications
        Generally, 461–485
        Consular absolutism, 469, 483
        Nonimmigrant and immigrant visas compared, 462 et seq.
        Refusals, review of, 468 et seq.
        Waiver program, 462
Battered self–petitioners, 453
Consular absolutism, 469, 483
Country–specific strategies, 885–886
Heightened scrutiny and delay, 886–887
Homeland Security, Dept. of, responsibilities, 5, 467, 886
Judicial review, 475 et seq.
National security considerations, 885–890

VISAS—Cont'd
Nonimmigrant and immigrant visas compared, 462 et seq.
Personal interviews with consular officers, 887
Post–September 11 procedures, 467
Refusals, review of, 468 et seq.
Review board, proposed, 473–475
Standing to challenge denial, 483
Technological innovation, 887
Visa bulletin, estimating waiting times, 251 et seq.
Waiver program
        Generally, 462
        Restrictions, 887–890

VISITORS
Tourists, this index
U.S. Visitor and Immigration Status Indication Technology System (US VISIT), 870–872

VOLUNTARY DEPARTURE
Generally, 617–622
Extended voluntary departure, 621, 1165–1166

VOTING RIGHTS
Citizenship, requirement of, 1353

WAGES
Employment, this index

WAIVER
Exclusion Grounds and Waivers, this index
National interest waivers, employment-based immigration, 294–295
Visa waiver program
        Generally, 462
        Restrictions, 887–890

WAR CLAUSE
Generally, 107

WARRANTS
Homeland Security, Dept. of, exercise of powers without search or arrest warrant, 634

WELFARE REFORM
Affidavits of support, 439–440
Citizenship requirements, 1353–1359
Personal Responsibility and Work Opportunity Reconciliation Act of 1996, 22

WITHHOLDING OF REMOVAL
Asylum, this index

WITNESSES
Deportation proceedings, 640–641